COMPETITION LAW SOURCE BOOK

Competition Law Source Book

EDITED BY

Tony O'Connor

VOLUME 1

ROUND HALL SWEET & MAXWELL

This book was typeset by
Gilbert Gough Typesetting for
ROUND HALL SWEET & MAXWELL
Kill Lane, Blackrock, Co. Dublin, Ireland.

A catalogue record for this book
is available from the British Library.

ISBN 1-85800-048-3

Printed in Ireland by
Betaprint, Dublin

TO THE MEMORY OF MY FATHER
THOMAS VALENTINE O'CONNOR (1916-1988)

The editor and publishers would like to express their appreciation and thanks for the help
and co-operation obtained from the Competition Authority, in particular
Ciarán Ó Cuinnegáin and his staff,
and for their kind permission to reproduce the Decisions in this book.

Foreword

Since the enactment of the Competition Act in 1991, the law has developed very rapidly. The Competition Authority has been active, and perhaps a surprising amount of litigation has occurred, and has been dealt with quickly. The time has come for a compilation of all this material, presented in a coherent and manageable way which is convenient for practitioners. This Tony O'Connor has done.

From a legal viewpoint, the Competition Act did several things. First, it gave Ireland an up-to-date law on restrictive practices and monopoly power comparable to that in most industrialised countries. This law is important for practising lawyers, and has given rise already to a substantial body of case law, which needs to be understood and made readily available. It is from this body of material that Tony O'Connor has selected, edited and presented in this book. Secondly it brought the Irish national competition law substantially into line with the competition law of the European Community, which until recently has been largely applied by the European Commission and the Community Courts in Luxembourg, but which is increasingly being applied by national courts and national competition authorities. This means that the Irish courts and the Irish Competition Authority do, and no doubt on occasions must, look to the case law of the Community Courts and of the Commission for guidance not only on Community law, when that is relevant, but also on the interpretation of the Irish competition legislation. There is therefore a considerable body of Community law material available, where this is mentioned in the book, citations are given, which is or may be useful to Irish lawyers handling Irish competition cases.

Underlying the cases set out here, there are the developing principles on cooperation between national authorities and the European Commission, and on the relationship between national competition law and Community competition law. This is a highly topical and multi-faceted area which involves the constitutional law of the Community, the sometimes complex relations between a national law very similar to EC law and EC law itself, and efficient and flexible cooperation (which of course can have legal effects for the companies concerned) between national competition authorities and the Commission. On these principles some of the cases reported have shed light, and in others it seems reasonable to see implicit assumptions which, if they are verified in due course, may have important implications for practitioners. The chapter on mergers in particular illustrates the issues which have already arisen, and which will no doubt continue to give rise to both litigation and controversy.

Tony O'Connor has therefore prepared a valuable and important collection of materials. He has also written useful practical introductions and comments. Irish practitioners and many lawyers outside Ireland concerned with Irish competition law e.g. because they have to notify a merger in Ireland, will find this book useful, convenient, practical and—if they have time to reflect—extremely interesting.

Dr. John TEMPLE LANG

Preface

This book seeks to assist practitioners, students, regulators, writers and researchers to access information available from official sources which is relevant to the domestic competition law of Ireland.

In deciding upon the format I have kept in mind the recognised means that facilitate research in the reports and textbooks on the competition law of the European Union.

I have included summaries and the full texts of judgments, decisions and notices which I consider to be the most significant. The list of all notifications from 1st October 1991 to 30th September 1995 with corresponding data on pages 1194 to 1314, refers to all Decisions of the Competition Authority in its first four years of operation. The annex contains the relevant domestic legislation together with published views of the Competition Authority as well as procedural Official Forms.

The chapter and sub-chapter headings were chosen with a view to correlating the relevant judgments, decisions and notices for comparison and review purposes. Each chapter introduction explains the chapter and sub-chapter lay-out. Introductions to chapters without particular sub-divisions explain the features of the judgments, decisions or notices which I have found noteworthy. The facts of each judgment and decision are summarised in a standard format. Category licences are reproduced without a summary because the operative part of a category licence is brief in any event. The summaries have headings which contain key words and embody the facts and the main elements in the judgment or decision. At the end of each summary is a list of the judgments and decisions which are mentioned in the reproduced text. These lists give more detailed citations than those which appear in the reproduced text and they also refer to the chapter number in which the decision or judgment may be found.

The list of notifications on pages 1194 to 1314 was compiled according to the numerical order of the reference number given to each notification by the Competition Authority. As each notification is received by the Competition Authority in any calendar year, the next number in sequence for that year of receipt is given as the appropriate reference number. Thus the first notification which will be received by the Competition Authority in 1996 will be 'CA/1/96' and in 1997 will be 'CA/1/97'. The list of notifications should assist researchers to identify in the decisions features of particular interest to them. The list is supplemented by an alphabetical index of the principal names in the notifications. This alphabetical index, which begins on page 1318, further enables the reader to identify decisions of the Competition Authority by reference to the principal name which is mentioned in any notification to the Competition Authority. A notification number which may be obtained from the alphabetical index will allow the reader to find details of the decision from the complete list on pages 1194 to 1314.

The list of Contents will give an overall view and the index at the end of the book may be used as another means of accessing information which may be of relevance.

The index uses *italics* for Decisions which are reported upon in the book and which are listed according to each name which is the subject of the notification leading to the Decision. Judgments of the Courts are similarly listed. Numbers in **bold** print indicate the beginning of the summary for each judgment or decision. Key words or concepts under the recognised headings used in the book are also listed in the index.

I hope that the book will contribute to the understanding and development of Irish Competition Law. I would be particularly pleased to hear from readers with suggestions for improvements, alterations or corrections which may be made in any further revised edition or supplement.

I would like to thank Mark Nicholas, Barrister-at-Law, for assisting most generously and particularly in preparing many draft summaries. Needless to say the summaries are not intended to be substitutes for the reproduced texts.

Eilis Maguire of the Round Hall Press is recommended as an expert counsellor because of her persistence and skills in ensuring that everyone maintained a good work momentum. I am deeply indebted to Kay Nugent who typed drafts and Gilbert Gough who did typesetting. Liam McMahon slaved at proofreading and has my everlasting gratitude. Nick Lundberg diligently compared the typeset with the original text.

The McMahon and O'Connor families have been extraordinarily encouraging and understanding while this book was being prepared.

The hours of labour tested their patience. I trust that the user of this book will benefit from that labour.

For the foreword I express my deep appreciation to John Temple Lang; himself a significant contributor to the development of European Competition law.

I commend Round Hall Sweet & Maxwell for publishing a source book on this subject.

Tony O'Connor, B.L.
Law Library Building,
158/159, Church Street,
DUBLIN 7

2nd November, 1995.

Contents

Table of Contents

VOLUME 1

CHAPTER 1 — UNDERTAKING

CHAPTER 2 — PROCEDURES

CHAPTER 3 — ACQUISITIONS

CHAPTER 4 — EXCLUSIVE PURCHASING/FRANCHISING

CHAPTER ONE

Undertakings

1.0 Introduction

The plural of the term 'undertaking' must be emphasised when considering section 4 of the Competition Act 1991. Before one can determine whether an agreement decision or concerted practice is prohibited under section 4 as opposed to section 5 two or more undertakings must be party to the agreement, decision or practice which is being reviewed under section 4.

Section 3(1) provides:

> 'Undertaking' means a person being an individual, a body corporate or an incorporated body of persons engaged for gain in the production, supply or distribution of goods or the provision of a service.

The decisions of the Competition Authority invariably identify each party which is considered to be an undertaking. One can avoid complex and protracted proceedings or a notification by identifying that there are not in fact two or more undertakings involved.

VHI case This approach was unsuccessfully used but expeditiously determined in the High Court and the Supreme Court in 1993 when those courts were requested to decide a preliminary issue about whether the VHI is engaged for gain and is thereby an 'undertaking'.[1] The High Court judgment of Costello J. was delivered *ex tempore* but the Supreme Court disagreed with the High Court's determination of the preliminary issue in its written judgment which is included in this book at 1.1.

Consumers On 10 July 1992 the Competition Authority published the following notice in the Irish Times:

> Notification CA/17/92E — Capital Holdings Ltd/Abbeysun; customers. Compulsory insurance for packaged holidays.
>
> The Competition Authority has rejected the above notification. The arrangements are not notifiable under section 7 of the Competition Act 1991 because

1. In *Sibra Building Company v. Palmerstown Centre Development Ltd* Keane J on 24 November 1992 stated that companies which only owned properties were not 'undertakings' because these types of companies were not engaged for gain in the production supply or distribution of goods or the provision of a service (reported at **7.1**, this case is under appeal). Costello P. on 27 February 1995 in *Greally v. Minister for Education* held that the Minister and the Association of Secondary Teachers were not "undertakings". In Decisions 288 and 289 the Competition Authority decided that University College Dublin and University of Limerick were 'undertakings' in the transaction notified (see reports at **7.12** and **7.13** below). In Decision 358 the Competition Authority decided that the Southern Health Board was an 'undertaking' in the property transaction notified (see report **7.16** below). In Decision 385 of 22 December 1994 in respect of Notification No. CA/32/94 — Irish Potato Marketing Ltd/Donegal Potatoes Ltd the Competition Authority considered that the liquidator of North Donegal Producers was an 'undertaking' in the notified acquisition agreement.

1.0 it is clear that customers who are consumers are not undertakings as required by section 4(1) of the Act.[2]

The Falcon Holidays/Ben McArdle decision of the Competition Authority is included in Part 2 of this chapter so that this rejection can be compared with the decision of the Competition Authority to proceed with a determination of the notification by a holiday company and an insurance broker for the provision of travel insurance to consumers. The holiday company and the insurance brokers are two 'undertakings' whereas in the rejection of the Capital Holdings Ltd/Abbeysun notification the Competition Authority only identified one undertaking.

Corporate groups Part 3 of this chapter concerns the question whether two parties constitute one economic unit. This may arise when the parties to an agreement, decision or concerted practice are part of the same corporate group. Decision 2 of the Authority concerns a reorganisation of an insurance company within the same corporate group and indicates the Competition Authority's view on what constitutes an economic unit. The other decision in this part has been inserted because of its relevance to the single economic unit reasoning.

Employees The Competition Authority's view on when an employee becomes a separate undertaking from his or her employer can be gleaned from Part 4 of this chapter headed 'Undertakings: Employees'. This Part could have formed part of chapter 3 on restrictions after termination of acquisition agreements because restrictions on officers and employees and shareholders are often necessary to secure the transfer of some or all of the assets under an acquisition agreement.[3] However the notice and decision of the Authority on restraints of trade on employees are contained in this chapter for the purpose of highlighting the importance of the term 'undertaking'.

Partnerships Part 5 of this chapter focuses on partnership arrangements and the effect of a sale of a business on quasi employer/employee agreements.

Commercial agents Part 6 of this chapter concentrates on which parties constitute separate undertakings. The decisions concerning agency agreements show a readiness of the Competition Authority to identify undertakings while dismissing any infringement of section 4 on the grounds that the commercial agent is an integral part of the principal's distribution business. The Competition Authority likens a commercial agency to an employee status as opposed to an independent trader.

Associations Part 7 of this chapter refers to a High Court judgment and Competition Authority decisions concerning Horizontal agreements arranged by or through the use of a group of undertakings. The distinction between an 'undertaking' on its own and a group of undertakings as one 'undertaking' is not an issue, apparently, which will allow an association of undertakings to avoid the effect of section 4(1) of the Competition Act.[4] The decision of Mr Justice Costello in an action taken by an

2. A notice in the *Irish Times* on 10 December 1993 also reads: 'The Authority has rejected the following notifications on the grounds that the arrangements are not undertakings within the meaning of section 3(1) of the Competition Act and subsequently are not notifiable under section 7 of the Act:
(a) CA/92/92E — Maxol Ltd; consumers; exclusive purchase agreement;
(b) CA/93/92E — Maxol Ltd; consumers; exclusive purchase agreement;
(c) CA/94/92E — Maxol Ltd; consumers; exclusive purchase agreement.
3. See footnote 8 at 3.0 below for comparisons.
4. The PRS/IMRO decisions are useful to note in this context also. See 1.3.2, 6.3 and 6.4.

association of electrical contractors and the decisions of the Competition Authority concerning groupings of separate undertakings which are included in this book concern Horizontal agreements in effect. 1.0

The tables of references and indices will allow the reader to avoid the strictures of the categories created for the form of the book. The decisions contained in this chapter should not only be useful for the purposes of clarifying the application of the term 'undertaking' but should also be relevant to the consideration of the many different markets, terms of agreement and effects of arrangements which are the subject of the decisions.

1.1 Statutory Boards

1.1.1 **Mary Deane, Nora Cronin, Kathleen Oliver Walsh and Anne Cody**, plaintiffs, **v. The Voluntary Health Insurance Board**, defendant [SC No. 148 of 1992], Supreme Court, 29 July 1992[1]

Competition – Dominant position – Undertaking – Supply of services – Body corporate established by statute to provide health insurance – Insurance cover provided in return for payment of subscriptions – Body corporate to collect only such revenue as necessary to meet its costs – Body corporate to contribute surplus funds to the Central Fund – Whether body corporate 'engaged for gain' – Whether body corporate 'undertaking' – Whether provisions of Competition Act 1991, applicable – Voluntary Health Insurance Act 1957 (No. 1), sections 3 and 4 – Competition Act 1991 (No. 24), sections 3 and 5 – Finance Act 1992 (No. 9), section 252

Statutory Interpretation – Statute expressed to be analogous with Articles 85 and 86 of European Economic Community Treaty 1957 – 'Engaged for gain' – Whether 'gain' restricted to 'profit' – Whether other articles of Treaty to be used as aid to construction – European Economic Community Treaty 1957, Articles 85, 86, 90, 92, 93 and 94 – Competition Act 1991 (No. 24), section 3

European Communities – European Economic Community Treaty 1957 – Competition – Whether undertaking providing public service formed for the object of making profit – Whether Articles of Treaty relevant – European Economic Community Treaty 1957, Articles 85, 86, 90, 92 and 94

The Competition Act 1991 is described in its long title as, *inter alia*,

> An Act to prohibit by analogy with articles 85 and 86 of the Treaty establishing the European Economic Community and in the interests of the common good the prevention restriction or distortion of competition and the abuse of dominant positions in trade in the State.

Section 5(1) of the Act of 1991 provides as follows:

> Any abuse by one or more undertakings of a dominant position in trade for any goods or services in the State or in a substantial part of the State is prohibited.

'Undertaking' is defined in section 3(1) of the Act of 1991 as meaning 'a person

1. This report is reproduced with the kind permission of the Incorporated Council of Law Reporting for Ireland and was first published in [1992] 2 IR at 319-332. This report concerns the determination of a preliminary issue. The judgments of the High Court and Supreme Court arising from the plenary hearing are set out at **8.1.5** and **8.1.6**.

being an individual, a body corporate or an unincorporated body of persons engaged for gain in the production, supply or distribution of goods or the provision of a service'. 1.1.1

Article 85 of the European Economic Community Treaty 1957, prohibits agreements between undertakings which have the aim of preventing, restricting or distorting trade.

Article 86 of the Treaty prohibits the abuse by an undertaking of a dominant position within the European Community or a substantial part thereof.

Article 90 of the Treaty exempts 'undertakings entrusted with the operation of services of general economic interest or having the character of a revenue producing monopoly' from the application of the rules relating to competition contained within the Treaty insofar as those rules would obstruct such undertakings in the performance of the particular task assigned to them.

Articles 92 93 and 94 of the Treaty deal with the circumstances in which state aids to industry are permitted.

The defendant was established pursuant to section 3 of the Voluntary Health Insurance Act 1957 to fulfil the functions therein assigned to it.

Section 4(1) of the Act of 1957 provides as follows:

> The Board shall make and carry out a scheme of voluntary health insurance for defraying to such extent as the Minister [for Health] may from time to time specify the costs of persons paying subscriptions to the Board in respect thereof and to dependents of such persons of such medical surgical hospital and other health services as the Minister may from time to time specify.

By virtue of section 4(2) of the Act of 1957 the Board may provide other schemes of voluntary health insurance subject to the consent of the Minister.

Section 4(4) of the Act of 1957 provides as follows with respect to the revenues of the Board:

> The Board shall so fix the subscriptions provided for by schemes under this section that taking one year with another the revenue of the Board from subscriptions together with its other revenues (if any) shall be sufficient but only sufficient (as nearly as may be) after the Board has made such allowances as it thinks proper for reserves depreciation and other like purposes, to meet the charges (including repayment of loans to the Minister) properly chargeable to revenue.

Section 252 of the Finance Act 1992 provides that the Voluntary Health Insurance Board shall pay a levy of £3,000,000 into the Central Fund on or before 30 June 1992 in respect of the year 1992.

The plaintiffs were trustees of a religious order and, in that capacity, the owners of a private hospital. Proceedings were issued concerning the continued inclusion of the plaintiffs hospital in the defendants schemes of health insurance and the payment of monies allegedly due for the treatment of the defendants' subscribers in the plaintiffs' hospital. The plaintiffs claimed *inter alia* that the defendant was in breach of a duty owed to them by virtue of section 5 of the Act of 1991. Prior to the hearing of the action, the defendant sought declarations that it was not an undertaking within

1.1.1 the meaning of section 3 of the Act of 1991 in that it was not engaged for gain and that the Act of 1991 therefore had no application to it. These declarations were granted in the High Court. On appeal by the plaintiffs it was

Held by the Supreme Court (Finlay CJ, Hederman and Egan JJ.) in allowing the appeal;

(1) That the word 'gain' was not limited to 'pecuniary gain' or 'profit'. *In re Arthur Average Association for British, Foreign and Colonial Ships* (1875) LR 10 Ch App 542 approved.

(2) That the true construction of section 3 of the Act of 1991 was that the words 'for gain' connoted an activity carried on or a service supplied in return for a charge or payment and that accordingly the defendant was an undertaking for the purposes of the Act of 1991.

(3) That had the word 'gain' been found to be ambiguous it would have been appropriate and desirable to consider the long title of the Act of 1991; and that had gain been limited to 'pecuniary gain' or 'profit' the probable consequence in Ireland would be that the Act of 1991 would be very limited indeed in its application.

(4) That none of the provisions of Articles 90, 92, 93 and 94 of the European Economic Community Treaty 1957, appeared to relate to questions as to whether or not authorities or undertakings providing public or national services were formed for the object of making profits or not.

Quaere whether it was possible to use Articles 90, 92, 93 and 94 as an aid to the construction of the Act of 1991.

(5) That what would be saved from the application of the Act of 1991 by the words 'engaged for gain' would be a charitable association for the spending of money or the supply of goods or services free of any charge or payment. *In re Arthur Average Association for British, Foreign and Colonial Ships* (1875) 10 LR Ch App 542 approved.

Cases mentioned in this report

In re Arthur Average Association for British, Foreign and Colonial Ships (1875) 10 LR Ch App 542

Vandyk v. Minister for Pensions and National Insurance [1955] 1 QB 29; [1954] 3 WLR 342; [1954] 2 All ER 723

Preliminary Issue

The plaintiffs commenced a number of actions concerning the continued inclusion of the plaintiffs' hospital in the defendant's schemes of health insurance, and the payment of monies allegedly due for the treatment of the defendant's subscribers in the plaintiffs' hospital. By order of the High Court (Costello J) made on 5 February 1992, the actions were consolidated. The statement of claim alleged *inter alia* that the defendant was in breach of the provisions of the Competition Act 1991, and of a duty owed under section 5 of the Act of 1991. By notice of motion dated 31 March 1992, the defendant sought *inter alia*:

(a) An order declaring the defendant not to be an 'undertaking' within the meaning of section 3 of the Act of 1991;

(b) An order declaring that the Competition Act 1991, did not apply to the defendant.

The motion came on for hearing before the High Court (Costello J) on 8 and 9 April 1992, and on the latter date an *ex tempore* judgment was delivered, in the course of which it was held that the words 'engaged for gain' were intended to mean that an undertaking, for the purpose of section 3 of the Act or 1991, had the object of gain. It was further held that the defendant's object was not that of gain, but the provision of a service in the public interest. the revenue of which met its costs. 1.1.1

The plaintiffs lodged a notice of appeal dated 6 May 1992. It was ordered by the Supreme Court that both parties should lodge a booklet of submissions on the appeal. The appeal came on for hearing before the Supreme Court (Finlay CJ, Hederman and Egan JJ) on 21 July 1992.

Nial Fennelly SC and William McKechnie SC (with them Dominick Hussey) for the plaintiffs: This Court is not concerned for the present with whether the defendant enjoys a dominant position, whether it is engaged in trade or whether it is engaged in the provision of services. These are all matters for the hearing of the action, and for the purposes of this appeal it must be assumed that each of these issues will be decided in the plaintiffs' favour.

There is no dispute that the defendant is a body corporate. If it had been intended by the Oireachtas to restrict the application of the Act of 1991 on the grounds that a body had been incorporated by statute or was a state sponsored body, it would have been easy to do so; for example, a list of exempted bodies corporate could have been appended as a schedule. But this was not done.

The expression 'for gain' is the sole basis of the defendant's case, and was accepted as such by the High Court. The defendant is no different from any private insurance company in that it charges a premium for the provision of insurance services. It enjoys a factual monopoly in the provision of health insurance services in Ireland. Sections 22, 23 and 24 of the Act of 1957 prohibit 'unlicensed business' in this field. The Minister for Health is charged with issuing such licences, but no such licence has ever been issued. Any licensed insurer under those sections would clearly be an undertaking within section 3 of the Act of 1991, even though its activity would be no different from that of the defendant.

The plaintiffs rely on the judgment of Jessel MR in *In re Arthur Average Association for British, Foreign and Colonial Ships*. In that case, the body concerned was a mutual marine insurance association dealing in cross-indemnities, and was not operating for gain.

Hederman J: Is it your contention that the learned trial judge erred in not adopting the definition of Jessel MR in that case?

Nial Fennelly SC: Yes. See also *Vandyk v. Minister for Pensions and National Insurance*. Halsbury's Law's of England (4th Ed) (Vol. 7(1)) at para. 20 states:

> Gain is not limited to pecuniary gain or confined to commercial profits only, and a company is formed for the acquisition of gain if it is formed to acquire something, as distinguished from a company formed for spending something.

Finlay CJ: Can you give an example of an undertaking not carrying on a trade for gain?

Nial Fennelly SC: Ministers of Government, or ministers corporate. Also, charities.

Finlay CJ: Do you say that the nominal or token returns to a charity fall outside what you say is 'gain'?

Nial Fennelly SC: Yes. Turning to section 4(4) of the Act of 1957, this means no more than that the defendant is obliged to balance its revenues with its expenditure, taking one year with another. The performance of this obligation is entirely internal to the defendant, and makes no difference to its behaviour in the market place. In practice, the defendant will make a profit in some years and a loss in others. When it makes a profit, the Government can take advantage of it.

Similar obligations are imposed on other State bodies — (e.g. section 21(2) of the Electricity Supply Act 1927). Section 11(1) of the Gas Act 1976, enables the Minister for Finance, from time to time, to give 'such general directives concerning the pricing policy as to the sale or supply of gas or the financial objectives of the Board as he considers appropriate. Does this mean that Bord Gais is an undertaking in some years but not in others, depending on whether the Minister applies the provisions of the Act of 1976?

1.1.1 Under sections 4, 7 and 8 of the Act of 1991, certain agreements must be notified to the Competition Authority. What will be the position with regard to agreements between private companies and state bodies? Will some agreements have to be notified and others not?

The Act of 1991 is intended to apply Articles 85 and 86 of the Treaty of Rome, 1957. If the defendant accepts that those Articles apply to it, how can it be said that the Act of 1991 applying those Articles does not apply? The use of the words 'for gain' is not sufficient to sustain such an argument. Under community law, state-owned corporations may be undertakings as may bodies entrusted by the state with particular tasks and quasi-governmental bodies which carry on economic activities.

Peter Shanley SC (with him John D. Cooke SC and Michael Cush) for the defendant: Subject to a small number of crucial changes, sections 4 and 5 of the Act of 1991 mirror the provisions of Articles 85 and 86 of the Treaty of Rome, 1957. It is true that in the context of those Articles, 'undertaking' has been given a wide construction in the jurisprudence of the Court of Justice of the European Community so as to encompass undertakings which carry on any form of economic or commercial activity, whether or not profit was an objective.

One of the most important and obvious distinctions between the provisions of the Treaty and the provisions of the Act is the deliberate introduction of a definition of 'undertaking' in the Act of 1991, and to the necessary ingredient of being 'engaged for gain'.

The introduction of such a distinction was both logical and necessary, having regard to the other distinctions between the Act and the Treaty. The Act mirrors only Articles 85 and 86 of the Treaty, whereas the Treaty competition rules are contained in Articles 85 to 94. In particular, the Act of 1991 does not contain anything corresponding to Article 90, which deals specifically with public undertakings to which Member States have granted special or exclusive rights.

It is clear that a deliberate policy decision was taken to apply the basic provisions of sections 4 and 5 (by analogy with Articles 85 and 86) to commercial undertakings, including those which happen to be owned by the State, but subject to the over-riding consideration that as 'undertakings' they must be engaged in their particular tasks for gain. Thus, various undertakings established at the instigation of the State and of which the State is frequently the major shareholder will be within the scope of the Act of 1991. But the purpose of the definition of 'undertaking' introduced by section 3 of the Act of 1991 is to distinguish between commercial enterprises, owned by the State, or otherwise, and those bodies such as the defendant established in order to provide a public service, rather than carrying on a gainful commercial enterprise.

Section 4(4) of the Act of 1957 fixes the financial parameters of the basis on which the defendant is to operate. It is, in effect, explicitly precluded from so arranging or conducting its affairs so as to pursue the accumulation of a surplus or any form of gain. Furthermore, it is excluded from the provisions of the Insurance Acts and from the European Communities (Non-Life Insurance) Regulations 1976 (SI No. 115 of 1976). The statutory scheme as a whole in relation to the position of the defendant in the insurance market is that it is not regarded as being a competitor of commercial enterprises such as would warrant it being brought within the regime for regulating competition in that sector. It is excluded because it is providing a public service on behalf of the State and doing so on a non-profit making basis.

Nial Fennelly SC in reply.

Cur. adv. vult.

Finlay CJ 29 July 1992

This is an appeal brought by the plaintiffs against an order made in the High Court on 9 April 1992 by Costello J upon a motion for the determination of a preliminary point of law in this action which declared that the defendant is not an 'undertaking' within the meaning of section

3 of the Competition Act 1991 and further declared that the said Act does not apply to the said defendant. 1.1.1

The facts

The plaintiffs are the trustees of the Congregation of the Franciscan Missionaries of Our Lady, and are the owners of St Francis Medical Centre, a private hospital situate at Ballinderry, Mullingar, County Westmeath.

The defendant is a statutory corporation created pursuant to the provisions of the Voluntary Health Insurance Act 1957. The plaintiffs have instituted proceedings against the defendant for various reliefs, including a claim arising from an alleged breach by the defendant of a duty owed by the defendant to the plaintiffs under the provisions of section 5(1) of the Competition Act 1991, and section 5(2)(a), (b) and (d) of the said Act.

The defendant by notice of motion sought a declaration that it was not an undertaking within the meaning of the Competition Act 1991, and that, accordingly, it owed no duty to the plaintiffs pursuant to the provisions of that Act, and sought a determination by way of preliminary issue, as a matter of law, of the issue thus arising. It was pursuant to that notice of motion that the order appealed against in this case has been made.

This Court is not, on the hearing of this appeal, concerned with any other issue and, in particular, is not concerned, if it were to find that the defendant was an undertaking within the meaning of the Act of 1991, as to whether the plaintiffs had established any other matter arising under that Act.

The long title of the Competition Act 1991, is as follows:

> An Act to prohibit by analogy with articles 85 and 86 of the Treaty establishing the European Economic Community and in the interests of the common good the prevention, restriction or distortion of competition and the abuse of dominant positions in trade in the State, to establish a competition authority, to amend the Mergers, Takeovers and Monopolies Control Act 1978, and to provide for other matters connected with the matters aforesaid.

Section 5(1) of the Act of 1991 provides:

> Any abuse by one or more undertakings of a dominant position in trade for any goods or services in the State or in a substantial part of the State is prohibited.

Subsection 2 of section 5 provides that without prejudice to the generality of subs. 1 such abuse may in particular consist of certain matters which are set out in subclauses.

Section 3(1) of the Act of 1991 provides that:

> 'Undertaking' means a person, being an individual, a body corporate or an unincorporated body of persons engaged for gain in the production, supply or distribution of goods or the provision of a service.

It is not in issue on the hearing of this appeal, nor was it in issue in the High Court, that the defendant is a body corporate and is engaged in the supply of a service.

The issue which arose in the High Court and which arises again in this Court is net and is the question as to whether, on the evidence consisting solely of the statutory provisions applicable to the defendant, the defendant is a body corporate engaged for gain in the supply of a service. The Voluntary Health Insurance Act 1957, at section 3, provides for the establishment of a board, to be styled and known as The Voluntary Health Insurance Board, to fulfil the functions assigned to it by the Act.

Section 4(1) provides that:

1.1.1 The Board shall make and carry out a scheme of voluntary health insurance for defraying, to such extent as the Minister may from time to time specify, the costs of persons paying subscriptions to the Board in respect thereof, and to dependents of such persons, of such medical, surgical, hospital and other health services as the Minister may from time to time specify.

Subsection 2 of section 4 provides that the Board may make and carry out such other schemes of voluntary health insurance as it may think fit, subject to the consent of the Minister in regard to the scope and extent of the benefits.

Section 4(4) provides as follows:

> The Board shall so fix the subscriptions provided for by schemes under this section that taking one year with another the revenue of the Board from subscriptions together with its other revenues (if any) shall be sufficient, but only sufficient (as nearly as may be), after the Board has made such allowances as it thinks proper for reserves, depreciation and other like purposes, to meet the charges (including repayment of loans to the Minister) properly chargeable to revenue.

It is on this subsection, and on this subsection alone, that the defendant claims that it falls outside the definition of an undertaking in that it does not supply the service of health insurance for gain.

No relevant amendment has been made to the Voluntary Health Insurance Act 1957 and, in particular, no amendment has been made to section 4(4) of that Act. Relevant, however, to a consideration of the issues arising is a provision contained in section 252 of the Finance Act 1992 which provides:

> The Voluntary Health Insurance Board shall pay a levy of £3,000,000 into the Central Fund on or before 30 June 1992 in respect of the year 1992.

The judgment of the High Court

In the course of his *ex tempore* judgment, Costello J in the High Court stated as follows:

> It is absolutely clear that the existing law of the European Community (which it is agreed is correctly stated in the passage quoted from the Butterworths' publication on Competition law which has been handed to me) is that an undertaking for the purposes of Articles 85 and 86 has been construed as extending to any form of undertaking regardless of whether it makes a profit. Clearly the definition in the Act of 1991 has deliberately departed from this. If it was intended to take over precisely the same meaning for the word in the Act, the Oireachtas would not have included the words 'engaged for gain', unless there was a deliberate intention to mean otherwise. I consider that this was a deliberate intention to depart from the meaning of Articles 85 and 86. If it had been intended to give a full effect to those Articles, the Oireachtas would not have included these words in the definition section.

I think that the statute is to be construed in the way I have stated. I should say I have considered whether I should follow the statement of Jessel MR in *In re Arthur Average Association for British, Foreign and Colonial Ships* (1875) LR 10 Ch App 542. I consider that the approach I have suggested is preferable. I think my view is the more correct one in view of the statute I am considering.

I agree with the submission made by Mr Cooke that the words 'engaged for gain' are intended to mean that the undertaking's object is that of gain. The defendant clearly does not engage for gain in that sense. It merely provides a service in the public interest. On the contrary its purpose is providing a scheme which, one year with another, will ensure that its revenues meet its costs'. 1.1.1

The submissions

Counsel on behalf of the plaintiffs has made, as a primary submission, the submission that the word 'gain' cannot he construed as equivalent to the word 'profits'. That its proper meaning is, in particular, when used as it is in this definition, in the singular, the acquisition of some tangible thing, that in so far as the defendant undoubtedly supplies health insurance and acquires by such supply from each subscriber a sum of money, be it called a subscription or a premium, that it is manifestly engaged in the supply of a service for gain. Whether it intends, hopes or actually succeeds in making a profit or not is, the submission says, immaterial. As a corollary to this submission it is contended on behalf of the plaintiffs that an undertaking supplying a service otherwise than for gain would he an undertaking supplying a service free or for some nominal return only whereby the activity would take place by way of spending and not gaining money.

The provisions of section 252 of the Finance Act 1992, are relied upon by the plaintiffs in the course of their submissions merely as an indication that by that time the defendant had gained as a result to the supply of the service of health insurance, a substantial sum of money which by statutory intervention it was obliged to pay into the Central Fund.

On behalf of the defendant it was submitted that 'undertaking' for the purpose of the provisions of Articles 85 and 86 of the European Economic Community Treaty 1957 has not been defined and in fact has been widely construed in European Community law so as to encompass undertakings which carried out any form of economic or commercial activity whether or not the activities were pursued with profit-making motive or objective.

Sections 4 and 5 of the Act of 1991, it is pointed out, mirror to a very large extent the restrictive and prohibitory provisions of Articles 85 and 86 and, accordingly, it is submitted that the legislature in not adopting the general phrase 'undertaking', or any definition of it equivalent to that which has evolved in European Community law but inserting into it the words 'engaged for gain', must be taken to have had a special purpose and that purpose was in effect to ensure that non-profit making institutions, being bodies corporate or otherwise, providing a public service should be excluded from the Competition Act 1991. It is conceded by counsel for the defendant that the interpretation of 'engaged for gain' which was laid down by Costello J in the High Court and which he seeks to uphold on the hearing of this appeal, makes the phrase 'for gain' equivalent in all respects to the phrase 'for profit'.

The decision

The only previous judicial definition of the word 'gain' of potential relevance to the issue arising on this appeal, to which we were referred, is that of Sir George Jessel MR in *In re Arthur Average Association for British, Foreign and Colonial Ships* (1875) LR 10 Ch App 542 referred to be Costello J in the course of his judgment.

The report of that decision is of the judgment on appeal from the Master of the Rolls, but the decision of the Master of the Rolls relevant to this issue did not form the subject matter of an issue arising on the appeal. The judgment of Jessel MR is, however, contained in the report, and the material portion of it deals with section 4 of the Companies Act 1862. That section provides as follows:

> No company, association or partnership consisting of more than twenty persons shall be formed after the commencement of this Act for the purpose of carrying on any other business [i.e. other than banking] that has for its object the acquisition of gain by the company, association or partnership, or by the individual members thereof, unless it is

1.1.1 registered as a company under this Act.

The provisions of this section are in fact contained in indistinguishable form in section 376 of the Companies Act 1963, which reads as follows:

> No company, association or partnership consisting of more than twenty persons shall be formed for the purpose of carrying on any business other than the business of banking that has for its object the acquisition of gain by the company, association or partnership, or by the individual members thereof unless it is registered as a company under this Act or is formed in pursuance of some other statute.

In the course of his judgment, at p. 546, Sir George Jessel MR stated as follows:

> The fourth section applies to companies or associations having for their object the acquisition of gain either by the company or association or the individual members thereof Now if you come to the meaning of the word 'gain', it means acquisition. It has no other meaning that I am aware of. Gain is something obtained or acquired. It is not limited to pecuniary gain. We should have to add the word 'pecuniary' so to limit it. And still less is it limited to commercial profits The word used, it must be observed, is not 'gains' but 'gain' in the singular. Commercial profits, no doubt, are gain but I cannot find anything limiting gain simply to a commercial profit. I take the words as referring to a company which is formed to acquire something or in which the individual members are to acquire something, as distinguished from a company formed for spending something and in which the individual members are similarly to give something away or to spend something and do not gain anything.

This appears to me to be a satisfactory and in so far as is relevant to the section of the Companies Act with which it was dealing and also to this section of the Act of 1991, a complete definition of the word 'gain'. I find it impossible to accept, as I would have to accept, if I were to uphold the interpretation placed upon this section in the High Court, that the word 'gain' was equivalent in this section of the Act of 1991 to the word 'profit'. If the legislature had intended that any undertaking which, though engaged in the supply of goods or services was not so engaged with a view to making profits, it seems to me it would unambiguously have said so, and the word we would see would be 'profit' instead of 'gain'.

I do not find the word 'gain' in this section ambiguous, but if it were to be so found, then it seems to me that it would be appropriate and desirable to look at the long title of the Act.

In that regard it is stated that the purposes of the Act include the prohibition by analogy with Articles 85 and 86 of the Treaty establishing the European Economic Community and in the interests of the common good the prevention, restriction or distortion of competition and the abuse of dominant positions in trade in the State. Articles 85 and 86 undoubtedly apply to a body corporate engaged in the supply of services even if it does not have as its object the making of commercial profits.

Reliance was placed by the defendant on the provisions of Article 90, para. 2 and Articles 92 to 94, inclusive, of the Treaty of Rome to the extent that it was suggested that the reflection of the provisions contained in those articles could be found in the exception provided in the Act of 1991 for bodies corporate engaged in the supply of services, otherwise than for gain, in so far as it would have the consequence of exempting from the provisions of the Act of 1991 such public service bodies corporate as the Voluntary Health Insurance Board and the Electricity Supply Board which, by virtue of section 21(1) of the Electricity Supply Act 1927, is subject to a restriction similar to that applied by section 4 of the Act of 1957 to the Voluntary Health Insurance Board. Even if such an aid to construction were possible, it seems to me to be ineffective. None of the provisions of Articles 90 or of Articles 92 to 94, inclusive, of the

Treaty would appear to relate to questions as to whether or not authorities or undertakings providing public or national services are formed for the object of making profits or not, and if the Construction of this section contended for by the defendant is correct, then it is probable that its consequence in Ireland would be be that the Act of 1991, so far from being a prohibition of distortion and abuse of dominant position by way of analogy to Articles 85 and 86, would be very extensively limited indeed, in its application of the provisions of those articles. **1.1.1**

I am, therefore, driven to the conclusion that the true construction of this section is that the words 'for gain' connote merely an activity carried on or a service supplied, as it is in this case, which is done in return for a charge or payment, and that, accordingly, the defendant does come within the definition of an undertaking in the Act of 1991. What would be saved from application of the Act, by reason of the insertion of the words 'engaged for gain' is, in my view, what is referred to in the judgment of Jessel MR in *In re Arthur Average Association for British, Foreign and Colonial Ships* (1875) LR 10 Ch App 542 namely, a charitable association providing the spending of money and the supply of goods or services free of any charge or payment. I would, therefore, allow this appeal, and vary the order of the High Court by declaring that the defendant does come within the definition of an undertaking contained in section 3 of the Competition Act 1991.

Hederman J.

I agree.

Egan J.

I agree.

Solicitors for the plaintiffs: *Nora Gallagher& Co.*
Solicitors for the defendant: *McCann Fitzgerald*

James Devlin, BL

1.2 Consumers

1.2.1 Competition Authority Decision No. 274, Falcon Holidays/Ben McArdle Ltd: 4 February 1994, Notification No. CA/31/92E

Oral arrangement – Tour operator obliges consumers purchasing package holidays to purchase the travel insurance policy of tour operator's broker – Insurance broker effectively acting as agent of tour operator in arranging insurance for customers – Compulsion to take policy changed to mandatory insurance requirement with option to take policy of tour operator's broker – Changed arrangement after statement of objections – View that the original arrangement was not indispensable to the aim of mandatory insurance requirement – Certificate that new arrangement does not offend against section 4(1) of Competition Act 1991 (No. 24), sections 3, 4 and 7

Facts: On 28 May 1992 notification was made to the Authority with a request for a certificate under section 4(4) of the Competition Act 1991, or failing that, a licence under section 4(2) in relation to an oral arrangement whereby Falcon Holidays made it mandatory for persons buying one of their package holidays to take travel insurance offered by the insurance broker Ben McArdle Ltd. The terms of the notified arrangement were amended after a Statement of objections had issued on 13 October 1993. On 26 November 1993 notice of intention to take a favourable decision along with an invitation to comment on the notification as described in an available summary was published.

Falcon Holidays is the trading name of Falcon Leisure Group (Overseas) Ltd ('Falcon'), a private company with its registered office in London, which carries on the business of providing package holidays in markets including the State. Ben McArdle Ltd, a private company incorporated in Ireland, is an insurance brokerage dealing with all forms of general and life insurance including travel insurance. Under the notified arrangement any customer purchasing a Falcon holiday is obliged to purchase a travel insurance policy from Ben McArdle Ltd. Each year Falcon approaches or is approached by various insurance brokers or companies in relation to the provision of holiday insurance for its travel customers and after consideration of the proposals from each of the tendering groups selects one insurance broker or company to offer insurance on a compulsory basis to all its travel customers. Falcon has a significant proportion of the Irish package holiday market and Ben McArdle Ltd estimated their share of the travel insurance market at about 20%. On the facts it appeared that the composite commission retained by Falcon, Ben McArdle Ltd and the relevant travel agent represented a significant percentage of the premium charged. The terms of the booking contract for any consumer purchasing a Falcon holiday required the consumer to be covered by the travel insurance arranged by Ben McArdle Ltd. The compulsory insurance policy covered risks such as cancellation and curtailment of holiday, medical and additional expenses, personal accident, personal baggage, personal money, travel delay and personal liability. Ben McArdle Ltd had similar arrangements with other large tour operators in the Irish market. 1.2.1

The Authority noted that in Northern Ireland, Falcon's booking form made it obligatory for the customer to have travel insurance cover but did not make it compulsory for the customer to purchase the insurance cover arranged by Falcon. An EC Directive (90/314) relating to package holidays, and not yet in force in Ireland, does not make holiday insurance mandatory but does make it mandatory for tour operators and/or travel agents to give to the customer before the start of the holiday information on insurance to cover the cost of cancellation by the customer or the cost of assistance, including repatriation, in the event of accident or illness. Following the issue of a statement of objections by the Authority to Falcon setting out why it would not be issuing a certificate or licence in respect of the notified arrangements Falcon agreed to amend the notified arrangement with effect from the 1 December 1993 to the effect that customers booking holidays with Falcon would have an option of taking Falcon's pre-arranged insurance policy or of making alternative insurance arrangements.

Decided by the Authority In issuing a certificate under section 4(4) of the Competition Act 1991 in respect of the notified arrangement that:

(1) Each of Falcon and Ben McArdle Ltd are 'undertakings' within the meaning of the Competition Act 1991.

(2) Notwithstanding that the arrangement was made orally the subject of the notification was within the scope of section 4(1) of the Competition Act 1991.

(3) Falcon in selecting Ben McArdle Ltd as its insurance broker was in effect appointing Ben McArdle Ltd as its agent to arrange travel insurance cover for Falcon customers. This in itself could not be considered to be any more anti competitive than the selection of an insurance intermediary for any other purpose.

(4) The requirement that customers of Falcon should be covered by insurance is a prudent and permissible requirement to be inserted into a contract and does not of itself offend against section 4(1) of the Competition Act 1991.

(5) The requirement that a particular insurance policy of the tour operator should be purchased offends against section 4(1) of the Competition Act 1991 because:

(i) Falcon customers are prevented from obtaining travel insurance from sources other than Ben McArdle Ltd;

(ii) customers who had adequate insurance cover through pre- existing or alternative arrangements were still obliged to take the Ben McArdle Ltd insurance policy;

(iii) the arrangement affected competition between insurance brokers and between insurers in that they were prevented from selling insurance to Falcon customers;

(iv) the arrangement prevented travel agents from selling travel insurance as had been the case heretofore;

(v) on the evidence it was established that Ben McArdle Ltd was the appointed compulsory insurance broker for other tour operators operating arrangements similar to the notified arrangement thus giving Ben McArdle Ltd a very substantial share of the travel insurance market and effectively excluding other insurance brokers and companies from the market.

(6) The amendment introduced by Falcon which retained the requirement for travel insurance but removed the compulsion to purchase the Falcon nominated insurance has the effect that the notified arrangement as amended does not offend against section

1.2.1 4(1) of the Competition Act 1991.

(7) The notified arrangements, prior to their amendment, would not have satisfied the requirements for licences as set out in section 4(2) of the Competition Act 1991 because while the effect of such an arrangement would be the provision to customers of adequate travel insurance, the requirement that such customers should compulsorily purchase the Falcon nominated insurance was not indispensable to the attainment of that aim.

Submissions of Parties

(A) Submissions made on behalf of Falcon

(1) The arrangement contributed to an improvement in the provision of services because in the event of emergency the Falcon representatives could offer full and immediate assistance in the knowledge that all customers had comprehensive travel insurance and therefore any assistance rendered by Falcon would be automatically refunded.

(2) By virtue of their experience in the travel business Falcon could negotiate a wider and more competitively priced insurance package than customers acting on their own behalf. By insisting on customers purchasing the pre-arranged insurance, Falcon was able to avoid litigation where customers had purchased an inferior insurance policy.

(3) The arrangement allowed the consumers a fair share of the resulting benefit because the policy negotiated by Falcon gave wider cover and had no exclusion by reference to age or ill-health, was priced competitively by virtue of being bought in large volume and gave the consumer the benefit of Falcon's negotiating strength in any dispute with the insurance company.

(4) Falcon did not have any long term agreement with Ben McArdle Ltd and tenders to provide insurance were invited on an annual basis. Thus the notified arrangements did not afford the possibility of eliminating competition in respect of the market for travel insurance.

(5) The requirement that consumers must take a holiday insurance policy was analogous to a tying arrangement and was fundamental to the overall package holiday arrangement.

(B) Submissions on behalf of Ben McArdle Ltd:

It was submitted that Ben McArdle Ltd did not impose mandatory insurance but simply arranged insurance cover at the request of tour operators which was imposed by those operators on a mandatory basis.

Competition Authority Decision of 4 February 1994 relating to a proceeding under section 4 of the Competition Act 1991

Notification No. CA/31/92E — Falcon Holidays/Ben McArdle

The facts

Introduction

1. On 28 May 1992, the tour operator Falcon Holidays notified the Competition Authority of an arrangement whereby they make it mandatory for persons buying Falcon package holidays to take the travel insurance offered by the insurance broker, Ben McArdle Ltd. The notification was made under section 7 of the Competition Act 1991 for a licence under section 4(2).

2. A Statement of Objections was issued to Falcon on 13 October 1993. On 8 November 1993, Falcon replied indicating their intention to amend the notified agreement. Notice of intention to issue a certificate to the amended agreement was published on 26 November 1993 and some submissions were received. **1.2.1**

Subject of the Notification

3. The notified agreement was concerned with a scheme of mandatory travel insurance whereby as a condition of every Falcon holiday package purchased, Falcon stipulated that the consumer buying the holiday was obliged to obtain travel insurance on the terms set out in the contract for the purchase of the holiday. Under an agreement with Ben McArdle Ltd, Falcon Holidays agreed the terms of an insurance policy which were set out in the holiday contract. The policy provided for a level of cover for the customers of Falcon at a price and for a duration agreed between Falcon and McArdle. Thus Falcon and McArdle agreed that all Falcon customers were obliged to obtain travel insurance through Ben McArdle Ltd.

The parties involved

4. The parties involved in this notification are Falcon Leisure Group (Overseas) Ltd trading as Falcon Holidays (Falcon) and Ben McArdle Ltd (McArdle).

Falcon

5. Falcon is the trading name of Falcon Leisure Group (Overseas) Ltd ('Falcon Overseas') a private limited company incorporated in the United Kingdom with its registered office in London. Falcon Overseas is a wholly-owned subsidiary of Owners Abroad plc ('Owners Abroad') a public limited company incorporated in the United Kingdom and having its registered office at the same address as that of Falcon Overseas. Owners Abroad carries on business through a number of wholly owned subsidiaries (the 'Group'). The Group is, broadly speaking, engaged in the travel business including the provision of retail services, inclusive holiday packages, aviation services, ground handling and foreign agency services. The total annual turnover of Falcon Overseas is Stg£23.5 million.

6. The wholly-owned subsidiary of Owners Abroad which carries on business in the State is the UK company Falcon Leisure Group (Overseas) Ltd which trades under the name Falcon Holidays. In Northern Ireland another wholly-owned subsidiary of Owners Abroad viz. Owners Abroad Tour Operations Ltd carries on business under the trading names 'Martyns Holidays' and 'Enterprise Holidays'.

7. Falcon is a tour operator which provides a package holiday product incorporating flights, accommodation, transfers and the services of a holiday representative. It has been operating in the State for over five years and is licensed by the Minister for Transport, Energy and Communications as a tour operator under the Transport Act 1982. Falcon specialises in providing package holidays and is not involved in the sale or marketing of any other form of travel product. Its holidays are marketed by the vast majority of licensed travel agents. Falcon is one of the top four operators operating within the State. Its annual turnover in respect of sales in the Republic of Ireland is IR£13 million. The Authority understands that consumers cannot book a holiday with Falcon directly and that they must always book through a travel agent.

McArdle

8. Ben McArdle Ltd is an insurance broker dealing with all forms of general and life assurance including travel insurance. The company does not specialise in the provision of any one form of insurance. It is a private limited company incorporated in Ireland.

9. Each year Falcon approaches or is approached by various insurance brokers/companies for example Durhams, D.G. Dunbar Ltd, Accident and General, AMEV and McArdle in relation to the provision of holiday insurance for its travel customers. Falcon considers the policies offered in terms of the level of cover, the cost of the policies and the service offered

1.2.1 and makes its decision as to the policy which it will choose accordingly. For the past few years Falcon has chosen the travel insurance policy offered by McArdle. McArdle acts on behalf of a number of tour operators providing travel insurance cover on a mandatory basis to some and on a non-mandatory basis to others. At each renewal McArdle contacts all insurers writing in the Irish market who might be interested in writing travel insurance business. They receive a number of quotations from interested insurers but the majority express no interest in quoting for this class of business. Having obtained a number of quotations from various insurers, McArdle then offers to their client (the holiday tour operators) the best package which combines cover levels and premium cost.

The product and the market

10. The product/service involved in this notification is package holiday travel insurance. It is a package policy underwritten by non-life companies. It includes elements of property, travel and personal accident insurance, with in some cases motor related cover. All Irish tour operators selling overseas holidays require their customers to have adequate insurance cover and in most cases this cover is arranged by the tour operators. The market is the market for travel insurance for package holidays. On the basis of information supplied to the Department of Transport, Energy and Communications by all tour operators, 175,000 passengers were carried to the sun spot destinations in the course of the tour operator summer season in 1991. Falcon themselves estimate that for the year 1991 (including both Winter and Summer Seasons) the total number of passengers was 190,000 and the total turnover in the market was IR£62.5m. The four major tour operators are Falcon, Budget Travel, Joe Walsh Tours and Abbey Sun (now Sunworld). Recent publicity* quoted a figure of £75m as the national package holiday market for the year up to September 1992, and estimated that both Falcon and Budget each had between 35% and 40% of the Irish package holiday market.

11. Total turnover in the market for travel insurance in the State for the year ended 31 December 1991, was estimated by McArdle to be IR£4m – IR£5m. McArdle estimated that their share of this market was about 20%. This included all travel insurance including sales to the retail travel agents and to tour operators who did not carry mandatory insurance. The principal authorised and approved competitors of McArdle who place travel insurance are Durhams, D.G. Dunbar Ltd, Accident and General (brokers) and AMEV (insurance company).

The arrangements

12. Prior to January 1991, travel insurance was mandatory in Ireland at the insistence of the tour operators but the travel agent through whom the particular holiday was being booked had a choice of offering either the policy negotiated by the tour operators or an alternative policy which accorded with the level of cover offered by the policy arranged by the tour operators. Since January 1991, Falcon has required all its customers to take out the insurance policy which they had negotiated with their insurance broker. Falcon stipulated that any customer purchasing one of its package holidays must take out travel insurance on the terms of the policy set out in its brochures.

13. Each year Falcon invites tenders and negotiates annually with a number of insurance brokers and selects what is, in its opinion, the best insurance policy available in terms of price and level of cover. The policy provides for a level of cover for the customers of Falcon at a price and for a duration agreed between Falcon and the insurance broker. The policy of insurance, the support of this notification, was that sold to Falcon by McArdle and for which McArdle tendered competitively. As a consequence of this arrangement, any customer who booked and purchased a Falcon holiday since January 1991 was obliged to obtain travel insurance on the terms agreed by Falcon and McArdle. The agreement between Falcon and McArdle was a verbal one. The agreement operated from the Winter season 1991-1992, of the

**Business and Finance,* 11 February 1993 and 26 August 1993.

Summer season 1992, the Winter season 1992-1993, the Summer season 1993 and was intended to operate for the Winter season 1993-1994. 1.2.1

14. For the 5-year period 1989 to 1993 the insurance premia charged by Falcon/McArdle for a 2 week sun package holiday to a European destination were as follows:

	Adult Price	*Children's Price*	*Total 2 Adults and 2 Children*
	IR£	IR£	IR£
1989	17.50	13.12	61.24
1990	18.50	19.50	74.00
1991	20.00	20.00	80.00
1992	24.00	12.00	72.00
1993	25.00	12.50	75.00

The cover provided by Falcon/McArdle was set out in the following sections of the 1991/1992 insurance policy:

(1) cancellations and curtailment up to holiday cost,
(2) medical and additional expenses – £500,000,
(3) personal accident — up to £40,000,
(4) personal baggage — £1,000,
(5) personal money — £100,
(6) travel delay,
(7) personal liability.

The insurance policy also set out general conditions, general exclusions and exclusions under each section. It stated that the insurance was underwritten by certain underwriters at Lloyds.

15. In all cases customers book holidays with Falcon through travel agents and the insurance premia are paid directly to travel agents as part of the deposit payable by the customer on the cost of the holiday. The travel agents retain IR£6.75 of the adult premium by way of commission and then remit the balance of monies received by them directly to Falcon. Under the agreement between Falcon and McArdle, Falcon retain approximately 40% of the adult premia paid by the holidaymakers before transferring the balance in relation to travel insurance to McArdle. Falcon absorb most of the 50% reduction in premium level in respect of children. Children can account for up to 33% of all passengers carried, and therefore the weighted average margin retained by Falcon is in the range of £6.75 – £7.00. Falcon claimed that, in addition, very considerable expense, including freight costs, is frequently absorbed by Falcon where emergencies occur while customers are on holiday and they have to be brought home quickly. Based on the 1993 adult premium of £25 and child premium of £12.50 for a 2 week package holiday, the breakdown of the premia payments is as follows:

	Adult	Child
	£	£
Travel Agent	6.75 (27%)	3.38 (27%)
Falcon	9.98 (40%)	0.85 (7%)
McArdle	8.27 (33%)	8.27 (66%)
	25.00	12.50

Since it may be presumed that part of the remittance is retained by McArdle, it appears that as little as 25% of the adult premium paid goes towards the insurance cover provided.

16. When a consumer booked a Falcon package holiday s/he was obliged to pay an insurance premium as part of the deposit for the holiday. The booking conditions formed part of the

1.2.1 booking form which had to be signed by the consumer. The booking conditions, *inter alia*, stated:

> No contract shall arise until the organiser has received this complete booking form together with a deposit or full payment for the holiday and has issued written confirmation of its acceptance to the retailer. The terms of contract are contained solely in this booking form, the organiser's confirmation, the organiser's brochure or other descriptive material, any airline or sailing ticket issued and the itinerary issued by the organiser.
>
> The holiday must be paid for in full at least 8 weeks before the schedule date of departure. If it is not paid by that date, the organiser shall have the option to cancel the holiday. If the organiser exercises that option or if the consumer cancels the holiday (which cancellation must be notified in writing to the organiser) the following cancellation charges are payable by the consumer:
>
> More than 6 weeks before the departure date any deposit paid shall be forfeited:

Within 6-4 weeks of departure:
30% of the cost of the holiday is forfeited.
Within 4-2 weeks of departure:
45% of the cost of the holiday is forfeited.
Within 2 weeks – 72 hours of departure:
60% of the cost of the holiday is forfeited.
Within 72 hours of departure:
100% of the cost of the holiday is forfeited.

> All cancellation charges apply to each person covered by a booking. Any insurance premium paid is not refundable.
>
> It is a condition of this contract that the consumer is covered by the travel insurance scheme arranged by the organiser. It is the responsibility of the consumer to check that the insurance scheme provides the consumer with his desired level of cover. In so arranging insurance cover for the consumer the organiser is acting as the agent of the relevant insurer and shall not be responsible to the consumer for any default by the insurer under that policy. All claims made against the insurance policy shall be made directly to the insurer. The consumer shall be responsible for making any special or increased insurance arrangements which he deems necessary.

The booking form for Falcon Holidays stated that 'holiday insurance is compulsory and is arranged automatically (and the premium added to your invoice)'.

17. The arrangements operated by Falcon were part of overall wider arrangements in the travel trade. According to the Irish Travel Agents Association, several tour operators, but not all had introduced mandatory travel insurance for approximately 10 years prior to January 1991. It was done on an individual basis by the tour operators. During this period, it is understood that a number of insurance brokers brought out a range of policies offering higher cover at a similar price to the tour operators and these were offered to holiday customers by the retail agents. According to an article in Irish Travel Trade News (ITTN) at the time the commission offered to retail agents by the insurance brokers was much higher than tour operators were paying the retail agents in commission of their travel insurance arrangements. The Retail Council and the Tour Operators Council of the ITAA met after the 1990 AGM on 12 December 1990 to discuss mandatory insurance and commission levels. The following is an extract from the Minutes of that meeting:

'it was acknowledged by everyone at the meeting that the question of MANDATORY insurance and the level of commission available on such insurance was a matter of vital importance to both tour operators and retail agents. Both sides approached the issue in a constructive manner, and it was clear from the outset that compromise was needed on both sides if a solution was to be found. Following difficult negotiations, it was agreed that the Tour Operators Council and Retail Council would adopt the following arrangements for the next two years. 1.2.1

— The insurance arranged by tour operators will be sold with all package holidays.

— Tour operators will pay £6.50 commission on the insurance element of every package.

— All tour operators will submit details of the cover provided in their insurance policies to the chief executive who will have them independently and professionally vetted, to ensure that they provide an acceptable level of cover and benefits.

The retail council representatives accepted that while the agreed arrangement was not an ideal solution, it was, nonetheless, a fair and reasonable outcome to an issue which is potentially very divisive and damaging for the entire industry. The Tour Operators Representatives, while stressing the negative revenue implications for wholesalers of the increased commission, were unanimous in their acceptance of the arrangement, and agreed to implement it fully in their own companies.

18. However, according to the Irish Travel Trade News' article mentioned above, in January 1991 the Dublin Chapter of the ITAA rejected the above arrangements but they were accepted or at least not rejected by all other chapters of the ITAA. In November 1991 the AGM of the ITAA rejected mandatory insurance by a majority of 4 to 1 according to ITTN. It was accepted and recommended by the ITAA also at the AGM in November 1991 that every client should have adequate travel insurance but the particular policy should be optional so as to allow for the best possible choice.

EC legislation

19. An EC Directive (90/314) on package travel, package holidays and package tours was adopted by the EC Consumer Affairs Ministers' Council on 13 June 1990. The Directive lays down obligations for package organisers/retailers and safeguards for the consumer. It applies to packages offered or sold in the territory of the community viz., any two combinations of transport, accommodation or 'other tourist service'. Both packages with a destination outside the EC and within the member states are affected. The Directive is expected to be brought into force by regulation in this country shortly by the Department of Transport, Energy and Communications. Enforcement will be the responsibility of the Director of Consumer Affairs.

20. Article 4.1(b)(iv) of the Directive provides that the organiser and/or retailer shall provide the consumer with the following information before the start of the journey:

> information on the optional conclusion of an insurance policy to cover the cost of cancellation by the consumer or the cost of assistance, including repatriation, in the event of an accident or illness.

The Directive, therefore, does not make holiday insurance mandatory. In addition, the approach of the Department of Transport, Energy and Communication will be to provide that the implementation regulations will require that the following should be supplied to the consumer before the start of the journey:

> information about an insurance policy which the consumer may, if he wishes, take out in order to cover the cost of cancellation by the consumer or the cost of assistance, including repatriation in the event of accident or illness except where the consumer is required as a term of the contract to take out an insurance policy in order to cover these risks in which case the information must be given before the contract is concluded.

This proposed 'amplification' of the Directive text by the Department of Transport, Energy

1.2.1 and Communications is in line with the Regulations made by the UK Authorities to implement the EC Directive in that country.

21. The proposed implementation of the Directive by the Department of Transport, Energy and Communication also elaborates on the information to be supplied to the consumer before the conclusion of the package holiday contract as follows:

> if applicable, the minimum level of insurance cover required by the organiser to cover the cost of cancellation by the consumer or the cost of assistance, including repatriation in the event of accident or illness, but so that nothing in these regulations authorises an organiser to make it compulsory for the intending consumer to purchase any specified insurance policy.

Northern Ireland situation

22. The booking form used in Northern Ireland by Falcon (using the trading names 'Martyns Holidays' and 'Enterprise Holidays') for the 1992 Summer season contains the following provisions in relation to insurance;

— Holiday insurance is arranged automatically (and the premium added to your invoice) unless you or your travel agent have arranged, and supplied us with details of, alternative comparable cover.

— If you have not taken out insurance please complete the following:
My/our insurers are:
24 hour emergency telephone:
with whom I have taken a policy giving comparable or greater cover than that offered in this brochure.
Signed:

It can be seen from the above that Northern Ireland customers have a choice of taking the insurance policy offered by Falcon or making their own insurance arrangements and notifying Falcon.

UK developments

23. In March 1993, the UK Office of Fair Trading (OFT) issued a press release warning holidaymakers to beware of the insistence by travel agents that clients take out travel insurance especially where the agents themselves marketed insurance policies. The OFT stated that the EC Directive which came into force on 31 December 1992 in the UK did not require holiday makers to take out travel insurance. While they considered it a wise precaution to take out such insurance, they advised customers to shop around and compare costs because insurance represented a significant proportion of the total price of a holiday.

24. The press release further stated that although there was no legal requirement for anyone to take out insurance when travelling abroad, most tour operators made it a condition of their contracts that holidaymakers arrange adequate cover. This was quite legal. It was a matter of company policy, rather than a legal requirement however. Customers could either take out the insurance offered by the operator or where possible make alternative arrangements. If a customer decided to arrange insurance independently, he or she might have to sign an undertaking to arrange cover which was comparable to that offered by the tour operator.

Summary

25. Falcon made it mandatory for persons buying Falcon package holidays to take the travel insurance offered by McArdle. Other tour operators acted in a similar fashion. Only a small proportion of the premium paid related to the actual cost of the insurance. EC Directive 90/314 provides that travel insurance should be optional and not mandatory. In implementing the Directive into Irish law, the Department of Transport, Energy and Communication are

proposing that travel insurance should be optional. While they recognise and accept that some tour operators make the taking out of travel insurance mandatory, the proposed regulations are not to be seen as authorising tour operators to make a specified insurance policy compulsory. In Northern Ireland the situation is that tour operators only provide travel insurance if the traveller has not arranged comparable cover himself. In the North, therefore, travel insurance is mandatory but the traveller has the choice of arranging cover himself or accepting the tour operators insurance cover. In the UK the situation is that travel insurance is not compulsory but is regarded by the authorities as being a wise precaution and it was perfectly legal for tour operators to make it a condition of the holiday contract that holidaymakers arrange adequate insurance cover either themselves or through the tour operators. **1.2.1**

Views of the parties

Falcon

26. Falcon stated that the introduction of mandatory insurance by them in January 1991 under which Falcon customers were obliged to take out the travel insurance policy which Falcon had negotiated with their insurance broker was motivated by developments in the industry and particularly by experiences in holiday resorts. This arrangement necessarily resulted in certain restrictions on the travel agents, through whom consumers booked holidays with Falcon, and on the consumers themselves. The arrangement prevented the travel agents and consumers from taking independent commercial decisions because:

— The travel agents were prevented from offering holidaymakers alternative schemes for travel insurance. In the absence of the Falcon mandatory insurance arrangement, travel agents could potentially negotiate with insurance brokers and arrange schemes for travel insurance separately from that provided by Falcon.

— Consumers similarly were not given any choice as to the form of travel insurance they could take or the broker or insurance company from whom they could obtain such travel insurance. The arrangement ensured that any customer booking a Falcon holiday took out the policy of travel insurance negotiated between Falcon and McArdle.

27. Falcon stated that the arrangement contributed to an improvement in the provision of services in a number of ways:

— As a consequence of the mandatory insurance provisions in its holiday packages, Falcon was assured that, in every case, customers purchasing Falcon package holidays had comprehensive travel insurance. Consequently, its representatives in the various resorts (a) were assured that in the event of an emergency e.g. death, serious injury or loss of money or property, the individual concerned had insurance cover upon which the premiums were fully paid, (b) immediately knew the identity of the insurance broker and company to contact and (c) were aware of the procedures to be put in place to provide medical or other assistance. Under the arrangements with McArdle the customer through Falcon was provided with 24 hour emergency assistance. Customers could therefore be offered full and immediate assistance should an emergency occur in the course of their holiday. In the absence of such an arrangement, Falcon would be reluctant to provide assistance to holidaymakers in the event of an emergency as it could not be assured that a customer had any or adequate holiday insurance and that any cost incurred by Falcon in providing assistance would automatically be refunded.

— Falcon, because it had negotiated the terms of the policy itself and on behalf of its customers, could be satisfied that its customers had purchased the widest available cover at the most competitive price, with no restrictions as to age or pre-existing disability and no onerous pre-conditions or exclusions. A customer acting on his own behalf might not have obtained such cover.

1.2.1 — Because of the mandatory insurance, there was no risk for Falcon that in selling the package holiday it would be identified with inadequate or defective travel insurance sold by the travel agent and there was, therefore, no danger that Falcon would thus have to defend costly litigation, in respect of matters not covered by such defective or inadequate holiday insurance, which could potentially arise.

— Because of the mandatory insurance, the travel agents, through whom holidays with Falcon were booked, reduced the risk of problems arising for themselves because the insurance policy which the customer might have had independently arranged might prove to be defective.

28. Falcon also stated that the arrangement allowed consumers a fair share of the resulting benefit for the following reasons:

— The fact that Falcon insisted on insurance being mandatory and in accordance with a previously agreed policy enabled Falcon to provide an immediate service to its customer should an emergency occur. This assistance was of obvious practical importance and benefit to the customer at a time of distress. If no travel insurance had been obtained by the customer or if travel insurance had been obtained elsewhere, Falcon would not be in the same position with regard to providing help and assistance and the customer might have difficulty in making contact with the travel agent or insurance broker who had arranged his policy.

— In booking a Falcon holiday, the consumer was assured of insurance cover regardless of his age or state of health as the policy which Falcon had arranged gave cover in wider circumstances with no exclusion of pre-existing disability. It was common for other policies of travel insurance to exclude claims arising from pre-existing disability.*

— The insurance policy provided by Falcon included cover for cancellation of the holiday. As the customer mandatorily acquired insurance at the time he booked the holiday, he was assured of cover should he, for whatever reason, be forced subsequently to cancel his holiday. Without mandatory insurance, there was a risk that the consumer might be forced to cancel his holiday before he had obtained travel insurance, and might therefore lose a substantial proportion of the cost of the holiday already paid.

— Consumers typically and understandably did not have enough experience or expertise in relation to insurance to be able to fully assess the merits of any particular policy of travel insurance. Consumers booking holidays with Falcon were provided with as comprehensive a policy as possible.

— The cost of the holiday to the consumer was reduced because the deduction which Falcon made from the insurance premium paid by the consumer enabled Falcon to reduce the cost of its holidays. Falcon was also enabled to negotiate a reduced premium for the insurance as it was, in effect, arranging for the buying in bulk from McArdle, which also had beneficial effects for consumers.

— In the event of any dispute arising with the insurance broker or company, the consumer had the benefit of the negotiating strength which Falcon had because of its position in the market. If McArdle wished to retain the contract with Falcon for the following year, it was in its interest to ensure a proper and efficient service to customers of Falcon.

— The cost of the travel insurance acquired by the consumer under his contract with Falcon was in line with the cost of travel insurance available elsewhere and was lower than that charged by a number of insurance companies.

*In relation to this particular point, the Competition Authority notes that the insurance policy between Falcon and McArdle *inter alia* confirms the following exclusions:

— Any claim arising from travel or holiday arrangements made against the advice of any medical practitioner.

— Any claim arising consequent upon pregnancy within five months of the expected date of delivery.

29. Falcon stated that the arrangements did not impose on the undertakings concerned terms which were not indispensable to the attainment of the objectives outlined above. The benefits with regard to improved service which were directly passed on to consumers could only be achieved if insurance was mandatory and by way of a pre-arranged comprehensive policy. 1.2.1

30. Falcon stated that the arrangements did not afford either Falcon or McArdle the possibility of eliminating competition in respect of the market for travel insurance. Falcon did not have any long term agreement or arrangement with McArdle. Tenders were invited on an annual basis for the provision of holiday insurance. McArdle was also not precluded from selling travel insurance to any consumer who approached it and wished to purchase travel insurance from it independently. Customers of Falcon were not precluded from purchasing extra holiday insurance cover elsewhere.

31. Falcon stated, that travel insurance by its nature and in accordance with commercial usage was inextricably linked with the subject of a package holiday. Falcon did not impose any supplementary obligations. In their view section 4(1) of the Competition Act did not apply to the notified arrangements.

32. Falcon referred to a number of block exemptions and decisions in EC law particularly to 'tying' arrangements which involved a 'tying product' for which the customer had a particular demand and a 'tied product' which was supplied on condition that the purchaser also bought the tying product. Falcon submitted that, while the EC had not specifically exempted arrangements equivalent to that which was the subject of this notification, the requirement that consumers take out mandatory holiday insurance when booking a Falcon package holiday was analogous to a tying arrangement and was fundamental to the overall package holiday arrangement.

McArdle

33. McArdle stated in its submission to the Competition Authority that as members of the Irish Broking Association, they complied with the requirements of the Insurance Act 1989. McArdle stated that it did not impose mandatory insurance but simply arranged insurance cover at the request of tour operators which was imposed by them on a mandatory basis. It was their understanding however that some brokers from the UK and a local Irish agent, who operated in the Irish market for travel insurance, were not authorised intermediaries under the Act; some of these intermediaries were also placing business into unauthorised insurance markets and, despite objections by McArdle to the Department of Enterprise and Employment, no action was taken according to McArdle.

Views of third parties

Irish Travel Agents Association (ITAA)

34. ITAA stated that no comprehensive survey had been conducted with each member of the Association to establish his or her views on the subject of mandatory insurance. However a majority of members present at the Association's annual general meeting in November 1991 appeared to express the view that travel insurance should be mandatory but with choice. The Association, incorporating the views of both travel agent and tour operator, felt very strongly that mandatory insurance should remain an integral part of the holiday package. In support of this view, the ITAA pointed out that many types of insurance cover on the market did not offer, for example, cancellation loss, whereby a holiday maker due to last minute change of plans for valid reasons would forfeit possibly the total cost if s/he could not go on holiday.

Irish Brokers Association (IBA)

35. The Association stated that its members were affected by the mandatory travel insurance arrangements in a number of ways. It denied some members of IBA the ability to compete in

1.2.1 terms of cover, price and service with the insurances provided on a mandatory basis by tour operators. IBA brokers had available to them comprehensive travel insurance packages, which allowed them to insure their clients on an all year round basis, for both their business and for their pleasure travel. It was a source of frequent aggravation and annoyance to some IBA brokers, and particularly to their clients, who had such cover, that, when they wished to purchase a package holiday, tour operators should force additional, unnecessary, and inferior cover on them. It was generally accepted that the mandatory travel insurance arrangements, operated by various tour operators, were frequently inferior to travel insurance packages which were available in the insurance market.

36. Many IBA members had complained that they, as insurance brokers, had been required to effect mandatory travel insurance arrangements by tour operators when they, as brokers, in their professional capacity, had the ability to arrange superior cover at competitive prices through their own businesses. However travel insurance was not regarded by brokers as core business and consequently did not represent a significant portion of their premium income.

37. IBA said that fundamentally they objected to the practice of mandatory travel insurance being arranged by tour operators, as it resulted in many persons who had comprehensive all year round cover being required to waste money on an unnecessary and inferior product. This practice also prevented insurance brokers from competing directly in this market with the products which were offered by a number of major insurers, which were both more cost competitive and more comprehensive in terms of protection afforded to the clients.

Irish Insurance Federation

38. The Federation stated that whenever any supplier of a service imposed a pre-selected, mandatory insurance cover on his client, he thereby restricted the consumer's freedom of choice, and from the point of view of insurers, a potential market was closed off. This was particularly the case where an independent, competitive market existed for the cover in question as it did for travel insurance. The existence of mandatory travel insurance arrangements operated by individual tour operators and, or travel agents therefore restricted the travel insurance market available to those of their members writing that type of policy.

39. The Federation also stated that their members were strongly of the view that the imposition of mandatory travel insurance on package holiday clients of tour operators or travel agents was wholly undesirable as being a reduction of consumer rights of choice and curtailment of the normal competitive and commercial life of the insurance market. It appeared that a substantial proportion of travel insurance business, particularly under the mandatory scheme, was in fact being written by unlicensed insurers. Therefore contracts of insurance taken out by clients of the tour operators involved were not enforceable, (e.g., in the event of a claim dispute) and indeed were illegal under insurance supervisory law.

Department of Enterprise and Employment

40. The policy of the Department was that persons purchasing holiday insurance should have a choice of insurer. Any insurance, compulsory or otherwise, should be placed through an insurer authorised to do business in the State. The provision of unauthorised insurance was a matter for that Department and allegations about difficulties in this regard in the travel insurance area were the subject of ongoing investigation.

The Consumers' Association of Ireland (CAI)

41. The Consumers' Association of Ireland (CAI) believed that the mandatory insurance arrangements operated by Falcon were restrictive and anti-competitive. While they considered that every person who travelled should be insured, they believed that customers should have the right to select their own insurance, tailored to their own personal needs. The Association expressed concern about the cost element of compulsory insurance. Their research had shown that despite the facts that insurance cover was on a 'bulk rate' basis to the tour operator, a fair

share of the resulting benefit was not passed on to the consumer. 1.2.1

42. A survey carried out and published in the CAI magazine 'Consumer Choice' in May 1992 compared the costs and benefits of travel insurance offered by 8 tour operators, 6 insurance companies and 2 charge card companies. The details related to one adult to a European destination. The premia varied from £17 – £24 per person for a period varying between 14 and 31 days. All the policies provided for personal accident to cover death and disability. The charge card companies provided the highest cover (£75,000 and £100,000). The policies provided for medical expenses varying from £1m. to an unlimited amount in many cases. There was provision in all the policies for baggage loss and baggage delays with most setting limits per item for loss. Loss of money or passport was not covered by the charge card companies. Cancellation was covered by all the policies with the exception of the charge cards and generally the amount varied from £1,500 to final invoice cost. Travel delays and public liability were also provided for. Many of the policies had other benefits which covered legal expenses, missed departure and hospital inconvenience cover abroad.

43. The CAI survey also makes reference to the then new VHI service for their members who became ill or have an accident abroad. The service known as 'VHI assist' was launched in March 1992. It is available to all VHI members with plans A to E cover, without payment of additional subscription as they renew their cover from 1 March 1992. On renewal, VHI members receive an identity card giving the telephone number of a medical emergency centre capable of giving immediate and expert assistance in any part of the world, on a 24 hours-a-day basis. The maximum benefit ranges from £3,750 (Plan A) to £13,500 (Plan E). The CAI survey also refers to Form E 111 which entitles persons travelling to an EC country except Britain, where it is not necessary, to free emergency health care. It gives some cover towards the cost of drugs, hospitalisation and general medical treatment in the event of injury or accident. The CAI survey states that Form E 111 should not be regarded as a substitute for private holiday insurance.

Director of Consumer Affairs (Director)

44. The Director of Consumer Affairs in a submission to the Authority stated that the decision to make certain travel insurance policies compulsory had been taken by the Irish tour operators themselves and the practice was of some concern to him. He believed that the booking conditions/contract (para. 16 above) which was standard to all ITAA members restricted the consumer and also restricted competition. While a great majority of consumers might opt for the organiser's own insurance package for the sake of convenience, the Director felt it would be unwise to assume that consumers should not have a choice or indeed want a choice or that competition was not possible in this area. There were for example, a number of insurance packages which were designed for the non-standard package holiday or for open-ended travel and it was absolutely certain that more packages could be designed and marketed in the event that exclusive insurance arrangements, like the Falcon/McArdle one, ceased.

45. The Director believed that the tour organiser was under no legal or contractual obligation to provide services to holidaymakers in the event of a problem arising in the course of a holiday. It was appreciated than in many cases tour operator representatives did help out but this could not be relied upon as a justification for a particular form of insurance being made compulsory. The Director had no objection to insurance, per se, being made compulsory for consumers buying package holidays or to a certain minimum level of cover being insisted upon.

46. The Director stated that it was not clear to what extent insurance companies provided insured travellers with services such as the arranging of flights home, but it was clear, however, that the tour operator took no responsibility because the contract stated that 'in so arranging insurance cover for the consumer the organiser is acting as the agent of the relevant insurer and shall not be responsible to the consumer for any default by the insurer under that policy. All claims made against the insurance policy shall be made directly to the insurer'.

47. The Director also stated that complaints had been received from consumers about extra

1.2.1 costs, lack of choice and possible reduced cover resulting from mandatory insurance. In some cases consumers had argued that they could get a standard insurance package cheaper than the compulsory package. In other cases consumers had already paid for insurance by way of annual policies or by having it included in their credit card arrangements (e.g. with gold cards). In a number of cases consumers had complained about the compulsory insurance over-rode earlier insurance (annual or credit card) and gave them less favourable insurance than they otherwise would have had. It was possible that compulsory insurance would not meet consumers' full needs. This was acknowledged in the standard booking conditions/contract where it was stated that 'it is the responsibility of the consumer to check that the insurance scheme provides the consumer with his desired level of cover'. Furthermore the standard booking conditions/contract states that 'the consumer shall be responsible for making any special or increased insurance arrangements which he deems necessary'. The Director points out that it was almost certainly more expensive to make travel insurance arrangements by means of two policies than it was with one policy only, e.g. administration charges would be doubled.

48. The Director considered that the agreement of December 1990 between the Retail Council and the Tour Operators Council of ITAA (para 17 above) changed the policy which had operated prior to that in relation to consumer contracts. This agreement became part of the standard ITAA booking conditions and applied to all ITAA members and appeared to be a concerted practice which restricted competition according to the Director. The Director also maintained that it had not been demonstrated that the practice contributed to improving the provision of services while allowing consumers a fair share of the resulting benefit. The Director, therefore, submitted that a licence should not be granted by the Competition Authority in respect of the Falcon/McArdle arrangements on mandatory travel insurance.

Consumer complaints to the Authority

49. There have been many complaints to the Competition Authority from members of the public who were forced to take the particular policy on offer by tour operators. In some cases customers were booking seats only. In other cases customers felt that they were adequately covered by private arrangements e.g. Premier Visa card, and, therefore, felt that the mandatory insurance being imposed on them by tour operators was unnecessary. Not all of these complaints referred to Falcon Holidays. It was pointed out that the Authority had no power to investigate arrangements which had not been notified to it.

Subsequent developments

50. Following the issue of the Statement of Objections by the Authority, Falcon agreed to amend the notified arrangements. Falcon agreed, by letter dated 8 November 1993, that customers booking holidays with Falcon would have the option of taking Falcon's pre-arranged insurance policy or of making alternative arrangements for insurance as and from 1 December 1993. They stated that customers might have to sign an undertaking that they would organise their own insurance cover. They also stated that it seemed to be implicit in the Statement of Objections that the Authority would have no objection to such arrangements.

51. Following publication on 26 November 1993 of its intention to take a favourable decision on the amended arrangements, the Authority received a number of observations from third parties. Joe Walsh Tours Ltd stated that under the existing mandatory insurance arrangement, the tour organiser was in a position to pay the cost of providing a linking service with the Assistance Company and the Underwriter from the gross profit earned from the sale of that insurance policy. In the event of a holidaymaker arranging an alternative policy to that arranged by the tour organiser, the tour organiser received no commission/handling fee to cover such costs. In the event of the Authority publishing its decision in the Falcon/McArdle case, JWT stated that they would propose charging a handling fee to the consumer/retailer to cover such costs. It has also come to the notice of the Authority that the tour operator Sunworld has instructed travel agents to charge an administrative fee of £6 per adult and £3 per child under

16 years, from 4 January 1994, to customers who opt for holiday insurance cover other than that provided under Sunworld's own policy. Falcon stated that one of its competitors charged an administration fee, another insisted that no bonus commission would be provided unless the travel agent purchased insurance from the travel company, and a third operated a similar scheme and, in addition, insisted that, to obtain their low family deposit on holidays, their insurance must be purchased. Falcon, however, have not imposed any such charges in order to keep to the spirit of the undertaking which it gave to the Authority. **1.2.1**

Assessment

(a) *Applicability of section 4(1)*

52. Section 4(1) of the Competition Act 1991 prohibits and renders void all arrangements between undertakings, decisions by associations of undertakings and concerted practices which have as their object or effect the prevention, restriction or distortion of competition in trade in any goods or services in the State, or in any part of the State.

(b) *The Undertakings*

53. The term 'undertaking' is defined in section 3(1) of the Competition Act 1991 as follows:

> a person being an individual, a body corporate or an unincorporated body of persons engaged for gain in the production, supply or distribution of goods or the provision of a service.

54. The parties to the arrangement, as notified, Falcon Holidays and Ben McArdle Ltd, are both corporate bodies engaged for gain in the provision of holiday travel and insurance services, respectively and are, therefore, undertakings as defined in the Competition Act.

(c) *The Agreement*

55. The agreement as notified was a verbal one between the parties relating to the Winter season 1991/1992, the Summer season 1992, the Winter season 1992/1993, the Summer season 1993 and was intended to operate for the Winter season 1993/1994. Even though it was not written it was still an agreement within the meaning of section 4(1) of the Act. It is clear from the facts outlined above that the arrangements also form part of a wider practice involving the travel trade generally because most of the other tour operators also insist that their customers take out the particular insurance policy contained in the contracts for the purchase of their holidays. In this decision, however, the Authority is only concerned with the Falcon/McArdle agreement, i.e. the agreement as notified whereby Falcon/McArdle agreed that all Falcon customers were obliged to obtain travel insurance through Ben McArdle Ltd, and its subsequent amendment.

(d) *Object and effects of the Agreement*

56. The State alone can impose a legal obligation on the public to take out insurance, e.g. motor insurance. Even then the State does not stipulate a particular insurance broker/company but leaves it to the member of the public affected to choose his own insurance broker/company. As mentioned previously the State imposes no obligation on a holidaymaker to take out holiday insurance when going abroad. Falcon and other tour operators in Ireland do however impose such an obligation on holidaymakers. While this restricts the freedom of choice of consumers as to whether they purchase insurance or not, the Competition Authority does not consider that that restriction offends against section 4(1) of the Competition Act because it does not prevent, restrict, or distort competition in the markets for holiday insurance or for package holidays. Indeed it seems logical and prudent for Irish holidaymakers going abroad to have adequate travel insurance. The imposition of a requirement to take out insurance implies that a minimum

1.2.1 level of cover would have to be specified.[1] This does not mean, however, that a tour operator's particular insurance policy should be imposed on its customers.

57. The arrangements as notified provided that holidaymakers booking Falcon package holidays were obliged to take out the travel insurance agreed between Falcon and McArdle. This was mandatory on the Falcon holidaymaker who had no choice in the matter and who was thus prevented from securing insurance from other sources. This clearly restricted competition in that Falcon customers were prevented from obtaining travel insurance other than from McArdle. Even customers who were satisfied that their private insurance arrangements were adequate to cover them while on holidays abroad were nevertheless obliged to take the Falcon/McArdle insurance policy. The arrangements also affected competition between insurance brokers and between insurers in that they were prevented from selling insurance to Falcon customers. It must be remembered that Falcon is one of the major tour operators in the State with a market share of around 20% of the package holiday market. This represents a significant share of the package holiday insurance market which was effectively foreclosed because Falcon customers were obliged to take the insurance policy offered by McArdle and were precluded from approaching other insurance brokers or insurers. In addition the Authority understands that McArdle had similar arrangements with the two tour operators Corona and Joe Walsh Tours and that in the past both Budget Travel and Abbey Sun had made the McArdle insurance package mandatory for their customers. A large part of the holiday insurance business was therefore provided exclusively by McArdles with the result that other insurance brokers and insurance companies had been virtually excluded from the market. This arrangement also prevented travel agents from selling travel insurance as they had done in the past. The Falcon/McArdle agreement, as notified, therefore, offended against section 4(1) of the Act.

58. In the Authority's view Falcon is perfectly entitled to offer its holiday insurance package to its customers provided it is made clear that there is no compulsion on the customer to take that particular insurance policy. This does not offend against section 4(1) of the Act.

59. The Authority appreciates that Falcon, in selecting McArdle as its insurance broker, was in effect appointing an agent to arrange travel insurance cover for its customers and on Falcon's behalf. This, in itself, cannot be considered to be anti-competitive any more than the selection of an insurance intermediary for any other purpose could be so considered. This does not offend against section 4(1).

60. While the Authority is only concerned with the notified agreement between Falcon and McArdle, it appears that almost all tour operators in the State operated a scheme of mandatory travel insurance. This made it feasible for Falcon to operate their particular scheme. Furthermore, the December 1990 agreement between the Retail Council and Tour Operators Council of ITAA (para. 17) specified that over the following two years, only the insurance policies arranged by the tour operators would be sold with their package holidays. As a result, holidaymakers were left with little or no choice in the selection of travel insurance. Even though the agreement referred to was rejected at the AGM of ITAA in November 1991 in favour of giving consumers a choice, this agreement continued to operate until recently as far as the Authority is aware.

Applicability of section 4(2)

61. Under section 4(2), the Competition Authority may grant a licence in the case of any agreement or category of agreements which, having regard to all relevant market conditions, contributes to improving the production of goods or provision of services or to promoting technical or economic progress, while allowing customers a fair share of the resulting benefit and which does not:

1. The minimum level of insurance would incorporate adequate medical and additional expenses cover, personal accident cover, personal luggage cover, personal money cover, personal liability cover, in addition to insurance against cancellation, curtailment and travel delay.

(i) impose on the undertakings concerned terms which are not indispensable to the attainment of those objectives;

(ii) afford undertakings the possibility of eliminating competition in respect of a substantial part of the products or services in question.

62. In order to qualify for a licence under the Competition Act, therefore, a notified agreement must satisfy all four criteria stipulated above. In the opinion of the Authority, the arrangements as notified did not fulfil at least two of the conditions provided for in section 4(2).

Indispensability

63. The effect of the arrangement was to ensure that Falcon customers were provided with adequate travel insurance and this was of benefit to them. It must be shown, however, that the requirement to take the insurance offered by Falcon was indispensable to secure these benefits. In the view of the Authority there is no reason why such benefits could not be obtained were consumers free to make their own travel insurance arrangements. It is highly relevant that Falcon customers booking holidays in Northern Ireland and in Britain have the option of taking Falcon's pre-arranged insurance policy or making alternative arrangements (paras. 22 to 25 above). The arrangements contained in the agreement as notified cannot, therefore, be regarded as indispensable.

Elimination of competition

64. As mentioned in para 57, the arrangements notified eliminated competition in relation to the holiday insurance which Falcon holidaymakers could take out. Furthermore, the Authority notes that the practice operated by Falcon was widespread throughout the Irish travel industry. In view of this it has to be concluded that the practice incorporated in the agreement as notified afforded the undertakings the possibility of eliminating competition in respect of a substantial part of the service in question (package holidays insurance).

(f) The amended arrangements

65. By letter dated 8 November 1993, Falcon agreed to discontinue the arrangements which were the subject of the original agreement as notified and from 1 November 1993 to give their customers the option of taking the Falcon/McArdle pre-arranged holiday insurance policy or making alternative arrangements for holiday insurance. Falcon had sought a licence for the original Falcon/McArdle agreement but confirmed to the Authority that a Certificate for the amended arrangements would be acceptable to them. In the Authority's opinion, the amended arrangements would not offend against section 4(1) of the Act. Neither would the arrangement whereby from 1 December 1993, onwards, Falcon customers may have to sign an undertaking that they will organise their own holiday insurance cover, offend against section 4(1) of the Act.

66. Falcon had discontinued the notified arrangements and allows its customers freedom to choose its policy or some alternative policy, and it has not instituted an administrative or other fee in the event of an alternative being chosen. The Authority is aware that some tour operators have imposed, or are proposing to impose, a fee if an alternative to the operator's own insurance policy is chosen, or have introduced other measures in an attempt to ensure that their insurance policy is sold. The Authority is concerned that such fees and measures may be an attempt to frustrate its intention of ensuring greater freedom of choice for customers in the area of holiday insurance, and may deny customers potential savings from selecting an alternative. The Authority would not have accepted such arrangements if they had been proposed by Falcon.

(g) *The decision*

67. Falcon Leisure Group (Overseas) Ltd trading as Falcon Holidays and Ben McArdle Ltd are undertakings within the meaning of section 3(1) of the Competition Act and the arrange-

1.2.1 ments between them on package holiday insurance constitute an agreement between undertakings. By letter of 8 November 1993, Falcon agreed that from 1 December 1993, they would discontinue the arrangements under which it was mandatory on their customers to take the Falcon/McArdle pre-arranged holiday insurance policy and give their customers the option of taking that policy or of making alternative holiday insurance arrangements. In the Authority's opinion, the amended arrangements which have operated since 1 December 1993, do not offend against section 4(1) of the Act.

The certificate

68. The Competition Authority has issued the following certificate:

The Competition Authority certifies that in its opinion, on the basis of the facts in its possession, the agreement between Falcon Leisure Group (Overseas) Ltd trading as Falcon Holidays and Ben McArdle Ltd, on package holiday insurance (Notification No. CA/31/92E), notified under section 7 of the Competition Act on 28 May 1992 and amended by letter of 8 November 1993, does not offend against section 4(1) of the Competition Act 1991.

For the Competition Authority

Des Wall
Member

4 February 1994

1.3 Corporate Groups

Competition Authority Decision No. 2, AGF/Irish Life Holdings plc: 14 May 1992, Notification No. CA/7/92 1.3.1

Agreement transferring activities between member companies of the same group – Article 85 of Treaty of Rome, EC Regulation 4064/89 Mergers, Takeovers and Monopolies (Control) Act 1978 and Competition Act 1991 (No. 24), section 3(1), 4 and 7.

Facts On 3 March 1992 notification was made to the Authority by AGF/Irish Life Holdings plc ('AGF') of arrangements which allocated non-life insurance businesses to two in the same corporate group. The notification was accompanied by a request for a certificate under section 4(4) of the Competition Act 1991 or, failing that a licence under section 4(2).

On 10 April 1992 notice of intention to take a favourable decision along with an invitation to comment on the notification as described in an available summary was published.

AGF, a public limited company registered in Ireland, is an investment holding company with no full time employees and is ultimately owned by Societe Centrale Des Assurance Generales de France and Irish Life plc The notified arrangements transferred commercial lines and commercial marine business from Church & General Insurance plc ('Church & General') to the Insurance Corporation of Ireland plc ('ICI'), both being wholly owned subsidiaries of AGF. Personal lines and aviation business transferred from ICI to Church and General. The effect of the notified arrangements was to rationalise the areas of operation of each of Church & General and ICI so that each company would then specialise in certain sectors of the non-life insurance market rather than each company covering every sector as was the case before the operation of the notified arrangements.

Decided by the Authority In issuing a certificate under section 4(4) of the Competition Act 1991 in respect of the notified arrangements that:

(1) Each of Church & General and ICI are 'undertakings' within the meaning of section 3(1) of the Competition Act. AGF is a holding company with no employees and while not directly engaged in the production, supply or distribution of a service it is engaged in economic activity through its subsidiary firms which it controls and is therefore an undertaking within the meaning of the Competition Act. The three companies while forming separate entities constitute a single economic entity.

(2) The notified arrangements constitute an agreement which has effect in the State.

(3) The notified arrangements do not prevent, restrict or distort competition in the meaning of section 4 of the Competition Act because:

1.3.1 (i) ICI and Church & General, being wholly owned subsidiaries of the same holding company, are not independent of each other. An economic entity does not compete with itself and ICI and Church & General are not therefore in competition with each other;
(ii) ICI and Church & General have no real freedom to determine their own course of action in the relevant market;
(iii) The arrangements merely re-allocate functions within the Group.

Cases, Decisions, Reports and Books mentioned

Beguelin Import Company v. EC Commission (Case No. 22/71), [1971] ECR 949, [1972] CMLR 81
ICI Ltd v. European Commission (Case Nos 48 to 57/69 – 1972) [1972] ECR 619, [1972] CMLR 557
Centrafarm BV and Adriaan de Peijper v. Sterling Drug Inc (Case No. 15/74), [1974] ECR 1147, [1974] 2 CMLR 480
Bodson v. Pompes Funebres Des Region Liberees SA (Case No. 30/87), [1988] ECR 2479, [1989] 4 CMLR 984
EC Commission Decision Christiani & Nielsen, Commission Decision No. 69/165 [1969] OJ L165/12, [1969] CMLR D36
EC Commission Decision Reuter/BASF [1976] 6254/40, [1976] 2 CMLR D44.
European Commission Fourth Report on Competition Policy 1974, para. 52
Competition Authority Decision No. 1 – Nallen/O'Toole (Belmullet), 2 April 1992 **at 3.3 below**.
Bellamy and Child, *Common Market Law of Competition* (Third Edition, para. 2-005).

Competition Authority Decision of 14 May 1992 relating to a proceeding under section 4 of the Competition Act 1991
Notification No. CA/7/92 — AGF/Irish Life Holdings

Introduction

1. Notification was made with a request for a certificate under section 4(4) of the Competition Act, 1991, or in the event of a refusal by the Competition Authority to issue a certificate, a licence under section 4(2), by AGF-Irish Life Holdings plc, on 3 March 1992 in respect of arrangements for the rationalisation of two wholly-owned subsidiaries of the notifying party.

2. Notice of intention to take a favourable decision was published in the 'Irish Times' on 10 April, 1992. No submissions were received from interested parties.

The Facts

(a) *The subject of the decision*

3. This decision concerns arrangements for the rationalisation of the operations of two companies which are both wholly-owned subsidiaries of a third company. The arrangements involve each subsidiary specialising in certain lines of the business concerned and transferring its other lines to the other subsidiary.

(b) *The undertakings concerned*

4. The parties to the arrangements are three companies, AGF — Irish Life Holdings plc (AGFILH), Church & General Insurance plc (CG) and The Insurance Corporation of Ireland plc (ICI). The notification was made on behalf of AGFILH, of which both CG and ICI are wholly-owned subsidiaries.

5. AGFILH is a public limited company registered in Ireland with a registered office in Dublin. It is an investment holding company with no full-time employees. It is owned to the extent of about 66% by AGF Holdings Ireland, about 30% by Irish Assurance plc and about 3% by other interests. The ultimate parent company of AGF Holdings Ireland is Societe

Centrale des Assurances Generales de France, the French holding company of the third largest life and general insurance company in France, which is about 78% owned by the French State. It has subsidiaries in forty countries and at the end of 1990 had total assets of about £21 billion. Irish Life Assurance plc is the largest Irish life assurance company. It is a wholly-owned subsidiary of Irish Life plc which is quoted on the stock exchange in Dublin and London with its principal shareholder being the Irish Minister for Finance with about 34% of the issued share capital; the Assurances Generales de France Group owns about 5% of Irish Life plc. Irish Life plc was privatised in 1991. **1.3.1**

6. ICI is a wholly-owned subsidiary of AGFILH which acquired the Irish business and name of the Insurance Corporation of Ireland plc from the Administrator of that company on 31 July 1990. ICI underwrites all classes of general insurance in both the Republic of Ireland and Northern Ireland. Its head office is in Dublin and it has seven branch offices in Ireland, including one in Northern Ireland. It has about 420 employees and the value of its gross premiums written in 1990 was £70m.

7. CG underwrites all classes of non-life insurance. All of its issued share capital was acquired by AGFILH on 27 June 1991. Its head office is in Dublin and it has seven branch offices in the same locations as those of ICI. It has about 340 employees and the value of its gross premiums written in 1990 was £61m.

8. At the time that AGFILH acquired CG, the EC Commission Merger Task Force formed the view that the transaction would not give rise to any concentration which had a 'Community dimension' within the meaning of Regulation (EEC) 4064/89. The transaction was notified in Ireland to the Minister for Industry and Commerce under the Mergers, Takeovers and Monopolies (Control) Act, 1978, and the Minister allowed the proposal to proceed without making it subject to any conditions.

9. Following the acquisition by AGFILH of the business of ICI and of CG, the directors of ICI and of CG are the same as the directors of AGFILH.

(c) *The products concerned*

10. ICI and CG are non-life insurance companies. Both are authorised in Ireland and in the UK to transact all classes of non-life insurance. Such insurance can be divided into seven categories:

— accident and health insurance,

— motor vehicle insurance,

— marine, aviation and transit insurance,

— fire and other damage to property insurance,

— liability insurance,

— miscellaneous pecuniary loss insurance,

— treaty reinsurance.

(d) *The market involved*

11. The market involved is the sale in Ireland of the non-life insurance products mentioned above. The market is regulated by the Insurance Acts and by EC harmonisation directives which have been implemented by Statutory Instruments. Authorised assurance and insurance companies are required to submit annual returns to the Minister for Industry and Commerce and returns are summarised in the Insurance Annual Report or 'Blue Book' produced by the Department.

12. The 1990 Blue Book lists 52 companies as holding authorisations to transact non-life insurance business in Ireland, with 24 having their head office in Ireland and a further 27 having their head office in other EC member states. Thirty six of these companies are shown to be active on the Irish domestic market. While some of these are specialists who would not transact

1.3.1 all classes of non-life insurance, it is understood that most transact all the major classes. The Second Non-Life Insurance Services Directive (of the EC) was implemented in Ireland in 1991. This allows insurers who are established in other member states, but who are not established in Ireland, to transact business directly in Ireland. It is understood that 53% of business is transacted through brokers and 47% of the market is direct, but these proportions vary widely for different classes of insurance. While there would be some differences between the cover offered by different companies, the basic cover offered by competitors within the various classes of insurance can be regarded as similar.

13. On the basis of net premiums written in 1990, the Blue Book indicates that ICI has a 6.8% share of the Irish market and CG a 5.9% share. The Blue Book also indicates the shares of the major companies, on the basis of gross premiums written, in each of the seven categories. The share of CG varies from negligible in the treaty reinsurance category to 13% of the marine and aviation category. The share of ICI ranges from 2.4% of the accident and health category to 50% of the marine and aviation category, with its next highest category share being 14.3% of the pecuniary loss category. (In the marine, aviation and transit category the market has been open for many years to foreign insurers to transact on a service basis).

(e) *The notified arrangements*

14. Following the acquisition of the subsidiaries, the Board of AGFILH is now seeking to make arrangements which would

(i) rationalise the administration side of the business by pooling common resources and thus facilitate more competitive future premium levels;

(ii) arrange for each operational company to specialise in distinctive lines of the Irish insurance market so that each subsidiary will be better able to concentrate on its main strengths and thereby become more competitive;

(iii) review the channels of distribution so that the commercial relationships with the customers, intermediaries and shareholders were preserved and even improved;

It is proposed that

'(i) personal lines business should transfer from Insurance Corporation to Church & General;

(ii) commercial lines business should transfer from Church & General to Insurance Corporation;

(iii) within the Marine and Aviation class, Aviation business should transfer from Insurance Corporation to Church & General while commercial marine business should transfer from Church & General to Insurance Corporation.'

As a result of the transfers of business, it is intended that Church & General will concentrate exclusively on religious social, personal lines and aviation business while Insurance Corporation will concentrate exclusively on commercial lines and marine insurance business.

15. It is envisaged that business would transfer at renewal time on an invitation basis, with the policyholder being invited to take out a new policy on terms at least equivalent with the other company; a portfolio transfer of the business of any class from one company to another is not planned. Customers would not be compelled to transfer and would be free to transfer to other companies. The transfer process is planned to be effected between July 1992 and June 1993. It is envisaged that the transfer of business will involve 60 to 70 staff moving between the two companies. The regional offices of ICI and CG, all in the same seven cities and towns, are to be consolidated while maintaining the separate identities of the companies.

Assessment

(a) *Section 4(1)*

16. Section 4(1) of the Competition Act states that 'all agreements between undertakings, decisions by associations of undertakings and concerted practices which have as their object

or effect the prevention, restriction or distortion of competition in trade in any goods or services in the State or in any part of the State are prohibited and void'. 1.3.1

(b) *The Undertakings*

17. The present decision concerns arrangements involving AGFILH, Church and General (CG) and Insurance Corporation (ICI) in the non-life insurance market. Section 3(1) of the Competition Act defines an undertaking as 'a person being an individual, a body corporate or an unincorporated body of persons engaged for gain in the production, supply or distribution of goods or the provision of a service.' CG and ICI are wholly owned subsidiaries of AGFILH engaged in the provision of different types of non-life insurance. Both CG and ICI are bodies corporate engaged for gain in the provision of services and are therefore undertakings within the meaning of section 3 of the Act.

18. AGFILH is a public limited company registered in the Republic of Ireland which trades as an investment holding company. AGFILH, being a holding company, is not directly 'engaged for gain in the production, supply or distribution of goods or the provision of a service.'

19. Decisions of the European Commission concerning the definition of an undertaking in a number of cases under Article 85(1) of the Treaty of Rome on which section 4(1) is based indicate that:

> The word 'undertaking' is a wide term which extends to almost any legal or natural person carrying on activities of an economic or commercial nature including, for example, limited companies, partnerships, trade associations, agricultural co-operatives, sole traders and State Corporations.[1]

20. The Authority recognises that there are some differences between Irish and EC competition law in respect of the definition of an undertaking. EC decisions may nevertheless provide some guidance on the question of undertakings. In particular the Authority accepts the EC view that the term undertaking should be interpreted widely. In the Authority's view AGFILH is engaged in economic activity, namely the provision of insurance services for gain, through subsidiary firms which it controls. It is, therefore, an undertaking within the meaning of section 3 of the Act. This is in accordance with the view of the Authority in a previous decision where it decided that individuals were undertakings within the meaning of the Act by virtue of engaging in economic activity through firms which were under their control.[2]

21. The essential issue in this case is the fact that both CG and ICI are wholly owned subsidiaries of AGFILH. The latter company owns 100% of the share capital in both CG and ICI. The Authority is not, therefore, dealing with several economically independent undertakings but rather with a group which constitutes a single economic entity.

(c) *The Agreement*

22. The present decision is concerned with arrangements whereby AGFILH is reorganising the activities of its two subsidiary companies so that each of them will specialise in particular segments of the non-life insurance market. Such an arrangement constitutes an agreement between undertakings within the meaning of section 4 of the Act. The agreement affects the operations of CG and ICI in the non-life insurance market in the State.

1. See C. Bellamy and G. Child (1987); *Common Market Law of Competition*, 3rd ed., Sweet and Maxwell, London, para. 2-003.
2. Notification no. CA/8/91, Nallen/O'Toole (Belmullet), decision of 2 April 1992. This decision was in line with the approach adopted by the EC Commission in the Reuter/BASF case. (Case no. 76/743/EEC, OJ L254, 17.9.76, p. 40).

1.3.1 (d) *Effect on Competition*

23. The principal question that arises is whether, given the group relationship which exists between AGFILH, CG and ICI, the present notified agreement between them can be regarded as preventing, restricting or distorting competition within the meaning of section 4(1) of the Competition Act.

24. A group relationship usually arises where there is common ownership or control of undertakings. The individual undertakings within a group would not normally enjoy commercial independence in such circumstances. The group would therefore normally be regarded as constituting a single economic entity even though it may be composed of a number of separate undertakings. Clearly an economic entity does not compete with itself.

25. The notion that members of a group do not compete with one another is implicitly recognised by legislation designed to control mergers and takeovers. A merger or takeover results in two or more separate independent undertakings being brought under common control in the context of a group relationship. It is recognised that the result of this will be to eliminate competition between undertakings which were previously operating in the same market. The elimination of competition resulting from a merger or takeover is one of the main reasons why legislation exists to control such activities in Ireland and elsewhere.

26. Neither CG nor ICI have any real commercial autonomy in their own right, although some autonomy may be delegated to them by AGFILH in order to improve overall efficiency within the group. The arrangements which are the subject of the present decision involve a reallocation of business between CG and ICI along the lines set out in paras 14 and 15. Rather than have both firms operate in all segments of the non-life insurance market, AGFILH is proposing that each should specialise in particular segments of the market in order to improve overall group efficiency. The object of these changes is to increase overall group efficiency by having CG concentrate on religious, social, personal lines and aviation business and ICI specialise in commercial lines and marine business.

27. CG and ICI, being wholly owned subsidiaries of AGFILH, and, therefore, part of a single economic entity, are not in competition with each other. While they are both undertakings they are not independent of each other but are really separate arms of the same organisation. The proposed arrangements merely involve a reallocation of functions within the group because, in the view of the group's management, this will be of benefit to it. For these reasons the Authority does not consider that the proposed arrangements prevent, restrict or distort competition within the meaning of section 4(1) of the Act.

28. The view adopted by the Authority is in accord with that taken by the European Commission and the European Court of Justice in a number of cases under Article 85(1) of the Treaty of Rome on which section 4(1) of the Competition Act is based.[3] While it was accepted that an agreement between a parent and a subsidiary or between two companies which are under the common control of a third may, strictly speaking, be an agreement between undertakings, agreements of this kind have been found not to offend against Article 85(1) if the 'undertakings' form an economic unit within which the subsidiary has no real freedom to determine its course of action on the market.[4]

29. In the *Christiani v. Nielsen* case, involving a market sharing agreement between a Danish company and its wholly owned Dutch subsidiary, the European Commission ruled that the agreement only constituted a 'division of labour within the same economic entity'. The Court of Justice endorsed the Commission view in the Beguelin Import and ICI (Imperial

3. *Christiani v. Nielsen* [1969] CMLR D36; *Beguelin Import Co. and Others v. SAGL Import Export and Others* [1971] ECR 949, *ICI Ltd v. European Commission* [1972] ECR 619; *Centrafarm BV and Adrian de Peijper v. Sterling Orug Inc.* [1974] ECR 1147; *Corinne Bodson v. Pompes funebres des regions liberees SA* [1988] ECR 2479.

4. C. Bellamy and G. Child (1987), *Common Market Law of Competition*, 3rd ed., para. 2-005, Sweet and Maxwell, London.

Chemical Industries) cases. This view was restated in the Centrafarm case where the Court ruled that: 1.3.1

> Article 85, however, is not concerned with agreements or concerted practices between undertakings belonging to the same concern and having the status of parent and subsidiary, if the undertakings form an economic unit within which the subsidiary has no real freedom to determine its course of action on the market, and if the agreements or practices are concerned merely with the internal allocation of tasks between the undertakings.[5]

The latter point is particularly relevant to the present decision which concerns the internal allocation of tasks between undertakings which are part of the same group.

30. The European Commission has, however, argued in the past that agreements concluded within a corporate group may be in breach of Article 85(1) if they have wider implications, for instance agreements which restrict the scope for non-member undertakings to penetrate a given market.[6] There is some doubt on this point as the Court of Justice does not appear to have accepted this view in the Centrafarm case. In the present case the Authority does not consider that the proposed arrangements would restrict any undertakings from outside the group from entering the relevant segment of the non-life insurance market.

31. More recently in the Pompes Funebres case the Court of Justice hinted that the mere fact of a parent/subsidiary relationship is not enough to take an agreement outside of Article 85(1). In deciding on the question of whether or not the parties involved in that case were caught by Article 85(1) the Court stated that:

> The mere fact that holders of concessions belong to the same group of undertakings is not decisive in that regard. Account must be taken of the relationship between the undertakings belonging to that group . . . it is not apparent that the undertakings pursue the same market strategy, which is determined by the parent company.[7]

32. It is clear that the present decision involves undertakings where market strategy is determined by the parent company. Indeed the notification concerns arrangements that CG and ICI should specialise in particular segments of the the market. The questions raised by the Pompes Funebres case do not therefore apply.

The Decision

33. AGFILH, CG and ICI are undertakings within the meaning of section 3 of the Competition Act and the arrangements notified constitute an agreement which applies within the State.

34. The Authority does not consider that the proposed arrangements prevent, restrict or distort competition within the meaning of section 4 of the Act because:

(i) ICI and CG, being wholly-owned subsidiaries of the same holding company, are not independent undertakings but are in fact separate arms of the same organisation and are not therefore in competition with each other;

(ii) ICI and CG have no real freedom to determine their course of action on the relevant market;

(iii) The proposed arrangements merely involve a reallocation of functions within the group.

5. Op. cit. at p. 1167. The point was restated in the more recent decision in the *Pompes Funebres* case
6. See European Commission, Fourth Report on Competition Policy, 1974 para. 52.
7. Op. cit. at p. 2513.

1.3.1 The Certificate

35. The Competition Authority has issued the following certificate:

> The Competition Authority certifies that, in its opinion, on the basis of the facts in its possession, the agreement between AGF-Irish Life Holdings, Church and General and Insurance Corporation of Ireland (CA/7/92), whereby Church and General and Insurance Corporation will each confine their activities to particular segments of the non-life insurance market, which was notified on 3 March 1992 under section 7, does not offend against section 4(1) of the Competition Act, 1991.

For the Competition Authority

Patrick Massey
Member

14 May 1992

1.3.2 Competition Authority Decision No. 5, Performing Right Society and Irish Music Rights Organisation: 30 June 1992, Notification No. CA/1/91E

Non-Profit making associations for benefit of members – Agreement between member companies of the same group transferring certain activities – Meaning of 'Undertaking' in Irish Competition Law – Competition Act 1991 (No. 24) sections 3(1), 4 and 7

Facts On 1 October 1991 the Performing Right Society ('PRS') and the Irish Music Rights Organisation ('IMRO') jointly notified to the Authority under section 7(2) of the Competition Act, 1991 an agreement of 29 December 1988 which transferred to IMRO the responsibility in the State for the licensing of the repertoire of PRS and the collection of royalties for the repertoire. The notification was accompanied by a request for a certificate under section 4(4) of the Competition Act or, failing that a licence under section 4(2).

On 10 April 1992 notice of intention to take a favourable decision along with an invitation to comment on the notification as described in an available summary was published.

PRS, a private company registered in England and Wales limited by guarantee and having no share capital, is an association of creators and publishers of musical works. The main objects of PRS are the exercise and enforcement on behalf of its members of the rights and remedies associated with copyright in the works of their members, including but not limited to its collection and distribution of royalties. PRS has also entered into agreements with other collecting societies throughout the world ('affiliated societies') to administer the rights of those societies within Ireland and the UK. IMRO is a registered private company limited by guarantee not having a share capital whose objects are broadly similar to those of PRS. Its main activities are the licensing of the performing rights in the State and the collection of royalties. Prior to the execution of the notified agreement PRS administered the rights of its members and of its affiliated societies in Ireland and the UK. The purpose of the notified agreement was to transfer these functions for Ireland to IMRO. 1.3.2

The relationship between PRS and IMRO is such that PRS controls every aspect of the business of IMRO, including the composition of its board of directors. The notified agreement assigned from PRS to IMRO the administration of the PRS repertoire of musical works in the Republic of Ireland. The agreement had already been considered under articles 85 (1) and 86 of the Treaty of Rome by the European Commission and in a letter of 11 April 1991 the Commission indicated that a preliminary examination had not revealed the existence of any grounds for further action.

Decided by the Authority In issuing a certificate under section 4(4) of the Competition Act 1991 in respect of the notified agreement that:

(1) PRS and IMRO are 'undertakings' within the meaning of section 3(1) of the Competition Act 1991. 'Engaged for profit' was used in the Mergers, Take-overs and Monopolies Act 1978 but section 3(1) of the Competition Act uses the term 'engaged for gain'. The term 'gain' means any consideration or reward for goods or services provided. The members of PRS derive gain from the activities of PRS/IMRO and that objective of gain is attributable to PRS and IMRO also.

(2) The notified agreement is an agreement between undertakings which has effect in the State.

(3) PRS effectively controls IMRO and a 'parent-subsidiary' relationship exists between PRS and IMRO. The two companies constitute a single economic entity. The notified agreement merely transfers functions from one member of a common group to another member. Accordingly the notified agreement does not have as its object or effect the prevention, restriction or distortion of competition in the State and does not offend against section 4(1) of the Competition Act.

Cases, Decisions and Books mentioned:

Competition Authority Decision No. 1 — Nallen/O'Toole (Belmullet) 2 April 1992 **3.3**
Competition Authority Decision No. 2 – AGF-Irish Life Holdings plc, 14 May 1992 **1.3.1**
Deane v. Voluntary Health Insurance Board, ex Tempore Judgement of Costello J, 9 April 1992 — Editor's note: This judgment was successfully appealed and the Supreme Court's judgement is reported at [1992] 2 IR 319-32 **1.1**
EC Commission decision ARD [1989] OJ L284/36, [1990] 4 CMLR 841
Hydrotherm v. Andreoli (Case 170/83) [1984] ECR 2999, [1985] 3 CMLR 224
Kerse C.S., EEC Antitrust Procedures (2nd ed., p. 4)
Bellamy and Child, *Common Market Law of Competition* (3rd ed., pp 45/46)
Van Bael and Bellis, *Competition Law of the EEC* (2nd ed., pp 23/24)

Submissions by Parties

(1) PRS and IMRO submitted that they were not 'undertakings' within the meaning of section 3(1) Competition Act 1991 as neither were profit making organisations and so were not engaged for gain in the services which they provided. Their objects were merely to give effect to the rights of the members of PRS (and affiliated societies worldwide) under copyright legislation.

(2) IMRO has no commercial independence from PRS because it is under the control of PRS. IMRO is simply continuing the arrangements of PRS in the State prior to the execution of the notified agreement. There is no intention or effect on competition in the State as a result of the notified agreement.

(3) The agreement does not restrict, distort or prevent competition because no

1.3.2 impediment existed to the formation of other performing right organisations in the State and because PRS is specifically free to terminate the agreement if it could advantageously administer its members' rights in any other way.

Editor's note: PRS and IMRO arrangements are also the subject of Decisions 326, 383 and 384 which are noted in chapter 6 of this book.

Competition Authority Decision of 30 June 1992 relating to a proceeding under section 4 of the Competition Act 1991
Notification No. CA/1/91E — Performing Right Society and Irish Music Rights Organisation

Introduction

1. On 1 October, 1991 Performing Right Society (PRS) and Irish Music Rights Organisation (IMRO) jointly notified to the Competition Authority, under section 7(2) of the Competition Act 1991, an agreement transferring functions between themselves dated 29 December 1988 for the purpose of obtaining a certificate under section 4(4) of the Act or, in the event of refusal by the Authority to issue a certificate, a licence under section 4(2) of the Act.

2. Notice of the intention of the Authority to take a favourable decision in relation to the agreement was published in the Irish Times on 10 April 1992. No substantive observations on this agreement were received from interested parties.

The facts

(a) *The subject of the decision*

3. The agreement transfers from PRS to IMRO responsibility for the licensing of the repertoire of PRS, and the collection of royalties in respect of this, in the Republic of Ireland. This decision does not concern any of the other agreements which have been notified by PRS/IMRO.

(b) *The parties involved*

PRS

4. PRS is an association of composers, lyricists (creators) and publishers which was incorporated in 1914 as a company registered in England and Wales. It is a private company limited by guarantee and not having a share capital.

5. The main objects of PRS are to exercise and enforce on behalf of its members all rights and remedies in relation to the exploitation of the copyright in their works; to collect and receive all royalties and fees payable in respect of their works; to restrain and recover damages for the infringement of the copyright; to obtain from members assignments of copyright; to distribute the net monies minus administration expenses to the members; to establish and support funds, trusts, associations or institutions for the benefit of its members or ex-members, to lend money to members and to invest the monies of the company not immediately required.

6. Copyright in relation to an original literary, dramatic, musical or artistic work is the exclusive right to do, or to authorise other persons to do, certain acts in relation to that work. Such acts include reproducing the work in any material form, publishing it, performing it in public, broadcasting it, causing it to be transmitted to subscribers to a diffusion service or making any adaptation of it. This type of copyright normally lasts during the lifetime of the creator and for fifty years after his death. The authorisation of other persons to use copyright material is normally by way of licence in return for payment of royalties to the copyright owner. Copyright is a form of property right which is protected and regulated by statute. The relevant legislation is the Copyright Acts 1963 and 1987.

7. Collective licensing and enforcement of copyright in relation to musical works is common throughout the world, wherever copyright is enforced. In effect, the copyright owners combine

to offer use of their works against payment of royalties. PRS accepts assignments from creators of the performing right in their musical works and then licenses the performance of those works through radio, television and public performances such as concerts and discos. Periodic royalty payments are made by PRS to the creators from the licence fees received. This system of copyright and its collective administration in practice can be said to involve two kinds of 'monopoly', first, the exclusive right to the use of the original musical work which is inherent in the notion of copyright itself and, secondly, the monopoly of the licensing rights assigned to and controlled by PRS which appears to be the only body engaged in the collective administration of the performing right in musical works in Ireland. **1.3.2**

8. The activities of PRS (and IMRO) relating to copyright licensing and royalty collection form part of a wider network involving reciprocal representation agreements with similar organisations in other countries. PRS represents in the State the interests of over 750,000 musical copyright owners of all nationalities. Its own membership is over 23,000, including 942 members in Ireland. The members of PRS in the Republic of Ireland are also generally members of the following bodies — Association of Irish Composers; Irish Association of Songwriters and Composers; and Republic of Ireland Music Publishers Association.

9. PRS, being a company not having a share capital, may not distribute dividends. Its income derives mainly from its licensing activities and, after deduction of expenses and taxation, it is distributed to members (apart from some funds placed in reserves). Its licence revenue in 1990 was in excess of Stg £123 million of which Stg £2.5 million represented payments to PRS by IMRO. The total licence revenue of IMRO in 1990 was IR £3.55m.

IMRO

10. IMRO is a registered private company limited by guarantee, not having a share capital. Its objects are broadly similar to those of PRS. Its main activities are the licensing of the performing right in the State and the collection of royalties. Prior to 1989, these activities were carried out by PRS itself. IMRO distributes its licence revenue less operating expenses to PRS and at year end 1990 showed net assets at nil. The company was registered with nine founding members, including PRS.

Relationship between PRS and IMRO

11. The applicants have stated that:

> Under the Articles of Association of IMRO, PRS controls the composition of its Board of Directors and PRS is the ultimate parent company of IMRO.

12. The following provisions are included in the Articles of Association of IMRO:

Article 2 — One of the members of IMRO is required to be PRS.

Article 4 — A resolution for cessation of membership must have the prior approval of PRS.

Article 12 — The presence of PRS is required for a quorum at a general meeting.

Article 19 — PRS can effectively veto a resolution at a general meeting to remove a director.

Article 21 — Nominations for directors require the written approval of PRS prior to any person being appointed as a director. The chairman of PRS and the Chief Executive Officer of PRS are ex-officio directors of IMRO and PRS has the right to appoint two other persons as directors. Any proposal to remove a director may not come before the members unless PRS has given its prior written consent to such a proposal. PRS has the right to remove any director of the company. PRS appoints the chairman and deputy chairman of IMRO.

Article 22 — The directors of IMRO may fill a casual vacancy on the board provided that PRS has consented in writing to the nomination.

Article 35 — A director nominated by PRS is required for the quorum of 3 at board meetings.

Article 53(1) — A Member's Voluntary Winding Up resolution cannot be proposed without the prior consent of PRS.

1.3.2 Article 53(2) — PRS has the right to propose at any time that the Company be wound up and for the purpose of any such resolution the votes cast by PRS shall be deemed to represent a majority consisting of three quarters of all such votes.

13. The PRS/IMRO agreement itself includes the following provisions:

(i) IMRO undertakes to use its best endeavours to enforce in the Territory the rights licensed hereunder and to do so within the limits of the legal protection afforded. (Para 6).

(ii) IMRO shall supply PRS with any information for which it is asked concerning the tariffs IMRO applies to different types of music use in the Territory. (Para 6).

(iii) If any legal or other situation arises in the Republic of Ireland or by virtue of EC law which PRS considers makes the exercise of PRS's rights less favourable to its members or other persons through whom it derives its rights than would be the case if this Agreement did not exist, PRS may terminate this Agreement forthwith by notice in writing without prejudice to any right of action accrued hereunder down to the date of termination. (Para 10(c)).

(iv) The Agreement shall continue from year to year subject to six months' written notice of termination from either party expiring on an anniversary of the commencement date. (Para 12).

(v) IMRO shall be entitled in each year of the Agreement to deduct from the gross sum due to PRS any sum set aside by IMRO as reserve for future contingencies subject to PRS's prior consent in writing. (Para 5 (3)).

(c) *The service and the market*

14. In the context of the present agreement the relevant market is the market in services relating to the management of the performing right in musical works. The main services involved are the accepting of assignments from creators of the performing right in their musical works and the licensing of the performing right to users such as radio and television organisations, discos, public houses and cinemas, who pay a royalty for licences. The geographic scope of the relevant market is the State. IMRO is the only body in the State which is engaged in the licensing of the performing right in musical works belonging to the PRS repertoire. As such, it has a monopoly of the provision of this service in the State, a position which was formerly occupied by PRS. This monopoly extends only to musical works included in the PRS repertoire. In 1990, IMR0 had 8,078 non- broadcast licensees, 24 radio licensees and 1 broadcast licensee (RTE), yielding royalties of IR£1.28m, IR£0.33m and IR£1.62m respectively (total IR£3.23m). IMR0 is also a party to copyright licence agreements with cable television companies, licence revenue from which amounted to IR £0.32m in 1990.

(d) *The agreement*

15. The Agreement assigns to IMRO the right to license exclusively the public performance of the PRS repertoire to users of musical works in the Republic of Ireland. The agreement also appoints IMRO to collect the royalties due from the users and obliges IMRO to remit to PRS all royalties and other monies collected less reasonable administration expenses, donations to Irish musical causes, reserves for future contingencies and taxes. IMRO is not entitled to assign any of its rights or obligations under the agreement to any other party. The agreement between PRS and IMRO came into force on 1 January 1989 for a period of 3 years and is automatically renewed yearly thereafter.

(e) *Submissions of the parties*

16. The parties have stated:

— It is submitted that PRS and IMRO may not be within the statutory definition of 'undertaking' in that neither company is engaged for gain in the service which it provides. It is submitted that 'gain', within the meaning of the Act, necessarily means gain to the undertaking and equally means only financial gain. Both companies are non-profit making and exist merely with the object of giving effect to the rights of the members of PRS (and affiliated organisations worldwide) under copyright legislation. There are no shares in the company, and consequently no dividends can be paid. 1.3.2

— It is no part of the intention or effect of the PRS/IMRO Agreement to affect competition in any goods or services in the State or in any part of the State.
— Competition is neither restricted, prevented nor distorted because no impediment exists to the formation of other performing right organisations in the State and because PRS would be free to terminate this Agreement (under Clause 10) if it could more advantageously administer its members' rights in any other way. In addition, IMRO has no commercial independence and is simply continuing the arrangements operated by PRS in the State before 1989.
— It is submitted that the PRS/IMRO Agreement should be regarded as transparent for the purposes of considering the other aspects of the Arrangements.

(f) *European Commission*

17. The Agreement has already been considered under Articles 85 (1) and 86 by the European Commission on the basis of a preliminary examination. In its administrative letter of 11 April 1991, the Commission indicated that the examination 'has not revealed the existence of any grounds . . . for further action on the part of the Commission in respect of the notified agreement.' The Authority understands that the reason for this decision was that the agreement involved no real change in relation to the position of third parties.

Assessment

(a) *The prohibition in section 4(1)*

18. Section 4(1) of the Competition Act 1991 prohibits and renders void all agreements between undertakings, decisions by associations of undertakings and concerted practices which have as their object or effect the prevention, restriction or distortion of competition in trade in any goods or services in the State, or in any part of the State.

(b) *The undertakings*

19. The term 'undertaking' is defined in section 3(1) of the Competition Act 1991 as follows:

> a person being an individual, a body corporate or an unincorporated body of persons engaged for gain in the production, supply or distribution of goods or the provision of a service.

20. Each of the parties is a body corporate engaged in the provision of a service. The services provided by PRS and IMRO include in the case of IMRO, the licensing of the PRS repertoire to users in the State and the collection of royalty payments and, in the case of PRS, the remittal of royalty payments to musical creators resident in the State.

21. The parties have submitted that neither of them may be within the statutory definition of 'undertaking' in that they are not engaged 'for gain' in the service which they provide.

22. The immediate issue raised by this submission relates to the interpretation of the words 'for gain' in the statutory definition of 'undertaking'. The term 'undertaking' is one of the pivotal terms in the Act and its interpretation is of considerable importance in defining the scope of the Act generally. Accordingly, the Authority considers that it should in the present decision outline its overall approach to the interpretation of the term undertaking as well as dealing with the immediate issues raised in the PRS/IMRO submission.

General considerations

23. The overall approach taken in the Competition Act 1991 was largely inspired by the competition provisions of the Treaty of Rome, particularly Articles 85 and 86. Indeed, the wording of those articles was followed almost verbatim in sections 4 and 5 of the 1991 Act

1.3.2 (the main difference being the omission in the Act of any reference to trade between Member States). The Authority, accordingly, gives full weight in its decisions under section 4 of the Act to the Community jurisprudence on Articles 85 and 86 of the Treaty, whenever relevant.

24. The concept of undertaking has been extensively defined in a number of EC cases. These cases have also been discussed in the leading text books. Kerse for example states:

> It is significant that Articles 85 and 86 do not refer to 'persons' but to 'undertakings', a much looser and wider concept. The Treaty does not define 'undertakings' for these purposes but, broadly speaking, 'undertaking' encompasses any body, whether company, partnership, sole trader, etc., carrying on economic activities. An economic rather than a legal approach is necessary. So the Court has said: 'In competition law, the term 'undertaking' must be understood as designating an economic unit for the purposes of the subject matter of the agreement in question even if in law that economic unit consists of several persons natural or legal'.[1] Autonomus commercial activity is more relevant than legal personality in this context and no useful distinction can be drawn from the different legal forms which a business may take, or its precise status under domestic law. Individuals may be 'undertakings'; for example, a self-employed inventor commercially exploiting his patents by licensing, a commercial adviser and even artistes when they commercially exploit their artistic performances. The term may include non-profit making bodies. An undertaking is an 'undertaking' for the purposes of Articles 85 and 86 even if it has its seat outside the Community.[2]

Bellamy & Child point out:

> The word 'undertaking' is a wide term which extends to almost any legal or natural person carrying on activities of an economic or commercial nature including, for example, limited companies, partnerships, trade associations, agricultural co-operatives, sole traders, and State corporations. Whether the undertaking is profit-making is immaterial, provided it carries out economic or commercial activities. Undertakings engaged in the supply of services are 'undertakings' within the meaning of Article 85(1) as well as undertakings engaged in the supply of goods. But it is essential that the 'undertaking' should carry on some economic or commercial activity; bodies which are not engaged in any such activity are not 'undertakings' within the meaning of Article 85(1).'[3]

Van Bael and Bellis state:

> The term 'undertaking' is not defined anywhere in the Treaty. According to the Commission the term 'undertaking' must be viewed in the broadest sense covering any entity engaged in economic or commercial activities such as production, distribution or the supply of services and ranging from small shops run by one individual to large industrial companies.' Indeed, from the cases it appears that virtually every natural or legal person participating in the economic process will qualify as an undertaking. For example, in addition to companies and associations of various kinds, individuals have likewise been held to constitute an undertaking within the sense of Article 85. The nationality or location of the undertaking has no bearing on the issue. Similarly, it is irrelevant whether the undertaking is privately or publicly owned. Even state-controlled trade organisations of East-European countries have been considered to fall within the scope of the undertaking concept.

1. *Hydrotherm v. Andreoli* (Case 170/83) [1984] ECR 2999.
2. Kerse, C.S., *EEC Antitrust Procedures* (2nd ed., p. 4) European Law Centre Ltd., 1987.
3. Bellamy, C.W. and Child, G.D., *Common Market Law of Competition* (3rd ed., pp. 45/46) Sweet & Maxwell Ltd. 1987.

Although the Member States as such do not qualify as 'undertakings' and are therefore not the addressees of Articles 85 and 86, these Treaty provisions coupled with Articles 3(f) and 5 of the Treaty are increasingly used by the Court to scrutinise the effects of national legislation upon competition.'[4] 1.3.2

25. Commission decisions also illustrate this broad approach to the interpretation of the term 'undertaking' in Community Law. For example, in a 1989 case dealing with television broadcasting organisations in Germany,[5] the Commission stated as follows:

> The functional concept of undertaking in Article 85(1) covers any activity directed at trade in goods or services irrespective of the legal form of the undertaking and regardless of whether or not it is intended to earn profits.

26. In its first decision[6] under section 4 of the Act, the Authority stated as follows:

> There is a difference between Irish and EC Legislation in that the Irish Act defines an undertaking as being 'engaged for gain.' In practice, this appears to differ very little from the EC view that an undertaking carries out economic or commercial activities.

27. The Authority is aware that the scope of the statutory definition of 'undertaking' was considered recently by the High Court in a case involving an alleged abuse of a dominant position by the Voluntary Health Insurance Board. In its judgment, which is not yet officially reported, the Court held that VHI did not come within the statutory definition because it was not engaged *for gain* in the provision of a service. It is understood that this decision is being appealed to the Supreme Court. The High Court decision confirms that there is some difference between the Irish and Community concepts of undertaking. The Authority remains of the view that the difference, in substance, between the two concepts is very small. In fact, the Authority believes that the definition of the term 'undertaking' in the Competition Act was seeking to do no more than to confirm that certain activities not normally regarded as 'economic activities' were not included within the scope of the Act. These activities include those carried out by local authorities, as well as certain activities carried out by entities not normally regarded as economic entities such as charitable or benevolent associations. The inclusion in the definition of the qualification 'for gain' ensured that such activities were not caught by the Act. This interpretation is supported by the fact that the Act, unlike most of the competition legislation which preceded it, contains no express exclusions for particular enterprises or activities. The Authority has also taken into account various statements on the matter made in the Houses of the Oireachtas by the Minister for Industry and Commerce during the passage of the Competition Bill. These confirm that the intended scope of the definition was to encompass all commercial activities whether in the public or private sectors or whether they relate to goods or to services. Furthermore, a narrow definition of undertaking might mean that certain public enterprises would be outside the scope of the Competition Act while other enterprises, with which they are in competition, would be caught by the Act. In addition, the situation might arise where such public enterprises would be caught by EC Competition Law but not by Irish Competition Law.

28. In the view of the Authority, it is immaterial whether 'profit', in the technical sense, actually occurs or not. The term 'gain' is clearly a wider one than 'profit'. In this connection, it is noted that the phrase 'engaged for profit' was used in the Mergers Act 1978 but this was not repeated in the 1991 Act. In the view of the Authority the term gain means any consideration or reward in return for the supply of a good or the provision of a service.

4. Van Bael, I. and Bellis, J.F., *Competition Law of the EEC* (2nd ed., pp. 23/24). CCH Editions Ltd., 1990.
5. Film purchases by German television stations, OJ L284 3.10.89, p. 36 (at p. 41).
6. Notification No. CA/8/91 — Nallen/O'Toole (Belmullet) — Decision No. 1 of 2 April, 1992.

1.3.2 The arguments of PRS/IMRO

29. The main activity carried out by PRS and IMRO is the licensing of the performing right in musical works to a multiplicity of users. Licences are granted in return for the payment of a consideration (a royalty) by the user. The amount of this royalty is determined by agreement between the parties. There is no essential difference between this transaction and the sale and purchase of any other good or service. There can be no doubt, therefore, that the licensing of the performing right in musical works constitutes an economic activity. On these grounds, the Authority is satisfied that PRS and IMRO are 'undertakings' within the meaning of the Act.

30. It is also necessary to consider the specific points raised by the notifying parties (see para. 16). These were (i) that the term 'gain' must be interpreted as meaning financial gain only and (ii) that it must mean gain to the undertaking in question.

31. The Authority accepts that financial or monetary gain, as the form of gain normally associated with the pursuit of economic activities, is the main form of gain envisaged in the statutory definition of undertaking. It does not accept, however, that this is the only form of gain envisaged or that an entity carrying out economic activities for other forms of reward or benefit is automatically excluded from the scope of the definition and, thereby, from the scope of the principal provisions of Part II of the Competition Act. It is not necessary to pursue this aspect further here since, in the Authority's view, 'gain' even in the narrower sense is, in fact, present in the case under consideration.

32. It is clear from the financial statements of PRS and IMRO that both derive financial gain from the activities which they carry out. In 1990, IMRO derived IR £3.55 million in licence revenue. It expended IR £0.78 million in defraying costs of administration. It remitted IR £2.76 million to PRS. No surplus of income over expenditure was recorded in that year but there is nothing to prevent surpluses occurring in the future. PRS had a licence revenue in 1990 in excess of Stg£123 million. It allocated Stg£100.3 million to its members and to affiliated societies. Costs of administration of Stg£23.7 million were defrayed. An appropriation of Stg£200,000 was made from their income and expenditure account to reserves bringing the total to Stg£1.3 million. IMRO's licence revenue includes monetary reward for the administration services which it provides under the cable television agreements which are the subject of separate notifications to the Authority.[7] These services, which are carried out on a commercial basis, clearly go beyond the object of merely giving effect to the rights of members of PRS.

33. It is recognised that the ultimate beneficiaries of the activities of PRS and IMRO are the members of PRS who, in fact, are the proprietors of the two bodies. This raises the question whether a body in respect of which all or most of the gain derived from its activities goes to its constituent members could be outside the scope of the statutory definition. Such an interpretation, if adopted, could have far-reaching consequences. It could be argued, for instance, that since any company exists ultimately for the benefit of its members rather than its own benefit, it should therefore be exempt from the Competition Act. Such an interpretation would deprive the whole Competition Act of any real meaning or effect.

34. The purpose of the system under which companies and certain other forms of association may be incorporated and registered is to enable individual persons to pursue, collectively, goals and objectives which would be difficult or impossible to pursue on their own. A body corporate, in itself, is merely a legal conception. Its purposes, objectives and activities are determined by individual human beings. To suggest some general distinction between a purpose of the body and a purpose of the constituent members is somewhat unreal. The purposes of a company and the purposes of its members, as members, are ultimately identical.

35. In the present case, it is clear that the individual members of PRS do derive gain from the activities of PRS/IMRO. That, indeed, is the reason for the existence of these bodies. But the pursuit of that objective must also be attributed to the two bodies themselves. In seeking gain for their members as members the bodies must by the same token be considered to be seeking gain for themselves.

7. Notifications Nos. CA/6/91E and CA/7/91E.

36. In sum, the Authority believes that PRS and IMRO provide a service for gain and are, therefore, undertakings within the meaning of the Competition Act. **1.3.2**

(c) *The agreement*

37. The agreement under consideration is a formal written agreement signed and sealed by PRS and IMRO and dated 29 December 1988. There can be no doubt that it constitutes an 'agreement' for the purposes of the Competition Act.

(d) *Restriction of competition*

38. The principal question that arises under this heading is whether, having regard to the relationship between PRS and IMRO, the agreement between them of December 1988 can be considered to be restrictive of competition within the meaning of section 4(1) of the Act.

39. In paragraphs 11-13 above, various provisions in the agreement under consideration and in the articles of association of IMRO which pertain to the relationship between IMRO and PRS were outlined. From these it is clear that PRS, by means of various rights vested in it, including those in relation to control of the composition of the board of directors of IMRO, is the parent company of IMRO and that a 'parent-subsidiary' or 'group' relationship exists between the two bodies. They, therefore, constitute a single economic entity.

40. In its decision in the AGF-Irish Life Holdings case,[8] the Authority considered that an agreement between member companies of the same group which provided for a reallocation of functions within the group did not offend against section 4(1). The reasoning stated in that decision is equally applicable in the present case because:

(i) PRS and IMRO, being a parent and a subsidiary, are not independent undertakings but are in fact separate arms of the same organisation and are not therefore in competition with each other;

(ii) IMRO has no real freedom to determine its own course of action on the relevant market;

(iii) The proposed arrangement merely involves a reallocation of functions within the same group.

Accordingly, the Authority considers that the present agreement does not have as its object or effect the prevention, restriction or distortion of competition in the State.

The decision

41. Both of the notifying parties, PRS and IMRO, are undertakings for the purposes of the Competition Act 1991 and the agreement of 29 December 1988 between them constitutes an agreement between undertakings for the purposes of section 4(1) of the Act.

42. The agreement of 29 December 1988 does not offend against section 4(1) because of the parent/subsidiary relationship which exists between the parties and because the agreement concerned involves no more than a transfer of functions between them.

The certificate

43. Accordingly, the Authority has granted the following certificate:

> The Competition Authority certifies that, in its opinion, on the basis of the facts in its possession, the agreement of 29 December 1988 between Performing Right Society and Irish Music Rights Organisation (CA/1/91E) which was notified under section 7 on 1 October 1991 does not offend against section 4(1) of the Competition Act 1991.

For the Competition Authority

E. Carey
Member

30 June 1992

1.4 Employees

1.4.1 Competition Authority notice: 'Employee agreements and the Competition Act' (published in *Iris Oifigiúil* No. 75, 18 September 1992)

The Competition Authority has received numerous requests regarding the position of employment contracts or agreements between employers and employees under the Competition Act. Since this indicates that many employment contracts may include non-competition clauses, the Authority considers that it would be useful to give some indication of its views regarding such agreements. The Authority points out that the interpretation of the provisions of the Competition Act is ultimately a matter for the Courts.

The prohibition in section 4(1) of the Competition Act relates to agreements between undertakings, decisions of associations of undertakings and concerted practices. Clearly most employers are undertakings. The Authority does not consider, however, that employees as such are undertakings within the meaning of the Act. Employees normally act on behalf of an undertaking and do not, therefore, constitute an undertaking themselves. This view is in accord with that expressed by the European Court of Justice in the *Suiker Unie* case, which involved Article 85(1) of the Treaty of Rome, upon which section 4(1) is based. The Court indicated that employees should be regarded as an integral part of the undertaking which employed them and were not therefore undertakings themselves. The view that employees are not undertakings was endorsed in a written answer to the European Parliament by the EC Commission in relation to professional soccer players which stated that:

> individuals participating in professional sports normally do so as employees of a club on the basils of an employment contract and as such are not undertakings.[1]

Although, there is a difference between Irish and EC legislation, in that the Irish Act defines an undertaking as being engaged for gain, the Authority believes that employees as such should not be regarded as undertakings under section 4 on the basis of the reasoning advanced by the Court of Justice in the Suiker Unie case.

As it does not consider that employees are undertakings, the Authority believes that an agreement between an employer and an employee is not an agreement between undertakings and is not therefore within the scope of section 4(1). It follows also that an employment agreement as such is not notifiable to the Authority, as sections 7(1) and (2) of the Act only provide for the notification of agreements of a kind described in section 4(1).

1. Written question no. 2391/83; OJ 1984 C222/21, 23.8.1984.

The position changes, however, once an employee leaves an employer and seeks to set up his or her own business. They would then be regarded as an undertaking. This view is in accord with EC treatment of such cases. As Van Bael and Bellis point out: **1.4.1**

> Employees are normally acting on behalf of an undertaking and therefore do not constitute an undertaking themselves. However, from the moment an employee pursues his own economic interests, and where they are different from his employer's interests, he might well become an undertaking within the sense of Article 85.[2]

At that stage the Authority would regard the agreement as an agreement between undertakings which could then be notified. If the former employer were to seek to enforce a non-competition clause in an employment contract in respect of an employee who had left and was seeking to establish his or her own business, the Authority believes that this would represent a restriction of competition within the meaning of section 4(1). While such an agreement between one individual and an employer may not have a substantial impact on competition, the existence of such agreements in many sectors of the economy means that their combined effect would be to greatly restrict competition. The Authority therefore believes that in these circumstances such agreements would offend against section 4(1) of the Competition Act. The Authority also believes that it would be difficult for such an agreement to satisfy the requirements specified for the grant of a licence in section 4(2) of the Act.

Should an employee in addition own or control the undertaking, the view of the Authority, expressed in several decisions, is that the individual can then be regarded as an undertaking.[3]

For the Competition Authority

Patrick M Lyons
Chairman

15 September 1992

2. I. Van Bael and J.F. Bellis, *Competition Law of the EEC*, 2nd ed., CCH Editions Ltd, 1990, point 206.
3. Notification nos. CA/9/91 — Nallen/O'Toole (Belmullet), decision of 2 April 1992, CA/9/91 — ACT/Kindle, decision of 4 September 1992 and CA/1/92 — Budget Travel/Phil Fortune, decision of 14 September 1992.

Editor's Notes:

A. Niamh Hyland in her article entitled 'Legal Status of Notices issued by the Competition Authority' makes interesting comparisons and observations about the positive and negative aspects of such notices. Published 1993 *ILT* 240-243.
B. James Bergeron's 'The Competition Act and Restraint of Trade in Employment Contracts' is an interesting article with reference to this notice. It is published at [1990-1993] 9 *JISLL* at p. 57 [*JISLL* = Journal of the Irish Society for Labour Law].
C. Paula O'Hare, legal adviser to the Competition Authority published an article entitled: 'The Competition Act 1991 and Employmnet Contacts' at [1990-1993] 9 *JISLL* at p. 80.

1.4.2 Competition Authority Decision No. 13, Peter Mark/Majella Stapleton: 18 February 1993, Notification No. CA/1011/92E

Employment contract containing restraint of trade clauses – Meaning of 'undertaking' – Employees are not separate undertakings from their employers – Clarification of Authority's notice – Employee agreements and the Competition Act for employees working for another employer – Whether commission payments have an effect on an employee's status as an undertaking – Authority's view that reasonable grounds for doubting that section 4(1) is offended must exist before certificate is requested – Competition Act 1991, sections 3, 4 and 7.

Facts: On 30 September 1992 notification was made to the Authority of a contract of employment made 16 July 1990 between Peter Mark, as employer and Majella Stapleton as employee, with the request for a certificate under section 4(4) of the Competition Act 1991 or, failing that a licence under section 4(2). Peter Mark, an unlimited Irish Company, carries on the business of hairdressing through 48 salons located throughout the State and Majella Stapleton is a hairstylist who was employed by Peter Mark in Sligo between July 1990 and September 1992 at which date she terminated her employment to take up a new position with David Martin Salon, also in Sligo. The notified agreement placed restrictions on Ms. Stapleton upon termination of the employment contract, for a period of six months, from setting up by herself or taking employment with any competitor within a range of one mile from the Peter Mark salon in Sligo.

In September 1992 Mr Justice Barron granted an interim injunction restraining Ms Stapleton from working for a David Martin salon which was a competitor of Peter Mark in Sligo. At the interlocutory hearing, the interim injunction was discharged and the interlocutory injunction application was refused upon Ms. Stapleton's undertaking to keep a list of her new customers up to the day of the trial of the action.

Decided by the Authority: In refusing to issue a certificate or grant a licence under ss. 4(4) and 4(2) respectively of the Competition Act 1991 that:

(1) The Authority's notice 'Employee Agreements and the Competition Act' was clear that an agreement between an employer and employee was not an agreement between undertakings.

(2) An agreement is not notifiable to the Authority if the agreement is not within the scope of section 4(1) because section 7(1) and (2) provide for the notification of an agreement described in section 4(1).

(3) There must be reasonable grounds for doubting whether an agreement offends against section 4(1) before a request for a certificate can be made.

(4) The Authority's notice on Employee Agreements did not deal with the question about whether an employee who works for another employer is a separate undertaking. Ms Stapleton's submission that she was a separate undertaking because of the commission payments which she receives from her new employer causes reasonable doubts concerning the application of the Competition Act to the notified agreement.

(5) Ms Stapleton is not an 'undertaking' within the meaning of section 3(1) of the Competition Act because her former position with Peter Mark and her current position with her new employer is solely that of an employee and the fact that in her new position she is paid partly on a commission basis is not sufficient to establish her as

an undertaking pursuing her own economic interest. 1.4.2

(6) The notified agreement is not an agreement between undertakings because Ms Stapleton was not at any material time an 'undertaking'.

(7) The Authority refuses to grant a certificate or licence because the agreement is not of a kind described in section 4(1) as required by section 7.

Cases and Other Authority Decisions referred to:
Suiker Unie v. EC Commission [1975] ECR 1663, [1976] 1CMLR 295
Competition Authority Notice on Employee Agreements and the Competition Act (Iris Oifigiúil No. 75 — 18 September 1992, pp. 632-3) **at 1.4.1 above**
Competition Authority Decision No. 11 — *Firestone/Grenfells Ltd and Thoroughbred Promotion & Development Company*, 5 November 1992 **at 3.9 below**

Submissions by Parties

(A) Peter Mark submitted that Ms Stapleton was not an undertaking within the meaning of the Competition Act in that she was an employee of Peter Mark's in the first instance and subsequently of David Martin and was therefore at no time conducting business on her own account.

(B) Submissions made on behalf of Ms Stapleton.

(1) The terms of Ms Stapleton's arrangement with David Martin's hair salon meant that she received profits from an increase in business which was attributable to her efforts and she was therefore an undertaking within the meaning of the Competition Act.

(2) The non-competition clause represented a significant barrier to entry into the hairdressing business.

Competition Authority Decision of 18 February 1993 relating to a proceeding under section 4 of the Competition Act 1991
Notification No. CA/1011/92E — Peter Mark/Majella Stapleton

Introduction

1. This decision concerns a contract of employment between Peter Mark and Ms Majella Stapleton, who is now a former employee of Peter Mark. The arrangements were notified to the Competition Authority on 30 September 1992 under section 7 of the Competition Act 1991 for the purpose of obtaining a certificate under section 4(4) or, in the event of a refusal by the Authority to issue a certificate, a licence under section 4(2). Both parties were given an opportunity of commenting upon the proposed decision before it was taken by the Authority. No response was received from either party.

The Facts

(a) *Subject of the Decision*

2. The decision concerns solely the contract of employment between Peter Mark and Ms Majella Stapleton.

(b) *The parties concerned*

Peter Mark

3. Peter Mark is an unlimited company carrying on the business of hairdressing. It is a subsidiary company of Glenberg, also an unlimited company which is a property holding company not involved in the hairdressing business.

1.4.2 *Majella Stapleton*

4. Majella Stapleton is a hair stylist who was employed by Peter Mark in Sligo as a stylist between July 1990 and September 1992. She is currently employed at a David Martin salon in O'Connell Street, Sligo. Ms Stapleton was trained by Skolars Training School, Thomas Street, Limerick, (a course of one year's duration which cost £2,800). She worked in a salon in Galway for six months and in a salon in London for one year prior to commencing employment with Peter Mark. Civil proceedings were instituted by Peter Mark to enforce the restraint provisions contained in her employment contract after she had left their Sligo salon.

(c) *The service and the market*

5. The service in this case is the provision of hairdressing and hairstyling services. The relevant geographic market is the Town of Sligo and its immediate environs. Peter Mark has one hairdressing salon in Sligo out of a total of some 30 salons. In the State as a whole, it is understood that there are approximately 3,000 to 3,500 hairdressing salons of which about 1,000 are in the Dublin area. Peter Mark have stated that they have 48 salons in the State.

6. There are no entry requirements to the hairdressing profession and anyone is free to set up a hairdressing salon, subject to compliance with planning, safety and health regulations. A salon over a period of time builds up a clientele. A salon located in a prime shopping centre or a high street position, where there is much passing trade, can build up its clientele much more quickly than salons in less favourable locations. It takes about six to twelve months for a new stylist to build up a personal clientele. It is claimed that the stylist becomes an asset of the salon having built up a personal clientele, and is in a position to bring those clients on leaving the salon since many clients tend to stay with the same stylist.

7. There are between 12,000 and 16,000 people employed in the hairdressing industry according to the Irish Hairdressers Federation which represents about 850 hairdressing businesses. The Federation considered that employment contracts were used only by the bigger firms and non-competition clauses were included in some written employment contracts but were considered difficult to enforce. It appears from enquiries made that the practice of using written employment contracts and of having non-competition restraints is not widespread in this industry.

(d) *The agreement*

8. The contract of employment between Peter Mark and their former employee, Majella Stapleton, was made on 16 July 1990 on commencement of her employment with Peter Mark. The relevant clauses in the notified agreement in these proceedings are clauses 4, 5 and 6 which provide as follows:

Clause 4 —'The Employee upon ceasing employment with the Employer shall not take up employment with any competitor of the Employer nor commence business in competition with the Employer within a radius of one mile of Peter Mark, Wine Street, Sligo for the term of six months from the date that such employment ceases'.

Clause 5 — 'As and from the termination of the employment the Employee shall not canvas, circularise or solicit business from the Employer's customers using the name Peter Mark'.

Clause 6 — 'In the event that the restraint provisions in this contract are-modified by any court, then such provisions as are considered reasonable by such court shall apply in lieu of the foregoing provisions.'

(e) *Submissions by the parties*

Peter Mark

9. Peter Mark submitted that Ms Stapleton was not and never became an undertaking as defined by the Act. Ms Stapleton was formerly an employee of Peter Mark and subsequently became an employee of David Martin. At no time was she conducting business on her own

account. They relied on the principles of the European Court of Justice in the *Suiker Unie* case[1] referred to in the Competition Authority Notice on Employee Agreements.[2] The *Suiker Unie* case was applied by Judge Esmond Smyth in the case between *Peter Mark v. Marcus Daly* in the Circuit Court (No. 14) on 21 July 1992 where he determined that Marcus Daly (a former employee of Peter Mark, Rathmines) was not an undertaking for the purposes of the Competition Act 1991. **1.4.2**

10. Peter Mark also presented arguments in support of their request for a certificate or a licence in respect of clauses 4, 5 and 6 of the notified agreement. Since the Authority accepts the submission that Ms Stapleton is not an undertaking for the purposes of the Act (see para. 17 below), it is not necessary to set out or consider these arguments.

Ms Majella Stapleton

11. The solicitors on behalf of Ms Stapleton submitted that Ms Stapleton is an undertaking within the meaning of the Act and profits from an increase in business which is attributable to her employment in David Martin's Hair Salon. They submitted that their client profited directly from an increase in business in the David Martin Salon through the payment of a commission rate on business and this rate would increase after she has worked for six months in the salon. She had not been requested to give a covenant to refrain from working or competing after termination of her engagement with the David Martin Salon.

12. They further submitted that it was their client's belief that Peter Mark and associated undertakings of Peter Mark sought to restrict all trainees and qualified staff in a manner similar to the restrictions in the notified agreement. The solicitors on behalf of Ms Stapleton claimed that significant barriers to entry in the hairdressing business had been created by those undertakings trading under the name 'Peter Mark' and other hairdressing businesses with substantial numbers of trainees and newly qualified personnel.

Peter Mark v. Majella Stapleton. High Court Proceedings

13. Peter Mark was refused an injunction implementing the non-competition clauses in Majella Stapleton's employment contract in the High Court in September 1992. Mr Justice Barron said that the main issue was the balance of hardship. He discharged the interim injunction on the basis of Ms Stapleton's undertaking to keep a list of new customers. The full case has yet to be heard.

Assessment

(a) *Section 4(1)*

14. Section 4(1) of the Competition Act 1991 prohibits and renders void all agreements between undertakings, decisions by associations of undertakings and concerted practices which have as their object or effect the prevention, restriction or distortion of competition in trade in any goods or services in the State, or in any part of the State.

(b) *The undertakings and the agreement*

15. Section 3(1) of the Competition Act defines an undertaking as 'a person being an individual, a body corporate or an unincorporated body of persons engaged for gain in the production, supply or distribution of goods or the provision of a service'.

Peter Mark

16. Peter Mark, an unlimited company and subsidiary of Glenberg, is a body corporate

1. *Suiker Unie & Others v. EC Commission* [1975] ECR 1663, p. 2007.
2. Competition Authority, 'Employee Agreements and the Competition Act', *Iris Oifigiúil*, No. 75, 18 September 1992, pp. 632-33.

1.4.2 engaged in the provision of hairdressing and hairstyling services for gain and is therefore an undertaking within the meaning of the Act.

Majella Stapleton

17. The Competition Authority in its Notice on Employee Agreements and the Competition Act outlined its views on the employee as an undertaking and on agreements between employers and employees. It is stated there that:

> the Authority does not consider, however, that employees as such are undertakings within the meaning of the Act. Employees normally act on behalf of an undertaking and do not, therefore, constitute an undertaking themselves: This view is in accord with that expressed by the European Court of Justice in the Suiker Unie case, which involved Article 85(1) of the Treaty of Rome, upon which section 4(1) is based. The Court indicated that employees should be regarded as an integral part of the undertaking which employed them and were not therefore undertakings themselves. The view that employees are not undertakings was endorsed in a written answer to the European Parliament by the EC Commission in relation to professional soccer players which stated that: 'individuals participating in professional sports normally do so as employees of a club on the basis of an employment contract and as such are not undertakings'.[3]
> Although, there is a difference between Irish and EC legislation, in that the Irish Act defines an undertaking as being engaged for gain, the Authority believes that employees as such should not be regarded as undertakings under section 4 on the basis of the reasoning advanced by the Court of Justice in the Suiker Unie case'. As it does not consider that employees are undertakings, the Authority believes that an agreement between an employer and an employee is not an agreement between undertakings and is not therefore within the scope of section 4(1). It follows also that an employment agreement as such is not notifiable to the Authority, as section 7(1) and (2) of the Act only provide for the notification of agreements of a kind described in section 4(1).

18. In its decision in the Aga Khan case[4] the Authority indicated that it:

> had also taken the view that the provisions of sections 4(1), 4(4), 7(1) and 7(2) taken together, imply that an agreement may be notified, and a certificate requested, where the parties are in some doubt as to whether that agreement would offend against section 4(1), but not otherwise. In the Authority's view, there must be reasonable grounds for such doubts.

19. In the Notice on Employee Agreements it was further indicated by the Authority that once an employee leaves an employer and seeks to set up his or her own business they would then be regarded as an undertaking. The Authority, however, did not deal directly with the question of an employee taking up employment with another employer in the Notice. It was also noted that Van Bael & Bellis, had in the context of Article 85, stated:

> However, from the moment an employee pursues his own economic interests, and where they are different from his employer's interests, he might well become an undertaking within the sense of Article 85.[5]

3. Written question No. 2391/83, OJ 1984 C222/21, 23.8.1984.
4. Notification No's CA/673/92E — Thoroughbred Promotion and Development Co Ltd./Grenfell Ltd. and CA/674/92E — Bertram and Diana Firestone/His Highness Karim Aga Khan.
5. I. Van Bael and J.F. Bellis, *Competition Law of the EEC*, 2nd Ed., CCH Editions Ltd, 1990, point 206.

20. Ms Stapleton's solicitors have claimed that she is an undertaking within the meaning of the Competition Act because she profits directly from an increase in the business of her employer through the payment of a commission. For these reasons the Authority believes that there was reasonable doubt in this instance, and it has considered the notified agreement in the context of the Competition Act 1991. 1.4.2

21. Majella Stapleton was employed by Peter Mark from July 1990 to September 1992 as a stylist. She left Peter Mark to take up employment in a competing hairdressing salon. Her position with Peter Mark was solely that of an employee. Her position with her new employer is also solely that of an employee. She had or has no ownership or control in her previous or present employment. The fact that Ms Stapleton is paid partly on a commission basis and, as a result, benefits directly from any increase in business, is not sufficient to establish, in the Authority's view, that she is an undertaking by virtue of pursuing her own economic interests. Accordingly, in the Authority's view she was not and is not an undertaking under section 3(1) of the Competition Act 1991.

22. The position would of course be wholly different if Ms Stapleton were seeking to set up her own business. As the notified agreement is, therefore, not an agreement between undertakings the arguments submitted by Ms Stapleton's solicitor in support of a certificate or a licence in relation to Clauses 4, 5 and 6 need not be considered by the Authority.

The decision

23. This decision applies solely to the contract of employment between Peter Mark and Ms Majella Stapleton, dated 16 July 1990. In the opinion of the Authority, that contract does not constitute an 'agreement between undertakings' for the purposes of the Competition Act 1991 because one of the contracting parties, Ms Stapleton, was not at any material time an 'undertaking' within the meaning of the Act. Accordingly, the agreement, not being 'of a kind described in section 4(1)', falls outside the scope of section 7 of the Act and the Authority refuses to grant a certificate or a licence under the Act.

For the Competition Authority

E. Carey
Member

18 February 1993

Competition Authority Decision No. 20, Apex Fire Protection Ltd/Mr Noel Murtagh: 10 June 1993, Notification No. CA/1130/92 1.4.3

Employment contract – Whether non-solicitation and confidentiality clauses in employment contract restrict, distort or prevent competition – Whether former employee is an undertaking – Amendment of originally notified agreement prior to decision – Refusal to grant a licence because not indispensable for the attainment of benefits achieved by agreement – Competition Act 1991 (No. 24) sections 3, 4 and 7

Facts: On 11 November 1992 Apex Fire Protection Ltd ('Apex') notified to the Authority a contract of employment dated 29 October 1991 between Apex and Mr

1.4.3 Noel Murtagh for the purpose of obtaining a certificate under section 4(4) of the Competition Act 1991 or, failing that, a licence under section 4(2).

Apex, a limited company registered in Ireland, provides fire prevention and protection products and services throughout the State. Mr Murtagh commenced employment with Apex on 1 February 1989 as a sales representative. Following promotion to field training supervisor Mr Murtagh signed the contract of employment which is the subject of this decision. Mr Murtagh left Apex on the 6 October 1992 and set up his own company A & A Fire Prevention Ltd which competes with Apex.

Under the notified contract of employment Mr Murtagh was restrained within the district which he worked for Apex for a period of two years from the date of the termination of his employment with Apex from soliciting business from persons who were customers of Apex within the two years immediately preceding Mr Murtagh's departure from Apex. The contract also required Mr Murtagh not to divulge any information gained as a result of his employment with Apex.

On 25 January 1993 the Dublin Circuit Court granted an interlocutory injunction enforcing the non solicitation and non disclosure clauses having decided that a fair issue was to be tried, that damages would not be an adequate remedy for Apex if it succeeded at the full hearing of the case and that the balance of convenience lay with granting the injunction in favour of Apex.

On 5 May 1993 the Authority issued a statement of objections to both parties setting out reasons why it could not issue a certificate or licence as requested. By letter of 28 May 1993 Apex offered to amend the non-solicitation clause so that it would apply to persons who were customers on the date of termination of Mr Murtagh's employment. The Authority objected on the grounds that the clause purported to exclude customers who had ceased to be customers before Mr Murtagh left his employment with Apex. Further, Apex suggested a period of 18 months for the non-solicitation of customers in reply to the Authority's objection to the duration of the restriction. Apex indicated that it would only use the non-disclosure clause to prevent Mr Murtagh from divulging information and that Mr Murtagh would not be prevented from entering the relevant market.

Decided by the Authority:

(A) In refusing to issue a certificate under section 4(4) of the Competition Act 1991:

(1) Both Apex and Mr Murtagh are undertakings within the meaning of section 3(1) of the Competition Act 1991.

(2) A restriction on soliciting customers is not a total prohibition of all forms of competition. The non-solicitation clause in this notification covers a small proportion of all customers in the relevant market.

(3) Mr Murtagh has confidential information concerning the requirements of, service dates for and prices charged to the customers of Apex because of his employment with Apex. Apex is therefore entitled to some protection from the competitive advantage which Mr Murtagh has acquired.

(4) No restriction on general advertising or passive sales which may arise because of an approach by a customer is intended to be enforced according to Apex and on that basis the Authority would not object to the non-solicitation clause.

(5) Dublin, which was identified by Apex as the ill-defined 'district' in the contract, was not an excessive area of restriction because of Mr Murtagh's former position in Apex as 'Field Training Officer'.

(6) The interpretation that Apex could prevent Mr Murtagh from seeking former customers of Apex who had ceased to be Apex customers before his departure from Apex was not restrictive of competition because of the assurance given by Apex that it would not enforce the clause in this way. **1.4.3**

(7) The effect of the non-solicitation clause which prevented Mr Murtagh from soliciting customers of Apex who had ceased to be customers during a period after the date of termination of his employment had no practical effect because Mr Murtagh would not be aware of his own knowledge that such former customers had ceased to be Apex customers.

(8) The two year duration and even the proposal of an eighteen month non-solicitation clause was not necessary for the protection of the legitimate interests of Apex. The two year restrictions in sales of businesses which are accepted by the Authority can be distinguished. The goodwill of Apex is not exclusively attributable to Mr Murtagh. In the sale of a business the purchaser is usually starting from a position that he does not have any of the goodwill of the business to be acquired. Mr Murtagh will have to convince customers that he is better than Apex which is one of the leading firms in the market. The Authority in rejecting the two year restriction acknowledged that it took into account that most customers would be contacted on an annual basis for their service needs and that the technical expertise of Mr Murtagh which was acquired in Apex must be taken into account when assessing the necessity of the two year restriction to protect the legitimate interests of Apex.

(9) The restrictions on divulging confidential information does not offend against section 4(1) provided that such provision is not used to prevent a party from re-entering the market after the expiry of a legitimate non-competition clause.

(B) In refusing to grant a licence under section 4(2) of the Competition Act, 1991 in respect of the notified agreement that:

(1) All four conditions set out in section 4(2) must be satisfied for a licence to be granted.

(2) The restriction on soliciting exceeds what is required for the legitimate commercial interests of Apex and it cannot be considered to be 'indispensable' within the meaning of section 4(2) of the Competition Act, 1991.

Cases, Competition Authority Decisions and Books referred to:

Suiker Unie & Others v. EC Commission (Case No. 40-48, 50, 54-56, 111, 113 and 114/75), [1975] ECR 1663, [1976] 1 CMLR 295

Remia v. Commission (Case No. 42/84), [1985] ECR 2545, [1987] 1 CMLR 1

Decision of EC Commission — Nutricia (Case No. 83/670/EEC) [1983] OJ L376/22, [1984] 2 CMLR 165

Competition Authority Decision No. 9 — Budget Travel/Phil Fortune, 14 September 1992 **at 3.7 below**

Competition Authority Decision No. 13 Peter Mark/Majella Stapleton, 18 February 1993 **at 1.4.2 above**

Competition Authority Decision No. 12, Scully Tyrell/Edberg Ltd, 29 January 1993 **at 3.10 below**

Competition Authority Notice on Employee Agreements and the Competition Act (*Iris Oifigiúil* No. 75, 18 September 1992, pp. 632-3) **at 1.4.1 above**

Stroud's 'Words and phrases legally defined', 3rd ed., p. 199

Forde, *Employment Law*, p. 96.

Editors note: Competition Authority Decision No. 27 Apex Fire Protection Ltd/William Brennan of 2 July 1993 — Notification No. CA/717/92 refers to a similar agreement between Apex and William Brennan who ceased to be an employee of

1.4.3 Apex in May 1992. In this one-page decision the Authority accepted the withdrawal of the notification having been notified that Apex did not intend to rely on its employment agreement with Mr Brennan and that Apex wished to withdraw the notification. **2.1.4**

Competition Authority Decision of 10 June 1993 relating to a proceeding under section 4 of the Competition Act 1991
Notification No. CA/1130/92 — Apex Fire Protection Ltd/Noel Murtagh

Introduction

1. This decision concerns a contract of employment between Apex Fire Protection Ltd and Mr Noel Murtagh. The arrangements were notified on 11 November 1992 under section 7(1) of the Competition Act 1991 for the purpose of obtaining a certificate under section 4(4) or, in the event of a refusal by the Authoritv to issue a certificate, a licence under section 4(2).

2. A Statement of Objections was issued to both parties on 5 May 1993. A response was received from Apex Fire Protection Ltd, and this has been taken into account in this decision, but an oral hearing was not requested. No response was received from Mr Murtagh.

The Facts

(a) *Subiect of the Decision*

3. The decision concerns an employment contract between Apex Fire Protection Ltd and Mr. Noel Murtagh a former employee of Apex, who has now set up his own business dealing in fire protection products and related services. The employment contract includes certain restrictions on the employee in the event of termination of employment.

(b) *The parties concerned*

Apex Fire Protection Ltd

4. Apex Fire Protection Ltd, of Apex House, Greenmount Industrial Estate, Harolds Cross Road, Dublin 12, was established in 1973. The company is involved in the provision of fire protection and detection products and related services throughout the Republic of Ireland. They employ 50-53 people full time and their staff turnover is approximately 50% per annum. They provide training courses for their employees. It has a customer base of several thousand with about 2,000 in the Dublin area alone.

Mr Noel Murtagh

5. Mr Noel Murtagh commenced employment with Apex Fire Protection Ltd on 1 February 1989 as a sales/service representative for 'the purpose of selling the goods, servicing and refilling equipment, collecting the accounts and furthering the commercial interests' of Apex. He was based in the Dublin area — city and county. He was promoted to a field training supervisor in October 1991 and following this promotion, he signed the contract of employment on 29 October 1991 with Apex. Mr Murtagh left Apex on 6 October 1992 and set up his own company called A & A Fire Prevention Ltd and currently employs one other person. Circuit Court proceedings were instituted by Apex to enforce the restraint provisions contained in the contract of employment of Mr Murtagh and an injunction, which is still in force, was obtained against him by Apex, (see para 24).

(c) *The product/service and the market*

6. The range of services provided by the various firms in this industry include the survey, design, installation, commissioning and maintenance of fire alarm and detection systems; the supply of fire extinguishers and fire equipment and the servicing, testing, repair and refurbish-

ing of equipment. The products involved in this case are portable fire equipment including fire extinguishers, spare parts and refills; fire hose reels and spare parts; fire extinguisher cabinets and covers; fire safety signs, push bars to open locks and key boxes. Maintenance of the products on an annual basis is also provided as part of the overall service. The relevant product market is the market for the sale and servicing of portable fire equipment. The relevant geographical market is the city and county of Dublin because that is the geographic area in which the restrictions under consideration apply. There are no reliable data available on the overall size of the market for the sale and servicing of portable fire equipment and the various companies' market shares. There are approximately forty companies involved in the industry in the greater Dublin area. The major companies apart from Apex are Champion Fire Ltd, Antifyre Ltd, George Angus & Company, Gendist Ltd and Chubb Fire and there are several smaller companies as well. 1.4.3

7. There are no legal entry requirements for a person seeking to enter the industry for the provision of goods and services for fire prevention purposes. Fire protection and the maintenance of fire equipment is now mandatory in the majority of buildings (other than private houses). Certain standards apply to various items of equipment used for these purposes such as fire extinguishers. The National Standards Authority of Ireland issued standards IS 290 and IS 291 covering portable fire extinguishers in order to regulate standards for the maintenance of fire equipment. Almost all fire extinguishers are required to be serviced on an annual basis. Apex said that about 3-5% of extinguishers would require maintenance at six monthly intervals under IS 291, in high risk circumstances.

(d) *The Agreement*

The contract of employment between Apex Fire Protection Ltd and their former employee, Mr Noel Murtagh, was made on 29 October 1991, on his promotion to the position of field training supervisor. The relevant clause in the notified agreement in these proceedings is Clause 15 which provides as follows:

Clause 15 — 'On the termination of this agreement howsoever occasioned, the representative shall not for the period of two years next after such termination within the district of which he has operated during the course of this agreement solicit any of the persons who were customers of the employer within two years immediately preceding the date of such termination and shall not divulge or disclose to any other party any information gained as a result of employment with the employer'.

(e) *Submissions by the Parties*

Apex Fire Protection Ltd

9. Apex submitted that Mr Noel Murtagh was not an undertaking in that he was now employed by a company known as A & A Fire Prevention Ltd. Mr Murtagh and another person were both employed by A & A Fire Prevention Ltd. In these circumstances, in accordance with the general direction of the Authority with regard to the definition of an undertaking, the decision of the European Court of Justice in the Unit Sugar case[1] the decision of the Circuit Court in the case of *Peter Mark v. Marcus Daly,*[2] and the decision of the Authority itself in the reference of the contract between Peter Mark and Majella Stapleton,[3] Mr Noel Murtagh was not an undertaking and therefore it was appropriate for the Authority to determine that the Act does not apply in this instance. Apex also submitted that either an individual was employed by a company in which he was not an undertaking, or the Authority must set some standard or

1. *Suiker Unie & Others v. EC Commission* [1975] ECR 1663, p. 2007.
2. *Peter Mark v. Marcus Daly*, Circuit Court (No. 14), 21 July 1992.
3. Notification No. CA/1011/92E — Peter Mark/Majella Stapleton, Competition Authority decision No. 13, 18 February, 1993.

1.4.3 rule defining when an individual (though merely a shareholder, director or employee of a company) was nonetheless deemed to be carrying on business and therefore an undertaking. They submitted that no such standard had been suggested by the Authority in this case.

10. Apex submitted that the purpose of their notification was to certify the validity of clause 15 of the Contract of Employment with Noel Murtagh of 29 October 1991. The company found it necessary to include this clause in the contract due to the incidence of representatives leaving the company and attempting to induce customers to do business with them.

11. Apex felt that clause 15 was reasonable since a former representative had gained knowledge of their customer base at the company's expense and that representatives capitalised on their former association with Apex and the high standing of its name whilst not necessarily working to the same standard required by Apex. They maintained that a very high percentage of representatives who went into business on their own failed in a very short space of time, but caused a lot of problems and thereby created a bad image for the industry. Some of the products supplied by Apex required specialist servicing and the company considered it important that this be done by a fully trained representative as failure to do so could result in very serious consequences for the consumer.

12. Apex submitted that they spent £35,700 on training new staff annually. They also stated that they were in the process of providing a modern training room complete with audio visual facilities which seated 40 people at a cost of £75,000 to the company. They also had a 2-3 week training programme for new trainees and provided a Field Training Supervisor to further assist the trainees. A weekly meeting was held for representatives in the Dublin area to introduce them to new products and services in the industry and a three monthly meeting was also held for all Apex staff.

13. The company submitted that they did not want to overly restrict any past employee, but they felt that past employees, such as Mr Murtagh, would have a distinct advantage through their knowledge of customer contact name and address; dates of service due; familiarity with existing customers and their requirements; and the relevant price that the company charged for each of its services.

14. Apex submitted that Mr Murtagh had worked for the company for nearly four years and during that time he would have had contact with at least 240 customers of Apex. In his capacity as a Field Training Supervisor, which involved liaison with a large number of new representatives, Mr Murtagh would have gained knowledge of and a personal introduction to some 15% to 20% of the pool of over 1,000 client accounts given to new representatives to help them get started in the business. It was Apex's view that as sales representatives naturally discussed their clients with each other they would be aware of the identities and individual needs of each others' customers. There were also the weekly meetings for all representatives at which the company's customer problems were discussed.

15. They submitted that Apex's market share was a small percentage of the potential available in Dublin city and county and they merely wished to protect the nature of the business and the standards to which they aspired. Without the restrictive clause any current employee would be free to leave and capitalise at the company's expense on the training and knowledge they gained through their employment with Apex. It had taken Apex 20 years to build up its customer base and the company did not want to be used as a training camp for people who trained with them and then set up their own business and profited from the knowledge of Apex's customer base.

16. Apex stated that any employee who wished to leave and start up in competition could do so provided they observed and abided by the restriction on soliciting Apex customers within the District/Territory that they had worked in previously. Furthermore, the restriction did not extend to canvassing Apex customers outside the district where they worked previously and this gave everybody a chance to compete fairly in the market place. They further stated that this was the very basic and minimum restriction that could be inserted into a contract such as this. The clause would not restrict competition from a person or persons who wished to conduct

themselves professionally, but would deter an opportunist who wanted to capitalise on the goodwill of the company which had invested many years in developing a professional approach and had a proven commitment in the industry. This was also for the benefit of the consumer who was guaranteed that qualified staff would supply, maintain and service the equipment that they had bought and thereby enabled the company to stand over the warranties that they had given in relation to their products. **1.4.3**

17. Apex also submitted that both the consumer and the employee benefited as a result of the efficacy of Clause 15 of the Agreement between Apex and Mr Murtagh. Because Apex was confident that it could restrict employees soliciting its customers, it could allow individual employees to become familiar with, and gain the trust of, Apex's customer base. This meant that those customers might go to the employee after he left, and it meant that the customer had a regular Apex employee in whom it could have confidence in respect of the servicing of its needs. Apex would have to put some other arrangement into place which might not be as beneficial for the employee or the customer if it did not have the protection of Clause 15. If this Clause was not operative Apex could continue to preserve its customer base by visiting customers in advance of any employee who was soliciting their business, or by offering promotions or discounts to those customers in order to prevent an employee taking Apex's business. It was pointed out that this would mean servicing customers more regularly than was warranted by good business practice or incurring extra costs (in promotion or otherwise) which were not strictly necessary. Ultimately, the customer would have to pay for this, and it could not be in the customer's interests to see an escalation on price in Apex or elsewhere in the industry (where similar clauses exist) simply because Apex had to take these extra steps to protect itself against former employees exploiting their knowledge of and familiarity with Apex's customer base.

18. With regard to the term 'soliciting' contained in Clause 15, Apex submitted that they relied on the definition of the word as contained in Stroud's 'Words and Phrases Legally Defined'[4] and the definition also contained therein as given by Mr Justice Hosking in the case of *Sweeney v. Astle* (1923) NZLR 1198 which stated as follows:

> The typical case of soliciting orders is where a trader or his traveller goes to some individual whom he selects to try and induce him to buy. If instead of doing this he sends a letter or circular inviting orders, and addressed individually to those whom it is thought worth while, that also would be to solicit orders. . . . It involves a selection of the persons to be appealed to.

The company considered an approach to a former customer or a written communication to a former customer to be soliciting. They did not consider the placing of an advertisement in the Golden Pages, for example, to be soliciting, but that of a direct approach or an appeal to a 'select group', i.e. Apex's customers was soliciting. The company submitted that the restriction (in Clause 15) was very limited and was not a blanket restriction.

19. On the issue of confidentiality, also contained in Clause 15, Apex submitted that every employee had a common law duty to his employer not to disclose any information that he had gained through the course of his employment. Dr Michael Forde in his book on Employment Law[5] stated as follows:

> Even where there is no express provision, by virtue of an employee's general duty of fidelity, it is an implied term of almost all Employment Contracts that employees will not disclose or use their employer's confidential information without letters of consent. The duty is broken, for instance, where the employee makes or copies the list of employer's customers for use by him when the employment ends or indeed where he memorises that very list for that purpose (*Robb v. Green*, 1895, 2QB315).

4. Stroud's, 'Words and Phrases Legally Defined', 3rd ed., 1990, p. 199.
5. Forde, Dr Michael, *Employment Law*, 1992, p. 96.

1.4.3 They also submitted that the confidentiality requirement in the Clause covered business secrets such as customer lists, pricing lists, proposed pricing lists, any information as to service techniques which would be unique to the company, details of the Company structure and internal financing and any other information that was not available to a competitor in the general market. The obligation not to disclose any confidential information was included in Clause 15 out of a sense of fairness to their employees so that they would be fully aware of their obligations.

20. The company stated that there had been other cases in which former employees of Apex had been in breach of Clause 15. They supplied copies of two letters which were sent to two former employees and they also referred to notification No. CA/717/92 — Apex Fire Protection Ltd and Mr William Brennan, another former employee of the company.

Mr Noel Murtagh

21. Mr Murtagh submitted that the restrictions concerned were excessive, particularly the two year restriction on soliciting. Mr Murtagh submitted that the restrictions in Clause 15 of the employment contract were substantial in scope and were unfair in their effect on his capability to earn his livelihood. He also submitted that the clause ran contrary to both the letter and spirit of the Competition Act. The time restrictions were inordinately long as the time aspect worked both backwards — the restriction related to all customers of Apex during the two years prior to the date of termination — and forwards — for a period of two years after termination during which Mr Murtagh could not solicit any of those customers.

22. Mr Murtagh submitted that it was patently unreasonable and unfair for Apex to restrict him from contact with Apex's 2,000 customers in the Dublin area even though he had contact with only 240 of those customers and maintained also that he did not receive a list of the 2,000 customers. Mr Murtagh also submitted that Apex seemed to have a dominant position in the market and sought to maintain this by means of the restrictive clause which was grossly disproportionate to any real risk to Apex.

23. Mr Murtagh claimed that because of the injunction he had to turn away potential customers because he felt restricted in being unable to respond to enquiries from ex-customers of his, which were also Apex customers. Mr Moore his legal adviser thought that the wording of the restriction on soliciting Apex customers for two years seemed to include even those customers who had left Apex during the course of the previous two years. Mr Murtagh felt strongly that the restriction had caused him and continued to cause him grave difficulties in exercising a basic right — that of earning his livelihood by means of his own initiative and labour. He submitted that for these reasons the Authority should not grant a certificate or a licence in any circumstances to Apex.

Apex Fire Protection Ltd v. Noel Murtagh. Circuit Court Proceedings

24. Apex Fire Protection Ltd obtained an injunction against Mr Murtagh in the Circuit Court on 25 January 1993. This prevented him from soliciting any of those persons who were clients, during the two years prior to 6 October 1992, in the Dublin area for a period of two years and restrained him from divulging or disclosing to anyone any information gained as a result of his employment with Apex for two years. Judge Kelly said that there was a fair issue to be tried, that damages would not be an adequate remedy and that the balance of convenience lay with granting the injunction to the Plaintiffs since there was a possibility of a certificate or a licence being granted in respect of the contract by the Competition Authority.

Subsequent Developments

25. In response to the Statement of Objections, a letter was received from Apex Fire Protection Ltd., on 28 May 1993. It was suggested that the wording of Clause 15 be amended by the substitution of the words 'who are customers of the employer at the date of the termination of employment' for the words 'who were customers of the employer within two

years immediately preceding the date of such termination'. Apex claimed, however, that the period of 12 months after termination proposed by the Authority, rather than two years, would not be adequate for the protection of Apex's legitimate interests. A number of reasons were given for this view, principally that 12 months would not allow sufficient time for a new representative to obtain the trust of a client, or even to visit the client. They suggested, however, that they would accept a reduction of the period to 18 months. 1.4.3

Assessment

(a) *Section 4(1)*

26. Section 4(1) of the Competition Act 1991 prohibits and renders void all agreements between undertakings, decisions by associations of undertakings and concerted practices which have as their object or effect the prevention, restriction or distortion of competition in trade in any goods or services in the State, or in any part of the State.

(b) *The Undertakings*

27. Section 3(1) of the Competition Act defines an undertaking as 'a person being an individual, a body corporate or an unincorporated body of persons engaged for gain in the production, supply or distribution of goods or the provision of a service'.

Apex Fire Protection Ltd

28. Apex Fire Protection Ltd is a limited company involved in the provision of fire protection and detection goods and services for various premises for gain and is therefore an undertaking within the meaning of the Act.

Mr Noel Murtagh

29. Mr Noel Murtagh, a former employee of Apex Fire Protection Ltd, set up his own business in October 1992 called A & A Fire Prevention Ltd. The Authority in its Notice on Employee agreements and the Competition Act[6] stated that it did not consider an employee to be an undertaking within the meaning of the Act and, as such, agreements between employers and employees did not come within the scope of the Act. It was further indicated that when an employee left an employer and set up his or her own business they would then be regarded as an undertaking. The Authority in its decision on Phil Fortune/Budget Travel[7] considered an ex-employee who acquired and became the proprietor of her former employer's business to be an undertaking. In this respect, the Authority has followed the approach taken under European Competition Law. For example, in the Nutricia Case[8] the Commission decided, and the Court of Justice agreed, that an individual who owns or controls a business is an undertaking. As Mr Murtagh now owns and controls his own business — A & A Fire Prevention Ltd which provides goods and services for gain — he is an undertaking within the meaning of section 3(1) of the Act.

(c) *The Agreement*

30. Apex Fire Protection Ltd and Mr Noel Murtagh, carrying on business under the name A & A Fire Prevention Ltd, are both undertakings within the meaning of the Act and consequently the agreement between Apex and Mr Murtagh is now an agreement between

6. Competition Authority, 'Employee Agreements and the Competition Act', *Iris Oifigiúil*, No. 75, 18 September, 1992, pp 632-3.
7. Notification No. CA/1/92 - Budget Travel/Phil Fortune, Competition Authority decision No. 9, 14 September, 1992.
8. Nutricia/De Rooij and Nutricia/Zuid Hollandse Conservenfabriek (83/670/EEC, OJ L 376, 31.12.83, p. 22), on appeal *Remia BV and Others v. European Commission*, Case 42/84, [1985] ECR 2545.

1.4.3 undertakings as defined in section 4(1) of the Competition Act 1991. The relevant product market is the market for the sale and servicing of portable fire equipment and the relevant geographical market is the city and county of Dublin.

(d) *Restriction of Competition*

31. The provisions of the notified agreement, other than clause 15, concerned matters appropriate to contracts of employment such as the duties of the employee, remuneration, working conditions etc. They are no longer operative since the employment has ceased.

32. In clause 15, two restrictions are imposed on the employee in the event of termination of the employment. These restrictions are to apply for a period of two years after termination. During that period, the employee may not, within the district in which he operated,

(a) solicit any of the persons who were customers of the employer within two years preceding the date of termination

(b) divulge or disclose to any other party any information gained as a result of the employment.

33. In its notice on 'Employee Agreements and the Competition Act'[9] the Authority has already given general guidance on the subject of non-competition clauses in contracts of employment. In that Notice the Authority stated as follows:

> If the former employer were to seek to enforce a non-competition clause in an employment contract in respect of an employee who had left and was seeking to establish his or her own business, the Authority believes that this would represent a restriction of competition within the meaning of section 4(1). While such an agreement between one individual and an employer may not have a substantial impact on competition, the existence of such agreements in many sectors of the economy means that their combined effect would be to greatly restrict competition. The Authority therefore believes that in these circumstances such agreements would offend against section 4(1) of the Competition Act. The Authority also believes that it would be difficult for such an agreement to satisfy the requirements specified for the grant of a licence in section 4(2) of the Act.

34. The Authority therefore believes that a restriction which seeks to prevent a former employee entering the market as a competitor offends against section 4(1). The restrictions in this instance are confined to soliciting the former employer's customers and to disclosing information confidential to the employer's business. The Authority considers that there is a difference between a restriction which seeks to prevent a former employee from entering the business and one which seeks only to protect the proprietary interests of the employer in his own business. The Authority believes that it is essential to employer/employee relationships that an individual should not be able to take up employment solely for the purpose of gaining an introduction to the employer's customers in order to solicit such customers. A restriction on soliciting the former employer's customers may therefore be regarded as essential both to protect the employer's proprietary interest in the goodwill of his business and to normal employer/employee relationships. Such a restriction must not, however, exceed what is absolutely necessary to protect the employer's interests or it would be regarded as an attempt to prevent competition by the ex-employee.

35. The Authority has considered carefully the arguments submitted by Apex in support of the proposition that the agreement does not restrict competition. These were summarised above in paras. 9-20. Insofar as the company are arguing that the non-solicit clause is necessary to protect the public from the provision of unsatisfactory goods or services, the Authority would say that this function is not one for private firms and that it cannot afford any justification for the imposition of clauses of the kind under consideration. It is clear that the main purpose of

9. Op. cit.

the clause is to protect the interests of the company itself from what it may consider to be unfair competition. The company is seeking by this clause to protect the goodwill in its customer base for a certain period in relation to a particular area. The company considers that the restrictions involved do not exceed reasonable limits. **1.4.3**

Restriction on soliciting

36. The Authority recognises that the restriction on soliciting in the present case is by no means a total prohibition of all forms of competition. The Authority understands, on the basis of the facts in its possession, that the restriction does not cover more than a small proportion of all customers in the relevant market. Mr Murtagh remains free to transact unsolicited business with Apex customers within the designated area, all business with Apex customers elsewhere, and all business with non-Apex customers everywhere. He may engage in normal forms of advertising to attract customers. After the expiry of the restriction, he will be completely free to carry on businiss everywhere without any restriction. It must be recognised that the clause places some restrictions on Mr Murtagh's commercial freedom. Mr Murtagh is seeking to earn a livelihood and build up a new business using the resources he has, including his knowledge and expertise of the business and his relationships with various customers, all acquired, admittedly while in the employment of Apex. He considers that he should be free to offer his services to any customer; it should be for the customer alone to decide whether to do business with him or Apex or any other firm.

37. Apex has provided important training to Mr Murtagh. He has had personal access to some of the customers of the company as well as access to information about the company's manner of operation. Besides having knowledge of the identity of Apex's customers, he also possesses confidential information concerning their requirements, the service dates and prices charged to them. His employment with the company has put him in possession of information which would place him at a competitive advantage *vis-à-vis* the company, were he to commence business himself (as he has done). The company is, in the Authority's view, entitled to some protection against its former employee in these circumstances.

Scope of restricted activities

38. The restriction applies to 'soliciting' certain customers. Two issues arise here (i) whether this could extend to general advertising e.g. an advertisement in the Yellow Pages and (ii) whether it could extend to 'passive' sales i.e. a sale resulting from an approach by the customer to the employee. The Authority understands the clause not to apply in either of these situations and Apex have confirmed that that is their interpretation also. On that basis, the Authority would raise no objection to this aspect of the clause.

Scope by reference to customers and area

39. The persons who may not be solicited by Mr Murtagh are those persons who were customers of Apex within two years of the termination of Mr Murtagh's employment. The reference to the area ('within the District of which he has operated') is somewhat ambiguous but it is understood (and Apex confirm) that the customers concerned are those who are based within the area of Dublin city and county only (and not the whole country) and this is unobjectionable as far as geographic scope is concerned. Of more significance is the determination of the class of customers affected. No distinction is drawn between customers with whom Mr Murtagh had dealings and other customers. It is mainly in relation to the former category that the arguments in favour of the restriction generally derive their force. The Authority accepts, however, that due account must be taken of the particular post occupied by Mr Murtagh in the Apex organisation. As a 'Field Training Supervisor', Mr Murtagh had access directly and indirectly to a wider range of customers than those dealt with previously by himself. Accordingly, the scope of the restriction in this respect does not appear to be excessive. A second difficulty which the Authority sees under this heading is that the class of customers, as

1.4.3 defined, includes persons who have ceased to be 'customers' of Apex before Mr Murtagh established his business as well as persons who chose to leave Apex during the period of the restriction. In the Authority's view, the company is not entitled to protection from solicitation of these persons. This conclusion does not apply, of course to persons who ceased to be customers as a result of soliciting by Mr Murtagh in breach of the clause. The Authority therefore concludes that the agreement offends against section 4(1) of the Act in that it applies to persons who are no longer customers of Apex other than as a result of soliciting by Mr Murtagh and this exceeds what is required for the legitimate commercial interests of Apex.

40. Apex offered to amend this clause, by letter of 28 May 1993, so as to apply only to those persons who were customers at the date of termination of employment. Since this would now permit Mr Murtagh to solicit those persons who ceased to be customers of Apex in the two years prior to the date when his employment ceased, the Authority considers that this aspect of the agreement no longer offends against section 4(1) of the Act. While this would still prevent Mr Murtagh from soliciting those persons who ceased to be customers during a period after his employment ceased, the Authority considers that this would have no real effect on competition, and that its removal would not lead to any practical difference in the situation since Mr Murtagh would not be aware, of his own knowledge, that such persons had ceased to be customers. In the circumstances, the Authority considers that the scope of the agreement by reference to customers, as amended, does not offend against section 4(1) of the Act.

Scope by reference to duration

41. In the view of the Authority, the company has not shown that a two year period after termination is necessary for the protection of its legitimate commercial interests. In coming to this view, the Authority has taken into account the fact that the period of time during which items of fire protection equipment normally require servicing is one year. A one year period of protection, in the view of the Authority, would provide the company with ample opportunity to confirm its business connection and goodwill with its existing customers prior to facing competition for those customers from Mr Murtagh subsequently. In reaching this conclusion the Authority has also taken account of the following factors:

(i) Insofar as the purpose of the restriction is to protect the company's goodwill, it must be admitted that only some of the goodwill in question is exclusively attributable to Mr Murtagh. Most of the goodwill must be attributable to the company itself and to the business reputation of its services, products and the back-up support provided by the company to its representatives.

(ii) In the case of sale of business agreements, the Authority accepted that a two year period of protection was normally necessary to protect the goodwill of the business being acquired. In such a case however, the starting position for the purchaser is one in which he normally possesses none of the goodwill. He has to secure all of that goodwill unlike the employer who already holds most of it. This consideration would suggest that a period of less than two years should normally be necessary in the case of employment contracts.

(iii) Notwithstanding his previous employment with Apex, Mr Murtagh is in a position somewhat akin to a new entrant into the market. He has to convince customers that the products and services he is offering are as good or better as those of others, including Apex, and that he is in a position to ensure adequate back-up service.

(iv) Apex is one of the leading firms in that market.

(v) While there is obviously some degree of technical expertise involved in the provision of the services concerned, that degree is not such as to justify a lengthy period of protection. 1.4.3

The Authority does not consider that the suggested period of 18 months, as proposed in the letter of 28 May 1993, is necessary to protect the legitimate interests of Apex.

42. The Authority therefore concludes that the agreement offends against section 4(1) of the Act in that it applies for a period of two years after the termination of the employment and exceeds what is required for the legitimate commercial interests of Apex.

Restriction on Divulging Information

43. In some previous cases concerning sale of business or shareholder agreements the Authority considered obligations not to disclose information. For example in the Budget Travel case,[10] the Authority accepted a clause preventing one party from using, disclosing or divulging information of a secret or confidential nature, following the sale of a business after the second party had given an undertaking not to use this clause to prevent the first party from re-entering the market. In another case, Scully/Tyrrell,[11] the Authority decided that a clause preventing the use and disclosure of confidential information did not offend against section 4(1) of the Act, after the parties involved had stated that the restriction would not be used to prevent the second party from competing in business. In those cases, the Authority was concerned to ensure that obligations of this kind were not used as a means of preventing or impeding a party from re-entering the market after the expiry of a non-competition clause. The restriction in the present case only involves disclosure. Apex have indicated that the clause under consideration will not be used in this way and will only be used to protect information covered by normal business confidentiality.

44. Unless confidentiality can be ensured, employer/employee relationships, and many others, just could not occur. This is relevant during the term of an agreement, and afterwards. It is akin to the goodwill being transferred as part of the sale of a business, but is probably even more important. It is hard to see how an employer would be prepared to give confidential information to employees if they were allowed to use this or disclose it to competitors when employment ceased. At the same time, it often has to be disclosed to employees for them to be able to do their job. Confidentiality may therefore be seen as ancillary in the sense of being fundamentally necessary for such relationships.

45. In the view of the Authority the restriction on disclosure does not offend against section 4(1) of the Act.

Applicability of section 4(2)

46. Under section 4(2), the Competition Authority may grant a licence in the case of any agreement or category of agreements which, 'having regard to all relevant market conditions, contributes to improving the production or distribution of goods or provision of services or to promoting technical or economic progress, while allowing consumers a fair share of the resulting benefit and which does not:

(i) impose on the undertakings concerned terms which are not indispensable to the attainment of those objectives;

(ii) afford undertakings the possibility of eliminating competition in respect of a substantial part of the products or services in question'.

47. As the restriction on soliciting exceeds what is required for the legitimate commercial interests of Apex, it cannot be considered to be 'indispensable' within the meaning of section

10. Notification No. CA/ 1/92 — Phil Fortune/Budget Travel Ltd, Competition Authority decision No. 9 of 14 September 1992.
11. Notification No. CA/57/92 — Scully Tyrrell & Company and Edberg Ltd, Competition Authority decision No. 12 of 29 January 1993.

1.4.3 4(2) of the Act. Since all of the four tests of the subsection must be met in order to qualify for a licence, it follows that the agreement in its present form cannot be granted a licence. It is not necessary to consider the position in relation to the other three requirements of section 4(2).

The Decision

48. Apex Fire Protection Ltd., and Mr Noel Murtagh are undertakings within the meaning of the Competition Act and the contract of employment between them, dated 29 October 1991 (CA/1130/92), is an agreement between undertakings. The agreement, as amended in the letter of 28 May 1993, offends against section 4(1) of the Act insofar as it contains a restriction on soliciting certain customers which exceeds what is required for the legitimate commercial interests of Apex in that it still applies for a period of 18 months after termination of employment. The agreement may not benefit from the provisions of section 4(2) of the Act because it contains terms which are not indispensable to the attainment of any benefits achieved by the agreement. The Authority therefore refuses to grant a licence to the agreement between Apex Fire Protection Ltd and Mr. Noel Murtagh.

For the Competition Authority

Patrick M. Lyons
Chairman

10 June 1993.

1.5 Partnership

Competition Authority Decision No. 333, Martin Doyle/Joseph Moffitt: 10 June 1994, Notification No. CA/1132/92 1.5.1

Arrangements for sale of interest in a rural partnership – Whether covenants restricting partners from specific work during and after the partnership restricts, distorts or prevents competition – How the Authority considers goodwill, geographic area, and duration protection. Competition Act 1991 (No. 24) sections 3, 4 and 7

Facts: On 24 November 1992 notification was made to the Authority of partnership arrangements and in particular a partnership deed of 1 January 1992 and a sale agreement which sought to allow one partner acquire most of the partnership goodwill over a period of ten years. The notification was accompanied with a request for a certificate under section 4(4) of the Competition Act, 1991 or, failing that, a licence under section 4(2) for the arrangements.

Mr Doyle and Mr Moffitt, the parties to the notified arrangements, are veterinary surgeons in the area of New Ross, Co. Wexford. Mr Doyle had been in practice in that area since 1965 and Mr Moffitt was employed by Mr Doyle in recent years as a veterinary assistant. Under the arrangements, the practice of Mr Doyle would be transferred to a partnership owned by both parties and Mr Moffitt would purchase the partnership over a period of ten years by paying annual instalments to Mr Doyle. The partnership would continue until 1 January 2003.

The sale agreement restrained Mr Doyle for a period of 5 years from 29 September 2002 from engaging in the private practice of veterinary surgeon within a radius of 20 miles from the town of New Ross. Mr Moffitt, the purchaser covenanted that he would not for a period of 5 years beginning the 29 September 2002 engage in equine or equestrian practice within a radius of 20 miles from the town of New Ross. Under the terms of the partnership deed each partner covenanted with the other that on his retirement from the partnership he would not, for a period of 5 years, within a twenty mile radius of New Ross:

(i) act for any party who was a client of the partnership within 2 years preceding his retirement;

(ii) seek to fill any veterinary vacancy which is capable of being filled by the continuing partner and, for which vacancy, the continuing partner has applied; or

(iii) do any act which may impair the goodwill of the practice of the continuing partner.

On 29 March the Authority issued a statement of objections indicating that a period of trade restriction in excess of two years might be justified in this case but five years could not be so justified. The Authority also suggested that the commencement date of the restriction should be more specific. No response was received from either of the parties.

1.5.1 **Decided by the Authority:**

(A) In refusing to issue a certificate under section 4(4) of the Competition Act 1991 in respect of the notified arrangements that:

(1) Each of the parties to the notified arrangements are 'undertakings' within the meaning of section 3(1) of the Competition Act 1991 and the notified arrangements constitute agreements between undertakings.

(2) The arrangements seek to give effect to the transfer of the business from the vendor to the purchaser and clauses within such agreements which place restrictions on the vendor competing with the purchaser do not offend against section 4(1) provided such clauses do not exceed in terms of their duration, geographic coverage and subject matter what is necessary to secure the transfer of the goodwill involved. The restrictions in the notified agreements in terms of geographic coverage and subject matter do not exceed what is necessary for this purpose but the duration of such restrictions being in excess of two years, which the Authority considers sufficient, offends against section 4(1). The restrictive covenants in the sale agreement operate for five years from September 2002 while those in the deed of partnership operate for five years from the date of the relevant partner's retirement. The combined result of these two restrictions is to have two separate periods one of which is totally un-related to any requirement for the protection of the goodwill of the business being transferred. Therefore the notified arrangements breach section 4(1) of the Competition Act.

(3) Protection against competition is only acceptable so long as it is necessary to secure the transfer of the goodwill.

(B) In refusing to grant a licence under section 4(2) of the Competition Act that: The non-competition clauses go beyond what is necessary to transfer the goodwill of the business and therefore cannot be considered as indispensable to the attainment of the objectives of the agreement.

Cases and Other Competition Authority Decisions referred to:
Competition Authority Decision No. 1 — Nallen/O'Toole (Belmullet), 2 April 1992 **3.3**
Competition Authority Decision No.12 — Scully/Tyrell, 29 January 1993 **3.10**
United States v. Addyston Pipe & Steel Company et al., 85 FED. 271, (6 cir. 1898)

Submissions It was submitted on behalf of the parties that the notified arrangements would result in a smooth transition of the practice initially to the partnership and thereafter to the purchaser which would benefit the clients and further that the retiring partner would still have opportunities to continue practice.

Competition Authority Decision of 10 June 1994 relating to a proceeding under section 4 of the Competition Act 1991 Notification No. CA/1132/92 — Martin Doyle/Joseph Moffitt

Introduction

1. Arrangements for the creation of a veterinary partnership and for the subsequent purchase of the business by one of the partners were notified to the Competition Authority on 24 November 1992. The notification requested a certificate, or in the event of a refusal by the Authority to grant a certificate, a licence.

The Facts

1.5.1

(a) *The Subject of the Notification*

2. The notification relates to an arrangement, dated 5 March 1992, between Martin Andrew Doyle of Priory Street New Ross (the vendor) and Mr Joseph Moffitt (the purchaser) of The Lodge, Mount Elliott, New Ross. The arrangement establishes a partnership for the purpose of a buy out of one of the partners by the other. This buy out is to be achieved over a period of 10 years. The purchase agreement and the associated partnership deed both include certain non-compete arrangements to apply from the time of the completion of the sale and the cessation of the partnership.

3. The Authority issued a Statement of Objections to both parties on 29 March 1993 expressing its concern with certain aspects of the non-compete provisions. The parties were given 28 days to respond and offered the opportunity of an Oral Hearing to present their case to the Authority. No reply was received from any of the parties.

(b) *The Parties*

4. Both Mr Doyle and Mr Moffitt are veterinary surgeons. Mr Doyle has a practice located in the town of New Ross County Wexford which he has operated since 1965. Mr Moffitt was employed by him as a veterinary assistant. Under the arrangements the parties will now operate the practice as a partnership with Mr Moffitt buying out Mr Doyle over a 10 year period.

(c) *The Product and the Market*

5. The business in which the parties are engaged is a rural veterinary practice located in the town of New Ross. The parties provide veterinary services of all descriptions within a radius of approximately 20 miles of New Ross and perhaps further. Services would include a small pet practice along with veterinary services provided for farmers with various types of livestock. Mr Doyle is a specialist in the equine/equestrian area. He has specifically excluded the equine practice from the sale agreement as he intendes to continue in this business.

6. The market therefore is that for the provision of various types of veterinary services. The parties have stated that there are a number of veterinary practices located in New Ross and the surrounding areas and that it is also possible for new suppliers to enter the market. They estimate that the practice accounts for about one quarter of the veterinary business in the area. Four veterinary practices including Mr Doyle's are listed in the latest edition of the Yellow Pages as being located in New Ross. In addition a number of others are located in adjoining towns. There were a total of 1,813 registered veterinary surgeons within the State on 1 January 1992.

(d) *The Arrangements*

7. The arrangements relate to the creation of a partnership between Mr Doyle and Mr Moffitt for the purpose of Mr Moffit purchasing the business of the veterinary practice previously owned by Mr Doyle over a period of 10 years. There are two related agreements one for the sale of the business over a period of 10 years and the other a deed of partnership which commenced on 1 January 1992 and will continue until 1 January 2003.

The Sale Agreement

8. The sale agreement provides for the purchase of the Practice formerly operated by Mr Doyle alone, including the goodwill attaching to it, over a period of 10 years. The purchase is being made in instalments on the basis of a schedule set out in the agreement under which a certain proportion of the business is to be transferred in return for payments by Mr Moffitt. The first payment was made on 1 January 1992. Thereafter Mr Moffitt will pay an annual sum on 1 January each year up to and including 1 January 2002.

9. Under clause 5 Mr Doyle and Mr Moffitt entered into a partnership agreement the terms of which are set out in an attached partnership deed.

1.5.1 Clause 7 provides that:

> the Vendor, will not within a period of five years engage in the private practice of Veterinary Surgeon within a radius of twenty miles from the town of New Ross such period to commence on the 29th day of September, 2002 accepting* any work done by the Vendor, as assistant to the Purchaser.'

Clause 8 provides that:

> the Purchaser will not within a period of five years from 29 September 2002 engage in equine or equestrian practice within a radius of twenty miles from the town of New Ross accepting* any work done by the Vendor, as assistant to the Purchaser.

The Partnership Deed

10. Clause 13.1.2 provides that each of the parties shall:

> devote his full time and attention to the Partnership diligently and faithfully employ himself in the Partnership and use his best skill and endeavours to carry on that business for the utmost benefit of the partnership.

11. Clause 19.1 provides that any partner may retire from the partnership on giving the other partners not less than 6 months notice in writing expiring on the last day of the financial year. Clause 24 requires an outgoing partner to deliver up to the continuing partners lists of clients correspondence and all other documents and papers which may have come into his possession while he was a partner and he shall not retain any copies of them.

12. Clause 26.1 contains a number of non-compete provisions which are set out below:

> Each Partner hereby covenants with all the other Partners that he shall not for a period of [5] years from the date of retirement from the Partnership within an area of twenty miles radius of the town of New Ross;
> (i) without the written approval of the Continuing Partners act for any person who shall have been a client [of] the Partnership within the preceding [2] years;
> (ii) seek apply for accept or hold any part-time profession* appointment whether honorary or paid by fees salaries or otherwise within the aforesaid area which is capable of being filled by a veterinary surgeon and for which the Continuing Partners or their nominees are applicants; or
> (iii) do any act or thing which may tend to destroy or impair the goodwill of the practice of the Continuing Partners.

(e) *Submissions of the Parties*

13. The parties have stated that there are a number of veterinary practices in New Ross and the surrounding areas and that it is presumably possible for new practices to commence. They have stated that, as the agreement concerns a small rural veterinary practice, the arrangements would not have the effect of preventing, restricting or distorting competition within the State in veterinary practices. They also made some arguments to justify the grant of a licence should a certificate be refused. Specifically they argued that the arrangements would result in the smooth transition of the practice, initially to a partnership and thereafter to the purchaser as a sole practitioner. They claimed that this would help the practice and that customers would benefit from the smooth transition and the continuation of the practice. They stated that the restrictions imposed would not interfere with the running of the practice and that the retiring partner would have some opportunities to continue in practice.

**Editor's note:* Typographical errors must have arisen in the original Sale Agreement or the transcription by the Competition Authority as 'accepting' ought to be 'excepting' and 'profession' should be 'professional'.

(f) *Subsequent Developments* 1.5.1

14. On 15 April the Authority wrote to Simon W. Kennedy solicitors, requesting certain additional information. It also indicated that, in its previous decisions relating to sale of business agreements, it had indicated in italics that non-compete clauses of more than two years duration would generally be regarded as offending against section 4(1) and not meeting the requirements for a licence under section 4(2) of the Competition Act. The parties were asked what justification there was for a longer period of restriction in this instance. On 22 June 1993 the Authority wrote again to the solicitors representing both parties as no reply had been received in response to its earlier letter.

15. The parties argued, in a letter dated 8 July 1993, that the non-compete provisions were purely for the benefit of Mr Moffit. They claimed that a restriction for more than two years was justified in this instance given the fact that Mr Doyle has operated the business for 28 years in New Ross, was well known within the locality and is closely identified with the practice by everyone in the locality.

16. The Authority issued a Statement of Objections to the parties on 29 March 1994 indicating that it intended to refuse a certificate or licence to the notified agreement and setting out the reasons why it intended to do so. It indicated in a letter to the parties that it accepted that a non-compete clause of more than two years duration might be necessary in this instance but it did not consider that a restriction for five years was justified. In addition it indicated that such a restriction should date either from the termination of the partnership or the date of completion of the sale and could not apply in both instances. No response was received from either of the parties.

Assessment

(a) *Section 4(1)*

17. Section 4(1) of the Competition Act states that 'all agreements between undertakings, decisions by associations of undertakings and concerted practices which have as their object or effect the prevention, restriction or distortion of competition in trade in any goods or services in the State or in any part of the State are prohibited and void.'

(b) *The Undertakings and the Agreement*

18. Section 3(1) of the Competition Act defines an undertaking as 'a person being an individual, a body corporate or an unincorporated body of persons engaged for gain in the production, supply or distribution of goods or the provision of a service.' The parties to the present agreement are Mr Doyle and Mr Moffitt who are engaged as partners in the provision of veterinary services for gain and are therefore undertakings within the meaning of the Act. This view is consistent with that taken by the Authority in its first decision where it decided that two individuals who had carried on an electrical goods business in partnership were undertakings.[1] The arrangements involving the sale of business agreement and the deed of partnership constitute an agreement between undertakings.

(c) *Applicability of section 4(1)*

The Sale Agreement.

19. The Authority has stated on a number of occasions that agreements for the sale of a business do not per se offend against section 4(1) of the Competition Act. The Authority believes that the agreement notified is purely concerned with the transfer of ownership of a business and, in the absence of any indication that such a transfer would of itself prevent, restrict or distort competition, does not believe that the sale offends against section 4(1).

1. Competition Authority decision no. 1, Nallen/O'Toole (Belmullet), 2 April 1992.

1.5.1 20. The arrangement is slightly unusual in that the sale is to take place in instalments over a period of 10 years. This gradual transfer of ownership is to be secured by the creation of a partnership involving both Mr Doyle and Mr Moffitt for that period. The Authority has indicated in previous decisions that it would take a negative view of any artificial arrangements designed to extend the period during which one or other of the parties were restrained from competing with the business being sold.[2] The Authority accepts that the present arrangement has not been designed with that object in view but that it constitutes an arrangement whereby the current owner can arrange for his future retirement and can sell his business to an individual who would not have the capital or resources to acquire it immediately.

21. The Authority has, in a number of decisions, indicated that in the case of a sale of business a restriction on the vendor competing with the business following the completion of the sale does not offend against section 4(1), provided it does not exceed what is necessary to secure the transfer of any goodwill involved, in terms of its duration, geographic coverage and subject matter. It has also stated on several occasions that it generally considers a period of two years sufficient to ensure the transfer of goodwill. Clause 7 provides for a restriction on the vendor competing with the business for a period of 5 years after completion of the sale. As only a transfer of goodwill is involved the Authority can see no reason for accepting such a long restriction and it believes that its effect will be not merely to secure the transfer of goodwill, but also to restrict competition. The restriction is confined to an area within 20 miles of the town of New Ross which is the area within which the practice operates. It is confined to the provision of veterinary services. Thus in terms of its geographic scope and subject matter it does not exceed what is necessary to protect the purchaser's interest in the goodwill of the business. Clause 7 of the sale agreement offends against section 4(1) since its duration exceeds what is necessary to secure the transfer of the goodwill of the business.

22. Clause 8 restricts the purchaser from providing certain equine and equestrian services within a radius of 20 miles of New Ross for a period of 5 years from 29 September 2002. Restrictions of this sort on the purchaser are unusual and would not normally be considered essential to the agreement. Effectively the vendor intends to continue in this business, so the intention is that this element of the partnership, with its associated goodwill, will be retained by him. In effect the sale involves the dissolution of the partnership with each party retaining a part of the business previously carried on jointly. Thus for reasons already outlined some restriction on the other partner, who is the purchaser in this instance, may be necessary to ensure that the vendor retains that part of the goodwill of the partnership. Such restrictions must, however, be subject to the limitations outlined in the previous paragraph. As in the case of clause 7 the Authority believes that the duration of clause 8 exceeds what is necessary to secure the transfer of the goodwill by virtue of its duration and it therefore also offends against section 4(1).

The Partnership Deed

23. The Authority has not previously considered a partnership arrangement. It did, however, indicate in Nallen/O'Toole that it 'does not regard partnerships as being in contravention of the Act *per se*. In certain circumstances, however, partnership agreements may be in breach of section 4(1).' It agrees with the views expressed by Mr Justice Taft in the Addyston Pipe case in the United States almost a century ago:

> Again, when two men became partners in a business, although their union might reduce competition, this effect was only an incident to the main purpose of a union of their capital, enterprise, and energy, to carry on a successful business, and one useful to the community. Restrictions in the articles of partnership upon the business activity of the

2. Competition Authority decision no. 12, Scully/Tyrrell, 29 January 1993.

members, with a view to securing their entire effort in the common enterprise, were, of course only ancillary to the main end of the union, and were to be encouraged.[3] 1.5.1

24. Consequently the requirement in clause 13.1.2 that each partner 'devote his full time and attention to the Partnership diligently and faithfully employ himself in the Partnership and use his best skill and endeavours to carry on that business for the utmost benefit of the partnership', cannot be said to offend against section 4(1). Indeed the Authority has already indicated in Scully Tyrrell that:

> It is clear, even if it is not explicitly stated, that an agreement between parties to carry on business together, implies that they will not compete against the business or against each other so long as they remain in business together.[4]

25. Similarly the Authority considers that the requirements in clause 19.1, to give notice of intention to retire from the partnership, and clause 24, to hand over correspondence and other information which rightly belongs to the partnership, do not offend against section 4(1).

26. Clause 26.1 contains a number of non-compete provisions which are to apply upon the dissolution of the partnership. These are related to the fact that the partnership is linked to the sale of the business. As already noted the purchaser of a business is entitled to protection against competition by the vendor where such protection is necessary to secure the complete transfer of the goodwill of the business. This applies equally where the vendor and purchaser have been engaged together as partners in a business. As stated, however, such protection must not exceed what is necessary to protect the transfer of the goodwill of the business.

27. Clause 26.1 restricts each partner for a period of 5 years from the date of retirement from the partnership, within an area of twenty miles radius of the town of New Ross from:

> (i) acting for any person who would have been a client of the partnership within the preceding two years without the written approval of the continuing partners;
> (ii) seeking, accepting or holding any part-time professional appointment whether honorary or paid which would be capable of being filled by a veterinary surgeon and for which the continuing partners or their nominees have applied; or
> (iii) doing anything to damage the goodwill of the practice of the Continuing Partners.

This restriction is confined to activities which may be engaged in by a veterinary surgeon within the area in which the partnership operates and in terms of its geographic scope and subject matter does not offend against section 4(1). In the Authority's view, however, the restriction for a period of 5 years exceeds what is necessary to secure the transfer of the goodwill to the continuing partners for the reasons already set out above and thus offends against section 4(1).

28. In addition the Authority has to consider the relationship between clause 26.1 of the partnership deed and clause 7 of the sale agreement. The latter contains a restriction of 5 years dating from September 2002. While the Authority accepts that it is the intention of the parties to operate the partnership until that time it must nevertheless recognise the possibility that one or other party may retire from the partnership before that date. In particular if Mr Doyle were to retire in September 1997, for example, the combined effect of the two clauses would be to prevent him from competing for a period of some 10 years after the partnership ceased. Should Mr Doyle retire from the partnership then the business and the goodwill attaching to it would remain with Mr Moffit. He would be entitled to be protected against Mr Doyle competing with the business for some period of time after he had retired in order to ensure that he acquired the

3. *United States v. Addyston Pipe & Steel Company et. al.*, 85 Fed. 271, (6th cir. 1898).
4. Para. 72.

1.5.1 full goodwill of the business. However, once that period had expired Mr Moffit would be entitled to no further period of protection. Thus in the event of Mr Doyle retiring before 2002, some restriction on his competing with the business for a period of time after he retired from the partnership would be acceptable, but in those circumstances a further period beginning in September 2002 when Mr Moffit would make the final payment for the business, would not. Protection against competition is only acceptable so long as it is necessary to secure the transfer of the goodwill. The transfer of the goodwill does not take place in instalments. The fact that the parties to a sale of business may agree to have the purchaser pay for the acquisition over a period of time does not, in the Authority's view, affect the period during which a non-compete clause can be regarded as not offending against section 4(1). For this reason the combined non-compete provisions also offend against section 4(1).

Applicability of section 4(2)

29. Under section 4(2), the Competition Authority may grant a licence in the case of any agreement or category of agreements which offends against section 4(1) but which, 'having regard to all relevant market conditions, contributes to improving the production of goods or provision of services or to promoting technical or economic progress, while allowing consumers a fair share of the resulting benefit and which does not—

(i) impose on the undertakings concerned terms which are not indispensable to the attainment of those objectives;

(ii) afford undertakings the possibility of eliminating competition in respect of a substantial part of the products or services in question.'

30. In the Authority's opinion the non-compete provisions contained in the notified arrangements go beyond what is necessary to secure the transfer of the business. Consequently, in the Authority's opinion, they cannot be regarded as indispensable to the attainment of the objectives of the agreement and so do not satisfy the requirements for a licence.

The Decision

31. In the opinion of the Competition Authority the agreement between Mr Martin Andrew Doyle and Mr Joseph Moffitt for the creation of a partnership between them and the eventual acquisition of the business by Mr Moffitt (Notification No. CA/1133/92) notified on 24 November 1992, under section 7(1), constitutes an agreement between undertakings. It considers that the restrictions in clauses 7 and 8 of the Share Purchase Agreement and in clause 26 of the partnership agreement offend against section 4(1) of the Competition Act and do not satisfy the requirements for a licence under section 4(2). Consequently the Authority refuses a certificate or licence in respect of this notification.

For the Competition Authority

Patrick Massey
Member

10 June 1994

1.6 Commercial Agents

Competition Authority Decision No. 286, Conoco Consignee Agreements: 25 February 1994, Notification No. CA/71/92E* **1.6.1**

Licence agreement – Licensee acting as licensor's agent in sale of licensor's motor fuel products – Licensee acting as independent contractor in sale of non-motor fuel products – Licensee remunerated on commission basis for agency services – Power of licensor to determine the suppliers to the licensee of non-motor fuel goods – Whether such provisions prevent, restrict, distort competition – Competition Act 1991 (No. 24) sections 3, 4 and 7

Facts On 7 September 1992 notification was made to the Authority with a request for a certificate under section 4(4) of the Competition Act 1991, or failing that, a licence under section 4(2) in respect of standard agreements between Conoco Ireland Ltd ('Conoco') and various licensees. Conoco, a wholly owned subsidiary of the US Company Conoco Inc., is engaged, *inter alia,* in the supply and distribution of motor fuels and other petroleum products in the State through a chain of retail outlets most of which are owned by independent dealers and some being owned by Conoco.

The notified agreement between Conoco and various licensees relates to the operation of those retail stations owned by Conoco. Under the terms of the notified agreement the licensee is given a licence by Conoco to occupy and make use of the service station premises subject to the terms of that agreement. The agreement has various obligations for the licensee in respect of his carrying on the business of a retail petrol filling station and also in respect to the running of a convenience shop located on the premises.

In regulating the relationship between the licensee and Conoco with regard to the sale of fuel products the agreement provided that all motor fuel products remained the propoerty of Conoco until they were sold, that the licensee shall sell the fuel at prices notified to the licensee by Conoco from time to time and that the proceeds from such sale less any commission payable to the licensee and any amounts due for VAT were to be lodged to a Conoco bank account on a daily basis. The agreement further provides that if the licensee fails to sell a specified quantity of motor fuels on a monthly basis the licensee will pay to Conoco agreed sum of liquidated damages. Paragraph 8.6 of the agreement expressly states that no relationship of partnership or agency exists between the party and that the licensee is for all purposes an independent contractor. The licensee is also responsible for the discharge of all overheads and for any fuel losses on the premises. The licensee also covenants not to carry on, directly

**Editor's note:* Chapter 4, which concerns exclusive purchasing arrangements, includes a number of decisions which are particularly relevant to motor fuel solus arrangements.

1.6.1 or indirectly, any business in which competing products are sold or offered for sale at or from a premises situated within a specified radius.

Appendix I of the notified agreement sets out specific provisions relating to the operation of the shop on the premises. In particular the licensee is permitted to sell products other than Conoco's motor fuel products in the shop provided such goods are supplied by suppliers approved by Conoco in writing. The licensee covenants to pay to Conoco monthly a fee equal to a percentage of the wholesale price of the products sold in the shops and to facilitate this covenants to keep accurate records for inspection from time to time by Conoco. The licensee also undertakes to present and merchandise the products in the shop in accordance with the initial layout configuration implemented by or on behalf of Conoco at the shop and the licensee also undertakes to conduct stock takes as directed by Conoco from time to time. The licensee is given an annual turnover figure for the shop and should he fail to meet that figure a fee is payable by the licensee to Conoco, which fee increases in line with the shortfall of the actual turnover from the targeted turnover.

In response to questions posed by the Authority, Conoco stated that in the sale of the fuel products, where ownership and financial risks remain with Conoco, the licensee may be regarded as a trade representative or commercial agent of Conoco rather than an independent trader. In the operation of the shop Conoco submitted that the licensee was clearly an independent trader and that any restrictions imposed on the licensee are for the purposes of the general operation of the service station on behalf of Conoco.

On 5 October 1993 the Authority wrote to Conoco expressing concern over the clause in the notified agreement that required the licensee to obtain supplies of the shop products from suppliers approved by Conoco in writing. The Authority stated that its concern would be removed by the addition in that clause of the following sentence; 'approval will be withheld only for objectively valid reasons which shall be disclosed to the licensee'. By letter dated 29 November 1993 Conoco agreed to amend the agreement by the addition of the said wording.

Decided by the Authority: In issuing a certificate under section 4(4) of the Competition Act 1991 in respect of the notified agreement that:

(1) Each of Conoco and the licensees are undertakings within the meaning of section 3(1) of the Competition Act in that they are both engaged in the sale of motor fuels for gain and the licensees are also engaged in the sale of other products for gain. The notified agreement is an agreement between undertakings in the relevant product markets are those for motor fuels and those for the products sold in the shop on the premises. The relevant geographic market is the State.

(2) The licensee is a self-employed intermediary between Conoco and the purchasers of motor fuels and he concludes the sale of fuel on behalf of Conoco, on a continuing basis, for up to ten years. The licensee does not own the motor fuel stocks, the resale prices are set by Conoco and the licensee lodges the proceeds of such sale, less any commission, to the credit of Conoco's bank account. While the licensee is responsible for the hiring and paying of employees the profits and losses of the motor fuel business as a whole accrue to Conoco and the licensee must obey Conoco's instructions and may undertake no autonomous behaviour in respect of the operation of the petrol station. The licensee, in operating the petrol station and selling Conoco products, is an auxiliary organ, forming an integral part of Conoco's distribution

business and in the sale of the motor fuels can be considered a commercial agent of Conoco. 1.6.1

(3) The licensee sells products other than Conoco's products in the shop for his own account and separately from and independent of the sale of the motor fuel products and although he pays a commission on sales to Conoco and is bound by certain obligations imposed by Conoco regarding the operation of the shop he is in no sense a commercial agent of Conoco in respect of the shop but is an independent trader.

(4) Undertakings are entitled to decide how to operate their distribution systems and, in particular, to appoint commercial agents to sell their goods on their behalf. Since a commercial agent is an auxiliary organ and similar to an employee an agreement between the princpal and a commercial agent does not in principle offend against section 4(1). The notified agreement insofar as it creates the relationship between a principal and a commercial agent does not offend against 4(1).

(5) The relationship of commercial agent is closer to being an employee than to being an independent trader and certain restrictions may be imposed upon a commercial agent without offending against section 4(1) of the Competition Act which would if they were imposed upon an independent trader would so offend.

(6) Only one of the provisions in the agreement relating to the shop has the object or effect of preventing restricting or distorting competition. The other restrictions reflect the fact that the shop is owned by Conoco and is licensed to the licensee for the purpose of enhancing earnings at the station for the mutual benefit of the owner and the licensee while ensuring that the reputation of Conoco and the brand name of the motor fuel is not damaged.

(7) The provision in the agreement relating to the shop whereby the licensee shall be free to obtain supplies of shop products from any supplier approved by Conoco in writing could be used to limit the freedom of the licensee to determine what products to sell and from whom he might obtain supplies which could affect the ability of the licensee to compete with other retailers in the area. Such a provision could also limit competition between suppliers to obtain the custom of the licensee. While the effect of this provision might have little effect upon competition in the case of an individual licensee the cumulative effect of this obligation in respect of all Conoco's licensees might not be insignificant and therfore this clause prior to its subsequent amendment in line with the Authority's letter of 5 October 1993, offended against section 4(1) of the Competition Act.

Cases, Decisions and Notices referred to:

Suiker Unie v. EC Commission [1975] ECR 1663, [1976] 1 CMLR 295

EC Commission notice on exclusive dealing contracts with commercial agents, [1962] OJ 139

EC directive relating to coordination of the laws of the Members States relating to self-employed commercial agents [1986] OJ L328

Competition Authority Decision No. 25, motor fuel category licence — 1 July 1993 **4.2**

Competition Authority Decision of 25 February 1994 relating to a proceeding under section 4 of the Competition Act 1991
Notification No. CA/71/92E — Conoco Consignee Agreements

Introduction

1. Notification was made with a request for a certificate or licence by Conoco Ireland Ltd on 7 September 1992 in respect of its standard agreement with consignees.

1.6.1 2. Notice of intention to take a favourable view of the agreement was published in the Irish Times on 14 January 1994. A submission was received from the Jet Retailers Association.

The facts

(a) *The subject of the notification.*

3. The decision concerns the standard consignee agreement between Conoco and the consignees at a number of its company owned petrol stations. Each agreement consists of a licence to operate the petrol station on behalf of Conoco and to sell only Jet motor fuel on the premises, and there are special provisions in the agreement in respect of a shop on the premises in which are sold products other than motor fuels and other Jet branded products, such as grocery goods, confectionery, cigarettes, newspapers, etc. The two parts of the agreement are dealt with separately in this decision.

(b) *The parties involved.*

4. Conoco is a wholly owned subsidiary of Conoco Inc., which is a wholly owned subsidiary of E.I. Du Pont de Nemours and Company, Inc., both being US companies. Conoco is involved, *inter alia*, in the supply and distribution of motor fuels and other petroleum products to the motoring public through a chain of retail outlets, most of which are owned by independent dealers, the remainder being owned by Conoco. Twenty-three of its company outlets are occupied by so called consignees, who operate the petrol station and a convenience shop. The consignees sell motor fuels for Jet Oil's account, but they operate the shop on their own account.

(c) *The products and the market.*

5. The product with which the main part of the notified agreements is concerned consists of motor fuels, that is petrol and diesel for use in mechanically propelled road vehicles. The market was described in detail in the motor fuels category licence (1).

6. The convenience shop primarily sells grocery goods, confectionery, newspapers, cigarettes, etc. The market consists of all retail outlets selling goods of a similar character.

(d) *The notified agreement*

(i) Conoco's motor fuels and other Conoco products.

7. The introduction states that the premises comprise and are adapted and intended for use wholly or mainly for the carrying on of the business of a retail petrol filling station and convenience shop. The consignee, referred to in the agreement as a licensee, has agreed to operate the premises for the purposes and in furtherance of Conoco's business objective of the sale by retail at and from the premises of the company's motor fuels and other products. For the purposes of such operation, the company has agreed to licence and permit the licensee to occupy and make use of the premises subject to the terms of the agreement.

8. Appendix V describes the relationship between the licensee and Conoco and sets out some of the licensee's responsibilities in respect of motor fuels. Regarding the product, it states as follows:

> 6. All the Company's Motor Fuel and the Company's products delivered by the Company to the Company to the Premises and entrusted to the custody of the Licensee for sale shall remain the property of the Company until sold in the way of normal retail trade from the Premises and the Licensee shall not charge, pledge or part with possession of the same save for the purposes of sale as aforesaid.

Notwithstanding para 6, it is stated in para 7 that 'all products delivered to the Premises shall be held at the sole and absolute risk of the licensee who shall be liable to pay the Company for the same . . . in certain circumstances. **1.6.1**

9. Appendix V also provides for the handling of receipts from the sale of motor fuels as follows:

> 1. The amount for which the Licensee shall be accountable and which shall be payable by the Licensee to the Company in respect of 'the Company's motor fuel' to be sold at the premises shall be the price which the Company shall from time to time notify to the Licensee as the price at which the same is/are to be sold by retail at and from the Premises and applicable at the date of such sale less the amount which the Licensee is authorised to deduct and retain by way of commission and Value Added Tax thereon as hereinafter provided and shall be computed and paid as provided below.
>
> 2. For the purposes of ascertaining the total amount to be paid by the Licensee and received by the Company and of accounting between the Company and the Licensee:
> 2.1 The quantity of each Motor Fuel sold each day shall be ascertained by provisional stock assessment each of which shall be recorded by the Licensee in the manner and form required by the Company, which shall have the right to inspect and to take copies of such records whenever so required.

According to para 2.2, the licensee has to pay the amount payable under para 1 in respect of the quantity sold into a bank account nominated by Conoco on each day it is open for business. A full reconciliation is made each month between the lodgments made and the amount due to be paid, on the basis of stocks and purchases during the month. Sufficient details to allow this must be furnished to Conoco. The commission rate, in terms of pence per gallon on minimum sales, and percentage of the retail margin on sales above a specified level, is included in the agreement.

10. Appendix V also provides that the quantity of motor fuels and the turnover value of the other products shall not fall below specified monthly values. If the quantity of motor fuels sold falls below that specified, an agreed sum of liquidated damages has to be paid by the licensee.

11. The body of the agreement provides that the licence does not create any relationship between the parties of landlord and tenant (clause 8.5), or any partnership or any contract of agency or service, and it is expressly agreed that, for all purposes, the licensee is an independent contractor (para 8.6).

12. Appendix 1 describes the obligations on the licensee in respect of the premises, some of which are as follows:

(a) to pay and discharge all outgoings of the type described (labour and insurance costs, losses of motor fuel, telephone and postage costs, and consumable items such as cleaning materials and shop bags) (clause 1 and Appendix VII);

(b) to keep the premises open during normal business hours as agreed (clause 2);

(c) to use every endeavour and due diligence to sell and promote the products (clause 3);

(d) to keep adequate stocks (clause 4);

(e) to be responsible for the conduct and operation of the premises, and to engage, at licensee's own expense, sufficient and satisfactory staff (clause 5);

(f) not to exhibit posters or signs on the premises without the company's approval (clause 12); and

(g) not to carry on or to be concerned or interested in any manner whatsoever directly or indirectly in the conduct or management of any business in or through which competing products are sold or offered for sale by retail at or from premises situate within the radius shown.

13. The agreement also makes provision for the duration of the licence, the obligations of Conoco (delivery of motor fuels, subject to ability to supply, and repairs), early termination, and minimum insurance requirements to be met by the licensee.

1.6.1 (ii) Obligations regarding the shop.

14. The agreement also contains obligations on the licensee in respect of the shop. The licensee is permitted to sell 'other products' in the shop, 'other products' being defined as 'such goods and products (not being the Company's motor fuel or Company's products) as the Product Supplier (as hereinafter defined) may from time to time provide or procure to be provided at and for the purpose of sale by retail from the premises. The term 'Product Supplier' means 'such Supplier of the "other products" as may be approved of from time to time by the Company'. (Clause 1)

15. Appendix 1 of the agreements deals with the shop in more detail, the main provisions being as follows:

1. The Licensee shall be free to obtain supplies of 'the other products' from any supplier approved of by the Company in writing.

1.1 Pay to the Company by monthly direct debit a fee equal to the aggregate of [ ] % of the wholesale price of all cigarettes and tobacco products and [ ] % of the wholesale price of all 'other products'.

1.2 At all times keep full and accurate records of all 'other products' purchased and sold by it (and furnish monthly a certificate certifying the gross turnover, and permit the company to inspect the books and records to verify the gross turnover).

2. Present and merchandise 'The Products' in accordance with the initial layout configuration and merchandising presentation implemented by or on behalf of the Company, at the shop.

3. Properly and effectively merchandise and promote 'The Products' with advice and selective assistance of the Company or its authorised representative.

4. Maintain point of sale and window material and introduce no additional material except with the approval of the Company.

6. Conduct physical stock-takes as directed by the company or its authorised representatives with or without the assistance of the Company or its authorised representatives.

1.3 Pay the Company annually in arrear the fee specified. (This fee is not payable if the annual turnover is equal to or greater than the specified minimum turnover but the fee increases the lower the turnover is compared to the specified minimum turnover).

The licensee is also obliged to maintain adequate stock levels, to maintain a retail environment, to ensure that the premises are kept clean and that the attendants are properly attired, to complete and return all relevant documentation to the company, and to try to ensure that petrol customers pay in the shop, and to pay the amounts due to the other product suppliers.

16. Appendix V contains certain other provisions relating to the shop, as follows:

1. The licensee and appropriate employees shall if so required by the company participate in any training and support programme in retail shop sales and interior systems which the company may arrange whether directly or by other parties on its behalf.

It is also stated that the company shall have no liability to the licensee in respect of the other products, and that the company is not the agent of the product supplier; that the licensee will indemnify the company in respect of the other products; and that, if the company terminates the agreement, the licensee shall remove the other products from the premises. (Similar provisions are included in Conoco's licence agreements, where the operator of the Conoco station is independent, and also in certain agreements for the operation of a Jet shop on premises owned by dealers who have a solus agreement for the sale of Jet motor fuels. These are the subject of separate notifications).

(e) *Submissions by Conoco.*

(i) Conoco's motor fuels.

17. In its initial submission, Conoco stated that the consignee stations were operated by Conoco/Jet Oil for its own account and under its operational control and direction. Other licensees, however, operated company stations in a way which enabled them to conduct their

own independent businesses for their own account, in much the same way as an independent dealer buying exclusively from Conoco. It went on to say that, in respect of the consignees, which it refers to as licensees: **1.6.1**

Conoco/Jet Oil engages the Licensee to undertake and perform services required by Conoco/Jet Oil for the purpose of operating a Company station in its own name and for its own account and in a manner in which it retains full ultimate control over the sale of motor fuels by retail to the motorist direct.

In this situation:

> (i) Conoco/Jet Oil is the retailer and the entity from which the motorist purchases his/her motor fuel; and
>
> (ii) the Licensee is a provider of services, for the purposes of which he is authorised and licensed by Conoco/Jet Oil to enter upon and to use the Company station on and subject to the terms of the LA [licence agreement].

For his services, the Licensee is remunerated by payment of a commission at a rate which is negotiated and agreed with each Licensee individually. However, an additional, integral and synergistic feature of the arrangement is that the Licensee is permitted to use the Shop for the sale of goods (other than motor fuels and Conoco/Jet Oil's other products, such as vehicle lubricants and anti-freeze) for his own account and separately from and independently of the business of the sale of Conoco/Jet Oil's motor fuels and other products. For this, Conoco/Jet Oil receives the benefit of a licence fee. . . .

While such licences in the past were subject to a Restrictive Practices Order and were usually granted for three years, the period for this licence was unlikely to exceed ten years.

18. Conoco also presented the following arguments for a certificate or a licence:

> Contract operation of Company stations enables Conoco/Jet Oil to engage in inter-retailer competition, and thereby to develop and pursue its own ideas for innovative and creative marketing more effectively than would be possible if its role were restricted to that of a wholesaler supplying petroleum products to retail operators. In particular, it enables and provides an incentive for Conoco/Jet Oil to develop and pursue and, by its own conduct and example, to influence and enhance within the retail sector generally standards and practices which
> (a) promote efficiency;
> (b) benefit the consumer by ensuring availability of quality assured products at competitive prices through attractive, well- maintained premises and facilities and providing a level of services dedicated to total customer care; and
> (c) better recognise and address topical operating issues, particularly those concerned with health and safety and with protection of the environment.
>
> The arrangement under notification is considered to have no material or perceptible effect on competition in trade within the relevant market and a certificate under section 4(1) is requested on that ground. The position resulting from this arrangement is that Conoco/Jet Oil maintains and exercises full and complete control of the marketing of the motor fuels which are being offered for sale at the contract operated station. The effect of this on competition is no different from that which would arise if the station was operated by Conoco/Jet Oil's direct employees.

Conoco also claimed that this was not affected by the restriction on the Licensee's engaging in a competing business within a specified radius, which was necessary in principle and reasonable in extent for the purpose of safeguarding Conoco/Jet Oil's interests in the Station.

1.6.1 (ii) *Concerning the shop*

19. Conoco made the following remarks about the shop:

> On a number of contract operated stations, the Shop facility has been upgraded and re-equipped to the high quality, modern standards established by Conoco/Jet Oil for its Jet Shops concept. . . . This has been undertaken as part of Conoco/Jet Oil's ongoing programme for enhancement of the scope and quality of customer services at Jet Oil branded service stations; and has required (and will continue to require) substantial investment. In these cases, the licence fee which Conoco/Jet Oil receives as consideration for the use of the Shop facility ('the Shop fee') is related to turnover of 'other products' but with a mechanism to ensure attainment of an agreed minimum annual fee. The level of the minimum fee is agreed with each Licensee individually and reflects the mutually agreed expectation of the profit earning potential for the Licensee of the separate business for which the Shop is to be used. Relating the fee to turnover also provides Conoco/Jet Oil with a reasonable opportunity to receive a fair return on its investment.

Conoco also stated that the obligation on the licensee to purchase other products from approved suppliers was:

> necessary and reasonable in order better to ensure that products are purchased only from reputable and reliable suppliers, thereby (i) better assuring the consumer availability of supply and of the quality and range of goods on offer for sale; and (ii) safeguarding the proprietary interests of Conoco/Jet Oil by avoiding any erosion of the reputation and good standing, as perceived and identified by the consumer, of the brand name 'JET' and of the 'JET Shop' identity where applicable.

(iii) *Concerning the status of the consignee.*

20. In response to questions posed by the Authority concerning the status of the consignee under the consignee agreement, Conoco replied as follows:

1. Jet Oil remains the retailer of, and the entity from which the motorist purchases motor fuels supplied at the contract operated station.

2. The Licensee is engaged to conduct the physical operation of that station and, as such, is a provider of services to Jet Oil on terms which authorise and license him to use the contract operated station not only for the purpose of fulfilling his obligations as a provider of services but also for the sale, through the Shop which is part of the station, of goods (other than motor fuels and Jet Oil's other products, such as vehicle lubricants and antifreeze; collectively 'Jet Oil products') for his own account and separately from and independently of the sale of Jet Oil products which the licensee undertakes in his capacity as a provider of services.

3. Thus, the Licensee operates in two capacities: as a provider of services in relation to the sale of Jet Oil products; and as an independent business man acting on his own account in relation to the sale of other goods through the station Shop.

4. In both capacities, the Licensee is an independent contractor, as is expressly recognised in Clause 8.6 of the Licence Agreement.

5. In relation to the sale of Jet Oil products (where, for emphasis, ownership and financial risks remain with Jet Oil, which also retains complete control over the determination of selling prices), we can readily agree and confirm that:

> (a) the Licensee sells in the name and for the account of Jet Oil;
> (b) The Licensee is obligated to carry out Jet Oil's instructions; and
> (c) In these circumstances, the Licensee is but an intermediary between Jet Oil and the consumer and, as such, may be regarded as forming an integral part of Jet Oil's

undertaking in much the same way as would be the case if the relationship were one of employer and employee. **1.6.1**

This leads us to conclude and accept that, for the purposes of the sale of Jet Oil products, the Licensee is a trade representative or commercial agent for Jet Oil rather than an independent trader.

6. However, in relation to the Licensee's activities relating to the sale of the 'other goods' for the purpose of which he is authorised to use the Shop:

(a) The Licensee is clearly an independent trader.

(b) If, as we would submit, the majority and 'essential trust' of the restrictions which are imposed upon the Licensee are properly to be regarded as relating to and arising from the services which he agrees to undertake and perform for the purpose of the sale of Jet Oil products and the general operation on behalf of Jet Oil of the contract operated station then the only remaining 'extraneous' restrictions (i.e. those which affect his activities as an independent trader) would appear to be those which are to be found in Part II of Appendix 1 of the Licence Agreement.

(c) Of those restrictions, the only one which might be regarded as being of any consequence is that which arises from paragraph 1: and then only if this was to be interpreted as a requirement that supplies of 'other products' were to be obtained only and exclusively from suppliers approved by Jet Oil.

Conoco pointed out that this issue had been covered in the initial submission, as set out in para 19.

Finally, Conoco stated that:

> If, in these circumstances, it is your considered view that the Consignee Licensee is not an 'undertaking' within the meaning of section 3[1] and/or that our arrangements do not otherwise need to be notified under section 7 then, we would not wish to argue to the contrary.

(f) *Subsequent developments*

21. The Authority wrote to Conoco on 5 October 1993 expressing concern in relation to clause l of Appendix l, which required the consignee to obtain supplies of 'the other products' from suppliers approved of by Conoco in writing. It stated that its concern would be removed by the addition of the following sentence: 'Approval will be withheld only for objectively valid reasons which shall be disclosed to the licensee'. The Authority considered that this would still adequately safeguard the legitimate interests of the company, while not impinging on the commercial freedom of the independent operator. By letter dated 29 November 1993, Conoco agreed to amend the agreement by adding the wording above and to notify all their consignees of the amendment.

(g) *EC Commission views on commercial agency.*

22. The EC Commission first gave its views on exclusive dealing contracts with commercial agents in a Notice published in 1962.[2] In this it stated that it considered that contracts made with commercial agents, who acted on behalf of an enterprise, did not fall under the prohibition

1. Motor fuels category licence, l July 1993, paras. 7 to 9.
2. EC Commission Notice on exclusive dealing contracts with commercial agents, OJ 139, 24.12.1962, p. 2921.

1.6.1 in Article 85(1) of the EC Treaty. It was essential that the commercial agent should not engage in activities proper to an independent trader. The decisive criterion, according to the Commission, was that the commercial agent should not assume any risk resulting from the transaction.

23. It has long been recognised, by the Commission and others, that the 1962 Notice is limited in scope, and that it no longer reflects economic reality and is also legally obsolete. It also needed revision in the light of the 1986 harmonisation Directive relating to self-employed commercial agents.[3] The Commission has been preparing, therefore, a revised Notice on commercial agents, which has not yet been finalised.

24. The EC Court of Justice considered the question of agency in the Suiker Unie case, where it stated:

> If such an agent works for his principal he can in principle be regarded as an auxiliary organ forming an integral part of the latter's undertaking bound to carry out the principal's instructions and thus, like a commercial employee, forms an economic unit with this undertaking.[4]

(h) *Submission by Jet Retailers Association*

25. Following the publication of the Authority's intention to take a favourable view of the agreement, a submission was received from the Jet Retailers Association, which is comprised of 26 Jet licensees. The general view was that the Association supported the issue of a certificate, but that the agreement did not accurately describe the relationship between the parties and it should be modified before a certificate was granted. It was stated that the notion of 'licensee' accurately described the relationship under land law, but it did not accurately describe the commercial relationship between the parties under competition law. The Association considered that its members were non-exclusive distributors for the shop products, but that they were effectively commercial agents of Conoco for motor fuels. It claimed that the agreement, in clause 8.6, denied this reality. It maintained that either this clause should be redrafted to state positively that there was a relationship of commercial agency subsisting between the parties, or that the phrase 'or any contract of agency or service' should be deleted. The Association stated that this was very important since, as agents, its members were entitled to rely on the EC Directive on Commercial Agents, including the right to compensation on termination of the agency in certain circumstances. The Association objected to the issue of a certificate for the agreement as currently drafted. The Authority has taken full account of the views of the Association in the following assessment of the agreement. It does not consider, however, that, for the purposes of the Competition Act, it is necessary to require that the position of the licensees as commercial agents should be specifically recognised in the agreement.

Assessment

(a) *Applicability of section 4(1)*

26. Section 4(1) of the Competition Act 1991 prohibits and renders void all agreements between undertakings which have as their object or effect the prevention, restriction or distortion of competition in trade in any goods or services in the State or in any part of the State.

27. Conoco and the consignees are engaged in the sale of motor fuels for gain, and the consignees are also engaged in the sale of other products for gain, and they are therefore undertakings within the meaning of section 3(1) of the Competition Act. The standard consignee agreement is an agreement between undertakings. The relevant product markets are

3. EC Directive of 18 December 1986 relating to the coordination of the laws of the Member States relating to self-employed commercial agents, OJ L382, 31.12.86, p. 17.
4. Judgment of the Court of Justice of 16 December 1975 — *Suiker Unie and Others v. Commission of the European Communities* [1975] ECR 1663 at p. 2007.

those for (a) motor fuels, and (b) the products sold in the shop on the petrol station premises. **1.6.1**
The relevant geographic market is the State.

(i) *The status of the consignee*

(1) In respect of the sales of motor fuels

28. In operating the petrol station premises and selling motor fuels, the consignee is not an employee of Conoco and there is no contract of employment or service between them. He is a self-employed contractor. At the same time, while the consignee is stated to be an independent contractor, the consignee does not purchase motor fuels from Conoco for resale to the public. Unlike the Conoco licensee or independent dealer, the consignee sells motor fuel, not on his own account, but on behalf of Conoco. He does not pay for the motor fuels, and the motor fuels remain the property of Conoco until they are sold at retail, even though they are held at the consignee's risk. All receipts from the sale of motor fuels, less the agreed commission, must be lodged daily to Conoco's bank account. Out of his commission, the consignee must pay for certain outgoings, such as labour and insurance costs, the balance representing the consignee's remuneration. The consignee is responsible for employing staff. Conoco determines the prices at which the motor fuels are to be sold. The petrol station is effectively under the operational control and direction of Conoco, and is operated for Conoco's own account, and the consignee is obliged to obey Conoco's instructions. The relationship between Conoco and the consignee is an ongoing one, and the agreement may have a duration of up to ten years.

29. The Authority considers that the question of agency is quite complex, and that each case must be examined on its own merits in relation to the Competition Act, in the light of certain general considerations. In the first place, it is not conclusive that one party is referred to as an 'agent' in the agreement, since he may not perform the functions of an agent in any real sense. Conversely, it does not matter if the agreement states that there is no relationship or contract of agency between the parties. This may be done, for example, to limit one party's ability to undertake binding obligations on behalf of the other, without the latter's knowledge or consent. From the point of view of the Competition Act, the Authority is concerned with whether the relationship between the two parties is such that one of them may be termed a 'commercial agent' of the other. It is not intended that the views of the Authority about whether a person is a commercial agent or not should have any implications for the legal relationship between the parties.

30. The Authority considers that a commercial agent is a self-employed intermediary between the principal and a purchaser or seller. The commercial agent concludes the sale or purchase of goods and services on behalf of the principal, on a continuing basis. The commercial agent is an auxiliary organ, forming an integral part of the principal's business, and is bound to carry out the instructions of the principal, and his position is similar to that of an employee. Being integrated into the principal's business, the commercial agent can undertake no autonomous commercial behaviour, under the agreement, and certain restrictions on him are fundamental to the relationship. The Authority considers that profits or losses essentially accrue to the principal and not to the commercial agent.

31. The relationship between Conoco and its consignees has been summarised in para. 28. The agreement also states that there is no contract of agency between the parties. Conoco has argued that, in respect of the sale of motor fuels, the consignee is an intermediary, and forms an integral part of Conoco, like an employee. They said that the effect on competition was no different to that which would have occurred if the station had been run by a direct employee of Conoco.

32. The consignee is a self-employed intermediary between Conoco and the purchasers of Jet motor fuels. He concludes the sale of goods on behalf of Conoco, on a continuing basis, for up to ten years. He does not own the stocks, the resale prices are set by Conoco, and the consignee lodges the proceeds of sale, less the commission, to the credit of Conoco's bank account. While the consignee accepts some risk, in relation to stock and cash losses, and is

1.6.1 responsible for hiring and paying employees, the profits and losses of the motor fuels business as a whole accrue to Conoco, and the consignee must obey Conoco's instructions and may undertake no autonomous behaviour in respect of the operation of the petrol station. The Authority considers that the consignee, in operating the petrol station and selling Conoco products, is an auxiliary organ, forming an integral part of Conoco's distribution business, and it concludes that he can be considered to be a commercial agent. This conclusion is not affected by the fact that the consignee also operates the shop supplied by Conoco on the same premises, since the operation of the petrol station constitutes a significant proportion of the whole business, and there is also a relationship between the consignee and Conoco in relation to the shop.

(2) In respect of the shop

33. The consignee sells products other than motor fuels and Jet products in the shop for his own account and separately from and independently of the sale of Jet Oil products. Although he pays a commission on sales to Conoco, and is bound by certain obligations imposed by Conoco regarding the operation of the shop, he is in no sense a commercial agent of Conoco in respect of the shop on the petrol station premises. He is an independent trader in the shop.

(ii) *The commercial agency agreement.*

34. The Authority considers that undertakings are entitled to decide how to operate their distribution systems, and, in particular, to appoint commercial agents to sell their goods on their behalf. Suppliers of motor fuels are free to choose to sell their products through independent dealers or through company-owned outlets; these latter may be operated by lessees, licensees, employees or by consignees and commercial agents. Since the commercial agent is an auxiliary organ, similar to an employee, the agreement between a principal and a commercial agent does not, in principle, offend against section 4(1) of the Competition Act.

35. In the present case, the Authority has concluded that the consignee is a commercial agent. It considers that the agreement between Conoco and the consignee, insofar as it creates a relationship between the principal and a commercial agent, does not offend against section 4(1).

36. Even though the basic arrangement of commercial agency might not offend against section 4(1), certain clauses in the agreement might occasionally do so. In the case of motor fuels agreements, the Authority has published a category licence, which permits the imposition of certain obligations upon resellers of motor fuels and upon their suppliers. The Authority considers that the obligations which are not regarded as offending against section 4(1) in the case of independent traders would equally not offend in the case of commercial agents. More fundamentally, the Authority recognises that there are certain features of commercial agency agreements which define and confirm the relationship, and are intrinsic to the commercial agency. Since the commercial agent is closer to being an employee than an independent trader, the Authority considers that certain restrictions may be imposed upon a commercial agent without offending against section 4(1), whereas they would offend against section 4(1) if they were imposed on an independent trader. In the Authority's opinion, none of the provisions in the notified agreement offend against section 4(1).

(iii) *The shop agreement*

37. In the opinion of the Authority, all but one of the relevant provisions regarding the shop in the notified agreement do not have the object or effect of preventing, restricting or distorting competition. They reflect the fact that the shop is owned by Conoco, and is licensed to the consignee for the purpose of enhancing earnings at the station, for the mutual benefit of the owner and the consignee, while ensuring that the reputation of Conoco and the Jet brand name is not damaged. Since a fee which is related to the turnover of different classes of goods is payable by the consignee, it is essential for accurate and detailed records to be furnished to

Conoco, and for Conoco to have power to verify these. Such provisions do not interfere with the freedom of the consignee to operate the shop and they do not interfere with competition. In the view of the Authority, they do not offend against section 4(1) of the Act. **1.6.1**

38. The Authority was concerned, however, with the clause which stated that 'the licensee shall be free to obtain supplies of "the other products" from any supplier approved of by the company in writing.' The Authority considered that this clause could be used to limit the freedom of the consignee to determine what products to sell and from whom he might obtain supplies. This could affect the ability of the consignee to compete with other retailers in the area. It could also limit competition between suppliers to obtain the custom of the consignee. The consignees would have no voice in deciding which suppliers they should deal with for their purchases. While the effect of this requirement to obtain Conoco's approval of every supplier might have little effect upon competition in the case of an individual consignee, the cumulative effect of this obligation in respect of all Conoco's consignees, licensees and dealers with a Jet shop, who are similarly bound, might not be insignificant. Since this practice might also be followed by other petrol companies in convenience shops attached to their company and dealer outlets, and since such convenience shops are growing rapidly in number and importance, the overall effect was thought likely to be considerable. The Authority considered that this clause offended against section 4(1) of the Act. (The Authority also considered that this clause would not satisfy, at least, the indispensability requirement of section 4(2) of the Act, and so would not qualify for the grant of a licence).

39. At the suggestion of the Authority however, as stated in para 21, Conoco have agreed to provide that approval of a supplier 'will only be withheld for objectively valid reasons which shall be disclosed to the licensee.' The Authority considers that this would adequately ensure the reputation and good standing of Conoco and of the Jet and Jet Shop tradenames, as required by Conoco, but in a less restrictive way. The Authority considers that the part of the agreement relating to the shop no longer offends against section 4(1).

The Decision

40. In the Authority's opinion, Conoco and its consignees are undertakings within the meaning of section 3(1) of the Competition Act, and the notified standard consignee agreement for the operation of a Conoco-owned petrol station and associated shop constitutes an agreement between undertakings. In the Authority's opinion, the consignee is a commercial agent of Conoco in the petrol station, and an independent operator in the shop, and the arrangements, as amended, do not have, as their object or effect, the prevention, restriction or distortion of competition. The standard Conoco consignee agreement, as amended by the letter of 29 November 1993, does not, in the Authority's opinion, offend against section 4(1) of the Competition Act 1991.

The Certificate

The Competition Authority has issued the following certificate:

The Competition Authority certifies that in its opinion, on the basis of the facts in its possession, the standard agreement between Conoco and its consignees for the operation of a Conoco-owned petrol station and shop (notification no CA/71/92E), notified on 7 September 1992 under section 7, and amended by Conoco in its letter of 29 November 1993, does not offend against section 4(1) of the Competition Act 1991.

For the Competition Authority

Patrick M. Lyons
Chairman

25 February 1994

1.6.2 Competition Authority Decision No. 303, Patrick Flynn/Wardell Roberts plc: 7 April 1994, Notification No. CA/120/92E

Commercial agency agreement – Constituents of a commercial agency agreement – Agent responsible for 10 percent of bad debts of his customers – Whether agent an undertaking for the purpose of the Competition Act 1991 – Whether agent forms intricate part of principal's business – Whether agency agreement offends against Competition Act 1991 – Competition Act 1991 (No. 24) sections 3, 4 and 7

Facts: On 25 September 1992 notification was made to the Authority by Patrick Flynn with a request for a certificate under section 4(4) of the Competition Act 1991, or failing that a licence under section 4(2) in respect of an agency agreement between Mr Patrick Flynn and Wardell Roberts plc. Wardell Roberts is an importer and wholesaler of wines and spirits and also a distributor of food products within the State. Mr Flynn, previously an employee of Woodford Bourne (a company subsequently acquired by Wardell Roberts) is an agent of Wardell Roberts engaged in the wholesaling of Wardell Roberts products to customers in an area designated in the notified agreement.

The notified agreement was made on 1 June 1983 and under its terms Woodford Bourne Ltd appointed Mr Flynn as it's sole selling agent for wine and spirits in five south eastern counties. On or about 31 May 1988 Woodford Bourne was acquired by Wardell Roberts and the benefit and obligations of Woodford Bourne under the notified agreement were assigned to Wardell Roberts. Under the terms of the agreement the agent is appointed the principal's sole selling agent in five south eastern counties with exclusive selling rights for the principal's brands of wines and spirits. The agent is required to use his best endeavour to promote and extend the sales of the goods and is paid a monthly commission on such sales. The agreement also provides that all distribution costs of goods delivered directly by the principal are to be borne by the principal and the principal is also responsible for keeping records and accounts. The agent is responsible for a maximum of 10 percent of bad debts.

Mr Flynn submitted that the price of the products and the credit terms afforded to customers was as determined by the principal. While Mr Flynn did keep some stocks in his own warehouse the ownership of such stocks remained with the principal. Mr Flynn further submitted that as an agent he was not an independent trading entity separate from his principal but was an auxiliary part of the principal's operation. Accordingly he submitted that the agreement was not one between undertakings.

Decided by the Authority: In issuing a certificate under section 4(4) of the Competition Act 1991 in respect of the notified agreement that:

(1) Wardell Roberts and Mr Flynn are engaged in the distribution of wines and spirits for gain and they are therefore undertakings within the meaning of section 3(1) of the Competition Act. The fact that Mr Flynn is an agent does not mean that he is not an undertaking, the position being similar to that of a parent firm and a subsidiary where, in the view of the EC Commission both are undertakings even though a restrictive agreement between them may not infringe provisions of Article 85(1) of the Treaty of Rome.

(2) The agency agreement is an agreement between undertakings and the relevant product market is that for wines and spirits and the relevant geographic market is the

five specified counties which are part of the State. 1.6.2

(3) A commercial agent is a self employed intermediary between the principal and the purchaser or seller who concludes the sale or purchase of goods and services on behalf of the principal and such purchaser or seller. Such commercial agent is an auxiliary organ forming an integral part of the principal's business and is bound to carry out the instructions of the principal and his position in this respect is similar to that of an employee. Profits or losses essentially accrue to the principal and not the commercial agent.

(4) Mr Flynn is a self employed intermediary between Wardell Roberts and the purchasers of its wines and spirits. He does not own the stocks, and resale prices are set by Wardell Roberts and while he accepts some risk in respect of bad debts the profit and losses in respect of the transactions accrue to Wardell Roberts and therefore Mr Flynn is an auxiliary organ, forming an intricate part of the Wardell Robert distribution business and as such can be considered to be a commercial agent.

(5) Undertakings are entitled to decide how to operate their distribution systems and, in particular, appoint commercial agents. Since a commercial agent is an auxiliary organ similar to an employee, an agreement between a principal and a commercial agent does not in principle offend against section 4(1) of the Competition Act. The notified agreement, insofar as it creates a relationship between the principal and the agent does not offend against section 4(1).

(6) There are certain features of the commercial agency relationship which define and confirm the relationship and are intrinsic to the commercial agency. A commercial agent is closer to being an employee than to being an independent trader and certain restrictions may be imposed upon a commercial agent without offending against section 4(1) whereas they will offend against such section if they are imposed upon an independent trader.

Decisions and Notice cited:
Competition Authority Decision No. 2 AGF — Irish Life, 14 May 1992 **1.3.1**
Competition Authority Decision No. 286 Conoco Consignee Agreement, 25 February 1994 **1.6.1**
EC Commission Notice concerning commercial agents [OJ 139/62]

Competition Authority Decision of 7 April 1994 relating to a proceeding under section 4 of the Competition Act 1991
Notification No. CA/120/92E — Patrick Flynn/Wardell Roberts plc

Introduction

1. Notification was made with a request for a certificate or, failing the issue of a certificate, a licence on 25 September 1992 by Mr Patrick Flynn in respect of an agency agreement with Wardell Roberts plc.

The Facts

(a) *The subject of the notification*

2. The notification concerns an agreement dated 1 June 1983 under which Woodford Bourne Ltd appointed Mr Patrick Flynn as its sole selling agent for wine and spirits in five south-eastern counties. On or about 31 May 1988, Woodford Bourne was acquired by Wardell Roberts plc, and the benefit and the obligations of Woodford Bourne were assigned by agreement of all parties to Wardell Roberts. Mr Flynn is now therefore the sole selling agent for Wardell Roberts in the specified territory.

1.6.2 (b) *The parties involved*

3. Wardell Roberts is an importer and wholesaler of wines and spirits and it distributes branded and private label food products. Mr Flynn had previously been employed directly by Woodford Bourne for about ten years acting as Sales Manager dealing with much the same type of customers as at present. Due to a re-organisation he became an agent in wholesaling the principal's products to the principal's customers. These customers are mainly restaurants/hotels, off-licences and cash and carry outlets.

(c) *The products and the market*

4. The products which are the subject of the notification are wines and spirits. The main competitors of Wardell Roberts are distributors such as Gilbeys, Grants, Dillons, Fitzgeralds and Barry/Fitzwilliam. Each distributor tends to have exclusive distribution agreements for different brands of wines and spirits, but these are generally in competition with each other.

(d) *The notified agreement*

5. Under the agreement, Mr Flynn was appointed sole selling agent of the principal in the counties of Waterford, Wexford, Kilkenny, Tipperary and Carlow, with exclusive selling rights for the sale of all of the principal's brands of wines and spirits. The agent is required to use his best endeavours to promote and extend the sales of the goods, and he is paid a monthly commission on sales. So long as the agent continues to promote and market the goods in a sufficient and workmanlike manner, the agreement shall not be determined by either party. All distribution costs of goods delivered directly by the principal are to be borne by the principal, and the principal is also responsible for keeping accounts and records. The agent is responsible for a maximum of 10% of bad debts.

6. According to the notifying party, the price of the products is set by the principal, who also determines what credit facilities are afforded to customers. It was also stated that, as a matter of practice, the agent only sold wines and spirits stocked by the principal. In addition, it was explained that the agent kept stocks at a warehouse owned by him in Waterford city, although the ownership of the stocks remained with the principal. While distribution was the responsibility of the principal, the agent maintained a small stock of wine for emergency deliveries.

(e) *Submissions by Mr Flynn*

7. The principal argument put forward in favour of a certificate by Mr Flynn was that, as an agent, he was not an independent trading entity separate and distinct from his principal. The agent, in economic terms, was part of the same undertaking as the principal, and no more than an auxiliary part of the principal's operation. Accordingly, the agreement between the parties was not an agreement between undertakings. The submission referred to the EC Notice of 1962 concerning commercial agents (OJ139, 24.12.1962, p. 2921). It was maintained that in this case the agent was no more than an intermediary as distinct from an independent trader. He was neither a purchaser from the principal nor a vendor to the customer and was not, therefore, an economic force in his own right. It was clear that, in both practice and as set out in the agreement, the financial risks in all transactions remained with the principal (except for the agent's liability for a maximum of 10% of bad debts, which, it was argued, was not an out-of pocket expense as such but rather a retrospective reduction in the agent's commission rate). The agent did not determine the selling price of the goods which was fixed by the principal and invoiced directly by the principal to the customer. While the agent carried a stock of products in his own premises, ownership of these stocks rested with the principal.

Assessment

(a) *Applicability of section 4(1)*

8. Section 4(1) of the Competition Act 1991 prohibits and renders void all agreements

between undertakings which have as their object or effect the prevention, restriction or distortion of competition in trade in any goods or services in the State or in any part of the State. **1.6.2**

9. Wardell Roberts and Mr Flynn are engaged in the distribution of wines and spirits for gain, and they are therefore undertakings within the meaning of section 3(1) of the Competition Act. The Authority does not accept the argument of Mr Flynn that an agent is not an undertaking or that there is any EU precedent for this view. In particular, neither the 1962 Notice, nor its draft revision, states that an agent is not an undertaking, and this is not the reason for regarding an agreement between a principal and an agent as not being in breach of Article 85(1). The position is similar to that of a parent firm and a subsidiary where the EU Commission has held that both are undertakings even through a restrictive agreement between them may not infringe Article 85(1). A similar view has been taken by the Authority in its decision in AGF-Irish Life (Decision No. 2, 14 May 1992). The agency agreement is an agreement between undertakings. The relevant product markets are those for wines and spirits, and the relevant geographic market is the five specified counties, which are a part of the State.

(i) The status of Mr Flynn

10. Mr Flynn is not an employee of Wardell Roberts, and there is no contract of employment or service between them. He is a self-employed contractor. At the same time, he does not purchase wines and spirits from Wardell Roberts for resale to customers. He sells these, not on his own account, but on behalf of Wardell Roberts. He does not pay for the products, and the stocks remain the property of Wardell Roberts until they are sold. Payments are made by customers to Wardell Roberts, and Mr Flynn receives a commission, out of which he must pay his business expenses. Wardell Roberts determines the prices at which the products are sold. The relationship is an ongoing one, and has been in existence for more than ten years.

11. The Authority summarised the views of the EU Commission on commercial agency, and outlined its own opinion on the subject, in its decision on the Conoco consignee agreement (Decision No. 286, 25 February 1994). The Authority considers that a commercial agent is a self-employed intermediary between the principal and a purchaser or seller. The commercial agent concludes the sale or purchase of goods and services on behalf of the principal and a purchaser or seller, on a continuing basis. The commercial agent is an auxiliary organ, forming an integral part of the principal's business, and is bound to carry out the instructions of the principal, and his position in this respect is similar to that of an employee. Being integrated into the principal's business, the commercial agent can undertake no autonomous commercial behaviour, under the agreement, and certain restrictions on him are fundamental to the relationship. The Authority considers that profits or losses essentially accrue to the principal and not to the commercial agent.

12. The Authority considers that Mr Flynn is a self-employed intermediary between Wardell Roberts and the purchasers of its wines and spirits. He concludes the sale of goods on behalf of Wardell Roberts on a continuing basis. He does not own the stocks, and resale prices are set by Wardell Roberts. While he accepts some risk in respect of bad debts, the profits and losses in respect of the transactions accrue to Wardell Roberts. The Authority considers that Mr Flynn is an auxiliary organ, forming an integral part of Wardell Robert's distribution business, and it concludes that he can be considered to be a commercial agent.

(ii) The commercial agency agreement

13. The Authority considers that undertakings are entitled to decide how to operate their distribution systems, and, in particular to appoint commercial agents to sell their goods on their behalf. Since the commercial agent is an auxiliary organ, similar to an employee, the agreement between a principal and a commercial agent does not, in principle, offend against section 4(1) of the Competition Act.

14. In the present case, the Authority has concluded that Mr Flynn is a commercial agent.

1.6.2 It considers that the agreement between Wardell Roberts and Mr Flynn, insofar as it creates a relationship between the principal and a commercial agent, does not offend against section 4(1).

15. Even though the basic arrangement of commercial agency might not offend against section 4(1), certain clauses in the agreement might occasionally do so. The Authority recognises that there are certain features of commercial agency relationships which define and confirm the relationship, and are intrinsic to the commercial agency. Since the commercial agent is closer to being an employee than to being an independent trader, the Authority considers that certain restrictions may be imposed upon a commercial agent without offending against section 4(1), whereas they would offend against section 4(1) if they were imposed on an independent trader. In the Authority's opinion, none of the provisions in the notified agreement offend against section 4(1).

The Decision

16. In the Authority's opinion, Wardell Roberts and Mr Flynn are undertakings within the meaning of section 3(1) of the Competition Act, and the notified agency agreement constitutes an agreement between undertakings. In the Authority's opinion, Mr Flynn is a commercial agent of Wardell Roberts, and the arrangements do not have, as their object or effect, the prevention, restriction or distortion of competition. The notified agreement does not, in the Authority's opinion, offend against section 4(1) of the Competition Act 1991.

The Certificate

The Competition Authority has issued the following certificate:

The Competition Authority certifies that, in its opinion, on the basis of the facts in its possession, the agency agreement between Wardell Roberts plc and Mr Patrick Flynn (notification no. CA/120/92E), notified on 25 September 1992 under section 7, does not offend against section 4(1) of the Competition Act 1991.

For the Competition Authority

Patrick M. Lyons
Chairman

7 April 1994

1.6.3 **Competition Authority Decision No. 325, Shell Appointment and Licence:** 5 May 1994, Notification No. CA/261/92E

Commercial agency agreement – What constitutes a commercial agency – Whether commercial agency agreements breach the Competition Act – Whether agent forms an integral part of principal's business – Whether agent an undertaking within the meaning of the Competition Act 1991 – Competition Act 1991 (No. 24) sections 3, 4 and 7

Facts: On 30 September 1992 notification was made to the Authority by Irish Shell Ltd ('Irish Shell') with a request for a certificate under section 4(4) of the Competition

Act 1991, or failing that, a licence under section 4(2) in respect of its standard agreement of appointment and licence with licensees. Irish Shell, whose ultimate parents are the Royal Dutch Petroleum Company and the Shell Transport and Trading Company Ltd, is engaged in the marketing of motor fuels through a chain of retail outlets, a small number of which are owned by Irish Shell, within the State. The notified agreement is the standard type agreement entered into between Irish Shell and the licensees who operate those retail outlets owned by Irish Shell. The product market relevant to the notified agreement is that for motor fuels for use in mechanical propelled road vehicles. 1.6.3

Under the terms of the notified agreement Irish Shell appointed a person as agent and licensee for the reception, storage, dispensing and sale at a specified site of the company's motor fuel products and for the purpose of rendering and supplying such other services and commodities as are commonly rendered and supplied at service stations. The period of appointment is three years and there are provisions for early termination, compensation and arbitration. The notified agreement places certain responsibilities on the licensee which include, *inter alia,* that the licensee must use the provided equipment solely for the purpose of the sale and distribution of Irish Shell fuel products, must not do anything that would damage the property or goodwill of Irish Shell, must hold on trust for Irish Shell all monies received from the sale of the products and lodge them to a designated Irish Shell bank account, must sell each grade of motor fuel on behalf of Irish Shell at such price as Irish Shell may notify to the licensee from time to time, must discharge all the normal overheads for the operation of the service station and pay for stock losses above a specified level. The agreement places certain responsibilities on Irish Shell which include, *inter alia,* the obligations to insure equipment on the site against loss or damage, to supply the licensee with stocks of Irish Shell products and to pay a commission to the licensee. The agreement states explicitly that it does not confer on the licensee an exclusive right to use the site or equipment nor does it create a landlord and tenant relationship.

Irish Shell made various submissions with the notification and on 25 February 1994 the Authority published in the Irish Times notice of its intention to take a favourable decision. A submission was also received from the Association of Shell Retailers.

Decided by the Authority: In issuing a certificate under section 4(4) of the Competition Act 1991 in respect of the notified agreement that:

(1) Irish Shell and the licensees are engaged in the sale of motor fuels for gain and they are therefore undertakings within the meaning of section 3(1) of the Competition Act. The submission by Irish Shell that an agent is not an undertaking is rejected, the position being similar to that of a parent firm and a subsidiary where, both are undertakings even though a restrictive agreement between them may not affect competition.

(2) The notified agreement is an agreement between undertakings, the relevant product market is that for motor fuels and the relevant geographic market is the State.

(3) A commercial agent is a self-employed intermediary between the principal and a purchaser or seller and concludes the sale or purchase of goods or services on behalf of the principal on a continuing basis. The commercial agent is an auxiliary organ forming an integral part of the principal's business and is bound to carry out the instructions of the principal, and his position is similar to that of an employee. Being

1.6.3 integrated into the principal's business, the commercial agent can undertake no autonomous commercial behaviour, under the agreement, and certain restrictions on him are fundamental to the relationship. Profits or losses essentially accrue to the principal and not the commercial agent.

(4) The licensee in the notified agreement is a self-employed intermediary between Irish Shell and the purchasers of Shell motor products and concludes the sale of goods on behalf of Irish Shell on a continuing basis. The licensee does not own the motor fuel stocks, the resale terms are set by Irish Shell and the proceeds from the sale of same are lodged to the credit of Irish Shell bank account. While the licensee accepts some risk in relation to stock losses and is responsible for hiring and paying employees the profit and losses of the motor fuel business as a whole accrue to Irish Shell and the licensee must obey Irish Shell's instructions and may undertake no autonomous behaviour in respect of the operation of the petrol station. The licensee is an auxiliary organ forming an integral part of Irish Shell's distribution business and therefore can be considered a commercial agent.

(5) Undertakings are entitled to decide how to operate their distribution systems and, in particular, appoint a commercial agent. Since a commercial agent is an auxiliary organ and similar to an employee an agreement between the principal and a commercial agent does not in principle offend against section 4(1). The notified agreement insofar as it creates a relationship between the principal and a commercial agent does not offend against section 4(1).

(6) While the basic arrangement of commercial agency might not offend against section 4(1) certain clauses might occasionally do so. Commercial agency agreements contain features which confirm and define the relationship and are intrinsic to such relationship. A commercial agent is closer to being an employee than an independent trader and certain restrictions may be opposed on a commercial agent without offending against section 4(1) of the Competition Act which would, if they were imposed on an independent trader, offend against such section.

Cases, Decisions, Notices and Order referred to:
ECJ Decision *Suiker Unie v. Commission* [1975] ECR 1663, [1976] 1 CMLR 295
ECJ Decision *Hydrotherm v. Compact* (Case No. 170/83), [1984] ECR 2999, [1985] 3CMLR 276
EC Commission Notice on exclusive dealing contracts with commercial agents [JO139/62]
EC Commission Decision ARG/Unipart [1987] OJ L45/34, 4 CMLR [1988] 513
EC Commission Decision Fisher Price [1987] OJ L49/19, 4 CMLR [1989] 553
EC Commission Decision Pittsburgh Corning [1972] OJ L272/35, [1973] CMLR D2
Competition Authority Decision No. 25, Motor Fuels category licence, 1 July 1993 **4.2**
Restrictive practices (motor spirit and motor vehicle lubricating oil) Order 1981
Competition Authority Decision No. 2, AGF — Irish Life Holdings plc, 14 May 1992 **1.3.1**

Competition Authority Decision of 5 May 1994 relating to a proceeding under section 4 of the Competition Act 1991
Notification No. CA/261/92E — Shell Appointment and Licence (1)

Introduction

1. Notification was made to the Competition Authority with a request for a certificate, or, failing the issue of a certificate, a licence, by Irish Shell Ltd on 30 September 1992 in respect of its standard agreement of appointment and licence with licensees.

2. The Authority published notice of its intention to take a favourable decision in relation to the agreement in the Irish Times on 25 February 1994. A submission was received from the Association of Shell Retailers.

The Facts **1.6.3**

(a) *The subject of the notification.*

3. The decision concerns the standard appointment and licence agreement between Shell and the licensees at a number of Shell-owned petrol stations. Under the agreement, Shell appoints the licensee for the purpose of the reception, storage, dispensing and sale at the site of Shell products, and for the purpose of rendering and supplying such services and commodities as are commonly rendered and supplied at filling or service stations. The agreement provides for the exclusive sale of Shell motor fuels, on behalf of Shell, and for the payment of commission on sales to the licensee.

(b) *The parties involved*

4. Irish Shell Ltd has as its ultimate parents The Royal Dutch Petroleum Company as well as The Shell Transport and Trading Company Ltd. Shell is primarily involved in the marketing of motor fuels through a chain of retail outlets, most of which are owned by independent dealers, the remainder being owned by Shell. Around 20 of its company outlets are occupied by licensees who operate the station under the notified agreement. A number of outlets which also include a shop are operated by licensees under a different agreement, which is the subject of a separate notification.

(c) *The product and the market*

5. The product with which the notified agreement is concerned consists of motor fuels, that is petrol and diesel for use in mechanically propelled road vehicles. The market was described in detail in the motor fuels category licence.[1]

(d) *The notified agreement*

6. Under the agreement, Shell appoints a person as agent and licensee for the reception, storage, dispensing and sale at a specified site of the company's products, particularly motor fuels, and generally for the purpose of rendering and supplying such other services and commodities as are commonly rendered and supplied at filling or service stations (recital (a), (d)(i)). The appointment is for a period not exceeding three years (recital (b)). Shell licenses the licensee to occupy and use the site and the equipment thereon, solely upon the conditions in the agreement ((d)(ii)). The main features of the agreement are as follows:

During the term of the Agreement, a licensee occupies and uses the site and equipment for the purpose of the reception, storage, dispensing, sale and distribution of Irish Shell's products (clause 2). A site may also be used for subsidiary and ancillary purposes provided Irish Shell gives prior written consent (clause 3).

The Agreement places certain responsibilities on the licensee:

(a) the licensee must use the equipment solely for the reception, storage, sale and distribution by the licensee of Irish Shell's products (clause 4(a));

(b) the licensee must use its best endeavours to develop and extend the sale at the site of Irish Shell's products in such manner as Irish Shell may from time to time suggest (clause 4(b));

(c) in order to ensure the effective running of the site, the licensee must employ such staff and take all necessary measures to ensure the smooth running of the site (clause 4 (c) (i));

(d) the licensee must attend at the site for a certain period of time (clause 4(c) (ii)) and must not introduce any other equipment or vehicles onto the site (clause 4(d));

(e) the licensee must not do anything which would injure or damage the property or goodwill of Irish Shell (clause 4(e));

(f) the licensee must hold on trust for Irish Shell all monies received and lodge them to a bank account (clause 4(f));

1. Motor fuels category licence, Decision No. 25, 1 July 1993, paras. 7 to 9.

1.6.3 (g) the licensee must maintain in good repair the equipment (clause 4(g));

(h) the licensee must keep records (clause 4(j));

(i) the licensee must indemnify Irish Shell against all actions and maintain adequate insurance cover (clause 4(k));

(j) the licensee must pay all charges for water, electricity, gas, telephone and other such public services and pay for stock losses above a specified level (clause 4(q));

(k) the licensee must notify Irish Shell of any change in the ownership of the licensee (clause 4(s));

(l) the licensee must sell each grade of motor fuel on behalf of Irish Shell at such price as Irish Shell may notify to the licensee from time to time (clause 4(v));

(m) the licensee must hold the proceeds of sale at its own risk (clause 4(y)) but lodge as soon as may be the proceeds of sale to a bank account (clause 4(x)); and

(n) the licensee must bear the risk in respect of motor fuels (clause 4(z)).

The Agreement also places certain responsibilities on Irish Shell such as to:

(a) insure and keep insured the equipment against loss or damage (clause 5(a));

(b) repair the equipment (clause 5(b));

(c) supply the licensee with stocks of Irish Shell products (clause 5(c));

(d) pay a commission to the licensee (clause 5(d)).

The Agreement does not confer any exclusive right on the licensee to use the site or equipment, nor does it create a landlord and tenant relationship (clause 7).

7. The agreement also makes provision for termination of the agreement before it has expired, notice by the company of such termination, refusal to renew the appointment of the licensee on termination of the agreement, and for compensation and arbitration. These provisions are largely based upon the 1981 Restrictive Practices Order for motor spirits,[2] which was repealed on 30 September 1991.

Submissions by Shell

8. Shell submitted the following arguments in support of its request for a certificate:

> The preamble to the Act clearly states that the Act is to be interpreted by analogy with Articles 85 and 86 of the Treaty of Rome. Article 85(1) sets out the prohibition on agreements which prevent, restrict or distort competition.

It is essential under Article 85 that there are two 'undertakings' acting in concert for the prohibition to operate. Undertaking has been given a broad meaning covering virtually every natural or legal person engaging in economic activity. Notices and decisions of the European Commission and decisions of the European Court of Justice indicate that the relationship of principal and agent in its normal economic context does not breach Article 85(1) as the agent is merely an auxiliary and extension of its principal and is not an undertaking, unlike an independent trader. In *Hydrotherm v. Compact*, the ECJ said:

> In competition law the term 'undertaking' must be understood as designating an economic unit . . . even if in law that economic unit consists of several persons legal or natural.

In 1962 the European Commission issued its Notice on Exclusive Dealing Contracts with Commercial Agents ('the Notice').[3] The purpose of the Notice is to set out the circumstances where the Commission considers Article 85(1) inapplicable to an agency contract. Certain requirements must be met in order for a contract to benefit from the Notice:

2. Restrictive Practices (Motor Spirit and Motor Vehicle Lubricating Oil) Order, 1981.
3. EC Commission Notice on exclusive dealing contracts with commercial agents, OJ 139, 24 December 1962, p. 2921.

(i) the commercial agent must not act as an independent trader during the course of commercial operations; **1.6.3**

(ii) financial risks related to the transaction must remain with the principal;

(iii) the commercial agent must not be required to keep a large stock of contract goods as its own property;

(iv) the commercial agent must not be required to organise, maintain or ensure at his own expense a substantial service to customers free of charge; and

(v) the commercial agent may not be vested with discretion to determine prices or business terms.

The over-riding element in a positive determination of agency in the Notice is the absence of risk on the agent's part when conducting business on behalf of the principal. The European Commission's decisions in Austin Rover Group (ARG)/Unipart and Fisher-Price/Quaker Oats — Toyco illustrate the importance of this point.

However, later developments show that assumption of risk is not the only criterion to be applied in deciding whether or not Article 85(1) is applicable. In Pittsburgh Corning Europe, the European Commission held that the use of the word 'agent' is not the critical factor and that economic reality took precedence over legal form especially where the so called agent was not in the position of economic dependence on the other party. In the Suiker Unie case the European Court of Justice followed this line of thinking in holding that traders who acted as agents for each other as well as principals on their own account in the same level of the sugar market could not benefit from an exemption from Article 85(1). Similarly, in VVR the Court rejected the idea that travel agents were auxiliary organs where they transacted business for a multitude of tour operators.

The European Commission published its Preliminary draft Notice on Commercial Agency Agreements ('the draft Notice') in 1990 as a first step to amending the Notice.

Under the guidelines the mere use of the label 'agent' is insufficient to judge whether an exemption should apply.

In assessing the relationship the Commission will disregard the general financial risk resulting from the conduct of the intermediary under the agreement, e.g. responsibility for personnel or professional liability. Instead the risks taken into account are those connected with the performance of the transactions negotiated by the intermediary in respect of the product in question. For an exemption to apply an intermediary must not assume primary responsibility for the performance of the transactions by his principal, i.e. profit or loss resulting from the performance of these transactions must, in the first place accrue to the principal.

A genuine agency relationship will not exist where the intermediary determines the principal's product and marketing strategy. Clauses obliging an agent to negotiate or conclude transactions on behalf of his principal only at prices, terms and conditions provided by the principal or subject to approval by the principal, do not restrict competition in the context of a genuine agency relationship.

The restrictions imposed by a principal on an agent can only be justified where the agent is integrated into the distribution or purchasing system of the principal. Integration means a situation where the agent has a particularly intensive link with the principal which leads him to subordinate his interests and to dedicate his operations in the field of the product covered by the agency agreement to those of the principal and which leaves customers or suppliers with whom the agent deals not to expect autonomous commercial behaviour from the agent but to identify him with the principal.

Where the agent has interests outside the agreement with its principal which do not prevent a close identification of the agent with the principal, the concept of integration will apply.

This will only occur where the outside interests are: (i) limited, and (ii) do not interfere with the subject matter of the agency agreement.

An obligation in an agency agreement on the part of the agent not to handle competing

1.6.3 products for the duration of the agreement does not infringe Article 85(1) where it is intended to achieve integration.

It is submitted that the appointment and licence constitutes an agency relationship and does not offend against section 4(1) of the Act.

The only 'undertaking' involved in the Arrangements within the meaning of section 4 of the Act is the Applicant as the Licensee is merely an auxiliary not having the status of an independent trader.

In regard to the parallel application of the Notice to section 4, clauses 4(a), 4(b), 4(f), 4(o), 4(t), 4(v) and 4(x) of the Licence prevent the Licensee from acting as an independent trader during the course of commercial operations.*

Recital (d) of the Licence by appointing the Licensee the Applicant's agent vests the financial risk for the sale of Motor Fuel in the principal vis a vis third parties.

The Licence provides that the Applicant is the owner of the site and Equipment (Clause 7) and accordingly the Licensee is not required to organise, maintain or ensure at its own expense a substantial service to customers free of charge.

The Licensee can not determine the price of Motor Fuel by virtue of Clause 4(v) of the Licence.

In overall terms, the Arrangements constitute an agency agreement between two parties each in different positions in the business chain. The Applicant has a turnover of [——] and the Licensee [——]. In terms of economic dependence the Licensee is bound to the Applicant and is incapable of influencing price or supply in the automotive fuel market. If the concept of agency defined in terms of economic dependence as set out in the European Court of Justice decisions in Pittsburgh Corning and VVR is applied to section 4(1), then it is submitted that the Arrangements do not infringe the said section.

The provisions of the draft Notice, if applied in parallel to section 4(1) of the Act, contains a number of criteria for determining whether an agency agreement is genuine and outside the scope of section 4(1).

The draft Notice considers it essential for the profit or loss resulting from the performance of the transactions with customers to accrue in the first place to the principal. The effect of Clauses 4(f) and 4(x) of the Licence requires the proceeds of sale of Motor Fuel to be lodged to the Applicant's bank account. It is only when this occurs that commission is paid to the Licensee.

The draft Notice does not envisage exemption of an agreement from the competition rules where the intermediary can determine the principal's product and marketing strategy. Under the Licence the Applicant determines the range of products for which the Licensee acts as agent and the Applicant outlines the marketing strategy (Clause 4(b)).

Clauses obliging an agent to negotiate or conclude transactions on behalf of its principal only at prices, terms and conditions provided by the principal and subject to approval by the principal, do not restrict competition in the context of a genuine agency relationship. This is clearly the situation under the Licence, for example, see Clauses 4(v) and 4(w).

One of the critical factors in the draft Notice for determining the competitive effect of an agreement is the concept of integration. Clause 4(a) of the Licence obliges the Licensee to use the Equipment on the Site solely for reception, storage, sale and distribution of the Company's products. This accords with the idea of dedicating operations to the sale of one particular brand.

For the reasons outlined above and by analogy with European Community Law, it is submitted that the Licence does not infringe section 4(1) of the Act. Shell also submitted arguments in support of the grant of a licence which are not relevant to this decision and are not considered here.

*4(o) relates to planning permission, and 4(t) relates to changing the name of the site, neither of which is regarded by the Authority as being relevant to this decision.

Response to Notice of Intention 1.6.3

9. The Association of Shell Retailers responded to the notice of intention. It claimed that its members were unable to confirm whether Shell regarded them as lessees, licensees, agents, partners or employees. While Shell might have notified a standard licence agreement, they believed that Shell were applying dissimilar conditions, in prices for example, which were not based on objective criteria. It claimed that Shell had the ability and were becoming more powerful to direct customers to particular sites. The Authority has taken account of the Association's comments insofar as they are relevant to the notified agreement.

Assessment

Applicability of section 4(1)

10. Section 4(1) of the Competition Act 1991 prohibits and renders void all agreements between undertakings which have as their object or effect the prevention, restriction or distortion of competition in trade in any goods or services in the State or in any part of the State.

11. Shell and the licensees are engaged in the sale of motor fuels for gain, and they are therefore undertakings within the meaning of section 3(1) of the Competition Act. The Authority does not accept the argument of Shell that an agent is not an undertaking, or that there is any EC precedent for this view. In particular, neither the 1962 Notice, nor its draft revision, states that an agent is not an undertaking, and this is not the reason for regarding an agreement between a principal and an agent as not being in breach of Article 85(1). The position is similar to that of a parent firm and a subsidiary, where the EC Commission has held that both are undertakings, even though a restrictive agreement between them may not infringe Article 85(1). A similar view has been taken by the Authority in its decision in AGF-Irish Life.[4] The standard licensee agreement is an agreement between undertakings. The relevant product market is that for motor fuels. The relevant geographic market is the State.

(i) The status of the licensee

12. In operating the petrol station premises and selling motor fuels, the licensee is not an employee of Shell and there is no contract of employment or service between them. He is a self-employed contractor. At the same time, the licensee does not purchase motor fuels from Shell for resale to the public. Unlike the Shell independent dealer, the licensee sells motor fuel, not on his own account, but on behalf of Shell. He does not pay for the motor fuels, and the motor fuels remain the property of Shell until they are sold at retail, even though they are held at the licensee's risk. All receipts from the sale of motor fuels must be lodged to Shell's bank account. Out of his commission, the licensee must pay for certain outgoings, such as labour, insurance and other costs, the balance representing the licensee's remuneration. The licensee is responsible for employing staff. Shell determines the prices at which the motor fuels are to be sold. The petrol station is effectively under the operational control and direction of Shell, and is operated for Shell's own account, and the licensee is obliged to obey Shell's instructions. The relationship between Shell and the licensee is an ongoing one, and the agreement may have a duration of up to three years.

13. The Authority considers that the question of agency is quite complex, and that each case must be examined on its own merits in relation to the Competition Act, in the light of certain general considerations. In the first place, it is not relevant that one party is referred to as an 'agent' in the agreement, since he may not perform the functions of an agent in any real sense. Conversely, it does not matter if the agreement states that there is no relationship or contract of agency between the parties. This may be done, for example, to ensure that one party is not empowered to undertake binding obligations on behalf of the other, without the latter's

4. Decision No. 2 — AGF-Irish Life Holdings plc (14 May 1992).

1.6.3 knowledge or consent. From the point of view of the Competition Act, the Authority is concerned with whether the relationship between the two parties is such that one of them may be termed a 'commercial agent' of the other. It is not intended that the views of the Authority about whether a person is commercial agent or not should have any implications for the legal relationship between the parties.

14. The Authority considers that a commercial agent is a self-employed intermediary between the principal and a purchaser or seller. The commercial agent concludes the sale or purchase of goods and services on behalf of the principal, on a continuing basis. The commercial agent is an auxiliary organ, forming an integral part of the principal's business, and is bound to carry out the instructions of the principal, and his position is similar to that of an employee. Being integrated into the principal's business, the commercial agent can undertake no autonomous commercial behaviour, under the agreement, and certain restrictions on him are fundamental to the relationship. The Authority considers that profits or losses essentially accrue to the principal and not to the commercial agent.

15. The relationship between Shell and its licensees has been summarised in para. 12. Shell has argued that the licensee is an auxiliary and that the agreement does not offend against section 4(1).

16. The licensee is a self-employed intermediary between Shell and the purchasers of Shell motor fuels. He concludes the sale of goods on behalf of Shell, on a continuing basis, for up to three years. He does not own the stocks, the resale prices are set by Shell, and the licensee lodges the proceeds of sale to the credit of Shell's bank account. While the licensee accepts some risk, in relation to stock losses, and is responsible for hiring and paying employees, the profits and losses of the motor fuels business as a whole accrue to Shell, and the licensee must obey Shell's instructions and may undertake no autonomous behaviour in respect of the operation of the petrol station. The Authority considers that the licensee, in operating the petrol station and selling Shell products, is an auxiliary organ, forming an integral part of Shell's distribution business, and it concludes that he can be considered to be a commercial agent.

(ii) The commercial agency agreement

17. The Authority considers that undertakings are entitled to decide how to operate their distribution systems, and, in particular, to appoint commercial agents to sell their goods on their behalf. Suppliers of motor fuels are free to choose to sell their products through independent dealers or through company-owned outlets; these latter may be operated by lessees, licensees, employees or by consignees and commercial agents. Since the commercial agent is an auxiliary organ, similar to an employee, the agreement between a principal and a commercial agent does not, in principle, offend against section 4(1) of the Competition Act.

18. In the present case, the Authority has concluded that the licensee is a commercial agent. It considers that the agreement between Shell and the licensee, insofar as it creates a relationship between the principal and a commercial agent, does not offend against section 4(1).

19. Even though the basic arrangement of commercial agency might not offend against section 4(1), certain clauses in the agreement might occasionally do so. In the case of motor fuels agreements, the Authority has published a category licence, which permits the imposition of certain obligations upon resellers of motor fuels and upon their suppliers. The Authority considers that the obligations which are not regarded as offending against section 4(1) in the case of independent traders would equally not offend in the case of commercial agents. More fundamentally, the Authority recognises that there are certain features of commercial agency agreements which define and confirm the relationship, and are intrinsic to the commercial agency. Since the commercial agent is closer to being an employee than an independent trader, the Authority considers that certain restrictions may be imposed upon a commercial agent without offending against section 4(1), whereas they would offend against section 4(1) if they were imposed on an independent trader. In the Authority's opinion, none of the provisions in the notified agreement offend against section 4(1).

The Decision 1.6.3

20. In the Authority's opinion, Shell and its licensees are undertakings within the meaning of section 3(1) of the Competition Act, and the notified standard licensee agreement for the operation of a Shell-owned petrol station constitutes an agreement between undertakings. In the Authority's opinion, the licensee is a commercial agent of Shell, and the arrangements do not have, as their object or effect, the prevention, restriction or distortion of competition. The standard Shell licensee agreement does not, in the Authority's opinion, offend against section 4(1) of the Competition Act 1991.

The Certificate

The Competition Authority has issued the following certificate:

> The Competition Authority certifies that in its opinion, on the basis of the facts in its possession, the standard agreement between Shell and its licensees for the operation of a Shell-owned petrol station (notification no CA/261/92E), notified on 30 September 1992, under section 7, does not offend against section 4(1) of the Competition Act 1991.

For the Competition Authority

Patrick M. Lyons
Chairman

5 May 1994

Competition Authority Decision No. 327, Shell Licence: 19 May 1994, Notification No. CA/263/92E 1.6.4

Licence agreement – Licensee acting as licensor's agent in the sale of licensor's motor fuel goods – Licensee acting as independent contractor in the sale of non motor fuel goods – Licensee remunerated on commission basis in respect of agency services – Power of licensor to oblige the licensee to cease selling non motor fuel products which it considers inappropriate – Whether licensee an undertaking within the meaning of Competition Act 1991 – Competition Act 1991 (No. 24) sections 3, 4 and 7

Facts: On 30 September 1992 notification was made to the Authority by Irish Shell Ltd ('Irish Shell') with a request for a certificate under section 4(4) of the Competition Act 1991 or, failing that, a licence under section 4(2) in respect of its standard licence agreement. Irish Shell whose ultimate parents are the Royal Dutch Petroleum Company and Shell Transport and Trading Company Ltd, is engaged in the marketing of motor fuels through a chain of retail outlets a small number of which are owned by Irish Shell, within the State. A number of the service stations owned by Irish Shell also contain a convenience shop and are occupied by licensees who operate the stations under the provisions of the notified agreement. The agreement came into effect after 1 October 1991.

The product market with which the main part of the notified agreement is concerned

1.6.4 consists of motor fuels for use in road vehicles and the market which that part of the agreement relating to the shop is concerned with is all retail outlets selling goods of a similar character. Under the terms of the notified agreement Irish Shell appoints licensees as its agent to sell motor fuels on its behalf for a period of three years. The licensee agrees, *inter alia,* not to sell or use the equipment for any competing motor fuel product, to operate the service station in accordance with Irish Shell's operation manual and to sell motor fuel on behalf of Irish Shell at such prices as Irish Shell may notify to the licensee from time to time. Irish Shell agrees, *inter alia,* to supply the licensee with motor fuel and to pay licensee a commission for such fuel sold. The agreement also provides for the prompt lodgement to Irish Shell's bank account of the receipts of sale of fuel and that the motor fuel shall remain the property of Irish Shell until such time as it is sold.

With regard to the shop products and services the agreement provides that the licensee shall pay to Irish Shell an amount in respect of shop products and services calculated in accordance with the agreement. Clause 9.5 provides that Irish Shell may oblige the licensee to withdraw from the service station upon demand any products, services, advertisements, displays or anything whatsoever which Irish Shell considers to be inappropriate at a service station.

In response to concerns raised by the Authority Irish Shell stated that the licensee was an independent undertaking in respect of the sale of goods other than petrol and that he was free to determine the re-sale prices of goods sold in the shop. Irish Shell had never used clause 9.5 of the agreement to oblige a licensee to remove any products. On 11 February 1994 the Authority wrote to Irish Shell outlining its concerns regarding clause 9.5, and intimated that those concerns would be dispelled by the addition in the relevant clause of the following sentence 'this clause would only be invoked for objectively valid reasons which shall be disclosed to the licensee'. By letter dated 1 March 1994 Irish Shell consented to the amendments of clause 9.5 and on 8 April 1994 the Authority published notice of its intention to make a favourable decision in relation to the notification.

Decided by the Authority: In issuing a certificate under section 4(4) of the Competition Act 1991 in respect of the notified agreement that:

(1) Each of Irish Shell and the licensees are engaged in the sale of motor fuels for gain, and the licensees are also engaged in the sale of other products for gain and they are therefore undertakings within the meaning of section 3(1) of the Competition Act. The submission by Irish Shell that an agent is not an undertaking is rejected, the position being similar to that of a parent firm and a subsidiary where both are undertakings even though a restrictive agreement between them may not affect competition.

(2) The notified agreement is an agreement between undertakings. The relevant product markets are those for (a) motor fuels and (b) the products sold in the shop on the petrol station premises and the relevant geographic market is the State.

(3) The licensee is a self employed intermediary between Irish Shell and the purchaser of Irish Shell motor fuels who concludes the sale of goods on behalf of Irish Shell on a continuing basis for up to three years. The licensee does not own the stocks, the retail prices are set by Irish Shell and the licensee lodges the proceeds of sale to the credit of Irish Shell's bank account. While the licensee accepts some risk in relation to stock losses and is responsible for hiring and paying employees, the profits

and losses of the motor fuels business as a whole accrue to Irish Shell and the licensee must obey Irish Shell's instructions and undertake no autonomous behaviour in respect of the operation of the petrol station. The licensee selling Irish Shell's fuel products is an auxiliary organ forming an integral part of Irish Shell's distribution business and therefore can be considered to be Irish Shell's commercial agent in respect of motor fuel sales. This conclusion is not effected by the fact that the licensee also operates shops supplied by Irish Shell since the operation of the petrol station constitutes a significant proportion of the whole business and there is also a relationship between the licensee and Irish Shell in relation to the shop. **1.6.4**

(4) The licensee sells products other than motor fuels in the shop for his own account and separately from the sales of the Irish Shell petrol products. Although the licensee pays a commission on the sale to Irish Shell and is bound by certain obligations imposed by Irish Shell regarding the operation of the shop he is in no sense a commercial agent of Irish Shell in respect of the shop but is an independent trader.

(5) Undertakings are entitled to decide how to operate their distribution systems and, in particular, to appoint commercial agents. Since a commercial agent is an auxiliary organ similar to an employee an agreement between the principal and the commercial agent does not in principle offend against section 4(1) of the Competition Act. The notified agreement insofar as it creates the relationship between a principal and a commercial agent does not offend against section 4(1).

(6) There are certain features of commercial agency agreements which define and confirm the relationship and are intrinsic to commercial agency. A commercial agent is closer to being an employee than an independent trader and certain restrictions may be imposed upon a commercial agent without offending against section 4(1) which would offend against such section if they were imposed on independent traders.

(7) Clause 9.5 of the agreement whereby Irish Shell could oblige the licensee to withdraw form the site on demand any product, services, advertisements, displays or anything whatsoever which Irish Shell consider to be inappropriate at a service station could, prior to its subsequent amendment, be used to limit the freedom of the licensee to determine what products to sell and from whom he may obtain supplies which could affect the ability of the licensee to compete with other retailers in the area. While the affect of this requirement might have little effect upon competition in the case of an individual licensee the cumulative effect of this obligation in respect of all Irish Shell licensees, and the fact that this practice might be followed by other petrol companies, might not be insignificant. Similarly such a clause would not have qualified for a license as it would not satisfy the indispensability requirement of section 4(2) of the Competition Act.

Cases, Decisions and Notice referred to:

ECJ Decision *Hydrotherm v. Compact* (Case No. 170/83), [1984] ECR 2999, [1985] 3 CMLR 276
ECJ Decision *Suiker Unie v. Commission* [1975] ECR 1663, [1976] 1 CMLR 295
Notice on exclusive dealing contracts with commercial agents [JO139/62]
Commission Decision ARG/Unipart [1987] OJ L45/34, 4 CMLR [1988] 513
Commission Decision Fisher Price [1987] OJ L49/19, 4 CMLR [1989] 553
Commission Decision Pittsburgh Corning [1972] OJ L272/35, [1973] CMLR D2
Competition Authority Decision No.25, Motor Fuels category licence, 1 July 1993 **4.2**
Restrictive practices (motor spirit and motor vehicle lubricating oil) Order, 1981 [SI No. 70 of 1981
Competition Authority Decision No. 2, AGF — Irish Life Holdings plc, 14 May 1992 **1.3.1**
Competition Authority Decision No. 325 Shell Appointment and Licence, 5 May 1994 **1.6.3**

1.6.4 Competition Authority Decision of 19 May 1994 relating to a proceeding under section 4 of the Competition Act 1991 Notification No. CA/63/92E — Shell Licence

Introduction

1. Notification was made to the Competition Authority with a request for a certificate, or failing the issue of a certificate, a licence, by Irish Shell Ltd on 30 September 1992 in respect of its standard licence agreement.

2. The Authority published notice of its intention to take a favourable decision in relation to the agreement as amended in The Irish Times on 8 April 1994. No submissions were received from interested parties.

The facts

(a) *The subject of the notification*

3. The decision concerns the standard licence agreement between Shell and the licensees at a number of Shell-owned petrol stations. Under the agreement, Shell appoints the licensee to be its agent to sell various goods and services on its behalf. It makes provision for the running and maintenance of the service station, the exclusive sale of Shell petroleum products, the sale of other goods and services and the payment of commission on sales of motor fuels to the licensee, although, in certain cases, a management fee may be paid to the licensee. There are special provisions in the agreement in respect of a convenience shop on the premises, in which are sold products other than motor fuels, such as grocery goods, etc. The two parts of the agreement are dealt with separately in this decision.

(b) *The parties involved*

4. Irish Shell has as its ultimate parents the Royal Dutch Petroleum Company as well as the Shell Transport and Trading Company Ltd. Shell is primarily involved in the marketing of motor fuels through a chain of retail outlets, most of which are owned by independent dealers, the remainder being owned by Shell. Around 20 of its company outlets are occupied by licensees who operate the station under the notified agreement, which only came into effect after 1 October 1991. A number of outlets which do not include a shop are operated by licensees under a different agreement, which is the subject of a separate decision.[1]

(c) *The product and the market*

5. The product with which the main part of the notified agreement is concerned consists of motor fuels, that is petrol and diesel for use in mechanically propelled road vehicles. The market was described in detail in the motor fuels category licence.[2]

6. The convenience shop primarily sells grocery goods, confectionery, newspapers, cigarettes, etc. The market consists of all retail outlets selling goods of a similar character.

(d) *The notified agreement*

(i) Motor fuels

7. Under the agreement, which is between Shell and the licensee, Shell licenses the person to enter and use the site and the equipment, and Shell appoints the licensee as its agent to sell motor fuel on its behalf. The main features of the agreement in respect of motor fuels are as follows:

> The licence provides that Shell is the owner of the land and buildings (known as the 'site') (clause 2.1). Shell has adapted the site to be used as a filling/service station (clause

1. Decision No. 325 — Shell Appointment and Licence (5 May 1994).
2. Motor fuels category licence, Decision No. 25, 1 July 1993, paras. 7 to 9.

2.2). Unless otherwise agreed to in writing, Shell owns or provides the fixtures, fittings, plant and equipment which are situate on the site (clause 2.3). The licensee may use the equipment on the site only for the purposes of the licence (clause 2.6). 1.6.4

The licence shall remain in force for three years (clause 3.1). Under the licence, Shell licenses the licensee to enter the site and use the equipment as licensee subject to the terms and conditions contained in the licence (clause 3.3).

Shell appoints the licensee as its agent to sell motor fuel on its behalf (clause 4.5). The licensee agrees to actively sell and promote the products (as defined in the licence) and actively render and supply the services (as defined in the licence) (clause 4.6). The licensee shall use the equipment on the site solely for the reception, storage, sale, distribution and provision of the product and services (clause 4.7). The licensee agrees not to sell or use the equipment for any motor fuel or petroleum product manufactured or distributed by a competitor of Shell (clause 4.8). The licensee may use the site for the

provision or sale of bulk automotive liquified petroleum gas but only on such terms and conditions consented to in writing by Shell from time to time (clause 4.9). The licensee shall keep the site open during such minimum hours as specified from time to time by Shell (clause 5.1). The site and equipment shall be used and operated strictly in accordance with the Operations Manual produced and amended from time to time (clause 6.1). This Operations Manual is annexed to the licence and forms an integral part of the licence.*

Shell agrees to supply the licensee with motor fuel (clause 7.1). The licensee shall sell motor fuel on behalf of Shell at such prices as Shell may notify to the licensee from time to time and the licensee shall set the pricing mechanisms of the several relevant dispensers on the site to record such notification (clause 7.2). The licensee shall sell motor fuel on behalf of Shell for cash, cheque, Euroshell or payment card of those companies whose payment cards are from time to time acceptable by Shell (clause 7.3). When any part of the motor fuel is sold by the licensee to a third party, the title to that part shall pass to the purchaser on leaving the dispenser on the site. The title to the remaining motor fuel shall remain vested in Shell (clause 7.4).

Shell shall pay to the licensee a commission for each litre of motor fuel sold by the licensee on the site (clause 8.10). There are various banking arrangements relating to the prompt lodgment to a bank of the receipts of sale (clause 8.2).

There are various operational matters relating to the level of service (clause 9.1), staff (clause 9.2) and sale of motor cars (clause 9.3).

The licensee agrees to use such a site management system as shall be nominated from time to time by Shell (clause 10.1). The licensee agrees to keep records (clause 10.2) and shall furnish to Shell such records on request (clause 10.3).

Shell may require the licensee to share the use of the site and/or the equipment with any other person nominated by Shell (clause 11.3).

No equipment shall be introduced on to the site by the licensee except with the prior consent of Shell (clause 12.7). The licensee pays charges for all water, electricity, gas, telephone and such other services as may be used on the site (clause 12.11).

The insurance of the site, the equipment and motor fuel against loss or damage by fire or explosion shall be for Shell (clause 13.1). The licensee shall maintain adequate insurance against all or any risks in relation to the running of or operating of the site and equipment including but not limited to such matters as public liability and employer's liability (clause 13.2). The insurance referred to in clause 13.2 must be with an insurance company acceptable to Shell (clause 13.3).

* There would appear to be nothing in the Operations Manual which is relevant to this decision.

1.6.4 The licensee shall comply with Shell's requirements in regard to intellectual property matters (clause 15.1).

Clause 16 refers to the fact that the parties agree to notify the agreement to the Competition Authority.

Clause 17 provides for termination of the licence.

Part I of the Second Schedule of the licence refers to the commission or management fee to be paid to the licensee.

(ii) Shop products and services

8. The agreement also relates to the operation of a shop selling 'shop products' (which are defined by clause 4.2 as 'Products that may from time to time be sold at filling/service stations excluding Motor Fuel, automotive lubricants and anti-freeze') and 'Services' (which are defined by clause 4.3 as 'such services as may from time to time be provided at filling/service stations including car wash and vacuum cleaning'). Under clause 8.3, the licensee agrees to pay to Shell an amount in respect of Shop Products and Services which shall be calculated in accordance with Part II of the Second Schedule to the agreement. The agreement provides for a mechanism for calculating these payments.

Clause 9.5 states as follows:

> The Licensee agrees that Shell reserves the right during the Term to oblige the Licensee to withdraw from the Site upon demand any Shop Products, Services or other goods, services advertisements, displays or anything whatsoever which Shell considers to be inappropriate at a filling/service station.

Submissions by Shell

9. Shell submitted the following arguments in support of its request for a certificate:

> The preamble to the Act clearly states that the Act is to be interpreted by analogy with Articles 85 and 86 of the Treaty of Rome. Article 85(1) sets out the prohibition on agreements which prevent, restrict or distort competition. It is essential under Article 85 that there are two 'undertakings' acting in concert for the prohibition to operate. 'Undertaking' has been given a broad meaning covering virtually every natural or legal person engaging in economic activity. Notices and decisions of the European Commission and decisions of the European Court of Justice indicate that the relationship of principal and agent in its normal economic context does not breach Article 85(1) as the agent is merely an auxiliary and extension of its principal and is not an undertaking, unlike an independent trader. In *Hydrotherm v. Compact*, the Court said:
>
> In competition law the term 'undertaking' must be understood as designating an economic unit . . . even if in law that economic unit consists of several persons, legal or natural.

In 1962 the European Commission issued its Notice on Exclusive Dealing Contracts with Commercial Agents ('the Notice').[3] The purpose of the notice is to set out the circumstances where the commission considers Article 85(1) inapplicable to an agency contract. Certain requirements must be met in order for a contract to benefit from the Notice:

> (i) the commercial agent must not act as an independent trader during the course of commercial operations;
> (ii) financial risks related to the transaction must remain with the principal;

3. EC Commission Notice on exclusive dealing contracts with commercial agents, OJ 139, 24.12.1962, p. 2921.

(iii) the commercial agent must not be required to keep a large stock of contract goods as its own property; 1.6.4
(iv) the commercial agent must not be required to organise, maintain or ensure at his own expense a substantial service to customers free of charge; and
(v) the commercial agent may not be vested with discretion to determine prices or business terms.

The over-riding element in a positive determination of agency in the Notice is the absence of risk on the agent's part when conducting business on behalf of the principal. The European Commission's decision in Austin Rover Group (ARG)/Unipart and Fisher-Price/Quaker Oats — Toyco illustrate the importance of this point. However, later developments show that assumption of risk is not the only criterion to be applied in deciding whether or not Article 85(1) is applicable. In Pittsburgh Corning Europe, the European Commission held that the use of the word 'agent' is not the critical factor and that economic reality took precedence over legal form especially where the so-called agent was not in the position of economic dependence on the other party. In the Suiker Unie case the European Court of Justice followed this line of thinking in holding that traders who acted as agents for each other as well as principals on their own account in the same level of the sugar market could not benefit from an exemption from Article 85(1). Similarly, in VVR the Court rejected the idea that travel agents were auxiliary organs where they transacted business for a multitude of tour operators.

The European Commission published its Preliminary draft Notice on Commercial Agency Agreements ('the draft Notice') in 1990 as a first step to amending the Notice. Under these guidelines the mere use of the label 'agent' is insufficient to judge whether an exemption should apply. In assessing the relationship, the Commission will disregard the general financial risk resulting from the conduct of the intermediary under the agreement, e.g. responsibility for personnel or professional liability. Instead the risks taken into account are those connected with the performance of the transactions negotiated by the intermediary in respect of the product in question. For an exemption to apply an intermediary must not assume primary responsibility for the performance of the transactions by his principal, i.e. profit or loss resulting from the performance of these transactions must, in the first place accrue to the principal.

A genuine relationship will not exist where the intermediary determines the principal's product and marketing strategy. Clauses obliging an agent to negotiate or conclude transactions on behalf of his principal only at prices, terms and conditions provided by the principal or subject to approval by the principal, do not restrict competition in the context of a genuine agency relationship.

The restrictions imposed by a principal on an agent can only be justified where the agent is integrated into the distribution or purchasing system of the principal. Integration means a situation where the agent has a particularly intensive link with the principal which leads him to subordinate his interests and to dedicate his operations in the field of the product covered by the agency agreement to those of the principal and which leaves customers or suppliers with whom the agent deals not to expect autonomous commercial behaviour from the agent but to identify him with the principal.

Where the agent has interests outside the agreement with its principal which do not prevent a close identification of the agent with the principal, the concept of integration will apply. This will only occur where the outside interests are:

(i) limited, and
(ii) do not interfere with the subject matter of the agency agreement.

An obligation in an agency agreement on the part of the agent not to handle competing products for the duration of the agreement does not infringe Article 85(1) where it is intended to achieve integration.

1.6.4 It is submitted that the Licence hereby notified constitutes an agency relationship and does not offend against section 4(1) of the Act.

The only 'undertaking' involved in the Arrangements within the meaning of section 4 of the Act is the Applicant as the Licensee is merely an auxiliary and does not have the status of an independent trader/undertaking. In regard to the parallel application of the Notice to section 4 of the Act, Clauses 2.3, 4.5, 4.6, 4.7, 4.8, 5.1, 6.1 and 7.2 of the Licence prevent the Licensee from acting as an independent trader during the course of commercial operations. Clauses 4.5, 4.6, 4.7, 4.8, 5.1 and 7.2 prevent the Licensee from acting as an independent trader during the course of commercial operations. Clause 4.5 appoints the Licensee as the Applicant's agent to sell motor fuel on its behalf. Clauses 4.6 and 4.7 oblige the Licensee to sell the Products and supply the services and to use the equipment solely for the reception, storage, sale, distribution and provision of the Products and services. Clause 4.8 forbids the Licensee from selling or using the Equipment in relation to competing products. Clause 5.1 states that the Applicant will stipulate the hours of opening of the site. Clause 7.2 that the Licensee shall sell motor fuel on behalf of the Applicant at such prices as the Applicant may notify to the Licensee from time to time. Clause 4.5 of the Licence by appointing the Licensee the Applicant's agent vests the financial risk for the sale of Motor Fuel in the principal vis a vis third parties. The Licensee is only obliged to stock such amount of Motor Fuel as the storage tanks on the Site can hold. The legal title in any of the Motor Fuel is vested in the Applicant and only passes to a customer on leaving the dispenser. At no time does the Licensee have any interest or title to that Motor Fuel (Clause 7.4), clearly showing the auxiliary nature of the Licensee. The Licence provides that the Applicant is the owner of the Site and Equipment and accordingly the Licensee is not required to organise, maintain or ensure at its own expense a substantial service to customers free of charge. The Licensee cannot determine the price of Motor Fuel by virtue of Clause 7.2 of the Licence. The Licensee has no discretion to dictate the terms of sale for Motor Fuel to customers by virtue of Clauses 7.3 and 7.4.

In overall terms, the Arrangements constitute an agency agreement between two parties each in different positions in the business chain. If the concept of agency defined in terms of economic dependence as set out in the European Court of Justice's decisions in Pittsburgh Corning and VVR is applied to section 4(1), then it is submitted that the Arrangements do not infringe the said section.

The provisions of the draft Notice, if applied in parallel to section 4(1) of the Act, contains a number of criteria for determining whether an agency agreement is genuine and outside the scope of section 4(1).

The draft Notice considers it essential for the profit or loss resulting from the performance of the transactions with customers to accrue in the first place to the principal. The effect of Clause 8.2 of the Licence requires the proceeds of sale of Motor Fuel to be lodged to a Shell bank account. It is only when this occurs that commission is paid to the Licensee.

The draft Notice does not envisage exemption of an agreement from the competition rules where the intermediary can determine the principal's product and marketing strategy. Under the Licence the Applicant determines the range of products for which the Licensee acts as agent (Clauses 4.1 & 4.5) and the Applicant outlines the marketing strategy by way of the Operations Manual.

Clauses obliging an agent to negotiate or conclude transactions on behalf of its principal only at prices, terms and conditions provided by the principal and subject to approval by the principal, do not restrict competition in the context of a genuine agency relationship. This is clearly the situation under the Licence, for example, see Clauses 7.2, 7.3 and 7.4.

Clause 4.8 of the Licence denies the Licensee the right to use the Equipment on the Site for the sale of any motor fuel or petroleum product manufactured or distributed by a competitor of the Applicant which accords with the idea of dedicating operations to the sale of one particular brand.

Where the agent has interests outside the agreement with its principal which do not prevent a close identification of the agent with the principal, the concept of integration will apply. However, it will only apply where the outside interests are limited and do not interfere with the subject matter of the agency agreement. While strictly speaking the Licensee has no interest outside the Licence which would prevent a close identification with the Applicant, the Licence itself provides for the Licensee selling goods and providing services on its own account which are unconnected to the automotive fuel market (Clauses 4.2 to 4.6 inclusive). However, this is on account of the Applicant's desire to provide a value added service to its customers at its filling stations so that not only will the customer be able to buy motor fuel but also have the opportunity and convenience of buying products that are normally sold at filling/service stations such as groceries and having their cars washed or cleaned. This provision of the Licence is an attempt to improve and strengthen the agency business so that the Licensee will have a greater opportunity to maximise his profit and in no way detracts from the core agency business of selling automotive fuel. **1.6.4**

For the reasons outlined above and by analogy with European Community Law, it is submitted that the Licence does not infringe section 4(1) of the Act and a Certificate ought to be granted.

Shell also submitted arguments in support of the grant of a licence which are not relevant to this decision and are not considered here.

Subsequent developments

10. In response to the Authority, Shell stated that a management fee was paid only when the volume of business on a site did not generate sufficient income for the Licensee/operator to pay outgoings. This was normally done only for new sites or new Licensees so as to initially stimulate business, and there were few sites where management fees were paid. Shell operates three stations through Donnybrook Self-Service Ltd in order to train its staff in the management and operation of retail outlets. Shell stated also that the Licensee was an independent undertaking in respect of the sale of goods other than petrol, and that he was free to determine the resale prices of goods sold in the shop. Shell had never asked any Licensee to remove products. If it were to use the power, then it would probably be for safety consideration (pending action by public authorities) or because the products were unsuitable for a filling station.

11. The Authority wrote to Shell on 11 February 1994 expressing concern in relation to clause 9.5 which permitted Shell to oblige the licensee to withdraw from the site upon demand any shop products, etc., which Shell considered inappropriate. It stated that its concern would be removed by the addition of the following sentence: 'This clause would only be invoked for objectively valid reasons which shall be disclosed to the licensee.' The Authority considered that this would still adequately safeguard the legitimate interests of the company, while not impinging on the commercial freedom of the independent operator. By letter dated 1 March 1994, Shell consented to the insertion of the addition to clause 9.5 as suggested by the Authority.

Assessment

Applicability of section 4(1)

12. Section 4(1) of the Competition Act 1991 prohibits and renders void all agreements between undertakings which have as their object or effect the prevention, restriction or distortion of competition in trade in any goods or services in the State or in any part of the State.

13. Shell and the Licensees are engaged in the sale of motor fuels for gain, and the Licensees are also engaged in the sale of other products for gain, and they are therefore undertakings within the meaning of section 3(1) of the Competition Act. The Authority does not accept the argument of Shell that an agent is not an undertaking, or that there is any EC precedent for this view. In particular, neither the 1962 Notice, nor its draft revision, states that an agent is not an undertaking, and this is not the reason for regarding an agreement between a principal and an agent as not being in breach of Article 85(1). The position is similar to that of a parent firm

1.6.4 and a subsidiary, where the EC Commission has held that both are undertakings, even through a restrictive agreement between them may not infringe Article 85(1). A similar view has been taken by the Authority in its decision in AGF-Irish Life.[4] The standard licensee agreement is an agreement between undertakings. The relevant product markets are those for (a) motor fuels, and (b), the products sold in the shop on the petrol station premises. The relevant geographic market is the State.

(i) *The status of the licensee*

(1) In respect of the sales of motor fuels

14. In operating the petrol station premises and selling motor fuels, the licensee is not an employee of Shell and there is no contract of employment or service between them. He is a self-employed contractor. At the same time, the licensee does not purchase motor fuels from Shell for resale to the public. Unlike the Shell independent dealer, the licensee sells motor fuel, not on his own account, but on behalf of Shell. He does not pay for the motor fuels, and the motor fuels remain the property of Shell until they are sold at retail, even through they are held at the licensee's risk. All receipts from the sale of motor fuels must be lodged daily to Shell's bank account. Out of his commission, or management fee, the licensee must pay for certain outgoings, such as labour, insurance and other costs, the balance representing the licensee's remuneration. The licensee is responsible for employing staff. Shell determines the prices at which the motor fuels are to be sold. The petrol station is effectively under the operational control and direction of Shell, and is operated for Shell's own account, and the licensee is obliged to obey Shells instructions and to follow the Operations Manual. The relationship between Shell and the licensee is an ongoing one, and the agreement may have a duration of up to three years.

15. The Authority considers that the question of agency is quite complex, and that each case must be examined on its own merits in relation to the Competition Act, in the light of certain general considerations. In the first place, it is not conclusive that one party is referred to as an 'agent' in the agreement, since he may not perform the functions of an agent in any real sense. Conversely, it does not matter if the agreement states that there is no relationship or contract of agency between the parties. This may be done, for example, to limit one party's ability to undertake binding obligations on behalf of the other, without the latter's knowledge or consent. From the point of view of the Competition Act, the Authority is concerned with whether the relationship between the two parties is such that one of them may be termed a 'commercial agent' of the other. It is not intended that the views of the Authority about whether a person is a commercial agent or not should have any implications for the legal relationship between the parties.

16. The Authority considers that a commercial agent is a self-employed intermediary between the principal and a purchaser or seller. The commercial agent concludes the sale or purchase of goods and services on behalf of the principal, on a continuing basis. The commercial agent is an auxiliary organ, forming an integral part of the principal's business, and is bound to carry out the instructions of the principal, and his position is similar to that of an employee. Being integrated into the principal's business, the commercial agent can undertake no autonomous commercial behaviour, under the agreement, and certain restrictions on him are fundamental to the relationship. The Authority considers that profits or losses essentially accrue to the principal and not to the commercial agent.

17. The relationship between Shell and its licensees has been summarised in para 14. Shell has argued that, in respect of the sale of motor fuels, the licensee is an auxiliary and that the agreement does not offend against section 4(1).

18. The licensee is a self-employed intermediary between Shell and the purchasers of Shell motor fuels. He concludes the sale of goods on behalf of Shell, on a continuing basis, for up

4. Decision No. 2 — AGF-Irish Life Holdings plc (14 May 1992).

to three years. He does not own the stocks, the resale prices are set by Shell, and the licensee lodges the proceeds of sale to the credit of Shell's bank account. While the licensee accepts some risk, in relation to stock losses, and is responsible for hiring and paying employees, the profits and losses of the motor fuels business as a whole accrue to Shell, and the licensee must obey Shell's instructions and may undertake no autonomous behaviour in respect of the operation of the petrol station. The Authority considers that the licensee, in operating the petrol station and selling Shell products, is an auxiliary organ, forming an integral part of Shell's distribution business, and it concludes that he can be considered to be a commercial agent. This conclusion is not affected by the fact that the licensee also operates the shop supplied by Shell on the same premises, since the operation of the petrol station constitutes a significant proportion of the whole business, and there is also a relationship between the licensee and Shell in relation to the shop. **1.6.4**

(2) In respect of the shop

19. The licensee sells products other than motor fuels and Shell products in the shop for his own account and separately from and independently of the sale of Shell petrol products. Although he pays a commission on sales to Shell, and is bound by certain obligations imposed by Shell regarding the operation of the shop, he is in no sense a commercial agent of Shell in respect of the shop on the petrol station premises. He is an independent trader in the shop.

(ii) *The commercial agency agreement*

20. The Authority considers that undertakings are entitled to decide how to operate their distribution systems, and, in particular, to appoint commercial agents to sell their goods on their behalf. Suppliers of motor fuels are free to choose to sell their products through independent dealers or through company-owned outlets; these latter may be operated by lessees, licensees, employees or by consignees and commercial agents. Since the commercial agent is an auxiliary organ, similar to an employee, the agreement between a principal and a commercial agent does not, in principle, offend against section 4(1) of the Competition Act.

21. In the present case, the Authority has concluded that the licensee is a commercial agent. It considers that the agreement between Shell and the licensee, insofar as it creates a relationship between the principal and a commercial agent, does not offend against section 4(1).

22. Even though the basic arrangement of commercial agency might not offend against section 4(1), certain clauses in the agreement might occasionally do so. In the case of motor fuels agreements, the Authority has published a category licence, which permits the imposition of certain obligations upon resellers of motor fuels and upon their suppliers. The Authority considers that the obligations which are not regarded as offending against section 4(1) in the case of independent traders would equally not offend in the case of commercial agents. More fundamentally, the Authority recognises that there are certain features of commercial agency agreements which define and confirm the relationship, and are intrinsic to the commercial agency. Since the commercial agent is closer to being an employee than an independent trader, the Authority considers that certain restrictions may be imposed upon a commercial agent without offending against section 4(1), whereas they would offend against section 4(1) if they were imposed on an independent trader. In the Authority's opinion, none of the provisions in the notified agreement relating to the sale of motor fuels offend against section 4(1).

(iii) *The shop agreement*

23. In the opinion of the Authority, all but one of the relevant provisions regarding the shop in the notified agreement did not have the object or effect of preventing, restricting or distorting competition. They reflect the fact that the shop is owned by Shell, and is licensed to the licensee for the purpose of enhancing earnings at the station, for the mutual benefit of the owner and the licensee, while ensuring that the reputation of the Shell brandname is not damaged. Since a fee which is related to the turnover of different classes of goods is payable by the licensee, it is essential for accurate and detailed records to be furnished to Shell, and for Shell to have

1.6.4 power to verify these. Such provisions do not interfere with the freedom of the licensee to operate the shop and they do not interfere with competition. In the view of the Authority, they do not offend against section 4(1) of the Act.

24. The Authority was concerned, however, with the clause whereby Shell reserved the right to oblige the licensee to withdraw from the site upon demand any shop products, services or other goods, services advertisements, displays or anything whatsoever which Shell considered to be inappropriate at a filling/service station (Clause 9.5). The Authority considered that this clause could be used to limit the freedom of the licensee to determine what products to sell and from whom he may obtain supplies. This could affect the ability of the licensee to compete with other retailers in the area. It could also limit competition between suppliers to obtain the custom of the licensee. The licensees would have no voice in deciding which suppliers they should deal with for their purchases. While the effect of this requirement might have little effect upon competition in the case of an individual licensee, the cumulative effect of this obligation in respect of all Shell's licensees, who are similarly bound, might not be insignificant. Since this practice might also be followed by other petrol companies in convenience shops attached to their company and dealer outlets, and since such convenience shops are growing rapidly in number and importance, the overall effect was thought likely to be considerable. The Authority considered that this clause offended against section 4(1) of the Act. (The Authority also considered that this clause would not satisfy, at least, the indispensability requirement of section 4(2) of the Act, and so would not qualify for the grant of a licence).

25. At the suggestion of the Authority however, as stated in para 11, Shell have agreed to provide that the obligation upon the licensee to withdraw from the site any shop products, etc. which Shell considered inappropriate 'would only be invoked for objectively valid reasons which shall be disclosed to the licensee'. The Authority considers that this would adequately safeguard the concerns of Shell with regard to safety considerations and unsuitable products, but in a less restrictive way. The Authority considers that the part of the agreement relating to the shop no longer offends against section 4(1).

The Decision

26. In the Authority's opinion, Shell and its licensees are undertakings within the meaning of section 3(1) of the Competition Act, and the notified standard licensee agreement for the operation of a Shell-owned petrol station and associated shop constitutes an agreement between undertakings. In the Authority's opinion, the licensee is a commercial agent of Shell in the petrol station, and an independent operator in the shop, and the arrangements, as amended, do not have, as their object or effect, the prevention, restriction or distortion of competition. The standard Shell licensee agreement, as amended by the letter of 1 March 1994, does not, in the Authority's opinion, offend against section 4(1) of the Competition Act 1991.

The Certificate

The Competition Authority has issued the following certificate:

> The Competition Authority certifies that in its opinion, on the basis of the facts in its possession, the standard agreement between Irish Shell Ltd and its licensees for the operation of a Shell-owned petrol station and shop (notification no. CA/263/92E), notified on 30 September 1992 under section 7, and amended by Shell in its letter dated 1 March 1994, does not offend against section 4(1) of the Competition Act 1991.

For the Competition Authority

Patrick M Lyons
Chairman.

19 May 1994

Competition Authority Decision No. 328, Esso Contractor Agreement: 19 May 1994, Notification No. CA/101/92E **1.6.5**

Commercial agency agreement – Agents remunerated on commission basis – Financial risk of venture residing with the principal – Whether agent forms an integral part of principal's business – Whether agent an undertaking within the meaning of the Competition Act 1991 – Competition Act 1991 (No. 24) sections 3, 4 and 7

Facts: On 22 September 1991 notification was made by Artane Service Station Ltd ('Artane') with a request for a certificate under section 4(4) of the Competition Act 1991, or failing that, a license under section 4(2) in respect of its standard contractor agreement. Artane, a wholly owned subsidiary of Esso Ireland Ltd, is engaged in the marketing of motor fuels through service stations owned by Esso Ireland. The notified contractor agreement provides for the engaging of a contractor to operate the Esso owned service stations on behalf of Artane and provides, for the exclusive sale of Esso petroleum products and other non motor fuel products through a shop situated at the service station.

The product market with which the notified agreement is concerned is (a) that for motor fuels for use in road vehicles and (b) the retail market selling goods similar to those sold in the shop.

The notified agreement places certain responsibilities on the contractor including, *inter alia,* that he may not carry out on the premises any business other than that as contractor for Artane, that he shall lodge to Artane's bank account all gross receipts received at the service station less any payments authorised under the terms of the agreement, that he shall keep proper books of account relating to the station and furnish to Artane details of the monthly operating costs, that he shall sell the motor fuels and other products at prices notified by Artane from time to time and where sales prices are not so notified by Artane, that he shall sell the products at the suppliers recommended retail prices. Artane undertake to pay the contractor a commission on sales at the end of each calendar month and is responsible for the insurance of buildings, equipment, public liability and engineering. Clause 10 of the agreement provides that a contractor shall not either during the term of the agreement or for a period of six months after its termination be associated whether as principal, agent or employee in the business of retail sales of petroleum products within a radius of three miles of the said service station without the prior consent of Artane.

In response to a letter from the Authority dated 23 November 1992 Esso submitted on 25 August 1993 that the contractor is a commercial agent and not an employee and that he is able to increase his earnings if he keeps his operating costs below the standard operating costs agreed with Artane and at the same time increases his sales, thereby increasing his commission. In response to a further letter from the Authority Esso confirmed that all goods, including those in shop, were purchased and sold for the account of Artane and not for the account of the contractor.

In response to a further letter from the Authority concerning the post-termination non-compete clause 10 of the agreement Esso submitted that such clause is necessary to give any new contractor an opportunity to establish a reputation with the customers and such clause is necessary as Artane risk the loss of its considerable investment in the business if the contractor were to set up a similar business immediately upon termination of the agreement within the same locality. Esso submitted that the

1.6.5 situation was similar to protection which might be reasonably required by the purchaser of a business.

The Authority published notice of its intention to make a favourable decision in relation to the notification to the Irish Times on 15 April 1994.

Decided by the Authority: In issuing a certificate under section 4(4) of the Competition Act 1991 in respect of the notified agreement that:

(1) Artane and the contractors are engaged in the sale of motor fuels for gain and they are also engaged in the sale of other products for gain and are therefore undertakings within the meaning of section 3(1) of the Competition Act. The notified agreement is an agreement between undertakings and the relevant product markets are those for (a) motor fuels and (b) products sold in the shop on the petrol station premises. The relevant geographic market is the State.

(2) The question of agency is quite complex and each case must be examined on its own merits in relation to the Competition Act in the light of certain general considerations. A commercial agent is a self-employed intermediary between the principal and a purchaser or seller and concludes the sale or purchase of goods or services on behalf of the principal on a continuing basis. The commercial agent is an auxiliary organ forming an integral part of the principal's business and is bound to carry out the instructions of the principal and his position is similar to that of an employee, being integrated into the principal's business the commercial agent can undertake no autonomous commercial behaviour and profit and losses of the business eventually accrue to the principal and not the commercial agent.

(3) A contractor, in operating the petrol station and the shop is acting as a commercial agent for Artane in that he is a self-employed intermediary between Artane and the purchasers of Esso motor fuels and the shop products, he concludes the sale of goods on behalf of Artane on a continuing basis and for an indefinite period, he lodges the proceeds of such sales to the credit of Artane's bank account and he must obey Artane's instruction and may undertake no autonomous behaviour in respect of the operation of petrol station and shop. While the contractor accepts some risks in relation to stock and cash losses and is responsible for hiring and paying of employees the profits and losses of the business as a whole accrue to Artane therefore making the contractor an auxiliary organ forming an integral part of Artane's distribution business.

(4) Undertakings are entitled to decide how to operate their distribution systems and, in particular, to appoint commercial agents. Since a commercial agent is an auxiliary organ similar to an employee of the principal an agreement between the principal and the commercial agent does not in principle offend against section 4(1) of the Competition Act. The notified agreement insofar as it creates the relationship between a principal and a commercial agent does not offend against section 4(1).

(5) There are certain features of commercial agency agreements which define and confirm the relationship and are intrinsic to commercial agency. A commercial agent is closer to being an employee than to being an independent trader and certain restrictions may be imposed upon a commercial agent without offending against section 4(1) which would if they were imposed upon an independent trader offend against such section.

(6) The non-compete provision on termination of the agreement contained in clause 10 does not in all the circumstances offend against section 4(1) as the clause

is limited to sale of motor fuels and does not include the shop products, is confined to a three mile radius from the relevant station and is for a period of six months after termination. The agreement provides for the payment of compensation to the contractor if the agreement is terminated by Artane for reasons other than those stated in the agreement. Only a small number of persons are affected by these non-compete clauses and a former contractor can enter into competition with Esso immediately after termination of the agreement outside the three miles radius and after six months within the radius. **1.6.5**

Cases, Decisions and Notices referred to:
ECJ judgment — *Suiker Unie v. Commission* [1975] ECR 1663, [1976] 1 CMLR 295
EC Commission Notice on exclusive dealing contracts with commercial agents [OJ 139/62 24.12.1962, p. 2921]
EU Council Directive on the coordination of the laws of member states relating to self employed commercial agents 86/653 OJ [1986] L 382/17. **Editor's Note:** Ireland implemented this directive by the European Communities (Commercial Agents) Regulations 1994 [SI 33 of 1994]
Restrictive Practices (motor spirit and motor vehicle lubricating oil) Order, 1981 [SI No. 70 of 1981]
Competition Authority Decision No. 25, Motor Fuels category licence, 1 July 1993 **4.2**
Competition Authority Decision No. 144 — licence for categories of exclusive distribution agreements, 5 November 1993 **5.1**
Competition Authority Notice on employee contracts and the Competition Act, *Iris Oifigiúil*, 18 September 1991, pp. 632/3 **1.4.1**
Competition Authority Decision No. 10 — GI Corporation/General Semi-conductor Industries Inc, 23 October 1993 **3.8**

Competition Authority Decision of 19 May 1994 relating to a proceeding under section 4 of the Competition Act 1991
Notification No. CA/101/92E — Esso Contractor Agreement

Introduction

1. Notification was made to the Competition Authority with a request for a licence by Artane Service Station Ltd on 22 September 1992 in respect of its standard agreement with contractors. On 23 February 1994, the notification was amended for the purposes of obtaining a certificate or, in the event of a refusal by the Authority to issue a certificate, a licence.

2. The Authority published notice of its intention to take a favourable decision in relation to the agreement in The Irish Times on 15 April 1994. No submissions were received from interested parties.

The Facts

(a) *The subject of the notification*

3. The decision concerns the standard contractor agreement between Artane Service Station and the contractors at a number of Esso-owned petrol stations. The contractor agreement provides for engaging the services of an independent contractor to carry on the operation of a service station on behalf of Artane, which leases the service station from Esso Ireland Ltd. It provides for the exclusive sale by the contractor of petroleum products and other goods which are the property of the company, and the contractor is remunerated on a commission basis related to the sales and profitability of the station. The other goods are sold in a convenience grocery shop which is situated on the petrol station premises.

(b) *The parties involved*

4. Artane Service Station Ltd is a wholly owned subsidiary of Esso Ireland Ltd, and is primarily involved in the marketing of motor fuels through the Esso chain of company owned service stations. Esso Ireland Ltd is one of the major suppliers of motor fuels in the State. It is

1.6.5 a wholly owned subsidiary of the Exxon Corporation of the USA. Esso is primarily involved in the marketing of petroleum products to the motoring public through a chain of retail outlets, most of which are owned by independent dealers, the remainder being owned by Esso. Artane occupies 41 Esso company stations under a tenancy agreement with Esso, these being the stations with a substantial volume potential. Each station is managed by an independent person referred to as a 'contractor' who is engaged by Artane, and who sells motor fuels for Artane's account.

(c) *The products and the market*

5. The product with which the main part of the notified agreement is concerned consists of motor fuels, that is petrol and diesel for use in mechanically propelled road vehicles. The market was described in detail in the motor fuels category licence.[1]

6. The convenience shop primarily sells grocery goods, confectionery, newspapers, cigarettes, etc. The market consists of all retail outlets selling goods of a similar character.

(d) *The notified agreement*

7. The introduction to the agreement between Artane and the contractor states that Artane is the legal occupier of the specified service station and is desirous of engaging the services of an independent contractor to carry on the operation of the business on its behalf, but so that the contractor shall in no way be regarded as an employee of Artane. The appointment is evergreen, but may be terminated subject to certain conditions.

Clause 1 states that the contractor is to be remunerated on a commission basis, and it provides that:

> The Contractor must at all times ensure the proper operation of the business at the Service Station and in this regard his duties may be delegated by him to other persons and for such time as Artane shall first approve. The Contractor may not carry on any business on or from the premises other than as Contractor for Artane in accordance with this Agreement.

Clause 2 obliges the contractor to maintain a bank account in his name through which he will transact all business expenditures. The contractor must allow Artane to inspect his books and records.

8. Clause 3 provides for accounts between Artane and the contractor, as follows:

A. The Contractor shall lodge to the credit of Artanes' Bank Account the gross receipts received at the Service Station less cash payments authorised by Artane in accordance with the terms of this Agreement. . . .

B. The Contractor shall be responsible for all expenses incurred in the operation of the Service Station except payments in respect of rates and such other items as are the liability of Artane as the legal occupier of the site.

Artane may at any time measure and check the stocks of all products kept at the Service Station. In the absence of any negligent act or omission of the Contractor or his staff, Artane will bear the cost of any motor fuels, monies, property and equipment belonging to Artane which are lost. . . .

C. The Contractor shall during the currency of this Agreement furnish an invoice to Artane in respect of his monthly operating costs hereunder. . . .

D. The Contractor shall keep proper books of account relating to the operation of the Service Station.

E. Artane will calculate the Contractor's commission in the terms of this Agreement as soon as possible following the calendar month end and will submit to the Contractor a statement of account. . . .

1. Motor Fuels Category Licence, Decision No. 25, 1 July 1993, paras. 7 to 9.

9. Clause 5 requires the contractor to pay the insurance costs discharged by Artane on his behalf. Clause 6 provides for the operation of the service station, as follows: **1.6.5**

> The Contractor shall employ persons of such a quality as to ensure a service of the highest standard. Such persons being employees of the Contractor, are subject to the Contractors control and direction and the Contractors shall be fully responsible for their acts or omissions and for any losses or damages resulting therefrom.

10. Under Clause 7A Artane and the Contractor may terminate the agreement at any time upon giving the specified period of notice. The rest of Clause 7 provides for the termination of the agreement without notice by Artane in the event of certain occurrences and provides for the contractor to leave the service station. It also provides for the payment of compensation if Artane terminates the agreement for reasons other than those stated, and for arbitration in case of dispute. These provisions are largely based upon the 1981 Restrictive Practices Order for motor spirits,[2] which was repealed on 30 September 1991.

11. Clause 8 provides for extended sick leave of the contractor, and Clause 10 states that:

> The Contractor shall not during the period of this Agreement or during the period of six months after the termination hereof for any reason whatsoever be associated whether as principal or agent or employee in the business of retail sales of petroleum products within a radius of three miles of the Service Station without the prior written consent of Artane.

Under Clause 11:

> This Agreement may not be assigned or transferred by the Contractor without the prior consent in writing of Artane. In the event of Artane not consenting to assignment or transfer of this Agreement no reason shall be furnished by Artane.

12. The First Schedule refers to products for resale, as follows:

> (i) Deliveries of motor fuels, and other products as shall be made by Esso Ireland Ltd ('Esso') and other named suppliers to the Service Station during normal hours of operation and in such quantities as to ensure that adequate supplies of product are available to meet the normal requirements of the Service Station.
> (ii) The Contractor shall sell those grades of motor fuels, and other products specified at prices notified by Artane to the Contractor from time to time. Where selling prices are not notified by Artane to the agent the Contractor shall sell products only at the suppliers recommended retail prices.
> (iii) No other product (petroleum or otherwise) or services whatsoever other than those supplied or approved by Artane shall be stored handled sold or distributed on or from the Service Station without the previous written consent of Artane.

The named supplier in (i) is a supplier named and authorised by Artane for the supply of goods to the service station.

13. The Second Schedule provides for insurance. Artane is responsible for the insurance of buildings, plant and equipment, public liability, and engineering. The contractor is liable for employer's liability, personal accident for the contractor, and for other persons undertaking duties connected with the business.

14. The Fourth Schedule specifies the rates of commission to be paid to the contractor in respect of the sales of motor fuels and other products and the turnover from the car wash with an allowance based on the image and appearance of the service station.

2. Restrictive Practices (Motor Spirit and Motor Vehicle Lubricating Oil) Order, 1981.

1.6.5 (e) *Submissions by Artane*

15. Artane made a number of submissions in respect of its request for a licence to be granted for the contractor agreements, but these are not considered here.

16. In response to a letter from the Authority on 23 November 1992, Esso made the following submission on 25 August 1993:

> It is submitted that notwithstanding that section 4(1) of the Competition Act is based upon Article 85(1) of the Treaty, Irish Competition Law stands alone and independent from E.C. Regulations and Decisions. The agreement, the subject of the notification, does not affect trade between Member States.
> The Authority did not regard, in our clients' view correctly, our clients exclusive purchasing agreements as a category of agreements exempted by E.C. Regulation 1984/83 being the Block Exemption relating to such agreements.
> Our clients submit that these agreements must be considered in the construction of the Competition Act and while E.C. Regulations and Decisions may give guidance, they need not necessarily be followed where trade between Member States is not involved.
> Our clients contend that the definition of 'undertaking' in the Act does not by itself exclude a commercial agent and the test is whether both parties to the agreement are engaged for gain in the production, supply or distribution of goods.
> The agreements are between Artane Service Station Ltd and the Contractor.
> We presume it is accepted that our clients are so engaged.
> Our clients contend that the Contractor who is a commercial agent and not an employee, is also so engaged.
> Notwithstanding that the Contractor does not keep a stock of his own and may deal in products supplied or approved by Artane only and he must sell the goods at prices specified by Artane, he is engaged in the business of operating and managing the business for his own benefit. He is responsible for operating expenses incurred in excess of such expenses approved by Artane and by promoting and fostering the business at the Service Station he is able to increase the commission earned. He is also able to increase his earnings by savings in the standard operating costs agreed with Artane. He is also able to conserve his commission by not allowing the operating costs exceed the amount allowed by Artane for such costs.
> The Contractor is in control of the business of operating the Service Station by selling the goods of Artane to his best possible advantage by increasing sales and reducing operating expenses thereby increasing his earnings by increased commission on sales and by a surplus on the standard operating expenses allowed by Artane.
> The Contractor accordingly benefits directly from any increase in the business and savings in the operating costs and is pursuing his own economic interests.
> It is submitted that on these facts the Contractor is engaged for gain in the distribution of goods though such goods may not be his own property.

17. In response to a further letter from the Authority on 8 September, Esso stated, in a letter of 25 November, that they confirmed that all goods for resale at the service station, including the convenience shop, were purchased and sold for the account of Artane, and not for the account of the contractor. In the absence of a specific instruction from Artane, goods were to be sold at the supplier's recommended retail price so that, in the absence of a specific instruction, the contractor was aware of the approved resale price. They emphasised that this provision was seldom used and the notified resale prices were determined in accordance with competition in the locality of each service station.

18. In response to another letter from the Authority on 11 February 1994, concerning the post-termination non-compete provision in clause 10 of the agreement, Esso suggested that the contractors were commercial agents, and not exclusive distributors or employees. They also

stated as follows: **1.6.5**

> In the case of the notified agreement the Contractor does not place his capital at risk as Artane provides the service station, the retail shop and also the motor fuels and shop products for resale. Artane accordingly risks a loss of its considerable investment in the business in the event that the Contractor sets up a similar business immediately upon termination of the Agreement and within the same locality. The Contractor by reason of being entrusted with the operation and management of the business for his own benefit creates, particularly if he is successful, a personal reputation with the customers. The post-termination non-compete clause which is for a period of 6 months and within a radius of three miles of the service station is not unduly restrictive on the Contractor and it gives Artane the opportunity of enabling the new Contractor to establish a reputation with the customers.

Esso submitted that the situation was similar to the protection which might be reasonably required by a purchaser of a business, and that this clause did not offend against section 4(1).

(f)*EC Commission views on commercial agency*

19. The EC Commission first gave its views on exclusive dealing contracts with commercial agents in a Notice published in 1962.[3] In this it stated that it considered that contracts made with commercial agents, who acted on behalf of an enterprise, did not fall under the prohibition in Article 85(1) of the EC Treaty. It was essential that the commercial agent should not engage in activities proper to an independent trader. The decisive criterion, according to the Commission, was that the commercial agent should not assume any risk resulting from the transaction.

20. It has long been recognised, by the Commission and others, however, that the 1962 Notice is limited in scope, and that it no longer reflects economic reality and is also legally obsolete. It also needed revision in the light of the 1986 harmonisation Directive relating to self-employed commercial agents.[4] The Commission has been preparing, therefore, a revised Notice on commercial agents, which has not yet been finalised.

21. The EC Court of Justice considered the question of agency in the Suiker Unie case, where it stated:

> If such an agent works for his principal he can in principle be regarded as an auxiliary organ forming an integral part of the latter's undertaking bound to carry out the principal's instructions and thus, like a commercial employee, forms an economic unit with this undertaking.[5]

Assessment

Applicability of section 4(1)

22. Section 4(1) of the Competition Act 1991 prohibits and renders void all agreements between undertakings which have as their object or effect the prevention, restriction or distortion of competition in trade in any goods or services in the State or in any part of the State.

23. Artane and the contractors are engaged in the sale of motor fuels for gain, and they are also engaged in the sale of other products for gain, and they are therefore undertakings within the meaning of section 3(1) of the Competition Act. The standard contractor agreement is an

3. EC Commission Notice on exclusive dealing contracts with commercial agents OJ 139, 24.12.1962, p. 2921.
4. EC Directive of 18 December 1986 relating to the coordination of the laws of the Member States relating to self-employed commercial agents, OJ L382, 31.12.86, p. 17.
5. Judgment of the Court of Justice of 16 December 1975 — *Suiker Unie and Others v. Commission of the European Communities* [1975] ECR 1663, at p. 2007.

1.6.5 agreement between undertakings. The relevant product markets are those for (a) motor fuels, and (b) the products sold in the shop on the petrol station premises. The relevant geographic market is the State.

(i) The status of the contractor

24. In operating the petrol station premises and selling motor fuels, the contractor is not an employee of Artane and there is no contract of employment or service between them. He is a self-employed contractor. At the same time, while the contractor is stated to be an independent contractor, he does not purchase motor fuels from Artane for resale to the public. Unlike the Esso licensee or independent dealer, the contractor sells motor fuel, not on his own account, but on behalf of Artane. He does not pay for the motor fuels, and the motor fuels remain the property of Artane until they are sold at retail, even though they are held at the contractor's risk. All gross receipts from the sale of motor fuels, less authorised cash payments, must be lodged to Artane's bank account. Out of his commission, the contractor must pay for certain outgoings, such as labour, insurance and other costs, the balance representing the contractor's remuneration. The contractor is responsible for employing staff. Artane determines the prices at which the motor fuels are to be sold. The petrol station is effectively under the operational control and direction of Artane, and is operated for Artane's own account, and the contractor is obliged to obey Artane's instructions. The relationship between Artane and the contractor is an ongoing one, and the agreement may have an indefinite duration.

25. The position is the same in respect of the operation of the convenience shop. The other goods are purchased and resold for Artane's account, at prices determined by Artane. Gross receipts, less authorised cash payments, are paid into Artane's bank account. While the contractor is responsible for employing and paying staff, the shop is under the operational control and direction of Artane. The relationship is ongoing, and lasts as long as the contractor operates the petrol station.

26. The Authority considers that the question of agency is quite complex, and that each case must be examined on its own merits in relation to the Competition Act, in the light of certain general considerations. In the first place, it is not conclusive that one party is referred to as an 'agent' in the agreement, since he may not perform the functions of an agent in any real sense. Conversely, it does not matter if the agreement states that there is no relationship or contract of agency between the parties. This may be done, for example, to ensure that one party is not empowered to undertake binding obligations on behalf of the other, without the latter's knowledge or consent. From the point of view of the Competition Act, the Authority is concerned with whether the relationship between the two parties is such that one of them may be termed a 'commercial agent' of the other. It is not intended that the views of the Authority about whether a person is a commercial agent or not should have any implications for the legal relationship between the parties.

27. The Authority considers that a commercial agent is a self-employed intermediary between the principal and a purchaser or seller. The commercial agent concludes the sale or purchase of goods and services on behalf of the principal, on a continuing basis. The commercial agent is an auxiliary organ, forming an integral part of the principal's business, and is bound to carry out the instructions of the principal, and his position is in this respect similar to that of an employee. Being integrated into the principal's business, the commercial agent can undertake no autonomous commercial behaviour, under the agreement, and certain restrictions on him are fundamental to the relationship. The Authority considers that profits or losses essentially accrue to the principal and not to the commercial agent.

28. The relationship between Artane and its contractors has been summarised in paras. 24 and 25. The agreement also states that there is no contract of employment between the parties. Artane has argued that the contractor is a commercial agent.

29. The contractor is a self-employed intermediary between Artane and the purchasers of Esso motor fuels and the convenience shop products. He concludes the sale of goods on behalf

of Artane, on a continuing basis, for an indefinite period which can be lengthy. He does not own the stocks, the resale prices are set by Artane, and the contractor lodges the proceeds of sale, less authorised cash payments, to the credit of Artane's bank account. While the contractor accepts some risk, in relation to stock and cash losses, and is responsible for hiring and paying employees, the profits and losses of the business as a whole accrue to Artane, and the contractor must obey Artane's instructions and may undertake no autonomous behaviour in respect of the operation of the petrol station and of the convenience shop. The Authority considers that the contractor, in operating both the petrol station and the convenience shop, is an auxiliary organ, forming an integral part of Artane's distribution business, and it concludes that he can be considered to be a commercial agent of Artane. **1.6.5**

(ii) The contractor agreement

30. The Authority considers that undertakings are entitled to decide how to operate their distribution systems, and, in particular, to appoint commercial agents to sell their goods on their behalf. Suppliers of motor fuels are free to choose to sell their products through independent dealers or through company-owned outlets; these latter may be operated by lessees, licensees, employees or by consignees and commercial agents. Since the commercial agent is an auxiliary organ, similar to an employee, the agreement between a principal and a commercial agent does not, in principle, offend against section 4(1) of the Competition Act.

31. In the present case, the Authority has concluded that the contractor is a commercial agent. It considers that the agreement between Artane and the contractors, insofar as it creates a relationship between the principal and a commercial agent, does not offend against section 4(1).

32. Even though the basic arrangement of commercial agency might not offend against section 4(1), certain clauses in the agreement might occasionally do so. In the case of motor fuels agreements, the Authority has published a category licence, which permits the imposition of certain obligations upon resellers of motor fuels and upon their suppliers. The Authority considers that the obligations which are not regarded as offending against section 4(1) in the case of independent traders would equally not offend in the case of commercial agents. More fundamentally, the Authority recognises that there are certain features of commercial agency agreements which define and confirm the relationship, and are intrinsic to the commercial agency. Since the commercial agent is closer to being an employee than to being an independent trader, the Authority considers that certain restrictions may be imposed upon a commercial agent without offending against section 4(1), whereas they would offend against section 4(1) if they were imposed on an independent trader. In the Authority's opinion, none of the provisions in the notified agreement, whether relating to the petrol station or to the convenience shop, offend against section 4(1).

33. The Authority, however, had some initial concerns in respect of the provision preventing the contractor from being engaged in the sale of petroleum products (but not other products), for a period of six months after the agreement terminates, within a radius of three miles of the petrol station. The Authority has tended to oppose the imposition of post-termination non-compete clauses in exclusive dealing agreements. They are not permitted under Article 5(f) of the motor fuels category licence, nor under Article 3(i) of the exclusive distribution category licence.[6] The Authority has indicated that such clauses in employment contracts would offend against section 4(1) where the former employee attempted to set up in business in competition with the former employer.[7] In the case of a sale of business, however, the Authority has accepted that a post-termination non-competition clause is essential to ensure the transfer of the goodwill. Provided that it is limited in terms of duration, geographic coverage and subject matter to what is necessary to ensure the transfer of the goodwill, such a clause would not offend against

6. Licence for categories of exclusive distribution agreements, Decision No. 144, 5 November 1993.
7. Notice on Employee Contracts and the Competition Act, *Iris Oifigiúil*, 18 September 1992, pp 632-3.

1.6.5 section 4(1). In General Semiconductor, the Authority considered that a restriction of two years would generally be regarded as being sufficient for the complete transfer of the goodwill of a business.[8]

34. The notified agreement is not an exclusive dealing agreement under the terms of the two category licences mentioned above, nor is it an employment contract. It is clearly not an agreement for the sale of business. At the same time, the Authority recognises that Esso is the owner of the petrol station, and it has invested a very large amount of money in the station. It also has a special relationship of commercial agency with the contractor. While the location of a petrol station is extremely important in securing sales of petrol, the operator can also have an influence in attracting customers. If the Esso contractor were permitted to be involved in the petrol business after his contract terminated in a station close to the one which he operated, he could initially attract a significant amount of custom away from the former station, thus having a significant adverse effect on the Esso investment. The Authority is aware that the EU Directive on commercial agents provides that, where a commercial agent is entitled to an indemnity after termination of the agency contract, there may be a 'restraint of trade clause'. Such a clause is valid so long as it relates to the geographical area or the group of customers and the geographical area entrusted to the agent and to the kind of goods covered by his agency, and provided it extends for not more than two years after termination of the contract.

35. In the Esso contractor agreement, the non-compete clause is limited to motor fuels (and does not cover shop products), it is confined to an area within a three-mile radius of the Esso station, and it is for a period of six months after termination. The agreement provides for the payment of compensation to the contractor if the agreement is terminated by Artane for reasons other than those stated in the agreement. Only a relatively small number of persons are affected by this non-compete clause. The former contractor can enter into competition with Esso for the sale of motor fuels immediately after termination of the agreement outside the three mile radius from the original station, and after six months within this area. In all the circumstances, the Authority concludes that this clause does not offend against section 4(1) of the Act.

The Decision

36. In the Authority's opinion, Artane and its contractors are undertakings within the meaning of section 3(1) of the Competition Act, and the notified standard contractor agreement for the operation of an Esso-owned petrol station and convenience shop constitutes an agreement between undertakings. In the Authority's opinion, the contractor is a commercial agent of Artane in both the service station and the convenience shop, and the arrangements do not have, as their object or effect, the prevention, restriction or distortion of competition. The standard Artane contractor agreement does not, in the Authority's opinion, offend against section 4(1) of the Competition Act 1991.

The Certificate

The Competition Authority has issued the following certificate:

The Competition Authority certifies that in its opinion, on the basis of the facts in its possession, the standard agreement between Artane and its contractors for the operation of an Artane-owned petrol station and convenience shop (Notification No. CA/101/92E), notified on 22 September 1992 under section 7, does not offend against section 4(1) of the Competition Act 1991.

For the Competition Authority
Patrick M. Lyons
Chairman
19 May 1994

8. Competition Authority Decision No. 10, GI Corporation/General Semiconductor Industries Inc, 23 October 1992.

1.7 Associations

Dermot Donovan, Liam Killeen, John Cortin, John O'Loughlin, John Cahill, Thomas Lenihan and **M.J. Marshall (Killarney) Ltd, Plaintiffs v. The Electricity Supply Board, Defendant:** [1992 No. 6452P], High Court, 5 May 1994; Supreme Court, 12 May 1994 (Costello J)* **1.7.1**

Competition – Dominant position – Monopoly supplier of electricity – Change in conditions of supply – Establishment of register of electrical contractors – Register ostensibly established to promote electrical safety – Electrical supply to be connected only on production of certificate of registered contractor or of inspector employed by body in charge of register – Trade rivals of plaintiffs having significant role in control of register – Publicity campaign against use of unregistered contractors – Whether producing anti-competitive effects – Whether criteria for enrolment too imprecise – Whether criteria for enrolment unnecessary for purposes of electrical supply – Whether absence of obligation to give reasons for refusal and absence of appeals procedure permitting arbitrary decisions – Whether abuse of dominant position – Competition Act 1991 (No. 24), section, 5

Competition – Dominant position – Abuse – Imposition of unfair trading conditions – Whether participation in anti-competitive agreement, decision or practice capable of constituting abuse of dominant position – Competition Act 1991 (No. 28), sections 4 and 5

Competition – Dominant position – Relevant market – Whether undertaking having monopoly in Ireland market capable of having dominant position in relevant market – Competition Act 1991 (No. 24), section 5

Competition – Statutory prohibition on anti-competitive agreements, decisions or practices – Competition Authority empowered to certify its opinion that matters notified to it not anti-competitive – Authority empowered to licence certain agreements, decisions or practices notwithstanding anti-competitive nature – Defendant

***Editor's Note:** This report has been reproduced with the kind permission of the Incorporated Council of Law Reporting for Ireland and was first published in [1994] 2 IR at 305 and 330.

By a notice published in the *Irish Times* on 9 December 1994 the Competition Authority stated: 'On the basis of its initial assessment, the Authority intends to issue a certificate in relation to section 4 of the Competition Act 1991 in respect of the following notification:

(a) . . . .
(b) . . . .
(c) . . . .
(d) CA/836/92E — ESB/RECI (amended)

Before doing so, the Authority invites interested third parties to send their observations within three weeks from the date of publication of this notice'.

1.7.1 *applying for certificate or licence if certificate refused – Whether matters notified appropriate for certification – Whether application should be treated as one for licence only – Whether notifying party entitled to amend matters notified pending determination of application for certificate – Whether abuse of dominant position not to await decision on application – Competition Act 1991 (No. 24), section 4 and 7*

Competition – Abuse of dominant position – Abuse unintentional – Whether damages recoverable for unintentional abuse — Competition Act 1991 (No. 24), sections 5 and 6

Facts Section 4(1) of the Competition Act 1991 provides *inter alia*:

> Subject to the provisions of this section, all agreements between undertakings, decisions by associations of undertakings and concerted practices which have as their object or effect the prevention, restriction or distortion of competition in trade in any goods or services in the State or in any part of the State are prohibited and void. . . .

Section 10(1) of the Act of 1991 establishes a body known as the Competition Authority. By virtue of section 4(2) and (3) of the Act of 1991, the Compeititon Authority may issue a licence which permits the doing of acts which would otherwise be prohibited and void under subsection 1, in respect of any agreement, decision or concerted practice of which it has been notified and meets certain criteria.

By section 4(4) of the Act of 1991, the Competition Authority may certify its opinion that an agreement, decision or concerted practice of which it has been notified does not offend against subsection 1.

Section 5 of the Act of 1991 provides that:

> Any abuse by one or more undertakings of a dominant position in trade for any goods or services in the State or in a substantial part of the State is prohibited.

Section 5(2)(a) provides that such abuse may consist of, *inter alia*, 'directly or indirectly imposing . . . unfair trading conditions.

There is no provision for the grant of a licence or certificate in respect of the matters prohibited by section 5.

Section 6(1) of the Act of 1991 confers a right of action on 'any person who is aggrieved in consequence' of any matters prohibited by sections 4 or 5, against any undertaking a party thereto, or guilty of an abuse of a dominant position. By section 6(3) a plaintiff in an action under section 6 may be granted injunctive relief, declaratory relief and damages, or any of those reliefs. However, by virtue of section 6(7), there is no right of action in respect of an agreement, decision or concerted practice to which section 7(2) applies (namely one in existence on 1 October 1991, and notified within one year thereof) until the Competition Authority has decided on an application and any appeal has been concluded.

The plaintiffs were electrical contractors. The defendant was a statutory body enjoying a monopoly in the generation, transmission and supply of electricity. Prior to 31 August 1992, the defendant's general conditions of supply would only permit a connection to the national grid if the electricial contractor who had carried out electrical installation work certified that the installation had been carried out in accordance with certain standards laid down by a body known as the Electro-Technical Council of Ireland (ETCI). Upon presentation of such a certificate, supply would be effected subject to the defendant's right to inspect the work to ensure that its network would not be adversely affected by connection. 1.7.1

From 1 September 1992, changes in the defendant's general conditions of supply came into effect. For some years the government had pressed for the introduction of a self-regulatory scheme in relation to standards for electrical work. In June 1991, a limited company known as 'Register of Electrical Contractors of Ireland Ltd' (RECI Ltd) had been established. The objects of that company included the promotion of safety standards and fair trading within the electrical contracting business and the maintenance of appropriate levels of business and technical competence and ethical behaviour. The members of the company were two associations of electrical contractors (to neither of which the plaintiffs belonged), the ETCI and the defendant, each of which could nominate two directors. The company established a register of electrical contractors and appointed inspectors to carry out spot-checks on the work of registered contractors and to inspect the work of unregistered contractors and, if appropriate, certify compliance with the ETCI standards. From 1 September 1992, the defendant would only permit connection on production of a certificate of compliance with ETCI standards from a registered contractor, or, in the case of an unregistered contractor, a certificate from an inspector employed by RECI Ltd.

Applicants seeking enrolment on the register had to sign a declaration agreeing to abide by the rules established by RECI Ltd, and offer proof of technical skills and experience, possession of suitable premises, specified levels of insurance and compliance with wages and pensions criteria. An applicant for registration could be refused without reasons being given, and no appeal lay against refusal. Reduced entry fees and annual fees were available to members of one of the founder members of the company. Standard fees for registered contractors were a £75 entry fee and an annual fee of £125, whereas unregistered contractors had to pay a fee of £85 per inspection.

Prior to the institution of proceedings the defendant had served a notification of matters relating to the establishment of RECI Ltd on the Competition Authority, seeking a certificate pursuant to section 4(4) or, in the event of refusal, a licence pursuant to section 4(2). The plaintiffs instituted proceedings seeking damages and injunctive relief pursuant to section 6, for a breach of sections 4 and 5, and obtained an interlocutory injunction on 2 November 1992, restraining the implementation of the new conditions of supply.

The plaintiffs contended that the defendant enjoyed a dominant position in the market for the supply of electrical contracting services in that it would determine the conditions under which a supply of electricity would be given to the customers of electrical contractors. While it was not disputed that the right of action for a breach of section 4 itself had been suspended pending the determination of the application for a certificate or licence, it was contended that the defendant had abused its dominant position by imposing 'unfair trading conditions' contrary to section 5(2) of the Act of 1991, in that it had entered into agreements amounting to a breach of the prohibition contained in section 4. In this regard the plaintiffs contended that the objects of RECI Ltd went beyond what was necessary for the promotion of electrical safety; that since control of the register lay with RECI Ltd, trade rivals of the plaintiffs could exercise considerable influence on membership of the register; that preferential treatment was

1.7.1 given to trade rivals of the plaintiffs; that unregistered contractors had difficulty competing with registered contractors due to the extra cost of obtaining the inspector's certificate for each installation; and that unregistered contractors had also suffered a competitive disadvantage due to a publicity campaign against the use of unregistered contractors.

With regard to the defendant's notification to the Competition Authority, the plaintiffs contended that although the application had in form been for a certificate or, in the event of refusal, a licence, the court should regard the application as one for a licence only, in that the only way in which the defendant could lawfully have imposed the new conditions of supply was if a licence had been granted in respect of the agreements leading to the establishment of RECI Ltd; that accordingly it was an abuse of a dominant position to introduce the new conditions of supply until the licensing procedures had been concluded; and that the plaintiffs were accordingly entitled to injunctive relief, notwithstanding the provision of section 6(7).

Subsequent to the issue of proceedings, amendments were made to the memorandum and articles of RECI Ltd. The reference to the maintenance of proper levels of technical and business competency and ethical behaviour were removed; all registered contractors became members of RECI Ltd, with the right to vote for two directors; and nomination of a chairman was to be by the appropriate Government Minister. Amendments were also made to the rules for enrolment on the register; the requirement in respect of suitable premises was deleted; reasons for refusal of an application had to be given; and an appeals procedure was introduced.

The defendant counterclaimed for a declaration that the supply of electrical power only on compliance with the new certification procedures was reasonable and *intra vires* its statutory powers.

Held by Costello J, in refusing injunctive relief, reserving the question of damages to a later date and refusing declaratory relief to the defendant:

(1) That the defendant was in a dominant position in the market for the supply of electrical contracting services.

(2) That if is was established that the defendant had entered into agreements, decisions or concerted practices of the type prohibited under section 4(1), that would amount to the imposition of unfair trading conditions within the meaning of section 5(2)(a) and therefore an abuse of that dominant position.

(3) That the defendant was an undertaking, and that RECI Ltd and the two trade associations involved in the establishment of RECI Ltd were associations of undertakings within the meaning of the Act of 1991.

(4) That the issue was not whether the plaintiffs' objections were objectively reasonable, but whether the matters of which they complained had either as their object or effect the prevention, restriction or distortion of competition.

(5) That, on the evidence, the object of the agreements entered into by the defendant leading to the establishment of RECI Ltd had not been to prevent, restrict or distort competition in the market for the supply of electrical contracting services, or in any market.

(6) That with regard to the position from 1 November 1992, until the amendment in the memorandum and articles of RECI Ltd and the rules of enrolment on its register:

(a) that the effect of the publicity campaign run by RECI Ltd had been to restrict the ability of unregistered contractors to compete;

(b) that the charge of £85 for the inspector's certification of work by unregistered contractors (which had to be passed on to their customers) had had the effect of restricting the ability of a small number of unregistered contractors to compete with registered contractors, who did not have to pay that fee. **1.7.1**

(7) That the foregoing anti-competitive effects would have been obviated had there not been unjustifiable restrictions on enrolments on RECI Ltd's register.

(8) That the restrictions were unjustifiable in that the criteria for enrolment were extremely imprecise; the absence of any obligation to give reasons for a refusal and the absence of an appeal procedure permitted arbitrary decisions; and at least one of the criteria for enrolment, namely the possession of suitable premises, was not reasonaly required for the maintenance of safety standards.

(9) That, accordingly, the defendant had not been unintentionally abusing its dominant position from 1 September 1992, until the injunction.

(10) That the fact that trade rivals of the plaintiff were among the controllers of RECI Ltd and its register did not of itself constitute a barrier to trade; that the lower subscription rates for members of one of the founders of RECI Ltd had been based on commercial considerations, and had had neither the aim nor effect of conferring a competitive advantage; and that the subscription costs and the requirements in respect of equipment, insurance and technical competence did not amount to breaches of the Act of 1991.

(11) That as a result of the amendment of the memorandum and articles of RECI Ltd and the criteria for enrolment on the register, there was no longer any restriction or distortion of competition, in that the criteria could be said to be unnecessary; the court was satisfied that the elements of the publicity campaign to which the plaintiffs objected would not recur; and that while the fee of £85 remained for the certification of the work of unregistered contractors, there were no longer any restrictions on registration constituting a barrier to trade.

(12) That the notification could not be regarded simply as an application for a licence, in that it was open to an applicant for a certificate to amend the matters notified before the Competition Authority had made its decision, in order to ensure that a certificate would be granted; and that, accordingly, the defendant had not abused its dominant position by introducing its new conditions of supply without awaiting a determination in respect of the application.

(13) That since the complaint had at all times been in relation to the conditions of supply and the new certification procedures in conjunction with the impugned decisions of RECI Ltd to implement them, rather than the condition of supply and the certificate procedures themselves, it would be otiose to make any declaration in relation to the conditions of supply and the certification procedures by themselves.

(14) That decisions of the European Court of Justice and of the European Commission in relation to Article 85 of the European Economic Community Treaty 1957, were of strong persuasive effect in construing the provisions of section 4 of the Act of 1991.

Held further by Costello J, having heard argument in regard to the form of the order and the question of damages:

(1) That the plaintiffs should be given declaratory relief in respect of the abuse of a dominant position from 1 September 1992, until the injunction, to make clear to the Competition Authority the meaning of the judgment.

1.7.1 (2) That the plaintiffs were entitled to damages in respect of the abuse of a dominant position notwithstanding that the abuse was unintentional; and that the court would assess the quantum if the parties were unable to reach agreement.

(3) That if there was reason to do so, the claim in respect of the breach of the prohibition in section 4 of the Act of 1991 could be re-entered after the Compeititon Authority had determined the application for a certificate and licence.

Cases referred to in judgment:
Association of Optometrists, Ireland Decision No. 16 CA/9/92E **1.7.2**
Sarabex Ltd, In re [1979] 1 CMLR 262

Plenary Summons The facts are summarised in the headnote and fully set out in the judgment of Costello J, *in fra.*

By plenary summons issued on 7 October 1992, the plaintiffs sought declaratory and injunctive relief and damages, including exemplary damages.

On 2 November 1992, it was ordered by the High Court (Lardner J) that:

The defendant be restrained pending the trial of this action from requiring as a condition of its contract for the supply of electricity the supplementary obligation that the plaintiffs or their customers or their employers subscribe to or obtain the approval of an association known as the Register of Electrical Contractors of Ireland Ltd.

The action was heard by the High Court (Costello J) on 8, 9, 10, 11, 15, 22 and 23 February 1994.

John Cooke SC and Henry Downing **for the plaintiffs**
James O'Reilly SC and Mel Christle **for the defendant**

COSTELLO J 5 May 1994 saying:

Introduction

The plaintiffs are electrical contractors carrying on business in the south west of Ireland. They bring this claim on their own behalf and on behalf of an association known as the 'Association of South Western Electrical Contractors' which has about 70 members. Their claim is that the Electricity Supply Board (a) entered into agreements, made decisions and engaged in concerted practices prohibited by section 4 of the Competition Act 1991 and (b) it abused its dominant position in the market for the supply of electrical contracting services, contrary to section 5 of the Act. They seek appropriate declaratory and injunctive relief. The claim arises from the introduction in September 1992 by the ESB of new conditions regulating the supply by the ESB of electricity to customers of contractors after they have carried out installation and other work to their customers' premises.

I can summarise the background to this dispute as follows:

The Electro Technical Council of Ireland (ETCI) was established in the year 1972 by a number of organisations concerned with electrical standards and electrical safety. It has now a membership of 20 bodies drawn from the government and semi-state sector, the private sector, local authorities, the universities and the industry itself. Its objects, according to its constitution, include the promotion of safety in electrical equipment and installations and the co-ordination of standardisation in all branches of electro technology in harmony with international agreements. It is a voluntary body and has been recognised as the body suitable to advise the Institute of Industrial Research and Standards and the government on matters relating to standards and codes of practice. In 1976 it adopted and promulgated the first National Rules for Electrical Installations and published an up-to-date edition in 1991. Its rules (generally known as the 'wiring rules') contain a form of certificate which electrical contractors should complete when an installation has been effected. The first paragraph of this 'completion certificate' contains a declaration by the contractor that the installation complies with the national rules for electrical installation. 1.7.1

The Electricity Supply Board is a statutory corporation endowed with wide powers and duties under the Electrical (Supply) Acts 1927-1988 relating to the generation, transmission and supply of electric power. In the course of their business electrical contractors necessarily are required to arrange for the connection to the national grid maintained by the ESB of installations, plant and equipment on the premises belonging to persons on whose behalf they have carried out electrical contracting work. The ESB will make a connection to the national grid and supply power to their customers only pursuant to its 'general conditions relating to supply'. Prior to 31 August 1992 its 'general conditions' provided that electrical contractors who had carried out electrical installation work should complete the ETCI's completion certificate and thereby certify that installation had been carried out in accordance with ETCI's national rules for electrical installations. The completed certificate together with an application for supply signed by the owner or occupier of the premises was then brought to the local office of the ESB and, subject to an inspection on behalf of the ESB, supply would then be effected. It was however made clear that the purpose of the inspection was to ensure that the ESB's network would not be adversely effected by the installation work and condition 4 of the board's 'general conditions' made it clear that the board took no responsibility for testing the customer's electrical installation — in common parlance it was not responsible for the wiring 'on the customer's side of the meter'. These procedures came to an end on 1 September 1992 and were replaced by new procedures. It is these which have given rise to the present action.

The Association of Electrical Contractors of Ireland (AECI) is a trade association comprising electrical contractors in the segment of the market for the supply of electrical services in which the plaintiffs also are mainly engaged, that is the market for low voltage contracts. Currently it has about 600 members. None of the plaintiffs are members of AECI. The Electrical Contractors Association of Ireland (ECA) is also a trade association, its members being mainly engaged in electrical contract work in the middle voltage segment of the market. It has currently a membership of about 300. None of the plaintiffs are members of the association. For some considerable time the absence of an adequate system of verification and certification of safety in electrical installations had been a source of concern both to the ETCI, the ESB, and the relevant government department. In 1989, at the instigation of the Department of Trade, the ETCI established a working group with a view to the establishment of a body which would promote and protect the interest of the public as users of electrical services. The working group comprised representatives both of the ETCI, the ESB, AECI and ECA. Its chairman was a former chairman of the ESB and a retired senior civil servant.

The department had made clear its opposition to a system which involved legislation and a statutory inspectorship and indicated that it favoured the establishment of a self-regulatory system. In accordance with these guidelines the working party drew up a report. The report proposed the establishment of a private company limited by guarantee, that its members would be the ETCI, the ESB, AECI and ECA, that the composition of the company would be based on an equal partnership of the participating organisations, that the directors of the company would comprise eight persons, two being nominated by each of the participating organisations. It proposed that the company would establish a register of electrical contractors. These proposals were accepted and implemented and a company was established known as the 'Register of Electrical Contractors of Ireland Ltd' and incorporated on 18 June 1991. This company has since been known by its acronym RECI. It set about organising the establishment of a register of electrical contractors and as part of the new self- regulatory regime it appointed inspectors. They were to fulfil two functions, (a) to carry out spot check inspections on the work of registered contractors and (b) to inspect installations carried out by non-registered contractors and certify (if such be the case) their compliance with the wiring rules. In 1992 the

1.7.1 ESB announced changes in its conditions of supply. From 1 September 1992 it stated that it would only supply electrical power to installations carried out by electrical contractors on the production of an ETCI completion certificate signed either by (a) an electrical contractor on RECI's register or (b) an inspector employed by RECI, in the case of installations completed by non-registered contractors.

The plaintiffs do not object in principle to a system of inspection of electrical contractors nor to the adoption by the industry of a self-regulatory system of inspection. There are however specific features of the new regime (detailed hereunder) and the manner in which it has been implemented to which strong objection is taken and which, the plaintiffs say, infringe the 1991 Act.

I propose to continue to use the acronym RECI. But it is a source of potential confusion as it has been used both to refer to the limited company known as the 'Register of Electrical Contractors of Ireland Ltd' and the register of electrical contractors which that company maintains. I will use it to denote the company. The 'rules of RECI' are the rules which the company drew up dealing with its register and it is of importance to bear in mind that originally contractors who were enrolled on the register did not thereby become members of the company. The 'RECI regime' is a compendious term which I will use to denote the state of affairs (both legal and practical) brought about by the ESB's conditions of supply, its agreement with RECI, RECI's memorandum and articles of association and RECI's rules relating to its register.

The proceedings

Subsequent to a meeting held to introduce the new regime to electrical contractors carrying on business in the south west of the country, the plaintiffs and some like minded contractors met and established the Association of South Western Electrical Contractors to voice their misgivings and objections. The association's solicitors wrote on 28 August 1992 setting out some of the plaintiffs' concerns and after some inconclusive correspondence a plenary summons was issued on 2 October 1992, followed by an application for an interlocutory injunction to restrain the implementation of the new regime. The plaintiffs were successful on this application and obtained interlocutory relief from Lardner J on 2 November. It is relevant to note that their detailed objections had been articulated in a very full affidavit grounding the application.

After the first letter of complaint had been written but before the proceedings had been instituted, the ESB had served a 'notification' on the competition authority established under the Competition Act 1991 in accordance with section 7 of the Act. This 'notification' features prominently in this case but I must defer its consideration for the moment. A further development requires to be noted. After the injunction had been obtained, amendments to RECI's memorandum and articles of association and its registration rules were effected. I infer that this was done in response to the criticism levelled against the original memorandum and articles of association and rules at the interlocutory hearing but without any admission that the Act had been infringed. Whilst Mr O'Reilly SC, on behalf of the ESB, is correct in his submission that the current memorandum and articles of association and the current rules are what the court must now consider nonetheless in order to understand fully, and adjudicate upon, the issues which arise, it is necessary to consider both the original RECI regime as well as the modified form. Before doing so, however, it will be helpful if I refer to the relevant provisions of the 1991 Act.

The Competition Act 1991

According to its preamble the 1991 Act is an Act 'to prohibit . . . the prevention, restriction or distortion of competition and the abuse of dominant positions in trade in the State' and, most remarkably, it states that this prohibition is to be 'by analogy with Articles 85 and 86 of the treaty establishing the European Economic Community'. Article 85 of the treaty prohibits agreements, decisions and concerted practices whose objects or effect is to prevent, restrict or distort competition, whilst Article 86 prohibits any abuse by one or more undertakings in a dominant position within the common market or a substantial part of it. These articles have direct effect in this State and are part of Irish domestic law but they relate to agreements, decisions and concerted practices and abuses which affect trade between member states. What the 1991 Act set out to do was by an enactment of the Irish parliament to make analogous provisions relating to trade within the State. 1.7.1

S. 4(1) of the Act adopts almost word for word Article 85(1) of the treaty. It provides that subject to the provisions of the section:

> All agreements between undertakings, decisions by associations of undertakings and concerted practices which have as their object or effect the prevention, restriction or distortion of competition in trade in any goods or services in the State or in any part of the State are prohibited and void.

The subsection then goes on to give examples of what are prohibited by providing that without prejudice to the generality of this subsection agreements, decisions and concerted practices are prohibited and void which:

> (a) directly or indirectly fix purchase or selling prices or any other trading conditions;
> (b) limit or control production, markets, technical development or investment;
> (c) share markets or sources of supply;
> (d) apply dissimiliar conditions to equivalent transactions with other trading parties thereby placing them at a competitive disadvantage;
> (e) make the conclusion of contracts subject to acceptance by the other parties of supplementary obligations which by their nature or according to commercial usage have no connection with the subject of such contracts.

S. 5(1) adopts Article 86 of the treaty by providing:

> Any abuse by one or more undertakings in a dominant position in trade for any goods or services in the State or in a substantial part of the State is prohibited.

The section then gives examples of abusive conduct by providing:

> (2) Without prejudice to the generality of subs. (1) such abuse may, in particular, consist in—
>
> (a) directly or indirectly imposing unfair purchase or selling prices or other unfair trading conditions;
> (b) limiting production, markets or technical development to the prejudice of consumers;
> (c) applying dissimilar conditions to equivalent transactions with other trading parties, thereby placing them at a competitive disadvantage;
> (d) making the conclusion of contracts subject to the acceptance by other parties of supplementary obligations which by their nature or according to commercial usage have no connection with the subject of such contracts.

The plaintiffs claim that the ESB has breached both ss. 4 and 5 of the Act.

A right of action is conferred by section 6 of the Act on any person aggrieved in consequence of any agreement, decision, concerted practice or abuse prohibited by ss. 4 and 5 and relief by way of injunction, declaration and/or damages may be granted to an aggrieved party. But there is one important exception contained in section 6 (7) which is of relevance in this case and which has the effect of suspending the right to relief in respect of claims under section 4 (but

1.7.1 not under section 5). The Act establishes a competition authority and empowers it to grant 'licences' and 'certificates'. I should explain what these are. Section 4(2) provides that the competition authority may grant a *licence* in the case of agreements, decisions and concerted practices which in its opinion:

> having regard to all relevant market conditions, contributes to improving the production or distribution of goods or provision of services or to promoting technical or economic progress, whilst allowing consumers a fair share of the resulting benefit and which does not—
>
> (i) impose on the undertakings concerned terms which are not indispensable to the attainment of those objectives;
> (ii) afford undertakings the possibility of eliminating competition in respect of a substantial part of the products or services in question.

S. 4(3) provides that a licence under subs. (2) shall 'permit the doing of acts which would otherwise be void under subs. (1)'. This means that, if satisfied that there exists the countervailing factors referred to in subs. (2), the competition authority may license the doing of acts which would otherwise be prohibited and void — in effect, the licence confers an exemption on the licensee. No cause of action for breaches of the prohibitions contained in section 4 therefore will exist in relation to acts protected by a licence. The licence may have retrospective effect to the date of notification to the competition authority and it may be granted for a specific period and subject to conditions (see section 7(1) and section 8(1)).

The role of *certificates* granted by the competition authority under the Act is an entirely different one. The authority may certify under section 4(4) that in its opinion, on the basis of the facts in its possession, an agreement, decision or concerted practice does not offend against section 4(1). This certificate does not have the effect of validating the agreement, decision or concerted practice to which it relates, which may still be condemned by a court in proceedings relating to them notwithstanding the existence of the certificate. But it has one significant legal effect; damages may not be awarded, in proceedings instituted after the issue of the certificate, for loss sustained while the certificate is in force (section 6(6)).

It is important to note that the competition authority has power only to grant licences and issue certificates in relation to anti-competitive agreements, decisions and concerted practices — it has no power to grant licences or issue certificates in relation to the conduct of an undertaking which may amount to an abuse of a dominant position contrary to section 5.

The Act's provisions relating to the procedures for obtaining a licence or a certificate are highly relevant in this case. The application for a section 4(2) licence or a section 4(4) certificate is made by a 'notification' to the competition authority under section 7. Notification of agreements, decisions and concerted practices existing when the Act came into force (1 October 1991) must be made within one year of that date (section 7(2)). In this case the ESB notified the competition authority under section 7(2) on 30 September 1992 of the agreements which are in controversy in this case. The nature of the notification it made and the nature of the application involved in the notification is a matter of considerable debate in this case, which I must consider later.

It is agreed that the effect of the ESB's notification was to suspend the plaintiffs' right of action for any breach of section 4 because the right of action does not apply after an agreement, decision or concerted practice has been notified to the authority until such time as the authority has decided to grant or refuse to grant a licence or certificate or until any appeal to the court has been concluded (section 6(7)). The plaintiffs accept (a) that as the authority has not yet made a decision pursuant to the notification, they presently have no claim under section 4, and (b) that their claim is limited to one under section 5. I turn now to the plaintiffs' submissions in support of that claim.

The plaintiffs' submissions in relation to the original RECI regime 1.7.1

Although RECI's memorandum and articles of association and its registration rules were amended after these proceedings were instituted, the plaintiffs' claim that the original RECI regime as it existed in September 1992 involved an abuse by the ESB of its dominant position is relevant for a number of reasons and so I must firstly consider it. In summary, the plaintiffs' case is as follows:

(a) Although the market with which this case is concerned is not the market in the supply of electrical power (in which the ESB enjoys a statutory monopoly), it is concerned with a market (namely the supply of electrical contracting services) in which the ESB, as monopoly supplier of electrical power, enjoys a dominant position. This dominant position arises from the fact that the ESB can determine the conditions under which the supply of electricity will be given to customers of electrical contractors, and so, in effect, determine what customers of electrical contractors will obtain electrical power and which will not.

(b) The ESB has abused, it is said, its dominant position in this market by imposing conditions under which it will supply electricity to customers of electrical contractors. This abuse arises because the ESB is imposing 'unfair trading conditions' within the meaning of section 5(2)(a). The trading conditions are 'unfair' because they constitute a breach of section 4. It is accepted that the right of action for breach of section 4 has been suspended, but the right of action for an abuse contrary to section 5 still subsists and it is submitted that if it can be shown that an undertaking in a dominant position has entered into anti-competitive agreements or decisions or engaged in anti-competitive practices which are prohibited by section 4, then these, being illegal and void, are also 'unfair' within the meaning of section 5(2)(a). By a side wind, as it were, section 4 is brought back into the case.

(c) Illegality arises in this case, it is said, because the agreements, decisions and concerted practices entered into by the ESB had as their object or had as their effect the restriction or distortion of competition in the supply of electrical contracting services. This restriction or distortion arises because of the combination of a number of the features in the ESB's new conditions of supply, in the memorandum and articles of association of RECI, in RECI's enrolment rules, and in the ESB's agreement with RECI, in the implementation by RECI of its rules, particularly in the promotion campaign it mounted.

Before I outline the matters of which the plaintiffs complain I should make one brief comment. The plaintiffs' objections have been strong and sincerely held but Mr Cooke SC, on their behalf, accepts that they must establish that these objections are also objectively reasonable. But even if this can be done this would not establish their case. The plaintiffs have to show that the features of the RECI regime of which they object either had as their object or had as their effect the prevention, restriction or distortion of competition.

The plaintiffs' objections to the original RECI regime

In the course of this case both in affidavit evidence and oral evidence at the trial, the plaintiffs expressed their objections taken to the RECI regime, objections more formally expressed in the pleadings and replies to notices for particulars. I can summarise the objections which appear to me to be relevant for present purposes as follows:

(a) It is claimed that the objects for which the new company was established go beyond the needs for promoting safety standards; that the objects clause of the company includes as an object the 'fair trading within the electrical contracting business' and the maintenance of 'appropriate levels of business competence and ethical behaviour', as well as the invocation of sanctions against 'unethical contractors'. These objectives are reflected in the rules relating to registration and it was pointed out that applicants must sign a declaration that they will abide by the rules set from time to time by RECI, that qualification for enrolment includes not only proof of technical skills and experience but the possession of suitable premises, specified levels of insurance cover and compliance with criteria relating to wage rates and pension arrange-

1.7.1 ments.

(b) The control of the register: The company, it was pointed out, controls the register. As originally established the only members of the company were the four founding organisations each of whom nominate two directors. This meant, it is submitted, that the trade rivals of the plaintiffs have considerable influence both on decisions, on applications for enrolment of the register, and on decisions in relation to criteria to be adopted in the future for the maintenance of membership. Particular attention was drawn to the fact that the company could by rule 7 reject any application for registration without assigning any reason and no appeal lay from this decision.

(c) It was claimed that preferential treatment was given by the company to the plaintiffs' rivals who were members of AECI as they were permitted to pay a reduced entry and annual membership fee.

(d) The effect on the ability of non-members to compete in conditions established by the new regime was adverted to. Under the rules members pay an initial subscription of £75 and an annual subscription of £125, and once on the register they complete their own completion certificates. Non-members however are required to pay in respect of every installation a fee of £85 to obtain a completion certificate signed by a RECI inspector. This fee of £85 was a significant cost factor to small traders in a very competitive market and as delays occur and are known to occur their ability to compete was further diminished by the delays in obtaining the attendance of RECI inspectors and certification. The ability of non-members to compete was affected in another way, it was claimed. In advertisements to the public in the print media, the public was urged to employ the services of registered contractors in order to ensure that they got a good service, the clear implication being that the employment of non-registered electrical contractors was inadvisable. This point was made more explicitly in a television advertisement which quite unambiguously suggested that unregistered contractors were 'cow-boys' whose services should be eschewed in favour of registered contractors. Non-members were thus placed at a competitive disadvantage.

Conclusions on these submissions

In the light of the evidence my conclusions are as follows:

(1) It seems to me that the ESB is in a dominant position in the market for the supply of electrical contracting services. I agree with Mr Cooke's submission (advanced on behalf of the plaintiffs) that if it could be shown that the ESB entered into agreements, decisions or concerted practices which were prohibited by section 4, this would amount to the imposition of unfair trading conditions within the meaning of section 5(2)(a) and therefore an abuse of its dominant position.

(2) The ESB is an 'undertaking' within the meaning of the 1991 Act. The AECI and ECA and RECI are all 'associations of undertakings' within the meaning of the Act.

(3) Agreements, formal and informal, which the ESB entered into which resulted in the establishment of RECI and the RECI regime were motivated by a desire to improve safety standards in the public interest. I am satisfied that the ESB did not intend to prevent, restrict or distort competition in the market for the supply of electrical contracting services or any market.

(4) RECI is a non-statutory company established to regulate the electrical contracting industry by those engaged in electrical contracting and organisations concerned with safety in electrical contracting matters. It can properly be regarded as a voluntary self-regulating body for the industry. Mr Moore McDowell, the expert economist called on behalf of the ESB, accepted that self-regulation raises serious questions as to the possible anti-competitive consequences that may arise. But as to the purpose of its establishment, I am quite satisfied that RECI was established in the utmost good faith and with no anti-competitive intent.

What falls, then, for consideration is whether the *effect* of the RECI regime was to restrict or distort competition by non-registered contractors. My conclusions on this point are as follows: 1.7.1

(5)(i) The promotion campaign undertaken by RECI in the manner complained of restricted, in my opinion, the ability of non- registered contractors to compete with registered contractors because of the public attitudes to non-registered contractors which such a campaign created.

(ii) The decision by RECI to charge an inspection fee of £85 to non-registered contractors was not motivated by any desire to restrict competition. But it did have the effect of restricting the ability of a significant number of small contractors to compete with registered contractors because of the extra costs involved which would have to be passed on to the customer by those bearing it.

(iii) The anti-competitive effects of the matters referred to at (i) and (ii) would be obviated if there were no restrictions on enrolment on the RECI register.

(6) The criteria for membership was extremely imprecise leaving a great deal of discretion in those deciding on applications for enrolment. In addition the rules relating to adjudication on applications permitted arbitrary decisions to be taken which were not appealable and in respect of which no reasons had to be given. Furthermore, at least one of the criteria for membership was not reasonably required for the purpose for which RECI was established, namely the maintenance of safety standards — the rule relating to possession by applicants of premises which RECI considered suitable was not required for such purpose.

I must now consider, in the light of the applicable legal principles, whether the findings of fact made at (5) and (6) above constitute a breach of section 4 of the Act.

S. 4 is in identical terms to Article 85 of the treaty, around which has grown up in the past thirty years a very considerable volume of case-law from decisions of the commission and the Court of Justice. These decisions are not binding on our courts but in view of (a) the provisions of the Act's preamble which declares that its object is to prohibit by analogy with Article 85 the prevention, restriction and distortion of competition, and the fact that (b) Article 85 of the treaty is part of Irish domestic law and the Irish courts are required to follow decisions of the Court of Justice in relation to it on inter-state trade, it seems to me that the decisions of both the commission and the Court of Justice on the construction of Article 85 should have very strong persuasive force. This view is, of course, subject to any qualifications which may arise where the statutory provisions are different from the treaty provisions (as, for example, the definition of what constitutes an 'undertaking' for the purposes of the statute).

The principles developed in community law relating to membership of trade associations can, in my judgment, be properly applied when considering the possible anti-competitive consequences under the 1991 Act of a self-regulatory body like RECI and, in particular, its rules relating to admission to membership. It is well established that the commission requires that rules of admission should be based on objective criteria with a proper appeal procedure. These views are illustrated in proceedings before the commission relating to the City of London Foreign Exchange Market (*In re Sarabex Ltd* [1979] 1 CMLR 262, noted in the commission's eighth report on competition policy (1978), paragraphs 35 to 37). Sarabex complained that it was unable to trade in certain scheduled currencies. The commission intervened and as a result the rules relating to the recognition of foreign exchange brokers in London were revised. Certain objective criteria which firms had to meet were established and a special appeals procedure in the event of the refusal of an application was introduced.

The application of community law in the context of the 1991 Act is seen in Decision No. 16 of the competition authority in this country on the *Notification of the Association of Optometrists of Ireland*. The association notified the authority of its memorandum and articles of association and its code of ethics and a certificate under section 4(4) was sought or in the event of a refusal a licence under section 4(2). In the course of its decision the authority pointed out (paragraph 82) that the EC decisions under Article 85(1) indicated that membership rules of professional and trade associations must be based on reasonable and objective standards and that whilst membership of the Optometrists Association is not compulsory in order to compete

1.7.1 in the relevant market 'it may be that individuals unable to join would be placed at a serious competitive disadvantage relative to members'. The decision went on, in a comment which is relevant to the facts of this case, to state:

> In particular if the public felt that non-members were in some sense less qualified than members, then restrictions on entry to the association could distort competition (paragraph 82).

The decision examined different aspects of the association's code of ethics including that portion of it which dealt with the guidelines relating to the premises in which members could carry on their profession. It drew attention to the report of the UK Director of General Fair Trading on similar guidelines issued by the UK Opticians Association which held that they were unnecessary because they were not related to clinical matters. The decision of the Irish competition authority expressed its agreement with these views but because the association had withdrawn all references to premises in its codes of ethics, the authority concluded that the question of a breach of section 4(1) no longer arose.

In my view the combination of factors referred to in paragraph (6) above (namely, the imprecision of the criteria for enrolment, the lack of objective standards for registration, the arbitrary power to refuse enrolment, the absence of any appeal procedure, the existence of a requirement for enrolment not required for the objects for which the register was formed) — imposed unjustifiable restrictions for enrolment on the register. These resulted in a restriction on competition in the electrical contracting trade because non-registered contractors had been placed at a competitive disadvantage for the reasons set out in paragraph 5(i) and (ii) above and faced restrictions on joining RECI which would have enabled them to overcome them.

Finally, as to two other objections taken, (a) I do not think that the fact that the four founding members of RECI controlled the company and the register was a factor which in itself constituted a barrier to trade and (b) the evidence satisfies me that there were commercial considerations which justified the lower entry and annual subscriptions charges available to members of AECI and the rule which allowed this was not intended to, nor did it in fact, give members of AECI a competitive advantage of any significance.

For a period therefore from September 1992 until the interlocutory injunction the ESB, albeit unintentionally, was abusing its dominant position in breach of section 5 because of the unfair trading conditions to which I have referred.

For reasons which I will now explain that situation had been rectified by April 1993.

Amendments to the RECI regime

Amendments were effected to the company's memorandum and articles of association in March 1993 and in the following month to the rules for registration. The amendments can be summarised as follows:

(a) *The company's objects.* Clause (2)(1)(d) of the original objects clause was deleted so that it no longer became an objective of the company 'to ensure that there are sufficient number of licensed and registered electrical contractors . . . properly qualified to meet the standards set by the company and who will maintain proper levels of technical and business competency and ethical behaviour.' There was a corresponding amendment to the objectives of the register as contained in the new rules in that it was no longer an objective of the register 'to maintain appropriate business competency and ethical behaviour'. Thus the original vague and imprecise criteria for registration were deleted from the rules.

(b) *The possession of suitable premises.* The requirement that an applicant for registration should be in possession of suitable premises was deleted from the qualifications for enrolment.

(c) *Adjudication on applicants for registration.* The original rule 7 was deleted and in its place it was provided that when applications for registration were rejected, reasons for doing so must be given and a right of appeal must be conferred. Thus the arbitrary aspect of the adjudication process was removed. 1.7.1

(d) *The control of the company and its register*. The articles of association of the company were changed and as a result all contractors enrolled on the register also became members of the company and 'independent members' as defined were entitled to vote for two directors of the company. Furthermore, provision was made for the nomination of an independent chairman by the appropriate minister. These amendments had the effect of ensuring that the possibility of arbitrary decisions relating to applications for membership and maintenance of members on the register would be avoided.

I must conclude therefore that these amendments succeed in overcoming the defects to which I have referred and as a result the rules dealing with applications for enrolment no longer constitute any barrier to entry and consequently competition is no longer distorted or restricted. The criteria for enrolment are now clear and reasonably precise. There are no requirements for membership which can be said to be unnecessary for the achievement of the aims of RECI. The rules of adjudication are fair and reasonable.

In my opinion from the date of the amendments it could not be said that the ESB was abusing its dominant position because of the imposition of 'unfair trading conditions' or for any other reason.

In reaching this decision it will be clear that I did not accept that a number of the objections taken by the plaintiffs both to the original and to the new regime (although no doubt genuinely held) established any further breaches of the Competition Act. I do not think that the registration rules imposed unnecessary costs on firms so as to create a barrier to entry on the register. The evidence satisfies me that the equipment which members are required to possess is reasonably required in the interests of safety. The insurance cover required is that which is now normal in the industry and does not constitute an unreasonable requirement. The initial and annual subscriptions are set at reasonable levels and are necessary to ensure that the objectives of RECI are realised. As to the complaint that RECI gave preferential treatment to members of AECI and ECA, the evidence establishes that slightly lower subscription rates were granted because of the saving in administrative expenses which were effected. Finally, the requirement in the rules by which applicants have to establish a certain level of technical competence is not an unreasonable one.

The features of the public information campaign to which the plaintiffs objected have been discontinued and I am satisfied that in the future RECI will not seek to suggest that non-registered contractors are less qualified or less competent than registered contractors. The inspection fee of £85 remains but the rules of RECI no longer constitute any restriction on enrolment or a barrier to trade.

One further point needs to be considered. The ESB not only supplies electricity but it also supplies electrical contracting services through its contracting division. It was alleged during the case that part of the object and desired effect of the establishment by the ESB of the new regime was to improve the financial and competitive position of the ESB itself in the market for the supply of electrical contracting services. The evidence, however, establishes that the market for the supply of electrical contracting services is a very segmented one and that the share of the ESB in the market for low voltage installations (which is the market in which the plaintiffs are mainly engaged and which is the relevant market for the purposes of this case) is extremely small (between 1% and 2¼%). The ESB is not a serious competitor in this market and I must conclude that neither the object nor the effect of the new regime was to improve the ESB's competitive position in the market for the supply of electrical contracting services.

The plaintiffs' final submissions

I turn now to the final submissions made by Mr Cooke on behalf of the plaintiffs in which the notification to the competition authority to which I referred at the beginning of this judgment features prominently. It is urged that the conclusions which I have just announced do not

1.7.1 deprive the plaintiffs of the right to an injunction and it is submitted that the ESB abused and still abuses the dominant position in the market. What is said is as follows. The imposition of new trading conditions by the ESB in September 1992 amounted to the imposition of unfair trading conditions within the meaning of section 5(2)(a) (because they breached the anti-competitive provisions of section 4) and therefore amounted to an abuse of its dominant position. The only way in which the ESB could lawfully and therefore fairly have imposed those conditions was by applying for a licence under section 4(2) which would have exempted them from the provisions of the section. It is submitted that although the form of application made to the competition authority was for a *certificate* under section 4(4), the application should properly be regarded by the court as an application for a *licence* because it cannot properly be treated as an application for a certificate. That being so it is suggested that it is an abuse by the ESB of its dominant position to introduce these new conditions before the procedures relating to applications for their exemption had been complied with. By introducing the new conditions without going through the proper procedures, the ESB, it is said, deprived the plaintiffs of the benefit of these statutory proceedings which would allow them to make representations to the competition authority and appeal, if necessary, should they be aggrieved by the decision of the authority. The introduction of the new trading conditions in September 1992 was an abuse, and the abuse is still continuing because the procedures have not yet concluded and accordingly the plaintiffs are entitled to injunctive relief.

This submission depends on the proper construction of the 'notification' of 30 September 1992. On that date a firm of competition consultants sent to the competition authority a form CA 'on behalf of the ESB and the Register of Electrical Contractors of Ireland' together with 13 items of information which it specified. Form CA is entitled:

> Notification under section 7 of the Competition Act 1991 to the competition authority of an agreement, decision or concerted practice for the purpose of obtaining a certificate under section 4(4) or a licence under section 4(2).

The first paragraph of the form is headed 'purpose of notification' and reads:

> 1. State whether the notification is for the purpose of obtaining,
> —a certificate only (section 4(4))
> —a licence only (section 4(2))
> —a certificate, or in event of refusal by the authority to issue a certificate, a licence.

The ESB in the form completed on 30 September answered this query as follows:

> This notification is for the purpose of obtaining a certificate or, in the event of a refusal of a certificate, a licence.

I cannot (as argued on the plaintiffs' behalf) regard this notification as an application for a licence by the ESB under section 4(4). It seems to me that I must give the words used in the form their ordinary and natural meaning. By applying for a *certificate* under section 4(4) the ESB is in effect claiming that the agreement to which it refers is not prohibited by section 4. By applying for a *licence* in the event of a refusal of a certificate, it is claiming that should the authority not concur with its view that the agreement is not prohibited then the authority should grant an exemption because the agreement comes within the criteria for a licence set out in section 4(2). When an application is made in this way, an applicant may, if so advised, modify or amend, in the course of the procedures before the authority, the agreements to which the notification relates so as to ensure that a certificate is granted. This is what the Association of Optometrists of Ireland did. The association submitted a notification under section 7 and applied for a *certificate* in respect of the notification and for a *licence* in the event of a refusal to grant a certificate. Whilst their application was pending modifications were made in its code of ethics. It is clear that in the absence of the modifications a certificate would have been refused but that as a consequence of their adoption a certificate was issued. These are the procedures followed by the ESB in this case. I must conclude, therefore, that the application made was for a *certificate* (and not for a *licence*) as was stated in the form it filed and that the ESB did not abuse its dominant position by introducing its new conditions of supply without waiting for an adjudication on its application of 30 September 1992, and it is not now abusing it. 1.7.1

In the event, therefore, the plaintiffs are not now entitled to injunctive or declaratory relief. For a limited time after September 1992 an unintentional abuse occurred. Whether the plaintiffs are entitled to maintain a claim for damages is a matter on which, if requested, I will hear submissions.

Counterclaim

The ESB raised a counterclaim seeking certain declaratory relief.

Part 6 of the rules of ETCI is headed 'verification and certification' and requires that every new installation and every major extension of an installation should be inspected and tested to verify that the requirements of the wiring rules have been fulfilled and further provides that following inspection and testing a completion certificate shall be issued by the contractor or person responsible for the work. What these rules require therefore is (a) *testing to verify* compliance with the rules and (b) *a completion certificate* which certifies that they do. There is no requirement for verification of the completion certificate itself. Nor is there any such requirement either in the rules of RECI or the ESB's conditions for supply. What is required under the new regime is the production of a *completion certificate* signed by the contractor registered with RECI or in the case of non-registered contractors, a completion certificate signed by an inspector appointed by RECI. The declaratory relief claimed in the counterclaim appears to be based on the view that the new regime involves the 'verification' of a 'completion certificate' because declarations are sought to the effect that the *verification of completion certificates* required by the ESB as a pre-condition to connection to its network (a) is in accordance with its general conditions, (b) is a reasonable requirement, (d) is not an abuse of its dominant position, (e) is a reasonable exercise of its statutory powers and (f) is *intra vires* those powers. And paragraph (c) seeks a declaration that the 'independent verification of completion certificates' is a reasonable requirement to request as a pre-condition to connection. It seems to me the ESB is not entitled to declarations in this form as they would not accord with the rules which do not provide for verification of completion certificates.

The declaratory relief seems to be intended to obtain declarations that the agreement to supply electrical power only on compliance with the new certification procedures was reasonable and *intra vires* the statutory powers of the ESB. But no issue has been raised that the agreement or the new certification procedures are in themselves invalid. The issue has been the validity of the agreement and the new certification procedures taken in conjunction with the impugned decisions taken by RECI to implement them. Accordingly, declarations only relating to the agreement and the certification procedures would be otiose and I do not think that any order on the counterclaim should be made.

On 12 May 1994, argument was heard on the question of damages and form of the order.

COSTELLO J

12 May 1994 saying:

The first matter that arises today is the claim advanced by Mr Cooke that in the light of my judgment the court should m ake a declaratory order in the form of the draft order handed into court.

In giving my judgment on 5 May 1994, I was concerned with the situation at the date of the trial. In that judgment I said that no declaratory or injunctive relief was called for. I did not advert in the judgment to the desirability of a declaration to deal with the situation which existed

1.7.1 from the beginning of September 1992, to March or April, 1993, when the rules of RECI were changed. Having heard the submission of Mr Cooke I think that there may be an advantage to such a declaration and that the plaintiffs were entitled to it.

While the position should be clear to anyone reading the judgment as to the conclusions I reached, I think that it may be of assistance to the Competition Authority to have the matter made clear in a declaration. That will make it clear beyond peradventure what my judgment meant.

The next matter concerns the application by the plaintiffs for liberty to re-enter the proceedings in respect of their claim under section 4 of the Competition Act 1991, after the application of the ESB has been dealt with by the Competition Authority. I am not clear what damages or other relief would arise in such circumstances that would not have been covered under the claim for abuse of a dominant position, but I am not making any further determination at this point. I will give liberty to either party to re-enter the matter when the proceedings before the Competition Authority are concluded if there should be reason to do so at that point.

The next question is the issue of damages. It is submitted by Mr O'Reilly that the plaintiffs are not entitled to damages for a limited period of two months from 1 September 1992, until 2 November 1992, because the abuse by the ESB of its dominant position was unintentional. Mr O'Reilly was not able to refer to any authority to substantiate that proposition and the submission seems to me to be unsustainable in the light of the clear provisions of the statute that the plaintiffs are entitled to damages if loss is suffered.

I would hope that the parties could reach agreement on the amount of damages to avoid a new hearing. If there is a fresh hearing in the absence of agreement I will bear in mind the attitude of the parties in failing to agree damages in determining the costs of such a hearing.

I therefore hold that the plaintiff who has suffered loss in the two month period of the infringement is entitled to damages. I will give liberty to the parties to re-enter the matter for the purposes of measuring damages if they have not been agreed.

The final matter is the very important question of the costs of the proceedings. The effect of my judgment is that I have found that the ESB had for a limited time after September 1992, unintentionally abused its dominant position. It is clear that the defendant must pay the costs of the initiation of the proceedings and the interlocutory injunction because at that time a wrong had been committed. The fact that I have decided that the wrong was remedied at the earliest opportunity by the defendant is not a justifiable ground for rewarding the ESB and not making an award for costs against it.

The difficult question I have to deal with is what order for costs would be just after April 1993. What happened was that RECI at the instigation of the ESB amended its rules, memorandum and articles of association. I have held that these amendments resulted in removing any form of abuse. I have to take into account the way in which the defendant met this case from then on. Had the defendant met the case on the basis that the wrong had been committed and subsequently remedied, in a way analogous to the practice of lodgments, the plaintiffs could be regarded as thereafter proceeding at their peril and the defendant would be entitled to its costs after that date.

But that is not what happened. It is true that some of the amendments were relied upon in the defence but it does not refer to all of the changes made. It refers to the memorandum and articles of association but does not refer to the admission criteria under the RECI rules. What occurred was that the defendant resolutely denied any wrongdoing at any time. The submission made by Mr O'Reilly was that I should not pay attention to what had occurred when the proceedings were initiated but should look at the situation as at the date of the hearing. Notwithstanding that this submission was made, there was no admission that wrongdoing had occurred at any stage. I have held that wrongdoing did occur and that the plaintiffs are entitled to damages.

The justice of the case requires that I order the defendant to pay all of the costs of the action. Had the defendant taken a different stance when the case opened, it would not have lasted eight days. The defendant was perfectly entitled to have denied that any wrongdoing occurred, but the hearing of the action was lengthened as a result and in all the circumstances the defendnat must pay all the costs of the action including all costs reserved and the costs of the interlocutory proceedings, and I will make an order in those terms. 1.7.1

[*Reporter's note:* By notice of appeal dated 4 August 1994, the defendants appealed from so much of the judgments and order of the High Court 'as determined that the plaintiffs . . . were entitled to declaratory relief in respect of an unintentional abuse on the part of the defendants and to damages for an unintentional abuse of a dominant position contrary to section 5(1) of the Competition Act 1991, together with an order for costs . . . and refused the defendants all relief on their counterclaim, in circumstances where the learned trial judge in the reserved judgment delivered on 5 May 1994, refused the plaintiffs the entire of the declaratory and injunctive relief sought in the within proceedings'.]

Solicitors for the plaintiffs: *Burke & Co.*
Solicitor for the defendant: *Martina Walsh*

James Devlin
Barrister

Competition Authority Decision No. 16, Association of Optometrists, Ireland; 29 April 1993, Notification No. CA/90/92E 1.7.2

Association of undertakings – Association of undertakings having restrictions on admission to membership – Code of ethics of the association containing restrictions on the work practices of its members – Restrictions on advertising by members of the association – Amendment of notified arrangements – Effect of Competition Act, 1991 on earlier specific legislation Competition Act, 1991 (No.24) ss. 3, 4, 7, and 8 – Opticians Act 1956 (No. 17) ss. 5, 18, 23, 24, 33, 47 and 49

Facts: On 6 March 1992 notification was made to the Authority of the Memorandum & Articles of Association and the Code of Ethics of the Association of Optometrists, Ireland with a request for a certificate under section 4(4) of the Competition Act, or failing that, a licence under section 4(2). The Association of Optometrists Ireland ('the Association') is an Irish registered company whose primary objects are the promotion of high standard of training, education and practice for optometrists and its membership consists almost entirely of ophthalmic opticians who are engaged in practice alone, in partnership or as employees of other members or other entities. The services provided by optometrists are eye examination, advice and where necessary the prescribing of spectacles and contact lenses.

The prescribing or dispensing of spectacles and contact lenses is regulated in the State by the Opticians Act 1956 and under the terms thereof only registered medical practitioners or registered opticians may prescribe spectacles, dispense prescriptions and sell spectacles. Section 5 of the Opticians Act provides for the establishment of the Opticians Board whose functions are the setting up and maintenance of the register of ophthalmic opticians and the register of dispensing opticians in the State and, pursuant to sections 51 and 52, the power to make penal rules for the regulation and control of prescribing, dispensing and selling spectacles and for the control of advertising by registered opticians.

1.7.2 Once an optician has undergone training and passed the examinations as prescribed by the Board he may apply for registration on the appropriate register. For registration as an ophthalmic optician an applicant must have a diploma in optometry from the Dublin Institute of Technology of which there are c.20 places per annum for c.1000 applicants.

The notified arrangements concern the Memorandum & Articles of Association of the Association and its Code of Ethics. The notification stated that the arrangements contained no restriction on members freedom to take individual commercial decisions other than the requirement that members abide by the provisions of the Opticians Act and the rules of the Board. Article 6 of the Articles of Association provides that to be admitted to membership the applicant must be nominated by two members which application is then sent to the Council of Management ('the Council') of the Association three quarters of whom must support the applicant if the applicant is to be successful. There are three classes of membership; Ordinary Membership, being Opticians who trained other than in Ireland and who have qualifications similar to the Irish Diploma in Optometry, Fellows who are persons who have an Irish Diploma in Optometry and dispensing members. The Articles provide that Fellows may affix and Ordinary members may use the phrase 'FAOI' and 'Member of the Association of Optometrists, Ireland' respectively on their stationery. Articles 21, 22 and 24 set out the procedure whereby a member may be expelled from the Association if his conduct, in the opinion of the Council, is derogatory of the profession or renders him unfit to remain a member of the Association. Article 24 provides a right of appeal to a general meeting of the Association.

The other notified agreement, the Code of Ethics which is binding on all members of the Association gives guidance to Optometrists in carrying out their professional services. The Code recommends that an Optician's practice be sited in consulting rooms without an external display or a display within the reception area and that it should be laid out in such manner that the patient is allowed adequate privacy during consultation. The Codes recommendations on advertising were revised on 30 October 1992 and provide that particular attention should be paid by members to the rules of the Opticians Board on advertising. The revised Code permitted media advertising only in the public press and placed restrictions on the content, style, and size of advertisements. It also restricted members from using their titles and qualifications in media articles or in the sponsorship of non-optical events and also restricted members from offering discounts to clubs or groups. Rule 31 of the Opticians Board, a penal rule made under section 52 of the Opticians Act, contained a prohibition on canvassing but allowed a limited form of advertising on condition that such advertising was to inform the public of the availability of optical services and not to make comparisons with or claim superiority over any other optical practice and that any such advertising should not be misleading or be regarded as likely to bring the profession of Opticians in to disrepute. The Code recommended that members should charge for their services on a professional fee system and also provided that members on leaving employment should not entice clients away from their former employer or set up in practice in the proximity of their employer for such purpose. The Code further provided that where a patient is referred by one member to a second member possessing extra skill that that second member should not carry out any work which the first member could carry out himself.

Following a meeting between the Authority and the Association at which the

Authority expressed concerns over certain aspects of the Code of Ethics, the Association indicated by letter dated 22 December 1992 it's intention to suspend pending the coming into effect of new rules, those sections of the Code: (a) which refer to the places of business of practices in a specific way, (b) which refer to methods of charging for services and appliances and (c) which refer to advertising and discounts. The revised rules of the Opticians Board were made on 21 December 1992 and removed the prohibition on price advertising in the media and on advertising in media other than newspapers which had prevailed theretofore but retained a restriction on canvassing. By letter dated 23 March 1993 the Association informed the Authority that the sections of the Code of Ethics relating to premises, advertising and fees and charges were suspended pending the re-writing of the entire Code of Ethics. During the investigation of the notified arrangements the Authority became aware that certain members had been suspended or threatened with suspension or expulsion from the Association for breach of the Code of Ethics as it related to advertising. 1.7.2

Decided by the Authority: In issuing a certificate under section 4(4) of the Competition Act, 1991 in respect of the notified arrangements (as amended) that:

(1) An association whose object is to represent the interests of its members as undertakings is an association of undertakings. Consequently the Association of Optometrists is an association of undertakings, as many of its members are undertakings, even though some members may be employees rather than undertakings.

(2) The Association's Memorandum & Articles of Association and its Code of Ethics constitute decisions of an Association. The requirement by the Association that its members abide by the provisions of the Opticians Act, 1956 and the rules of the Opticians Board constitute decisions by the Association and the notified arrangements therefore include the provisions of the Opticians Act and the rules of the Opticians Board insofar as members of the Association are obliged to observe such rules.

(3) The protection and promotion of members interests as envisaged by Article 3(2) of the Articles of Association is a legitimate activity for a professional association to engage in. Article 3(2) does not *per se* offend against section 4(1) but where measures to protect members interests extend to include restrictions on competition they are prohibited under 4(1).

(4) The provisions of the Opticians Act which restrict entry into and competition in the market for the prescription and sale of spectacles do not come within the scope of the Competition Act as they are enshrined in separate legislation and therefore the requirement by the Association that it's members abide by the provisions of the Opticians Act does not offend against section 4(1). The Association's requirement that its members observe the rules of the Opticians Board (without prejudice as to whether the Opticians Board is itself subject to the provisions of the Competition Act) would offend section 4(1) if those rules were in conflict with that section.

(5) Entry into the particular market is restricted by the provisions of the Opticians Act. Given such legal restrictions any additional restrictions would constitute a serious restriction on competition. Articles 6 and 15 set out criteria for membership. While membership of the Association is not compulsory in order to compete in the relevant market individuals who may be unable to join are placed at a serious competitive disadvantage relative to members. The fact that only one applicant for membership has been refused during the past five years indicates that Articles 6 and 15 have not been operated in such a way as to restrict competition and consequently they do not

1.7.2 offend against section 4(1).

(6) The restriction on admission to fellowship to those who obtained a diploma in Optometry in Ireland does not offend against section 4(1) provided the Association does not seek to create the impression that fellows of the Association are more highly skilled than overseas trained Optometrists, thereby giving 'fellows' a competitive advantage.

(7) Articles 21, 22 and 24 which deal with procedures relating to the expulsion of members from the Association do not *per se* offend against section 4(1). If however expulsion or the threat of expulsion effectively represented a means of enforcing anti-competitive practices such expulsion or threat would offend against section 4(1).

(8) The Board is empowered by the terms of the Opticians Act to establish rules for courses of training and examinations to be taken by candidates in order for them to be registered as opticians. Rule 21 of the Board provides that to be registered as an ophthalmic optician a person must pass the prescribed examination held by Dublin VEC. Only c.20 applicants out of c.1000 are accepted each year for the Dublin VEC diploma in optometry. The number is restricted to 20 due to the shortage in the number of teaching staff available and because the college authorities felt that 20 per year represented the number of optometrists required. While student intake cannot be increased without an increase in resources the notion that intake is being decided on the basis of perceived demand would cause concern. If such an intake limit reflected the view of the Association on the perceived requirements this would represent a serious restriction on competition.

(9) The provision in the Code of Ethics whereunder a practitioner who receives a referral from a colleague should not carry out any work which that colleague could carry out himself does not offend section 4(1) as the provision serves to encourage Opticians to refer patients to specialist colleagues which is for the public benefit and nothing in this provision prevents a patient from deciding to change Opticians.

(10) The restrictions contained in the Code of Ethics setting out guidelines relating to premises and layout of practices, had they not been suspended on 23 March 1993, would have been found in breach of section 4(1) in that they can prevent new entrants or existing practitioners from offering services in an innovative way or a manner more convenient to the customer. While the rules of the Opticians Board could prevent, restrict or distort competition they do not appear to have been interpreted in a restrictive way and have not prevented a number of innovative developments.

(11) The restrictions contained in the Code of Ethics on advertising whereby members were restricted in media advertising and subject to restrictions on content, style and size of advertisements but for their suspension would have been found in breach of section 4(1) and would not have qualified for a licence under section 4(2) of the Competition Act. Provisions in the Code of Ethics that practitioners should charge on a professional fee system and the prohibition on members granting group discounts represents a restriction on members freedom to charge as they choose and but for the suspension of this provision would have been found offensive to section 4(1).

(12) The requirement that members determine fees in a particular manner and the restriction on the offering of discounts, had they not been subsequently deleted, would have offended against section 4(1).

(13) The restriction in the Code of Ethics on a member when leaving employment in a practice from enticing customers from that practice or from setting up in proximity to that practice so as to entice customers does not offend section 4(1) in that a restriction on former employees from directly enticing customers of former employers is not anti-competitive. 1.7.2

Cases and Decisions referred to:

IAZ International Belgium (Navewa) v. EC Commission (Case No. 96/102, 104, 105, 108 and 110/82), [1983] ECR 3369, [1984] 3 CMLR 276

EC Commission Decision – Milchfoerderungsfonds (Case No. 85/76/EEC), [1984] OJ L35/35, [1985] 3 CMLR 101

Competition Authority Decision No. 1 – *Nallen v. O'Toole*, 2 April 1992 **3.3**

Competition Authority Decision No. 4 – Esso Solus and related agreements, 25 June 1992 **4.1**

Competition Authority decision of 29 April 1993 relating to a proceeding under section 4 of the Competition Act 1991
Notification No. CA/90/92E — Association of Optometrists, Ireland

Introduction

1. The Memorandum, Articles of Association and Code of Ethics of the Association of Optometrists, Ireland, were notified to the Competition Authority on 6 March 1992. A certificate in respect of the notification was sought. In the event of a refusal by the Authority to grant a certificate, a licence was also sought. Following discussions with the Authority, certain aspects of the notified arrangements were amended.

2. Notice of the intention of the Authority to take a favourable decision in relation to the arrangements was published in the Irish Times on 12 February 1993. No substantive submissions were received from third parties in response.

The Facts

(a) *Subject of the Notification*

3. This notification concerns the Memorandum, Articles of Association (the Articles) and Code of Ethics (the Code) of the Association of Optometrists, Ireland. These documents provide a framework for the operation of the Association and the behaviour of its members. Members of the Association are required to give an undertaking to observe and be bound by the Association's Articles, Rules and Regulations and Code of Ethics and practice.

(b) *The Parties Concerned*

4. The Association of Optometrists (the Association), formerly called the Association of Ophthalmic Opticians, has been in existence for 85 years. The primary stated objective of the Association is to promote high standards of training, education and practice for optometrists (ophthalmic opticians) for the public good.

5. There are three categories of members in the Association; ordinary, fellows and dispensing. Membership figures are as follows:

	1987	1992
Ordinary	17	10
Fellows	270	315
Dispensing	6	5
Totals	293	330

A fellow of the Association is a member who has passed the Association's clinical

1.7.2 examinations in optometry, has applied and has been admitted to the fellowship of the Association. A dispensing member means a member of the Association who holds, by examination, the Association's dispensing certificate or is otherwise entitled to be in the Register of the Opticians Board. This certificate is no longer being issued. The ordinary category of membership dates from a time when many optometrists practising in Ireland received their training and education in the United Kingdom. Essentially optometrists who have not passed the Association's clinical examinations but who are eligible for inclusion in the Opticians Board Register of ophthalmic opticians may apply for ordinary membership.

(c) *The Products Concerned*

6. The services provided by optometrists are eye examination, advice and, where necessary, the prescribing of spectacles and contact lenses. Visual assessment and certification for occupational and other purposes is also provided. Goods provided by optometrists are spectacles and contact lenses. Accessories for these products are also sold.

(d) *Legislation*

7. The prescribing of spectacles and contact lenses and the dispensing of such goods is regulated by the Opticians Act 1956. Under the Opticians Act, only a registered medical practitioner or a registered ophthalmic optician can prescribe spectacles. Similarly, only a registered medical practitioner or a registered optician can dispense prescriptions for spectacles. The relevant provisions in the Act are as follows:

> 47(1) A person shall not, on or after the appointed day, prescribe spectacles unless he is a registered medical practitioner or a registered ophthalmic optician.
> (2) A person shall not, on or after the appointed day, dispense prescriptions of registered medical practitioners or registered ophthalmic opticians for spectacles unless he is a registered medical practitioner or a registered optician. . . .

8. Section 49 of the Act prohibits the sale of spectacles unless it is done by or on behalf of a registered medical practitioner or a registered optician:

> 49(1) A person shall not, on or after the appointed day, sell spectacles unless —
>
> (a) in case the person is not a body corporate, the person is a registered medical practitioner or a registered optician or, if the sale is conducted on behalf of the person by another person that person is a registered medical practitioner or a registered optician, or
> (b) in case the person is a body corporate, the sale is conducted by a registered medical practitioner or a registered optician. . . .

9. Section 5 of the Act provides for the establishment of the Opticians Board as regulatory body for opticians. Sections 23 and 32 of the Opticians Act provide for the setting up and maintenance of the Register of Ophthalmic Opticians and the Register of Dispensing Opticians by the Board.

10. Practitioners may get their names placed on the Register if they have undergone and passed specified training courses.

The relevant provisions in the Act are as follows:

> 24. The Board shall, in accordance with rules, register in the Register of Ophthalmic Opticians a person who applies for such registration and who has undergone such courses of training and passed such examination (being courses of training and examinations under Part V of this Act) as are specified for the purposes of this section in the rules.

33. The Board shall, in accordance with rules, register in the Register of Dispensing Opticians a person who applies for such registration and who had undergone such courses of training and passed such examinations (being courses of training and examination under Part V of this Act) as are specified for the purposes of this section in the rules. **1.7.2**

The Opticians Board

11. The Opticians Act provides for the establishment of the Opticians Board, which has responsibility, inter alia, for the registration of Ophthalmic Opticians and Dispensing Opticians and for making rules regulating their activities.

12. The Opticians Board (the Board) was established under section 5 of the Opticians Act. It was empowered under section 18 of the Act to make rules (the Board's rules) relating to any matter referred to in the Act and generally for carrying the Act into effect. Sections 51 and 52 of the Act give the Board power to make penal rules for the regulation and control of prescribing, dispensing and sale of spectacles by registered opticians and for the control of advertising by registered opticians. Rules 28, 29, 30 and 31 of the Board, which relate to premises and advertising, are stated to be penal rules under the above mentioned sections of the Act, the contravention of which would leave the registered optician liable on summary conviction to be fined. Under sections 23 and 32 of the Act, the Board is required to set up Registers of Ophthalmic Opticians and Dispensing Opticians. Ophthalmic opticians can prescribe and dispense prescriptions for spectacles.

Dispensing opticians dispense prescriptions of registered medical practitioners or registered ophthalmic opticians.

13. Rule 30 of the Opticians Board deals with the regulation and control of sales of spectacles by registered opticians. It states that:

(b) Save as provided for in the next sub-paragraph no registered optician shall sell or offer for sale any spectacles save on a prescription issued following an examination by a registered medical practitioner or by a registered ophthalmic optician or by way of replacement of broken spectacles or lenses;

(c) Notwithstanding the preceding sub-paragraph a registered optician may sell spectacles without prescription for an adult person where the spectacles have two single vision lenses of the same positive spherical power not exceeding four dioptres and where the spectacles are intended to correct, remedy or relieve the condition known as presbyopia.

14. The functions of the Board include providing for the training of opticians and control of the practice of optics, in accordance with rules made by the Board with the approval of the Minister for Health. The Board's rules provide for a limited form of advertising by practitioners.

15. The Board consists of eleven members. Four of these are registered medical practitioners appointed by the Minister for Health; five are registered Ophthalmic Opticians and one is a registered Dispensing Optician — these members are elected by registered Opticians; one other person is appointed to the Board by the Minister.

Entry and Training

16. The examinations provided for under rule 21 of the Board in the case of candidates for registration on the Register of Ophthalmic Opticians are as follows:

(a) Such examinations as are prescribed by the City of Dublin Vocational Education Committee with the approval of the Board.

(b) Such examination in clinical practice as is approved by the Board.

Where a person satisfies the Board that he has passed a qualifying examination of a standard not lower than that which the Board requires candidates to pass, the Board may

1.7.2 exempt such person seeking registration from any examination or from any part of an examination.

In the case of candidates for registration in the Register of Dispensing Opticians, the following examinations are prescribed under rule 22:

(a) Such examinations as are prescribed by the City of Dublin Vocational Education Committee with the approval of the Board.
(b) Such examination in clinical practice as is approved by the Board.
Where a person satisfies the Board that he has passed a qualifying examination of a standard not lower than that which the Board requires candidates to pass, the Board may exempt such person seeking registration from any examination or from any part of an examination.

17. The course for optometrists is of four years full-time duration, leading to a diploma with honours classification of the Dublin Institute of Technology (DIT) which is under the control of the City of Dublin Vocational Education Committee (CDVEC). The course, which is considered to be of degree standard, is run at DIT Kevin Street, a constituent college of DIT, also known as the College of Technology, Kevin Street. This is the only course approved by the Opticians Board for the purposes of registration on the Register of Ophthalmic Opticians. Completion of this course, and of subsequent clinical examinations set by the Association of Optometrists Ireland (AOI), provides entitlement to register with the Opticians Board. However, other qualifications deemed by the Board to be equivalent to the above are acceptable for registration.[1] The clinical examination of the Association is the only one approved by the Opticians Board as fulfilling its requirements under Rule 21(b).

18. The course for Dispensing Opticians is the Certificate in Optical Dispensing. This is a three-year part-time course run at DIT Kevin Street, and requires attendance for the equivalent of two days per week. Students are required to be working as trainee dispensing opticians, under the supervision of a registered optician, for the remainder of the week. The course has been accepted by the Opticians Board as fulfilling its requirements for the training of dispensing opticians. Those who complete the course and pass professional examinations are entitled to register with the Opticians Board. As graduates from the first course for the Certificate in Optical Dispensing to be held in Ireland are not due to sit their final examinations until 1993, the application of rule 22(b) has not yet arisen.

19. The minimum standards required for entry to the courses at DIT Kevin Street are set out below. Admission is on a competitive basis, on the CAO/CAS system.

Diploma in Optometry:

(a) Irish Leaving Certificate in 6 subjects with grade C or higher in at least 2 Higher Level papers; subjects (at either level) must include English and Mathematics, or
(b) Such qualification as the College may deem equivalent.

Certificate in Optical Dispensing:

(a) Irish Leaving Certificate in 5 subjects (at either level) which must include Mathematics and English, or
(b) Such qualification as the College may deem equivalent.

20. There have been approximately 1000 applicants per year for the Diploma in Optometry. 14 applicants were accepted in 1987 and 1988, 20 have been accepted each year since then. It was stated by the Director of the DIT Course, who is a member of the Association, that the

1. Applicants from overseas could be accepted on to the Register under this provision.

number of places was limited to 20 per year due to shortages in the number of staff available to teach the relevant courses. It was also indicated that the College Authorities felt that 20 per year represented the number of optometrists required. In relation to the Certificate in Optical Dispensing, the course was started, in its present form, in January 1991. Recruitment is on a tri-annual basis. The number of applicants in the first year was 32 and 20 of these were admitted onto the course. 1.7.2

(e) *The Market*

21. The market in this instance is that for the provision of eye examinations, visual assessments, the prescription of spectacles and contact lenses, the sale of such goods and other services provided by optometrists. Detailed statistics on the market are not readily available. Almost everybody needs lenses at some stage of their lives - spectacles have a bigger share of the market than contact lenses. 40% of people in Western Europe have corrective lenses. Half of these are sold to over-40s. Only optometrists or medical practitioners may conduct eye examinations and prescribe spectacles or contact lenses. Both these groups together with dispensing opticians may dispense prescriptions and sell spectacles. A number of medical practitioners such as ophthalmologists and ophthalmic surgeons conduct eye examinations and prescribe spectacles. They generally do not sell spectacles but refer patients to ophthalmic opticians or dispensing opticians to have their prescriptions filled.

22. The numbers of practitioners included on each of the registers of the Optician's Board are as follows:

	Registered Ophthalmic Opticians	Registered Dispensing Opticians	Totals
1992	327	147	474
1990	324	149	473
1989	315	149	464
1988	300	166	466
1987	298	169	467

Having regard to Para. 5 above, which sets out membership details for the Association, it is evident that (a) virtually all practitioners on the Board's Register of Ophthalmic Opticians are members of the Association and (b) very few of those in the Register of Dispensing Opticians belong to the Association.

23. The form of business practice for optometrists varies. The majority of members practice as sole traders, other members are in partnerships, some are engaged as employees of members and some are employees of companies having more than one outlet. One of the features of the Irish market in recent years has been the entrance of large foreign owned companies. These companies have relied heavily on large advertising budgets and price discounting as competitive tools.

(f) *The Notified Arrangements*

24. The Association notified its Memorandum, Articles of Association and Code of Ethics. Observance of the Code, which derives mainly from the Rules of the Opticians Board, is binding on members of the Association. The main objectives of the Association as set out in its Memorandum of Association are as follows:

(1) The encouragement of (a) the Science of Optics, and (b) the art of the application of the Science of Optics to the improvement of Human Vision.

(2) The protection of the Members of the Association from influences inimical to the prosperity of the profession of an Optician.

The notification states that the arrangements contain no restrictions on members' freedom

1.7.2 to take individual commercial decisions 'other than a requirement that members abide by the provisions of the Opticians Act 1956 and the Rules of the Opticians Board'.

Articles of Association

25. The Articles of Association provide for the conduct of Annual General Meetings, Special General Meetings and procedures relating to election and operation of the Council of Management.

The Articles also contain provisions relating to entry to and expulsion from the Association. The relevant Articles relating to entry to the Association are as follows:

> 5. The Association shall consist of all persons whose names are registered in the Register of Members of the Association of Ophthalmic Opticians Ireland prior to the registration of the Association and of all persons who shall thereafter be admitted members.
> 6(a) Subject to Article 5 hereof no person shall be admitted as a Member of the Association unless he is duly elected in accordance with the provisions of this Article.
> (b) Every Applicant seeking admission to membership of the Association shall be over twenty-one years of age.
> (c) A Candidate may apply to be elected to Membership of the Association and the application for election shall be proposed and seconded in writing by two Members and the name, address and place of practice together with the names of his Proposer and Seconder shall be placed on the Notice convening the Meeting of the Council at which his application for admission is to be considered.
> (d) The election shall be carried out by ballot of the members of the Council present at the Meeting. If three-fourths of the members present ballot in favour of the Applicant he shall be declared duly elected and thereupon entitled to apply for admission to membership.
>
> 7(a) The members of the Association including those members who were admitted to the Association prior to the date of the registration of the Association shall consist of three classes, namely, (1) Fellows (2) Dispensing Members (3) Ordinary Members.
> (b) Subject to the provisions of these articles an ordinary member may be granted and may hold for so long as he continues to be a member of the Association a Certificate of Membership. An ordinary member shall not use the initials of the Association in connection with his practice or in any other way whatsoever but may indicate his membership by printing in reasonable small type on his letter headings or other business forms the words 'Member of the Association of Optometrists, Ireland' without contraction or abridgement.
> (c) A Member who has passed the Association's examinations in Optometry may apply to the Council to be admitted to the Fellowship of the Association and on application shall be admitted to the Fellowship and entitled to use the affix F.A.O.I. . . .
>
> 15. No person shall be admitted a member of the Association unless he is first approved by the Council and the Council shall have full discretion as to admission of any person to membership.

26. A number of Articles also relate to professional obligations and conduct. In this connection the following are of relevance:

> 19. Every member shall be bound to further to the best of his ability the objects interests and influence of the Association and to observe the ethical principles and the Regulations of the Association agreed to by the members in General Meeting.
> 20. No member of the Association shall advertise his connection with the Association

for trade or business purposes, but nothing herein shall operate to prevent any member so long as he remains a member from using the crest of the Association on his stationery. 1.7.2

27. Articles 21, 22 and 24 are concerned with procedures relating to expulsion of a member. Article 21(a) provides that:

> A member who is guilty of conduct which in the opinion of the Council is derogatory of the profession of Optics or renders him unfit to be allowed to remain a member of the Association may be excluded from membership.
>
> 21(b) provides that a member associated with a person guilty of such conduct shall also be deemed to be guilty of such conduct. Article 22 provides that at least 21 days' notice must be given to a member of any allegation that a member has engaged in such conduct, and provides the member with a right to be present and be heard at a meeting of the Council where such allegations are considered. Article 24 provides a right of appeal against suspension or expulsion to a Special General Meeting. A majority of three fourths of the members present at such a meeting is needed to overturn such a decision by the Council.

Code of Ethics

28. The Code of Ethics, which is binding on all members of the Association, gives guidance to optometrists in carrying out their professional services. Details of the Code are outlined below under various headings.

Premises and Advertising

29. The Code contains provisions relating to publicity under the headings 'Premises' and 'Advertising'. In addition certain rules of the Opticians Board are relevant in this context given that the Association requires its members to abide by these rules.

> PREMISES
> It is recommended that practices be sited in consulting rooms or offices without an external display, or a display within the initial reception area.
> The display of a dignified professional plate is recommended. The display of illuminated signs stating 'Eye Centre' or 'Contact Lens Centre' or such like are unprofessional, and are in contravention of the Rules of the Opticians Board.
> Practices should be laid out in such a way that the patient is allowed adequate privacy during waiting or consultations.

Rules 28 and 29 of the Opticians Board state that when not provided in the patient's home, services should be provided in a suitable apartment or space used primarily for such purposes and situated or constructed so as to ensure reasonable privacy for the customer.

> ADVERTISING
> Members should attract patients to their practices only by their professional skill and quality of service.
> Particular attention should be paid to the Rules of the Opticians Board on advertising. However, the Council feel that any form of window display is unprofessional. For guidance see Association resolution on voluntary abolition of window display.
> The declaration at the public level such as press, radio or television of name and profession, is unprofessional. The inclusion of a practitioner's title and qualifications in credits or lists of sponsors for non-optical events is unprofessional. Offering of discounts to clubs or organisations is unprofessional.

1.7.2 A revised code on advertising was issued to members of the Association in June 1989. The Authority only became aware of this revision on 30 October 1992. The revised code is as follows:

> Members should attract patients to their practices by their professional skill and quality of service. Particular attention should be paid to the Rules of the Opticians' Board on advertising.
> It is unethical and illegal under the present rules to make use of media features or articles to advertise, invite custom or promote a particular name, practice, business or company. Media advertising is permissible only in the public press as specified in the Rules of the Board and should be in the style of a business card, not more than 3.5 by 2 inches and in accordance with the Rules.[2] Thus, no art-work, drawings, illustrations or photographs shall be used in advertisements.
> The inclusion of a practitioner's title and qualifications in credits or lists of sponsors for non-optical events is unprofessional. Offering of discounts to clubs or organisations is unprofessional.

30. The rules of the Board on advertising which members are requested to observe are made under section 52 of the Opticians Act which gives the Board the power to make provision for the control of advertising. Rule 31 of the Board deals with restrictions on advertising. It contained a prohibition on canvassing but allowed a limited form of advertising subject to the following principles:

> — the purpose of such advertising shall be to inform the public of the availability of optical services and shall not seek to make comparisons with other optical practices nor claim any superiority over any other optical practice or business;
>
> — any such advertising shall not be misleading or untruthful or of a character that could reasonably be regarded as likely to bring the professions of ophthalmic optician or dispensing optician into disrepute.

The following forms of advertising were permitted under Rule 31(2)(ii):

> Subject to the preceding principles 'Responsible persons may:
> (a) exhibit at their practice or business premises:
>
> — signs giving their registered name and occupation;
>
> — notices that they are Optical Benefit Opticians or Medical Card Scheme Opticians, as the case may be;
>
> — notices that they supply and fit contact lenses.
>
> (b) display at their practice or business premises, spectacles, spectacle frames, contact lens accessories, spectacle cases, and illustrated cards displaying spectacles and spectacle frames. Prices may also be displayed and where prices are displayed it shall be clearly indicated what the prices include;
> (c) advertise in the public press and in directories and medical publications, and such advertisements shall not contain any photographs or illustrations or references to prices;
> (d) exhibit one small illuminated sign at their practice or business premises showing only their occupation as ophthalmic optician or dispensing optician, as entitled;

2. The Opticians Board indicated in a letter dated 24 February 1993, that they do not issue instructions on the size of advertisements in the public press.

(e) stamp or print their names, addresses and occupations on billheads, envelopes, notepaper, the case or box in which spectacles are sold or on any material provided for cleaning spectacles. **1.7.2**

This is stated to be a penal rule in accord with section 52 of the Opticians Act (see above).

31. Revised rules on advertising were introduced by the Board on 21 December 1992. A copy of the revised rules were received by the Authority on 26 January 1993. These rules are set out in the section on 'Subsequent Developments', at para. 62.

Fees and Charges

32. The provisions of the Code in respect of 'Fees and Charges' are as follows:

(1) Practitioners should charge for their service on a professional fee system, e.g. fee for examination, fee for dispensing, plus the cost of appliances or material supplied.
(2) Patients should be entitled to an explanation or breakdown of professional charges.

Restriction on establishment of practices by 'Employees'

33. The Code of Ethics provides that employees, on leaving employment, shall not strive to entice clients away from their former employer. It goes on to state that:

Proximity of premises to his former employers for the purpose of enticing patients is unethical.

Referral of Clients

34. The areas of optometrists' relationships with the patient's family doctor and with their colleagues are also covered by the Code:

Where a patient is referred to a colleague possessing extra skills or knowledge, e.g. orthoptist or contact lens practitioner, the referral should be done by a proper exchange of case history. The second practitioner should not take advantage of the trust placed in him by his colleague, by carrying out any work which the referring practitioner could carry out himself.

Submissions of the Association

35. The Association has supported the provisions of its code in respect of advertising as follows:

The opinion of Optmetry is that patients should be attracted to a practitioner mainly by the quality of the examinations and advice expected and usually by recommendation. It has been recognised in more recent times that the public has a right to more information about the spectacles they may need and so, as already indicated, the Association took the initiative in seeking a liberalisation of publicity and display rules.

The restrictions on advertising contained in Rule 31 of the Board are intended to prevent misleading and false information being advertised to the public and, as such, must be in the public interest. These restrictions are subject to review, as indicated, and have been subject to advice and comment from the Director of Consumer Affairs. The purpose of the Opticians Act is the protection of the public and that must be the continuing principle behind any liberalisation of advertising Rules or codes of ethics.

In addition, they have submitted that they do not regard the code on premises 'as a rule of the Association - rather as a recommendation. . . . It arose from a belief at the time of its discussion that the public should not be seduced by lavish frame displays in seeking a professional eye-care service which, in our view, should be provided without the overtones of

1.7.2 the fashion aspects of whatever appliances might result from the consultation. . . .'

In relation to the restriction on price advertising in the media, the Association have also stated that 'the restriction is, as we understand it, the law of the land, determined by the Opticians Board, and imposed under the authority of the Minister for Health. We feel, therefore that we have no option but to abide by those Rules. . . .'

In defence of the prohibition on discounts to clubs and associations, the Association have added that 'the prohibition on group discounts sprang from a belief that fees for professional services could not be subject to 'discounts'. Any person providing such services is at liberty to modify his fees or waive them in the face of the patient's circumstances and that has always been the case in health service professions. Health professions may well be considering this matter at this time. . . .'

In relation to fees and charges, the Association have submitted that:

> In line with the Association's view of the importance of unbiased advice, both in the consultation and in any spectacle dispensing which might follow, it is believed that the remuneration of optometrists should arise from fees for their professional services. This should apply both to consultation and dispensing services and the use of a 'mark-up' margin on appliances should be avoided. This enables objective advice on choice to be given, without monetary overtones.
>
> . . . This recommendation was introduced at a time when the fashion aspects of spectacle frames were developed, with corresponding spread of frame costs. It was our view that the work, time and expertise involved in dispensing spectacles had little direct relationship to the cost of frames and that a 'mark-up' system of determining charges to a patient created inordinately high prices and an incentive to recommend more costly frames unnecessarily. Many would still hold that view and the belief that the public is afforded more protection by our recommendation than otherwise. . . .

The Association made the point that it 'does not lay down any guidelines as to what constitutes proximity, nor has it taken any action against any member in such circumstances'.

Having regard to the Association's ethics on the referral of clients, they have stated that:

> The reasons for the provisions in the Code of Ethics are precisely the same as those which govern referral of patients by doctors or dentists for specialist opinion or treatment. Such patients are normally returned to the referring practitioner for the provision of such assessments and treatment as are within the competence of that practitioner. It is essential for the welfare of patients and for the most suitable assessment of their special needs that health care practitioners should make such referrals. The patient remains the patient of the referring practitioner.

In relation to Article 20 of the Articles of Association, the notifying parties have stated that this is a prohibition on advertising of Council membership, membership of a committee or some special form of membership in order to suggest some professional superiority over other practitioners.

36. An editorial in the Association's newsletter for January 1992 referred to the danger of bringing the profession into disrepute by means of advertising practices. This article stated inter alia that:

> Bringing the profession into disrepute (to use the legal sounding phrase) is a betrayal of colleagues, vocation and undertaking. On rare occasions this can occur through carelessness or stupidity, but all too often the act is deliberate and material by selfishness in an effort to steal a march on the colleagues of the perpetrator and gain some advantage,

usually imagined. **1.7.2**

Reneging from the recognised parameters as agreed by the professional group as a whole is the more shabby and selfish when it employs advertising trickery and gimmickry. This style of conduct damages the reputation of the profession by cheapening the dispensing role and taking the emphasis off the vision-care function of optometrists.

If our association is really determined to maintain the public image of the profession as one of integrity, then we must all act as exemplary representatives of our profession and close ranks against attempts to bring us into disrepute.

(g) *Views of Third Parties*

NPC Enquiry

37. The National Prices Commission (NPC) conducted an investigation into the price of spectacles in the early 1980's.

It concluded that:

> We are concerned at the lack of competition and consequently the implication from a price control standpoint which results from (i) the monopolistic situation, arising from the Opticians Act 1956, which makes it illegal for any person other than opticians to test sight or to supply spectacles or contact lenses, and (ii) the rules made by the Opticians Board under the same Act which prevent opticians from advertising their services or displaying their prices.

Investigation by the Examiner of Restrictive Practices

38. Following the publication of the NPC Report, an investigation was carried out by the Examiner of Restrictive Practices (The Examiner) in 1983/84 into the restrictions imposed by the Opticians Act 1956 on the supply and distribution of spectacles. The Examiner's investigation concerned two aspects of the Act: confining the sale of spectacles to registered medical practitioners or opticians and restrictions on advertising by opticians.

39. The Examiner considered that non-opticians should be allowed to sell spectacles in certain circumstances, excluding the sale of spectacles to children and the fitting of contact lens. He also concluded that the restrictions on advertising by opticians should be removed, to allow the consumer to be more aware of the prices, locations, services available, speed of dispensing, product guarantee and specialised services offered by opticians. The Examiner conveyed his recommendations for amendments to the Act to the Department of Health in March 1984.

40. The Opticians Board amended some of its rules in 1987. The Examiner welcomed these changes particularly the proposals to permit price displays at premises. He also made the point that while he would not at present urge that price advertising in the media be permitted, he would tend to favour such advertising, within limits.

U.K. Investigation

41. The impetus for the investigations by the NPC and by the Examiner was provided by similar investigations which had been carried out in the UK.

42. In 1982, the Director General of Fair Trading in the UK published a report of a review[3] concerning certain aspects of the UK Opticians Act 1958. The review was requested by the UK Minister of State for Consumer Affairs. The report found that the publicity rules which were in force at the time led to higher prices for spectacles and reduced the efficiency of opticians; it also suggested that the restrictions on the sale of spectacles could be lifted, but observed that there was a risk of eye disease going undetected. It concluded that restrictions

3. Opticians and Competition — a report by the Director General of Fair Trade on sections 21 and 25 of the Opticians Act 1958. Published by her Majesty's Stationery Office.

1.7.2 on the location of practices within department stores was not justified on clinical grounds and that such restrictions should be removed. It also concluded that the advertising restrictions result in prices being significantly higher and efficiency significantly lower than would otherwise be the case.[4]

43. Subsequent to that report, the opticians' monopoly on the sale of spectacles was ended on 10 December 1984 when the Sale of Optical Appliances Order came into effect, enabling ordinary retailers to sell complete spectacles, separate lenses and empty frames as long as appliances containing lenses or the lenses themselves are in accordance with a prescription from an ophthalmic optician which was not more than two years old. Under the Health and Medicines Act 1988, it became legal for ready-made reading glasses (which have simple magnifying lenses) to be sold over the counter without a prescription from 1 April 1989. The restrictions on advertising by opticians have also now been somewhat relaxed. Price advertising is allowed provided the advertisements are not unprofessional, unethical or misleading.

Director of Consumer Affairs

44. On 31 October 1990, complaints were received by the Director of Consumer Affairs and Fair Trade from solicitors representing Mr. Stephen Keough of Specsavers, Dublin and Messrs. Austin Kelly and Michael O'Connor of Specsavers, Cork. The complaints concerned the restrictions on advertising contained in Rule 31 of the Opticians Board which the complainants contended were unfair under restrictive practices legislation.

45. Mr. Keough had commenced his practice in January/February of 1990 and carried out an extensive advertising campaign to inform the public of his services and the availability of spectacles at 'keen' prices. Mr. Keough was contacted by the Opticians Board and was informed that his advertising was in breach of the advertising rules as prescribed by the Board.

46. The practice commenced by Messrs. Kelly and O'Connor was also widely advertised in the public press. They were also contacted by the Board and their attention was drawn to Rule 31, specifically to the prohibition on advertising in the public press and in directories and medical publications with advertisements which contained illustrations, photographs, reference to prices and the overriding principle that advertisements should not seek to make comparisons with other optical practices.

47. The Opticians Board submitted to the Director that selling spectacles was not like selling commercial products such as television sets, washing machines and cereals, which came in standard weights and sizes and could be compared in press advertisements.

48. The Board made the point that it was not just representative of the opticians profession, it was the statutory body appointed by the Minister for Health to act in the public interest in the carrying out of its functions under the Opticians Act and included in its membership persons appointed by the Minister who were not opticians. It claimed that its advertising rules were not unreasonable and did not constitute unfair practices. The Rules were stated to be in the interests of proper professional standards and the real difficulty was in getting other practitioners to abide by them in view of the deliberate and repeated breaches by Specsavers.

49. Mr. Keough, one of the complainants, stated that the ban on advertising photos and illustrations made an advertisement less useful and interesting and he could not see how such advertisements could harm the consumer. On the matter of prices, Mr. Keough considered that the absence of price information reduced competition and that opticians had been able to charge as much as they liked, due to the lack of consumer awareness. Until now, Specsavers advertised the price of frames and contact lenses, only, but he did not preclude the possibility of advertising the price of their services. He acknowledged that there was no such thing as a 'standard eye test' as testing would depend on the professional opinion of the optician. There were a number of other variables which he acknowledged could make a standard 'all-in' price meaningless, such as the variations in the sight test, the type of lens considered necessary and dispensing

4. Ibid., para. 14.19.

charges, nevertheless he was satisfied that some prices could be illustrated. 1.7.2

50. As regards whether there were any grounds for concern that standards could drop, Mr. Keough pointed out that Specsavers operated under the highest standards. Their operation depended on getting repeat business, therefore their services, products and equipment had to be top quality. The volume of sales enabled Specsavers to afford the best equipment.

51. The Director concluded that consumers should have access to as much information as possible in order to make a reasoned choice. He saw price advertising as an important element in this respect. He added that the restrictions on advertising were a restraint on competition and that they might exclude new entrants to the profession or at the very least make it more difficult to establish a new practice. He did not see any basis for the contention that the lifting of the restrictions on advertising would lead to a lowering of standards. He was of the view that the maintenance of standards was a separate issue from the question of advertising and competition.

52. The Director recommended a change in the Rules to remove the restrictions on specific advertising, i.e. press advertising, shop advertising, signs, letterheads, etc. As regards canvassing, he recommended that the rules should not prohibit the distribution of advertising material. He accepted, however, the recommendation of the Fair Trade Commission that professional bodies should be allowed to retain a degree of control over their members' advertising to ensure that the profession was not brought into disrepute and therefore recommended the same criteria as those established in the case of the accountancy profession.[5] The Opticians' Board might, therefore, provide that advertisements placed by their members:

— should not be such as would bring the profession into disrepute;

— should not be false or misleading in any respect;

— should not be in bad taste;

— should not reflect unfavourably on other persons in the profession.

In taking this decision, the Director was satisfied that the provisions of the Consumer Information Act 1978 and the assistance of the Advertising Standards Authority of Ireland (ASAI) would provide deterrents to any optician intending to abuse the new system. Furthermore, there were adequate sanctions in the Act should anyone publish a misleading advertisement.

53. The Department of Health was informed of the views of both Specsavers and the Board and the Director's concern that the Board's Rules were anti-competitive. It was indicated to the Director that the chief medical officer of the Department was not opposed to a liberalisation of the advertising rules.

Opticians Board

54. New Rules on Advertising have been approved by the Minister for Health. The text of the new requirements is set out in para. 62. These amendments have the effect of lifting many of the restrictions in the present Rule 31 on advertising.

55. These revised Rules allow price advertising provided that it is clearly indicated what precisely is included in the price quoted.

56. The Authority's attention was also drawn to proceedings instituted by the Opticians Board in 1991 against Specsavers for infringement of the Board's rules on advertising. Specsavers argued in reply that the Board's rules on advertising infringed Articles 85(1) and 86 of the Treaty of Rome and the Restrictive Practices Acts. The Opticians Board indicated to each registered optician in a letter of 13 March, 1991, that it had withdrawn from pursuing this prosecution for breaches of the advertising rules. In its letter the Board explained that 'what was becoming the issue was not whether there was a breach of the Rules but the legality of the

5. Restrictive Practices Commission (1987(a)); Report of Study into Concerted Fixing of Fees and Restrictions on Advertising in the Accountancy Profession 1987. Pl. 4862.

1.7.2 Rules themselves and that a referral of this issue to the European Court of Justice would be sought during the pending court proceedings. At the same time the Board was aware that these same issues had been referred to the Office of the Director of Consumer Affairs and Fair Trade for investigation. . . . It was in these circumstances the Board decided, on legal advice, not to embark on what could be very costly legal proceedings pending the clarification of the legality of the Board's Rules'.

Donal MacNally Opticians Ltd

57. Donal MacNally Opticians Ltd submitted to the Authority that the Association's rules on advertising and discounts contained in the Code of Ethics restrict competition within the meaning of section 4(1) of the Act.

58. The comments of Donal Mac Nally Opticians Ltd on advertising are set out below:

> The present Association rules on advertising are based on those of the Opticians Board. Both sets of rules have been in force, substantially unchanged, for the last thirteen years or so. The original purpose of the rules was to prevent any form of advertising which could possibly encourage members of the public to choose an optometrist on any basis other than that he was a qualified practitioner.
>
> In the past it was felt that, as all optometrists had to achieve a common standard of education before registration as an optometrist, the quality of the sight test offered would be the same, whichever practitioner was chosen. The sight test was seen as the primary function of optometrists whilst the spectacle frames, which ultimately hold the corrective lenses, were purely functional. The dispensing of spectacles was thus a secondary function and it was felt that promotion of this function would cause patients to choose their optometrist for the 'wrong' reason.
>
> The current situation is dramatically different. Spectacle frames are now very much fashion accessories. In addition, there is a wide choice of lenses in different forms, different materials and with different surface treatments. The average member of the public demands information, the right to make an informed choice and to buy from a competitive retailer. This situation will be brought about more quickly by the use of advertising and promotions, as it would any other high fashion retail sector, but will happen whether advertised or not. The advertising can then be controlled by the sort of general control imposed by the Advertising Standards Authority, in just the same way as any other retail function.
>
> The Association's rules on advertising have, therefore, the effect of seriously restricting competition in the optical market in Ireland, particularly given the recent changes in the market. Advertising is a vital element of competition. However, the rules permit advertising in only very limited circumstances. By restricting members of the Association from advertising and, therefore, competing with each other, the Company believes that the rules of the Association are in breach of section 4(1).

59. Donal Mac Nally Opticians Ltd stated that the entry into the Irish market of large foreign companies had intensified competition and placed Irish companies in a position where they had to respond or their market position would be undermined. They pointed to the fact that two of the Company's branches had to be closed as evidence of this. In these circumstances, the company decided to introduce an advertising campaign at the end of 1991 in an attempt to maintain market share. Subsequently, the Council of the Association took proceedings against Mr. MacNally alleging that the advertisements in question constituted a breach of the Code of Ethics. Donal Mac Nally Opticians Ltd claimed that if the Association were to expel a member, the optometrist concerned would have to arrange his own professional indemnity insurance and could expect to incur premium costs in excess of those presently negotiated by the Association on behalf of its members. They also claimed that this rule would appear to place

practitioners who were not members of the Association at an advantage as they could advertise without fear of any legal action from the Association for breach of its rules. **1.7.2**

60. In relation to discounts, the company submitted that:

> The Association has also complained about certain discount vouchers which the Company has offered. . . . The Council is alleging that the vouchers breach the Code of Ethics.
>
> Discounts are an important element of competition, as much as prices, terms and conditions of sale, payment periods, credit facilities, etc. Consequently, the Company believes that any restriction on discounts is also a breach of section 4(1) of the Act.

Lynx Optique

61. In a submission of 3 July 1992, Lynx Optique, a company with 65 optical outlets internationally, stated that:

> Where we can wholeheartedly accept certain restrictions on advertising, we do feel it is unprofessional to deprive the consumer of a minimum of information. . . . The consumer has a right to a minimum of information to guide his choice of eye-care specialist.

Subsequent Developments

62. The Authority expressed its concerns to the Association in respect of certain aspects of its code of ethics and, following a meeting with the Authority, the Association indicated by letter dated 22 December 1992, its intention to amend its code as follows:

> Those sections of the Code of Ethics which:
> (a) specify the siting of practices in a specific way,
> (b) recommend a particular method of charging for services and appliances, and
> (c) the entire section on advertising, including the reference to discounts,
> should be suspended pending the coming into effect of new Rules on Advertising through the Opticians Board and the consequential and necessary re-writing of the entire Code of Ethics. . . .

They also stated that 'those Members who have been suspended are now free to resume full Membership should they so wish. . . .'

63. The revised advertising rules of the Opticians Board were made on 21 December 1992. They are as follows:

> 31 The following is the Rule under section 52(1) of the Act for the control of advertising.
> (1) The Rule applies to
> (a) a registered optician in relation to the dispensing of prescriptions for spectacles or the sale of spectacles
> (b) a registered optician in relation to the prescribing of spectacles or the provision of orthoptic treatment and
> (c) every person (including a corporate body) whether a registered optician or not in relation to the sale of spectacles conducted by a registered optician.
>
> (2) Registered opticians, and corporate bodies or other bodies employing the services of registered opticians shall not canvass for business whether on their own behalf or on behalf of any other person or body corporate. Communication with, or issue of reminders to persons who have previously been provided with services or optical appliances shall not be regarded as canvassing.
> (3) (i) Registered opticians, and corporate bodies or other bodies employing the services of registered opticians, may publicise their businesses or practices in relation to the

1.7.2 prescribing, display or sale of spectacles, subject to the overriding principle that the main purpose of such publicity shall be to inform the public of the availability of optical services and the nature of the services provided.
(ii) Prices may be advertised or displayed, and if so it shall be clearly indicated what precisely is included in the price quoted.
(iii) Spectacles, spectacle frames, contact lens accessories, spectacle cases, and illustrated cards displaying spectacles and spectacle frames may only be displayed at practice premises.
(iv) Any publicity engaged in shall not

(a) be false or misleading in any respect;
(b) be of a character that could reasonably be regarded as being in bad taste or likely to bring the professions of ophthalmic optician or dispensing optician into disrepute;
(c) seek to make comparisons with other optical practices or claim superiority over or reflect unfavourably on other optical practices or businesses.

(4) All practices shall show in their windows or on nameplates, at their practice or business premises the names and designation of the registered opticians providing services at those premises, and if the registered opticians are not in attendance on a full time basis, the days and times at which they provide services at those premises.
This Rule is hereby stated in accordance with section 52 (2) of the Act, to be a penal rule.

64. The Association, by letter of 27 January 1993, stated that '. . . a circular is being prepared, and will issue to members shortly, suspending those sections of the present Code referred to in our letter of 22 December 1992 (see para. 61). I am also to inform you that those members suspended during the past year have indicated their wish to resume full membership and the matter will come before the Council at its February meeting'.

64. The Association informed the Authority by letter of 23 March, 1993, that the circular referred to in Para. 64 was issued to members in February 1993. This letter stated inter alia that:

> The Council has therefore decided to suspend the following sections of the Code, pending a re-writing of the entire document:
> (1) PREMISES
> (2) ADVERTISING
> (3) FEES AND CHARGES

Assessment

(a) *Section 4(1)*

65. Section 4(1) of the Competition Act states that 'all agreements between undertakings, decisions by associations of undertakings and concerted practices which have as their object or effect the prevention, restriction or distortion of competition in trade in any goods or services in the State or in any part of the State are prohibited and void'.

(b) *The Parties*

66. The present arrangements involve the Memorandum and Articles of Association along with the Code of Ethics of the Association of Optometrists Ireland, which is incorporated as a limited company. The Association is a representative body established primarily to promote the interests of its members.[6]

6. See, for example, Competition Authority Decision No. 1, Nallen/O'Toole (CA/8/91), 2 April 1992.

67. The present notification differs from those previously dealt with by the Authority in that it concerns the activities of a professional association. The members of the association are optometrists registered with the Opticians Board in accordance with the Opticians Act 1956. The members include optometrists who are self-employed operating their own practice as well as optometrists employed either in the practice of another member or by a company. Section 3(1) of the Act defines an undertaking as 'a person being an individual, a body corporate or an unincorporated body of persons engaged for gain in the production, supply or distribution of goods or the provision of a service.' The provision of ophthalmic and dispensing services by optometrists constitutes the provision of services while the selling of spectacles and other lenses clearly constitutes the supply of goods. Optometrists who are self-employed or running their own practice are clearly engaged for gain in the provision of goods and services and are undertakings. The Authority has previously stated in a number of decisions that individuals who own or control a business constitute undertakings within the meaning of the Act. 1.7.2

68. EC precedents under Article 85 of the Treaty of Rome, on which section 4(1) is based, offer some guidance concerning the definition of associations of undertakings. Many of these have involved trade associations. Van Bael and Bellis define a trade association as follows:

> A trade association is an organisation that reflects, encourages and promotes the interests of a given industry or economic sector. In its 'typical' form a trade association is composed of undertakings — usually competitors — that have come together to share experiences and ideas which may contribute to a general improvement of the industry.[7]

69. Under EC law, as Bellamy and Child point out:

> Although trade associations of various kinds are the commonest 'associations of undertakings' the word 'associations' is not limited to any particular type of association. It includes agricultural co-operatives, associations without legal personality, non-profit making associations, associations of associations and an association outside the Community.[8]

The legal form of the association has been found to be irrelevant.[9]

70. The Authority recognises that a professional association differs in some respects from a trade association. In its view, however, there is no reason to treat a professional association any differently under the Competition Act to any other type of association. The view that professional associations were by their nature exempt from competition laws was rejected by the US Supreme Court.[10] An association whose object is to represent the interests of its members as undertakings is, in the Authority's view, an association of undertakings. Consequently the Association of Optometrists is an association of undertakings within the meaning of section 4(1), as some of its members are undertakings and its object is to promote its members' professional interests.

(c) *The Arrangements*

71. The Association's Memorandum and Articles of Association, together with its Code of Ethics, constitute a decision or decisions of an association. This view is also supported by EC precedents:

7. I. Van Bael and J.F. Bellis (1990); 'Competition Law of the EEC', 2nd ed., CCH Editions Ltd, para. 702.
8. C. Bellamy and G. Child (1987); 'Common Market Law of Competition', 3rd ed., Sweet & Maxwell, London, para. 2-032.
9. See Milchforderungsfonds, 85/76/EEC, OJ L35/35, 7.2.85.
10. See, *Goldfarb., et. us. v. Virginia State Bar et. al.*, (1975).

1.7.2 The concept of 'decision' includes the rules of the association in question, decisions binding upon the members and recommendations. Agreements implemented within the framework of the association concerned may be analysed either as 'decisions' of that association or 'agreements' between the members.[11]

72. As pointed out in para 24 the notification states that the arrangements contain no restrictions on members' freedom to take individual commercial decisions 'other than a requirement that members abide by the provisions of the Opticians Act 1956 and the Rules of the Opticians Board.' The Code of Ethics expressly states that; 'Particular attention should be paid to the Rules of the Opticians Board on advertising.' Both these requirements also constitute a decision by an association of undertakings and the notified arrangements, therefore, include the provisions of the Opticians Act and the Rules of the Opticians Board in so far as members of the Association are obliged to observe such rules. This is in line with previous decisions where the Authority regarded arrangements which constituted part of the notified agreement as being part of that agreement.[12] The Authority's view is supported by the fact that in applying Article 85 of the Treaty of Rome on which section 4(1) of the Competition Act is based, the EC Commission and Court of Justice have accepted that: 'A series of connected agreements will be read together as one agreement'.[13]

73. The Opticians Act restricts the prescribing of spectacles and dispensing of prescriptions for spectacles to registered opticians and medical practitioners and generally regulates trade in such goods and services. A number of the Act's provisions, including the restriction on entry, restrict competition in the market for spectacles. The Authority does not believe, however, that these restrictions offend against section 4(1) of the Competition Act as they are enshrined in separate legislation and do not constitute an agreement between undertakings, a decision by an association of undertakings or a concerted practice between undertakings. The Association's requirement that members abide by the terms of the Opticians Act does not offend against section 4(1) of the Competition Act.

74. The Opticians Act allows the Board to establish rules for the profession. The Authority, however, takes the view that the Association's requirement that its members observe the Rules of the Board would offend against section 4(1) of the Competition Act, if those rules were in conflict with that section. This decision is without prejudice to any view as to whether the Opticians Board is itself subject to the provisions of the Competition Act.

(d) *Applicability of section 4(1)*

75. The Competition Act does not contain any blanket prohibition on the existence of trade or professional associations or on their activities. It is only decisions of associations of undertakings which have as their object or effect the prevention, restriction or distortion of competition which are prohibited under section 4(1).

> 'As a general rule, activities that are lawful when engaged in by competitors acting jointly are lawful for trade associations. Conversely, activities that are unlawful when engaged in by individuals acting together are quite simply unlawful when undertaken by trade associations.'[14]

76. The Association claimed that its Code of Ethics merely set out recommendations for its members. The European Court of Justice has ruled however, that:

11. Bellamy and Child at para. 2-031.
12. See, for example, Competition Authority Decision No. 4 — Esso Solus and Related Agreements (CA/11-14/91E), 25 June 1992, where the Authority decided that the practices of informing solus dealers of proposed retail price changes constituted part of the notified arrangements.
13. Bellamy and Child, at para. 2-017.
14. Van Bael and Bellis at para. 703.

> A recommendation of an association of undertakings, even if it has no binding effect, cannot escape that article [85(1)] where compliance with the recommendations by the undertakings to which it is addressed has an appreciable influence on competition in the market in question.[15] **1.7.2**

Consequently the claim that the Code merely contains recommendations does not put it outside the scope of section 4(1).

Memorandum and Articles of Association

77. Article 3(2) of the Memorandum of Association provides that one of the objects of the Association is:

> The protection of the Members of the Association from influences inimical to the prosperity of the profession of an Optician.

The Authority recognises that the protection and promotion of its members' interests is a legitimate activity for a professional association to engage in, and, in general, such activities are not anti-competitive. The Authority notes, however, that anti-competitive activities are frequently justified on the grounds that they are necessary to protect the interests of those engaging in them or the broader public interest. The Authority has no reason to believe that this Article has been used or interpreted in that way. The Authority considers that the Article does not offend against section 4(1) of the Competition Act per se, but notes that where measures to protect members interests extend to include restrictions on competition, they are prohibited under 4(1).

78. Entry to this particular market, as already stated, is restricted by the provisions of the Opticians Act. Given such legal restrictions, however, the Authority considers that any additional restrictions on entry would constitute a serious restriction on competition.

79. Article 6 of the Articles of Association outlines the procedures for admission to membership of the Association. In particular, Article 6(d) specifies that three-fourths of the Council members present must vote in favour of an applicant to be elected to membership of the Association. In addition Article 15 provides that: 'No person shall be admitted a member of the Association unless he is first approved by the Council and the Council shall have full discretion as to admission of any person to membership.'

80. Virtually all optometrists are members of the Association.[16] 315 of the 330 members of the Association are fellows. The Association has indicated that only 1 applicant for membership was refused in the past 5 years. It indicated that this applicant was refused due to the lack of a qualified proposer and seconder.

81. Membership of the Association is not compulsory in order for an individual to practise as an optician. Van Bael and Bellis point out, however, that under EC competition law membership of a trade association should be open to any interested party in that sector on the grounds that an association normally serves to represent the interests of an entire industry.[17] Again, while noting that there are differences between a trade association and a professional association, the Authority considers that membership of such bodies should generally be open to all those engaged in the profession.

82. EC decisions under Article 85(1) indicate that membership rules must be based on

15. *NV IAZ International Belgium and Others v. EC Commission,* Case Nos. 96-102, 104, 105, 108 and 110/82 [1983] ECR 3369-3430, point 3. This restated a view that the Court had expressed in a number of previous cases. These views echo those expressed by the US Supreme Court in Goldfarb v. Virginia State Bar.
16. The Association indicated that it has 325 Fellows and ordinary members, while the Board stated that there are 327 opthalmic opticians on its register. In addition the Association has 5 dispensing members.
17. Van Bael and Bellis at para. 701.

1.7.2 reasonable and objective standards.[18] In the Cauliflowers case, the European Commission decided that a requirement that a majority of the Board of Directors of an association be in favour before a new member could be admitted was in breach of Article 85(1), on the grounds that a new entrant would be competing with the directors who would therefore be unlikely to agree to admit the applicant. In that case, however, only members of the association concerned could operate in the market in question. While membership of the Optometrists' Association is not compulsory in order to compete in the relevant market it may be that individuals unable to join would be placed at a serious competitive disadvantage relative to members. In particular if the public felt that non-members were in some sense less qualified than members, then restrictions on entry to the Association could distort competition. Members also enjoy some advantage over non-members as a result of the lower rates of professional liability insurance that the Association has negotiated. This could also place non-members at a competitive disadvantage.

83. The fact that only one application for membership has been refused during the past 5 years indicates that this Article has not been operated in such a way as to restrict competition. Consequently the Authority does not believe that Articles 6 and 15 offend against section 4(1).

84. Article 7 provides for three classes of members; ordinary, dispensing and fellows. The Association has stated that the distinction between ordinary members and fellows dates from a time when many optometrists received their training and qualifications overseas. Admission to fellowship is restricted to those who have passed the Association's clinical examination in Optometry. As the Association's clinical examination constitutes one of the requirements for qualification for inclusion on the Opticians Board register of opticians, all Irish trained optometrists are entitled to be elected as fellows. The Board may admit to the Register anyone who can establish that they have passed an examination of equivalent standard. Consequently individuals with overseas qualifications which are deemed to be the equivalent of the Association's examination will be registered by the Board. Yet such individuals may only be admitted as ordinary members and not as fellows of the Association despite having qualifications which the Board deems to be equivalent to those required for admission to fellowship.

85. The Association have claimed that individuals who qualified overseas may sit for the Association's clinical examination and, if they pass, they will be admitted to Fellowship. The Association has also argued that individuals who hold recognised overseas qualifications are entitled to cite such qualifications. Provided the Association does not seek to create the impression that Fellows of the Association are more highly skilled than overseas trained optometrists, thereby placing the latter group at a competitive disadvantage, the Authority believes that the restriction of the title of Fellow to those who have passed the Association's examination does not offend against section 4(1).

86. Article 7(b) provides that an ordinary member may not use the initials of the Association in connection with his practice or in any other way whatsoever but may indicate his membership by printing in reasonable small type on letter headings or business forms the words 'Member of the Association of Optometrists, Ireland'. Article 7(c) provides that fellows are entitled to use the suffix F.A.O.I. Article 20 then provides that no member shall advertise his connection with the Association for trade or business purposes. The Association has indicated that the latter restriction only applies to individuals advertising their membership of the council of the association or of a particular committee or working party set up by the association. It is to ensure that members of such groups do not seek to convey the impression to the public that they offer a superior service by virtue of such membership. The Authority has considered the wider issue of advertising restrictions included in the Code of Ethics. It does not believe that the restrictions in articles 7 and 20 offend against section 4(1).

18. See, for example, Central Bureau voor de Rijwielhandel, 78/59/EEC, OJ L20, 26.1.78, p. 18, Cauliflowers, 78/66/EEC, OJ L21, 26.1.78, p. 23, Papiers peints de Belgique, 74/431/EEC, OJ L237, 29.8.74, p. 3, Gas water-heaters and bath-heaters, 73/2323/EEC, PJ L217, 6.8.73, p. 237.

87. Articles 21, 22 and 24 are concerned with the procedures relating to the expulsion of a member. Article 21(a) provides that: 1.7.2

> A member who is guilty of conduct which in the opinion of the Council is derogatory of the profession of Optics or renders him unfit to be allowed remain a member of the Association may be excluded from membership.

21(b) provides that a member associated with a person guilty of such conduct shall also be deemed to be guilty of such conduct. Article 22 provides that at least 21 days notice must be given to a member of any allegation that he has engaged in such conduct, and provides the member with a right to be present and be heard at a meeting of the Council where such allegations are considered. Article 24 provides a right of appeal against suspension or expulsion to a Special General Meeting. A majority of three fourths of the members present at such a meeting is needed to overturn such a decision by the Council.

88. Again the Authority does not consider that these Articles per se offend against section 4(1) of the Competition Act. If, however, expulsion or the threat of expulsion effectively represented a means of enforcing anti-competitive practices, then it would take the opposite view. It is relevant, in this context, that certain acts described in the Association's Code of Ethics as unprofessional or unethical are, in the Authority's view, anti-competitive. The Association have indicated that unprofessional or unethical behaviour could be regarded as being in breach of Article 21(a) although it would depend on the form of the conduct and its duration or persistence. It has been submitted to the Authority that some members have in fact been suspended and threatened with expulsion for breaching the Association's rules on advertising and offering discounts. As the Authority regards these rules as anti-competitive, it believes that the suspension or expulsion of a member for breaking such rules offends against section 4(1).

89. The Board is empowered under the terms of the Opticians Act to establish rules for the courses of training and examinations to be taken by candidates in order to be registered as ophthalmic or dispensing opticians. Rule 21 of the Board provides that to be admitted to the register of ophthalmic opticians an individual must pass the examination held by the City of Dublin VEC, who provide the training course prescribed by the Board for such candidates, and an examination in clinical practice approved by the Board. The Association of Optometrists is the only body recognised to conduct the Board's clinical examination for ophthalmic opticians, and this is also the examination specified in Article 7(c) as a requirement for admission to Fellowship of the Association.

90. The Authority notes that only 20 new applicants are accepted each year by the DIT for the diploma in optometry course from a total of 1,000 applicants. This serious mismatch between the number of applicants and the number of places available is a matter of some concern to the Authority as it suggests that many individuals who would like to enter the profession are being denied the opportunity of doing so. The number of places was said to be limited to 20 per year due to shortages in the number of staff available to teach the relevant courses and because the College Authorities felt that 20 per year represented the number of optometrists required. The Authority accepts that without an increase in resources the level of student intake could not be increased. It is concerned, however, at any notion that intake is being decided on the basis of perceived demand. Certainly if such a limit reflected a view of the Association on perceived requirements, the Authority would regard this as a serious restriction on competition.

91. The views expressed by the Fair Trade Commission in its Report on the Legal Profession are particularly relevant in this context.[19] It noted specifically that:

19. Fair Trade Commission (1990); 'Report of Study into Restrictive Practices in the Legal Profession', Dublin, Stationery Office.

1.7.2 The fact that each profession, however, exercises complete control over the numbers of persons admitted to the profession, and their qualifications, is clearly of direct and critical relevance to the Commission. Barriers to entry are one of the most important factors in the analysis of competition. If the barriers to entry are set at a very high level, with relatively few entrants as a consequence, there tends to be a lessening of competitive pressures, and a weakening, in particular, of price competition. As a group or individually, members of a profession may be enabled to exercise market power, to raise prices above competitive levels, and to enjoy monopoly profits. Within the scope of the practices listed in the 1972 Act, referred to in para. 3.37, restrictions on the numbers entering imposed by a profession itself appear to the Commission to be designed to exclude new entrants to the profession, and they appear to restrict or to be likely to restrict the exercise by any person of his freedom of choice as to what services he will supply. Such entry restrictions are likely also to secure a substantial or complete control of the provision of a class of services, and are likely to have the effect of limiting or restraining free and fair competition, and of being in restraint of trade.[20]

92. The Commission went on to state that:

The great danger arising from a situation where the existing members of a profession can determine precisely how many new entrants are admitted to the profession, in the opinion of the Commission, is that the number admitted might be restricted to a level which was believed to match the perceived requirements of the profession, and not of the public. If the power of controlling entry to the profession is exercised in the light of the profession's own perception of the demand for members of the profession, this is quite likely to lead to a situation where the protection and promotion of the interests of those already within the profession becomes paramount, however much this might be claimed to be in the public interest. The Commission considers that such self-protection would amount to both a restrictive practice and an abuse of a dominant position which would be seriously disadvantageous to the common good. In principle, the Commission favours freedom of entry to a profession, consistent with the maintenance of acceptable, but not excessive, standards, with the market for professional services being allowed to determine the numbers of practitioners.[21]

The Code of Ethics

93. A number of the provisions of the Code of Ethics raise questions from a competition perspective. These are now considered.

(i) *Relationships with our colleagues*

94. The Code provides that where a member refers a patient to a colleague possessing extra skills or knowledge, e.g. contact lens specialist, the second practitioner 'should not take advantage of the trust placed in him by his colleague, by carrying out any work which the referring practitioner could carry out himself.' It could be argued that this prevents patients from obtaining all of their requirements from the more highly qualified practitioner, albeit at a possibly higher cost. It is claimed by the Association that it is essential for the welfare of patients and for the most suitable assessment of their special needs that health care practitioners should make such referrals. The Authority accepts this point and would regard it as detrimental to patients' welfare if in fact practitioners were to be discouraged from referring patients to more specialised colleagues for necessary treatment because they would lose the patient's custom. Similarly it may be that if only a small number of practitioners can provide specialist

20. Para. 7.128.
21. Para. 7.129.

services, it is in the overall interests of consumers that they specialise in the provision of such services and not offer services available from the general body of practitioners. In the Authority's view this requirement does not offend against section 4(1). 1.7.2

95. The Code also provides that a practitioner should not deal professionally with a patient whilst the patient is currently receiving attention from a colleague. Provided this is not interpreted in such a way that the patient is effectively denied the option of changing from one optician to another, if dissatisfied with the service offered, the Authority believes that it would not offend against section 4(1).

(ii) *Premises*

96. The Code as notified set out certain guidelines relating to premises. In particular, it recommended that practices be sited in consulting rooms or offices without an external display, or a display within the initial reception area. (The question of displays is considered in the context of the restrictions on advertising below). It also provided that practices should be laid out in such a way that the patient is allowed adequate privacy during consultation.

97. These guidelines reflect requirements set out in the Rules of the Opticians Board. Rules 28 and 29 provide that examination, refraction, fitting and all consultations should either be carried out in the patient's home or in a suitable apartment or space used primarily for such purposes, so situated or constructed as to ensure reasonable privacy of the patient. These are penal rules under section 51 of the Opticians Act which allows the Board to make rules for the regulation and control of the prescribing, dispensing and sale of spectacles by registered medical practitioners, or registered opticians.

98. As pointed out in para 42 the UK Director General of Fair Trading found that guidelines issued by the relevant UK opticians' associations concerning the siting of optical practices were unnecessary. These guidelines related to the siting of practices within department stores and set out minimum standards, including reference to the need for privacy and comfort along with a requirement that the practice should be a fully enclosed unit with doors capable of being made secure. The Report argued that such restrictions might prevent new or existing practices from offering services in a new or innovative way, or in a manner or setting which would be more convenient to the customer. It also argued that such restrictions were not related to clinical matters but were instead concerned with the levels of privacy preferred by patients, which patients could decide for themselves.

99. The Authority agrees with the sentiments expressed in the UK report, that such restrictions are unnecessary, and are not concerned with clinical practice but with matters of patient privacy. Patients are quite capable of deciding for themselves to what extent they require privacy when obtaining such services. Such rules may in fact prevent, restrict or distort competition in so far as they could prevent new entrants or existing practitioners from offering services in a new or innovative way, or in a manner or setting which would be more convenient to the customer. The Authority notes that any attempts to provide such innovative services could not succeed unless there was a demand for them. As the Association have indicated that they are withdrawing the references to premises from their Code of Ethics, the question of offending against section 4(1) no longer arises.

100. As pointed out the Authority is only concerned with the Board's rules in so far as the arrangements notified by the Association of Optometrists require members to abide by such rules. It recognises, however, that even without such a requirement, optometrists face a strong incentive to observe the Board's rules where such rules are designated as penal rules which involve penalties for breaching them. The Authority believes that individuals or firms offering a particular service should be largely free to decide upon the type and location of premises they wish to operate from. The location of the premises combined with its lay-out and other features are a component part of the various factors which attract consumers to a particular supplier and are therefore a means by which suppliers compete with one another in attracting customers. Rules 28 and 29 of the Opticians Board concerning premises could prevent, restrict or distort

1.7.2 competition. Admittedly the Rules do not appear to have been interpreted in a restrictive way and have not prevented a number of innovative developments such as the location of optometrists premises in high street retail outlets, in offices adjoining other types of retail premises or the provision of services in business premises to any employee of such business who wishes to avail of them. The Authority believes, however, that a less restrictive rule may be possible.

(iii) *Advertising*

101. The Code, as originally notified to the Authority, contained a number of restrictions on advertising. Members were also required to adhere to the Board's Rules on advertising. During the proceedings the Authority was informed that this section of the Code had been amended by a letter dated June 1989. Details of the amendments are given in para 29 above. The Authority is concerned that considerable time was devoted to considering obsolete rules since amendments made to these rules had not been notified.

102. The Authority believes that the restrictions on advertising set out in the Code of Ethics involved a serious restriction on competition. In particular it considers that individuals should be free to advertise their qualifications and the services offered in whatever manner they think fit. Consequently in its view restrictions on the content, type and size of advertisements, together with restrictions on members' names, titles and professions being referred to in media articles, and in the sponsorship of non-optical events, restrict competition and offend against section 4(1). In addition the requirement to observe the Board's rules by which members of the Association were precluded from (a) advertising in media other than newspapers, (b) quoting prices in media advertisements and (c) from using signs which did not conform to certain specifications, also constituted a restriction of competition which offended against section 4(1).

103. The Authority also believes that restrictions on advertising generally serve to prevent new entrants from becoming established in the market and that they therefore protect existing undertakings from competition. It is significant, in this regard, that in recent years one third of newly qualified graduates are estimated to have emigrated. While it has been suggested that this reflects the fact that there is insufficient demand for additional practitioners, the Authority believes that it may indicate that it is extremely difficult for new entrants to establish themselves in the business due to the restrictions on advertising. It is relevant in this context that UK based firms have successfully entered the market as a result of extensive advertising campaigns.

104. Specific restrictions on advertising prices represent, in the Authority's view, a further serious restriction on competition. Such a restriction by denying important information to consumers makes it difficult for them to choose an optometrist. In addition, the Authority notes that overseas evidence indicates that restrictions on price advertising by health care service providers, and by optometrists in particular, have been found to result in higher prices to consumers than would otherwise be the case.[22]

105. The Authority does not consider that there is any good reason for preventing price advertising. Indeed the fact that the Board has allowed window displays, including prices since 1981, indicates that price advertising is possible. The Authority welcomes the fact that restrictions on price advertising in the media have now been abolished by the Board.

106. Advertising, including the quoting of prices is, in the Authority's view, a legitimate means of attracting business. The Authority also believes that, in general, restrictions on price advertising represent a serious restriction on competition which cannot be justified. In this

22. This was the conclusion of the Report of the UK Director General of Fair Trading on opticians. In the United States in Massachusetts Board of Registration in Optometry (110 FTC 549 (1988)), it was found that restrictions on advertising raised prices to anti-competitive levels. Economic analysis in support of this is provided by J.A. Langenfeld and J.R. Morris; 'Analyzing Agreements Among Competitors: What does the future hold?', The Antitrust Bulletin, Vol. XXVI No. 3, Fall 1991, pp. 651-679.

respect its view is in accord with those expressed by the Fair Trade Commission in its reports on the legal,[23] engineering[24] and accountancy professions.[25] In particular the Authority agrees with the views expressed in the latter report to the effect that: **1.7.2**

> If a practitioner cannot advertise his fees, there is less incentive for him to engage in fees competition, and clients are not likely to become aware very rapidly that lower fees are available. If price competition is allowed, then it is virtually axiomatic that advertising of fees should not be forbidden, and in most cases, freedom to advertise fees is essential for effective price competition.[26]

107. The Authority notes that the Board, in a letter dated 13 March 1991, indicated to opticians that it had withdrawn actions against certain firms after they had claimed that the restriction on advertising might be in breach of Articles 85 and 86 of the Treaty of Rome, and that, following complaints to the Director of Consumer Affairs regarding the restrictions on price advertising, the Board proposed to amend its rules so as to allow optometrists to advertise in all forms of newsmedia and to quote prices in such advertisements. In spite of this the Association suspended some members who were alleged to have breached these rules.

108. It was claimed to the Authority that expulsion from membership of the Association could have adverse effects on the businesses concerned by increasing the cost of insurance. In addition, given that the vast majority of optometrists are members, non-members may be regarded by the public as offering inferior services. A report that a member had been suspended could adversely affect the member's business since the public might consider that the member must have been guilty of improper behaviour in order to merit such action.

109. The Association claimed that it felt it right to take action against members who were in breach of the law as it understood it. The legality of the Board's rules had been challenged and, as the Board decided not to pursue the case, the exact legal position was unclear. In the Authority's view the Board has responsibility for enforcing such rules and it is not for a private organisation to seek to ensure compliance with rules whose legality has been challenged. The Association suspended members for breaching rules of the Board, which the Board had not sought to enforce following a challenge to their legality, and at a time when the Board had stated that it was amending such rules. The fact that the Association took such action to try and dissuade members from advertising prices suggests that the provisions of the Code in relation to advertising cannot be regarded as mere recommendations. Rather such actions must be seen as an attempt to dissuade members from advertising their prices.

110. The Authority's attention was also drawn to the editorial contained in the Association's newsletter of January 1992 (see para 36x above). The editorial criticised what it described as bringing the profession into disrepute although no specific activity was mentioned. It stated *inter alia* that:

> Reneging from the recognised parameters as agreed by the professional group as a whole is the more shabby and selfish when it employs advertising trickery and gimmickry.

It also stated that:

> all too often the act is deliberate and material by selfishness in an effort to steal a march on the colleagues of the perpetrator and gain some advantage. . . .

23. Fair Trade Commission (1990), op. cit.
24. Restrictive Practices Commission (1987)(b)); 'Report of Study into Concerted Fixing of Fees and Restrictions on Advertising in the Engineering Profession', Pl. 4993, Dublin, Stationery Office.
25. Restrictive Practices Commission (1987(a)), op. cit.
26. Ibid., para. 5.30.

1.7.2 111. In sum the Authority believes that restrictions on the content, type and size of advertisements, together with restrictions on members' names, titles and professions being referred to in media articles, and in the sponsorship of non-optical events contained in the Code of Ethics as amended by the letter of June 1989, offended against section 4(1) of the Competition Act. In addition the Authority believes that the requirement to observe the Board's rules which precluded advertising in media other than newspapers, the quoting of prices in media advertisements while setting out specifications for the type of signs which may be used, together with the implementation of sanctions by the Association for alleged breaches of those rules also constituted restrictions of competition which offended against section 4(1).

112. Rule 31 of the Board also forbids canvassing by optometrists. It has been indicated to the Authority that this is primarily aimed at preventing door-to-door selling or cold calling, (unsolicited telephone approaches), while allowing distribution of promotional material by direct mail and other means. Cold calling, it is argued, is an objectionable practice while also being something of a nuisance to consumers. Consequently it is claimed that such behaviour brings the profession into disrepute. If in fact consumers object to such selling methods then they are likely to prove counterproductive and it is not clear that restrictions of this kind are necessary.

113. The Authority believes that a requirement that advertisements not be misleading or untruthful or of a character that could reasonably be regarded as likely to bring the profession into disrepute, as exists in Rule 31(2)(i) of the Board would not normally be anti-competitive. It does not believe that a requirement to adhere to such a rule offends against section 4(1). The Authority would be concerned if such a rule were to be interpreted in a way that sought to restrict competition or to prevent innovative marketing of services by members of the profession.

114. The Association indicated to its members by letter dated February 1993, that it had suspended all references to advertising from its Code of Ethics.[27]

115. As has been stated the Authority is not concerned with the Rules of the Opticians' Board *per se*. It, however, welcomes the decision by the Board to amend Rule 31, thereby removing the prohibition on price advertising in the media and on advertising in media other than newspapers, which in the Authority's view were anti-competitive. The Authority notes, however, that there is still a restriction on canvassing, although it believes that this will be limited to door to door selling and cold calling. It nevertheless believes that this still restricts competition to some degree as such activities are legitimate forms of advertising. If consumers object to such activity then it will not benefit any individual to engage in such practices.

(iv) *Restrictions on Price Competition*

116. The Association's Code of Ethics required that practitioners should charge on a professional fee system e.g. fee for examination, fee for dispensing, plus the cost of appliances and material supplied. It was submitted by them that the rationale for this was that by avoiding a system of mark-ups on materials it removed the incentive for members to sell more expensive types of frames.

117. This requirement of the Association did not, as far as the Authority is aware, involve actual agreements between members on the scale of fees to be charged for different services. The Authority would regard any such agreement which eliminated or greatly reduced price competition as an anti-competitive practice of the most serious kind, which is specifically cited in the Act as offending against section 4(1).

118. In Esso[28] the Authority indicated that it would regard even the exchange of price information by competitors as a breach of the prohibition on anti-competitive behaviour

27. Had this action not been taken, the Authority would have been likely to hold that the restrictions on advertising would not have qualified for a licence under section 4(2) of the Act.
28. Op. cit., para. 58.

contained in section 4(1) of the Competition Act. In this case the Authority can see no reason why members should not be free to set charges in any way they choose. It is concerned that requiring members to set charges in a particular way could facilitate agreements between some or all of the members of the Association on prices. For this reason it believes that the requirement to set charges in the manner prescribed in the Code of Ethics may prevent, restrict or distort competition. 1.7.2

119. The Code also prohibited the granting of group discounts by members as unprofessional. It was submitted to the Authority that members who had offered such discounts were suspended and/or threatened with expulsion from the Association. The Authority regards such a rule and the actions taken to enforce it as a restriction on price competition. It is relevant in this context that it has been found in EC cases that:

> the prohibition of Article 85(1) covers not only 'prices' in the narrow sense but also discounts, margins, rebates and credit terms.[29]

120. The requirement to determine fees in a particular manner and the restriction on the offering of discounts also prevented, restricted or distorted competition and offended against section 4(1). As the Association has deleted these provisions from the Code, it no longer offends against section 4(1).

(v) *Restrictions on Employees*

121. The Code states that a practitioner employed in a practice shall not, on leaving such employment, strive to entice patients away from his former employer. Proximity of premises to his former employers for the purpose of enticing patients is unethical.

122. If this requirement were to be used to restrict former employees from competing with the business of their former employers the Authority would regard it as offending against section 4(1). The Authority has indicated in its notice on employee agreements that it would regard a restriction on a former employee setting up his own business in competition with his former employer as offending against section 4(1) and it would generally not grant a licence to such an agreement. In the Authority's view, employees generally should be free to enter the market on the same basis as any other new competitor and this implies that they should be free to do business with customers of their former employer. The Authority accepts, however, that an employee may not use information which is properly confidential to the employer, such as lists of customer names and addresses, to set up in competition with his former employer. In this instance the Authority also accepts that a restriction on former employees directly soliciting their former employers' customers is not of itself anti-competitive.[30]

The Decision

123. The Association of Optometrists is an association of undertakings within the meaning of the Competition Act. The Memorandum and Articles of Association together with the Code of Ethics of the Association constitute decisions by an association of undertakings within the meaning of section 4(1) of the Competition Act.

124. The Authority believes that the rules on premises, advertising, fee determination and discounts originally contained in the Association's Code of Ethics had the effect of preventing, restricting or distorting competition and offended against section 4(1). As the Association has indicated by letter dated 22 December 1992 that the offending provisions have been deleted

29. Bellamy and Child at para. 4-003.
30. In some cases, however, it may be that an individual could only enter the market by approaching the customers of his former employer, e.g. where there were only a small number of potential customers, all or most of whom transacted business with the former employer, and where the normal method of entering the market would entail approaching such customers and informing them that one was entering the business.

1.7.2 and that members suspended for breaching such provisions are now free to resume full membership, the Memorandum and Articles of Association and Code of Ethics no longer offend against section 4(1) of the Competition Act 1991.

125. The Authority considers that certain other rules could be interpreted and used in such a way as to prevent, restrict or distort competition. The Authority found no evidence that they had been used in this way. If this were to happen the Authority has power to revoke this certificate under section 8(6).

The Certificate

126. The Competition Authority has issued the following certificate:

> The Competition Authority certifies that in its opinion, on the basis of the facts in its possession, the Memorandum and Articles of Association and the Code of Ethics of the Association of Optometrists, (notification no. CA/9/92E), notified on 6 March 1992 under section 7 and amended by letter of 22 December 1992, do not offend against section 4(1) of the Competition Act 1991.

For the Competition Authority

Patrick Massey
Member

29 April 1993

1.7.3 **Competition Authority Decision No. 335, Irish Stock Exchange rules in relation to dealings in Irish Government securities:** 10 June 1994, Notification No. CA/199/92E

Rules of an association of undertakings governing dealings in particular government securities – Provision in such rules for the charging of a mandatory minimum commission on all transactions – Restrictions in such rules on any member of the association of undertakings transacting business in the relevant government securities other than as agent – Whether the rules of the association of undertakings prevent, restrict or distort competition – Statement of objections – Competition Act 1991 (No. 24) sections 3, 4 and 7 – The Act for better regulation of Stockbrokers 1799 – Stockbrokers (Ireland) Act 1918

Facts: On 29 September 1992 notification was made to the Authority with a request for a certificate under section 4(4) of the Competition Act 1991 or, failing that, a licence under section 4(2) in respect of the rules of the Irish Stock Exchange ('ISE') in relation to dealings by its members in Irish government securities. The ISE, the Irish branch of the International Stock Exchange of the United Kingdom and Republic of Ireland Ltd, is owned by its member firms throughout Ireland and the UK. The notified rules govern ISE member firms in their dealings with medium and long term government securities (i.e. gilts with maturity dates over five years).

Under the rules the member firm may only deal in such securities as an agent and not as a principal. The members are also obliged to charge a certain fixed level of commission which can be reduced in certain circumstances to a lesser but yet fixed amount. Investors transacting business in the relevant securities need not use stock-brokers and can deal in the market without the payment of the mandatory commission. **1.7.3**

The Act for the Better Regulation of Stockbrokers 1799 provided that a licensed broker shall not buy or sell government stocks or securities on his own account when employed by any person who is not a stockbroker. The Stockbrokers (Ireland) Act 1918 provides that the Dublin Stock Exchange could set maximum rates of fees which may be charged by a licensed broker on the sale or purchase of any government stock subject to the approval of the Minister for Finance now.

On 10 March 1994 the Authority issued a statement of objections to ISE stating that it intended to refuse a certificate or licence in respect of the notified arrangements on the grounds that the rules setting out the minimum commissions and prohibiting brokers acting as principals were anti-competitive. In response the ISE agreed to abolish its rule requiring the payment of minimum commissions on all transactions in the relevant securities and announced its intention to change the rule permitting member firms to deal with the securities only as an agent.

Decided by the Authority:

(A) In refusing to issue a certificate under section 4(4) of the Competition Act 1991 that:

(1) The rules of ISE as notified constitute a decision by an association of undertakings.

(2) The rules providing for fixed commission rates in transactions involving the securities, which must be adhered to by all member firms, eliminate the possibility for brokers to compete on price in that market. The alternatives to transacting through brokers do not represent realistic options as evidenced by the overwhelming number of transactions conducted through brokers and the fact that brokers did not have to depart from fixed commissions as a result of competition from those alternatives.

(3) The rules are not recommendations of commission rates because ISE have threatened the use of sanctions against members who attempt to charge lower rates of commission.

(4) The argument of ISE that the abolition of the fixed commissions might result in a market establishing a similar commission level is no defence to the maintenance of fixed commissions. There is a fundamental difference between a price set by competitive market forces and one based on agreement between competitors or on a rule of an association.

(5) Price fixing is anti-competitive regardless of the level at which it is set and cannot be justified on the basis that the price fixed is reasonable.

(6) The arguments that the abolition of fixed commission would lead to a breakdown of agency broking, even if sustainable, is not relevant as section 4(1) is designed to protect competition and not competitors.

(7) The Stockbrokers (Ireland) Act 1918 provides for the setting by the Stock Exchange of maximum rates of fees. The Act did not concern the practice of setting minimum commissions and therefore did not exclude the notified practice from the scope of section 4(1) of the Competition Act.

(8) The requirement that ISE member firms could only deal as agents in respect of

1.7.3 the relevant securities operates to prevent broking firms acting as market makers and appears to prevent any other entity operating as a market maker since such an entity would be operating outside the market. The absence of such restriction would have some impact in competition in the securities market and therefore the restriction offends against section 4(1).

(9) The 1799 Stockbrokers Act which provides that brokers must not buy or sell government securities on their own account when employed by a non stockbroker does not prevent a broker acting other than as agent when not employed by some other person.

(10) The changes to the notified arrangements whereby the ISE abolished its fixed minimum commission on transactions involving the relevant securities and its proposal to amend the requirement that members only act as agents in such transactions have not been formerly notified under section 7 and therefore are not considered in this application.

(11) The Authority's role is to consider whether arrangements notified to it by the parties involved offend against section 4(1) and when they do so offend, whether they meet the requirements for a licence. *Semble:* The Authority will not consider proposals for arrangements.

(B) In refusing to grant a licence under section 4(2) of the Competition Act 1991 in respect of the notified arrangements that:

(1) The fixed minimum commission does not meet the requirements set out in section 4(2) and the requirements that the stockbrokers only act as agents, while arguably capable of contributing to technical and economic progress in the relevant market, is not indispensable for such a development.

Cases, Decisions, Notices and Books cited:

Cementhandelaren v. EC Commission (Case No. 8/72), [1972] ECR 977, [1973] CMLR 7
NAVEWA v. EC Commission (Case No. 96-102/82) [1983 ECR 3369, [1984] 3 CMLR 276
EC Commission Decision Milchforderungsfond (Case No. 85/76/EEC), [1985] OJ L35/35, [1985] 3 CMLR 101
EC Commission Decision London Sugar Futures Market, [1985] OJ L369/25, [1988] 4 CMLR 138
EC Commission Decision IFTRA Aluminium (Case No. 75/497/EEC), [1975] OJ L228/32, [1975] 2 CMLR D20
EC Commission Decision Uniform Eurocheques, [1984] OJ L35/43, [1985] 3 CMLR 434
EC Commission Decision Nuovo CEGAM, [1984] OJ L99/29, [1984] 2 CMLR 484
EC Commission Decision London Cocoa Terminal Market Association Ltd, [1985] OJ L369/28, [1988] 4 CMLR 143
EC Commission Decision Coffee Terminal Market Association of London Ltd, [1985] OJ L369/31, [1988] 4 CMLR 155
EC Commission Decision London Rubber Terminal Market Association Ltd, [1985] OJ L369/34, [1988] 4 CMLR 149
EC Commission Decision GAFTA Soya Bean Meal Futures Association, [1987] OJ L19/18-30, [1989] 4 CMLR 287
EC Commission Decision London Grain Futures Market, [1986] OJ L19/22, [1989] 4 CMLR 294
EC Commission Decision The London Potatoes Futures Association Ltd, [1986] OJ L19/26, [1989] 4 CMLR 301
EC Commission Decision The London Meat Futures Exchange Ltd, [1986] OJ L19/30, [1989] 4 CMLR 308
United States v. Trenton Potteries Company et. al., 273 US 392 (1927)
United States v. Socomy-Vacuum Oil Company, Inc. et. al., 310 US 150 (1940)
Bellamy and Child (1987) 'Common Market Law of Competition' (3rd ed.) Sweet & Maxwell, London
Van Baels and Bellis, 'Competition Law of the EEC', (2nd ed.) CCH Editions Ltd.

Submissions by the Parties 1.7.3

Submissions on behalf of behalf of ISE

(1) Abolishing fixed commissions would ultimately result in the emergence of a market making system which would have the effect of reducing liquidity and turnover in the market and raise costs while the adherence to the agency rules ensures transparency in every trade.

(2) The restrictions contained in the rules were ameliorated by the freedom of the investors to deal directly with each other without the use of brokers, by the existence of alternatives to the gilt market, by the freedom of entry into the broking business and by the requirement that commission rates be approved by the Department of Finance.

(3) Even if the restrictions offend section 4(1), a licence under section 4(2) was justified in that stock brokers had contributed to the development of secondary trading in the relevant securities and this was only made possible by the transparency in the market due to fixed commissions. If these restrictions were abolished the market would move fairly swiftly into one of competing market makers in which there would only be two or three domestic banking groups with the required level of capital to carry out that role thus necessitating bringing in outside finance houses and so transferring employment and value added abroad.

Competition Authority Decision of 10 June 1994 relating to a proceeding under section 4 of the Competition Act 1991
Notification No. CA/199/92E — Irish Stock Exchange rules in relation to dealings in Irish Government securities

Introduction

1. The rules of the Irish Stock Exchange in relation to dealings in Irish Government Securities (Gilts) were notified to the Competition Authority on 29 September 1992. The notification requested a certificate, or in the event of a refusal by the Authority to grant a certificate, a licence. On 10 March 1994 the Authority issued a Statement of Objections to the Stock Exchange indicating that it intended to refuse its request for a certificate or licence. The Authority specifically objected to two aspects of the rules namely those setting minimum commissions for transactions in gilts and providing that stockbrokers act only as agents in respect of such transactions. On 6 April 1994 the Stock Exchange indicated that it had decided not to challenge the Authority's objections to the fixed commission regime. It indicated that it did not accept the Authority's views on the agency rule and requested an Oral Hearing. On 16 May 1994 the Stock Exchange informed the Authority that the rules on minimum commissions would be abolished with effect from 17 May 1994. On 27 May 1994 the Stock Exchange informed the Authority that it was withdrawing its request for an Oral Hearing having decided not to contest the Authority's objections in respect of the agency rule. It subsequently announced its intention to change this rule, subject to the approval of the Minister for Finance.

The Facts

(a) *The Subject of the Notification*

2. The notification relates to the rules of the Irish Stock Exchange in relation to dealings in Irish Government Securities (Gilts) by member firms dated January 1987. The rules set out the basis on which member firms of the Exchange may deal in Irish Gilts. In particular they provide that brokers may operate in an agency capacity only and prohibit brokers from competing on the basis of commission levels by setting out fixed commissions to be charged by all member

1.7.3 firms in respect of gilts with over five years to maturity. The rate of commission has been approved by the Minister for Finance.

(b) *The Parties*

3. The parties involved in the arrangements are the Irish Stock Exchange and its member firms. The Irish Stock Exchange is presently constituted as an administrative unit, being in effect the Irish branch of the International Stock Exchange of the United Kingdom and the Republic of Ireland Ltd., which is owned by its member firms throughout Ireland and the UK. Its functions include the regulation of its member firms. There are currently 12 member firms of the Irish Stock Exchange and they are listed in Annex I.[1] The Authority is aware that there are proposals to establish the Irish Stock Exchange as a separate entity independent of the UK Stock Exchange.

4. The Stock Exchange has submitted that none of these firms has a shareholding in any of the other firms listed or any right to control, manage or influence the board or partnership of another. Some of the stockbroking firms are however, subsidiaries of, or partly owned by, other companies.

5. Stockbroking firms act as intermediaries in the gilt and equity markets. They are also engaged in a number of other activities including *inter alia* the provision of advice to investment clients and the organising of share placings for corporate clients.

(c) *The Product and the Market*

6. A gilt is an Irish Government security. The Government issues or sells gilts in order to fund its borrowing requirements. Gilts generally offer a fixed rate of interest for a number of years and have a specific redemption date. Such gilts are usually bought by institutional investors such as insurance companies, pension funds and banks. Private investors account for an almost negligible part of gilt sales.

7. Gilts were traditionally issued by the Department of Finance although this role has now been assumed by the National Treasury Management Agency (NTMA). The NTMA creates new stocks with a particular maturity date and coupon from time to time. They might issue only a relatively small amount initially but further amounts may be issued or 'tranched' as the need for funds and the market demand for stock allows. Tranches of existing stocks may also be created.

8. As an inducement to investors to hold gilts the Department of Finance undertook to buy back stock at a price set from time to time. Increased budget deficits from the mid 1970s onwards led to a substantial increase in the amount of Government gilts held by institutions. In addition as investors became more willing to trade their gilt portfolios, opportunities for brokers arose to find sellers and buyers of gilts. This resulted in the development of a secondary market for gilts. Gilts are bought and sold by investors on the secondary market between their issue and redemption date. Most transactions on the secondary market are arranged by stockbroking firms with the vast majority of transactions conducted by telephone. Secondary market trading now dominates overall turnover so that the Department of Finance's role as a market maker diminished over time. The relevant market is the secondary gilt market. The relevant geographical market is the State.

9. The total value of Government stock or gilts outstanding at the end of 1993 was over £14bn. (See Table 1). The main holders of gilts are financial institutions. These can be divided into two broad classes. Banks and building societies tend to hold gilts for investment purposes on their own account and also, in the former case, to comply with liquidity ratio requirements imposed by the Central Bank of Ireland. Such institutions tend mainly to hold short dated gilts. Life assurance and pension funds effectively invest in gilts on behalf of their policyholders and would largely invest in medium and long dated gilts. The tendency for the different institutions

1. Within the past few weeks one of the smaller broking firms has announced that it is relinquishing its seat on the Exchange.

to operate largely in different areas of the market reflects the differing maturity ranges of their respective liabilities. Insurance companies were the largest domestic holders of gilts accounting for almost 29% of stock outstanding. The personal and corporate sectors hold a very small proportion of outstanding gilts. In effect the personal sector is a major holder of gilts indirectly through life assurance and pension policies. 1.7.3

10. In recent years overseas institutions, particularly German institutions, have become major holders of gilts. At the end of 1991 non-resident gilt holdings accounted for almost 30% of stock outstanding. This fell sharply during 1992, due largely to the currency crisis. By the end of 1993 non resident holdings of gilts was more than £4bn, just £120m below the end 1991 level, representing almost 29% of gilts outstanding.

Table 1: Government Stock — Nominal Holding £M

	1993	1992
Government Departments	262.9 (1.9)	441.6 (3.3)
Central Bank	180.0 (1.3)	240.0 (1.8)
Associated Banks	2157.3 (15.3)	2049.6 (15.5)
Non-Associated Banks	625.7 (4.4)	1023.1 (7.7)
Building Societies	427.4 (3.0)	838.1 (6.3)
Insurance Companies	4035.9 (28.5)	3702.8 (27.9)
Pension Funds	1115.0 (7.9)	1139.5 (8.6)
Unit and Investment Trusts	306.5 (2.2)	288.1 (2.2)
Commercial Companies	299.6 (2.1)	375.0 (2.8)
Personal Sector	359.7 (2.5)	447.7 (3.4)
Other	327.1 (2.3)	387.1 (2.9)
Non-Resident Holdings	4047.3 (28.6)	2320.7 (17.5)
Total	14144.4 (100.0)	13253.3 (100.0)

Figures in parentheses are percentage shares

Source: Central Bank; Quarterly Bulletin, Summer 1994, Table D2.

11. Gilts may be divided into three broad categories according to their maturity date. Those maturing in less than 5 years would be described as shorts, those with a maturity date of between 5 to 15 years are mediums, while those with a maturity of over 15 years are long gilts. At end 1992 there were a total of 31 stock issues.[2] Table 2 illustrates that 45% of the gilts outstanding are shorts. This proportion has fallen in recent years.

Table 2: Maturity Range of Gilts (% distribution)

	1991	1992	1993
Stocks due to mature in			
less than 5 years	51.7	50.0	45.4
5-15 years	39.8	40.5	45.8
15 years or more	8.4	9.6	8.8

Source: Central Bank Quarterly Bulletin Summer 1994, Table D2

2. The number of stock issues has fallen sharply in recent years. At the end of 1990 there were 47 stock issues.

1.7.3 12. Stockbroking firms are engaged *inter alia* in arranging the purchase and sale of gilts on behalf of investors on the secondary market. These firms are only allowed by the Stock Exchange to act in an agency capacity and must have on their staff individuals licensed by the Minister for Finance to deal in gilts for commission.

Table 3: Gilt Market Turnover £m

	Under 5 years to Maturity	Over 5 years to Maturity	Total
1990	28180	7917	36097
1991	17026	18456	35482
1992	21093	26809	47902
1993	30281	36107	66388

Source: Central Bank Quarterly Bulletin Summer 1994, Table C20

13. Total turnover has increased sharply since 1991. Apart from 1990 more than half of total turnover involved stock with more than five years to maturity. There were over 19,000 bargains involving gilts with more than five years to maturity in 1993, 55% of all gilt bargains. The Irish Times reported that total gilt commissions paid to stockbrokers in 1993 by Irish institutions alone amounted to £4.5m. This was 22% up on the 1992 total.

14. The market is in fact a highly concentrated one with just four firms accounting for the bulk of gilt market transactions. According to a report in the Irish Times, Davy Stockbrokers accounted for almost 31% of gilt market transactions, while the top four firms accounted for almost 90% of the market. (See Table 4). In effect many of the smaller stockbroking firms are not heavily involved in the gilt market, with most of their business being accounted for by private clients. During 1993 two smaller firms have managed to secure a significant increase in their market share. In one case they did so, according to newspaper reports, by offering a partial rebate of commissions to institutions if and when the current scale of fixed commissions is revised.

Table 4: Gilt Commissions Paid to Stockbrokers

	1991	1992	1993
	%	£m %	£m %
Davy Stockbrokers	29.3	1.19 (32.3)	1.45 (31.0)
Goodbody	21.4	0.79 (21.2)	0.90 (20.0)
NCB	21.6	0.86 (23.1)	0.86 (19.0)
Riada	20.8	0.61 (16.6)	0.81 (18.0)
Bloxham	—	—	0.23 (5.0)
MMI	—	—	0.23 (5.0)
Others	6.9	0.25 (6.7)	0.09 (2.0)

Note: Separate figures for Bloxham and MMI were not published for 1991 and 1992 and they are included in the total for others

Source: Irish Times 7 April 1993 and 17 February 1994

(d) *The Arrangements*

15. The notified arrangements involved the Stock Exchange Rules as they applied to transactions in Government gilts. They provided that stockbrokers may only act in an agency

capacity in respect of Irish Government securities and were obliged to charge a fixed rate of commission on transactions in gilts with more than five years to maturity. These conditions were set out in the 'Rules and Regulations of the Irish Stock Exchange'. The relevant rules are set out below. **1.7.3**

49.1 'A Member firm shall only deal as an agent in respect of any security issued or guaranteed by the Government of the Republic of Ireland.'

75.1(1) 'The Rules and Regulations of the Stock Exchange relating to Commission shall apply *in toto* on bargains on Securities issued or guaranteed by the Government of the Republic of Ireland, a broker who is subject to the jurisdiction of the Republic of Ireland shall charge his client Commission at not less than the rates laid down in Appendix II to these unit rules and no reduction thereof may be allowed except as authorised by the provisions of the Rules and Regulations of The Stock Exchange.'

77.1 'A broking firm shall charge commission in respect of every bargain made on a client's behalf and in respect of every service for which a charge is prescribed.'

78.1 'In the case of securities issued by the Government of Ireland, the commission chargeable by a Broking Firm shall be at not less than the rates adopted by the Irish Administrative Unit and set out in Appendix II — Irish Government Funds of these rules, except to the extent authorised by these Rules.'

16. Rule 79.1 and 2 provides for lower, albeit fixed rates of commission to be applied in respect of a new security issue with a maturity date of more than ten years on transactions effected within three months of the first day of dealings done for the same principal in such a new issue. Rule 80 allows brokers to waive commissions in certain limited circumstances. Rule 81 allows for certain reductions in the case of a change from one security to another for the same principal.

17. Details of the rates of commission specified in Appendix II of the Stock Exchange Rules are set out in Table 5 below.

Table 5: Scale of Minimum Commissions
(for Irish Government Funds)

0.52% on the first £2500 consideration

0.1625% on the next £15500 consideration

0.0813% on the next £232000 consideration

0.065% on the next £750000 consideration

0.0585% on the next £3000000 consideration

0.026% on the next £6000000 consideration

0.013% on the excess.

18. The Irish Times reported on 7 November 1992 that one of the smaller stockbroking firms, MMI, had announced plans to offer discounts of up to 20 per cent on gilt deals. MMI was formed early in 1992 when MMI moneybrokers acquired Doak & Company a small stockbroking firm. The Stock Exchange reportedly objected to the MMI proposal to charge less than the minimum commissions set in its rules. The Irish Times report also claimed that a Japanese broking house had decided to make a market in Irish gilts from its London trading room although it appears that they subsequently withdrew from the market.

1.7.3 (e) *Submissions of the Parties*

19. The Irish Stock Exchange has argued that the arrangements do not have as their object or effect the prevention, restriction or distortion of competition in trade in any goods or services in the State or in any part of the State within the meaning of section 4(1) of the Competition Act. They have argued that fixed commissions are required because banks who are large holders and traders of gilts may also be owners or controllers of broking operations. Without fixed commissions they could obtain the services of a subsidiary broker at a nominal charge. Other buyers of gilts would recognise this possibility and would treat brokers as principals quickly leading to a situation where the major participants in the market were principal traders and there would emerge a market making system. The Exchange argued that this would reduce liquidity and turnover in the market and raise costs. The Stock Exchange also argued that a 'standard' rate of commission would emerge even in the absence of fixed commission arrangements, given the nature of the market involved. Thus they submitted that the arrangement merely formalised the structure that would emerge under a negotiated commission regime, except that it preserved the agency broking structure of the market, thus ensuring the transparency of every trade.

20. It was claimed that the agency broking system benefited investors and Government through improved liquidity and lower overall dealing costs. It was argued that the commission levels prevailing resulted in bid-offer spreads which were quite narrow. The parties stated that: 'A reduction of commission levels, if it reduced competition in the broking market, would be offset many times by wider spreads.' They also stated that any restrictions were greatly ameliorated by the freedom of investors to deal direct without the use of brokers, by the existence of alternatives to the gilt market (i.e. futures), by the freedom of entry into broking and by the requirement that the commission rates be approved by the Department of Finance.

21. The Exchange also argued that, even if the fixed commission rules could be considered to offend against section 4(1), a licence was justified. It was stated that the primary objective of the fixed commission rules was to implement the provisions relating to the licence to deal in Government securities on a commission basis which must be obtained from the Minister for Finance. The Exchange submitted that brokers had contributed to the development of the secondary trading in gilts and an increase in the liquidity of the market. It indicated that without fixed commissions it would be impossible to distinguish between an agency transaction and a principal transaction and that this would lead to a deterioration in the quality of the market. It was claimed that this would cause a significant number of investors, especially overseas investors, to cease to trade. Competitive broking would therefore disappear.

22. The Stock Exchange argued that the elimination of fixed commissions would cause the market to evolve fairly quickly into one of competing market-makers. They claimed, however, that there were only two or three domestic banking groups with the high level of capital required for adequate market-making and that it was therefore unlikely that a competitive market making system could be put in place. They also submitted that to increase the number of competitive market makers it would be necessary to attract foreign houses, 'so transferring employment and value added abroad.'

23. The Exchange argued that broking was essential to the maintenance of market liquidity. They also submitted that any change to the system could damage market confidence which would be difficult to re-establish. They stated that domestic market participants did not consider that gilt commissions were a particularly important factor. They went on to state that:

> The abolition of fixed commission rates would lead rapidly to a fundamental change in the structure of the gilt market and would lead to a less competitive, less liquid market dominated by larger financial institutions whose market making capacity would have to be supported by the Authorities.
>
> We believe there is a grave danger that in the absence of agency broking — which would disappear without a minimum commission regime — the liquidity of the market

would dwindle and its continuing attraction to foreign investors would be greatly reduced. 1.7.3

The reduction in liquidity would be reflected in wider spreads which would far outweigh any potential savings in commission levels currently required by the voluntary use of an agency broker.

24. In support of its request the Stock Exchange submitted a simulation exercise on Market Making on Long Bonds prepared by Mr Barry Dillon of Davy Stockbrokers. This claimed that market making would require relatively wide spreads thereby reducing liquidity in the market. A separate study entitled The Development of the Irish Bond Market prepared by Mr Jim O'Leary and Mr Tony Garry, also of Davy Stockbrokers concluded that while spreads on Irish long gilts appeared relatively high, this was attributable to a number of factors including *inter alia* the size of the market and the degree of stock dispersion. It rejected arguments that the replacement of the present agency broking system with a market making system would have a positive effect on market liquidity.

(f) *Legislation*

25. The Act for the Better Regulation of Stock Brokers 1799 provides *inter alia* that any licensed stockbroker shall not buy or sell Government stocks or securities on his own account when employed by any person not being a broker. In 1918 the Stockbrokers (Ireland) Act was enacted which provided that the Dublin Stock Exchange could set maximum rates of fees which may be charged by a licensed stockbroker in Ireland on the sale or purchase of any Government stock or securities, subject to the approval of the Lord Lieutenant. Responsibility for approving such rates now lies with the Minister for Finance.

(g) *Views of Third Parties*

National Treasury Management Agency

26. Under the National Treasury Management Agency Act 1990 the NTMA is responsible for the management of the national debt a function previously discharged by the Department of Finance. The NTMA has effectively assumed the Department's role of financing maturing debt and the Exchequer Borrowing Requirement (EBR) through the issue and sale of new gilts In addition the NTMA is also engaged in actively promoting depth and liquidity in the gilt market through active intervention in the secondary market. This latter function is in contrast with the approach adopted by the Department in the past when the development of the secondary market was due purely to the activities of stockbrokers. The NTMA in its submission to the Authority stated that it had 'a vital and unique interest in any matter relating to Government securities, including the rules of the Irish Stock Exchange pertaining to those securities.'

27. The NTMA went on to state that:

> In the Agency's view the minimum fixed rate commission arrangement is not necessary for the proper functioning of the gilt market. Moreover, the arrangement does not allow of a competitive broking system in as much as all investors, regardless of size, are obliged to pay the same price irrespective of the level or quality of service. The Agency does not accept the Stock Exchange's assertion that the deregulation of commission rates would necessarily lead to a fundamental change in the structure of the market, in the form of market making, and to reduced liquidity.

It noted that equity market transactions continue to be conducted on an agency-only broker basis although negotiable commissions have applied since 1986. It then stated that:

> In any event, even if some form of market making were to be introduced in the gilt

1.7.3 market following the abolition of fixed rate commissions, such a development, which would be in line with practice in most other European markets, would be welcomed in principle by the Agency.

28. The NTMA also argued that, while it was true that buyers and seller of gilts were free to deal directly with one another and avoid paying commissions, the Exchange had the unique characteristics of prudential regulation and investor protection, so that the vast bulk of investors did not deal outside of it, giving brokers a *de facto* monopoly. It pointed out that institutions who were actually managing funds on behalf of individual and corporate investors were under an obligation to those investors to deal at the best price. By not dealing through the market they would be exposed to claims that they had not done so. The NTMA also indicated that the Stock Exchange simulation, showing that market making in long gilts would reduce liquidity, was seriously flawed.

Irish Association of Investment Managers

29. The Irish Association of Investment Managers (IAIM) represents institutional investors in the Irish market. IAIM indicated that it had 18 corporate members who between them held 35-40% of the total Irish gilt market with a considerably higher share of the medium and long end of the market to which fixed commission rates apply. They claimed that IAIM members had paid £4.5m in commission on gilt transactions to Irish brokers in 1993.

30. IAIM stated that it was opposed to the Stock Exchange's application for a certificate on the basis that the system of fixed gilt commissions contravened section 4 of the Competition Act. It was also opposed to the Exchange's application for a licence as it believed that this would institutionalise an anti- competitive practice which was not in the interests of the market and was unnecessary for the maintenance of an agency broking system.

31. IAIM submitted that commission rates were payable to agency brokers for their services as intermediaries. Commission rates include payment for the basic service of matching buyers and sellers and any added value provided by the broker over and above that basic role. The latter includes the provision of research, advice, ability to deal in size, knowledge of international markets etc. These demand a higher payment than would be the case for the basic service. They argued that fixed commissions incorporated payments for a composite service and that it was anti-competitive as it prevented new or existing brokers from offering a mix of one or more of these services to clients at appropriate commissions. It forced investors to buy a composite service and meant that brokers competed only on the basis of services offered, rather than on the basis of price and/or services offered.

32. IAIM argued that an efficient market was not characterised by the existence of fixed commissions and that it could be argued that, with negotiable commissions, turnover and consequently liquidity would be increased. In addition they submitted that the abolition of fixed commissions would not have the effect claimed by the Stock Exchange. Specifically IAIM indicated that the move to a market making system was not an inevitable result of the abolition of fixed commissions. They noted that the abolition of fixed commissions for equities had not resulted in a move to dual capacity. Similarly they argued that the Exchange's claim that certain banks would use their position as owners or controllers of certain broking firms to obtain their services at nominal charges, thus leading to market making was not sustainable. In support of this argument they pointed out that banks were the most active players in the short end of the market where commissions are negotiable and their involvement has not affected broking in shorts. In addition it was claimed that, if such practices were to occur, the banks would realise that other investors would not deal with the broker concerned, thus undermining its viability. They also claimed that banks with broking subsidiaries should be indifferent to commission levels as they were simply a transfer from one area of operations to another.

33. In conclusion IAIM argued that the introduction of market making was not related to the issue of fixed commissions. They did not accept the claim that the possibility of principals

dealing directly outside the Exchange ensured that brokers did not have a monopoly. However, they considered that the emergence of overseas brokers willing to compete on price and not bound by minimum commission rules had the potential to break the stockbroking monopoly. **1.7.3**

Other Submissions

34. A Mr Frank Kelleher complained that the system of fixed commissions was anti-competitive and that the granting of a licence for such a practice would not be in the interests of the country. Mr Kelleher indicated that he was currently involved in a venture that proposed to set up a technology driven trading organisation in Dublin and that the Stock Exchange had indicated that any attempt by an organisation to undercut the minimum commission rates would result in its membership being revoked. He claimed that as his organisation aimed to undercut the current minimum level of commissions in order to attract clients, it was unlikely that the Exchange authorities would recommend that his organisation be granted membership, if and when, sought.

(h) *UK Experience*

35. As pointed out above the Irish Stock Exchange is an administrative unit of the International Stock Exchange of the United Kingdom and Ireland. Prior to October 1986, the UK Stock Exchange also required UK stockbrokers to charge minimum fixed commissions. On 9 February 1979 the UK Director General of Fair Trading referred the Stock Exchange rules to the UK Restrictive Practices Court. Among the main anti-competitive restrictions cited by the Director General in announcing the reference was the provision preventing stockbrokers from providing services below specified minimum rates of commission. The reference also cited certain other restrictions such as the provision that jobbers could not act as brokers and the requirement for all deals to be put through a jobber.

36. On 27 July 1983 the UK Secretary of State for Trade and Industry announced that the Stock Exchange was to amend its rules. In particular it proposed to dismantle in stages the rules which prescribed minimum scales of commission, with this process to be completed by 31 December 1986. As a result the Government amended the UK Restrictive Practices Act to exclude the rules of the Stock Exchange from its provisions. In fact the move from minimum to negotiated commissions was completed on 27 October 1986. At that time minimum commissions for both equities and short gilts were also abolished in Ireland. The Minister for Finance announced, however, that such commissions would be retained in Ireland in the case of dealings in medium and long term government gilts, although the rate of commission was reduced considerably.

(h)* *Subsequent developments*

37. In a report in the Irish Times on 3 January 1994, it was stated that the NTMA were anxious to see a change in the operation of the gilt market. In particular the NTMA was reported to be seeking a move to a 'market-making' system in gilts. Mr John Corrigan of the NTMA was reported as expressing the view that such a system would improve liquidity in the market and would thereby lower the gap between Irish and German bond yields. A report in the Sunday Business Post of 6 February again indicated that the NTMA were anxious to see a change to a market making system. According to the report the IAIM were opposed to such a change.

38. On 10 March 1994 the Authority issued a Statement of Objections to the Stock Exchange indicating that it intended to refuse to issue a certificate or grant a licence in respect of the notified arrangements. In particular the Authority stated that, in its opinion, the rules setting minimum commissions for gilt transactions and requiring that brokers act only as agents in respect of such transactions were anti-competitive and offended against section 4(1) of the Competition Act. It also indicated that, in its view, none of these rules satisfied the requirements

**Editor's Note*: The lettering for the paragraphs are as per original text.

1.7.3 for a licence set out in section 4(2) of the Act. On 6 April 1994 the Stock Exchange indicated that it had decided not to challenge the Authority's objections to the fixed commission regime. It indicated that it did not accept the Authority's views on the agency rule and requested an Oral Hearing. On 16 May 1994 the Stock Exchange informed the Authority that the rules on minimum commissions would be abolished with effect from 17 May 1994. A report in the Sunday Business Post on 29 May 1994 indicated that gilt commissions had fallen significantly as a result of the abolition of minimum commissions and the introduction of negotiated commissions for all gilt transactions. On 27 May 1994 the Stock Exchange informed the Authority that it was withdrawing its request for an Oral Hearing having decided not to contest the Authority's objections in respect of the agency rule. It subsequently announced its intention to change this rule, subject to the approval of the Minister for Finance. The IAIM wrote requesting that the Authority indicate in its decision whether the arrangements which IAIM would like to see introduced in place of the agent only rule would meet the requirements for a certificate or licence.

Assessment

(a) *Section 4(1)*

39. Section 4(1) of the Competition Act states that 'all agreements between undertakings, decisions by associations of undertakings and concerted practices which have as their object or effect the prevention, restriction or distortion of competition in trade in any goods or services in the State or in any part of the State are prohibited and void.'

(b) *The Parties*

40. The notified arrangements involve certain rules of the Irish Stock Exchange. The Irish Stock Exchange is constituted as an administrative-unit of the International Stock Exchange of the United Kingdom and the Republic of Ireland Ltd. It is owned by its members which are stockbroking firms. Section 3(1) of the Act defines an undertaking as 'a person being an individual, a body corporate or an unincorporated body of persons engaged for gain in the production, supply or distribution of goods or the provision of a service.' Stockbroking firms are engaged in the provision of services for gain. Consequently the Irish Stock Exchange is an association of undertakings within the meaning of section 4(1), as its members are undertakings. This view is supported by EC law, as Bellamy and Child point out:

> Although trade associations of various kinds are the commonest 'associations of undertakings' the word 'associations' is not limited to any particular type of association. It includes agricultural co-operatives, associations without legal personality, non-profit making associations, associations of associations and an association outside the Community.[3]

The legal form of the association has been found to be irrelevant.[4]

(c) *The Arrangements*

41. The notified arrangements involved the Stock Exchange Rules as they apply to transactions in Government gilts. They provided that stockbrokers may only act in an agency capacity in respect of Irish Government securities and must charge a fixed rate of commission on transactions in medium and long gilts. These conditions were set out in the 'Rules and Regulations of the Irish Stock Exchange'. The Rules constituted a decision by an association of undertakings. This view is also supported by EC precedents.

3. C. Bellamy and G. Child (1987); 'Common Market Law edition', 3rd ed., Sweet & Maxwell, London, para. 2-032.
4. See Milchforderungsfonds, case no, 85/76/EEC, OJ L35/35, 7.2.85.

> The concept of 'decision' includes the rules of the association in question, decisions binding upon the members and recommendations. Agreements implemented within the framework of the association concerned may be analysed either as 'decisions' of that association or 'agreements' between the members.[5] **1.7.3**

The Rules of the Exchange and the Rules relating to minimum commissions also constitute an agreement between undertakings since they were agreed by the Member Firms which, as already pointed out, are undertakings. Each of the relevant rules is now considered.

(d) *Applicability of section 4(1)*

(i) Minimum Commissions

42. Rules 75.1(1) and 78.1 provided that brokers must charge no less than the rates adopted by the Irish Administrative Unit and set out in Appendix II of the Rules. Lower rates were permitted under the Rules in certain limited circumstances. The requirement in both of these Rules that brokers should not charge less than the rate of commission fixed by the Irish Exchange on transactions in Irish Government Gilts prevented price competition between stockbrokers in respect of such transactions. The vast majority of transactions in Irish Government Gilts were conducted using stockbrokers.

43. Theoretically it might have been possible for principals to by-pass brokers and deal directly with one another. The notifying parties in this instance had sought to argue that the arrangements were not anti-competitive as investors did not have to deal through brokers. It was argued in other submissions that this is not a practical alternative for a number of reasons. Clearly if institutions by-passed brokers they could avoid paying commission altogether. The fact that the overwhelming majority of transactions are conducted through brokers implies that direct dealing is not a viable alternative. Similarly while transactions could also be channelled through the futures exchange, the fact that there is so little activity in that market again suggests that it is not a viable alternative. It is clear, therefore, that such alternatives do not represent a realistic alternative to brokers and that brokers did not have to depart from the fixed commissions as a result of competition from such alternatives.

44. It was pointed out above that transactions in short dated gilts were not subject to fixed commissions. The Authority believes that short dated gilts are not sufficiently close substitutes for mediums and longs to be regarded as part of the same market. Consequently it does not believe that the absence of fixed minimum commissions on short gilts means that their application to mediums and longs did not amount to a restriction of competition. Quite simply the Stock Exchange could not discriminate in this fashion between the commission rules applying to the different types of gilts if they were in fact substitutes for one another. The rule prescribing fixed minimum commissions to be charged by brokers on transactions in Irish Government Gilts prevented brokers from competing on price, and this amounted to a restriction of competition within the State.

45. Price fixing agreements have been consistently regarded as in breach of Article 85(1) of the Treaty of Rome. Bellamy and Child point out that:

> Since price is the main instrument of competition, Article 85(1)(a) expressly prohibits agreements, which 'directly or indirectly fix purchase or selling prices or any other trading conditions.' An agreement to fix prices by its very nature constitutes a restriction on competition within the meaning of Article 85(1).[6]

46. They go on to state that:

5. Bellamy and Child, at para. 2-031.
6. Ibid. at para. 4-002.

> 1.7.3 Article 85(1) is infringed by an explicit agreement between suppliers to fix prices, and also by a concerted practice to restrict price competition, for example informal concertation on the dates and amounts of price increases or the exchange of price information. Similarly the prohibition of Article 85(1) covers not only 'prices' in the narrow sense but also discounts, margins, rebates and credit terms.[7]

47. Van Bael and Bellis point out that:

> Although there exist no *per se* rules in EEC competition law, horizontal price fixing arrangements have always been held incompatible with Article 85(1) and have generally been denied an exemption.[8]

In the US horizontal price fixing agreements have generally been regarded by the courts as a *per se* violation of the antitrust statutes.

48. In a number of decisions relating to the rules and regulations of a number of the London Futures Exchanges, the EU Commission decided that rules, which set minimum net rates of commission to be charged by members, infringed Article 85(1). In the London Sugar Futures Market case, for example, the Commission stated that:

> The Rules and Regulations as originally notified specified the minimum net rates of commission which could be charged by a member. The Committee had powers to suspend or expel offending members. The minimum commission rates varied according to who was paying and who was receiving the commission. . . . The Commission considered the above described system of specified minimum commission rates as a form of price-fixing that violated Article 85(1) of the EEC Treaty. The LSFM was requested to abandon the system of fixed minimum rates. The system has now been abolished as such. References to the system in the Rules and Regulations have been deleted. The rules now provide that business concluded on the floor of the market between Full Members may be transacted free of commission. Commission must be charged on all other transactions between members and non-members. The Commission believes that this obligation is not appreciably restrictive of competition because it only entails the obligation to charge 'a' commission without any reference to the rate. It follows that complete freedom exists to negotiate the commission rates.[9]

The Commission took an identical view in a number of other cases where negative clearances were granted after the provisions specifying minimum rates of commission were dropped.[10]

49. There are also a number of Commission decisions and judgments of the European Court of Justice in other cases which found that price-fixing agreements infringed Article 85(1) and which are relevant to the present notification. In IFTRA[11] the EC Commission found that an

7. Ibid. at para. 4-003.
8. I. Van Bael and J.F. Bellis, 'Competition Law of the EEC', 2nd ed., CCH Editions Ltd, para. 802.
9. Commission Decision of 13 December 1985, OJ L369/25, 31.12.85. The omitted section of the quotation describes the actual commission rates set.
10. See, for example, Commission Decisions of 13 December 1985 in respect of; London Cocoa Terminal Market Association Ltd, Coffee Terminal Market Association of London Ltd and London Rubber Terminal Market Association Ltd, OJ L369/28 et. seq., 31.12.85. See also Commission Decisions of 10 December 1986 in respect of; The GAFTA Soya Bean Meal Futures Association, The London Grain Futures Market, The London Potato Futures Association Ltd and the London Meat Futures Exchange Ltd, OJ L19/18 et. seq., 21.1.87.
11. Case no. 75/497/EEC, OJ L228/3, 29.8.75.

agreement between producers of virgin aluminium not to sell below their published prices was in breach of Article 85(1). The Commission found that the arrangements 'provide the parties with means of shelter from competition to the extent that price stability is increased and that the parties are enabled to predict each other's price policy with a reasonable degree of certainty'.[12] 1.7.3

It went on to state that:

> '. . . every producer should have complete discretion to establish his own policy in these matters without risking the accusation that he is violating the spirit of an agreement. The contractual organisation of a system requiring adherence to various existing prices and whereby price stability is encouraged by the recommendations which are made to the parties to use and adhere to price lists . . . constitutes a major restriction of competition, both in its object and its effect.[13]

50. In Cementhandelaren the European Court of Justice ruled that:

> The fixing of a price, even one which merely constitutes a target, affects competition, because it enables all the participants to predict with a reasonable degree of certainty what the pricing policy pursued by their competitors will be.[14]

51. In the present context it is also relevant that the European Court of Justice has ruled that:

> A recommendation of an association of undertakings, even if it has no binding effect, cannot escape that article [85(1)] where compliance with the recommendations by the undertakings to which it is addressed has an appreciable influence on competition in the market in question.[15]

It is clear, however, that the rules of the Stock Exchange go beyond being mere recommendations. As pointed out above when one of the smaller stockbroking firms attempted to offer lower commissions on gilts to clients, the Exchange threatened to expel it. The use or threatened use of sanctions to ensure compliance with the system of fixed minimum commissions supports the view that they are anti-competitive.

52. The Stock Exchange argued that a 'standard' rate of commission would emerge even in the absence of fixed commission arrangements, given the nature of the market involved. Thus they submitted that the arrangement merely formalised the structure that would emerge under a negotiated commission regime, except that it preserved the agency broking structure of the market, thus ensuring the transparency of every trade. The Authority rejects this argument. It is true that in the absence of fixed minimum commissions a uniform rate of commission might emerge as a result of competition. In a truly competitive market homogeneous products would tend to sell at a uniform price. There is, however, a fundamental difference between a price which is set by competitive market forces and one which is based upon an agreement between competitors or upon the rule of an association.

53. The Authority also wishes to point out that, in its view, price fixing is anti competitive regardless of the level at which prices may be fixed. It has long been recognised under US competition law, for example, that price fixing arrangements cannot be justified on the basis

12. Ibid., p. 10.
13. Ibid., p. 12.
14. Case no. 8/72 [1972] ECR 977, point 23
15. *NV IAZ International Belgium and Others v. EC Commission*, Case nos. 96-102, 104, 105, 108 and 110/82, [1983] ECR pp. 3359-3430, point 3. This restated a view which the Court had expressed in a number of previous cases.

1.7.3 that the prices set were 'reasonable'. Thus, for example in Trenton Potteries[16] Mr Justice Stone noted that:

> The aim and result of every price-fixing agreement, if effective, is the elimination of one form of competition. The power to fix prices, whether reasonably exercised or not, involves power to control the market and to fix arbitrary and unreasonable prices. The reasonable price fixed today may through economic and business changes become the unreasonable price of tomorrow.

A similar view was taken in *Socony Vacuum Oil*[17] where the Supreme Court's judgment, as delivered by Mr Justice Douglas outlining why the reasonableness of prices could not serve to justify price-fixing stated:

> The reasonableness of prices has no constancy due to the dynamic quality of business facts underlying price structures. Those who fixed reasonable prices today would perpetuate unreasonable prices tomorrow, since those prices would not be subject to continuous administrative supervision and readjustment in light of changed conditions.

54. The Stock Exchange argued that the abolition of fixed commissions would lead to the breakdown of the agency broking system and the present arrangements would be replaced by a system of competing market makers. They submitted that this would reduce liquidity and turnover in the market and raise costs. The claim that the abolition of fixed minimum commissions would lead to the end of an agency broking system was disputed by both the IAIM and the NTMA. Section 4(1) of the Act prohibits anti-competitive agreements. It is designed to protect competition not competitors. The Authority in considering whether an arrangement offends against section 4(1) is required to decide whether or not it prevents, restricts or distorts competition. It may be that the removal of anti-competitive arrangements will result in a market structure very different to that which exists under such arrangements. In particular it may well change the nature of the entities operating in the market. It is not, however, for the Authority to express a preference for one type of system over another. Rather it must decide whether a particular arrangement is or is not anti-competitive.

55. The Authority is not convinced that the abolition of fixed commissions would lead inevitably to a move to a system of market makers. In taking this view it notes the views expressed by the IAIM and the NTMA. It also notes that the absence of fixed minimum commissions in the equity market and in the case of short dated gilts has not resulted in a move to market making. It is also relevant that attempts to offer discounts on gilts have been made by one of the smaller broking firms which would be unlikely to have the resources necessary to engage in market making.

56. The Stock Exchange also argued that the restrictions in respect of commissions did not restrict competition as brokers competed in other ways such as quality of service provided to clients. Many brokers provide a wide range of back-up services to their clients including detailed economic analysis and advice. Such services are financed out of commission income. While minimum commissions financed such services, they meant that investors are prevented from deciding which services they want. Many of the larger institutional investors have the resources to carry out their own detailed research and do so. Yet they were obliged, under the notified arrangements, to pay for such services which they might not want.

57. The Exchange did not argue that the commission arrangements were designed to prevent free riding although there may be some scope for this. For example, if commissions varied depending on the level of back-up services offered by brokers, then investors could obtain detailed analysis and advice from the broker providing such services, but then deal through a

16. *United States v. Trenton Potteries Company et. al.*, 273 US 392 (1927).
17. *United States v. Socony-Vacuum Oil Company, Inc. et. al.*, 310 US 150 (1940).

broker charging a lower commission and not providing such services. There appears to be no reason why brokers offering detailed research and analysis to their clients could not specifically charge for such services thereby avoiding the free rider problem. Indeed it is possible that if cross subsidisation of such services were eliminated a situation might arise whereby specialist firms decided to offer such services to meet the demands of gilt market investors. **1.7.3**

58. In sum therefore the Authority believes that the setting of fixed minimum commissions by the Stock Exchange for transactions in Irish Government securities, which had to be adhered to by all member firms, eliminated the possibility for stockbrokers to compete on price in the secondary market for such securities. In the Authority's opinion the elimination of price competition in this way prevents competition in the relevant market. Agreements to fix selling prices are listed as a specific example of the type of agreement prohibited by section 4(1) of the Act. Consequently in the Authority's opinion the rule requiring Stock Exchange members to charge minimum rates of commission on Irish Government securities offended against section 4(1).

59. Rule 79.1 and 2 provided for lower, albeit fixed rates of commission to be applied in respect of a new security issue with a maturity date of more than ten years on transactions effected within three months of the first day of dealings done for the same principal in such a new issue. Again, in the Authority's opinion this rule offended against section 4(1) since it fixed a minimum rate of commission to be charged on such transactions. The fact that this was lower than the normal rates applied under Rule 78.1 is irrelevant for the purpose of determining whether or not it offends against section 4(1).

60. Rule 81 allowed for certain reductions in the case of a change from one security to another for the same principal. Again, however, as this specified the reductions which may be offered from the standard rates it also offended against section 4(1).

61. The 1918 Stockbrokers (Ireland) Act provides for the setting by the Stock Exchange of a maximum rate of fees which may be charged by licensed stockbrokers on gilts. The Rules which were considered in the preceding paras relate to the fixing of minimum rates of commission. The Authority does not believe that the fixing of minimum commission rates was permitted by that Act thereby excluding such a practice from the scope of section 4(1) of the Competition Act.

(ii) The Agent Only Rule

62. Rule 49.1 provides that Stock Exchange member firms could only deal as an agent in respect of any security issued or guaranteed by the Government of the Republic of Ireland. If this restriction were removed certain types of institutions which currently operate as principals might be interested in offering broking services. In reality a number of large financial institutions have stockbroking firms as wholly owned subsidiaries and there appears to be nothing to stop any institution setting up its own broking subsidiary or acquiring one. Consequently the restriction would not appear to have the effect of preventing new entrants from coming into the market for stockbroking services.

63. The Authority must also consider whether the restriction on brokers acting as principals prevents, restricts or distorts competition in the gilt market itself. The Authority has accepted the view that the abolition of fixed commissions will not automatically lead to a system of market making and that in such circumstances brokers may continue to operate in an agency only capacity. Indeed they would be required to do so if Rule 49.1 remained. Clearly this rule prevented brokers from operating as buyers and sellers of gilts in the gilt market The rule requiring brokers to act only as agents prevented them operating as market makers should they wish to, and indeed appeared to prevent any other entity from operating as a market maker, since such an entity would in effect be operating outside of the market. In the absence of such a restriction some broking firms could conceivably decide to operate as market makers. This would obviously have some impact on competition in the gilt market itself.

64. The Authority accepts that the establishment of a market making operation would

1.7.3 require a considerable capital investment and that this would appear to be beyond the existing resources of most brokers. Thus it may be that only a small number of brokers might establish themselves as market makers, while the others would continue to act as agents, or that agent only brokers might not survive. It might also be that the removal of the agency restriction might cause a number of smaller brokers to establish links with overseas institutions in order to set up a market making operation. Indeed this appeared to be a concern of the Stock Exchange which submitted that to increase the number of competitive market makers it would be necessary to attract foreign houses, 'so transferring employment and value added abroad.' Again the entry of such overseas entities would appear likely to enhance competition in the market and the Authority would point out that anti-competitive arrangements cannot be justified on the basis that they keep foreign competitors out of a market. Essentially the agency only rule prevented the emergence of market makers which might otherwise be expected to operate in the gilt market and other forms of dealing enterprise. Competition on the gilt market may therefore be said to have been distorted to a degree, by the requirement that brokers act only as agents. Consequently this provision also offended against section 4(1).

65. The Authority notes that the 1799 Stock Brokers Act provides that brokers must not buy or sell on their own account when employed by any person not being a broker. This restriction does not prevent them acting as other than an agent when not employed by some other person. On balance therefore the Authority concludes that the obligation contained in Rule 49.1 that brokers act only as agents offended against section 4(1).

(e) *Applicability of section 4(2)*

66. Under section 4(2), the Competition Authority may grant a licence in the case of any agreement or category of agreements which offend against section 4(1) but which, 'having regard to all relevant market conditions, contributes to improving the production of goods or provision of services or to promoting technical or economic progress, while allowing consumers a fair share of the resulting benefit and which does not —

(i) impose on the undertakings concerned terms which are not indispensable to the attainment of those objectives;

(ii) afford undertakings the possibility of eliminating competition in respect of a substantial part of the products on services in question.

(i) Minimum Commissions

67. The requirement that brokers charge fixed minimum commissions on transactions in Irish Government Gilts did not satisfy the criteria set out in section 4(2) of the Act for a licence, in the Authority's view. The Authority does not believe that the rule on fixed minimum commissions contributes to improving the distribution of goods or provision of services or to promoting technical or economic progress. On balance it tends to accept the argument that the abolition of fixed commissions would enhance the degree of liquidity in the market. Consequently minimum commissions may actually hinder the further development of the market. It accepts that brokers have in the past contributed to the development of the market particularly when official agencies may not have been actively developing such business. In particular it accepts that they played a major role in attracting overseas investors into the market. It does not believe, however, that fixed commissions were essential for that purpose. Given that the Authority does not consider that the arrangements lead to any efficiency benefits, consumers, in this instance the clients of stockbrokers, by definition, do not benefit from such gains. In fact orthodox economic theory indicates that price- fixing agreements are detrimental rather than beneficial to consumer interests because cartels are inefficient and lessen consumer welfare.

68. The Authority does not believe that a system of fixed commissions is indispensable to the continued development of the gilt market. In addition as the vast bulk of transactions in government gilts is conducted through stockbrokers the arrangements afford the undertakings

involved the possibility of eliminating competition in respect of a substantial part of the market in question. As all four elements of section 4(2) must be satisfied before a licence may be granted the notified arrangements do not meet the requirements for a licence. **1.7.3**

69. In coming to the conclusion that the fixed minimum commission rules do not satisfy the criteria for a licence the Authority took account of the fact that over a period of 30 years the EU Commission has virtually never exempted price-fixing arrangements from the prohibition contained in Article 85(1).[18] It can see no reason for departing from well established EU precedents in the present case. It is also relevant that price-fixing is generally prohibited under the competition laws of most developed economies.

(ii) The Agent Only Rule

70. In the case of Rule 49.1 that brokers act only as agents the Authority considers that this can contribute to technical and economic progress and indeed accepts that the agency system contributed to the development of the market over the past decade. It believes that consumers in the form of investors have shared in such benefits. It does not, however, believe that the restriction is essential for the development of the market and so it cannot be regarded as indispensable. The Authority does not believe that the restriction affords the undertakings concerned the possibility of eliminating competition in respect of a substantial part of the market. Nevertheless as it did not meet all four of the requirements specified for the grant of a licence, the Authority was unable to grant a licence to this restriction.

The Decision

71. The Irish Stock Exchange is an association of undertakings since all of its member firms are themselves undertakings being engaged in the provision of services for gain, The Rules and Regulations of the Irish Stock Exchange, including those relating to transactions in Irish Government Securities, constitute decisions of an association of undertakings and agreements between undertakings. In the Authority's opinion the following Rules, namely:

> Rule 49.1 which required that brokers act only as agents in respect of transactions in Irish Government securities;
> Rule 75.1 which required brokers to charge fixed minimum rates of commission on such transactions;
> Rule 78.1 which set out fixed minimum rates of commission which had to be applied to such transactions;
> Rule 79.1 and 2 and Rule 81 which provided for lower rates of commission in certain limited circumstances;

had as their object and effect the prevention, restriction or distortion of competition in the market for Government securities within the State and thus offended against section 4(1). They did not, in the opinion of the Authority, satisfy the requirements for a licence set out in section 4(2). Consequently the Authority refuses to issue a certificate or grant a licence to the Irish Stock Exchange Rules in respect of Irish Government securities, (CA/199/92E), notified on 29 September 1992.

72. The rule on fixed commission has now been abolished by the Irish Stock Exchange. The present decision is not concerned with any new rules which might be introduced by the Irish Stock Exchange in respect of dealings in Government Gilts as no such arrangements have been notified to it. The Authority has not considered the proposals made by the Irish Association of Investment Managers to replace Rule 49.1. The Authority's role is to consider whether

18. In Uniform Eurocheques an exemption was granted for an agreement on uniform commission charges among the banks operating the Eurocheque system, (OJ 1985 L35/43 [1985] CMLR 434). In Nuovo Cegam an exemption was granted to an agreement between Italian engineering insurers on basic premiums to be charged, for exceptional reasons, but this did not extend to total premiums (OJ 1984 L99/29 [1984] 2 CMLR 484).

1.7.3 arrangements notified to it by the parties involved offend against section 4(1) and, when they do, whether they meet the requirements for a licence under section 4(2).

For the Competition Authority

Patrick Massey
Member

10 June 1994

Annex 1: Irish Stock Exchange Member Firms

B.C.P. Stockbrokers
72 Upper Leeson Street
Dublin 2

Bloxham Stockbrokers
9-12 Fleet Street
Dublin 2

Butler & Briscoe
3 College Green
Dublin 2

Campbell O'Connor & Co.
8 Cope Street
Dublin 2

Davy Stockbrokers
49 Dawson Street
Dublin 2

Goodbody Stockbrokers
5 College Green
Dublin 2

Money Markers International
Stockbrokers Ltd
26 Lower Baggot Street
Dublin 2

W & R Morrogh
74 South Mall
Cork

NCB Stockbrokers Ltd.
45/53 Lower Mount Street
Dublin 2

O'Brien Stokes Stockbrokers
36 Dame Street
Dublin 2

Riada Stockbrokers
1 College Green
Dublin 2

Solomons Stockbrokers
Stephen Court
18/21 St Stephen's Green
Dublin 2

Competition Authority Decision No. 336, Net Book Agreement: 10 June 1994, Notification Nos. CA/23-30/92E **1.7.4**

Arrangements between UK book publishers having an effect on trade in the State – Resale price maintenance – Horizontal restraints – Arrangements whereby an association of undertakings monitors and enforces adherence to such arrangements – Unfair competitive advantage to some booksellers – Request to delay decision pending appeal decision of ECJ on similar arrangements – Statement of Objections – Oral hearing – Competition Act 1991 (No. 24) sections 3, 4 and 7

Facts: On 20 May 1992 notification was made to the Authority with a request for certificate under section 4(4) of the Competition Act 1991 or, failing that, a licence under section 4(2) in respect of arrangements comprising of eight agreements providing for the imposition by UK publishers of minimum net prices for the majority of their books sold within the State.

The notified arrangements (hereinafter referred to 'the net book arrangements') comprise; (i) Net Book Agreement (members version); (ii) Net Book Agreement (non-members version); (iii) Book Club Regulations 1985; (iv) Library Licence; (v) Book Agent's Licence; (vi) Quantity Book Buying Scheme; (vii) National Book Sale conditions; and (viii) Primary and Secondary School Licence. The terms of the net book arrangements are administered and monitored by the Publishers Association, a UK based association of publishers. Under the terms of the Net Book Agreement (members and non-members versions) books which are designated net books by publishers cannot be sold at less than the net published prices except in very restricted circumstances. There is no obligation on the publisher to designate a book a 'net book' but in practice most do and circa 75% of the books imported from the UK and Ireland are designated net books.

Under the terms of the net book arrangements the Publishers Association is appointed to act on behalf of the publishers in the monitoring of breaches of such price restrictions by booksellers and the publishers agree that when informed by the Publishers Association of such breaches they will enforce their contractual rights against such booksellers. The book club regulations regulate the sale of net books through book clubs under licence and contain restrictions on the terms on which such clubs can offer net books to their members including restrictions on advertising the books available. The library licence and the book agent's licence permit booksellers to give specified discounts to library and agents holding such a licence on the condition that, *inter alia,* the licensee purchases from a specified bookseller and in the case of library licensee that the books so purchased are not resold and in the case of the agent licensee that the books so purchased are not re-sold below the net published price. The quantity book buying scheme provides that large orders of net books may be sold by booksellers at specified rates of discount on the condition that such books are not re-sold by the purchaser. The primary and secondary school licence provides that schools which satisfy certain requirements will be issued a licence which will permit them, upon depositing that licence with a bookseller, to a discount from such bookseller (not exceeding 10%) in the purchase of net school books for use in that licensed school. The net book arrangements provide that net books may be sold to the public at less than the net published price during the national book sale. The terms of the national book sale limit the national sale to a specified duration (usually

1.7.4 one month per annum) during which period booksellers may participate for any length of time within that period in the sale of net books at reduced prices subject to the further restrictions on the books that are so sold.

Under the terms of the notified arrangements the publishers appoint the Publisher Association to act on their behalf in collecting information concerning breaches of contract by persons selling net books. The publishers agree to enforce their contract rights when called upon to do so by the Publishers Association.

On 28 October 1993 the Authority issued a statement of objections indicating that it intended to refuse a certificate or licence in respect of the notified arrangements. At an oral hearing on 10 May 1994 the Publishers Association in addition to making further submissions requested that the Authority would not make a final decision in respect of the notified arrangements pending the outcome of an appeal to the European Court of Justice in relation to similar agreements following the EC Commissions refusal to grant an exemption to the arrangements under Article 85(3) of The Treaty of Rome.*

Decided by the Authority

(A) In refusing to issue a certificate under section 4(4) of the Competition Act 1991 in respect of the notified arrangements that:

(1) The parties to the notified agreement are publishers and are engaged for gain in the production and publication of books and are therefore 'undertakings' within the meaning of the Competition Act.

(2) The net book agreement (members and non-members versions) constitute agreements between undertakings relating to the standard conditions of sale for UK published books within the State and also constitute decisions of an association of undertakings. The other related arrangements notified which set out the conditions upon which publishers supply books to different category of buyers constitute an agreement between those publishing undertakings and also decisions of an association of undertaking within the meaning of the Competition Act.

(3) While the publishing undertakings to the notified arrangements are based in the UK, the arrangements apply in respect of the sale of net books within the State and therefore are within the scope of the Competition Act.

(4) Re-sale price maintenance is generally restrictive of competition and arrangements involving re-sale price maintenance will generally offend against section 4(1).

(5) While the net book arrangements might not amount to a full horizontal price fixing arrangement it does go some considerable way towards reducing uncertainty regarding competitor's pricing decisions which uncertainty is normally an essential part of the competitive process. As most books which are sold are UK published books and are books which are subject to the notified arrangements price competition between retailers is restricted in a substantial part of the market. The net book arrangements thus have the object and the effect of restricting competition in the market for books within the State.

(6) While publishers may choose not to include a book in the arrangements, 75% of UK published books are so designated. Once so designated a publisher is bound to apply the standard considerations governing the sale of net books. This aspect of the

**Editor's Note:* On 17 January 1995 [Case C-360/92P OJ No. C54 4.3.1995] the Court of First Instance's confirming judgment of the EC Commission decision was set aside by the European Court of Justice. The original EC Commission decision in 1988 is reported at [1988] OJ L22/12; [1989] 4 CMLR 825.

arrangement restricts competition in the market for books in the State and offends against section 4(1) of the Act. The publishers' option not to apply the arrangements to every book is not sufficient to avoid the scope of section 4(1). 1.7.4

(7) The provisions under the arrangements whereby the Publishers Association collects information on breaches of the arrangements by sellers of net books and the undertaking by the publishers to enforce those breached contractual rights when so called upon by the Publishers Association reinforces the restrictions on competition and is designed to ensure a more efficient surveillance of compliance with the agreement and rules. These provisions are designed to ensure adherence to arrangements which offend against section 4(1) and therefore these provisions also offend against section 4(1).

(8) The book club regulations, while applicable to UK book clubs, operate within the State to the extent that they prevent UK based book clubs selling net books in the State other than in accordance with the terms of the regulations has the object of restricting competition between book clubs and other booksellers in the State.

(9) The requirement in the library licence and book agent's licence that the licensees must purchase from a particular bookseller to avail of specified discounts restricts competition in the supply to those licensed libraries and agent's thereby offending section 4(1).

(10) The provisions of the national book sale which allow booksellers to offer net books for sale only during a specified period and by limiting the range of books which may be sold during such period have as their object and effect the prevention, restriction, and distortion of competition.

(11) The provisions of the primary and secondary school licence, fixes maximum discounts and ensures that schools will not sell books below the set price. Booksellers which supply schools and which benefit from a licence have an unfair competitive advantage over other booksellers.

(12) The quantity book buying scheme offends section 4(1) of the Competition Act because it limits the circumstances in which booksellers may offer discount rates and the purpose of such restrictions is to support the resale price maintenance provisions of the agreement.

(B) In refusing to grant a licence under section 4(2) of the Competition Act in respect of the notified arrangements that:

(1) In the absence of the notified arrangements there would be discounting of the more popular book titles. This implies that the arrangements result in higher prices for popular books which permits cross-subsidisation of less popular titles. Cross-subsidisation results in a misallocation of resources since customers do not bear the true cost of the individual products. A misallocation of resources reduces efficiency and so cannot be claimed to increase technical or economic progress.

(2) The possibility that the elimination of the restrictive practices set out in the net book arrangements might have the effect of harming smaller or specialist booksellers to the advantage of larger booksellers cannot be used to justify the continuance of a restrictive practice for the essence of the Competition Act is to protect competition and not competitors and to the extent that the notified arrangements prevent the emergence of new competitors and innovative methods of retailing, such as discounting, it cannot be said to result in any improvement in the distribution of goods or in the promotion of economic progress in the relevant market.

1.7.4 (3) Insofar as the notified arrangements do not contribute to improving the production of goods or provision of services or to promoting technical or economic progress there is no benefit in which consumers can be said to share and since the majority of the books imported from the UK are 'net' books the restrictions contained in the arrangements can be said to eliminate competition in respect of a substantial part of the relevant market.

(4) The primary aim of the ancillary agreements notified with the net book agreements is to ensure the effective operation of the resale price maintenance provisions set out in the 'net' book agreements and for that reason they also fail to satisfy the requirements for a licence.

Case and Decision referred to:

EC Commission Decision Net Book Agreements (Case No. 89/44/EEC), [1988] OJ L22/12, [1989] 4 CMLR 825

VBVB/VBBB v. EC Commission (Case No. 43 and No. 63/82), [1984] ECR 19, [1985] 1 CMLR 27

Competition Authority Decision of 10 June 1994 relating to a proceeding under section 4 of the Competition Act 1991

Notification Nos. CA/23-30/92E — Net Book Agreement

Introduction

1. Arrangements for the imposition by UK publishers of a minimum net price on most of their books sold within the State were notified to the Authority on 20 May 1992. The arrangements comprising 8 agreements in total are known as the Net Book Agreement and have operated in their present form since 1957. The notification requested a certificate, or in the event of a refusal by the Authority to grant a certificate, a licence.

2. The Authority issued a Statement of Objections to the notifying parties on 28 October 1993 informing them that the Authority intended to refuse to issue a certificate or licence to the notified agreements. An Oral Hearing was held on 10 May 1994.

(a) *The Subject of the Notification*

2. The notification concerns an arrangement known as the Net Book Agreement (NBA). This is a voluntary agreement administered by the Publishers Association (PA), whereby UK book publishers impose a minimum net price on the sale of most of their publications in the U.K. and the Republic of Ireland. The notification also contains a number of ancillary agreements providing for limited exemptions from the provisions of the NBA for specified groups of book purchasers.

(b) *The Parties Concerned*

3. The NBA is a voluntary agreement administered by the PA. The parties to it are a number of UK book publishing companies. The notification lists 197 publishers who are PA members and over 200 publishers who are not members of the PA who are party to either the members or non-members version of the NBA.

(c) *The Product and the Market*

5. The notified arrangements are concerned with the retail sale of books to the general public and the sale of books by publishers to schools, book clubs, libraries and retail outlets. The products concerned are books of various types. To some degree each individual book title may be considered an individual product. Some consumers are interested in particular types of books, e.g. thrillers, while others may have a preference for a particular author. A DIY title is not a close substitute for a romantic novel. Nevertheless there is scope for a considerable degree of substitutability between book titles. It is possible, however, to distinguish between school-

books and other types of books as these categories cannot be considered to be close substitutes for one another. The Net Book Agreement is an agreement involving UK book publishers who are the chief suppliers of general books to the Irish market. The principal market involved therefore is that for the sale of books other than schoolbooks in the State. **1.7.4**

5. A study of the Irish book market estimated that the total value of retail sales of books in 1985 was £56m, of which £16m (28.6%) was spent on schoolbooks.[1] It estimated that Irish publishers supplied 85% of the domestic market for schoolbooks and 12% of that for all other publications. Thus the non-schoolbook market was estimated at about £40m of which £35m was imported. Imported books accounted for 88% of the non-schoolbook market or 67% of all books purchased in Ireland. Total household expenditure on books other than schoolbooks was estimated at £25m. The study figures suggest a total retail value of £37.4m for imported books in 1985. According to the CSO book imports in 1985 amounted to £33.3m.[2] Allowing for mark-ups by domestic distributors and retailers, this suggests that the study estimates for book imports may be slightly on the low side. Whether this is because it underestimated imports' share of the market or the overall side of the market is unclear. Nevertheless even allowing for some error in the study figures it is clear that imports account for the majority of books sold within the State.

Table 1: Estimated Market for Books 1985

	£ million	%
Household expenditure		
— on school books	16.0	28.6
— on other books	25.0	44.6
Libraries (public and academic)	4.5	8.1
Other corporate expenditure	5.5	9.8
Expenditure by non-residents	5.0	8.9
Total	56.0	100.0

Source: Fishwick

6. Book imports in 1991 amounted to £59.8m (Table 2), an increase of almost 80% on the 1985 figure. It is not possible to establish whether imported books' market share had risen in the intervening period. Nevertheless it is clear that imports continue to account for a large proportion of the Irish book market. Imports of books from Great Britain and Northern Ireland accounted for 79% of book imports in 1991. In sum the majority of books sold in Ireland are imported and the majority of imported books are published in the UK.

Table 2: Book Imports by Country

	1991		1990	
Country	(£000)	(%)	(£000)	(%)
Great Britain	45,047	(75.3)	41.271	(73.9)
Northern Ireland	2,121	(3.5)	1,980	(3.5)
U.S.A.	7,493	(13.4)	4,268	(7.8)
Other Cos.	5,138	(9.2)	6,892	(12.7)
Total	59,799	(100)	54,411	(100)

1. The Market for Books in the Republic of Ireland — Francis Fishwick, MA(Econ) PhD, Reader in Managerial Economics at the Cranfield School of Management.
2. Central Statistics Office Trade Statistics, December 1986.

1.7.4 7. According to the 1988 Census of Services, there were 370 retail outlets involved in the sale of books and stationery with 1659 persons engaged. Total turnover of bookshops in 1988 was £79m according to the Census, of which Dublin outlets accounted for £35.7m (45.4%).[3] The number of bookshops had increased by 130 since the 1977 census. Of the 370 outlets, 111 were located in Dublin with the rest of Leinster accounting for an additional 102. This compares with the 1977 figure of 72 and 41 respectively. The province of Munster had 115 outlets in 1988 compared with 84 in 1977. Of the 1988 total 37 were located in Cork 17 in Limerick and 8 in Waterford. Connacht had 31 bookshops compared to 25 in 1977. The Ulster counties of Donegal, Monaghan and Cavan had a combined total of 11 outlets which represented a decrease on the 1977 figure of 18.

Table 3: Book and Stationery Retail Outlets

	No. of outlets		Gross Turnover	
	1988	1977	1988 **	1977
	%	%	%	%
Leinster	213 (57.6)	113 (47.1)	52.3 (66.5)	12.1 (66.5)
Munster	115 (31.1)	84 (35.0)	22.2 (28.3)	2.2 (28.9)
Connacht	31 (8.4)	25 (10.4)	3.0 (3.7)	0.5 (2.6)
Ulster	11 (3.0)	18 (7.5)	1.2 (1.5)	0.3 (2.0)
State	370 (100)	240 (100)	78.6 (100)	18.1 (100)
Dublin	111 (30.0)	72 (30.0)	35.7 (45.4)	10.8 (59.6)
Cork	37 (10.0)	24 (10.0)	10.5 (13.4)	2.4 (13.4)
Limerick	17 (4.6)	9 (3.8)	4.1 (5.2)	1.0 (5.3)
Waterford	8 (2.2)	7 (2.9)	2.2 (2.8)	0.4 (2.3)
Galway	10 (2.7)	*	1.3 (1.7)	*
Total	183 (49.5)	112 (46.7)	53.8 (68.4)	14.6 (80.6)

* Figures not available

Source: Census of Services (CSO) 1988 and 1977

8. Table 4 shows that the average size of retail bookshops in 1988 was almost 900 square feet. Overall average size in 1983 was 8% higher than in 1977. There were considerable regional variations. The average size of bookshops in Dublin was 1300 square feet compared with 700 square feet outside of Dublin. The average bookshop in Connacht/Ulster was less than half the size of the average Dublin shop, while the average Munster bookshop was only 60% as large. It is clear, however, that the average size of bookshops outside of Dublin increased over the 1977-88 period.

3. Some of these stores may specialise in stationery although it is likely that there would be relatively few of those. Consequently the figures from the Census of Distribution for book and stationery stores probably provide a good indication of the number of retail book outlets. In addition some shops included in other categories of the Census may also sell some books e.g. newsagents. The Authority has not attempted to reconcile this figure with those contained in the Fishwick study.

***Editor's note*: The totals and percentages for 1977 Gross Turnover do not add up to the figures quoted according to the editor's calculations. See Table 2 in Decision 348 at 1.7.5 also. Pg 236.

Table 4: Average Size of Book and Stationery Outlets (Sq-Ft) **1.7.4**

	1988	1977
Leinster	1013	1048
Munster	788	776
Connacht	539	360
Ulster	645	300
Dublin	1304	1369
Rest of Ireland	716	592
State	892	825

Source: Census of Services (CSO) 1988 and 1977

9. Libraries, both public and academic, account for a significant proportion of book purchases. It was estimated by Dr Fishwick in his publication that, in 1985, libraries (both private and those operated by local authorities) accounted for 8.1% of total book sales representing an expenditure of £4.5m (Table 7). CSO figures show that expenditure on book acquisitions by public libraries in 1985 amounted to £3.2m.[4] By 1989 this figure had fallen to £2.3m but subsequently increased to £3m in 1991.

The Arrangements

10. The Net Book Agreement, 1957, is an agreement between firms of publishers on the standard conditions of sale for net books published by them in the UK and Ireland. There are two net book agreements — one for members of the PA, the other for non-members. The Net Book Agreement first came into force in 1900, following massive price cutting in the book trade. Its terms were revised in 1957 to bring it into line with the UK Restrictive Trade Practices Act 1956.

Net Book Agreement — members version

11. The basic clause in the Net Book Agreement, contained in clause (i), provides that, except in specified circumstances, net books cannot be sold at less than the net published prices. These prices are determined by the individual publishers.

(i) Except as provided in clauses (ii) to (iv)

hereof and except as we may otherwise direct net books shall not be sold or offered for sale or caused or permitted to be sold or offered for sale to the public at less than the net published prices.

A net book is defined in clause (vi) as a book which is published at a net price, i.e. at a price fixed by the publisher below which the net book shall not be sold to the public.

12. The exceptions to the requirement in clause (i) are set out in clauses (ii), (iii) and (iv) and refer to net books which have been in stock for a considerable time, second-hand books and net books sold to libraries, book agents, quantity buyers and authorised institutions. The clauses are as follows:

> (ii) A net book may be sold or offered for sale to the public at less than the net published price if
> (a) it has been held in stock by the bookseller for a period of more than twelve months from the date of the latest purchase by him of any copy hereof and
> (b) it has been offered to the publisher at cost price or at the proposed reduced price whichever shall be the lower and such offer has been refused by the publisher.

4. Although this is somewhat lower than the Fishwick figure, the latter includes private libraries.

1.7.4 (iii) A net book may be sold or offered for sale to the public at less than the net published price if it is second-hand and six months have elapsed since its date of publication.

(iv) A net book may be sold at a discount to such libraries, book agents (including Service Unit libraries), quantity buyers and institutions as are from time to time authorised by the Council of The Publishers Association of such amount and on such conditions as are laid down in the instrument of authorisation. Such amount and conditions shall not initially be less or less favourable than those prevailing at the date of this Agreement.

These clauses are dealt with in more detail in other agreements which are described below.

Enforcement

13. The publishers also agree, under the National Book Agreement, to appoint the Council of the PA to act on their behalf in relation to breaches of the standard conditions of sale of net books. In this respect, the Council collects information concerning breaches of contract by booksellers and keeps each individual publisher informed of such breaches. The publishers agree that they will enforce their contractual rights under the UK Restrictive Trade Practices Act, 1956, which refers to a statutory right to enforce a minimum resale price condition in respect of certain goods including books and to obtain an injunction to restrain breach of the conditions. The funds of the Association may be used to cover legal expenses in pursuing actions for breach of the standard conditions of sale. The PA stated that:

> In practice, there have been few if any cases of alleged breach in Ireland, any problems that might arise being resolved by explaining the conditions of sale to the bookseller and seeking assurances for the future. The NBA has a very high level of acceptance in the Irish book trade because of the clear benefits it gives to the public and to the book trade in Ireland.

Net Book Agreement, 1957 – non members version

14. This agreement is the same as the members version with one exception. Under the members version, the members of the PA who are signatories to the members agreement are indemnified by the Association in respect of the costs of action for reinforcement. No such provision is included in the non members agreement.

Book Clubs Regulations

15. The stated objective of these regulations, set out in Clause 2, is to regulate the operation of book clubs in the public interest. Clause 6 states that:

> These Regulations shall apply to, and only to, titles the trade editions of which are published as net books. They shall not apply to the sale of net books at not less than the net price.

16. By virtue of Clause 14, Book Clubs are required to notify the trade in advance of offering any books to members:

> At least, four months before offering a title, book clubs shall send to the Publishers Association a list of all their forthcoming titles which the Publishers Association shall cause to be published forthwith in the trade press. This notification shall include the following details: (a) title; (b) author; (c) licensing publisher.

17. Under clause 17 every book offered by a book club has to have on the title page, cover and on the binding, its own imprint, crest or legend to indicate that it is a book club edition. The exceptions to this requirement are as follows:

(a) in exceptional cases where there proves to be an inadequate supply of such copies bearing the book club imprint the trade edition may be used up to a maximum number of copies equivalent to 20 per cent of the order for the copies bearing the book club imprint. **1.7.4**

(b) when a book club does not have exclusive book club rights to a title, the licensing publisher may permit the use by book clubs of not more than a total of 5,000 copies of the trade edition or 50 per cent of the licensing publisher's print order (whichever is the lower).

18. Book clubs must, under Clause 13, have the consent of the licensing publisher before disposing of surplus stock as remainders. Clauses 12 and 16 relate to the supply of books to members. In this connection a premium is a book offered as an inducement to join a book club.

12. Book clubs shall supply book club choices only to registered members, and premiums only to persons applying to become members.

16. A title shall not be offered as a premium until at least six months after its first issue as a trade edition.

19. Advertising restrictions on book clubs are contained in Clauses 15 and 18:

15. Book clubs shall not make any announcement to the public or to members that a title is to be offered as a book club choice or as a premium until three months before the intended date of issue of the book club choice or of the premium as the case may be.

18. (a) In advertising book club choices or premiums, any comparison with the price of the trade edition issued by the licensing publisher shall be only in the following form:

Publisher's price £x
(Book Club) price £y

(b) Advertisements and publicity material relating to the offer of a book club choice or premium shall not suggest or indicate in any way, in particular by the showing of an imprint, that the copies to be supplied by the club are physically identical with the trade edition.

20. Members of book clubs are required under Clause 11 to purchase at least 3 books within a specified period of time, usually a year.

11. Book clubs shall lay down a minimum period of membership which shall be not less than six months and members shall be required to purchase not less than three book club choices (excluding premiums) within the first year of membership, (or such shorter period as may be appropriate).

21. The PA stated that the Book Club Regulations apply only to book club operations within the UK and have no application to trade in books between EC Member States. They apply only to titles the trade editions of which are published as net books. The PA also indicated that book club licences confer either exclusive or non-exclusive licences on a club allowing it to make and issue copies of the work. The book clubs have signed a 'concordat' limiting the duration and extent of exclusive licences so as to protect the interests of smaller clubs, with licensing publishers recommended by the Council of the PA not to license rights to book clubs which did not subscribe to, and honour, the concordat.

Library Licence

22. The terms and conditions under which net books are supplied to libraries are detailed

1.7.4 in a document entitled 'Library Licence'. Booksellers are entitled by virtue of condition (iv) of the Standard Conditions of Sale of Net Books, Net Book Agreement, 1957, to supply libraries with net books at a discount not exceeding 10% of their net published prices subject to the following conditions:

> 1. Discount on net books may be allowed only in return for prompt settlement of invoices.
> 2. Discount may not be allowed on net books on which the Bookseller receives a discount of less than sixteen and two-thirds per cent plus five per cent.
> 3. Discount may be allowed only so long as the Library's total annual purchases of net books solely for the use of the library is not less than £100.
> 4. No consideration in cash or in kind, other than the granting of a discount permitted under this Licence, shall be offered or given by the Bookseller or sought or accepted by the Library in respect of or in connection with the supply of net books by the Bookseller to the Library.
> 5. Without prejudice to the generality of the last foregoing Condition, supplementary services (such as card-indexing, stamping, reinforcement of binding, the supply and fitting of plastic jackets etc.), if provided by or on behalf of the Bookseller to the Library, shall be charged and paid for at not less than the actual cost thereof to the Bookseller.
> Books purchased under this Licence shall be purchased solely for the use of the Library and not for resale.
> This Licence is revocable by the Council of the Publishers Association at any time but, unless revoked on account of a breach of the Standard Conditions of Sale referred to above, not less than three months previous notice shall be given.

Book Agent's Licence

23. Book agents are individuals not carrying on the business of selling books as their main activity, e.g. a school principal who maintains a small supply of books for sale to pupils. Under Clause (iv) of the standard conditions of sale, Net Book Agreement 1957, book agents may purchase net books at a discount. A book agent's licence may be granted where the book agent agrees to give the following undertaking:

> (i) not to offer for sale or to sell any new net book or books at less than the full net published price, either directly or indirectly or by way of settlement discount;
> (ii) not to ask for or to accept any allowance upon new net books except from the bookseller named upon this Licence or upon any endorsement thereof.

Once this undertaking is given, the book agent becomes authorised to purchase new books from a specified bookseller for resale to the public at the full published price.

24. The bookseller is authorised to allow the book agent an allowance not exceeding 50% of the retail discount given to the book seller by the publisher in respect of each new book supplied to the book agent.

25. The Licence may be revoked by the Publishers Association in the event of a breach of its terms and/or conditions. The licence may also be withdrawn by giving 3 months notice to the Licensee.

Quantity Book Buying Scheme

26. A net book may be sold at a discount to quantity buyers under the standard conditions of sale of the Net Book Agreement. This scheme is designed to extend the large scale purchase of net books by individual and commercial enterprises. The scheme covers large single orders for net books of an aggregate value of £250 or more, regardless of the number of copies of any one title contained in the order.

For an order for assorted titles worth £250 or more: 1.7.4

Value of order	Discount
£250 — £349	5%
£350 — £449	6%
£450 — £549	7%
£550 — £649	8%
£650 — £749	9%
£750 — and over	10%

(b) For an order for a large quantity of one title (minimum 12), to a total value of £25 or more:

A flat 10 per cent discount.

28. Licences for the granting of discounts as set out above are issued by the Publishers Association subject to the following conditions:

> (a) The books must be required for gift or presentation in connection with the purchaser's business, or for philanthropic or propaganda purposes. The provision of a library, whether recreational or educational, for use by the purchaser's own employees, free of charge, would qualify.
> (b) The books are not to be offered for sale by the purchaser, nor is their use or distribution to be made subject by him to any charge or other consideration.
> (c) The order will be delivered in one consignment and paid for in cash on receipt.
> (d) No discount shall be allowable on books on which the bookseller himself does not receive from the publisher a discount of at least 25 per cent. The value of any such books shall be deducted from the total value of any order coming under this scheme before application is made for discount to be allowed.
> (e) Licences issued by the Publishers Association under this scheme shall apply to one order only and shall not be valid for repeat orders (although application may be made for fresh licences in respect of repeat orders that qualify on their own account).

National Book Sale

29. The Net Book Agreement provides that net books may be sold to the public at less than the net published price during the national book sale. In relation to national book sales, certain conditions apply and they must be observed by all participating publishers, wholesalers and retailer booksellers. Books available in these sales can be from one of three sources — bookseller's overstocks, publisher's overstocks and wholesaler's overstocks. The sale has a limited specified duration — in 1992, it lasted from 27 June to 25 July. Booksellers may participate in the sale for any length of time within the period of the sale.

30. Where retail booksellers have not ordered a copy of books within the preceding twelve months, they are allowed to sell these titles at a discount of 33% or more during the period of the sale [condition 2]. However, publishers have the right to exclude all of their titles from the sale but no publisher can exclude selected titles only. Similarly books that are already reduced in price in accordance with clause (ii) of the standard conditions of the Sale of Net Books cannot be excluded [condition 3].

31. Publishers taking part in the sale arrange for lists of their overstocks to be sent to a marketing company for mailing to licensed booksellers. Condition 5 provides for the terms on which publishers' overstocks should be offered:

> 5. Publishers' overstocks shall be offered on the following terms: at 50 per cent off the Sale Price, the Sale price being fixed by the publisher. Sale prices shall not be more than half the published price. Not less than three copies may be ordered of books of a sale price of 50p or less.

1.7.4 32. Booksellers are permitted, under condition 6, to fix their own prices for publishers overstocks during the last week of the sale. No advance announcement of the intended further reductions is permitted. Publishers' overstocks which remain unsold revert to their original full price on conclusion of the sale. These books can be sold at any price in subsequent national sales by the bookseller without reference to the publishers. [condition 7]. Publishers are prohibited from issuing titles offered at reduced prices during the sale, at prices lower than those which obtained prior to the sale, for a period of six months after the sale period [condition 8]. Booksellers are restricted in accepting publications of a non-participating publisher at a reduced price for the sale [condition 9].

33. Under condition 12, Wholesale booksellers are permitted to offer participating retail booksellers:

> (i) any title in their stocks, a copy of which has not been ordered or added to stock during the previous twelve months (provided it has not been excluded from the sale by the publishers under condition 3), and
> (ii) any title in their stock, which is not being offered as an overstock by publishers.

Wholesalers fix the sale prices for their overstocks subject to the proviso that they cannot be more than half the published price [condition 13]. Prices of books to be included in the sale cannot be advertised at these prices more than 21 days in advance of the sale [condition 14].

Primary and Secondary school Licence

34. Under the standard conditions of Sale of Net Books, a net book may be sold at a discount to institutions such as primary and secondary schools subject to authorisation by the Council of the PA. The organisations who benefit under this arrangement are given a licence — the 'Primary and Secondary School Licence'. These organisations are described as principal licensees in the 'Terms of Licence' and Clause 2 sets out the requirements to be satisfied by a principal licensee:

> 2. The requirements to be satisfied by a principal licensee are that it must be:
> (a) a primary and/or secondary school teaching a full curriculum to full-time students and accepted as such by the appropriate authorities; or
> (b) a local education authority responsible for schools as defined in (a).

35. A subsidiary licensee may also benefit under the arrangement. Where the principal licensee is a local education authority, schools which satisfy the requirements of Clause 3 may attain subsidiary licensee status.

> 3. The requirements to be satisfied by a subsidiary licensee are as follows:
> (a) it must be a school as defined in Clause 2(a) above;
> (b) it must be a school for which the principal licensee is responsible;
> (c) it must agree to be bound by the conditions of this licence and must communicate such agreement to the principal licensee; and
> (d) its name must be included in a list, to be provided to booksellers in accordance with Clause 7 below, in which the principal licensee certifies the school's compliance with (a) to (c) above.

36. Certain procedures must be complied with before discounts can be granted. This provision is included in Clause 7 of the Terms of Licence.

> 7. No discount shall be granted by a bookseller to a licensee pursuant to this Licence unless the licensee has first deposited with the bookseller:

(a) a copy of this Licence; 1.7.4

(b) where the principal licensee is a local education authority, an accurate list of names and addresses of schools certified by the authority to qualify as subsidiary licensees (which list shall be updated as necessary).

Clause 5 indicates how organisations benefit from holding a licence:

> 5. The License permits (but does not require) a bookseller to supply net books to a licensee at a discount not exceeding 10 per cent of their net published prices, subject to other conditions of this Licence and of the Standard Conditions of Sale of Net Books, but otherwise on such terms and conditions as may be agreed.

Clause 6 sets out the extent of the benefits available:

> 6. The Licence permits such discounts to be granted only in respect of net books supplied to a licensee for use within the Licensee's own school or schools (or, in the case of supply to a licensed local education authority, for use within the schools which are that authority's subsidiary licensees) for the purposes of primary and/or secondary education.

37. Clause 13 provides that:

> Any breach of the conditions of this Licence constitutes a breach of the Standard Conditions of Sale of Net Books and, without prejudice to whatever other remedies may be available will render the Licence liable to immediate revocation.

The notification stated that such licences has not yet been applied in Ireland. The PA subsequently indicated that the school licences had never been used in Ireland. In a letter dated 25 May 1994 the PA indicated that, if the Authority were minded to grant a licence, the PA would seek to bring the arrangements into operation in Ireland as soon as possible.

Directory

38. The Net Book Agreement was notified to the EC in 1973. This notification alluded to a directory consisting of a list of booksellers who confirmed, *inter alia*, that they were in receipt of the standard conditions of sale of net books and who gave an undertaking absolutely to observe these conditions. This directory was maintained by the Association. At the time of the EC notification, the Association stated that this listing was an information service to publishers and booksellers — it was not a recommendation by the Association to supply or not to supply a particular bookseller. The Association have indicated that the Directory was discontinued during the course of the proceedings with the EC Commission.

(d) *Submissions of the Parties*

39. The PA submitted that the NBA operates to the benefit of the consumer by ensuring that booksellers are enabled to stock a wide range of books on varying subjects which, in the absence of the NBA, would not be available for reasons of economic viability. In support of this contention, the PA referred to the judgments of the UK Restrictive Practices Court in 1962, 1964 and 1968 which concluded that abrogation of the Net Book Agreement would lead to fewer and less well equipped book shops, higher prices and fewer available titles. It claimed that a 1989 investigation by the UK Office of Fair Trading into all relevant aspects of the NBA concluded that the judgments of the RPC in 1962, 1964 and 1968 were just as relevant in present circumstances and for this reason did not request it to reconsider the agreement. It was submitted that the judgment conferred the same benefits on Ireland as on the UK. The PA also submitted

1.7.4 a copy of a letter from the Department of the Taoiseach dated 27 January 1987 which stated that the Minister of State for Arts and Culture would be concerned if Ireland, with its limited publishing industry, was to be denied the benefits of resale price maintenance for books. Reference was also made to a communication issued by the European Commission entitled 'The European Dimension with regard to books' in which it was stated that the Commission had found that price fixing arrangements applying to books in member states were operating satisfactorily and that the majority of governments wished to see them continue.

40. A copy of proof of evidence of Mr P.W.S. Andrews, Lecturer in Economics at the University of Oxford to the UK Restrictive Practices Court in 1962 was also submitted. Mr Andrews, after a detailed analysis, concluded that under the NBA the consumer had the benefit of a larger number and more varied selection of book titles and at lower prices. It was submitted by the parties that if the NBA was not to continue, a situation would be created in which larger book stores would sell best-selling titles at discounted prices. This would have the effect of eliminating the smaller retailer from the market and also of increasing the retail price of the less popular titles which would become less readily available. It was also submitted that operation of the NBA had stimulated growth in book sales while keeping prices within general inflation levels. Output of titles had also increased.

41. The PA also submitted that the availability of a wide range of titles to meet different social needs, the value of libraries, the importance of books in education, were all of cultural and democratic importance to a country such as Ireland and that the continuance of the NBA was essential for the protection of such an arrangement. Reference was also made to a resume of the case for resale price maintenance for books prepared by Dr Fishwick, entitled 'The Economic Case for the New Book Agreement.' Dr Fishwick concluded that operation of the NBA was to the benefit of both publishers and consumers and that the benefits conferred were as applicable to Ireland as they were to the UK.

(e) *Overseas Cases*

42. The Net Book Agreement as it operated between Ireland and the UK was also notified to the EC on 12 June 1973. The EC Commission initiated proceedings on 8 October 1986 and took a final decision on 12 December 1988.[5] It found that the agreement offended against Article 85(1) and refused an exemption under Article 85(3). This decision was subsequently appealed.

43. The Commission found that the arrangements were agreements between undertakings although certain aspects were also deemed to be decisions of an association of undertakings. The Commission concluded that the arrangements had as their object and effect the restriction of competition within the EC.[6] The Commission found that once publishers had decided to impose a fixed resale price they were almost totally prevented from adapting the conditions governing its application and from offering more freedom than the agreements provide to resellers. The requirement to impose on resellers the standard conditions of sale specified in the agreements was also found to have a restrictive effect on price competition between booksellers as far as net books were concerned as they restricted the reseller's freedom to depart from the fixed resale price. The publication and application of a code of allowances was found to contribute to maintaining the net price system and to reinforce it.

44. The book club regulations were also found to offend as they involved restrictions on book clubs thereby restricting the possibilities for competition between booksellers and book clubs. The provisions relating to the 'annual book sale' were also found to contribute to maintaining the net price system and its restrictive effects as effectively as possible. Similarly the conditions for being mentioned in the directory of booksellers were found to have restrictive effects. The Commission decided that the restrictive effects were reinforced by the enforcement mechanism provided in the rules.

5. Case no. 89/44/EEC, OJ L22/12, 26.1.89.
6. Point 50.

45. The Commission concluded that: **1.7.4**

> . . . the agreements are not indispensable to the attainment of their objectives. Since an agreement, in order to be exempted from the prohibition contained in Article 85(1), fulfil all conditions of Article 85(3), they cannot be exempted. It is therefore not necessary to examine whether the agreements meet the other conditions of Article 85(3).[7]

46. The PA appealed the decision.[8] The Court of First Instance gave its judgement on 9 July 1992. Essentially it upheld the Commission decision. Most of the issues dealt with by the court were points of law and procedural issues. The appeal against the finding of an infringement of Article 85(1) was primarily on the grounds of the effect on trade between member states, i.e. the Commission view that the agreements were anti-competitive was not challenged. The PA subsequently appealed to the European Court of Justice.

47. The NBA has also been the subject of proceedings under the UK Restrictive Practices Act, before the Restrictive Practices Court.[9] The Court found that the NBA was not in breach of UK legislation. The UK legislation at the time permitted anti-competitive agreements where they could be shown to be in the public interest. The NBA had been amended following the introduction of the UK RPA in 1956. Essentially the amendment involved the publishers agreeing to take action against retailers who sold the book below the net price, with the costs of such actions being met by the association. Prior to 1957 the publishers boycotted retailers who breached the agreement.

48. The UK court took a very different view from that subsequently taken by the Commission and the Court of First Instance. It distinguished between maintaining retail price stability and price fixing. It also accepted the publishers' arguments that if price competition was allowed, specialist bookshops would have to lower prices on popular titles, they would not be able to cross-subsidise back-up services, and the holding of stocks of unpopular titles. Consequently the number of specialist shops would fall, overall prices would rise and fewer books would be published. It also concluded that consumers benefited from the availability of a greater diversity of books. Further proceedings were taken in the UK under amended legislation in 1964 and 1968 but with the same result.

49. The Director General of Fair Trade (DGFT) may apply to the Court for leave to have its decisions reconsidered if there is *prima facie* evidence of a material change in circumstances relevant to the original reasoning of the Court in finding the agreement not to operate against the public interest. An investigation into the effects of the agreement was carried out by the DGFT in 1989 but it was decided at that time not to apply to the Court. On 23 November 1993 the DGFT announced that the NBA was to be examined again. Announcing this fresh review the DGFT stated *inter alia* that:

> There have been many changes in the general economic structure of the country and in the economics of book publishing and retailing during that time, and we must now consider the possibility that the Court would reach a different judgment today on the effects of the agreement. . . .
>
> An investigation into the effects of the agreement was carried out . . . in 1989. It was decided then not to apply to the Court partly because it was expected that the Government would introduce new legislation in the near future to replace the Restrictive Practices Act and enactment of the new law would have required all restrictive agreements previously upheld by the Court to be reviewed.[10]

7. At para. 86.
8. Judgement of Court of First Instance 9 July 1992, [1992] 5 CMLR 120.
9. Judgement of UK Restrictive Practices Court, 30 October 1993.
10. Office of Fair Trading, Press release of 23 November 1993.

1.7.4 (f) *Subsequent*

50. On 19 August 1992 the Authority wrote seeking clarification from the PA of its intentions in the light of the decision of the European Court of First Instance to uphold the EC Commission decision that the agreement infringed Article 85(1) and did not merit exemption. On 22 September 1993 the PA replied indicating that it was pursuing an appeal to the European Court of Justice. It also indicated that in the interim it had decided to suspend the operation of the NBA in Ireland and had advised publishers to make similar interim amendments to their conditions of supply.

51. On 28 October 1993 the Authority issued a Statement of Objections to the PA, indicating that it intended to refuse a certificate or a licence to the notified agreements. As the PA is based in the UK, and as it had to consult with its members prior to formulating its response, the Authority allowed it until 31 January 1994 to respond to the Statement of Objections. An Oral Hearing was subsequently held on 10 May 1994.

52. In their response to the Statement of Objections the PA argued that the Authority should not take a final decision in respect of the notified arrangements as these were the subject of an appeal to the European Court of Justice following the EC Commission's refusal to grant an exemption to the arrangements under Article 85(3). It claimed that if the Authority went ahead with its decision a conflict of jurisdiction might arise. It also claimed that the NBA was a very unrestrictive agreement and that even if it came within section 4(1), the minimal nature of the restrictions made it easier to justify under section 4(2). In addition the PA argued that all four of the criteria in section 4(2) were satisfied, that the NBA led to the wider availability of books at lower prices than would otherwise be the case and that it encouraged publishers to publish more books. The PA claimed that it therefore contributed to improving the production and distribution of books, that consumers benefited from a healthy book industry, that no less restrictive system had ever been proposed which would be workable in practice and offer such benefits and that no question of the elimination of competition could arise in respect of such an unrestrictive agreement.

53. The PA indicated that it stood by the submissions already made in support of the notified arrangements although it did not intend to restate them. It argued that one of the principal objects of the NBA was to promote the continued existence of a vibrant retail sector for books in Ireland and the UK with a wide range of booksellers selling a wide range of books at low prices. It argued that the distribution of books was dependent on a strong network of stockholding bookshops in Ireland and that the NBA was necessary for the continued existence of such bookshops It also argued that, while Irish publishers were not party to the arrangements, they also benefited from them.

54. The PA conceded that it had failed to make the position with respect to the school licence clear in its notification. It indicated that such licences had never in fact been operated in Ireland and therefore had no actual or potential effects in Ireland. The PA claimed therefore that it did not come within the jurisdiction of the Authority and should not be the subject of any adverse finding.

55. The PA argued that the NBA was a voluntary arrangement in that no publisher was compelled to become a party to the agreement and any publisher could decide to opt out of the arrangements at any time. Similarly publishers were free in the case of every book published to decide whether or not to classify it as a net book and to decide independently what net price to set. It concluded that:

> As a matter of economic reality, the effect of the NBA is to enable publishers individually to practise maintenance of their books, if and to the extent that, in their individual discretion, they choose to do so.
>
> If one is against publishers having the ability to practise resale price maintenance of their books (if and to the extent that they, in their individual discretion, choose to do so),

then one will be against the NBA. If, on the other hand, one believes that, having regard to the unique characteristics of books, the existence of the ability in question results in major public interest benefits, then the case in favour of the NBA is overwhelming. In any event, that is the area within which, as the PA believes, the justifiability of the NBA falls to be debated. 1.7.4

The PA also pointed out that it was accepted by the UK Restrictive Practices Court and agreed between the parties to the court hearing that individual RPM would not survive without the NBA.

56. The PA stated that it did not dispute the general propositions of law and economics contained in the Statement of Objections but claimed that the Authority's objections failed to take into account the very special characteristics of the NBA, and the unique features of the book trade. It argued that all competition law analysis has to be related to the particular market in which the allegedly restrictive conduct takes place. The PA disputed that the arrangements involved an element of collective as well as individual RPM on the grounds that it was up to individual publishers to decide whether or not to net a book. The PA also claimed that the Authority had misunderstood certain aspects of the arrangements. In addition it submitted that it was wrong to argue that the NBA restricted price competition between books since the publisher in setting a net price had to take account of competition in the market.

57. The PA disputed the Authority's conclusions that all four of the requirements of section 4(2) were not satisfied. It claimed *inter alia* that the Authority had misunderstood certain aspects of the arrangements. It also argued that the fact that other authorities, such as the EC Commission, had found the arrangements to be beneficial implied that the Authority might have reached incorrect conclusions. The PA relied extensively on the conclusions of the UK Restrictive Practices Court in the 1962 case concerning the NBA to show that the arrangements were beneficial. The PA also included submissions from the Cle, the Irish publishers association and the Booksellers Association of Great Britain and Ireland — Irish Branch, in support of the continued operation of the NBA.

58. In support of its arguments the PA also submitted a report on the effects of the removal of RPM for books in a number of other countries specifically Australia, Belgium and Sweden. The author of the report, Dr Fishwick stated that the observations on the first two countries were based mainly on research visits undertaken by himself, while those on Sweden were based on other published information. The study argued that the characteristics of books and the nature of the book market meant that price discounting would tend to be relatively limited in the absence of RPM. It was claimed that margins in Australia were relatively high but that within the last few years a new discount chain had entered the market capturing a significant market share. It was claimed that, as a result, discounting of popular titles was now widespread especially in outlets other than stockholding bookshops and that consequently, there had been a reduction in the number of bookshops, additional mark-ups on less popular titles, charges for special orders and fewer staff and less service. It was claimed that the abolition of RPM in Belgium had led to a decline in the number of bookshops as a result of discounting. In Sweden RPM for books was abolished in 1970. Traditional book shops had lost market share to other types of outlet. The report claimed that the abolition of RPM had a serious effect on the book trade on the basis that book sales over a period of time increased by less than in the UK.[11]

59. At the Oral Hearing on 10 May 1994 the representative of the PA restated many of the points already made in written submissions to the Authority. He indicated that in fact the PA accepted that the NBA offended against section 4(1) but argued that it satisfied the requirements for a licence. In particular he argued that the abolition of the NBA would, the PA believed, lead to a fall in the number of bookshops, reduction in stock holding, higher book prices and argued that such developments would be detrimental. He indicated that this was a view based

11. In the Authority's opinion such a conclusion is highly tenuous.

1.7.4 on the PA's knowledge and experience of the industry. He was questioned regarding other studies which disputed the PA's claims and also as to whether the abolition of RPM in respect of books in other countries had been detrimental as the PA claimed. It was pointed out that a study of the NBA published by the Institute of Economic Affairs disputed most of the claims of the PA.[12] This study indicated that in recent years, in the absence of RPM, there had been a significant growth in book selling chains in the US carrying very extensive ranges of stock. He argued that this was only true of large cities. It was pointed out that the IEA study indicated that the abolition of RPM in France led to the opening of more bookshops in smaller towns and that these had closed following the re-imposition of RPM in 1981. He disputed these findings.[13]

Assessment

(a) *Section*

60. Section 4(1) of the Competition Act states that 'all agreements between undertakings, decisions by associations of undertakings and concerted practices which have as their object or effect the prevention, restriction or distortion of competition in trade in any goods or services in the State or in any part of the State are prohibited and void.'

(b) *The Undertakings and the Agreement*

61. Section 3(1) of the Competition Act defines an undertaking as 'a person being an individual, a body corporate or an unincorporated body of persons engaged for gain in the production, supply or distribution of goods or the provision of a service.' The parties to the PA agreements are book publishers based in the UK. The majority of these publishers are corporate bodies. The publishers are engaged for gain in the production and publication of books and are therefore undertakings within the meaning of the Act.

62. There are two Net Book Agreements, one for members of the PA and the other for non-members. These agreements constitute agreements between undertakings relating to the standard conditions of sale for UK published books within the State. They also constitute decisions of an association of undertakings. In addition to the two versions of the Net Book Agreement the PA has notified a series of related arrangements. These are:

(a) the book club regulations;
(b) the library licence;
(c) the book agent's licence;
(d) the quantity book buying scheme;
(e) the primary and secondary school licence.

These set out the conditions upon which publishers supply books to different categories of buyer. In addition the association has drawn up a set of conditions for a national book sale. Each of these documents constitutes an agreement between undertakings (the publishers), setting out the terms upon which net books may be sold below the net published price to certain categories of customer. These arrangements also constitute decisions of an association of undertakings within the meaning of section 4(1).

63. While the publishers who are parties to the agreement are based in the UK, the notified arrangements apply in respect of the sale of UK published books within the State. They affect the distribution and sale of UK published books within the State. As pointed out up to 80% of books sold in the State are imported from the UK.

12. W. Allen and P. Curwen, (1991); 'Competition in the Publishing Industry', Institute for Economic Affairs, London.
13. The Authority also notes that the Australian Trade Practices Commission has recently recommended that restrictions on parallel importing of books should be abolished having rejected arguments that price competition in the book trade would prove harmful.

(c) *Applicability of Section 4(1)* **1.7.4**

Resale Price Maintenance

64. Resale Price Maintenance (RPM) describes a practice whereby a supplier agrees to supply retailers on condition that they sell the goods at a price specified by the supplier. The arrangements notified involve a form of RPM. Such arrangements restrict the ability of retailers to determine their own prices. They also eliminate price competition between retailers for the suppliers/ products, assuming that the supplier applies arrangements to all retailers handling his products.

65. There is some disagreement among economists as to whether or not RPM is an undesirable practice. Over the past 25 years or so, the so-called 'Chicago school' economists have challenged traditional economic thinking concerning most forms of vertical restrictions[14] including RPM. Essentially their argument is that manufacturers will not impose vertical restraints such as RPM unless they increase output and hence profits. Specifically it is argued that RPM causes the retailer to devote greater efforts to selling the manufacturer's goods through promotional efforts and/or increased service, in the form of information about the product, instruction in its use, the holding of larger stocks and the like. It is argued that retailers would not provide such services in the absence of RPM since consumers would avail of such free services and then purchase the goods in question from lower cost outlets which would effectively 'free ride' on the services provided by others. According to the Chicago approach consumers benefit from increased service levels resulting from RPM and sales are increased resulting in greater output of the goods in question. Consequently RPM should not be seen as anti-competitive, but as a mechanism for increasing distribution efficiency to the benefit of consumers, retailers and suppliers.

66. The Chicago approach is, however, strongly challenged by other economists. Scherer and Ross[15], for example, argue that relatively few products are susceptible to 'free riding' which RPM is supposed to prevent. Many consumers know what they want and do not need pre-sales service. Similarly consumers will only go to lower priced outlets, having availed of the free pre sales service provided in the more expensive outlet, in the case of goods which are expensive, and where the cost saving is significant. They also argue that it is not clear why RPM is necessary to cause retailers to provide a greater level of service anyway. Thus, in response to the Chicago claim that without RPM discount retailers would 'free ride', many would argue that a lot of products are not susceptible to free riding and that free rider arguments can only apply in respect of pre- sale services.

67. Scherer and Ross show that RPM may inhibit competition in a number of ways. It can inhibit the entry of discount outlets and thus prevent retailing innovations. Manufacturers who have relied on RPM in order to encourage product promotion by retailers and increase sales may be unwilling to dispense with such arrangements long after the need to promote new products has ended. Where many manufacturers engage in RPM it may be difficult for one to end the practice since retailers may simply cease stocking the firm's products. They conclude that, on balance, the evidence suggests RPM is likely to restrict competition and result in prices being higher and output lower than would otherwise be the case.

68. While economic theory suggests that there may be circumstances in which RPM may increase overall economic welfare, most goods and services do not appear to satisfy the necessary conditions for such a result. In addition other methods are available to induce greater efforts by retailers to sell the manufacturers' products. On balance therefore, economic arguments indicate that RPM is generally harmful and restricts competition.

14. A vertical restriction is one applied by a firm at one level of production/distribution chain to one operating at a different level. Generally these apply between manufacturers/suppliers and retailers.
15. F.M. Scherer and D. Ross, (1990); 'Industrial Market Structure and Economic Performance', 3rd ed., Houghton Mifflin, New York, p. 550.

1.7.4 69. RPM has been prohibited under the competition laws of most developed countries. Legislation which permitted RPM was repealed in the United States in 1976 and the Supreme Court has regarded RPM as a *per se* violation of the antitrust rules.[16] Legislation prohibiting RPM was enacted in Canada in 1951, in France in 1953 and in the UK in 1964. The UK Competition Act is generally neutral with respect to most forms of anti-competitive behaviour, in that it only prohibits practices which are shown to be against the public interest, and there is no presumption one way or the other as to whether practices are against the public interest. RPM, however, is specifically prohibited by statute. While the latter legislation allows for exemption, there have only been four requests for such exemption, and in only two instances, one involving the Net Book Agreement, has such an exemption been granted.

70. The Authority considers that the weight of evidence indicates that RPM is generally restrictive of competition. Consequently, in its view, agreements involving RPM will generally offend against section 4(1).

Net Book Agreement — Members Version

71. Clause (i) provides that, except in specified circumstances, net books cannot be sold at less than the net published price. Such net prices are determined by individual book publishers who must also decide whether or not to classify a particular book as a net book. The agreement provides that in certain circumstances a net book may be sold below the net price. These apply where the book has been in stock for some considerable time and to second hand copies of net books. In addition the agreement allows net books to be sold below the net published price to certain classes of customer subject to certain conditions, in particular relating to prices.

72. Individual RPM refers to a situation in which an individual supplier sets resale prices for his products. Collective RPM relates to a situation where a number of suppliers agree to set resale prices for their products. The agreement, according to the PA, is designed to enable publishers to operate a system of individual RPM. Thus it involves a mixture of individual and collective RPM. The Net Book Agreement eliminates price competition between retailers in respect of every book which has been designated a net book by its publisher. To the extent that each individual book title constitutes a unique product, price competition at the retail level is therefore eliminated in respect of any book designated a net book. The Authority believes that to some degree certain books are substitutes for one another. While some consumers will wish to buy a particular book by a particular author, others are looking for a particular type of book, whether a thriller or one on gardening, and will therefore choose from among the range of titles available in that particular category. As the majority of UK published books are net books, price competition between retailers in respect of different titles is also restricted. It is true that not all books of a particular type retail at a uniform price, but where books which could be considered substitutes are designated net books the possibility of retailers offering discounts on such books is eliminated and so competition is restricted between different titles.

73. Price fixing agreements have been consistently regarded as in breach of Article 85(1) of the Treaty of Rome. Bellamy and Child point out that:

> Since price is the main instrument of competition, Article 85(1)(a) expressly prohibits agreements, which 'directly or indirectly fix purchase or selling prices or any other trading conditions'. And agreement to fix prices by its very nature constitutes a restriction on competition within the meaning of Article 85(1).[17]

74. The agreement requires the publishers to apply the standard conditions of sale on their

16. This view was restated in Sylvania where the court distinguished between RPM and other forms of vertical restraint.
17. C. Bellamy and G. Child, (1987); 'Common Market Law of Competition', 3rd ed., Sweet and Maxwell, London, at para. 4-002.

resellers. This restricts price competition between retailers as far as net books are concerned by curtailing the freedom of resellers to depart from the fixed resale price by offering discounts in order to increase their sales. The agreement also restricts competition between publishers as all the publishers who are parties to the agreement must apply uniform terms in respect of the resale of all books designated by them as net books. In addition once a book is designated as a net book by a publisher, the publishers of rival titles can set their prices in the knowledge that the designated book will not be sold below the designated net price. Consequently the agreement reduces the element of uncertainty regarding a competitor's response to a firm's marketing strategy which is an essential feature of competitive markets. Allen and Curwen, for example, argued that: 1.7.4

> In general, given the existence of the NBA, we would expect publishers to price similar products as though they were operating a cartel. The fact that they can fix the price of a specific title at any level they wish is very far from what is meant by 'conditions of free competition'. In conditions of free competition there would be constant downward pressure upon prices in order to clear the market, so that over time prices, on average, would rise more slowly than elsewhere in the economy where free competition did not exist.[18]

While the Authority does not consider that the NBA necessarily amounts to a fully fledged horizontal price fixing arrangement, it nevertheless believes that it does go some considerable way towards reducing uncertainty regarding competitors' pricing decisions in the publishing industry and that such uncertainty is normally an essential part of the competitive process. As the vast bulk of UK published books are net books and these account for the majority of books sold within the State, price competition between retailers and between publishers is restricted in respect of a substantial part of the book market within the State. The net book agreement therefore has the object and effect of restricting competition in the market for books within the State.

75. The PA in its response to the Statement of Objections, claimed that:

> (a) the Authority had not made any criticism of the operation that is specific to its effects in Ireland but had instead made a general attack on the NBA; and
> (b) the sole ground for the Authority asserting jurisdiction in respect of the NBA was that it affects inter-State trade between the UK and Ireland and therefore has effects within Ireland. It argued that the Authority was wrong to assert jurisdiction in this way.

The Authority rejects such claims. It is clear from the preceding paras that the Authority, in finding that the NBA offends against section 4(1), has based its decision on its assessment of the effects of the NBA on competition within the State. The Authority has never introduced the issue of inter-state trade. Section 4(1) of the Competition Act refers to agreements which prevent, restrict or distort competition within the State. The PA's claim that the Authority cannot assert jurisdiction over the notified agreement amounts to a claim that the Competition Act does not apply in respect of goods which are imported into the State.

76. The Authority's view that the NBA restricts competition is in accord with that of the EC Commission which stated in the case of the Net Book Agreement:

> Thus, the agreements and rules have facilitated and contributed to the maintenance or introduction of fixed book prices by a large number of publishers and continue to do so.[19]

18. Op. cit., p. 25.
19. Point 62.

1.7.4 Commission found that the arrangements had the object and effect of restricting competition within the EC. This view was subsequently upheld by the Court of First Instance following an appeal by the PA.

77. In *VBVB/VBBB v. EC Commission* the Court of Justice upheld an EC Commission decision that an agreement between two associations of publishers and booksellers, one based in Holland and the other in Belgium, that books could not be sold in Belgium or the Netherlands at prices below those fixed by the Dutch or Belgian publishers infringed Article 85(1).

78. Agreements between Dutch and Belgian publishers and booksellers involving RPM in respect of books were also the subject of proceedings in the national courts. The Amsterdam district court made an order on 26 May 1977 which provided that books published in the Netherlands, which had been bought abroad, could be sold at a price below that set by the publisher. This was confirmed by the Dutch Supreme Court on 18 May 1979.[20] The Commercial Court in Brussels by order dated 18 June 1979, in a dispute between the Flemish Association and a department store chain, ordered the association to cease making the sale of Dutch language books conditional on the store being obliged to conform to the retail price fixed by the supplier. The Court found that the rules infringed Article 85(1) and it had not been shown that there was any great probability that the Commission would grant an exemption.

79. While the NBA does not require that the publishers designate any particular book or even the majority of their books as net books, in practice the publishers involved in the agreement do so designate the vast majority of books published by them. It was conceded that up to 75% of books published are designated net books. The publishers are free not to designate any particular book a net book. Having designated a book to be a net book, however, the publisher is bound to apply the standard conditions governing net books including the terms upon which discounts can be granted in respect of such a book i.e. the only circumstances in which a net book may be sold at below the specified net price are those specified in clauses (ii) to (iv) of the agreement. This aspect of the arrangements also restricts competition in the market for books within the State and offends against section 4(1). It is not sufficient to put arrangements outside the scope of section 4(1) that publishers are not compelled to designate every book a net book. The purpose of the NBA, according to the PA, is to enable all book publishers to operate a system of RPM.

80. Again the EC Commission decided in respect of the Net Book Agreement that:

> Neither the freedom for publishers to decide whether to make a net book or not or to end the net character of the book or not, nor their freedom to determine the level of the net price prevent the agreements and implementing rules from being restrictive. The fact that, if a publisher decides to impose a fixed price for a book, he is then bound to impose almost wholly uniform conditions . . . upon resellers as to the discounts they may give to their customers, is sufficient to make the agreements and implement rules restrictive.[21]

81. The Authority notes that, in its appeal to the Court of First Instance against the Commission decision that the agreement infringed Article 85(1), the PA only sought to show that the agreement did not affect trade between member states and did not challenge the finding that it restricted competition. Indeed it was conceded at the Oral Hearing by the PA's representative that the arrangements offended against section 4(1).

82. Under the agreement the publishers have agreed to appoint the PA to act on their behalf in relation to collecting information concerning breaches of contract by persons selling or offering for sale net books, breaches of the agreement and keeping each publisher informed of breaches in respect of such net books as are published by him. This reinforces the extent of the restriction on competition contained in the basic agreement as it is designed to ensure more

20. Nederlandse Jurisprudentie 1979, no. 480.
21. Point 52.

efficient surveillance of compliance with the agreements and rules. 1.7.4

83. The parties also agree to enforce such contractual rights if called upon to do so by the PA, provided that they are indemnified by the Association in respect of any costs of such action incurred by them or by the Council of the Association on their behalf. Under these provisions the parties agree to take action against any retailer who sells a net book below the net price where he has contractually agreed not to. The purpose of this provision is to ensure effective adherence to the net prices as specified by the publishers. While no individual contractual arrangement with any bookseller in the State has been notified to the Authority, any such agreement which required that the retailer not sell below the net price specified by the publisher would offend against section 4(1). The enforcement provisions are therefore designed to ensure adherence to arrangements which offend against section 4(1). For that reason the agreement by the publishers to enforce such agreements also offends against section 4(1).

84. The parties' submission concedes that the arrangements involve resale price maintenance but argues that such arrangements are beneficial in the case of books. In VBVB/VBBB v. Commission the European Court of Justice found that:

> The special features of the book trade do not permit national associations of publishers and booksellers in two Member States to set up, in their mutual relations, a restrictive system whose effect is to deprive distributors of all freedom of action as regards the fixing of selling price up to the level of the final price to the consumer. Such an arrangement infringes Article 85(1)(a) which expressly prohibits all agreements which 'directly or indirectly fix purchase or selling prices'. Furthermore, where the system of resale price maintenance laid down in the agreement allows each of the two association to control outlets as far Member State from the point of view of thus to make impossible the introduction capable of allowing consumers to economically more favourable conditions, the associations are also brought into conflict with Article 85(1)(b).[22]

The parties' claim that RPM is beneficial in the case of books does not, therefore, prevent the agreement from offending against section 4(1).

85. Clauses (ii), (iii) and (iv) set out circumstances in which a net book may be sold below the net price. Under clause (ii) a net book may be sold below the net price if the bookseller has held it in stock for a period of more than 12 months from the date of purchase and he has offered it to the publisher at either the lower of cost price or the proposed reduced price and such offer has been rejected by the publisher. Clause (iii) allows the bookseller to sell a book below the net price if it is second- hand and more than 6 months have elapsed since publication. Clause (iv) allows for net books to be sold to libraries, book agents, quantity buyers and other institutions as are from time to time authorised by the Council of the Association on such conditions as are laid down in the instrument of authorisation.

86. While allowing the bookseller some scope to sell below the net price, these clauses seriously restrict the circumstances in which he may do so and generally set maximum levels of discount. They therefore also have the effect of restricting in competition in the market for books within the State. By limiting the circumstances in which net books may be sold below the net price these clauses reinforce the RPM arrangements contained in clause (i). Consequently these clauses also offend against section 4(1).

Non-members Version

87. As already pointed out the non-members' version of the NBA is the same as the members' version save that there is no provision for indemnifying non-members in respect of the costs of court actions to enforce the terms of the agreement on booksellers. The non-members Version of the Net Book Agreement also offends against section 4(1) as its object

22. Point 9.

1.7.4 and effect is to prevent, restrict or distort competition in the market for books within the State. Clauses (i), (ii), (iii) and (iv) which are identical to the corresponding clauses in the Members version all offend against section 4(1) as their object and effect is to restrict competition in the market for books within the State. The provision whereby publishers who are not members have agreed to appoint the PA to act on their behalf in relation to collecting information concerning breaches of the agreement by booksellers and keeping each publisher informed of breaches in respect of such net books as are published by him reinforces the extent of the restriction on competition contained in the basic agreement. Similarly the provision whereby the publishers have agreed to take action against any retailer who sells a net book below the net price where he has contractually agreed not to, also offends against section 4(1).

Book Club Regulations

88. The book club regulations set out the terms and conditions upon which the PA permit book clubs to sell book club editions of net books at below the net price. The PA argued that the Regulations apply only within the UK and that the Authority has no jurisdiction to examine such arrangements. Nevertheless the restrictions apply within the State to the extent that they prevent UK book clubs selling books within the State other than on the terms set out in the Regulations. They therefore offend against section 4(1) since they have the object and effect of preventing, restricting or distorting competition in the market for books within the State. The PA claimed that, while the regulations restricted the right of book clubs to sell books to individuals within the State, arguing that this offended against section 4(1) was akin to arguing that, because an Irish resident who travelled to the UK might buy a book there, which would be subject to the NBA, the NBA in the UK also offended against section 4(1). The Authority rejects this argument, as the actual restriction on book clubs selling to individuals in Ireland restricts competition within the State while the hypothetical situation described by the PA clearly does not. It is relevant that the EC Commission in its decision on the NBA found that the Book Club Regulations infringed Article 85(1) implying that they restricted the sale of books outside of the UK. In particular the restriction of offers to members (clause 12), requirements that membership be for a period of six months and that members purchase at least three club choices within the first year (clause 11) are designed to restrict book clubs from competing with other booksellers in selling books to the general public within the State. The restrictions on advertising by book clubs (clauses 15 and 18) have the same objective. The requirement that every book offered by a book club has to carry the book club's crest or title and that book clubs may not supply copies of a trade edition (clause 17) has a similar objective. The requirement in clause 13 that book clubs must have the consent of the licensing publisher before disposing of surplus stock as remainders and the requirement in clause 16 that a title not be offered as a premium (introductory book) until at least six months after its first issue as a trade edition are further restrictions since they limit the commercial freedom of book clubs to compete with other booksellers within the State.

The Library Licence

89. The library licence sets out the terms upon which the PA permits booksellers to sell net books to the library specified in the licence at a discount to the net published price. It constitutes an agreement between the publishers and a decision by the Association which offends against section 4(1).

90. As each library licence specifies that only the bookseller named therein may offer a discount to a particular library, it restricts the ability of other booksellers to supply that library. The Association have argued that licensees are free to choose any supplier or suppliers they wish so long as such suppliers are prepared to supply then at a discount in accordance with the terms of the licence. The licence, however, names a specific bookseller. The existence of a network of library licences, each restricting the right to supply books to the named library at a discount to the bookseller named in the licence means that competition between booksellers

throughout the State to supply libraries is restricted. The provision that booksellers may only give a maximum discount of up to 10% also restricts competition between booksellers. Indeed it was admitted at the hearing before the UK Restrictive Practices Court, that the object of this arrangement was to prevent specialist library suppliers undercutting bookshops in respect of sales to libraries. Several other provisions of the library licence also offend against section 4(1), namely: 1.7.4

> the requirement that booksellers may only offer a discount when they themselves have received a certain level of discount in respect of the books concerned, (clause 2);
> the requirement that discounts may only be allowed so long as the library's total annual purchases of net books solely for the use of the library is not less than £100, (clause 3);
> the requirement that booksellers may not provide any other consideration in cash or in kind, (clause 4);
> the requirement that booksellers may only provide services such as card-indexing to libraries provided they charge them no less than the cost price of such service (clause 5).

91. Each of these requirements restricts competition between booksellers to supply libraries. They mean that libraries cannot obtain books on better terms than those specified in the licence from any other bookseller and remove any incentive for libraries to seek a licence to purchase from another bookseller. Bellamy and Child point out that:

> the prohibition of Article 85(1) covers not only 'prices' in the narrow sense but also discounts, margins, rebates and credit terms. Other agreements which directly or indirectly restrict price competition include agreements not to submit quotations without prior consultation, not to deviate from published prices, not to make public any deviations from published prices, not to quote other than delivered prices, not to give other than cost related rebates, and not to sell 'below cost'.[23]

92. The provision of additional services either free or below cost, or offering other forms of consideration represents an alternative to offering discounts. Consequently booksellers could, in the absence of this restriction, compete for library business by offering such services free or at a low cost in lieu of any discount. The object of this provision is to ensure that booksellers do not offer any hidden discounts to libraries in this way, thereby exceeding the maximum discounts permitted under the licence. Such restrictions on competition also offend against section 4(1).

The Book Agent's Licence

93. The book agent's licence sets out the terms and conditions upon which the publishers have agreed to allow booksellers to supply net books to book agents. The agent's licence also offends against section 4(1) since it is designed to ensure that book agents will not sell books below the net price. The fact that the Association may revoke the licence in the event of any breach of any of its terms and conditions ensures that book agents do not sell net books at less than the net published price. Thus its object and effect is to prevent competition between book agents and other booksellers. The licence also restricts competition between booksellers to supply book agents since the maximum discount which they may give to such an agent is fixed by the licence and since the agent is not permitted to seek or obtain any discount from any bookseller other than the one nominated in the licence.

National Book Sale

94. The rules governing the national book sale set out the terms and conditions upon which

23. Ibid. at para. 4-003.

1.7.4 the PA permit net books to be sold below the net price during the annual national book sale. The regulations relating to the national book sale also offend against section 4(1) as their object and effect is to prevent, restrict or distort competition in the sale of books within the State. In particular, by only allowing booksellers to offer books for sale during a specific period of the year and by limiting the range of books which may be sold at below the net published price to overstocks, the regulations limit the ability of booksellers to compete with one another by offering discounts on a broad range of book titles.

95. A number of the conditions applying to the national book sale also restrict competition and offend against section 4(1) namely;

> Condition 3 which enables individual publishers to exclude all of their titles from the sale as it enables publishers to prevent price competition in respect of their book titles;
>
> Condition 5 which allows publishers to fix the sale price of publishers' overstocks;
> Condition 6 which allows booksellers to set the price of publishers overstocks during the last week of the sale provided they may make no advance announcement of intended reductions;
> Condition 8 which restricts publishers from issuing titles offered at reduced prices during the sale at prices below those which obtained prior to the sale for a period of six months afterwards;
> Condition 9 which prevents booksellers from accepting publications of non-participating publishers at a reduced price for the sale;
> Condition 12 which restricts the titles which wholesalers may offer to participating retail booksellers;
> Condition 13 which allows wholesalers to set the price for their overstocks subject to the proviso that they cannot be more than half the published price;
> Condition 14 that prices of books to be included in the sale cannot be advertised more than 21 days in advance.

The Quantity Book Buying Scheme

96. The quantity book buying scheme sets out the conditions upon which booksellers may give discounts in respect of the purchase by a buyer of a large quantity of net books. A scale of the discounts allowable is set out in the licence. The Quantity Book Buying Scheme also offends against section 4(1). In particular it restricts competition within the State by limiting the circumstances in which booksellers may offer discounts to customers purchasing net books in large quantities and by specifying the rates of discount which may be given in respect of such orders. This eliminates price competition between booksellers for this type of order. The restriction on offering any discounts in respect of books on which the bookseller has not himself received a discount of at least 25% (clause d) also offends against section 4(1) since booksellers should be free to decide for themselves which books they wish to offer discounts on. The requirement that such books may only be purchased as gifts or for presentations in connection with the purchaser's business or for philanthropic or propaganda purposes (clause a) and the ban on the purchaser offering such books for resale (clause b) are designed to restrict competition in the sale of books and offend against section 4(1).

The Primary and Secondary School Licence

97. The schools licence sets out the terms and conditions upon which the publishers have agreed to allow booksellers to supply net books to schools. The PA, in notifying the schools licence, indicated that it had not yet been implemented in Ireland. It subsequently indicated that the licence had never operated within Ireland but that if it were licensed by the Authority they would seek to introduce it. The school licence restricts competition between booksellers to supply schoolbooks by fixing the maximum discount which booksellers may give to schools

(clause 5). The requirement that the licence be deposited with the bookseller before any discount may be given (clause 7), also restricts competition as it prevents the school from obtaining discounts from any other bookseller, thus placing other booksellers at a competitive disadvantage in terms of supplying books to a particular school. In addition the requirement that books be solely for use by the school for educational purposes (clause 6) is designed to ensure that schools will not resell net books below the net price and its object is to reinforce the restrictions contained in the Net Book Agreement itself. It is clear that its object is to restrict competition. 1.7.4

Applicability of section 4(2)

98. Under section 4(2), the Competition Authority may grant a licence in the case of any agreement or category of agreements which offends against section 4(1) but which, 'having regard to all relevant market conditions, contributes to improving the production of goods or provision of services or to promoting technical or economic progress, while allowing consumers a fair share of the resulting benefit and which does not

(i) impose on the undertakings concerned terms which are not indispensable to the attainment of those objectives;

(ii) afford undertakings the possibility of eliminating competition in respect of a substantial part of the products or services in question.

99. The PA claimed that the Authority, in its Statement of Objections, had argued that because the first requirement was not satisfied the other three were actually not satisfied. In making this argument the PA appear to be misreading the provisions of section 4(2). Firstly all four tests must be met before a licence can be granted. Secondly, however, the tests are not disjunctive, they are cumulative. Thus an agreement must first of all contribute to improving the production of goods or provision of services or to promoting technical or economic progress. If it does so, it must allow consumers a fair share of the resulting benefit, i.e. a fair share of the benefit which satisfies the first test. Similarly if it meets both of these requirements it must not impose on the undertakings concerned terms which are not indispensable to the attainment of those objectives, and, finally, it must not afford the undertakings the possibility of eliminating competition in respect of a substantial part of the products or services in question. Clearly if an agreement does not satisfy the first test it cannot satisfy the second since there is no resulting benefit. Conversely, however, an agreement which satisfies the first test may well not satisfy the second, third or fourth test.

100. It was submitted by the PA that the various restrictions involved in the Net Book Agreement and associated arrangements satisfied the requirements for a licence. In particular it argued that the restrictions in the Net Book Agreement, by preventing discounting, enabled specialist bookshops to provide a comprehensive service to consumers which includes, *inter alia*, services such as ordering particular titles as well as general advice. In addition it was argued that preventing discounting allows bookshops to stock a wide range of less popular titles, thereby providing consumers with a wider choice of book titles.

101. In the absence of the price restrictions contained in the Net Book Agreement it was submitted that non-specialist shops and some discount booksellers would offer popular titles at reduced prices. This would force specialist booksellers to reduce their prices on such titles. The reduction in margins on popular titles would reduce the ability of specialist booksellers to provide back-up services such as ordering for which they do not charge. In addition they would have to recoup the loss in margin on more popular books by increasing their margins on less popular titles or by reducing their stock of such titles. The effect of this, it was claimed, would be to eliminate a number of smaller booksellers while reducing the range of titles currently available to consumers.

102. It was further argued that in the absence of RPM the risks involved in publishing books would be increased and this in turn would make publishers less willing to publish titles by new or less popular authors and on subjects which were of minority interest. Many of these

1.7.4 arguments were advanced by the Association in the 1962 hearing before the UK Restrictive Practices Court and before the EC Commission and the Court of First Instance. In particular the PA has argued that the decision of the UK Restrictive Practices Court indicates that the NBA meets the requirements of section 4(2). The Authority does not accept this claim. In the first place there is a fundamental difference between Irish and UK legislation. Under the UK legislation it is necessary to establish that restrictive arrangements are not in the public interest. Under the Competition Act, the onus is on the parties to establish that the specific requirements of section 4(2) are satisfied. More fundamentally, however, the Authority does not believe that a decision based on the conditions prevailing in the UK book trade over thirty years ago is applicable to the conditions prevailing in the Irish market today. The PA claimed that the DGFT had re- examined the NBA in 1989 and had found that it was still in the public interest. In fact the DGFT announced in 1993 that the NBA was being re-examined because there had been significant changes in the book trade since 1962 and that the decision not to refer it back to the Court in 1989 was prompted, in part, by an expectation that UK legislation would change and that all restrictive agreements would have to be re-assessed in the light of new legislation.

103. Undoubtedly in the absence of RPM the price of some book titles at least would be reduced. The Authority accepts that some stores may well discount the more popular titles in order to increase their sales. It may be also that many non-specialist bookshops will offer such discounts while stocking only a limited range of books. The effect may well be to increase sales of such books. Consequently the abolition of RPM would to this extent benefit consumers, those retailers offering discounts, and authors who would benefit from an increase in sales of their works. The Authority agrees with the views of the EC Commission in the Dutch Books case that:

> It would be possible to reach fresh categories of purchaser by liberalising price competition.

The Commission went on to dismiss claims that RPM in the case of books contributed to improvements in distribution or technical or economic progress.

104. The PA's case is that, in the absence of the NBA, there would be limited discounting of the most popular book titles. Shops would have to raise the prices of less popular book titles to counter such discounting. In effect this implies that RPM results in higher prices of popular book titles than would otherwise be the case, but that this permits cross-subsidisation of less popular titles and of back-up services provided by specialist booksellers. It is widely recognised in economic theory that cross-subsidisation results in a misallocation of resources since consumers do not bear the true cost of individual products. A misallocation of resources reduces efficiency and so cannot be claimed to increase technical or economic progress. The PA claim that in the longer run the effect of discounting would be to increase the risks in publishing thereby raising costs and leading to higher overall book prices. The Authority does not accept this argument. The economics of the publishing business have changed significantly due to technological developments over the past thirty years and it is no longer the case that producing shorter print runs will result in much higher book prices.

105. It may be that price discounting of books will result in a loss of business by specialist bookshops to other types of retail outlet, or that larger bookshops will gain at the expense of smaller ones. The purpose of the Competition Act is to protect competition not competitors. The essence of competition is that competitors will seek to take custom away from their rivals. At the heart of the view that competition is desirable is the judgment that such activity benefits consumers and enhances overall economic welfare. Consequently the fact that some competitors may be harmed by the elimination of a particular restrictive practice cannot justify the continuance of such a practice. To the extent that RPM prevents the emergence of new competitors and of innovative methods of retailing such as discounting, it cannot be said to result in any improvement in the distribution of goods or in the promotion of economic progress.

The PA have argued that, as a result of the NBA, the number of specialist booksellers is greater than it would otherwise be, and that without it, many rural bookshops would close. It pointed to the increase in the number of bookshops between 1977 and 1988 as evidence of the favourable effects of the NBA. While the number of bookshops certainly increased over this period, much of the increase occurred in the larger urban centres. In contrast in the three Ulster counties the number of bookshops fell sharply. It was pointed out at the Oral Hearing that there was evidence that the abolition of RPM in France led to an increase in the number of rural bookshops there and that many of these subsequently closed following its re-imposition. The PA disputed this. 1.7.4

106. The claim that discounting will cause booksellers to reduce the range of titles covered also appears unrealistic. Rural bookshops are, as was noted earlier, considerably smaller than those in Dublin. By definition therefore they carry a far more limited range of stock and presumably concentrate on the more popular titles anyway. Consequently even if the argument regarding stocks was valid, it would only apply to some bookshops in Ireland. The validity of the argument itself is questionable. As the EC Commission noted in the Dutch Books case:

> As the holding of stock is the essential characteristic of a bookshop it would be illogical to consider reducing it; bookshops might usefully improve their efficiency by specialising.[24]

The abolition of the Net Book Agreement may result in the closure of some shops but these are likely to be replaced by new entrants.

107. The Authority does not believe that the abolition of RPM would have serious adverse effects on the availability of minority interest books. The price of such books may well increase reflecting the slower turnover and higher costs of stocking such titles. Those wishing to purchase such books will have to pay higher prices because they are no longer being subsidised by purchasers of more popular titles. The subsidisation of a minority of consumers by the majority cannot be regarded as efficiency enhancing or contributing to the promotion of economic or technical progress.

108. It may be that the abolition of RPM will mean that specialist booksellers will have to introduce specific charges to cover the cost of back-up services such as ordering titles which are out of stock. Authority does not believe that the type or pre-sales services provided by book shops is conducive to free riding. In simple terms it does not believe that consumers will go into specialist bookshops in order to obtain detailed advice concerning a particular book and then go to a discount outlet to purchase it. Particular services such as ordering out of stock titles are not prone to free riding anyway. Indeed if consumers must pay a charge to order a book they are likely to come back and buy the book. Under the present system consumers may order a book but subsequently obtain it elsewhere in which case the first store has suffered a loss by ordering the book.

109. Nor is the Authority persuaded by the argument that the abolition of RPM in the Net Book Agreement will lead to fewer books being published. As already stated modern technological developments have greatly altered the economics of the book publishing industry. 'Desk-top publishing' technology has greatly eased the task of publishing books. The Authority notes that as a result of such technological advances many new small scale specialist book publishers have emerged in the UK in recent years. Many are engaged in publishing books which have a very limited minority appeal and which would not previously have been published by mainstream publishers. Desk top publishing has also enabled many authors particularly in the academic field to publish their own works. It has been claimed that the cost of producing a book using desk top publishing techniques may be as low as stg£1. The low cost of desk top publishing greatly reduces the risk of publishing minority interest books. The fact that new

24. *VBVB and VBBB v. Commission*, p. 40.

1.7.4 technology has enabled the publication of many titles which would not have been published by established UK publishing firms under the Net Book Agreement undermines the argument that in the absence of the NBA fewer books would be produced. It is advances in publishing technology rather than the NBA which have enabled an ever growing range of titles to be published.

110. The Authority notes that if an agreement fails to meet any of the requirements specified in section 4(2), a licence cannot be granted to it. The primary objective of the NBA is to establish a system of RPM in respect of UK published books in Ireland. RPM does not in the Authority's view contribute to improving the production of goods or provision of services or to promoting technical or economic progress. Consumers cannot therefore be said to share in such benefits and the restrictions cannot be regarded as indispensable to the achievement of such objectives. UK published books account for a substantial portion of books sold in Ireland. As most UK books are net books the restrictions contained in the NBA eliminate competition in respect of a substantial part of the relevant market. Consequently the Net Book Agreement, both members non-members versions, do not satisfy any of the requirements for a licence set out in section 4(2) of the Competition Act. The primary aim of the remaining agreements is to ensure the effective operation of RPM. Thus they also fail to satisfy the requirements for a licence.

111. The PA argued that the Authority, in deciding that all four requirements for a licence were not met, had taken a view which was directly at odds with the EC Commission. In particular it claimed that the Commission accepted that the NBA produced benefits which were shared with consumers. On the contrary the Commission, as already noted in para 45, stated that:

> . . . the agreements are not indispensable to the attainment of their objectives. Since an agreement, in order to be exempted from the prohibition contained in Article 85(1), has to fulfil all conditions of Article 85(3), the agreements cannot be exempted. It is therefore not necessary to examine whether the agreements meet the other conditions of Article 85(3).[25]

In the Dutch Books case the Commission specifically decided that a system of RPM for books failed all four tests for exemption under Article 85(3). These tests are the same as those contained in section 4(2).

112. The PA also claimed that the Authority was wrong in finding that the NBA failed the fourth test under section 4(2), arguing that competition was not eliminated by the NBA. The Authority wishes to point out that the specified test is whether the arrangements afford the undertakings concerned the possibility of eliminating competition in respect of a substantial part of the products in question. As UK published books account for the vast bulk of books sold within the State, and, as the overwhelming majority are net books, the Authority believes that net books constitute a substantial part of the products in question, and that price competition, which is particularly important in the case of books, is eliminated by the NBA in the case of the majority of imported books.

113. The book club regulations are designed to prevent book clubs competing with other booksellers by delaying the offering of books at reduced prices to the general public and by imposing restrictions designed to limit book clubs ability to sell books. Their object is to reinforce the restrictions contained in the Net Book Agreement itself. Consequently in the Authority's view the Book Club Regulations do not satisfy any of the requirements for a licence set out in section 4(2) of the competition Act.

114. The library licence specifies the terms and conditions including the maximum discounts which booksellers may provide to libraries approved by the PA. The Authority does not believe that the restrictions contained in the library licence, in particular the setting of maximum

25. At para 86.

levels of discount and the requirement that books be purchased from a particular bookseller contribute to improving the production of goods or provision of services or to promoting technical or economic progress. Such restrictions provide no benefit to consumers and cannot be regarded as indispensable to the achievement of such objectives. Again as the restrictions apply to the majority of books sold within the State, they eliminate competition in respect of a substantial part of the relevant market. Consequently the Library Licence does not satisfy the requirements for a licence set out in section 4(2) of the Competition Act. **1.7.4**

115. The book agent's licence sets out the terms and conditions upon which booksellers may supply book agents approved by the PA. The arrangement is designed to prevent book agents from selling books below the net published price, while it also specifies the maximum discounts which they may be given by booksellers. As with the restrictions contained in the NBA itself, the Authority does not believe that the Book Agent's Licence satisfies any of the requirements for a licence set out in section 4(2) of the Competition Act.

116. The quantity book buying scheme limits the circumstances in which booksellers may offer discounts to customers purchasing net books in large quantities and specifies the rates of discount which may be given in respect of such orders. It restricts the offering of discounts in respect of books on which the bookseller has not himself received a discount of at least 25% and provides that such books may only be purchased as gifts or for presentations in connection with the purchaser's business or for philanthropic or propaganda purposes, while preventing the purchaser offering such books for resale. In the Authority's view the purpose of such restrictions is to maintain the RPM provisions in the Net Book Agreement itself. The quantity book buying scheme does not satisfy any of the requirements for a licence set out in section 4(2) of the Competition Act.

117. The rules governing the national book sale set out the terms and conditions upon which the PA permit net books to be sold below the net price during the annual national book sale. While the rules permit net books to be sold below the net published price in certain limited circumstances, their main object and effect is to greatly restrict competition in the market for books, and to reinforce the restrictions contained in the Net Book Agreement. Consequently the rules governing the National Book Sale do not satisfy any of the requirements for a licence set out in section 4(2) of the Competition Act.

118. The primary and secondary school licence fixes the maximum discount which booksellers may give to schools, prevents the school from obtaining discounts from any other bookseller and is designed to ensure that schools will not resell net books below the net price. Its object is to reinforce the restrictions contained in the Net Book Agreement itself. Consequently the Primary and Secondary School Licence does not satisfy any of the requirements for a licence set out in section 4(2) of the Competition Act.

119. The PA argued in its reply to the Statement of Objections that the Authority had failed to specify the reasons for finding that the Book Club Regulations the Library Licence, the Book Agents Licence, the Quantity Book Buying Scheme, the National Book Sale and the Primary and Secondary Schools Licence failed to meet the requirements of section 4(2). Again the Authority rejects this claim. As pointed out in the preceding paras the Authority believes that the restrictions contained in all these arrangements are essentially designed to underpin the system of RPM for books. Consequently as RPM for books does not meet the requirements for a licence, these related arrangements equally do not satisfy such requirements for the same reasons.

120. The PA requested the Authority to defer its decision pending the outcome of its appeal against the EU Commission decision to the European Court of Justice. At the time the notification was made, the PA had indicated that it wanted a speedy decision to influence the Court of First Instance. No action may be taken against the notified arrangements under the Competition Act until the Authority has taken a decision. The Authority does not believe that it should extend the protection against court action afforded by the Act by deferring a decision.

121. In the Competition Authority's opinion the book publishers, who are party to the

1.7.4 notified arrangements, are undertakings as they are engaged for gain in the production of goods. The Net Book Agreement (1957) Members Version is an agreement between undertakings. Similarly the Net Book Agreement (1957) Non Members Version is an agreement between undertakings. The Authority is also of the opinion that the Book Club Regulations, the Library Licence, The Book Agent's Licence, the Quantity Book Buying Scheme, The Rules for the National Book Sale and the Primary and Secondary School Licence constitute agreements between the members of the Publishers Association setting out the terms on which members and non-members, who are signatories of the Net Book Agreement, will sell books to certain groups and/or permit certain reductions on the price of net books, and that these arrangements also constitute agreements between undertakings. The various arrangements also constitute decisions of an association of undertakings. Further, in he Authority's opinion each of these agreements has as its object or effect the prevention, restriction or distortion of competition in the market for books within the State insofar as they provide for a system of resale price maintenance in respect of UK published books and impose other restrictions on both publishers and book sellers in respect of the discounts they may offer in respect of books and certain other services. It therefore refuses to issue a certificate in respect of the notified agreements listed below. The Authority considers that the agreements do not satisfy any of the requirements of section 4(2). Consequently the Authority refuses to grant a certificate or licence in respect of the following notifications:

CA/23/92E — Net Book Agreement (Members Version);

CA/24/92E — Net Book Agreement (Non-Members Version);

CA/25/92E — Book Club Regulations 1985;

CA/26/92E — Library Licence;

CA/27/92E — Book Agent's Licence;

CA/28/92E — Quantity Book Buying Scheme; CA/29/92E — National Book Sale Conditions; and

CA/30/92E — Primary and Secondary School Licence;

also collectively known as the Net Book Agreement, notified under section 7(2) of the Competition Act on 20 May 1992.

For the Competition Authority

Patrick Massey
Member

10 June 1994

Competition Authority Decision No. 348, The Booksellers Association (Currency Conversion Agreement): 2 December 1994, Notification No. CA/904/92E 1.7.5

Practice by the members of an Association of Undertakings to convert the sterling prices on books imported from the UK in to Irish pounds at the same exchange rate – Whether such practice amounts to an agreement to fix prices – Arrangements ancillary to an agreement involving re-sale price maintenance – Witness summons – Statement of Objections – Competition Act 1991 (No. 24) sections 3,4 and 7

Facts On 30 September 1992 notification was made to the Authority of a currency conversion chart for calculating the Irish price of UK published books together with a request for a certificate under section 4(4) of the Competition Act 1991, or failing that, a licence under section 4(2). The notification is an arrangement between members of the Booksellers Association of Great Britain and Ireland, Irish branch, ('the Association') for determining the exchange rate to be applied to the cover price of books imported from the UK into Irish pounds for sale to consumers. These arrangements involve the preparation of a currency conversion chart by the Association which was circulated to members. The Association stated that there was no written agreement.

The parties to the notified arrangements are the Association and the individual booksellers in Ireland. The product market with which the notification is concerned is essentially that for the sale of books other than school books in the State. The Authority noted that 79% of all book imports into the State came from Great Britain and Northern Ireland and such books account for in excess of 50% of the relevant book market in the State. There are 370 retail outlets selling books in the State.

The currency conversion chart was notified on 30 September 1992 with the statement that further information requested by the Authority would be supplied in due course. The currency conversion chart enclosed was dated May 1982. It included a column headed UK price under which a series of UK prices of regular intervals from 25 pence upwards were arranged. The chart also contained a series of columns showing the appropriate Irish pound price for various Irish pound/Sterling exchange rates. The conversion rates as published included an add-on of 15% for VAT. A letter dated 6 July 1990 with a revised conversion chart was also submitted which was similar to the 1982 version save that it covered a wider band of exchange rates. It is to be noted that the 1990 chart gave one Irish pound exchange rate to cover a band of UK rates (e.g. Irish pound I = Sterling pound 0.87-0.899)7 in one case the Sterling band being a Stg£0.0599 wide. An exercise comparing the price of a Stg£20 UK book when converted using the conversion chart as against an actual exchange revealed that the price per the conversion chart was in general more expensive.

The Authority wrote to the Association requesting a copy of the annex to the notification which was not submitted with the chart. No reply was received. After further letters from the Authority, the Authority on 24 March 1994 issued a summons to the Chairman of the Association requiring him to appear before the Authority and produce certain documents. The Chairman appeared before the Authority and while the documents which were produced did not constitute a complete record they provided considerable information regarding the nature of the arrangement. The documents produced consisted of various meeting reports of the Association, meeting reports of the executive committee of the Association, various letters to and from

1.7.5 officers of the Association and various copies of the Association's newsletters. Much of this documentation dealt with an attempt by the Association to establish a pricing formula governing the pricing in Irish Pounds of UK books which would be acceptable to all of the membership. Excerpts from the Association newsletter advised that in fixing prices in the fluctuating Irish pound/Sterling environment the important thing was to maintain margins. In the minutes of the Associations committee meeting on 15 June 1993 the chairman emphasised the importance of the Association's members acting as one retail body.

On 22 June 1994 the Authority issued a Statement of Objections and offered the Association the option of an oral hearing. On 6 July 1994 the Association replied indicating that it did not wish to have an oral hearing and stated that the Authority's decision to refuse a certificate or licence to the Net Book Agreement nullified any currency conversion mechanism.

Decided by the Authority In refusing to issue a certificate or grant a licence under section 4(4) and section 4(2) of the Competition Act respectively in respect of the notified arrangements that:

(1) The parties to the notified arrangements are booksellers located throughout the State who are engaged for gain in the resale of books and are therefore undertakings within the meaning of the Act.

(2) The notified arrangements involved an arrangement between booksellers who are members of the Association to employ a common mechanism for converting Sterling prices into Irish pounds and while there is no formal agreement between the members there is at least a concerted practice whereby the members approve the conversion chart and use it to price hooks imported from the UK.

(3) The conversion rates are determined by the Association which, because its members are undertakings is an association of undertakings. The arrangements therefore also constitute a decision by an association of undertakings.

(4) The arrangements do not fix specific prices but provide for an uniform method of calculating the amount to be added to the UK publishing price in order to arrive at the retail price. If booksellers buy foreign currency at a different rate then it is possible, under the arrangement, for the price of the same book to differ between different bookshops. This however does not alter the fact that the object and, for the most part, the effect of the arrangement is to greatly reduce price competition between retailers in respect of the imported books.

(5) To the extent that each individual book title constitutes an unique product, price competition at the retail level is eliminated in respect of each book title imported from the UK. Price competition between retailers in respect of different titles is also restricted in that the possibility of retailers offering discounts on such books is eliminated.

(6) The conversion chart means that retailers can set their prices in the knowledge that other retailers are likely to charge the same price. Consequently the arrangements reduce the element of uncertainty regarding a competitors response to a rival firm's marketing strategy which is an essential feature of competitive market.

(7) Adherence to the conversion chart has the effect of fixing prices which are higher than would be justified on the basis of the actual exchange rate and this coupled with the reality that UK published books are generally sold at the same price by the majority of bookshops suggests that the notified arrangements are adhered to by a

substantial proportion of the booksellers operating in the relevant market. This has the affect preventing price competition in that market. **1.7.5**

(8) It is not necessary to show that agreement results in higher prices than would otherwise be the case for it to offend against section 4(1). It is the agreement to fix prices per se which is prohibited by that section and by agreeing to fix prices the parties can remove the essential element of competition. Such an agreement may not be justified on the basis that the prices fixed are claimed to be fair or reasonable. Nor can such an arrangement he justified on the basis that it is in the public interest.

(9) The arguments submitted by the Association that the conversion chart merely sets out recommendations for its members is rejected. Even if the chart was a recommendation it is clear that compliance with such a recommendation by the members has an appreciable influence on competition in the market in question. It is also relevant that before various versions of the chart were put into practice it was circulated to the members for comment and in a sense for approval.

(10) The arrangements were drawn up to facilitate the operation in Ireland of the net book agreement, an agreement between most UK book publishers which involves re-sale price maintenance. Retail price maintenance restricts the ability of retailers to determine their own prices and is generally restrictive on competition. Consequently an agreement designed to facilitate the operation of retail price maintenance offends against section 4(1).

(11) The notified arrangements do not contribute to improving the production of goods or provision of services or to promoting technical or economic progress and consumers cannot therefore be said to share in such benefits and the restrictions cannot be regarded as indispensable to the achievement of such objective. UK published books account for a substantial portion of books sold in Ireland and consequently the arrangement affords the parties involved the possibility of eliminating competition in respect of a substantial part of the relevant market. The arrangements do not therefore satisfy any of the requirements for a licence set out in section 4(2).

Cases and Decisions referred to

Cementhandelaren v. EC Commission (Case No. 8/72), [1972] ECR 977, [1973] CMLR 7
NAVEWA v. EC Commission (Case No. 96-102/82), [1983] ECR 3369, [1984] 3 CMLR 276
EC Commission Decision IFTRA Aluminium (Case No. 75/497/EEC:) [1975] OJ L228/32, [1975] 2 CMLR D20
EC Commission Decision Netbook Agreements [1988] OJ L22/127 [1989] 4 CMLR 825
United States v. Addyston Pipe & Steel Company et. al. 85 Fed 271 (6th Circuit 1898)
United States v. Trenton Potteries Co. et. al. 273, US 392 (1927)
Competition Authority Decision No. 336, Netbook Agreements — 10 June 1994 **1.6.4**
Competition Authority Decision No. 16, Association of Optometrists, Ireland — 29 April 1993 **1.6.2**

Competition Authority Decision of 2 December 1994 relating to a proceeding under section 4 of the Competition Act 1991

Notification No. CA/904/92E — The Booksellers Association (Currency Converstion Agreement)

Introduction

1. Arrangements involving a currency conversion chart for calculating the price of UK published books were notified to the Authority by the Irish Branch of the Booksellers Association on 30 September 1992. The notification requested a certificate, or in the event of

1.7.5 a refusal by the Authority to grant a certificate, a licence. The Authority issued a Statement of Objections to the Association on 22 June 1994. On 6 July 1994 the Association replied indicating that they did not wish to have an Oral Hearing and stating that the Authority's decision on the Net Book Agreement[1] nullified any currency conversion mechanism.

The Facts

(a) *The Subject of the Notification*

2. The notification concerns an arrangement between members of the Booksellers Association of Great Britain and Ireland — Irish Branch, (the Association), for determining the exchange rate to be applied to the cover price of books imported from the UK into Irish pounds for sale to consumers. These arrangements involve the preparation of a currency conversion chart by the association which is circulated to members. The Association stated that there was no written agreement.

(b) *The Parties Concerned*

3. The Booksellers Association of Great Britain and Ireland is an association of booksellers with members in Ireland and the UK. The parties to the notified arrangements are individual booksellers in Ireland. The notification stated that it related 'to the practice of members of the Association, comprising booksellers in Ireland, in relation to determining the exchange rate to be applied to the cover price of books imported from the United Kingdom for conversion into Irish pounds for sale to consumers'.

(c) *The Product and the Market*

4. The product concerned in the notification is books encompassing the retail sale of books to the general public through retail outlets located throughout the State. To some degree each individual book title may be considered an individual product. Some consumers are interested in particular types of books, e.g. thrillers, while others may have a preference for a particular author. A DIY title is not a close substitute for a romantic novel. Nevertheless there is scope for a considerable degree of substitutability between book titles. It is possible, however, to distinguish between schoolbooks and other types of books as these categories cannot be considered to be close substitutes for one another. The arrangements concern books imported from the UK. As most schoolbooks are not imported, the principal market involved is that for the sale of books other than schoolbooks in the State. The agreement also affects the schoolbook market within the State to the extent that some schoolbooks are imported from the UK.

5. Book imports in 1991 amounted to £59. 8m (Table 1). Imports of books from Great Britain and Northern Ireland accounted for 79% of book imports in 1991. Imports of books from Great Britain and Northern Ireland accounted for almost 1% of total imports from these countries. Imports account for a large proportion of the Irish book market. For example in its decision on the Net Book Agreement, the EC Commission stated that books imported from the UK accounted for slightly more than 50% of total book sales in Ireland.[2] A significant proportion of the books sold within the State are schoolbooks and the majority of these are published by Irish publishers. Thus imports from the UK account for well in excess of 50% of the relevant market, i.e. books other than schoolbooks.

1. Competition Authority Decision No. 336, 10 June 1994.
2. Commission Decision of 12 December 1988, OJ L22/12, 26.1.89, para 42.

Table 1: Irish Imports of Books

Country	1991 (£000)	(%)	1990 (£000)	(%)
Great Britain	45,047	(75.3)	41,271	(75.9)
Northern Ireland	2,121	(3.5)	1,980	(3.6)
U.S.A.	7,493	(12.5)	4,368	(7.8)
Other Cos.	5,138	(8.6)	6,892	(12.7)
Total	59,799	(100)	54,411	(100)

Source: CSO; Trade Statistics

6. According to the 1988 Census of Services, there were 370 retail outlets involved in the sale of books and stationery with 1659 persons engaged. Total turnover of bookshops in 1988 was £79m according to the Census, of which Dublin outlets accounted for £35.7m (45.4%).[3] The number of bookshops had increased by 130 since the 1977 census. Of the 370 outlets, 111 are located in Dublin with the rest of Leinster accounting for an additional 102. This compares with the 1977 figure of 72 and 41 respectively. The province of Munster had 115 outlets in 1988 compared with 84 in 1977. Of the 1988 total 37 were located in Cork, 17 in Limerick and 8 in Waterford. Connacht had 31 bookshops, of which 10 were located in Galway, compared to 25 in 1977. The Ulster counties of Donegal, Monaghan and Cavan had a combined total of 11 outlets which represented a decrease on the 1977 figure of 18.

Table 2: Book and Stationery Retail Outlets

	No. of Outlets 1988	%	1977	%	Gross Turnover (£m) 1988	%	** 1977	%
Leinster	213	(57.6)	113	(47.1)	52.3	(66.5)	12.1	(66.5)
Munster	115	(31.3)	84	(35.0)	22.2	(28.2)	2.2	(28.9)
Connacht	31	(8.4)	25	(10.4)	3.0	(3.7)	0.5	(2.6)
Ulster	11	(3.0)	18	(7.5)	1.2	(1.5)	0.3	(2.0)
State	370	(100)	240	(100)	78.6	(100)	18.1	(100)
Dublin	111	(30.0)	72	(30.0)	35.7	(45.4)	10.8	(59.6)
Cork	37	(10.0)	24	(10.0)	10.5	(13.4)	2.4	(13.4)
Limerick	17	(4.6)	9	(3.8)	4.1	(5.2)	1.0	(5.3)
Waterford	8	(2.2)	7	(2.9)	2.2	(1.7)	0.4	(2.3)
Galway	10	(2.7)	*		1.3	(2.8)	*	
Total	183	(49.5)	112	(46.7)	51.6	(65.6)	14.6	(80.6)

*Figures not available

Source: Census of Services (CSO) 1988 and 1977

3. Some of these stores may specialise in stationery although it is likely that there would be relatively few of those. Consequently the figures from the Census of Distribution for book and stationery stores probably provide a good indication of the number of retail book outlets. In addition some shops included in other categories of the Census may also sell some books e.g. newsagents. The Authority has not attempted to reconcile this figure with those contained in the Fishwick study.

***Editor's note*: In table 3 for Decision No. 336 [at 1.7.4] the total figures for 1988 are '53.8 (68.4)'. There

1.7.5 7. Table 3 shows that the average size of retail bookshops in 1988 was almost 900 square feet. Overall average size in 1988 was 8% higher than in 1977. There were considerable regional variations. The average size of bookshops in Dublin was 1300 square feet compared with 700 square feet outside of Dublin. The average bookshop in Connacht and Ulster was less than half the size of the average Dublin shop, while the average Munster bookshop was only 60% as large. It is clear, however, that the average size of bookshops outside of Dublin increased over the 1977-88 period.

Table 3: Average size of Book and Stationery Outlets

	1988 (sq ft)	1977 (sq ft)
Leinster	1013	1048
Munster	788	776
Connacht	539	360
Ulster	645	300
Dublin	1304	1369
Rest of Ireland	716	592
State	892	825

Source: Census of Services (CSO) 1988 and 1977

(d) *The Arrangements*

8. The arrangements relate to the practice of members of the Association comprising booksellers in Ireland, in relation to converting the cover price of books imported from the UK into Irish Pounds for sale to consumers. They are described in the notification form as an 'agreement/decision/concerted practice in relation to conversation [sic] rates applicable to sales of books in Ireland originating from England.' The notification included what was described as a typical conversion chart and stated that there was no written agreement as such to be notified. The notification stated that it was being submitted 'without the further information requested by the Authority in order to ensure that the Association complies with the deadline of 30 September 1992 laid down by section 7(2) of the Competition Act 1991. The further information will be supplied in due course.'

9. The conversion chart enclosed was dated May 1982. It included a column headed UK price with a series of prices from 25p to £3 and a series of columns showing the appropriate Irish pound price for various exchange rates ranging from IR£1 = stg£0.69 to IR£1 = stg£0.8399. The chart described the prices as 'Selling Prices at the Following Exchange Rates'. The chart also stated that to calculate selling prices for prices not shown various percentage add-ons should be added to the UK price, ranging from 23.5% to 48%. (The Association subsequently pointed out that these conversion rates included an add-on of 15% due to VAT). A letter dated 6 July 1990 with a revised conversion chart was also submitted. The letter states as follows.

> Dear Member,
> Following the issuing of the revised Ready-Reckoner there have been a great number of complaints from booksellers on the decision to drop scales C (11%) and E (19%).
> I have discussed the matter with some members of the Executive and in the circumstances, it has been decided to restore Scales C and E with immediate effect. The revised Scales are attached for your information.

Editor's note contd.: also appears to be an incorrect calculation for 1977 figures in the right hand column. See editor's note for table 3 in Decision No. 336. Pg 204.

The letter is signed by the Chairman of the Association. The attached chart is similar to the 1982 version except that it now provides conversion rates for exchanges rates varying from IR£1 = stg£0.75 to IR£1 = stg£0.9899. 1.7.5

10. The exchange rates in the 1990 chart are broken down into intervals of stg£2.99p in all cases bar one i.e. the same conversion rate applies, for example, for an exchange rate of IR£1 = stg£0.87-0.8999. In one case the same conversion rate applies for a range of stg5.99p, so that the same conversion rate is applied in the event of the Irish pound being worth 98.99p sterling as when it is worth 93p sterling. The chart also includes a note that for an exchange rate in the range IR£ = stg0.99-1.04, the UK price column should be used for pricing. The chart then states that to calculate selling prices not known above the following percentages should be added to the UK price. The Association stated that, in its view the bands were relatively narrow and were adjusted quite regularly and this ensured that the trade was seen to act responsibly in the light of exchange rates. They also stated that the 1990 chart was misleading since it was superseded as soon as it was issued.[4]

75 — 77.99	Add 33%
78 — 80.99	Add 28%
81 — 83.99	Add 23.5%
84 — 86.99	Add 19%
87 — 89.99	Add 15%
90 — 92.99	Add 11%
93 — 98.99	Add 7.5%

Table 4 gives an example of the Irish pound price given by the chart for a book priced at stg£20 for various exchange rates and compares it with the price calculated on the basis of the actual exchange rate. The add-ons listed in the conversion chart for each exchange rate band are those which would be necessary to convert the sterling price into Irish pounds for the bottom rate of the band, i.e. for any exchange rate between IR£1 = stg93p and stg98.99p the conversion gives the Irish pound price which would apply for a rate of 93p sterling. Thus at the extreme, at an exchange rate of IR£1 = stg98.99p, the chart gives an Irish pound price of £21.50 when the correct price would be £20.30.

Table 4: Irish Price of a Book with a UK Price of stg£20.

IR£/stg£ exchange rate	Price in IR£ per chart	per actual exchange rate
IR£1 = stg90p	22.22	22.20
IR£1 = stg92.5p	21.62	21.20
IR£1 = stg93p	21.50	21.51
IR£1 = stg98.99p	21.50	20.30

11. It is relevant to the present notification that many UK publishers are party to an agreement, known as the Net Book Agreement (NBA). This agreement has also been notified to the Authority and is the subject of a separate decision. The NBA is a voluntary agreement administered by the Publishers Association (PA) whereby UK book publishers impose a minimum net price on the sale of most of their publications in the U.K. and Republic of Ireland.

4. This chart was one of the two examples submitted to the Authority as part of the original notification, with no indication that it had in fact been promptly withdrawn.

1.7.5 It includes a number of ancillary agreements providing for limited exemptions from the provisions of the NBA for specified groups of book purchasers.

12. The NBA was also notified to the EC Commission. The Commission refused an exemption to the NBA under Article 85(3) of the Treaty of Rome. The decision was upheld by the Court of First Instance on appeal and the PA subsequently appealed to the European Court of Justice. The Commission, in its decision on the NBA, stated that:

> A special situation prevails in Ireland, where the ending of parity between the Irish punt and the British pound following Ireland's joining the European Monetary System, had made the pricing of books and the enforcement of the standard conditions of sale more difficult, as was reported by the Association. These problems were discussed by the Association and the Irish book trade at meetings in Dublin in 1981, as a result of which various measures were recommended to members. In particular, the Irish branch of the Booksellers Association of Great Britain and Ireland introduced a currency conversion schedule, which enables Irish booksellers to convert book prices expressed in British pounds easily into Irish punts.[5]

(e) *Submissions of the Parties*

13. The Association stated that it did not believe that the arrangements were anti-competitive. They had decided to notify them merely as a precautionary measure.

(f) *Subsequent Developments*

14. The Authority wrote to the Association's solicitors on 11 May 1993 requesting a copy of the Annex to the notification. No reply was received. On 23 June 1993 the Authority wrote to the Association's solicitors drawing their attention to the reference in the EC Commission decision in respect of the NET Book Agreement (see above) to the introduction of the currency conversion chart by the Association following discussions with the UK Publishers Association regarding problems with the enforcement of the NBA in Ireland. They were specifically asked if the notified arrangements related to the currency conversion chart specified in the Commission decision. No response was received. The solicitors concerned informed the Authority that they have no record of such letters. The parties were subsequently asked for specific information relating to the operation of the arrangements. On 10 March 1994 the Authority informed the Association that, if certain documentation relevant to its examination of the notified arrangements was not furnished within 7 days, it would summon a representative of the Association to appear before it and produce said documents. The Association responded objecting to the limited time given to it to compile the information requested. It indicated that in the time available it had been possible to locate one letter from the Association to its members on the subject of the arrangements. It indicated that it would do its best to locate the remainder of the information sought by the Authority. On 24 March 1994 the Authority issued a summons to the Chairman of the Association requiring him to appear before it on April 18 1994 and to produce any of the following documents:

> (i) All records of discussions between the Booksellers Association and UK Publishers' Association, and all correspondence between the two bodies in connection with the notified conversion chart;
> (ii) All correspondence and records of discussions between the Irish and UK branches of the Booksellers Association in connection with the chart;
> (iii) All correspondence and records of all discussions between the Booksellers Association, Irish branch, in connection with the chart;

5. Point 37.

(iv) All records of the work of the working group set up in January 1993 and referred to in the Associations' letter to its members of 30 November 1992. **1.7.5**

At the request of the Association, the Authority agreed to defer the date for the appearance of Mr O'Mahony to 20 April 1994. At that time Mr O'Mahony produced a number of the requested documents, indicating that these were all the relevant documents which he had managed to find. While the documents produced by Mr O'Mahony did not constitute a complete record they nevertheless provide considerable information regarding the nature of the arrangements.

15. On 22 June 1994 the Authority issued a Statement of Objections to the Association indicating its intention to refuse its request for a certificate or licence in respect of the notified arrangements. The Association was given 28 days to respond in writing and were offered the option of an Oral Hearing. On 6 July 1994 the Association replied indicating that it did not wish to have an Oral Hearing and stating that the Authority's decision to refuse a certificate or licence to the Net Book Agreement nullified any currency conversion mechanism.

(h) *Additional Information*

16. As stated in para 14, the Authority issued a summons to Mr O'Mahony, the Chairman of the Association, requiring him to produce specific documents which the Authority considered necessary for it to come to a decision in respect of the notified arrangements. The material provided includes records of meetings and correspondence concerning the arrangements. These provide a more detailed picture of the notified arrangements. It was unclear when exactly the currency conversion arrangements were first established. The documents submitted by Mr O'Mahony in cluded a report of a meeting between the Executive Committee of the Booksellers Association and a number of UK paperback publishers, including the Chairman of the Publishers Association Home Sales Committee (PAHSC) on 14 October 1980. It was noted that a Mr Williams of Pan (a UK publisher) had visited Ireland in July and had submitted a note which was discussed by the PAHSC at a meeting on 15 September. The report went on to refer to an initial report prepared by a Mr Harold Clarke in July 1980, and the banding tables by which a bookseller was able to price up his books based on the prevailing value of the Irish pound. It was also noted that a Mr Davies, described as a Director of the Booksellers Association, had visited Ireland in July and that it was envisaged that, as a result of this, a report would be sent to the Publishers Association after which a meeting would be arranged. The meeting of 14 October arose as the proposed report had not been prepared and the paperback publishers felt that they as a group should investigate what could be done in the future. Among the main topics discussed at the meeting were the fact:

> That, due to the currency differentials, the Irish Trade is now suffering a drop in gross profit.

It was suggested at the meeting that 'it would be a good idea that an official Booksellers Association sticker be used which would be virtually 'unpeelable' so that the public would know that this was an official price.' The report also notes the suggestion that, 'in common with other export markets, the Irish Trade should set their own price, was received with less than enthusiasm.' The publishers agreed to explore the matter further and possibly to have a further meeting with the Irish Trade in London.

17. A report of a meeting held in 31 South Anne Street, Dublin on Thursday 19 March 1981 at 4.00 pm notes that, at the AGM of the Irish Branch of the Booksellers Association in Kilkenny in March, the problem of pricing UK published books was seen to be causing great difficulty. It went on to state that:

> The Executive Committee was instructed to approach British publishers as soon as

1.7.5 possible to endeavour to work out a pricing formula which would be acceptable to the public, the trade and the Prices Commission.

As a result the new executive appointed a sub-committee to investigate the situation with a view to meeting a delegation from the Publishers Association at the earliest opportunity. This note is a record of a meeting of the sub-committee.

18. In a letter to members dated 15 April 1981, Mr Frank O'Mahony, then Chairman of the Booksellers Association Irish Branch, proposed that a small group of people would meet the UK publishers having agreed with the executive committee in advance the points to be discussed with them. It was suggested that the following points should be discussed with the Publishers Association.

> 1. Books should come unpriced if possible but with an agreed code — UK price visible is a great disincentive.
> 4. Books sent for review should be unpriced with approximate Irish Price given perhaps let P.A. distribute our chart to their members.'

Apart from discussions on rounding up of conversion rates, the Association provided no further records up to 1990. Mr David O'Mahony informed the Authority that he was not aware of any meeting between the Booksellers Association and the UK Publishers Association to discuss the currency conversion chart. He indicated that he had not been heavily involved in the Booksellers Association at that time. He subsequently informed the Authority that he raised the matter of whether such a meeting occurred with the Chief Executive of the Publishers Association and had been informed that no formal meeting took place between the two associations but that there had been a meeting between the Booksellers Association and a number of paperback publishers purely to discuss pricing in Ireland. Mr O'Mahony stated that the currency conversion chart had to take cognisance of the relationship with the NBA.

19. A revised ready reckoner for converting sterling into Irish pounds when pricing books was issued on 29 June 1990. It stated that:

> The broadening of some of the bands will allow for greater stability of pricing and avoid the need to change bands frequently.

It also stated that:

> The Executive Committee of the Booksellers Association have agreed to introduce this Reckoner from Wednesday, 27 June 1990.

20. The minutes of a meeting of the Booksellers Association on 28 August 1990 record that:

> The Bands agreed for the sterling charts at the meeting of 20 June had been changed. The agreed bands had been sent out on 29 June. The reaction of booksellers had been monitored between 29 June and 6 July. As a result of strong representations from booksellers (who felt they could not stand over some of the bands), the Chairman had consulted with several committee members and had drawn up another pricing chart in line with the views expressed to him. This had been circulated on 9 July. Some committee members expressed their concern at the arbitrary way in which the revised scale was drawn up. An E.G.M. should possibly have been called to discuss the changes. It was proposed and agreed that a sub-committee on prices would be set up. . . . It was suggested that representative from another trade together with a financial person would also serve on such a pricing sub-committee. It was agreed that any future changes would be circulated and discussed at the next A.G.M.

These appear to be references to the chart referred to in para 10 above which had been submitted with the original notification. 1.7.5

21. Draft minutes of the March 1991 AGM of the booksellers Association record discussions of a proposal for a draft agreement between booksellers and publishers for a system of resale price maintenance (RPM). It noted that a discussion document had been circulated to all Irish Branch members in advance of this meeting proposing a draft RPM agreement. According to the minutes the proposal was discussed and a number of modifications were agreed by consensus.

22. At a meeting of the Booksellers Association Committee held on 18 June 1991 a Mr John Davey proposed that the sterling pricing chart should be changed to reflect the changes brought on by the EMS. After a full discussion it was agreed that a letter would be sent to members outlining the following proposal:

88p — 89.99p — 15%
90p — 91.99p — 12%
92p — 93.99p — 10%

A letter to this effect was sent by Mr Davey to the members of the Association on 21 June 1991. It stated, *inter alia*, that the '11% we are currently adding is not enough to cover our costs, particularly when bank charges are taken into account.' It goes on to state that before the committee would recommend the implementation of these proposals it would welcome comments before 5 July. At a meeting of the Committee on 28 August 1991 Mr Davey recommended as a result of consensus among members that the sterling chart should be changed as per the June letter. Following discussions it was agreed that Mr Davey would draft the chart. The minutes of the following meeting held on 25 September 1991 record that Eason & Son along with some other members had objected against the circulation of the new chart but it had been adopted by a majority of those at the meeting.

23. The minutes of the 1992 AGM of the Booksellers Association held on 13 March 1992 records that the Association had until 30 September to notify the NBA (Net Book Agreement) to the Authority for the purpose of obtaining a licence. It was stated that in the meantime a draft of a system of RPM for Ireland was being prepared in case the European Court decided against the NBA.

24. In a letter dated 16 November 1992, Ms. Gemma Barry of the Bray Bookshop (then Chairwoman of the Booksellers Association Irish Branch) wrote to Mr David O'Mahony. The letter stated inter alia that Ms. Barry was waiting on Eason's come back to her on the currency situation. She expressed the view that if they had not done so by the end of the week the current conversion chart should be withdrawn immediately. It went on to state that:

> The situation is getting quite tricky in Dublin. Hodges are at -3% and say they will go to -5%. Eason's are 'officially' at -3%.

At this time the Irish Pound was above parity with sterling.

25. On 30 November 1992 Ms. Barry, as Chairwoman of the Association, wrote to the members. The letter indicated that the Committee had been reviewing the question of 'how members might wish to price in Irish pounds books which members have purchased from UK publishers.' It argued that if members simply translated the sterling retail price directly into Irish pounds at the current exchange rate, they were likely to suffer a substantial reduction in profitability compared with the situation before sterling weakened and devalued. It stated that the Committee had decided to set up a working party as of January 1993 to review the whole question. It pointed out that the Committee's preliminary analysis suggested that pricing guidelines along the basis outlined in the attached discussion note would maintain the profitability of booksellers. The note in question argues that profitability had been reduced

1.7.5 following the weakening of sterling. In particular it stated that previous practice which involved adding 12% to the retail price when sterling was at 91p when compared with the then current practice of subtracting 3% from the retail price of a book when sterling was at £1.08p resulted in lower margins. It went on to state that 'It is also possible to determine what rate should be applied to the sterling price to maintain previous levels of profitability'. It then stated that this procedure would give the following translation rates:

98 — 101.99	+6%
102 — 105.99	+4%
106 — 109.99	+2%
110 — 113.99	0%
114 — 117.99	-2%

The summons issued to Mr O'Mahony requested that he produce the records of the working party referred to in this letter. He stated that it had not been set up and that therefore there were no such records.

26. The Booksellers Association Irish Branch Newsletter for February 1993 stated that the Competition Act had come into effect on 30 September 1992 and that anyone 'operating a price controlled system and who wished to continue to do so was required to submit details of their pricing system and to make an application for a licence which would exempt them from the requirements of the Competition Act.' It stated that the association had fulfilled those requirements on behalf of booksellers. The present notification is the only one made to the Authority by the Association. The newsletter reported that a sub-committee had been set up 'to examine possible pricing structures which would allow us to maintain our existing margins and at the same time address the serious marketing problems that the present pricing structure is causing.'

27. In April 1993 the newsletter stated that the currency situation had changed dramatically since the Association had last written to people. It stated that:

> We advise our members to use the last conversion chart as a guideline only. It is basically up to each bookseller to convert at whatever rate they see fit. The most important consideration is maintaining profitability and reducing customer queries.

In June the newsletter stated that:

> It is very important that the trade act fully together and not be wholesale' led. They have slightly different operations criteria than the retail trade so remember stick to maintaining margin.

The September issue observed that most people were still operating on a 10% price differential to take account of the exchange rate. It went on:

> It may be wise to continue the 10% for another two weeks but if the exchange rate rests at around 0.94/0.95 you would need to be putting on a minimum of 7.5% to maintain margin.

It also referred to some UK publishers now putting Irish pound prices on their Irish editions and observed that:

> It is great to see a number of English publishers finally meeting our request going back many years but it is important to ensure that this pricing arrangement has no effect on your margin.

28. The minutes of the Association committee meeting on 15 June 1993 refers to a member stating that he 'would like to see consistent pricing in bookshops as there was emerging a 'wholesale' type situation. . . .' The Chairman emphasised the importance of acting together as one retail body. 1.7.5

29. In addition the Authority was also provided with a wholesale sterling ready-reckoner. Another undated copy of the currency conversion chart stated that:

> To calculate prices not shown above add appropriate percentages and round to nearest 5p. The basis for the sterling rate is the 60 day forward retail bank rate. Rates are set on the 1st Wednesday of the month and are held for the month.

30. In his letter of 6 July 1994 the Chairman of the Association stated that the references made in the various documents indicated the difficulty in pricing and maintaining the principles of the NBA at the same time. He stated that the pricing chart was only meant to act in the public interest and showed the tremendous concern of the Association with pricing consistencies. He argued that if anything the book trade was too responsive to currency matters as most other trades set their prices at the beginning of the year with an inbuilt cushion to account for estimated exchange fluctuations. He also stated that, the chart was introduced so as to insure minimum disparities in the retail price of books in Ireland and so would be consistent with the principles of the NBA. He stated that it was only introduced as a guideline and was always perceived as such.

Assessment

(a) *Section 4(1)*

31. Section 4(1) of the Competition Act states that 'all agreements between undertakings, decisions by associations of undertakings and concerted practices which have as their object or effect the prevention, restriction or distortion of competition in trade in any goods or services in the State or in any part of the State are prohibited and void.'

(b) *The Undertakings and the Agreement*

32. Section 3(1) of the Competition Act defines an undertaking as 'a person being an individual, a body corporate or an unincorporated body of persons engaged for gain in the production, supply or distribution of goods or the provision of a service.' The parties to the arrangements are booksellers located throughout the State and include sole traders and corporate bodies. Booksellers are engaged for gain in the resale of books and are therefore' undertakings within the meaning of the Act. The notified arrangements involve an arrangement between booksellers who are members of the Association to employ a common mechanism for converting sterling prices into Irish pounds. It appears from the documents obtained from Association that the proposed conversion charts were circulated to members for discussion before being formally adopted. While there is no formal agreement between the members it appears to the Authority that there is at least a concerted practice whereby the members approve the chart and use it to price books imported from the UK. It is relevant in this context that the notification specifically describes the notified arrangements as an 'agreement/decision/concerted practice in relation to conversation rates applicable to sales of books in Ireland originating from England.'

33. The conversion rates are determined by the Association which is an association of undertakings as its members are undertakings. The arrangements also therefore constitute a decision by an association of undertakings. The Authority noted in its decision on the Association of Optometrists that according to EC precedents:

> The concept of 'decision' includes the rules of the association in question, decisions

1.7.5 binding upon the members and recommendations. Agreements implemented within the framework of the Association concerned may be analysed either as 'decisions' of that association or 'agreements' between the members.[6]

The notified arrangements apply in respect of the sale of UK published books within the State. They affect the import, distribution and sale of UK published books within the State. As pointed out the majority of books other than schoolbooks sold in the State are imported from the UK.

34. A question also arises as to whether the arrangements also involved some form of agreement or concerted practice between the Association's members and the members of the UK Publishers Association to ensure the operation of system of Resale Price Maintenance for UK books in Ireland. As pointed out the EC Commission stated in its decision on the Net Book Agreement that the arrangement was introduced following a meeting with the UK Publishers Association in Dublin in 1981 to facilitate the operation of the Net Book Agreement in Ireland. Mr David O'Mahony indicated that he had not been involved in the Booksellers Association in 1981 and so was not aware of what might have happened at that time. It is clear from the documents which the Authority has obtained that the Booksellers Association met certain UK publishers and representatives of the UK Publishers Association. At various meetings of the Booksellers Association proposals were advanced for formal meetings with the Publishers Association. Mr David O'Mahony told the Authority that he could find no record of meetings between the two associations and claimed that the conversion chart was a purely internal matter.

(c) *Applicability of section 4(1)*

35. The essential feature of the notified arrangements is that the Association issues a chart to its members to enable them to convert UK prices into Irish pounds. The arrangements have both horizontal and vertical aspects. It is a decision by an association of undertakings and a concerted practice to directly or indirectly fix retail selling prices throughout the State of books imported from the UK. Such an agreement is specifically prohibited under section 4(1)(a) of the Competition Act.

36. The arrangements do not fix specific prices but provide for a uniform method of calculating the amount to be added to the UK publishers' price in order to arrive at the retail price. If booksellers buy foreign currency at different rates then it is possible, under the arrangements, for the price of the same book to differ between different bookshops. Nevertheless this does not alter the fact that the object and, for the most part, the effect of the arrangements is to greatly reduce price competition between retailers in respect of imported books. Indeed in his letter replying to the Statement of Objections the Chairman of the Association states that:

> The pricing chart was introduced so as to ensure minimum disparities in the retail price of books in Ireland and so would be consistent with the principles of the NBA.

37. To the extent that each individual hook title constitutes a unique product, price competition at the retail level is therefore eliminated in respect of each book title imported from the UK. The Authority believes that to some degree certain books are substitutes for one another. While some consumers will wish to buy a particular book by a particular author, others are looking for a particular type of book, whether a thriller or one on gardening, and will therefore choose from among the range of titles available in that particular category. Price competition between retailers in respect of different titles is also restricted. It is true that not all books of a particular type retail at a uniform price. Nevertheless the possibility of retailers offering discounts on such books is eliminated and so competition is restricted between different titles.

6. Bellamy and Child, at para. 2-031.

38. In addition the conversion chart means that retailers can set their prices in the knowledge that other retailers are likely to charge the same price. Consequently the arrangements reduce the element of uncertainty regarding a competitor's response to a firm's marketing strategy which is an essential feature of competitive markets. As UK published books account for the majority of books sold within the State, price competition between retailers is restricted in respect of a substantial part of the book market within the State. It is also relevant that a number of the letters issued to members advocated the use of the conversion rates in order for them to maintain or improve margins. **1.7.5**

39. It is well established under competition law in other countries that horizontal price fixing agreements are anti-competitive. Price fixing agreements have been consistently regarded as in breach of Article 85(1) of the Treaty of Rome. Bellamy and Child point out that:

> Since price is the main instrument of competition, Article 85(1)(a) expressly prohibits agreements, which 'directly or indirectly fix purchase or selling prices or any other trading conditions.' An agreement to fix prices by its very nature constitutes a restriction on competition within the meaning of Article 85(1).[7]

40. They go on to state that:

> Article 85(1) is infringed by an explicit agreement between suppliers to fix prices, and also by a concerted practice to restrict price competition, for example informal concentration on the dates and amounts of price increases or the exchange of price information. Similarly the prohibition of Article 85(1) covers not only 'prices' in the narrow sense but also discounts, margins, rebates and credit terms. Other agreements which directly or indirectly restrict price competition include agreements not to submit quotations without prior consultation, not to deviate from published prices, not to make public any deviations from published prices, not to quote other than delivered prices, not to give other than cost related rebates, and not to sell at below cost'.[8]

41. Van Bael and Bellis point out that:

> Although there exist no *per se* rules in EEC competition law, horizontal price fixing arrangements have always been held incompatible with Article 85(1) and have generally been denied an exemption.[9]

42. In IFTRA 10 the EC Commission found that an agreement between producers of virgin aluminium not to sell below their published prices was in breach of Article 85(1). The Commission found that the arrangements 'provide the parties with means of shelter from competition to the extent that price stability is increased and that the parties are enabled to predict each other's price policy with a reasonable degree of certainty'.[10]

It went on to state that:

> . . . every producer should have complete discretion to establish his own policy in these matters without risking the accusation that he is violating the spirit of an agreement. The contractual organisation of a system requiring adherence to various existing prices and

7. C. Bellamy and G. Child, (1987); 'Common Market Law of Competition', 3rd ed., Sweet and Maxwell, London, at para. 4-002.
8. Ibid. at para. 4-003.
9. I. Van Bael and J.F. Bellis, 'Competition Law of the EEC', 2nd ed., CCH Editions Ltd, para. 802.
10. Case no. 75/497/EEC, OJ L228/3, 29.8.75.

1.7.5 whereby price stability is encouraged by the recommendations which are made to the parties to use and adhere to price lists . . . constitutes a major restriction of competition, both in its object and its effect.[12]

43. In Cementhandelaren the European Court of Justice ruled that:

> The fixing of a price, even one which merely constitutes a target, affects competition, because it enables all the participants to predict with a reasonable degree of certainty what the pricing policy pursued by their competitors will be.[13]

The Court upheld the Commission's decision that such an agreement was in breach of Article 85(1) despite evidence that competition from other suppliers meant that the parties to the agreement did not necessarily abide by the agreed target prices. The Commission had argued that:

> The possible malfunctioning of a cartel cannot serve as a criterion for deciding whether or not it falls within Article 85(1).[14]

44. In the US horizontal price fixing agreements are generally regarded by the courts as a *per se* violation of the antitrust statutes. This view was originally set out in Addyston Pipe.[15] In Trenton Potteries[16] Stone J, giving the judgment of the US Supreme Court stated that:

> The aim and result of every price-fixing agreement, if effective, is the elimination of one form of competition. The power to fix prices, whether reasonably exercised or not, involves the power to control the market and to fix arbitrary and unreasonable prices.

45. Section 4(1) relates to agreements which have as their object or effect the prevention, restriction or distortion of competition. In the Authority's view the object of the arrangements is to prevent or restrict price competition in respect of UK published books. The European Court of Justice Decision in Cementhandelaren confirms that such an arrangement is prohibited by Article 85(1) even if it does not have the effect of preventing, restricting or distorting competition either because the members of the cartel fail to abide by the terms of an agreement or because they are forced to respond to discounting by non-members. In reality UK published books are generally sold at the same price by the majority of bookshops. It was noted in para 10 above that the conversion chart involves fixing prices which are higher than would be justified on the basis of the actual exchange rate, e.g. where the exchange rate is IR£1 =stg98p, the chart applies a rate of IR£ = stg93p. In the Authority's view it would be extremely difficult for an agreement to raise prices in this fashion unless it was adhered to by a substantial proportion of the firms operating in the relevant market. Thus the effect of the arrangements is to prevent price competition in the market for such books.

46. The Authority wishes to state that in its view it is not necessary to show that an agreement results in higher prices than would otherwise be the case for it to offend against section 4(1). It is the agreement to fix prices per se which is prohibited by that section. By agreeing to fix prices the parties remove an essential element of competition. Such an agreement may not be justified on the basis that the prices fixed are claimed to be fair or reasonable. Nor can the

11. Ibid., p. 10.
12. Ibid., p. 12.
13. Case no. 8/72, [1972], ECR 977, point 23.
14. Ibid., p. 984.
15. *United States v. Addyston Pipe & Steel Company et. al.*, 85 Fed. 271 (6th Cir. 1898).
16. *United States v. Trenton Potteries Company et. al.*, 273 US 392 (1927).

Authority accept the argument advanced by the Association in its letter of 6 July 1994 that the arrangement was only meant to act in the public interest. In enacting the Competition Act the Oireachtas has decided that the public interest is best served by competition. It is not for private parties to decide that the public interest is best served by their entering into anti-competitive arrangements. **1.7.5**

47. The Association claimed that the chart merely set out recommendations for its members. The Authority noted in its decision on Optometrists that:

> As a general rule, activities that are lawful when engaged in by competitors acting jointly are lawful for trade associations. Conversely, activities that are unlawful when engaged in by individuals acting together are quite simply unlawful when undertaken by trade associations.[17]

It also noted that the European Court of Justice he ruled that:

> A recommendation of an association of undertakings, even if it has no binding effect, cannot escape that article [85(1)] where compliance with the recommendations by the undertakings to which it is addressed has an appreciable influence on competition in the market in question.[18]

There is no indication in the notification or the conversion chart that the prices indicated by the conversion rates are recommended. Even if they were, however, it is clear that compliance with such recommendations by the members has an appreciable influence on competition in the market in question. It is also relevant that before various versions of the code were put into practice they were circulated to the members for comment. Thus in a sense the conversion chart was approved by the members.

48. The arrangements were drawn up to facilitate the operation in Ireland of the NBA an agreement between most UK book publishers which involves Resale Price Maintenance. Resale Price Maintenance (RPM) describes a practice whereby a supplier agrees to supply retailers on condition that they sell the goods at a price specified by the supplier. Such arrangements restrict the ability of retailers to determine their own prices. They also eliminate price competition between retailers for the suppliers' products, assuming that the supplier applies such arrangements to all retailers handling his products.

49. While economic theory suggests that there may be circumstances in which RPM may increase overall economic welfare, most goods and services do not appear to satisfy the necessary conditions for such a result. In addition other methods are available to induce greater efforts by retailers to sell the manufacturers' products. On balance therefore economic arguments indicate that RPM is generally harmful and restricts competition. RPM has been prohibited under the competition laws of most developed countries. Legislation which permitted RPM was repealed in the United States in 1976 and the Supreme Court has held that RPM constitutes a *per se* violation of the antitrust rules.[19] Legislation prohibiting RPM was enacted in Canada in 1951, in France in 1953 and in the UK in 1964. The UK Competition Act is generally neutral with respect to most forms of anti-competitive behaviour, in that it only prohibits practices which are shown to be against the public interest, and there is no presumption one way or the other as to whether practices are against the public interest. RPM, however, is specifically prohibited by statute. While the latter legislation allows for exemption, there have

17. Van Bael and Bellis, at para. 703.
18. NV IAZ International Belgium and Others v. EC Commission, Case nos. 96-102, 104, 105, 108 and 110/82, [1983] ECR pp. 3369-3430, point 3.
19. This view was restated in Continental T.V., inc. et al. V. GTE Sylvania inc., (1977) where the court distinguished between RPM and other forms of vertical restraint.

1.7.5 only been four requests for such exemption, and in only two instances, one involving the Net Book Agreement, has such an exemption been granted. On 23 November 1993 the UK Director General of Fair Trading announced, however, that the NBA was to be re-examined given the changes which had occurred since the decision to exempt the NBA was taken in the 1960s. The Director General subsequently announced that the agreement had been referred back to the Court.

50. The Authority considers that the weight of evidence indicates that RPM is generally restrictive of competition. Consequently an agreement involving RPM or designed to facilitate the operation of RPM, in its view, offends against section 4(1).

51. The notified arrangements, which involve an arrangement between booksellers for converting the price of UK books to Irish pounds and a decision by an association of undertakings, have as their object and effect, the prevention, restriction or distortion of competition in the market for books, other than schoolbooks, within the State, and thus offend against section 4(1). There is some conflict regarding the possible involvement of UK book publishers in the arrangements. It is not necessary for the Authority to decide whether they were in fact parties to the arrangements.

Applicability of section 4(2)

52. Under section 4(2), the Competition Authority may grant a licence in the case of any agreement or category of agreements which offends against section 4(1) but which, having regard to all relevant market conditions, contributes to improving the production of goods or provision of services or to promoting technical or economic progress, while allowing consumers a fair share of the resulting benefit and which does not —

(i) impose on the undertakings concerned terms which are not indispensable to the attainment of those objectives;

(ii) afford undertakings the possibility of eliminating competition in respect of a substantial part of the products or services in question.'

53. The notifying parties advanced no reasons to support their request for a licence. In the Authority's opinion the arrangements do not satisfy the requirements for a licence as set out in section 4(2). The Authority notes that if an agreement fails to meet any of the requirements specified in section 4(2), a licence cannot be granted to it. In the Authority's view the notified arrangements which involve the restriction of price competition in the book market do not contribute to improving the production of goods or provision of services or to promoting technical or economic progress. Consumers cannot therefore be said to share in such benefits and the restrictions cannot be regarded as indispensable to the achievement of such objectives. UK published books account for a substantial portion of books sold in Ireland. Consequently the arrangements afford the parties involved the possibility of eliminating competition in respect of a substantial part of the relevant market. They do not therefore satisfy any of the requirements for a licence set out in section 4(2) of the Competition Act.

54. It may be that the abolition of such arrangements will result in a loss of business by specialist bookshops to other types of retail outlet or that larger bookshops will gain at the expense of smaller ones. The purpose of the Competition Act is to protect competition not competitors. The essence of competition is that competitors will seek to take custom away from their rivals. At the heart of the view that competition is desirable is the judgment that such activity benefits consumers and enhances overall economic welfare. Consequently the fact that some competitors may be harmed by the elimination of a particular restrictive practice cannot justify the continuance of such a practice. Orthodox economic theory indicates that price-fixing agreements are detrimental rather than beneficial to consumer interests. Breit and Elzinga observed that:

> Economists are almost unanimous in their condemnation of cartels, especially those engaged in price fixing, because no expert has satisfactorily established that consumers

will benefit from price fixing. On the contrary economic analysis can show that cartels are inefficient and lessen consumer welfare. It is, therefore, not surprising that antitrusters have the closest meeting of minds on the baleful influence of cartels.[20] **1.7.5**

The decision

55. The Authority concludes that booksellers are undertakings within the meaning of the Competition Act and that the Booksellers Association of Great Britain and Ireland — Irish Branch, is an association of undertakings. The notified arrangements constitute an agreement and/or a concerted practice between undertakings, namely the booksellers who are members of the Association. They also constitute a decision by an association of undertakings. In the Authority's opinion the arrangements have, as their object and effect, the prevention, restriction or distortion of competition in the market for books within the State and therefore offend against section 4(1). They do not satisfy any of the requirements for a licence under section 4(2). The Authority therefore refuses to issue a certificate or grant a licence to the Booksellers Association of Great Britain and Ireland (Irish Branch) Currency Conversion Chart, Notification No. CA/904/92E, notified to the Authority on 30 September 1992 under section 7 of the Competition Act 1991.

For the Competition Authority

Patrick Massey
Member

2 September 1994

20. W. Breit and K.G. Elzinga, (1989); 'The Antitrust Casebook: Milestones in Economic Regulation', 2nd ed., Dryden Press, New York, p. 12.

[illegible] will be taken into account [illegible] in the context [illegible] can show that [illegible] and less [illegible] [illegible] the [illegible] not [illegible]

The decision

[illegible] company [illegible] within the [illegible] and [illegible] sellers [illegible] in [illegible] [illegible] of [illegible] [illegible] decision [illegible] [illegible] [illegible] have [illegible] [illegible] [illegible] [illegible] [illegible] [illegible] of the [illegible] [illegible] [illegible] [illegible] [illegible] in the [illegible] [illegible] [illegible] [illegible] [illegible] [illegible] [illegible]

[illegible]

[illegible]

[illegible]

[illegible]

CHAPTER TWO

Procedures

2.0 Introduction

Section 7 of the Competition Act 1991 provides for the notification of agreements, decisions and concerted practices of a kind described in section 4(1) of the same Act. Thus the Competition Authority is not empowered to accept a notification of an abuse of a dominant position of itself unless it is requested by the Minister under section 14 of the Competition Act 1991. The Authority has also reported upon the dominant position of Independent Newspapers in its report to the Minister which was requested under section 11.[1]

It needs to be emphasised that only agreements, decisions or concerted practices described in section 4(1) of the Competition Act 1991 can be notified to the Competition Authority. The Authority in Decision No. 35 — ICC Bank plc/Navenby Ltd — decided that a particular notification was 'invalid' because there was not an agreement between undertakings in existence at, or since the time the Competition Act 1991 came into force. A similar decision was made in respect of Decision No. 219 — Cadbury Ireland Ltd; Chivers & Sons Ltd.[2] The Competition Authority has also rejected a notification because the subject thereof was authorised under Article 65 of the ECSC Treaty.[3]

The Competition Authority has issued certificates that an agreement does not offend against section 4(1) where the agreement clearly does not affect trade in the State or where the agreement clearly does not have an object or effect of preventing, restricting or distorting competition. In decision 31 — Energy Control Systems Ltd/Erinova Ltd/Belton Engineering Works Ltd, the Authority issued a certificate relating to an exclusive distribution agreement for territories outside the State.[4] The Authority in this decision reiterated its view in Decision No. 11 — B & D Firestone/Grenfells Ltd & Thoroughbred Promotion and Development Company[5] when it stated that it is questionable whether an agreement which clearly does not offend

1. The Interim Report of Study on the Newspaper Industry which was not published by the Government Publications Service is available @ £5 from the Department of Enterprise and Employment. The report was requested by the Minister under section 11 of the Competition Act. The *Irish Times* of 31 May 1995 reported on the unsuccessful application of Irish Press plc to the High Court for an order directing the Minister for Enterprise and Employment to supply Irish Press plc with an unedited copy of the report. Mr Justice Keane in his judgment noted that the Minister could either institute proceedings under section 6 or use the provisions of section 14 to deal with any perceived abuse. If the Minister adopted either of these measures, the interests or rights of Irish Press plc were not diminished by the availability of an edited report. Mr Justice Keane said 'the obligations of the Competition Act 1991 would be seriously impaired if the Competition Authority could not ensure the confidentiality of commercially sensitive material supplied to the Authority by business people or firms who expected that that confidence would be respected'. [See page 291 also]
2. Summarised at 2.2.1 and 2.2.2.
3. The Competition Authority Notice in the *Irish Times* of 9 June 1995 gave notice of this rejection in relation to CA/503/92E — Irish Coal Importers/joint purchasing agreement.
4. Summarised and text at 5.2
5. Summarised and text at 3.9.

2.0 against section 4(1) can be notified under section 7 of the Competition Act 1991 in the first place.

Competition Authority Decision No. 13 — Peter Mark/Majella Stapleton and Competition Authority Decision No. 20 APEX Fire Protection Ltd/Noel Murtagh are decisions which indicate the Competition Authority's view about when employees become an 'undertaking' and more significantly when an agreement between an employer and an employee may be considered to be subject to section 4(1) and consequently notifiable under section 7(1) of the Competition Act 1991.[6]

Agreements, decisions and understandings which were in existence on 1 October 1991 may not be notified now and the parties could only have sought a licence or certificate by notifying the Competition Authority on or before 30 September 1992.[7]

A Notification is a voluntary act on the part of the notifying party and there is no legal requirement to notify the Competition Authority of what can be notified under section 7 of the Competition Act 1991. Greater benefits were afforded to those who notified agreements which were in existence when the Act was commenced on 1 October 1991 than to those who notify agreements now.[8] Only the grant of a licence will preclude an aggrieved party from claiming damages, exemplary damages, an injunction or a declaration for a breach of section 4 of the Competition Act 1991. Agreements, decisions or understandings which come into existence after 1 October 1991 may be granted a licence with retrospective effect to the date upon which the Authority was notified of the agreement. A certificate will merely disentitle an aggrieved person to damages in respect of the period covered by the certificate for a contravention of section 4 (1) if the proceedings were instituted after the issue of the certificate. It is difficult to conceive how the subject of a certificate of the Authority could be the basis of a claim for damages in respect of the period prior to the issue of a certificate. Nevertheless it will be noted that no statutory provision exists for the issue of certificates with specific retrospective application as licences may provide.

In September 1993 the Authority commenced to accept the withdrawal of notifications without making a decision. Previously in Decisions 14 and 15 the Authority indicated its acceptance of withdrawals because of the liquidation or the cessation of trade of one of the parties to an agreement. In Decision 23 the Authority accepted the withdrawal of a notification of an agreement which had been terminated and in Decision 27 the Authority decided to accept the withdrawal of a notification on the expressed intention of the notifying party that it did not intend to rely on the employment contract notified. More recently the Authority indicates in its published notices of withdrawals if the withdrawal has arisen as a result of the termination of the subject of the notification.[9]

The only prescribed procedure under section 7(6) by the legislature for the notification process is Statutory Instrument No. 250 of 1991 which provides that a

6. Summarised and text at 1.4.2 and 1.4.3.
7. The Authority nevertheless has shown its willingness to accept alterations to Notifications of Agreements which may have been in existence prior to the commencement of the Competition Act. 'NC' in the List of Notifications and more particularly under 'Decision No.' column in this book identify potential examples.
8. The List of Notifications with columns of details in this book indicate which agreements may so benefit by footnote 1 after CA/1124/92E in the list of notifications in this book (page 1298).
9. The decisions referred to in this paragraph are summarised in 2.1. The 1994 Annual report of the Authority, notes that 55 notifications were withdrawn in 1994, 'in many cases after the issue of a Statement of Objections'.

fee of £100 must be paid with each notification to the Competition Authority.[10] **2.0**

The Authority in its 'A Guide to Irish Legislation and Competition' (PL9199) describes the procedures of the Authority under section 4. The Authority refers to its powers under paragraph 7(1) of the Schedule to the Competition Act 1991 whilst submitting that the principle of proportionality suggests that no more onerous a procedure should be adopted than is strictly necessary when the Authority is exercising its investigatory powers.[11]

The Competition Authority's guide states that if a decision is favourable concerning a notification, notice of the Authority's intention to grant a certificate or a licence is published in a daily newspaper and interested third parties will be entitled to obtain a summary of the notification from the Authority for a small fee.[12] This has not been the universal practice of the Authority as evidenced particularly by the issue of certificates in respect of notifications concerning shopping centre leases without the publication of an intention to make a decision in each such decision.

Paragraphs 3.26 and 3.27 of the Competition Authority's guide outlines the manner of dealing with notifications for which an unfavourable decision may be taken. Discussions between the Authority and the notifying parties may result in the subject of the notification being changed in order to overcome the objections of the Authority. The list of notifications contained in this book can be quickly scanned to see where notifications have been changed before a decision has been made by the Authority and which show the cases in which the Authority and the notifying parties may have discussed ways in which a favourable decision could be achieved prior to the making of a decision.

No publication of the Competition Authority's intention to refuse a certificate or a licence is made other than to the notifying parties. A formal statement of objections is transmitted to the notifying parties which may result in a request and the acceptance or refusal of that request for an oral hearing. The summary and description of the notification no. CA/1080/92E — Eason/Newspread which was first published in the 1993 Annual Report of the Competition Authority gives a published example of how the Authority can deal with notifying parties who may resist the objections of the Authority to a request for a certificate or a licence.[13]

The Competition Authority has also decided that it may issue a licence for a category of agreements even though some of the agreements may not have been notified to the Authority. The Authority has described the latter as the equivalent of the 'block exemption' given by the European Commission.[14] In *Cronin v. Competition Authority and others* Costello J in an *ex tempore* judgment rejected the claim of the Plaintiff that the Authority acted unfairly and unconstitutionally in granting the Motor Fuels Category Licence. This case which is under appeal to the Supreme Court also involves a challenge to the constitutionality of the grant of the extensive powers to the Authority to grant licences in respect of categories of agreements, the form and consequence of which may never be known or reviewed by the Competition Authority.[15]

10. See Annex A.2.
11. See Annex A.8.
12. See para. 3.23 of the Competition Authority Guide at Annex A.8.
13. Summarised and text at 2.3.1.
14. See para. 3.31 of the Competition Authority Guide at Annex A.8.
15. Summarised and text at 2.3.2.

2.0 That statutory instrument was revoked but effectively reinstated with a provision that publication in *Iris Oifigiúil* of a licence or certificate which covers a category of agreements, decisions or concerted practices will be sufficient notice to every body to which the licence or certificate relates.[16]

Section 9 of the Competition Act 1991 enables any undertaking or any person aggrieved by a licence or a certificate to appeal to the High Court within 28 days of the publication of the licence or certificate. The editor suggests that in the absence of prescribed appeal procedures, an appellant would be required to issue and serve a Plenary Summons with the necessary Indorsement of Claim followed by the delivery of a Statement of Claim if required by the Competition Authority. No statutory provision exists for an appeal to the High Court from a refusal of the Authority to grant a certificate or licence, from the Authority's rejection of a notification or from the Authority's acceptance of a withdrawal of a notification.[17]

16. See Statutory Instruments in Annex A.2 and more particularly SI No. 76 of 1992 and SI No. 293 of 1993.
17. 'EC Antitrust Procedure' (3rd ed.) by C.S. Kerse and published by Sweet & Maxwell in 1994 is a most useful book. The procedures of the European Commission are explained. The book is the ideal source for the reader who may wish to compare Irish and EC Antitrust procedure.

2.1 Withdrawal of Notifications

Competition Authority Decision No. 14, Palace Video Ltd/Abbey Films Ltd: 19 February 1993, Notification No. CA/1111/92E **2.1.1**

Oral agreement – Notifying party now in liquidation – Acceptance of request for withdrawal of notification – Competition Act 1991 (No. 24) sections 4 and 7.

Facts: On 30 September 1992 Palace Video Ltd notified an oral agreement concerning the distribution of films with a request for a certificate or a licence under section 4 of the Competition Act 1991. On 17 December 1992 the Competition Authority was notified that Palace Video Ltd was now in administration in the United Kingdom and requested the withdrawal of the notification. By order dated 13 January 1993 Palace Video Ltd was placed in liquidation.

Decision by the Authority: Having regard to the fact that the agreement is the subject of another notification and on the basis that Palace Video Ltd is now in liquidation the Authority accepted the withdrawal of the notification.

Competition Authority Decision of 19 February 1993 relating to a proceeding under section 7 of the Competition Act 1991
Notification No. CA/1111/92E — Palace Video Ltd/Abbey Films

1. An oral agreement between Palace Video Ltd and Abbey Films Ltd concerning the distribution of films was notified to the Competition Authority on 30 September 1992 by Palace Video Ltd. The notification requested a certificate, or in the event of a refusal by the Authority to grant a certificate, a licence.

2. On 17 December 1992 the notifying party's legal representatives informed the Authority that Palace Video Ltd was now in administration in the United Kingdom and stated that they had been requested, by the administrator, to withdraw the notification. In response to a query by the Authority the notifying party's legal representatives stated, in January 1993, that they wished to withdraw the notification on the grounds that Palace Video Ltd, which was no longer in administration, was due to go into liquidation shortly. The legal representatives stated that as the notified agreement was also the subject of another notification — No. CA/1054/92 E — none of the parties to the agreement would be prejudiced by the withdrawal of Notification No. CA/1111/92E. The legal representatives also stated that they had been instructed by the administrator to cease working on behalf of Palace Video Ltd.

3. The Authority has established that, by order of the High Court in the United Kingdom, dated 13 January 1993, Palace Video Ltd is now in liquidation.

The Decision

4. The Competition Authority has decided, on the basis that Palace Video Ltd is in liquidation and having regard to the fact that the same agreement is the subject of Notification

2.1.1 No. CA/1054/92E, to accept withdrawal of Notification No. CA/1111/92E — Palace Video Ltd/Abbey Films Ltd.

For the Competition Authority

Patrick M. Lyons
Chairman

19 February 1993

2.1.2 **Competition Authority Decision No. 15, The 'Old Bushmills' Distillery Co. Ltd/Joseph B Casey:** 19 February 1993 — Notification No. CA/976/92E

Party to notified agreement ceases to trade – Request for withdrawal of notification – Competition Act 1991 (No. 24) sections 4 and 7

Facts: On 30 September 1992 a trademark usership agreement was notified to the Authority with a request for a certificate or a licence under section 4 of the Competition Act 1991. On 11 February 1993 the Old Bushmills Distillery Co. Ltd and the notifying party informed the Authority that Joseph Casey had ceased trading and requested the withdrawal of the notification.

Decided by the Authority: On the basis that Joseph Casey had ceased to trade the withdrawal of the notification was accepted.

Competition Authority Decision of 19 February 1993 relating to a proceeding under section 7 of the Competition Act 1991
Notification No. CA/976/92E — The 'Old Bushmills' Distillery Co. Ltd/Joseph B. Casey

1. A trade mark usership agreement between the 'Old Bushmills' Distillery Co. Ltd and Joseph B. Casey was notified to the Competition Authority on 30 September 1992 by the 'Old Bushmills' Distillery Co. Ltd. The notification requested a certificate, or in the event of a refusal by the Authority to grant a certificate, a licence.

2. On 11 February 1993 the notifying party's legal representatives informed the Authority that Joseph B. Casey had ceased trading and requested withdrawal of the notification.

The Decision

3. The Competition Authority has decided, on the basis that Joseph B. Casey has ceased trading, to accept withdrawal of Notification No. CA/976/92E — The 'Old Bushmills' Distillery Co. Ltd.

For the Competition Authority

Patrick M. Lyons
Chairman

19 February 1993

Competition Authority Decision No. 23, Spar (Ireland) Ltd/BWG Foods Ltd/ Sancroft Ltd: 11 June 1993, Notification No. CA/982/92E 2.1.3

Termination of notified agreement prior to decision of the Competition Authority – Withdrawal of notification of agreement to Competition Authority – Competition Act 1991 (No. 24) sections 4 and 7

Facts: On 30 September 1992 an equipment supply and merchandising agreement between Spar (Ireland) Ltd, BWG Foods Ltd and Sancroft Ltd was notified to the Authority with a request for a certificate or a licence under section 4 of the Competition Act 1991. On 25 May 1993 the parties informed the Authority that the notified agreement terminated on 17 February 1993 and requested that the notification be withdrawn.

Decided by the Authority: In accepting the withdrawal of the notification that since the notified agreement has terminated no agreement now exists between undertakings and accordingly no certificate or licence shall issue.

Competition Authority Decision of 11 June 1993 relating to a proceeding under section 7 of the Competition Act 1991
Notification No. CA/982/92E — Spar (Ireland) Ltd; BWG Foods Ltd; Sancroft Ltd

1. An equipment supply and merchandising agreement between Spar (Ireland) Ltd, BWG Foods Ltd and Sancroft Ltd was notified to the Competition Authority on 30 September 1993. The notification requested a licence.

2. On 25 May 1993 the notifying parties' legal representatives informed the Authority that the notified agreement was terminated on 17 February 1993 and requested withdrawal of the notification.

The Decision

3. The Competition Authority has decided, on the basis that the notified agreement was terminated and that no agreement between undertakings now exist, that it will not be issuing a licence in respect of Notification No. CA/982/92E. The Authority, therefore, accepts the withdrawal of Notification No. CA/982/92E — Spar (Ireland) Ltd, BWG Foods Ltd and Sancroft Ltd.

For the Competition Authority

Patrick M. Lyons
Chairman

11 June 1993

2.1.4 Competition Authority Decision No. 27, Apex Fire Protection Ltd/Mr William Brennan: 2 July 1993, Notification No. CA/717/92

Post-employment contract term non-soliciting provisions – Request for withdrawal of notification – Competition Act 1991 (No. 24) sections 4 and 7

Facts: On 30 September 1992 an employment contract with post-term non-soliciting provisions was notified to the Competition Authority by Apex Fire Protection Ltd with a request for a certificate or a licence under section 4 of the Competition Act 1991. In May 1992 Mr Brennan ceased to be an employee and established his own business in June 1992. In March 1993 Apex Fire Protection Ltd informed the Competition Authority that it did not intend to rely on the employment contract and requested the withdrawal of the notification. The non-soliciting provisions are similar to those included in the agreement which was included in Notification No. CA/1130/92 — Apex Fire Protection Ltd/Mr Noel Murtagh and the subject of Decision No. 20.

Decided by the Authority: As Apex Fire Protection Ltd does not intend to rely on the employment contract and the Competition Authority would not issue a certificate or licence, the Competition Authority accepts the withdrawal of the notification.

Competition Authority Decision of 2 July 1993 relating to a proceeding under section 7 of the Competition Act 1991
Notification No. CA/717/92 — Apex Fire Protection Ltd/Mr William Brennan

1. An employment contract between Apex Fire Protection Ltd and Mr William Brennan was notified to the Competition Authority on 30 September 1992 by Apex Fire Protection Ltd. The notification requested a certificate, or in the event of a refusal by the Authority to grant a certificate, a licence.

2. Mr Brennan ceased to be an employee of Apex Fire Protection Ltd in May 1992 and had established his own business in June 1992.

3. On 26 March 1993 the notifying party's legal representatives informed the Authority that Apex Fire Protection Ltd did not intend to rely on its employment contract with Mr Brennan and requested withdrawal of the notification.

4. The Authority has decided that non-solicit provisions similar to those involved in this agreement offended against section 4(1) of the Competition Act and did not satisfy the requirements for a licence under section 4(2) (Decision No. 20 of 10 June 1993 — Notification No. CA/1130/92 — Apex Fire Protection Ltd/Mr Noel Murtagh.

The Decision

5. The Competition Authority has decided, on the basis of its views on employment contracts expressed in Decision No. 20 and the fact that Apex Fire Protection Ltd does not intend to rely on the employment contract, that it will not be issuing a certificate or a licence in respect of Notification No. CA/717/92. The Authority, therefore, accepts the withdrawal of Notification No. CA/717/92 — Apex Fire Protection Ltd/Mr William Brennan.

For the Competition Authority

Patrick M. Lyons
Chariman

2 July 1993

2.2 Rejections

Competition Authority Decision No. 35, ICC Bank plc/Navenby Ltd/Savage Plastic Packaging Ltd/Savpak Ltd: 24 September 1993, Notification No. CA/864/92E 2.2.1

Acquisition of entire share capital in 1989 – Non-compete clause expiring in April 1991 – Validity of notification – Competition Act 1991 (No. 24) sections 3, 4 and 7

Facts: On 30 September 1992 an agreement for the sale of the entire issued share capital of two companies was notified to the Authority with a request for a certificate or licence under section 4 of the Competition Act 1991. The agreement contained a non-compete clause which prevented the vendors from becoming involved in any business which competed with those sold for a period which expired on 28 April 1991. The agreement provided for the consideration to be given to the vendors in shares of the company which acquired the entire issued share capital of two companies to the agreement.

Decided by the Authority:

1. The vendors and the company which now own the entire issued share capital of two other companies in the transaction are undertakings within the meaning of section 3(1) of the Competition Act 1991.

2. As the entire agreement had expired before 1 October 1991 the notified agreement constitutes an agreement which was not in existence at the time of or since the Competition Act 1991 came into force and therefore the agreement cannot be validly notified under section 7(1) or section 7(2) of the Competition Act 1991.

Decisions and Notice referred to:
Competition Authority Decision No. 8 — ACT Group plc and Kindle Group **3.6**
Competition Authority Decision No. 12 — Scully Tyrell/Edberg Ltd **3.10**
'Notice in respect of Mergers and Takeovers which predate the Competition Act' **3.1**

Competition Authority Decision of 28 September 1993 relating to a proceeding under section 4 of the Competition Act 1991
Notification No. CA/864/92E — Navenby Ltd/Savage Plastic Packaging Ltd/Savpak Ltd/Nocl Savage and Others

Introduction

1. An agreement between Navenby Ltd (Navenby) and Noel Savage, Kevin Savage, Christopher Kiernan, and Industrial Credit Corporation (the vendors) containing a non-compete clause pursuant to the sale of the entire issued share capital of Savage Plastic Packaging Ltd (Savage) and Savpak Ltd (Savpak) was notified to the Competition Authority on 30 September 1992. The notification requested a certificate or, in the event of a certificate being refused, a licence.

2.1.1 The facts

(a) *The subject of the notification*

2. The notification relates to an agreement dated 28 April 1989 between the vendors and Navenby whereby the vendors agree to sell the entire issued share capital of Savage and Savpak to Navenby. The agreement also contains a non-compete provision.

(b) *The parties*

3. Savage and Savpac are limited companies incorporated in the State. Prior to its sale, the vendors had a 100% interest in both companies. Navenby is a limited company with registered offices at 41-45 St Stephen's Green, Dublin 2. As part of the sale agreement, the vendors have received shares in Navenby by way of consideration for the sale of Savage and Savpak.

(c) *The arrangements*

4. The notification relates to an agreement, dated 28 April 1990, for the sale of the entire share capital of Savage and Savpac to Navenby. The agreement contained a non-compete clause which prevented the vendors from becoming involved in any business which competed with those sold for a period of two years from the date of completion. This period expired on 28 April 1991.

Assessment

(a) *Section 4(1)*

5. Section 4(1) of the Competition Act states that 'all agreements between undertakings, decisions by associations of undertakings and concerted practices which have as their object or effect the prevention, restriction or distortion of competition in trade in any goods or services in the State or in any part of the State are prohibited and void'.

(b) *The undertakings and the agreement*

6. Section 3(1) of the Competition Act defines an undertaking as 'a person being an individual, a body corporate or an unincorporated body of persons engaged for gain in the production, supply or distribution of goods or the provision of a service'. The parties to the present agreement are the vendors and Navenby. Navenby is a limited company with registered offices in Dublin. It is engaged for gain through its interest in Savage and Savpak, both of which are engaged for gain in the packaging business. Prior to completion of the agreement, the vendors were the beneficial owners of the companies and were therefore undertakings within the meaning of the Act at the time of the agreement. This is consistent with the Authority's decision in ACT/Kindle and Scully/Tyrrell.[1]

(c) *Applicability of section 4(1)*

7. As the sale of business was completed prior to 1 October 1991, the date on which the Competition Act came into force, this element of the agreement had been discharged by performance before the Act commenced. The property which was the subject of the agreement had been transferred. In the Authority's view, the prohibition in section 4(1) only applies to a current or continuing contractual commitment or one entered into subsequent to the coming into force of the Act.[2] As the merger or sale element of the 1991 transactions was discharged

1. Competition Authority Decision No. 8, ACT Group plc and Kindle Group (CA/9/91), 4 September 1991 and No. 12, Scully Tyrrell & Co. and Edberg Ltd (CA/57/92), 29 January 1993.
2. 'Notice in respect of Mergers and Takeovers which predate the Competition Act' — Competition Authority, *Iris Oifigiúil*, 14 May 1992, p. 367.

prior to the commencement of the Act, that aspect of the arrangements does not come within the scope of section 4(1). 2.2.1

8. The non-compete clause had also expired before the Act came into force. Thus, in the Authority's view, there was not an agreement between undertakings in existence at, or since, the time the Act came into force. The notification is therefore invalid and the authority is unable to grant a certificate or licence.

The decision

9. In the Authority's opinion, Navenby Ltd, Noel Savage, Kevin Savage, Christopher Kiernan, and Industrial Credit Corporation are undertakings within the meaning of section 3(1) of the Competition Act. As the entire agreement had expired before 1 October 1991, the notified arrangements do not constitute an agreement which was in existence at the time, or since, the Act came into force; it cannot be validly notified under section 7(1) or 7(2) of the Competition Act and the Authority cannot issue a certificate or licence in respect of the notification.

For the Competition Authority

Patrick Massey
Member

24 September 1993

Competition Authority Decision No. 219, Cadbury Ireland Ltd/Chivers & Sons Ltd: 3 December 1993 — Notification No. CA/521/92E 2.2.2

Exclusive distribution agreement containing restrictions on competition – Agreement terminated prior to commencement of the Competition Act 1991 – Whether such agreement can be validly notified – Competition Act 1991 ss. 2, 3, 4 and 7

Facts: On 30 September 1992 notification was made to the Authority by Cadbury Ireland Ltd of an exclusive distribution agreement made 13 May 1986 between Schweppes Ltd and L. Rose & Company Ltd of the one part and Chivers & Sons Ltd of the other part with a request for a certificate under section 4(4) of the Competition Act 1991 or, failing that, a licence under section 4(2). Cadbury Ireland Ltd is a fellow subsidiary with Schweppes Ltd and L. Rose & Co. Ltd of Cadbury Schweppes plc the UK based food and beverages group. Under the terms of the notified agreement Chivers was appointed, subject to certain restrictive covenants, exclusive distributor of particular Schwepps and Rose products within the State. The notified agreement expired on or about 1 January 1991.

Decided by the Authority: In refusing to issue a certificate or a licence under sections 4(4) and 4(2) respectively of the Competition Act 1991 in respect of the notified agreement that since the notified agreement expired before 1 October 1991, it was not an agreement which was in existence at the time or since the coming into force of the Competition Act and thus it cannot validly be notified under section 7(1) or 7(2) of the Act.

2.2.2 Decision referred to:
Competition Authority decision No. 144 — Category Licence for Exclusive Distribution Agreements — 5 November 1993 **5.1**

Competition Authority Decision of 3 December 1993 relating to a proceeding under section 4 of the Competition Act 1991
Notification No. CA/521/92E — Cadbury Ireland Ltd/Chivers & Sons Ltd

Introduction

1. An exclusive distribution agreement between Schweppes Ltd (Schweppes) and L. Rose & Co Ltd (Rose) and Chivers & Sons Ltd (Chivers) was notified by Cadbury Ireland Ltd (Cadbury) to the Competition Authority on 30 September 1992. The notification requested a certificate or, in the event of a certificate being refused, a licence.

The Facts

(a) *The subject of the notification*

2. The notification relates to an agreement dated 13 May 1986 between Schweppes and Rose and Chivers whereby Chivers was appointed exclusive distributor in the State of certain Schweppes and Rose products, namely the Kia-Ora range of whole-fruit drinks and Roses squashes and cordials.

(b) *The Parties*

3. Cadbury is an Irish-registered company, engaged in the manufacture and distribution of food and beverages, whose ultimate parent is Cadbury Schweppes plc, of the U.K. Schweppes and Rose are wholly owned subsidiaries of Cadbury Schweppes plc. Chivers is an Irish-registered company which is engaged in the manufacture, distribution and sale of, among other things, beverages.

(c) *The Arrangements*

4. The notification relates to an exclusive distribution agreement, dated 13 May 1986. Chivers was appointed exclusive distributor of the products in the State. The supplier agreed not to appoint any other distributor in the State, to sell exclusively to the distributor, and to refer enquiries in the territory to Chivers. Chivers agreed to purchase all its requirements of the products from the supplier, to promote sales and to supply the products in the packages in which they were supplied. Chivers was prevented from seeking customers or establishing any depot outside the territory. Chivers agreed to maintain adequate and suitably qualified staff, and not to divulge confidential information, during the agreement and after termination. Chivers was bound, during the agreement and for one year thereafter, not to deal in competing products, except those being handled at the date of the agreement. Sales targets were to be agreed. The agreement was to continue in force for five years, and yearly thereafter, subject to 12 months' notice of termination. The agreement was replaced by a subsequent agreement between Cadbury Beverages Ltd and Chivers, covering the same products, dated 9 May 1991, which has been notified by each party separately (CA/506/92E and CA/509/92E).

Assessment

(a) *Section 4(1)*

5. Section 4(1) of the Competition Act states that 'all agreements between undertakings, decisions by associations of undertakings and concerted practices which have as their object or effect the prevention, restriction or distortion of competition in trade in any goods or services in the State or in any part of the State are prohibited and void.'

(b) *The Undertakings and the Agreement* 2.2.2

6. Section 3(1) of the Competition Act defines an undertaking as 'a person being an individual, a body corporate or an unincorporated body of persons engaged for gain in the production, supply or distribution of goods or the provision of a service.' Schweppes, Rose and Chivers were each engaged in the manufacture and distribution of goods for gain, and they were therefore undertakings within the meaning of the Act. The agreement was an agreement between undertakings.

(c) *Applicability of section 4(1)*

7. The Authority considers that an exclusive distribution agreement such as that between Schweppes, Rose and Chivers, offends against section 4(1) of the Act, for the reasons stated in its category licence for exclusive distribution agreements (Decision No. 144 of 5 November 1993, para 14).

8. The agreement, however, was replaced by a new agreement dated 9 May 1991 and effective from 1 January 1991. The notified agreement, therefore, had expired before the Act came into force. Thus, in the Authority's view, there was not an agreement between undertakings in existence at, or since, the time the Act came into force. The notification is therefore invalid and the Authority is unable to grant a certificate or licence.

The Decision

9. In the Authority's opinion, Schweppes Ltd, L. Rose & Co Ltd and Chivers & Sons Ltd were undertakings within the meaning of section 3(1) of the Competition Act. As the entire agreement had expired before 1 October 1991, the notified arrangements do not constitute an agreement which was in existence at the time, or since, the Act came into force; it cannot be validly notified under section 7(1) or 7(2) of the Competition Act and the Authority cannot issue a certificate or licence in respect of the notification.

For the Competition Authority

Patrick M. Lyons

Chairman

3 December 1993

2.3 Judicial Review

2.3.1 **Proposed Competition Authority Decision, Easons and Newspread:** Notification No. CA/1080/92E

Agreement between wholesalers/distributors of UK magazines in the State on the conversion of the price of such magazines from Sterling to Irish Pounds – Agreement between wholesalers as to their margins on the sale of such magazines – Distribution by both wholesalers to retailers of identical ready-reckoners to enable retailers work out the recommended retail price for UK magazines – Horizontal re-sale price maintenance – Statement of objections – Injunction – Oral hearing – Termination of notified agreement – Withdrawal of notification – Competition Act 1991 (No. 24) ss. 3, 4 and 7

Facts: On 30 September 1992 notification was made to the Authority with a request for a certificate under section 4(4) of the Competition Act 1991, or failing that, a licence under section 4(2) in respect of arrangements between Eason & Sons Ltd ('Easons') and Newspread Ltd ('Newspread') relating to the calculation of Irish Pound prices for UK magazines distributed in the State.

Easons, a private Irish company, is engaged in retail and wholesale newspaper and magazine distribution in Ireland. Newspread is a subsidiary of Independent Newspapers Ltd which distributes newspapers, periodicals and magazines in Ireland. Easons and Newspread supply around 3,500 and 5,000 retail newsagents respectively. Easons distribute some 1,900 magazine titles and Newspread distributes some 1,200 magazine titles and both companies distribute many of the same UK magazines.

UK magazines is the product concerned in the notified agreement and the service is the distribution by wholesalers of magazines published in the UK to retail newsagents in Ireland. Few newsagents have space to carry more than 75 to 100 of the nearly 2,000 titles and within these titles the magazines fall into distinct categories in which they compete with each other.

The initial notification referred to the agreement between Easons and Newspread on the forward purchase of Sterling and the application of exchange rate factors to determine the retail selling prices of UK magazines to be recommended to newsagents. The annex to the notification, submitted by Easons in January 1993, made it clear that in addition to the currency purchasing agreement that there was an arrangement between the two firms to ensure that each recommended the same re-sale price for the same magazine to newsagents. Easons submitted that substantial adjustments were required to the UK price in order to arrive at the cover price appropriate for Ireland so as to take account of the exchange rate prevailing between Sterling and the Irish Pound, VAT at 21% chargeable in Ireland (and not chargeable in the UK) and a higher margin for the Irish wholesaler in order to cover the higher distribution costs and the costs associated with distributing to a small, widely scattered population.

Under the arrangements, Easons and Newspread each independently agree a purchase price for a particular magazine with the UK publishers which respective purchase prices may be different. These prices are based on a discount from the UK retail price on the cover of the magazine and are expressed and paid for in Sterling. Purchase prices have then to be converted into the equivalent in Irish currency. Both Easons and Newspread agreed to buy Sterling forward for six months in advance (and more recently three months in advance) and to use the same exchange rate for their Irish Pound price calculation. The forward purchase of foreign currency is a means whereby the wholesalers can reduce risks to their profitability arising from fluctuations in exchange rates and it permits a single exchange rate to be applied to magazine price calculations for the relevant 6 month period. Once the UK publishers price was converted to Irish Pounds at the agreed exchange rate Easons and Newspread added on an agreed wholesalers margin, an agreed and identical retailers margin and VAT at the appropriate rate to give an identical final re-sale price for each magazine which was recommended by both Easons and Newspread to the retailers. Even if the two firms did not always agree the detailed calculations each recommended the same retail price to newsagents, each allowed the same standard 25% margin to such newsagents and each applied the same rate of VAT for a particular magazine the consequences of which meant that the sale price to newsagents by both firms had to be identical. Easons also submitted that in practice an alternative calculation had been used by both parties whereby the UK magazine cover price was converted at the agreed exchange rate to Irish pounds to which was then added an additional margin of 5% to cover the extra costs of the Irish wholesaler and the relevant rate for VAT. Using this method the parties found that over time the 5% additional margin to cover the increased distribution costs in Ireland reduced in real cash terms as the Irish Pound strengthened against Sterling. Consequently they adjusted this 5% distribution margin as the exchange rate varied so as to maintain in real cash terms the same margin to cover these distribution costs. 2.3.1

Given the large number of magazines involved the wholesaler until recently did not specify the actual price to be charged by the retailer for each. Instead each retailer was provided with a simple ready-reckoner which showed the recommended retail price in Irish currency at the relevant VAT rate for a number of cover prices in Sterling. For each magazine the retailer ascertained the Sterling price from the cover, checked the ready-reckoner for the Irish price, and put the latter on the magazine. The ready-reckoners supplied by Easons and Newspread produced identical results in terms of an Irish price for a given UK cover price. Easons stated that they made the calculations and these were followed by Newspread. Copies of the ready-reckoners supplied by Easons from November 1992 onwards referred to the prices being 'recommended Irish selling price for UK magazines'. The Newspread ready-reckoner contains similar language from May 1993 but both wholesalers informed retailers that certain publications were to be sold at the Irish Pound price printed on the cover. This was later changed in the case of Newspread to say that the relevant publications 'are recommended to be retailed at the indicated Irish Pound cover price'. A practice had also recently developed whereby the Delivery Note which accompanied each batch of magazines delivered to the newsagent set out an actual Irish Pound cover price (including VAT) for each separate UK magazine and retailers tended to rely on these rather than the ready-reckoners. In the Newspread case the Delivery Note contained no indication that the Irish Pound price was recommended or suggested while the

2.3.1 Easons Delivery Note contained the statement that 'the determination of the retail price of each publication is a matter to be decided by each retailer'.

While retailers were encouraged to charge appropriate prices Easons claimed that there was nothing in their standard terms and conditions which required them to charge these prices. Easons stated that it might draw a retailers attention to the fact that incorrect prices were being charged but it could not enforce adherence to the prices which it wished to see charged and it had not withdrawn supplies from suppliers for selling at another price.

A Statement of Objections was sent to both parties on 2 March 1993 and a response was received from Easons on 8 April. No response had been received from Newspread by 11 June and the Authority proceeded to take a decision refusing to grant a licence to the notified agreement. Before the decision could be published Newspread was granted an injunction by Mr. Justice Flood on 17 June preventing the publication of the decision and was also granted an entitlement to have their response considered and to have an oral hearing. Newspread was also granted leave to apply for judicial review of the Authority's decision. On 27 July 1993 Mr. Justice Carney quashed the Authority's decision and extended time for the delivery of the response to the Statement of Objections and the request for an oral hearing. The oral hearing with Newspread was held on 13, 14 and 20 September 1993. On 22 December 1993 Easons informed the Authority that it had terminated the agreement and no longer required any certificate, licence or decision for the notification.

Views of the Authority: Prior to the termination of the agreement and the withdrawal of the notification the Authority concluded that the notified agreement offended against section 4(1) of the Competition Act 1991 and satisfied none of the conditions for a licence laid down in section 4(2).

(a) *Applicability of section 4(1)*

1. Easons and Newspread are engaged in the distribution of magazines for gain and are therefore undertakings within the meaning of section 3(1) of the Competition Act.

2. The agreement between Easons and Newspread concerning the forward purchase of Sterling and the determination of relevant exchange rates, although unwritten, was an agreement between undertakings. These exchange rates were used by Easons and Newspread to determine the retail selling prices of UK magazines to be recommended to newsagents and involved an arrangement between the two parties to sell each magazine at the same price to newsagents and to recommend the same retail price to such newsagents. While these arrangements were also unwritten they constituted agreements between undertakings.

3. The arrangements between Easons and Newspread which involved agreement on purchase prices for foreign exchange, an agreed addition for wholesaler margins, and the same standard selling price to newsagents for each magazine constituted the fixing of prices, a practice which is specifically mentioned as being prohibited under section 4(1). The agreement on the purchase of foreign exchange and on foreign exchange rates to be used in calculating prices was an integral part of the pricing arrangements. The arrangements represented a serious restriction on competition and virtually eliminated price competition between the only two magazine wholesalers in the State and as such clearly offended against section 4(1) of the Act.

4. The arrangements between the parties to maintain their wholesale margin as constant in cash terms was itself anti-competitive. By agreeing a wholesale cash margin to be used in calculating retail prices Easons and Newspread effectively removed any uncertainty as to how they as rivals might adjust their margins in response to exchange rate movements. Such measures were anti-competitive since their purpose was clearly to prevent or restrict in some way the normal operation of competitive market forces and as such offended against section 4(1). **2.3.1**

5. The agreement on currency purchases by Easons and Newspread resulted in their producing the same ready-reckoner and the same re-sale price for a particular magazine on their advice notes. It also resulted in their charging the same price for a particular magazine to the vast majority of retailers. Indications on the ready-reckoners that retailers were free to set their own prices have only appeared in the recent past and such indications were not given on the Newspread advice note, the advice note now being widely used as a means of setting prices. The whole arrangement differed little from a full blown system of re-sale price maintenance with procedures for enforcement.

6. The two firms agreed on the price at which they recommended newsagents to sell the magazines since both firms used a ready-reckoner which gave the same results. There was also almost total adherence to these prices by newsagents thus completely eliminating price competition between newsagents for a particular magazine. The system led to ossification of the price structure and hence to higher prices and as such offended against section 4(1).

(b) *Applicability of section 4(2)*

1. The arrangements had an adverse effect rather than an improving effect on the distribution of magazines because they eliminated any price competition for a particular magazine at wholesale and at retail level. There was only limited competition between different magazine titles and competition in the price of a particular magazine was an important means of rationalising and improving the distribution system for magazines.

2. There was no evidence that consumers benefited from the fact that a particular magazine was sold at the same price in all outlets in their area or throughout the State. If one distributor could buy currency cheaper than another or save in the purchase price or distribution costs, or if a retailer received discounts or achieved cost savings, there was no benefit to the consumer because these savings were not passed on to the consumer by way of reduced prices.

3. The collusion on exchange rates between Easons and Newspread was not indispensable for the effective distribution of imported magazines but rather was indispensable for the recommendation of the same re-sale prices to retailers.

4. While newsagents could engage in competition with each other through ordering a wider range of magazine titles or having longer opening hours the fact that price competition was eliminated at both the wholesale and the retail levels in the magazine market eliminated competition in respect of a substantial part of the products in question.

Cases, Decisions and Notice referred to:

ICI v. EC Commission (Case No. 48/69), [1972] ECR 619, [1972] CMLR 557

Agence et Messageries de la Presse v. Binion (Case No. 243/83) [1985] ECR 2015, [1985] 3 CMLR 800

2.3.1 *VBVB and VBBB v. EC Commission* (Case No. 43 & 63/82) [1984] ECR 19, [1985] 1 CMLR 27
Court of First Instance Decision, *Publishers Association v. EC Commission* (Case No. T-66/89) II [1992] ECR 1995 and 5 [1993] CMLR 120
EC Commission Decision, Net Book Agreements [1988] OJ L22/12, [1989] 4 CMLR 825
EC Commission Decision, GERO-Fabriek [1976] OJ L16/1618, [1977] 1 CMLR D35
EC Commission Decision, VBBB/VBVB [1981] OJ L54/36, [1982] 2 CMLR 344
Competition Authority Decision No. 4 — Esso Solus and related agreements, 25 June 1992 **4.1**
Notice pursuant to Art. 19(3) of Reg. No. 17 — Agence et Messageries de la Presse OJ L164 23 June 1987

Notification No. CA/1080/92E — Easons and Newspread

Introduction

1. Notification was made by Eason & Son Ltd. on 30 September 1992 with a request for a certificate under section 4(4) of the Competition Act 1991 or, in the event of a refusal by the Competition Authority to grant a certificate, a licence under section 4(2) in respect of an agreement between Easons and Newspread Ltd. on the forward purchase of sterling and the application of exchange rate factors to determine the retail selling prices of UK magazines to be recommended to newsagents.

2. A Statement of Objections was sent to both parties on 2 March 1993. A response was received from Easons on 8 April. No request was made for an oral hearing. No response had been received from Newspread by 11 June, and the Authority proceeded to take a decision refusing to grant a licence to the notified agreement. Before the decision could be published, Newspread was granted an injunction by Mr Justice Flood on 17 June preventing publication of the decision. Newspread was also granted entitlement to have its response considered and to have an oral hearing, and was granted leave to apply for a judicial review. On 27 July the Authority consented to an Order by Mr Justice Carney quashing the refusal decision, and extending the time for the delivery of the response to the Statement of Objections and request for an oral hearing. The response by Newspread to the Statement of objections was received by the Authority on 17 June and an oral hearing with Newspread was held on 13, 14 and 20 September 1993. Easons informed the Authority on 22 December 1993 that it had terminated the agreement and no longer required any certificate, licence or decision on the notification.

The Facts

(a) *The subject of the notification*

3. Under an agreement which originated in 1979, following the breaking of unitary parity between the Irish pound and sterling, Easons and Newspread separately purchased forward from their bankers, at around the same time, the anticipated amount of sterling required for the payment of UK publishers who supplied them with magazines during the ensuing six month period. Since May 1993, the arrangement was on a three-monthly basis. In order to arrive at their standard selling prices and recommended resale prices, which were the same for each company for a particular magazine, each company utilised the same relevant exchange rate and the same additional cash margin required to recover the extra costs of distribution in Ireland, and the same retailer margin. The arrangement was verbal and contained no other terms as to duration or otherwise. In addition, retailers were expected to resell the magazines at the prices recommended by the two wholesalers.

(b) *The parties involved*

4. Eason & Son Ltd. is a private Irish company which is engaged in retail and wholesale newspaper and magazine distribution in Ireland. The group also operates in Northern Ireland, and it includes Easons Advertising Service Ltd., Irish Representation Ltd. and Easons Library Supplies Ltd. Easons distributes UK daily and Sunday newspapers, with some exceptions, and Irish provincial newspapers, as well as UK and foreign magazines. It does not distribute Irish

daily or Sunday newspapers, or certain UK and other foreign magazines. It distributes some 1,900 magazine titles, weekly or monthly, obtained from about 140 publishers. It supplies around 3,500 retail newsagents. 2.3.1

5. Newspread Ltd. is a subsidiary of Independent Newspapers Ltd. It distributes Irish periodicals, the Farmers' Journal, Anois, the Sunday World, the Sunday Business Post and the Sunday Tribune, the Star, the Daily and Sunday Express, and the Observer, mainly on an exclusive basis. It distributes many of the same UK magazines as Easons, although it handles only some 1,200 titles. It delivers to over 5,000 agents in total, and to some 3,200 on a daily basis. It delivers about I million copies of magazines a week, in 55,000 parcels.

6. Both Easons and Newspread deliver throughout the State, except for North Donegal, which is serviced by Menzies of Derry. Each may supply a newsagent on an exclusive basis, or they may each supply different UK magazines to a single newsagent. Each may also deliver some copies of the same magazine to the same newsagent. Foreign, non-UK, magazines are obtained through the UK, and are treated as UK magazines. While newspapers are delivered every day of the week, magazines are delivered on five days each week. There are other, smaller wholesalers in operation, who deal primarily in newspapers, especially UK Sunday newspapers. The Irish newspaper publishers, except in the case of the Sunday World, the Sunday Tribune and the Sunday Business Post, do not utilise the distributors or wholesalers.

(c) *The product and the market*

7. The product concerned in the notified agreement was UK magazines, and the service was the distribution by wholesalers, Easons and Newspread, of magazines published in the UK to retail newsagents in Ireland. Newspapers were not covered by the notified agreement. UK publications may also be obtained by consumers direct from the publishers by post on a subscription basis. Easons estimated that turnover in the market was £30 million, divided approximately 60% and 40% between Easons and Newspread. Imports of newspapers and journals, which did not appear at least four times a week, were valued at £27.9m. in 1991 according to official trade statistics. In addition to magazines, this figure includes UK Sunday newspapers, which are substantial in terms of both volume and value.

8. Newspapers and magazines, whether published in Ireland or abroad, are all, in some sense, substitutes for each other, and they combine to form the total market for printed publications, except books. Not all such publications, however, are perfect, or even close, substitutes for any others. In its report of the investigation into the proposed increase in the shareholding by Independent Newspapers in the Tribune Group, the Authority commented as follows:

> It would appear that no newspaper is a perfect substitute for any other newspaper. . . . While there is much similarity between newspapers within a single market segment, there is a considerable difference between a 'quality' upmarket paper and a popular down-market paper. Nevertheless, potential purchasers are faced with a large degree of choice in deciding which newspaper to buy. . . . The Authority accepts that there is some overlap between the market for daily newspapers and that for Sunday newspapers . . . the Authority considers that daily papers are not a perfect, or even a close, substitute for Sunday papers. . . . With considerable reservations, the Authority considers that the market for Irish Sunday newspapers should be the primary focus of concern in the present investigation.[1]

9. There is a very wide range of magazines, most of which are designed for a specific

1. Competition Authority Report of the investigation about the proposal whereby Independent Newspapers plc would increase its shareholding in the Tribune Group from 29.99% to a possible 53.09%. Pl 8795. March 1992, pp. 19-21.

2.3.1 audience. A particular magazine may be bought regularly by an individual, or may be purchased sporadically or only once merely on an impulse. While newsagents display many different magazines, few have the space to carry more than 75 to 100 out of nearly 2,000 titles. While there is thus still a wide choice, a customer who wishes to purchase a woman's magazine will not regard a motor magazine as a reasonable substitute, and a person wanting to buy the latter will not have equal regard for a magazine about computers or pets. Similarly, a person wanting up-to-date daily news will not regard a magazine, even a news magazine, as an acceptable substitute for a daily newspaper. While accepting an amount of overlap, the Authority considers that magazines generally constitute a separate and distinct market from that of newspapers. Magazines also fall into distinct categories in which they compete with each other, and some Irish magazines compete with their UK counterparts. The Authority considers that imported magazines constitute a major segment of the market for magazines.

10. Easons and Newspread distribute throughout Ireland, except in North Donegal, and retailers are free to buy from either wholesaler or from both. It is understood, however, that the prices of magazines are the same in the Menzies territory as elsewhere in the State, although Easons stated that they had no formal contact with Menzies. The relevant geographic market therefore is the State.

(d) *The distribution system*

11. The distribution system for newspapers and magazines was described at length in a 1979 report by the Restrictive Practices Commission.[2] The physical characteristics of the system have not changed a great deal since that date. A major change, however, has been the development of Newspread. It was set up in 1971 as a service company to distribute newspapers, the *Farmers Journal* and certain Irish magazines. In the early 1980's it started to distribute UK newspapers and magazines. In brief, Easons and Newspread tender with UK magazine publishers for the distribution of their titles in Ireland. Purchase prices, based on a discount from the sterling price which is printed on the magazine, are negotiated independently, and are paid in sterling, and Easons and Newspread may purchase the same magazine at a different price. Following their transmission to Ireland, by sea or air, the magazines are arranged according to the titles and numbers required for each newsagent. Parcels for each customer are then delivered throughout the country on five days each week by various methods. It is necessary for magazines to be delivered before the publication date printed on each issue. Newsagents place an indication of the sales price recommended by the wholesaler on each copy, and display the magazines from the appropriate date. Magazines, which are fairly perishable in nature, along with other publications, are sold on a sale or return basis, so unsold copies are sent back to the wholesalers. The latter credit the newsagent for unsold copies, and themselves receive a compensatory credit from the publishers. It is estimated that some 25% of magazines distributed are returned as unsold, and dealing with them is a major task for the wholesalers. Newsagents are generally invoiced on a weekly basis, and attempts are made to obtain payment weekly.

(e) *The notified arrangements*

12. The initial notification referred to the agreement between Easons and Newspread on the forward purchase of sterling and the application of exchange rate factors to determine the retail selling prices of UK magazines to be recommended to newsagents. The Annex to the notification, submitted by Easons in January 1993, made it clear that, in addition to the currency purchasing agreement, there was an arrangement between the two firms to ensure that each recommended the same resale price for the same magazine to newsagents.

13. It has long been the practice worldwide for magazines (and newspapers) to carry the

2. Restrictive Practices Commission. Report of Enquiry into the supply and distribution of daily and Sunday newspapers published in Ireland, and of newspapers, periodicals and magazines distributed by wholesalers. Prl 8380. May 1979, pp. 12-19.

retail price on the cover. Thus each UK magazine has on its cover the retail price in sterling. In the UK, wholesalers buy at a certain discount from the publishers, they resell to newsagents at a higher price, to cover the wholesaler's distribution costs and profit margin, and the retailers sell at the cover price. It is understood that, in the UK, about one third of the total margin accrues to the wholesaler, and two-thirds to the retailer. **2.3.1**

14. Quite substantial adjustments are required to the UK prices according to Easons, in order to arrive at the cover price appropriate for Ireland, as follows:

(a) account has to be taken of the exchange rate between sterling and the Irish pound, since purchases are made in sterling;
(b) VAT has to be included in the Irish price, currently almost always at 21%, whereas there is no VAT on magazines in the UK; and
(c) there is a higher margin needed for the Irish wholesaler in order to cover the higher distribution costs compared to the UK, in terms of higher wages, higher transport costs (vehicles, fuel, insurance, etc.), and the costs associated with distributing to a small, widely-scattered population.

15. Easons and Newspread each independently agree a purchase price for a particular magazine with the UK publishers, and these purchase prices may be different. These prices are based on a discount from the UK retail price of the magazine, and are expressed and paid for in sterling. Purchase prices then have to be converted to the equivalent in Irish currency. Both firms had agreed to buy sterling forward for six months in advance, (more recently three months in advance), and to use the same exchange rate for their price calculations. The forward purchase of foreign currency is a means whereby importers reduce risks arising from fluctuations in exchange rates. It involves the importer making arrangements with his bankers to purchase specified amounts of foreign currency at a particular date in the future. The foreign currency will be supplied at a particular rate which is agreed on the date on which the arrangement is made. The particular rate reflects market expectations concerning the likely course or exchange rates over the period.

16. In this case, each firm agreed with its bankers around the same time to buy a given amount of sterling for each of the following six months at a particular rate of exchange each month. These exchange rates were averaged over the six months, and a single exchange rate for both firms was calculated which was applied to magazine price calculations for the whole period. Thus, for six consecutive months, the same exchange rate was used in determining Irish prices for UK magazines, irrespective of the actual exchange rate at any particular time during the period. (This operation was more recently performed on a three-monthly basis).

17. Once the agreed exchange rate was applied to the UK publisher's price, and the price was expressed in terms of Irish currency, the firms agreed to add on a wholesale margin so as to produce the same standard selling price to newsagents for each magazine. To this was added an agreed and identical retail margin and VAT at 21%, to give an identical final resale price which was recommended by both Easons and Newspread. While this might appear to mean that the two firms colluded in agreeing on margins, this is slightly misleading. They tended to agree on an average purchase price of magazines in sterling, they agreed the six- month exchange rate, they agreed on a wholesale margin (which might be above or below the actual margin they achieved, depending on the price which they paid to the UK publisher), they each allowed the retailer a margin of around 25% on the VAT-exclusive price, and each had to include the same VAT rate. This produced the same recommended resale price for retailers. Even if the two firms did not always agree to the detailed calculations, it is clear that each recommended the same resale price to newsagents, each allowed the same standard 25% margin to retailers, and the VAT rate was the same for a particular magazine. Simple arithmetic demonstrates that their standard selling prices to newsagents had to be identical. These calculations could also be done by means of an alternative approach which produced the same result.

2.3.1 18. Based on a hypothetical UK purchase price of [62p]* sterling, with a retail price of £1.00 sterling, the build-up of the Irish price would be as follows, at an exchange rate of IR£1=85p sterling:

	Stg	IR£
UK retail price	£1.00	—
UK price to wholesaler	[ ]	—
Price to Irish wholesaler at 85p	—	[ ]
Wholesaler margin	—	[ ]
Retailer margin	—	[ ]
VAT exclusive retail price	—	123.5p
VAT at 21%	—	25.9p
Recommended retail price	—	149.4p

Thus a magazine with a cover price of £1 sterling, at this exchange rate, would have an Irish retail price of £1.49p, which could be directly compared by the purchaser with the sterling price. (The ratio of wholesale to retail margins in the UK is lower than in Ireland).

19. Easons stated that, in practice, an alternative calculation had been used which involved applying the agreed exchange rate to the UK cover price, adding an additional margin of 5% to cover the extra costs of the Irish wholesaler, and then adding the VAT. This produced the same recommended retail price as before, and the same wholesaler and retailer margins.

*Certain information, indicated by [ ], is omitted on the grounds of commercial confidentiality.

20. Easons claimed that the 5% alternative method penalised the wholesaler in particular as the Irish pound exchange rate against sterling improved The cash margin available to the wholesaler would decrease, resulting in lower revenue for the wholesaler, whereas the costs of distribution would remain unchanged.

21. Accordingly, the calculation was done so as to ensure that the wholesaler's cash margin remained unchanged, and that the retailer received the same percentage of the VAT-exclusive price, as follows:

	Stg	IR£
UK retail price	£1.00	—
UK price to wholesaler	[ ]	—
Price to Irish wholesaler at 103p	—	[ ]
Wholesaler margin	—	[ ]
Retailer margin	—	[ ]
VAT-exclusive retail price	—	106.5p
VAT at 21%	—	22.4p
Recommended retail price	—	128.9p

Compared to the situation where the exchange rate was 85p, the price at an exchange rate of IR£1=Stg£1.03 was 20.5p lower, the purchase price being [ ] less, the retailer margin [ ] less and VAT 3.5p lower The wholesaler cash margin, however, was unchanged at [ ].

22. To obtain the same result using the alternative approach, an agreed addition of 9.7% was required to the UK cover price, rather than 5%.

23. Based upon a UK cover price of £1, therefore, the alternative approach utilised an agreed additional wholesaler margin of 5% at an exchange rate of 85p, rising to an additional 9.7% at a rate of 103p, and higher percentages at rates over 103p. Conversely, an additional margin of less than 5% was needed at exchange rates below 85p.

24. Given the large number of magazines involved, the wholesaler until recently did not specify an actual price to be charged by the retailer for each. Instead, each retailer was provided

with a simple ready reckoner, which showed the recommended retail price in Irish currency at a VAT rate of 21% for a number of cover prices in sterling. (There were also prices at VAT rates of 10%, for newspapers and newspaper-type magazines, and 0%, for occasional zero-rated items). For each magazine, the retailer ascertained the sterling price from the cover, checked the ready reckoner for the Irish price, and put the latter on the magazine, in writing or by means of a printed sticker. The ready reckoners supplied by Easons and Newspread produced identical results in terms of an Irish price for a given UK cover price. Easons stated that they performed the calculations, and these were followed by Newspread. 2.3.1

25. The Eason ready reckoner from November 1992 referred to 'recommended Irish selling price for UK magazines.' In May 1993, this was amended to 'suggested Irish selling price for UK magazines.' In August 1983, the following wording was used—'This Ready Reckoner contains suggested prices only. The determination of the retail price of each publication is a matter to be decided by each retailer. This list is therefore offered for guidance only.' The Newspread ready reckoner, however, for May and August 1993 states 'Magazine Ready Reckoner Incorporating Sterling Differential and VAT,' though there was a reference to 'Recommended Irish selling price' in the August ready reckoner. In addition, the Eason ready reckoner, on all three occasions, stated that:

'Please note the following are sold at the printed Irish Selling Price:

All Irish Publications	Newsweek	Economist
All UK Dailies	Universe	
All Partworks	Catholic Herald'.	

The introduction was changed in November 1993 to read: 'Please note that the publishers have printed an Irish Selling Price on the following:'. The Newspread ready reckoner for May 1993 stated that:

> The following publications — Time, Life, Fortune and all Part Works must be retailed at the indicated IR£ cover price'. This was changed in the August 1993 ready reckoner to:
>
> '. . . are recommended to be retailed at the indicated IR£ cover price'.

26. At the oral hearing, Newspread stated that both wholesalers had recently started to include an actual IR£ cover price including VAT for each separate UK magazine on the Delivery Note which accompanied each parcel of magazines. It appears that newsagents now tend to refer to the advice note in order to place the Irish selling price on each magazine, rather than use the ready reckoner. There was no indication on the Newspread delivery note that the Irish price was 'recommended' or 'suggested', or that the retailer was free to set his own resale prices. On the Eason's delivery note, however, it was stated that 'The determination of the retail price of each publication is a matter to be decided by each retailer'. Easons also produce a document entitled 'Trade News for its customers, which contains details of specific publications, special issues, promotions, etc. This also carried the above wording, and also stated that the 'Ready Reckoner contains suggested prices only'.

27. While retailers were encouraged to charge the appropriate prices, Easons claimed that there was nothing in their standard terms and conditions which required them to charge these prices. Easons might draw a retailer's attention to the fact that incorrect prices were being charged, but it could not enforce adherence to the prices it wished to see charged, and had not withheld supplies from retailers for selling at another price. It appeared, however, that there was almost invariable adherence to recommended resale prices.

28. Besides the fact that the two wholesalers may pay different prices to the UK publishers for the same magazine, it appeared that the larger Irish retailers were able to negotiate larger discounts from the wholesalers, and so they paid the wholesalers less for their supplies than

2.3.1 the majority of newsagents who received only the standard discount. Some retailers also received longer credit terms than others. The wholesalers also imposed a weekly service charge on newsagents, which is understood to vary from £1.50 to £14. The normal service charge of Newspread was stated to be £5. It is important to note that foreign currency may be bought forward not only by means of the method described above, but also by using a forward options contract. This gives the holder the right, but not the obligation, to buy currency at an agreed rate at a future date. If it is more beneficial to buy currency at the spot rate, on the due date, this can be done. By this means, exchange rate losses can still be avoided, but exchange rate gains can be secured, though a fee is charged for the option right.

(f) *Submissions by the Parties and other developments*

29. Easons initially submitted arguments in support of their request for a certificate and for a licence, and a brief submission was made by Newspread. In response to the Statement of Objections, Easons made a lengthy submission. Following the initiation of legal proceedings, Newspread also submitted a detailed response to the Statement of Objections. At the oral hearing in September 1993, Newspread presented arguments and evidence from its own representative and its legal advisers. Newspread also called, as witnesses, a bank official, two retail newsagents, a representative of the UK magazine publishers and an Irish magazine publisher. Further submissions were received from the Periodical Publishers Association Ltd of the UK and from a legal representative of Newspread. At the oral hearing, Newspread stated that the agreement on the forward purchase of currency had been notified by them to the EC Commission a few days prior to the hearing. In a letter dated 22 December 1993, Easons informed the Authority that they had written to Newspread terminating the currency purchasing arrangements, since they had taken the commercial view that there was no obvious need to continue the arrangements. Easons also stated that they would not require a licence or a certificate, and they would not require any decision upon the application, if a decision on a non-existent agreement was technically feasible.

Views of the Authority

(a) *Applicability of section 4(1)*

30. Easons and Newspread are engaged in the distribution of magazines for gain. They are therefore undertakings within the meaning of section 3(1) of the Competition Act.

31. The agreement between Easons and Newspread concerning the forward purchase of sterling and the determination of relevant exchange rates, although unwritten, was an agreement between undertakings. These exchange rates were used by Easons and Newspread to determine the retail selling prices of UK magazines to be recommended to newsagents. This involved an arrangement between the two parties to sell each magazine at the same price to virtually all newsagents, and to recommend the same resale price to newsagents. While these were also unwritten, they constituted agreements between undertakings. The sole purpose of the agreement on forward purchasing of sterling, on Easons' own admission, was to ensure that changes in exchange rates did not lead to any divergences in the prices charged to newsagents or in resale prices charged by newsagents.

32. Even if the information in the Easons' submissions had not been made available, the Authority would have found it necessary to deal with the currency agreement between Easons and Newspread in the context of the whole arrangements in order to assess whether or not it had the object or effect of preventing, restricting or distorting competition. An agreement on the purchase of currency, in particular, would be pointless except as part of an agreement to ensure that magazines were sold at the same price at both wholesale and retail level. As is clear from the submissions by Easons, the above agreements formed part of an overall arrangement whereby there was an understanding that specific resale prices for UK magazines be charged.

33. It was clear to the Authority that, in the absence of an agreement on the exchange rate

to be applied in order to calculate prices of UK magazines, an agreement on magazine prices would be extremely difficult to operate. In particular, if the two wholesalers were to purchase sterling separately and use the actual exchange rate from such transactions, this would probably lead to price divergences at wholesale and possibly retail level. Neither party could be sure that the divergence in prices was due solely to differences in the purchase price of sterling, rather that to attempts by the other party to undercut its prices. The EC Commission noted in its decision on the Net Book Agreement that: **2.3.1**

> A special situation prevails in Ireland, where the ending of the parity between the Irish punt and the British pound following Ireland's joining the European Monetary System, had made the pricing of books and the enforcement of the standard conditions of sale more difficult, as reported by the Association. These problems were discussed by the Association and the Irish book trade at meetings in Dublin in 1981, as a result of which various measures were recommended to members. In particular, the Irish branch of the Booksellers Association of Great Britain and Ireland introduced a currency conversion schedule, which enables Irish booksellers to convert book prices expressed in British pounds easily into Irish punts.[3]

34. The Authority stated in its decision on the Esso solus agreements that, even though a certain practice was not part of the written terms of the agreements notified, it was considered to form 'part of the total relationship between the supplier and its solus dealers, and that it should be considered in this context'.[4] The Authority's view is supported by the fact that, in applying Article 85 of the Treaty of Rome, on which the Competition Act is based, the EC Commission and the EC Court of Justice have accepted that: 'A series of connected agreements will be read together as one agreement'.[5] The Authority had to consider the overall commercial and economic context in which the currency agreement operated, in order to assess its object and effect.

35. The overall arrangements had both horizontal and vertical effects. In the first place, irrespective of the price at which they each purchased magazines from the UK publishers, and irrespective of the exchange rate at which they did or might purchase their requirements of sterling, Easons and Newspread agreed to incorporate in their price calculations a fixed margin for the retailer. These resulted in an agreement that each charge the same price for a particular magazine to every newsagent, with the exception that a few larger newsagents could negotiate lower purchase prices or extended terms of credit.

36. In the view of the Authority, the arrangements between Easons and Newspread, which involved agreement on purchase prices for foreign exchange, an agreed addition for wholesaler margins, and the same standard selling price to newsagents for each magazine, notwithstanding the fact that a small minority of newsagents could negotiate lower purchase prices, constituted the fixing of prices, a practice which is specifically mentioned as being prohibited under section 4(1). The Authority emphasises that, in its opinion, the agreement on the purchase of foreign exchange and on the exchange rates to be used in calculating prices was an integral part of the pricing arrangements, and the notified agreement on forward currency purchases had to be examined in that light. The arrangements represented a serious restriction on competition, and virtually eliminated price competition, between the only two magazine wholesalers in the State. As such, it clearly offended against section 4(1) of the Act. Each party was prevented from passing onto newsagents any savings it might have achieved compared to the other in the price which it paid the publisher, in securing a more favourable exchange rate, or in lower costs of distribution.

3. Commission decision of 12 December 1988 under Article 85 — Publishers Association — Net Book Agreements. OJ L22, 26 January 1989, p. 12 at p. 16.
4. Decision No. 4 of 25 June 1992 — Esso solus and related agreements, para. 57.
5. Bellamy and Child, *Common Market Law of Competition*, 3rd ed., Sweet & Maxwell, 1989, para. 2-017.

2.3.1 37. Since price is the main instrument of competition, Article 85(1)(a) of the Rome Treaty expressly forbids price fixing agreements, and its wording is followed verbatim in section 4(1)(a), as quoted above. According to Bellamy and Child; 'An agreement to fix prices by its very nature constitutes a restriction on competition within the meaning of Article 85(1). Hitherto an exemption under Article 85(3) has been granted only in exceptional circumstances in certain service industries'.[6] Quoting several cases, they point out that 'It is also a serious infringement of Article 85(1) for distributors to agree prices among themselves. . . .'[7] As early as 1972, in one of the Dyestuffs cases, the EC Court of Justice stated that:

> '. . . it is contrary to the rules on competition contained in the Treaty for a producer to cooperate with his competitors, in any way whatsoever, in order to determine a co-ordinated course of action relating to a change of prices and to ensure its success by prior elimination of all uncertainty as to each other's conduct regarding the essential elements of that action, such as the amount, subject-matter, date, and place of such changes'.[8] In a case involving the distribution of newspapers and periodicals, the Court held that: 'Provisions which fix the prices to be observed in contracts with third parties constitute, of themselves, a restriction of competition within the meaning of Article 85(1)'.[9]

38. The parties indicated that their recommended resale prices included an additional agreed wholesale cash margin. The Authority noted also that the parties decided in 1990 to vary the way in which retail prices were calculated so that the wholesale margin would remain constant in cash terms. It was claimed that the wholesale margin was estimated on the basis of what it would have been under an exchange rate of IR£1=Stg£0.85, which the parties stated had been the average over the 1983-90 period. It was not for the Authority to decide the appropriate level of wholesale margins. It noted, however, that over the previous four years the average exchange rate had been significantly higher than the rate chosen by the parties. In the Authority's view the agreement on the wholesale cash margin was itself anti competitive. A firm in a competitive market faced with a decline in its cash margin due to a change in the exchange rate would be faced with several possible responses. It could decide to maintain its existing cash margin. It could decide to accept a reduction in its cash margin and seek to make savings in its costs. It could decide on some combination of the two, effectively accepting some reduction in its margin and its costs. In deciding which course to follow it would have to take account of how its competitors might react. In a competitive market the likelihood was that the firm would be under pressure to improve efficiency and absorb some decline in cash margins. By agreeing a wholesale cash margin to be used in calculating retail prices, however, Easons and Newspread had effectively removed any uncertainty as to how their rival might adjust its margins in response to exchange rate movements. Such measures were anti-competitive since their purpose was clearly to prevent or restrict in some way the normal operation of competitive market forces. This also offended against section 4(1).

39. The arrangements resulted in an agreement whereby both Easons and Newspread ensured that the same resale price was recommended to all newsagents for each magazine, after taking the VAT rate of 21% into account. No evidence was forthcoming that retailers charged anything but the same price for a particular magazine throughout the State, with minor exceptions, so that the effect of these arrangements was that recommended resale prices were maintained. The agreement on currency purchases by the wholesalers resulted in their produc-

6. Ibid., para. 4-002.
7. Ibid., para. 4-009.
8. Judgment of the Court of 14 July 1972 in the case of *Imperial Chemical Industries Ltd v. Commission of the European Communities* [1972] ECR 621.
9. Judgment of the Court of 3 July 1985 in the case of *SA Binon and Cie v. SA Agence et Messageries de la Presse* [1985] ECR 2015, at p. 2046.

ing the same ready reckoner, and the same resale price for a particular magazine on their advice notes. It also resulted in their charging the same price for a particular magazine to the vast majority of retailers. The Authority considered that this agreement contributed significantly to the fact that individual magazines were sold at a uniform price. Indeed, the latter could not happen in the circumstances unless the wholesalers agreed on currency purchases and agreed to use the same ready reckoner and to recommend the same resale prices. Indications on the ready reckoner that retailers were free to set their own prices have only appeared in the recent past, and such indications were not given on the Newspread advice note, the advice note now being widely used as a means of setting prices. The Authority considered that the effect of the whole arrangement differed little, if anything, from a full-blown system of resale price maintenance with procedures for enforcement. 2.3.1

40. According to Bellamy and Child: 'A horizontal agreement whereby suppliers collectively agree to operate a system of resale price maintenance infringes Article 85(1)'.[10] Article 85(1) may also be infringed by price 'recommendations', according to Bellamy and Child.[11] Furthermore, 'An agreement between a supplier and a customer whereby the former agrees or imposes a minimum resale price may also infringe Article 85(1)'.[12] The Authority also considers that resale price maintenance, whether on a collective or an individual basis, offends against section 4(1) of the Act.

41. As the Commission stated in the GERO-Fabriek case,

> Likewise, the system of imposed retail prices makes it impossible for dealers to fix their own retail prices by reference to their own costs and commercial policy. The free formation of prices and the ability to pass on to purchasers any possible resulting benefits are hindered or at least substantially reduced. The system is thus clearly contrary to the prohibition in Article 85(1).[13]

42. In the case involving VBBB and VBVB, which concerned collective resale price maintenance on books, the Commission stated that:

> It prevents efforts at price competition for a single title between booksellers in the two countries. This means that booksellers are prevented from increasing their market shares through their own independent competitive efforts, by selling books at below the prices fixed by their publishers and by passing on the benefits of the rationalisation to consumers. The scheme also restricts the freedom of action of publishers and importers. They are prevented from promoting in one country the sale of books published in the other by making temporary or permanent reductions in the price, and from passing on the benefits of any cuts in costs to consumers in the former country.[14]

43. The EC Court of Justice dismissed the appeal against the decision of the Commission in this case, and said:

> Its view is however that the special features of that market do not permit the two associations to set up, in their mutual relations, a restrictive system whose effect is to deprive distributors of all freedom of action as regards the fixing of the selling price up to the level to the final price to the consumer. Such an arrangement would indeed infringe Article 85(1)(a), which expressly prohibits all agreements which 'directly or indirectly

10. *Op. cit.*, para. 4-016.
11. *Op. cit.*, para. 4-004.
12. *Op. cit.*, para. 4-017.
13. Commission decision of 22 December 1976 under Article 85 — GERO-fabriek. OJ L16, 19 January 1977, p. 8 at p. 11.
14. Commission decision of 25 November 1981 under Article 85 — VBBB/VBVB. OJ L54, 25 February 1982, p. 35 at p. 45.

2.3.1 fix purchase or selling prices'. Furthermore the system of resale price maintenance laid down in the agreement allows each of the two associations to control outlets as far as the last stage in the other Member State from the point of view of price-fixing and thus to make impossible the introduction of sales methods capable of allowing consumers to be supplied in economically more favourable conditions, which brings the applicant associations also into conflict with the contents of Article 85(1)(b). . . . The submission put forward by the applicants must therefore be dismissed.[15]

44. More recently, the Commission took a similar view in deciding upon the Net Book Agreements, which involved resale price maintenance for UK-published books sold in Ireland.[16] In an appeal on that case, the Court of First Instance accepted that Article 85(1) applied to the Net Book Agreements.[17] The Authority regarded all the above EC precedents as lending considerable support to its view that the arrangements in question offended against section 4(1) of the Act.

45. The Authority was not expressing any view upon whether an individual importer/distributor should purchase forward its requirements of foreign currency, or on the period forward for which foreign currency is purchased. Its concern was solely with the agreement to apply a uniform exchange rate in order to calculate resale prices. The two firms sold magazines at the same price to the vast majority of newsagents, thus almost entirely eliminating price competition between themselves. This offended against section 4(1).

46. In addition, the two firms agreed on the price at which they recommended newsagents to sell the magazines, since both firms used a ready reckoner which gave the same results. There was also almost total adherence to these prices by newsagents, thus completely eliminating price competition between newsagents for a particular magazine. Indications to the retailer that he was free to charge prices different from those derived from the ready reckoner were a fairly recent development. Newsagents did not attempt to improve their competitive position and increase their sales by reducing the price of magazines, and any efficiencies in the manner in which they operated their business were not passed on to consumers by way of lower prices. Even the few large newsagents who benefited from higher discounts did not share any of these benefits by way of lower prices to consumers, but simply retained the increased margins. The system led to ossification of the price structure, and hence to higher prices. For these reasons also, the agreement offended against section 4(1).

(b) *Applicability of section 4(2)*

47. The Authority did not consider that the agreement on forward purchasing of foreign currency and exchange rates fulfilled the conditions for a licence specified in section 4(2).

(i) Improvements in production or distribution

48. It was maintained that the arrangements led to a proper and orderly distribution of magazines, for which consistent pricing was necessary. It ensured the certainty and reliability of the service and the supply of perishable products throughout the State.

49. The Authority accepted that the distribution system operated by Easons and Newspread ensured the supply of imported magazines throughout Ireland on the appropriate day every week or every month. It was a complex system which required careful organisation and control. In order to satisfy the first condition of section 4(2), however, it was essential to demonstrate that the restrictive practices led to an improvement in distribution. That is, according to the EC Commission in the VBBB/VBVB case, the restrictions must 'objectively achieve improve-

15. Judgment of the Court of 17 January 1984 in the case of *VBVB and VBBB v. Commission of the European Communities* [1984] ECR 19 at p. 66.
16. *Op. cit.*, p. 19.
17. Court of First Instance judgment of 9 July 1992 in the case of *Publishers Association v. Commission of the European Communities* [1992] 5 CMLR 120 at pp. 134-136.

ments over the situation which would exist without them'.[18] There was no evidence that the exchange rate agreement produced the required improvements in the distribution of magazines. 2.3.1

50. Even if there were any objective improvements as a result of the arrangements, the Authority considered that these would not outweigh the anti-competitive effects of the collusion. Indeed, the Authority believed that the arrangements had an adverse effect on the distribution of magazines, because they eliminated any price competition for a particular magazine at wholesale and at retail level. There was only limited competition between different magazine titles, and competition in the price of a particular magazine was an important means of rationalising and improving the distribution system for magazines. This was also the view of the EC Commission in the VBBB/VBVB case.[19]

(ii) Fair share of benefit for consumers

51. It was claimed that consumers were ensured certainty and reliability of the service, that is the regular supply of magazines. It was claimed that certainty and stability of cover prices was an integral part of the proper and orderly distribution system. The arrangements ensured that a magazine was available everywhere at the same price, and they eliminated the haphazard and unforeseen effects on prices of changes in exchange rates. The benefits of the system outweighed the apparent short-term gains from price-cutting and loss leading.

52. The Authority again accepted that imported magazines were regularly available throughout the State, and that this was of benefit to consumers. The Authority did not accept that this would not be the case in the absence of an exchange rate agreement, nor did it believe that newsagents would not continue in business and display a range of imported magazines without such a system, which also guarantees them specific margin on each copy sold. As before, the customer could not benefit from the advantages of any rationalisation which might take place in the magazine trade. For many consumers, the price of the product is an important element in their decision to purchase, and the Authority considered that, since prices were the same in all outlets, consumers were not receiving a fair share of any benefits resulting from the arrangements. There was no evidence that consumers benefited from the fact that a particular magazine was sold at the same price in all outlets in their area, or throughout the State. The Authority could see no reason why changes in exchange rates, which are an essential element of cost like other factors, should not be reflected directly in selling prices. If one distributor could buy currency cheaper than another, or save in purchase prices or distribution costs, or if a retailer received discounts or achieved cost savings, there was no benefit to the consumer if these could not be passed on to the consumer by way of reduced prices. The Authority considered that price-cutting was a real, not an apparent, gain for consumers, and was not necessarily a short-term phenomenon. The Authority rejected the suggestion that price competition was the same thing as loss-leading. The latter, or selling below cost, might be anti-competitive if it was engaged in by a firm in a dominant position for predatory reasons. There was no suggestion of such an abuse in the case of newsagents, and ordinary price competition was far removed from loss-leader selling, and was desirable in itself.

(iii) Indispensable nature of the restrictions

53. It was claimed that the agreement on currency purchases and the maintenance of prices were indispensable to secure a proper and orderly distribution system for imported magazines, and to ensure a certain and reliable supply. It was also argued that price maintenance was necessary in the context of a sale or return system.

54. As is clear from the foregoing, the Authority did not believe that collusion on exchange rates was indispensable for the effective distribution of imported magazines. Rather, it was indispensable for the recommendation of the same resale prices. There was no evidence to suggest that uniform wholesale prices or a system which amounted to resale price maintenance

18. *Op. cit.*, p. 47
19. *Op. cit.*, p. 47

2.3.1 were the sole means of ensuring that magazines were distributed regularly and reliably throughout the State, or that improvements in publication and distribution could not he achieved by the use of less restrictive methods. It might well be that resale price maintenance for magazines and newspapers was long-established in Ireland and elsewhere, and the outcome of alternatives had not been tested. This was not to say that alternative approaches would not be viable and satisfactory. Indeed, in the case of all other goods where resale price maintenance was prevalent, and in spite of strong protestations from the trades involved, the abolition of price maintenance has not produced a curtailment of widespread availability of the products concerned. Invariably, it has led to immediate benefits to consumers by way of price competition, and this has led to even further benefits as this competition produced improvements to the distribution system. The Authority had no grounds to think that the situation would be any different in the case of magazines, which are more discretionary for consumers than was the case for necessities where price maintenance has been abolished.

55. The EC Commission did not consider that resale price maintenance was indispensable in the VBBB/VBVB case,[20] nor did it consider it to be indispensable in the Net Book Agreement case.[21] Both decisions were upheld by the Court in subsequent appeals.

(iv) Substantial elimination of competition

56. It was argued that the two wholesalers competed in the efficiency and pricing of the service they offered to publishers. It was said that price competition between publishers would be distorted by arbitrary price changes caused by rate of exchange changes. Exchange rates were a non-competitive factor, and the arrangement was not a restraint on competition but was the removal of a fortuitous and unpredictable influence upon true competition. At the retail level, it was claimed that there was no elimination of competition. Magazines could be purchased direct from the publishers by retailers, or they could be purchased by consumers on subscription.

57. In the view of the Authority, however, the most important features of the system were that:

(a) the two distributors did not compete with each other in terms of standard prices charged to newsagents, irrespective of any differences in the distributors' purchase prices, currency purchases or distribution costs; and
(b) newsagents were given a guaranteed margin on each magazine, and they did not compete on selling prices for any magazine.

The other forms of competition in which newsagents could engage — range of titles, opening hours or willingness to order certain magazines — were, in the view of the Authority, secondary to price competition. This was particularly true from the perspective of the consumer who was often not especially interested in selecting from a wide range of magazines, but who either wanted to buy a particular magazine or type of magazine, or who bought on impulse. It was clear to the Authority that, because price competition was eliminated at both the wholesale and the retail levels, competition was eliminated in respect of a substantial part of the products in question. This accords with the view of the EC Commission in the VBBB/VBVB case.[22]

58. Even if there was competition between the two distributors regarding the price they paid to the publishers, this did not mean that competition elsewhere in the distribution chain was not eliminated, especially since any competitive advantage gained was not passed on to newsagents or to consumers by way of lower prices. The Authority could not accept that exchange rate changes resulted in arbitrary price changes, or that exchange rates were a non-competitive, fortuitous and unpredictable influence upon 'true competition'. Exchange

20. *Op. cit.*, p. 49.
21. *Op. cit.*, p. 23.
22. *Op. cit.*, p. 49.

rates are an integral part of the price structure of imports and therefore an important element in price determination and thereby in competition. Each distributor carries a very large and similar range of magazines from each UK publisher. Even if they incorporated different exchange rates into their price calculations, the purchase price relativities of magazines of different publishers would be unchanged within the range of magazines each distributed when exchange rates were altered, and any difference in relative price differences at retail level because of exchange rate differences between Easons and Newspread would be fairly small. Prices should be determined in the market by the free play of competitive forces between publishers, distributors and newsagents, and not by anti-competitive agreements on costs, margins and exchange rates. 2.3.1

59. The Authority rejected the claim that there was no elimination of competition at retail level. Price competition had been in fact non-existent. While it accepted that magazines could in theory be purchased direct from the publishers by retailers, the Authority did not consider that this represented a practical element of potential competition. An individual retailer would be unlikely to buy from publishers more cheaply than did the distributors. He might need to buy minimum quantities which would be larger than he needed, and he would have to bear the cost of transporting the magazines from many different sources, the cost of dealing with a large number of publishers, and exchange rate risks. This was not a viable alternative source of competition. While consumers could purchase from publishers on subscription, and a small number did so, again this could provide no significant element of competition to distributors and newsagents. The cost was not always cheaper than buying from a newsagent, the consumer would not be immune to exchange rate risks, and this ignored the position of the vast number of consumers who bought on impulse and who did not wish to subscribe a relatively large sum in advance for a specific magazine over a lengthy period.

EC Considerations

60. Newspread placed great emphasis on the 1987 notice of the EC Commission to take a favourable view of resale price maintenance in the AMP case.[23] Besides the fact that the Commission has not taken a final decision in this case after more than six years, the Authority considered that it had no relevance to the notified agreement in this case. The AMP case related to a single distributor in Belgium, whereas the notified agreement was one whereby competing distributors agreed on exchange rates, and other matters, and where competitors produced the same recommended resale price for a particular magazine.

61. Newspread also maintained that, because of its notification of the agreement to the EC Commission, the Authority should stay its decision or issue a certificate or licence. The Authority noted that the notification to the Commission was made only a few days before the oral hearing with Newspread. Since the Authority considered that it was unlikely that the EC Commission would grant a negative clearance or an exemption to the agreement in question, it did not consider that it was in any way estopped from taking an unfavourable decision in this case. Indeed, the Authority does not believe that the notification of an agreement to the Commission automatically estops the Authority from taking a decision in respect of the agreement.

Conclusions

62. Prior to the termination of the agreement and the withdrawal of the notification, the Authority had concluded, for the reasons outlined above, that the agreement between Easons and Newspread in respect of purchases of foreign exchange offended against section 4(1) of the Competition Act 1991. In the opinion of the Authority, the notified agreement satisfied none of the conditions laid down in section 4(2) of the Act, and a licence could not be granted in respect of the agreement.

23. Notice pursuant to Article 19(3) of Regulation No. 17 — Agence et Messageries de la Presse. OJC 164, 23 June 1987, p. 2.

2.3.2 **Declan Cronin, applicant v. The Competition Authority, the Minister for Enterprise and Employment, Ireland and the Attorney General, respondents and Texaco (Ireland) Ltd, notice party** [Judicial Review 1993 No. 242] High Court 24 June 1994

Licence in respect of motor fuels, Decision No. 25 of the Competition Authority – Applicants association requesting notifications and information – Proper exchange of views – Reasonableness of procedures adopted – One essential issue – Sections 4(1), 4(2), 7(6) and 23 of the Competition Act 1991

Judicial Review – Certiorari – *Decision of Competition Authority – Whether Applicant has locus standi – Issue of licence for categories of agreements – Whether Competition Authority adopted fair procedure for reasons advanced by Applicant – Rejection of claim for certiorari and other declaratory reliefs*

Facts: On 30 March 1992 the Competition Authority published a notice that it had received notification from Texaco (Ireland) Ltd of five different types of agreement. On 6 November 1992 a further notification was made by Texaco (Ireland) Ltd of a new version of an agreement. On 20 November 1992 the Applicant's solicitor requested information concerning the notification referred to in the advertisement of 6 November 1992. The Applicant's solicitor was informed by the Competition Authority that a notification is confidential until a summary of the facts of the notification is published by the Authority and it was suggested to the solicitor to seek details of the notification from Texaco (Ireland) Ltd. The solicitors for Texaco (Ireland) Ltd declined to give a copy of the notification on the grounds that it contained confidential information and business secrets of Texaco.

On 11 December 1992 the Competition Authority advertised to the public that it was intending to grant a category licence and a draft of the category licence was made available to the public. The Competition Authority in respect of this draft category licence was not only taken into account the agreements notified by Texaco (Ireland) Ltd but also 57 other types of agreements from 11 different oil companies. The Applicant's representative association made a detailed submission concerning the draft category licence. On 9 July 1993 the category licence was granted and the Applicant in these proceedings sought to quash the decision.

Held by Costello J:

(1) The failure to provide copies of the agreements notified to the Applicant or his representative association caused no harm to the Applicant.

(2) The failure to provide copies of the notification or a summary of the notification made by Texaco (Ireland) Ltd did not cause any harm to the Applicant.

(3) The Applicant was not placed in any difficulty in commenting upon the views of the Competition Authority and he was not damnified by the procedures adopted by the Competition Authority.

(4) The procedures adopted by the Competition Authority were eminently fair and reasonable.

(5) As a result of the finding that the procedures adopted were fair the other issues raised in the proceedings need not be commented upon.

(6) The constitutional issue raised by the Applicant does not arise because of the

way in which the Competition Authority met the case. The Competition Act 1991 is not unconstitutional upon the ground that it permitted a non constitutional decision to be made. **2.3.2**

(7) Despite not making any conclusion about whether the applicant had locus standi in this application, the applicant was very concerned at the position which the Competition Authority might take and he would have a strong case on locus standi if there was an abuse of fair procedures.

(8) Section 23 of the Competition Act 1991 does not require the Minister to make regulations because it is a permissive provision. The Competition Authority can carry out its functions even if the Minister does not prescribe procedures because paragraph 6(3) of the Schedule to the Competition Act 1991 allows the Authority to regulate its own procedures.

(9) The Applicant's claim is rejected.

COSTELLO J delivered his ex tempore judgment on 24 June 1994 saying: The applicant in this case is Declan Cronin who is the licensee of a petrol filling station at Blackrock, County Dublin, and who brings this application for judicial review both on his own behalf and on behalf of the members of the Texaco Retailers Association of which he is one.

The company with which he has an agreement is Texaco (Ireland) Ltd and it has been joined as a notice party in the proceeding.

The first named respondent is the Competition Authority established under the Competition Act 1991.

The principal relief sought by the applicant is an order of *certiorari* in relation to a decision made by the Competition Authority in July 1993 to grant a category licence under section 4(2)(a) of the Act of 1991. A further claim is made against the Minister that he failed to carry out a mandatory duty upon him under the Act to make regulations prescribing procedures to be followed by the Competition Authority.

The brief facts which form the background to the proceeding are as follows:

On 13 March 1992 an advertisement appeared in the newspapers of the fact that the Competition Authority had received notification of five different types of agreement by Texaco (Ireland) Ltd. It is clear that these were notifications made under section 7(2) as agreements which were already in existence. The notification with which we are concerned is the notification by Texaco of their new licence agreement.

This is the one in which the applicant was directly concerned because it is the agreement of Texaco with licensees.

It may or may not be of significance that Mr Cronin and his associates took no step in relation to this notification of the existing agreement. It may have been appreciated by Mr Cronin and his colleagues that this was a notification in relation to existing agreements, but I am not deciding anything in relation to that.

I think Mr Cronin and his colleagues were alerted by the next advertisement which appeared on 6 November 1992 as a notification to the new version of the agreement in which he was interested. While he was subject to an existing agreement, Mr Cronin and his colleagues were obviously interested in this new version as he clearly had a hope or expectation that when it expired he would be offered a new agreement so that the attitude which the Competition Authority was going to take to the new agreement was of concern to him.

On 20 November 1992 the solicitor acting on behalf of the Association wrote to both the Competition Authority and to Texaco with a specific request to be supplied with a copy of the notification which had been advertised on 6 November. On 3 November 1992 the Competition Authority replied saying:

> Details of a notification are confidential until a summary of the facts of the notification

2.3.2 is published by the Authority at the notice of intention stage, with an invitation to interested parties to make submissions. At this stage it is open to you to seek details of the notifications from the notifying party.

On 9 December solicitors on behalf of Texaco had replied saying that the notification contained confidential information and business secrets of Texaco and saying:

> As you may be aware, once the Authority had made an initial assessment, it has been the Authority's practice to publish a summary of the notification and to make that available to members of the public inviting submissions. Texaco welcomes any useful contribution which your clients can make to the Authority's consideration of the agreements which have been notified.

It should be pointed out that when reference is made to a 'notification' it is a reference to a great deal more than a mere covering letter sending the agreement to the Competition Authority. As the guide published by the Authority indicating its approach to the legislation and the form CA to be used for notifications shows applicants give a great deal of very detailed information and this is, in effect, the submission which is made to the Authority.

In any event, on 11 December 1992 the Authority advertised to the public its intention to grant a category licence and a draft of the licence was made available to interested parties including the Applicant.

The draft licence is a great deal more than the mere licence. The draft was produced after a very detailed appraisal was made by the Competition Authority of the operation of the Act on existing contracts and of the proposals for new agreements which might be entered into. It then gave its appraisal of these factors and set out the proposed form of the category licence which was to be issued.

It is very important to understand the nature of this document. Interested parties can see from it the view which the Competition Authority has taken of the different views given in the submissions which it has received. The Competition Authority was not only taking into account the agreements notified by Texaco, by taking into account 27 different types of agreement in all from 11 different oil supply companies.

This is a very detailed appraisal of the submissions that had been made to the Authority. The applicant availed of the opportunity which had been given by the Competition Authority and a detailed written submission was made to it.

On 9 July 1993 notice was given that a category licence had been granted pursuant to the decision of the Competition Authority taken on 1 July. It is this decision No. 25 which the applicant seeks to quash in this proceeding.

As in a lot of cases where a great number of points have been raised, the ultimate issue can and frequently is reduced to a very simple one.

The issue is not whether the Competition Authority had a duty to adopt fair procedures — the Authority accepts that it has such a duty — but whether it failed for the reasons advanced on behalf of the applicant to exercise that duty in this case. Those reasons fall into a very narrow compass indeed.

The first is that the Competition Authority was notified by five agreement types in March 1992 and of the new version of the agreement identified in 6 November 1992 advertisement and that it was in breach of the rules of fair procedures in that the applicant did not get copies of these agreements or a summary of these agreements.

The second reason is that the applicant did not get a copy of the notification made by Texaco or a summary of that notification.

The third reason is that there should have been some form of exchange of views so that the submissions that Texaco had made could be replied to.

In my view the procedures adopted were eminently fair and reasonable and no breach of its duty on the part of the Competition Authority occurred. 2.3.2

The failure to provide copies of these documents in no way caused any harm to the applicant.

I take the same view in relation to the failure to provide copies of the notification or a summary of the notification.

It is to be borne in mind that the issue of fair procedures depends entirely upon the circumstances of the administrative decision that has to be made.

In this case the decision was one under section 4(2) of the Act in relation to the grant of a category licence. What it did was to consider all existing and proposed agreements that has been sent to it. It considered whether they constituted an infringement of section 4(1) and then considered whether to grant a licence under section 4(2) in accordance with the criteria laid down and the conditions, if any, to be attached thereto.

The Competition Authority having made its appraisal then issued a draft of its tentative and preliminary views of what had been submitted and gave everyone an opportunity of considering that. The applicant availed of the opportunity to comment.

The applicant was not placed in any difficulty in responding because the one agreement which was relevant to his position he already had. In relation to the new version of the agreement, he had the views of the Competition Authority on it and how it proposed to deal with it.

So in commenting upon the licence he was not at any disadvantage. The applicant was not damnified in any way by these procedures. He was given an opportunity to comment and availed of it in a very detailed document.

In my judgment the criticism of the procedure is unfounded and I must therefore reject the claim for certiorari and for the declaratory reliefs.

A number of other issues were raised in the proceedings and in view of the decision I have come to I do not need to express my views on them.

It was claimed that the applicant had no *locus standi* in the matter. I have not come to any conclusive view on this point but it seemed to me that he was very concerned indeed at the position which the Competition Authority might make. If he had been able to satisfy the Court that there was an abuse of fair procedures he might have had a strong case on locus standi.

For the same reason it seems to me that the issue of the discretionary nature of the relief does not arise. Similarly the constitutional issue does not arise because of the way in which the Competition Authority has met the case. The Act is not unconstitutional upon the ground that it permitted an unconstitutional decision to be made.

The last issue concerns the alleged breach by the Minister of his duty to make regulations under the Act in relation to procedures. Section 23 of the Act provided that 'the Minister may by regulations provide for any matter referred to in this Act as prescribed or to be prescribed'. On first reading that provision is clearly permissive and not mandatory.

Section 7(6) provided 'the functions of the Authority under this Act shall be carried out in accordance with such procedures, if any, as may be prescribed'.

It is perfectly clear that the Oireachtas contemplated that the Competition Authority could carry out its functions even if the Minister did not prescribe procedures and clearly this section did not impose any mandatory duty to prescribe that had to be adopted. The Oireachtas provided in the Schedule to the Act at paragraph 6(3): 'Subject to this Act, the Authority may regulate its own procedure', and this is what has happened.

Accordingly, I must reject this claim.

CHAPTER THREE

Acquisitions and Mergers

3.0 Introduction

THE REGULATORY AUTHORITIES

Acquisitions, mergers and take-overs raise a number of questions in the context of national legislation such as the Mergers, Take-Overs and Monopolies (Control) Act 1978 as amended, the Central Bank Act 1989 and the Competition Act 1991. The annex to this book contains a consolidated version of the Mergers, Take-Overs and Monopolies (Control) Act 1978 as amended along with a list of the statutory instruments made pursuant to that legislation and the note published by the Department of Enterprise and Employment for the notification of mergers. The annex to this book also contains the relevant part of the Central Bank Act 1989 which includes provisions for the notification of acquisitions and mergers which have a direct investment by or in the holder of a licence from the Central Bank.[1]

SECTIONS 5, 11 AND 14

The relevance for mergers and acquisitions of section 5 of the Competition Act which seeks to control the abuse of a dominant position by undertakings in the State or in a substantial part of the State is not within the scope of the Competition Authority functions unless the Minister for Enterprise and Employment requests a study and report from the Competition Authority under section 11 or section 14 of the Competition Act 1991. In October and November 1994 the Minister requested the Authority under section 11 of the Competition Act to study and report on the supply and distribution of newspapers in the State, trans-frontier competition in the Irish newspaper industry and the implications arising from the acquisition of a 24.9% interest in Irish Press Newspapers Ltd. and Irish Press Publishing Ltd. by Independent Newspapers plc. In an interim report published at the end of April 1995 the Competition Authority quite forcefully opines that the acquisition of a minority shareholding by a dominant newspaper undertaking in a competitor was in that instance an abuse of a dominant position which breached section 5 of the Competition Act. Furthermore, the Competition Authority refers to the possibility that the arrangements between the various undertakings connected with the minority shareholding acquisition have breached section 4 of the Competition Act. Such is the conviction of the Competition Authority that breaches of sections 4 and 5 of the Competition Act have occurred in the newspaper industry that it 'strongly recommends that the Minister exercise his power under section 6 of the Competition Act to take an action seeking an injunction

1. The editor, Tony O'Connor, has written an article entitled 'Notifying the Irish Regulatory Authorities of a merger or takeover' in *Commercial Law Practitioner*, 1994, Vol. 16, No. 6, pp. 156-159 which summarises the effects of not notifying the relevant regulatory authorities.

3.0 and/or a declaration prohibiting these arrangements on the grounds that they are prohibited under sections 4 and 5'.[2]

SECTION 4

The decisions of the Competition Authority included in this chapter along with the High Court decision in the case *RGDATA Ltd. v. Tara Publishing Co. Ltd.* address some of the following issues which arise under section 4 of the Competition Act 1991 for acquisitions and mergers:

(a) When persons and entities forming a merger cease or remain separate undertakings;
(b) The effect of an acquisition on the relevant market;
(c) The purpose of the acquirer in the acquisition, take-over or merger;
(d) The purpose and effect of the ancillary restrictions in the acquisition arrangements;
(e) The necessity and reasonableness of the restrictions which are ancillary to the acquisitions;
(f) Whether the commencement of restrictions after an acquisition can be delayed until another agreement such as a service agreement terminates.

The determination of the Competition Authority to apply the Competition Act to mergers and acquisitions does not reflect the considerable debate and doubts about the application of Article 85 (upon which section 4 is based) to mergers prior to the introduction of the merger regulation.[3] Earlier editions of the leading text books on EEC Competition Law usefully trace the debate on the application of Articles 85 and 86 to mergers.[4]

2. Quote is from Paragraph 8.64 of the Competition Authority's 'Interim Report of Study on the Newspaper Industry' which does not have a Government Publication number and is at present only available from the Department of Enterprise and Employment, Dublin 2 @ £5.00.
3. Regulations OJ 4064/89 [1989] L 395/1; [1990] 4 CMLR 286. An article by Keane and Walsh in (1990) *ILT* at 181 explains the background and possible future application of this regulation.
4. Whish in his book 'Competition law' (2nd ed.) published by Butterworths in 1989, pp. 737-750 explains concisely the evolution of the judicial and European Commission views on the application of Articles 85 and 86 to mergers. In the 3rd edition of the same book published in 1993 on pp. 702-705 Whish summarises the historical basis to the implementation of the merger regulation which seeks to render the issue of the application of Article 85 to mergers more certain. Ritter Braun and Rawlinson in 'EEC Competition Law: A Practitioner's Guide', compact edition published by Kluwer in 1993 give in Chapter VI a good overall view of the application of Articles 85 and 86 to mergers and concisely explain the merger regulation. Similarly Van Bael and Bellis in 'Competition Law of the European Community' (3rd ed.) published by CCH Europe in 1994 explain in Part 6 the relevance of Articles 85 and 86 whilst giving useful footnotes of cases which are relevant to the issues arising. Goyder in his book 'EC Competition Law' (2nd ed.) published by Oxford University Press in 1993 gives in chapter 20 an interesting historical account of events leading up to the merger regulation. Bellamy and Child in 'Common Market Law of Competition' (3rd ed.) published by Sweet & Maxwell in 1987 make interesting assertions in chapter 9 arising from the European Commission's utterances about the application of Article 85 to mergers prior to the merger regulation. The authors also usefully summarise relevant decisions of the European Commission about common provisions of acquisition agreements. Chapter 6 of the fourth and latest edition of this book (1993) deals with the Merger regulation in great detail.

Mergers which pre-date the Competition Act **3.1** **3.0**

The Notice of the Competition Authority entitled 'Notice in Respect of Mergers and Takeovers which predate the Competition Act' states the Authority's view that an acquisition which has been completed prior to the commencement of the Competition Act cannot be prohibited or rendered void by the operation of section 4.

RGDATA Ltd. v. Tara Publishing Co. Ltd. **3.2**

When the Competition Authority is requested to make a decision in respect of a notification requesting a certificate or a licence it must take the agreement as agreed between the parties. Decisions of the Competition Authority indicate the willingness of the Authority to enter into negotiations with the notifying party for the deletion of clauses of an agreement which may offend against section 4 of the Competition Act in the Authority's view. The list of notifications prepared for this book[5] indicate those decisions in which alterations have been made to a notified arrangement prior to the making of the decision of the Competition Authority by including 'NC' in the columns opposite the notification number. If the notifying parties do not agree to delete a clause from a notified arrangement which may offend section 4 according to the Authority the Authority has no ability to sever the offending clause when making its decision.

The High Court, however, by virtue of the common law and by virtue of section 4(7) of the Competition Act 1991 may sever provisions of an acquisition agreement which may offend the Competition Act 1991 or the common law restraint of trade doctrine. The judgment of Murphy J in *RGDATA v. Tara Publishing Co. Ltd.* is particularly noteworthy because the High Court after striking out a prohibited clause gave effect to what the court determined was the agreement between the parties.

Nallen/O'Toole (Belmullet) **3.3**

This was the first decision of the Competition Authority and is often referred to by the Competition Authority in its later decisions. The decision concerns the sale of a business in Belmullet, County Mayo with ancillary restraints on the vendor from competing within a defined territory with the business sold for a period of 3 years. In issuing a certificate the Competition Authority noted that the Competition Act did not exclude small undertakings and did not incorporate a *de-minimis* exclusion for agreements which have little effect on competition. The Competition Authority emphasised the importance of effect on potential competition and not merely actual competition when assessing the compatibility of the arrangements with section 4 of the Competition Act. Reference is made in the decision to the recognition in other jurisdictions of the need for competition restrictions in respect of a sale of business. In this particular instance the Authority accepted the need for a 3 year competition restriction in order to secure the complete transfer of the goodwill sold.

Athlone Travel Ltd/Michael SteinTravel **3.4**

The Competition Authority issued another certificate for the sale of this business with competition restrictions which are limited geographically and to a period of two years. The Authority stated that restrictions in excess of two years in a sale of business agreement can rarely be justified as being necessary to secure the transfer of goodwill.

Woodchester Bank Ltd/UDT Bank Ltd **3.5**

This decision concerns the sale of the entire share capital of a company with ancillary

5. See pages 1194–1317.

3.0 restrictions in order to secure the transfer of the goodwill in the company which is the subject matter of the sale agreement. The Competition Authority states that section 4(1) of the Competition Act 1991 impacts upon mergers. The Authority recognises that the subject of a decision in a share sale agreement may be monitored and controlled under the Mergers, Take-Overs and Monopolies (Control) Act 1978 as amended or the Central Bank Act 1989. In the Authority's view before a merger offends against section 4(1) of the Competition Act it must be shown that it would or would be likely to result in an actual diminution of competition in the relevant market. The ancillary restrictions on the vendor of the share in the company sold did not offend against section 4 of the Competition Act according to the Authority.

ACT Group Ltd/Kindle Group Ltd **3.6**
Vendors who become employees of the acquired company are separate undertakings when entering into restrictive covenants which secure the transfer of the business according to the Competition Authority in this decision. The extension of the normally accepted two year period for restrictions for businesses involving know-how is also first mentioned by the Competition Authority in this decision. Shareholders and subscription agreements are discussed for the first time.[6]

Budget Travel Ltd/Phil Fortune **3.7**
The original notification of an agreement for the sale by Budget Travel Ltd. of their entire share capital in a subsidiary company specialising in the arrangement of tours for groups was amended because of restrictions by the Competition Authority that the originally notified agreement had reservations which extended beyond what was necessary to secure the transfer of the goodwill with the shares. The parties ultimately agreed to reduce the vendor's covenant not to solicit employees of the company sold to a period of 3 years and the vendor's covenant not to compete in the group to a period of 2 years. The Authority qualified its acceptance of the confidentiality covenant of the vendor by stating that such confidentiality clauses should not be used to impede re-entry into the market by the vendor.

G.I. Corporation/General Semiconductor Industries Inc **3.8**
The arguments that a merger which is reviewable under the Mergers, Take-Overs and Monopolies (Control) Act 1978 or which involves an undertaking with a dominant position within the meaning of section 5 of the Competition Act preclude the application of the Competition Act were rejected by the Competition Authority in this decision. This particular decision also deals with the need for lengthy restrictions on the use of know how when the subject of a share sale agreement involves the transfer of know how.

Firestone/Grenfell Ltd **3.9**
The Competition Authority comments that a notifying party ought to have reasonable doubts that the subject of a notification offends against section 4 of the Competition Act before seeking a certificate or licence. It remarks that a literal interpretation of section 4 (1) could result in any business agreement being found to be prohibited since

6. An interesting decision to refuse a certificate for a shareholders agreement is Decision 417 of 8 September 1995 "Prince of Wales Ltd/Share Subscription and Shareholders Agreement 1990".

a party entering an agreement chooses the other party over others. The entering into another agreement is thereby precluded. In this decision the sale of stud farms and shares in a bloodstock auctioneering company without ancillary restrictions were not affected by the prohibition in section 4(1). 3.0

Scully Tyrell & Co./Edberg Ltd **3.10**
This decision is significant because it indicates the Competition Authority's views about mergers in concentrated markets and the ability to impose restrictions on shareholders while they retain shares and after they have disposed of their interests. The ability to enter the relevant market after an acquisition and the ability of customers to provide the relevant market's services are considered significant factors in assessing the effect of a merger. Mergers which exceed the thresholds of the Herfindahl-Hirschman index as used in the United States or which increase the merged undertaking's market share above the four firm concentration ratio of 40% merit close scrutiny according to the Competition Authority in this decision.

Chemical International Finance Ltd/Irish Life **3.11**
No geographic limitation on the restrictive covenants was contained in this notified arrangement for the sale of three subsidiary companies and their businesses from Irish Life. The covenant by Irish Life not to compete in the relevant market for a period of two years was thought to be necessary to give effect to the sale of the businesses which was the subject of the notification in the decision.

Cambridge ACT/Imari **3.12**
The necessity for venture capitalists to secure their investments by tying the main personnel to the investment is ancillary to the acquisition of shares. The Competition Authority in this decision acknowledges that many such restrictive provisions which protect the venture capitalist do not offend against section 4 of the Competition Act. Typical provisions in a shareholders agreement which could relate to a joint venture or investment acquisition were contained in the notified arrangements leading to this decision. The Authority sets out many of the clauses in its lengthy decision and comments on the overall effect of the restrictions eventually.

Food Industries/Norish plc **3.13**
The difference in the subject of this decision from other share acquisition agreements which were notified to the Competition Authority is that the purchaser delays in obtaining full control of the acquired company from the vendor until the purchaser exercises its option to purchase the entire share capital. Nevertheless the Competition Authority decided that effective control of the business of the company sold was transferred when the purchaser obtained 66% of the share capital pursuant to the agreement prior to the commencement of the Competition Act. In that respect the acquisition itself was not reviewable. The Authority then proceeded to accept the necessity for a covenant from the vendor not to compete for a period of two years from the date of the exercise by the purchaser of its right to purchase the remaining shares in the company. The Authority cautioned that artificial arrangements which would seek to delay the commencement of non-compete provisions by staggering the purchase of shares will be noted and will not merit a certificate of compliance from the Authority. In this particular instance the Authority accepted the authenticity and lack of artificiality of the arrangements notified.

3.0 *PJD Investment/Fitzwilton plc* **3.14**
A share purchase agreement completed prior to the commencement of the Competition Act was outside the scope of section 4. The share purchase agreement imposed a 5 year covenant on the vendors not to compete in the State and in specified countries in order to secure the transfer of the goodwill. These restrictions would in any case have ceased to operate in April 1994 but the parties on being notified of the Authority's reservations on the period of the restrictions agreed that all restrictions on the vendors other than to maintain confidentiality would cease on 1 October 1993. Consequently on 27 October 1993 the Authority issued a certificate as requested.

Spring Grove (Ireland) Ltd/Initial Services (International) Ltd **3.15**
Considerable discussions appear to have taken place between the Authority and the party involved in the share purchase agreement which is the subject of this decision. The Authority reiterated its views that section 4 can apply to mergers and acquisitions and rejected the submission that the maxim *generalia specialibus non derogant* had any application to the issue about whether the Mergers, Take-Overs and Monopolies (Control) Act 1978 being a specific Act of regulation precluded the application of the Competition Act to mergers. In examining mergers the Authority repeated its view in the Scully Tyrrell decision that an acquisition merits close scrutiny where the merger or take-over gave rise to the four firm concentration ratio exceeding 40%. The Authority also indicated its willingness to apply the Herfindahl-Hirschman Index when assessing the concentration arising from a merger or take-over.

The Authority stated that it will examine a merger in detail if the 40% threshold in the four firm concentration ratio is exceeded by the merged entity. It also indicated that it may apply the Herfindahl-Hirschman Index as used by the US Department of Justice to evaluate mergers.

It appears that the Authority will rely on market shares estimated by the notifying parties and that market shares in certain industries are very difficult to establish. In this particular decision the Authority opined that the concentration arising from the merger would not hinder new entrants to the relevant market. The Authority adverted to the possibility of customers providing the services themselves as an in-house operation and that this fact is an element to be taken into account when assessing the effect of a merger on the relevant market.

Both the purchaser and the vendor covenanted not to use trademarks and other intellectual property rights associated with the company which was being sold and this did not offend against section 4(1) according to the Authority.

The decision coupled with Competition Authority Decision No. 12 – Scully Tyrrell & Co./Edberg Ltd are useful for the purpose of ascertaining the manner by which the Authority will examine the effects of a merger on the market relevant to the merger.

Irish Distillers plc/Cooley Distillery plc **3.16**
This decision to refuse to issue a certificate or a licence in respect of the acquisition by Irish Distillers of Cooley Distillery is particularly noteworthy because of the Authority's decision to look at the purpose of the acquirer in the acquisition agreement. Apart from observations and submissions made by the parties and a third party the Authority refers to newspaper reports of statements made by representatives of the relevant party when deciding that the purpose of the acquisition was anti-competitive. The Authority when commenting upon the argument based on the *failing*

firm defence sets out extracts from the Guidelines of the US Department of Justice about this type of defence. The Authority in this decision shows its reluctance to accept an argument that the acquired company has no option but to merge with the larger competitor unless all other avenues of keeping the acquired company going have been explored. 3.0

Rohan Construction Ltd/Rohcon Ltd **3.17**
The asset and goodwill sale agreement which is the subject of this decision required the chairman director who is not a shareholder to enter into various restrictions in order to secure the transfer of the goodwill. The Authority teases out the issue of when an employee or director is an undertaking separate from the employer. The Authority noted that this particular acquisition did not require the originally agreed five year restriction on the chairman but did need a four year restriction on the chairman in order to secure the transfer of the goodwill of the business. The reasoning in this decision can usefully be compared with the decisions of the Authority concerning the applicability of section 4(1) to post-termination covenants in employee agreements.[7]

Barlo Group plc/Kingspan Group plc **3.18**
The acquisition of the entire assets and goodwill of a competing firm despite the high concentration in the relevant market of the merged enterprise did not offend against section 4(1) of the Competition Act according to the Authority in this decision. Representations from the Minister for Enterprise and Employment were made to the Authority concerning the necessity for this merger in order to maintain employment and the competitiveness of the acquiring company. The Authority refers to the *failing firm defence* and decided that the relevant market in the State could be accessed in any event by one of the larger competitors of the acquiring company in Europe if any of those competitors so decided.

Sedgwick Overseas Group Ltd/Dineen **3.19**
An employment agreement entered into by a vendor of shares in the undertaking which prevented the vendor from soliciting customers after termination of his employment for one year did not offend against section 4(1) because the Competition Authority opined that soliciting customers was not essential to enter the relevant market. The Authority noted that a non compete clause would not be acceptable.

IAWS (Agri) Society/Unigrain Ltd **3.20**
Restrictions on competition by vendors who remained on as employees of the acquired company were not considered to be necessary for the purpose of transferring the business to the purchaser according to the Authority in this decision. Restrictions for a period of 3 years concerning the soliciting of employees or customers of the acquired company were thought to be reasonable. This decision can be usefully compared with Competition Authority Decisions No. 13, 20, 142 and 301 and 373.[8]

7. See in particular the Competition Authority notice and the Competition Authority Decisions Nos. 13 and 20 set out at 1.4 above.
8. 12 – Scully Tyrrell/Edberg Ltd **3.10**; 13 – Peter Mark/Stapleton **1.4.2**; 20 – Apex/ Murtagh **1.4.3**; 24 – Cambridge/ACT/Imari **3.12**; 142 – PJD Investment Fitzwilton **3.14**; 301 – Rohan/Rohcon **3.17**; 373 – Dairygold/Cotter **3.23**.

3.0 *Kantoher Food Products Ltd/Carton Brothers Ltd* **3.21**
The Authority in this decision rejected the submissions that know how brought to the merged enterprise by the purchaser could justify the extension of the period for non-competition beyond the normally acceptable two years. The Authority acknowledged that a transfer of know how might require periods of restriction for up to five years but it did not accept that any know how transferred in the agreement which is the subject of this decision, justified such an extension of the normally acceptable period of two years.

Hickson International plc/Angus Fine Chemicals Ltd **3.22**
In this decision the Competition Authority accepted that the transfer of know how did justify lengthy periods of restriction in excess of the normally acceptable two year period to secure the transfer of the business. In addition to this aspect of the arrangements which are the subject of this decision it is interesting to note the secrecy arrangement in order to allow the purchaser exploit and develop the raw material which would continue to be supplied by the vendor. The possible abuse of a dominant position in giving effect to the acquisition arrangements does not in the Authority's view preclude the application of section 4 of the Competition Act.

Dairygold Cooperative Society Ltd/Cotter **3.23**
The sale of a milk round which is the subject of this decision did not necessitate the vendor who continued to operate the milk round to give a covenant on the termination of his employment not to compete with the purchaser of the milk round. The Authority believes that the purchaser in this instance, if it wished to secure the transfer of the goodwill, could require the vendor not to compete with the business in the defined territory for a given period after the date of acquisition. However if the vendor remained on as an employee of the purchaser, the purchaser took the consequences of that decision which included the prohibition of a post-term restriction on competition in the service agreement of the vendor. Again, it is interesting to compare this decision with the IAWS/Unigrain decision and the decisions mentioned in footnote 6.

Post-term restrictions on milk roundsmen and wholesale deliverers were the subject of two notifications which were substantially amended by deleting the restrictions before the Competition Authority issued certificates in decisions dated 12 April 1995 and which are entitled 'Notification No. CA/55/92 – Premier Milk Distributors Agreement – Decision No. 391' and 'Notification No. CA/394/92E – Premier Wholesale Delivery Agreement – Decision No. 392'.[9]

OTHER RELEVANT DECISIONS

Two decisions which are contained in Chapter 7 concerning property are relevant to acquisitions in particular and which are as follows:

'Notification No. CA/1127/92 – Adsites Ltd/David Allen Holdings Ltd –

9. These decisions are not contained in this book but they are available from the Competition Authority, Block 4, Irish Life Centre, Talbot Street, Dublin 1.

Decision No. 381' [7.19] which is a decision to refuse a certificate or a licence to an agreement giving an option to the only other principal competitor in the relevant market to purchase the competitor's assets for the relevant market. **3.0**

'Notification No. CA/8/93 – RHM Ltd/Naresa Ltd – Decision No. 394' **7.20** which is a decision to refuse a certificate in respect of the surrendering provisions in a property lease. The particular surrendering provision states that on the payment of certain sums the landlord would not compete with the lessee. The lessee could then bring the business long-established in the leased premises to another part of the town in which both parties had their places of business.

3.1

Competition Authority
Notice in Respect of Mergers and Takeovers which predate the Competition Act

1. In the year to 30 September 1992 the Competition Authority received a number of notifications in respect of mergers and sale of business agreements which had been concluded prior to the coming into force of the Competition Act. Most such notifications were received shortly before the deadline for the notification of existing agreements under section 7(2). The number of such agreements notified indicates some degree of uncertainty concerning the position of such agreements under the Competition Act. The Authority therefore considers that it would be useful to give some indication of its views regarding such agreements. The Authority points out that the interpretation of the provisions of the Competition Act is ultimately a matter for the Courts.

2. Section 4(1) of the Competition Act states that 'all agreements between undertakings, decisions by associations of undertakings and concerted practices which have as their object or effect the prevention, restriction or distortion of competition in trade in any goods or services in the State or in any part of the State are prohibited and void'.

3. Where a merger or sale of business was completed prior to 1 October 1991, the date on which the Competition Act came into force, then, even if the transaction were the result of an agreement between undertakings at the time of its completion, that element of the agreement had been discharged by performance before the Act commenced. The property which was the subject of the agreement will have been transferred. In the Authority's view the prohibition in section 4(1) only applies to a current or continuing contractual commitment or one entered into subsequent to the coming into force of the Act. As the merger or sale element of pre-October 1991 transactions was discharged prior to the commencement of the Act, that aspect of the arrangements does not come within the scope of section 4(1).

4. This notice is without prejudice to any view the Authority may take of non-compete provisions or other ancillary clauses in such agreements, since it may be that in some instances such clauses would involve current or continuing contractual commitments on the part of the parties. These aspects of the notifications will be considered on an individual basis.

For the Competition Authority

Patrick M. Lyons
Chairman

4 May 1993

3.2 RGDATA Ltd (plaintiffs) v. Tara Publishing Co. Ltd. (defendant): [1993] No. 4983P, High Court, 21 December 1994

Asset sale – Whether restriction for over 20 years on vendor is enforceable – Declaration sought – principles applying to severance – Whether vendor using a description has infringed the severed restriction – Article 85(1) of the Treaty of Rome – Competition Act 1991 (No. 24) section 4

Facts: Since 1950 members of RGDATA which is a company representing the interests of independent retailers were circulated with a magazine called 'Retail News'. In or about 1980 Retail News was printed and published as a joint venture between RGDATA Ltd. ('the plaintiff') and Tara Publishing Co. Ltd. ('the defendant'). The profit which arose exclusively from fees for advertisements inserted in the magazine were shared equally by the plaintiff and the defendant.

By an agreement dated 1 June 1985 the plaintiff sold to the defendant the interest of the plaintiff in Retail News and another publication called 'Retail News Year Book'. The agreement contained the following clause which was the subject of these proceedings seeking a declaration that it was void, prohibited and unenforceable:

> RGDATA hereby covenants and agrees and undertakes not to publish or to assist or cause or permit others to publish or assist, for a term of 20 years renewable for a further 5 year period and one year periods thereafter, in publication of any other publications in the Republic of Ireland. . . .

The plaintiff in these proceedings sought a declaration that the relevant restrictions were void by virtue of section 4(1) of the Competition Act 1991. The defendant counterclaimed that a publication of the plaintiff entitled 'How to Manage your Shop' was in breach of the 1985 agreement which caused the defendant to lose advertising revenue.

The defendant conceded that the restrictions could not be justified even under the common law principles if the sale related simply to goodwill and assets. The defendant argued that RGDATA was selling the assurance given to its members and that Retail News was 'the official magazine of RGDATA serving the independent grocer'. Both parties accepted that the applicable legal provisions were correctly stated in *Remia BV v. Commission of the European Communities*: 'Non-competition clauses incorporated in an agreement for the transfer of an undertaking in principle have the merit of ensuring that the transfer has the effect intended. By virtue of that very act they contribute to the promotion of competition because they lead to an increase in the number of undertakings in the market in question. Nevertheless, in order to have the beneficial effect on competition, such clauses must be necessary to the transfer of the undertaking concerned and their duration and scope must be strictly limited to that purpose'.

Held: by Murphy J in granting a declaration that the relevant clause should be severed and allowing the counterclaim of the defendant:

(1) Even the limiting of the restriction to publications which resembled the magazines which were the subject of the agreement could not be validly upheld.

(2) A restraint on trade for a period of 20 years could only be justified to protect

the defendant purchaser's property right in the title themselves or the title that the magazine was 'the official publication of RGDATA'. 3.2

(3) The relevant restraint should be severed in accordance with well established principles at common law and recognised in the Competition Act 1991 in positive terms to the effect that 'the Retail News' magazine should be the only official publication for RGDATA.

(4) The magazine entitled 'How to Manage your Shop' which was circulated with the description: 'An RGDATA publication' constituted a breach of the asset sale agreement.

(5) No specific computation of the damages having been made the damages to be awarded to the defendant and counterclaimant were assessed at £7,500.

Case referred to in judgment:
Remia BV v. The Commission of European Communities [1985] 4 ECR 2545; [1987] 1 CMLR 1

MURPHY J delivered his judgment on 21 December 1994 saying: In this case the plaintiffs claim a declaration that Clause 2 of an Agreement dated 1 June 1985 made between RGDATA Ltd of the one part and the above named defendants, Tara Publishing Company Ltd, of the other part was rendered void by section 4(1) of the Competition Act 1991. The defendants counterclaim for damages for the alleged breach of the said Agreement by the plaintiffs.

By the said Agreement dated 1 June 1985 (the 1985 Agreement) RGDATA sold to Tara Publishing Company Ltd ('Tara') the interest of RGDATA in the title and ownership of two publications, namely, 'Retail News' and 'Retail News Yearbook' for a purchase price of £21,000 and subject to the terms and conditions therein contained which included a covenant by Tara to invest sufficient funds and make improvements in the magazines aforesaid over a twelve month period so as to obtain within that period 'the overall objective of achieving and maintaining a standard of publication of the said magazines that is equivalent and comparable to other quality trade publications'. The undisputed evidence was to the effect that this investment was made and amounted to approximately £25,000.

The 1985 Agreement, which is deceptively simple in its terms, includes two restrictive covenants, one dealing with the nature and the other with the duration of the restriction. These are Clauses 2 and 7 which provide as follows:

> 2. RGDATA hereby covenants and agrees and undertakes not to publish or to assist or cause or permit others to publish or assist, during the currency of this agreement, in publication of any other publications in the Republic of Ireland PROVIDED ALWAYS that this will not restrict RGDATA in issuing and supplying press releases and photographs to other publications not under the control nor in the ownership of Tara Publishing. Further, RGDATA covenants and agrees and undertakes to give equitable treatment to 'Retail News' in supplying photographs and press releases and further, that 'Retail News' shall during the currency of this agreement, be the only official publication for RGDATA PROVIDED ALWAYS that Tara Publishing adheres to the terms and conditions of this agreement.
>
> 7. This agreement shall remain in force for a term of 20 years from the date hereof and shall renew automatically for a 5 year period thereafter unless and until terminated by either party by not less that 1 year's written notice to the other, expiring on any such renewal date.

The Competition Act 1991, section 4(1), so far as material to these proceedings provides

3.2 as follows:

> 4(1) Subject to the provisions of this section, all agreements between undertakings, decisions by associations of undertakings and concerted practices which have as their object or effect the prevention, restriction or distortion of competition in trade in any goods or services in the State or in any part of the State are prohibited and void, including in particular, without prejudice to the generality of this subsection those which—
> (b) limit or control production, markets, technical development or investment.

Counsel on behalf of Tara rightly and necessarily accepted that the apparently wide ranging and long running covenants in restraint of competition contained in Clauses 2 and 7 (above) could not be justified even under the common law principles established prior to the enactment of the Competition Act 1991 if the sale related simply to the goodwill and assets consisting in the title of a newspaper or magazine. The essence of the defendants' case was that the plaintiffs were selling and Tara purchasing a magazine or magazines which had been long established as the official publication for RGDATA and was circulated to all 3,500 or so members of that Association as part of their entitlement by virtue of their subscription with the reassurance that it was 'the official magazine of RGDATA serving the independent grocer'. The importance of this fact is noted in Clause 2 where it provides that 'Retail News' shall be the *only official publication* for RGDATA during the continuance of the agreement.

The first problem in the present case is to construe the 1985 Agreement and particularly the above quoted clauses. In this context both parties recognised that it is a case in which the much invoked 'factual matrix' was highly material.

Apparently 'Retail News' was first published in or about the 1950's for circulation among the independent grocers who were members of the plaintiff Association. In the early 1980's the magazine was printed and published as a joint venture between the plaintiffs and the defendants. They divided the profits equally between them. These profits derived exclusively from fees paid by persons placing advertisements in the magazine. Whilst a price was placed on 'Retail News' and comparable magazines, sales thereof represented an insignificant proportion of the income which they generated. Income was generated by the sale of the advertising space and not of the magazine itself. Clearly the concept of publications of this type is for a publisher to establish a magazine which is of an appropriate quality, content or authority to attract or compel a circulation within a defined group of potential customers whom suppliers may wish to target with their advertisements. The members of RGDATA are a clearly defined and no doubt valuable market but it was not one which RGDATA had or has a monopoly in exploiting. For many years magazines similar to 'Retail News' have been circulated free of charge to members of the plaintiff Association and they have been facilitated in so doing by RGDATA who provide to such publishers a list of their membership. On the other hand, no doubt there is a particular relationship between RGDATA and its members and perhaps there would be a reasonable expectation amongst potential suppliers to the grocery industry that, other things being equal, members of RGDATA would be more likely to read the official publication of their own organisation in preference to other publications. Clearly this was an important consideration for both parties to the 1985 Agreement. RGDATA were selling not only a well established title but they were selling to Tara the right to represent the title as the *official publication* of RGDATA.

What is on the face of it surprising is that when the plaintiffs granted to Tara the right to represent the magazine published by them as such an official publication they did not expressly reserve any control over the content or quality of the magazine or impose any specific obligations on Tara in relation to its publication or circulation. It seems to me that such terms must be inferred.

In the context in which the Agreement was excecuted it is clear that Tara accepted an obligation to circulate the magazines at their own expense to the members of RGDATA at appropriate intervals. It is also clear that Tara accepted an obligation to invest in the magazines in such a way as not merely to achieve but also to maintain a particular standard of publication. Moreover, it would seem that of its very nature the official publication of an organisation would be required to support, or at any rate refrain from attacking, the organisation whose imprimatur it bears. The 1985 Agreement does not attempt to define any such duties. This may be explained by the prior knowledge which both parties had of the publication or by the fact that market forces would compel Tara to produce a magazine of high quality which was acceptable in its content and production to RGDATA and more particularly its members. Whilst Tara's immediate concern is to attract advertising revenue, that objective could hardly be achieved if they alienated the readership which they acquired by virtue of their status as the official publication of RGDATA. The conclusion that there are continuing obligations imposed on Tara is supported by the proviso to Clause 2 aforesaid which provides that the undertakings given by RGDATA are conditional upon Tara adhering to the terms and conditions of the Agreement. Furthermore, the inclusion (at Clause 6) of an arbitration clause suggests that the parties foresaw continuing commitments to each other. 3.2

In fact the parties themselves accepted that their obligations were more extensive than they appeared to be under the terms of the 1985 Agreement. Mr. Farrell, the proprietor of Tara, understood that Clause 2 aforesaid precluded RGDATA from publishing a magazine financed by advertising revenue which might otherwise have been secured for 'Retail News' or the annual yearbook. RGDATA not merely accept this interpretation but contend that it demonstrates the argument on which they rely. It is argued that this is a clear and excessive restrictive covenant or anti-competition provision which offends both at common law and under the 1991 statute.

Counsel on behalf of each party accepted that the applicable legal provisions were correctly stated in *Remia B.V. v. The Commission of European Communities* [1985] 3 ECR 2545 at p. 2571 in the following terms:

> It should be stated at the outset that the Commission has rightly submitted — and the Applicants have not contradicted it on that point — that the fact that non-competition clauses are included in an agreement for the sale of an undertaking is not of itself sufficient to remove such clauses from the scope of Article 85(1) of the Treaty.
>
> In order to determine whether or not such clauses come within the prohibition in Article 85(1), it is necessary to examine what would be the state of competition if those clauses did not exist.
>
> If that were the case, and should the vendor and the purchaser remain competitors after the transfer, it is clear that the agreement for the transfer of the undertaking could not be given effect. The vendor, with his particularly detailed knowledge of the transferred undertaking, would still be in a position to win back his former customers immediately after the transfer and thereby drive the undertaking out of business. Against that background non-competition clauses incorporated in an agreement for the transfer of an undertaking in principle have the merit of ensuring that the transfer has the effect intended. By virtue of that very fact they contribute to the promotion of competition because they lead to an increase in the number of undertakings in the market in question.
>
> Nevertheless, in order to have that beneficial effect on competition, such clauses must be necessary to the transfer of the undertaking concerned and their duration and scope must be strictly limited to that purpose. The Commission was therefore right in holding that where those conditions are satisfied such clauses are free of the prohibition laid down in Article 85(1).

It seems to be that that principle could be viewed in circumstances such as the present at three different levels as follows:

1. Insofar as a vendor is selling the goodwill attaching to a named publication it would be

3.2 justifiable to require the vendor to covenant against competing in the same business for such reasonable period as might be necessary to ensure that the purchaser achieved the goodwill in the enterprise which he had purchased.

2. Insofar as the particular title itself was purchased it would be reasonable to include covenants precluding the vendor indefinitely from publishing a comparable magazine under the same title though he could not be precluded indefinitely from engaging in the business of publishing magazines generally.

3. Where a purchaser acquires, as in the present case, not merely the right to the goodwill in a magazine under a particular title but purchases the right to represent that magazine as the only official publication of the vendor to its members, that too would constitute a concluded property transaction which might be lawfully sustained by covenants precluding the vendor from purporting to publish any other comparable magazine either under the same title or under any other title in the context of its being 'the official publication of RGDATA'. Again, however, it seems to me that such covenants could not lawfully prevent the vendor after a reasonable interval of time from publishing any other magazine provided it did not offend in either of those respects.

The fact that the vendors in a notional case or RGDATA in the present case would be precluded from publishing a magazine under a particular title or with a particular accolade may in theory restrict competition but only in the sense that the vendor cannot reclaim and exploit the asset of which he has disposed. Any additional restriction which would impose wider restrictions of a lengthy nature would offend the Treaty of Rome, the 1991 Act and at common law.

Clearly the opening phrase of paragraph 2 aforesaid if literally interpreted precludes RGDATA from publishing or assisting in the publication of any publication for a minimum period of twenty years. In the light of the views expressed above, clearly such a provision would be unsustainable. It may be that one could give to the particular phrase a more restrictive interpretation. Certainly, it would seem reasonable to limit the restriction to publications which bore some relationship to the magazines which were the subject matter of the agreement.

Notwithstanding the wide expressions used, I believe it would be proper to conclude that the clause did not extend to newsletters or other communications between the organisation and its members but, even so restricted, it seems to me that the validity of this part of the clause could not be upheld. In my view a restraint for a period of twenty years could only be justified to protect the purchaser's property right in the titles themselves or the very nature of the magazines as the official publication of RGDATA.

In accordance with the principles well established at common law and recognised in the 1991 Act, I conclude that I should sever the covenant precluding publication of magazines generally from the covenant expressed in positive terms to the effect that the 'Retail News' should be the only official publication for RGDATA. In that context I should add that I understand the 1985 Agreement as indicating that both the 'Retail News' and 'Retail News Yearbook' are *the* official publication for this purpose, even though only 'Retail News' was expressly referred to in Clause 2.

In effect, therefore, the plaintiffs are free to publish or assist in publishing magazines or other publications whether or not relying upon advertising revenue for their profitability if but only if the magazines or publications are not described, represented or held out to be official publications of RGDATA.

In these circumstances the publication by RGDATA of the magazine 'How to manage your shop' with the description 'An RGDATA publication' (with an introduction by the Director General of that organisation) constituted a breach of the 1985 Agreement in respect of which the defendants have claimed damages. These damages were computed on the basis that advertising revenue was lost as a result of the competition from the RGDATA publication. That loss was assessed by Tara and its witnesses at some £15,000. Counsel on behalf of Tara properly conceded that this was not specific computation of special damages but rather an indication of the loss which flowed from the unlawful competition. I think in the circumstances that if I assessed damages at £7,500 it would meet the justice of the case. 3.2

I will hear the parties as to the remainder of the Order to be made herein.

Competition Authority Decision No. 1, Nallen/O'Toole (Belmullet): 2 April 1992, Notification No. CA/8/91 3.3

Agreement for the sale of business – Meaning of undertaking – Economic effect of agreement – Three-year restriction in agreement preventing vendor from competing with the business for a specified period in a specified area – Whether restrictions exceed that necessary to ensure the transfer of the goodwill in the business – Competition Act 1991 (No. 24) sections. 3, 4 and 7

Facts: On 21 November 1991 notification was made to the Authority with a request for a certificate under section 4(4) of the Competition Act, or failing that, a licence under section 4(2) in respect of an agreement whereunder Mr O'Toole sold his interest in a business to Mr Nallen. Up to the date of the notified agreement Mr Nallen and Mr O'Toole carried on in partnership the business of the sale, repair and rental of televisions, video recorders and hi-fi equipment and also of video film rentals. The business drew its customers from the town of Belmullet and the surrounding rural areas.

The market relevant to the notified agreement is that for the sale of the relevant electrical goods, that for the rental of the relevant electrical goods, and that for the rental of video tapes. There were three other undertakings carrying on the same business in Belmullet with each undertaking having an estimated 20-30% of the market. Nallen and O'Toole did not have exclusive distribution rights with respect to any particular brand and did not confine themselves to dealing with particular brands of products.

Under the terms of the notified agreement, which was effective from 1 October 1991, Mr Nallen purchased Mr O'Toole's interest in the business. Under the agreement Mr O'Toole undertook not to engage in the relevant business within a radius of 20 miles of the town of Belmullet for a period of three years commencing on 1 October 1991. He further undertook not to directly or indirectly solicit any such business from the public on his own behalf or on behalf of any other party. Since the date of the notified agreement Mr O'Toole is engaged in the repair and sale of general and specialist radio and audio equipment especially in connection with the fishing industry in the Belmullet area and both parties agree that this does not breach the terms of the notified agreement.

On 12 March 1992 the Authority published in the Irish Times a notice of intention to take a favourable decision. No submissions were received from interested parties.

Decided by the Authority: In issuing a certificate under section 4(4) of the Competition Act 1991, in respect of the notified agreement that:

(1) Mr Nallen and Mr O'Toole were and are engaged for gain in the provision of

3.3 services and are therefore undertakings within the meaning of section 3 of the Competition Act. The notified arrangements are concerned with the acquisition by Mr Nallen of Mr O'Toole's share in what had been a jointly owned business and various undertakings given by Mr O'Toole. The arrangements constitute an agreement between undertakings which applies to a part of the State.

(2) There is no provision in the Competition Act which would exclude small undertakings from the provisions of the Act on a *de minimis* basis and given the size and distribution of population in Ireland it is possible that a number of relatively small undertakings could, by acting together, prevent, restrict or distort competition in a part of the State. The present agreement therefore cannot be regarded as outside the scope of the Act.

(3) The number of competitors and the level of competition in the relevant market in Belmullet will remain unchanged as a result of the notified agreement.

(4) While partnerships *per se* do not contravene the Act, partnership agreements may, in certain circumstances breach section 4(1) by virtue of certain restrictive clauses contained in them.

(5) Economic theory stresses the importance of potential as opposed to actual competition in a particular market. In the market relevant to the notified agreement there appears to be few if any barriers to entry and there are no legal impediments which prevent new competitors from entering the market. Mr Nallen does not have any exclusive distribution rights over particular brands and the cost of entry into that market appears to be relatively low. The only apparent reason why additional competitors have not entered into the relevant market in Belmullet is that it is already regarded as operating competitively and there is perceived to be no scope for a new competitor to enter the market by under-cutting those already there. In the absence of barriers to other new entrants the agreement cannot be regarded as having any real effect on competition in this market.

(6) It is widely recognised in competition law in other countries and in common law that some restraint on a party disposing of all or part of his interests in a business is essential for the proper transfer of the goodwill of the business to take place, and that without the transfer of such goodwill, the transfer of ownership would be incomplete. Without such a restraint no proper transfer of goodwill could take place. The restraint must, however, be limited in terms of its duration, geographical coverage and subject matter to that which is necessary to secure the adequate transfer of the goodwill. Provided this is the case, then clearly the intention of such a restraint is not to restrict competition in the market in question.

(7) Consumers tend to purchase the products relevant to the notified agreement infrequently and in the particular business close personal contact with customers was a major factor. In addition Mr O'Toole is still active in business within the area and for these reasons it would appear the period of three years specified in the agreement is no more than is required to secure the complete transfer of the goodwill.

(8) The restraint also applies to an area with a radius of twenty miles from the town of Belmullet which appears to correspond to the area within which Mr Nallen and Mr O'Toole previously carried on business. The restriction applies only to those lines of business in which Mr O'Toole was previously engaged in partnership with Mr Nallen and the restrictions involved are no more than are necessary to ensure the adequate transfer of the goodwill of the business and are not in breach of section 4(1) of the Competition Act.

Cases, Decisions and Notice Referred to: 3.3
Volk v. Vervaecke (Case No. 5/69) [1969] ECR 295, [1969] CMLR 273
Remia v. EC Commission (Case No. 42/84) [1985] ECR 2545, [1987] 1 CMLR 1
Orr (John) Ltd v. Orr [1987] ILRM 702
United States v. Addyston Pipe & Steel Company et. al., 85 Fed. (6th Circuit) (1898)
EC Commission Decision Reuter/BASF [1976] OJ L254/40, [1976] 2 CMLR D44
EC Commission Decision Nutricia [1983] OJ L376/22, [1984] 2 CMLR 165
EC Commission Decision Mecaniver — PPG [1985] OJ L35/54, [1985] 3 CMLR 359
EC Commission Notice on agreements of minor importance [1986] OJ C 231/2, 3 September 1986

Competition Authority Decision of 2 April 1992 relating to a proceeding under section 4 of the Competition Act 1991
Notification No. CA/8/91 — Nallen/O'Toole (Belmullet)

Introduction

1. Notification was made with a request for a certificate under section 4(4) of the Competition Act 1991 or, in the event of a refusal by the Competition Authority to issue a certificate, a licence under section 4(2), by Mr Nallen and Mr O'Toole, Belmullet, on 21 November 1991 in respect of an agreement to transfer a business interest.

2. Notice of intention to take a favourable decision was published in 'The Irish Times' on 12 March 1992. There were no submissions from interested parties.

The Facts

(a) *The subject of the notification*

3. This notification concerns an agreement between the vendor and the purchaser of an interest in a business in which they had previously been partners. In the agreement the vendor agrees, as part of the arrangements in selling his share of the business to his partner, to refrain from engaging in the business concerned for a specific period in a defined geographical area.

(b) *The undertakings concerned*

The parties to the agreement are Mr Thomas J. Nallen and Mr Edward O'Toole who had carried on business in partnership with one another in the town of Belmullet, Co. Mayo.

(c) *The products and services concerned*

5. The business carried on was the sale, repair and provision for rent of televisions, video recorders and hi-fi equipment, commonly referred to in the electrical trade as 'brown goods'. They also provided video films for rent and there was particular emphasis on providing televisions, video recorders and video films for rent. They were engaged in this business for a period of three years. While in partnership both serviced the business more or less equally, with no staff being employed, and they therefore both knew their customers and dealt with them on a personal basis. They travelled around the area collecting rents and had a premises in the town of Belmullet where they stored equipment, carried out repair work and provided products for sale and rent. They dealt with customers who were resident in the town of Belmullet or who lived in the surrounding rural area.

(d) *The market involved*

6. The market can be seen as sub-dividing into three elements, the sale of brown goods, the provision of the same goods for rent, and the provision of video tapes for rent. Consumers face a choice between buying and renting certain brown electrical goods such as TVs and video recorders. The purchase of such goods is a one-off transaction involving a substantial outlay for most consumers. Renting may represent a more viable option for those unable to undertake such a large outlay. The choice between purchasing and renting, however, involves a choice between consuming different types of product. A rental agreement includes repair and service

3.3 of the goods. An individual who purchases a TV or video recorder must purchase such services separately. Thus the sale and rental of brown electrical goods constitute two separate but related markets. The rental of video tapes is a third distinct market.

7. There are three other undertakings carrying on the same business in Belmullet. The four undertakings are each estimated to have a market share in the range of twenty to thirty per cent. They deal in the same range of products and engage in the same three functions, i.e. sale, repair and rental, except that one undertaking does not provide goods for rent. The list of licensed video rental outlets in the office of the Film Censorship Board indicates that Mr Nallen is licensed in respect of two such outlets in Belmullet, Belmullet TV in Upper Barrack Street and Video City in Main Street. In addition to Nallen/O'Toole, one of the other undertakings is a relatively recent entrant to the market, having replaced another undertaking which left the market. Consumers in the area also have access to the same products and services in other towns close to the area concerned, in Crossmolina, Ballina and Castlebar which are respectively thirty one, thirty nine and forty seven miles from Belmullet. Nallen and O'Toole did not have exclusive distribution rights with respect to particular brands and did not confine themselves to dealing in particular brands of products.

(e) *The Agreement*

8. With effect from 1 October 1991, Mr Nallen purchased Mr O'Toole's interest in the business. As part of the arrangements associated with the transfer of Mr O'Toole's interest to Mr Nallen, the parties made the agreement, which is the subject of this notification, on 1 November 1991.

9. In the agreement, Mr O'Toole undertook not to engage in the relevant business within a radius of twenty miles of the town of Belmullet for a period of three years commencing on 1 October 1991. He would not directly or indirectly solicit any such business from the public on his own behalf or on behalf of any other party. Clause 3a of the Agreement states:

> Mr O'Toole hereby undertakes and covenants with Mr Nallen, that he will not, for a period commencing on 1 October 1991, and terminating three years thereafter, be engaged in the relevant business in any capacity whatsoever, and without prejudice to the generality of the foregoing, that he shall not be engaged, either as principal, partner, agent, servant, employee, director (including shadow director) or otherwise howsoever, whether directly or indirectly carry on, help, or assist in carrying on or be associated with the relevant business within a radius of 20 (twenty) miles, of the town of Belmullet, in the County of Mayo, and that during the same period, within the same area, Mr O'Toole shall not directly or indirectly solicit from the public, any business connected with the relevant business, nor shall he solicit or endeavour to obtain business for any other party, carrying on the same or similar business in the same area, during the same period.

Mr O'Toole also agreed to pay, by way of damages, specified sums of money to Mr Nallen in the event of any breach of the agreement by Mr O'Toole.

10. Mr O'Toole is now engaged in the repair and sale of general and specialist radio and audio equipment, especially in connection with the fishing industry in the Belmullet area, ship to shore radio, sonar, depth finders and the like. Mr Nallen and Mr O'Toole consider that this does not compete with the relevant business as defined in the agreement.

Assessment

(a) *Section 4(1)*

11. Section 4(1) of the Competition Act states that 'all agreements between undertakings, decisions by associations of undertakings and concerted practices which have as their object

or effect the prevention, restriction or distortion of competition in trade in any goods or services in the State or in any part of the State are prohibited and void'. **3.3**

12. As this is the first notification on which the Authority has taken a decision some general outline of the Authority's views on section 4(1) might be appropriate at this stage. Both the European Commission and the Court of Justice have decided against interpreting Article 85(1) literally. If section 4(1) were to be interpreted literally then virtually every form of business agreement could be argued to prevent, restrict or distort competition because any agreement effectively prohibits others from concluding the very same contract with the original parties. Such an interpretation would render it virtually impossible for business to operate.

13. The present notification concerns arrangements whereby an individual has bought out his former partner's interest in a business and is seeking to impose restrictions designed to prevent his former partner setting up business in competition with him for a period of time, by means of what may be best described as a 'non-competition clause'. In deciding whether the agreement is in breach of section 4(1) of the Competition Act, the Authority first of all examines its overall economic impact and then considers the specific question of the non-competition clause.

(b) *The Undertakings and the Agreement*

14. Section 3(1) of the Competition Act defines an undertaking as 'a person being an individual, a body corporate or an unincorporated body of persons engaged for gain in the production, supply or distribution of goods or the provision of a service.' The section explicitly states that individuals may come within the definition of undertakings if they are 'engaged for gain in the production, supply or distribution of goods or the provision of a service.'

15. Prior to the conclusion of this agreement Mr Nallen and Mr O'Toole as business partners were engaged for gain in the supply and distribution of goods, namely televisions, videos and hi-fi equipment, and in the provision of a service, namely the rental and repair of televisions and rental of video films in the town of Belmullet and its environs. Having bought out Mr O'Toole, Mr Nallen has continued to trade in the same business. Mr O'Toole has continued in business in his own right repairing and servicing radio, radar and navigation equipment on fishing vessels.

16. The European Commission has ruled on the definition of an undertaking in a number of cases under Article 85(1) of the Treaty of Rome on which section 4(1) is based.

> The word 'undertaking' is a wide term which extends to almost any legal or natural person carrying on activities of an economic or commercial nature including, for example, limited companies, partnerships, trade associations, agricultural co-operatives, sole traders and State Corporations. Whether the undertaking is profit-making is immaterial, provided it carries out economic or commercial activities.[1]

17. The Commission ruled in the Reuter/BASF case[2] that an individual could be regarded as an undertaking by virtue of engaging in economic activity through firms which were under his control, by exploiting the results of his own research and as commercial adviser to third parties. Similarly in the Nutricia case[3] the Commission decided that individuals were undertakings by virtue of their being the future proprietors of a business.

18. There is a difference between Irish and EC legislation in that the Irish Act defines an undertaking as being 'engaged for gain'. In practice, this appears to differ very little from the EC view that an undertaking carries out economic or commercial activities.

1. See C. Bellamy and G. Child (1987); *Common Market Law of Competition*, 3rd ed., Sweet and Maxwell, London, para. 2-003.
2. Case No. 76/743/EEC (OJ L254, 17.9.76, p. 40).
3. Nutricia/de Rooij and Nutricia/Zuid Hollandse Conservenfabriek, case no. 83/670/EEC (OJ L376, 31.12.83, p. 22).

3.3 19. Mr Nallen and Mr O'Toole were and are engaged for gain in the provision of services and are therefore, undertakings within the meaning of section 3 of the Act. The arrangements notified to the Authority in this case are concerned with the acquisition by Mr Nallen of Mr O'Toole's share in what had been a jointly owned business and various undertakings given by Mr O'Toole. The arrangements constitute an agreement between undertakings which applies to a part of the State.

(c) *Economic effects of the Agreement*

20. The present notification involves an agreement between two quite small undertakings. Following the Court of Justice decision in the *Volk v. Vervaecke* case,[4] the European Commission has taken the view that undertakings below a certain size are not subject to the competition rules on the grounds that they cannot, by virtue of their small side, be regarded as having any significant impact on competition.[5] This 'de-minimis' provision was an administrative response to the Court's decision in the Volk case that

> an agreement falls outside the scope of Article 85 when it has only an insignificant effect on the markets, taking into account the weak position which the persons have on the market of the product in question.

21. There is no provision in the Competition Act which would exclude small undertakings from the provisions of the Act. Section 4(1) of the Act prohibits agreements, decisions and concerted practices 'which have as their object or effect the prevention, restriction or distortion of competition in trade in any goods or services in the State or in any part of the State'. Given the size and distribution of population in Ireland it is possible that a number of relatively small undertakings could, by acting together, prevent, restrict or distort competition in a part of the State. The exclusion of small undertakings from the provisions of the Act could deny consumers in parts of the State the protection against anti-competitive activities which the Act provides. The present agreement cannot, therefore, be regarded as outside the scope of the Act on the grounds that it concerns undertakings which are so small that they cannot have any significant effect on competition.

22. There are currently four undertakings engaged in the retailing and rental of brown electrical goods in Belmullet. One of these, the ESB is a large State company which, *inter alia*, has a nationwide chain of stores retailing white and brown electrical goods. Apart from the ESB, the undertakings concerned are also engaged in the rental of brown electrical goods and of video films. Mr Nallen operates a separate video rental business in Belmullet. In many areas garages, grocers and various other outlets compete in the market for video film rentals. The number of competitors and the level of competition in the brown electrical goods market in Belmullet will remain unchanged as a result of this agreement.

23. The partnership arrangement between Mr Nallen and Mr O'Toole, which had ceased to operate prior to the coming into force of the Competition Act, may itself have reduced the number of competitors in the market. The Authority was not concerned with examining the partnership agreement in this case and, to date, no partnership agreements have been notified to it. The Authority does not regard partnerships *per se* as being in contravention of the Act. In certain circumstances, however, partnership agreements may be in breach of section 4(1) by virtue of certain restrictive clauses contained in them.

24. While the Authority is primarily concerned in this case with the market in the town of Belmullet and its environs, competition is not confined to this area. Traders based in Belmullet cannot prevent consumers from purchasing such goods elsewhere. There are undertakings engaged in this business in a number of nearby towns, namely; Crossmolina, Ballina and

4. *Volk v. Vervaecke* [1969] ECR 295.
5. Notice on agreements of minor importance, 1986 (OJ C231, 12.9.86, p. 2).

Castlebar. Many electrical discount stores based in Dublin advertise the prices of such appliances extensively in the national newspapers, so that there is no reason to suppose that consumers would be ignorant of the prices pertaining elsewhere. Similarly, as pointed out, one of the undertakings located in Belmullet operates on a nationwide basis. There is anecdotal evidence that consumers were in the past prepared to travel long distances to avail of cheaper prices for such items in Northern Ireland. An important consideration here is the fact that most of these items are relatively expensive and constitute 'one-off' purchases for households. It could not, for example, be reasonably argued that consumers in Belmullet have the option of going to Dublin or elsewhere to purchase bread.[6] 3.3

25. Undertakings located in Belmullet may face less competition from suppliers outside the area in the rental market as it may not be possible to rent brown electrical goods from suppliers outside the area. While the ESB is not involved in the rental of such goods it does sell them on attractive credit terms. It is claimed that the purchase of electrical goods on such terms from the ESB represents an alternative to renting for low income households and that there is some overlap between the retail and rental market as a result.

26. The European Commission has interpreted the term 'competition' to refer not only to actual competition but also to potential competition.[7] In the case of joint ventures the Commission has stated that 'the degree of potential competition depends largely on the nature of the product manufactured or the services offered by the joint venture.'[8] In general a restriction of competition arises if, in the absence of the restriction, there would have been a real likelihood of the restricted party engaging in the activity in question.[9] The restraint placed on Mr O'Toole by this agreement may be viewed as preventing a new competitor from entering the market.

27. The Commission view is in accord with modern economic theories of competition which stress the importance of potential as opposed to actual competition in a particular market.[10] The main conclusion of such theories is that, provided it is relatively easy for new competitors to enter and leave a market, this will be sufficient to produce competitive behaviour within that market. As the US Federal Trade Commission pointed out:

> the threat of new entry can be as potent a procompetitive force as its realisation.[11]

28. The threat of potential competition does not apply in all cases. Experience has shown that some markets where such considerations were thought to apply and which were thought to be 'contestable' are not in fact. The main advocates of 'contestability theory', as it is known in the economics literature, have themselves indicated that 'before anyone can legitimately use the analysis to infer that virtue reigns in some economic sector and that interference is therefore unwarranted, that person must first provide evidence that the arena in question is, in fact, highly contestable.'[12]

29. If incumbent firms perceive that new entry is unlikely and act with disregard for potential

6. This view is consistent with that expressed in the European Commission's notice on Agreements of Minor Importance that where the cost of transport is expensive relative to the value of the product this would tend to reduce the geographic extent of the market.
7. On this point see I. Van Bael and J.F. Bellis (1990); *Competition Law of the EEC*, 2nd ed., CCH Editions Ltd, para. 216.
8. European Commission (1983); 'Thirteenth Report on Competition Policy', para. 55.
9. See Bellamy and Child, op. cit., para. 5-012.
10. See in particular W.J. Baumol, J.C. Panzar and R.O. Willig (1982); 'Contestable Markets and the Theory of Industry Structure', San Diego University Press.
11. Echlin Manufacturing Corporation case.
12. See W.J. Baumol and R.O. Willig, 'Contestability: Developments Since the Book' in D.J. Morris, P.J.N. Sinclair, M.D.E. Slater and J.S. Vickers (eds.), 'Strategic Behaviour and Industrial Competition', Oxford University Press, 1986.

3.3 competitors, then it is not to the point that new entry is feasible. It follows that if the threat of potential entry is sufficiently strong to deter anti-competitive behaviour by undertakings in a particular market, the existence of restrictive practices such as price fixing or market sharing is, *a priori*, an indication that the threat of entry is unlikely or perceived to be unlikely by existing firms, and that the market is therefore not a contestable one.

30. Economic research has indicated that the prospect of entry is considerably reduced if entry costs are high and it is believed that such costs will not be recovered if a new entrant is forced to leave the market.

31. Contestability arguments would not apply where:

(a) impediments imposed by law or convention limited the scope for potential entry;

(b) arrangements existed which would prevent a potential new entrant from obtaining supplies required by them in order to enter the market;

(c) the costs of entry and the risk of losses entailed in having to withdraw from the market effectively deterred potential new entrants;

(d) the behaviour of undertakings within the market indicated that they regarded the threat of entry as unlikely.

32. In the case of this agreement the Authority is concerned with the market for the sale and rental of brown electrical goods and video films in the Belmullet area. This is a market where there appear to be few if any barriers to entry. There are no legal impediments which would prevent new competitors from entering the market. Mr Nallen has indicated that he does not have any exclusive distribution rights over particular brands. The costs of entry would appear to be relatively low. An undertaking need only rent relatively small premises and purchase a limited number of appliances for sale or rental. The bulk of such costs could be recouped relatively easily by selling the appliances somewhere else, so that the risk of suffering a major loss through having to withdraw from the market is slight.

33. It would appear therefore that anyone who wants to could enter this market relatively easily. Such a view of the business is supported by frequent references in trade journals complaining about the constant inflow of new entrants who are alleged to undermine the position of incumbent undertakings. The only apparent reason why additional competitors have not entered the market in Belmullet is that it is already regarded as operating competitively, and there is perceived to be no scope for a new competitor to enter the market by undercutting those already there. One undertaking has ceased to operate in Belmullet within the past three years, but it has been replaced by a new entrant.

34. This agreement will have no effect on the actual level of competition within the market as the number of competitors in Belmullet and adjacent towns will not be affected. The exclusion of Mr O'Toole may appear to involve some reduction of potential competition but only for a limited period. Indeed the longer term effect may be to increase the level of competition in the market if Mr O'Toole decides to re-enter the business in his own right at the end of three years. In the absence of barriers to other new entrants the agreement cannot be regarded as having any real effect on competition in this market.

(d) *The Non-Competition Clause*

35. The Authority now turns to the specific issue of the non-competition clause which is a key element of the present agreement. There are a series of EC cases dealing with similar agreements under Article 85(1).[13] The Commission view, which has been confirmed by the European Court of Justice, is that arrangements of this type are essential to secure the transfer of the goodwill of a business to a new owner. They are regarded as not involving any restriction on competition but as essential to allow the full transfer of ownership, provided their duration

13. Reuter/BASF, Nutricia/de Rooij and Nutricia/Zuid Hollandse Conservenfabriek, and Mecaniver-PPG (85/78/EEC) (OJ L35, 7.2.85, p. 54). The European Court of Justice dealt with an appeal in the Nutricia case, see *Remia BV and Others v. European Commission*, Case 42/84, [1985] ECR 2545.

and extent is only that which is necessary to secure the full transfer of the goodwill. If an agreement satisfies these criteria it has been found not to be in breach of Article 85(1). **3.3**

36. In the Nutricia and Reuter/BASF cases the Commission ruled that the agreements were in breach of Article 85(1) of the Treaty of Rome. The Commission decision was, however, based on the view that the duration of the non-competition clause was longer than was necessary for the proper transfer of the goodwill of the business to the new owner. It is clear from both decisions that a shorter non-competition clause would have been acceptable. Indeed in the Nutricia case, although the agreements had operated since 1979, the Commission ruled that the infringement only dated from 1983, four years after the agreement came into effect. The Commission decision in this case was upheld by the Court of Justice. In the Mecaniver-PPG case the Commission granted a negative clearance to the agreement for a specified period of time.

37. It is clear from the Commission's decisions that the length of time necessary for the full transfer of the goodwill of a business will vary from industry to industry.

> In general, the assessment under Article 85(1) of non-competition obligations imposed on sellers of businesses will depend on the particular circumstances of each individual case and no universal rule can therefore be established as to the permissible duration of such clauses.[14]

38. Thus what may be regarded as a reasonable length of time for a non-competition clause in one case may be regarded as excessive in another. In the former case such a clause would not be regarded as a breach of Article 85(1) whereas in the latter it would.

> In the absence of circumstances which deviate greatly from those in the Reuter/BASF or Nutricia cases, these decisions, however, indicate as [a] general guide that where the transfer of a business also involves the transfer of good-will and know-how, a period of approximately five years will normally be acceptable, whereas a period of approximately two years will normally apply if the sale involves only the transfer of good-will.[15]

39. In the Nutricia case the Commission indicated that among the factors to be taken into account in evaluating the duration of such clauses were:

(i) how frequently consumers in the relevant market change brands and type (in relation to the degree of brand loyalty shown by them),

(ii) for how long, after the sale of the business, the seller, without a restrictive clause, would be able to make a successful comeback to the market and regain his old customers.

40. The European Commission also decided in the Nutricia case that:

> The geographical scope of a non-competition clause also has to be limited to the extent which is objectively necessary to achieve the aforementioned goal. As a rule, it should therefore only cover the markets where the products concerned were manufactured or sold at the time of the agreements.

41. The view that such arrangements are essential in order to secure the transfer of the goodwill of a business and that they do not, therefore, involve a restriction of competition, appears to be well established under both US competition law and common law in the UK and Ireland. Such a view has prevailed in the US for almost one hundred years, following the decision of Judge Taft in the Addyston Pipe case which stated that:[16]

14. European Commission (1983); 'Thirteenth Report on Competition Policy', para. 88.
15. European Commission (1983); 'Thirteenth Report on Competition Policy', para. 88.
16. *United States v. Addyston Pipe & Steel Company et. al.*, 1898. See W. Breit and K. Elzinga (1989);

3.3 It was equally for the good of the public and trade, when partners dissolved, and one took the business, or they divided the business, that each partner might bind himself not to do anything in trade thereafter which would derogate from his grant of the interest conveyed to his former partner. Again, when two men became partners in a business, although their union might reduce competition, this effect was only an incident to the main purpose of a union of their capital, enterprise, and energy to carry on a successful business, and one useful to the community. . . . For the reasons given, then, covenants in partial restraint of trade are generally upheld as valid.

42. The EC competition rules are themselves based on US antitrust legislation.

43. The courts in Ireland and the UK have tended to take a favourable view of restraint clauses of this nature in the past. Such views were based on common law rather than competition legislation.

> The purchaser of a business can restrict the seller from engaging in similar enterprises in the future. The need to impose such a restriction is accepted by the courts because the proprietary interest in the goodwill of the business may be worthy of protection. But such restrictions will not be upheld should they be deemed to be wider than are reasonably necessary for that protection.[17]

44. In deciding whether the restraint imposed is reasonable, the courts have regarded two factors as particularly relevant. Firstly the buyer must establish a proprietary interest which the clause is seeking to protect. Secondly the clause must be reasonable in the light of all the circumstances of the case. In this respect the restraint must not go further than reasonably necessary for the protection of the purchaser's interest in point of space, time or subject-matter.[18]

45. It is therefore widely recognised in competition law in other countries and in our own common law that some restraint on a party disposing of all or part of his interest in a business is essential for the proper transfer of the goodwill of the business to take place, and that without the transfer of such goodwill, the transfer of ownership would be incomplete. Without such a restraint no proper transfer of goodwill could take place. The Authority agrees with this view. The restraint must, however, be limited in terms of its duration, geographical coverage and subject matter to that which is necessary to secure the adequate transfer of the goodwill. Provided this is the case, then clearly the intention of such a restraint is not to restrict competition in the market in question.

46. The restraint on Mr O'Toole in this agreement is for a period of three years, although the agreement involves a transfer of goodwill only. While the Authority would tend to agree at this stage with the EC view that a period of two years would generally be sufficient for the complete transfer of the goodwill of a business, it believes that a longer period is justified in this case. Consumers tend to purchase the products in question infrequently. In addition, in this case, close personal contact with customers was a major factor in the business. This is a small rural community where most consumers would know, or at least know of, Mr O'Toole as someone engaged in the particular business. In addition, Mr O'Toole is still active in business within the area. For these reasons it would appear that the period specified in the agreement is no more than is required to secure the complete transfer of the goodwill.

47. In this case the restraint applies to an area with a radius of 20 miles from the town of Belmullet and appears to correspond to the area within which Mr Nallen and Mr O'Toole

'The Antitrust Casebook: Milestones in Economic Regulation', 2nd ed., Dryden Press, New York, pp. 17-23.

17. B. Doolan (1989); 'A Casebook of Irish Contract Law', p. 254. See also the decision of Costello J in the case of *John Orr Ltd. v. Orr*, High Court 1987.

18. See E. McKendrick (1990); 'Contract Law', Macmillan, London.

previously carried on their business. Finally the restriction applies only to the lines of business in which Mr O'Toole was previously engaged in partnership with Mr Nallen. The restrictions involved are no more than are necessary to ensure the adequate transfer of the goodwill of the business to Mr Nallen and on those grounds are not in breach of section 4(1) of the Competition Act. 3.3

The Decision

48. Mr Nallen and Mr O'Toole are undertakings within the meaning of section 3 of the Competition Act and the arrangements in question constitute an agreement which applies within a part of the State.

49. The Authority believes that in this case the agreement cannot be said to prevent, restrict or distort competition as it involves no reduction in the number of actual competitors in the market in question, and does not reduce the threat of potential competition within this market.

50. In any case, on the specific issue of the non-competition clause, which is at the heart of this agreement, the Authority believes that such a clause is essential in the event of the sale of a business for the transfer of the goodwill of the business to the purchaser. Without such a restraint the purchaser could not be sure of obtaining all of the goodwill of the business for which he had paid and the seller would be unable to benefit by disposing of his share in a business which he had helped to build up. In the Authority's view therefore, such a clause is not in breach of section 4(1) of the Competition Act provided that the restrictions contained in such a clause or clauses are limited in terms of time, geographical coverage and subject matter to those which are necessary to secure the adequate transfer of the goodwill. The Authority believes that the present agreement between Mr Nallen and Mr O'Toole satisfies these criteria and that it does not offend against section 4(1) of the Competition Act 1991.

The Certificate

51. The Competition Authority has issued the following certificate:

> The Competition Authority certifies that in its opinion, on the basis of the facts in its possession, the agreement for the transfer of a business interest between Mr Nallen and Mr O'Toole of Belmullet, notified under section 7, does not offend against section 4(1) of the Competition Act 1991.

For the Competition Authority

Patrick Massey
Member

2 April 1992

3.4 Competition Authority Decision No. 3, Athlone Travel Ltd/Michael Stein Travel Ltd: 4 June 1992, Notification No. CA/12/92

Agreement for sale of business – Restriction on vendor competing with business for a period of three years – Whether such restriction necessary for the complete transfer of the goodwill of the business being sold – Competition Act 1991 (No. 24), sections 3, 4 and 7.

Facts: On 13 April 1992 notification was made to the Authority with a request for a certificate under section 4(2) of the Competition Act in respect of the sale by Athlone Travel Ltd ('Athlone') of the business of Blackpool Holidays to Michael Stein Travel Ltd ('Stein').

Athlone and Stein are tour operators and travels agents based in Ireland and engaged in the package tour and holiday business. Blackpool Holidays was a trade name used by Athlone for specialising in organising tours to Blackpool.

The product market is the sale of tours to Blackpool which market is part of the overall packaged tour/holiday market. While Blackpool Holidays had to compete with other tour operators for the Blackpool business, it must also compete with other holiday destinations. The notified agreement for the sale and purchase of the goodwill of Blackpool Holidays was made on 23 March 1992 and under its terms Athlone agreed not to engage in the business of organising tours to Blackpool, either directly or indirectly, for a period of three years from the date of the agreement. Notice of intention to make a favourable decision was published in the *Irish Times* on 8 May 1992 and no submissions were received from interested parties.

Decided by the Authority: In issuing a certificate under section 4(4) of the Competition Act in respect of the notified agreement that:

(1) Each of Athlone and Stein are undertakings within the meaning of the Competition Act and the agreement is an agreement between undertakings within the meaning of the Act.

(2) In the sale of a business some restriction on the seller re-entering the market is necessary in order to ensure the complete transfer of the goodwill of the business. If the restriction is limited in terms of its duration, geographical coverage and subject matter to that which is necessary for the complete transfer of the goodwill that restriction will not be in breach of section 4(1). In general a time limit of two years is considered adequate for transfer of goodwill but a restriction of longer duration would be accepted where it could be shown that such was necessary to secure the complete transfer of goodwill. A period of three years is justified in the current case on the basis that consumers tend to purchase the products in question infrequently and personal contact with the customer is an important factor of the business. The business of Athlone is relatively small and it only began operating tours to Blackpool in May 1991. It might therefore be relatively easy for Athlone to recapture quickly its former customers if it were to resume offering tours to Blackpool and for these reasons it would appear that the period specified in the agreement is no more than is required to secure the complete transfer of the goodwill.

(3) The restrictions are limited in terms of their geographical cover and subject matter to that which is necessary for the transfer of the goodwill and so the clause does not offend against section 4(1).

Case and Decisions Referred to **3.4**
Remia v. EC Commission (Case No. 42/84), [1985] ECR 2545, [1987] 1 CMLR 1
EC Commission Decision Reuter/BASF [1976] OJ L 254/40, [1976] 2 CMLR D44
EC Commission Decision Nutricia [1983] OJ L 376/22, [1984] 2 CMLR 165
EC Commission Decision Mecaniver/PPG [1985] OJ L 35/54, [1985] 3 CMLR 359
Competition Authority Decision No. 1, Nallen/O'Toole (Belmullet) – 2 April 1992 **3.3**

Competition Authority Decision of 4 June 1992 relating to a proceeding under section 4 of the Competition Act 1991
Notification No. CA/12/92 — Athlone Travel Ltd/Michael Stein Travel Ltd

Introduction

1. Notification was made with a request for a certificate under section 4(2) of the Competition Act 1991 by Athlone Travel Ltd. in respect of the sale of the business of Blackpool Holidays to Michael Stein Travel Ltd., on 13 April 1992.

2. Notice of intention to take a favourable decision was published in the Irish Times on 8 May 1992. No submissions were received from interested parties.

The Facts

(a) *The parties involved*

J. Athlone Travel and Michael Stein Travel are tour operators and travel agents based in Ireland and engaged in the package tour/holiday business. Blackpool Holidays was a trade name used by Athlone Travel for specialising in organising tours to Blackpool. Athlone Travel had operated this business since May 1991 with outlets in Athlone and at 12 Upper O'Connell Street, Dublin. Michael Stein Travel has its principal place of business at 77 Lower Camden Street, Dublin.

(b) *The product and the market*

The agreement concerns the sale of the business of tours to Blackpool. Blackpool Holidays arranged for travel to and from Blackpool and accommodation there for its clients. This service is a part of the overall package tour-holiday market in the sense that Blackpool is one out of a large number of places that consumers may choose to go for a holiday. There are a number of other firms who compete in providing tours to Blackpool. These include P.A.B. Travel, Quay Travel and Arrow Tours. Travel agents would book trips to Blackpool for their clients through one of these tour operators. In addition it is of course possible for consumers to arrange trips to Blackpool themselves, by purchasing boat or plane tickets directly and booking their own accommodation. Blackpool has to compete, for example, with other British destinations and with package deals to sun holiday destinations. It has been suggested by the parties that up to 10,000 people may go to Blackpool from Ireland. In 1991 Blackpool Holidays arranged trips for approximately 800 people.

The Agreement

The agreement for the sale and purchase of the goodwill of Blackpool Holidays was made on 23 March 1992. Under the terms of the agreement Athlone Travel has agreed not to engage in the business of organising tours to Blackpool for a period of three years. This provision is set out in clause 3.4 which states:

> that the Assignor will not during the period of three years from the date hereof directly or indirectly carry on or be concerned or interested in the business to which the Goodwill in Ireland relates and the Assignor will use its best efforts to secure to the Assignee the benefit of the connection and custom thereof but not so as to be required to waive any

3.4 expense in so doing. It is agreed by the assignor that the restrictive covenant hereon is reasonable and necessary for the legitimate protection of the Goodwill hereby acquired by the Assignee.

6. The First Schedule to the agreement defines the term Goodwill as follows:

> All the Goodwill attaching to the Business Blackpool Holidays including the Business and Trade Name 'Blackpool Holidays' together with all the Intellectual Property Rights belonging to the business Blackpool Holidays including all intellectual and industrial property rights including, without limitation, the trade marks, registered designs, copyrights and business names in any part of the world and copyright in all drawings, plans, specifications, design and computer software owned by the Assignor and used in and for the purposes of the business and all know how and confidential information so owned and used.

Assessment

(a) *Section 4(1)*

7. Section 4(1) of the Competition Act states that 'all agreements between undertakings, decisions by associations of undertakings and concerted practices which have as their object or effect the prevention, restriction or distortion of competition in trade in any goods or services in the State or in any part of the State are prohibited and void'.

(b) *The Undertakings and the Agreement*

8. Section 3(1) of the Competition Act defines an undertaking as 'a person being an individual, a body corporate or an unincorporated body of persons engaged for gain in the production, supply or distribution of goods or the provision of a service.' The present decision involves two limited companies engaged in the business of selling package tours/holidays on the Irish market. They are both undertakings within the meaning of the Act. The agreement for the sale and purchase of the business of Blackpool Holidays is an agreement between undertakings within the meaning of the Act.

(c) *Restraints on Competition*

9. In the Authority's view the only issue arising under the Competition Act in respect of this agreement relates to clause 3.4 which restricts Athlone Travel from re-entering the market for tours/holidays to Blackpool. The Authority has previously set out its views on such clauses in its decision on Nallen/O'Toole.[1] In that decision the Authority indicated that in the case of the sale of a business some restriction on the seller re-entering the market was necessary in order to ensure the complete transfer of the goodwill of the business. It stated that, provided the restriction was limited in terms of its duration, geographical coverage and subject matter to that which was necessary for the complete transfer of the goodwill, then the restriction was not in breach of section 4(1) of the Act. In this respect the Authority's decision was in line with that taken by the European Commission in a number of cases under Article 85 of the Treaty of Rome on which section 4 of the Competition Act is based.[2]

10. The Authority indicated that it would normally regard a time-limit of two years as being adequate for the transfer of goodwill. It went on to state, however, that it would accept a

1. Notification no. CA/8/91 — Nallen/O'Toole (Belmullet), decision of 2 April 1992.
2. Reuter/BASF (76/743/EEC, OJ L254, 17.9.76, p. 40), Nutricia/deRooji and Nutricia/Zuid Hollandse Conservenfabriek (83/670/EEC, OJ L376, 31.12.83, p. 22), and Mecaniver-PPG (85/78/EEC, OJ L35, 7.2.85, p. 54). The European Court of Justice dealt with an appeal in the Nutricia case. See *Remia BV and Others v. European Commission*, Case 42/84, [1985] ECR 2545.

restriction of longer duration, where it could be shown that this was necessary to secure the complete transfer of goodwill. In Nallen/O'Toole it accepted a restriction of three years. 3.4

11. The present agreement involves a restriction for three years as in Nallen/O'Toole. The Authority believes that a period of three years is justified in this case for similar reasons to those outlined in Nallen/O'Toole. Consumers tend to purchase the products in question infrequently perhaps once a year. In addition personal contact with customers is an important factor in the business. The business is relatively small and claims to have had only 800 customers during 1991. In addition, although Athlone Travel only began operating tours to Blackpool in May 1991, it is still active in the travel business. It might therefore be relatively easy for it to recapture quickly its former customers if it were to resume offering tours to Blackpool. For these reasons it would appear that the period specified in the agreement is no more than is required to secure the complete transfer of the goodwill.

12. The restriction is limited in terms of its geographical coverage and subject matter to that which is necessary for the transfer of the goodwill. Clause 3.4 of the agreement requires that Athlone Travel not 'directly or indirectly carry on or be concerned or interested in the business to which the Goodwill in Ireland relates'.

13. Athlone Travel and Michael Stein Travel are undertakings within the meaning of section 3 of the Competition Act and the arrangements in question constitute an agreement which applies within the State.

14. The Authority believes that the present agreement cannot be considered to prevent, restrict or distort competition in the State or any part of the State.

15. In the case of a sale of business, some restriction on the seller is essential in order to ensure the complete transfer of the goodwill for which the purchaser has paid. A non-competition clause in a sale of business agreement which is limited in terms of duration, geographic coverage and subject matter to what is necessary to ensure the complete transfer of the goodwill of the business does not, in the Authority's opinion, prevent, restrict or distort competition. The Authority believes that the non-competition clause in the present agreement between Athlone Travel Ltd and Michael Stein Travel Ltd satisfies the above criteria and that it does not offend against section 4(1) of the Competition Act 1991.

The Certificate

16. The Competition Authority has issued the following certificate:

> The Competition Authority certifies that, in its opinion, on the basis of the facts in its possession, the agreement between Athlone Travel Ltd. and Michael Stein Travel Ltd. (CA/12/92), for the sale of the business Blackpool Holidays, notified on 13 April 1992 under section 7, does not offend against section 4(1) of the Competition Act 1991.

For the Competition Authority

Patrick Massey
Member

4 June 1992

3.5 Competition Authority Decision No. 6, Woodchester Bank Ltd/UDT Bank Ltd: 4 August 1992, Notification No. CA/10/92

Share sale agreement – Vendors covenant that its related companies will not engage in the State in instalment credit or vehicle leasing for one year – Definition of market – Segment of lending market – Whether mergers affected by section 4(1) – Recognition of uncertainty – Intention of legislature – When a merger offends against section 4(1) – Whether restrictions necessary to ensure the complete transfer of the goodwill – Articles 85 and 86 of the Treaty of Rome, EC Regulation 4064/89, Article 3 – Central Bank Act (No. 24) 1971, section 9 – Mergers, Take-overs and Monopolies (Control) Act (No. 17) 1978 sections 1 and 3 – Central Bank Act (No. 16) 1989 and Competition Act (No. 24) 1991 sections 3, 4, 5 and 7

Facts: On 20 March 1992 notification was made to the Competition Authority of an agreement between Hill Samuel & Co. BV ('HSBV') and Woodchester Bank Ltd ('Woodchester Bank') for the sale of UDT Bank Ltd ('UDT') together with the request for a certificate under section 4(4) of the Competition Act or failing that a licence under section 4(2).

Woodchester Bank is a wholly owned subsidiary of Woodchester Investments plc which was founded in 1977 and is now a listed company on the Stock Exchange. 45% of its shares are owned by a subsidiary of Credit Lyonnais. Woodchester Bank is licensed under the Central Bank Acts.

UDT is a bank licensed under the Central Bank Acts also and is a wholly owned subsidiary of HSBV a subsidiary of the UK listed TSB Group plc.

Both Woodchester and UDT operate largely in the market for wholesale deposits and both Woodchester and UDT offered a range of personal and commercial lending services. Leasing, instalment credit and hire purchase arrangements were offered in particular by both UDT and Woodchester. Links between leasing companies and motor car dealers are apparent in the market.

The agreement whereby Woodchester would purchase the share capital of UDT from HSBV required HSBV to undertake that its related companies would not engage in the State in the instalment credit or motor vehicle leasing business for one year. In addition a three year restriction on the soliciting of orders from any person, firm or company who has been a customer of UDT during the three years prior to completion was also imposed. The employment of employees of UDT by HSBV and its related companies was the subject of an additional covenant given by HSBV to Woodchester. A three year restriction on the use of the business names of UDT by HSBV and its related companies was also undertaken by HSBV.

Submissions The notifying parties argued that the acquisition agreement was not reviewable under the Competition Act 1991 because it had been approved under the Mergers Act and the Central Bank Acts. It was also submitted that the acquisition of the entire share capital of a company could only be reviewed as a 'concentration' and therefore only under section 5 of the Competition Act 1991. The notifying parties argued that the restrictions in any event were fair and reasonable.

Decided by the Authority: In issuing a certificate:

(1) Hill Samuel & Co. BV is engaged for gain in the provision of services through

its subsidiaries and both parties to the notified agreement are undertakings. **3.5**

(2) A merger or take-over may prevent, restrict or distort competition.

(3) Mergers frequently include a number of ancillary clauses which restrict competition and the Authority does not believe that the legislature intended that these restrictions would escape the prohibition of section 4(1).

(4) The thresholds which are applicable to the notification of a merger under the Mergers, Take-overs and Monopolies (Control) Act 1978 are not relevant to the application of the Competition Act to mergers.

(5) A merger between two licensed banks is not notifiable under the Mergers, Take-overs and Monopolies (Control) Act 1978.

(6) EC Regulation 4064/89 does not require that an undertaking acquire a 100% shareholding in another undertaking for it to constitute a concentration.

(7) The reduction in the number of competitors arising from a merger does not necessarily restrict competition contrary to section 4(1). The economic circumstances in the relevant market must be taken into account in any such assessment.

(8) Before a merger offends against section 4(1) it must be shown that it would, or would be likely to result in an actual diminution of competition in the market concerned. A merger whereby competition would lessen and thereby allow the merged undertaking to raise prices would offend against section 4(1). Other factors could also be taken into account in assessing a merger such as the ease of entry into the relevant market from new competitors.

(9) The apparent 40% share of the Irish car leasing market held by Woodchester raised some concern for the Authority in assessing the merger. The availability of alternative finance for vehicle purchasing suggests that the motor vehicle leasing market should not be regarded as a separate market.

(10 The restraint of trade provisions (described in the facts) do not breach section 4(1) of the Act. The restrictions are limited to that which is necessary to ensure the complete transfer of the goodwill.

Cases, Decisions and Reports referred to

BAT & Reynolds v. Commission (known as *Philip Morris* case – 142 & 156/84) [1987] ECR 4487; [1988] 4 CMLR 24

Deane v. Voluntary Health Insurance Board [1992] 2 IR 319 **1.1**

EC Commission Decision – Mecaniver/PPG – 12.12.84 [1985] OJ L35/54; [1985] 3 CMLR 359

Competition Authority Decision No. 1 – 2.4.1992 – Nallen/O'Toole (Belmullet) **3.3**

Competition Authority Decision No. 2 14.5.1992 – AGF/Irish Life Holdings plc. **1.3.1**

EC Commission [1988] 17th Report on Competition Policy – para. 101

EC Commission [1991] 20th Report on Competition Policy – para. 118

Fair Trade Commission Report of Competition Law, April 1991, para. 12.1 (pl 7080)

Competition Authority Decision of 4 August 1992 relating to a proceeding under section 4 of the Competition Act
Notification No. CA/10/92 — Woodchester Bank Ltd./UDT Bank Ltd.

Introduction

1. An agreement between Hill Samuel & Co. B.V. and Woodchester Bank Ltd for the sale of UDT Bank Ltd was notified to the Competition Authority on 20 March 1992. While the notified agreement is between Hill Samuel & Co. BV and Woodchester Bank Ltd, the

3.5 notification includes Hill Samuel Bank Ltd and Woodchester Investments plc, which are the parents of the main parties. The notification was in respect of a certificate, or in the event of refusal by the Authority to issue a certificate, a licence.

2. Notice of intention to take a favourable decision was published in 'The Irish Times' on 3 July 1992. No submissions were received from interested parties.

The Facts

The Parties

3. The Woodchester Group was founded in 1977. It initially concentrated on the business of leasing office equipment. The Company's development was seen to be limited by capital constraints and so a decision was taken to float Woodchester on the Unlisted Securities Market (USM) in 1982 to raise additional capital. Woodchester raised further capital when it was floated on the USM in London in 1983. Woodchester took over 2 Cork based motor finance companies in 1984. In 1986, it acquired Hamilton Leasing Ireland which was the biggest non-bank leasing company in Ireland.

4. In 1987 Woodchester expanded into the banking sector with the acquisition of Bowmaker Bank. It has continued its policy of expansion into the banking sector with the acquisition of Trinity Bank in 1988 and Mercantile Credit in 1991. The company has also expanded into the UK market by purchasing a licensed bank and a leasing company.

5. Woodchester Investments plc (Woodchester) is a public limited company incorporated in Ireland. It is a holding and investment company with a number of subsidiaries and associated companies operating in Ireland, Woodchester Bank Ltd, and the UK. Its shares are listed on the Dublin and London Stock Exchange; 45% of its issued share capital is owned by Campagnie Rhodanienne de Gestion, a subsidiary of the French bank, Credit Lyonnais. The other major shareholders are Irish Life Assurance plc., AIB Investment Managers Ltd and the Standard Life Assurance Company. Pre-tax profits in 1991 were £39.6m, an increase of 34% over the previous year's figure.

6. Woodchester Bank Ltd (Woodchester Bank) is a wholly owned subsidiary of Woodchester of which it is the principal subsidiary operating in Ireland. It is a licensed bank under the Central Bank Acts 1942-84. It was acquired by Woodchester in 1987 when it traded as Bowmaker Bank Ltd.

7. UDT Bank Ltd (UDT) was founded in 1937 and is a licensed bank under the Central Bank Acts. In 1989 UDT acquired from the Bank of Nova Scotia the entire issued share capital of First Southern Bank Ltd. The business of First Southern was similar to UDT except that it focused on small to medium sized companies. Its business had arisen in large part from personal contacts.

8. UDT Bank Ltd is a wholly owned subsidiary of Hill Samuel & Co. B.V. which is in turn a subsidiary of Hill Samuel Bank Ltd, and ultimately of the UK TSB Group plc. UDT's principal subsidiaries in Ireland are UDT Leaseline Ltd which provides lease finance and United Dominions Trust (Ireland) Ltd which provides residential mortgages.

9. Hill Samuel & Co. B.V. is a company incorporated in Holland which is the immediate parent of UDT. It exists solely as a holding company. Its ultimate holding company is TSB Group plc., a public limited company incorporated in the UK, whose shares are listed on the London and Dublin Stock Exchange.

10. Hill Samuel Bank Ltd is a limited company incorporated in the UK. It trades in the UK as a licensed bank. Its ultimate holding company is TSB Group plc. Hill Samuel Bank (Ireland) Ltd is a licensed bank under the Central Bank Acts engaged in banking business in Ireland.

The Products

11. The activities of Woodchester Bank are general banking activities including deposits, secured and unsecured lending, foreign exchange transaction, commercial paper, personal

loans, sales aid finance, leasing of office equipment and vehicles, instalment credit and farm finance. 3.5

12. The services offered by UDT include the acceptance of deposits, instalment credit to business and to the public, leasing, hire purchase and bank loans.

The Market

13. Banks may be regarded as multi-product firms, which accept deposits and make loans. Admittedly this is something of a simplification as both of these activities may be broken down into a number of distinct markets. It nevertheless represents a useful starting point for considering the relevant market. Banks also provide a third type of product namely cash transmission services which are considered later.

14. Traditionally the Irish financial system was composed of a variety of different types of institution each confined primarily by regulation to a particular range of activities. The main financial groupings comprised the associated and non-associated banks, the building societies, the Trustee Savings Banks and other State owned institutions. The latter group included the Post Office Savings Banks, the ACC and the ICC. In addition, the life assurance companies operated in some areas of the financial services market.

15. The associated banks are essentially clearing banks which provide a broad range of retail and wholesale banking services and were traditionally responsible for the money transmission system. The name derives from a provision of the 1942 Central Bank Act and is a carry over from the banks' status as shareholders in the Currency Commission, the forerunner of the Central Bank. A series of mergers during the 1960s reduced the number of associated banks from eight to four. Two of these are Irish owned institutions while the other two, which are much smaller in terms of size, are subsidiaries of overseas banking groups. Entry to retail banking was effectively inhibited other than by means of a takeover.

16. In the 1960s there were virtually no controls on the establishment of branches or subsidiaries by foreign banks who wished to concentrate on wholesale banking. In the decade up to 1975 a number of major European and North American banks opened branches in Ireland. The success of such institutions in capturing business from the associated banks, caused the latter to establish non-associated bank subsidiaries of their own. The initial development of the non-associated banks was prompted by the failure of the associated banks to respond adequately to the growing demand for new types of product. The non-associated banks entered the market to provide the specialised lending and deposit services which the associated banks had failed to supply.

17. The Spring 1992 Central Bank Bulletin lists 23 non-associated banks among its list of reporting institutions in the merchant and commercial banks category with a further 8 in the industrial banks category. Some banking groups have both industrial and merchant and commercial banking subsidiaries. Woodchester Investment Bank is included in the latter category while Woodchester Bank and UDT are listed as industrial banks.

18. Building societies traditionally specialised in the business of raising funds from members and depositors for lending to members largely for house purchase by way of a mortgage. The societies have been very successful in attracting deposits at the expense of the banks. The assets of the largest society are believed to exceed the assets within the State of the two smaller associated banks. Until relatively recently societies were not permitted to engage in unsecured lending and were thus not regarded as competing with banks in the lending market. There are 8 societies included in the Central Bank's list of reporting institutions.

19. State owned financial institutions may be divided into three groupings, the Trustee Savings Banks (TSBs), the Post Office Savings Bank and the ACC and ICC. The latter two institutions were originally established to provide credit in order to encourage the development of particular sectors, namely agriculture and small business. The Post Office Savings Bank traditionally confined itself to attracting deposits from small savers and lent virtually all of its resources to the Exchequer.

3.5 Since the 1960s the TSBs have gradually expanded their branch network. Over the same period their number has declined as a result of a series of amalgamations. Recently the two remaining TSB groups combined to form a single entity. Traditionally TSBs were legally obliged to lend most of their resources to the Exchequer.

20. Some idea of the relative size of the different types of institutions can be gauged from their respective shares of total assets which is given in Table 1.

Table 1: Assets of Credit Institutions *vis-à-vis* residents

	%
Associated Banks	40.2
Non-Associated Banks	36.5
Building Societies	15.9
Others	7.4

The data is for 31 December 1991. Others in this case includes the ACC, ICC and the TSB. Source: Central Bank bulletin, Spring 1992.

21. The associated banks account for over 40% of the assets of credit institutions with the non-associated banks having almost 37% and building societies 16%. The combined assets of Woodchester Bank and UDT represent 2.7% of the total assets of credit institutions. The Business and Finance listing of the top 1000 Irish companies for 1991 ranked Woodchester Investments as the ninth largest financial institution in terms of assets. UDT was ranked 36.

22. The life assurance companies also compete in the market for savings. Although their products are not close substitutes for deposits with banks or building societies, fiscal incentives have in the past favoured savings with life assurance companies.

23. Hire purchase companies also compete in the lending market. Such companies may generally be regarded as engaging in personal lending and in small scale commercial lending. There are 33 companies listed as hire purchase companies in the Central Bank's list of reporting institutions.

24. During the past decade many of the distinctions between the different types of institution have begun to break down. Building societies are now permitted to engage in unsecured lending up to certain limits while the obligation on the TSB to lend the bulk of its resources to the Exchequer has been relaxed, allowing it to compete in the market for personal and corporate loans. The ACC and ICC have shifted toward providing a broader range of banking services to a greater number of customers. The associated banks have become far more active in the home mortgage market.

25. The development of Woodchester and UDT is described in paras 3-8 above. The parties have indicated that the market in which Woodchester Bank and UDT compete is the market for banking services within the State. The principal services provided by them include deposits, personal and commercial loans, lease and hire purchase finance.

26. As already pointed out banks may generally be described as being in the business of accepting deposits and making loans. In reality the market is somewhat more differentiated than this, although as para 24 above indicated, these distinctions are becoming less important over time.

27. Woodchester Bank has a network of ten branches throughout the country, while UDT has a small branch network located principally in the Munster region. Thus on the deposit side both institutions effectively operate in the market for wholesale rather than retail deposits. Wholesale deposits include commercial and personal deposits which must generally exceed a certain amount and be placed on deposit for a specified period of time. Retail deposits in contrast involve no minimum amount and may be withdrawn virtually on demand. Both associated and non-associated banks have traditionally competed in the wholesale deposit

market. More recently state institutions such as the ACC and ICC have entered this market along with the building societies. Societies offer higher interest rates for deposits above a certain size in an attempt to attract funds of this type and have begun to pay higher rates on funds deposited for fixed periods. 3.5

28. Both Woodchester Bank and UDT offer a range of lending products including personal and commercial loans, lease and hire purchase finance, personal and commercial mortgages, and term loans. All licensed banks compete in the market for commercial loans. The easing of restrictions on building societies' permitted activities has allowed them to enter this market also. In addition larger companies have always had the option of borrowing overseas. There has also been a growing tendency for large companies to lend directly to other large companies so that in the market for large commercial loans Irish based banks face competition from non-banks and foreign based institutions.

29. The personal lending market was traditionally distorted by quantitative credit guidelines and other controls. These led both to credit rationing and disintermediation. The latter term describes the process by which regulations divert business from regulated institutions to less regulated or unregulated competitors. Credit guidelines have not been applied since the mid 1980s. Together with the removal of restrictions on unsecured lending by the building societies and the easing of the obligation on the TSBs to lend most of their resources to the Exchequer, this has increased competition in the personal lending market.

30. Data on total lending and deposits of credit institutions is included in the Central Bank's quarterly bulletins. The distribution of non government deposits and lending by the different types of institution is given in Table 2.

Table 2: Private Sector Loans and Deposits by Credit Institution

	% Deposits	% Loans
Associated Banks	43.2	35.5
Non-Association Banks	22.1	32.2
Societies	25.9	20.7
Hire Purchase Companies	—	3.6
Other	8.8	8.0
Total	100.0	100.0
Woodchester	2.0	2.2
UDT	1.8	1.1
Woodchester & UDT	3.8	3.3

Data relate to 31.12.1991

Others include the TSB, ACC and ICC.

Woodchester's share of the deposit market is based on the figure for deposits in the consolidated balance sheet of Woodchester Investments plc.
Source: Central Bank bulletin Spring 1992 and Woodchester Investments Annual Report 1991.

31. The four associated banks accounted for 43% of non Government deposits and 36% of non Government lending in 1991. The non– associated banks accounted for 22% of deposits but their share of lending was almost as large as that of the associated banks at 32%. Building societies accounted for 26% of deposits and 21% of lending. Woodchester accounted for 2.0% of non-Government deposits with credit institutions in 1991 while UDT accounted for a further 1.8%. On this basis the enlarged Woodchester Group would have 3.8% of the total non-Government deposit market. In para. 27 it was indicated that Woodchester and UDT operated

3.5 largely in the market for wholesale deposits although UDT does have a branch network in the Munster region which may be regarded as operating to some extent in the retail deposit market. It is not possible to obtain separate information on the value of wholesale deposits. Nevertheless it would appear that its share of the market is relatively small.

32. The table does not include deposits with the Post Office Savings Bank. Clearly the POSB is in competition with other financial institutions in seeking to attract deposits. At the same time some POSB savings schemes involve placing funds on deposit for a lengthy period of time and they cannot, therefore, be regarded as close substitutes for deposits with a bank or a building society. If deposits with the POSB were included then Woodchester's share of the deposit market would be reduced.

33. Woodchester Bank accounted for 2.2% of total loans and advances in 1991 while UDT had a market share of just over 1%. This would give the enlarged group a market share of just over 3.3%. The lending market is somewhat more fragmented than the deposit market, however, with some institutions specialising mainly in particular areas of business.

34. Woodchester Investments plc originally developed as a leasing company. Essentially under a leasing arrangement the finance company rents the asset in question to the lessee while retaining ownership of that asset. Leasing is frequently regarded as an alternative to instalment credit or hire purchase although it differs from such finance in a number of respects. Traditionally the bulk of the leasing business of Woodchester Investments plc involved office equipment and motor vehicles with most of the customers being commercial organisations. In recent years there has been a growing trend toward motor vehicle leasing by private individuals and it has come to be regarded as an alternative means of 'buying' a car.

35. Historically the leasing company, as the owner, could avail of capital allowances on the asset, thereby reducing its tax liabilities. Leasing arrangements can appear attractive. They may appear lower than repayments on a conventional loan but it has to be kept in mind that they are in effect only rental payments so that it is difficult to make comparisons between the two. The cost may also be lower than loan repayments because, as the leasing company retains ownership of the asset, the risk of default is considerably reduced.

36. There appear to be some links between leasing companies and motor car dealers. In some instances for example, leasing companies may finance dealers' stocks. Such arrangements are not a part of the present notified agreement. The Authority regards any such arrangements which may exist as constituting entirely separate agreements which have not been notified. The present assessment, therefore, offers no view as to whether or not such arrangements offend against section 4(1) of the Competition Act.

37. In sum, banks operate in the markets for deposits and lending. Both these markets may be further broken down into different segments. On the deposits side both Woodchester and UDT concentrated on the wholesale deposit market although UDT was also active in the retail deposit market. On the lending side both institutions offered a wide range of personal and commercial lending services. Both operated in the leasing business while UDT was also engaged in the residential mortgage market.

The Agreement

38. The agreement for the sale and purchase of UDT was made on 10 March 1992. Clause 3 of the agreement provides that:

> Subject to the terms and conditions hereof and for the consideration hereinafter appearing the Vendor as beneficial owner hereby agrees to sell or procure the sale and the Purchaser hereby agrees to purchase all the Shares with effect on and from the Completion Date free from all options, charges, liens or encumbrances and with all rights now or hereinafter attaching thereto including rights to all dividends and distributions declared, made or paid on the Shares or applicable to or deriving from such rights thereafter.

39. The agreement also includes several non-competition provisions. Clause 9.01 states that: 3.5

The Vendor hereby undertakes and covenants to the Purchaser:

9.01.1 that it will not and will procure that all the Related Companies will not within the Republic of Ireland during the period of one year after Completion carry on or be involved directly or indirectly or be engaged involved or interested whether as principal, shareholder (including as a shareholder in a company which is itself a shareholder in a company engaged, involved or interested in the undermentioned businesses), partner, employee, agent, or otherwise in the business of Instalment Credit or Motor Vehicle Leasing except (i) as a shareholder in a public company whose shares are quoted or dealt in any recognised Stock Exchange and holding not more than 5% of the share capital of such public company or (ii) in respect of shareholdings held by the Related Companies which shareholdings are not beneficially owned by or held in trust for any of the Related Companies;

9.01.2 that it will not and will procure that all the Related Companies will not within the Republic of Ireland during the period of three years after Completion either on their own account or on behalf of any other person firm or company knowingly solicit orders in connection with Instalment Credit or Motor Vehicle Leasing from any person firm or company who has been a customer of the Company during the three years immediately prior to Completion;

9.01.3 that it will not and will procure that all the Related Companies will not within the period of three years after Completion solicit, endeavour to entice away, employ, offer to employ or engage any executive or employee other than clerical or secretarial employees of the Company at the date hereof provided that this Clause 9.01.3 shall not be construed so as to prevent or restrict the Related Companies from employing any such person who approaches it or initiates a request to it for employment without direct solicitation on its part or so as to prevent or restrict it from soliciting or initiating an offer of employment to any such person whose employment with the Company has been terminated or whose employment will terminate on the expiration of any notice period in relation to which notice of termination had been served at such time or from employing any person who applies to a Related Company for employment in response to a public advertisement offering employment within such Related Company;

9.01.4 that it will not and will procure that all Related Companies will not within the period of three years after Completion carry on or be concerned engaged or interested as aforesaid in any business in the Republic of Ireland under the name or style of 'UDT', 'United Dominions Trust', 'First Southern Bank' or 'Endeavour Securities' or any variation, derivative or abbreviation thereof or any misleadingly similar name in any corporate name, sign, logo, emblem, letterhead, advertisement or promotional material.'

Views of the Parties

40. The notifying parties have stated that the acquisition is not reviewable under the Competition Act 1991, because it has already been notified and approved under the Mergers Act. They argue that an acquisition reviewable under the latter Act is not reviewable under the Competition Act. They also state that if such transactions were reviewable under the Competition Act this would introduce serious uncertainty into commercial transactions. The acquisition has been notified to and approved by the Minister for Industry and Commerce and the Central Bank under the Mergers and Central Bank Acts respectively.

3.5 41. They also state that 'where the acquisition is of a one hundred percent interest in another company and this results in a concentration, then, subject to EC Council Regulation 4069/89, the acquisition may only be reviewed under Article 86 of the Treaty. . . . By analogy, as sections 4 and 5 of the Competition Act are essentially identical to Articles 85 and 86 of the Treaty, an acquisition of a one hundred percent interest in another company which results in a concentration may only be reviewed under the Competition Act (if at all) under section 5 of the Act'.

> . . . the parties submit that the acquisition by Woodchester of the entire issued share capital of UDT constitutes a concentration and, therefore, may only be reviewed under the Competition Act (if at all) under section 5 of the Act. On this basis, the parties submit that the acquisition is not subject to review by the Competition Authority under the Competition Act. In particular, on notifications under the Competition Act, the Competition Authority reviews agreements in the context of section 4 of the Competition Act and not section 5'.

42. The notifying parties have stated that 'The restrictions in section 9 of the agreement are fair and reasonable, and do not have either as their object or effect the prevention, restriction or distortion of competition in the markets to which they relate, so that the restrictions do not infringe section 4(1) of the Competition Act 1991.' They referred to EC case law in support of their arguments.

Assessment

(a) *Section 4(1)*

43. Section 4(1) of the Competition Act states that 'all agreements between undertakings, decisions by associations of undertakings and concerted practices which have as their object or effect the prevention, restriction or distortion of competition in trade in any goods or services in the State or in any part of the State are prohibited and void'.

(b) *The Undertakings*

44. Section 3(1) of the Competition Act defines an undertaking as 'a person being an individual, a body corporate or an unincorporated body of persons engaged for gain in the production, supply or distribution of goods or the provision of a service.' Woodchester Bank is a body corporate engaged for gain in the provision of banking services and is therefore an undertaking within the meaning of the Act. Hill Samuel & Co. BV is a holding company. It is a body corporate which is a subsidiary of Hill Samuel Bank. The Authority decided in AGF/Irish Life Holdings[1] that a holding company was an undertaking within the meaning of section 3(1) of the Act, as it was engaged for gain in the provision of services through its subsidiaries. Hill Samuel & Co. BV is an undertaking.

(c) *The Agreement*

45. The notified arrangements concern an agreement whereby Woodchester Bank has acquired from Hill Samuel the shares of UDT Bank Ltd. The agreement also includes a number of 'non- competition' provisions. The arrangements constitute an agreement between undertakings within the State.

(d) *Applicability of section 4(1) to an Acquisition*

Interpretation of the Act

46. The parties have argued that the arrangements constitute a 'merger or takeover' within the meaning of section 5 of the Mergers, Takeovers and Monopolies (Control) Act 1978 (the

1. Notification No. CA/7/92 — AGF/Irish Life Holdings, decision of 14 May 1992.

Mergers Act) as amended by the Competition Act for reasons already given in paras 40-41. **3.5**

47. The present notification raises some complex questions regarding the treatment of mergers under the Competition Act and the relationship between that Act and the Mergers Act on which the Authority is required to give its views.

48. The FTC report on Competition Law[2] specifically addressed the mergers issue in recommending a law based on Articles 85 and 86 of the Treaty of Rome and stated that:

> In addition a merger or a takeover is often an agreement which may have the effect of restricting or distorting competition. Such mergers would be prohibited under the provisions of Article 85. Other mergers might be prohibited under Article 86. If separate merger and take-over provisions are to continue, there must be a specific exclusion for mergers and take-overs which would otherwise be caught by Articles 85 or 86.

49. It is clear to the Authority that a merger or takeover may, on occasion, prevent, restrict or distort competition. Indeed this is one of the reasons why there are legislative controls in relation to mergers. The parties have argued for a number of reasons that it cannot have been the legislature's intention that mergers, which had been notified to, and approved by, the Minister, would be reviewable under the rules of competition as set out in the Competition Act. The Authority considers that there is some merit to this argument. The important point, however, is that section 4(1) specifically refers to 'all agreements'. There are no exceptions provided for in the Section. In arguing that mergers are not reviewable under section 4 of the Competition Act the parties are implying that the Section be read as 'all agreements except mergers subject to review under the Mergers Acts'. In the Authority's opinion the legislature's intention is clear from the form of words chosen. Having specified 'all agreements', it seems reasonable to conclude that the legislature would have specified exceptions if that had been its intention. It is relevant in this context that in a recent Supreme Court decision which ruled that the VHI was an undertaking within the meaning of section 3(1) of the Competition Act, Finlay CJ stated that: 'If the legislature had intended that any undertaking which, though engaged in the supply of goods or services, was not so engaged with a view to making profits, it seems to me that it would unambiguously have said so, and the word we would see would be 'profit' instead of 'gain'.'[3] It is relevant in this regard that the Competition Act is a significant new departure in Irish law which was designed to introduce a blanket prohibition on all anti-competitive agreements.

50. Mergers frequently include a number of ancillary clauses which may themselves involve some restriction on competition. If notifiable mergers are not reviewable under the Competition Act, then a number of practices which would be prohibited in other circumstances under section 4(1) would escape that prohibition if they were part of a merger agreement. The Authority does not believe that this was the legislature's intention.

51. A further complication arises by virtue of the fact that mergers involving firms below a certain size are not subject to review under the Mergers Act. If the parties argument were accepted it could mean that mergers above the thresholds set in the Mergers Act were outside the Competition Act while those below the threshold were subject to it. This in turn could mean that, where a merger below the threshold prevented, restricted or distorted competition, aggrieved parties would have a right of relief under section 6 of the Competition Act but no such relief would exist in the case of a merger which had been notified to, and approved by, the Minister. This would appear highly inconsistent as the latter case would appear likely to give rise to more serious restrictions of competition than the former.

52. The Minister must take account of the effects on competition of any notified merger before approving it. While this is so, the Minister might approve a merger which had adverse

2. Pl 7080, April 1991, para 12.1.
3. *Mary Deane and Others v. Voluntary Health Insurance Board* (29 July 1992).

3.5 effects on competition because he believed that it was in the common good. While section 4(2) of the Competition Act allows the Authority to grant a licence to an anti-competitive agreement exempting it from the prohibition contained in section 4(1), strict criteria must be satisfied before such a licence can be granted. Section 4(2) does not allow a licence to be granted to an agreement on the grounds that it is in the interests of the common good. Thus, if the parties' argument was accepted, and section 4 was not to apply in the case of mergers notifiable under the Mergers Act, this would create a further inconsistency in the treatment of large and small mergers. The Authority believes that such an inconsistency was not intended.

53. The parties have argued that, if mergers are reviewable under sections 4 and 5 of the Competition Act, this would create considerable uncertainty for business. The Authority accepts that this may be the case. It is frequently the case that the enactment of new legislation results in uncertainty for business. Such uncertainty tends only to be eliminated over time as a result of court decisions which clarify the meaning of legislation. It has been claimed in some quarters that the entire Competition Act has created considerable uncertainty for business as people do not know exactly what sort of activities are prohibited by the legislation. The Authority cannot accept the view that it was not the legislature's intention that mergers would be subject to the Rules of Competition simply because this would create uncertainty.

54. It is relevant to the present case that the notified arrangements involve a merger between two licensed banks. Section 1(3)(a) of the Mergers Act states that:

> For the purposes of this Act, but subject to section 3, a merger or take-over shall be taken to exist when two or more enterprises, at least one of which carries on business in the State, come under common control.

55. Section 1(1) defines an enterprise as 'a person or partnership engaged for profit in the supply or distribution of goods or the provision of services'. A service is deemed not to include 'any service provided by the holder of a licence under section 9 of the Central Bank Act 1971'.

56. Thus a merger between two licensed banks, not being a merger between enterprises, appears not to be notifiable under the Mergers Act. To the extent, however, that the merger is between holding companies which are the parents of licensed banks it would appear, to come within the scope of the Mergers Act. If the parties arguments are accepted, however, a merger involving two licensed banks would presumably come within the scope of the Competition Act by virtue of the fact that it is not an agreement to which the Mergers Act applies. This would appear to create a further anomaly which the Authority does not believe was the legislature's intention.

EC Precedents

57. The parties have further argued that, by analogy with EC law, the acquisition does not come within the scope of section 4(1). In this they have sought to rely on the decision of the European Court of Justice in the Philip Morris case.[4] The parties have claimed that the Court's decision in this case implies that where an undertaking acquires 100% of the shares in another undertaking, Article 85 of the Treaty of Rome and hence section 4(1) of the Competition Act do not apply.

58. Prior to the Philip Morris case it was believed that Article 85 did not apply to mergers. In the Philip Morris case, the Court decided that the acquisition by one company of an equity interest in a competitor might fall within Article 85(1) where the acquirer obtained legal or *de facto* control of the commercial conduct of the other company.[5] It is argued by the parties,

4. *BAT and Reynolds v. Commission, Cases 142 and 156/84*, [1987] ECR 4487.
5. C. Bellamy and G. Child (1991); 'Common Market Law of Competition', First supplement to the third edition, Sweet and Maxwell, London, para. 9-004.

however, that this only applies to an acquisition of less than 100% of the share capital in the company. **3.5**

59. In its decision the Court stated that: 'The main issue in these cases is whether and in what circumstances the acquisition of a minority shareholding in a competing company may constitute an infringement of Articles 85 and 86 of the Treaty.'[6] In other words the Court specifically stated that it was only considering the issue of the acquisition of a minority shareholding. It is difficult to see therefore how the Court's decision can be interpreted as implying that a 100% acquisition is not caught by Article 85(1) since the Court did not address this issue. The Court went on to state that:

> Since the acquisition of shares in Rothmans International was the subject of agreements by companies which have remained independent after the entry into force of the agreements, the issue must be examined first of all from the point of view of Article 85. (Point 31)

60. It is argued by the parties that the key issue is whether the parties to the agreement can be said to have remained independent after it has come into force and that in the case of an acquisition of 100% of the shares there are no longer two independent undertakings. In the case of the present agreement both Hill Samuel & Co. B.V. and Woodchester Bank remain as independent undertakings.

61. The Court then went on to assess whether or not an acquisition of shares infringed Article 85(1).

> Although the acquisition by one company of an equity interest in a competitor does not in itself constitute conduct restricting competition, such an acquisition may nevertheless serve as an instrument for influencing the commercial conduct of the companies in question so as to restrict or distort competition on the market on which they carry on business. (Point 37)

62. The judgment (points 38 and 39) implies that where the acquisition gave the purchaser legal or *de facto* control, or indeed where it created the possibility of it doing so at a later stage, the agreement would be in breach of 85(1). This view is supported by the fact that the Court stated that in the market circumstances which prevailed in this instance:

> any attempted take-over and any agreement likely to promote commercial cooperation between two or more of those dominant companies is liable to result in a restriction of competition. (Point 44)

63. It appears that an agreement to acquire shares in a competitor which would give the purchaser legal or *de facto* control would be in breach of Article 85(1). The Authority does not believe that the decision can be construed in such a way as to imply that the acquisition of a shareholding in a competitor which gave the purchaser legal or *de facto* control could only be in breach of Article 85(1) if the acquisition involved less than 100% of the shares.

64. Commenting on the decision the EC Commission stated that:

> As the share purchase had been the subject of agreements between undertakings which remained independent after the agreement had taken effect, the Court looked at the question primarily from the angle of Article 85. . . . Not only the immediate consequences, but also the potential effects of the agreement had to be considered, including the possibility that the agreement was part of a long-term plan.'[7]

6. Philip Morris, op. cit. at point 30.
7. EC Commission (1988); 'Seventeenth Report on Competition Policy', Brussels, para. 101.

3.5 65. Significantly the EC Commission went on to state that:

> The judgment has far-reaching implications. It underlines the need for an economic approach in interpreting and applying Articles 85 and 86. Conduct cannot cease to be anti-competitive merely by reference to the legal form in which it is presented. Even purchases of blocks of shares in a company may in particular circumstances infringe the competition rules.
>
> The judgment also makes important statements about the scope of Articles 85 and 86. Agreements on the acquisition of shareholdings in competitors fall within Article 85 where they influence the market behaviour of the firms concerned so that competition between them is restricted or distorted. For this to occur it is not necessary for the agreement specifically to provide for or to facilitate commercial cooperation between the competitors. It is sufficient if the result of the acquisition of the shareholding is to give one company legal or *de facto* control over the commercial policy of the other company. It does not matter whether the holding necessary for control is acquired in one go or successively in a series of operations. These rulings by the Court mean that contrary to the hitherto accepted view, certain transactions involving the acquisition by an undertaking of shares in a competitor may be caught by Article 85.[8]

66. Subsequent to the Philip Morris decision the EC Commission in Carnaud/ Sofreb examined the acquisition of a 66.6% shareholding in a company under Article 85 following a complaint by a minority shareholder. Carnaud then offered to buy the remaining shares and the complaint was withdrawn. The Commission saw no objection to a full takeover of Sofreb as the acquisition only marginally increased Carnaud's share of the relevant market.[9] In this case, Article 85 was applied to the acquisition of a majority shareholding and there is no reference to Article 85 ceasing to apply in the event of a 100% acquisition.

67. In the case of a subsequent notification the EC Commission issued a comfort letter in respect of agreements notified by the Compagnie Internationale des Wagons Lits et du Tourisme and Volkswagen AG concerning the merger of their respective car rental subsidiaries, Europcar and InterRent, and providing for the organisation of a joint network of affiliated companies. The Commission stated that the agreements did not infringe Article 85(1). Since the two undertakings were not competitors the arrangement did not restrict competition. Two clauses had been regarded as unacceptable but these had been removed.[10] This decision again indicates that the EC Commission does not regard mergers as automatically outside the scope of Article 85 as the parties have sought to argue.

68. If the notifying parties' arguments were correct, then undertakings could, by exchanging ownership of subsidiary companies, engage in practices which would otherwise be prohibited under section 4(1). The Authority does not consider that such an interpretation is correct. It agrees with the EC Commission view that it is the economic effect rather than the legal form of agreement which must be considered in deciding whether or not arrangements offend against section 4(1).

69. Further clarification is given by the European Commission's decision in PPG/Mecaniver. In this case the EC Commission was concerned with an agreement between Mecaniver, a Belgian holding company, which was 78% owned by BSN-Gervais Danone and PPG Industries Inc. The latter firm was the largest glass producer in the US. The decision involved a share purchase agreement whereby Mecaniver sold 67% of the shares in a wholly owned subsidiary to PPG. The agreement also provided for PPG to subscribe to an increase in the share capital of the company in question thereby increasing its shareholding to 81%. The agreement also

8. Ibid.
9. Ibid. at para 70.
10. EC Commission (1991); Twentieth Report on Competition Policy, para. 118.

gave PPG an option of purchasing Mecaniver's remaining 19% holding in the company during the period from two to four and a half years after the closing date and, if PPG did not exercise the option, it gave Mecaniver the option in the six months following the expiry of PPG's option of obliging PPG to purchase its remaining shareholding. 3.5

70. The Commission made the following decision in respect of the share purchase agreements:

> The share purchase agreement and the ancillary agreements of 17 December 1981 between the companies of the BSN-Mecaniver group and PPG are agreements between undertakings.

71. It went on to state that, in the absence of a risk of co-ordination of competitive behaviour:

> The sale constituting the mere transfer of a business [did] not in itself and in the absence of any indications to the contrary give rise to any restriction of competition and as such did not fall within the scope of Article 85(1).'[11]

72. The clear implication is that the sale of a business which gave rise to any restriction of competition would come within the scope of 85(1). By analogy, therefore, such an agreement would offend against section 4(1) of the Competition Act which is based on Article 85 of the Treaty of Rome. The Commission cleared the transaction in that particular case since it also could not be said to have strengthened a dominant position such that it could be regarded as an abuse under 86.

73. The parties have argued that EC Regulation 4064/89 (the 'Merger' regulation) implies that an acquisition of a one hundred percent interest in another company results in a concentration which may only be reviewed under Article 86. By analogy therefore it is only subject to review under section 5 of the Competition Act. Article 3 of the EC Merger Regulation states that a concentration shall be deemed to arise where:

> (a) two or more previously independent undertakings merge, or
> (b) one or more persons already controlling at least one undertaking or,
> one or more undertakings
> acquire, whether by purchase of securities or assets, by contract or by any other means direct or indirect control of the whole or parts of one or more other undertakings.[12]

The regulation does not require that an undertaking acquire a one hundred percent shareholding in another undertaking for it to constitute a concentration. It is relevant also that the EC Commission has explicitly stated that it does not intend to apply Articles 85 and 86 of the Treaty to mergers covered by the merger control regulation other than by means of this regulation. The Commission has also stated that it does not intend to take action in respect of mergers below certain limits which are below the thresholds in the merger regulation, on the grounds that below such levels a merger would not normally significantly affect trade between Member States.[13] Third parties are not, however, thereby precluded from taking a private action against a merger under Articles 85 or 86 in the national courts.

The View of the Authority

74. The Authority recognises that, if mergers are subject to section 4 of the Competition Act, this will create considerable uncertainty for business. It also recognises that the prospect

11. Case No. 85/78/EEC, OJ L35/54, 7.2.85.
12. OJ 1990, L257/14.
13. Community merger control law, *Bulletin of the European Communities Supplement 2/90*, p. 25.

3.5 of having to notify a merger to two separate bodies, the Authority and the Minister, can impose a significant burden on the parties to a proposed merger. The Authority, however, has to operate on the basis of its interpretation of the Act. Even if the Authority considered that mergers are not subject to the Act, this would not prevent a challenge by a third party in the High Court in respect of section 4 or section 5. In this instance the parties have notified an acquisition to the Authority and requested a certificate for it. In the Authority's view such arrangements do not enjoy any automatic exemption from the provisions of section 4(1).

75. The present agreement is between Woodchester Bank and Hill Samuel & Co. B.V., both of which will continue as independent undertakings. There is, therefore and by analogy with PPG/Mecaniver, an agreement between undertakings. The result of the agreement is that two previously competing financial institutions, Woodchester Bank and UDT Bank, have become a single entity. The question is whether such an arrangement may be viewed as preventing, restricting or distorting competition in the market. The Authority has indicated in previous decisions that the prohibition in section 4(1) is not to be interpreted literally.[14] In its decision on Nallen/O'Toole it stated that:

> If section 4(1) were to be interpreted literally then virtually every form of business agreement could be argued to prevent, restrict or distort competition because any agreement effectively prohibits others from concluding the very same contract with the original parties.

76. As pointed out earlier a merger may, on occasion, prevent, restrict or distort competition. The primary objective of a merger may in fact be the elimination of a competitor and a lessening of competition. Having concluded that a merger may come within the scope of section 4 of the Competition Act, the Authority believes that it is desirable that it should set out its views on when a merger might be found to offend against section 4(1) of the Act or not.

77. A merger will frequently result in a reduction in the number of competitors in a market. The Authority does not believe that this necessarily restricts competition. If section 4(1) were in fact to be interpreted in this way, it would amount to a *per se* prohibition of mergers. The Authority does not believe that this was the legislature's intention. It has already indicated in Nallen/O'Toole that an agreement which excluded an undertaking from a particular market for a period of time would not necessarily amount to a restriction of competition. That decision indicated that the economic circumstances prevailing in the market in question had to be taken into account before deciding whether or not the agreement was anti-competitive.

78. The Authority believes, therefore, that, before a merger can be found to offend against section 4(1) of the Competition Act, it must be shown that it would, or would be likely to, result in an actual diminution of competition in the market concerned. A reduction in the number of competitors or the fact that a merger will result in the merged entity having a larger share of the market than that previously held by either of the merged undertakings individually are not, of themselves, sufficient to establish that such a diminution of competition has occurred or would be likely to occur. A merger would, in the Authority's opinion, offend against section 4(1) where it resulted in, or would be likely to result in, a lessening of competition in the relevant market such as would allow, for example, the merged undertaking or all of the remaining firms in the market to raise their prices. Other factors, such as the ease with which new competitors could enter the market, would also be relevant in assessing the merger in the Authority's view.

Woodchester Bank and UDT

79. Woodchester Bank and UDT both competed in the overall market for banking services within the State whilst specialising in particular segments of the market. The impact of the

14. Notification No. CA/8/91 – Nallen/O'Toole (Belmullet), decision of 2 April 1992.

acquisition on a number of separate markets must, therefore, be taken into account in order to establish whether it offends against section 4(1) of the Competition Act. 3.5

80. Data on total lending and deposits of credit institutions were given in Table 2. This showed that the combined share of Woodchester Bank and UDT Bank in both markets was relatively small. The Authority believes that there is considerable competition from a large number of other financial institutions in the wholesale deposit market which has been the main area of the deposit market in which Woodchester Bank has tended to operate. It has also been indicated to the Authority that, having acquired UDT's retail branch network, Woodchester Bank intends to expand its activities in this area. The entry of a stronger group into the retail banking market would actually increase competition in that sector so that the agreement is in some respects pro-competitive.

81. The lending market is somewhat more fragmented than the deposit market, however, with some institutions specialising mainly in particular areas of business. Nevertheless while these may all represent separate markets to some extent, it seems that in areas such as commercial lending there is a large number of competitors in the market and that the acquisition by Woodchester Bank of UDT will not therefore prevent, restrict or distort competition.

82. UDT is involved in the residential mortgage business to some degree. Here again there are a large number of competitors in the market. In recent years the associated banks have captured a significant share of the market from the building societies which had dominated the market. The growing diversity in the range of mortgage products now available to consumers is further evidence of the extent to which there is competition in this market. Here again the Authority does not believe that this acquisition will reduce competition in the relevant market. This view is reinforced by the fact that the vendor may, under the terms of the agreement, continue to operate in the market for all banking services other than motor vehicle leasing and instalment credit.

83. Following the acquisition Woodchester's share of the deposit and lending markets is quite small. While it has increased its market share as a result of such acquisitions, the Authority does not believe that the increase in market share could be regarded as preventing, restricting or distorting competition. There are still a large number of competing institutions active in all areas of the lending and deposit markets. The Authority does not believe that the acquisition has resulted, or would be likely to result, in a diminution of competition for various types of financial services. It is also relevant that, while regulations restricted the entry of new institutions in many areas of financial services in the past, the advent of the single market at the end of 1992 will allow institutions from other EC Member States to provide financial services in Ireland thereby opening up the market to a large number of new entrants.

84. As pointed out, some banks also operate in the market for money transmission services. Traditionally this market has been confined to the big four associated banks because this business required a large retail branch network. It was also regarded as a loss making activity which the associated banks cross– subsidised from profits on their other activities. For this reason it was not an attractive proposition for other financial institutions. In recent years technological developments have changed this picture. The introduction of Automated Teller Machines (ATM's) and other developments has made it possible to provide a wide range of money transmission services without the need for an extensive branch network. As a result, building societies, for example, now provide certain money transmission services. Neither Woodchester Bank nor UDT were really active in this market so the arrangements do not have any adverse implications for competition in this area. Indeed to the extent that the enlarged group might enter into retail banking this would make it a potential competitor in this sector so that the effect on competition might be positive.

85. The one segment of the market where the Authority had some concerns was in respect of motor vehicle leasing. This was due to the fact that Woodchester was reported to have held a significant share of this market and the acquisition of UDT was claimed to have increased this significantly. In particular a report in Business and Finance claimed that the acquisition

3.5 would increase Woodchester's share of the Irish car leasing market to over 40%.[15] An acquisition which increased market share to this level might prevent, restrict or distort competition.

86. The total of outstanding leasing finance from credit institutions and hire purchase companies as at 31 December 1991 amounted to £912m. Of this total £519m or 57% was accounted for by hire purchase companies. Central Bank figures show a rapid increase in leasing by hire purchase companies from a total of £194m in December 1989. Over the same period there has been some decline in leasing by other credit institutions. A further £310m was outstanding in instalment credit and hire purchase finance, of which hire purchase companies accounted for £135m or 43%. As pointed out leasing is frequently regarded as an alternative to the latter type of finance. These figures indicate that there are a large number of firms competing in the overall leasing market.

87. Turning to the specific area of motor vehicle leasing the essential issue in this regard is whether or not this can be regarded as a distinct market. Certainly leasing differs from other forms of finance for car purchase. Indeed, as pointed out, leasing essentially amounts to renting a car although it appears that consumers may not always appreciate this. The issue is whether there are other products which may be regarded as sufficiently close substitutes for leasing as a form of car purchase finance. Banks, hire purchase companies and other leasing companies all provide alternative means of financing the purchase of a new car. The number of institutions which provide credit for motor vehicle purchase has increased significantly with the entry of the building societies to this market.

88. New cars leased by Woodchester and UDT as a proportion of new private car registrations increased up to 1989 although they account for a relatively small proportion of the total. Since then their share has levelled off. Indeed focusing on new private car registrations may, if anything, overstate the market share held by Woodchester and UDT as some of their leased vehicles may in fact be registered as commercial vehicles. The relatively low proportion of new car registrations accounted for by Woodchester and UDT combined tends to support the view that there are a wide number of alternatives means of financing the purchase of a new car available to consumers and that these are substitutes for leasing.

89. It may be argued that certain classes of consumer may not be able to avail of other forms of finance and may have little option other than leasing if they wish to obtain a new car. There are a number of firms other than Woodchester in the leasing business. In addition such consumers may be more likely to purchase a second-hand as opposed to a new car. The Authority believes that the option of buying a second hand car represents a substitute to leasing for individuals who might have difficulty obtaining the necessary credit to buy a new car.

90. The Authority believes therefore that there are a number of substitutes to leasing available and that motor vehicle leasing should not be regarded as a separate market. In sum the Authority does not believe that the acquisition by Woodchester Bank of UDT could be regarded as preventing, restricting or distorting competition within the State or in any part of the State and does not therefore offend against section 4(1).

(e) *Restraints on Trade*

91. Section 9 of the agreement sets out a number of restrictions on the conduct by the vendors of their business in Ireland.

92. Clause 9.01.1 prevents the vendors from engaging in the instalment credit or motor vehicle leasing business in Ireland for a period of one year. Clause 9.01.2 prevents the vendors soliciting orders from ex-customers in connection with the instalment credit or motor vehicle leasing business in Ireland for a period of three years. Clause 9.01.3 prevents the vendors from enticing their former executives away from Woodchester Bank for a period of three years. This restriction does not apply where the executive approaches the vendors with a view to

15. 20 February 1992, p. 35.

employment or where the executive applies to the vendors for employment in response to a public advertisement. Clause 9.01.4 prevents the vendors using trade names, for example 'UDT', for a period of three years. 3.5

93. The Authority has set out its views on clauses similar to 9.01 in previous decisions such as Nallen/O'Toole. In this decision the Authority indicated that, in the case of the sale of a business, some restriction on the seller was generally necessary in order to ensure the complete transfer of the goodwill of the business. It stated that provided the restriction was limited in terms of its duration, geographical coverage and subject matter to that which was necessary for the complete transfer of the goodwill, then the restriction was not in breach of section 4(1) of the Act. In this respect the Authority's decision was in line with that taken by the European Commission in a number of cases under Article 85 of the Treaty of Rome on which section 4 of the Competition Act is based.

94. In these previous decisions, non-competition clauses of three years were accepted by the Authority. Clause 9.01.1 involves a restriction for a period of one year. This restriction is limited to the Irish market and it relates solely to the instalment credit and motor leasing business. It is evident that this clause is not in breach of section 4(1) of the Act having regard to the Authority's earlier decisions.

95. A restriction on the vendors soliciting orders from their ex-customers in order to ensure the proper transfer of goodwill in the case of a sale of business is acceptable in principle. Clause 9.01.2 is limited to the instalment credit and motor leasing business in Ireland and its duration is for a period of three years.

96. The Authority has indicated in its decision on Nallen/O'Toole that it would normally regard a time-limit of two years as being adequate for the transfer of goodwill. It went on to state, however, that it would accept a restriction of longer duration, where it could be shown that this was necessary to secure the complete transfer of goodwill.

97. Clause 9.01.2 involves a restriction for three years. The market sectors in which the restriction applies are those in which UDT and Woodchester Bank have traditionally competed and in which UDT has built up substantial goodwill. In addition, the restriction on solicitation reflects the fact that much of the custom of UDT has been acquired by personal contacts. In these circumstances the period specified in this clause is no more than is required to secure the complete transfer of the goodwill. In addition, the scope and geographical coverage of this clause are not in breach of section 4(1) of the Act.

98. There is little doubt that ex-UDT executives have become familiar with the various facets of their business over a number of years and will be efficient in dealing with them. Accordingly, it is the Authority's view that the expertise of the UDT executives represents an important part of the goodwill of the company and that the purchasers are entitled to seek to protect this element of the goodwill. The restriction in clause 9.01.3 is for a period of three years. Under the terms of the restriction, ex-UDT executives may approach their former employers with a view to obtaining employment. In addition, these executives may respond to public notices from their former employers who advertise positions in their organisations. The restriction in clause 9.01.3 does not have the effect of tying UDT executives to Woodchester Bank, and the Authority is satisfied that no breach of section 4(1) of the Act arises.

99. The restriction in clause 9.01.4 relates to the trade names such as 'UDT' used by the vendors prior to the agreement. It prevents the use of such names in Ireland by the vendors for a period of three years. It is necessary to prevent the vendors passing themselves off to their customers or suppliers as representing UDT or some other organisations previously owned by the vendors, in the event that they should decide to compete against Woodchester. This restraint does not involve any restriction on competition within the State or any part of the State and does not offend against section 4(1).

The Decision

100. Woodchester Bank and Hill Samuel and Co. B.V., are undertakings within the meaning

3.5 of Section 3 of the Competition Act and the arrangements in question constitute an agreement which applies in the State.

101. The Authority believes that the agreement for the purchase and sale of UDT Bank Ltd does not offend against section 4(1) of the Competition Act 1991.

102. In the case of a sale of business, some restriction on the seller is generally essential in order to ensure the complete transfer of the goodwill for which the purchaser has paid. If these restrictions are limited to that which is necessary to ensure the complete transfer of the goodwill of the business, then, in the Authority's opinion, they do not prevent, restrict or distort competition. The restrictions in clause 9.01 of the notified agreement satisfy these criteria.

The Certificate

The Competition Authority has issued the following certificate:

> The Competition Authority certifies that, in its opinion, on the basis of the facts in its possession, the agreement between Hill Samuel & Co. B.V. and Woodchester Bank Ltd, for the purchase and sale of UDT Bank Ltd, notified on 20 March 1992, under section 7, does not offend against section 4(1) of the Competition Act 1991.

For the Competition Authority

Patrick Massey
Member

4 August 1992

3.6 **Competition Authority Decision No. 8, ACT Group plc/Kindle Group Ltd:** 4 September 1992, Notification No. CA/9/91

Share sale arrangements – Consideration for sale comprising cash and shares in purchasing entity – Restrictive covenants imposed on executive shareholders of target company – Restrictions on executive shareholders from utilising or disclosing confidential information and 'know-how' for a period of 5 years – Whether vendors who become employees are separate undertakings – Restrictions having world-wide effect for the relevant market – Amendment of notified arrangements – EC Regulation No. 556/89, Art.1 – Mergers, Take-overs and Monopolies (Control) Act (No. 17) – Competition Act 1991 (No. 24) sections 3, 4 and 7

Facts: On 26 November 1991 notification was made to the Authority with a request for a certificate under section 4(4) of the Competition Act 1991 or, failing that, a licence under section 4(2) in respect of arrangements for the acquisition by ACT Group plc ('ACT') of the entire issued share capital of Kindle Group Ltd ('Kindle').

The parties concerned with the notified arrangements are ACT, Kindle and various executives of Kindle. ACT, a publicly quoted company in the UK, which specialises in software solutions for the health care, financial and public sectors provides systems integration and support services for the wider computer market. Kindle, an Irish registered company, is engaged in the development and sale of an integrated range of software packages for the banking and financial services industry. Various senior executives of Kindle ('the Executives') held in excess of 50% of the share capital of Kindle and were also party to the notified arrangements. **3.6**

Companies in the financial sector use either main frame computer systems or a system of network personal computers ('PCs'). Kindle operates largely in the market for PC banking software which is the market relevant to the notified arrangement. ACT does not compete in either of these markets in Ireland. Sales of Kindle and ACT products on the Irish market represent a very small fraction of the total business. The majority of ACT's sales arise in the UK and a significant part of Kindle sales are generated in the UK, Asia, Africa and Eastern Europe.

A number of agreements giving effect to the acquisition of Kindle were submitted with the notification. Under the terms of a Deed of Irrevocable Undertakings and Warranties the Executives accepted a number of restrictions on their future business activities. In particular the Executives undertook not to: (i) solicit or deal with Kindle's customers or solicit Kindle's suppliers; (ii) carry on business in competition with Kindle in relation to certain specified products and services; (iii) solicit Kindle's senior employees; (iv) reveal confidential information about Kindle other than as required by law; (v) commence business using any of the business names utilised by Kindle; and (vi) attempt, or knowingly assist or procure any other person to do any of the foregoing matters. Restrictions (i), (ii) and (iii) were referable to those persons who were Kindle's customers, suppliers or employees in the 12 month period prior to completion of the take over and the duration of such restrictions was to last for three years from the date of completion. No time limit was specified in respect of restriction (iv) save that it would cease to apply when such relevant information came into the public domain. The agreement also contained a clause whereby the Executives gave an undertaking not to dispose, for a period of 12 months from the date they were allotted, the shares in ACT which formed part of the consideration for the acquisition.

By letter dated 28 May 1992 ACT agreed, at the request of the Authority, to amend restriction (iv) set out above such that the restriction in that clause applied for a period of five years from the date of completion of the take over.

Decided by the Authority: In issuing a certificate under section 4(4) of the Competition Act 1991 in respect of the notified agreement that:

(1) ACT is a publicly quoted company on the London Stock Exchange engaged in the production and distribution of computer software and is clearly an undertaking within the meaning of section 3 of the Competition Act. The Executives effectively controlled Kindle prior to its sale to ACT and were therefore engaged for gain in the supply and distribution of goods and the provision of support services and are therefore undertakings within the meaning of the Competition Act 1991. The arrangements therefore represent an agreement between a number of undertakings for the transfer of ownership of Kindle, an undertaking which operates within the State.

(2) A merger would only offend against section 4(1) of the Competition Act if it resulted in, or was likely to result in, a diminution of competition in the relevant market. A reduction in the number of competitors is not, in itself, evidence of a reduction in competition as this will amount to a prohibition on mergers *per se*. It has been submitted that no other ACT company competes directly or indirectly with

3.6 Kindle in the market affected by the proposed arrangements and on that basis the transfer of ownership involves no diminution in the level of actual competition in the relevant market in Ireland.

(3) Competition includes potential as well as actual competition. The question therefore is whether there was a real likelihood that ACT would have entered the Irish market in competition with Kindle if this takeover had not arisen. On the evidence there appears no reason to believe that there was a real likelihood that ACT would have entered the market and for this reason the takeover of Kindle by ACT does not involve a restriction on competition within the State in accordance with section 4(1) of the Competition Act 1991.

(4) The restrictions on competition imposed on the Executives under the terms of the Deed of Irrevocable Undertakings and Warranties are of a three year duration save that the undertaking not to use or disclose confidential information survives for five years. While such clauses are necessary to secure the transfer of the goodwill of the business to a purchaser their scope must be strictly limited to that purpose. A period of two years would generally be sufficient with a complete transfer of the goodwill of a business. The notified arrangements are concerned with more than just the transfer of goodwill in that the creation, development and application of computer software involves a degree of technical 'know-how'.

(5) The software products developed by Kindle embody a substantial amount of detailed technical 'know-how' and some protection against competition from the Executives of Kindle who are familiar with such 'know-how' is justified. In the case of a transfer of technical 'know-how' such protection can be justified for a longer period than in a case where only goodwill is being transferred. In such cases a time limit of five years is acceptable. Technical 'know-how' must satisfy the criteria set out in the EC Know-How Licensing Regulations. The restriction on the use or disclosure of confidential information for a period of five years is reasonable in the circumstances as being necessary for ACT to familiarise itself with the technical 'know-how' involved and does not offend against section 4(1) of the Competition Act 1991.

(6) Non-competition clauses in the sale of a business must be restricted in terms of geographical coverage and subject matter to what is necessary to secure a complete transfer of the goodwill of the business. The restraints apply world-wide and relate to the business of software development, marketing and sales. As this represents the geographic market and product market in which Kindle operates the restraint is reasonable in terms of geographic coverage and subject matter.

(7) The clause in the notified arrangements whereby the Executives may not sell their ACT shares for a period of 12 months from the completion of the sale does not prevent, restrict or distort competition in trade in any goods or services in the State and is not in breach of section 4(1) of the Competition Act.

Cases, Decisions and report referred to:
Reuter/BASF [1976] OJ L254/40, [1976] 2 CMLR D44
Remia BV v. EC Commission (Case No. 42/84) [1985] ECR 2545; [1987] 1 CMLR 1
Competition Authority Decision No. 1 – Nallen/O'Toole, 2 April 1992 **3.3**
Competition Authority Decision No. 6 – Woodchester Bank/UDT Bank, 4 August 1992 **3.5**
European Commission (1983) '13th Report on Competition Policy', para. 88

Competition Authority Decision of 4 September 1992 relating to a proceeding under section 4 of the Competition Act 1991 Notification No. CA/9/91 — ACT Group plc and Kindle Group Ltd 3.6

Introduction

1. On 26 November 1991 ACT Group plc and Kindle Group Ltd notified to the Competition Authority, under section 7(2) of the Competition Act 1991, arrangements for the acquisition by ACT of the entire issued share capital of Kindle for the purpose of obtaining a certificate under section 4(4) of the Act or, in the event of a refusal by the Authority to issue a certificate, a licence under section 4(2) of the Act.

2. Notice of the intention of the Authority to take a favourable decision in relation to the arrangements was published in the Irish Times on 10 July 1992. No observations were received from interested parties.

The facts

The subject of the Notification

3. The notification concerns an agreement between ACT Group plc and Messrs. Kilduff, Nagle, Kinsella and Downey, DCC Ltd., and Elmbank Ltd., whereby ACT has acquired the full share capital of Kindle. The agreement also contains a number of non-competition provisions.

The parties concerned

4. The individual companies which form ACT are based for the most part in the UK where they employ 1,600 people. They are a publicly quoted company with an authorised share capital of 120m ordinary shares of 10p each. For the year ending 31 March 1991, ACT achieved profits after taxation of £8.9m sterling on a turnover of £98m sterling. The employment figures and the authorised share capital also relate to the year ending 31 March, 1991. ACT has one subsidiary based in Ireland — DDT Maintenance (Ireland) Ltd. This company is active in the maintenance of computer systems and micro computers. One of ACT's subsidiaries — ACT Financial Systems Ltd — is involved in the provision of applications software and associated services to the financial services sector; however, their products are not considered to be competitive with those of Kindle and no sales of these products have been made in Ireland.

5. Kindle has its registered offices in Dublin. It employs 183 people.

6. 'The Executives' are Mr A. Kilduff, Mr K. Nagle, Mr C. Kinsella and Mr R. Downey. These individuals each had shareholdings in Kindle before the acquisition. Mr Kilduff was the Chairman of the Group and the combined shareholding of 'The Executives' exceeded 50% of Kindle Group shares.

7. DCC Ltd are an investment company registered in Ireland. They held approximately 28% of Kindle's shares prior to the acquisition.

8. Elmbank Ltd are a private investment holding company registered in the Isle of Man. They held approximately 4% of Kindle's shares before the acquisition.

The products

9. ACT specialises in software solutions for the healthcare, financial and public sectors, and provides systems integration and support services for the wider computer market.

10. The principal activity of Kindle is the development and sale of an integrated range of software packages for the banking and financial services industry.

Market information

11. Companies in the financial sector may use main frame computers or a network of personal computers (PCs). Different software is necessary for these two computer environments. The majority of Kindle's sales within Ireland are to customers who use PCs. The cost

3.6 of purchasing a mainframe machine is such that companies are unlikely to substitute PCs for a mainframe in order to obtain software products designed for use with a PC. Software for mainframes and software for PCs are not, therefore, substitute products. There are, in effect, two distinct markets for banking computer software. ACT do not compete in either of these markets in Ireland. Kindle operate largely in the market for PC banking software and this is the market involved in the present notification.

12. Sales of Kindle and ACT products on the Irish market represent a very small fraction of their total business. The majority of ACT's sales arise in the UK. A significant part of Kindle's sales are also generated in the UK. In addition, Asia, Africa, and Eastern Europe are important markets for Kindle.

The arrangements

13. A number of agreements giving effect to the acquisition of Kindle were submitted to the Authority. Under one agreement Kindle shareholders could opt to receive new ACT shares or to receive cash in lieu of any of these shares. A separate agreement was made for the acquisition of a block of Kindle's shares owned by DCC Ltd. The consideration involved in this agreement was a combination of new ACT shares and guaranteed loan notes.

14. Additional consideration became due under each of the agreements if Kindle's profits for 1991/92 exceed certain levels.

15. By virtue of a Deed of Irrevocable Undertakings and Warranties 'the Executives' accepted a number of restrictions on their future business activities. The restrictions, with one exception, were for a period of three years. They are included in Clause 6.1 of the Deed under which the 'Executives' referred to above are obliged not to:

6.1.1 'canvass or solicit orders from any person who was a customer of any Group Member at any time during the twelve months preceding the date of this deed for the supply of relevant products.'

6.1.2 'deal for the purpose of supplying relevant products with any person who was a customer of any Group Member at any time during the twelve months preceding the date of this deed.'

6.1.3 'solicit or entice away from any Group Member any supplier to any Group Member who had supplied goods and/or services to any Group Member at any time during the twelve months immediately preceding the date of this deed if such solicitation or enticement causes or would cause such supplier to cease supplying, or materially to reduce its supply of those goods and/or services to any Group Member.'

6.1.4 ' in relation to any relevant products work be engaged or interested in any trade or business.'

6.1.5 'solicit or entice away from any Group Member any employee of any Group Member employed at the date of this deed in a senior managerial, supervisory, technical, sales or administrative post.'

6.1.6 'use, or reveal to any person any of the trade secrets (save to the extent required by the order of any court of competent jurisdiction), secret or confidential operations, processes or dealings or any other confidential information concerning any Group Member or any client or customer of any Group Member, including but not limited to customer lists and names, sales targets and statistics, market share statistics, surveys and reports and pricing information relating to sales and purchases by any Group Member until such time as the same fall into the public domain otherwise than by reason of a breach of this undertaking.' This restriction is not limited in terms of duration.

6.1.7 'use in connection with any trade or business any name which includes the name of any Group Member or any colourable imitation of it; or'

6.1.8 'attempt, or knowingly assist or procure any other person, to do any of the foregoing things.'

16. The deed also includes restrictions in Clause 7.1 on the disposal of new ACT shares by 'the Executives' and Elmbank Ltd. (the holders of 4% of Kindle's shares) whereby they gave an undertaking not to, for a period of twelve months from the date on which the shares are allotted, 'dispose of or create or agree to dispose of or create any interest in more than half of the number of' ACT shares allotted to them. Notwithstanding this undertaking, 'the Executives' and Elmbank Ltd. also agreed to notify ACT in writing of any intention to dispose of their shares in ACT. These restrictions relate to approximately 2m new ACT shares. **3.6**

Submissions of the parties

17. The parties have stated that Kindle will bring to ACT a new range of high value added products in a niche market of the financial sector, with little overlap with ACT's existing product range. Kindle should benefit from the opportunity for further international business made available to it as a result of its becoming part of ACT. In addition, Kindle's expertise in the emerging markets of Eastern Europe and the Far East should enable ACT's existing business to expand into these markets. Considerable scope should also exist for cross selling of products between the customer bases of both companies. The enlarged group represents a major financial software business in the UK and Europe.

18. It was also stated by the parties that the combined market share of Kindle and ACT in Ireland in banking industry software is negligible. The parties claimed that the limited restrictions imposed would not enable them post-completion to eliminate competition in a substantial part of the market.

19. The parties stated that the restrictions imposed on certain of the vendors were fair and reasonable given the nature of the transaction. They cited EC cases in support of their argument that restrictions on the sellers of business competing in that business were justified.

20. ACT sought to justify the restriction in 6.1.6 as follows:

> It is generally considered that an arbitrary time limit is not appropriate for such a restriction because if the information is still secret at the point where the time limit expires, its disclosure at that time is still capable of causing damage to the business acquired by the purchaser.
>
> Furthermore, the restriction is limited only to the period during which the relevant information has not fallen into the public domain. The persons accepting the restriction will not, therefore, be prohibited from using information once third parties are also entitled to use it.
>
> To this extent, the parties consider that the restriction goes no further than is reasonably necessary to protect the legitimate business interest of the purchaser following its acquisition.

21. The following case was advanced by ACT in support of the restrictions outlined in Clause 7.1:

> The parties do not consider that the proposed restriction on the disposal of certain of the new ACT shares has either the object or effect of preventing, restricting or distorting such competition.
>
> Given that the restriction applies to shares, the market relating to the provision of software and related services in Ireland will not be affected.
>
> The parties consider that this restriction is common in transactions where the consideration is satisfied (in whole or in part) by the issue of shares in the purchasing company, its purpose being to prevent any de-stabilisation in the market for those shares, such as might otherwise arise if all were to be sold immediately. They also consider that this restriction is fair and reasonable and is directly related to the transaction.
>
> It might also be noted that the parties accepting the restriction did have a choice

3.6 concerning the extent to which they would each accept shares rather than take a cash alternative.

22. At the request of the Authority, by letter dated 2 March 1992, ACT agreed, by letter dated 28 May 1992, to amend Clause 6.1.6 of the agreement (see para. 15). ACT now propose to apply the restriction in this clause for a period of five years. Effect was given to this amendment in the form of a Deed of Variation which was executed by the parties to the Agreement.

Assessment

(a) *Section 4(1)*

23. Section 4(1) of the Competition Act states that 'all agreements between undertakings, decisions by associations of undertakings and concerted practices which have as their object or effect the prevention, restriction or distortion of competition in trade in any goods or services in the State or in any part of the State are prohibited and void'.

(b) *The parties concerned and the Agreement*

24. The present decision concerns an agreement between ACT, 'The Executives', Elmbank Ltd and DCC Ltd. section 3(1) of the Competition Act defines an undertaking as 'a person being an individual, a body corporate or an unincorporated body of persons engaged for gain in the production, supply or distribution of goods or the provision of a service.' ACT is a public company quoted on the London stock exchange, engaged in the production and distribution of computer software. ACT is clearly an undertaking within the meaning of section 3 of the Act.

25. DCC is a company which *inter alia* provides venture and development capital to small and medium sized enterprises in return for shares. This constitutes the provision of a service for gain and DCC is therefore an undertaking within the meaning of the Act. Elmbank being a private investment holding company is also an undertaking.

26. 'The Executives' were shareholders in Kindle and constituted the group's management team. Between them they effectively controlled Kindle. The Authority has decided in a previous case that individuals who either own or control a business are undertakings for the purposes of section 3 of the Competition Act.[1] This decision was based on the fact that individuals are included in the definition of undertakings in section 3 provided they are 'engaged for gain in the production, supply or distribution of goods or the provision of a service.' The Authority's approach in this respect is similar to that adopted by the European Commission in a number of cases under Article 85(1) of the Treaty of Rome on which section 4(1) is based.

27. 'The Executives' owned more than 50% of the shares in Kindle between them and effectively controlled the company prior to its sale to ACT. They were, therefore engaged for gain in the supply and distribution of goods, namely computer software products designed for use in the banking industry, and the provision of support services for this software. Kindle was engaged in this business in a number of countries throughout the world.

28. 'The Executives' are therefore undertakings within the meaning of section 4(1) of the Act. The notification relates to arrangements for the transfer of ownership of Kindle, an undertaking which operates within the State. These arrangements therefore represent an agreement between a number of undertakings within the meaning of section 4(1) of the Act.

(d) *Effect of the Arrangements*

The Kindle Takeover

29. The arrangements notified are essentially concerned with the transfer of ownership of

1. Notification No. CA/8/92 — Nallen/O'Toole (Belmullet), Decision of 2 April 1992.

Kindle from 'The Executives' to ACT. Such arrangements constitute a merger within the meaning of the Mergers, Takeovers and Monopolies (Control) Acts. The present merger has already been approved by the Minister for Industry and Commerce under the terms of the latter Act. 3.6

30. The Authority considered the relationship between section 4 of the Competition Act and the Mergers Act at some length in its decision on Woodchester Bank.[2] It concluded that mergers were not automatically exempt from the provisions of section 4 of the Competition Act. It indicated its view that a merger might, on occasion, offend against section 4(1) of the Competition Act. The Authority went on to state, however, that in its view a merger would only offend against section 4(1) if it resulted in, or was likely to result in, a diminution of competition in the relevant market. In particular, the Authority stated that it did not consider that a reduction in the number of competitors was, in itself, evidence of a reduction in competition as this would amount to a prohibition on mergers *per se*.

31. The Kindle group specialises in the development, marketing, installation and on-going support of a suite of computer software packages for banking. These software packages go under the tradenames 'Bankmaster', 'Branchpower' and 'Linkmaster'.

32. The notification states that the business of ACT and its subsidiaries is the supply of computer software and services. One of ACT's subsidiaries — ACT Financial Services Ltd (ACT FS) — is primarily involved in the provision of applications software and associated services to the financial services sector.

33. There are several other international firms competing with Kindle in the PC software market. In addition it is argued by the notifying parties that a number of users, particularly banks, develop their own software and/or commission customised solutions, whereas others buy packaged solutions of the type offered by Kindle and its competitors. The market would appear to be a competitive one.

34. The notification states that, although ACT Computer Support Ltd may have banking industry clients, it is concerned with providing hardware and operating systems maintenance. It is claimed that, while ACT FS has banking industry products, these are not considered to be competitive with Kindle's products and in any event no sales of these products have been made in Ireland. It is also stated that no other ACT Group company competes directly or indirectly in the market affected by the proposed arrangements. On that basis the transfer of ownership involves no diminution in the level of actual competition in the relevant market in Ireland.

35. The Authority indicated in Nallen/O'Toole that it interpreted 'competition' as including potential as well as actual competition in line with the views adopted by the European Commission. In general a restriction of competition arises if, in the absence of the restriction, there would have been a real likelihood of the restricted party engaging in the activity in question.

36. The question is whether there is a real likelihood that ACT would have entered the Irish market in competition with Kindle if this takeover had not arisen. It is submitted by the parties that ACT's products do not compete with those of Kindle. Kindle operates on a worldwide basis with only a small proportion of its business in Ireland. ACT is engaged in producing a different range of products. It is always possible that, in the absence of a takeover, ACT might, at some time, have developed products to compete with Kindle in the Irish market. There is no reason, however, to believe that there is a real likelihood that ACT would have entered the market. For this reason the Authority does not believe that the takeover of Kindle by ACT involves a restriction on competition within the State in accordance with section 4(1) of the Competition Act.

Non-Competition Clauses

37. The agreement contains a number of what may be termed non competition clauses.

2. Notification No. CA/10/92 — Woodchester Bank/UDT Bank, Decision of 4 August 1992.

3.6 These are contained in clause 6.1 of the Deed of Irrevocable Undertakings and Warranties. This clause requires 'The Executives' to give undertakings not to:

> (i) solicit or deal with Kindle's customers or solicit Kindle's suppliers, (6.1.1, 6.1.2 and 6.1.3)
> (ii) carry out business in competition with Kindle in relation to certain specified products and services, (6.1.4)
> (iii) solicit Kindle's senior employees, (6.1.5)
> (iv) reveal confidential information about Kindle other than as required by law, (6.1.6)
> (v) commence business using any of the business names utilised by Kindle, (6.1.7) and
> (vi) attempt, or knowingly assist or procure any other person, to do any of the foregoing things (6.1.8).

38. Restrictions (i) to (iii) apply for a period of three years from completion of the takeover arrangements. No limit was specified in respect of (iv) and (v) save that it is provided that it shall not apply in the case of information which has come into the public domain. At the request of the Authority clause 6.1.6 was amended by way of a deed of variation to provide for a time limit of 5 years from the date of the deed. In addition 'The Executives' are required to retain a proportion of the ACT shares which they are to receive as part of the consideration for the sale of their Kindle shares, for a period of 12 months following completion of the takeover.

39. The restriction in 6.1.7 is to the use of the Kindle name. The latter restraint does not involve any restriction on competition within the State or any part of the State. It is necessary to prevent 'The Executives' passing themselves off to Kindle's customers or suppliers as representing Kindle, in the event that they should decide to compete against ACT or Kindle.

40. The Authority has previously given its views on non-competition clauses in Nallen/O'Toole. These views were restated in a number of subsequent decisions. In Nallen/O'Toole the Authority stated that:

> In any case, on the specific issue of the non-competition clause, which is at the heart of this agreement, the Authority believes that such a clause is essential in the event of the sale of a business for the transfer of the goodwill of the business to the purchaser. Without such a restraint the purchaser could not be sure of obtaining all of the goodwill of the business and the seller would be unable to benefit by disposing of his share in a business which he had helped to build up. In the Authority's view therefore, such a clause is not in breach of section 4(1) of the Competition Act provided that the restrictions contained in such a clause or clauses are limited in terms of time, geographical coverage and subject matter to those which are necessary to secure the adequate transfer of the goodwill.

41. The Authority view is consistent with that adopted by the EC Commission and the European Court of Justice in similar cases. In particular the Court of Justice stated in the Remia case that:

> In order to determine whether or not such clauses come within the prohibition in Article 85(1), it is necessary to examine what could be the state of competition if those clauses did not exist.
>
> If that were the case, and should the vendor and the purchaser remain competitors after the transfer, it is clear that the agreement for the transfer of the undertaking could not be given effect. The vendor, with his particularly detailed knowledge of the transferred undertaking, would still be in a position to win back his former customers immediately after the transfer and thereby drive the undertaking out of business. Against that background non-competition clauses incorporated in an agreement for the transfer of an undertaking in principle have merit of ensuring that the transfer has the effect

intended. By virtue of that very fact they contribute to the promotion of undertakings in the market in question. **3.6**

Nevertheless, in order to have that beneficial effect on competition, such clauses must be necessary to the transfer of the undertaking concerned and their duration and scope must be strictly limited to that purpose. The Commission was therefore right in holding that where those conditions are satisfied such clauses are free of the prohibition laid down in Article 85(1).[3]

42. The Authority also indicated that it would tend to agree with the EC view that a period of two years would generally be sufficient for the complete transfer of the goodwill of a business.

43. The restraint on 'The Executives' in clauses 6.1.1 to 6.1.5 of the Deed of Irrevocable Undertakings and Warranties is for a period of three years. Clause 6.1.6 as amended provides for a time limit of five years. The Authority believes that in this instance the arrangements are concerned with more than just the transfer of goodwill. It is satisfied that the creation, development and application of computer software involves a degree of technical 'know-how'.

44. 'The Executives' who are parties to this agreement and the senior employees referred to in 6.1.5 possess this know-how, having themselves developed it. Possession of this know-how would allow them to attract Kindle customers if they were allowed to compete against Kindle or ACT. The period of three years specified in clauses 6.1.1 to 6.1.5 appears reasonable in the circumstances.

45. Clause 6.1.6, which prevents the disclosure of confidential information, appears to cover two types of information namely commercial information about Kindle Group companies, e.g. customer names, prices e.g. and technical know-how e.g. trade secrets, processes. The Authority's only concern was in respect of the know-how aspects of the clause.

46. The arguments raised by the parties were quite similar to those raised in the Reuter/BASF case. In the latter case the European Commission in its decision argued as follows:

> It is further recognised that it may be necessary in certain cases to provide additional safeguards to ensure the effective performance of an agreement in cases where technical knowledge, constituting an important part of the value of a transferred undertaking, is placed at the disposal of the transferee. As in the case of goodwill, it must be possible to prevent the transferor for a certain time from using such knowledge in a manner which would prevent the transferee from acquiring the undertaking with its market position undiminished.
>
> Here too, the protection afforded to the transferee should be limited in time, since the transfer of legally unprotected know-how confers no exclusive rights on the purchaser. Contrary to the contention of BASF, the transfer of technical know-how in connection with the sale of an undertaking does not automatically preclude any further activity on the part of the seller based on such know-how. The opportunity of using such know-how which is unknown to competitors is, like goodwill, a competitive advantage. This advantage can be diminished by the development of third party competitors of their own know-how in the particular field of research. Unlike third parties the transferor of an undertaking remains aware of the contents of any transferred know-how, since he cannot divest himself of his own knowledge. For this reason it appears legitimate to protect the transferee in order for a certain time to enable him to acquire the undertaking with its competitive position undiminished. This need to protect the competitive position of the undertaking provides the justification for and prescribes the time limits to any non-competition clause involved.[4]

3. *Remia BV and Others v. European Commission*, Case No. 22/84 [1985] ECR 2545.
4. Reuter/BASF 76/743/EfC (OJ L254, 17.9.76, p. 40).

3.6 47. The Commission went on to state that:

> In no circumstances may an obligation to keep know-how secret from third parties, imposed on the transfer of an undertaking, be used to prevent the transferor, after the expiry of the reasonable term of a non-competition clause, from competing with the transferee by means of new and further developments of such know-how.

The Commission ruled in this case that 8 years was too long for a non-competition clause where a transfer of technical know-how was involved and that in fact the agreement which had been in existence for 5 years at the time of the decision was in breach of Article 85(1) and could not be exempted under Article 85(3).

48. The Commission subsequently indicated that:

> In the absence of circumstances which deviate greatly from those in the Reuter/BASF or Nutricia cases, these decisions, however, indicate as general guide that where the transfer of a business also involves the transfer of good-will and know-how, a period of approximately five years will normally be acceptable, whereas a period of approximately two years will normally apply if the sale involves only the transfer of good-will.[5]

49. The present notification raises some question as to what might be regarded as technical know-how. The EC Regulation on know-how licensing states in Article 1(7)(1) that 'know-how means a body of technical information that is secret substantial and identified in the appropriate form'.[6] Know-how is only protected as long as it is secret. The regulation provides that the know-how must be substantial to ensure that know-how licensing agreements and the restrictions contained in them are not a disguised way of restricting competition by licensing worthless and trivial know-how. Article 1(7)(4) provides that know-how must be 'described or recorded' in such a manner as to make it possible to verify that the first two conditions are fulfilled, and to 'ensure that the licensee is not unduly restricted in his exploitation of his own technology. In order to be identified the know-how can either be set out in the licence agreement or in a separate document or recorded in any other appropriate form.'

50. It is clear to the Authority that the 'trade secrets' and 'processes' referred to in clause 6.1.6 in so far as they relate to specifications of computer software packages, constitute know-how, and that the restriction in clause 6.1.6 applies both to technical know-how concerning products of the Kindle Group, as well as financial and other information. To afford the purchaser unlimited protection against the use of technical know-how by the seller would, in the Authority's view, restrict competition since such an unlimited restriction would go beyond what is necessary to secure the complete transfer of the business to the purchaser. As in the Reuter/BASF case it appears reasonable to limit such protection to the time required to allow the purchaser to obtain full control of the undertaking. Once such a reasonable time has elapsed, however, the purchaser is no longer entitled to be protected against competition by the seller. As pointed out, the European Commission has indicated that 'where the transfer of a business also involves the transfer of goodwill and know-how, a period of approximately five years will normally be acceptable'. The Authority could find no good reason to depart from EC guidelines on this first occasion on which it considered a non-competition clause relating to technical know-how.

51. The product market involved here, namely the market for PC banking software is

5. European Commission 1983; ' Thirteenth Report on Competition Policy', para. 88.
6. Regulation No. 556/89 on the application of Article 85(3) of the Treaty to certain categories of know-how licensing agreements, OJ L61, 4 March 1989, p. 1.

constantly developing with the range and capabilities of products available growing at a rapid rate. As in the Reuter case, if the individuals concerned were excluded from the market for an excessive length of time, it might be very difficult for them to re-enter as viable competitors. **3.6**

52. It is also relevant that the EC regulation on know-how licensing provides that where licensees modify or develop the know-how they are allowed to use such developed know-how themselves beyond the termination of the licence agreement, provided they give details of the modifications to the licensor.

53. Where the transfer of know-how is part of a sale of a business, the purchaser is entitled to protection for some length of time against the seller in order for the complete transfer of ownership to take place. As in the Reuter case, however, such protection cannot be any longer than is necessary for the completion of such transfer.

54. The Authority accepts that the software products developed by Kindle embody a substantial amount of detailed technical know-how and that some protection against competition from the 'executives' of Kindle who are familiar with such know-how is justified. It also accepts that in the case of a transfer of technical know-how such protection can be justified for a longer period than in a case where only goodwill is being transferred. At this stage the Authority agrees with the EC Commission view that a time limit of 5 years is acceptable where technical know-how is involved. It believes that technical know-how must satisfy the criteria set out in the EC know-how licensing regulation as outlined in para 49 above. It does not consider that knowledge concerning a particular line of business can be regarded as constituting technical know-how. The Authority believes the 5 year restriction contained in the amended clause 6.1.6 is reasonable in the present circumstances as being necessary for ACT to familiarise itself with the technical know-how involved.

55. The Authority indicated in Nallen/O'Toole that non-competition clauses in the sale of a business must also be restricted in terms of geographical coverage and subject matter to what was necessary to secure the complete transfer of the goodwill of the business. In this respect it was following the approach taken by the EC Commission in the Nutricia case and by Irish and UK courts at common law.

56. No specific geographical area is specified in the various clauses in the present agreement. The fact is that the Kindle Group operates on a worldwide basis. The fact that the restraints apply worldwide is, therefore, reasonable in the case of clauses 6.1.1 to 6.1.6. The restraints relate to the business of software development, marketing and sales. As this represents the market in which Kindle operates, the restraint is reasonable in terms of subject matter.

57. The restrictions contained in clauses 6.1.1 to 6.1.7 do not, in the Authority's view prevent, restrict or distort competition and do not therefore offend against section 4(1) of the Competition Act. The restriction in clause 6.1.8 is in respect of the sellers knowingly assisting or procuring any other person to do any of the things covered in clauses 6.1.1 to 6.1.7. As those clauses do not, in themselves, offend against section 4(1), clause 6.1.8 cannot be regarded as offending against that section.

(c) *The Shareholding Arrangements*

58. Clause 7 of the notified agreement restricts the amount of ACT shares which Kindle shareholders, who are due to receive them in part consideration for the sale of their Kindle shares, may sell within a period of 12 months of the completion of the sale. Clause 7.2.1 provides that this provision will not have effect until it has been notified to the Competition Authority in accord with section 7 of the Competition Act and until any relevant licence has been obtained in respect thereof.

59. This clause of the agreement is not considered to be in breach of section 4(1) of the Competition Act as it does not prevent, restrict or distort competition in trade in any goods or services in the State or in any part of the State.

3.6 The Decision

60. ACT, 'The Executives', Elmbank and DCC are undertakings within the meaning of section 3 of the Competition Act and the arrangements in question constitute an agreement between undertakings which applies within the State.

61. The Authority believes that the agreement for the purchase and sale of Kindle does not offend against section 4(1) of the Competition Act.

62. The Authority has previously stated that, in the case of a sale of business, some restriction on the seller competing with the purchaser is normally justified in order for the purchaser to acquire the complete goodwill of the business. A non-competition clause which is limited in terms of duration, geographic coverage and subject matter to what is necessary to secure the complete transfer of the goodwill of the business does not prevent, restrict or distort competition within the meaning of section 4(1) of the Competition Act. The Authority believes that similar considerations may apply where the sale of business involves the acquisition of technical know-how. While the Authority has accepted that a restriction for two years would generally be acceptable in the case of the transfer of goodwill, it agrees with the EC Commission that a restriction for five years is acceptable in a case where the sale involves the acquisition of technical know-how. In the Authority's view the restrictions in clause 6.1 of the present agreement, as amended by the letter of 28 May 1992 from ACT's solicitors, do not prevent, restrict or distort competition in the State or any part of the State.

63. The present agreement for the transfer of ownership of Kindle Group Ltd. between ACT Group Ltd. and Messrs Kilduff, Nagle, Kinsella and Downey, Elmbank Ltd. and DCC Ltd. does not, in the Authority's opinion offend against section 4(1) of the Competition Act 1991.

The Certificate

64. The Competition Authority has issued the following certificate:

The Competition Authority certifies that in its opinion, on the basis of the facts in its possession, the agreement between ACT Group Ltd. and Messrs Kilduff, Nagle, Kinsella and Downey, Elmbank Ltd. and DCC Ltd. for the transfer of the shares in Kindle Group Ltd., notified on 26 November 1991 under section 7 and amended by letter of 28 May 1992, does not offend against section 4 (1) of the Competition Act 1991.

For the Competition Authority

Patrick Massey
Member

4 September 1992

Competition Authority Decision No. 9, Phil Fortune/Budget Travel Ltd: 14 September 1992, Notification No. CA/1/921 3.7

Share sale arrangement – Restrictive clauses to transfer entire worth of company sold – Application for licence and subsequent request for certificate – Non-compete for two years – Non-solicit for four years and confidential information covenant – Discussions with Authority – Reduce non-solicit to three years – Undertaking not to use confidentiality covenant to prevent reentry to market – Whether lack of geographic limits affects Authority's decision – Whether scope of restriction goes beyond what is necessary for the transfer of the goodwill – Competition Act 1991 (No. 24), sections 3, 4 and 7

Facts: On 17 January 1992 notification was made to the Competition Authority with a request for a licence under section 4(2) of the Competition Act 1991 in respect of an agreement for the sale of the entire issued share capital of Budget Travel Schools Abroad Ltd ('BTSA') from Budget Travel Ltd ('Budget') to Phil Fortune, an employee of BTSA. It was subsequently stated that the parties would be satisfied with a certificate if the Authority considered that a certificate could issue under section 4(1).

BTSA had six employees and was engaged in organising tours for school and adult groups. The market for this tour market catered for about 20,000 to 25,000 passengers per year and there are four principal competitors to BTSA.

The share sale agreement contained one clause with three particular restrictions which according to the notifying parties sought to secure the transfer of BTSA's worth. Budget which is one of the largest tour operators in the State covenanted not to compete with BTSA in the relevant group tour market for two years. In addition Budget covenanted not to solicit any employee of BTSA for four years and not to use or divulge any confidential information about the business of BTSA.

Following discussions with the Authority Phil Fortune agreed to reduce the non soliciting provision to a period of three years and to undertake that the confidentiality clause would not be used to prevent the reentry of Budget to the relevant market.

Decided by the Authority: In issuing a certificate under section 4(4) of the Competition Act 1991 in respect of the notified agreement that:

(1) The purchaser although an employee of the company being sold was a separate undertaking from the Vendor who previously owned the company being sold. The agreement was an agreement between undertakings which applies within the State.

(2) The sale cannot prevent restrict or distort competition because the purchaser was not in competition previously.

(3) Some restraint on a vendor may be necessary to ensure the adequate transfer of goodwill of a business. Although no geographic limits are imposed on the non competition clause the Authority accepts the argument that the vendor could undermine the transfer of goodwill by establishing in Northern Ireland. The competition restriction did not go beyond what is necessary for the transfer of the goodwill.

(4) The restrictions on soliciting and engaging in business the employees of BTSA for three years is justified by the need to transfer the goodwill because of the familiarity of the employees with the business of BTSA. This familiarity is not the same as know how but it is a form of expertise.

(5) The Authority's concern that confidentiality clauses may be used to prevent

3.7 reentry of Budget to the relevant market have been allayed by the undertaking given by Phil Fortune not to use this covenant in such a manner.

Case and Decisions referred to:
Remia BV v. EC Commission (Case No. 42/84) [1985] ECR 2545; [1987] 1 CMLR 1
EC Commission Decision — Nutricia/De Rooij and Nutricia/Zuid Hollandse — 12 December 1983 [1983] L376/22; [1984] 2 CMLR 165
Competition Authority Decision No. 1 — Nallen/O'Toole, 2 April 1992 **3.3**
Competition Authority Decision No. 6 — Woodchester Bank/UDT Bank, 4 August 1992 **3.5**
Competition Authority Decision No. 8 — ACT Group plc/Kindle Group, 4 Septemebr 1992 **3.6**

Competition Authority Decision of 14 September 1992 relating to a proceeding under section 4 of the Competition Act 1991
Notification No. CA/1/92 — Phil Fortune/Budget Travel Ltd

Introduction

1. An agreement for the sale by Budget Travel Ltd of their shares in Budget Travel Schools Abroad Ltd (hereinafter referred to as BTSA) to Phil Fortune, a former employee of BTSA, was notified to the Competition Authority on 17 January 1992 for the purposes of obtaining a licence under section 4(2) of the Competition Act 1991. It was subsequently stated by the Company that 'if the Authority considers that it is in a position to issue a certificate that the agreement in this instance does not offend against subsection 4(1) of the Competition Act 1991, we are more than satisfied to accept such a certificate'.

2. Notice of intention to take a favourable decision was published in the Irish Times on 24 July 1992. No submissions were received from interested parties.

The Facts

The subject of the Notification

3. This decision concerns the transfer of ownership of BTSA from Budget Travel Ltd. to Phil Fortune, an employee of BTSA up to the time of the agreement. The sale of business agreement includes a non competition clause.

The parties concerned

4. The vendor, Budget Travel Ltd, is a subsidiary of the UK publicly quoted Granada group. It is one of the largest tour operators and travel agents in Ireland. Budget Travel Ltd has been in operation since 1975. It acquired the Aer Lingus Holiday travel companies at the end of 1990.

5. The purchaser, Phil Fortune, was a senior employee in BTSA up to the time of the agreement.

6. BTSA is the subject of the agreement. The company organises overseas tours for school and adult groups. It has six employees. Prior to the agreement Budget Travel Ltd owned the entire issued share capital of BTSA.

The products

7. The service provided by BTSA involves organising accommodation as well as travel arrangements directly with carriers and hotels and through various agents for groups (10 or more people) wishing to travel abroad.

The Market

8. The Irish holiday travel industry is estimated to cater for 250,000 people travelling abroad

each year. The majority of such travellers avail of an inclusive tour package marketed by a tour operator or travel agent which relieves them of the burden of arranging the many details associated with going on a foreign holiday. Tour operators pre-book airline flights and accommodation at 'sun holiday' destinations and then attempt to sell these as 'package holidays'. Package holidays normally cater for individuals or small family groups. The service provided by BTSA is for groups of 10 or more people. Many of these would be school groups. Normally such a group will approach the tour operator and ask them to arrange a group tour, perhaps indicating particular extras. Generally such tours do not go to 'sun holiday' locations and such groups do not go on 'package holidays'. The services offered by BTSA are the arranging of tours to meet the requirements of the specific groups. Accordingly, the market in which BTSA is involved—the market for group tours—is a niche market within the overall holiday travel industry. It is a separate and distinct market from the overall holiday travel market. 3.7

9. The market for group tours in which BTSA is active caters for between 20,000 and 25,000 passengers per year. BTSA has a substantial share of this market. Its main competitors are Student and Group Travel Ltd, Group and Educational Travel Ltd, Funtrek and Campotel.

The agreement

10. The agreement for the sale and purchase of BTSA was made on 7 November 1991. Under the agreement, Budget Travel Ltd. agreed to sell BTSA to Phil Fortune and to accept a number of restrictions on their future activity in the market for group tours. Specifically, Budget Travel Ltd. gave undertakings in Clause 13(b) of the Agreement not to:

> (i) For a period of two years from Completion be directly or indirectly interested or concerned in or assist in carrying on any business, undertaking, company or firm actively marketing, promoting, or selling, tours or holidays catering for school or academic institutions, PROVIDED ALWAYS that nothing in this clause shall prevent the Vendor from accepting group bookings from school and other academic institutions for holidays the nature of which the Vendor presently promotes, or
>
> (ii) For a period of four years from Completion either on their own or each of their own account or on behalf of any person, firm or company solicit the employment of or enter into partnership with or appoint as consultant any person who is at Completion or who has within the six months prior to Completion [been] an officer or employee of the company or,
>
> (iii) At any time hereafter make use of or disclose or divulge to any third party any information of a secret or confidential nature relating to the business of the Company.

Submissions of the parties

11. Phil Fortune was asked to justify the restrictions in Clause 13 (b) of the agreement.

12. In relation to 13(b)(i), Phil Fortune submitted that it was 'entirely justifiable' because it has as its objective 'only the transfer of the entire worth of the company'. In addition, the purchaser stated that the ambit of this clause was justifiable 'on the grounds that unless such a clause was included in the manner in which same is now included it would be possible for the Vendor to establish a Company either in Northern Ireland or England and retain Sales Persons on a commission or other basis in this jurisdiction to compete directly' with BTSA.

13. The restriction in 13(b)(ii) was justified by Phil Fortune on the following basis:

> In order for the Company to succeed, the Company must retain its qualified and trained staff, who constitute one of its principal assets. The restriction imposed by Clause 13(b)(ii) merely prevents the Vendor Company 'soliciting' the employment of certain

3.7 officers or employees of the Company. We submit that the restrictions imposed by this clause are justified by section 4 of the Competition Act 1991, on the same grounds as Vendor and Purchaser covenants are justified in European law, in that same are 'essential to the preservation of the transferred worth of the undertaking'. The only rationale behind the 'four year' and 'two year' terms is that same were so negotiated between the parties.

14. Following discussions with the Authority, Phil Fortune agreed by letter dated 22 June 1992, to accept a lesser period of three years for the duration of this clause.

15. The case advanced by Phil Fortune in support of 13(b)(iii) was as follows:

> Clause 13(b)(iii) of the Agreement is entirely justifiable on the same grounds as the earlier paragraphs of this clause, namely that they have as their objective only the transfer of the entire worth of the company. We respectfully submit that it is inconceivable that a vendor of shares in a company should be permitted, after the sale thereof, to disclose business information of a secret or confidential nature to any third party. Such disclosure would undoubtedly undermine the present stability and future viability of the company.

16. Phil Fortune also gave an indication of the type of information that was meant to be covered by the Clause:

> . . . it is clear that information pertaining to the business operated by Budget Travel Schools Abroad Ltd, relating, for example, to that company's profits, margins, turnover, overheads and other financial information not in the public domain, must be covered by such expressions. On the other hand, information which is clearly in the public domain, such as accounts disclosed pursuant to the Companies Act, prices and locations disclosed in brochures and other literature, are clearly not included in the aforementioned expressions.

17. In a letter dated 22 June 1992, Phil Fortune stated that 'she will not use or attempt to use this clause in any manner which would prevent the Vendor re-entering the market after the period provided by Clause 13(b)(i) has expired'.

Assessment

(a) *Section 4(1)*

18. Section 4(1) of the Competition Act states that 'all agreements between undertakings, decisions by associations of undertakings and concerted practices which have as their object or effect the prevention, restriction or distortion of competition in trade in any goods or services in the State or in any part of the State are prohibited and void'.

(b) *The Undertakings and the Agreement*

19. The Authority is concerned with an agreement between Phil Fortune and Budget Travel Ltd. Section 3(1) of the Competition Act defines an undertaking as 'a person being an individual, a body corporate or an unincorporated body of persons engaged for gain in the production, supply or distribution of goods or the provision of a service.'

20. Budget Travel Ltd. is a subsidiary of the U.K. publicly quoted Granada group. It acts as a tour operator on the Irish market and is clearly an undertaking within the meaning of section 3 of the Act. Prior to this agreement Budget Travel Ltd. was the owner of BTSA.

21. Phil Fortune, a former employee of BTSA, has bought the company from Budget Travel Ltd. Section 3 of the Act explicitly states that individuals may come within the definition of undertakings if they are 'engaged for gain in the production, supply or distribution of goods

or the provision of a service.' **3.7**

22. The Competition Authority has decided in previous cases that individuals who either own or control a business are undertakings for the purposes of the Act[1] provided they are engaged for gain in the production, supply and distribution of goods and services through the firms which they control.

23. In this respect the Authority has followed the approach taken by the European Commission which has ruled in a number of cases under Article 85(1) of the Treaty of Rome, on which section 4(1) of the Act is based, that individuals can be undertakings in certain circumstances. In the Nutricia case the Commission decided, and the European Court of Justice agreed, that individuals were undertakings by virtue of their being the future proprietors of a business.[2] This ruling is of particular relevance to the present agreement as Phil Fortune became the owner of BTSA under the agreement.

24. For the reasons detailed above, Budget Travel Ltd. and Phil Fortune are considered to be undertakings within the meaning of section 4(1) of the Act. The present arrangements constitute an agreement between undertakings which applies within the State as both parties to the agreement operate within the State.

(c) *Effect of the Arrangements*

(i) The Sale Agreement

25. The arrangements notified are essentially concerned with the transfer of ownership of BTSA from Budget Travel to Phil Fortune, a former manager in BTSA. BTSA specialise in organising tours for school and adult groups.

26. In a previous decision, the Authority indicated that an agreement for the sale and purchase of a business may come within the scope of section 4(1) of the Competition Act.[3] The present agreement involves the purchase of a business by an individual who was previously an employee of that business. The purchaser was not, therefore, in competition with the business concerned prior to this agreement, and the sale of the business of itself cannot, therefore, prevent, restrict or distort competition within the State or any part of the State and does not offend against section 4(1). It is possible that competition may become more intense if Budget Travel Ltd. decide to re-enter the market when the restriction on their participation in it expires.

(ii) Restraints on Competition

27. The agreement contains a number of provisions which may be described as non-competition clauses. These are contained in Clause 13(b) of the agreement. In this Clause Budget Travel Ltd. gives undertakings not to:

(i) carry on business in competition with the purchaser in the relevant market for a period of 2 years, (13(b)(i));
(ii) solicit, appoint as consultants or enter into partnership with employees of BTSA for a period of 4 years, (13(b)(ii));
(iii) reveal secret or confidential information relating to the business of BTSA, (13(b)(iii)).

28. The Authority has given its views on non-competition clauses in Nallen/O'Toole and a number of other decisions. In these cases the Authority took the view that some restraint on

1. Notification Nos. CA/1/91 — Nallen O'Toole (Belmullet), decision of 2 April 1991 and CA/9/91 — ACT/Kindle, decision of 4 September 1992.
2. Nutricia/De Rooij and Nutricia/Zuid Hollandse Conservenfabriek (83/670/EEC, OJ L376, 31.12.83, p. 220, on appeal *Remia BV and Others v. European Commission, Case 42/84* [1985] ECR 2545.
3. Notification No. CA/10/92 — Woodchester Bank Ltd/UDT Bank Ltd, decision of 4 August 1992.

3.7 the business activities of the vendors may be necessary to ensure the adequate transfer of the goodwill of the business concerned. The Authority decided that the restraint must be limited in terms of its scope, duration and geographical coverage to that which is necessary to fully secure the transfer of the goodwill. Provided this is the case, then such a restraint does not restrict competition in the market in question. In this respect the Authority has followed the views of the EC Commission in respect of similar agreements under Article 85(1) which have been endorsed by the European Court of Justice.

29. The Authority accepts that in the present case some restriction on Budget Travel competing in the relevant market is necessary to secure the complete transfer of the goodwill of BTSA. The issue therefore is whether the restrictions in the notified agreement are limited to what is necessary to secure the transfer of the goodwill.

Clause 13(b)(i)

30. In Clause 13(b)(i), Budget Travel Ltd. have undertaken not to become involved in the relevant market for a period of two years. The Authority has indicated in previous decisions that it would normally regard a time limit of two years as being adequate for the transfer of goodwill. This clause, does not, therefore, offend against section 4(1) of the Act by virtue of its duration.

31. On the question of the geographical scope of the non-competition clause in 13(b)(i), no specific geographical area to which it applies is specified.

32. The European Commission ruled in the Nutricia case that:

> The geographical scope of a non-competition clause also has to be limited to the extent which is objectively necessary to achieve the aforementioned goal. As a rule, it should therefore only cover the markets where the products concerned were manufactured or sold at the time of the agreements.

33. The Authority took a similar view in the Nallen/O'Toole and ACT/Kindle cases. In the latter case, no specific geographical area was mentioned in the restrictive clauses. This was found to be acceptable by the Authority given that, prior to the agreement, Kindle was operating on a worldwide basis.

34. It has been argued that Budget could compete directly with BTSA by establishing a company either in Northern Ireland or England and retaining sales persons on a commission or other basis. Accordingly, the application of the non-competition clause in 13(b)(i) was not limited to the Irish market. The Authority accepts the validity of this argument and does not consider that this restriction offends against section 4(1) of the Act.

35. In relation to the scope of the clause, Budget Travel Ltd. are required not to compete in the market for group tours which is the market in which BTSA was involved at the time of the agreement. Therefore, the scope of the restriction does not restrain the vendors from being active in any market outside of the one served by BTSA. It is evident that the scope of the restriction does not go beyond what is necessary for the transfer of the goodwill and does not offend against section 4(1) of the Act.

Clause 13(b)(ii)

36. This Clause prevents Budget Travel Ltd. from soliciting into employment, entering into partnership with or appointing as consultants employees of BTSA for a period of 4 years.

37. The justification advanced for the restriction was that it was essential for BTSA to 'retain its qualified and trained staff, who constituted one of its principal assets', and that it was 'essential to the preservation of the transferred worth of the undertaking'.

38. There is little doubt that BTSA employees who have worked in this area over a number of years have become familiar with the various facets of the business and will be efficient in dealing with them. However, this knowledge does not constitute technical know-how as

defined by the Authority in ACT/Kindle. Accordingly, it is the Authority's view that the expertise of the employees of BTSA represents primarily part of the goodwill of the company. **3.7**

39. In principle, there is nothing wrong with preventing the vendors from soliciting the services of BTSA employees for a period of time. Such a restriction ensures that the goodwill of the company being purchased is transferred.[4] In this case, however, the original clause may have gone beyond what was required to secure the transfer of the goodwill of BTSA because of its duration. Phil Fortune has agreed to accept a lesser period of three years. The Authority believes that, given the fact that personal contacts are quite important in this business, Ms Fortune, despite her background in the business, will need some time to establish a reputation for the newly managed entity, and that the restriction on Budget Travel competing in the group tour market is for only 2 years, the three years duration now proposed for this clause is acceptable and does not offend against section 4(1).

Clause 13(b)(iii)

40. This Clause prevents Budget Travel Ltd. from using, disclosing or divulging information of a secret or confidential nature about BTSA. The restriction is not limited in terms of its duration.

41. In advancing a case to support this Clause a distinction was made by Phil Fortune between business information in the public domain and other business information such as profits, margins, turnover, overheads and other financial matters not in the public domain. The intention is to prevent the disclosure and use of the latter type of information. Phil Fortune's main argument in relation to this Clause was that it was essential to 'transfer the entire worth of the company'.

42. Confidential business information may constitute an important part of the value of the transferred undertaking. The use of such information may confer a competitive advantage on the vendor. Nonetheless, the value of the type of confidential business information referred to in this case will be eroded over time. Eventually, it will be worthless and restrictions on its disclosure or use will become meaningless.

43. The Authority is concerned, however, that such a clause should not be used to impede any possible re-entry into the market by Budget once the two year non-competition clause in 13(b)(i) has expired. In particular, the Authority would be concerned that the effect of this could be to prevent Budget using its knowledge of the market for group tours if they decided to engage in that market in the future. The Authority accepts Phil Fortune's undertaking not to 'use or attempt to use this clause in any manner which would prevent the Vendor re-entering the market after the period provided by clause (b)(i) has expired'. In the light of this undertaking the Authority considers that this clause does not offend against section 4(1) of the Act.

The Decision

44. Phil Fortune and Budget Travel Ltd. are undertakings within the meaning of section 3 of the Competition Act and the arrangements in question constitute an agreement which applies within the State.

45. The Authority believes that the agreement for the sale of BTSA does not prevent, restrict or distort competition in the State or in any part of the State.

46. In the case of a sale of business, some restriction on the seller is essential in order to ensure the complete transfer of the goodwill for which the purchaser has paid. The Authority believes that the non-competition clause in the present agreement between Phil Fortune and Budget Travel Ltd. as amended by, and with the undertaking regarding clause 13(b)(iii) given in the letter of 22 June 1992, is limited to what is necessary to ensure the complete transfer of the goodwill of BTSA and that it does not offend against section 4(1) of the Competition Act 1991.

4. The Authority took a similar view in Woodchester Bank/UDT Bank.

3.7 The Certificate

47. The Competition Authority has issued the following certificate:

> The Competition Authority certifies that, in its opinion, on the basis of the facts in its possession , the agreement between Phil Fortune and Budget Travel Ltd (CA/1/92) for the sale of Budget Travel Schools Abroad Ltd, notified on 17 January 1992 under section 7, as amended by, and with the undertaking regarding clause 13(b)(iii) given in the letter of 22 June 1992, does not offend against section 4(1) of the Competition Act 1991.

For the Competition Authority

Patrick Massey
Member

14 September 1992

3.8 Competition Authority Decision No. 10, G.I. Corporation/General Semiconductor Industries Inc.: 23 October 1992, Notification Nos. CA/51/92 and CA/52/92

Multi-national acquisition agreement – Sale of entire share capital in Irish company – Five year restriction on vendor from competing in EC and North America – One year restriction on soliciting employees – Restriction on negotiation with other parties pending completion – Whether acquisition agreement reviewable under Competition Act – Whether restrictions in excess of two years are justified where know-how is transferred – Articles 85 and 86 of the Treaty of Rome – EC Council Regulation 4069/89, EC Council Regulation 556/89 – Mergers, Take-overs and Monopolies (Control) Act, (No. 17) 1978, section 5 – Competition Act (No. 24) 1991, sections 3, 4, 5 and 7

Facts: On 18 June 1992 notification was made to the Authority of a worldwide asset acquisition agreement and a share acquisition agreement for a certificate under section 4(4) of the Competition Act, or failing that, a licence under section 4(2). General Semiconductor Ireland ('GSI') is an unlimited company incorporated in Ireland and which is a subsidiary of General Semiconductor Inc. which is in turn a subsidiary of Schneider SA listed on the Paris Stock Exchange. G.I. Corporation is a subsidiary of General Instrument Corporation ('G.I.') a public corporation incorporated in the United States.

GSI manufactures and sells protection devices for electronic circuitry in Ireland. G.I. corporation has no manufacturing facility for such devices in Europe but does sell such devices in Europe.

Under the arrangements G.I. Corporation purchased the entire share capital of GSI. General Semiconductor Inc. and its affiliates covenanted for the benefit of G.I. Corporation to comply with restrictions in the multi-national acquisition agreement. One quite intricate restriction effectively precluded General Semiconductor Inc. and its affiliates for a period of five years in the EEC and North America from carrying on business which was conducted by GSI. This restriction was subject to the right of General Semiconductor Inc. to manufacture and to subcontract the manufacture of specified products. In addition General Semiconductor Inc. was precluded from conducting other sale negotiations relating to the subject of the acquisition agreement while the parties awaited the conclusion of the acquisition agreement. General Semiconductor Inc. also covenanted not to solicit employees for one year after the completion of the agreement. 3.8

Submissions: The parties notifying the arrangements submitted:

(1) The agreements were not reviewable under the Competition Act 1991 because the agreements are notifiable under the Mergers Act.

(2) An agreement for the acquisition of the entire share capital of another company is a concentration and is not affected by section 4 of the Competition Act by analogy with EC Council Regulation 4069/89 and Article 86 of the Treaty of Rome.

(3) The periods for the restrictions are related to the time during which a potential competitor would be able to build a market position equivalent to the life span of the goodwill and know how of GSI.

(4) The five year competition restriction is a reasonable period because the agreements concern the transfer of know-how.

Decided by the Authority: In issuing a certificate under section 4(4) of the Competition Act 1991 in respect of the notified arrangements that:

(1) The share acquisition agreement and the restrictive clauses contained in a separate notification constitute agreements between undertakings which have effect within the State.

(2) The relevant market is the manufacture and supply of protection devices for electronic circuitry.

(3) The rejection in the Woodchester/UDT decision of the argument that section 4 of the Competition Act does not apply to mergers is reiterated. The acquisition of the entire share capital of a company may be affected by section 4.

(4) The sales of the protection devices for electronic circuitry in this State represent small percentages of the worldwide sales of those devices by both the vendor and the purchaser. The vendor and purchaser hold less than 5% of the relevant Irish market.

(5) Two strong competitors of the vendor and purchaser in the relevant market indicate a high degree of concentration. The considerable number of small suppliers indicate the relative ease with which new competitors can enter the market. The share acquisition agreement does not offend against section 4(1).

(6) Restrictions in excess of 2 years can be justified where a transfer of technical know-how and goodwill occurs as was decided in the Authority's decision, ACT/Kindle. The know-how transferred in the notified arrangements meet the know-how requirements specified in ACT/Kindle and the EC Council Regulation on know-how licensing.

(7) The covenant not to negotiate pending the closing of the acquisition agreement was for a brief period and no longer has effect. Such provisions do not offend against section 4(1) of the Competition Act.

(8) The limited restriction on the soliciting of employees by a vendor does not offend against section 4(1) when as stated in the Woodchester/UDT decision 'exper-

3.8 tise is an integral part of the goodwill of the company being sold. . . . The restriction on soliciting employees which does not prevent employees from responding to advertisements does not offend against section 4(1)'.

Cases and Decisions referred to:
Remia v Commission (Case No. 42/84) 11.7.85. [1985] ECR 2545; [1987] 1 CMLR 1
EC Commission Decision — Reuter/BASF – 26.7.76. [1976] OJ L254/40; [1976] 2 CMLR D44
Competition Authority Decision No. 1 Nallen/O'Toole 2 April 1992. **3.3**
Competition Authority Decision No. 3 Athlone Travel/Michael Stein Travel Ltd – 4 June 1992 **3.4**
Competition Authority Decision No. 6 Woodchester/UDT Bank Ltd – 4 August 1994 **3.5**
Competition Authority Decision No. 8 ACT Group plc/Kindle Group Ltd. – 4 September 1992 **3.6**
Competition Authority Decision No. 9 Phil Fortune & Budget Travel Ltd – 14 September 1992 **3.7**

Competition Authority Decision of 23 October 1992 relating to a proceeding under section 4 of the Competition Act 1991 Notification Nos. CA/51/92 and CA/52/92 — G.I. Corporation/General Semiconductor Industries Inc.

Introduction

1. Arrangements for the acquisition of General Semiconductor Ireland, a Cork based manufacturer of electrical devices, and certain assets of its parent company, General Semiconductor Industries Inc., by G.I. Corporation, a multinational company based in the US, were notified to the Competition Authority on 18 June 1992. The arrangements were notified for the purposes of obtaining a certificate under section 4(4) of the Competition Act 1991 or, in the event of a refusal by the Authority to issue a certificate, a licence under section 4(2) of the Act. The acquisition and restrictive clauses included in the arrangements were notified separately. The Authority is considering these notifications together for the purposes of this decision.

2. Notice of the intention of the Authority to take a favourable decision in relation to the arrangements was published in the Irish Times on 14 August 1992. No observations were received from third parties.

The Facts

(a) *The subject of the decision*

3. This decision concerns the acquisition of General Semiconductor Ireland by G.I. Corporation. Restrictive clauses are included in the arrangements for the acquisition.

(b) *The parties concerned*

4. The parties to the agreement are G.I. Corporation, General Semiconductor Industries Inc. and Square D Company. G.I. Corporation is the principal operating subsidiary of General Instrument Corporation (G.I.) of Chicago, Illinois. G.I. is a publicly held company. It is a holding company with no assets or operations other than through G.I. Corporation.

5. The gross value of the assets of G.I. Corporation, as it appears from its latest audited consolidated accounts to 31 December 1991, is US$1,783m. The turnover of G.I. Corporation, excluding payments in respect of value added tax on sales, for the 10 month period ended 31 December 1991, is US$785m.

6. General Semiconductor Ireland was incorporated in Ireland on 10 December 1981 under the name General Semiconductor Ireland Ltd and was subsequently re-registered as an unlimited liability company on 5 December 1988 under the name of General Semiconductor Ireland. It is a wholly owned subsidiary of General Semiconductor Industries Inc. General Semiconductor Industries Inc is in turn a wholly owned subsidiary of Square D Investment Company which is in turn a wholly owned subsidiary of Square D Company. The ultimate parent is Schneider SA public company with its shares quoted on the Paris Stock Exchange. **3.8**

7. General Semiconductor Ireland has an authorised share capital of IR£10,000,000 divided into 10,000,000 ordinary shares of IR£1 each of which 1,895,000 ordinary shares of IR£1 each have been issued and allotted. General Semiconductor Industries Inc is the beneficial owner of all of the issued share capital of General Semiconductor Ireland. Square D Company is a nominee on behalf of General Semiconductor Industries Inc in respect of one share in General Semiconductor Ireland.

(c) *The products and the market*

8. General Semiconductor Ireland is a manufacturer of avalanche transient voltage suppressors for the home and export markets. These products protect sensitive electronic systems from voltage and current surges induced by such phenomena as lightning, load switching, electrostatic discharges, etc. They operate by clamping the transient voltage and redirecting the energy away from sensitive components. Such protection devices exist in all electrical systems and therefore the market for these devices covers all electronic end use sectors including the automotive, computer, consumer, industrial and telecommunications industries. The parties have claimed that similar protection devices are inductors, capacitors, carbon blocks, Metal Oxide Varistors, zener diodes and thyristors. The market can be described as the market for protection devices for electronic circuitry.

9. The value of sales of protection devices for electronic circuitry in Ireland is estimated by the parties to be IR£4m annually. They estimate that General Semiconductor Ireland and G.I. Corporation each has less than 5% of the Irish market. Other major suppliers are Motorola, Thomson, Toshiba and Microsemi. Entry costs are low and therefore a large number of smaller suppliers operate in the market. According to the parties Motorola and Thomson each have over 30% of the market.

10. General Semiconductor Ireland sells to a broad range of industrial sectors in Ireland. G.I. Corporation has no manufacturing facility in Europe, it sells its products through various agents.

11. The parties estimate that total worldwide sales of protection devices in 1990 was US$570m approx. G.I. Corporation supplies protection devices to the automotive, computer, consumer, industrial and telecommunications sectors and in particular to the cable and satellite television industry.

The arrangements

12. Two agreements known as the 'Main Acquisition Agreement' and the 'Irish Agreement' give effect to the arrangements. Under the agreements, General Semiconductor Industries Inc and its nominee, who own all of the issued and outstanding shares of par value IR£1 per share in General Semiconductor Ireland, agree to sell the shares and the assets specified in the Main Acquisition Agreement to G.I. Corporation. The Irish agreement deals only with the acquisition of the shares.

13. Section 1.01(ii) of the 'Main Acquisition Agreement' sets out the assets being purchased by G.I. Corporation. These assets include:

> . . .(b) all technical, manufacturing or marketing information, new development, inventions or ideas, know-how and trade secrets used or held for use in connection with the Products or the Business and all documentation thereof, including related papers,

3.8 parts drawings, blueprints and specification sheets, tool drawings, chemical compositions, formulae, diaries, notebooks, specifications, methods of manufacture, data processing cards, discs and tapes and all data contained therein or thereon and all rights thereto;

(c) all customer files, customer lists, collection and credit records, purchasing records, supplier lists, parts lists, bills of material, catalogues, advertising literature, vendor lists, and all rights or claims in or under customers' and suppliers' contracts used or held for use in connection with the Products or the Business;

(d) all patents, copyrights, and applications and registrations therefor used or held for use in connection with the Products or the Business, including, without limitation, those listed in Schedule 1.01(d);

(e) the trademarks and service marks and registrations therefor used or held for use in connection with the Products or the Business, including, without limitation, those listed in Schedule 1.01(e);

(f) all patent, trade secrets, technology licenses or other licence agreements, software designs, machine readable data, drawings, unpatented designs or processes, formulae, know-how, technical assistance or other proprietary rights of Seller used or held for use in connection with the Products or the Business, including, without limitation, those listed in Schedule 1.01(f);

(o) the name 'General Semiconductor Industries, Inc.', 'GSI' or any similar name and any trade names, trademarks, service names, service marks or corporate symbols or logos utilising such name or any similar name; . . .

14. The provisions of the 'Main Acquisition Agreement' were incorporated into the 'Irish Agreement' by reference. The relevant provision in the 'Irish Agreement' is as follows:

3. The Seller has agreed to sell and the Purchaser has agreed to purchase certain assets described in the Main Agreement and to purchase the Shares free from all Encumbrances, for the consideration stated in the Main Agreement. The purpose of this Agreement is to evidence the Agreement to sell the Shares and the consideration relating thereto shall be paid on Closing and the allocation of the consideration to such Shares shall be determined by the Purchaser in accordance with the Main Agreement.

15. The 'Main Acquisition Agreement' also contained a number of restrictive covenants accepted by the vendors:

8.10 Non-competition by Seller and Parent

(a) Seller and Parent[1] hereby agree that, subject to the consummation of the transactions herein provided for, neither they nor any Square D Affiliate will, prior to the fifth anniversary of the Closing Date, directly or indirectly, and whether as principal or agent or otherwise, alone or in association with any Person, engage, anywhere in North America or the European Economic Community, in the business carried on by GSI Ireland or the Business (or any business which is substantially similar therewith) at any time during the three years preceding the Closing Date (the 'Restricted Period'); provided, however, that Parent may itself manufacture or subcontract the manufacture of the following products (the 'Excluded Products') solely for the purpose of including

1. Square D Company.

the same as components in Parent's products: (i) trilliant surge arrestors, (ii) SP 1175, (iii) SP 3650 and (iv) any other similar surge arrestors; provided, further, however, that Parent may not manufacture any component used in such Excluded Products if such component was manufactured by Seller or GSI Ireland during the Restricted Period (but may subcontract or license the manufacture or otherwise have made any such component solely for use in the Excluded Products; provided that such subcontracting, licensing, manufacturing or having made such components will not violate or infringe upon any Intellectual Property which is a Purchased Asset). Notwithstanding the foregoing, the restrictions contained in this section 8.10(a) shall not be applicable to the purchase by a Square D Affiliate, solely for the purposes of investment, of up to 10% of the outstanding equity securities of a corporation, some or all of the operations of which would otherwise violate the foregoing prohibitions. **3.8**

(b) If any court of competent jurisdiction determines that section 8.10(a), or any clause therein, is unenforceable because of the duration or geographic scope of section 8.10(a), such court shall have the power to reduce the duration or scope of such clause, as the case may be, and, in its reduced form, such clause shall then be enforceable. Each of Seller and Parent acknowledges that Purchaser may have no adequate remedy at law if Seller, Parent or any Seller Affiliate violates any of the terms contained in section 8.10(a). In such event, Purchaser shall have the right, in addition to any other rights it may have, to obtain in any court of competent jurisdiction injunctive relief to restrain any breach or threatened breach hereof or otherwise to specifically enforce any of the provisions in section 8.10(a).

8.11 No-Shop. Between the date of this Agreement and the Closing, none of Seller, Parent or any of their respective representatives shall, directly or indirectly, solicit or engage in discussions or negotiations with or provide any information to, or otherwise cooperate with any Person which seeks to acquire, or expresses an interest in acquiring, all or any part of the Business or the Purchased Assets, or for the purpose of otherwise effecting a transaction inconsistent with the transactions contemplated by this Agreement. It is understood that this section 8.11 does not restrict the activities of Seller or Parent with respect to the sale of assets other than the Purchased Assets or GSI Ireland or businesses other than the Business.

8.12 No Raiding. For a period of one year from and after the Closing, neither Seller nor any Seller Affiliate will solicit to employ or hire any Person listed on Schedule 6.19 or any employee of GSI Ireland retained by GSI Ireland after the Closing Date, except for employees (i) whose employment has been terminated by Purchaser or GSI Ireland, as the case may be, or (ii) who respond to general, non-directed, employment solicitations through an independent employment agency or advertisement.

Submission of the parties

16. The notifying parties have argued that the acquisition is not reviewable under the Competition Act 1991, because it is notifiable under the Mergers Act. In addition, they have submitted that:

> . . . whilst the Competition Act amended certain aspects of the Mergers Act, it was not the intention of the legislature that transactions notified under the Mergers Act might also be reviewed under the Competition Act.

17. The notifying parties also argued that 'if transactions notified under the Mergers Act could also be reviewed under the Competition Act, this would introduce a serious degree of

3.8 uncertainty into commercial transactions. . . .' It was acknowledged by the notifying parties at a subsequent meeting with the Authority that lesser significance might be applied to this particular argument that mergers cannot be reviewed under section 4 of the Competition Act than to the argument referred to in Para. 18.

18. The parties also argued that:

> Where the acquisition is that of a 100% interest in another company and this results in a concentration, then subject to EC Council Regulation 4069/89, the acquisition is only reviewable under Article 86 of the Treaty. By analogy, an acquisition of a 100% interest in another company which results in a concentration may only be reviewed under the Competition Act (if at all) under section 5 of the Act. . . .
>
> . . . the parties submit that the acquisition by G.I. Corporation of the entire issued share capital of General Semiconductor Ireland and certain assets of General Semiconductor Industries Inc constitutes a concentration and, therefore, may only be reviewed under the Competition Act (if at all) under section 5 of the Act. On this basis, the parties submit that the acquisition is not subject to review by the Competition Authority under the Competition Act. In particular, on notifications under the Competition Act, the Competition Authority reviews agreements in the context of section 4 of the Competition Act and not section 5. . . .

19. The notifying parties have submitted the following arguments in support of the inclusion of the restrictive covenants at 8.10, 8.11 and 8.12 of the 'Main Acquisition Agreement':

> It is submitted that, by analogy with the criteria adopted in the *Reuter/BASF* Decision, the *Remia* judgement and the Decision of the Authority in *Nallen/O'Toole*, the restrictions in Clauses 8.10, 8.11 and 8.12 of the Main Agreement should not be held to infringe section 4(1) of the Act. The periods during which the restrictions are to apply are related to the time during which a potential competitor would be able to build up a market position equivalent to the lifespan of the goodwill and know-how of General Semiconductors Ireland protected by Clauses 8.10, 8.11 and 8.12 of the Main Agreement.
>
> In particular, as the transfer of the business involves the transfer of goodwill and know-how a period of five years as under clause 8.10 is reasonable in the circumstances and does not have as its object or effect the prevention, restriction or distortion of competition in trade in any goods or services in the State or any part of the State. The know-how which is being transferred with the business involves formulae and technology required to manufacture the products. The provisions in clauses 8.11 and 8.12 are less restrictive and operate for shorter periods of time than those in clause 8.10. These provisions should also be considered as reasonable and necessary to protect the value of the know-how being transferred in particular the knowledge of employees of General Semiconductor Ireland in relation to the products manufactured at the Macroom plant.

Assessment

(a) *Section 4(1)*

20. Section 4(1) of the Competition Act states that 'all agreements between undertakings, decisions by associations of undertakings and concerted practices which have as their object or effect the prevention, restriction or distortion of competition in trade in any goods or services in the State or in any part of the State are prohibited and void'.

(b) *The Undertakings*

21. Section 3(1) of the Competition Act defines an undertaking as 'a person being an individual, a body corporate or an unincorporated body of persons engaged for gain in the production, supply or distribution of goods or the provision of a service.' The parties involved

in the present notification, G.I. Corporation and General Semiconductor Industries Inc., are both corporate bodies engaged for gain in the electronic industry and are therefore undertakings within the meaning of the Act. **3.8**

(c) *The Agreements*

22. Under the agreements G.I. Corporation has acquired certain assets of General Semiconductor Industries Inc., as provided for in the 'Main Acquisition Agreement' and the entire issued share capital of General Semiconductor Ireland, as provided for in the 'Irish Agreement'.

The agreements include a number of restrictive covenants. They constitute agreements between undertakings which have effects within the State.

(d) *The Acquisition*

23. The parties have argued that the arrangements constitute a 'merger or takeover' within the meaning of section 5 of the Mergers, Takeovers and Monopolies (Control) Act 1978 (the Mergers Act) as amended by the Competition Act. They have indicated that the acquisition has been notified and approved under the Mergers Act and therefore they claimed that it should not be reviewable under the Competition Act. The arguments advanced by the notifying parties in support of their position are similar to those set out in the Woodchester/UDT decision.[2] Briefly these arguments are as follows:

— it was not the intention of the legislature that transactions notified under the Mergers Act might also be reviewed under the Competition Act;

— if transactions notified under the Mergers Act were reviewable under the Competition Act, a serious degree of uncertainty would be introduced into commercial transactions;

— it would be inconsistent to have an acquisition approved by the Minister for Industry and Commerce under the Mergers Act subject to review under the Competition Act.

— on the basis of EC precedents, the acquisition of a 100% interest in a company can only be reviewed under section 5 of the Competition Act, if at all.

24. The Authority concluded in its Woodchester/UDT decision that the arrangements notified for the acquisition of UDT did not enjoy any automatic exemption from the provisions of section 4(1) of the Competition Act. In arriving at this conclusion the Authority noted that section 4(1) specifically referred to 'all agreements' without exception. In addition, the Authority stated that ancillary clauses, forming part of merger agreements and containing restrictions on competition, could escape scrutiny under section 4(1) if merger agreements were not reviewable under the Competition Act. The Authority added that it would be inconsistent for the Competition Act not to apply to agreements notified under the Mergers Act when it could apply to mergers that were below the thresholds set for notifications under that Act. The Authority rejected the argument put forward by the notifying parties that section 4 of the Competition Act could not be applied where the acquisition of a 100% interest in a company was involved in its decision in respect of Woodchester/UDT.

25. The present agreements are between General Semiconductor Industries Inc., its parent Square D Company and G.I. Corporation.

The result of the agreements is that General Semiconductor Ireland will now be owned by G.I. Corporation and that one competitor will be eliminated from the Irish market. The Authority indicated in its decision on Woodchester/UDT that it did not consider that a reduction in the number of competitors, of itself, constituted a restriction of competition. The question is whether such an arrangement may be viewed as preventing, restricting or distorting competition in the market. Accordingly, the impact of the acquisition on the market for

2. Notification no. CA/10/92 – Woodchester Investments plc. and Woodchester Bank Ltd., UDT Bank Ltd., decision of 4 August 1992

3.8 protection devices for electronic circuitry in Ireland must be considered.

26. The principal activity of General Semiconductor Ireland is the manufacture of avalanche transient voltage suppressors for the electronics industry. The vast majority of the company's sales are achieved on worldwide markets with 2% of sales generated in Ireland. G.I. Corporation is a major supplier of systems and equipment (including electronic protection devices) to the cable and satellite television market. Its sales of protection devices for electronic circuitry in Ireland represent a negligible percentage of its overall sales. According to the parties' estimates General Semiconductor Ireland and G.I. Corporation each held less than 5% of the Irish market which is estimated to be worth $4m.

27. The products supplied as protection devices are numerous — inductors, capacitors, carbon blocks, ziener diodes, etc. The Authority has accepted the parties' claim that these products are substitutes for the voltage suppressors supplied by General Semiconductor Ireland as they carry out the same function and can be used in electronic devices found in a broad range of industries. Accordingly, the provision of voltage suppressors should not be regarded as a separate market.

28. While the acquisition of General Semiconductor Ireland will increase G.I. Corporation's share of the Irish market for protection devices for electronic circuitry, the Authority does not believe that the increase in market share of itself could be regarded as preventing, restricting or distorting competition, as it will amount to less than 10%. There are a considerable number of strong competitors such as Motorola and Thomson supplying the market to ensure against such a possibility. The cumulative share of the market held by these two companies is claimed to be about 60% which implies that a high degree of concentration exists in this market. The cost of becoming involved in this business is relatively small and this accounts for the large number of small suppliers who are involved in it. In addition, there is considerable competition from imports in this market. In these circumstances, the Authority does not believe that the acquisition of General Semiconductor Ireland by G.I. Corporation offends against section 4(1) of the Act.

(e) *Restraints on competition*

29. Clauses 8.10, 8.11 and 8.12 of the 'Main Acquisition Agreement' contain restrictions on the activities of the vendors.

30. Under Clause 8.10, the vendors undertake not to engage in the business carried on by General Semiconductors Ireland for a period of five years.

31. The Authority has set out its views on clauses similar to 8.10 in a series of previous decisions.[3] In these decisions the Authority indicated that in the case of the sale of a business some restriction on the seller may be necessary in order to ensure the complete transfer of the goodwill of the business. It stated that, provided the restriction was limited in terms of its duration, geographical coverage and subject matter to that which was necessary for the complete transfer of the goodwill, then the restriction was not in breach of section 4(1) of the Act. The Authority's decisions are in line with those of the European Commission in a number of cases under Article 85 of the Treaty of Rome on which section 4 of the Competition Act is based. The Authority has stated that it generally regards a restriction of two years as sufficient to ensure the complete transfer of the goodwill of a business. Having now considered several such agreements the Authority can see no reason for altering this view, and, where only the transfer of goodwill is involved, it will generally not accept a restriction on competition of more than two years.

3. Notification No. CA/8/91 — Nallen/O'Toole (Belmullet), decision of 2 April 1992; CA/12/92—Athlone Travel/Michael Stein Travel Ltd., decision of 4 June 1992; CA/10/92—Woodchester Investments plc. and Woodchester Bank Ltd.; UDT/Bank Ltd., decision of 4 August 1992; CA/1/92—Phil Fortune and Budget Travel Ltd, decision of 14 September 1992; CA/9/91 — ACT Group plc./Kindle Group Ltd, decision of 4 September 1992.

32. In its decision in ACT/Kindle, the Authority indicated that it believed a longer restriction on a seller of a business competing with a purchaser was justified where the sale included the transfer of technical know-how as well as goodwill. The Authority stated that 'It appears unreasonable to afford the purchaser unlimited protection against the use of technical know-how by the seller. As in the Reuter/BASF case it appears reasonable to limit such protection to the time required to allow the purchaser to obtain full control of the undertaking. Once such a reasonable time has elapsed, however, the purchaser is no longer entitled to be protected against competition by the seller. As pointed out the European Commission has indicated that 'where the transfer of a business also involves the transfer of goodwill and know-how, a period of approximately five years will normally be acceptable'. The Authority could find no good reason to depart from EC guidelines on this first occasion on which it considered a non-competition clause relating to technical 'know-how'.' The know-how transferred in this case meets the know-how requirements specified in ACT/Kindle and detailed in the EC Regulation on know-how licensing. The Authority concludes that the five year non-competition clause is justified. 3.8

33. The effect of clause 8.10 is confined to North America and the EEC. General Semiconductor Ireland operates on a worldwide basis therefore the geographical restraint of the clause does not, in the opinion of the Authority, exceed what is necessary to secure the complete transfer of the goodwill and know-how. The restraints relate to protection devices for use in electronic circuits. As this is the market in which General Semiconductor Ireland operates, the subject matter of the restraint does not, in the opinion of the Authority, exceed what is necessary to secure the complete transfer of the goodwill and know-how. Accordingly, the Authority is satisfied that clause 8.10 does not offend against section 4(1) of the Act.

34. Clause 8.11 provides that, having agreed to sell the business of General Semiconductor Ireland, the vendor cannot, before completion, enter into negotiations with or attempt to sell it to another party. The vendor is also prevented from entering into arrangements which would in any way alter the nature of the business being sold. The purpose of these provisions was to ensure that completion of the agreement would not be frustrated by specific actions of the vendors. The provisions were in existence for only a brief period of time and they are no longer in effect, since the contract for sale has been completed. In the Authority's view such provisions do not prevent, restrict or distort competition, and do not offend against section 4(1).

35. Clause 8.12 prevents the vendors from soliciting the employment of former employees for a period of 1 year. This restriction does not apply where the employees respond to advertisements or to general employment solicitations by independent employment agencies.

The Authority has considered similar clauses in its decision in Woodchester/UDT and Phil Fortune/Budget Travel. In Woodchester/ UDT, the vendors, UDT, were prevented from enticing their former executives away from Woodchester for three years. The restriction had no effect where the executives approached UDT with a view to employment or if they responded to a public advertisement from their former employers. The Authority concluded that no breach of section 4(1) had arisen because 'expertise is an integral part of the goodwill of the company being sold and the restriction . . . does not have the effect of tying UDT executives to Woodchester Bank'.

In Phil Fortune/Budget Travel, the vendors, Budget Travel were prevented from soliciting into employment employees of Budget Travel Schools Abroad Ltd. (BTSA—the sale of which was the subject of the agreement) for a period of four years. The Authority found that this clause had gone beyond what was necessary to secure the transfer of the goodwill of BTSA because of its duration. Phil Fortune agreed to accept a lesser period of three years and the Authority concluded that this was acceptable '... given that Ms Fortune, despite her background in the business, will need some time to establish a reputation for the newly managed entity. . . .'

36. The notifying parties have submitted that this clause is 'necessary to protect the value of the know-how being transferred in particular the knowledge of employees of General

3.8 Semiconductor Ireland in relation to the products manufactured at the Macroom plant.' The Authority accepts that this clause is necessary to ensure the complete transfer of the goodwill and know-how of General Semiconductor Ireland. It applies for a period of one year which is not considered to be excessive. In addition, the employees affected by the clause may respond to advertisements and to independent employment agencies during this time. In the circumstances, the Authority considers that clause 8.12 does not offend against section 4(1) of the Act.

The Decision

37. G.I. Corporation, General Semiconductor Industries Inc., Square D Company and General Semiconductor Ireland are undertakings within the meaning of section 3 of the Competition Act and the arrangements in question give effect to agreements which apply within the State.

38. The Authority believes that the agreements for the purchase and sale of assets of General Semiconductor Industries Inc and the issued share capital of General Semiconductor Ireland do not offend against section 4(1) of the Competition Act 1991.

39. In the case of a sale of business, some restriction on the seller is essential in order to ensure the complete transfer of the goodwill for which the purchaser has paid. If these restrictions are limited to that which is necessary to ensure the complete transfer of the goodwill of the business, then, in the Authority's opinion, they do not prevent, restrict or distort competition. For the same reasons the Authority believes that a restriction on competition may be necessary to ensure the complete transfer of all technical know-how. Again such a restriction may not exceed the period necessary to achieve that end. The Authority believes that the restrictive covenants in this agreement satisfy these requirements and that they do not offend against section 4(1) of the Competition Act 1991.

The Certificate

The Competition Authority has issued the following certificate:

> The Competition Authority certifies that, in its opinion, on the basis of the facts in its possession, the agreements between General Semiconductor Industries Inc., Square D Company and G.I. Corporation (CA/51/92 and CA/52/92), for the purchase and sale of assets of General Semiconductor Industries Inc and the issued share capital of General Semiconductor Ireland, including clauses which restrict the vendors from competing with the purchaser, notified on 18 June 1992 under section 7, do not offend against section 4(1) of the Competition Act 1991.

For the Competition Authority

Patrick Massey
Member

23 October 1992

Competition Authority Decision No. 11, Firestone/Grenfell Ltd and Thoroughbred Promotion & Development Company: 5 November 1992, Notification No. CA/673- 4/92E 3.9

Agreement for the sale of Stud Farms and shares in bloodstock auctioneering company – No restrictions on the vendor or purchaser in the arrangements – Whether reasonable doubt that agreement offends section 4 of the Competition Act before notifying under section 7 of the Competition Act – Mergers, Takeovers and Monopolies (Control) Act 1978 (No. 17) – Competition Act 1991 (No. 24) sections 3, 4 and 7

Facts: On 30 September 1992 arrangements for the purchase of two Stud Farms by Grenfell Ltd ('Grenfell') and the purchase of certain shares in Robert J Goffs plc by Thoroughbred Promotion & Development Company ('TPDC') from Mr. and Mrs. Firestone as vendors in each case were notified to the Authority with a request for a certificate under section 4(4) of the Competition Act or, failing that, a licence under section 4(2).

The parties to the notified arrangements were Mr. and Mrs. Firestone, as vendors (the 'Vendors') and TPDC and Grenfell as purchasers. The Vendors owned and operated two Stud Farms in Ireland and also owned a Stud Farm in the USA. TPDC and Grenfell are corporate bodies ultimately owned and controlled by His Highness the Aga Khan through a series of Luxembourg registered companies. The Aga Khan owns two other Stud Farms in the State and also has significant interests in the French bloodstock industry. Grenfell's business consists of owning and renting out Stud Farms to another company owned by the Aga Khan engaged in the operation of stud farms. TPDC's business consists of holding shares in Goffs. It was noted that the Aga Khan already owned 34.72% of the shares in Goffs through the cumulative holdings of his two companies Bravo Romeo Ltd and TPDC.

The market relevant to Stud Farming is the market for the sale of nominations for stallions standing at the Stud and for bloodstock sales. In the case of Goffs the product is a provision of bloodstock auctioneering and ancillary services. This is an international market in which a small number of firms located throughout the world are engaged.

Under the terms of the notified arrangement the Vendor sold two stud farms in Ireland to Grenfell and 4,242,362 Ordinary Shares in Goffs bearing 9.56% of the voting rights to TPDC. Under the terms of the arrangements the Firestones were to issue redundancy notices to all the staff at the two Stud Farms and the arrangements therefore related only to the farms themselves and not to the businesses on the two Farms. The agreements contained no restrictive clauses. The transfer of the shares in Goffs constituted a merger within the meaning of the Mergers, Takeovers and Monopolies (Control) Act 1978 (as amended). It was indicated that the merger had been notified to the Minister for Industry and Commerce under the terms of that Act on 20 August 1992 and was approved by the Minister by letter dated 30 October 1992.

Decided by the Authority: In issuing a certificate under section 4(4) of the Competition Act in respect of the notified arrangements that:

(1) Grenfell is a body corporate engaged in the business of owning and renting Stud Farms. TPDC, a holding company is an undertaking within the meaning of the

3.9 Competition Act because it is engaged in economic activity through subsidiary firms which it controls and the Vendors are also undertakings within the meaning of the Act as they were engaged in the business of owning and operating Stud Farms in Ireland and are still engaged in this business in the United States.

(2) The notified arrangements constitute an agreement between undertakings.

(3) The provisions of sections 4(1), 4(4), 7(1) and 7(2) of the Competition Act taken together, imply that an agreement may be notified, and a certificate requested, where the parties are in some doubt as to whether that agreement would offend against section 4(1), but not otherwise, and there must be reasonable grounds for such doubt. A literal interpretation of section 4(1) could result in almost any business agreement being found to be prohibited, since once a party enters into an agreement with another, it is prevented from concluding the self-same agreement with someone else. It is clear that the intention of the Competition Act is not to prohibit all business agreements, nor to require that all agreements be notified.

(4) The notified arrangements do not involve the acquisition of the business of the Stud Farms but relate only to the acquisition of property and land on which the purchaser intends to establish it's own business. This does not prevent or restrict any other party who so wishes, from engaging in the business of Stud Farming within the State or any part of it and cannot therefore be deemed to offend against section 4(1).

(5) In the case of the acquisition of the additional shares in Goffs by the Aga Khan through TPDC there is no question of a merger between competitors as neither the Aga Khan nor TPDC are involved in any business which is a competitor of Goffs. While it could be argued that were TPDC and the Aga Khan to acquire actual or *de facto* control over Goffs this could be used to restrict access to bloodstock auctioneering services for other horse breeders, there does not seem to be any real likelihood of such a development and there would appear to be adequate alternative outlets for breeders.

Decisions referred to:

Competition Authority Decision No. 1 – Nallen/O'Toole (Belmullet), 2 April 1992 **3.3**
Competition Authority Decision No. 2 – AGF/Irish Life Holdings, 14 May 1992 **1.3.1**
Competition Authority Decision No. 6 – Woodchester Bank Ltd/UDT Bank Ltd, 4 August 1992 **3.5**

Competition Authority Decision of 5 November 1992 relating to a proceeding under section 4 of the Competition Act 1991
Notification Nos. CA/673/92E — Thoroughbred Promotion Development Co. Ltd./Grenfell Ltd. and CA/674/92E — Bertram and Diana Firestone/His Highness Karim Aga Khan

Introduction

1. Arrangements for the purchase of two stud farms by Grenfell Ltd (Grenfell) and of shares in Robert J. Goff plc by Thoroughbred Promotion & Development Co. (TPDC) were notified to the Competition Authority on 30 September 1992. The arrangements were notified both by TPDC and Grenfell (CA/673/92E) and by Bertram and Diana Firestone (CA/674/92E) on the same day. Both notifications requested a certificate, or in the event of a refusal by the Authority to grant a certificate, a licence.

2. The Authority has not previously published any notice of intention to take a favourable decision in relation to this notification.

The Facts 3.9

(a) *The Subject of the Notifications*

3. The notifications relate to an agreement between Mr and Mrs Firestone (the Firestones) and His Highness Karim Aga Khan for the sale of two stud farms in Ireland along with 4,242,362 Ordinary Shares in Robert J. Goff plc (Goffs), bearing 9.56% of the voting rights in the company to the Aga Khan. The farms are being acquired by Grenfell and the shares by TPDC both of which are ultimately owned by the Aga Khan. Goffs is a firm which primarily carries on the business of bloodstock auctioneering and ancillary activities, such as providing bloodstock valuations, bloodstock financing and which also runs a theatre and exhibition centre. The arrangements were the subject of lengthy court proceedings which resulted in the grant of an order for specific performance.

(b) *The Parties*

4. The parties to the notified arrangements are Mr and Mrs Firestone (the vendors) and TPDC and Grenfell. The Firestones owned and operated two stud farms in Ireland, Gilltown and Sallymount in County Kildare. The Firestones also own a stud farm at Waterford, Virginia, USA.

5. TPDC and Grenfell are corporate bodies. They are ultimately owned and controlled by His Highness, the Aga Khan through a series of Luxembourg registered companies. The parties stated that the Aga Khan owned two other stud farms in Ireland and also had significant interests in the French bloodstock industry. Grenfell's business consists of owning and renting out stud farms to HHAKS, another company owned by the Aga Khan, which owns bloodstock and operates stud farms. The parties have stated that TPDC's business consisted of holding shares in Goffs. The parties indicated that the Aga Khan already owned 34.72% of the shares of Goffs through Bravo Romeo Ltd and TPDC.

The Product and the Market

6. A stud farm derives its income primarily from the sale of nominations for stallions standing at the stud, the nominations being owned by, or available for, the benefit of the stud, and the sale of bloodstock produced on the stud farm either at public auction or by private sale. The market is the market for stallion nominations, the services concerning the physical keep and support for the stallions concerned and for bloodstock sales.

7. In the case of Goffs the product is the provision of bloodstock auctioneering and ancillary activities. This is stated to be an international market in which a small number of firms located throughout the world are engaged. There is one other firm engaged in this market located in Ireland. In addition the parties have stated that in their view the value of private sales transactions equal those at auction.

The Arrangements

8. The agreement relates to the sale by the Firestones of Gilltown and Sallymount stud farms to Grenfell, together with the sale of 4,242,362 Ordinary Shares in Goffs, bearing 9.56% of the voting rights in that company, to TPDC. The original agreements were entered into some time ago. A dispute arose, however, which led to lengthy legal proceedings. These resulted in a court order which required that the agreement be completed by 9 October 1992 or within 7 days of the Minister for Industry and Commerce indicating his approval for the merger, whichever was the later.

9. Under the terms of the agreement the Firestones were required to issue redundancy notices to all of the staff at the two stud farms and to pay them their statutory redundancy entitlements and this has been done. The arrangements therefore relate only to the two farms themselves and not to the businesses of the two farms. The agreements contain no restrictive clauses. The parties stated that the transfer of the shares in Goffs constituted a merger within the meaning

3.9 of the Mergers Act 1978 (as amended). They indicated that the merger had been notified to the Minister for Industry and Commerce under the terms of that Act by letter dated 20 August 1992. The merger was approved by the Minister by letter dated 30 October 1992.

Submissions of the Parties

10. TPDC and Grenfell submitted that, although the Aga Khan has increased his shareholding in Goffs by virtue of the agreement, this increase did not prevent, restrict or distort competition in the relevant market since the number of competitors in the market was not affected and it would not result in the diminution of actual or potential competition in the market for the services provided by the company. They have also argued that:

> His Highness has not obtained legal or de facto control over the commercial policy of . . . the Company (a factor the relevance of which was stressed in *BAT and Reynolds v. Commission*, Cases 142 and 156/84, [1987] and referred to in the Woodchester decision at pages 13 and 15.

11. In the case of the stud farms the parties have argued that the acquisition would lead to improvements in the supply and quality of services available due to the application of the Aga Khan's expertise. They submitted that such advantages would not accrue were the sale of the stud farms to be to anyone else.

12. Both parties indicated that the notification was prompted by the Authority's decision in Woodchester[1] and stated that as the present agreements constituted a merger they had decided to notify it to the Authority.

Assessment

(a) *Section 4(1)*

13. Section 4(1) of the Competition Act states that 'all agreements between undertakings, decisions by associations of undertakings and concerted practices which have as their object or effect the prevention, restriction or distortion of competition in trade in any goods or services in the State or in any part of the State are prohibited and void.'

(b) *The Undertakings and the Agreement*

14. Section 3(1) of the Competition Act defines an undertaking as 'a person being an individual, a body corporate or an unincorporated body of persons engaged for gain in the production, supply or distribution of goods or the provision of a service.' The parties to the present agreement are the Firestones, TPDC and Grenfell.

15. Grenfell is a body corporate engaged in the business of owning and renting stud farms. Renting a stud farm constitutes the provision of a service for gain and so Grenfells is an undertaking within the meaning of the Act. TPDC, a body corporate, is, in effect, a holding company. In a previous decision the Authority indicated that a holding company was an undertaking within the meaning of the Act because it was engaged in economic activity through subsidiary firms which it controlled.[2] This is the case with TPDC, and so it is also an undertaking. The Firestones were engaged in the business of owning and operating stud farms in Ireland and are still engaged in this business in the United States. They therefore constitute an undertaking within the meaning of the Act.

1. Notification No. CA/10/92 — Woodchester Bank Ltd/UDT Bank Ltd, Competition Authority Decision No. 6, 4 August 1992.
2. Notification No. CA/7/92 — AGF Irish Life Holdings, Competition Authority Decision No. 2, 14 May 1992.

(c) *Applicability of section 4(1)* 3.9

16. The present arrangements therefore constitute an agreement between undertakings. The Authority emphasises, however, that the prohibition in section 4(1) relates only to agreements between undertakings 'which have as their object or effect the prevention, restriction or distortion of competition within the State or any part of the State'. Furthermore it notes that sections 7(1) and 7(2) provide that agreements, decisions and concerted practices 'of a kind described in section 4(1)' and in respect of which the parties seek or request a licence or certificate shall be notified to the Authority. Clearly not all agreements between undertakings are prohibited under section 4(1), only those which have as their object or effect the prevention, restriction or distortion of competition. Similarly, in the Authority's view, every agreement between undertakings is not notifiable under sections 7(1) and 7(2), only those of a kind described in section 4(1).

17. Section 4(4) of the Act provides that the Authority may 'certify that in its opinion . . . an agreement, decision or concerted practice . . . does not offend against section 4(1)' A literal interpretation would suggest that, as only agreements of a kind described in section 4(1) may be notified, it would be somewhat difficult for the Authority to issue a certificate saying the arrangements do not offend against section 4(1). Indeed strictly speaking such an interpretation would mean that, unless an agreement offended against section 4(1), it could not be notified with a request for a certificate in the first place. In the Authority's opinion this reinforces the views expressed in its first decision,[3] that section 4(1) ought not to be interpreted literally. It can happen that arrangements which at first sight appear to have the object or effect of preventing, restricting or distorting competition, may, after careful analysis, be found not to do so in practice. The Authority believes that this is consistent with well established practice under competition law in the European Community and the United States.

18. The Authority has also taken the view that the provisions of sections 4(1), 4(4), 7(1) and 7(2) taken together, imply that an agreement may be notified, and a certificate requested, where the parties are in some doubt as to whether that agreement would offend against section 4(1), but not otherwise. In the Authority's view, there must be reasonable grounds for such doubts. Again in Nallen/O'Toole it pointed out that a literal interpretation of section 4(1) could result in almost any business agreement being found to be prohibited, since once a party enters into an agreement with another, it is prevented from concluding the self same agreement with someone else. It is clear to the Authority that the intention of the Act is not to prohibit all business agreements, nor to require that all agreements be notified to the Authority. The Authority in this instance accepts the parties' claim that they felt, in the light of its decision in Woodchester and as the agreement constituted a merger within the definition of the Mergers Act, it should be notified under the Competition Act.

19. The Authority considers that its decision in Woodchester should not be interpreted in this way. The Authority did not indicate in that decision, as has been widely reported, that all mergers had to be notified to the Authority. It simply stated that, in its view, there was no provision in the Competition Act which would automatically exclude a merger, which was notifiable to the Minister for Industry and Commerce under the Mergers Act, from the scope of the Competition Act.

20. It found in Woodchester that the notified arrangements for the acquisition of UDT Bank by Woodchester Bank constituted an agreement between undertakings and the question therefore, was whether this had the object or effect of preventing, restricting or distorting competition, within the State or any part of the State. As the merger in Woodchester involved the acquisition by a firm of one of its competitors there was a possibility at least, that the object or effect was the restriction of competition. The Authority found, after a detailed analysis, that the arrangement did not offend against section 4(1). It indicated that before a merger could be

3. Notification No. CA/8/91 — Nallen/O'Toole (Belmullet), Competition Authority Decision No. 1, 2 April 1992.

3.9 found to offend against section 4(1) it would have to be shown that it would, or would be likely to result in a lessening of competition in the relevant market(s).

21. The Authority considered first of all the acquisition of the two stud farms by Grenfell. The arrangements do not involve the acquisition of the business of the stud farms but relate only to the acquisition of property and land on which the purchaser intends to establish its own business. In the Authority's view this does not prevent or restrict any other party who so wishes, from engaging in the business of stud farming within the State or any part of it. It cannot therefore be deemed to offend against section 4(1).

22. In the case of the acquisition of the additional shares in Goffs, the Authority notes from the submission on behalf of TPDC, that neither they nor the Aga Khan, who is the ultimate owner of TPDC, own or are involved in any business which is a competitor of Goffs. There is therefore, no question of a merger between competitors. It could be argued that, were TPDC and the Aga Khan to acquire actual or de facto control over Goffs, this could be used to restrict access to bloodstock auctioneering services by other horse breeders. The Authority does not believe that there is any real likelihood of such a development, that there would in any case appear to be adequate alternative outlets for breeders, and considers that such parties would have protection under the Competition Act if such a situation were to arise. The arrangements therefore represent nothing more than an agreement for the purchase of shares in a business. Consequently the Authority can see no reason to believe that the acquisition of the shares in Goffs offends against section 4(1).

23. There were no restrictive clauses in the agreement.

The Decision

24. Grenfell, TPDC and the Firestones are undertakings within the meaning of section 3 of the Competition Act, and the notified arrangements constitute an agreement between undertakings. In the Authority's opinion the agreement for the purchase of Gilltown and Sallymount stud farms and of 4,242,362 Ordinary Shares in Goffs do not have as their object or effect the prevention, restriction or distortion of competition within the State or any part of the State. The notified agreement does not therefore, in the Authority's opinion, offend against section 4(1) of the Competition Act.

The Certificate

The Competition Authority has issued the following certificate:

> The Competition Authority certifies that in its opinion, on the basis of the facts in its possession, the agreement between Mr and Mrs Firestone of Waterford, Virginia, USA and Grenfell Ltd. and Thoroughbred Promotion & Development Company for the purchase of 2 stud farms (Gilltown and Sallymount in County Kildare) and of 4,242,362 Ordinary Shares in Robert J. Goff & Co. plc, notified on 30 September 1992 under section 7 (CA/673/92E and CA/674/92E), does not offend against section 4(1) of the Competition Act 1991.

For the Competition Authority

Patrick Massey
Member

5 November 1992

Competition Authority Decision No. 12, Scully Tyrrell/Edberg Ltd: 29 January 1993, Notification No. CA/57/92 **3.10**

Series of agreements for acquisition of business and control thereafter – Whether vendors becoming employees are separate undertakings from acquirer and employer – Whether post-termination restrictions in service agreements are necessary and reasonable to complete the transfer of the goodwill – Whether relevant markets are easily entered – Whether the degree of concentration after acquisition raises reasonable concerns – Whether Herfindahl-Hirschman Index assists in examination of the effects after acquisition – Amendment of agreements after discussion with the assurance that confidentiality covenant will not prevent competition – Acceptance of undertaking by the parties concerning application of confidentiality covenants – Article 85(1) of the Treaty of Rome – Competition Act 1991 (No. 24) sections 3, 4 and 7

Facts: On 31 July 1992 notification was made to the Competition Authority of an acquisition and shareholders agreement with related agreement with a request for a certificate under section 4(4) of the Competition Act 1991 or failing that, a licence under section 4(2). Under the notified agreements Edberg Ltd ('Edberg') acquired the loss adjusting business of Scully Tyrrell & Co. ('STC'). The partners in STC as a result of the arrangements acquired 38% of the shareholding in Edberg Ltd with specified minority protection rights. The balance of the shares in Edberg continued to be held by its holding company Robins Holdings Ltd ('RHL') which had already acquired the business of Robins Davies (Ireland) Ltd ('RDI') which was also engaged in loss adjusting in Ireland.

The relevant market concerns the provision to the insurance industry of monitoring surveying and handling services in respect of risks projects and claims. The estimated market share in the State of STC was 26.5% and 2.5% for RDI.

The cumulative effect of the notified arrangement required the vendor to covenant in respect of the United Kingdom and the State for a period of 3 years after completion or 2 years after termination of their contracts of employment which commenced after completion not to engage in loss adjusting. Similar provisions for the same period and territory were also included concerning the soliciting of customers and employees.

The shareholders agreement provided that a majority of the vendors on the one hand and the main shareholders on the other would need to agree before a number of decisions could be made including those concerning:

(1) When Distributable profits could be retained by Edberg;
(2) The issue of new shares;
(3) When reserves of Edberg could be distributed;
(4) The disposal of certain assets and incurring of expenditure;
(5) The commencement of new businesses and offices and the closing of any office;
(6) The borrowing or lending by Edberg;
(7) The amalgamation of Edberg with other businesses.

The option agreement allowed RHL to purchase the shares of a vendor in Edberg when that vendor's service contract terminated.

The service agreement entered into by all but one vendor provided for periods of notice for termination, the confidentiality of Edberg's affairs and a two year non-compete provision after termination.

3.10 **Submissions** The parties submitted:

(1) The business acquisition was a concentration to which section 4 of the Competition Act 1991 does not apply.

(2) The vendors by becoming employees and directors are not undertakings distinct from Edberg and they form an integral part of the same economic undertaking as Edberg.

(3) Entry to the relevant market is relatively easy and competition is not affected by the acquisition.

(4) The restrictive covenants are necessary and reasonable to complete the transfer of the goodwill of the business to Edberg.

Following discussions with the Authority the parties entered into a supplemental agreement dated 18 December 1992 whereby the combined competition restrictions in all agreements were limited to a two year period from the date of disposal of the vendors in Edberg.

Decided by the Authority: In issuing a certificate under section 4(4) of the Competition Act 1991 in respect of the notified arrangements:

(1) Prior to the completion of the agreements the vendors were not employees of the acquiring company and the arrangements constitute an agreement between a separate undertaking.

(2) Under the notified arrangements the vendors would not simply be employees and they will continue to be separate undertakings. Once an employee pursues his own economic interests which differ from his employer he may well become an undertaking.

(3) The notified connected agreements should be read together as one agreement.

(4) Acquisition agreements may affect competition.

(5) The degree of concentration in the relevant market causes concern although the four firm concentration ratio following the merger is less than 40% of the relevant market.

(6) The Herfindahl-Hirschman Index ('HHI') which is the sum of the squares of the shares of all firms in a market when applied to the given facts in the notification indicates that the arrangements merit further examination. *[Editor's note: see paragraphs 55 and 56 of the decision in particular]*

(7) In a small economy such as the Irish market, concentration ratios in many sectors may be higher than those which exist in larger economies. The Authority does not state that high market concentration restricts competition. Nevertheless it will conduct a more detailed examination of a merger when a relatively high degree of concentration in a market occurs after an acquisition.

(8) The threat of entry of new firms in the relevant market indicates that the relevant market is in fact 'contestable' although the Authority noted that new entrants would be limited to those already involved in insurance or to foreign loss adjusting firms.

(9) The goodwill purchased which is attributable also to other employees rewarded by commission does not require the lengthy periods for the restriction proposed in the notified arrangements.

(10) The parties for so long as they work together in the relevant business can be restricted from competing with each other.

(11) The combined two year restriction after the termination of the service agreements and the disposal of shares is no more than is necessary to secure the

transfer of the goodwill of the vendors to the purchaser. 3.10

(12) Given the representation by the parties that the confidentiality provision would not be used to prevent competition, the confidentiality clause in the notified arrangements does not offend against section 4(1) of the Competition Act.

Cases, Decisions, Notices, Report and Book referred to:
BAT and Reynolds v. EC Commission and Philip Morris (case no. 142 and 156/84) [1987] ECR 4487; [1988] 4 CMLR 24
High Court judgment: *Masterfoods Ltd. v. HB Ice Cream Ltd* [1993] ILRM 145 213; **8.2.2**
EC Commission Decision: Reuter/BASF [1976] OJ L 254/40; [1976] 2 CMLR D44
EC Commission Decision: Vaessen/Moris [1979] OJ L 19/32; [1979] 2 CMLR 511
Competition Authority Decision No. 1; Nallen/O'Toole **3.3**
Competition Authority Decision No. 3; Athlone Travel/Michael Stein Travel Ltd **3.4**
Competition Authority Decision No. 5; Woodchester Bank Ltd./UDT Bank Ltd **3.5**
Competition Authority Decision No. 8; ACT/Kindle **3.6**
Competition Authority Decision No. 9; Budget Travel Ltd./Phil Fortune **3.7**
Competition Authority Decision No. 10; GI Corporation / General Semiconductor Industries **3.8**
Competition Authority Notice 'Employee Agreements and the Competition Act', *Iris Oifigiúil*, 18 September 1992 **1.4.1**
EC Commission '17th Report on Competition Policy' Para. 101
Bellamy & Child [1987] 'Common Market Law of Competition' [3rd edition] paragraph 2.017

Competition Authority Decision of 29 January 1993 relating to a proceeding under section 4 of the Competition Act 1991
Notification No. CA/57/92 — Scully Tyrrell & Company/Edberg Ltd

Introduction

1. Arrangements for the purchase of Scully Tyrrell & Company by Edberg Ltd were notified to the Competition Authority on 31 July 1992. The notification requested a certificate, or in the event of a refusal by the Authority to grant a certificate, a licence. Following discussions with the Competition Authority, certain aspects of the notified arrangements were amended by a supplemental agreement dated 18 December 1992 and received by the Authority on 14 January 1993.

2. Notice of the intention of the Authority to take a favourable decision in relation to the arrangements was published in the Irish Times on 18 December 1992. No observations were received from third parties.

The Facts

(a) *The Subject of the Decision*

3. The decision concerns a series of related agreements namely;

— The STC Agreement or the Irish Business Sale Agreement;

— The Option Agreement;

— The Putman Sale Agreement;

— The Shareholders Agreement;

— A number of Service Agreements.

Under these agreements Edberg Ltd (Edberg) acquired the business of Scully Tyrrell & Co (STC) which was engaged in the business of loss adjusting. Edberg is a subsidiary of Robins

3.10 Holdings Ltd. (RHL) and had already acquired the business of Robins Davies (Ireland) Ltd. (RDI), a subsidiary of RHL which was engaged in loss adjusting in Ireland. A number of the former partners in STC acquired a 38% shareholding in Edberg with the balance being held by RHL. The arrangements give the STC partners a degree of control over Edberg. The arrangements also include a number of non-competition provisions.

The Parties

4. Edberg is a private limited company registered in Ireland. It was incorporated on 18 June 1992, for the purpose of acquiring the business and assets of RDI, insurance loss adjusters, and STC. Edberg is a wholly owned subsidiary of RHL, a private limited company engaged, *inter alia*, in the loss adjusting business in the UK, which had previously owned RDI. The parent company of RHL is a Swiss company, SGS Societe Generale De Surveillance Holding SA (SGS). Its principal activities are inspection and monitoring concerning trading and shipping of raw materials, petroleum and petrochemical, agricultural produce, consumer goods and industrial equipment. A significant part of the activities of SGS is the provision of loss adjusting services for insurance companies through its subsidiaries RHL and GAB. According to the 1991 Annual Report of SGS 'the division is one of the largest property loss adjusters in the world.'[1] RHL subsidiaries are engaged in loss adjusting in many countries throughout the world.

5. RHL carried on business in the insurance loss adjusting sector in Ireland indirectly through RDI which was established in September 1985. RDI had accumulated losses of £424,000 as of 31 December 1991.

6. STC was a partnership of eight individuals engaged in the business of insurance loss adjusters and related services to the insurance industry in Ireland. They employed 55 people of whom 31 were loss adjusters. The vast bulk of its business was in the property/fire sectors. The instructing principals for STC were almost exclusively insurance companies. The STC partners who are parties to the present arrangements are listed below.

Table 1: STC Partners

D.P. Scully	J.M. Tyrrell	T.P. Crawford	D.F. Herbert
W. Sleater	T.F. Conroy	M. O'Donoghue	D. Putman

The Product and the Market

7. This notification relates to the provision of a range of loss adjusting services to the insurance industry. Services covered by the notification include risk monitoring, claims investigation, project monitoring, risk surveying, valuation, revaluation, estate reinstatement, claims handling and surveying in respect of claims for fire and property damage. Loss adjusting in respect of fire and property damage claims constitutes a distinct market from other types of loss adjusting and this is the market in which STC and RDI are engaged.[2]

8. Some insurance companies employ inspectors to assess claims. When, however, the claim involves amounts in excess of £5,000, it is the practice for insurance companies to engage a company from their panel of loss adjusters to facilitate the processing of the claim. It is the function of loss adjusters to check the claim made by the insured parties, making any enquiries necessary to agree fair values within the terms of the policy. Should adjustments—either upwards or downwards—be required, the adjuster will bring these to the attention of the insured. After agreement of the proposed settlement figure with the insured, the adjuster will report to the insurers with a recommendation for payment. The instructions under which an

1. Societe General de Surveillance Holding SA; Annual Report, 1991, p. 27.
2. Unless otherwise stated references to loss adjusting in the present decision relate to loss adjusting in respect of fire and property insurance claims.

adjuster works do not allow him to commit his principals to the payment of a particular sum. His duty is to report the facts and to recommend the amount which he considers is representative of their liability. The final decision on payment then rests with the insurers. Loss adjusters are generally paid a proportion of the final settlement figure calculated on a sliding scale. The parties stated that in the past loss adjusters' fee scales were based on scales recommended by the Chartered Institute of Loss Adjusters (CILA). This practice was abandoned some time ago and now each individual firm sets its own scale of fees. While it appears that virtually all loss adjusters operate a sliding scale of fees based on the final settlement figure, the Authority discovered at least one firm which charges on the basis of time involved in each particular case. The Authority checked with a number of leading insurance companies who confirmed that loss adjusting firms' fees differ. **3.10**

9. Insurance claims paid in respect of fire and property damage in Ireland amounted to £117.8m in 1990. Almost all of this was paid by firms with head offices in Ireland with the balance attributable to overseas firms. In general, overseas companies will employ locally based loss adjusters unless the policy nominates a specific firm for this purpose.

10. Loss adjusting firms in Ireland are either partnerships or small companies. STC is the largest loss adjusting company based in Ireland. Its major competitors are Farrells, Thornton & Partners, McLarens and Astons. RDI has a negligible share of the market. Foreign loss adjusting companies can and do provide services to principals in Ireland through subsidiaries based here or through intermediaries.

11. The notifying parties have stated, and the Authority accepts, that it is difficult to obtain accurate information on market shares held by the various loss adjusting firms, as many are partnerships or private companies, and do not publish accounts. They have suggested that the number of loss adjusters engaged by each firm as a proportion of the total number of loss adjusters engaged, could be used as a proxy for the market share of STC. The Authority recognises that this is not an ideal measure of market share, but believes nonetheless, that it provides some guide to the market shares of the various firms.

Table 2: Loss Adjusting Firms Located in Ireland

Name of Firm	Number of Loss Adjusters Engaged	Estimated Market Share (%)
STC	31	26.5
Farrells	20	17.1
Thornton & Partners	14	12.0
McLarens*	13	11.1
Astons	11	9.4
Thomas Howell*	7	6.0
Toplis Hume*	7	6.0
Thornton Adjusters	4	3.4
RDI*	3	2.5
Others (3)	7	6.0
Total	117	100.0

* Denotes subsidiaries of UK firms.

Market share figures are estimated on the basis of the number of loss adjusters engaged by each firm as a proportion of the total number of loss adjusters engaged by all firms in the market. The figures in the table on the number of loss adjusters engaged by each firm were supplied by STC. The Authority checked these figures with each of the other named firms and while it

3.10 found some discrepancies, it is satisfied that the figures shown are broadly representative of the actual position.

12. There are 12 firms operating in the loss adjusting market. Four of these are subsidiaries of UK firms. Six firms have entered the market within the past 10 years. In many instances these new firms were established by individuals who had previously worked for one of the incumbent firms.

13. RDI accounts for 2.5% of all loss adjusters engaged according to the figures submitted by the parties. More importantly, comparing STC's turnover with that of RDI, would imply that RDI's market share was around 2%, assuming that the STC share is estimated correctly. While recognising the shortcomings of calculating market shares on the basis of employment shares, the Authority believes that estimates of market shares for all firms should be made on a consistent basis, and so it has adopted a figure of 2.5% for RDI's market share.

14. The arrangements were not subject to notification under the Mergers Act because the relevant turnover and value of assets figures did not exceed the thresholds for notification.

The Arrangements

15. The notification involves a series of related agreements. On 24 July 1992 Edberg, (the purchaser), and D.P. Scully & Others, (the 'Vendors'),[3] entered into an agreement for the sale and purchase of the business and assets of STC, ('the STC Agreement'), whereby, Edberg agreed to acquire the business of loss adjusters carried on by the Vendors in partnership under the name of Scully Tyrrell & Company. The consideration to be paid pursuant to the terms of the STC Agreement comprised both cash and the issue of shares in Edberg to the Vendors. On completion of the sale and purchase of the business and assets of STC, and payment of the purchase consideration by Edberg, RHL will be the beneficial owner of 62% of the Edberg share capital and the Vendors will be the beneficial owners of the remaining 38%. All of the Vendors, (except Mr. Putman), are to become directors of Edberg under the terms of the Shareholders Agreement which gives them a considerable degree of control over the business. They have also agreed to continue working for the company for a minimum period of 3 years.

16. Mr. Putman, who was a partner in STC based in the UK, will not remain involved with Edberg. The Edberg shares paid to him in respect of his interest in STC are the subject of a separate agreement between Mr. Putman and RHL, (the 'Putman Sale Agreement'), whereby RHL has agreed to purchase Mr. Putman's shares. There are no non-compete clauses or other restrictive provisions in this agreement.

17. The STC Agreement requires the parties thereto to enter into a number of other agreements on completion of the matters provided for therein:

(a) a shareholders agreement between RHL and the Vendors, (other than Mr. Putman), who, following completion of the matters provided for in the Putman Sale Agreement, will be the beneficial owners of the entire share capital of Edberg, with RHL owning 62% and the Vendors, (other than Mr. Putman), owning the remaining 38%, (the 'Shareholders Agreement');

(b) an option agreement between the Vendors, (other than Mr. Putman), and RHL, (the 'Option Agreement'), whereby the Vendors, (other than Mr. Putman), grant an option to RHL to purchase all their equity share capital in Edberg upon the terms and conditions set out therein;

(c) service agreements between each of the Vendors, (other than Mr. Putman), and Edberg, (the 'Service Agreements'), pursuant to which each of the Vendors will agree to act as a director and become an employee of Edberg for three years, with effect from

3. 'The Vendors' are named in Table 1.

completion of the matters provided for in the STC Agreement, and continuing after the three year period on a rolling basis, subject to termination on six months notice. **3.10**

The STC Agreement

18. Clause 12 of the STC Agreement as notified contains a number of restrictions on the future activities of the Vendors. These are:

12.1 The Vendors hereby severally covenant to the Purchaser that each such Vendor shall not during the longer of (i) a period of 3 years from Completion and (ii) the Second Period (as hereinafter defined), in the Republic of Ireland or Northern Ireland or England or Wales or Scotland or the Channel Islands or the Isle of Man either solely or jointly with or as officer, employee manager adviser consultant or agent of any other person firm or corporation directly or indirectly (other than by way of bona fide investments or holding of shares not exceeding 5 per cent in nominal value of any class or share capital of a company whose share or loan capital is quoted or listed or regularly dealt in on a recognised Stock Exchange) carry on or be engaged or concerned or interested in any business competing with the business of loss adjusting. 'The Second Period' means the period of 2 years from the date of termination of the relevant Vendor's employment with the Purchaser, except that:
(a) if such employment is terminated by the Purchaser in breach of the terms thereof, there shall be no Second Period;
(b) if such employment is terminated by notice in accordance with Clause 2.2 of the Service Agreement (or any provision agreed by the relevant Vendor and the Purchaser in substitution therefor), the Second Period shall be the period of 6 months from the date of termination of the relevant Vendor's employment with the Purchaser.

12.2 The Vendors hereby severally covenant with the Purchaser that each such Vendor shall not during the longer of a period of 3 years from Completion or a period of 2 years from the termination of the relevant Vendor's employment with the Purchaser either on his own account or jointly with or as officer employee manager adviser consultant or agent for any person firm or corporation directly or indirectly:
(a) canvass solicit orders from in relation to the business of loss adjusting interfere with or endeavour to entice away from the Purchaser any person firm or company with which he has had dealings and who or which has in the period of two years prior to Completion or the date of termination of employment (as the case may be) been a client or employee of the Business or the Purchaser;
(b) use at any time after Completion together as all or part of a name or as a trade or service mark or part thereof or use to trade under the words 'Scully' or 'Tyrrell' or 'Scully Tyrrell' or any colourable imitation thereof (in each case whether or not such words are separated by other words) in relation to any business which is competitive with the business of the Purchaser. . . .'

The Shareholders Agreement

19. Several provisions in the Shareholders Agreement grant powers to the Vendors. These are as follows:

3.1 Subject to the terms of this Agreement, the Vendors shall be responsible for the day to day management of the Business subject to the overall control of the chief executive of Robins.

Clauses 5.1 and 8.2 provide that the quorum at board meetings and general meetings requires one representative from each of Robins and the Vendors.

Clause 6.1 requires the approval of Robins and the majority of the Vendors for a wide range of matters including:

— the creation or issue of any shares or the grant or agreement to grant by the Company any

3.10 option over shares or uncalled capital of the Company or the issue of any loan capital convertible into shares;

— the distribution of any amount standing to the credit of any reserve of the Company;

— the sale or disposal of any assets of the Company having an aggregate book value in excess of IR5,000 or the purchase of any assets for an aggregate consideration in excess of IR5,000;

— the amalgamation or merger of the Company;

— any expenditure in excess of an aggregate of IR10,000 or the making of any capital commitment in excess of IR10,000;

— the commencement of any new type of business;

— the borrowing of any moneys;

— the lending of any moneys;

— any change to the terms of employment of the Vendors and all employees and former employees of the Company and the appointment, removal or remuneration of any employee or consultant of the Company;

— the opening or closing of any office.

> 7.1 Each of the Vendors shall, for so long as he remains a Shareholder of the Company, be entitled to be a Director of the Company. Robins shall be entitled to appoint such number of Directors of the Company as it shall in its absolute discretion determine. The initial Directors shall be as follows:

The Vendors:	Appointed by Robins:
D.P. Scully	P. Gregg
J.M. Tyrrell	M. Creed
T.P. Crawford	C. Carter
D.F. Herbert	R. Binning
W. Sleater	
T.F. Conroy	
M. O'Donoghue	

In addition Clause 10 provides that all of the distributable profits in any financial period up to 31 December 1994 shall be distributed by way of dividend unless Robins and a majority of the Vendors agree otherwise.

20. Clause 14.1 of the Shareholders Agreement provides for an undertaking by the shareholders relating to the disclosure of confidential information as follows:

> Each of the Shareholders undertakes to the other and to the Company that he will not and the Shareholders will procure that the Company will not at any time hereafter without the prior consent of the Shareholders divulge or communicate to any person (other than to officers or employees of the Company or its subsidiaries whose province it is to know the same or to Robins or to any subsidiary of Robins or when required by law) any confidential information concerning the business, accounts, finance or contractual arrangements or other dealings, transactions or affairs of the Company or any of the Shareholders which may come to his knowledge as a shareholder in, or through a director of, the Company and he shall use all reasonable endeavours to prevent the publication or disclosure of any confidential information concerning such matters and these obligations shall survive the termination of this Agreement.

The Option Agreement 3.10

21. Under the terms of the Option Agreement RHL has an option on the Vendors' shares in Edberg. The agreement includes the following clauses:

> 3.1 To the extent that the Option has not been exercised under Clause 3.2 the Purchaser may exercise the Option in respect of all but not some only of the Option Shares held by each Vendor (and so that the Purchaser may at its sole discretion exercise the Option in respect of any one or more of the Vendors) by serving notice in writing at any time during the period from 1st April 1995 to 31st October 1995 ('The Option Period').
>
> 3.2 If prior to 31st December 1994 (or, in the case of Mr. Scully, 31st December 1993):
> (a) the contract of employment of any of the Vendors with the Company is terminated in circumstances where the Vendor is at fault, that is, either:
> (i) the contract is terminated by the Company on any of the grounds set out in sub-clauses (a) to (e) of Clause 12.1 of the Vendor's service agreement; or
> (ii) the contract is terminated by the Vendor in circumstances where he was not entitled to do so; or
> (b) any of the Vendors is in breach of Clause 12 of the Business Sale Agreement; or
> (c) any of the Vendors becomes bankrupt or makes an arrangement or composition with his creditors;
> then the Purchaser shall be entitled to serve on that Vendor within three calendar months from the date of such event coming to the knowledge of the Purchaser, a written notice exercising the Option in respect of all but not some only of the Option Shares held by that Vendor.

22. Schedules 5, 6 and 7 of the Option Agreement provide for the calculation of the consideration payable to the Vendors on termination of their employment contracts. The consideration involved will differ depending on how and when the employment contracts are terminated. If the option is exercised under clause 3.1 of the 'Option Agreement' i.e. after 3 years, the consideration is a proportion of the value of Edberg Ltd, calculated by reference to the ratio of the shares held by the Vendors to the entire issued share capital of the company. Where the contract of employment is terminated within 3 years for a reason other than as referred to in clause 3.2(a) above, the consideration payable to the Vendors will be a fraction of that payable under Clause 3.1. This fraction will be based on the number of days worked as a fraction of the number of days to be worked under the employment contract (3 years or 1096 days). If the option is exercised in accordance with any other part of clause 3.2, the consideration payable to the Vendors will be the sum of £1.

The Service Agreements

23. The Service Agreements provide (in clause 2.2) that the individuals concerned will be employed by Edberg 'for a period of 3 years and thereafter unless and until determined by either party giving to the other no less than 6 months prior written notice expiring on or at any time after the third anniversary hereof.' Clause 2.4 provides that if either party should give notice of termination to the other pursuant to clause 2.2, then the Company is not obliged to provide work and may require the individual concerned not to attend at any of its premises nor to undertake any work for the company during the period of such notice.

24. The Service Agreements also contain the following provisions relating to confidentiality and restrictions on competition:

> *Confidentiality*
> 11.1 The Appointee shall not (except in the proper course of his duties hereunder) either during or at any time after the termination of the Employment divulge to any person

3.10 whomsoever and shall use his best endeavours to prevent the unauthorised publication or disclosure of and shall not use for his own purposes or for any purposes other than those of the Company any knowledge or information relating to any trade secret, process or invention or concerning the business or finances of the Company or any dealings, transactions or affairs of it or of any officers or employees of the Company or any other information of a confidential character (including confidential information belonging to or relating to any third party) which may come to his knowledge during or in the course of the Employment. Such restrictions shall not apply to any knowledge or information which is or may become (otherwise than through the default of the Appointee) available to the public generally.

11.2 All notes memoranda and records made or used by the Appointee in relation to any of the knowledge or information referred to in Clause 11.1 shall be and remain the property of the Company and shall be delivered together with all copies thereof, to the Company or as it shall direct from time to time on demand or forthwith when the Appointee leaves the service of the Company.

Restrictive Covenants

14.1 Subject as hereinafter provided the Appointee shall not either during the Employment or for a period of 2 years from the date of termination of the Employment in the Republic of Ireland, Northern Ireland, England, Wales, Scotland, the Channel Islands or the Isle of Man either solely or jointly with or as officer, employee, manager, adviser, consultant or agent of any other person firm or corporation directly or indirectly (other than by reason of such shareholdings as are permitted by Clause 5.1 hereof) carry on or be engaged, concerned or interested in any business competing with the business of loss adjusting as carried on by the Company at the date of the termination of the Employment. If the Employment is terminated by the Company:

(a) in breach of the terms set out herein, the said covenant shall not apply;

(b) by notice in accordance with Clause 2.2 (or any provision agreed by the Company and the Appointee in substitution therefor), the period of 2 years shall be reduced to a period of 6 months from the date of termination of the Employment.

14.2 The Appointee hereby covenants with the Company that he will not either during the Employment or for a period of 2 years after the termination of the Employment either on his own account or jointly with or as officer, employee, manager, adviser, consultant or agent of any other person firm or corporation directly or indirectly canvass solicit interfere with or endeavour to entice away from the Company any person firm or company with which he has had dealings and who or which has in the period of 2 years prior to the date of termination of the Employment been a client or employee of the Business or the Company.

25. Clause 12.1 of the Service Agreements sets out the basis on which Edberg Ltd may terminate the appointment of the Vendors. The relevant provisions are:

The Company may at any time by notice in writing to the Appointee forthwith terminate the Employment and the Appointee shall have no claim against the Company in respect of such termination, if the Appointee shall:

(a) commit any material breach of this Agreement other than such a breach which is capable of remedy and is remedied by the Appointee within 14 days of the Company requesting the same in writing, or continue (after being given a written warning stating that continuance or repetition of the breach could lead to the Appointee's contract of employment with the Company being terminated) any other breach of any of his obligations (whether under this Agreement or otherwise) to the Company;

(b) be guilty of any fraud or grave misconduct or be convicted of any indictable criminal offence (other than a motoring offence not resulting in a custodial sentence); 3.10
(c) become bankrupt or compound or make any arrangement with his creditors;
(d) be guilty of conduct which might reasonably be considered to be likely to bring himself or the Company into disrepute;
(e) be or become prohibited by law from being a director;
(f) be, for any cause, incapacitated from efficiently performing his duties hereunder for 26 consecutive weeks, or for periods aggregating 130 working days in any period of 52 weeks; or
(g) become a patient for any purpose of any legislation relating to mental health.

Submissions of the Parties

26. It was stated that RHL made an initial takeover approach to STC in the mid 1970s but nothing had come of this. The parties indicated that the initiative for the present arrangements had come from STC as it wished to expand outside of Ireland and considered that such a link-up made sense given the advent of the Single European Market.

27. The notifying parties have asserted that the STC Agreement does not fall within the ambit of section 4 of the Competition Act for the following reasons:

> (i) The sale and transfer of the business pursuant to the STC Agreement is tantamount to a 'concentration' within the meaning of the decisions and practice of the Commission. It is well established that Article 85(1) of the Treaty of Rome does not apply to 'Concentrations'. Accordingly as the sale and transfer of the business pursuant to the STC Agreement is tantamount to a 'Concentration' as outlined above, it does not fall within the ambit of section 4 CA 91.
> (ii) The STC Agreement and the provisions of clause 12 thereof do not constitute an agreement between 'Undertakings' within the meaning of section 3(1) CA 91 in view of the fact that the Vendors have agreed to act as and become directors and employees of and/or minority shareholders in Edberg as and with effect from completion of the transfer of the business to Edberg and in their capacity as such must be treated as forming an integral part of the same economic undertaking as Edberg.

28. The notifying parties also argue that the STC Agreement does not have as its object or effect the prevention, restriction or distortion of competition because:

> . . . the Vendors will become directors, employees and minority shareholders of Edberg, and as such form an integral part of the same economic unit or undertaking as Edberg, the Vendors cannot be said to be competitors or potential competitors of Edberg and, in the absence of the restrictions contained in clause 12 of the STC Agreement, there cannot be said to be any real likelihood of the Vendors engaging in the insurance loss adjusting business [in] competition with Edberg.
> Notwithstanding that Edberg will have acquired the business of RDI prior to the acquisition of the business of STC, with an apparent reduction in the number of competitors in the market after completion of these acquisitions, there will in fact be no effect or no real or appreciable effect on competition in the market because the insurance loss adjusting business in the Republic of Ireland is a very competitive and fluid market with numerous competitors, fragmented market share and no material cost or other impediments or barriers to market entry or exit.

29. It is submitted that the insurance loss adjusting business in the Republic of Ireland is relatively easy for new competitors to enter and leave and is therefore highly 'contestable' and that the STC Agreement and clause 12 thereof cannot be regarded as having any effect or any

3.10 real or appreciable affect on competition in this market in accordance with the economic rationale of the 'contestability theory' and the criteria highlighted in the Nallen/O'Toole Decision. . . . Insurance loss adjusting services can also be freely provided across international borders and this is occurring on an increasing basis. Insurers generally spread business amongst a number of loss adjusters who compete with each other for the business at competitive rates.

30. Accordingly, even if the restrictive covenants in clause 12 of the STC Agreement could be construed as apparently falling within the parameters of section 4 CA 91, the covenants do not infringe section 4 CA 91 since they do not have any effect or any real or appreciable affect on competition in the insurance loss adjusting business in the Republic of Ireland or in any part thereof. . . .

31. In relation to the restrictive covenants included in Clause 12 of the STC Agreement, the notifying parties argue that:

> The covenants contained in clause 12 of the STC Agreement do not involve a restriction on competition as they are limited in terms of duration, geographical scope and subject matter to that which is necessary and reasonable in all the circumstances to complete the transfer of the full commercial value of the goodwill of the business of Edberg pursuant to the STC Agreement. Accordingly, the covenants contained in clause 12 of the STC Agreement do not contravene section 4(1) CA 91.

This submission is clearly supported by the decisions and practice of the Commission and the ECJ . . . by Irish common law and by the previous decisions of the Competition Authority in similar cases. . . .

This submission is further supported by analogy with the policy underlying the EC Mergers Regulation as interpreted by the Commission . . . on the basis that, to the extent that the covenants in clause 12 of the STC Agreement may constitute restraints on the Vendors such restraints are directly related and necessary to the implementation of the 'Concentration' and are therefore properly ancillary to the 'Concentration' and not in breach of section 4(1) CA 91 since they are reasonable in duration, geographical scope and subject matter.

It is submitted that the covenants contained in clause 12 of the STC Agreement do not restrict competition in the insurance loss adjusting business and do not therefore offend against section 4(1) CA 91 as they are a legitimate means of ensuring the performance of the Vendors' contractual obligations to effectively complete the sale and transfer of the full commercial value of the business to Edberg and are of a duration, geographical scope and nature which is reasonable and objectively necessary in all the circumstances to complete the proper transfer of the goodwill of the business.

We would submit that in the context of the importance of customer/client relations and the considerable degree of consumer/client loyalty which has been built up over the years by the Vendors in relation to the business carried on by STC, the duration of the covenants in clause 12 of the STC Agreement is the minimum that is objectively necessary for Edberg to assume, by active competitive behaviour, the place in the market previously occupied by the Vendors through STC and therefore satisfies the criteria applied by the Commission in the Nutricia case and endorsed by the Competition Authority in the Nallen/O'Toole Decision and the Athlone Travel Decision.

This analysis is not affected by the fact that the duration of the covenants in clause 12 may potentially, in certain circumstances, exceed three years since the 'Second Period' of protection afforded by clause 12 is equally objectively necessary to protect and preserve the value of the investment by SGS and Edberg in the STC business in view of the nature of the business as a service business where customer/client loyalty is invaluable and persists for a period which may well exceed three years. . . .

It is also submitted that as regards the application of CA91 and the Competition Authority's jurisdiction thereunder in relation to competition in the Republic of Ireland the geographical scope of the covenants in clause 12 of the STC Agreement is limited to the extent which is objectively necessary for Edberg to assume, by active competitive behaviour, the place in the market in the Republic of Ireland previously occupied by the Vendors through STC. Insofar as the geographic scope of the covenants extends beyond the Republic of Ireland this is outside the ambit of CA91 which governs competition only in the Republic of Ireland. . . . 3.10

It is further submitted that the subject matter of the covenants in clause 12 of the STC Agreement does not restrict competition within the meaning of section 4(1) CA 91 as it is confined to the business of insurance loss adjusting carried on by the Vendors through STC at the date of the STC Agreement. . . .

32. In relation to the Service Agreements with each of the Vendors (other than Mr. Putman), the notifying parties have submitted that:

> It is generally accepted by the ECJ that employees acting in their capacity as such are not 'undertakings' within the meaning of Article 85(1) . . . the rationale being that an employee can in principle be regarded as an auxiliary organ forming an integral part of the employer's undertaking bound to carry out the employer's instructions and thus forms an economic unit with the employer. It is submitted that this reasoning applies with equal force to section 4(1) CA 91 and that the Service Agreements do not therefore fall within the ambit of, or otherwise contravene or offend against section 4(1) CA 91 as they do not constitute agreements between 'undertakings' within the meaning of CA91.
>
> The fact that the Vendors are also minority shareholders in Edberg does not render the[m] 'undertakings' within the meaning of section 3(1) CA 91 since none of the Vendors will control Edberg. This submission is entirely consistent with the decisions of the Commission in Reuter v. BASF (op. Cite.) and H. Vaessen v. Alex Morris (Commission Decision 79/86/EEC [1979] 1 CMLR 511).
>
> It will be noted that the provisions of clause 2.4 and 14 of the Service Agreement come into operation only in connection with or upon termination of the Service Agreements. Even if an employee entering into covenants with his employer to take effect in connection with or subsequent to the termination of the employment relationship is regarded as an 'undertaking' within the meaning of section 3(1) CA 91, neither clause 2.4 nor clause 14 of the Service Agreements contravene or offend against section 4(1) CA 91 since they are reasonable in subject matter, duration and geographical scope of application in the context of the STC business being acquired by Edberg and the importance of personal relationships and customer loyalty and goodwill in such a business.

33. At a meeting with the Authority the parties indicated that a number of the provisions of the Shareholders' Agreement were designed to protect the Vendors' interests. They also indicated that they were designed to ensure that RHL exercised its option to acquire the Vendors' 38% shareholding in Edberg after 3 years thus buying out the Vendors' interest in the business.

Subsequent Developments

34. In a subsequent letter dated 19 October 1992 the parties restated many of their arguments. In particular they argued that the EC Commission has maintained that there is a fundamental distinction between restrictive practices relating essentially to the conduct of companies and to mergers/acquisitions which relate essentially to the structure of a market. They claimed that the Commission would only examine mergers or acquisitions under Article 85 where the merger or acquisition agreements extended beyond acquisition of ownership of shareholdings to encompass contractual obligations facilitating a co-ordination of market behaviour or commercial policies between the relevant parties. They cited the European Court

3.10 of Justice decision in the Philip Morris case.[4] They also argued that the notified arrangements differed from those in Woodchester[5] as they did not constitute an agreement between undertakings since the Vendors would not be undertakings following completion.

35. The parties also argued that the arrangements would not result in any diminution of competition as RDI had less than 1% of the market. In addition they argued that the loss adjusting market was highly competitive as there were a sizeable number of firms in the market, rates were competitive, the consumers of loss adjusters' services had considerable bargaining power, there were no restrictions on market entry and contracts were concluded on an ad-hoc basis with no long term contracts or retainers between insurers and loss adjusters.

Amendments to the Agreements

36. Following discussions with the Authority the parties made amendments to the agreements in a Supplemental Agreement dated 18 December 1992. The parties agreed to delete clause 12.1 of the Irish Business Sale Agreement (referred to above as the STC Agreement) and the first paragraph of clause 12.2, (see para 18 above), and substitute the following.

> 12.1 The Vendors hereby severally covenant to the Purchaser that each such Vendor shall not for so long as such Vendor remains an employee of or a shareholder in the Purchaser and for a period of 2 years from the date of disposal of the relevant Vendor's shares in the Purchaser, in the Republic of Ireland or Northern Ireland or England or Wales or Scotland or the Channel Islands or the Isle of Man either solely or jointly with or as officer, employee manager adviser consultant or agent of any other person firm or corporation directly or indirectly (other than by way of bona fide investments or holding of shares not exceeding 5 per cent in nominal value of any class or share capital of a company whose share or loan capital is quoted or listed or regularly dealt in on a recognised Stock Exchange) carry on or be engaged or concerned or interested in any business competing with the business of loss adjusting, save that where the relevant Vendor's employment with the Purchaser is terminated by the Purchaser in breach of the terms thereof the restrictive covenants shall cease to be binding on such Vendor immediately upon such termination.
>
> 12.2 The Vendors hereby severally covenant with the Purchaser that each such Vendor shall not for a period of 2 years from the date of disposal of the relevant Vendor's shares in the Purchaser either on his own account or jointly with or as officer employee manager adviser consultant or agent for any person firm or corporation directly or indirectly: . .

The parties also agreed to delete Clauses 14.1 and 14.2 of the Service Agreements (see para 24 above) and to replace them as follows.

> 14.1 Subject as hereinafter provided the Appointee shall not during the Employment in the Republic of Ireland, Northern Ireland, England, Wales, Scotland, the Channel Islands or the Isle of Man either solely or jointly with or as officer, employee, manager, adviser, consultant or agent of any other person firm or corporation directly or indirectly (other than by reason of such shareholdings as are permitted by Clause 5.1 hereof) carry on or be engaged, concerned or interested in any business competing with the business of loss adjusting as carried on by the Company at any time during the continuance of the Employment.

4. *BAT and Reynolds v. EC Commission*, cases 142 and 156/84 [1987] ECR 4487.
5. Notification No. CA/10/92 — Woodchester Bank Ltd/UDT Bank Ltd, Competition Authority Decision No. 6, 4 August 1992.

14.2 The Appointee hereby covenants with the Company that he will not during the Employment either on his own account or jointly with or as officer, employee, manager, adviser, consultant or agent of any other person firm or corporation directly or indirectly canvass solicit interfere with or endeavour to entice away from the Company any person firm or company with which he has had dealings and who or which has been or is at any time during the continuance of the Employment a client or employee of the Business or the Company. 3.10

The parties agreed that para 7 of Schedule 2 of the Option Agreement (see para 22 above) should be deleted in its entirety and the following substituted therefor:

7.1 If the Option is exercised in accordance with Clause 3.2(a) the Consideration payable to the Vendor in respect of the Option Shares purchased from him shall be the price determined by the Auditors to be the market value, on the basis of a willing seller and a willing buyer and that the Option Shares constitute a minority shareholding, less an agreed discount of [5%].

Clause 3.2(a) (see para 21) refers to the termination of the Vendor's employment contract, by the company, where he was at fault, or by the Vendor where he was not entitled to do so.

7.2 If the Option is exercised in accordance with Clause 3.2(b) or (c) the Consideration payable to the Vendor in respect of the Option Shares purchased from him shall be the aggregate sum of 1.

Clause 3.2(b) relates to a breach by the Vendor of Clause 12 of the STC Agreement, while clause 3.2(c) relates to a situation where the Vendor becomes bankrupt or makes an arrangement with his creditors.

The parties also indicated by letter dated 23 November 1992 that the confidentiality provisions in clause 15 of the STC Agreement, clause 14.1 of the Shareholders Agreement and clause 11.1 of the Service Agreements 'are not intended or designed to prevent the Vendors from competing with the business carried on by Edberg but rather are intended and designed simply to prohibit a Vendor from using or abusing information that is confidential to Edberg or any of the Edberg shareholders.'

Assessment

(a) *Section 4(1)*

37. Section 4(1) of the Competition Act states that 'all agreements between undertakings, decisions by associations of undertakings and concerted practices which have as their object or effect the prevention, restriction or distortion of competition in trade in any goods or services in the State or in any part of the State are prohibited and void.'

(b) *The Undertakings*

38. Section 3(1) of the Competition Act defines an undertaking as 'a person being an individual, a body corporate or an unincorporated body of persons engaged for gain in the production, supply or distribution of goods or the provision of a service.' The parties involved in the notified arrangements are:

— 'D P Scully and Others' (the Vendors), who carried on in partnership the business of loss adjusters under the name 'Scully Tyrrell & Company' (STC);

— Edberg Ltd, a private limited company which has acquired the business and assets of RDI, a firm of insurance loss adjusters;

3.10 — Robins Holdings Ltd (RHL), a private limited company, which is engaged in the business of insurance loss adjusting and the provision of other services in the insurance industry in the UK. Edberg Ltd is a wholly owned subsidiary of RHL. As a result of these arrangements RHL retain 62% of the shares in Edberg with an option to purchase the remainder on certain conditions.

Both Edberg and RHL are undertakings within the meaning of the Act since they are engaged for gain in the provision of loss adjusting services to insurance companies.

39. The notifying parties have argued that the agreement relating to the purchase of STC does not constitute an agreement between undertakings within the meaning of the Act, because the Vendors have agreed to act as, and become directors, employees, and minority shareholders in Edberg, and must be treated as forming an integral part of the same economic undertaking as Edberg. The Vendors clearly owned and controlled the business of STC prior to the conclusion of this agreement and were, therefore, undertakings at the time of the agreement.[6] The Authority is satisfied therefore that the present arrangements constitute an agreement between undertakings within the meaning of section 4(1).

40. The Authority also believes that under the notified arrangements the Vendors will not become simply employees of Edberg. The Authority has stated that in line with EC precedents it does not consider employees to be undertakings.[7] It noted, however, that EC precedents indicate that once an employee pursues his own economic interests and these differ from those of his employer he may well become an undertaking within the meaning of Article 85 and, by analogy, of section 4(1). In addition to becoming employees of Edberg under the notified arrangements, the Vendors will also acquire 38% of Edberg Ltd. The Authority has concluded in previous decisions that individuals who either own or control a business are undertakings. In particular in Budget/Phil Fortune it decided that an individual who had purchased a business was an undertaking, a view which is again consistent with EC precedents.[8]

41. The Vendors are minority shareholders and this might not be sufficient in itself to regard them as undertakings. They have, however, been granted extensive powers under various clauses of the Shareholders Agreement. They are able to exert control over many, including the most important, facets of Edberg's operations by virtue of these clauses. Clause 6, for example, requires the approval of the majority of the Vendors concerning a wide range of matters including:

— the creation or issue of any shares, or the grant or agreement to grant any option over shares or uncalled capital, or the issue of any loan capital convertible into shares;

— the distribution of any amount standing to the credit of any reserve of the Company;

— the sale/disposal of any assets worth in excess of 5,000 or the purchase of any assets for an aggregate consideration in excess of 5,000;

— the amalgamation or merger of the Company;

— the commencement of any new type of business;

— any expenditure in excess of an aggregate of 10,000 or the making of any capital commitment in excess of 10,000;

— the borrowing of any moneys;

— lending of any moneys;

6. This view is consistent with earlier decisions by the Authority which found that individuals who owned or controlled a business prior to its sale were undertakings. See, for example, Notification No. CA/9/91 — ACT/Kindle, Competition Authority decision no. 8, 4 September 1992.

7. Competition Authority; 'Employee Agreements and the Competition Act', *Iris Oifigiúil*, 18 September 1992, p. 632.

8. Notification No. CA/1/92 — Budget Travel/Phil Fortune, Competition Authority decision no. 9, 14 September 1992.

— any change to the terms of employment of the Vendors and all employees and former employees of the Company and the appointment, removal or remuneration of any employee or consultant of the Company, etc.; 3.10

— the opening or closing of any office.

It is incorrect to claim therefore that the Vendors will not control Edberg.

42. The parties have stated that clause 6 exists to protect the Vendors' shareholding and maximise the value of Edberg in the light of the option held by RHL to buy out that shareholding in 1995. Decisions which are in the long-term interests of the business may reduce the firm's short-run profits, thereby reducing the amount to be paid as dividends to the Vendors in accord with clause 10 of the Shareholders Agreement, and the amount they would receive from RHL for their shares in Edberg, if it exercises its option to buy them after 3 years, in accord with clause 3.1 of the Option Agreement. Accordingly, the interests of the Vendors and of Edberg and RHL differ in that measures which are in the long-term interests of the business are not in the Vendors' interest. The fact that one of the objectives of clause 6, according to the Vendors, is to provide RHL with a strong incentive to buy out the Vendors' shareholding in Edberg after 3 years, implies that they do not regard the relationship as permanent. As pointed out it is recognised under EC law that once an employee pursues his own economic interests and these differ from his employers, he may well become an undertaking. In addition, unless a majority of the Vendors agree, all of the profits of the business in the period up to 3 December 1994, must be distributed by way of dividends to the shareholders under Clause 10. It is clear that the Vendors will exercise considerable control over the business. They cannot be regarded as mere employees bound to carry out their employer's instructions.

43. The Authority concludes that because the Vendors have a substantial share in Edberg, exercise extensive control over its operations and could pursue interests which differ from those of the company, they can continue to be regarded as undertakings following completion of the notified arrangements.

(c) *The Agreement*

44. The arrangements involve a series of related agreements between undertakings with effects within the State. The Authority considers that the agreements are so closely related that they may be read together as a single agreement. In this respect it is following the practice adopted by the EC Commission and the European Court of Justice that: 'A series of connected agreements will be read together as one agreement.'[9]

(d) *Applicability of section 4(1)*

(i) The Agreement for the Purchase of STC

45. The notifying parties have also argued that the agreement for the purchase of STC is tantamount to a 'concentration' within the meaning of the decisions and practice of the EC. They assert that Article 85(1) of the Treaty does not apply to 'concentrations' and therefore this agreement does not fall within the ambit of section 4 of the Competition Act 1991.

46. The arrangements involved in the present notification are rather complex. Two enterprises (Scully Tyrrell and RDI) have come under common control and this constitutes a merger as defined in the Mergers Act. The Authority has already indicated in Woodchester/UDT that it does not believe that a merger which has been notified and approved by the Minister is automatically excluded from the prohibition contained in section 4(1) of the Competition Act. In this instance the merger is below the thresholds set for notification under the Mergers Act. The Authority believes, for similar reasons to those outlined in its decision on Woodchester,

9. See C. Bellamy and G. Child (1987); 'Common Market Law of Competition;, 3rd edition, Sweet and Maxwell, London, para. 2-017.

3.10 that the present arrangements are not automatically outside the scope of section 4(1) simply because they constitute a merger. The arrangements represent an agreement between undertakings and the issue therefore is whether or not that agreement has the object or effect of preventing, restricting or distorting competition.

47. The arguments made by the parties that EC precedents indicate that such arrangements do not come within the scope of section 4(1) were also dealt with at length in the Woodchester decision and are not restated here. The Authority, however, notes the views expressed by the EC Commission following the European Court of Justice decision in the Philip Morris case:

> The judgement has far-reaching implications. It underlines the need for an economic approach in interpreting Articles 85 and 86. Conduct cannot cease to be anti-competitive merely by reference to the legal form in which it is presented. Even purchases of blocks of shares may in particular circumstances infringe the competition rules.[10]

In effect the parties' argument seeks to exclude any consideration of economic circumstances and contends that the arrangements do not offend against section 4(1) because they constitute a merger.

48. RHL has been involved in the Irish market for the provision of loss adjusting services through RDI. This company has already been acquired by Edberg Ltd, a subsidiary of RHL. RDI held a very small share of the market. The effect of the transaction will be that STC and RDI who were competitors in the Irish market will be replaced by Edberg.

49. The Vendors, however, have, under the arrangements, acquired a considerable shareholding in, and a substantial degree of control over Edberg. Indeed in effect Edberg will be jointly controlled by RHL and the Vendors for at least 3 years under the arrangements. The arrangements in some respects resemble a cooperative joint venture rather than a merger, as normally, in the case of a merger or takeover, the former owners or management leave the business. The Authority does not believe that the present arrangements constitute a joint venture as the Vendors will no longer carry on business in their own right and Edberg cannot, therefore be regarded as jointly owned by undertakings which continue to operate in other markets. It therefore considers that the arrangements should properly be regarded as a merger.

50. The Authority indicated in Woodchester that the agreement did not offend against section 4(1) as the arrangements had not resulted, and were not likely to result, in a diminution of competition in the relevant market. The Authority in that decision restated the view expressed in its first decision that the prohibition contained in section 4(1) ought not to be interpreted literally. In adopting such a view the Authority has followed the approach of the EC Commission and the European Court of Justice. Such an approach is well established in competition law following the US Supreme Court decision in the Standard Oil case in 1911. In that case, (which involved a merger), White CJ, in delivering the opinion of the Court, rejected the view that the blanket prohibition in section 1 of the Sherman Act applied to every contract in restraint of trade and imposed the plain duty of applying its prohibitions to every case within its literal language. The US Supreme Court decision in that case was cited by Keane J in the Mars/HB case when considering the correct interpretation of Article 85(1) of the Treaty of Rome on which section 4(1) is based.[11]

51. In Woodchester the Authority stated that:

> before a merger can be found to offend against section 4(1) of the Competition Act, it must be shown that it would, or would be likely to, result in an actual diminution of competition in the market concerned. A reduction in the number of competitors or the fact that a merger will result in the merged entity having a larger share of the market

10. EC Commission (1988); 'Seventeenth Report on Competition Policy', Brussels, point 101.
11. Judgment of 28 May 1992, *Masterfoods Ltd trading as Mars Ireland v. HB Ice Cream Ltd*, unreported.

than that previously held by either of the merged undertakings individually, are not, of themselves, sufficient to establish that such a diminution of competition has occurred or would be likely to occur.[12] **3.10**

52. Among the factors which the Authority believes need to be considered in order to decide whether a merger would result, or would be likely to result in a diminution of competition are the actual level of competition in that market, the degree of market concentration and how it is affected by the merger, the ease with which new competitors may enter the market and the extent to which imports may provide competition to domestic suppliers.

53. The market share figures set out in Table 2 would imply that the arrangements will result in Edberg having a market share of 29% (assuming that it retains the shares previously held by STC and RDI). The parties have argued that the impact of the acquisition on competition will be insignificant as RDI had only a very small share of the market.

54. Although the parties contend that this is a highly fragmented market, the figures in Table 2 indicate that it is in fact highly concentrated. The top two firms accounted for almost 44% of the market, while the top four accounted for 67%. The four firm concentration ratio (the aggregate market share of the four largest firms) is a standard measure of market concentration used in economics. The Authority believes that it would generally be accepted that a market where the four firm concentration ratio fell below 40 percent was effectively competitive. The degree of concentration in this market, however, is such as to give some cause for concern. The present arrangements will not greatly increase the four firm concentration ratio. Nevertheless the Authority believes that in a highly concentrated market a merger which results in even a relatively small increase in the market share of one of the larger firms merits closer examination. It follows from this that, if the four firm concentration ratio following a merger is less than 40 percent, the Authority would regard it as unlikely that the merger would prevent, restrict or distort competition and hence offend against section 4(1).

55. An alternative measure of market concentration is the Herfindall-Hirschman Index (HHI). The HHI is the sum of the squares of the shares of all firms in a market. The HHI is used by the US Department of Justice to evaluate mergers and its guidelines classify markets into three categories.[13] Where the post-merger HHI is below 1000 the market is regarded as unconcentrated and mergers in such markets are considered unlikely to have adverse effects on competition. Where the post merger HHI lies between 1000 and 1800 the market is regarded as moderately concentrated. Mergers which increase the HHI by more than 100 points in such markets are considered to potentially raise significant competitive concerns depending on other factors. When the HHI exceeds 1800 the market is regarded as highly concentrated, although even in this case, a merger raising the HHI by less than 50 points is considered unlikely to have adverse competitive consequences.

56. The Table 2 figures indicate that, in the loss adjusting market, this merger will increase the HHI by about 130 points to over 1600. Clearly this places it within the range where a merger would be subject to further examination under US Department of Justice guidelines. Thus the data on both the four firm concentration ratio and the HHI suggests that the present arrangements merit further examination. The Authority recognises that in a small economy such as Ireland market concentration ratios in many sectors may be high relative to those which exist in much larger economies. Nor is the Authority stating that where market concentration following a merger is found to be relatively high the merger is likely to restrict competition. It is merely stating that, in considering a merger notified to it, where the degree of concentration in a market post-merger is relatively high it will conduct a more detailed examination of the agreement than would otherwise be the case. While recognising that the thresholds applied in

12. Op cit., para. 78.
13. United States Department of Justice Merger Guidelines, issued 14 June 1984.

3.10 this instance were developed for larger economies it nevertheless considers that they provide a useful guide.[14]

57. It is also relevant in this instance that the merger is not simply one involving a large domestic firm and a much smaller competitor. RDI is a subsidiary of a large multinational organisation with an extensive involvement in loss adjusting throughout the world. Thus both RDI and, more importantly, its parent, must be regarded as a major potential competitor in the Irish market. According to its latest Annual Report, RHL employs 369 loss adjusters compared with an estimated total of 117 employed by all firms in Ireland.

58. RDI has been operating in the loss adjusting market in Ireland since September 1985. During this time it has failed to secure more than a very small share of the Irish market. It had accumulated losses of 400,000 in the period to end December 1991. During this period other firms have successfully established themselves in the market. The Authority accepts therefore, that RHL had sought to enter the market in its own right.

59. It has been submitted by the parties that the loss adjusting market in Ireland is highly competitive. The quality of service and the prices charged are stated by the parties to be the key considerations when obtaining business from insurance companies. As stated earlier, the Authority has confirmed with several major insurance companies that they believe prices quoted by loss adjusting firms are competitively determined.

60. The parties have also submitted that the market for loss adjusting services is a highly contestable one, that there are no barriers to entry and that the costs of entry are relatively low and are unlikely to deter new entrants. The Authority noted in Nallen/O'Toole[15] that recent theoretical developments in the economics literature indicated that in 'contestable markets' the threat of entry by new firms was sufficient to ensure that the market operated competitively. The Authority noted, however, that before such arguments can be relied upon it was necessary to establish that a market was in fact contestable. The experience of RDI, a subsidiary of a major multinational, is not, at first sight, consistent with a view that the loss adjusting market is contestable. As stated earlier, however, five firms, other than RHL, have successfully entered this market since 1984. Some of these have grown to become quite significant in the market within a relatively short period of time. Indeed it would appear that one of these is now the second largest in the market. These firms have indicated to the Authority that entry costs, in their view, did not constitute a significant entry barrier.

61. The parties also stated that there were no legal or other qualifications required for entry and that not all the individuals engaged as loss adjusters were members of the relevant professional body (CILA). The Authority does not believe, however, that virtually anybody could enter this business. Insurance claims inspectors who carry out similar work in-house for their employers, albeit involving smaller claims, could, however, set up in the market since they would have both relevant experience of the business and some contacts among the principals who employ loss adjusters. It would appear that such individuals, together with existing employees of loss adjusting firms, and CILA members currently resident in the UK, together constitute a significant source of potential competition to incumbent firms. The Authority also considers that overseas based loss adjusting firms could enter the market either by establishing subsidiaries in Ireland or by offering their services directly to Irish insurance companies.

62. It is also relevant, as the parties have argued, in assessing the present arrangements to take account of the position of users of loss adjusters' services, namely insurance companies. There were 32 insurance companies operating in the fire and property risk business in Ireland according to the 1990 Blue Book. Many of these are large companies, including subsidiaries

14. The Authority also recognises that it may not always be possible to obtain detailed information on market shares in order to compute these ratios or indices.

15. Notification No. CA/8/91—Nallen/O'Toole (Belmullet), Competition Authority Decision No. 1, 2 April 1992.

of overseas firms. Data on premium income suggests that this market is also fairly concentrated, implying in turn that the bulk of loss adjusters' business would be accounted for by a relatively small number of insurers. In such circumstances it would appear that the users of loss adjusting services would have considerable bargaining power and that this would impose significant pressure on loss adjusting firms to compete. **3.10**

63. In addition insurers already obtain some of these services in-house, as their own claims inspectors perform a similar function in respect of claims below a certain level. Insurers therefore have the option of increasing the extent to which such services could be obtained in-house and presumably would do so if such a move made commercial sense. In-house services are therefore, to some extent, a substitute for the services provided by loss adjusters and this is also likely to ensure that adjusters are forced to compete with each other.

64. Taking all of these factors into account the Authority believes that, in spite of the highly concentrated nature of the market, the merger of STC and RDI is unlikely to lessen competition in the market. Consequently it believes that the overall arrangement does not offend against section 4(1).

65. In the light of its decision in Woodchester, the Authority wishes to point out that, while it believes that a merger is not automatically outside the scope of section 4(1), this is not the same as stating that a merger offends against section 4(1). The present decision seeks to clarify the Authority's views in this area. In general, the Authority believes that a merger, per se, between competitors would not prevent, restrict or distort competition and thereby offend against section 4(1) unless the market is, or will as a result of the merger become, highly concentrated.

If the market were highly concentrated following the merger the Authority believes that it would be unlikely to prevent, restrict or distort competition where

— there were no significant impediments preventing new competitors from entering the market, and/or,

— there was effective competition from overseas suppliers.

(ii) Restraints on Competition

66. Many of the restrictive provisions included in the STC Agreement were repeated in the Service Agreements of the Vendors. Accordingly, the same arguments can be applied to both sets of provisions. Consideration is given to the effect of these restrictions below.

67. Collectively the Vendors have retained a significant shareholding (38%) in Edberg Ltd as part of the agreement for the sale of STC. RHL have acquired the option to buy this shareholding from the Vendors in 1995. In the interim, it is proposed that the Vendors be employed in Edberg for an initial period of three years under clause 2.2 of the Service Agreement. Their employment may be terminated thereafter by either party giving not less than six months written notice to the other.

68. If any of the Vendors terminated their employment contract before the initial three years had expired, they would have been deemed to have breached that contract and RHL could have exercised the right to acquire their shares in Edberg within three months. The consideration payable to the vendor in these circumstances would have been £1.

69. Clause 12 of the STC Agreement set out restrictions on the future activities of the Vendors. 12.1 contained a non-competition clause which applied to the Vendors for a period of the longer of (i) 3 years from completion and (ii) a second period. The second period was 2 years from termination of the vendor's employment with the purchaser if such termination occurred within 3 years of completion. This non-competition provision was also included in Clause 14.1 of the Service Agreement. After the initial 3 year period had elapsed there would be no second period if the vendor's employment was terminated by the purchaser in breach of the terms thereof. The second period would be six months if the vendor's employment was terminated by notice in accordance with Clause 2.2 of the Service Agreement.

3.10 70. It is evident that termination by the Vendors of their employment within the first three years was not a feasible option in the light of the return on their shareholding provided for under the Option Agreement. The Vendors were therefore tied to Edberg for an initial period of three years. In these circumstances the additional six months provided for under Clause 12.1(b) of the STC Agreement (the second period) meant that the duration of the non-competition clause was effectively a minimum of three and a half years.

71. In relation to the duration of the non-competition clause, the purchasers had stressed the importance of customer/client loyalty built up over the years by the Vendors. They argued that the duration of the clause was the minimum that was objectively necessary for Edberg to assume, by active competitive behaviour, the place in the market previously occupied by the Vendors through STC. They added that 'the duration of the covenants in Clause 12 may potentially, in certain circumstances, exceed three years since the 'Second Period' of protection afforded by Clause 12 was equally objectively necessary to protect and preserve the value of the investment by SGS and Edberg in the STC business in view of the nature of the business as a service business where customer/client loyalty was invaluable and persisted for a period which might well exceed three years.'

72. The Authority's view on the duration of non-competition clauses in the case of the sale of a business has been stated in several previous decisions. Its view is that some restriction on the seller is generally necessary in order to ensure the complete transfer of the goodwill of the business. It stated that provided the restriction was limited in terms of its duration, geographical coverage and subject matter to that which was necessary for the complete transfer of the goodwill, then the restriction did not offend against section 4(1) of the Act. Most recently in General Semiconductor, the Authority indicated that, having had an opportunity to consider a number of such agreements, it would generally consider a non-competition clause exceeding two years in a sale of business agreement to offend against section 4(1).[16]

73. Given its previous decisions, the Authority regarded the non-competition clauses in the notified arrangements, which were effectively for a minimum of three and a half years, as being more than was necessary to secure the complete transfer of goodwill. It is relevant that insurers would be dealing with the firm frequently and in such circumstances a period of two years was considered sufficient for the new owners to acquire the complete goodwill. It must also be considered that figures for commission paid to the Vendors in respect of fee income earned by them in 1991, indicated that a lot of the company's business was attributable to its other employees.

74. In this case it was not clear that the arrangements could be viewed as a simple sale of business, since the Vendors are to remain on as shareholders and employees following the sale. This raised the question of the date from which the non-compete clause should have effect. The arrangements could be viewed as akin to the creation of a partnership involving RHL and the Vendors. An agreement between parties to engage in business together could not operate if the parties were free to compete with the business or with each other. The Authority believes that individuals could not jointly engage in business together if they were free to compete with each other. It is clear, even if it is not explicitly stated, that an agreement between parties to carry on business together implies that they will not compete against the business or against each other so long as they remain in business together.

75. Where individuals agree to engage in business together as part of a single economic entity and not to compete with one another, the Authority believes there is a case for not regarding such arrangements, of themselves, as offending against section 4(1). Indeed such arrangements may be pro-competitive in that the combined entity may be in a better position to compete with other undertakings in the relevant market. The position changes, however, if the parties are prevented from withdrawing from such arrangements. If a party wishes to

16. Competition Authority decision no. 10, notification nos. CA/51/92 and CA/52/92 — GI/General; Semiconductor Industries, 23 October 1992.

withdraw from such arrangements then measures designed to prevent him doing so may restrict competition. In the event that one of the parties to such an arrangement decides to withdraw then, given the Authority's views in Nallen/O'Toole, where one partner bought out the other partner's share in the business, a provision which restricts the vendor from competing with the business for a time may be justified in order to allow the purchaser obtain the goodwill of the business for which he had paid. 3.10

76. In the present case Edberg has purchased the business of STC from the Vendors, who are to become shareholders in, and employees of Edberg. The Authority believes that in such circumstances the Vendors could not be expected to compete with Edberg for so long as they continue to be significant shareholders and enjoy a degree of control over the running of the business and that in such circumstances any agreement not to compete does not offend against section 4(1). The Authority does not believe that such a restriction would be acceptable if the shareholding was held for purely investment purposes or if it was part of an artificial arrangement which had the object or effect of evading the prohibition contained in section 4(1).

77. The original restrictions went beyond what was necessary to secure the complete transfer of the goodwill of the business to the extent that they did not just prevent the Vendors competing with the business while they remained involved in it, but sought to tie them to the business for a minimum period of time. The Vendors were effectively tied to Edberg for at least three years by virtue of the service and option agreements. In addition they would have been prevented from competing with Edberg for a further six months if they then left. The combined effect of the non-compete clauses, the option agreement and related provisions therefore was to exclude potential competitors—the Vendors— from the market for at least three and a half years. This period exceeded what the Authority generally regards as necessary to secure the transfer of the goodwill of a business and the Authority therefore considered that the effect of the arrangements was to prevent competition. The restrictions, therefore, offended against section 4(1).

78. Clause 12.2(a) of the STC Agreement prevented the Vendors canvassing orders from clients of Edberg. This restriction applied for the 'longer of a period of three years from completion or a period of 2 years from termination of the relevant vendor's employment with the purchaser. . . .' As already explained, it was not in the Vendors' interests to break their three year service contracts. Therefore, the duration of this clause was effectively a minimum of five years. Given the nature of the business, in particular the relatively small number of users of loss adjusters' services, the Authority believes that a restriction on canvassing former clients would make it extremely difficult if not impossible to compete in this market. In the Authority's opinion, this clause would have served to reinforce the duration of the other non-competition provisions in the arrangements and would have had the effect of preventing the Vendors from competing with Edberg for an excessive period of time. Clause 14.2 of the Service Agreements also included this restriction. The Authority concluded that both of these clauses offended against section 4(1) of the Act for the reasons outlined in the previous paragraph.

79. On balance the Authority believes that in a case such as this a restriction on competition should be limited to the period during which the Vendors remain as shareholders, employees and enjoy a degree of control over the business. Should they sell their shareholding at some stage then a restriction on their competing with the business may be justified to enable the purchaser to acquire the remaining goodwill of the business. Such a restriction generally ought not to exceed two years from the time of such sale.

80. In a Supplemental Agreement dated 18 December 1992, the parties amended the offending provisions of the agreement. Under the amended agreement the Vendors agree not to compete with Edberg for so long as they remain shareholders and/or employees of Edberg and for a period of 2 years after they dispose of their shareholding in accord with the terms of the option agreement. In addition the Option Agreement has been amended to provide that, in the event that the Vendors leave Edberg before 31 December 1994, the buy out price pursuant to clause 3.2 (a) of that agreement would be 'such sum as equals the price determined by the auditors of Edberg to be the market value on the basis of a willing seller and a willing buyer

3.10 and on the basis that the relevant shares constitute a minority shareholding less an agreed discount of 5 percent.'

81. The Authority believes that while the Option Agreement as amended means that there may still be some disincentive for the Vendors to leave the business before 31 December 1994, this is not now so great as to effectively exclude such a possibility. The Authority considers that a restriction on the Vendors competing with the business for so long as they remain employees and shareholders and for a further 2 years after they dispose of their shareholding is acceptable in such circumstances as being no more than is necessary to secure the transfer of the goodwill of the business to the purchaser. For these reasons the Authority considers that the amended provisions do not offend against section 4(1).

82. The Authority wishes to make clear that the restrictions contained in the arrangements as amended were acceptable in the context of the parties having agreed to engage in business together as part of a single economic entity. As stated above, in its view a restriction on individuals competing with a business in which they were shareholders would offend against section 4(1) where such shareholding was purely for investment purposes or was an artificial arrangement whose object or effect was to evade the prohibition contained in that Section. It would take a similar view of an employment contract that was an artificial arrangement whose object or effect was to evade the prohibition contained in that Section.

83. The scope of Clause 12.1 is limited to the business of loss adjusting. Accordingly, the scope of the restriction does not offend against section 4(1) of the Competition Act 1991. It applies to Ireland, Northern Ireland, England, Wales, Scotland, the Channel Islands and the Isle of Man. In view of the fact that insurance loss adjusting services can be easily provided across international borders, the Authority is satisfied that the geographical impact of the clause is limited to that which is necessary for the transfer of the goodwill of STC.

84. Clause 12.2(b) of the STC Agreement prevents the Vendors using the words 'Scully' or 'Tyrrell' or 'Scully Tyrrell' as a trade name or mark in the relevant market. It is necessary to prevent the possibility of the Vendors passing themselves off to their customers or suppliers as representing STC in the event that they should decide to compete against the purchasers. This restraint does not involve any restriction on competition within the State or any part of the State and does not offend against section 4(1).

85. Clause 15 of the STC Agreement, clause 14.1 of the Shareholders Agreement and Clause 11.1 of the Service Agreements involve undertakings by the Vendors concerning the disclosure or use of confidential information and related matters. These clauses prevent the Vendors from disclosing or making use of trade secrets. There is no time limit on these clauses. The Authority has considered the question of preventing the use of non-technical know-how in Budget Travel. As in that case, the Authority was concerned that such a clause should not be used to impede any possible re-entry into the market by the Vendors once the non-competition clauses had expired. The parties indicated by letter dated 23 November 1992 that the confidentiality provisions in clause 15 of the STC Agreement, clause 14.1 of the Shareholders Agreement and clause 11.1 of the Service Agreements 'are not intended or designed to prevent the Vendors from competing with the business carried on by Edberg but rather are intended and designed simply to prohibit a Vendor from using or abusing information that is confidential to Edberg or any of the Edberg shareholders.' In these circumstances, the Authority finds that these clauses do not offend against section 4(1) of the Act.

The Decision

86. Edberg, RHL and the Vendors are undertakings within the meaning of section 3(1) of the Competition Act and the notified arrangements for the sale of the business of STC to Edberg constitute an agreement between undertakings which applies within the State.

87. The Authority believes that the agreement for the purchase and sale of STC does not offend against section 4(1) of the Competition Act.

88. The Authority has previously stated that, in the case of a sale of business, some

restriction on the seller competing with the purchaser is normally justified in order for the purchaser to acquire the complete goodwill of the business. A non-competition clause which is limited in terms of duration, geographic coverage and subject matter to what is necessary to secure the complete transfer of the goodwill of the business does not prevent, restrict or distort competition within the meaning of section 4(1) of the Competition Act. In this instance the Vendors have decided to remain on and effectively agreed to engage in business with the purchaser as part of a single economic entity. The Authority believes that, in such circumstances, an agreement by the Vendors not to compete with Edberg for so long as they remain shareholders and employees of that company does not offend against section 4(1) of the Competition Act, provided the shareholding is not held for purely investment purposes and provided that the arrangements are not an artificial construction whose object or effect is to evade the prohibition contained in that section. **3.10**

89. The Authority believes that the restriction on the Vendors competing with Edberg for 2 years after they sell their shares is limited in terms of duration, geographic coverage and subject matter to what is necessary to secure the complete transfer of the goodwill of the business following such a sale. In the Authority's view the restrictions contained in the various agreements, as amended by the Supplemental Agreement of 18 December 1992, together with the undertaking in respect of the confidentiality clauses in the letter of 23 November 1992, do not prevent, restrict or distort competition in the State or any part of the State.

90. The present agreement for the transfer of ownership of Scully Tyrrell & Co. between Robins Holdings Ltd, Edberg Ltd and Messrs Scully, Tyrrell, Crawford, Herbert, Sleater, Conroy, O'Donoghue and Putman does not, in the Authority's opinion offend against section 4(1) of the Competition Act 1991.

The Certificate

91. The Competition Authority has issued the following certificate:

> The Competition Authority certifies that in its opinion, on the basis of the facts in its possession, the agreement between Robins Holdings Ltd, Edberg Ltd and Messrs Scully, Tyrrell, Crawford, Herbert, Sleater, Conroy, O'Donoghue and Putman, for the transfer of ownership of Scully Tyrrell & Co., (Notification No. CA/57/92), notified on 31 July 1992 under section 7, as amended by the Supplemental Agreement of 18 December 1992, together with the undertaking in respect of the confidentiality clauses in the letter of 23 November 1992, does not offend against section 4(1) of the Competition Act 1991.

For the Competition Authority

Patrick Massey
Member

29 January 1993

3.11 Competition Authority Decision No. 17, Chemical International Finance Ltd/Irish Life Assurance plc: 29 April 1993, Notification No. CA/10/93

Arrangements for the sale of business – Deed of Covenant made between vendor and purchaser wherein vendor enters into restrictive covenants in favour of purchaser – Restrictive covenants two years in duration – No geographic limitation on restrictive covenants – Competition Act 1991 (No. 24) sections 3, 4 and 7

Facts On 2 March 1993 notification was made to the Authority of a Deed of Covenant between Irish Life Assurance plc ('Irish Life') and Chemical International Finance Ltd ('CIF') with a request for a certificate under section 4(4) of the Competition Act 1991 or failing that, a licence under section 4(2).

The notified Deed of Covenant was entered into pursuant to an agreement by CIF to acquire the entire issued share capital of three subsidiary companies from Irish Life ('the subsidiaries'). The notified Deed contained a number of non- compete covenants given by Irish Life as part of the sale of business arrangements.

CIF, a wholly owned subsidiary of US Bank Chemical Banking Corporation, is engaged in the provision of financial services in both the US and internationally. Irish Life, a publicly quoted company in London and Dublin, is the largest provider of life assurance in the State.

The Subsidiaries which are being acquired by CIF provide a broad range of services to investment businesses located within the International Financial Services Centre, Dublin, which services include, *inter alia*, fund accounting, dividend collection, shareholder registration, calculation of brokers commissions, settlement of purchases and sales of stock, preparation of interim and final fund management accounts, acting as company secretary and arrangement of board meetings (collectively referred to as 'management services'). The relevant market is for the provisions of such a management service to firms operating in the IFSC and such services are also provided on a global basis by firms located in different financial centres throughout the world.

Under the terms of the notified agreement Irish Life covenants to CIF that it will not for a period of two years from completion of the sale of the subsidiaries be engaged in the carrying on of business of providing management services other than to existing funds or new funds to which Irish Life is the principal sponsor within the European Community. Irish Life also covenanted for a period of two years from the date of completion not to solicit any client of the subsidiaries for the purpose of providing such management services or to solicit any employee of such subsidiary.

Decided by the Authority: In issuing a certificate under section 4(4) of the Competition Act 1991 in respect of the notified agreement that:

(1) Each of Irish Life and CIF are corporate bodies engaged in the provision of goods and services for gain and are therefore undertakings within the meaning of the Competition Act.

(2) The notified arrangements constitute an agreement between undertakings whereby Irish Life has agreed not to compete in certain types of business for a period of two years pursuant to an agreement to sell the subsidiaries to CIF.

(3) The notified agreement is part of the arrangement for the sale of a business. Non-compete provisions of the kind contained in the notified agreement do not offend against section 4(1) where they are essential to the sale of a business but were they

not part of an overall sale of business arrangement such an agreement not to compete would offend against section 4(1). Consequently the agreement notified cannot be considered purely in isolation but must be regarded as part of the sale of a business. A series of related agreements may, in certain circumstances, be regarded as a single agreement. **3.11**

(4) The notified agreement is part of an arrangement for the transfer of ownership of businesses and, in the absence of any indication to the contrary, such an arrangement to transfer ownership does not offend against section 4(1) of the Competition Act.

(5) A restriction on a vendor competing with the business transferred does not offend against section 4(1) of the Competition Act 1991 provided it does not exceed what is necessary to secure the transfer of any goodwill involved, in terms of its duration, geographic coverage and subject matter. Generally a period of two years is sufficient to ensure the transfer of goodwill. The notified arrangements do not exceed two years. No geographic area is specified in the notified agreement but if the restriction was applied only to a specific geographic area this would not suffice to prevent Irish Life from competing in the market and retaining the goodwill of the subsidiaries. The notified arrangements do not offend against section 4(1) of the Competition Act.

Decisions referred to:
EC Commission Decision PPG/Mecaniver, 12.12.84 [1985] OJ L 35/54; [1985] 3 CMLR 359
Competition Authority Decision No. 1 Nallen/O'Toole, 2 April 1992 **3.3**
Competition Authority Decision No. 3 Athlone Travel Ltd./Michael Stein Travel Ltd, 4 June 1992 **3.4**
Competition Authority Decision No. 8 ACT Group plc/Kindle Group Ltd, 4 September 1992 **3.6**
Competition Authority Decision No. 9 Phil Fortune/Budget Travel Ltd, 14 September 1992 **3.7**
Competition Authority Decision No. 12 Scully Tyrrell & Co./Edberg Ltd, 29 January 1993 **3.10**

Competition Authority Decision of 29 April 1993 relating to a proceeding under section 4 of the Competition Act 1991
Notification No. CA/10/93 — Chemical International Finance Ltd/Irish Life Assurance plc.

Introduction

1. A deed of covenant between Irish Life Assurance plc (Irish Life) and Chemical International Finance Ltd. (CIF), containing a number of non-compete clauses, entered into pursuant to a sale of business agreement, was notified to the Competition Authority on 2 March 1993. The notification requested a certificate, or in the event of a refusal by the Authority to grant a certificate, a licence.

The Facts

(a) *The Subject of the Notifications*

2. The notification relates to a deed of covenant dated 1 January 1993, between Irish Life and CIF. The covenant was entered into pursuant to an agreement by CIF to acquire the entire issued share capital of three subsidiary companies (the companies) from Irish Life. The

3.11 companies in question are, Fund Administration, Custody and Trustee Services Ltd ('FACTS'), Irish Life International Investment Management Ltd, ('ILIML'), and Irish Life Investment Fund Managers Ltd, ('ILIFML'). The covenant contains a number of non-compete covenants given by Irish Life as part of the sale of business arrangement.

(b) *The Parties*

3. CIF is a wholly owned subsidiary of Chemical Banking Corporation, a US bank. Chemical and its subsidiaries provide financial services both in the US and internationally. Chemical Banking Corporation shares are quoted on the New York and London stock exchanges.

4. Irish Life is a company with shares quoted on the London stock exchange. It is the largest provider of life assurance in Ireland.

The Product and the Market

5. The companies which are being acquired by CIF provide a range of services to investment businesses located within the International Financial Services Centre, (IFSC). These services fall into four broad categories:

(i) Fund administration services;
(ii) Custody services;
(iii) Financial and administrative services;
(iv) Trustee services.

These services include a wide range of activities such as fund accounting, dividend collection, shareholder registration, calculation of brokers' commissions, settlement of purchases and sales of stock, preparation of interim and final fund and management accounts and of reports to regulators, acting as company secretary and arranging board meetings. The market is that for the provision of such services to firms operating in the IFSC. Such services are provided on a global basis by firms located in different financial centres throughout the world.

The Arrangements

6. The notification relates to a deed of covenant entered into pursuant to an agreement for the sale of the companies by Irish Life to CIF. The deed of covenant contains a number of non-compete provisions. These are contained in clause 2.1 of the deed which provides as follows.

> Life covenants and undertakes with Chemical and its successors in title in relation to the Shares as trustee for itself and each of the Companies that:
> (a) for the period of two years after Completion Irish Life will not either on its own behalf or in conjunction with or on behalf of any person, firm or company carry on or be engaged or interested in carrying on the businesses of providing securities custody, trustee, settlement, clearing, valuation, administration or back office services or registrar services other than to existing funds or new funds to which Irish Life are the principal sponsor (and other than as a holder of shares or debentures listed on The Stock Exchange or dealt in on the Unlisted Securities Market) within the European Community (as constituted from time to time);
> (b) for the period of two years after Completion Irish Life will not either on its own behalf or in conjunction with or on behalf of any person, firm or company solicit or endeavour to solicit any Existing Client of the Company for the purposes of providing such client with such services as are provided or are capable of being provided to an Existing Client by any Company;
> (c) for the period of two years after Completion Irish Life will not either on its own behalf or in conjunction with or on behalf of any person, firm or company solicit or entice away from any of the Companies any officer, manager or servant whether or not

such person would commit a breach of his contract of employment by reason of leaving service; **3.11**

(d) Irish Life shall procure that no company owned or controlled by Irish Life (and insofar as Irish Life is able to ensure the same none of its subsidiaries or associated companies) shall act in such a way as would be in contravention of the obligations contained in this paragraph if Irish Life were itself to so act.

Submissions of the Parties

7. The parties have argued that restrictions on the vendor of the kind contained in the deed of covenant entered into pursuant to a sale of business have been regarded as acceptable in competition law in other jurisdictions. They also referred to a number of previous decisions in which the Authority had certified that non- compete clauses in the case of a sale of business did not offend against section 4(1), provided they were limited in terms of duration, scope and subject matter to what was necessary to secure the transfer of any goodwill attaching to the business being sold, to support their request for a certificate.[1] They pointed out that in Nallen/olToole and Phil Fortune/Budget Travel, the Authority had indicated that a period of two years would normally, in its view, suffice to ensure the transfer of such goodwill. In addition they referred to the fact that in ACT/Kindle and Phil Fortune/Budget Travel the Authority had accepted a restriction which applied to no specific geographical area, given the nature of the businesses involved. They argued that as the market in which the businesses being sold was global, a similar unspecified geographical restriction was justified in this instance. They also submitted that the restrictions were confined to the businesses carried on by the companies being sold and thus were acceptable in terms of subject matter.

Assessment

(a) *Section 4(1)*

8. Section 4(1) of the Competition Act states that 'all agreements between undertakings, decisions by associations of undertakings and concerted practices which have as their object or effect the prevention, restriction or distortion of competition in trade in any goods or services in the State or in any part of the State are prohibited and void.'

(b) *The Undertakings and the Agreement*

9. Section 3(1) of the Competition Act defines an undertaking as 'a person being an individual, a body corporate or an unincorporated body of persons engaged for gain in the production, supply or distribution of goods or the provision of a service.' The parties to the present agreement are Irish Life and CIF. They are both corporate bodies engaged in the provision of goods and services for gain and are therefore undertakings within the meaning of the Act.

(c) *Applicability of section 4(1)*

10. The present arrangements therefore constitute an agreement between undertakings whereby Irish Life has agreed not to compete in certain types of business for a period of two years, pursuant to an agreement to sell companies engaged in such lines of business to CIF. The Authority has previously stated its views on non-compete provisions in sale of business agreements in a number of previous decisions. It does not therefore propose to restate at length its views in the present decision.

11. The present notification differs from most of those previously considered by the Authority as only the deed of covenant incorporating the non-compete arrangements was

1. Competition Authority Decision No. 1, Nallen/O'Toole (Belmullet), (CA/8/91), 2 April 1992; No. 3, Athlone Travel Ltd/Michael Stein Travel Ltd, (CA/12/92), 4 June 1992; No. 8, ACT Group plc/ Kindle Group Ltd, (CA/9/91), 4 September 1992; and No. 9 Phil Fortune/Budget Travel Ltd, (CA/1/92), 14 September 1992.

3.11 specifically notified. In its previous decisions the Authority has concluded that non-compete provisions of the kind contained in the present notified agreement do not offend against sectlon 4(1) where they are essential to the sale of a business. Were they not part of an overall sale of business arrangement, such an agreement not to compete would offend against section 4(1). Consequently the agreement notified cannot be Considered purely in isolation but must be regarded as part of the broader sale of business arrangement. The Authority indicated in Scully/Tyrrell[2] that a series of related agreements may be regarded as a single agreement.

12. The Authority has stated on a number of occasions that agreements for the sale of a business are not automatically outside the scope of section 4(1) of the Competition Act. It would, however, agree with the views expressed by the EC Commission in PPG/Mecaniver that, in the absence of a risk of co-ordination of competitive behaviour,

> The sale constituting the mere transfer of a business [did] not in itself and in the absence of any indications to the contrary give rise to any restriction of competition and as such did not fall within the scope of Article 85(1).[3]

The Authority believes that the agreement notified is part of an arrangement for the transfer of ownership of businesses and, in the absence of any indication to the contrary, does not believe that such an arrangement offends against section 4(1).

13. As noted by the parties, the Authority has, in a number of decisions, indicated that in the case of a sale of business a restriction on the vendor competing with the business transferred does not offend against sectioh 4(1), provided it does not exceed what is necessary to secure the transfer of any goodwill involved, in terms of its duration, geographic coverage and subject matter. It has also stated on several occasions that it generally considers a period of two years sufficient to ensure the transfer of goodwill. The present arrangement clearly meets the criteria set out in those earlier decisions. The restriction on Irish Life is for a period of two years and is confined to the businesses in which the companies being sold are engaged. No geographic area is specified. The Authority is satisfied that firms located outside of the State can and do provide such services to firms operating in the IFSC. Consequently if the restriction applied only to a specific geographic area, this would not suffice to prevent Irish Life competing in the market and retaining the goodwill of the businesses which now properly belongs to the purchaser. In sum the notified arrangements do not, in the Authority's opinion, offend against section 4(1).

The Certificate

14. The Competition Authority has issued the following certificate:

> The Competition Authority certifies that in its opinion, on the basis of the facts in its possession, the deed of covenant between Chemical International Finance Ltd and Irish Life Assurance plc, entered into pursuant to Chemical International finance having purchased certain businesses from Irish Life (Notification No. CA/10/93), notified on 2 March 1993 under section 7(1), does not offend against section 4(1) of the Competition Act 1991.

For the Competition Authority

Patrick Massey
Member

29 April 1993

2. Competition Authority Decision No. 12, Scully Tyrrell & Company/Edberg Ltd, (CA/57/92), 29 January 1993.
3. Case No. 85/78/EEC, OJ L35/54, 7.2.85.

Competition Authority Decision No. 24, Cambridge Investments Ltd/ACT/ Imari Ltd: 21 June 1993, Notification No. CA/8/92E 3.12

Share subscription and shareholders agreement – Provisions whereby venture capital shareholder could veto and regulate business of the company – Provision whereby managing director and promoter of the company was restricted from competing with the company for five years from the date of the agreement or two years from the date of his cessation of employment whichever was later – Provision preventing the managing director and promoter of the company from transferring his shares without the prior approval of the venture capital shareholder – Whether managing director and promoter is an undertaking – Whether investment by venture capitalist deemed a concentration or merger agreement – Whether ancillary restrictive clauses in the agreement are essential in order to achieve the main purpose of the agreement – Whether the restrictions imposed on the promoter and managing director went further than was necessary to achieve the legitimate end of the agreement – Amendment of notified agreement – EC Merger Regulation 4064/89 – Competition Act 1991 (No. 24) sections 3, 4 and 7

Facts: On 6 March 1992 notification was made to the Authority of a share subscription and shareholders agreement made 25 October 1991 between Mr Timothy O'Neill ('O'Neill'), Cambridge Investments Ltd. ('Cambridge'), Imari Ltd. ('Imari') and Allied Combined Trust Ltd. ('ACT') together with a request for certificate under section 4(4) of the Competition Act 1991 or, failing that, a licence under section 4(2). The notified agreement provided for the acquisition by Cambridge of 19% of the shares in Imari and it also provided for the regulation of matters between the shareholders of Imari.

O'Neill, the managing director of Imari, was with the company since its foundation in 1987 and held approximately 19% of the entire issued share capital of the company. Imari, an Irish registered private holding company, operated through its subsidiaries in the shipping, transport, freight forwarding and port services industries. Cambridge, an Irish registered company, was involved in the business of *inter alia* fund management and the provision of venture capital. ACT, an Irish investment holding company, provided venture and development capital to companies in Ireland and the UK.

The Imari group is engaged in the shipping, transport, freight forwarding and port services businesses through a number of wholly owned subsidiaries which include general haulage and specialist haulage services both within the State and internationally. Cambridge and ACT provide venture capital to small businesses which they believe have development potential, by acquiring usually a shareholding in the hope of making a capital gain on their shareholding at a future date.

Under the terms of the notified agreement Cambridge was allotted 24,000 shares in the capital of Imari (circa 19% of the issued shares). The agreement also contained provisions regulating the management of Imari and certain restrictions on Imari and O'Neill for the benefit of Cambridge and ACT. In particular clauses 6.9 and 6.10 regulated the type of business which Imari could carry on and limited the amount of expenditure which Imari could incur during the period when either of Cambridge or ACT held 10% or more of the ordinary shares in the capital of Imari. Under clause 6.14 Imari covenanted to fully enforce the provisions of its employment contract with O'Neill and not to rescind, terminate or amend such agreement without the prior

3.12 written consent of each of Cambridge and ACT. Clause 8 imposed restrictions on O'Neill for a period of five years from the completion date or the second anniversary of the date upon which he ceased to be employed by Imari (whichever was later) from:

(a) Carrying on or being engaged in any business in Ireland which competes with any company in the Imari Group;

(b) Doing business with any person who was a customer or supplier of any company within the Imari Group during the two years preceding his cessation of employment;

(c) Interfering with the continuance of supplies to the Imari Group from companies who were suppliers to Imari during the two years preceding his cessation of employment;

(d) Soliciting or offering employment to any person who was an employee of the Imari Group during the two years preceding his cessation of employment;

(e) Entering into a partnership with or appointing as consultant/adviser any person who was an employee of the Imari Group during the two years preceding the completion date;

(f) Using or adopting the name of any company of the Imari Group. Clause 9 of the notified agreement prohibited O'Neill from transferring or otherwise disposing of his shares in Imari without the prior consent in writing of Cambridge and ACT.

Submissions The parties submitted, *inter alia,* that the notified agreement was tantamount to a concentration and as such any restraints contained therein are ancillary to the investments constituting the concentration and by analogy with EU law did not infringe section 4 of the Competition Act. It was further submitted that the undertakings associated with the notifying parties did not carry on business directly or indirectly in competition with the Imari Group and therefore the agreement does not interfere with competition. In addition the parties submitted that the restrictions on O'Neill did not fall within section 4 of the Competition Act because:

(a) O'Neill was not an undertaking within the meaning of section 3 of the Competition Act;

(b) The restrictive covenants in clause 8 are ancillary restraints of a nature, duration and scope which are reasonable in all the circumstances to protect the value of Cambridge and ACT's investments in Imari;

(c) The restrictive covenants are given by O'Neill not to Imari but to Cambridge and to ACT neither of whom are competitors of O'Neill or Imari and therefore they do not interfere with competition;

(d) Even if the restrictive covenants in clause 8 were construed as potentially affecting competition they were unlikely to have any effect or any appreciable or significant effect on competition in the market where Imari or any other parties to the agreement operates.

Amendments By letter dated 21 May 1992 the parties stated that clause 8.1(ii) would not be invoked to prevent O'Neill entering the business but only to stop him using any confidential information. In response to the Authority's concerns in relation to the scope of clause 8 an amendment to the notified agreement was submitted on 1 March 1993. In particular the amendment provided that the restrictions in clause 8 would apply to a period commencing on the completion date and expiring on the later of (i) 950 days after O'Neill ceased to beneficially own any shares in the capital of

Imari and (ii) the date on which O'Neill ceased to be an employee of Imari. 3.12

Decided by the Authority: In issuing a certificate under section 4(4) of the Competition Act in respect of the notified agreement that:

(1) Each of Cambridge, ACT and Imari are body corporates engaged in the provision of services for gain and are therefore undertakings within the meaning of the Competition Act. O'Neill is an undertaking engaged for gain in the provision of services because he exercises considerable *de facto* control over the business of Imari by being a part owner and managing director of Imari.

(2) The notified agreement constitutes a series of arrangements involving Cambridge, ACT, Imari and O'Neill which constitute an agreement between undertakings. Imari is engaged in providing international freight transport and other services within the State and between the State and other countries and the relevant market is that for the provision of such services throughout the State.

(3) The notified arrangements do not constitute a concentration within the meaning of the EC Merger Regulation and do not include a merger within the meaning of the Mergers, Takeovers and Monopolies (Control) Act 1978 as two or more previously independent enterprises are not coming under common control within the meaning of the Mergers, Takeovers and Monopolies (Control) Act 1978. The proportion of shares being acquired by Cambridge is below the level at which enterprises are deemed to come under common control under the Mergers Act 1978 as amended by the Competition Act. A merger agreement does not automatically fall outside the scope of section 4(1) of the Competition Act.

(4) The primary object of venture capitalists in acquiring shares in small and medium sized businesses is investment. The object of the business into which the investment goes is to finance for expansion. While such an arrangement is not a partnership, it nevertheless represents an arrangement by two or more parties to participate together in a business venture, with one providing the necessary capital and the other the business knowledge. The object of such an arrangement is not to prevent, restrict or distort competition. The effect is likely to help competition. The investment arrangements do not offend against section 4(1) of the Competition Act.

(5) While the notified agreement is not of its nature anti-competitive consideration must also be given as to whether any of the provisions of the agreement have the object or effect of preventing, restricting or distorting competition. Where the provisions of the agreement are ancillary to the main purpose of the agreement they should not be considered to offend against section 4(1) of the Competition Act. In order to decide whether individual clauses of an agreement should be properly regarded as merely ancillary to the main purpose of the agreement it must be established that they are necessary, but no more than is absolutely necessary to achieve such ends. Where individual restrictive clauses in an agreement go beyond what is absolutely necessary to achieve a legitimate end then they can no longer be regarded as merely ancillary to that end but must be considered as having the object of seeking to prevent, restrict or distort competition.

(6) The restrictions on the management of Imari in Clauses 6.9 and 6.10 which last while either Cambridge or ACT hold 10% of the shares of Imari are restrictions which are designed to protect the venture capital investment and such restrictions may be regarded as no more than are necessary to achieve the aims of the overall agreement and do not therefore offend against section 4(1) of the Competition Act.

3.12 (7) Clause 6.14 is designed to ensure that Imari retains the services of O'Neill, that he continues to devote his efforts to the promotion of Imari's interests and that he does not compete with Imari so long as he remains involved with the company. As such this clause is a legitimate means for Cambridge and ACT to protect their investment and it cannot be said to offend against section 4(1).

(8) In general a restriction on the parties involved in a business competing with that business for so long as they remain part of the business does not offend against section 4(1) but if the parties are prevented from withdrawing from such arrangements this may represent a restriction on competition.

(9) The restrictions on O'Neill for the later of five years after the investment or two years after termination of his service contract in clause 8.1 (before they were subsequently amended) went further than was necessary to protect Cambridge and ACT's investment in Imari because all of the restrictions in the arrangements together were designed to prevent O'Neill from leaving Imari and seeking to establish himself as a competitor. The effect of clause 8.1 (before subsequent amendment) was to prevent O'Neill leaving and setting up in competition with Imari either on his own or in partnership or from taking up employment with another competing company for an unduly long period of time and these provisions had the object or effect of preventing, restricting or distorting competition in certain transport services within the State and offended against section 4(1) of the Competition Act.

(10) The amended clause 8.1 provides that the restrictions on O'Neill shall apply from the completion date until the later of 915 days after the date upon which O'Neill ceases to beneficially own any shares in Imari or the date upon which he ceases to be an employee of Imari. The amended clause 8.1 provides for a restriction of two and a half years from the date of the sale of the shares in the business and, given the importance of O'Neill to the business and the size of the investment by Cambridge, a period of six months longer than the general norm is acceptable in this instance and therefore the amended clause 8.1 does not offend against section 4(1) of the Competition Act.

(11) Clause 8.1(ii) whereby O'Neill is prohibited from making use for his own purposes of any confidential information belonging to Imari does not offend against section 4(1) of the Competition Act because the parties have indicated in writing that this clause would not be invoked to prevent O'Neill from entering the business.

(12) The protection of the interests of Cambridge and ACT justifies the restriction contained in clause 9.1 which prevent O'Neill from disposing of his shareholding in Imari without the consent of Cambridge and ACT. However, the withholding of consent in order to prevent O'Neill from leaving and competing with Imari would represent a restriction on competition.

Cases, Decisions, Notice and Report referred to:

Suiker Unie v. Commission (Case Nos. 40-48, 50, 54-56, 111, 113 and 114/73) [1975] ECR 1663; [1976] 1 CMLR 295

Remia BV v. European Commission (Case No. 42/84) [1985] ECR 2545; [1987] 1 CMLR 1

BAT v. EC Commission and Philip Morris (Case Nos. 142 & 156/84) [1987] ECR 4487; [1988] 4 CMLR 24

Volk v. Vervaecke (Case No. 5/69) [1969] ECR 295; [1969] CMLR 273

United States v. Addyston Pipe & Steel Co. et. al., 85 F 271 (6th Cir 1898)

EC Commission Decision Reuter/BASF [1976] OJ L 254/40, [1976] 2 CMLR D44

EC Commission Decision Nutricia [1983] OJ L 376/22, [1984] 2 CMLR 165

EC Commission Decision Odin (Elopak/Metal Bod) [1990] OJ L209/15; [1991] 4 CMLR 832

Competition Authority Decision No. 1 Nallen/O'Toole, 2 April 1992 **3.3** **3.12**
Competition Authority Decision No. 2 AGF/Irish Life Holdings, 14 May 1992 **1.3.1**
Competition Authority Decision No. 6 Woodchester Bank/UDT Bank, 4 August 1992 **3.5**
Competition Authority Decision No. 8 ACT/Kindle, 4 October 1992 **3.6**
Competition Authority Decision No. 9 Budget Travel/Phil Fortune, 14 October 1992 **3.7**
Competition Authority Decision No. 12 Scully Tyrrell/Edberg, 29 January 1993 **3.10**
Competition Authority Decision No. 13 Peter Mark/Majella Stapleton, 18 February 1993 **1.4.2**
Competition Authority Notice on Employee Agreements and Competition Act **1.4.1**
Competition Authority Report of Investigation of the proposal whereby Independent Newspapers plc would increase the shareholding in Tribune Group (PL. 8795)

Competition Authority Decision of 21 June 1993 relating to a proceeding under section 4 of the Competition Act 1991
Notification No. CA/8/92E — Cambridge-ACT/Imari

Introduction

1. On 25 October 1991, Mr Timothy O'Neill, Cambridge Investments Ltd, Imari Ltd and Allied Combined Trust Ltd (ACT) entered into a Share Subscription and Shareholders Agreement to regulate the terms on which the Cambridge Equity Fund would acquire approximately 19% of the entire issued ordinary share capital of Imari Ltd and the terms on which ACT's previous investment in the Company would be regulated. The arrangements were notified to the Authority on 6 March 1992. A certificate was sought in respect of the notification. In the event of a refusal by the Authority to grant a certificate, a licence was sought. Following discussions with the Authority certain aspects of the notified arrangements were amended. These amendments were notified on 1 March 1993.

2. Notice of the intention of the Authority to take a favourable decision in relation to the arrangements was published in the Irish Times on 14 May 1993. No submissions were received from third parties in response.

The Facts

(a) *Subject of the Notification*

3. This notification concerns the investment by Cambridge Equity Fund and Allied Combined Trust Ltd in Imari Ltd, a company dealing mainly in the shipping transport business. Under the arrangements d number of restrictions were placed on Mr Timothy Joseph O'Neill, the managing director of Imari.

(b) *The Undertakings*

4. The parties to the agreement are Mr Timothy Joseph O'Neill, Cambridge Investments Ltd (Cambridge), Allied Combined Trust Ltd (ACT) and Imari Ltd (Imari).

5. Mr O'Neill is the Managing Director of Imari and is responsible for the day to day management of the company. He has been with the company since its foundation in 1987. He is referred to as 'the covenantor' in the agreement. Mr O'Neill holds approximately 23% of the issued ordinary share capital and 19% of the entire issued share capital of Imari.

6. Imari is a private limited holding company incorporated and managed in Ireland with a number of subsidiaries and an associated company which operate in the shipping, transport, freight forwarding and port services industries. The number of people employed by the company in 1990 was 88. Imari is referred to as 'the Company' in the agreement.

7. Cambridge is a private limited company incorporated and managed in Ireland and involved in the business of fund management. It is the manager of the Cambridge Investment

3.12 Equity Fund referred to as 'the Fund' in the agreement and is a wholly owned subsidiary of Cambridge Group plc., the core business of which is asset financing (leasing and hire) and confirming (financing the working capital requirements of small to medium sized companies) but which is also involved in corporate finance and international financing activities. Cambridge is referred to as 'the Manager' in the agreement.

8. ACT is a private limited investment holding company incorporated and managed in Ireland and involved in providing venture and development capital to companies in Ireland and the UK. 60.8% of the company is owned by Allied Irish Banks plc. ACT's profits are derived principally from dividends from investments and from gains made on the disposal of investments.

(c) *The Products and Markets Concerned*

9. Cambridge Investments act as providers of venture capital to small businesses which they believe have development potential, usually by acquiring a shareholding in such businesses, in the hope of being able to sell their shareholding and make a capital gain. In the absence of such a source of capital the development of such businesses may be hindered by lack of capital. The existing owners may lack the resources to provide additional equity capital so that the only alternative source of finance would be by way of loans from a bank. By obtaining funds from a venture capital firm the business avoids the interest costs associated with loan finance. A key factor in the venture capital firm's assessment of the development potential of the business will be the managerial and entrepreneurial skills of the owner of the business.

10. In simple terms the venture capitalist provides a source of equity capital to the owner of a small business to enable him to develop the business. The owner retains a significant degree of control subject to restrictions designed to protect the investment of the venture capitalist, with the payback to the latter coming about through the realisation of a capital gain on the subsequent disposal of its shareholding in the business. Where the venture capitalist raises funds from investors it pays a proportion of the capital gains to them and retains some proportion for itself.

11. The Imari Group is engaged in the shipping, transport, freight forwarding and port services businesses. The following companies in Imari are involved in servicing the following markets:

- James Scott & Co. (Dublin) Ltd. (JSC) and Bestglen Shipping Ltd Agencies Ltd (Bestglen) operate in the 'lo-lo' business (i.e. loading on and off shipping containers) between Ireland and continental Europe. The Imari Group estimate the size of this market to be approximately £40m. The principal competitors to JSC and Bestglen are B&I, BEU Lines, Dublin Maritime and Rhine Tainer. This market was claimed to be extremely competitive by the notifying parties.
- Dublin Container and Transport Services Ltd (DCATS) is involved in the storage, repair and manufacture of containers in Ireland. The principal users of the service include shipping lines and container leasing companies. The Irish market is estimated to be worth £3m. The principal competitors to DCATS are Storecon, FSK and Container Specialists. This market was claimed to be extremely competitive and to be very sensitive to price adjustments.
- Donesk Ltd (Donesk) is in the road haulage business in Ireland focusing on the provision of driver accompanied trailer services and also using subcontract services. There are a very large number of small operators in this market and Donesk is in this category. Major competitors are CIE, Murphy International Ltd, Frank Barrett and Nestor.
- Tanktrans Ltd (Tanktrans) is a bulk-tank operator between Ireland and the UK offering specialist bulk liquid/powder service. It is a highly specialist market with considerable emphasis on quality and customer service. Market value is approximately £20m. The major competitors to Tanktrans include Haulage Services Ltd, Hoyer Ireland Ltd and Tank Freight

(Ireland) Ltd. In order to compete effectively in this market, an operator requires high specification specialised tanks and specialist market knowledge. 3.12

— Wildcoast International Ltd (Wildcoast) operates as a consolidator (a company which makes up loads for groups) operating between Ireland and The Far East and between Ireland and Finland. Turnover in these markets is estimated to be £13m and £2m respectively. The notifying parties claim that the Far Eastern market is particularly competitive. P&O and Mersk are major competitors in this market. The only other Irish competitor in the Finnish market is Meadows Freight Ltd. It is claimed that there is substantial competition between the two principal competitors.

— TSS Translink Shipping Services Ltd (TSS), Translink USA Inc. (TSA) and Translink Air (TA). TSS and TSA are specialist freight service companies operating in the Irish/US freight forwarding market. They are involved in air and sea freight services to and from the US and arrange transportation from door to door between Ireland and the US. TA provides air freight services to TSS. This is a highly specialised market with an important emphasis on flexibility and customer service. It is estimated that the turnover of the US to Ireland market is £6m. Others engaged in this business include IPS, Aseco and National Coa's.

— Roadferry Ltd (Roadferry) operates as a trailer operator in the door to door dry freight unit load market between Ireland and the UK. The value of the market is estimated to be £256m. Pandoro, Dukes, Woodside, Riley Transport and Montgomery are the major competitors to Roadferry.

(d) *The Agreement*

12. On 25 October 1991, Mr O'Neill, Imari, Cambridge and ACT entered into a Share Subscription and Shareholders Agreement to regulate the terms of the investment by the Cambridge Equity Fund ('the Fund') and the terms on which ACT's previous investment would be regulated.

13. The agreement is stated to be of a form commonly used in Ireland for investments by venture or development capital funds in private companies with growth potential.

14. By virtue of the agreement, the Fund now holds 19% of the ordinary share capital of Imari with ACT holding approximately 35%. Shareholdings in Imari before and after the Cambridge Investment are set out in the following table:

	Pre-investment No. of shares held	Post-investment No. of shares held
Cambridge	—	24000 (19%)
ACT	44000 (44%)	44000 (35%)
Mr O'Neill	29000 (29%)	26000 (21%)
Sidarta Inv. Ltd.	13000 (13%)	16000 (13%)
Maunsell Regus Co. Ltd.	14000 (14%)	14000 (12%)

15. The agreement contains certain restrictions on Imari and on Mr O'Neill. The relevant parts of these clauses are detailed below:

'6.4 *Management of the Company*

The business of the Company shall be controlled by the Board and the Company shall not enter into any contract arrangement or transaction whereby any of its business would be controlled otherwise than by the Board.

6.5 *Board of Directors of the Company*

(a) The Board shall be constituted in accordance with the provisions of this clause 6.5.

(b) Each of the Manager and ACT shall during the continuance of this Agreement be entitled

3.12 to appoint one person as a director of each company in the Imari Group and to remove and/or replace any such person from time to time'.

It is specified that the directors appointed by Cambridge and ACT are non-executive directors.

'6.9 *Restricted Transactions*

(i) The Company hereby covenants with and undertakes to the Manager that for so long as the Subscriber and/or any Permitted Transferee of the Subscriber holds in aggregate 10% or more of the ordinary shares in the capital of the Company in issue from time to time the Company shall not without the prior consent in writing of the Manager:

(a) carry on any business other than the Business or make any material change in the scope or nature of its business or operations which would or would be likely to have a material adverse effect on its assets, business or financial condition;
(b) (except in respect of loans or credit provided to any member of the Imari Group) make any loan or provide any credit (other than normal trade credit given in the ordinary course of business);
(c) create or issue or agree to create or issue any share or loan capital or instrument carrying rights of conversion into any share or loan capital or give or agree to give any option in respect of any share or loan capital or redeem, purchase, re-issue or convert or agree to redeem, purchase, re-issue or convert any of its share or loan capital;
(d) consolidate, divide, sub-divide or alter in any respect any of the rights attaching to any of its shares or reduce its share capital or capital reserve account or repay any amount standing to the credit of any share premium account or credit redemption reserve or otherwise reorganise its share capital in any way or create any new class of shares;
(e) incur or permit to subsist any borrowings of any nature whatsoever in excess of an amount equal to 100% of Shareholder Funds.
(f) otherwise than for borrowing permitted by Clause 6.9(e) hereof create or permit to subsist any mortgage or charge whether floating or specific on the whole or part of its undertakings, property or assets or give any guarantee or indemnity or enter into any arrangement guaranteeing or securing the obligations of any person or become surety for any person;
(g) enter into any contract, transaction or arrangement otherwise than in the ordinary course of its business and upon an arms length and commercial basis or whereby it would receive less than a fair commercial price for any of its goods or services or would pay more than a fair commercial price for any goods or services supplied to it (less customary trade discounts and allowances in each case);
(h) pass any resolution amending or altering its memorandum or articles of association.

(ii) The Company hereby covenants with and undertakes to ACT that for so long as ACT and/or any Permitted Transferee of ACT holds in aggregate 10% or more of the ordinary shares in the capital of the Company in issue from time to time the Company shall not (and shall procure that each company in the Imari Group shall not) without the prior consent in writing of ACT (which consent shall not be unreasonably withheld) do, permit, suffer or enter into any of the transactions or matters specified in clause 6.9(i)(a) to (h) inclusive.

6.10 (i) The Company hereby covenants with and undertakes to the Manager that for so long as the Subscriber and/or any Permitted Transferee of the Subscriber holds in aggregate 10% or more of the ordinary shares in the capital of the Company in issue from time to time the Company shall not without the prior approval of the Board:

(a) enter into any onerous contract, arrangements or understanding or any contract materially affecting its business or assets;
(b) incur any capital expenditure which would result in the capital expenditure of the Imari Group exceeding ____________ in aggregate in any one Financial Year of the Company;
(c) change its auditors or the date of the end of its Financial Year;
(d) alter the basis of the accounting principles upon which its accounts have been consistently

prepared for all prior years; or

(e) incur expenditure which would result in the expenditure incurred by the Imari Group exceeding ____________ in aggregate within any twelve month period in acquiring any share or loan capital of any company or entering into any partnership, joint venture or profit sharing arrangement with any person.

(ii) The Company hereby covenants with and undertakes to ACT that for so long as ACT and/or any Permitted Transferee of ACT holds in aggregate 10% or more of the ordinary shares in the capital of the Company in issue from time to time the Company shall not (and shall procure that each company in the Imari Group shall not) without the prior approval of the Board do, permit, suffer or enter into any of the transactions or matters specified in clause 6.10(i)(a) to (e) inclusive.'

'6.14 *Service Agreement*

(a) The Company shall fully enforce the provisions of any contract of employment with the Covenantor and all other subsisting service agreements for executives of the Imari Group and shall not rescind, terminate or make any change in any of the material terms thereof without the prior written consent of each of the Manager and ACT.

(b) The Covenantor hereby covenants with and undertakes to each of the Company, the Manager and ACT during the continuance of this Agreement to (unless prevented by illness) devote substantially the whole of his time attention and abilities to the promotion and development of the business of the Imari Group.'

'8. *Restrictive Covenants*

8.1 In further consideration of, and as a further inducement to, the Manager and ACT entering into this Agreement the Covenantor hereby covenants with and undertakes to each of the Manager and, as a separate covenant and undertaking, to ACT that:

(i) he shall not during the period commencing on the Completion Date and expiring on the fifth anniversary of the Completion Date or the second anniversary of the date upon which he ceases to be employed by the Company (whichever is the later), either alone or jointly or in conjunction with or on behalf of or through the agency of any person and whether as principal, agent, partner, shareholder, director, manager, adviser, consultant, employee or otherwise howsoever and whether directly or indirectly:

(a) carry on or participate or assist to be engaged or concerned or interested in any business in Ireland which competes with any business carried on by any company in the Imari Group at the time of such expiry;

(b) procure or seek to procure orders from or to do business with or procure directly or indirectly any other person to procure orders from or do business with any person who has been at any time during the period of two years immediately preceding his cessation of employment with any company within the Imari Group a customer of or supplier to any company in the Imari Group;

(c) interfere or seek to interfere or take such steps as may interfere with the continuance of supplies to any company in the Imari Group (or the terms relating to such supplies) from any suppliers who have been at any time during the period of two years immediately preceding his cessation of employment with any company within the Imari Group supplying materials, components, products, goods or services to any company in the Imari Group;

(d) solicit or entice away or offer employment to or endeavour to solicit or entice away or offer employment to any person who has at any time during the period of two years immediately preceding his cessation of employment with any company within the Imari Group been an employee, officer or manager of any company in the Imari Group whether or not such person would commit a breach of contract by reason of leaving the employment, office or service of any company in the Imari Group;

(e) enter into partnership with or appoint as a consultant or adviser any person who has been

3.12 at any time during the period of two years preceding the Completion Date an employee, officer or manager of any company in the Imari Group;

(f) use or adopt or purport to use or adopt the name of any company or trade name of the Imari Group for any purpose other than for the benefit of the Imari Group in the proper performance of his duties under his Service Agreement.

(ii) he shall not knowingly at any time after Completion disclose or cause to be disclosed to any person or use for his own purposes or for any purposes other than those of the Imari Group any Confidential Information and he shall use all reasonable endeavours to prevent the publication or disclosure of any such Confidential Information.

8.2 Each of the parties hereto hereby acknowledge and agree that each of the undertakings contained in clause 8.1 constitute entirely separate and severable and independent restrictions and that the duration, extent and application of the respective restrictions in clause 8.1 hereof are no greater than is reasonable and necessary for the protection of the legitimate interests of the Manager and of ACT respectively but that if any such restriction shall be adjudged by any court or regulatory authority or agency of competent jurisdiction to be void or unenforceable but would be valid if part of the wording thereof was deleted and/or the period thereof was reduced and/or the geographical area dealt with thereby was reduced, the said restriction shall apply within the jurisdiction of that court or regulatory authority or agency with such modifications as may be necessary to make it valid, effective and enforceable to the greatest extent permissible within the jurisdiction of such court or regulatory authority or agency.

9. *Transfer of Shares*

9.1 The Covenantor hereby covenants with and undertakes to each of the Manager and ACT that he shall not transfer or otherwise dispose of any interest (whether legal or equitable) in or create any Encumbrance over any of his shares in the capital of the Company except with the prior consent in writing of the Manager and ACT and in compliance with the provisions of this Agreement and the Articles of Association PROVIDED ALWAYS HOWEVER that:

(a) the consent of the Manager and ACT to any such transfer or disposal shall not be taken as a waiver of any pre-emption rights to which the Subscriber or ACT or any Permitted Transferee may be entitled in respect of such transfer; and

(b) the Covenantor shall be entitled, without requiring the prior consent of the Manager or ACT, to transfer or otherwise dispose of any interest (whether legal or equitable) in up to, in aggregate:

(i) 5,800 ordinary shares in the capital of the Company; or

(ii) (in the event that the Covenantor has subscribed for 7,000 ordinary shares in the capital of the Company pursuant to an Option Agreement on 16 February 1990 between the Covenantor and the Company) 7,200 shares in the capital of the Company.'

Submissions of the Parties

16. The notifying parties have advanced a number of reasons why a certificate should be issued by the Authority in respect of this agreement. Some of these points relate to the agreement as a whole, others relate to specific clauses.

17. The notifying parties have asserted that the agreement is tantamount to a concentration or concentrative joint venture. In this context, they submit that:

> It is well established in the EC that as regards Article 85(1) of the Treaty of Rome, being the equivalent of section 4 CA 91, restraints ancillary to the establishment of a joint venture which is not itself anti-competitive do not fall within Article 85(1) (Elopak/Metal Box (Odin) OJ 1990 L209/15). Accordingly, to the extent that any provisions of the agreement are construed as restraints they are ancillary to the investments constituting the concentration or concentrative joint venture and by analogy do not therefore infringe Section 4 CA 91.

This proposition is further supported by analogy with the policy of the EC Commission in respect of mergers, acquisitions and joint ventures as illustrated by the Commission Notice and the EC Commission's Notice (90/C 203) regarding restrictions ancillary to concentrations ('the Ancillary Restraints Notice') which clearly provide that restrictions which are ancillary to a concentration between undertakings, including non-competition clauses, do not fall within Article 85(1) and therefore by analogy do not fall within the ambit of section 4 CA 91. **3.12**

18. They also submit that any undertakings associated with the notifying parties do not:

carry on business directly or indirectly in competition with any business of any Irish member of the Imari Group.

In these circumstances, it is submitted that:

the investments by the Fund and ACT in the Company, both of which are now regulated by the Agreement, do not and could not foreseeably prevent, restrict or distort competition in any of the markets in which any of the parties operate as the Agreement is not an agreement between competitors or potential competitors and does not provide a framework for co-operation or coordination of market behaviour between competitors or potential competitors. Section 4 CA 91 does not therefore apply to the Agreement.

19. The notifying parties have submitted that Clause 8 of the agreement, which imposes restrictions on Mr O'Neill, does not fall within section 4 of the Act for the following reasons:

(a) Mr O'Neill is not an 'undertaking' within the meaning of section 3(1) CA 91 since he is not engaged for gain in the production, supply or distribution of goods or the provision of a service.

Mr O'Neill is a director, employee and only a minority shareholder in the Company and is not engaged or interested in any other business which directly or indirectly competes with any business carried on by any member of the Imari Group.

Mr O'Neill is simply an auxiliary organ forming an integral part of the Company's undertaking bound to carry out the Company's instructions and thus forms an economic unit with the Company (See, for example Cases 40/73 etc. *Suiker Unie v. Commission* [1974] ECR 1663 1007 at paragraph 539).

(b) Without prejudice to our submission under paragraph (d) above, the restrictive covenants in clause 8 are ancillary restraints of a nature, duration and scope which is reasonable in all the circumstances to protect the value of the Fund's and ACT's substantial investments in the Company and their legitimate interests as minority shareholders. The provisions of clause 8 are legitimate means of ensuring the performance of Mr O'Neill's contractual obligations to protect the goodwill of the Company and its customer relations and loyalty, the expertise and know-how of the Company and the full commercial value of the Fund's and ACT's investments in the Company.

(c) Without prejudice to our submissions under paragraphs (d) and (b) above, the restrictive covenants in clause 8 of the Agreement do not have the 'object or effect' of preventing, restricting or distorting competition since the covenants are given only to the Manager and to ACT neither of whom are competitors or potential competitors of Mr O'Neill (the Covenantor) or indeed of the Company which employs Mr O'Neill. The restrictive covenants In clause 8 are not enforceable by the Company.

3.12 (d) Without prejudice to our submissions under paragraphs (a), (b) and (c) above, even if the restrictive covenants in clause 8 could be construed as potentially affecting competition within the meaning of section 4 CA 91, they do not infringe section 4 since by analogy with the decision of the ECJ in *Volk v. Vervaecke* (Case 5/69 [1969] ECR 295), they are unlikely to have any effect or any appreciable or significant effect on competition in any market where the Company or any other party to the Agreement operates.

Subsequent Developments

20. The parties indicated by letter dated 21 May 1992, that clause 8.1(ii) would not be invoked to prevent Mr O'Neill entering the business only to stop him using any confidential information. In particular, they have stated that:

> We confirm that the only restriction accepted by Mr O'Neill under Clause 8.1(ii) is that he will not use or abuse information that is confidential to the Imari group for his own or for any other purposes. Clause 8.1(ii) is expressly limited to the use or disclosure of 'Confidential Information' as defined in Clause 1.1. This does not prevent Mr O'Neill using his general knowledge of the relevant business for his own or any other purposes to the extent that such knowledge is not strictly confidential to the Imari Group.

21. The Authority's concerns in relation to clause 8 of the Agreement were conveyed at a meeting with the notifying parties on 7 October 1992. An amendment to the Share Subscription and Shareholders Agreement was submitted to the Authority on 1 March 1993. The amendment related to the duration of the non-compete provisions contained in clause 8 and a new clause 8.1 was included with minor consequential changes in the rest of the clause. The full revised clause is as follows:

'8. RESTRICTIVE COVENANTS

8.1 For the purposes of this clause 8 the expression 'Relevant Period' shall mean the period commencing on the Completion Date and expiring on the later of:

(i) the nine hundred and fifteenth day after the day upon which the Covenantor ceases to hold or beneficially own or be entitled to any shares in the capital of the Company; and
(ii) the date upon which the Covenantor ceases to be an employee of the Company.

8.2 In further consideration of, and as a further inducement to, the Manager and ACT entering into this Agreement the Covenantor hereby covenants with and undertakes to each of the Manager (on behalf of itself on behalf of the Subscriber as trustee of the Fund) and, as a separate covenant and undertaking, to ACT that:

(i) he shall not during the Relevant Period either alone or jointly or in conjunction with or on behalf of or through the agency of any person and whether as principal, agent, partner, shareholder, director, manager, adviser, consultant, employee or otherwise howsoever and whether directly or indirectly:

(a) carry on or participate or assist to be engaged or concerned or interested (except as the holder or beneficial owner for investment purposes of not more than 5% in nominal value of any class of securities listed or dealt in on a recognised stock exchange) in any business in Ireland which competes with any business carried on by any company in the Imari Group at the time of such expiry;
(b) procure or seek to procure orders from or to do business with or procure directly or

indirectly any other person to procure orders from or do business with any person who has been at any time during the period of two years immediately preceding his cessation of employment with any company within the Imari Group a customer of or supplier to any company in the Imari Group; 3.12

(c) interfere or seek to interfere or take such steps as may interfere with the continuance of supplies to any company in the Imari Group (or the terms relating to such supplies) from any suppliers who have been at any time during the period of two years immediately preceding his cessation of employment with any company within the Imari Group supplying materials, components, products, goods or services to any company in the Imari Group;

(d) solicit or entice away or offer employment to or endeavour to solicit or entice away or offer employment to any person who has at any time during the period of two years immediately preceding his cessation of employment with any company within the Imari Group been an employee, officer or manager of any company in the Imari Group whether or not such person would commit a breach of contract by reason of leaving the employment, office or service of any company in the Imari Group;(e) enter into partnership with or appoint as a consultant or adviser any person who has been at any time during the period of two years preceding the Completion Date an employee, officer or manager of any company in the Imari Group;

(f) use or adopt or purport to use or adopt the name of any company or trade name of the Imari Group for any purpose other than for the benefit of the Imari Group in the proper performance of his duties under his Service Agreement.

(ii) he shall not knowingly at any time after Completion disclose or cause to be disclosed to any person or use for his own purposes or for any purposes other than those of the Imari Group any Confidential Information and he shall use all reasonable endeavours to prevent the publication or disclosure of any such Confidential Information'.

8.3 Each of the parties hereto hereby acknowledge and agree that each of the undertakings contained in clause 8.2 constitute entirely separate and severable and independent restrictions and that the duration, extent and application of the respective restrictions in clause 8.2 hereof are no greater than is reasonable and necessary for the protection of the legitimate interests of the Manager and of ACT respectively but that if any such restriction shall be adjudged by any court or regulatory authority or agency of competent jurisdiction to be void or unenforceable but would be valid if part of the wording thereof was deleted and/or the period thereof was reduced and/or the geographical area dealt with thereby was reduced, the said restriction shall apply within the jurisdiction of that court or regulatory authority or agency with such modifications as may be necessary to make it valid, effective and enforceable to the greatest extent permissible within the jurisdiction of such court or regulatory authority or agency.

Assessment

(a) *Section 4(1)*

22. Section 4(1) of the Competition Act states that 'all agreements between undertakings, decisions by associations of undertakings and concerted practices which have as their object or effect the prevention, restriction or distortion of competition in trade in any goods or services in the State or in any part of the State are prohibited and void'.

(b) *The Undertakings*

23. In this instance the Authority considered arrangements involving (i) Cambridge Investments Ltd, (ii) ACT, (iii) Imari and (iv) Mr Timothy O'Neill. Section 3(1) of the Competition Act defines an undertaking as 'a person being an individual, d body corporate or

3.12 an unincorporated body of persons engaged for gain in the production, supply or distribution of goods or the provision of a service.'

24. Cambridge Investments is a private limited company incorporated in Ireland and engaged in the business of fund management and the provision of venture and development capital. It is engaged in the management of funds on behalf of investors. It uses such funds *inter alia* to provide venture and development capital to small and medium sized businesses. specifically by acquiring equity in such businesses with a view to earning a capital gain by selling such equity at a future date. Such gains accrue to investors and to Cambridge Investments itself. Fund management and the provision of funds to small and medium sized businesses constitute the provision of services in which Cambridge is engaged for gain.

25. ACT is a private limited investment holding company incorporated and managed in Ireland and involved in providing venture and development capital to companies in Ireland and the UK. ACT is effectively engaged in the provision of funds to small and medium sized firms for gain and is therefore an undertaking.

26. Imari is a private limited holding company incorporated in Ireland with a number of subsidiaries and an associated company which operate for gain in the shipping, transport, freight forwarding and port services industries. The Authority decided in AGF-Irish Life that a holding company, although not directly 'engaged for gain in the production, supply or distribution of goods or the provision of a service', was an undertaking by virtue of its being engaged for gain in such activities through subsidiary firms which operate for gain and which it controls.[1] Imari is therefore an undertaking within the meaning of the Act since its subsidiary companies are engaged in the provision of services for gain.

27. The parties have submitted that Mr O'Neill is not an undertaking as he is an employee. Section 3 of the Act clearly provides that an individual is an undertaking if he/she is 'engaged for gain in the production, supply or distribution of goods or the provision of a service'. The Authority has previously indicated that, in its view, employees as such, are not undertakings, since they normally act on behalf of an undertaking and do not, therefore, constitute an undertaking themselves.[2] The Authority has also taken the view, however, that individuals who either own or control a business are undertakings for the purposes of section 3 of the Competition Act.[3] Similarly it has indicated that once an employee pursues his own economic interests and these differ from his employer's interests, he may well become an undertaking within the meaning of section 3(1).[4] Such views are consistent with the EC Commission decision in Reuter/BASF.[5]

28. Mr O'Neill is a shareholder in the Imari Group as well as being employed as managing director of the firm. The mere fact of being a shareholder in a company is not, in the Authority's view, sufficient grounds for regarding an individual as an undertaking.[6] In ACT/Kindle, however, the Authority decided that as a group of individuals who were parties to the agreement had held between them the majority shareholding in Kindle and had effectively controlled that business, they were undertakings. In Scully/Tyrrell, the Authority concluded that individuals who between them held a minority shareholding, were nevertheless undertakings, since the agreement in question afforded them a significant degree of control over the business and their interests differed from those of the company.

29. Some consideration of relevant EC cases under Article 85(1) of the Treaty of Rome on

1. Competition Authority Decision No. 2, AGF/Irish Life Holdings (CA/7/92), 14 May 1992.
2. See Competition Authority Notice on Employee Agreements and the Competition Act, *Iris Oifigiúil*, 14 September 1992, pp. 632/3. This view was confirmed in Competition Authority Decision No. 13, Peter Mark/Majella Stapleton (CA/1011/92E), 18 February 1993.
3. Competition Authority Decision No. 1, Nallen/O'Toole (Belmullet) (CA/8/91), 2 April 1992.
4. Competition Authority Decision No. 12, Scully/Tyrrell (CA/57/92), 29 January 1993.
5. Case No. 76/743/EEC, OJ L254 16.9.76, p.40.
6. Competition Authority Decision No. 8, ACT Group plc/Kindle Group Ltd (CA/9/91), 4 September 1992.

which section 4(1) is based is also relevant to this question.[7] In Reuter/BASF the EC Commission decided that Dr Reuter was an undertaking by virtue of engaging in economic activity through firms which were under his control, by exploiting the results of his own research and as commercial adviser to third parties. Similarly in the Nutricia case the Commission decided that an individual was an undertaking by virtue of being the future proprietor of a business. That decision was the subject of an appeal to the European Court of Justice. The Court, in its decision, upheld the view that the individual concerned was an undertaking but went somewhat further than the Commission in setting out the reasons for this view. 3.12

30. The applicants had argued that Article S of the Commission decision should be declared void on the grounds that Mr de Rooij was not an undertaking either in his private capacity or in his capacity as a signatory to the agreement in question. The court ruled that:

> That argument cannot be accepted. As the Commission rightly points out, Mr de Rooij was a contracting party to the agreement, which grants him, particularly in clauses 5 and 7, rights peculiar to him and distinct from those of Remia.

The Court pointed out that the applicants themselves had previously referred to Mr de Rooij as an undertaking. It went on to state that:

> It must therefore be inferred that Mr de Rooij played a part in his own right both in the conclusion of the transfer agreement and as a signatory of the non-competition clause and that that justified his being made an addressee of the contested decision.[8]

31. Mr O'Neill is the managing director of Imari and prior to the conclusion of the present agreement he held approximately 29% of the shares in the businesses. As a result of the issuing of additional shares to Cambridge and other transactions arising out of this agreement he retains a 21% shareholding in Imari. Mr O'Neill cannot be regarded as controlling the business by virtue of his holding the majority of the shares. It is widely recognised, however, that it is not essential for an individual or firm to hold the majority of shares in a business in order to enjoy some degree of control over that business. The Mergers Acts, as amended by the Competition Act, provide that the acquisition of more than a 25% shareholding in an enterprise constitutes control. The European Court of Justice recognised in its decision in the Philip Morris case that the acquisition of a minority shareholding in an undertaking could allow the purchaser to exercise control over that undertaking.[9]

32. In practice individuals who do not hold a majority shareholding in a business may effectively control that business if, for example no other shareholder or allied group of shareholders holds any significant block of shares, or if the majority of shares is held by institutional investors. For example, in its report on the proposed takeover of Tribune Group Newspapers by the Independent Group the Authority noted that, although Dr A.J.F. O'Reilly owned less than 28% of the total shares in the latter group, 'He is widely regarded as having the controlling interest in the Independent'.[10]

33. The Imari group began when Mr O'Neill took over the business of James Scott, which is now one of the Imari group of companies. Mr O'Neill is the managing director of Imari. ACT provided much of the financial backing necessary for Mr O'Neill to acquire and develop

7. Reuter/BASF and Nutricia/De Rooij and Nutricia/Zuid Hollandse Conservenfabriek, 83/670/EEC, OJ L376, 31.12.83, p.22. The Commission view in the latter case was confirmed by the European Court of Justice in the case of *Remia BV and Others v. European Commission*, Case No. 42/84, [1985] ECR 2545.
8. P. 2579.
9. *BAT Ltd. & Reynolds v. EC Commission*, Case Nos. 142 & 156 84, [1987] ECR 4487.
10. Report of Investigation of the proposal whereby Independent Newspapers plc would increase its shareholding in the Tribune Group from 29.99% to a possible 53.09%, Pl. 8795 at para 2.14.

3.12 this business and it, in return, acquired a sizeable shareholding in the organisation. With the financial support of ACT, Mr O'Neill has developed the business to its present stage. The object of the present agreement is to obtain additional funding to allow for the further expansion and development of the Imari Group, the hope being that it will eventually become a publicly quoted company. The acquisition of the business was essentially Mr O'Neill's idea and he, with the financial backing of ACT, has built it up to its current position. Apart from the restrictions imposed to protect themselves against a dilution of the value of their investment, both ACT and Cambridge are content to allow Mr O'Neill along with the rest of the board of Imari to run the business.

34. Clause 6.4 of the agreement provides that the business of Imari will be controlled by the Board. Clause 6.5 allows ACT and Cambridge to each appoint one non-executive director to the Board. There are four directors including Mr O'Neill in addition to those appointed by ACT and Cambridge. Two of these are employees of Imari. To the extent that the business of Imari is controlled by the board Mr O'Neill enjoys the same degree of control as both Cambridge and ACT. The Authority believes that in the case of Imari it is reasonable to conclude that Mr O'Neill is able to exercise a significant degree of control over the business. Indeed if he was, in fact, only a minority shareholder with little control, clauses 6.9 and 6.10 of the agreement, restricting what the company can do without the prior approval of Cambridge and ACT, would not be necessary.

35. The provision of venture and development capital to small businesses in return for the acquisition of a shareholding in the business essentially involves an arrangement between the venture capitalist and the owners of the business to engage in a particular business venture together. The owners provide the necessary expertise and knowledge of the business, while the venture capitalist provides funds necessary for the development of the business. It is not a partnership arrangement, nor is it a joint venture. It is nevertheless an arrangement to participate together in a particular business venture. Such an arrangement is not akin to that between an employer and an employee. Mr O'Neill has a considerable stake in the business and has a major say in the control of the business.

36. Mr O'Neill is party to the agreement by virtue of his being part owner of Imari. As in the case of Mr de Rooij, Mr O'Neill 'played a part in his own right both in the conclusion of the transfer agreement and as a signatory of the non-competition clause'. The agreement imposes a series of obligations on Mr O'Neill in respect of the other parties. These obligations arise under a number of other clauses besides clause 8. The agreement confers no explicit benefits on Mr O'Neill. It is clear, however, that he is a beneficiary of the agreement by virtue of the fact that the agreement provides him with the opportunity to further develop the Imari Group. His interest in the development of the business is primarily as a joint owner rather than as an employee. This view is supported by the parties' statement in a letter dated 21 May 1992 that 'the investment by the Cambridge Equity Fund in the Imari Group is as much an investment in Mr O'Neill as it is an investment in the Imari Group.' The position of Mr O'Neill is, in the Authority's view, similar to that of Mr de Rooij.

37. In sum Mr O'Neill is an undertaking by virtue of the fact that he is a part owner and managing director of Imari, he exercises considerable *de facto* control over the business and is therefore engaged for gain in the provision of services.

The Agreement

38. The present notification constitutes a series of arrangements involving Cambridge, ACT, Imari and Mr O'Neill, whereby Cambridge has invested funds in Imari. These arrangements constitute an agreement between undertakings. Imari is engaged in providing international freight, transport and other services within the State and between the State and other countries, so that the relevant market is that for the provision of such services throughout the State.

Applicability of section 4(1) 3.12

39. The parties have submitted that the present agreement does not come under section 4 of the Competition Act on the grounds that the arrangements are analogous to a concentration or concentrative joint venture and that, as EC precedents indicate such arrangements are outside the scope of Article 85(1), then they should also be outside the scope of section 4(1) which is based on 85(1). In addition they argued that as restrictions which are ancillary to a concentration between undertakings, including non-competition clauses, do not come within the scope of Article 85(1) by virtue of the EC's ancillary restraints notice, they are also outside the scope of section 4(1).[11]

40. Article 3 of the EC Merger Regulation[12] defines a concentration as arising where:

(a) two or more previously independent undertakings merge, or
(b) — one or more persons already controlling at least one undertaking, or
— one or more undertakings acquire, whether by purchase of securities or assets, by contract or by other means, direct or indirect control of the whole or parts of one or more other undertakings.

Section 1(3)(a) of the Mergers Act as amended provides that:

> a merger or takeover shall be taken to exist when two or more enterprises, at least one of which carries on business in the State, come under common control.

Section 1(3)(c) as amended by section 15(2) of the Competition Act provides that where an enterprise holds more than 25 percent of the voting rights in another enterprise the enterprises are deemed to be under common control.

41. The present notification does not, in the Authority's view, involve a concentration within the meaning of the EC Merger Regulation nor does it constitute a merger within the meaning of the Mergers Act. Two or more previously independent undertakings are not coming under common control. The proportion of shares being acquired by Cambridge is below the level at which enterprises are deemed to have come under common control under the Mergers Act 1978, as amended by the Competition Act. Cambridge has acquired a minority shareholding in Imari. The European Court of Justice decision in Philip Morris indicates that the acquisition of a minority shareholding may come within the scope of Article 85(1). The analogy with a concentration under the EC Merger Regulation does not therefore apply. The Authority has already indicated, however, that it does not regard a merger agreement as being automatically outside the scope of section 4(1) of the Competition Act.[13]

42. The Authority does not consider that the arrangements in this case can be regarded as a concentrative joint-venture. ACT and Cambridge have invested funds in Imari in order to enable Imari to expand and develop, in the hope that they will be able to resell their shareholdings and secure a capital gain. Cambridge's only link with ACT and Imari is as a minority shareholder and provider of development funds. The Authority does not believe that such an arrangement can be regarded as constituting a concentrative joint-venture. As pointed out the arrangement involves the parties participating together in a particular business venture. It is clear, however, that the motivation for participating in such a venture on the part of Cambridge is for purely investment purposes, although the expectation is that it may be some time before any return on this investment is realised.

43. The parties have also argued that the restrictive provisions relating to Mr O'Neill contained in clause 8 of the agreement do not offend against section 4(1) of the Act by virtue

11. Commission Notice Regarding Restrictions Ancillary to Concentrations, OJ C203/05, 14.8.90.
12. Regulation 4064/89 (OJ L257/14, 21.9.90).
13. Competition Authority Decision No. 6, Woodchester Bank Ltd/UDT Bank Ltd (CA/10/92), 4 August 1992.

3.12 of the fact that Mr O'Neill is not an undertaking. They claimed that clause 8 in fact constitutes a separate agreement solely involving Mr O'Neill and Cambridge which, given their view that Mr O'Neill is not an undertaking, is not an agreement between undertakings. The fact that the overall agreement is an agreement between undertakings does not, in their view, alter the fact that clause 8 is a separate agreement which is not an agreement between undertakings.

44. For the reasons given in paras 27-37 above the Authority believes that Mr O'Neill is an undertaking and therefore rejects the argument advanced by the parties. In addition the Authority believes that no agreement could have arisen between Mr O'Neill and Cambridge, restricting Mr O'Neill's rights to engage in the transport business, other than as part of the broader agreement by which Cambridge has agreed to invest in Imari. It is equally clear to the Authority that the restrictions being imposed on Mr O'Neill by clause 8 were a central element in Cambridge agreeing to invest in Imari. This is evident from reading clause 8.1 which states that it is 'In further consideration of, and as a further inducement to, the Manager [Cambridge] and ACT entering into this agreement. . . .' In addition the rationale behind such restrictions is that they are necessary to protect Cambridge's investment in Imari. Clause 8 cannot therefore be regarded as constituting a separate agreement, even if it was deemed to constitute a separate agreement the Authority notes that in applying Article 85 of the Treaty of Rome on which the Competition Act is based, the EC Commission and Court of Justice have accepted that: 'A series of connected agreements will be read together as one agreement'.[14]

The purchase of Imari shares by Cambridge.

45. As already pointed out the Authority does not consider that the share purchase arrangements give rise to a concentration. The parties have submitted that neither Cambridge, nor any member of Cambridge Group plc, nor any company in which any member of Cambridge Group plc has a significant shareholding, nor, so far as the directors of Cambridge Group are aware, any investor in the Fund, carry on business directly or indirectly in competition with any business of any Irish member of the Imari Group. Similarly, neither ACT, nor any member of the AIB Group, nor any company in which any member of the AIB Group has a significant shareholding, carry on business directly or indirectly in competition with any business of any Irish member of the Imari Group.

46. The acquisition of a minority shareholding in an undertaking of itself cannot be viewed as preventing, restricting or distorting competition. This view is consistent with the European Court of Justice decision in the Philip Morris case. The primary object of venture capitalists in acquiring shares in small and medium sized businesses is investment, while the object of the business is to obtain additional funding to enable it to expand further. While such an arrangement is not akin to a partnership, it nevertheless represents an arrangement by two or more parties to participate together in a business venture, with one providing the necessary capital, and the other the entrepreneurial skills and business knowledge. Thus the object of such an arrangement is not, in the Authority's view, to prevent, restrict or distort competition. In the absence of indications to the contrary the Authority also believes that such arrangements generally do not have the effect of preventing, restricting or distorting competition. Indeed to the extent that they assist the development of small and medium sized businesses, their long term effect may be pro-competitive. The investment by Cambridge Investments in Imari by means of the acquisition of a minority shareholding in the Imari Group, does not therefore, in the Authority's opinion, offend against section 4(1).

Subordinate Clauses

47. While the agreement is not of its nature anti-competitive, the Authority nevertheless must also consider whether any of the provisions of the agreement have the object or effect of

14. See C. Bellamy and G. Child (1987); *Common Market Law of Competition*, 3rd ed., Sweet and Maxwell, London, para. 2-017.

preventing, restricting or distorting competition. In considering such provisions, the Authority believes that the correct approach is to consider whether they are essential in order to achieve the main purpose of the agreement. Where the provisions are ancillary to the main purpose of the agreement, then the Authority believes that they should not be considered to offend against section 4(1). The Authority believes that this approach is consistent with that taken by it in considering restrictive clauses in sale of business agreements. It is also consistent with the view taken by the EC Commission and the European Court of Justice in such cases. In the case of restrictions in sale of business agreements the European Court of Justice stated in its decision in Remia that: **3.12**

> In order to determine whether or not such clauses come within the prohibition in Article 85(1), it is necessary to examine what would be the state of competition if those clauses did not exist.[15]

Such an approach has long been adopted by the US courts in competition cases.

48. In order to decide whether the individual clauses of an agreement should be properly regarded as merely ancillary to the main purpose of the agreement the Authority believes that it must be established that they are necessary, but no more than is absolutely necessary to achieve such ends. Where individual restrictive clauses in an agreement go beyond what is absolutely necessary to achieve a legitimate end, then, in the Authority's view, they can no longer be regarded as merely ancillary to that end, but must be considered as having the object of seeking to prevent, restrict or distort competition. As Judge Taft noted in the Addyston Pipe case in the United States almost a century ago:

> no conventional restraint of trade can be enforced unless the covenant embodying it is merely ancillary to the main purpose of a lawful contract, and necessary to protect the covenantee in the enjoyment of the legitimate fruits of the contract, or to protect him from the dangers of an unjust use of those fruits by the other party.[16]

Clause 6.9.

49. Under clause 6.9 of the agreement Imari has agreed with Cambridge and ACT that, for so long as either Cambridge or ACT hold 10% or more of the ordinary share capital of Imari, Imari, (and each of the companies included in the Imari Group), will not do certain things without the prior consent of Cambridge or ACT. Such consent cannot be unreasonably withheld.

50. Cambridge and ACT are in the business of providing venture and development capital to companies. They undoubtedly need to take some steps to protect their investment and to ensure that the money provided is not used for a quite different purpose to what they had intended. Without such protection it is difficult to see how venture and development capital companies could operate, as the risks involved would greatly increase. In such circumstances it may also prove difficult to attract the necessary funds from investors given the higher risk which would attach to such investments. It is clear that the absence of such venture/development capital would seriously hinder the development of many small and medium sized businesses within the economy and that this would restrict the strengthening and development of competition in many sectors of the economy. The Authority believes, therefore, that providers of venture/development capital are entitled to take some steps to protect their investment.

15. Point 18
16. Judgment in the case of *United States v. Addyston Pipe & Steel Company et. al.*, (1898), as reproduced in W. Breit and K. Elzinga; *The Antitrust Casebook: Milestones in Economic Regulation*, 2nd ed., Dryden Press, New York 1989, p. 19.

3.12 51. Given that neither Cambridge nor ACT have any other involvement either directly or indirectly in the markets in which Imari operates, it is clear that the restrictions in clause 6.9 are designed to protect their investment. In other words the provisions contained in clause 6.9 may be regarded as no more than is necessary to achieve the aims of the overall agreement. Therefore the Authority does not regard the provisions in clause 6.9 as offending against section 4(1) of the Competition Act.

Clause 6.10

52. Clause 6.10 restricts Imari from carrying out certain activities without the prior consent of the Board. As in the case of 6.9 these apply for so long as either Cambridge or ACT hold 10% or more of the share capital of Imari. The Authority considers these restrictions to be similar in nature to those contained in clause 6.9 and for the same reasons believes that they do not offend against section 4(1).

Clause 6.14

53. Clause 6.14 requires that Imari fully enforce the provisions of any contract of employment with Mr O'Neill, that no changes can be made to that contract without the prior written consent of Cambridge and ACT, and that Mr O'Neill devote substantially the whole of his time, attention and abilities to the promotion and development of the business of the Imari Group. Clause 6.14 is designed to ensure that Imari retains the services of Mr O'Neill, that he continues to devote his efforts to the promotion of Imari's interests and that he does not compete with it, so long as he remains involved with the company. Again this clause is considered by the Authority as a legitimate means for Cambridge to protect their investment and it cannot be said to offend against section 4(1).

Clause 8

54. Clause 8 involves various restrictions on Mr O'Neill which are set out in para. 15. As originally notified, the restrictions applied for a period of 5 years from the Completion Date or the second anniversary of the date upon which he ceased to be employed by Imari, whichever was the later. Under these restrictions Mr O'Neill was prohibited for that period of time from:

(a) carrying on or being engaged in any business in Ireland which competes with any company in the Imari Group;
(b) doing business with any person who was a customer or supplier of any company within the Imari Group during the 2 years preceding his cessation of employment;
(c) interfering with the continuance of supplies to any company in the Imari Group from any undertakings which supplied any company in the Imari Group during the 2 years preceding his cessation of employment;
(d) soliciting or offering employment to any person who was an employee of the Group during the 2 years preceding his cessation of employment;
(e) entering into partnership with or appointing as consultant or adviser any person who was an employee of the Group during the 2 years preceding the Completion Date;
(f) using or adopting the name of any company in the Group other than for the benefit of the Group in the proper performance of his duties under his Service Agreement.

55. The restriction in 8.1(i)(f) relates to the use of the Imari name or the name of any member of the Group. The Authority has already indicated in previous decisions that such a provision does not involve any restriction on competition within the State or any part of the State. It is necessary to prevent Mr O'Neill passing himself, or any undertaking under his control, off to Imari customers or suppliers as representing Imari, in the event that he should decide to go into business in competition with Imari. It therefore does not offend against section 4(1).

56. The parties have argued that the businesses of the Imari Group rely heavily on the

considerable degree of loyalty which has been built up over the years. Mr O'Neill's connection is seen as critical in this regard. The parties have argued that such ancillary restraints do not infringe section 4(1) as they are in pursuit of legitimate commercial objectives which are not *per se* anti-competitive. They have cited a series of EC Commission and Court of Justice decisions in support of this argument.[17] 3.12

57. The Authority has already indicated in para. 47 above that it accepts, as a broad principle, that restrictive clauses which are merely ancillary to a legitimate agreement should not be regarded as offending against section 4(1). It has also stated, however, that to be regarded as ancillary to a legitimate agreement such clauses should be no more than is absolutely necessary to facilitate the object of that agreement. In Nallen/O'Toole it accepted that, in the case of a sale of business some restriction on the seller's ability to re-enter the market is necessary in order to ensure the complete transfer of the goodwill of the business to the purchaser. It decided that such restrictions must be limited in terms of their duration, geographical coverage and subject matter to what is necessary for the complete transfer of the goodwill of the business and indicated that it would normally regard a restriction of two years as sufficient to secure the transfer of the goodwill. In Woodchester Bank and Budget Travel/Phil Fortune[18] the Authority accepted that, in the case of a sale of business, some restriction on the ability of the seller to solicit key employees was legitimate in order to secure the complete transfer of the goodwill of the business. Again such a restriction had to be limited in duration to what was necessary to secure the complete transfer of the goodwill. In addition the restriction in that instance only prevented the seller from soliciting such staff, who were of course free to obtain employment with another undertaking competing in the business, to set up in the business themselves, or to obtain employment with the vendor provided the vendor had not solicited any application for employment from them.

58. The Authority has accepted that restrictions which are necessary to protect the investment by Cambridge in Imari should be regarded as ancillary. In the absence of such protection, such an investment, which may be desirable, might not have taken place. The issue then is simply whether a non-competition clause is necessary to protect that investment and, if so, whether its content and duration goes beyond what is necessary for that purpose.

59. As already stated the agreement constitutes an arrangement between the parties to engage jointly in a particular business venture. Such an arrangement could not operate if the parties were free to compete with the business or with each other. For example, when two or more individuals come together to form a partnership, they agree not to compete with one another. The Authority indicated in Nallen/O'Toole that it did not 'regard partnerships *per se* as being in contravention of the Act.'[19] Where individuals agree to engage in business together and not to compete with one another the Authority does not regard such arrangements of themselves, as offending against section 4(1). Indeed such arrangements may be pro-competitive in that the combined entity may be in a better position to compete with other undertakings in the relevant market. The Authority believes that, in general, a restriction on the parties involved in a business competing with it for so long as they remain part of the business, does not offend against section 4(1). The position changes, however, if the parties are prevented from withdrawing from such arrangements. If a party wishes to withdraw from such arrangements then measures designed to prevent him doing so may restrict competition.

60. Mr O'Neill retains a significant shareholding in, and is employed as managing director of Imari. The Authority believes that, for so long as that remains the case, there is no question of Mr O'Neill competing with Imari. Indeed it would not appear to be in his interest to set up in competition with Imari so long as he retains a significant shareholding in that business. It is

17. *Reuter/BASF, Remia v. EC Commission Mecaniver/PPG*, Case No. 85/78/EEC, OJ L35, 7.2.85, p. 54.
18. Competition Authority Decision No. 9, Budget Travel/Phil Fortune (CA/1/92), 14 September 1992.
19. Para 23.

3.12 also relevant that clause 6.14 provides further protection to Cambridge inasmuch as it requires that Imari fully enforce the provisions of any contract of employment with Mr O'Neill, that no changes can be made to that contract without the prior written consent of Cambridge and ACT, and that Mr O'Neill devote substantially the whole of his time, attention and abilities to the promotion and development of the business of the Imari Group.

61. If Mr O'Neill were to sell his shareholding in the business then, given the Authority's previous decisions concerning sale of business agreements, some restriction on his competing with Imari would almost certainly be acceptable. The Authority has stated in all its previous decisions involving such arrangements that it would generally regard two years as the appropriate duration for such a restriction on competition.

62. In the Authority's view the restrictions in clause 8.1(i)(a), (b), (c), (d) and (e) went beyond what was necessary to protect the value of Cambridge's investment in Imari. It is relevant that some protection is afforded to Cambridge by clauses 6.9, 6.10, 6.14 and 9.1. The latter clause prevents Mr O'Neill from disposing of his shareholding in Imari without the prior consent of Cambridge and ACT. In addition the Authority considers that a restriction on Mr O'Neill competing with Imari for so long as he remains an employee and/or shareholder of the business is necessary to protect the interest of Cambridge. It also believes that a restriction on Mr O'Neill competing with Imari for a period after he had disposed of any shareholding in the business is necessary to protect Cambridge. Taking all of these factors into account, the Authority believes that the restrictions originally included in clause 8.1(i), which were for the later of 5 years from the completion date and 2 years after Mr O'Neill ceased to be employed by Imari, went beyond what was absolutely necessary to protect the investment by Cambridge in Imari and could not be regarded as merely ancillary to the primary purpose of the agreement.

63. The Authority accepts the arguments advanced by the notifying parties that Mr O'Neill has played a major part in developing the business of Imari in the past, and that, as a result, Imari's future prospects will be enhanced if it retains Mr O'Neill's services in the future. It could reasonably be argued that Mr O'Neill's undoubted expertise in the business was a factor behind Cambridge's decision to invest in Imari and that the retention of his services would enhance the prospect of Cambridge making a capital gain on this investment. For these reasons it may be considered logical that the parties would seek to ensure that Mr O'Neill remains with Imari and that measures designed with this end do not prevent, restrict or distort competition.

64. Investment in a business is, by its very nature, a risky undertaking subject to considerable uncertainty. In deciding whether or not to invest in a company an investor will be influenced by a number of considerations, including the company's past performance, his assessment of its future prospects, of the overall economic outlook and of the quality of the company's management. The company may not perform in line with the investor's prior expectations for a number of reasons. The economy may not develop as he had anticipated, the company may perform poorly, key staff, including management may be enticed away to a competing firm or may set up in business for themselves.

65. Increased competition in the relevant market could have adverse consequences for Imari in terms of profitability, its long-term development and attractiveness to investors, thereby reducing the potential gain on the investment made by Cambridge and ACT. To the extent that this is so, both Cambridge and ACT would benefit if a potential competitor were prevented from competing. All anti-competitive agreements are designed to benefit those participating in them, and by extension, their shareholders, largely by securing higher profits for the participants than would otherwise accrue. The benefits expected to accrue to the participants cannot be accepted as justifying restrictions on competition. If Cambridge or ACT were to enter into an agreement with a competitor of Imari whereby it agreed not to compete against Imari, then this would constitute an anti-competitive agreement and would be both prohibited and void under section 4(1). The same would apply to an agreement between them and a potential competitor.

66. The Authority rejects the parties claim that the restrictions in clause 8.1(i) did not

prevent, restrict or distort competition on the grounds that neither Cambridge nor ACT is either **3.12**
directly or indirectly in competition with any member of the Imari Group, as irrelevant. It has previously indicated in Nallen/O'Toole that competition is to be interpreted as meaning potential as well as actual competition. The Authority's interpretation of competition in this respect is in line with that of the European Commission.[20] The part played by Mr O'Neill in the development of Imari and the claim by the parties that they see Mr O'Neill as having a key role in the group's future development indicates that they clearly believe that he would provide strong competition to the Imari group, were he to take up employment with a competing firm, or to set up in business on his own account, or in partnership with someone else. Clause 8.1 by seeking to prevent Mr O'Neill from working for another company or setting up in business either alone or in partnership for a minimum of five years from the completion of the notified agreement seeks to restrict potential competition in the markets in which Imari operates. The fact that Cambridge and ACT are not engaged directly in the market concerned does not alter the fact that the object or effect was to restrict competition. Such a restriction offends against section 4(1) of the Competition Act since it went beyond what was necessary to protect the investment made by Cambridge in the Authority's view.

67. The parties have also claimed that the arrangements notified 'are unlikely to have any effect or any appreciable or significant effect on competition in any market where the company or any other party to the Agreement operates.' They cited the European Court of Justice decision in *Volk v. Vervaecke* in support of this argument.[21]

68. The Authority indicated in Nallen/O'Toole that the prohibition in section 4(1) of the Act should not, in its view, be interpreted literally. It went on to state that the agreement notified in Nallen/O'Toole would have no effect on the actual level of competition in the market and that in the absence of barriers to other new entrants, (besides Mr O'Toole), the agreement could not be regarded as having any real effect on competition in the relevant market.

69. The Authority does not believe that such arguments are valid in the case of the present agreement. It is true that in some of the markets in which Imari operates e.g. road freight, there are a large number of competitors, that many of these are small scale operators and owner-drivers, and that entry to the market is relatively easy. In such circumstances the views expressed by the Authority in Nallen/O'Toole, that it would not regard a restriction on a single individual competing in the market as preventing, restricting or distorting competition, would apply.

70. Other markets in which Imari is involved, namely the provision of international freight and shipping services, are, by the parties own admission, highly specialised businesses. The number of undertakings in Ireland with the knowledge and resources to enter such businesses is, in the Authority's view, quite limited. It is again significant in this regard that Mr O'Neill's proven track record in the business is a key factor behind Cambridge's decision to invest in the business. The amount of money being invested by Cambridge for a minority stake in Imari indicates that the cost of getting into this business for a new entrant would be quite high. The risk of losing most or all of such monies would be equally high. It is well recognised in economic theory that where the costs of entry to a market are high and the threat of losses are significant, the prospect of new firms entering a market is greatly reduced. Mr O'Neill with his proven track record constitutes a significant potential competitor in the market. While it could be argued that foreign firms could always enter the market, the Authority does not regard the likelihood of such entry as sufficiently strong to outweigh the restriction on competition entailed by the restriction on Mr O'Neill.

71. The restrictions contained in clause 8.1(i) must be considered in a wider context. The effect of the restrictions cannot be considered in isolation as, if all such agreements were

20. On this point see I. Van Bael and J.F. Bellis (1990); *Competition Law of the EEC*, 2nd ed., CCH Editions Ltd, para. 216.
21. Case No. 5/69 [1969] ECR 295.

3.12 considered in isolation, it could be argued that their effects were minimal. If such restrictions were to apply generally throughout the economy, however, their combined effect on competition would be considerable. There are indications from reported court cases and from other notifications to the Authority that they are fairly widespread. Certainly if the Authority were to decide that such a restriction was acceptable in isolation, then the likelihood is that they would become a standard feature of such arrangements.

72. In the Authority's view the restrictions in clause 8.1(i)(a),(b),(c),(d) and (e) went further than was necessary to protect Cambridge's investment in Imari since:

(i) Clauses 6.9 and 6.10 already restricted the ability of Imari to engage in a number of activities without Cambridge's approval, thereby reducing the risk of Cambridge suffering a loss as a result of poor management decisions;
(ii) Clause 6.14 provided that Imari shall not alter or rescind any of the material terms of Mr O'Neill's contract of employment without the prior written consent of Cambridge and ACT and that Mr O'Neill would devote substantially the whole of his time attention and abilities to the promotion and development of the business of the Imari Group and thereby prevents him competing with Imari so long as he remains involved with the company;
(iii) Clause 9.1 provided that Mr O'Neill could not dispose of his shareholding in Imari without the prior consent of Cambridge and ACT;
(iv) If Mr O'Neill were to sell his shares in Imari either to the other shareholders or to a third party, some restriction on his competing with Imari would appear to be justified, given the Authority's previous decisions;
(v) The proposed duration of the non-competition clause, namely the later of 5 years from the completion date or two years from the date of cessation of employment, is designed to prevent Mr O'Neill from leaving Imari and seeking to establish himself as a competitor to it and were he to attempt to do so such restrictions would be excessive.

73. In addition it was admitted that ACT and Cambridge could jointly decide to terminate Mr O'Neill's employment at any time. If, in fact, ACT and Cambridge should decide to terminate Mr O'Neill's employment with the Imari group they could hardly expect to be protected against his competing with Imari.

74. The effect of clause 8.1(i) (a),(b),(c),(d) and (e) was to prevent Mr O'Neill leaving and setting up in competition with Imari either on his own or in partnership with someone else or from taking up employment with another competing company for an unduly long period of time. These provisions, in the Authority's view, had the object or effect of preventing, restricting or distorting competition in certain transport services within the State and offended against section 4(1) of the Act.[22]

75. Clause 8.1(i)(d) in addition restricted Mr O'Neill from soliciting or offering employment to any person who was an employee of Imari during the two years prior to Mr O'Neill leaving the business. In Budget Travel and Woodchester the Authority accepted a restriction on the vendor of a business soliciting the employment of its former employees. Thus a restriction on Mr O'Neill offering employment to a former employee, where the offer was initiated by Mr O'Neill, would not in the Authority's view offend against section 4(1), but this would not apply to an offer of employment where the request for employment was originated by the employee. The Authority does not believe, however, that an absolute prohibition on

22. As the restrictions are deemed to go beyond what was necessary to achieve the primary purpose of the agreement, they would fail at least one of the requirements for a licence in section 4(2), that they must be indispensable to the achievement of any benefit provided by the arrangement and so would not qualify for a license.

offering employment to former employees is normally justified and it would regard such a restriction as offending against section 4(1). **3.12**

76. The parties have amended clause 8.1(i) by an amending agreement dated 4 February 1993 which was submitted to the Authority on 1 March 1993. The amended agreement provides that the restrictions originally contained in clause 8.1 shall apply from the completion date until the later of, (a) the 915th day after the date upon which Mr O'Neill ceases to hold or beneficially own or be entitled to any shares in the capital of Imari, or (b) the date upon which he ceases to be an employee of Imari.

77. As already stated, the Authority believes that a restriction on an individual competing with a business for so long as he remains an employee and/or shareholder in that business is essential to enable individuals to engage in business together and such a provision does not offend against section 4(1). The Authority indicated in Scully/Tyrrell that it would take a different view if the individual held only a nominal shareholding for investment purposes, or if the shareholding or employment arrangements were an artificial arrangement, designed to escape the provisions of section 4(1). It does not believe that this is the object of the amended arrangements. The Authority has also accepted in Nallen/O'Toole that a restriction on a party to a business competing with it for a period after he has disposed of his interest in the business does not offend against section 4(1). It has stated, in a number of cases that it would generally regard a restriction of two years as sufficient for this purpose. The arrangements as amended provide for a restriction of 2.5 years from the date of a sale of shares in the business. The Authority believes that, given the importance of Mr O'Neill to the business, the size of the investment by Cambridge, a period of 6 months longer than the general norm is acceptable in this instance. Therefore clause 8.1 does not offend against section 4(1) of the Act. While 8.1(i)(d) could be interpreted as preventing Mr O'Neill offering employment to a former Imari employee where the employee had sought such employment, the Authority believes that such a restriction could only be regarded as anti-competitive inasmuch as it prevents Mr O'Neill from competing with Imari by employing individuals whom he knows to be familiar with the businesses in which Imari operates. As Mr O'Neill is prevented from competing with Imari for the period during which clause 8.1(i)(d) is effective, the Authority does not believe that clause 8.1(i)(d), as amended, restricts competition or offends against section 4(1).

78. Clause 8.1(ii) is designed to prevent Mr O'Neill from disclosing or making use of, for his own purposes, any confidential information. Confidential information is defined in clause 1.1 as 'any information relating to the organisation, business, finances, prices, customers, suppliers, transactions or affairs of any company in the Imari Group.' The Authority has accepted in ACT/Kindle and Budget Travel/Phil Fortune that a restriction on disclosure of confidential information is not generally regarded as in breach of section 4(1). It has also decided in those cases that a restriction on making use of information cannot be employed to prevent the seller of a business re-entering the market once sufficient time has passed for a purchaser to have acquired the complete goodwill of the business. The parties have indicated by letter of 21 May 1992, that the clause would not be invoked to prevent Mr O'Neill entering the business only to stop him using any confidential information. The Authority believes that in the light of this commitment, clause 8.1(ii) does not offend against section 4(1).

Clause 9

79. As pointed out clause 9.1 prevents Mr O'Neill from disposing of his shareholding in Imari without the consent of Cambridge and ACT. The Authority believes that such a restriction can be justified to protect the interests of Cambridge. Cambridge has invested in Imari partly on the assumption of Mr O'Neill's continued involvement with the company. The Authority is concerned, however, that such consent may be withheld in order to prevent Mr O'Neill leaving Imari and thereby prevent him competing with it. It would regard the withholding of consent in such circumstances as restricting competition.

3.12 The Decision

80. In the Authority's opinion, Cambridge Investments Ltd, ACT, Imari and Mr Timothy O'Neill are undertakings within the meaning of section 3(1) of the Competition Act, and the notified arrangements for the acquisition by Cambridge of shares in Imari, constitute an agreement between undertakings which applies within the State.

81. The Authority believes that the agreement for the purchase of shares in Imari by Cambridge Investments Ltd. does not prevent, restrict or distort competition within the State, since it merely represents an arrangement by a number of parties to engage in a particular business venture together, whereby certain parties agree to invest money in the business.

82. The Authority believes that, where the primary purpose of the agreement is legitimate under the Competition Act, any restrictive clauses contained in such an agreement do not offend section 4(1), provided they are ancillary to the main purpose of the agreement. To be regarded as ancillary the Authority believes that such restrictions should be necessary, but no more than is absolutely necessary to achieve the primary purpose of the agreement. Restrictions which go beyond what is absolutely necessary for the achievement of that purpose would offend against section 4(1).

83. The restrictions contained in clause 8.1(i) of the agreement as originally notified, in the Authority's opinion, went beyond what was absolutely necessary to protect the investment being made in Imari by Cambridge and therefore went beyond what was necessary to enable the parties to engage in the business venture together. The Authority believes that the restrictions contained in clauses 6.9, 6.10, 6.14, 8.1(i), as amended by the agreement of 4 February 1993 and with the undertaking given in the letter of 21 May 1992, and clause 9.1 are ancillary to the main purpose of the agreement which is to engage in a form of joint business venture. Consequently such restrictions, in the Authority's opinion, do not prevent, restrict or distort competition in the State or any part of the State.

84. The agreement of 25 October 1991 for the acquisition of shares in Imari Ltd. between Cambridge Investments Ltd, ACT Ltd, Imari Ltd. and Mr Timothy O'Neill, as amended by the agreement between the parties of 4 February 1993 and with the undertaking given in the letter of 21 May 1992, does not, in the Authority's opinion, offend against section 4(1) of the Competition Act 1991.

The Certificate

85. The Competition Authority has issued the following certificate:

> The Competition Authority certifies that in its opinion, on the basis of the facts in its possession, the agreement of 25 October 1991 for the acquisition of shares in Imari Ltd. between Cambridge Investments Ltd, ACT Ltd, Imari Ltd. and Mr Timothy O'Neill, (notification no. CA/8/92E), notified on 6 March 1992 under section 7 and amended by the agreement between the parties of 4 February 1993 and with the undertaking given in the letter of 21 May 1992 does not offend against section 4(1) of the Competition Act 1991.

For the Competition Authority

Patrick Massey
Member

21 June 1993

Competition Authority Decision No. 138, Food Industries plc/Norish plc: 20 October 1993, Notification No. CA/672/92E **3.13**

Share sale agreement with option for the purchase of the remaining shares – Whether non-competing and non-soliciting provision after the option exercise is required for the transfer of the goodwill – Effect of a five year non-compete clause in an agreement executed three years prior to the Competition Act – Competition Act 1991 (No. 24) sections 3, 4 and 7

Facts: On 30 September 1992 notification was made to the Competition Authority of an agreement between Food Industries plc ('Food Industries') and Norish plc ('Norish') for the sale of 66.6% of the share capital in a company called Gyrtna which was later called 'Norish (Eirfreeze) Ltd. ('Eirfreeze'). The notification was made with a request for a certificate under section 4(4) of the Competition Act 1991 or failing that a licence under section 4(2).

Food Industries is involved in the food processing business while Norish and Eirfreeze provide and maintain food refrigeration equipment.

Under the terms of the share purchase and option arrangement notified Food Industries was prevented for a period of five years from competing in the same business and from soliciting the customers of Eirfreeze and the employees of Eirfreeze. On 16 September 1992 Norish acquired the remaining one third share capital of Eirfreeze. Both parties confirmed to the Authority that the restriction would expire on 31 July 1994.

Decided by the Authority: In issuing a certificate:

(1) Effective control of the business transferred in the agreement which predated the coming into force of the Competition Act had been transferred prior to the commencement of the Act. The merger therefore is not affected by section 4(1) of the Competition Act.

(2) Although the Competition Authority has indicated in a number of decisions that a two year non compete clause is normally sufficient for the complete transfer of goodwill in a sale of business, the acquiring company only acquired full control of the target in September 1992 and the remaining two year non compete period would be acceptable.

(3) In the notified agreement the parties were not seeking to extend the two year acceptable period for non compete clauses. The Authority would nevertheless be concerned with artificial arrangements such as a share sale agreement by instalment which would prolong the normally acceptable two year period for non compete clauses.

Notice and Decision referred to:

Competition Authority Notice dated 4 May 1993 entitled 'Notice in respect of mergers and takeovers which predate the Competition Act' **3.1**

Competition Authority Decision No. 12 — Scully Tyrrell & Co./Edberg Ltd, 29 January 1993 **3.10**

3.13 Competition Authority Decision of 20 October 1993 relating to a proceeding under section 4 of the Competition Act 1991 Notification No. CA/672/92E — Food Industries plc/Norish plc

Introduction

1. An agreement between Food Industries plc (Food Industries) and Norish plc (Norish), for the purchase and sale of shares in Gyrtna Ltd (Gyrtna) containing a non-compete clause was notified to the Competition Authority on 30 September 1992. The notification requested a certificate or, in the event of a certificate being refused, a licence.

The Facts

(a) *The Subject of the Notification*

2. The notification relates to an agreement dated 1 May 1989 between Food Industries and Norish whereby Food Industries agreed to sell a portion of its entire share capital holding in Gyrtna to Norish. The agreement also contains a non-compete provision.

(b) *The Parties*

3. Food Industries and Norish are limited companies incorporated in the State. Food Industries is involved in the food processing business while Norish and Gyrtna are engaged in the provision and maintenance of food refrigeration equipment. Gyrtna is also a limited company registered in the State and, as a result of a separate agreement of the same date as that notified, is the parent company of Eirfreeze Ltd (Eirfreeze). Following the acquisition, Gyrtna became known as Norish (Eirfreeze) Ltd.

(c) *The Arrangements*

4. The notification relates to an agreement, dated 1 May 1989, for the sale by Food Industries of two-thirds of the share capital of Gyrtna to Norish. Under the terms of the agreement, Norish had the option of acquiring the remaining third of the company. Clause 6.03(a) of the agreement prevents the vendors from competing in the same business as that sold for a period of five years from the date of completion of the agreement. Clause 6.03(b) of the agreement prevents the vendors from soliciting or enticing orders, for the same period, from any persons or companies who were customers of Gyrtna on, or twelve months prior to, the date of completion. This clause also prevents the vendors from soliciting employees from Gyrtna for the same period of time.

(d) *Subsequent Developments*

5. The parties advised the Authority by letter dated 31 August 1993 that on 16 September 1992, Norish had exercised its option to acquire the remaining one-third of the share capital of Gyrtna. They submitted that, in order to secure the full transfer of the goodwill, a restriction on the vendors competing with the purchaser for 2 years from that date would be justified. They indicated that the original non-compete clause would expire on 31 July 1994 and that this was less than two years from the time of the acquisition of the balance of the shares by virtue of the exercise of the option. Consequently they considered it should not be regarded as offending against section 4(1).

Assessment

(a) *Section 4(1)*

5. Section 4(1) of the Competition Act states that 'all agreements between undertakings, decisions by associations of undertakings and concerted practices which have as their object

or effect the prevention, restriction or distortion of competition in trade in any goods or services in the State or in any part of the State are prohibited and void'. 3.13

(b) *The Undertakings and the Agreement*

6. Section 3(1) of the Competition Act defines an undertaking as 'a person being an individual, a body corporate or an unincorporated body of persons engaged for gain in the production, supply or distribution of goods or the provision of a service.' Both Food Industries and Norish are corporate bodies engaged for gain in the provision of goods and services and are, therefore, undertakings.

(c) *Applicability of section 4(1)*

7. The agreement for the acquisition of the majority shareholding in the business and the grant of the option to acquire the balance predates the coming into force of the Competition Act. Effective control of the business which was the subject of the agreement had been transferred prior to the Act. In the Authority's view, the prohibition in section 4(1) only applies to a current or continuing contractual commitment or one entered into subsequent to the coming into force of the Act.[1] As the merger or sale element of the 1991 transaction was discharged prior to the commencement of the Act, that aspect of the arrangements does not come within the scope of section 4(1).

8. The agreement contains a five-year non-compete clause which applied from the 31 July 1989. The Authority has indicated in a number of previous decisions that it normally regards a two-year non-compete clause as being sufficient for the complete transfer of goodwill in a sale of business. In the case of this notification, however, the Authority believes that as Norish only acquired *full* control of Gyrtna on 16 September 1992, a two-year period from that date would have been acceptable. This is consistent with its decision in Scully/Tyrrell.[2]

9. The Authority, however, generally considers that a non-compete clause in the event of a sale of business, where a transfer of goodwill rather than technical know-how is concerned, should be limited to two years from the date of completion. It does not believe that an extension of such limits would generally be acceptable by virtue of the fact that the acquisition of the business takes place in stages over a period of time. In particular it would be concerned that such an arrangement might be regarded as a means of extending the duration of non-compete clauses beyond the period which the Authority would normally consider necessary to secure the transfer of the goodwill. The Authority is satisfied that this was not the object of the present agreement. The parties have pointed out that the non-compete clause will expire on 31 July 1994 and that this is less than two years from the time of the acquisition of the balance of the shares. As it is satisfied that it was not an artificial arrangement to extend the duration of the non-compete clause the Authority does not consider that it has the object or effect of preventing, restricting or distorting competition.

The Decision

10. In the Authority's opinion, Food Industries and Norish are undertakings within the meaning of section 3(1) of the Competition Act, and the notified arrangements for the acquisition of Gyrtna constitute an agreement between undertakings. In the Authority's opinion, the arrangements do not have, as their object or effect, the prevention, restriction or distortion of competition. The agreement of 1 May 1989 between Food Industries plc and Norish plc, for the purchase and sale of shares in Gyrtna Ltd, does not, in the Authority's opinion, offend against section 4(1) of the Competition Act 1991.

1. 'Notice in respect of Mergers and Takeovers which predate the Competition Act' — Competition Authority.
2. Competition Authority Decision No. 12, Scully Tyrrell & Company/Edberg Ltd, 29 January 1993.

3.13 The Certificate

11. The Competition Authority has issued the following certificate:

> The Competition Authority certifies that in its opinion, on the basis of the facts in its possession, the agreement between Food Industries plc and Norish plc, for the purchase and sale of shares in Gyrtna Ltd (CA/672/92E), notified on 30 September 1992 under section 7, does not offend against section 4(1) of the Competition Act 1991.

For the Competition Authority

Patrick Massey
Member

20 October 1993

3.14 Competition Authority Decision No. 142, PJD Investment Company/P.J. Donohoe & Paul S. Power/Fitzwilton plc.: 27 October 1993, Notification No. CA/651/92E

Share Purchase Agreement containing five year restrictive covenant regarding competition – Whether such restriction necessary – Amendment of duration of restriction in response to Authority concerns – Restriction on competition in foreign countries – Competition Act 1991 (No. 24), sections 3, 4, 7 and 8

Facts: On 30 September 1992 notification was made to the Authority of a Share Purchase Agreement between, *inter alia*, P.J. Donohoe and Paul S. Power as vendors, and Fitzwilton plc, as purchaser, together with a request for a certificate under section 4(4) of the Competition Act, 1991 or, failing that a licence under section 4(2). P.J. Donohoe and Paul S. Power were the sole shareholders in PJD Investment Company, an investment holding company whose wholly owned subsidiaries Press-O-Matic Ltd and Novum (Overseas) Ltd are engaged respectively in the manufacture and export of domestic appliances. Fitzwilton plc is an Irish registered holding company. Under the terms of the notified share purchase agreement dated 26 April 1989, Fitzwilton plc purchased 80% of the shares in PJD Investment Company from Messrs Donohoe and Power. Under the terms of the agreement the vendors covenanted for a period of five years not to: (i) compete in the same business as the purchaser in Ireland or in certain other foreign countries; (ii) not to solicit any customers or employees of the purchaser and; (iii) not to disclose certain confidential information. The Authority expressed concern at the duration of the restriction on competition and suggested that two years was generally considered sufficient for the transfer of the goodwill in the sale of a business. In a letter dated 7 September 1993 the parties agreed that the restrictive clauses other than that relating to confidential information would cease to apply from 1 October 1993.

Decided by the Authority: In issuing a certificate under section 4(4) of the Competition Act 1991 that:

(1) All the parties to the notified agreement were 'undertakings' within the meaning of the Competition Act 1991 and such agreement was an agreement between undertakings. **3.14**

(2) The prohibition in section 4(1) only applies to a current or continuing contractual commitment or to one entered into subsequent to the coming into force of the Competition Act and therefore the purchase of shares under the terms of the notified agreement, having been discharged by performance prior to the commencement of the Competition Act, was outside the scope of the Act.

(3) While the restrictive covenants, being continual contractual commitments, were within the scope of the Competition Act they did not (after their duration was amended) exceed what was necessary in order to secure the transfer of the goodwill of the business being purchased.

(4) The restriction on disclosing confidential information, being unlimited in time does not offend section 4(1) provided it is not used to prevent the vendors competing in the market. Such a use could lead to a revocation of the certificate under section 8(6) of the Act.

Decision and Notice referred to:

Competition Authority Decision No. 10, 23 October 1992 — GI Corporation/General Semi-conductor Industry Inc. **3.8**

Competition Authority Notice in respect of Mergers and Takeovers which pre-date the Competition Act **3.1**

Competition Authority Decision of 27 October 1993 relating to a proceeding under section 4 of the Competition Act 1991
Notification No. CA/651/92E — PJD Investment Company/Fitzwilton Public Ltd Company/P.J. Donohoe, Paul S. Power/Press-O-Matic Ltd and Novum (Overseas) Ltd

Introduction

1. An agreement between P.J. Donohoe and Paul S. Power (the vendors), PJD Investment Company, Fitzwilton plc (the purchaser), Press-O-Matic Ltd and Novum (Overseas) Ltd was notified to the Competition Authority on 30 September 1992. The agreement provided for the sale of 80% of the shares in PJD Investment Company to the purchaser. The notification requested a certificate, or, in the event of a refusal to issue a certificate, a licence.

The Facts

(a) *The Subject of the Notification*

2. The notification relates to an agreement dated 26 April 1989, between the purchaser and P.J. Donohoe and Paul S. Power whereby the vendors agreed to sell 80% of the shares in PJD Investment Company.The agreement also contained a non-compete provision.

(b) *The Parties*

3. PJD Investment Company is an investment holding company. Fitzwilton plc is a limited liability company incorporated in the State. Press-O-Matic Ltd is a subsidiary of PJD Investment Company and is involved in the business of the manufacture and sale of deep freezers under various brand names. Novum (Overseas) Ltd is also a subsidiary of PJD Investment Company and is engaged in the export of domestic appliances. P.J. Donohoe and Paul Power were both directors and shareholders of PJD Investment Company.

3.14 (c) *The arrangements*

4. The notification related to a Share Purchase Agreement dated 26 April 1989, for the sale of 80% of the shares in PJD Investment Company. Clause 8 of the agreement contained a non-compete clause in which the vendors covenanted:

(i) Not to compete in the same business as the purchaser in the Republic of Ireland, China, Iraq, or any other country where the company or its subsidiaries were doing business for a period of five years from the date of the agreement;

(ii) Not to use or disclose any confidential information relating to the business or affairs of the company;

(iii) Not to solicit any of the customers of the purchaser, for a period of five years from the date of completion; and

(iii) Not to solicit any of the employees of the purchaser, for a period of five years from the date of completion.

Subsequent Developments

5. The Authority expressed concern at the duration of the non-compete clauses, on the basis that in general a two year non-compete period is considered sufficient for the tranfer of good will in the sale of a business. This view was expressed by the Authority in General Semiconductor.[1] In a letter to the Authority dated 7 September 1993, the parties agreed that the restrictive clauses, other than that in respect of confidential information would cease to apply from 1 October 1993. In a subsequent letter dated 7 October, the vendors confirmed their acceptance of this change.

Assessment

(a) *Section 4(1)*

6. Section 4(1) of the Competition Act states that 'all agreements between undertakings, decisions by associations of undertakings and concerted practices which have as their object or effect the prevention, restriction or distortion of competition in trade in any goods or services in the State or in any part of the State are prohibited and void'.

(b) *The Undertakings and the Agreement*

7. Section 3(1) of the Competition Act defines an undertaking as 'a person being an individual, a body corporate or an unincorporated body of persons engaged for gain in the production, supply or distribution of goods or the provision of a service'. The parties to this particular agreement are the vendors and Fitzwilton Public Ltd Company. At the time of the agreement the vendors were the beneficial owners of Press-O-Matic and Novum, both limited companies engaged for gain in the manufacturing and distribution of refrigerators, freezers and associated products. The vendors were therefore undertakings. Fitzwilton plc is a limited liability company engaged for gain and is therefore an undertaking. The arrangements therefore constitute an agreement between undertakings.

(c) *Applicability of section 4(1)*

8. The share purchase agreement itself was completed prior to 1 October 1991, the date on which the Competition Act came into force, consequently, this element of the agreement had been discharged by performance before the Act commenced. The property which was the subject of the agreement had been transferred. In the Authority's view, the prohibition in section 4(1) only applies to a current or continuing contractual commitment or one entered into subsequent to the coming into force of the Act.[2]

1. Notification No. CA51/92, Competition Authority Decision No. 10 — GI Corporation/General Semiconductor Industries Inc., 23 October 1992.
2. Notice in respect of Mergers and Takeovers which predate the Competition Act — Competition Authority, *Iris Oifigiúil*, 14 May 1993, p. 367.

9. The Authority considered that the duration of the restrictions in clause 8 exceeded what was necessary to secure the complete transfer of the goodwill of the business. In its view such restrictions would offend against section 4(1) and would not satisfy the requirements for a licence under section 4(2). It considered that the geographic scope of the restriction insofar as it applied to the State did not exceed what was necessary to secure the transfer of the goodwill. As the Authority is only asked to consider whether or not an agreement prevents, restricts or distorts competition within the State, the fact that the restrictions apply also to China and Iraq was not considered. **3.14**

10. In letters to the Authority dated 7 September and 7 October 1993, the notifying parties undertook to cease applying the restrictions with effect from 1 October 1993. Consequently in the Authority's opinion the agreement no longer offends against section 4(1). The restriction on using or disclosing confidential information is unlimited in time. In the Authority's view such a restriction does not offend against section 4(1) provided it is not used to prevent the vendors competing in the market. If that were to happen the Authority would have to consider revoking the certificate under section 8(6) of the Act.

The Decision

11. In the Authority's view P.J. Donohoe, Paul S. Power and Fitzwilton plc are undertakings within the meaning of section 3(1) of the Competition Act. In the Authority's opinion The Share Purchase Agreement, between P.J. Donohoe, Paul S. Power and Fitzwilton plc dated 26 April 1989, as amended by the letters of 7 September and 7 October 1993, does not offend against section 4(1).

The Certificate

12. The Competition Authority has issued the following certificate:

> The Competition Authority certifies that in its opinion, on the basis of the facts in its possession, the agreement of 26 April 1989, between P.J. Donohoe, Paul S. Power, PJD Investment Company, Fitzwilton plc, Press-O-Matic Ltd and Novum (Overseas) Ltd for the sale and purchase of 80% of the shares in PJD Investment Company (notification no. CA/651/92E), notified on 30 September 1992, under section 7, and amended by the letters of 7 September and 7 October 1993, does not offend against section 4(1) of the Competition Act 1991.

For the Competition Authority

Patrick Massey
Member

27 October 1993

3.15 Competition Authority Decision No. 148, Spring Grove Ireland Ltd/Initial Services (International) Ltd/P&O Services Group/BET plc: 18 November 1993, Notification No. CA/1135/92

Purchase of entire share capital – Merger notified to the Minister for Industry and Commerce – Whether the maxim 'generalia specialibus non derogant' excludes application of Competition Act in a notified merger – Whether three years restriction for non-competition covenant necessary for the transfer of goodwill – Whether ten year protection for industrial property rights restricts market entry – Application of 'four firm concentration ratio' – Application of Herfindahl-Hirschman Index without sufficient information – Relevance of self-provision in the relevant market – Reduction of three year restriction to two years by supplemental agreement – Mergers, Take-Overs and Monopolies (Control) Act 1978 (No. 17) – Competition Act 1991 (No. 24) sections 3, 4 and 7

Facts: On 30 December 1992 notification was made to the Competition Authority of a share purchase agreement with a request for a certificate under section 4(4) of the Competition Act 1991 or failing that, a licence under section 4(2).

The notified agreement dated 27 November 1992 concerned the transfer of the entire issued share capital of Conkenner from Initial Services (International) Ltd to Spring Grove Ireland Ltd. ('Spring Grove'). The provision of textile rental was deemed by the Competition Authority to be the relevant market. The parties gave estimates of market shares in the State of the relevant company. The agreement provided that Spring Grove would not use defined industrial property rights such as trademarks for a period of ten years from the date of completion. The vendors on the other hand covenanted not to licence the use of the industrial property rights in the State for a period of ten years from completion.

The vendors also covenanted for a period of 3 years not to engage in any competing enterprise or to solicit customers from Conkenner and its group. A similar restriction on the soliciting of supervisors employed by Conkenner was also included.

A confidentiality provision was also included concerning Conkenner and its customers.

Submissions

(1) The parties submitted that the period of three years for the restrictions were reasonable and that the restrictions did not restrict competition in the relevant market.

(2) The Competition Authority's decision in Woodchester/UDT was wrong because the maxim *generalia specialibus non derogant* meant that the merger when examined under the mergers legislation precluded the application of section 4(1) of the Competition Act.

(3) The merger could not offend against section 4(1) because the markets were highly competitive.

Following discussions with the Authority the parties notified the Authority by letter dated 6 December 1993 that the non-competition clause would be limited to two years and that the non solicitation of customers on the date of completion of Conkenner would be restricted to three years.

Decided by the Authority: In issuing a certificate under section 4(4) of the Competition Act 1991 in respect of the notified share acquisition agreement: **3.15**

(1) The Woodchester/UDT decision of the Competition Authority is correct. If the submission which relies on the maxim *generalia specialibus non derogant* was correct all non compete clauses in a share acquisition agreement would be excluded from the scope of section 4(1) of the Competition Act.

(2) There is no obligation on the parties to notify agreements under the Competition Act. The implication of the notifier's argument is that the agreement should not have been notified because section 4(1) has allegedly no application to the notified agreement.

(3) The relevant markets are fairly highly concentrated and in one particular sector the merged entity will have a market share of almost 40%. This triggers a more detailed examination by the Competition Authority of the notified arrangement. The indications are that the threshold according to the Herfindahl-Hirschman Index as discussed in the Scully Tyrrell decision of the Competition Authority has also been exceeded.

(4) The market should include substitutable products and should include the fact that the relevant services could be substituted by customer. The acquisition when examined does not offend against section 4(1).

(5) The three year restriction on competition has been reduced to two years and as such does not offend against section 4(1).

(6) The restrictions on the use of the intellectual property rights by the vendor and the purchaser would not prevent the vendor from re-entering the market and do not offend against section 4(1).

(7) The non-solicitation of customers on the date of completion for a period of three years does not offend against section 4(1).

(8) The restriction on the use of confidential information about the company sold and its customers would not prevent the vendor from re-entering the relevant market.

Cases and Decisions referred to:

BAT v. Commission and Philip Morris (Case No. 142 and 156/84) [1987] ECR 4487; [1988] 4 CMLR 24
The Vera Cruz (1884) 10 Appeal Cases 59
Director of Public Prosecutions v. Grey [1986] IR 317
Deane & Others v. Voluntary Health Insurance Board [1992] 2 IR 319 **1.1**
EC Commission Decision; Reuter/BASF [1976] OJ L 254/40; [1976] 2 CMLR D44
EC Commission Decision; Penney [1978] OJ L 60/19; [1978] 2 CMLR 100
Competition Authority Decision No. 1; Nallen/O'Toole **3.3**
Competition Authority Decision No. 6; Woodchester Bank Ltd./UDT Bank Ltd **3.5**
Competition Authority Decision No. 8; ACT/Kindle **3.6**
Competition Authority Decision No. 9; Budget Travel Ltd/Phil Fortune **3.7**
Competition Authority Decision No. 12; Scully/Tyrrell/Edberg Ltd **3.10**
Competition Authority Decision No. 29; Carrolls Catering/Sutcliffe

Competition Authority Decision of 18 November 1993 relating to a proceeding under section 4 of the Competition Act 1991
Notification No. CA/1135/92 — Spring Grove/Conkenner

Introduction

1. Arrangements for the purchase of the entire issued share capital of Conkenner Ltd (Conkenner) by Spring Grove Ireland Ltd (Spring Grove) from Initial Services (International)

3.15 Ltd (ISIL), were notified to the Competition Authority on 30 December, 1992. The notification requested a certificate, or in the event of a refusal by the Authority to grant a certificate, a licence.

The Facts

(a) *The Subject of the Notification*

2. The notification relates to an agreement, dated 27 November 1992, between ISIL, BET plc (BET) and Spring Grove and the P&O Services Group for the sale and purchase of the entire issued share capital of Conkenner. The arrangements include a number of non-compete provisions together with restrictions on the use of certain industrial property rights (mainly trade marks). The arrangements were notified to, and approved by, the Minister for Industry and Commerce under the Mergers Act.

(b) *The Parties*

3. ISIL is a company incorporated in England and Wales. It is a wholly owned subsidiary of BET. Prior to the completion of the notified agreement Conkenner was a wholly owned subsidiary of ISIL. Conkenner is engaged in the provision of textile rental and associated services throughout the State. ISIL is engaged *inter alia* in the provision of such services in the UK.

4. Spring Grove is a private limited company incorporated in Ireland. It is a wholly owned subsidiary of Spring Grove Services which in turn is a wholly owned subsidiary of The P&O Services Group Ltd. The ultimate parent is The Peninsular and Oriental Steam Navigation Company (P&O), a company listed on the London Stock Exchange.

The Product and the Market

5. Conkenner is engaged in the business of providing textile rental and associated services throughout the State on a contract basis to offices, schools and factories and other establishments. Prior to this agreement Conkenner operated under the trade names 'Initial Services', 'Swastika Laundry Ltd' and 'M Laundries Ltd'. The latter two are trading subsidiaries of Conkenner. The services provided to clients include:

(a) the provision of hand drying facilities, i.e. the sale or rental of warm air hand dryers, hire of wall cabinets containing continuous towels, the provision of paper towels and the hire or sale of cloth towels;
(b) workwear rental, being the hire, largely to employers, of items such as boiler suits, chefs' jackets and trousers, overalls and uniforms. The parties have indicated that: 'Such garments are normally sized and marked for particular wearers';
(c) dustmat rental, such mats being entrance or corridor mats, either impregnated with fluids or of special material or weave designed to remove dirt and dust from shoes;
(d) linen rental, being the hire of sheets, pillowcases, hand towels, bath towels, bath mats, table cloths and napkins to hotels, restaurants, caterers and hospitals. Spring Grove is engaged in the first three activities.

6. The market is that for the provision of textile rental and associated services as described in the previous paragraph to offices, schools, factories and other establishments. There are several other firms engaged in this business. These include Celtic Linen, Connaught and Court Group and a number of others. The notifying parties have estimated the breakdown of market shares as follows.

Parties Estimate of Market Shares 3.15

%

	Hand Drying Facilities	Workwear Rental	Dustmat Rental	Linen Services
Spring Grove	10	17	14	0
Conkenner	18	21	25	27
Spring Grove/Conkenner Total	28	38	39	27
Connaught & Court	14	33	29	47
Celtic	9	10	14	19
Others	49	19	18	7

(All columns add to 100% after rounding up or down)

7. In addition the parties have indicated that many firms and institutions provide such services in-house and that specialist suppliers account for only a relatively small share of the market in each case. According to the parties in-house provision accounts for 75% or more of total use of such products and some customers regularly switch to in-house provision when contracts come up for renewal.

The Arrangements

8. The agreement relates to the sale by ISIL of the entire issued share capital of Conkenner to Spring Grove. The agreement, as notified, included a number of non-compete provisions which are summarised below.

9. Clause 5 provides that, for a period of 10 years from Completion, Spring Grove shall not use and procure that no group company shall use the industrial property rights or any other marks similar to or likely to be confused with them, and not to represent, and procure that no group company should represent, that they have any right in or to such industrial property rights. The industrial property rights means the trade marks and trade names of the business. Clause 5(2) provides for a number of exceptions to this provision. These essentially operate for a period of months from completion and are designed to give the purchaser time to remove such trade marks and logos from vehicles, staff uniforms, name boards etc.

10. Clause 7(1)(a) provided that for a period of 3 years from the date of completion, ISIL, BET or its subsidiaries, (the vendors), would not without the prior written consent of the purchaser:

(i) be engaged or concerned in any Competing Enterprise, (save as the holder of not more than 5% of the shares of a quoted company);
(ii) through any competing enterprise, transact business with any person who was a customer of a Conkenner Group Company during the 12 months preceding completion;
(iii) knowingly canvass or solicit orders for competing enterprises from any person who was a customer of a Conkenner Group Company during the 12 months preceding completion.

Essentially a competing business is defined in the agreement as one competing with the business of Conkenner. Clause 7(1)(b) provides that ISIL and BET or its subsidiaries will not for a period of 10 years from Completion, use any one or more of the industrial property rights to do any of the things specified in 7(1)(a).

11. Clause 7(2) provides that ISIL, BET or its subsidiaries will not without the prior written consent of the purchaser assign licence or permit in the State the use of any one or more of the

3.15 industrial property rights by any person interested directly or indirectly in any competing enterprise for a period of 10 years from Completion.

12. Clause 7(3) provided that, for a period of 3 years from completion, neither BET nor any of its subsidiaries would, without the prior written consent of the purchaser, knowingly solicit or entice away from any Conkenner group company any supplier who had supplied goods to it during the previous 12 months if this would adversely affect the supply of goods or services by the supplier to that company. Clause 7(4) provided that neither BET nor any of its subsidiaries would solicit or entice away from any Conkenner Group Company any manager or supervisor employed by it upon Completion, for a period of 3 years from that date, without the purchaser's prior written permission.

13. Clause 7(5) provided that neither, ISIL, BET nor any of its subsidiaries, would without the prior written consent of the purchaser, use or reveal to any person any of the trade secrets, secret or confidential operations, processes or dealings or any other confidential information concerning any Conkenner group company or its customers. Such information includes customer lists and names, sales statistics, reports on pricing, and information relating to sales by any group company, until such time as they should fall into the public domain.

14. Clause 7(6) provides that each of the covenants and undertakings contained in clauses 7(1) to (5) shall be construed as a separate covenant and undertaking. Clause 7(8) provides that if the Competition Authority indicates that but for the duration, extent or scope of clause 5 or 7, it would issue a certificate in respect of the agreement, the parties shall forthwith in writing agree that provision with the minimum variation or modification so as to give the provision the maximum duration extent or scope permissible but so as to procure such certificate.

Submissions of the Parties

15. The parties referred to the decision of the EC Commission in Reuter/BASF[1] and the European Court of Justice decision in Remia[2] to support the view that the restrictions contained in the agreement did not prevent, restrict or distort competition and therefore merited a certificate. They also quoted extensively from the Authority's first decision in Nallen/O'Toole,[3] where it granted a certificate in respect of a sale of business agreement incorporating non-competition clauses. They stated that the periods during which the restrictions would apply were 'related to the period during which a potential competitor would be able to build up a market position relevant to the life span of the goodwill'. They also claimed that the period of three years specified under clause 7 was reasonable in the circumstances and that it did not prevent, restrict or distort competition in trade in any goods or services in the State or in any part of the State.

16. They argued that it had effectively been agreed that for a period of 10 years the industrial property rights will be used by neither party in a competing enterprise. They claimed that this did not restrict competition but rather regulated the use of certain intellectual property rights. They stated that such considerations applied in respect of clauses 5, 7(1)(b) and 7(2).

17. The parties also claimed that the acquisition itself, as distinct from the ancillary restrictive clauses, might not be properly reviewable under section 4(1) of the Competition Act. While recognising that the Authority had given its views on the applicability of section 4(1) to mergers and acquisitions in Woodchester,[4] the parties argued that the Authority's decision was essentially wrong in law. Specifically they submitted that the maxim *generalia specialibus non derogant* was applicable. They cited certain court judgements in support of this.[5] They also argued that the Competition Act did not contain any specific direction that the

1. *Reuter/BASF* OJ L254, 17.9.76, p.40.
2. *Remia BV and Others v. European Commission*, Case 42/84 [1985] ECR 2545.
3. Competition Authority Decision No. 1, Nallen/O'Toole (Belmullet), (CA/8/91), 2 April 1992.
4. Competition Authority Decision No. 6, Woodchester Bank/UDT Bank, (CA/10/92), 4 August 1992.
5. The Vera Cruz (1884) 10 App. Cas. 59, 68 and *DPP v. Grey* [1986] IR 317, 327

jurisprudence at Community level was to be used and that such omission suggested that the Oireachtas did not intend that such jurisprudence was to be given any particular weight. They also claimed that EC precedents indicated that mergers and acquisitions were not subject to Article 85(1). **3.15**

18. The parties also submitted that the acquisition satisfied the test set by the Authority in Woodchester for establishing whether or not a merger could offend against section 4(1). Specifically they stated that the markets were highly competitive with all of the users being competitors or potential competitors and consequently the acquisition could not be said to have resulted in, or be likely to result in a lessening of competition.

Subsequent Developments

19. Following discussions with the Authority the parties presented further arguments in support of the arrangements. They contended that BET possessed secret trading information which would allow it, at the end of two years, to solicit lucrative business away from Conkenner.

20. The parties indicated, however, by letters dated 6 July and 23 September 1993, that they would amend a number of the provisions of clause 7 by means of a supplemental agreement. These amendments are as follows. Clause 7(1) as amended provides that:

(a) for a period of 2 years from the date of completion, ISIL, BET or its subsidiaries, will not without the prior written consent of the purchaser:

> (i) be engaged or concerned in any Competing Enterprise, (save as the holder of not more than 5% of the shares of a quoted company);
> (ii) through any Competing Enterprise, transact business with any person who was a customer of a Group Company at or about the date of Completion;
> (iii) knowingly canvass or solicit orders for Competing Enterprises from any person who was a customer of a Group Company at or about the time of Completion;

(b) for a period of three years immediately following the date of completion:

> (i) through any competing enterprise, transact business with any person who was a customer of a Group Company at or about the date of completion where such transaction or dealing arises directly or indirectly as a consequence of any canvassing or solicitation of orders as set out in subclause B below;
> (B) knowingly canvass or solicit orders for competing enterprises from any person who was a customer of a Group Company at or about the date of completion;

For the purpose of subclause 7(1)(b), canvassing or soliciting orders shall include contacting customers directly or indirectly with a view to informing customers that BET or any of its subsidiaries is operating/doing business in the Republic of Ireland or with a view to securing business from them.

Clause 7(1)(b), dealing with the use of Industrial Property rights, now becomes 7(1)(c).

Clause 7(1)(d) defines the term 'at or about the time of completion' as a period of two months prior to the date of completion.

Clause 7(4) as amended provides that neither BET nor any of its subsidiaries will solicit or entice away from any Conkenner Group Company any manager or supervisor employed by it upon Completion, for a period of 2 years from that date, without the purchaser's prior written permission.

Clause 7(5), which relates to confidential information, was amended by the addition of the following.

> The foregoing provisions of this subclause shall not apply to the extent that
> (i) BET or a subsidiary of BET is required by law to reveal the same; or

3.15 (ii) BET or a subsidiary of BET would, by virtue of such provisions be deemed to be prohibited itself from doing any one or more of the acts matters or things referred to in the foregoing subclauses of this clause 7 after the expiry of the respective periods of time specified in those subclauses.

The parties confirmed by letter dated 27 October 1993, that both sides had agreed to the text of the supplemental agreement and that they were prepared to execute it as soon as practicable subject to a satisfactory response from the Authority. In a letter to the Authority dated 6 December 1993, the parties indicated that arrangements had been made to have the supplemental agreement executed.

Assessment

(a) *Section 4(1)*

21. Section 4(1) of the Competition Act states that 'all agreements between undertakings, decisions by associations of undertakings and concerted practices which have as their object or effect the prevention, restriction or distortion of competition in trade in any goods or services in the State or in any part of the State are prohibited and void.'

(b) *The Undertakings and the Agreement*

22. The parties to the present agreement are Spring Grove, ISIL and BET. Each of these is a body corporate which is engaged in the provision of a service or services for gain. Consequently they are undertakings within the meaning of section 3(1). The present arrangement is, in the Authority's view, an agreement between undertakings.

(c) *Applicability of section 4(1)*

The Sale Agreement

23. Under the agreement Spring Grove has purchased Conkenner from ISIL. The Authority has given its views for believing that mergers are not automatically excluded from the prohibition in section 4(1) at length in its decision on Woodchester. It does not propose to restate those here. To the extent that the parties have raised issues not covered in that decision the Authority proposes to deal with them briefly.

24. The parties have claimed that the Authority's interpretation of the Act in Woodchester is wrong in that an acquisition *per se*, as distinct from the ancillary restrictive clauses, is not subject to section 4(1), since specific provisions for dealing with acquisitions are provided under the Mergers Act. In the Authority's view it is inconsistent to claim that an acquisition agreement is not subject to section 4(1) but that certain clauses of such an agreement are subject to such provisions. The Authority does not believe that the legislation could be interpreted as implying that certain aspects of an agreement are subject to section 4(1) while others are not. Thus if the parties interpretation is correct then all aspects of the acquisition should properly be regarded as not reviewable under section 4(1) and non compete clauses regardless of their duration or extent would not be subject to its provisions.

25. The parties have argued that the Act does not include any specific direction that the jurisprudence at Community level was to be used and that such omission suggests that the Oireachtas did not intend that such jurisprudence was to be given any particular weight. The Authority, however, notes the comments of Finlay CJ in VHI.[6] Having relied upon the definition of gain established in Arthur Average he went on to state that, although he did not find the word 'gain' in section 3(1) of the Competition Act ambiguous,

6. *Mary Deane & Others v. Voluntary Health Insurance Board*, Supreme Court judgement of 29 July 1992, unreported.

> if it were so found it would be appropriate to look at the long title of the Act, where it was stated that the purposes of the Act included the prohibition by analogy with Articles 85 and 86 of the Treaty establishing the European Economic Community, and in the interests of the common good, the prevention, restriction or distortion of competition and the abuse of dominant positions in trade in the state. Articles 85 and 86 undoubtedly applied to a body corporate engaged in the supply of services even if it did not have as its objects the making of commercial profits. **3.15**

In the Authority's view such sentiments appear to indicate that where there is any ambiguity in the legislation, one should look to the long title of the Act and, as that provides that it is an Act to do certain things by analogy with Articles 85 and 86, EC decisions under those Articles should be considered.

26. The Authority also notes that, in decisions where it found that restrictive clauses in sale of business agreements infringed Article 85(1), the EC Commission stated that it was the sale agreement and not the restrictive clauses which constituted an agreement between undertakings.[7] The Authority believes that the exclusion of the acquisition and the associated restrictive clauses would mean that the provisions of the Competition Act differed substantially from those of Articles 85 and 86 and it considers this to be inconsistent with the long title to the Act and the interpretation placed on that in the VHI judgment.

27. There is no obligation on parties to notify agreements under the Competition Act. If the parties' arguments are accepted then the present agreement is not an agreement of a kind described in section 4(1) and it may not be notified. The Authority could not issue a certificate or licence in respect of such an agreement since it can only issue these in respect of notified agreements. Since a certificate or licence can only be granted in respect of an agreement, the Authority could not issue one in respect of the non-compete provisions in the present agreement since, if the parties were correct, they are part of an agreement which could not be notified. Indeed the implication of the parties argument is that they should not have notified this agreement. The Authority considers that, on balance, the reasons stated in Woodchester for concluding that mergers are not automatically excluded from the scope of the Act remain valid.

28. The parties' figures on market share imply that the relevant markets are fairly highly concentrated and that the degree of concentration would increase significantly as a result of this agreement. In two instances, namely workwear and dustmat rental, the merged entity will have a market share of almost forty percent according to these figures, while in hand drying and linen services its share will be 28 and 27 percent respectively. In the latter case admittedly the agreement has no impact on concentration, since Spring Grove was not engaged in this market.

29. The Authority indicated in Scully Tyrrel[8] that, where the four firm concentration ratio post merger was below 40%, it believed an acquisition would be unlikely to have any adverse effect on competition and in such circumstances it would generally find that the acquisition did not offend against section 4(1). It indicated, however, that, where the four firm concentration ratio exceeded this threshold, it would conduct a more detailed examination of the arrangements. The parties figures would place this agreement into the latter category. While the detailed information needed to estimate the Herfindahl Hirschman Index (HHI)[9] is not available from the table, it is clear that in some, if not all, of the relevant markets the threshold set by the Authority in Scully Tyrrell is also exceeded on this measure.

30. The parties have submitted that many businesses provide the relevant products themselves. Clearly an alternative to renting workwear from the parties is for a firm to buy it themselves and supply it to their employees and let them make their own cleaning arrange-

7. See for example the Commission's decision in Reuter/BASF.
8. Competition Authority Decision No. 12, *Scully Tyrrell/Edberg* (CA/57/92), 29 January 1993.
9. This is an alternative measure of market concentration which was also applied in *Scully Tyrrell.*

3.15 ments. Similarly businesses and institutions can purchase and install hand dryers, or cloth or paper towels on their premises and likewise in the case of dustmats. Indeed the parties have submitted that the vast majority of businesses and institutions do just this and that some proportion of their customers decide, each year, to provide such services themselves, rather than continue to obtain them from the notifying parties.

31. The important issue here is the question of the definition of the market. Specifically should the market be defined to include only sales by firms specialising in providing such products to others or should it include the self provision of such products by the users. A similar issue has arisen in respect of other notifications, including one involving the purchaser's parent company.[10] The market should properly be defined so as to include those products which are close substitutes and important competitors to the products in question. Clearly the range of products which may properly be regarded as close substitutes or important competitors will be confined within quite narrow limits. Products to which only a relatively small number of users might switch in the event of a variation in price ought not to be considered close substitutes. In Carrolls Catering the Authority stated that:

> In the Authority's view it is unlikely that contract catering firms either individually or collectively are in a position to exercise market power. It seems likely that if they attempted to do so, users of catering services would respond by providing such services in-house. In the Authority's view the costs of switching to in-house provision of such services would not represent a deterrent. Consequently it would appear legitimate to regard self operated services as sufficiently close substitutes for bought-in catering services for them to be regarded as part of the same market.

The Authority has previously considered that insurance companies could substitute in-house provision of services for those of loss adjusters.[11]

32. The Authority believes that the argument advanced in Carrolls Catering could also be applied in this instance to justify regarding self-provision of the products by users as constituting a part of the market. Specifically the Authority believes that, were the enlarged firm to attempt to exercise market power, many of its customers would choose to provide such products in-house. Indeed the parties have indicated that the vast majority of firms and institutions do in fact rely on in-house provision. Allowing for the level of in-house provision suggests that specialist providers of such services account for a quarter or less of the relevant markets. This indicates that in-house provision is a sufficiently close substitute for bought-in services for it to be considered part of the same market. The inclusion of in-house provision indicates that post-merger levels of concentration are considerably below the thresholds at which the Authority believes a merger might pose problems for competition and therefore merit closer examination. Consequently the Authority concludes that the present acquisition does not offend against section 4(1).

Non-Compete Provisions

33. The agreement as notified contained a number of non-compete provisions. These included restrictions on the vendor competing with the business for a period following completion as well as restrictions in relation to industrial property rights. The former type of restriction has been dealt with on a number of occasions by the Authority. The Authority has indicated that in the case of a sale of business it normally regards a restriction on the vendor competing with the business following completion as necessary to secure the complete transfer of the goodwill of the business. It has stated that provided the restriction on the vendor is limited

10. Competition Authority Decision No. 29, *Carrolls Catering/Sutcliffe* (CA/1136/92), 9 September 1993.
11. See *Scully Tyrrell.*

in terms of duration, geographic scope and subject matter to what is necessary to achieve that purpose, then it does not, in the Authority's view offend against section 4(1). The Authority has indicated that it regards a period of two years as sufficient to secure the transfer of goodwill. **3.15**

34. Clause 7(1)(a) as notified restricted the vendor from being engaged in a competing enterprise, from transacting business with any former customers through a competing enterprise and from soliciting orders from former customers for any competing enterprise for a period of 3 years from completion. The duration of this restriction went beyond what was necessary to secure the transfer of the goodwill of the business as the Authority does not believe that a restriction of more than 2 years was justified in this instance. In this context it is relevant that Spring Grove is already active in the relevant markets and that the combined business would operate under the Spring Grove name. The Authority concluded that clause 7(1)(a) as notified offended against section 4(1).

35. The duration of the restriction on being engaged in a competing enterprise has now been reduced to 2 years by an amending agreement submitted to the Authority and no longer offends against section 4(1). The restriction on doing business with or soliciting customers (now clause 7.1(b))is now limited to those firms or individuals who were customers at or about the date of completion as opposed to those who were customers at any time during the 12 months preceding completion. The parties argued strongly, however, that a period of three years from completion was justified for this restriction as a significant proportion of Conkenner's customer contracts would not come up for renewal for more than two years and BET would be free to approach such customers knowing that their contracts were due to expire. By letters dated 6 July and 23 September 1993, the parties indicated their intention to amend the clause so that the three year restriction on the vendor preventing it from transacting business with persons who were customers at or about the time of the agreement only applied 'where such transaction or dealing arises directly or indirectly as a consequence of any canvassing or solicitation of orders. . .'. Canvassing or soliciting orders is defined as including '. . . contacting customers directly or indirectly with a view to informing customers that BET or any of its subsidiaries is operating/doing business in the Republic of Ireland or with a view to securing business from them'. The Authority remains of the view that a restriction of 2 years on a vendor competing with a business which he has sold is normally adequate to secure the complete transfer of the goodwill and provide sufficient protection to the purchaser. However, the Authority considers that a three year restriction on soliciting former customers may be necessary in this case. Therefore, clause 7(1)(c), as amended, does not, in the Authority's opinion, offend against section 4(1).

36. Clause 7(1)(c)[12] restricts the vendor and BET from being engaged in a competing enterprise, from transacting business with any former customers through a competing enterprise and from soliciting orders from former customers for any competing enterprise for a period of 10 years, using any of the industrial property rights of the business. Clause 7(2) provides that the vendor and BET will not licence or permit the use by any competing enterprise of any of the industrial property rights for a period of 10 years from completion. The Authority has accepted in previous decisions that a restriction of unlimited duration on the vendor of a business using any of the trade names associated with the business is necessary to prevent the vendor from representing itself as being associated with the business.[13] In the Authority's view this restriction would not prevent the vendor re entering the market or markets involved following the expiry of a legitimate non-competition clause on the same basis as any other new entrant. Consequently it has neither the object or effect of preventing, restricting or distorting competition and does not offend against section 4(1).

37. Clause 7(3) provides that, for a period of 3 years, neither the vendor nor BET will knowingly solicit or entice away any supplier to the business, without the purchaser's prior

12. This was clause 7(1)(b) in the original agreement.
13. Competition Authority Decision No. 8, ACT/Kindle (CA/9/91), 4 September 1992.

3.15 written agreement, if the effect of such a move would be to reduce the supplier's supply of goods and/or services to the business. This provision does not, in the Authority's view prevent the vendor or BET doing business with such suppliers or from re-entering the market once a legitimate non-competition clause has expired and hence does not offend against section 4(1).

38. Clause 7(4), as notified, restricted the vendor and BET soliciting or enticing away from any group company any manager or supervisor employed by the business upon completion for a period of 3 years. The Authority has already accepted in a number of decisions that a restriction on a vendor soliciting former employees to take up employment with it may be necessary to secure the transfer of the goodwill of the business being sold. It has previously accepted a restriction of 3 years in such clauses were necessary in certain decisions.[14] The Authority has already indicated in para 35 that it considers a period of 2 years sufficient to secure the transfer of goodwill in this instance. Consequently clause 7(4), as notified, offended against section 4(1). As it has now been amended so as to reduce the duration of this restriction to two years, the Authority considers that it no longer offends against section 4(1).

39. Clause 7(5) is a restriction on the vendor and BET using or revealing to anyone any confidential information relating to the business being sold. While it refers to trade secrets and processes, the Authority does not believe that any 'technical know-how' is covered by this provision but that it simply relates to confidential business information. The Authority has stated in previous decisions that such restrictions are acceptable provided it is not intended that they be used to prevent the vendor re-entering the relevant market once a legitimate non-competition clause has expired.[15] Clause 7(5), as notified, included no such provision and, in the Authority's opinion, it offended against section 4(1). Clause 7(5) as amended, however, does not offend against section 4(1).

40. Clause 5 provides that, following an initial period designed to afford the purchaser the opportunity to remove the name and logos of the business from its vehicles, staff uniforms etc., the purchaser will not use any of the vendor's industrial property rights. Such rights are defined to include the trade marks, logos and other marks which were the property of Conkenner. The Authority does not believe that this restriction is designed to or will have the effect of impairing the purchaser's ability to compete in the relevant markets since the purchaser is already well established in those markets. The European Court of Justice has indicated that an agreement not to market goods under a trademark infringes Article 85(1) if the purpose is to secure market protection.[16] In Penneys[17] the Commission granted a negative clearance to an agreement which involved one party agreeing not to make use of a disputed trade mark for 5 years, in a situation where the party restrained was already carrying on business successfully under other names. This case involved a dispute concerning trade marks and the Commission accepted that the agreement was the least restrictive solution to a genuine dispute. In the Authority's view clause 5 does not offend against section 4(1).

The Decision

41. The agreement between Spring Grove Ireland Ltd and Initial Services (International) Ltd and BET plc for the sale of the entire issued share capital of Conkenner Ltd is an agreement between undertakings since the parties to the agreement are undertakings.

42. In the Authority's opinion, the sale of the business of Conkenner Ltd does not have the object or effect of preventing, restricting or distorting competition within the State or any part of the State and does not offend against section 4(1). The restrictions contained in clause 5 and in clause 7, as amended by a Supplemental Agreement, do not offend against section 4(1) of the Competition Act.

14. [Editor: This is blank in original decision issued by CA]
15. See Budget Travel.
16. *BAT v. EC Commission* [1985] ECR 365.
17. 0J L60/19, . . 78.

The Certificate 3.15

43. The Competition Authority has issued the following certificate:

> The Competition Authority certifies that in its opinion, on the basis of the facts in its possession, the agreement of 27 November 1992 between Spring Grove Ireland Ltd, P&O Services Group Ltd, Initial Services (International) Ltd and BET plc for the acquisition of the entire issued share capital of Conkenner Ltd by Spring Grove, (Notification No. CA/1135/92), notified on 30 December 1992 under section 7 as amended by a Supplemental Agreement, does not offend against section 4(1) of the Competition Act 1991.

For the Competition Authority

Patrick M. Lyons
Chairman

18 November 1993

Competition Authority Decision No. 285, Irish Distillers Group plc/Cooley Distillery plc: 25 February 1994, Notification No. CA/62/93 3.16

Share acquisition agreement – Definition of relevant product and geographic market – Review of decisions concerning mergers – Whether 'failing firm defence doctrine' applies – Whether object or effect prevents, restricts or distorts competition – Disjunctive reading of 'object or effect' – Refusal to issue a certificate – Unsatisfactory nature of a licence for a merger – Article 85(1) of the Treaty of Rome – Competition Act 1991 (No. 24) sections 3, 4 and 7

Facts: On 14 October 1993 notification was made to the Authority with a request for a certificate under section 4(4) of the Competition Act 1991 or, failing that, a licence under section 4(2) in respect of a letter of agreement dated 5 October 1993 whereby Irish Distillers Group plc ('IDG') agreed to purchase the entire share capital of Cooley Distillery plc ('Cooley'). IDG which is a wholly owned subsidiary of Pernod Ricard SA produces and distributes several brands of Irish whiskey. Cooley was incorporated in 1987 and developed a distillery with finance raised under the business expansion scheme.

In 1992 IDG had an annual turnover of IR£302m. and a turnover within the State of IR£200m. IDG itself was formed by the amalgamation of three Irish distilleries and a subsequent distillery in the North of Ireland between 1972 and 1974. IDG was acquired by Pernod Ricard in 1988.

Cooley acquired its first alcohol plant in 1987 and acquired other distilleries between 1989 and 1990. Cooley launched its first brand of whiskey in September 1992 under the 'Tyrconnell' brand name. Distilling closed down in early 1993 due to

3.16 financial problems but at that stage 5.8 million litres of whiskey had been distilled and warehoused.

Submissions: Both IDG and Cooley submitted:

(1) The share acquisition had no actual or potential adverse effect on competition because Cooley's absence from the relevant market would be insignificant.

(2) Cooley was unlikely to become a competitor within the foreseeable future and no increase in market concentration would occur as a result of the agreement.

(3) If Cooley was left to suffer its financial difficulties sub standard whiskey stocks would flood the market and would have an adverse effect on IDG.

The Authority referred to a submission made on behalf of employees of Cooley who argued against the monopoly in Irish whiskey which would be created as a result of the takeover. The submission on behalf of employees concluded that IDG's participation in the share acquisition was to eliminate competition in the market for Irish whiskey. Two Irish residents, a German company and two US parties made similar submissions to the Authority. Paragraphs 46 to 51 of the decision indicate the Authority's review of media attention to the proposed acquisition.

A statement of objections was issued on 2 December 1993 and at an oral hearing held between 24 and 26 January 1994 IDG and Cooley disputed the definition of the relevant market made by the Authority. The parties also argued against the proposition that Cooley was an actual or potential competitor of IDG.

Decided by the Authority: In refusing to issue a certificate or to grant a licence:

(1) The agreements between IDG and the shareholders of Cooley constituted an agreement between undertakings.

(2) The fact that the proposed merger was below the threshold for the control of mergers under separate legislation did not raise a presumption that the proposed merger was not anti-competitive.

(3) The relevant market is primarily that for Irish whiskey within the State despite the implications for the broader whiskey and white spirits market in the State and abroad.

(4) The arrangement will have an impact on competition because of the significant impediments to entry in the relevant market and because the elimination of a new entrant does have an impact on competition in a market.

(5) Cooley is clearly a potential competitor and there is a reasonable prospect that an overseas drinks producer would acquire Cooley.

(6) The 'failing firm' defence as outlined by the US Department of Justice Merger Guidelines 1984 is not satisfied because it was not established to the satisfaction of the Authority that another party would purchase Cooley at a price in excess of the liquidation value. The US Department of Justice Merger Guidelines describes the main features of the 'failing firm defence' as follows:

> The failing firm defence is a long established, but ambiguous, doctrine under which an anti-competitive merger may be allowed because one of the merging firms is 'failing'. Because the defence can immunize significantly anti-competitive mergers, the Department will construe its elements strictly.

The Department is unlikely to challenge an anti- competitive merger in which one of the merging firms is allegedly failing when: (1) the allegedly failing firm probably would be unable to meet its financial obligations in the near future; (2) it would probably not be able to reorganise successfully under chapter 11 of the Bankruptcy Act; and (3) it has made unsuccessful good faith efforts to elicit reasonable alternative offers of acquisition of the failing firm that would both keep it in the market and pose a less severe danger to competition than does the proposed merger.' **3.16**

(7) 'Object or effect' referred to in Article 85(1) of the Treaty of Rome is to be read disjunctively according to Keane J in the Mars/HB decision. The agreement nevertheless has the effect and object of preventing restricting and distorting competition.

(8) Despite the viewpoint that a licence is not satisfactory for a merger the Authority is obliged to assess the application for a licence according to the criteria set out in section 4(2) of the Competition Act. The present arrangements do not contribute to improving the production of goods or the provision of services or to promoting technical or economic progress. The arrangements will not produce any benefits which can be shared with consumers and the arrangements will afford IDG the possibility of eliminating competition in respect of a substantial part of the products in question.

Cases, Decisions and Books referred to:

Aerospatiale-Alenia/de Havilland [1991] OJC 334/42; [1992] 4 CMLR-M2
Masterfoods Ltd T/A Mars Ireland v. HB Ice Cream [1993] ILRM 145 **8.2.2**
European Commission Notice on Agreements of Minor Importance — OJ C 231 12.9.86, p.2
EC Commission Decision; Bell & Sons Ltd – OJ L 235/15, 26.8.78 [1978] 3 CMLR 298
EC Commission Decision; Whiskey & Gin [1985] L369/19 – 13.12.85. [1986] 2 CMLR 664
Competition Authority Decision No. 1 Nallen/O'Toole **3.3**
Competition Authority Decision No. 6 Woodchester Bank Ltd./UDT Bank Ltd. **3.5**
Competition Authority Decision No. 12 Scully Tyrrell & Co./Edberg Ltd. **3.10**
Scherer & Ross [1990] 'Industrial market structure and economic performance', 3rd edition Houghton Mifflin p.186
Werden [1992] 'Four suggestions on market delineation', anti-trust bulletin, vol. XXXVII, no. 1, p. 112

Competition Authority Decision of 25 February 1994 relating to a proceeding under section 4 of the Competition Act 1991
Notification No. CA/62/93 — Irish Distillers Group plc/Cooley Distillery plc.

Introduction

1. An arrangement involving a letter of agreement dated 5 October 1993, between Irish Distillers Group plc (IDG) and Cooley Distillery plc (Cooley), whereby IDG agreed to make an offer for the whole of the existing share capltal of Cooley subject to certain conditions, was notified to the Competition Authority on 14 October 1993. The arrangement would have had the ultimate effect of IDG acquiring the assets and property, including the goodwill, of Cooley. The notification requested a certificate, or in the event of a refusal by the Authority to grant a certificate, a licence.

2. The Authority issued a Statement of Objections to the parties on 2 December 1993 indicating the reasons why, in its opinion, the notified arrangement offended against section 4(1) of the Competition Act and did not satisfy the requirements for the grant of a licence set out in section 4(2). Both IDG and Cooley replied disputing a number of the points made in the Authority's Statement of Objections. An oral hearing was held on 24-26 January 1994 which

3.16 was attended by representatives of both IDG and Cooley. The Authority refused a request by a third party to attend the hearing.

The Facts

(a) *The Subject of the Notifications*

3. The notification relates to an agreement, in the form of a letter of agreement dated 5 October 1993, between IDG and Cooley, whereby IDG agreed to make an offer for the whole of the existing share capital of Cooley, subject to obtaining valid acceptances for shares representing more than 50% of such issued share capital and to certain other conditions. The letter of agreement was 'agreed and accepted for and on behalf of Cooley Distillery plc' by Dr John Teeling and Messrs. Donal Kinsella, Paul Power and Lee Mallaghan, being directors and shareholders of Cooley. A share offer document was issued to all Cooley shareholders on 5 November 1993. It states that:

> The Boards of Cooley and IDG have reached agreement on the terms of a recommended Offer to be made by IBI Corporate Finance on behalf of IDG for all of the Issued Share Capital of Cooley.

(b) *The Parties*

4. IDG is a wholly owned subsidiary of Pernod Ricard S.A. IDG is comprised of companies which are engaged, *inter alia*, in the distilling and sale of whiskey and other spirits, and in the distribution of spirits, non-alcoholic beverages. It also has subsidiaries in other businesses including an annual turnover of £302m in the year ended December 1992 with pre-tax profits of £30.3m. Its turnover within the State was £200m. IDG produces and distributes several brands of Irish and whiskey including Bushmills, Jameson, Powers, Paddy and Middleton Reserve. Its turnover from distilling and agency activities in 1992 was £139. 7m. It is the major producer of Irish whiskey. Indeed, prior to the advent of Cooley, IDG was the only producer of Irish whiskey for many years. IDG which was for formed in 1966 was initially made up of Power's, Jameson and Cork Distilleries. IDG acquired a minority stake in Bushmills Distillery in Northern Ireland in 1972. Bushmills became a fully owned subsidiary in 1974. IDG operates a distillery at Midleton in County Cork which distils whiskey as well as grain neutral spirit for gin, vodka and other alcoholic beverages. It operates a second distillery at Bushmills in Northern Ireland where malt whiskey is distilled.

5. IDG was acquired by the French drinks producer Pernod Ricard in 1988. Pernod Ricard was formed in 1975 as a result of the merger of France's two largest anise-based spirits producers. The group includes fifty companies in the spirits, wines and non-alcoholic beverages and products sectors. In addition to IDG, Pernod-Ricard's wholly owned subsidiaries include three Scotch whisky producers and a US based distiller. These subsidiaries produce and market whisky under the Clan Campbell, White Heather, Aberlour and Bourbon Wild Turkey labels. The group also includes amongst its brands Karinskaya vodka along with Epsom and BlackJack gins. In addition it holds concession rights in respect of Cutty Sark whisky, Stolichnaya vodka and Gilbey's gin.

6. IDG owns a minority 33.3% stake in Edward Dillon, a firm engaged, *inter alia*, in the importing and distribution of alcoholic drinks. In addition to distributing IDG products under the Bushmills brand name, Dillons distribute five scotch whisky brands and two US whiskey brands. They also distribute Zamoyski vodka and Gordon's and Tanqueray gins.

7. Cooley was incorporated on 30 September 1987 and acquired the alcohol plant owned by Ceimici Teo at Cooley, Co. Louth in November of that year. Since then it has operated a distillery at the plant producing whiskey. It also acquired the plant and certain business assets of Adam Miller & Company Ltd. and in 1989 purchased and partly refurbished the John Locke distillery premises at Kilbeggan Co. Westmeath. A pot still malt whiskey distillery was opened

in 1989 and a column grain distillery came on stream in mid 1990. The development of the 3.16
Cooley distillery was in large part financed by the establishment of associate companies which raised equity finance under the Business Expansion Scheme (the BES Companies).

8. In all, seven companies were launched to raise equity finance under the BES scheme for the Cooley operation. The first of these, Whiskey Manufacturing plc, was set up in March 1989 and raised £2.451m under the BES. Kilbeggan Whiskey plc raised a further £1m while the remaining five companies, (Inishowen Distilleries plc; Locke's Distillery plc; Tyrconnell Distillery plc; Brosna Whiskey plc; and Carlingford Whiskey plc), raised a further £2.496m. Essentially Cooley sold whiskey to such firms and they stored it until maturation. After a period of five years the BES companies were to sell the matured whiskey back to Cooley and distribute the proceeds to investors. Cooley has an option to purchase such whiskey owned by the BES companies. If the option is not exercised by Cooley, then the BES companies can call on Cooley to buy the whiskey or they can sell it to any third party. Another company called Riverstown Animal Feeds plc was also established under the BES scheme. Cooley leased certain equipment to Riverstown and agreed to sell certain by-products to it, which it used to produce animal feeds. The funding raised by such companies under the BES scheme effectively provided the initial source of working capital for Cooley to produce and mature its whiskey. Changes introduced to the BES regulations in 1991 prevented Cooley and the BES companies from raising further funds from this source. As a result both Cooley and the BES companies had to rely on bank borrowings for their ongoing working capital requirements.

9. Cooley was established to produce Irish whiskey. While it also imports alcohol which it blends to vodka, gin and rum and has sold whiskey on a bulk basis, its main business is the distilling of whiskey for sale as Irish whiskey. Given the requirement to mature the product for a number of years before it can be sold as Irish whiskey, only a limited amount of Cooley Irish whiskey has come onto the market to date. Cooley's first branded whiskey was launched in September 1992 under the Tyrconnell brand name at a price of £15.50 per bottle.[1] It subsequently introduced two brands of single malt whiskey on selected markets in the early part of 1993. Its 1992 Annual Report stated that its blended whiskies were to begin entering the market in the Autumn of 1993. It also sold some of its whiskey in bulk to IDG and to overseas producers for blending with other whiskey. The distilling operations were closed down in early 1993 due to the company's financial problems. At that stage 5.8m litres of whiskey had been distilled and warehoused.[2]

Table 1: Breakdown of Cooley Fixed Assets £m
as at 31 December 1992.

Intangible Assets		0.09
Tangible Assets		
Land and Buildings	0.671	
Plant and Equipment	2.807	
Office Equipment	0.017	
Motor Vehicles	0.005	
		3.50
Financial Assets		0.04
Total Fixed Assets		3.63

Source: Cooley Distillery plc Annual Report 1992.

1. Licensing World, 15 August 1993.

3.16 10. Cooley's annual report for 1992 gives its turnover for that year as £3.6m on which it incurred operating losses of £71,000. The domestic market accounted for 70% of total turnover. Total losses up to December 1992 were £695,000. The accounts valued Cooley's fixed assets as at 31 December 1992 at £3.6m. (See Table 1). In addition stocks and debtors amounted to a further £690,000.

Table 2: % Distribution of Cooley's Case Sale[3]

	Tyrconnell	Non-Whiskey
Dunnes Stores	[	
Quinnsworth		
Kelly's		
Leyden's		
McCambridge		
Export		
Others		]

11. A breakdown of Cooley's sales is given in Table 2. This indicates that more than one third of its sales of Tyrconnell whiskey went to export markets. All of its non whiskey products were sold on the domestic market. Its principal customers for such products included some of the major multiple and cash and carry groups.

The Product and the Market

12. IDG and Cooley are both engaged in the distilling of alcoholic drinks, notably Irish whiskey and certain other spirits including gin and vodka.[4] Whiskey is sold both as a branded product after bottling by the producer and as a bulk product. The bottled product is distributed to retail outlets in Ireland and overseas and is also sold to licensed premises for resale and consumption on such premises. Whiskey producers also buy and sell product between themselves in bulk form. Such product is blended with other whiskey as part of the production process before bottllng.

13. The definition of the relevant market is particularly important in this instance. In this respect the Authority notes the views of the EC Commission which has stated that:

> A relevant product market comprises in particular all those products which are regarded as interchangeable or substitutable by the consumer, by reason of the products' characteristics, their prices and their intended use

in situations ranging from application of the merger control Regulation to the Notice on Agreements of Minor Importance.[5] The Authority also notes the views expressed by the US Supreme Court on the issue of market definition in Times Picayune where it stated that:

2. This information is contained in the Share Offer document.
3. In the published version of the decision certain information, indicated by [ ], is omitted on the grounds of commercial confidentiality.
4. Strictly speaking Cooley does not distill any spirits other than whiskey; as pointed out, it imports alcohol which it blends to produce vodka, gin and rum.
5. See, for example, Commission decision of 2 October 1991 declaring the incompatibility with the common market of a concentration — Aerospatiale — Alenia/de Havilland (OJ L334, 5.12.91, p.44) and Commission Notice on agreements of minor importance which do not fall under Article 85(1) of the Treaty, (OJ C231, 12 September 1986, p. 2).

> For every product substitutes exist, but a relevant market cannot meaningfully encompass that infinite range, the circle must be drawn narrowly to exclude any other products to which, within reasonable variations in price, only a limited number of buyers will turn.[6] **3.16**

14. Some additional insights into the question of market definition are provided by the US Department of Justice merger guidelines which include guidelines on defining the relevant market in order to establish whether a merger is likely to have anti-competitive effects. These provide that:

> Specifically, the Department will begin with each product (narrowly defined) produced or sold by each merging firm and ask what would happen if a hypothetical monopolist of that product imposed a 'small but significant and nontransitory' increase in price.[7] If the price increase would cause so many buyers to shift to other products that a hypothetical monopolist would not find it profitable to impose such an increase in price, then the Department will add to the product group the product that is the next-best substitute for the merging firm's product and ask the same question again. This process will continue until a group of products is identified for which a hypothetical monopolist could profitably impose a 'small but significant and nontransitory' increase in price. The Department generally will consider the relevant product market to be the smallest group of products that satisfies this test.[8]

15. The Irish Whiskey Act 1980 sets out specific requirements which must be satisfied before a product can be described as Irish whiskey. These include, *inter alia*, a requirement that spirits be distilled in the state or in Northern Ireland from a mash of cereals and that they be matured in wooden casks in a warehouse in the State or in Northern Ireland for a period of not less than three years. Thus Irish whiskey is, to some extent, a unique product.

16. In looking at the final product market it might appear to consider all alcoholic drinks as substitutes for one and consequently part of the same market. In practice, however, it appears somewhat unrealistic to regard all alcoholic drinks as perfect substitutes for each other. Personal tastes and preferences appear to be extremely important, and to lead to a fairly clear demarcation within the overall drinks market. Many drinkers will tend inevitably to consume either beer or spirits, or a category within these, or even confine themselves to a specific brand. There is, without doubt, a degree of interchangeability, over time and particularly among newer drinkers, and there is no rigid separation of the market into very small segments. Nevertheless, competition between drinks categories and brands can best be described as imperfectly competitive. Support for such a view is offered by the behaviour of the main drinks suppliers, who are increasingly involved in producing and/or distributing a wide range of drinks and who place heavy emphasis on branding products. The Authority also notes the views expressed by Werden that:

> There is always some competition from other products and consumers can do without. Thus, one should not conclude that a product or area is in the relevant market just because there is some competition or substitutability between it and, products or areas for which one is trying to delineate the relevant market.[9]

17. It seems reasonable to conclude that there are definable and separate markets for beer

6. 345 U.S. 594, 612 (1953).
7. In general the test applied is whether a price increase of 5% could be sustained for 12 months or more.
8. US Department of Justice Merger Guidelines, 1984, section 2.1.
9. G.J. Werden, (1992); 'Four Suggestions on Market Delineation', *Antitrust Bulletin*, Vol. XXXVII No. 1, p. 112.

3.16 and spirits. Within the spirits sector there are somewhat less clearly defined markets for the major categories — whiskey, gin, vodka, rum and brandy. The Authority does not believe that other spirits could be considered to be sufficiently close substitutes for whisk(e)y to be considered part of the same product market. In other words it believes that in the event of a small increase in whisk(e)y prices relative to that of other spirits, there would be a very limited shift in consumption away from whisk(e)y to such products. Consequently the Authority does not believe that there is a single spirits market.

18. The Authority believes that in Ireland, although perhaps not elsewhere, Irish whiskey and Scotch whisky may constitute separate markets. Such a view is supported by a number of factors. In the Authority's view a small increase in the price of Irish whiskey would not lead to any significant shift in consumption from Irish to Scotch whisk(e)y. The Authority believes that the entry of a new Irish whiskey producer onto the market would have a far greater impact on the price and level of sales of IDG's products than would the entry of a new brand of imported whisky. It is relevant in this context that a number of media reports on the arrangements have indicated that the entry of Cooley would lead to a fall in Irish whiskey prices. IDG have stated that the market for whiskey in Ireland is highly brand oriented with customers specifying particular brands when buying whiskey. In addition they cited the potential harm which the release of sub-standard Cooley products could have on the image of, and demand for, Irish whiskey. The Authority accepts that any damage arising as a result of such developments would be confined to Irish whiskey and that the demand for Scotch whisky both in Ireland and overseas would not be adversely effected. This point, however, tends to reinforce the view that Irish and Scotch are not part of the same relevant product market. The Authority also notes the EC Commission decision in the case of Bells, a major Scotch whisky producer, where it found that a prohibition on exports affected the structure of competition on the Scotch whisky or non-Scotch whisky market', indicating that Scotch whisky constituted a separate market to other whiskeys.[10] In sum the Authority believes that the notified arrangements will mainly affect the Irish whiskey market, while noting that they may also have implications for the wider whisk(e)y market. As both IDG and Cooley are engaged in producing other spirits, i.e. vodka and gin, the arrangements also have some implications for those markets. The parties in their replies to the Authority's Statement of Objections and in their arguments at the Oral Hearing have strongly disputed the Authority's definition of the market. These points are returned to below.

19. The Authority also believes that there is a bulk whisk(e)y market which can be distinguished from the final product market. In consldering the present notification the Authority is concerned primarlly with the final product market for reasons which are outlined, below. Various products are sold from time to time in the bulk market. These include new fillings of malt (pot still) and grain whiskey and mature malt and grain whiskey, together with blends of the two. The bulk trade is stated to be driven largely by supply and demand conditions in Scotland and is claimed to be notoriously cyclical. The bulk trade is primarily export orientated. The market is said to have been soft for the past two years with grain whiskey trading at around stg£1.50 per litre of pure alcohol and malt at around stg£3 or less.

20. According to the Checkout Yearbook 1.8m cases of spirits were sold in Ireland in 1991. Details of sales of the main categories of spirits are given in Table 3. Almost 840,000 cases of whisk(e)y were sold in 1991, with Irish whiskey accounting for almost 72% of this total. IDG accounted for 100% of the sales of Irish whiskey in both years. Imported produce accounted for 28.4% of whisk(e)y sales in 1991, down slightly on the previous year. Scotch whiskies are the main imports. Checkout reported that Scotch whisky had continued to decline during the past year, while noting that the Scotch sector was increasingly splintered, with Teachers being the leading brand. The only whiskeys sold at that time were those produced by IDG. In addition to Scotch there were also some imports of whiskey from the US and Canada, with brands such

10. OJ L235/17; 26 August 1978, p. 17.

as Southern Comfort, distributed by Dillons, a company partly owned by IDG, reported to be growing in popularity. The Checkout yearbook also reported that Cork' Dry Gin from Irish Distillers was the market leader in the Gin sector. Gordon's Gin which is distributed by Dillons was reported to be showing strong growth. Smirnoff which is distributed by Gilbey's was reported to have a 70 share of vodka sales. 3.16

Table 3: Sales of Selected Spirits in Ireland (Cases)

1992*	1991	1990
Home Produced		
Whiskey	601,630	589,127
Gin	123,982	128,637
Vodka	396,956	392,882
Imported		
Whisky	238,586	241,223
Brandy	214,255	212,424
Rum	98,074	95,822
Vodka	28,951	28,852

Source: Checkout Yearbook 1993.

Note: Home produced whiskey figures include Bushmills

21. Table 4 provides some more recent figures on market share provided by IDG. The figures are broadly consistent with those given in Table 3, although they suggest that IDG's share of the whiskey and gin markets is slightly higher than the Checkout figures indicate. Cooley's whiskey sales to date have been quite small and its share of the Irish whiskey market is slight. IDG also indicated that it had 76% of the market for all whisk(e)ys, i.e. Irish and others, with Cooley having a negligible market share. Most of the remaining 24% is accounted for by various Scotch whisky producers, with US and Canadian brands having a relatively small market share. IDG accounted for over 72% of sales of gin in the Irish market. IDG claimed that its products accounted for almost 47% of total sales of spirits while Cooley accounted for less than 1%.

Table 4: % Market Shares

	IDG	Cooley
Irish whiskey	99.7	0.3
All Whisk(e)y	76.0	0.2
Gin	72.2	0.4
Vodka	26.5	1.4
Others	10.0	0.3
All Spirits	46.9	0.6

Note: The Cooley figures may be slightly understated as they refer only to the first nine months of the year.

The Arrangements

22. The notification relates to an agreement, in the form of a letter of agreement dated 5

**Editor's note*: The positioning of the years which is contained in this text copies the original but there appears to be an error.

3.16 October 1993, between IDG and Cooley, whereby IDG agreed to make an offer for the whole of the existing share capital of Cooley subject to obtaining valid acceptances for shares representing more than 50% of the whole of the issued share capital of Cooley. The letter of agreement was agreed and accepted for and on behalf of Cooley by Dr John Teeling and Messrs. Donal Kinsella, Paul Power and Lee Mallaghan, being directors and shareholders of Cooley.

23. The letter also set out a number of conditions which would have to be met prior to making the offer. These included, *inter alia*, requirements:

> (i) to execute new trading agreements between Cooley and each of Whiskey Manufacturing plc, Kilbeggan Whiskey plc, Lockes Distillery plc, Carlingford Whiskey plc, Inishowen Distilleries plc, Brosna Whiskey plc and Tyrconnell Distillery plc (the 'BES Companies') in terms acceptable to IDG, Cooley and the relevant BES company and to change the trading status of Riverstown Animal Feeds plc ('Riverstown') in terms acceptable to IDG, Cooley and Riverstown;
> (ii) not to contravene the Irish Whiskey Act in relation to the maintenance/maturation of the whiskey in the possession or under the control of Cooley;
> (iii) that Cooley and IDG enter into an Inventory Purchase Agreement in terms acceptable to both parties which will provide for the purchase of whiskey by IDG from Cooley.

In addition the agreement provides that the offer will be constructed so as to preserve the BES status of all Cooley shareholders.

24. The letter of agreement also states that:

> In signing this Letter of Agreement:
> — Cooley and IDG are agreeing to use all reasonable endeavours to complete the sale as soon as possible; and
> — the Directors of Cooley are agreeing to deal exclusively with IDG prior to and during the Offer period.

The agreement is also stated to be conditional on obtaining the approval of the Competition Authority for the purchase/sale of Cooley. Schedule D of the letter provides that Cooley will continue to supply its existing customer base in the State with:

> (a) cased goods other than whiskey;
> (b) bulk alcohol;
> (c) The Tyrconnell.

It also provides that Cooley will not supply any export orders from the date of the letter and will withdraw all salesmen with the exception of a representative in the North West who is described as an order taker. It goes on to state that Cooley sales levels in November/December are 3-4 times that of October noting that two products, Zara Vodka and Millars Gold were growing rapidly from a small base and that sales of those products to Dunnes and Quinnsworth could be at significant levels in December. Cooley also agree to 'attempt to minimise dry goods stock levels by placing some, although not all, of the bottles, and cutting down packaging and label orders' for Lockes and Kilbeggan.

25. A share offer document was issued to all Cooley shareholders on 5 November 1993. This states that:

> The Boards of Cooley and IDG have reached agreement on the terms of a recommended Offer to be made by IBI Corporate Finance on behalf of IDC for all of the Issued Share Capital of Cooley.

It also states that the directors of Cooley and certain other shareholders have given irrevocable undertakings to accept the offer in respect of 3,079,330 Cooley Shares (representing 58.63 per cent of the issued share capital). These undertakings will become effective over a period of time up to June 1995. The share offer document also provides for the purchase of shares from BES investors to be spread over time so as to allow those investors to retain the shares until the 5 year period necessary for them to qualify for tax relief under the BES scheme has expired. IDG has agreed to honour Cooley's commitments to purchase whiskey currently being stored by the various BES companies. Once such purchases have been completed those companies will be wound up. 3.16

26. The offer document states that in the event of the Offer being declared unconditional in all respects, the following has been agreed:

(i) a thirty five year lease, entered into in 1990 by Cooley, with shareholders' approval, for a warehouse at Tullamore, County Offaly will be terminated on financial terms acceptable to both parties. (The warehouse will be surplus to IDG's requirements for Cooley);
(ii) a quantity of whiskey, the purchase of which was procured in 1992 by the Directors of Cooley from a BES Company in order to facilitate the ongoing financing of Cooley, will be purchased by Cooley in accordance with the original arrangements;
(iii) within five business days thereafter, IDG will procure that Cooley purchases sufficient whiskey from the BES Companies to ensure the release of personal undertaking given to banks by the Directors of Cooley put in place at the time to facilitate the ongoing financing of Cooley; and
(iv) the directors of Cooley will enter into a covenant with IDG not to compete in whiskey manufacturing to the extent permitted by law.

27. The agreements with the BES companies have been amended as follows. There is no further obligation on Cooley to supply raw materials to such firms and, as a result, a fixed price has been agreed for the resale of the existing stocks held by the companies. Cooley has agreed to purchase upfront sufficient stock to discharge the bank indebtedness of the BES companies. The put and call option to purchase the remainder of the stock is now on the basis of fixed prices within the limits of the BES scheme.

28. Under the terms of the arrangement IDG will effectively pay £24.5m to acquire Cooley. This consists of a payment of £9.5m to Cooley shareholders for their shares, equivalent to £1.80 per share. The shares were originally placed in different tranches at prices of 10p, 20p, 35p 105p and 315p between 1987 and 1990. Individuals purchasing the shares would have obtained tax relief at their marginal tax rate under the BES scheme, thereby reducing the effective price of the shares considerably. In addition IDG will pay £4m to clear Cooley's outstanding debts to the BES companies and £1.5m to clear its bank debts. It will also pay £450,000 to secure termination of a long term leasing agreement for a warehouse owned by a number of Cooley directors. There are revised trading agreements whereby Cooley, under the control of IDG, will purchase the whiskey stocks held by the BES companies at a total cost of £9m. The total cost to IDG will be £24.5m which compares with IDG's 1992 pre-tax profits of £30.3m. The arrangements also provided that, in the event of the agreement not proceeding, IDG would purchase whiskey to the value of £600,000 from Cooley between October and December 1993. There have been some further purchases since then.

Submissions of the Parties

29. The parties stated that they were strongly of the view that the Agreement to purchase a majority interest in Cooley did not give rise to any restriction or distortion of competition in the State or in any part of the State. They argued that there was no actual or potential adverse effect on competition arising, either directly or indirectly, from the acquisition initially of a

3.16 majority stake in Cooley, or the eventual acquisition of the remaining interests in Cooley, for the purpose of achieving the objectives of the transaction from IDG's standpoint. They argued that the figures on market share indicated that any effect on competition in the relevant markets due to Cooley's absence would be insignificant. They have claimed that Cooley's sales in Ireland to date have been insignificant and that it had no brands currently capable of competing in the market. They also indicated that the market for whiskey in Ireland was very much brand oriented and that customers specified particular brands when buying whiskey. The main competitors to IDG in the whiskey market in Ireland were stated to be international brands, mainly from Scotland but also from the USA and Canada.

30. The parties also submitted that the acquisition of Cooley would not increase the degree of market concentration to any significant extent and that any merger which did not increase concentration significantly or result in a concentrated market did not offend against section 4(1) of the Competition Act. They also argued that the arrangements would not either directly or indirectly result in

— fixing purchase or selling prices or any other trading terms;
— limiting or controlling production (given the absence therein of Cooley), markets, technical development or investment;
— sharing markets or sources of supply;
— the application of dissimilar conditions to equivalent transactions with other trading parties thereby placing them at a competitive disadvantage;
— making the conclusion of contracts subject to the acceptance by other parties of supplementary obligations which by their nature or according to commercial usage have no connection with the subject of such contracts.

It was also submitted that the very serious nature of Cooley's financial position established that they were not a competitor and were unlikely to become a competitor within the foreseeable future. Consequently it was argued that there would not be any diminution of competition in the market.

31. The parties argued that Cooley was in financial difficulties and that it had been for sale at various stages since 1991. They submitted a number of articles from various newspapers in support of these claims. They submitted that the working capital requirements for maturing whiskey stocks were particularly onerous. Although Cooley had made extensive use of the BES scheme to finance its operations, changes in the legislation had forced it to incur substantial borrowings and its ability to obtain additional funding was severely constrained. It was argued that to obtain markets and contracts for its new brands Cooley would have required considerable additional financial resources. In this context Dr Teeling is reported to have stated on a number of occasions that up to £9m would have been needed. Its efforts to find a partner or to secure additional long term funding had not proved successful and, given its obligations to the BES companies, this had encouraged the directors to negotiate the current sale.

32. IDG expressed concern that the financial difficulties besetting Cooley could lead to the disposal of whiskey stocks which could be sub standard and that this would damage the image of Irish whiskey overseas, thereby having an adverse effect on IDG itself. According to IDG:

> IDG is proceeding with the proposed acquisition of Cooley in order to contain the anticipated serious adverse impact on IDG itself, to protect its extensive investment in promotion of Irish Whiskey, its existing stock inventory and the traditional image of Irish whiskey with consumers internationally.

The Authority asked why the scheduled launch of Cooley's blended whiskey had not gone ahead. IDG's response stated that:

Owing to Cooley's pressing financial circumstances the launch of the Locke's brand name was scheduled for the earliest date possible in the latter part of 1993. . . . However the effective launch would have required considerable additional marketing expenditure and the deteriorating financial position of Cooley over the year made the prospects of achieving this remote. The necessary funds did not materialise and in the event agreement was reached with IDG for the purchase of Cooley's shares. **3.16**

33. IDG argued that Cooley, together with the BES companies, had accumulated substantial stocks of whiskey for which no significant market had been developed. They stated that in their view the stock was not suitable for any purpose other than sale as a bulk ingredient product due to the fact that it was not triple distilled. IDG's stated intention was that the Cooley plant should remain closed. The warehouses at Kilbeggan were stated to be surplus to IDG's needs and would be phased out. They indicated that they would respect the existing leasing arrangement for the shop, museum and restaurant facility. The operation of the old distillery visitors unit would be reviewed with the Kilbeggan Preservation and Development Association. IDG also stated its intention to phase out the rented warehouse in Tullamore. In sum the bulk of the Cooley operation, including its distilling plant, would be closed down.

34. IDG stated that it would honour the trading agreements between Cooley and the various BES whiskey manufacturing companies and would do nothing to compromise their BES structure. They also stated that the arrangements would enable Cooley and the BES companies to honour their liabilities to financial institutions.

Views of third parties

35. The Authority received a submission prepared on behalf of some of the employees of Cooley arguing against the grant of a certificate or licence to the agreement. It stated that the takeover would recreate a monopoly. It pointed out that as the Cooley distillery was the only one in Ireland not currently controlled by IDG, any new entrant would have to build a new distillery. The time taken to build such a plant coupled with the requirement that the plant would have to operate for a number of years before any product would be ready for sale meant that it would take at least five years before any new competitor could enter the market. In addition it was suggested that entry costs were high, both because of the need to build a new plant, and because it would take several years from the time production commenced before any sales revenue could be achieved. It was argued therefore that the high level of finance required before any sales could be achieved represented a further barrier to entry.

36. The submission argued that Irish whiskey was a separate and distinct market from Scotch whisky as there was almost no cross elasticity of demand between the two products. In addition it was claimed that IDG would not purchase the company at a price substantially in excess of its book value in order to close it down unless Irish whiskey constituted a separate market. It was also claimed that gin, vodka, rum and other spirits were not substitutes for whiskey.

37. The submission rejected any claim that Cooley products were inferior, pointing out that Cooley's products satisfied all of the requirements of the Irish Whiskey Act. It stated that although the Cooley products were different they were not inferior.

38. The submission rejected the view that Cooley would have ceased operating anyway in the absence of the takeover. It was submitted that Cooley management had succeeded in September 1993 in making an arrangement, subject to final agreement with a named German distributor, to distribute Cooley's products in Germany. In addition it was claimed that similar arrangements had been entered into with an American and a French distributor, while arrangements had also been agreed with a major French supermarket chain to produce a private label whiskey. It stated that the total advance payments of £1.5m which would have been received under such arrangements would have assured Cooley's future. The submission also claimed that Cooley's blended whiskey brand 'Lockes' was scheduled to have been launched

3.16 at the ANUGA drinks fair in the week beginning October 9.

39. Indeed it was claimed that the takeover was motivated by the success of Cooley. It was argued that the shareholders believed that Cooley was worth more to IDG, the existing monopolist, than to anyone else but that IDG would not be prepared to pay a premium for the business unless it was likely to succeed. It was claimed therefore that the shareholders had not had serious discussions with any other buyer or that potential bidders were aware that regardless of the price they offered, IDG would have last refusal. The submission also suggested the possibility that some of the founding shareholders may never have intended to be long-term investors but to sell at the first available opportunity once the five year period for qualification under the BES scheme had been satisfied. It was also claimed that even if the agreement did not succeed, Cooley would suffer damage as a result of the agreement as the company was at a crucial stage in its development.

40. The submission also rejected the IDG claim that the takeover was prompted by a desire to avoid having sub-standard whiskey come on the market, thereby damaging IDG's brand name products. It argued that in the event that Cooley went into receivership, IDG could have bought such products as, presumably, it would have been prepared to offer a higher price else. It also arqued that IDG's brands would not have been harmed by the appearance of other products on the market.

41. The submission concluded that IDG did not wish to see a competitor to its virtual monopoly on the Irish market and that it would have been particularly concerned that, once such a competitor was established, it might be acquired by a major overseas firm which would offer real competition. It was therefore submitted that no certificate should be given. It also argued against the grant of a licence on the basis that the agreement would produce no benefits in terms of production or distribution, that consumers would not benefit and that it would permit IDG to eliminate competition in the market for Irish whiskey.

42. A Mr Denis Buckley wrote to the Authority following a report on the RTE programme 'Marketplace'. Mr Buckley claimed to have secured orders in France for Cooley's products. He also stated that despite his meetings with Dr Teeling and Mr John Harte (the marketing manager of Cooley), his orders had not been passed on to the distillery. Mr Buckley argued that the acquisition would have detrimental long-term effects on the economy and on business development in Ireland.

43. Mr Pat Hogan a director of the Molloy group and general manager of its liquor store outlets also wrote to the Authority. He argued that real competition was needed in the marketing of Irish whiskey on the domestic and world market. He pointed out that all the existing major Irish whiskey brands were marketed by IDG. He claimed that the Cooley brands were known to whiskey aficionados and that Cooley's Tyrconnell brand was on the market and attracting a premium price. In reply to a request for information from the Authority, Mr Hogan indicated that the Molloy Group had been selling Cooley's Tyrconnell whiskey since early 1993 in its off licence outlets. He indicated that Cooley whiskey was available in the major population centres. He stated that as Cooley whiskey products were in their infancy, substantial sales had not been achieved but would guess that they accounted for 1% of the Group's Irish whiskey sales and 0.5% of all its whisk(e)y sales.

44. The Authority was informed by a German company, which claimed to be one of the largest spirits distributors in Germany, of its interest in securing distribution rights in Germany for Cooley whiskey and indicating that it had expressed a willingness to invest in purchasing inventory for many years in advance and in promotion of the products. The Authority also received two submissions from parties in the US. One of these, a distilling company, stated that they believed that a market existed in the US for Cooley whiskey. They stated that they had been negotiating a distribution agreement with Cooley for the US and to purchase quantities of Cooley whiskey. The other submission claimed also that markets existed in the US and that contracts for up to half of Cooley's production capacity could be secured. It also indicated that certain parties in the US had expressed an interest in purchasing the Cooley business in the

early part of 1993 following reports that it was in financial difficulties. It was claimed that the Cooley directors showed no interest in this proposal. 3.16

45. All of the submissions disputed the claim that Cooley's whiskey was in any way an inferior product to those produced by IDG. Reference was made to the views expressed in the RTE programme marketplace by a well known restaurant critic that it was a good whiskey. The Authority was also referred to a review in the Sunday Telegraph of 14 March 1993 by Mr Jim Murray. This article stated, *inter alia*, that:

> However, Cooley has a number of things in its favour. Its single malt is a delicate distillate of some finesse the three-year-old soft and sweet, reminiscent of an eight-year-old Scottish Lowland (though the four-year-old is a bit metallic in the finish).
> The grain whiskey — to go into the John Locke blend which is on the way — is among the most flavoursome and beautifully textured I have tasted. But Cooley's greatest coup is its peated Irish malt, the only new one in living memory, which is a masterpiece — though it is only 18-months old and has that time again to mature before it can legally be added to the malt or blend.

46. The arrangements have also been the subject of considerable media attention. Writing in the Sunday Tribune of 17 October 1993, Mr Frank Fitzgibbon, the paper's business correspondent wrote:

> How can Irish Distillers Group justify spending £22 million on Cooley, a company which has few products worth speaking of and a bleak future? And is Irish Distillers' branding so weak and anonymous that it seriously feared that world famous names like Jameson and Bushmills would be threatened by the temporary appearance of immature whiskey in some third world market?

He went on:

> By agreeing to shell out this extraordinary sum IDG boss Richard Burrows has contributed handsomely to the John Teeling legend, illustrating the latter's ability to extract himself from seemingly terminal positions.

In a report in the Irish Times on October 9 1993 it was stated that:

> This move by Irish Distillers is purely defensive, and its chief executive, Mr Richard Burrows, said that IDG had no plans to keep Cooley trading. He added that 'Cooley has no future once it has met its obligatlons' to the seven whiskey-maturing companies from which Cooley has already agreed to buy matured whiskey.

The report went on to quote Mr Burrows as follows:

> We are cleaning up what has turned into a very nasty situation; Cooley started off with a lot of enthusiasm but has now run out of cash. That could have resulted in immature whiskey coming on to the market and would have damaged the image and credibility of Irish whiskey.
> Cooley has been up for sale for two years but has failed to find a buyer because people were not prepared to put cash into the company and build up a brand from scratch. Once the whiskey stocks have been run down, Cooley has no future, there has been no distilling at the company for the past eight months and we have no plans to recommence distilling. . . . We would have preferred not to have had to spend this money.

3.16 48. Writing in the *Irish Times* on 15 October 1993, Mr John Maher stated that:

> IDG had watched with mounting concern as Cooley's whiskey reached maturity and the distillery prepared to launch its product.

The report indicates that Cooley whiskey might have been expected to retail at about two thirds the price of IDG's brands.

49. A report in the Dundalk Argus dated 15 October 1993 reported that Dr Teeling had visited the Cooley distillery in order to meet with the workforce. Dr Teeling reportedly claimed that he had not realised some of the pitfalls involved in setting up a distillery. Dr Teeling is also reported to have indicated that Cooley had good responses to marketing abroad and that they had very strong contacts in France, Germany and America but that it would take three to four years to get up the necessary level of sales to make it viable. Dr Teeling was also quoted as saying that he had not realised that IDG were planning to close the plant and indicated that while he accepted that it would not be used to produce whiskey he had asked IDG to sell it or lease it for use for other purposes so that jobs would be saved. (This point was subsequently disputed by IDG who stated that they had made it clear to the Cooley directors from an early stage of their discussions that they intended to cease distilling at the Cooley plant.) The paper also reported a spokesperson for the workforce claiming that the only reason why IDG had moved to take over the company was that it was in a position to become viable. It was claimed that a number of major distributors were being lined up including Borco in Germany. The spokesperson is also reported to have claimed that bottling of the Kilbeggan brand for the German market was to have begun the following week and that a distributor in Europe and another in America were willing to put up £1.5m to support the product.

50. The arrangements were also the subject of a report by Ms. Aileen O'Toole in the Sunday Business Post of October 17 1993. This states that:

> Cooley Distillery was finalising agreements with overseas distributors, which would have given the company a cash injection of at least £1.5 million, when Irish Distillers (IDG) announced its bid for the company.

It went on:

> The Sunday Business Post has learned that agreements were close to completion with a large distributor, Borko, which also handles Carolans Irish cream liqueur, to market Cooley brands on the German market. A consignment of 12,000 bottles of whiskey was due to be shipped to Germany to the ANUGA fair last week but was halted because of the IDG bid.
>
> A US company was also at an advanced stage of negotiation about a US distribution deal and talks were underway with a potential French distributor.
>
> Together, these distributors were prepared to commit over £1.5 million to the company which would have helped the company overcome its severe cash crisis.

The Report went on to cite Mr Richard Burrows of IDG as indicating that he was 'not aware' that the company was on the verge of signing various distribution agreements. He is also reported as stating that £1.5m was 'infinitesimal' compared with what the company needed.

51. The report states that Dr Teeling dismissed allegations of collusion with IDG. He is reported to have confirmed that funds of more than £1.5 million would have been made available to Cooley by the overseas distributors but claimed that much more would have been necessary. Dr Teeling was also reported to have indicated that progress was being made with the development of Cooley's brands and that its Locke's brand would have been launched in Ireland by the end of the month if the IDG bid had not happened. He is reported to have claimed

that IDG was aware that the Cooley brands had the potential to 'wreck' its products and could have led to a drop in its whiskey prices of as much as £2 per bottle. Dr Teeling is also reported to have confirmed that there had been several abandoned attempts by IDG to take over the company. He claimed there had been at least two other sets of negotiations but a deal had not been agreed because of the price. He stated that they had started out at £25 million but had ended up with £9.5 million.[11] The report concluded by stating that: 3.16

> Teeling explained that the primary motivation of the board was to protect the 900 shareholders who had invested in the company.
> IDG, on the other hand, had to weigh up the risk of allowing Cooley to launch its whiskeys and depress prices of its own brands.

Subsequent Developments

52. The Authority issued a Statement of Objections to the parties on 2 December 1993. Both IDG and Cooley responded to the Statement of Objections. An oral hearing was held on 24-26 January 1994. The Authority refused a request by a third party to attend the hearing.

53. The parties argued that the notified arrangements lay outside the scope of section 4(1) of the Competition Act. In particular they claimed that what had been notified was not an agreement for the acquisition of Cooley by IDG, but rather was an agreement whereby IDG undertook to make an offer for the Cooley shares provided certain conditions were satisfied. They claimed that any agreement for the acquisition of the Cooley shares was in fact an agreement between IDG and the individual shareholders and that any such agreement had not been notified and was not anyway an agreement between undertakings.

54. Both parties strongly disputed the Authority's view that the relevant market was primarily that for Irish whiskey in Ireland and that for all whisk(e)y in Ireland. It was submitted that the perceptions of the parties themselves was a key factor in determining what the relevant market was. In addition they cited the EU Commission decision in the Distillers case[12] where the relevant market was found to be that for whisk(e)y. The parties, however, disagreed as to the market they were operating in. At the oral hearing Dr Teeling claimed that Cooley saw the market as being the world spirits market, while Mr Burrows (Chief Executive of IDG) stated that IDG regarded the market as being the world whisk(e)y market.

55. Dr Teeling said he had to sell a Scotch' which had a lighter, sweeter taste than traditional Irish whiskey. He went on to state that it appeared that whiskey was becoming known as Scotch, so Cooley wanted to produce a similar product to Scotch. With the help and advice of Burns Stewart and other Scotch manufacturers, including senior Scottish consultants Cooley designed and developed their product. He claimed that the market was becoming a generic Scotch market. Scotches were becoming more and more dominant and it was what people wanted whereas traditional Irish whiskey did not satisfy that demand. He indicated that the position was different in Ireland as it had a traditional market for whiskey going back hundreds of years. In most other markets Scotch was the only whisk(e)y available.

56. Mr Burrows indicated that if IDG were to engage only in the whiskey business, their competitive situation would be seriously damaged. If they reduced their portfolio, wholesalers and others could import products and damage IDG. Economics required white spirit to be sold in the country in which it was produced; it was difficult to make a profit on exports and money was not spent in developing outside sales. White spirits were very successful in Ireland and it was important to be able to offer and supply a range of products to retailers. Consumers had a portfolio of products which they wanted. He stated that IDG did not target white spirit at different consumers. Irish whiskey, gin and vodka were stated to be quite interchangeable between consumers at different times of the day.

11. The latter figure excludes monies to be paid to the BES companies for whiskey stocks.
12. OJ L369/19, 31 December 1985.

3.16 57. IDG also produced a report prepared for them by the Henley Centre in support of their claim that Irish whiskey was not the relevant product market. The Report contained data from a number of market research surveys. It showed that over time there had been a reduction in consumption of brown spirits and a shift to drinking white spirits and wine. In addition it included data which showed that individuals who indicated that they had drunk Irish whiskey during the past month had consumed various other drinks including beer, wine, fruit juice and mineral water. The figures indicated, *inter alia*, that of those who had consumed Irish whiskey in the past month 52% had consumed stout in the past week while 47% had consumed fruit juice and 39% other soft drinks. In contrast only 9% had consumed scotch during the past month while 8% had consumed vodka and 7% gin. The author of the report argued that such figures indicated that Irish whiskey drinkers consumed a wider range of drinks than just Irish whiskey and that all alcoholic drinks should be considered to be part of the market.

58. The Report also included data from a second market research study. This distinguished individuals on the basis of what they drink most often among Irish whiskey, Scotch, other IDG spirits and non IDG spirits. Of those drinking Irish whiskey most often, while 47% had drunk Scotch at some time in the past, only 14% had drunk it in the past 12 months, while 31% reported drinking other IDG spirits and 27% non-IDG spirits during that time. This survey also showed that of those Irish whiskey drinkers who had drunk Scotch at some time over the previous 12 months, 77% had drunk it less often than once a month. Put another way of all those individuals in the survey who cited Irish whiskey as the drink consumed most often, less than 2% had drunk Scotch once a month or more frequently. 78% of those drinking other IDG spirits and 86% drinking non IDG spirits in the past year did so less often than once a month.

59. Cooley claimed in its submission that declining sales of Scotch occurred because its price had risen relative to that of Irish whiskey. At the oral hearing the consultant retained by IDG produced data which showed that the average price per bottle of Irish whiskey in a number of selected supermarket outlets was more than 10% higher than that of Scotch in four out of the past five years. (See Table 5). The figures also showed that the price differential narrowed sharply in 1991 but had since widened significantly in favour of Scotch. Yet IDG stated that Irish whiskey accounted for 66% of off licence whisk(e)y sales and there was no evidence that the adverse price movement since 1991 had resulted ln any significant loss of market share to Scotch. In fact while the price of Irish whiskey in 1993 was 6.1% higher than in 1991, the price of Scotch in 1993 was 1.3% below its 1991 level.[13] IDG stated at the oral hearing that in the UK once the price of Irish whiskey exceeded that of Scotch by more than about 5%-7% sales dried up. In Ireland, however, a price differential of around 10% in the off licence sector appears sustainable.

Table 5: Comparisons of Whisk(e)y Prices

	Irish	Scotch	Price Ratio Irish/Scotch
1989	12.84	11.69	109.8
1990	12.67	11.18	113.3
1991	11.54	11.20	103.0
1992	12.14	10.65	114.0
1993	12.24	11.06	110.7

Notes: The average prices are for a range of Irish and Scotch whisk(e)y brands in 4 multiple supermarket chains.
Source: Report prepared for IDG by The Henley Centre.

13. The figures must be treated with some caution. In particular changes in VAT and bottle size mean

60. Both parties argued that the relevant geographical market was not confined to the State. IDG stated that it sold its whiskey worldwide and that this was the relevant market. Similarly Cooley argued that it could never have concentrated on just selling in Ireland and that the relevant market was the world spirits market. It was also claimed that the advent of the single EU market meant that the State could no longer be considered to be the market. **3.16**

61. The parties then proceeded to argue that Cooley could not be regarded as a potential competitor. They stated that its financial position meant that it was not in a position to compete on the market and that it would not be able to successfully enter the market. It was pointed out that the plant had a production capacity which was relatively large compared to potential sales and that unit costs were higher than those of Scottish distilleries. It was also claimed that the cost of developing and marketing a new international spirits brand could be as high as £50m. Goodbody stockbrokers stated that its corporate finance division had made extensive efforts to find a buyer for Cooley. Beginning in late 1991 it had approached a number of leading drinks companies throughout the world but none had shown much interest. IDG had been among the firms initially approached at that stage. It had indicated its interest in acquiring Cooley but indicated it had subsequently changed its mind when it became fully aware of the level of Cooley's indebtedness.

62. At the oral hearing Mr Burrows stated that he did not view Cooley as a competitor. When it was suggested that Cooley's whiskey stocks were over-valued at £9.5 million, Mr Burrows confirmed that IDG planned to sell them on the bulk market over time. His view was that Scotch whisky prices were falling at present, but it was extremely difficult to project prices in 1995. He admitted that by comparison with comparable Scotch whisky, stocks were over valued. When it was suggested that the total cost of £24.5 million involved in the take over was a lot to pay for a plant which IDG did not want and overvalued stocks, Mr Burrows said IDG was concerned that Cooley would be continuing under capitalised and that the reputation of Irish whiskey sold into key markets at home and abroad could be damaged. Mr Burrows said IDG was concerned about the damage that might be done to it by the appearance of Cooley's products. People who were not familiar with Irish whiskey might taste Cooley product first and be disappointed and this would put them off the image of Irish whiskey for all time. The risk of allowing that to happen outweighed the opportunity of acquiring Cooley. Mr Burrows stated that Cooley had managed to keep going in the past, in spite of being in seemingly impossible situations, and that it could not be ruled out that they would continue in some way for a number of years. He argued, however, that they would not be able to survive on a permanent basis. In the event of Cooley collapsing, the BES companies would be left with the stocks. In such a scenario, Mr Burrows agreed that it would be reasonable to suggest that IDG would be the most likely buyers but indicated that merely acquiring the stocks would not overcome IDG's concerns and that they wanted to acquire the plant also. He stated that they had no need for the distillery but they were buying it so that nobody else could do so.

63. It was argued on behalf of IDG that a firm could only be regarded as a potential competitor if it was likely to be able to enter the market and survive on a permanent basis. It was submitted that Cooley could not survive in the market on a permanent basis given its financial position and that even though it might be able to struggle on for some time, it should not be regarded as a potential competitor. It was also submitted that Cooley could not survive unless it was purchased by a major international drinks company and that it had tried to find such a buyer for over two years but that no one other than IDG had come forward.

64. The parties referred to the report by the Henley Centre. This purported to show that Irish whiskey prices in supermarkets had fallen over the past few years and that such behaviour was not consistent with that of a firm which was sheltered from competition. It was pointed

that the figures do not compare like with like over time. Such statistical problems do not, however, invalidate comparisons of the relative price trend of the two products.

3.16 out to the parties that any fall in prices could be explained by cuts in VAT and by a reduction in bottle size and that when these factors were taken into account the price had in fact risen. The Report also included some estimates of income and own price elasticities for spirits. It argued that these showed that increases in income only resulted in a relatively small increase in consumption of spirits while increases in the price of spirits would result in a proportionately greater decline in sales thereby making it futile for IDG to attempt to raise its prices.

Assessment

(a) *Section 4(1)*

65. Section 4(1) of the Competition Act states that 'all agreements between undertakings, decisions by associations of undertakings and concerted practices which have as their object or effect the prevention, restriction or distortion of competition in trade in any goods or services in the State or in any part of the State are prohibited and void'.

(b) *The Undertakings and the Agreement*

66. Section 3(1) of the Competition Act defines an undertaking as 'a person being an individual, a body corporate or an unincorporated body of persons engaged for gain in the production, supply or distribution of goods or the provision of a service.' The parties to the present agreement are IDG and Cooley. They are both corporate bodies engaged in the provision of goods and services for gain and are therefore undertakings within the meaning of the Act. The notified arrangements therefore constitute an agreement between undertakings.

67. IDG submitted that the agreement they had notified was not an agreement for a merger or takeover. Their submission was that the actual takeover or merger would be effected by the individual agreements between IDG and each shareholder; and that these agreements had, firstly, not been notified, and secondly were not notifiable because the shareholders were not themselves undertakings. The agreement which had been notified had no effect on competition and therefore should be certified.

68. If IDG had in fact done what they submitted they had done, i.e. isolated arrangements peripheral to their merger with no anti-competitive effect, and notified only those, then the Authority would consider that a waste of time, and if deliberate, an abuse of its procedure. However, the agreement, the subject matter of this notification, is the agreement which binds IDG to making the takeover offer, and which specifies the terms on which that offer will be made. The agreement has no other object or effect than that the takeover should result. This was also the parties' view when they made their original notification which makes its case throughout by reference to the effect on competition of the taking over of Cooley. The letter of agreement also refers to the Competition Authority approval of the purchase/sale of Cooley as a condition precedent.

69. It was submitted on behalf of IDG that the existing mergers legislation, using competition as one criterion for permitting or disallowing a merger, and with its lower threshold was a legislative indication that mergers below the threshold were *per se* not anti-competitive. For the sake of clarity, the Authority states that it did not accept this submission. The Authority's consideration of mergers does not begin from a presumption about whether they are anti-competitive or not.

(c) *The Definition of the Market.*

70. As pointed out the parties argued, both in their written response to the Statement of Objections, and in the submissions made at the Oral Hearing, that the relevant market in this instance is not that for Irish whiskey within the State, nor indeed that for all types of whisk(e)y. It was submitted that the market should be defined as being the one in which the parties considered themselves to be competing. The Authority recognises that in some circumstances the perception of undertakings concerning the market in which they are operating may affect

their behaviour. It does not, however, believe that the view of the undertakings involved is the only factor which should be taken into account in defining the relevant market. 3.16

71. The parties in this instance disagreed as to what the relevant market was, IDG arguing that the relevant market was the world whisk(e)y market and Cooley that it was the world spirits market. The Authority rejects the parties' claims that the relevant geographical market is the whole world rather than the State. This claim appears to be based primarily on the fact that IDG exports much of its whiskey output and also on the fact that it would not have been viable for Cooley to sell whiskey only on the Irish market. The fact that the parties are involved in selling their products in a number of different countries does not mean that all of those countries are part of the same market. The fact is that the price of Irish whiskey and indeed other alcoholic drinks differs greatly between different countries. In large part such differences are due to differences in the amount of tax levied on alcoholic drink by the relevant national authorities. Nevertheless such price differentials could not be sustained over a prolonged period if, in fact, there was a single world market. The reality is that there are restrictions on the ability of Irish consumers to import such products from non EU countries thereby partitioning the market. Since 1 January 1994 restrictions on consumers importing alcoholic drink from other EU countries have been greatly reduced. There is no limit, for example, on the amount that individuals may import for their own personal use. Consumers still face other obstacles. In particular they must incur the financial and temporal costs involved in travelling to another country. Such costs are sufficiently high that it would require quite a slzeable price differential to exist before it would be worthwhile for consumers to do so. The one exception in this instance arises with respect to Northern Ireland as the costs involved are much lower. Nevertheless factors such as the time and cost involved in travelling to another country do fragment the market as they allow significant price differentials to persist between different countries. The fact that Jameson whiskey can be purchased in Dublin, Paris, New York and Sydney does not mean that all four cities are part of the same market. Thus the Authority concludes that the relevant geographlc market is the State and not the World.

72. The parties also argued that the relevant product market was wider than that for Irish whiskey. In fact most of the evidence produced by them tended, if anything, to support the view that Irish whiskey was the relevant product market. IDG indicated, for example, that in order to compete it had to produce and market a wide range of different alcoholic drinks. If in fact all spirits were sufficiently close substitutes for one another so that they could be considered to form a single market there would appear to be little need to produce such a range of products. In addition they indicated that the economics of the business largely ruled out the possibility for exporting white spirits, indicating that market conditions in this instance are rather different to those pertaining in the whisk(e)y business.

73. Dr Teeling told the Authority that Cooley was attempting to produce a Scotch type product because this was what consumers in international markets wanted. In terms of its taste and other characteristics Scotch was what consumers in most countries wanted. In contrast relatively little Irish whiskey was consumed and it was seen to be a different product. He also indicated that the position was different in Ireland as it had a traditional market for whiskey going back hundreds of years.

74. The market research data produced by the Henley Centre also purported to show that the market was much broader than that for Irish whiskey alone. This was on the basis of statistics which indicated that individuals who had consumed Irish whiskey in the past month had also consumed a range of other drinks during the past week or month. In the first place the study defined Irish whiskey drinkers as anyone who had consumed Irish whiskey in the past month. By so doing it included individuals who would only occasionally drink Irish whiskey but who would regularly drink something else. It is therefore not surprising that it found many so called 'Irish whiskey drinkers' had also consumed other drinks. Even allowing for this, however, the data showed that only a very small minority of such individuals had consumed other spirits during the previous month. The figures were as follows; Scotch 9%, gin 7%, vodka 8% and

3.16 brandy 10%. In sum the vast majority of 'Irish whiskey drinkers' do not consume other types of spirits or even other types of whisk(e)y.

75. In contrast 52% of 'Irish whiskey drinkers' had consumed stout during the previous week, 47% fruit juice and 39% other soft drinks. The Authority does not believe that two or more products can be regarded as substitutes because they are consumed by the same individuals at different times and it does not therefore believe that fruit juice and other soft drinks are substitutes for Irish whiskey. The figures offer no support for the view that Scotch and other spirits constitute substitutes for Irish whiskey, quite the opposite in fact. Indeed this becomes clearer when one considers the statistics from the second market research study cited in the report which identified those individuals who classified Irish whiskey as the drink they consumed most often. Only 14% of such individuals had drunk Scotch in the past 12 months and less than 2% reported drinking Scotch once a month or more; 31% reported drinking other IDG spirits and 27% non-IDG spirits during that time; 78% of those drinking other IDG spirits and 86% drinking non-IDG spirits in the past year did so less often than once a month.

76. In addition the Henley Centre study indicates that in retail supermarkets the price of Irish whiskey has consistently been 10% or more above that of Scotch (see Table 5 above). It also indicated that since 1991 Irish whiskey prices had risen relative to those of Scotch. Yet there was no indication that this had led to a loss of market share. Indeed one of the parties had claimed that Scotch sales had fallen because its relative price had risen. This again indicates that Scotch is not a close substitute for Irish whiskey. The wholesale price of Irish whiskey was also stated to be 10% higher than that for Scotch, though this is not reflected in pub prices.

77. Finally the Henley Centre study included some estimates of own price elasticities to show that if IDG were to increase its prices this would be more than offset by a reduction in sales. The data, however, related to all spirits. Secondly the estimates were based on annual observations for a period of ten years, whereas a far greater number of observations would generally be required in order to obtain reliable results from such an analysis. In fact the ESRI had carried out such an exercise using data over a much longer timespan.[14] That study found, however, that due to data deficiencies caused by cross border trade in spirits in the early 1980s, the price elasticities for spirits did not make sense. The results in fact indicated a spirits own price elasticity of almost zero. Such results cast serious doubt over the reliability of the results contained in the Henley Centre study.

78. Thus contrary to the claims made by the parties, the evidence indicates that Irish whiskey drinkers do not, by and large consume Scotch or other spirits. Price differentials in off licence outlets do not indicate that Irish and Scotch are perceived as substitutes. Dr Teeling's evidence indicates that, in contrast to other countries where consumers prefer Scotch because of its taste and other characteristics, in Ireland the opposite situation prevails. IDG conceded that it would not be possible to compete in the market by concentrating on whiskey only but that it is necessary to produce a range of different products. In addition on the supply side the economics of the whisk(e)y and white spirits businesses are rather different. Thus on the basis of the evidence submitted by the parties the Authority can see no reason to change its view that the relevant market is primarily that for Irish whiskey within the State. It recognises that the arrangement may also have implications for the broader whisk(e)y market. In addition it believes that the arrangements have effects on the white spirits market since Cooley also sells vodka and gin.

(d) *Applicability of section 4(1)*

79. The Authority has given its views on mergers in a number of previous decisions. In Woodchester it stated that:

14. D. Conniffe and D. McCoy, (1993); 'Alcohol Use in Ireland: Some Economic and Social Implications', ESRI, Research Paper No. 160.

> before a merger can be found to offend against section 4(1) of the Competition Act, it must be shown that it would, or would be likely to, result in an actual diminution of competition in the market concerned. A reduction in the number of competitors or the fact that a merger will result in the merged entity having a larger share of the market than that previously held by either of the merged undertakings individually, are not, of themselves, sufficient to establish that such a diminution of competition has occurred or would be likely to occur.[15] **3.16**

80. The Authority clarified its position further in Scully Tyrrell where it stated that:

> Among the factors which the Authority believes needs to be considered in order to decide whether a merger would result, or would be likely to result in a diminution of competition is the actual level of competition in that market, the degree of market concentration and how it is affected by the merger, the ease with which new competitors may enter the market and the extent to which imports may provide competition to domestic suppliers.[16]

It then went on:

> The Authority believes that it would generally be accepted that a market where the four firm concentration ratio fell below 40 percent is effectively competitive.... Nevertheless the Authority believes that in a highly concentrated market a merger which results in a relatively small increase in the market share of . the larger firms merits closer examination. It follows from this that, if the four firm concentration ratio following a merger is less than 40 percent, the Authority would regard it as unlikely that the merger could prevent, restrict or distort competition and hence offend against section 4(1).[17]

The Authority also indicated that it might use an alternative measure of market concentration, namely the Herfindahl Hirschman Index (HHI) which is used by the US Department of Justice to evaluate mergers.

81. In Scully Tyrrell the Authority found that the data on both the four firm concentration ratio and the HHI suggested that the arrangements merited further examination. Having concluded in Scully Tyrrell that the merger in question did not prevent, restrict or distort competition the Authority stated that:

> The present decision seeks to clarify the Authority's views in this area. In general the Authority believes that a merger *per se* between competitors would not prevent, restrict or distort competition and thereby offend against section 4(1) unless the market is, or will as a result of the merger become, highly concentrated.
> If the market were highly concentrated following the merger the Authority believes that it would be unlikely to prevent, restrict or distort competition where
> —there were no significant impediments preventing new competitors from entering the market, and/or
> —there was little effective competition from overseas suppliers.'[18]

82. The figures given in Tables 3 and 4 indicate that the relevant market in this instance is highly concentrated. IDG accounts for virtually 100% of the Irish whiskey market, for 76% of

15. Competition Authority Decision No. 6, Woodchester Bank Ltd./UDT Bank Ltd, 4 August 1992, para. 78.
16. Competition Authority decision no. 12, Scully Tyrrell & Company/Edberg Ltd, 29 January 1993, para. 52.
17. Para. 54.
18. Para. 65.

3.16 the whisk(e)y market, 72% of gin sales and 46% of all spirits. Given the Authority's views in Scully Tyrrell, such a situation requires a detailed examination.

83. There are no other Irish producers of whiskey apart from IDG and Cooley. The establishment of Cooley was facilitated by the availability of a disused alcohol plant which it was able to acquire at a relatively modest price. The Authority accepts the view that, as the arrangement would bring all the existing distilleries within the State under the control of IDG, the only way for a new entrant to commence producing whiskey in Ireland would be through the construction of a new plant on a greenfield basis. The Authority considers that this would involve substantial costs. Such costs would be considerably higher than those incurred by Cooley. Dr Teeling indicated that, in his view, such an exercise would cost £15m. In addition it accepts that the level of working capital necessary for entry is high due to the long lead time involved between the commencement of production and the availability for sale of the finished product. It believes that the start-up costs represent a significant barrier to entry in this market. It is significant in this respect that, although Cooley was able to raise a considerable amount of the finance required to enter the market, the mechanism it used to do so, namely the BES scheme, has been altered in such a way as to prevent this route being used in future.

84. The Authority also considers that the costs which would be incurred in building a distillery and in holding stocks of whiskey until maturity would constitute sunk costs, in that, if a new producer had to cease its operations, it would be unable to recoup a large part of such costs. Modern economic theories of industrial structure and performance tend to place greater emphasis on the question of whether or not costs are 'sunk', rather than on the absolute level of entry costs, in establishing whether or not such costs are likely to restrict entry. The Authority does not believe that the Irish whiskey market could be considered to be contestable. Consequently the Authority believes that there are significant impediments to entry in the relevant market.

85. The arrangements will, as pointed out lead to the elimination of Cooley from the market. It is true that Cooley's sales of whiskey to date have been relatively small. This is effectively attributable to the long lead time involved between the commencement of production and the availability of the finished product for sale. Cooley is only now an effective new entrant to the market. The Authority rejects the claim that the arrangements will have no impact on competition because Cooley's present level of sales is low. Such an argument is tantamount to a claim that the elimination of a new entrant has no impact on competition in a market. It must therefore be rejected as wrong.

86. As the Authority indicated in Nallen/O'Toole,[19] competition includes potential as well as actual competition. In the Authority's view, Cooley is clearly a potential competitor in the Irish whiskey market. Given Cooley's production capacity it has the potential to capture a significant share of the Irish whiskey market. Dr Teeling indicated that Cooley had hoped to achieve sales of 50,000 cases of whiskey per annum on the domestic market after four years, equivalent to about 8% of Irish whiskey sales in 1992. Undoubtedly the situation is complicated by Cooley's financial difficulties. Nevertheless, it is certain that if the arrangement proceeds any possibility of Cooley becoming a competitor will be eliminated, while the barriers to entry highlighted above make it unlikely that any other new entrant would emerge. In the Authority's view if Cooley were to survive this would certainly enhance competition in the whiskey market. The present arrangements would have the effect of preventing a new competitor (Cooley) entering the market and would thus effectively prevent competition, given the nature of the market. The Authority also believes as already stated that the entry of Cooley would have some effect on Irish whiskey prices and the arrangements therefore would permit prices to be higher than they might otherwise be.

87. IDG has indicated publicly that it intends to close the Cooley distillery and not to produce or market any of its products. Thus the only Irish whiskey producer not controlled by IDG and

19. Competition Authority Decision No. 1, Nallen/O'Toole (Belmullet), 2 April 1992.

ultimately by its parent Pernod-Ricard will be eliminated. IDG has argued that Cooley's financial difficulties mean that it is unlikely to remain in business and therefore should not be regarded as a potential competitor. The Authority accepts that Cooley requires additional finance if it is to continue. Undoubtedly the conclusion of distribution agreements for major overseas markets would provide one means of securing Cooley's future. There was evidence that a number of such agreements were close to finality and a number of overseas firms have indicated to the Authority their interest in concluding such agreements with Cooley. The parties have claimed that such arrangements were not finalised and were anyway inadequate as many more would be needed to provide sufficient revenue for Cooley's survival. The Authority believes that such arrangements would have assisted Cooley in its attempts to survive. **3.16**

88. An alternative would be a sale of the business or a part of it to an overseas drinks producer. While it is true that Cooley has, over the past two years, failed to attract a partner to provide the necessary funds to develop its business, the reality is that Cooley is worth more to IDG than to any other drinks producer. The failure to conclude an agreement may be due to the fact that other parties placed a lower value on Cooley than IDG and they were being asked to pay a price which they regarded as too high. This does not mean that if the present arrangement did not go ahead no other buyer would be found for Cooley and it would inevitably close. Obviously that might happen. Howeyer, in the Authority's opinion, there is a reasonable prospect that an overseas drinks producer would be interested in having an Irish whiskey operation within its portfolio of activities. If IDG were not a potential buyer, there is a distinct possibility of Cooley being acquired by another firm, albeit at a lower price. Indeed the fact that IDG is prepared to pay what appears to be an inflated price to acquire Cooley and its assets and the fact that among the reasons given by its Chief Executive for doing so is to ensure that no one else can acquire the plant, suggests that IDG at least, considers that there is a possibility of Cooley being purchased by someone else. On balance, while the Authority recognises that the survival of Cooley is by no means certain, it remains a distinct possibility and Cooley cannot therefore be dismissed as a potential competitor to IDG. (This point is returned to below).

89. Mergers which have an adverse effect on competition have been permitted under US law under the 'failing firm defence doctrine' in the US since the 1930s.[20] The US Department of Justice Merger Guidelines 1984 outline the main features of the 'failing firm' defence.

> The 'failing firm defense' is a long-established, but ambiguous, doctrine under which an anti-competitive merger may be allowed because one of the merging firms is 'failing'. Because the defense can immunize significantly anticompetitive mergers, the Department will construe its elements strictly.
>
> The Department is unlikely to challenge an anticompetitive merger in which one of the merging firms is allegedly failing when: (1) The allegedly failing firm probably would be unable to meet its financial obligations in the near future; (2) it would probably not be able to reorganize successfully under Chapter 11 of the Bankruptcy Act; and (3) it has made unsuccessful good faith efforts to elicit reasonable alternative offers of acquisition of the failing firm that would both keep it in the market and pose a less severe danger to competition than does the proposed merger.[21]

The guidelines state that the fact that an offer is less than the proposed transaction does not make it unreasonable. Indeed any offer to purchase the assets of the failing firm for a price above the liquidation value of those assets will be regarded as a reasonable alternative offer. It is also necessary to show that, in the absence of the acquisition, the assets of the failing firm would leave the relevant market. Although Cooley has failed to flnd any partner in recent years it is not clear that the assets would not be purchased for a price above the liquidation value but

20. See F.M. Scherer and D. Ross (1990); 'Industrial Market Structure and Economic Performance', 3rd edition, Houghton Mifflin, p. 186.
21. Section 5.1.

3.16 below the price which IDG is prepared to pay. In addition the arrangements will not prevent Cooley's assets leaving the market but rather will ensure that they do so. Thus while the parties submitted that the present arrangements would satisfy the failing firm defence, in the Authority's opinion, they would not do so.

90. There is undoubtedly competition in the whisk(e)y market in Ireland from imports. As noted such products account for almost 24% of that market. At the same time the Authority considers that the level of competition from imports is limited by several factors. The imports are split between several different manufacturers. While some imported brands are produced by major multinational companies, many are produced by smaller firms which would not be in a position to offer strong competition to IDG in the Irish market. The small market share accounted for by individual overseas producers relative to the very large market share held by IDG again suggests that the ability of overseas producers to offer strong competition to IDG is somewhat limited. It is also relevant that some of these competing products are distributed by a firm in which IDG is a minority shareholder.

91. In sum, given the concentrated nature of the market, the absence of any other domestic competitors, the barriers to entry which exist, the fact that other domestic firms are unlikely to enter the market and the limited competition to IDG from overseas producers, the Authority considers that the effect of the notified agreement would be to prevent, restrict or distort competition in the market for Irish whiskey and in the broader whisk(e)y market within the State. Specifically the Authority believes that the arrangements would have the effect of limiting or controlling production and markets contrary to section 4(1)(b) of the Act. It believes, for similar reasons, that the arrangements would have an adverse effect on competition in the market for certain other drinks, e.g. gin, albeit to a lesser extent. The Authority does not believe that the arrangements would have any effect on competition in the bulk whiskey market.

92. Section 4(1) prohibits an agreement which has as its object or effect the prevention, restriction or distortion of competition within the State. In Mars/HB, Keane J made clear that the term object or effect' in Article 85(1) of the Treaty of Rome was to be read disjunctively.[22] Thus, once it is shown that an agreement has as its effect the prevention, restriction or distortion of competition, it offends against section 4(1).

93. IDG has claimed that its decision to purchase Cooley is prompted by the fact that Cooley's adverse financial position could result in inferior Irish whiskey coming onto the market thereby harming the image of its products. Were Cooley to collapse IDG could of course seek to purchase the stocks in question from any receiver that might be appointed. Alternatively it could offer to purchase the whiskey from the BES companies. Both options would appear likely to cost IDG a lot less than the present arrangement.

94. IDG's claim that Cooley's product could harm its own appears to some degree to be based on the fact that Cooley's whiskey is double distilled while IDG's is triple distilled. Most Scotch whiskies are also double distilled. It is not clear that the difference in production methods means that Cooley's product is inferior to that of IDG. It is relevant that the Irish Whiskey Act sets out legal requirements which must be satisfied in order for a product to be described as Irish whiskey. As far as the Authority is aware, Cooley's products comply with the requirements of the Act.

95. The purchase price being paid by IDG of £9.5m for Cooley shares is considerably higher than the book value of Cooley's assets. It is relevant that IDG does not propose to utilise any of these assets but has stated publicly that it intends to close them. Thus the premium being paid by IDG cannot be explained on the basis that the assets are more valuable to it, in use at least, than their stated book value in Cooley's accounts. The Authority notes also that this agreement has been reached just at the point where Cooley's main brand, Locke's, was scheduled to be launched. Despite IDG claims that there was no market for Cooley's products,

22. Masterfoods Ltd trading as *Mars Ireland v. H.B. Ice Cream Ltd*, judgment of 28 May 1992, unreported.

both the staff and others have claimed that distribution agreements for Cooley were close to finality for major markets in Europe and the US, a point which Dr Teeling apparently conceded in a newspaper interview and confirmed at the Oral Hearing. The price at which IDG has agreed to purchase the whiskey currently held by the BES companies appears to be significantly higher than the prevailing price of bulk whiskey, although IDG has stated that this is the only use to which such product can be put. Again it is relevant that the terms of the letter of agreement oblige Cooley to cease supplying export orders. The claims that there was no market for Cooley's products, that the finances necessary to launch its brands were not available and that its products were inferior are in marked contrast to the submissions received by the Authority indicating a considerable degree of interest among overseas buyers in securing distribution rights for such products and the indications that Cooley was close to securing agreements which would have provided it with a sum in excess of £1.5m. **3.16**

96. IDG and Cooley both submitted at the oral hearing that there could not be in their agreement an object or effect to prevent restrict or distort competition unless there was either competition or potential competition to be prevented, restricted or distorted; and they both submitted that the Authority could not correctly find that there was potential competition unless there was evidence before the Authority identifying a specific investor or investors capable of sustaining Cooley not just as a short term proposition but to be a competitor in at least the medium term.

97. For the sake of clarity the Authority is stating its position on this submission. The Authority agrees that, in finding that behaviour has the *effect* of preventing restricting or distorting competition or potential competition, it must see strong evidence of the potential competition which is being affected, i.e. prevented. On the other hand, in finding that behaviour has the *object* of preventing, restricting or distorting competition, the Authority does not consider that it has to be satisfied that, were it not for the behaviour being examined, the potential competition would successfully metamorphose into real and continuing competition. It need only be satisfied that the threat of the potential competition is sufficiently real to form the motivating force in the anti-competitive behaviour.

98. IDG in their written submission and at the oral hearing gave evidence as to what their object was in seeking to take over Cooley. They stated that they were concerned that Cooley would collapse, either now or in the near future. Since it would be unable to meet the contracts to buy back whiskey stocks from the BES companies, the bank creditors would force the BES companies to sell the stocks on the open market. This would be harmful to the image of Irish whiskey, and therefore to IDG brands which incorporated Irish as part of their brand image; therefore, IDG to protect their brand names, needed to control the Cooley stocks.

99. The Authority does not disbelieve that this is an object of the takeover. The Authority considers that the object of protecting the IDG brand names is not objectionable in itself, but does not justify behaviour which is anti-competitive. The object of protecting the image of 'Irish whiskey' as inextricably identified with the style and taste of IDG whiskeys is anti-competitive insofar as it inhibits the emergence of another Irish whiskey producer, producing whiskey in another style. The Authority does not, in any case, believe that the protection of the image of IDG brands is the sole object of the takeover.

100. IDG did not give evidence of where they thought the whiskey stocks would end up but the danger posited could only happen if the buyer of the stocks, instead of using it as bulk whiskey for any non-Irish brand, bottled and sold it as Irish whiskey.

101. The takeover will involve IDG paying of the order of £24.5m in total, which will give them control of the whiskey stocks, the Cooley plant, and the Cooley brand names. IDG have said that they will not use the Cooley plant; that if they wanted to they could not, without huge expenditure, on effluent disposal; and that, although they might sell it, this would only be to a business other than a distiller. IDG do not intend to use the brand names Tyrconnel and Lockes. Under the whiskey option contracts, Cooley or their assignee would have to pay significantly more than the market price for the whiskey stocks. Richard Burrows, presenting IDG's position,

3.16 was asked by the Authority to explain why, if the object was solely to control the whiskey stocks, IDG had chosen to pay a total of £24.5m for plant it would not use, brand names it would not use, and whiskey stocks which they expected would inevitably come on the market at a lower price. He stated that the risk being bought was the risk that Cooley would continue, undercapitalised, and selling whiskeys different in style to IDG brands, into IDG markets, damaging the image of Irish whiskey. Later, but in this context, he stated that this did not mean that he regarded Cooley as a competitor; it could damage IDG but that was by damage to the image of Irish whiskey and IDG brands, not by actually taking away customers. He was asked why IDG did not simply wait and buy the stocks when they, inevitably, came onto the market. He said that IDG also wanted the plant. He agreed that IDG did not need and could not use the plant, but wanted to stop anyone else using it.

102. Schedule D of the Letter of Agreement contains specific restrictions on Cooley's activities from the date of the letter. In particular it provides that Cooley will not supply any export orders from the date of the letter and will withdraw all salesmen with the exception of a representative in the North West who is described as an order taker. The requirement that Cooley withdraw all salesmen with one exception has the effect of preventing or restricting competition within the State since it impedes Cooley from obtaining new orders or new customers for its products. In addition the restriction on supplying any export orders also has the effect of restricting or distorting competition within the State. This is because some level of export sales is essential to the long-term viability of Cooley. By preventing it from exporting its products, this restriction hampers the development of Cooley, thereby limiting its ability to compete in the domestic market.

Applicability of section 4(2)

103. Under section 4(2), the Competition Authority may grant a licence in the case of any agreement which offends against section 4(1) but which, 'having regard to all relevant market conditions, contributes to improving the production of goods or provision of services or to promoting technical or economic progress, while allowing consumers a fair share of the resulting benefit and which does not

(i) impose on the undertakings concerned terms which are not indispensable to the attainment of those objectives;

(ii) afford undertakings the possibility of eliminating competition in respect of a substantial part of the products or services in question.

104. It may be argued that a licence is not very satisfactory for a merger as it can only apply for a limited period of time. Admittedly a licence may be extended but this nevertheless means that the merger is always subject to some degree of uncertainty. The Authority is aware of such viewpoints but points out that a decision on whether or not to grant a licence must be based on an assessment of whether or not the criteria set out in section 4(2) of the Act are satisfied.

105. In the Authority's view the present arrangements will not contribute to improving the production of goods or provision of services or to promoting technical or economic progress. In fact the arrangements will result in a reduction in the production of Irish whiskey. Cooley uses a different process to produce its whiskey compared to IDG, double rather than triple distilling. Without adjudicating on the relative merits of the different processes, the Authority concludes that the introduction of new or alternative methods of production would constitute a form of technical progress which would be prevented by the arrangements. The arrangements will produce no benefits which can be shared with consumers. In fact the arrangements will deny consumers the benefit which they might obtain from the availability of a new source of Irish whiskey. In addition as IDG accounts for almost 100% of Irish whiskey sales and over 76% of all whisk(e)y, the arrangements, in the Authority's view, afford the undertakings the possibility of eliminating competition in respect of a substantial part of the products in question. As all four of the licence criteria must be satisfied before a licence may be granted, a licence cannot be granted in respect of the notified arrangements.

The Decision 3.16

106. IDG and Cooley are undertakings within the meaning of the Competition Act. The letter of agreement dated 5 October 1993, between Irish Distillers Group plc (IDG) and Cooley Distillery plc (Cooley) whereby IDG agreed to make an offer for the whole of the existing share capital of Cooley subject to certain conditions, which would have had the ultimate effect of IDG acquiring the assets and property, including the goodwill of Cooley, is an agreement between undertakings. In the Authority's opinion the notified agreement has both the object and the effect of preventing, restricting or distorting competition in the markets for Irish whiskey, for whisk(e)y generally, and for certain other spirits, within the State and offends against section 4(1) of the Competition Act. It does not meet the requirements for a licence specified in section 4(2). The Authority therefore refuses to issue a certificate or grant a licence in respect of the notified arrangements.

For the Competition Authority

Patrick Massey
Authority Member

25 February 1994

Competition Authority Decision No. 301, Rohan Construction Ltd./Rohcon Ltd: 3.17
25 March 1994, Notification No. CA/15/93

Asset and goodwill sale agreement – Whether chairman director but non shareholder is a separate undertaking from his employer and vendor of the assets – Whether four year non compete restriction is necessary to secure the transfer of the goodwill – Whether proposed liquidation of vendor has a bearing on decision – Amendment of restriction from five years to four years – Decision to issue certificate for amended notification – Mergers, Take Overs and Monopolies (Control) Act (No. 17), 1978 – Competition Act (No. 24) 1991 sections 3, 4 and 7

Facts: On 18 April 1993 notification was made to the Competition Authority of an asset acquisition agreement between Rohan Construction Ltd. as the vendor of the assets and Rohcon Ltd. which had been specifically incorporated for the purchase of the assets by Ascon Ltd. The notification was made with a request for a certificate under section 4(4) of the Competition Act or failing that a licence under section 4(2). The arrangements had been notified to the Minister for Enterprise and Employment under the Mergers, Take Overs and Monopolies (Control) Act 1978 but no order had been made.

Another party to the notified arrangement was a Mr Kenneth Rohan who until 1987 had a large shareholding in the parent company of Rohan Construction Ltd. In 1987 the entire share capital of the parent company was sold but Mr Rohan continued on as chairman and director of Rohan Construction Ltd.

The relevant market to the notified arrangements was that for construction and specifically that for commercial and industrial building work.

The notified arrangement included a number of non compete clauses and particu-

3.17 larly one which required Rohan Construction Ltd. not to compete for an unlimited period of time. Mr Rohan had agreed that for a period of 5 years he would not trade in Ireland or the UK using the name Rohan Construction Ltd. and would not enter the general contracting business in Ireland or the UK.

Submissions: The parties submitted that Rohan Construction Ltd. was unable to tender for new business because its parent company had been placed in liquidation. Rohan Construction Ltd. would be liquidated when outstanding contracts had been completed. Mr Kenneth Rohan was firmly identified in the public mind with Rohan Construction Ltd. even though he did not have any beneficial ownership of the shares in Rohan Construction Ltd. The purchaser required Mr Kenneth Rohan to enter into non compete provisions in order to secure the transfer of the goodwill nevertheless.

The Competition Authority noted its concern about the non compete clause and the parties suggested that the five year period of restriction on Mr Kenneth Rohan would be reduced to four years.

Decided by the Authority: In issuing a certificate in respect of the asset purchase agreement as amended that:

(1) Although Mr Kenneth Rohan enjoyed a considerable degree of managerial autonomy ultimate control of Rohan Construction Ltd. still rested with its parent company and Mr Rohan was not therefore 'an undertaking' within the meaning of section 3(1) of the Competition Act.

(2) The relatively small market share of Rohan Construction Ltd. and Ascon Ltd. in the commercial building market meant that the impact on market concentration by the acquisition was relatively slight. The sale of the business would not have any anti-competitive effect on the relevant market.

(3) The EC Commission factors in the Nutricia case: '(i) how frequently consumers in the relevant market change brands and type (in relation to the degree of brand loyalty shown by them); (ii) for how long, after the sale of the business, the seller, without a restrictive clause, would be able to make a successful come back to the market and regain his old customers' were relevant. The Authority agreed that the vendor in the notified agreement would be able to make a successful comeback to the market within the normally acceptable two year restriction period notwithstanding the stated intention to liquidate the vendor company. In this exceptional instance the Competition Authority considered that a period of four years is no more than is necessary to secure the transfer of the goodwill of the business being sold.

(4) If a vendor ensures that certain of its employees become party to non compete provisions in a sale agreement such clauses may offend against section 4(1) if they go beyond what is necessary to secure the transfer of the goodwill of the business being sold. In this exceptional instance Mr Rohan who is not a separate undertaking is so closely identified with the vendor company that the amended period of restriction from five years to four years is necessary to secure the transfer of the goodwill of the business being sold.

Decisions and Report referred to:
European Commission Decision 12.12.83 – Nutricia [1983] L376/22; [1984] 2 CMLR 165
EU Commission (1983) Thirteenth Report on Competition Policy – paragraph 88
Competition Authority Decision No. 6 – Woodchester Bank Ltd./UDT Bank Ltd **3.5**

Competition Authority Decision of 25 March 1994 relating to a proceeding under section 4 of the Competition Act 1991 Notification No. CA/15/93 — Rohan Construction Ltd/Rohcon Ltd 3.17

Introduction

1. Arrangements for the acquisition by Rohcon Ltd (Rohcon) of certain assets, including the goodwill, of Rohan Construction Ltd (Rohan), were notified to the Competition Authority on 18 April 1993. The arrangements included a number of non-compete clauses. The notification requested a certificate, or in the event of a refusal by the Authority to grant a certificate, a licence. The Authority informed the parties of its concerns with certain aspects of the arrangements by letter dated 31 August 1993. The arrangements had been notified to the Minister for Enterprise and Employment under the Mergers Acts and no Order was issued.

The Facts

(a) *The subject of the Notifications*

2. The notification relates to an agreement, dated 19 February 1993, between Rohan (the vendor), Mr Kenneth Rohan, Rohcon (the purchaser) and Ascon Ltd for the purchase by Rohcon of certain of the assets, including the goodwill of Rohan. In addition to the goodwill of Rohan, the assets being purchased included equipment, vehicles and existing contracts. The arrangements included certain non-compete provisions which were amended.

(b) *The Parties*

3. Rohcon was incorporated in February 1993 for the specific purpose of acquiring the existing contracts and other assets of Rohan. It is a wholly owned subsidiary of Ascon, a private limited company established in Ireland in 1959, which is engaged in the construction industry, primarily in the business of civil engineering contractor. It had a reported turnover of £59m in the year to May 1993.[1] Ascon in turn is wholly owned by a Dutch company which is part of the Hollandshe Breton group. Ascon has three operating divisions consisting of Ascon Ltd. which is engaged in civil engineering and heavy industrial construction, Rohcon which is engaged in building contracting and Ascon Excavation Ltd which is engaged in site development and earthworks. Ascon had its own building division prior to the purchase of the Rohan business. This division was combined with Rohan in establishing Rohcon.

4. Rohan is a private limited company which was engaged in building and construction, in particular commercial and industrial building. It had a turnover in 1992 of £16m. It was part of the Rohan group of companies but the ultimate owner was Cabra Estates Ltd (Cabra), a company incorporated in the UK which is now in liquidation. Mr Rohan is a director and chairman of Rohan. Until 1987 he held a 13% shareholding in Rohan Group plc, Rohan's parent company. At that time the entire share capital of the Rohan Group was purchased by Phoenix Properties & Finance plc, a UK registered company. Since then he has held no shares in Rohan or the Rohan Group but continued to act as a director and chairman of the company. Mr Rohan had an agreement with Cabra Estates, who subsequently purchased the share capital of the Rohan group which entitled him to retain the name Rohan Construction Ltd for future use.

(c) *The Product and the Market*

5. The construction industry can be broken down into two broad categories, namely civil engineering and building. The former category includes construction of infrastructure such as roads, bridges and water and sewage systems. The latter includes the construction of all types of buildings ranging from private houses to factories and office buildings. Rohan was

1. Sunday Business Post: Top 500 companies.

3.17 specifically engaged in the commercial and industrial building sector. Ascon was primarily engaged in civil engineering, although it had a building division with a very small market share. The relevant market in this instance is that for construction, specifically that for commercial and industrial building work.

6. Detailed information on the construction industry and on its principal components can be obtained from the Census of Building and Construction. The latest published Census date are for 1991. Summary details are given in Table 1.

Table 1: Building and Construction — Summary of Activity

	Buildings*		All Construction	
	1990	1991	1990	1991
Number of Firms	150	149	296	295
Persons Engaged ('000)	6.6	6.9	15.6	16.0
Turnover (£m)	567.9	654.5	1202.7	1272.7

*This consists of NACE industrial category 501 which is defined as comprising the construction of flats, office blocks, hospitals and other buildings, both residential and non-residential. It is comprised mainly of general building contractors together with specialist contractors involved in construction of buildings, including scaffolding erectors. Only firms employing 20 or more are included.

Source: CSO, Census of Building and Construction 1991, Irish Statistical Bulleting, December 1993

7. The table shows that in 1991 there were 149 firms employing 20 or more persons in the building sector. Between them these firms employed almost seven thousand people, both directly and indirectly, and had a combined turnover of almost £655m. Of this total £630m was due to work done as a principal contractor. It is also possible to get a breakdown of the latter figure which provides some further insight into the type of work done. Details for the building sector was given in Table 2.

Table 2: Details of Turnover as Principal Contractor (£m)

	Buildings		All Construction	
	1990	1991	1990	1991
New Construction				
Dwellings	138.5	222.5	173.9	250.4
Other Buildings	376.2	364.7	598.8	575.9
Other Work	18.7	29.4	216.2	230.7
Total	533.3	616.5	988.8	1056.9
Repair and Maintenance				
Dwellings	2.8	0.6	20.9	36.4
Other Buildings	11.3	12.4	18.1	18.8
Other Work	0.4	0.8	2.2	6.4
Total	14.5	13.8	41.2	61.7
Overall Total	547.8	630.3	1030.0	1118.6

Source: As for Table 1.

8. The figures in Table 2 show that the vast bulk of turnover of building firms is accounted for by new buildings. Almost 60% of such work is accounted for by non-residential building, 36% is attributable to construction of dwellings with the remainder due to other work. There is some degree of specialisation in the building sector with some firms concentrating largely or exclusively on house building while others would concentrate in the commercial and, which was the area where Rohan was principally involved. In effect therefore not all of the 149 firms classified as being engaged in building would operate in the non-residential building sector. As against this Table 2 indicates that firms in the building category of the Census accounted for only 63% of non-residential building. A significant proportion (32%) was accounted for by firms classed in the Census as engaged in general building and engineering, of which there were 16 in 1991. 3.17

(d) *The Arrangements*

9. The agreement relates to the purchase by Rohcon of certain assets of Rohan. The assets being purchased included equipment, vehicles, existing contracts and goodwill. In effect the arrangement will result in Rohcon acquiring the on-going business of Rohan. Certain Rohan contracts were excluded from the arrangements. A number of non-compete clauses were included in the notified agreement. In particular clause 14.1 provided that Rohan would not engage in the business of building contractors or otherwise compete directly or indirectly with Rohcon for an unlimited period of time from the completion date. Rohan also agreed to use its best endeavours to prevent the formation within the State of a company under the name of Rohan Construction Ltd or any similar name, save where such company was formed by Mr Rohan. Under Clause 14.2 Mr Rohan agreed that for a period of five years from completion he would not trade in Ireland or the UK using the name Rohan Construction Ltd and would not enter the general contracting business in Ireland or the UK.

(e) *Submissions of the Parties*

10. The parties stated that as result of the placing in liquidation of its parent company, Cabra, Rohan was unable to tender for new business. In particular it encountered extreme difficulty in securing the performance bonds which were essential for tenders in the construction industry. They argued that if the jobs of Rohan's employees were to be protected it was essential that Rohan be acquired by another building contractor, as otherwise Rohan would be perceived as having lost its ability to compete for contracts. Accordingly the directors and shareholders of Rohan had concluded that they had no option but to sell the business promptly as a going concern. Rohan itself would be wound up once work on outstanding contracts is completed. They argued that the non-compete provisions were justified by the fact that Rohcon could not acquire the goodwill of the business in its entirety if Rohan, or another party using its name, were to set up in business as a building contractor. It was claimed that Rohan was firmly identified in the public mind, and with those with whom it had done business over the past twenty years, with Mr Kenneth Rohan. They pointed out that he was not a shareholder in Rohan but that Rohcon were not prepared to complete the agreement unless he agreed to limit his activities in the manner set out in clause 14.

(f) *Subsequent developments*

11. The Authority wrote to the parties expressing its concern with the duration of the non-compete clauses in the agreement. Rohcon replied by letter dated 31 August 1993. They stated that, while they accepted that the period of two years normally considered sufficient by the Authority to secure the transfer of the goodwill of a business was adequate in most circumstances, they believed that a longer period was justified in this instance. They argued that Rohan had been engaged in the construction industry for 20 years and that, if Mr Rohan were free to set out in business in competition with Rohcon after two years, his close association with Rohan would be likely to attract business which should properly accrue to Rohcon by

3.17 virtue of it having purchased the goodwill of Rohan. They stated that goodwill in the construction business is reflected in the form of invitations to tender for projects. Rohan had been involved in major projects for clients who would not necessarily be involved in similar projects on an ongoing basis. It was therefore conceivable that a client who had previously employed Rohan would prefer them to Rohcon even after an interval of two or three years. Rohcon indicated, however, that they accepted that the goodwill would have substantially passed to them after four years, and they would be willing to undertake to waive the benefit of clause 14, to the extent that it provided that neither Rohan nor Mr Rohan would compete with Rohcon for a period in excess of four years.

Assessment

(a) *Section 4(1)*

12. Section 4(1) of the Competition Act states that 'all agreements between undertakings, decisions by associations of undertakings and concerted practices which have as their object or effect the prevention, restriction or distortion of competition in trade in any goods or services in the State or in any part of the State are prohibited and void'.

(b) *The Undertakings of the Agreement*

13. Section 3(1) of the Competition Act defines an undertaking as 'a person being an individual, a body corporate or an unincorporated body of persons engaged for gain in the production, supply or distribution of goods or the provision of a service'. The parties to the present agreement are Rohcon, Ascon, Rohan and Mr Rohan. Rohcon, Ascon and Rohan are corporate bodies which were engaged in the construction business for gain and are therefore undertakings within the meaning of the Act. Mr Rohan is a director and chairman of Rohan. He ceased to be a shareholder of the company and its parent in 1987. He did not own or control the company. Although he may have enjoyed a considerable degree of managerial autonomy, ultimate control resided with Rohan's parent company. Consequently, Mr Rohan is not, in the Authority's view, an undertaking.

(c) *Applicability of section 4(1)*

14. The present arrangements therefore constitute an agreement between undertakings whereby Rohcon has purchased the assets of the business from Rohan. The Authority has indicated in previous decisions[2] that such a sale of business *per se* does not offend against section 4(1). In the present case Rohcon's parent Ascon was active in the construction industry although primarily in the civil engineering side of the industry. It is clear, however, from the figures in Tables 1 and 2 that there are a large number of firms engaged in the relevant market. The combined market share of Rohan and Ascon in the commercial building market would appear to be relatively small when their turnover figures are judged against figures for total turnover in that market. The impact on market concentration would be relatively slight. In addition the Authority accepts that Rohan should not have continued as an independent competitor in the market given its inability to secure performance bonds which are essential to compete for business. Consequently the Authority does not believe that the sale of the business will have an anti-competitive effect on the relevant market and so it does not offend against section 4(1)

15. Clause 14 of the agreement, as notified, contained certain non-compete provisions. The Authority has stated on numerous occasions that such provisions in sale of business agreements do not offend against section 4(1), provided they are limited in terms of duration, geographic scope and subject matter to what is necessary to secure the transfer of the goodwill of the business being sold. It generally regards a period of two years as adequate for this purpose.

2. Competition Authority Decision No. 6, Woodchester Bank Ltd/UDT Bank Ltd, 4 August 1992.

Under clause 14.1, as notified, Rohan was prevented from competing in the construction business for an unlimited period of time. Such a restriction offended against section 4(1). Rohcon have now stated that they will waive that restriction to the extent that it prevents Rohan competing in the market for more than four years. The four year period exceeds what the Authority generally considers necessary to secure the transfer of the goodwill of a business although the Authority has accepted that a longer period of restriction may be necessary in certain circumstances. 3.17

16. The Authority notes that, while the EU Commission has generally adopted the view that non-compete clauses of more than two years would infringe against Article 85(1) of the Treaty of Rome, it also has accepted that a longer restriction may be justified in certain circumstances. Indeed it is clear from the Commission's decisions that the length of time necessary for the full transfer of the goodwill of a business will vary from industry to industry.

> In general, the assessment under Article 85(1) of non-competition obligations imposed on sellers of businesses will depend on the particular circumstances of each individual case and no individual rule can therefore be established as to the permissible duration of such clauses.[3]

Thus what may be regarded as a reasonable length of time for a non-competition clause in one case may be regarded as excessive in another. In the former case such a clause would not be regarded as a breach of Article 85(1) whereas in the latter it would. In the Nutricia case the Commission indicated that among the factors to be taken into account in evaluating the duration of such clauses were:

> (i) how frequently consumers in the relevant market change brands and type (in relation to the degree of brand loyalty shown by them),
> (ii) for how long, after the sale of the business, the seller, without a restrictive clause, would be able to make a successful comeback to the market and regain his old customers.[4]

The Authority considers that such factor should be taken into account when considering the object and the effect of non-compete clauses in individual cases.

17. It remains firmly of the view, however, that a restriction of two years would provide adequate protection in the vast majority of cases. In this instance, however, the Authority accepts that buyers in the market only purchase the products in question infrequently and that having awarded a construction contract to a firm it may be several years before they seek to award further contracts. It therefore accepts that, in this market, the seller would be able to make a successful comeback to the market and regain his old customers, by virtue of the goodwill of the business previously owned, after a period of two years. In this instance the Authority considers that a period of four years is no more than is necessary to secure the transfer of the goodwill of the business being sold. Consequently it believes that the provision, as amended, no longer offends against section 4(1).[5]

18. Clause 14.2, as notified prevented Mr Rohan from competing in the relevant market for five years after completion. As pointed out above, Mr Rohan is not an undertaking. Clause 14.2 is, however, part of an agreement between undertakings. Rohcon have stated that they

3. EU Commission (1983), 'Thirteenth Report on Competition Policy', para. 88.
4. Nutricia/de Rooij and Nutricia/Zuid Hollandse Conservenfabriek, OJ L376, 31.12.83.
5. Although the parties stated that it was the intention that Rohan be wound up and, consequently, the duration of any non-compete clause in respect of Rohan might appear academic, there is no guarantee that this would actually happen. The Authority does not consider it to be appropriate to issue certificates in respect of an unlimited non-compete clause simply because the parties state that the entity affected by them will be wound up.

3.17 would not have purchased the business unless Mr Rohan were restricted from competing by means of such a clause. Thus the restriction was essential to the agreement between Rohcon and Rohan for the sale of the business. The Authority believes that, if, as part of a sale of business agreement, the vendor ensures that certain of its employees become party to the non-compete provisions in an agreement, such clauses offend against section 4(1) if they go beyond what is necessary to secure the transfer of the goodwill of the business being sold. In this instance the Authority considers that a restriction for five years offended against section 4(1), but as in the case of clause 14.1 it accepts that a restriction for up to four years is necessary, and concludes that clause 14.2, as amended, does not offend against section 4(1).

The Decision

19. In the Authority's opinion, Rohcon, Ascon and Rohan are undertakings within the meaning of section 3(1) of the Competition Act, and the notified arrangements for the acquisition by Rohcon of the assets and goodwill of Rohan, constitute an agreement between undertakings. The Authority believes that in the light of the amendments proposed to the agreement in the letter of 31 August 1993, the restrictions in the agreement are no more than is necessary to secure the transfer of the goodwill of the business to Rohcon. The agreement of 19 February 1993 between Rohan Construction Ltd, Mr Kenneth Rohan, Rohcon Ltd and Ascon Ltd for the purchase by Rohcon of certain of the assets, including the goodwill, of Rohan, as amended by the letter of 31 August 1993, does not, in the Authority's opinion, offend against section 4(1) of the Competition Act 1991.

The Certificate

20. The Competition Authority has issued the following certificate:

> The Competition Authority certifies that in its opinion, on the basis of the facts in its possession, the agreement of 19 February 1991 between Rohan Construction Ltd, Mr Kenneth Rohan, Rohcon Ltd and Ascon Ltd for the purchase of Rohcon of certain of the assets, including the goodwill, of Rohan Construction Ltd (Notification No. CA/15/93), notified on 18 April 1991 under section 7, and amended by the letter of 31 August 1993, does not offend against section 4(1) of the Competition Act 1991

For the Competition Authority

Patrick Massey
Member

25 March 1994

Competition Authority Decision No. 302, Barlo Group plc/Kingspan Group plc: **3.18**
25 March 1994, Notification No. CA/2/94

Asset purchase agreement by competitor of vendor – Whether acquisition within the scope of the Mergers Act – Representations from Minister for Enterprise and Employment concerning the necessity of merged enterprise and maintenance of employment – Application of four firm concentration ratio – Measure of market concentration according to the Herfindahl-Hirschman Index – Whether 'failing firm defence doctrine' has an application – Difference from other decision which referred to failing firm defence – Mergers, Take-Overs and Monopolies (Control) Act 1978 (No. 17) – Competition Act 1991 (No. 24) sections 3, 4 and 7

Facts: On 8 February 1994 notification was made to the Competition Authority of an asset purchase agreement dated 7 February 1994 with a request for a certificate under section 4(4) of the Competition Act 1991.

Kingspan Veha Ltd ('Veha') manufactured radiators. Barlo Group plc ('Barlo') through its subsidiaries also manufactures radiators and heating equipment. Under the notified arrangements a subsidiary of Barlo was the purchaser of the assets. The parties estimated that Barlo had 35% of the relevant market and Veha had 38% of the relevant market.

Submissions

(1) Barlo submitted that the relevant market was intensely competitive and that the acquisition would enable it to compete with larger European firms and would not confer any more market power on Barlo.

(2) The acquisition of additional manufacturing facilities was necessary for Barlo to achieve the economies of scale necessary to compete in the European market. Barlo would increase the capacity of the purchased facility in order to boost its output even further.

(3) The Minister for Enterprise and Employment indicated his concern about safe-guarding the employment of those in the plant being acquired and his belief that the acquisition would enable Barlo to compete effectively against larger European manufacturers.

Decided by the Authority: In issuing a certificate under section 4(4) of the Competition Act 1991 in respect of the notified acquisition agreement:

(1) Applying the four firm concentration ratio and using the Herfindahl-Hirschman Index the Authority noted the high concentration in the relevant market. Such a high concentration required the Authority to give a detailed examination of the notified acquisition.

(2) By virtue of the acquisition the acquirer will have a preponderant share of the relevant market. Any abuse by the acquirer of a dominant position would allow for action to be taken to prevent a breach of section 5 of the Competition Act.

(3) The presence of other radiator manufacturers in other European Union States to which the merged enterprise will be exporting the bulk of its produce, is sufficient to maintain competition. The acquisition by virtue of the agreement will not restrict competition within the State in the relevant market.

(4) There is little prospect of the plant which is being sold under the agreement

3.18 continuing in operation unless the acquisition proceeds. After referring to the failing firm defence as described in the US Department of Justice Merger Guidelines, 1984 the Competition Authority stated its belief that the acquisition did not have as its object the restriction of competition within the State.

(5) The restriction on soliciting customers and employees and the disclosure of confidential information for two years is necessary to protect the goodwill of the business sold and does not offend against section 4(1).

Decisions referred to:
Competition Authority Decision No. 6; Woodchester Bank Ltd/UDT Bank Ltd **3.5**
Competition Authority Decision No. 12; Scully Tyrrell & Co./Edberg Ltd **3.10**
Competition Authority Decision No. 285; Irish Distillers Group plc/Cooley Distillery plc **3.16**

Competition Authority Decision of 25 March 1994 relating to a decision under section 4 of the Competition Act 1991
Notification No. CA/2/94 — Barlo Group plc/Kingspan Group plc

Introduction

1. Arrangements for the acquisition by Barlo Group plc, (Barlo), of the assets and property, including the goodwill, of Kingspan Veha Ltd, (Veha), from Kingspan Group plc, (Kingspan), were notified to the Competition Authority on 8 February 1994. The notification requested a certificate. Notice of intention to issue a certificate was published in the Irish Times on 18 March 1994.

The Facts

(a) *The Subject of the Notifications*

2. The notification relates to an agreement, dated 7 February 1994, between Barlo, Mellstock Ltd, Veha and Kingspan for the sale by Veha of the assets and property, including goodwill, of its business located in Wicklow to Mellstock. Mellstock is a wholly owned subsidiary of Barlo and the arrangements effectively involve the acquisition by Barlo of Veha's radiator manufacture and design business. Veha is a wholly owned subsidiary of Mildenhall which is an associate company of Kingspan.[1] The business being acquired is defined in the agreement as that heretofore carried on by Veha 'comprising the design, manufacture, distribution and sale of radiators and other heating equipment.' The assets being acquired are the 'Agency Agreements, the Computing Assets, the Consumable Stores, the Contingent Rights, the Contracts, the Goodwill, the Intellectual Property, the Investments, the Leased Assets, the Motor Vehicles, the Plant, the Prepayments, the Property, the Records, the Shares and the Stocks.' The arrangements include certain non-compete provisions. The acquisition does not appear to come within the scope of the Mergers Acts although Barlo has disputed this point.

(b) *The Parties*

3. Mellstock is a wholly owned subsidiary of Barlo. Barlo is a manufacturing based company which is engaged *inter alia* in radiator production and processing of plastic products for both domestic and export markets. It owns radiator manufacturing plants in Clonmel, Belgium and the UK. It had a turnover of £49.7m in the year to March 1993.

4. Veha is a private limited company which manufactures domestic radiators at premises situated in Wicklow Town. The plant was originally established by Veha B.V., a Dutch company, in the mid 1950s. In 1962 both the Dutch parent and the Irish subsidiary went into

1. Kingspan owns 49.9% of the shares in Mildenhall, the rest are owned by BES investors, but Kingspan has an option to acquire these shares, and may be required to purchase them.

liquidation. It was acquired from the liquidator by a management buy out in 1964. An industrial dispute which began in 1984 resulted in the closure of the plant. In 1988 the business was again put into liquidation. It was sold by the liquidator to Brackenglen, which subsequently changed its name to Kingspan Veha. At the time Brackenglen was wholly owned by Kingspan. BES investors acquired a 50.1% stake in Mildenhall, Veha's holding company in 1989, but Kingspan has an option to purchase those shares and may be required to purchase them. According to Veha's accounts it recorded losses of £155,000 in the year ending 31 December 1992. At that stage it had accumulated losses of £426,000. Kingspan is a public company engaged in the building products sector. In the year ending 31 December 1992 it had a turnover of £53.1m. **3.18**

(c) *The Product and the Market*

5. Veha is engaged in the business of manufacturing and designing panel radiators, i.e. radiators for use in conjunction with central heating systems mainly in private households and commercial premises. Most household central heating systems use boilers to heat water which is pumped to radiators located in individual rooms within the house. The boilers in such systems are fuelled by either oil, solid fuel, natural gas or LPG. The same type of radiators can be used for any of these fuels. Electrical central heating systems and certain warm air systems do not use radiators.

6. The relevant market is that for radiators for use in central heating systems in households and commercial premises. There are two main sources of demand for installation of household central heating systems and hence for radiators, namely, new houses and existing houses. By and large radiators tend to have a fairly long life and so there is only a very limited demand for replacement or upgrading of radiators once installed.

7. Trends in house building have changed considerably over the past 20 years or so, with the result that most new houses now have central heating installed when they are being built, in contrast to the situation which prevailed prior to 1970. Essentially most new houses are built by private speculative builders and they effectively make the decision as to which type of heating to install. They also decide on the type or brand of radiators to use. The actual central heating systems may be installed by sub-contractors employed by the main builder, in which case they may make the decision as to which brand of radiator to install. Both groups purchase these radiators from builders' suppliers who in turn are supplied by manufacturers and/or importers. The individual house buyer is effectively not involved in the decision as to which brand of radiator will be installed.

8. The number of new house completions has been rising steadily over the past 5 years although the 1992 total was lower than that recorded during the early 1980s. Over 22,000 houses were completed in 1992 and, as stated earlier, the vast majority would have had central heating installed. According to the 1991 Census of Population there were a total of 1,029,000 private households in the State.

Table 1: Number of New House Completions

	Private	Local Authority	Total
1988	14204	1450	15654
1989	17300	768	18068
1990	18536	1003	19539
1991	18472	1180	19652
1992	20982	1482	22464

Note: 1992 figures are provisional. Source: Department of the Environment; Annual Housing Statistics Bulletin 1992.

3.18 9. A significant proportion of the total housing stock is more than 25 years old and, as pointed out, such houses were generally not built with central heating systems. Over the past number of years, however, many such households have had central heating systems installed. In spite of this a significant proportion of the existing housing stock still does not have central heating systems. It is to be expected, however, that a continuing number of existing households will install central heating over time. Obviously as the number of houses without heating systems declines, the number of existing houses in which central heating systems are being installed will also decline. In the case of existing houses central heating systems are typically installed by specialist firms engaged in this business. In this instance the actual householder may have a greater input into the decision as to the brand of radiator used, although, in the vast majority of cases, this decision is likely to be taken by the firm or individual carrying out the installation work. Again they purchase the radiators from builders' suppliers.

10. Of course the decision as to whether or not radiators will be installed depends to some extent on the type of heating system chosen. Thus in a sense non radiator heating systems are substitutes for radiator based systems. It would appear that the radiator based systems are far more common than other types of system. Electrical central heating is used in only a relatively small number of households while warm air heating systems are also relatively unpopular. The parties have indicated, however, that electrical heating systems are popular in older houses. In practice the relative costs of fuels and the particular features of the system, e.g. cleanliness, storage requirements etc. are far more likely to be the decisive factors in the decision as to the type of system chosen. The cost of radiators is unlikely to result in a preference for one type of system over another. Once a decision has been made to install a water based system then one must use radiators. Consequently the relevant market is that for radiators for use in household and commercial heating systems.

11. According to the parties Barlo and Veha are the two main suppliers of radiators to the domestic market. Both firms were stated to have a market share of more than 30%. No other supplier holds more than 10% of the market. A large proportion of radiators produced in Ireland is exported while imports have a sizeable share of the home market.

Table 2: Market Shares in Panel Radiators

	%
Veha	38
Barlo	35
Myson	10
Rettig	5
Others	12

Source: Notifying Parties' Estimates

(d) *The Arrangements*

12. The agreement relates to the sale by Veha of its business of designing and manufacturing radiators to Barlo. It is located at Wicklow town. Under the terms of the sale Barlo are purchasing the property, business assets and goodwill of the business together with the benefit of certain contracts but not the actual company or its liabilities. The business assets essentially consist of the plant and equipment of the business.

13. Clause 2 of the agreement provides that it is conditional on a number of conditions being fulfilled prior to 21 February 1994 or such later date as the parties may agree. Among the conditions to be fulfilled is the receipt of a certificate from the Competition Authority. In this instance the Authority notes that the parties only notified the agreement on 8 February 1994 having set 21 February as the original deadline for obtaining a certificate from the Authority. Notification of agreements under the Competition Act is not compulsory, although obviously

the parties to an agreement notify it requesting a certificate or licence because they perceive a benefit in so doing. The Authority is required to give a detailed consideration to any agreement notified to it before reaching a decision and it follows certain procedures in the interests of fairness and justice to the notifying parties and others. While the Authority recognises the need for prompt decisions particularly when a sale of business is involved, it believes that it must follow fair procedures, and cannot accept the setting of deadlines for a decision by the parties involved. **3.18**

14. Clause 9 contains a number of restrictive provisions. Specifically Kingspan and the vendor[2] agree that they will not for two years in any capacity either be engaged in the relevant business, solicit former customers on their own or anyone else's account or solicit or obtain the services of any employees of the business. In addition they agree not to use or disclose any confidential information relating to the business at any time.

(e) *Submissions of the Parties*

15. Barlo argued that the radiator market was an intensely competitive one. They claimed that the acquisition would not confer any market power on Barlo but would enable it to compete with larger European firms. They pointed out that the product was by its nature a standard one built to common specifications, and that the product could move freely throughout the EU. They argued that the acquisition of additional manufacturing facilities was necessary for Barlo to achieve the economies of scale necessary to compete in the European market. They indicated that their aim would be to use the Wicklow plant to export to the UK and that Barlo planned to increase production at the plant by 40-50% thereby increasing efficiency at the plant and enhancing employment prospects at the plant. The parties pointed out that the products moved freely into and out of Ireland so that the Irish market would remain competitive after the acquisition. They pointed out that major European producers were active in this market and that Rettig, one of the leaders in the European market had a plant located in Ireland which exported approximately 90% of its output to Germany.

(f) *Views of Third Parties*

16. The Minister for Enterprise and Employment wrote to the Authority following the announcement of the receipt of the notification. He indicated that his main concern was safeguarding employment but that he was also concerned to see the growth and strengthening of Irish companies which would permit them to compete successfully in Europe and world markets. He believed that the acquisition would enable Barlo to achieve the necessary economies of scale to compete against larger European manufacturers, considering such economies of scale to be a crucial success factor in this industry. He also pointed out that Veha had been in a loss making situation for some years and that if the takeover did not proceed there would be a serious danger that jobs would be in jeopardy. He believed that Barlo was committed to investing the necessary resources in the plant to develop it into a profitable operation.

Assessment

(a) *Section 4(1)*

17. Section 4(1) of the Competition Act states that 'all agreements between undertakings, decisions by associations of undertakings and concerted practices which have as their object or effect the prevention, restriction or distortion of competition in trade in any goods or services in the State or in any part of the State are prohibited and void.'

(b) *The Undertakings and the Agreement*

18. Section 3(1) of the Competition Act defines an undertaking as 'a person being an individual, a body corporate or an unincorporated body of persons engaged for gain in the production, supply or distribution of goods or the provision of a service'. The parties to the

2. Kingspan Veha (Veha) is the vendor in the agreement.

3.18 present agreement are Barlo, Mellstock, Veha and Kingspan. Barlo, Veha and Kingspan are corporate bodies engaged in the provision of goods and services for gain and are therefore undertakings within the meaning of the Act. As Mellstock is acquiring the business of Veha it is also an undertaking. The notified arrangements therefore constitute an agreement between undertakings.

(c) **Applicability of section 4(1)**

The Acquisition

19. The Authority has given its views on mergers in a number of previous decisions. In Woodchester it stated that:

> before a merger can be found to offend against section 4(1) of the Competition Act, it must be shown that it would, or would be likely to, result in an actual diminution of competition in the market concerned. A reduction in the number of competitors or the fact that a merger will result in the merged entity having a larger share of the market than that previously held by either of the merged undertakings individually, are not, of themselves, sufficient to establish that such a diminution of competition has occurred or would be likely to occur.'[3]

20. The Authority clarified its position further in Scully Tyrrell where it stated that:

> The Authority believes that it would generally be accepted that a market where the four firm concentration ratio fell below 40 percent is effectively competitive . . . the Authority believes that in a highly concentrated market a merger which results in even a relatively small increase in the market share of one of the larger firms merits closer examination.[4]

The Authority also indicated that it might use an alternative measure of market concentration, namely the Herfindahl Hirschman Index (HHI) which is used by the US Department of Justice to evaluate mergers.

21. In Scully Tyrrell the Authority found that the data on both the four firm concentration ratio and the HHI suggested that the arrangements merited further examination. Having concluded in that instance that the merger in question did not prevent, restrict or distort competition the Authority stated that:

> The present decision seeks to clarify the Authority's views in this area. In general the Authority believes that a merger per se between competitors would not prevent, restrict or distort competition and thereby offend against section 4(1) unless the market is, or will as a result of the merger become, highly concentrated.
>
> If the market were highly concentrated following the merger the Authority believes that it would be unlikely to prevent, restrict or distort competition where
> —there were no significant impediments preventing new competitors from entering the market, and/or
> — there was effective competition from overseas suppliers.[5]

22. The figures given in Table 2 indicate that the relevant market in this instance is highly concentrated. Both Barlo and Veha account for more than 30% of the market and their combined market share exceeds 70%. No other supplier accounts for more than 10% of the market. Given the Authority's views in Scully Tyrrell, such an arrangement requires a detailed examination. A similar conclusion would emerge on the basis of the HHI estimates.

3. Competition Authority Decision No. 6, Woodchester Bank Ltd/UDT Bank Ltd, 4 August 1992, para. 78.
4. Competition Authority Decision No. 12, Scully Tyrrell & Co./Edberg Ltd, 29 January 1993, para. 54.
5. Para. 65.

23. In the Authority's opinion there are no particular barriers to entry in this market. Radiators which conform to legal standards set down in other EU countries can be freely imported. It accepts the parties' claim that the product is by its nature a standard one built to common specifications. Nor does the Authority believe that, in this instance, transport costs would be such as to create a barrier to entry for imported products. It is relevant that Veha and Barlo export a significant proportion of their output to other EU countries and that a significant proportion of sales in Ireland is attributable to imports. In addition the Authority notes that there is another radiator manufacturer located in Ireland with only a small share of the domestic market which exports the vast bulk of its output to other EU countries. The Authority believes therefore that the presence of other producers located within Ireland and in other EU countries would be sufficient to maintain competition in spite of the fact that, following the acquisition, Barlo would have a preponderant share of the market. Should Barlo abuse a dominant position contrary to section 5 of the Competition Act, action can be taken to prevent this. In addition it believes that the customers in this market are capable of obtaining supplies from abroad. The Authority does not believe that the acquisition will have the effect of preventing, restricting or distorting competition within the State. **3.18**

24. The Authority also notes that Veha is in financial difficulties and that Kingspan is disposing of the business because it does not wish to incur further losses. In the absence of the sale of the business to Barlo, the closure of the plant is a likely prospect. Were Veha to close then the degree of market concentration would increase anyway although perhaps not to the same degree as is likely as a result of the acquisition.[6]

25. Mergers which have an adverse effect on competition have been permitted under US law under the 'failing firm defence doctrine' since the 1930s.[7] The US Department of Justice Merger Guidelines 1984 outline the main features of the 'failing firm' defence:

> The 'failing firm defense' is a long-established, but ambiguous, doctrine under which an anti-competitive merger may be allowed because one of the merging firms is 'failing'. Because the defense can immunise significantly anti-competitive mergers, the Department will construe its elements strictly. The Department is unlikely to challenge an anti-competitive merger in which one of the merging firms is allegedly failing when: (1) The allegedly failing firm probably would be unable to meet its financial obligations in the near future; (2) it would probably not be able to reorganise successfully under Chapter 11 of the Bankruptcy Act; and (3) it has made unsuccessful good faith efforts to elicit reasonable alternative offers of acquisition of the failing firm that would both keep it in the market and pose a less severe danger to competition than does the proposed merger.[8]

The guidelines state that the fact that an offer is less than the proposed transaction does not make it unreasonable. Indeed any offer to purchase the assets of the failing firm for a price above the liquidation value of those assets will be regarded as a reasonable alternative offer. It is also necessary to show that, in the absence of the acquisition, the assets of the failing firm would leave the relevant market.

26. In the present circumstances of continuing losses, were Veha not to be acquired by Barlo then it is likely to face imminent closure. The plant has had a chequered history, with a number of owners having failed to operate it profitably. In these circumstances the Authority believes that there is little prospect of the plant being acquired by someone other than Barlo or of it continuing in operation under its present ownership. In addition the Authority believes that the

6. This is based on the assumption that were Veha to close, some, but not all, of its business would go to Barlo, while if it is acquired by Barlo it is assumed that all of its business would go to Barlo.
7. See F.M. Scherer and D. Ross (1990), *Industrial Market Structure and Economic Performance*, Houghton Mifflin, p. 186.
8. US Department of Justice, 'Merger Guidelines 1984', section 5.1.

3.18 acquisition of Veha by Barlo would result in the assets of the business being retained in the radiator industry.[9] The Authority also believes that Barlo's existing Irish operations will continue in production. Consequently the Authority does not believe that the acquisition has as its object the prevention, restriction or distortion of competition within the State and so does not offend against section 4(1).

The Non-Compete Provisions.

27. Clause 9 of the agreement imposes a number of restrictions on the vendor and Kingspan. They are both prevented for two years from being engaged in any capacity in the relevant business, from soliciting former customers on their own or anyone else's account or from soliciting or obtaining the services of any employees of the business. In addition they agree not to use or disclose any confidential information relating to the business at any time.

28. The Authority has considered similar restrictions in a number of previous decisions and they can be dealt with briefly here. The Authority has stated previously that a restriction on a vendor competing with the purchaser of a business may be necessary to protect the goodwill of the business being sold and where such a restriction does not exceed what is necessary for the protection of that goodwill in terms of its duration, geographic coverage and subject matter, it does not offend against section 4(1). It has stated that it would normally regard a period of two years as adequate for such purposes. It has also stated that restrictions on soliciting customers and former employees for a like period do not offend against section 4(1).

29. The Authority has also stated in previous decisions that a restriction on the vendor using or revealing to anyone any confidential information relating to the business being sold are acceptable provided that they are not used to prevent the vendor from re-entering the relevant market once a legitimate non-competition clause has expired. Were it to be used in such a way the Authority would regard it as offending against section 4(1).

The Decision

30. In the Authority's opinion, Barlo, Mellstock, Kingspan and Veha are undertakings within the meaning of section 3(1) of the Competition Act, and the notified arrangements for the acquisition by Barlo of the business of Veha constitutes an agreement between undertakings. In the Authority's opinion, the agreement does not have, as its object or effect, the prevention, restriction or distortion of competition and does not offend against section 4(1) of the Competition Act 1991.

The Certificate

31. The Competition Authority has issued the following certificate:

> The Competition Authority certifies that in its opinion, on the basis of the facts in its possession, the agreement of 7 February 1994 between Barlo Group plc, Mellstock, Kingspan Group plc and Kingspan Veha Ltd. for the acquisition by Barlo Group plc of the radiator manufacturing and design business of Kingspan Veha Ltd. in Wicklow town (Notification No. CA/2/94), notified on 8 February 1994 under section 7, does not offend against section 4(1) of the Competition Act 1991.

For the Competition Authority

Patrick Massey
Member

25 March 1994

9. This is in contrast to the situation which prevailed in the case of the proposed acquisition of Cooley Distillery plc by Irish Distillers Group plc where the purchaser's stated intention was to close the plant down. Competition Authority Decision No. 285, 25 February 1994.

Competition Authority Decision No. 349, Sedgwick Overseas Group Ltd/PJ Dineen: 6 September 1994, Notification No. CA/14/94 3.19

Share sale agreement – Restriction in agreement on vendor from competing with business or soliciting employees or customers for a period of two years – Related post sale employment agreement – Restriction in employment agreement on vendor from soliciting employees or customers of the company for a period of one year after termination of his employment – Whether vendor an undertaking for the purpose of the Competition Act – Competition Act 1991 (No. 24) sections 3, 4 and 7

Facts: On 25 February 1994 notification was made to the Authority with a request for a certificate under section 4(4) of the Competition Act 1991 or, failing that, a licence under section 4(2) in respect of an option agreement between Sedgwick Overseas Group Ltd ('Sedgwick') and Mr Dineen whereunder Sedgwick obtained an option to acquire from Mr Dineen his 20% shareholding in the capital of Sedgwick Dineen Group Ltd ('SDGL'). The notification also contained an employment agreement between SDGL and Mr Dineen setting out the terms of Mr Dineen's employment following completion of the sale. Both the agreements contained non-compete provisions.

Sedgwick, a limited company incorporated under the laws of England and Wales, is engaged in the business of risk consultancy, insurance broking, employee benefit schemes and other financial services. SDGL, its Irish subsidiary, is engaged primarily in the provision of life assurance and disability benefits, services for employees of corporate bodies. Mr Dineen was one of the founding members of SDGL.

The relevant market is the personal financial services market as it relates to the provision of advice to individuals (as opposed to corporate bodies) on the purchase of life assurance and investment products. It was submitted that the market is extremely competitive and that there are no significant barriers to entry into the market.

The notified option agreement was made on 25 February 1994 between Sedgwick and Mr Dineen and under its terms Sedgwick have an option to acquire from Mr Dineen his 20% shareholding in SDGL. The option had to be exercised between 10 April and 10 July 1994 and was in fact exercised on 18 April 1994. The agreement contains a clause preventing Mr Dineen for a period of two years from completion of the agreement from competing directly or indirectly with the business of SDGL or from soliciting any client or employee of SDGL. The notified employment agreement which regulates Mr Dineen's post sale employment with SDGL contains a clause restricting Mr Dineen for a period of one year after cessation of employment from soliciting any client or employee of SDGL.

Decided by the Authority: In issuing a certificate under section 4(4) of the Competition Act 1991 in respect of the notified arrangement that:

(1) Sedgwick is an undertaking within the meaning of the Competition Act. Mr Dineen at the time of the agreement was the owner of 20% of the shares in the business and was not merely an auxiliary organ bound to carry out his employers instructions and was in a position to pursue his own economic interests and is therefore also an undertaking for the purpose of the Competition Act. The arrangements constitute an agreement between undertakings.

3.19 (2) As Sedgwick already owned 80% of the shares in the business the acquisition of the remaining shares had no implications from a competition perspective and does not offend against section 4(4).

(3) A restriction on a vendor competing with a business following its sale is necessary to secure the complete transfer of the goodwill of that business. If the restriction on the vendor is limited in terms of duration, geographic scope and subject matter to what is necessary to achieve that purpose it would not offend against section 4(1). The restriction on the vendor in the option agreement for a period of two years from completion does not exceed what is necessary to secure the transfer of goodwill and such non-compete provision does not offend against section 4(1) of the Act.

(4) The employment agreement between SDGL and Mr Dineen was an essential part of the overall agreement and must be regarded as part of the agreement between undertakings. The restriction on soliciting customers for one year after termination of employment does not offend against section 4(1). However a different view would be taken if soliciting customers was essential in order to enter the market. The similar restriction on soliciting employees for a period of one year does not offend against section 4(1).

Case and Decisions referred to:

Suiker Unie v. EC Commission (Case No. 40 etc /75) [1975] ECR 1663, [1976] 1 CMLR 295
Competition Authority Decision No. 1, Nallen/O'Toole (Belmullet) — 2 April 1992 **3.3**
Competition Authority Decision No.12, Scully Tyrell & Company/Edberg Ltd — 29 January 1993 **3.10**
Competition Authority Decision No. 20, Apex/Murtagh — 10 June 1993 **1.4.3**
Competition Authority Decision No. 29, John D. Carroll Catering Ltd/Sutcliffe Ireland Ltd — 9 September 1993

Competition Authority Decision of 6 September 1994 relating to a proceeding under section 4 of the Competition Act 1991
Notification No. CA/14/94 — Sedgwick Overseas Group Ltd/PJ Dineen

Introduction

1. Arrangements for the purchase of approximately 20% of the issued share capital of Sedgwick Dineen Group Ltd (SDGL) by Sedgwick Overseas Group Ltd (Sedgwick) from Mr P.J. Dineen were notified to the Competition Authority on 7 June 1994. The notification requested a certificate or, in the event of a certificate being refused, a licence.

The Facts

(a) *The Subject of the Notification*

2. The notification concerns an Option Agreement dated 25 February 1994 between Sedgwick and Mr Dineen whereby Sedgwick obtained an option to acquire from Mr Dineen his shareholding (about 20%) in SDGL to Sedgwick. Sedgwick already held 80% of the shares, a shareholding which had been built up since its first involvement in 1973. The notification also contained an Employment Agreement pursuant to SDGL's retention of Mr Dineen as an employee following completion of the sale. Both agreements contain non-compete provisions.

(b) *The Parties*

3. Sedgwick Overseas Group Ltd is a limited company with registered offices in London. It is engaged in the business of risk consultancy, insurance broking, employee benefits schemes, consultancy and financial services. Sedgwick Dineen Group Ltd is its Irish subsidiary which

is engaged, primarily, in the provision of pensions, life assurance and disability benefits services for employees of corporate bodies. Mr P.J. Dineen was one of the founding members of Sedgwick Dineen. Prior to the agreement, he was the owner of approximately 20% of the share capital of SDGL. 3.19

(c) *The Product and the market*

4. The arrangement relates to the financial services sector, in particular, the personal financial services and employee benefits markets. The personal financial services market refers to the provision of advice to individuals (as opposed to corporate bodies) on the purchase of life assurance and investment products. In its submission to the Authority the parties explained that the products falling into this category would include term assurance, whole life and endowment policies, permanent health insurance, personal accident insurance, personal pensions, unit linked funds, unit trusts and, annuities. According to the parties, the size of the market is difficult to quantify. In its Annual Report the Department of Industry and Commerce indicated that the total single premiums amounted to IR£662 million with total annual premiums of IR£861 million for 1991. These amounts would include employer-sponsored pension schemes which should properly be excluded to arrive at a relevant assessment of market size. In addition, it would be necessary to add the amount invested in unit trusts. Statistics are not readily available but according to the parties these items may reduce the annual premium market to IR£550 million approximately) and the single premiums market to IR£700 million approximately).

5. The services in the employee benefits sector which SDGL provide relate mainly to pensions, life assurance and disability benefits for employees of corporate bodies. Advice is occasionally rendered on profit-sharing schemes. According to the parties, other services which may be considered to be part of the employee benefits market are the remuneration and fringe benefits provided to employees. In general, Sedgwick Dineen Group does not advise on these; the main purveyors of these services would be accountancy firms, management consultants, and recruitment consultants. It is difficult to quantify this market but the parties estimated that it is between £30 million and £40 million in terms of fees/commissions.

6. There is a significant number of sellers in the personal financial services market in Ireland including banks and building societies as well as insurance and pension brokers. The buyers are mainly corporate bodies who would have a very high level of sophistication, in terms of their understanding of the market, knowledge of the available services and purchasing power. Individuals rarely use these services.

7. According to the parties, it is difficult to estimate the turnover of the Irish financial services market but they indicated that it is in excess of IR£1 billion. The employee benefits market is worth between IR£30 million and IR£40 million.

8. According to the parties the market is extremely competitive. There are many competitors in the market including many new entrants such as the banks which have established separate divisions in-house for these areas of business.

9. There are no significant barriers to establishment in this market. No actuarial valuations are required nor are government licences normally required. There is no equivalent in Ireland to the 1992 Financial Services Act.

(d) *The Arrangements*

10. The notification relates to an agreement, known as the Option Agreement, dated 25 February 1994, between Sedgwick and Mr Dineen. Under the terms of the agreement Sedgwick obtained an option to acquire from Mr Dineen his shareholding (approximately 20%) in SDGL. The option had to be exercised between 10 April and 10 July 1994. The option was exercised on 18 April 1994. Clause 4.2 of the agreement prevents Mr Dineen, for a period of two years from completion, from acquiring an interest in, or becoming engaged or employed by persons or companies with an interest in, any activity which operates in the insurance business in

3.19 competition with SDGL. The agreement also prevents Mr Dineen, for the same period, from soliciting the business of any client of SDGL on his own behalf or that of any other party and also from seeking to entice or persuade any employee of SDGL to take up employment with any person or company operating in competition with SDGL. The restriction also prevents Mr Dineen from collaborating with any other employees of SDGL to leave the group and become involved in the activities outlined above.

11. The notification also contained a related Employment Agreement pursuant to Mr Dineen's post-sale employment with SDGL. Under the conditions of the employment agreement, Mr Dineen is prevented, for the duration of his employment and for a period of one year after the cessation of employment, from soliciting the business of any client of SDGL on his own behalf or that of any other party and also from seeking to entice or persuade any employee of SDGL to take up employment with any person or company operating in competition with SDGL. The restriction also prevents-Mr Dineen from collaborating with any other employees of SDGL to leave the group and become involved in the activities outlined above.

(e) *Submissions of the Parties*

12. The parties made lengthy submissions justifying both the acquisition of the shares and the non-compete clauses. The arguments made in support of the acquisition of the shares were not considered to be relevant by the Authority. In support of the request for a certificate the parties referred to a number of EC decisions and previous decisions by the Authority under the Competition Act that non-compete clauses in sale of business agreement were not anti-competitive.

Assessment

(a) *Section 4(1)*

13. Section 4(1) cf the Competition Act states that 'all agreements between undertakings, decisions by associations of undertakings and concerted practices, which have as their object or effect the prevention, restriction or distortion of competition in goods or services in the State or in any part of the State are prohibited and void'.

The Undertakings and the Agreement

14. Section 3(1) of the Competition Act defines an undertaking as a person being an individual, a body corporate or an unincorporated body of persons engaged for gain in the production, supply or distribution of goods or the provision a service.' Sedgwick Overseas Group Ltd is a limited company engaged for gain in the business of risk consultancy, insurance broking, employee benefits schemes, consultancy and financial services and is therefore an undertaking within the meaning of the Act. Sedgwick Dineen Group plc is its Irish subsidiary which is engaged, primarily, in the provision of pensions, life assurance and disability benefits services for employees of corporate bodies. Mr Dineen was the owner of approximately 20% of the shares in the business at the time of the agreement, having previously held a much larger shareholding in the business. He owned a sizeable stake in the business and had a significant influence on its day-to-day operations. He is also involved in a number of other business activities. In the Authority's view his position is not analogous to that of an employee, as described by the ECJ in the Suiker Unie case,[1] who is an auxiliary organ bound to carry out his employer's instructions. Indeed as Van Bael and Bellis point out from the moment an employee pursues his own economic interests, and where they are different from his employer's interests, he might well become an undertaking within the sense of Article 85.[2] Thus in the Authority's view, Mr Dineen is not merely an auxiliary organ bound to carry out his employer's

1. *Cooperatieve Vereninging Suiker Unie UA v. EC Commission* [1975] ECR 1663.
2. J.F. Bellis, (1990), *Competition Law of the EEC*, 2nd edition, CCH Editions Ltd, point 208.

instructions. He is clearly in a position to pursue his own economic interests and indeed the sale of his shares clearly is an example of his doing just that. Thus, in the Authority's opinion, he is an undertaking. 3.19

Applicability of section 4(1)

15. The present arrangements constitute an agreement between undertakings whereby Sedgwick has secured an option to purchase from Mr Dineen his 20% shareholding in SDGL. As Sedgwick already owns 80% of the shares in the business the acquisition of the remaining shares has no implications from a competition perspective and does not offend against section 4(1).

Non-Compete Clause

16. Clause 4.2 of the Option Agreement prevents Mr Dineen from competing with SDGL for a period of two years from the date of completion of the agreement. The Authority has indicated in a number of previous decisions[3] that in the case of the sale by a partner in a business of his interest in the business to the other partner(s), it normally regards a restriction on the vendor competing with the business following completion as necessary to secure the complete transfer of the goodwill of the business. It has stated that provided the restriction on the vendor is limited in terms of duration, geographic scope and subject matter to what is necessary to achieve that purpose, it would not, in the Authority's view, offend against section 4(1). The Authority has indicated that it generally regards a period of two years as sufficient to secure the transfer of goodwill in such circumstances. As the duration of the non-compete period in this notification does not exceed this accepted period, the Authority does not consider that the non-compete provision of the agreement offends against section 4(1) of the Act.

Employment Agreement

17. The employment agreement between Sedgwick and Mr Dineen was entered into as part of the sale agreement. It was expressly included as part of the notified arrangements. The Authority's views on notification of employment agreements as part of wider sale of business agreements were expressed in its decision in Carroll Catering/Sutcliffe.[4] In the Authority's view the employment agreement between Sedgwick and Mr Dineen was an essential part of the overall agreement and it must be regarded as part of that agreement between undertakings.

18. Under the conditions of the employment agreement, Mr Dineen is prevented, for a period of one year, from soliciting the business of any client of SDGL on his own behalf or that of any other party and also from seeking to entice or persuade any employee of SDGL to take up employment with any person or company operating in competition with SDGL. The restriction also prevents Mr Dineen from collaborating with any other employees of SDGL to leave the group and become involved in the activities outlined above. In Carrolls Catering/Sutcliffe, the Authority acknowledged that where the vendor agrees to become an employee of the business, he should not compete with it for so long as he remains an employee. However, a restriction on his competing after he has ceased to be an employee is not acceptable. On this occasion, however, Mr Dineen is not prevented from competing with the business after the cessation of his employment. He is prevented from soliciting customers and other employees of the business for one year after cessation of employment. The Authority indicated in APEX/Murtagh that it does not regard a restriction on soliciting customers for one year after termination of employment as offending against section 4(1).[5] It would take a different view if soliciting customers was essential in order to enter the market. The Authority takes a similar view of the restriction

3. See for example, Competition Authority decision No. 1, Nallen/O'Toole (Belmullet), 2 April 1992.
4. See, for example, Decision No. 29 John D. Carroll Catering Ltd/Sutcliffe Ireland Ltd, 9 September 1993 Decision No. 12, Scully Tyrrell & Company/Edberg Ltd.
5. Competition Authority decision no. 20, 10 June 1993.

3.19 on soliciting employees and, in this instance, does not consider that it would prevent Mr Dineen from competing in the market following cessation of his employment. Therefore, this aspect of the notified arrangements does not offend against section 4(1).

The Decision

19. In the Authority's opinion, Sedgwick Overseas Group Ltd and Mr P.J. Dineen are undertakings within the meaning of section 3(1) of the Competition Act and the notified arrangements for the purchase by Sedgwick of Mr Dineen's 20% shareholding in Sedgwick Dineen Group Ltd constitutes an agreement between undertakings. In the Authority's opinion, the arrangements do not have, as their object or effect, the prevention, restriction or distortion of competition. The Option agreement of 25 February 1994 between Sedgwick and Mr Dineen does not, in the Authority's opinion, offend against section 4(1) of the Competition Act 1991.

The Certificate

20. The Competition Authority has issued the following certificate:

> The Competition Authority certifies that in its opinion, on the basis of the facts in its possession, the Option Agreement between Sedgwick Overseas Group Ltd and Mr P.J. Dineen whereby Sedgwick Overseas Group Ltd obtained an option to acquire Mr. Dineen's shareholding in Sedgwick Dineen Group Ltd (Notification No. CA/14/94), notified on 7 June 1994 under section 7, does not offend against section 4(1) of the Competition Act 1991.

For the Competition Authority

Patrick Massey
Member

6 September 1994

3.20 **Competition Authority Decision No. 351, IAWS Agri-Society Ltd/Unigrain Ltd:** 6 September 1994, Notification No. CA/691/92E

Share sale agreement – Provisions in agreement preventing vendors of business competing with purchasers for a period of three years – Arrangements whereby certain of the vendors continued in their contracts of service with the purchased company as part of the sale agreement – Whether such vendors are undertakings for the purpose of the Competition Act – Statement of objections – Competition Act 1991 (No. 24) sections 3, 4 and 7

Facts On 30 September 1992 notification was made to the Authority of an agreement between IAWS — Agri Society Ltd ('IAWS') and Messrs Ronan Fitzpatrick, Michael Farrington, Edward Gilmartin Snr, John Farrington, Martin Murphy and T & J Farrington Ltd (collectively 'the vendors') for the purchase and sale of the entire issued share capital of Unigrain Dublin Ltd and Unigrain Foynes Ltd with a request for a certificate under section 4(4) of the Competition Act 1991, or failing that, a licence under section 4(2).

IAWS, a public limited company quoted on the Irish Stock Exchange, operates in the Irish agricultural and food market particularly in fish processing, fertilizers, animal feed, energy products and foods. Unigrain Dublin Ltd and Unigrain Foynes Ltd are limited companies registered in the State and prior to the completion of the notified agreement were wholly owned by the vendors. **3.20**

Under the terms of the notified agreement which was made on 12 January 1989 the vendors sold the entire issued share capital of Unigrain Dublin Ltd and Unigrain Foynes Ltd to IAWS. The notified agreement contained a non-compete clause which prevented the vendors from competing with the business or soliciting employees of IAWS or its subsidiaries for a period of three years from the completion date. This expired on 11 January 1992. The notified agreement also contained a clause whereby Messrs. Fitzpatrick and Murphy, who entered into service contracts with IAWS companies, were not to compete with the business or solicit its employees for the duration of their employment in the business and for three years after cessation of such employment.

On 15 July 1993 the Authority wrote to the parties expressing concerns about the inclusion of post employment restrictions on Messrs Fitzpatrick and Murphy. In response it was stated that Mr Fitzpatrick's employment with IAWS had terminated on 31 March 1990 and that the post employment restriction had therefore expired on 31 March 1993. The Authority issued a statement of objections on 27 June 1994 indicating its intention to refuse a request for a certificate or licence. In a letter dated 19 July 1994, IAWS responded stating that in his capacity as vendor of his interest in the business Mr Murphy was acting as an undertaking while the non-compete provisions imposed on him for three years after his termination of employment with IAWS were entered into by Mr Murphy not as an undertaking but as an employee.

Decided by the Authority: In refusing to issue a certificate or grant a licence under sections 4(4) and 4(2) respectively of the Competition Act 1991 in respect of the notified agreement that:

(1) Each of IAWS, Unigrain Dublin Ltd and Unigrain Foynes Ltd are engaged for gain in the production, supply or distribution of goods or the provision of a service and are undertakings within the meaning of the Competition Act. At the time of the agreement the vendors were beneficial owners of the Unigrain companies and were also undertakings. The arrangements therefore constitute an agreement between undertakings.

(2) The prohibition in section 4(1) of the Competition Act only applies to a current or continuing contractual commitment or one entered into subsequent to the coming in to force of the Act. As the sale aspect of the agreement was discharged prior to 1 October 1991, the commencement date of the Act, that aspect of the arrangement does not come within the scope of section 4(1).

(3) The provision in the notified agreement which prevented the vendors from competing with or soliciting employees from IAWS for a period of three years from the completion date was designed to secure the transfer of the goodwill of the business and did not offend against section 4(1).

(4) The provisions facing restrictions on the vendors Messrs Fitzpatrick and Murphy for the duration of their continued employment with IAWS and for three years after cessation of such employment do offend against section 4(1) of the Act. Where a vendor enters into a service agreement with a purchaser and such an

3.20 agreement is an important part of the overall sale of the business, as was the case here, it must be considered part of that agreement between undertakings. The submissions by IAWS would classify Mr Murphy as an undertaking for part and an employee for a different part of the same agreement.

(5) The restrictive clause affecting Mr Murphy prevents him from competing with the business for three years after termination and from soliciting customers or employees of the business for a like period. While restrictions on soliciting customers or employees for up to one year after termination of employment would not offend against section 4(1) the restrictions in the present case clearly go beyond this and therefore offend against section 4(1). While the restriction in the case of Mr Fitzpatrick expired on 31 March 1993 it offended against section 4(1) from 12 January 1992 up to that time.

(6) Where, as part of a sale of a business agreement, a vendor becomes an employee of the business, a post-employment non-compete clause does not satisfy the requirement for a licence under section 4(2) since such clause is not necessary to secure the transfer of the goodwill of the business and is therefore not indispensable to the attainment of that objective.

Decisions and Notices referred to:
Competition Authority Decision No. 29, John D. Carroll Catering Ltd/Sutcliffe Ireland Ltd
Competition Authority Decision No. 12, Scully Tyrell & Company/Edberg Ltd **3.10**
Competition Authority Decision No. 20, Apex Fire Protection Ltd/Mr Noel Murtagh **1.4.3**
Competition Authority Notice on Employee Agreements and the Competition Act **1.4.1**
Competition Authority Notice in respect of Mergers and Takeovers which pre-date the Competition Act **3.1**

Competition Authority Decision of 6 September 1994 relating to a proceeding under section 4 of the Competition Act 1991
Notification Authority No. CA/691/92E — IAWS Agri Society Ltd/Unigrain Ltd

Introduction

1. An agreement between IAWS-Agri Society Ltd (IAWS) and Messrs Ronan Fitzpatrick, Michael Farrington, Edward Gilmartin Snr, John Farrington, Martin Murphy and T & J Farrington Ltd (collectively the Vendors) for the purchase and sale of the entire issued share capital of Unigrain Dublin Ltd and Unigrain Foynes Ltd (collectively the Unigrain companies) containing certain non-compete provisions, was notified to the Competition Authority on 30 September 1992. The notification requested a certificate or, in the event of a certificate being refused, a licence. The Authority issued a Statement of Objections to the parties on 27 June 1994 indicating its intention to refuse their request for a certificate or a licence. IAWS responded in a letter dated 19 July 1994. They did not request an Oral Hearing.

The Facts

(a) *The Subject of the Notification*

2. The notification relates to an agreement dated 12 January 1989 between IAWS and the Vendors whereby the Vendors agreed to sell the entire issued share capital of the Unigrain companies to IAWS. The agreement also contains a non-compete provision.

(b) *The Parties*

3. IAWS is a public limited company quoted on the Irish Stock Exchange. It has, through its subsidiaries, been a major supplier of material and services to the Irish agricultural and food

industries for over 90 years. The groups' principal operating businesses consist of fish processing, fertilisers, animal feed, energy products and food. Its turnover for the year ended 31 July 1993 was £402m. Unigrain Dublin Ltd and Unigrain Foynes Ltd are limited to companies registered in the State. Prior to the completion of the agreement, the Vendors collectively owned the entire issue share capital of the Unigrain companies. **3.20**

(c) *The Arrangements*

4. The notification relates to an agreement, dated 12 January 1989, for the sale by the Vendors of the entire share capital of the Unigrain companies to IAWS. Clause 6.01 of the agreement contains a non-compete clause which prevented the vendors from competing with the business or from soliciting employees of IAWS or its subsidiaries for a period 3 years from the completion date. This period expired on 11 January 1992. Clause 6.02 provides that Messrs Fitzpatrick and Murphy should not compete with the business or solicit its employees for the duration of their employment in the business and for three years after cessation of such employment.

(d) *Subsequent Developments*

5. The Authority wrote to the parties on 15 July 1993 expressing concerns at the inclusion of post-employment restrictions on Messrs Fitzpatrick and Murphy. In a letter of reply dated 3 August 1993, the parties stated that Mr Fitzpatrick's employment with IAWS had terminated on 31 March 1990 and that the post-employment restriction had therefore expired on 31 March 1993. They also referred to the Authority's notice in relation to employee agreements,[1] from which they assumed that the Authority would refuse to accept notification of the restrictive covenants affecting Mr Murphy.

6. The Authority issued a Statement of Objections to the parties on 27 June 1994 indicating its intention to refuse their request for a certificate or licence. IAWS responded in a letter dated 19 July 1994. In their reply they stated that they disagreed with the Authority's view as expressed in its decision in Carroll's Catering that where a vendor of a business enters into a service agreement with the purchaser it is an important part of the overall sale of business agreement and must be considered part of an agreement between undertakings.[2] They went on:

> We would point out that clearly in the agreement the subject matter of this notification, the employment aspect and the restrictions relating thereto were an important part of the overall sale of business agreement. However whilst in the sale of his interest in his business Mr Murphy was acting as an undertaking, we would respectively submit that the capacity in which the restrictive covenant under discussion would have bound him was not as an undertaking but as an employee and as the Authority itself has confirmed employees are not undertakings *per se* . . . we would submit for the purposes of these particular provisions Mr. Murphy entered into them not as an undertaking but as an employee.
>
> . . . In our particular case it was essential from our client's point of view that in acquiring the business it also acquired the services of Martin Murphy. The consideration which our client paid for the acquisition . . . related directly to this being part of the transaction and also to Mr Murphy agreeing to restrictions should his employment with the company be terminated. Our client would not have been prepared to pay the price it paid had this not been part of the equation and indeed might not have gone ahead at all with this particular acquisition.

1. Competition Authority — Employee Agreements and the Competition Act 15 September 1992.
2. Decision No. 29, John D. Carroll Catering Ltd/Sutcliffe Ireland Limlted, 9 September 1993.

3.20 They further argued that it was not within the power of the Authority to retrospectively impose different conditions on the parties from those they had entered into in 1989 and stated that if a restriction were not placed on Mr Murphy for a period following termination of his employment untold damage could be caused to the business. Mr Murphy replied in a letter dated 21 July 1994 indicating that he was prepared to accept the Authority's proposed decision. None of the parties availed of the opportunity for an Oral Hearing offered to them by the Authority.

Assessment

(a) *Section 4(1)*

7. Section 4(1) of the Competition Act states that 'all agreements between undertakings, decisions by associations of undertakings and concerted practices which have as their object or effect the prevention, restriction or distortion of competition in trade in any goods or services in the State or in any part of the State are prohibited and void'.

(b) *The Undertakings and the Agreement*

8. Section 3(1) of the Competition Act defines an undertaking as 'a person being an individual, a body corporate or an unincorporated body of persons engaged for gain in the production, supply or distribution of goods or the provision of a service.' IAWS is a corporate body engaged for gain and is therefore an undertaking. Unigrain Dublin Ltd and Unigrain Foynes Ltd are also registered in the State and are also engaged for gain. At the time of the agreement, the Vendors were the beneficial owners of the Unigrain companies and are also, therefore, undertakings. The arrangements therefore constitute an agreement between undertakings.

(c) *Applicability of section 4(1)*

Sale of Business

9. As the sale of business was completed prior to 1 October, 1991, the date on which the Competition Act came into force, this element of the agreement had been discharged by performance before the Act commenced. The property which was the subject of the agreement had been transferred. In the Authority's view, the prohibition in section 4(1) only applies to a current or continuing contractual commitment or one entered into subsequent to the coming into force of the Act.[3] As the merger or sale element of the 1991 transaction was discharged prior to the commencement of the Act, that aspect of the arrangements does not come within the scope of section 4(1).

Non-Compete Clauses

10. Clause 6.01 of the agreement contains a non-compete provision which prevented the Vendors from competing with IAWS for a period cf three years from the completion date and from soliciting employees of the company or its subsidiaries for the same period. The Authority believes that this restriction was designed to secure the transfer of the goodwill of the business and did not offend against section 4(1). Clause 6.02 imposes similar restrictions on Messrs Fitzpatrick and Murphy for the duration of their employment with IAWS and for three years after cessation of such employment. (As Mr Fitzpatrick's employment with IAWS ceased on 31 March 1990 and the non-compete clause applied up to 31 March 1993, he is no longer subject to any restrictions. The provision continues to apply to Mr Murphy who is still employed by IAWS.)

3. 'Notice in respect of Mergers and Takeovers which predate the Competition Act' — Competition Authority, 4 May 1993.

11. IAWS argued that as Mr. Murphy is now an employee, the post-employment restrictions do not constitute an agreement between undertakings and, therefore, the restrictive covenants of the agreement do not come within the scope of the Competition Act and should not be considered by the Authority. However the Authority considers that, in the case of a sale of business, where a vendor enters into a service agreement with the purchaser, such an agreement is an important part of the overall sale of business agreement and must be considered part of that agreement between undertakings. Indeed in their response to the Statement of objections IAWS clearly indicated that the agreement of the vendors to remain as employees was an essential element of the sale agreement. In this instance, the post employment non-compete provisions are included as part of the sale agreement. In arguing that Mr Murphy should be considered to be an employee per se and not an undertaking for the purposes of the post-employment restrictions, IAWS are arguing that Mr Murphy was both an undertaking and not an undertaking within the context of the same agreement. The Authority has previously indicated[4] that in such circumstances, a restriction on competing after termination of employment offends against section 4(1) of the Competition Act as it goes beyond what is necessary to secure the transfer of the goodwill of the business. In addition to preventing Mr Murphy from competing with the business for three years after termination of employment, clause 6.02 also prevents him from soliciting customers or employees of the business for a like period. The Authority has indicated that a restriction on soliciting customers or employees for up to one year after termination of employment would not offend against section 4(1). The restrictions in this case clearly goes beyond that. In the Authority's opinion, therefore, clause 6.02 of the agreement offends against section 4(1). While the restriction in the case of Mr Fitzpatrick expired on 31 March 1993, it offended against section 4(1) from 12 January 1992 up to that time. **3.20**

(d) *Applicability of section 4(2)*

12. Under section 4(2), the Competition Authority may grant a licence in the case of any agreement or category of agreements which offend against section 4(1) but which, having regard to all relevant market conditions, contributes to improving the production of goods or provision of services or to promoting technical or economic progress, while allowing consumers a fair share of the resulting benefit and which does not:

(i) impose on the undertakings concerned terms which are not indispensable to the attainment of those objectives;
(ii) afford undertakings the possibility of eliminating competition in respect of a substantial part of the products or services in question.

13. The Authority believes that where, as part of a sale of business agreement, a vendor becomes an employee of the business, a post-employment non-compete clause does not satisfy the requirements of a licence under section 4(2) since it is not necessary to secure the transfer of the goodwill of the business and it is therefore not indispensable.

The Decision

14. In the Authority's opinion, IAWS-Agri Society Ltd, Messrs Ronan Fitzpatrick, Michael Farrington, Edward Gilmartin Snr, John Farrington, Martin Murphy and T & J Farrington Ltd are undertakings within the meaning of section 3(1) of the Competition Act, and the notified arrangements for the purchase and sale of the entire issued share capital of Unigrain Dublin Ltd and Unigrain Foynes Ltd constitute an agreement between undertakings. For the reasons given above, the Authority believes that the restrictions on Mr Fitzpatrick and Mr Murphy

4. 'Competition Authority — Employee Agreements and the Competition Act', 15 September 1992 Decision No. 12 — Scully Tyrrell & Company/Edberg Ltd, 29 January 1993, Decision No. 20 — Apex Fire Protection Ltd./Mr Noel Murtagh, 10 June 1993.

3.20 competing with the business after they cease(d) to be employed by it had or have the effect of preventing, restricting or distorting competition within the State. The agreement therefore offends against section 4(1) of the Competition Act 1991 and does not satisfy the conditions necessary for the grant of a licence set out in section 4(2). The Competition Authority has refused to issue a certificate or grant a licence to the agreement of 12 January 1989, between IAWS-Agri Society Ltd (IAWS) and Messrs Ronan Fitzpatrick, Michael Farrington, Edward Gilmartin Snr, John Farrington, Martin Murphy and T & J Farrington Ltd (collectively the Vendors), for the purchase and sale of the entire issued share capital of Unigrain Dublin Ltd and Unigrain Foynes Ltd (collectively the Unigrain companies), (CA/691/92E), notified on 30 September 1992 under section 7 of the Competition Act 1991.

For the Competition Authority

Patrick Massey
Member

6 September 1994

3.21 **Competition Authority Decision No. 352, Kantoher Food Products Ltd/Carton Bros. Ltd:** 7 September 1994, Notification No. CA/1107/92E

Agreement for the sale of equipment and business – Agreement made before commencement of Competition Act but completion to take place after commencement of the Act – Restriction on competition imposed on vendor for three years from the date of completion – Transfer of goodwill of business – Transfer of technical know-how – Competition Act 1991 (No. 24) sections 3, 4 and 7 – EC Regulation No. 556/89

Facts: On 30 September 1992 notification was made to the Authority with a request for a certificate under section 4(4) of the Competition Act 1991 or, failing that, a licence under section 4(2) in respect of an arrangements for the sale by Kantoher Foods Products Ltd ('KFP') of a turkey processing line to Carton Bros. (Processing) Ltd ('CBPL').

The notified agreement was made on 29 July 1991 between KFP, CBPL and Carton Bros. Ltd ('Cartons') for the sale by KFP of the processing equipment and the goodwill of a turkey processing plant located at Killeedy, Co. Limerick to CBPL. The agreement contained a non-compete provision.

The Carton group of companies is involved in the production, rearing, processing and sale of chickens and poultry products. In November 1990 CBPL, a subsidiary of Cartons, acquired 76% of the shares of KFP from Kantoher Co-operative Agricultural and Dairy Society Ltd. In July 1991 CBPL, due to financial difficulties at KFP sold its 76% shareholding in KFP to Donal Flynn, a former manager of KFP. Immediately following the sale of that shareholding KFP sold the turkey processing equipment to CBPL on a deferred delivery basis which agreement is the subject of this notification. In December 1991 a liquidator was appointed to KFP and its assets were acquired by Grove Turkeys Ltd. The liquidator of KFP together with Grove Turkeys Ltd instituted legal proceedings against CBPL, Cartons and others seeking to have the contract of 29 July 1991 declared void.

The product market involved in the notification is that relating to the chicken and poultry meat products. The factory value of the processed poultry market was 180 million pounds per annum, 85% of the chicken market being concentrated with the top five companies and 75% of the turkey market being dominated by the Kerry Group (which includes the Grove Turkey Group). **3.21**

Under the terms of the notified agreement the turkey processing equipment was not to be removed by CBPL until 30 April 1993 (the transfer date) and until such date KFP were licensed to use the equipment and to process turkeys for both KFP and CBPL until that date. Clause 4 of the notified agreement contained a non-compete provision restricting KFP from competing with CBPL in the production of turkey products in Ireland for a period of three years from the transfer date.

The Authority by letter dated 15 July 1993 expressed its concerns in relation to the non-compete clause. Cartons submitted that the seasonal nature of the turkey market and the fact that the product was purchased infrequently justified such a clause. Cartons also argued that they brought considerable expertise to KFP which expertise included technical know-how and that they had installed their own computerised systems on the turkey processing line. They further stated that KFPs share of the turkey processing market was only 2.5% and that their exclusion from the market for three years would only have very minimal effect on competition. Cartons also submitted that the agreement to sell the turkey processing line had effectively been made prior to the sale by CBPL of its shareholding in KFP, at the time of such decision both CBPL and KFP were not economically independent but a group constituting a single economic entity and that the agreement amounted to a reallocation of an asset and a function within the group. Cartons did not avail of the opportunity of an oral hearing.

Decided by the Authority: In refusing to issue a certificate or grant a licence under sections 4(4) and 4(2) respectively of the Competition Act 1991 in respect of the notified agreements that:

(1) Each of CBPL and KFP are undertakings within the meaning of the Competition Act as both at the time of the agreement were bodies engaged for gain in the turkey and chicken processing business. Consequently the notified arrangements constitute an agreement between undertakings.

(2) While the sale of the business agreement was initiated prior to 1 October 1991, the commencement date of the Competition Act, the equipment the subject matter of the agreement was not to be transferred until 30 April 1993. The prohibition under section 4(1) applies to a current or continual contractual commitment, or to one entered into subsequent to the coming into force of the Act. The notified agreement is a continuing contractual commitment and therefore comes within the scope of the Act. The sale of a business *per se* does not offend against section 4(1) and in this particular case the respective market shares of Cartons and KFP being 6.2% and 2.5% do not result in any significant increase in concentration in the market.

(3) In the sale of a business a restriction does not offend against section 4(1) provided it does not exceed what is necessary to secure the transfer of the goodwill in terms of its duration, geographic cover and subject matter. The transfer of goodwill is not an issue in the notified arrangement as prior to the date of the notified agreement CBPL owned 76% of KFP and sold that shareholding to Mr. Flynn and then immediately bought the turkey processing line from KPF. CBPL had therefore already

3.21 acquired at least a part of the goodwill in the business. The turkeys which were processed by KFP under the equipment licenced to it by CBPL were considered by consumers to be CBPL products and the goodwill associated with the turkey processing business had in fact accrued to CBPL. In such circumstances a non-compete clause for three years from the date of the transfer of the equipment is not justified. Irrespective of the duration of such clause the fact that it only began to operate long after the date of the agreement also causes problems. Consequently the non-compete restriction offends against section 4(1).

(4) The infrequency of sales in the relevant market due to its seasonal nature is not an issue in this case as turkey processors operate largely by building up long term supply contracts with major multiples, butchers and caterers.

(5) A longer restriction on competing with the purchaser of a business is afforded where the purchase involves a high degree of technical know-how to afford the purchaser the opportunity to become familiar with the know-how and to be in a position to exploit it fully. Such considerations do not arise in this case since if there was any technical know-how involved it was the purchaser who supplied it in the first place and it does not therefore need additional time to become familiar with such know-how.

(6) The fact that the decision to transfer the turkey processing line from KFP to CBPL was made at a time when KFP was under the control of CBPL and therefore constituted a decision of a single economic entity does not render the arrangement inoffensive to section 4(1). Arrangements which were acceptable and not considered offensive under section 4(1) while the parties constitute a single economic entity might offend once the undertaking has become independent. In this case the parties no longer constitute a single economic entity and thus a restriction on competition offends against section 4(1).

(7) A restriction on KFP from competing with CBPL for three years from the transfer date goes beyond what is necessary to secure the transfer of the goodwill of the business as CBPL had already acquired the goodwill prior to the agreement. Consequently such restriction cannot be regarded as indispensable to the attainment of the objectives of the agreement and so does not satisfy the requirements for a licence.

Decisions and Notice referred to:
EC Commission Decision Reuter/BASF [1976] OJ L254/40, [1976] 2 CMLR D44
Competition Authority Decision No. 1, Nallen/O'Toole (Belmullet) — 2 April 1992 **3.3**
Competition Authority Decision No. 2 AGF/Irish Life **1.3.1**
Competition Authority Decision No. 3, Athlone Travel Ltd/ Michael Stein — 4 June 1992 **3.4**
Competition Authority Decision No. 8, ACT Group/Kindle Group — 4 September 1993 **3.6**
Compa Authority Decision No. 10, GI Corporation/General Semiconductor — 23 October 1992 **3.8**
Notice in respect of mergers and take-overs which pre-date the Competition Act **3.1**

Competition Authority Decision of 7 September 1994 relating to a proceeding under section 4 of the Competition Act 1991
Notification No. CA//1107/92E — Kantoher Food Products Ltd/Carton Bros. Ltd

Introduction

1. Arrangements for the sale by Kantoher Food Products Ltd (the vendor), of a turkey processing line located at Killeedy, Co. Limerick, to Carton Brothers (Processing) Ltd (the purchaser) were notified to the Authority on 30 September 1992. The notification requested a

certificate or, in the event of a refusal to issue a certificate, a licence. The Authority issued a Statement of Objections to the parties on 5 July 1994, indicating its intention to refuse their request for a certificate or a licence. Carton Bros. responded in a letter dated 2 August 1994. They did not request an Oral Hearing. **3.21**

The Facts

(a) *The subject of the Notification*

2. The notification concerns an agreement dated 29 July 1991 between Kantoher Food Products Ltd (KFP), Carton Brothers (Processing) Ltd (CBPL) and Carton Brothers Ltd (Cartons), for the sale by KFP of the equipment and the goodwill of a turkey processing plant, located at Killeedy, Co. Limerick to CBPL. The agreement contained a non-compete provision.

(b) *The Parties*

3. The Carton group of companies (Cartons) was established in the early 1920's and is involved in the production, rearing, processing and sale of chickens and poultry products. On 16 November 1990, CBPL a subsidiary of Cartons acquired 76% of KFP. Prior to the the takeover by Cartons KFP was a wholly owned subsidiary of Kantoher Co-Operative Agriculture and Dairy Society Ltd (the Co-Op). In July 1991, due to financial difficulties at the plant, CBPL was no longer in a position to support KFP and sold the entire shareholding (76%) of CBPL to Donal Flynn, a former manager of KFP. Mr Flynn undertook to procure substantial investment of new funds into KFP. Immediately following the purchase of the shareholding, KFP sold the turkey processing equipment to CBPL. This sale is the subject of the notification In December 1991, a liquidator was appointed to KFP and its assets acquired by the Kerry/ Grove Group. The liquidator of KFP together with Grove Turkeys Ltd subsequently instituted legal proceedings against CBPL, Cartons and others seeking to have the contract of 29 July 1991 declared void on several grounds.

(c) *The product and the market*

4. The products involved in this instance are chicken and poultry meat products. The 1989 Census of Industrial Production indicates that the factory gate value of sales of processed poultry was £118m. According to Cartons, the Irish market for chickens is highly concentrated with the top five companies having 85% of the market. They claimed that the turkey market was dominated by Kerry Group and Grove Turkey Group which are part of the same operation and control 75% of the market. The chicken business has a steady year round trade while the turkey business is seasonal with the bulk of the trade taking place at Christmas and other holidays. According to Cartons there is also a growing business for value-added turkey products.

5. Cartons submitted that the main customers for both chicken and turkey products, are the major multiples, the butcher and catering trades. The key to both markets is the ability of the processor to negotiate long term supply contracts. Cartons traditionally operated in the Dublin wholesale turkey market (up to 1976), but have now concluded contracts to process turkeys for smaller contractors.

(d) *The Arrangements*

6. The notification relates to an agreement made in July 1991 of the sale by KFP of a turkey processing line to CBPL. Although the agreement was made in July 1991 the equipment which was the subject of the sale was not due to be removed by CBPL until 30 April 1993 (the transfer date). Under the terms of a licence contained in clause 3 of the sale agreement, CBPL licensed KFP to use the equipment until the transfer date. KFP processed turkeys both for CBPL and for itself under the licence agreement. Clause 4 of the agreement contained a non-compete provision restricting KFP from competing with the purchaser in the production of turkey

3.21 products in Ireland for a period of three years from the transfer date. A liquidator was appointed to KFP in December 1991, and its assets were acquired by the Kerry/Grove Group. The liquidator together with Grove Turkeys Ltd subsequently took legal proceedings against CBPL seeking to have the contract of 29 July declared void.

(e) *Arguments in support of a certificate*

7. Cartons submitted that no restraint on competition was placed on KFP. Mr Flynn was getting out of the turkey business and had no intention of competing therein after the transfer date. No restriction was placed on KFP until after the transfer date. In addition the restriction only applied to producing or processing turkeys and did not prevent KFP from selling or marketing turkey products not processed by it. At the time of the agreement KFP were in urgent need of investment. A substantial part of the consideration for the equipment was paid on closing while leaving the equipment in the possession of KFP and allowing them to use it until the transfer date. The joint running of turkey and chicken processing operations had caused substantial difficulties for KFP and an essential part of the company's rationalisation plan was to concentrate solely on chicken production. Cartons submitted that CBPL was responsible for the removal expenses of the equipment. In addition the agreement and price were negotiated at 'arms length' with both parties having their own individual legal advice throughout.

8. In support of the three year non-compete clause, Cartons referred to the Authority's decision in Nallen/O'Toole and in particular to the fact that a non-compete clause is essential for the transfer of the goodwill in the sale of a business. They submitted that the restrictions were limited in terms of time, geographic coverage and subject matter. They also referred to the decision of the European Commission in Reuter/BASF and to the Commission's conclusion that provisions restricting the vendor of a business competing with the business sold could be found to be legitimate and not to contravene Article 85(1).

(f) *Arguments in support of a licence*

9. Cartons submitted that, due to the intention of Mr Flynn that KFP would no longer engage in the processing and production of turkeys, the purchase of the plant equipment to be utilised to produce and process turkeys contributed to improving production with a consequent resulting benefit to consumers. It was also argued that the takeover would secure the survival of competition due to Mr Flynn's intention not to continue to process turkeys. It was submitted that the three year non-compete clause was reasonable to secure the purchase of the business and goodwill of KFP and imposed upon KFP terms which were necessary to the attainment of the objectives.

(g) *Subsequent Developments*

10. The Authority communicated its concern regarding the non-compete clause in a letter to the parties, dated 15 July 1993. In a reply dated 11 August 1993 Cartons reiterated much of what they had already submitted in their original notification. In addition they indicated that, as in the Nallen/O'Toole and Athlone Travel cases, the seasonal nature of the turkey market justified the non-compete clause as the product was purchased infrequently. They argued that Cartons had brought considerable expertise and experience to KFP, including the training of personnel and the restructuring of the turkey processing line. They submitted that the expertise included technical know-how and they had installed their own computerised system of box weighing order processing and a computerised debtor system. They claimed that in line with the Authority's decision No. 10 GI Corporation/General Semiconductor, a period of five years was justified where technical know-how was involved. They stated the belief that it would be relatively easy for KFP to re-enter the turkey market after three years, having already established itself in the poultry business and having benefited from CBPL's involvement. Cartons had also given KFP the benefit of its poultry patent which it left with KFP. In addition Cartons submitted that KFP had benefited from CBPL's considerable repertoire of customer

contacts during its involvement. As most turkeys were exported due to the infrequency of turkey sales, export contracts were very valuable. In conclusion Cartons submitted that KFP has only a 2.5% share of the turkey processing market and their exclusion from the market for three years would only have a very minimal effect on competition. 3.21

11. On 5 July 1994 the Authority issued a Statement of Objections to the parties indicating its intention to refuse their request for a certificate or a licence. In a reply dated 2 August 1994 the solicitors acting on behalf of Carton Bros. argued that the notified agreement which was the subject of the notification should be considered in the context of the overall rescue plan put in place to ensure the survival of KFP. They stated that the sale of the turkey processing line was an essential pre-requisite of this plan designed to provide KFP with a cash injection and to phase out turkey production which was causing KFP a substantial loss. Its object was not to restrain competition but to ensure the survival of KFP which was unable to compete in both the chicken and turkey businesses. They also argued that the agreement to sell the turkey processing line was contemporaneous to the agreement by CBPL to sell its shareholding in KFP to Mr Flynn. They went on to argue that it had been agreed by both Mr Flynn and CBPL prior to the sale of the shares that KFP would sell the turkey processing line and goodwill to CBPL immediately following the sale of shares to Mr Flynn. The decision to sell the turkey processing line was, according to them, effectively made prior to the sale to Mr Flynn and therefore at a time when KFP was in the control of CBPL. They argued that the notified agreement therefore involved an agreement between undertakings which were not economically independent but rather a group constituting a single economic entity and that the agreement amounted to a re-allocation of an asset and a function within the group. They cited the Authority's decision in AGF-Irish Life Holdings that an agreement between members of the same group which provided for a re-allocation of functions within the group did not offend against section 4(1).

12. They further argued that, although KFP had acquired a majority shareholding in KFP eight months prior to the agreement, this was an inadequate period for them to have acquired the goodwill of the business, that the goodwill had reverted back to KFP during the period up to the transfer date when it had operated the turkey processing line, and that the non-compete provisions were therefore justified. They also argued that Mr Flynn's long standing service to KFP meant that much of the goodwill of the business attached to him. They also argued that the seasonal nature of the business justified a three year non-compete clause. In addition they stated that the line included equipment not commonly found in the turkey processing business which included technical know-how which would justify a non-compete restriction for up to five years.

13. In a letter dated 11 July 1994 solicitors acting on behalf of the liquidator of KFP stated that the liquidator supported the Authority's proposed decision and indicated that they considered a three year restriction to be excessive, particularly in the light of the Authority's guidelines set out in its decision in Nallen/O'Toole. None of the parties availed of the opportunity of an Oral Hearing afforded to them by the Authority.

Assessment

(a) *Section 4(1)*

14. Section 4(1) of the Competition Act states that 'all agreements between undertakings, decisions by associations of undertakings and concerted practices, which have as their object or effect the prevention, restriction or distortion of competition in goods or services in the State or in any part of the State are prohibited and void'.

(b) *The Undertakings and the Agreement*

15. Section 3(1) of the Competition Act defines an undertaking a 'a person, being an individual, a body corporate or an unincorporated body engaged for gain in the production,

3.21 supply or distribution of goods or the provision of a service.' CBPL is a corporate body engaged for gain in the rearing, processing and sale of poultry products. At the time of the agreement KFP was a corporate body engaged for gain in the turkey and chicken processing business. Consequently the notified arrangements constitute an agreement between undertakings.

(c) *Applicability of section 4(1)*

16. While the sale of business agreement was initiated prior to 1 October, 1991, the date on which the Competition Act came into force, the equipment, which was the subject of the agreement was not transferred until 30 April 1993. In the Authority's view, the prohibition under section 4(1) applies to a current or continuing contractual commitment, or one entered into subsequent to the coming into force of the Act.[1] In this instance the Authority considers that the notified agreement is a continuing contractual commitment and therefore comes within the scope of the Act. In the Authority's opinion, a sale of business *per se* does not offend against section 4(1). In this particular case, Cartons and KFP only had 6.2% and 2.5% shares respectively of the turkey market and the acquisition did not result in any significant increase in concentration in the market.

17. The non-compete provision in clause 4 of the agreement prevents the vendor from competing with the purchaser for a period of three years from the date of the transfer of the equipment. The Authority has given its view on non-compete clauses in sale of business agreements in a number of previous decisions. In the Authority's opinion, provided such a restriction does not exceed what is necessary to secure the transfer of the goodwill in terms of its duration, geographic coverage and subject matter, then it does not offend against section 4(1). The Authority believes however that the transfer of goodwill is not an issue in this instance as Cartons owned 76% of the entire shareholding of KFP prior to July 1991, when they sold it to Mr Flynn and then bought the turkey processing line.[2] Therefore they had already acquired at least part of the goodwill of the business. They then sold the shareholding in the overall business and on the same day bought back a part of that business, while licensing the vendor to operate the equipment involved for up to three years after the sale. During that time the vendor has processed turkeys for CBPL which were sold under its name. No evidence was advanced to suggest that the vendor or Mr Flynn acted on CPBL's behalf in dealing with customers. Thus the Authority is satisfied that the turkeys processed by the vendor using the equipment licensed to it were considered by those customers to be CPBL's products and the goodwill associated with KFP's turkey processing business has in fact accrued to CPBL. In the circumstances, the Authority considers that a non-compete clause for three years from the date of the transfer of the equipment is not justified. More importantly it is not just the duration of the non-compete clause but the fact that it only began to operate long after the date of the agreement which is problematical. Consequently the Authority considers that the restriction in clause 4 offends against section 4(1).

18. In their submission to the Authority, Cartons indicated that the three year restriction was justified in line with the Authority's decision in Nallen/O'Toole and Athlone Travel, as the seasonal nature of the turkey market resulted in the product being purchased infrequently. The Authority does not believe that infrequency of sales is an issue in this case. Turkey processors operate largely by building up long term supply contracts with major multiples, butchers and caterers. As stated in the previous paragraph, the Authority believes that the transfer of the relevant goodwill had taken place by the time of the transfer of the equipment. Consequently the Authority cannot accepts Cartons' submission in this regard.

19. Cartons also submitted that there was technical know-how involved. They argued that

1. Notice in respect of Mergers and Takeovers which predate the Competition Act — Competition Authority, *Iris Oifigiúil*, 14 May 1993, p. 367.
2. In the case of a straightforward sale of business a non-compete clause should be effective from the completion date.

in re-structuring the turkey processing line Cartons installed their own computerised system of box weighing order processing and a computerised debtor system. The EC Regulation on know-how licensing defines know-how as 'a body of technical information that is secret, substantial and identified in appropriate form'.[3] The Authority indicated in its decision in ACT/Kindle that it would accept such a definition of technical know-how.[4] In this instance the equipment was installed by Cartons and was subsequently transferred back to them with the other equipment. The purchaser of a business is afforded a longer period where the purchase involves a high degree of technical know-how to afford the purchaser the opportunity to become familiar with the know-how and to be in a position to exploit it fully. Again, however, such considerations do not arise in this case, since, if there was any technical know-how involved, it was the purchaser who supplied it in the first place and it does not therefore need additional time to become familiar with such know-how. Therefore the Authority does not accept Cartons submission in this regard. 3.21

20. Finally Cartons argued that the agreement did not offend against section 4(1) since it was effectively, if not in fact, concluded at a time when KFP was under the control of CPBL and it therefore constituted an agreement between a parent and a subsidiary. Irrespective of the actual time at which the agreement is concluded agreements between a parent and a subsidiary which result in their not competing with each other are not considered to be anti-competitive as they are regarded as part of a single economic entity. However, this ceases to apply if and when the undertakings cease to be part of a single economic entity. Arrangements which were acceptable and not considered offensive under section 4(1) while the parties constitute a single economic entity, might offend once the undertakings become independent. In this case the parties no longer constituted a single economic entity and thus a restriction on competing with one another offends against section 4(1).

(d) *Applicability of section 4(2)*

21. Under section 4(2), the Competition Authority may grant a licence in the case of any agreement or category of agreements which offends against section 4(1) but which, 'having regard to all relevant market productions, contributes to improving the production of goods or provision of services or to promoting technical or economic progress, while allowing consumers a fair share of the resulting benefit and which does not:

(i) impose on the undertakings concerned terms which are not indispensable to the attainment of those objectives;

(ii) afford undertakings the possibility of eliminating competition in respect of a substantial part of the products or services in question.'

22. The restriction on the vendor competing for three years from the transfer date in clause 4 of the agreement is considered to go beyond what was necessary to secure the transfer of the goodwill of the business as Cartons had already acquired the goodwill prior to the agreement. Consequently, in the Authority's opinion, it could not be regarded as indispensable to the attainment of the objectives of the agreement and so does not satisfy the requirements for a licence.

The Decision

23. In the opinion of the Competition Authority, the agreement between Kantoher Food Products Ltd and Carton Brothers (Processing) Ltd relating to the purchase of the turkey processing line at Killeedy, Co. Limerick by Carton Brothers (Processing) Ltd (Notification No. CA/1107/92E) notified on 30 September 1992, under section 7, constitutes an agreement between undertakings. It considers that the restriction in clause 4 of the agreement on the

3. Regulation No. 556/89 on the application of Article 85(3) of the Treaty to certain categories of know-how licensing agreements [1989] OJ L61/1.
4. Competition Authority No. 8, ACT Group plc and Kindle Group Ltd, 4 September 1992.

3.21 vendors competing with the purchaser, for three years from the date of the transfer of the equipment, offends against section 4(1) of the Competition Act and does not satisfy the requirements for a licence under section 4(2). Consequently the Authority refuses to issue a certificate or grant a licence in respect of the said notified agreement.

For the Competition Authority

Patrick Massey
Member

7 September 1994

3.22 **Competition Authority Decision No. 353, Hickson International plc/Angus Fine Chemicals Ltd:** 7 September 1994, Notification No. CA/56/92

Arrangements for the sale of a business – Clause in the share purchase agreement restricting vendor from competing with the undertaking being sold for a period of four years – Clauses in share purchase agreement restricting the vendor from utilising or disclosing technical know-how and other confidential information associated with the undertaking being sold for an unlimited period – Product supply agreement whereunder the undertaking being sold agreed to purchase 90% of an essential product from the vendor for a period of three years – Know-how license agreement whereunder vendor agreed in very restrictive circumstances to license to the undertaking being sold certain know-how relating to the manufacture of a particular product – Secrecy agreement whereunder the undertaking being sold agreed to keep secret for a period of ten years know-how supplied by the vendor in order to enable the undertaking being sold to produce certain products for the vendor – Statement of objections -Amendment of notified arrangements – EC Regulation 556/89 – Mergers, Take-Overs and Monopolies (control) Act 1978 (No. 17) – Competition Act 1991 (No. 24) sections 3, 4 and 7

Facts: On 29 July 1992 notification was made to the Authority of arrangements between Hickson International plc ('Hickson'), as Purchaser, and Angus Chemical Company, the Vendor for the sale and purchase of Angus Fine Chemicals Ltd ('AFCL'), a Cork based chemical company with the request for a certificate under section 4(4) of the Competition Act or, failing that, a licence under section 4(2).

Hickson is an international chemical company whose headquarters are in the UK and whose main activities can be divided into four categories: fine chemicals, performance chemicals, applied chemicals and protections and coatings. Angus, a USA based company whose ultimate parent is Alberta Natural Gas Company Ltd was until the notified arrangement the parent company of AFCL. Angus produces and markets nitroparaffin based chemicals, fine chemicals and pharmaceutical intermediaries.

AFCL, an Irish registered company based in Cork, makes high value organic chemicals to order for major pharmaceutical companies. AFCL is a highly specialised company engaging in custom fine chemical manufacturing. This involves the manufacture of higher value organic chemicals to the order of customers who provide the greater part of the know-how necessary for the production of such chemicals. AFCL's products constitute raw materials which are subsequently processed to an active drug ingredient or to a pharmaceutical intermediate. It has six customers and one main customer ('the Main Customer') for whom it supplies a chemical NMSM. This Main Customer accounts for 40% of AFCL's business. A product called nitromethane, which AFCL obtains from its former parent Angus is used to produce NMSM. Angus is the leading producer of nitromethane in the world with only three other companies, all of which are located in the Peoples Republic of China, also producing the chemical. 3.22

The market in which AFCL operates is for the manufacture of custom fine chemicals. There are no substitutes for the goods which it produces and therefore the relevant market is not that for the particular products produced by AFCL but the market for custom fine chemical production generally. This market cannot be analyzed in terms of an Irish market but it is to be considered as a global market due to the location of competitors throughout the world. Transportation costs are not a factor in this market as the products being dealt with are high in value and small in volume.

The arrangements notified involve a number of agreements which are inter-related of which only four are relevant for review under the Competition Act. These are; a share purchase agreement, an exclusive supply agreement, a know-how licensing agreement and a secrecy agreement. All of these agreements were dated 8 July 1992 with the exception of the secrecy agreement which was dated 22 June 1992.

The share purchase agreement provided for the 100% acquisition of AFCL by Hickson. Clause 9.1 of the agreement contained a number of restrictive covenants made by Angus and binding Angus and other members of the Angus Group. Clause 9.1 (i) provided that Angus would not for a period of four years following completion canvass or solicit orders from persons who were customers of AFCL at any time within three years prior to completion. Clause 9.1 (ii) provided that Angus would not for a period of four years following completion supply or manufacture any relevant products for any person who had been a customer of AFCL at any time within three years prior to completion. Clause 9.1 (iii) provided that for a period of two years following completion, Angus would not seek to induce particular employees to become employed by Angus or other members of the Angus Group. Under clause 9.1 (iv) and (v) Angus undertook not to use or reveal to any person any of the know-how or trade secrets or any other confidential extra information owned by and exclusive to AFCL unless the relevant licensor or any joint owner thereof shall have consented in writing to Angus so doing. In addition Angus agreed not to use or reveal to any person any of the foregoing which have been licensed to AFCL or which are jointly owned by AFCL and a third party until such time as such know-how falls into the public domain otherwise than by a breach of this undertaking or is made available to Angus by a third party other than in breach of any duty of confidentiality.

Under the terms of the supply agreement Angus agreed to supply to AFCL nitromethane for the duration of the agreement on condition that AFCL purchased from Angus such quantities of nitromethane as necessary to satisfy 90% of AFCL requirements of such product for the production and sale of NMSM to its Main Customer. The agreement is for a period of three years terminating on 31 December 1994 but is reviewable on an annual basis thereafter and may be terminated by either party on 60 days written notice prior to the end of the term.

Under the terms of the know-how license agreement Angus agreed to license technology to AFCL with which AFCL could manufacture the nitromethane itself in

3.22 the event of a shortfall in supply and only in order to enable AFCL to produce the NMSM for its Main Customer. The license granted is a personal and non- transferable right to use the technology and AFCL is obliged to use its best endeavours to minimise the possibility of this license becoming operative and to minimise the period during which it is operative. In essence the purpose of this license is to ensure continuation of supply for AFCL in the event of supply from Angus being interrupted by some unforeseen event such as a fire or accident at the Angus plant. The agreement contains stringent obligations on the part of AFCL with regard to confidentiality of the know-how so revealed and a further obligation to return the information and all related documents and materials upon written request from Angus. The agreement will expire on the earlier of the termination of the contract between AFCL and the Main Customer or the termination of the supply agreement.

Under the terms of the secrecy agreement AFCL agreed to treat as confidential for a ten year period certain technical information disclosed to it by Angus to enable AFCL to produce certain products for Angus. The secrecy agreement will not apply to any portion of the secret information which comes into the public domain through no fault of AFCL or is disclosed to AFCL by a third party who has a right to make such disclosure.

The notifying parties submitted that the acquisition by Hickson amounts to a merger or takeover for the purpose of section 5 of the Mergers, Takeovers and Monopolies (Control) Act 1978 and having already been cleared by the Minister for Industry and Commerce should not be reviewable under the Competition Act. They further submitted that the acquisition of 100% interest in AFCL could only be reviewed under the Competition Act, if at all, under section 5 of the Competition Act which deals with abuses of a dominant position.

The Authority expressed concerns about certain aspects of the notified arrangements and additional information was sought. The parties replied on 8 April 1993. In relation to the restrictions on disclosure of confidential information contained in clauses 9.1 (iv) and (v) of the share purchase agreement the parties argued that this could be distinguished from EC Commission precedents on the basis that the covenants contained therein did not prevent Angus from engaging in other businesses. They also submitted that the restriction not being for a fixed term was reasonable and most effectively reflected the legitimate commercial aspirations of the parties. It was also submitted that 90% of the know-how involved was either owned by a customer exclusively or jointly by AFCL and a customer. The Authority issued a statement of objections to the parties on 11 April 1994 indicating that the non-compete provisions in clauses 9.1 (iv) and (v) offended against section 4(1) of the Competition Act and did not satisfy the requirements for a license. By letter dated 1 June 1994 the parties indicated that they would amend the provisions of clause 9.1 (iv) and (v) such that there would remain an unlimited restriction on the use or disclosure by Angus of know-how which was owned by third parties or owned jointly by AFCL and third parties. The restriction on Angus from using or disclosing know-how which is the exclusive property of AFCL is to be subject to the proviso that such restriction would not prevent Angus from engaging in manufacturing, supplying or soliciting orders for products in competition with AFCL once four years had elapsed since completion. A supplemental agreement recording the amended clauses was signed on 1 September 1994 and distinguishes between technical know-how belonging in whole or in part to customers of AFCL and that technical know-how which belongs to AFCL itself.

Decided by the Authority: 3.22

(A) In issuing a certificate under section 4(4) of the Competition Act in respect of the share sale agreement, the know- how license agreement and the secrecy agreement that:

(1) Each of Hickson, Angus and AFCL are undertakings within the meaning of the Competition Act and consequently the notified arrangements constitute agreements between undertakings.

(2) The arrangements, insofar as they constitute a concentration, are not automatically excluded from the scope of section 4(1). Where a notified arrangement constitutes an agreement between undertakings the issue to be decided is whether it has the object or effect of preventing, restricting or distorting competition. The stated object of the notified arrangements is to transfer ownership of the business of AFCL from Angus to Hickson which object does not *per se* offend against section 4(1).

(3) AFCL is a custom fine chemical producer which is a market in which other Hickson subsidiaries are also engaged. As a result of the acquisition the number of competitors in the relevant market will be reduced. An agreement which leads to a reduction in the number of competitors does not *per se* prevent, restrict or distort competition. The object of section 4(1) is to protect competition and not competitors. The reduction in the number of competitors does not necessarily result in a reduction of competition.

(4) The sale of AFCL is unlikely to have any effect in competition in the relevant market due to the fact that the relatively low transport costs do not represent a barrier to competition from overseas producers and also that a number of customers could produce there own requirements in-house if such became necessary. While the costs of establishing a plant to produce such products are not insignificant they are within the ability of a large number of chemical and pharmaceutical firms which would have the necessary skills and resources to enter the market.

(5) The notification involves the sale of a business engaged in the production of high grade organic chemicals which clearly involves technical know-how. The restrictions in clauses 9.1 (i) and (ii) which are of four years duration, do not exceed what is necessary for the complete transfer of the business where technical know-how is involved. The restrictions are limited to certain products and to dealing with anyone who was a customer of AFCL during the previous three years so that in terms of geographic scope and subject matter they involve no more than is necessary to secure the complete transfer of the business. These clauses do not offend against section 4(1) of the Competition Act.

(6) The restriction in clause 9.1 (iii) of the share sale agreement on Angus from soliciting employees of AFCL is necessary to protect the goodwill of the business being sold. The restriction in this case being two years in duration is sufficient to ensure the transfer of the goodwill and does not offend against section 4(1) of the Competition Act.

(7) The situation with regard to clauses 9.1 (iv) and (v) which set out unlimited restrictions on Angus from utilising the know-how of AFCL is complex. The business in which AFCL is engaged, being the operation of a custom fine chemical production plant, involves a degree of technical know-how. There is also another different element of technical know-how involved where AFCL produces chemicals in accordance with the specifications of its customers. This latter know-how belongs to those AFCL customers who have effectively licensed it to AFCL and these two categories

3.22 of know-how must be treated differently.

It is legitimate for customers who supply technical know-how to AFCL in order for AFCL to produce products to their specifications, to restrict AFCL from using such know-how for any other purpose. Such know-how is the property of AFCL's customers and was not, and is not the property of AFCL or of Angus. Consequently to the extent that the restrictions in clauses 9.1 (iv) and (v) related to technical know-how provided to AFCL by one of its customers, in order to enable it to supply that customer, they do not offend against section 4(1).

Technical know-how regarding the operation of a custom fine chemical plant itself is different. In this instance an obligation to keep know-how secret from third parties imposed on the transferor of an undertaking may not be used to prevent the transferor after the expiry of a reasonable term of a non- competition clause, from competing with the transferee by means of new and further developments of such know-how. To the extent that they have this effect clauses 9.1 (iv) and (v), as notified, offended against section 4(1) because they went beyond what was necessary to secure the transfer of the business being sold.

The amendments to clauses 9.1 (iv) and (v) concerning the restriction on using know-how and other confidential information, the exclusive property of AFCL will not prevent Angus from engaging in manufacturing or supply or soliciting orders for products in competition with AFCL after the four year non-compete clause has elapsed. There is no longer an unlimited restriction on the use of such know-how such as would prevent the transferor ever re-entering the market. Consequently such restrictions do not now offend against section 4(1) of the Act.

(8) The provision in the supply agreement whereunder AFCL is required to purchase 90% of its requirement of nitromethane for the production of NMSM for its Main Customer restricts competition for the supply of nitromethane to AFCL. While there may only be a small number of suppliers of the product throughout the world the provision restricts competition by obliging AFCL to purchase 90% of its requirements from a single supplier which is stated to be dominant in the market for that product. In addition the provision would prevent new suppliers from competing for AFCL's business and consequently it restricts competition in the market for the product within the State and offends against section 4(1).

(9) Under the terms of the know-how license agreement AFCL may use the know-how to produce NMSM during periods when it is unable to obtain supplies from Angus or any other source. The know-how belongs to Angus and they are not under an obligation to supply such know-how to AFCL. The arrangement is designed purely to ensure that in the event of any disruption of supplies AFCL will be able to produce its own supplies of nitromethane in order to continue producing NMSM. While EC know-how licensing regulation 556/89 provides that a license may not restrict the quantities which the licensee may produce, the present arrangement is not a standard know-how license but is an arrangement designed to deal with a particular contingency, which may never arise. Consequently the license agreement does not offend against section 4(1) of the Competition Act.

(10) The secrecy agreement notified is concerned with preserving confidential information, essentially technical know-how, which Angus had previously supplied to AFCL, to enable AFCL to produce certain products for Angus. While such information was not provided as part of a know-how license arrangement it was in many respects a similar type of arrangement, albeit one between a parent and a

subsidiary. As in the case of licensed know-how, the know-how is the property of the parent, and it is entitled to be protected against its disclosure to any third party. Consequently, the secrecy agreement does not offend against section 4(1) of the Competition Act. 3.22

(B) In granting a licence for a period of five years under section 4(2) of the Competition Act in respect of the supply agreement that:

(1) The fact that there are only a small number of suppliers of the product in question in the world, that Angus is the dominant producer, that access to supplies is essential for AFCL to produce certain products in order to supply its customers, that in the absence of such provision there could well be a disruption of supplies to AFCL with the result that AFCL would lose a valuable customer accounting for one third of its output, are all circumstances which made a guaranteed supply of the product essential for Hickson in agreeing to acquire AFCL at the price paid. Consequently the supply agreement may be indispensable to AFCL for a time.

(2) The supply agreement does not afford the undertaking the possibility of eliminating competition in respect of a substantial part of the market in question. The supply agreement therefore satisfies the requirements of section 4(2). In the circumstances the restrictions in the supply agreement are only necessary to avoid disruption to supplies in the short term and therefore the license is to be limited to a period of five years from the date of the notification.

Cases and Decisions referred to:

Remia v. EC Commission (Case No. 42/84) [1985] ECR 2545; [1987] 1 CMLR 1
BAT & Reynolds v. EC Commission and Philip Morris (Case No. 142 & 156/84) [1987] ECR 4487; [1988] 4 CMLR 24
EC Commission Decision – Reuter/BASF [1976] OJ L254/40 [1976] 2 CMLR D44
Competition Authority Decision No.1, Nallen/O'Toole – 2 April 1992 **3.3**
Competition Authority Decision No.6, Woodchester Bank Ltd/UDT Bank Ltd – 4 August 1992 **3.5**
Competition Authority Decision No. 8, ACT/Kindle – 4 September 1992 **3.6**
Competition Authority Decision No. 9, Budget Travel/Phil Fortune – 14 September 1992 **3.7**
Competition Authority Decision No. 10, GI Corporation/General Semiconductor Industries Inc., 23 October 1992 **3.8**

Competition Authority Decision 7 September 1994 relating to a proceeding under section 4 of the Competition Act 1991
Notification No. CA/56/92 — Hickson International plc/Angus Fine Chemicals Ltd

The Facts

(a) *Subject of the Notification*

1. The notified arrangements concern the acquisition of Angus Fine Chemicals Ltd (AFCL), a Cork based company, by Hickson International plc (Hickson), an English company based in West Yorkshire, from ANGUS Chemical Company (ANGUS), the US based parent company of AFCL. The arrangements include a number of related agreements. The Authority issued a statement of objections to the parties on 11 April 1994, indicating its intention to refuse to issue a licence or grant a certificate to the notified arrangements. In a letter dated 1 June 1994, the parties indicated that they would amend the offensive provisions in the arrangements. Notice of intention to grant a certificate and licence was published in the *Irish Times* on 24 June 1994.

3.22 No submissions were received in response to the notice. The Supplemental Agreement giving effect to the proposed amendments was signed on 1 September 1994.

(b) *The Parties concerned*

2. The parties to the acquisition are Hickson International plc and ANGUS Chemical Company of Illinois, USA. AFCL is the subject of the acquisition agreement. It is a party to some of the related agreements.

3. Hickson International plc is an independent group of businesses specialising exclusively in the provision of high quality chemical products for manufacturing industries and markets worldwide. It is a publicly quoted company. In 1991 it had a turnover of STG£379m, of which STG£79m was attributed to fine chemicals. The company's business activities can be put into four categories: Fine Chemicals, Performance Chemicals, Applied Chemicals and Protections and Coatings. Its sales in Ireland for 1991 amounted to STG£529,000 consisting solely of sales of surfactants and timber treatment products.

(i) Fine Chemicals: This division is currently made up of two companies, Hickson and Welch based at Castleford, England and Hickson Danchem, based in Virginia, USA. Hickson and Welch is the world's largest merchant manufacturer of nitrotoluene derivatives which are sold into the detergent, textile, paper, dyestuff and agrochemical markets. It is also a custom manufacturer of chemicals i.e. it manufactures higher value organic chemicals to the order of its customers who may provide the necessary know-how or rely on Hickson and Welch to develop it. Hickson Danchem is a toll chemical manufacturer: i.e. it sells its manufacturing skills to provide customers with their specific requirements.

(ii) Protections and Coatings: This division sells varnishes and lacquers for coating of wood furniture, stains for wood products and chemicals for the protection of wood against fire, insect attack and rot. It manufactures these chemicals in England, Italy, Holland and France.

(iii) Applied Chemicals: This division sells wood protection chemicals in North America and sulphur containing chemicals into the agricultural market as fertiliser and into the mining and other industries for a range of uses including mineral processing. Its companies trading in this field are Hickson Corporation, Kerley and Koppers-Hickson (joint venture, 49%).

(iv) Performance Products: This division sells surface active chemicals or 'surfactants' to the detergent and personal care industries from manufacturing plants in England and South Africa. It also sells a range of organic and inorganic chemicals to diverse industries from plants in South Africa. Its companies operating in this area are Manro, Hickson Timber Products and Hickson Surface Coating.

4. ANGUS Chemical Company is a Delaware based company which is a wholly owned subsidiary of Canstates Holdings Inc., whose ultimate parent is the Alberta Natural Gas Company Ltd of Alberta, Canada, a company quoted on the Toronto Stock Exchange. Angus produces and markets nitroparaffin based chemicals, fine chemicals and pharmaceutical intermediaries. Nitroparaffins are produced at the company's plant located at Sterlington, Louisianna. During 1991 this plant was damaged in an explosion and fire. The company also has a wholly-owned subsidiary Angus Chemie GmbH operating in the Federal Republic of Germany. In 1991 it had a turnover of $112m.

5. AFCL makes value organic chemicals to order for major pharmaceutical companies. Following its acquisition by Hickson, its name was changed to Hickson Pharmacem Ltd. It incurred a net loss of £4.3m. in 1991 on an annual turnover of £17m. It has 160 employees. The plant was damaged in an explosion and fire during 1993.

(c) *The Product*

6. AFCL is a custom fine chemical manufacturer. By custom fine chemical manufacture is meant the manufacture of higher value organic chemicals to the order of customers who provide the greater part of the know-how necessary for the production of such chemicals. AFCL's products constitute raw materials which are subsequently processed to an active drug ingredient

or to a pharmaceutical intermediate. AFCL currently produces chemicals for a relatively small number of firms. It has 6 customers of which 3 are on formal long term contracts. Its contracts include one for the supply of [ ] NMSM to [ ][1] This accounts for 40% of AFCL's business. A product called nitromethane, which AFCL had obtained from its former parent Angus, is used to produce NMSM. NMSM is used to manufacture Zantac, a popular anti-ulcer drug registered by the Food and Drug Administration (FDA) of the USA.

(d) *The market*

7. The market in which AFCL operates is that for the manufacture of custom fine chemicals. There are no substitutes for the goods produced by AFCL in the sense that it produces specific products for particular customers. Although the chemical products produced by AFCL are goods, in reality it appears that AFCL is engaged in providing a service, namely the production of such chemicals to the customer's specifications. It competes with other similar producers for contracts to produce such goods. The buyers of such products provide the necessary know-how to produce them and, in effect, they are contracting out the task of producing the raw materials which they require. Producers of custom fine chemicals such as AFCL compete for the business of producing such chemicals. Thus, in considering whether the arrangements have the effect of preventing, restricting or distorting competition, the focus of attention is not on the market for the particular products currently being produced by AFCL, but on the market for custom fine chemical production generally.

8. Competition in this market is provided in the main by the in- house divisions of potential pharmaceutical industry customers and other suppliers located throughout the world. It was claimed that competing firms located in Ireland include Newport Pharmaceuticals, Athlone Chemicals, Irish Fehr, Plaistowe and S.I.F.E. It was also claimed that there were a number of competitors in the UK including Sterling Organics (Eastman Kodak), Fine Organics (Laporte), MTM plc., Ibis (Shell) and Robinson Brothers. Transportation costs are not a factor in this market as the products being dealt with are high in value and small in volume. The notifying parties claim therefore that competition is truly global. The notifying parties claimed that, as there was no particular Irish market for customs fine chemicals, it was not possible to calculate figures for such a market. The custom fine chemical market worldwide is estimated at US$50 billion annually of which pharmaceutical chemical demand constitutes 40% to 50%.

9. The production of NMSM is a particularly significant part of AFCL's business. There are only two purchasers of NMSM worldwide, [ ] and another purchaser of whom it was claimed purchases approximately 10% of the quantity purchased by [ ]. There are four suppliers of the raw material needed to manufacture NMSM, nitromethane. These are Angus and three companies operating in the People's Republic of China. The arrangements notified include an agreement between AFCL and Angus for the purchase of Nitromethane. The combined production capacity of the Chinese companies is substantially less that of Angus. AFCL is the only user of nitromethane in Ireland, although there are many other users of the product worldwide, given the diverse nature of the end products which it is used to produce. The notifying parties have indicated that there are no effective substitute products available for either NMSM or nitromethane.

10. According to the 1989 Census of Industrial Production (CIP), the gross output of the chemical industry in Ireland was £2,282.6m. At that time, the industry employed 12,923 people in 216 establishments.[2] Of these 155 had a workforce of less than 50. Only 54 establishments employed more than 100 people, but these accounted for 63.3% of gross output. The estimated turnover for the industry in 1989 was £2235m.[3] The CIP figures indicate that there were 112 firms in the chemical sector in 1989 compared with 90 in 1981. According to the IDA there

1. The complete formula for NMSM and the customer's name are business secrets.
2. An establishment is effectively an individual plant or factory.
3. Estimated as gross output +/– changes in stocks.

3.22 were 277 chemical firms operating in Ireland in 1991 of which 110 were foreign owned.[4] The CIP figures for the chemical industry include 72 pharmaceutical establishments in Ireland in 1989 with a gross output of £1,328m. The number of pharmaceutical firms in 1989 was 51 compared with 33 in 1981.

11. There is no specific information on the number of custom fine chemical producers. It is believed that a number of the firms included under the broad chemicals classification in official statistics are engaged in the production of such goods. It is likely that a number of the pharmaceutical firms purchase raw materials from fine chemical producers whether in Ireland or elsewhere, while others may produce their requirements in-house.

12. A high percentage of what is produced by Irish chemical companies is exported, with few companies depending solely on the domestic market. The value of chemical exports in 1991 was £2,657.5m. Imports of chemical products are also relatively high, amounting to £1,707.5m in 1991. Imports of organic chemicals in 1991 amounted to £349.4m, 20.5% of all chemical imports. Again it is not possible to establish how much of these imports could be classed as custom fine chemicals, although much of what is imported consists of raw materials for further processing. Nevertheless it would appear that transportation costs do not constitute an impediment to competition from overseas suppliers of custom fine chemicals.

(e) *The arrangements*

13. The notified arrangements involve a number of agreements as follows:

— a share purchase agreement,

— an exclusive supply agreement,

— a know-how licensing agreement,

— two consultancy agreements,

— a vendor agreement,

— a deed of agreement,

— a secrecy agreement,

— an agreement to transfer invention rights,

— an inventory value agreement,

— an accounting memorandum.

All of the agreements were dated 8 July 1992, with the exceptions of the secrecy agreement and the agreement to transfer invention rights which were dated 22 June 1992 and the consultancy agreements which were dated 4 August 1992.

14. The share purchase agreement specifically provides at clause 13.3 that:

> This Agreement (including all documents to be executed pursuant to Clause 4), the Exit Deed, the Disclosure Letter, the Accounting Memorandum and the In-4 Agreement contain the whole agreement between the parties relating to the subject matter of this Agreement. . . .[5]

Clause 12.1 provides that:

> The parties shall immediately on the execution hereof notify this Agreement and the documents to be executed pursuant to this Agreement to the Competition Authority of the Republic of Ireland pursuant to and in compliance with the provisions of the

4. IDA Annual Report 1991. It is important to note that the CSO and IDA figures are not directly comparable.

5. Clause 4 refers to the Nitromethane Licence Agreement, the Supply Agreement and the Consultancy Agreements.

Competition Act 1991, with a view to obtaining a certificate or a licence in respect of the provisions of this Agreement and such documents. 3.22

Notwithstanding this, the Authority only received all of the agreements on 2 December 1992 following several requests.

Share Purchase Agreement

15. The Share Purchase Agreement, (Share Agreement), provides for the 100% acquisition of AFCL by Hickson through the purchase of all the issued and outstanding shares in the company. Clause 9.1 of the agreement contains a number of restrictive clauses. Specifically it provides that neither the Vendor hereby nor any other member of the Vendor Group will:

> (i) for a period of 4 years immediately following completion canvass or solicit orders for the supply of Restricted Products (as defined) to, or for the manufacture of Restricted Products for, any person who was a customer of AFCL at any time within the three year period prior to completion; or
> (ii) for a period of 4 years immediately following completion, supply or manufacture Restricted Products to or for any person who has been a customer of AFCL at any time within the three year period prior to completion; or
> (iii) for a period of 2 years immediately following completion, induce or seek to induce any particular employee of AFCL at completion (including certain named individuals who have employment arrangements with ANGUS but who are regarded as employees of AFCL for this purpose) to become employed whether as employee or consultant or otherwise, by ANGUS or other members of its group; or
> (iv) use, or reveal to any person, any of the know-how or the trade secrets, techniques or processes owned by and exclusive to AFCL or unless the relevant licensor or any joint owner thereof shall have consented in writing to ANGUS so doing, use or reveal to any person any of the foregoing which have been licensed to AFCL, or which are jointly owned by AFCL and a third party, until such time as the same fall into the public domain otherwise than by reason of a breach of this undertaking or is made available to ANGUS or any other member of its group by a third party other than in breach of any duty of confidentiality owed by that third party to AFCL; or
> (v) disclose to any person any other confidential extra information of AFCL or of any customer of AFCL (other than where ANGUS is authorised by such customer in writing to do so), until such time as the same shall fall into the public domain otherwise than by reason of a breach of this undertaking or is made available to ANGUS or any other member of its group by a third party other than in breach of any duty of confidentiality owed by that third party to AFCL; or
> (vi) knowingly assist, or procure any other person to do any of the foregoing things.

16. Clause 9.4 provides for the amendment of any part of Clause 9 should it be considered void in its present form.

Nitromethane Supply Agreement

17. To take effect concurrent with the Acquisition, AFCL entered into a long term contract with ANGUS for the supply of nitromethane. This is the 'Nitromethane Supply Agreement' (the Supply Agreement). Clause 1 provides that:

> (a) Subject to the provisions of clause (c), during the term of this Agreement, ANGUS shall sell and deliver to Buyer and Buyer shall purchase and accept from ANGUS quantities of Product necessary to satisfy ninety percent (90%) of Buyer's requirements of Product for the production and sale of [ ] ('NMSM') to [ ] and [ ] being

3.22 collectively referred to hereinafter as [ ], as the same may be amended, renewed, extended or otherwise modified or replaced from time to time (the [ ] Agreement).[6]

18. AFCL has the option of purchasing additional quantities of nitromethane. The agreement provides, however, that Angus is under no obligation to sell and deliver more than 400,000 pounds of Nitromethane per annum under the terms of this Agreement although if the quantities to be supplied exceed that limit it has the option of supplying such quantities upon the terms and subject to the conditions set forth in the agreement.

19. Clause 3 provides that the agreement is for a period of three years commencing January 1, 1992 through December 31, 1994. It also provides that the agreement will be automatically renewed on an annual basis thereafter unless one of the parties terminates it by written notice to the other at least sixty (60) days prior to the end of the term.

Nitromethane Licence Agreement

20. In addition ANGUS agreed to licence technology by which AFCL could manufacture this material itself in the event of a shortfall in supply. This is the 'Nitromethane Licence Agreement' (the Licence Agreement). Under the terms of this agreement, ANGUS agrees to grant to AFCL a limited right and license to use the technology that ANGUS possesses to produce Nitromethane. Clause 2 provides that, if, after full compliance by all parties with section 4(a) of the [ ] Agreement, AFCL and [ ] are unable to obtain Nitromethane for use in producing NMSM to fulfil the [ ] Agreement, Angus will grant, subject to any required compliance with applicable export laws and regulations, AFCL a personal, non-transferable right and licence to use the technology at its current plant located in Cork, solely in connection with the production by AFCL of chemically synthesised Nitromethane for use in producing NMSM pursuant to the [ ] Agreement. AFCL is obliged to use its best efforts to minimise the possibility of this licence becoming operative and to minimise the period during which it is operative.

21. In addition AFCL may only use the technology during those limited periods in which AFCL and [ ] cannot obtain Nitromethane as contemplated by section 4(a) of the [ ] Agreement and is therefore required to chemically synthesise Product pursuant to section 4(b) of the [ ] Agreement Title to the technology which may be licensed to AFCL and any other information (as hereafter defined) is not conveyed to AFCL by the licence granted. The agreement also provides that title to any improvements made to the technology by AFCL at any time that the licence granted hereunder is operative shall be owned by AFCL. AFCL hereby grants to ANGUS an irrevocable non-exclusive royalty- free personal right and license to use such improvements.

22. Clause 3 provides that AFCL must notify ANGUS in writing that it requires the technology, setting forth in sufficient detail the facts and circumstances surrounding such requirement. Angus is then required to make the technology available to AFCL as soon as reasonably practicable and in any case not later than twenty (20) days after the written notification. AFCL is also required to notify ANGUS in writing as soon as it no longer requires the technology to produce nitromethane in accord with the agreement.

23. Clause 4 states that:

> (a) *Obligations:* AFCL shall maintain in strict confidence and shall not disclose to any third party any Technology or other information disclosed by ANGUS to AFCL, including, without limitation, information disclosed by ANGUS personnel to AFCL pursuant to section 3(b) of this Agreement (collectively, the 'Information'). In addition, AFCL shall not use the Information except solely for the purposes contemplated herein.

6. This is an agreement between AFCL and one of its customers. It is not part of the present notification and has not been notified separately. This decision does not apply to this agreement.

AFCL shall limit disclosure of Information to only those employees of AFCL who have a need to know such Information solely for purposes contemplated herein. AFCL shall require that, as a condition to an AFCL employee's receipt of any Information, each AFCL employee shall expressly agree to be bound by the confidentiality and use terms of this Agreement. AFCL shall bear full responsibility and liability for breach of this Agreement by its current or former employees. **3.22**

(b) *Limitations:* The obligations of section 4(a) shall not apply to information which:
(1) is now or shall in the future become available to the general public through no fault or action of AFCL;
(2) is disclosed to AFCL subsequent to the date hereof by a party other than ANGUS without obligation of confidentiality; or
(3) is developed by AFCL subsequent to the date hereof independent of any past or future disclosure from ANGUS.

(c) *Disclosure:* If disclosure of Information is sought by any third party pursuant to court process or otherwise; or (ii) required to be disclosed to a governmental body under law, AFCL shall notify ANGUS immediately in writing and before making any such disclosure. Thereafter, AFCL shall, after consultation with ANGUS, take all reasonable steps requested by ANGUS to assist ANGUS in procuring a confidentiality order, confidential treatment or otherwise avoiding any public disclosure of Information.

(d) *Return of Information:* Upon ANGUS' written request, AFCL agrees to return any and all documents or other materials containing or reflecting Information. AFCL agrees to give ANGUS whatever reasonable assurances ANGUS requires that all documents or other materials containing or reflecting Information have been returned.

(e) *Injunction:* AFCL acknowledges that ANGUS may suffer irreparable harm if any Information is disclosed or used in violation of the terms hereof, and that remedies at law may be inadequate to protect ANGUS against a breach or threatened breach of this Agreement. AFCL agrees that ANGUS shall be entitled to appropriate equitable relief, including injunctive relief if necessary, in addition to any legal damages or other remedy provided by law.

(f) *Survival:* The survival of the parties obligations with respect to section 4 shall survive the expiration or termination of this Agreement for any reason.

24. Clause 5 provides that the agreement shall expire upon the earliest to occur of the following:

(1) the termination of the [ ] Agreement, or any extension or renewal thereof; and
(2) the termination of the Supply Agreement.

In addition ANGUS may terminate the agreement immediately if AFCL breaches either section 2 or 4 of this Agreement. Either party may terminate the agreement in the event of a default by either party.

Consultancy Agreements
25. Under the terms of the consulting agreements, ANGUS agrees to provide Hickson with consulting advice relating to technical matters necessary for the continuance of two separate contracts. The agreements are identical, except for the names of the customers and consultants and duration of the consultancy.

3.22 **Vendor Agreement**

26. The Vendor Agreement is an agreement between ANGUS and Lazard Brothers & Co. Ltd, whereby Lazard Brothers has undertaken to act as agent in the sale of shares in Hickson International which were paid to Angus as consideration for the acquisition of AFCL.

Deed of Agreement

27. The Deed of Agreement records the obligations to, or rights and remedies against, the other party in the event of termination of the Acquisition Agreement.

Secrecy Agreement

28. Under the terms of the Secrecy Agreement, AFCL agree to treat as confidential, certain technical information disclosed to it by ANGUS prior to the sale for a period of ten years. The relevant extracts of the agreement are as follows:

> In consideration of the opportunity afforded to AFCL to manufacture products for ANGUS by utilising the ANGUS technical information, AFCL promised, prior to receiving the information disclosed, to preserve the ANGUS technical information identified in Exhibit A in strict secrecy within its own company organisation, and further agreed not to reveal the information to any third party by oral or written communication for a period of ten (10) years. AFCL further promised to inform its employees that they are so obliged to preserve the ANGUS technical information. AFCL has, in fact, so preserved the information disclosed by ANGUS thus far, and promises to continue to preserve that information. This agreement shall not apply to any portion of the information that comes into the public domain through no fault on the part of AFCL, or that is disclosed to AFCL by a third party who has a right to make such disclosure, or for which a written release is obtained from ANGUS.
>
> In the event that AFCL does not manufacture a product for ANGUS, AFCL will return the written technical information pertaining to the product and any product samples to ANGUS.

Agreement to Transfer Invention Rights

29. ANGUS, through its subsidiary AFCL, founded a fellowship for the development of nitroalkanes at University College Cork from which AFCL was granted an exclusive license by UCC to any inventions and patent rights participating to the development. Under the terms of this agreement AFCL has agreed to transfer such rights to ANGUS in return for which Angus has agreed to reimburse it for the payments to date and for all future payments, if any.

IN4 Agreement

30. The IN4 agreement is an agreement between ANGUS and Hickson which determines the value and payment mechanism in respect of certain items of inventory, namely stocks of IN4 which are used in the manufacture of chemicals for a particular company.

Accounting Memorandum

31. The Accounting Memorandum determined the specific meaning of the accounting terms used in the context of the overall agreement.

(f) *Submissions of the parties*

32. The notifying party argued that, by analogy with the criteria adopted in the Reuter/BASF European Commission decision,[7] the Remia European Court of Justice judgment,[8] and the

7. Case No. 76/743/EEC, OJ L254/40, 17.9.76.
8. *Remia BV and others v. EC Commission*, Case 42/84 (1985) ECR 2545.

Competition Authority's decision in Nallen/O'Toole,[9] the restrictions in clause 9 of the Share Purchase Agreement should not be held to infringe section 4(1) of the Competition Act. **3.22**

33. It was further argued that as the acquisition constitutes a 'merger or take-over' for the purposes of section 5 of the Mergers, Take-over and Monopolies (Control) Act 1978, having already been cleared by the Minister for Industry and Commerce, it should not be reviewable under the Competition Act. They also submitted that, by analogy with EC Commission review of mergers and acquisitions under Articles 85 and 86 of the Treaty of Rome, the acquisition of 100% interest in a company could only be reviewed under the Competition Act, if at all, under section 5 of the Act which deals with abuse of a dominant position. Reference was made to the European Court of Justice judgment in *BAT and Reynolds v. Commission*[10] in support of this view. As the Share Purchase Agreement represents a 100% acquisition, it was argued that this Agreement should be dealt with in a similar manner. It is submitted that the Competition Authority's main purpose is to review agreements which come within the scope of section 4 of the Act and not section 5.

34. The parties stated that the supply agreement arose because AFCL needed supplies of the raw material nitromethane in order to ensure the continued supply of a certain chemical intermediate product to one of its customers [ ]. It was claimed that there were only two producers of this raw material and that the agreement secured supplies for AFCL and could not be considered to constitute a restriction of competition.

(g) *EU Regulation 556/89, Know-how Licensing Agreement*

35. EEC Regulation No. 556/89 of 30 November 1988[11] is a block exemption treaty which applies Article 85(3) of the Treaty of Rome to categories of know-how licensing agreements. It came into force on 1 April 1989 and applies until 31 December 1999. Know-how, for the purpose of this regulation, is defined as 'a body of technical information that is secret, substantial and identified in any appropriate form'.

36. The regulation has the effect of exempting agreements involving the transfer of know-how from the provisions of Article 85(1). It recognises the increasing economic importance of non-patented technical information such as description of manufacturing processes, recipes, formulae and drawings. The regulation recognises that such agreements are pro-competitive and have beneficial effects on the economy by facilitating the transfer of technology and boosting innovation. They may, however, in some circumstances, inhibit competition by imposing territorial restrictions. The regulation also provides greater legal certainty for agreements of this nature, given that the transfer of know-how is frequently irreversible.

37. The regulation lists obligations of a restrictive nature that benefit from automatic exemption pursuant to Article 85(3) of the Treaty. A know-how licensing agreement to which only two undertakings are party and which contains one or more of these obligations is exempt from the provisions of Article 85(1). Among them is an obligation on the licensee to limit his production of a licensed product to the quantities he requires in manufacturing his own products, provided that such quantities are freely determined by the licensee. Other obligations include requirements that the licensee does not divulge the know-how to third parties, grant sub-licenses, assign the licence or exploit the know-how where it remains secret after the termination of the agreement. A number of obligations involving territorial rights and protection are also contained.

38. The regulation also provides for an obligation on the licensee to advise the licensor of any developments made in exploiting the licensed technology within the period of the agreement and to grant him a non-exclusive license in respect of them. This is on condition

9. Competition Authority Decision No. 1, 2 April 1992.
10. Cases 14 and 156/84, [1987] ECR 4487.
11. Regulation 556/89, OJ L61/1, 4.3.89.

3.22 that the licensee is not prevented from exploiting his improvements, in so far as they can be exploited with the licensors original know-how remaining secret.

(h) *Subsequent developments*

39. The Authority expressed concerns about certain aspects of the notified arrangements to the notifying parties and additional information was sought. They replied on 8 April 1993, and made the following observations.

40. In relation to the restrictions on disclosure of confidential information contained in clause 9.1(iv) of the Share Purchase Agreement, the following additional argumentation was submitted

> . . . that the current notification in Hickson/Angus can be distinguished from the Decision in Reuter/BASF on a number of grounds, as follows:
>
> The facts of Reuter/BASF involved a personal non competition covenant, backed by a personal obligation to maintain knowhow as confidential. The scope of the covenants was so wide as to prevent the covenantor, Reuter, from undertaking any business at all. In the instant case Angus are not so prevented from undertaking other businesses. Clause 9 of the Share Purchase Agreement makes this clear.
>
> In Reuter/BASF the knowhow restriction also covered non-commercialised research and development. In the present case, the restriction only applies in respect of what has commercial value.
>
> In Reuter/BASF, Reuter was prevented from keeping in touch with scientific and technical progress by doing any further research and development. As such, he was effectively eliminated from becoming a potential competitor at any time in the future. This is not the case here, where Angus is engaged in a variety and range of other businesses which are highly successful.
>
> In the present circumstances it is submitted that the confidential information restrictions are reasonable, given that they only subsist until the information falls into the public domain. Given that the information in question constitutes a pivotal part of the assets acquired by virtue of the Acquisition Agreement it is submitted that this type of restriction, as opposed to a restriction limited by a fixed term, as reasonable, and most effectively reflects the legitimate commercial aspirations of the parties.
>
> The European Competition Authorities have long held that in the absence of any harmonisation of the laws relating to confidential information each country is entitled to unilaterally protect confidential information. Such protection is not, in the absence of any harmonisation provisions, in itself anti-competitive. See section 22 of the Treaty of Rome. Furthermore the protection of confidential information goes, it is submitted, to the very existence of the right and should be unimpeachable under European competition law, see *Magill TV Guide v. Radio Telefís Éireann*, case 70/1989.
>
> . . . It is submitted that, as in relation to Reuter/BASF referred to above, the ACT/Kindle matter specifically referred to personal non competition covenants, and that many of the same distinctions enumerated above in the context of Reuter/BASF are substantially applicable, in particular the issue that Angus carries on a number of businesses and is not, by virtue of the Share Purchase Agreement with Hickson, effectively prevented from carrying on other commercial activity.

41. In a further submission dated 20 September 1993 the parties again claimed that clauses 9(iv) and 9(v) were not anti-competitive. They stated that the wording of clause 9(iv) made it clear that it was not a disguised non-competition clause. They pointed out that 90% of the know-how involved was either owned by a customer exclusively or jointly by AFCL and the customer. They argued that the circumstances differed from those in Reuter/BASF. In particular

they claimed that the Reuter/BASF decision was only concerned with a non-compete clause of excessive duration and not with the issue of a restriction on use or disclosure of confidential information. In addition they stated that the confidentiality obligation is no more than has been accepted by the EU Commission in the Know-How Licensing Regulation. It was pointed out that the Regulation states that an obligation on the licensee not to divulge the know-how communicated by the licensor is generally not restrictive of competition' and allows the licensee to be held to such an obligation after the licence has expired. They drew an analogy with a bottling firm licensed to manufacture Coca-Cola under licence and argued that if such a company were sold the vendor would not be entitled to exploit the Coca-Cola formula or commercial know-how which had been obtained through the licence. It was stated that the purchaser could not and would not object to the vendor competing with them after four years in making identical products and selling them to AFCL's customers as long as the vendor had not used the know-how owned by AFCL or by AFCL and the customer jointly. 3.22

42. Concerning the obligation on the purchaser to obtain at least 90% of its nitromethane from the vendor, the notifying parties argued that the 90% supply obligation in respect of nitromethane was not in fact a restriction of competition adversely affecting AFCL. They argued that AFCL's requirement for nitromethane arose in respect of its obligations under contract to supply to [ ] quantities of NMSM and that the purpose of this obligation was to guarantee to AFCL an ongoing reliable supply of nitromethane, which would allow it to meet its contractual obligations to [ ]. It was a question of ensuring security of supply as, in their view, the purpose and effect of the Agreement was to oblige Angus to supply this volume of material, not to prevent AFCL from dealing elsewhere.

43. They stated that consideration had been given to obliging Angus to supply to AFCL 100% of the latter's requirements of nitromethane. Ultimately, however, it was felt by the purchaser's side in the negotiations that AFCL should retain an effective option to source up to 10% of its nitromethane requirements elsewhere, lest another producer of nitromethane appeared on the world scene and AFCL wished to check on the quality and suitability of the material produced by such an alternative supplier. They also argued that the agreement had had a negligible effect on competition since, prior to the purchase by Hickson of AFCL, AFCL was supplied with virtually all of its nitromethane by Angus.

44. On the question of restricting the licensee's freedom to produce nitromethane under the Nitromethane Licence Agreement, the parties stated that the purpose of the Licence Agreement was to provide a safety net for AFCL in the event that Angus could no longer supply the substance in the event, for example, that the premises of Angus might be destroyed. Within the past couple of years Angus' plant in the USA was the location of a major industrial accident which caused several fatalities and which appears to have been caused due to the volatility of the substances being manufactured there. It was consciousness of this history and the danger of another such incident that prompted the purchaser, in the instant case to seek, in defined circumstances, access to the technology of Angus, to allow AFCL to produce nitromethane itself on an emergency and temporary basis, in order to maintain its contractual obligations to [ ], pending the recommencement of production of nitromethane by Angus following any unfortunate incident such as was envisaged.

45. It was also argued that the technology which Angus has related to a continuous process production of nitromethane. If the licence agreement were triggered, Angus would give to AFCL a subset of that technology which would enable AFCL to produce nitromethane on a batch process. This batch process would not be an economically efficient as the continuous process used by Angus and would, by its very nature, be an interim or temporary solution to a problem such as is envisaged above. They also pointed out that prior to the current arrangements between the parties AFCL had no right of access to the nitromethane technology of Angus.

> As a matter of competition law it is therefore submitted that it would be incorrect to state that AFCL are subject to a restriction, since AFCL had no rights to use the technology

3.22 prior to the Agreement. Furthermore, there is nothing in and of the agreements which restricts AFCL from becoming a nitromethane producer using appropriate technologies should it wish in the future to do so. It must be stated however that it is extremely unlikely that AFCL would ever wish to become such a producer.

46. The Authority issued a Statement of objections to the parties on 11 April 1994 indicating that, in its view, the non-compete provisions in Clauses 9.1(iv) and 9.1(v) offended against section 4(1) of the Competition Act and did not satisfy the requirements for a licence under section 4(2). The parties were informed that the Authority therefore intended to refuse to issue a licence or grant a certificate in respect of the notified arrangements. They were given 28 days to respond and offered the chance of an Oral Hearing. The parties subsequently sought an extension of the 28 day period stating that they were examining ways of amending the clauses in question in order to satisfy the Authority's concerns. In a letter dated 1 June 1994 the parties indicated that they would amend the provisions of clause 9.1 as follows:

For the purpose of assuring to the Purchaser the full benefit of the Company, the Vendor hereby undertakes to the Purchaser that the Vendor will not, and will procure that no other member of the Vendor Group will:
(i) for a period of four years immediately following Completion canvass or solicit orders for the supply of Restricted Products to, or for the manufacture of Restricted Products for, any person who was a customer of AFCL at any time within the three year period prior to completion; or
(ii) for a period of four years immediately following completion, supply or manufacture Restricted Products to or for any person who has been a customer of AFCL at any time within the three year period prior to completion; or
(iii) for a period of two years immediately following completion, induce or seek to induce any particular employee of AFCL at completion (including. . .[12]) to become employed whether as employee or consultant or otherwise, by the vendor or any other members of the Vendor Group; or
(iv) use, or reveal to any person, any of the know-how or the trade secrets, techniques or processes licensed to the Company or jointly owned by the Company and a third party unless the relevant licensor or any joint owner thereof shall have consented in writing to the Vendor so doing until such time as the same fall into the public domain otherwise than by reason of a breach of this undertaking or is made available to the Vendor or any other member of the Vendor Group by a third party other than in breach of any duty of confidentiality owed by that third party to the Company; or
(v) use, or reveal to any person, any of the know-how or the trade secrets, techniques or processes owned by and exclusive to the Company until such time as the same fall into the public domain otherwise than by reason of a breach of this undertaking or is made available to the Vendor or any other member of the Vendor Group by a third party other than in breach of any duty of confidentiality owed by that third party to the Company PROVIDED that such undertaking shall not prevent the Vendor from doing those things set out in clauses 9.1(i) and 9.1(ii) above after the expiry of the time periods contained in those sub-clauses; or
(vi) disclose to any person any other confidential information of the Company or of any customer of the Company (other than where the Vendor is authorised by such customer in writing to do so), until such time as the same shall fall into the public domain otherwise than by reason of a breach of this undertaking or is made available to the Vendor or any other member of the Vendor group by a third party other than in breach of any duty of confidentiality owed by that third party to AFCL PROVIDED that such undertaking

12. Certain named individuals were specified here.

shall not prevent the Vendor from doing those things set out in clause 9.1(i) and 9.1(ii) above after the expiry of the time periods contained in those sub-clauses; or **3.22**
(vii) knowingly assist, or procure any other person to do any of the foregoing things.

47. The Supplemental Agreement was finally signed on 1 September 1994. This proposed amendment distinguished between technical know-how belonging in whole or in part to customers and licensed them to AFCL and that technical know-how which relates to the business sold itself. It provides that a limitation on using the latter type of technical know-how must be limited in time.

Assessment

(a) *Section 4(1)*
48. Section 4(1) of the Competition Act states that 'all agreements between undertakings, decisions by associations of undertakings and concerted practices which have as their object or effect the prevention, restriction or distortion of competition in trade in any goods or services in the State or in any part of the State are prohibited and void'.

(b) *The Parties*
49. The parties to the share purchase agreement are Hickson International and Angus Fine Chemicals both of which are corporate bodies engaged in the provision of goods and services for gain and are therefore undertakings within the meaning of the Act. AFCL is a party to some of the subsidiary agreements. It is also an undertaking within the meaning of the Act.

(c) *Applicability of section 4(1)*

The Share Purchase Agreement

(i) The Acquisition
50. The present arrangements constitute an agreement between undertakings whereby Hickson has purchased the business of AFCL from Angus. The parties have argued that as the agreement constitutes a merger which has been approved by the Minister for Industry and Commerce under the Mergers Act, it does not come within the scope of section 4(1). They also argued by analogy with EC law that the arrangements constitute a concentration which is not within the scope of Article 85(1). These arguments have been dealt with in previous Authority decisions where the Authority indicated that it did not believe such agreements were automatically excluded from the scope of section 4(1).[13] In the Authority's view, where a notified arrangement constitutes an agreement between undertakings, the issue to be decided is whether it has the object or effect of preventing, restricting or distorting competition. The stated object of the notified arrangements is to transfer ownership of the business of AFCL from Angus to Hickson. The Authority indicated in Woodchester that such an object *per se* does not offend against section 4(1).
51. AFCL, as already stated, is a custom fine chemical producer, i.e. it makes high grade organic chemicals to order for its customers. Other Hickson subsidiaries are also engaged in the relevant market so that the number of competitors will be reduced as a result of the arrangements. Again in Woodchester the Authority stated that it did not consider that an agreement, which led to a reduction in the number of competitors, prevented, restricted or distorted competition *per se*. The object of section 4(1) is to protect competition not competitors

13 Competition Authority Decision No. 6, Woodchester Bank Ltd./UDT Bank Ltd, 4 August 1992. The arguments presented by the parties here are almost identical to those which the Authority rejected in GI/General Semiconductor, Decision No. 10, 23 October 1992, and so they are not dealt with at length in this decision.

3.22 and, in the Authority's view, a reduction in the number of competitors does not necessarily result in a reduction of competition.

52. The Authority believes that the sale is unlikely to have any effect on competition in the relevant market. As pointed out AFCL effectively manufactures chemical products to order for customers. Any firm within the State which is currently purchasing products from AFCL or which wishes to have fine chemical products manufactured to its specifications will be able to obtain them from other custom fine chemical producers either in Ireland or elsewhere. The Authority considers that transport costs in the case of such products are relatively low and do not represent a barrier to competition from overseas producers. It is relevant in this context that much of AFCL's current output is exported, in some cases to customers in the Far East. The nature of the market is such that purchasers of such products located in Ireland can choose to have their requirements manufactured by producers located almost anywhere in the world.[14]

53. In addition the Authority accepts the argument that a number of customers could produce their own requirements in-house rather than buy them, if, in fact, Hickson tried to exercise any market power. It would appear to the Authority that new suppliers would also be likely to enter the market in such circumstances. The Authority recognises that the costs of establishing or converting a plant to produce such products are not insignificant, but believes that such costs are within the compass of a large number of chemical and pharmaceutical firms which would have the necessary skills and resources to enter this market. Nor does the Authority believe that the arrangement will have any adverse effect on competition on the supply side, i.e. in its view the arrangement will not have any detrimental impact on other Irish-based firms' ability to supply the products in question. Although Hickson was clearly a potential competitor on the Irish market, the Authority concludes that, having taken all relevant market factors into account, the sale of the business of AFCL to Hickson will not have the effect of preventing, restricting or distorting competition in the State or in any part of the State and so it does not offend against section 4(1).

(ii) Non-compete provisions

54. Clause 9 contains a number of non-compete provisions. The Authority has indicated its views on such restrictive agreements in a number of previous decisions. In ACT/Kindle[15] the Authority indicated that it believed that a restriction on the vendor of a business competing with it for up to five years may be necessary to secure the complete transfer of the business where technical know-how was involved. The Authority, in ACT/Kindle referred to the definition of technical know-how contained in the EC Regulation on Know-How Licensing. The Authority believes that for a non-compete clause to be regarded as essential to protect technical know-how, the know-how would have to satisfy the requirements set out in Article 1(7)(1) of the Regulation.

55. The present notification involves the sale of a business engaged in the production of high grade organic chemicals and the Authority believes that this clearly involves technical know-how. Given the Authority's decision in ACT/Kindle, the restrictions in clause 9.1(i) and 9.1(ii), which are for four years duration, do not exceed what is necessary for the complete transfer of the business. They are limited to certain products and to dealing with anyone who was a customer of AFCL during the previous three years so that in terms of geographic scope and subject matter they involve no more than is necessary to secure the complete transfer of the business. Consequently, in the Authority's view, the restrictions in clauses 9.1(i) and (ii) do not offend against section 4(1) of the Competition Act.

56. The Authority has also considered the question of restrictions on vendors soliciting

14. In such circumstances measuring concentration in the Irish market would not appear to be very relevant. In addition as Hickson was not previously engaged in supplying such products to Irish based firms, technically the agreement has no implications for market concentration.
15. Competition Authority Decision No. 8, ACT/Kindle, 4 September 1992.

employee to leave the business and take up employment with them. It stated that it regarded **3.22**
such restrictions as necessary to protect the goodwill of the business being sold and that, provided such a restriction was limited in time to what was necessary to secure the transfer of that goodwill, it was not objectionable. In this instance the restriction is for two years, which the Authority regards as sufficient to ensure the transfer of goodwill. Consequently in its opinion clause 9.1(iii) does not offend against section 4(1) of the Act.

57. The Authority also gave its views on restrictions on use or disclosure of technical know-how in ACT/Kindle. In particular it noted the views expressed by the EC Commission in Reuter/BASF that:

> In no circumstances may an obligation to keep know-how secret from third parties, imposed on the transfer of an undertaking, be used to prevent the transferor, after the expiry of the reasonable term of a non-competition clause, from competing with the transferee by means of new and further developments of such know-how.

The Authority then went on to state that:

> To afford the purchaser unlimited protection against the use of technical know-how by the seller would, in the Authority's view, restrict competition since such an unlimited restriction would go beyond what is necessary to secure the complete transfer of the business to the purchaser. As in the Reuter/BASF case it appears reasonable to limit such protection to the time required to allow the purchaser to obtain full control of the undertaking. Once such a reasonable time has elapsed, however, the purchaser is no longer entitled to be protected against competition by the seller.

58. Hickson sought to rely on the above passage from Reuter/BASF, in particular, the reference to 'new and further developments of such know-how' to claim that the restrictions in the agreement as originally notified differed to those in Reuter/BASF. In effect they claimed that it was only restrictions on new and further developments of the know-how which were not permitted. The Authority does not agree with this view. The Commission stated in Reuter/BASF that:

> It is further recognised that it may be necessary in certain cases to provide additional safeguards to ensure the effective performance of an agreement where technical knowledge, constituting an important part of the value of a transferred undertaking, is placed at the disposal of the transferee. As in the case of goodwill, it must be possible to prevent the transferor for a certain time from using such knowledge in a manner which would prevent the transferee from acquiring with its market position undiminished.
>
> Here too, the protection afforded to the transferee should be limited in time, since the transfer of legally unprotected know-how confers no exclusive rights on the purchaser. Contrary to the contention of BASF, the transfer of technical know-how in connection with the sale of an undertaking does not automatically preclude any further activity on the part of the seller based on such know-how. The opportunity of using know-how which is unknown to competitors is, like goodwill, a competitive advantage. This advantage can be diminished by the development by third party competitors of their own know-how. Unlike third parties the transferor of an undertaking remains aware of the contents of any transferred know-how, since he cannot divest himself of his own knowledge. For this reason it appears legitimate to protect the transferee in order for a certain time to enable him to acquire the undertaking with its competitive position undiminished. This need to protect the competitive position of the undertaking provides

16. See Competition Authority Decision No. 9, Budget Travel/Phil Fortune, 14 september 1992.

3.22 the justification for and prescribes the time limits to any non-competition clause involved.

In determining the duration of the non-competition clause, the factors particularly to be taken into account are the nature of the transferred know-how, the opportunities for its use and the knowledge possessed by the purchaser. It is also reasonable to assume that the transferee will actively exploit the assets transferred. A distinction must be made between know-how existing at the date of transfer and new or further developments by the transferor based on or in connection with the transferred know-how. A non-competition clause extending to new or further developments can be of shorter duration.[17]

59. The Commission clearly indicated that the transfer of technical know-how in connection with the sale of an undertaking does not automatically preclude any further activity on the part of the seller based on *such know-how*. In drawing a distinction between the know-how existing at the time of the sale and new or further developments of the know-how, it indicated that a longer non-compete clause could apply in respect of the existing know-how. Thus, in the Authority's opinion, the Commission's views in Reuter/BASF do not support the arguments made by the parties.

60. In this instance the position with respect to 'know-how' is somewhat more complex. The Authority believes that the business in which AFCL is engaged, i.e. that of operating a custom fine chemical production plant, involves a degree of technical know-how'. The Authority also recognises, however, that there is another element of technical know-how' involved here. AFCL produces chemicals in accord with the specifications of its customers. The know-how involved in producing the specific products belongs to those customers, who have effectively licensed it to AFCL. These two categories of 'know-how' must be treated differently.

61. In the latter case the Authority regards it as legitimate for customers who supply technical 'know-how' to AFCL in order for it to produce goods to their specifications, to restrict AFCL from using such know-how for any other purpose. Such know-how is the property of AFCL's customers, and was not, and is not the property of AFCL or of Angus. Consequently, to the extent that the restriction in clauses 9.1(iv) and (v), as notified, related to technical know-how provided to AFCL by one of its customers, in order to enable it to supply that customer, they do not offend against section 4(1). This was always the Authority's position and the Authority had never suggested that a restriction on the use or disclosure of such 'know-how' was anti-competitive.

62. The position with respect to technical 'know-how' regarding the operation of a custom fine chemical plant itself is different. In this instance the Authority agrees with the EC Commission view in Reuter/BASF that an obligation to keep know-how secret from third parties, imposed on the transfer of an undertaking, may not be used to prevent the transferor, after the expiry of the reasonable term of a non-competition clause, from competing with the transferee by means of new and further developments of such know-how. To the extent that they have this effect clauses 9.1(iv) and (v), as notified, offended against section 4(1) as they went beyond what was necessary to secure the transfer of the business being sold.

63. In seeking to justify such a restriction, the parties, in the Authority's view, were asking it to take a different view to that of the Commission in Reuter/BASF for no good reason. In particular they argued that in the latter case the Commission view was prompted by the fact that the offensive clauses would have prevented the vendor, an individual, from earning a livelihood. In the Authority's view that is an incorrect interpretation of the Reuter/BASF decision, which found that a similar restriction was anti-competitive, as it prevented a vendor re-entering a particular business after a certain period of time. The Authority also rejects the

17. Point 3(b).

claim that the Reuter/BASF decision was only concerned with a non-compete clause which was excessively long and not with the restrictions on the use of confidential information. Such an interpretation is inconsistent with what the Commission said as known in above. In the Authority's opinion this requires that Angus be free to use any 'know-how' relating to the operation of a custom fine chemical plant which they possessed as the former owner of AFCL, to re-enter that market four years after completion of the sale. **3.22**

64. In respect of other confidential information the Authority has indicated in ACT/Kindle and Budget Travel that a restriction on using or revealing confidential information of a non-technical nature could not be used to prevent the vendor from re-entering the market following the expiry of an acceptable non-compete clause. In the latter decision the Authority accepted the restriction subject to an undertaking by the purchaser that the clause would not be used in this way. The Authority therefore believes that the restrictions contained in clauses 9.1(iv) and 9.1(v), as notified, could have been used to prevent the vendor from re-entering the market and for this reason also they offended against section 4(1).

65. The parties have now amended the specific clauses in question. In particular the new clause 9.1(iv) provides for an unlimited restriction on the use or disclosure of 'know-how' which was owned by third parties or was owned jointly by the company and a third party, without the permission of that third party. For reasons already stated above the Authority does not believe that such a provision offends against section 4(1). The new Clauses 9.1(v) and 9.1(vi) prevent the vendor using or disclosing know-how which is the exclusive property of the business and other confidential information subject to the proviso that such restrictions will not prevent it from engaging in manufacturing or supplying or soliciting orders for products in competition with the company once four years have elapsed since completion. The Authority believes that this no longer represents an unlimited restriction on the use of the 'know-how' such as would prevent the vendor ever re-entering the market. Consequently, in its opinion, such restrictions do not offend against section 4(1).

The Supply Agreement

66. The Supply Agreement is an arrangement under which AFCL agrees to purchase 90% of its requirements of a particular product (nitromethane) which is used in producing NMSM under contract for one of its customers. The agreement is for a period of 3 years and is subject to automatic renewal on an annual basis thereafter unless one or other of the parties gives written notice of termination to the other.

67. This arrangement obliges AFCL to obtain 90% of its requirements from Angus thereby preventing it from obtaining the bulk of its supplies from other suppliers and also preventing such other suppliers from selling the product in question to AFCL. The parties have claimed in their defence that the only other sources of supply are three firms based in the Peoples' Republic of China. They have argued that it makes sense for AFCL to purchase its requirements from Angus rather than obtain supplies elsewhere, as the quality of such supplies might not be satisfactory to the customer who purchases the NMSM produced from the Nitromethane. In addition they have argued that the provision is designed to ensure supplies to AFCL from Angus which is the dominant producer of Nitromethane, and not to oblige AFCL to purchase from Angus.

68. Similar arrangements have been found to be in breach of EC competition rules. Although many of these cases have been regarded as infringements of Article 86, some were also found to infringe Article 85(1) In Billiton/M&T an agreement by M&T to purchase all of its requirements of tin tetrachloride, used in its production of tin cans, from Billiton, was found to infringe 85(1) as well as Article 86.1.[18] Similarly in Soda Ash I the EC Commission insisted on the deletion of such restrictive arrangements.[19] In Carlsberg[20] the Commission found that

18. See EC Commission (1978), 'Seventh Report on Competition Policy', points 13-16 and 131.
19. See EC Commission (1982), 'Eleventh Report on Competition Policy', points 73-76.
20. OJ L207/26.

3.22 an agreement by Grand Metropolitan to purchase large quantities of lager from Carlsberg for a period of 11 years, where the quantity involved represented over half of Grand Metropolitan's lager requirements, infringed Article 85(1) on the grounds that it prevented the purchaser from producing this quantity itself, or from obtaining it from other producers. In Industrial Gases, the Commission secured an amendment whereby clauses requiring customers to obtain all or a fixed percentage of the requirements from one supplier were replaced by commitments to purchase quantities falling within a fixed minimum-maximum.[21] In Moosehead/Whitbread, however, the Commission found no infringement of Article 85(1) in the case of an exclusive purchasing obligation for yeast, on the grounds that it was necessary to ensure satisfactory exploitation of know-how and trademarks licensed under the agreement.

69. While accepting that Angus is a dominant producer of Nitromethane and that some provisions are required to ensure supplies to AFCL so that it may continue to produce NMSM, the Authority nevertheless considers that such a provision restricts competition for the supply of Nitromethane to AFCL. It may be, as the parties claim, that there are only a small number of suppliers of the product throughout the world. Nevertheless the provision restricts competition by obliging AFCL to purchase 90% of its requirements from a single supplier which is stated to be dominant in the market for that product. In addition the provision would prevent new suppliers from competing for AFCL's business. Consequently it restricts competition in the market for the product within the State and offends against section 4(1).

The Licence Agreement

70. The licence agreement provides that, should AFCL be unable to obtain supplies of Nitromethane from Angus or any other source, Angus will provide it with the necessary know-how to produce its requirements of the product itself. The agreement provides that the know-how only be used to produce the product for use as a raw material in the production of NMSM, which AFCL has a long term agreement to supply to a customer. AFCL will have the title to any improvements which it makes to the know-how and grants Angus an irrevocable non-exclusive, royalty free perpetual right and license to such improvements. AFCL is prohibited from disclosing the licensed know-how to third paries except where it has come into the public domain or it had obtained the know-how from another source or is developed independently by AFCL.

71. The Licence Agreement is a form of 'know-how' licence agreement. Certain restrictions e.g. those on disclosure, in the agreement are necessary to protect the secret know-how which is the lawful property of Angus. Unless such know-how were protected, then Angus would almost certainly not provide the know-how necessary for the production of the product concerned to AFCL. Without the licence AFCL might not be able to supply NMSM to its client.

72. AFCL may only use the know-how to produce NMSM during periods when it is unable to obtain supplies from Angus or any other source. The 'know-how' belongs to Angus. They are under no obligation to supply such 'know-how' to AFCL. Angus is not licensing the 'know-how' to AFCL to enable it to engage in the production of nitromethane generally. It cannot restrict competition since in the absence of the licence AFCL could not produce nitromethane. The arrangement is designed purely to ensure that, in the event of any disruption of supplies, AFCL will be able to produce its own supplies of nitromethane in order to continue producing NMSM. While the EC Know-How licensing Regulation provides that a licence may not restrict the quantities which the licensee may produce, the Authority considers that the present arrangement is not a standard know-how licence but is an arrangement designed to deal with a particular contingency, which may never arise. Consequently, in the Authority's view the licence agreement does not offend against section 4(1).

21. EC Commission (1990), Nineteenth Report on Competition Policy'.

The Secrecy Agreement 3.22

73. The Secrecy Agreement is concerned with preserving confidential information, essentially technical know-how, which Angus had previously supplied to AFCL, to enable AFCL to produce certain products for Angus. While such information was not provided as part of a know-how licence arrangement, it was in many respects a similar type of arrangement, albeit one between a parent and subsidiary. As in the case of licensed know-how, the know-how is the property of the parent, and it is entitled to be protected against its disclosure to third parties. Consequently, in the Authority's opinion, the Secrecy Agreement does not offend against section 4(1).

74. The remaining agreements involve a variety of diverse arrangements, including provisions for the valuation of stocks, the transfer of rights over technological developments stemming from a University Research Programme funded by AFCL when it was an Angus subsidiary, arrangements for the issue and sale of Hickson shares by Lazard to fund the purchase of AFCL, and consultancy agreements whereby Angus agrees to supply the services of certain staff to assist AFCL in the development of technology for use in the production of certain products for supply to AFCL's customers. In the Authority's opinion none of these agreements[22] have either the object or effect of preventing, restricting or distorting competition within the State or any part of the State, and do not offend against section 4(1).

Applicability of section 4(2)

75. Under section 4(2), the Competition Authority may grant a licence in the case of any agreement which offend against section 4(1) but which, 'having regard to all relevant market conditions, contributes to improving the production of goods or provision of services or to promoting technical or economic progress, while allowing consumers a fair share of the resulting benefit and which does not —

(i) impose on the undertakings concerned terms which are not indispensable to the attainment of those objectives;

(ii) afford undertakings the possibility of eliminating competition in respect of a substantial part of the products or services in question.'

76. Clauses 9.1(iv) and 9.1(v) of the sale agreement, as notified, relating to the use and disclosure of confidential information went beyond what was necessary to secure the transfer of the goodwill of AFCL. They could not therefore be regarded as indispensable and consequently they did not satisfy the requirements for a licence under section 4(2).

77. The supply agreement provides AFCL with the raw material necessary to produce certain products under contract for [ ]. It therefore contributes to improving the production of goods. The customers of AFCL benefit from this to the extent that they obtain supplies of the finished products as a result. Supply agreements of this type are dealt with in the EC Commission Notice on Restrictions Ancillary to Concentrations.[23] The notice recognises that it may be necessary, at least for a transitional period, to maintain a supply arrangement between the purchaser and the vendor because the transfer of the business may entail the disruption of traditional lines of internal procurement and supply arising from the previous integration of operations. The Commission's view is that there is no general justification for exclusive purchase and supply obligations. The notice states that:

> Save in exceptional circumstances, for example, resulting from the absence of a market or the specificity of products, such exclusivity is not objectively necessary to permit the implementation of a concentration in the form of a transfer of an undertaking or part of an undertaking.[24]

22. The Consultancy Agreements; The Vendor Agreement; The Deed of Agreement; The UCC Agreement; The IN4 Agreement; The Accounting Memorandum.
23. OJ C203/05 14.8.90.
24. Article IIIC3.

3.22 It also states that the duration of such provisions 'must be limited to a period necessary for the replacement of the relationship of dependency by autonomy in the market. The duration of such a period must be objectively justified'.[25]

78. The Authority notes that, in this instance, there are only a small number of suppliers of the product in question worldwide, and that Angus is the dominant producer. It also recognises that access to supplies is essential for AFCL to produce certain products in order to supply its customers. It accepts that in the absence of such a provision there could well be a disruption of supplies to AFCL. Were AFCL to be denied access to supplies, there is a significant possibility that it would not be able to produce NMSM. Were this to happen AFCL would lose a valuable customer accounting for one third of its output. The Authority believes that, in such circumstances, guarantees of supply were essential to Hickson agreeing to acquire AFCL at the price paid. Consequently the Authority believes that such a provision may be indispensable for a time.

79. The Authority does not believe that the supply agreement affords the undertakings the possibility of eliminating competition in respect of a substantial part of the market in question. The supply agreement therefore satisfies the requirements of section 4(2). In the circumstances the Authority considers that as it regards the restrictions in the agreement as only necessary to avoid disruption to supplies in the short-term, the licence should be limited to a period of 5 years from the date of notification.

The Decision

80. In the Authority's opinion, Hickson International, Angus Fine Chemicals and AFCL are undertakings within the meaning of section 3(1) of the Competition Act, and the notified arrangements for the acquisition by Hickson of the business of AFCL, together with the related agreements involving Hickson, Angus and AFCL constitute an agreement between undertakings.

81. In the Authority's opinion the agreement for the sale of AFCL by Angus Fine Chemicals to Hickson International, as amended by the Supplemental Agreement of 1 September 1994 does not offend against section 4(1) of the Competition Act. The Supply Agreement between AFCL and Angus offends against section 4(1). The remaining agreements do not, in the Authority's opinion, offend against section 4(1). In the Authority's opinion, the Supply Agreement satisfies the requirements for a licence. The Authority believes that a licence for a period of five years from the date of notification, i.e. 29 July 1992, is justified in this instance.

The Certificate

82. The Competition Authority has issued the following certificate:

> The Competition Authority certifies that, in its opinion, on the basis of the facts in its possession, the agreement of 8 July 1992 between Angus Chemical Company and Hickson International plc for the sale to Hickson of Angus Fine Chemicals Ltd (CA/56/92), notified on 29 July 1992, under section 7, and amended by the Supplemental Agreement of 1 September 1994, does not offend against section 4(1) of the Competition Act 1991.

For the Competition Authority

Patrick Massey
Member

7 September 1994

25. Article IIIC4.

The Licence 3.22

83. The Competition Authority has granted the following licence:

> Pursuant to section 4(2) of the Competition Act 1991, the Competition Authority hereby grants a licence to the agreement of 8 July 1992 between Angus Chemical Company and Angus Fine Chemicals Ltd for the supply of Nitromethane by Angus Chemical Company to Angus Fine Chemicals Ltd, which was entered into pursuant to the sale of Angus Fine Chemicals Ltd. to Hickson International plc, (CA/56/92), notified on 29 July 1992, under section 7. This licence shall apply from 29 July 1992 to 28 July 1997.

For the Competition Authority

Patrick Massey
Member

7 September 1994

Competition Authority Decision No. 373, Dairygold Co-Operative Society Ltd/ CMP Dairy/Michael Cotter: 17 November 1994, Notification No. CA/720/92E 3.23

Sale of milkround – Appointment of vendor as distributor by the purchaser – Whether restrictions on competition and soliciting customers after termination of distribution agreement prohibited – Whether procuring of goodwill can justify competition restrictions after a distribution agreement entered into immediately after the sale agreement – Whether resale maximum price maintenance is prohibited – Whether restrictions are indispensable to the attainment of the objective of the agreement – Whether agreement contributes to the improvement in distribution promotion of progress and the conferring of benefits on consumers – Significance of the negotiation of other similar agreements. EC Commission Regulation 1983/83, Competition Act (No. 24) 1991, sections 3, 4 and 7

Facts: On 30 September 1992 notification was made to the Authority with a request for a certificate under section 4(4) of the Competition Act 1991 or, failing that, a licence under section 4(2) in respect of an agreement dated 10 April 1990 under which Mr Cotter sold his milk round in Cork City to the predecessor of Dairygold Co-operative Society Ltd ('Dairygold'). At the same time Mr Cotter entered into an exclusive type distribution agreement for the same milk round with Dairygold's predecessor. The relevant market concerned liquid milk, cream and potted products. Dairygold came into existence as a result of the amalgamation of two co-operative societies, one of which had entered into the agreements. Dairygold at the time of notification serviced the City and County of Cork, West Waterford, South Tipperary and parts of Limerick County.

Under the agreement Mr Cotter covenanted not to sell products which compete with Dairygold products within a half mile of any customer of his milk round for a period of three years after the termination of the distribution agreement. Mr Cotter also agreed not to solicit any customer who was a customer within the past two years

3.23 for a period of 3 years after the termination of the distribution agreement. The agreement also provided that Mr Cotter would not sell products in excess of the maximum price set by the supplier to the distributor.

The Competition Authority by letter dated 16 July 1993 expressed concern about the competition restriction and the maximum price resale maintenance provisions. Dairygold argued that the purchase of the milk round necessitated such a post-term restriction in the exclusive distribution agreement because of Mr Cotter's long established relationship with his customers.

On 29 April 1994 a statement of objections was issued to the parties and both Dairygold and Mr Cotter argued that the restrictions were not anti-competitive. Dairygold expressed its willingness in its answer to the statement of objections to reduce the period for the restraint of trade to one year and agreed to eliminate any restrictions on the retail prices of its products.

At an oral hearing on 11 October 1994 Dairygold argued that it did not acquire the goodwill until the exclusive distribution agreement was terminated. Whilst accepting that Mr Cotter did not have an exclusive territory under the distribution agreement Dairygold argued that Mr Cotter had a specific and exclusive customer base.

Decided by the Authority:

(A) In refusing to issue a certificate:

(1) Mr Cotter was not an employee and acted as a distributor of Dairygold. The notified agreement was an agreement between 'undertakings'.

(2) The sale of the business under the notified agreement was completed prior to the commencement of the Competition Act. As the Competition Act only applies to a current or continuing contractual commitment the prohibition under section 4(1) does not apply to that part of the agreement concerning the sale of the milk round.

(3) Mr Cotter was a distributor of the owner of the milk round.

(4) A purchaser of goodwill is not entitled to a longer period for competition restrictions because the purchaser fails to secure the business associated with the goodwill. In this case the purchaser, the predecessor of Dairygold, chose to operate the business after the acquisition through a distribution agreement with the vendor of the milk round.

(5) A period of even less than one year after the termination of the distribution agreement could not be justified. The Competition Authority's category licence for exclusive distribution agreements and the EC block exemption on exclusive distribution agreements do not provide for competition restrictions after termination of a distribution agreement.

(6) The agreement on its own might not have a significant impact on competition. Dairygold however stated that it was negotiating similar agreements with other roundsmen and the effect of such agreements would lead to a significant restriction on competition in the relevant market.

(7) The resale maximum price maintenance terms of the agreement are prohibited by section 4(1). The imposition of maximum prices creates a real danger that these prices become minimum prices.

(B) In refusing to grant a licence:

(1) The restrictions on competition and the soliciting of customers go beyond what is necessary to secure the proprietary interests of Dairygold. The restrictions are not

'indispensable to the attainment of the objectives of the agreement'. 3.23

(2) The resale maximum price provisions do not contribute to any improvement in distribution, to promoting technical or economic progress or to conferring any benefits on consumers.

Case, Decisions and Notice referred to:
Remia v. Commission (Case No. 42/84) 11.7.85 [1985] ECR 2545; [1987] 1 CMLR 1
EC Commission Decision – Reuter/BASF 26.7.76 [1976] OJ L254/40; [1976] 2 CMLR D44
Competition Authority Decision No. 1 Nallen/O'Toole – 2 April 1992 **3.3**
Competition Authority Decision No. 144 Licence for categories of exclusive distribution agreements – 5 November 1993 **5.1.1**
Competition Authority Decision No. 301 Rohan Construction/Rohcon – 25 March 1994 **3.17**
Competition Authority 'Notice in Respect of Mergers and Take-overs which predate the Competition Act' – *Iris Oifigiúil*, 14 May 1993, P. 367 **3.1**

Competition Authority Decision of 17 November 1994 relating to a proceeding under section 4 of the Competition Act 1991
Notification No. CA/720/92E — Dairygold Co-Operative Society Ltd/C.M.P. Dairy/Mr Michael Cotter

Introduction

1. This decision concerns an agreement between Mitchelstown Export Company Ltd and Mitchelstown Co-Operative Agricultural Society Ltd (the predecessor in title to Dairygold Co-Operative Society Ltd (Dairygold)), together trading as C.M.P. Dairy and Mr Michael Cotter, notified on 30 September 1992, whereby the latter sold his milkround to Dairygold and undertook to promote the sale of C.M.P. products in and around Cork city. The notification requested a certificate or in the event of a refusal to issue a certificate, a licence. The Authority issued a Statement of Objections to the parties on 29 April 1994 indicating that it intended to refuse their request for a certificate or licence. An Oral Hearing was held on 11 October 1994.

The Facts

(a) *The subject of the notification*

2. The notification concerns an agreement dated 10 April 1990, between Mitchelstown Export Company Ltd and Mitchelstown Co-Operative Agricultural Society, together trading as C.M.P. Dairy (C.M.P.) and Mr Michael Cotter. Under the terms of the agreement C.M.P. purchased a milk round which was at the time owned by Mr Cotter. In addition C.M.P. appointed Mr Cotter as exclusive distributor of its products in and around the Mayfield area of Cork City (the existing milk round). The agreement contained a number of non-compete clauses.

(b) *The Parties*

3. Dairygold was incorporated on 1 October 1990, having come into existence as a result of the amalgamation of Mitchelstown Co-Operative Agricultural Society Ltd and Ballyclough Co-Operative Creamery Ltd. Dairygold is a multi-purpose co-operative, engaged in a wide range of activities including *inter alia* dairy and meat processing, the sale of dairy and meat products on the domestic and export markets, the manufacture and sale of animal feed, grain trading, shop retailing and the supply of farm equipment. At the time of the agreement Michael Cotter owned a milk round in the vicinity of the Mayfield area of Cork city which he subsequently sold to Dairygold and which is the subject of this agreement.

3.23 (c) *The product and the market*

4. The products concerned in this agreement are liquid milk, cream and potted products. There are a significant number of suppliers operating in this market including, Dairygold, Waterford Co-Op, Central Dairies, Dungarven, Avonmore Co-op, Thurles Co-Op Creamery, Shannon Dairies, Golden Vale Co-Op, North Cork Creameries, Dawn Dairies, Strand Dairies and Miltown Farm. The market which is serviced by Dairygold includes the greater part of Cork city and county, part of West Waterford, a significant part of South Tipperary and parts of South and East Limerick, (excluding Limerick city). According to Dairygold the market is highly competitive with no restrictions on new suppliers coming into the market. Buyers in the market consist of independent agents, supermarkets, convenience stores and shops, door step consumers and institutions i.e. hospitals.

(d) *The arrangements*

5. The notification relates to an agreement dated 10 April 1990 for the sale by Mr Michael Cotter of the milk round which he owned in the Mayfield area of Cork city to Dairygold, trading as C.M.P. dairies. As part of the purchase agreement, C.M.P. appointed Mr Cotter as exclusive distributor of its products for its existing milk round. Clause 2 of the agreement prevented Mr Cotter, for a period of three years from the termination of the distribution agreement, from becoming involved in a business engaged in the sale, marketing or distribution of products similar to, or competing with C.M.P., within a distance of a half mile of any customer, who had been a customer of the existing milk round in the year prior to termination. In addition, clause 2.1 (ii) prevented Mr Cotter for a period of three years from termination, from enticing any person, firm or company who had been a customer or was in the. habit of dealing with C.M.P. in the two years prior to the date of termination. Clause 4 of the agreement stated that Mr Cotter was obliged to deliver and sell C.M.P. products at a price not exceeding the retail price recommended by C.M.P. for those products.

(e) *Subsequent Developments*

6. The Authority communicated its concerns regarding the non-compete and the pricing clauses in a letter to the parties dated 16 July 1993. In a reply dated 31 August 1993, Dairygold argued strongly for the necessity of the non-compete clauses. They submitted that the relationship which existed between C.M.P. and Mr Cotter was one of supplier/independent distributor and not employer/employee. According to Dairygold, Mr Cotter earned his living by buying products from C.M.P. and reselling them at a profit rather than receiving a salary from C.M.P. Consequently they argued that the principles which apply to employer/employee contracts could not be applied to this arrangement. Mr Cotter was paid valuable consideration by Dairygold for the purchase of the milk round which he now operates as an exclusive distributor, therefore the terms of clause 2 were inextricably linked to the purchase by Dairygold of the milk round operated by Mr Cotter. Consequently, Dairygold submitted that the principles which the Authority applied to restrictions on a vendor following the sale of a business should apply in this case. The restrictions on Mr Cotter competing with Dairygold were necessary to protect Dairygold's interests in the event of Mr Cotter ceasing to operate the distribution agreement and seeking to take over the goodwill of the round himself. Due to Mr Cotter's long and established relationship with the customers of the milk round he would be in a very strong position to compete with Dairygold and in the circumstances it was reasonable that he should be prevented from competing for a limited period. In addition, Dairygold argued that because the vendor was well known in the area he could effectively continue to run the business hence a non-compete clause for a period of three years, rather than the two years normally accepted by the Authority, was justified (see paragraphs 12-14 below). Regarding the pricing restrictions contained in clause 4, Dairygold acknowledged that Article 3(f) of the Draft Licence for Categories of Exclusive Distribution Agreement indicated that it would not apply where a supplier obliges the exclusive distributor to sell at a fixed price, or not less than a minimum

price or not more than a maximum. They stated that clause 4 had the effect of obliging Mr Cotter not to sell at more than the maximum price recommended by C.M.P. **3.23**

7. On 29 April 1994, the Authority issued a Statement of Objections to the parties indicating its intention to refuse to issue a certificate or grant a licence in respect of the notified agreement. On 26 May 1994 Dairygold replied arguing that the non- compete provisions contained in clause 2 of the agreement were not anti-competitive rather they argued that the restrictions were essential to protect the goodwill of the milk round which Dairygold had purchased from Mr Cotter. They cited the decision of the EU Commission in *Reuter/BASF*[1] and of the European Court of Justice in *Remia*[2] in support of their arguments. In addition they referred to the Authority's decisions in *Nallen/O'Toole*[3] and *Rohan Construction/Rohcon.*[4] Dairygold also indicated that it was prepared to reduce the period of restraint to one year from the termination of the distribution agreement. Dairygold also stated that it was prepared to amend clause 4 so as to eliminate any restrictions on retail prices. Mr Cotter also responded arguing that the restrictions were not anti-competitive.

8. On 11 October 1994 the Authority held an Oral Hearing at which Dairygold presented further arguments in support of the non- compete provisions contained in clause 2 of the agreement. In particular they argued strongly that they had not acquired the goodwill at the time of the sale as Mr Cotter remained on in the business as an exclusive distributor. Consequently a non-compete clause following the termination of the exclusive distribution agreement was essential to enable them to acquire the goodwill. They pointed out that while Mr Cotter did not operate in an exclusive territory, he did have a specific customer base, and in the circumstances a non-compete clause relating to the customers which he dealt with was justified. Dairygold also explained that the agreement which they had concluded with Mr Cotter was not unusual insofar as they were currently in the process of negotiating similar agreements with three or four other Dairygold roundsmen. In addition they restated their proposal to reduce the period of restraint in clause 2 to one year from the termination of the distribution agreement.

Assessment

(a) *Section 4(1)*

9. Section 4(1) of the Competition Act states that 'all agreements between undertakings, decisions by associations of undertakings and concerted practices, which have as their object or effect the prevention, restriction or distortion of competition in goods or services in the State or in any part of the State are prohibited and void'.

The Undertakings and the Agreement

10. Section 3(1) of the Competition Act defines an undertaking as 'a person, being an individual, a body corporate or an unincorporated body engaged for gain in the production, supply or distribution of goods or the provision of a service.' Dairygold is a corporate body engaged for gain in the production and sale of dairy and meat products. Mr Cotter was, at the time of the agreement, the beneficial owner of the milk round and subsequently operated it as an exclusive distributor and is therefore an undertaking. In a submission to the Authority, Dairygold submitted that:

> the contractual relationship between CMP and Mr Cotter is not one of employer/employee but rather one of supplier/independent distributor. In particular, Mr Cotter earns his living by buying products from CMP which he then resells and makes a profit on

1. OJ L254/40. 17.9.76.
2. *Remia BU and Others v. European Commission,* Case 42184 [1993] ECR 2545.
3. Competition Authority Decision No. 1, 2 April 1992.
4. Competition Authority Decision No. 301, 25 March 1994.

3.23 the margin rather than receiving a salary from CMP. Consequently, the principles which may apply to an employer/employee situation do not apply to the agreement.

Consequently the notified arrangements constitute an agreement between undertakings.

Applicability of section 4(1)

11. As the sale of business was completed prior to 1 October 1991, the date on which the Competition Act came into force, this element of the agreement had been discharged by performance before the Act commenced. In the Authority's view, the prohibition under section 4(1) only applies to a current or continuing contractual commitment, or one entered into subsequent to the coming into force of the Act.[5] The milk round which was the subject of the agreement had been transferred before the Act came into force.

12. The non-compete provisions in clause 2 of the agreement prevented the vendor from competing with Dairygold, for a period of three years from the termination of the distribution agreement, within a half mile radius of any customer of the milk round, who had been a customer in the previous year. Under the terms of that clause he was also prevented for the same period, within a half mile radius of any customer of the existing milk round, from soliciting any person, firm or company who had been a customer of C.M.P. in the two years prior to termination. The Authority considers that following the sale of the business, Mr Cotter was an exclusive distributor who was appointed by Dairygold in order to distribute certain dairy products in a specified territory i.e the Mayfield area of Cork. He did not own the milk round, having sold it to Dairygold who subsequently appointed him as its distributor.

13. The Authority has accepted in the case of a sale of business that a restriction on the vendor competing with the business for some time after the sale does not offend against section 4(1). Under the terms of this agreement, however, the purchaser decided to appoint the vendor as its exclusive distributor for the area in which the business operated, and is seeking to prevent the vendor competing with the business for a period of three years after the termination of the distribution agreement. Such a restriction restricts competition. The Authority has accepted in numerous decisions involving a sale of business that a restriction on the vendor competing with the business is not anti-competitive provided it does not exceed what is necessary to enable the purchaser to secure the goodwill of the business. The emphasis is on what is necessary to enable the purchaser to secure the goodwill. In the Authority's opinion, a purchaser is not entitled to a longer period of restriction if, because of the way he chooses to operate the business, he fails to secure the goodwill. Dairygold purchased the business in April 1990 and a restriction on Mr Cotter competing with Dairygold for some time after completion would not be considered anti-competitive. Dairygold, having purchased the business, is clearly entitled to operate it as it sees fit and in this instance it chose to appoint Mr Cotter as its distributor. Having taken that decision it is not open to Dairygold to claim that it has not acquired the goodwill of the business which it bought and that it is entitled to protection against competition by the former owner for a period of three years starting from an, as yet unknown, date in the future. In the Authority's opinion even a lesser period of restraint of one year from the termination of the agreement, as proposed by Dairygold, cannot be justified in such circumstances. In effect, while Dairygold are claiming that the restriction is justified by virtue of their purchasing the business, they are also claiming that the goodwill attaches to the former owner as he operates as their distributor. Both the Authority's Category Licence for Exclusive Distribution Agreements and the EC Block Exemption for such agreements do not allow post-term non-compete provisions. While the Authority does not consider that this agreement alone would have a significant impact on competition, it is relevant that Dairygold indicated at the Oral Hearing that they were in the process of negotiating similar agreements with a number of other roundsmen. In the Authority's

5. Notice in respect of Mergers and Takeovers which predate the Competition Act — Competition Authority, *Iris Oifigiúil*, 14 May 1993, p. 367.

opinion, the combined effect of such agreements would lead to a significant restriction on competition in the Cork area. Having considered the arguments presented by the parties, it can see no reason for accepting such a restriction in this instance. Consequently in the Authority's opinion, the restrictions in clause 2 offend against section 4(1). **3.23**

14. Under the terms of Clause 4 of the agreement, Mr Cotter is obliged to sell C.M.P. products at a price not exceeding the price recommended by C.M.P. for those products. In the Licence for Categories of Exclusive Distribution Agreements, the Authority stated its views regarding pricing restrictions.[6] In particular it stated that any limitations on the exclusive distributor in determining his own resale prices were considered as serious infringements of the prohibition in section 4(1). In regard to the setting of maximum retail prices the Authority stated that this practice is in itself anti-competitive and there is a real danger that the maximum price imposed on a supplier would become, at the same time, the effective minimum price charged by the resellers. In their submission to the Authority, Dairygold acknowledged that Article 3(f) of the Category Licence, stated that the licence would not apply where the supplier obliges the exclusive distributor to sell at a fixed price, or not less than a minimum price or more than a maximum. The EC Block Exemption for Exclusive Distribution Agreements requires that distributors be free to set their own resale prices. Consequently the Authority considers that the restriction on pricing in clause 4 offends against section 4(1). It notes, however, that Dairygold had offered to remove this restriction.

Applicability of section 4(2)

15. Under section 4(2), the Competition Authority may grant a licence in the case of any agreement or category of agreements which offends against section 4(1) but which, 'having regard to all relevant market conditions, contributes to improving the production of goods or provision of services or to promoting technical or economic progress, while allowing consumers a fair share of the resulting benefit and which does not —

(i) impose on the undertakings concerned terms which are not indispensable to the attainment of those objectives;

(ii) afford undertakings the possibility of eliminating competition in respect of a substantial part of the products or services in question.'

16. The restrictions on competing and enticing customers in clause 2 of the Agreement go beyond what is necessary to secure the proprietary interests of Dairygold. Consequently, in the Authority's opinion, they can not be regarded as indispensable to the attainment of the objectives of the agreement and so do not satisfy the requirements for a licence. Similarly, the restriction on resale pricing in clause 4 does not contribute to any improvement in distribution or to promoting technical or economic progress, it does not therefore confer any benefits on consumers and cannot be considered to be indispensable. It therefore fails to meet the requirements for a licence.

The Decision

17. In the opinion of the Competition Authority, the agreement between Dairygold, C.M.P. Dairy and Michael Cotter relating to the sale of the milkround in Mayfield, Cork City by Michael Cotter to Dairygold and the subsequent appointment of Mr Cotter as an exclusive distributor of C.M.P. products (Notification No. CA/720/92E) notified on 30 September 1992, under section 7(2), constitutes an agreement between undertakings. It considers that the restriction in clause 2 of the Agreement on the vendor competing with the business and enticing customers of the milk round following termination of the distribution agreement and the restriction on pricing in clause 4 offend against section 4(1) of the Competition Act and do not

6. Competition Authority, Licence for Categories of Exclusive Distribution Agreements, Decision No. 144, 5 November 1993.

3.23 satisfy the requirements for a licence under section 4(2). Consequently the Authority refuses to issue a certificate or grant a licence in respect of the notified agreement.

For the Competition Authority

Patrick Massey
Member

17 November 1994

CHAPTER FOUR

Exclusive Purchasing/Franchising

4.0 Introduction

Distinction of Exclusive Arrangements
Exclusive purchasing as opposed to exclusive distribution or franchising of its nature suggests that the only obligation which may restrict competition is a reseller's promise or covenant to purchase a range of goods from an agreed source. Exclusive distribution and franchising generally grants to the reseller selling rights which may not be available to every reseller. Exclusive distribution and franchising arrangements may impose other restrictions on the reseller which may affect competition.

European Attitude
The European Court of Justice initially took a relaxed attitude to exclusive purchasing agreements.[1] Eventually the European Commission recognised restrictions of competition which can arise when powerful market players enter into a series of exclusive purchasing arrangements. Such arrangements could eliminate or substantially reduce competition in respect of a substantial part of the products and services covered by the exclusive purchasing arrangements. Commission Regulation No. 67/67/EEC of 22 March 1967[2] was the initial response of the European Commission to the need for an exemption from Article 85(1) of the Treaty of Rome to exclusive dealing arrangements. This block exemption expired on 30 June 1983 and was replaced by a block exemption specifically for exclusive purchasing agreements and a block exemption for exclusive distribution agreements.[3]

This Chapter
This chapter contains the decisions of the Competition Authority concerning exclusive purchasing agreements. Interestingly no general exemption from section 4(1) of the Competition Act has yet been granted by the Competition Authority in a manner similar to the European Commission's block exemption on exclusive purchasing. The Competition Authority has shown its preference to analyse and examine the economic sectors in which exclusive purchasing arrangements are found.

CATEGORY LICENCES

Motor Fuels Category Licence 4.2
The first category licence granted by the Competition Authority concerns the motor fuels industry and the common solus arrangements in that industry. The Authority on

1. A concise history of European competition policy in this area is contained in D.G. Goyder, *EC Competition Law* (2nd ed.) at pp. 232-236.
2. OJ 57, 25 March 1967, p. 849/67.
3. Commission Regulation (EEC) No. 1983/83 concerning exclusive distribution agreements and Commission Regulation (EEC) No. 1984/83 concerning exclusive purchasing agreements.

4.0 11 December 1992 published its intention to grant a motor fuels category licence and requested comments from the public on the draft category licence which was contained on the last six pages of a 42 page draft decision. The pages preceding the actual draft licence described the Authority's finding of facts and reasoning in making such a category licence. By decision no. 25 of 1 July 1993 the Authority granted a licence in practically identical terms to the draft category licence, save for the inclusion of Article 1(2) concerning ancillary contracts and Article 7(4) which included a refusal to grant a licence to notified agreements which do not fulfil the terms of the category licence. This chapter contains all of the findings of fact and the reasoning of the Authority with the ultimate category licence. This category licence did not identify which agreements do actually benefit from the category licence. The publication of the decision in *Iris Oifigiúil* does however contain the list of agreements which is described as 'a list of exclusive purchasing agreements for motor fuels which have been notified to the Authority'. The Authority continues on to state in respect of the list that 'this does not imply that they satisfy the requirements of the category licence'.[4]

The list of notifications of exclusive purchasing agreements for motor fuels which the Competition Authority mention as having been notified and which is contained at the end of the official publication in *Iris Oifigiúil* of the Competition Authority's decision is also reproduced separately in this book apart from being referred to in the tables of the notifications. The date of the decision granting a category licence is noted at the beginning of every category licence. In the columns opposite the description of the notifications which are set out in the exhaustive list in this book, the reader will find the date of publication of every category licence in *Iris Oifigiúil*. It is stressed that the date of the decision of the Competition Authority corresponds with the date of the commencement of each category licence to date and not with the date of publication in *Iris Oifigiúil*.

LPG Category Licence 4.8

Decision No. 364 of 28 October 1994 of the Competition Authority granted a licence to a category of exclusive purchasing agreements in respect of cylinder liquified petroleum gas and is termed as the 'cylinder LPG category licence'. This particular category licence took the same format and procedure as the motor fuels category licence. On 24 June 1994 the Authority published a draft. The actual category licence contained at the end of the published decision is the same as the draft category licence contained at the end of the draft decision except that no reference is made in the final version of the category licence to the retrospective effect of the category licence to agreements which were in existence on the commencement of the Competition Act and notified prior to the first anniversary of that commencement.[5] In addition the dates for the commencement and expiration of the category licence along with the date on which reports from suppliers need to be submitted were contained in the final version of the category licence. Whereas the category licence concerning motor fuels will remain in force for 15 years without any obligation on suppliers to submit information to the Authority, the LPG category licence will expire on 31 October 1999, 5 years

4. The Notification 'CA/72/92E — Conoco Ireland Ltd; licensees. Licence agreement' was deemed to come within the terms of the Category Licence according to a Notice published on 26 November 1993.
5. Article 5(1) of the Draft Category Licence.

after the Authority's decision. In addition there is an obligation on suppliers benefiting from the category licence to submit reports about the market each year.[6] The LPG category licence did not contain a list of notified agreements which came within its ambit but did identify three agreements in respect of which the Authority had decided to refuse the request for a licence or a certificate.[7] 4.0

INDIVIDUAL DECISIONS

ESSO 4.1

Decision No. 4 of 25 June 1992 concerned the notification of standard solus agreements with ancillary equipment and financing agreements between ESSO and dealers in motor fuels who entered into such agreements. The Competition Authority acknowledged that one solus agreement might be insignificant but it was the network of ESSO outlets which introduces a degree of rigidity into the market. In that context the Authority considered that the standard ESSO solus agreement offended against section 4(1) of the Competition Act. In granting a licence to the ESSO standard agreements the Authority identified the return for the reseller, the supplier and the consumer in allowing exclusive purchasing arrangements for a period of 10 years for motor fuels considering the costs and investment on the part of a supplier like ESSO. The Authority's disapproval of resale price maintenance by a supplier was articulated in this decision. Subsequent decisions including the category licences leads one to conclude that the Authority will not approve of a supplier stipulating the price at which a reseller can sell products which may be sold to the reseller by the supplier.

Musgraves 4.3 and 4.5

Decisions 304 and 354 concerning notifications by Musgraves Ltd in relation to group purchasing arrangements for toys and grocery products respectively are noteworthy because of the rejection by the Authority of any semblance of resale price maintenance by a supplier, whether that resale price maintenance relates to the minimum or maximum prices which may be charged by a reseller.

Burmah Castrol 4.4, 4.6 and 4.7

Decision 324 refers to an agreement which seeks to ensure that a reseller will be able to freely display advertising and stock of a loan provider. This decision is inserted in this part of the book to show types of arrangements acceptable to the Authority which ensure sales points for a supplier's goods without imposing exclusive purchasing obligations.

Decision 361 is a decision to refuse a certificate or a licence to hire purchase agreements which impose exclusive use provisions in respect of the equipment being purchased. The exclusivity is designed to guarantee sales points and has the effect of reducing sales points for competitors.

6. Article 7 of the Category Licence makes this provision.
7. See Article 5 which identifies dealer agreements notified by Flogas (Ireland) Ltd under CA/14/92E, Calor Teo under reference CA/213/92E and Blugas Ltd under reference CA/538/92E.

4.0 Franchising Category Licence 4.9

Franchising is included in this part of the book because it is a form of exclusive purchasing. An exclusive purchasing agreement may not require the supplier to fulfil any conditions other than to supply the goods or services. Franchising of its nature requires the giving of something intellectual whether that consists of property, trademarks or know-how. Nevertheless such agreements typically require a reseller to enter into restrictions for the sources of the reseller's supplies. Decision 354 in respect of a notification by Musgraves Ltd concerning its SuperValu and Centra shops throughout the State concerned a type of franchise agreement.

On 8 July 1994 the Competition Authority published notification of its intention to grant a category licence in respect of franchise agreements. The category licence contained at the end of the 20 page decision was published in Iris Oifigiuil on 9 December 1994 and at the end of this publication the Authority included the following: 'The Authority considers that, on the basis of the information supplied to it, the following notified franchise agreements come within the scope of the category licence and satisfy its condition. In the circumstances, the effect of Article 7 of the category licence is that the category licence constitutes the grant of a licence in respect of these agreements:

CA/243/92E — Quality Hotel;
CA/1092/92E — Mothercare Ireland Ltd; Mothercare UK Ltd;
CA/21/94 — Office Team Supplies Ltd; Kelly Office Supplies Ltd.

No reference is made to a refusal to grant a licence to franchise agreements which may have been notified.

Franchising was considered in great depth by the European Commission which recognised it in its 1985 report on competition policy as 'a rapidly developing form of distribution and commercialisation in Europe'.[8] The Authority summarises its perception of the 'EU treatment of franchise agreements' at paragraphs 7 and 8 whilst usefully noting the differences between the category licence and EU Regulation 4087/88 in paragraphs 33, 34 and 35 of the Category Licence's preamble.

GENERAL

Only when the courts have adjudicated upon the applicability of section 4(1) of the Competition Act to exclusive purchasing obligations and franchising agreements with and without the benefit of the category licences which have been granted by the Competition Authority, will the full impact of section 4(1) of the Competition Act on the ever increasing numbers of such agreements, be more certain. The judgment and reasoning of Keane J in the *HB v. Mars* case which principally concerned the allegation of an abuse of a dominant position does however indicate the willingness of the High Court to use a 'rule of reason' when assessing the enforceability and

8. Point 25 of the 15th Report on Competition Authority. D.G. Goyder in his book, *EC Competition Law* (2nd ed.) at pp. 260-269 gives a useful history of franchising and the reaction by regulatory authorities to its development. Valentine Korah in Franchising and the EEC Competition Rules Regulation 4087/88 sets out a very useful analysis and critique of the applicable European Commission block exemption to franchising now.

prohibition of exclusive purchasing clauses. This type of approach casts a considerable onus of proof onto a claimant making an allegation of a contravention of the Competition Act and especially concerning the effects on competition by the subject of the complaints. The development of the Courts' jurisprudence in this area will be carefully watched. 4.0

Competition Authority Decision No. 4, Esso Solus and related agreements: 25 June 1992, Notification Nos. CA/11-14/91E 4.1

Solus and related agreements containing exclusive purchasing covenants – Ten year duration on exclusive arrangements – Foreclosure effect of such agreements – Practice by supplier of issuing recommended retail price to retailers – Whether such agreements improve distribution of product and give consumers a fair share of resulting benefit – Whether terms of agreements indispensable to securing benefits for the consumer – Competition Act 1991 (No. 24) sections 3, 4 and 7 – EEC Regulation 1984/83

Facts: On 19 December 1991 notification was made to the Authority with a request for a licence under section 4(2) of the Competition Act, by Esso Ireland Ltd ('Esso') in respect of standard solus and related agreements made between Esso and independent motor fuel dealers.

The notified agreements were entered into between Esso, an Irish incorporated company which is engaged in the supply of motor fuels and oils in the State and which is a wholly owned subsidiary of Exxon Corporation in the United States, and various independent dealers who are engaged in the business of, *inter alia,* selling motor fuels and oils in the State. While Esso, in common with the other major fuel suppliers in the State, does own and operate some petrol stations the notified arrangements apply only to independent dealers operating from their own premises.

The agreements notified included a standard solus agreement, a standard dealer equipment loan agreement, a standard dealer loan agreement and a deed of charge.

Under the terms of the standard solus agreement the dealer agrees to purchase all motor fuels required for consumption or sale at the service station (or at any other premises owned by the dealer within a one mile radius of that service station) exclusively from Esso for a period of ten years from the date thereof, the dealer only being free to purchase from other suppliers in the event of Esso withholding, reducing or suspending deliveries. Annexed to the solus agreement was the Esso Dealer Co-operation Plan which required solus dealers to trade during all reasonable hours, to support Esso sales promotions and to give preference to the sale of Esso motor oils. Esso for its part undertakes to supply the dealer with the dealer's total fuel requirement for a period of ten years and agrees to pay to the dealer a rebate on motor fuels delivered by Esso. The dealer agrees to take delivery of a certain minimum amount of fuel and to operate his service station as far as possible in accordance to the principles of the Esso dealer cooperation plan.

Under the terms of the standard dealer equipment loan agreement, which is

4.1 ancillary to the solus agreement, Esso agrees to provide equipment to the dealer for a maximum period of ten years, such agreement being determinable by Esso in the event of, *inter alia*, the dealer ceasing to retail Esso motor fuels or failing to carry out its obligations under any supply agreement.

Under the terms of the dealer loan agreement Esso agrees to loan money to any dealer for the purpose of developing his site, such loan to be interest bearing and repayable over a period not exceeding fifteen years and such agreement containing the same exclusive purchase covenants as contained in the solus agreement.

The standard deed of charge is executed in favour of Esso by those dealers who borrow under a standard dealer loan agreement and under its terms the dealer mortgages in favour of Esso as security for its obligations under such loan his interest in the service station.

EEC regulation No. 1984/83, a block exemption regulation under Article 85(3) of the Treaty of Rome, gives exemption to categories of exclusive purchasing agreement (including solus agreements) on the condition that the agreement does not exceed ten years in duration. While a dealer may covenant not to sell fuels of other suppliers he may not be prevented from selling motor oils supplied by other firms.

During the investigation of the notified agreements the Authority became aware that shortly before any change in the wholesale price of its products Esso circulated a newsletter to its solus dealers advising them of the change in wholesale prices and of the maximum recommended retail price for each grade of motor fuel. This practice was explained by Esso as being a carry over from the days prior to the Competition Act when dealers could not exceed prices set by the maximum prices order. In response to the Authority's concerns Esso undertook to discontinue the practice.

It was submitted on behalf of Esso that the amount of investment required to modernise and develop service stations was prohibitive for most dealers and was only economically viable for Esso on the basis of the solus arrangements and for a period of not less than ten years, which period had been accepted by the EC under regulation 1984/83. Further it was submitted that the upgrading of the service station as part of the solus arrangement included the provision of larger storage capacity to take deliveries in economic load sizes which resulted in financial advantages and savings in delivery costs. The solus arrangement also allowed for long term planning of sales and consequently cost effective organisation of distribution. In addition it was submitted that the extension of the exclusive purchase and non- competition requirement to a radius of one mile from the relevant service station was necessary as a safeguard against the catastrophic effect of a dealer developing a competing virgin site in the very proximity of the relevant station. The minimum delivery requirement was stated to be necessary to guarantee efficiency of the delivery operation.

Decided by the Authority:

(A) In refusing a certificate under section 4(4) of the Competition Act 1991 that:

(1) Each of the parties to the notified agreements are 'undertakings' within the meaning of section 3(1) of the Competition Act, the agreements are agreements between undertakings and the relevant geographical market is the State.

(2) The primary feature of the solus agreement is that the solus dealer is obliged to purchase his requirements of motor fuels exclusively from Esso for a period not exceeding ten years and this limits the commercial freedom of the dealer to obtain supplies and the freedom of other suppliers to supply him and is a restriction on

competition within the terms of section 4(1) of the Competition Act 1991. While the effect of one agreement might be insignificant, Esso and other major suppliers have similar such agreements with several hundred dealers which tends to introduce a considerable degree of rigidity into the market and makes it difficult for any new entrant to enter the market on any significant scale. The standard solus agreement therefore offends against section 4(1) and since the three related agreements (the deed of charge, the equipment loan and the loan agreements) also involve an exclusive purchase commitment or are dependant on an agreement containing such an obligation they also come within the prohibition of section 4(1) of the Act. **4.1**

(3) Of the other obligations in the solus agreement the obligation on Esso to supply the dealer with his total requirements is a corollary of the exclusive purchase requirement on the dealer and it offends against section 4(1) of the Act. The extension of the exclusive purchasing obligation on the dealer to include an area within a one mile radius from the relevant service station prevents the dealer from selling competing motor fuels in that area. Competition in petrol sales appears to be a very localised phenomenon as it would not be economic for a motorist to drive very far to buy cheaper petrol at another station and therefore this provision breaches section 4(1) of the Competition Act 1991.

(4) The agreement (in some cases) to provide a loan is a reward to the dealer for accepting the exclusive agreement and insofar as it cannot be used to extend the life of the exclusive agreement beyond 10 years does not offend against section 4(1) of the Act. The payment of the rebate to solus dealers, another reward for exclusivity, is not within the terms of section 4(1) of the Act. The minimum delivery requirement in the solus agreement, provided it is not unreasonable, does not of itself restrict the dealer from obtaining supplies from another supplier and does not offend against section 4(1). The obligations in the dealer cooperation plan to give preference to Esso lubricating oils and other products does not prevent the dealer from selling competing products and is therefore not in breach of section 4(1). The requirements to give Esso a chance of introducing a purchaser in the event of a sale of the station does not restrict the dealer's freedom to sell the station and does not therefore offend against section 4(1) of the Act.

(5) The equipment loan agreement comes within the scope of section 4(1) as it is subsidiary to and dependant on the solus agreement which is itself prohibited by section 4(1). The equipment loan does not have a period of effectiveness beyond the solus agreement and cannot be used to artificially extend the ten year exclusivity period and the length of the loan does not offend against section 4(1) of the Act. The loan agreement, being virtually identical to the solus agreement is prohibited by section 4(1). The deed of charge is related to the loan agreement and contains an exclusive purchase requirement which brings it within the scope of the prohibition in section 4(1).

(6) The practice of Esso advising solus dealers of a maximum recommended retail price for each grade of motor fuel when advising of changes in wholesale prices was, on the facts, a breach of section 4(1). While advising dealers who are free to set their own resale prices of recommended prices does not, in the ordinary course, breach the Competition Act, in this case the fact was that the recommended retail price was also the price at which Esso, as a competitor of the solus dealers, proposed to charge at its company owned stations. This had the effect of eliminating price uncertainty in intra-brand competition and was therefore in breach of section 4(1).

4.1 (B)In granting unconditional licences up to 24 June 2002 under section 4(2) of the Competition Act 1991 in respect of the notified agreements that:

(1) The solus arrangements produce an appreciable improvement in distribution of motor fuels in which consumers are allowed a fair share of the resulting benefit and but for these arrangements independent dealers would not be able to afford to modernise and improve their services to customers with the result that supplier owned petrol stations would dominate. The solus arrangements permit long term planning of sales and consequently a cost effective organisation of production and distribution. The reduced costs of distribution of large volumes of fuel to a smaller dedicated group of dealers leads to cost savings which can be passed on to the customer. The extension of the exclusive purchase requirement to all premises of the relevant dealer within a one mile radius from the relevant service station is important if this improvement in distribution is to be secured because otherwise the dedication of the dealer to maximising the sales of Esso motor fuels would be likely to be adversely affected.

(2) The advantages produced by the solus arrangements cannot with any certainty be achieved to the same extent in any other way and the exclusive purchase and non-competition obligations imposed on the dealer are indispensable for the attainment of these advantages and are only confined to the purchase of motor fuels and not to other products. The duration of the exclusive arrangement to ten years is sufficient to produce these advantages while maintaining the dealers' commercial freedom to change supplier. Any lesser period would significantly reduce the incentive for suppliers to invest in dealer outlets to the detriment of dealers and consumers. Having regard to the motor fuel market as a whole and the inter-brand and intra-brand competition made possible by the removal of price control legislation, the freedom of dealers to change their supplier on the expiry of solus arrangements which occurs on a continuous basis, ensures that there is no possibility of the parties being afforded the possibility of eliminating competition for a substantial part of the products in question.

Cases and Decisions referred to:

Brasserie De Haecht v. Wilkin (No. 1 case) (Case No. 23/67), [1967] ECR 407, [1968] CMLR 407

Texaco (Ireland) Ltd v. Thomas Farrell (High Court, unreported decision of Blayney J, 1 May 1991)

EC Commission decision, BP Kemi/DDSS [1979] OJ L286/32, [1979] 3 CMLR 684

Competition Authority decision of 25 June 1992 relating to a proceeding under section 4 of the Competition Act 1991
Notification Nos. CA/11/91E, CA/12/91E, CA/13/91E and CA/14/91E — Esso Solus and Related Agreements

Introduction

1. Notification was made with a request for a licence under section 4 of the Competition Act 1991 by Esso Ireland Ltd on 19 December 1991 in respect of the standard Esso solus agreement with independent dealers, and its dealer loan equipment and dealer loan agreements, and its deed of charge/mortgage.

2. Notice of intention to take a favourable decision was published in 'The Irish Times' on 29 May 1992. There were no submissions from interested parties.

The Facts 4.1

(a) *The Subject of the decision*

3. This decision concerns the standard Esso solus agreement, which provides for the exclusive purchase by an independent dealer of Esso motor fuels for resale, for a maximum period of ten years, and the following related agreements:

— the dealer loan equipment agreement, which relates to the provision of service station equipment on loan to the dealer;

— the dealer loan agreement, which is used when an interest-bearing loan is made available to the dealer for redevelopment of the outlet; and

— the deed of charge/mortgage, which is used to provide security for the loan to the dealer.

Each notified agreement is a standard agreement which Esso employs with the dealers in its independent dealer network throughout the State. While each independent dealer is a party to the solus agreement, not all dealers are party to the other three agreements.

(b) *The parties involved*

4. Esso Ireland Ltd is one of the major suppliers of motor fuels and oils in the State. It is a wholly-owned subsidiary of the Exxon Corporation of the USA. Esso is primarily involved in the marketing of petroleum products, which includes the supply and distribution of motor fuels to the motoring public through a chain of retail outlets. Esso imports its products, usually from an Esso refinery in the UK, through various Irish ports where it has storage facilities. From there, retail outlets are supplied by road tanker. The Esso retail network consists of a number of company owned outlets, mostly operated by Artane Service Station Ltd, and several hundred dealer owned outlets which operate under the Esso brand.

5. Most of the Esso branded dealers purchase motor fuels from the company under exclusive supply agreements. The remaining dealers are not contracted to Esso, and purchase their motor fuels without being tied by formal supply agreements. The Esso dealer network accounts for more than half of the Esso branded sales volume. Esso dealer stations are located in almost every county in the State, and they have a wide range of annual sales (throughput). A higher proportion of company owned than dealer owned stations is located in the major centres of population. Esso exclusive (solus) dealers are independent resellers of motor fuels, and this operation may be combined with car repairs, car sales or a shop selling, among other items, grocery products.

(c) *The product*

6. The product with which the notified agreements are concerned consists of motor fuels, that is petrol and diesel for use in mechanically-propelled road vehicles.

(d) *The market*

7. While some motor fuels are sold direct by Esso to commercial users, and a large proportion is sold through Esso company owned outlets, this Decision relates only to sales of motor fuels through dealer owned outlets. Besides Esso, there are ten other suppliers to the dealer market in the State:

B.P. Ireland Ltd	Irish Shell Ltd
Burmah Castrol Ireland	McMullan Bros. Ltd
Campus	Morris of Fiddown
Conoco Ireland Ltd	Tedcastle Oil Products Ltd
Estuary	Texaco (Ireland) Ltd

8. According to the Report of Enquiry into the Supply and Distribution of Motor Fuels by the Fair Trade Commission in 1989 (PL. 7951), total sales of petrol through retailers in 1988

4.1 were 1,090 million litres, while total retail sales of autodiesel were 187 million litres. In 1988, there were 3,227 retail petrol outlets, of which 447 were company owned, or 13.9%. The proportion of total petrol sales through company owned outlets was, however, 41.6%; 36.3% of dealer outlets sold less than 20,000 gallons of petrol per year (90,920 litres) and only 4.6% sold more than 200,000 gallons (909,200 litres). The respective figures for company stations were 4.1% and 57.2%. Company outlets had a higher average annual throughput than solus dealers, who had a higher average throughput than non-solus dealers. The average throughput of all outlets in Ireland was only about one-quarter of the EC average.

9. Each oil company sells motor fuels through independent dealers, both solus and non-solus, and almost all also own company stations.

10. Since dealer stations are located throughout the State, the appropriate geographic market in this case is the State.

11. Up to 30 September 1991, the motor fuels sector was subject to strict price control and to the provisions of the Restrictive Practices (Motor Spirit and Motor Vehicle Lubricating Oil) Order, 1981. Both the Order and price control were removed on the coming into force of the Competition Act on 1 October 1991.

(e) *The notified agreements*

(i) The standard Esso solus agreement

12. The standard solus agreement which Esso has with each of its independent solus dealers is the basic agreement, and it provides for the exclusive supply of Esso motor fuels for resale for a period not exceeding 10 years. It makes provision for an interest-free loan and provides for a rebate on fuels purchased. The loan is unsecured and the rebate earnings can be offset against the loan, which is the usual procedure. The agreement contains the following main provisions:

Clause 3(a) — The Dealer agrees with Esso 'To purchase all motor fuels required for consumption or sale at the Service Station exclusively from Esso for a period of ten years from the date hereof and not during the said period of ten years to purchase, receive or sell or knowingly permit to be purchased received or sold at the Service Station any motor fuels other than such as shall be purchased from Esso.'

Clause 1(c) — 'Motor fuels shall mean all motor fuels including motor diesel fuel. . . .'

Clause 1(d) — 'The Service Station shall for all the purposes of this Agreement mean and include the said Service Station known as ____________________ and any other Service Station or premises owned, occupied or used by the Dealer for the retail of motor fuels at the date of this Agreement or at any time during the continuance thereof within an area comprised by a circle having a radius of one mile from the said Service Station.'

Clause 2(a) — Esso agrees with the Dealer 'To sell to the Dealer at Esso's wholesale schedule price to Dealers ruling on the date of delivery the Dealer's total requirements of motor fuels for resale at the Service Station for a period of ten years from the date hereof.'

Clause 2(b) — Esso agrees with the Dealer 'To pay to the Dealer a loan of . . . to assist the Dealer . . . towards the cost of improvements at the Service Station consisting of. . . .'

Clause 2(c) — Esso agrees with the Dealer 'To pay to the Dealer a rebate on motor fuels delivered by Esso . . . calculated at the prevailing rebate rate. . . .' (which is 0.156p per gallon, or 0.034p per litre).

Clause 3(e) — The Dealer agrees with Esso 'To take deliveries of motor fuels in quantities of not less than . . . litres.'

Clause 3(f) — The Dealer agrees with Esso 'To operate the Service Station as far as possible in accordance with the principles of the Esso Dealer Co-operation Plan. . . .'

Clause 3(j) — The Dealer agrees with Esso 'Not to sell or offer to sell the Service Station or the business carried on there during the said period of ten years without first giving Esso the opportunity to introduce a purchaser and to use the Dealer's best endeavours to ensure that any purchaser, assignee or transferee of the Service Station or the business will enter into an agreement with Esso similar to this Agreement including this clause.' **4.1**

Clause 4(b)(ii) — 'In the event of Esso withholding, reducing or suspending deliveries . . . the Dealer shall be free to purchase from other suppliers any quantities which Esso after request by the dealer fails to deliver. . . .'

13. In respect of an option being exercised by the dealer upon the expiration of the Agreement to postpone repayment in respect of an unpaid balance of a loan, clause 7(e) states that 'The provision of this option herein shall not be deemed or construed to impose any present undertaking or obligation on the Dealer extending beyond the period of ten years from the date hereof and this Agreement shall be construed accordingly.'

14. The Esso Dealer Co-operation Plan, contained in the Schedule to the Agreement, contains the following clauses:

> '5. To keep the Service Station open at all reasonable hours for the sale of Esso Motor Fuels and Esso Motor Oils.
> 6. To participate in advertising and sales promotion plans and provide a mailing list for circulation to customers and prospective customers.
> 7. To give preference to the sale of Esso Motor Oils and other products.'

(ii) The Dealer Equipment Loan Agreement

15. The dealer equipment loan agreement is subsidiary to and dependent upon the solus agreement. Almost all dealers with a solus agreement are also party to the equipment loan agreement. Title to the equipment remains with Esso, and the loan is for a maximum period of 10 years. The agreement is used in tandem with the solus agreement when a dealer first signs, and thereafter when new or reconditioned equipment is being installed on site on a loan basis. Among the terms of the agreement are:

Clause 1(i) — 'Subject to the provisions of this Agreement Esso will loan for a period of . . . years ('the loan period') commencing from the date of completion of installation as specified in the Schedule hereto the item of equipment ('the equipment') together with the cost of installation ('installation cost') as set out in the Schedule. The equipment shall remain Esso's property.'

Clause 3 — 'Esso may during the loan period without prior notice determine the loan of the equipment . . . in the event of the Dealer ceasing for any reason whatsoever to occupy the Service Station or ceasing to carry out there the business of retailer of Esso Motor Fuels or failing to carry out any of the obligations hereunder or under any Supply Agreement. . . .'

Clause 4 — 'The Dealer agrees with Esso:

(i) To keep the equipment in his possession and control at the Service Station and not to remove it to any other premises and to permit Esso Ireland Ltd from time to time to inspect it and where the equipment includes or consists of storage or dispensing equipment to use such storage and dispensing equipment exclusively for the storage and supply of Esso Motor Fuels and to permit Esso Ireland Ltd:

(1) to take samples of the contents and

(2) to place a lock & seal on the tank during the continuance of this Agreement and the Dealer undertakes not to interfere with or remove such lock or seal.'

(iii) The Dealer Loan Agreement

16. The dealer loan agreement is used when an interest bearing loan is paid to the dealer for redevelopment. The loan is secured by mortgage and is repayable over a period not exceeding 15 years. The agreement is virtually identical to the Esso solus agreement, with the clauses contained in (i) above, including the 10 year exclusive purchasing clause. One additional provision is:

Clause 3(f) — The Dealer agrees with Esso 'To grant to Esso or its nominee as security for

4.1 the loan and interest a . . . mortgage on the Service Station. . . .'

17. About one third of Esso solus dealers are party to the dealer loan agreement.

(v) Deed of Charge/Mortgage

18. The deed of charge/mortgage is supplemental to the dealer loan agreement, and it is used to provide security for the loan advanced to the Dealer. Among its provisions are:

Clause 1(i) — 'In consideration of the sum of £.... paid by Esso to the Dealer . . . the Dealer hereby covenants with Esso that the Dealer will repay the loan with interest as hereinafter provided to Esso on demand and in the meantime . . . to pay to Esso equal monthly payments of £.... each. . . .'

Clause 6 — 'The Dealer hereby attorns and becomes tenant at will to Esso of the Mortgaged Premises at a pepper corn rent during such times as the loan or any part thereof shall remain owing on this security but nothing in this clause contained shall prevent Esso from at any time entering on and taking possession of the Mortgaged Premises and so determining the tenancy hereby created.'

Second Schedule. Clause 2 — 'To occupy the Mortgaged Premises and personally to conduct and keep the same open for business as a retailer of motor fuels.'

Clause 3 — 'To purchase exclusively from Esso all motor fuels which the Dealer shall require for consumption or sale on the Mortgaged Premises or any other premises owned, occupied or used by the Dealer within an area comprised by a circle with a radius of one mile from the Mortgage Premises so long as Esso shall be ready to supply the same for a period of ten years from the date of the Loan Agreement and not during the said period to buy, receive or sell or knowingly permit to be bought, received or sold on the Mortgaged Premises or any other premises owned, occupied or used by the Dealer within an area comprised by a circle with a radius of one mile from the Mortgaged Premises any motor fuels other than such as shall be purchased from Esso.'

Third Schedule. Clause 4 — 'The Dealer will not without the previous consent in writing of Esso grant or agree to grant (whether in exercise or independently of any Statutory Power) any lease or tenancy of the Mortgaged Premises.'

19. All dealers with a loan agreement are also subject to the deed of charge/mortgage.

(f) *EEC Regulation 1984/83*

20. EEC Regulation No. 1984/83, of 22 June 1983, is a block exemption regulation which applies Article 85(3) of the Treaty of Rome to categories of exclusive purchasing agreements. It includes special provisions for service station agreements, that is for solus agreements and for agreements relating to company owned stations. The regulation entered into force on 1 July 1983 and it expires on 31 December 1997.*

21. The regulation applies to agreements involving only two parties whereby one party, the reseller, agrees with the other, the supplier, to purchase specified goods only from the supplier, or from a connected undertaking or one entrusted by the supplier with the sale of his goods.

22. In the case of agreements for the supply of petroleum-based motor vehicle fuels, or for these and other fuels, for resale in a specified service station, special commercial or financial advantages may be accorded by the supplier to the reseller. In such cases, the exclusive purchasing agreement may be for a period not exceeding ten years, and the reseller may be obliged not to sell fuels supplied by other undertakings. The reseller may also be obliged not to use lubricating oil supplied by other firms in equipment financed or made available by the supplier, but he may not be prevented from selling oil supplied by other firms. These exclusive purchasing agreements may refer to no other goods, nor to services (except in connection with the servicing of equipment owned or financed by the supplier). Some general provisions of the regulation also apply, such as permitting the reseller to be obliged to purchase minimum

*OJ No. L173, 30. 6. 83, p. 5

quantities of goods, to sell the goods under trademarks and to advertise. The benefits of exemption may be withdrawn by the Commission in a particular case where it considers that the conditions of Article 85(3) are not satisfied, where, for example, effective competition is lacking. There are special transition provisions for existing service station agreements. Service station agreements cannot be combined with general exclusive purchasing agreements involving the same parties. **4.1**

(g) *Submissions of the parties and others*

Esso

23. Esso stated that the high proportion of sales through the dealer network emphasised the importance of the independent sector in the distribution of retail motor fuels. Thus Esso supported each dealer in maintaining and improving the business by providing investment funding commensurate with the volume potential of each station. The investment required to maintain or improve even a basic service station facility was substantial, and there was a need to build in safeguards to ensure that a reasonable return was achieved on the investment. The arrangements were beneficial to consumers in that they provided for the safe distribution of motor fuels to the motoring public, in a cost-effective and efficient manner.

24. Esso claimed that its investment policy was geared toward providing modern and purpose-built facilities which offered the highest standards of consumer service, by implementing a branded image at service stations. The considerable investment also had to ensure adherence to the safety and environmental legislation governing the industry. Each retail investment was considered a joint venture with the dealer which should be capable of generating an adequate financial return to both Esso and dealer. The level of investment differed in each case, depending on the individual circumstances of the dealer, the physical aspects of the proposed development and the volume potential of the location. The minimum cost of a basic facility, according to Esso, was substantial, including tanks, pumps, pipework and tank gauges, civil works, a canopy and service station equipment. A modern, fully equipped station, with a car wash and a convenience store, would cost a considerable amount.

25. Esso claimed that the initial investment for even the basic facility would place an inordinate strain on the finances of the independent dealer. Independents generally did not have the capital resources or access to such resources to provide new facilities or develop existing facilities, and the available margin from trading was inadequate to fund such investment. Over the last five years, Esso had invested a large amount of money in the dealer network, and the investment programme was continuing.

26. Esso argued that, to safeguard its considerable investment in the dealer network, the economically viable period for the exclusive purchase agreement was ten years, because of the relatively low level of average throughput pertaining in Ireland. It noted that, when the agreement expired, the dealer was free to negotiate a new supply agreement with any wholesale supplier of his choosing. Competition among wholesalers for untied dealers was very intense and a significant amount of brand switching took place.

27. Esso maintained that the arguments in favour of having ten- year supply agreements in the retail motor fuel market had already been accepted by the EC, and had been ratified under Regulation 1984/83. It pointed out that the Fair Trade Commission did not consider that the maximum 10 year period operated against the common good, but that any shorter period would substantially lessen the incentive for wholesalers to invest in dealer outlets to the detriment of dealers and consumers.

28. Esso stated that the solus agreement provided financial assistance to independent operators for the provision of modern, safe and efficient facilities for the retail sale of motor fuels and in return an assured outlet for the wholesaler. The investment included the provision of adequate storage capacity to take deliveries in economic load sizes. This resulted in savings in the substantial delivery costs. The commercial and financial advantages conferred by the

4.1 supplier made it significantly easier to establish, modernise, maintain and operate a service station. The ban on dealing in competing products incited the reseller to devote all his resources to the sale of the contract goods, which allowed the parties to improve or maintain the quality of the contract goods and of the services to the customer. The agreements allowed long term planning of sales and consequently a cost-effective organisation of distribution.

29. Esso claimed that consumers benefited from these improvements as they were assured supplies of goods of satisfactory quality at fair prices and conditions while being able to choose between the products of different suppliers. Consumers had available a choice of modern, safe and efficient outlets for the purchase of motor fuels at a price which reflected the reduced cost of distribution. The only obligation imposed upon the retailer was to purchase motor fuels exclusively from the wholesaler for a ten-year period. This was required in order to justify the considerable investment involved. The obligation related to a particular outlet only. Motor fuels supplied by other wholesalers were available to the motoring public at other outlets in close proximity to the assured outlet.

30. Esso stated that the exact location of a service station was not easy to define and the intention of including any other outlet within a one-mile radius was to include all such facilities owned or used by the retailer in connection or association with the main outlet. They considered a radius of one mile to be a reasonable distance which did not impose an undue restraint on the retailer. It was intended only as a safeguard against the catastrophic effect of a retailer developing a competing virgin site in the very proximity of the subject site. The minimum delivery quantity was incorporated into the agreement to guarantee the efficiency of the delivery operation. The Cooperation Plan was merely a guide to the proper and efficient operation of a service station, and the obligation was not absolute and was not enforced. The obligation in respect of opening was at all reasonable hours and no specific hours were or had been specified. In locations where there was an opportunity, Esso might recommend a retailer to extend his usual hours on a trial basis. For some time, there had not been any joint advertising or sales promotions and, in the past, any such promotions had been with the full agreement of the retailer.

31. Esso stated that they considered it normal business practice that, where equipment was provided by a supplier, it could only be used for that supplier's goods. The usual period of the Dealer Equipment Loan agreement was ten years. The few dealers without such an agreement had such an agreement in the past which had expired. While the equipment was written off over the ten year period of the agreement, in reality it had a longer useful life. In addition to the basic solus agreement which provided for the payment of rebate in advance by way of interest free loan, further financial assistance could be requested by the retailer in the form of an interest bearing loan. The usual period for such a loan was 15 years, but it could be repaid at any time at the discretion of the dealer. The clause in the Deed of Charge/Mortgage restricting letting by the retailer without consent was stated by Esso to be a normal requirement of a lender whose security could be depreciated by a letting at a rent less than the market rent.

32. Esso stated that solus dealers were free to set their own retail prices, and Esso did not influence or enforce a retail price. In their communication advising wholesale price changes, they informed dealers of the revised retail prices which would apply at their company-operated sites. In fact, in the retailer newsletter which advises of any change in wholesale prices, Esso include, for information, the maximum recommended retail price for each grade of motor fuel, effective some days ahead. Esso explained that this had been done in the past in order to advise dealers of the maximum prices which could be charged under the Maximum Prices Order. The practice was continued after the MPO had been repealed for information purposes, and not to influence prices charged by dealers, since, in its absence, all their dealers would telephone to enquire about the prices which Esso would charge in their company stations. At the request of the Authority, Esso agreed, by letter dated 13 May 1992, not in future to inform solus retailers in advance of pump price changes at company stations operated by Artane Service Station Ltd.

Society of the Irish Motor Industry

33. The Society of the Irish Motor Industry (SIMI), which has a number of Esso solus dealers among its members, stated that there appeared to be a significant amount of price competition, as was evidenced by the wide variation in prices displayed at filling stations. With regard to autodiesel, SIMI understood that from time to time dealers could avail themselves of very competitive prices from wholesale suppliers other than their usual petrol company supplier, and this arrangement was helpful from the point of view of enhancing competition. SIMI understood that Esso suggested pump prices to their solus dealers, but they were not aware of any insistence that solus dealers had to comply with these suggested prices. SIMI considered that, depending on the proximity of a company owned station to a dealer, the dealer might wish to protect his sales volume by pricing competitively with the company owned station.

34. SIMI stated that any agreement whereby retailers were required to source their supplies from one supplier was, by definition, restrictive of competition. However, apart from other considerations, solus agreements did provide the stability to enable petrol retailers to develop and retain a reasonable sales volume. Of itself, the solus agreement need not necessarily inhibit price competition, as was clear from the present market place. SIMI supported, as a matter of general principle, and without reference to any individual solus agreement, the granting of a licence in respect of solus agreements.

35. While the provision of loans for improvements or equipment might tend to prolong the exclusive purchase requirement beyond ten years, SIMI considered that the retailer was normally a free agent in this regard and had the option of exploring more favourable arrangements for raising any additional capital required. Without the availability of loans from petroleum companies, SIMI considered that it was very unlikely that many petrol retailers would be successful in raising the necessary capital for improvements and additional equipment, having regard to the very low profit margins as traditionally associated with the sale of petrol by retail. Since the repeal of the Restrictive Practices Order, SIMI had not received any complaints about unreasonable pressure on petrol retailers in relation to advertising and promotion. SIMI were not in favour of advertising or promotional schemes which involved the petrol retailer in additional costs which, inevitably, had to be passed on to purchasers.

Assessment

(a) *Applicability of section 4(1)*

36. Section 4(1) of the Competition Act 1991, prohibits and renders void all agreements between undertakings which have as their object or effect the prevention, restriction or distortion of competition in trade in any goods or services in the State or in any part of the State.

37. Esso Ireland Ltd and the independent Esso solus dealers are engaged in the sale of motor fuels for gain, and they are therefore 'undertakings' within the meaning of section 3(1) of the Competition Act. The solus and related agreements are agreements between undertakings. The relevant product market is that of motor fuels for resale to the public. Since there are Esso solus dealers in all but one county, the relevant geographical market is the State.

(i) *The solus agreement — exclusive purchasing requirement*

38. The primary feature of the basic solus agreement is that the solus dealer is obliged to purchase his requirements of motor fuels exclusively from Esso for a period not exceeding ten years (clause 3(a)). The solus dealer, therefore, is not permitted to purchase any motor fuels from a supplier other than Esso during the period of the agreement, and no supplier other than Esso may supply the dealer during that period. This limits the commercial freedom of the dealer to obtain supplies, and the freedom of others to supply him, and is a restriction upon competition within the terms of section 4(1) of the Competition Act.

4.1 39. While the effect of a single agreement between Esso and an independent dealer might be insignificant, each agreement must be considered in the economic context of the retail market for motor fuels.* Esso alone has solus agreements with several hundred dealers, and it operates through its own outlets, all of which can only purchase Esso motor fuels for a lengthy period at least. Together, the network of Esso dealer and company stations accounts for a not insignificant proportion of total retail sales of motor fuels, and it comprises Esso stations with the largest throughputs. In addition, all the other major suppliers operate a similar system of dealer stations with ten-year solus agreements and large numbers of company stations. The smaller suppliers also have solus dealers, with a few company outlets. The net result is that a high proportion of all retail outlets, and almost all of the largest ones, are either owned by a supplier or are operated on a ten-year solus agreement. None of these can purchase motor fuels for a long period from any other supplier.

40. This tends to introduce a considerable degree of rigidity into the market, and makes it difficult for a new entrant to enter the market on any significant scale, since the most important potential customers are not available, at least in some cases until their solus agreements have expired.

41. The Authority considers, therefore, that the standard Esso solus agreement has the object and the effect of preventing, restricting or distorting competition in goods in the State, and therefore offends against section 4(1) of the Competition Act 1991. Since the three related agreements — concerning equipment loan, loan and deed of charge/mortgage — also involve an exclusive purchasing commitment for ten years, or are dependent on an agreement containing such an obligation, they also come within the prohibition of section 4(1) of the Act.

(ii) *The solus agreement — other requirements*

42. The obligation in the solus agreement upon Esso to supply the dealer with his total requirements (clause 2(a)), is a corollary of the exclusive purchase obligation on the dealer, and it comes within the prohibition of section 4(1). It is qualified to the extent that the dealer is permitted to purchase supplies in certain circumstances if Esso withholds, reduces or suspends deliveries (clause 4(b)(ii)). The extension of the exclusive purchasing requirement to include the sale of motor fuels by the dealer at any premises within a one mile radius of the designated service station (clause 1(d)), prevents the dealer from selling competing motor fuels at any premises within that area. At the public enquiry held by the Fair Trade Commission in 1989, it was widely held in evidence that the location of a service station was very important in attracting motorists, and that, because of the high price of petrol, it would not be economic for a motorist to drive very far in order to buy petrol cheaper in another service station, because any consequent saving would be offset by the cost of fuel consumed. Competition would therefore appear to be a localised phenomenon. The obligation not to deal in competing motor fuels within a one mile radius of the designated station is a restriction on competition which is prohibited by section 4(1).

43. The agreement to provide a loan (clause 2(b)), which is not applicable in all agreements, is a reward to the dealer for accepting the exclusive agreement, and is not caught by section 4(1). It is important that the existence of a loan cannot be used to extend the life of the exclusive purchase agreement beyond ten years (clause 7(e)). The payment of a rebate to the dealer (clause 2(c)), which is a small amount per litre and is not payable to non-solus dealers or to company owned operators, is a further recompense for exclusivity, and is not within the terms of section 4(1). The rebate is usually paid as a lump sum in advance by way of a loan under clause 2(b), and amounts to the estimated rebate over the ten years of the solus agreement. The minimum delivery requirement (clause 3(e)), provided that it is not unreasonable, does not itself restrict the dealer from obtaining supplies from another supplier, since he is prevented

*This is the view of the Court of Justice in the *Brasserie de Haecht*, No. 1 Case, No. 23/67 [1967] ECR 407.

from doing so by the exclusive purchasing requirement in clause 3(a). It is not restrictive of competition and does not offend against section 4(1). The requirements in the Dealer Cooperation Plan to open at reasonable hours (clause 5) and to participate in advertising and sales promotion (clause 6), provided that the requirements in a particular case are not unreasonable, do not restrict the dealer in deciding upon his own opening hours nor do they restrict the dealer in engaging or not in his own forms of advertising and promotion. They are not restrictive of competition and are not prohibited by section 4(1). The obligation to give preference to Esso lubricating oils and other products (clause 7), does not prevent the dealer from selling competing products, and is not restrictive of competition and is not caught by section 4(1). The requirements to give Esso the chance of introducing a purchaser to the dealer and for the dealer to try to ensure that any purchaser will continue to deal with Esso (clause 3(j)), do not restrict the dealer's freedom to sell the station, and are not prohibited by section 4(1).* **4.1**

(iii) *The dealer equipment loan agreement*

44. The dealer equipment loan agreement comes within the scope of section 4(1) since it is subsidiary to and dependent upon the solus agreement which is itself prohibited by section 4(1). The equipment loan agreement does not have a period of effectiveness beyond that of the solus agreement (clause 1(i)), and cannot be used to extend the ten-year period of exclusivity by artificial means, and the length of the loan is not a restriction on competition within the meaning of section 4(1).

The ability of Esso to determine the agreement in the event of the dealer ceasing to operate the station or failing to carry out his obligations (clause 3), is a normal consequence of the supply agreement and of the fact that the equipment is the property of Esso, and does not restrict competition in the sense of section 4(1). The requirements to allow Esso to inspect the equipment, for the dealer to use the equipment exclusively for Esso products, and for Esso to take samples and lock and seal the tanks (clause 4(1)), reflect the solus agreement and the ownership of the equipment by Esso, and do not restrict competition and are not caught by section 4(1).

(iv) *The loan agreement*

45. The loan agreement, being virtually identical to the solus agreement, is prohibited by section 4(1) for the same reasons as set out above, while many clauses are not caught by section 4(1) as before. The obligation on the dealer to grant a mortgage in return for the loan (clause 3(f)), which cannot be used to extend the period of exclusivity, is a normal requirement for the granting of a loan, and is not a restriction on competition within the meaning of section 4(1).

(v) *The deed of charge/mortgage*

46. The deed of charge/mortgage is related to the loan agreement, and it also contains an exclusive purchase requirement (Second Schedule, clause 3), which brings it within the scope of the prohibition in section 4(1). The requirements to repay the loan (clause 1(i)), to become a tenant at will (clause 6), to keep the premises open for the sale of petrol (Second Schedule, clause 2), and not, without the consent of Esso, to grant any lease or tenancy (Third Schedule, clause 4), are normal requirements of loan and mortgage agreements, and they do not restrict competition and so they do not offend against section 4(1).

*The Authority has considered the implications of the judgment of the High Court on 1 May 1991 in the case of *Texaco (Ireland) Ltd v Thomas Farrell and Esso Ireland Ltd.* Blayney J held that a pre-emption clause in a solus agreement, whereby the dealer had first to offer his premises for sale to Texaco, was in restraint of trade and was void. He held that Texaco were adequately protected by the clause which required the dealer to secure purchaser's written agreement with Texaco to be bound by the solus agreement. The Authority considers that the Esso agreement does not give any similar pre-emption right to Esso, and that it does not even oblige the dealer to secure the purchaser's agreement to be bound by the solus agreement, only to try to secure such agreement.

4.1 (b) *Applicability of section 4(2)*

47. Under section 4(2), the Competition Authority may grant a licence in the case of any agreement or category of agreements which, 'having regard to all relevant market conditions, contributes to improving the production of goods or provision of services or to promoting technical or economic progress, while allowing consumers a fair share of the resulting benefit and which does not —

(i) impose on the undertakings concerned terms which are not indispensable to the attainment of those objectives;

(ii) afford undertakings the possibility of eliminating competition in respect of a substantial part of the products or services in question.'

48. In the opinion of the Authority, the solus and related agreements notified by Esso fulfil the conditions provided for in section 4(2).

49. Solus agreements in the motor fuels sector differ from other exclusive purchase agreements in that the supplier confers on the reseller special commercial or financial advantages by contributing to his financing, granting him a loan on favourable terms, and providing him with equipment, while the reseller enters into a long-term exclusive purchasing obligation which is accompanied by a ban on dealing in competing products and the supplier agrees to supply the reseller's total requirements of motor fuels.

50. The solus agreements produce an appreciable improvement in distribution in which consumers are allowed a fair share of the resulting benefit. The commercial and financial advantages conferred by the supplier on the retailer make it significantly easier to establish, modernise, maintain and operate service stations. A high level of investment is needed to provide adequate facilities and to meet safety standards, and Esso has invested heavily in its company owned stations. Independent dealers would have insufficient resources for the necessary investment without substantial support from the supplier, otherwise company stations would become dominant. They are able to provide a range of services which they would otherwise be unable to offer. The exclusive purchasing obligation and the ban on dealing in competing products imposed on the reseller encourage the reseller to devote all the resources at his disposal to the sale of motor fuels, while retaining his independence and freedom to run the business as he sees fit. Solus agreements lead to durable cooperation between the parties, allowing them to improve or maintain the quality of the motor fuels and of the services to the customer and the sales efforts of the reseller. The investment by the supplier ensures security of supply by providing assured outlets for its product, and retailers are guaranteed regular supplies. This allows long-term planning of sales and consequently a cost-effective organisation of production and distribution. The costs of distributing motor fuels to a limited number of exclusive outlets which purchase in large quantities are lower than delivering smaller volumes to a large number of outlets selling two or more brands at the one service station. The pressure of competition between different brands of motor fuel obliges the undertakings involved to determine the number and characteristics of service stations in accordance with the wishes of consumers.

51. The solus agreement includes a clause extending the exclusive purchasing requirement to include the sale of motor fuels by the dealer at any premises within a one-mile radius of the designated service station. The Authority accepts that competition in the sale of motor fuels is a fairly localised phenomenon. Motorists do not tend to travel any great distance to buy at a cheaper price, since the cost of so doing would soon eliminate any savings made. The dedication of the dealer to maximising sales of Esso motor fuels at the designated outlet would be likely to be adversely affected if he were permitted to sell another brand at a station owned or operated by himself within one mile of the designated station. Without such a requirement, the improvement in distribution would not be secured. The dealer is free, however, to sell competing motor fuels outside the one mile radius.

52. Consumers benefit from these improvements especially because they are ensured supplies of motor fuel of satisfactory quality while being able to choose between different

brands of motor fuel. The solus system leads to more efficient distribution and to better facilities and services at dealer stations, to the benefit of consumers. They have a choice between stations offering differing degrees and types of service. The system should ensure both intra-brand and inter-brand competition, including price competition. **4.1**

53. The advantages produced by solus agreements cannot be achieved to the same extent and with the same degree of certainty in any other way. The exclusive purchasing obligation on the reseller and the non-competition clause imposed on him are essential components of such agreements and are indispensable for the attainment of these advantages. These obligations are confined to the purchase of motor fuels for resale, and do not extend to other products. The limitation of the period of the exclusive agreement to ten years is sufficient to produce the advantages, while maintaining the reseller's commercial freedom to change supplier and to ensure access to the retail level of distribution on the part of other suppliers. Any shorter period would substantially lessen the incentive for suppliers to invest in dealer outlets, to the detriment of dealers and consumers. This is especially so in the State, where the average throughput in petrol stations is only about one quarter of the EC average.

54. There are large numbers of Esso solus, company and non-solus outlets, and there are many other outlets of these types which sell motor fuels under other brand names. There is a high degree of competition between outlets, both intra-brand and inter-brand, and, with the removal of price control, there is scope for price competition, in particular, since solus and non-solus dealers are free to determine their own selling prices. While the long-term nature of the exclusive supply contracts limits the possibilities for a new entrant to secure outlets, all dealers are free to change their supplier at the expiry of the contract, and this does occur, and agreements are expiring on a continuous basis. In addition, a new supplier entrant would be likely to want the security offered by long-term solus agreements before making the sizeable investment necessary to enter the market in the first place. There is thus no possibility of the undertakings being afforded the possibility of eliminating competition for a substantial part of the products in question.

55. It will be apparent that, in its assessment, the Authority has had regard to EC Regulation No. 1984/83, which exempts certain exclusive purchasing agreements, including service station agreements, from the prohibition of Article 85(1) of the Treaty of Rome (see paras. 20 to 22).

(c) *Recommended Prices*

56. During the course of its investigation of the notified agreements, the Authority became aware that, shortly before any change in the wholesale price of its products, Esso circulated a newsletter to its solus retailers advising them of the change in wholesale prices and of the maximum recommended retail price for each grade of motor fuel. It was explained by Esso, and was accepted by the Authority, that this had been done in the past in order to try to ensure that its retailers did not exceed the maximum prices which could be charged under the Maximum Prices Order, price control only being abolished on 30 September 1991. The subsequent continuance of this practice, according to Esso, was not designed to influence prices charged by independent solus dealers nor was it aimed at ensuring resale price maintenance.

57. This practice was not part of the written terms of the agreements notified. Nevertheless, the Authority considered that it formed part of the total relationship between the supplier and its solus dealers, and that it should be considered in this context. In most circumstances, provided that independent resellers are free to set their own resale prices, and that they are aware of this, the informing of resellers by suppliers of recommended, or recommended maximum, resale prices does not, in the opinion of the Authority, amount to resale price maintenance, and is not therefore caught by the prohibition in section 4(1). (This might not be the case, however, if a considerable degree of price similarity were observed in the market).

58. Esso tends to differ from other oil wholesalers in that its company-owned stations are operated by the company itself, through Artane Service Station Ltd, and Esso sets the resale prices at these company stations. Such stations are in competition with Esso solus stations in

4.1 the vicinity. Esso is an operator on the market like its solus dealer outlets. In BP Kemi/DDSF, the EC Commission condemned an information exchange agreement between a supplier and his distributor where the supplier himself competed in the distributor's territory.* In effect, Esso, by informing its solus dealers of a maximum recommended price, was informing them of the price which would be charged in Esso company operated stations. Its action amounted to informing solus dealers in advance about the prices which would be charged by their competitors, competitors who accounted for a large proportion of total retail sales of Esso products. The Authority was concerned that this could have the effect of eliminating uncertainty and of distorting intra-brand competition between Esso outlets. In response to this concern, Esso, as pointed out in para 32, readily agreed not in future to inform solus retailers in advance of pump price changes at company stations operated by Artane Service Station Ltd, that is at Esso company-operated stations. The Authority believes that,in general, the exchange of price information by competitors would offend against section 4(1) and it does not believe that a licence under section 4(2) could be justified for such a practice.

The decision

59. Accordingly, the Authority is of the opinion that all the conditions set out in section 4(2) of the Competition Act are fulfilled.

60. The Authority therefore grants a licence under section 4(2) in respect of each of the notified Esso agreements. Since each notification relates to a category of standard agreements, each licence is granted in respect of that category of notified Esso agreements.

61. The licences shall apply from the date of this decision, that is 25 June 1992. Given the ten-year duration of the notified agreements, it seems appropriate that the period specified for the licences should be ten years also, that is until 24 June 2002. It is not considered necessary to attach any conditions to the licences.

62. A copy of the licences is annexed to this decision.

For the Competition Authority

Patrick M. Lyons
Chairman

25 June 1992

Annex: The licences
(a) *The standard Esso solus agreement*

Article 1

The provisions of section 4(1) of the Competition Act 1991 are declared inapplicable to the category of standard Esso solus agreements notified to the Competition Authority on 19 December 1991 (CA/14/91E), on the grounds that, in the opinion of the Authority, all the conditions of section 4(2) of the Competition Act 1991 have been fulfilled. This licence shall apply from 25 June 1992 to 24 June 2002.

Article 2

This licence is addressed to: Esso Ireland Ltd, Stillorgan, Co. Dublin.

For the Competition Authority

Patrick M. Lyons
Chairman

25 June 1992

*BP Kemi/DDSF (OJ L286, 14.11.79, p. 32).

(b) *The Dealer Equipment Loan Agreement* 4.1

Article 1 The provisions of section 4(1) of the Competition Act 1991 are declared inapplicable to the category of Esso dealer equipment loan agreements notified to the Competition Authority on 19 December 1991 (CA/13/91E), on the grounds that, in the opinion of the Authority, all the conditions of section 4(2) of the Competition Act 1991 have been fulfilled. This licence shall apply from 25 June 1992 to 24 June 2002.

Article 2

This licence is addressed to: Esso Ireland Ltd, Stillorgan, Co. Dublin.

For the Competition Authority

Patrick M. Lyons
Chairman

25 June 1992

(c) *The Dealer Loan Agreement*

Article 1

The provisions of section 4(1) of the Competition Act 1991 are declared inapplicable to the category of Esso dealer loan agreements notified to the Competition Authority on 19 December 1991 (CA/12/91E), on the grounds that, in the opinion of the Authority, all the conditions of section 4(2) of the Competition Act 1991 have been fulfilled. This licence shall apply from 25 June 1992 to 24 June 2002.

Article 2

This licence is addressed to: Esso Ireland Ltd, Stillorgan, Co. Dublin.

For the Competition Authority

Patrick M. Lyons
Chairman

25 June 1992

(d) *Deed of Charge/Mortgage*

Article 1

The provisions of section 4(1) of the Competition Act 1991 are declared inapplicable to the category of Esso deed of charge/mortgage agreements notified to the Competition Authority on 19 December 1991 (CA/11/91E), on the grounds that, in the opinion of the Authority, all the conditions of section 4(2) of the Competition Act 1991 have been fulfilled. This licence shall apply from 25 June 1992 to 24 June 2002.

Article 2

This licence is addressed to: Esso Ireland Ltd, Stillorgan, Co. Dublin.

For the Competition Authority

Patrick M. Lyons
Chairman

25 June 1992

4.2 Competition Authority Decision No. 25, Motor Fuels Category Licence — Preamble

Competition Authority Decision of 1 July 1993 granting a licence under section 4(2) of the Competition Act 1991, to a category of exclusive purchasing agreements in respect of motor fuels.

Introduction

1. Under section 4(2) of the Competition Act 1991, the Competition Authority may grant a licence for the purposes of section 4 of the Act to any category of agreements:

> which in the opinion of the Authority, having regard to all relevant market conditions, contributes to improving the production or distribution of goods or provision of services or to promoting technical or economic progress, while allowing consumers a fair share of the resulting benefit and which does not—
> (i) impose on the undertakings concerned terms which are not indispensable to the attainment of those objectives;
> (ii) afford undertakings the possibility of eliminating competition in respect of a substantial part of the products or services in question.

2. A number of agreements have been notified to the Authority concerning long-term exclusive purchasing arrangements for the resale of petroleum products in service stations. Since agreements have been notified, in accordance with section 7(3) of the Act, the Authority may grant a licence, including a category licence, under section 4(2) of the Act. The Authority has already granted licences in respect of the Esso solus and related agreements.[1] It has also carefully examined notifications from other companies relating to exclusive purchasing agreements for both independent dealer and company-owned outlets. The experience of the Authority enables it to define a category of agreements and concerted practices which can be regarded as normally satisfying the conditions laid down in section 4(2).

3. Notice of intention to grant a category licence for motor fuels was published on 11 December 1992, and submissions were invited from interested parties. A number of submissions was received on the draft category licence, and full account was taken of these prior to finalising this decision.

The Subject of the Decision

4. This decision concerns the long-term supply and exclusive purchasing agreements between suppliers of motor fuels and their tied service station retailers, subsequently referred to as resellers. The majority of independent resellers operate under exclusive purchasing, or solus, agreements, which have a maximum term of ten years. Most company-owned outlets are operated under licence or in accordance with a lease. This decision applies only to such solus agreements, licences and leases. Some independent dealers, while tending to buy from a single supplier, do not do so in accordance with any formal long-term agreement, and consequently are not covered by this decision. Some company-owned outlets are operated, directly or indirectly, by the supplying companies. Since the relationship between supplier and reseller in these cases is that of parent/subsidiary or employer/employee, and the Authority has already indicated that, in such circumstances, any relevant agreements are not caught by section

1. Decision No. 4 of 25 June 1992 — Notification Nos. CA/11/91E, CA/12/91E, CA/13/91E and CA/14/91E — Esso Solus and Related Agreements.

4(1) of the Act, they are also outside the scope of this decision.[2] This decision only covers agreements for the resale of motor fuel. It does not cover agreements for the sale of motor fuels direct to commercial users, or for the resale or sale of aviation, marine or other petroleum-based fuels. **4.2**

5. The agreements with solus dealers are often accompanied by other agreements, which either contain an exclusive purchasing obligation for motor fuels or are dependent upon an agreement which contains such an obligation. These other agreements may also contain different restrictive provisions. The more important of these other agreements are in connection with:

(a) the loan of equipment to the dealer;
(b) the payment of rebates in advance by way of an interest-free loan to the dealer;
(c) the loan of money to the dealer;
(d) a deed of charge or mortgage, as security for a cash loan to the dealer;
(e) a hire purchase agreement for equipment purchased by the dealer.

Agreements relating to equipment may cover that for the sale of motor fuels (tanks, pumps, etc.), lubricating oil equipment, or civil construction at the service station (the forecourt, canopies, a service bay, a car wash, or a shop).

The Products Concerned

6. The products with which this decision is concerned consist of motor fuels, that is petrol and diesel for use in mechanically-propelled motor vehicles, and other petroleum-based motor fuels, such as liquefied petroleum gas (LPG) and kerosene. Insofar as they are supplied to motor fuel resellers, lubricants and related petroleum-based products, such as greases, additives and brake fluids, are also covered by this decision.

The Market

7. Motor fuels are imported into Ireland by a number of suppliers, usually from refineries in the UK, through various Irish ports where they have storage facilities. Each supplier must obtain 35% of its total product from the State-owned Whitegate refinery. The suppliers are primarily concerned in Ireland with the marketing of petroleum products, that is with the supply and distribution of motor fuels to the motoring public through a chain of retail outlets, though some product is sold directly to commercial customers. From the storage depots, retail outlets are supplied by road tanker. A number of the suppliers are subsidiaries of multi-national oil companies, while the newer entrants, which are small, are Irish-owned. The main suppliers of motor fuel to resellers are:

Burmah Castrol Ireland
Campus Oil Ltd
Conoco Ireland Ltd
Esso Ireland Ltd
Estuary Fuel Ltd
Irish Shell Ltd
McMullan Bros. Ltd
Morris Oil Company Ltd
Statoil Ireland Ltd
Tedcastle Oil Products Ltd
Texaco (Ireland) Ltd

McMullans trades under the trademarks Maxol and Ola. B.P. Ireland Ltd was taken over by Statoil Ireland Ltd in mid-1992. There are a number of smaller companies which also supply small numbers of retail petrol outlets. They do not import the product but obtain it from one of the above-named suppliers. The retail outlets display their brand name. These companies vary from time to time, but among the small suppliers known to the Authority to be, or to have

2. See Decision No. 2 of 14 May 1992 — AGF-Irish Life Holdings and Decision No. 5 of 30 June 1992 — PRS/IMRO and the guidance note on Employee Agreements and the Competition Act, *Iris Oifigiúil*, 18 September 1992, pp. 632-3.

4.2 been recently, trading are the following: Delta (associated with Campus), Ryan Oil, Falcon, Togher, Primo, Phoenix, Torc and Amber.

8. Each supplier supplies motor fuel to resellers who comprise independent solus dealers, who have an exclusive purchasing agreement, non-solus dealers, without such an agreement, and, usually, company-owned outlets. Company-owned outlets may be operated in several different ways. They may be licensed to an operator on a short-term basis, or leased to an operator on, usually, a long-term basis, or managed by an employee of the company or by a commission agent. Licensees and lessees tend to have a greater degree of freedom in their commercial activities than managers or commission agents in company-operated stations. As stated in para 4, however, this decision only covers solus dealers, licensees and lessees. Dealer and company-owned stations are located throughout the State, but the latter tend to be located in the major centres of population. The sale of motor fuels through service stations may be combined with car repairs and servicing, car sales, or a shop selling, among other items, grocery products. (Motor fuels may also be sold from outlets ancillary to other businesses, such as grocery shops or public houses, though, because of their small sales, these tend not to have solus agreements with their suppliers).

9. According to the Report of Enquiry into the Supply and Distribution of Motor Fuels by the Fair Trade Commission in 1989 (PL. 7951), total sales of petrol through retailers in 1988 were 1,090 million litres, while total retail sales of autodiesel were 187 million litres. In 1988, there were 3,227 retail petrol outlets, of which 447 were company owned, or 13.9%, and 2,017 were solus outlets, or 62.5%. Non-solus dealers accounted for 23.6% of total outlets. The proportion of total petrol sales through company-owned outlets was, however, 41.6%, with 51.5% through solus outlets and 7.0% through non-solus outlets 36.3% of dealer outlets sold less than 20,000 gallons of petrol per year (90,920 litres) and only 4.6% sold more than 200,000 gallons (909,200 litres). The respective figures for company stations were 4.1% and 57.2%. Company outlets had a higher average annual throughput than solus dealers, who had a higher average throughput than non-solus dealers. The average throughput of all outlets in Ireland was only about one-quarter of the EC average.

10. Since petrol outlets are located throughout the State, the appropriate geographic market in this case is the State.

11. Up to 30 September 1991, the motor fuels sector was subject to strict price control and to the provisions of the Restrictive Practices (Motor Spirit and Motor Vehicle Lubricating Oil) Order, 1981. Both the Order and price control were removed on the coming into force of the Competition Act on 1 October 1991.

EEC Regulation 1984/83

12. EEC Regulation No. 1984/83, of 22 June 1983, is a block exemption regulation which applies Article 85(3) of the Treaty of Rome to categories of exclusive purchasing agreements. It includes special provisions for service station agreements, that is for solus agreements and for agreements relating to company owned stations. The regulation entered into force on 1 July 1983 and it expires on 31 December 1997.[3]

13. The regulation applies to agreements involving only two parties whereby one party, the reseller, agrees with the other, the supplier, to purchase specified goods only from the supplier, or from a connected undertaking or one entrusted by the supplier with the sale of his goods. The supplier may be obliged not to distribute the goods or competing goods in the reseller's principal sales area and at the reseller's level of distribution. For goods generally, the exclusive distribution agreement may be for no longer than five years.

14. In the case of agreements for the supply of petroleum-based motor vehicle fuels, or for these and other fuels, for resale in a specified service station, special commercial or financial

3. OJ No. L173, 30.6.83, p. 5, as corrected in OJ No. L281, 13.10.83, p. 24, and Explanatory Notice, OJ No. C101, 13.4.84, p. 2.

advantages may be accorded by the supplier to the reseller. In such cases, the exclusive purchasing agreement may be for a period not exceeding ten years, and the reseller may be obliged not to sell fuels supplied by other undertakings. If the service station is let to the reseller by the supplier, the ban on dealing in competing products may be imposed for the whole period during which the reseller operates the station. The reseller may also be obliged not to use lubricating oil supplied by other firms where equipment is financed or made available by the supplier, but he may not be prevented from selling oil supplied by other firms. 4.2

These exclusive purchasing agreements may refer to no other goods, nor to services (except in connection with the servicing of equipment owned or financed by the supplier). Where the reseller (in this case the independent dealer) sells his outlet, he may not be obliged to impose the exclusive purchasing obligation on his successor for a longer period than the reseller would remain tied to the supplier. Some general provisions of the regulation also apply, such as permitting the reseller to be obliged to purchase minimum quantities of goods, to sell the goods under trademarks and to advertise and promote the goods. The benefits of exemption may be withdrawn by the EC Commission in a particular case where it considers that the conditions of Article 85(3) are not satisfied, where, for example, effective competition is lacking. There are special transition provisions for existing service station agreements. Service station agreements cannot be combined with general exclusive purchasing agreements involving the same parties.

Assessment

(a) *Applicability of section 4(1)*

15. Section 4(1) of the Competition Act 1991, prohibits and renders void all agreements between undertakings which have as their object or effect the prevention, restriction or distortion of competition in trade in any goods or services in the State or in any part of the State.

16. The suppliers of motor fuels, the independent solus dealers, and the licensees and lessees of company stations, are all engaged in the supply and distribution of motor fuels for gain, and they are therefore 'undertakings' within the meaning of section 3(1) of the Competition Act. The solus and related agreements, the licences and the leases are all agreements between undertakings. The relevant product market is that of motor fuels and other petroleum-based products for resale to the public. The relevant geographical market is the State.

(i) The exclusive purchasing requirement

17. The primary feature of the basic solus agreement is that the solus dealer is obliged to purchase his requirements of motor fuels from one supplier, or a person appointed by the supplier, for a period not exceeding ten years. In the case of licences and leases, the exclusive purchasing requirement lasts for the full term of the agreement, which can be as long as thirty or more years for a lease. The solus dealer, licensee or lessee, therefore, is not permitted to purchase any motor fuels from a supplier other than the other party to the agreement (except in certain circumstances, see para 24) during the period of the agreement, and no supplier other than the other party may supply the dealer, licensee or lessee during that period. This limits the commercial freedom of the dealer or operator to obtain supplies, and the freedom of other suppliers to meet his requirements, and is a restriction upon competition which offends against section 4(1) of the Competition Act.

18. While the effect of a single agreement between a supplier and an independent dealer or operator of a company station might be insignificant, each agreement must be considered in the economic context of the retail market for motor fuels.[4] As is clear from para 9, outlets

4. This is the view of the EC Court of Justice in the Brasserie de Haecht No. 1 Case, No. 23/67, [1967] ECR 407.

4.2 subject to an exclusive purchasing tie — solus dealers and company stations — accounted for 76.4% of all retail petrol outlets, including almost all of the larger stations, and for 93.1% of total retail sales of petrol, petrol being the most important motor fuel sold by retailers. The vast bulk of petrol sales, therefore, is through tied outlets, which are precluded from purchasing motor fuels from any other supplier over a long period.

19. This tends to introduce a considerable degree of rigidity into the market, and makes it difficult for a new entrant to enter the market on any significant scale, since the most important potential customers are not available, at least in some cases until their solus agreements have expired. All company stations are tied indefinitely to the supplier who owns them.

20. The Authority considers, therefore, that the basic solus agreements, the licences and leases, have the object and effect of preventing, restricting or distorting competition in goods in the State, and thus they offend against section 4(1) of the Competition Act 1991. Agreements related to the solus agreement which either contain an exclusive purchasing commitment or are dependent on an agreement containing such an obligation, are also regarded by the Authority as coming within the prohibition of section 4(1) of the Act.

(ii) Other restrictive clauses

(a) Geographical extent of exclusivity

21. The exclusive purchasing requirement in motor fuel agreements, particularly in solus agreements, may extend to include not only the designated service station but also any land or premises adjoining or in close proximity to the station. For the reasons given above, such a restriction also offends against the prohibition of section 4(1) of the Act.

22. The exclusive purchasing requirement may also be extended to include the sale of motor fuels by the dealer at any premises within a given radius of the designated service station, for example, within a one-mile radius. This prevents the dealer from selling competing motor fuels at any premises within the specified area. At the public enquiry held by the Fair Trade Commission in 1989, it was widely held in evidence that the location of a service station was very important in attracting motorists, and that, because of the high price of petrol, it would not be economic for a motorist to drive very far in order to buy petrol cheaper in another service station, because any consequent saving would be offset by the cost of fuel consumed. Competition would therefore appear to be a localised phenomenon. The obligation not to deal in competing motor fuels within, say, a one mile radius of the designated station is a restriction on competition which is prohibited by section 4(1). The Authority considers that any restriction on a dealer from dealing in competing fuels in any wider area, including a prohibition covering the whole State, is also a restriction on competition which offends against section 4(1).

(b) Post-term limitations

23. Agreements can contain restrictions upon dealers in relation to their activities after the agreement has terminated. These could involve, for example, a requirement that a further solus agreement should be concluded after the first agreement has terminated at the end of the ten-year period, or that exclusive purchasing continue after this period. There might also be some restriction upon the dealer, or a licensee or lessee, engaging in the sale of competing motor fuels after the agreement has terminated. Any such clauses interfere with competition, and offend against section 4(1).

(c) Obligation to supply

24. As a corollary to the obligation upon the dealer to purchase his total requirements of motor fuels from the supplier, there is an obligation upon the supplier to supply the dealer's total requirements. This obligation is usually qualified by a provision that the supplier is not bound to supply in certain circumstances, such as when it is prevented from supplying some or all of the requirements. It may be provided that the supplier will use its best endeavours to

procure supplies from some other source. Should the supplier fail to meet the supply obligation, the dealer is permitted to seek and purchase from another supplier during the period when supply is disrupted. Such provisions do not constitute limitations upon competition and so they do not offend against section 4(1). 4.2

(d) Resale price maintenance

25. Agreements might contain a requirement that the reseller sells at a price fixed by the supplier, or at a price not less than or not more than that indicated by the supplier. Alternatively, while not being specified in the agreement, it might be the practice of suppliers to issue price notices of this nature as part of the arrangements with their exclusive purchasers. Even if these are not binding, resellers might be of the belief that they were binding or that they should be followed. The Authority regards anything which enforces, or is conducive to, resale price maintenance as a serious restriction upon competition, and indeed to an elimination of price competition, and therefore as a serious infringement of the prohibition in section 4(1).

26. As the Authority stated in its decision on the Esso solus agreements, 'In most circumstances, provided that independent resellers are free to set their own resale prices, and that they are aware of this, the informing of resellers by suppliers of recommended, or recommended maximum, resale prices does not, in the opinion of the Authority, amount to resale price maintenance, and is not therefore caught by the prohibition in section 4(1). (This might not be the case, however, if a considerable degree of price similarity were observed in the market).'[5]

27. Where a supplier itself operates some of its company stations, however, the issuing of price recommendations may present some difficulties. This happens when the prices recommended in advance to dealers are known to be those which will be charged at the company-operated stations. The latter are in competition with solus and other dealers who are tied to the supplier, and the supplier is an operator on the market like these others. In BP Kemi/DDSF, the EC Commission condemned an information exchange agreement between a supplier and his distributor where the supplier himself competed in the distributor's territory.[6] As the Authority stated in its Decision concerning the Esso solus and related agreements: 'In effect, Esso, by informing its solus dealers of a maximum recommended price, was informing them of the price which would be charged in Esso company operated stations. Its action amounted to informing solus dealers in advance about the prices which would be charged by their competitors, competitors who accounted for a large proportion of total retail sales of Esso products. The Authority was concerned that this could have the effect of eliminating uncertainty and of distorting intra-brand competition between Esso outlets.'[7]

The Authority considers that, in general, the exchange of price information by competitors offends against section 4(1) of the Act.

(e) Lubricants, etc.

28. The suppliers of motor fuels also supply petroleum-based lubricating products, such as lubricating oils and greases, additives and brake fluids, which carry the supplier's brand name. There are some specialist oil products, admittedly produced by suppliers of motor fuels, which are widely available outside the suppliers' networks of service stations. A requirement on the exclusive purchaser of motor fuels to purchase, stock and sell exclusively lubricants and related products supplied by the supplier is a restriction on competition which offends against section 4(1).

29. An obligation in an agreement to give preference to the supplier's lubricants, provided

5. Decision No. 4, at para 57.
6. BP Kemi/DDSF, OJ L286, 14.11.79, p. 32.
7. Decision No. 4, at para 58.

4.2 it does not prevent the dealer from selling competing products, is not restrictive of competition and so does not offend against section 4(1).

(f) Other Products

30. Agreements may contain obligations to stock and sell other products obtained exclusively from the supplier, such as tyres, batteries and other motoring products, or other products. On occasion, it may be a requirement of an equipment loan agreement that the equipment be purchased from the supplier, or not purchased from someone else without the supplier's permission. Such exclusive purchasing requirements offend against the prohibition of section 4(1). Where there is merely a non-exclusive requirement or encouragement to stock and sell such products, or to purchase such equipment, this does not offend against section 4(1). A restriction by suppliers on the types of motor fuel storage and dispensing equipment used by resellers, provided that this is on objectively justified qualitative grounds, does not offend against section 4(1).

(g) Commercial and Financial Assistance

31. Suppliers of motor fuels almost invariably provide commercial and financial assistance to their exclusive purchasers. In the case of solus dealers, the assistance can take one or more of the following forms:

— payment of solus rebates on purchases of motor fuels;

— payment of the solus rebate in advance for up to ten years, by way of an interest-free loan;

— outright grants for the purchase of equipment or for construction work on the station (buildings, canopies, lubrication bays, car wash, a shop, etc.);

— long-term loans for the above purposes, at favourable rates of interest;

— the loan of equipment, such as storage tanks and petrol pumps, which may become the property of the dealer after some years;

— the arrangement of hire purchase financing for equipment;

— the provision of loan guarantees.

Where loans are made available, especially large loans, some security may be required from the dealer, such as the grant of a mortgage on the premises. Such financial assistance is often essential to the dealer in order for him to be able to erect, maintain or modernise his station, and to enable him to compete with other stations, particularly those owned by suppliers. Such assistance is both an encouragement to the dealer to become party to a long-term exclusive purchasing agreement, and a reward to him for doing so. While associated with the exclusive purchasing agreement, such financial assistance is not in itself restrictive of competition, and so does not offend against section 4(1). It is essential, however, that no loan arrangement should be capable of extending the life of the exclusive purchasing agreement beyond a maximum period of ten years.

32. In the case of stations which are owned, but not operated, by the supplier, the granting of a licence or a lease to the operator is itself a valuable form of financial assistance, since it enables the operator to trade in the retail motor fuels business without having to provide the substantial amount of capital to erect a modern service station. Such arrangements do not offend against section 4(1) of the Act.

Restrictions on the sale of a station

33. Solus agreements may contain certain conditions relating to the dealer's freedom to sell his station. There may be, for example, a requirement that the dealer must first offer the station for sale to the supplier, or that any purchaser must be approved by the supplier. There may be a requirement that the dealer must procure that the purchaser enter into a new ten-year solus agreement with the supplier, or that the purchaser undertake to be bound for the remaining

period of the solus agreement. Such obligations place restrictions upon the dealer's freedom to sell his premises, and upon the freedom of another person to buy the premises. They constrain exit from and entry to the trade in the retail sale of motor fuels, and they therefore affect competition in the trade. They offend against section 4(1) of the Act. 4.2

34. Other agreements merely require the dealer to give the supplier the chance of introducing a purchaser to the dealer, and/or that the dealer use his best endeavours to try to ensure that any purchaser will continue to deal with the supplier. Such obligations do not impose any restriction upon the dealer or any potential purchaser, they do not limit exit from or entry to the trade, and so they do not offend against section 4(1).

35. Since a licensee has no equity interest in the station which he operates under licence, he cannot dispose of any interest to another person, and no clauses restricting to whom he may sell are found in licence agreements.

36. In the case of lease agreements, however, the lessee does have an interest in the property, and he may normally dispose of this interest. He is usually required not to dispose of all or part of his interest without previously obtaining the consent of the supplier, who is the lessor, and he is required to ensure that the purchaser accept all the covenants in the original lease. It may be specified that the consent of the supplier will not be unreasonably withheld. The station is owned by the supplier, and he is exercising rights which are inherent in his ownership of the property. The Authority considers that the exercise of property rights by means of restrictions such as those described does not offend against section 4(1). Mortgage agreements, where there is a loan to a solus dealer, also require that no lease or tenancy be created without the consent of the mortgagee (the supplier), and such requirements likewise do not offend against section 4(1).

Other Restrictions in the Agreements

37. *Minimum delivery.* There is usually a minimum size of delivery of motor fuels specified in the exclusive purchase agreements. This is generally discussed with the reseller. Such a requirement does not in itself restrict the dealer from obtaining supplies from another supplier, which might happen in other circumstances, since he is already prevented from purchasing from another supplier by the exclusive purchasing requirement. A minimum delivery requirement, in these circumstances, provided that it is not discriminatory, is not restrictive of competition and does not offend against section 4(1).

38. *Opening hours.* The agreement usually specifies the hours at which the station shall be open for the sale of motor fuels. Actual hours may be specified, differing on weekdays, Sundays and holidays, and are normally discussed with the dealer, or the requirement may be to 'open during normal business hours' or 'at reasonable hours'. Provided that the hours are agreed with the dealer, such requirements do not restrict the dealer in deciding upon his own opening hours and they are not restrictive of competition. They do not offend against section 4(1).

39. Lease and licence agreements may also stipulate that the operator should not discontinue, whether wholly or in part, the business of selling motor fuels at the station. This is a consequence of the ownership of the station by the supplier, and does not offend against section 4(1).

40. *Advertising.* Agreements may prohibit the advertising of competing motor fuels at the station. Since these may not be sold at the station, this restriction in itself does not limit competition, and so does not offend against section 4(1).

41. Dealers may be required to advertise and engage in sales promotion. These requirements generally do not restrict the dealer in engaging or not engaging in his own forms of advertising and promotion. They do not restrain competition, and they do not offend against section 4(1).

42. Licensees and lessees may be required to obtain the permission of the supplier for on-site advertising. The station is owned by the supplier, and such obligations cannot be regarded as unduly limiting the operator's freedom to advertise, provided such permission is not unreasonably withheld, and thus they do not restrict competition in a manner which offends against section 4(1).

4.2 43. Certain agreements, particularly licences and leases, forbid the advertising of competing lubricating oils and other products on the premises. Such restrictions limit the ability of the reseller to advertise and compete, and so they offend against section 4(1).

44. *Termination and Expiry of Licences.* In accordance with the provisions of the 1981 Restrictive Practices Order, (Articles 25 to 33), licence agreements had to contain provisions governing the termination of a licence during its currency or on its expiry, and requiring that licences should be for a term of three years. They had to provide that termination shall only be for specified reasons, and they had to deal with compensation, arbitration and notice of termination. The RPO was designed to give licensees a degree of security of tenure and certain rights, without giving them rights of assignment or an equity interest in the premises. The Authority considers that such clauses do not amount to restraints upon competition which offend against section 4(1).

45. The repeal of the RPO, however, means that it is not mandatory to include such provisions in licence agreements any longer. Some suppliers have indicated their intention to remove these provisions in future. There would appear to be no grounds under the Competition Act 1991 for making such provisions mandatory in licence agreements, since their omission would not prevent, restrict or distort competition.

46. *Locking and sealing of tanks, sampling of contents, etc.* Exclusive purchasing agreements usually contain clauses which require the reseller to allow the supplier to lock and seal storage tanks, to sample the contents of tanks, to inspect stocks and to take readings. These requirements are designed, among other things, to ensure that the exclusive purchasing requirement is not being breached. In themselves, they do not restrict competition, and so they do not offend against section 4(1).

47. *Identification signs and globes.* Agreements often contain requirements to allow the company to erect an identification sign and to place identification globes on the petrol pumps. These requirements are designed to ensure that the reseller trades under the trademark of the supplier and that the consumer knows what brand of motor fuel is being sold at the premises. They do not restrict competition, and they do not offend against section 4(1).

48. *Adequate service and staff.* Agreements usually contain an obligation for the reseller to provide adequate service at the station and to employ adequate and efficient staff. Since the reseller is largely free to determine his own levels of staffing and service, these obligations do not offend against section 4(1).

49. *Inspection of equipment.* Agreements often require the reseller to permit the supplier to inspect equipment at the station, particularly where the equipment has been supplied or financed by the supplier. Since the supplier is entitled to inspect his own property, to ensure that it is installed where it should be and is being securely maintained, such requirements do not offend against section 4(1).

50. *Keep premises in good repair and insured.* Licence agreements and leases oblige the operator to keep the premises in good repair and fully insured. Since the main purpose of such requirements is to secure the property owned by the supplier, they do not offend against section 4(1).

51. *Maintain the number of pumps.* Licences and leases require the operator not to reduce the number of pumps nor to change the manner of operating the station. Since the supplier is entitled to ensure that the value of his property as a motor fuel station is not diminished, such requirements do not offend against section 4(1).

52. *Not to use the premises for other Purposes.* Licences and leases often forbid the operator from parking vehicles on the forecourt or from engaging in other motor-related businesses, such as car sales, car hire, taxi operator, or motor vehicle repairer (though some vehicle servicing is usually permitted). These are designed to prevent access to the pumps being blocked, or to ensure that the operator concentrates on sales of motor fuels rather than engaging in other activities. Since the station was made available by the supplier expressly for the purpose of selling motor fuels, such requirements do not restrict competition and do not offend against

section 4(1). **4.2**

53. *Keep records.* The licensee may be required to keep such records as are required by the supplier. This is so that the licensee will control his business properly and to comply with the requirements of the Revenue Commissioners. It does not restrict competition, and so does not offend against section 4(1).

(b) *Applicability of section 4(2)*

54. Under section 4(2), the Competition Authority may grant a licence in the case of any agreement or category of agreements which, 'having regard to all relevant market conditions, contributes to improving the production of goods or provision of services or to promoting technical or economic progress, while allowing consumers a fair share of the resulting benefit and which does not (i) impose on the undertakings concerned terms which are not indispensable to the attainment of those objectives; (ii) afford undertakings the possibility of eliminating competition in respect of a substantial part of the products or services in question.'

55. In the opinion of the Authority, arrangements for the exclusive purchasing of motor fuels, in general, are likely to fulfil the conditions provided for in section 4(2) and qualify for the grant of a category licence.

(i) The exclusive purchasing and related requirements

56. Solus agreements in the motor fuels sector differ from other exclusive purchasing agreements in that the supplier confers on the reseller special commercial or financial advantages by contributing to his financing, granting him a loan on favourable terms, and providing him with equipment, while the reseller enters into a long-term exclusive purchasing obligation which is accompanied by a ban on dealing in competing products and the supplier agrees to supply the reseller's total requirements of motor fuels. Another important difference between the distribution system for motor fuels and that for other products is that a large number of outlets, accounting for over 40% of total retail sales, is owned by the supplying undertakings. The licensee or lessee, not having to pay the capital cost of the station, is given even greater commercial or financial advantages than the solus dealer, in return for which the exclusive purchasing requirement lasts as long as the operator occupies the station, and indeed for as long as the supplier owns the station.

57. While recognising that exclusive purchasing agreements generally restrict competition, the Authority accepts that they may produce benefits which outweigh the detriments to competition. This is the case only if the exclusive purchasing obligation is limited in respect of the period of time for which it is imposed. Upon expiry of the period of exclusive purchasing, the reseller may seek supplies from another supplier, and others may attempt to win his custom, or he may enter into another agreement with the same supplier, possibly on better terms. At least at this time, competition is completely unfettered.

58. In the case of exclusive purchasing agreements in the motor fuels sector, however, where the reseller receives special commercial or financial advantages, the Authority considers that a longer, but still limited, period is justified for the exclusive purchasing requirement than otherwise would be the case. Under Regulation 1984/83, the EC Commission has indicated that five years is normally the maximum period for which an exclusive purchasing agreement is justified, but it has allowed a maximum period of ten years in the case of motor fuels. The Authority considers that, in the case of solus dealers, the maximum period of the agreement should not exceed ten years, but there should be no prohibition on the renewal of the agreement at the end of this period. (For company owned stations, see para 63). Indeed, the Authority considers that the making available of such special commercial or financial advantages is a necessary condition for the imposition of the long-term exclusive purchasing obligation. Without the provision of such advantages, exclusive purchasing agreements for motor fuels do not benefit from the exemption from the prohibition in section 4(1) of the Competition Act conveyed by this category licence. At the same time, commercial and financial advantages,

4.2 such as loans, should not be used to extend the exclusive purchasing obligation beyond 10 years, otherwise the category licence does not apply.

59. The exclusive purchasing agreements produce an appreciable improvement in distribution in which consumers are allowed a fair share of the resulting benefit. The commercial and financial advantages conferred by the supplier on the retailer make it significantly easier to establish, modernise, maintain and operate service stations. A high level of investment is needed to provide adequate facilities and to meet safety standards, and the suppliers have invested heavily in their company owned stations. Independent dealers would have insufficient resources for the necessary investment without substantial support from the supplier, otherwise company stations would become completely dominant. They are able to provide a range of services which they would otherwise be unable to offer. Most, if not all, licensees and lessees would not be able to enter the trade, and certainly not in such very expensive premises, unless the stations were provided for them by the suppliers.

60. The exclusive purchasing obligation and the ban on dealing in competing products imposed on the reseller encourage the reseller to concentrate on the sale of a particular brand of motor fuel, while retaining his independence and freedom to run the business as he sees fit. Exclusive purchasing agreements lead to durable cooperation between the supplier and the reseller, allowing them to improve or maintain the quality of the motor fuels and of the services to the customer and the sales efforts of the reseller. The investment by the supplier ensures security of supply by providing assured outlets for its product, and retailers are guaranteed regular supplies provided that they comply with the terms of the agreement. This allows long-term planning of sales and consequently a cost-effective organisation of production and distribution. It also allows suppliers to undertake the necessary investment in storage and shipping facilities. The costs of distributing motor fuels to a limited number of exclusive outlets which purchase in large quantities are lower than delivering smaller volumes to a large number of outlets selling two or more brands at the one service station. The pressure of competition between different brands of motor fuel obliges the undertakings involved to seek to design outlets in a way which attracts customers.

61. Exclusive purchasing agreements may include a clause extending the exclusive purchasing requirement to include the sale of motor fuels by the reseller at adjoining or adjacent premises, or at any premises within a one-mile radius of the designated service station. The Authority accepts that competition in the sale of motor fuels is to some degree a localised phenomenon. Motorists do not tend to travel any great distance to buy at a cheaper price, since the cost of so doing would soon eliminate any savings made. The dedication of the dealer to maximising sales of the supplier's motor fuels at the designated outlet would be likely to be adversely affected if he were permitted to sell another brand at a station owned or operated by himself within one mile of the designated station. Without such a requirement, the improvement in distribution would not be secured. The dealer is free, however, to sell competing motor fuels outside the one mile radius. Any greater geographical restraint, particularly one covering the entire State, would preclude the application of this category licence. (It should be noted that, since a restriction of this type is not specifically permitted under Regulation 1984/83, agreements which contain such a clause might not benefit from the exemption afforded by that Regulation).

62. Consumers benefit from these improvements especially because they are ensured supplies of motor fuel of satisfactory quality in a safe and environmentally secure environment while being able to choose between different brands. The exclusive purchasing system leads to more efficient distribution and to better facilities and services at dealer and company stations, to the benefit of consumers. They have a choice between stations offering differing degrees and types of service. The system should ensure both intra-brand and inter-brand competition, including price competition.

63. The advantages produced by exclusive purchasing agreements cannot be achieved to the same extent and with the same degree of certainty in any other way. The exclusive

purchasing obligation on the reseller and the non-competition clause imposed on him are essential components of such agreements and are indispensable for the attainment of these advantages. These obligations are confined to the purchase of motor fuels and other petroleum-based products for resale, and do not extend to other products. The limitation of the period of the exclusive agreement to ten years for solus dealers is sufficient to produce the advantages, while maintaining the reseller's commercial freedom to change supplier and to ensure access to the retail level of distribution on the part of other suppliers. This is because, on average, roughly 10 per cent of solus agreements will expire in a given year, and new suppliers may seek to recruit some or all of these. Any shorter period would substantially lessen the incentive for suppliers to invest in dealer outlets, to the detriment of dealers and consumers. This is especially so when the average throughput in petrol stations in the State is only about one quarter of the EC average. In the case of company owned outlets which are licensed or leased, because of the substantial investment made by the company in the station which is its own property, and because of the generally long-term nature of the agreement between the supplier and the occupant of the station, it appears appropriate to permit the exclusive purchasing obligation to continue for as long as the operator occupies the station. In many cases, of course, there is a licence agreement, which, while it may be renewed, has a duration of much less than ten years. 4.2

64. There are large numbers of solus, non-solus and company owned outlets which sell motor fuels under the different brand names. There is a high degree of competition between outlets, both intra-brand and inter-brand, and, with the removal of price control, there is scope for price competition, in particular, since solus and non-solus dealers and most company outlets are free to determine their own selling prices. While the long-term nature of the exclusive supply contracts limits the possibilities for a new entrant to secure outlets, all solus dealers are free to change their supplier at the expiry of the contract, and this does occur, and agreements are expiring on a continuous basis. In addition, a new supplier entrant would be likely to want the security offered by long-term solus agreements before making the sizeable investment necessary to enter the market in the first place. There is thus no possibility of the undertakings being afforded the possibility of eliminating competition for a substantial part of the products in question, even though company outlets are tied to the supplier virtually indefinitely.

(ii) Other restrictions

65. The Authority considers that the exclusive purchasing requirement should apply only in the case of the supplier's motor fuels. An exclusive purchasing obligation for the supplier's lubricants and related products, or a requirement that they be used exclusively in equipment owned by the reseller, cannot be shown to produce benefits in the distribution of motor fuels which could be shared with consumers. Such a restriction does not fulfil the conditions required under section 4(2), and is therefore prohibited under section 4(1).

66. Where lubricating equipment or a lubrication bay has been supplied or financed by the supplier, however, the Authority considers that a requirement on the reseller not to use competing lubricants and related products on the premises can benefit from the provisions of section 4(2). The supplier has provided essential and costly equipment, and the reseller benefits from such installations, and these benefits can be shared with consumers. The possibility for the supplier to impose such obligations on the reseller acts as an incentive for the supplier to undertake such substantial investment, and thus may be regarded as indispensable to obtain the objectives. Nevertheless, in these circumstances, the reseller, whether a solus dealer, a licensee or a lessee, must be permitted to stock and sell competing lubricants at the premises, and to supply them for topping up on the forecourt when requested by customers, in order to ensure that competition is not eliminated.

67. Since the selling of competing lubricants must be allowed, and there are no discernable benefits from preventing the advertising of these at the service station, any provision which prevents such advertising does not fulfil the conditions of section 4(2), and offends against

4.2 section 4(1). Such advertising, however, may be limited to the proportion which sales of competing lubricants bear to total sales in the station.

68. The same considerations apply in the case of other goods which may be sold by the reseller which are not subject to an exclusive purchasing obligation. A complete prohibition on advertising does not satisfy the conditions of section 4(2) and advertising must be permitted in proportion to sales of other goods compared to total sales.

69. A requirement that a solus dealer who wishes to sell his station must procure that the purchaser undertake to be bound for the remaining period of the solus agreement is regarded by the Authority as being indispensable for the achievement of the benefits of the long term exclusive purchasing agreement. It ensures that, irrespective of the change in ownership, the supplier is assured of a ten year exclusive purchasing agreement, without which the supplier would not have provided the initial special commercial and financial advantages. The benefit of section 4(2) can be accorded to such a requirement. Such purchaser may require to be approved by the supplier, but such approval should not be unreasonably withheld.

70. Where the requirement is that the supplier be given first option to purchase the station, or where the obligation would secure that the purchaser would be bound for a longer period than the reseller himself, there are no demonstrable benefits which could be shared with consumers, and such requirements are not indispensable. While this issue was raised in a number of submissions, the Authority is concerned that the implementation of first option to purchase clauses could lead to a situation where a significant number of important dealer outlets would be acquired by the suppliers, to the detriment of competition. This category licence does not therefore extend to such arrangements.

71. Any clause in an agreement which requires that a further solus agreement should be concluded after the end of the ten-year term, or that exclusive purchasing should continue after this period, or which restricts the freedom of the solus dealer, licensee or lessee from engaging in the sale of competing motor fuels after the agreement has terminated, falls under the prohibition of section 4(1). Such clauses do not produce any benefit which could be shared by consumers, and they are not indispensable for the exclusive purchasing agreement. They do not satisfy the criteria specified for a licence in section 4(2). This category licence does not therefore extend to such arrangements.

72. Any clause in an exclusive purchasing agreement, or any associated practice, which enforces or is conducive to the maintenance of resale prices, whether fixed, maximum or minimum resale prices, would not constitute an improvement in distribution. A restriction of this nature upon price competition would not convey any benefit upon consumers, but rather the reverse. It is not indispensable to the exclusive purchasing obligation, and it would tend to eliminate competition in respect of a substantial part of the products in question. No licence under section 4(2) could be justified for anything which constitutes or amounts to resale price maintenance, and this category licence does not extend to such arrangements.

73. Where a company operates its own stations, and informs solus dealers in advance of price changes at those stations, this constitutes the exchange of price information between competitors. This activity, also, does not produce an improvement in distribution or benefit consumers, and it is not indispensable to an exclusive purchasing agreement. It cannot be granted a licence under section 4(2), and this category licence does not extend to such arrangements.

74. Obligations to stock and sell products other than motor fuels and lubricants obtained exclusively from the supplier, or to purchase equipment only from the supplier, do not produce improvements in the distribution of motor fuels which can be shared by consumers, nor are they indispensable to the agreements. They cannot benefit from the exemption granted from the prohibition of section 4(1) and this category licence does not extend to such arrangements.

Miscellaneous Considerations

75. This category licence applies to agreements to which only two undertakings are party

— the supplier and the reseller. The benefit of the licence is not lost if the supplier enters into exclusive purchase agreements with many different resellers. The category licence also applies if the agreements do not contain some of the permitted restrictions, or if the arrangements are less restrictive than those specified, e.g. if the period of exclusive purchasing is less than ten years. **4.2**

76. In accordance with section 4(3)(b) of the Competition Act, where a licence covers a category of agreements, agreements within that category which comply with the terms of the licence need not be notified under section 7 to benefit from the licence while it is in force. Nevertheless, where there is real doubt, in a particular case, an undertaking may request the Authority to declare whether its agreements comply with this category licence. This would have to be done by way of full notification under section 7.

77. Any action by, or by agreement with, the supplier to prevent the reseller exercising his rights would entail the loss of the category licence. In these circumstances, it makes no difference whether the reseller's freedom is restricted by contract, informal understanding, economic pressures or other practical measures.

78. This category licence, being granted in accordance with section 4(2) of the Competition Act, does not exclude the application of section 5 of the Act.

79. This category licence applies only to agreements whereby the reseller undertakes with the supplier to purchase motor fuels and other petroleum-based products only from the supplier. Since some aspects relevant to exclusive purchasing of motor fuels may take the form of concerted practices rather than of agreements, the category licence applies to such practices as well as to agreements between undertakings. The licence does not apply where, in addition to the exclusive purchasing obligation on the reseller, the supplier undertakes with the reseller to supply only to the reseller certain goods for resale in the whole or in a defined part of the State. Such an agreement would constitute an exclusive distribution agreement rather than an exclusive purchasing agreement.

80. Section 8(3) of the Competition Act states:

> Where the Authority is of the opinion that, having regard to the requirements of section 4(2) and to the basis upon which a licence under that subsection was granted —
> (a) there has been a material change in any of the circumstances on which the decision was based,
> (b) any party commits a breach of any obligation attached to the decision,
> (c) the licence was based on materially incorrect or misleading information, or
> (d) any party abuses the permission granted to it by the licence,
> the Authority may revoke or amend the licence and, without prejudice to the generality of this subsection, may in particular insert in a licence conditions the effect of which is to prohibit specific acts by any party thereto which would otherwise be authorised pursuant to such a licence.

The Authority considers that it also has the power, in accordance with section 8(3), to withdraw the benefit of the category licence in individual cases. This would be the case where an individual agreement had effects incompatible with section 4(2), particularly where:

(a) the motor fuels are not subject to effective competition;
(b) access by other suppliers to the different stages of distribution is made difficult to a significant extent; or
(c) the supplier, without any objectively justified reason:

(i) refuses to supply resellers who cannot obtain the motor fuels elsewhere on reasonable terms, or applies to them differing prices or conditions of sale;
(ii) applies less favourable prices or conditions of sale to resellers bound by an

4.2 exclusive purchasing obligation as compared with other resellers at the same level of distribution.

The situations described above are meant as illustrations of the sort of situations in which the Authority can withdraw a category licence in the case of an individual agreement. There may well be other situations in which the Authority might exercise this power.

81. It is to be anticipated that suppliers of motor fuels who wish to benefit from this category licence in future will ensure that new exclusive purchasing agreements satisfy the conditions specified in the licence. They will also presumably seek to amend existing agreements so as to satisfy the conditions of the licence, especially in the case of agreements which were in existence on the date of commencement of the Act, that is agreements which were entered into prior to 1 October 1991. Appropriate provisions are necessary in the circumstances.

82. In the case of agreements which were in existence on 1 October 1991, and which have been notified to the Authority before 1 October 1992, this licence shall have effect from 1 July 1993, where the agreements already fulfil the conditions of the licence or where they are amended so as to fulfil those conditions before 1 July 1993. Where such notified agreements do not fulfil the conditions of the licence, or where they are not amended to fulfil the conditions before 1 July 1993, they do not qualify for the benefit of the licence, and the grant of this licence constitutes a refusal to grant a licence to such existing agreements. Where such notified agreements are amended to fulfil the conditions of the licence, the licence shall have effect from the date when the conditions of the licence are fulfilled.

83. In the case of agreements which were in existence on 1 October 1991, and which were not notified to the Authority before 1 October 1992, this licence shall have effect from 1 July 1993, where the agreements already fulfil the conditions of the licence or where they are amended so as to fulfil those conditions before 1 July 1993. Where such non-notified agreements are amended to fulfil the conditions of the licence in the future, the licence shall have effect from the date when the conditions of the licence are fulfilled. Where such non-notified agreements do not fulfil the conditions of the licence, they do not qualify for the benefit of the licence until the date when the conditions of the licence are fulfilled.

84. In the case of agreements which came into existence after 1 October 1991, and which have been notified to the Authority before 1 July 1993, this licence shall have retroactive effect from the date of notification, if the agreements already fulfilled the conditions of the licence, or from the date, being not earlier than the date of notification, when the conditions of the licence were fulfilled. For other agreements which came into existence after 1 October 1991, and which have not been notified, or those which come into existence in the future, this licence shall have effect from the date, at or after the date of grant of the licence, upon which its conditions are fulfilled.

85. The sole requirement for motor fuel agreements to enjoy the benefit of the category licence is that they be brought into line with the provisions of the licence. It is left to the undertakings concerned as to how they do this. One way is for the parties to agree to amend the original agreement, while another is for the supplier unilaterally to release the reseller from all obligations that would prevent the application of the category licence after it comes into operation. The Authority considers that this category licence constitutes a refusal to grant a licence to agreements which have been notified but which do not fulfil the conditions of the licence.

86. Given that the maximum term of the exclusive purchasing agreement is ten years, the Authority considers that the specified period for the category licence should be fifteen years. At the end of this period, following a review by the Authority, the period of the category licence may be extended, with or without amendments to the licence, if it is considered by the Authority that the requirements of section 4(2) continue to be fulfilled. The category licence shall enter into force on 1 July 1993. It shall expire on 30 June 2008. The category licence is at the end of this Decision.

Divergences from EC Regulation 1984/83 4.2

87. This Decision and the category licence itself are based very largely upon Title III and the other relevant provisions of EC Regulation 1984/83, which grants a block exemption from the prohibition of Article 85(1) of the Treaty of Rome to certain categories of exclusive purchasing agreements for service stations. Given that most, if not all, such agreements in the State are within the scope of Article 85(1), motor fuels being largely imported from other Member States, it is desirable that exemptions from Article 85(1) of the Treaty and licences under section 4(2) of the Act in respect of the same agreements should correspond to the greatest extent possible. Where divergences occur, the Authority does not consider that they are such as would frustrate the achievement of the objectives of Regulation 1984/83, nor would they prejudice the uniform application of Community competition law throughout the common market.

88. The main difference between this Decision and the Regulation is in its method of construction. The Regulation is in two sections, the Recitals, which give some justification for, and explanation of, the operative part, and the Regulation itself. There is also a subsequent explanatory Notice related to the Regulation. This Decision follows more closely the approach of the Authority in individual licence decisions. The justification and explanations are given in a form different from that in EC-type recitals, and they avoid the need for a separate explanatory note. As with the Recitals, however, this part of the Decision is vital to the operative part of the licence, which is identical in form to the corresponding section of the Regulation.

89. Article 1.2 of this category licence makes clear that, where some or all of the special commercial or financial advantages are granted in the form of a separate contract or contracts, these are considered together with the exclusive supply agreement to form 'the agreement' for the purposes of the category licence. Such a provision is not included in Regulation 1984/83, but the Authority considers that its approach is in accordance with EC precedents.

90. Articles 3 to 5 of Regulation 1984/83 relate mainly to situations where manufacturers of identical or equivalent goods enter into reciprocal or non-reciprocal exclusive purchasing agreements between themselves in respect of such goods. Such situations have not occurred in the State in respect of motor fuels, and the Authority does not consider that similar provisions are required in this category licence. The definition of 'connected undertakings' in Article 4 of the Regulation is deleted since references to 'connected undertakings' which appear elsewhere in the Regulation do not appear in the category licence. The Authority considers that the term 'another undertaking entrusted by the supplier' includes connected undertakings.

91. The Regulation extends the permitted exclusive purchasing requirement to other fuels, such as heating oil, bottled gas and paraffin. No such requirements have been found in agreements notified to the Authority, and it is not considered necessary to include them in this category licence, which is therefore confined to motor fuels.

92. In Article 11(d) of the Regulation, restrictions on equipment owned or financed by the supplier being serviced by an undertaking other than the supplier are exempted under Article 85(3). The agreements notified to the Authority have not contained such an obligation, and it is not considered necessary to include this requirement in the category licence.

93. Article 17 of the Regulation states that the exemption does not apply to agreements for the exclusive purchase of motor fuels and other non petroleum-based goods. No such agreements have been notified, and it is not considered necessary to include any reference to them in this category licence. Nevertheless, this category licence only applies to agreements for the exclusive purchase of motor fuels and other petroleum-based products.

94. For the sake of clarity, the Authority lists in more detail than is found in the Regulation provisions in agreements which do not offend against section 4(1), and others which may or may not be permitted under section 4(2). These are:

(a) *not offending against section 4(1)*

(i) obligations on resellers to take minimum deliveries, to open during agreed hours and to allow the supplier to lock and seal the fuel storage tanks, and to take samples and readings from

4.2 them, and to allow the supplier to inspect equipment supplied or financed by the supplier.

(ii) in the case of leased and licenced stations, obligations on the reseller not to discontinue the business of selling motor fuels, to keep the premises in good repair and fully insured, to maintain the number of pumps, not to change the manner of operating the station, not to use the premises for purposes other than the sale of motor fuels, not to allow access to the pumps to be impeded, and to keep adequate records.

(b) *not Permitted under section 4(2)*

(i) the supplier restricts the freedom of the reseller to sell the premises, particularly by:

— requiring the reseller to give the right of first refusal to the supplier,

— requiring the reseller to secure the approval of the purchaser by the supplier, unless it is also provided that such approval shall not be unreasonably withheld;

(ii) restrictions on the reseller after the date of expiry of the agreement, and in particular obligations:

— to conclude a further exclusive purchasing agreement,

— not to engage in the purchase and resale of competing goods;

(iii) the supplier obliges the reseller to sell at a fixed price, or above a minimum price or below a maximum price;

(iv) the supplier recommends to the reseller a specified, or specified maximum, resale price, unless the reseller is informed that he is free to determine his own resale prices; and

(v) the supplier informs resellers in advance of changes in prices at service stations operated by the supplier.

(c) *Permitted under section 4(2)*

(i) obligations on resellers not to sell competing motor fuels adjoining or adjacent to, or within a one-mile radius of, the designated premises.

(ii) the obligation not to use competing lubricants in the station where a lubrication bay or other lubrication equipment has been made available or financed by the supplier is only allowed provided that the reseller is permitted to stock and sell such products and to supply them for topping up on the forecourt when requested by customers.

(References in the Regulation to obligations to maintain a sales network and to provide guarantee services have been omitted from the category licence since they are not relevant to the resale of motor fuels).

95. The arrangements for notified agreements differ between this Decision and the Regulation because of the different treatment of provisional validity for such agreements in the Competition Act and in Regulation 17/62, the regulation implementing Articles 85 and 86. In particular, the Authority cannot grant a licence which applies retrospectively to agreements which were in force on 1 October 1991 which have been duly notified before 1 October 1992. In addition, the Regulation was, in a sense, an extension of a previous block exemption, Regulation 67/67, while this category licence has not been preceded by any other.

96. Notwithstanding the fact that this category licence is closely based upon Regulation 1984/83, the fact that an agreement satisfies the conditions of this category licence does not necessarily mean that it benefits from the exemption afforded by the Regulation.

The Decision

97. The Competition Authority considers that long-term exclusive purchasing arrangements for the resale of petroleum products in service stations constitute agreements between undertakings which have the object and effect of preventing, restricting or distorting competition in goods in the State, and thus they offend against section 4(1) of the Competition Act 1991. In the opinion of the Authority, having regard to all relevant market conditions, such agreements generally satisfy all the conditions required for the grant of a category licence under section 4(2) of the Competition Act. Accordingly, the Competition Authority grants a licence to the specified category of agreements, subject to the specified period and specified conditions as required under section 8(1) of the Competition Act, as follows:

The Category Licence 4.2.1

Article 1

1. Pursuant to section 4(2) of the Competition Act 1991, and subject to the provisions of this licence, the Competition Authority grants a category licence to agreements to which only two undertakings are party and whereby one party, the reseller, agrees with the other, the supplier, in consideration for the according of special commercial or financial advantages, to purchase only from the supplier, or another undertaking entrusted by the supplier with the distribution of his goods, certain petroleum-based motor-vehicle fuels specified in the agreement for resale in a service station designated in the agreement.

2. Where some or all of the special commercial or financial advantages are granted by the supplier in the form of a separate contract or contracts, these are considered together with the exclusive supply agreement to form 'the agreement' for the purposes of this category licence.

Article 2

No other restriction of competition shall be imposed on the supplier than the obligation not to distribute the contract goods or goods which compete with the contract goods in the reseller's principal sales area and at the reseller's level of distribution.

Article 3

Apart from the obligation referred to in Article 1, no restriction on competition shall be imposed on the reseller other than:

(a) the obligation not to sell motor-vehicle fuels which are supplied by other undertakings in the service station designated in the agreement;

(b) the obligation not to sell motor-vehicle fuels which are supplied by other undertakings in premises adjoining or adjacent to, or within a one-mile radius of, the service station designated in the agreement;

(c) the obligation to advertise goods other than motor fuel supplied by other undertakings within or outside the service station designated in the agreement only in proportion to the share of these goods in the total turnover realised in the service station.

(d) the obligation not to use lubricants or related petroleum-based products which are supplied by other undertakings within the service station designated in the agreement where the supplier has made available to the reseller, or financed, a lubrication bay or other motor-vehicle lubrication equipment, provided that the reseller is permitted to stock and sell such products and to supply them for topping up on the forecourt when requested by customers.

Article 4

1. Article 1 shall apply notwithstanding that the reseller undertakes any or all of the following obligations:

(a) to purchase complete ranges of goods;

(b) to purchase minimum quantities, or to take minimum deliveries, which are subject to the exclusive purchasing obligation;

(c) to sell the contract goods under trademarks, or packed and presented as

4.2.1 specified by the supplier;

(d) to take measures for the promotion of sales, in particular:

— to advertise,

— to maintain a stock of goods,

— to provide customer services,

(e) to allow the supplier to lock and seal the fuel storage tanks, and to take samples and readings from them, and to allow the supplier to inspect equipment supplied or financed by the supplier.

2. Where the agreement relates to a service station which the supplier lets to the reseller, or allows the reseller to occupy on some other basis, in law or in fact, Article 1 shall apply notwithstanding that the reseller undertakes any or all of the following obligations:

(a) not to discontinue the business of selling motor fuels;

(b) to keep the premises in good repair and fully insured;

(c) to maintain the number of pumps;

(d) not to change the manner of operating the station;

(e) not to use the premises for purposes other than the sale of motor fuels;

(f) not to allow access to the pumps to be impeded;

(g) to keep adequate records.

Article 5

1. Article 1 shall not apply where:

(a) the supplier imposes on the reseller exclusive purchasing obligations for goods other than motor-vehicle fuels or for services;

(b) the supplier restricts the freedom of the reseller to obtain from an undertaking of his choice goods or services for which under the provisions of this licence neither an exclusive purchasing obligation nor a ban on dealing in competing products may be imposed;

(c) the agreement is concluded for an indefinite duration or for a period of more than ten years;

(d) the supplier obliges the reseller to impose the exclusive purchasing obligation on his successor for a longer period than the reseller would himself remain tied to the supplier;

(e) the supplier, without prejudice to paragraph (d), restricts the freedom of the reseller to sell his premises, and in particular by:

— requiring the reseller to give first refusal for the purchase of the premises to the supplier,

— requiring the reseller to secure the approval of the purchaser by the supplier, unless it is also provided that such approval shall not be unreasonably withheld;

(f) the supplier imposes any restriction on the reseller after the date of expiry of the exclusive purchasing agreement, and in particular imposes an obligation:

— to conclude a further exclusive purchasing agreement for a fixed or indefinite period, or

— not to engage in the purchase and resale of competing goods;

(g) the supplier obliges the reseller to sell at a fixed price, or at not less than a minimum price or at not more than a maximum price;

(h) the supplier recommends to the reseller a specified resale price or a specified maximum resale price, unless the reseller is informed that he is free to determine his own resale prices;

(i) the supplier informs resellers in advance of changes in prices at service stations operated directly or indirectly by the supplier.

2. Where the agreement relates to a service station which the supplier lets to the reseller, or allows the reseller to occupy on some other basis, in law or in fact, exclusive purchasing obligations or bans on dealing in competing products specified in this licence may, notwithstanding paragraph 1(c) of this Article, be imposed on the reseller for the whole period for which the reseller in fact operates the premises.

Article 6

The Authority may withdraw the benefit of this category licence pursuant to section 8(3) of the Competition Act 1991, when it finds in a particular case that an agreement which is exempted by this licence nevertheless has certain effects which are incompatible with the conditions set out in section 4(2) of the Competition Act, and in particular, but not only, where:

(a) the contract goods are not subject to effective competition from identical goods or goods considered by users as equivalent in view of their characteristics, price and intended use,

(b) access by other suppliers to the different stages of distribution is made difficult to a significant extent;

(c) the supplier, without any objectively justified reason:

(i) refuses to supply resellers who cannot obtain the contract goods elsewhere on reasonable terms, or applies to them differing prices or conditions of sale,

(ii) applies less favourable prices or conditions of sale to resellers bound by an exclusive purchasing obligation as compared with other resellers at the same level of distribution.

Article 7

1.(a) As regards agreements which were in existence on 1 October 1991, and were notified before 1 October 1992, this category licence shall have effect from 1 July 1993, where the agreements already fulfil the conditions of the licence or where they were amended so as to fulfil those conditions before 1 July 1993.

(b) As regards agreements which were in existence on 1 October 1991, and were notified before 1 October 1992, and which do not fulfil the conditions of the licence, but which are later amended to fulfil the conditions of the licence, this category licence shall have effect from the date when those conditions were fulfilled.

2(a) As regards agreements which were in existence on 1 October 1991, and were not notified before 1 October 1992, this category licence shall have effect from 1 July 1993, where the agreements already fulfil the conditions of the licence or where they were amended so as to fulfil those conditions before 1 July 1993.

(b) As regards agreements which were in existence on 1 October 1991, and were not notified before 1 October 1992, and which do not fulfil the conditions of the licence, but which are later amended to fulfil the conditions of the licence, this category licence shall have effect from the date when those conditions were fulfilled.

3. As regards agreements which came into existence after 1 October 1991, and

4.2.1 which were notified before 1 July 1993, this category licence shall have retroactive effect from the date of notification where the agreements already fulfil the conditions of the licence, or from the date, being not earlier than the date of notification, when the agreements were amended so as to fulfil those conditions.

4. This category licence constitutes a refusal to grant a licence to notified agreements which do not fulfil its conditions.

Article 8

This category licence shall not apply to agreements by which the supplier undertakes with the reseller to supply only to the reseller certain goods for resale, in the whole or in a defined part of the State, and the reseller undertakes with the supplier to purchase these goods only from the supplier.

Article 9

This category licence shall apply *mutatis mutandis* to the categories of concerted practices defined in Article 1.

Article 10

This category licence shall enter into force on 1 July 1993. It shall expire on 30 June 2008.

For the Competition Authority

Patrick M. Lyons
Chairman

1 July 1993

Notifications within the scope of the motor fuel category licence 4.2.2

The following is a list of exclusive purchasing agreements for motor fuels which have been notified to the Authority. This does not imply that they satisfy the requirements of the category licence:

CA/11/91E	Esso Ireland Ltd; deed of charge/mortgage
CA/12/91E	Esso Ireland Ltd; loan agreement
CA/13/91E	Esso Ireland Ltd; equipment loan agreement
CA/14/91E	Esso Ireland Ltd; solus agreement
CA/2/91E	Texaco (Ireland) Ltd; standard licence agreement
CA/3/92E	Texaco (Ireland) Ltd; solus agreement
CA/4/92E	Texaco (Ireland) Ltd; lease of service station
CA/5/92E	Texaco (Ireland) Ltd; equipment loan agreement
CA/6/92E	Texaco (Ireland) Ltd; cessation of agreement undertaking
CA/13/92E	Estuary Fuels Ltd; exclusive purchase (solus) agreement
CA/32/92E	Burmah Castrol (Ireland) Ltd; dealer supply agreement
CA/33/92E	Burmah Castrol (Ireland) Ltd; equipment loan agreement
CA/34/92E	Burmah Castrol (Ireland) Ltd; licence agreement
CA/35/92E	Burmah Castrol (Ireland) Ltd, lease
CA/39/92E	Burmah Castrol (Ireland) Ltd; mortgage
CA/40/92	Burmah Castrol (Ireland) Ltd; dealer supply agreement (new)
CA/41/92	Burmah Castrol (Ireland) Ltd; equipment loan agreement (new)
CA/42/92	Burmah Castrol (Ireland) Ltd; licence agreement (new)
CA/46/92	Burmah Castrol (Ireland) Ltd; mortgage (new)
CA/49/92E	Esso Ireland Ltd; licence agreement
CA/70/92E	Conoco Ireland Ltd; dealer agreement
CA/72/92E	Conoco Ireland Ltd; licensees (as amended)
CA/77/92	Texaco (Ireland) Ltd; licence agreement (new)
CA/83/92E	Maxol Ltd; solus agreement (new)
CA/84/92E	Maxol Ltd; bailment agreement
CA/85/92E	Maxol Ltd; solus agreement (old)
CA/86/92E	Maxol Ltd; loan agreement
CA/87/92E	Maxol Ltd; deed of charge
CA/88/92E	Maxol Ltd; hire purchase agreement
CA/89/92E	Maxol Ltd; licence agreement
CA/90/92E	Maxol Ltd; lease agreement

4.2.2

CA/106/92E	Conoco Ireland Ltd; Jet Oil image agreement
CA/107/92E	Conoco Ireland Ltd; dealer support and loan agreement
CA/108/92E	Conoco Ireland Ltd; mortgage
CA/167/92E	Ola Teoranta; solus agreement
CA/168/92E	Ola Teoranta; equipment agreement
CA/169/92E	Ola Teoranta; bailment agreement
CA/170/92E	Ola Teoranta; mortgage
CA/258/92E	Irish Shell Ltd; loan equipment agreement
CA/260/92E	Irish Shell Ltd; exclusive purchase (solus) agreement
CA/262/92E	Irish Shell Ltd; loan agreement for tank storage
CA/264/92E	Irish Shell Ltd; publicity allowance agreement
CA/265/92E	Irish Shell Ltd; temporary licence agreement
CA/266/92E	Irish Shell Ltd; licence agreement (old)
CA/441/92E	Statoil lreland Ltd; standard sales agreement
CA/442/92E	Statoil Ireland Ltd; loan agreement
CA/443/92E	Statoil Ireland Ltd; HP loan agreement
CA/444/92E	Statoil lreland Ltd; exclusivity payment agreement
CA/445/92E	Statoil lreland Ltd; licence and trial licence agreement
CA/446/92E	Statoil lreland Ltd; lease agreement
CA/447/92E	Statoil lreland Ltd; deed of charge/mortgage
CA/751/92E	Campus Oil Ltd; licence agreement
CA/752/92	Campus Oil Ltd; mortgage agreement
CA/753/92E	Campus Oil Ltd; loan
CA/754/92E	Campus Oil Ltd; equipment loan agreement
CA/755/92E	Campus Oil Ltd; petrol pump agreement
CA/756/92E	Campus Oil Ltd; solus agreement
CA/969/92E	Tedcastle Oil Products Ltd; exclusive distribution agreement

**Editor's note*: The numerically based lists of notifications in this book will give more up-to-date information. See pages 1194-1358.

Competition Authority Decision No. 304, Musgraves Ltd — 'SuperToys': 21 April 1994, Notification No. CA/20/92E 4.3

Group purchasing agreement – Resale price maintenance – Exclusive purchasing obligations – Significant defect – Toy market – Discussions with Competition Authority – Statement of objections – Oral Hearing – Amendments of notified arrangements – Certificate – Competition Act 1991 (No. 24) sections 3, 4 and 7

Facts: On 30 April 1992 notification was made to the Authority with a request for a certificate under section 4(4) of the Competition Act 1991 or, failing that, a licence under section 4(2) by Musgraves Ltd ('Musgraves') and a number of independent toy retailers who trade using the symbol 'SuperToys'. The agreement which allowed the use of the symbol also obliged retailers to purchase certain toys exclusively from suppliers with whom Musgraves negotiated the terms of supply.

Musgraves, an Irish company, is primarily a wholesale distributor of grocery goods to independent grocery retailers in the State. In 1985 Musgraves established a SuperToys with 11 retailers. The 11 retailers commenced to sell toys under the trade name SuperToys whilst undertaking to purchase a range of toys from suppliers nominated by Musgraves.

Under the notified arrangements Musgraves negotiated the range and terms of supply of toys from suppliers. Musgraves also organised the production of two catalogues annually of the toys and the prices at which the toys would be sold. The range and the prices were decided upon by Musgraves in conjunction with the Council of Retailers of SuperToys who generally approved the decision of Musgraves.

Each new application for membership of the SuperToys retailing group is considered by the existing retailer members for acceptance or rejection. Members are free to terminate their agreement at any time and without any penalty. Musgraves directly received a percentage of the bulk purchase discount offered by suppliers for organising the arrangements.

The Authority was dissatisfied with the insertion of catalogue prices and the adherence to those prices by the retailers. It was stated that no objection would be taken to a retailer selling catalogued items at less than the recommended price in response to competition within the retailers area subject to the condition that such reduction in price was not advertised nationally. Musgraves submitted that in order to compete successfully with the multiples in the toy market (Quinnsworth and Dunnes Stores) that the products and corresponding prices had to be advertised nationally and for this to be effective the prices would have to be agreed amongst and applied by the members of SuperToys in general.

In response to the concerns expressed by the Authority Musgraves proposed removing the ban on advertised prices below the catalogue prices. However, the Authority were not satisfied and issued a Statement of Objections on 15 February 1993. Following an oral hearing on 22 October 1993 Musgraves informed the Authority that the SuperToys agreement would be amended to enable retailers to sell at prices different from those listed in the catalogue and that the cover of the catalogue would indicate that the prices in the catalogue of toys were only recommended prices.

Decided by the Authority:

(A) In issuing a certificate under section 4(4) of the Competition Act 1991 that:

(1) Musgraves and each retailer which are parties to the notified arrangements are

4.3 each 'undertakings' within the meaning of section 3(1) of the Competition Act 1991.

(2) The retailers involved in the group purchasing arrangements are competitors of each other.

(3) The retailers relevant market share is the whole purchasing group arranged by Musgraves and not the market share of each retailer. The relevant market is therefore not the local area of each retailer who participates in the group purchasing arrangements.

(4) Price fixing within the SuperToys purchasing group does have a significant effect on competition.

(5) Independent retailer outlets cannot agree uniform prices despite the setting of uniform prices for the outlets of a competing retail multiple. The setting of such prices for the outlets of a multiple does not involve two or more undertakings.

(6) The arrangements notified originally and prior to the amendments following discussions with the Competition Authority included a concerted practice by all SuperToys retailers to observe the prices set out in the catalogues and only to sell at lower prices when local competition demands it.

(7) The provisions of the agreement notified other than the exclusive purchasing obligation and the binding obligation to abide by the lists and prices in the catalogues and promotion of SuperToys, are merely essential to the achievement of the agreement's objectives and are therefore not anti-competitive and in breach of section 4(1).

(8) The obligation on the retailer to purchase from specific suppliers the range of toys does not offend against section 4(1) of the Competition Act because:

The retailers are free to buy competing products from other suppliers while remaining part of the group and the retailers are not obliged to buy any product in the range;

The retailers are free to leave the SuperToys group at any time without penalty;

Competing suppliers of toys may recruit SuperToys retailers who can participate in the notified arrangements for as long as it suits those retailers.

(9) The arrangements, as amended, whereby the catalogue prices are recommended prices permit retailers to set their own prices and no longer offends section 4(1).

(10) The notified arrangements prior to their amendment would not have satisfied the conditions set out for the grant of a licence under section 4(2) because the agreement on prices did not contribute to improving the distribution of goods or the provision of services or to promoting technical or economic progress.

Cases, Decision and Reports referred to:

Consten and Grundig v. Commission (Case No. 56 and 58/64) [1966] ECR 299; [1966] CMLR 418
Cement Dealers v. Commission (Case No. 8/72) [1972] ECR 977; [1973] CMLR 7
Papiers Peints v. Commission (Case No. 73/74) [1975] ECR 1491; [1976] 1 CMLR 589
Hasselblad v. Commission (Case No. 86/82) [1984] ECR 883; [1984] 1 CMLR 559
EC Commission Decision — Intergroup [1975] OJ L212/23; [1975] 2 CMLR D20
EC Commission Decision — IFTRA Aluminium [1975] OJ L228/3; [1975] 2 CMLR D14
EC Commission Decision — National Sulphuric Acid Association I [1980] OJ L260/25; [1980] 3 CMLR 429
EC Commission Decision — Vimpoltu [1983] OJ L200/44; [1983] 3 CMLR 619
EC Commission Decision — Nuovo-CEGAM [1984] OJ L99/29; [1984] 2 CMLR 484
EC Commission Decision — Uniform Eurocheques [1985] OJ L35/43; [1985] 3 CMLR 434
EC Commission Decision — National Sulphuric Acid Association II [1989] OJ L190/22; [1989] 4 CMLR 612
Competition Authority Decision No. 4 — Esso Solus and Related Agreements **4.1**
Fair Trade Commission Report (1991); 'Study of Competition Law'

Competition Authority Decision of 21 April 1994 relating to a proceeding under section 4 of the Competition Act 1999 Notification No. CA/20/92E — SuperToys 4.3

Introduction

1. This decision relates to arrangements between Musgrave Ltd (Musgraves) and a number of independent toy-retailers which were notified to the Competition Authority on 30 April 1992. Under the terms of the agreement the retailers agree to purchase certain toys exclusively from suppliers nominated by Musgraves. The retailers also distribute a catalogue which includes details of prices of a selected range of products.

2. The Authority had discussions with Musgraves which set out its concerns with certain aspects of the arrangements. As these discussions failed to resolve the Authority's concerns, it issued a statement of objections on 15 February 1993, indicating its intention to refuse a certificate or licence. An oral hearing was held on 22 October 1993. Musgraves subsequently indicated their intention to make specific amendments to the arrangements and an amended agreement was completed on 13 April 1994.

3. Notice of intention to grant a certificate was published in the Irish Times on 11 February 1994. No submissions were received.

The Facts

(a) *Subject of the notification*

4. The agreement involves an arrangement between Musgrave Ltd (Musgraves) and a number of independent toy-retailers. Musgraves operates a central billing system for toys purchased by the retailers and retains a fee from the Long Term Allowance rebate as a payment for the service. There is an obligation on the retailers to purchase a range of toys from certain suppliers.

(b) *The parties concerned*

5. The parties to the agreement are Musgraves Ltd and a number of independent toy retailers trading under the name of SuperToys. The principal activity of the Musgrave Group is the wholesale supply of groceries to retailers. Musgrave Ltd the holding company, operates the trade in the State while Musgrave Distribution Ltd a wholly-owned subsidiary of Musgrave Ltd carries on the business in Northern Ireland. Since 1979, the Musgrave Group has operated exclusive-purchasing agreements with a number of independent retailers trading under the Musgraves owned SuperValu/Centra names. Musgraves have been involved in the toy industry since 1982.

6. The SuperToys trade name is used as a symbol by a number of independent toy retailers who have undertaken to purchase a certain range of toys from suppliers nominated by Musgraves with most of the retailers trading under their own name. SuperToys commenced its operation in 1985 with 11 members. This had increased to 32 at the time of the notification, although a small number of members left subsequently. SuperToys is a wholly-owned division of SuperValu and Centra Distribution Ltd which is itself a wholly-owned division of Musgrave Ltd.

(c) *The Product and the Market*

7. Supertoys outlets are in the business of selling toys to the consumer on a 12 month basis. Consequently the market concerned is that for childrens' toys. The parties have stated that there are no independent market research figures available to assess the value of the toy market. It was estimated by the parties at the time of the notification to be in the region of £70m at retail prices including value added tax. There are no definitive figures on market share. The parties estimated the market shares of the major competitors in the market as follows:[1]

1. In the published version of the decision certain information indicated by [ ] is omitted for reasons of commercial confidentiality.

4.3

	%
Dunnes Stores	[ ]
Quinnsworth	[ ]
SuperToys	[ ]
Toymaster	[ ]
Roches Stores	[ ]
Arnotts	[ ]
All others	[ ]

8. At the time of the notification, Supertoys claimed to be the third largest seller of toys in the State. They believed that the two largest supermarket multiples were the two largest toy retailers. SuperToys substantial share of the market was mainly due to increases in the number of SuperToys outlets. Other parties in the market include independent newsagents who sell what are known as 'pocket money' toys, i.e. toys which children would purchase themselves as opposed to larger toys which would normally be bought by adults for children. Musgraves subsequently indicated that SuperToys market share had fallen significantly due to some retailers leaving and increased competition by one of the multiples during the Christmas 1992 period.

9. The toy market is one which, because of its nature and developments in technology, is subject to constant change. As trends are constantly changing it is relatively easy for new suppliers to enter the market. Sales to the retailers are principally carried out at toy fairs, at which new suppliers are a common feature. No one supplier appears to enjoy a significant percentage of the market. Musgraves claimed that Hasbro Bradley UK, considered the biggest toy supplier to the Irish market, supplied only a small proportion of the total business of SuperToys.

(d) *The notified agreement*

10. Under the terms of the agreement, Musgraves permit the retailers to operate as SuperToys outlets and undertake to negotiate with suppliers on their behalf for the provision of a range of toys. They also supervise the twice-yearly production of SuperToys catalogues and other advertising material. In return, the retailers undertake to display the SuperToys fascia sign in a prominent position on the premises. They also agree to purchase a range of toys from the nominated suppliers and to distribute locally the advertising catalogue. The use of SuperToys marketing materials (carrier bags, etc.) is also an obligation as is a contribution from the retailers towards the marketing costs of SuperToys. Each new application for membership is considered by the existing members who decide whether or not the application should be accepted or rejected. Members are free to terminate their agreement at any time without penalty. There is no time limit involved in the agreement. Musgraves are paid by way of a percentage of the LTA (long term allowance) offered by the suppliers, i.e. a percentage of the discount offered by the supplier in return for a bulk purchase.

11. Apart from a relatively small budget for television advertising, SuperToys only advertising is in the form of a catalogue distributed locally by each of the retail outlets. This catalogue takes the form of a display of many of the items on sale in all of the stores, accompanied by a prominent price display. The notification stated that the prices quoted were decided on by an elected council of SuperToys retailers and approved at a meeting of all of the members.

12. The relevant extracts of the agreement are as follows:

> 2. The Wholesaler agrees as follows:
> (a) To permit the Retailer to operate as a 'SuperToys' outlet.
> (b) To provide to the Retailer a range of toy and associated merchandise at the terms negotiated by the wholesaler on behalf of 'SuperToys', from such suppliers nominated

from time to time by the wholesaler.
(c) To supervise the production of annual 'SuperToys' catalogues, and other marketing material.
(d) To arrange for national media advertising on behalf of the 'SuperToys' group.
(e) To arrange regular Council and General meetings as may be required.
(f) To supply at cost to the Retailer a 'SuperToys' fascia sign, which cost is defrayed by a non-refundable entry fee, less any subsidy as may be applied from time to time.

3. The Retailer agrees as follows:
(a) To display the authorised 'SuperToys' fascia sign in a prominent position on the premises.
(b) To support and to purchase a range of toys and associated merchandise from those suppliers with whom terms have been negotiated by the Wholesaler on behalf of 'SuperToys'.
(c) To support the 'SuperToys' Group promotional programme including the following:

(i) To distribute the 'SuperToys' catalogue throughout his trading area.
(ii) To use the 'SuperToys' marketing materials including carrier bags, point of sale cards, and hanging signs.
(iii) To contribute towards 'SuperToys' marketing costs.

(d) To pay the Wholesalers account by Direct Debit within the credit periods stipulated. This is currently 28th of the month following the month in which the Musgrave invoice is issued.
(e) To maintain adequate insurance cover under normal Commercial Policies, especially to protect stock supplied through 'SuperToys', but not yet paid for.
(f) To support training programmes for management and staff provided by the Wholesaler from time to time.
(g) To observe and uphold the standard and quality required of a 'SuperToys' retailer.
(h) To treat as private and confidential all information divulged by the Wholesaler in relation to the operation of 'SuperToys' and the sale or purchase of products, and not to communicate or disclose whether by his servants, agents or howsoever otherwise any of such confidential information to any person at any time without the prior written consent of the wholesaler.
(i) To provide all audited accounts and requirements as required by the Wholesaler.

(e) *Submissions of the Parties*

13. Musgraves argued that the restrictions contained in the agreement did not have the effect of preventing, restricting or distorting competition in any goods or services in the State or part of the State, and that because the agreements were pro-competitive in their effects, were caught by section 4 of the Act only in a technical sense.

14. Musgraves submitted that the agreement resulted in greater cost-effectiveness among SuperToys suppliers as a reduced number of accounts meant more efficient administration for suppliers. The reduced costs which they are then in a position to offer, allows SuperToys' individual toy retailers to survive in competition with the multiple grocery retailers who would otherwise have a virtual dominance of the toy market. It was submitted that as a result of the agreement, the consumer had the benefit of lower prices, particularly in non-urban areas. It also ensured the survival of the independent toy-retailers, thus providing the consumer with a year round professional toy service which would otherwise be unavailable.

15. In support of the contention that toy prices had fallen because of the emergence of such groups, Musgraves submitted a letter from one of its retailers claiming that the average mark-up on toys was now 40% plus VAT compared with 50% in the early 1980s.

16. Musgrave submitted that the agreement contained only two restrictions both of which

4.3 were indispensable to the attainment of the objective of improving the distribution of goods. The first of these was a purchasing restriction, whereby retailers who wished to purchase from certain listed suppliers were obliged to do so through SuperToys (Musgraves) which earned its income by retaining a fee from the Long Term Allowance rebate. The combined purchasing power of the individual retailers enabled the best possible prices to be obtained from the suppliers, thus increasing the retailers ability to compete. If any individual retailer does not support the voluntary group arrangement, the group is weakened and the viability of all may be impaired. Musgraves further submitted that retailers would not in any event be able to negotiate more favourable terms as individuals and that compliance with the agreement therefore was in their best interest. Acceptance of the arrangements also allowed them to devote more time to achieving sales and providing adequate service to customers.

17. The agreement also contained a sales price restriction in relation to items advertised in a nationally distributed catalogue. The catalogue advertises a number of items which have been chosen by a council of retailers for national promotion. The annex stated that once items had been selected for inclusion in the catalogue, the council of retailers agreed upon the price at which the advertised item was to be sold, this was then agreed by all of the retailers and was included in the catalogue. All of the SuperToys retailers were prohibited by the agreement from selling at prices in excess of those displayed, but were allowed to sell at a lower price provided it was within the retailer's own area and not advertised nationally. In practice, the majority sold the items at the agreed price according to the annex.

18. This aspect of the arrangements was described in the annex to the notification as follows:

> A significant part of the SuperToys promotional activity is concerned with the production of two catalogues annually, for Summer and for Christmas. The production of this catalogue involves the agreement by the Council of the retailers of SuperToys of prices for about 80 products in Summer and 150 at Christmas. These prices, and therefore the margins, are decided on by the Council and then are submitted to a general meeting of all retailers for approval. The inclusion of these items in the catalogue means that these are the promoted items. (para 3.8)
>
> It is understood by the retailers that they can reduce their prices below the catalogue levels in response to local pressure but they cannot advertise their reduction nationally. (para 3.9)
>
> The retailers have freedom on selling prices for non catalogue items. The price restriction only applies to the promoted items. For the vast majority of items there is, therefore, no agreement on price. The agreement on price for the catalogue items is indispensable to the arrangements for the reasons below:
>
> > . . . In practice, the majority of retailers sell them at the recommended prices. SuperToys has no objection of any kind to the retailer selling the products at less than the recommended price to meet competition, provided it is within the retailers area and is not advertised nationally.
> >
> > . . . If the price is to be included in the catalogue then prices have to be agreed between the members of the voluntary group.
> >
> > . . . Similarly if the products are to be advertised nationally it is essential that price should be quoted in the advertisement. For this to be done, prices have to be agreed and, in general, adhered to. (para 5.8)

19. It was argued that such an arrangement was necessary if the concept of a nationally distributed catalogue was to work. The inclusion of prices enabled consumers to assess the products in relation to their ability to spend. As the catalogue was distributed nationwide, it was considered essential that the prices be adhered to. It was further submitted that such price advertising was, in fact, pro-competitive. Given SuperToys market share, it was argued that the existence of the agreement has not had the effect of eliminating competition. All SuperToys

outlets, regardless of location, were subject to some form of competition. **4.3**

20. Musgraves submitted that the obligation on the retailers to maintain insurance cover was because, in many cases, stock might not yet be paid for. It was essential that Musgraves be assured that adequate insurance was held by the retailer. It was also submitted that rather than being in competition with each other, the SuperToys retailers operate collectively in opposition to all other toy retailers, including the multiples.

21. Reference was made to the EC Block Exemption Regulations for Exclusive Distribution,[2] Exclusive Purchasing,[3] Know-how Licensing,[4] and Franchising agreements in support of the application. The Know-how Licensing Regulation came into force on 1 April 1989 and applies until 31 December 1999. Know-how, for the purpose of this regulation, is defined as 'a body of technical information that is secret, substantial and identified in any appropriate form.' The regulation has the effect of exempting agreements involving the transfer of know-how from the provisions of Article 85(1).

22. The regulation lists obligations of a restrictive nature that benefit from automatic exemption pursuant to Article 85(3) of the Treaty. A know-how licensing agreement to which only two undertakings are party and which contains one or more of these obligations is exempt from the provisions of Article 85(1). Among them is an obligation on the licensee to limit his production of a licensed product to the quantities he requires in manufacturing his own products, provided that such quantities are freely determined by the licensee. Other obligations included are requirements that the licensee does not divulge the know-how to third parties, grant sub-licenses, assign the license or exploit the know-how where it remains secret after the termination of the agreement.

23. EEC regulation number 4087/88 of 30 November 1988[5] is a block exemption regulation which applies Article 85(3) of the Treaty of Rome to categories of franchising agreements. It came into force on 1 February 1989 and remains in force until 31 December 1999. Franchising agreements essentially consist of licences of industrial or intellectual property rights (trade-marks or names or know-how) to be exploited for the purpose of selling goods or providing services to end-users in premises of uniform appearance and with the same business methods.

24. The Regulation applies to agreements which contain at least one of a number of specified restrictions including that of territorial protection granted by the franchisor and the obligation on the franchisee not to deal in goods competing with those manufactured by the franchisor or bearing its trademark. The regulation also contains a list of restrictions which, if present in an agreement, prevent the application of the exemption. This applies in particular to market sharing between competing manufacturers, clauses unduly restricting the franchisees choice of suppliers or customers and to cases where the franchisee is restricted in determining its prices.

Subsequent developments

25. After the Authority expressed its concern regarding the setting of catalogue prices it was indicated that, contrary to what was stated in the annex, the prices contained in the twice-yearly catalogue were, in fact, proposed by Musgraves. They were then submitted to the Council of SuperToys retailers and, in the vast majority of cases, accepted. Musgraves therefore proposed at a meeting on 12 October 1992 to amend section 3.8 of their initial submission to read as follows:

> 3.8 A significant part of the SuperToys promotional activity is concerned with the production of two catalogues annually, for Summer and for Christmas.

2. Regulation 1983/83, OJ L173/1, 30.6.83. See Competition Authority Licence for Categories of Exclusive Distribution Agreements, Decision No. 144, 5 November 1993, for a summary of the main provision of the Regulation.
3. Regulation 1984/83, OJ L173, 30.6.83, p. 5. See Competition Authority, Motor Fuels Category Licence, Decision No. 25, 1 July 1993, for a summary of the main provisions of the Regulation.
4. Regulation 556/89, OJ L61/1, 4.3.89.
5. Regulation 4087/88, OJ 359, p. 46, 28.12.88.

4.3 The items for inclusion in the catalogue which are 80 in the Summer and 150 at Christmas, are pre-selected by Musgraves, and the final product list is agreed with the membership. Prices are decided upon by Musgraves and are recommended prices.

26. In a subsequent letter dated 19 October 1992, Musgraves restated their proposal to amend para 3.8 of their annex and indicated that they proposed to drop para 3.9 which stated that SuperToys retailers were prohibited from advertising nationally if they sold toys for less than the catalogue price. The Authority considered that the proposed amendments did not satisfy its concerns. A Statement of Objections was issued to the parties on 15 February 1993 indicating that the Authority intended to refuse a certificate or licence for the notified arrangements. An oral hearing was held on 22 October 1993 at which Musgraves responded to the Statement of Objections.

27. Musgraves argued that the arrangements did not constitute a price-fixing agreement. They argued that the catalogue prices were merely recommendations. They also stated that the catalogue prices were very competitive to begin with and that in the period from 8 December to Christmas the multiples tended to reduce their prices and SuperToys retailers were forced to do likewise. Musgraves argued that wholesalers should be able to recommend prices. They restated their view that the retailers were in fact competing with other outlets including the multiples, rather than with each other. In addition they claimed that the pricing arrangements allowed smaller retailers to compete with the multiples. They argued that, as only a small proportion of all of the toys sold by SuperToys outlets were included in the catalogue, the arrangements had a negligible effect on competition. They argued that a catalogue without prices would be useless. It was neither practical nor effective for individual retailers to either include their own price list with the catalogue or to have different catalogues printed with the prices of each retailer. They also claimed that the prices included were merely maximum prices and that the setting of maximum prices was not anti-competitive.

28. Musgraves subsequently indicated their intention to make specific amendments to the notified arrangements. In a letter dated 14 November 1993 Musgraves informed the Authority that they were prepared to amend section 3(c)(i) of the SuperToys agreement to provide that the retailer would undertake:

> To distribute the above catalogue throughout his trading area, noting that the retailer is free to sell at prices different from those listed in the catalogue. The retailer is, however, recommended by the wholesaler not to sell at higher prices than those included in the catalogue or in any other advertising or promotion.

In a subsequent letter, dated 13 December 1993, SuperToys indicated that future catalogues would indicate, on the cover, that the prices were recommended prices.

Assessment

(a) *Section 4(1)*

29. Section 4(1) of the Competition Act states that 'all agreements between undertakings, decisions by associations of undertakings and concerted practices which have as their object or effect the prevention, restriction or distortion of competition in trade in any goods or services in the State or in any part of the State are prohibited and void'.

(b) *The Undertakings and the Agreement*

30. The notified arrangements involve Musgrave plc and a number of independent retailers. Musgrave plc is a body corporate engaged in the wholesale distribution of grocery goods mainly to independent grocery retailers. It also provides a central billing service for its grocery customers and for independent toy retailers, whereby suppliers deliver goods directly to the retailer but invoice Musgraves. Musgraves is engaged for gain in the supply of goods and the

provision of services and is therefore an undertaking within the meaning of the Act. The other parties to the notified arrangements are independent retailers who are either sole traders or corporate bodies who are also undertakings within the meaning of the Act. 4.3

The Arrangements

31. The notified agreement involves arrangements for the joint purchasing of toys from suppliers and for the advertising and pricing of these products. This constitutes an agreement between undertakings. As the retailers are located nationwide the arrangements affect the market for toys within the State.

32. There were two key aspects to the notified agreement. Firstly the retailers agree to support and to purchase a range of toys from those suppliers with whom terms have been negotiated by Musgraves on behalf of Supertoys retailers. Secondly the retailers agreed to support the Supertoys Group promotional programme. This included distributing the Supertoys catalogue throughout their trading area and agreeing on, and abiding by, the prices quoted in the catalogue. The Authority concluded that the other provisions of the agreement were merely essential to the achievement of its objectives, were not anti-competitive and therefore did not offend against section 4(1).

(c) *Applicability of section 4(1)*

33. The agreement requires the retailer to support and purchase from those suppliers with whom Musgraves has negotiated a central billing arrangement. The agreement does not apply for a specific period. Although clause 7 provides for certain procedures to be followed upon termination of the agreement, there is no express provision in the agreement setting out the basis on which either party may terminate the agreement. It was stated that the arrangement was somewhat looser than that between Musgraves and retailers in the grocery sector, and that, as a result, a number of issues were not covered by the agreement. It was subsequently indicated that members were free to terminate the agreement at any time without penalty. Since the agreement was notified a small number of retailers had in fact terminated their agreements with Musgraves.

(i) Exclusive Purchase Restriction

34. Under the agreement the retailer is not permitted to purchase toys covered by the agreement, which includes a wide range of toys, from suppliers other than those who have concluded agreements with Musgraves. The arrangement is not strictly speaking an exclusive purchasing agreement as the retailer is only committed to buy, via the central billing arrangement, the products for which Musgraves have agreements with suppliers, from those suppliers. In a sense they do not have to buy those products and they are free to buy other products from other suppliers. To some extent these other products could be considered substitutes for those products for which Musgraves has agreements with suppliers so that the agreement is not an exclusive purchase agreement. The arrangement is in fact more akin to a group purchase scheme than an exclusive purchase agreement. The object is to enhance the buying power of the retailers by operating together thereby obtaining a significant degree of purchasing power.

35. It has been indicated that the retailers obtain between 50% and 66% of their requirements through Supertoys. It is presumably in Musgraves interest to conclude agreements with as many suppliers as possible and to have the retailers purchase as much as possible of their requirements through them. The high proportion of retailers requirements sourced through Musgraves indicates that Musgraves have been successful in concluding agreements for those toys which are popular. As Musgraves claims that Supertoys accounted for [ ] of the total toy market, this implies that the agreement relates to between [ ] and [ ] of total toy sales.

36. This requirement means that the retailer cannot obtain those products which are the subject of agreements between Musgraves and suppliers from any other source. In addition this restriction applies to a large proportion of the retailers' requirements and restricts access to retail outlets which account for a sizeable share of the total market.

4.3 37. The Authority has taken account of EC decisions regarding buying group arrangements. In Intergroup[6] the EC Commission ruled that there were no grounds for action under Article 85(1) in respect of such an arrangement. The Commission decision was based on the fact that (a) the members were free not to use Intergroup's services when making purchases and (b) the arrangements did not have any substantial effect on competition since purchases through Intergroup represented only a small proportion of the members turnover and only a small proportion of turnover in the relevant market within the EC.[7] In contrast, in the Sulphuric Acid case,[8] the EC Commission found that a buying agreement offended against Article 85(1), but granted an exemption, where the members were required to obtain a minimum of 25% of their requirements through the buying arrangement. If any member purchased less than 25% of their requirements from the pool, they were deemed to have withdrawn from it. There was no penalty for withdrawal in such circumstances and the member concerned was free to rejoin, commencing on 1 January or 1 July, on giving 12 months notice of their intention to do so. In its decision granting an extension of the exemption, the Commission stated that nearly all members of the pool had continued to purchase all of their requirements through the pool.[9]

38. The agreement contains no provisions for termination. The Authority accepts, however, that in the absence of any specific termination provision, the retailers are free to terminate at any time without any penalty. Consequently they have the right to leave the group at any time if they feel they can obtain toys on better terms from suppliers or from other wholesalers or buying groups. Similarly other suppliers of the products covered by the Musgraves joint purchase agreement are free to seek to recruit those retailers who are members of Supertoys. In practice, however, it would be difficult for an individual supplier who could only offer a limited range of toys to entice a retailer to leave the group.

39. The proportion of the retailers supplies which they obtain through the group buying arrangement and the combined market share of the retailers involved would indicate that the arrangement could not be considered to conform to the situation in the Intergroup case. It is relevant, however, that the retailers are free to quit the group at any time without incurring any penalty and are also free to purchase competing products from other suppliers while remaining members of the group. In effect the retailers are only committed to obtain supplies through the group buying arrangement for so long as it suits them. In such circumstances the Authority believes that, on balance, the group buying agreement per se, does not offend against section 4(1).

(ii) Pricing Restriction

40. Clause 3(c) of the agreement required the retail members of SuperToys to support the Supertoys promotional programme. This included an obligation to distribute the Supertoys catalogue which was produced twice yearly throughout their trading area. It also required, although it was not explicitly stated in the actual agreement, that retailers agree to abide by the prices specified in the catalogue.

41. It was stated in the annex to the notification that the production of the catalogue 'involves the agreement by the Council of the retailers of Supertoys of prices for about 80 products in Summer and 150 at Christmas. These prices, and therefore the margins, are decided on by the Council and then are submitted to a general meeting of all retailers for approval'. Retailers were allowed to sell the products included in the catalogue at prices below those quoted therein,

6. Case No. 75/482/EEC, OJ L212/23, 9.8.75.
7. In respect of the main products involved Intergroup purchases accounted for a maximum of less than 6% of the turnover of the product into the Member States of destination. Imports througn Intergroup accounted for less than 1% of the turnover of all the wholesalers affiliated to the retail chains concerned while the total turnover affiliated wholesalers represented less than 4% of the retail trade in the relevant market in Member States.
8. National Sulphuric Acid Association, Case No. 80/917/EEC, OJ L260/24, 3.10.80.
9. Case No. 89/408/EEC, OJ L190/22, 5.7.89.

'in response to local pressure', but they could not advertise their reduction nationally. The parties confirmed this arrangement at a meeting on 16 June 1992. Following a letter indicating the Authority's concern about the manner in which prices for a range of toys were set, the parties indicated, (at a meeting on 12 October 1992), that Musgraves proposed a list of prices to be included in the catalogue to the Council. Once these were agreed by the Council they were then put to a full meeting of the members and agreed. It was stated that Musgraves proposed prices were accepted in the vast majority of cases. Musgraves argued that the catalogue prices were, in effect, recommended prices and that, in some cases, retailers sold items listed in the catalogue below the catalogue price. **4.3**

42. The notification indicated that the retailers agreed the prices of the items which were to be included in the promotional catalogue and they agreed to abide by those prices. The retailers were allowed to reduce their prices in response to local competition but they could not advertise such price reductions nationally. The arrangements described involved an agreement between retailers, who were competitors, on the prices which they proposed to apply to a range of products and an understanding that none of the retailers would depart from such agreed prices except in response to local competition. In the Authority's opinion, such an arrangement amounts to an agreement to fix the retail selling prices of such goods. The fact that the agreed prices were suggested to the Council of Supertoys and the members by Musgraves indicates that the agreement also includes some element of vertical price fixing or resale price maintenance. Agreements to fix selling prices are expressly cited in section 4(1) of the Competition Act as an example of the type of agreement which is prohibited under that section.

43. The parties subsequently argued that the arrangements did not constitute a price-fixing agreement. The fact is that prices were suggested to the Council of the retailers by Musgraves and, following approval by the Council, were then put to a meeting of all of the retailers before their inclusion in the catalogue. The annex describing the agreement submitted with the notification specifically stated inter alia that:

> The production of this catalogue involves the agreement by the Council of the retailers of SuperToys of prices for about 80 products in Summer and 150 at Christmas. These prices, and therefore the margins, are decided on by the Council and then are submitted to a general meeting of all retailers for approval. . . .
> It is understood by the retailers that they can reduce their prices below the catalogue levels in response to local pressure but they cannot advertise their reduction nationally. The retailers have freedom on selling prices for non catalogue items. The price restriction only applies to the promoted items. *For the vast majority of items there is, therefore, no agreement on price. The agreement on price for the catalogue items is indispensable to the arrangements for the reasons below*:
>
> > *In practice, the majority of retailers sell them at the recommended prices*. SuperToys has no objection of any kind to the retailer selling the products at less than the recommended price to meet competition, provided it is within the retailers area and is not advertised nationally.
> > *If the price is to be included in the catalogue then prices have to be agreed between the members of the voluntary group.*
> > *Similarly if the products are to be advertised nationally it is essential that price should be quoted in the advertisement. For this to be done, prices have to be agreed and, in general, adhered to.* (Emphasis added)

44. Musgraves suggested prices for inclusion in the catalogue and all the prices to be included were considered and approved by the retailers. The arrangement is described in the annex as an agreement on prices and it is stated that the prices had not only to be agreed but, 'in general, adhered to'.

4.3 EU Precedents

45. Price fixing agreements have been consistently regarded as in breach of Article 85(1) of the Treaty of Rome. Bellamy and Child point out that:

> Since price is the main instrument of competition, Article 85(1)(a) expressly prohibits agreements, which 'directly or indirectly fix purchase or selling prices or any other trading conditions.' An agreement to fix prices by its very nature constitutes a restriction on competition within the meaning of Article 85(1).[10]

46. They go on to state that:

> Article 85(1) is infringed by an explicit agreement between suppliers to fix prices, and also by a concerted practice to restrict price competition, for example informal concertation on the dates and amounts of price increases or the exchange of price information. Similarly the prohibition of Article 85(1) covers not only 'prices' in the narrow sense but also discounts, margins, rebates and credit terms. Other agreements which directly or indirectly restrict price competition include agreements not to submit quotations without prior consultation, not to deviate from published prices, not to make public any deviations from published prices, not to quote other than delivered prices, not to give other than cost related rebates, and not to sell 'below cost'.[11]

47. Van Bael and Bellis point out that:

> Although there exist no per se rules in EEC competition law, horizontal price fixing arrangements have always been held incompatible with Article 85(1) and have generally been denied an exemption.[12]

In the US horizontal price fixing agreements, agreements by competitors to exchange price information and vertical price restrictions involving resale price maintenance have generally been regarded by the courts as a per se violation of the antitrust statutes.

48. In IFTRA[13] the EC Commission found that an agreement between producers of virgin aluminium not to sell below their published prices was in breach of Article 85(1). The Commission found that the arrangements 'provide the parties with means of shelter from competition to the extent that price stability is increased and that the parties are enabled to predict each other's price policy with a reasonable degree of certainty'.[14]

It went on to state that:

> . . . every producer should have complete discretion to establish his own policy in these matters without risking the accusation that he is violating the spirit of an agreement. The contractual organisation of a system requiring adherence to various existing prices and whereby price stability is encouraged by the recommendations which are made to the parties to use and adhere to price lists . . . constitutes a major restriction of competition, both in its object and its effect.[15]

49. In Cementhandelaren the European Court of Justice ruled that:

10. C. Bellamy and G. Child (1987), *Common Market Law of Competition*, 3rd ed., Sweet & Maxwell, London at para. 4-002.
11. Ibid. at para. 4-003.
12. I. Van Bael and J.F. Bellis, *Competition Law of the EEC*, 2nd ed., CCH Editions Ltd, para. 802.
13. Case No. 75/497/EEC, OJ L228/3, 29.8.75.
14. Ibid., p. 10.
15. Ibid., p. 12.

> The fixing of a price, even one which merely constitutes a target, affects competition, because it enables all the participants to predict with a reasonable degree of certainty what the pricing policy pursued by their competitors will be.[16] 4.3

The Court upheld the Commission's decision that such an agreement was in breach of Article 85(1) despite evidence that competition from other suppliers meant that the parties to the agreement did not necessarily abide by the agreed target prices. The Commission had argued that:

> The possible malfunctioning of a cartel cannot serve as a criterion for deciding whether or not it falls within Article 85(1).[17]

50. In Papiers peints de Belgique the Court of Justice upheld a Commission decision that an agreement between wallpaper manufacturers, which required retailers to display the lists of prices fixed jointly by the manufacturers, and not to make any public announcement of rebates on these prices, while allowing them to grant rebates in particular cases on a regular basis, was in breach of Article 85(1).[18] In Hasselblad the Court upheld the Commission decision that measures designed to restrict price advertising were in breach of Article 85(1).[19] In Vimpoltu the EC Commission found that recommended retail prices fixed independently by importers and arrangements for the exchange of price lists between importers could restrict competition and these arrangements were found to be in breach of Article 85(1).[20]

51. The Court of Justice decision in Pronuptia indicates that the communication by the supplier to the retailer of recommended prices does not contravene Article 85(1) 'provided that there is no agreement or concerted practice that the distributor observe those prices'.[21]

The exclusive distribution and purchase block exemptions provide that the distributor or reseller must be free to determine prices and terms of resale.[22] Similarly the franchise block exemption allows the franchisor to recommend prices but provides that the franchisee must be free to determine prices. In the Intergroup case the retailers set their own selling prices.

Views of the Authority

52. The Authority accepts that not all toys sold by the retailers were included in the brochure. The parties indicated that about 80 items were included in the Summer brochure and 150 in the Christmas brochure. It was argued that a large number of toys were not covered by the agreement. The Authority does not consider the fact that the arrangements only extended to a particular number of products is particularly relevant. The toy market is one where tastes change rapidly from year to year. As a result there tends to be a particularly strong demand for a limited range of toys at any given time. If, as is the case, the products are chosen as part of a national advertising campaign, then it is reasonable to conclude that they will include the more popular products accounting for a high proportion of total sales. The fact, therefore, that not all toys sold by the retailers were covered by the price agreement does not alter the fact that such an agreement on prices restricts competition.

53. The Authority has already indicated in Esso[23] that it would regard the mere communication in advance of information regarding price changes or pricing intentions to competitors as offending against section 4(1) because, as in Esso and Cementhandelaren, such behaviour reduces uncertainty regarding competitors' pricing intentions which is an essential element of

16. Case No. 8/72 [1972] ECR 977, point. 23.
17. Ibid., p. 984.
18. Case No. 73/74 [1975] ECR 1491.
19. Case No. 86/82 [1984] ER 883.
20. Case No. 83/361/EEC, OJ L200/44, 23.7.83.
21. Bellamy and Child, *op. cit.*, para. 6-033.
22. Commission Notice concerning Regulation No. 1983/83 and No. 1984/83, OJ C101/2, 1984.
23. Competition Authority Decision No. 4, Esso Solus and Relate Agreeements, 25 June 1992.

4.3 competition. The Authority considers the fact that prices for the catalogue were discussed and approved by the retailers in advance went far beyond the mere exchange of price information involved in Esso. As in Cementhandelaren the fact that the retailers involved might, on occasion, have been forced to reduce prices in response to competition does not negate the restriction on competition involved in the arrangement. Similarly as in Papiers peints de Belgique and Hasselblad, the requirement that retailers do not make known any reductions they may make on the catalogue price through advertising nationally also represents a restriction of competition.

54. The fact that the catalogue prices in this instance were agreed by all the retailers meant that they could not simply be regarded as recommended prices. As in IFTRA, any retailer deviating from the catalogue prices which had been agreed by all of the retailers, risked the accusation that he was violating the spirit of the agreement. It was suggested to the Authority that if member retailers were free to sell below the catalogue prices generally the discipline necessary for the promotion and development of the group would break down. Indeed the annex states that it was essential, if the group was to advertise prices that those prices be agreed and generally adhered to. The notified arrangement also fails the requirement set by the Court of Justice in Pronuptia which allowed suppliers to recommend prices 'provided that there is no agreement or concerted practice that the distributor observe those prices'.

55. Musgraves put forward a number of arguments to justify their pricing arrangements. These were:

— that Supertoys retailers ought not to be regarded as competitors because of their location;
— that they were not in competition with one another but rather were competing with multiple supermarket outlets;
— that they could not compete in the market unless they were allowed advertise by way of a catalogue which included prices, since this was how some of their competitors advertised;
— that their share of the market meant that the arrangements did not restrict competition.

Each of these points is now considered.

56. The retailers involved are independent undertakings, although, because of their geographical location, not all of the retailers will be in direct competition with one another. All of the retail outlets involved traded under their own name while displaying the 'Supertoys' logo. The fact that they participated in a joint purchasing arrangement which allowed them to obtain the benefits of purchasing from suppliers in large quantities does not alter the fact that they are prohibited by section 4(1) of the Competition Act from entering into agreements not to compete with one another. Nor does the Authority accept the argument that, because of their location, the stores could not be considered to be in competition with one another. In a number of cases the stores concerned were located reasonably close to one another and their customers would come from the same catchment area.[24] The Authority does not therefore accept the argument that the location of the stores precludes their being regarded as competitors. In the Authority's view it is not necessary that every party to an horizontal agreement should be in direct competition with every other party to it. Musgraves had argued that the departure of certain members meant that the incidence of SuperToys stores being located in the same catchment area had been reduced.

57. The Authority does not accept the view that the retailers cannot be regarded as competing with one another because they are in competition with the multiple supermarket groups. The

24. The Authority considers that in establishing whether outlets can be regarded as coming within the same catchment area the length of time taken to travel from one location to another or the availability of public transport linking the two locations is important. It believes that where the journey time is reasonably short or there are public transport links that consumers would be influenced by differences in price to choose, one outlet in preference to another. Indeed, the Authority believes that in the case of toys, particularly at Christmas time, consumers would be prepared to travel much greater distances to avail of lower prices.

multiple supermarket groups undoubtedly sell a very wide range of goods extending beyond the range of food and other household necessaries normally regarded as grocery goods and they do compete with Supertoys outlets. Undoubtedly the large size of the two major multiple groups gives them some advantages over smaller competitors. The Authority could not, however, accept the argument that small undertakings should be excused from having to compete with one another solely because there were some undertakings competing in the market who happened to have a large share of that market. Section 4(1) prohibits anti-competitive agreements between undertakings regardless of their size. **4.3**

58. Musgraves claimed that because some other undertakings competing in the toy market produce a catalogue illustrating their products and prices, SuperToys retailers could not compete unless they were able to produce their own catalogue including prices. In essence they were arguing that unless they have a catalogue with a common set of prices they could not compete. Again the Authority does not accept such arguments.

59. All of the retailers could do their own advertising illustrating their prices. They could do this in any way they wish, via the national media, in local newspapers, in freesheets, on local radio, by delivering fliers to households within the area or by their own shop displays. It is relevant in this context that, where individual retailers offered lower prices, they were prevented from advertising them nationally. This restriction implies both that the retailers could undertake their own advertising at a national level, and that such advertising would have a competitive effect on other members.

60. It is relevant that in making their case Musgraves claimed that they had to compete with catalogue shops which are located outside of the State. Such stores offer a vast range of goods in outlets which are effectively large warehouses, with a relatively small reception area where consumers can examine the catalogues. They have developed this particular form of operation because it appears to allow them to sell at keen prices and they attract customers in this way. The Authority does not accept the argument that the existence of such stores can justify the present arrangements. The fact that the parties cited these outlets as competitors indicates to the Authority that, in this market, competition is not a localised phenomenon, that consumers are prepared to travel considerable distances in order to avail of lower prices, and this serves to undermine their earlier argument that, because of their location, Supertoys retailers should not be regarded as competitors.

61. Multiple store groups can obviously charge uniform prices in all of their outlets if they so wish, and advertise such prices in whatever way they wish because the group is under common ownership. The Authority again cannot accept an argument which essentially states that, because undertakings with multiple outlets can advertise uniform prices, independent retail outlets should be allowed agree uniform prices.

62. The Authority does not accept the proposition advanced by the parties that their share of the market meant that the pricing arrangements did not prevent, restrict or distort competition. Musgraves claimed that their retailers had a combined market share of [ ]. An arrangement to apply uniform prices between undertakings with such a market share cannot be regarded as having no significant effect on competition. It is relevant in this context that the former Fair Trade Commission, while favouring a 'de-minimis' provision in the Competition Act, recommended that such 'provisions should not apply to price fixing agreements.[25]

In addition under EC law 'de minimis' provisions only apply in respect of agreements between undertakings with an aggregate market share of less than 5%.

63. There are a number of other factors which should be taken into account. Musgraves have claimed that the two multiple supermarket groups between them have over [ ] of the toy market. They have also submitted, while claiming that margins have fallen, that the average gross mark-up of one of their members on toys was 40%. The Authority does not consider that a mark-up of this order of magnitude is necessarily consistent with a market in which there is

25. Fair Trade Commission (1991); 'Study of Competition Law', para. 9.29.

4.3 intense competition. The present agreement represents, in the Authority's view, a significant restriction on competition between a number of retailers who between them account for a significant share of the market. Such a restriction cannot be justified on the grounds that other undertakings have a larger market share especially when the difference in market share is small.

64. The arrangements involved some restriction of intra-brand competition. The Authority agrees with the views of the European Court of Justice which stressed the importance of intra-brand competition in the Grundig case.

> The principle of freedom of competition concerns the various stages and manifestations of competition. Although competition between producers is generally more noticeable than that between distributors of products of the same make, it does not thereby follow that an agreement tending to restrict the latter kind of competition should escape the prohibition of Article 85(1) merely because it might increase the former.[26]

65. In the Authority's view, toy purchases, particularly at Christmas, represent major outlays for most consumers. In such circumstances the Authority believes that consumers do shop around and compare prices between outlets. It also believes that they will be prepared to travel significant distances in order to benefit from lower prices. This view is supported by the parties claim that outlets located outside the State are competitors, and the experience of the mid 1980s, when trips by consumers to Northern Ireland to avail of lower prices, particularly in the pre-Christmas period, occurred on a large scale. The tradition of consumers travelling to Dublin from many rural areas on 8th December to do their Christmas shopping also indicates that competition in this market is not a localised phenomenon. This further undermines the parties claim that the Supertoys outlets are not in competition with one another.

66. The Authority believes therefore that the pricing arrangements, as notified, which were both between the retailers and Musgraves and between the retailers themselves had the effect of restricting price competition and therefore offended against section 4(1). The Authority also believes that the requirement not to deviate from such prices, except in response to local competitive pressures and not to advertise any such price deviations at national level also had the effect of restricting competition and offended against section 4(1). The Authority considers therefore that the notified agreement had the object and the effect of preventing price competition on a significant range of goods within the State. It also had the effect of restricting or distorting competition in the supply of such goods within the State. For these reasons it offended against section 4(1) of the Competition Act 1991.

Proposed Amendment

67. The parties responded to the Authority's expressed concern regarding the pricing arrangements by proposing that Musgraves would in future decide upon the prices to be included in the catalogue and that these would be 'recommended prices'. As pointed out, EU cases indicate that suppliers are allowed recommend prices, but that retailers must be free to set prices independently. In particular the Pronuptia case makes clear that recommended prices are only allowed 'provided that there is no agreement or concerted practice that the distributor observe those prices.' The Authority was not satisfied that the proposed amendments would in fact overcome the restriction on competition inherent in the arrangement. It merely removed the requirement that the retailers formally agree to the catalogue before publication. In particular the Authority was concerned that:

— a concerted practice to adhere strictly to the catalogue prices would simply be maintained;

— there would be a strong incentive for retailers to adhere to these prices as, given the existing arrangement, any retailer deviating from the catalogue price would risk the accusation that he was violating the spirit of the Supertoys arrangement;

26. *Consten and Grundig v. EC Commission* [1966] ECR 299, p. 342.

— past behaviour would lead retailers to conclude that other members would abide by the prices thereby greatly reducing uncertainty.

68. The position in this instance was quite different to that in Esso. In that case the Authority was satisfied that the exchange of price information between Esso and independent solus dealers was a practice that had developed in order to ensure that maximum prices orders were not breached. In addition the fact that the arrangement involved several hundred resellers, there was no indication that it had been part of a concerted practice and there were hundreds of other competing resellers, all indicated that requiring Esso to stop informing its solus dealers in advance of planned retail prices in company owned stations would be sufficient to overcome any restriction on price competition in that instance. For the reasons given above, the Authority was not satisfied that the amendments originally proposed by the parties in this case would be adequate to bring to an end the agreement to have uniform prices between the Supertoys retailers.

69. Musgraves indicated, in a letter dated 14 November 1993, that they would amend section 3(c)(i) of the SuperToys agreement to provide that SuperToys retailers undertake:

> To distribute the above catalogue throughout his trading area, noting that the retailer is free to sell at prices different from those listed in the catalogue. The retailer is, however, recommended by the wholesaler not to sell at higher prices than those included in the catalogue or in any other advertising or promotion.

In a subsequent letter dated 13 December SuperToys indicated that future catalogues would indicate, on the cover, that the prices were recommended prices.

70. Clause 3(c)(i) as amended makes clear that retailers are free to set their own prices. In addition they are merely recommended not to exceed the prices included in the catalogue. This latter point is in accord with amendments which the EC Commission accepted in Pronuptia. It is relevant that SuperToys is not a toy wholesaler and that the notified arrangements involve some elements of franchising. The Authority believes that Musgraves should be entitled to include prices in their catalogue, provided it is clear that such prices are only recommended and that retailers are free to set prices themselves. This allows SuperToys to compete in the toy market. The inclusion on the cover of the catalogue of the fact that the prices included in it are merely recommendations clarifies the true nature of the prices which are quoted therein. The agreement as amended by the addition to section 3(c)(i) and, given the indication on the catalogue cover that the prices contained therein are recommended, no longer offends against section 4(1).

(c) *Applicability of section 4(2)*

71. The pricing arrangements which were part of the originally notified agreement did not satisfy the criteria set out in section 4(2) of the Act for a licence, in the Authority's view. The Authority's reasons for this conclusion are set out here in order to clarify its position on such arrangements.

72. Under section 4(2), the Competition Authority may grant a licence in the case of any agreement or category of agreements which offend against section 4(1) but which, 'having regard to all relevant market conditions, contributes to improving the production of goods or provision of services or to promoting technical or economic progress, while allowing consumers a fair share of the resulting benefit and which does not — (i) impose on the undertakings concerned terms which are not indispensable to the attainment of those objectives; (ii) afford undertakings the possibility of eliminating competition in respect of a substantial part of the products or services in question'.

73. The Authority does not believe that the agreement on prices contributed to improving the distribution of goods or provision of services or to promoting technical or economic progress. Given that the Authority does not consider that the price-fixing arrangement led to

4.3 any efficiency benefits, consumers, by definition, did not benefit from such gains. In fact orthodox economic theory indicates that price-fixing agreements are detrimental rather than beneficial to consumer interests.

> Economists are almost unanimous in their condemnation of cartels, especially those engaged in price fixing, because no expert has satisfactorily established that consumers will benefit from price fixing. On the contrary economic analysis can show that cartels are inefficient and lessen consumer welfare. It is, therefore, not surprising that antitrusters have the closest meeting of minds on the baleful influence of cartels.[27]

74. It was claimed that the inclusion of prices in the catalogue saved consumers time in phone calls and visits to retail outlets. The Authority does not believe that such arrangements could be accepted on the grounds that they saved consumers the bother of having to shop around. As all four elements of section 4(2) must be satisfied before a licence may be granted the notified arrangements did not meet the requirements for a licence.

75. In coming to the conclusion that the pricing arrangements did not satisfy the criteria for a licence the Authority took account of the fact that over a period of 30 years the EC Commission has virtually never exempted price-fixing arrangements from the prohibition contained in Article 85(1).[28] It could see no reason for departing from well established EC precedents in the present case. It is relevant that price-fixing is generally prohibited under the competition laws of most developed economies.

The Decision

76. Musgraves and the independent retailers involved in the Supertoys agreement are undertakings within the meaning of the Competition Act and the arrangements constitute an agreement between undertakings within the State. The joint purchasing element of the agreement does not offend against section 4(1). The effect of the agreement on prices, which was an integral part of the promotion arrangements, was to restrict competition within the State and it therefore offended against section 4(1) of the Competition Act. The agreement as notified did not satisfy the requirements specified for the grant of a licence in section 4(2) as it did not contribute to improving the production or distribution of goods or to promoting technical progress and consequently conferred no benefit on consumers. As the amendments to the agreement provide that Musgraves may recommend prices but that the retailers are free to set their own prices and, as future catalogues will indicate that the prices contained therein are recommended, the agreement, as amended, no longer offends against section 4(1).

The Certificate

77. The Competition Authority has issued the following certificate:

The Competition Authority certifies that in its opinion, on the basis of the facts in its possession, the SuperToys agreement between Musgraves and independent toy retailers, (notification no. CA/20/92E), notified on 30 April 1992, under section 7, as amended by the agreement of 13 April 1994, does not offend against section 4(1) of the Competition Act 1991.

For the Competition Authority
Patrick Massey
Member
21 April 1994

27. W. Breit and K.G. Elzinga (1989), The Antitrust Casebook: Milestones in Economic Regulation, 2nd ed., Dryden Press, New York, p. 12.

28. In Uniform Eurocheques an exemption was granted for an agreement on uniform commission charges among the banks operating in Eurocheque system (OJ L35/43 [1985] CMLR 434). In Nuovo Cegam an exemption was granted to an agreement between Italian engineering insurers on basic premiums to be charged, for exceptional reasons, but this did not extend to total premiums (OJ 1984 L99/29 [1984] 2 CMLR 484).

Competition Authority Decision No. 324, Burmah Castrol (Ireland) Ltd — Loan Agreement: 5 May 1994, Notification No. CA/36/92E 4.4

Loan agreements from distributor of a product to retailers containing negative covenant – Whether restrictions prohibited – Competition Act 1991 (No. 24), sections 3, 4 and 7

Facts: On 8 June 1992 notification was made to the Authority by Burmah Castrol (Ireland) Ltd ('Burmah') of a standard loan agreement made between Burmah and various retailers with a request for a certificate under section 4(4) of the Competition Act 1991, or failing that, a licence under section 4(2). The parties to the notified agreement were Burmah and various retailers. Burmah, an Irish registered company engaged in the manufacture, importation and distribution in the State of various petroleum products, is a subsidiary of Burmah Castrol Plc, a company engaged worldwide in all stages of production and supply of petroleum products. The retailers include persons engaged in the maintenance and service of motor vehicles. The notified agreement is a standard cash loan agreement made between Burmah and various retailers whereunder Burmah loans money to finance the purchase of motor vehicle lubricating facilities and/ or equipment and it contains, *inter alia*, a covenant by the retailer not to enter into any arrangement with any other entity, the effect of which would place a fetter of any kind upon the retailer from freely displaying, advertising, stocking and selling the Burmah products. The loan advanced under the notified agreement is immediately repayable if this condition is breached.

Decided by the Authority: In issuing a certificate under section 4(4) of the Competition Act 1991 in respect of the notified agreement that:

(1) Each of the parties to the notified agreement are 'undertakings' within the meaning of section 3(1) of the Competition Act 1991 and the notified agreements are agreements between undertakings which have effect in the State.

(2) The object of the negative covenant in the loan agreement is to prevent other agreements being entered into by the retailer which restrict the sale of Burmah products on the relevant premises and does not prevent or hinder the sale of any competing products and as such does not have as its object or effect the prevention, restriction or distortion of competition.

Competition Authority Decision of 5 May 1994 relating to a proceeding under section 4 of the Competition Act 1991
Notification No. CA/36/92E — Burmah Castrol (Ireland) Ltd

Existing cash loan agreement

The Facts

(a) *Subject of the notification*

1. The notification relates to existing agreements concerning the lending of money to finance the purchase of lubricating oil facilities and/or equipment by Burmah Castrol (Ireland) Ltd to certain resellers of lubricating oils notified under section 7 of the Competition Act 1991 on 8 June 1992.

4.4 (b) *The parties involved*

2. Burmah Castrol (Ireland) Ltd is an Irish registered company engaged in the manufacture, importation, marketing and distribution in the State of various petroleum products. The company is a subsidiary of Castrol Ltd, registered in the UK, and its ultimate holding company is Burmah Castrol plc. The parent company is engaged worldwide in all stages of the production and supply of petroleum products. The Burmah retail motor fuel network consists of a number of company-owned outlets and a number of dealer-owned outlets operating under the Burmah brand. In addition, lubricating products are supplied to a large number of other outlets, including petrol stations supplied by other wholesalers and other outlets, and other customers.

3. The other parties to the notified agreements are car franchise main dealers, who undertake guarantee and servicing work, including servicing and oil changes, and other non- franchise vehicle workshops which undertake car servicing. These dealers generally do not sell petrol. At the end of September 1992, 28 customers had cash loans under the existing agreement. In addition, over 200 other customers had agreements providing for the supply of lubricating oil equipment on loan or hire purchase, which are not dealt with in this decision. Approximately six hundred similar customers were supplied without such agreements, but on Burmah's standard terms and conditions.

(c) *The product*

4. The product with which the notified agreements are concerned consists of lubricants, that is any oil-based product which is used for the lubricating of a motor vehicle. Almost all Burmah lubricating products are sold under the trade name 'Castrol'. While lubricating oils are to some extent interchangeable, the product is usually differentiated as follows:

(a) top engine oils;
(b) other multigrades;
(c) monogrades; and
(d) two-stroke oils.

Top engine oils appears to be the largest category of sales.

(d) The market

5. Besides Burmah Castrol, all the other main wholesalers of petroleum products in the State also market lubricating products. In addition to supplying lubricants to their company-owned and dealer-owned petrol stations, the wholesalers also supply motor franchise dealers and other motor workshops, motor accessory shops, other retail outlets, and direct to industrial and agricultural users.

6. Overall, according to its own confidential estimates, Burmah Castrol has a significant presence on the lubricating oils market as a whole and in important sectors of it. This is despite the fact that Burmah Castrol has only a small share of the petrol market and relatively few company and tied dealer outlets, where it could expect to sell mainly Castrol oils. It has over 20% of the total market for all engine oils supplied by the main firms. Its market share in the total and top engine oils markets is about twice that of the next largest supplier. Most of its sales consist of multigrades, by far the largest selling products in the sector. In respect of franchised vehicle workshops, it is sold at a high proportion of all outlets. It supplies a large number of these outlets under the different types of notified agreements. Of the non-franchised workshops, Burmah Castrol supplies a very high proportion under the different agreements. Burmah Castrol is regarded as the market leader and occupies a strong position in the market for lubricating oils generally, and in the top engine oils and franchised and non-franchised vehicle workshops segments of that market.

7. Since outlets retailing lubricants are located throughout the State, the appropriate geographical market in this case is the State.

8. Up to 30 September 1991, part of the motor lubricants sector was subject to the provisions of the Restrictive Practices (Motor Spirit and Motor Vehicle Lubricating Oil) Order 1981. The Order was repealed on the coming into force of the Competition Act on 1 October 1991.

(e) *The existing cash loan agreements* **4.4**

9. Burmah Castrol had made cash loans for the purchase of lubricating equipment to 28 customers as at 30 September 1992. The size of loan ranged from £2,500 to £25,000 and attracted a low rate of interest. Eleven loans were to be repaid over a five year period, and 17 over 10 years.

10. The cash loan agreement is used where Burmah Castrol lends money to finance the purchase of motor vehicle lubricating facilities and/or equipment. The agreement provides for the amount of the loan, the interest rate, and payment on a quarterly basis over a specified period. Other clauses are as follows:

(a) The company (the purchaser) agrees not to enter into any agreement or arrangement with any other individual firm or company, the effect of which would place a fetter of any kind upon it from freely displaying, advertising, stocking and selling the products of your company (Burmah Castrol) in our workshops and stores. (Clause 2).

(b) The company also agrees that in the event of disposal, selling or ceasing to carry on our business, or in the event of any breach by us of any term contained in this agreement, the company will forthwith repay Burmah Castrol (Ireland) Ltd the whole amount of the loan that may be outstanding at the date of such disposal, sale, ceasing to carry on business or breach of aforesaid. (Clause 3).

(c) This agreement shall remain in force until the entire loan shall have been discharged in the manner aforesaid. If however, immediate cash repayment of the balance outstanding is required at any time, such repayment shall be made at the request of either party giving to the other, one month's clear notice in writing, to this effect and at the expiration of the time specified in the said notice, the full amount shall be payable to Burmah Castrol (Ireland) Ltd (Clause 4).

(f) *Views of Burmah Castrol*

11. Burmah Castrol made the following observations on the notified agreements:

> It is submitted that the agreements, viewed individually or as a network, are not intended to prevent, restrict or distort competition. The intention of the agreements is to increase the sales of the Company's products, improve distribution and reduce costs and to maintain quality control and protect against environmental risks.

12. In a further submission, following a meeting with the Authority, Burmah Castrol stated that:

> It is again submitted that none of the markets into which the company sells are foreclosed to any significant degree. Of the market segments listed in the first page of the market plan extract, it is considered that, apart from petrol service stations, which are to be subject to a different regime, only the franchised car and commercial vehicle work shops market (if it constitutes a separate market) is to any extent tied up. Burmah Castrol have agreements with 100 franchise dealers. The company estimates that about 50% of the dealers in this segment are not subject to any tie whatsoever and that of the remainder, the operation of the five year rule means that an average of 20% of those become free every year. The company estimate, therefore, would be that at any time only 40% of the segment is subject to a tie at any one time. . . . In any event, the company does not accept that the franchise dealer network can be regarded as a separate market and believes that the market as a whole is not foreclosed to access by acquisition or otherwise and that, as a result, the Authority should certify its opinion that the arrangements do not offend against section 4(1).

4.4 Assessment

Applicability of section 4(1)

13. Section 4(1) of the Competition Act 1991, prohibits and renders void all agreements between undertakings which have as their object or effect the prevention, restriction or distortion of competition in trade in any goods or services in the State or in any part of the State.

14. Burmah Castrol and the resellers who are party to the notified agreements are all engaged in the supply and distribution of lubricating oils for gain, among other activities, and they are therefore 'undertakings' within the meaning of section 3(1) of the Act. The notified agreements are all agreements between undertakings. The relevant product market is that of lubricating oils for resale, and particularly that part which is supplied to franchised and non-franchised motor vehicle workshops. The relevant geographical market is the State.

15. The existing cash loan agreement provides that the recipient will not enter into any agreement or arrangement with any other individual, firm or company, the effect of which would place a fetter of any kind upon it from freely displaying, advertising, stocking and selling Castrol in the recipient's workshops and stores. The object of this requirement is to ensure that no other agreement will be entered into which would restrict the sale of Castrol on the premises. Its effect is to permit the sale of Castrol, and not to prevent or hinder the sale of any competing lubricating oils. The Authority considers therefore that this requirement has neither the object nor the effect of preventing, restricting or distorting competition. This agreement, therefore, does not offend against section 4(1).

The Decision

16. Burmah Castrol and their customers who are party to the existing cash loan agreements are undertakings within the meaning of the Competition Act. The notified agreements are agreements between undertakings, and they operate within the State. The Authority considers that, on the basis of the facts in its possession, the existing cash loan agreement, which merely requires that there be no fetter on dealing in Burmah Castrol products arising from any other agreement, does not offend against section 4(1) of the Competition Act. A certificate may therefore be issued in respect of this agreement.

The Certificate

The Competition Authority has issued the following certificate:

The Competition Authority certifies that in its opinion, on the basis of the facts in its possession, the existing cash loan agreement between Burmah Castrol (Ireland) Ltd and certain of its customers of lubricating oils, notified under section 7 on 8 June 1992 (notification No. CA/36/92E), does not offend against section 4(1) of the Competition Act 1991.

For the Competition Authority

Patrick M. Lyons
Chairman

5 May 1994

Competition Authority Decision No. 354, Musgraves Ltd — Licensee and Franchisee Agreements: 19 September 1994, Notification Nos. CA/18/92E and CA/19/92E 4.5

Exclusive purchasing agreement – Approval of recommended prices – rejection of maximum resale price maintenance – Post termination restrictions – Call option on purchase of premises – Multiple amendments to agreements notified during decision process – Refusal to grant a certificate or a licence – Competition Act 1991 (No. 24) sections 3, 4 and 7; Commission Regulations Nos. 1983/83, 1984/83, 4087/88 and 556/89

Facts: On 30 April 1992 notification was made to the Authority with a request for a certificate under section 4(4) of the Competition Act 1991 or, failing that, a licence under section 4(2) by Musgraves Ltd ('Musgraves') of two types of standard agreements for the operation of grocery retail outlets. The agreements allowed retailers to trade under the name of and to benefit from the marketing and promotion of the retail chain known as 'SuperValu' and 'Centra'. The retailer becomes obliged to support suppliers nominated by Musgraves. The prices and discounts offered by those nominated suppliers are negotiated by Musgraves. The retailer also agrees to support the promotional programme for SuperValu and Centra.

Musgraves, an Irish company, is primarily a wholesale distributor of grocery products to independent grocery retailers in the State; 352 independent retailers who own their own stores entered into a licence agreement which was virtually identical to the notified licence agreement. The notified franchise agreement related to 18 agreements which were virtually identical and which related to shops owned by Musgraves. Each agreement specifies which of the two names, SuperValu or Centra, could be used in the outlet.

The notified licence agreement required the retailer to support promotional campaigns and to stock and display products branded with the tradenames of Musgraves at prices recommended by Musgraves. An option was also given to Musgraves to purchase the retailers outlet on any sale of the retail premises. After termination of the agreement which could be effected by either party giving three months notice, the retailer was precluded from selling grocery products within a radius of one mile from the outlet for one year.

The franchise agreement described the retailer as a 'manager' and included an obligation similar to the licence agreement to take grocery products from suppliers approved by Musgraves. Promotional campaigns were to be supported in a similar manner by the franchisee and on termination of the franchise agreement the management covenanted not to engage in the grocery business within a one mile radius of the outlet if it was situated in a city and five miles of a premises if it was situated outside a city.

Estimated market shares based on figures published in 'Checkout Year Book 1993' were cited by the Authority to indicate that Musgraves had an estimated 16% of the grocery market in the State. Many amendments were proposed to the notified agreement both before and after the issue of a statement of objections on 26 April 1994 and an oral hearing on 28 June 1994. after a series of changes the ultimate notified clauses for determination required the retailer not to exceed the recommended price of products when they were nationally advertised but the retailer was free to set

4.5 his own prices in relation to all other products. The post termination covenants were changed so that the retailer would allow Musgraves to bid on the same terms as any other bidder for the premises.

The Authority decided

(A) In refusing to issue a certificate under section 4(4) of the Competition Act 1991 that:

(1) Musgraves and the licensees are engaged for gain in the grocery business and are 'undertakings'. The franchisees are also engaged for gain since they keep any profit made after meeting costs and they assume risk when buying stock.

(2) The obligation to purchase form nominated suppliers restricts to an appreciable extent the freedom of choice in the supply and distribution of grocery goods.

(3) The network of restrictive agreements as opposed to a single individual agreement introduces considerable rigidity into the market. The exclusive purchasing obligation offends against section 4(1) of the Competition Act.

(4) Although recommending prices is not anti-competitive per se the obligation to stock and display SuperValu brands at the price recommended by Musgraves offends against section 4(1) of the Act because retailers are not entirely free to set their own prices.

(5) The desire of Musgraves to maintain standards does not justify the requirement of Musgraves that retailers purchase all equipment and computer systems from suppliers nominated by Musgraves.

(6) The amended proposal of Musgraves which restricts the retailer after termination from continuing to sell groceries and the obligation on the retailer to allow Musgraves to purchase the premises on the same terms as all other parties is not justified by Musgraves desire to protect its 'know how'. Even a restriction for six months would offend against section 4(1) of the Competition Act.

(7) The proposed amendment of Musgraves that a retailer should not operate from any other premises without Musgraves' consent is designed to prevent retailers from using know how supplied by Musgraves and therefore does not offend against section 4(1) of the Competition Act.

(8) The compulsion under the notified franchise agreement on a manager to purchase stocks solely from Musgraves is not a restriction which offends against section 4(1) of the Competition Act because Musgraves cannot be compelled to grant access to their stores to competitors when they have made a significant investment in those stores.

(9) The obligations on franchisees to apply recommended prices offends against section 4(1) of the Competition Act.

(10) The requirement to purchase equipment from suppliers nominated by Musgraves is designed to ensure a standard format and quality in the shops owned by Musgraves and therefore does not offend against section 4(1) of the Competition Act.

(11) The original restriction on franchisees from making their own stock insurance arrangements would have offended against section 4(1) of the Competition Act but the amended obligation whereby franchisees could chose their own insurers subject to satisfying Musgraves that adequate insurance arrangements are in place does not offend against section 4(1) of the Competition Act.

(12) The payment of a service charge under the standard franchise agreement does not offend against section 4(1) of the Competition Act.

(13) The accounting requirements, inspection rights of Musgraves, opening hours and repair clauses of the franchise agreements do not offend against section 4(1) of the Competition Act. **4.5**

(14) The restriction on a franchisee from competing with SuperValu or Centra while a franchisee, does not offend against section 4(1) of the Competition Act. However, the similar restriction which was limited to one year and one mile after termination of the franchise agreement is not warranted and offends against section 4(1) of the Act. The franchisee should be allowed to benefit from the goodwill generated by the franchisee during the course of the agreement.

(15) The original clause restricting the franchisee from using know how acquired during the course of the franchise agreement could allow Musgraves to prevent the franchisee from entering the grocery retail market on the termination of the agreement. The subsequent proposal of Musgraves to exclude know how which is easily accessible would mean that the clause would not offend against section 4(1) of the Competition Act.

(B) In refusing to grant a licence under section 4(2) of the Competition Act 1991:

(1) Exclusive purchasing arrangements which offend against section 4(1) of the Competition Act contribute to reducing costs and improves the distribution of grocery goods. This enables the retailer to compete more effectively.

(2) Consumers benefit from the competition which Musgraves has provided to the supermarket multiples.

(3) The purchasing obligation is indispensable to the attainment of having a viable purchasing group.

(4) The purchasing requirements does not afford Musgraves the possibility of eliminating competition in respect of a substantial part of the market because of the competition which exists in the retail grocery market.

(5) The finite period of the exclusive purchasing obligation means that the requirements for a licence in respect of the exclusive purchasing obligation are satisfied.

(6) The obligation to stock and display brands at recommended prices does not contribute to an improvement in the provision of services or the promotion of technical and economic progress. Such pricing obligations are not indispensable to the objects of the agreement.

(7) The safeguarding of the identity of the SuperValu name by obliging retailers to purchase equipment from suppliers nominated by Musgraves can be achieved in a less restrictive manner. The proposed amendment which included the obligation to purchase equipment from one of two suppliers in relation to the computer system would meet the requirements of section 4(2) of the Competition Act.

(8) The post term restrictions on licensees do not contribute to improving the distribution of goods or the provision of services or to promoting technical or economic progress. There is no gain and no benefit derives to consumers.

(9) The Authority rejects the argument that the post term non compete clause is designed to protect the know how of Musgraves.

Cases, Decisions and Report referred to:

Texaco (Ireland) Ltd v. Farrell and Esso Ireland Ltd (unreported, High Court, judgment of Blayney J of 1 May 1991)

Papiers Peints v. Commission (Case No. 73/74) [1975] ECR 1491; [1976] 1 CMLR 589

4.5 *Hasselblad v. Commission* (Case No. 86/82) [1984] ECR 883; [1984] 1 CMLR 559
EC Commission Decision — Intergroup [1975] OJ L212/23; [1975] 2 CMLR D14
EC Commission Decision — National Sulphuric Acid Association I [1980] OJ L260/25; [1980] 3 CMLR 429
Competition Authority Decision No. 144 — Category Licence for Exclusive Distribution Agreements **5.1**
Competition Authority Decision No. 25 — Motor Fuels Category Licence **4.2**
FTC Report of Review of the Restrictive Practices (Groceries) Order 1987 (Pl 8304)

Competition Authority Decision of 19 September 1994 relating to a proceeding under section 4 of the Competition Act 1991 Notification Nos. CA/18/92E and CA/19/92E — Musgraves Ltd — Licensee and Franchisee Agreements

Introduction

1. Musgraves Ltd (Musgraves) notified two types of standard agreement relating to the operation of grocery retail outlets on 30 April, 1992. These agreements involve Musgraves, trading as SuperValu and Centra Distribution (Musgraves), and 352 licensees (licensee agreements) on the one hand and Musgraves and 18 franchisees (franchise agreements) on the other.

The facts

(a) *Subject of the Notification*

2. The notifications involve two types of standard agreements between Musgraves and a number of individual grocery retailers. The essential feature of the arrangements is that the retailers undertake to purchase all of their requirements from the range of merchandise offered by Musgraves. All of the retailers trade under either the SuperValu or Centra name. There are actually four standard agreements. Two of these are with retailers who own their own stores and these are referred to as licence agreements. There is a separate licence agreement for SuperValu and Centra retailers, although the two agreements are virtually identical The other two agreements are with retailers who operate stores which are owned by Musgraves. These are referred to as franchise agreements. Again while there are different agreements for Super Valu and Centra stores, the agreements are virtually identical. There are over 350 licence agreements and less than 20 franchise agreements.

(b) *The Parties*

3. The parties to these agreements are Musgraves, 352 independent retailers (the licensees) and 18 franchisees. Musgraves is a holding company. Its divisions trade almost exclusively in the grocery business. Musgraves Distribution Ltd a wholly owned subsidiary of Musgraves, carries on the business in Northern Ireland.

4. At the retail end of the grocery market, retailers linked to Musgraves operate under the SuperValu and Centra names. SuperValu and Centra are known as Symbol Groups i.e. groups of independent retailers who operate under a common group name.

SuperValu and Centra Distribution division of Musgraves acts as a wholesaler supplying the retail outlets from two warehouses in Cork and Galway and a central billing system is in operation. Musgraves also operate nine cash and carry outlets.

(c) *The Product and the Market*

5. Musgraves provides a wholesale service, including central billing arrangements, for grocery goods to independent retailers. The retailers buy directly from Musgraves or alternatively they purchase their requirements under the central billing system from suppliers nominated by Musgraves.

The Wholesale Market 4.5

6. According to the Fair Trade Commission,[1] there were four major wholesale groupings in 1991. These groups were members of the Irish Association of Distributive Trades (IADT). IADT members represented 54 wholesale companies which operated 140 warehouses in 1990. Of these 39 were delivered and the remaining 101 were cash and carry outlets. In addition, the ADM/Londis group operates a wholesale company which is owned by retailers, and a number of smaller wholesalers.

7. The delivered warehouses are largely concerned with servicing symbol shops in the various retail symbol groups. Cash and carry outlets represent a source of supply for independent grocers. In the 1991 review there was evidence to suggest that the cash and carry business was becoming less significant with a growing demand from retailers for wholesalers to provide credit and delivery services.

8. Musgraves also operates a central billing arrangement with its symbol group retailers. Under this system, goods are delivered by suppliers to individual retailers rather than to the wholesaler's warehouse for onward delivery. The supplier then bills the wholesaler for all deliveries to the symbol shops. The wholesaler pays the supplier and collects the money from its individual retail customers. The advantage of this arrangement to the wholesalers is that it allows them to trade in goods of a relatively short shelf-life which could not be stored indefinitely in their warehouse. For the retailers, it gives some of the benefits of bulk-buying which they would not otherwise be in a position to avail of.

The Retail Market

9. Retail grocery outlets include both independent small retailers, retailers connected to particular wholesalers as well as outlets owned by the supermarket multiples. Details of the number of retail outlets associated with symbol groups as well as retail outlets operated by the multiples are given in Table 1.

Table 1: Numbers of Retail Outlets

	1986	1990	1991
Multiples			
Dunnes	41	51	50
Powers	69	68	69
Superquinn	11	12	13
L & N	14	16	18
Roches Stores	6	7	7
H Williams	33	—	—
Total	174	154	157
Symbols			
ADM Londis	78(a)	85(a)	90(a)
Musgraves	380	370	371
Associated National Distributors (Mace)	320	193	(b)
BWG Foods (Spar) Wisebuy, Family Value)	425	406	(b)
Total Symbols	1203	1054	999

Notes: (a) Londis symbol shops only. (b) Separate figures for these groups were not available.
Source: FTC, (1991) and Checkout Yearbook (1993).

1. Fair Trade Commission: Report of Review of the Restrictive Practices (Groceries) Order, 1987, Stationery Office, Dublin, 1992), P1 8304.

4.5 (i) Multiples

10. There are five multiple groups which between them operated 157 retail outlets in 1991. These are Quinnsworth, Dunnes Stores, Superquinn, L&N and Roches Stores. Only two of these, Quinnsworth and Dunnes could be regarded as operating nationally. In terms of turnover and market share these two are far larger than the other three multiple groups who operate on a regional basis and have far fewer stores.

(ii) Symbol Groups

11. Symbol group shops are groups of independent retailers who operate under a common group name. Among the major symbol groups operating in the grocery trade are SuperValu, Centra, Mace, Spar, and Wisebuy. There were almost 1,000 symbol group stores in the State in 1991. The symbol group shops are organised by a wholesaler or group of wholesalers, from which the retail members purchase a large part of their supplies. The retail members of symbol groups benefit from membership in a number of ways, such as being able to get and offer cheaper prices arising from bulk purchasing by the group members as a whole, combined advertising, other group promotions and the benefits of a common logo. There are over 370 stores attached to the two Musgrave symbol groups. This total has changed very little since the mid 1980's. There has been a change in membership of the groups. SuperValu stores tend to be larger than Centra ones. Roughly 35% of the Musgrave affiliated stores trade as SuperValu outlets with the balance operating under the Centra name.

(iii) Independents and Other Retailers

12. The majority of independently owned grocery outlets do not belong to any of the symbol groups. While most of these are single shop operations this category includes some operators with a number of stores. Independent stores range in size from small corner stores to supermarkets comparable in size to those operated by the multiples.

13. There are in addition a sizeable number of stores specialising in certain foodstuffs. These include butchers, greengrocers and tobacco, sweets and newspaper shops (TSNs). These are not grocery stores in the strictest sense. It is clear, however, that grocery stores are in competition with butchers and greengrocers for particular segments of the food market. Similarly there has been an increased tendency for TSNs to stock a small but significant range of grocery products. Many petrol stations now have forecourt shops which also stock a range of grocery products. These latter two groups would certainly appear to be competing in the convenience store segment of the grocery market.

Table 2: Estimated Market Shares December 1992

Quinnsworth	10.0
Crazy Prices	10.5
Powers Total	20.5
Dunnes Stores	24.0
Superquinn	4.0
L & N	3.5
Roches Stores	2.0
Total Multiples	54.0
SuperValu	12.0
Centra	4.0
Musgrave Total	16.0

Spar	4.0
Mace	3.0
Londis & Other	
Symbols	4.0
Total Symbols	27.0
Other Outlets	19.0

Source: Checkout Yearbook 1993.

14. No accurate assessment of market shares within the grocery trade is easily attainable. However, estimated market shares included in the Checkout yearbook for 1993 indicate that the five multiple groups accounted for 54% of the total national grocery trade. Three of the five groups have a share of less than 5% with Dunnes and Powers accounting for 44.5% of the market. The symbol groups accounted for 27% of the market at the end of 1992 with the Musgraves affiliated SuperValu/Centra stores, the largest symbol group, having 16% of the total, of which 12% was attributed to SuperValu stores. Their market share is far higher than that of the other symbol groups which between them had only 11% of the market. Of the multiples, only Dunnes Stores and the Powers Group have a larger share of the market. Musgraves indicated that they did not know the source of the Checkout data and produced alternative figures suggesting that their market share was lower than stated in the Checkout Yearbook.

(d) *The arrangements*

15. Musgraves notified four agreements — the standard SuperValu and Centra licensee agreements and the standard SuperValu and Centra franchisee agreements.

The SuperValu Licensee Agreement

16. The licensee agreements are entered into with independent retailers who own their own stores and agree to undertake the obligations in the licensee agreements. The most important provisions in the standard SuperValu licensee agreement are detailed below.

17. Under the agreement Musgraves, trading as SuperValu undertakes:

— to allow the retailer to operate as a SuperValu outlet,

— to supply a SuperValu fascia sign,

— to sell to the retailer the range of merchandise which Musgraves Ltd stocks at the scheduled wholesale price ruling at the date of delivery, and

— to provide the retailer with promotional material on a regular basis.

18. The retailer's obligations under the agreement are contained in Clause 3. The most important of these are:

(a) pay an entrance fee of [ ] to the wholesaler

(b) to display the authorised SuperValu fascia sign in a prominent position on the premises

(c) purchase all his/her/its requirements from the range of merchandise offered by the wholesaler

(d) to support those suppliers nominated by the wholesaler from whom there is a group discount available on a Central Billing and Retail Rebate Scheme.

(e) support the SuperValu Group promotional programme including the following;

(i) To display all point of sale material supplied by the Wholesaler in the manner stipulated by the Wholesaler.

4.5 (ii) To pay a weekly contribution towards SuperValu marketing costs, the amount to be decided by Musgraves Ltd trading SuperValu & Centra Distribution and the Retailer to be bound by all such decisions in all respects absolutely.

(iii) To stock and display all SuperValu brands at the price recommended by the wholesaler.

19. Clause 5 of the standard licensee agreement provides for purchasing fixtures and fittings for the SuperValu and Centra outlets:

> The retailer agrees to purchase all equipment (fixtures and fittings) from suppliers nominated and approved by the Wholesaler, and used in his premises, and further agrees to use the SuperValu corporate colours as specified by the Wholesaler.

20. Clause 12 contains restrictions relating to the sale of the licensee's premises.

> In further consideration of the financial, commercial and trading assistance given by the Wholesaler to the Retailer, the Retailer further agrees and covenants with the Wholesaler as follows:
>
> (i) Not to transfer, sell, assign, let, sub-let, or otherwise dispose of the premises or the retail business carried out therein to a competitor of the Wholesaler.
>
> (ii) In the first instance if he/she/it decides to dispose of his/her/it's interest in the premises to offer to the Wholesaler the first option to purchase the premises at a price to be agreed between the parties. In default of agreement the price shall be determined by an independent valuer nominated by the Wholesaler and approved by the Retailer, such price to be determined on the basis of the then prevailing market value for the premises, with vacant possession having regard to the location of the premises. The Wholesaler shall have one month from the determination of the price as aforesaid to enter into Agreement for sale to purchase the same.
>
> (iii)After termination of this Agreement, not to carry on the trade or business of retailer of the type of goods commonly sold by the Retailer from the premises for a period of one year from the date of termination within a radius of one mile from the premies. . . .

21. Clause 14 provides for termination of the Agreement:

> (a) Either party shall be entitled to terminate this Agreement by giving three months notice in writing to the other party, which termination shall not affect the accrued rights up to the date of termination of either party under the Agreement.
>
> (b) In the event of the Retailer exercising his rights as aforesaid the Retailer shall be immediately bound by all provisions of Clause 12 hereof.

22. The standard Centra licensee agreement is identical to this apart from the omission of clause 3(a) (see para. 18).

The Franchisee Agreements

23. The standard franchisee agreements deal with the situation where Musgraves owns the store and enters into a type of tenancy agreement with the franchisees. Franchisees are termed 'Managers' in the agreements. The SuperValu and Centra franchisee agreements are identical.

24. The franchisees are required to comply with the provisions of the standard licensee agreements in addition to the undertakings given in the franchisee agreements.

25. The franchisees give a series of undertakings to Musgraves. These undertakings deal with, *inter alia*, exclusive purchasing, promotion, insurance, service charges, trading laws, non-compete clauses and repairs. The following provisions are included:

2(ii) To take all supplies of grocery products and all other allied products at all times for sale in the business to be carried on hereunder from a supplier or suppliers approved by the Company. **4.5**
(iii) To take from the Company or a supplier or distributor authorised by the Company, all supplies and other commodities such as advertising material, trade notices, items, paper products and packaging bearing a trade mark or logo of the Company, and miscellaneous equipment incidental to the preparation, advertisement supply or presentation of the business as the Company may prescribe same to be willingly supplied by the Company at prices, which shall at all times be reasonable having regard to the cost thereof to the Company. If payment of any Invoice due to the Company is overdue all other Invoices and payments due by the Manager to the Company shall immediately become due and payable and interest on such unpaid amounts shall accrue at the rate of 1.5% per month. . .
(v) The Company shall insure and keep insured throughout the term of this Agreement with an Insurance Company of repute the premises together with all stock thereon, and all equipment and fixtures and fittings therein, and shall also insure against all claims for Public Liability and Employers Liability together with such consequential loss, together with cash in transit and on the premises at a level which shall be fixed at the discretion of the Company and shall further insure and continue to keep insured such risks as the Company may at its sole discretion deem to be prudent and practical in the circumstances of this Agreement and in the circumstances of the ownership and operation of the shop. The company shall furnish to the Manager copies of the Insurance Agreements entered into by it and shall also furnish to the Manager the amount of the Premiums payable in respect of such Insurance it shall arrange. The Manager shall pay to the Company on presentation of the said premiums the amount which has been discharged by the Company in respect of same and this sum shall not be deemed to form any part or portion of the Management Charge herein referred to.
(vi) The Manager shall pay to the Company a Service Charge representing a percentage of the total sales of the Manager exclusive of V.A.T. on the premises during each accounting month. The Service Charge shall be the percentage amount agreed between the Company and the Manager and shall be paid, together with V.A.T. thereon at the rate of [ ] within ten days of the end of each accounting month. If the payment of the Service Charge is overdue, all other Invoices and payments due by the Manager to the Company shall immediately become due and payable and interest on such unpaid amounts shall accrue at the rate of 2% per month. In the event of the Manager and the Company failing to agree as to the percentage figure which is to be the Service Charge within a period of twenty one days the Company may forthwith and without further notice to the Manager, terminate this Agreement and same shall be forthwith determined and void and of no effect. . .
(x) The Company has the right to nominate the accountant to act for the manager to ensure proper books of account are kept. The Accountant nominated will be acceptable to Company and Manager and will at all times be the Managers accountant.

The rate of service charge is subject to alteration in line with fluctuations in the AA bank rate.

The service charge rate can be based on either of the following:

(a) % of turnover excluding VAT

(b) Interest at AA rates on total cost of premises, renovations, equipment and fees outlaid by the Company.

This Agreement is for a period of ________________ after which the manager has the option to purchase the property at a cost to include original cost of premises including fees, renovations, equipment and fees on sale. This option will be at the discretion of the Company.

4.5 (xi) To allow the company or its Accountants or other duly authorised Agents of the company to examine during business hours at its own expense the books and records of the Manager. The Manager will keep complete and accurate books and records of the operation of the business at the Managed Premises, and will keep them available for the Company to inspect upon request for 24 months. In the event of such examination disclosing an error in the computation of the total gross sales made from or on the Managed Premises to an extent in excess of 2% the Manager shall bear the expenses of the examination forthwith, and shall forthwith pay any deficiency on the Service Charge which may be disclosed on such examination, together with any interest payable thereon.

(xii) To allow the Company's authorised personnel to enter the Managed Premises at all times during business hours to inspect and examine the Manager's stock, operations and facilitate for the purpose of determining whether the Manager has complied with his obligations under this agreement and with the standard prescribed by the Company.

(xv) Diligently and continuously to perform the services forming part of the operational system prescribed by the Company for the Managed premises in strict compliance with the provisions of this Agreement.

(xvi) To keep the Managed Premises open and in normal operation each and every day of the week including Saturdays and Sundays for such hours as shall be agreed between the Company and the Manager or in the event of disagreement such hours as the Company may reasonably direct.

(xix) Not except as herein authorised during the continuance of this agreement either alone or in association with or in the employment of any other person engage or be concerned directly or indirectly in any business or employment in the field of the grocery business or businesses allied or associated thereto except with the express authority in writing of the Company which authority shall not be reasonably withheld.

(xx) Not for a period of one year from the determination of this Agreement either alone or in association with or in the employment of any other person to engage or be engaged directly or indirectly in any business in the field of the sale of groceries or any business allied thereto within a radius of one mile of the Managed Premises, where the Managed Premises is in a a city and five miles of the Managed Premises where the managed Premises is elsewhere other than a city.

(xxii) To have and use on the Managed Premises only such cash registers as are supplied thereto by the Company. The said cash registers shall remain and always be the exclusive property of the Company. The said cash registers shall have two keys, one of which shall be retained by and be the exclusive property of the Company. The Manager hereby agrees not in any way to interfere with the mechanism or working of the said cash registers, and by virtue of the execution of this Agreement acknowledges that the Company and/or its designated representative may at any time have access to the said cash registers for the purposes of checking same, and in particular, for the purposes of checking the tally rolls thereon, then such checking and inspection shall be carried out in the presence of the Manager or in the presence of a representative to attend such inspection or checking of the cash registers shall not in any way preclude the Company or its designated representative from carrying out such checking and examination. The property in the said cash registers shall vest totally in the Company and the Company shall insure same in the full replacement value, and shall be at liberty from time to time or any time to remove whatever cash registers are placed in the managed Premises and to replace same with other cash registers. No other cash registers whatsoever shall be kept or used on the Managed Premises.

(xxv) The Company shall, at it's own discretion, carry out such repairs and renewals which it shall deem fit, proper and reasonable in order to maintain the Managed Premises at the standards which would be appropriate for such premises. Prior to carrying out such repairs and renewals the Company shall agree same with the Manger, but in the event of the Manager disagreeing with the Company as the necessary repairs and renewals shall be carried out with the least possible disturbance to the Manager. The costs of the said repairs and renewals shall be a charge against the accounts of the Manager, and shall be payable on presentation of the Invoices in respect of same. **4.5**

26. Clause 3 of the standard agreements set out the circumstances in which the agreements shall cease to have effect. Such a situation could arise if the franchisee fails to observe the stipulations and agreements contained in Clause 2. Bankruptcy and default in payment for goods and other matters would also bring about a termination of the agreement. There is also a limit on the duration of the agreements:

This agreement shall cease and determine upon the happening of any of the following events, without notice being served by either party, namely;

(a) The affluxion of 10 years from the date hereof, provided however, and it is hereby agreed between the Company and the Manager that this Agreement shall continue so long only as the Manager holds his appointment as Manager of the SuperValu Franchise of the Company.

27. Post-termination provisions are also included in this Clause:

> On the determination of this Agreement whether by affluxion of time or otherwise, the Manager shall forthwith discontinue any or all use of the name SuperValu and any other of the trade marks or logos referred to in this Agreement or any equipment or items bearing the name or trade mark of the Company or the logo thereof, and shall forthwith remove from display all advertisements, signboards or name plates supplied or used in connection with the exploitation of this Agreement, and shall not in any way whatsoever use the name of nor similar kind or routine service or method of selling grocery products whereby the public could be misled into believing that are in any way associated with the marketing from the Managed Premises or any other Premises.

(e) *Submissions of the Parties*

28. Musgraves submitted that the agreements were pro-competitive in their effects on the market and did not prevent, restrict or distort competition in any goods or services in the State. The agreements were stated to be pro-competitive because they allowed retailers supplied by Musgraves to compete effectively against the multiples. The undertakings given by the licensees and franchisees were said to be necessary to facilitate the success of the operation.

29. Musgraves submitted that the arguments they presented in support of an application for a licence were also applicable to the application for a certificate. They stated that they believed that the agreements between Musgraves and its licensees and franchisees contributed to improving the distribution of goods and to economic progress. They claimed that this was supported by the fact that they had increased the market share in recent years. This increase in share was due, inter alia, to the competitiveness of the retailers when compared with the multiples. The agreements improved the efficiency of the distribution of goods by bringing about a close and mutually beneficial relationship between the wholesaler and the retailers. The cost of transferring goods from the suppliers to consumers was reduced as a result of the agreements.

30. The benefits of technical and economic progress were brought to many small rural communities and were not confined to urban areas. The relationship brought about by the agreements has allowed the development of expertise in scanning, re-ordering of stocks and handling of goods, which was appropriate for operation by independent retailers. It had been possible, by making these agreements, to bring the benefits of modern technology to many independent businesses who would have found it very difficult to avail of these benefits on their own and would have been at risk of experimenting with untried, and over costly, or unsuitable systems.

31. Consumers in remote areas gained because they were able to obtain their groceries at the same prices as those in urban areas. Before the advent of the type of trading exemplified in the agreements, there was a significant variation in the prices paid for many grocery items

4.5 in urban and rural areas. Consumers in urban areas gained from the proximity to them of many of the SuperValu retailers thus obviating the cost and time of travelling to a multiple. Consumers gained from a greater diversity of services from supermarkets than had been available. These included:

(a) the willingness to deliver goods which have benefited many consumers,

(b) longer opening hours including Sunday opening which has benefited many persons,

(c) the generally higher standard of service resulting from the presence of the owner of the enterprise in the store.

32. Consumers also gained from the vigorous competition which Musgraves had provided for the multiples and had forced multiples to compete strongly on price and to improve their services. This was particularly important in the period since the demise of H. Williams and Tesco when there were only two national multiples. The agreements could not be shown to have eliminated competition in a substantial part of the market given their market share. Even in the convenience sector there were many competitors, including other symbol groups such as Spar, Mace, Londis as well as many independent traders and the petrol retailers. While the market share of Musgraves varied from place to place, the effect of the agreements did not eliminate competition in any part of the country. In all parts of the country there was competition to Musgraves. Nor was there any products or product range where Musgraves had a monopoly of the market. Musgraves submitted detailed argumentation in support of a number of the restrictions contained in the agreements.

Exclusive Purchasing — Clause 3(c)

33. In relation to the exclusive purchasing requirements, Musgraves stated that the wholesaler earned its income from sales to the retailers. There was no other payment by the retailer other than the payment by the retailer for the goods (apart from the payment by the eighteen franchisees of a sum equal to the interest on the value of the premises occupied by them). The payment for the goods comprised the price of the goods, which was the same to all retailers, and a handling charge, which was on a scale and had a slight advantage for larger outlets to recognise economies of scale. About half the margin before the Long Term Allowance was earned from the handling allowance. If the retailer did not purchase the goods, the wholesaler was not remunerated for the services provided to the retailer.

34. The essence of the concept was that the combined purchasing power of the retailers enabled the best possible prices to be obtained from suppliers. This enabled the retailers to compete more effectively. If any individual retailer purchased separately from the wholesaler, the whole group was weakened and the viability of all might be threatened. No individual retailer would be able to purchase more cheaply than Musgraves across the range of merchandise. By attempting to do so, retailers would put their viability at risk.

Support Suppliers — Clause 3(d)

35. In connection with the requirement to support suppliers nominated by them, Musgraves stated that there were many products where it was more practicable to have them delivered direct to the retailer than to be delivered from a central warehouse. Examples of these were fruit and vegetables, dairy products and fresh products generally. These could be centrally billed. It was possible for Musgraves to negotiate arrangements with suppliers of many of these products which incorporated service levels, quality standards, promotion schemes, lower credit risk, reduced sales representative cost, lower interest cost on outstanding debt, etc. which could be shared between the wholesaler and the retailer and which would enable the retailer to obtain the goods at lower prices than would be possible if the retailer purchased separately. Musgraves were also able to negotiate credit terms, thus allowing the retailer proper working capital to expand and develop the business. Retailers purchasing independently from suppliers often obtained little or no credit, which impacted heavily on their development and expansion opportunities. The central billing arrangements with suppliers encouraged them to deliver to

remote areas. Central billing resulted in a substantial reduction in a retailer's administration costs, as the vast majority of the work was done centrally by Musgraves thus allowing the retailer to be more competitive in retail price levels. 4.5

Pricing — Clause 3(c)(iii)

36. Musgraves stated that the requirement to stock and display all SuperValu (or Centra) brands at the price recommended by the wholesaler applied to own brands with the Musgraves names rather than the supplier's name on the product. These tended to be known value items. These products were nationally advertised and were chosen in order to compete with the remainder of the trade. It was essential that the products should be sold at the prices advertised nationally. If they were not, the image of the symbol would be devalued to consumers. In practice, because these tended to be low margin items, the majority of retailers sold them at the recommended price. Musgraves had no objection of any kind to the retailer selling the products at less than the recommended price. The restriction was on selling at more than the recommended price for the reasons given above. It was believed that this restriction was also indispensable to the success of the concept.

37. The Authority queried Musgraves in connection with an article in the October 1992 edition of Retail News. This involved an interview with Mr. Pat Herlihy, described as operations director at Musgraves. In this interview Mr. Herlihy described how retailers order their stock from Musgraves using hand held computer terminals. The report then stated that:

> These display the relevant product, price and margin information on each of the lines in the warehouse'. Musgraves were asked how this conformed with earlier information provided by them that retailers were free to set their own prices and margins. In their reply they indicated that the prices shown were only recommended prices and that retailers were free to set their own prices. They also claimed that this was similar to the long accepted practice of suppliers recommending prices to the trade. They indicated that this differed from the arrangements in respect of own brands which are dealt with elsewhere. Musgraves indicated that Retailers were provided with suggested retail prices and suggested gross margins for all goods sold, but were free to sell below these prices if they so wished, so long as the item was not on promotion (i.e. nationally advertised). In a letter dated 6 April, 1993, Musgraves indicated that the arrangements in relation to pricing which applied to a licensee also applied to a franchisee.

Equipment — Clause 5

38. Musgraves submitted that they in all cases nominated two suppliers for the retailer to choose from. The reason for this clause was to ensure that the equipment obtained by the retailer met the standards required from a Musgraves retailer. The service was also valuable because it prevented the retailer from purchasing unsuitable equipment or purchasing from unsuitable suppliers. The combined experience of the group was made available to any new retailer or to any retailer updating the equipment.

Restriction on Re-sale of Premises — Clause 12

39. Musgraves argued that these clauses were to protect the wholesaler in the event of the retailer deciding to end the agreement. They were similar in their effect to clauses found in many employment contracts. In addition to protecting the wholesaler they also protected the other retailers as any significant reduction in the number of retail outlets would mean a reduction in the viability of the whole group. Essentially, Musgraves invested in the Musgraves symbol brand names. These names, because of their reputation, brought customers to the shops. They considered that it was reasonable for Musgraves to protect its investment by restricting the retailer from disposing of the premises to a competitor of Musgraves. The second part of the clause, obliging the retailer to give Musgraves first refusal on the premises, was fair to the

4.5 individual retailer while ensuring that Musgraves was able to protect their investment. The third part of the clause ensured that the retailer was not able, after receiving a fair price for his/her business, to restart the business again within a mile from the premises sold.

40. Musgraves argued that a number of EU block exemptions were relevant to these agreements. These were:

(1) 1983/83 Exclusive distribution
(2) 1984/83 Exclusive purchasing
(3) 4087/88 Franchising
(4) 556/89 Know-how licensing

They stated that, while in many respects, the Musgraves agreements could be classified as exclusive distribution agreements or exclusive purchasing agreements, it was apparent that these regulations were intended to apply to manufactured goods being distributed by exclusive distributors. Nevertheless many of the arguments made by the EU in justifying these block exemptions applied equally in the case of the notified agreements. Similarly, the Franchise Regulation had a general applicability to the form of agreements being notified but not all of the requirements of the Regulation were met by the agreements. The know-how licensing regulation had also some relevance for this notification. In effect, it was the know-how of Musgraves which was being made available to the retailers and which, inter alia, ensured their success.

Franchise Agreement

41. In relation to clause 2(v) of the standard franchise agreement, which provides for the organising of insurance by Musgraves, it was submitted that adequate insurance on stock was essential in Musgraves' interests. Musgraves nominated a small number of insurance brokers to provide insurance services to their franchised outlets. The use of these brokers was supported by the notifying parties on the basis that it was more convenient and efficient to obtain insurance services in this manner. In order to ensure that the nominated broker remained competitive, Musgraves sought quotes every 2/3 years from a number of brokers, the one deemed to provide the best cover, having regard to rates and quality of service, was then recommended to all retailers, not just the franchisees. Approximately one-third of the licensees insured through the recommended broker although they were not obliged to do so.

42. Musgraves reserved the right to inspect the franchisee's stock at any time under Clause 2(xii). Musgraves stated that as the franchisee does not make any form of capital investment, some assurance of compliance with trading conditions was essential. It has claimed that the 'operational system' referred to in clause 2(xv), involved conditions relating to standards of hygiene, point-of-sale materials as well as assurances that all legal requirements were being met. There was no separate document setting out the operational system.

(f) *EU Regulations*

43. EU Regulation No. 1983/83, of 22 June 1983, is a block exemption regulation which applies Article 85(3) of the Treaty of Rome to categories of exclusive distribution agreements. The regulation entered into force on 1 July 1983 and it expires on 31 December 1997.[2] The main features of the regulation are summarised in the Authority's Category Licence for Exclusive Distribution Agreements.[3] The regulation applies to agreements involving only two parties in which one agrees to supply only the other with certain goods for resale within the whole or a defined area of the common market. The exclusive distributor — the purchaser may undertake to purchase complete ranges or minimum quantities of the goods, to sell the goods under trademarks or packed and presented as specified by the supplier, and to engage in sales promotion, involving advertising, maintaining a sales network or stock of goods. The Regulation provides that distributors must be free to set their own prices.

2. Commission Regulation No. 1983/83, OJ L173 30.6.1983, P1.
3. Competition Authority Decision No. 144, 5 November 1993.

44. EU Regulation No. 1984/83, of 22 June 1983, is a block exemption regulation which applies Article 85(3) of the Treaty of Rome to categories of exclusive purchasing agreements. The regulation entered into force on 1 July 1983 and it expires on 31 December 1997.[4] The main features of the regulation are summarised in the Authority's Motor Fuels Category Licence.[5] The general provisions regarding what is and is not permissible are very similar to those of Regulation 1983/83. The exclusive purchasing agreement, however, must have a maximum duration not exceeding five years, although it may be renewed, and it must not cover more than one type of goods which are not connected to each other either by their nature or by commercial usage. Under the terms of the Regulation the reseller must be free to set prices. 4.5

45. EU Regulation No. 556/89 of 30 November 1988, is a block exemption regulation which applies Article 85(3) of the Treaty of Rome to categories of know-how licensing agreements. It came into force on 1 April 1989 and applies until 31 December 1999.[6] Know-how, for the purpose of this regulation, is defined as 'a body of technical information that is secret, substantial and identified in any appropriate form'.

46. The regulation exempts agreements involving the transfer of know-how from the provisions of Article 85(1). The regulation recognises that such agreements are pro-competitive and have beneficial effects on the economy by facilitating the transfer of technology and boosting innovation. The regulation lists obligations of a restrictive nature that benefit from automatic exemption pursuant to Article 85(3) of the Treaty. A know-how licensing agreement to which only two undertakings are party and which contains one or more of these obligations is exempt from the provisions of Article 85(1). Obligations included are requirements that the licensee not divulge the know-how to third parties, grant sub-licenses, assign the license or exploit the know-how where it remains secret after termination of the agreement. A number of obligations involving territorial rights and protection are also included.

47. EU Regulation number 4087/88 of 30 November 1988 is a block exemption regulation which applies Article 85(3) of the Treaty of Rome to categories of franchising agreements. It came into force on 1 February 1989 and remains in force until 31 December 1999.[7] Franchising agreements essentially consist of licences of industrial or intellectual property rights (trade-marks or names or know-how) to be exploited for the purpose of selling goods or providing services to end-users in premises of uniform appearance and with the same business methods.

48. The Block Exemption applies to agreements which contain at least one of a number of specified restrictions including that of territorial protection granted by the franchisor and the obligation on the franchisee not to deal in goods competing with those manufactured by the franchisor or bearing its trademark. The regulation also contains a list of restrictions which, if present in an agreement, prevent the application of the exemption. This applies in particular to market sharing between competing manufacturers, clauses unduly restricting the franchisee's choice of suppliers or customers and to cases where the franchisee is restricted in determining its prices.

(g) *Subsequent Developments*

49. Following a meeting with representatives of the Authority on 16 June 1992, Musgraves proposed the following amendments to the licence agreement. In relation to clause 3(e)(iii), Musgraves submitted that the wording of the clause should be amended to read:

> To stock and display all SuperValu brands, either at or below the price recommended by the Wholesaler.

4. Commission Regulation No. 1984/83, OJ 173, 30.6.1983 P5.
5. Competition Authority Decision No. 25, 1 July 1993.
6. Commission Regulation No. 556/89, OJ L461, 4.3.1989, P1.
7. Commission Regulation No. 4087/88, OJ L359, 28.12.1988, P46.

4.5 50. Musgraves proposed the insertion of an additional clause in the standard licensee agreement as follows:

> The retailer hereby covenants with the Wholesaler so long as this Agreement is in force (a) to carry on his business as Supermarket Operator from the premises (b) and further that he shall not, without the consent of the Wholesaler, which consent shall not be unreasonably withheld, carry on the business of Supermarket Operator in another premises in the Republic of Ireland. In consideration of the terms of this Agreement, the retailer acknowledges and agrees that such restriction is reasonable and valid.

51. The Authority informed Musgraves of its concerns regarding several aspects of the agreements. Following discussions, Musgraves proposed a number of further amendments to the licencee agreements in a letter dated 16 November 1993. These are set out below.

Clause 3(e)(iii) 'To stock and display all SuperValu brands. The retailer can set his own retail prices, the prices being circulated by the wholesaler being merely suggestions. The retailer, is, however, recommended not to exceed the recommended prices.'

Clause 5 '(i) in order to ensure compatibility with the wholesaler's computer based systems, to purchase all equipment which interfaces with the computer systems from one of two suppliers nominated by the wholesaler,

(ii) for all other equipment, to comply with the wholesaler's standards and specifications for the equipment and the presentation of the contract premises and transport.'

Clause 12 It was proposed to retain the existing clause 12(i) which prevented the transfer of sale of the premises to a competitor of Musgraves. In addition the following amendments were proposed:

12(ii) 'the licensee undertakes that if he wishes to sell the premises he will inform the wholesaler of his intention and allow the wholesaler to offer to purchase the premises on the same terms as all other parties.'

(iii) the licensee agrees to give the one year's notice of his intention to sell the premises to a competitor of the wholesaler.'

In place of the old clause 12(iii) which included a one year post term ban it was proposed to include a new clause 12(iv) which stated that:

> the licensee agrees not to engage, directly or indirectly for six months after the expiry or termination of this agreement, in any similar business in the same area [or in any other area where he would be in competition with another SuperValu outlet].'

In the case of the franchise agreements Musgraves proposed the following amendments: Musgraves proposed amending clause 2(v), so as to allow the franchisees to arrange their own insurance, subject to a requirement that Musgraves determine the appropriate level of insurance required and for the franchisee to produce evidence of insurance. Clause 2(x), would be amended to allow the franchisees to appoint their own auditors subject to Musgraves agreement which would not be unreasonably withheld. Musgraves proposed reducing the post-term non-compete provision in clause 2(xx), from 12 to 6 months and its scope from 5 miles to 1 mile in country areas, thereby making it the same as in city areas. Musgraves proposed adding to the end of clause 3(i), the words 'except where the know-how has become generally known or easily accessible.'

52. It was indicated to Musgraves that most of the proposed amendments were acceptable to the Authority. It was pointed out, however, that as Musgraves recommended prices for most of the goods sold by the retailers and as the retailers could not exceed such prices for goods on promotion, clause 3(e)(iii) as amended should apply to non-own brand goods also. It was also indicated that while a six month post-termination non-compete clause was acceptable the remaining provisions of clause 12 were not. It was also pointed out to the parties, that while

they had sought to justify these provisions on the grounds that Musgraves had borne the cost of building and developing the stores and should therefore be protected against their being sold to competitors, in fact the vast majority of stores were owned by the retailers themselves and it was they who had paid for their construction and development. 4.5

53. Musgraves then submitted further amendments to the agreement in a letter dated 14 February 1994. These were as follows:

Licensee Agreements

Clause 3(e)(iii) — To stock and display all SuperValu brands. The Wholesaler provides recommended selling prices as guidelines. The Retailer is, however, recommended not to exceed the recommended prices of SuperValu and other brands when they are on promotion.

Clause 5 — To substitute for existing clause 5.

(i) In order to ensure compatibility with the wholesaler's computer systems to purchase all equipment which interfaces with the computer systems from one of two suppliers nominated by the Wholesaler,

(ii) for all other equipment, to comply with the Wholesaler's standards and specifications for the equipment and the presentation of the contract premises and transport.

Clause 12 To substitute for the existing clause 12:

In further consideration of the financial, trading and commercial assistance given by the Wholesaler to the Retailer, the Retailer further agrees and covenants as follows:

(a) where the Retailer has purchased the site or premises from the Wholesaler, or where the Wholesaler has made the site or premises available to the Retailer,

(i) If it is decided to dispose of the Retailer's interest in the premises in the ten years after purchase, to offer to the Wholesaler the first option to purchase the premises at a price to be agreed between the parties. In default of agreement the price shall be determined by an independent valuer nominated by the Wholesaler and approved by the Retailer, such price to be determined on the basis of the then prevailing market value for the premises, with vacant possession having regard to the location of the premises. The Wholesaler shall have one month from the determination of the price aforesaid to enter into an Agreement for Sale to purchase the same.

(ii) after the expiry of ten years, the Retailer undertakes that if he wishes to sell the premises he will inform the Wholesaler of his intention and allow the Wholesaler to offer to purchase the premises on the same terms as all other parties.

(b) where the Retailer has not purchased the site or premises from the Wholesaler,

(i) the Retailer undertakes that if he wishes to sell the premises, within ten years after the date of this agreement, he will inform the Wholesaler of his intention and allow the Wholesaler to offer to purchase the premises on the same terms as all other parties.

(ii) after the expiry of ten years from the date of this agreement, if the Retailer sells the premises without allowing the Wholesaler to offer to purchase the premises the Retailer undertakes to give one year's notice of the determination of this agreement.

(c) the Retailer agrees not to engage, directly or indirectly, for a period of one year after the expiry of this agreement, in any similar business within one mile of the Premises.

Additional clause 13(b) existing clause becomes clause 13(a). The Retailer hereby covenants with the Wholesaler so long as this agreement is in force (a) to carry on his business as Supermarket Operator from the premises, (b) and further that he shall not, without the consent of the Wholesaler, which consent shall not be unreasonably withheld, carry on the business of Supermarket Operator in another premises in the Republic of Ireland. In consideration of the terms of this agreement the Retailer hereby acknowledges and agrees that restriction is reasonable and valid.

54. The Authority wrote to Musgraves on 21 February 1994 asking for an explanation for the change in the proposed wording of clause 3(e)(iii). In a reply, dated 4 March 1994, Musgraves stated that they had re-considered the wording proposed in their letter of 16

4.5 November 1993. They now felt that such wording would have a considerable effect on the group and they could not accept it. The wording of 16 November stated that retailers were free to set their own prices but were recommended not to exceed the recommended price of SuperValu own brands when they were on promotion. Musgraves argued that although the revised wording did not explicitly state that retailers were free to set their own prices it was implied. Nevertheless they went on to state that the reason for changing the proposed wording was because Musgraves wished the recommended prices in the case of goods on promotion to be maximum prices. They advanced various arguments to justify their setting maximum prices.

Franchise Agreements

55. Clause 2(v) — in substitution for existing clause 2(v).

(i) The franchisee shall insure and keep insured throughout the term of this agreement with an insurance company of repute, all stocks in the premises and all equipment and fixtures and fittings therein, and shall also insure against all claims for Public Liability and Employers Liability together with such consequential loss, together with cash in transit and on the premises, at a level which shall be fixed at the discretion of the Company and shall further insure and continue to keep insured such risks as the Company may at its sole discretion deem to be prudent and practical in the circumstances of this agreement and in the circumstances of the ownership and operation of the shop.

(ii) The Manager shall furnish to the Company a copy of the policies and the acknowledgement that cover is in place for a period of 12 months, at least two weeks before the renewal date of the policy. If the Manager fails to provide the required evidence of insurance, the Company may insure all of the franchisee's risks temporarily and all charges arising from such insurance shall be paid to the Company by the manager on presentation of an invoice for such charges. Such charges shall not be deemed to form any part of the Management Charge herein referred to.

Clause 2(x) — in substitution for existing clause 2(x).

The appointment of an Auditor by the Manager shall be subject to the agreement of the company which agreement shall not be unreasonably withheld.

Clause 2(xx) — in substitution for clause 2(xx).

Not for a period of one year from the determination of this agreement either alone or in association with or in the employment of any other person to engage or be engaged directly or indirectly in any business in the field of sale of groceries or any business allied thereto within a radius of a mile of the Managed Premises.

Clause 3(i) — in substitution of second paragraph of clause.

On the determination of this agreement whether by affluxion of time or otherwise, the Manager shall forthwith discontinue any or all use of the name SuperValu and any other of the trade marks or logos referred to in this Agreement or any other of the trade marks or logos referred to in this agreement or any equipment or items bearing the name or trade mark of the Company or the logo thereof, and shall forthwith remove from display all advertisements, signboards or name plates supplied or used in connection with the exploitation of this agreement, and shall not in any way whatsoever use the name of nor similar kind or routine service or method of selling grocery products whereby the public could be misled into believing that they are in any way associated with the marketing from the Managed Premise or any other Premises except where the know-how has become generally known or easily accessible.

56. The Authority issued a Statement of Objections to Musgraves on 26 April 1994 indicating its intention to refuse their request for a certificate or licence in respect of the notified agreements. Musgraves responded in a letter dated 26 May 1994 with further arguments in support of their request. An Oral Hearing was held on 28 June 1994 at which further arguments were advanced by Musgraves.

57. With regard to clause 3(e)(iii) Musgraves argued that it was absolutely essential in their view, for the competitiveness of the SuperValu and Centra stores, that Musgraves should be

able to specify the maximum prices of goods on promotion regardless of whether they were own brand or suppliers' brands. They considered that there was nothing anti-competitive in a supplier or a wholesaler being able to determine a maximum price. They then proposed a further amendment to clause 3(e)(iii) as follows: **4.5**

To stock and display all SuperValu brands. The wholesaler provides recommended selling prices as guidelines. The retailer must not exceed the recommended price of the SuperValu and other brands when they are a nationally advertised promotion.

Musgraves stated that if they or any of the other wholesalers with symbol groups could not set maximum prices for goods on promotion, there would be no meaningful future for group trading.

58. In relation to the proposed amendments to clause 12 Musgraves argued that it did not give them an option to purchase but merely allowed them to bid for the premises in a fair way. They submitted that it would provide them with a minimum protection against a takeover of outlets by stealth without their ever having the opportunity to purchase the outlet.

Assessment

59. The Authority is charged with deciding whether to issue a certificate or a licence to agreements notified to it. It accepts amendments to notified agreements and, where such amendments have been made, it decides whether the amended agreement satisfies the criteria for a certificate or licence. In this instance the parties have proposed a large number of possible amendments following indications from the Authority that certain clauses in the notified agreements did not, in its view, meet the requirements for a licence. These various proposals have not fully dealt with the Authority's concerns. The Authority has therefore taken a decision in respect of the notified agreements as these are the agreements before it. For purposes of clarity it gives its views concerning a number of the proposed amendments. Considerable time has been expended in dealing with the present notifications. In particular the parties have been given numerous opportunities to propose amendments. It will not be possible to repeat this in future cases.

(a) *Section 4(1)*

60. Section 4(1) of the Competition Act states that 'all agreements between undertakings, decisions by associations of undertakings and concerted practices which have as their object or effect the prevention restriction or distortion of competition in trade in any goods or services in the State or in any part of the State are prohibited and void'.

(b) *The Parties and the Agreements*

61. The notified agreements involve Musgraves plc and a number of independent retailers — 'the licensees', and 'the franchisees'. The latter group operate SuperValu or Centra outlets which are owned by Musgraves. Musgraves and the licensees are engaged for gain in the grocery business and are therefore undertakings within the meaning of section 3(1) of the Competition Act. The franchisees are engaged for gain in the supply of grocery goods and the provision of associated services since they keep any profit made after meeting costs and paying the service charge to Musgraves. Franchisees are risk takers — they are involved in buying stock for resale with no guarantee that a profit will be generated from turning over the stock acquired. In the Authority's view, franchisees are also undertakings within the meaning of the Act.

(c) *Applicability of section 4(1)*

Standard SuperValu Licensee Agreement

Purchasing Requirements

62. The primary feature of the agreement, which is contained in Clause 3, is that the licensee

4.5 is obliged to purchase his requirements from Musgraves or a supplier appointed by Musgraves. Therefore this provision constitutes an exclusive purchasing arrangement which lasts for the duration of the agreement. The Agreement is of indefinite duration although there is provision for its termination. Clause 14 allows either party to terminate the agreement by giving three months' notice in writing to the other party.

63. Under Clause 3(c) and 3(d), licensees are required to purchase from Musgraves or from suppliers nominated by them. In this respect it should be noted that SuperValu/Centra are the third largest retail grocery operation in Ireland behind Dunnes Stores and Powers (see table 2) with outlets throughout the State. The exclusive purchasing requirement has a twofold effect. It restricts retailers from buying from anyone other than Musgraves or suppliers approved by Musgraves, thereby preventing licensees in the Musgraves operation from obtaining goods on more favourable terms than they can get through Musgraves. In addition, it denies many suppliers of grocery goods and allied products and services the opportunity of dealing with a considerable proportion of the retail grocery market other than through Musgraves. Freedom of choice in the supply and distribution of grocery goods is, in the Authority's view, restricted to an appreciable extent as a result of these agreements. The Authority considers, therefore, that these provisions have the object and effect of preventing, restricting or distorting competition in goods in the State, and offend against section 4(1) of the Act.

64. The Authority believes that an exclusive purchasing agreement must be considered in its economic and legal context and as part of a network of such agreements by one supplier, and if necessary, as part of a series of networks of several suppliers.

65. While each individual agreement might generally have relatively little effect on competition, all the licence agreements together form a network of restrictive agreements for the distribution of grocery and associated products and services. No licensee can purchase their requirements from anyone other than Musgraves, or a supplier recommended by them, for a relatively long period of time. This tends to introduce a considerable degree of rigidity into the market and makes it more difficult for a new entrant to the market to trade successfully. Musgraves stated that they listed all national suppliers and supported many local suppliers so that many suppliers had the opportunity of selling to the group's retailers.

66. Essentially, this notification concerns exclusive purchasing, however, elements of group buying are also involved. In this context, the EU Commission, in its decision on the National Sulphuric Acid Association,[8] found that the rules of a joint buying pool for the purchase of sulphur infringed Article 85(1) of the Treaty but exempted the arrangements under Article 85(3). Under these rules, each member was required to purchase at least 25% of its sulphur requirements from the pool. The Commission stated that:

> Each member of the Pool, to the extent he is committed to purchasing through the Pool, is prevented from competing with other Pool members to obtain more favourable terms from the suppliers than those obtained by the management committee.
>
> To whatever amount the member is committed, he is deprived of the choice to negotiate terms and conditions with the suppliers. . . .

67. The Commission also noted the effect of such arrangements on suppliers stating that because Pool members were committed to purchasing through the Pool, suppliers in the Community were excluded from selling directly to those members and therefore at least 21% of all sulphur imported by UK acid-makers would be supplied to one outlet, i.e. the Pool. In this case suppliers are prevented from negotiating for business directly with the SuperValu and Centra retailers — they must deal with a single purchaser, Musgraves.

68. In the Intergroup Decision[9] the EU found that Article 85(1) did not apply to an

8. Commission Decision of 29 July 1980, OJ L260, 3.10.1980, P24.
9. Commission Decision of 14 July, 1975, OJ L212, 9.8.75.

arrangement whereby an intermediary known as Intergroup acted on behalf of national SPAR chains in purchasing and selling goods. The Commission noted that the Spar chains were free not to use Intergroup's services when making purchases and they were free to determine their prices and resale terms. The Commission concluded that the agreements did not have substantial effects on competition and that the freedom of choice in both supply and demand in respect of the products concerned was not affected by the agreements to any appreciable extent. In that instance, however, purchases by Intergroup accounted for a very small proportion of sales of Spar stores. Such considerations do not apply here. Consequently, the exclusive purchasing arrangements offend against section 4(1). **4.5**

Pricing Provisions

69. Clause 3(e) of the standard licensee agreement provides that the SuperValu retailers supported the Promotional Programme. Clause 3(e)(iii) requires the licensee to stock and display all SuperValu brands at the price recommended by Musgraves. Musgraves own brand goods account for 15% of dried goods sold by the retailers.

70. Musgraves submitted that SuperValu brands are usually low margin items which are nationally advertised. They stated that they had no objection to retailers selling the products at less than the recommended prices — the restriction was on selling at more than the recommended price. The clause, however, states that the retailer is obliged to stock and display all SuperValu brands at the recommended prices. If a retailer was not to comply with this obligation, he could be considered to be in default of the agreement and Musgraves would have grounds for termination under Clause 7. In these circumstances, the scope for retailers to sell SuperValu brands at anything other than the recommended price is extremely limited. While Musgraves claimed that they had no objection to retailers selling such items at a lower price, clause 3(e)(iii) specifically required retailers to display the goods at the recommended price. Retailers cannot sell at lower prices while observing this clause. Even if these prices were not binding, resellers might believe that they were binding or that they should be followed given the wording of this clause. The Authority regards anything which enforces, or is conducive to, resale price maintenance as a serious restriction on competition.

71. The Court of Justice decision in Pronuptia indicates that the communication by the supplier to the retailer of recommended prices does not contravene Article 85(1) 'provided that there is no agreement or concerted practice that the distributor observe those prices.' The exclusive distribution and exclusive purchase block exemptions provide that the distributor or reseller must be free to determine prices and terms of resale. Similarly the franchise block exemption allows the franchisor to recommend prices but provides that the franchisee must be free to determine prices.

72. In Papiers peints de Belgique the Court of Justice upheld a Commission decision that an agreement between wallpaper manufacturers, which required retailers to display the lists of prices fixed jointly by the manufacturers, and not to make any public announcement of rebates on these prices, while allowing them to grant rebates in particular cases on a regular basis, was in breach of Article 85(1).[10] In Hasselblad the Court upheld the Commission decision that measures designed to restrict price advertising were in breach of Article 85(1).[11]

73. The arrangements involve an agreement between a wholesaler and a large number of retailers on the prices which apply to a range of products. In the Authority's view, the obligation on the retailers to display own label products at the recommended prices is likely to result in selling at those recommended prices and this is a form of resale price maintenance and therefore offends against section 4(1). It also restricts the retailers' ability to advertise lower prices and for this reason also offends against section 4(1).

74. National promotions may include non-own brand products as well as own label products.

10. Case No. 73/74 [1975], ECR 1491.
11. Case No. 86/82, [1984], ECR 883.

4.5 Musgraves have submitted that 'retailers are provided with suggested retail prices and suggested gross margins, but are free to sell below these prices if they so wish, so long as the item is not on promotion . . .'. The retailers are, in effect, required to adhere to the prices set by Musgraves for goods that are on promotion. This applies to both own brand and non-own brand products. Therefore the points made above in relation to own label goods apply equally to non-own brand products and the pricing policy used by Musgraves in respect of these products while on national promotion offends against section 4(1). In the Authority's opinion this provision is tantamount to a form of resale price maintenance for such goods and it offends against section 4(1).

75. As pointed out Musgraves also include recommended prices for all other goods stocked in their warehouse on their hand-held computer terminals (see para. 37). Although this practice is not specifically provided for in the notified agreement, the Authority believes that it forms part of the total relationship between the parties and that it should be considered in this context. This agreement is not between a supplier and its distributors. Musgraves is a wholesaler and organises a central billing arrangement for the SuperValu and Centra retailers. The only reason advanced to justify the recommending of prices by Musgraves is that the recommending of prices by suppliers is a long accepted practice. The Groceries Order, while allowing suppliers to recommend prices, does not allow wholesalers to do so. Consequently the arrangement is not in line with long accepted practice. The Authority accepts that Musgraves is not acting purely as a wholesaler in the context of the notified agreements. It is to a degree akin to a franchisor in that it has established and developed a uniform system for grocery retailing under the SuperValu and Centra names. The Authority believes therefore that there is nothing anti-competitive in Musgraves recommending prices per se in the context of these agreements. It notes, however, that under EU law, suppliers are only allowed recommend prices provided there is no concerted practice that retailers observe these prices. Given that retailers are required by the agreement to display own brand items at the recommended price, and to adhere to recommended prices for all items on promotion, the Authority is concerned that they might also believe that they had to observe the 'recommended prices' for other goods. Such provisions also offend against section 4(1).

76. Musgraves proposed amending clause 3(e)(iii) to provide that the retailer would stock and display all SuperValu brands, be free to set his own prices but would be recommended not to exceed the recommended prices for such goods. In the Authority's opinion such a provision would not offend against section 4(1) since it leaves retailers free to set their own prices. The wording is in line with that accepted by the EU Commission for franchise agreements in Pronuptia.

77. Musgraves then changed their proposal. Specifically the reference to retailers' freedom to set their own prices was dropped. The new proposal referred to Musgraves providing recommended prices as guidelines and retailers being recommended not to exceed these in the case of SuperValu brands and others when they were on promotion. When asked why they were making this further change Musgraves stated that they wished to be able to fix the maximum prices at which their retailers could sell. They claimed that otherwise the group's image would be damaged. They also referred to the speed with which individual prices could change in the grocery business and the requirement that as a competitor they would need to respond to this. They stated that: 'Musgraves has the ability, by using its computer system, to inform all its retailers of the new maximum price while ensuring that the retailers are still obtaining an overall margin which allows them to stay in business.' They referred to a report prepared for the OECD Secretariat which stated inter alia that there was a difference between fixing minimum and maximum prices and that maximum prices could be used to eliminate double mark-up problems thereby increasing efficiency.[12]

78. The Authority believes that such a provision would offend against section 4(1) since,

12. OECD (1994); Competition Policy and Vertical Restraints: Franchising Agreements, OECD, Paris.

according to Musgraves, its aim is to enable Musgraves to set maximum prices, which means that retailers are not entirely free to set their own prices. In the Authority's opinion the setting of maximum prices in this fashion by a wholesaler such as Musgraves constitutes a form of price fixing which is anti-competitive. The independent retailers must be free to set prices, as setting prices on the basis of their own commercial judgment is an essential feature of the competitive process. In seeking to set maximum prices, Musgraves are going beyond what the EU Commission accepted as legitimate for a franchisor in Pronuptia i.e. they may recommend retailers not to exceed the recommended price. The Authority notes Musgraves statement that their computer system allows them to inform retailers of new maximum prices while ensuring that they are still obtaining an overall margin which allows them to stay in business. If Musgraves arrangements allows them to lower the maximum prices of some goods and ensure adequate margins for the retailers, this implies that other prices must rise to maintain the overall margin. It is for the individual retailer to decide upon the appropriate prices for the products he sells and upon his margins. The State has abolished price controls including the setting by it of maximum prices, relying instead on the competitive process to ensure that prices to the consumer are kept as low as possible. The Authority believes that in such circumstances, wholesalers or any other third party cannot be allowed to establish maximum retail prices for those retail outlets supplied by them. 4.5

79. There is also a danger that a maximum price could quite easily become the minimum price. This reinforces the problems caused by allowing a wholesaler to set maximum prices. Musgraves referred to a study prepared for the OECD Secretariat to justify the setting of maximum prices. The report on franchising indicates that three of the twenty four members of the OECD allow franchisors to set maximum prices. The study also points out, for example, that:

> All countries are very suspicious of restrictions that aim to limit the franchisee's freedom to choose their own price, and it is difficult to find another topic where there is such unanimity. Resale price maintenance isvirtually always unlawful. Only more limited restrictions — such as the use of recommended prices — are tolerated and even then sometimes only in exceptional circumstances such as promotional campaigns for the introduction of new products.[13]

80. The present arrangement is not a pure franchise agreement although Musgraves dispute this point. Musgraves themselves have pointed out that the agreement does not satisfy all the criteria of the EU Franchise Regulation. Therefore, the propositions advanced in the study are not directly applicable. The Authority does not in any case accept the arguments made in the study cited by Musgraves. The Authority believes that its views on setting maximum prices are consistent with those of competition authorities in the vast majority of OECD countries.

Equipment — Clause 5

81. Clause 5 of the standard licensee agreement as notified, requires retailers to purchase all fixtures and fittings from suppliers nominated and approved by Musgraves. Musgraves submitted that they nominated two suppliers for the retailer to choose from. Musgraves indicated that this clause was included to ensure that equipment obtained by the retailer met the standards required from a SuperValu/Centra retailer.

82. This requirement had the effect of restricting the retailer in selecting suppliers to carry out work in the retail outlet. On the supply side, it denied suppliers, other than those already approved by Musgraves, access to business available in SuperValu outlets. These suppliers have the opportunity to become approved by Musgraves every 2/3 years. To the extent that this happens there is a possibility that competition could arise. The Authority accepts that

13. P.162.

4.5 Musgraves are entitled to seek to maintain standards in those retail outlets affiliated to their symbol group. However, it considered that SuperValu retailers should be free to choose suppliers of these services provided the products supplied conform to Musgraves standards especially as ownership of the equipment rests with the licensee. In the Authority's view this clause offended against section 4(1).

83. Musgraves have proposed amending clause 5. Except in the case of equipment which interfaces with their computer system the retailers may purchase equipment from any supplier. The only requirement is that such equipment comply with Musgraves specifications and standards. Such a provision does not offend against section 4(1). The retailers would still have to obtain equipment which interfaces with the computer system from one of two suppliers named by Musgraves. This provision offends against section 4(1) for the same reasons as the original clause 5.

Post-termination Restrictions — Clause 12

84. Clause 12 as notified required the licensee (i) not to sell the business to a competitor of Musgraves, (ii) to give Musgraves first option to purchase the business and (iii) not to compete in the grocery trade within a limited radius of the business for one year. Clause 12 makes selling the business to competitors of Musgraves impossible and it seeks to enforce a non-compete clause of one year on the licensee. The licensee is also bound by this clause if he terminates the agreement under clause 14.

85. The effect of the requirement not to dispose of the business to a competitor of Musgraves is to prevent competitors, whether existing ones or new entrants, from acquiring retail outlets and thereby extending market share. Its object therefore is to prevent, restrict or distort competition. This requirement is unlikely to affect competition to any significant degree in the short term as the likelihood is that only a small number of retailers will want to sell their business at any one time. Nonetheless, over time this requirement could have a significant effect on competition. Once an outlet becomes a SuperValu outlet, it is likely to remain under that name as long as it continues as a grocery outlet. This introduces a considerable amount of rigidity into the market and makes it difficult, in particular, for new entrants to successfully enter the market. It is relevant that the restriction applies to almost 400 grocery outlets located nation-wide, with an estimated 16% of the grocery market. Musgraves argued that it was misleading to aggregate the SuperValu and Centra stores in this way. Nevertheless the fact remains that the total number of SuperValu and Centra stores is more than twice the number of stores currently owned by all of the multiple groups combined. While some of these outlets may be small, together they represent a significant proportion of all the supermarket outlets within the State. The number of SuperValu stores alone is greater than the numbers of the two largest multiples combined. The Authority does not believe that Musgraves are entitled to seek to prevent the stores being acquired by a competitor in this way. In the case of licensees, Musgraves do not own the stores. The object of this clause is to ensure that outlets which have become part of the SuperValu group are not subsequently acquired by another group or multiple, and thus it has both the object and the effect of restricting or distorting competition and offends against section 4(1).

86. Clause 12(ii) requires the retailers to give Musgraves first option on the purchase of premises being disposed of. In this connection, the Authority has considered the implications of the judgment of the High Court on 1 May, 1991, in the case of *Texaco (Ireland) Ltd v. Thomas Farrell and Esso Ireland Ltd.* Blayney J held that a pre-emption clause in a solus agreement, whereby the dealer had first to offer his premises for sale to Texaco, was in restraint of trade and was void. It should be noted that Musgraves do not make any major investment in the licensees' shops and therefore should not be in a position to dictate how these outlets are used once the licensee agreement is terminated.

87. If the retailer cannot sell the outlet to a competitor of Musgraves under 12(i) and the premises has been designed as a grocery outlet, its value to potential buyers in other markets

may not be as great as it would be to people in the grocery trade. This reduces the likelihood of the licensee getting a fair price for the premises and increases the probability that the outlet will continue within the Musgraves operation. Clause 12(ii) reinforces the restriction contained in clause 12(i). It also offends against section 4(1). **4.5**

88. Clause 12(iii) requires the retailers not to carry on the trade or business within a radius of one mile from the outlet for a period of one year. The one year non-compete clause would be acceptable where Musgraves had purchased the business including goodwill. The Authority has ruled in a number of decisions relating to the sale of a business that a non-compete clause of two years duration is acceptable. However, if Musgraves have not purchased the business they should not be permitted to keep the licensee out of the market by virtue of this provision. They may prevent him using the SuperValu name — to the extent the goodwill of the business is associated with that name, it belongs to Musgraves. Clause 12(iii) provided that the retailer could not operate as a grocery retailer from the premises for twelve months after termination of the agreement. The Authority considers that such a post-term restriction represents a restriction on competition which offends against section 4(1). It notes that EU Exclusive Purchase and Exclusive Distribution Block Exemptions do not allow such post-term restrictions. The Authority can see no reason for allowing such a restriction in this case. In the Authority's opinion the retailer is entitled to operate as a grocery retailer following termination of the agreement whether as an independent or as part of another symbol group. In the Authority's view clause12 and each of its parts restrict competition and offend against section 4(1) of the Act.

89. Musgraves have proposed a number of amendments to clause 12. Firstly they proposed that the licensee would be required to inform Musgraves of any intention to sell the premises and to allow it to purchase the premises on the same terms as all other parties and to require the licensee to give one year's notice of intention to sell to a competitor. As the original clause 12(i) remained under this proposal, the amendment appeared superfluous. Its object and its likely effect is to prevent competitors acquiring those premises and thus to restrict competition. It therefore, would offend against section 4(1). They also proposed reducing the post-term non-compete clause to 6 months. They sought to justify this on the grounds that the EU franchise Regulation allows a post-term non-compete clause for up to one year for the purpose of preventing former franchisees exploiting the know-how of the franchisor which had been provided under the terms of the agreement. While the Authority accepts that the arrangements have some elements of a franchise agreement, it does not believe that the know-how provided to the retailers by Musgraves is sufficient to justify a post-term non-compete clause. Thus even a six month restriction would, in the Authority's view, offend against section 4(1).

90. Musgraves subsequently proposed an alternative amendment to clause 12. This would distinguish between premises sold or provided to the retailer by Musgraves and those which were not. In the former case, the retailer would, if he decided to sell the premises within ten years of acquiring it, be required to give Musgraves first option to purchase the premises. After ten years if the retailer wished to sell he would have to inform Musgraves and allow them to offer to purchase the premises at the same price as anyone else. The Authority accepts that, where Musgraves have sold premises to retailers, they have invested substantially in the development and/or construction of such premises in the expectation that they would benefit from such premises being operated as part of their symbol group for some period of time. Consequently, the Authority does not believe that a requirement that the retailer would have to give Musgraves first option to buy back the premises if he wished to sell within ten years, would offend against section 4(1). After ten years the Authority can see no reason for restricting the retailer's freedom to sell to whoever he chooses. There is no justification for allowing Musgraves any advantage over any other would be buyer. The object is to try to prevent other retail groups from purchasing the store and this would-be its most likely effect. Thus it would offend against section 4(1).

91. In the case of premises not acquired from Musgraves they proposed that, where the

4.5 retailer sells the premises within ten years of the commencement of the agreement, he must inform Musgraves, and allow them to offer to purchase the premises on the same terms as anyone else. After ten years if they do not inform Musgraves of their intention to sell they must give one year's notice of intention to terminate the agreement. The Authority again concludes that the object, and the most likely effect, of such a provision is to prevent Musgraves competitors from acquiring the premises. Thus it would also offend against section 4(1).

92. Musgraves then proposed that the post-term non-compete clause remain at 12 months as originally notified. The Authority has already stated that such a restriction would offend against section 4(1).

93. Musgraves also indicated that they wished to amend the licensee agreement by inserting an additional clause 13(b) under which the licensee agreed to operate his business from the premises and not, without Musgraves consent, which should not be unreasonably withheld, carry on the business of supermarket operator in another premises in the State. The Authority accepts that such a restriction is designed to prevent retailers from using know-how supplied by Musgraves or commercial information relating to prices, promotions and other activities other than as part of the SuperValu or Centra symbol group. It would not therefore, in the Authority's opinion, offend against section 4(1).

Standard Centra Licensee Agreement

94. Clauses 3(b), 3(c) and 3(d)(iii), of the Centra licensee agreement are identical to clauses 3(c), 3(d) and 3(e)(iii) respectively of the SuperValu licensee agreement. Similarly clauses 5 and 12 in both agreements are identical. Each of these provisions offends against section 4(1) for the reasons set out in the previous paragraphs.

Standard SuperValu and Centra Franchisee Agreements

95. Clause 2(ii) of the standard franchisee agreements contain the purchasing restrictions. Under this clause the franchisees are obliged to purchase all their requirements from Musgraves or suppliers approved by Musgraves. The franchisee agreements, and therefore this requirement, last for a period of ten years. Musgraves own these outlets. They could operate these stores themselves in which case supplies would be obtained exclusively from Musgraves. They cannot be compelled to grant access to their stores to competitors as they have made a significant investment in such stores. If Musgraves choose to grant to someone else the right to operate one of their stores then a requirement for that individual to obtain their supplies through Musgraves does not offend against section 4(1).

Pricing Arrangements

96. The pricing provisions contained in clauses 3(d)(iii) and 3(e)(iii) of the Centra and SuperValu licensee agreements respectively also apply to SuperValu and Centra franchisees, i.e. they must stock and display all Musgraves own brands at the price recommended by the wholesaler. The arrangements relating to non-own brand products on national promotion and to the prices of all other goods also apply to franchisees. As already stated such arrangements offend against section 4(1) of the Act.

Supply of Equipment

97. Clause 2(iii) requires franchisees to take 'all supplies and other commodities such as advertising material, trade notices, items, packaging material, bearing a trade mark or logo of the company, and miscellaneous equipment incidental to the preparation, advertisement, supply or presentation of the business' from Musgraves or a supplier or distributor authorised by Musgraves. Musgraves have submitted that such an arrangement is designed to ensure standard format and quality. In addition they have stated that these goods can be obtained from one of three suppliers who are obliged to tender for the provision of these goods every 2/3 years. This does not offend against section 4(1) for the same reason as in the case of clause 2(ii).

Insurance

98. Clause 2(v) of the standard franchise agreement provides for the provision of insurance services. These services are organised by Musgraves and paid for by the franchisees. Musgraves have a right, as owners of the premises, to make the necessary insurance arrangements for them. As they are extending credit to the franchisees on stock supplied they are entitled to satisfy themselves as to the adequacy of insurance cover on such stock. However, this Clause restricts suppliers of insurance services, other than those approved by Musgraves, from dealing with the individual retailers. In addition, the franchisees are prevented from making their own stock insurance arrangements and from trying to negotiate better terms with insurance companies. The Authority believes that the franchisees should be free to do so, subject to satisfying Musgraves that the stock is adequately insured, and therefore this Clause offends against section 4(1) of the Act. Musgraves have proposed to amend this clause to enable the franchisees to choose their own insurer subject to satisfying Musgraves that adequate insurance arrangements for stock are in place. Such a provision would not offend against section 4(1).

Service Charges

99. Under Clause 2(vi) of the standard franchisee agreements, the franchisee is required to pay a service charge to Musgraves based on a percentage of total sales during each month. Musgraves have stated that this payment is to cover the interest charges on the franchisees' premises. The Authority is satisfied that this provision does not offend against section 4(1).

Accounting Requirements

100. Clause 2(x) provides for the nomination of an accountant by Musgraves to act on behalf of the franchisee. The accountant nominated must be acceptable to both Musgraves and the franchisee. Franchisees are independent operators and as such should be allowed to appoint accountants to act on their behalf subject to the provision that these individuals are acceptable to Musgraves. Accordingly, the Authority is of the view that clause 2(x) offends against section 4(1). Musgraves proposed to amend this clause to allow the franchisee to appoint an auditor of their choice, subject to Musgraves approval and in that case it would no longer offend against section 4(1). Clause 2(xi) allows Musgraves to examine the franchisees' books and records during business hours. These clauses allow Musgraves to monitor their investment in the franchisees' business. They also require franchisees to maintain proper records thereby facilitating the operation of a successful business. They do not restrict competition and so do not offend against section 4(1).

Inspection of Business

101. Clause 2(xii) allows Musgraves to inspect and examine the franchisee's stock and operation. Clause 2(xv) requires franchisees to perform the services forming a part of the operational system prescribed by Musgraves. Musgraves are entitled to inspect their own premises and to seek to ensure that the standards prescribed in the agreement are being adhered to. Accordingly, these clauses do not restrict competition and do not offend against section 4(1).

Opening Hours

102. Clause 2(xvi) of the standard franchise agreement provides that the retail outlet shall remain open every day, the hours of opening to be agreed between Musgraves and the retailer. In the event of dispute, Musgraves' view on opening hours will prevail. There is a possible restriction on the dealer in deciding his own opening hours, however, it is in the interests of both parties to agree on the optimum opening hours as both the retailer and Musgraves stand to benefit from such an agreement. Provided that the hours are agreed with the franchisee, this provision does not restrict the franchisee in determining opening hours, and does not offend against section 4(1).

4.5 Non-involvement in Grocery Business

103. Clause 2(xix) provides that franchisees cannot be involved, except with the approval of Musgraves, in the grocery business otherwise than as a manager of a SuperValu or Centra outlet for the duration of the agreement. Implicit in this provision is the concept that the franchisees should not compete against the business of which they are an integral part. This clause restricts the freedom of franchisees by preventing them setting up as competitors of SuperValu/Centra in the grocery business. However, it ensures that the franchisees devote all their efforts to the running of the franchise retail outlet. In addition, the small number of franchisees means that the potential effect of this restriction on competition is negligible. Therefore this clause does not offend against section 4(1).

104. Clause 2(xx) of the standard franchisee agreement provides that once the agreement has been terminated, the franchisee cannot be engaged in the grocery business for a period of one year within a one mile radius of the outlet, in a city, or a five mile radius, if the outlet is located in a rural area. It should be noted that there is no sale of business involved here and that the franchisee cannot operate from his previous place of business because this is owned by Musgraves and in all likelihood will continue to be operated as a Musgraves retail outlet by another franchisee or licensee. Accordingly, any goodwill generated by use of the Musgraves trade marks, logos, etc., will work to the benefit of the new retailer. The franchisee may have generated goodwill of a personal nature through knowledge of and dealings with local people. The Authority is of the view that this element of the goodwill properly belongs to the franchisee and that he should be allowed to benefit from his efforts in this respect and that a non-compete clause is not warranted in this instance. Accordingly, this provision offends against section 4(1) of the Act. Musgraves proposed to reduce the duration of this clause to 6 months, but subsequently changed their mind. They also proposed reducing its geographic scope to a one mile radius of the premises in country areas. Such proposals would still offend against section 4(1).

Cash Registers

105. Clause (xxii) provides that only cash registers which are supplied by Musgraves may be used and they shall remain the property of Musgraves. Each cash register has two keys, one of which is retained by Musgraves. Musgraves reserve the right to obtain access to the cash registers at any time for the purposes of checking the tally roll and can also remove them at any time and replace them with other cash registers. In the Authority's opinion this clause does not offend against section 4(1).

Repairs and Renewals

106. Clause 2(xxv) provides for the repair and renewal of franchisees' premises by Musgraves. Musgraves may insist on this work being carried out if the franchisee disagrees about the need for it. The cost of the work is borne by the franchisee. As owners of the outlets the Authority believes that Musgraves are entitled to make provision for the repair and renewal of their premises. Accordingly, this clause does not offend against section 4(1) of the Act.

Termination

107. Clause 3 of the standard franchisee agreements contains provisions for the termination of the agreements as well as post termination provisions. The Agreements may cease to have effect if the franchisee fails to observe the stipulations set out in Clause 2. Bankruptcy and default in payment for goods would bring about termination of the agreement. They may also lapse after a 10 year period. If an agreement between Musgraves and a franchisee lapses, Musgraves as owners of the premises would be likely to enter into a subsequent agreement with another franchisee for the operation of the outlet. Therefore the competitive situation would remain unchanged. The provisions in clause 3 relating to cessation of the agreements do not offend against section 4(1).

108. Clause 3 also includes post-agreement provisions. One of these provisions seeks, in the future, to prevent franchisees from using a method of selling grocery goods similar to that operated under the SuperValu/Centra names. Know-how acquired by the franchisees over the duration of the agreement could be generic in nature therefore it would not belong, in any technical sense, to Musgraves and they could not seek to enforce a provision on this basis. This provision is acceptable to the extent that the SuperValu/Centra method of selling grocery products is unique to that operation. Van Bael and Bellis note, in relation to the EU block exemption on franchising agreements that 'it is forbidden to prevent the franchisee from continuing to use the licensed know-how after termination of the agreement, where the know-how has become generally known or easily accessible'.[14] In the Authority's opinion, this provision may have the effect of unfairly restricting franchisees in any subsequent attempts they might make to re-enter the grocery business by preventing them from using knowledge of a generic nature gained through operating a SuperValu or Centra outlet. Accordingly, it offends against section 4(1) of the Act. Musgraves have proposed to amend this clause to exclude know-how which is easily accessible. Such a proposal would not offend against section 4(1). **4.5**

Applicability of section 4(2)

109. Under section 4(2), the Competition Authority may grant a licence in the case of any agreement or category of the agreements which, 'having regard to all relevant market conditions, contributes to improving the production of goods or provision of services or to promoting technical or economic progress, while allowing consumers a fair share of the resulting benefit and which does not —

(i) impose on the undertakings concerned terms which are not indispensable to the attainment of those objectives;

(ii) afford undertakings the possibility of eliminating competition in respect of a substantial part of the products or services in question'.

Standard SuperValu Licensee Agreement

Exclusive Purchase Requirement

110. The exclusive purchase arrangements in clauses 3(c) and (d) of these agreements contribute to reducing cost and improving the distribution of grocery goods. The combined purchasing power of the retailers through Musgraves enables the best possible price to be obtained from suppliers. This enables the retailers to compete more effectively.

111. Consumers benefit to the extent that some part of the savings accruing to the retailers is passed on in the form of lower prices. They also benefit from the provision of additional services such as free delivery provided by SuperValu/Centra stores. The Authority accepts that consumers have gained from the competition which Musgraves has provided for the multiples particularly in rural areas.

112. Musgraves earns its income from sales to the retailers. There is no payment by the retailer other than payment for the goods. If the retailers order stock other than through Musgraves, the whole group is weakened and its viability would be threatened. Accordingly, the Authority believes that the purchasing obligation is indispensable to the attainment of the objectives of the agreement.

113. Musgraves has a significant share of the retail grocery market, 16%. Nevertheless, others, e.g. Dunnes Stores and Powers, have larger market shares and there are numerous other competitors in the market. The Authority's view therefore is that the purchasing requirements do not afford Musgraves the possibility of eliminating competition in respect of a substantial part of the market.

14. Competition Law of the EEC, second edition, Van Bael and Bellis, P169.

4.5 114. The exclusive purchase agreement will last for as long as an agreement between Musgraves and a licensee is in force. The standard licensee agreement can be terminated at any time by the licensee although there is no specific duration for the agreement. The Authority agrees with the view of the EU Commission that if exclusive purchase agreements were of indefinite duration, this would effectively block competing suppliers and distributors access to any retail outlets permanently. However, given the fact that provision is made for the termination of the licensee agreement, the requirements for a licence in section 4(2) are satisfied.

Pricing Practices

115. The Authority does not believe that the requirement in Clause 3(e)(iii) to stock and display all SuperValu own brands at the price recommended by Musgraves contributes to an improvement in the provision of services or to promoting technical or economic progress. It believes that such benefits essentially derive from the purchasing arrangements and the associated central billing system. Given that the Authority does not consider that the pricing provisions lead to any efficiency benefits, consumers, by definition, do not benefit from such gains. The Authority also concludes that the requirements are not indispensable for SuperValu to derive the benefits from operating as a symbol group. Accordingly, the requirements for granting a licence under section 4(2) are not satisfied. Similarly the Authority considers that the requirement to sell those goods which are on national promotion at the price set by Musgraves also amounts to resale price maintenance. This requirement does not satisfy the requirements for a licence for the reasons given above.

116. In coming to the conclusion that the price arrangements do not satisfy the criteria for a licence the Authority has taken account of the fact that, in over 30 years, the EU Commission has virtually never exempted such arrangements from the prohibition contained in Article 85(1). It can see no good reason for departing from well established EC precedents in the present case.

117. Franchise agreements do not benefit from the EU block exemption on such agreements if the franchisee is restricted in determining prices. On this basis, the licensee agreement would not be exempt under EU regulations. The Authority believes for the same reasons that the proposed amendment, which would allow Musgraves to set maximum prices, would not satisfy the requirements for a licence.

Equipment

118. The arrangements for the provision of fixtures and fittings in Clause 5 of the Agreement is important to the efficient operation of the Musgraves organisation. In view of the experience of Musgraves in arranging for the provision of this type of service, it is likely that the retailers will be helped rather than hindered in their efforts to modernise, maintain and operate retail outlets by the involvement of Musgraves. Consumers may benefit from the economies of scale involved in organising these services for a large number of retail outlets as opposed to their provision on an independent basis.

119. The arrangements help to safeguard the identity and reputation of the network symbolised by the SuperValu name. However, the Authority does not believe that these obligations are indispensable to the attainment of the objectives of the agreement. It believes that the standards Musgraves seek to attain can be achieved in a less restrictive manner.

120. While these requirements have an effect on suppliers of fixtures and fittings in any attempts they make to generate business in the Musgraves outlets, the Authority believes that it is likely that they do not result in the elimination of competition in a substantial part of the market in question. Nonetheless, all the requirements in section 4(2) are not satisfied and a licence cannot be granted.

121. Under the proposed amendment to clause 5 only the restriction requiring retailers to purchase equipment which would interface with the computer system from one of two suppliers

would offend against section 4(1). The Authority believes that this would meet the requirements of section 4(2). 4.5

Post Agreement Provision — Clause 12

122. Clause 12 of the licence agreement sets out the post agreement provisions which prevent (1) licensees selling their premises to competitors of Musgraves, (2) require that first option on the purchase of the premises be given to Musgraves and (3) prevent licensees trading as independents in the locality for a period of one year.

123. In the Authority's view this clause does not contribute to improving the distribution of goods or provision of services or to promoting technical or economic progress. As there are no clear gains in efficiency, no benefit derives to consumers. The Authority does not regard these clauses as indispensable to the overall arrangement.

124. Although the EU block exemption on franchising agreements allows a post term non-compete clause of up to 1year to protect the franchisee's know-how, the Authority considers that the provision in this agreement is designed to prevent competition and not to protect know-how. Accordingly, it would not benefit from the EU block exemption even if it came within its scope. The exclusive purchase block exemption does not permit such clauses. Clause 12 fails to meet the requirements of section 4(2). The Authority believes that this is also true of the various amendments proposed to clause 12 which were found to offend against section 4(1).

Standard Centra Licensee Agreement

125. The Authority concludes, for the same reasons given in connection with the standard SuperValu licensee agreement, that:

(i) the exclusive purchasing requirement in Clause 3 satisfies the requirements for the issuing of a licence under 4(2) of the Act;

(ii) the pricing arrangements in Clause 3(d)(iii), the provisions relating to fixtures and fittings in Clause 5 and the post agreement provisions in Clause 12 fail to meet the criteria in 4(2).

Standard Franchisee Agreements

126. The pricing requirements for licensees also apply to franchisees. The Authority considers that for the same reasons outlined in paras. 115-117, the arrangements as they apply to franchisees do not satisfy the requirements of 4(2).

127. Clause 2(xx) of the standard franchise agreements prevent franchisees from engaging in the grocery business for one year within a limited radius of the premises. This provision seeks to ensure that any new Musgraves franchisee does not face competition from the outgoing franchisee for at least one year. This has the effect of restricting competition which is not in the interests of consumers. The benefits that arise from the overall arrangements will not be adversely affected by the removal of this provision. The Authority's view therefore is that it is not indispensable to the overall arrangements. This clause does not fulfil all the requirements of section 4(2).

The decision

128. Musgraves and the SuperValu and Centra licensees and franchisees are all undertakings and the notified agreements between Musgraves and the various licensees and franchisees are agreements between undertakings. The requirement that the licensees obtain all of their supplies from Musgraves or a supplier nominated by them offends against section 4(1). The exclusive purchase obligation, however, satisfies the requirements for a licence. The following provisions of the notified agreements also offend against section 4(1) for the reasons set out above:

4.5 The SuperValu Licensee Agreement

— Clause 3(e)(iii)

— Clause 5

— Clause 12

The Centra Licensee Agreement

— Clause 3(d)(iii)

— Clause 5

— Clause 12

The Franchisee Agreements

— Clause 2(v)

— Clause 2(x)

— Clause 2(xx)

— Clause 3

The Authority considers that none of these provisions satisfy the requirements for a licence as set out in section 4(2).[15] The Authority therefore refuses to issue a certificate or grant a licence to the licensee agreement between Musgraves Ltd and the SuperValu and Centra licensees, (CA/18/92E) and to the franchise agreement between Musgraves Ltd and the SuperValu and Centra franchisees, (CA/19/92E), notified on 30 April 1992 under section 7 of the Competition Act.

For the Competition Authority

Patrick Massey
Member

19 September 1994

15. The Authority believes however, that the proposed amendments to clause 5 of the licence agreements would meet the requirements for a licence. Similarly the proposed amendments to clauses 2(v), 2(x) and 3 of the franchisee agreement would not offend against section 4(1).

Competition Authority Decision No. 361, Burmah Castrol (Ireland) Ltd — Hire Purchase and Equipment Loan Agreements: 13 October 1994, Notification Nos. CA/37-38/92E 4.6

Equipment loan agreement – Equipment hire purchase agreement – Equipment to be used only in conjunction with products supplied by the supplier of the equipment – Exclusive purchasing commitment – Foreclosure effect of such agreements – Whether possibility of elimination of competition in respect of a substantial part of the products in question – Whether terms in agreements indispensable to securing benefits to the consumer – Amendment of notified agreements – Statement of Objections – Refusal of certificate and licence – Competition Act 1991 (No. 24) sections 3, 4 and 7 – EEC Regulation 1984/83

Facts: On 8 June 1992 notification was made to the Authority with a request for certificates under section 4(4) of the Competition Act 1991 or, failing that, licences under section 4(2) in respect of a standard loan of equipment agreement and a standard hire purchase equipment agreement entered into between Burmah Castrol (Ireland) Ltd ('Burmah') and the various purchasers of its lubricating oils.

Burmah, a subsidiary of Burmah Castrol plc, is an Irish registered company engaged in the manufacture, importation, marketing and distribution of various petroleum products in the State. The other parties to the notified agreements are car servicing outlets which undertake the maintenance and servicing of motor vehicles.

In addition to Burmah all the main wholesalers of petroleum products in the State also market lubricating products. Consumers purchase lubricating oil either by topping up the oil sump on a visit to a petrol station or by way of a complete oil change during an overall engine service. In the latter case the consumer is not usually present when the oil is supplied and appears to have little choice in the selection of the brand used. Topping up and a full service with oil change cannot be regarded as a close substitute for each other.

Burmah has well over 20% of the total market for all engine oils supplied by the main firms and its market share in the engine oil market is about twice that of the next largest supplier. As the outlets retailing lubricants are located throughout the State the appropriate geographical market is the State.

The notified arrangements include a standard equipment loan agreement and a standard hire purchase of equipment agreement entered into between Burmah and various retailers of its products. In each case the value of the equipment the subject of the agreement ranges from c. £500 to c. £40,000. Under the terms of the equipment loan agreement the relevant borrower agrees that the equipment shall be used exclusively for the dispensing of Burmah products and that the equipment shall be returned should the borrower cease to purchase his total requirements of lubricating oils and greases from Burmah. The agreement also contains standard covenants to keep the equipment in good repair and fully insured. Under the terms of the standard hire purchase agreement the hirer, during the currency of the agreement, agrees to stock and supply to customers only Burmah products. The rate of interest applicable to such agreements ranges from 0% to 5% with the hire periods varying from 1 to 10 years.

EEC Regulation No. 1984/83, a block exemption regulation relating to exclusive purchasing agreements, applies to agreements involving only two parties whereby one party, the reseller, agrees with the other, the supplier, to purchase specified goods from

4.6 that supplier. The supplier may be obliged not to distribute the goods or competing goods in the reseller's principal sales area and the reseller may be obliged not to manufacture or distribute goods which compete with the contract goods. The regulation states that such exclusive distribution agreements should be no longer than 5 years.

Following meetings and correspondence with the Authority Burmah agreed to amend the notified arrangements to address the concerns of the Authority. The proposed amendments were not acceptable to the Authority and a statement of objections was issued to Burmah on 27 June 1994 in response to which Burmah proposed further amendments. With regard to the equipment loan agreements of five years duration or longer Burmah proposed amending those agreements by giving the user of the equipment an option within six months from the date of the amendment to buy the equipment outright, return the equipment or retain the equipment on the same terms with the exception of the obligation to return the equipment if the user ceased to purchase their entire product requirement from Burmah. With regard to those loan agreements which had been in existence for less than 5 years Burmah proposed amending same such that for a period of 5 years from the date of the agreement the equipment shall be used exclusively for dispensing Burmah products and that on the fifth anniversary of the agreement the user would be given an option to return the equipment or purchase the equipment at its fully discounted value. Burmah further proposed to amend the hire purchase agreement where the term of hire was longer than 5 years in such manner that the exclusive use of Burmah products restriction would cease to apply on the fifth anniversary of the agreement.

Decided by the Authority

(A) In refusing to issue a certificate under section 4(4) of the Competition Act in respect of the notified agreements that:

(1) Burmah and the resellers who are party to the notified arrangements are all engaged, *inter alia*, in the supply and distribution of lubricating oils for gain and they are therefore 'undertakings' within the meaning of section 3(1) of the Competition Act 1991. The notified agreements are all agreements between undertakings, the relevant product market is that of lubricating oils for resale and the relevant geographical market is the State.

(2) The equipment supplied under the terms of the equipment loan agreement is at all times owned by Burmah who therefore has a significant proprietorial interest in such equipment. S. 4(1) of the Competition Act does not call into question the existence of a property right but the exercise of a property right may be anti-competitive in nature and may therefore fall within the scope of the activity prohibited by section 4(1).

(3) The essential feature of the arrangements under review is that Burmah supplies equipment to another party in return for which the latter agrees to use the equipment exclusively for Burmah products. An obligation on a reseller to use equipment supplied by the supplier only for the storage and sale of the supplier's goods would not *per se* offend against section 4(1) unless it had the effect of ensuring that only the goods of that supplier could be sold by the reseller. If exclusive use of equipment meant, in a particular set of circumstances, that the goods of only one supplier could be handled by the reseller, this would amount to exclusive purchasing which generally offends against section 4(1).

(4) In the present case the requirement that the equipment be used only for Burmah products does not necessarily have the object or effect that the user must purchase lubricating oils exclusively from Burmah. However some workshops would only have space for the installation of one set of equipment and even where additional space is available it may be used for better commercial purposes. The existing equipment may be geared to the workshop's entire output and it cannot be expected that sales of lubricants will increase because additional equipment is installed. While workshops could return the loaned equipment they face strong disincentives to doing so. In these circumstances the exclusive use of equipment requirement would in many cases represent an exclusive purchasing requirement and therefore offends against section 4(1) of the Competition Act 1991. 4.6

(5) The equipment loan agreement is of indefinite duration thus giving Burmah products a long period of preference and there is no clear provision for termination by the user. In the circumstances the agreement is likely to amount to foreclosure of the products of competitors and therefore offends against section 4(1).

(6) The obligation on the user to return the equipment if he ceases to purchase his total requirements of lubricants from Burmah carries the clear implication that, if the equipment is to be retained, there must be exclusive purchase of Burmah products. While short term exclusive purchasing agreements with a single customer would be unlikely to have much impact in the market for lubricants, a network of such agreements with many major customers with an indefinite duration would have a significant impact. The effects are reinforced when the agreements concern the leading firm and by far the largest supplier in the market and when other major suppliers also have exclusive purchasing requirements. The obligation to return the equipment unless all requirements of lubricants are obtained from Burmah offends against section 4(1) of the Competition Act 1991.

(7) The amendments proposed by Burmah following the issue of the statement of objections still involve exclusive use of Burmah products in the equipment and therefore still offend against section 4(1).

(8) In the case of the notified hire purchase agreements the provision for the exclusive use of Burmah products with the equipment amounts, in the circumstances, to an exclusive purchasing requirement which offends against section 4(1) of the Competition Act 1991.

(B) In refusing to grant a licence under section 4(2) of the Competition Act in respect of the notified arrangements that:

(1) The requirement in the existing equipment loan agreement to return the equipment if the user ceases to purchase its total requirements of lubricating oils from Burmah constitutes an exclusive purchasing requirement. While restraints in vertical agreements such as exclusive purchasing can produce efficiency gains such benefits do not automatically result from such agreements. On the facts of the case the notified arrangements produce a minimal, if any, reduction in distribution costs which could be shared with the consumers. While the provision by Burmah of high quality equipment does promote technical progress which benefits the consumers these benefits do not derive from the exclusive purchasing obligation. While the notified agreements only apply to a small part of the total servicing operation carried out in the market there is a risk that this type of restriction, if permitted, would be applied in all cases leading to a situation of foreclosure against new suppliers. Such agree-

4.6 ments therefore could afford undertakings the possibility of eliminating competition in respect of a substantial part of the products in question and therefore fails an essential condition of section 4(2).

(2) Under the terms of the notified arrangements high quality equipment has been supplied and high quality services are provided by Burmah which benefit the consumers. Burmah would have been unlikely to provide such equipment if it could be used freely for competing products. In this respect exclusive use for a period of time can be regarded as indispensable to securing the benefits from the supply of the equipment, which may be shared fairly with the consumer. However, the notified agreements still have a foreclosure effect because they represent exclusive purchasing and thus have the possibility of substantially limiting competition.

(3) If, in the case of the Hire Purchase Agreement, the period of exclusive use of equipment was limited to the period of the term of hire purchase or to 5 years, whichever was the shorter, this would not afford the possibility of eliminating competition to a substantial degree and in all the circumstances the conditions of section 4(2) would be fulfilled. An exclusive use requirement for any longer period however would not satisfy all the conditions of section 4(2) since it would afford the possibility of eliminating competition and would not be indispensable and would not be licensed.

(4) Under the terms of the equipment loan agreement, unlike the hire purchase agreement, the equipment never becomes the property of the retailer and can never be used for products of a competitor. The equipment itself can be replaced from time to time thus extending the period of exclusive use and hence of exclusive purchase. This presents the danger of long term foreclosure of the market to competitors' products. It could be argued that the equipment loan is not indispensable since Burmah could ensure the provision of equipment by way of cash or hire purchase so that the workshops could purchase the equipment themselves. The equipment loan agreement therefore fails to satisfy all the requirements of section 4(2) and cannot be granted a licence.

(5) The possibility of eliminating competition might be avoided if a five year limit were placed upon the equipment loan agreement whereafter the retailer would have the option of purchasing the equipment at its written down value or of returning the equipment to Burmah. The amendments to the notified arrangements proposed by Burmah allow the retailer an option to purchase or return the equipment at the expiration of five years but only upon request. At the end of the five year term Burmah appears not to be obliged to give the option to the retailer but the retailer must request that this option be given. In the absence of this request the agreement continues in existence. The suggested amendment therefore would not satisfy the conditions of section 4(2) of the Competition Act since they would involve exclusive use of the equipment for a period in excess of 5 years.

Cases, Decisions and Report referred to:

Masterfoods Ireland Ltd v. HB Ice Cream Ltd (High Court, Keane J, 28 May 1992) [1993] ILRM 145 **8.1.4**

Delimitis v. Henninger Brau (case no. 234/89), [1991] 1 ECR 935, [1992] 5 CMLR 210

EC Commission Decision Scholler Lebensmittel GmbH & Co. KG, 1993 OJ L183/1 [1993] 2 CCH 101

EC Commission Decision Langnese-Iglo GmbH, 1993 OJ L183/19 [1993] 2 CCH 123

Competition Authority Decision No. 4, ESSO Solus and related agreements, 25 June 1992 **4.1**

Competition Authority Decision No. 324 Burmah Castrol (Ireland) Ltd **4.4**

FTC Report of Enquiry into the Supply and Distribution of Motor Fuels, 1989 (Pl 7951)

Competition Authority Decision of 13 October 1994 relating to a proceeding under section 4 of the Competition Act 1991 Notifications Nos. CA/37/92E and CA/38/92E — Burmah Castrol (Ireland) Ltd 4.6

Introduction

1. Notification was made to the Competition Authority on 8 June 1992 of two standard form agreements, one regarding the loan of equipment the other regarding a hire purchase loan by Burmah Castrol (Ireland) Ltd to purchasers of its lubricating oils. The notifications requested certificates under section 4(4) of the Competition Act 1991, or, in the event of a refusal by the Competition Authority to issue certificates, licences under section 4(2). The Authority issued a Statement of Objections to Burmah Castrol on 27 June 1994. In response, Burmah Castrol proposed certain amendments to the agreements which were not acceptable to the Authority.

The Facts

(a) *Subject of the notification.*

2. These notifications relate to existing standard form agreements concerning the supplying of lubricating equipment on hire purchase terms and the loan of lubricating equipment by Burmah Castrol (Ireland) Ltd to certain resellers of lubricating oils. An existing cash loan agreement was also notified to the Authority (Notification No. CA/36/92E). Since it did not offend against section 4(1) of the Competition Act, the Authority issued a certificate in respect of the agreement.[1] A new cash loan agreement was also notified to the Authority, and this is the subject of a separate decision.

(b) *The Parties Involved*

3. Burmah Castrol (Ireland) Ltd., is an Irish registered company engaged in the manufacture, importation, marketing and distribution in the State of various petroleum products. The company is a subsidiary of Castrol Ltd, registered in the UK, and its ultimate holding company is Burmah Castrol plc. The parent company is engaged worldwide in all stages of the production and supply of petroleum products. The Burmah retail motor fuel network consists of a number of company-owned outlets and a number of dealer-owned outlets operating under the Burmah brand. In addition, lubricating products are supplied to a large number of other outlets, including petrol stations supplied by other wholesalers and other outlets, and other customers.

4. The other parties to the notified agreements are car franchise main dealers, who undertake guarantee and servicing work, including servicing and oil changes, and other non-franchise vehicle workshops which undertake car servicing. These dealers generally do not sell petrol. At the end of September 1992, over 100 customers had equipment loans and less than 100 had hire purchase loans. Each customer was a party to one of the existing agreements. About 30 other customers had cash loans from Burmah. Approximately six hundred similar customers were supplied without such agreements, but on Burmah's standard terms and conditions.

(c) *The Product*

5. The product with which the notified agreements are concerned consists of lubricants, that is any oil-based product which is used for the lubricating of a motor vehicle. Almost all Burmah lubricating products are sold under the trade name 'Castrol'. While lubricating oils are to some extent interchangeable, the product is usually differentiated as follows:

(a) top engine oils;
(b) other multigrades;
(c) monogrades; and
(d) two-stroke oils.

1. Decision No. 324 of 5 May, 1994

4.6 Top engine oils appears to be the largest category of sales.

(d) *The market*

6. Besides Burmah Castrol, all the main wholesalers of petroleum products in the State also market lubricating products. In addition to supplying lubricants to their company-owned and dealer-owned petrol stations, the wholesalers also supply motor franchise dealers and other motor workshops, motor accessory shops, other retail outlets, and direct to industrial and agricultural users.

7. According to the Report of Enquiry into the Supply and Distribution of Motor Fuels by the Fair Trade Commission in 1989 (PL. 7951), total sales of lubricating oil through retailers in 1988 were 14.8m. litres, while commercial sales amounted to 24.4m. litres. Major end-users in the commercial sector purchase lubricants direct from the wholesalers, and the retail and commercial sales of lubricants constitute distinct sections of the total lubricants market.

8. The main wholesalers supply figures of sales to Stokes Kennedy Crowley, which produces estimates of total sales of the different petroleum and oil products. The estimate of total sales of engine oils in the consumer market, that is through resellers, in 1991 amounted to over 11m. litres. Burmah Castrol, however, considers that this represented only about 85% of the full consumer lubricant market, due to the omission of suppliers who do not contribute data to Stokes Kennedy Crowley. Burmah Castrol estimates that total multigrades account for almost 90% of the sales of 11m. litres, and monogrades for 9% of the total. According to Burmah Castrol, the number of outlets of different kinds is as follows:

Type of Outlet	No. of Outlets
Franchise vehicle workshops	729
Other vehicle workshops	561
Petrol service stations	1,740
Oil and lube shops, etc.	8
Supermarkets, etc.	850
Accessory shops	53
Motorcycle shops	221
Agricultural dealers, etc.	507
Wholesale distributors	291
Fuel distributors	160
Total	5,120

Note: The number of petrol stations is much less than the total number of outlets in the State selling petrol. Many of the latter do not sell lubricating oil, and these are excluded from the figures in the Table.

Burmah Castrol estimates that each of the first three types of outlet accounts for between 15 and 20% of total sales of engine oils.

9. Consumers who purchase lubricating oil do so either:

(a) for topping up the oil sump on the forecourt of a petrol station or as a do-it-yourself operation; or

(b) for a complete oil change, usually at a motor workshop or in a lubrication bay attached to a petrol station; or

(c) for a complete oil change as part of an overall engine service, usually at a motor workshop.

In the latter case, consumers will go to the place where they purchased a new vehicle for any service under guarantee, and will often go to the same place or to another outlet franchised for their make of vehicle for subsequent maintenance and service, including oil changes. Where there is an oil change involved, consumers have little or no choice of brand, and the three activities above are so separate as to constitute quite distinct market segments. **4.6**

10. Oil may be sold in cans or plastic packages marked with the brand name of the supplier. It may also be sold by way of a bulk oil container, in which case the consumer has no way of knowing for certain which brand of oil has been supplied. Oil from bulk containers is often used for oil changes, whether or not as part of a complete service operation, and the customer is not usually present when the oil is supplied. Again, the consumer appears to have little choice of the brand of oil and cannot know which brand, or even grade, has actually been supplied. In addition, the cost of oil is usually only a small part of the cost of a complete service, and the customer is unlikely to choose an outlet for a service on the basis of the brand of oil supplied, or its price. Topping up, a single oil change, and a full service with oil change cannot be regarded as close substitutes for each other.

11. Franchised vehicle workshops are shown separately in the market estimates compiled by Burmah Castrol, and it appears that, since customers tend to go regularly to the same outlet for servicing, they can be regarded to some extent as a separate market category. The same is true to a lesser extent of other vehicle workshops. To the extent that a customer patronises the same outlet, any restraint upon the oil which may be sold there reduces the customer's freedom of choice of oil products.

12. Overall, according to its own confidential estimates, Burmah Castrol has a significant presence on the lubricating oils market as a whole and in important sectors of it. This is despite the fact that Burmah Castrol has only a small share of the petrol market and relatively few company and tied dealer outlets, where it could expect to sell mainly Castrol oils. It has well over 20% of the total market for all engine oils supplied by the main firms. Its market share in the total and top engine oils markets is about twice that of the next largest supplier. Most of its sales consist of multigrades, by far the largest selling products in the sector. In respect of franchised vehicle workshops, it is sold at a high proportion of all outlets. It supplies almost 14% of these outlets under the notified agreements. Of the non- franchised workshops, Burmah Castrol supplies a very high proportion, nearly 25% of these being supplied under the agreements. Burmah Castrol is certainly the market leader and occupies a strong position in the market for lubricating oils generally, and in the top engine oils and franchised and non-franchised vehicle workshops segments of that market.

13. Since outlets retailing lubricants are located throughout the State, the appropriate geographical market in this case is the State.

14. Up to 30 September 1991, part of the motor lubricants sector was subject to the provisions of the Restrictive Practices (Motor Spirit and Motor Vehicle Lubricating Oil) Order, 1981. The Order was repealed on the coming into force of the Competition Act on 1 October, 1991.

(e) *Financial details of the existing agreements.*

(i) Lubricating equipment loan agreement.

15. Burmah Castrol had made loans of lubricating equipment to 146 customers at 30 September 1992. The value of the equipment loaned ranged from £410 to £40,000. The equipment consisted of one or more of garage lifts, compressors, oil reels, grease reels, air reels, water reels, oil pumps, grease pumps, waste oil pumps, bulk lube oil tanks, waste oil tanks, oil flow meters, and oil monitoring units. The equipment is capable of being loaned for an indefinite period, though Burmah Castrol claimed that the borrower would presumably be entitled to terminate the loan on giving reasonable notice.

(ii) Hire purchase agreement

16. Burmah Castrol had hire purchase agreements for the purchase of lubricating equipment with 72 customers, covering 86 agreements at 30/9/92. The size of loan ranged from £600 to £40,000. The rate of interest varied from 0 to 5%. The loans had varying repayment periods,

4.6 from one to ten years. The equipment concerned was of the same type as that listed in respect of the equipment loan agreements. At a certain stage of the repayment process, in accordance with the law on hire purchase, ownership of the equipment passes from the company which provides the loan to the hirer.

(f) *The notified agreements*

(i) Loan agreement (lube oil equipment) — existing version

17. The arrangements provide for Burmah Castrol to lend lubricating oil equipment to the reseller, the hirer. In return, the hirer agrees that the equipment shall be used exclusively for the dispensing of Burmah Castrol products, and that the hirer will return the equipment if he ceases to purchase his total requirements of lubricating oils and greases from Burmah Castrol. It contains the following main provisions:

(a) The owner will lend to the hirer from the date hereof the equipment specified in the Schedule to this agreement. (Clause 1)

(b) The hirer agrees that during the continuance of this agreement, the equipment shall be used exclusively for the dispensing of 'Castrol' products, and any other types of lubricating oils and greases distributed by the owners, or any associated company of the owners from time to time. Should the hirer, for any reason, cease to purchase his total requirements of lubricating oils and greases from the owners, the hirer shall return the equipment at the hirers risk and expense as specified in Clause 2 hereof. (Clause 4)

The agreement also provides that the hirer keep the equipment in good order and repair, and that he will keep the equipment insured for a specific replacement value. It permits the company to have access to the equipment at all reasonable times in order to inspect its state of repair and maintenance. Provision is made for the owner to terminate the agreement, on seven days' notice, and to take possession of the equipment, and for the hirer to be responsible for all costs and expenses of repair and reinstatement to his property. The Schedule lists the equipment and its value.

(ii) Hire purchase agreement — existing version

18. This agreement is used where Burmah Castrol supplies equipment on hire purchase terms. It provides for the initial payment and monthly rentals. It provides that the equipment shall remain the property of the owner until a certain sum has been paid, when it becomes the property of the hirer. It also requires the hirer to keep the equipment at a specified address and not to dispose of it, and to keep it insured for the full hire purchase price, and for inspection by Burmah Castrol. It contains standard terms in hire purchase agreements concerning the right of the hirer to terminate the agreement and a restriction on the owner's right to recover the goods. The Schedule lists the equipment and details of the financial arrangements. If the equipment is for use with lubricants, its use is restricted as follows:

> Where the garage equipment or any part thereof is for use with lubricants the hirer shall during the currency of this agreement use and stock therein and supply therefrom to customers only the lubricants manufactured by the owner which shall be purchased direct from the owner and do his utmost to dispose of such lubricants in the ordinary course of business and shall not keep or allow to be kept in the garage equipment or any part thereof or use or allow to be used therewith anything whatever except such lubricants as aforesaid. (Clause 7)

(g) *EEC Regulation 1984/83*

19. EEC Regulation No. 1984/83, of 22 June 1983, is a block exemption regulation which applies Article 85(3) of the Treaty of Rome to categories of exclusive purchasing agreements.[2]

2. OJ No. L173, 30.6.83, p. 5, and Explanatory Notice, OJ No. C101, 13.4.84, p.2.

The regulation entered into force on 1 July 1983 and it expires on 31 December 1997. **4.6**

20. The regulation applies to agreements involving only two parties whereby one party, the reseller, agrees with the other, the supplier, to purchase specified goods only from the supplier, or from a connected undertaking or one entrusted by the supplier with the sale of his goods. The supplier may be obliged not to distribute the goods or competing goods in the reseller's principal sales area and at the reseller's level of distribution. For goods generally, the exclusive distribution agreement may be for no longer than five years. Besides the exclusive purchasing requirement, the only other restriction of competition that may be imposed on the reseller is the obligation not to manufacture or distribute goods which compete with the contract goods. The reseller may also undertake to purchase complete ranges or minimum quantities of the goods, to sell the goods under trademarks or packed and presented as specified by the supplier, and to engage in sales promotion, involving advertising, maintaining a sales network or stock of goods, providing customer and guarantee services, and employing staff with specialised or technical training. The benefit of the exemption may be withdrawn from a specific agreement in certain circumstances where, for example, effective competition is lacking, or market access is made difficult, or where less favourable prices are made available to exclusive purchasers than to other purchasers for resale.

21. Lubricating oil is mentioned in Title III of the Regulation, which applies solely to agreements for the supply of petroleum-based motor vehicle fuels for resale in a specified service station. Where special commercial or financial advantages have been accorded by the supplier to the reseller, the exclusive purchasing obligation for motor fuels may be imposed for a maximum period of ten years. In such service station agreements, but only in such agreements, the reseller may also be obliged not to use lubricating oil supplied by other firms where equipment is financed or made available by the supplier, but he may not be prevented from selling oil supplied by other firms.

(h) *Views of Burmah Castrol.*

22. Burmah Castrol made the following observations on the notified agreements:

> Leaving aside ancillary elements, the essential nature of the provisions of these agreements which might be regarded as restrictive is that, in return for the provision by the Company of equipment or cash to purchase equipment, the customer agrees:
> 1 to use the equipment exclusively for the Company's products; and either
> 2 to purchase the customer's entire requirements of lubricant products from the Company; or
> 3 to stock for use and use on the customer's business premises only the Company's lubricant products.

It is submitted that these restrictions do not have the object or effect of preventing, restricting or distorting competition in trade in any goods or services in the State or any part of the State.

It is submitted that the agreements, viewed individually or as a network, are not intended to prevent, restrict or distort competition. The intention of the agreements is to increase the sales of the Company's products, improve distribution and reduce costs and to maintain quality control and protect against environmental risks.

The Authority is referred in general to the decision of the High Court in *Masterfoods Ireland Ltd v. HB Ice Cream Ltd* (unreported, Keane J, 28 May 1992). As regards improving distribution, the provision of storage and dispensing equipment enables larger volumes of the Company's lubricants to be stored, thus decreasing the frequency of drops required. This could not be achieved if the customer was allowed to use the storage for products of competitors. As regards increase in quality control and the management of environmental risks, the provision by the Company of specific types of equipment enables the Company to ensure that only top quality equipment is used, thus significantly reducing chances of contamination. The exclu-

4.6 sivity is required in order to ensure that the Company can be satisfied that inferior quality products are not mixed with the products of the Company. This reduces the Company's exposure to liability claims. It should be pointed out that, except where the agreement is terminable by reasonable notice, no prohibition is placed on the customer selling competing products; the only restriction is on the use of those products. To the extent that this limits the use of the equipment, it is submitted that this is necessary for quality control and to the extent that the use of other lubricant products on the premises is prohibited, this is necessary to give effect to the prohibition on use of other lubricant products through the equipment. Essentially, there is no other effective way of policing the obligation in regard to the equipment.

The Authority is referred to the decision of the Court of Justice of the European Communities in case 234/89 *Delimitis v. Henninger Brau* [1991] 4 CMLR. At paragraph 13, the Court pointed out that if agreements providing for exclusive purchase obligations do not have the objective of restricting competition, it is nevertheless appropriate to verify whether or not they have the effect of hindering it, restricting it or distorting its interplay. In order to assess this, it is necessary to examine the agreements in their legal and economic context. In paragraph 27, the Court held that an exclusive purchasing obligation would infringe article 85(1) of the EEC Treaty if (to paraphrase) (a) the national product market concerned is difficult to gain access to for competitors which might become established in this market or increase their share of this market and (b) it is necessary that the contract in dispute contributes significantly to the blocking effect produced by the network of contracts in their legal and economic context. It is submitted that the Authority should adopt this as its basis for considering the exclusive and limited purchase obligations contained in the agreements. It is submitted that these agreements do not have any effect on entry to or increasing penetration in this market. The market is not characterised by any significant barriers to entry. The Company is of the opinion that there is a substantial market not currently tied by the provision of equipment to any supplier. The figures [supplied] for new customers during 1992 illustrate this. In addition, the Authorities attention is drawn to the successful entry into the market in the last few years of the Kuwait Petroleum Company which carries on business of selling lubricating oil. This indicates that the market remains penetrable. It is submitted that the length of the tie in this regard is not necessarily relevant and that, in this regard, the provisions of article 3(d) of regulation 1984/83/EEC should not be regarded as conclusive.

In addition, it is submitted that the exclusivity is necessary to protect the Company's property rights in the equipment, in the same way as for instance the insurance obligation, and that the Act should not be interpreted as permitting interference with these rights.

If the Authority does not accept the above submissions it is submitted in the alternative that a licence should be granted for the continuance of these arrangements on the basis that they fulfil the conditions set out in section 4(2) of the Act.

The Authority is referred to the recitals to regulation 1984/83/EEC. It is submitted that the benefits identified by the Commission as generally found in exclusive purchasing arrangements are applicable to the exclusive purchasing obligations contained in the agreements. The Authority is also referred to [the above] which discusses the benefits in terms of distribution costs arising from these agreements. It is accepted that, as regards agreements to which Title I of Regulation 1984/83 applies, the maximum term of such agreements is five years. The Company would intend to inform its customers that the restriction on purchasing other lubricants for resale does not apply beyond 5 years from the commencement of the agreement, where Title I rather than Title III applies.

The proportion of total sales covered by these agreements is approximately 7.5%. The Company does not believe that this in any way implies that the agreements do not bring about the suggested improvements in distribution in respect of that proportion of its sales.

As regards the fact that equipment supplied under hire purchase does not remain the Company's property, this is a necessary consequence of the Hire Purchase Acts'.

Burmah Castrol further explained that, in the existing agreements, the restriction on the use of other lubricant products was interpreted by the company and its legal advisors to refer only to use through the lubricating equipment. The reference to 'exclusive requirements' in the existing equipment loan agreement was not interpreted by the company as giving them exclusivity of supply. It was possible for workshops to have more than one lubricating bay, financed by more than one supplier. **4.6**

23. In a further submission, following a meeting with the Authority, Burmah Castrol stated that:

> The company confirms that, to the extent that it is obliged under the Competition Act not to apply dissimilar conditions to equivalent transactions with other trading parties thereby placing them at a competitive disadvantage, it complies fully with this obligation.

As regards the Authority's impression [stated at the meeting] that the investments represent a poor return and could therefore be regarded as having been entered into merely for the purposes of foreclosure, the company, while admitting that the restrictions placed on the dealer in these agreements is valuable, does not regard these investments as bad investments. The figures derived by the Authority do not take account of the fact that a large number of the agreements in any one year are new agreements and therefore the value of those agreements for a full year would be up to 90% greater later. In addition, many of the businesses in which investments are made will be new businesses which will take time to mature and provide the appropriate return.

It was suggested at our meeting that the cash loan and hire purchase methods may not involve financing the purchase of equipment. While we accept that provision of low cost loans or goods on hire purchase is not the same as providing the equipment, the two methods of assisting dealers are it is submitted permitted by the block exemption regulation. In our view, there is nothing on the face of the block exemption or the explanatory notice to suggest that financing must be on such terms as to be equivalent to providing the equipment. In our view, they can be clearly interpreted as alternatives to each other. We are instructed that this method of financing represents normal practice in the industry throughout Europe. Therefore, it is submitted that both forms of investment involve financing the purchase of lubricating bay or other lubricating equipment.

It is again submitted that none of the markets into which the company sells are foreclosed to any significant degree. Of the market segments listed in the first page of the market plan extract, it is considered that, apart from petrol service stations, which are to be subject to a different regime, only the franchised car and commercial vehicle work shops market (if it constitutes a separate market) is to any extent tied up. Burmah Castrol have agreements with 100 franchise dealers. The company estimates that about 50% of the dealers in this segment are not subject to any tie whatsoever and that of the remainder, the operation of the five year rule means that an average of 20% of those become free every year. The company estimate, therefore, would be that at any time only 40% of the segment is subject to a tie at any one time. The company believes that the criterion to be used in determining whether or not an agreement or bundle of agreements restrict competition within the meaning of section 4(1) of the Competition Act should be the same as those identified by the European Court of Justice in the Delimitis decision at paragraph 23 which reads:

> If an examination of all similar contracts entered into on the relevant market and the other factors relevant to the economic and legal context in which the market must be examined shows that the agreements do not have the cumulative effect of denying access to that market to new national and foreign competitors, the individual agreements comprising the bundle of agreements cannot be held to restrict competition within the meaning of Article 85(1) EEC. They do not, therefore, fall under the prohibition laid down in that provision.

4.6 While it is accepted that Article 85(1) is slightly different from section 4(1), the company does not believe that the difference is material in this context.

The company also point out that, as shown by the Statoil acquisition of BP Ireland, there are real concrete opportunities to acquire market share by acquisition.

In any event, the company does not accept that the franchise dealer network can be regarded as a separate market and believes that the market as a whole is not foreclosed to access by acquisition or otherwise and that, as a result, the Authority should certify its opinion that the arrangements do not offend against section 4(1).

The company believes that consumers receive a fair share of the benefits of these agreements. With a few exceptions, the retail customers in all market segments, including motor vehicle franchisees, are single operations although in some cases they are backed by motor importers. It is not the practice of such motor importers to invest in equipment for the retailer. The retailers themselves would evidently not have the resources to make or finance investments of the type provided by the company. Effectively, therefore, it is only through investments of the type made by the company and its competitors that the consumer can obtain the benefit of the equipment which the company supplies. This equipment is, as far as possible, maintained at a state of the art level and includes a wide range of special products to respond to the increasing wave of new technical requirements. The company provides technical services and consultancy services and also laboratory and analytical services, many of which are unique in Ireland. In addition, Burmah Castrol has been awarded the ISO9002 Standard for its services. While the consumer may not appreciate the benefits which are thus supplied, they do in fact enable the retailer to provide a better service to the consumer than would otherwise be the case'.

Subsequent developments

24. Following further meetings and correspondence with the Authority, Burmah Castrol agreed by letter of 8 April 1994 to amend its agreements in order to address the concerns of the Authority. Since the amendments proposed were not acceptable to the Authority, a Statement of Objections was issued to Burmah Castrol on 27 June 1994. In response, Burmah Castrol proposed further amendments. In respect of the equipment loan agreement, they enclosed two draft letters, one for agreements entered into less than five years ago and another for agreements with a term of greater than five years to run. They stated that there was a distinction between agreements which were more than five years old and those which were less than five years old. In the former case, a proposed option could now be exercised.

25. The draft letter for agreements entered into five years ago or more contained the following:

> 'Following discussions with the Competition Authority, we have agreed that these Agreements will be modified so that, after 5 years from the start of the Agreement, the customer would have the option of purchasing the equipment at its written down value or returning it to Burmah Castrol. . . .
>
> If within 6 months from the date of this letter, you either buy the equipment or return it, your obligations under the Agreement will end on purchase or return. Otherwise, the agreement will remain in full force and effect except the obligation to return the equipment if you cease to purchase your entire requirements from us'

26. The draft letter for agreements entered into less than 5 years ago contained the following:

> We have agreed to amend clause 4 of the Agreement by replacing the entire existing clause 4 with the following:—
>
>> The Hirer agrees that for a period of five years from the date of this Agreement, the equipment shall be used exclusively for the dispensing of 'Castrol' products and any

other type of lubricating oils and greases distributed by the owners or any associated company of the owners from time to time. **4.6**

Clause 1 will also be altered to read:

> The Owner will lend the Hirer, for a period of 5 years from the date of this Agreement, the equipment specified in the Schedule to this Agreement.
>
> At the end of 5 years from the original date of your agreement, you will be given, on request, the option to return the equipment to us or to purchase it from us at its fully discounted value. The rest of the Agreement as at the date hereof is confirmed and is unaffected by these changes.

27. Burmah Castrol also enclosed a draft letter to be sent to customers with Hire Purchase Agreements which were for a term of longer than 5 years. They stated that the Hire Purchase Agreement contained options to purchase equipment and options to return the equipment to the Company, which were regulated by the Hire Purchase Acts. The only change was that the 'exclusive use' restriction ceased to apply five years from the date of the agreement. As this would be the case in any event for agreements which were entered into for periods of less than five years, no amendment was necessary to such agreements. In a letter of 8 April 1994, however, Burmah Castrol had stated that:

> . . . the equipment in the case of a hire purchase agreement becomes the property of the hirer under the terms and conditions of the Hire Purchase Acts, 1946-1960 (as the law now stands). Within the balance of the five year term, the Company would propose to have the exclusive use of the equipment for its products.

Assessment

28. The Authority is charged with deciding whether to issue a certificate or a licence to agreements notified to it. It accepts amendments to notified agreements and, where such amendments have been made, it decides whether the amended agreement satisfies the criteria for a certificate or licence. In this instance the parties have proposed some amendments following indications from the Authority that certain clauses in the notified agreements did not, in its view, meet the requirements for a licence. These various proposals have not fully dealt with the Authority's concerns. The Authority has therefore taken a decision in respect of the notified agreements as these are the agreements before it. For purposes of clarity it gives its views concerning the proposed amendments.

(a) *Applicability of section 4(1).*

29. Section 4(1) of the Competition Act 1991, prohibits and renders void all agreements between undertakings which have as their object or effect the prevention, restriction or distortion of competition in trade in any goods or services in the State or in any part of the State.

30. Burmah Castrol and the resellers who are party to the notified agreements are all engaged in the supply and distribution of lubricating oils for gain, among other activities, and they are therefore 'undertakings' within the meaning of section 3(1) of the Act. The notified agreements are all agreements between undertakings. The relevant product market is that of lubricating oils for resale, and particularly that part which is supplied to franchised and non-franchised motor vehicle workshops. The relevant geographical market is the State.

(i) The equipment loan agreement — existing version

31. The two main restrictions in the existing equipment loan agreement are:

(a) the equipment shall be used exclusively for the dispensing of Castrol products; and

(b) the equipment shall be returned should the recipient cease to purchase his total requirements of lubricating oils and greases from Castrol.

4.6 32. The equipment which is the subject of the loan agreements is owned by Burmah Castrol, is loaned to the dealer, and may be reclaimed by Burmah Castrol if the agreement is terminated, or if the dealer ceases to purchase Castrol products exclusively. While no time limit has been placed upon the duration of the agreement, Burmah Castrol have claimed that it could be terminated by the dealer at any time after giving reasonable notice. While the value of the equipment is fairly small in some cases, it is substantial in others.

33. Since the equipment supplied is owned at all times by Burmah Castrol, they have a significant proprietorial interest in the equipment. The Authority quite clearly accepts that section 4(1) does not call into question the existence of the property right. The exercise of a property right, however, may be anti-competitive in nature, and may therefore fall within the scope of the activity prohibited by section 4(1).

34. Suppliers of goods for resale do not usually also supply equipment for the storage of the goods or from which they are dispensed or sold. Where such equipment is supplied, however, there is often a requirement that the equipment be used exclusively for the supplier's goods, and not for other goods, particularly competing goods. Recent cases in respect of Article 85 of the Rome Treaty have involved the exclusive use of ice cream freezer cabinets and are of considerable relevance. The producers of Mars ice cream complained to the EC Commission that the two main German ice cream manufacturers were preventing access by Mars to the market by requiring resellers to sell their products exclusively from freezer cabinets supplied and owned by the suppliers, and also by requiring that dealers purchase exclusively from one supplier. In Ireland, Mars brought an action against HB Ice Cream Ltd (a subsidiary of Unilever, as is one of the German firms) alleging infringements of Articles 85 and 86 of the Treaty because of the requirement of freezer exclusivity by HB. (HB also brought a counter-claim against Mars). The EU Commission, by decision of 25 March 1992, took interim measures against the German firms, primarily against the exclusive purchasing requirement. This decision was not published in the Official Journal, and is the subject of an appeal to the EU Court of First Instance. Final decisions in the cases were taken by the EU Commission on 23 December 1992, ruling against the exclusive purchasing requirements.[3]

35. In the High Court cases, judgment was delivered by Keane J On 28 May 1992 (not yet reported), in the course of which he said:

> At the outset, two points should be noted. First, the fact that the impugned term is unarguably intended to prohibit the retailer from stocking other products in the cabinet does not of itself mean that the term is automatically void under Article 85(2). . . .

In the case of the agreements in issue here, one of the principal objects is to ensure that HB's competitors do not obtain an advantage over them by obtaining cabinet space for the display and storage of their products for which they have not had to pay and which is provided to them free of charge by HB. This cannot be regarded as an inherently anti-competitive objective. . . .

Again, in this context, the fact that the agreements do not prevent the retailers from selling competing products is of great importance, since in outlets where there is room for more than one cabinet the exclusivity term of itself cannot have the effect of excluding competitors. Even in outlets where there is room for only one cabinet, there is nothing to prevent the retailer from terminating the agreement at any stage and either buying a cabinet himself to stock any brands he wishes or obtaining a cabinet from another supplier. . . .

Far from being a supplementary obligation which has no connection with the subject of such a contract, the exclusivity term is of the essence of the contract, since where the cabinet is supplied free of charge the whole purpose of the contract would be frustrated from the supplier's point of view if such a term were not to be included.

3. Commission decisions of 23 December 1992 under Article 85 — Scholler Lebensmittel GmbH & Co. KG, OJ L183, 26.7.93, p.1; and Langnese-Iglo GmbH, OJ L183, 26.7.93, p. 19.

I have, accordingly, come to the conclusion that Mars have failed to establish that the agreements in question are prohibited by Article 85(1) and that hence they are not void by reason of Article 85(2).... **4.6**

The cabinets are supplied by HB for one purpose alone, the storage and display of their products. If they were available to all comers without restriction, then it seems to me that their property rights would have been very significantly eroded indeed'.[4]

It is understood that the judgment has been appealed to the Supreme Court.

36. In the EU decisions on exclusive purchase agreements for ice cream, mentioned in para. 34, the Commission referred in the following manner to exclusive use of freezer cabinets:

> (134) An exhaustive account of all the barriers to entry to the relevant market will not be attempted here (other examples would be the technology and know-how needed for the production of impulse ice-cream and the consumer preferences which have built up after many years of experience and advertising); but special mention should be made of the insulating effect on the relevant market as a whole of the restrictions on the use of the freezer cabinets which are everywhere supplied to retailers by the established manufacturers (recital 55).
>
> (135) Clearly, retailers are allowed the use of these freezer cabinets, which are needed for the sale of impulse ice-cream, without having to bear the cost, or at any rate the entire cost, so that by giving up their commercial freedom they avoid having to make the corresponding investments themselves. Even competitors who are ready and willing to follow this customary trade practice are restricted in the competition they can allow. They must persuade dealers either to replace their freezer cabinet or to install further cabinets.
>
> (136) A trader who replaces his freezer cabinet must give up selling the products of his current supplier. He will not do so if the current supplier, like SLG, is strong on the market, and the competitor is less well known or offers only a partial range which does not provide a full alternative to the earlier one.
>
> (137) The possibility of installing further cabinets is limited: there may be no space available, or what space there is may be used for commercial purposes other than the sale of ice-cream. In the traditional trade there will be many sales outlets with no space for further cabinets. It might be thought that in other shops space could surely be found somewhere for a freezer cabinet, even if only a small one, as a general rule; but in fact this view seriously misjudges the constraints under which grocery retailing in particular operates. Firstly, impulse ice-cream cannot be put on offer just 'somewhere'; it is intended for immediate consumption, and must be displayed very close to the check-out desk. And every section of the total surface of a retail store generally has a specific function. The existing freezer cabinets are already geared to the outlet's total requirements. Nor can it generally be expected that sales of ice-cream will increase substantially if further cabinets are installed. The effort and space devoted to a new cabinet is lost to other commercial purposes, without securing additional turnover.[5]

37. The essential feature of the arrangements under review is that Burmah Castrol supplies equipment to another party in return for which the latter agrees to use the equipment exclusively for Castrol products. An obligation on a reseller to use equipment supplied by the supplier only for the storage and sale of the supplier's goods would not, in the view of the Authority, per se offend against section 4(1), unless it had the effect of ensuring that only the goods of that

4. The High Court. Cases between Masterfoods Ltd trading as Mars Ireland and HB Ice Cream Ltd, and between HB Ice Cream Ltd, and between HB Ice Cream Ltd and Masterfoods Ltd trading as Mars Ireland. Judgment of Keane J delivered on 28 May 1992, not yet reported.
5. Scholler Lebensmittel, op. cit., pp 15 and 16.

4.6 supplier could be sold by the reseller. The use of equipment for the goods of a competitor results in the latter getting a 'free ride' in, and a competitive advantage from, the use of equipment for which the competitor did not pay. If exclusive use of the equipment, however, meant, in a particular set of circumstances, that the goods of only one supplier could be handled by the reseller, this would amount to exclusive purchasing. The reseller could not purchase competing goods from other suppliers, nor could competitors sell to that reseller. As in the Esso[6] case the Authority considers that exclusive purchasing agreements generally offend against section 4(1) (see also para. 40). There can be no general presumption under the Competition Act either in favour or against exclusive use of equipment obligations, and each case must be examined on its merits in the light of the prevailing economic circumstances.

38. In the present case, the requirement that the equipment only be used for the dispensing of Castrol products, while it means that it cannot be used for the products of competitors, does not necessarily have the object or effect that the user of the equipment must purchase lubricating oils exclusively from Castrol. While in many workshops there would be space for the installation of equipment for storing and dispensing the oil of one or more competitors, equally, in many instances there would not. What space there is may be better used for other commercial purposes. The existing equipment may be geared to the outlet's total requirements, and it cannot be expected that sales of lubricants would increase if additional equipment were installed. While workshops could return the loaned equipment, they face strong disincentives to doing so. It would be possible to stock the products of competitors which are supplied in small containers, but this might not provide effective competition to oil from dispensing equipment, since it would be less convenient and would be more costly. In these circumstances, the Authority considers that the exclusive use of equipment requirement would in many cases represent an exclusive purchasing requirement. The agreement to supply equipment provided it is used exclusively for Castrol lubricants, therefore, offends against section 4(1). (See also para 40). In addition, the Authority is concerned that the equipment loan agreement with the exclusive use of equipment provision appears to be of indefinite duration, and that there are no provisions for early termination by the workshop. Burmah Castrol has stated that the borrower would presumably be entitled to terminate the loan on giving reasonable notice. In the circumstances, given the preference which would be likely to be afforded to Castrol products by virtue of the loan of the equipment, the Authority considers that the agreement, which is of indefinite length and has no clear and brief period of notice for termination, is likely to amount to foreclosure of the products of competitors, and so for these reasons also it offends against section 4(1).

39. The second part of the restriction goes much further than requiring exclusive use of equipment supplied by Burmah Castrol. It obliges the customer to return the equipment should he cease to purchase his total requirements of lubricants from Castrol. This carries the clear implication that, if the equipment is retained, there must be exclusive purchase of Castrol lubricants. Since Castrol lubricants could still be obtained on a non- exclusive basis if the equipment had been removed, or had not been supplied by Burmah Castrol in the first place, the net effect is that the loan of the equipment by Burmah Castrol has the effect of securing the exclusive purchase of Castrol products, according to the wording of the agreement. This view is reinforced by the fact that the equipment is not vital for the storage and sale of lubricants, as evidenced by the fact that many resellers do not have such equipment, and it is not necessary for it to be provided only by the lubricant supplier.

40. As mentioned above, the Authority stated in the Esso case (p. 11) that a solus dealer is not permitted to purchase any motor fuels from a supplier other than Esso during the period of the agreement, and no supplier other than Esso may supply the dealer during that period. This limits the commercial freedom of the dealer to obtain supplies, and the freedom of others to

6. Decision No. 4 of 25 June 1992 — Esso Solus and Related Agreements, p. 11.

supply him. Furthermore, in the case of lubricating oil, consumers go to the workshops in question primarily to have their car serviced, and the supply of oil is only incidental. They do not select a workshop on the basis of the oil supplied, but, once they have chosen the outlet, they have no choice of oil brands where the outlet must purchase one brand exclusively. Such a restriction on consumer choice also constitutes a restriction on competition. Notwithstanding the fact that resellers are free to return the equipment at any time, there would be a disincentive for them to do so, even if they were aware of the possibility, since it is of value to them and might have to be replaced at their expense. The exclusive purchasing tie is not limited in duration, and lasts for as long as the equipment is loaned, which could be a very long period, particularly if it is replaced from time to time. In addition, sizeable numbers of important customers (146) are party to the loan agreements (and many others are party to the other Castrol agreements). While a short-term exclusive purchasing agreement with a single customer would be unlikely to have much impact in the market for lubricants, a network of such agreements with many major customers with an indefinite duration would have a significant impact. The effects are reinforced when the agreements concern the leading firm, and by far the largest supplier, in the market, and when other major suppliers, according to Burmah Castrol, also have exclusive purchasing requirements. The Authority considers that the obligation to return the equipment unless total requirements of lubricants are obtained from Castrol is a restriction upon competition and therefore offends against section 4(1). Burmah Castrol has stated, however, that it has not interpreted this clause as giving exclusivity of supply, but the wording nevertheless remains in the agreement. **4.6**

41. In their submissions, Burmah Castrol drew attention to the judgment of the Court of Justice in the case of Delimitis v. Henniger Brau.[7] The Authority agrees with the Court that an exclusive purchasing agreement must be considered in its economic and legal context, and as part of a network of such agreements by one supplier, and, if necessary, as part of a series of networks of several suppliers, as part of its overall assessment. It agrees with the view of the Court that access to the market or increasing market share by competitors must be made difficult, because of the cumulative nature of such agreements, and that the agreement in question must make a significant contribution to the sealing-off effect produced by the totality of these agreements, in order for Article 85(1), and therefore section 4(1), to be applicable. Following this judgment, the EU Commission modified the notice concerning Regulations 1983/83 and 1984/83 by providing that beer supply agreements would not fall under Article 85(1) if, in particular, the market share of the individual brewer did not exceed more than 1 per cent of the national market for the resale of beer in on-licensed premises.[8]

42. It is clear that, however narrow or broad a definition is adopted of the market for lubricating oil, Burmah Castrol has a market share vastly in excess of 1 per cent. It occupies the leading position without question in the supply of lubricating oil. The agreement has the effect of securing to Burmah Castrol the exclusive right to supply a significant proportion of both franchised and non-franchised outlets, and thereby of denying access to them by competitors for a lengthy period. Burmah Castrol has stated that other suppliers of lubricants also have exclusive arrangements, and, notwithstanding the fact that a number of workshops might have no exclusive arrangements, a sizeable number would be tied to one or other of the major suppliers of lubricants, including, in all probability, the most important outlets, for a lengthy period of time. The Authority does not consider that the Henniger Brau judgment provides any grounds for considering that the notified arrangements do not offend against section 4(1).

43. Burmah Castrol, having been made aware of the Authority's concerns, made suggestions for amendments to the equipment loan agreement, but these were not regarded as acceptable.

7. Judgment of the Court of Justice of 28 February 1991 in the case of *Stergios Delimitis v. Henniger Brau AG.* [1991] ECR I-935.

8. Commission notice modifying the notice concerning Regulations No. 1983/83 and No. 1984/83. OJ C121, 13.5.92, p. 2.

4.6 Following the issue of the Statement of Objections, Burmah Castrol suggested further amendments. Since these would still involve exclusive use of Castrol products in the equipment, they also would offend against section 4(1). The deletion of the clause requiring return of the equipment if total requirements are not purchased from Burmah Castrol, however, would satisfy the concerns of the Authority in respect of this matter.

(ii) The hire purchase agreement — existing version

44. The main feature of the existing hire purchase agreement is that the equipment shall be used exclusively for stocking and supplying only Castrol products purchased direct from the owner, and the hirer shall not keep or allow to be kept in the equipment, or use or allow to be used with the equipment, any lubricants other than Castrol.

45. The equipment which is the subject of these agreements is initially supplied by Burmah Castrol, but is supplied on foot of a hire purchase agreement. The hirer makes regular payments to Castrol, and eventually bcomes outright owner of the equipment. While most hire purchase agreements last for five years or less, almost a quarter have a duration of ten years. All agreements carry a low rate of interest, varying from 0% to 5%, which is very low compared with standard hire purchase interest rates. The loans vary from the small to the large. The customer might otherwise be unable to borrow such sums, and would certainly face a much higher rate of interest, and often a shorter repayment period, both contributing to much higher loan repayments.

46. Exclusivity relates to the use of the equipment solely for Castrol lubricants. Since, in the circumstances, this represents an exclusive purchasing requirement, the exclusive use requirement is regarded by the Authority as offending against section 4(1)for the reasons stated earlier.

47. The amendments proposed by Burmah Castrol in response to the Statement of Objections would still involve exclusive use of the equipment, and so the agreements would continue to offend against section 4(1).

(b) *Applicability of section 4(2).*

48. Under section 4(2), the Competition Authority may grant a licence in the case of any agreement or category of agreements which, 'having regard to all relevant market conditions, contributes to improving the production of goods or provision of services or to promoting technical or economic progress, while allowing consumers a fair share of the resulting benefit and which does not —

(i) impose on the undertakings concerned terms which are not indispensable to the attainment of those objectives;

(ii) afford undertakings the possibility of eliminating competition in respect of a substantial part of the products or services in question'.

49. In the opinion of the Authority, the existing equipment loan and hire purchase agreements do not fulfil the conditions necessary for the grant of a licence under section 4(2) of the Act. As indicated above, the Authority considers that the following provisions in these agreements offend against section 4(1):

(a) obligations which constitute exclusive purchasing of lubricants; and

(b) obligations to use the equipment exclusively for Castrol products.

At the same time, the Authority considers that these agreements would fulfil the conditions for a licence if there were no provision for exclusive purchase of Castrol products, and if the period of exclusive use of equipment were limited in duration.

(i) Exclusive purchasing requirements

50. The Authority considers that the requirement in the existing equipment loan agreement to return the equipment, if the workshop ceases to purchase its total requirements of lubricating oils from Burmah Castrol, constitutes an exclusive purchasing requirement. The Authority

recognises that restraints in vertical agreements, that is, for example, in agreements between buyers and resellers, can have pro-competitive features. Restraints such as exclusive purchasing can produce efficiency gains, more effort from retailers into selling products and thus higher sales, the provision of expert advice, and the provision of costly equipment and improved levels of service, among others. These benefits do not, however, automatically result from vertical agreements. **4.6**

51. In the case of the Burmah Castrol agreement, the Authority does not consider that there are any benefits in the way of economies of bulk distribution, since the agreements relate to only a small proportion of Burmah Castrol's lubricants for resale and deliveries appear to be in relatively small volumes. There would appear to be no, or only a minimal, reduction in distribution costs which could be shared with consumers. The Authority recognises, however, that in some cases high quality equipment has been supplied on foot of these agreements, and that Burmah Castrol does provide a high quality of technical services. These promote technical progress. The Authority considers, however, that these benefits, part of which accrues to consumers, do not derive from the exclusive purchasing obligation. The equipment could be supplied by the workshop itself, and Castrol supplies many outlets, the majority in fact, and provides its technical services, without supplying any equipment or finance, and without requiring exclusive purchasing. In addition, two existing agreements — the cash loan and hire purchase agreements — do not contain any explicit exclusive purchase requirement. Such a requirement, therefore, is not indispensable to secure any benefits from the supply of lubricants or the provision of equipment. While recognising that these agreements only apply to a minority of outlets, and that lubricating oil forms only a small part of the total servicing operation carried out by these workshops, the Authority nevertheless considers that there is a risk that this type of restriction, if permitted, would be applied in all Burmah Castrol agreements, and in those of other suppliers, leading to a situation of foreclosure against new suppliers. The Authority considers that such agreements could afford undertakings the possibility of eliminating competition in respect of a substantial part of the products in question. Since the essential conditions of section 4(2) have not been satisfied, a licence cannot be granted in respect of the notified equipment loan agreements.

(ii) Exclusive use of equipment requirements

52. Both the existing equipment loan and hire purchase agreements contain an explicit requirement that the equipment be used exclusively for Castrol lubricants. As explained above, the Authority considers that such exclusive use of equipment requirements, in the circumstances, represent exclusive purchasing requirements in return for the loan of equipment or money. Nevertheless, the Authority can take a more favourable view of such arrangements than of exclusive purchase arrangements on their own.

53. As before, the Authority does not consider that equipment exclusivity produces any economies in distribution. It accepts that in some cases high quality equipment has been supplied, and that high quality technical services are provided by Burmah Castrol, and that these benefit consumers. An interest rate subsidy is provided in the case of the hire purchase loan, and equipment is provided in the other case. It is likely that the particular equipment supplied or financed would not have been installed in the workshops unless exclusive use of the equipment had been a requirement. Burmah Castrol would have been unlikely to provide such loans or equipment if they could have been used freely for competitive products. In this respect, exclusive use for a period of time can be regarded as indispensable to securing the benefits from the supply of the equipment, which may be shared fairly with consumers.

54. Nevertheless, the two agreements still have a foreclosure effect, because they represent exclusive purchasing, and thus they have the possibility of substantially limiting competition. In the case of the hire purchase agreement, however, the problem of foreclosure is considerably reduced since the equipment becomes the property of the workshop once the agreement has terminated. At that stage, the equipment can be used for any lubricants of the workshop's

4.6 choosing. The Authority considers therefore that if the period of the exclusive use of equipment requirement were limited to the period of the hire purchase loan, or to five years, whichever was the shorter, this would not afford the possibility of eliminating competition to a substantial degree. In these circumstances, since all the conditions of section 4(2) would have been fulfilled, a licence could be granted for the agreement. An exclusive use requirement for any longer period, however, would not satisfy all the conditions of section 4(2), since it would afford the possibility of eliminating competition and would not be indispensable, and could not be licensed.

55. On the other hand, the position differs in respect of the equipment loan agreement. This is granted without a definite duration, and with no provision for termination by the workshop. The equipment never becomes the property of the workshop, and can never be used for the products of a competitor. It can be replaced from time to time, thus extending the period of exclusive use, and hence of exclusive purchase. In the view of the Authority, this presents the danger of long-term foreclosure of the market to competitors' products. It applies in a large number of cases, and cannot be regarded as insignificant in its effects. Indeed, it can be argued that the loan of equipment is not indispensable, since Castrol could ensure the provision of equipment by making a loan to the workshops by way of cash or hire purchase, so that the workshops could purchase the equipment themselves. In the view of the Authority, therefore, the equipment loan agreement fails to satisfy all the requirements of section 4(2), and cannot be granted a licence.

56. The Authority, however, considers that this possibility of eliminating competition might be avoided if a five year time limit were placed upon agreements for the loan of equipment, after which the workshop would have the option of purchasing the equipment at its written down value or of returning the equipment to Burmah Castrol. A new agreement could be made at the end of the five year period, with an exclusive requirement on the use of the equipment when new equipment is installed. There is unlikely to be as much competition to secure an arrangement with a workshop on the expiry of an oil agreement as there is for petrol dealers on the expiry of a solus agreement, which is why the Authority considers that the option to purchase the equipment is important. Burmah Castrol may, in addition, supply equipment free, with no exclusive use obligation, or supply it on cash or hire purchase loan terms, where the exclusive use tie could last for a maximum of five years, after which the equipment would become the property of the workshop and could be used for Castrol products or the lubricants of any competitor. The conclusion of the Authority that the equipment loan agreement does not satisfy the conditions of section 4(2), therefore, does not mean that Castrol cannot supply equipment to the workshops in question.

57. While the amendments proposed by Burmah Castrol in response to the Statement of Objections have gone some way to meet the concerns of the Authority, they are not sufficient, after a lengthy period of negotiation, to satisfy the requirements of section 4(2). In the case of equipment loan agreements which have already been in existence for five years or more, Burmah Castrol has proposed that, if the option to purchase or return the equipment is not exercised, the agreement and the exclusive use of equipment requirement would remain in force for as long as the equipment was on loan. In addition, Burmah Castrol proposed that the workshops be given six months to exercise this option. The Authority considers that any agreement which involves exclusive use of equipment should be terminated no later than at the end of five years from the date of its commencement, and that agreements of a longer duration cannot be licensed. In the case of those equipment loan agreements which were made less than five years ago, Burmah Castrol has proposed that the exclusive use requirement should be limited to five years, which is, at first sight, acceptable to the Authority. They propose, however, to allow the option of purchase or return only upon request. At the end of the five year term, therefore, Burmah Castrol appears not to be obliged to give the option to the workshop, but the latter must request that this option be given. In the absence of the request, the agreement continues in existence. It is possible, at least, that the workshop would consider

itself bound to use the equipment exclusively for Burmah Castrol products after the expiry of the five-year period. The Authority considers that the suggested amendments would not satisfy the conditions of section 4(2), since they would involve exclusive use of the equipment for a period in excess of five years.

58. In the case of the hire purchase agreements, Burmah Castrol has proposed to limit the period of exclusive use of equipment to five years where the agreement was for a period of five years or longer. This would be acceptable to the Authority. In the case of agreements with a shorter duration, however, Burmah Castrol has proposed to have the exclusive use of its equipment 'within the balance of the five year term'. They would appear to be requiring exclusive use for five years, even where the agreement was for a lesser period, and after it has become the property of the hirer. The Authority considers that these suggested amendments also would not satisfy the conditions of section 4(2) in respect of the standard hire purchase agreement.

The Decision

59. Burmah Castol and their customers who are party to the standard equipment loan and hire purchase agreements are undertakings within the meaning of the Competition Act. The notified agreements are agreements between undertakings, and they operate within the State. The Authority considers that the notified agreements have the object or effect of preventing, restricting or distorting competition, that they offend against section 4(1) of the Act, and that they do not satisfy the conditions set out in section 4(2) of the Act, in the following respects:

(i) the existing equipment loan agreement

— the requirement that the equipmnt shall be used exclusively for the dispensing of Burmah Castrol products; and

— the requirement to return the equipment if the borrower ceases to purchase his total requirements of lubricants from Burmah Castrol; and

(ii) the existing hire puchase agreement

— the obligation in some agreements for exclusive use of Burmah Castrol lubricants in the equipment for a period which exceeds five years.

Accordingly, the Authority refuses to issue a certificate or grant a licence in respect of the existing equipment loan agreement (CA/38/92E) and the existing hire purchase agreement (CA/37/92E) notified on 8 June 1992 under section 7 of the Competition Act 1991 by Burmah Castrol (Ireland) Ltd.

For the Competition Authority.

Patrick M. Lyons
Chairman

13 October 1994

4.7 Competition Authority Decision No. 380, Burmah Castrol (Ireland) Ltd — Loan Agreement (New Version): 15 December 1994, Notification No. CA/43/92

Low interest loan agreement from supplier of a product enabling the borrower to purchase certain equipment – Borrower to stock and use only the supplier's products during currency of loan agreement – Exclusive purchasing commitment – Foreclosure effect of such agreements – Whether possibility of elimination of competition in respect of a substantial part of the market in question – Whether terms in agreements indispensable to securing benefits to the consumer – Amendment of notified agreement – Statement of objections – Competition Act 1991 (No. 24) sections 3, 4 and 7 – EEC Regulation 1984/83

Facts: On 8 June 1992 notification was made to the Authority with a request for a certificate under section 4(4) of the Competition Act 1991 or, failing that, a licence under section 4(2) in respect of a standard form loan agreement entered into between Burmah Castrol (Ireland) Ltd ('Burmah') and the various purchasers of its lubricating oils.

Burmah, a subsidiary of Burmah Castrol plc, is an Irish registered company engaged in the manufacture, importation, marketing and distribution of various petroleum products in the State. The other parties to the notified agreements are car servicing outlets which undertake the maintenance and servicing of motor vehicles.

The product relevant to the notified agreement is oil based lubricants for motor vehicles. Burmah has over 20% of the total market for all engine oils and its market share in the engine oil market is about twice that of the next largest supplier. The appropriate geographical market is the State because the outlets retailing lubricants are located throughout the State.

The notified agreement is a cash loan agreement whereunder Burmah loans money to various car maintenance outlets ('the Borrower') so that the Borrower can purchase lubricating equipment. The agreement provides for the amount of the loan, the interest rate and the repayment schedule. It also provides for the exclusive use of Burmah products by the Borrower on his premises. The duration of the agreement may vary but Burmah stated that the maximum period of the loan agreement is five years.

EEC Regulation No. 1984/83, a block exemption regulation regulating exclusive purchasing agreements, applies to agreements involving only two parties whereby one party, the reseller, agrees with the other, the supplier, to purchase specified goods from that supplier. The supplier may be obliged not to distribute the goods or competing goods in the reseller's principal sales area and the reseller may be obliged not to manufacture or distribute goods which compete with the contract goods. The regulation provides that where special commercial or financial advantages have been accorded to a reseller exclusive purchasing obligations on the reseller may be imposed for a maximum period of ten years.

Following meetings and correspondence with the Authority, Burmah agreed to amend the notified arrangements to address the concerns raised by the Authority. The proposed amendments were not acceptable to the Authority and a statement of objections was issued to Burmah on 27 June 1994. In response to the statement of objections Burmah proposed amending the notified agreement so that the clause prohibiting the Borrower from using on its premises lubricants other than those supplied by Burmah would be deleted and in its place the Borrower would covenant that for the duration of the agreement the borrower would use the equipment and facilities purchased with the loan for dispensing Burmah products exclusively. 4.7

Decided by the Authority

(A) In refusing to issue a certificate under section 4(4) of the Competition Act in respect of the notified agreements that:

(1) Burmah and the resellers who are party to the notified agreement are all engaged, *inter alia*, in the supply and distribution of lubricating oils for gain and they are therefore 'undertakings' within the meaning of section 3(1) of the Competition Act 1991.

(2) The notified standard agreements are all agreements between undertakings and an agreement as amended between two undertakings following meetings with the Authority was entered into on 14 October 1994.

(3) The relevant product market is that of lubricating oils for resale and the relevant geographical market is the State.

(4) The essential feature of the notified loan agreement is that, in return for a cash loan at a reduced rate of interest the Borrower would use exclusively on the premises lubricants supplied by Burmah during the term of the agreement. This amounted to an exclusive purchasing agreement and must be examined on its own merits. While a short term exclusive purchasing agreement with a single customer would be unlikely to have much impact on the market for lubricants, a network of similar agreements with many major customers with a long duration would have a significant impact. The effects are reinforced when the agreements concern the leading firm and by far the largest supplier in the market and when other major suppliers also have exclusive purchasing requirements. For these reasons the notified agreements offend against section 4(1) of the Competition Act.

(5) The amendments proposed by Burmah deletes the requirement of exclusive use of Burmah products on the premises and substitutes a requirement that the equipment which was financed by a loan from Burmah should be used exclusively for dispensing Burmah products. An obligation on the Borrower to use equipment supplied or financed by the supplier only for the storage and sale of the supplier's goods would not *per se* offend against section 4(1) unless it had the effect of ensuring that only the goods of that supplier could be sold by the Borrower. If exclusive use of the equipment meant, in the particular circumstances, that the goods of only one supplier could be handled by the Borrower, this would amount to exclusive purchasing arrangements which generally offends against section 4(1).

(6) In the amended agreement the requirement that the equipment only be used for dispensing of Burmah products does not necessarily have the object or effect that the user of the equipment must purchase only Burmah products. While many workshops would have space for the installation of equipment of one or more competitors there are many workshops which would not have such space and even where space was available it may be better used for other commercial purposes. Further, the existing equipment may be geared to the workshop's entire output and it cannot be expected that sales of lubricants will increase because additional equipment is installed. Workshops could terminate their loan arrangements for the equipment but they face 'strong disincentives' to doing so. In the circumstances the exclusive use of equipment requirement would in many cases represent an exclusive purchasing requirement and therefore it offends against section 4(1) of the Competition Act 1991.

4.7 (B) In granting an unconditional licence valid from 14 November 1994 to 30 November 2004 under section 4(2) of the Competition Act in respect of the notified agreement that:

(1) The original requirement in the loan agreement for exclusive use of Burmah products on the premises constitutes an exclusive purchasing requirement. While restraints in vertical agreements such as exclusive purchasing can produce efficiency gains such benefits do not automatically result from such agreement. The notified agreement produces a minimal, if any, reduction in distribution costs which could be shared with the consumers. While the high quality equipment which has been part financed under the notified agreement and the high quality technical services provided by Burmah do promote technical progress which benefit in part the consumers, these benefits do not derive from the exclusive purchasing obligation. Further, such a requirement is not indispensable to secure the benefits from the supply of the lubricants or the provision of the equipment. While the notified standard agreement only applies to a small part of the total servicing operation carried out in the market there is a risk that this type of restriction, if permitted, would be applied in all cases leading to a situation of foreclosure against new suppliers. Such agreements, therefore, could afford an undertaking the possibility of eliminating competition in a substantial part of the products in question and therefore fails to satisfy the essential condition of section 4(2).

(2) Under the terms of the notified standard agreement high quality equipment has been financed at subsidised interest rates and high quality technical services are provided by Burmah both of which benefit consumers. Burmah would have been unlikely to provide such loans if the equipment could be freely used for competitors' products. In this respect exclusive use for a period of time can be regarded as indispensable to securing the benefits from the supply of the equipment, which may be shared fairly with the consumer.

(3) The notified agreement has a foreclosure effect because it represents exclusive purchasing and thus has the possibility of substantially limiting competition. If the agreements last for a long period of time, the foreclosure effect would be considerable. In the case of the agreements as amended, however, the problem of foreclosure is considerably reduced since once the agreement terminates at the end of 5 years or less the equipment can be then used for any lubricants of the workshop's choosing. In these circumstances provided that the period of exclusive use of the equipment does not exceed the period of the loan and that the loan does not exceed 5 years in duration, the agreement as amended, would not afford the possibility of eliminating competition to a substantial degree and all the conditions of section 4(2) are fulfilled.

Cases and Decisions referred to

Masterfoods Ireland Ltd v. HB Ice Cream Ltd (High Court, Keane J) 28 May 1992; [1993] ILRM 145 **8.1.4**

Delimitis v. Henniger Brau (case no. 234/89), [1991] 1 ECR 935, [1992] 5 CMLR 210

EC Commission Decision Scholler Lebensmittel GmbH & Co. KG, 1993 OJ L183/1 [1993] 2 CCH 101

EC Commission Decision Langnese-Iglo GmbH, 1993 OJ L183/19 [1993] 2 CCH 123

Competition Authority Decision No. 4, ESSO Solus and related agreements, 25 June 1992

Competition Authority Decision No. 24 — Motor Fuels Category Licence **4.2**

Competition Authority Decision No. 324 — Burmah Castrol (Ireland) Ltd **4.4**

Competition Authority Decision No. 361 — Burmah Castrol (Ireland) Ltd **4.6**

Competition Authority Decision of 15 December 1994 relating to a proceeding under section 4 of the Competition Act 1991 Notification No. CA/43/92 — Burmah Castrol (Ireland) Ltd 4.7

Introduction

1. Notification was made to the Competition Authority on 8 June 1992 of a standard form agreement regarding the loan of cash by Burmah Castrol (Ireland) Ltd to purchasers of its lubricating oils. The notification requested a certificate under section 4(4) of the Competition Act 1991, or, in the event of a refusal by the Competition Authority to issue a certificate, a licence under section 4(2). The Authority issued a Statement of Objections to Burmah Castrol on 27 June 1994. In response, Burmah Castrol proposed certain amendments to the agreement which are acceptable to the Authority. Notice of intention to grant a licence was published in the Irish Times on 11 November 1994. There were no submissions from interested parties.

The Facts

(a) *Subject of the notification*

2. The notification relates to a new standard form agreement concerning a cash loan for the purchase of lubricating equipment provided by Burmah Castrol (Ireland) Ltd to certain resellers of lubricating oils. The earlier version of the cash loan agreement. was also notified to the Authority. Since it did not offend against section 4(1) of the Competition Act, the Authority issued a certificate in respect of that version of the agreement.[1] Agreements relating to the supply of equipment on hire purchase and the loan of equipment by Burmah Castrol were also notified the Authority, and these are the subject of a separate decision refusing the issue of a certificate or the grant of a licence.[2]

(b) *The Parties Involved*

3. Burmah Castrol (Ireland) Ltd., is an Irish registered company engaged in the manufacture, importation, marketing and distribution in the State of various petroleum products. The company is a subsidiary of Castrol Ltd, registered in the UK, and its ultimate holding company is Burmah Castrol plc. The parent company is engaged worldwide in all stages of the production and supply of petroleum products. The Burmah retail motor fuel network consists of a number of company-owned outlets and a number of dealer-owned outlets operating under the Burmah brand. In addition, lubricating products are supplied to a large number of other outlets, including petrol stations supplied by other wholesalers and other outlets, and other customers.

4. The other parties to the notified standard agreements are car franchise main dealers, who undertake guarantee and servicing work, including servicing and oil changes, and other non-franchise vehicle workshops which undertake car servicing. These dealers generally do not sell petrol. By January 1993, three new loan agreements, had been made, two of them with workshops which had existing agreements. At the end of September 1992, about 250 customers had cash loans, equipment loans or hire purchase terms from the company. A further six hundred customers were also being supplied on Burmah's standard terms and conditions.

(c) *The Product*

5. The product with which the notified agreement is concerned consists of lubricants, that is any oil-based product which is used for the lubricating of a motor vehicle. While the agreement refers to 'additives' as well, Burmah has stated that it does not sell additives. Almost all Burmah lubricating products are sold under the trade name 'Castrol'. While lubricating oils are to some extent interchangeable, the product is usually differentiated as follows:

1. Decision No. 324 of 5 May, 1994.
2. Decision No. 361 of 13 October 1994.

4.7 (a) top engine oils;
(b) other multigrades;
(c) monogrades; and
(d) two-stroke oils.

Top engine oils appears to be the largest category of sales. Other lubricating products and additives, with much smaller sales, include transmission fluids, brake fluids, anti-freeze and greases.

(d) *The market*

6. Besides Burmah Castrol, all the other main wholesalers of petroleum products in the State also market lubricating products. In addition to supplying lubricants to their company-owned and dealer-owned petrol stations, the wholesalers also supply motor franchise dealers and other motor workshops, motor accessory shops, other retail outlets, and direct to industrial and agricultural users.

7. According to the Report of Enquiry into the Supply and Distribution of Motor fuels by the Fair Trade Commission in 1989 (PL. 7951), total sales of lubricating oil through retailers in 1988 were 14.8m. litres, while commercial sales amounted to 24.4m. litres. Major end-users in the commercial sector purchase lubricants direct from the wholesalers, and the retail and commercial sales of lubricants constitute distinct sections of the total lubricants market.

8. The main wholesalers supply figures of sales to Stokes Kennedy Crowley, which produces estimates of total sales of the different petroleum and oil products. The estimate of total sales of engine oils in the consumer market, that is through resellers, in 1991 amounted to over 11m. litres. Burmah Castrol, however, considers that this represented only about 85% of the full consumer lubricant market, due to the omission of suppliers who do not contribute data to Stokes Kennedy Crowley. Burmah Castrol estimates that total multigrades account for almost 90% of the sales of 11m. litres, and monogrades for 90% of the total. According to Burmah Castrol, the number of outlets of different kinds is as follows:

Type of Outlet	No. of Outlets
Franchise vehicle workshops	729
Other vehicle workshops	561
Petrol service stations	1,740
Oil and lube shops, etc.	8
Supermarkets, etc.	850
Accessory shops	53
Motorcycle shops	221
Agricultural dealers, etc.	507
Wholesale distributors	291
Fuel distributors	160
Total	5,120

Note: The number of petrol stations is much less than the total number of outlets in the State selling petrol. Many of the latter do not sell lubricating oil, and these are excluded from the figures in the Table.

Burmah Castrol estimates that each of the first three types of outlet accounts for between 15 and 20% of total sales of engine oils.

Consumers who purchase lubricating oil do so either:

(a) for topping up the oil sump on the forecourt of a petrol station or as a do-it-yourself operation; or

(b) for a complete oil change, usually at a motor workshop or in a lubrication bay attached to a petrol station; or

(c) for a complete oil change as part of an overall engine service, usually at a motor workshop. In the latter case, consumers will go to the place where they purchased a new vehicle for any service under guarantee, and will often go to the same place or to another outlet franchised for their make of vehicle for subsequent maintenance and service, including oil changes. Where there is an oil change involved, consumers have little or no choice of brand, and the three activities above are so separate as to constitute quite distinct market segments. **4.7**

10. Oil may be sold in cans or plastic packages marked with the brand name of the supplier. It may also be sold by way of a bulk oil container, in which case the consumer has no way of knowing for certain which brand of oil has been supplied. Oil from bulk containers is often used for oil changes, whether or not as part of a complete service operation, and the customer is not usually present when the oil is supplied. Again, the consumer appears to have little choice of the brand of oil and cannot know which brand, or even grade, has actually been supplied. In addition, the cost of oil is usually only a small part of the cost of a complete service, and the customer is unlikely to choose an outlet for a service on the basis of the brand of oil supplied, or its price. Topping up, a single oil change, and a full service with oil change cannot be regarded as close substitutes for each other.

11. Franchised vehicle workshops are shown separately in the market estimates compiled by Burmah Castrol, and it appears that, since customers tend to go regularly to the same outlet for servicing, they can be regarded to some extent as a separate market category. The same is true to a lesser extent of other vehicle workshops. To the extent that a customer patronises the same outlet, any restraint upon the oil which may be sold there reduces the customer's freedom of choice of oil products.

12. Overall, according to its own confidential estimates, Burmah Castrol has a significant presence on the lubricating oils market as a whole and in important sectors of it. This is despite the fact that Burmah Castrol has only a small share of the petrol market and relatively few company and tied dealer outlets, where it could expect to sell mainly Castrol oils. It has well over 20% of the total market for all engine oils supplied by the main firms. Its market share in the total and top engine oils markets is about twice that of the next largest supplier. Most of its sales consist of multigrades, by far the largest selling products in the sector. In respect of franchised vehicle workshops, it is sold at a high proportion of all outlets. It supplies almost 14% of these outlets under the various notified agreements. Of the non-franchised workshops, Burmah Castrol supplies a very high proportion, nearly 25% of these being supplied under these agreements. Burmah Castrol is certainly the market leader and occupies a strong position in the market for lubricating oils generally, and in the top engine oils and franchised and non-franchised vehicle workshops segments of that market.

13. Since outlets retailing lubricants are located throughout the State, the appropriate geographical market in this case is the State.

14. Up to 30 September 1991, part of the motor lubricants sector was subject to the provisions of the Restrictive Practices (Motor Spirit and Motor Vehicle Lubricating Oil) Order, 1981. The Order was repealed on the coming into force of the Competition Act on 1 October, 1991.

(e) *The notified agreement*

15. The new cash loan agreement is used where Burmah Castrol lends money to finance the purchase of lubricating equipment. The agreement provides for the amount of the loan, the interest rate and repayment over a specified period. It also provides for exclusive use of Burmah Castrol lubricating oil and other products on the premises. The first of the agreements made is dated 2 September 1992. Its main provisions are as follows:

(1) The company carries on and intends hereinafter to carry on the business of vehicle servicing and maintenance at: ('the premises') which expression means all that part of the said land now used or intended to be used for the purpose of the said business and includes any adjoining or neighbouring land which shall during the currency of this Agreement be used for

4.7 the servicing and maintenance of vehicles by or for the benefit of the company. (Clause 1)

(2) The company agrees that this loan money advanced by Burmah Castrol (Ireland) Ltd is to be used by the company to finance motor vehicle lubrication facilities, including lubrication equipment, to be used by the company to carry on the business of servicing and maintenance of motor vehicles at the premises. (Clause 2)

(3) During the currency of this agreement the company shall use exclusively on the premises, lubricants, additives and brake fluids ('lubricant products') supplied by Burmah Castrol (Ireland) Ltd and shall not cause, allow, permit or procure any other company or person to use or stock for use at the premises, lubricant products obtained from any other supplier. (Clause 3)

(4) The company also agrees that in the event of disposal, selling or ceasing to carry on our business, or in the event of any breach by us of any term contained in this agreement, the company will immediately on written demand by Burmah Castrol (Ireland) Ltd repay Burmah Castrol (Ireland) Ltd the whole amount of the loan that may be outstanding at the date of such disposal, sale, ceasing to carry on business or breach of aforesaid. (Clause 5)

(5) This agreement shall remain in force for a period of years from the date hereof. (Clause 6) (Burmah Castrol has stated that the maximum period of the new loan agreement is five years).

(f) *EEC Regulation 1984/83*

16. EEC Regulation No. 1984/83, of 22 June 1983, is a block exemption regulation which applies Article 85(3) of the Treaty of Rome to categories of exclusive purchasing agreements.[3] The regulation entered into force on 1 July 1983 and it expires on 31 December 1997.

17. The regulation applies to agreements involving only two parties whereby one party, the reseller, agrees with the other, the supplier, to purchase specified goods only from the supplier, or from a connected undertaking or one entrusted by the supplier with the sale of his goods. The supplier may be obliged not to distribute the goods or competing goods in the reseller's principal sales area and at the reseller's level of distribution. For goods generally, the exclusive distribution agreement may be for no longer than five years. Besides the exclusive purchasing requirement, the only other restriction of competition that may be imposed on the reseller is the obligation not to manufacture or distribute goods which compete with the contract goods. The reseller may also undertake to purchase complete ranges or minimum quantities of the goods, to sell the goods under trademarks or packed and presented as specified by the supplier, and to engage in sales promotion, involving advertising, maintaining a sales network or stock of goods, providing customer and guarantee services, and employing staff with specialised or technical training. The benefit of the exemption may be withdrawn from a specific agreement in certain circumstances where, for example, effective competition is lacking, or market access is made difficult, or where less favourable prices are made available to exclusive purchasers than to other purchasers for resale.

18. Lubricating oil is mentioned in Title III of the Regulation, which applies solely to agreements for the supply of petroleum-based motor vehicle fuels for resale in a specified service station. Where special commercial or financial advantages have been accorded by the supplier to the reseller, the exclusive purchasing obligation for motor fuels may be imposed for a maximum period of ten years. In such service station agreements, but only in such agreements, the reseller may also be obliged not to use lubricating oil supplied by other firms where equipment is financed or made available by the supplier, but he may not be prevented from selling oil supplied by other firms.

(g) *Views of Burmah Castrol*

19. Burmah Castrol made the following observations in relation to all its notified agree-

3. OJ No. L173, 30.5.83, p. 5, and Explanatory Notice, OJ No. C101, 13.4.84, p. 2.

ments: 'Leaving aside ancillary elements, the essential nature of the provisions of these agreements which might be regarded as restrictive is that, in return for the provision by the Company of equipment or cash to purchase equipment, the customer agrees: 4.7

1, to use the equipment exclusively for the Company's products; and either

2. to purchase the customer's entire requirements of lubricant products from the Company; or

3. to stock for use and use on the customer's business premises only the Company's lubricant products.

It is submitted that these restrictions do not have the object or effect of preventing, restricting or distorting competition in trade in any goods or services in the State or any part of the State.

It is submitted that the agreements, viewed individually or as a network, are not intended to prevent, restrict or distort competition. The intention of the agreements is to increase the sales of the Company's products, improve distribution and reduce costs and to maintain quality control and protect against environmental risks.

The Authority is referred in general to the decision of the High Court in *Masterfoods Ireland Ltd v. HB Ice Cream Ltd* (unreported, Keane J, 28 May 1992). As regards improving distribution, the provision of storage and dispensing equipment enables larger volumes of the Company's lubricants to be stored, thus decreasing the frequency of drops required. This could not be achieved if the customer was allowed to use the storage for products of competitors. As regards increase in quality control and the management of environmental risks, the provision by the Company of specific types of equipment enables the Company to ensure that only top quality equipment is used, thus significantly reducing chances of contamination The exclusivity is required in order to ensure that the Company can be satisfied that inferior quality products are not mixed with the products of the Company. This reduces the Company's exposure to liability claims. It should be pointed out that, except where the agreement is terminable by reasonable notice, no prohibition is placed on the customer selling competing products; the only restriction is on the use of those products. To the extent that this limits the use of the equipment, it is submitted that this is necessary for quality control and to the extent that the use of other lubricant products on the premises is prohibited, this s necessary to give effect to the prohibition on use of other lubricant products through the equipment. Essentially, there is no other effective way of policing the obligation in regard to the equipment.

The Authority is referred to the decision of the Court of Justice of the European Communities in case 234/89 *Delimitis v. Henninger Brau* [1991] 4 CMLR. At paragraph 13, the Court pointed out that if agreements providing for exclusive purchase obligations do not have the objective of restricting competition, it is nevertheless appropriate to verify whether or not they have the effect of hindering it, restricting it or distorting its interplay. In order to assess this, it is necessary to examine the agreements in their legal and economic context. In paragraph 27, the Court held that an exclusive purchasing obligation would infringe article 85(1) of the EEC Treaty if (to paraphrase) (a) the national product market concerned is difficult to gain access to for competitors which might become established in this market or increase their share of this market and (b) it is necessary that the contract in dispute contributes significantly to the blocking effect produced by the network of contracts in their legal and economic context. It is submitted that the Authority should adopt this as its basis for considering the exclusive and limited purchase obligations contained in the agreements. It is submitted that these agreements do not have any effect or, entry to or increasing penetration in this market. The market is not characterised by any significant barriers to entry. The Company is of the opinion that there is a substantial market not currently tied by the provision of equipment to any supplier. The figures [supplied] for new customers during 1992 illustrate this. In addition, the Authorities attention is drawn to the successful entry into the market in the last few years of the Kuwait Petroleum Company which carries on business of selling lubricating oil. This indicates that the market remains penetrable. It is submitted that the length of the tie in this regard is not necessarily relevant and that, in this regard, the provisions of article 3(d) of regulation 1984/83/EEC should

4.7 not be regarded as conclusive.

In addition, it is submitted that the exclusivity is necessary to protect the Company's property rights in the equipment, in the same way as for instance the insurance obligation, and that the Act should not be interpreted as permitting interference with these rights.

If the Authority does not accept the above submissions it is submitted in the alternative that a licence should be granted for the continuance of these arrangements on the basis that they fulfil the conditions set out in section 4(2) of the Act.

The Authority is referred to the recitals to regulation 1984/83/EEC. It is submitted that the benefits identified by the Commission as generally found in exclusive purchasing arrangements are applicable to the exclusive purchasing obligations contained in the agreements. The Authority is also referred to [the above] which discusses the benefits in terms of distribution costs arising from these agreements. It is accepted that, as regards agreements to which Title I of Regulation 1984/83 applies, the maximum term of such agreements is five years. The Company would intend to inform its customers that the restriction on purchasing other lubricants for resale does not apply beyond 5 years from the commencement of the agreement, where Title I rather than Title III applies.

The proportion of total sales covered by these agreements is approximately 7.5%. The Company does not believe that this in any way implies that the agreements do not bring about the suggested improvements in distribution in respect of that proportion of its sales.

Burmah Castrol further explained that, in the existing agreements, the restriction on the use of other lubricant products was interpreted by the company and its legal advisors to refer only to use through the lubricating equipment. The reference to 'exclusive requirements' in the existing equipment loan agreement was not interpreted by the company as giving them exclusivity of supply. It was possible for workshops to have more than one lubricating bay, financed by more than one supplier.

20. In a further submission, following a meeting with the Authority, Burmah Castrol stated that:

> The company confirms that, to the extent that it is obliged under the Competition Act not to apply dissimilar conditions to equivalent transactions with other trading parties thereby placing them at a competitive disadvantage, it complies fully with this obligation.

As regards the Authority's impression that the investments represent a poor return and could therefore be regarded as having been entered into merely for the purposes of foreclosure, the company, while admitting that the restrictions placed on the dealer in these agreements is valuable, does not regard these investments as bad investments. The figures derived by the Authority do not take account of the fact that a large number of the agreements in any one year are new agreements and therefore the value of those agreements for a full year would be up to 90% greater later. In addition, many of the businesses in which investments are made will be new businesses which will take time to mature and provide the appropriate return.

It was suggested at our meeting that the cash loan and hire purchase methods may not involve financing the purchase of equipment. While we accept that provision of low cost loans or goods on hire purchase is not the same as providing the equipment, the two methods of assisting dealers are it is submitted permitted by the block exemption regulation. In our view, there is nothing on the face of the block exemption or the explanatory notice to suggest that financing must be on such terms as to be equivalent to providing the equipment. In our view, they can be clearly interpreted as alternatives to each other. We are instructed that this method of financing represents normal practice in the industry throughout Europe. Therefore, it is submitted that both forms of investment involve financing the purchase of lubricating bay or other lubricating equipment.

It is again submitted that none of the markets into which the company sells are foreclosed to any significant degree. Of the market segments listed in the first page of the market plan extract, it is considered that, apart from petrol service stations, which are to be subject to a different regime, only the franchised car and commercial vehicle work shops market (if it constitutes a separate market) is to any extent tied up. Burmah Castrol have agreements with 100 franchise dealers. The company estimates that about 50% of the dealers in this segment are not subject to any tie whatsoever and that of the remainder, the operation of the five year rule means that an average of 20% of those become free every year. The company estimate, therefore, would be that at any time only 40% of the segment is subject to a tie at any one time. The company believes that the criterion to be used in determining whether or not an agreement or bundle of agreements restrict competition within the meaning of section 4(1) of the Competition Act should be the same as those identified by the European Court of Justice in the Delimitis decision at paragraph 23 which reads: **4.7**

> If an examination of all similar contracts entered into on the relevant market and the other factors relevant to the economic and legal context in which the market must be examined shows that the agreements do not have the cumulative effect of denying access to that market to new national and foreign competitors, the individual agreements comprising the bundle of agreements cannot be held to restrict competition within the meaning of Article 85(1) EEC. They do not, therefore, fall under the prohibition laid down in that provision.

While it is accepted that Article 85(1) is slightly different from section 4(1), the company does not believe that the difference is material in this context.

The company also point out that, as shown by the Statoil acquisition of BP Ireland, there are real concrete opportunities to acquire market share by acquisition.

In any event, the company does not accept that the franchise dealer network can be regarded as a separate market and believes that the market as a whole is not foreclosed to access by acquisition or otherwise and that, as a result, the Authority should certify its opinion that the arrangements do not offend against section 4(1).

The company believes that consumers receive a fair share of the benefits of these agreements. With a few exceptions, the retail customers in all market segments, including motor vehicle franchisees, are single operations although in some cases they are backed by motor importers. It is not the practice of such motor importers to invest in equipment for the retailer. The retailers themselves would evidently not have the resources to make or finance investments of the type provided by the company. Effectively, therefore, it is only through investments of the type made by the company and its competitors that the consumer can obtain the benefit of the equipment which the company supplies. This equipment is, as far as possible, maintained at a state of the art level and includes a wide range of special products to respond to the increasing wave of new technical requirements. The company provides technical services and consultancy services and also laboratory and analytical services, many of which are unique in Ireland. In addition, Burmah Castrol has been awarded the ISO9002 Standard for its services. While the consumer may not appreciate the benefits which are thus supplied, they do in fact enable the retailer to provide a better service to the consumer than would otherwise be the case'.

(h) *Subsequent developments*

21. Following further meetings and correspondence with the Authority, Burmah Castrol agreed by letter of 8 April 1994 to amend its agreements in order to address the concerns of the Authority. Since the amendments were not acceptable to the Authority, a Statement of Objections was issued to Burmah Castrol on 27 June 1994. In response, Burmah Castrol proposed further amendments to the new cash loan agreement. They enclosed a draft letter, which contained the following:

'Following discussions with the Competition Authority, we have agreed to amend clause

4.7 3 of the Agreement. As currently drafted, clause 3 prohibits you from using on the premises lubricant products supplied by anyone other than the Company.

The new provision is as follows:

'During the currency of this Agreement the Company shall use the equipment and facilities purchased pursuant to clause 2 exclusively for dispensing lubricants and brake fluids ('lubricant products') supplied by Burmah Castrol (Ireland) Ltd'. The rest of the Agreement as at the date hereof is confirmed and is unaffected by these changes.'

Burmah Castrol also stated that the notified standard form agreement did not indicate the term. This was to give them a flexibility to enter into agreements for less than 5 years. All of the existing agreements were for 5 years, and no amendment was necessary in this regard. On 22 November 1994 Burmah Castrol provided evidence that the amendments had been agreed with a named reseller (Carroll and Kinsella Motors (Churchtown) Ltd) in 14 November 1994.

Assessment.

(a) *Applicability of section 4(1)*

22. Section 4(1) of the Competition Act 1991, prohibits and renders void all agreements between undertakings which have as their object or effect the prevention, restriction or distortion of competition in trade in any goods or services in the State or in any part of the State.

23. Burmah Castrol and the resellers who are party to the notified agreements are all engaged in the supply and distribution of lubricating oils for gain, among other activities, and they are therefore 'undertakings' within the meaning of section 3(1) of the Act. The notified agreements are all agreements between undertakings. The relevant product market is that of lubricating oils for resale, and particularly that part which is supplied to franchised and non-franchised motor vehicle workshops. The relevant geographical market is the State.

(i) The notified agreement

24. The essential feature of the new cash loan agreement is that, in return for a cash loan at a reduced rate of interest, the recipient shall use exclusively on the premises lubricants supplied by Burmah Castrol during the term of the agreement, and shall not use or stock for use lubricants obtained from any other supplier. The agreement is limited to a period of five years. While only three such agreements had been made up to early January 1993, it is understood that this agreement will replace the existing cash loan agreement in the future.

'Premises' is defined as the whole premises occupied by the workshop, and the agreement covers additives as well as lubricants.

25. The existing agreement contained no restriction of any kind on the recipient, but the new version amounts to an exclusive purchasing agreement for Castrol lubricants, and implicitly it involves exclusive use of the equipment which has been bought on foot of the loan. The equipment is quite clearly the property of the customer, though there is a contribution to its financing by Burmah Castrol. Equally clearly, the wording has been derived from Regulation 1984/83, where such a restriction was permitted, but only in the context of an exclusive purchasing agreement for motor fuels which satisfied the conditions of the Regulation. The present agreement is not associated with such an agreement for motor fuels, and must be examined on its own merits.

26. While the Regulation permits a requirement of exclusive use within the service station of lubricating equipment which has been made available or financed by the petrol company, the dealer must be allowed to sell competing lubricants. In adopting this approach in the category licence for motor fuels, the Authority has explained that it understands that the Regulation does not permit the use of competing lubricants for servicing of cars or for regular topping up on the forecourt, but that competing lubricants may be sold to the motorist for

topping up if specifically requested, and they may be sold for use by the motorist elsewhere.[4] **4.7**
The dealers involved in these Castrol agreements, however, do not usually sell petrol, or oil for topping up, and their primary business is servicing cars, including oil changes, and so the restriction on the use of competing lubricants is virtually absolute.

27. The new agreement effectively requires exclusive purchase of Castrol products. Since competing lubricants cannot be used in the premises for the primary business of the dealer — the servicing of motor vehicles — they cannot be purchased by the dealer either. The Authority stated in the Esso decision[5] that a solus dealer is not permitted to purchase any motor fuels from a supplier other than Esso during the period of the agreement, and no supplier other than Esso may supply the dealer during that period. This limits the commercial freedom of the dealer to obtain supplies, and the freedom of others to supply him. Furthermore, in the case of lubricating oil, consumers go to the workshops in question primarily to have their car serviced, and the supply of oil is only incidental. They do not select a workshop on the basis of the oil supplied, but, once they have chosen the outlet, they have no choice of oil brands where the outlet must purchase the brand exclusively. Such a restriction on consumer choice also constitutes a restriction on competition. While a short-term exclusive purchasing agreement with a single customer would be unlikely to have much impact in the market for lubricants, a network of similar agreements with many major customers with a long duration would have a significant impact. The effects are reinforced when the agreements concern the leading firm, and by far the largest supplier, in the market, and when other major suppliers, according to Burmah Castrol, also have exclusive purchasing requirements. For these reasons, in the opinion of the Authority, the notified agreements offend against section 4(1) of the Competition Act.

28. The agreement defines premises as being the whole premises used or to be used for the purpose of the business of motor vehicle servicing and maintenance. If a lubricating bay or equipment is financed by means of this cash loan agreement the exclusive use is not confined to the bay or the equipment, but it applies to the whole premises. Contrary to the claim by Burmah Castrol, it would not be possible in these circumstances for there to be, in the same premises, one lubrication bay supplied with the assistance of Burmah Castrol and one financed by another supplier, or indeed one financed by the reseller where competing products were used. In addition, Burmah Castrol has submitted that the restriction of the use of other lubricants on the premises is necessary to give effect to the exclusive use of equipment provision, there being no other effective way of policing the latter provision (see para 19).

29. In their submissions, Burmah Castrol drew attention to the judgment of the Court of Justice in the case of *Delimitis v. Henniger Brau.*[6] The Authority agrees with the Court that an exclusive purchasing agreement must be considered in its economic and legal context, and as part of a network of such agreements by one supplier, and, if necessary, as part of a series of networks of several suppliers, as part of its overall assessment. It agrees with the view of the Court that access to the market or increasing market share by competitors must be made difficult, because of the cumulative nature of such agreements, and that the agreement in question must make a significant contribution to the sealing-off effect produced by the totality of these agreements, in order for Article 85(1), and therefore section 4(1), to be applicable. Following this judgment, the EC Commission modified the notice concerning Regulations 1983/83 and 1984/83 by providing that beer supply agreements would not fall under Article 85(1) if, in particular, the market share of the individual brewer did not exceed more than 1 per cent of the national market for the resale of beer in on-licensed premises.'

30. It is clear that, however narrow or broad a definition is adopted of the market for lubricating oil, Burmah Castrol has a market share vastly in excess of 1 per cent. It occupies

4. Category licence for motor fuels, 1 July 1993. *Iris Oifigiúil*, 9 July 1993, pp. 513-515, at Article 3(d).
5. Decision No. 4 of 25 June 1992 — Esso Solus and Related Agreements, p. 11.
6. Judgment of the Court of Justice of 28 February 1991 in the case of *Stergios Delimitis v. Henniger Brau AG* [1991] ECR I-935.

4.7 the leading position without question in the supply of lubricating oil. While only three new loan agreements have been made to date, Burmah Castrol has indicated that this restrictive clause will be included in all future cash loan agreements, and also in amended versions of the equipment loan and hire purchase agreements. Such a policy would have the effect of securing to Burmah Castrol the exclusive right to supply a significant proportion of both franchised and non-franchised outlets, and thereby of denying access to them by competitors for a lengthy period — five years being proposed by Burmah Castrol. Burmah Castrol has stated that other suppliers of lubricants also have exclusive arrangements, and, notwithstanding the fact that a number of workshops might have no exclusive arrangements, a sizeable number would be tied to one or other of the major suppliers of lubricants, including, in all probability, the most important outlets, for a lengthy period of time. The Authority considers that the Henninger Brau judgment does not provide any grounds for considering that the notified arrangements do not offend against section 4(1).

31. While the new cash loan agreement relates primarily to lubricants, it also refers to additives, even though Burmah Castrol has stated that it does not supply additives. The agreement thus has the effect of obliging the reseller to purchase additives exclusively from Burmah Castrol because Burmah Castrol has assisted in the financing of equipment for lubricating oils. This would appear to fall under section 4(1)(e) of the Act, which prohibits agreements which 'make the conclusion of contacts subject to acceptance by the other parties of supplementary obligations which by their nature or according to commercial usage have no connection with the subject of such contracts'. Since Burmah Castrol does not supply additives, the obligation has no meaning. Nevertheless, it is included in the agreement and the Authority considers that this obligation offends against section 4(1).

(ii) *The amended agreement*

32. Under the amended agreement, the clause requiring exclusive use of Castrol lubricants on the premises is deleted and is replaced by a requirement that the equipment whose purchase is financed by the loan should be used exclusively for dispensing lubricant products supplied by Burmah Castrol. This requirement is similar to that in other Burmah Castrol agreements, particularly those under which they have loaned equipment to the workshop. In those cases, the equipment is owned at all times by Burmah Castrol and they have a significant proprietorial interest in the equipment. In the new loan agreements, however, the equipment is owned by the workshop at all times, and Burmah Castrol has merely provided a cash loan, at a low rate of interest, which must be repaid within five years.

33. Suppliers of goods for resale do not usually also supply equipment, or help to finance the purchase of equipment, for the storage of the goods or from which they are dispensed or sold. Where such equipment is supplied or financed, however, there is often a requirement that the equipment be used exclusively for the supplier's goods, and not for other goods, particularly competing goods. Recent cases in respect of Article 85 of the Rome Treaty have involved the exclusive use of ice cream freezer cabinets and are of some relevance. The producers of Mars Ice cream complained to the EU Commission that the two main German ice cream manufacturers were preventing access by Mars to the market by requiring resellers to sell their products exclusively from freezer cabinets supplied and owned by the suppliers, and also by requiring that dealers purchase exclusively from one supplier. In Ireland, Mars brought an action against HB Ice Cream Ltd (a subsidiary of Unilever, as is one of the German firms) alleging infringements of Articles 85 and 86 of the Treaty because of the requirement of freezer exclusivity by HB. (HB also brought a counter-claim against Mars). Reference was made to this case by Burmah Castrol. The EU Commission, by decision of 25 March 1992, took interim measures against the German firms, primarily against the exclusive purchasing requirement.

7. Commission notice modifying the notice concerning Regulations No. 1983/83 and No. 1984/83. OJ C121, 13.5.92, p. 2.

This decision was not published in the Official Journal, and is the subject of an appeal to the EU Court of First Instance. Final decisions in the cases were taken by the EU Commission on 23 December 1992, ruling against the exclusive purchasing requirements.[8] **4.7**

34. In the High Court cases, judgment was delivered by Keane J on 28 May 1992 ([1393] ILRM 145), in the course of which he said:

> 'At the outset, two points should be noted. First, the fact that the impugned term is unarguably intended to prohibit the retailer from stocking other products in the cabinet does not of itself mean that the term is automatically void under Article 85(2). . . .
> In the case of the agreements in issue here, one of the principal objects is to ensure that HB's competitors do not obtain an advantage over them by obtaining cabinet space for the display and storage of their products for which they have not had to pay and which is provided to them free of charge by HB. This cannot be regarded as an inherently anti-competitive objective. . . .
> Again, in this context, the fact that the agreements do not prevent the retailers from selling competing products is of great importance, since in outlets where there is room for more than one cabinet the exclusivity term of itself cannot have the effect of excluding competitors. Even in outlets where there is room for only one cabinet, there is nothing to prevent the retailer from terminating the agreement at any stage and either buying a cabinet himself to stock any brands he wishes or obtaining a cabinet from another supplier. . . .
> Far from being a supplementary obligation which has no connection with the subject of such a contract, the exclusivity term is of the essence of the contract, since where the cabinet is supplied free of charge the whole purpose of the contract would be frustrated from the supplier's point of view if such a term were not to be included.
> I have, accordingly, come to the conclusion that Mars have failed to establish that the agreements in question are prohibited by Article 85(1) and that hence they are not void by reason of Article 85(2). . . .
> The cabinets are supplied by HB for one purpose alone, the storage and display of their products. If they were available to all comers without restriction, then it seems to me that their property rights would have been very significantly eroded indeed'.[9]

It is understood that the judgment has been appealed to the Supreme Court.

35. In the EU decisions on exclusive purchase agreements for ice cream, mentioned in para. 33, the Commission referred in the following manner to exclusive use of freezer cabinets:

> '(134) An exhaustive account of all the barriers to entry to the relevant market will not be attempted here (other examples would be the technology and know-how needed for the production of impulse ice-cream and the consumer preferences which have built up after many years of experience and advertising); but special mention should be made of the insulating effect on the relevant market as a whole of the restrictions on the use of the freezer cabinets which are everywhere supplied to retailers by the established manufacturers (recital 55).
> (135) Clearly, retailers are allowed the use of these freezer cabinets, which are needed for the sale of impulse ice-cream, without having to bear the cost, or at any rate the entire cost, so that by giving up their commercial freedom they avoid having to make the corresponding investments themselves. Even competitors who are ready and willing to

8. Commission decisions of 23 December 1992 under Article 85 — Scholler Lebensmittel GmbH & Co.KG, OJ L183, 26.7.93, p. 1; and Langnese-Iglo GmbH, OJ L183, 26.7.93, p. 19.

9. The High Court. Cases between Masterfoods Ltd trading as Mars Ireland and HB Ice Cream Ltd, and between HB Ice Cream Ltd and Masterfoods Ltd trading as Mars Ireland. Judgment of Keane J, delivered on 28 May 1992, [1993] ILRM, p. 145.

4.7 follow this customary trade practice are restricted in the competition they can offer. They must persuade dealers either to replace their freezer cabinet or to install further cabinets. (136) A trader who replaces his freezer cabinet must give up selling the products of his current supplier. He will not do so if the current supplier, like SLG, is strong on the market, and the competitor is less well known or offers only a partial range which does not provide a full alternative to the earlier one.

> (137) The possibility of installing further cabinets is limited: there may be no space available, or what space there is may be used for commercial purposes other than the sale of ice-cream. In the traditional trade there will be many sales outlets with no space for further cabinets. It might be thought that in other shops space could surely be found somewhere for a freezer cabinet, even if only a small one, as a general rule; but in fact this view seriously misjudges the constraints under which grocery retailing in particular operates.
>
> Firstly, impulse ice-cream cannot be put on offer just 'somewhere'; it is intended for immediate consumption, and must be displayed very close to the check-out desk. And every section of the total surface of a retail store generally has a specific function. The existing freezer cabinets are already geared to the outlet's total requirements. Nor can it generally be expected that sales of ice-cream will increase substantially if further cabinets are installed. The effort and space devoted to a new cabinet is lost to other commercial purposes, without securing additional turnover'.[10]

36. The essential feature of the arrangements under review is that Castrol helps to finance the purchase of equipment by another party in return for which the latter agrees to use the equipment exclusively for Castrol products. An obligation on a reseller to use equipment supplied or financed by the supplier only for the storage and sale of the supplier's goods would not, in the view of the Authority, *per se* offend against section 4(1), unless it had the effect of ensuring that only the goods of that supplier could be sold by the reseller. The use of equipment for the goods of a competitor results in the latter getting a 'free ride' in, and a competitive advantage from, the use of equipment for which the competitor did not pay. If exclusive use of the equipment, however, meant, in a particular set of circumstances, that the goods of only one supplier could be handled by the reseller, this would amount to exclusive purchasing. The reseller could not purchase competing goods from other suppliers, nor could competitors sell to that reseller. As in the Esso case, the Authority considers that exclusive purchasing agreements generally offend against section 4(1). There can be no general presumption under the Competition Act either in favour or against exclusive use of equipment obligations, and each case must be examined on its merits in the light of the prevailing economic circumstances.

37. In the amended agreement, the requirement that the equipment only be used for the dispensing of Castrol products, while it means that it cannot be used for the products of competitors, does not necessarily have the object or effect that the user of the equipment must purchase lubricating oils exclusively from Castrol. While in many workshops there would be space for the installation of equipment for storing and dispensing the oil of one or more competitors, equally, in many instances there would not. What space there is may be better used for other commercial purposes. The existing equipment may be geared to the outlet's total requirements, and it cannot be expected that sales of lubricants would increase if additional equipment were installed. While workshops could return the loaned equipment, they face strong disincentives to doing so. It would be possible to stock the products of competitors which are supplied in small containers, but this might not provide effective competition to oil from dispensing equipment, since it would be less convenient and would be more costly. In these circumstances, the Authority considers that the exclusive use of equipment requirement would in many cases represent an exclusive purchasing requirement. The agreement to finance the

10. Scholler Lebensmittel, op. cit., pp. 15 and 16.

purchase of equipment, provided it is used exclusively for Castrol lubricants, therefore, offends against section 4(1). **4.7**

38. The notified agreement required the exclusive use of additives, which was considered to offend against section 4(1) The deletion of the reference to additives eliminates the concerns of the Authority in this regard.

(b) *Applicability of section 4(2)*

39. Under section 4(2), the Competition Authority may grant a licence in the case of any agreement or category of agreements which, 'having regard to all relevant market conditions, contributes to improving the production of goods or provision of services or to promoting technical or economic progress, while allowing consumers a fair share of the resulting benefit and which does not—

(i) impose on the undertakings concerned terms which are not indispensable to the attainment of those objectives;

(ii) afford undertakings the possibility of eliminating competition in respect of a substantial part of the products or services in question'.

40. In the opinion of the Authority, the new cash loan agreement notified by Burmah Castrol did not fulfil the conditions necessary for the grant of a licence under section 4(2) of the Act. The amended agreement, however, is regarded as satisfying the conditions for a licence.

(i) The notified agreement

41. As stated above, the Authority considers that the requirement in the new cash loan agreement for the exclusive use of Castrol lubricants on the premises constitutes an exclusive purchasing requirement. The Authority recognises that restraints in vertical agreements, that is, for example, in agreements between buyers and resellers, can have pro-competitive features. Restraints such as exclusive purchasing can produce efficiency gains, more effort from retailers into selling products and thus higher sales, the provision of expert advice, and the provision of costly equipment and improved levels of service, among others. These benefits do not, however, automatically result from vertical agreements.

42. In the case of the Burmah Castrol new cash loan agreement, the Authority does not consider that there are any benefits in the way of economies of bulk distribution, since the agreements relate to only a small proportion of Burmah Castrol's lubricants for resale and deliveries appear to be in relatively small volumes. There would appear to be no, or only a minimal, reduction in distribution costs which could be shared with consumers. The Authority recognises, however, that high quality equipment has been part-financed on foot of these agreements, and that Burmah Castrol does provide a high quality of technical services. These promote technical progress. The Authority considers, however, that these benefits, part of which accrues to consumers, do not derive from the exclusive purchasing obligation. The equipment could be supplied by the workshop itself, and Castrol supplies many outlets, the majority in fact, and provides its technical services, without supplying any equipment or finance, and without requiring exclusive purchasing. In addition, two of the existing agreements — the cash loan and hire purchase agreements — do not contain any explicit exclusive purchase requirement. Such a requirement, therefore, is not indispensable to secure any benefits from the supply of lubricants or the provision of equipment. While recognising that these agreements only apply to a minority of outlets, and that lubricating oil forms only a small part of the total servicing operation carried out by these workshops, the Authority nevertheless considers that there is a risk that this type of restriction, if permitted, would be applied in all Burmah Castrol agreements, and in those of other suppliers, leading to a situation of foreclosure against new suppliers. The Authority considers that such agreements could afford undertakings the possibility of eliminating competition in respect of a substantial part of the products in question. Since the essential conditions of section 4(2) have not been satisfied, a licence can not be granted in respect of the notified agreements.

4.7 (ii) The amended agreement

43. The amended new cash loan agreement provides that the equipment which is financed by the Burmah Castrol loan should be used exclusively for the dispensing of Castrol lubricants during the currency of the agreement, which has a term of no more than five years. As explained above, the Authority considers that such exclusive use of equipment requirements, in the circumstances, represent exclusive purchasing requirements in return for the loan of money. Nevertheless, the Authority can take a more favourable view of such arrangements than of exclusive purchase arrangements on their own.

44. As before, the Authority does not consider that equipment exclusivity produces any economies in distribution. It accepts that high quality equipment has been supplied, and that high quality technical services are provided by Burmah Castrol, and that these benefit consumers. An interest rate subsidy is provided in the case of the cash loans. It is likely that the particular equipment would not have been installed in the workshops unless exclusive use of the equipment had been a requirement. Burmah Castrol would have been unlikely to provide such loans if the equipment could have been used freely for competitive products. In this respect, exclusive use for a period of time can be regarded as indispensable to securing the benefits from the supply of the equipment, which may be shared fairly with consumers.

45. Nevertheless, the new cash loan agreement still has a foreclosure effect, because it represents exclusive purchasing, and thus it has the possibility of substantially limiting competition. If the agreements lasted for a long period of time, the foreclosure effect would be considerable. In the case of the amended agreements, however, the problem of foreclosure is considerably reduced since, once the agreement terminates at the end of five years or less, the equipment can then be used for any lubricants of the workshop's choosing. In these circumstances, provided that the period of exclusive use of the equipment does not exceed the period of the loan and that the loan does not exceed five years in duration, the Authority considers that this would not afford the possibility of eliminating competition to a substantial degree. Since all the conditions of section 4(2) have been fulfilled by the amended new cash loan agreement, a licence can be granted for the agreement. An exclusive use requirement for any longer period, however, would not satisfy all the conditions of section 4(2), since it would afford the possibility of eliminating competition and would not be indispensable, and could not be licensed.

Duration of the licence

46. Given that agreements of up to five years' duration are involved, the Authority considers that the appropriate period for the licence should be ten years. Since the agreement was notified under section 7(1), in accordance with section 7(3) the licence can be made retrospective to the date when it satisfied the conditions of section 4(2), that is the date on which the amendments were made. The licence shall apply from 14 November 1994 to 13 November 2004. It is not considered necessary to attach any conditions to the licence.

The Decision

47. Burmah Castrol and their customers who are party to the standard form new cash loan agreement are undertakings within the meaning of the Competition Act. The notified agreement is an agreement between undertakings, and it operates within the State. The Authority considers that the notified new cash loan agreement offended against section 4(1) of the Competition Act, and that it did not satisfy the conditions set out in section 4(2) of the Act. The Authority considers, however, that the agreement, as amended to provide for exclusive use of the equipment for Castrol products for a limited period, not exceeding five years, offends against section 4(1) of the Act but that it satisfies the requirements of section 4(2). Accordingly, the Authority grants a licence to the standard form new Burmah Castrol cash loan agreement, as amended, for a ten year period from the date when the agreement was amended to satisfy the requirements of section 4(2) of the Act.

The licence 4.7

48. The Competition Authority grants the following licence:

> The Competition Authority grants a licence to the new standard form Burmah Castrol cash loan agreement (Notification No. CA/43/92), notified on 8 June 1992, under section 7(1), as amended by the agreement of 14 November 1994 between Burmah Castrol and Carroll and Kinsella Motors (Churchtown) Ltd, on the grounds that, in the opinion of the Authority, all the conditions of section 4(2) of the Competition Act 1991 have been fulfilled. This licence shall also apply in respect of the new standard form Burmah cash loan agreement where it has been amended to accord with the Carroll and Kinsella agreement.

This licence shall apply from 14 November 1994 to 13 November 2004.

For the Competition Authority

Patrick M. Lyons
Chairman

15 December 1994

Competition Authority Decision No. 364 — Cylinder LPG Category Licence — Preamble 4.8

Competition Authority Decision of 28 October 1994 granting a licence under section 4(2) of the Competition Act 1991, to a category of exclusive purchasing agreements in respect of cylinder liquified petroleum gas.

Introduction

1. Under section 4(2) of the Competition Act 1991, the Competition Authority may grant a licence for the purposes of section 4 of the Act to any category of agreements:

> which in the opinion of the Authority, having regard to all relevant market conditions, contributes to improving the production or distribution of goods or provision of services or to promoting technical or economic progress, while allowing consumers a fair share of the resulting benefit and which does not —(i) impose on the undertakings concerned terms which are not indispensable to the attainment of those objectives,
> (ii) afford undertakings the possibility of eliminating competition in respect of a substantial part of the products or services in question.'

2. Several agreements have been notified to the Authority concerning exclusive purchasing arrangements for the resale of cylinder liquified petroleum gas (LPG) by dealers. The Authority issued Statements of Objections to two suppliers in respect of their notified agreements. Having considered certain notified agreements at length and the relevant market, the Authority has decided to grant a category licence under section 4(2) of the Act. The Authority published a draft of the category licence on 24 June 1994, and several submissions were received.

4.8 The Subject of the Decision

3. This decision concerns the supply and exclusive purchasing agreements between suppliers of cylinder LPG and resellers at the retail level, subsequently referred to as dealers. It does not cover agreements for the exclusive distribution of cylinder LPG to dealers, nor to agreements for the purchase of bulk LPG by end-users.

The Product Concerned

4. LPG is the term commonly used to describe butane or propane gases or a mixture of both. These gases can be readily liquified by applying moderate pressure. This gives LPG its unique advantage — it has the clean-burning characteristics of a gaseous fuel while at the same time it can be transported and stored as a concentrated liquid with a high energy content. LPG has a very broad range of applications including domestic and commercial cooking, heating and water-heating; process heating, space and water-heating in industry; the rearing of poultry and farm animals; atmospheric growth enrichment of plants; vehicle propulsion, power generation and finally as a chemical feedstock. LPG is supplied in cylinder or bulk form, cylinder LPG being mainly used for domestic cooking and heating. It is a volatile fuel, and is subject to stringent safety Regulations in storage, handling and use.

The Market

5. LPG forms part of the overall market for energy in Ireland. There is a wide variety of energy products including LPG, oil, coal, turf, electricity and natural gas. The consumption of the different fuels in recent years is shown in Table 1.

Table 1
Final Energy Consumption in Ireland

Fuel	Tons of Oil Equivalent (000's)		Percent of Total	
	1988	1991	1988	1991
Coal	976	845	14.9	11.5
Peat	679	659	10.3	9.0
Oil	3,343	3,966	50.9	54.0
LPG	146	153	2.2	2.1
Gas	485	644	7.4	8.8
Electricity	934	1,084	14.2	14.7
Town Gas	1	—	*	—
TOTAL	6,564	7,351	100.0	100.0

Source: Department of Energy

*Negligible

Oil accounts for well over 50% of final energy consumption in Ireland, and electricity for over 14%, while the share of LPG in the total is only around 2%. While total energy consumption has increased between 1988 and 1991, this is largely due to an increase in oil consumption. Consumption of LPG was slightly higher in 1991 compared to 1988.

6. The Authority agrees with the often stated view of the EC Commission that 'A relevant product market comprises in particular all those products which are regarded as interchangeable or substitutable by the consumer, by reason of the products' characteristics, their prices and their intended use', in situations ranging from application of the merger control Regulation to

the Notice on agreements of minor importance.[1] The substitutes for LPG depend to some extent upon the usage to which the energy is put. For domestic cooking, electric cookers and, where the product is available, natural gas cookers are alternatives to LPG, as are oil-fired and solid fuel cookers. For domestic heating, the alternative fuels are also electricity, natural gas, oil and solid fuel, by means of central heating installations or single appliances or fireplaces. Two or more fuels may be used in a single household. While most fuels are substitutes in the medium to long run, there appears to be a much lesser degree of interchangeability in the short term. Once a particular appliance or system has been purchased, only one form of fuel can normally be used. Thus, for example, only LPG can be used in an LPG cooker or heater. In many households, cylinder LPG is used as a supplementary heating fuel. Some households have more than one appliance or system, each using a different fuel, though this can be costly. Over time, any appliance or system can be replaced by one using a different fuel. If a person wishes to use a cylinder LPG appliance, there is no substitute for a cylinder of LPG. In addition, safety obligations and a cylinder distribution system impose significant extra costs on LPG suppliers compared to other fuels, putting LPG at a relative price disadvantage compared to these fuels. Over the past 12 years, the price of other energy sources, according to Calor, has fallen in relation to LPG. Nevertheless, while mindful of the fact that LPG forms part of the total energy market, the Authority considers that cylinder LPG constitutes a distinct product market on its own. 4.8

7. The total consumption of LPG in Ireland since 1975 is shown in Table 2.

Table 2
LPG Consumption in Ireland ('000 tonnes)

Year	Consumption	Year	Consumption
1975	148	1983	170
1976	148	1984	145
1977	168	1985	147
1978	149	1986	146
1979	166	1987	136
1980	169	1988	130
1981	163	1989	130
1982	176	1990	133

Source: Flogas, Davy Stockbrokers, November 1991.

Note: The above figures relate to tonnes of LPG, as compared to tonnes of oil equivalent in Table 1.

While changes in consumption of LPG as a whole have been marked in some years compared with the previous year, over the period there appears to have been an upward trend in consumption from 1975 to a peak in 1982, with a decline thereafter, so that 1990 consumption was more than 10% below that in 1975 and around 25% lower than the peak level in 1982. A number of reasons was advanced for the fall in LPG consumption over the last ten years, the

1. See, for example, Commission Decision of 2 October 1991 declaring the incompatibility with the common market of a concentration — Aerospatiale-Alenia/de Havilland, (OJ L334, 5.12.91, p. 42, at p.44); and Commission Notice on agreements of minor importance which do not fall under Article 85(1) of the Treaty (OJ C231, 12.9.86, p.2).

4.8 demand for cylinder LPG for domestic purposes, in particular, having suffered a substantial decrease.

8. The structure of the LPG market has changed over the years. The first supplier was Calor, which entered the Irish market in 1936. Kosangas entered in 1951, and Calor took over Kosangas in 1971. That year also, Ergas (later associated with Shell) commenced operations, followed by Flogas in 1978 and Tervas in 1987. Flogas acquired Ergas in 1989, and in 1990 Blugas entered the market, Blugas being formed by three distributors of Esso products.

9. The main suppliers in the market at present are Calor Teoranta, Flogas Ireland Ltd and Blugas Ltd. Calor, which also owns Kosangas, has four import terminals — at Dublin, Cork, Whitegate and New Ross — and distribution terminals at Claremorris and Sligo, and its LPG cylinders are filled at Dublin and Cork. Flogas, which also owns Ergas, has three terminals in the State — at Drogheda, Cork and Ballyhaunis. From these, Flogas supplies a network of distributors, mainly by road tanker, and the distributors 'bottle' the gas in cylinders. Blugas was founded by three firms which were all involved in the oil distribution business. Its LPG is mainly supplied by Esso, and is stored at a terminal in Dublin, where it is bottled. Distribution was initially done by the three founder members, but Blugas itself has now replaced one of these. These three suppliers operate nationwide. Tervas operates mainly in the Cork area, with a small market share. Another firm, Trugas, was reportedly operating in the Drogheda area. Most LPG is imported, with some supplies being obtained from the INPC refinery at Whitegate.

10. The main suppliers have invested heavily in storage and filling equipment at depots, in road tankers and other delivery vehicles, and in small and medium-sized cylinders and bulk storage tanks. Part of the reason for this is that LPG is highly flammable, and has been designated a dangerous substance and is subject to extensive regulation and supervision. LPG is bottled centrally or locally, and is distributed by the supplier or by exclusive distributors to a large number and variety of retail outlets for resale to final consumers. Retail outlets include hardware, grocery, fruit and vegetable shops, builders' providers, newsagents, domestic appliance sales centres, garage forecourts, fuel depots and roundsmen of various sorts, e.g. milk, coal, etc.

11. It is understood that Calor sells through some 3,000 dealers, Flogas through some 3,400, and Blugas through over 1,000, although there was some dispute over these figures. A sizeable number of dealers sell small quantities of LPG, on average less than 10 cylinders a week. Generally each dealer has an exclusive purchase agreement with the supplier, even if supplies are obtained from distributors. Dealers are usually tied to a brand for five years, and are subject to certain safety standards. Suppliers have invested in dealer outlets in the form of hardware, such as cylinders, signs and storage cages, and they provide marketing, technical advice and safety support systems.

12. It is generally accepted that Calor is the market leader, with a share of the total market for LPG in excess of 60%, followed by Flogas with over 30% of the market. Blugas is considered to have a market share of more than 5%, with Tervas having under 1%.

13. LPG can only be used in specific appliances, and suppliers usually insist on approving these. Appliances can use any brand of LPG, although a special adaptor is needed in the case of Ergas.

14. Up to January 1986 the retail price of cylinder LPG was subject to strict price control by way of a Maximum Prices Order. Since then, there has been no statutory control of retail prices for LPG.

The Dealer Agreements

15. According to the notifications received, each dealer in cylinder LPG has an exclusive purchase agreement with its supplier. The dealer is required to purchase cylinder LPG exclusively from the supplier, or from a distributor appointed by the supplier, and is required not to engage, directly or indirectly, in the sale, distribution or advertising of any other brand or brands of LPG. The dealer is also obliged not to sell the product from any premises other

than the premises specified in the agreement. In the case of the Calor (and Kosangas) and Blugas agreements, the agreement remains in force for a period of five years, with no period specified for notice of termination. The Calor agreement, where it has expired, has been replaced by an agreement which provides for such alternative period of exclusive purchase as may be licensed or certified under the Competition Act. (Previous versions of the Calor agreement provided that the agreement would remain in force indefinitely until terminated by either party giving 12 months' notice). The Flogas (and Ergas) agreement provides that the agreement remains in force for two years, and from year to year thereafter, subject to the right of either party to terminate the agreement on giving 12 months' notice, provided that the agreement terminates after five years. All agreements may be renewed after they have been terminated. The agreements do not confer any exclusive territorial rights on the dealer. None of the agreements contain a post-termination non-compete clause, though previous versions of the Calor agreement prohibited the dealer, for 3 months after termination of the agreement, from selling other brands of LPG within a one mile radius of the premises. **4.8**

16. While not explicitly stated in the agreements, dealers are only appointed by the three main suppliers if they meet certain safety standards, as provided in Irish safety standards, I.S. 3213 of 1987, concerning the storage of LPG cylinders and cartridges.

17. Under the terms of the notified agreements, dealers are required not to engage in any activity which might prejudice the promotion and sale of the supplier's brand. They are also required to promote sales and to obtain new customers. Dealers are required to display approved signs, both outside and inside the premises, identifying the dealer as an approved dealer of the supplier. Dealers may be required to display advertising and publicity material, and only to advertise and publicise the product in a form approved by the supplier. They may be required to provide window space to display approved appliances. Dealers are required to sell cylinders under the supplier's trademark.

18. Dealers agree to keep stocks of cylinders and regulators, and in some cases, recognised appliances. They are required to provide suitable storage facilities and to allow access to the premises by the supplier. They may be required not to supply any customer unless that customer has signed an agreement with the supplier. Dealers are required to maintain an up-to-date list of the names and addresses of all customers, which may be inspected by the supplier at any time on request, although this requirement largely does not operate in practice.

19. Dealers may be required not to permit any other person, who is not authorised, to engage in the sale, delivery or service of the product. They may be required to ensure that cylinders are not filled by unauthorised persons. Dealers are required to comply with statutory safety provisions, and with specified standards, and with regulations established by the supplier. Dealers accept that the cylinders and regulators remain the property of the supplier at all times, and that they may not sell or transfer the cylinders other than in accordance with the agreement. Dealers agree that they are not constituted agents or servants of the supplier, though they may describe themselves as authorised dealers. They are required to maintain insurance, including public liability insurance.

20. All the notified agreements provided that the supplier would furnish the dealer with a notification showing the current retail price of the product, and that the dealer was obliged to display this notice in a prominent place on the dealer's premises. The Calor/Kosangas agreements provided that the dealer was required not to exceed the official retail prices in effect at the time of the delivery. (A similar provision was included in the previous Flogas/Ergas agreements).

21. The Calor and Flogas agreements provided that the dealer was not to permit their cylinders to be used other than in recognised appliances. The Calor agreement required the dealer not to sell or advertise appliances other than those recognised by Calor, and not to purchase appliances other than from Calor. The Flogas agreement required the dealer not to sell or advertise appliances which Flogas had notified were unsuitable for use with Flogas or for use in association with or close to Flogas.

4.8 EEC Regulation 1984/83

22. EEC Regulation No. 1984/83, of 22 June 1983, is a block exemption regulation which applies Article 85(3) of the Treaty of Rome to categories of exclusive purchasing agreements. The regulation entered into force on 1 July 1983 and it expires on 31 December 1997.[2]

23. Exemption is granted to agreements involving only two parties whereby the reseller agrees to purchase specified goods only from the supplier, or from a connected undertaking or one entrusted by the supplier with the sale of his goods. No exclusive territory is allotted to the reseller, but the supplier may be obliged not to distribute the contract goods or competing goods in the reseller's principal sales area and at the reseller's level of distribution. There are general provisions regarding what is and is not permissible. The exclusive purchasing agreement must have a definite duration which may not exceed five years, although it may be renewed, and it must not cover more than one type of goods which are not connected to each other either by their nature or by commercial usage. The reseller must be allowed freedom to determine his resale prices. The benefit of exemption may be withdrawn by the Commission from an individual agreement, if the conditions of Article 85(3) are not satisfied.

24. In this latter connection, the decision in 1992 of the EU Commission in the Scholler and Langnese-Iglo cases is of considerable relevance.[3] These German ice-cream manufacturers had exclusive purchasing agreements with a large number of retail outlets. Each had a leading position and a substantial share of the market. The Commission found, inter alia, that the agreements restricted inter-brand competition and restricted the choice available to consumers. There were barriers to entry, and there was not effective competition on the relevant market. The Commission accordingly refused to exempt the Scholler agreements under Article 85(3) of the Rome Treaty, and withdrew the benefit of the block exemption in Regulation 1984/83 from the Langnese agreements.

Subsequent developments

25. Following publication of the draft category licence, a number of submissions was made to the Authority. Calor and Flogas maintained that a licence should be granted for five-year exclusive purchasing agreements. Blugas and Tervas, however, argued that there should not be any exclusive purchasing agreements with LPG dealers. The conflicting arguments are dealt with in the assessment below, and account has been taken of other points made in the submissions.

Assessment

Applicability of section 4(1)

26. Section 4(1) of the Competition Act 1991 prohibits and renders void all agreements between undertakings which have as their object or effect the prevention, restriction or distortion of competition in trade in any goods or services in the State or in any part of the State.

(i) Agreements between undertakings

27. According to section 3(1) of the Act, 'undertaking means a person being a body corporate or an unincorporated body of persons engaged for gain in the production, supply or distribution of goods or the provision of a service.' The suppliers are corporate bodies engaged for gain in the supply and distribution of LPG, both to resellers and to final consumers. Accordingly, the suppliers are undertakings within the meaning of the Act. The dealers may

2. OJ No. L173, 30.6.83, p.5, as corrected in OJ No. L281, 13.10.83, p. 24, and Commission Notice concerning the Regulation, OJ No. C101, 13.4.84, p. 2.
3. Commission decisions of 23 December 1992 under Article 85 — Scholler Lebensmittel GmbH & Co. KG, OJL 183, 26.7.93, p 1; and Langnese-Iglo GmbH, OJL 183, 26.7.93, p. 19.

be either bodies corporate, unincorporated bodies of persons or sole traders, all of whom purchase LPG for resale to consumers, and they are thus engaged in the supply and distribution of LPG for gain. They also are undertakings within the meaning of the Act. The dealer agreements are agreements between undertakings. The relevant product market is that for cylinder LPG. Since the product is distributed, and the dealers are located throughout the State, the relevant geographical market is the State. **4.8**

(ii) The exclusive purchasing requirement

28. The essential feature of the notified agreements is that the dealer must purchase LPG exclusively from the supplier for a specified period, generally for five years, although, in the case of Flogas, the agreement may be terminated after two years, provided that 12 months' notice of termination is given. This exclusive purchasing requirement is accompanied by an obligation not to deal in LPG supplied by another supplier. The exclusive purchasing requirement limits the freedom of the dealer to obtain supplies of LPG from other suppliers, and of other suppliers to supply him, and denies him supplies unless he accepts the exclusive purchase requirement. The arrangements restrict competition in a number of ways. Given the bulky nature of the product, the market is essentially a localised one. This is in contrast to the view taken by the Authority in the case of shopping centres. Consequently, the requirement that the retailer purchase LPG from only one supplier limits competition, particularly in rural and certain suburban areas where there are relatively few other outlets. The Authority accepts that in many instances other brands of LPG may be available from other retail outlets nearby. In many instances, however, this will not be true and the restriction means that the consumer's choice as to which brand of LPG to buy will be greatly limited.

29. While each individual agreement might generally have relatively little effect upon competition, all the agreements together form a network of restrictive agreements for the distribution of each brand of LPG at the dealer level. A significant proportion of all retail outlets in the State is obliged to purchase LPG only from a particular supplier by virtue of these agreements thereby restricting competition throughout the State. In addition, the large number of retailers tied to a specific brand means that in some instances competing retail outlets may be tied to the same brand, effectively reinforcing the restriction on competition in the particular area of the individual agreements. Finally, each supplier's agreements are themselves part of a wider restrictive system for distribution in the cylinder LPG market as a whole. No dealer can purchase LPG from anyone other than the exclusive supplier for a relatively long period of time. This tends to introduce a considerable degree of rigidity into the market, and it makes it difficult for a new entrant to enter the market quickly on any significant scale since a large number of retail outlets for LPG, including most if not all of the best outlets, are not available, at least until their exclusive agreements have expired. The fact that retailers are tied to a particular supplier for up to five years may also prevent other suppliers gaining access to retail outlets in particular local markets. The Authority considers, therefore, that the standard LPG dealer agreements have the object and the effect of preventing, restricting or distorting competition in goods in the State, and thus they offend against section 4(1). This view of the Authority applies whether the exclusive purchasing requirement applies for a fixed number of years only, or whether it applies for a fixed or indefinite number of years subject to a lengthy period of notice to terminate the agreement.

30. This view about exclusive purchasing agreements is consistent with that taken by the Authority in the Esso decision,[4] and also with that in US and EU cases. In the US, for example, the Supreme Court ruled in *Standard Fashion v. Magrane-Houston*[5] that an exclusive purchasing agreement was illegal under section 3 of the Clayton Act which prohibits such arrangements if their effect is to 'substantially lessen competition or tend to create a monopoly'. In that case,

4. Decision No. 4 of 25 June 1992, Esso solus and related agreements, para. 57.
5. *Standard Fashion Co v. Magrane-Houston Co.*, 258 US 346 (1922).

4.8 40% of retailers of the products in question were covered by such agreements. Scherer and Ross report that subsequent court decisions found exclusive purchase agreements involving lower market shares to be illegal.[6] In addition, the Authority agrees with the judgment of the EU Court of Justice in the case of *Delimitis v. Henniger Brau.*[7] The Court stated that an exclusive purchasing agreement must be considered in its economic and legal context, and as part of a network of such agreements by one supplier, and as part of a series of networks of several suppliers, as part of its overall assessment. The Court decided that access to the market or increasing market share by competitors must be made difficult, because of the cumulative nature of such agreements, and that the agreement in question must make a significant contribution to the sealing-off effect produced by the totality of these agreements in order for Article 85(1) to be applicable. The Authority believes that such considerations apply in this instance and consequently, in its view, exclusive purchase agreements for cylinder LPG have the effect of restricting competition within the State. In addition, the Authority believes that the object of the agreements is to restrict competition within the State by restricting dealers to selling only one brand of LPG and preventing other suppliers from gaining access to retail outlets. The Authority also considers that any period of notice to terminate an agreement which lasts for a fixed period of time, and which must terminate at the end of that period, inhibits the freedom of the dealer in deciding whether or not to renew the agreement. For these reasons the exclusive purchase agreements notified by Calor, Flogas and Blugas and any other exclusive purchase agreements for cylinder LPG offend against section 4(1).

(iii) Selection of dealers

31. While the criteria for the selection of dealers were not included in the notified agreements, they do form an integral part of the arrangements for the distribution system of LPG. As in the Esso and other Authority decisions, and in line with the views of the EU Commission and the Court of Justice, the Authority considers that related arrangements should be considered together as one.

32. It appears that not every dealer who wishes to sell a particular brand of LPG will be appointed, and that the arrangements have some of the features of a selective distribution system. In the Metro (No. 1) case, the EU Court of Justice upheld the view of the EU Commission that selective distribution systems based on objective qualitative criteria were not contrary to Article 85(1). The Court said: 'selective distribution systems [constitute], together with others, an aspect of competition which accords with Article 85(1), provided that resellers are chosen on the basis of objective criteria of a qualitative nature relating to the technical qualifications of the reseller and his staff and the suitability of his premises and that such conditions are laid down uniformly for all potential resellers and are not applied in a discriminatory fashion.'[8] The Authority considers that a selective distribution system which is based on objective qualitative criteria does not offend against section 4(1), provided these criteria are not applied in a discriminatory fashion.

33. The Authority considers that refusal to appoint a dealer unless the dealer's premises comply with the Irish safety standards for the storage of LPG is an objective qualitative criterion. A requirement for the dealer to have a reasonable commercial presence in the locality and to have minimum financial capabilities, provided these criteria are not applied discriminatorily, are also accepted as objective qualitative criteria. Given the bulky nature of the product, a requirement that dealers in areas where delivery is necessary should have the ability

6. F.M. Scherer and D. Ross (1990): Industrial Market Structure and Economic Performance, Houghton Mifflin, Boston.
7. Judgment of the Court of Justice of 28 February 1991 in the case of Stergios Delimitis v. Henniger Brau A.G. [1991] ECR I-935.
8. Judgment of the Court of Justice of 25 October 1977 in the case of Metro v. EC Commission [1977] ECR 1875, at p. 1904.

to deliver LPG cylinders is also considered to be an objective criterion. It is relevant that, despite an element of selection of dealers being present, a large number of dealers in LPG has been appointed. None of these requirements is considered to offend against section 4(1). **4.8**

34. Requirements that the dealer has the ability to generate a minimum turnover and that appointments be commercially viable for the dealer do, however, represent quantitative criteria which, by excluding some potential dealers from obtaining supplies of LPG, restrict them in exercising complete freedom to operate their business. Where such restrictions are imposed as part of an agreement or concerted practice between a supplier and other dealers, they represent restrictions on competition which offend against section 4(1). This accords with the judgment of the Court of Justice in the Binon case where it held that 'a selective distribution system . . . is prohibited by Article 85(1) of the Treaty if resellers are chosen on the basis of quantitative criteria.'[9]

(iv) Price Maintenance

35. The notified agreements contained a clause requiring the dealer not to exceed the supplier's official retail prices, and to display prominently a notice showing the current retail prices. These notices did not indicate that the prices were recommended, or that they were not binding on the dealer, or that the dealer was free to set resale prices. The specification of a fixed or a maximum price limits the freedom of the dealer to set prices in accordance with his own judgment. It is not for suppliers to take it upon themselves the role of setting fixed or maximum resale prices for their product. Setting a maximum price on its own can lead to the situation where this becomes the minimum price also, and thus to the only price being charged. Thus the requirement not to exceed the official retail price offends against section 4(1) in the Authority's opinion. The requirement to display prominently the supplier's notice showing the current retail price represents a further restriction of competition. In the Authority's opinion the object of this requirement is to try to ensure that this is the price charged by dealers thereby leading to uniform retail prices for cylinder LPG. These views are supported by considerable evidence that most dealers charge the price on the supplier's display notice most of the time. This price appears, frequently at least, to have been the same for all LPG suppliers in the market. The requirement to display this price virtually ensures that it is the price which will be charged. The Authority regards anything which constitutes, or which enforces or is conducive to, resale price maintenance as a serious restriction upon competition, indeed as the elimination of price competition, and therefore as a serious infringement of the prohibition in section 4(1) of the Act. It tends to ossification of the price structure, and hence to higher prices. This is in line with the general attitude of the EC to resale price maintenance. In the GERO-Fabriek case, for example, the Commission stated that:

> Likewise, the system of imposed retail prices makes it impossible for dealers to fix their own retail prices by reference to their own costs and commercial policy. The free formation of prices and the ability to pass on to purchasers any possible resulting benefits are hindered or at least substantially reduced. The system is thus clearly contrary to the prohibition in Article 85(1).[10]

Thus, requirements to display a notice containing the supplier's current retail prices, and requirements not to exceed the supplier's recommended prices, offend against section 4(1).

36. As it stated in the Esso decision,[11] the Authority does not regard the recommending of

9. Judgment of the Court of Justice of 3 July 1985 in the case of SA Binon and Cie V SA Agence et Messageries de la Presse [1985] ECR 2015, at p. 2044.
10. Commission decision of 22 December 1976 in the case of GERO-Fabriek, OJ No. L16, 19.1.77, p. 8, at p. 11.
11. Op. cit. at para. 57.

4.8 resale prices by the supplier as amounting to resale price maintenance, provided that there is no agreement or concerted practice that the dealer observe these prices, and provided that the dealer is informed that he is free to set his own prices, and it considers that this does not offend against section 4(1). Unless these conditions are satisfied, the recommendation of prices by a supplier would offend against section 4(1).

(v) Post-termination clauses

37. Some older agreements imposed an obligation on the dealer not to compete with the supplier by selling another brand of LPG for a stated period after termination of the agreement. Such a non-compete clause offends against section 4(1).

(vi) Sale of appliances

38. While dealers may be required to purchase LPG exclusively from one supplier, and may be required to sell only approved appliances, they must be free to purchase appliances from any source. Any obligation on dealers to purchase appliances only from the LPG supplier, or from a source specified by the LPG supplier, limits the freedom of the dealer to purchase appliances, and limits the ability of appliance suppliers to supply dealers, and interferes with competition. Such a requirement offends against section 4(1).

(vi) Other clauses

39. The Authority considers that none of the other clauses in the notified agreements come within the scope of the prohibition in section 4(1) of the Act, and in particular:

(a) an obligation on the dealer to operate from specified premises in an area which may be designated by the supplier, since the premises must be approved by the supplier on safety grounds, and since the dealer is not given exclusive rights in any area;

(b) obligations on the dealer to promote sales of the product, to seek new customers and not to prejudice the promotion of the brand, and to keep adequate stocks of LPG cylinders (and appliances where applicable), and to sell under trademarks, do not restrict competition, but rather encourage it;

(c) obligations on the dealer to display signs and to provide display space for appliances, and to secure the supplier's approval for advertising material, do not restrict the dealer's ability to advertise and compete;

(d) obligations on the dealer to ensure that no cylinder will be refilled other than by the supplier or distributor, and to ensure that cylinders are only issued on a service basis, or for the purposes of the agreement, and that the dealer will not dispose of or decant any cylinders, reflect the fact that the supplier is entitled to ensure that its product is used exclusively in its equipment. They also ensure that its property rights are not infringed, that competing products do not get a 'free ride' in equipment for which other suppliers have not had to pay, thus giving them a competitive advantage, and that there is adherence to safety factors. These do not restrict competition within the meaning of section 4(1);

(e) the acceptance that the dealer is not a servant or agent of the supplier, and that appliance customers are customers of the supplier not of the dealer, are designed to limit the liability of the supplier, on safety grounds;

(f) an obligation on the dealer to ensure that each new customer signs a cylinder service agreement reflects the relationship between the supplier and the customer, and does not restrict competition;

(g) an obligation on the dealer to keep a list of names and addresses of customers for inspection by the supplier could be used for anti-competitive purposes, for example to ensure the integrity of a distribution system which offended against section 4(1). The Authority considers that this is not the object or effect of the requirement in the LPG agreements, but rather for reasons of ensuring safety. In case of a complaint or an accident, it is necessary for the supplier to be able to ascertain the source from which the customer obtained the cylinder in question. In addition, the obligation appears rarely to have been enforced, and is virtually redundant, and it does not affect competition; **4.8**

(h) an obligation on the dealer not to permit others to deal in the product is imposed for reasons of safety, and does not affect competition;

(i) obligations to provide suitable storage facilities and to allow access to these by the supplier, to comply with statutory safety provisions, standards and regulations of the supplier, and to maintain insurance, including public liability insurance, do not affect competition; and

(j) obligations on the dealer to sell only approved appliances or not to sell unsuitable appliances, and to ensure that cylinders are used only in recognised appliances, are for reasons of safety, and do not interfere with competition.

Applicability of section 4(2)

40. Under section 4(2), the Competition Authority may grant a licence in the case of any agreement or category of agreements which satisfies all the requirements of the section, as quoted in para 1 above.

41. In the Authority's opinion, exclusive purchasing agreements by dealers for cylinder LPG for a lengthy period of time do not fulfil the conditions set out in section 4(2) and cannot therefore qualify for a licence. Any benefits and efficiencies produced by such arrangements are, in the Authority's view, quite limited in this instance, and a lengthy period of exclusivity is not essential for their attainment. The Authority believes that exclusive purchase agreements for a limited period of time, i.e. no more than two years, may satisfy the requirements for a licence, although it considers that, given the nature of the trade, the operation of such more limited restrictions would need to be closely monitored to ensure that the requirements of section 4(2) are in fact met.

(i) The exclusive purchasing and related requirements

(a) Improvements in distribution and benefits to consumers

42. There are a large number of LPG dealers in the State, most of whom sell only a fairly small number of cylinders. Very many dealers sell, on average, less than ten cylinders a week. There would thus not appear to be any economic or efficiency gains as a result of the exclusive purchasing arrangements. The Authority accepts that there may be some limited improvements in the distribution system arising from the agreements to the extent that they facilitate forward planning by the suppliers. It also recognises that the agreements may contribute to technical progress by virtue of adherence to safety standards. It accepts that LPG is distributed throughout the country, although it believes it would continue to be distributed throughout the State in the absence of any exclusive purchase agreements. The Authority believes that there is some benefit from the agreements in which consumers can share, although these would seem to be rather limited.

(b) Indispensability of the arrangements

43. The Authority does not consider, however, that five year exclusive distribution agreements are indispensable to achieve the limited benefits described above. The Authority accepts that the suppliers have made a substantial investment in terminals, equipment, transport, cylinders and storage tanks. It does not consider that this investment can only be viable if the distribution system for cylinder LPG relies upon exclusive purchase by dealers of the product of one supplier for a five-year period, especially for well-established firms. In the case of many other products, suppliers undertake substantial investments without imposing such exclusive requirements on their customers. It is relevant also that cylinder LPG represents only about 40% of total LPG sales. While exclusive purchasing agreements for a long period might be helpful for a new entrant, as stated in Regulation 1984/83, this does not apply to firms which have become established in the market. It would be more advantageous for consumers, and for

4.8 the suppliers themselves, if suppliers attempted to justify their investment by competing for customers rather than by tying dealers for lengthy periods.

44. The Authority does not believe that regular, stable and convenient supplies of LPG would not be made available to consumers on a widespread basis were exclusive purchasing agreements to be limited to a two-year period. Indeed, competition for market share by suppliers, and attempts to sell to dealers who had formerly been tied to another brand, and increased competition by dealers, could all produce significant benefits to consumers, especially in terms of price, if dealers were free to change supplier more frequently than at present. The Authority considers that market forces should be permitted to determine which LPG brands are sold through which dealer outlets. Any disadvantage to a supplier from the risk of losing a dealer at the end of a two-year period of exclusive purchasing would be offset by its access to other dealers who would only be tied to other suppliers for two years.

45. The Authority does not accept that an exclusive purchasing system is indispensable to ensure adherence to adequate safety standards. Dealers may be selected on the basis of Irish safety standards, as laid down in I.S. 3213 of 1987, and be subjected to the same degree of surveillance thereafter as they have been in the past. There are other ways of ensuring adherence to safety standards than by means of restrictive trading agreements. The Health and Safety Authority, following representations from two of the suppliers, has given its view that the storage of LPG cylinders from more than one supplier in a retail premises should not represent a greater hazard than storage from a single supplier, provided there is adherence with the Regulations and the Approved Code of Practice. The H.S.A. has also stated that the Regulations have no requirements in respect of single, as opposed to multiple, sources of supply, requiring primarily safe storage. The Authority is also aware that some LPG suppliers, and the retailers' association RGDATA, have expressed opposition to exclusive purchasing arrangements for cylinder LPG. The Authority believes that whatever limited benefits are provided by exclusive purchase agreements for cylinder LPG can be achieved with a much shorter period of exclusivity. In particular it can see no reasons why an exclusive purchase requirement for more than two years is necessary to secure such benefits. Thus it concludes that, while some period of exclusivity may well be necessary to achieve such benefits, an exclusive purchasing requirement for more than two years is not indispensable for the achievement of the limited benefits which such arrangements bring about.

(c) Elimination of competition

46. Given the structure of the LPG industry, the Authority considered carefully whether five year exclusive purchasing agreements represented a significant barrier to entry which could result in the foreclosure of new entrants. The long-established firms, Calor and Flogas, have a combined market share of around 90%. Between them, they have exclusive purchase agreements with well over 6,000 dealers. Not surprisingly, these dealers are considered to be those best suited to sell LPG. Establishment of a presence in the market as a supplier of LPG is an expensive operation. Nevertheless, in spite of the fact that the LPG market has been dominated by only one or two firms since its establishment nearly 60 years ago, the Authority considers that the following facts are also relevant:

(a) while some 8,000 dealers are bound under the notified agreements to purchase exclusively from one supplier for up to five years, there are a significant number of other potential outlets available to a new entrant for the sale of LPG, even though many might not be as attractive as the tied outlets;

(b) it might be expected that, on average, up to 20% of the tied agreements expire every year, and the dealer would be free to sign a new agreement with the existing supplier or with another supplier, although it appears than many existing agreements have been signed recently and will not expire for some years, and will then expire at around the same time;

(c) in the case of Flogas, every agreement can be terminated from the end of the second year of the agreement, although the need to give 12 months' notice of termination reduces the scope for taking advantage of this possibility; **4.8**

(d) when an outlet is sold to a new owner, the latter is not bound by the supply agreement, and the dealer is free to obtain supplies from any supplier;

(e) it has been claimed that dealers are changing suppliers more readily, or are negotiating better deals before renewing an agreement, with competition between suppliers for dealers becoming more intense; and

(f) the industry has been marked by the occasional successful entry of new suppliers, such as Ergas in 1971, Flogas in 1978, Tervas in 1987 and Blugas in 1990. Although Ergas ceased to exist as a supplier independent of Flogas in 1989, Blugas appears to have built up a widespread network of dealers and to have achieved a not insignificant market share in a relatively short period. It was undoubtedly better placed to do so given its links with distributors of one of the major oil companies.

The Authority concludes, therefore, that, while the existence of networks of tied dealers with exclusive purchasing agreements for five years makes it more difficult to enter the LPG market than in the absence of such arrangements, access to the retail market is not entirely ruled out and the exclusive purchasing systems do not operate to absolutely foreclose new entry. At the same time, the establishment of a large exclusive dealer network by Blugas, when viewed in conjunction with the Calor and Flogas networks, has made it more difficult for another supplier to enter the market than it was for Blugas to enter. On balance, the Authority considers that there is a significant risk that such five-year arrangements as are contained in the notified agreements could afford the undertakings the possibility of eliminating competition in respect of a substantial part of the products in question. A two-year exclusive purchasing agreement, however, would ensure that all dealer agreements had to be renewed over a two year period rather than over five years, and it would be much easier for a new supplier to enter the market, thus easing the concerns of the Authority in this regard. The Authority considers that two year agreements would not afford the possibility of the substantial elimination of competition.

(d) *Notice of termination*

47. A period for notice of termination, particularly one as long as 12 months, and in the context of a two year agreement, would appear to make it difficult for a dealer to change supplier, and it confers no benefit which could be shared with consumers. A dealer who terminated the agreement at the end of two years could be replaced by a dealer who had been tied to another company but whose agreement had also expired, and, according to the submissions by the two main suppliers, there are a large number of other potential dealers. A period of notice of termination, in the Authority's opinion, is not indispensable. There would, of course, be nothing to prevent the supplier from attempting to negotiate a new agreement before the current agreement had expired.

(e) *Summary*

48. The Authority considers that exclusive purchasing agreements for five years in respect of cylinder LPG do not satisfy the conditions specified in section 4(2), and a licence may not be granted for such agreements. Agreements which contain a period for notice of termination do not satisfy the conditions of section 4(2), and a licence cannot be granted for these either. The Authority considers that LPG dealer agreements which oblige the dealer to purchase exclusively from the supplier for not longer than two years, and not to deal in competing products for the same period, and which do not oblige the dealer to give prior notice of termination before the end of the agreed period, satisfy the conditions of section 4(2), and they may be made the subject of the grant of a category licence.

(ii) Selection of dealers

49. The Authority has indicated above that suppliers are entitled to refuse to supply a dealer who does not satisfy safety requirements without offending against section 4(1). It has

4.8 indicated, however, that, in certain circumstances selection of dealers on a quantitative, subjective or discriminatory basis may offend against section 4(1).The Authority does not consider that selection of dealers on such grounds conveys any benefits which may be shared with consumers, or that it is indispensable. Since the conditions of section 4(2) are not satisfied, arrangements of this nature do not benefit from this category licence.

(iii) Price Restrictions

50. Dealer agreements have required the dealer not to exceed the supplier's official retail prices and to display a notice showing the current retail prices in a prominent place, and some have obliged the dealer not to exceed a specified price. Such clauses in agreements can produce no benefit which could be shared with consumers, they are not indispensable to the exclusive purchasing obligation, and they tend to eliminate competition in respect of a substantial part of the products in question. They satisfy none of the conditions required for a licence under section 4(2) of the Act, and this category licence does not apply to agreements which contain any such requirements.

(iv) Post-term non-compete clauses

51. Agreements which contain any obligation on the dealer not to compete with the supplier after termination of the agreement produce no benefits which can be shared with consumers, and they are not indispensable. They do not satisfy the conditions of section 4(2), and this category licence does not apply to such agreements.

(v) Limitations on dealing in appliances

52. Agreements which contain any obligation on the dealer to purchase appliances only from the LPG supplier, or only from an undertaking specified by the supplier, produce no benefits which can be shared with consumers, and they are not indispensable. They do not satisfy the conditions of section 4(2), and this category licence does not apply to such agreements.

Miscellaneous considerations

Only two undertakings party

53. This category licence applies to agreements to which only two undertakings are party — the supplier and the exclusive purchaser. The benefit of the licence is not lost if the supplier enters into exclusive purchase agreements with many different resellers. The licence also applies if the supplier has delegated certain functions, such as filling cylinders with LPG and/or distributing cylinders to dealers, to connected or independent undertakings. The category licence also applies if the agreements do not contain some of the permitted restrictions, or if the arrangements are less restrictive than those specified, provided that the essential exclusive purchasing nature of the agreements remains.

Withdrawal of the category licence

54. Section 8(3) of the Competition Act states:

> Where the Authority is of the opinion that, having regard to the requirements of section 4(2) and to the basis upon which a licence under that subsection was granted —
> (a) there has been a material change in any of the circumstances on which the decision was based,
> (b) any party commits a breach of any obligation attached to the decision,
> (c) the licence was based on materially incorrect or misleading information, or
> (d) any party abuses the permission granted to it by the licence,
> the Authority may revoke or amend the licence and, without prejudice to the generality

of this subsection, may in particular insert in a licence conditions the effect of which is to prohibit specific acts by any party thereto which would otherwise be authorised pursuant to such a licence. **4.8**

The Authority considers that it also has the power, in accordance with section 8(3), to withdraw the benefit of the category licence in individual cases. This would be the case where an individual agreement had effects incompatible with section 4(2).

Section 5 of the Act

55. This category licence, being granted in accordance with section 4(2) of the Competition Act, does not exclude the application of section 5 of the Act.

Exclusive distribution

56. The licence does not apply where, in addition to the exclusive purchasing obligation on the reseller, the supplier undertakes with the reseller to supply only to the reseller certain goods for resale in the whole or in a defined part of the State. Such an agreement would constitute an exclusive distribution agreement rather than an exclusive purchasing agreement.

Entry into force of category licence

57. The Authority considers that the notified agreements would all have to be amended in order to satisfy the conditions of the category licence, at least to ensure that the maximum term of each agreement does not exceed two years. From now on, any new agreement should have a maximum term of two years, in order to benefit from the category licence. Many agreements which are already in existence have not yet been in effect for more than two years. Each of these would need to be amended so as to expire not more than two years after they were made. Such agreements would terminate over the next two years, after which new agreements will have to be negotiated. Most existing agreements, however, have already been in effect for more than two years. On the coming into force of the category licence, such agreements, since they do not satisfy the conditions for a licence, including this category licence, would have to be terminated forthwith. They could, of course, be replaced by a new two-year agreement with the same supplier. The category licence shall enter into force on 28 October 1994.

Notification

58. In accordance with section 4(3)(b) of the Competition Act, where a licence covers a category of agreements, agreements within that category which comply with the terms of the licence need not be notified under section 7 to benefit from the licence while it is in force.

59. The Authority hopes that suppliers of LPG who wish to benefit from this category licence in future will ensure that new exclusive purchasing agreements satisfy the conditions specified in the licence. Agreements which were in existence on 1 October 1991, and which have been notified to the Authority before 1 October 1992, but which do not fulfil the conditions of the licence, do not qualify for the benefit of the licence, and the grant of this licence constitutes a refusal to grant a licence to such existing agreements.

Duration of category licence

60. The Authority considers that the operation of this category licence should be subject to early review. The specified period for the category licence should be five years. At the end of this period, the duration of the category licence may be extended, with or without amendments to the licence, if it is considered that the requirements of section 4(2) continue to be fulfilled. The category licence shall expire on 31 October 1999.

Reporting conditions

61. In order to facilitate this early review of the category licence, the Authority considers that it is necessary to attach certain reporting conditions to the licence. The suppliers will be

4.8 required to make an annual report to the Authority, at the end of each calendar year, in respect of dealers supplied and sales of cylinder LPG to dealers, so that the Authority can monitor developments in the market. Thus all suppliers who take advantage of the category licence will be required, every year before the end of [June],[1] to send a report to the Authority covering the preceding year. [The first of these reports shall be submitted before the end of March 1995].[1] The reports shall contain the following information:

(a) the total number of dealer LPG agreements in operation at the end of the preceding year;
(b) the total number of new dealer agreements made during the preceding year;
(c) the total number of dealer agreements terminated during the preceding year; and
(d) the total volume of sales, in tonnes, to dealers in standard domestic cylinders (i.e. 11.343 kg) during the preceding year.

The Decision

62. The Competition Authority considers that exclusive purchasing agreements by dealers for cylinder LPG constitute agreements between undertakings which have the object and effect of preventing, restricting or distorting competition in goods in the State, and thus they offend against section 4(1) of the Competition Act 1991. In the opinion of the Authority, having regard to all relevant market conditions, such agreements, provided that they are of fairly short duration, that is not more than two years, generally satisfy all the conditions required for the grant of a category licence under section 4(2)of the Competition Act. Accordingly, the Competition Authority grants a licence to the specified category of agreements, subject to the specified period and specified conditions as required under section 8(1) of the Competition Act, as follows:

The Category Licence

Article 1

Pursuant to section 4(2) of the Competition Act 1991, and subject to the provisions of this licence, the Competition Authority grants a category licence to agreements to which only two undertakings are party and whereby one party, the reseller, agrees with the other, the supplier, to purchase only from the supplier, or from another undertaking entrusted by the supplier with the distribution of his goods, cylinder liquified petroleum gas (LPG) for resale.

Article 2

1. Apart from the obligation referred to in Article 1, no restriction on competition shall be imposed on the reseller other than the obligation not to sell cylinder LPG which is supplied by other undertakings in the premises designated in the agreement while the agreement is in force.

2. Article 1 shall apply notwithstanding that the reseller undertakes any or all of the following obligations:

(a) to purchase minimum quantities, or to take minimum deliveries, of goods which are subject to the exclusive purchasing obligation;

(b) to sell the contract goods under trademarks, or only in cylinders owned by the supplier;

(c) to take measures for the promotion of sales, in particular:

— to advertise;

1. 'June' was inserted for March and the sentence in square brackets was deleted by Decision 402 of 19 June 1995.

— to maintain a stock of LPG cylinders and regulators and, where relevant, of LPG appliances;
— to provide customer services;
— to provide display space for appliances.

(d) to sell only from the premises specified in the agreement;

(e) to meet safety standards, and to comply with statutory safety provisions, specified standards, and regulations laid down by the supplier;

(f) to provide suitable storage, and to allow access by the supplier;

(g) not to prejudice the promotion and sale of the goods;

(h) not to permit any other person to deal in the goods;

(i) to ensure that cylinders are not filled by unauthorised persons;

(j) to maintain adequate insurance;

(k) to supply only customers who have signed an agreement with the supplier;

(l) to maintain a list of names and addresses of customers, for inspection by the supplier;

(m) to sell only recognised appliances and not to sell unsuitable appliances; and

(n) to permit LPG cylinders to be used only in recognised appliances.

Article 3

Article 1 shall not apply where:

(a) the agreement is concluded for an indefinite duration or for a period of more than two years;

(b) the supplier agrees with resellers to limit the number of resellers selected for reasons other than those related to objective grounds of safety, and in particular where dealers are selected on the basis of quantitative, subjective or discriminatory criteria;

(c) the supplier imposes on the reseller exclusive purchasing obligations for goods other than cylinder LPG, or for services;

(d) the supplier imposes any restriction on the reseller after the date of expiry of the exclusive purchasing agreement, and in particular imposes an obligation:

— to conclude a further exclusive purchasing agreement for a fixed or indefinite period, or
— not to engage in the purchase and resale of competing goods.

(e) the supplier obliges the reseller to sell at a fixed price, or at not less than a minimum price or at not more than a maximum price;

(f) the supplier recommends to the reseller a specified resale price or a specified maximum resale price, unless the reseller is informed that he is free to determine his own resale prices;

(g) the supplier obliges the reseller to display a list of resale prices notified by the supplier;

(h) the supplier obliges the reseller to give any advance notice of termination of the agreement.

Article 4

The Authority may withdraw the benefit of this category licence, pursuant to section 8(3) of the Competition Act 1991, when it finds in a particular case that an agreement which is exempted by this licence nevertheless has certain effects which are incompatible with the conditions set out in section 4(2) of the Competition Act.

4.8 *Article 5*

This category licence constitutes a refusal to grant a licence to notified agreements which do not fulfil its conditions. In particular, the following agreements, as notified, do not fulfil these requirements:

CA/14/92E — Flogas Ireland Ltd/dealer agreement;
CA/213/92E — Calor Teo/dealer agreement; and
CA/538/92E — Blugas Ltd/dealer agreement.

Article 6

This category licence shall not apply to agreements by which the supplier undertakes with the reseller to supply only to the reseller cylinder LPG, or LPG for use in cylinders, for resale, in the whole or in a defined part of the State, and the reseller undertakes with the supplier to purchase these goods only from the supplier.

Article 7

[Suppliers who take advantage of this category licence are required, every year before the end of March, to send a report to the Competition Authority in respect of the following:][1]

(a) the total number of dealer LPG agreements in operation at the end of the preceding year;

(b) the total number of new dealer agreements made during the preceding year;

(c) the total number of dealer agreements terminated during the preceding year; and

(d) the total volume of sales, in tonnes, to dealers in standard domestic cylinders (i.e. 11.343 kg) during the preceding year.

[The first of these reports shall be submitted before the end of March 1995].[2]

Article 8

This category licence shall enter into force on 28 October 1994. It shall expire on 31 October 1999.

For the Competition Authority

Patrick M. Lyons
Chairman
28 October 1994

1. The sentence in square brackets was substituted by 'It is a condition of this category licence that suppliers are required every year before the end of June to sent a report to the Competition Authority in respect of the following:' consequent upon Decision 402 of 19 June 1995.
2. This sentence was deleted and he following added 'For the avoidance of doubt. Failure by a supplier to comply with this condition shall have the effect that the agreements of that supplier do not benefit from this category licence' consequent upon Decision No. 402 of 19 June 1995.

Competition Authority Decision No. 372 — Franchise Agreement Category Licence — Preamble 4.9

Competition Authority Decision of 17 November 1994 granting a licence under section 4(2) of the Competition Act 1991, to categories of franchise agreements.

Introduction

1. Under section 4(2) of the Competition Act 1991, the Competition Authority may grant a licence for the purposes of section 4 of the Act to any category of agreements:

> which in the opinion of the Authority, having regard to all relevant market conditions, contributes to improving the production or distribution of goods or provision of services or to promoting technical or economic progress, while allowing consumers a fair share of the resulting benefit and which does not—
> (i) impose on the undertakings concerned terms which are not indispensable to the attainment of those objectives;
> (ii) afford undertakings the possibility of eliminating competition in respect of a substantial part of the products or services in question.

2. A large number of notifications has been made to the Authority concerning franchise agreements for the sale of products or the supply of services. Having considered the notified agreements in detail, the Authority has decided to grant a category licence under section 4(2) of the Act. A draft of the category licence was published on 8 July 1994. Several submissions were received, and these have been taken into account by the Authority.

The subject of the Decision

3. This decision concerns arrangements whereby one of the parties supplies goods or provides services to end users under a franchise agreement. A franchise agreement consists essentially of a licence of industrial or intellectual property rights relating to trade marks or signs and know-how, which can be combined with restrictions relating to the supply or purchase of goods. The licence usually includes restrictions in relation to the assignment or use of industrial property rights, and the agreement usually involves also the exclusive distribution or exclusive purchase of goods. According to Bellamy & Child:

> Each franchisee remains an independent trader bearing his own financial risk, but pays royalties to the franchisor. The franchisor's aim is to create a chain of franchisees using a uniform presentation and selling products or services of uniform quality; to the outside observer the outlets look like subsidiaries or branches of the franchisor. To achieve that uniformity the franchisor normally requires the franchisee to obtain his stock from the franchisor or from sources nominated by him or to produce it in accordance with the franchisor's specifications; the franchisor provides know-how and commercial assistance and a marketing image which usually has proven market appeal. He usually retains the right to supervise the location, layout and decor of the premises. In general terms, the franchising relationship involves a greater degree of co-operation and a greater involvement of the supplier in the licensed enterprise than is found in other kinds of vertical agreement.[1]

4. This decision covers franchise agreements between two undertakings, the franchisor and the franchisee, for the retailing of goods or the provision of services to end users, or a

1. Bellamy & Child, *Common Market Law of Competition*, 4th ed., Sweet & Maxwell 1993, para 7-163.

4.9 combination of these activities, such as the processing or adaptation of goods to fit specific needs of their customers. It also covers cases where the relationship between franchisor and franchisees is made through a third undertaking, the master franchisee. The decision does not cover wholesale franchise agreements or industrial franchise agreements.

The Products and the Market

5. Franchise agreements operate in many lines of business. A very wide variety of goods and services forms the subject matter of the notified agreements, there being more than one notification of a particular agreement in some cases. These include the selling of groceries, builders' materials, posters, jeans and babywear; fast food and catering services; hotels; health and fitness; the cleaning of vehicles, carpets and video display units; vehicle tuning; video rental; and sharpening of knives and blades. Given the large number and the heterogeneous nature of the products and services concerned, and of those which may also be included in other agreements which have not been notified or which may be made in future, it is not possible to describe the relevant market conditions which prevail. It is not necessary to do so in the case of this category licence, however, in particular because the benefit of the category licence may be withdrawn in the case of an individual agreement if it is found that it does not satisfy all the conditions prescribed in section 4(2), especially where competitive conditions in the market are inadequate.

6. Most of the notified agreements stipulate the territory concerned, this being either the whole or a part of the State, though the territory sometimes includes Northern Ireland. This decision covers agreements which relate to the State or any part of the State.

EU Treatment of Franchise Agreements

7. In 1986, the European Court of Justice issued an important judgment on franchise agreements in the Pronuptia case.[2] The Court recognised that there were different forms of franchise agreements and indicated that it was only concerned with what it termed 'a distribution franchise'. The Court held that franchise agreements, which brought benefits to both parties, were not as such restrictive of competition. They often enabled a franchisor to exploit the expertise he had acquired, without having to invest in a retail network. They also gave inexperienced retailers access to trading methods which had already proved successful while enabling them to remain independent. The Court held that obligations in the agreement which were necessary to support the essential ingredients of the franchising relationship did not fall within Article 85(1) of the Treaty of Rome, but that certain other clauses could do so. One essential ingredient for a franchise system to work was that the franchisor had to be able to give the franchisee his know-how and assistance without fearing that the information would benefit competitors. A second essential ingredient was that the franchisor had to have sufficient control over the operation of the retail outlet to enable him to protect the common identity and reputation of the network trading under the franchisor's name. Clauses which were necessary to achieve these objectives, according to the Court, fell outside Article 85(1). The Court stated, however, that clauses which did not relate to these essential ingredients might fall within Article 85(1), especially where these concerned market-sharing or limitations on price competition. Some of these restrictive clauses might be capable of exemption under Article 85(3).

8. Following this judgment, and some individual decisions on franchise agreements, the EU Commission, in 1988, made a block exemption regulation, Regulation 4087/88, granting exemption under Article 85(3) to categories of franchise agreements.[3] The Regulation applies from 1 February 1989, and expires at the end of 1999. The Regulation exempts agreements to

2. Judgment of the Court of Justice of 28 January 1986 in the case of *Pronuptia de Paris GmbH v Pronuptia de Paris Irmgard Schillgalis* [1986] ECR 353

3. Commission Regulation (EEC) No. 4087/88 of 30 November 1988 on the application of Article 85(3) of the Treaty to categories of franchise agreements, OJ L359, 28.12.88, p.46.

which only two firms are party and whereby one firm, the franchisor, enters into an agreement with another firm, the franchisee, under which the latter is granted the right to exploit a franchise for the purposes of marketing specified types of goods and/or services. It does not cover industrial or wholesale franchise agreements. The Regulation specifies which clauses the franchise agreement can contain and which must not be included if it is to benefit from the block exemption. The obligations which are not normally restrictive of competition include those which are essential either to preserve the common identity and reputation of the network or to prevent the know-how made available and the assistance given by the franchisor from benefiting competitors. It is necessary, however, that parallel imports remain possible. The Regulation exempts the territorial protection granted by the franchisor to the franchisee, the location clause imposed on the franchisee and the obligation on the latter not to sell contract products outside the franchise network. It also exempts an obligation for the franchisee to resell exclusively the franchisor's goods which form the essential subject of the franchise, and a post-term non-competition obligation for a reasonable period not exceeding one year. Resale price maintenance is specifically prohibited, but recommended prices are allowed. An accelerated opposition procedure is provided for dealing with franchise agreements containing clauses not specified among those expressly exempted or prohibited. Benefit of the exemption may be withdrawn in any particular case where an agreement has effects which are incompatible with the conditions laid down in Article 85(3), particularly where competition is significantly restricted because of the structure of the relevant market. 4.9

Assessment

(a) *Applicability of section 4(1)*

9. Section 4(1) of the Competition Act 1991, prohibits and renders void all agreements between undertakings which have as their object or effect the prevention, restriction or distortion of competition in trade in any goods or services in the State or in any part of the State.

10. The franchisors, whether they are located outside or inside the State, are engaged in the supply of goods and/or the provision of services for gain, and the same applies to the franchisees, including master franchisees. Both franchisors and franchisees are therefore undertakings within the meaning of section 3(1) of the Competition Act. The franchise agreements are agreements between undertakings. The relevant product or service in each case is as specified in the individual agreement. The relevant geographic market is the State or a specific part of the State, depending on the agreements concerned. This decision only applies to agreements to which only two undertakings are party — the franchisor and the franchisee. Several undertakings forming one economic unit (such as the franchisee and its owner acting as guarantor) count as one undertaking for the purposes of this decision.

(i) The franchise agreement as a whole

11. The Authority considers that, for the purposes of this decision, it should adopt the definitions of 'franchise' and 'franchise agreement' used in Regulation 4087/88. There, a 'franchise' is defined to mean:

> a package of industrial or intellectual property rights relating to trade marks, trade names, shop signs, utility models, designs, copyrights, know-how or patents, to be exploited for the resale of goods or the provisions of services to end users.

A 'franchise agreement' is defined as:

> an agreement whereby one undertaking, the franchisor, grants the other the franchisee, in exchange for direct or indirect financial consideration, the right to exploit a franchise

4.9 for the purposes of marketing specified types of goods and/or services; it includes at least obligations relating to:

— the use of a common name or shop sign and a uniform presentation of contract premises and/or means of transport,

— the communication by the franchisor to the franchisee of know-how,

— the continuing provision by the franchisor to the franchisee of commercial or technical assistance during the life of the agreement.

The Authority also adopts the definition of 'know-how' in the Regulation, whereby 'know-how' means:

> a package of non-patented practical information, resulting from experience and testing by the franchisor, which is secret, substantial and identified.

It also adopts the definitions of 'secret', 'substantial' and 'identified' contained in the Regulation, as well as the other definitions therein.

12. The Authority also agrees with the view of the Court of Justice that a franchise agreement differs from an exclusive distribution agreement in that, for example, it imposes obligations regarding the use of a business name and methods and the provision of know-how. For this reason, the Court held that franchise agreements did not come within the block exemption for exclusive distribution agreements. Likewise, the Authority considers that franchise agreements do not come within the scope of its category licence for exclusive distribution agreements.[4]

13. The Authority agrees with the view of the Court that franchise agreements as such are not restrictive of competition, nor are obligations in franchise agreements which are necessary to support the essential ingredients of the franchising relationship, namely clauses that:

(a) are essential to prevent the know-how made available and the assistance given by the franchisor from benefiting competitors; or

(b) that provide for the control essential to preserve the common identity and reputation of the network trading under the franchisors' name.

Franchise agreements which contain only obligations of this nature do not, in the Authority's opinion, have as their object or effect the prevention, restriction or distortion of competition, and so they do not offend against section 4(1) of the Competition Act. Many franchise agreements, however, contain obligations which go beyond these parameters, and they may therefore offend against section 4(1). Individual obligations under each heading are described below.

(ii) Clauses which do not offend against section 4(1)

14. The Authority considers, in the first place, that certain obligations on the franchisor do not offend against section 4(1), because they form part of the basic services the franchisor provides to the franchisee. These include obligations on the franchisor to assist the franchisee with selecting the site and premises, shopfitting, promotion and advertising, training, news of products, innovations, etc.

15. The Authority considers that the following obligations on the franchisee are in conformity with the two parameters described above:

(a) to sell, or use in the course of the provision of services, exclusively goods matching minimum objective quality specifications laid down by the franchisor;

(b) to sell, or use in the course of the provision of services, goods which are manufactured only by the franchisor or by third parties designated by it, where it is impracticable, owing to the nature of the goods which are the subject matter of the franchise, to apply objective quality

4. Licence for Categories of Exclusive Distribution Agreements, Decision No. 144, 5 November 1993.

specifications; 4.9

(c) not to engage, directly or indirectly, in any similar business in a territory where it would compete with a member of the franchised network, including the franchisor; the franchisee may be held to this obligation after termination of the agreement, for a reasonable period which may not exceed one year, in the territory where it has exploited the franchise;

(d) not to acquire financial interests in the capital of a competing undertaking, which would give the franchisee the power to influence the economic conduct of such undertaking;

(e) to sell the goods which are the subject-matter of the franchise only to end users, to other franchisees and to resellers within other channels of distribution supplied by the manufacturer of these goods or with its consent;

(f) to use its best endeavours to sell the goods or provide the services that are the subject-matter of the franchise; to offer for sale a minimum range of goods, achieve a minimum turnover, plan its orders in advance, keep minimum stocks and provide customer and warranty services;

(g) to pay to the franchisor a specified proportion of its revenue for advertising and itself carry out advertising for the nature of which it shall obtain the franchisor's approval.

Accordingly, such obligations do not offend against section 4(1).

16. The Authority considers that the following obligations on the franchisee also do not offend against section 4(1), that is obligations:

(a) not to disclose to third parties the know-how provided by the franchisor; the franchisee may be held to this obligation after termination of the agreement;

(b) to communicate to the franchisor any experience gained in exploiting the franchise and to grant it, and other franchisees, a non-exclusive licence for the know-how resulting from that experience;

(c) to inform the franchisor of infringements of licensed industrial or intellectual property rights, to take legal action against infringers or to assist the franchisor in any legal actions against infringers;

(d) not to use know-how licensed by the franchisor for purposes other than the exploitation of the franchise; the franchisee may be held to this obligation after termination of the agreement;

(e) to attend or have its staff attend training courses arranged by the franchisor;

(f) to apply the commercial methods devised by the franchisor, including any subsequent modification thereof, and use the licensed industrial or intellectual property rights;

(g) to comply with the franchisor's standards for the equipment and presentation of the contract premises and/or means of transport;

(h) to allow the franchisor to carry out checks of the contract premises and/or means of transport, including the goods sold and the services provided, and the inventory and accounts of the franchisee;

(i) not without the franchisor's consent to change the location of the contract premises;

(j) not without the franchisor's consent to assign the rights and obligations under the franchise agreement.

(iii) Clauses which offend against section 4(1)

17. The Authority considers that in certain circumstances the following obligations may involve a restriction upon competition:

(a) an obligation on the franchisor, in the State or in a defined area of the State, the contract territory, not to:

- grant the right to exploit all or part of the franchise to third parties,
- itself exploit the franchise, or itself market the goods or services which are the subject-matter of the franchise under a similar formula,
- itself supply the franchisor's goods to third parties;

(b) an obligation on the franchisee to exploit the franchise only from the contract premises;

4.9 (c) an obligation on the franchisee to refrain, outside the contract territory, from seeking customers for the goods or the services which are the subject-matter of the franchise;

(d) an obligation on the franchisee not to manufacture, sell or use in the course of the provision of services, goods competing with the franchisor's goods which are the subject-matter of the franchise.

The first three of these obligations could involve market sharing between the franchisor and the franchisee or between franchisees. The effect of these obligations is to protect each franchisee from competition from the franchisor or from other franchisees. The last obligation prevents the franchisee from dealing in competing goods. Where such restrictions restrict competition, they also, in the Authority's opinion, offend against section 4(1).

18. Any provisions in a franchise agreement which restrict the franchisee's freedom to determine his own prices would always offend against section 4(1), in the Authority's opinion. The franchisor is, however, entitled to recommend prices to franchisees, provided there is no concerted practice whereby franchisees are expected to abide by such prices.

(b) *Applicability of section 4(2)*

19. Under section 4(2), the Competition Authority may grant a licence in the case of any agreement or category of agreements which satisfies all the requirements of the section, as quoted in para. 1 above.

20. In the opinion of the Authority, franchise agreements, in general, are likely to fulfil the conditions provided for in section 4(2) and qualify for the grant of a category licence.

21. Franchise agreements which are covered by this decision normally improve the distribution of goods and/or the provision of services as they give franchisors the possibility of establishing a uniform network with limited investments, which may assist the entry of new competitors on the market, particularly in the case of small and medium-sized undertakings, thus increasing interbrand competition. They also allow independent traders to set up outlets more rapidly and with a higher chance of success than if they had to do so without the franchisor's experience and assistance. They have therefore the possibility of competing more efficiently with large distribution undertakings.

22. As a rule, franchise agreements also allow consumers and other end users a fair share of the resulting benefit, as they combine the advantage of a uniform network with the existence of traders personally interested in the efficient operation of their business. The homogeneity of the network and the constant cooperation between the franchisor and the franchisees ensures a constant quality of the products and services. The favourable effect of franchising on interbrand competition and the fact that consumers are free to deal with any franchisee in the network guarantees that a reasonable part of the resulting benefits will be passed on to the consumers.

23. In order to satisfy the requirements of the category licence, only specific obligations which are restrictive of competition may be included in franchise agreements. This is the case in particular for the granting of an exclusive territory to the franchisees combined with the prohibition on actively seeking customers outside the territory, which allows them to concentrate their efforts on their allotted territory. The same applies to the granting of an exclusive territory to a master franchisee combined with the obligation not to conclude franchise agreements with third parties outside that territory. Where the franchisees sell, or use in the process of providing services, goods manufactured by the franchisor or according to its instructions, and/or bearing the franchisor's name or trade mark, an obligation on the franchisees not to sell, or use in the process of the provision of services, competing goods, makes it possible to establish a coherent network which is identified with the franchised goods. However, this obligation should only be accepted with respect to the goods which form the essential subject-matter of the franchise. It should notably not relate to accessories or spare parts for these goods. The obligations referred to above thus do not impose restrictions which are not necessary for the attainment of the above mentioned objectives. In particular, the limited

territorial protection granted to the franchisees is indispensable to protect their investment. **4.9**

24. The category licence must specify the conditions which must be satisfied for the licence to apply. To guarantee that competition is not eliminated for a substantial part of the goods which are the subject of the franchise, it is necessary that there should not be absolute territorial protection for franchisees. Therefore, cross deliveries between franchisees should always be possible. Furthermore, where a franchise network is combined with another distribution system, franchisees should be free to obtain supplies from authorized distributors.

25. The category licence must also specify restrictions which may not be included in franchise agreements if these are to benefit from the exemption granted by the licence, by virtue of the fact that such provisions are restrictions falling under section 4(1) for which there is no general presumption that they will lead to the positive effects required by section 4(2). This applies in particular to market sharing between competing manufacturers, to clauses unduly limiting the franchisee's choice of suppliers or customers, and to cases where the franchisee is restricted in determining its prices. However, the franchisor should be free to recommend prices to the franchisees to the extent that it does not lead to concerted practices for the effective application of these prices.

(c) *Miscellaneous considerations*

Withdrawal of the category licence

26. Section 8(3) of the Competition Act states:

> Where the Authority is of the opinion that, having regard to the requirements of section 4(2) and to the basis upon which a licence under that subsection was granted:
> (a) there has been a material change in any of the circumstances on which the decision was based,
> (b) any party commits a breach of any obligation attached to the decision,
> (c) the licence was based on materially incorrect or misleading information, or
> (d) any party abuses the permission granted to it by the licence,
>
> the Authority may revoke or amend the licence and, without prejudice to the generality of this subsection, may in particular insert in a licence conditions the effect of which is to prohibit specific acts by any party thereto which would otherwise be authorised pursuant to such a licence.

The Authority considers that it also has the power, in accordance with section 8(3), to withdraw the benefit of the category licence in individual cases. This would be the case where an individual agreement had effects incompatible with section 4(2).

Duration of the Category Licence

27. As in the case of exclusive distribution agreements, the Authority considers that the specified period for the licence should be five years, so as to allow the possibility for early review. At the end of this period, the period of the category licence may be extended, with or without amendments to the licence, if it is considered by the Authority that the requirements of section 4(2) continue to be fulfilled. The Authority considers that the category licence should expire on the same date as Regulation No. 4087/88. The category licence shall enter into force on 17 November 1994. It shall expire on 31 December 1999. The category licence is at the end of this Decision.

Notification

28. In accordance with section 4(3)(b) of the Competition Act, where a licence covers a category of agreements, agreements within that category which comply with the terms of the

4.9 licence need not be notified under section 7 to benefit from the licence while it is in force. Nevertheless, where there is a real doubt, in a particular case, an undertaking may request the Authority to declare whether its agreements comply with this category licence. This would have to be done by way of full notification under section 7.

29. It is expected that franchisors and franchisees who wish to benefit from this category licence in future will ensure that new franchise agreements satisfy the conditions specified in the licence. Parties to agreements which have been made prior to the coming into force of the category licence will also presumably seek to amend these agreements if necessary so as to satisfy the conditions of the licence, especially in the case of agreements which were in existence on the date of commencement of the Act, that is agreements which were entered into prior to 1 October 1991. Appropriate provisions are necessary in the circumstances.

Agreements already notified

30. In the case of franchise agreements which were in existence on 1 October 1991, and which have been notified to the Authority before 1 October 1992, this licence shall have effect from 17 November 1994 where the agreements already fulfil the conditions of that licence. Where such notified agreements do not fulfil the conditions of the licence, they do not qualify for the benefit of the licence. The Authority will inform notifying parties whether their agreement fulfils the conditions of the licence, and, if it does not, the reasons for this. Where such notified agreements are amended to fulfil the conditions of the licence, the licence shall have effect from the date when the conditions of the licence are fulfilled.

31. In the case of franchise agreements which came into existence after 1 October 1991, and which have been notified to the Authority before 17 November 1994, this licence shall have retroactive effect from the date of notification, if the agreements already fulfilled the conditions of the licence, or from the date, being not earlier than the date of notification, when the conditions of the licence were fulfilled. The Authority will inform the parties whether their agreement fulfils the conditions of the licence or not. For other agreements which came into existence after 1 October 1991, and which have not been notified, or those which come into existence in the future, this licence shall have effect from the date, at or after the date of grant of the licence, upon which its conditions are fulfilled.

Other category licences

32. Agreements may benefit from the provisions either of this category licence or of another category licence, according to their particular nature and provided that they fulfil the necessary conditions of application. They may not benefit from a combination of the provisions of this category licence with those of another category licence.

Divergences from EU Regulation 4087/88

33. This Decision and the category licence itself are based to a very large extent upon EU Regulation 4087/88, which grants a block exemption from the prohibition of Article 85(1) of the Treaty of Rome to certain categories of franchise agreements. One difference between the category licence and the Regulation, however, is that references to the common market or to a defined area of the common market in the Regulation are altered to the State or to a defined area of the State in the category licence. In addition, references to exemption and the Regulation are altered to references to the category licence.

34. The main difference is that the category licence omits Article 6 of the Regulation which provides for an accelerated opposition procedure. This allows for agreements which contain clauses not specifically covered by the Regulation to be notified to the EU Commission and for exemption to follow provided that the Commission does not oppose the application for exemption within a specified period of time (six months). The Authority does not consider that there is a need for such a procedure in the case of this category licence. The procedure appears to have been of little practical use, and it is significant that the Commission is proposing to

eliminate similar procedures from revised block exemption Regulations for intellectual property licences. Consequently, Article 7 of the Regulation, which imposes an obligation of secrecy upon the Commission and the authorities of the Member States in connection with this procedure, is also omitted from the category licence. 4.9

35. In addition, unlike the Regulation, which contains no transition provisions, the category licence has to make provision for agreements which have been notified to the Authority, which are contained in Article 7 of the category licence. Finally, the Authority does not consider it necessary to include the following parts of the Regulation in the category licence:

(i) Article 2(b), which permits an obligation on the master franchisee not to conclude franchise agreements outside its contract territory (because in general the contract territory in such agreements covers the whole State);

(ii) Article 4(b) and (c), which impose conditions for the application of the exemption, namely concerning the honouring of guarantees by franchisees and the indication by a franchisee of its status as an independent undertaking; and

(iii) Article 8 where specific examples are given of the circumstances in which the benefit of the Regulation may be withdrawn in a particular case.

Any franchise agreement, however, which comes within the scope of Article 85(1) of the Treaty would have to satisfy the conditions of the Regulation in order to benefit from the block exemption afforded by the Regulation, irrespective of whether it satisifies the conditions for this category licence.

The Decision

36. The Competition Authority considers that franchise agreements, which contain certain clauses which restrict competition, constitute agreements between undertakings which have the object and effect of preventing, restricting or distorting competition in goods and/or services in the State, and thus they offend against section 4(1) of the Competition Act 1991. In the opinion of the Authority, having regard to all relevant market conditions, such agreements generally satisfy all the conditions required for the grant of a category licence under section 4(2) of the Competition Act. Accordingly, the Competition Authority grants a licence to the specified category of agreements, subject to the specified period and specified conditions as required under section 8(1) of the Competition Act, as follows:

The Category Licence 4.9.1

Article 1

1. Pursuant to section 4(2) of the Competition Act 1991, and subject to the provisions of this licence, the Competition Authority grants a category licence to franchise agreements to which two undertakings are party, which include one or more of the restrictions listed in Article 2.

2. The category licence provided for in paragraph 1 shall also apply to master franchise agreements to which two undertakings are party. Where applicable, the provisions of this category licence concerning the relationship between franchisor and franchisee shall apply mutatis mutandis to the relationship between franchisor and master franchisee and between master franchisee and franchisee.

3. For the purposes of this category licence:

(a) 'franchise' means a package of industrial or intellectual property rights relating to trade marks, trade names, shop signs, utility models, designs, copyrights, know-how or patents, to be exploited for the resale of goods or the provision of services to end users;

4.9.1 (b) 'franchise agreement' means an agreement whereby one undertaking, the franchisor, grants the other, the franchisee, in exchange for direct or indirect financial consideration, the right to exploit a franchise for the purposes of marketing specified types of goods and/or services; it includes at least obligations relating to:

— the use of a common name or shop sign and a uniform presentation of contract premises and/or means of transport,

— the communication by the franchisor to the franchisee of know-how,

— the continuing provision by the franchisor to the franchisee of commercial or technical assistance during the life of the agreement;

(c) 'master franchise agreement' means an agreement whereby one undertaking, the franchisor, grants the other, the master franchisee, in exchange for direct or indirect financial consideration, the right to exploit a franchise for the purposes of concluding franchise agreements with third parties, the franchisees;

(d) 'franchisor's goods' means goods produced by the franchisor or according to its instructions, and/or bearing the franchisor's name or trade mark;

(e) 'contract premises' means the premises used for the exploitation of the franchise or, when the franchise is exploited outside those premises, the base from which the franchisee operates the means of transport used for the exploitation of the franchise (contract means of transport);

(f) 'know-how' means a package of non-patented practical information, resulting from experience and testing by the franchisor, which is secret, substantial and identified;

(g) 'secret' means that the know-how, as a body or in the precise configuration and assembly of its components, is not generally known or easily accessible; it is not limited in the narrow sense that each individual component of the know-how should be totally unknown or unobtainable outside the franchisor's business;

(h) 'substantial' means that the know-how includes information which is of importance for the sale of goods or the provision of services to end users, and in particular for the presentation of goods for sale, the processing of goods in connection with the provision of services, methods of dealing with customers, and administration and financial management; the know-how must be useful for the franchisee by being capable, at the date of conclusion of the agreement, of improving the competitive position of the franchisee, in particular by improving the franchisee's performance or helping it to enter a new market;

(i) 'identified' means that the know-how must be described in a sufficiently comprehensive manner so as to make it possible to verify that it fulfils the criteria of secrecy and substantiality; the description of the know-how can either be set out in the franchise agreement or in a separate document or recorded in any other appropriate form.

Article 2

The category licence provided for in Article 1 shall apply to franchise agreements which include some or all of the following restrictions, notwithstanding the fact that, in some circumstances, these may not constitute restrictions of competition:

(a) an obligation on the franchisor, in the State or in a defined area of the State, the contract territory, not to:

— grant the right to exploit all or part of the franchise to third parties,

— itself exploit the franchise, or itself market the goods or services which are the subject-matter of the franchise under a similar formula, 4.9.1

— itself supply the franchisor's goods to third parties;

(b) an obligation on the franchisee to exploit the franchise only from the contract premises;

(c) an obligation on the franchisee to refrain, outside the contract territory, from seeking customers for the goods or the services which are the subject-matter of the franchise;

(d) an obligation on the franchisee not to manufacture, sell or use in the course of the provision of services, goods competing with the franchisor's goods which are the subject-matter of the franchise; where the subject-matter of the franchise is the sale or use in the course of the provision of services both certain types of goods and spare parts or accessories therefor, that obligation may not be imposed in respect of these spare parts or accessories.

Article 3

1. The category licence provided for in Article 1 shall apply notwithstanding the presence of any of the following obligations on the franchisee, in so far as they are necessary to protect the franchisor's industrial or intellectual property rights or to maintain the common identity and reputation of the franchised network, since these are not deemed to constitute restrictions of competition in such circumstances:

(a) to sell, or use in the course of the provision of services, exclusively goods matching minimum objective quality specifications laid down by the franchisor;

(b) to sell, or use in the course of the provision of services, goods which are manufactured only by the franchisor or by third parties designated by it, where it is impracticable, owing to the nature of the goods which are the subject matter of the franchise, to apply objective quality specifications;

(c) not to engage, directly or indirectly, in any similar business in a territory where it would compete with a member of the franchised network, including the franchisor; the franchisee may be held to this obligation after termination of the agreement, for a reasonable period which may not exceed one year, in the territory where it has exploited the franchise;

(d) not to acquire financial interests in the capital of a competing undertaking, which would give the franchisee the power to influence the economic conduct of such undertaking;

(e) to sell the goods which are the subject-matter of the franchise only to end users, to other franchisees and to resellers within other channels of distribution supplied by the manufacturer of these goods or with its consent;

(f) to use its best endeavours to sell the goods or provide the services that are the subject-matter of the franchise; to offer for sale a minimum range of goods, achieve a minimum turnover, plan its orders in advance, keep minimum stocks and provide customer and warranty services;

(g) to pay to the franchisor a specified proportion of its revenue for advertising and itself carry out advertising for the nature of which it shall obtain the franchisor's approval.

2. The category licence provided for in Article 1 shall apply notwithstanding the presence of any of the following obligations on the franchisee:

4.9.1 (a) not to disclose to third parties the know-how provided by the franchisor; the franchisee may be held to this obligation after termination of the agreement;

(b) to communicate to the franchisor any experience gained in exploiting the franchise and to grant it and other franchisees a non-exclusive licence for the know-how resulting from that experience;

(c) to inform the franchisor of infringements of licensed industrial or intellectual property rights, to take legal action against infringers or to assist the franchisor in legal actions against infringers;

(d) not to use know-how licensed by the franchisor for purposes other than the exploitation of the franchise; the franchisee may be held to this obligation after termination of the agreement;

(e) to attend or have its staff attend training courses arranged by the franchisor;

(f) to apply the commercial methods devised by the franchisor, including any subsequent modification thereof, and use the licensed industrial or intellectual property rights;

(g) to comply with the franchisor's standards for the equipment and presentation of the contract premises and/or means of transport;

(h) to allow the franchisor to carry out checks of the contract premises and/or means of transport, including the goods sold and the services provided, and the inventory and accounts of the franchisee;

(i) not without the franchisor's consent to change the location of the contract premises;

(j) not without the franchisor's consent to assign the rights and obligations under the franchise agreement.

3. In the event that, because of particular circumstances, obligations referred to in paragraph 2 fall within the scope of section 4(1), they shall also be licensed even if they are not accompanied by any of the obligations licensed by Article 1.

Article 4

The category licence provided for in Article 1 shall apply on condition that the franchisee is free to obtain the goods that are the subject-matter of the franchise from other franchisees; where such goods are also distributed through another network of authorized distributors, the franchisee must be free to obtain the goods from the latter.

Article 5

The category licence provided for in Article 1 shall not apply where:

(a) undertakings producing goods or providing services which are identical or are considered by users as equivalent in view of their characteristics, price and intended use, enter into franchise agreements in respect of such goods or services;

(b) without prejudice to Article 2 (d) and Article 3 (1)(b), the franchisee is prevented from obtaining supplies of goods of a quality equivalent to those offered by the franchisor;

(c) without prejudice to Article 2 (d), the franchisee is obliged to sell, or use in the process of providing services, goods manufactured by the franchisor or third parties designated by the franchisor and the franchisor refuses, for reasons other than protecting the franchisor's industrial or intellectual property rights, or maintaining the common identity and reputation of the franchised network, to designate as authorized manufacturers third parties proposed by the franchisee;

(d) the franchisee is prevented from continuing to use the licensed know-how after termination of the agreement where the know-how has become generally known or easily accessible, other than by breach of an obligation by the franchisee; **4.9.1**

(e) the franchisee is restricted by the franchisor, directly or indirectly, in the determination of sale prices for the goods or services which are the subject-matter of the franchise, without prejudice to the possibility for the franchisor of recommending sale prices;

(f) the franchisor prohibits the franchisee from challenging the validity of the industrial or intellectual property rights which form part of the franchise, without prejudice to the possibility for the franchisor of terminating the agreement in such a case;

(g) franchisees are obliged not to supply within the State the goods or services which are the subject-matter of the franchise to end users because of their place of residence.

Article 6

The Competition Authority may withdraw the benefit of this category licence where it finds in a particular case that an agreement nevertheless has certain effects which are incompatible with the conditions laid down in section 4(2) of the Competition Act.

Article 7

1.(a) As regards agreements which were in existence on 1 October, 1991, and were notified before 1 October 1992, this category licence shall have effect from 17 November 1994, where the agreements already fulfil the conditions of the licence.

(b) As regards agreements which were in existence on 1 October 1991, and were notified before 1 October 1992, and which do not fulfil the conditions of the licence, but which are later amended to fulfil the conditions of the licence, this category licence shall have effect from the date when those conditions were fulfilled.

2. As regards agreements which came into existence after 1 October 1991, and which were notified before 17 November 1994, this category licence shall have retroactive effect from the date of notification where the agreements already fulfil the conditions of the licence, or from the date, being not earlier than the date of notification, when the agreements were amended so as to fulfil those conditions.

Article 8

This category licence shall enter into force on 17 November 1994. It shall expire on 31 December 1999.

For the Competition Authority

Patrick M. Lyons
Chairman

17 November 1994

[illegible] from continuing to use the licensed know-how [illegible] the agreement [illegible] has become [illegible] publicly known [illegible] than by [illegible] on the part of the licensee [illegible]

[illegible] is [illegible] by the [illegible] or indirectly [illegible] in the determination of sale prices for the goods, [illegible] in the [illegible] [illegible] to the [illegible] for the [illegible] of recommending [illegible]

[illegible] the franchisee [illegible] the [illegible] industrial or intellectual property rights [illegible] part of the [illegible] to the possibility for the franchisor of terminating the agreement [illegible]

[illegible] not to supply within the [illegible] the [illegible] services which are the subject-matter of the franchise [illegible] place in [illegible]

The [illegible] may withdraw the benefit of this [illegible] in a case where [illegible] particular case that an agreement [illegible] this [illegible] has certain effects which are incompatible with the conditions laid down in [illegible] of the [illegible]

[illegible] agreements which were in force on [illegible] 1991 [illegible] of [illegible] this [illegible] [illegible] 1991 [illegible] the date [illegible] agreements which [illegible] December 1991 [illegible] which do not fulfil the conditions of [illegible] [illegible]

[illegible] agreements [illegible] 1991 [illegible] from the date of notification [illegible] than the date [illegible]

[illegible] 1999.

[illegible]

COMPETITION LAW SOURCE BOOK

Competition Law Source Book

EDITED BY

Tony O'Connor

VOLUME 2

ROUND HALL SWEET & MAXWELL

This book was typeset by
Gilbert Gough Typesetting for
ROUND HALL SWEET & MAXWELL
Brehon House, 4 Upper Ormond Quay, Dublin 7.

A catalogue record for this book
is available from the British Library.

ISBN 1-85800-048-3

Printed in Ireland by
Betaprint, Dublin

Contents

COMPETITION LAW SOURCE BOOK

VOLUME 1

(For a more detailed Table of Contents please see Volume 1)

Table of Contents

VOLUME 2

CHAPTER 5 — DISTRIBUTION AGREEMENTS

CHAPTER 6 — INTELLECTUAL PROPERTY

CHAPTER 7 — PROPERTY

CHAPTER 8 — IRISH COURT DECISIONS

NOTIFICATIONS TO THE COMPETITION AUTHORITY

ANNEX

CHAPTER FIVE

Distribution Agreements

5.0 Introduction

Agreements concerning purchasing, franchising and distribution share a common objective of trying to provide a system which allows a manufacturer or supplier to sell its goods. The lack of consistency in the use of agency, distribution, franchising and purchasing concepts does not facilitate a clear definition of what may be considered a distribution agreement. This chapter seeks to concentrate on those type of arrangements which have been considered by the Authority and which do not fall within the agency, purchasing and franchising concepts which are the themes of other chapters in this book.

Vertical Agreements — EC

Text books on the application of the European Union competition rules categorise distribution agreements as vertical agreements.[1] Unless a manufacturer or supplier arranges through its employees and agents the sales of its products or services, some form of agreement which will impose vertical restraints will need to be entered into by that manufacturer or supplier. Vertical restraints refer to terms of agreements which may restrict the manufacturer or supplier on the one hand or the wholesaler or retailer on the other hand. Such restraints of themselves may not particularly contravene section 4(1) of the Competition Act. The decisions contained in this chapter indicate that the policy of the Competition Authority will resemble the policy of the European Commission. In common with the European Commission the Authority is critical of resale price maintenance and prohibitions on sales of products and services. Restrictions on the marketing of products and services can be countenanced by the Authority.

Description of Agreements

It is emphasised that agreements which may be called agency, purchasing, or distribution agreements, may not be such a type of agreement when considered in the overall context of the arrangements between the parties. Identifying the restrictions and benefits to each party will enable one to identify whether the name of the agreement is accurate in its description. An agency agreement will typically provide for the payment of commission on the sales of products by the manufacturer or the supplier which have been arranged by the agent. An agent will have some authority to bind the supplier or manufacturer and will not become the legal owner of the goods which may be sold pursuant to the agency agreement. In contrast a distribution

1. (i) Bellamy & Child, 'Common Market Law of Competition', 4th ed. (1993), edited by Vivien Rose, chapter 7.
   (ii) Richard Whish, 'Competition Law', 3rd ed. (1993), chapter 17.
   (iii) Van Bael & Bellis, 'Competition Law of the European Community', 3rd ed. (1994) Part II.
   (iv) D.G. Goyder, 'EEC Competition Law', 2nd ed. (1993), chapter 12.

5.0 agreement will typically provide for the ownership of the goods by the distributor and the distributor will be a separate economic entity to the manufacturer or supplier.

Assessment of Distribution Options

A supplier or manufacturer which engages a distributor will have various reasons to appoint a distributor. A supplier may not have the resources to engage a direct sales and delivery force and may not have sufficient local knowledge to ensure that the relevant market is penetrated. A distributor may have access to an experienced sales channel for the market targeted. In addition the risks of the supplier in establishing a market by using a distributor may be capped and a distributor may have more incentive to apply resources to the marketing and sales of the relevant products or services if the distributor is given guaranteed rights. The decision to appoint a distributor, to use an exclusive purchasing arrangement, to use franchising or to use agents will be determined by a multitude of factors. The prohibition of entering into agreements or arrangements which may offend the Competition Act may be relevant. The decisions of the Competition Authority which are summarised and contained in this book should assist the assessment of this last mentioned factor.

EXCLUSIVE DISTRIBUTION

Variations from Draft Category Licence

On 9 July 1993 the Competition Authority published notice of its intention to grant a category licence for exclusive distribution agreements.[2] Decision No. 144 of 5 November 1993 incorporates the category licence as originally drafted but made amendments arising from the Competition Authority's assessment of submissions made. The changes to the draft category licence were as follows:

(a) Article 3(d) of the draft was qualified by inserting the right of a supplier to restrict sales of a reseller to 'unsuitable dealers';

(b) The sub-paragraphs of Article 3 which list those terms of an agreement which may disapply the benefit of the category licence were abbreviated in the final version of the Category Licence. The draft category licence disapplied the category licence if the exclusive distributor was prohibited from challenging intellectual property rights of the supplier and if the period of notice for termination of the exclusive distribution agreement exceeded 12 months. These black-listed clauses are not contained in the final version of the category licence;

(c) The draft category licence contained a provision that the category licence constituted a refusal to grant a licence to notified agreements which did not fulfil its conditions. Article 6 (3) of the final version of category licence and which is contained in this book, was modified by giving the opportunity to those notifying parties who did not benefit from the category licence to persuade the Competition Authority otherwise in relation to their agreements provided individual consideration was requested before 17 December 1993;

(d) Article 7 of the final version of the category licence introduced a provision that the category licence does not apply to agreements which are part of a 'selective

2. Vincent Power in "How to comply with the Irish licence for categories of Exclusive Distribution Agreements" in *Commercial Law Practitioner*, Vol. 3, No. 2, explains the application of this Category Licence with the use of a flow chart.

distribution system'. Most commonly this would relate to exclusive distribution and dealership agreements entered into regarding the sales of motor vehicles; **5.0**

(e) The draft category licence proposed a 15 year period for the duration of the licence. The final version reduced that period to 5 years after the Authority accepted various submissions.

(f) In an effort to put the matter beyond doubt, the Competition Authority in the final version of the category licence at Article 8 provides that the category licence does not authorise any exclusive distribution agreement which may infringe Article 85(1) of the Treaty of Rome unless the agreement has been exempted under the Block Exemption, EC Regulation 1983/83 or specifically exempted.

Variations from 1983/83 Regulation
Paragraphs 65 to 74 of the reasoning of the Competition Authority prior to the actual category licence summarises the divergences from EC Regulation 1983/83.

Restrictions on Competition
Apart from the interest which may arise from the disapplication of section 4(1) of the Competition Act to exclusive distribution agreements which fall within the ambit of the category licence, Decision No. 144 identifies the terms of an exclusive distribution agreement which in the opinion of the Competition Authority, constitutes a restriction upon competition and which thereby offends against section 4(1) of the Competition Act. Paragraphs 14 to 31 of the reasoning of the Competition Authority in issuing the category licence indicate common terms of an exclusive distribution agreement which in the opinion of the Authority offend against section 4(1) of the Competition Act. These paragraphs do not purport to be an exhaustive list of the terms of such an agreement which would be considered to restrict competition. The list of terms arising from these paragraphs must be viewed from the circumstances giving rise to the decision of the Authority to issue a category licence. The Authority has tracked the approach of the European Commission. The Authority could not anticipate future developments in distribution which may give rise to other types of express and implied restrictions which those developments may introduce. The benefit of Decision No. 144 apart from the disapplication of section 4(1) to agreements which fall within the ambit of the category licence is that the present approach of the Competition Authority to vertical restraints in distribution can be gleaned. The editor suggests that the Competition Authority is not bound to follow its previous assessments of restrictions which may have an effect on competition and the reasoning must be so read.

List of Notifications within Scope
The published version of the category licence in *Iris Oifigiúil* on 19 November 1993 does not contain the paragraphs in Decision 144 prior to the category licence. However, at the end of the published version of the category licence in *Iris Oifigiúil* is a list of agreements notified to the Authority which in the opinion of the Authority come within the scope of the category licence. This list has been supplemented by subsequent decisions of the Authority to include other notified agreements which were amended after the issue of the category licence and which the Authority subsequently decided could benefit from the category licence. The complete list of those notified agreements are contained in this book and can also be identified from the list of notifications under the heading 'Relevant Decision in Book'.

5.0 INDIVIDUAL DECISIONS

Energy Control Systems Ltd 5.2
Decision 31 is noteworthy for the principal reason that it refers to an exclusive distribution agreement with effects outside the State. In Decision No. 11 the Authority had already indicated some reluctance to accept a notification under section 7 of the Competition Act 1991 when it is unlikely in the first place that the notified agreement could offend section 4(1) of the Competition Act.

Sigma Wireless Communications/Motorola 5.3
This decision is principally concerned with an asset purchase agreement but it has been included in this chapter because of the interesting decision by the Authority that the exclusive distribution arrangement was necessary to transfer the goodwill and business which was the subject matter of the agreement.

Rhone Poulenc/Shell 5.4
In this decision the Competition Authority granted a certificate in respect of an asset purchase agreement which was conditional upon the appointment of the vendor as an exclusive distributor of the purchaser. No detailed assessment of the exclusive distribution arrangement was described in the decision however.

Campus Oil/Delta 5.5
In Decision No. 319 licences were granted by the Authority in respect of arrangements which were ancillary to an exclusive distribution agreement which were deemed to come within the scope of the exclusive distribution category licence. The Authority decided that the ancillary agreements underpin the exclusive distribution agreement and thereby offended against section 4(1) of the Competition Act. Being ancillary and without containing further restrictions the terms of the licence for the related exclusive distribution agreement could be applied to these agreements also.

Decision No. 321 is a similar type arrangement involving a different oil company, Statoil Ireland Ltd.

Reflex/Storage Technology Ltd 5.6
By the time the Authority made its decision in this case the agreement had been terminated. The Authority decided that it could not in any event have granted a retrospective licence because of the wording of section 7 of the Competition Act which enabled a licence to be made retrospective. In any event the Authority would not have granted a licence because of the absolute territorial protection given to the distributor and the restrictions on the distributor to choose its own customers and its own resale prices.

Mount Juliet/David Leadbetter 5.7
The covenants given by a golf course management to an instruction academy that no one else would be appointed as an instructor at the golf course was considered by the Authority not to affect competition. A restriction on the Academy not to provide services in other golf courses was similarly found acceptable to the Authority. The Authority expressed a view that such instruction facilities which were the subject of the agreement could be offered elsewhere by other competitors.

Cable & Wireless/Irish Telephone Rentals 5.8 5.0
This long decision which is partly due to the complexity of the arrangements notified concerns restrictions which were found acceptable to the Authority arising from equipment, rental and maintenance agreements.

Statoil Distributor Agreement 5.9
This decision is similar to Decision Nos. 319 and 321 mentioned above. It is interesting to note that Statoil in obtaining the licence in this agreement agreed that the notification should be changed to refer only to agreements with its exclusive distributors. It is not clear whether a similar equipment loan agreement between Statoil and its other customers are still in existence and whether the Competition Authority would grant a certificate or issue a licence in respect of those agreements if they still exist.

Murphy Brewery/Clada Soft Drinks 5.10
The original notification made to the Authority refers to a distributorship agreement which was later clarified to be a delivery type agreement. Clada soft drinks was appointed to distribute the products of Murphy Brewery in a certain region but it was clarified that Clada soft drinks did not purchase and later resell the goods. In that respect such a distributor agreement which may be better termed a delivery agreement would not offend against section 4(1) of the Competition Act according to the Authority.

Gill & Macmillan/Various Publishers 5.11
After the agreement of the parties to omit any reference to direct or indirect resale price maintenance the Authority issued a certificate in respect of these arrangements which concern a major book publisher and distributor giving its services to other small publishers for agreed charges. The Authority ultimately decided that the notified arrangements were a type of delivery and commercial agency agreement.

Johnson Brothers/Campbell Grocery Products 5.12
Under the agreement giving rise to this decision a manufacturer of grocery products appointed a distributor to sell its goods in the State. No exclusivity provision or restrictions were accepted by either party. Thus the Competition Authority had no difficulty in issuing a certificate.

Farmers Journal/Newspread 5.13
Decision No. 369 refers to another type of delivery agreement. The delivering party or the distributor was obliged to sell the Farmers Journal at a specified price and the Competition Authority found this acceptable because the distributor was not reselling the product but merely acting on behalf of the publisher in an agency type capacity.

The 1994 Annual Report of the Authority which was made available in September 1995 refers to the withdrawal of a notification by Raleigh of its standard terms and conditions. The annual report discloses that the Authority issued a Statement of Objections which objected to the manner of recommending minimum retail prices and the provision of quantity rebates which were not related to a single order. [paras. 2.138–2.142]

5.1 **Competition Authority Decision No. 144,** Licence for Categories of Exclusive Distribution Agreements

Competition Authority Decision of 5 November 1993 granting a licence under section 4(2) of the Competition Act 1991, to categories of exclusive distribution agreements.

Introduction

1. Under section 4(2) of the Competition Act 1991, the Competition Authority may grant a licence for the purposes of section 4 of the Act to any category of agreements:

> which, in the opinion of the Authority, having regard to all relevant market conditions, contributes to improving the production or distribution of goods or provision of services or to promoting technical or economic progress, while allowing consumers a fair share of the resulting benefit and which does not
>
> (i) impose on the undertakings concerned terms which are not indispensable to the attainment of those objectives;
> (ii) afford undertakings the possibility of eliminating competition in respect of a substantial part of the products or services in question.

2. A large number of agreements have been notified to the Authority concerning exclusive distribution arrangements for the resale of products. Since such agreements have been notified, the Authority may grant a licence, including a category licence, under section 4(2) of the Act, in accordance with section 7(3). The Authority has carefully examined all of the notified agreements. The Authority is therefore able to define a category of agreements and concerted practices which can be regarded as normally satisfying the conditions laid down in section 4(2).

3. Notice of intention to grant a category licence for exclusive distribution agreements was published on 9 July 1993, and submissions were invited from interested parties. A large number of submissions was received on the draft category licence, and full account was taken of these prior to finalising this decision.

The Subject of the Decision

4. This decision concerns agreements for the exclusive distribution of goods for resale. The essential feature of such agreements is that the manufacturer or supplier (the supplier) agrees to supply certain goods for resale to only one party, the exclusive distributor, within a defined territory. Within that territory, no other party will be supplied with the goods for resale by the supplier. The agreements usually contain other restrictions, as well as clauses which are not restrictive.

5. A large number of the notified agreements relate to imported products, where the supplier is located outside the State and supplies the goods to, usually, a single exclusive distributor who undertakes the distribution of goods within the State to resellers. A considerable proportion of the agreements, however, is in respect of Irish manufactured products where the manufacturer, rather than distribute the goods himself, entrusts distribution to another party, who is usually a specialist distributor. While the exclusive territory in these cases is often the State, it may be confined to a part, sometimes a small part, of the State on occasion. A number of distributors have exclusive distribution agreements with several different suppliers, either for imported products or domestic products or both. Some suppliers may entrust the distribution of different products to different exclusive distributors.

The Products and the Market

6. A very wide variety of products forms the subject matter of the notified agreements. These include foodstuffs, other grocery products, consumer durable goods, pharmaceuticals,

petroleum products, products for the agricultural and industrial sectors, and many others. Given **5.1**
the large number and the heterogeneous nature of the products concerned, and of those which may also be included in other agreements which have not been notified or which may be made in future, it is not possible to describe the relevant market conditions which prevail. It is not necessary to do so in the case of this category licence, however, in particular because the benefit of the category licence may be withdrawn in the case of an individual agreement if it is found that it does not satisfy all the conditions prescribed in section 4(2), especially where competitive conditions in the market are inadequate.

7. Most of the notified agreements stipulate that the territory concerned is the State, or a wider area, including, for example, Northern Ireland. Where the territory is a part of the State, there are usually several parallel agreements which, in combination, cover the State. In some cases, however, only a part of the State is covered by the agreement. This decision relates to agreements which relate to the State or to any part of the State.

EEC Regulation 1983/83

8. EEC Regulation No. 1983/83, of 22 June 1983, is a block exemption regulation which applies Article 85(3) of the Treaty of Rome to categories of exclusive distribution agreements. The regulation entered into force on 1 July 1983 and it expires on 31 December 1997.[1] This replaced a previous block exemption for exclusive distribution agreements, Regulation 67/67.[2]

9. Exemption is granted to agreements involving only two parties in which one agrees to supply only the other with certain goods for resale within the whole or a defined area of the common market. The only other obligation allowed upon the supplier is not to supply the goods to users in the contract territory. The exclusive distributor—the purchaser—may be obliged not to manufacture or distribute competing goods, to obtain the goods only from the supplier, and to refrain from active marketing outside the contract area, that is, he may be required not to seek customers, establish any branch or maintain any distribution depot outside his own territory. He may also undertake to purchase complete ranges or minimum quantities of the goods, to sell the goods under trademarks or packed and presented as specified by the supplier, and to engage in sales promotion, involving advertising, maintaining a sales network or stock of goods, providing customer and guarantee services, and employing staff with specialised or technical training. Exclusive agreements for the supply of services rather than the resale of goods are not covered by the Regulation.

10. The exemption does not apply where competing manufacturers enter into reciprocal agreements, that is, where each agrees to supply the other exclusively. Where at least one of the competing manufacturers has a total annual turnover below 100m ECU, however, a non-reciprocal agreement is allowed, that is, one may agree to supply the other exclusively. Benefit of the exemption is denied also where users can obtain the goods only from the exclusive distributor, with no alternative source of supply outside the contract territory, or where one or both of the parties makes it difficult for intermediaries or users to obtain the goods from dealers inside or outside the common market by, for example, the exercise of industrial property or other rights. Agreements for the resale of drinks in premises used for the sale and consumption of drinks or for the resale of petroleum products in service stations are not allowed the benefit of exemption under this Regulation.

11. An essential feature of the Regulation is that there must be no attempt to create absolute territorial protection for the exclusive distributor, that is there must always be the possibility of parallel imports into the contract territory (and the distributor must always be free to sell to dealers or users in another distributor's exclusive territory). The benefit of the exemption may

1. OJ No. L173, 30.6.83, p. 1, as corrected in OJ No. L281, 13.10.83, p. 24, and Explanatory Notice, OJ No. C101, 13.4.84, p. 2.
2. OJ No. 57, 25.3.67, p. 849 (Special Edition 1967, p. 10).

5.1 be withdrawn from a specific agreement in certain circumstances, where, for example, effective competition is lacking. Exclusive distributors must be free to choose their own customers and to decide upon their own resale prices.

Assessment

(a) *Applicability of section 4(1)*

12. Section 4(1) of the Competition Act 1991, prohibits and renders void all agreements between undertakings which have as their object or effect the prevention, restriction or distortion of competition in trade in any goods or services in the State or in any part of the State.

13. The suppliers of goods, whether they are located outside or inside the State, are engaged in the supply of goods for gain. The exclusive distributors in the State are engaged in the distribution of goods for gain. Both suppliers and exclusive distributors are, therefore, undertakings within the meaning of section 3(1) of the Competition Act. The exclusive distribution agreements are agreements between undertakings. This decision also applies to exclusive distribution arrangements which are operated by undertakings but which take the form of concerted practices rather than of a legally-binding agreement. The relevant product or products in each case is or are as specified in the individual agreement. The relevant geographic market is the State or a part of the State, as specified in the individual agreement. This decision only applies to agreements to which only two undertakings are party—the supplier and the exclusive distributor. Both the products and the area of distribution concerned must be specified in the agreement.

(i) *The exclusive distribution requirement*

14. The primary feature of an exclusive distribution agreement is that the supplier agrees to supply certain goods for resale only to the exclusive distributor within a defined territory. Such an agreement may be made for a very long time, or it may have an indefinite duration, which may also be lengthy in practice. This prevents the supplier from supplying the goods which are the subject of the agreement for resale to any other distributor in the territory for as long as the agreement endures, and it prevents any other distributor in the territory from obtaining the goods from the supplier for resale in the territory for the same period. This limits the commercial freedom of the supplier to supply for resale other distributors, and the freedom of other distributors to obtain the goods for resale from the supplier. It introduces a degree of rigidity into the market, since distribution arrangements are established for long or relatively long periods of time, and since many goods are already tied under such agreements. The fact that the products are available only from a single source in the territory also tends to restrict intra-brand competition. An exclusive distribution agreement, therefore, constitutes a restriction upon competition which offends against section 4(1) of the Competition Act.

(ii) *Other restrictive clauses*

(a) *Restrictions on the supplier*

15. Besides the obligation on the supplier not to supply the goods to other distributors in the territory, there may be a requirement for the supplier not to supply users, that is final purchasers, in the territory. Since such an obligation prevents suppliers from dealing directly with users, and prevents users from obtaining supplies directly from the supplier, this represents a restriction upon competition which offends against section 4(1) of the Competition Act.

(b) *Restrictions on the exclusive distributor which affect competition*

16. Agreements often contain clauses which oblige the exclusive distributor:

(1) not to manufacture or distribute goods which compete with the contract goods;

(2) to obtain the contract goods for resale only from the supplier; 5.1

(3) to refrain, outside the contract territory and in relation to the contract goods, from seeking customers, from establishing any branch and from maintaining any distribution depot.

Each of these restrictions is dealt with below, along with other possible restrictions on competition.

Dealing in competing goods and dealing only with the supplier

17. The obligation not to manufacture or distribute competing goods limits the freedom of the exclusive distributor in choosing which goods to handle, and it prevents suppliers of competing goods from supplying, or availing of the services of, that distributor. The requirement to obtain the goods only from the supplier prevents the exclusive distributor from obtaining them from another source, in particular from exclusive distributors in other territories where they might be obtained more cheaply. These obligations restrict competition and they offend against section 4(1) of the Act.

Active competition outside territory

18. The obligation to refrain from seeking customers, etc. outside the allotted territory, prevents the exclusive distributor from engaging in active competition outside his territory, that is from directly seeking customers in the territory or territories contracted to other exclusive distributors. It affords a degree of territorial protection to exclusive distributors. Where the agreement is one of a series, each of which applies to a different part of the State, an obligation of this nature restricts competition within the State, and offends against section 4(1) of the Act. Where the agreement relates to the whole State, such an obligation prevents the exclusive distributor from actively competing outside the State. It does not represent, *prima facie*, a restriction upon competition within the State. The Authority is concerned that such an agreement could be one of a series of standard agreements which the supplier has with exclusive distributors in a number of different countries, particularly in the various EC Member States. The presence of an identical or similar clause in these other agreements would prevent active competition in Ireland from exclusive distributors in other countries, and, in the circumstances, this would effectively represent a restriction upon competition. Clauses of this nature may well come within the scope of Article 85(1) of the Rome Treaty.

Passive competition outside territory

19. An obligation on the exclusive distributor to refrain from supplying any customers who are located outside the allotted territory, however, that is one which forbids even passive competition and the responding to unsolicited orders from outside the territory, is an even more serious restriction upon competition. This may also take the form of requiring the distributor not to supply anyone who might resell the products outside the territory. Where the agreement is one of a number for different territories, each with the same requirement, this provides each exclusive distributor with absolute territorial protection. They are assured that they are the only source of supply of the products in the territory, and that other resellers and users are unable to obtain the products from any source whatsoever outside the territory. This effectively eliminates any competition to the exclusive distributor in respect of the contract products. Again, where the agreement is one of a series, each of which applies to a different part of the State, an obligation of this nature restricts competition within the State, and offends against section 4(1) of the Act. The same type of territorial problem arises as in the case of prohibitions on active competition where the specified territory is the State. Such clauses also may well come within the prohibition of Article 85(1) of the Rome Treaty.

Freedom to choose customers

20. Any limitation on the freedom of the exclusive distributor to choose his own customers is generally restrictive of competition, and offends against section 4(1) of the Act. In certain

5.1 circumstances, however, the exclusive distributor may be forbidden to supply the goods to unsuitable dealers. This is acceptable provided that admission to the distribution network is based on objectively justifiable criteria of a qualitative nature relating to the professional qualifications of the owner of the business or his staff or the suitability of his business premises, if the criteria are the same for all potential dealers, and if the criteria are applied in practice in a manner which is non-discriminatory. To this extent, such an obligation would not offend against section 4(1) of the Act. This category licence, however, does not apply to exclusive distribution agreements which are part of a selective distribution system, including those for motor vehicles.

Freedom to appoint agents and sub-distributors

21. Any limitation on the freedom of the exclusive distributor to appoint agents and sub-distributors to distribute the products likewise is generally restrictive of competition, and offends against section 4(1) of the Act. If the supplier reserves the right to approve the appointment of agents or sub-distributors by the exclusive distributor, the supplier must not be allowed to withhold approval arbitrarily. If the supplier withholds consent from the exclusive distributor to conclude, alter or terminate such sub-agreements only for objectively valid reasons, this would not offend against section 4(1) of the Act.

Freedom to determine prices

22. A limitation on the exclusive distributor in determining his own resale prices and conditions of sale is also a restriction on competition. In particular, the exclusive distributor might be required to sell at a price fixed by the supplier, or at a price not less than or more than that indicated by the supplier. The Authority regards such clauses as limitations upon the reseller's freedom to determine his own prices, and to represent the enforcement of, or being conducive to, resale price maintenance. It considers these as being a serious restriction upon competition, and, therefore, as a serious infringement of the prohibition in section 4(1). It was argued in several submissions that suppliers should be allowed to impose maximum resale prices. The Authority disagrees with these arguments. While the Government is entitled to specify maximum prices for any product, this is not the prerogative of private undertakings; the setting of maximum resale prices is, in itself, an anti-competitive practice; and there is the real danger that any maximum price imposed by a supplier would become, at the same time, the effective minimum price charged by resellers. The Authority does not, however, regard the recommending of resale prices to the distributor by the supplier as amounting to resale price maintenance, provided that there is no agreement or concerted practice that the distributor observe such prices, and provided also that the distributor is informed that he is free to set his own prices. In these circumstances, the recommending of resale prices to the distributor by the supplier would not offend against section 4(1) of the Act.

Dealers' resale prices

23. The Authority takes the same view concerning the freedom of the person who purchases from the distributor, if that purchaser is a reseller, to determine his own resale prices. Any limitation upon such a purchaser (a dealer) imposed by the supplier or the exclusive distributor would offend against section 4(1) of the Act. The recommending of resale prices to the dealer, in the terms outlined above, whether by the supplier or the exclusive distributor, would not be regarded by the Authority as offending against section 4(1).

Post-term limitations

24. Any restrictions upon competition, and indeed other limitations as well, which apply after the termination of the agreement also generally offend against section 4(1). The only exception to this concerns the keeping confidential of secret information.

(c) *Restrictions on the exclusive distributor which do not affect competition* 5.1

Promotion of sales

25. The exclusive distributor may undertake to do any or all of the following:

(1) to purchase complete ranges of goods or minimum quantities;

(2) to sell the contract goods under trade marks, or packed and presented as specified by the supplier;

(3) to take measures for the promotion of sales, in particular:

- to advertise,
- to maintain a sales network or stock of goods,
- to provide customer and guarantee services,
- to employ staff having specialised or technical training.

The Authority considers that these are examples of clauses which generally do not restrict competition, and the list is not comprehensive. They relate to matters which are usually an integral part of the function of distributing goods for resale on behalf of the supplier. They are needed in order to ensure an adequate performance by the exclusive distributor, and they provide the rationale for employing an exclusive distributor in the first place. Without them, it is possible that distribution of the goods might not occur at all, which itself would be deleterious to competition. The Authority believes that such clauses generally do not offend against section 4(1) of the Act. The minimum quantity may relate to a single delivery or to purchases over a period, and it may include the setting of sales or turnover targets.

26. It is possible, however, that obligations of this nature might be formulated or applied in a fashion such that they take on the character of restrictions of competition, in which case they would offend against section 4(1) of the Act.

Keeping of records, etc.

27. A number of other obligations may also be imposed on the exclusive distributor, such as:

(1) to provide reports and returns of information relating to customers, sales, prices, stocks, competitive conditions, the activities of competitors, etc;

(2) to keep accounts, records etc, for inspection;

(3) to keep lists of names of customers, or serial numbers on products, for inspection;

(4) to provide suitable premises;

(5) to store products in suitable conditions;

(6) to allow inspection of premises, storage and stocks;

(7) to permit the supplier to approve the content of advertisements and promotional material.

For the reasons given above, the Authority considers that such clauses also do not generally restrict competition and so do not offend against section 4(1) of the Act. If they were to be formulated or applied in a way which did restrict competition, they would offend against section 4(1). This would apply, in particular, if any requirement on the exclusive distributor to supply information resulted in a limitation of his freedom to set prices. The circulation of such information, by the supplier, to exclusive distributors would also offend against section 4(1).[3]

3. This is consistent with the EC Commission decision in Hasselblad, OJ No. L161, 12.6.82, p. 18, at p. 27.

5.1 **Challenge to validity of trademarks, etc.**

28. Exclusive distribution agreements may contain an obligation on the distributor not to challenge the validity of the supplier's trademark or other industrial or commercial property, during and/or after termination of the agreement. Such an obligation does not generally offend against section 4(1) of the Act. If the supplier does not prohibit the distributor from challenging such validity, but allows the possibility of terminating the agreement in the event of any challenge, this does not offend against section 4(1) of the Act.

Confidentiality Provisions

29. Exclusive distribution agreements may contain obligations on the distributor (and sometimes on the supplier as well) to keep secret confidential information. There can be a requirement to use such information only for the purposes of the agreement, and a prohibition on disclosing or divulging such information to any other person. The confidential information may include that relating to products, processes, business, accounts, etc. The confidentiality provisions may also have to be made binding on employees and subsidiary and affiliated companies, and occasionally on customers. While the confidentiality provisions, if any, are always applicable during the course of the agreement, they often continue after the agreement is terminated.

30. The Authority considers that such provisions on confidentiality during the period while the agreement is in operation are integral features of the relationship between the supplier and the exclusive distributor and they usually relate to proprietary information. Without them, the agreement might well not be made, and the goods might not be distributed. They do not restrain competition between the two parties, since there is none under the overall terms of the agreement. Such obligations on confidentiality during the period of the agreement are not regarded by the Authority as offending against section 4(1) of the Act.

31. Confidentiality provisions which apply after termination of the agreement, particularly those concerned with proprietary information, are also considered by the Authority to be generally integral to the original agreement. To the extent that they are not used to prevent either party competing after termination of the agreement, they are not regarded as offending against section 4(1) of the Act. If they were to be used to prevent competition after termination, they would offend against section 4(1) of the Act.

(b) *Applicability of section 4(2)*

32. Under section 4(2), the Competition Authority may grant a licence in the case of any agreement or category of agreements which, 'having regard to all relevant market conditions, contributes to improving the production of goods or provision of services or to promoting technical or economic progress, while allowing consumers a fair share of the resulting benefit and which does not:

(i) impose on the undertakings concerned terms which are not indispensable to the attainment of those objectives;

(ii) afford undertakings the possibility of eliminating competition in respect of a substantial part of the products or services in question.'

33. In the opinion of the Authority, exclusive distribution agreements, in general, are likely to fulfil the conditions provided for in section 4(2) and qualify for the grant of a category licence.

(i) *The exclusive distribution and related requirements*

(a) *Improvements in distribution*

34. Exclusive distribution agreements generally lead to an improvement in distribution because the supplier is able to concentrate his sales activities and he does not need to maintain numerous business relations with a large number of dealers. Particularly in the case of

international trade, difficulties resulting from linguistic, legal and other differences are more easily overcome by the appointment of a distributor located in the territory. In the case of domestic firms, it is often preferable for the supplier to concentrate on production and to delegate the distribution function to a specialist distributor who already possesses the necessary organisation and dealer contacts. 5.1

35. Exclusive distribution agreements facilitate the promotion of sales of a product and lead to intensive marketing and to continuity of supplies while at the same time rationalising distribution. They stimulate competition between the products of different manufacturers. The appointment of an exclusive distributor who will take over sales promotion, customer services and carrying of stocks is often the most effective way, and sometimes indeed the only way, for the manufacturer to enter a market and compete with other manufacturers who are already present. This is particularly so in the case of small and medium-sized undertakings. It must be left to the parties, however, to decide whether and to what extent they consider it desirable to incorporate in the agreements terms providing for the promotion of sales.

(b) *Fair share to consumers*

36. As a rule, such exclusive distribution agreements also allow consumers a fair share of the resulting benefit as they gain directly from the improvement in distribution, and their economic and supply position is improved as they can obtain products, particularly those manufactured in other countries, more quickly and more easily.

(c) *Indispensability, Exclusive supply, etc.*

37. The exclusive supply obligation, which involves the supply of the goods for resale only to the exclusive distributor in the territory, and the obligation on the supplier not to supply the goods to users in the territory, the obligations on the distributor not to deal in competing products, to obtain the goods only from the supplier, and to refrain from active sales outside the territory, are indispensable to the attainment of these objectives. They produce a clear division of functions between the parties and compel the exclusive distributor to concentrate his sales on the contract goods and the contract territory. The Authority believes that, where they are limited to the duration of the agreement, such restrictions are generally necessary in order to attain the improvement in the distribution of goods sought through exclusive distribution. A post-termination restriction on competition is not indispensable. Consumers will be assured of a fair share of the benefits only if there is no absolute territorial protection for the exclusive distributor.

Passive sales

38. An obligation to refrain from passive sales outside the territory, where the territory comprises only part of the State, is not indispensable to achieve the benefits, and does not fulfil the conditions of section 4(2) of the Act. It cannot be granted the benefit of this category licence. An obligation to refrain from passive sales outside the territory, when the territory is the State, as explained, creates some difficulty under the Competition Act since it does not directly affect competition within the State. To the extent that it is part of a series of similar agreements which prevent passive sales into the State it would restrict competition within the State. It would produce no benefits and would not be indispensable (and would tend to eliminate competition) and would not fulfil the conditions of section 4(2) of the Act. Such restrictions are not permitted under Regulation 1983/83. (See also para. 74).

Choice of customers

39. An obligation which limits the exclusive distributor's choice of customers, except where the exclusive distributor is forbidden to supply the goods to unsuitable dealers on objectively justifiable grounds, in the conditions described in para. 20, offends against section 4(1). Such an obligation produces no benefit and is not indispensable, and so does not fulfil the conditions of section 4(2) and cannot be granted the benefit of this category licence.

5.1 **Appointment of agents and sub-distributors**

40. A provision which limits the exclusive distributor's freedom to appoint agents and sub-distributors, without objectively valid reasons on the part of the supplier, offends against section 4(1). Such a provision produces no benefits, and is not indispensable, and so does not fulfil the conditions of section 4(2), and cannot be granted the benefit of this category licence.

Price determination

41. A limitation on the freedom of the exclusive distributor to determine his prices and conditions of sale offends against section 4(1) and, since it produces no benefits and is not indispensable, it does not fulfil the conditions of section 4(2), and cannot be granted the benefit of this category licence. The position is the same where the customer of the distributor, who is the reseller, is not free, or is not informed that he is free, to determine his resale prices. Such a restriction on competition also cannot be granted the benefit of this category licence.

Post-term restrictions

42. The restrictions on competition which are permitted under this category licence are only permitted for the duration of the agreement. Restrictions which continue after the termination of the agreement produce no benefits and are not indispensable, and so they fail to fulfil the conditions of section 4(2), and do not benefit from this category licence. While certain confidentiality provisions which continue after termination of the agreement do not offend against section 4(1), this is the case only if they are not used to prevent competition. If they were to be used in this way, this would produce no benefit and would not be indispensable and would not fulfil the conditions of section 4(2). Such provisions cannot benefit from this category licence.

Other obligations

43. To the extent that obligations on the supplier of the kind described in paras. 25 and 27 are formulated or applied in a way which restricts competition, they offend against section 4(1). They produce no benefits and are not indispensable, and do not fulfil the conditions of section 4(2). They also cannot benefit from this category licence.

(d) *Elimination of competition*

44. Since competition at the distribution stage is ensured by securing that there is no absolute territorial protection for the exclusive distributor, the exclusive distribution agreements covered by this category licence will not normally afford any possibility of eliminating competition in respect of a substantial part of the products in question. This would not be the case if an exclusive distributor had exclusive agreements in respect of a substantial range of competing products, insofar as these afforded the possibility of eliminating competition in respect of a substantial part of the products in question. This licence would not apply in such circumstances.

Competing manufacturers

45. The category licence should be reserved for agreements for which it can be assured with sufficient certainty that they satisfy the conditions of section 4(2) of the Act. It is not possible, without a case-by-case examination, to conclude that adequate improvements in distribution occur where a manufacturer entrusts the distribution of his goods to another manufacturer with whom he is in competition. This applies whether the agreement is on a reciprocal or a non-reciprocal basis. Such agreements are, therefore, excluded from this category licence. They require an individual decision by the Authority.

No absolute territorial protection

46. Consumers will be assured of a fair share of the benefits only if absolute territorial protection is not permitted. Thus agreements relating to goods which the user can obtain only

from the exclusive distributor should be excluded from this category licence. In addition, the parties cannot be allowed to abuse industrial property rights or other rights in order to create absolute territorial protection. 5.1

(ii) *Miscellaneous considerations*

Only two undertakings party

47. This category licence applies to agreements to which only two undertakings are party —the supplier and the exclusive distributor. Several undertakings forming one economic unit count as one undertaking for the purposes of this category licence. The benefit of the licence is not lost if the supplier enters into exclusive purchase agreements with several resellers. The category licence also applies if the agreements do not contain some of the permitted restrictions, or if the arrangements are less restrictive than those specified, provided that the essential exclusive distribution nature of the agreements remains.

48. The supplier may delegate the performance of his contractual obligations to a connected or independent undertaking which he has entrusted with the distribution of his goods, so that the reseller has to purchase the contract goods from the latter undertaking. The involvement of undertakings other than the contracting parties must be confined to the execution of deliveries. The parties may accept exclusive supply only for themselves and not impose them on third parties since otherwise more than two undertakings would be party to the agreement. The obligation on the parties to ensure that the obligations they have accepted are respected by connected undertakings is, however, covered by this category licence.

For resale

49. The notion of resale requires that the goods concerned be disposed of by the purchasing party to others in return for consideration. Agreements on the supply of goods which the purchasing party transforms or processes into other goods or uses or consumes in manufacturing other goods are not agreements for resale. The same applies to the supply of components which are combined with other components into a different product. The criterion is that the goods distributed by the reseller are the same as those the other party has supplied to him for that purpose. The economic identity of the goods is not affected if the reseller merely breaks up and packages the goods in smaller quantities, or repackages them, before resale. Where the reseller performs additional operations to improve the quality, durability, appearance or taste of the goods (including the dilution of a concentrated extract with water or another liquid and bottling before resale), the position will mainly depend on how much value the operation adds to the goods. Only a slight addition in value can be taken not to change the economic identity of the goods.

Goods

50. Exclusive agreements for the supply of services rather than the resale of goods are not covered by this category licence. The licence still applies, however, where the reseller provides customer or after-sales services incidentally to the resale of the goods. Nevertheless, a case where the charge for the service is higher then the price of the goods would fall outside the scope of this licence.

Exclusive Obligation

51. The exclusive supply obligation does not prevent the supplier from providing the contract goods to other resellers who afterwards sell them in the exclusive distributor's territory. It makes no difference whether the other dealers concerned are established outside or inside the territory. The supplier is not in breach of his obligation to the exclusive distributor provided that he supplies the resellers who wish sell the contract goods in the territory only at their request and that the goods are handed over outside the territory. It does not matter whether the reseller takes delivery of goods himself or through an intermediary, such as a freight forwarder.

5.1 Supplies of this nature are only permissible, however, if the reseller and not the supplier pays the transport costs of the goods into the contract territory.

52. This category licence does not apply where the exclusive distributor is restricted to supplying only certain categories of customers (e.g. specialist retailers) in his contract territory and prohibited from supplying other categories (e.g. department stores), which are supplied by other resellers appointed by the supplier for that purpose.

Restriction on competition by the supplier

53. The restriction on the supplier himself supplying the contract goods to final users in the exclusive distributor's contract territory need not be absolute. Clauses permitting the supplier to supply certain customers in the territory—with or without compensation to the exclusive distributor—are compatible with the category licence provided that the customers in question are not resellers. The supplier remains free to supply the contract goods outside the contract territory to final users based in the territory.

No absolute territorial protection

54. The category licence cannot be claimed for agreements that give the exclusive distributor absolute territorial protection. If the situation described in Article 3(b) of this category licence obtains, the parties must ensure either that the contract goods can be sold in the contract territory by other undertakings or that users have a real possibility of obtaining them from undertakings outside the contract territory, at the prices and on the terms there prevailing. The supplier can represent an alternative source of supply for the purpose of this provision if he is prepared to supply the contract goods request to final users located in the contract territory. Article 3(c) of this licence is chiefly intended to safeguard the freedom of dealers and users to obtain the contract goods from outside the territory.

55. This category licence ceases to apply as from the moment that either of the parties takes measures to impede sales into the contract territory from outside. Agreements in which the supplier undertakes with the exclusive distributor to prevent his other customers from supplying into the contract territory are ineligible from the outset. The inapplicability of the category licence follows from the mere fact that the agreement contains restrictions on competition which are not covered by Article 2.1 of this category licence.

Withdrawal of the category licence

56. Section 8(3) of the Competition Act states:

> Where the Authority is of the opinion that, having regard to the requirements of section 4(2) and to the basis upon which a licence under that subsection was granted:
>
> (a) there has been a material change in any of the circumstances on which the decision was based,
>
> (b) any party commits a breach of any obligation attached to the decision,
>
> (c) the licence was based on materially incorrect or misleading information, or
>
> (d) any party abuses the permission granted to it by the licence,
>
> the Authority may revoke or amend the licence and, without prejudice to the generality of this subsection, may in particular insert in a licence conditions the effect of which is to prohibit specific acts by any party thereto which would otherwise be authorised pursuant to such a licence.

The Authority considers that it also has the power, in accordance with section 8(3), to withdraw the benefit of the category licence in individual cases. This would be the case where an individual agreement had effects incompatible with section 4(2), particularly where:

(a) the contract goods are not subject, in the contract territory, to effective competition from identical goods or goods considered by users as equivalent in view of their characteristics, price and intended use; **5.1**

(b) access by other suppliers to the different stages of distribution within the contract territory is made difficult to a significant extent;

(c) for reasons other than those referred to in Article 3(b) and (c) of this category licence it is not possible for intermediaries or users to obtain supplies of the contract goods from dealers outside the contract territory on the terms there customary;

(d) the exclusive distributor, without any objectively justified reason, either refuses to supply in the contract territory categories of purchasers who cannot obtain contract goods elsewhere on suitable terms or applies to them differing prices or conditions of sale.

The situations described above are meant as illustrations of the sort of situations in which the Authority can withdraw a category licence in the case of an individual agreement. There may well be other situations in which the Authority might exercise this power.

Service station agreements

57. This category licence does not apply to agreements for the resale of petroleum products in service stations, since these relate only to exclusive purchasing. They are subject to a separate category licence.

Section 5 of the Act

58. This category licence, being granted in accordance with section 4(2) of the Competition Act, does not exclude the application of section 5 of the Act.

Duration of category licence

59. A number of submissions suggested that the specified period for the licence should be five years, so as to allow the possibility for early review. The Authority considers that there is merit in such arguments, and that the specified period for the category licence should be five years. At the end of this period, on the application of a party to a request under section 7 of the Act, the period of the category licence may be extended, with or without amendments to the licence, if it is considered by the Authority that the requirements of section 4(2) continue to be fulfilled. The category licence shall enter into force on 5 November 1993. It shall expire on 31 December 1998. The category licence is at the end of this Decision.

Notification

60. In accordance with section 4(3)(b) of the Competition Act, where a licence covers a category of agreements, agreements within that category which comply with the terms of the licence need not be notified under section 7 to benefit from the licence while it is in force. Nevertheless, where there is real doubt, in a particular case, an undertaking may request the Authority to declare whether its agreements comply with this category licence. This would have to be done by way of full notification under section 7.

61. It is expected that suppliers and exclusive distributors who wish to benefit from this category licence in future will ensure that new exclusive distribution agreements satisfy the conditions specified in the licence. Parties to agreements which have been made prior to the coming into force of the category licence will also presumably seek to amend these agreements if necessary so as to satisfy the conditions of the licence, especially in the case of agreements which were in existence on the date of commencement of the Act, that is agreements which were entered into prior to 1 October 1991. Appropriate provisions are necessary in the circumstances.

Agreements already notified

62. In the case of exclusive distribution agreements which were in existence on 1 October

5.1 1991, and which have been notified to the Authority before 1 October 1992, this licence shall have effect from 5 November 1993 where the agreements already fulfil the conditions of the licence. Where such notified agreements do not fulfil the conditions of the licence, they do not qualify for the benefit of the licence. The grant of this licence constitutes a refusal to grant a licence to such agreements, unless individual consideration by the Authority is requested before 17 December 1993. Where such notified agreements are amended to fulfil the conditions of the licence, the licence shall have effect from the date when the conditions of the licence are fulfilled.

63. In the case of exclusive distribution agreements which came into existence after 1 October 1991, and which have been notified to the Authority before 5 November 1993, this licence shall have retroactive effect from the date of notification, if the agreements already fulfilled the conditions of the licence, or from the date, being not earlier than the date of notification, when the conditions of the licence were fulfilled. For other agreements which came into existence after 1 October 1991, and which have not been notified, or those which come into existence in the future, this licence shall have effect from the date, at or after the date of grant of the licence, upon which its conditions are fulfilled.

64. The sole requirement for exclusive distribution agreements to enjoy the benefit of the category licence is that they be brought into line with the provisions of the licence. It is left to the undertakings concerned as to how they do this. One way is for the parties to agree to amend the original agreement, while another is for the supplier unilaterally to release the exclusive distributor from all obligations that would prevent the application of the category licence after it comes into operation.

Divergences from EC Regulation 1983/83

65. This Decision and the category licence itself are based to a very large extent upon EC Regulation 1983/83, which grants a block exemption from the prohibition of Article 85(1) of the Treaty of Rome to certain categories of exclusive distribution agreements. A large number of the notified agreements are within the scope of Article 85(1), and it is desirable that exemptions from Article 85(1) of the Treaty and licences under section 4(2) of the Act in respect of the same agreements should correspond to the greatest extent possible. These agreements should also be treated in the same way as purely domestic agreements which do not fall within the scope of Article 85(1). Where divergences occur, the Authority does not consider that they are such as would frustrate the achievement of the objectives of Regulation 1983/83, nor would they prejudice the uniform application of Community competition law throughout the common market.

66. The main difference between this Decision and the Regulation is in its method of construction. The Regulation is in two sections, the recitals, which give some justification for, and explanation of, the operative part, and the Regulation itself. There is also a subsequent explanatory Notice related to the Regulation. This decision follows more closely the approach of the Authority in individual licence decisions. The justification and explanations are given in a form different from that in EC-type recitals, and they avoid the need for a separate explanatory note. As with the recitals, however, this part of the decision is vital to the operative part of the licence, which is identical in form to the corresponding section of the Regulation.

67. References to the common market or to a defined area of the common market in the Regulation are altered to the State or to a defined area of the State in the category licence (Articles 1 and 3(c) of the licence).

68. Article 3(b) of the Regulation allows manufacturers of competing goods to enter into a non-reciprocal exclusive distribution agreement if one or both has a total annual turnover of no more than 100 million ECU. It is not proposed to include an equivalent *de minimis* provision in the category licence. The Authority considers that any such agreements, which might have a significant effect on the domestic economy, should be subject to individual decisions. As a consequence, Article 5 of the Regulation, which relates to the ECU and the calculation of total

turnover, is not necessary in this category licence. Article 4.1 of this category licence also omits the reference to Article 3(b) in the Regulation. 5.1

69. Article 3 of the category licence contains a number of clauses which are not included in the operative part of the Regulation, as follows:

(1) Article 3(d) prohibits any restriction on the reseller's freedom to choose customers, with one exception. This is covered, however, in the notice relating to the Regulation;

(2) Article 3(e) does not permit the supplier to withhold consent from the exclusive distributor appointing agents or sub-distributors, except for objectively valid reasons. While not referred to in the Regulation, such a provision is found in the EC block exemption Regulation for motor vehicle distribution and servicing agreements;[4]

(3) Articles 3(f)(g) and (h) refer to the imposition of fixed prices and to recommended prices, to distributors and to dealers. The preamble to the Regulation states that the distributor must have freedom to determine his prices. The category licence spells this out specifically and in more detail in the case of exclusive distributors, and applies it also to dealers. This latter is in accordance with Article 85(1) and with EC precedents in individual decisions;

(4) Article 3(i) prohibits any restriction on the distributor after termination of the agreement, except in the case of confidential information provided that the distributor is not restrained from competing. The preamble and the Notice clearly states that any restrictions may be imposed only for the duration of the agreement. The reference to confidential information is not believed to be in contradiction with EC precedent, provisions prohibiting the disclosure of secret know-how after termination being found, for example, in the EC block exemption Regulations for patents,[5] and know-how licences;[6]

(5) Article 3(j) refuses the benefit of the category licence where the exclusive distributor has exclusive agreements in respect of a substantial range of competing products, which afford the possibility of eliminating competition in respect of a substantial part of the products in question. While this is not specifically referred to in Article 3 of the Regulation, the Authority is concerned that such a situation could arise to the detriment of competition, given the size of the domestic economy, since it might lead to a restriction of inter-brand competition. It is not considered to be in contradiction with the principles underlying the Regulation.

70. Article 5 of the category licence is identical to Article 6 of the Regulation, except that references to the EC are changed to references to the Authority and the Competition Act, and that the reference to the charging of excessive prices has been omitted. The Authority considers that excessive prices could only be charged where the exclusive distributor possesses market power, and thus where Article 5(a) would already be applicable.

71. Article 7 of the Regulation contains transitional provisions for agreements which previously benefited from Regulation 67/67. Since there has been no previous category licence in the State, such transitional provisions are not needed in the category licence. Certain provisions are needed for agreements which have been notified, however, and these are contained in Article 6 of the licence. This is particularly necessary because the Authority cannot grant a licence which applies retrospectively to agreements which were in force on 1 October 1991 and which have been duly notified before 1 October 1992.

72. Article 8 of the Regulation stated that it did not apply to agreements for the sale of drinks on on-licensed premises or for the sale of petroleum products in service stations, there being a separate Regulation relating to these. Since there is no equivalent category licence for drinks, but there is for petroleum products, the reference to drinks is omitted from Article 7 of the category licence, but the reference to petroleum products is retained. Article 7 of the category licence states that this licence does not apply to exclusive distribution agreements which are

4. Commission Regulation (EEC) No. 123/85, OJ L15, 18.1.85, p. 16, at Article 5.1(2)(a).
5. Commission Regulation (EEC) No. 2349/84, OJ L219, 16.8.84, p. 15, and Corrigendum, OJ L280, 22.10.85, p. 32, at Article 2.1(7).
6. Commission Regulation (EEC) No. 556/89, OJ L61, 4.3.89, p. 1, at Article 2(1)1.

5.1 part of a selective distribution system, including those for motor vehicles. The EC Commission considers agreements in respect of each selective distribution system separately, and it has a special block exemption Regulation in respect of the distribution of motor vehicles.

73. Apart from different commencement and expiry dates in Article 10 of the category licence compared to Article 10 of the Regulation, the rest of the category licence is the same as the Regulation.

74. Notwithstanding the fact that this category licence is closely based upon Regulation 1983/83, the fact that an agreement satisfies the conditions of this category licence does not necessarily mean that it benefits from the exemption afforded by the Regulation. This category licence cannot authorise exclusive distribution agreements which infringe Article 85(1) and which do not satisfy the requirements of Regulation 1983/83. This point is included as Article 8 of the category licence, and there is no corresponding provision in the Regulation.

The Decision

75. The Competition Authority considers that exclusive distribution agreements constitute agreements between undertakings which have the object and effect of preventing, restricting or distorting competition in goods in the State, and thus they offend against section 4(1) of the Competition Act 1991. In the opinion of the Authority, having regard to all relevant market conditions, such agreements generally satisfy all the conditions required for the grant of a category licence under section 4(2) of the Competition Act. Accordingly, the Competition Authority grants a licence to the specified category of agreements, subject to the specified

5.1.1 period and specified conditions as required under section 8(1) of the Competition Act, as follows:

The Category Licence

Article 1

Pursuant to section 4(2) of the Competition Act 1991, and subject to the provisions of this licence, the Competition Authority grants a category licence to agreements to which only two undertakings are party and whereby one party, the supplier, agrees with the other, the exclusive distributor, to supply certain goods for resale within the whole or a defined area of the State only to that other.

Article 2

1. Apart from the obligation referred to in Article 1 no restriction on competition shall be imposed on the supplier other than the obligation not to supply the contract goods to users in the contract territory.

2. No restriction on competition shall be imposed on the exclusive distributor other than:

(a) the obligation not to manufacture or distribute goods which compete with the contract goods;
(b) the obligation to obtain the contract goods for resale only from the other party;
(c) the obligation to refrain, outside the contract territory and in relation to the contract goods, from seeking customers, from establishing any branch, and from maintaining any distribution depot.

3. Article 1 shall apply notwithstanding that the exclusive distributor undertakes all or any of the following obligations:

(a) to purchase complete ranges of goods or minimum quantities;
(b) to sell the contract goods under trade marks, or packed and presented as

specified by the other party; 5.1.1

(c) to take measures for the promotion of sales, in particular:
- — to advertise,
- — to maintain a sales network or stock of goods,
- — to provide customer and guarantee services,
- — to employ staff having specialised or technical training.

Article 3

Article 1 shall not apply where:

(a) manufacturers of identical goods or of goods which are considered by users as equivalent in view of their characteristics, price and intended use enter into reciprocal exclusive distribution agreements between themselves, or into a non-reciprocal exclusive distribution agreement between themselves, in respect of such goods;

(b) users can obtain the contract goods in the contract territory only from the exclusive distributor and have no alternative source of supply outside the contract territory;

(c) one or both of the parties makes it difficult for intermediaries or users to obtain the contract goods from other dealers in other countries, in particular where one or both of them:

1. exercises industrial property rights so as to prevent dealers or users from obtaining outside, or from selling in, the contract territory properly marked or otherwise properly marketed contract goods;
2. exercises other rights or takes other measures so as to prevent dealers or other users from obtaining outside, or from selling in, the contract territory contract goods.

(d) the supplier imposes any restriction on the reseller's freedom to choose customers, except where the reseller is forbidden to supply unsuitable dealers on objectively justifiable grounds;

(e) the supplier is entitled, without objectively valid reasons, to withhold consent from the exclusive distributor to conclude, alter or terminate agreements with agents and sub-distributors;

(f) the supplier obliges the exclusive distributor to sell at a fixed price, or at not less than a minimum price or at not more than a maximum price;

(g) the supplier recommends to the exclusive distributor a specified resale price or a specified maximum or minimum resale price, unless the reseller is informed that he is free to determine his own resale prices;

(h) the above subsections (f) and (g) shall apply *mutatis mutandis* to obligations upon and recommendations to any reseller supplied by the exclusive distributor;

(i) the supplier imposes any restriction on the reseller after the date of termination of the agreement, except in the case of prohibiting the use or disclosure of confidential information, provided that such prohibition does not prevent the exclusive distributor from competing after such termination;

5.1.1 (j) the exclusive distributor has exclusive agreements in respect of a substantial range of competing products, which afford the possibility of eliminating competition in respect of a substantial part of the products in question.

Article 4

1. Article 3(a) shall also apply where the goods there referred to are manufactured by an undertaking connected with a party to the agreement.

2. Connected undertakings are:

(a) undertakings in which a party to the agreement, directly or indirectly:
— owns more than half the capital or business assets, or
— has the power to exercise more than half the voting rights, or
— has the power to appoint more than half the members of the supervisory board, board of directors or bodies legally representing the undertaking, or
— has the right to manage the affairs;

(b) undertakings which directly or indirectly have in or over a party to the agreement the rights or powers listed in (a);

(c) undertakings in which an undertaking referred to in (b) directly or indirectly has the rights or powers listed in (a).

3. Undertakings in which the parties to the agreement or undertakings connected with them jointly have the rights or powers set out in paragraph 2(a) shall be considered to be connected with each of the parties to the agreement.

Article 5

The Authority may withdraw the benefit of this category licence, pursuant to section 8(3) of the Competition Act 1991, when it finds in a particular case that an agreement which is covered by this licence nevertheless has certain effects which are incompatible with the conditions set out in section 4(2) of the Competition Act, and in particular, but not only, where:

(a) the contract goods are not subject, in the contract territory, to effective competition from identical goods or goods considered by users as equivalent in view of their characteristics, price and intended use;

(b) access by other suppliers to the different stages of distribution within the contract territory is made difficult to a significant extent;

(c) for reasons other than those referred to in Article 3(b) and (c) it is not possible for intermediaries or users to obtain supplies of the contract goods from dealers outside the contract territory on the terms there customary;

(d) the exclusive distributor, without any objectively justified reason, either refuses to supply in the contract territory categories of purchasers who cannot obtain contract goods elsewhere on suitable terms or applies to them differing prices or conditions of sale.

Article 6

1. (a) As regards agreements which were in existence on 1 October 1991, and were notified before 1 October 1992, this category licence shall have effect from 5 November 1993, where the agreements already fulfil the conditions of the licence.

(b) As regards agreements which were in existence on 1 October 1991, and were notified before 1 October 1992, and which do not fulfil the conditions of the licence, but which are later amended to fulfil the conditions of the licence, this category licence shall have effect from the date when those conditions were fulfilled. 5.1.1

2. As regards agreements which came into existence after 1 October 1991, and which were notified before 5 November 1993, this category licence shall have retroactive effect from the date of notification where the agreements already fulfil the conditions of the licence, or from the date, being not earlier than the date of notification, when the agreements were amended so as to fulfil those conditions.

3. This category licence constitutes a refusal to grant a licence to exclusive distribution agreements which have been notified before the coming into force of this category licence and which do not fulfil its conditions, unless individual consideration by the Authority is requested before 17 December 1993.

Article 7

This category licence shall not apply to agreements entered into for the resale of petroleum products in service stations, or to exclusive distribution agreements which are part of a selective distribution system, including those for motor vehicles.

Article 8

Nothing in this category licence may be taken as authorising any exclusive distribution agreement which infringes Article 85(1) of the Treaty of Rome and fails to satisfy the requirements of EC Regulation 1983/83, unless the agreement has been specifically exempted by the EC Commission under Article 85(3).

Article 9

This category licence shall apply *mutatis mutandis* to concerted practices of the type defined in Article 1.

Article 10

This category licence shall enter into force on 5 November 1993. It shall expire on 31 December 1998.

For the Competition Authority

Patrick M. Lyons
Chairman

5 November 1993

5.1.2 Notifications which satisfied the conditions of the exclusive distribution category licence

The Authority considers that, on the basis of the information supplied to it, following notified exclusive distribution agreements come within the scope of the category licence and satisfy its conditions. In these circumstances, the effect of Article 6 of the category licence is that the category licence constitutes the grant of a licence in respect of these agreements.*

CA/53/92E	Crown Equipment Ireland/Hydraulic Services Ltd
CA/59/92	Rank Xerox (Ireland) Ltd/concessionaires
CA/91/92E	Maxol Ltd/area distributors
CA/128/92E	Esso Ireland Ltd/distributors
CA/140/92E	Esso Ireland Ltd/Irish Tar + Bitumen Ltd (as amended) (Irish Times, 13.1.95)
CA/141/92E	Esso Ireland Ltd/Blugas Ltd
CA/149/92E	HSI Ltd/Hoover plc
CA/150/92E	Dimpco Ltd/Sharp Electronics (UK) Ltd
CA/156/92E	Beaver Distribution Ltd/Balay SA
CA/157/92E	Beaver Distribution Ltd/Scintilla AG
CA/159/92E	Beaver Distribution Ltd/Blaupunkt Werke GmbH
CA/160/92E	Beaver Distribution Ltd/Robert Bosch (as amended) (Irish Times, 24.6.1994)
CA/161/92E	Beaver Distribution Ltd/Robert Bosch GmbH
CA/195/92E	Player & Wills (Ireland) Ltd/Henry Wintermans Sigarenfabrieken BV
CA/196/92E	Player & Wills (Ireland) Ltd/R.J. Reynolds Tobacco (GB) Ltd
CA/218/92E	Wardell Roberts plc/Williams & Humbert Ltd
CA/219/92E	Wardell Roberts plc/Lofthouse of Fleetwood Ltd
CA/237/92E	International Coatings Ltd/Power Adhesives Ltd
CA/238/92E	International Coatings Ltd/ISF Group Ltd
CA/239/92E	International Coatings Ltd/System Devpack Ltd
CA/247/92E	Johnson Bros Ltd/United Biscuits (UK) Ltd
CA/248/92E	Ciba-Geigy Ireland Ltd/Cahill May Roberts Ltd
CA/249/92E	Ciba-Geigy Ireland Ltd/Pemberton Marketing International Ltd
CA/250/92E	Ciba-Geigy Ireland Ltd/SDS Biotech UK Ltd
CA/252/92E	Johnson Bros Ltd/Combe International Ltd
CA/259/92E	Irish Shell Ltd/distributors
CA/277/92	Greencore Foodsales Ltd/Major International Ltd (Irish Times, 4.2.1994)
CA/283/92E	Tedcastle Engineering Ltd/MAN

*Reference to Irish Times and date means the date of publication in the Irish Times of the announcement that the Notification benefits from the Category Licence.

CA/284/92E	Tedcastle Engineering Ltd/Atlas Weyhausen GmbH
CA/285/92E	Tedcastle Engineering Ltd/Orienstein & Koppel Ltd
CA/286/92E	Tedcastle Engineering Ltd/JI Case Europe Ltd
CA/287/92E	Tedcastle Engineering Ltd/Jacty Engineering Co. Ltd
CA/288/92E	The Nestle Co. Ltd/Clayton Love Distribution Ltd
CA/293/92E	Irish Ropes Ltd/Koltec B.C. (Irish Times, 15.4.1994)
CA/303/92E	M & R Martini & Rossi Ltd/Grants of Ireland Ltd
CA/304/92E	Grants of Ireland Ltd/L & P Antinori SPA
CA/322//92E	Masterfoods Ld/Shamrock Foods (Distributors) Ltd (as amended) (Irish Times, 10.3.1995)
CA/365/92E	Sigma Wireless Communications Ltd/Motorola AS
CA/366/92E	Sigma Wireless Communications Ltd/Motorola Ltd (Irish Times, 9.9.1994)
CA/382/92E	Natureline Ltd/Jackel International Ltd
CA/387/92E	Unifood Ltd/DCL (Yeast) Ltd
CA/388/92	Unifood Ltd/John F. Renshaw & Co. Ltd (as amended) (Irish Times, 27.5.1994)
CA/389/92E	Irish Biscuits Ltd/Jacobs Suchard Manufacturing GmbH (as amended) (Irish Times, 6.5.1994)
CA/390/92E	Unifood Ltd/DCA Industries Ltd
CA/396/92E	Masterfoods Ltd/JC Distribution Ltd
CA/405/92E	Cahill May Roberts Ltd/Mates Healthcare Ltd
CA/406/92E	Cahill May Roberts Ltd/Kabipharmcia Ireland Ltd
CA/408/92E	Cahill May Roberts Ltd/Fisons Pharmaceuticals Ireland Ltd
CA/411/92E	Cahill May Roberts Ltd/Eurocetus UK Ltd
CA/413/92E	Cahill May Roberts Ltd/Clini-Med Ltd
CA/414/92E	Cahill May Roberts Ltd/Merck Sharp & Dohme Ltd
CA/416/92E	Wiggins Teape Ireland Ltd/KNP Fine Paper
CA/417/92E	Wiggins Teape Ireland Ltd/Collins Stationery & Diary Ltd
CA/418/92E	Irish Ropes Ltd/Mobil Plastics Europe Inc
CA/419/92E	Irish Ropes Ltd/Rosenlaw Emballage AB
CA/420/92E	Irish Ropes Ltd/Werra Plastics GmbH
CA/421/92E	Irish Ropes Ltd/Itipack SRL
CA/422/92E	Irish Ropes Ltd/British Twines Ltd
CA/448/92E	Statoil Ireland Ltd/distributors
CA/462/92	JC Distribution Ltd/Prestige Group plc
CA/463/92	JC Distribution Ltd/Kopex International Ltd
CA/464/92	JC Distribution Ltd/H Vesshoff & Co. GmbH

5.1.2

CA/466/92	JC Distribution Ltd/Vileda LP
CA/468/92	JC Distribution Ltd/Dietzel GmbH
CA/478/92E	B M Browne Ltd/Roche Products Ltd
CA/481/92E	B M Browne Ltd/Dia Med AG
CA/482/92E	B.M. Browne Ltd/Stratex Medical Ltd (as amended) (Irish Times, 24.6.1994)
CA/505/92E	Chivers & Sons Ltd/Tate & Lyle Industries Ltd
CA/506/92E	Chivers & Sons Ltd/Cadbury Beverages Ltd
CA/509/92E	Cadbury Beverages Ltd/Chivers & Sons Ltd
CA/528/92E	Gilbeys of Ireland Sales Ltd/Hermann Kendermann GmbH
CA/530/92E	Gilbeys of Ireland Sales Ltd/Veuve Clicquot Ponsardin (Irish Times, 4.2.1994)
CA/543/92E	Gilbeys of Ireland Sales Ltd/Matthew Gloag (UK) Ltd
CA/545/92E(a)	Kitchen Accessories Ltd/Franke UK Ltd
CA/545/92E(b)	Kitchen Accessories Ltd/NEF Ltd
CA/545/92E(c)	Kitchen Accessories Ltd/Paini SpA
CA/545/92E(d)	Kitchen Accessories Ltd/Elica SpA
CA/545/92E(e)	Kitchen Accessories Ltd/Emerson Electrical Corp
CA/545/92E(f)	Kitchen Accessories Ltd/Hera GmbH
CA/545/92E(g)	Kitchen Accessories Ltd/Merloni Electricadomecstica
CA/545/92E(h)	Kitchen Accessories Ltd/Schlautecnik
CA/545/92E(i)	Kitchen Accessories Ltd/ASKO
CA/545/92E(j)	Kitchen Accessories Ltd/Fulgar SpA
CA/552/92E	United Drug plc/Pentax Europe NV
CA/562/92E	United Drug plc/Nycomed (UK) Ltd
CA/575/92E	United Drug plc/Pharma Services
CA/576/92E	United Medical/Clement Clarke International Ltd
CA/577/92E	United Medical Ltd/Haag Streit AG (Irish Times, 15.4.1994)
CA/580/92E	Pemberton Marketing International Ltd/Nevinar Ltd
CA/583/92E	Pemberton Marketing International Ltd/Ilford Ltd
CA/585/92E	Pemberton Marketing International Ltd/Ciba-Geigy Ireland Ltd
CA/616/92E	TEIS Ltd/Landis & Gyr Lake Ltd
CA/617/92E	TEIS Ltd/Case Communications Ltd
CA/618/92E	TEIS Ltd/Infotron Systems Ltd
CA/619/92E	T.E.I.S./MDS Telephone Systems Ltd (as amended) (Irish Times, 24.6.1994)
CA/620/92E	T.E.I.S./Sharptext Ltd (as amended) (Irish Times, 24.6.1994)

CA/621/92E	T.E.I.S./Siemens Ltd (as amended) (Irish Times, 24.6.1994)
CA/628/92E	Gilbeys of Ireland Sales Ltd/Rothschild SA
CA/629/92E	Estuary Fuel Ltd/distributors (as amended) (Irish Times, 24.6.1994)
CA/641/92E	TEIS Ltd/Mitel Telecom Ltd
CA/658/92E	Technical Equipment Co. Ltd/Holex BV (as amended) (Irish Times, 15.4.1994)
CA/659/92E	Technical Equipment Co. Ltd/Leyland & Birmingham Rubber Co. Ltd
CA/660/92E	Technical Equipment Co Ltd/BTR Hose Ltd
CA/661/92E	Technical Equipment Co Ltd/Digi-Table Ltd
CA/662/92E	Technical Equipment Co Ltd/Jumo Instrument Co. Ltd
CA/663/92E	Technical Equipment Co. Ltd/Eaton Ltd (as amended) (Irish Times, 15.4.1994)
CA/664/92E(a)	Technical Equipment Co Ltd/Keyence Corp
CA/664/92E(b)	Technical Equipment Co Ltd/Flash SA
CA/664/92E(c)	Technical Equipment Co Ltd/Thomas & Betts
CA/664/92E(d)	Technical Equipment Co Ltd/Staubli SA
CA/664/92E(e)	Technical Equipment Co Ltd/AG Petzatakis SA
CA/664/92E(f)	Technical Equipment Co Ltd/Willcox Hose Ltd
CA/664/92E(g)	Technical Equipment Co Ltd/Enerpac Ltd
CA/664/92E(h)	Technical Equipment Co Ltd/IVG Colbachine SpA
CA/664/92E(i)	Technical Equipment Co. Ltd/Felten Guilleaume
CA/675/92E	Allied Foods Ltd/Spendgrade Ltd
CA/676/92E	Allied Foods Ltd/Van den Broeke (Foods) (UK) Ltd
CA/677/92E	Allied Foods Ltd/U B (Ross Young's) International Ltd
CA/678/92E	Allied Foods Ltd/Goosens BV
CA/704/92E	Tennant & Ruttle Distribution Ltd/United Biscuits
CA/706/92E	Tennant & Ruttle Distribution Ltd/Kinnerton Confectionery Co. Ltd
CA/707/92E	Tennant & Ruttle Distribution Ltd/Duracell UK Ltd
CA/708/92E	Tennant & Ruttle Distribution Ltd/Greensleeves Confectionery Ltd
CA/709/92E	Tennant & Ruttle Distribution Ltd/Lindt & Sprungli (UK) Ltd
CA/711/92E	Tennant & Ruttle Distribution Ltd/The Wrigley Co. Ltd (Irish Times, 15.4.1994)
CA/727/92E	Beaumark Ltd/Russell Hobbs Tower Ltd
CA/728/92E(a)	Beaumark Ltd/Toastess Ltd
CA/728/92E(b)	Beaumark Ltd/Goblin Ltd
CA/728/92E(c)	Beaumark Ltd/Berry Magicoal Ltd
CA/728/92E(d)	Beaumark Ltd/Payer Ltd
CA/729/92E	Waterford Foods Ireland Ltd/Avondale Foods Ltd

5.1.2

CA/735/92E	Clayton Love Distribution Ltd/Nestle Co. Ltd
CA/737/92	Walker Air Conditioning Ltd/Vokes Ltd
CA/738/92	Walker Air Conditioning Ltd/Condair AG
CA/765/92E	Campus Fuels Ltd/distributors
CA/897/92E	Jotun-Henry Clarke Ltd/Marinco Ltd
CA/900/92E	Burmah Castrol (Ireland) Ltd/Distributors (as amended) (Irish Times, 11.3.1994)
CA/902/92E	Burmah Castrol (Ireland) Ltd/Liffey OilLtd (as amended) (Irish Times, 11.3.1994)
CA/903/92E	Burmah Castrol (Ireland) Ltd/Kingdom Oil Co. (as amended) (Irish Times, 4.2.1994)
CA/905/92E	Brown Thomas & Co Ltd/Extravert Design Ltd
CA/917/92E	Brooks Thomas Ltd/Servicised Ltd (as amended) (Irish Times, 4.2.1994)
CA/940/92E	PJ Carroll & Co. Ltd/Le S.E.I.T.A. (Irish Times, 4.2.1994)
CA/950/92E	Maguire & Paterson Ltd/G. & M. Ltd
CA/951/92E	Maguire & Paterson/Irish Dog Foods Ltd (Irish Times, 9.9.94)
CA/952/92E	Maguire & Paterson/JADT Cosmetics (as amended) (Irish Times, 13.1.1995)
CA/955/92E	Maguire & Paterson/Wilkinson Sword (Irish Times, 16.9.1994)
CA/956/92E	Maguire & Paterson Ltd/Conros Corporation
CA/957/92E	Fannin Ireland Ltd/Vernon & Co. (Pulp Products) Ltd (as amended) (Irish Times, 11.3.1994)
CA/958/92E	Fannin Ltd/Portex Ltd
CA/959/92E	Fannin Ltd/Hospicare Ltd
CA/960/92E	Fannin Ltd/Kendall Co. (UK) Ltd
CA/961/92E	Fannin Ltd/Eschmann Bros & Walsh Ltd
CA/965/92E	ESM Paper Ltd/Du Pont (UK) Ltd
CA/966/92E	ESM Paper Ltd/Iggesund Paperboard Ltd
CA/1032/92E	Musicmaker Ltd/Vie Firth Inc
CA/1033/92E	Musicmaker Ltd/Roland (UK) Ltd
CA/1034/92E	Musicmaker Ltd/Pearl Musical Instrument Co.
CA/1035/92E	Musicmaker Ltd/Young Chang Akki Europe GmbH
CA/1036/92E	Musicmaker Ltd/Paul Reed Smith Guitars
CA/1037/92E	Musicmaker Ltd/Marshall Amplification plc
CA/1038/92E	Musicmaker Ltd/Freestyle Music Products
CA/1039/92E	Musicmaker Ltd/D'Andre Mfg. Co. Ltd
CA/1040/92E	Musicmaker Ltd/GMS Corp
CA/1041/92E	Musicmaker Ltd/Sabian Ltd

CA/1042/92E	Musicmaker Ltd/TEAC UK Ltd
CA/1043/92E	Musicmaker Ltd/Trace-Elliot Ltd
CA/1054/92E	Palace Video Ltd/Abbey Films Ltd/Mayfair Entertainment UK Ltd
CA/1058/92E	Allegro Ltd/Wander Ltd (Irish Times, 15.4.1994)
CA/1060/92E	Allegro Ltd/Northern Foods Ltd (as amended) (Irish Times, 13.1.1995)
CA/1061/92E	Allegro Ltd/Del Monte Foods International Ltd
CA/1062/92E	Allegro Ltd/Kimberly-Clark Corporation
CA/1063/92E	Allegro Ltd/Albright & Wilson Ltd
CA/1073/92E	T P Whelehan Son & Co Ltd/AmericanCyanamid Co.
CA/1074/92E	T P Whelehan Son & Co Ltd/AmericanCyanamid Co.
CA/1075/92E	T P Whelehan Son & Co Ltd/Carter-Wallace Ltd
CA/1076/92E	T P Whelehan Son & Co Ltd/Rohm & Haas (UK) Ltd
CA/1082/92	E Dillon & Co Ltd/Jas Hennessy & Co. Ltd (Irish Times, 9.9.1994)
CA/1083/92E	E Dillon & Co Ltd/The Old Bushmills Distillery Co. Ltd (as amended) (Irish Times, 8.4.1994)
CA/1084/92E	E Dillon & Co Ltd/Grants of St James's
CA/1085/92E	E Dillon & Co Ltd/United Distillers plc (as amended) (Irish Times, 15.4.1994)
CA/1086/92E	E Dillon & Co Ltd/Maison Bouchard Pere & Fils
CA/1087/92E	E Dillon & Co Ltd/Hedges & Butler Ltd
CA/1088/92E	E Dillon & Co Ltd/Vintners International Co. Inc
CA/1089/92E	E Dillon & Co Ltd/Seagram UK Ltd
CA/1090/92E	E Dillon & Co Ltd/H Sichel Sohne GmbH
CA/1091/92E	E Dillon & Co Ltd/Bacardi International Ltd
CA/1103/92E	Tambrands Inc/David Mayrs Ltd
CA/1125/92	JCB Sales Ld/ECI (as amended) (Irish Times, 14.10.1994)
CA/1131/92	Precision Heating Equipment Ltd/Bentone Electro Oil AB
CA/2/93	Butler Manufacturing Services Ltd/Melvin Pumps Ltd
CA/29/93	Tate & Lyle Industries Ltd/Co-Operative Animal Health Care Ltd (as amended) (Irish Times, 4.2.1994)
CA/40/93	Celmac Ltd/Protim (Ireland) Ltd
CA/41/93	Kiddie Products Inc/UPC Co. Ltd
CA/58/93	Warner Lambert Distributors (Irl) Ltd/Johnson Brothers Ltd (as amended) (Irish Times, 12.8.1994)
CA/3/94	T Sheridan Sales and Marketing Ltd/St Ives Laboratories Ltd (as amended) (Irish Times, 13.1.94)
CA/5/94	T Sheridan Sales and Marketing Ltd/Beauty International Ltd (as amended) (Irish Times, 11.11.94)

5.2 Competition Authority Decision No. 31, Energy Control Systems Ltd/Erinova Ltd/Belton Engineering Works Ltd: 9 September 1993, Notification Nos. CA/31/93 and CA/32/93

Exclusive distribution agreement governing distribution of products outside the State – Whether such agreements have effect on competition within the State – Competition Act 1991 (No. 24) sections 3, 4 and 7

Facts: On 13 July 1993 notification was made to the Authority by Energy Controls Systems Ltd ('ECS') of two exclusive distribution agreements it had entered into with Erinova Ltd and Belton Engineering Works Ltd respectively, with a request for a certificate under section 4(4) of the Competition Act 1991 or, failing that, a licence under section 4(2). ECS is an Irish registered company with an expertise in the construction of hydro-electric facilities and each of Belton Engineering Ltd and Erinova Ltd are small Irish engineering companies which manufacture water turbines. Under the terms of the notified agreements ECS was appointed by each of Erinova Ltd and Belton Engineering Ltd as exclusive distributor of water turbines for territories outside the State.

Decided by the Authority: In issuing a certificate under section 4(4) of the Competition Act 1991 in respect of the notified agreements that:

(1) Each of the parties to the notified agreements are 'undertakings' within the meaning of section 3(1) of the Competition Act 1991 and the agreements were agreements between undertakings.

(2) The object of the agreements is to provide for exclusive distribution outside the State and do not have as their object or effect the prevention, restriction or distortion of competition in the State or any part of the State.

(3) The non-extension of the ECS exclusive distribution rights within the State does not affect competition in the State as ECS has no entitlement to such rights and the manufacturers are free to determine how their products are to be distributed in the State.

(4) Agreements which clearly do not offend against section 4(1) of the Competition Act ought not to be notified since it is not necessary to obtain either a certificate or a licence in order to implement such agreement.

Decision referred to:

Competition Authority Decision No. 11—Firestone/Grenfells Ltd and Thoroughbred Promotion and Development Company **3.9**

Competition Authority Decision of 9 September 1993 relating to a proceeding under section 4 of the Competition Act 1991

Notification No. CA/31/93 — Energy Control Systems Ltd/Erinova Ltd, and No. CA/32/93 — Energy Control Systems Ltd/Belton Engineering Works Ltd

Introduction

1. Notifications were made with a request for a certificate under section 4(4) of the Competition Act, 1991 or, in the event of a refusal by the Competition Authority to issue a certificate, a licence under section 4(2), by Energy Control Systems Ltd on 13 July 1993 in respect of two exclusive distribution agreements it had entered into with Erinova Ltd and Belton Engineering Works Ltd, respectively.

The Facts 5.2

(a) *The subject of the notification*

2. These notifications concern agreements whereby two Irish manufacturers of water turbines have each appointed another Irish firm as exclusive distributor of these products for territories outside the State.

(b) *The undertakings concerned*

3. Energy Control Systems (ECS), of Newbridge, Co. Kildare, is a six-person operation which has developed an expertise in producing control systems for hydroelectric schemes. Its main business has been in Ireland, where it has several agreements with landowners for the construction of hydroelectric facilities to generate electricity. It has no market share in Ireland in the distribution of water turbines. Erinova Ltd, of Pearse Street, Dublin, is a small engineering company with three employees. It has sold three water turbines in Ireland and none abroad. Belton Engineering Works Ltd (Belton), of Ardagh, Co. Longford, is a small family-run mechanical engineering company with six employees. It has sold about 50 small water turbines in Ireland over the last 15 years and none abroad.

(c) *The product and the markets concerned*

4. The product is a water turbine which is used for the generation of electricity in small-scale hydroelectric installations. In both agreements, ECS is appointed exclusive distributor for water turbines outside the State, and accordingly no analysis is required concerning the market for water turbines in the State.

(d) *The notified agreements*

5. The agreement between ECS and Erinova is dated 2 June 1993, and that between ECS and Belton is dated 21 January 1993. The two agreements are identical in their terms, except for the territory allocated to the exclusive distributor. The main clauses of the agreements are as follows:

1. The manufacturer appoints the distributor and the distributor accepts the appointment as the sole and exclusive distributor for ten years from the date of this agreement of all water turbines produced by the manufacturer and any subsidiary, associated company, licensee or agent of the manufacturer ('the products').

2. The distributor may not assign transfer or sublet its rights and responsibilities under this agreement to an exclusive sub-distributor without the written consent of the manufacturer.

3. The manufacturer and the distributor will negotiate the pricing and general terms and conditions for the supply of the products by the manufacturer to the distributor on an individual project basis.

Erinova agreement

4. The manufacturer may not appoint another distributor and may not itself supply products to users in the United Kingdom, Australia, New Zealand, Thailand, Indonesia, Malaysia, Philippines, Germany, Austria and Switzerland during the term of this agreement.

Belton agreement

4. The manufacturer may not appoint another distributor and may not itself supply products to users in the world other than Ireland and Northern Ireland for the term of this agreement.

Assessment under section 4(1)

6. Section 4(1) of the Competition Act states that 'all agreements between undertakings, decisions by associations of undertakings and concerted practices which have as their object or effect the prevention, restriction or distortion of competition in trade in any goods or services in the State or in any part of the State are prohibited and void'.

7. ECS, Erinova and Belton are all corporate bodies engaged in the supply and distribution

5.2 of goods or the provision of services. They are all, therefore, undertakings within the meaning of section 3 of the Competition Act 1991. The agreements are agreements between undertakings.

8. Under the agreements, ECS has been appointed exclusive distributor of water turbines produced by the other parties for territories outside the State, in one case for ten other countries, and in another for the rest of the world excluding Northern Ireland. The object of the agreements is to provide for exclusive distribution outside the State and to regulate the relations between the manufacturers and the exclusive distributor. The agreements do not apply to the State and they do not have the object of affecting competition within the State or in any part of the State. The restrictions in the agreements only have effects in the territories concerned, which are outside the State. The agreements have no effects in the domestic market, and they do not effect competition within the State or in any part of the State. The fact that the manufacturers do not extend exclusive distribution rights in the State to ECS does not affect competition, since ECS has no entitlement to such rights and the manufacturers are free to determine how their products are to be distributed in the State. Since the agreements have neither the object nor the effect of preventing, restricting or distorting competition in the State or in any part of the State, they do not offend against section 4(1) of the Competition Act 1991.

9. The Authority has stated in the past that it is not necessary to notify an agreement which clearly does not offend against section 4(1), since it is not necessary to obtain a certificate in order to implement such an agreement. Indeed it is questionable whether such an agreement can be notified under section 7 of the Competition Act in the first place, since it is not an agreement 'of a kind described in section 4(1)', that is an agreement which has as its object or effect the prevention, restriction or distortion of competition in the State. (See Decision No. 11 of 5 November 1992—B. and D. Firestone/Grenfells Ltd and Thoroughbred Promotion and Development Company). In this case the notifying parties had some concern about whether any restriction on their selling outside the State could effect production, and thus come within the scope of the Competition Act. Agreements whose only effects on competition are in markets outside the State do not come within the scope of the Act, and, in the Authority's opinion, are not capable of being notified under section 7.

The Decision

10. ECS, Erinova and Belton are all undertakings and the notified agreements are agreements between undertakings. Since the agreements relate to exclusive distribution by ECS outside the State, they have neither the object nor the effect of preventing, restricting or distorting trade in the State or in any part of the State, and so they do not offend against section 4(1) of the Competition Act 1991 and certificates may be issued in respect of the agreements.

The Certificates

11. The Competition Authority has issued the following certificates:

(a) The Competition Authority certifies that in its opinion, on the basis of the facts in its possession, the exclusive distribution agreement of 2 June 1993 between Energy Control Systems Ltd and Erinova Ltd (Notification No. CA/31/93) notified on 13 July 1993 under section 7, does not offend against section 4(1) of the Competition Act 1991.

For the Competition Authority

Patrick M. Lyons
Chairman

9 September 1993

(b) The Competition Authority certifies that in its opinion, on the basis of the facts in its possession, the exclusive distribution agreement of 21 January 1993 between Energy

Control Systems Ltd and Belton Engineering Works Ltd (Notification No. CA/32/93) notified on 13 July 1993 under section 7, does not offend against section 4(1) of the Competition Act 1991. 5.2

For the Competition Authority

Patrick M. Lyons
Chairman

9 September 1993

Competition Authority Decision No. 143, Sigma Wireless Communications Ltd/ Motorola Ireland Ltd: 27 October 1993, Notification No. CA/364/92E 5.3

Asset sale agreement including exclusive distribution rights of vendor containing non-compete clause – Whether such clause and agreement in compliance with Irish Competition Law – Competition Act 1991 (No.24) sections 3, 4 and 7

Facts: On 30 September 1992 notification was made to the Authority of an asset sale agreement containing a non-compete clause between Sigma Wireless Communications Ltd ('Sigma') as purchaser and Motorola Ireland Ltd ('Motorola') as vendor with a request for a certificate under section 4(4) of the Competition Act 1991 or, failing that, a licence under section 4(2). Sigma is a limited liability company incorporated in Ireland which is engaged in the sale and distribution of mobile communication products. Motorola is a subsidiary of Motorola Inc., a worldwide corporate group engaged in the manufacture and supply of advanced electronic communication systems. Under the terms of the notified agreement, which was made on 1 July 1991, Sigma acquired Motorola's Irish distribution business and by virtue of clause 9 thereof Motorola undertook to comply with an exclusive distribution arrangement entered into with Sigma whereunder Sigma was appointed exclusive distributor for two years in the State for Motorola's products. In addition Motorola was prevented from soliciting employees from the business sold to Sigma.

Decided by the Authority: In issuing a certificate under section 4(4) of the Competition Act 1991 in respect of the notified arrangements that:

(1) Each of the parties to the notified arrangements are 'undertakings' within the meaning of section 3(1) of the Competition Act 1991 and the arrangements constitute an agreement between undertakings.

(2) The arrangements relating to the sale of the assets were completed prior to 1 October 1991, the commencement date for the Competition Act and are therefore not reviewable. Section 4(1) only applies to a current or continual contractual commitment or one entered into subsequent to the coming into force of the Competition Act.

(3) Clause 9 of the notified agreement whereunder Sigma was appointed Motorola's exclusive distributor for a period of two years and the restriction on Motorola soliciting staff from the transferred business are forms of non-compete clauses which in the circumstances are necessary to secure the transfer of the goodwill of the business and whose object is not to prevent, distort or restrict competition (Competition Authority Decision No. 10, *GI/General Semiconductor*, 23 October 1992 referred to).

5.3 **Decision and Notice referred to:**
Competition Authority Notice in respect of mergers and takeovers which pre-date the Competition Act (*Iris Oifigiúil*, 14 May 1993 p. 367) **3.1**
Competition Authority Decision No. 10—GI/General Semiconductor, 23 October 1992 **3.8**

Competition Authority Decision of 27 October 1993 relating to a section under section 4 of the Competition Act 1991
Notification No. CA/364/92E—Sigma Wireless Communications Ltd/Motorola Ireland Ltd

Introduction

1. An agreement between Sigma Wireless Communications Ltd (Sigma) and Motorola Ireland Ltd (Motorola) containing a non-compete clause, pursuant to the purchase and sale of certain assets and exclusive distribution rights of Motorola was notified to the Competition Authority on 30 September 1992. The notification requested a certificate or, in the event of a certificate being refused, a licence.

The Facts

(a) *The Subject of the Notification*

2. The notification relates to an asset purchase agreement dated 1 July 1991 between Sigma and Motorola whereby Sigma purchased Motorola's distribution business in Ireland. The agreement was initiated by Motorola's parent company, Motorola Ltd (U.K.) (Motorola U.K.) which decided to remove the Irish distribution rights from its wholly-owned subsidiary. The agreement contained non-compete provisions.

(b) *The Parties*

3. Sigma is a limited company registered in the State. It is a subsidiary of Sigma Communications Group Ltd and is engaged in the sale and distribution of mobile communications products such as cellular phones, paging equipment, etc. Motorola UK forms part of Motorola Inc., a worldwide group of companies based in Chicago, Illinois engaged in the manufacture and supply of advanced electronic and communications systems.

(c) *The Arrangements*

4. The notification relates to an agreement, dated 1 July 1991 whereby Sigma acquired Motorola's Irish distribution business from Motorola (Ireland) Ltd, a wholly-owned subsidiary of Motorola U.K. Clause 9 of the agreement requires the vendor to adhere to the exclusivity provisions of certain exclusive distribution agreements entered into at the time of the sale, for a period of two years from the date of completion.[1] In effect this meant that Sigma acted as Motorola's exclusive distributor in Ireland for that period. In addition the vendors were prevented from soliciting employees of the business for a similar period of time. These provisions expired on 1 July 1993.

Assessment

(a) *Section 4(1)*

5. Section 4(1) of the Competition Act states that 'all agreements between undertakings, decisions by associations of undertakings and concerted practices which have as their object or

1. The present decision is not concerned with those agreements which were notified separately as all notified exclusive distribution agreements were considered in the context of the Authority's proposed category licence for exclusive distribution agreements.

effect the prevention, restriction or distortion of competition in trade in any goods or services in the State or in any part of the State are prohibited and void'. 5.3

(b) *The Undertakings and the Agreement*

6. Section 3(1) of the Competition Act defines an undertaking as 'a person being an individual, a body corporate or an unincorporated body of persons engaged for gain in the production, supply or distribution of goods or the provision of a service.' Sigma is a limited company registered in the State engaged for gain in the sale and distribution of mobile communications products. It is therefore an undertaking within the meaning of the Act. Motorola (Ireland) Ltd was engaged for gain in the manufacture and supply of advanced electronic and communications systems and was also an undertaking within the meaning of the Act. The arrangements constitute an agreement between undertakings.

(c) *Applicability of section 4(1)*

7. As the sale of assets was completed prior to 1 October 1991, the date on which the Competition Act came into force, this element of the agreement had been discharged by performance before the Act commenced. The property which was the subject of the agreement had been transferred. In the Authority's view, the prohibition in section 4(1) only applies to a current or continuing contractual commitment or one entered into subsequent to the coming into force of the Act.[2] As the merger or sale element of the 1991 transaction was discharged prior to the commencement of the Act, that aspect of the arrangements does not come within the scope of section 4(1).

8. Clause 9 required the vendor to adhere to the terms of the agreements under which it appointed Sigma as its exclusive distributor for a period of two years. This represents a form of non-compete clause. The business which was sold was the vendor's distribution operation within the State. Consequently this requirement was necessary to secure the transfer of the goodwill of the business and did not offend against section 4(1). The restriction on the vendors soliciting Sigma staff was also necessary to secure the transfer of the goodwill of the business and similarly did not offend against section 4(1).[3]

The Decision

9. In the Authority's opinion, Sigma Wireless Communications Ltd and Motorola Ireland Ltd are undertakings within section 3(1) of the Competition Act and the notified arrangements for the purchase and sale of certain assets and exclusive distribution rights of Motorola to Sigma constitute an agreement between undertakings.

10. The Authority believes that as the sale element of the transaction was discharged prior to the commencement of the Competition Act, the agreement for the purchase and sale of certain assets and exclusive distribution rights of Motorola does not come within the scope of section 4(1) of the Act. As the restrictions in the agreement were necessary to secure the transfer of the goodwill of the business being sold, the agreement did not offend against section 4(1).

The Certificate

11. The Competition Authority has issued the following certificate:

> The Competition Authority certifies that in its opinion, on the basis of the facts in its possession, the agreement for the purchase of certain assets, between Sigma Wireless

2. Notice in respect of Mergers and Takeovers, which predate, the Competition Act—Competition Authority, *Iris Oifigiúil*, 14 May 1993, p. 367.
3. This view regarding restrictions on the vendor in a sale of business agreement is in accord with a number of previous Authority decisions. See, for example, Competition Authority Decision No. 10, GI/General Semiconductor (CA/51/92 and CA/52/92), 23 October 1992.

5.3 Communications Ltd and Motorola Ireland Ltd (Notification No. CA/364/92E), notified on 30 September 1992, under section 7, did not offend against section 4(1) of the Competition Act 1991.

For the Competition Authority

Patrick Massey
Member

27 October 1993

5.4 Competition Authority Decision No. 273, Rhone Poulenc Ireland Ltd/Shell Chemicals Ireland Ltd: 3 February 1994, Notification No. CA/98/92

Agreement for sale and transfer of business – Conditional upon appointment of Exclusive distributor – Competition Act 1991 (No. 24) sections 3, 4 and 7

Facts: On 18 September 1992 notification was made to the Authority in respect of arrangements between Rhone Poulenc Ireland Ltd ('RPI') and Shell Chemicals Ireland Ltd ('Shell') whereunder RPI purchased certain assets from Shell, with the request for a certificate under section 4(4) of the Competition Act 1991 or, failing that, a licence under section 4(2). Shell, a private company registered in Ireland and a subsidiary of Royal Dutch Petroleum Company and the Shell Transport and Trading Company Ltd, is engaged in the marketing of industrial chemicals, polymers and agricultural pesticides in the State. RPI, a private company registered in Ireland and a subsidiary of Rhone Poulenc is engaged in the importation and distribution of chemical and animal health products in the State. The product market relevant to this notification was the seed treatment business wherein seed assemblers treat their products with chemicals in order to make them disease resistant and it is a market in which many of the multi-national chemical companies are engaged in the State. The notified agreement relates to the purchase by RPI of the seed treatment business of Shell in the State and under the terms thereof Shell is restricted for a period of 4 years from the date of transfer of the business from competing in Ireland either directly or indirectly with RPI in that business, from soliciting persons who were clients of the transferred business during the period 2 years immediately proceeding the transfer or from soliciting any employee of RPI. The vendor further covenants in the notified agreement not to disclose any confidential information relating to the transferred business and not to cause the termination of any arrangement or agreement relating to the business. The entire sale of the business from Shell to RPI was conditional upon RPI appointing Shell its exclusive distributor within the State in relation to a certain chemical cereal herbicide.

Decided by the Authority: In issuing a certificate under section 4(4) of the Competition Act 1991 in respect of the notified arrangements that:

(1) Each of the parties to the notified arrangements are 'undertakings' within the meaning of section 3(1) of the Competition Act 1991.

(2) Contrary to the submissions by the parties, the notified agreement is an agreement between undertakings which is reviewable against the criteria set out in section 4(1) of the Competition Act. 5.4

(3) Having regard to the number of large multinational firms competing in the relevant market and the parties' submissions that the entry barriers into the market are low, the acquisition aspect of the notified agreement is unlikely to have any anti-competitive effects.

(4) The restriction on competition for a period of 4 years while exceeding that period generally approved by the Authority (2 years), in this case, due to the degree of technical know how involved in the business being transferred, does not exceed what is necessary to secure the complete transfer of the goodwill in the business.

(5) The restriction on the vendor disclosing confidential information to third parties does not offend against section 4(1) provided that such restriction is not used to prevent the vendor, after the expiry of legitimate non-competition period, from competing with the purchaser by means of new and further developments of such secret technical knowledge.

Editor's Note: The Authority did not refer in its certifcate to the condition of the agreement that Shell would be the sole and exclusive distributor of a certain chemical cereal herbicide. The Authority noted that the agreement had been terminated.

Cases and Other Authority Decisions referred to:

BAT v. EC Commission and Philip Morris (Case No. 142 & 156/84), [1987] ECR 4487, [1988] 4 CMLR 24

EC Commission Decision—Reuter/BASF [1976] OJ L254/40, [1976] 2CMLR D44

Competition Authority Decision No. 1—Nallen/O'Toole (Belmullet), 2 April 1992 [3.3]

Competition Authority Decision No. 3—Athlone Travel Ltd/Michael Stein Travel Ltd, 4 June 1992 **3.5**

Competition Authority Decision No. 6—Woodchester Bank Ltd/UDT Bank Ltd, 4 August 1992 **3.5**

Competition Authority Decision No. 9—Budget Travel Ltd/Phil Fortune, 14 September 1992 **3.7**

Competition Authority Decision No. 12 — Scully Tyrell & Company/Edberg Ltd, 29 January 1993 **3.10**

Submissions: Submissions made on behalf of both parties:

(1) Under the notified agreement RPI was acquiring assets, know-how and goodwill from Shell in relation to the seed treatment business from which Shell was withdrawing and the agreement therefore amounted to a concentration rather than an arrangement for the coordination of commercial conduct in the market and so did not fall within ambit of section 4(1) of the Competition Act.

(2) The notified arrangements were not anti-competitive when considered against the relevant market where entry barriers were low and competition keen between several large multinational chemical companies.

(3) The clauses restricting competition in the notified agreements were not in breach of section 4(1) of the Competition Act in that they did not go beyond what was necessary to secure the transfer of the goodwill of the business been sold.

(4) The distribution agreement was not anti-competitive as it satisfied the requirements for the licence set out in section 4(2) of the Competition Act and the require-

5.4 ments of the EC block exemption (regulation 1983/83) for exclusive distribution agreements.

Competition Authority Decision of 3 February 1994 relating to a proceeding under section 4 of the Competition Act 1991
Notification No. CA/98/92 — Rhone Poulenc Ireland Ltd/Shell Chemicals Ireland Ltd

Introduction

1. Arrangements for the purchase of a seed treatment business by Rhone-Poulenc Ireland Ltd (RPI) from Shell Chemicals Ireland Ltd (Shell) were notified to the Competition Authority on 18 September 1992. The agreement was conditional on Shell and RPI entering into an agreement appointing Shell as sole and exclusive distributor of certain RPI products within the State at or before completion. The agreement also included a number of non-compete provisions. The notification requested a certificate, or in the event of a refusal by the Authority to grant a certificate, a licence.

The Facts

(a) *The Subject of the Notification*

2. The notification relates to an agreement, dated 6 August 1992, between RPI and Shell for the sale and purchase of the Shell seed treatment business. At the time of the sale and purchase, Shell and RPI were to enter into an agreement appointing Shell as sole and exclusive distributor of certain RPI products within the State.

(b) *The Parties*

3. Shell is a private limited company engaged in the marketing of a wide range of industrial chemicals, polymers and agricultural pesticides in the State. It has, as its ultimate parents, The Royal Dutch Petroleum Company and The Shell Transport and Trading Company Ltd. RPI is a private limited company registered in Ireland and engaged in the importation and distribution of a wide range of chemical, agrochemical and animal health products. It is a subsidiary of the international company Rhone Poulenc.

(c) *The Products and the Market*

4. The products concerned are those used in the seed treatment business within the State. Essentially seed assemblers treat their products in order to make them disease resistant. The parties have submitted that the following companies produce the following products for seed treatment in Ireland:

Company	Product
Rhone Poulenc	Panoctine 30
	Panoctine Plus
	Rappor
	Rappor Plus
Shell	New Kotol
ICI	Vincit
	Ferrax
Bayer	Raxil
	Baytan
Janssen Pharmaceutical	Fungazil
DowElanco	Wireworm FS

In addition they have indicated that the following companies distribute the following products: 5.4

Company	Product
RPI	Panoctine 30
	Panoctine Plus
Shell	New Kotol
	Vincit
ICI	Ferrax
Bayer	Raxil
	Baytan
Duphar	Fungazil
	Rappor
	Rappor Plus
	Wireworm FS

5. According to the parties the seed treatment market is highly competitive and new products are being developed by firms such as ICI, Bayer and Ciba-Geigy, the latter being a new competitor in the market.

6. There are a number of firms engaged in the seed assembly business in Ireland and they all treat their products in order to increase their resistance to disease. Specialised seed treatment dressing machines are used by seed assemblers for seed treatment. According to the parties most of these machines are leased to the seed assemblers for a nominal annual charge. The machines are maintained serviced and calibrated by the owner companies which are mainly producers\distributors of seed treatment chemicals. A number of these leasing agreements are included among the assets of the business being acquired by the company. The parties have stated that these leasing agreements provide that only products supplied by Shell may be used, unless otherwise agreed in writing by Shell. The parties stated that:

> The existence of this type of clause has historically made access to machinery important in order to access the cereal treatment market and may have inhibited chemical producers from penetrating the seed treatment market without alternative access to machinery.

They also pointed out that, following problems with certain products in Autumn 1991 and Spring 1992, Shell granted RPI permission for its products to be used in Shell machines. In addition the parties have stated that upon completion of the acquisition, RPI deleted this form of clause from the standard Shell leasing agreements. The parties have claimed that assemblers remain reluctant to assume the responsibility of owning their own machines although they are freely available and are relatively inexpensive.

7. Detailed figures on the size of the seed treatment market are difficult to obtain. According to the CSO, the total value of seeds purchased by farmers in 1991 was £42.3m. The relevant market is the State.

(d) *The Arrangements*

8. The agreement relates to the acquisition by RPI of the seed treatment business of Shell. It includes in clause 10 a number of restrictive provisions which are summarised below. Clause 10.01 restricts the vendors for four years from completion from:

(i) carrying on or assisting or being engaged concerned or interested in any business within Ireland which competes with any part of the business;

(ii) soliciting the custom within Ireland in relation to any services of the same type as those provided in the ordinary course of the Business of any person who at any time during the period of two years immediately preceding Completion was a customer or client of the Business;

5.4 (iii) soliciting any employee or consultant to the Purchaser;

Clause 10.02 provides that the vendor shall not at any time after completion, either on its own account or jointly with or on behalf of another person, either directly or indirectly cause or seek to cause to be terminated or adversely affected or otherwise interfere with any agreement or arrangement of any kind relating to the business. Clause 10.03 restricts the Vendor from disclosing any information of a secret or confidential nature or any know-how relating to the organisation, business, affairs, finances, customers, suppliers, employees or transactions of the business and from using to the detriment of the business any information which it has obtained or received in confidence in the course of or as a result of having owned the business, except to the extent required by law and then only after prior consultation with the purchaser.

9. Clause 3.01 (c) provides that the completion of the agreement is conditional upon a distribution agreement being executed and exchanged between the purchaser and the vendor at or before completion. Under the terms of the distribution agreement RPI has appointed Shell as its sole and exclusive distributor in the State of a certain chemical cereal herbicide. Such products are sprayed on plants at an early stage of growth to protect them against weed infestation. Clause 3.01 (g) provides that completion is conditional upon Shell being released from its obligations to Bayer (Ireland) Ltd on foot of its existing distribution agreements in relation to the product commonly known as Raxil. This agreement was subsequently terminated.

(e) *Submissions of the Parties*

10. The parties argued that as the acquisition agreement was tantamount to a concentration it did not fall within the ambit of section 4(1) of the Competition Act. They submitted that the position in this instance was different to that which arose in either the *Philip Morris*[1] case or in *Woodchester*[2] as RPI was not acquiring legal or *de facto* control over Shell but rather was acquiring certain assets, know-how, technology and goodwill from Shell in relation to the seed treatment business. It was argued that, as Shell was withdrawing completely from the market, there was no question of the arrangement serving as an instrument for the co-ordination of the commercial conduct of either Shell or RPI so as to restrict or distort competition in the seed treatment market. In addition it was submitted that the arrangements could not be regarded as anti-competitive given that there were several large multinational enterprises competing in the market, barriers to entry were low and competition was strong. In support of this they claimed that RPI's success in the market had encouraged other firms to accelerate the development of new products for the market.

11. The parties also submitted that the restrictions in clause 10 were not anti-competitive as they did not go beyond what was necessary to secure the transfer of the goodwill of the business being sold. A number of EC Commission decisions and judgments of the European Court of Justice were submitted in support of this claim as were the Authority's decisions in *Nallen/O'Toole*[3] and *Athlone Travel.*[4]

12. It was stated that the distribution agreement was not anti-competitive since it related to a different product market and because the grant of distribution rights to Shell increased competition in that market. It was also submitted that this agreement satisfied the requirements for a licence set out in section 4(2) and the requirements of the EC Block Exemption for exclusive distribution agreements.[5]

1. *BAT v. EC Commission*, Cases 142 and 156/84.
2. Decision No. 6, Woodchester Bank Ltd/UDT Bank Ltd, 4 August 1992.
3. Decision No. 1, Nallen/O'Toole (Belmullet), 2 April 1992.
4. Decision No. 3, Athlone Travel Ltd/Michael Stein Travel Ltd, 4 June 1992.
5. Regulation 1983/83, OJ L 173/1, 30 June 1983.

Assessment

(a) *Section 4(1)*

13. Section 4(1) of the Competition Act states that 'all agreements between undertakings, decisions by associations of undertakings and concerted practices which have as their object or effect the prevention, restriction or distortion of competition in trade in any goods or services in the State or in any part of the State are prohibited and void.'

(b) *The Undertakings and the Agreement*

14. Section 3(1) of the Competition Act defines an undertaking as 'a person being an individual, a body corporate or an unincorporated body of persons engaged for gain in the production, supply or distribution of goods or the provision of a service.' The parties to the present agreement are Shell and RPI. They are both corporate bodies engaged in the provision of goods and services for gain and are therefore undertakings within the meaning of the Act.

(c) *Applicability of section 4(1)*

The Sale Agreement

15. The present arrangements therefore constitute an agreement between undertakings whereby RPI has purchased Shell's seed treatment business. The Authority indicated in *Woodchester* that an agreement giving rise to a merger or concentration was not, in its opinion, outside the scope of section 4(1). It has restated this view on a number of occasions. The Authority does not accept the claim by the parties that, as the present agreement is for the sale of a business only, it lies outside the ambit of section 4(1). As the Authority indicated in *Woodchester* the prohibition in section 4(1) relates to any agreements between undertakings which have as their object or effect the prevention, restriction or distortion of competition in trade in any goods or services in the State or in any part of the State. It does not provide that certain types of agreements are not by their nature, subject to that provision. Thus in the Authority's view, the issue which it must decide upon in the case of any notified agreement, is whether it is an agreement between undertakings which has as its object or effect the prevention, restriction or distortion of competition within the State or within any part of the State. In *Woodchester* the Authority, while stating that the acquisition of a business did not offend against section 4(1) *per se*, indicated that in certain circumstances it might. In order to clarify its views it outlined in *Scully Tyrrell*[6] the circumstances in which it might find the acquisition of a business to be anti-competitive.

16. In this instance the Authority does not have detailed information on market shares which would allow it to measure the impact of the arrangements on the degree of market concentration which would normally be the first issue to be considered in assessing whether or not the acquisition can be regarded as anti-competitive. The Authority notes that there are a number of large firms competing in the relevant market. In addition it notes the claim that entry barriers are low. In such circumstances the Authority believes that the acquisition is unlikely to have an anti-competitive effect and hence it does not offend against section 4(1).

Non-Compete Provisions

17. The agreement as notified contained a number of non-compete provisions which have been outlined above. Specifically under clause 10.01 the vendor may not engage in the relevant business or solicit customers or employees of the business for a period of four years from completion. Such restrictions have been dealt with on a number of occasions by the Authority and so it is only necessary to deal with them briefly in this decision. Specifically the Authority has indicated that in the case of a sale of business it normally regards a restriction on the vendor

6. Decision No. 12, Scully Tyrrell & Co./Edberg Ltd, 29 January 1993.

5.4 competing with the business following completion as necessary to secure the complete transfer of the business. It has stated that provided the restriction on the vendor is limited in terms of duration, geographic scope and subject matter to what is necessary to achieve that purpose, then it does not, in the Authority's view offend against section 4(1). The Authority has indicated that it regards a period of two years as sufficient to secure such a transfer where only goodwill is involved while a restriction of up to five years may be acceptable where technical know-how is involved. The Authority considers that the particular business involving the production and preparation of chemicals for use in seed treatment involves a degree of technical know-how. Consequently, in its opinion, the restrictions in clause 10.01 do not offend against section 4(1).

18. The Authority's decision is not concerned with the seed assembly machinery leases directly as it considers that these constitute separate agreements between the business and its customers which have not been notified. It notes that the existing Shell agreements provided that the lessees could only use Shell products in the machines. Clause 10.02 of the acquisition agreement provided that the vendor should not cause or seek to cause to be terminated any agreement relating to the business. There is no time limit on this clause. If the exclusive use provisions of the leasing agreements were retained, then clause 10.02 would prevent Shell from re-entering the seed treatment business after the expiry of the provisions in clause 10.01. This would arise because the lessees could not use Shell's products in the machines and Shell could only sell its products if the lessees terminated the assembly machine leases. RPI indicated that it intended to remove the exclusive use provisions from the lease agreements. As a result of the amendment to the machine leases, Clause 10.02 does not prevent Shell re-entering the market for seed treatment chemicals and so it does not, in the Authority's opinion offend against section 4(1).

19. Clause 10.03 prevents the Vendor from disclosing any information of a secret or confidential nature or any know-how relating to the organisation, business, affairs, finances, customers, suppliers, employees or transactions of the business and shall not use to the detriment of the business any information which it has obtained or received in confidence in the course of or as a result of having owned the business, except to the extent required by law and then only after prior consultation with the purchaser.

20. The Authority has stated in previous decisions that such restrictions are acceptable provided it is not intended that they be used to prevent the vendor re-entering the relevant market once a legitimate non-competition clause has expired.[7] In particular the Authority wishes to draw attention to the views expressed by the European Commission in the *Reuter/BASF* case with which it fully agrees.

> It is further recognised that it may be necessary in certain cases to provide additional safeguards to ensure the effective performance of an agreement in cases where technical knowledge, constituting an important part of the value of a transferred undertaking, is placed at the disposal of the transferee. As in the case of goodwill, it must be possible to prevent the transferrer for a certain time from using such knowledge in a manner which would prevent the transferee from acquiring the undertaking with its market position undiminished.
>
> Here too, the protection afforded to the transferee should be limited in time, since the transfer of legally unprotected know-how confers no exclusive rights on the purchaser. Contrary to the contention of BASF, the transfer of technical know-how in connection with the sale of an undertaking does not automatically preclude any further activity on the part of the seller based on such know-how. The opportunity of using such know-how which is unknown to competitors is, like goodwill, a competitive advantage. This advantage can be diminished by the development of third party competitors of their own know-how in the particular field of research. Unlike third parties the transferrer of an

7. See Budget Travel Ltd/Phil Fortune, Decision No. 9, 14 September 1992.

undertaking remains aware of the contents of any transferred know-how, since he cannot divest himself of his own knowledge. For this reason it appears legitimate to protect the transferee in order for a certain time to enable him to acquire the undertaking with its competitive position undiminished. This need to protect the competitive position of the undertaking provides the justification for and prescribes the time limits to any non-competition clause involved.[8] 5.4

21. The Commission went on to state that:

In no circumstances may an obligation to keep know-how secret from third parties, imposed on the transfer of an undertaking, be used to prevent the transferrer, after the expiry of the reasonable term of a non-competition clause, from competing with the transferee by means of new and further developments of such know-how.

In this instance the Authority believes that the restriction on the vendor disclosing technical know-how to third parties does not offend against section 4(1) provided it is not used to prevent the transferrer, after the expiry of the provisions contained in clause 10.01, from competing with the transferee by means of new and further developments of such know-how.

The Decision

22. In the Authority's opinion, Shell and RPI are undertakings within the meaning of section 3(1) of the Competition Act, and the notified arrangements for the acquisition by RPI of the seed treatment business of Shell, constitute an agreement between undertakings. The Authority believes that the acquisition of the business does not offend against section 4(1). The restrictions in the agreement are no more than is necessary to secure the transfer of the business to RPI. The agreement of 6 August 1992 for the acquisition of the seed treatment business of Shell by RPI between Shell Chemicals Ireland Ltd and Rhone Poulenc Ireland Ltd does not, in the Authority's opinion, offend against section 4(1) of the Competition Act 1991.

The Certificate

23. The Competition Authority has issued the following certificate:

The Competition Authority certifies that in its opinion, on the basis of the facts in its possession, the agreement of 6 August 1992 for the acquisition of the seed treatment business of Shell by RPI between Shell Chemicals Ireland Ltd and Rhone Poulenc Ireland Ltd, (Notification No. CA/98/92), notified on 18 September 1992 under section 7, does not offend against section 4(1) of the Competition Act 1991.

For the Competition Authority

Patrick Massey
Member

3 February 1994

5.5 **Competition Authority Decision No. 319, Campus Oil Ltd/Delta Distributor Agreements:** 21 April 1994, Notification Nos. CA/759/92E, CA/760/92E, CA/761/92E, CA/762/92E, CA/763/92E, CA/764/92E

Arrangments ancillary to exclusive distribution agreement – Whether arrangements prevent, distort or restrict competition – Competition Act 1991 (No. 24) sections 3, 4 and 7

Facts: One 30 September 1992 notification was made to the Authority by Campus Oil Ltd ('Campus') and Delta Fuels Ltd ('Delta') of six agreements, which agreements related to an exclusive distribution agreement, with the request for certificates under section 4(4) of the Competition Act 1991 or, failing that, licences under section 4(2). The parties to the notified agreements were either of Campus and Delta and various distributors of oil products within the State. The notified standard agreements were: (i) a guarantee made between Campus/Delta and the owner of the relevant distributor company whereunder the owner guarantees payment to Campus/Delta by the Distributor Company for all goods supplied; (ii) Standard Licence type 1 made between Campus/Delta and a distributor whereunder Campus/Delta gives to the Distributor a non-exclusive licence over property owned by Campus/Delta for the purposes of carrying on the business of oil distribution; (iii) Standard Licence type 2 whereunder the distributor grants Campus/Delta an exclusive licence for a period of ten years to enter upon the premises owned by the distributor should the distributor breach the terms of the related exclusive distribution agreement; (iv) Two standard debentures made between Campus/Delta and the distributor whereunder the distributor charges certain assets in favour of Campus/Delta in support of its obligations to pay for the goods supplied; (v) Standard equipment loan agreement made between Campus/Delta and the distributor whereunder Campus/Delta leases to the Distributor certain equipment for a nominal rent. Each of the licences and the equipment loan agreement terminate on the expiration of the related exclusive distribution agreement. The related exclusive distribution agreement was notified separately to the Authority (CA/765/92E) and was held to satisfy the conditions of the category licence for exclusive distribution agreements (Decision No. 144, 5 November 1993).

Decided by the Authority: In granting licences under section 4(2) of the Competition Act 1991 in respect of the notified agreements that:

(1) Each of the parties to the notified agreements are 'undertakings' within the meaning of section 3(1) of the Competition Act 1991.

(2) All the notified agreements offend against section 4(1) of the Competition Act 1991 as they underpin an exclusive distribution agreement which itself offends against section 4(1).

(3) The notified agreements, being ancilliary to a related exclusive distribution agreement, satisfy the four conditions for the granting of a licence set out in section 4(2) of the Competition Act for the same reasons as that related exclusive distribution agreement. (See the decision of Competition Authority No. 144, 5 November 1993).

Decision referred to:

Competition Authority Decision No. 144, 5 November 1993, Category licence for exclusive distribution agreements **5.1**

Competition Authority Decision of 21 April 1994 relating to a proceeding under section 4 of the Competition Act 1991 5.5
Notification Nos. CA/759/92E, CA/760/92E, CA/761/92E, CA/762/92E, CA/763/92E, CA/764/92E — Campus/Delta Distributor Agreement

Introduction

1. Notification was made of six agreements by Campus Oil Ltd/Delta Fuels Ltd on 30 September 1992 with a request for certificates under section 4(4) of the Competition Act 1991 or in the event of a refusal by the Competition Authority to issue certificates, a request for licences under section 4(2).

The Facts

(a) *The subject of the decision*

2. The decision concerns four types of documents signed by Campus/Delta and some of their exclusive distributors namely a Guarantee Agreement, a Licence Agreement (two forms), a Debenture Agreement (two forms) and an Equipment Agreement.

(b) *The parties involved*

3. The suppliers involved in the notified agreements are Campus Oil Ltd/Delta Fuels Ltd, two companies in the Clashfern Group. These companies are limited companies which supply petroleum products. The other parties to the arrangements are distributors of oil used for home heating purposes, agricultural oil and oil for commercial purposes (fuel oils). In the case of the guarantee agreement the other parties involved are the owners of the distribution companies.

(c) *The products and the market*

4. The products involved are fuel oils. The oil companies involved in this market generally use distributors to deliver to final customers and do not use their own staff as in the past.

(d) *The notified agreements*

5. The arrangements notified are those between two companies in the Clashfern Group of companies (namely Campus Oil Ltd and Delta Fuels Ltd) and their distributors of fuel oils. These arrangements are embodied in a standard distribution agreement for a term of ten years, which every distributor has executed. The Authority has already concluded that the standard distribution agreement (CA/765/92E) satisfies the conditions of the category licence for exclusive distribution agreements (Decision No. 144 of 5 November 1993). In addition to the exclusive distribution agreement, there are four other documents, which are the subject of this decision, namely, an equipment agreement, a debenture, a guarantee and a licence. The details of these are given below.

(a) *Guarantee.* In return for Campus having agreed to supply petroleum products to the distributor, the individual owner (or owners) guarantees payment to Campus by the distributor for all goods supplied. The guarantee has been executed by 17 persons.

(b) *Licence 1.* Campus or Delta owns a site, and it licences the distributor to use the site for the business of oil distribution. The owner licences the non-exclusive use of the property and the assets, but the owner retains full access to and rights to use the property and the assets at all times, for any purpose whatsoever. The licence is of even date with the exclusive distribution agreement, and lasts for a set number of years or until the distribution agreement is terminated, whichever is the sooner. The licence is stated not to be a landlord/tenant relationship, nor a partnership. Two such licences are in existence.

(c) *Licence 2.* Under this agreement, the distributor owns the site and grants Campus a licence to use the site, in consideration for Campus having spent a specified sum in construction works on the site. Campus is granted an exclusive licence to enter on and use the site in the event of the distributor failing to use the site in accordance with the exclusive distribution agreement of

5.5 even date. The distributor is entitled to use the site until the termination of the distribution agreement, and the licence is granted for ten years, but the distributor is not entitled to use the site for the period between the expiration of the agreement and the expiration of the licence. There is one such licence in existence.

(d) *Debenture 1.* This debenture creates a first floating charge on all assets of the company, and it takes the form of a resolution to the effect that the company will pay on demand to Campus all such sums as are or will be due whether in respect of monies advanced or paid to or for the use of the company or in respect of goods sold and delivered by Campus to the company. This debenture agreement has been obtained from six distributors.

(e) *Debenture 2.* This debenture states that all monies owing now or in the future to Delta shall be secured in a manner and on the terms specified. The company covenants with the supplier that it will pay all sums of money which are or may become due under the distribution agreement. There is one such debenture in existence.

(f) *Equipment loan agreement.* In order to enable the distributor to carry out his obligations under the exclusive distribution agreement, Campus agrees to provide the distributor with certain machinery and equipment by way of lease at a nominal rent. The equipment remains the property of Campus, and the distributor is obliged to keep it in good repair, pay for servicing, ensure it is operated by competent persons, keep it in the distributor's possession and not remove it from the premises, allow Campus to inspect it, indemnify Campus and insure the equipment, and allow Campus' name to be affixed to the equipment. The distributor is not permitted to sell or assign the equipment, nor to sell the premises without giving Campus prior notice and allowing Campus to repossess the equipment, nor to alter the equipment without permission. The agreement terminates on the expiration of the exclusive distribution agreement, or on Campus giving one month's notice to the distributor. There are nine such agreements in existence.

Assessment

Applicability of section 4(1)

6. Section 4(1) of the Competition Act 1991 prohibits and renders void all agreements between undertakings which have as their object or effect the prevention, restriction or distortion of competition in trade in any goods or services in the State or in any part of the State.

The Undertakings

7. Section 3(1) of the Competition Act defines an undertaking as 'a person being an individual, a body corporate or an unincorporated body of persons engaged for gain in the production, supply or distribution of goods or the provision of a service.' Campus/Delta and the distributors are engaged in the sale of oil products for gain, and are therefore undertakings within the meaning of section 3(1) of the Competition Act. In the case of the Guarantee Agreements, the owners of the distribution companies own and control the business and, in line with previous Authority decisions, they are also undertakings.

The Agreements

8. All the notified agreements are connected with, and dependent upon, the exclusive distribution agreements, they form part of the exclusive distribution arrangements and, in some cases, they strengthen those arrangements. In the opinion of the Authority, while the agreements might contain some provisions which by themselves could offend against section 4(1), all the notified agreements offend against section 4(1) of the Competition Act because they underpin an exclusive distribution agreement which itself offends against section 4(1) of the Competition Act for the reasons given in the category licence for exclusive distribution agreements.

Applicability of section 4(2) 5.5

9. Under section 4(2), the Competition Authority may grant a licence in the case of any agreement or category of agreements which, 'having regard to all relevant market conditions, contributes to improving the production or distribution of goods or provision of services or to promoting technical or economic progress, while allowing consumers a fair share of the resulting benefit and which does not—(i) impose on the undertakings concerned terms which are not indispensable to the attainment of those objectives; (ii) afford undertakings the possibility of eliminating competition in respect of a substantial part of the products or services in question'.

10. The Authority has decided that the basic Campus/Delta standard exclusive distribution agreement satisfies the conditions of the category licence. It is of the opinion that the notified related agreements also satisfy the conditions of the category licence, for the same reasons, and thus they also satisfy the requirements of section 4(2) of the Competition Act. This applies also to any exclusivity provisions specifically included in the notified agreements. A licence may therefore be issued in relation to each of these agreements. The licences come into effect on 21 April 1994. They will expire on the date of expiry of the category licence for exclusive distribution agreements, that is on 31 December 1998.

The Decision

11. In the Authority's opinion, Campus/Delta and the other parties to the agreements are undertakings. The notified agreements between the parties are agreements between undertakings. The Authority considers that the notified agreements offend against section 4(1) of the Competition Act 1991. The Authority considers that the notified agreements satisfy the conditions of section 4(2) of the Competition Act. It has therefore decided to issue a licence to each of the notified agreements, and these licences shall apply from 21 April 1994 to 31 December 1998. It is not considered necessary to attach any conditions to the licences.

The Licences

12. The Competition Authority has issued the following licences:

The provisions of section 4(1) of the Competition Act 1991 are declared inapplicable to the following agreements notified to the Competition Authority by Campus Oil Ltd/Delta Fuels Ltd on 30 September 1992, on the grounds that, in the opinion of the Authority, all the conditions of section 4(2) of the Competition Act 1991 have been fulfilled:

(a) Distributor Agreement (Guarantee).....................CA/759/92E
(b) Distributor Agreement (Licence)....................CA/760/92E
(c) Distributor Agreement (Licence)....................CA/761/92E
(d) Distributor Agreement (Debenture)...............CA/762/92E
(e) Distributor Agreement (Debenture)................CA/763/92E
(f) Distributor Agreement (Equipment)................CA/764/92E

These licences shall apply from 21 April 1994 to 31 December 1998.

For the Competition Authority

Patrick M. Lyons
Chairman

21 April 1994

5.6 Competition Authority Decision No. 329, Reflex Investments plc/Storage Technology Ltd: 19 May 1994, Notification No. CA/750/92E

Exclusive distribution agreement — Termination of notified agreement after notification — Whether licence can be made retrospective to the date of the notification for an agreement notified under section 7(2) — Competition Act 1991 (No. 24), sections 3, 4 and 7

Facts: On 30 September 1992 notification was made to the Authority of an exclusive distribution agreement made 4 April 1991 between Storage Technology Ltd, as supplier, and Reflex Investments Plc ('Reflex'), as distributor, with a request for a certificate under section 4(4) of the Competition Act 1991 or, failing that, a licence under section 4(2).

Reflex, an Irish registered company, is engaged in the business of the sale and lease of computer systems and Storage Technology Ltd, a UK based company is engaged in the sale and maintenance of computer equipment manufactured by its US parent Storage Technology Corporation.

Under the terms of the notified agreement Reflex was appointed exclusive distributor in the State of certain computer products of Storage Technology Ltd which agreement was conditional upon, *inter alia,* Reflex not selling other products without the consent of Storage Technology Ltd and Reflex's obligation to pay to Storage Technology Ltd 50% of the monthly maintenance fees charged by Reflex for all computers installed. While Storage Technology Ltd could reject any order placed by Reflex, Reflex was obliged to supply any customer nominated by Storage Technology. For its part Storage Technology undertook to prevent the infringement of Reflex's rights under the notified agreement by any of its other agents or distributors. By letter dated 7 February 1994 Reflex informed the Authority that the notified agreement had been terminated on or about 31 May 1993.

Decided by the Authority: In refusing to issue a certificate or grant a licence under sections 4(4) and 4(2) respectively of the Competition Act 1991 in respect of the notified agreement that:

(1) Each of the parties to the notified agreement are 'undertakings' within the meaning of section 3(1) of the Competition Act 1991 and the arrangement was an agreement between undertakings.

(2) The notified agreement offends against section 4(1) of the Competition Act for the reason set out in the Authority's category licence for exclusive distribution agreement *(Competition Authority Decision No. 144*—5 November 1993).

(3) Section 7(3) of the Competition Act provides that no licence or certificate may be granted until an agreement has been notified. The section further states that a licence notified under section 7(1) may be made retrospective to the date of the notification. Section 7(1) provides for the notification of agreements which come into existence after the commencement of section 4(1); being 1 October 1991. The notified arrangement was in existence prior to that date and was notified under section 7(2). The agreement expired on or about 31 May 1993 and consequently a licence cannot be made retrospective in this case even if the conditions for a licence were satisfied.

(4) The notified agreement would not have satisfied the requirements of the category licence for exclusive distribution agreements nor the conditions of section

4(2) due to: 5.6

(a) the supplier agreeing to safeguard the distributor's rights conferred absolute territorial protection on the distributor;
(b) the distributor accepting the supplier's orders and the supplier being entitled to accept or reject orders limited the freedom of the distributor to choose his own customers; and
(c) the delivery of the invoice to the distributor and payment of 50% of the list maintenance price restricted the freedom of the distributor to set his own prices.

Decision referred to:
Competition Authority Decision No. 144, Category licence for exclusive distribution agreements, 5 November 1993 **5.1**

Competition Authority Decision of 19 May 1994 relating to a proceeding under section 4 of the Competition Act 1991
Notification No. CA/750/92E — Reflex Investments plc/Storage Technology Ltd

Introduction

1. An exclusive distribution agreement between Reflex Investments plc and Storage Technology Ltd was notified by Reflex to the Competition Authority on 30 September 1992. The notification requested a certificate or, in the event of refusal by the Authority to issue a certificate, a licence.

2. The Authority issued a Statement of Objections to the parties concerned in respect of the notified agreement on 25 March 1994. No response was received from either of the parties.

The Facts

(a) *The subject of the notification*

3. The notification relates to an agreement dated 4 April 1991 between Reflex and Storage Technology whereby Reflex was appointed exclusive distributor in the State of certain computer products.

(b) *The parties involved*

4. Reflex is an Irish-registered company which distributed certain STC computer products and is engaged in the sale and lease of other computer systems and the provision of related technical advice. Storage Technology is a UK company engaged in the sale and maintenance of computer equipment which is manufactured in the US by Storage Technology Corporation (STC).

(c) *The arrangements*

5. The notification relates to an exclusive distribution agreement dated 4 April 1991. Reflex was appointed sole and exclusive dealer of the products in the State (and in Northern Ireland). The distributor was not to deal in competing goods, except where necessary to supply competing IBM goods in preference to the supplier's products. The distributor was not to seek end-users, or to supply or install the products, or to establish any branch or depot, or enter into third party maintenance agreements, outside the territory. Minimum purchase requirements were specified. The distributor was obliged to promote sales, engage in advertising, provide maintenance staff and undertake maintenance, to keep records, and was to sell under trademarks. The distributor was not to sell other products without permission, and was to sell the products as principal, not as agent. The supplier agreed to safeguard the distributor's rights, including preventing the

5.6 infringement of those rights by other distributors and agents of the supplier. The distributor was to accept the supplier's orders for the products for onward sale to end-users, and the supplier was entitled to accept or reject each order. The price payable by the distributor was in Schedule 1 of the agreement, and an invoice in respect of products sold was to be delivered to the distributor at the time the products were delivered. The distributor was to pay the supplier a percentage of its then current list maintenance price each month for each machine installed. In Schedule 2, it was specified that the distributor should pay the supplier 50% of the maintenance price each month. The agreement was deemed to take effect from 7 April 1991, for an initial period of three years, and thereafter from year to year, subject to six months' notice. By letter of 7 February 1994, Reflex informed the Authority that the agreement had been terminated on or about 31 May 1993.

Assessment

(a) *Section 4(1)*

6. Section 4(1) of the Competition Act states that 'all agreements between undertakings, decisions by associations of undertakings and concerted practices which have as their object or effect the prevention, restriction or distortion of competition in trade in any goods or services in the State or in any part of the State are prohibited and void'.

(b) *The undertakings and the agreement*

7. Section 3(1) of the Competition Act defines an undertaking as 'a person being an individual, a body corporate or an unincorporated body of persons engaged for gain in the production, supply or distribution of goods or the provision of a service.' Reflex is engaged in the distribution of goods for gain, and Storage Technology is engaged in the sale and maintenance of goods for gain, and they are therefore undertakings within the meaning of the Act. The arrangement was an agreement between undertakings.

(c) *Applicability of section 4(1)*

8. The Authority considers that an exclusive distribution agreement such as that between Reflex and Storage Technology offends against section 4(1) of the Act, for the reasons stated in its category licence for exclusive distribution agreements (Decision No. 144 of 5 November 1993, para. 14).

(d) *Applicability of section 4(2)*

9. Under section 4(2), the Competition Authority may grant a licence in the case of any agreement or category of agreements which offends against section 4(1) but which, 'having regard to all relevant market conditions, contributes to improving the production of goods or provision of services or to promoting technical or economic progress, while allowing consumers a fair share of the resulting benefit and which does not: (i) impose on the undertakings concerned terms which are not indispensable to the attainment of those objectives; (ii) afford undertakings the possibility of eliminating competition in respect of a substantial part of the products or services in question'.

10. Section 7(3) of the Act provides that no licence or certificate may be granted until an agreement has been notified. It goes on to provide that 'any such licence may in the case of an agreement, decision or concerted practice to which subsection (1) applies be made retrospective to the date of notification under that subsection.' Section 7(1) provides for the notification of agreements which come into existence after the commencement of section 4(1), i.e. after 1 October 1991. The present arrangement was in existence prior to that date and was notified under section 7(2). The notified agreement expired on or about 31 May 1993. Consequently a licence cannot be made retrospective in this case even if the conditions for the grant of a licence were satisfied. In this instance it appears to the Authority that:

(a) the supplier agreeing to safeguard the distributor's rights conferred absolute territorial protection on the distributor; 5.6

(b) the distributor accepting the supplier's orders, and the supplier being entitled to accept or reject orders, limited the freedom of the distributor to choose his own customers; and

(c) the delivery of the invoice to the distributor, and payment of 50% of the list maintenance price restricted the freedom of the distributor to set his own prices.

These restrictions would not have satisfied the requirements of the category licence for exclusive distribution agreements nor would they have satisfied the conditions of section 4(2).

The Decision

11. In the opinion of the Authority, the exclusive distribution agreement between Reflex Investments plc and Storage Technology Ltd (Notification No. CA/750 /92E) notified on 30 September 1992, under section 7(2) of the Competition Act, constituted an agreement between undertakings. It considers that the agreement offended against section 4(1) of the Competition Act and therefore it refuses to issue a certificate. The agreement expired on or about 31 May 1993. The Authority is not empowered to grant a licence with retrospective effect in the case of an agreement notified under section 7(2). In any case the limitation on the freedom of the distributor to set its own resale prices and the other limitations in the agreement would have precluded the Authority from granting a licence as these would not have satisfied the conditions of section 4(2) of the Competition Act. Accordingly, the Authority refuses to grant a licence in respect of the notified agreement.

For the Competition Authority

Patrick M. Lyons
Chairman.

19 May 1994

Competition Authority Decision No. 355, Mount Juliet/David Leadbetter Golf Academy Inc: 19 September 1994, Notification No. CA/8/94 5.7

Service supply agreement — Undertaking by supplier of service not to supply service elsewhere in the State during term of agreement — Confidentiality clause — Non-solicitation of employees clause — Competition Act 1991 (No. 24) sections 3, 4 and 7

Facts: On 31 March 1994 notification was made to the Authority with the request for a certificate under section 4(4) of the Competition Act 1991 or, failing that, a licence under section 4(2) in respect of an agreement between Mount Juliet and David Leadbetter Golf Academy Inc. ('DLGA') relating to the establishment of a golf school at Mount Juliet, Thomastown, Co. Kilkenny.

Mount Juliet, an unlimited company, is the owner and operator of a hotel, leisure centre and golf course at Mount Juliet, County Kilkenny. DLGA, an Ohio based corporation operates golf schools in many countries throughout the world and David Leadbetter, an employee of DLGA, ranks to the fore of golf instructors in the world.

The market relevant to the notified arrangements is that for the provision of golfing

5.7 instruction. Golfers who require instruction generally have recourse to their club professionals, golf driving ranges or golf instructors outside clubs. In recent years there has been a substantial investment in over 70 new golf courses the majority of which cater primarily for the tourist and corporate visitor sector. Mount Juliet falls into this latter category.

Under the terms of the notified agreement made 8 February 1994 DLGA agreed to provide at Mount Juliet a separate golf instructional academy to be operated by DLGA. The agreement is for a five year term from the date of its execution but it may be terminated earlier in the event of default on money payments or other conditions of the agreement or the insolvency of either party. Clause 6.1 provides that DLGA shall be the sole provider of golf tuition at Mount Juliet. Under clause 6.2 Mount Juliet agrees that upon termination of the agreement it will not engage the services of any of the Academy Directors or any of the Academy instructors for a period of eighteen months from the date of such termination. Under clause 6.3 Mount Juliet agrees to keep confidential and to procure that it's employees keep confidential information relating to the 'Leadbetter method' or other information of DLGA which is by it's nature clearly confidential. Clause 9 of the agreement provides that during the term of the agreement DLGA will not provide the services specified in the agreement to any third party located within Ireland and Northern Ireland.

The parties submitted that the fact that DLGA would be the sole provider of golf tuition at Mount Juliet did not offend against section 4(1) of the Competition Act because it would be clearly impractical to have two different operations providing golf tuition in a small area and further that the restriction in Clause 9 which prevented DLGA from providing its services elsewhere in Ireland or Northern Ireland did not offend against section 4(1) because it would be unreasonable to Mount Juliet that DLGA would be entitled to set up another academy in a country as small as Ireland in view of the size of its investment.

Decided by the Authority: In issuing a certificate under section 4(4) of the Competition Act 1991 in respect of the notified arrangements that:

(1) Each of Mount Juliet and DLGA are undertakings within the meaning of section 3(1) of the Competition Act and the notified agreement is an agreement between undertakings which has effect within the State.

(2) There is nothing anti-competitive where the operator of a leisure facility enters into an agreement with a supplier of services to provide services at that facility rather than supply that service himself. As the notified agreement is concerned largely with regulating the contract for the supply of those services its general provisions do not *per se* raise issues under the Competition Act.

(3) While clause 6.1 will prevent the possibility of any other professional tutor providing tuition at Mount Juliet on a commercial basis it does not prevent the possibility of such person establishing a golf tuition service nearby in competition to DLGA. Furthermore it would be impractical to have more than one golf tuition operation in any golf club and therefore the provisions of clause 6.1 do not offend against section 4(1). Clause 9 of the notified agreement whereunder DLGA may not offer its services in other facilities throughout Ireland does not prevent other golf courses establishing golf tuition centres elsewhere in the State but merely DLGA from participating in such activities. In these circumstances clause 9 does not offend against section 4(1).

(4) Clause 6.2 whereunder Mount Juliet agrees not to engage the services of DLGA employees for a period of eighteen months after termination of the agreement and clauses 6.3 and 21 dealing with non-disclosure of confidential information are not restrictive of competition as they do not prevent Mount Juliet or, another party, from operating its own golfing school within the Mount Juliet facilities after termination of the agreement. The purpose of the restrictions is to protect know-how which is the property of DLGA and without this protection DLGA would not be prepared to enter into such arrangement. In such circumstances clauses 6.2, 6.3 and 21 of the notified agreement do not offend against section 4(1). 5.7

Competition Authority Decision of 19 September 1994 relating to a proceeding under section 4 of the Competition Act 1991
Notification No. CA/8/94 — Mount Juliet/David Leadbetter Golf Academy Inc

Introduction

1. Notification was made jointly by Mount Juliet and David Leadbetter Golf Academy Inc on 31 March 1994 with a request for a certificate under section 4(4) of the Competition Act 1991 or, in the event of a refusal by the Competition Authority to issue a certificate, a licence under section 4(2), in respect of an agreement between Mount Juliet and David Leadbetter Golf Academy Inc relating to the establishment of a golf school at Mount Juliet, Thomastown, Co. Kilkenny.

The Facts

(a) *Subject of the notification*

2. The notification concerns an agreement for the establishment by the David Leadbetter Golf Academy Inc of a golf instruction school at Mount Juliet.

(b) *The parties involved*

3. Mount Juliet is an unlimited company and is the owner and operator of a hotel, leisure centre and golf course at Mount Juliet. David Leadbetter Golf Academy Inc (DLGA) is an Ohio corporation and operates golf schools in many countries world wide. David Leadbetter, who is an employee of the corporation, is regarded as probably the best known golf teacher in the world and numbers many of the top ranking professional golfers among his students.

(c) *The Market*

4. The David Leadbetter Golf Academy is engaged in the provision of golfing instruction. Most club golfers have probably had little or no formal instruction by way of golfing school but those that require instruction generally have recourse to their club professionals, golf driving ranges or golf instructors outside clubs. The Yellow Pages list 17 such instructors in the greater Dublin area. Up to the middle 1980s, the vast majority of golf courses were those owned by golf clubs whose use was largely confined to club members most of whom resided within a reasonable distance of the course. In more recent years there has been substantial investment in over 70 new golf courses many of which cater primarily for the tourism and corporate visitor sector. Mount Juliet falls into this latter category with its extensive hotel and leisure and golfing complex, some distance from the more densely populated areas in the State. The Mount Juliet golf course is considered to be among the best in Europe and hosted the 1994 Irish Open Golf Championship which attracted 80,000 spectators. Since the mid 1980s the number of golfing tourists have doubled with over 120,000 annually now visiting Ireland.

5.7 (c) *The notified arrangements*

5. The notified agreement was made on 8 February 1994 between Mount Juliet and DLGA to provide the arrangements for the opening of a separate golf instructional academy at Mount Juliet to be operated by DLGA. The agreement provides for the consultancy/advisory services to be provided by DLGA both for the preopening/development stage and the operational stage, the appointment of DLGA employees as chief instructor (Director) and other instructors and the financial arrangements relating thereto. Mount Juliet is to provide premises for the academy, specific numbers of golf holes and practice tees, covered areas, equipment and accommodation for employees. The agreement provides for the financial arrangements between the parties including remuneration and revenues. DLGA agrees to procure that David Leadbetter subject to availability shall provide his services personally at Mount Juliet for a specified maximum number of days annually. Mount Juliet is permitted to use DLGA trademarks in promoting the academy subject to specific approval of DLGA in each instance. The trade mark remains the sole and exclusive property of DLGA. The agreement contains confidentiality and competition clauses set out under. The agreement is stated specifically not to be a joint venture and neither party can bind the other in that regard. The agreement is effective from date of signature and will terminate 5 years from the date the academy opens with provision for earlier termination in the event of default on money payments or other conditions of the agreement or insolvency of either party. The further performance of the agreement is contingent on the parties applying for and getting a licence for the exclusivity arrangements in clause 6.1 and 9 of the agreement. The exclusivity provisions and confidentiality provisions of the agreement are as follows:

> 6.1 DLGA shall be the sole provider of golf tuition at Mount Juliet
> 9. EXCLUSIVITY During the term DLGA will not provide the services specified herein to any third party located within Ireland and Northern Ireland.
> 6.2 . . . The company (Mount Juliet) agrees that, upon termination of this agreement, it will not engage the services of any of the Academy Directors, or any of the Academy Instructors for a period of 18 months from the date of such termination. . . .
> 6.3 . . . If any of the Company's employees (i.e. employees of Mount Juliet) are trained in the 'Leadbetter Method', the Company (Mount Juliet) agrees to procure that such employees sign declarations of confidentiality . . . such employees undertake to keep confidential, and not use for their own benefit or for the benefit of any third party, the information that they have been provided with and the method of tuition that they have been taught in relation to the 'Leadbetter Method'.
> 21. The Company (Mount Juliet) shall treat as confidential all information supplied by DLGA which is designated as confidential by DLGA or which is by its nature clearly confidential. The Company agrees not to divulge any of DLGA's confidential information to any person or body unless authorised by DLGA. In the event of termination of this Agreement, the Company shall return any confidential information and all copies thereof (including all database information) to DLGA at its registered office.

(e) *Submission by the Parties*

6. The parties accept that the notified agreement contains two exclusivity arrangements in clauses 6.1 and 9. However, they maintain that the agreement does not have as its object or effect the prevention, restriction or distortion of competition in trade in any goods or services in the State or in any part of the State. The parties argue that the restriction in clause 6.1, whereby DLGA Inc will be the sole provider of golf tuition at Mount Juliet, does not offend against section 4(1) of the Competition Act because it would clearly be impractical to have two different operations providing golf tuition in what is a relatively small area. The parties also argue that the restriction in clause 9, whereby DLGA Inc. is prevented from providing its services to any third party within Ireland or Northern Ireland during the term of the notified agreement, does not offend against section 4(1) because it would be unreasonable to Mount Juliet that the David

Leadbetter Golf Academy would be entitled to set up another academy in a country as small as Ireland in view of the investment being made by Mount Juliet. The David Leadbetter organisation has opened an academy in England and academies in a number of European countries and in one or two Asian countries. 5.7

Assessment

(a) *Applicability of section 4(1)*

7. Section 4(1) of the Competition Act 1991 prohibits and renders void all agreements between undertakings, decisions by associations of undertakings and concerted practices which have as their object or effect the prevention, restriction or distortion of competition in trade in any goods or services in the State, or in any part of the State.

(b) *The Undertakings*

8. Section 3(1) of the Competition Act defines an undertaking as 'a person being an individual, a body corporate or an unincorporated body of persons engaged for gain in the production, supply or distribution of goods or the provision of a service'.

9. Mount Juliet is engaged for gain in the provision of a service i.e. the operation of a hotel and leisure facilities including golf, at Mount Juliet. DLGA is also engaged for gain in the provision of a service i.e. golf tuition. The notified agreement is an agreement between undertakings and has effect within the State.

(c) *The Agreement*

10. The Authority accepts that there is nothing anti-competitive in Mount Juliet, the owner and operator of tourism/leisure facilities, to choose to enter into an agreement with a supplier of services to provide services at Mount Juliet rather than supply them itself. As the agreement is largely concerned with regulating the contract for the supply of those services its general provisions, *per se*, do not raise issues under the Competition Act.

11. Clause 6.1 ensures that for the duration of the agreement David Leadbetter Golf Academy Inc will be the sole provider of golf tuition at Mount Juliet. This will prevent the possibility of any professional golfer, qualified tutor or any other golf academy from providing tuition at Mount Juliet on a commercial basis. However, it would not prevent the possibility of them establishing a golf tuition service nearby to Mount Juliet in competition to the DLGA. Members and patrons are not forced to use the services of David Leadbetter Golf Academy at Mount Juliet. They are free to avail of similar services provided by other golf clubs. The Competition Authority accepts that it would be impractical to have more than one golf tuition operation in any golf club. In the opinion of the Competition Authority the provisions of Clause 6.1 do not therefore offend against section 4(1).

12. Clause 9 provides that for the duration of the Agreement the David Leadbetter Golf Academy will not provide golf instruction services to any third party located within Ireland or Northern Ireland. This is an arrangement which has been equally accepted by both parties to the agreement. Mount Juliet is supplying exceptional facilities to attract a world name, the DLGA, to Mount Juliet. It seems unlikely that DLGA would locate their academy at Mount Juliet in the absence of such facilities but the capital investment by Mount Juliet would not have proceeded without some assurance of exclusivity from DLGA. The DLGA organisation has only one academy in the UK and it seems improbable that, considering the much smaller size of the Irish market, they would wish to dilute their custom at Mount Juliet or the international standing of their name by establishing other academies within the State, at least in the relatively short term of 5 years which is covered by the agreement. In any event, because of the personal services of David Leadbetter to be supplied at Mount Juliet under the contract, it would appear that the completion of similar agreements by DLGA elsewhere in the State would not be very practicable. The agreement does not prevent other golf courses establishing golf tuition centres elsewhere in the State. It merely prevents DLGA from participating in such

5.7 activities. The Competition Authority, therefore, considers that clause 9 of the agreement does not offend against section 4(1).

13. Under clause 6.2 Mount Juliet agrees not to engage the services of any of the Academy directors or instructors for a period of 18 months from the date of termination of the agreement while clause 6.3 and clause 21 prevent the disclosure of confidential information relating to DLGA or its tuition methods by Mount Juliet or its employees. The Authority does not regard these restrictions as being restrictive of competition as they do not prevent Mount Juliet, or another party, from operating its own golfing school within the Mount Juliet facilities after termination of the agreement. The purpose of the restriction is to protect know-how which is the property of DLGA and without this protection DLGA would not be prepared to enter into such arrangements. In these circumstances the Competition Authority considers that clause 6.2, clause 6.3 and clause 21 of the notified agreement do not offend against section 4(1).

The Decision

14. Mount Juliet and David Leadbetter Golf Academy Inc are undertakings within the meaning of section 3(1) of the Competition Act 1991 and the notified agreement is an agreement between undertakings. In the Authority's opinion the notified agreement between Mount Juliet and David Leadbetter Golf Academy Inc does not offend against section 4(1) of the Competition Act 1991.

The Certificate

15. The Competition Authority has issued the following certificate:

> The Competition Authority certifies that in its opinion, on the basis of the facts in its possession, the agreement dated 8 February 1994 between Mount Juliet and David Leadbetter Golf Academy Inc. notified under section 7 on 31 March 1994 (Notification No. CA/8/94) does not offend against section 4(1) of the Competition Act 1991.

For the Competition Authority

Des Wall
Member

19 September 1994

5.8 **Competition Authority Decision No. 356, Cable & Wireless Ltd/Irish Telephone Rentals Ltd/Sound Systems Ltd:** 19 September 1994, Notification No. CA/132-139/92E and CA/175-191/92E

Equipment rental agreements – Duration of agreements – Maintenance of equipment to be carried out only by the supplier – Prohibition on customer repairing or replacing any of the equipment – Prohibition on additions, alterations or extensions to the equipment without the suppliers written consent – Protection of copyright – Amendment of notified arrangements – Notice of intention to issue a certificate – Submission by third party – Competition Act 1991 (No. 24), sections 3, 4 and 7

Facts: On 25 and 29 September 1992 notifications were made by Cable & Wireless

Ltd ('C&W') with a request for certificates under section 4(4) of the Competition Act 1991 or, failing that, licences under section 4(2) in respect of 25 standard rental agreements with their customers relating to telecommunications, staff location, time control and security service equipment. **5.8**

From 1 April 1991 the business of Irish Telephone Rentals Ltd ('ITR') was transferred to Sound Systems Ltd ('SS') which company subsequently changed its name to Cable & Wireless (Ireland) Ltd and later in May 1992 changed its name to Cable & Wireless Ltd. The notified agreements, depending on the date of their execution, are in the name of one or other of these companies. The parties involved are C&W (and its predecessors ITR and SS) of the one part and organisations such as industry and business users, hotels, other commercial undertakings, hospitals, government departments, including schools and churches of the other part. C&W is an Irish registered company wholly owned by Cable & Wireless Plc, a UK registered public company, which is engaged in a wide range of telecommunication services on a global basis.

The products involved in the notifications are: (i) telecommunications related equipment, (ii) staff location equipment, (iii) time control equipment, and (iv) security service equipment. The telecommunication related equipment consists of telephone systems and ancillary equipment, facsimile machines, telephone answering systems and network management systems. There are approximately 40 suppliers in the market with an estimated annual turnover of IR£45 million. Staff location equipment consists of paging, public address and intercom systems. There are approximately 50 suppliers in the market with an annual estimated turnover of IR£4.5 million. The time control equipment consists of time monitoring devices for the workplace and there is an estimated 15 suppliers active in the Irish market which has an estimated annual turnover of IR£2.8 million. The security service equipment consists mainly of fire alarms and watchman's clocks. C&W are no longer active in this market and are only servicing old contracts which were concluded some time ago.

Customers seeking communications equipment have the option of purchasing, leasing or renting the equipment. In a rental agreement the customer pays a quarterly or annual charge to the equipment supplier for a defined number of years. The customer never attains ownership of the equipment and the supplier contracts to support and maintain the equipment for the duration of the rental agreement. C&W advise that of the three options rental is the least common representing less than 10% of the equipment market. The twenty five notified agreements are all concerned with rental of equipment.

Under the terms of the notified agreements C&W agrees to supply, install and let on hire the relevant equipment for a fixed term of years. The rental is adjustable annually by reference to a percentage proportionate to movement in electrician wage rates. Unless determined by mutual agreement in writing the term of the contract is for a stated number of years and thereafter until one of the parties gives six months' notice expiring at a year's end. The equipment remains the property of C&W who undertake to execute without charge during normal working hours all repairs and replacements arising from fair wear and tear. No additions or extensions to the installation may be made without a C&W's written consent and the customer may not repair or replace any part of the installation. If the customer repudiates the contract, and C&W agrees, the customer will pay a formulated amount by way of liquidated damages.

5.8 The main provisions in each of the twenty five notified agreements are concerned with rental and maintenance terms relating to the equipment on hire to the customer. These in general do not raise issues under the Competition Act. The restrictive provisions that have to be considered from the competition aspect are as follows:- (i) the long duration of some of the agreements which have minimum periods ranging from five to fourteen years and the notice period for termination thereafter; (ii) the incorporation of both hire and maintenance in the same agreement; (iii) the restriction on the customer's ability to repair or replace all or any part of the installation; (iv) the restriction on the customer's ability to add to, alter or extend the equipment without the written consent of C&W; (v) the restriction on the customer passing on intellectual property such as software to third parties; (vi) the requirement to purchase batteries for transceivers from C&W.

On 28 April 1994 the Authority wrote to C&W expressing concern in relation to the prohibitions in the agreements on additions, alterations or extensions without the written consent of C&W and the requirement in three agreements that batteries for pocket transceivers must be purchased from C&W. By letter dated the 26 May 1994 C&W agreed to remove the requirement in relation to the purchase of batteries from the three relevant agreements and to amend all agreements to provide the consent for additions, alterations or extensions to rented equipment will only be withheld for objectively valid reasons which shall be disclosed to the customer. Following publication on 15 July 1994 of its intention to issue a certificate the Authority received a submission from a telephone systems consultant in relation to the repudiation penalty clause contained in the standard agreement. The submission stated that the users of C&W systems found that this clause restricted those customers in choosing a replacement system.

Decided by the Authority: In issuing a certificate under section 4(4) of the Competition Act 1991 in respect of the notified arrangements that:

(1) C&W (and its predecessors in title ITR and SS) are companies engaged for gain in the sale, hire, provision and maintenance within the State of equipment and are therefore undertakings under section 3(1) of the Competition Act. The other parties to the rental contracts are organisations within the State such as industrial and business users, hotels, other commercial undertakings, hospitals, government departments and other bodies including churches and schools. Most of these organisations are undertakings within the meaning of the Competition Act because they are engaged for gain in the production supply or distribution of goods or the provision of service. A number of the organisations may not come within this definition of an undertaking and are not therefore covered by the Competition Act. This decision does not apply to those agreements and with the exception of those agreements the rental agreements notified are agreements between undertakings which have effect within the State.

(2) In the light of the choice that is freely available to the customer at the time of acquisition of the equipment to purchase outright, to lease or to rent, the rental sector cannot be regarded as a separate market but as part of the overall market for the equipment in question.

(3) The provision of rental facilities by C&W as an alterative to purchase or leasing for the acquisition of the equipment must be regarded as pro-competitive because it provides an additional facility to enable customers to acquire the equipment. The fact that C&W's customers have a free choice at the time of acquisition to either purchase,

lease or rent the equipment from C&W or to go to any of its competitors means that the rental agreements cannot be regarded as offending against section 4(1) of the Competition Act. 5.8

(4) The notified agreements are for varying periods ranging from five to fourteen years with a further provision of up to twelve months notice of termination by either party after the end of the fixed term. A number of agreements also provide for strict terms for repudiation of agreements involving the payment of a liquidated sum by way of damages. The rental agreements *per se* are not anti-competitive. A customer on entering into his original contract with C&W (or its predecessors) made his decision freely on the basis of his own economic criteria when he chose to rent rather than purchase or lease. Unlike the purchaser who may have to contract for the maintenance of his installations at periodic intervals, the rental customer is covered by a long term rental/maintenance package. In its initial negotiations with its customer on rentals/maintenance terms including the duration of the agreement C&W has no special market power and the duration fixed in the agreement is that agreed by the customer. For its part C&W has to provide through rental payments, for the recovery of the cost of the installation, as well as its financing charges, and for the projected cost of maintenance which they are committed to provide over the full term of the contract. In concluding its leases C&W had no special or exclusive rights to market the products involved and had offered rental only as an option to other forms of acquisition.

C&W's rental share of the relevant market for each of the three product categories involved in less than 10% and a proportion of this would be represented by agreements of five years duration as well as a number of older agreements which by now can be terminated with a maximum of twelve months notice. The five year rental agreement cannot be regarded as representing any degree of foreclosure since an alternative purchaser (or customer under a leasing agreement) would be unlikely to seek to replace the equipment within five years of acquisition. The basic installations are of a type which are normally replaced by the customer only after long periods of use and therefore it is not clear why competition should be effected by the length of such leases. Furthermore the share of the annual market effected by the longer term rental agreements must be well below 10% and therefore the duration aspect of even the long term rental agreements could not have any significant effect on competition. For these reasons the duration aspect of the agreements do not offend against section 4(1).

(5) It seems clear from the agreements furnished that where the maintenance charge is not shown separately it has effectively been built into the rental payable particularly in those agreements which provide for an annual inflation adjustment with regard to electrician pay rates. The incorporation of maintenance into the rental agreement means that no other company may compete against C&W for the maintenance of the equipment. While it could offend against section 4(1) of the Competition Act to make a purchase transaction conditional on a long term maintenance contract with the original supplier the situation is different in regard to rental contracts. In a rental agreement the ownership of the property remains with the supplier and the customer is required to return it to the supplier on termination. The customer in a rental agreement acquires a package consisting of the equipment and a prompt maintenance service to keep it fully operational and the supplier has a proprietary interest in maintaining the value of their property and a contractual obligation to keep it in good working order. It seems essential therefore that to protect their property the supplier

5.8 must be in a position of control over the maintenance of their equipment and therefore the incorporation of maintenance with the rental terms in the case of the notified agreements does not offend against section 4(1).

(6) Most of the notified agreements specifically prohibit the repair or replacement by the customer of any part of the installation. The effect of this provision is that the customer is prohibited from engaging any of C&W competitors to have the equipment repaired or replaced. This restriction on repairs by other seems necessary to protect C&W position in the light of their proprietary interest in the equipment and their contractual obligation in relation to maintenance and does not therefore offend against section 4(1) of the Competition Act.

Three of the notified agreements provided that batteries for paging receivers must be purchased from the supplier ostensibly to prevent damage to the instrument resulting in the use of unsuitable batteries. Given the wide availability of batteries it should be possible for customers to purchase batteries to the correct specifications from sources other than the supplier and while the impact of this requirement might not be significant, the restriction involved, prior to its subsequent deletion from the relevant agreements, offended against section 4(1).

(7) Many of the notified agreements contained a provision that no additions, alterations or extensions were to be made to the installations without the written consent of the supplier. These clauses in these agreements could be used to prevent the customer seeking an alternative supplier for additional compatible equipment for use with the existing rented installation even though the additional equipment was not the subject of the original contract. Furthermore by the operation of these clauses other suppliers with the capability to supply and install compatible equipment would be prevented from tendering for this business and therefore these provisions offended against section 4(1) of the Competition Act and would not have satisfied the requirements of section 4(2). C&W since the notification have agreed to amend these clauses by providing that their consent to additions, alterations or extensions will only be withheld for objectively valid reasons which shall be disclosed to the customer and these clauses, as amended, no longer offend against section 4(1).

(8) A number of the notified agreements require the customer not to pass on copyright material including software to any third party without the written consent of the supplier. The software like the hardware remains the property of the rental company and these clauses which are inserted to protect the proprietary interest of the rental company do not offend against section 4(1).

Cases referred to:

United States v. United Shoe Machinery (1953) 110 F. supp. 295

Irish Telephone Rentals Ltd v. Irish Civil Service Building Society Ltd [1991] ILRM 880, High Court decision of Costello J, 8 February 1991

Notification Authority Decision No. 356 of 19 September 1994 relating to a proceeding under section 4 of the Competition Act 1991

Notifications Nos. CA/132/92E to CA/139/92E and CA/175/92E to CA/191/92E — Cable & Wireless Ltd/Irish Telephone Rentals Ltd/ Sound Systems Ltd

Introduction

1. Notifications were made by Cable & Wireless Ltd on 25 and 29 September 1992, with requests for certificates under section 4(4) of the Competition Act 1991 or, in the event of

refusals by the Competition Authority to issue certificates, licences under section 4(2) in respect of 25 standard rental agreements with their customers relating to telecommunications, staff location, time control and security service equipment. Notice of intention to issue a certificate was published on 15 July, 1994 and a submission was received. **5.8**

The Facts

(a) *Subject of the Notifications*

2. The notifications concern rental contracts for the supply, installation and maintenance of the following equipment (the equipment) to commercial and other non-household users:

(i) telecommunication-related equipment (11 notifications);

(ii) staff location, paging and public address systems (5 notifications);

(iii) time control equipment for monitoring working hours and staff deployment (5 notifications);

(iv) equipment for use in the security service industry, such as fire alarms and watchman's clocks (4 notifications);

3. Three of the notified agreements are in the name of Cable & Wireless (Ireland) Ltd. Fourteen of the notified agreements are in the name of Irish Telephone Rentals Ltd (ITR) and eight are in the name of Sound Systems Ltd (SS). From 1 April 1991 the business of ITR was transferred to SS and SS changed its name first to Cable and Wireless (Ireland) Ltd and later in May 1992 to Cable and Wireless Ltd (C&W). The notifications are in respect of both current contracts and earlier versions of those contracts which are still in force.

(b) *The Parties involved*

4. The parties involved are C&W and its predecessors, ITR and SS, on the one part and organisations such as industry and business users, hotels, other commercial undertakings, hospitals, Government Departments, and other bodies including churches, schools, etc.

Cable and Wireless Ltd

5. C&W is an Irish registered company wholly owned by Cable and Wireless plc, a UK registered public company which had a total turnover of Stg. £3,176.2m in 1991. The UK parent company employs over 38,000 people and is engaged in world wide activities in the transmission of data and satellite communication, providing a wide range of telecommunications services, networks and equipment to business and residential customers internationally.

Irish Telephone Rentals Ltd/Sound Systems Ltd

6. ITR was engaged in the sale, rental and maintenance of the equipment in the State for over 20 years until its business was transferred to SS in March 1991. In 1990/1 ITR had a turnover of £4.7m and its accounts at end March 1991 showed that the value of its installations on rental was £8.6m less £2.4m accumulated depreciation. ITR is now a wholly owned subsidiary of C&W with its activities limited to property holding. SS has also been engaged for over 20 years in the sale, maintenance and rental of The Equipment within the State and following its acquisition of the business of ITR continues to trade under the name of Cable and Wireless Ltd. Since 1991 therefore, all the sales/rental business of ITR and SS has been transacted by C&W.

Other Subsidiaries of C&W

7. At the time of notification, C&W had 3 other subsidiaries operating in the Irish market. Irish Time Systems Ltd was a supplier of time control equipment, fire alarm systems and devices for monitoring security patrols of premises. Sound Productions Ltd was a supplier of staff location equipment. C&W stated that it regarded these two companies to be among its competitors in the market for those particular products even though they were subsidiaries of

5.8 C&W. However, the Directors' Report with C&W's accounts for 1991/2 indicates that a decision was taken to wind down the activities of these 2 subsidiaries. In October 1993, these two companies were sold to a third party. A further C&W subsidiary, Cardio Ltd, trades in the data communications market which entails products totally different to those specified at paragraph 2.

Turnover of C&W

8. In the year ended 31 March 1992 the C&W Group had a turnover of £14.8m. Its accounts also showed that the value of installations on rental by the C&W company (including those transferred from ITR) was £10.571m less £3.8m for accumulated depreciation while the value of rented installations for the Group (including the £10.571m above) was £10.7m less £3.93m for depreciation. Additions to the rent roll in 1991/2 were valued at £1.183m. The major part of the Company's turnover arises from sales, rental and maintenance of Telecommunications Equipment.

(c) *The Products*

9. The products involved in these notifications (i.e. the equipment) are as follows:

(i) Telecommunications-related Equipment.

(ii) Staff Location Equipment

(iii) Time Control Equipment

(iv) Security Service Equipment

Telecommunication-Related Equipment

10. Telecommunication-related equipment, known in the trade as Customer Premises Equipment (CPE), consists of private automatic branch exchange telephone systems, key telephone systems, automatic call distribution systems, dealerboards, telephone instruments, bells, loud speakers, facsimile machines, telephone answering systems and network management systems.

11. CPE suppliers on the Irish market fall into two categories:

(a) CPE manufacturers, such as Ericsson, Siemens, etc almost all of whom supply and support customers directly, generally via wholly owned local subsidiaries, and

(b) independent distributors such as C&W, TEIS, etc who buy CPE from a range of manufacturers and then offer both products and services (including maintenance) to their customers.

12. There are approximately 40 suppliers of CPE equipment in the Irish market of whom only 4 or 5 are also manufacturers. C&W are not manufacturers. C&W claim to be the only suppliers of telephone equipment produced by manufacturers such as Panasonic, GEC, Melco Labs, Tie and Picture Tel, and also claim to be the only distributor with specifically trained and qualified staff for the maintenance of such equipment. The major suppliers are TEIS , C&W (incorporating SS), LM Ericsson, Technico, GPT, Digital Telephones, Siemens, and Allied Telephones. C&W's estimate of the annual market is £45m. The 4 largest suppliers are estimated to hold 63% of the market.

Staff Location Equipment

13. Staff location equipment is stated to comprise wide area network pagers, on-site short range radio paging systems, public address systems and intercom systems.

14. C&W state that there are at least 50 suppliers selling into the Irish market for these products. In general the suppliers do not manufacture the equipment themselves. The major suppliers besides C&W are Sigma Wireless, SKS, Sound Productions Ltd, Sound Communications and Peats. C&W estimate that total market turnover is £4.5m. per annum. The 4 largest suppliers are estimated to hold 74% of the market.

Time Control Equipment

15. Time control equipment includes time monitoring devices for the work place (enabling employees' hours to be calculated); central clock control systems and secondary clocks for use throughout premises; time systems for monitoring flexible working arrangements; time and date stamps and devices for monitoring security patrols on premises.

16. C&W estimate that there are approximately 15 suppliers active in the Irish market. The major suppliers apart from C&W are Flexitime, Compuplan and Irish Time Systems Ltd. C&W estimate that total market turnover is £2.75m. per annum. The 3 largest suppliers are estimated to hold 74% of the market.

Security Service Equipment

17. The products covered by this heading are mainly fire alarms and watchmen's clocks. C&W are no longer active in the fire alarm area and by this stage are servicing the remainder of contracts most of which were concluded 10/15 years ago. Their estimate of the Irish market for security service equipment is around £5m per annum with about 40 companies involved.

(d) *The Market*

18. In summary while there is a substantial degree of market concentration in each of the main product areas there are a large number of suppliers active in each sector. In the telecommunications sector up to November 1992, a licence from the Department of Transport, Energy and Communications was required to engage in the business of supplying, installing and maintaining equipment for attachment to the telephone network. However the qualification for licences was based on competency factors and by 1992, 300/400 companies or persons had been licensed for these purposes. Since 1992 the only requirement remaining is that the equipment should be type approved by the Department. There were therefore apparently no significant barriers to market entry by other competitors.

The market situation is summarised below :

Equipment market	Estimated Annual Market	No. of suppliers
Telephone	£45.0m	40
Staff location	£ 4.5m	50
Time control	£ 2.8m	15
Security service	£ 5.0m	40

19. Customers seeking communications equipment have a number of options available to them when considering how best to satisfy their requirements i.e. to purchase the equipment outright, to take the equipment under a leasing agreement, or to rent it. In many cases the customer will also require post-installation support and maintenance. In general the equipment is supplied on terms that incorporate maintenance as an integral part of the product. In a sale agreement the customer pays up front the capital sum to acquire ownership of the equipment, and after the termination of the warranty period will make his own arrangements for ongoing repairs and maintenance. The customer owns the equipment. If a maintenance agreement has been offered to and accepted by the customer the responsibility of the supplier to continue such maintenance service is limited to any notice necessary (generally 3 months) from either the supplier or customer to terminate the maintenance agreement. In a lease agreement the customer reaches an agreement with a leasing company that the latter will pay the capital sum to the equipment supplier. The customer repays the capital cost to the leasing company over a number of years but from the end of the seller's warranty period is free to make his own arrangements for maintenance. In a rental agreement the customer pays a quarterly or annual charge to the equipment supplier for a defined number of years. The customer never attains ownership of the equipment. The supplier contracts to support and maintain this equipment for the duration of the rental agreement. C&W advise that, of the 3 options, rental is the least common

5.8 representing less than 10% of The Equipment market.

20. The 25 notified agreements are all concerned with the rental of equipment. C&W advise that apart from themselves, suppliers in general do not offer rental contracts. Currently around 200 CPE, 30/40 time control and 150/200 staff location rental agreements are concluded by C&W annually. A significant, though minority element of the turnover of the C&W Group is derived from rental contract revenues. C&W claim to be the dominant supplier in the rental side of each market with their rental business representing less than 10% of each product market, excepting the security equipment market where their share is minuscule.

21. The relevant product markets in which the above mentioned goods and services are supplied could be characterised as a homogeneous market for the supply and maintenance of such equipment. Within the relevant product markets, a wide range of substitute products are readily available from sources other than C&W. The operational functional equivalent of everything supplied is available from other sources. To a large extent the equipment supplied by other suppliers is largely interchangeable with similar products supplied by C&W and C&W claim that, where consent for such substitution is required of C&W, it is readily given. The relevant geographic market is the State.

(e) *The Notified Arrangements*

22. The standard agreements notified, which were in use at different time periods but which are still in force, are as follows:

(i) *Current Agreements—Cable & Wireless Ireland Ltd*

Telecommunications equipment	— CA/133/92E
Staff location equipment	— CA/137/92E
Time control equipment	— CA/138/92E

All 3 agreements have identical clauses.

Under this standard contract, which is currently used for new agreements, C&W (the company) agrees to supply, instal and let on hire the equipment set out in the schedule, including cabling, at the customer's premises for a fixed term of years. The customer agrees to pay the labour cost of installation and an annual rental for the hire of the installation and its maintenance. The rental is adjustable annually by reference to a percentage proportionate to movements in electrician wage rates. Unless determined by mutual agreement in writing the term of the contract is for a stated number of years and thereafter until one or other of the parties gives 6 months notice expiring at a year end*. The installation remains the property of the company and the company undertakes to execute without charge during normal working hours all repairs and replacements arising from fair wear and tear. No additions or extensions to the installation may be made without the company's written consent. The customer may not repair or replace any part of the installation. If the customer repudiates the contract, and the company agrees, the customer will pay all amounts due and also a sum equal to the present value on a 5% per annum basis of the remaining rentals that would have been payable less a 25% deduction to cover the estimated cost of future maintenance and the value of the installation which has to be surrendered. The sum shall be payable as liquidated damages, it being an agreed estimate of the loss the company would suffer. Copyright and other industrial/intellectual property rights including software operating programmes remain vested in the company and the customer undertakes not to pass on such material to any third party. The customer may have the installation transferred at his own expense to any other premises within the area in which the Company operates. The customer shall not assign the contract without the prior written consent of the Company, such consent not to be unreasonably withheld.

*C&W have stated that the actual duration of the contract is a matter for negotiation but that the average period in more recent agreements has been 6 years.

(ii) *Earlier agreements concluded by ITR and SS* **5.8**

The other 22 standard agreements notified are earlier versions of the contracts used by ITR and SS in different years. These agreements are basically similar to the C&W current contracts with some minor differences. Details are as follows:

Sound Systems Ltd

Reference	Product	Year used	Term	**Notice	features
CA/187/92E	Telephone	1959	12 yrs.	6mth	A
CA/190/92E	do.	1962	7 yrs.	do.	A
CA/183/92E	Security	1966	10 yrs.	12mth	A
CA/177/92E	Time control	1970	10 yrs.	do.	A
CA/188/92E	Telephone	1976	14 yrs.	do.	B
CA/189/92E	Telephone	1980	14 yrs.	do.	B
CA/178/92E	Telephone	1988	14 yrs.	3mth	B
CA/136/92E	Telephone	1990	5 yrs.	3mth	B

Irish Telephone Rentals

Reference	Product	Year Used	Term	**Notice	Features
CA/175/92E	Telephone	1974	14 yrs.	6mth	A
CA/184/92E	Staff location	1972	14 yrs.	6mth	A
CA/182/92E	Time control	1979	14 yrs.	6mth	C
CA/191/92E	Staff location	1987	—	N/A	CM
CA/176/92E	Telephone	1987	—	6mth	C
CA/180/92E	Security	1987	12 yrs.	6mth	C
CA/135/92E	Staff location	1989	—	6mth	CM
CA/181/92E	do.	1989	—	6mth	CM
CA/134/92E	Telephone	1989	10	6mth	C
CA/179/92E	do.	1989	10	6mth	C
CA/132/92E	Time control	1989	—	6mth	C
CA/186/92E	do.	1989	—	6mth	C
CA/185/92E	Security	1989	—	6mth	C
CA/139/92E	do.	1989	—	6mth	C

**This relates to the period set for notice of termination after the end of the fixed rental period

Special features

A—no separate charge for maintenance no inflator
B—separate annual charge for maintenance with annual inflator
C—no separate charge for maintenance—inflator applies to 50% of annual rental
M—includes requirement to purchase batteries for pocket transceivers from the company

23. While 25 separate standard agreements were notified the provisions in each are broadly similar. The main provisions which are common to each of the 25 agreements notified are concerned with the rental and maintenance terms relating to the equipment on hire to the customer. These in general do not raise issues under the Competition Act. The restrictive provisions that have to be considered from the competition aspect are as follows:—

5.8 (i) The long duration of some of the agreements which have minimum periods ranging from 5 to 14 years and the notice period for termination thereafter.

(ii) The incorporation of both hire and maintenance in the same agreement. The current C&W agreement provides in para. 2 'The Subscriber will pay to the company for the hire of the installation and its maintenance during the continuance of this contract a total of IR. . . . .' while para. 6(a) provides that 'The company shall . . . guarantee to execute without charge in the Company's normal working hours all repairs and replacements arising solely from fair wear and tear. . . .' Similar provisions are in the other 24 agreements although some provide for a separate annual charge for maintenance.

(iii) The restriction on the customer's ability to repair or replace all or any part of the installation. The current C&W agreement provides in para. 5 'The Subscriber agrees to notify the Company immediately any fault occurs in the installation or any repairs become necessary. . . . The subscriber shall not repair or replace or cause to be repaired or replaced any part of the installation.' The ITR agreements state at para. 8 'The installation shall not in any way be interfered by the subscriber. . . .' Provisions similar to those above are in all agreements.

(iv) The restriction on the customer's ability to add to, alter or extend the equipment without the written consent of the company. The C&W and SS agreements (with the exception of a 1959 SS agreement) provide at para. 8 'No additions alterations or extensions of any kind are to be made to the installation without the written consent of the Company and if any additions, alterations or extensions are made without the written consent of the company, it shall, if it thinks it in any way prejudices the operation of the installation be at liberty to remove such additions, alterations or extensions and the Subscriber agrees to indemnify the Company for such costs as may be involved. Any alterations or extensions to the Installation necessary shall be carried out by the Company at the Subscribers expense.' The ITR agreements provide at clause 8 'Any alterations or extensions to the Installation necessary or requested by the Subscriber shall be carried out by the Company at the Subscriber's expense.' A similar provision is inserted in the 1959 SS agreement.

(v) The restriction on the customer passing on intellectual property such as software to third parties. The 3 C&W agreements and the 10 latest ITR agreements provide at para. 14 'Copyright and all other forms of ownership including industrial and intellectual property rights in all documents including operating programs for software-operated systems . . . remain vested in the Company. The Subscriber undertakes not to pass such material or any part thereof or copies of the whole or any part thereof to any third party without the written consent of the Company'.

(vi) The requirement to purchase batteries for transceivers from the company.

(f) *Submissions of the Parties.*

24. In a comprehensive submission C&W put forward a number of arguments as to why a certificate should be issued viz.

(i) That the object of the notified agreements was to ensure that the customer who opted to rent rather than buy or lease equipment from C&W had at all times fully functional equipment and an optimal repair and maintenance service throughout the duration of the rental period. In particular, the provisions of certain clauses in the agreements did not have as their object or effect the restriction of competition in the Republic of Ireland or any part of it.

(ii) That it was standard practice for customers to choose the supplier on the strength of its after installation service. The customer expected all comparable suppliers in the market to offer the same or a substantially similar product. Accordingly, the combination of initial installation and subsequent support and maintenance was something which the customer would seek and deliberately choose. In all but the most unusual circumstances the customer required both elements of the product from a single source even when given the option of separating the installation and maintenance between different suppliers. As a result, it was clear that the acceptance by the customer in a rental contract of terms relating to the maintenance of the product by C&W, did not impose supplementary obligations which by their nature or commercial usage had no connection with the subject of such contract. 5.8

(iii) That it was recognised that a customer might not have the necessary expertise to enable it to determine whom it should engage for the maintenance and repair of such equipment and that a customer would not normally wish to be concerned with engaging an independent contractor in this regard. One of the objects of C&W was therefore to relieve the customer of this responsibility and provide an integrated rental and maintenance service which accorded with the normal expectation in the market place for customers renting or indeed, as in the vast majority of cases, buying, such equipment. In providing maintenance with the rental of the equipment, C&W was not restricting the customer's ability to shop around but was simply offering a composite service in common with several other suppliers within the market.

(iv) That given the level of capital expenditure incurred by C&W in the purchase of the equipment and the fact that it was not in C&W's possession during the rental period, the protection afforded to C&W by the arrangement could not be regarded as a supplementary obligation and was an essential element of the rental contract.

C&W also submitted arguments in support of the grant of a licence which are not relevant to this decision and are not considered here.

25. In regard to certain specific clauses in the agreements C&W provided added comments viz.:

(i) In relation to the prohibition on additions or extensions to the installation C&W stated that this clause '. . . does not have as its object the prevention, restriction or distortion of competition. It provides that no additions, alterations or extensions are to be made to rented equipment without the written consent of C&W and has as its object the protection of C&W's investment. Pursuant to the arrangement C&W parts with possession of the rented equipment which at all times belongs to it. In view of the fact that C&W has continuing obligations under the contract to ensure that the CPE equipment is maintained to a reasonable functional standard the limited prohibition in clause 7 is also designed as a protective measure, having regard at all times to ensure the proper functioning and operation of the telecommunications equipment supplied by it. In seeking to control the people who handle and operate CPE equipment and any additions to it C&W is furthering this object. The supplier's capital investment in sensitive equipment is also protected'.

(ii) In relation to the requirement that any alterations or extensions to the Installation shall be supplied by the Company C&W have pointed out the significant benefit to customers of this provision i.e. 'The customer does not have to make any capital investment. . . . Sound Systems, in addition to accepting the obligation to finance and execute any such additional work, waive any opportunity to exploit such a situation by agreeing in advance that any additional equipment to be provided will be supplied on the terms and conditions of the original contract . . . Therefore the provision in question is not a restriction in any manner but rather represents a facility of which customers are often glad to benefit.'

(iii) The requirement that 'only batteries supplied by the company be used in paging receivers' is justified on the following basis:

> Rather than simply pass to the customer the responsibility for damage caused by the use of incorrect batteries the company adopted the pre-emptive and preventative measure. In the interest of protecting both parties to the agreement and to ensure that the equipment is not damaged by the use of incorrect materials, the company undertook to stock and supply the correct types of batteries for supply to rental customers at normal prices. This practice was designed to ensure that incorrect types of batteries would not be used, damage would not be caused, and neither party would suffer any abnormal cost or loss.

(g) *Subsequent Developments*

26. The Authority wrote to C&W on 28 April 1994 expressing its concern in relation to the

5.8 prohibitions in the agreements on additions, alterations or extensions without the written consent of the company and the requirement in three agreements that batteries for pocket transceivers must be purchased from the company. In a letter dated 26 May 1994 C&W agreed to remove the requirement relating to the purchase of batteries from the three relevant agreements and to amend all agreements to provide that consent for additions, alterations or extensions to rented equipment will only be withheld for objectively valid reasons which shall be disclosed to the customer. C&W also stated that they would write to all their contracted customers advising them of the amendments.

27. Following publication on 15 July 1994, of its intention to issue a certificate, the Authority received a submission from a Telephone Systems Consultant in relation to the penalty clause contained in the standard agreements. The submission stated that users of the systems found that this clause restricted them in choosing a replacement system. A copy of a Judgment of Mr. Justice Costello delivered on 8 February 1991 in the matter of a High Court action between ITR, the plaintiff, and the Irish Civil Service Building Society Ltd, the defendant, was also enclosed. The action arose out of a decision by the defendant to seek to prematurely terminate rental contracts relating to telephone and broadcasting equipment. The issue arising in the contract for broadcasting equipment was whether ITR was entitled to an award under the repudiation clause (i.e. clause 11, see para. 22) or whether this clause was a penalty clause. Mr. Justice Costello *inter alia* found as follows:

> I have come to the conclusion that the formula contained in clause 11 does not produce a liquidated sum that can properly be regarded as a genuine pre-estimate made at the date of the contract of the loss which the Plaintiff would suffer should the contract be prematurely determined and that it is in the reality a penalty and therefore unenforceable.

Damages in a much reduced amount were awarded to the plaintiff.

28. The submission did not make the further argument that the penalty clause was thereby restrictive of competition. The Authority, as stated at paragraph 23(i), consider that the long duration of the contracts is a competition issue and this is dealt with at paras. 39 and 40 below.

Assessment

(a) *Section 4(1)*

29. Section 4(1) of the Competition Act 1991 prohibits and renders void all agreements between undertakings, decisions by associations of undertakings and concerted practices which have as their object or effect the prevention, restriction or distortion of competition in trade in any goods or services in the State, or in any part of the State.

(b) *The Undertakings*

30. The term 'undertaking' is defined in section 3(1) of the Act, as 'a person being an individual, a body corporate or an unincorporated body of persons engaged for gain in the production, supply or distribution of goods or the provision of a service'.

31. The rental contracts notified are in the names of Cable and Wireless (Ireland) Ltd, now known as Cable and Wireless Ltd (C&W), Irish Telephone Rentals Ltd and Sound Systems Ltd (which was since renamed Cable and Wireless Ltd). ITR were and SS, now named Cable and Wireless Ltd, are, companies engaged for gain in the sale, hire, provision and maintenance within the State of The Equipment and are therefore undertakings under the Act.

32. The other parties to the rental contracts are organisations within the State, such as industrial and business users, hotels, other commercial undertakings, hospitals, Government Departments, and other bodies including churches, schools, etc. Most of these organisations are undertakings within the meaning of the Competition Act because they are engaged for gain in the production, supply or distribution of goods or the provision of a service. A number of

the organisations may not come within this definition of an undertaking and are not therefore covered by the Act. This decision does not apply to those agreements. With the exception of these agreements, the rental agreements notified to the Authority by C&W are agreements between undertakings. The agreements have effect within the State. 5.8

(c) *The Market*

33. The Authority does not believe that the rental segments of each of the product markets involved could be regarded as separate markets. At the time the equipment is acquired by the customer it may be purchased outright, it may be leased under a leasing contract or it may be rented. While purchase involves cash up front, both leasing and rental involve deferred payments on the part of the customer. If the customer is reluctant or unable to pay the full price up front he still has the options of leasing or rental. The method of acquisition is a matter of choice for the customer to decide having regard to his own economic criteria or convenience at the time he seeks to acquire the equipment. The larger part of C&W's turnover derives from the sale of equipment rather than rental and it would be too extreme to regard them as catering for 2 separate markets for each of the product areas based on the method of acquisition eventually decided by their customer. In the light of the choice that is freely available at the time of acquisition of the equipment the Authority does not regard the rental sector as a separate market but as part of the overall market for the equipment in question.

(d) *Applicability of section 4(1)*

Provision of Rental

34. The provision of rental facilities by C&W, *per se*, as an alternative to purchase or leasing for the acquisition of the equipment must be regarded as pro-competitive because it provides an additional facility to enable customers to acquire the equipment. The acquisition of this equipment can be a substantial expenditure factor for companies and the availability of rental enables them to obtain modern equipment to improve their productivity at a lesser immediate cost. In some cases customers might not otherwise be able to obtain the equipment. On the other hand the customer, at the time he seeks to acquire the equipment, has the choice whether to rent, obtain under leasing or purchase. In *US v. United Shoe Machinery* (1953)* the US Government charged that United Shoe maintained its market share of 75% to 85% of the American shoe machinery market primarily through its practice of refusing to sell its machinery, agreeing only to lease it. However in this instance C&W's market share is much smaller and its customers have a free choice at the time of acquisition to either purchase, lease or rent the equipment from C&W or go to any of its competitors. In these circumstances the Authority would not regard the provision of rental facilities *per se* as offending against section 4(1) of the Competition Act.

Duration of Agreements

35. C&W have stated that each of the standard agreements notified, which have been used in their varying forms since 1959, are for varying periods ranging from 5 to 14 years with a provision for up to 12 month's notice of termination by either party after the end of the fixed or minimum term. While, at the shorter end, a rental period of 5 years is in line generally with normal leasing periods for many categories of office and industrial equipment, a period of 14 years is more akin to lettings of property rather than equipment. A number of the agreements also provide for strict terms for repudiation of agreements, i.e. that if the customer repudiates the agreement, and if C&W accept this repudiation, C&W may remove the installation with the customer obliged to pay rentals to date plus a discounted value of rental for the remainder of the full term of the contract less 25% to cover the estimated cost of maintenance and the value of the recovered material. The attention of the Authority was drawn to a court case

*110. F. supp. 295 (1953)

5.8 involving the repudiation clause in a contract and which was found to be unenforceable (see paras. 27 and 28). The Authority notes that the determination of the Court that the penalty clause is unenforceable affects the ease or otherwise of exit from the contract for customers. This is relevant as a competition issue insofar as the duration of the agreements is a competition issue. This is dealt with in paragraphs 39 and 40. Other agreements allow for mutual determination but in all cases C&W are in a position to require that the rental agreements be continued for their full term if they so wish.

36. In addition to the minimum term, the agreements continue thereafter until either party gives notice of termination which expires at the end of a calendar year. The period of the notice required varies from 3 to 12 months. This can effectively extend the contract from anything from 3 months to almost 24 months depending on the notice period provided and the time of year the notice is made.

37. Customers who have satisfied their equipment requirements under a rental agreement are effectively out of the market for this equipment from other equipment suppliers. This is no different to the position of customers who have recently purchased equipment since these are similarly out of the market for some considerable time. However since maintenance is included in the rental contracts, other persons who provide maintenance are effectively excluded for the full period of the rental contract from competing for the maintenance of the equipment also. Because of the restrictions in the agreements against additions or extensions to the installations without the consent of C&W, competitors of C&W may also be excluded from a significant element of such additional business. By reason of the rental contracts therefore competitors of C&W may be excluded from part of the market for supply, maintenance and additions for some very extensive periods.

38. C&W have indicated that they are the only company to any degree involved in the renting of the equipment with their rental business representing a significant though minority element of their turnover in each category or less than 10% of each product market, excepting the security equipment market where their share is miniscule and not relevant in this context.

39. The Authority does not believe that the rental of equipment, *per se*, is anti-competitive. The Authority would accept that the customer on entering into his original contract with C&W, or its predecessors, made his decision freely on the basis of his own economic criteria when he chose to rent rather than purchase or lease. Apart from the lower up front costs, other customer benefits might have been the fact that future rental/maintenance payments are set for the long term (which facilitates financial planning), and the security of a satisfactory maintenance/repair service with the ability to withhold rental payments if the maintenance service contracted for is not provided. Unlike the purchaser who may have to contract for the maintenance of his installations at periodic intervals, the rental customer is covered by a long term rental/maintenance package. In its initial negotiations with its customer on rental/maintenance terms including the duration of the agreement, C&W has no special market power and the duration fixed in the agreement is that agreed by the customer. C&W appear to be meeting a market need. On its part, C&W has to provide, through rental payments, for the recovery of the cost of the installation, as well as its financing charges, and for the projected cost of maintenance which they are committed to provide over the full period of the contract. It should follow that the longer the rental term, the lower the annual amortisation charge. The Authority does not see its role as second guessing commercial decisions made by companies. Its concern is whether arrangements have the object or effect of interfering with competition within the State.

40. In *US v. United Shoe Machinery Corporation*, the US Court ruled that United Shoe's 10 year leases were 'so drawn and so applied as to strengthen United's power to exclude competitors' but this was in the context of a company which had refused to allow its machinery (which was generally regarded as superior) to be purchased and which held 75/85% of the relevant market. In concluding its leases in the first place, C&W (or its predecessors SS and ITR) had no special or exclusive rights to market the products involved and had offered rental

only as an option to other forms of acquisition. Furthermore C&W's rental share of the relevant market for each of the 3 product categories involved is less than 10% and a proportion of this would be represented by agreements of 5 years'duration, as well as by pre-1978 agreements, which by now can be terminated with a maximum of 12 months notice, if either party thereto so chooses. In this regard the Authority would not regard a 5 year rental agreement as representing any degree of foreclosure since an alternative purchaser (or customer under a leasing agreement) would be unlikely to seek to replace the equipment within 5 years of acquisition. In view of the wide date spread of past rental agreements managed by C&W, a significant number could be expected to finish their minimum term each year with the customer then free to terminate the agreement, if he so wishes, and re-enter the market. Since the basic installations are of a type which are normally replaced by the customer only after long periods of use it is not clear why competition should be affected by the length of such leases. In any event the share of the annual market affected by the longer term rental agreements must be well below the 10% mentioned above and the Authority therefore considers that the duration aspect of even the long term rental agreements could not have any significant effect on competition. For these reasons the duration aspect of the agreements does not offend against section 4(1). **5.8**

Maintenance and Repairs

41. Each of the 25 agreements notified provides that the Company shall for the duration of the contract execute without charge all repairs and replacements arising solely from fair wear and tear. It seems clear from the agreements furnished that where the maintenance charge is not shown separately it has effectively been built into the rental payable particularly in those later agreements which provide for an annual inflation adjustment having regard to electrician pay rates. The incorporation of maintenance in the rental agreement means that no other company may compete against C&W for the maintenance of the equipment. While the Authority considers that it could offend against section 4(1) of the Competition Act to make purchase transactions conditional on a long term maintenance contract with the original supplier, the situation is different in regard to rental contracts. In the former situations, the ownership of the equipment passes from the supplier when it is acquired by the customer, but, under a rental agreement, the ownership of the property remains with the supplier with the customer required to return it to the supplier on termination. The customer in a rental agreement acquires a package consisting of the equipment and a prompt maintenance service to keep it fully operational. The nature of the equipment is such that in many cases any malfunction would add costs to business far greater than the immediate cost of repair. Effectively the customer under the rental agreement is paying for an early response maintenance service. C&W have a proprietary interest in maintaining the value of their property and a contractual obligation to keep it in good working order. If the equipment does not function satisfactorily the customer may refuse to continue rental payments. It seems essential therefore that to protect their property C&W must be in a position of control over the maintenance of their equipment. The Authority therefore does not consider that the incorporation of maintenance with rental terms, in the case of these agreements, offends against section 4(1).

Repairs by Customer

42. Most of the agreements notified also specifically prohibit the repair or replacement by the customer of any part of the installation. The effect of this provision is that the customer is prohibited from approaching any of C&W's competitors to have the equipment repaired or replaced. As a result of this clause C&W can ensure that the equipment is maintained by itself to both its satisfaction and that of the customer. In the opinion of the Authority, an integrated rental and maintenance contract, without the involvement of a third party, is a more practical arrangement from the point of view of both supplier and subscriber. Furthermore under the notified contracts C&W guarantee to execute without charge in the company's normal working

5.8 hours all repairs and replacements arising from fair wear and tear in order to maintain the equipment in efficient working order. In these circumstances it seems more likely that the supplier and owner of the equipment would provide a more satisfactory service to the subscriber than a third party especially if the third party was a competitor of the supplier/owner. If, in the absence of this provision, the equipment was inadequately serviced or repaired by a third party which resulted in the equipment not functioning satisfactorily the rental company could be responsible for putting it right. The restriction on repairs by others seems necessary to protect C&W's position in the light of their proprietary interest in the equipment and their contractual obligation in relation to maintenance. The Authority therefore considers that this provision does not offend against section 4(1).

Purchase of Batteries

43. Three older staff location equipment agreements concluded by ITR contained a requirement that consumables, i.e. batteries for paging receivers, must be purchased from the company. The company claimed that the purpose of this requirement was to prevent damage to the instrument that might be caused by the use of unsuitable batteries. The Authority however took the view that considering the wide availability of batteries, it should be possible for customers to purchase batteries to the correct specification from other sources if they so wished. While the impact of this requirement in the ITR agreements on competition, if it is practicable to enforce, may not be very significant, the Authority considered that the restriction involved offended against section 4(1). The Authority also noted that this restriction was not incorporated in the current agreements used by C&W. However as C&W has now agreed to amend the three agreements by the deletion of this clause, this aspect no longer offends against section 4(1).

Prohibition on Additions, Alterations and Extensions

44. The C&W agreements and 10 SS agreements contained a provision that no additions, alterations or extensions were to be made to the installation without the written consent of the Company. The ITR agreement and the 1959 SS agreement provided that any alterations or extensions to the installation necessary or requested by the customer shall be carried out by the Company at the subscriber's expense. Over the past decade in particular there have been rapid technological advances in the capability and range of functions of communications equipment, which, combined with normal growth in businesses, would have led to increased demand from existing customers for additions, alterations or extensions to their existing installations. With recent advances in technology there is the capability to significantly upgrade existing installations by the addition of new equipment compatible with the original equipment. This can involve major new investment. Much of the new equipment on the market can be mutually compatible with existing systems with equipment from other suppliers largely interchangeable with that supplied by C&W. C&W claimed that where their consent to such substitution had been sought it had been readily given. Nevertheless the Authority was concerned that the relevant clauses in the agreements could be used to prevent the customer seeking an alternative supplier for additional compatible equipment for use with an existing rented installation even though the additional equipment was not the subject of the original contract. The Authority were also concerned that, by the operation of these clauses, other suppliers with the capability to supply and instal compatible equipment would be prevented from tendering for this business. The Authority therefore considered that this provision offended against section 4(1) of the Competition Act and would not have satisfied the requirements of section 4(2) in the Authority's opinion.

45. The Authority does not consider, however, that C&W should have to permit additions, alterations or extensions which would damage or inhibit the effective working of the existing installation. They accept that C&W should have a concern to protect their proprietary interest in the rented installation and their position under the maintenance element of the contract. It considers however that this could be adequately ensured in a less restrictive way which would

not offend against section 4(1). C&W has now agreed to amend these clauses by providing that their consent for additions, alterations or extensions will only be withheld for objectively valid reasons which shall be disclosed to the customer. The amended clause on this basis no longer offends against section 4(1). **5.8**

46. The C&W agreements also provide that C&W may remove at the customer's expense any unauthorised addition, alteration or extension to the rented installation if C&W thinks it in any way prejudices the operation of the installation. Similar clauses are inserted in the other two C&W standard contracts and in the SS contracts. The effect of these clauses was to provide C&W with additional powers to enforce the prohibition on unauthorised additions, alterations and extensions. Since the amended agreement provides that C&W's consent to such additions, alterations or extensions will only be withheld for objectively valid reasons which shall be disclosed to the customer, this clause no longer offends against section 4(1).

(e) *Copyright*

47. A number of the agreements require the customer not to pass on copyright material, including software to any third party without the written consent of the Company. In more recent years software programmes have become a major feature of large telephone installations. The software, like the hardware, remains the property of the rental company and the Authority would not consider these measures, which are inserted to protect the proprietary interest of the rental company, as offending against section 4(1).

(f) *The Decision*

48. Cable and Wireless (Ireland) Ltd, Irish Telephone Rentals Ltd, (ITR) and Sound Systems Ltd, (SS) now known as Cable and Wireless Ltd, (C&W) are undertakings within the meaning of section 3(1) of the Competition Act. Most of the other parties are also undertakings and the rental contracts constitute agreements between undertakings. In the Authority's opinion, the notified agreements, as amended by letter dated 26 May 1994, do not offend against section 4(1) of the Competition Act 1991.

The Certificate

49. The Competition Authority has issued the following certificate:

The Competition Authority certifies that in its opinion, on the basis of the facts in its possession, the agreements set out below in respect of standard rental contracts notified on 25 and 29 September, 1992 under section 7, and amended by letter of 26 May, 1994, do not offend against section 4(1) of the Competition Act 1991:

(a) notification nos. CA/133/92E, CA/137/92E, CA/138/92E—current contracts relating to telecommunication-related, staff location, and time control equipment between Cable and Wireless Ltd, and business users,

(b) notifications nos. CA/132/92E, CA/134/92E, CA/135/92E, CA/139/92E, CA/175/92E, CA/176/92E, CA/179/92E, CA/180/92E, CA/181/92E, CA/182/92E, CA/184/92E, CA/185/92E, CA/186/92E, and CA/191/92E—old contracts relating to telecommunication-related, staff location, time control and security equipment between Irish Telephone Rentals Ltd (now Cable and Wireless Ltd) and business users, and

(c) notifications nos. CA/136/92E, CA/177/92E, CA/178/92E, CA/183/92E, CA/187/92E, CA/188/92E, CA/189/92E and CA/190/92E—old contracts relating to telecommunication-related, staff location, time control and security equipment between Sound Systems Ltd (now Cable and Wireless Ltd) and business users.

For the Competition Authority

Des Wall
Member

19 September 1994

5.9 Competition Authority Decision No. 357, Statoil Distributor Agreement (Equipment Loan): 20 September 1994, Notification No. CA/450/92E

Equipment loan agreement ancillary to exclusive distribution agreement – Related exclusive distribution agreement licenced under a category licence – Competition Act 1991 (No. 24) sections 3,4 and 7

Facts: On 30 September 1992 notification was made to the Authority by Statoil Ireland Ltd ('Statoil') with a request for a licence under section 4(2) of the Competition Act 1991 in respect of a standard equipment loan agreement. The notification indicated that the equipment loan agreement was made between Statoil and its exclusive distributors and its commercial customers. By letter dated 22 August 1994 Statoil requested that the notification be considered by the Authority only in respect of agreements with exclusive distributors and that the notification in respect of agreements with commercial customers be withdrawn. This notification therefore, is linked to the Authority Decision No. 321 dated 21 April 1994 concerning Statoil Distributor agreements in relation to cash advances and loans.

Statoil is a limited company engaged in the supply of oil products, both retail and commercial and the other parties to the notified arrangements are exclusive distributors of petroleum products. The products involved in the notification are motor fuel oils.

Statoil notified its exclusive distribution agreement for fuel oils (CA/448/92E) which agreement was considered by the Authority to satisfy the conditions of the category licence for exclusive distribution agreements (Authority Decision No. 144). Statoil also notified the equipment loan agreement which is ancillary to the exclusive distribution agreement and is the subject of this decision.

The equipment loan agreement relates to a standard loan agreement for tank storage and equipment whereby Statoil loans to its distributors items of equipment for a period of ten years. During this period, the distributor is required to confine purchases to be stored in or handled through the equipment to brands approved by Statoil, and not to use the equipment for or in connection with any other brand. The distributor is required to maintain and repair the equipment for ten years even though it remains the property of Statoil and Statoil is entitled to lock and seal the equipment and to place identification marks on the equipment and the distributor may not interfere with, or obscure, these marks.

Decided by the Authority: In granting a licence under section 4(2) of the Competition Act 1991 in respect of the notified agreement that:

(1) Each of Statoil and the distributors who are party to the notified agreement are undertakings within the meaning of section 3(1) of the Competition Act. The notified agreement is connected with and dependent upon the exclusive distribution agreement and it forms part of the exclusive distribution arrangements and in some respects strengthens those arrangements. While the agreement might contain some provisions which by themselves could offend against section 4(1) of the Competition Act the notified agreement offends against section 4(1) because it underpins an exclusive distribution agreement which itself offends against section 4(1) of the Competition Act for the reasons given in the category licence for exclusive distribution agreement.

(2) Under section 4(2) of the Competition Act the Authority may grant a licence

in the case of any agreement or category of agreements which meet the criteria set out in that section. The basic Statoil standard exclusive distribution agreement satisfied the conditions of the category licence and the notified related agreement also satisfies the conditions of the category licence for the same reasons and thus it also satisfies the requirement of section 4(2) of the Competition Act. This applies also to any exclusivity provisions specifically included in the notified agreement. 5.9

(3) A licence may be issued in respect of the Statoil distributor equipment loan agreement with effect from 20 September 1994 and expiring on the date of expiry on the category licence for exclusive distribution agreements, that is 31 December 1998.

Decision referred to:
Competition Authority Decision No. 144, Exclusive Distribution Category Licence, 5 November 1993 **5.1**

Competition Authority Decision of 20 September 1994 relating to a proceeding under section 4 of the Competition Act 1991
Notification No. CA/450/92E — Statoil Distributor Agreement (Equipment Loan)

Introduction

1. Notification was made of an agreement by Statoil Ireland Ltd on 30 September 1992 with a request for a licence under section 4(2) of the Competition Act 1991 in respect of its Equipment Loan Agreement. The notification indicated that the Equipment Loan Agreement was made with both exclusive distributors and with commercial customers. By letter of 22 August 1994 Statoil's solicitors requested that the notification be considered by the Competition Authority only in respect of agreements with exclusive distributors and that the notification in respect of agreements with commercial customers be withdrawn. This notification is, therefore, linked to the Competition Authority's decision of 21 April 1994 concerning Statoil Distributor Agreements in relation to Cash Advances and Loans (Decision No. 321).

The Facts

(a) *The subject of the notification*

2. The decision concerns a document signed by Statoil and some of its distributors namely an Equipment Loan Agreement.

(b) *The parties involved*

3. Statoil Ireland Ltd is a limited company engaged in the supply of oil products, both retail and commercial. The other parties to the arrangements are exclusive distributors of petroleum products.

(c) *The products and the market*

4. The products involved are fuel oils. The oil companies involved in this market generally use distributors to deliver to final customers and do not use own staff as in the past.

(d) *The notified agreement*

5. Statoil notified its exclusive distribution agreement for fuel oils (CA/448/92E), and the Authority considered that the agreement satisfied the conditions of the category licence for exclusive distribution agreements (Decision No. 144 of 5 November 1993). Statoil also notified the Equipment Loan Agreement which is associated with the exclusive distribution agreement and which is the subject of this decision.

The Equipment Loan Agreement relates to a standard loan agreement for tank storage and

5.9 equipment whereby Statoil makes available to its distributors items of equipment on loan for a period of ten years. During this period, the distributor is required to confine purchases to be stored in or handled through the equipment to brands approved by Statoil, and not to use the equipment for or in connection with any other brands. The distributor is required to maintain and repair the equipment for ten years, even though it remains the property of Statoil. Statoil is entitled to lock and seal the equipment, and to place identification marks on the equipment, and the distributor may not interfere with, or obscure, these marks.

Assessment

Applicability of section 4(1)

6. Section 4(1) of the Competition Act 1991 prohibits and renders void all agreements between undertakings which have as their object or effect the prevention, restriction or distortion of competition in trade in any goods or services in the State or in any part of the State.

The Undertakings

7. Section 3(1) of the Competition Act defines an undertaking as 'a person being an individual, a body corporate or an unincorporated body of persons engaged for gain in the production, supply or distribution of goods or the provision of a service.' Statoil Ireland Ltd and the distributors are engaged in the sale of motor fuels for gain, and are therefore undertakings within the meaning of section 3(1) of the Competition Act.

The Agreement

8. The notified agreement is connected with, and dependent upon, the exclusive distribution agreement, it forms part of the exclusive distribution arrangements and in some respects it strengthens those arrangements. In the opinion of the Authority, while the agreement might contain some provisions which by themselves could offend against section 4(1), the notified agreement offends against section 4(1) of the Competition Act because it underpins an exclusive distribution agreement which itself offends against section 4(1) of the Competition Act for the reasons given in the category licence for exclusive distribution agreements.

Applicability of section 4(2)

9. Under section 4(2), the Competition Authority may grant a licence in the case of any agreement or category of agreements which, 'having regard to all relevant market conditions, contributes to improving the production or distribution of goods or provision of services or to promoting technical or economic progress, while allowing consumers a fair share of the resulting benefit and which does not—

(i) impose on the undertakings concerned terms which are not indispensable to the attainment of those objectives;

(ii) afford undertakings the possibility of eliminating competition in respect of a substantial part of the products or services in question.'

10. The Authority has decided that the basic Statoil standard exclusive distribution agreement satisfies the conditions of the category licence. It is of the opinion that the notified related agreement also satisfies the conditions of the category licence, for the same reasons, and thus it also satisfies the requirements of section 4(2) of the Competition Act. This applies also to any exclusivity provisions specifically included in the notified agreement. A licence may therefore be issued in relation to the Statoil Distributor Equipment Loan Agreement. The licence comes into effect on 20 September 1994. It will expire on the date of expiry of the category licence for exclusive distribution agreements, that is on 31 December 1998.

The Decision

11. In the Authority's opinion, Statoil Ireland Ltd and the other parties to the agreement are

undertakings . The notified agreement between the parties is an agreement between undertakings. The Authority considers that the notified agreement offends against section 4(1) of the Competition Act 1991. The Authority considers that the notified agreement satisfies the conditions of section 4(2) of the Competition Act. It has therefore decided to issue a licence in respect of the notified agreement, and the licence shall apply from 20 September 1994 to 31 December 1998. It is not considered necessary to attach any conditions to the licence. 5.9

The Licence

12. The Competition Authority has issued the following licence:

> The Competition Authority grants a licence under section 4(2) of the Competition Act 1991 to the equipment loan agreement between Statoil Ireland Ltd and its distributors (Notification No. CA/450/92E) notified under section 7 on 30 September 1992, on the grounds that, in the opinion of the Authority, all the conditions of section 4(2) of the Competition Act 1991 have been fulfilled.

The licence shall apply from 20 September 1994 to 31 December 1998.

For the Competition Authority

Patrick M. Lyons
Chairman

20 September 1994

Competition Authority Decision No. 362, Murphy Brewery Ireland Ltd/Clada Soft Drinks Ltd: 13 October 1994, Notification Nos. CA/212/92E and CA/427/92E 5.10

Delivery agreement – Term of agreement giving the deliverer exclusive delivery rights within a specified territory – Undertaking by owner of goods not to permit other deliverers to deliver the goods within the specified territory – Title to goods at all material times residing with the owner – EC Regulation 1983/83 – Competition Act 1991 (No. 24) sections 3, 4 and 7.

Facts: On 29 and 30 September 1992 notification was made to the Authority of a distributorship agreement between Murphy Brewery Ireland Ltd ('Murphys') and Clada Soft Drinks Ltd ('Clada') with a request for a certificate under section 4(4) of the Competition Act 1991 or, failing that, a licence under section 4(2).

Murphy, an Irish registered company and subsidiary of the Dutch company Heineken NV, is involved in the brewing, marketing and distribution of beers in the State. Clada, an Irish company located in Galway, is engaged in the manufacture of soft drinks, juices and bottled waters, and in the distribution of its own products and the products of other manufacturers.

Under the terms of the notified agreement made on 23 September 1992 Clada was appointed what was described as 'an exclusive distributor' of Murphy products in a territory covering Connacht and the counties of Cavan, Donegal, Longford and parts

5.10 of Westmeath and Offaly. Under the terms of the agreement all enquiries received by Murphy from the territory were to be referred to Clada and Murphy was not to supply any of its other agents with the relevant products who knowingly and wilfully supplied those products to customers within the relevant territory. Clada was precluded from seeking customers of the said products outside the territory and undertook to support the products in order to achieve agreed annual sales targets, keep proper books and records and allow for their inspection and not to engage in advertising or other expenditure without authorisation by Murphy. For its services Clada receives an annual fee from Murphy. The notified agreement further set out that title in the said products is retained at all times by Murphy and that no brand or identification for the products may be changed or defaced in any way. The initial term of the agreement was 10 years to be followed by two additional periods of 5 years, unless six months notice of termination is given by either party before the end of the 15th year of the agreement.

In response to questions from the Authority in August 1993 Clada stated that the agreement was not one for the purchase and resale of goods and that Clada was remunerated only in respect of the warehousing and distribution costs which it incurred. Clada submitted and Murphy agreed that the agreement was purely a delivery agreement.

Decided by the Authority: In issuing a certificate under section 4(4) of the Competition Act 1991 in respect of the notified agreement that:

(1) Murphy is engaged in the production and distribution of goods and Clada is engaged in the distribution of goods and they are therefore both undertakings and the agreement is an agreement between undertakings which has effect within the State.

(2) The essential feature of the notified agreement is that Clada delivers Murphy products to Murphy customers for which Clada receives a fee. The agreement does not involve the purchase and resale of the products by Clada and is not an exclusive distribution agreement as defined in the category licence for exclusive distribution agreements. While Clada is required to do some advertising, the agreement does not confer any continuing authority on Clada to negotiate the sale or purchase of goods on behalf of Murphy and Clada cannot be considered to be a commercial agent of Murphy.

(3) The agreement involves merely the delivery of Murphy products by Clada within a defined territory on an exclusive basis. Undertakings are entitled to decide how their products shall be distributed to their customers and Murphy has decided that, rather than deliver its goods itself in most parts of the State, to use Clada and other distributors. Distribution agreements involving delivery only do not offend against section 4(1) of the Competition Act 1991.

(4) While a delivery agreement might not *per se* offend against section 4(1), certain clauses in the agreement might so offend. None of the clauses in the notified agreement between Murphy and Clada offend against section 4(1).

Decision referred to:

Competition Authority Decision No. 144, Category Licence for Exclusive Distribution Agreements, 5 November 1993 **5.1**

Competition Authority decision of 13 October 1994 relating to a proceeding under section 4 of the Competition Act 1991 5.10
Notifications Nos. CA/212/92E and CA/427/92E — Murphy Brewery/ Clada Soft Drinks

Introduction

1. Notifications were made by each party separately of the distributorship agreement between Murphy Brewery Ireland Ltd and Clada Soft Drinks Ltd on 29 and 30 September 1992, with a request for a certificate under section 4(4) of the Competition Act 1991 or, in the event of a refusal by the Competition Authority to issue a certificate, a licence under section 4(2).

The Facts

(a) *The subject of the notifications*

2. The notifications concern an agreement between Murphy Brewery and Clada, whereby Clada is appointed what is termed 'exclusive distributor' of Murphy draught and kegged products within a specified territory.

(b) *The parties involved*

3. Murphy Brewery is an Irish registered company, located in Cork, whose ultimate parent company is Heineken N.V. of the Netherlands. It is involved in the brewing, marketing and distribution of beers. Clada is a company which is located in Galway and is involved in the manufacture of soft drinks, juices and bottled water, and in the distribution of fruit and vegetables, soft drinks, Murphy Brewery keg products and the bottled beers of other manufacturers.

(c) *The products and the market*

4. The products involved in the agreement are draught and kegged Heineken Lager Beer and draught and kegged Murphys Irish Stout. Murphy Brewery estimates that it has the second highest share in the market for beer, lager and stout in the State, but this is very much smaller than that of the market leader, Guinness. The service involved is the distribution of these products to the licenced trade. Murphy Brewery delivers directly to the licenced trade in Cork and Dublin, and elsewhere it uses various distribution companies, including Clada. Murphy Brewery stated that there were a large number of actual and potential suppliers of distribution services for this market.

(d) *The notified agreement*

5. The agreement between Murphy Brewery and Clada was made on 23 September 1987. Clada was appointed what is termed an 'exclusive distributor' of the products in the territory outlined in a map, the territory covering Connacht, the counties of Cavan, Donegal and Longford, and parts of Westmeath and Offaly. All enquiries received by Murphy Brewery from the territory are to be referred to Clada, and Clada will be given exclusive rights in the territory for any new products. Clada is not permitted to seek customers or promote the products outside the territory, nor stock the products in any branch or distribution warehouse outside the territory. Murphy Brewery agrees not to supply any of its agents with draught products, who knowingly and wilfully supply the products in their draught form to customers within the territory, and it will use its best endeavours to ensure such a situation does not arise (clause 2.0). Clada agrees to actively support the products in order to achieve agreed annual sales targets; to keep proper books and records and allow their inspection; and not to engage in advertising or other expenditure without authorisation. Clada is paid a fee for warehousing and distributing the products. The fee is to be agreed annually or from time to time as may be agreed but in the event of failure to agree shall not be less than a fixed percentage of the pretax selling price to

5.10 retail customers. The agreement may not be assigned by Clada without consent. No brand or identification for the products may be changed or defaced in any way. Title in the products is retained at all times by Murphy Brewery and the products at all times remain the property of Murphy Brewery. The initial term of the agreement is ten years, followed by two additional periods of five years, unless 6 months' notice of termination is given by either party before the end of the fifteenth year of the agreement.

(e) *Submissions by the parties*

6. No submissions or arguments for a certificate or licence were made by Clada. Murphy Brewery, however, stated that the exclusive nature of the agreement could be regarded as anti-competitive, but this was contemplated by EU Regulation 1983/83, and was justified by the circumstances of the market. Clause 2 was only in some of the agreements where it was believed necessary in the interest of maintaining a network, and it was contemplated by Article 2 of the Regulation. Murphy Brewery submitted that the distributor was effectively an agent rather than a distributor, and the agreement should be entitled to a certificate since such a relationship did not restrict competition. Reference was made to the 1962 Notice on agents by the EU Commission. The distributor bore no financial risk and constituted an agent. It was argued that the arrangements would facilitate the development of new, and the maintenance of existing, competitors in the market to stimulate further competition by offering high quality service. There was a relatively high number of competitors and this number would not be significantly reduced. The arrangements allowed for the creation and maintenance of new competitors in the geographical market because of the ability to use a local distributor with local contacts and distribution arrangements. Murphy Brewery stated that it believed that the agreement did not appreciably affect trade in the State. Murphy Brewery also presented arguments in support of its request for a licence, but these are not relevant to this decision.

7. In response to questions from the Authority in August 1993, Clada stated that the agreement was not one for the purchase and resale of goods, and that Clada was remunerated only in respect of the warehousing and distribution costs which it incurred. Drawing on the EU Commission's draft notice on commercial agency agreements as a guide to interpretation, Clada suggested that the agreement was a pure delivery agreement. Clada essentially handled the physical distribution on behalf of Murphy Brewery, rather than being engaged in negotiating or concluding transactions on behalf of Murphy Brewery. Murphy Brewery stated that the agreement was merely agency whereby the 'agent' merely collected the goods and delivered them, and prepared a delivery docket; Murphy Brewery invoiced the customer. It also stated that the agreement was a pure delivery agreement.

Assessment

Applicability of section 4(1)

8. Section 4(1) of the Competition Act 1991 prohibits and renders void all agreements between undertakings which have as their object or effect the prevention, restriction or distortion of competition in trade in any goods or services in the State or in any part of the State.

The Undertakings

9. Section 3(1) of the Competition Act defines an undertaking as 'a person being an individual, a body corporate or an unincorporated body of persons engaged for gain in the production, supply or distribution of goods or the provision of a service'. Murphy Brewery is engaged in the production and distribution of goods, and Clada is engaged in the distribution of goods. They are both undertakings, and the agreement is an agreement between undertakings. It has effect within the State.

The notified agreement 5.10

10. The essential feature of the notified agreement is that Clada delivers Murphy Brewery products to Murphy Brewery customers; in return for the performance of this service, Clada is paid a fee by Murphy Brewery. The agreement does not involve the purchase and resale of the products by Clada, and it is not an exclusive distribution agreement as defined in the category licence for exclusive distribution agreements (Decision No. 144, of 5 November 1993), nor as defined in EU Regulation 1983/83. While Clada is required to do some advertising, the agreement does not confer any continuing authority on Clada to negotiate the sale or purchase of goods on behalf of Murphy Brewery, and Clada cannot be considered to be a commercial agent of Murphy Brewery. The Authority considers that the agreement involves merely the delivery of Murphy Brewery products by Clada within a defined territory on an exclusive basis. It considers that undertakings are entitled to decide how their products shall be distributed to their customers. Murphy Brewery has decided that, rather than deliver its goods itself in most parts of the State, it should use Clada and other distributors. Distribution agreements involving delivery only do not, in the Authority's opinion, offend against section 4(1) of the Competition Act.

11. While a delivery agreement might not *per se* offend against section 4(1), certain clauses in the agreement might offend. The Authority considers that none of the clauses in the notified agreement with Clada offend against section 4(1). In particular, the supplier is entitled to determine the duration of any agreement to deliver its goods, whether for a short or long period, without the term of the agreement affecting competition. Likewise, the supplier is entitled to determine the remuneration paid to those persons who deliver the goods. Murphy Brewery delivers its goods itself in some areas, it has the goods delivered by Clada in a defined area of the State, and it utilises commercial agents to deliver its goods in other defined areas. Neither Clada nor the agents sell Murphy Brewery products on their own account, and they are required to sell to customers within the territory allocated to them. In these circumstances, the restrictions in Clause 2, whereby Clada must not actively sell outside its territory and is protected from other customers outside the territory selling into the territory, do not, in the opinion of the Authority, effect competition, and so they do not offend against section 4(1).

The Decision

12. Murphy Brewery and Clada are undertakings, and the notified agreement is an agreement between undertakings. In the Authority's opinion, the notified agreement is a delivery agreement, and it does not have the object or effect of preventing, restricting or distorting competition.

The Certificate

13. The Competition Authority has issued the following certificate:

> The Competition Authority certifies that in its opinion, on the basis of the facts in its possession, the delivery agreement between Murphy Brewery Ireland Ltd and Clada Soft Drinks Ltd notified under section 7 on 29 and 30 September 1992 (notification nos. CA/212/92E and CA/427/92E) does not offend against section 4(1) of the Competition Act 1991.

For the Competition Authority

Patrick M. Lyons
Chairman

13 October 1994

5.11 Competition Authority Decision No. 366, Gill & Macmillan/Attic Press, Brandon Book Publishers, Lilliput Press, Irish Academic Press, Four Courts Press, The Round Hall Press, O'Brien Press, Wolfhound Press and Townhouse & Country House Publishers Ltd: 28 October 1994, Notification Nos. CA/804-812/92E

Agreement whereby a publisher undertakes to deliver books of a competitor publisher within the State – Provision in the agreement for the provision of administrative services – Resale price maintenance clause – Statement of objections – Amendment of notified agreement – Competition Act 1991 (No. 24) sections 3, 4 and 7

Facts: On 30 September 1992 notification was made to the Authority by Gill & Macmillan Ltd of nine agreements with various Irish publishers together with the request for a certificate under section 4(4) of the Competition Act 1991 or, failing that, a licence under section 4(2).

Gill & Macmillan Ltd ('G&M') is an Irish based company engaged in the publication and distribution of books in Ireland. It also distributes books produced by a number of other Irish Publishers. The other parties to the notified agreements being, Attic Press, Brandon Book Publishers, Lilliput Press, Irish Academic Press, Four Courts Press, The Round Hall Press, O'Brien Press, Wolfhound Press and Townhouse & Countryhouse Publishers Ltd are all small scale specialist publishers in Ireland.

The service concerned with the notification is the distribution of books produced by Irish publishers to booksellers throughout the State and other ancillary services. G&M commenced distributing other publishers books in 1984 and it distributes books on behalf of the majority of the Irish publishers in the State.

Under the terms of the notified agreements G&M, apart from the physical delivery of books, provides storage, stock control, invoicing, credit control, debt recovery and royalty calculation services. G&M also undertakes liability for bad debts. Each publisher undertakes to accept G&M's decision on how each account is to be operated and G&M undertakes not to treat any publisher's books differently from its own books. The agreements state that the word 'seller' printed on the conditions of sale of the distributor's invoices shall mean the relevant publisher and not G&M. Clause 16 of the conditions of sale on the distributor's invoice states that 'books supplied by the seller are supplied on condition that they are to be offered for sale and sold at a retail level in Ireland at not less than the unit price indicated on the invoice by the seller without the sellers' specific consent. . . .'

Other than some minor changes all agreements are virtually identical save that the service charge levied on each publisher is not the same in each case. The various agreements commenced at different dates from 1 July 1987 to 1 January 1991 and all agreements are for an indefinite term subject to six months notice of termination.

On 7 June 1994 in response to questions from the Authority G&M submitted that the service provided was essentially a storage and order fulfilling service rather than a distribution or commercial agency service in that at no stage did G&M purchase the books or acquire title to them so there was no question of resale as envisaged in the category licence for exclusive distribution agreements. G&M does not act as an intermediary between the publishers and retail outlets or have any authority from the publishers to negotiate or conclude sale agreements akin to that undertaken by commercial agents.

On 22 June 1994 the Authority issued a statement of objections in respect of the standard terms and conditions of sales on the basis that clause 16 of the conditions of sale represented resale price maintenance. G&M responded saying that they intended to delete clause 16 from the standard terms and conditions of sale. The Authority also questioned the differential in service charges levied on each publisher and G&M responded stating that the commission rates were assessed and charged in accordance with turnover and that the rate reflected the cost of handling each list. G&M emphasise that there was no question of discrimination between client companies, the varying commission rates reflecting only the economy of scale which could be gained by increased turnover. **5.11**

Decided by the Authority: In issuing a certificate under section 4(4) of the Competition Act 1991 in respect of the notified arrangements that:

(1) Each of G&M and the various publishers are undertakings within the meaning of section 3(1) of the Competition Act and the agreements are agreements between undertakings which have effect within the State.

(2) Contrary to the initial submission by G&M the notified agreements do not involve the purchase and resale of books by the distributor, and ownership remains with the publisher and not the distributor, and they are therefore not exclusive distribution agreements and do not come within the scope of the category licence for exclusive distribution agreements.

(3) The essential feature of the arrangement is that G&M supplies this service of storage and physical distribution of books on behalf of the publishers. This amounts to something more than the provision of a delivery service because G&M provide additional services such as credit control and debt collection. At the same time the arrangements do not amount to commercial agency agreements since G&M does not conclude the sale or purchase of goods or services on behalf of a principal which is a fundamental feature of a commercial agency agreement. The notified arrangements fall somewhere between a simple delivery agreement and a commercial agency agreement.

(4) Undertakings are entitled to decide how their products shall be distributed and distribution arrangements do not, in principle, offend against section 4(1) of the Competition Act. The publishers are small in size and while it is essential that their books are distributed to booksellers throughout the State they would find it difficult and probably uneconomic to deliver the books themselves and so they utilise the spare capacity available from G&M. The situation is not altered by the fact that G&M is a competing publisher. It provides little more than a delivery service and it does not sell the books on behalf of the other publishers nor does it determine the re-sale price of the book. In addition G&M may not discriminate in favour of its own books. While the provision of this service means that G&M has access to information about deliveries of its competitors' books to booksellers and probably information about sales to consumers there is no evidence that this confers a competitive advantage upon G&M.

(5) The clauses relating to storage, invoicing, credit control, debt recovery, royalties, financial information, returns and order stocks form a necessary part of the overall service provided and they do not offend against section 4(1). The distributor undertakes liability for bad debts and so allowing the distributor to determine whether an account should be opened or closed when it may not discriminate in favour of its own books it does not offend against section 4(1). The notified agreements imply

5.11 acceptance of the standard conditions of sale of G&M and these included, as clause 16 a resale price maintenance requirement. But for the deletion of this clause 16 a certificate would not have been issued or a licence been granted. Since clause 16 has been removed from the conditions of sale it no longer presents an impediment to issuing certificates for these delivery agreements.

(6) Having examined the figures supplied by G&M and having considered the explanation given there are no grounds for believing the differences in the service charges levied on each publisher are not objectively justified and so they do not offend against section 4(1) of the Act.

Decisions referred to:

Competition Authority Decision No. 144, Category Licence for Exclusive Distribution agreements, 5 November 1993 **5.1**

Competition Authority Decision No. 286, Conoco Consignee agreement, 25 February 1994 **1.6.1**

Competition Authority Decision No. 365, Gill and MacMillan Terms and Conditions, 28 October, 1994.

Competition Authority Decision of 28 October 1994 relating to a proceeding under section 4 of the Competition Act 1991
Notification Nos. CA/804-812/92E — Gill & Macmillan Ltd/Attic Press, et al.

Introduction

1. Notification was made on 30 September 1992 by Gill and Macmillan Ltd of nine agreements with various Irish publishers. The notification requested certificates under section 4(4) of the Competition Act 1991 or, in the event of a refusal by the Competition Authority to issue certificates, licences under section 4(2). Notice of intention to issue a certificate was published in the Irish Times on 16 September 1994. No submissions were received from interested parties.

The Facts

(a) *The subject of the notification*

2. The decision concerns agreements whereby Gill and Macmillan agrees to act as sole distributor for books produced by nine other Irish publishers. The terms and conditions under which Gill and Macmillan supplies booksellers were notified separately, and are the subject of another decision.

(b) *The parties involved*

3. Gill and Macmillan is an Irish based firm which is engaged *inter alia* in the publication of books including general, academic, professional and educational books for second and third level students. It is associated through the Macmillan publishers group, which owns 49.9% of the issued share capital, with publishers throughout the world. It is, according to the notification, one of the largest Irish book publishers. Gill and Macmillan also distributes books produced by a number of other Irish publishers. These publishers are the other parties to the agreements, namely Attic Press, Brandon Book Publishers, Lilliput Press, Irish Academic Press, Four Courts Press, Round Hall Press, O'Brien Press, Wolfhound Press, and Townhouse and Countryhouse Publishers Ltd. They are mainly small-scale, specialist publishers.

(c) *The product and the market*

4. The product concerned in the notification is books, specifically those books produced by

those publishers whose books Gill and Macmillan distributes. The service concerned is the distribution of books produced by Irish publishers to booksellers throughout the State. This involves, besides the physical distribution of the books, the provision of storage, stock control, invoicing, credit control and debt recovery, calculation of royalties and financial information. According to the 1988 Census of Services, there were 370 retail outlets involved in the sale of books and stationery. The market is the service of distributing Irish-published books to booksellers. The market for books was described at length in the decision in the Net Book Agreement case (Decision No. 336 of 10 June 1994). 5.11

5. Gill and Macmillan stated that it effectively entered the market in 1984 at the request of existing publishers who were clients of Irish Book Handling, which had become insolvent. They were not in a position to handle their own needs, because of the economics of the book trade. It believed itself to be the only firm offering a full book distribution service for all titles of a publisher, although certain other distributors, such as Eason and Newspread, did occasionally distribute whole editions of a given work. Of the larger Irish publishers, only Poolbeg Press and Mercier Press were not clients of their distribution service.

(d) *The notified agreements*

6. In all cases, Gill and Macmillan has been appointed sole distributor in Ireland for the publisher, and also for other territories. It charges a standard service charge, which is reduced, it was stated, for clients with higher sales.

7. The distribution agreement is virtually a standard agreement, as epitomised by the agreement between Gill and Macmillan, the distributor, and Attic Press, the publisher. Under the agreement, the distributor undertakes:

(a) to store the publisher's book stocks for two years (after which additional charges are made);

(b) to provide proper stock control;

(c) to provide a complete invoicing and debt collection service. The distributor informs the publisher of any accounts on stop, and undertakes liability for bad debts. A dispatch service is provided for titles supplied on a consignment basis, which is charged separately;

(d) to pack and dispatch books, including normal carriage charges;

(e) to provide a service which will calculate the royalties due on each title;

(f) to provide monthly sales reports by title and territory; and

(g) to record orders for titles which are temporarily unavailable.

8. The publisher undertakes to accept the distributor's decision whether an account is to be opened or stopped; not to supply stock to any stopped accounts; to appoint the distributor as its sole distributor within Ireland to the wholesale and retail book trade and to all book trade accounts regularly supplied by the distributor; to accept the distributor's decision as to means of delivering books (and the distributor shall treat publisher's books no differently from their own books); and to be responsible for the authorisation of returns and overstocks.

9. The agreement makes provision for payments by the distributor to the publisher. In the case of the Attic Press agreements, it is clear that Gill and Macmillan acts as distributor for the State, the UK and the rest of the world. The publisher is charged for the services provided at a percentage of invoice value, excluding postage, service and VAT charges. It is stated that the ownership of the book stock and other goods shall remain with the publisher who shall be responsible for insurance of the books and goods held on the distributor's premises. The agreement was to operate for a period of 18 months from 1 July 1992. It was to be renewed automatically thereafter unless otherwise agreed in writing. Six months' notice of termination was required. The agreement is still in existence.

10. The agreement states that the word 'seller' printed on the conditions of sale on the distributor's invoices shall mean the publisher and not Gill and Macmillan, particularly in relation to clauses 4, 13 and 14. By implication, therefore, the publishers have accepted the conditions of sale of Gill and Macmillan, including clause 16, which states:

5.11 Books supplied by the seller are supplied on condition that they are to be offered for sale and sold at retail level in Ireland at not less than the unit price indicated on the invoice by the seller without the Sellers' specific consent. . . .

11. The other eight notified agreements are virtually the same as that described above. The only differences are:

(a) in one case, the publisher has existing distribution arrangements in the UK and US. In all others, the agreement covers distribution throughout the world;

(b) the service charge differed somewhat between publishers;

(c) in four cases, the initial period of the agreement was 18 months, in three cases it was 12 months, and in one case it was 21 months; and

(d) the agreements commenced at different dates from 1 July 1987 to 1 January 1991.

12. The initial period of each agreement has now expired, and so they are all for an indefinite term, subject to six months' notice of termination. All the agreements appoint Gill and Macmillan as their sole distributor in the State.

(e) *Submissions by Gill and Macmillan*

13. In its initial submission, Gill and Macmillan stated that it was one of the largest Irish publishers and had invested considerable resources in developing a state of the art distribution service. Having extra capacity, it acceded to the requests of the clients to provide distribution services for them. It was not aware of any other similar network in Ireland. It treated its client's books and its own equally in all respects.

14. In support of its request for a certificate, Gill and Macmillan argued that the present arrangements were not designed to exclude new competitors from the market, whether a distributor or publisher. On the contrary, they had been established to promote the more effective distribution of books and maintain a greater diversity of titles available. The existence of the distribution system offered by the Company acted, if anything, as an incentive to new publishers to publish new and more specialised titles, who were assured of an effective distribution outlet, without the necessity of investing scarce resources in distributing their products. The territorial exclusivity and other ancillary restrictions contained in the distribution agreements were necessary for the Company to protect its investment, which to-date had been considerable. On the one hand, it was agreed that the company did not put the distribution system in place in order to keep competitors out of the market and take advantage of other operators in the market place, but acted in response to the clients' request. Shared distribution was a universal practice among the international book trade and unilateral abandonment of this practice would simply enable the company's competitors to make use of its capital investment to their own benefit. For these reasons, the arrangements had an objective commercial justification.

15. Gill and Macmillan further submitted that competition was not actually or potentially restricted as the clients would not have been able to penetrate the market in the absence of the present agreements. This was corroborated by the fact that the clients approached the company to establish the distribution system. The clients did not have nor presently had the necessary financial and technical resources to set up their own distribution systems and a centralised network such as the distribution network operated by the company permitted the clients to concentrate on their publishing activities, without having to set aside valuable financial and other facilities for the purposes of distributing their products. The books market in Ireland was small as was each of the client's share of the overall market in terms of the number of titles published, and a nationwide distribution system was the only way for each of them to ensure effective and efficient distribution of their products, at more competitive prices.

16. Gill and Macmillan also claimed that the restrictive clauses were ancillary restraints of a nature, duration and scope which were reasonable in all the circumstances to protect the value of the company's investment in setting up the distribution network. The clauses were of a type

not uncommon in the book trade worldwide. The duration of the restrictions was limited to six months. The restrictive clauses were a legitimate means of ensuring the full commercial value of the company's investment, and in return, passing on the envisaged benefits to the clients and the booksellers and consumers. The territorial exclusivity granted to the company was a necessary inducement to the company to enter into the distribution agreements as without this protection the company would not have been prepared to make the investment. Furthermore, absence of territorial exclusivity would have prohibited the clients from achieving the market penetration presently enjoyed under existing arrangements. Gill and Macmillan also presented arguments in support of its request for a licence, which are not relevant to this decision. **5.11**

(f) *Subsequent developments*

17. In a further submission on 7 June 1994 in response to questions from the Authority, Gill and Macmillan submitted, contrary to its earlier submissions, that the service provided should be viewed in competition law terms as essentially a storage and order fulfilling service rather than a distribution or commercial agency service. Gill and Macmillan at no stage purchased the books or acquired title to them, so there was no question of resale as envisaged in the category licence for exclusive distribution agreements. Neither did it act as an intermediary between the publishers and retail outlets or have any authority from the publishers to negotiate or conclude sale agreements akin to those undertaken by commercial agents. The service provided to the publishers was limited to that of storage, stock control, stockholding, delivery to retail outlets, invoicing and debt collection, for which it was remunerated by way of a service charge calculated as a fixed percentage of invoice value. It had no function in influencing or concluding sales to retail outlets. The individual publishers exercised complete autonomy as regards marketing, price setting, negotiating with retail outlets on volume of sales, etc.

18. Gill and Macmillan also submitted that the object of the arrangement was solely to ensure an efficient storage, distribution and payment system on behalf of publishers who, because of their scale of operation and the particular features of the Irish book publishing market, were simply not in a position to provide these services economically for themselves. The trade was also very seasonal, due to the influence of school book sales. Some pooling of storage facilities, therefore, made sound economic sense, without giving rise to any coordination of competitive behaviour between publishers. The service was strictly a commercial one which allowed Gill and Macmillan to make efficient use of spare capacity which it enjoyed when the arrangements were established at the suggestion of the other publishers. There was no pressure on publishers to take up this service, and the publishers were completely free to seek out alternative storage and order fulfilling services at relatively short notice. On these grounds, it was submitted that the agreements merited a certificate.

19. On 22 June 1994, the Authority issued a Statement of Objections in respect of the Gill and Macmillan Standard Terms and Conditions of Sale. The Authority considered that clause 16 represented resale price maintenance, and it indicated that it intended to refuse a certificate or a licence to the agreement. On 7 July 1994, Gill and Macmillan wrote that they intended to delete clause 16 from the Standard Terms. Accordingly, on 28 October 1994, the Authority granted a certificate to the amended agreement. Reference to the conditions of sale of Gill and Macmillan in the agreements which are the subject of this decision therefore now relates to the conditions of sale as amended by the deletion of clause 16.

20. On 21 June 1994, the Authority wrote questioning the differential service charges. Gill and Macmillan, in its reply, stated that commission rates were assessed and charged in accordance with turnover, and the rate reflected the cost of handling each list. The rates were negotiable annually at the initiative of clients. It said that it should be noted that there was a considerable variance in the average price per unit of books sold between client companies. The cost of provision of an identical service was the same for a book with an average price of £12.96 as that with an average price of £2.83, but the net commission was considerably less. It maintained that it had to be emphasised that there was no question whatever of discrimination

5.11 between client companies. The varying commission rates reflected only the economy of scale which could be gained by increased turnover.

Assessment

Applicability of section 4(1)

21. Section 4(1) of the Competition Act 1991 prohibits and renders void all agreements between undertakings which have as their object or effect the prevention, restriction or distortion of competition in trade in any goods or services in the State or in any part of the State.

The Undertakings

22. Section 3(1) of the Competition Act defines an undertaking as 'a person being an individual, a body corporate or an unincorporated body of persons engaged for gain in the production, supply or distribution of goods or the provision of a service'. Gill and Macmillan is engaged in the production and distribution of books for gain, and the other publishers are engaged in the production of books for gain. All the parties involved are therefore undertakings, and the agreements are agreements between undertakings. The agreements have effect within the State.

The agreements

23. Under the notified agreements, Gill and Macmillan is appointed sole distributor in the State of books produced by each of the nine publishers. This operation was undertaken, according to Gill and Macmillan, at the request of the publishers some years ago when the handling firm which distributed their books became insolvent. The services provided are book storage, physical distribution, invoicing, credit control, debt recovery, calculation of royalties, provision of financial information, and the handling of returns and overstocks. In return, Gill and Macmillan imposes a service charge related to sales. While the agreements were for an initial period of 18 months, they are now for an indefinite period subject to six months' notice of termination. Ownership of the books remains with the publisher, who is responsible for insurance while they are on the distributor's premises. The agreements involve acceptance of Gill and Macmillan's conditions of sale. The distributor may decide whether to open or stop a bookseller's account, and undertakes liability for bad debts. It is required to treat the publisher's books no differently from its own books. The publishers determine the prices at which the books are sold to resellers.

24. Contrary to the initial submission by Gill and Macmillan, the agreements do not involve the purchase and resale of books by the distributor, and ownership remains with the publisher and not the distributor, and they are therefore not exclusive distribution agreements. They do not come within the scope of the category licence for exclusive distribution agreements (Decision No. 144 of 5 November 1993).

25. Subsequently, Gill and Macmillan claimed that the arrangements amounted to a storage and order fulfilling service, rather than to a commercial agency service. Unlike commercial agents, it did not negotiate or conclude sale agreements on behalf of the publishers. The Authority considers that the essential feature of the arrangements is that Gill and Macmillan supplies the service of storage and physical distribution of books on behalf of the publishers. It considers that this amounts to something more than the provision of a delivery service, however, because Gill and Macmillan provides additional related services, such as credit control and debt collection, and because it can determine whether an account is to be opened or closed, none of which are normally undertaken by suppliers of delivery services. At the same time, the Authority does not consider that the arrangements amount to commercial agency agreements (as described in Decision No. 286—Conoco Consignee agreement—of 25 February 1994), since Gill and Macmillan does not conclude the sale or purchase of goods or services on behalf of a principal, which is the fundamental feature of a commercial agency agreement.

In the opinion of the Authority, the notified arrangements fall somewhere between a simple delivery agreement and a commercial agency agreement. 5.11

26. The Authority considers that undertakings are entitled to decide how their products shall be distributed, that is whether they distribute the goods themselves, or make use of firms providing delivery services, or whether they operate through commercial agents or exclusive distributors. In all except the last case, the Authority considers that distribution arrangements do not, in principle, offend against section 4(1) of the Competition Act. The publishers are fairly small in size and, while it is essential that their books are distributed to booksellers through the State, they would find it difficult and probably most uneconomic to deliver the books themselves. In the past, they had used a specialist book handling firm, and, when this firm became insolvent, they decided to utilise the spare capacity available from Gill and Macmillan, which distributed its own titles.

27. The situation in this case is not altered by the fact that Gill and Macmillan is a competing publisher of books. It provides what is little more than a delivery service, and it does not sell the books on behalf of the other publishers, nor does it determine the resale price of the books. In addition, under the agreements, Gill and Macmillan is obliged to treat their books no differently from its own books, and it may not discriminate in favour of its own books. Admittedly, provision of this service means that Gill and Macmillan has access to information about deliveries of its competitor's books to booksellers, and possibly also some information about sales to consumers. There is no evidence, however, that this confers a competitive advantage upon Gill and Macmillan.

28. Even though the basic distribution arrangement might not offend against section 4(1), certain clauses in the agreement might do so. In the Authority's opinion, the clauses relating to storage, invoicing, credit control, debt recovery, royalties, financial information, returns and overstocks, form a necessary part of the overall service provided, and they do not offend against section 4(1). The distributor undertakes liability for bad debts, so that allowing the distributor to determine whether an account should be opened or closed, when it may not discriminate in favour of its own books, does not offend against section 4(1).

29. The notified agreements imply acceptance of the conditions of sale of Gill and Macmillan. These included, as clause 16, a resale price maintenance requirement. For the reasons stated in the Authority's decision in the case of those conditions of sale (Decision No. 365, of 28 October 1994), the Authority would not have issued a certificate or granted a licence to an agreement which contained such an obligation. The same situation would have prevailed in respect of the agreements which are the subject of this present decision. Since clause 16 has been removed from the conditions of sale of Gill and Macmillan, it no longer presents any impediment to issuing certificates for these delivery agreements.

30. The Authority was initially concerned that the different rates of service charge might amount to unfair discrimination between publishers, contrary to Article 4(1)(d) of the Act. Having examined the figures supplied by Gill and Macmillan, and having considered the explanation given, the Authority has no grounds for believing that differences in service charges are not objectively justified, and so they do not offend against section 4(1) of the Act.

The Decision

31. In the Authority's opinion, Gill and Macmillan and the other publishers who are parties to the agreements are undertakings. The notified agreements are agreements between undertakings. The Authority considers that the sole distribution agreements do not have, as their object or effect, the prevention, restriction or distortion of competition. They do not, in the Authority's opinion, offend against section 4(1) of the Competition Act 1991.

The Certificate

32. The Competition Authority has issued the following certificate:

5.11 The Competition Authority certifies that in its opinion, on the basis of the facts in its possession, the following sole distribution agreements between Gill and Macmillan and various publishers, notified on 30 September 1992, do not offend against section 4(1) of the Competition Act 1991:

(a) Attic Press CA/804/92E
(b) Brandon Book Publishers Ltd CA/805/92E
(c) The Lilliput Press CA/806/92E
(d) Irish Academic Press CA/807/92E
(e) Four Courts Press CA/808/92E
(f) The Round Hall Press CA/809/92E
(g) The O'Brien Press CA/810/92E
(h) Wolfhound Press CA/811/92E
(i) Townhouse & Countryhouse Publishers Ltd CA/812/92E

For the Competition Authority

Patrick M. Lyons
Chairman
28 October 1994

5.12 **Competition Authority Decision No. 368, Johnson Brothers Ltd/Campbell Grocery Products Ltd:** 28 October 1994, Notification No. CA/290/92E

Non-exclusive distribution agreement – Distributor restricted from handling goods competing with those of the supplier without the prior consent of the supplier – Competition Act 1991 (No. 24) sections 3, 4 and 7

Facts: On 30 September 1992 notification was made to the Authority with the request for a certificate under section 4(4) of the Competition Act 1991 or, failing that, a licence under section 4(2) in respect of a distribution agreement made between Johnson Brothers Ltd ('Johnson') and Campbell Grocery Products Ltd ('Campbell').

Johnson is a private limited company which warehouses and distributes fast moving consumer goods to the grocery and confectionery trades and Campbell is a UK company engaged in the manufacture of grocery products. The products specified in the notified agreement are foodstuffs such as canned soups, stews and sauces which are sold to grocery retailers.

Under the terms of the notified distribution agreement dated 24 March 1983 between Campbell and Johnson, Campbell agrees to supply products for re-sale in the State to Johnson the distributor. The notified agreement expressly permits Campbell to sell directly or indirectly any of the relevant goods to persons within the State and Johnson, while required to indicate that it is acting as distributor for Campbell, is not permitted to describe itself as 'sole distributor' or 'the distributor' of Campbell. Johnson is required under the agreement to promote sales and maintain stocks and to sell the relevant goods. Johnson has autonomy over its pricing policy. Clause 9(a) states that Johnson shall not have the right to handle competitive products without the

prior written consent from Campbell, such consent not to be unreasonably withheld. 5.12
The agreement is of indefinite duration subject to twelve months notice of termination. By letter dated 10 September 1993 to the Authority Johnson stated that other distributors for re-sale can be appointed in the territory but none have been so appointed.

Decided by the Authority: In issuing a certificate under section 4(4) of the Competition Act 1991 in respect of the notified agreement that:

(1) Each of Campbell and Johnson are undertakings within the meaning of section 3(1) of the Competition Act and the notified agreement is an agreement between undertakings which has effect within the State.

(2) The notified agreement is for the purchase and resale of grocery goods and the object of the agreement is not to make Johnson the exclusive distributor within the specified territory since the supplier reserves the right to supply into the territory directly or indirectly and because Johnson may not refer to itself as 'the sole distributor'. The agreement does not have the effect of giving the distributor exclusivity for, even if Johnson is the only distributor at present, Campbell is at liberty to appoint another and it is open for other distributors to approach Campbell at any time for supplies. The agreement is not therefore an exclusive distribution agreement as defined in the category licence for exclusive distribution agreement (Authority Decision No. 144).

(3) The notified agreement does commit Johnson to a form of exclusive purchase from Campbell in that Johnson has an obligation not deal in competing goods without Campbell's consent, which shall not be unreasonably withheld. This requirement does not itself restrict competition as it does not prevent re-sellers from obtaining supplies of Campbell products from a source other than Johnson nor does it prevent the suppliers of competing products from gaining access from the grocery market in the State. In the circumstances the agreement does not offend against section 4(1).

Decision referred to:

Competition Authority Decision No. 144, Category Licence for Exclusive Distribution Agreements, 5 November 1993 **5.1**

Competition Authority Decision of 28 October 1994 relating to a proceeding under section 4 of the Competition Act 1991
Notification No. CA/290/92E — Johnson Brothers/Campbells

Introduction

1. Notification was made of an agreement between Johnson Brothers Ltd (Johnson) and Campbell Grocery Products Ltd (Campbell) on 30 September 1992 with a request for a certificate under section 4(4) of the Competition Act 1991 or, in the event of a refusal by the Competition Authority to issue a certificate, a request for a licence under section 4(2). Notice of intention to issue a certificate was published in the Irish Times on 16 September 1994. No submissions were received from interested parties.

The Facts

(a) *The subject of the notification*

2. The notification concerns a distribution agreement whereby Campbell appoints Johnson as distributor of its products in the State.

5.12 (b) *The parties involved*

3. Johnson is a private limited company based in Walkinstown, which warehouses and distributes fast-moving consumer goods to the grocery, confectionery and allied trades. Campbell is a UK company which manufactures grocery products in England.

(c) *The products and the market*

4. The products specified in the agreement are foodstuffs such as canned soups, meatballs, stews, sauces and vegetable juice which are sold to grocery retailers.

(d) *The notified agreement*

5. The arrangement notified is an agreement dated 24 March 1983 between Campbell and Johnson. Under the agreement Campbell agrees to supply products for resale in the State to Johnson, the distributor. It is stated in clause 1(b), however, that:

> Campbell reserves to itself the right notwithstanding anything to the contrary herein contained to sell directly or indirectly to any persons firms or bodies corporate in the Territory.

In addition, under clause 2(a)(v), the distributor is required to indicate that it is acting as distributor for Campbell 'provided that the Distributor shall not have the right to describe itself as "Sole Distributor" or "The Distributor" of Campbell'. The distributor is required to promote sales, to maintain stocks, to sell the goods under the trademarks, to act as principal, to purchase its requirements of the products only from Campbell, and to assist in protecting Campbell's intellectual property. Campbell is responsible for certain advertising. The distributor is to review with Campbell the advertising and promotional plans, which are subject to the approval of Campbell, but this does not apply to the distributor's pricing policy. The distributor must not alter trademarks or numbers on the products. Under clause 9(a), 'The distributor shall not have the right to handle competitive products without prior written consent from Campbell's—this is not to be withheld unreasonably—and is not now handling such products'. The agreement is of indefinite duration, subject to 12 months' notice of termination. By letter of 10 September 1993, Johnson stated that 'other distributors for resale can be appointed in the territory but none have been so appointed'.

Assessment

Applicability of section 4(1)

6. Section 4(1) of the Competition Act 1991 prohibits and renders void all agreements between undertakings which have as their object or effect the prevention, restriction or distortion of competition in trade in any goods or services in the State or in any part of the State.

The Undertakings

7. Section 3(1) of the Competition Act defines an undertaking as 'a person being an individual, a body corporate or an unincorporated body of persons engaged for gain in the production, supply or distribution of goods or the provision of a service'. Campbell is engaged in the production and distribution of grocery products for gain, and Johnson is engaged in the distribution of grocery products for gain, and they are undertakings. The agreement is an agreement between undertakings, and it has effect within the State.

The Agreement

8. The distribution agreement is for the purchase and resale of grocery goods. The Authority considers that it is not the object of the agreement to make Johnson the exclusive distributor within a specified territory, since the supplier reserves the right to supply into the territory

directly or indirectly, and because Johnson may not refer to itself as 'sole distributor' or 'the distributor'. Neither does the Authority consider that the agreement has the effect of giving the distributor exclusivity. Even if Johnson is the only distributor at present, the supplier is at liberty to appoint another, and it is open to other distributors to approach Campbell at any time for supplies. The agreement is not, in the opinion of the Authority, an exclusive distribution agreement as defined in the category licence for exclusive distribution agreements (Decision No. 144, of 5 November 1993). **5.12**

9. The notified agreement, however, commits Johnson to a form of exclusive purchase from Campbells. Johnson has an obligation not to deal in competing goods without the supplier's consent, which will not be unreasonably withheld. In the opinion of the Authority, this requirement does not in itself restrict competition. It does not prevent resellers from obtaining supplies of Campbell products from a source other than Johnson, nor does it prevent the suppliers of competing products from gaining access to the grocery market in the State. In the circumstances, the Authority considers that the agreement does not offend against section 4(1).

The Decision

10. In the Authority's opinion, Campbell and Johnson are undertakings. The notified agreement is an agreement between undertakings. The Authority considers that the distribution agreement does not have, as its object or effect, the prevention, restriction or distortion of competition. It does not, in the Authority's opinion, offend against section 4(1) of the Competition Act 1991.

The Certificate

11. The Competition Authority has issued the following certificate:

> The Competition Authority certifies that in its opinion, on the basis of the facts in its possession, the distribution agreement between Campbell Grocery Products Ltd and Johnson Brothers Ltd (Notification No. CA/290/92E) notified on 30 September 1992 under section 7, does not offend against section 4(1) of the Competition Act 1991.

For the Competition Authority

Patrick M. Lyons
Chairman

28 October 1994

5.13 Competition Authority Decision No. 369, The Agricultural Trust/Newspread Ltd: 28 October 1994, Notification No. CA/469/92E

Agreement between a publisher and a distributor for the delivery of publication within the State – Price of the publication determined by the publisher – Competition Act 1991 (No. 24) sections 3, 4 and 7

Facts: On 30 September 1992 notification was made to the Authority with the request for a certificate under section 4(4) of the Competition Act 1991 or, failing that, a licence under section 4(2) in respect of arrangements for the distribution of the *Farmers Journal* between The Agricultural Trust ('The Trust') and Newspread Ltd ('Newspread').

The Trust is a charitable trust established to further the interests of Irish agriculture through, *inter alia,* the promotion of good farm practice and its activities include the publication of the *Farmers Journal.* Newspread is a subsidiary of Independent Newspapers which is engaged in the distribution of newspapers and magazines in the State.

The *Farmer's Journal* is a newspaper aimed primarily at farmers and members of the rural community generally. Some of the daily newspaper include weekly supplements which deal with agricultural matters and there is also a publication, the *Farmer's Monthly*, which is aimed specifically at the same target audience.

The notified arrangements relate to an agreement dated 31 December 1987 between the Trust and Newspread for the distribution of the Farmers Journal and under the terms of that agreement the Trust gives to Newspread the entire and total franchise for the sale and distribution of the *Farmers Journal* for the entire State excluding Donegal for a period of ten years commencing 1 January 1988. Newspread is required under these arrangements to invoice each newsagent and customer supplied by it and to collect the sums due on all such invoices. Newspread is required to sell the paper at the list price less a percentage unless otherwise agreed.

Decided by the Authority: In issuing a certificate under section 4(4) of the Competition Act 1991 in respect of the notified arrangements that:

(1) The Trust is engaged in *inter alia* the publication of the *Farmers Journal* for gain and is therefore an undertaking within the meaning of the Competition Act. Newspread is engaged for gain in the distribution of newspapers, magazines and periodicals and is also an undertaking. The notified agreement therefore constitutes an agreement between undertakings.

(2) The essential feature of the arrangement is that Newspread delivers the *Farmers Journal* to retailers throughout the State on behalf of the Trust. The agreement does not involve the purchase and resale of the product by Newspread and it is not an exclusive distribution agreement as defined in the category licence for exclusive distribution agreement (Authority Decision No.144). Undertakings are entitled to decide how their products shall be distributed to their customers and distribution agreements involving delivery only do not offend against section 4(1).

(3) While the delivery agreement might not *per se* offend against section 4(1) certain clauses in the agreement might do so. None of the clauses in the notified agreement offend against section 4(1). In particular the requirement that Newspread sell to retailers at a price specified by the Trust is not anti-competitive since in this

case Newspread is merely providing a delivery service for the Trust and is not acting as a re-seller as the Trust is selling the products to the retailers it is entitled to set the price at which the papers should be sold to them. This is in contrast to the position in Easons/Newspread notification where competing wholesalers entered into arrangements to ensure a uniform selling price to retailers of imported magazines and also recommended uniform retail prices on such magazines. **5.13**

Decisions referred to:
Competition Authority Decision No. 144, Category Licence for Exclusive Distribution Agreements, 5 November 1993 **5.1**
Notification No. CA/1080/92E — Easons and Newspread , Annex 5 of Competition Authority Annual Report 1993 **2.3.1**

Competition Authority decision of 28 October 1994 relating to a proceeding under section 4 of the Competition Act 1991
Notification No. CA/469/92E — The Agricultural Trust/Newspread Ltd

Introduction

1. Arrangements for the distribution of the Irish Farmers Journal between the Agricultural Trust and Newspread Ltd were notified to the Authority on 30 September 1992. The notification requested a certificate, or in the event of a refusal by the Authority to grant a certificate, a licence.

The Facts

(a) *The Subject of the Notification*

2. The notification concerns an agreement dated 31 December 1987 between The Agricultural Trust and Newspread whereby the latter is appointed as sole distributor of the Irish Farmer's Journal for a period of 10 years. The Farmers Journal is a weekly newspaper which is published by the Agricultural Trust. As its name implies its target audience is farmers and the rural community generally. Under the terms of the agreement Newspread distributes copies of the Journal to retailers located throughout the State. The agreement is for a period of ten years commencing on 1 January 1988.

(b) *The Parties Concerned*

3. The Agricultural Trust is a charitable trust established to further the interests of Irish agriculture *inter alia* through the promotion of good farm practice. Its activities include inter alia publication of the Farmers Journal. Newspread is a subsidiary of Independent Newspapers which is engaged in the distribution of newspapers and magazines.

(c) *The Product and the Market*

4. The product concerned in the notification is the Farmers Journal a weekly newspaper aimed primarily at farmers and members of the rural community generally. The market therefore is that for news publications aimed specifically at such a target audience. The Authority does not believe that daily newspapers constitute a sufficiently close substitute to the product in question to be considered to be part of this market. It is relevant, however, that a number of daily newspapers do actually include weekly supplements which deal with agricultural matters. The Farmer's Monthly is another publication aimed specifically at the target audience. Sales of the Farmers Journal are estimated at 70,000 per week. The Farmer's Monthly is estimated to sell approximately 24,000 copies per month. The Labour Force survey indicates that there were 150,000 people engaged in agriculture in 1992.

5.13 (d) *The Arrangements*

5. The arrangements relate to an agreeement dated 31 December 1987 between The Agricultural Trust and Newspread for the distribution of the Farmers Journal. Under the terms of the agreement the Trust gives Newspread the entire and total franchise for the sale, distribution and dissemination of the Journal for the entire State excluding Donegal, for a period of ten years commencing on 1 January 1988. Newspread is required to provide a complete distribution service at least equivalent to that already being provided by them. Newspread are required to invoice each newsagent and customer supplied by them and to collect the sums due on all such invoices. Newspread are required to sell the paper at the list price less a percentage unless otherwise agreed. Newspread is required to pay the Trust a percentage of the full retail value of its net sales (after returns and bad debts (if any)), six weeks after the publication date of each issue. Newspread is required to use its best endeavours to keep returns from newsagents below ten per cent and is entitled to credit for such returns. Newspread is not responsible for exceptional returns due to factors outside of its control.

6. Under the agreement Newspread delivers copies of the Farmers Journal to approximately 3,000 newsagents located throughout the State excluding Donegal. They take packed and labelled parcels for overnight delivery to the retailers every Thursday morning, take back returns and record sales. They reimburse the Trust in accordance with the provisions of the agreement.

(e) *Submissions of the Parties*

7. The parties submitted that the extent of the business involved was such that one distribution company was more than adequate to cater for it and for a small operation of 70,000 copies per week it would not make sense to divide the business. They stated that it did not in any way restrict the purchaser's access to the product as it was available in many different outlets.

Assessment

(a) *Section 4(1)*

8. Section 4(1) of the Competition Act states that 'all agreements between undertakings, decisions by associations of undertakings and concerted practices which have as their object or effect the prevention, restriction or distortion of competition in trade in any goods or services in the State or in any part of the State are prohibited and void.'

(b) *The Undertakings and the Agreement*

9. Section 3(1) of the Competition Act defines an undertaking as 'a person being an individual, a body corporate or an unincorporated body of persons engaged for gain in the production, supply or distribution of goods or the provision of a service.' The parties to the arrangements are The Agricultural Trust and Newspread. The Trust is engaged *inter alia* in the publication of the Farmers Journal for gain and is therefore an undertaking within the meaning of the Act. Newspread is a corporate body which is engaged for gain in the distribution of newspapers, magazines and periodicals and is also an undertaking. The notified agreement therefore constitutes an agreement between undertakings.

Applicability of section 4(1)

10. The essential feature of the agreements is that Newspread deliver the Farmers Journal to retailers throughout the State with the exception of Donegal on behalf of the Agricultural Trust. The agreement does not involve the purchase and resale of the product by Newspread and it is not an exclusive distribution agreement as defined in the category licence for exclusive distribution agreements.[1] The Authority believes that undertakings are entitled to decide how their products shall be distributed to their customers. The Agricultural Trust has decided to retain Newspread to deliver the Farmers Journal to retailers rather than deliver the paper itself.

Distribution agreements involving delivery only do not, in the Authority's opinion, offend against section 4(1). 5.13

11. While a delivery agreement might not *per se* offend against section 4(1), certain clauses in the agreement might do so. Such an arrangement does not prevent other firms entering the market for the delivery of newspapers and periodicals throughout the State. None of the other clauses in the agreement offend against section 4(1). In particular the requirement that Newspread sell to retailers at a price specified by the Trust is not anti-competitive since in this case Newspread is merely providing a delivery service for the Trust and is not acting as reseller. As the Trust is selling the products to the retailers it is entitled to set the price at which the papers should be sold to them. (This is in contrast to the position in Easons/Newspread where competing wholesalers entered into arrangements to ensure a uniform selling price to retailers of imported magazines and also recommended uniform retail prices of such magazines.)[2]

The Decision

12. In the Authority's opinion, The Agricultural Trust and Newspread are undertakings within the meaning of section 3(1) of the Competition Act, and the notified arrangements for the distribution by Newspread of the Irish Farmers Journal constitute an agreement between undertakings. In the Authority's opinion, the agreement does not have, as its object or effect, the prevention, restriction or distortion of competition and does not offend against section 4(1) of the Competition Act 1991.

The Certificate

13. The Competition Authority has issued the following certificate:

> The Competition Authority certifies that in its opinion, on the basis of the facts in its possession, the agreement of 31 December 1987 between The Agricultural Trust and Newspread Ltd for the distribuion by Newspread Ltd of the Irish Farmers Journal, (Notification No. CA/469/92E), notified on 30 September 1992 under section 7, does not offend against section 4(1) of the Competition Act 1991.

For the Competition Authority

Patrick Massey
Member

28 October 1994

1. Competition Authority Decision No. 144, 5 November 1993.
2. See Annex of Competition Authority Annual Report 1993.

CHAPTER SIX

Intellectual Property

6.0 Introduction

This chapter concerns the decisions of the Competition Authority which have considered restrictions in copyright and trademark agreements. Competition Authority Decision No. 5—Performing Right Society and Irish Music Rights Organisation [at 1.3.2 above] decided that the transfer of arrangements between a company which controlled the other company to the arrangements was a matter of internal group organisation which did not offend against section 4(1) of the Competition Act 1991.

IRISH DISTILLERS/SOUVENIR MANUFACTURERS **6.1**

The Competition Authority in Decision No. 284 referred to the lack of guidance from the EU Commission on the compatibility of typical restrictions in a trademark licence agreement with the prohibition of Article 85(1). Ultimately the covenant not to challenge the validity of Irish Distillers' licence or trademark and the quality related termination provision were acceptable to the Competition Authority.

IRISH DISTILLERS/FOOD MANUFACTURERS **6.2**

This decision reiterates the views of the Competition Authority in Decision No. 284 described above. In addition the Competition Authority accepted the restriction on the manufacturer from referring to 'Irish Whiskey' in their produce on the termination of their notified agreements.

PRS/CREATORS AND PUBLISHERS **6.3**

The collection of royalties for music through collecting societies has been examined by the EU Commission more under Article 86 than under Article 85. This decision is significant from this aspect because the Authority in its role for notifications may only examine notifications with reference to section 4 of the Competition Act.

It was argued on behalf of the notifying party of the copyright assignments from the creators and publishers to PRS, that the arrangements as notified had to continue in order to ensure that creators of music were remunerated. The Competition Authority at the oral hearing prior to the making of the decision and in the decision accepted that the monopoly and exclusivity arrangements which would normally be anti-competitive merited a licence because of the unique nature of the music industry. However, the Competition Authority refused to issue a certificate or licence in respect of the notified arrangements surrounding the assignments of copyright to the monopolistic collecting organisation PRS because of the considerable difficulty posed by PRS to creators in seeking alternative arrangements to collect royalties and to licence

6.0 public performances of their works. The Authority indicated apparently to PRS that the relaxation of restrictions on creators could lead to the grant of a licence but PRS informed the Authority that their arrangements were uniform throughout the European Union and changes to comply with Irish competition law could not be facilitated as a result. The decision elaborately describes the operations of PRS on behalf of creators and the manner by which creators recover copyright royalty payments. Apart from the importance attaching to the failure of PRS to obtain a licence for assignments to it of copyright, this decision contains a useful view of the Authority's perception of its role and scope when making a decision in respect of a notification under section 7 of the Competition Act.

IMRO/CABLE AND MMDS OPERATORS 6.4

This decision, No. 383, also concerns the collective licensing arrangement for copyright. The Authority having decided that the monopolistic collective licensing arrangements did offend against section 4(1), was satisfied that all of the requirements for the grant of a licence under section 4(2) existed. The licence, therefore, was granted in respect of the notified licensing arrangement for copyright in television broadcasts until the year 2004. Decision 384 which concerns similar collective licensing arrangements on behalf of copyright holders in UK television programmes adopts similar reasoning for the grant of a licence for the notified arrangements giving rise to this decision.

Competition Authority Decision No. 284, Irish Distillers Ltd/Celtic Glass and Others: 7 February 1994, Notification Nos. CA/972/92E, CA/973/92E, CA/974/92E, CA/979/92E, CA/981/92E, CA/978/92E 6.1

Non-exclusive trademark usership agreements – Restrictive pledge clause – Whether no challenge clause contributes to an unjustified barrier to market entry – whether termination for quality reason is a justified entitlement for licensor – Competition Act 1991 (No. 24), sections 3, 4 and 7

Facts: On 30 September 1992 notification was made to the Competition Authority by Irish Distillers Group Plc of six trademark and design usership agreements with various parties with a request for certificates under section 4(4) of the Competition Act 1991 or, failing that, licences under section 4(2). The notified agreements contained two agreements between Irish Distillers Ltd and Celtic Glass Ltd, three further agreements between Irish Distillers Ltd and each of Lough Derg Handcrafts Ltd, LLEDO Plc and Tobler Suchard Ltd and one final agreement between Old Bushmills Distillery Company Ltd and Celtic Glass Ltd. Both Irish Distillers Ltd ('IDL') and Old Bushmills Ltd ('Bushmills') are wholly owned subsidiaries of Irish Distillers Plc and both companies engage in distilling, blending and distribution of whiskey in the State. Celtic Glass Ltd, an Irish registered company is engaged in design, production and sale of glassware products. Lough Derg Handcrafts Ltd, an Irish registered company is engaged in the production and sale of wooden finished polyester resin models. LLEDO Plc is an English company engaged in the production and sale of miniature models of vintage motor vehicles and Tobler Suchard Ltd, an English company is engaged in the manufacture and sale of chocolate products, including liqueur chocolates. Under the terms of each of the notified agreements IDL or Bushmills, as the case may be, grant non-exclusive licences to use certain trademarks and designs relating to whiskies brewed by IDL or Bushmills. Five out of the six agreements contained a clause whereunder the user of the trademark recognised the title of IDL/Bushmills to the trademark and undertook not to challenge or to claim any interest in the relevant trademark. All agreements provided that the grant of the licence to the user was subject to the products exhibiting the trademark and conforming to a standard of quality satisfactory to IDL/Bushmills and further that there will appear on the products an acknowledgement that ownership of the copyright and the trademark is vested in IDL/Bushmills. The agreements also provided that if the standard of any of the products do not meet with the requirements of IDL/Bushmills those products shall be withdrawn from distribution.

Submissions: Irish Distillers Group Plc (the holding company of IDL and Bushmills) submitted that the notified agreements do not offend against section 4(1) of the Competition Act because:

(i) the agreements are not with competing manufacturers;

(ii) the agreements do not restrict the users from normal commercial activity but only regulate the use of the IDL/Bushmill property;

(iii) IDL/Bushmills acquire no direct economic advantage from the notified agreements (with the exception of royalties with respect to the Celtic Glass Ltd agreements) whereas the users derive economic benefits by associating their products with the high quality standards associated with the IDL/Bushmill brand names.

6.1 **Decided by the Authority:** In issuing a certificate under section 4(4) of the Competition Act 1991 in respect of the notified agreements that:

(1) Each of the parties to the notified agreement are 'undertakings' within the meaning of the Competition Act 1991 and the notified agreements are agreements between undertakings which have effect within the State.

(2) Under the terms of the notified agreements IDL/Bushmills do not place restrictions on the production or marketing by the users of other products similar to those covered by the licences but only place restrictions on those products exhibiting the licensed trademark and the object of such restriction is to protect the quality and image of the IDL/Bushmill products sold under that trademark. Such restrictions do not represent a breach of section 4(1) of the Competition Act.

(3) The provision in five of the six notified agreements that the user will not challenge IDL/Bushmills title to the relevant trademark does not constitute a breach of section 4(1) of the Competition Act because ownership of the trademark only gives the holder an exclusive right to sell products under that name and does not restrict other parties from selling the product in question under a different trademark.

Decisions referred to:
EC Commission Decision — Campari [1978] OJ L70/69, [1978] 2 CMLR 397
EC Commission Decision — Moosehead Whitbread [1990] OJ L100/32, [1991] 4 CMLR 391

Competition Authority Decision of 7 February 1994 relating to a proceeding under section 4 of the Competition Act 1991
Notification Nos. CA/972/92E — Irish Distillers Ltd/Celtic Glass Ltd; CA/973/92E — Irish Distillers Ltd/Celtic Glass Ltd; CA/974/92E — Old Bushmills Distiller Ltd/Celtic Glass Ltd; CA/979/92E — Irish Distillers Ltd/Lough Derg Handcrafts Ltd; CA/981/92E — Irish Distillers Ltd/LLEDO plc; CA/978/92E — Irish Distillers Ltd/Tobler Suchard Ltd

Introduction

1. Notification was made by Irish Distillers Group plc (IDG) on 30 September 1992 with a request for certificates under section 4(4) of the Competition Act 1991 or in the event of a refusal by the Competition Authority to issue certificates, a request for licences under section 4(2) in respect of 6 trade mark/design usership agreements between companies within the IDG group and 4 other parties.

The Facts

(a) **Subject of Notification**

2. The notification concerns trade mark/design usership agreements, whereby companies within the group, the owners of the trademarks and designs relating to their whiskey brands, have granted non-exclusive licences to a number of companies to use the trade marks or designs in connection with the manufacture and marketing of other products within the State.

(b) **The Parties involved**

3. Irish Distillers Group plc is a wholly owned subsidiary of Groupe Pernod SA and is comprised of companies engaged in the distilling of whiskey and other spirits and in the distribution of spirits, wines and other beverages. Other businesses include grocery wholesale. IDG's annual turnover in 1992 was £302m, of which turnover within the State was £200m. Its wholly owned subsidiary Irish Distillers Ltd (IDL), which is party to 5 of the Usership

agreements, is engaged in the distilling, blending and distribution of whiskey including its main brands, Jameson, Powers and Paddy and at the time the agreements were made, Tullamore Dew. Another IDG subsidiary, Old Bushmills Distillery Co. Ltd, Bushmills, Co. Antrim which distils the Bushmills and Black Bush brands of whiskey in Northern Ireland and markets them within the State, is party to the other usership agreements. **6.1**

4. The user parties to each of the six notified agreements are as follows:

(i) Celtic Glass Ltd, Stillorgan, Co Dublin which is engaged in the design, production and sale of glassware products. Three of the six notified agreements are between IDL/OBD and Celtic Glass Ltd.

(ii) Lough Derg Handcrafts Ltd, Sandymount, Dublin which is engaged in the production and sale of wooden finish polyester resin models.

(iii) LLEDO plc, Middlesex, England which is engaged in the design, production and sale of miniature models of vintage motor vehicles.

(iv) Tobler Suchard Ltd, Bedfordshire, England which is engaged in the manufacture, production and sale of chocolate products, including liqueur chocolates.

(c) **The Notified Agreements**

Irish Distillers Ltd/Celtic Glass Ltd

5. The Usership Agreement made on 19 August 1991 provides for the grant of a non-exclusive licence by IDL, the owner, to Celtic Glass Ltd, the user, to use certain trademarks and designs relating to the Jameson, Powers, Paddy and Crested Ten brands in connection with the manufacture in Ireland and sale within Ireland, UK, Germany, France, Italy and USA (the Territory) of glassware products viz. tumblers, tankards etc. (the Products). The main provisions of the agreement are as follows:

(a) Under clause 1 the user recognises that all right, title and interest in and the exclusive right to use the Designs and Trade Marks is vested in IDL and under clause 2 the user agrees 'not to challenge the validity of, or IDL's ownership of the Designs, Trade Mark or any copyright in the representation thereof'.

(b) Under clause 3 the user agrees 'It shall not claim or acquire the ownership of, a licence to, or any right itself to licence the Designs, Trade Marks or any brand name, trade mark, trade name, patent, emblem, design, copyright, device, label, model or other industrial or intellectual property right of IDL, or any company related to it. . . .

(c) Under clause 4 IDL grants to User a non-exclusive licence to reproduce and use the Designs for the sole purpose of the manufacture of the products in Ireland and sale of the Products in the Territory, under the supervision and control of IDL and in a manner and form which shall be approved in writing by IDL and such a grant of licence shall be subject to the conditions that:

> (i) the Products shall conform to such standard of quality, design, workmanship and materials (hereinafter called the 'Standard of Quality') as IDL may from time to time prescribe. . . .
>
> (ii) the Designs will include in the main line of vision . . . an acknowledgement that ownership of the copyright is vested in IDL, such acknowledgement to be in the following form. . . .

(d) Clause 10 provides that 'In the event that any Products shall at any time fail to meet the Standard of Quality, user shall immediately withdraw same from distribution and sale. . . . In the event that IDL determines that the Products or any part thereof fails to meet the Standard of Quality it may terminate this agreement by written notice to user and User shall cease any use of and to use the Designs within 30 days of such notice'.

6.1 (e) Under clause 13 the agreement '. . . shall continue in full force and effect until terminated by either party by three months' notice in writing to the other, with or without cause'.

(f) Clause 15 provides that IDL shall have the right to terminate the Agreement forthwith by giving written notice to the user if the user commits a material breach of the agreement, or if there is a change in control of user or if user enters into liquidation, receivership etc.

(g) Clause 5 provides for certain purchases of the Products each year by IDL in such quantities as may be mutually agreed and also provides for payment of royalties by Celtic Glass to IDL.

Irish Distillers Ltd/Celtic Glass Ltd

6. The usership agreement dated 23 July 1992 involved the grant of a non-exclusive licence to Celtic Glass to reproduce and use the designs relating to the 'Tullamore Dew' brand for the sole purpose of the manufacture of its glassware products in Ireland and sale in the Territory. The agreement is in similar terms to that dated 19 August 1991 at para. 5 above.

Old Bushmills Distillery Ltd/Celtic Glass Ltd

7. The usership agreement made on 26 August 1991 between The Old Bushmills Distillery Company Ltd, Bushmills, Co Antrim and Celtic Glass involves the grant of a non-exclusive licence to Celtic Glass to use the trade marks and designs relating to the Black Bush and Bushmills Brands in the production and sale of glassware. The agreement is in similar terms to that dated 19 August 1991 at para. 5 above.

Irish Distillers Ltd/Lough Derg Handcrafts Ltd

8. The Usership Agreement notified was made on 21 April 1986 and provides for the grant of a non-exclusive licence by IDL, the owner, to Lough Derg Handcrafts Ltd, to reproduce a particular IDL Design/Concept involving a model of a cooper using a hammer and a drive to position hoops around a cask. The original model is situated in the Irish Whiskey Corner, Bow Street, Dublin. Under the agreement Lough Derg Handcrafts are also allowed to use the 'Jameson' Trade Mark in association with the models it produces for sale including models other than the IDL designed cooper. The agreement is in similar terms to that between IDL and Celtic Glass except that there are no provisions for the purchase of the product by IDL and no royalties are payable.

Irish Distillers Ltd/LLEDO plc

9. The Usership Agreement notified was made on 30 December 1991 and provides for the grant of a non-exclusive licence by IDL, the owner, to LLEDO plc, the user, to use certain IDL Designs associated with 'Jameson' Whiskey in the production of miniature model reproductions of the Model 'T' Ford Van which it produces for sale. In, addition the Agreement also allows LLEDO to use the Design in connection with the manufacture of that model van in England and in connection with the sale of the model van on a worldwide basis. The agreement is in similar terms to that between IDL and Celtic Glass at para. 5 above except that there are no provisions for the purchase of the product by IDL nor are royalties payable.

Irish Distillers Ltd/Tobler Suchard

10. The Usership Agreement notified is dated 1 October 1987 and provides for the grant of a non-exclusive licence by IDL, the owner, to Tobler Suchard, the user, to use the 'Jameson' Trade Marks to identify and promote the Goods (liqueur chocolates) that the user will manufacture and/or sell in the Territory (the UK, Channel Islands and the State). The agreement is in similar terms to the other agreements above except that 12 months notice in writing is required to enable either party to terminate it voluntarily and there is no provision for royalty payments.

The Product and the Market

11. The property that is the subject of the Usership Agreement is the property right attaching to IDL's or OBD's trade marks or designs. These are the only products being 'handed over' under the agreements by the owners to another person to use.

12. Under the usership agreement a non-exclusive licence to use designs/trade marks has been granted to four users. The users are not engaged in the marketing of Irish whiskey but in totally separate products of which only one, liqueur chocolates, may contain whiskey as an ingredient. The users are not therefore in competition with IDL or OBD or with one another. The usership agreements relate to the use of IDL/OBD designs and trade marks in the manufacture and marketing of glasses, models or liqueur chocolates. By the use of the designs and trademarks the users seek to enhance the marketability and range of their own products through familiar whiskey brand names but the markets in which they operate are the separate markets for glasses, model figures/cars and chocolates. In essence therefore the Authority considers that, while the licensing of IDL/OBD designs or trade marks are the subject of the agreements, the relevant markets, where competition issues might arise, are the separate markets for the particular products manufactured by the users. Since the Competition Act 1991 only relates to competition within the State or part of the State, the Authority is therefore only concerned with the market for these products within the State.

(d) Submissions of the Parties

13. Irish Distillers Group plc maintain that the six notified agreements do not have as their object or effect the prevention, restriction or distortion of competition in the State or in any part of the State for the following reasons:

(a) The agreements are not with competing manufacturers and the parties involved are not connected in any respect.

(b) The agreements relate solely to the use of IDL/OBD property and do not restrict the users involved from normal commercial conduct or activity other than in the use of IDL/OBD property.

(c) The users derive economic benefits from identifying their products with the high quality standards associated by consumers with the IDL/OBD brand names and images. The requirement in the agreements to indicate that the Trade Marks/Designs are used under licence further reinforces this association in the minds of consumers.

(d) The association of the products of small producers such as the users involved in the notifications with international brand names such as IDL/OBD products, enables the users to build up market share more quickly and to compete more effectively in the market place than might otherwise be the case without the association.

(e) There is no direct economic advantage to IDL accruing from the notified agreements (with the exception of the 3 agreements with Celtic Glass where IDL/OBD derive royalties).

(f) the use of the IDL/OBD brand names on the products of the users is complimentary to the product's image and secures its attractiveness to consumers.

(g) The notified agreements are indispensable if the users involved wish to associate their particular products with IDL/OBD trade marks and designs.

EC Position on Trade Mark Licences

14. Very few cases involving trade mark licences have been the subject of an EU Commission decision and the decisions recorded related to cases which also involved the manufacture and sale by the licensees of products similar to those produced by the original owners of the trade marks. Restrictions in the Campari[1] licensing agreement which were found not to come within the prohibition of Article 85(1) included requirements relating to the suitability of plant, the quality of the product and the purchase of certain secret raw materials

1. Campari OJ 1978, L70/69

6.1 for incorporation in the final product. In the Moosehead/Whitbread[2] decision, which related to an exclusive licence to Whitbread to produce and market Moosehead beer within the UK, the EU Commission decided that certain obligations on the licensee to maintain certain qualitative standards and the trade mark no challenge clause did not fall within Article 85(1). The aspects of these Agreements deemed by the Commission to fall within Article 85(1)—but capable of exemption under Article 85(3)—were the exclusivity of the trade mark licence and the prohibition on the licensee both in relation to active sales outside the UK and on the production and marketing of other Canadian beers.

Assessment

15. Section 4(1) of the Competition Act 1991 prohibits and renders void all agreements between undertakings, decisions by associations of undertakings and concerted practices which have as their object or effect the prevention, restriction or distortion of competition in trade in any goods or services in the State, or in any part of the State.

The Undertakings

16. Section 3(1) of the Competition Act defines an undertaking as 'a person being an individual, a body corporate or an unincorporated body or persons engaged for gain in the production, supply or distribution of goods or the provision of a service'. Irish Distillers Group and its subsidiaries, Irish Distillers Ltd and Old Bushmills Distillery Ltd, and the four user companies, Celtic Glass Ltd, Lough Derg Handcrafts Ltd, LLEDO plc and Tobler Suchard are all engaged for gain in the production, supply and distribution of goods and are therefore undertakings. The notified agreements are agreements between undertakings. The agreements have effect within the State.

Applicability of section 4(1)

17. Designs and trade marks are property rights which are normally used by the owner for ready market recognition, as a guarantee of quality and for publicity/advertising purposes in relation to the marketing of the product. The design/trade mark is often synonymous with the product itself and can represent a very considerable investment by its promoter in the development of the brand image and of its recognition and acceptance by the general consumer public. In the case of many branded consumer products, including beverages such as whiskey, the promotion of the brand name can be one of the main marketing tools in the promotion of the product. In effect a trade mark, particularly one related to a widely sold consumer product, can represent a very valuable asset with the rights to it strongly preserved by its owner.

18. The owner of a trade mark is normally under no obligation to permit its use by another trader. He may allow its use by another trader whether by way of a patent licensing agreement which would involve the production of a product similar or identical to his branded product or by way of a usership agreement to a manufacturer of a product which need not bear a particular relationship to the branded product. The latter situation applies to the usership agreements in this instance. The usership agreements state that IDL's (or OBD's) primary benefit from the users' use of the designs or trade marks will be an indirect benefit from the advertisement of IDL's products and that it is of the utmost importance to IDL that the quality image of its products be protected.

19. The Trade Mark/Design usership agreement between Irish Distillers Ltd or Old Bushmills Distillery Ltd and the four users are not exclusive licences nor do they contain any prohibition on the production or marketing by the licensees of other products similar to those covered by the licences. The obligations on the licensees from the usership agreements only apply to the products of the licensees which carry the IDL/OBD trade marks. Since the basic products involved i.e. glasses, models or liqueur chocolates are basically non-whiskey prod-

2. Moosehead/Whitbread 90/186/EEC OJ L100, 20.4.90, p. 32/37.

ucts, the licensee is free to produce and market them without any licence restrictions as long as it does not carry or is not marketed under the IDL/OBD trade marks or designs. **6.1**

20. Clause 2 in five of the notified agreements (excepting the agreement with Tobler Suchard) requires the Trade Mark user not to challenge the validity of IDL/OBD's ownership of the Trade Mark/Design or the copyright in any representation thereof. The notifying party has explained that IDL/OBD are the exclusive owners of the Trade Marks/Designs set out in the relevant Usership Agreements and that expenditure is incurred in promoting the quality and image associated with its products. In this regard IDG has a policy which is aimed at protecting its Trade Marks and it does not permit the use of its Trade Marks or Designs without written agreement. In entering into such Trade Mark Usership Agreements the users are required to conform with certain criteria and also to preserve the integrity of the relevant Trade Mark. IDL/OBD, in entering into such Trademark Usership Agreement provides an opportunity for the user to derive economic benefit from the use of the relevant Mark in association with a particular product. In consideration of IDL entering into such arrangements IDL/OBD requires its Marks to be protected and the validity to be preserved. In this respect IDL/OBD requires the relevant user to acknowledge its ownership of the relevant Mark and not to undermine or challenge the Mark.

21. In relation to a trade mark non-challenge clause the EU Commission in the Moosehead/Whitbread case stated:

> A clause in an exclusive trademark licence agreement obliging the licensee not to challenge the ownership of a trademark . . . does not constitute a restriction on competition within the meaning of Article 85(1). Whether or not the licensor or licensee has the ownership of the trademark, the use of it by any other party is prevented in any event, and competition would thus not be affected.
>
> The validity of a trademark may be contested on any ground under national law, and in particular on the grounds that it is generic or descriptive in nature. In such an event, should the challenge be upheld, the trade mark may fall (in) the public domain and may thereafter be used without restriction by the licensee and any other party.
>
> Such a (non-challenge) clause may constitute a restriction of competition within the meaning of Article 85(1), because it may contribute to the maintenance of a trademark that would be an unjustified barrier to entry into a given market.
>
> Moreover, in order for any restriction to fall under Article 85(1) it must be appreciable. The ownership of a trademark only gives the holder the exclusive right to sell products under that name. Other parties are free to sell the product in question under a different trademark or treatment. Only where the use of a well-known trademark would be an important advantage to any company entering or competing in any given market and the absence of which therefore constitutes a significant barrier to entry, would this clause which impedes the licensee to challenge the validity of the trademark, constitute an appreciable restriction of competition within the meaning of Article 85(1).

22. As indicated in paragraph 12 the relevant markets affected by the usership agreement are those for the particular products of the licensees, i.e. glasses, model figures and cars and liqueur chocolates. All these products are being freely marketed without IDL/OBD designs and brand names and the Authority therefore takes the view that the IDL/OBD designs or trade marks could not provide any significant barrier to entry to those markets. In these circumstances the Authority does not consider the 'no challenge' clauses in the agreements as offending against section 4(1) of the Competition Act.

23. Each of the usership agreements also provide, that in the event that IDL (or OBD) determines that the product fails to meet a particular standard of quality it may terminate the agreement by written notice to the user and that the user shall cease its use of the designs or trade marks within 30 days of such notice. In view of the importance to IDL/OBD of the quality

6.1 image of their products associated with the promotion of their trade marks at very considerable cost to IDL/OBD the Authority could accept that IDL/OBD are entitled to protect the value of their trade marks by measures to ensure that they are not associated with an inferior product. The Authority does not regard the withdrawal of a licence in such circumstances as offending against section 4(1).

The Decision

24. In the Authority's opinion, Irish Distillers Group plc, Irish Distillers Ltd and Old Bushmills Distillery Co Ltd and the users, Celtic Glass Ltd, Lough Derg Handcrafts Ltd, LLEDO plc and Tobler Suchard Ltd are undertakings and the notified usership agreements between these parties are agreements between undertakings.

25. The Authority considers that the notified agreements do not have the object or effect of preventing, restricting or distorting competition in trade in any goods or services in the State or any part of the State. The Authority therefore considers that the notified agreements between Irish Distillers Ltd and Celtic Glass Ltd, Lough Derg Handcrafts Ltd, LLEDO plc and Tobler Suchard, and between Old Bushmills Distillery Co. Ltd and Celtic Glass Ltd do not offend against section 4(1) of the Competition Act 1991.

The Certificate

26. The Competition Authority has issued the following certificate:

> The Competition Authority certifies that in its opinion, on the basis of the facts in its possession, the agreements set out below in relation to design/trade mark usership notified under section 7 on 30 September 1992 do not offend against section 4(1) of the Competition Act 1991:

(i) Irish Distillers Ltd/Celtic Class Ltd — CA/972/92E

(ii) Irish Distillers Ltd/Celtic Glass Ltd — CA/973/92E

(iii) Old Bushmills Distillery Ltd/Celtic Glass Ltd — CA/974/92E

(iv) Irish Distillers Ltd/Lough Derg Handcrafts Ltd — CA/979/92E

(v) Irish Distillers Ltd/LLEDO plc — CA/981/92E

(vi) Irish Distillers Ltd/Tobler Suchard Ltd — CA/978/92E

For the Competition Authority

Des Wall
Member

7 February 1994

Competition Authority Decision No. 287, Irish Distillers Ltd/Peadar O'Lionaird and Others: 25 February 1994, Notification Nos. CA/970/92E, CA/975/92E, CA/980/92E, CA/971/92E 6.2

Non-exclusive trademark usership agreements – Restrictive pledge clause – Whether no challenge clause contributes to an unjustified barrier to market entry – whether termination for quality reason is a justified entitlement for licensor – whether licensee's covenant not to use designation 'Irish Whiskey' after termination will have perceptible effect – Competition Act 1991 (No. 24), sections 3, 4 and 7

Facts: On 30 September 1992 notification was made to the Authority by Irish Distillers Group plc of various non-exclusive licence agreements between Irish Distillers Ltd and four other parties with a request for certificates under section 4(4) of the Competition Act 1991 or, failing that, licences under section 4(2). Irish Distillers Ltd ('IDL') a wholly owned subsidiary of Irish Distillers Group plc, is engaged in the business of distilling, marketing and distributing spirits in markets including the State. The four counter-parties to the notified agreements, Mr Ó Lionaird, Mr Thompson, Mileeven Ltd and Lakeshore Foods Ltd manufacture various food products using IDL products. Under the terms of the notified agreements IDL grant a non-exclusive licence to each of the users to use a trademark of a particular IDL product in connection with the manufacture and marketing of the users food product. Under the terms of the notified agreements each of the parties acknowledges IDL's title in the particular trademark and covenant not to challenge, claim or acquire ownership or otherwise of the particular trademark. Each of the users further covenants that they will produce their product to a standard of quality acceptable to IDL, that the labelling of the product shall contain an acknowledgement that the IDL trademark is used under licence and that in the event of the user failing to meet IDL standard of quality the user shall immediately withdraw the product from the market and IDL may terminate the agreement by written notice to the user who shall upon receipt of such notice cease in its use of the relevant trademark and the designation of Irish whiskey within 30 days.

Submissions: Irish Distillers Group plc (Parent company of IDL and Bushmills) submitted that the notified agreements do not offend against section 4(1) of the Competition Act because:

(i) the agreements are not with competing manufacturers;

(ii) the agreements do not restrict the users from normal commercial activity but only regulate the use of the IDL/Bushmill property;

(iii) IDL/Bushmills acquire no direct economic advantage from the notified agreements (with the exception of royalties with respect to the Celtic Glass Ltd agreement) whereas the users derive economic benefits by associating their products with the high quality standards associated with the IDL/Bushmill brand names.

Decided by the Authority: In issuing a certificate under section 4(4) of the Competition Act 1991 that:

(1) Each of the parties to the notified agreements are 'undertakings' within the meaning of section 3(1) of the Competition Act 1991 and the notified agreements are agreements between undertakings having effect within the State.

6.2 (2) The notified agreements do not confer exclusive licences to the licensees nor do they contain, while in force, any prohibition on the production or marketing by the licensees of other products similar to those covered by the licences and the obligations on the licensees arising out of the notified agreement only apply to those products of the licensees which carry the IDL trademark and therefore the notified agreements do not offend against section 4(1) of the Competition Act.

(3) The covenant by the licensees not to challenge IDL's title in, or claim for themselves any title in the relevant trademark does not offend against section 4(1) of the Competition Act in that parties who do not have ownership of the trademark are still free to sell the product in question under a different trademark or treatment.

(4) The requirement by IDL that on termination of any agreement due to the product failing to meet IDL standards that the licensee cease to use the non-trademark generic 'Irish Whiskey' on its products does not offend against section 4(1) of the Competition Act. The licensees would initially gain substantial benefit in the promotion and marketing of their product because of the public association of the product with the IDL trademark and there will be a risk that this association would continue even after the IDL trademark was removed. The object of this provision therefore was to protect the image of the IDL products and not to prevent, restrict or distort competition.

Decisions referred to:
EC Commission Decision—Campari [1978] OJ L70/69, [1978] 2 CMLR 397
EC Commission Decision—Moosehead Whitbread [1990] OJ L100/32, [1991] 4 CMLR 391

Competition Authority Decision of 25 February 1994 relating to a proceeding under section 4 of the Competition Act 1991
Notifications Nos. CA/970/92E—Irish Distillers Ltd/Peadar O'Lionaird; CA/975/92E —Irish Distillers Ltd/Phil Thompson; CA/980/92E—Irish Distillers Ltd/Mileeven Ltd; CA/971/92E—Irish Distillers Ltd/Lakeshore Foods Ltd

Introduction

1. Notification was made by Irish Distillers Group plc (IDG) on 30 September 1992 with a request for certificates under section 4(4) of the Competition Act 1991 or in the event of a refusal by the Competition Authority to issue certificates, a request for licences under section 4(2) in respect of 4 Trade Mark Usership agreements between Irish Distillers Ltd and 4 other parties.

The Facts

(a) **Subject of Notification**

2. The notification concerns trade mark usership agreements, whereby Irish Distillers Ltd, the owner of the trade marks relating to its whiskey brands, has granted non-exclusive licences to four parties to use the trade marks in connection with the manufacture and marketing of certain food products within the State.

(b) **The parties involved**

3. Irish Distillers Ltd (IDL) is a wholly owned subsidiary of Irish Distillers Group plc (IDG) which in turn is a wholly owned subsidiary of Groupe Pernod SA. IDG is comprised of companies engaged in the distilling of whiskey and other spirits and in the distribution of spirits, wines and other beverages. Other businesses include grocery wholesale. IDG's annual turnover

in 1992 was £302m, of which turnover within the State was £200m. IDL is engaged in the distilling, blending and distribution of whiskey including its main brands, Jameson, Powers and Paddy. 6.2

4. The user Parties to each of the notified agreements are as follows:

(i) Mr Peadar Ó Lionaird, Macroom, Co Cork who is a producer of preserves and is engaged in the manufacture, promotion and sale of Irish Whiskey marmalade.

(ii) Mr Phil Thompson, Carrigaline, Co Cork who is also a producer of preserves and like Mr Ó Lionaird is engaged in the manufacture, promotion and sale of Irish Whiskey Marmalade.

(iii) Mileeven Ltd, Piltown, Co Kilkenny which is a producer of preserves and honey products and is engaged in the manufacture, promotion and sale of Irish Whiskey Honey.

(iv) Lakeshore Foods Ltd, Nenagh, Co Tipperary, which is engaged in the manufacture, production and sale of prepared mustards.

(c) **The Notified Agreements**

Irish Distillers Ltd/Peadar Ó Lionaird

5. The Usership Agreement notified was made on 18 May 1990 and provides for the grant of a non-exclusive licence by IDL, the owner, to Peadar O'Lionaird, the user, to use the Jameson trademarks in connection with the manufacture and marketing of Irish Whiskey marmalade in Ireland. The main provisions of the agreement are as follows:

(a) Under clause 1 the user recognises that all right, title and interest in and the exclusive right to use the trademark is vested in IDL and under clause 2 the user agrees 'not to challenge the validity of, or IDL's ownership of the Trade Mark or copyright in the presentation thereof'.

(b) Under clause 3 the user agrees 'It shall not claim or acquire the ownership of, a licence to, or any right itself to licence the Trade Mark or any brand name, trade mark, trade name, patent, emblem, design, copyright, device, label, model or other industrial or intellectual property right of IDL, or any company related to it. . . .'

(c) Under clause 4 IDL grants to the user a non-exclusive licence to reproduce and use the trade marks in the Territory (Ireland) for the sole purpose of the manufacture and sale of the Product in a manner and form which shall be approved in writing by IDL subject to the following conditions:

(i) User shall use Jameson Whiskey exclusively for production of the product;
(ii) The product will conform to such standard of quality, design etc as IDL may prescribe (the Standard of Quality)
(iii) The labelling of the product shall contain an acknowledgement that the Jameson mark of IDL is used under licence.

(d) Clause 9 provides that 'In the event that any product shall at any time fail to meet the Standard of Quality, user shall immediately withdraw same. In the event that IDL determines that the product fails to meet the Standard of Quality it may terminate this agreement by written notice to user and user shall cease its use of the Trade Mark and the designation Irish Whiskey within 30 days of such notice'.

(e) Clause 14 provides that IDL shall have the right to terminate the Agreement forthwith by giving written notice to the user if the user commits a material breach of the agreement, or if there is a change in control of user or if user enters into liquidation, receivership etc.

(f) Under clause 12 the agreement '. . . shall continue in effect until terminated by either party by three months' notice in writing expiring on any date'.

There is no provision in the agreement for the payment of royalties.

Irish Distillers Ltd/Phil Thompson

6. The Usership Agreement notified is dated 26 April 1989 and provides for the grant of a

6.2 non-exclusive licence by IDL, the owner, to Phil Thompson, the user, to use 'Paddy' Trade Marks in connection with the manufacture and marketing of Irish Whiskey marmalade within Ireland. The agreement is similar to that between IDL and Peadar Ó Lionaird except for a requirement on Phil Thompson to use Paddy Whiskey exclusively in the product.

Irish Distillers Ltd/Mileeven Ltd

7. The Usership agreement notified is dated 13 September 1990 and provides for the grant of a non-exclusive licence by IDL, the owner, to Mileeven Ltd, the User, to use the 'Jameson' Trade Marks in connection with the manufacture and marketing of Irish Whiskey Honey in Ireland and elsewhere. The agreement is in similar terms to that made between IDL and Peadar Ó Lionaird.

Irish Distillers Ltd/Lakeshore Foods Ltd

8. The Usership Agreement notified is dated 18 December 1990 and provides for the grant of a non-exclusive licence by IDL, the owner, to Lakeshore Foods Ltd, the user, to use the 'Jameson' Trade Mark in connection with the manufacture of mustards in the State and marketing mustards in Ireland, UK, Canada and USA. The agreement is in similar terms to that between IDL and Peadar Ó Lionaird.

The Product and the Market

9. The property that is the subject of the Usership Agreements is the property right attaching to IDL's Jameson and Paddy trade marks. These are the only products being 'handed over' under the agreements by the owners to other persons to use.

10. Under the usership agreement a non-exclusive licence to use trade marks has been granted to 4 users. The users are not engaged in the marketing of Irish whiskey but in products which contain whiskey as a minor ingredient. The users are not, therefore, in competition with IDL. The usership agreements relate to the use of IDL trade marks in the manufacture and marketing of food products containing Irish whiskey. By the use of the trademarks the users seek to enhance the marketability and range of their own products by the use of familiar whiskey brand names but the markets in which they operate could be regarded as small specialist sub-sectors of overall markets for preserves or mustard aimed primarily at the tourism trade. In essence therefore the Authority considers that, while the licensing of Jameson and Paddy trade marks is the subject of the agreement, the relevant markets, where competition issues might arise, are the tourism-related specialist segments of the markets for preserves and mustard.

(d) **Submissions of the parties**

11. Irish Distillers Group plc maintain that the notified agreements do not have as their object or effect the prevention, restriction or distortion of competition in the State or in any part of the State for the following reasons:

(a) The agreements are not with competing manufacturers and the parties involved are not connected in any respect;

(b) the agreements relate solely to the use of IDL property and do not restrict the users involved from normal commercial conduct or activity other than in the use of IDL property;

(c) the users derive economic benefits from identifying their products with the high quality standards associated by consumers with the IDL brand names and images. The requirement in the agreements to indicate that the Trade Marks are used under licence further reinforces this association in the minds of consumers;

(d) the association of the products of small producers such the users involved in the notification with international brand names such as IDL products, enables the user to build up market share more quickly and to compete more effectively in the market place than might otherwise be the case without the association;

(e) there is no direct economic advantage to IDL accruing from the notified agreements;

(f) the use of the IDL brand names on the products of the users is complimentary to the product's image and secures its attractiveness to consumers; **6.2**

(g) the notified agreements are indispensable if the users involved wish to associate their particular products with IDL trade marks and designs.

EU Position on Trade Mark Licences

12. Very few cases involving trade mark licences have been the subject of an EU Commission decision and the decisions recorded related to cases which also involved the manufacture and sale by the licensees of products similar to those produced by the original owners of the trade marks. Restrictions in the Campari[1] licensing agreement which were found not to come within the prohibition of Article 85(1) included requirements relating to the suitability of plant, the quality of the product and the purchase of certain secret raw materials for incorporation in the final product. In the Moosehead/Whitbread[2] decision, which related to an exclusive licence to Whitbread to produce and market Moosehead beer within the UK, the EU Commission decided that certain obligations on the licensee to maintain certain qualitative standards and the trade mark no challenge clause did not fall within Article 85(1). The aspects of these Agreements deemed by the Commission to fall within Article 85(1)—but capable of exemption under Article 85(3)—were the exclusivity of the trade mark licence and the prohibition on the licensee both in relation to active sales outside the UK and on the production and marketing of other Canadian beers.

Assessment

13. Section 4(1) of the Competition Act 1991 prohibits and renders void all agreements between undertakings, decisions by associations of undertakings and concerted practices which have as their object or effect the prevention, restriction or distortion of competition in trade in any goods or services in the State, or in any part of the State.

The Undertakings

14. Section 3(1) of the Competition Act defines an undertaking as 'a person being an individual, a body corporate or an unincorporated body of persons engaged for gain in the production, supply or distribution of goods or the provision of a service'. Irish Distillers Group and its subsidiary Irish Distillers Ltd and the four user parties, Peadar Ó Lionaird, Phil Thompson, Mileeven Ltd and Lakeshore Foods Ltd are all engaged for gain in the production, supply and distribution of goods within the State and are therefore undertakings. The notified agreements are therefore agreements between undertakings. The agreements have effect within the State.

Applicability of section 4(1)

15. Designs and trade marks are property rights which are normally used by the owner for ready market recognition, as a guarantee of quality and for publicity/advertising purposes in relation to the marketing of the product. The design/trade mark is often synonymous with the product itself and can represent a very considerable investment by its promoter in the development of the brand image and of its recognition and acceptance by the general consumer public. In the case of many branded consumer products, including beverages such as whiskey, the promotion of the brand name can be one of the main marketing tools in the promotion of the product. In effect a trade mark, particularly one related to a widely sold consumer product, can represent a very valuable asset with the rights to it strongly preserved by its owner.

16. The owner of a trade mark is normally under no obligation to permit its use by another trader. He may allow its use by another trader whether by way of a patent licensing agreement which would involve the production of a product similar or identical to his branded product or

1. Campari OJ 1978, L70/69.
2. Moosehead/Whitbread 90/186/EEC OJ L100, 20.4.90, p. 32/37.

6.2 by way of a usership agreement to a manufacturer of a product which need not bear a particular relationship to the branded product. The latter situation applies to the usership agreements in this instance. The usership agreements state that IDL's primary benefit from the users' use of the designs or trade marks will be an indirect benefit from the advertisement of IDL's products and that it is of the utmost importance to IDL that the quality image of its products be protected.

17. The Trade Mark/Design usership agreements between Irish Distillers Ltd and the 4 users are not exclusive licences nor do they contain, while in force, any prohibition on the production or marketing by the licensees of other products similar to those covered by the licences. The obligations on the licensees from the usership agreements only apply to the products of the licensees which carry the IDL trade marks. Since the basic products involved i.e. marmalade, honey or mustard are basically non-whiskey products, the licensee is free to produce and market them, even if whiskey is an added ingredient, without any licence restrictions as long as it does not carry or is not marketed under the IDL trade marks or designs.

18. Under clause 2 in the agreement with Peadar Ó Lionaird an obligation is imposed on the user not to challenge the validity of IDL's ownership of the Trade Mark. A similar obligation appears in the other 3 agreements notified. The notifying party has explained that IDL is the exclusive owner of the Trade Marks/Designs set out in the relevant Usership Agreements and that expenditure is incurred in promoting the quality and image associated with its products. In this regard IDL has a policy which is aimed at protecting its Trade Marks and it does not permit the use of its Trade Marks or Designs without written agreement. In entering into such Trade Mark Usership Agreements the users are required to conform with certain criteria and also to preserve the integrity of the relevant Trade Mark. IDL, in entering into such Trademark Usership Agreement provides an opportunity for the user to derive economic benefit from the use of the relevant Mark in association with a particular product. In consideration of IDL entering into such arrangements IDL requires its Marks to be protected and the validity to be preserved. In this respect IDL requires the relevant user to acknowledge its ownership of the relevant Mark and not to undermine or challenge the Mark.

19. In relation to a trademark non-challenge clause the EU Commission in the Moosehead/Whitbread case stated:

> A clause in an exclusive trademark licence agreement obliging the licensee not to challenge the ownership of a trademark . . . does not constitute a restriction on competition within the meaning of Article 85(1). Whether or not the licensor or licensee has the ownership of the trademark, the use of it by any other party is prevented in any event, and competition would thus not be affected.
>
> The validity of a trademark may be contested on any ground under national law, and in particular on the grounds that it is generic or descriptive in nature. In such an event, should the challenge be upheld, the trade mark may fall (in) the public domain and may thereafter be used without restriction by the licensee and any other party.
>
> Such a (non-challenge) clause may constitute a restriction of competition within the meaning of Article 85(1), because it may contribute to the maintenance of a trademark that would be an unjustified barrier to entry into a given market.
>
> Moreover in order for any restriction to fall under Article 85(1) it must be appreciable. The ownership of a trademark only gives the holder the exclusive right to sell products under that name. Other parties are free to sell the product in question under a different trademark or treatment. Only where the use of a well-known trademark would be an important advantage to any company entering or competing in any given market and the absence of which therefore constitutes a significant barrier to entry, would this clause which impedes the licensee to challenge the validity of the trademark, constitute an appreciable restriction of competition within the meaning of Article 85(1).

20. As indicated in paragraph 10 the relevant markets affected by the usership agreements

are those for the particular products of the licensees, i.e. small specialised tourism-related segments of the markets for marmalade, honey or mustard, all containing whiskey as a minor ingredient. These products, whether or not they contain Irish whiskey as an ingredient, may be freely marketed without an IDL brand name and the Authority therefore takes the view that the IDL trade marks could not provide any significant barrier to entry to those markets. **6.2**

21. Under clause 4(i) of the Usership agreement involving Ó Lionaird there is an obligation on the licensee to use a particular brand of Irish Whiskey, Jameson Irish Whiskey, as an ingredient in the product. Since the product is being marketed under this trade mark and brand name the Authority would not regard such an obligation as anti-competitive. In fact since the particular brand is shown in the labelling of the product as an ingredient it would be a breach of consumer legislation not to use the brand. The same position applies to each of the other 3 agreements which all contain similar clauses although in the agreement relating to Phil Thompson the obligation relates to the use of Paddy Whiskey.

22. Clause 9 of the usership agreement involving Peadar Ó Lionaird provides, that in the event that IDL determines that the product fails to meet the standard of quality it may terminate the agreement by written notice to the user and that the user shall cease its use of the trade mark and the designation Irish whiskey within 30 days of such notice. A similar provision is inserted in the other 3 user agreements. In view of the importance to IDL of the quality image of their products associated with the promotion of their trade marks at very considerable cost to IDL, the Authority could accept that IDL are entitled to protect the value of their trade marks by measures to ensure that they are not associated with an inferior product. In these circumstances the Authority does not regard the withdrawal of a licence and a requirement to cease the use of the trade mark as offending against section 4(1).

23. In the event of IDL terminating the agreement with Peadar Ó Lionaird in accordance with clause 9, there would also be a requirement on Ó Lionaird to cease use of the designation 'Irish Whiskey' on its products. A similar requirement is in the other 3 agreements. However the designation 'Irish Whiskey' is a generic term defined in the Irish Whiskey Acts and is not the property of IDL. The exercise of the prohibition under clause 9 would therefore require the users to cease using a designation on their products which they would otherwise have been able to use if they had not entered into the usership agreements. In considering this aspect the Authority had regard to the fact that by use of the IDL trade marks the users gain substantial benefit in the promotion and marketing of their products while the benefit to IDL is at best very marginal. There is the real risk that an inferior non-whiskey product bearing an IDL trade mark could impact unfavourably on the value and image of the trade mark and, because of a past association of the product with the trade mark, there is some risk that this would continue even if the IDL trade mark was removed but the designation of Irish whiskey retained. In any event the restriction on the use of the designation would only arise if the product failed to meet the quality standards prescribed by IDL. The Authority does not therefore believe that the object of this provision is to prevent, restrict or distort competition. The Authority is also of the view that the restriction on the use of the designation in the circumstances is unlikely to have any perceptible effect on competition and does not offend against section 4(1).

The Decision

24. In the Authority's opinion, Irish Distillers Group plc, Irish Distillers Ltd and the users, Peadar Ó Lionaird, Phil Thompson, Mileeven Ltd and Lakeshore Foods Ltd are undertakings and the notified usership agreements between these parties are agreements between undertakings.

25. The Authority considers that the notified agreements do not have the object or effect of preventing, restricting or distorting competition in trade in any goods or services in the State or any part of the State. The Authority, therefore, considers that the notified agreements between Irish Distillers Ltd and Peadar Ó Lionaird, Phil Thompson, Mileeven Ltd and Lakeshore Foods Ltd do not offend against section 4(1) of the Competition Act 1991.

6.2 The Certificate

26. The Competition Authority has issued the following certificate:

The Competition Authority certifies that in its opinion, on the basis of the facts in its possession, the agreements set out below in relation to trade mark usership notified under section 7 on 30 September 1992 do not offend against section 4(1) of the Competition Act 1991:

(i) Irish Distillers Ltd/Peadar Ó Lionaird—CA/970/92E

(ii) Irish Distillers Ltd/Phil Thompson—CA/975/92E

(iii) Irish Distillers Ltd/Mileeven Ltd—CA/980/92E

(iv) Irish Distillers Ltd/Lakeshore Foods Ltd—CA/971/92E

For the Competition Authority

Des Wall
Member

25 February 1994

6.3 Competition Authority Decision No. 326, Performing Right Society and individual creators and publishers (Assignment of Copyright): 18 May 1994, Notification No. CA/2/91E

Copyright – Provision of musical works and rights – Whether creators, publishers and collecting organisation are undertakings – Access and withdrawal of membership conditions – Whether prescribed forms of assignment restrict competition – Whether income distribution system offends against section 4 of Competition Act – Whether objects of collecting agency are anti-competitive – Sacrifice of earnings for creators whose works fall in popularity – Whether conditions exist for the grant of a licence – Improvement of provision of service – Fair share of benefit for consumers – Indispensability of restrictions – Request for delay of decision and impact upon remedies under section 6 – Application of decision to foreign revenue – No review under section 5 – Whether Authority has power to grant a conditional licence for a suggested agreement which may be withdrawn under section 8 – Copyright Act 1963 (No. 10), sections 22, 25 and 47 – Competition Act 1991 (No. 24), sections 3, 4, 5, 6, 7 and 8

Facts: On 3 October 1991 notification was made by The Performing Right Society ('PRS') and Irish Music Rights Organisation ('IMRO') to the Authority of three standard form agreements with a request for a certificate under section 4(4) of the Competition Act 1991 or failing that, a licence under section 4(2). The standard forms provide for the assignment by individual creators and publishers of the performing right in their musical works to PRS. The Authority already issued a certificate for the assignment of PRS's rights to licence its repertoire in the State to IMRO in Decision No. 6 (see 1.3.2). IMRO is an Irish registered company and a wholly owned subsidiary of PRS but it is not party to the notified agreements. PRS is an English private company limited by guarantee and its main objects are to exercise and enforce the copyright of its members. PRS not having share capital distributes its income to its members. A composer or author of a musical work is one type of member of PRS and publishers are another type of member. The General Council lays down the division of copyright royalties collected by PRS. In order to avail of the collecting services of PRS, the composer and publisher join PRS and undertake to assign all rights to PRS for the whole world unless otherwise decided by the General Council. Provision is made for temporary arrangements to avoid the effects of the complete assignment. Returns from broadcasters and analyses of performances form the basis of allocating the royalties amongst composers and publishers which have been collected by PRS. Termination of membership of PRS by a member requires three months' notice of termination on the expiration of three years. If no royalties are received within specified periods membership of PRS may lapse. 6.3

The Authority issued a Statement of objections, convened an oral hearing and allowed time for PRS and IMRO to consider amending their arrangements. PRS refused to amend and asked for a conditional licence.

Submissions: PRS submitted:

1. It would be impossible for Irish creators to obtain a just reward for their works unless their collecting system operated.

2. The assignment merely substituted one owner for another.

3. Although PRS would seek to persuade members otherwise it was possible to subdivide rights and to allow the original creators to licence performances. Pop groups are admittedly refused by PRS to licence performances for valid reasons.

4. The allocation of revenue system adopted by PRS provided a cushion for composers against falling income and was a practicable allocation in view of administration costs for any other system.

5. A non-exclusive licensing system would complicate legal enforcement of copyright and would increase costs.

6. Section 4 of the Competition Act did not apply to the notified agreements because the effect of the arrangements arose because of the unilateral act or acts of PRS. Section 5 was therefore applicable.

7. The termination restrictions provided stability and security for its members.

8. There was little demand for licensing by composers or publishers themselves.

9. The changes suggested by the Authority to facilitate licensing by composers to a limited extent and the reduction of the termination period were not capable of change because the system notified was uniform throughout Europe. Changes for this State only would cause chaos.

10. A negative decision of the Authority to the request of the notifying parties for a licence would give rise to legal uncertainty and make it impossible for PRS to enforce its licensing system. The grant of a licence subject to conditions could be revoked if PRS failed to comply with the licence.

11. The Republic of Ireland Music Publishers Association which represents music publishers in the State commented that the maximum payment of 50% of returns to publishers was originally adopted by PRS to balance the economic strength of

6.3 composers and publishers. It suggested that publishers were now not as strong as before and that the maximum should be reviewed. The Concert Promoters and Venue Association argued that PRS's insistence on taking a percentage of gross box office receipts restricted the market. Concert promoters were hampered by PRS's inflexibility concerning payments. Representatives of vintners, newsagents and grocers commented that it was not necessary that assignments be made to one collecting organisation and stated that IMRO's charges were excessive.

Decided by the Authority:
(A) In refusing to issue a certificate under section 4(4) of the Competition Act 1991 that:

(1) Each composer and publisher is an undertaking and the assignments to PRS another economic entity are restrictive of competition in the State because they:

(a) preclude members of PRS from administering their performing rights;

(b) restrict copyright users from purchasing performing rights from suppliers other than PRS;

(c) restrict competition in the supply of performing rights between members of PRS;

(d) maintain uniform rates of royalties.

(2) The relevant market is the provision of musical works and the performing right therein in the State.

(3) The objects of PRS do not restrict competition provided they are not used to pursue acquisitions to maintain a dominant position.

(4) Access to membership of PRS is based on objective criteria which are applied in a non-discriminatory way.

(5) The restriction on terminating membership for three years offends against section 4(1).

(6) The division of rights and the practice of restricting the return of rights to composers and publishers offend against section 4(1) because it is a prescribed form and practice to be used in all which affects competition.

(7) The system of allocating royalties does not affect competition because any restrictive effect can be avoided by making provision in the writer/publisher contract. The sacrifice of earnings by the equalisation system is a voluntary donation by creators for fellow members of PRS whose income has fallen due to falling popularity of their music.

(B) In refusing to grant a licence under section 4(2) of the Competition Act 1991 that:

(1) The Authority accepted at the oral hearing and in its decision that collecting organisations were the only practicable means of recovering royalties and thereby contributed to improving the provision of service.

(2) Collective copyright arrangements allow consumers a fair share of the benefit of the arrangements because there is a greater supply and variety of musical works as a result.

(3) The licensing exclusivity given to PRS is not necessary as can be seen from the situation in the US where exclusivity is prohibited and collective organisations can licence the works of another collective organisation.

(4) The prescription of forms of assignments, the restrictions on dividing rights by category or country and the termination restrictions are not indispensable for the

effective operation of PRS, notwithstanding the EU Commission's decision in the GEMA case. The GEMA case concerned the compatibility of similar arrangements with Article 86 and the decision does not rule out the application of national competition law. The reduction of the terminating period to one year would satisfy the concerns of the Authority on these objections however. 6.3

(5) The special nature of the music market does not afford the possibility of eliminating competition in respect of a substantial part of the services in question despite the significant restrictions on competition between creators and publishers on prices.

(6) The Authority cannot grant a licence specifying the type of agreement it would like to see when no such agreement exists.

(7) The request of IMRO to delay the making of a decision until alternative arrangements are established cannot be accommodated. The Authority noted that until a decision is made the notifying parties are immune from action under section 6 of the Competition Act arising from the operation of section 6(7).

(8) Whether the Authority's decision applies to revenue derived outside the State is a matter of general law and not for the Authority to decide upon. The scope of the Authority's decision is co-extensive with the scope of the Competition Act whilst also recognising that the decision does not concern Section 5 of the Act.

Case and decisions referred to:
BRT (Belgische Radio en Televisie) v. SABAM (Case No. 127/73) 27.3.74 — [1974] ECR 313
EC Commission Decision—GEMA I—2.6.71 [1971] OJ L 134/15. [1971] CMLR D 35
EC Commission Decision—GEMA II—6.7.72 [1972] OJ L L166/22 [1972] CMLR D 115
Competition Authority Decision 6—30.6.1992. PRS/IMRO **1.3.2**

Competition Authority Decision of 18 May 1994 relating to a proceeding under section 4 of the Competition Act 1991
Notification No. CA/2/91E — Performing Right Society and individual creators/publishers (Assignment of Copyright)

Introduction

1. On 3 October 1991 The Performing Right Society Ltd (PRS) and the Irish Music Rights Organisation Ltd (IMRO) jointly notified to the Competition Authority, under sections 7(1) and 7(2) of the Competition Act 1991, three standard form agreements, relating to the assignment of copyright in musical works with a request for a certificate under section 4(4) of the Act or, in the event of a refusal by the Authority to issue a certificate, a licence under section 4(2).

2. The Authority issued a Statement of Objections to PRS on 4 March 1993, indicating why, in its opinion, the agreements offended against section 4(1) of the Competition Act and did not satisfy the requirements for the grant of a licence set out in section 4(2). An oral hearing was held on 7/8 March 1994, which was attended by representatives of PRS and IMRO. PRS were given some time to consider an amendment to their arrangements but at a further meeting on 4 May 1994, PRS informed the Authority that they were not prepared to make any amendment and requested a conditional licence from the Authority.

The Facts

(a) **Subject of the Notification**

3. The standard form agreements provide for the assignment by individual creators (composers and authors) and publishers of the performing right in their musical works to PRS

6.3 which, directly or through its subsidiary IMRO, administers on their behalf the performing right in the State and in the UK and, through affiliated societies, throughout the world wherever copyright is recognised. The Authority has already considered and approved (by certificate) an agreement transferring from PRS to IMRO responsibility for the licensing in Ireland of the repertoire of PRS, and the collection of royalties in respect of this.[1]

The Authority has under consideration a number of other PRS/IMRO notifications which relate to the licensing agreements between IMRO and various users. The present notification does not directly concern any of these notifications.

(b) **The Parties involved**

4. The parties involved are (i) PRS (ii) IMRO and (iii) individual creator and publisher members of PRS.

(i) *PRS*

5. Set up in 1914, PRS is an association of composers, authors (creators) and publishers for the United Kingdom and Republic of Ireland. It is a private company limited by guarantee and not having a share capital. The main objects of PRS are to exercise and enforce on behalf of its members all rights and remedies in relation to the exploitation of the copyright in their works; to collect and receive all royalties and fees payable in respect of their works; to restrain and recover damages for the infringement of the copyright; to obtain from members assignments of copyright; to distribute the net monies minus administration expenses to the members; to establish and support funds, trusts, associations or institutions for the benefit of its members or ex-members, to lend money to members and to invest the monies of the company not immediately required.

6. PRS, being a company not having a share capital, may not distribute dividends. Its income derives mainly from its licensing activities and, after deduction of expenses and taxation, it is distributed to members (apart from some funds placed in reserves). Its licence revenue in 1991 was Stg£130.3m. comprising Stg£3.5m. from the Republic of Ireland (IMRO), Stg£87.1m. from Great Britain and Stg£39.7m. from Overseas Territories. For the same period, the net distributable revenue by PRS in the Republic of Ireland was Stg£3.1m. The net distributable revenue was Stg£64.3m. in the UK and Stg£38.7m. overseas.

(ii) *IMRO*

7. IMRO is not a party to the notified agreements. It is a registered private company limited by guarantee, not having a share capital. Its main activities are the licensing of performing rights in the State and the collection of royalties. PRS controls the composition of the Board of Directors of IMRO. IMRO distributes its license income less operating expenses to PRS. The income and expenditure account of IMRO for the year ended 31 December 1991 showed that total licence revenue amounted to IR£4.8m consisting of IR£2.6m. from broadcasting and IR£2.2m from public performance. Total administration costs amounted to IR£1.0m. leaving IR£3.8m. for royalty payments for transmission to PRS.

(iii) *Individual Creator and Publisher Members of PRS*

8. The members of PRS include composers of musical works, authors of any literary or dramatic works, publishers of any such musical literary or dramatic works or other proprietors of the copyright of such works. PRS membership totals around 25,000 including approximately 1,000 Irish members. Through affiliation with similar societies overseas, PRS represents more than 750,000 copyright owners throughout the world. By virtue of reciprocal agreements with such societies, PRS, until 1 January 1989, administered the rights in the United Kingdom and Ireland of creators of music resident throughout the world. Since 1 January 1989, IMRO, a

1. PRS/IMRO—Decision No. 5 of 30 June 1992.

subsidiary of PRS, has taken over the licensing of the performing right and collection of royalties in Ireland but members of PRS resident in Ireland have remained members of PRS which continues to be responsible for the distribution of all royalties collected. PRS is also a member of CISAC, the International Confederation of Authors' Societies. **6.3**

9. The membership provisions and arrangements of PRS involve an important distinction between two types of member. First, there is the composer or author of a musical work. This person is also referred to as the 'creator' or 'writer'. The lyricist, i.e. the writer of the words accompanying a musical work, is also a creator. Secondly, there is the publisher of a musical work. When a musical work is composed, all copyright in it belongs to its creators. The creator usually makes a full assignment of the copyright in any musical work to the publisher although this is subject to the rights of PRS. The function of the publisher is to publish the work and generally to promote and exploit it commercially. When a publisher is involved in the promotion of a musical work, both the creator and the publisher have an interest in the work and in the performing right therein. In recognition of this, PRS accept publishers into their membership.

10. The activities of music publishers in Ireland include the publication in printed form of music and song sheets of their composers' works, the securing of the recording of their composers' music and lyrics and more particularly promoting the maximum possible exploitation of these works. The relationship between writer and publisher is usually formalised by means of a contract which normally specifies the services to be provided by the publisher and provides for the allocation of earnings arising from the exploitation of the musical work. The Rules and Regulations of PRS also provide for the division of copyright earnings payable by PRS. The 'normal basis of division' means the basis laid down by the General Council from time to time to regulate the apportionment of the net fees between two or more persons interested in the same work. The divisions are in every case subject to any modification that may be agreed upon in writing between the persons interested, except that in no case, other than in certain grades of arrangements of non-copyright music, may the share of the publisher, or the combined share of all the publishers and performing right owners, other than the creator, concerned with a particular work, exceed one half of the total distributable fees. The normal division under the Society's rules is 8/12ths to the writer and 4/12ths to the publisher. The PRS yearbook, which is supplied to every member, sets out in detail the different arrangements in relation to the division of fees. There is, for example, provision for division on an equal basis between composer, lyric writer and publisher in the case of published vocal works and between composer and lyric writer in the case of unpublished vocal works.

11. The members of PRS in Ireland are generally also members of one or other of the following bodies who represent their interests: Association of Irish Composers (AIC); Irish Association of Songwriters and Composers (IASC) and the Republic of Ireland Music Publishers Association (RIMPA).

(c) **Copyright**

12. Copyright in relation to an original literary, dramatic, musical or artistic work is the exclusive right to do, or to authorise other persons to do, certain acts in relation to that work. Such acts include reproducing the work in any material form, publishing it, performing it in public, broadcasting it, causing it to be transmitted to subscribers to a diffusion service or making any adaptation of it. This type of copyright normally lasts during the lifetime of the creator and for fifty years after his death. The authorisation of other persons to use copyright material is normally by way of licence in return for payment of royalties to the copyright owner. The performing right is part of the copyright which is a property right which initially vests in its creator who is entitled to remuneration for its use by others. It is protected in most jurisdictions including Ireland where the relevant legislation is the Copyright Acts 1963 and 1987. Ireland is also bound by International Conventions which require mutual recognition and protection of the performing right.

6.3 13. Collective licensing and enforcement of copyright in relation to musical works is common throughout the world, wherever copyright is enforced. The Copyright Act 1963 recognises the role of collective licensing bodies. Part V of the Act contains general provisions relating to the jurisdiction of the Controller of Industrial and Commercial Property in determining disputes between licensing bodies and persons requiring licences. It defines a licensing body as 'a society or other organisation which has its main object, or one of its main objects, the negotiation or granting of (such) licences, either as owner or prospective owner of copyright or as agent for the owners or prospective owners thereof'. Section 22 of the Act provides for action by the owner of copyright for infringements.

14. Section 47 of the Copyright Act 1963 provides for the total or partial assignment of copyright. It states: 'An assignment of copyright may be limited in any one of the following ways or in any combination of two or more of these ways, that is to say:

(i) so as to apply to one or more, but not all, of the classes of acts which by virtue of this Act the owner of the copyright has the exclusive right to do (including any one or more classes of acts not separately designated in this Act as being restricted by the copyright, but falling within any of the classes of acts so designated),
(ii) so as to apply to any one or more, but not all, of the countries in relation to which the owner of the copyright has by virtue of this Act the exclusive right,
(iii) so as to apply to part, but not the whole, of the period for which the copyright is to subsist'.

(d) **The Product and the Market**

15. The product involved in this notification is the musical work and the performing right therein. The definition of 'musical work' as set out in Clause 1 of the assignment agreement is given in para. 17. The 'performing right' is the right of public performance, broadcasting and cable diffusion of these works. Copyright legislation does not define what constitutes a performance in public. The general rule which has emerged from courts over the years, is to the effect that any performance which takes place outside the domestic circle is to be regarded as 'public' for this purpose, regardless of the nature of the entertainment and the nature of the premises at which the performance takes place and irrespective of whether a charge for admission is made. For example performances at clubs in which attendance is restricted to members, and performances in factories, have been found to be public performances. The market is the market for the performing right. In theory, an individual member of PRS could administer his performing right himself but it is understood that no individual member does so. In practice, members assign their performing right to PRS or an equivalent body who then license it to music users in return for the payment of a royalty. Creators and publishers are not obliged to join or assign their rights to PRS and could, for example, join any collecting society in the EC with whom PRS has reciprocal agreements or form their own society in Ireland. The reality however is that the overwhelming majority of creators resident in Ireland are members of PRS. PRS is a monopoly and its reciprocal arrangements mean that it has a monopoly in all copyright music. The users consist mainly of radio and television broadcasters, hotels, restaurants, public houses, retail shops and industrial premises, dance halls, concert halls, cinemas and theatres who buy the product through IMRO. The geographic scope of the relevant market is the State.

(e) **The arrangements**

16. Three standard form deeds of assignment were notified by PRS. One of these is used by creators. The other two standard deeds are used by publishers, one for publishers who are individual persons and the other for publishers having corporate status. The only difference in substance between the three standard form deeds relates to the scope of the warranty in Clause 4. This difference, which is explained in para. 21 below is not material for present purposes.

The full import of the contents of the assignment agreements are not fully apparent or evident from these documents in themselves. The assignment agreements have no life without the Articles of Association and Rules of PRS and the applicants in their notification drew specific attention to these. In addition, there is a considerable body of other more detailed regulation, practice and usage to which reference is necessary. These are set out generally in the PRS 'Yearbook', the 1990-91 version of which was included with the notification. In some cases, further clarification and elaboration was required from PRS by the Authority. The following paragraphs set out or summarise those arrangements which the Authority considers to be covered by the present notification or to be relevant for the purposes of deciding whether the arrangements are certifiable or licensable under the Competition Act. 6.3

17. A musical work is defined in Clause 1 of the assignment as 'any musical work whether now existing or hereafter composed and such words (if any) as are associated with any musical work and shall include (without prejudice to the generality of the expression 'musical work') the vocal and instrumental music in any cinematograph films, the words and/or music of any monologue having a musical introduction and/or accompaniment, the musical accompaniment of any non-musical play, and any part of any work, words, music or accompaniment as aforesaid.'

18. Under Clause 2 of the assignment, the assignor assigns to the Society 'All the undermentioned rights in musical works which now belong to or shall hereafter be acquired by or be or become vested in the assignor during the continuance of the assignor's membership of the Society and all such parts or shares (whether limited as to time, place, mode of enjoyment or otherwise) of, and all such interests in, any such rights as so belong to or shall so be acquired by or be or become vested in the assignor' and agrees 'to hold the same unto the Society for its exclusive benefit during such time as the rights assigned continue to subsist and (in accordance with the provisions of the Articles of Association of the Society for the time being in force) remain vested in or controlled by the Society'.

19. The term performing right means the right (a) to perform the work in public, (b) to broadcast a work or to include it in a cable programme service. PRS also takes an assignment from its writer members of the film synchronisation right in every work composed or written by the member primarily for the purpose of being recorded on the sound track of a particular film or films in contemplation when such work was commissioned. The rights assigned to PRS in the case of publishers are usually all performing rights for all parts of the world. PRS have indicated to the Authority that their members are free to divide their rights by reference to category (e.g. public performance) and also by country. This freedom is exercisable at 3 yearly intervals only (as in the case of the right of the member to leave PRS altogether).

20. Under Clause 3 of the deed of assignment, PRS 'covenants with the assignor, that the Society shall from time to time pay to the assignor such sums of money out of the monies collected by the Society in respect of the exercise of the rights assigned to the Society in the works of its members as the assignor shall be entitled to receive . . .' in accordance with PRS's rules. These rules are adopted by the members of PRS in general meetings.

21. Clause 4 contains a warranty of title and, for composers and authors only, a warranty that no breach of copyright will be involved in the assignment or the exercise of the performing right. The reason for the difference between creators and publishers is that publishers do not create the works and would not, therefore, be in a position to provide a warranty of originality.

22. The applicants stated that the assignment must be considered in conjunction with the Articles of Association and Rules of PRS, as membership is a precondition to the administration by PRS of the performing right on behalf of a creator. In the preamble to the assignment agreements express reference is made to the assignor 'pursuant to its membership of the Performing Right Society Ltd'. The following provisions are included in the Memorandum and Articles of Association of PRS.

23. The objects for which the company is established as set out in the Memorandum of Association include the following:

6.3 3(h) To acquire or undertake the whole or part of the business, property or liabilities of any person or company carrying on any undertaking or business which the company is authorised to carry on or possessed of property suitable for the purposes of the company.
3(k) To take or otherwise acquire and hold shares in any other company having objects altogether or in part similar to those of this company or carrying on any business capable of being conducted so as directly or indirectly to benefit this company.

24. Provisions for access to membership are set out in Articles 2-5 of the Articles of Association of PRS. They provide for 3 categories of membership i.e. provisional, associate and full member. New applicants are usually admitted at first to provisional membership. Article 5(b) states that the General Council shall have full and unrestricted power to refuse any application without assigning any reason for such refusal. The criteria governing admission to provisional membership for composers and lyricists, as prescribed from time to time, at present are 3 works which must each have been either (a) commercially recorded or (b) broadcast within the past 2 years or (c) performed in public on at least 12 occasions within the last 2 years and commercially published. There are also a number of alternative criteria for writer applicants. A publisher must have a catalogue of 15 works of which at least 10 have been commercially recorded. In addition, the writers of the 15 qualifying works must be members of PRS, or of one of its affiliated societies. The publisher must have acquired rights in at least 10 of the works for a territory within the EC. In a case where the catalogue of works consists entirely of works recorded on the sound-tracks of films, such catalogues must not consist only of works recorded on the sound-track of one film and the works must be of not less than 30 minutes duration in aggregate as recorded on such sound-tracks. Copies of all assignments between the applicant and the writers in respect of the works concerned must be supplied. The minimum qualifying criteria for associate membership are 1 year's provisional membership and certain aggregate PRS earnings over a period not exceeding 3 years. Associate members have one vote on a show of hands or on a poll or postal ballot.

25. For promotion to full member, earnings criteria are also prescribed. The figures are automatically adjusted each year in line with changes in the total revenue distributed to PRS members. Full members have 1 vote on a show of hands 10 votes on a poll or postal ballot plus 10 additional votes if their average annual earnings through PRS either over the preceding 2 years or over the preceding 20 years reach specified levels. The purpose of the provisions regarding voting rights is to ensure, having regard to the large number of members whose activities are limited and whose income is low, that a preponderant voice in the affairs of PRS may be exercised by its members who rely on it for their livelihood to a reasonably significant extent. The category of membership to which a writer or publisher is admitted does not affect in any way the share of royalties which he is entitled to receive. The heirs of deceased composers or authors are usually admitted to associate membership; they are not normally eligible to become full members.

26 Article 7 states:

7(a) Every Member shall, on election, or at any time thereafter if requested by the Society, assign or cause to be assigned to the Society all rights to be administered on his behalf by the Society.
7(b) Every assignment to the Society pursuant to this Article shall be in such form as the General Council may from time to time prescribe and shall operate for and during the period of the assignor's membership. . . . For films exhibited in the USA, PRS negotiates a theatrical performance licence with the production company for PRS members' music incorporated in the soundtrack.
7(c) The rights to be administered by the Society on behalf of a Member are:

(i) the performing right;

(ii) in the case of writer Members only, the film synchronisation right in every work composed or written by the Member primarily for the purpose of being recorded on the soundtrack of a particular film or films in contemplation when such work was commissioned; 6.3

(iii) such other rights, or such parts of the rights mentioned in subparagraphs (i) and (ii), as the General Council may direct,

for the whole world or such part or parts of the whole world as the General Council may direct, in all or any works or parts of works, present and future of which the Member is the writer, publisher or proprietor.

Article 7(d) provides for temporary arrangements and ceases to have effect on execution of the assignments. It allows PRS to exercise the rights of creators and allows creators to be paid by PRS before the assignment:

7(e) The Society may exercise and enforce the rights of members of any affiliated societies pursuant to the terms of any contract now existing or which may hereafter be made between the Society and such affiliated societies.

7(f) The Society may, by notice in writing to any member, decline to exercise the whole or any part of the performing right in any particular work or works of which such member is the composer, author, publisher or proprietor, and thereupon the provisions of sub-clauses (a) and (d) of this Article shall cease to apply to such right, and any assignment thereof already made to the Society by such member shall be determined by the Society. Provided always that the Society may at any time, and from time to time, by further notice in writing to such member, withdraw such notice in respect of all or any of the rights comprised therein, whereupon the provisions of sub-clauses (a) and (d) of this Article shall again apply to such right or rights.

27. Under the Article 7(f) procedure, the Society may, on request, return to members the whole or any part of the performing right in any of their works, to enable members, copyright owners or authorised third parties to license certain performances themselves in particular circumstances, examples of which are compilation shows, interpolated music in plays, music theatre, cantata musicals, and specially written music accompanying silent films. Once a member has made a request to the Society, and the terms are agreed, the procedure is that the Society gives formal notice to the member or members concerned, pursuant to Article 7(f) that it 'declines to exercise' the relevant part of the performing right in the works in question. During the period 1977 to 1992 use has been made of the provisions of this Article in about 60 instances. It has been used solely for the purpose of facilitating the direct licensing by members of works not originally written for theatrical performance but which are then used in theatrical compilation shows.

28. Where PRS is requested to apply the Article 7(f) procedure in respect of works to be performed in a compilation show it invariably accedes to such a request by giving formal notice to the member that it declines to exercise the relevant part of the performing right in the works in question. PRS does, as a matter of policy, apply two conditions to the granting of the request which do not appear in Article 7(f) itself:

(a) the royalty to be charged is not less than the appropriate PRS tariff rate, and

(b) the producer of the show is granted an exclusive licence by the copyright owner (in a defined context) for the performances which are the subject of the Article 7(f) notice.

29. Article 9 states that:

9(d) the membership of a provisional member may at any time be terminated without notice and without the assignment of any reason thereof, either by the General Council

6.3 or in accordance with such general directions as the General Council may from time to time give.

9(e) Any full or associate member may be given notice by the General Council determining his membership at the expiration of fourteen days from the date of such notice, and his membership shall cease accordingly.

9(f) 'Any member may, by giving three months' notice in writing to the Secretary, terminate his membership:

—three years after the date with effect from which he was first elected to membership,* and

—thereafter, on any third anniversary of that date.'

30. Provisional writer membership is terminated if no royalties at all are credited to the writer over a 3 year period, and the membership of provisional publisher members whose royalties have not exceeded an aggregate of £250 over 3 years is also terminated. Associate membership is terminated after a period of 5 years in which no royalties have been credited. Membership ceases on death but all royalties to which the deceased would have been entitled are payable to the personal representative of the deceased.

31. PRS stated that in practice they would only exercise their right to terminate provisional membership in the event that a provisional member was no longer earning any money. This was in the interests of the Society as a whole. If the member's name was kept on the files and he was no longer earning any royalties the cost of administration would increase and a lower standard of service provided to the remaining members would result. There were no rights of appeal. If a provisional member was no longer earning royalties he did not need the services of PRS and, in any event, if he did qualify for admission again he would always be welcomed. In the case of full or associate members however, they may appeal in writing and have the question of their continuance of membership put before the members at an Extraordinary General Meeting. Not until the members in the EGM had approved the action would membership cease.

32. Clause 3(d) of the Memorandum of Association and Article 54 of the Articles of Association empower the Society, through its General Council, to make 'rules' for regulating various matters, including the manner in which the net monies received by the company are to be divided and apportioned among members. These rules provide in more detail for PRS to exercise and enforce the statutory rights and remedies in relation to the performing right. They contain *inter alia* provisions relating to the distribution of money; deduction of expenses; notification of musical work in a prescribed manner; misleading or incorrect information; appointment of a disciplinary panel to hear and determine complaints and impose penalties; disputes regarding infringement or ownership of copyright and legal proceedings.

33. The general policy governing the distribution of fees to members is set out in Rule 2(c) which provides *inter alia* that all sums remaining after authorised deductions shall be distributed among the persons interested in the several works in such manner and in such proportions as the General Council may from time to time determine. Clearly this confers considerable discretionary power on the General Council in relation to distribution policy. The General Council is of course elected by and is accountable to the general membership of the Society. Under rule 2(f),** the royalty share paid by PRS to a publisher may not exceed one half of the net fee, although PRS cannot as a practical matter exercise control over contractual arrangements between the publisher and the creator, outside the PRS rules, which may prescribe different divisions of the royalty.

34. This and the following paragraphs (35-38), which are based on material submitted by PRS, summarise what happens in practice as regards distribution of royalty income. IMRO

*Amended at EGM of PRS by special resolution on 9 June 1992.

**As amended at EGM on 9 June 1992.

obtains from broadcasters and selected other music users licensed by IMRO, programme details of the music which has been broadcast or publicly performed. Generally speaking, broadcasting stations in the United Kingdom and in the State submit complete returns of all music used. The only exceptions are local radio stations which can, by special arrangement, submit sample returns in respect of broadcasts which have taken place using commercial recordings or 'stock' records. They are however, required to supply complete returns of all music which is broadcast 'live' from the studio or at an outside event or specially recorded in the studio. IMRO monitors the output of radio and television stations on a random sample basis and checks the results against the returns submitted. In the case of other music users, e.g. hotels, dance halls, restaurants, bars, etc., IMRO have stated that despite the express provisions of its licence, IMRO does not require returns for performances, recognising that this would place an undue burden on the users concerned as well as a massive administrative burden on IMRO. IMRO is able to do this, because of its ability to grant blanket licences of the entire PRS repertoire. IMRO also claimed that this procedure would not be effective if the PRS repertoire were non-exclusively held by PRS and IMRO were not in a position to grant such a licence. 6.3

35. Up to and including 1991, programmes were required to be submitted by public performance licensees only in respect of:

(a) concerts and recitals of 'classical music' (extended to include 'light-classical' music);
(b) concerts (including a series of concerts at a single venue and tours where the same works are performed on each occasion) for which the royalty payable is £200 or more;
(c) other 'live' musical events which are licensed on a 'per occasion' basis and where an identifiable separate royalty of £200 or more is payable by the licensee.

36. Royalties for live or recorded performances of copyright music in hotels, public bars etc., are usually paid under an annual blanket licence issued by IMRO to the proprietor of each venue. Over the years IMRO (and its predecessor PRS) encountered many problems in their attempt to obtain accurate and representative programme information about public performances of copyright music. Until 1964, PRS endeavoured with limited success, to collect programme returns for all such performances. In 1964 sampling was introduced and this has continued in one form or another since then. However, it was found that even on this limited basis, inadequate programme information was obtained.

37. In 1976 the Republic of Ireland Music Publishers Association made representations to PRS in relation to the live performances of copyright music in Ireland. It was felt that because of the inadequacies of the programme information being received in respect of performances of live music in Ireland, an alternative method of distributing some of those royalties should be considered. As a result a system was introduced whereby details of work frequently performed live and by recorded means were sought from Irish PRS members and a certain portion of the royalties collected in respect of live and recorded performances was set aside to be distributed on the basis of the details received from the members. Until recently, it was the practice of IMRO to write to all PRS members resident in Ireland in December each year to seek from them the details of the works popularly performed, either live or by way of recorded music. Such information was normally verified by music publishers but where no music publisher was involved a composer member could obtain verifying information from the venues at which performances of their works took place. In the case of the performance of recorded music, details of record sales involving Irish works were obtained from the members and used as a basis for the distribution of a certain portion of the royalties collected in respect of the performances of recorded copyright music. This system was found to be unsatisfactory so MRBI was commissioned to carry out a survey of actual live performances in significant venues throughout the country on a trial basis. Since January 1993 these details are being used to make appropriate royalty payments to creators whose works are performed live. The MRBI survey was to continue until September 1993.

6.3 38. Programme material received by the Society is analysed so as to identify the musical works which have been broadcast or publicly performed and in which a PRS member or one of the affiliated societies has an interest as a composer, lyric writer or publisher. It is not always feasible for all this material to be fully analysed; in that event analysis is carried out on a sample basis. This is applied, e.g., to the programme material supplied by most local radio stations and from RTE in respect of their TV services. Royalties received from broadcasting and general performance are kept separate and each of these separate categories of royalties is then further broken down into distribution pools usually referred to as 'sections' relating to specific sources of public performance or broadcasting e.g. RTE radio, RTE TV, discotheques, juke boxes. Each of the works identified as a result of the analysis of programme details for a particular section of revenue receives 'points', the number of which varies depending upon the number of times performed, the duration of the work and in some cases other factors, for example the level of royalties collected and the classification of a performance. When programmes have been analysed only on a sample basis, the number of points accruing to each 'sampled' performance is multiplied by the sample factor so as to take account of the fact that each 'sampled' performance represents a greater number of actual performances. The total number of points which have been awarded to works within a particular section is then calculated and divided into the distributable revenue for that section. This establishes the value of a point in each section at that distribution and, consequently, the amount of money each work is to receive from that pool. The value of a point thus varies from section to section and distribution to distribution. The point award plans and rules are applied without discrimination to all works which can be identified as coming under the control of PRS.

39. PRS operates an earnings equalisation scheme for the purpose of providing a form of financial 'cushioning' for long established members of the Society whose works, because of changes in musical fashion or for other reasons, cease to be publicly performed or broadcast to the same extent as may once have been the case.

(f) **Views of the Parties**

40. PRS stated that the purpose of the arrangements was to give effect to the rights of creators granted by the Copyright Acts 1963 and 1987. They considered that the arrangements afforded the mechanism for bringing to consumers, through the users, the benefits of the artistic achievements of the creators, in the most effective manner. In the absence of the arrangements in their present form, it would be impossible for Irish creators to obtain a just reward for their achievements and it would also be impossible for creators based abroad to be remunerated for Irish performance of their work.

41. PRS stated that the assignment involved an absolute transfer of property from one owner to another, on the basis that the property could be more efficiently managed by the second. The substituted owner acquired an equally exclusive right to that enjoyed by the previous owner, no more and no less. There was, therefore, no effect on competition.

42. According to PRS, effective protection of the performing right was extremely labour intensive involving considerable expenditure on administration and monitoring procedures. The development of the market in its present form had been entirely natural and was inevitable in the absence of effective and affordable legal remedies. Without the arrangements as presently constituted, most creators would be forced out of the market. While in some product or service markets this could lead to efficiency and increased competition, it was self-evident that in the market for musical works, this would be catastrophic for all concerned.

43. PRS considered that the arrangements were also beneficial to the listening public and that they were indispensable for the attainment of the objectives of the Copyright Acts and for securing a proper balance of benefit between creators, users and the ultimate consumers.

44. PRS said that the 50% rule was for the protection of the creator so that the publisher would not get too much or all of the royalties on their works. Creators have been forced to take Court action against their publishers on a number of occasions. Details of some well publicised

cases were provided. In continental Europe the actual divisions between the publishers and the writers are prescribed. They claimed that the PRS system was the least restrictive of all the European systems in force. The divisions were specified in the statutes and in the regulations of the societies. The publisher's share was limited to one third and they only got 50% in special circumstances. PRS were not aware of any society which permitted the publisher to get more than 50%. In the USA the royalties are split 50/50 between the creator and the publisher. 6.3

45. It appeared from the terms of the assignment that the freedom of PRS members to divide their rights by category or by country was very restrictive if not non-existent while the assignment was in force (paras. 18 and 19). PRS confirmed that its members were free to divide by category and by country but no member had ever asked to subdivide except by territory. In recent years, it had become relatively frequent for PRS to accept, on request, an assignment of territory comprising less than the whole world. The most frequent exclusion was the United States but there had, in recent years, been at least one case of a writer becoming a member of GEMA (the German collecting society), and therefore transferring his performing right to GEMA, for GEMA's territory of administration. In respect of PRS as a whole, of the admissions for the years 1989, 1990 and 1991 (approx. 1,400 per year), the number of writer applications to exclude any territory amounted to 4, 6 and 11 respectively. Thus only a minute proportion of applicants for membership requested and were granted membership for a territory comprising less than the whole world. The number of requests granted to existing PRS writer members to modify their territory of representation was 10, 12 and 8 in each of the three years respectively.

46. PRS stated that it was legally possible to subdivide by reference to category (e.g. public performance, broadcasting, film synchronisation), and a member who wished to do so would be accepted provided any permissible subdivision as set out in the GEMA cases (see para. 61 below) was not exceeded. Members had not asked for such a subdivision and were they to do so, PRS would attempt to dissuade them from this course of action. PRS would not feel bound to agree similar terms with non EU residents or nationals (under the GEMA decision).

47. Article 7(f) states 'the Society may by notice in writing to any member decline to exercise the whole or part of the performing right...' The applicants explained that PRS did not administer 'grand rights' i.e. rights in operas, ballets or pantomimes in so far as they consisted of words and music written expressly for them (although since 1 January 1992, PRS has administered grand rights for cable diffusion). On the other hand they administered 'small rights' i.e. the rights in the individual musical works and associated literary works such as songs. There was a category of works, the rights in which fell on the borderline between grand rights and small rights. The category consisted of those songs which were not written for theatrical productions but which had subsequently been used by the producer of a show and which usually, but not always, depicted the life or career of a particular composer or performer. Such shows were known as compilation shows.

48. PRS stated that Article 7(f) enabled an individual creator to carry out a licensing function himself in certain circumstances. The original reason for the inclusion of Article 7(f) in the PRS Articles was not known but in practice it had, over the past 25 years or so, been used solely for the purposes of facilitating the direct licensing by members of works not originally written for theatrical performance but which were then used in theatrical compilation shows. A further reason for the application of Article 7(f) to theatrical performances was that there was an uncertainty in the case of some works of American origin as to whether PRS did, in fact, control the rights. This was because the composers were normally members of ASCAP or affiliates of BMI, (the performing rights societies in the US) and the extent of the non-exclusive mandate granted to those organisations by their members was not the same as that of the assignment to PRS by its members. In many cases there was a PRS member sub-publisher for the PRS territory who assigned to PRS such rights as he had, but the sub-publisher did not always have full rights to assign to PRS. Owners of the copyright in songs and other works of American origin sometimes claimed that the use of such works in compilation shows constituted a dramatic

6.3 performance falling outside the scope of the mandate given to the US performing right organisation to which they belonged and in consequence PRS had no authority to license such use. Article 7(f) therefore facilitated direct licensing via the UK sub-publisher and prevented a damaging argument as to PRS's ability to license such rights.

49. PRS indicated that they invariably acceded to requests for the application of the Article 7(f) procedure in the case of compilation shows. They did, in these cases insist on compliance with the two conditions referred to in paragraph 28 above i.e. the tariff must not be lower than the appropriate PRS tariff and the licence granted to the producer of the show must be an 'exclusive' one. The main reason for insisting on the first condition was to avoid any undercutting of the relevant PRS tariff which could lead to pressure from users (and perhaps from the price regulatory authorities) for a reduction in that and perhaps other PRS tariffs. PRS also indicated that, in practice, this condition was largely redundant since the member concerned would not request the procedure if he did not think that he could license the public performance at a rate greater than the relevant PRS tariff. The second condition, relating to exclusivity, was to help the theatrical producer himself. Some producers required a degree of exclusivity to protect them from the possibility of a similar show being presented in competition with them.

50. PRS said that there have been some instances of pop groups, whose members are also composers, seeking to operate the Article 7(f) procedure in relation to pop concerts. Such requests have invariably been refused for a number of reasons. Pop concerts could be quite spontaneous events and the precise songs to be performed were not necessarily fixed in advance. Furthermore the condition regarding exclusivity could not be complied with. In effect since the main attraction at a pop concert was usually the performers themselves, the need for protection from similar events (and hence the need for exclusivity) did not arise. Accordingly the exclusivity condition is not really relevant to pop concerts.

51. PRS said that there were a number of problems which would be difficult to overcome if PRS ever acceded to such a request by a pop group. Firstly the request was likely to be made in respect of a given tour by the group and if a number of different countries were involved then PRS would have the task of trying to negotiate its reciprocal representation agreements with the local society in each of the different countries in which the group was to perform. PRS would have granted to those societies the right to authorise every public performance of works in the PRS repertoire. For PRS to decline to exercise the performing right in certain works in its repertoire would require the group in question to license its rights subject to the prior licences granted by PRS to the foreign societies (which would render the effect of Article 7(f) practically useless) or, alternatively, for the foreign societies to agree that the rights could be licensed directly by the group. There would be no particular reason for them to agree at all. The foreign societies would gain nothing from the arrangement and their own credibility in licensing the performances of foreign groups could be called into question.

52. Secondly, according to PRS almost always a tour by a prominent group would involve support acts. These acts would either perform their own works or other works within the repertoire of PRS. If the headline act were permitted to license the public performance of its own works directly, PRS would still be required to grant a licence for the public performance of other works to be performed by the support acts (or even by the headline act itself if it proposed to perform works written by others) and the cost of such licensing would be borne unfairly by the other members of PRS. The headline act would not bear its fair share of the normal PRS administrative costs arising out of the concert.

53. Thirdly, according to PRS there was undoubtedly in some instances of requests by pop groups to invoke the Article 7(f) procedure a conflict of interest which meant that the request was not necessarily made to benefit them as composers. PRS stated that it attempted to set licensing tariffs which ensured a reasonable rate of return for all members. To create a 'free market' in royalties for pop concerts might act to the detriment of the weaker members, who might, in the absence of effective protection, be induced to avail of Article 7(f) for a lesser

consideration.

54. Finally there was a further practical matter in that pop concerts provided a forum for young support bands and an arrangement which allowed pop groups to use the Article 7(f) procedure would not necessarily be in the interests of the support acts. It would be open to a headline act to decline to use any support acts to try to circumvent PRS's argument that it would still have to license the concert anyway. If support acts were no longer used, this would be a disincentive to young composers and performers and in itself would be a restriction on competition.

55. As regards the returns of programme details from hotels, restaurants, bars, etc (see para. 34), IMRO stated that it would not be practicable for them to require returns to be submitted from such users for all performances, and even if they were obtained, the cost of analysing them would consume so much of the royalties collected, that there would be little left to distribute.

56. PRS stated that in essence the earnings equalisation scheme referred to at para. 39 was close to being a pension scheme; however the 'pension' only became payable if the current PRS earnings of the member who had qualified under it fell below a level which was determined by reference to the level of his past earnings through the Society. The scheme, therefore, provided a 'cushion' against income falling below a given level.

(g) **Views of Representative Bodies**

57. The three associations representative of authors, composers and publishers referred to at para. 11 were invited to furnish observations on the assignment arrangements. One of the bodies, Republic of Ireland Music Publishing Association (RIMPA), made a submission. RIMPA represents virtually all trading music publishers in Ireland and its members belong to PRS. Its activities involve the promotion of the musical compositions of their composers including by way of performance on radio and television. These composers are also normally members of PRS. The position regarding distribution of performing royalties by PRS to these members is that a maximum of 50% may be paid to the publisher. RIMPA said that the reason for this maximum limit was to protect composers from selling out their interest in their compositions completely to music publishers who might be in a stronger economic position. RIMPA said that publishers generally were not in as strong an economic position as before and that the maximum limit should be reviewed accordingly.

(h) **Views of Third Parties**

58. A submission, on behalf of the Concert Promoters and Venue Owners Association, stated that the Association was formed in November 1991 for the specific purpose of representing concert promoters and venue owners in their dealings with PRS/IMRO. It was the understanding of the Association that once copyright in the performing right had been assigned to PRS, a member had no control thereafter as to how such copyright was disposed of. The result of this was that even where the composers were the performers of the music, as was commonly the case with popular artists, those composing and performing artists were not in a position to negotiate with the concert promoter as to how much the concert promoter was to be charged for the public performance of the composer's work. Instead, PRS insisted that a percentage of the gross box office be paid to them as the copyright owners in the performing rights in the music. The Association felt that it ought to be possible for them to negotiate directly with composer-performers 'on a free market basis'.

59. A submission on behalf of The Vintners' Federation of Ireland Ltd, RGDATA, Licensed Vintners' Association, National Federation of Retail Newsagents, Irish Retail Newsagents Association and Irish Hardware Association stated that they did not know the content of the agreements (CA/1, 2 and 3) and reserved the right to make a further submission on seeing the preliminary decision of the Authority. They felt that the system whereby they could only obtain licences from IMRO (a situation resulting from the combined effect of the assignments) was

6.3 fundamentally anti-competitive and contrary to section 4 of the Act. They had no objection to the idea of collecting copyright organisations as such. They did not accept that it was necessary for the assignments to result in only one such collecting organisation. In their view, IMRO's charges were excessive.

(i) **Collecting Societies and EU Law**

60. EU law imposes certain restrictions on the freedom of collecting societies in respect of their terms of membership and activities. This is because collecting societies usually operate as *de facto* monopolies in Member States and consequently, they occupy a dominant position within a substantial part of the EU within the meaning of Article 86 of the EEC Treaty and any abuse of this position is prohibited under EU law. The EU Commission have investigated the practices of a number of European collecting societies under Article 86 of the Treaty and there have been several EU Court of Justice judgments in respect of such societies. The rules and practices of performing right societies have not been examined by the EU Commission under Article 85 of the Treaty, which relates to anti-competitive agreements, decisions of associations and concerted practices. The Court of Justice made it clear in *BRT v. SABAM and FONIOR*,[2] that collecting societies, in drawing up internal rules must take account of all relevant interests in such a way that a balance is ensured between 'the requirement of maximum freedom for authors, composers, and publishers to dispose of their works and that of the effective management of their rights'.

61. The most detailed examination of the internal regulations of a collecting society from the viewpoint of EU competition rules was made in the 1971 GEMA[3] decision. In this decision the Commission ruled *inter alia* that, as far as relationships with members were concerned, GEMA had abused its dominant position (a) by discriminating against nationals of other Member States and (b) by binding its members with excessive obligations. It stated that members should be free to withdraw from GEMA the administration of certain categories (of which there were 7) at the end of each year. GEMA found that the right of annual resignation was too difficult to live with and negotiated further with the Commission. In 1972, the Commission accepted the right of GEMA[4] to extend the minimum length of membership to three years, on condition that the range of rights which had to be assigned during that period was narrowed, thus allowing members greater freedom in dividing up the responsibility for collection of royalties around different societies. They accordingly defined 12 'forms of utilisation' (e.g. the general performance right; the public performing right of broadcast works; the public performing right of televised works; the right of mechanical reproduction and distribution) within which the complete assignment of rights could be required for a given country. The Rules of PRS have been challenged under Articles 85 and 86 in a case currently before the High Court in London.

(j) **US law on Collecting Societies**

62. The operations of Music Performing Rights Associations in the USA have been the subject of several anti-trust actions principally under the Sherman Act 1890. There are three main licensing associations operating in the US viz. The American Association of Composers, Authors and Publishers (ASCAP—hose members are composers, lyricists and music publishers), Broadcast Music Inc (BMI—whose stock is owned by broadcasters) and the much smaller privately owned SESAC. All the associations operate under anti-trust constraints arising in particular from an amended consent decree accepted by ASCAP in 1950 and a consent judgment accepted by BMI in 1966. Under the 1966 decree judgment BMI was, *inter alia*, enjoined and restrained from

2. [1974] ECR 317.
3. OJ L134, 20.6.71, p. 15.
4. OJ L166, 24.7.72, p. 22.

(A) Failing to grant permission on the written request of all writers and publishers of a musical composition including the copyright proprietor thereof, allowing such persons to issue to a music user making direct performances to the public a non-exclusive licence permitting the making of specified performances of such musical composition by such music user directly to the public, provided that the defendant shall not be required to make payment with respect to performances so licensed.

63. The consent decree accepted by ASCAP in 1950 included, *inter alia*, a more restrictive enjoinment and restraint on ASCAP from:

(A) Holding, acquiring, licensing, enforcing or negotiating concerning any rights in copyrighted musical compositions other than rights of public performance on a non-exclusive basis;
(B) Limiting, restricting or interfering with the right of any member to issue to a user non-exclusive licenses for rights of public performance.

64. As a result of these consent decrees, creators/publishers in the US have the right to license the public performance of their works even though they are members or affiliates of collecting societies. In a number of cases, the US Supreme Court has held that the ASCAP and BMI arrangements, as amended by the consent decrees, do not constitute a collective price fixing arrangement *per se* and so do not infringe the provisions of the Sherman Act.[5]

Subsequent Developments

65. The Authority issued a Statement of Objections (SO) to PRS and IMRO on 4 March 1993. A written response was received on 23 April 1993. An oral hearing was held on 7/8 March 1994, and a further meeting with PRS took place on 4 May 1994. Notification of their arrangements was made by PRS to the EU Commission on 4 February 1994 seeking negative clearance under Articles 85(1) and 86 or alternatively an exemption under Article 85(3).

66. In its submissions and at the oral hearing, PRS disputed that the arrangements constituted an agreement between undertakings within the meaning of section 4(1) of the Competition Act. They considered that PRS, as distinct from its individual members, could not be considered as an economic undertaking independent of the other party, i.e. its members. In 1992 PRS had approximately 25,500 members of which 12,700 were provisional members with no vote 10,200 were associate members with 1 vote each and 2,600 full members with 10 votes each. PRS said that section 5 of the Act was designed to capture unilateral behaviour by one player and in this case there was just one player involved. PRS also stated that only the deeds of assignment had been notified to the Authority and not its Memorandum and Articles of Association and rules. They considered that section 5 of the Act, in respect of which the Authority had no function, was the proper focus for these.

67. PRS stated that sections 22 and 25 of the Copyright Act 1963 limited the rights to enforce copyright to the owner (PRS) and an exclusive licensee of the owner (IMRO). Ability to enforce within the framework of the Copyright Act was an essential element of the collection system. A rule of reason approach to the interpretation of section 4 of the Competition Act should take account of the unique aspects of music creation and marketing as well as of constraints on enforcement imposed by the Copyright Act, bearing in mind that copyright itself was created by statute. A non-exclusive licencing system would substantially complicate legal enforcement of copyright and increase its costs, e.g. in specific cases PRS would have to sue jointly with named members with any relief granted confined to the particular works cited. The cumulative effect of widespread non-exclusivity would be to so increase costs as to make enforcement

5. *Broadcast Music Inc. et al. v. Colombia Broadcasting Systems et al.*, 441 USI (1979), and *Colombia Broadcasting System Inc. v. ASCAP et. al.*, 620 F2d 930 (1980), and 450 US 970 (1981).

6.3 uneconomic and lead to a collapse in the licensing system. They stated that there was a difference between enforcement in the sense of being able to sue and licensing in the sense of being able to issue a licence. A non-exclusive licensee could issue a licence but he could not sue. PRS at present sought a wide injunction in respect of the full portfolio of the works they were entitled to license. That did not necessarily mean that PRS would sue on all of them.

68. PRS argued that the licencing environment in the USA was very different from that in the UK or Ireland, i.e. on a per head basis there were four times more licensed users in Ireland than in the US and in the US many types of public performance were exempted by law. Figures supplied by PRS showed that while revenue from live performance in Ireland represented 40% of public performance revenue (and for Great Britain and Ireland 30%), in the US (for one collection society) live performance revenue was only 5%. Under its consent decree ASCAP was required to permit the members themselves license performances of their works but the incidence of live performance licensing in the USA was low with the major share of revenue derived from broadcasting. with regard to the BMI consent decree, PRS said that they did not know whether there was an assignment or a non-exclusive licence but there was a transaction and creators and publishers could administer their own rights if they wished. Basically all persons involved in a composition had to send a written request to BMI which BMI could not refuse. PRS said that because non-exclusivity applied in the US, the Authority should not proceed on the basis that it should also work in this country. The practices operated in the EU countries, where exclusivity was the norm, were more relevant to, and comparable with, the Irish situation.

69. PRS said that the non-exclusivity of the US system did not prevent the inclusion of US works in their enforcement proceedings in Ireland. Currently PRS sued for breaches on the basis of a number of named works but sought an injunction in respect of their full portfolio. They said that with the exception of concerts there was no perceived demand from its members to exercise the performing rights themselves. In practice a creator might be able to collect royalties from his own performances but wider collection would not be practicable. The main concern of PRS was to avoid giving users another excuse for non-payment and creating uncertainty even for broadcasting where they could no longer guarantee exclusivity. A study undertaken by PRS showed that if some Irish song titles were non exclusive to PRS there would be a diminution in PRS income from public performance and a very substantial increase in costs largely due to increased monitoring of users resulting in a sharp decline in net revenue for distribution to members.

70. On the question of Rules 7(b) and 7(c), which required a three year assignment of rights, PRS in its written submission argued that this was the minimum period deemed necessary for the stability and security of membership necessary to achieve their objectives. At the oral hearing PRS stated that its Council would propose to reduce this period to 1 year at their AGM in September 1994.

71. At the oral hearing, the Authority accepted that PRS/IMRO could not operate if creators granted them a non-exclusive licence instead of an assignment in respect of their works, since this would make it extremely difficult for PRS/IMRO to take court actions for breach of copyright. It suggested that it should be possible to devise alternative arrangements which could satisfy the indispensability test in section 4(2) of the Competition Act and still protect the integrity of the collection/enforcement system. It was noted that Article 7(f) of their Articles of Association already enabled PRS to return the whole or any part of the performing right to a member although currently this was entirely at the discretion of PRS. It was indicated to PRS that if certain amendments were made to the Articles of Association, the arrangements would be acceptable to the Authority. In particular it was suggested that a variant of Article 7(f) whereby PRS would be required, in response to a request by all of the creators/publishers of a work, to allow members to license the use of their works to individual users within the State on a non-exclusive basis, (i.e. on the lines of the BMI consent decree), would be acceptable. PRS were given time to consider this proposal but subsequently informed the Authority on 4

May 1994 that they did not intend to make any amendments to their Articles of Association along the lines discussed. 6.3

72. PRS said that Article 7(f) was only used in respect of the return of compilation rights which were in the grey area between grand rights (which PRS did not hold) and small rights. Where this rule was invoked for a particular performance at a particular place PRS could still retain enforcement rights for other performances of the works involved. PRS argued that the PRS collecting system required that exclusive licensing rights remain with PRS. Broadcasting licences were for 3/5 year periods and premature return of broadcast rights to members for particular songs would damage the integrity of the PRS warranty to broadcasters on their full portfolio. The collective loss to PRS members from the loss of exclusivity, leading to increased collection costs, increased opportunities of evasion and uncertainty in relation to the scope of the PRS warranty, would far outweigh the individual gain. Anybody opting out of the system would cause chaos. PRS stated that legal differences existed between a non-exclusive licence and an assignment where some rights were given back and that the latter would not deprive IMRO (PRS) of its enforcement rights. The wider operation of a provision similar to 7(f) would damage the creation of music in Ireland especially in relation to support bands. It would not be practical for support bands with small repertoires to perform only their own music. Creators performing their own music would seek to maximise their income by cutting out support bands.

73. Following further consideration PRS informed the Authority on 4 May 1994 that they could not agree to the amendment to the Articles of Association as proposed at the oral hearing. They requested instead that a licence be issued subject to conditions as provided for in section 8(1) of the Act, i.e. that the licence would operate with the amendment suggested and that PRS would be given a time limit to comply with the condition imposed. This would minimise the damage that would result from a negative decision. It would also give PRS and other parties an opportunity to comply with, or appeal, the licence. Should the Authority subsequently decide on the basis of evidence submitted to it that PRS was not complying with the conditions imposed, it could amend or revoke the licence under section 8(3) of the Act. A negative decision would give rise to legal uncertainty and make it impossible for PRS to enforce its licensing system.

74. PRS stated that it would not be acceptable to them to have two sets of rules for one member, i.e. one set which would apply in Ireland and one applying elsewhere. Any changes in relation to Ireland would lead to great pressure for a change in the system with regard to other countries. They urged the Authority to defer a decision in this case until the EU, having looked at the arrangements from a European dimension, had made its decision. A decision by the Authority could be reversed by the EU and would have caused unnecessary chaos.

75. At the oral hearing, PRS also stated that discussions were taking place between PRS and IMRO on the question of IMRO becoming a separate membership organisation in Ireland during 1994. Currently PRS members in Ireland had little option to join other European societies because of the language difficulties. PRS stated that if IMRO was established as an independent membership society, members would be free to move between societies which would create competition and give members a choice of remaining with PRS or of joining IMRO. Subsequent to the oral hearing IMRO wrote to the Authority requesting that the Authority should not take a decision in respect of the notification until IMRO had been established as an independent body.

76. A number of other issues raised in the PRS submission and at the oral hearing relating to factual details and clarifications have been incorporated in this decision.

Assessment

(a) *Applicability of section 4(1)*

77. Section 4(1) of the Competition Act 1991 prohibits and renders void all agreements between undertakings, decisions by associations of undertakings and concerted practices which

6.3 have as their object or effect the prevention, restriction or distortion of competition in trade in any goods or services in the State, or in any part of the State.

(b) *The undertakings*

78. The term 'undertaking' is defined in section 3(1) of the Competition Act 1991 as follows: 'a person being an individual, a body corporate or an unincorporated body of persons engaged for gain in the production, supply or distribution of goods or the provision of a service.'

79. In its decision in the PRS/IMRO agreement, the Authority concluded that PRS was an undertaking within the meaning of the Act. That conclusion applies in the present case also. The individual composer, author, lyricist or publisher of music is also an undertaking since each is engaged in the provision of a service, i.e. the composition, writing or publishing of musical works, for gain. The primary purpose of the assignment is to facilitate the obtaining of financial gain from the exploitation of the copyright which arises from the musical composition.

(c) *The Agreements*

80. The assignment agreements under consideration are formal written agreements in standard form constituting categories of agreement between undertakings for the purposes of the Competition Act. The Authority also takes into consideration the Memorandum, Articles, Rules and related practices of PRS as the assignment agreements in isolation from these would have no life of their own, i.e. the assignment is in pursuance of the assignees' membership of PRS with membership a precondition to the administration by PRS of the performing right on their behalf. For the purposes of this decision, these are regarded as being part of the overall agreement between undertakings. In other circumstances, these latter might be viewed as decisions of an association of undertakings. While PRS might not be considered as an economic entity independent of the totality of its members, particularly the 10% of members, who, as full members, have voting control of its affairs, the assignment agreements are between PRS and particular individual members, each of whom operates as a separate independent undertaking. Individual members are pursuing their own economic interest when they create/publish musical works. They are competing to have their works used in preference to those of other creators/publishers in order to maximise their income. The members and PRS cannot be regarded as a single economic entity with common interests.

(d) *Restriction of Competition*

Arrangements generally

81. The essential feature of the assignment arrangements is that they involve a transfer of ownership of property (the performing right) from the creator or publisher to PRS, thereby granting PRS the exclusive right necessary to exploit the copyright (Clause 2 of the Assignment; Article 7(a) of Articles). Generally, the assignments cover the performing right in all works for the whole world. As such, the arrangements preclude the member from administering the performing right himself, e.g. by granting an individual right to individual users, or from engaging the services of any other collecting organisation. It is understood that most, if not all, active musical creators and publishers in Great Britain and Ireland are members of, and enter into these arrangements with, PRS. The arrangements also involve a restriction on the freedom of copyright users to purchase the performing right from any supplier other than PRS. They also have the effect of restricting competition in the supply of performing right between individual members and they involve the establishment and maintenance of uniform rates of royalty and other conditions in relation to the exploitation of the performing right thereby eliminating price competition. In effect, the arrangements, taken in their collective context, constitute an exclusive collective copyright enforcement system involving independent undertakings and, as such, are restrictive of competition within the State and offend against section 4(1) of the Competition Act.

Deed of Assignment 6.3

82. The main clause of the Deed which operates to carry out the assignment is Clause 2 and, accordingly, it offends against section 4(1) as it has the object and effect of preventing, restricting and distorting competition between individual creators and between individual publishers.

83. Clauses 1 and 4 which relate to definitions and to the giving of a warranty that the assignment itself does not involve breach of copyright are clearly not anti-competitive and do not offend against section 4(1).

84. Clause 3 provides for the making of payments to the assignor out of the royalties collected by PRS. As such, the clause, *per se*, does not offend against section 4(1). However, the amounts payable to members are determined in accordance with the Rules of the society and these are further considered in paras. 95 and 96 below.

Memorandum of Association

85. The objects of PRS, as set out in Clause 3 of the Memorandum, include the acquisition of the business or property of any company carrying on activities similar to those of PRS (Clause 3(h)) as well as the acquisition of shares in such a company (Clause 3 (k)). The main purpose of these clauses, apart from empowering PRS to make such acquisitions, is to ensure that PRS keeps within its main functional area. As such, these clauses do not have the object of restricting competition. As regards their effect, they could, in conjunction with relevant provisions of the articles, afford a basis for acquisitive activities intended to maintain the dominant position of PRS in the market for performing right. However, following enquiries with PRS in regard to the actual use of these provisions, it is clear that these provisions have not been used in this way. Accordingly, the Authority does not consider that these provisions offend against section 4(1).

Articles of Association

Access to Membership

86. Income derived from performing right royalties represents an important part of the livelihood of musical creators and publishers. While membership of PRS is not, in itself, essential to enable a person to pursue a livelihood in this field (since a creator or publisher could join another collecting society in the EU or attempt to collect royalties individually), exclusion from membership would involve considerable competitive disadvantages arising from additional delays in obtaining royalties and from additional administrative costs. The provisions of the Articles of Association relating to access to membership are outlined in paras. 24 and 25 above. The basic qualifying criteria are based on a minimum level of published or public output/work. Advancement from the lowest grade of membership (provisional member) to that of associate and full membership is conditional on the attainment of certain earnings levels. These distinctions as to membership are reflected also in the voting arrangements. The main perspective from which the Authority views these membership conditions is whether they might involve any unreasonable restrictions on the freedom of creators/publishers to enter into the profession of musical composition, writing and publishing. In the view of the Authority in these circumstances, the conditions relating to membership set out in Articles 2 to 5 of the Articles of Association are based on objective criteria which are applied in a non-discriminatory way. They do not involve any restriction on competition and, therefore, do not offend against section 4(1) of the Act.

Termination of Membership

87. For the same reason as that set out in the preceding paragraph, the Authority considers that Clauses 9(d) and 9(e) relating to termination of membership on the initiative of PRS do not offend against section 4(1).

6.3 88. A less sanguine view must be taken of the provisions of Article 9(f) under which the freedom of the member himself to terminate his membership is considerably limited. Under this article, the member is given an opportunity to leave, in effect, only at three-yearly intervals. This represents a significant impediment to the member to leave at all, if he were minded to do so, and to make other arrangements such as to administer his performing right himself, to join another collecting organisation or to seek, with others, to establish a new collecting organisation. It also represents a significant barrier to the possible entry of new collecting organisations into the performing right market. PRS has indicated that its Council is to propose an amendment to this rule at their AGM September 1994 to introduce a one year interval with 3 months' notice expiring at end year required. However, the agreements notified to the Authority provide for 3 yearly periods and, for the reasons stated above, the Authority is of the view that Article 9(f) offends against section 4(1).

Assignment of Rights

89. Article 7(a), which provides for a member of PRS to assign his rights to PRS, offends against section 4(1) for the reasons indicated in para. 81 above.

90. Article 7(b) offends against section 4(1) in two respects, (a) inasmuch as it prescribes the 'form' of the assignment agreement and (b) inasmuch as it prescribes, in conjunction with Article 9(f) (see para. 88 above), the duration of the assignment agreement.

91. Article 7(c) offends against section 4(1) inasmuch as it forms the legal basis for the imposition of the restriction relating to dividing up rights referred to in para. 19 above, i.e. the right to divide rights by category or country is exercisable on joining and thereafter at 3 year intervals only.

92. Article 7(d) which provides for transitional arrangements pending the ordinary assignment of rights pursuant to Article 7 offends against Article 4(1) inasmuch as it provides for or permits the imposition of terms or conditions similar to those in other clauses which do offend against Article 4(1), e.g. in relation to the basic assignment and duration of assignment.

93. Article 7(e) is an enabling provision under which PRS/IMRO may enforce, in the State, the rights of members of societies in other countries with which PRS is affiliated. This is provided for further in contracts between PRS and the affiliated societies. No such contracts have been notified to the Authority under the Competition Act and, accordingly, this decision does not apply to them. Since Article 7(e) is merely an enabling provision, it does not offend against section 4(1).

94. Article 7(f) empowers PRS to return to the member all or part of the performing right which he originally assigned to the Society. On the face of it, this provision appears to be pro-competitive. It represents a derogation from the restrictive ties of the assignment agreement. It is necessary, however, to consider how the provision operates in practice. It is clear from the material in paras. 49 to 54 that the provision is actually operated in a very restrictive way. Derogations are permitted only in very restricted circumstances. Applications from creators/performers to license their own concerts are invariably refused. Even if a request is granted, two further restrictions, which do not appear in the Article itself, are imposed. These require that the appropriate PRS tariff be respected and that an exclusive licence only be granted. PRS may also withdraw the derogation at any time. The manner in which Article 7(f) is operated reinforces the view that the assignment arrangements generally are indeed restrictive of competitive activity. In the Authority's view Article 7(f), as operated at present, offends against section 4(1).

Rules and related practices

95. Rule 2(c) of the Rules forms the legal basis for the value to be assigned to musical works for distributable purposes. In this regard, the operation of the point system as described in para. 38 is non-discriminatory and does not offend against section 4(1).

96. Rule 2(f) of the Rules provides that the share of the publisher and/or proprietor of the

performing right shall not exceed one half of the net fee. This rule sets a limit of 50% on the share of income payable directly by PRS to the publisher. However, the arrangements between the writer and publisher are also governed by the writer/publisher contracts which can, *inter alia*, provide that royalty payments to the writer are paid over to the publisher. Effectively any restrictive effect in this rule can be by-passed by the arrangements agreed in the creator/publisher contracts. Price competition between publishers in the provision of publishing services is, therefore, not affected and consequently this rule does not offend against section 4(1). **6.3**

97. The Authority considered whether the 'Earnings Equalisation Scheme', described in para. 39 above, might represent a form of 'tied sale' from the point of view of the ultimate users of the performing right. In the Authority's view, the scheme involves a voluntary donation by creators for fellow members whose earnings have fallen because their music is no longer popular. As such, it may be seen as a sacrifice of a small proportion of their earnings by the general membership and not involving the payment of additional royalties by users. The total amount paid out by PRS in 1991 in respect of the EES. was £619,000 Sterling or 0.5% of total royalty income. The Authority does not consider that these activities offend against section 4(1) of the Act.

Summary under section 4(1).

98. In the view of the Authority, the following features of the arrangements offend against section 4(1):

— the whole exclusive assignment agreement with PRS;

— the basic assignment provisions, including their exclusivity (Clause 2 of Deed of Assignment and Article 7(a) of the Articles of Association);

— Article 7(b) inasmuch as it prescribes the form and duration of the assignment agreement;

— Article 7(c) of the Articles insofar as it forms the legal basis for restricting the times at which the member may divide rights by category or by country;

— Article 7(d) insofar as it provides for restrictive arrangements on a temporary basis;

— Article 9(f) which imposes restrictions on termination of membership by a member;

— Article 7(f) and the operation of the two conditions attaching to it allowing individual members to administer the performing right themselves.

(e) *Applicability of section 4(2)*

99. Under section 4(2), the Competition Authority may grant a licence in the case of any agreement or category of agreements 'which in the opinion of the Authority, having regard to all relevant market conditions, contributes to improving the production of goods or provision of services or to promoting technical or economic progress, while allowing consumers a fair share of the resulting benefit and which does not

(i) impose on the undertakings concerned terms which are not indispensable to the attainment of those objectives;

(ii) afford undertakings the possibility of eliminating competition in respect of a substantial part of the products or services in question'.

100. In the opinion of the Authority, the notified arrangements do not fulfil all the conditions provided for in section 4(2).

Improvement in the provision of services

101. The notifying parties advanced a number of arguments in support of their claim that the arrangements notified met the above condition. These arguments may be summarised as follows. Effective protection of performing right is extremely labour intensive involving

6.3 considerable expenditure on administrative and monitoring procedures. In view of the practical difficulties and expense involved, it is only through collective action that creators may ensure effective protection of their performing right. In the absence of the present arrangements, it would be impossible for creators to obtain a just reward for the performance of their works and, in that event, the incentive to produce musical works would be very significantly reduced, or licences to perform music might not so readily be made available, and these would be to the detriment of licensed users and of the general public, as ultimate consumers.

102. The Authority accepts this reasoning. There are considerable practical difficulties involved in the administration and enforcement of performing rights, particularly in relation to the multiplicity of smaller users, and these difficulties do point to the need for a central collective licensing/enforcement system on behalf of creators and publishers many of whom are based outside the State. Substantial additional transaction costs would clearly be involved in any multiplicity of systems of administration of performing right based on licensing by individual creators. Compliant users would require a large number of licences while the cost of pursuit for non-compliance by individual creators/publishers would make this activity totally uneconomic except in the case of major users or events. The pursuit of breaches of copyright by smaller users would become totally uneconomic.

103. The Authority, therefore, accepts that a collective system of performing right administration involves efficiencies and these would be significant in the generality of cases. Assignment of the performing right to PRS is accepted as improving the provision of services.

Allowing consumers a fair share of the resulting benefit

104. Users benefit from the improved provision of services. Licensees (i.e. the users, such as radio and television broadcasters, discos, public houses, etc.) benefit from access to the PRS repertoire and from the avoidance of additional transaction costs which would be involved if they had to deal with a multiplicity of licensors. The ultimate consumers, the listening public, also share in this benefit as consumers of the various services, of which music forms part, provided by the intermediary undertakings. Consumers also benefit to the extent that a collective copyright arrangement has resulted in a greater supply and variety of musical works being available than would otherwise be the case. The Authority, therefore, considers that the collective copyright arrangements allow consumers a fair share of the benefit.

Indispensability

105. When a member assigns his performing right to PRS, he does so on an exclusive basis i.e. the rights which he has assigned may not, thereafter, be exercised by him as an individual apart from the Article 7(f) procedure in respect of which PRS has full discretion whether to apply it or not and which is applied very seldom in practice. This is in contrast with the situation in the US where either exclusivity is prohibited in the case of one society or where affiliates of another society must be granted permission to license individual users themselves. Essentially they, therefore, can individually license public performance of their works. This system has operated in the US for the past 50 years. There is no evidence that preventing members from granting non-exclusive licences to individual users for particular purposes is essential to achieve the efficiency gains generated by a collective copyright enforcement system. Even though licensing on an individual basis appears to be rarely used in the US, it is clear that a collective copyright enforcement system which allows such freedom can operate satisfactorily.

106. A mechanism for creators/publishers to assign their works to PRS is necessary to enable PRS to be in a position to license its repertoire. Those provisions, without which PRS could not exist at all, are clearly indispensable. The Authority believes that preventing the members from granting non-exclusive licences to individual users for particular purposes is not essential for PRS to operate effectively as a collective copyright enforcement agency. In the Authority's view such a restriction is not indispensable for the achievement of the efficiencies and other benefits which a collective copyright system produces. The experience

in the US over the past 50 years indicates that collective administration of performing right is not incompatible with allowing creators/publishers to grant individual non-exclusive licences. The Authority considers that members of PRS should have the freedom to choose whether to allow PRS alone to administer all or part of the performing right, or to administer it themselves on individual occasions. At the oral hearing the Authority indicated to PRS its view as to how this could be effected in a manner which could meet the indispensability test under section 4(2) without impinging on the integrity of the current licensing and enforcement system. Since it is likely that few would choose to exercise this option, the Authority believes that the efficient operation of PRS does not require the existing arrangements. 6.3

107. The Authority is also not convinced that the following provisions are indispensable for the effective operation of PRS:

— Article 7(b) which prescribes the duration and form of the assignment agreement,
— Article 7(c) which forms the legal basis for restricting the times at which a member may divide rights by category or by country,
— Article 9(f) which imposes restrictions on termination of membership by a member.

It is accepted that these restrictions are compatible with the GEMA decisions but compatibility with a Commission decision under Article 86 does not rule out the application of national competition law. It is also accepted that only a limited number of members may be interested in these freedoms. However, in the Authority's view, the three year period is, in the context of the present arrangements, excessive and should be reduced to such period as can be shown, objectively, to be indispensable for the efficient operation of PRS. In this regard the Authority noted the intention of the Council of PRS to recommend a reduction of this period to 1 year at their AGM in September 1994. A reduction of the period to one year would satisfy the concerns of the Authority in relation to Articles 7(b), 7(c) and 9(f).

Elimination of competition

108. It is clear from all of the foregoing that the assignment arrangements do involve significant restrictions on competition between creators and between publishers, especially in relation to price. Since each item of the PRS repertoire is essentially available at the same price, price competition is entirely eliminated by virtue of these arrangements. A creator cannot break into the market by offering his product at a lower price. The exclusive nature of the assignment contributes greatly to these restrictions. The Authority, however, believes that there is some degree of non-price competition between creators which is not eliminated by the arrangements. The Authority believes that normally arrangements which eliminate price competition would not satisfy the requirements for a licence. It considers on balance however that, taking into account the special nature of the market in music, the arrangements do not afford the possibility of eliminating competition in respect of a substantial part of the services in question.

Conditional licence

109. At its meeting with the Authority on 4 May 1994 PRS requested that, in the event of the Authority coming to a negative conclusion on their notifications, a conditional licence should be issued. The Authority is empowered to grant licences to agreements which meet the requirements of section 4(2) of the Act. It cannot grant a licence specifying the type of agreement it would like to see when no such agreement exists. In addition as PRS has already indicated that they were not prepared to amend the arrangements the Authority does not consider that a conditional licence would be appropriate. IMRO also requested the Authority not to take a decision until a planned new independent Irish based collection society with its own rules had been established. No action under the Competition Act can be taken in respect of the notified agreements under the terms of the Competition Act until the Authority has decided upon them, by virtue of section 6(7). The Authority does not believe that it should extend the protection of section 6(7) by deferring a decision in respect of a notified agreement

6.3 in these circumstances. Any new independent Irish collective copyright agency can notify its arrangements to the Authority in the future if it chooses to. A party which has notified an agreement to the Authority may withdraw it prior to the Authority taking a decision. By so doing it loses the benefit of section 6(7). The Authority does not believe, therefore, that there is any justification for it deferring a decision when the effect of such a deferral would be to deprive third parties of a right to take action under the terms of the Competition Act.

Scope of application of decision.

110. PRS has asked the Authority to state the scope of its decision, i.e. by specifying whether it applies to revenue derived outside the State. The Authority considers that the scope of any of its decisions is co-extensive with the scope of the Act, which is a matter of general law, rather than a matter to be determined by the Authority.

111. It is important to stress that the present proceeding and decision relates solely to section 4 of the Act. The Authority has not considered the present arrangements under section 5 since it is not empowered to do so.

The Decision

112. The Performing Right Society Ltd, and the individual creators and publishers who are parties to the notified standard assignment agreements under consideration are undertakings within the meaning of the Competition Act. The notified standard assignment agreements are agreements between undertakings. In the Authority's opinion, the notified agreements offend against section 4(1) of the Act. In its opinion also, the notified agreements do not qualify for a licence under section 4(2) of the Act because they do not meet all of the conditions required for the granting of a licence. The Authority, therefore, refuses to grant a certificate or a licence in respect of the PRS standard assignment of copyright in musical works, (CA/2/91E), notified to the Authority under section 7 of the Competition Act 1991 on 3 October 1991.

For the Competition Authority

Des Wall
Member

18 May 1994

Competition Authority Decision No. 383, Irish Music Rights Organisation Ltd/ UK Television Companies and Other Copyright Holders/Cable & MMDS Operators: 16 December 1994, Notification No. CA/7/91E* 6.4

Intellectual property – licence agreement between holders of copyright in television broadcasts and cable/MMDS operators – agreement four years in duration – appointment by separate competing broadcasters of same collecting agency to administer the copyright in their works – provision whereby licensees can request additional broadcasters to be included in the notified agreement – whether arrangements improve the provision of services – whether the arrangements benefit the consumer – whether the arrangements afford the possibility of eliminating competition within a substantial part of the services – amendment of notified arrangements – third party objections – subsequent notification of notified agreement to EU Commission – Competition Act, 1991 (No. 24), sections 3, 4 and 7

Facts: On 3 October 1991 notification was made to the Authority with a request for a certificate under section 4(4) of the Competition Act, 1991 or failing that, a licence under section 4(2) in respect of a standard agreement between Irish Music Rights Organisation ('IMRO'), various UK television companies, other copyright holders and cable and multi-point microwave distribution system (MMDS) operators relating to the licensing and retransmission and rebroadcasting within the State of television programmes originating in the UK.

IMRO, an Irish registered company and a wholly owned subsidiary of the UK company, Performing Right Society, is a collecting society the main activities of which are the licensing of performing rights for musical works in the State and the collection of royalties. The television companies to the notified agreement include BBC Enterprises Ltd, companies within the Independent Television Association, Channel 4 Television Corporation and the Welsh Fourth Channel Authority. Other copyright holders which are party to the notified agreement include specialist copyright administration and collection agencies. The cable and MMDS operators to the notified agreement are all corporate bodies engaged in the retransmission of television programmes broadcast from inside and outside the State to their subscribers within the State.

The service, the subject of the notification, is the retransmission of UK broadcasts to cable/MMDS service subscribers in their homes and premises. Irish operators of cable and MMDS networks in Ireland require licences to operate from the Department of Transport, Energy and Communication. In addition the rights of the broadcasters and the owners of copyright in the programmes for retransmission cannot be infringed. Individual broadcasters enter into arrangements which preclude them from authorising retransmission of their entire broadcast works. The conclusion of an agreement involving both broadcasters and other copyright owners is designed to overcome difficulties arising from these circumstances by providing a comprehensive blanket licence to the cable operators lawfully to transmit all broadcasts. The relative geo-

*Decision No. 384 Irish Music Rights Organisation Ltd/UK Television Companies/Copyright Holders which concerns the collective licensing of copyright in UK television programmes for cable and MMDS systems contains another licence and the reasoning is similar to this decision.

6.4 graphic market is those areas of the State which are served by the cable and MMDS system.

Under the standard notified agreement the licensors grants to the licensee (the cable company) a non-exclusive licence to transmit or rebroadcast to the licensee's subscribers in the State the defined programme services. The licence limits such rebroadcasting to the use of terrestrial equipment and consisting of only simultaneous and unabridged transmissions of the broadcaster's unaltered programmes. The term of the agreement is four years from 1 January 1991. Other terms of the notified agreement provide, *inter alia*, that a particular channel should be allocated by the licensee in the cable system for each of the programme services licensed and that the licensee will transmit as much of the programme services as commercially possible but a minimum of eight uninterrupted hours of each programme service every twenty-four hour period. The licensee may cease retransmission of any one or more of the programme services provided three months notice in proper terms is given. In addition, in exceptional circumstances either the licensor or the licensee may stop the retransmission on a particular programme on giving at least forty-eight hours notice to the other. At all times the licensors agree to indemnify the licensee against any claims or actions brought by a third party against the licensee in respect of the programme services. Clause 15 (as amended) of the notified agreement allows for the entry of new broadcasters to the notified agreement at the request of the licensee together with provisions for the amendment of the financial provisions of the agreement.

The notified agreement was notified to the EU Commission by BBC Enterprises Ltd on 6 December 1991 and the Commission came to the conclusion that the agreement, as notified, fell within Article 85(1) but could not benefit from an exemption under Article 85(3) of the EU Treaty. Several amendments to the notified agreement were agreed with the Commission following which the Commission issued an interim comfort letter indicating that sufficient *prima facie* justification had been provided for an exemption to be granted by the Commission pursuant to Article 85(3). The amendments were also notified to the Authority.

Decided by the Authority:
(A) In refusing to issue a certificate under section 4(4) of the Competition Act, 1991 that:

(1) Each of IMRO, BBC Enterprises Ltd, Channel 4 Television Corporation, the Welsh Fourth Channel Authority, and certain specialists collecting agencies are corporate bodies engaged for gain in the exploitation of copyright works and are, therefore, undertakings within the meaning of the Competition Act. The Independent Television Association and AGICOA (a specialist collecting agency) signed the notified agreement on behalf of its members who are undertakings. The cable/MMDS companies are engaged in the provision of a service to the general public for gain and are also undertakings. The notified agreement is an agreement between undertakings and the agreement has effect within the State.

(2) Collective licensing arrangements where actual or potential competitors in the market join forces for the collective licensing of their respective services for a global fee to be divided on an agreed basis restricts competition. Such arrangements eliminate the possibility of each television service competing on price against the others for the right to supply a retransmitted programme via cable or MMDS systems within the State and they, therefore, offend against section 4(1) of the Competition Act 1991.

(3) Clause 5 of the notified agreement provides that the licensee is to provide a particular channel in the cable network for each programme service. Clause 5 as amended gives the licensee the right to withdraw any one or more of the programme services during the term of the agreement by giving a three month notice in writing and clause 15 (as amended) also allows new broadcasters to become parties to the agreement. In such circumstances any possibility of foreclosure of cable channels by reason of the notified agreement does not arise and these clauses do not offend against section 4(1) of the Competition Act 1991. 6.4

(B) In granting an unconditional licence from 16 December 1994 to 15 December 2004 under section 4(2) of the Competition Act 1991 in respect of the notified agreement that:

(1) Because of the number and diversity of the copyright holders involved in the retransmitted television programmes the most effective and efficient way of operating a business of retransmission is through the collective licensing system provided for under the notified agreement. The alternative for the cable companies would be the negotiation of an agreement with each of the copyright holders in respect of each retransmitted programme service and this would involve extra costs for the cable company and the consumer. The collective nature of the arrangement which has enabled the provision of the full UK national programme services through cable has thus contributed to the development of the cable services and network and the collective arrangement also provides a blanket indemnity to cable companies against claims for infringement of copyright on retransmitted material which would not otherwise be available. In these circumstances the arrangements notified involve efficiencies and have improved the provision of the services.

(2) Because of the arrangements subscribers have a wider selection of television programme services and they benefit from the competition created between overseas and local broadcasters.

(3) The notified agreements do not impose on the undertakings concerned any conditions which are not indispensable to the attainment of the benefits.

(4) The notified agreement (as amended) enables the addition of other broadcasters to the notified agreement. Individual consumers can opt for satellite dishes or, in many parts of the country, can have their own television aerial as a potential source of competition and in these circumstances the notified agreements do not afford the possibility of eliminating competition in respect of a substantial part of the services in question.

Competition Authority Decision of 16 December 1994, relating to a proceeding under section 4 of the Competition Act 1991
Notification No. CA/7/91E—Irish Music Rights Organisation Ltd/UK Television Companies and other Copyright holders/Cable Relay and MMDS operators

Introduction

1. Notification was made on 3 October 1991 with a request for a certificate under section 4(4) of the Competition Act 1991 or, in the event of refusal by the Competition Authority to issue a certificate, a licence under section 4(2) in respect of a standard agreement between Irish Music Rights Organisation (IMRO), UK Television Companies and other copyright holders and cable relay and MMDS (Multipoint Microwave Distribution Systems operators relating to

6.4 the licensing of re-transmission and re-broadcast of foreign broadcast television programmes. Notification of this agreement was also made by BBC Enterprises Ltd to the EU Commission in December 1991. Following an examination of this notification by the EU Commission amendments were made to the notified agreement which were submitted to the Authority in December 1992. Notice of intention to issue a licence was published in the Irish Times on 11 November 1994. One submission was received by the Authority.

The Facts

(a) *Subject of the notification*

2. The notified agreement relates to the licensing, by IMRO, UK television companies and other holders of copyright in TV programmes, of the re-transmission, by cable companies and MMDS operators to subscribers of television programmes broadcast from outside the State.

(b) *The parties involved*

3. The parties to the notified agreements are IMRO and the following companies:

Television Companies BBC Enterprises Ltd, companies within The Independent Television Association (representing UK independent regional Television broadcasters/licensees), Channel Four Television Corporation,[1] The Welsh Fourth Channel Authority.

Other Copyright Holders Association De Gestion Internationale Collective Des Oeuvres Audiovisuelles (AGICOA), Authors' Licensing and Collecting Society Ltd (ALCS), Design and Artists Copyright Society Ltd (DACS) and Phonographic Performance (Ireland) Ltd (PPI).

Cable Relay Companies Cablelink Ltd, Cablelink (Waterford) Ltd, Cablelink (Galway) Ltd, Cork Communications Ltd, Westward Cables Ltd, Horizon TV Distribution Ltd, Suir Nore and Independent Wireless Cable Ltd. Similar agreements have since been concluded with a number of MMDS (Multipoint Microwave Distribution Systems) operators within the State.

IMRO

4. IMRO is an Irish registered private company limited by guarantee, not having a share capital. IMRO is a collecting society and its main activities are the licensing of performing rights for musical works in the State and the collection of royalties. At the time of notification it was a wholly owned subsidiary of the UK Performing Right Society (PRS) which controlled the composition of the Board of Directors of IMRO. Under an agreement with PRS, IMRO administered the PRS Performing rights in musical works in the State by the issue of licences for public performances, domestic radio and television broadcasts as well as cable re-transmission of foreign television services and collected royalties arising from these activities. IMRO distributes its license income less operating expenses to PRS. The income and expenditure account of IMRO for the year ended 31 December 1991 showed that total licence revenue amounted to IR£4.8m consisting of IR£2.6m from broadcasting and IR£2.2m from public performance. Total administration costs amounted to IR£1.0m leaving IR£3.8m for royalty payments for transmission to PRS.

5. (i) *BBC Enterprises Ltd*

BBC Enterprises Ltd, London, is the wholly-owned commercial trading subsidiary of the British Broadcasting Corporation, (BBC), which is engaged in the production, supply and distribution of television programmes and programme-related products.

(ii) *Independent Television Association*

Independent Television Association (ITVA), is an organisation representing the Independent Television companies in the UK. The companies represented by ITVA are Anglian

1. Known as Channel Four Television Co. Ltd at the time of notification.

Television Group plc, Border Television plc, Central Independent Television plc; Channel Island Communications (Television) Ltd; Grampian Television plc; Granada Group plc; HTV Group plc; LWT (Holdings) plc; Scottish Television plc; Tyne Tees Television Holdings plc; Ulster Television plc and Yorkshire Television Holdings plc. ITVA also represents the new Channel 3 licensees (now GMTV, Meridian, Carlton and West Country). 6.4

(iii) *Other Television Companies*

The other television companies which are signatories to the agreement are Channel Four Television Corporation, Sianel Pedwar Cymru (formerly named The Welsh Fourth Channel Authority).

Other copyright holders

6. AGICOA represents the producers and distributors of films and television programmes acquired by broadcasters for inclusion in their broadcasting services, where the relevant rights have not been acquired by the broadcasters. ALCS is engaged in the licensing of the public performance, broadcasting and transmission to subscribers to diffusion services of literary and dramatic works. DACS is engaged in the licensing of the broadcasting and transmission to subscribers to diffusion services of artistic works. PPI is an organisation representative of record companies engaged in the licensing for gain of the public performance of sound recordings in the State.

Cable companies

Cablelink Ltd, Cablelink (Waterford) Ltd and Cablelink (Galway) Ltd are 60% owned by Telecom Éireann. These companies as well as the other cable and MMDS operator companies simultaneously and subsequently licensed under the standard agreements, are corporate bodies engaged in the re-transmission of television programmes, broadcast from inside and outside the state, to their subscribers within the State.

(c) *The service and the market*

8. The service is the re-transmission of UK terrestrial broadcasts through a cable/MMDS service to subscribers homes or premises. Irish operators of cable and MMDS networks, in addition to having to obtain the necessary licences from the Department of Transport, Energy and Communications, also require the authorisation of both the broadcasters and the owners of copyright for the re-transmission within the State of TV programmes broadcast outside the State. Because of copyright difficulties the individual broadcasters based abroad may not themselves alone have the authority to authorise retransmission of all their broadcast works. The conclusion of an agreement involving both broadcasters and other copyright owners is designed to overcome these difficulties by providing a comprehensive blanket licence to the cable operators for the contents of the television programme services, to enable them lawfully to transmit the broadcasts.

9. The market is, therefore, that for the provision of TV programmes by means of a cable or MMDS service to consumers. Cable and MMDS operators provide a service ancillary to national television by the re-transmission of a range of programmes broadcast from abroad including terrestrial broadcasts from the UK and satellite programmes. The geographic market for cable/MMDS television services is the State or more specifically the areas of the country that are served by the cable and MMDS systems.

10. As television developed since the early 1950's householders and others located on the eastern seaboard and the northern border counties of Ireland were enabled by means of outdoor aerials to receive UK national television programme services due to overspill signals from the UK and particularly from Northern Ireland. Cable television developed as an alternative means of receiving these television programme services with improved reception quality and the elimination of the need for individual outside aerials. The cable networks which developed in

6.4 the cities and towns along the east coast have been available to cable viewers for over 20 years Cable television is now available in all major urban areas in the State. In more recent years the Government has authorised the introduction of MMDS operators on an exclusive basis as a means of making available multi-channel TV choice in areas outside the range of the overspill signals and there has subsequently been widespread development of these services. MMDS involves a re-broadcast by the MMDS operator through signals received by a small aerial in the subscriber's premises. In more recent years a further alternative for receiving foreign broadcast television has emerged where consumers can receive signals outside a cable/MMDS system by installing a satellite dish.

11. The number of homes owning at least one television set as indicated by the number of television licences issued to householders is approximately 900,000. About 350,000 of these are connected to cable networks licenced by the Department of Transport, Energy and Communications. According to IMRO/PRS cable operators serving more than 280,000 subscribers in Ireland are now covered by agreements similar to that notified. The value of the annual market for cable television services is estimated at over £30m.

(d) *The Notified Agreements*

12.(i) Under the standard agreement notified the licensors (i.e. IMRO, the television companies and other copyright holders representing to be the owners and controllers of all relevant copyright) grant to the licensee (the cable company) a non-exclusive licence and authority to transmit or re-broadcast by the technical means known as MMDS to the licensee's subscribers in the State certain defined programme services. The licence is subject to such re-broadcasting being limited to the use of terrestrial equipment and consisting of only simultaneous and unabridged transmissions of the broadcasters unaltered programmes. The programme services are defined as those of BBC1, BBC2, TVAM (now GMTV) and one each from UTV/HTV and Channel 4/S4C. The term of the agreement is 4 years from 1 January 1991.

(ii) Under Clause 3, the licence specifically excludes re-transmissions to outside the State and public performance and the licensee is prohibited from making recordings of the programmes or the issue of copies to the public. Clause 4 requires the licensee to ensure that a reference be entered in its standard subscriber agreements that it is unlawful for a subscriber to copy or record any part of the re-transmitted programme services. To overcome concerns of the EU Commission the previous sentence was altered in an amendment to the agreement to read 'Clause 4 requires the licensee to ensure that a reference be entered in its standard subscriber agreements that it *may be* unlawful. . . .'

(iii) Under Clause 5 the licensee is required to have regard to the concern of the licensors that a particular channel should be allocated in the cable system for each of the programme services but may allow for sharing of channels at those times when the broadcaster is not providing a programme service. The subscriber is to be advised clearly of the identity and source of each programme re-transmitted. The licensee will transmit as much of the programme services as commercially possible but as a minimum eight uninterrupted hours of each programme serviced in every twenty-four hour period. Such re-transmission shall be simultaneous, complete and unabridged. To overcome the concerns of the EU Commission the amended agreement also includes the provision that the licensee may cease re-transmission of any one or more of the programme services provided three months' notice in proper terms is given.

(iv) The agreement also provides that the broadcasters will provide information on programmes to the licensee. In exceptional circumstances, the licensors reserve the right to prohibit certain re-transmissions and the licensees reserve the right not to re-transmit such programmes and each are obliged to advise the other party about such instances giving at least forty-eight hours notice before the programme is due to be transmitted. The licensors agree to indemnify the licensee against any claims or actions brought by a third party against them in respect of the programme services and the licensees must notify the licensors' nominee (IMRO), in writing, of any such claims. 6.4

(v) Clause 9 provides for the amounts payable by the licensee which includes flat sums payable quarterly in the initial years going on to a royalty basis in 1993 involving a flat annual sum per subscriber to the cable network. The royalty increases each year by reference to the Consumer Price Index. In consideration of these payments the licensors waive any other claims for royalty income from the broadcast material. All payments are to be made to IMRO it being the licensors' duty to apportion the amounts paid between themselves. The licensors are given the right to examine the licensee's records to verify payments.

(vi) Clause 15 of the Agreement provided that if the licensors at any time during the term of the agreement entered into a similar agreement with a third party on terms that on a per subscriber basis are less favourable to the licensors than the terms of the notified agreement, the licensee 'shall be entitled to call upon the licensors to review with the licensee the terms as to payment contained herein with the intent that the said terms should be adjusted to conform to the terms agreed with such third party'.

(vii) To overcome the concerns of the EU Commission in relation to Clause 15, a new Clause '15 bis' was included in the revised agreement, as follows:

'15 bis *Additional broadcaster*

If at any time during the term the licensee requests that a broadcaster other than those mentioned in Clause 1 should become a party to this Agreement in order that the licensee may acquire the right to transmit, re-transmit or re-broadcast a programme service of that broadcaster when such programme service is broadcast from terrestrial transmitters situated either in the United Kingdom or in another country for reception in the United Kingdom or such other country respectively but the signals from which transmitters are directly receivable off-air in Ireland then, provided that the licensee notifies the licensors that it is prepared to pay reasonable additional remuneration to the licensors in respect of its acquisition of such right, the licensee together with such other broadcaster shall be entitled to call upon the licensors to review the terms of Clause 1 and Clause 9(a), (b) and (c) of the Agreement accordingly'.

Note Clause 1 relates to definitions while clauses 9(a) to (c) relate to the amounts payable and dates of payment.

(viii) Clause 16 provides that the licensee may not assign, sub-license, etc. any of its rights or obligations without the prior written consent of the licensors, such consent not to be unreasonably withheld. The licensee may, however, assign its rights to a third party holding a licence from the Department of Transport, Energy and Communications provided that the licensee has fulfilled all its obligations to the licensor prior to the assignment and that the licensee procures that the assignee will contract directly with the licensors to perform all the further obligations under the agreement.

(ix) Clause 17 allows the licensors to terminate the agreement in the event of the licensee company going into receivership, managership or liquidation, if the licensee ceases to carry on business or if the licensee is in breach of a material term of the Agreement, in particular those relating to payment arrangements. The licensors or the licensees may also terminate the Agreement in the event of certain legislative changes in the State. Clause 25 provides that as soon as practicable after completion the agreement shall be notified to the EU Commission.

(e) *EU Notification*

13. The notified agreement was also notified to the EU Commission by BBC Enterprises Ltd on 6 December 1991. On the basis of information supplied the Commission came to the conclusion that the Agreement as notified fell within Article 85(1) and in its then form could not benefit from exemption under Article 85(3) of the EU Treaty The Commission stated *inter alia* that collective royalty arrangements with the participation of actual or potential competitors clearly fell within Article 85(1). Several amendments to the notified arrangements were agreed

6.4 between the Commission and the BBC. Some other amendments were made to the notified agreement in order to accommodate changes in the contracting independent TV companies and Channel 3 licensees. Following the amendments to the agreement, the EU Commission issued an interim comfort letter indicating that sufficient *prima facie* justification had been provided for an exemption to be granted by the Commission pursuant to Article 85(3). A formal decision granting an exemption under Article 85(3) was not considered necessary.

(f) *Submissions of the parties*

14. IMRO submitted that the intention and effect of the arrangements was to give effect to the rights of the creators/licensors/broadcasters granted by the Copyright Acts, 1963 and 1987 while securing for consumers their proper share of the benefits. They said that a mechanism had already been provided for regulating the market between copyright owners and the persons requiring licences. This mechanism was provided in Part V of the Copyright Act 1963, which entrusts these functions to the Controller of Patents, Trade Marks and Designs.

Subsequent Developments

15. Following publication on 11 November 1994 of its intention to grant a licence in respect of the notified agreement, the Authority received a submission from a third party, Nolan and Company, Solicitors, New Ross, on behalf of Trace Lite International Ltd and Padraig Fitzgerald objected to the granting of a licence by the Competition Authority. They stated that a consortium was being established to set up a rival television distribution system to that offered by the cable relay and MMDS operators to deliver the same television programmes to customers in competition to the cable relay and MMDS operators. Equality in dealings with the copyright owners and programme suppliers was essential. They felt that granting a licence for the notified agreement would inhibit them from competing with the cable relay and MMDS operators. The points made by Nolan and Company on behalf of Trace Lite International Ltd and Padraig Fitzgerald are covered in the assessment which follows.

Assessment

(a) *Section 4(1)*

16. Section 4(1) of the Competition Act 1991 prohibits and renders void all agreements between undertakings, decisions by associations of undertakings and concerted practices which have as their object or effect the prevention, restriction or distortion of competition in trade in any goods or services in the State, or in any part of the State.

(b) *The Undertakings*

17. The term 'undertaking' is defined in section 3(1) of the Act as 'a person being an individual, a body corporate or an unincorporated body of persons engaged for gain in the production, supply or distribution of goods or the provision of a service'. IMRO, BBC Enterprises Ltd, Channel Four Television Corporation, The Welsh Fourth Channel Authority, ALCS, DACS and PPI are corporate bodies engaged for gain in the exploitation of copyright works and are, therefore, undertakings. The Independent Television Association signed the agreement on behalf of its members, the independent television companies in the UK, who are undertakings. AGICOA signed the agreement on behalf of its members, producers and distributors of films and television programmes, who are undertakings. The cable/MMDS companies are engaged in the provision of a cable television or MMDS re-transmission service to the general public for gain and are also undertakings. The notified agreement is an agreement between undertakings. The agreement has effect within the State.

(c) *The Agreement*

18. The notified agreement is stated to be the standard form of several agreements whereby

the owners of copyright in television programmes, broadcast from outside the State, license the live re-transmission of TV programmes by cable companies to cable subscribers. For these services, royalties are payable to the licensors. It involves a collective licensing system whereby a number of television companies who are otherwise in competition with one another, and other holders of copyright on broadcast material, have joined together as licensors in these agreements. The agreements also contain a number of restrictive clauses whose effect on competition must be considered. **6.4**

Collective licensing and royalty provisions

19. The Authority takes the view that collective licensing arrangements *per se*, where actual or potential competitors in the market join together for the collective licensing of their separate services for a global fee to be divided on an agreed basis, restricts competition. Such arrangements eliminate the possibility of each television service competing on price against the others for the right to supply re-transmitted programmes via cable or MMDS systems within the State. Such arrangements therefore offend against section 4(1) of the Competition Act.

Allocation of channels by the licensee

20. Clause 5 requires the licensee to allocate a particular channel in the cable network for each programme service and that a minimum uninterrupted 8 hours per 24 hours on the cable channel has to be devoted to broadcasts of each particular service. Modern television sets have the capacity to carry 100 or more channels. Since the number of channels covered by the agreement is 4 there remains very substantial leeway to accommodate the rapid development of private satellite broadcasting. The amended agreement gives the licensee the right to withdraw any one or more of the programme services during the term of the agreement, by giving three months' notice in writing and also allows new broadcasters to become parties to the agreement. In these circumstances any possibility of foreclosure of cable channels by reason of the notified agreement does not arise and this clause, as amended, does not offend against section 4(1).

Exclusions from licence

21. Clause 3 of the agreement expressly excludes the licensee from retransmitting programmes capable of lawfully being received by members of the public outside the State or programmes for public performance and from making recordings for issue to the public. This geographical exclusion does not affect competition within the State and does not, therefore, offend against section 4(1). Similarly the copyright licence relates to the provision of cable television services and that alone. Copyright in respect of public performance or the making of recordings is not licensed under the agreement and the express exclusion of these activities does not, therefore, offend against Section 4(1).

Applicability of section 4(2)

22. Under Section 4(2), the Competition Authority may grant a licence in the case of any agreement or category of agreements 'which in the opinion of the Authority, having regard to all relevant market conditions, contributes to improving the production of goods or provision of services or to promoting technical or economic progress, while allowing consumers a fair share of the resulting benefit and which does not

(i) impose on the undertakings concerned terms which are not indispensable to the attainment of those objectives;
(ii) afford undertakings the possibility of eliminating competition in respect of a substantial part of the products or services in question'.

In the opinion of the Authority, the notified arrangements fulfil the conditions provided for in section 4(2).

6.4 Improvement in the provision of services

23. Because of the number and diversity of the copyright holders involved in the re-transmitted television programmes the Authority believes that the most effective and efficient way of operating a business of re-transmission of UK terrestrial broadcasts is through the collective licensing system provided under the agreements. The alternative for the cable companies would be the negotiation of an agreement with each of the copyright holders in respect of each re-transmitted programme service. This would involve extra costs for the cable company and the consumer. Prior to the introduction of cable television many viewers on the East coast and Northern parts of the State were accustomed to receiving the signals from the full range of the UK national channels by way of outdoor aerials and would have been unlikely to subscribe to a service which did not include the full UK terrestrial national range. The collective nature of the arrangement which has enabled the provision of the full UK national programme services through cable has thus contributed to the development of cable services and networks. The collective arrangement also provides a blanket indemnity to cable companies against claims for infringement of copyright on re-transmitted material which would not otherwise be available. The Authority therefore accepts that the arrangements notified involve efficiencies and have improved the provision of the service.

Benefit to the Consumer

24. The consumers in question are the subscribers to cable and MMDS systems in the State. Because of the arrangements, the Authority believes that subscribers have a wider selection of television programme services and that they benefit from the competition created between overseas and the local broadcaster. Because of the participation of all those who own copyright in the broadcast material, consumers' rights to receive and enjoy re-transmitted programmes are not likely to be hampered by legal disputes concerning the cable or MMDS operators' rights to re-transmit.

Indispensability

25. In the Authority's opinion the notified agreement does not impose on the undertakings concerned any conditions which are not indispensable.

Elimination of Competition

26. Following the notification to the EU Commission Clause 15 of the agreement was amended by the addition of Clause 15 bis as set out at para. 12 (vii) above. The amendment allows for the entry of new broadcasters to the agreement at the request of the licencee together with provisions for the amendment of the financial provisions of the agreement. In practice the agreement has not prevented other broadcasters, particularly satellite companies, from negotiating their own re-transmission agreements with the cable companies. Nevertheless the amendment enables the addition of other broadcasters to the notified agreement. Individual consumers can opt for satellite dishes or, in many parts of the country, can have their own television aerial as potential sources of competition. In all these circumstances the Authority considers that the agreements do not afford the possibility of eliminating competition in respect of a substantial part of the services in question.

The Decision

21. In the Authority's opinion, Irish Music Rights Organisation, BBC Enterprises Ltd, the companies represented by The Independent Television Association, Channel Four Television Corporation, The Welsh Fourth Channel Authority, Association De Gestion Internationale Collective Des Oeuvres Audiovisuelles, Authors' Licensing and Collecting Society Ltd, Design and Artists Copyright Society Ltd and Phonographic Performance (Ireland) Ltd and the cable companies are undertakings. The notified standard agreement between the parties is an agreement between undertakings. The Authority considers that the notified agreement

offends against section 4(1) of the Competition Act 1991. The Authority considers that the notified agreement satisfies the conditions of section 4(2) of the Competition Act. It has therefore decided to issue a licence in respect of the notified agreement, and the licence shall apply from 16 December 1994 to 15 December 2004. A ten year licence is appropriate because the notified standard agreement operates for a four year period. It is not considered necessary to attach any conditions to the licence. **6.4**

The Licence

28. The Competition Authority has issued the following licence:

The Competition Authority grants a licence under section 4(2) of the Competition Act 1991 to the standard agreement between Irish Music Rights Organisation, BBC Enterprises Ltd, the companies represented by The Independent Television Association, Channel Four Television Corporation, The Welsh Fourth Channel Authority, Association De Gestion Internationale Collective Des Oeuvres Audiovisuelles, Authors Licensing and Collecting Society Ltd, Design and Artists Copyright Society Ltd and Phonographic Performance (Ireland) Ltd and the cable companies in relation to the re-transmission and re-broadcast of UK television programmes, notified under section 7 on 3 October 1991 (Notification No. CA/7/91E), on the grounds that, in the opinion of the Authority, all the conditions of section 4(2) of the Competition Act 1991 have been fulfilled.

The licence shall apply from 16 December 1994 to 15 December 2004.

For the Competition Authority

Des Wall
Member

16 December 1994

Des [illegible]
Member
16 December 1994

CHAPTER SEVEN

Property

7.0 Introduction

Background

The unreported judgement of Keane J of 24 November 1992, *Sibra Building Company Ltd and others v. Palmerstown Centre Development Ltd and another*,* which is contained in this chapter anticpated the attitude of the Competition Authority to property restrictions. Interestingly the Competition Authority has never adverted to this judgement in its decisions. The view of Keane J that property holding companies are not 'undertakings' because they are not engaged in the production, supply or distribution of goods or the provision of a service must be identified as a judgement which was delivered after the Supreme Court's judgement that the Voluntary Health Insurance Board was an 'undertaking'.

Prior to the deadline, 30 September 1992, for the making of notifications to the Competition Authority in respect of agreements or practices and understandings which were in existence on the date of the commencement of the Competition Act, the Authority received many notifications of agreements concerning restricted user clauses in property transactions. Most commonly those clauses appeared in agreements and leases involving shopping centres. Landlords and managers of shopping centres usually impose restrictions on the tenant or purchaser of a unit in a shopping centre concerning the type of shop or outlet for which a unit in the shopping centre could be used. The Authority before issuing any decision to issue a certificate in respect of a restricted user clause, published a notice dated 2 September 1993 in the edition of 10 September 1993 of Iris Oifigiúil entitled 'Notice in Respect of Shopping Centre Leases'.

Shopping Centre Leases 7.3

The Authority identified restricted user clauses as intending to prevent or restrict the operation of another outlet from engaging in various businesses but it comments in this notice that 'such clauses do not normally offend against section 4(1) of the Competition Act'. The Authority continues to rely on its statement in Nallen/O'Toole that the Competition Act 'should not be interpreted literally since to do so would mean that "virtually every form of business agreement could be argued to prevent, restrict or distort competition. . . . Such an interpretation would render it virtually impossible for business to operate".' The Authority seeks to invoke a 'rule of reason' when assessing such restricted user type clauses.

The Authority accepts that a restricted user clause may restrict competition in a shopping centre which is a part of the State. However, it proceeds to determine that 'the relevant geographic market for each shopping centre' covers a much wider area than the centre's location. In this notice and in the decisions concerning property transactions the Authority reiterates that competing traders may establish their businesses outside the shopping centre subject to planning restrictions. On this basis the

*This case has been appealed and awaits a hearing

7.0 Authority concludes that 'the restricted user, exclusive user or permitted user clause, and the restriction and change of user in shopping centre leases do not generally have as object or effect the prevention, restriction or distortion of competition in trade in any goods or services in the State or in any part of the State'.

The notice at paragraph 18 deals with other common lease type obligations and concludes that such clauses which require the payment of rates and compliance with legislation do not restrict competition.

At paragraph 21 the Competition Authority emphasise that the notice is merely its interpretation and that the interpretation of the courts of any particular set of circumstances will prevail.

Murray/O'Connells 7.2

This was the first decision of the Competition Authority concerning a restricted user clause in a property transaction. The O'Connells as tenants were restricted from using the premises which they lease for businesses other than for insurance, investment and financial services. The consent of the landlord could not be unreasonably withheld to an application by the O'Connells for a change of use. The Authority having decided that each party were undertakings decided to issue a certificate because the O'Connells could carry on any business outside the leased premises and in any event the landlord could not unreasonably withhold his consent to an application by the O'Connells to change the use of the leased premises.

Roches Stores/Peter Mark 7.4

This was the first shopping centre notification in respect of which a certificate was issued by the Authority. In common with all other decisions to issue certificates for shopping centre restrictions the Authority referred to the notice in respect of shopping centre leases. Apart from the restricted use to which the leased hairdressing salon could be used by the tenant, Roches Stores also committed itself not to allow any trade to be over-represented in the shopping centre and where possible to allow only one unit in respect of each trade. The Authority in issuing a certificate reiterated its opinion that any person wishing to operate a trade which may be carried on in the centre could do so outside the centre.

Fuel Distributors/Enright 7.5

This decision of the Competition Authority to issue a certificate concerned an agreement under which the purchaser of a property covenanted not to use the premises as it had been used by the vendor.

Melincourt/Horkan 7.6

The Competition Authority issued a certificate in respect of arrangements whereby a newsagent tenant of Huntstown Shopping Centre could be assured that his exclusive user restrictions would not be interrupted or interfered with by another tenant of the shopping centre. The Competition Authority's notice in respect of shopping centre leases was relied upon in support of the reasoning to issue a certificate.

Tenants of The Square Town Centre 7.7

The Square Town Centre in Tallaght is the largest shopping centre in the State. Decision No. 206 concerns the notification of arrangements between the landlords in the shopping centre which allowed a board of the management company for the shopping centre, discretion on the use to which the units in the centre could be used. An application for a change of use could not be unreasonably withheld but the board of management would have ultimate decision on the question of reasonableness. The Authority in relying upon the reasoning in respect of shopping centre leases issued a certificate for the arrangements notified. 7.0

Aviette/Firhouse Shopping Centre Tenants 7.8
Restricted and exclusive user clauses were also contained in the agreements which were notified and which led to this decision. The additional feature of the notified arrangements was an undertaking given by the landlord not to permit any other unit to be used as a general supermarket within 21 years from the date of the undertaking. The Authority again relied upon the reasoning in its notice in respect of shopping centre leases to issue a certificate.

Elkinson/Bushe 7.9
This decision concerns a restriction on the landlord in particular not to lease adjoining premises for a trade which would compete with the business of the tenant. The Authority in its decision does not identify the extent of the premises which the landlord owns and leases. The Competition Authority issued a certificate along the same lines of reasoning as that used in respect of shopping centre leases. The Authority contends that any undertaking which wished to compete with the tenant in the transaction could establish in the vicinity and would not be affected by the restrictions.

Grant/Power Leisure Ltd 7.10
This decision by the Authority to issue a certificate is included in this book because of the covenant by the landlord in favour of the tenant not to permit adjoining premises to be used as a betting office. The decision reiterates the Authority's view in these types of notifications that any competitor could establish within the same vicinity.

Green Property plc/Tenants at Northside Shopping Centre 7.11
This decision was the first decision of the Authority which referred to a restriction on tenants of shopping centres from operating in premises outside the shopping centre also. The Authority mentioned its reservations to the lessor and in reply the lessor confirmed that the restriction would be deleted from the standard lease. The Authority then proceeded to issue a certificate in respect of the shopping centre lease arrangement.

UCD/Bank of Ireland 7.12
Apart from identifying that University College Dublin is an undertaking, this decision is noteworthy because of its covenant in favour of the Bank of Ireland that no other financial institution could be established within the substantial campus of the university. The Authority issued a certificate on the basis that competing financial institutions could operate and did operate within a radius of two miles of the university and thus offered competition.

University of Limerick/Bank of Ireland 7.13
In addition to the benefits which were granted to the Bank of Ireland by University

7.0 College Dublin, the University of Limerick also undertook not to allow advertisements to be placed on the campus in favour of other financial institutions. The University of Limerick was identified as an undertaking and concluded that the competition offered outside the campus of the university meant that section 4(1) of the Competition Act was not breached by the arrangements.

McMullan Brothers/Powers Supermarkets Ltd 7.14

This decision to issue a certificate concerned a covenant by the company trading as Quinnsworth not to use premises as a petrol filling station. The covenant was in favour of the company which trades with the name Maxol and which continued to own a petrol filling station adjoining the site sold. The Competition Authority repeats that if Powers Supermarkets wished to retail petrol it was free to enter this business at other sites in the vicinity.

Grittar/Bolger 7.15

In this decision the Authority decided to issue a certificate in respect of arrangements which precluded the establishment of a large supermarket in the area of Lucan, County Dublin which was sold. It is not apparent from the decision the extent of the area sold by a subsidiary of Powers Supermarkets and the effect of the restriction on potential supermarkets in the area. The structure of the arrangements to ensure that Powers Supermarkets could continue to benefit from the restrictions had to contend with the restriction on the creation of ground rents for new residences. This is not stated in the decision but it appears that the freehold of each house would be conveyed as each house was built. The restrictions continued to operate in respect of that part of the estate sold by the subsidiary of Powers Supermarkets and on which houses were not erected or planned to be erected.

FBD Developments (Cork) Ltd/Southern Health Board 7.16

The decision that the Southern Health Board is an 'undertaking' because it receives income other than by way of grants is the most notable point arising from this decision. The Competition Authority reiterates its view even more concisely that the leasing of premises cannot offend against section 4(1) and the normal restrictions on user and assignability do not constitute infringements of section 4(1) of the Competition Act.

Powers Supermarkets/Whytes 7.17

The Competition Authority issued a certificate for a premises sale agreement in Mullingar which precluded the purchasers from allowing the premises sold to be used as a large retail shop. The vendors could therefore maintain the small size of the units sold. In deciding to issue a certificate the Authority noted that if the purchasers wished to acquire property which could be merged into a large retail outlet, they could do so by acquiring other properties.

David Allen Holdings Ltd/Adsites 7.18

The Authority in this decision refused to issue a certificate or to grant a licence which concerned the licensing of the use of advertising panels throughout the State. The reasoning leading to the conclusion by the Authority that large size posters constitutes a distinct market segment of the outdoor advertising product market is interesting and of useful guidance in product market definition. The Authority decided that the two

parties to the arrangements were direct competitors and the combination of the 7.0
marketing forces which would arise as a result of the arrangement would indeed have effects on competition. The Authority thereby concluded that the arrangements clearly offended against section 4(1) of the Competition Act.

The Authority could not identify any of the factors which would allow for a licence to be granted and commented that in any event all of the requirements needed to be satisfied before a licence could be granted.

Adsites Ltd/David Allen Holdings Ltd 7.18
This decision would possibly be better located in the chapter concerning acquisitions. However, it is contained in this chapter because it is a corollary to the attempt by the parties to enter into arrangements concerning their outdoor advertising capacity. The decision concerns an option which was given by Adsites to David Allen Holdings Ltd to purchase all of its advertising panels. The Authority refused to issue a certificate or to grant a licence because of the significance of each of the parties in the relevant market and the diminution in competition which would arise as a result of any effect being given to the options. From the property viewpoint the decision might be of relevance in the future where other large operators of a particular property segment may conclude joint arrangements.

Conclusion
The rule of reason approach adopted by the Competition Authority and which seems to be primarily based on the fact that competition can be offered by the acquisition of other properties in each particular vicinity could lead one to believe that the Competition Authority will not find any transaction concerning restrictions on the use of property to offend against section 4(1) of the Competition Act. It should be noted that the ultimate decision on whether restricted user clauses combined with other arrangements in a locality may be restrictive of competition 'in a part of the State' and thereby offend against section 4(1) of the Competition Act rests with the Courts. The onus of proof, however, could be quite burdensome for any challenger of arrangements in a locality which would be based on section 4(1) of the Competition Act.

Sibra Building Co. Ltd, Silver Birch Estates Ltd and Bunker Estates Ltd (plaintiffs) v. Palmerstown Centre Development Ltd and Luke Moriarty (defendants): (1991 No. 11920P), High Court, 24 November 1992* 7.1

Restrictive Covenant – Purchaser not to construct, erect or have a licensed premises on the property sold – Meaning of 'licensed premises' – Reference to turf accountant and auctioneer – Whether refers to off-licence in spirits and beer – Equitable jurisdiction – Acquiesence – Possibility of increasing sale price of land in the absence of a restriction – Restraint of trade doctrine – Whether section 4(1) of the Competition Act 1991 renders void – whether each of the plaintiffs were 'an undertaking'

Facts: A special condition in a contract between the first named plaintiff, a building company, and the second named defendant provided: 'The purchaser hereby cove-

*This case has been appealed and awaits a hearing.

7.1 nants (which covenant shall be binding on the purchaser, his successors, administrators and assigns) not to construct or erect or to have a public house or licensed premises of any nature on the property herein so long as Frank Towey, his successors or assigns, remain the proprietor of the public house opposite the site or so long as any company or individual holds the said public house on his behalf. This covenant shall extend to the administrator, successors and assigns of the said Frank Towey. Licensed premises shall include a licensed restaurant'.

The defendants established and maintained a supermarket and the plaintiffs never seriously objected to the defendants carrying on the off-licence trade in wine. The plaintiffs were not aware of an application by the defendants for a declaration concerning the commencement of an off-licensed trade in the defendants supermarket. The plaintiffs applied for an interlocutory injunction as soon as they became aware that the defendants were intending to change their premises in order to accommodate an off licence trade in spirits and beer.

Submissions: The defendants contended:

(1) The definition of licensed premises should be construed narrowly and that an off-licence should have been specifically mentioned in the restrictive covenant if it was to be enforced to prevent the opening of an off-licence.

(2) The benefit of the restrictive covenant was for Frank Towey and the general reference to successors and assigns was not enforceable.

(3) The plaintiffs' conduct constituted an act of acquiesence to the opening of an off-licence by the defendants.

(4) The clause is in restraint of trade and is unenforceable.

(5) Section 4(1) of the Competition Act 1991 renders void agreements which are anti-competitive.

Held by Keane J in granting an injunction restraining the sale of beer and spirits at the premises by the defendants:

(1) Although it would be inconceivable to prohibit under the relevant restrictive covenants the business of a turf accountant and an auctioneer, a sensible reading of the clause would apply the restrictive covenant to an off-licence business.

(2) The benefit of the clause for Frank Towey his successors and assigns was clearly intended to cover the plaintiff companies which were in existence at the time.

(3) The plaintiffs took steps by way of an application for an interlocutory injunction as soon as they became aware that the defendants were proceeding to commence an off-licence trade in spirits and beer. They were not aware of an application for the commencement of such a business in the District Court made by the defendants. The plaintiffs did not allow the defendants to incur loss or expense before asserting their right to enforce the restrictive covenant.

(4) *Esso v. Harpers* [1968] AC 269 constitutes good law and common sense in respect of the enforceability of such a restrictive covenant. If the restrictive covenant was not contained in the sale agreement the defendants might have had to pay an extra £50,000 or £100,000. The restriction was agreed between the parties and did not in any way reduce the number of outlets in the shopping centre. The condition was one which the purchaser could take or leave.

(5) Only one of the plaintiff companies could be considered to be engaged in the production, supply or distribution of goods or the provision of a service. The other

two plaintiff companies do not come within the meaning of an undertaking. The provisions of the Competition Act 1991 have no application to the circumstances of the plaintiff's application. 7.1

Case mentioned in this report
Esso v. Harpers [1968] AC 269.

Brian McCracken SC and Bernard McDonagh **for the plaintiffs**
Ercus Stewart SC and Roddy Horan **for the defendants**

KEANE J delivered his judgment on (24 November 1992) saying: I have some sympathy for the defendant in this case because I am quite satisfied that what the plaintiffs had in the forefront of their mind when the various agreements were entered into was to prevent him from carrying on the business of a licensed bar in the shopping centre which he was proposing to construct. Given the difficulties that business people face today, it is understandable that the defendant should have taken somewhat of a risk in the circumstances and proceeded with the off-licence business in the hope (in vain, as it turned out) that the plaintiffs would not have any great practical objection to it. Another reason why I have some sympathy for the defendant is that he fairly faced up to the matter in the witness box. He was aware, I am quite sure, that his answers were not doing him much good when he said unequivocally that he was on the wrong side when going ahead but that he did not think of it as a matter that would be in the forefront of the mind of the plaintiffs. These are matters which evoke one's sympathy but the case has to be decided in accordance with the law and not in accordance with where one's sympathy might lie.

In the first place the case turns on the construction of condition 6 of the special conditions in the first contract between Sibra Building Company Ltd and the defendant. However, for all practical purposes the agreements are identical and it is immaterial which contract one takes for this purpose. Condition 6 provides:

> The purchaser hereby covenants (which covenant shall be binding on the purchaser his successors, administrators and assigns) not to construct or erect or have a public house or licensed premises of any nature on the property herein so long as Frank Towey his successors or assigns remain the proprietor of the public house opposite the site or so long as any company or individual holds the said public house on his behalf. This covenant shall extend to the administrators successors and assigns of the said Frank Towey. Licensed premises shall include a licensed restaurant.

The defendant correctly says that 'licensed premises' is an expression which is not necessarily confined in its application to premises licensed for the sale of intoxicating liquor and that in this very shopping centre there are premises which do require licences of various sorts such as a turf accountant and an auctioneer. It would seem inconceiveable to prohibit those businesses and it was obviously not the intention to prohibit the carrying on of those businesses. Since 'licensed' cannot be construed in that way, it is suggested that the whole clause must be construed somewhat narrowly against the Plaintiffs.

It is contended, and correctly so, that the agreement was proferred to the purchaser and that the relevant clause was designed solely for the vendor's benefit. It is restrictive in its nature and that might suggest that it should be read against the party from whom it emanated under the contra proferentem rule. Even allowing that that is so, the phrase 'licensed premises' was not intended to apply to premises such as a bookmaker's premises and so on, and one has to ask what was the intention of the parties as inferred from the language which they used. I think it is clear that they had in mind a premises of the same nature as a public house, that a premises

7.1 which dealt in intoxicating liquor and which required a licence, and there is no reason why it would not include an off-licence. If the parties had intended to exclude such a premises they should have used specific language to indicate that intention but they did not do so. The only premises apart from an off-licence which can comply with that expression is a restaurant licensed under the applicable code to sell wine or spirits for consumption on the premises. So to restrict the expression 'licensed premises' is clearly not possible because at the end of the clause it says 'licensed premises shall include a licensed restaurant', and that clause is quite unnecessary if in fact the restriction was intended to cover only that form of licensed premises. Obviously the parties intended the phrase 'licensed premises' to be given some wider meaning not simply a licensed restaurant. Within that meaning there would obviously be included a premises for the sale of intoxicating liquor to be consumed off the premises. I think that that is the only sensible reading of the clause.

The clause goes on to say that the covenant is to remain in force 'so long as Frank Towey his successors or assigns remain the proprietor of the public house opposite the site or so long as any company or individual holds the said public house on his behalf. This covenant shall extend to the administrators successors and assigns of the said Frank Towey'. The evidence establishes that the Frank Towey referred to in the clause whose sons seem to have taken over the running of the public house business on a day-to-day basis is the holder of the largest individual shareholding in the three plaintiff companies. While the expression 'proprietor' has no precise meaning in law it seems to me to be apt to apply it to the situation of Mr Towey as the largest shareholder in these three companies. In any event the clause goes on to say 'This covenant shall extend to the administrators successors and assigns of the said Frank Towey.' That was clearly intended to cover the companies which were in existence at the time and in which Mr Towey although not the majority shareholder, was in fact the principal shareholder. So I am satisfied that the intention of the parties was that so long as this public house remained in the ownership of the Towey family and so long as Mr Frank Towey retained the principal interest in the premises, the covenant was to remain in force. Of course, if the premises were simply sold to another party and the Towey family retained a minority interest, the situation would be different. I have no doubt whatever that the intention was that the clause would be binding for so long as the present plaintiffs remained the owners of the public house. That being so, the covenant is prima facie binding on the defendant.

However, the defendant raises three points which, it is said, should prevent an injunction being granted. In the first place it is said that the plaintiffs have acquiesced in the conduct by the defendant of the off-licence. It is not seriously disputed that the plaintiffs never raised any serious objection to the carrying on of the off-licence trade in wine, even though that might also have been in breach of the covenant. If they came here simply looking for an injunction to restrain the defendant from doing that, they would not have been heard by the court because they undoubtedly did not take any steps although they must have known that wine was being sold in the defendant's supermarket. But they have made it clear that their objection is to the off-licence trade in spirits and beer. I am satisfied that the plaintiffs took steps by way of an application for an interlocutory injunction as soon as they became aware that this matter was going ahead. They did not, it would seem, object to the application for the necessary declaration under the Act in the District Court but they were not aware of the application being made.

If the defendant had attempted to steal a march on the plaintiff by going ahead with the work on the premises and incurring expenses thereby creating a situation which the court might find difficult to undo, then the court would grant relief. I am satisfied that matters here did not reach that stage, but undoubtedly the defendant went ahead in the knowledge that he was doing something which was at least arguably in breach of the contract. If the plaintiffs had simply allowed the defendant to incur a lot of expense and had waited until the last moment to move by way of restraining him, the court might say that it would be inequitable, but I am satisfied that that is not the situation here. So in my view it is not a case in which acquiescence affords any defence to the plaintiffs' claim in so far as they seek to restrain the defendant from selling spirits and beer under an off-licence licence. 7.1

The next point taken by the defendant is that this is a clause in restraint of trade. It is to be borne in mind that this clause was introduced into the contract by the owners of the land. The owners of the land did not have to sell the land. They were perfectly entitled to keep the land and to continue running their public house on the land. If that had been their attitude, there would have been no other licensed premises on the land the subject matter of these proceedings. The plaintiffs elected to sell the land to the defendant and they included this clause which, it must be assumed, led to the consequence that the consideration for the property was thereby affected. In other words, if the attitude of the defendant had been not to agree with that clause and not agree to buy the land unless he was allowed to have a bar in the supermarket or shopping centre, the plaintiffs might very well have said to the defendant that it would cost him an extra £50,000 or £100,000. If this were a case in which the plaintiffs were seeking to restrain the defendant from carrying on a bar trade in flagrant defiance of the covenant, no court would entertain the defence that it was in restraint of trade. In my opinion the restriction was mutually agreed between the parties and did not in any way reduce the number of outlets in the shopping centre. It was a condition which the purchaser could take or leave; if he took it he must comply with it.

I respectfully adopt what was said in *Esso v. Harpers* [1968] AC 269, to which Mr McCracken referred. It seems good law and common sense.

The final point on which the defendant relies relates to the provisions of the Competition Act 1991. That Act, as is well known imports into our law provisions relating to anti-competitive agreements which are in similar terms to the provisions of the relevant Articles of the European Community Treaties.

Now, the question might very well arise as to whether this type of agreement, which comes within section 4(1) of the 1991 Act, was intended to be rendered void under the Act. However, the Act applies only to undertakings as defined by section 3(1):

> 'undertaking' means a person being an individual, a body corporate or an unincorporated body of persons engaged for gain in the production, supply or distribution of goods or the provision of a service.

In this case the covenant was entered into with each of the three plaintiff companies. Only one of those companies, Bunker Estates Ltd, which runs the public house, could be reasonably regarded as a body engaged in the production, supply or distribution of goods or the provision of a service. The function of the other two companies was simply to hold land and to dispose of the land and they are not in any sense within the meaning of that section bodies engaged in the production, supply or distribution of goods or the provision of a service.

I am satisfied that the Act has no application to the circumstances of the present case and that the plaintiffs are entitled to the relief sought. An injunction will therefore be granted in the terms of the concluding paragraph of the Statement of Claim, subject to one matter which I will hear the parties on.

I take it, Mr McCracken, that the plaintiffs will be satisfied with an injunction restraining the sale of beer and spirits?

Mr McCracken: I have no absolute instructions. I can see the force of it, my Lord.

Solicitors for the plaintiffs: *Hugh J. O'Hagan Ward & Co.*
Solicitors for the defendants: *Porter Morris & Co.*

7.2 **Competition Authority Decision No. 30, J. Murray/L. & J. O'Connell:** 9 September 1993, Notification No. CA/27/93

Restricted user clause in property lease agreement – Competition Act 1991 (No. 24) sections 3, 4 and 7

Facts: On 2 July 1993 notification was made to the Authority by James Murray of an agreement to lease made 17 June 1993 and a draft 35 year lease which are both between James Murray, as landlord, and the O'Connells as tenants, with a request for a certificate under section 4(4) of the Competition Act 1991 or, failing that, a licence under section 4(2). James Murray carries on the business of a grocer and the O'Connells are in the business of providing insurance brokerage, investment and financial services. Each of the notified agreements contain a restricted user clause whereunder the tenants could not use the demised premises for any purpose other than for the business of providing insurance, investment and financial services without the prior consent of the landlord.

Decided by the Authority: In issuing a certificate under section 4(4) of the Competition Act 1991 in respect of the notified agreements that:

(1) Each of the parties to the notified agreements are undertakings within the meaning of section 3(1) of the Competition Act 1991 and the notified agreements were agreements between undertakings having effect within part of the State.

(2) The object of the restricted user clause was for good estate management and did not operate to prevent the tenants or any other party from engaging in any other business in the vicinity and further the landlord undertook not to unreasonably withhold consent to an application for change of user by the tenant.

Competition Authority Decision of 9 September 1993 relating to a proceeding under section 4 of the Competition Act 1991
Notification No. CA/27/93 — J. Murray/L. and J. O'Connell

Introduction

1. Notification was made by James Murray, Main Street, Baltinglass, Co. Wicklow on 2 July 1993 with a request for a certificate under section 4(4) of the Competition Act, 1991 or, in the event of a refusal by the Competition Authority to issue a certificate, a licence under section 4(2), in respect of a tenancy agreement and proposed lease with Len and John O'Connell.

The Facts

(a) *The subject of the notification*

2. The notification concerns the lease of a premises at Main Street, Baltinglass, Co. Wicklow between James Murray, landlord, and Len O'Connell and John O'Connell, tenants. The premises consists of a lock-up shop, with a residence overhead.

(b) *The parties involved*

3. James Murray owns the premises at Main Street, Baltinglass, and he also operates a grocery shop in the town. Len and John O'Connell are in the business of providing services as insurance brokers, investment brokers and financial advisors.

(c) *The notified arrangements*

4. The notified agreement for the letting of a business premises was made on 17 June 1993

for a period of 6 months from 18 June 1993. This was accompanied by a draft lease in respect of the same premises for 35 years from 14 June 1993, provided that planning permission was received for the development. The agreement for letting contains the following restricted user clause: 7.2

> 2. The tenant agrees with the landlord as follows:(g) Not to use or occupy the premises or permit the same to be used or occupied otherwise than for the purpose of the Tenant's business as Insurance Brokers, Investment Brokers and Financial Advisors. . . .

Under the draft lease, the tenant covenants with the landlord:

> 3.16 Not to use or permit the demised premises or any part thereof to be used for any purpose other than:
> 3.16.1 Insurance Broker, Investment Broker and Financial Advisors without the Landlord's consent in writing to the change of use of the premises, which said consent shall not be unreasonably withheld.

In addition, there are a number of other standard restrictive covenants and obligations in the agreement and the lease.

Assessment — The applicability of section 4(1)

5. The Authority considers that James Murray is an undertaking, within the meaning of section 3 of the Competition Act, by virtue of providing suitable accommodation in which persons can carry on a business in return for rental payments, and because he operates a grocery shop. Len and John O'Connell provide certain services for gain, and they also are undertakings. The notified agreement for letting and the draft lease are agreements between undertakings. The agreements have effect within a part of the State.

6. The Authority considers that the notified agreements, and their restricted user clauses and the other standard restrictive clauses and obligations, do not have the object or effect of preventing, restricting or distorting competition in trade or in services in the State or in any part of the State. The restricted user clause prevents the premises being used by the tenants for any purpose other than that specified. The object of the restriction is for good estate management. The tenants, should they wish to engage in any other line of business, could do so in many other premises, both in the vicinity and throughout the State, and so the effect of the agreements is not anti-competitive. Similarly, the agreements do not prevent any other person engaging in any form of business activity in any part of the State. In addition, there can be a change of user for the premises, for which the landlord's consent may not be unreasonably withheld. The Authority therefore considers that the notified agreements between James Murray and Len and John O'Connell do not offend against section 4(1) of the Competition Act 1991.

The Certificate

7. The Competition Authority has issued the following certificate:

> The Competition Authority certifies that in its opinion, on the basis of the facts in its possession, the agreements between John Murray and Len and John O'Connell in relation to the tenancy agreement and draft lease of the premises at Main Street, Baltinglass, Co. Wicklow, (Notification No. CA/27/93), notified on 2 July 1993 under section 7, do not offend against section 4(1) of the Competition Act 1991.

For the Competition Authority

Patrick M. Lyons
Chairman

9 September 1993

7.3 Competition Authority — Notice in respect of Shopping Centre Leases

1. The Competition Authority has received a large number of notifications of shopping centre leases. Most of these notifications were made at the end of September 1992, after which agreements made before the Competition Act 1991 came into operation could no longer be notified. The notified agreements have been carefully scrutinised by the Authority. In this Notice, the Authority gives its view concerning shopping centre leases generally and section 4(1) of the Competition Act. The main relevant feature of such leases in relation to the Competition Act is the so-called 'restricted user' clause.

Shopping Centres

2. Shopping centres, which first appeared in the late 1960's, have grown to become a very important part of the retail sector in the State. As of July 1990 there were one hundred and eight shopping centres in excess of 20,000 square feet within the State. Fifty-three of these were located in the Dublin Region with fifty-five elsewhere. A number of additional centres have opened since that time.[1] A shopping centre is designed to ensure that there is a variety of retail outlets within the same precinct. While it is usually developed by a single developer, eventually ownership of the different retail units may pass to several different landlords, or to a single investor, or may be acquired by the original tenants. The retail units are leased to individual traders. The developers or landlords do not usually operate any of the retail units themselves, though some large retail organisations have developed, or now own, shopping centres in which they also trade at retail level themselves. An almost invariable feature of shopping centres is that there is an 'anchor tenant' and a range of other shops. In the larger centres, the anchor tenant, who is designed to be the main means of attracting customers to the centre as a whole, is a large grocery supermarket, operated by one of the multiple organisations or by a symbol group retailer. Only nine of the one hundred and eight large shopping centres which were in existence in 1990 did not have an anchor tenant.[2] In the smaller centres, however, the anchor tenant may be a newsagent with grocery goods or a convenience grocery store. The other retail outlets consist of some or the whole range of retail outlets, including food shops, chemists, department stores, clothing and footwear shops, hardware, electrical goods, and newsagents, depending on the size of the centre. Other retail outlets might also provide services, such as hairdressing, medical services, video shops, and printing, and part of the centre may also be used as offices.

3. Shopping centres vary widely in size, from those with only two or three units to the Tallaght Town Centre with around two hundred units and three multiple supermarket tenants. The agreements notified to the Authority include both small and large centres. Shopping centres, especially the larger ones, have large areas of car parking space, and they are designed to attract customers from a hinterland surrounding the centre. Usually, the larger the centre, the larger the hinterland from which it is expected to attract customers, sometimes from a very considerable distance. Shopping centres are now found throughout the State, with small centres even in small towns, and two or more centres in larger towns and cities and in their suburbs. Shopping centres generally require a substantial capital investment in order to permit their development.

The Undertakings

4. Each shopping centre lease is basically an agreement between two parties—the landlord and the tenant—though some may also involve a head landlord and/or a management company. Section 3(1) of the Competition Act defines an undertaking as 'an individual, a body corporate or an unincorporated body of person's engaged for gain in the production, supply or distribution

1. Centre for Retail Studies, UCD, Fact Sheet 91/1.
2. UCD, op. cit.

of goods or the provision of a service'. The letting of shopping centre units is clearly a commercial activity for gain. Shopping centre landlords provide retailers with suitable accommodation in which to carry on their business in return for rental payments. In addition, they ensure the attraction of complementary retail users to the centre to the mutual benefit of each of the individual retailers, managing the allocation of tenancies so as to ensure a mix of different types of outlet along with the provision of car parking and other facilities in order to attract customers. These activities are an essential element of shopping centre lease agreements. All this constitutes the provision of a service for gain. The Authority considers that the shopping centre landlord is an undertaking within the meaning of the Act. In addition, the shopping centre landlord provides managerial and other services, such as cleaning, security, etc., for which there is a service charge levied on the tenants. Those shopping centre landlords who are engaged primarily in investing funds in the centres on behalf of others, such as pension funds, provide the service of managing these funds and they charge for the service accordingly. It is well established under EC law that the concept of undertaking in Article 85(1) on which section 4(1) is based 'extends to almost any legal or natural person carrying on activities of an economic or commercial nature . . .'[3] The Authority has no doubt that the business of shopping centre landlords is an economic or commercial activity and that shopping centre landlords are undertakings within the meaning of section 4(1). It takes this view also of head landlords and management companies where they provide any of the above mentioned services for gain. The individual tenants are individuals, bodies corporate or unincorporated bodies who supply goods or provide services for gain (including the occupants of offices in the centre) and they also are undertakings. The leases between shopping centre landlords and tenants, and others where appropriate, are therefore, in the view of the Authority, agreements between undertakings within the meaning of section 4(1) of the Competition Act. Such agreements operate within the State. 7.3

Restricted User Clauses

5. The fundamental principle of a shopping centre is that it provides consumers with the opportunity of obtaining a wide range of goods and services in a single location. In order to do this it is essential that there should be a balanced mixture of different types of retail outlet in the centre. This implies that the landlord tries at all times to ensure that there is a wide variety of outlets to satisfy consumer demand for different goods and services within the centre. The provision of too many outlets of the same type would reduce the number and scope of other types of outlet and would therefore reduce the attractiveness of the centre to consumers and retailers. This variety of outlets is achieved by means of the inclusion in leases of a restricted user clause, also referred to as an 'exclusive user' or 'permitted user' clause.

6. Such clauses come in a variety of forms but essentially they oblige the tenant to engage only in a specified line or lines of business. In addition, there may be a clause granting the tenant the sole right to engage in the specified activity or stating that no other tenant will have such a right. Even where this is not stated explicitly, it is achieved in practice because all other tenants in the centre are similarly obliged to engage only in a specified activity or activities, these usually being different from each other. In some cases, the exclusion may not be total, in that, for example, the supermarket lease may permit other tenants to operate a food shop not exceeding a certain limited site, or allowing only one other greengrocer, butcher, breadshop, and so on. In this way, the landlord ensures a diversity of retail outlets, and can ensure also a specific layout for the centre so as to avoid having identical or similar types of shop, where they are permitted, in close proximity to each other.

7. The landlord also needs to ensure that this diversity of outlet types is maintained in the future when tenants wish to change their business or when tenancies change hands. Tenants

3. See C. Bellamy and G. Child (1987); 'Common Market Law of Competition', 3rd edition, Sweet and Maxwell, London, para 2-003.

7.3 have certain statutory rights, not only to occupy the premises and to renewal of their leases, but also generally to dispose of or to assign their interest in the lease. Thus there is usually a clause in the lease requiring the landlord's consent to any change of use, either by the tenant or on assignment or sub-letting. Such consent, however, 'may not be unreasonably withheld', as is required under sections 67(1) and (2) of the Landlord and Tenant (Amendment) Act 1980. It is understood that this still enables the landlord to withhold consent from certain changes of use in order to ensure the diversity of units in the centre and the attractiveness of the centre for consumers.

Section 4(1) of the Competition Act

(i) Restricted User Clause

8. Section 4(1) of the Competition Act prohibits and renders void all agreements between undertakings 'which have as their object or effect the prevention, restriction or distortion of competition in trade in any goods or services in the State or in any part of the State'. Notwithstanding the fact that a restricted user clause in a Shopping centre lease tends to prevent or restrict the operation of another outlet engaged in the same kind of business within the confines of the shopping centre, the Authority is of the view that such clauses do not normally offend against section 4(1) of the Competition Act.

9. The Authority has stated in its first decision, that of Nallen/O'Toole,[4] that it considered that section 4(1) of the Act should not be interpreted literally, since to do so would mean that 'virtually every form of business agreement could be argued to prevent, restrict or distort competition. . . . Such an interpretation would render it virtually impossible for business to operate' The Authority considers that it should apply a rule of reason to all agreements and, in this case, specifically to shopping centre leases.

10. The principal object of the development of a shopping centre is to ensure that the shops, usually leased to individual tenants, comprise a balanced range of outlets offering different goods and services in order to attract the maximum amount of custom given the assured mix of outlets and the attractiveness of the centre, this encourages tenants to lease the units, and, without an assurance that this mix existed and would be maintained, the units would be less likely to be leased. The Authority considers that the object of the development of a shopping centre is pro-competitive rather than anti-competitive, and that the restricted user provisions are essential to ensure such developments.

11. It is also relevant, in the view of the Authority, to consider what the state of competition would be in the absence of restricted user clauses. (This is in line with the approach of the EC Commission and the Court of Justice towards 'non-compete' clauses). The Authority considers that, without the freedom for the landlords to decide upon the precise types of outlet in the shopping centres, by means of the restricted user clause, such centres would be unlikely to be developed, and competition would be significantly less that if shopping centres were established.

12. From a strictly literal point of view, the effect of the restricted user clause is to restrict competition in the individual shopping centre, which is a part of the State. The Authority considers that this is too narrow an interpretation of the real effect of such clauses. The relevant geographic market for each shopping centre covers a much wider area than the centre alone. In many urban areas there are two or more shopping centres located reasonably close to each other, serving the same catchment area. These centres, and their supermarket anchor tenants, are in effective competition with each other. There are also, almost invariably, supermarkets and other shops in the vicinity of shopping centres, but not themselves located in shopping centres, but which are also in competition with the shops in the centre. Many customers travel

4. Competition Authority Decision No. 1 of 2 April 1992, Notification No. CA/8/91—Nallen/O'Toole at para 12.

by car, and they have a wide choice of centres and other shops; others can use public transport and they have a degree of choice also; those who must travel on foot have some choice besides the shopping centre. Even in smaller towns, with only a single shopping centre, local residents and those in the hinterland of the towns have the possibility of frequenting other shops in the town or shopping centres in other towns. 7.3

13. Advertising of shopping centres and individual outlets in them is not confined to the immediate vicinity of the centres. It is placed in national or local newspapers, or appears on local radio, and reaches a much wider audience than that living in close proximity to the centre alone. The Authority does not regard it as being essential for the attainment of effective competition that competing retail outlets should be located in virtually the same place. Even if shoppers who travel on foot have a lesser degree of choice than those who can make use of a car or public transport, they suffer no discrimination or disadvantage by virtue of being largely confined to one shopping centre. Its shops are in competition with shops elsewhere, and the retailers do not have the market power to increase their prices to all customers without fear of losing their more mobile customers, nor can they charge one price to these customers and a higher price to those who are less able to transfer their custom elsewhere.

14. In addition, even within a single shopping centre there is usually some degree of competition. The supermarket faces competition, for example, from the butcher, the greengrocer, the baker and, to a degree, from the newsagent and the chemist. In the larger centres, there may be more than one outlet of a particular type, including even two or three different supermarkets. (Even where a particular class of goods is sold in only one outlet, there is usually a competing outlet in the neighbourhood). It is relevant also that the restriction is not absolute, in that there can be a change of user, for which the landlord's consent may not be unreasonably withheld.

15. It is true that, where only one unit in a shopping centre is permitted to engage in a particular line of business, competing traders may not operate in the same centre. There is no restraint, however, save that of obtaining planning permission, on competing traders from setting up anywhere else in the whole State, including a location in the vicinity of the centre.

16. The Authority concludes therefore that the restricted user, exclusive user or permitted user clause, and the restriction on change of user, in shopping centre leases do not generally have as object or effect the prevention, restriction or distortion of competition in trade in any goods or services in the State or in any part of the State. Such agreements in the opinion of the Authority, on the basis of the facts in its possession, do not generally offend against section 4(1) of the Competition Act 1991.

17. Should any shopping centre lease infringe the prohibition in section 4(1) in a particular case, then any person aggrieved has a right of action for relief under section 6 of the Competition Act. Should a certificate have been issued by the Authority in respect of a particular agreement, it is open to any person to request the Authority to revoke the certificate in accordance with section 8(6) of the Competition Act.

(ii) Other Clauses

18. Shopping centre leases may also contain a number of other obligations, besides the restricted USCI clause, which the Authority considers do not generally restrict competition, and so do not offend against section 4(1). The tenant may be obliged to undertake or to do or not to do any or all of the following:

(a) to pay the rent, and other outgoings;
(b) to pay insurance premiums;
(c) to pay rates and taxes, ESB charges, etc.;
(d) to pay maintenance and service charges;
(e) to carry out certain works;
(f) to maintain the premises and keep them in good repair;
(g) to keep the premises tidy and clean;

7.3 (h) not to alter the premises;
(i) to maintain the appearance of the premises;
(j) to permit inspection of the premises by the landlord;
(k) to permit necessary work by the landlord;
(l) to keep open during the normal hours of business of the centre,
(m) to keep the premises insured;
(n) not to overload the structure;
(o) not to cause any nuisance or inconvenience;
(p) not to affix signs without consent;
(q) not to hold any auction;
(r) not to hold a 'fire sale' or a 'bankruptcy sale';
(s) not to use for illegal or immoral purposes;
(t) not to cause any obstruction;
(u) not to contravene the planning acts;
(v) not to use as a dwelling house;
(w) not to allow loud music or noise;
(x) not to use for betting or gambling;
(y) not, without consent, to erect any new building, etc., on the premises; and
(z) to comply with statutory provisions.

The Authority considers that these are examples of clauses which generally do not restrict competition, and the list is not comprehensive. Such clauses relate to the proper operation of the shopping centre.

19. The Authority considers, however, that any clause in a shopping centre lease which imposes any restriction on the tenant engaging in any form of business activity after the termination of the lease would be likely to offend against section 4(1) of the Act.

The Consequences of this Notice

20. In the case of shopping centre leases already notified to the Authority, certificates will be issued individually after examination except where the agreement appears to offend against section 4(1). In the latter situation, further consideration by the Authority will be necessary.

21. This Notice is without prejudice to any interpretation that may be given by the Courts.

For the Competition Authority

Patrick M. Lyons
Chairman

2 September 1993

Competition Authority Decision No. 37, Roches Stores, Dublin Ltd/Peter Mark: **7.4**
5 October 1993, Notification No. CA/1016/92E

Lease agreement of a unit in a shopping centre containing restricted user clauses – Undertaking by lessor to lessee to limit number of competing traders in the shopping centre – Competition Act 1991 (No. 24), sections 3, 4 and 7

Facts: On 30 September 1992 notification was made to the Authority by Peter Mark with a request for a certificate under section 4(4) of the Competition Act 1991 or, failing that, a licence under section 4(2) in respect of a lease agreement made between Roches Stores Dublin Ltd and Peter Mark on 25 November 1989. Roches Stores Dublin Ltd, a private company registered in Ireland, carries on the business of supermarket and department store operator in the State and Peter Mark is engaged in the business of hairdressing through approximately 48 outlets in the State. The notified lease, between Roches Stores Dublin Ltd as lessor and Peter Mark, as lessee contained restricted user clauses whereunder the lessee covenanted with the lessor that, save with the consent of the lessor to the contrary, the lessee would; (i) utilise the demised premises for a particular purpose only, and (ii) not alienate its interest or part with possession or occupation of the demised premises, in both cases the consent of the lessor not to be unreasonably withheld. The lessor, by letter to the lessee, gave a commitment to the lessee that no trade would be over represented in the shopping centre and, where possible, that there would be only a single unit in the centre for any particular trade.

Decided by the Authority: In issuing a certificate under section 4(4) of the Competition Act that:

(1) Each of the lessor and lessee are 'undertakings' within the meaning of Competition Act and the notified lease agreement is an agreement between undertakings which has effect within the State.

(2) The restrictions within the lease and the commitment given by the lessor do not have the object or effect of preventing, restricting or distorting competition in trade in any goods or services in the State or in any part of the State *(Notice of Authority in respect of Shopping Centre Leases, 2 September 1993 (Iris Oifigiúil, 10 September 1993, pp. 665-67) applied).*

Notice referred to:
Notice of Authority in respect of Shopping Centre Leases, 2 September 1993 (*Iris Oifigiúil*, 10 September 1993, pp. 665-67) **[7.3]**

Competition Authority Decision of 5 October 1993 relating to a proceeding under section 4 of the Competition Act 1991
Notification No: CA/1016/92E — Roches Stores Dublin Ltd/Peter Mark.

Introduction

1. Notification was made on 30 September 1992 by Peter Mark with a request for a certificate under section 4(4) of The Competition Act 1991 or, in the event of a refusal by the Competition Authority to issue a certificate, a licence under section 4(2), in respect of a lease between Roches Stores Dublin Ltd and Peter Mark.

7.4 The Facts

(a) *The subject of the notification*

2. The notification concerns the lease of a shop unit, Unit 1, Frascati Shopping Centre, Blackrock, Co Dublin, between Roches Stores Dublin Ltd as landlord and Peter Mark as tenant.

(b) *The parties involved*

3. Roches Stores Dublin Ltd trades as a supermarket and department store and is engaged in the letting of shop units at Frascati Shopping Centre. Peter Mark trades as a hairdresser with approximately 48 outlets in the State including the salon at Frascati Shopping Centre.

(c) *The subject of the notification*

4. The notified shopping centre lease was made on 25 November 1989 for a period of 30 years from 1 September 1989. The restricted user clauses in the lease are as follows:

> (a) In clause 4.11.2 the tenant covenants with the landlord 'Not without the prior consent in writing of the Landlord or its Agency thereunto lawfully authorised to use or to permit or suffer or allow the Demised Premises or any part or parts thereof to be used for any purposes other than as a retail shop for the Permitted business and for no other purpose or purposes whatsoever .... PROVIDED ALWAYS AND IT IS HEREBY AGREED AND DECLARED that upon any application by the Tenant or any authorised under-tenant of the Tenant for liberty to alter or change the Permitted Business the Landlord shall not unreasonably withhold its consent to such proposed change of user. . . .'

Clause l defines 'the Permitted Business' as 'The retail trade or business of Ladies & Gents Hairdressing Salon, and for the sale of beauty products and for carrying out beauty treatment including sunray treatment and as a Solarium.'

> (b) In Clause 4.25.1 the tenant covenants with the landlord 'Not to assign, transfer, underlet, ...or part with the possession or occupation of the Demised Premises or any part thereof or ....as concessionaire BUT SO THAT NOTWITHSTANDING the foregoing the Landlord shall not unreasonably withhold its consent to an assignment, transfer under-letting, charging, mortgaging or encumbering of the entire of the Demised Premises ......'.

In addition there are a number of other standard restrictive covenants and obligations in the lease.

Peter Mark has also advised that by way of side letter the Landlord has given a commitment that no one trade would be over represented at the centre and where possible only a single shop unit in the centre would be used for a single trade.

Assessment—The Applicability of section 4(1)

5. The Authority considers that Roches Stores Dublin Ltd and Peter Mark are undertakings and that the notified lease is an agreement between undertakings. The agreement has effect within the State.

6. The Authority considers that the notified agreement, and its restricted and exclusive user clauses and the other restrictive clauses and obligations, does not have the object or effect of preventing, restricting or distorting competition in trade in any goods or services in the State or in any part of the State, for the reasons given in the Notice of the Authority of 2 September 1993 in respect of shopping centre leases (*Iris Oifigiúil*, 10 September 1993, pp. 665-667). The Authority therefore considers that the notified agreement between Roches Stores Dublin Ltd and Peter Mark, does not offend against section 4(1) of the Competition Act 1991.

The Certificate 7.4

7. The Competition Authority has issued the following certificate.

> The Competition Authority certifies that in its opinion, on the basis of the facts in its possession, the agreement between Roches Stores Dublin Ltd and Peter Mark in relation to the lease of a premises at Unit 1 Frascati Shopping Centre, Blackrock, Co Dublin, notified under section 7 on 30 September 1992 (Notification No. CA/1016/92E), does not offend against section 4(1) of the Competition Act 1991.

For the Competition Authority

Des Wall
Member

5 October 1993.

Competition Authority Decision No. 145, Fuel Distributors Ltd/J. Enright: 18 November 1993, Notification No. CA/61/93 7.5

Restrictive covenant for future use in an agreement for sale of property — Competition Act 1991 (No. 24) sections 3, 4 and 7

Facts: On 11 October 1993 notification was made to the Authority by Fuel Distributors Ltd of a property sale agreement made 6 October 1993 between Fuel Distributors Ltd as vendors and Joseph Enright as purchaser with a request for a certificate under section 4(4) of the Competition Act 1991 or, failing that a licence under section 4(2). Fuel Distributors Ltd, an Irish registered limited company and wholly owned subsidiary of Consolidated Holdings Ltd, is engaged in the business of importation and distribution of fuel products within the State and Mr. Joseph Enright was stated in the notification to be involved in the scrap business. The notified sale agreement contained a restrictive covenant prohibiting Mr. Enright from using the purchased property for the purpose of the sale, marketing or otherwise of solid fuels, this being the purpose for which the premises had been used by Fuel Distributors Ltd prior to the sale.

Decided by the Authority: In issuing a certificate under section 4(4) of the Competition Act 1991 in respect of the notified agreement that:

(1) Each of the parties to the notified agreement are undertakings within the meaning of section 3(1) of the Competition Act 1991 and the agreement is an agreement between undertakings having effect within a part of the State.

(2) The notified agreement including the restrictive covenant does not have the effect of preventing, restricting or distorting competition in the solid fuel market in the State or any part of the State as should Mr. Enright wish to engage in such business there is nothing in the notified agreement to prevent him from so doing in some other premises in the same locality or elsewhere in the State.

7.5 Competition Authority Decision of 18 November 1993 relating to a proceeding under section 4 of the Competition Act 1991 Notification No. CA/61/93 — Fuel Distributors Ltd/J Enright

Introduction

1. Notification was made by Fuel Distributors Ltd on 11 October 1993 with a request for a certificate under section 4(4) of the Competition Act 1991 or, in the event of a refusal by the Competiton Authority to issue a certificate, a licence under section 4(2), in respect of a sale of property agreement with Joseph Enright.

(a) *The subject of the notification*

2. The notification concerns the sale of property at Le Fanu Road, Ballyfermot, Dublin by Fuel Distributors Ltd to Joseph Enright. The premises consists of a large yard, offices and a number of sheds, and was previously used as a fuel and coal storage depot.

(b) *The parties involved*

3. Fuel Distributors Ltd is a wholly owned subsidiary of Consolidated Holdings Ltd, an Irish private limited company. It is engaged in the importation and distribution of fuel products, including coal, anthracite and smokeless coal and the distribution of oil and oil products. Mr Joseph Enright is stated by Fuel Distributors Ltd to be involved in the scrap business.

(c) *The notified arrangement*

4. The notified agreement for the sale of property at Le Fanu Road, Ballyfermot, Dublin was made on 6 October 1993. The sale of property agreement contains a restrictive covenant prohibiting Joseph Enright from using the premises at Le Fanu Road, Ballyfermot, Dublin for the sale or marketing, whether by wholesale or retail, of coals, anthracites, turf or other solid fuels.

Assessment

Applicability of section 4(1)

5. The Authority considers that Fuel Distributors Ltd is an undertaking, within the meaning of section 3 of the Competition Act, as it is engaged in the importation, distribution and sale of fuel products. Joseph Enright is involved in the buying and selling of scrap, and is also considered an undertaking within the meaning of section 3 of the Act. The agreement is therefore between undertakings, and it has effect within a part of the State.

6. In the Authority's view agreements for the sale of property *per se* do not come within the scope of section 4(1). In addition, the Authority considers that restrictions on the future use of property do not generally offend against section 4(1). In this case the Authority considers that the notified agreement, including the restrictive covenant, does not have the object or effect of preventing, restricting or distorting competition in the solid fuel market in the State or in any part of the State. The restrictive covenant prevents the premises being used as a wholesale or retail outlet for solid fuel. Mr Enright is not engaged in the solid fuel business at present and, should he wish to, he can do so in many other premises, both in the vicinity or elsewhere in the State. Similarly, the agreement does not prevent any other person engaging in the solid fuel business in any part of the State. The effect of the agreement is not, therefore, anti-competitive. The Authority considers that the notified agreement between Fuel Distributors Ltd and Joseph Enright does not offend against section 4(1) of the Competition Act 1991.

The Certificate

7. The Competition Authority has issued the following certificate:

The Competition Authority certifies that in its opinion, on the basis of the facts in its possession, the agreement between Fuel Distributors Ltd and Joseph Enright in relation to the purchase of property at Le Fanu Road, Ballyfermot, Dublin, (Notification No. CA/61/93), notified on 11 October 1993 under section 7, does not offend against section 4(1) of the Competition Act 1991. 7.5

For the Competition Authority

Patrick M. Lyons
Chairman

18 November 1993

Competition Authority Decision No. 179, Melincourt Ltd/D. Horkan Ltd: 3 December 1993, Notification No. CA/817/92E 7.6

Lease of a unit in shopping centre – Restriction on partial alienation of the leased property – Covenant by tenant to utilise demised premises for a particular use – Undertaking by landlord not to permit other tenants in the shopping centre to use their premises in competition with the tenants permitted use – Competition Act 1991 (No. 24) sections 3, 4 and 7

Facts: On 30 September 1992 notification was made to the Authority with a request for a certificate under section 4(4) of the Competition Act 1991 or, failing that, a licence under section 4(2) in respect of a lease between Melincourt Ltd ('the Landlord') and D. Horkan Ltd ('the Tenant').

The Landlord is engaged in the business of owning and renting property at Huntstown Shopping Centre, County Dublin, and the Tenant trades as Huntstown Newsagency in the said shopping centre.

The notified lease was made 28 September 1990. In addition to the standard restrictive covenants in the notified lease the Tenant undertook not to alienate or part with possession of part only of the demised unit. The Tenant also covenanted with the Landlord not to use or permit the demised unit or any part thereof to be used for any purpose other than the use permitted under the terms of the lease and the Landlord undertook that should an application be made by the Tenant (or any under-tenant) for a change of user that the Landlord would not unreasonably withhold its consent. The permitted user under the lease was that of newsagent, including groceries, confectionery, tobacco, toys, cards and ancillary services. The Landlord and the management company of the shopping centre undertook under the terms of the notified lease to ensure that the Tenant enjoyed his exclusive user without interruption during the term of the lease and they further undertook not to permit any part of the shopping centre to be used for any purpose which would interrupt or interfere with the Tenant's exclusive user.

Decided by the Authority: In issuing a certificate under section 4(4) of the Competition Act 1991 in respect of the notified agreement that:

7.6 (1) Each of the Landlord and the Tenant are undertakings in the meaning of the Competition Act 1991 and the notified lease is an agreement between undertakings which has effect within the State.

(2) The notified agreement and it's restrictive and exclusive user clauses and the other standard restrictive clauses do not have the object or effect of preventing, restricting or distorting competition in trade in any goods or services in the State.

Notice referred to:
Competition Authority notice of 2 September 1993 in respect of shopping centre leases (*Iris Oifigiúil* — 10 September 1993, pp. 665-67) **[7.3]**

Competition Authority Decision of 3 December 1993 relating to a proceeding under section 4 of the Competition Act 1991
Notification No: CA/817/92E — Melincourt Ltd/D. Horkan Ltd

Introduction

1. Notification was made by D. Horkan Ltd on 30 September, 1992 with a request for a certificate under section 4(4) of the Competition Act 1991 or, in the event of a refusal by the Competition Authority to issue a certificate, a licence under section 4(2), in respect of a lease between Melincourt Ltd and D. Horkan Ltd.

The Facts

(a) *Subject of the notification*

2. The notification concerns the lease of Unit No. 1 at Huntstown Shopping Centre, Pinewood House, Huntstown Road, Mulhuddart, Co. Dublin between Melincourt Ltd as Landlord and D. Horkan Ltd as tenant.

(b) *The parties involved*

3. D. Horkan Ltd trading as Huntsdown Newsagency is engaged in the business of Newsagent at Unit 1. Melincourt Ltd is the landlord of the shopping centre.

(c) *The notified arrangements*

4. The notified lease was made on 28 September, 1990 for a period of 500 years from 1 August, 1990. The restricted user clauses in the lease are as follows:

(a) Under clause 6.24.1 the tenant covenants with the landlord 'Not to assign, transfer, underlet or part with possession or occupation of part only of the Demised Unit'.

(b) Under clause 6.25.1 the tenant covenants with the landlord 'Not without the prior consent in writing of the Landlord or its agent thereunder lawfully authorised which consent shall not be unreasonably withheld or delayed to use or to permit or suffer or allow the Demised Unit or any part or parts thereof to be used for any purpose other than as set forth in Part II of the First Schedule hereto and for no other purpose or purposes whatsoever. . . . Provided Always And It Is Hereby Agreed And Declared that upon any application by the Tenant or any under-tenant of the Tenant for liberty to alter or change the aforesaid permitted user of the Demised Unit the Landlord shall not unreasonably withhold its consent. . . .'

(c) Under clause 11 the Landlord covenants with the tenant that:

> 1. The Permitted User set out in Paragraph II of the First Schedule hereto is exclusive to the Tenant where so indicated and the Landlord and the Management Company hereby covenant and undertake with the Tenant to ensure that such exclusivity (where indicated) continues without interruption or interference throughout the term of this Lease.

2. The Landlord and the Management Company hereby covenant and undertake with the Tenant that they shall not cause or permit any part of the Estate to be used for any purpose which would interrupt or interfere with the Tenant's exclusivity (where appropriate) as aforesaid. 7.6

(d) In the First Schedule, Part II, of the lease the permitted user is defined as follows:

(a) *Exclusive User:* Newsagents, including groceries, confectionery, tobacco, toys, cards, lottery and Dublin Bus Agents.
(b) *Non-exclusive User:* Cakes, software, books, stationery and photocopying services.

In addition, there are a number of other standard restrictive covenants and obligations in the lease.

Assessment — The applicability of section 4(1)

5. The Authority considers that D. Horkan Ltd and Melincourt Ltd are undertakings and that the notified lease is an agreement between undertakings. The agreement has effect within the State.

6. The Authority considers that the notified agreement, and its restricted and exclusive user clauses and the other standard restrictive clauses and obligations, does not have the object or effect of preventing, restricting or distorting competition in trade in any goods or services in the State or in any part of the State, for the reasons given in the Notice of the Authority of 2 September 1993 in respect of shopping centre leases (*Iris Oifigiúil*, 10 September 1993, pp. 665-667). The Authority therefore considers that the notified agreement between D. Horkan Ltd and Melincourt Ltd does not offend against section 4(1) of the Competition Act 1991.

The Certificate:

7. The Competition Authority has issued the following certificate:

The Competition Authority certifies that in its opinion, on the basis of the facts in its possession, the agreement between D. Horkan Ltd and Melincourt Ltd in relation to the lease of the premises at Huntstown Shopping Centre, Huntstown Road, Mulhuddart, Co. Dublin notified under section 7 on 30 September 1992 (Notification No. CA/817/92E), does not offend against section 4(1) of the Competition Act 1991.

For the Competition Authority

Des Wall
Member

3 December 1993

7.7 Competition Authority Decision No. 206, The Square Management Ltd/L & C Properties Ltd and Others/Tenants of the Square Towncentre: 3 December 1993, NOTIFICATION No. CA/886/92E

Agreement between landlords of shopping centre regulating the management of the centre – Restricted user clauses in leases of shop units in shopping centre – effect of agreement between landlords on the restricted user clauses – Competition Act 1991 (No. 24) section 4

Facts: On 30 September 1992 notification was made to the Authority by The Square Management Ltd in respect of agreements relating to the lease of shop units at The Square shopping centre, Tallaght, and other agreements regulating the management of the shopping centre with a request for a certificate under section 4(4) of the Competition Act 1991 or, failing that, a licence under section 4(2). The parties to the notified agreements are The Square Management Ltd which is the manager and freeholder of the Square shopping centre, Guardian Assurance plc and L & C Properties Ltd which are the holders of the leasehold interest in the Square shopping centre, all the other landlords of the shopping centre (twenty two in all) and the tenants of the 177 units in the shopping centre. The notified arrangements include: a shareholders agreement dated 22 October 1990 made between the Square Management Ltd and all the landlords to units in the shopping centre (other than those owner occupied units), a deed of assignment dated 19 October 1990 made between The Square Management Ltd on the one part and Guardian Assurance plc and L & C Properties Ltd on the other part under which all common areas in the Shopping Centre were assigned to the Square Management Ltd and a standard lease agreement made between a landlord and a tenant in respect of a unit in the Shopping Centre. Under the terms of the shareholders agreement the board of the Square Management Ltd must approve the permitted uses of the units in the Centre or to any alterations of such permitted uses and the landlords covenant which each other and with The Square Management Ltd not to agree to a permitted use or to a change of permitted use without the prior approval of the Square Management Ltd. Under the deed of assignment Guardian Assurance plc and L & C Properties Ltd (as owners of all lettable premises at that time) covenanted to The Square Management Ltd to use each unit for a set use and covenant it to regulate it in each of the lease agreements with the tenants. Under the terms of the standard lease each tenant covenants to use the premises solely for the permitted use. Further the landlord and the Square Management Ltd agrees with the tenant not to unreasonably withhold consent to any application for a change of user and the tenant further covenants not to alienate the demised premises in any way without the prior consent of the landlord, such consent not to be unreasonably withheld.

Decided by the Authority: In issuing a certificate in respect of the notified agreements under section 4(4) of the Competition Act 1991 that:

(1) Each of the parties to the notified agreements are 'undertakings' within the meaning of the Competition Act 1991.

(2) The restricted and exclusive user clauses in the notified standard leases do not have the object or effect of preventing, restricting or distorting competition for the reasons set out in the Notice of the Authority of 2 September 1993 in respect of

shopping centre leases (*Iris Offigiúil*, 10 September 1993, pp. 665-67). **7.7**

(3) The restricted user clauses in the notified deed of assignment are similar to those set out in the standard leases and for the same reasons do not offend against section 4(1) of the Competition Act 1991.

(4) The shareholders agreement does not offend against section 4(1) of the Competition Act 1991 as it is a fundamental principle of a shopping centre that it provides consumers with a wide range of goods and services in a single location and where, as in this case, there are a large number of landlords the regulation of a permitted user policy can only be achieved through such an agreement (Notice of Authority dated 2nd September 1993 in respect of Shopping Centre leases referred to and applied).

Notice referred to:

Notice of Authority dated 2 December 1993 in respect of Shopping Centre Leases (*Iris Oifigiúil*, 10 September 1993, pp. 665-67) **[7.3]**

Competition Authority Decision of 3 December 1993 relating to a proceeding under section 4 of the Competition Act 1991
Notification No: CA/886/92E—The Square Management Ltd/L & C Properties Ltd and others/Tenants of The Square, Towncentre

Introduction

1. Notification was made by The Square Management Ltd on 30 September 1992 with a request for a certificate under section 4(4) of the Competition Act 1991 or, in the event of a refusal by the Competition Authority to issue a certificate, a licence under section 4(2) in respect of agreements relating to the leases of shop units at The Square, Towncentre, Tallaght.

The Facts

(a) *Subject of the notification*

2. The notification concerns the leases relating to shop units in The Square, Towncentre, Tallaght, Dublin 24 between The Square Management Ltd as Freeholder, L&C Properties and others as Landlords, and the tenants. It also concerns associated agreements relating to the management of the centre.

(b) *The parties involved*

3. The Square Management Ltd is the Freeholder of The Square, Towncentre, Tallaght, Dublin 24. Guardian Assurance plc and L & C Properties Ltd, were the holders of the long leasehold and the sub leasehold interest respectively in October 1990, and are landlords. Other landlords include Salix Trust Ltd, AIB Investment Nominees, IBI Nominees Ltd, IBI Property Nominees, Ricarton Ltd, Airspace Investments Ltd, Aviette Ltd and 13 other individuals or partnerships. The tenants of the 177 shop units involved are engaged in various retail and service activities at the shopping centre.

(c) *The notified arrangements*

4. The agreements notified are as follows:

— Shareholders Agreement dated 22 October 1990

— Deed of Assignment dated 19 October 1990

— Standard leases

7.7 Shareholders Agreement

5. The shareholders of The Square Management Ltd are the several landlords of units and the Shareholders Agreement was entered into on 22 October 1990 by the earlier landlords to regulate matters between them and to ensure an orderly provision of services and diversity of use within the shopping centre. Shares in the company may only be held by the initial shareholders (L&C Properties, Guardian Assurance, AIB Investment Nominees, IBI Nominees, IBI Property Nominees Ltd and Salix Trust Ltd) and future landlords of leased units (excluding owner occupied units). The agreement provides for the regulation of the company business including the following viz.

> (i) . . . (the Boards) business shall include:
> 6.1.3 The approval or otherwise by the Board of the permitted uses of the units in the centre and the approval or otherwise of any proposals to alter the said permitted uses or any subsequent variations.
> 6.1.5 The approval of the annual Service Charge budget for the centre
> (ii) The Shareholders hereby covenant with the company and mutually covenant with one another.
> 13.2.6 Not to agree to a change of use of any Unit without first obtaining the companys consent and in particular not to agree to the establishment of a use (in respect of units unlet at the date hereof) or to the change of any use as disclosed by the Disclosure Booklet where such establishment or change of use would result in same being in conflict with any of the exclusivity undertakings granted to Tenants of Units as disclosed by the Disclosure Booklet.

Deed of Assignment

6. The deed of assignment dated 19 October 1990 was made between The Square Management Ltd as Landlord and Guardian Assurance (holder of the lessee interest in the Superior lease) and L&C Properties Ltd (holder of the lessee interest in the Sub-Lease and Licence). Under this deed all the common parts of the shopping centre were assigned to The Square Management Ltd and the assignees as owners of all the lettable premises at that time covenanted to use each unit for a set use and inter alia covenanted to the covenants in the agreed standard lease set out at para.7 under.

Standard Lease

The standard shopping centre lease furnished in draft form contains the following restricted user clauses viz.

(i) Under clause 3.2(3) the tenant covenants with the Freeholder and the landlord 'Not without the prior consent in writing of the Landlord and the Freeholder or their respective Agents thereunto lawfully authorised, to use or permit or suffer to allow the Demised Premises or any part thereof, to be used for any purpose other than PROVIDED ALWAYS AND IT IS HEREBY AGREED AND DECLARED that upon any application by the Tenant, or any Undertenant of the Tenant, for liberty to alter or change the aforesaid permitted use of the Demised Premises the Landlord and the Freeholder shall not unreasonably withhold their consent. . . .'

(b) Under clause 3.2(5) the tenant covenants with the freeholder and the landlord 'Not to assign transfer, mortgage, charge or part with the possession or occupation of the Demised Premises or any part thereof or suffer any person to occupy the Demised Premises or any part thereof as a licensee or concessionaire except with the previous consent in writing of the Landlord and the Freeholder BUT SO THAT NOTWITHSTANDING the foregoing the Landlord and the Freeholder shall not unreasonably withhold its consent. . . .'

In addition, there are a number of other standard restrictive covenants and obligations in the lease.

Permitted/Exclusive User 7.7

The Square Management Ltd has supplied details of the permitted user under clause 3.2(3) attaching to each lease whereby the tenant is restricted to particular specified retail or service activities. In addition particulars of exclusive user attaching to 36 tenancies have been supplied.

Assessment—The Applicability of section 4(1)

9. The Authority considers that The Square Management Ltd, the Landlords and the tenants are undertakings and that the notified leases and agreements are agreements between undertakings. The agreements have effect within the State.

10. The Authority considers that the notified leases, and their restricted and exclusive user clauses and the other standard restrictive clauses and obligations, do not have the object or effect of preventing, restricting or distorting competition in trade in any goods or services in the State or in any part of the State, for the reasons given in the Notice of the Authority of 2 September 1993 in respect of shopping centre leases (Iris Oifigiúil of 10 September 1993, pp. 665-667). The Authority therefore considers that the notified leases between The Square Management Ltd, the Landlords and the tenants do not offend against section 4(1) of the Competition Act 1991.

11. The restricted user clauses in the Deed of Assignment are identical to those in the standard lease. The Authority would therefore take the view that these clauses do not offend against section 4(1) of the Competition Act 1991.

12. As regards the Shareholders Agreement the Authority must take into consideration the fact that with over 170 shopping units The Square shopping centre is the largest in the State and that it has 22 separate landlords. The Authority in its notice on shopping centre leases stated:

> The fundamental principle of a shopping centre is that it provides consumers with the opportunity of obtaining a wide range of goods and services in a single location. In order to do this it is essential that there should be a balanced mixture of different types of retail outlets in the centre. This implies that the Landlord tries at all times to ensure that there is a wide variety of outlets to satisfy consumer demand for different goods and services within the centre.

In fact, in this case, the arrangements provide for the location of competing outlets within the centre so no question of a restriction on competition arises.

With 22 landlords letting units at the centre it would seem essential that there should be a mechanism to ensure this diversity of use and this is achieved by means of the shareholders agreement. This agreement allows the application of permitted user and exclusive user clauses on a common basis throughout the shopping centre. The Authority considers that such clauses do not offend against section 4(1). Similarly an agreement between landlords at the centre to enable common application of the clauses would not offend. The Authority therefore takes the view that the Shareholders Agreement does not offend against section 4(1) of the Competition Act 1991.

The Certificate

13. The Competition Authority has issued the following certificate:

> The Competition Authority certifies that in its opinion, on the basis of the facts in its possession, the agreements between The Square Management Ltd, and Guardian Assurance plc, L & C Properties Ltd, Salix Trust Ltd, AIB Investment Nominees Ltd, IBI Nominees Ltd, IBI Property Nominees Ltd, Riccarton Ltd, Airspace Investments Ltd, Aviette Ltd and other landlords and the tenants in relation to the lease of premises at The Square Towncentre, Tallaght, Dublin 24, notified under section 7 on 30 September

7.7 1992 (Notification No. CA/886/92E), do not offend against section 4(1) of the Competition Act 1991.

For the Competition Authority

Des Wall
Member

3 December 1993

7.8 Competition Authority Decision No. 267, Aviette Trust Company Ltd/Tenants of Firhouse Shopping Centre: 15 December 1993, Notification No. CA/871/92E

Leases of units in a shopping centre containing restricted and exclusive user clauses and other restrictions – Whether such restrictions prevent, restrict or distort competition – Competition Act 1991 sections 3, 4 and 7

Facts: On 30 September 1992 notification was made to the Authority by Aviette Trust Company Ltd in respect of various lease agreements made between Aviette Trust Company Ltd, as landlord of Firhouse Shopping Centre, Dublin and fourteen individual tenants, with a request for a certificate under section 4(4) of the Competition Act 1991 or, failing that, a licence under section 4(2). Aviette Trust Company Ltd is engaged in the business of letting units in the Firhouse Shopping Centre, Dublin and each of the tenants is engaged in various retail and service activities at the shopping centre. The notified agreements included six standard shopping centre leases each of which contained restricted and exclusive user clauses and a restriction on the tenant alienating his interest in the demised premises without the prior consent of the landlord. In addition the notified lease in respect of the tenant operating a supermarket in the shopping centre contained, by way of supplementary letter, an undertaking by the landlord for a period of 21 years from the date thereof not to permit any other unit to be used as a general supermarket.

Decided by the Authority: In issuing a certificate in respect of the notified agreements under section 4(4) of the Competition Act 1991 that:

(1) Each of the parties to the notified agreements are 'undertakings' within the meaning of the Competition Act 1991 and that the notified leases are agreements between undertakings having effect within the State.

(2) The notified agreements and their restrictive and exclusive user clauses and other standard restrictive clauses and obligations do not have as their object or effect the preventing, restricting or distortion of competition and do not offend against section 4(1) of the Competition Act 1991. (Notice of Authority dated 2 September 1993 in respect of shopping centre leases applied)

Notice referred to

Notice of Authority dated 2 September 1993 in respect of shopping centre leases (*Iris Offigiúil*, 10 September 1993, pp. 665-67) **[7.3]**

Competition Authority Decision of 15 December 1993 relating to a proceeding under section 4 of the Competition Act 1991 — 7.8
Notification No: CA/871/92E — Aviette Trust Company Ltd/Tenants of Firhouse Shopping Centre

Introduction

1. Notification was made by Aviette Trust Company Ltd on 30 September 1992 with a request for a certificate under section 4(4) of the Competition Act 1991 or in the event of a refusal by the Competition Authority to issue a certificate, a licence under section 4(2) in respect of leases between Aviette Trust Company Ltd and its tenants at Firhouse Shopping Centre.

The Facts

(a) *Subject of the notification*

2. The notification concerns the leases in respect of shop units in the Firhouse Shopping Centre, Tallaght, Dublin 24 between Aviette Trust Company Ltd as landlord and 14 tenants.

(b) *The parties involved*

3. Aviette Trust Company Ltd is the owner and landlord of the Firhouse Shopping Centre, Tallaght, Dublin 24. The tenants are engaged in various retail and service activities at the shopping centre.

(c) *The notified arrangements*

4. 6 standard shopping centre leases were notified viz.

(i) The standard lease relating to 1, 1A, 8 and 15 has the following restricted user clauses viz.

(a) Under clause 3.2(3) the tenant covenants with the landlord 'To keep the Demised Premises for the use Provided Always that the premises or any part thereof shall not be used for the sale, vending, consumption or otherwise of any type of food stuffs on the said premises for human or animal consumption only and, not without the Landlord's prior consent in writing, which shall not be unreasonably withheld, to use or permit or suffer the same or any part thereof to be used for any other purpose.'

(b) Under clause 3.2(5) the tenant covenants with the landlord 'Not to assign transfer or underlet or part with the possession or occupation of the demised premises or any part thereof or suffer any person to occupy the demised premises or any part thereof as a licencee BUT SO THAT NOTWITHSTANDING the foregoing the Landlord shall not unreasonably withhold its consent to an assignment of the entire or a suitable portion thereof (hereinafter called "a portion") or underletting of the entire or a portion of the demised premises. . . .'

(c) Under clause 3.10 the tenant covenants 'Subject to the provisions of 3.2(3) hereof, the tenant . . . hereby covenants with the Landlord not to use or permit to be used the Demised Premises or any part thereof for the sale of food or food products'.

(ii) The lease notified for unit 4 has a term of 35 years. The restricted user clauses in the lease are as follows:

(a) Under clause 12(a) the tenant covenants with the landlord: '. . . and not to use or permit the premises hereby demised to be used for any purpose other than for the sale and hire of videos and ancillary electrical goods specifically related to videos and excluding televisions and radios. . . .'

(b) Under clause 30 the tenant covenants with the landlord

(a) Not to assign, underlet or part with or share the possession of any part of the demised premises.

(b) Not, without the consent of the Lessor, to assign, underlet or part with or share the possession of the whole of the demised premises except to a suitable and solvent Lessee. . . .

7.8 (iii) The lease notified for unit 13 has a term of 35 years. The restricted user clauses in the lease are as follows:

(a) Under clause 12 the tenant covenants with the landlord '. . . and not to use or permit the premises hereby demised to be used for any purpose other than a Dry Cleaning Service.

(b) Under clause 30 the tenant covenants with the landlord not to assign, underlet or part with or share the possession of any part of the demised premises,

not to assign, underlet or part with or share the possession of the whole of the demised premises except to a suitable and solvent tenant and subject to the consent of the Lessor Provided Always. . . .

(iv) The lease notified for units 5/6 has a term of 10,000 years. The restricted user clauses in the lease are as follows:

(a) Under clause l2 the tenant covenants with the landlord '. . . and not without the prior written consent of the Lessor which consent shall not be unreasonably refused or withheld to use or permit the premises hereby demised to be used for any purpose other than for the sale of haberdashery, soft furnishings, linens, household linens, furniture, carpets, curtain rails, wallpaper and paint.

(b) Under clause 31 the tenant covenants with the landlord 'Not to assign, underlet or part with or share the possession of all or any part of the demised premises without the consent of the Lessor which shall not be unreasonably refused or withheld.'

(v) The lease notified in respect of the supermarket unit has a term of 9,980 years from 1 December 1991. The restricted user clauses in the lease are as follows:

(a) Under clause 3.2(2) the tenant covenants with the landlord 'Not without the prior consent in writing of the Landlord or its agent thereunto lawfully authorised, to use or to permit or suffer or allow the Demised Premises or any part thereof, to be used for any purpose other than as a general supermarket and ancilliary goods or services or other retail trades or businesses which do not require planning permission for change of use. . . . PROVIDED ALWAYS AND IT IS HEREBY AGREED AND DECLARED that upon any application by the Tenant or any under-tenant of the Tenant for liberty to alter or change the aforesaid permitted use of the Demised Premises the Landlord shall not unreasonably withhold its consent to such proposed change of user.'

(b) In a supplementary letter to the lease the landlord confirmed to the tenant subject to the existing uses granted in the Centre . . . 'that you, your successors and assigns shall have the exclusive right from the date hereof to use the entire of the Demised Premises as a General Supermarket and we hereby undertake not to let or sell any other unit in the Centre for a period of 21 years which would entitle the occupant to use same for the business of a General Supermarket or unit for the sale of Liquor, Wines or Spirits off the premises subject to the proviso herein contained and we will not permit any Tenant occupying any unit in the Centre or any Assignee of the Tenant within the Centre to use any unit or part thereof for such purposes. . . .'

(vii) The standard lease notified in respect of units 2, 3, 7, 9, 10/11, 12 and 14 contains the following restricted user clauses viz.

(a) Under clause 12 the tenant covenants with the landlord '. . . and not to use or permit the premises hereby demised to be used for any purpose other than .'

(b) Under clause 30 the tenant covenants with the landlord Not to assign, underlet or part with or share the possession of any part of the demised premises

Not, without the consent of the Lessor, to assign, underlet or part with or share the possession of the whole of the demised premises. . . .'

In addition, there are a number of other standard restrictive covenants and obligations in all the leases.

5. Aviette has supplied details of the permitted user attaching to each tenancy whereby the tenant is restricted to particular specified retail or service activities. In addition details of exclusive user granted in respect of Unit 12 as a Sports/Leisure/Hobby shop has been supplied.

Assessment—The Applicability of section 4(1) 7.8

6. The Authority considers that Aviette Trust Company Ltd and its tenants are undertakings and that the notified leases are agreements between undertakings. The agreements have effect within the State.

7. The Authority considers that the notified agreements, and their restricted and exclusive user clauses and the other standard restrictive clauses and obligations, do not have the object or effect of preventing, restricting or distorting competition in trade in any goods or services in the State or in any part of the State, for the reasons given in the Notice of the Authority of 2 September 1993 in respect of shopping centre leases (Iris Oifigiúil of 10 September 1993, pp. 665-667). The Authority therefore considers that the notified agreements between Aviette Trust Company Ltd and its tenants does not offend against section 4(1) of the Competition Act 1991.

The Certificate

8. The Competition Authority has issued the following certificate:

> The Competition Authority certifies that in its opinion, on the basis of the facts in its possession, the agreements between Aviette Trust Company Ltd and its tenants in relation to the lease of premises at Firhouse Shopping Centre, Tallaght, Dublin 24, notified under section 7 on 30 September 1992 (Notification No. CA/871/92E), do not offend against section 4(1) of the Competition Act 1991.

For the Competition Authority

Des Wall
Member

15 December 1993

Competition Authority Decision No. 276, Cecil and Bella Elkinson, Adeline Jacob & Ivor Elkinson/Damien and Mary Bushe: 4 February 1994, Notification No. CA/99/92E 7.9

Restricted user clauses in property lease agreement – Restriction for adjoining properties on landlord – Whether such clauses are anti-competitive – Landlord and Tenant Act 1980 (No. 10) – Competition Act 1991 (No. 24) sections 3, 4 and 7

Facts: On 21 September 1992 notification was made to the Authority by the Bushes of a property lease agreement between the Elkinsons, as landlords, and the Bushes, as tenants, together with a request for a certificate under section 4(4) of the Competition Act 1991, or failing that a licence under section 4(2). The Elkinsons were in the business of letting properties and the Bushes carried on business as newsagents in the demised property. The notified lease was made on 4 June 1994 and contained certain restrictive clauses. Under clause 3.19 the tenant covenanted not to use the demised premises for any purpose other than a newsagency and light grocery save with the landlord's consent, and the landlord undertook in return not to permit the adjoining

7.9 properties of the landlord to be used for the business of a newsagency or light grocery. Clause 3.21 contained restrictions on alienation of the demised premises by the tenant but the landlord undertook not to unreasonably withhold their consent to any assignment or underletting of the entire demised premises.

Decided by the Authority: In issuing a certificate under s.4(4) of the Competition Act 1991 in respect of the notified agreement that:

(1) Both parties are 'undertakings' for the purposes of the Competition Act 1991 and the notified lease is in agreement between undertakings which has effect in the State.

(2) The restrictions in the notified lease, other than the restricted user clause, are necessary for the maintenance of the relationship of landlord and tenant in respect of the tenancy and do not raise issues under the Competition Act.

(3) The restricted user clause is based on the use suggested by the tenant and is governed by considerations such as the physical characteristics of the premises, the requirements of the planning acts and the landlord's policy regarding the premises and does not have as its object or effect the prevention, restriction or distortion of competition.

(4) The undertaking by the landlord to the tenant not to lease adjoining premises to businesses in competition with the tenant does not prevent competitors of the tenant setting up in other premises in the area and therefore can not be regarded as preventing distorting or restricting competition.

Competition Authority Decision of 4 February 1994 relating to a proceeding under section 4 of the Competition Act 1991
Notification No: CA/99/92E — Cecil and Bella Elkinson, Adeline Jacob and Ivor Elkinson/Damien and Mary Bushe

Introduction

1. Notification was made by Damien and Mary Bushe on 21 September 1992 with a request for a certificate under section 4(4) of the Competition Act 1991 or, in the event of a refusal by the Competition Authority to issue a certificate, a licence under section 4(2), in respect of a lease between Cecil and Bella and Ivor Elkinson and Adeline Jacob (the Elkinsons) and Damien and Mary Bushe (the Bushes).

The Facts

(a) *Subject of the notification*

2. The notification concerns the lease of a shop at 173 Lower Rathmines Road, Dublin 6 between the Elkinsons as landlord and the Bushes as tenant.

(b) *The parties involved*

3. The Elkinsons are engaged in the letting of shops at Lower Rathmines Road. The Bushes, under the name Bonanza Newsagents, trade is newsagents at 173 Lower Rathmines Road.

(c) *The notified arrangements*

4. The notified lease was made on 18 December 1984 for a term of 35 years from 4 June 1984. The restricted user clauses in the lease are as follows:

(a) Under clause 3.19 the tenant covenants:

> Not to use or permit the demised premises or any part thereof to be used for any purpose other than as newsagency and light grocery and the sale of ice cream, sweets, confectionery and toys *and* for no other purposes save with the landlord's written consent which consent shall not be unreasonably refused. . . . 7.9

while it is also stated in this clause:

> The landlords will not permit their adjoining premises to be used for the business of newsagency light grocery or sale of ice cream sweets and confectionery. On no account will the tenant use the premises for the sale of shoes as long as there is a shoe shop adjoining or the sale of second-hand clothes. . . .

(b) Under clause 21 the tenant covenants:

> Not to assign transfer or underlet or part with the possession or occupation of the demised premises or any part thereof or suffer any person to occupy the Demise Premises. . . . BUT SO THAT NOTWITHSTANDING the foregoing the landlord shall not unreasonably withold its consent to an assignment of the entire or underletting of the entire of the demised premises subject to the following provisions. . . .

In addition there are a number of other standard restrictive covenants and obligations in the lease.

Assessment — The applicability of section 4(1)

5. The Authority considers that the Elkinsons and the Bushes are undertakings and that the notified lease is an agreement between undertakings. The agreement has effect within the State.

6. The lease agreement contains standard restrictions and obligations on both landlord and tenant which are necessary for the maintenance of the landlord/tenant relationship in respect of the tenancies. These do not raise issues under the Competition Act. In addition each agreement also provides, by way of the permitted user clause 3.19, restrictions on the use of the premises and those adjoining but which effectively allows the premises to be used for the purpose of the business of the tenant. Such permitted user clauses are normally based on the user proposed by the tenant at the time the lease is first executed but are also governed by considerations such as the physical characteristics of the premises, the requirements of the Planning Acts and the landlord's own policy, when granting the lease, on how the premises should be used. The Authority considers that such user restrictions in the letting of premises do not have the object or effect of preventing, restricting or distorting competition in the State or any part of the State.

7. The very act of leasing the premises to a particular tenant prevents competitors of the tenant from using those premises to compete with the tenant. Clearly this cannot be regarded as preventing, restricting or distorting competition since it would imply that the leasing of a commercial premises in order to carry on a business therein was prohibited unless licensed under section 4(2) of the Competition Act. Clause 3.19 also prevents the landlords from leasing their adjoining premises to anyone for the purposes of operating a business in competition with that of the tenant. In the Authority's opinion, however, this also cannot be regarded as preventing, restricting or distorting competition within the State or any part of it. Anyone wishing to operate a business in competition with the tenants may do so by occupying any other premises within the same catchment area. The tenants are prevented from operating a business which would compete with those operating from the landlord's adjoining premises. Again such a restriction would not prevent the tenant or anyone else from operating such a business from another premises within the same catchment area. In taking up the lease the tenant negotiates the permitted user required for his business. This is reflected in the lease but if he were subsequently to seek a change of user he could in most instances have recourse to the provisions

7.9 of the Landlord and Tenant Act 1980 which provide that a landlord cannot unreasonably withhold consent to a change of user requested by a tenant. The object or effect of such permitted user clauses in lease agreements are not therefore anti-competitive. The Authority therefore considers that the notified agreement between Cecil, Bella and Ivor Elkinson and Adeline Jacob and Damien and Mary Bushe does not offend against section 4(1) of the Competition Act 1991.

The Certificate

8. The Competition Authority has issued the following certificate:

> The Competition Authority certifies that in its opinion, on the basis of the facts in its possession, the agreement between Cecil, Bella and Ivor Elkinson and Adeline Jacob and Damien and Mary Bushe in relation to the lease of premises at 173 Lower Rathmines Road, Dublin 6 notified under section 7 on 21 September 1992 (Notification No. CA/99/92E), does not offend against section 4(1) of the Competition Act 1991.

For the Competition Authority

Des Wall
Member

4 February 1994

7.10 **Competition Authority Decision No. 278, Michael and Veronica Grant/Power Leisure Ltd:** 4 February 1994, Notification No. CA/313/92E

Restricted user clauses in property lease agreement – Landlord's undertaking not to rent adjoining premises to competitor of tenant – Whether arrangements anti-competitive – Competition Act 1991 (No. 24) sections 3, 4 and 7

Facts: On 30 September 1992 notification was made to the Authority by Power Leisure Ltd of a property lease agreement between the Grants, as landlords, and Power Leisure Ltd, as tenant, with a request for a certificate under section 4(4) of the Competition Act 1991, or failing that a licence under section 4(2). The Grants are in the business of letting premises and Power Leisure Ltd (trading as Paddy Power) is a licenced bookmaker with over seventy outlets throughout the country. The notified lease was executed on 1 November 1986 for a term of ten years and contained certain restrictive clauses. Under clause 8.1 the tenant covenanted to use the demised premises as a betting office and under clause 8.5 not to use the demised premises for the sale of hardware, plumbing, or building supplies. Clause 13.1 contained restrictions on alienation of the demised premises by the tenant but the landlord undertook not to unreasonably withhold consent to assignment or underletting of the entire demised premises. The landlord also covenanted with the tenant not to permit the landlord's adjoining premises to be used as a bookmaking office.

Decided by the Authority: In issuing a certificate under section 4(4) of the Competition Act 1991 that:

(1) Both the landlord and tenant are 'undertakings' for the purposes of the

Competition Act 1991 and the notified lease is an agreement between undertakings which has effect in the State. 7.10

(2) The standard restrictions and obligations contained in the notified lease (other than the restricted user clauses) are necessary for the maintenance of the relationship of landlord and tenant in respect of the tenancy and do not raise issues under the Competition Act.

(3) The restricted user clause is based on the use suggested by the tenant and is governed by consideration such as the physical characteristics of the premises, the requirements of the planning acts and the landlord's policy concerning the premises and does not have as its object or effect the prevention, restriction or distortion of competition. Further should the tenant at a later date wish to have a change of user he would have recourse to the provisions of the Landlord and Tenant Act 1980 which provides that a landlord cannot unreasonably withhold consent for a change of user requested by a tenant.

(4) The undertaking by the landlord not to lease adjoining premises to competitors of the tenant does not prevent those competitors from setting up in other premises in the area and therefore cannot be regarded as preventing, distorting or restricting competition.

Competition Authority Decision of 4 February 1994 relating to a proceeding under section 4 of the Competition Act 1991
Notification No: CA/313/92E — Michael and Veronica Grant/Power Leisure Ltd

Introduction

1. Notification was made by Power Leisure Ltd on 30 September 1992 with a request for a certificate under section 4(4) of the Competition Act 1991 or, in the event of a refusal by the Competition Authority to issue a certificate, a licence under section 4(2), in respect of a lease between Michael and Veronica Grant (the Grants) and Power Leisure Ltd.

The Facts

(a) *Subject of the notification*

2. The notification concerns the lease of shop premises at Duffry Hill, Enniscorthy, Co. Wexford between the Grants as Landlord and Power Leisure Ltd as tenant.

(b) *The parties involved*

3. The Grants are engaged in the letting of shops at Duffry Hill. Power Leisure Ltd (trading as Paddy Power) is a licensed bookmaker with over 70 outlets throughout the country.

(c) *The notified arrangements*

4. The notified lease was executed on 1 November 1986 for a term of 10 years from 1 November 1986. The restricted user clauses in the lease are as follows:

> (a) Under clause 8.1 of Schedule IV the tenant covenants 'To use the premises as a Betting Office . . .' while under clause 8.5 the tenant covenants 'Not to use the demised premises for the sale of new or second hand hardware, plumbing or building supplies. . . .'
> (b) Under clause 13.1 of Schedule IV the tenant covenants 'Not to assign, charge underlet . . . part only of the Premises' while under clause 13.3 he covenants 'Not to assign, charge underlet nor part with possession of the whole of the premises except with the previous written consent of the Landlord which shall not be unreasonably witheld. . .'
> (c) Power Leisure has also advised that the Landlords have covenanted with the tenant not to allow the Landlord's adjoining premises to be used as a bookmaking office.

7.10 In addition there are a number of other standard restrictive covenants and obligations in the lease.

Assessment—The Applicability of section 4(1)

5. The Authority considers that the Grants and Power Leisure are undertakings and that the notified lease is an agreement between undertakings. The agreement has effect within the State.

6. The Lease agreement contains standard restrictions and obligations on both landlord and tenant which are necessary for the maintenance of the landlord/tenant relationship in respect of the tenancy. These do not raise issues under the Competition Act. In addition the notified agreement also provides, by way of the permitted user clause 8.1 and 8.5 of Schedule IV and a landlord covenant restrictions on the use of the premises and those adjoining but which effectively allow the premises to be used for the purposes of the business of the tenants. Such permitted user clauses are normally based on the user proposed by the tenant at the time the lease is first executed but are also governed by considerations such as the physical characteristics of the premises, the requirements of the Planning Acts and the landlord's own policy, when granting the lease, on how the premises should be used. The Authority considers that such user restrictions in the letting of premises do not have the object or effect of preventing, restricting or distorting competition in the State or any part of the State.

7. The very act of leasing the premises to a particular tenant prevents competitors of the tenant from using those premises to compete with the tenant. Clearly this cannot be regarded as preventing, restricting or distorting competition since it would imply that the leasing of a commercial premises in order to carry on a business therein was prohibited unless licensed under section 4(2) of the Competition Act. Anyone wishing to operate a business in competition with the tenants may do so by occupying any other premises within the same catchment area. The tenants are prevented from operating a business which would compete with those operating from the landlord's adjoining premises. Again such a restriction would not prevent the tenant or anyone else from operating such a business from another premises within the same catchment area. In taking up the lease the tenant negotiates the permitted user required for his business. This is reflected in the lease but if he were subsequently to seek a change of user he could in most instances have recourse to the provisions of the Landlord and Tenant Act 1980 which provides that a Landlord cannot unreasonably withhold consent to a change of user requested by a tenant. The object or effect of such permitted user clauses in lease agreements are not therefore anti-competitive. The Authority therefore considers that the notified agreement between Michael and Veronica Grant and Power Leisure Ltd do not offend against section 4(1) of the Competition Act 1991.

The Certificate

8. The Competition Authority has issued the following certificate:

> The Competition Authority certifies that in its opinion, on the basis of the facts in its possession, the agreement between Michael and Veronica Grant and Power Leisure Ltd in relation to the lease of premises at Duffry Hill, Enniscorthy, Co. Wexford notified under section 7 on 30 September 1992 (Notification No CA/313/92E), does not offend against section 4(1) of the Competition Act 1991.

For the Competition Authority

Des Wall
Member

4 February 1994

Competition Authority Decision No. 283, Green Property plc/Tenants — Northside Shopping Centre: 4 February 1994, Notification No. CA/423/92 7.11

Leases of units in shopping centre containing exclusive user covenants – Restriction on lessee from engaging in any other retail operation within a radius of 2.5 miles of the relevant shopping centre – Amendment of notified agreement – Competition Act 1991 (No. 24) sections 3, 4 and 7

Facts: On 30 September 1992 notification was made to the Authority with a request for a certificate under section 4(4) of the Competition Act 1991 or, failing that, a licence under section 4(2) in respect of a standard lease agreement between Green Property plc ('the Lessor') and its tenants at Northside Shopping Centre ('the Lessees').

The Lessor, an Irish listed public company is involved in investment and development of property in the State and is the owner of Northside Shopping Centre. The Lessees are engaged in various retail and service activities at the said shopping centre.

The notified agreement provided that the Lessee would not without the written consent of the Lessor:

(1) use the demised premises for a purpose other than as agreed;

(2) transfer the whole or part of the demised premises;

(3) operate or be concerned with any other general retail store within a radius of 2.5 miles of the Northside Shopping Centre.

Other common and standard restrictive clauses were also included in the leases.

The Lessor submitted that the restriction on the Lessees from operating other retail stores within a radius of 2.5 miles of the Northside Shopping Centre was not *de facto* anti-competitive because the lessor would on request delete this clause should any Lessee so request and further the Lessor has never brought an action seeking to enforce the terms of the said clause. The Authority was nevertheless concerned that the effect of this clause was to restrict tenants of the Centre from being involved in any retail business elsewhere within a radius of 2.5 miles from the shopping centre which area represented almost 20 square miles of the outer suburbs of Dublin City. The Lessor, by letter dated 5 January 1994, confirmed that the said clause in the standard lease would be deleted.

Decided by the Authority: In issuing a certificate under section 4(4) of the Competition Act 1991 in respect of the notified agreement that:

(1) The Lessor and the Lessees are undertakings within the meaning of the Competition Act and the notified lease is an agreement between undertakings which has effect within the State.

(2) The notified standard agreement, as amended, and its restricted user clauses and the other standard restricted clauses and obligations do not have the object or effect of preventing, restricting or distorting competition in trade in any goods or services in the State or any part of the State and consequently does not offend against section 4(1) of the Competition Act 1991.

Notice referred to:

Notice of Authority in respect of shopping centre leases, 2 December 1993 (*Iris Oifigiúil,* 10 September 1993, pp. 665-67) **[7.3]**

7.11 Competition Authority Decision of 4 February 1994 in relation to a proceeding under section 4 of the Competition Act 1991 Notification No: CA/423/92 — Green Property plc

Introduction

1. Notification was made by Green Property plc on 30 September 1992 with a request for a certificate under section 4(4) of the Competition Act 1991 or, in the event of a refusal by the Competition Authority to issue a certificate, a licence under section 4(2), in respect of a standard lease between Green Property plc and its tenants at Northside Shopping Centre.

The Facts

(a) *Subject of the notification*

2. The notification concerns the standard lease relating to the shop units at Northside Shopping Centre, Coolock, Dublin 5 between Green Property plc as lessor and 70 tenants.

(b) *The parties involved*

3. Green Property PLC is a publicly quoted company involved in investment and the development of property and it is the owner of the Northside Shopping Centre. The tenants are engaged in various retail and service activities at the shopping centre.

(c) *The notified arrangements*

4. The standard shopping centre lease notified contains the following restricted user clauses viz.

(a) Under clause 3.10 of section III the tenant covenants with the landlord:

(i) To use the demised premises for the purpose of _________ and not without the lessor's consent in writing to use or permit or suffer the same or any part thereof to be used for any other purpose and not to permit any business to be operated in or from the demised premises by any concessionaire or licensee without the prior written consent of the lessor.

(ii) Not without the previous consent in writing of the lessor to operate manage or be concerned in the operation or management of any other general retail store within a radius of two and a half miles of the Northside Shopping Centre it being recognised that to do so might be detrimental to the interests of the Northside Shopping Centre and the lessees and traders therein.

(b) Under clause 3.12(a) of section III the tenant covenants with the landlord:

Not to assign, sub-let, part with or share possession of the demised premises or any part thereof without the consent in writing of the Lessor (such consent in the case of an assignment or sub-letting of the entire of the demised premises not to be unreasonably withheld) AND provided the under lessee shall enter into a direct covenant with the Lessor to perform and observe all the covenants (other than for payments of rent) and conditions herein contained including a covenant not to further assign or underlet or part with possession of the premises or any part thereof in any manner which shall be inconsistent with the provisions of this covenant.

In addition, there are a number of other standard restrictive covenants and obligations in the standard lease.

Submission of the Parties

5. In its comprehensive submission Green Property argued that the standard lease does not have as its object or effect the prevention, restriction or distortion of competition in any trade

in goods or services in the State. As regards clause 3.10(ii) the company stated: **7.11**

> With regard to the restriction in clause 3.10(ii), Green firstly submits that, in practice, should any tenant coming in to the Centre request the deletion of this clause, Green consents to such deletion. It must be assumed that where a tenant does not request that the clause be deleted, that tenant does not intend operating or managing a retail store within two and a half miles of the Centre. Consequently the clause has no practical effect, anti-competitive or otherwise. Secondly, Green submits that it has never brought an action to enforce the clause and would not envisage doing so. Consequently once again, Green submits that the clause does not therefore have an anti-competitive effect within the meaning of section 4(1) of the Act.

6. Despite these arguments the Authority was concerned that the effect of this clause in the standard lease was to restrict tenants of the centre from being involved in any retail business elsewhere within a radius of two and a half miles from the shopping centre. This is represented an area of almost 20 square miles of the outer suburbs of Dublin city. Following correspondence with the Authority Green Property plc, by letter of 5 January 1994, confirmed that clause 3.10(ii) in the standard lease would be deleted.

Assessment — The applicability of section 4(1)

7. The Authority considers that Green Property plc and the tenants are undertakings and that the notified lease is an agreement between undertakings. The agreement has effect within the State.

8. The Authority considers that the notified standard agreement, as amended, and its restricted user clauses and the other standard restrictive clauses and obligations, does not have the object or effect of preventing, restricting or distorting competition in trade in any goods or services in the State or in any part of the State, for the reasons given in the Notice of the Authority of 2 September 1993 in respect of shopping centre leases (*Iris Oifigiúil* of 10 September 1993). The Authority therefore considers that the amended standard agreement between Green Property plc and its tenants does not offend against section 4(1) of the Competition Act 1991.

The Certificate

9. The Competition Authority has issued the following certificate:

> The Competition Authority certifies that in its opinion, on the basis of the facts in its possession, the standard agreement between Green Property plc and its tenants (Notification No. CA/423/92) in relation to the lease of premises at Northside Shopping Centre, Coolock, Dublin 5, notified under section 7, and as amended by letter of 5 January 1994, does not offend against section 4(1) of the competition Act 1991.

For the Competition Authority

Des Wall
Member

4 February 1994

7.12 Competition AuthorityDecision No. 288, University College Dublin/The Governor and Company of the Bank of Ireland: 10 March 1994, Notification No. CA/332/92E

Exclusive concession agreement – Whether such agreement compatible with Irish Competition Law – Competition Act 1991 (No. 24) sections 3, 4 and 7

Facts: On 30 September 1992 notification was made to the Authority by The Governor and Company of the Bank of Ireland ('Bank of Ireland') of an exclusive concession agreement between University College Dublin and Bank of Ireland with a request for certificate under section 4(4) of the Competition Act 1991 or, failing that, a licence under section 4(2). Bank of Ireland is the second largest commercial bank in Ireland with a network of 290 branches within the State and University College Dublin, a constituent college of the National University of Ireland having a large degree of autonomy, earned in 1992 income of *c.*£30 million excluding governmental grants. Under the terms of the notified agreement which was made on 1 October 1979 and supplemented by agreement dated 19 September 1984, University College Dublin granted to Bank of Ireland, subject to the payment of a licence fee, a sole concession to operate a bank branch on the University Campus in premises provided rent free by University College Dublin.

Decided by the Authority: In issuing a certificate under section 4(4) of the Competition Act 1991 in respect of the notified agreement that:

(1) Both parties to the notified agreement are 'undertakings' within the meaning of section 3(1) of the Competition Act 1991 and the agreement is an agreement between undertakings which has effect within the State. (*Deane v. Voluntary Health Insurance Board*, Supreme Court Decision [1992] 2 IR 319, applied)

(2) The general conditions (other than the exclusive concession condition) in the notified agreement are necessary for the maintenance of a proper relationship in regard to the operation of the concession and the occupation of the premises and do not raise issues under the Competition Act.

(3) The exclusivity of the concession to Bank of Ireland does not offend against section 4(1) of the Competition Act because while Bank of Ireland is the only bank situated within the university campus there are a significant number of competing financial institutions within a radius of two miles of the University (Competition Authority Notice in respect of Shopping Centre leases, 2 September 1993 applied)

Case and Notice referred to

Deane v. Voluntary Health Insurance Board, Supreme Court [1992] 2 IR 319 **1.1**

Competition Authority Notice in respect of Shopping Centre leases dated 2 September 1993 (*Iris Oifigiúil*, 10 September 1993 pp. 665-67) [**7.3**]

Competition Authority Decision of 10 March 1994 relating to proceeding under section 4 of the Competition Act 1991 Notification No. CA/332/92E — University College Dublin/The Governor and Company of the Bank of Ireland 7.12

Introduction

1. Notification was made by The Governor and Company of the Bank of Ireland (Bank of Ireland) on 30 September 1992 with a request for a certificate under section 4(4) of the Competition Act 1991 or, in the event of a refusal by the Competition Authority to issue a certificate, a licence under section 4(2), in respect of a concession agreement between University College Dublin and the Bank of Ireland.

The Facts

(a) *The subject of the notification*

2. The notification concerns the grant by University College Dublin of a sole concession to the Bank of Ireland to operate a bank branch on the university campus at Belfield, Dublin 4.

(b) *The parties involved*

3. The Bank of Ireland is the second largest commercial bank in Ireland with a network of 290 branches within the State. University College Dublin (UCD) is a constituent college of the National University of Ireland, which was established under the National University Act and incorporated by charter in 1908. UCD enjoys a large degree of autonomy with its own Governing body and is primarily engaged in the provision of third level education and in research. In addition to Government grants of £39m, UCD had an income in 1992 of £19m from academic fees and £11.6m from other sources.

(c) *The notified arrangements*

4. The notified agreement was made on 1 October 1979 for a period of 16 years and extended for a further 10 years from 1 March 1989 by way of supplemental agreement dated 19 September 1984. Under the agreement, University College Dublin, granted a sole concession to Bank of Ireland to operate a bank branch on the University campus in premises provided rent free by UCD. The agreement also provides for the calculation of an annual licence fee as well as several clauses relating to the occupation and maintenance of the premises. It also specifically provides '. . . it is hereby mutually agreed that nothing herein contained shall create the relationship of Landlord and Tenant between the College and the Bank in respect of the said premises.'

Assessment—The applicability of section 4(1)

5. Section 4(1) of the Competition Act 1991 refers to agreements between undertakings and section 3(1) of the Act defines undertaking as a 'person being an individual, a body corporate or an unincorporated body of persons engaged for gain in the production, supply or distribution of goods or the provision of a service.' According to the judgment of the Supreme Court in the VHI case, as delivered by Finlay CJ, the words 'for gain' connote merely an activity carried on or a service supplied, as in this case, which is done in return for a charge or payment'. UCD is engaged in the provision of the services of third level education and research for which it receives substantial revenue by way of fees etc and it is therefore an undertaking engaged for gain in the provision of a service. Bank of Ireland is an undertaking engaged for gain in the provision of banking and other financial services. The notified agreement is therefore an agreement between undertakings. The agreement has effect within the State.

6. The agreement notified contains standard restrictions and obligations on both parties which are necessary for the maintenance of a proper relationship in regard to the operation of

7.12 the concession and the occupation of the premises. These do not raise issues under the Competition Act. The agreement also provides for exclusivity in relation to the operation by Bank of Ireland of the banking concession. In a number of earlier decisions the Authority has already indicated its view that exclusive user clauses in the letting of premises in a particular shopping centre or building complex do not offend against section 4(1) of the Competition Act. For similar reasons this view also applies in relation to the grant of an exclusive concession to use premises in a building complex for the purposes of a business. In this instance while Bank of Ireland is the only bank situated within the university campus, Allied Irish Banks has a branch at the gate of the campus. There are also six branches of competitor banks and 2 ATM machine sites within a radius of two miles of the university while four building societies have eleven branches within the same radius. The Authority therefore considers that the notified agreement between University College Dublin and the Bank of Ireland does not offend against section 4(1) of the Competition Act 1991.

The Certificate

7. The Competition Authority has issued the following certificate:

> The Competition Authority certifies that in its opinion, on the basis of the facts in its possession, the agreement between University College, Dublin and the Governor and Company of the Bank of Ireland, in relation to a banking concession at University College, Dublin, notified under section 7 on 30 September 1992 (Notification No. CA/332/92E), does not offend against section 4(1) of the Competition Act 1991.

For the Competition Authority
Des Wall
Member

10 March 1994

7.13 **Competition Authority Decision No. 289, University of Limerick/The Governor and Company of the Bank of Ireland:** 10 March 1994, Notification No. CA/330/92E

Concession agreement – Agreement between a bank and a university whereby university grants to the bank sole concession to carry on banking business within a certain part of the university – University agrees to restrict advertising by other banks or institutions within the agreed area – Competition Act 1991 (No. 24) sections 3, 4 and 7

Facts: On 30 September 1992 notification was made to the Authority with a request for a certificate under section 4(4) of the Competition Act 1991 or, failing that, a licence under section 4(2) in respect of a concession agreement between the University of Limerick ('UL') and the Bank of Ireland.

Bank of Ireland is the second largest commercial bank in Ireland having a network of 290 branches within the State. UL, as successor to the National Institute for Higher Education Limerick ('NIHE') and Thomond College, is an independent university established under the University of Limerick Act 1989 and is primarily engaged in the provision of third level education and research with a campus revenue of c. £28m. in 1992/1993. 7.13

The notified agreement was made on 25 October 1984 between the then NIHE and the Bank of Ireland and under its terms NIHE granted to Bank of Ireland the sole concession of carrying on the ordinary business of a branch bank for a term of 20 years from 1 September 1985 and also agreed to let premises to the Bank of Ireland subject to the payment of rent. The parties agreed that the agreement shall be deemed to be a licence only and not a lease or letting agreement within the meaning of the Landlord and Tenant Acts. Under the agreement the Bank may not assign, transfer or underlet or part with possession or occupation of the concession to any person or other institution. NIHE undertook not to allow advertisements to be placed on the campus in favour of any other bank or building society.

Decided by the Authority: In issuing a certificate under section 4(4) of the Competition Act 1991 in respect of the notified agreement that:

(1) UL is engaged in the provision of the services of third level education and research for which it receives substantial revenue by way of fees and it is therefore an undertaking engaged for gain in the provision of a service. Bank of Ireland is an undertaking engaged for gain in the provision of banking and other financial services and the notified agreement is therefore an agreement between undertakings which has effect within the State.

(2) The notified agreement contains standard restrictions and obligations on both parties which are necessary for the maintenance of a proper relationship in regard to the operation of a concession and the occupation of the premises. These do not raise issues under the Competition Act.

(3) The notified agreement provides for exclusivity in relation to the operation by Bank of Ireland of the banking concession within the former NIHE area of the college. AIB Bank plc has a similar exclusive concession in relation to the former Thomond College area of the university and in addition there are branches of four competitor banks and four building societies located within a radius of three miles from the university. In these circumstances and for the reasons set out in earlier decisions regarding exclusive user clauses in shopping centre leases this clause does not offend against section 4(1) of the Competition Act.

(4) Under the terms of the agreement UL agrees not to allow advertising or canvassing on the campus in favour of any other bank or building society. In the light of the location involved this is not regarded as having an effect on competition.

Case referred to

Deane and others v. Voluntary Health Board, Supreme Court 1992 2 IR 319 **1.1**

Competition Authority Decision of 10 March 1994 relating to a proceeding under section 4 of the Competition Act 1991

Notification No. CA/330/92E — University of Limerick/The Governor and Company of the Bank of Ireland

Introduction

1. Notification was made by The Governor and Company of the Bank of Ireland (Bank of Ireland) on 30 September 1992 with a request for a certificate under section 4(4) of the

7.13 Competition Act 1991 or, in the event of a refusal by the Competition Authority to issue a certificate, a licence under section 4(2), in respect of a concession agreement between the University of Limerick and the Bank of Ireland.

The Facts

(a) *The Subject of the Notification*

2. The notification concerns the grant of a sole concession by the University of Limerick to the Bank of Ireland to carry on the business of a branch bank within the former NIHE area of the University.

(b) *The Parties involved*

3. The Bank of Ireland is the second largest commercial bank in Ireland with a network of 290 branches within the State. The University of Limerick, as successor to NIHE Limerick and Thomond College, is an independent university established under the University of Limerick Act 1989. It is primarily engaged in the provision of third level education and research with a campus revenue of £28.7m in 1992/3.

(c) *The notified arrangements*

4. The notified agreement was made on 25 October 1984 between the National Institute for Higher Education, Limerick (NIHE) and the Bank of Ireland. Under the agreement NIHE grants to the bank the sole concession of carrying on the ordinary business of a branch bank for a term of 20 years from 1 September 1985 and also agrees to let premises subject to a provision for rent. The parties agree that the agreement shall be deemed to he a licence only and not a lease or a letting within the meaning of the Landlord and Tenant Act. Under the agreement Bank of Ireland may not 'assign, transfer or underlet or part with possession or occupation or assign its interest in this concession to any person, hank or other institution' while NIHE agrees 'Not to allow advertisements to be placed on the Campus or any form of advertising or canvassing on the campus in favour of any other bank or building society'.

The Agreement also includes a number of standard provisions relating to the occupation and maintenance of the premises.

Assessment — The applicability of section 4(1)

5. Section 4(1) of the Competition Act, 1991 refers to agreements between undertakings and section 3(1) of the Act defines an undertaking as a 'person being an individual, a body corporate or an unincorporated body of persons engaged for gain in the production, supply or distribution of goods or the provision of a service'. According to the judgment of the Supreme Court in the VHI case, as delivered by Finlay CJ, the words 'for gain' connote merely an activity carried on or a service supplied, as in this case, which is done in return for a charge or payment. University of Limerick is engaged in the provision of the services of third level education and research for which it receives substantial revenue by way of fees etc. and it is therefore an undertaking engaged for gain in the provision of a service. Bank of Ireland is an undertaking engaged for gain in the provision of banking and other financial services. The notified agreement is therefore an agreement between undertakings. The agreement has effect within the State.

6. The agreement notified contains standard restrictions and obligations on both parties which are necessary for the maintenance of a proper relationship in regard to the operation of the concession and the occupation of the premises. These do not raise issues under the Competition Act. The agreement also provides for exclusivity in relation to the operation by Bank of Ireland of the banking concession within the former NIHE area of the college. In a number of earlier decisions the Authority has already indicated its view that exclusive user clauses in the letting of premises in a particular shopping centre or building complex do not

offend against section 4(1) of the Competition Act. For similar reasons this view also applies in relation to the grant of an exclusive concession to use premises in a building complex for the purposes of a business. In this instance AIB has a similar exclusive concession in relation to the former Thomond College area of the university. In addition there are branches of 4 competitor banks and 4 building societies located within a radius of 3 miles from the university. Under the agreement, University of Limerick has also agreed not to allow advertising or canvassing on the campus in favour of any other bank or building society. In the light of the location involved the Authority would not regard this restriction as having any effect on competition. The Authority therefore considers that the notified agreement between University College Dublin* and the Bank of Ireland does not offend against section 4(1) of the Competition Act 1991. 7.13

The Certificate

7. The Competition Authority has issued the following certificate:

> The Competition Authority certifies that in its opinion, on the basis of the facts in its possession, the agreement between the University of Limerick and the Governor and Company of the Bank of Ireland in relation to a banking concession at the University of Limerick notified under section 7 on 30 September 1992 (Notification No. CA/330/92E), does not offend against section 4(1) of the Competition Act 1991.

For the Competition Authority

Des Wall
Member

10 March 1994

**Editor's note*: The original refers to 'Dublin' but this would seem to be a typographical error for 'of Limerick'.

Competition Authority Decision No. 308, McMullan Bros. Ltd/Power Supermarkets Ltd: 21 April 1994 — Notification No. CA/511/92E 7.14

Property sale agreement containing mutual restricted user clauses — Competition Act 1991 (No. 24) sections 3, 4 and 7

Facts: On 30 September 1992 notification was made to the Authority by Power Supermarkets Ltd ('Power') in respect of a property sale agreement between McMullan Bros. Ltd ('McMullan'), as vendor, and Power, as purchaser, with a request for a certificate under section 4(4) of the Competition Act 1991 or, failing that, a licence under section 4(2). McMullan, an Irish registered company, is engaged in the distribution of motor fuels and Power, also an Irish registered company, trades as a supermarket with outlets throughout the State. The notified agreement, made 3 April 1969 provided for the sale of part of a site owned by McMullan to Powers. Under the terms of the agreement Powers covenanted not to use or permit to be used the premises as a petrol station or premises for the sale of motor vehicles and McMullan covenanted with Power not to permit McMullan's retained portion of the premises to be used for business in competition with Powers grocery business.

7.14 Decided by the Authority: In issuing a certificate under section 4(4) of the Competition Act 1991 in respect of the notified agreement that:

(1) The notified agreement is an agreement between 'undertakings' which has effect within the State.

(2) Restricted user clauses covenanted by each party for the benefit of the other do not offend against section 4(1) of the Competition Act in that they permitted each party to use the premises for the original intended use and there was nothing in the agreements to prevent either party from setting up elsewhere in the vicinity a business which was prohibited on the premises the subject matter of the notified agreement.

Competition Authority Decision of 21 April 1994 relating to a proceeding under section 4 of the Competition Act 1991
Notification No. CA/591/92E — McMullan Bros Ltd/Power Supermarkets Ltd

Introduction

1. Notification was made by Power Supermarkets Ltd on 30 September 1992 with a request for a certificate under section 4(4) of the Competition Act 1991 or in the event of a refusal by the Competition Authority to issue a certificate, a licence under section 4(2), in respect of a sale agreement between McMullan Bros Ltd and Power Supermarkets Ltd.

The Facts

(a) *Subject of the notification*

2. The notification concerns an agreement relating to the sale of part of the site of the former Naas Railway Station, Naas, Co. Kildare between McMullan Bros Ltd as Vendor and Power Supermarkets Ltd as Purchaser.

(b) *The parties involved*

3. McMullan Bros Ltd is engaged in the distribution of motor fuels and was the owner of a petrol filling station on the retained part of the Naas site. Power Supermarkets Ltd trades as a supermarket with outlets throughout the State.

(c) *The notified arrangements*

4. The notified agreement was made on 3 April 1969. The agreement provided for the sale of part of the site to Powers. The agreement also included the following restrictive covenants viz.

(a) Under clause 3 (A) the purchaser covenants with the vendor:

> Not to use or permit to be used Powers premises or any part thereof as a petrol filling or service station, Garage or Show Room for the sale of petrol motor oils or greases (other than the Vendor's products) or mechanically propelled vehicles and not in any way to compete or allow others to compete with the Vendor its Tenants Lessees or Licencees in the sale of any of these products which are sold at the adjoining petrol filling station of the Vendor.

(b) Under clause 4(f) the Vendor covenants with the purchaser:

> Not to use or permit to be used McMullan's premises or any part thereof for any of the businesses of a retailer of groceries or provisions seller of beer wine or spirits for consumption on or off the premises Cafe or Restaurant Baker Confectioner Butcher

Victualler Fish-Monger Shoe Shop Draper of any description Jeweller Hardware Shop or Supermarket of any description.

The restricted user clauses above are binding on assignees and successors of each party. The agreement also contains a number of provisions concerning access, maintenance, prevention of nuisance, boundaries, buildings, etc.

Assessment — The applicability of section 4(1)

5. The Authority considers that McMullan Bros Ltd and Power Supermarkets Ltd are undertakings and that the notified sale agreement is an agreement between undertakings. The agreement has effect within the State.

6. The sale agreement contains standard restrictions and provisions relating to each party's occupancy and sharing of the site which do not raise issues under the Competition Act. In addition it contains restrictive user clauses on both the Vendor and the Purchaser. The vendor has covenanted not to use his premises on the site for the purpose of retailing groceries or provisions (which is the business of Power Supermarkets), and the purchaser has covenanted not to use his adjoining premises for the purpose of a petrol filling or service station or garage (which is the business of McMullan Bros Ltd). In the Authority's opinion, the inclusion of exclusive user clauses in agreements for the sale of an adjoining premises cannot be regarded as preventing, restricting, or distorting competition within the State or any part of it. Powers purchased the premises for its intended use i.e. the business of supermarket. If Powers sought to enter the business of petrol retailing it is free to enter this business at other sites in the near vicinity or elsewhere in the State. Similarly while McMullans are prevented from engaging at the site in retailing of the type of goods sold at supermarkets they are free to engage in this form of retailing at other premises either in the near vicinity or elsewhere in the State. Similarly any other undertaking wishing to operate a business in competition with either the purchaser or the vendor is not restricted from doing so in the immediate vicinity or elsewhere in the State. The Authority therefore considers that the notified agreement does not offend against section 4(1) of the Competition Act 1991.

The Certificate

7. The Competition Authority has issued the following certificate:

> The Competition Authority certifies that in its opinion, on the basis of the facts in its possession, the agreement between McMullan Bros Ltd and Power Supermarkets Ltd in relation to the sale of a premises at Naas Railway Station, Naas, Co. Kildare notified under section 7 on 30 September 1992 (Notification No. CA/591/92E), does not offend against section 4(1) of the Competition Act 1991.

For the Competition Authority

Des Wall
Member

21 April 1994

7.15 **Competition Authority Decision No. 345, Grittar/David J. Bolger:** 23 June 1994, Notification No. CA/605/92E

Agreement for the transfer of property – Transfer by way of lease to transferee – Condition in agreement whereby transferor must assign the freehold to the transferee should the transferee obtain certain planning permissions – Restriction in lease agreement on transferee utilising or permitting to utilise the lands for the sale of food and drink products – Competition Act 1991 (No. 24) sections 3, 4 and 7

Facts: On 30 September 1992 notification was made to the Authority with a request for a certificate under section 4(4) of the Competition Act 1991, or, failing that, a licence under section 4(2) in respect of a sale by way of a lease agreement between Grittar ('the Vendor') and David J. Bolger ('the Purchaser').

The Vendor is a subsidiary of Power supermarkets which trades as a supermarket with outlets throughout the State. The Purchaser is engaged in the business of property development.

The notified agreement was made on 15 February 1991. The agreement provided that the sale would be carried out by way of a 500 year lease to be granted by the Vendor to the Purchaser but that in the event of the Vendor [*sic*]* obtaining planning permission for a housing development the Vendor would be bound without further consideration to transfer to the Purchaser the freehold title to the reversion of the said lease on a phased basis as the housing development was completed. Any restrictive covenant in the lease would cease to apply in respect of which the freehold was transferred. Under the terms of the lease the Purchaser covenanted with the Vendor that it would not at any time sell, supply or stock any food products or drinks, or permit same to be sold, supplied or stocked, in an area exceeding 1,000 square feet on the lands the subject of the lease (excluding restaurant, licensed premises and hotel sales). Subsequent to the agreement 88% of the plot was used for housing construction and a transfer of the freehold in lieu of a lease in respect of this portion of the land was effected.

Decided by the Authority: In issuing a certificate under section 4(4) of the Competition Act 1991 in respect of the notified agreement that:

(1) Each of the Vendor and the Purchaser are undertakings within the meaning of the Competition Act 1991 and the notified agreement is an agreement between undertakings which has effect within the State.

(2) The agreement contains a number of standard conditions relating to the sale of the property which do not raise issues under the Competition Act.

(3) The inclusion of restrictive and exclusive user clauses in agreements for the sale of land cannot normally be regarded as preventing, restricting or distorting competition within the State or any part of it. The Purchaser acquired the land for his particular housing development purposes and if he seeks to develop a larger premises for the sale of food or alcoholic drink or seeks to enter into this business himself he is free to do so at any other premises in the locality or elsewhere within the State, subject to the grant of planning permission. Similarly any other undertaking wishing

*Editor's Note: The original decision refers to Vendor when it might be anticipated that it should refer to 'purchaser'.

to compete with either the Vendor or Purchaser is not restricted by this agreement from doing so in the vicinity or elsewhere in the State and therefore the notified agreement does not offend against section 4(1) of the Competition Act 1991. 7.15

Competition Authority Decision of 23 June 1994 relating to a proceeding under section 4 of the Competition Act 1991
Notification No: CA/605/92E — Grittar/David J. Bolger

Introduction

1. Notification was made by Grittar on 30 September 1992 with a request for a certificate under section 4(4) of the Competition Act 1991 or, in the event of a refusal by the Competition Authority to issue a certificate, a licence under section 4(2), in respect of a sale by way of lease agreement between Grittar and David J. Bolger.

The Facts

(a) *Subject of the notification*

2. The notification concerns the agreement for a sale by way of lease of a plot of ground at Tandy's Lane, Lucan, Co Dublin between Grittar as Vendor and David J. Bolger as purchaser. Subsequently 88% of the plot has been used for housing construction and a transfer in lieu of a lease has been granted in respect of this portion.

(b) *The parties involved*

3. Grittar is a subsidiary of Power Supermarkets which trades as a supermarket with outlets throughout the State. David J. Bolger is engaged in property development.

(c) *The notified arrangements*

4. The notified sale agreement was executed on 15 February 1991. The agreement consists of the general conditions of sale as well as special conditions. The special conditions provide that the sale will be carried out by way of a 500 year lease (the draft of which accompanies the sale agreement) and that provided, *inter alia*, that the vendor obtains planning permission for housing development, the Vendor shall be bound without further consideration to transfer to the Purchaser freehold title to the reversion to the said lease on a phased basis as housing and ancillary works on the plot are completed. The special conditions require the purchaser to enter into the covenant set out under but also provide that "...in the event of the Purchaser completing the conditions set out above and requiring the Vendor to transfer freehold title then the question of granting a lease relating to property so transferred with freehold title shall not arise and in the transfer of such freehold title no restrictive covenant of any nature shall then apply. . . .'

5. The covenant set out in the sale agreement to be included in the lease is as follows: 'The lessee hereby further covenants with the Lessor as the owner of the supermarket in Lucan Shopping Centre, Lucan, County Dublin not at any time to sell supply, stock or keep groceries food foodstuffs, food products or drinks in an area exceeding one thousand square feet in the demised premises or suffer or permit any such action or activity save that use of the demised premises or part thereof as a Restaurant licensed premises, hotel or guest house shall be permissible and not to make any transfer, letting subletting or grant any licence to use or part with or share the possession of the said demised premises or any part thereof save on the basis that any such party shall first covenant under seal with the Lessor in manner similar to this covenant'

Assessment — The Applicability of section 4(1)

6. The Authority considers that Grittar and David J. Bolger are undertakings and that the

7.15 notified sale agreement is an agreement between undertakings. The agreement has effect within the State.

7. The agreement contains a number of standard conditions relating to the sale of the property which do not raise issues under the Competition Act. In addition the special conditions to the sale require the purchaser in certain circumstances to enter into a lease with restrictive conditions relating to the use of the land i.e. that if the plot is not used for housing or development ancillary to housing other buildings on the plot in excess of 1,000 square feet cannot be used for the sale of food or alcoholic drinks (excluding restaurant/licensed premises/hotel sales). Already 88% of the site has been used for housing purposes and title transferred without any lease.

8. In the Authority's opinion, the inclusion of restrictive and exclusive user clauses in agreements for the sale of land cannot normally be regarded as preventing, restricting, or distorting competition within the State or any part of it. The purchaser acquired the land for his particular purposes, i.e. housing development. If he seeks to develop a larger premises for the sale of food or alcoholic drink or seeks to enter into this business himself, he is free to do so at other premises in the locality or elsewhere within the State, subject to the grant of planning permission. Similarly any other undertaking wishing to compete with either the vendor or purchaser is not restricted by the agreement from doing so in the vicinity or elsewhere in the State. The Authority therefore considers that the notified agreement does not offend against section 4(1) of the Competition Act 1991.

The Certificate

9. The Competition Authority has issued the following certificate:

> The Competition Authority certifies that in its opinion, on the basis of the facts in its possession, the agreement between Grittar and David J. Bolger in relation to the sale by way of lease of the plot of ground at Tandy's Lane, Lucan, Co. Dublin, notified under section 7 on 30 September 1992, (Notification No. CA/605/92E) does not offend against section 4(1) of the Competition Act 1991.

For the Competition Authority

Des Wall
Member

23 June 1994

Competition Authority Decision No. 358, FBD Developments (Cork) Ltd/ Southern Health Board: 12 October 1994, Notification No. CA/311/92E 7.16

Leasing of property – Standard restrictions in lease agreement – Restricted use for tenant – Landlord and Tenant (Amendment) Act, 1980 (No. 10) – Competition Act 1991 (No. 24) ss. 3, 4 and 7

Facts: On 30 September 1992 notification was made to the Authority with a request for a certificate under section 4(4) of the Competition Act, 1991 or, failing that, a licence under section 4(2) in respect of the lease of office premises at Wilton, Cork from FBD Developments (Cork) Ltd to the Southern Health Board.

The Southern Health Board is a statutory corporate body responsible for the administration of health services in the Counties of Cork and Kerry and provides hospital services through over 30 hospitals in the area. Its revenue is generated from government grants, receipts from hospitals and other miscellaneous income.

The notified agreement was a lease made on the 28th February 1977 for a term of 25 years. The Southern Health Board under the lease, covenants not to use the premises for any purpose other than that of offices.

Decided by the Authority: In issuing a certificate under section 4(4) of the Competition Act, 1991 in respect of the notified lease that:

(1) FBD Developments (Cork) Ltd and the Southern Health Board are engaged in the letting of premises and the provision of hospital services respectively. Both parties to the lease are undertaking to an agreement which has effect within the State.

(2) Leasing premises prevents competitors of the tenant from using those premises to compete with the tenant. This cannot be regarded as preventing, restricting or distorting competition. Anyone wishing to operate a business in competition with the tenant may do so by occupying any other premises within the State.

(3) The restrictions on the use of the premises are normally governed by considerations such as physical characteristics of the premises, the requirements of the Planning Acts and the landlord's own policy. Such user restrictions do not have the object or effect of preventing, restricting or distorting competition. Change of use is in any event facilitated by the provisions of the Landlord and Tenant Act 1980.

Competition Authority Decision No. 358 of 12 October 1994 relating to a proceeding under section 4 of the Competition Act 1991

Notification No. CA/311/92E — FBD Developments (Cork) Ltd/Southern Health Board

Introduction

1. Notification was made by FBD Developments (Cork) Ltd on 30 September 1992 with a request for a certificate under section 4(4) of the Competition Act 1991 or, in the event of a refusal by the Competition Authority to issue a certificate, a licence under section 4(2) in respect of leases between FBD Developments (Cork) Ltd and the Southern Health Board.

The Facts

(a) *Subject of the notification*

2. The notification concerns the lease of premises at the Cork Farm Centre, Wilton, Cork between FBD Developments (Cork) Ltd as lessor and the Southern Health Board as lessee.

7.16 (b) *The parties involved*

3. FBD Developments (Cork) Ltd, a subsidiary of FBD Insurances PLC, is the owner and landlord of the Cork Farm Centre, Wilton, Cork. The Southern Health Board is a statutory corporate body responsible for the administration of health services in the counties of Cork and Kerry and is also engaged in the provision of hospital services through over 30 hospitals within this area. Its accounts for 1990 show that it had a revenue of £163.8m in that year of which £149m was represented by Government grants and the balance represented by receipts from hospital and other charges as well as other income.

(c) *The notified arrangements*

4. Three leases were notified. One was made on 28 February 1977 for a term of 25 years from 1 January 1976, another was made on 23 September 1977 for a similar term and the other lease was made on 23 December 1982 for a term of 20 years from 1 January 1981. Each notified lease is in similar terms and each contains a restricted user clause 12 as follows:

> Not to use the premises for any purpose other than that of offices and for meetings in connection with the business of the Lessee with ancillary staff canteen and not to use the said parking spaces for any purpose other than the parking of private motor vehicles and light commercial vehicles.

In addition, there are a number of other standard restrictive covenants and obligations in the leases including a restriction on the lessee from assigning or sub-letting the premises, without the consent of the lessor, which consent shall not be unreasonably withheld.

Assessment

(a) *Section 4(1)*

5. Section 4(1) of the Competition Act 1991 prohibits and renders void all agreements between undertakings, decisions by associations of undertakings and concerted practices which have as their object or effect the prevention, restriction or distortion of competition in trade in any goods or services in the State, or in any part of the State.

6. The term 'undertaking' is defined in section 3(1) of the Act, as 'a person being an individual, a body corporate or an unincorporated body of persons engaged for gain in the production, supply or distribution of goods or the provision of a service'. FBD Developments (Cork) Ltd is engaged in the letting of premises for gain and is therefore an undertaking. While the main activities of the Southern Health Board are State funded, the Board is also engaged for gain in the provision of hospital and other services for which charges are made to the general public. It is therefore an undertaking engaged for gain in the provision of a service. The notified leases are agreements between undertakings. The agreements have effect within the State.

7. The lease agreements contain standard restrictions and obligations on both the lessor and lessee which are necessary for the maintenance of the landlord/tenant relationship in respect of the tenancy. These do not raise issues under the Competition Act. The very act of leasing the premises to a particular tenant prevents competitors of the tenant from using those premises to compete with the tenant. Clearly this cannot be regarded as preventing, restricting or distorting competition since it would imply that the leasing of a commercial premises in order to carry on a business therein was prohibited unless licensed under section 4(2) of the Competition Act. Anyone wishing to operate a business in competition with the tenant may do so by occupying any other premises within the State.

8. In addition the agreements also provide, by way of the permitted user clause 12, restrictions on the use of the premises but which effectively allow the premises to be used for the purpose of the business of the tenant. Such permitted user clauses are normally based on the user proposed by the tenant at the time the lease is first executed but are also governed by

considerations such as the physical characteristics of the premises, the requirements of the Planning Acts and the landlord's own policy, when granting the lease, on how the premises should be used. The Authority considers that such user restrictions in the letting of premises do not have the object or effect of preventing, restricting or distorting competition in the State or in any part of the State. In taking up the lease the tenant negotiates the permitted user required for his business. This is reflected in the lease but if he were subsequently to seek a change of user he could in most instances have recourse to the provisions of the Landlord and Tenant Act 1980 which provide that a landlord cannot unreasonably withhold consent to a change of user requested by the tenant. In addition the tenant is free to undertake other businesses in many other premises, both in the vicinity or elsewhere in the State. The object or effect of such permitted user clauses in the lease agreements are not therefore anti-competitive. The Authority therefore considers that the notified agreements between FBD Developments (Cork) Ltd and the Southern Health Board do not offend against section 4(1) of the Competition Act 1991. 7.16

The Certificate

9. The Competition Authority has issued the following certificate:

> The Competition Authority certifies that in its opinion, on the basis of the facts in its possession, the agreements between FBD Developments (Cork) Ltd and the Southern Health Board in relation to the lease of premises at Cork Farm Centre, Wilton, Cork notified under section 7 on 30 September 1992 (Notification No. CA/311/92E) do not offend against section 4(1) of the Competition Act 1991.

For The Competition Authority

Des Wall
Member

12 October 1994

Competition Authority Decision No. 377, Power Supermarkets Ltd/Richard and Susan Whyte: 21 November 1994, Notification No. CA/1115/92E 7.17

Property Sale Agreement – Post sale restrictive covenants given by the purchasers in favour of the vendor – Competition Act 1991 (No. 24) sections 3, 4 and 7

Facts: On 30 September 1992 notification was made to the Authority with a request for a certificate under section 4(4) of the Competition Act 1991 or, failing that, a licence under section 4(2) in respect of a property sale agreement between Power Supermarkets Ltd ('the Vendor") and Richard and Susan Whyte ('the Purchasers').

The Vendor is engaged in the supermarket business with a large number of outlets throughout the State including one in Mullingar which is approximately one half mile distance from the premises sold. The Purchasers are engaged in the business of letting property in Mullingar.

The notified agreement made on 24 September 1989 provides for the sale of a premises containing nine shop units in Mullingar by the Vendor to the Purchasers. In

7.17 particular the notified agreement contains a covenant on the part of the Purchasers and their assigns that they would not, without the prior consent in writing of the Vendor, assign, lease or permit to be used any shop or unit in the property sold as a retail shopping outlet with an area containing or totalling more than 2,500 square feet.

Decided by the Authority: In issuing a certificate under section 4(4) of the Competition Act 1991 in respect of the notified agreement that:

(1) Each of the Vendor and the Purchasers are undertakings within the meaning of the Competition Act 1991 and the notified sale agreement is an agreement between undertakings which has effect within the State.

(2) The sale of the premises was completed prior to 1 October 1991, and therefore that element of the agreement was discharged by performance before the Competition Act came into force. The prohibition under section 4(1) of the Competition Act only applies to a current or continuing contractual commitment or one entered into subsequent to the coming into force of the Competition Act. As the sale element was discharged prior to the commencement of the Act that aspect of the arrangements does not come within the scope of section 4(1).

(3) The covenant on the part of the Purchasers and their assigns not, without the prior written consent of the Vendor, to allow any part of the property sold to be used as a retail shopping outlet with an area totalling more than 2,500 square feet constitutes a continuing contractual commitment. The Purchasers acquired the property which was laid out as nine small shop units. If the Purchasers wished to acquire properties which could be used as retail units in excess of 2,500 square feet they were free to do so elsewhere in Mullingar subject to planning permission considerations. Similarly, any other undertaking wishing to compete with either the Vendor or with the Purchasers is not restricted by the agreement from doing so in the vicinity and therefore the notified agreement does not offend against section 4(1) of the Competition Act 1991.

Competition Authority Decision of 21 November 1994 relating to a proceeding under section 4 of the Competition Act 1991
Notification No. CA/1115/92E — Power Supermarkets Ltd/Richard and Susan Whyte

Introduction

1. Notification was made by Power Supermarkets Ltd on 30 September 1992 with a request for a certificate under section 4(4) of the Competition Act 1991 or, in the event of a refusal by the Competition Authority to issue a certificate, a licence under section 4(2) in respect of a sale agreement between Power Supermarkets Ltd and Richard and Susan Whyte.

The facts

(a) *Subject of the notification*

2. The notification concerns an agreement relating to the sale of premises containing 9 shop units at 12 Austin Friar's Street, Mullingar, Co. Westmeath between Power Supermarkets Ltd as the vendor and Richard and Susan Whyte as purchasers.

(b) *The parties involved*

3. Power Supermarkets Ltd is engaged in the supermarket business with a large number of outlets throughout the State. It operates a supermarket at Fairgreen, Mullingar, which is

approximately one half mile distance from the premises sold. Richard & Susan Whyte are the landlords of, and are engaged in the letting of a number of shop units at 12 Austin Friar's Street, Mullingar, Co. Westmeath. 7.17

(c) *The notified arrangements*

4. The notified agreement which was executed on 24 September 1989, provides for the sale of the premises by Power Supermarkets Ltd to Richard and Susan Whyte for a substantial consideration. Under the agreement the Purchasers covenant to keep the vendor indemnified against any breaches of earlier agreements between the vendor and a number of previous owners of part of the properties involved. The agreement also contains the following covenant on the part of the purchasers:

> The Purchasers hereby for themselves and their Assigns covenant and each of them hereby for himself and his assigns covenants separately with the Vendor not without the prior consent in writing of the Vendor to grant, convey, assign, lease or let or permit to be granted, conveyed, assigned, leased, let, subleased or sublet or suffer or permit to be used or occupied any shop or unit in the property sold as a retail shopping outlet with an area containing or totalling more than 2,500 square feet.

Assessment — Applicability of section 4(1)

(a) *Section 4(1)*

5. The Authority considers that Power Supermarkets Ltd and Richard & Susan Whyte are undertakings and that the notified sale agreement is an agreement between undertakings. The agreement has effect within the State.

6. As the sale of the premises was completed prior to 1 October 1991, the date the Competition Act came into force, that element of the agreement was discharged by performance before the Act came into force. The property that was the subject of the agreement has been transferred. In the Authority's view, the prohibition under section 4(1) only applies to a current or continuing contractual commitment or one entered into subsequent to the coming into force of the Act. As the sale element was discharged prior to the commencement of the Act, that aspect of the arrangements does not come within the scope of section 4(1). In any event the Authority would not consider the sale, *per se*, of a property as raising any issues under the Competition Act.

7. The sale agreement contains a continuing contractual commitment on the part of the purchasers and their assigns in that they have covenanted not to allow any part of the property sold to be used as a retail shopping outlet with an area totalling more than 2,500 square feet without first obtaining the consent of the Vendor.

8. In the Authority's opinion the inclusion of restrictive user clauses in agreements for the sale of a particular property cannot normally be regarded as preventing, restricting or distorting competition within the State or any part of the State. The purchasers acquired the property, which was laid out as 9 shop units for a particular purpose i.e., the letting of smaller shop units. If the purchasers wished to acquire properties which could be used as retail units in excess of 2,500 square feet, they were free to do so elsewhere in the town of Mullingar, subject to the grant of planning permission. Similarly any other undertaking, wishing to compete with either the vendor (whose nearest place of business is one half mile away) or with the purchaser is not restricted by the agreement from doing so in the vicinity. The Authority therefore considers that the notified agreement between Power Supermarkets Ltd and Richard and Susan Whyte does not offend against section 4(1) of the Competition Act 1991.

The Certificate

9. The Competition Authority has issued the following certificate:

7.17 The Competition Authority certifies that in its opinion, on the basis of the facts in its possession, the agreement between Power Supermarkets Ltd and Richard and Susan Whyte in relation to the sale of premises at 12 Austin Friar's Street, Mullingar, Co. Westmeath notified under section 7 on 30 September 1992 (Notification No. CA/1115/92E), does not offend against section 4(1) of the Competition Act 1991.

For The Competition Authority

Des Wall
Member

21 November 1994

7.18 **Competition Authority Decision No. 378, David Allen Holdings Ltd/Adsites Ltd/ Licence Agreement:** 21 November 1994, Notification No. CA/1128/92

Exclusive licence agreement between two competing companies – agreement whereby one company markets a particular product on behalf of both companies – Whether outdoor advertising is a separate 'product market' – Combined market share of companies in excess of 60% – Third party submissions – Statement of objections – Refusal to issue certificate or grant licence – Competition Act 1991 (No. 24) sections 3, 4 and 7

Facts: On 30 October 1992 notification was made to the Authority with a request for a certificate under section 4(4) of the Competition Act 1991 or, failing that a licence under section 4(2) in respect of an exclusive licence agreement made between David Allen Holdings Ltd ('DAH') and Adsites Ltd ('Adsites'). Under the terms of this agreement DAH obtained from Adsites an exclusive licence to market and sell in respect of outdoor advertising panels owned by Adsites for a period of 3 years.

DAH, an English registered company which operates in Ireland through a branch, is engaged in the business of providing space for use in outdoor advertising. Adsites, an Irish registered company, comprises Adsites Ltd, Campaign Poster Sites Ltd and Adsites (Northern Ireland) Ltd and is also engaged in the business of providing space for use in outdoor advertising. The advertising market in Ireland is, based on statistics from Advertising Statistics Ireland Ltd, divided as follows: National Press 45%; Regional Press 3%; Consumer Press 5%; Television and Radio 41%; Outdoor 5% and Cinema 1%. Outdoor and poster advertising can be divided into three different categories namely road side, transport and other. Road side advertising includes posters, which are displayed on the side of the road or in pedestrian areas while transport posters are those which are displayed on buses, railways and taxis. Posters come in various sizes and are attached to structures known as panels. The 48- sheet poster is the predominant large poster size sited on panels and accounts for approximately 40% of the total outdoor advertising market. It is the 48-sheet poster panels which are relevant to the notified licence agreement.

Poster contractors own the panels on which the posters are displayed and have rights to use the sites on which they are located. Generally the sites are not owned by the contractors but are rented from the owner. There are three principal ways in which poster panels are booked. A contractor may sell individual panels for a particular advertising campaign, or the contractor may allocate a group of panels into pre-selected campaigns or packages for a single period sale or the contractor may accept long-term bookings for a panel. 7.18

All advertising media may be considered to be substitutes for each other to some degree. Clients decide which medium to chose based on cost, audience and the product sought to be advertised. The extent to which other media are substitutes for road side posters will vary according to the product being advertised and to the nature of the campaign. Poster advertising is often used in conjunction with another medium to reinforce the message which the advertiser is seeking to portray and to this extent posters can be regarded as complements rather than substitutes to other forms of advertising. On balance it appeared that the outdoor advertising market does constitute a distinct product market and that larger size posters constitute a distinct market segment within the overall outdoor advertising sector.

The notified arrangements relate to 48-sheet posters and DAH acknowledged that the notified agreement would combine its 56% of that market with the 8% held by Adsites to give it a total of 64% of the relevant market. The recent move in the relevant market to a poster network concept and the requirement for planning permission for the erection of poster panels has the effect of making it difficult for new entrants to enter into the relevant market.

Under the terms of the notified agreement Adsites gave to DAH an exclusive right to market and sell all Adsites 48-sheet advertising panels within the 32 counties of Ireland for the 3 year period up to 31 December 1994 in return for which DAH would pay to Adsites all of the rental revenue from each panel less the costs involved in selling the advertising and less a 10% commission for DAH. The notified agreement also provided that any new 48-sheet sites acquired by Adsites during the currency of the agreement would at DAH's discretion be included in the arrangement.

The Authority received a submission from a competing outdoor advertising company stating that the notified agreement gave DAH control of the 48-sheet market and that this dominance enabled DAH to dictate prices and availability. The submission further stated that the cost of advertising would be likely to rise and that this cost should be passed onto the consumer.

On 13 September 1994 the Authority issued a Statement of Objections to the parties indicating its intention to refuse to issue a certificate or grant a licence on the basis of the information available to it concerning the agreement. An oral hearing was held on 27 October 1994 during the course of which DAH conceded that the licence agreement offended against section 4(1) of the Competition Act.

Decided by the Authority: In refusing to issue a certificate or grant a licence under sections 4(4) and 4(2) respectively of the Competition Act 1991 in respect of the notified agreement that:

(1) Each of DAH and Adsites are companies engaged for gain in the business of providing outdoor advertising space and are therefore undertakings within the meaning of the Competition Act and the arrangements constitute an agreement between undertakings.

(2) The notified agreement essentially involves two competitors deciding to cease competing with one another in respect of a particular product and instead to allow one

7.18 to have sole responsibility for the joint marketing of that product, namely 48-sheet advertising panels. The arrangement applies to 64% or more of the 48-sheet poster advertising market and there can be no question but that the object and the effect of such an agreement is to prevent, restrict or distort competition within the State. Adsites cannot compete with DAH by acquiring new sites since DAH under the terms of the notified agreement has exclusive rights to such new sites unless it specifically chooses not to exercise those rights. There is no doubt therefore that the notified licence agreement is anti-competitive and clearly offends against section 4(1) of the Competition Act 1991.

(3) The notified agreement does not contribute to improving the production of goods or the provision of services or to promoting technical or economic progress and not convincing arguments have been offered to show how the notified agreement would produce such benefits or that consumers would receive any share of these benefits. Since the agreement does not satisfy all the requirements of section 4(2) of the Competition Act, no licence may be granted in respect of it.

Competition Authority Decision of 21 November 1994, relating to a proceeding under section 4 of the Competition Act 1991
Notifications No. CA/1128/92 — David Allen Holdings Ltd/Adsites Ltd — Licence Agreement

Introduction

1. Two related agreements involving David Allen Holdings Ltd (DAH) and Adsites Ltd (Adsites), were notified to the Authority on 30 October 1992, with a request for a certificate or a licence. Under the terms of these agreements, DAH obtained from Adsites an exclusive licence to market and sell in respect of advertising panels owned by Adsites up to 31 December 1994, and an option to purchase such panels from Adsites, at any time up to and including 12 noon on 30 September 1994, provided DAH complied with its obligations under the terms of the licence agreement. The present decision concerns the exclusive licence agreement. The option agreement is the subject of a separate notification (CA/1127/92). The Authority issued a Statement of Objections to the parties in respect of the notified agreements on 13 September 1994 and an Oral Hearing was held on 27 October 1994.

The Facts

(a) *The subject of the Notification*

2. The notification concerns a Licence Agreement dated 2 January 1992 between DAH and Adsites. The Licence Agreement grants DAH an exclusive right to market and sell advertising space on the Adsites panels referred to in the agreement up to 31 December 1994.

(b) *The Parties*

3. DAH is an English registered company established in 1859 and is part of the Avenir Havas Media Group. DAH has operated through a branch (David Allen) in Ireland since 1859. It is an outdoor advertising contractor and is involved in the business of providing space for use in outdoor advertising. It negotiates a site rental with a property owner, constructs and maintains an advertising structure on the property and rents the space to advertisers in fortnightly units. Up until 1991 outdoor advertising contractors gave exclusive rights to other companies known as poster specialists to perform their sales function and contracted with them rather than with the advertising company. It was claimed that this had the effect of distorting the market as access to particular sites depended on which specialist had exclusive rights. Following the collapse of the largest company in that area, contracts are now made directly with the advertising agency.

4. The Avenir Havas Media Group (AHM), is a Paris based multinational, whose shares are publicly quoted. It is 97% owned by Havas which was established in 1835 and which is now France's largest media and communications group. Havas is also engaged in seven major business areas in France and worldwide, including publishing, tourism and audiovisual. Havas' total revenue in 1992 was FF28 billion. Adsites comprises Adsites Ltd, Campaign Poster Sites Ltd and Adsites (Northern Ireland) Ltd. Adsites is an outdoor advertising company whose registered office is at Lynwood House, Ballinteer Road, Dublin 16. 7.18

(c) *The Product and the Market*

5. The agreement relates to large panels which are used for poster advertising. There are a large number of alternative media available for firms wishing to advertise their products to consumers. In its submission to the Authority DAH argued that the market could be broken down into two expenditure categories, i.e. traditional forms of media and 'below-the-line' expenditure. Media advertising includes television, radio, press and outdoor advertising. According to DAH, industry estimates indicated that expenditure in this sector in Ireland for 1991 was £170m. 'Below-the-line' activity refers to sponsorships, supermarket tasting and any other activity which does not involve employing a media company. It is difficult to assess the level of expenditure in this area but according to DAH it was in the region of £100m. Table 1 below indicates the level of advertising expenditure in Ireland in 1993. It is based on figures which the Authority has obtained on the national advertising market from Advertising Statistics Ireland Ltd. (ASI), a company which specialises in monitoring the overall advertising market. Their figures are not wholly accurate since their estimates of newspaper advertising in particular are based on the 'rate card' whereas it is widely acknowledged that newspapers regularly give significant discounts from these rates. According to these figures the total expenditure on media advertising in Ireland in 1993 was £235.3m. The national press were estimated to account for 45% of this with television representing a further 31%. Outdoor advertising, including posters, was estimated to account for just 5% of the total.

Table 1: The Advertising Market in Ireland.

Media	£m	% Market Share
National Press	105.9	45
Regional Press	8.1	3
Consumer Press	12.3	5
Television	72.1	31
Radio	22.9	10
Outdoor	12.8	5
Cinema	1.2	1
Total	235.3	100

Source: ASI

6. DAH submitted that the buyers in the market are advertisers and advertising agencies. The method of advertising chosen is influenced by factors such as cost per thousand of audience, size of the audience and the number of times it can be reached, target audience and availability. The sellers in the market are the media owners or advertising contractors.

7. Outdoor or poster advertising can be divided into three different sectors namely roadside, transport and other. Roadside advertising includes posters displayed by the side of the road and in pedestrian areas, while transport posters are those which are displayed on buses, railways

7.18 and taxis. Posters may also be displayed at airports, sporting events or on vehicles in various locations. Outdoor advertising may also include neon lights and other special structures. The market is geographical and seasonal. Demand for outdoor advertising was highest for sites located in urban areas. The greatest demand occurred in the summer during the long daylight hours, with the six months from October to March accounting for only 30% of annual turnover. This situation is changing as a result of the increasing number of sites which are illuminated.

8. Posters come in various sizes and are attached to structures which are known as panels. This panel is placed, possibly with other panels on a poster site. The main sizes of posters in use are as follows:

(a) 4-sheet (5' x 3'4"). This small sized panel is aimed at pedestrians and is often found in shopping centres.

(b) 6-sheet (1.8m x 1.2m).* Often referred to as 'superlites', these are mainly located on bus shelters and are aimed at motorists as well as pedestrians. They are often back-lit to improve night time effect.

(c) 12-sheet (5' x 10')

(d) 16-sheet (10' x 6'8"). These posters are often attached to the sides of buildings.

(e) 32-sheet (10' x 13'4"). Again posters of this size are often attached to the sides of buildings.

(f) 48-sheet (10' x 20'). The predominant large poster size, sited on panels. Such posters are aimed at both motorists and pedestrians.

(g) 64-sheet (10' x 26'8"). This is a variant on the 48-sheet.

48 sheet posters account for 40% (approximately) of the total outdoor advertising market. The other most commonly used poster sizes are 4-sheet and superlites.

9. Poster contractors own the panels on which the posters are displayed and have rights to use the sites on which they are displayed. In general the sites are not owned by contractors but are rented from the owner. The advertiser pays the contractor for the use of the panels and also pays the production costs of his poster. Advertising agencies design a campaign to meet the needs and objectives of a particular manufacturer or supplier. Outdoor specialists occupy an intermediate position between the contractor and the advertising agency. They act for advertisers and advertising agencies as planners and/or buyers of poster campaigns. The advertising agency and the outdoor specialist receive their remuneration by way of a commission from the poster contractor.

10. There are three principal ways in which poster panels are booked. A contractor may sell individual panels for a particular advertising campaign, a form of short-term spot selling known as line-by-line sales. Alternatively the contractor may collect a group of panels into 'pre-selected campaigns' or 'packages' for a single period sale. Thirdly, a contractor may accept long term bookings for a panel for at least a year or possibly for an indefinite period.

11. According to DAH two specialist companies operated in the Irish market up until 1991, Outdoor Advertising Services Ltd, (OAS) and Poster Management Ltd (PML). Their respective market shares were 70% and 30%. The specialists were treated as principals by the outdoor contractors. These specialists negotiated exclusive rights to sell the plant of some of the contractors thus causing distortion in the market as access to sites depended on which specialist was used. In August 1991, OAS went into liquidation. Following the liquidation the poster contractors revised their terms and conditions of trading to establish the advertiser/advertising agency as principal. Payment is now arranged through the advertising agency. According to DAH there are three specialists currently operating within this system, PML, PosterPlan Ltd and PosterLink Ltd.

12. All of the advertising media may be considered to be substitutes, to some degree, with clients deciding which forum to choose based on cost, audience and product. The extent to which other media are substitutes for roadside posters will vary according to the product being

Editor's Note: In feet and inches this is 5'10" x 3'7".

advertised and to the nature of the campaign and over time. In general an advertiser makes use of more than one advertising medium and may use various media to portray different messages or concentrate on particular aspects of a product. In choosing which media to use an advertiser will take into account a broad range of factors. Television advertising, although expensive, is capable of portraying a strong image, reaches a wide audience and has a high impact inside the home. Press advertising includes national newspapers, local and regional newspapers and specialist periodicals. It costs less than television and may be aimed at different population segments or particular groups. Posters are relatively cheap, and large sized panels in particular offer strong visual impact. They may be used close to the point of sale and can be geographically directed. Posters are often used in conjunction with another medium to reinforce the message which the advertiser is trying to portray. To this extent posters should be regarded as complements rather than substitutes to other forms of advertising. 7.18

13. Pricing is a significant factor in determining the substitutability of posters by other media. Posters tend to be significantly cheaper than other forms of media advertising. Expenditure on poster advertising also tends to constitute a relatively small proportion of an advertiser's total marketing expenditure. In such circumstances it might be expected that it would require a significant increase in the cost of poster advertising before users would switch to other forms of advertising. Two other factors must also be considered in defining the market. Firstly there are legal restrictions in respect of certain types of advertising in specific media, e.g. tobacco advertising is banned on television. Such restrictions limit the number of alternative outlets available to advertisers of such products. In addition the UK Monopolies and Mergers Commission found that poster advertising appeared to be favoured more by advertisers of particular products.[1] A similar pattern is also true of Ireland with poster advertising more frequently used by some advertisers than others.

14. Within the outdoor advertising medium substitutes also include the size of the poster. There is a degree of overlap between roadside posters of different sizes as well as some complementarity in their use. The value to an advertiser of particular panels depends upon their location as well as other factors such as design features in terms of angle to passing traffic, illumination and the number and size of panels on a site. On balance the Authority believes that the outdoor advertising market does constitute a distinct product market and that larger size posters constitute a distinct market segment within the overall outdoor advertising sector. The arrangements in this notification relate to 48 sheet posters. In their submission DAH indicated the breakdown of 48-sheet panel holdings was as follows:

Table 2: % Distribution of 48 Sheet Advertising Panels

David Allen	1,425 (56%)	
Adsites	207 (8%)	
Sub-Total	1,632	64%
MOF Adshel Ltd	311	12%
Metro Advertising Ltd	176	7%
Computer Advertising Network	278	11%
Summerbrook Ltd	140	6%
Total	2,537	100%

Source: DAH

1. Monopolies and Mergers Commission (1991); Avenir Havas Media SP and Brunton Curtis Outdoor Advertising: A Report on the acquisition by Avenir Havas Media SA of Brunton Curtis Outdoor Advertising, cm 1737.

7.18 15. The operation of the poster market depends on the availability of sites. No advertisement can be displayed without first obtaining planning permission from the local authority. DAH submitted that entry to the market requires that a contractor negotiate for advertising rights with a property owner, obtain planning permission for an advertising display and erect an advertising structure. This would cost £2,000 per 48 sheet site. The planning regulations, which limit the number of new structures that can be erected, significantly constrain the extent to which a new entrant can construct panels or a small firm can expand. The past decade has also seen a shift towards the development of poster networks. The AHM Annual Report for 1991, for example, stated that the development by it of the network concept meant that outdoor advertising had become a powerful new mass medium. The network concept involves thinking 'no longer in terms of single billboards but in terms of sets of billboards which target groups of people.'[2] The Report points out that a poster network was made up of a set of billboards linked by the same marketing idea, with local networks for cities, for urban areas, for regions or even national networks. This tends to imply that effective entry to the market would require a firm to establish a widespread range of poster sites. Technical advances within the industry, the growth of packages by leading firms and other improved services tend to make it more difficult and more expensive for smaller firms to compete.

(d) *The arrangements*

16. The Licence Agreement gave DAH an exclusive right to market and sell all Adsites 48 sheet advertising panels within the 32 counties of Ireland, in respect of which Adsites was the freehold owner or licensee with the right of outdoor advertising up to 31 December 1994. The agreement applied to a minimum of 262 panel sites, of which 200 are located within the State. Clause 4.2 provided that DAH could compete with Adsites. Clause 5 set out the level of payments to be made by DAH to Adsites. Essentially DAH were to pay Adsites all of the rental revenue less all of the costs involved in selling the advertising and less a 10% commission for DAH, although this commission only applied provided the revenue due to Adsites exceeded the guaranteed minimum specified in the agreement. Clause 8.1 provided that any new panels signed up by Adsites would be treated in the same way as existing Adsites panels. Clause 8.2 provided that if Adsites wished to acquire or develop a new panel, it would notify DAH giving full details including anticipated revenue to be derived from the panel, and that DAH would have the right within 30 days to decline the inclusion of the panel upon giving reasonable grounds in writing. Clause 9 provided that if at any time the agreement was referred to any relevant authority which determined that it was void, it would terminate immediately. Clause 11 provided that either party could terminate the agreement by giving notice in writing in certain circumstances such as the other party being in breach of the agreement or becoming insolvent.

(e) *Submissions of the parties*

17. DAH argued that the agreements were not anti-competitive since they were for a fixed period with no post-term non-compete restrictions, that although DAH made certain payments the majority of these would be variable, that DAH was not restricted by the agreement, that DAH was required to sell and market the panels on the best terms so therefore it could not but market them in a competitive manner. They also argued that it had only one fixed price, the others being variable, it only limited the marketing of panels for a particular period, that it did not place Adsites at a competitive disadvantage and the agreement did not contain any conditions or provisions which had no commercial usage.

18. DAH submitted that outdoor advertising had experienced decline in relation to other media fora in recent years due to innovations in other media and lack of investment in this area of the market. They stated their intention to concentrate on broadening the base of advertisers using outdoor advertising. They pointed out that the market was subject to variations that arose

2. AHM, Annual Report 1991, p. 18.

from such a highly competitive industry. Competition took place at media expenditure level, between owners of different sizes of outdoor advertising sheets and between different owners of 48 sheets and also between transport advertising, press, radio and TV. In order to compete with other media, outdoor advertising had to be able to sell audiences to advertisers/advertising agencies. While other media fora could advise advertisers of viewing figures there were at present, no figures indicating measurement of the outdoor advertising audience. Therefore other forms of advertising had an advantage over outdoor advertising. DAH submitted that the use of Adsites sites and their investment would improve the service available and make it more efficient and competitive, thus increasing the quality of the market and the product available and resulting in benefit to the consumer. **7.18**

19. DAH submitted that the purpose of the arrangement was to provide a sound commercial base for investment in the medium. The beneficiaries of the arrangement would be users and owners of the medium. Users would have a medium that could compete effectively with other forms of media while owners would benefit when market share for outdoor advertising had been regained. DAH concluded that the arrangements were not regarded as being anti-competitive and would effectively develop outdoor advertising to a higher standard so that it would be in a position to compete with other fora with higher market shares of advertising.

(f) *Views of third parties*

20. The Authority received a submission from an outdoor advertising company [ ],[3] in which they claimed that DAH, by marketing the outdoor sites of Adsites, had achieved control of the 48 sheet market and currently had a 70% market share. They claimed that in addition to Adsites, DAH had also acquired approximately 100 x 48 sheet sites from More O'Ferrall in exchange for regional bus shelter sites and had also acquired Phoenix Poster Sites which had a small number of 48 sheet sites.

21. [ ] argued that DAH's dominance in the market enabled them to dictate prices and availability. It was likely that the cost of advertising would rise and the cost would be passed on to the consumer. In addition it was claimed that DAH were in a position to dictate rents paid to landowners/siteowners thereby ensuring that small contractors were unable to compete on rental offers for sites. It was claimed that this eliminated competition and minimised the income potential of the landlord.

(g) *Other Relevant Factors*

22. The AHM Annual Report states that one of its subsidiaries, Mills and Allen, which operated in the outdoor poster advertising market in the UK, had acquired another firm operating in that market. This acquisition had been investigated by the MMC and had been found likely to operate against the public interest. The MMC Report found that, while outdoor advertising represented only a small proportion of total advertising, it nevertheless constituted a distinct product market. It also found that large outdoor posters constituted a separate market from other forms of outdoor advertising. Although the acquisition would have increased Mills and Allen's share of the market to 33.8 per cent, the MMC found that this was likely to reduce competition and choice of supply in the relevant market and would in time lead to higher prices. While it found that Mills and Allen had introduced improvements to the industry which were beneficial it concluded that there were unlikely to be sufficient benefits from the merger to offset the adverse effects identified and that it would therefore offend against the public interest. An earlier investigation of a previous acquisition by Mills and Allen had reached similar conclusions but had been permitted on condition that Mills and Allen divest itself of a substantial number of panels.[4] The later acquisition would have given it control of these panels.

3. The company's name is confidential.
4. Monopolies and Mergers Commission (1987); MAI plc and London and Continental Advertising Holdings plc: A Report on the merger, cm 258.

7.18 (h) *Subsequent Developments*

23. On 13 September 1994 the Authority issued a Statement of Objections to the parties indicating its intention to refuse to issue a certificate or grant a licence on the basis of the information available to it concerning the agreement. DAH submitted that the arrangements were not anti-competitive. They argued that 48 sheet poster panels did not constitute a separate market and that the market was at least that for all outdoor advertising and could be viewed as all forms of media advertising. They also argued that they had not pushed up their advertising prices during the period in which the agreement had operated. Adsites replied indicating that they accepted the Authority's views as set out in the Statement of Objections.

24. An Oral Hearing was held on 27 October 1994. During the course of the hearing DAH conceded that the licence agreement offended against section 4(1).

Assessment

(a) *Section 4(1)*

25. Section 4(1) of the Competition Act states that 'all agreements between undertakings, decisions by associations of undertakings and concerted practices, which have as their object or effect the prevention, restriction or distortion of competition in goods or services in the State or in any part of the State are prohibited and void'.

(b) *The Undertakings and the Agreement*

26. Section 3(1) of the Competition Act defines an undertaking as 'a person, being an individual, a body corporate or an unincorporated body engaged for gain in the production, supply or distribution of goods or the provision of a service.' DAH is a corporate body engaged for gain in the business of providing outdoor advertising space. Adsites is also an outdoor advertising company and is engaged for gain. Therefore, they are both undertakings and the arrangements constituted an agreement between undertakings.

(c) *Applicability of section 4(1)*

27. The Licence Agreement grants DAH a three year exclusive licence to market and sell Adsites 48 sheet outdoor advertising space. In return DAH pays Adsites all revenue received from renting such sites less all of the costs involved and less a commission for DAH, although the commission is only paid provided Adsites receives a certain guaranteed income. Essentially the agreement involves two competitors deciding to cease competing with one another in respect of a particular product and instead to allow one to have sole responsibility for joint marketing of that product, namely 48 sheet advertising panels. The arrangement applies to 64% or more of the 48 sheet poster advertising market. There is no question, in the Authority's opinion, but that the object and the effect of such an agreement is to prevent, restrict or distort competition within the State. This would apply even if the market were that for all outdoor advertising. Under the agreement Adsites gives DAH exclusive rights to market and sell all advertising space on all of its large poster panel sites within the State in return for a specified schedule of payments. Thus DAH and Adsites, by virtue of this agreement, effectively agree not to compete with one another in the market. Nor can Adsites compete by acquiring new sites, since DAH also has exclusive rights to such sites unless it specifically chooses not to exercise them. The Authority has no doubt therefore that the Licence Agreement is anti-competitive and clearly offends against section 4(1).

(d) *Applicability of section 4(2)*

28. Under section 4(2), the Competition Authority may grant a licence in the case of any agreement which offends against section 4(1) but which, 'having regard to all relevant market conditions, contributes to improving the production of goods or provision of services or to promoting technical or economic progress, while allowing consumers a fair share of the resulting benefit and which does not —

(i) impose on the undertakings concerned terms which are not indispensable to the attainment of those objectives; 7.18
(ii) afford undertakings the possibility of eliminating competition in respect of a substantial part of the products or services in question.'

29. The Authority does not believe that the notified agreement contributed to improving the production of goods or the provision of services or to promoting technical or economic progress. The parties have offered no convincing arguments to show how the notified agreement would produce such benefits nor that consumers receive any share of these. Since the agreement did not satisfy all the requirements of section 4(2), no licence may be granted in respect of it.

The Decision

30. In the Authority's opinion DAH and Adsites are undertakings within the meaning of section 3(1) of the Competition Act and the notified arrangements constitute an agreement between undertakings. In the Authority's opinion the Licence Agreement dated 2 January 1992, whereby David Allen Holdings Ltd is granted an exclusive right to market and sell Adsites Ltd advertising panels has both the object and effect of preventing, restricting or distorting competition and consequently offends against section 4(1). The Authority does not believe that the agreement satisfies the requirements for a licence set out in section 4(2). The Authority therefore refuses to issue a certificate or grant a licence to the Licence Agreement of 2 January 1992 between David Allen Holdings Ltd and Adsites Ltd (Notification No. CA/1128/92), notified on 30 October 1992 under section 7 of the Competition Act 1991.

For the Competition Authority

Patrick Massey
Member

21 November 1994

Competitin Authority Decision No. 381, Adsites Ltd/David Allen Holdings Ltd/ Option Agreement: 15 December 1994, Notification No. CA/1127/92 7.19

Option agreement whereunder one undertaking could acquire a business of a competing entity – Combined market share of companies in excess of 60% – Herfindahl – Hirschman Index – Further acquisition restricts competition – Whether acquisition produces benefits which can be shared with the consumer – Third party submissions – Statement of objections – Oral hearing – Refusal to issue certificate or grant licence – Competition Act 1991 (No. 24) sections 3, 4 and 7

Facts: On 30 October 1992 notification was made to the Authority with a request for a certificate under section 4(4) of the Competition Act 1991 or, failing that, a licence under section 4(2) in respect of an option agreement made between David Allen Holdings Ltd ('DAH') and Adsites Ltd ('Adsites') whereunder Adsites gave DAH an option to purchase all of its 48-sheet advertising panels at any time up to 30 September 1994.

DAH, an English registered company which operates in Ireland through a branch,

7.19 is engaged in the business of providing space for use in outdoor advertising. Adsites, an Irish registered company, is also engaged in the business of providing space for use in outdoor advertising. The advertising market in Ireland is, according to statistics from Advertising Statistics Ireland Ltd, divided as follows: National Press 45%; Regional Press 3%; Consumer Press 5%; Television and Radio 41%; Outdoor 5% and Cinema 1%. Outdoor and poster advertising can be divided into three different categories namely road side, transport and other. Roadside advertising includes posters, which are displayed on the side of the road or in pedestrian areas while transport posters are those which are displayed on buses, railways and taxis. Posters come in various sizes and are attached to structures known as panels. The 48-sheet poster is the predominant large poster size sited on panels and is the poster size relevant to the notified option agreement.

Poster contractors own the panels on which the posters are displayed and have rights to use the sites on which they are located. Generally the sites are not owned by the contractors but are rented from the owner. There are three principal ways in which poster panels are booked. A contractor may sell individual panels for a particular advertising campaign, may allocate a group of panels into pre-selected campaigns or packages for a single period or may accept long-term bookings for a particular panel.

Within the outdoor advertising medium there are a number of alternative products. Of the different poster sizes the large 48-sheet panels are the most popular outdoor advertising medium accounting for almost 46% of such advertising. Smaller sized posters account for approximately one third of outdoor advertising with transport advertising accounting for the remaining 21%.

Under the terms of the notified option agreement which was made on 2 January 1992 Adsites gives to DAH an option to acquire all of Adsites' 48-sheet panels at any time up to and including 30 September 1994. DAH has exercised the option under the terms of the option agreement. Adsites 48-sheet poster sites were at all times during the option period marketed by DAH under the terms of a separate licence agreement. The exercise of the option under the option agreement increased the share of DAH in the 48-sheet outdoor advertising market from 56% to 64% which represents 29% of all forms of outdoor advertising or 37% of all poster advertising. Evidence presented indicated that the prices which advertisers will pay for large posters varied depending on the specific location and other features of the relevant poster panels which variation was considerable in Dublin and other urban environments as opposed to rural locations.

While all advertising media may be considered to be substitutes for each other to some degree the extent to which other media or substitutes for roadside posters will vary according to the product being advertised and the nature of the campaign. Poster advertising is often used in conjunction with another medium to reinforce the message which the advertiser is seeking to portray and to this extent posters complements rather than substitutes for other forms of advertising. On balance it appears that the outdoor advertising market does constitute a distinct product market and that larger poster sites constitute a distinct market segment within the overall outdoor advertising sector. In the Authority's view the relevant market was that for a large (48-sheet) outdoor advertising panel. Smaller outdoor advertising panels are only substitutes to this market to a limited degree and other advertising media are not sufficiently close substitutes to be regarded as in the same market as large outdoor panels. The Authority received a submission from a competing outdoor advertising company stating that the notified agreement gave DAH control of the 48-sheet market and that this dominance enabled DAH to dictate prices and availability. 7.19

On 13 September 1994 the Authority issued a Statement of Objections to the parties in respect of the notified agreement. At an oral hearing held on 27 October 1994 DAH argued, *inter alia* that the relevant market was not that for large size posters but rather was that for all forms of advertising since these were substitutes for one another and further that section 4(1) of the Competition Act was not applicable in the case of the notified agreement which was effectively an acquisition. They submitted that while the arrangements might result in DAH achieving a dominant position in the market any abuse of such a dominant position was not a matter coming within section 4(1) of the Act.

Decided by the Authority: In refusing to issue a certificate or grant a licence under sections 4(4) and 4(2) respectively of the Competition Act 1991 in respect of the notified agreement that:

(1) Each of DAH and Adsites are companies engaged for gain in the business of providing outdoor advertising space and are therefore undertakings within the meaning of the Competition Act 1991 and the notified agreement is therefore an agreement between undertakings.

(2) The sale of a business *per se* does not offend against section 4(1). However, where such a sale is likely to result in a significant diminution of competition in the market it would be regarded as offending against section 4(1). As a result of the acquisition DAH has increased its market share of the 48-sheet panels to 64%. Where there are only relatively few competitors and one firm has a large market share the elimination of a competitor and its acquisition by the largest firm may be expected to restrict or at the very least to distort competition unless there are off-setting factors at work. Even if all outdoor posters were deemed to constitute the relevant market the level of market concentration would be sufficiently high for the acquisition by one of the largest firms to have adverse implications for competition. In addition the requirement to obtain planning permission for the siting of panels and the cost involved in assembling a large number of suitable poster panel sites represents a significant barrier to entry into the market. In the circumstances, therefore, the notified arrangements result in a significant diminution of competition in the relevant market.

(3) Arising out of the notified agreement it would be possible for DAH to increase prices significantly for the rental of large poster sites. During the period DAH controlled *de facto* 64% of the market by reason of the licence agreement entered into between DAH and Adsites, the average DAH price increased by almost 10% which was double the rate of inflation for the period. In all the circumstances of the case the notified option agreement therefore offends against section 4(1) of the Competition Act 1991.

(4) The notified agreement will not contribute to improving the production of goods or the provision of services or to promoting technical or economic progress and no convincing argument has been offered to show how the notified agreement would produce such benefits. Since all four of the tests set out in section 4(2) of the Competition Act must be satisfied in order for a licence to be granted the fact that the agreement fails to satisfy this requirement is of itself sufficient for a licence to be refused. In addition the notified agreement produces no benefit in which consumers may share and the large share of the relevant market afforded to DAH by virtue of

7.19 the notified agreement means that it affords the undertaking the possibility of eliminating competition in respect of a substantial part of the products in question.

Decisions referred to
Competition Authority Decision No. 6 – Woodchester/UDT [**3.5**]
Competition Authority Decision No. 12 – Scully Tyrell/Edberg [**3.10**]
Competition Authority Decision No. 378 – David Allen Holdings Ltd/Adsites Ltd/Licence Agreement [**7.18**]

Competition Authority decision of 15 December 1994 relating to a proceeding under section 4 of the Competition Act 1991
Notification No. CA/1127/92 — Adsites Ltd/David Allen Holdings Ltd

Introduction

1. This decision concerns an Option Agreement between David Allen Holdings Ltd (DAH) and Adsites Ltd (Adsites), which was notified to the Authority on 30 October 1992, with a request for a certificate or a licence. The agreement gave DAH an option to purchase some 200 48 sheet advertising panels from Adsites, at any time up to and including 12 noon on 30 September 1994, provided DAH complied with its obligations under the terms of a related licence agreement. DAH has exercised the option under the terms of the agreement. Under the terms of the licence agreement DAH obtained from Adsites an exclusive licence to market and sell the advertising panels owned by Adsites up to 31 December 1994. The Authority refused the request for a certificate or licence in respect of that agreement.[1] The Authority issued a Statement of Objections to the parties in respect of the notified agreement on 13 September 1994 and an Oral Hearing was held on 27 October 1994.

The facts

(a) *The subject of the Notification*

2. This decision concerns an Option Agreement between DAH and Adsites dated 2 January 1992 under which DAH acquired the option of purchasing Adsites right, estate or title in the 48 sheet outdoor advertising panels owned by Adsites and marketed by DAH under the exclusive licence agreement referred to earlier, at any time up to and including 12 noon on 30 September 1994. Some 200 48 sheet advertising panels located throughout the State were covered by this agreement. DAH exercised its option to acquire the panels in early September 1994.

(b) *The Parties*

3. DAH is an English registered company established in 1859 and is part of the Avenir Havas Media Group. DAH has operated through a branch (David Allen) in Ireland since 1859. It is an outdoor advertising contractor and is involved in the business of providing space for use in outdoor advertising. It negotiates a site rental with a property owner, constructs and maintains an advertising structure on the property and rents the space to advertisers in fortnightly units.

4. The Avenir Havas Media Group (AHM), is a Paris based multinational, whose shares are publicly quoted. It is 97% owned by Havas which was established in 1835 and which is now France's largest media and communications group. Havas is also engaged in seven major business areas in France and worldwide, including publishing, tourism and audio-visual. Havas' total revenue in 1992 was FF28 billion. Adsites is an outdoor advertising company which comprises Adsites Ltd, Campaign Poster Sites Ltd and Adsites (Northern Ireland) Ltd.

(c) *The Product and the Market*

5. The agreement relates to large (48 sheet) panels which are used for poster advertising.

1. Competition Authority decision No. 378, 21 November 1994.

There are a large number of alternative media available for firms wishing to advertise their products to consumers. In its submission to the Authority DAH argued that the market could be broken down into two expenditure categories, i.e. traditional forms of media and 'below-the-line' expenditure. Media advertising includes television, radio, press and outdoor advertising. According to DAH, industry estimates indicated that expenditure on traditional forms of advertising in Ireland in 1991 was IR170m. 'Below-the-line' activity refers to sponsorships, supermarket tasting and any other activity which does not involve employing a media company. It is difficult to assess the level of expenditure in this area but according to DAH it was in the region of IR100m. Table 1 below indicates the level of advertising expenditure in Ireland in 1993. It is based on figures which the Authority has obtained on the national advertising market from Advertising Statistics Ireland Ltd. (ASI), a company which specialises in monitoring the overall advertising market. Their figures are not wholly accurate since their estimates of newspaper advertising in particular are based on the 'rate card' whereas it is widely acknowledged that newspapers regularly give significant discounts from these rates. According to ASI total expenditure on media advertising in Ireland in 1993 was £235.3m. The national press was estimated to account for 45% of this with television representing a further 31%. Outdoor advertising, including posters was estimated to account for just 5% of the total. 7.19

Table 1: The Advertising Market in Ireland

Media	£m	% Market Share
National Press	105.9	45%
Regional Press	8.1	3%
Consumer Press	12.3	5%
Television	72.1	31%
Radio	22.9	10%
Outdoor	12.8	5%
Cinema	1.2	1%
Total	235.3	100

Source: ASI

6. DAH submitted that the buyers in the market are advertisers and advertising agencies. The method of advertising chosen is influenced by factors such as cost per thousand of audience, size of the audience and the number of times it can be reached, target audience and availability. The sellers in the market are the media owners or advertising contractors.

7. Outdoor or poster advertising can be divided into three different sectors namely roadside, transport and other. Roadside advertising includes posters displayed by the side of the road and in pedestrian areas, while transport posters are those which are displayed on buses, railways and taxis. Posters may also be displayed at airports, sporting events or on vehicles in various locations. Outdoor advertising may also include neon lights and other special structures. The market is geographical and seasonal. Demand for outdoor advertising is highest for sites located in urban areas. The greatest demand occurs in the summer during the long daylight hours, with the six months from October to March accounting for only 30% of annual turnover.

8. Posters come in various sizes and are attached to structures which are known as panels. This panel is placed, possibly with other panels on a poster site. The main sizes of posters in use are as follows:

(a) 4-sheet (5' x 3'4"). This small sized panel is aimed at pedestrians and is often found in shopping centres.

(b) 6-sheet (1.8m x 1.2m). Often referred to as 'superlites', these are mainly located on bus shelters and are aimed at motorists as well as pedestrians. They are often back-lit to improve

7.19 night time effect.

(c) 12-sheet (5' X 10')

(d) 16-sheet (10' X 6'8"). These posters are often attached to the sides of buildings.

(e) 32-sheet (10' x 13'4"). Again posters of this size are often attached to the sides of buildings.

(f) 48-sheet (10' x 20'). The predominant large poster size, sited on panels. Such posters are aimed at both motorists and pedestrians.

(g) 64-sheet (10' x 26'8"). This is a variant on the 48-sheet.

48 sheet posters account are the most common size of outdoor advertising posters. The other most commonly used poster sizes are 4-sheet and superlites. In recent times there has been a move away from 4-sheet sites towards superlites. A DAH representative referred to the 4 sheet posters as a dying product.

9. Poster contractors own the panels on which the posters are displayed and have rights to use the sites on which they are displayed. In general the sites are not owned by contractors but are rented from the owner. The advertiser pays the contractor for the use of the panels and also pays the production costs of his poster. Advertising agencies design a campaign to meet the needs and objectives of a particular manufacturer or supplier. Outdoor specialists occupy an intermediate position between the contractor and the advertising agency. They act for advertisers and advertising agencies as planners and/or buyers of poster campaigns. The advertising agency and the outdoor specialist receive their remuneration by way of a commission from the poster contractor.

10. There are three principal ways in which poster panels are booked. A contractor may sell individual panels for a particular advertising campaign, a form of short-term spot selling known as line-by-line sales. Alternatively the contractor may collect a group of panels into 'pre-selected campaigns' or 'packages' for a single period sale. Thirdly, a contractor may accept long term bookings for a panel for at least a year or possibly for an indefinite period.

11. According to DAH two specialist companies operated in the Irish market up until 1991, Outdoor Advertising Services Ltd, (OAS) and Poster Management Ltd (PML). Their respective market shares were 70% and 30%. The specialists were treated as principals by the outdoor contractors. These specialists negotiated exclusive rights to sell the plant of some of the contractors thus causing distortion in the market, according to DAH, as access to sites depended on which specialist was used. In August 1991, OAS went into liquidation. Following the liquidation the poster contractors revised their terms and conditions of trading to establish the advertiser/advertising agency as principal. Payment is now arranged through the advertising agency. According to DAH there are three specialists currently operating within this system, PML, PosterPlan Ltd and PosterLink Ltd.

12. Within the outdoor advertising medium there are a number of alternative products. These include different poster sizes along with advertising on buses. It can be seen from Table 2 that large 48 sheet panels are the most popular outdoor advertising medium accounting for almost 46% of such advertising. Smaller size posters account for about one third of outdoor advertising with transport advertising (primarily buses) accounting for the remaining 21%.

Table 2: % Distribution of Outdoor Advertising

48 sheet panels	45.8
Bus shelters	25.0
4 Sheets	8.3
Transport advertising	20.9
Total	100.0

Source: DAH

13. The arrangements in this notification relate to 48 sheet posters. In their submission DAH indicated the breakdown of 48-sheet panel holdings was as follows: 7.19

Table 3: % Distribution of 48 Sheet Advertising Panels

David Allen	1,425 (56%)	
Adsites	207 (8%)	
Sub-Total	1,632	64%
MOF Adshel Ltd	311	12%
Metro Advertising Ltd	176	7%
Computer Advertising Network	278	11%
Summerbrook Ltd	140	6%
Total	2,537	100%

Source: DAH

14. The exercise of the Option Agreement increased the share of DAH in the 48 sheet outdoor advertising market from 56% to 64%. This represents 29% of all forms of outdoor advertising or 37% of all poster advertising. It is also relevant that there are only a relatively small number of firms engaged in the overall poster advertising business. The top two poster advertising firms each account for more than 30% of poster sites of all sizes, while the top four have in excess of 90%. While David Allen has a large share of the the 48 sheet market, the other main firm engaged in outdoor advertising has around 90% of the smaller posters. There are a number of smaller poster advertising firms but they each have only a tiny share of the poster business.

15. There is a degree of overlap between roadside posters of different sizes as well as some complementarity in their use. The value to an advertiser of particular panels depends upon their location as well as other factors such as design features in terms of angle to passing traffic, illumination and the number and size of panels on a site. Indeed evidence presented by DAH indicated that the prices which advertisers will pay even for large posters vary considerably depending on the site of the poster. There is considerable variation not only between Dublin and other parts of the country but prices can also vary depending upon the specific location and other features of poster panels even within Dublin. The price of the top grade of poster in Dublin, according to the DAH rate card is more than five times that of the cheapest grade. In contrast price differentials for the same grade vary far less between geographic locations. The rate card also indicates that price changes for different grades and in different geographic areas have varied considerably over the past 3 years raising some question as to whether all 48 sheet panels should be regarded as substitutes for one another. In fact it would appear that a 48 sheet panel in a rural location is not a substitute for a 48 sheet panel in a prime location in Dublin City suggesting that there are a number of separate market segments in the case of 48 sheet panels.

16. The operation of the poster market depends on the availability of sites. No advertisement can be displayed without first obtaining planning permission from the local authority. DAH submitted that entry to the market requires that a contractor negotiate for advertising rights with a property owner, obtain planning permission for an advertising display and erect an advertising structure. This would cost £2,000 per 48 sheet site. The planning regulations which limit the number of new structures that can be erected, significantly constrain the extent to which a new entrant can construct panels or a small firm can expand. The past decade has also seen a shift towards the development of poster networks. The AHM Annual Report for 1991,

7.19 for example, stated that the development by it of the network concept meant that outdoor advertising had become a powerful new mass medium. The network concept involves thinking 'no longer in terms of single billboards but in terms of sets of billboards which target groups of people.'[2] The Report points out that a poster network was made up of a set of billboards linked by the same marketing idea, with local networks for cities, for urban areas, for regions or even national networks. This tends to imply that effective entry to the market would require firms to establish a widespread range of poster sites. Technical advances within the industry, the growth of packages by leading firm and other improved services tend to make it more difficult and more expensive for smaller firms to compete.

17. All of the advertising media may be considered to be substitutes, to some degree, with clients deciding which forum to choose based on cost, audience and product. The extent to which other media are substitutes for roadside posters will vary according to the product being advertised and to the nature of the campaign and over time. In general an advertiser makes use of more than one advertising medium and may use various media to portray different messages or concentrate on particular aspects of a product. In choosing which media to use an advertiser will take into account a broad range of factors. Television advertising, although expensive is capable of portraying a strong image, reaches a wide audience and has a high impact inside the home. Press advertising includes national newspapers, local and regional newspapers and specialist periodicals. It costs less than television and may be aimed at different population segments or particular groups. Posters are relatively cheap, and large sized panels in particular offer strong visual impact. They may be used close to the point of sale and can be geographically directed. Posters are often used in conjunction with another medium to reinforce the message which the advertiser is trying to portray. To this extent posters should be regarded as complements rather than substitutes to other forms of advertising. Thus the Authority believes that outdoor advertising constitutes a distinct advertising medium.

18. Pricing is a significant factor in determining the substitutability of posters by other media. Posters tend to be significantly cheaper than other forms of media advertising. Expenditure on poster advertising also tends to constitute a relatively small proportion of an advertiser's total marketing expenditure. In such circumstances it might be expected that it would require a significant increase in the cost of poster advertising before users would switch to other forms of advertising. Two other factors must also be considered in defining the market. Firstly there are legal restrictions in respect of certain types of advertising in specific media, e.g. tobacco advertising is banned on television. Such restrictions restrict the number of alternative outlets available to advertisers of such products. In addition the UK Monopolies and Mergers Commission found that poster advertising appeared to be favoured more by advertisers of particular products. A similar pattern is also true of Ireland with poster advertising more frequently used by some advertisers than others.

19. The Authority believes that the relevant market is primarily that for large (48 sheet) outdoor advertising panels. It considers that smaller outdoor advertising panels may, to some extent, constitute substitutes to larger panels. However, in its view they are only substitutes to a limited degree, since they do not have the same visual impact as larger size posters. Other advertising media are also not sufficiently close substitutes to be regarded as in the same market as large outdoor panels.

(d) *The arrangements*

20. The Option Agreement gave DAH an option to acquire from Adsites 200 48 sheet advertising panels located throughout the State.[3] These panels had been marketed by DAH under the licence agreement since early 1992. DAH exercised the option to acquire the panels

2. AHM, Annual Report 1991, p. 18.
3. The agreement also covers a number of panels in Northern Ireland but these are not considered relevant to the present decision.

in September 1994. Clause 6.1 requires Adsites to notify DAH if it acquired any new panels, giving full details of such acquisitions including the anticipated revenue to be derived from them and DAH has the right within 30 days to decline to include such panels in the agreement. 7.19

(e) *Submissions of the parties*

21. DAH argued that the agreement was not anti-competitive since there were no post-term non-compete restrictions. DAH submitted that outdoor advertising had experienced decline in relation to other media fora in recent years due to innovations in other media and lack of investment in this area of the market. They stated their intention to concentrate on broadening the base of advertisers using outdoor advertising. They pointed out that the market was subject to variations that arose from such a highly competitive industry. Competition took place at media expenditure level, between owners of different sizes of outdoor advertising sheets and between different owners of 48 sheets and also between transport advertising, press, radio and TV. In order to compete with other media, outdoor advertising had to be able to sell audiences to advertisers/advertising agencies. While other media forums could advise advertisers of viewing figures there were at present no figures indicating measurement of the outdoor advertising audience. Therefore other forms of advertising had an advantage over outdoor advertising. DAH submitted that the use of Adsites sites and their investment would improve the service available and make it more efficient and competitive, thus increasing the quality of the market and the product available and resulting in benefit to the consumer.

22. DAH submitted that the purpose of the arrangement was to provide a sound commercial base for investment in the medium. The beneficiaries of the arrangement would be users and owners of the medium. Users would have a medium that could compete effectively with other forms of media while owners would benefit when market share for outdoor advertising had been regained. DAH concluded that the arrangements were not regarded as being anti-competitive and would effectively develop outdoor advertising to a higher standard so that it would be in a position to compete with other fora with higher market shares of advertising.

(f) *Views of third parties*

23. The Authority received a submission from an outdoor advertising company [ ], in which they claimed that DAH, by marketing the outdoor sites of Adsites, had achieved control of the 48 sheet market and currently had a 70% market share. They claimed that in addition to Adsites, DAH had also acquired approximately 100 x 48 sheet sites from More O'Ferrall in exchange for regional bus shelter sites and had also acquired Phoenix Poster Sites which had a small number of 48 sheet sites.

24. [ ] argued that DAH's dominance in the market enabled them to dictate prices and availability. It was likely that the cost of advertising would rise and the cost would be passed on to the consumer. In addition it was claimed that DAH were in a position to dictate rents paid to landowners/siteowners thereby ensuring that small contractors were unable to compete on rental offers for sites. It was claimed that this eliminated competition and minimised the income potential of the landlord.

(g) *Other Relevant Factors*

25. The AHM Annual Report states that one of its subsidiaries, Mills and Allen, which operated in the outdoor poster advertising market in the UK, had acquired another firm operating in that market. This acquisition had been investigated by the MMC and had been found likely to operate against the public interest. The MMC Report found that, while outdoor advertising represented only a small proportion of total advertising, it nevertheless constituted a distinct product market. It also found that large outdoor posters constituted a separate market from other forms of outdoor advertising. Although the acquisition would have increased Mills and Allen's share of the market to 33.8 per cent, the MMC found that this was likely to reduce competition and choice of supply in the relevant market and would in time lead to higher prices. While it found that Mills and Allen had introduced improvements to the industry which were

7.19 beneficial it concluded that there were unlikely to be sufficient benefits from the merger to offset the adverse effects identified and that it would therefore offend against the public interest. An earlier investigation of a previous acquisition by Mills and Allen had reached similar conclusions but had been permitted on condition that Mills and Allen divest itself of a substantial number of panels.[4] The later acquisition would have given it control of these panels.

(h) *Subsequent Developments*

26. The Authority issued a Statement of Objections to the parties in respect of the notified agreement on 13 September 1994 and an Oral Hearing was held on 27 October 1994. DAH argued that the arrangements were not anti-competitive. They stated that the relevant market was not that for large size posters but rather was that for all forms of advertising since they claimed that these were all substitutes for one another. They stated that the ability of poster firms to raise their prices was constrained by the ability of customers to switch to other forms of advertising. They also submitted that at the very least the relevant market should be regarded as that for all outdoor advertising.

27. DAH submitted that there was no evidence that they had been able to secure significant price increases since they secured the right to market Adsites poster panels under the licence agreement in early 1992. They stated that their prices had only increased in line with inflation and that this showed that they were not in a position to impose significant price increases on their customers.

28. DAH argued that section 4(1) of the Competition Act was not applicable in the case of an agreement such as this which was effectively an acquisition. They argued that Article 85(1) did not apply to mergers and acquisitions and by analogy section 4(1) should not apply to them either. They claimed that while the arrangements might result in DAH achieving a dominant position in the market any abuse of such a dominant position was not a matter coming within section 4(1) of the Act and so the arrangements could not be regarded as anti-competitive for this reason. DAH also argued that the position in Ireland was somewhat different to that applying in the UK and that therefore the conclusions of the MMC Reports in the case of Mills & Allen were not applicable. They also stated that advertisers in the UK were preparing a submission to the OFT disputing the MMC definition of the market. It was put to DAH that the agreement to swop their smaller poster sites for 48 sheet panels with one of the other major outdoor advertising firms appeared to contradict their contention that small and large posters were part of a single market. In response the former MD of DAH stated that in his view, this arrangement had been a mistake.

29. In a written reply to the Statement of Objections, Adsites stated that they agreed with the Authority's assessment. They stated that DAH had raised prices since the licence agreement first came into force. They also argued that the rate card had been revamped and that the effect of this had also been to raise prices. They also claimed that DAH were incorrect in stating that there were no audience figures available for outdoor advertising thereby placing it at a disadvantage relative to other media, since extensive research had been undertaken in this area in recent years and the results were known to market participants.

Assessment

(a) *Section 4(1)*

30. Section 4(1) of the Competition Act states that 'all agreements between undertakings, decisions by associations of undertakings and concerted practices, which have as their object or effect the prevention, restriction or distortion of competition in goods or services in the State or in any part of the State are prohibited and void'.

4. Monopolies and Mergers Commission, (1987); MAI plc and London and Continental Advertising Holdings plc: A report on the merger, cm 258.

(b) *The Undertakings and the Agreement* 7.19

31. Section 3(1) of the Competition Act defines an undertaking as 'a person, being an individual, a body corporate or an unincorporated body engaged for gain in the production, supply or distribution of goods or the provision of a service.' DAH is a corporate body engaged for gain in the business of providing outdoor advertising space. Adsites is also an outdoor advertising company and is engaged for gain. Therefore, they are both undertakings and the arrangements constituted an agreement between undertakings.

(c) *Applicability of section 4(1)*

32. Under the Option Agreement DAH has an option to acquire all of the large poster panel sites of Adsites. DAH have argued that such an arrangement does not come within the scope of section 4(1) The Authority has given its views on this point in a number of earlier decisions and it is not necessary to restate its views at length for the purposes of the present decision. The Authority has stated in a number of previous decisions that, in its opinion, a sale of business *per se* does not offend against section 4(1).[5] It has indicated, however, that where such an agreement is likely to result in a significant diminution of competition in the market it would be regarded as offending against section 4(1). Specifically the Authority has stated that, where in the aftermath of an acquisition the level of concentration as measured by the four firm concentration ratio or the Herfindahl-Hirschman Index exceeded certain thresholds, a detailed examination of the arrangements would be necessary to establish whether or not it could be considered anti- competitive.[6]

33. The effect of the acquisition by DAH of the Adsites 48 sheet panels is to increase DAH's share of such panels to 64%. The market is therefore a highly concentrated one and the effect of this agreement is to increase that level of concentration. According to figures supplied by DAH there are five other outdoor advertising companies operating in the 48 sheet poster market, but these all have much smaller market shares. Where there are only relatively few competitors and one firm has a large market share, the elimination of a competitor and its acquisition by the largest firm may be expected to restrict or at the very least distort competition unless there are offsetting factors at work. Even if all outdoor posters were deemed to constitute the relevant market, the level of market concentration would be sufficiently high for an acquisition by one of the largest firms to have adverse implications for competition. This is particularly so given that one firm accounts for a major portion of small posters.

34. As pointed out earlier there are significant regional variations even within the large advertising panel market. A firm with a large number of sites in rural areas would not constitute an effective competitor to one with a large number of sites in Dublin. As a result of the agreement DAH now has over 700 large panels in Dublin and more than 400 in the other main urban centres. It has increased the number of panels it has in Dublin by more than 20%. Thus although the Authority does not have a detailed breakdown of market shares within the Dublin region, it is clear that the arrangements result in the elimination of a significant competitor within that region and a considerable increase in the market share of the largest firm. Urban centres and, in particular, Dublin are very important in the outdoor advertising business. The arrangements also restrict and/or distort competition within Dublin.

35. In this instance the Authority believes that there are significant barriers to entry. The requirement to obtain planning permission and the cost involved in assembling a large number of suitable poster panel sites reduce the threat of new entry. DAH have argued that some poster site developments do not need planning permission. Nevertheless the Authority believes that in most instances planning permission would be required and that this would constitute a significant barrier to entry. Poster advertising by its nature is not subject to competition from

5. See for example, Competition Authority Decision No. 6, Woodchester/UDT, 4 August 1992.
6. Competition Authority Decision No. 12, Scully-Tyrrell/Edberg, 29 January 1993.

7.19 imports. The Authority therefore concludes that the arrangements will result in a significant diminution of competition in the relevant market. This would still be the case even if it considered that all outdoor posters came within the definition of the market since it would still be a highly concentrated one and the arrangements result in one of the two largest firms increasing its market share.

36. DAH had sought to argue that the relevant market was that for all advertising media. While the availability of other media outlets for advertising would represent some constraint on the ability of DAH to exercise market power, the Authority believes that this would be somewhat limited as it does not believe that the relevant market includes all media fora. In particular it believes that it would be possible for DAH to increase prices significantly for the rental of large poster sites. DAH has submitted an extensive amount of material on price changes over the past few years in support of its arguments that prices have not increased significantly. In particular DAH claimed that in many instances poster prices had fallen since 1991 and that it had only increased rate card prices by about 3% per annum since it had started marketing Adsites panels. The position is complicated by the fact that DAH has changed the basis on which it sets its poster rates since 1991. Rates are now related to periods of 14 rather than 28 days. In addition the classification of posters was revised in 1992 so that in comparing prices in 1994 with 1991 it is difficult to ensure that one is comparing like with like. This is important since the claim that poster prices have not increased to any significant extent is highly dependent on the figures quoted by DAH for 1991. These suggest that prices for many poster categories fell between 1991 and 1992, some quite sharply. Direct comparisons are possible for the past two years and these are summarised in Table 4 below.

Table 4: % Increases in Poster Rates

	1993	1994	Cumulative
Dublin	5.3	5.2	10.9
Other Urban	5.2	5.3	10.8
Regional	4.4	0.0	4.4
Total	5.1	4.1	9.4

Note: Posters are graded into five categories. The price changes shown above are a weighted average for the 5 poster categories for each region.

Source: DAH

37. Over the past two years the national average DAH base card rate has increased by almost 10%. This is almost double the rate of inflation over the period. Increases in urban areas have been greater running at almost 11% over the two years. In the case of the most common poster categories the rates of increase have been even greater with some poster categories showing increases of almost 17% in Dublin. The increases in the rate card do not fully capture what has happened to prices. There have been some changes to the rates of discount offered so that average prices for the year as a whole in 1994 increased by between 1 and 3% more than the rate card figure. In addition some areas previously included within the regional category up to 1993 now come within the other urban rate, implying a significant increase in the case of those sites, which admittedly are rather limited in number. Nevertheless the substantial increase in poster sites in urban areas, particularly in the case of the most common categories, together with other changes in the rates of discount offered and the re-classification of certain sites from regional to other urban do not, in the Authority's view, support claims that competition from other media sources has imposed a serious constraint on DAH increasing its prices. When questioned about the figures DAH executives stated that, while some prices increased by more than others, they were obliged to keep their overall price increases in line with inflation or face

the prospect of losing business to other media. **7.19**

38. As pointed out DAH have pioneered the concept of poster campaigns whereby advertisers purchase a number of poster sites as part of a package rather than renting individual sites. In effect only DAH have a sufficient number of 48 sheet sites to offer such a package. In the case of some of these campaigns the price per site has increased by a considerable amount over the past two years, (20% or more in some instances). When asked to comment on this DAH stated that this was attributable to an improvement in the quality of the sites available. DAH stated that about 50% of their sites are included in campaigns. In the case of Dublin the ratio may be much higher since the total number of Dublin sites available for inclusion in campaigns accounts for 74% of DAH's Dublin sites. (The fact that sites are available for inclusion in campaigns does not mean that all such sites are booked for campaigns at any given point in time).

39. It is relevant that the MMC in the UK found that an acquisition by another member of the same group which would have given it a much lower share of the relevant market would reduce competition. In the Authority's opinion the extent of competition, both national and local, from other media in the form of television, radio, national and local newspapers would be likely to be much greater in the UK given the larger number of firms in those markets. The Authority therefore concludes that the Option Agreement offends against section 4(1).

(d) *Applicability of section 4(2)*

40. Under section 4(2), the Competition Authority may grant a licence in the case of any agreement which offends against section 4(1) but which, 'having regard to all relevant market conditions, contributes to improving the production of goods or provision of services or to promoting technical or economic progress, while allowing consumers a fair share of the resulting benefit and which does not —

(i) impose on the undertakings concerned terms which are not indispensable to the attainment of those objectives;

(ii) afford undertakings the possibility of eliminating competition in respect of a substantial part of the products or services in question.'

41. The Authority does not believe that the notified agreements will contribute to improving the production of goods or the provision of services or to promoting technical or economic progress. The parties have offered no convincing arguments to show how the notified agreements would produce such benefits. Since all four of the tests must be satisfied in order for a licence to be granted the fact that the agreements fail to satisfy this requirement is of itself sufficient for the Authority to refuse a licence. Nevertheless the Authority believes that it should set out its views in respect of the other tests for purposes of clarity. In the Authority's view the agreement produces no benefit in which consumers may share. Essentially, as the agreements themselves are anti-competitive and do not produce any benefits, the question of the indispensability of individual terms does not arise. The large share of the relevant market afforded to DAH by virtue of the notified agreement means that it affords the undertakings the possibility of eliminating competition in respect of a substantial part of the products in question. The Authority considers that 64 per cent of the market constitutes a substantial part of the market.

The Decision

42. In the Authority's opinion DAH and Adsites are undertakings within the meaning of section 3(1) of the Competition Act and the notified arrangements constitute agreements between undertakings. In the Authority's opinion the Option Agreement dated 2 January 1992, whereby DAH secured the option to acquire all of Adsites 48 sheet advertising panels has the object and effect of preventing, restricting or distorting competition and consequently offends against section 4(1). The Authority does not believe that the agreement satisfies the requirements for licence set out in section 4(2). The Authority therefore refuses to issue a certificate or grant a licence to the Option Agreement of 2 January 1992 between David Allen Holdings

7.19 Ltd and Adsites Ltd (Notification No. CA/1127/92), notified on 30 October 1992 under section 7 of the Competition Act 1991.

For the Competition Authority

Patrick Massey
Member

15 December 1994

7.20 **Competition Authority Decision No. 382, Carlow Developments Ltd/Naas Holdings Ltd:** 16 December 1994, Notification No. CA/458/92E

Lease agreement – covenant by lessee not to use property in an area larger than the demised premises for specified uses – whether restriction concerning area outside demised premises offends against section 4(1) – continuing contractual commitment – Competition Act 1991 (No. 24) ss. 3, 4 and 7

Facts: On 30 September 1992 notification was made to the Authority by Carlow Developments Ltd with a request for a certificate under section 4(4) of the Competition Act 1991 or, failing that, a licence under section 4(2) in respect of a property sale agreement between Carlow Developments Ltd ('the vendor') and Naas Holdings Ltd ('the transferee').

Both the vendor and transferee are engaged in the business of developing and letting property.

The notified agreement which was made on 14 September 1982 provided for rights of access to the remainder of the site retained by the vendor. Particularly the transferee covenanted not to erect retail units on the property which was sold exceeding a certain area, which was in effect the town of Carlow.

Following concerns expressed by the Authority the solicitors for the vendor agreed to inform the transferee that it would not seek to enforce the covenant in so far as it purported to effect land in Carlow other than the property which had been the subject of the sale.

Decided by the Authority: In issuing a certificate under section 4(4) of the Competition Act 1991 in respect of the notified agreement that:

(1) The prohibition under section 4(1) only applies to a current or continuing contractual commitment and the sale element of the notified agreement does not raise issues under the Competition Act.

(2) Restrictive user clauses cannot normally be regarded as preventing, restricting or distorting competition within the State or in any part of the State. Such a sale agreement does not prevent the purchaser from acquiring other property in the vicinity.

(3) A construction of the agreement suggests that the restriction on the transferee extended to the town of Carlow. In view of the notification that this construction would

not be enforced by the vendor the Authority considers that the notified agreement does not offend against section 4(1). 7.20

Competition Authority Decision of 16 December 1994 relating to a proceeding under section 4 of the Competition Act 1991
Notification No. CA/458/92E — Carlow Developments Ltd/Naas Holdings Ltd

Introduction

1. Notification was made by Carlow Developments Ltd on 30 September, 1992 with a request for a certificate under section 4(4) of the Competition Act 1991 or, in the event of a refusal by the Competition Authority to issue a certificate, a licence under section 4(2), in respect of a sale agreement between Carlow Developments Ltd and Naas Holdings Ltd.

The Facts

(a) *Subject of the notification*

2. The notification concerns the agreement for the sale of a plot of land, which was part of an area being developed as a shopping centre, at Burrin Street, Carlow between Carlow Developments Ltd as transferor and Naas Holdings Ltd as transferee.

(b) *The parties involved*

3. Carlow Developments Ltd and Naas Holdings Ltd are both engaged in the business of the development and letting of commercial properties.

(c) *The notified arrangements*

4. The notified sale agreement was made on 14 September 1982. Apart from the standard matters relating to the transfer of the property, the agreement provides for access through and car parking facilities for customers of the transferee on the part of the remainder of the site retained by the transferor. It also provides for access for customers of the transferor through the premises of the transferee as well as the use of electrical, telephone, water and sewer connections through the transferees land. The Fourth Schedule to the Agreement contains the following restricted user clauses which are binding on the transferee and his successors to the propelty viz.

> The transferee doth hereby for itself and its assigns and, to the intent and so as to bind not only itself personally but also all persons deriving Title under it and all further owners and tenants for the property in the First Schedule or any part thereof and to bind such property into whosoever hands the same may come, covenants with the Transferor its successors and assigns the owner or owners for the time being of the property comprised in Folio 9859F County Carlow retained by the Transferor as follows:
> 1. Not to use or permit or suffer to be used the premises described in the First Schedule hereto or any buildings erected thereon or the area edged green on the Map annexed hereto or any buildings erected thereon for the purposes of carrying on the following:
> (a) Sale of meat, pork and bacon;
> (b) Sale of fruit and vegetables.
>
> 2. Not to erect or suffer or permit to be erected any Retail Units on the property hereby transferred or the property edged green on any other lands in the Town of Carlow in the ownership of the Purchaser exceeding 1,100 square feet and not to grant convey assign lease or let or permit to be granted conveyed assigned leased let sub-leased or sub-let or permit to be used as any one or more Retail Units or any part or parts either adjoining

7.20 each other or otherwise of the property hereby transferred the property edged green on the Map annexed hereto or any other property in Carlow acquired by the Transferee as retail shopping outlets with a gross area containing or totalling more than 1,100 square feet to any person.

(d) *Subsequent developments*

5. Followings concerns expressed by the Authority, the solicitors for Carlow Developments confirrned, by way of letter dated 1 November 1994, that the company had agreed to inform Naas Holdings that they would not seek to enforce the covenant in paragraph 2 of the 4th schedule insofar as it purports to affect lands in Carlow other than the properties edged green and red in the map attached to the Transfer. A letter to this effect was issued by Carlow Developments Ltd to Naas Holdings Ltd on 29 November 1994.

Assessment

(a) *Section 4(1)*

6. Section 4(1) of the Competition Act 1991 prohibits and renders void all agreements between undertakings, decisions by associations of undertakings and concerted practices which have as their object or effect the prevention, restriction or distrotion of competition in trade in any goods or services in the State, or in any part of the State.

(b) *The Undertakings*

7. Section 3(1) of the Competition Act defines an undertaking as 'a person being an individual, a body corporate or an unincorporated body of persons engaged for gain in the production, supply or distribution of goods or the provision of a service'.

(c) *The Agreement*

8. The Authority considers that Carlow Developments Ltd and Naas Holdings Ltd which are both engaged in the letting of property for gain, are undertakings and that the notified sale agreement is an agreement between undertakings. The agreement has effect within the State.

9. As the sale of the premises was completed prior to 1 October 1991, the date the Competition Act came into force, that element of the agreement was discharged by performance before the Act came into force. In the Authority's view, the prohibition under section 4(1) only applies to a current or continuing contractual commitment or one entered into subsequent to the coming into force of the Act. In any event the authority would not consider the sale, *per se*, of a property as raising any issues under the Competition Act.

10. The sale agreement contains a continuing contractual commitment on the part of the purchasers and their assigns in that they have covenanted not to use or permit any of the premises transferred to be used tor the purposes of the sale of meat, fruit or vegetables. They have also covenanted not to erect or allow to be erected any retail units on the site with an area greater than 1,100 square feet or use or permit to be used more than 1 unit as a retail outlet with a joint area in excess of 1,100 square feet.

11. In the Authority's opinion the inclusion of restrictive user clauses in agreements for the sale of a particular property cannot normally be regarded as preventing, restricting or distorting competition within the State or in any part of the State. The purchasers acquired the property, which in this case was mainly land, for a particular purpose i.e., the erection of smaller shop units. Where the restriction applies to the particular property sold, but only to that property, the Authority takes the view that it does not offend against section 4(1)of the Competition Act. The purchaser gets what he pays for i.e. premises whose use is subject to some restriction. Such a purchase does not prevent him acquiring other property in the vicinity, which can be used for other purposes. Neither does it prevent any other undertaking from competing with the purchaser or the vendor.

12. In this instance a construction of the agreement could suggest that the restriction on the purchaser extended not only to the property sold, and its immediate environs, but also to any other property in Carlow owned or acquired by the transferee. This, in the Authority's opinion offended against section 4(1) of the Competition Act. As the transferor has agreed by way of letter dated 1 November 1994 not to enforce this element of the covenant, and has so advised the transferee by letter dated 29 November 1994, the restriction no longer offends against section 4(1) of the Competition Act. The Authority therefore considers that the notified agreement between Carlow Developments Ltd and Naas Holdings Ltd, as amended by way of letter dated 1 November 1994, does not offend against section 4(1) of the Competition Act 1991. 7.20

The Certificate

13. The Competition Authority has issued the following certificate:

> The Competition Authority certifies that in its opinion, on the basis of the facts in its possession, the agreement between Carlow Developments Ltd and Naas Holdings Ltd in relation to the transfer of property at Burrin Street, Carlow notified under section 7 on 30 September, 1992 (Notification No. CA/458/92E), and amended by way of letter dated 1 November 1994, does not offend against section 4(1) of the Competition Act 1991.

For the Competition Authority

Des Wall
Member

16 December 1994

Competition Authority Decision No. 394, RHM Ltd/Naresa Ltd: 12 April 1995, Notification No. CA/8/93

7.21

Lease with option to surrender – Whether terms of surrender restricting lessor from establishing a newsagency in competition with the lessee after the surrender offends against section 4(1) – Whether the payment on surrender is equivalent to the purchase of the goodwill – Whether the transfer of the goodwill on surrender requires the one year restriction on the lessor – No response to statement of objections – Landlord and Tenant (Amendment) Act 1980 (No. 10) – Competition Act 1991 (No. 24) sections 3, 4 and 7

Facts: On 24 February 1993 notification was made to the Competition Authority by Naresa Ltd of a lease between RHM Ltd ('the lessor') and Naresa Ltd ('the lessee') with a request for a certificate under section 4(4) of the Competition Act 1991

The lessor by lease dated 1 February 1993 for a period of 35 years leased a shop in Ballina, County Mayo, to the lessee for the purposes of a newsagency. A clause which is quoted in the published decision attempts to require the lessor on the surrender of the lease in accordance with the terms of the lease not to carry on any business which would compete with the business carried on by the lessee in the demised premises on the date of surrender. The geographic location was limited to a

7.21 two mile radius from Ballina post office.

The lessee indicated in its notification that the premises had been used as a newsagency for upwards of 40 years and that the payment by the lessee of two years rent on the surrender was effectively an acquisition agreement relating to the goodwill in the newsagency. In effect Naresa Ltd could surrender the lease and transfer the goodwill of the newsagency to another location with the benefit of a covenant that the premises in which the newsagency was operated could not continue to be a newsagency.

No response to a statement of objections issued by the Competition Authority to the lessor and the lessee was received.

Decided by the Authority: In refusing to issue a certificate in respect of the notified lease that:

(1) The standard restrictions which are necessary for the maintenance of the landlord and tenancy relationship do not raise issues under the Competition Act.

(2) Leasing the premises prevents competitors from using the premises to compete with the tenant but this cannot be regarded as preventing, restricting or distorting competition. Anyone wishing to operate a business in competition with the tenant may do so by occupying any other premises in Ballina.

(3) The restrictions on the use of the premises are not anti-competitive in view of the statutory stipulation that an application for a change of use cannot unreasonably be withheld and the fact that the tenant could use other premises for any proposed alternative use.

(4) Although the Authority has indicated that a restriction of two years would be regarded as sufficient for the complete transfer of the goodwill of a business the Competition Authority in this case believes that the lessee acquired the goodwill on taking up the lease and that the object of the non-competition clause on the operation of the surrender provisions in the lease offends against section 4(1).

Decisions referred to

Competition Authority Decision No. 1 – Nallen/O'Toole [**3.3**]

Competition Authority Decision No. 10 – GI Corporation/General Semiconductor Industries Inc. [**3.8**]

Competition Authority Decision No. 394 of 12 April 1995 relating to a proceeding under section 4 of the Competition Act, 1991
Notification No: CA/8/93 — RHM Ltd/Naresa Ltd

Introduction

1. Notification was made by Naresa Ltd on 24 February 1993 with a request for a certificate under section 4(4) of the Competition Act 1991 in respect of a lease between RHM Ltd and Naresa Ltd. The Authority issued a Statement of Objections to both parties and no formal response to the Statement was received.

The Facts

(a) *Subject of the notification*

2. The notification concerns the lease of a shop at Pearse Street, Ballina, Co. Mayo between RHM Ltd as lessor and Naresa Ltd as Lessee.

(b) *The parties involved* 7.21

3. RHM Ltd is the owner and landlord of the shop at Pearse Street, Ballina. Naresa Ltd trades as a newsagent at the premises.

(c) *The notified arrangements*

4. The notified lease was made on 1 February 1993 for a term of 35 years from 1 October 1992. The restricted user clauses in the lease are as follows:

(a) Under clause 7 of the Second Schedule the lessee covenants 'To use the premises for the lessee's business as a Newsagency, Tobacconist and Confectioner. . . .'

(b) Under clause 8 of the Second Schedule the lessee covenants 'Not to assign, sub-let or part with or share the possession of the Demised Premises or any part thereof or permit any other person or Company to occupy the demised premises as a licensee without first obtaining the consent in writing of the Lessors which consent shall not be unreasonably withheld'.

(c) The lease also contains a number of other standard restrictive covenants and obligations relating to the letting of the premises.

(d) In addition the agreement provides for an early surrender of the lease by the lessee including the following clause D1(b)

'That the Lessee at anytime during this demise shall, on giving one months notice to the Lessor of its intention;

(i) to surrender the term then unexpired created by this demise and of its intention.

(ii) within 12 months from the date of surrender and within a radius of two miles of Ballina Post Office to carry on or be associated by any means directly or indirectly with a business to be carried on which will be in competition with the business at the date of such notice been carried on in the demised premises.

be entitled, on payment to the Lessor of all arrears of rent and other outgoings due pursuant to the terms of this demise up to the date of actual surrender and on payment to the Lessor in addition of a sum equal to the equivalent of twice the then current rent. To surrender to the Lessor the residue then unexpired of the term demised hereunder and the Lessor on compliance by the Lessee of these terms and on payment of the said moneys as aforesaid shall accept a surrender of the said term and shall enter into a suitable covenant with the Lessee that it shall not directly carry on or indirectly be engaged in or associated by any means with any business carried on by any person or Body in competition with the business carried on in the demised premises at the time of such surrender within a radius of two miles from Ballina Post Office for a period of twelve months from the date of such surrender'.*

(d) *Submission of the Parties*

5. In its submission Naresa stated 'The premises in question have in fact been used as a newsagency for upwards of forty years but the range of goods on sale has expanded recently. . . . In view of the position of the premises in the town and its long use as a general newsagents there is goodwill attached to the premises as a newsagents. During the term of the Lease Naresa Ltd on giving notice and on paying the equivalent of two years rent to RHM Ltd can surrender the Lease and can seek to move the goodwill to an alternative premises. In that event RHM Ltd is prohibited from using the existing premises as a newsagency for twelve months and further

**Editor's Note*: This is indeed an accurate copy desite the difficulty which the reader may have in understanding the clause.

7.21 is prohibited from carrying on a similar business in an alternative premises within two miles of Ballina Post Office during this same twelve month period. In short, the applicant Naresa Ltd can buy the goodwill and seek to transfer to an alternative premises in the knowledge that it will have a reasonable opportunity to build up the business in a new location.' Naresa also stated that there were six similar businesses within 400 yards of the premises.

Assessment

(a) *Section 4(1)*

6. Section 4(1) of the Competition Act 1991 prohibits and renders void all agreements between undertakings, decisions by associations of undertakings and concerted practices which have as their object or effect the prevention, restriction or distortion of competition in trade in any goods or services in the State, or in any part of the State.

(b) *The Undertakings*

7. Section 3(1) of the Competition Act defines an undertaking as 'a person being an individual, a body corporate or an unincorporated body of persons engaged for gain in the production, supply or distribution* of goods or the provision of a service'. RHM is engaged in the letting of premises for gain and is therefore an undertaking. Naresa is trading as a newsagent and is also an undertaking. The notified lease is an agreement between undertakings. The agreement has effect within the State.

(c) *Applicability of section 4(1)*

8. The lease agreement contains standard restrictions and obligations on both landlord and tenant which are necessary for the maintenance of the landlord/tenant relationship in respect of the tenancy. These do not raise issues under the Competition Act. The very act of leasing the premises to a particular tenant prevents competitors of the tenant from using those premises to compete with the tenant. Clearly this cannot be regarded as preventing, restricting or distorting competition since it would imply that the leasing of a commercial premises in order to carry on a business therein was prohibited unless licensed under section 4(2) of the Competition Act. Anyone wishing to operate a business in competition with the tenant may do so by occupying any other premises within the town of Ballina.

9. In addition the agreement also provides, by way of the permitted user clause 7 in the Second Schedule, restrictions on the use of the premises but which effectively allow the premises to be used for the purposes of the business of the tenant. Such permitted user clauses are normally based on the user proposed by the tenant at the time the lease is first executed but are also governed by considerations such as the physical characteristics of the premises, the requirements of the Planning Acts and the landlord's own policy, when granting the lease, on how the premises should be used. The Authority considers that such user restrictions in the letting of premises do not have the object or effect of preventing, restricting or distorting competition in the State or any part of the State. In taking up the lease the tenant negotiates the permitted user required for his business. This is reflected in the lease but if he were subsequently to seek a change of user he could in most instances have recourse to the provisions of the Landlord and Tenant Act 1980 which provide that a Landlord cannot unreasonably withhold consent to a change of user requested by a tenant. In addition the tenant is free to undertake other businesses in many other premises, both in the vicinity or elsewhere in the State. The object or effect of such permitted user clauses in lease agreements are not therefore anti-competitive. The Authority therefore considers that these clauses do not offend against section 4(1) of the Competition Act 1991.

**Editor's Note*: The word 'distortion' is in the original decision but this would appear to be a typographical error.

10. Clause 1(b) provides that where the lessee seeks to surrender the lease before its expiry date with the intention of opening a similar business within a radius of 2 miles from Ballina, the lessor would accept this surrender on payment of a sum equivalent to twice the then current rent. The lessor would also enter a covenant not to become engaged in any way or associated with a competing business in the premises or within the same 2 mile radius for a period of 12 months from the date of such surrender. It has been argued that this clause, if exercised, would enable Naresa to purchase the goodwill and seek to transfer it to an alternative premises in the knowledge that it will have a reasonable opportunity to build up the business in a new location. **7.21**

11. The Authority has dealt with restrictions on the vendor following the sale of a business on a number of occasions. In its first decision, *Nallen/O'Toole*,[1] the Authority stated that it regarded some restrictions on the seller of a business as being essential in order to ensure the adequate transfer of the goodwill of the business. In its opinion provided such restrictions were limited in terms of their duration, geographic coverage and subject matter to what was necessary to secure the transfer of the goodwill of the business, they would not be in breach of section 4(1) of the Act. In *G.I. Corporation/General Semiconductor*,[2] the Authority considered that a restriction of 2 years would generally be regarded as sufficient for the complete transfer of the goodwill of a business.

12. In this instance however the Authority is of the view that, on taking up the lease, the lessee had already acquired the goodwill of the business, which was attached to the premises in Ballina and that the object of clause D1(b) is to prevent and restrict competition by ensuring that RHM Ltd may not compete with or allow its premises to be used to compete with Naresa for a period of one year after any exercise of the option. The Authority therefore considers that this clause offends against section 4(1).

The Decision

13. In the opinion of the Authority, RHM Ltd and Naresa Ltd are undertakings within the meaning of section 3(1) of the Competition Act 1991 and the notified lease agreement constitutes an agreement between undertakings. In the Authority's opinion the notified agreement offends against section 4(1) of the Act. The Authority therefore refuses to issue a certificate in respect of the lease agreement between RHM Ltd and Naresa Ltd (Notification No. CA/8/93), notified on 24 February 1993, under section 7(1) of the Competition Act 1991.

For the Competition Authority

Des Wall
Member

12 April 1995

1. Competition Authority Decision No.1, 2 April 1992.
2. Competition Authority Decision No. 10, 23 October 1992.

CHAPTER EIGHT

Irish Court decisions

8.0 Introduction

The case law of the courts in Ireland concerning the application of competition law in Ireland is the most definitive interpretation which one can obtain concerning Irish law. This chapter contains judgments of the Supreme Court and High Court concerning matters and issues which will continue to be of relevance.

Kerry Co-Operative Ltd v. Bord Bainne and Others **8.1.1 and 8.1.2**
The reorganisation of Bord Bainne in such a manner as to encourage co-operatives to use the marketing and distributing services of An Bord Bainne were challenged by two of the largest co-operatives in Ireland, Kerry Co-Operative Creameries Ltd and Avonmore Creameries Ltd in High Court proceedings. The High Court judgment (at 8.1.1) traces the history of the co-operative movement in Ireland and the establishment of a milk marketing board called An Bord Bainne in a very useful historical summary. The legal issues in the case concerned:

(1) The amendment of the rules of a co-operative society;
(2) The alteration of the capital structure of a co-operative society;
(3) The right to expel members from a co-operative society;
(4) The class rights of various members of a co-operative society;
(5) The preemption rights in a co-operative society;
(6) The enforceability of a contractual obligation to trade with a co-operative society;
(7) The rights, if any, of a shareholder in a co-operative society to invoke the constitutional right to property and the principle of equality before the law;
(8) The restraint of trade doctrine;
(9) The powers of the board of a co-operative society;
(10) The applicability of Articles 85 and 86 of the Treaty of Rome in the context of a specific European Community Council Regulation granting exemptions to national dairy marketing organisations.

The discussion of the restraint of trade doctrine and the applicability of Articles 85 and 86 in the context of an exempting regulation will be of particular interest to those concerned with competition law. The judgment of Costello J (who is now President of the High Court) is set out in a succinct manner which facilitates the reader in identifying the judge's reasoning in respect of each of these issues. The use of headings throughout the judgment is of tremendous assistance.

The Supreme Court judgment which is contained in this chapter at 8.1.2 is of particular interest to the competition lawyer because of the Supreme Court's finding as a court of final appeal that it is obliged to refer under Article 177 of the Treaty of Rome to the European Court of Justice issues of law which are necessary to enable judgment to be given.

The review of the common law restraint of trade doctrine is also noteworthy and will be of significant guidance in any future case which may involve this doctrine.

8.0 Again the headings throughout each of the judgments affords the reader the opportunity of accessing the parts of the judgment relevant to the legal issues with which the reader may be concerned.

HB Ice Cream Ltd v. Masterfoods Ltd T/A Mars Ireland **8.1.3 and 8.1.4**
The judgment of Lynch J at 8.1.3 of this book concerning the granting of an interlocutory injunction in order to maintain the status quo may be used in the future as a support for the holder of a dominant position to benefit from the dominant position pending a full hearing despite the allegations of abuses of a dominant position and breaches of the Restrictive Practices (Groceries) Order, 1987. This case concerned the attempt by Masterfoods Ltd T/A Mars to gain access to cabinet freezers in small shops throughout Ireland for its products. Cabinet freezers in many of the shops were owned by the manufacturers of HB Ice Cream which precluded the retailer from stocking competing goods.

The judgment arising from the plenary hearing which is contained at 8.1.4 is a judgment of the utmost importance in the Irish competition law context. The interaction between Articles 85 and 86, the standard and requirement of proof of alleged infringements of Articles 85 and 86, the relationship between Articles 85 and 86 on the one hand and the property rights envisaged by Article 222 of the Treaty of Rome on the other and the enforceability of the Restrictive Practices (Groceries) Order, 1987 are the principal issues of competition law.

The definition of the relevant market and the judicial approach to expert economic evidence can be gleaned from this most comprehensive judgment which also employs the use of headings which greatly facilitates any reader's task.

Deane and Others v. Voluntary Health Insurance Board **8.1.5 and 8.1.6**
Arising from the determination of the preliminary issue that the Voluntary Health Insurance Board was an 'undertaking' the trial judge in this plenary hearing, Keane J, ultimately declined to accept the allegations that the VHI abused a dominant position but determined that the VHI exercised its power in a manner which lacked 'reason and equity' and thus breached its statutory duty to the plaintiffs. Again the relevant issues will be easily accessed by the reader because of the style adopted by Keane J in delivering his judgment. The rejection that the VHI had abused any dominant position which it might hold is supported by a purposive interpretation of the relevant provisions of the Competition Act. The competition lawyer will note the reference to the distinction between 'monopsonist' and 'monopolist'.

This judgment was appealed and the Supreme Court's judgments are contained in this book at 8.1.6. Ultimately the Supreme Court determined the issues between the parties based on contract law findings and the breach of statutory duty by the VHI to act fairly and reasonably. The Supreme Court deliberately refrained from commenting upon the allegation of an abuse of a dominant position because the disputes between the parties had been resolved under the contract law and statutory duty headings.

Interlocutory reliefs
Part II of this chapter contains a number of judgments arising from applications for interlocutory relief in cases which involved competition law matters.

Leanort and Others v. Southern Chemicals Ltd and Others **8.2.1** **8.0**
Blayney J in this case made an interlocutory order restraining all of the relevant parties from selling particular material for the construction industry 'at unreasonably low prices' pending the determination of the issues of fact. In this case the plaintiffs alleged that the defendant reduced their prices with a view to putting the plaintiffs out of business. Evidence was adduced on affidavit that the plaintiffs could not become members of an association of which the defendants were members also. Blayney J concluded in granting the injunction that the plaintiffs would cease to exist if an injunction was not granted.

Paramount Pictures Corporation and Others v. Cablelink Ltd **8.2.2**
The plaintiffs who were film producers sought an injunction restraining the defendants from infringing their copyright without paying the royalties which the plaintiffs sought to be recovered. The defendant alleged that the plaintiffs abused their dominant position by discriminating against the defendant in the charges which were sought to be recovered. The plaintiffs counter-argued that the defence based on Articles 85 and 86 was unstateable and that the defence should be struck out as 'an abuse of the process of the court'.

Murphy J on noting that the defendant had agreed to pay certain monies every month into a bank account in respect of its use of copyright of the plaintiffs refused to grant an injunction. Applying the balance of convenience test along with the finding that damages would be an adequate remedy Murphy J refused to grant an interlocutory injunction in favour of the copyright owners.

Dunlea v. Nissan (Ireland) Ltd **8.2.3**
The judgment which is contained at 8.2.3 of this book is an example of how a condition included in a European Commission Regulation, European Commission Regulation 123/85/EEC, was used by a motor car dealer to ensure that he obtained 12 months notice of termination. Barr J did not find conclusively that such a term was part of the arrangement between the plaintiff and the defendant but he granted an interlocutory injunction restraining the termination of the contract between the parties because there was a serious issue to be tried and because the balance of convenience rested with the plaintiff.

Mantruck Services Ltd and Another v. Ballinlough Electrical Refrigeration Co. Ltd **8.2.4**
The Supreme Court's judgment in allowing the appeal from the refusal of the High Court to grant an injunction restraining the defendant from selling the product manufactured by an entity of which the plaintiffs were sole distributors in the State is an example of the crucial nature of the balance of convenience test. The defendant alleged that the sole distributorship agreement from which the plaintiffs benefited precluded the defendant from being a 'parallel importer'. The Supreme Court ordered that pending the determination of the plenary hearing the defendant would be restrained from holding itself out as an authorised agent or distributor but the defendant could deal in the product.

8.0 *Curust Financial Services Ltd and Another v. Loewe Lack Werk Otto Loewe GmbH* **8.2.5**

The Supreme Court in this judgment which is set out at 8.2.5 of this book allowed the appeal from the order of the High Court granting an interlocutory injunction which restrained the first named defendant from licensing the manufacture of its products by another. The High Court referred to the principle of maintaining the status quo whereas the Supreme Court concentrated on the effects of granting or refusing an interlocutory injunction for the parties. The plaintiffs sought to enforce an exclusive manufacturing licence and were met with a defence that the agreement was void and prohibited by Article 85(1) of the Treaty of Rome. In addition the defendants alleged that the plaintiffs were in breach of contract which entitled them to terminate the agreement. The plaintiffs made averments on affidavit to the effect that the agreement was not one to which the provisions of Article 85(1) applied because it was an agreement of minor importance which had no material effect on intercommunity trade. Ultimately the Supreme Court found that the plaintiffs if successful at the plenary hearing would recover damages for breach of contract and no compelling reason was given to restrain the licensing of another manufacturer in the State.

8.1 The Courts

Kerry Co-Operative Creameries Ltd and Patrick James O'Connell v. An Bord Bainne Co-Operative Ltd and Registrar of Friendly Societies 8.1.1
Avonmore Creameries Ltd and Avonmore Foods plc and John Duggan v. An Bord Bainne Co-Operative Ltd and Registrar of Friendly Societies: High Court 1989 Nos. 4083P and 4101P (Costello J) 22 June 1990*

Industrial and provident society – Power to manage affairs – Power to alter capital – Power to amend rules – Industrial and Provident Societies Act 1893 (56 & 57 Vict., c. 39), sections 10, 21 & 22

Industrial and provident society – Property rights of shareholders – Rights of shareholders in or over assets of society – Industrial and Provident Societies Act 1893 (56 & 57 Vict., c. 39)

Contract – Restraint of trade – Whether rules of an industrial and provident society which benefit members who trade with that society over those who prefer not to do so are in restraint of trade

European Community – Competition – Agriculture – Application of competition rules to the activities of farmers' co-operatives – Whether exemption available under Council Regulation 26/62/EEC – Jurisdiction of Irish courts to apply Council Regulation 26/62/EEC – EEC Treaty, Articles 38, 39, 42, 85 & 86 – Council Regulation 26/62/EEC of 6 April 1962, Arts. 1 & 2

Industrial and provident society – Function of Registrar of Friendly Societies – Duties with regard to the registration of rules – Industrial and Provident Societies Act 1893 (56 & 57 Vict., c. 39), section 10(3)

Facts: An Bord Bainne Co-Operative Ltd ('the Bord') was established as an industrial and provident society in 1972 with the purpose of marketing Irish dairy produce abroad. Its membership consisted of co-operative societies of farmer producers. Members made a nominal subscription for shares calculated by reference to the value of milk intake in their respective creameries in the previous year. The rest of the Bord's capital was raised by means of levies, the issue of deferred shares or loans. With the full consent of its members, Bord Bainne never paid any dividends on its members' shares, maximised prices for the produce it bought and adopted a policy of using profits to reward those members who traded with it.

*The report first appeared in [1990] ILRM 664-739.

8.1.1 The members of Bord Bainne agreed upon a set of operating principles which provided, *inter alia*, that each member would get the same price for products of similar quality produced at the same time regardless of the ultimate market in which the product was sold and irrespective of when it was sold. Whilst members were obliged to sell export dairy products to the board and any breach of this obligation made them liable to have their membership terminated, no member had been expelled and there was no effective sanction to force members to fulfil their obligations. By means of waiver of the 1975 rules rather than any amendment thereof new purchasing arrangements were adopted by the Bord in 1981 to allow members a freer choice as to whether to use the Bord's services or to export products directly.

In 1987, the board of directors of Bord Bainne commenced discussions with its members concerning the future structure of the Bord. These led to the adoption of new rules aimed at improving the position of members which traded exclusively with the Bord over those members who chose to dispose of products for export themselves. At a special general meeting held on 15 November 1988 the members of Bord Bainne adopted certain amendments of its rules by a two-thirds majority. These provided for changes concerning membership and the expulsion of members, the manner in which bonus shares were to be issued, voting rights and the composition and election of the board of directors of Bord Bainne.

The plaintiffs in both proceedings had traded extensively with the Bord up until 1987, when they began to reduce the amount of dairy products sold thereto. They unsuccessfully opposed the adoption of the new rules by the Bord and subsequently sought to prevent them being registered by the Registrar of Friendly Societies. The allocation of bonus shares by the Bord under the new rules was restrained by an interlocutory order of the High Court made on 26 April 1988. The plaintiffs challenged the rules on the basis that (a) the suggested system for the allotment of bonus shares diluted a non-trading member's shareholding in the Bord and constituted an expropriation of its property; (b) any exercise of a power to terminate membership for failure to trade with the Bord and to return only the amount paid up on a member's shares would constitute a breach of property rights; (c) the rules relating to the allocation of bonus shares, termination of membership for non-trading and those having voting rights and the composition of the board of directors on the amount of trade with the Bord amounted to an unlawful restraint of trade; (d) their adoption was *ultra vires* both the members' powers to amend the rules and the provisions of the Industrial and Provident Societies Act 1893 and (e) the rules infringed Articles 85 and 86 of the EEC Treaty.

Held by the High Court (Costello J) in dismissing the claims against both defendants in both actions:

(1) Members of an industrial and provident society registered under the Industrial and Provident Societies Act 1893 are virtually free to manage the affairs of the society as they see fit. Whilst there is no statutory restriction on the manner in which the share capital may be altered, a majority may not abuse the power to amend the rules of a society since that power is confined to the internal rights of members and matters within the contemplated scope of the original venture. In determining whether an amendment is *intra vires* a society, an objective view is taken of the venture at the time a member joined. *Hole v. Garnsey* [1930] AC 472 applied.

(2) Assets acquired by an industrial and provident society are the property of the

society and no shareholder has a legal right to any specific portion thereof. In so far as a shareholder has property rights in the assets of an industrial and provident society, the nature and extent of those rights fall to be ascertained by reference to the contract entered into with the society the terms of which are contained in its rules. *Attorney General v. Jameson* [1904] 2 IR 644 at 669-70 *per* Kenny J applied. **8.1.1**

(3) An industrial and provident society is free to issue shares to new members or to allot new shares to existing members even though the effect is to reduce the fractional interest of existing members in the capital of the society. There is no implied term in the contract between a shareholder and the society of which he is a member that the fractional interest he has in the society's share captital will remain constant. *Mutual Life Insurance Co. of New York v. Rank Organisation Ltd* [1985] BCLC 11 considered.

(4) Rules of an industrial and provident society which benefit members who trade with that society over those who prefer not to do so are reasonable and not in restraint of trade. *McEllistrim v. Ballymacelligott Co-operative Agricultural and Dairy Society* [1919] AC 548 and *Tipperary Creamery Society v. Hanley* [1912] 2 IR 586 considered.

(5) Where a *prima facie* case is made out by a party for an exemption under Council Regulation 26/62/EEC from the application of Articles 85 and 86 of the EEC Treaty the Irish courts will allow that exemption unless good reason is shown as to why an application to that effect was not brought before the European Commission by the party alleging the exemption does not apply.

(6) The sole function of the Registrar of Friendly Societies is to consider whether rules proposed for registration conflict with the provisions of the 1893 Act. He is not obliged to consider whether rules proposed for registration are contrary to law. Where there is such a conflict the Registrar commits no actionable wrong in registering such rules. *Irish Civil Service Building Society v. Registrar of Friendly Societies* [1985] IR 167 followed.

Cases refered to in judgment:

Attorney General v. Jameson [1904] 2 IR 644
Hoffman-La Roche v. EC Commission (Case 85/76) [1979] ECR 461; [1979] 3 CMLR 211
Hole v. Garnsey [1930] AC 472; 99 LJ (Ch) 243; 46 TLR 312; 143 LT 153
Irish Civil Service Building Society v. Registrar of Friendly Societies [1985] IR 167
McEllistrim v. Ballymacelligott Co-operative Agricultural and Dairy Society [1919] AC 548
Michelin v. EC Commission (Case 322/81) [1983] ECR 3461; [1985] 1 CMLR 282
Mutual Life Insurance Co. of New York v. Rank Organisation Ltd [1985] BCLC 11
Private Motorists' Provident Society Ltd v. Moore [1983] IR 339; [1984] ILRM 88
Schroeder Music Publishing Co. Ltd v. Macaulay [1974] 3 All ER 616; [1974] 1 WLR 1308
Stenhouse Australia Ltd v. Phillips [1974] AC 391; [1974] 2 WLR 134; [1984] 1 All ER 117; [1974] 1 Lloyd's Rep 1
Stohmenger v. Borough of Finsbury Permanent Investment Building Society [1897] 2 Ch 469
Tipperary Creamery Society v. Hanley [1912] 2 IR 586; 46 ILTR 249

T.K. Liston SC, Daniel O'Keeffe SC and Paul Gallagher **for the plaintiffs in the Kerry Co-Operative proceedings**
Dermot Gleeson SC, Daniel O'Keeffe SC and Paul Gallagher **for the plaintiffs in the Avonmore Creameries proceedings**
Nial Fennelly SC, John D. Cooke SC and John Trainor **for the first named defendant**
Michael Collins **for the second named defendant**

8.1.1 INTRODUCTION

COSTELLO J delivered his judgment on 22 June 1990 saying: I have heard two actions together in both of which An Bord Bainne Co-operative Ltd, a co-operative society registered under the provisions of the Industrial and Provident Societies Act 1893 is a defendant. I will refer to this defendant as 'Bord Bainne' or where more appropriate 'the society' or 'the board'. The first named plaintiff in the first action is Kerry Co-operative Creameries Ltd, also a registered co-operative society. I will refer to this plaintiff by the name by which it is widely known, 'Kerry Co-op'. The second named plaintiff in that action is a director of and shareholder in Kerry Co-op. The first named plaintiff in the second action is Avonmore Creameries Co-operative Ltd, also a registered co-operative society, which I will call 'Avonmore Co-op'. The second named plaintiff in that action is a public limited company called Avonmore Foods plc which has been established by Avonmore Co-op. The third named plaintiff is the chairman of both Avonmore Co-op and Avonmore Foods plc and is a shareholder in both. Both Kerry Co-op and Avonmore Co-op are members of Bord Bainne, as are all the other dairy co-operatives in the country and some of the important manufacturers of dairy products. The second named defendant in both actions is the Registrar of Friendly Societies who has statutory functions relating to the registration of amendments to the rules of registered co-operative societies.

Although the facts in both actions are not identical the legal issues are and this enables me to give my conclusions determining both actions in a single judgment. The issues relate to amendments of the rules of Bord Bainne effected by a meeting of its members by the requisite two thirds majority at a special general meeting held on 15 November 1988. By resolution the members adopted a new set of rules only some of which amended the previous rules and only some of which are challenged in these actions. In summary the plaintiffs challenge the validity of a rule:

(a) empowering Bord Bainne to issue out of current profits bonus shares to its members rateably on the basis of trade done by its members with the board;

(b) empowering the board of directors to expel a member who has not traded for a period of two years with the board and return to the member no more than the amount paid up on its shares;

(c) empowering the board of directors to terminate the membership of a member who offends against the society's rules and return to the member no more than the amount paid up on its shares;

(d) which changes the voting rights of members from rights based on their milk intake to rights based on the volume of their sales to the board;

(e) by which voting for membership of the board of directors is based on volume of sales to the board rather than on the milk intake of members, and by which an eligibility test involving a commitment to trade with the board in a specific way is imposed.

The validity of these rules is challenged on a considerable number of different grounds in the plaintiffs' statements of claim, the principal claims being:

(a) a claim that an allotment of bonus shares based on the volume of sales to the board would, by diluting a non-trading member's shareholding in the board, constitute an expropriation of its property, an infringment of its property rights and that the members' adoption of the rule permitting this to be done amounted to a 'constitutional conspiracy';

(b) a claim that the exercise of a power to terminate membership for non-trading with the board and to return only the amount paid up on a member's shares would constitute a breach of constitutionally protected property rights;

(c) a claim that rules relating to the power to allocate bonus shares, terminate membership for non-trading and base entitlement to voting rights and a seat on the board of directors on volume of trade with the board amount to an unlawful restraint of trade and are therefore invalid;

(d) a claim that the impugned rules are invalid because their adoption was *ultra vires* the powers of the members to amend the rules and *ultra vires* the provisions of the 1893 Act; **8.1.1**

(e) a claim that the impugned rules infringe Articles 85 and 86 of the Treaty of Rome in that they constitute an agreement which has as its object and effect the restriction and distortion of competition within the EEC and affect trade between member states, and that their adoption and implementation constitute an abuse by Bord Bainne of its dominant position within a substantial part of the EEC and affects trade between member states.

Before the members' meeting of 15 November 1988 both Kerry Co-op and Avonmore Co-op wrote to Bord Bainne objecting to the adoption of certain of the rules at the proposed meeting, and their representatives at the special general meeting argued against their adoption. Notwithstanding this opposition the meeting adopted the new rules. On 24 November 1988 the plaintiffs' solicitor wrote to the Registrar of Friendly Societies objecting to the registration of the rules under the 1893 Act. After correspondence passing between them the Registrar wrote on 3 April 1989 informing the plaintiffs' solicitor that he had been advised that he could properly register the rules under the Act. These proceedings were then commenced on 7 April. An interim injunction temporarily restraining registration was obtained but on 26 April interlocutory relief restraining registration pending trial was refused and subsequently the new rules were registered under the Act. The plaintiffs have joined the Registrar as a defendant in these proceedings claiming that he had no jurisdiction to register the new rules, that by so doing he had infringed their constitutional rights and they seek appropriate declaratory orders against him and a mandatory injunction directing him to rectify the register.

In anticipation of their registration Bord Bainne had taken steps to implement rule 9 of the new rules and was preparing to allot 50,000 fully paid up £1 bonus shares in accordance with its provisions. At the interlocutory hearing an order restraining the issue of these shares until the trial of the action was made and in an amended statement of claim the plaintiffs plead as a separate ground of complaint and distinct from the challenge to the validity of the rules that the resolutions passed to issue and allot these bonus shares were invalid and claim declarations to that effect.

Although I have heard a great deal of evidence in this case the conflicts of fact are not many. It is, however, necessary for me to draw attention to the facts established which are relevant to the legal issues which have been raised as well as to determine some controversial issues. Accordingly I propose in Part I of this judgment to examine the structure of Bord Bainne and its predecessor, the statutory board established under an Act of 1961, and those developments in its trading and its relations with its members which are relevant to the issues in this case. In Part II I will consider the structure of Kerry Co-op, Avonmore Co-op and certain aspects of their trading history, as well as the role of the other plaintiffs in the case. In Part III I will examine the board's 1972 and 1975 rules, the steps taken to adopt the new ones and the new 1988 rules themselves. In Part IV I will consider the relevant provisions of the 1893 Act and then in Part V I will examine the legal issues in the light of the relevant facts, my conclusions on disputed facts and these statutory provisions.

PART I

(1) *Bord Bainne as a statutory board*

'Bord Bainne' is a name which has been and is still applied to two entirely different legal entities, firstly to 'An Bord Bainne' a statutory board established by the Dairy Produce Marketing Act 1961 and later to the co-operative society established in 1973 and registered under the 1893 Act and called 'An Bord Bainne Co-operative Ltd', the defendant in these actions.

The statutory board was established in the following circumstances. From 1936 there had been in existence an organisation called the Butter Marketing Committee to co-ordinate the export and marketing of creamery butter from this country. It was dissolved by the Dairy

8.1.1 Produce Marketing Act 1961 which established in its place a statutory board ('An Bord Bainne') with much greater powers over dairy exports. The board had no shareholders and comprised nine members nominated and appointed in the manner prescribed in the Act. It was in law and in fact a central market organisation empowered to export milk and milk products as the Minister for Agriculture should specify. In addition it had statutory powers to fix levies on producers and was under a duty to purchase at officially fixed prices butter offered to it by registered creameries. Power to prohibit the export of dairy produce otherwise than through the board was conferred on the Minister.

As explained by the Minister for Agriculture in moving the second reading of the Dairy Produce Marketing Bill 1961 in the Dáil:

> The board will take over the present functions of the Butter Marketing Committee in regard to purchase, storage, sale, etc of creamery butter. The government will provide the board with an annual grant, the amount of which will be negotiated each year, and the board will be authorised to collect levies from the producers to meet the balance of its requirements.
>
> The board will, in principle, become the sole exporter of all dairy products, but, as some exceptions to this are desirable in the interests of the dairy industry as a whole, the Bill empowers the Minister for Agriculture to delegate from time to time export marketing functions for particular products to the manufacturer concerned. At the outset, it is proposed to leave to the individual manufacturers the export of all chocolate crumb to Britain and the six counties; milk powder, non-creamery butter, and some special lines of cheese. The board will be the sole exporter of creamery butter, fresh cream, canned cream, condensed milk, and cheese other than some special lines, and will also handle the export of chocolate crumb to destinations other than Britain and the six counties'.

I draw attention to the reference in the Minister's speech to certain exceptions to the general requirement that all dairy products should be exported through the board. These exceptions came to be called 'special arrangements' or 'house to house arrangements' and they came to assume considerable significance in the years ahead. But in the early 1960's they were not of very great importance and by 1964 the board had a virtual monopoly of the sales of Irish dairy products abroad. Its efforts as a marketing agency met with considerable success. In 1962 it launched in connection with butter on the English market its trademark 'Kerrygold' which subsequently was applied in connection with other dairy products and is now widely known and of great commercial value. Total exports of butter from Ireland to the United Kingdom (the principal market for dairy products at that time) rose from 3,516 tons in 1960 to 38,295 tons in 1973.

(2) *Bord Bainne as a Co-operative*

Prudently, when it became clear that Ireland was likely to accede to the Rome Treaty and become a member of the European Economic Community, Bord Bainne took legal advice and not surprisingly was advised that it was probable that the 1961 Act and the regime relating to the export of dairy produce established under it infringed the Rome Treaty and the common agricultural policy established under it. It was accordingly decided to wind up the statutory board and to alter fundamentally the whole system for the export of dairy produce. At government level it was considered highly desirable and necessary to retain a central marketing organisation for the export of dairy products but it was concluded that this organisation should now be managed and controlled by a co-operative society whose members would be the dairy co-operatives throughout the country. To give effect to these decisions (whose implementation depended on the whole hearted support of the Irish dairy industry) a new society called 'An Bord Bainne Co-operative Ltd' was established and registered under the 1893 Act on 14 September 1972. At the same time legislation was introduced and subsequently enacted as the

Dairy Produce (Miscellaneous Provisions) Act 1973. Although I have no evidence on the point, I think I can safely assume that Bord Bainne's legal advisers were well aware that community law granted by Regulation 26 exemption to associations of farmers' co-operatives from some of the Treaty provisions on competition rules (an exemption considered later in section 3 of Part V of this judgment) and that this regulation must have considerably influenced the nature of the legal structure of the new board. 8.1.1

The 1973 Act provided for the dissolution of the old statutory board (section 4) and the transfer of its assets and liabilities to the new society (section 3). The Act referred to these assets as 'the specified assets' and placed a statutory obligation on the new society to use the 'specified assets' for the orderly marketing and distribution of dairy produce for the benefit of the dairy industry. The new society was prohibited from disposing of the 'specified assets' without the consent of the Minister for Agriculture and in the event of the society winding-up it was provided that these 'specified assets' must be disposed of for the benefit of the dairy industry as the minister should direct. It is of relevance to note that the 'specified assets' include the valuable 'Kerrygold' trademark.

The new co-operative was not established by the 1973 Act nor was it in any way subject to any statutory controls by the 1973 Act (other than those just noted relating to 'the specified assets'). It is free of all ministerial direction and runs its affairs as it thinks proper. It has, however, the benefit of a ministerial guarantee (up to a statutory limit which has been increased over the years) in relation to loans it may wish to raise. All the co- operatives in the dairy industry throughout the country were approached and asked to join the new co-operative and use it as a central marketing organisation for their dairy exports.

I should say a brief word about these co-operatives. The manufacture and marketing of dairy products by co-operative societies of farmer producers has long been a feature of the Irish dairy industry. The first co-operative was established in 1889. Shortly afterwards the Irish Agricultural Society Organisation (which subsequently changed its name to the Irish Co-operative Organisation Society) was established to promote amongst farmers the co-operative ideal. Its efforts in the dairy industry were remarkably successful and within ten years of its establishment 876 co-operative societies throughout the country had been set up. The movement continued to prosper and although there were some privately owned creameries and factories making dairy products the vast majority of the dairy farmers in the country were organised into co-operatives. In 1973 all the dairy co-operatives in the country agreed to become members of Bord Bainne and in addition a small number of companies, manufacturing dairy products, which were not co-operatively owned also joined as members. Membership of Bord Bainne has altered over the years with amalgamations and mergers of co-operative societies. There are now 56 members of the board of which 48 are co-operatives registered under the 1893 Act. From its inception Bord Bainne has been in law and in fact a co-operative whose purpose was to help the dairy farmers of the country. As stated in its publication *The Bord Bainne Story* (at p. 44) it regarded as its primary responsibility 'the loyalty and answerability to the Irish dairy farmer in ensuring that he/she gets the maximum return per gallon of milk'.

It is a highly significant and relevant fact that co-operatives asked to join the new society were only requested to make a nominal subscription for shares. This subscription was worked out by reference to the value of milk intake in the members' creameries in the previous twelve months. By this criterion there were in the country six major co-operatives, each of whom was requested to subscribe £1,000 for ordinary shares, all the other societies subscribing lesser sums. As a result only £17,000 was subscribed by the initial shareholders of the society. The rest of the board's capital, as we shall see, was raised by means of levies and the issue of deferred shares, or from loans.

It has long been a feature of Irish dairy co-operatives that their members are contractually bound to supply the milk they produce to the society of which they are members. An analogous obligation was a feature, until recently, of Bord Bainne's relationship with its members. Under

8.1.1 the original rules the members of Bord Bainne were required to provide to the society all their dairy produce destined for export unless otherwise agreed in writing with the society and this basic obligation was strengthened and underlined by amendments to the rules adopted by the members two years later in 1975. From its inception however the need to permit some of its members to enter into special arrangements by which some of its dairy produce could be traded outside the board was recognised, but it was clearly understood at the time that such special arrangements were exceptional. All (that is, the department, the board and all the dairy co-operatives in the country) were then agreed that the board would act as a central marketing organisation for exporting the great bulk of dairy produce from this country.

(3) *Bord Bainne's capital structure*
Originally it was provided that the capital of the society would consist of ordinary shares of £1 each but this was altered by amendments adopted in 1975. Since then the capital of the society has been divided into four different classes of ordinary shares 'A', 'B', 'C' and 'D', and a further class of 'deferred shares'. The 'A' shares were issued to registered dairy co-operatives, the 'B' shares to licensed manufacturers of dairy products other than co-operatives, the 'C' shares to co- operatives or companies not eligible under the previous rules and the 'D' shares to certain subsidiaries of co-operatives or companies. The holders of 'A' and 'B' shares could vote at general meetings but the holders of the 'C' and 'D' shares had no voting rights (subject to a power to authorise voting in the case of the holders of 'C' shares, vested in the board of directors) . The holders of the 'A' and 'B' shares were entitled, in the event of the society being wound up, to participate in the distribution of the society's assets other than the 'specified assets' referred to in the 1973 Act. The holders of the 'C' and 'D' shares were not entitled to participate in any distribution. The holders of the deferred shares were entitled in the event of a winding-up to participate with the holders of the 'A' and 'B' ordinary shares in the distribution of assets other than the specified assets but they had no right to the surplus assets which would remain after payment off of the whole of the paid up capital including that paid up on the deferred shares. The holders of deferred shares had no right to attend or vote at general meetings of the society.

The issue and allotment of deferred shares arose in the following way. The 1975 amendments empowered the directors to create a capital reserve fund and for this purpose to impose a levy on the holders of the 'A' shares (that is on the members who were co-operatives) in respect of each gallon of milk received in the creameries owned by the holders of the 'A' shares. Each member paying the levy then became entitled to such number of fully paid up deferred shares as should correspond to the total amount of the levy paid. Between 1975 and 1981 (when the capital levy scheme was discontinued) the society obtained £14.1 million from its members and issued to the holders of 'A' shares 14.1 million deferred shares according to the contributions each had made. At the present time the issued share capital of the company is as follows:

'A'	ordinary shares of one pound each	£12,600
'B'	ordinary shares of one pound each	£3,200
'C'	ordinary shares of one pound each	£410
'D'	ordinary shares of one pound each	£210
'E'	deferred shares of one pound each	£14,110,738
	TOTAL	£14,127,158

It should be noted that the £14.1 million which was contributed to Bord Bainne by means of the capital levy was in fact paid by individual farmer members of the co-operatives by means of a deduction from the price of milk paid to them by their co-operatives. This fact became of importance in the discussions which took place in 1987 and 1988 relating to the amendment of the society's rules and the new share structure which the society might adopt. But what is of central importance to all the issues in the case are the rights of the holders of the 14,000 'A' ordinary shares of which Kerry Co-op and Avonmore Co-op each own 1,000.

(4) *Operating principles between Bord Bainne and its members* **8.1.1**
In the years immediately following the establishment of the new society a set of operating principles governing the relationship between the board and its members was adopted, their object being to provide equity between the members and develop stable marketing conditions for the anticipated growth in milk production. The basis of these principles was a pooling arrangement based on the averaging of income 'over products over market over time'. They have been described by the board as follows:

> 1. Each member would get the same price for product of similar quality produced at the same time regardless of the ultimate market in which the product was sold and irrespective of when it was sold (averaging over time and averaging over markets).
> 2. Products would be pooled in groups so that members could decide product mix based on their own capacity and the relative economics of the product in question (averaging over groups).
> 3. A system of contracting was developed (eventually five year contracts) so that the board could enter into sales agreements overseas, confident in the knowledge that the product would be available at the scheduled delivery time.
> 4. Common minimum standards for product and packaging applied to all manufacturers enabling the board to fulfil all but very specialised orders from a number of processing plants. This system had strong commercial advantages in terms of holding, shipping, and loading costs and as well as that it provided a buffer against the decline in milk production levies which might affect the ability of the board to fulfil an order if it had related a single customer to a single supplier.
> 5. Where 'special arrangements' existed prior to February 1973 members were obliged to arrange supply of product to both marketing outlets on an equitable basis (*e.g.* every second day's production) to avoid distortion in the pool return.
> 6. In general the period over which averaging took place was one year's production.
> (*The Bord Bainne Story* p. 39).

The board of directors also adopted another operating principle which turned out to have certain significant and unforeseen consequences. It decided that contracts entered into between the board and its members should be negotiated between the society's executives and individual members and should remain confidential so that not even the directors knew the terms of members' contracts, what quantities each member was bound to supply to the board and what exemptions from the obligation to supply were permitted to individual members.

In 1981 a major revision in the society's purchasing arrangements with its members was effected. In a memorandum prepared for the benefit of new members of the board of directors in 1986 the then managing director explained the reasons for the 1981 changes as follows:

> By 1973 many co-operatives had special arrangements of one kind or another with multinational companies and all such arrangements were 'exempted' or 'excluded' from the exclusivity envisaged for Bord Bainne. This arrangement gave rise to many jealousies. Co-operatives who did not have such arrangements felt aggrieved that they were now precluded from doing so under Bord Bainne membership rules. This perception of inequity of treatment led to various skirmishes in the early years and a continuing element of discontent with the arrangements. After a number of frustrating years, major changes were made in the purchasing arrangements in 1981 that sought to eliminate the reasons for the unrest. In summary form, the new purchasing arrangements sought to;
>
> (i) provide more flexibility and freedom to members for individual initiative;
> (ii) preserve the fabric of central marketing in key product areas where fragmentation could achieve nothing but poorer market returns;

8.1.1 (iii) eliminate the need for penalties for rules breached;

(iv) place relationship between the board and members on a more commercial footing.

The views expressed in this memorandum were confirmed and developed in the evidence before me. It was pointed out that in the years prior to 1981 a great deal of time had been spent by the board's executives and its directors in trying to encourage members to abide by the rules and to fulfil their commitment to export through the board, and that apart from the friction caused by the existence of authorised 'special arrangements' there existed the problem of members deliberately breaking their contracts with the board and without authorisation exporting directly themselves when profitable opportunities offered. Furthermore, by 1981 some of the members of Bord Bainne wished to develop new business arrangements and a consensus developed pointing to a need to liberalize the purchasing regime so as to allow members a freer choice as to whether to use the board's services or export directly themselves. Finally, there was a further factor. Although members were contractually obliged to sell their export dairy products to the board (unless exempted in writing from doing so) and although breach of this contractual obligation could in theory have led to termination of the membership of the recalcitrant member, no member had in fact ever been expelled from the society and there was in reality no effective sanction forcing members to fulfil their contractual obligations.

The new purchasing arrangements adopted by the board of directors were as follows. Dairy products to be purchased by the board from its members were divided into product groups, and the obligation to trade was stated to be, as follows:

(a) *Group One*

This product group comprised, butter, oil, skim milk powder, and whole milk powder. Members were required to sell *all* their exportable output of these products to the board. These products constituted a high percentage of the board's total sales and of the industry's total output. This group was established (a) because of the need for the board to present itself as Ireland's sole supplier of major dairy products, particularly with government agencies in third world countries and (b) because of the need to obtain supplies at short notice, to achieve favourable freight rates, and to obtain the best benefits from Community payments.

(b) *Group Two*

This product group comprised one product, cheese. Members were free to trade or not to trade with the board in this product as they thought fit.

(c) *Group Three*

This product group comprised casein and caseinates. Members were free to trade or not to trade with the board as they thought fit in these products.

(d) *Group Four*

This product group comprised fat filled milk and whey. Members were free to trade or not to trade with the board as they thought fit in these products.

(e) *Group Five*

This product group comprised all consumer packaged products, in respect of which members were free to trade or not to trade with the board as they thought fit.

In relation to the *Group One* products the arrangements provided that each member got the same price for a product of a similar quality produced at the same time regardless of the ultimate market in which the product was sold and irrespective of the time the sale by the board ultimately took place, thus enshrining the principle of pooling income from different markets and of pooling returns over time periods. A guaranteed basic price was offered to all members equivalent to the Community intervention price plus a bonus fixed in advance at the beginning of the production year, a price which could be varied upwards by adding any EEC or Green Rate devaluations that might subsequently occur. It was explained that these arrangements, by fixing prices in advance, were designed to help manufacturers to adopt a systematic approach to production and planning. From the board's point of view they enabled it to enter into contracts with greater certainty that supplies to fulfil them would be available. Bonuses were to be paid at the end of the year but an important part of the arrangement was that bonuses would be forfeited if members failed to fulfil their obligation to provide all their Group One products manufactured for export to the board. 8.1.1

The legal consequences of these new arrangements are important and need to be understood. According to the *rules* which existed in 1981 and which constituted a contract between each member and the society every member was required to market through the society all its dairy products destined for export unless otherwise specifically exempted by an agreement in writing. These rules were not formally amended in 1981 but the board of directors decided that henceforth members would be required only to comply with their contractual obligations in respect of Group One products and it dispensed with the need to get written permission to export products in the other groups outside the board. In effect, it waived from that date full compliance of the contractual obligations contained in the 1975 rules.

(5) *Bord Bainne as a Marketing Organisation*

Economic developments since 1972 in the dairy industry have a relevance to the legal issues in the case as they affected the relationship between the board and its members. In 1972 the average price of milk in this country was 16p per gallon; in 1981 it was 60p. In 1972, the year before Ireland's entry into the European Community, the annual total of milk supply in the country was 563 million gallons, in 1981 it was 820 million gallons. In 1972 there were 1,141,000 creamery cows in the country; in 1981 there were 1,268,613. These figures naturally had a profound effect not only on all the farmers' co- operatives in the country (including the plaintiffs') but also on Bord Bainne. The home market for dairy produce was a finite one and the vast expansion in milk production could only be successfully marketed by marketing abroad dairy products manufactured from it. The growth in milk production continued until 1984 when it was abruptly stopped by the quota restrictions imposed in April of that year by the Council of Ministers of the EEC, and production was actually cut back by later restrictions so that in 1988 milk supplies were reduced by 4% on the previous year.

Bord Bainne's role in the dairy industry has been succinctly stated in the introduction to its 1988 accounts as follows:

> The basic business of An Bord Bainne and its subsidiaries is the export marketing of dairy products. The board is a farmer's co-operative whose members consist of all the dairy manufacturing co-ops and some private concerns. As the central marketing organisation for the dairy industry its principal objective is to market the produce of its members so as to generate the maximum return for the primary producers. Its secondary task is to reflect nationally and internationally a favourable image of the Irish dairy industry.

There are certain points in this summary which I should briefly develop.

(a) Bord Bainne is entirely dependent on its members for the products it sells abroad — it does not (unlike some of its major competitors in Europe) manufacture dairy products itself.

(b) Bord Bainne does not sell on the home market — it buys on the home market in this country only and sells abroad.

(c) Because it regards itself as a co-operative principally concerned with the welfare of the dairy farmers in the country it has, with the full consent of all its members, never paid any dividends on its members' shares, and has followed a policy of maximising prices for the

8.1.1 produce it buys. Any retained profits have been put in reserves for future development. Since its establishment it has with the approval of its members adopted a policy of using profits to reward those members who trade with it rather than those who contributed capital to it.

(d) The board sells a full range of dairy products, including a variety of butters, cheeses, creams, milk powders, casein. These are marketed either in bulk or in branded form. Its trademark 'Kerrygold' was launched in 1962 originally in relation to butter sold on the United Kingdom market but is now used on a wide range of dairy products on a worldwide basis. Large sums of money have been expended in making the mark internationally known. It is now a most valuable asset.

(e) In 1988 16% of its export sales went to the United Kingdom and 38.1% to the rest of the EEC. Thus the EEC accounts for nearly 50% of its exports. South America (with 19.9%) and North America (with 12.5%) are its next most important markets.

(f) Whilst Bord Bainne has been described as a 'central marketing organisation' developments over recent years would suggest that (as its managing director pointed out in evidence) it might now be more accurate to refer to it as a co-operative marketing organisation. In 1979 it handled approximately 75% (in value terms) of all dairy exports but by 1988 (for a variety of reasons which it is unnecessary here to detail) this figure had declined to 60% and in 1989 to about 49%. There are now a considerable number of companies and, in addition, a number of Bord Bainne's own members, who are engaged in the export of Irish dairy products in competition with Bord Bainne on foreign markets.

(g) Bord Bainne, having no manufacturing capability, depends entirely on its sales from its members in order to fulfil the contracts which it enters into abroad. Early in its existence the board had established a common form of contract which it requested (with mixed success) its members to execute on a five yearly basis. This common form of contract recited the then existing rule 34 (which required members to enter into contracts with the board in respect of their dairy products destined for sale outside the State) and went on:

> Fundamental to this agreement is the recognition by the board of its desire
> (1) to provide for a good return to the member for the products manufactured and supplied by the member to the board
> (2) to encourage the usage of milk in the products most profitable to the board and its members
> (3) to guarantee continuity in the supply of the products to customers of the board
> (4) to have full and regular consultation on the marketing of dairy products as the member may reasonably require.

This system of contracting on a five yearly basis has now been discontinued and I draw attention to its existence for the purpose of contrasting the old regime with the regime which presently exists under the new 1988 rules.

There is another aspect of the arrangements which the board entered into with its members which needs to be noted. The board enters into purchase agreements with its members under which title to the product passed to the board on production of an appropriate certification from the Department of Agriculture. The goods are then invoiced to the board although the product remains in the member's warehouse thereafter, and are only dispatched on receipt of shipping instructions from the board. Payment is made by the board on production of the invoices and the board then arranges the export of the dairy produce it has purchased from its members. These facts are to be borne in mind when the issues of Community law fall for consideration. A legal relationship of vendor and purchaser and not that of forwarding agent and shipper arises between the board and its members, and it is not an organisation advising and helping exporters sell their products abroad; (it is not the Coras Trachtala of the dairy industry). The board buys its members' products — it does not supply a service to its members. Thus, the board is in the market of buying and selling dairy produce and not in the market of supplying specialist services for exporters. 8.1.1

I come now to certain other aspects of the board's role as a central marketing organisation which require to be noted.

The board not only imposed the capital levy to which reference has already been made but in addition it established a market development fund in 1985 which was financed by another levy on its members. This fund had raised £10 million by the end of 1988 and this was used to help increase the performance and penetration of dairy products in a number of selected markets abroad. 75% of the fund was spent on market development and the balance on research for the development of market study.

In the course of the case certain advantages which it was said the board enjoyed over competitors or prospective competitors who might wish to purchase dairy products on the Irish market and export them to EEC markets were stressed.

(a) Reference was made to Bord Bainne's 'Kerrygold' trademark to which I have already referred. This has been widely used on a variety of dairy products and I am sure that its success enures considerably to the board's benefit. The evidence clearly establishes that the cost of establishing a mark of similar worth and commercial advantage would now be very considerable and well outside the financial capabilities of most if not all of its competitors in this country.

(b) Bord Bainne has built up a very considerable network of employees abroad to assist it market Irish dairy products. None of its members or its Irish competitors has a comparable organisation.

(c) As I have already pointed out the Minister for Agriculture may guarantee the repayment of money borrowed by the board. None of its competitors has a similar facility. The evidence, however, establishes, that for the last five years approximately the board has not utilised this facility and that it now no longer exists.

Bord Bainne has continued to expand in recent years, as will be seen in the following table taken from the board's latest annual report and accounts.

	1988 IR£'000	1987 IR£'000	1986 IR£'000	1985 IR£'000	1984 IR£'000
(Historical values)					
Turnover	892,873	732,824	725,822	822,842	808,611
Net current assets	79,712	48,636	43,436	38,873	35,779
Operating surplus	8,813	8,597	5,581	3,916	2,427
Net worth	88,847	71,815	61,369	56,228	46,631

These figures are taken from the consolidated accounts of the board and its subsidiaries. The growth in turnover speaks for itself. But there is one figure in the table which has figured prominently in the case and to which I should draw particular attention. The concept of a company's 'net worth', as referring to the excess of its assets over its outside liabilities is an accounting one in everyday use. It will be noted that the 'net worth' of the Bord Bainne group is stated to be £88.8m in 1988. Kerry Co-op and Avonmore Co-op claim that by trading over the years with the board they have contributed to the growth of the board's net worth both by assisting it in its profitable trading activities and by agreeing, along with other members, to the retention of profits in reserves (revenue reserves in 1988 stood at £65.6m). The question of the proprietorial interest (if any) Kerry Co-op and Avonmore Co-op now are entitled to in the board's net worth was much discussed throughout the case and it is one to which I will return in Part V. For the moment I need only draw attention to the fact that the figure for the board's net worth shown in this table as standing at £71.8m in 1987 is one which appears in the plaintiffs' statement of claim.

Because the acquisition of foreign subsidiaries by the board formed part of counsel's submissions at the hearing I should record, in brief summary, what has occurred. In 1972 the

8.1.1 board acquired a controlling interest in, later acquiring full ownership of, an English-based company called Adams Butter which later changed its name to Adams Foods. The object of this acquisition was to 'provide the most cost effective route for Irish dairy products in the UK and to provide adequate returns from UK-based business'. Later Adams Foods acquired two biscuit companies, a company called Lloyds Dairies (which was constituted into a drinks division) and it started cheese manufacture and acquired a cheese manufacturing company. Adams Foods also acquired a controlling interest in a distribution company in Northern Ireland called Cregagh Foods.

In 1985 the board decided to reduce its non-dairy investments in Adams Foods to facilitate new investment in Europe and the United States. It sold off the biscuit division and acquired a 30% interest in a Belgian distribution company called Yoko Fresh Foods and launched 'Kerrygold' dairy products through it. Later that year it acquired another Belgian company engaged in the manufacture of butteroil and ghee from butter. In 1988 its Belgian subsidiaries were integrated into a company called IDB (Benelux) SA and in 1989 two further Belgian distribution companies were purchased. The combined sales of the board's subsidiaries in Belgium are in excess of IR£100m and make the board the largest food distribution company in the Benelux countries.

Having acquired foreign distribution subsidiaries in the United Kingdom and mainland Europe the board early this year announced the acquisition of an 80% share in a large food distributor in the United States of America called 'Distribution Plus' . The final price for acquisition has not yet been worked out but it will be between 56m and 70m US dollars. It is anticipated that within five years 10% of the total sales of this company will be Irish dairy products, its total sales now being about 350m US dollars per annum. In view of the criticisms that were made of this purchase I should record my finding that I am quite satisfied on the evidence that the decision taken by the directors to acquire this subsidiary was, like earlier decisions in relation to other subsidiaries, taken in order to develop the retail sales of Irish dairy products on the US market, and for the sole purpose of furthering the interests of the dairy farmers of this country. Its acquisition, in my view, in no way derogates from its status as a farmers' association for the purpose of Community law.

Finally, there are certain features of the board's trading in the EEC to which I must refer. Based on the turnover figures of a league of 25 of the largest marketeers of dairy produce in the world (prepared by an authoritive Dutch source) Bord Bainne is 22nd. In a league of European suppliers of dairy products (prepared by an authoritive French source) Bord Bainne is 13th, again based on turnover figures. But turnover is only one indicator of the size of a firm and its competitive advantage and when competing in the EEC Bord Bainne differs in one particular and critical respect from its principal competitors in that it is purely a marketing organisation and carries on no manufacturing itself. One of its principal competitors in the EEC market is the Danish firm N.D. Foods (formerly 'Dairy Denmark') which controls 80% of the total milk intake in Denmark (which is roughly the same total as the Irish milk intake) but it is an organisation which manufactures as well as markets a full range of dairy products. Competition from Holland came from until recently four large co-operatives. But two have recently merged to form a single organisation with a milk intake much greater than the milk equivalent of the product purchased by Bord Bainne. These three Dutch organisations all manufacture as well as market dairy products. The same applies to Bord Bainne's French competitors, there are several very large co-operatives dominating the market in France, one of whom has a milk intake of 900m gallons. In the United Kingdom the Milk Marketing Board controls the total milk production in the country and is closely linked to 'Dairy Crest' which processes it. What is of importance about Bord Bainne's competitors on European markets therefore, is not just their size but also the fact that (a) they are integrated organisations with a guaranteed supply of products available to them and (b) instead of marketing a large amount of low value products, as Bord Bainne does, they have a better mix of more profitable products available to sell.

Bord Bainne also adduced evidence to show that the market in dairy produce in Europe is very much a seller's market, dominated by a few very large chains of supermarkets. In several of the countries of the EEC the top four or five of the biggest supermarket chains account for 60% or more of the total grocery sales. These are in a position to make many demands on their suppliers both as to the quality and quantity of goods supplied, and in relation to the sale of branded goods to require that the supplier promote them by appropriate advertising. To compete effectively in such a market producers are required to have very large resources, particularly for the sale of branded products. 8.1.1

In addition to the special features of the EEC markets to which I have referred evidence was given to show how important a guaranteed supply of products was to the board in competing in Latin American markets. This evidence is relevant, the board says, to the issue of the reasonableness of the present contract between the board and its members effected by the new rules. It was established that contractual supply commitments to the governments and governmental agencies of the states of Latin America entered into by Bord Bainne were supported by very stringent penalty clauses and that a failure to meet these obligations could have most serious financial consequences for the board. The board needs, it was claimed, a regular supply of product to enable it to contract successfuly in these markets.

PART II

The plaintiffs

(a) *The High Court 1989 No. 4083P*
The origins of the first-named plaintiffs in these proceedings, Kerry Co-op, can be traced to the establishment in 1972 of a company registered under the Companies Act 1963 called North Kerry Productions Ltd. At that time there were no milk processing plants in the North Kerry area and skimmed milk was returned to the farmers by the creameries to whom milk had been supplied. To provide a production outlet for this skimmed milk the new company was formed. Nine independent creameries had federated into a company called North Kerry Co-operative Creameries and it together with the Dairy Disposal Board and an American company called Erie Casein Ltd established North Kerry Productions Ltd to manufacture casein (which is the protein extracted from skimmed milk) for export to the American market. In 1973 Kerry Co-op was established as a co-operative society and registered under the 1893 Act. The new society acquired the assets of the Dairy Disposal Board (including its shares in North Kerry Productions Ltd) and of five of independent creameries (including their shares in that company) and thus obtained a holding of 60% in the company which it still retains. The acquisition of these assets was *inter alia* financed by the issue of £1.1m shares in Kerry Co-op. Approximately 6,000 persons became shareholders in the Co-op, of whom about 5,000 were dairy farmers (a figure which has now been reduced to approximately 3,000).

The expansion of Kerry Co-op has been quite extraordinary and dramatic. Its turnover increased from £21m in 1974 to £180m in 1984, to £397m in 1988. It expanded into meat products and the production of agricultural inputs and of the total turnover of £397m in 1988, £166m was attributable to dairy products, £128m to meat products, £39m to agricultural inputs, £44m to sales of liquid milk on the home market and £20m to the sale of an American company it acquired in that year. It acquired over the years a number of companies both in this country and abroad. In 1988 its largest foreign acquisition occurred when it purchased (for US$130m) the shares in Beatreme Food Ingredients. In 1988 its pre-tax profits, at £12.3m, had increased by 52% on its previous year's profits. In 1987 the Kerry Co-op Group employed 1,903 persons in this country and abroad.

In 1986 to facilitate the introduction of outside shareholders and to get a stock market listing a new company called Kerry Group plc was established. It acquired the undertaking, property and assets of Kerry Co-op (but not its shareholding in Bord Bainne) in exchange for shares in

8.1.1 the new company. As a result Kerry Co-op now describes itself as an investment holding company. There were private placings as well as public placings of the shares in the new plc. In the event Kerry Co-op now has 90m shares in the new company whilst other shareholders own 60m.

I have heard a considerable amount of evidence both about the history of the development of Kerry Co-op and of its relations over the years with Bord Bainne (which at times have been quite turbulent). I have been told of the disagreements between Kerry Co-op and Bord Bainne in recent years about the manufacture and marketing of low fat butter. But I need not detail these matters or adjudicate on the rights and wrongs of the disputes which have been related because it is not necessary to do so to determine the legal issues which are now for decision. However, certain of the statistical evidence relating to Kerry Co-op's trading with the board should be noted. In the early years of the board's history a significant percentage of the total purchases made by the board from its members were made from Kerry Co-op: 11.1% in 1975, 7.9% in 1976, 8.3% in 1977, 7.4% in 1978, 4.9% in 1979, 6.5% in 1980, 5.7% in 1981 and 7.1% in 1982. The total value of the sales made by Kerry Co-op to the board increased from £16.1m in 1975 to £47.5m in 1986. But thereafter there was a sudden drop, to £30.7m in 1987 and to a mere £6.0m (or 1.1% of total purchases made by the board) in 1988. This came about because of developments in the product range Kerry Co-op manufactured, its growing financial and commercial strength, the development of overseas contacts and the conclusion it reached that exporting directly rather than through the board could be more profitable. In 1983 nearly 50% of the value of the dairy products it exported were exported through Bord Bainne; in 1988 only 5% of its total exports (of £130,682,000) were so exported.

I should also make a brief reference to some of the rules of Kerry Co-op. Co-operative creameries, of course, depend for their successful management on a regular supply of milk and in line with other co-operatives, Kerry Co-op has a rule (rule 74) which imposes an obligation on every member who keeps or grazes cows in a defined area to sell to Kerry Co-op all the milk produced unless the farmer requires it for domestic consumption or for the use of livestock on his farm. But a member by serving a six months notice is entitled to free himself of this obligation. The power of Bord Bainne to expel its members is the subject of one of the issues in this case. It is relevant to note that rule 6 of Kerry Co-op's rules allows it to expel a member found guilty of conduct detrimental to the society. The evidence establishes that in recent years this power has been invoked in respect of 40 members who, in the course of one of the periodic milk wars that break out between neighbouring co-operatives, supplied their milk to a rival co-operative and were thus found guilty of conduct detrimental to Kerry Co-op. The rights of members of Bord Bainne on expulsion is also an issue in the case and it is, accordingly, relevant to note how this subject is dealt with in the rules of Kerry Co-op. The plaintiffs complain that on cancellation of membership the expelled member of Bord Bainne is entitled to be repaid the amount paid for his shares and no more. But rule 8 of Kerry Co-op's rules makes a similar provision and the expelled members of Kerry Co-op to whom I have referred were returned the capital they had subscribed, but no more.

The second-named plaintiff in the proceedings I am now considering is a dairy farmer and a director of and shareholder in Kerry Co-op and also a director of Kerry Foods plc. He claims that the new rules infringe his constitutionally guaranteed rights and he has been joined as a plaintiff to advance this claim. The plaintiff's legal advisers were of course aware it was open to the defendants to submit not only that no breach of constitutional rights were involved in the adoption of the new rules but that this part of Kerry Co-op's claim must fail because the Constitution did not guarantee the constitutional right in issue to bodies corporate. This latter defence would not be open should it be established that an individual shareholder of Kerry Co-op had suffered damage as a result of a breach of a right guaranteed to individuals by the Constitution — hence the need to join the second-named plaintiff in this action.

(b) *The High Court 1989 No. 4101P* 8.1.1

Avonmore Co-op, the first named plaintiff herein is a co-operative society registered under the provisions of the 1893 Act. Its history began in 1967 with a federation of 36 co-operative societies in County Kilkenny and neighbouring counties. This federated group shortly afterwards entered into a partnership arrangement, through a jointly owned subsidiary, with Unigate (a large English manufacturer and distributor of dairy products) and through this company established a milk processing plant at Ballyragget to manufacture butter and skim milk powder. This gave Avonmore Co-op access to the English markets for its dairy products (which were then subject to a rigid quota system), which were, however, marketed in England under Unigate's brand names. This arrangement was made with the permission of Bord Bainne and it affords an example of the type of exempted export of Irish dairy products which existed under the old statutory board prior to 1973. Later Avonmore Co-op purchased Unigate's interest in the joint company and Ballyragget is now operated by a wholly owned subsidiary in the Avonmore group of companies and is the largest dairy processing plant in the country. In 1973 a further merger of 20 co-operative societies occurred, 230,622 shares in Avonmore Co-op being then issued to the amalgamating societies. Avonmore Co-op now has about 13,000 shareholders of whom 4,000 are milk suppliers and 3 are co-operatives which directly supply milk to Avonmore Co-op for processing.

Like Kerry Co-op, Avonmore Co-op has grown spectacularly over the years and has remained one of the big six dairy co-operatives in the country. Milk intake between 1973 and 1983 doubled. It engages in grain production as well as manufacturing dairy products and its grain intake increased from 20,000 tonnes in 1973 to 150,000 in 1980. It also engages in the manufacture of pig meat. In 1988 it slaughtered 640,000 animals accounting for 37% of the total pig kill in the country. Its total workforce is 2,223 in this country, and in subsidiaries in the United States and the United Kingdom it has a further 193 employees. Its total annual milk intake is now 139m gallons and in 1988 its group accounts showed a turnover of £295.4m with a pre-tax profit of £9.5m.

In 1988 for a variety of reasons which it is unnecessary to detail it decided to establish a public liability company called Avonmore Foods plc (the second named plaintiff in the action). Avonmore Co-op transferred substantially all its undertaking property and assets to Avonmore Foods plc in exchange for cash and an allotment of 'B' shares in the plc. As a result Avonmore Co-op now owns 72% of the issued share capital of the plc and only retains ownership of a building, Avonmore House, which is the headquarters of the group of companies, a small parcel of land and a small staff. Like Kerry Co-op it is an investment corporation. In transferring all its assets to the Avonmore Foods plc it also agreed to transfer its shares in Bord Bainne. This explains why it was considered desirable to join Avonmore Foods plc as a plaintiff in these proceedings. But the transfer has never been registered and Avonmore Co-op is still a shareholder in Bord Bainne. As it has not been argued that Avonmore Co-op has no *locus standi* in these proceedings I can ignore the consequences of this agreement for the purposes of considering the legal issues in the case and treat Avonmore Co-op rather than the public limited company as enjoying the rights attached to its shareholding in Bord Bainne.

A number of incidents arising out of Avonmore Co-op's trading with Bord Bainne were dealt with in the course of the evidence, as were aspects of its trading and commercial experience outside the board, which I do not think is necessary here to discuss in detail except as follows. Avonmore Co-op has been a major supplier of Bord Bainne and has been scrupulous in complying with the board's trading rules over the years. Purchases from Avonmore Co-op by Bord Bainne were £9.4m in 1974. They increased to £79.5m in 1984. In 1987 they declined to £51.8m, and further declined to £33.3m in 1988. In the early 1980's sales by Avonmore amounted to approximately 12% of all sales by its members to Bord Bainne. The decline in sales since 1984 arose partly because Avonmore began to export directly its casein production instead of selling it to the board. In 1988, sales to the board of butter whey and skimmed milk powder also declined arising from decisions to export some of these products directly. This

8.1.1 followed deliberate commercial decisions taken in 1984. To assist in the new strategy Avonmore has acquired foreign companies. In 1989 it acquired Roys Dairy Inc. in the United States and two companies in the United Kingdom, Golden Dairy Co. Ltd and Glen Mills Dairy Ltd to enable it to export directly rather than through the board.

I must also refer to a takeover battle waged in 1989 between Avonmore Co-op, Avonmore Foods plc and Food Industries plc for the acquisition of Westmeath Co-operative Agricultural and Dairy Society Ltd. Avonmore Co-op and Avonmore Foods plc made an offer to the shareholders in Westmeath Co-op which included the following terms: an offer of £73 cash for each share; an offer to each shareholder who was not a milk supplier of the right to use part of the cash offer to acquire shares in Avonmore Co-op at their nominal value of £1 each (subject to a stated maximum). They offered to the milk suppliers of Westmeath Co-op a right to subscribe for shares in Avonmore Co-op by a contribution paid on the price of milk they would supply in the future. This offer involved the possible acquisition of 328,750 shares by new shareholders in Avonmore Co-op with a total estimated value of £3.62m. The relevance of the willingness of Avonmore Co-op to admit a considerable number of new members and allot them additional shares in its capital will be considered later when I examine the criticisms it has made of Bord Bainne's new rule which permits it to issue new bonus ordinary shares.

Three of the Avommore Co-op's rules are also relevant. Rule 6 (in its original and amended form) empowers the suspension of a member and a cancellation of his shares. On cancellation the member has no right to any payment from the Co-op other than the amount paid up on his shares. Rule 86 refers to the obligation of members who operate a premises of any kind receiving milk. Such members are contractually bound to sell all milk received (subject to certain limited exceptions) to Avonmore Co-op. A power to issue bonus shares is given by rule 84 and a very wide discretion as to the class of shareholders to whom the shares are to be allotted is conferred.

The third named plaintiff in these proceedings is Mr John Duggan the chairman of both Avonmore Co-op and Avonmore Foods plc and a shareholder in both. He claims that the new rules of Bord Bainne infringe the personal property rights conferred on him by the Constitution. He has been joined for the same reasons which prompted the joining of Mr O'Connell in the other proceedings to which I have referred.

In 1972 none of the dairy co-operatives in the country was capable of exporting profitably all their dairy products manufactured for sale outside Ireland and all, including Kerry Co-op and Avonmore Co-op, gladly availed of the marketing arrangements established by Bord Bainne. What has emerged from the evidence is that Kerry Co-op no longer needs the services of the central market organisation it had helped to establish and expand and that it has now developed an export capability of its own as a result of which it has virtually ceased to trade with Bord Bainne. In the case of Avonmore Co-op similar developments have occurred but not quite to the same extent. Avonmore Co-op has developed an export capability and has considerably reduced its sales to the board. But it still intends to utilise the board for the purpose of marketing some of its products, but to a much lesser extent than heretofore. These developments explain their main objection to the new rules for if bonus shares are to be allotted rateably on the basis of a member's trade with the board (as is proposed in new rule 9(d)) then Kerry Co-op will receive none, unless it changes radically its current trading policies, and Avonmore Co-op will only receive a small percentage of the total issued if it maintains its present trading patterns.

These developments should be contrasted with those of another of the big six co-operatives, Ballyclough Co-operative Creameries Ltd. Founded in 1908 it now has an annual turnover of over £190m with 4,600 shareholders of which 3,400 are milk suppliers. Over the years it has supplied between 9 and 10% of Bord Bainne's total purchases from one of the biggest milk intakes in the country, of over 100m gallons per annum. It produces a wide range of dairy products, including whole milk powder (of which it is the largest manufacturer in the country), butter, butteroil, low fat butter, dairy spreads, milk powders, cheese, liquid milk, skim milk;

40% of its total sales go to Bord Bainne and virtually all of its products destined for export are exported through Bord Bainne. Although of comparable financial strength to the plaintiff companies and societies it finds it profitable to continue to use Bord Bainne as its export arm rather than developing one of its own. 8.1.1

PART III

The Industrial and Provident Societies Act 1893
Bord Bainne (like Kerry Co-op and Avonmore Co-op) is registered as an 'industrial and provident society' under the provisions of the 1893 Act. The name 'industrial and provident society' was a name originally applied in the nineteenth century to those societies whose purpose was to make profits by the personal exertion of their members and to distribute them by way of provident provision for their members' future. Originally such societies were regarded as friendly societies and regulated by the statutes dealing with such societies but in 1852 special legislation was enacted to permit the registration of industrial and provident societies and to regulate their affairs, corporate status being granted to them in 1862. The 1852 and 1862 Acts were amended by further legislation until finally the consolidating Act of 1893 provided a unified code. Co-operative societies established for different purposes were a feature of nineteenth century social life in this country and in Great Britain and all such societies were registered under the Industrial and Provident Societies Acts. For the purposes of these proceedings only some of the provisions of the 1893 Act are relevant and to these I will now briefly refer:

— Registration of a society under the 1893 Act confers corporate status on the society (section 21);

— Registration of a society vests in it all property for the time being vested in any person in trust for it (section 21);

— Registration of a society limits the liability of its members to pay in event of the society being wound-up only the amount due on issued shares (section 21);

— The rules of a registered society bind the society and all its members to the same extent as if each member had subscribed his name and affixed his seal thereto and there was contained in such rules a covenant on the part of such member to conform thereto, subject to the provisions of the Act (section 22).

I draw particular attention to these features of the Act to show that a society registered under the 1893 Act bears certain important similarities to a company registered under the 1963 Act. Both have corporate status; both are legal entities distinct from their members; the liability of the members of both for the debts of the corporate entity of which they are members is limited; membership of both constitutes a contract between the member and the corporate entity which, in the case of a registered society, is to be found in its rules and, in the case of a registered company, is to be found in its memorandum and articles of association (section 25 of the Companies Act 1963). But the dissimilarities are also of importance. The affairs of registered companies are regulated in much greater detail by statute than are the affairs of registered societies, the members of a registered society being virtually free to manage their own affairs. In particular the 1893 Act contains no provisions regulating in any way the manner in which a society may increase or decrease its capital.

The following provisions are also to be noted:

(a) Originally it was provided by the 1893 Act that no member of a registered society could have any interest in the shares of a registered society exceeding £200, a figure later increased to £20,000. But this restriction on the amount which an individual could invest in a registered society did not apply if the member was itself a registered society.

(b) The rules of a registered society are required to contain provisions in respect of the several matters mentioned in the Second Schedule to the Act (section 10(1)). The wording of this section is of importance; the Act did not specify what the rules are to contain, it merely

8.1.1 sets out in the Second Schedule twelve matters for which provisions *must be made* in the rules of every society. The rules of Bord Bainne make provision in respect of all the matters specified.

(c) In addition to the matters specified in the Second Schedule the rules must make provision for profits being appropriated to any purpose stated therein or determined in such manner as the rules direct (section 10(6)). Thus the Act does not regulate how profits are to be appropriated — it merely requires that provision for appropriation be made in the rules. The rules of Bord Bainne have complied with this subsection.

(d) A registered society may be dissolved by a winding-up order made under the Companies Acts or by an instrument of dissolution signed by three-fourths of its members (section 58). The instrument of dissolution must make provision for the division of the funds and property of the society (section 61). A registered society is empowered to convert itself into a company or to amalgamate with or transfer its engagements to a company (section 54).

(e) The rules must make provision as to whether shares are transferable (Second Schedule, para. 7). Bord Bainne's rules like the rules of Kerry Co-op and Avonmore Co-op provide that shares can only be transferred with the consent of the board of directors. The rules must also make provision as to whether a member can withdraw from the society (Second Schedule, para. 9). Bord Bainne's rules provide that a member cannot withraw from the society.

(f) A society may amend its rules. But an amendment is not to be valid until it has been registered under the Act for which purpose two copies must be sent to the Registrar of Friendly Societies, who is now the Registrar for the purposes of the Act (section 10(2)).

(g) The duties of the Registrar are described as follows:

> The Registrar shall, on being satisfied that any amendment of a rule is not contrary to the provisions of this Act, issue to the society an acknowledgment of registry of the same, which shall be conclusive evidence that the same is duly registered (section 10(3)).

The extent and nature of the statutory duty thus imposed is of particular relevance when considering the plaintiffs' claim against the Registrar and I will refer to it in section 5 of Part V.

Finally, I should record that it is accepted that the amendment effected by the members of Bord Bainne at their meeting of 15 November 1988 was adopted in accordance with the board's existing rules.

PART IV

I come now to a consideration of the rules whose validity is challenged in these proceedings. Bord Bainne was registered on 14 September 1972 with a set of rules which very shortly afterwards, in 1975, were considerably amended. Because the plaintiffs, along with most of its current members, joined the society when the 1972 rules applied I must refer firstly to them as the plaintiffs contend that they are relevant to their claim that the new rules are *ultra vires*. Having done so, I will then consider the 1975 rules which, as amended in 1978 and 1979, were the rules in force immediately prior to the adoption of the new rules in November 1988. I will then examine the steps Bord Bainne took to amend the rules and then turn to the new rules themselves. Of course only seven of the new rules are challenged in the amended statement of claim (those dealing with the obligations of new members, the power to terminate membership, the power to expel members, the power to issue bonus shares, and certain of the provisions relating to voting rights and membership of the board of directors) but to resolve the issues in the case it is necessary to refer in addition, but briefly, to some others.

(1) *The 1972 rules*: 8.1.

(a) *Objects* (rule 4)
The objects of the society were declared, *inter alia*, to be the improvement and development of the marketing of milk and milk products, to promote and encourage the development of the marketing of milk and milk products to perform such functions in regard to the central marketing of Irish dairy products as were previously performed by An Bord Bainne under the 1961 Act as would be consistent with the other objects of the society. They clearly show that it was intended that the society would be a co-operative whose object was to help Irish dairy farmers by the establishment of a central marketing organisation for the export of dairy products.

(b) *Membership* (rule 5)
Those who had signed the original application for registration of Bord Bainne under the 1893 Act were referred to in the 1972 rules as the *special members*. Rule 5 provided that the society was to consist of *special members* and of such societies registered under the 1893 Act, and companies as were registered proprietors of creameries and cream separating stations, as the special members and subsequently the board of directors should admit to membership. But the rule contained an important qualification on the power to admit members to the society. Only those societies or companies who were 'prepared to market through the society or by agreement with the society all their dairy products destined for sale outside the State' could become members. Thus the combined effect of this rule and of the operation of the 1893 Act was to impose a contractual obligation on all new members of the Society to sell to the society their produce manufactured for export unless otherwise agreed to by the society.

(c) *Expulsion* (rule 6)
A member 'if found guilty of conduct detrimental to the society' could be expelled provided certain procedures were carried out. An expelled member was entitled to be repaid all sums paid on shares held by it in the society but no more. Readmission was only possible by a two-thirds majority vote of members at a general meeting (rule 7). 'Conduct detrimental to the interests of the society' is a phrase which would embrace a wide range of acts and omissions. As obviously the obligation to trade with the society in the manner required by rule 5 was an important obligation it seems to me that a member who failed to fulfil this obligation could have been expelled under rule 6.

(d) *Capital* (rule 9 to 13)
The capital of the society was to consist of ordinary shares of £1 each. Dividends could be paid on ordinary shares as determined by the society in general meeting. Shares could only be transferred on consent of the board of directors and were not withdrawable. The consideration for a transfer of a share could not exceed the amount paid up on the share.

(e) *Voting rights* (rule 30)
Members at general meeting of the society were entitled to a number of votes based on their annual valuation of milk and milk products. This rule should be understood in the context of the obligations of members under rule 6. It was to be anticipated that if members fulfilled their rule 6 obligations then those members with the largest milk intake were likely to be the major users of the board. Thus from the very start of its operations voting strength was linked to trade with the board.

(f) *Board of directors* (rule 32)
The board of directors was to consist of a maximum of 15 persons elected or appointed as

8.1.1 follows: (a) Six members with the highest annual valuation of milk and milk products as determined by the board of directors should each appoint one director, (b) the Dairy Disposal Board (should it become a member) was to appoint one director, (c) all other members were to elect six directors, the country for this purpose being divided into two regions, (d) the board of directors was empowered to co-opt two extra directors.

(g) *Amendment of rules* (rule 57)
The rules could be amended by a majority of two-thirds of the members present and voting at a special general meeting provided the written consent of the Irish Agricultural Organisation Society Ltd to the proposed amendments had been obtained. The approval of the IAOS to rule changes is a clear indication that the society regarded itself as an association of dairy co-operatives.

(h) *Allocation of surplus funds, the payment of bonuses, and the issue of bonus shares* (rules 61 and 63)
The net profit of the society, after payment of interest on loan capital, could be allocated in such amount as the members in general meeting on the recommendation of the board of directors should decide to a reserve fund. It could also be allocated in payment of a dividend on the ordinary shares, or in the payment of a bonus to members 'in proportion to their sales to the society at a rate which shall be determined by the board (*ie* the board of directors) and calculated on the amount of their sales to the society during the period to which the bonus relates'. It is important to note that from the very inception of the board it was envisaged that trading profits could be used to remunerate members who traded with the board (by paying them cash bonuses based on their level of trade) rather than employing them to remunerate capital (by paying dividends on members' subscriptions). In practice this is what occurred — no dividends have ever been paid on capital subscribed and members who traded have been rewarded with bonuses based on the level of trade.

In addition to the payment of *bonuses* calculated by reference to member's sales a power to issue *bonus shares* was conferred on the members in general meeting. Rule 63 declared that it would be lawful for the society in general meeting to apply the amount standing to the credit of the reserve funds to the allocation of additional fully paid up bonus shares in the society 'upon such terms and subject to such conditions as the society may think proper'. A complete discretion was given as to the allocation of these fully paid shares.

(2) *The 1975 rules* (as amended)
In 1975 the members adopted a new set of rules. These were the society's rules (having subsequently been twice amended) which existed prior to adoption by the members of the new rules in November 1988. A number of changes were made in the 1972 rules as detailed hereunder. I have assumed, in the absence of any evidence to the contrary, that they were agreed to by both Kerry Co-op and Avonmore Co-op.

(a) *Objects* (rule 4)
These were the same as under the 1972 rules.

(b) *Membership* (rule 5)
This new rule provided that the society was to consist of (a) present members, (b) co-operatives which were subsidiaries of existing members, (c) the proprietors of registered creameries or cream separating stations which had paid a levy to the statutory board, An Bord Bainne, under the 1961 Act and who 'agree to market through the society, or by agreement in writing with the society, all its dairy products destined for sale outside the State'. Other manufacturers of dairy products and co-operatives not eligible under other rules engaged in a business which

was sufficient to justify membership and which also agreed to market through the society, or by agreement in writing with the society, all its dairy products destined for sale outside the State were also eligible for membership. Thus the obligation to trade with Bord Bainne as established in the 1972 rules was maintained and strengthened in the 1975 rules. **8.1.1**

(c) *Expulsion* (rule 6)
Somewhat wider disciplinary powers were conferred by this rule. The board of directors was empowered to reprimand, suspend or expel any member who offended against the rules of the society or who was guilty of conduct detrimental to the society or whose conduct renders the member unfit for membership. A right of appeal to the society in general meeting against a decision of the board was given. An expelled member was entitled to a return of all sums paid up on shares held by it but no more. Expelled members could only be readmitted by a two-thirds majority of members at a general meeting (rule 7). A failure to enter an agreement to trade as required by the rules or to fulfil one which had been made would have, in my view, justifed expulsion under this rule.

(d) *Capital*
The 1975 rules effected a considerable alteration in the capital structure of the society. It provided that the capital of the society was to consist of:

> 'A' Shares of £1 each allotted to members referred to in rule 5(c)(i), that is to proprietors of registered creameries or cream separating stations which had paid a levy under the 1961 Act and who had agreed to market through the society their export products, as therein provided.
>
> 'B' Shares of £1 each allotted to members referred to in rule 5(c)(ii), that is to manufacture dairy products not eligible under 5(c)(i) who had agreed to market through the society their export products as therein provided.
>
> 'C' Shares of £1 each allotted to members referred to in rule 5(c)(iii) that is other co-operatives or companies admitted to membership by the directors who had agreed to market through the society their export products as therein provided.
>
> 'D' Shares of £1 each allotted to members referred to at rule 5(b), that is subsidiaries of members.

The 'A' and the 'B' shares were to rank *pari passu* save that the holders of the 'B' shares were to make a contribution to cover the use of the 'specified assets' of the society referred to in section 4 of the 1961 Act (that is the assets transferred from the old statutory board to the society). In the event of the society being wound up only the holders of the 'A' and 'B' shares were to be entitled to participate in any distribution of assets. Neither however was to be entitled to participate in the 'specified assets' (which, it will be recalled, could only be disposed of by the consent of the Minister for Agriculture). The holders of the 'C' shares had no right to attend or vote at meetings of the society unless expressly authorised by the board of directors. The holders of 'D' shares had no right to attend or vote at meetings of the society.

It is important to bear in mind that from 1975 only the holders of the 'A' shares (a group comprising all the dairy co-operatives in the country) and the holders of 'B' shares (a small group comprising companies manufacturing dairy products) could participate in a surplus in a winding-up. That is the situation under the new rules.

In addition, the 1975 rules made provision for the allotment of deferred shares. Rule 21 empowered the directors to create a capital reserve fund from levies imposed on members

8.1.1 holding the 'A' ordinary shares based on their milk intake and to allot to each member who has paid the levy such number of deferred shares treated as fully paid as should correspond to the total amount of levy paid. In the event of the society being wound up rule 9 provided that the holders of the deferred shares would be entitled to participate with the holders of the 'A' and 'B' ordinary shares in the distribution of the assets (other than the 'specified assets') but with no right to share in a distribution of any surplus assets. As has been seen, a considerable number of deferred shares were issued and allotted under this rule.

(e) *Voting rights* (rule 35)
Only the holders of the 'A' and 'B' ordinary shares had voting rights conferred on them by the rules. As in the 1972 rules they were entitled to a number of votes according to a determination made by the board of directors based on the quantity of their milk intake.

(f) *Board of directors* (rule 37)
The board was to consist of a maximum of 15 members elected or appointed as follows:

(a) Six members of the society who had paid levies and which had the highest annual gallonage of whole milk intake as determined by the board of directors were each entitled to appoint one director. But there was a pre-condition; each member was required to have agreed to market through the society or by agreement in writing with the society, all its dairy products destined for sale outside the State.
(b) All other levy-paying members other than those referred to above were to elect six directors. For this purpose the country was divided into four regions. The number of votes to which each member was entitled was determined by reference to this milk intake. Again membership of the board was conditional upon the member agreeing to market its export products through the society or by an agreement in writing as referred to at (a) above.
(c) Two members admitted under rule 5(c)(ii), that is, proprietory manufacturers with the highest annual valuation of production of dairy products in excess of £5m sterling and which complied with certain other requirements should each appoint one director. But again, this power of appointment was subject to a requirement that the member should agree to market through the society or by agreement with the society all its dairy products destined for sale outside the State.
(d) A power of co-option in certain specified circumstances was conferred on the board of directors.

Two aspects of these provisions should be noted. Firstly, the power to appoint members of the board was determined by reference to the milk intake of members, as was the number of votes by those members entitled to elect board members. Secondly, all elected or appointed members of the board were to be from members' organisations which had agreed to market their export products through the society unless they had reached a different agreement with the society.

(g) *Specific obligation to contract with the society* (rule 40)
This rule contained a new provision not to be found in the 1972 rules. It provided that every member manufacturing dairy products destined for sale outside the State was required to enter into contracts with the society for the supply and marketing of such dairy products by the society. The supply contracts were to provide for the submission by members of a forecast of its export sales, its annual export statistics and an on-account payment to the member by the society.

(h) *Amendment to rules* (rule 64) 8.1.1

The power to amend the rules was similar to that in the 1972 rules, *i.e.* by a two-thirds majority of members present and voting at a general meeting, provided they had been previously approved by the ICOS.

(i) *Allocation of surplus funds, payment of bonuses, and the issue of bonus shares* (rules 68 and 70)

The 1975 rules relating to the application of net profits were the same as those in the 1972 rules, so that for 15 years prior to the adoption of the 1988 amendments part of the net profits could be paid out in cash bonuses to members in proportion to their sales to the society, and the members in general meeting were empowered to apply the amount in any reserve fund in the allocation of bonus shares 'upon such terms and subject to such conditions as the society may think proper'.

(3) *The adoption of the new rules*

Before turning to the new 1988 rules and the circumstances in which they were adopted it would be as well to recall the legal position that existed after the adoption of the 1981 *trading* rules to which reference has already been made. Every member was contractually bound to supply, and to enter into formal contracts for this purpose, all its export dairy products to the board unless specifically exempted from doing so in writing and no person could be appointed or elected to the board of directors unless the co-operative or company of which he was a member had agreed to trade with the society. These contractual obligations were waived by the board of directors in relation to products other than 'Group I products' (as specified in 1981) and from that time in respect of the products other than Group I products members were free to trade outside the board. It is to be stressed that they remained under a contractual obligation to supply to the board all their Group I products manufactured by them and destined for export.

On 16 September 1987 the directors of Bord Bainne formally entered into discussions about the board's future role in the industry and the need to enact new rules. Their deliberations centered on a discussion paper entitled *Preparing for Change* presented by the board's chief executive. The need for change was outlined in the discussion paper, reference being made to changes in EEC agricultural policies, the effect of the introduction of quotas in 1984 and subsequent restrictions on milk output. Particular stress was laid on a document prepared by the ICOS which had put forward proposals for the restructuring of the dairy industry generally and Bord Bainne's role in it in particular. It was acknowledged that this document required a response from the board, and that it raised 'fairly fundamental problems' associated with the board's present structure. Briefly, the discussion paper supported the ICOS's concept of the need for further amalgamations and mergers amongst co-operatives in the dairy industry. It suggested that Bord Bainne as the national marketing organisation should find ways of facilitating this process and suggested that it should invest £30m in the share capital of those merging groups which were committed to the board in all product areas for export. Amongst its proposals were important changes in the method of electing and appointing the board's directors and eligibility for membership of the board of Directors. Six members would be appointed but not by the six largest co-operatives as determined by their milk intake but by the members representing the six largest suppliers who exclusively supplied butter, butteroil, skim milk powder and whole milk powder to the board. Two should be appointed by members representing the largest exclusive suppliers of all products which it specified. Four regional members representing suppliers who exclusively supply butter, butteroil, skim milk powder and whole milk powder for export and three members representing the IFA, the ICMSA and the ICOS. The concept behind these proposals was that the composition of the board of directors should be changed to give more representation to those who exclusively dealt with Bord Bainne.

8.1.1 For analogous reasons it was also proposed that the voting rights attached to existing shares should be altered and should in the future be determined by the volume exported through the board rather than on the milk intake of each member.

The directors meeting was followed by a round of discussions and consultations undertaken between the board's chairman and its executive officers and individual members. These were reported on in an addendum to the discussion paper dated 18 November 1987. It was reported that the main proposals relating to the investment by the board in merging co-operatives had not met with anything like general approval but that no objection had been raised to the concept of representation on the board of directors based on volume of trade with the board and as to the proposals for altering voting rights so as to base them on the volume of products exported through the board. It was stated that 'it was universally agreed that this was the correct approach'. After further discussions at board level it was agreed that consultation should take place with representatives of farm bodies. In a memorandum to the board of 16 December the managing director reported on what had been said to him, recording that the view that the change in voting arrangements was felt to be realistic 'giving as it does the voting power to those who are doing most trading with the board.'

A consensus at board level as to the best way forward was difficult to achieve and so further options were put before the directors by the managing director in a second discussion paper dated 16 March 1989 and entitled *Making Some Change*. It referred to the inability or the unwillingness of members to make any decision in relation to the earlier proposals, to the urgent need to deal with the problems facing the board, to the recent developments involving the takeover of an existing co-operative by a large private interest, to the fact that the road ahead would be 'dramatically curtailed if the shareholding and voting structure of Bord Bainne forever prevents recommendations from the executive from being implemented'. In summary, a complete reorganisation of the share structure of the society was proposed. Individual co-operatives and companies should cease to be members of the Society and instead, in order to ensure that the register of shareholders should more closely represent the board's suppliers, the existing share capital should be repaid, the board should be capitalised on the basis of the existing deferred shares and for this purpose new shares would be issued to individual farmers who had paid, through a deduction in the price paid for their milk, the capital levy subscribed by the Society's members. Furthermore, the Society should become a public limited company with listings on the London and Dublin exchanges. It is clear that this paper helped powerfully to concentrate the minds of the board of directors. It was discussed at meetings of 19 March and 20 April. At its meeting of 18 May it was decided to establish a rules sub-committee. This sub-committee met regularly and had detailed. discussions. Substantial progress was made and the chairman was able to report to the board at its meeting of 17 July that agreement had been reached on all changes with the exception of the new rule 9 relating to the issue of new bonus shares. A new revision of rule 9 was then circulated and it was pointed out by the managing director that the purpose of the proposal was to give greater acknowledgment to those who actually traded with the board and for board membership to reflect this fact. At this meeting it was formally decided that Bord Bainne should not become a public limited company. The directors met again on 21 September and approved the draft rules prepared by the rules sub-committee and fixed 15 November for the special meeting to adopt them.

Notwithstanding objections raised by the representatives of Kerry Co-op and Avonmore Co-op the rules were adopted at this meeting by the necessary two-thirds majority. Prior to their adoption formal approval from the ICOS as required by rule 64 had been obtained. An order for interim relief temporarily stopped their registration, but this was effected on 29 April 1989 after the Plaintiffs' application for interlocutory injunction to restrain registration was refused.

I can briefly summarise my views on these developments as follows: In adopting the new rules the members decided not to adopt the far-reaching proposal suggested in *Preparing for Change* (the first discussion paper) that Bord Bainne should itself engage in manufacturing dairy products by investing £30m in merging co-operatives. They also rejected the equally far-reaching proposal made in *Making Some Change* (the second discussion paper) to alter the whole existing basis of the society's capital structure and allot shares to levy-paying farmers. Instead they concentrated, in the main, on making significant changes in the relationship between the society and its members. **8.1.1**

In its annual report and accounts for 1988 the board explained the rule changes as follows:

> The proposals for a revision of the board's structure were the basis for a significant revision of the rules and were adopted by a substantial majority at a special meeting of the members on 15 November 1988.
> Broadly speaking the changes comprise:
>
> — Composition of the board of directors
> — Voting entitlements
> — Share structure
>
> The aim is to ensure that the organisation is controlled by and for the members trading with it in proportion to their level of trade. The new rules, which are now registered, were the outcome of considerable discussion by the board and the industry.

The documentary and oral evidence at the trial satisfies me that these statements are a correct summary of what was done. In adopting the new rules the members sought to achieve a number of different associated objectives. It was considered desirable that control of the board of directors should vest in those who traded most extensively with the society and who were not major competitors of the society on overseas markets. It was also considered desirable that decisions by the members in general meeting should be based on voting rights which reflected the level of trade with the society. But no major change of policy was involved. Because the contractual obligation to trade with the board was also reduced, the size of the members' milk intake would no longer reflect the level of trade with the board, the new rules became necessary. Furthermore it was considered proper that the ownership of the 'A' ordinary shares (which conferred voting rights and rights in a winding-up) should reflect the commitment of members to the society and for this reason it was proposed that fully paid up shares should from time to time be allotted out of current profits to members based on their level of trade with the society.

Because of certain matters pleaded, orally submitted and given in evidence I should conclude this part of my judgment by making the following findings of fact. The new rules were adopted by the members in the belief *bona fide* held by those voting for them that it was in the interest of the society and its members that they should be adopted. Their adoption was not aimed at depriving any member of its property rights, or for the purpose (by expelling members and reducing the society's capital) of enhancing the interests of existing members, or for any other ulterior purpose, or to force members to trade with the society, or for the purpose of restricting competition in export markets by members with the board, or to attempt to coerce members to abandon their constitutional rights. Nor were they adopted as a 'ruse' directed against any individual member. The new rules were adopted only after the most detailed discussion and wide consultation. Obviously it would be very difficult to get complete agreement on the proposed changes and a small dissentient minority was to be expected. I am satisfied that those who have brought their dissent to the courts have acted *bona fide* and in the belief that their rights were infringed in doing so, just as those who adopted the new rules acted in the belief that their actions were fully justified and in the interests of their society. These conclusions do not, of course, determine the case in the defendants' favour because, acting as they thought best in the interests of the society and its members as they undoubtedly did, they may unwittingly have adopted invalid rules. Before deciding whether they did so or not I must analyse those provisions of the new rules which the plaintiffs now challenge.

8.1.1 (4) *The new rules*
The new rules, adopted as an amendment to the 1975 rules which they replaced, contain a number of changes which are relevant to the issues in this case and so must be examined in some detail, as well as a number which, although referred to in the course of the proceedings, are not the subject of legal challenge and so need only be briefly touched on.

(a) *The objects* (rule 4)
Some changes were made in the objects clause. Whilst the general objective of improving the marketing of milk and milk products was retained there was added the object of engaging in business 'including manufacturing' which might be conducive to the interests of the society. The power to engage in manufacturing was inserted on legal advice because of certain packaging activity the society carried out and does not constitute any change in the society's functions or its policies. As in its previous rules, the society had as one of its objects the engaging in any business which the society considered conducive to the interests of its members but there was omitted as an objective 'the encouragment of individual initiative' which had been included in the earlier rules. This omission was in my view of no significance and did not indicate any change in policy on the part of the society. The society still maintains as one of its objectives the performance of the functions of a central marketing organisation for Irish dairy products.

(b) *Membership* (rule 5)
A significant change in the rules relating to new applicants for membership is effected in the first two sub-paragraphs of rule 5. They provide:

> The society shall consist of:
> (a) The present members of the society
> (b) Such of the following as apply for and are admitted to membership of the society by the board:
>
> (i) Any society registered under the Acts which has agreed to market dairy products through the society, in accordance with the board's purchasing policy as decided by the board from time to time and notified to the member.
> (ii) Any manufacturer of dairy products licensed under the provisions of s. 13 of the Creamery Act 1928 or any amendment or re-enactment thereof and not eligible for membership under paragraph 5(b)(i) of this rule which has agreed to market dairy products through the society in accordance with the board's purchasing policy as decided by the board from time to time and notified to the member.
> (iii) Any other society, company, body corporate, individual or organisation not eligible for membership under paragraphs b(i) or b(ii) of this rule, but which in the opinion of the board is engaged in a business which is sufficient, in accordance with the objects of the society to justify membership and which by resolution of the board is admitted to membership, and which has agreed where appropriate in the opinion of the board to market dairy products through the society as in (i) above.

This rule will have little practical effect as all the co-operatives in the country are already members of the board. But it reflects the change in the contractual obligations between members and the board which is marked elsewhere in the new rules. It should be construed in the context both of the other rules which had been adopted and of the trading arrangements existing when it was adopted. It has been suggested that this imposes an obligation on new members to market all their dairy produce through the society but when read in context with the other new rules and existing practices I think it becomes clear that it is merely an obligation to market such dairy products as a new member decides to sell to the board in accordance with the board's existing purchasing policies. The new rules relating to the 'A' and 'B' shares have deleted any express obligation on their holders to agree to sell all products destined for export (unless otherwise agreed) to the society, and as I will explain in a moment, impose a limited obligation merely to 'trade' with the society and not one to sell all products manufactured and destined for export. The rule was passed when the members must have fully appreciated the changes effected by the trading policies adopted in 1981 and the effect of the product grouping involved in them. Finally the evidence of the managing director (to which I can have regard when construing the rule) was to the effect that the object of the new rules was to give members almost total freedom to decide whether they wanted to use the board or not, the only requirement being what he termed the 'nominal' one contained in rule 8 to which I will refer in a moment. I am satisfied therefore, that the contractual obligation imposed on new members to supply dairy products to the board is much less onerous than that imposed on members under the 1972 and 1975 rules. **8.1.1**

(c) *Expulsion* (rules 6, 7 and 8)
Rule 6 of the 1975 rules was headed 'Expulsion'. This rule, with one change of some significance, has been reproduced in rule 6 of the new rules under the more anodyne heading of 'Termination of Membership'. The only change in the previous provision is that the repayment of a member's subscription for shares is at the discretion of the board of directors who must satisfy themselves that any repayment would not jeopardise the financial stability of the society. As the most that any member has ever subscribed to the society has been £1,000 it is unlikely that this addition is of any practical significance.

Rule 7, relating to the terms of readmission of a member whose membership has been terminated is the same as rule 7 of the 1975 rules.

A new power of expulsion which has featured prominently in the plaintiffs' arguments is given by rule 8(c) which provides that:

> Where the board is of the opinion that a member who is a manufacturer of dairy products has not traded with the society for a period of two years the board shall cause a notice to be served on such member by registered prepaid letter post at his address on the society's register intimating that the board proposes to consider the removal of the member from the register of the society at a board meeting to be held not less than one month after the posting of the said notice.
> Then at the board meeting referred to in the said notice or at any adjournment thereof it shall be lawful and competent for the board by resolution to that effect passed by a two-thirds majority of members of the board present and voting to remove the name of said member from the register of the society and upon such resolution having been passed the shares or share of such member shall be deemed for all purposes to have been cancelled and annulled and an entry shall be made in the society's register to that effect.

As in the case of termination of membership under rule 6, a member expelled under rule 8 is entitled only to a return on sums prescribed by it for shares but this right is subject to the board likewise being satisfied that repayment will not jeopardise the society's financial stability.

There are three comments to be made on these rules. Firstly, because rule 8(c) allows the board of directors to expel a member who has not traded for two years with the board I think that it must follow that there is to be implied in this rule an obligation on members 'to trade' with the board. I think that the scope of the obligation 'to trade' must be construed as an obligation to supply products to the board on a reasonably regular basis as I think that a member who merely sporadically sells products to the board could not be regarded as 'trading' with it bearing in mind the nature of the board's operations. But it is clear that there is no obligation to sell any given quantity of dairy produce destined for export and no level of trading or

8.1.1 percentage of the product available for export is specified or to be implied. This means that once the member is prepared to sell dairy products to the board on a regular basis, then, even though the quantity involved is small, the obligation is satisfied. Should this obligation not be fulfilled for a two- year period the member may then be expelled. Secondly, the member whose membership is terminated under rule 6 or who is expelled under rule 8 is only entitled to be repaid, at most, what had been paid up on its shares. This is the same as in previous rules and also is the same as the entitlement under the rules in Kerry Co-op and Avonmore Co-op. It is a feature of the rule strongly criticised by the plaintiffs and I will return to it. Thirdly, I do not think that the power to expel under rule 8(c) is any more extensive than had previously existed as under the earlier rules a member who failed to fulfil its trading obligations for two years could, in my view, have also been expelled.

(d) *Capital* (rule 9).
As under the previous rules it is provided that the capital of the company was to consist of 'A', 'B', 'C', 'D' shares as follows:

> 'A' Shares of £1 each which shall be allotted to the members referred to in rule 5(a) and rule 5(b)(i) or issued in accordance with the provisions of rule 9(d)(i) and (ii).
>
> 'B' Shares of £1 each which shall be allotted solely to the members referred to in rule 5(b)(ii).
>
> 'C' Shares of £1 each which shall be allotted solely to the members referred to in rule 5(b)(iii).
>
> 'D' Shares of £1 each which are currently allotted to the holders thereof.

The reference to rule 5 means that the members to whom these shares are allotted are only required to agree to market dairy produce through the society in 'accordance with the board's purchasing policy' so that it is no longer a condition for the allotment of shares that a member should have agreed to supply all its export products to the society, unless exempted from doing so.

The rule goes on to provide that the society's capital should also consist of deferred shares of £1 each allotted to levy-paying members as under the earlier rules and to provide that the 'A', 'B', 'C' and 'D' shares would have the same rights under the new rules as they had under the old ones.

By subsection (d) a new provision relating to the issue of bonus shares was made. It has been the subject of the plaintiffs' principal criticisms in this case and I should quote it in full. It provides as follows:

> (d) (i) Subject to and in accordance with the provisions of this sub-rule, the board shall be entitled in each year to apply net profits of the group otherwise available for payment of dividend (hereinafter called the 'annual bonus fund') in issuing to shareholders additional 'A' shares (hereinafter called 'bonus shares') and convertible loan stock rateably according to the value (as determined by the board) of the sales of products including all and any production aid paid to processors pursuant to the common agricultural policy made by such shareholders to or through the board in the immediately preceding financial year.
>
> (ii) The annual bonus fund shall be such sum as the board shall decide to make available for the purpose out of the net profits of the group after provision for taxation and after providing for such allocations (if any) as may be decided to be made in the ways provided

for under rule 74. **8.1.1**

(iii) The annual bonus fund shall be applied in issuing as fully subscribed bonus shares and units of convertible loan stock in the ratio of one (1) share for each ninety-nine (99) units of stock and the same shall be issued to holders of 'A' and 'B' shares provided that where an allocation of bonus shares would cause the number of 'A' shares held to exceed the maximum permitted to a shareholder by law, that shareholder may renounce any excess shares in favour of any other member of the society entitled to accept the same or, in the alternative, to opt to take convertible loan stock in lieu thereof.

(iv) A member entitled to an allocation of bonus shares and a proportionate allocation of convertible loan stock may elect to be paid in lieu of such allocation a sum equal to the aggregate nominal value of such bonus shares and loan stock provided he has first subscribed in cash for and taken up an equal amount of 'A' shares and convertible loan stock.

(v) Convertible loan stock issued by the board under this rule:

— shall carry no entitlement to any interest thereon unless the board shall so declare when issuing the same;
— shall be convertible into ordinary shares in the event of the society resolving to be converted into a company and according to such conversion ratio as may be resolved by the society upon such conversion.
— shall be redeemed at nominal value in the event of the winding-up of the society *pari passu* with the repayment of capital on deferred shares;
— shall not be transferable save with the consent of the board.

(vi) At any time after the expiry of five (5) years from the date of any issue of a unit of loan stock, the holder thereof may apply to the board to have the same redeemed and the board shall have a discretion as to whether and to what extent the same may be redeemed provided that the board shall be at liberty to pay the redemption value thereof in instalments of 50% in the 1st year and 10% in each of the following five (5) years as the board shall consider appropriate in the interests of the society.

(vii) Convertible loan stock in respect of which an application for redemption has been made shall not thereafter be eligible for conversion into shares pursuant to paragraph v. above but all sums outstanding upon such redemption shall be paid prior to the conversion of the society into a company. In the event of the winding-up of the society such unpaid amount shall rate *pari passu* with the repayment of capital on deferred shares.

The following should be noted about this new rule:

(a) The 'annual bonus fund' which the board may establish is to be established from the net products of 'the group', that is the net profits derived not just from Bord Bainne's operations but also from those of all its subsidiaries. Although the evidence establishes that it is extremely unlikely that the board would apply the net profit of foreign subsidiaries for the purposes contemplated by this rule undoubtedly the power to do so exists.

(b) The rule gives effect to the policy that those who trade with the board should be rewarded for doing so. As I have already pointed out this policy is not new as under the 1972 and 1975 rules the net profits could be allocated in payment of cash bonuses to members in proportion to their sales to the society. What is new, is that trading is to be rewarded by bonus *shares* rather than by a *cash bonus*.

8.1.1 (c) This rule gives effect to the policy that the ownership of the 'A' ordinary shares should reflect the commitment of members to the society as demonstrated by the use it makes of the society.

(d) The convertible loan stock is to be redeemed at nominal value in the event of a winding-up *pari passu* with the repayment of capital on deferred shares, but with no right to share in any surplus assets. This is the crucial distinction between the convertible stock and the bonus 'A' shares to be allotted under the new rule. For the owners of the 'A' shares have a right to share in a surplus on a winding-up. The plaintiffs have no objection to that part of the new rule which allows the directors to issue units of convertible loan stock rateably according to the value of members' sales to the board. What they object to is the issue of bonus 'A' shares allotted on this basis because of the 'dilution' effect of such allotment on the holdings of 'A' shares of those members who do not trade with the board or only partially trade with the board in the year in which bonus shares are issued.

One final general point about the rights of shareholders is to be noted: shares cannot be transferred without the consent of the board of directors and they are not withdrawable (rules 13 and 14).

(e) *Voting rights* (rule 42)

An important change was effected by this rule in voting rights of those members entitled to vote at general meetings. If a ballot is demanded then:

> Each member present and voting shall have one vote plus a number of votes which shall be determined by reference to each member's annual valuation of milk products sold to the board.

The rule provided how this calculation was to be made and that in the case of a special resolution under section 51 of the 1893 Act voting would be on the basis of one vote per member.

It will be recalled that under the 1972 and 1975 rules voting rights were determined by the size of the member's milk intake. But, as already pointed out, once the contractual obligation to trade through the board is greatly reduced it would not follow that a member's milk intake would reflect the level of its trade with the board. To give effect to the policy which existed from 1972 that those who most used the board should have most control of its affairs this change becomes necessary.

(f) *Board of directors* (rule 44)

A further important change was made in the manner in which members of the board of directors are to be nominated or elected to the board of directors. The rule provides as follows:

> 44. The board will consist of a maximum of 15 members of which 13 shall be elected or appointed with the following provisions:
>
> (a) Six members each supplying the largest volume of product as measured by value for export as measured by the board shall each appoint one director to the board of the society. To be eligible they shall exclusively supply butter, butteroil, skim milk powder and whole milk powder destined for sale outside the State and at least 50% by value of all other specified products destined for sale outside the State or such other higher percentage as the board may decide from time to time, provided always that the value referred to shall be a minimum of 6% by value of the total quantity purchased by the board from its members.
> Other specified products for this purpose are casein, caseinates, cheddar cheese, and such other products as the board may decide from time to time.

> The board shall ensure that the foregoing export requirements are complied with and in particular are not abused through the movement of whole or skimmed milk. 8.1.1
> In determining volume of product the aggregate supplied by subsidiaries and affiliates shall be taken into account.
> (b) A maximum of four members will be elected by all other members who supply product to the board. The country shall be divided into regions for the purpose of this election. The regions will be determined by the board on an equitable basis.
> Members' voting entitlement shall be determined by the board in accordance with the voting procedure outlined in rule 42.
> To be eligible for election a candidate shall be a member of the board or committee or employed by an eligible member in the region in which he seeks election. A candidate shall also be eligible for election if he is a milk supplier to any member in the region in which he seeks election and holds shares in the society and is eligible for election to the board or council of his society.
> For the purposes hereof an eligible member shall be one who shall exclusively supply butter, butteroil, skim milk powder and whole milk powder for export and at least 50% by value of all other specified products destined for sale outside the State or such other higher percentage as the board may decide from time to time.

Provision was made enabling three members to be appointed, one each by the ICMSA, ICOS and the IFA, and the board of directors is empowered to co-opt two further members.

Furthermore sub-paragraph (i) of these rules provides that if the volume of product supplied to the board by a member exceeds 16% of the total volume of product purchased by the board then that member shall be entitled to two seats on the board and each additional 10% will entitle the member to an extra seat.

The effect of this rule is perfectly clear: the six members entitled to nominate directors of the society, are to be calculated by reference to their trade with the society and not, as heretofore, by reference to the size of their milk intake. In addition they must pass an eligibility test: they must comply with the 1981 policy requirements relating to Group 1 products and in addition supply at least 50% of other specified dairy products to the society. This rule is to give effect to the policy that the day-to-day affairs of the society should be controlled by those who most use the society. Again, it seems to me that once the contractual obligation to supply was diminished then a rule such as this would be required to make such a policy effective.

(g) *Amendments to the rules* (rule 70)
The power of amendment of the new rules is the same as that in the 1975 rules (rule 64) and the written consent of the ICOS is still required before any future amendments to the current rules can be made.

(h) *Allocation of surplus funds* (rule 74)
Amendments consequential on the new provisions in rule 9(d) relating to the power to establish an 'annual bonus fund' were made in the rules relating to the allocation of surplus funds. The previous provision (in rules 68 and 70 of the 1975 rules) relating to bonus payments to members out of current profits and the allocation of fully paid up bonus shares out of past profits retained in reserve funds are deleted.

(i) *Obligation to contract*
It will be recalled that rule 40 of the 1975 rules provided that every member manufacturing dairy products for sale outside the State was required to enter into contracts with the society for the supply and marketing of such products by the society. This rule has been deleted in the new rules. Bearing this in mind and also the fact that the obligation of the holder of the 'A' and 'B' ordinary shares to agree to sell their export products to the board has also been deleted it

8.1.1 is clear that under the new rules the contractual obligation to sell to the board is now considerably less onerous. The only contractual obligation is that implied by rule 8, namely an obligation to 'trade' with the board which, as explained already, imposes no obligation to supply any specified quantity of product to the board. In place of the previous contractual obligation incentives are now offered to members, in the form of extra voting rights and the allotment of bonus shares to encourage trade with the board. But if a member wishes to qualify for membership of the board of directors, however, very specific commitments to trade with the board must be given.

I am now in a position to consider the criticisms to which these rules have been subjected and the legal issues to which these criticisms give rise. I will do this in the part of this judgment which follows.

PART V

Constitutional issues

(a) *Infringement of property rights*

The plaintiffs' constitutionally protected rights, it is claimed, have been infringed by the new rules; in particular their constitutionally protected property rights in Bord Bainne have been breached because their property in the board has been expropriated. Kerry Co-op and Avonmore Co-op as shareholders in the board have a contractual right in the event of the board being wound-up (i) to be repaid the amount they subscribed for their shares and (ii) to share in the distribution of any surplus assets as provided in the rules. Both these rights can properly be regarded as property rights. But the new rules in no way infringe the right of members to a return of their capital in the event of a winding-up or the right of the holders of the 'A' and 'B' ordinary shares to share in a distribution of surplus assets. The plaintiffs' claim is that membership of the board has conferred property rights additional to those just mentioned and that these have been infringed. I propose to examine firstly whether this claim is well founded because if it is not then the question whether any of the plaintiffs have property rights which are *constitutionally protected*, would not arise. To do so, I will consider how the claim is formulated in the pleadings that Kerry Co-op and Avonmore Co-op have property rights in Bord Bainne which have been infringed and I will then consider how they were propounded in the evidence and in the oral submissions. As the pleadings in both actions are identical for ease of reference I will refer to High Court No. 4083P of 1989.

The statement of claim (paragraph 7), having referred to Kerry Co-op's holding of £1,000 'A' shares, to its holding of deferred shares pleads that through the supply of its products and the provision of expertise that Kerry Co-op has over the years contributed to the 'capital' and 'value' of Bord Bainne. It is claimed that by reference to the board's balance sheet as of 2 January the board has 'a present value' of £71,815,000 excluding the value of the 'Kerrygold' brand name and that the 'Kerrygold' brand name is worth approximately £50m. It is then claimed that the value of Kerry Co-op's shareholding in Bord Bainne is worth in excess of £11m.

There are several points to note about the claim in this paragraph;

(a) The reference to a contribution to the 'capital' of Bord Bainne is obviously not a reference to the plaintiffs' contribution to the board's share capital; it is a reference to the capital assets acquired by the board;

(b) The reference to the 'value' of the board is obviously a reference to the value of the board's entire undertaking and not merely a reference to the value of the capital subscribed;

(c) What is advanced is a claim that by trading with the board Kerry Co-op contributed to the growth of the board's underlying assets;

(d) The figure of £71,815,000 is taken from the board's annual report for the year 1987 and is the figure for the board's 'net worth' which appears therein. The term 'net worth' is widely used throughout this case to refer to the difference between the board's outside liabilities and the book value of its assets as shown in its balance sheet; 8.1.1

(e) The evidence establishes that the claim that Kerry Co-op's shareholding is worth in excess of £11m is arrived at by adding (i) the board's net worth at that time and (ii) the value of the 'Kerrygold' trade mark as suggested by the plaintiff and (iii) by calculating what 6% of that total is. 6% is the percentage of the issued 'A' ordinary shares which Kerry Co-op holds in the issued capital. Thus what it is claimed is that the value of its shareholding can be ascertained by reference to (i) the board's net worth and (ii) its percentage of the issued ordinary shares. Since the statement of claim was filed the board's annual report for 1988 has been published which establishes that the board's net worth is £89.8m and that figure, sometimes rounded up to £90m, has been extensively used to base a valuation of the plaintiffs' shares. The validity of this method of valuing these shares is considered in section 2(a) of this part.

In several places throughout the statement of claim it is pleaded that the new rules amount to an 'unlawful expropriation' of Kerry Co-op's property rights in Bord Bainne (see paragraphs 13 (xxi), 22(c) and 28), a point repeated in the oral submissions. The first explicit reference to a property right which has been expropriated is in paragraph 13(iii). With reference to the power of expulsion given by rule 8(c) it is pleaded that this rule permits the board to repay to expelled members only the amount which they have paid up on their shares and it is claimed that as a consequence the expelled member is deprived of the 'substantial assets constituted by its ownership of the shares and in particular of its just and rightful share in the accumulated value of the first named defendant' (*ie* Bord Bainne). Kerry Co-op's 'rightful share in the accumulated value' of Bord Bainne is clearly a reference to the 6% share referred to in paragraph 7. What is therefore pleaded (and repeated forcibly in counsel's submissions) is that if Kerry Co-op is expelled under rule 8(c) it would be deprived of £11m, which is the value of the share in the net worth to which it claims to be entitled arising from the fact that as a shareholder it has contributed, by trading with the board, to the increase in the board's underlying assets. An expulsion, it is said, would involve an expropriation of this valuable property right. This plea can only be valid if Kerry Co-op is legally entitled to a right of property in the underlying assets of Bord Bainne derived from its status as a shareholder in the board, and its trading record with the board.

A similar claim forms the basis of the plaintiffs' attack on rule 9(d), which allows bonus shares to be allotted rateably on the basis of a member's trading record with the board. It is claimed (paragraph 13(xiv)) that the 'new rules' (clearly a reference to rule 9(d)) provide a means of depriving selected members (clearly a reference to those members who do not trade with the board or who only trade to a small extent with the board) of a return on their investments in the capital of Bord Bainne 'and in the contribution made by them to the value' of Bord Bainne. The same point is made later (paragraph 22(b)) and somewhat expanded. In a further reference to rule 9(d) it is again pleaded that this rule will deprive selected members of a return on their investment and the contribution made to the value of Bord Bainne and it is added the new rules 'thereby unlawfully and unjustly attack the property rights' of the plaintiffs. This means that Kerry Co-op claims (a) that it has contributed to the increase in the 'value' of Bord Bainne's underlying assets; (b) that it contributed by trading with Bord Bainne over the years; (c) as a consequence it has acquired property rights in the underlying assets of Bord Bainne; (d) these property rights will, by the operation of rule 9(d) be expropriated.

I must now go into a little more detail as to what it is said are the consequences of the operation of rule 9(d) and how the claimed expropriation is said to arise. To do so I will begin by referring to the evidence in Avonmore's case.

In Avonmore's case a table and schedules were produced to illustrate what has been referred to throughout this case as the 'dilution effect' on the operation of this rule. It is important to be clear that this has been used to describe two distinct concepts. When in a company or a registered society new shares are issued (either to new subscribers or as fully paid up) unless

8.1.1 the new shares are allotted *pari passu* to existing shareholders the new issue will alter the fractional interest which each shareholder has in the issued capital of the company or society. In this case Avonmore Co-op and Kerry Co-op each own about 6% of the issued 'A' and 'B' ordinary shares in Bord Bainne. If Bord Bainne were to admit new members and issue 50,000 £1 ordinary shares to them this would mean that the percentage which each of the plaintiff Co-ops owns in the increased share capital would be less than the percentage it owns in the existing share capital. Their percentage shareholding in the issued capital would be 'diluted'. Exactly the same would happen if 50,000 bonus shares are issued under rule 9(d) and they do not qualify for any of them or only qualify for less than 6%. But the term has also been used by the plaintiffs in connection with the claim that they have an interest in the assets of Bord Bainne. It is assumed that the percentage shareholding which each presently has in the issued 'A' and 'B' shares confers the same percentage interest in the board's net worth and then reference is made to the 'dilution effect' on the plaintiffs' 6% property interest in the board's net worth and to the fact that their property rights are diluted.

The table produced a number of columns and column headings. It showed the number of 'A' shares held by Avonmore as being 1,000, the total number of 'A' and 'B' shares issued at 16,000, and that Avonmore Co-op's percentage share of the issued capital was in 1989 6.02%. Under a column headed 'Projected net assets' for 1989 it gives a figure of £98m. It explains this figure in an accompanying note by stating that in 1988 the board's 'net assets' 'attributable to shareholders' at 31 December 1988 was £88,447,000 and that it had been assumed that the board would earn a surplus of £9m in 1989. It is clear therefore that the column headed 'net assets' is a column giving figures for what has elsewhere been referred to as the board's 'net worth'. The table then has a column headed 'Avonmore's share of net assets' and it gives this share as 6.02% in 1989 assuming no bonus issues were issued in that year. The table then shows what will happen to this percentage share assuming (a) that in 1989 Avonmore supplied 2.3% of the board's total purchases from its members and 3% in the years 1990 to 1998, and (b) and that in each year from 1989 to 1998 rule 9(d) was operated and £50,000 applied each year in the issue of bonus shares. What the table does is to illustrate what it suggests is the 'dilution effect' of the issues of bonus shares on the given assumptions and in doing so it further assumes that because the percentage of the total issued shares owned by Avonmore will be reduced there will be a corresponding diminution on what is called 'Avonmore's share' in the net assets. It calculates that an allotment of 50,000 bonus shares in 1989 would result in a diminution of its percentage share in the net assets to 3.23%, and by 1998 it would be 3.03% assuming the allocations and trading figures to which I have referred.

In a note attached to the table the basis of the plaintiffs' objection to rule 9(d) is succintly stated and the property right claimed identified. It states:

> If it is taken that the percentage shareholding of 'A' and 'B' ordinary shares represent the proportion of the members' *ownership* of ABB's net worth then this dilution would have the effect of rapidly reducing the value of Avonmore's shareholding in ABB. To put this in monetary terms, Avonmore's *share in ABB's net worth* would be reduced from £5.9m to £3.3m simply by the issuing of bonus shares in 1989 (emphasis added).

A similar exercise was carried out to show the dilution effect in Kerry Co-op's case, but making somewhat different assumptions. The table refers to the number of 'A' and 'B' shares in Bord Bainne in 1987 as being 17,000 of which Kerry Co-op held 1,000 and under a column headed 'Kerry's % of equity in Bord Bainne' (which I understand to be a reference to the ordinary shares carrying voting and participation rights) it is pointed out that Kerry Co-op held 5.88%. The table then shows what happens if in each of the years 1989 and 1990 50,000 bonus shares were issued and allotted in accordance with rule 9(d), it being assumed that (a) Kerry only supplied 1.09% of Bord Bainne's total purchases in 1988 and no product in each of the following years. The result would be that Kerry's share in the 'equity' would decline to 2.31%

in 1988, to 1.32% in 1989 and to 0.93% in 1990. (In passing, I think I should comment on the inappropriate, indeed the inherently misleading, reference to the 14,000 issued 'A' ordinary shares as the 'equity' capital of the society. This is a term usually used in the affairs of commercial companies to refer to the risk capital subscribed for shares on which dividends are paid out of profits after provision has been made for payment on fixed interest-bearing shares — hardly an accurate description of the nominal sums paid in this case by members on joining Bord Bainne.) **8.1.1**

I turn now to a different claim. As I have pointed out, rule 8(c) is challenged because in permitting repayment only of sums paid up on shares an expelled member is deprived of the property rights in the accumulated value, or net worth of the board; rule 9(d) is challenged because in reducing the percentage owned by non-trading members in the total issued capital it deprives those members of property rights in the accumulated net assets of the board. But rule 9(d) is also challenged on another ground which, again, is based on the premise to which I have earlier referred. It is pointed out that the rule permits the funding of bonus shares from the profits of the group of companies of which Bord Bainne is parent, so that they may be funded not only from profits made by Bord Bainne from its trade in dairy products purchased from members but also profits from its subsidiaries, including foreign subsidiaries who may be trading in both dairy products and other goods. It is said that because bonus shares can be allotted under the rule on the basis of trade with the board out of profits derived from previously acquired assets that the rule is invalid in that it infringes the property rights of Kerry Co-op and Avonmore Co-op. This is because these plaintiffs, along with others, have traded since 1973 with Bord Bainne and by so doing have contributed to the annual profits which the board has made. Figures were produced to show that their proportionate share of the board's total purchases from its members has been over the years greater than their proportionate shareholding in the board's issued capital. It was pointed out that the profits thus earned and in which the plaintiffs were entitled to share were not paid out in dividends but were retained and used to acquire further assets including profit-bearing foreign subsidiaries, and it was claimed that to fund bonus shares from such profits and to allot them on the basis of current trading was to deprive the plaintiffs of their rightful share of the income derived from assets acquired by past contributions made by them. Implicit in this argument there is again a claim that the plaintiffs have property rights in the assets of the board's profit-making subsidiary companies as otherwise no legal grounds for this particular complaint would exist.

To assist in a consideration of these claims I must refer to some basic, indeed trite, principles of company law, principles which regulate with equal force the rights of shareholders in societies registered under the 1893 Act.

(a) A registered company is a body corporate with a legal personality distinct from its members. A registered society is also a body corporate with a distinct legal personality.

(b) The assets acquired by a company are in the legal ownership of the company and no shareholder in the company has a legal right to any specific portion of the company's assets. As pointed out by Keane J in *Company Law in the Republic of Ireland* para. 16.01):

> Where a company has a share capital, each of the members owns at least one *share* of that capital and is consequently a *shareholder* in the company. This does not mean that he is the owner of any part of the company's assets or that he owns them jointly with his fellow shareholders.

This principle applies to the relationship between a member of a registered society and its members. The members own no part of the assets of a registered society. Whilst they own a percentage of the issued capital of a registered society it is not correct to say that they thereby own a similar percentage of the assets of the society. If the rules so provide they will have a contractual right to share in a distribution of surplus assets in the event of the society's liquidation in the same proportion as their shares bear to all the shares with participation rights.

8.1.1 (c) The rights of a shareholder in relation to the assets of the company of which he is a member have been explained as follows:

> The assets of the company, its premises, stock in trade etc are all capable of being disposed of without limitation or fetter of any sort. No shareholder has a right to any specific portion of the company's property, and save by, and to the extent of, his voting power at a general meeting of the company, cannot curtail the free and proper disposition of it. He is entitled to a share of the company's capital and profits, the former, in the words of Farwell J, being measured by a sum of money which is taken as the standard for the ascertainment of his share of the profits. If the company disposes of its assets, or if the latter be realised in a liquidation, he has a right to a proportion of the amount received after the discharge of the company's debts and liabilities. In acquiring these rights — that is, in becoming a member of the company — he is deemed to have simultaneously entered into a contract under seal to conform to the regulations contained in the articles of association. . . . There is no interest in the land, legal or equitable, vested in the defendants by reason of their testator's membership in their company. His property in the company was represented by contractual rights that created no such interest (Kenny J, *Attorney General v. Jameson* [1904] 2 IR 644 at 669-670.)

These same principles apply in relation to the rights of a shareholder in a registered society. The shareholder has rights which can properly be regarded as property rights (*Private Motorists' Provident Society Ltd v. Moore* [1984] ILRM 88) but their nature and extent are to be ascertained by reference to the contract it has entered into with the society whose terms are contained in the society's rules.

(d) There is no implied term in the contract between a member and the company of which he is a member that the fractional interest he has in the company's issued share capital will remain constant and will not be altered by the issuing of additional shares. This principle was confirmed in *Mutual Life Insurance Co. of New York v. Rank Organisation Ltd* [1985] BCLC 11. That was a case in which the Rank Organisation had offered for sale to the public 20 million 'A' ordinary shares, half of which were made available on a preferential basis to existing Rank 'A' ordinary shareholders except those resident in the United States or Canada. They were excluded because of the operation of the securities legislation in those countries. The plaintiffs were some of the American holders of the existing 'A' shares and claimed that they were discriminated against, basing their claim on a term which it was alleged could be implied into their contracts with the company. The claim failed. The court ruled that they had not been treated unfairly, in that their exclusion from participation did not affect the existence of their shares or of the rights attached to them. In the course of his judgment Goulding J pointed out (at p. 24) that no shareholder in Rank had 'any right to expect that his fractional interest in the company will remain forever constant'.

This principle applies to the contract between members of a registered society and the society of which they are members. There is no contractual obligation express or implied on a registered society not to 'dilute' its members' shareholding in the society and a registered society is free to obtain new members and issue shares to new members or to allot new shares to existing members even though the effect is to reduce the fractional interest in the capital of the society which existing members enjoy.

(e) The power to increase and reduce the capital of a *registered company* is subject to considerable statutory regulation. In particular, the recent Companies (Amendment) Act 1983 contains a provision designed to protect existing shareholders against the dilution of their holdings by the issue of new shares by conferring pre-emptive rights on existing shareholders when what are called 'equity securities' are issued (a term which does not include bonus shares). But none of this legislation applies to societies registered under the 1893 Act. There are no statutory restrictions on the manner in which *registered societies* may increase or decrease their share capital. They may decrease their capital, as Kerry Co-op did when it expelled members in the manner to which I have earlier referred and repaid them the capital they had contributed. They may increase their capital by taking in new members, as Avonmore Co-op proposed to do in its takeover battle in relation to Westmeath Co-op. When new shares are paid for, the society may acquire assets and in the event of a winding-up existing shareholders who own a smaller percentage of the enlarged issued capital may not suffer financially beacuse of this. But assets may be lost and if so the members whose shareholding has been diluted by the allotment of new shares will be adversely affected. But no legal wrong will have been committed. 8.1.1

(f) The terms 'net worth' and 'net assets' (frequently employed throughout this case) are terms used by accountants to refer to the difference between a company's outside liabilities and the book value of its assets. They refer to an abstract figure and there is no group of assets which can be designated 'the net worth' or the 'net assets' of the company and no property right can reside in a balance sheet figure of a registered society designated in the balance sheet as its 'net worth'.

The application of these principles to the facts of these cases inevitably leads to the conclusion that the claims that Kerry Co- op and Avonmore Co-op have property rights in the assets or in the 'net worth' of Bord Bainne fails;

(a) There is no term in their contracts as shareholders or members which confers any property rights in any of the underlying assets of Bord Bainne nor in what has been referred to as the board's 'net worth' or 'net assets'. They did not acquire any percentage of the board's net worth by virtue of their ownership of ordinary shares either by reference to the percentage of the ordinary shares they own or otherwise. It follows that by operating rule 8(c) so as to expel a member and return only the capital it paid up, or by operating rule 9(d) so as to reduce the percentage shareholding of a member in the total issued share capital of the society the board does not infringe any property right of the member or involve the expropriation of any member's property.

(b) Nor can it be said that by trading over the years with the board and by contributing at least in part to the net profits made from which assets were acquired that they acquired a proprietorial interest in any of the board's assets. The assets thus acquired became the board's property and no shareholder has any property in them either alone or jointly with others. Rule 9(d), by which profits from foreign subsidiaries may theoretically be used to fund an issue of bonus shares is not for this reason invalid, as it infringes no property right of any member.

The claim that the new rules amount to an expropriation of the plaintiffs' property rights in the board was supported by three additional and/or alternative arguments which I must now consider.

It was submitted that the operation of rule 9(d) would amount to an *expropriation* of the plaintiffs' *shareholding* in the board; indeed it was said that the operation of the rule would be the same as if the majority of shareholders in a company passed a resolution expropriating without compensation the shares of a minority. There would be, it was said, a 'transfer of ownership' effected by 'dilution' because by allotting new 'A' ordinary bonus shares only to members who traded with the board a 'transfer of ownership' of the company will be effected from those members who do not trade with the company to those who do. I cannot agree with this analysis. If Kerry Co-op and Avonmore Co-op do not trade with the board and so do not qualify for new bonus shares they will each still own 1,000 'A' ordinary shares after the allotment has been made. Their shareholding in the board will remain exactly the same and their property in their shares will be unaffected. All that happens is that their percentage of the total issued 'A' ordinary shares will be reduced, but that does not involve any transfer of their property in the shares. Secondly, it was argued that there was an expropriation of their property in Bord Bainne because the *value of their shareholding* in the board would be reduced by the operation of Rule 9(d). It was said that if they did not trade with the board and so obtained no new 'A' bonus shares the value of their existing 1,000 'A' ordinary shares would be reduced

8.1.1 to virtually nothing and that this amounted to an infringement of their property rights as shareholders. I hope to show in section 2(a) of this Part that no diminution in value of their shareholding in the board as alleged will in fact occur, but even if it did no property of the plaintiffs would be thereby expropriated. If X does an act which causes a reduction in the value of property owned by Y (whether corporeal and incorporeal) the diminution in value does not in itself establish that X has infringed Y's property rights. In this case new 'A' shares can be issued and allotted under rule 9(d) without infringing any statutory provision, and without infringing any of the contractual or proprietorial rights the members enjoy as shareholders in the board, and the mere fact that a diminution in the value of their existing shares might result does not in itself establish an infringement of such rights or the expropriation of the difference between the value of their shares before the allotment of new bonus shares and their post-allotment value.

The new rules, I am satisfied, therefore do not infringe any property right of Kerry Co-op or Avonmore Co-op in Bord Bainne. It must follow that no property right of any of their co-plaintiffs is infringed, and that the members of the society at their meeting which adopted the new rules did not engage in any 'constitutional conspiracy'. It is therefore unnecessary to consider whether, if such infringement had been established, a constitutional wrong had been committed which conferred a right of action on any of the plaintiffs.

(b) *Equality before the law*

The remaining constitutional issue which was pleaded did not figure largely at the hearing. Article 40.1 of the Constitution provides that all citizens shall as human persons be held equal before the law. It was pleaded that the new rules infringed this article because they were unconstitutionally discriminatory. Prescinding from the question as to whether bodies corporate could claim the benefit of this article it seems to me that rule 9(d) (which is the rule which is said to be discriminatory) does not infringe any constitutional guarantee given by this article. Invalidity, it is said, arises because the rule allows bonus shares to be allotted rateably on the basis of a member's trading; they should, it is said, be allotted on a *pari passu* basis. But the rules of Bord Bainne (like the rules of Kerry Co-op) have always permitted the directors to reward those who traded with the society by paying them rateably a *cash bonus* out of profits and these have not been challenged. It seems to me that a rule which allows bonus *shares* to be allotted rateably to members on the basis of a member's current trading is equally not an invidiously discriminating one. This challenge to the rules must also fail. Accordingly, I must reject the claim that the rules are invalid because they infringed the Constitution.

(2) *Common Law issues*

(a) *Restraint of Trade*

The first issue now to be considered is whether any of the new rules are illegal as being in restraint of trade. The principle applicable, long accepted in these courts, is that:

> A contract which is in restraint of trade cannot be enforced unless (a) it is reasonable as between the parties; (b) it is consistent with the interests of the public (*McEllistrim v. Ballymacelligott Co-operative Agricultural and Dairy Society Ltd* [1919] AC 548 at 562).

So, if it can be said of any of the impugned rules that it is one in 'restraint of trade' (a concept whose definition and application may give rise to problems) then it is illegal unless it passes the test of reasonableness and consistency to which I have referred. It is, moreover, well established that although a contract or a term of a contract may not explicitly restrain trade the prohibition against restraints may be infringed if the *effect in practice* of implementing a contractual term is to restrain trade: *Stenhouse Australia Ltd v. Phillips* [1974] AC 391. The time for testing whether a contract is illegal is the date on which the restraint was imposed: *Schroeder Music Publishing Co. Ltd v. Macaulay* [1974] 3 All ER 616. This means that the plaintiffs are entitled to argue, as they have done, that even though the rules may not explicitly restrain their trading activities their practical effect is that they will do so when implemented; so they are illegal. **8.1.1**

If the new rules are looked at firstly with a view to seeing what *express* stipulations they contain restraining the plaintiffs' freedom to trade it will be seen that there are none. It will be recalled that under the 1972 rules a member had to agree to market through Bord Bainne all its dairy products destined for sale outside the State before it could be admitted to membership, and that a similar obligation was imposed under the 1975 rules. In addition under the 1975 rules the ordinary shares would not be allotted unless the proposed allottee had similarly agreed and an agreement in writing to do so was a condition precedent to membership of the board of directors. The full vigour of these stipulations had been waived by the board of directors in 1981 so that from that date only in respect of Group I products was a member still bound to supply all its export dairy products to the board. Even that obligation was abolished by the new rules. From these has been removed any *express* obligation to enter into an agreement to supply dairy products to the board. What has been substituted is an *implied* obligation to 'trade' with the board under rule 8(c).

I have already explained how I think the implied obligation imposed by rule 8(c) should be construed; the only obligation is to supply dairy products to the board on a reasonably regular basis, an obligation met by even a small supply. I very much doubt that such an obligation can be regarded as a 'restraint of trade' but even if it can be so regarded it seems to me to be a reasonable one as between the parties. In considering reasonableness I look first to the legitimate interests of the board the restraint is designed to protect. In this connection it should be borne in mind that the board depends entirely on its members to fulfil its foreign contracts and that it is important for it to know the quantity and type of dairy products which will be available to it from its members. To require them to help the co-operative effort by supplying at least some of their products to the board on a regular basis so as to enable it to trade with confidence abroad seems to me a perfectly reasonable requirement. Furthermore the board is, it must be stressed, a co-operative whose members have entered into moral obligations with one another for mutual assistance and it is entirely reasonable that some legal obligation, even of a very limited kind, should be imposed on members to fulfil them. On the other hand, the hardship imposed on the plaintiffs by this obligation is almost non-existent. They are free to trade as they like on the home market; they are free to export as they like on foreign markets, subject to a requirement that at least some portion of their product available for export be sold instead to the board. If they suffer any loss of profit by having to do so such loss would be minimal and insignificant. Finally, the obligation clearly infringes no public interest; indeed it seems to me to be one which serves the interest of farmers and the public in general.

It is instructive to compare the contractual requirement now imposed by the new rules on members of Bord Bainne with those imposed on the members of agricultural co-operatives which were considered, and condemned, by the courts in this country and in England in the early years of this century. In *Tipperary Creamery Society v. Hanley* [1912] 2 IR 586 a rule was held to be invalid as being in unlawful restraint of trade which provided that as long as he should remain a member every milk-supplying member was required to deliver to the society's creamery on every working day all the milk produced from his cows (except such as might be required for use in his household). There was no provision for voluntary withdrawal except on transfer of shares (to which the consent of the committee of the co-operative was required). The Court of Appeal in Ireland in condemning the rule pointed out that there was no limitation on the locality of the lands in which the members' cows were to be found, that as the words of the rule applied to the whole country it concluded that it was not possible to place any bounds on the rule and that its scope and operation went beyond what was reasonable for the protection of the society.

8.1.1 Following this judgment co-operatives amended their rules on the advice of the IAOS. In *McEllistrim v. Ballymacelligott Co-operative Agricultural and Dairy Society Ltd* [1919] AC 548 members under the amended rules were required to supply all their milk to the society, subject to a similar exception as in *Hanley*, but the obligation was in respect of the produce of cows within a defined area rather than from the whole of the country. But this amendment did not save the rule. The House of Lords held that it was not necessary for the protection of the society that its members be tied to it for life. Thus the combination of the duty to supply exclusively its total milk supply with the indefinite duration of the duty rendered the stipulations in the contract an unreasonable restraint. Kerry Co- op in this case is able to avoid legal censure of its rules because although an obligation similar to that in *McEllistrim* is imposed it is one which can be terminated by notice. Bord Bainne is able to escape legal censure because their members' obligation, unlike the obligation in *McEllistrim*, allows extensive freedom to trade outside their society even though the obligation is of indefinite duration. I have no hesitation in concluding that the implied obligation under rule 8(c) to trade is not in itself an illegal one.

I come now to what I conceive to be the plaintiffs' principal ground of complaint in this part of the case, which is that certain of the new rules will *operate in practice* to restrain their freedom to trade and are for this reason illegal.

It was argued that as a member expelled for non-trading under rule 8(c) would only be repaid at most the sum subscribed (in the case of Kerry Co-op and Avonmore Co-op — £1,000 each) this rule would operate to impose an enormous 'penalty' on them. To avoid this 'penalty' they would be coerced into trading with the board against their will and contrary to their commercial interests. The 'penalty' was expressed in different ways throughout the case. It was suggested that, as members had contributed to the board's business in the past and had agreed not to take dividends from the resulting profits which had contributed to the growth in the board's assets, would now be forced to 'turn their backs' on the 'investment' or their 'interest' in the accumulated capital of the board if they did not trade. For reasons already explained the plaintiffs have, in my view, no 'investment' in Bord Bainne other than the £1,000 they subscribed for their shares (plus, of course, their subscription to the deferred shares which plays no part in the submissions I am now considering) and as it cannot be said that they have any interest in the assets which the board accumulated over the years there is no property right which the plaintiffs are compelled to protect by enforced trading with the board.

The second argument was this. In Avonmore's case it was submitted that the *value of its 'A' and 'B' shares* in Bord Bainne was 'in the region' of £10m or possibly more. And so if it did not trade with the board and as a result was expelled under rule 8(c) it would only receive £1,000. Rather than suffer the loss of £10m it would be obliged to trade against its will and so the rule operated as an illegal restraint of trade. A similar argument was advanced on behalf of Kerry Co-op. To consider this argument I will examine the pleadings, submissions and evidence relating to the value of the £1,000 'A' shares which each now has in Bord Bainne.

It will be recalled that in paragraph 7 of the plaintiffs' statements of claim it was pleaded that as Bord Bainne had according to its balance sheet as of 31 December 1988 a value in excess of £88,847,000 excluding the value attached to the 'Kerrygold' mark, that as the value of the 'Kerrygold' mark was 'in excess' of £50m that the value of shareholding of Avonmore Co-op and Kerry Co-op in the board was in excess of £8m. As I have pointed out this valuation of their 1,000 shares was arrived at by calculating what 6% was of the 'net worth' of Bord Bainne as disclosed in the balance sheet. This suggested valuation was repeated in the submissions made at the hearing in support of the attack on rule 8(c). It was urged that the current value of the plaintiffs' shareholding in Bord Bainne was between £5 and £10m, and that if a member was expelled under rule 8(c) it would lose a sum in this region. To avoid this loss it would be compelled to trade with the board.

It is, I believe, well established that in valuing shares in a case like the present one it is not correct to base a valuation on the book values of assets and liabilities as set out in a balance sheet. This view was confirmed by the expert witness called by the plaintiffs, Mr Glover. His estimate of the value of Avonmore Co-op's shares was arrived at by methods of valuation which were entirely different to that adopted in the pleadings. Although it related to Avonmore Co-op's shares I was asked to apply the same principles in valuing Kerry Co-op's shares. **8.1.1**

He set out firstly to assess the value of Bord Bainne in its entirety and then to consider how that value enures to the benefit of Avonmore Co-op. He pointed out that Bord Bainne would have a different value in different circumstances and that there was a range of likely values. He set out to consider (a) the value of the board on the basis of the board's likely capitalisation if its shares were currently listed on the stock exchange (b) the price a purchaser would pay for acquiring the entire issued share capital of the board and (c) the amount receivable by the members in a voluntary winding up. Having done this he then considered how likely each of these possible outcomes were and in the light of this he assessed the value to be attributed to Avonmore's shareholding under the old rules and under the new rules.

Whilst it is not necessary for me to explain in detail how he arrived at his different valuation some points are to be noted. He observed that the board in its present form could not get a stock exchange listing but that it could convert itself into a limited company and thereby obtain a listing. But he felt that this was extremely unlikely (a view with which I agree) as it would involve a radical change in the board's status and render its profits liable to tax. However, he suggested that it could follow the route taken by Avonmore Co-op and Kerry Co-op and establish a public limited company which would become a subsidiary of the board. He suggested that this subsidiary would acquire the shares of a new co-operative society to which Bord Bainne had transferred its undertaking and that a listing could be sought for the new plc. By this means a stock exchange price could be placed on the board's business. To assess the likely value of the board's business undertaking for the purpose of the stock exchange flotation he considered that it was proper to review the market price of comparable quoted companies. Having done so he concluded that the notional stock market capitalisation would be between £160m – £200m. I need express no view on this estimate except to point out that it must be a very tentative one and that it is open to a number of possible objections. In particular it is arrived at by assuming that dividends would be paid on the shares (which would be entirely contrary to the board's whole history) and that the figure for the board's profits has been inflated by adding back the bonuses paid to members from the pre-tax surplus.

As to possibility (b), a valuation was made based on the price which might be obtained in the sale of the entire 'equity' capital of the board. This valuation started by using the notional market capitalisation figures to which I have referred. A valuation for the purchase of the entire business was then given between £200m and £250m. As to possibility (c), based on the balance sheet as of 31 December 1988 he put forward a winding-up value of £75m on the board's undertaking.

Turning, then, to the value of Avonmore's shares, even though the value of Bord Bainne's undertaking had a value of between £75m and £250m he concluded that Avonmore's shares had no *market value*. He observed that the board has paid no dividends in the past and that there is no prospect that it would do so in the future and because of this and the impossibility of transferring shares otherwise than on terms acceptable to the board of directors there was no justification for attributing any substantial value to the shares. Taking 'market value' to mean the price which property will fetch when sold then Avonmore's shareholding has no value since to all intents and purposes it cannot be sold.

However, he said that it would be wrong to conclude that Avonmore's shares were worthless. If there was a reasonable probability either (a) there would be a stock exchange listing in the future, or (b) that its entire capital would be acquired by an outside purchaser, or (c) that the company would be wound up then there was a justification for imputing a value to Avonmore's shareholding. This value would not be market value but the 'value to the owner' of the shares. (The 'owner value' it was explained is identical to the 'deprival value', by which is meant the 'adverse consequences both direct and indirect for the owner if he were deprived of the property.') This 'owner value' would depend on which of the three different outcomes

8.1.1 were most probable and this, he admitted, involved a 'highly subjective judgment'. He concluded that 'that there was a strong likelihood', 'very much a probability', that the board would seek a stock exchange listing, that the likelihood of a sale of the entire share capital was smaller and would be some years away, and that the winding up of the board was not even remotely probable.

The 'owner value' was then based on the figure earlier given for the value of the undertaking based on a stock exchange listing within the next five years. The figure which had been given would have to be discounted to give this future expectation a present value. Doing this, and assuming Avonmore Co-op's percentage of the equity is 6.3% then the present 'owner value' of its 1,000 shares is between £6.1m and £7.6m he said.

An exercise was undertaken to show what would happen if 50,000 new bonus 'A' shares were issued and none were allotted to Avonmore Co-op because it did not trade with the board. It was pointed out that the total number of issued 'A' and 'B' ordinary shares would be increased from 15,800 (the present number which have been issued) to 65,800, and that Avonmore's percentage of the issued capital would be reduced from 6.3% to 1.5%. This would bring about a reduction in the value of its shares from £7m to £1.7m he said. Assuming the issuing of bonus shares would be an annual event this would bring about a 'massive dilution' of its shareholding interest. As a result the value of its shares would only be their nominal value of £1,000.

Because I cannot agree that the basic assumption underlying this valuation is correct I cannot accept the conclusions based on it. I certainly agree that there is not any reasonable prospect either that there will be a takeover of Bord Bainne by an outside purchaser of its shares or that Bord Bainne will be wound up and so it would be entirely wrong to suggest that the shares of Kerry Co-op and Avonmore Co-op have an 'owner value' based on the likelihood of the occurrence of either event. But I have had the benefit of a great deal of evidence as well as the minutes of meetings of members of Bord Bainne and of its board of directors not available to Mr Glover and I am satisfied that there is no 'strong likelihood' as he said or even a reasonable possibility that Bord Bainne will seek a stock exchange listing in the next five years. If there is no reasonable prospect of such an eventuality then the shares cannot have any 'owner value'.

I have reached this conclusion for several reasons. There are a number of factors which suggest that it is extremely unlikely that the members of Bord Bainne will decide to alter fundamentally the structure and status of the board in the manner envisaged in Mr Glover's evidence or to establish a corporate structure in some other way which would enable it to obtain a stock exchange listing. Firstly, there is no financial reason for it to do so, as there is no evidence to suggest that there is any need for it to raise equity capital by means of a public subscription in order to fund future development. Secondly, to carry out its functions as a central marketing organisation for the export produce of the dairy farmers of this country by means of a listed public company would involve a considerable alteration in the basic policy which has guided the board over the years and there is no evidence to show that the members would agree to such a change. That policy has been to pay the highest possible price for the dairy products of its members and not to operate so as to create profits to pay dividends to its shareholders. There might, it is true, be some immediate financial gain to the member societies and companies of the board if a decision to adopt the proposed new structure was taken but I think it is very unlikely that members would sacrifice the long term interests of Irish dairy farmers to obtain it. Thirdly, the whole future of the board was discussed by the members and debated in the media over many months before the decisions were taken at the meeting of 15 November 1988. Those decisions involved the rejection of an option involving the establishment of a public limited company with a stock exchange listing, which would have created a corporate status more beneficial to the individual dairy farmers than would the corporate framework envisaged in the evidence I am now considering. I think it is very unlikely that the question of the future structure of the board will be a live issue again for some considerable time and I believe that the corporate structures established in 1988 will remain in place for the foreseeable future.

I conclude therefore that it cannot be said that the shares of the members of Bord Bainne have any 'owner value' and as it is agreed that they have no market value it follows that their only value is their nominal one. This view gains support from the fact that the report and accounts of Kerry Co-op and Avonmore Co-op were prepared by two different highly experienced firms of accountants neither of whom placed any value on their clients 1,000 shares in Bord Bainne in the balance sheets they prepared. 8.1.1

If the shares owned by the members have no value other than their nominal value then it follows that rule 8(c) does not operate to restrain trade in the way suggested and is not illegal.

Rule 9(d) was also attacked because it was claimed that its operation would coerce members into trading with the board. In this connection the dilution effect of the rule was relied on, the principal argument in this connection being that to protect their property rights in the board or what was referred to as their 'investment' in the board from the possible diluting effect of rule 9(d) that members would be forced to trade with the board. I have already answered this argument in the conclusions which I expressed in section (1) of this part. For the reasons explained, the members have no property rights in the board's assets and so it is incorrect to regard Kerry Co-op or Avonmore Co-op as having a 6% property right which would be diluted by the issue of bonus shares if they did not trade with the board.

A further argument was advanced based on the valuation evidence to which I have just referred. Even if an issue of bonus shares did not expropriate their property, it was said that the *value of their shares* would be reduced if they did not qualify themselves for bonus shares by trading with the board and to preserve this value they would be coerced into trading with it. As, for the reasons given, the shares have no market value and no 'owner's value' this argument also fails.

A further criticism of this rule is also answered by the conclusion I have just expressed. It was said that members like the plaintiffs whose own milk supply is inadequate for their production needs and who obtain significant quantities from other members will be adversely affected because those other members will be forced to trade with the board rather than with them in order to protect their property rights. But this argument proceeds on the misapprehension of the legal effects of the operation of rule 9(d) to which I have referred and it cannot support a claim that the rule is illegal as being in unlawful restraint of trade. As no other criticisms of the rule were advanced under this part of the case I can declare that both rules 8(c) and 9(d) are not illegal.

I now turn to consider the claims that rules 42 and 44 are illegal. Rule 42 provides that each member present and voting at a meeting shall have one vote plus a number of votes determined by reference to the annual valuation of milk products sold to Bord Bainne. It is claimed that this imposes a trade restraint because it forces members to trade with the board in order to maintain or obtain voting power at members' meetings. But it seems to me that this rule is not a 'restraint' within the meaning of the doctrine which I am now considering as it does not force members to trade against their will; it requires them to make a commercial decision as to benefits of trading with the board (including the benefits of acquiring voting rights) and the benefits of trading outside the board (including the profits to be made and the opportunities for further beneficial contracts that may be afforded). But even if I am wrong in this it seems to me that this rule is both reasonable and fair. The new rules have abolished the previous obligation to sell all export products to the board and in view of the very limited obligation which has been substituted and the need to ensure a supply of products to assist the board in fulfilling its role of providing markets for its members' products not sold on the home market, it is perfectly reasonable to attempt to encourage members to trade with it by rewarding them with extra votes for so doing. I do not think that any great detriment is suffered by the operation of the rule by those members who prefer to seek greater profits by sales outside the board and as it imposes no detriment to the public interest I think it is not illegal.

For similar reasons I think rule 44 is not illegal. This, it will be recalled, provides that eligibility for membership of the board of directors be based on the fulfilment of certain trading

8.1.1 obligations to the board. Even if the operation of this rule could be regarded as a 'restraint', which I do not think it is, the protection of the board's legitimate interests justifies it. The members' view is that the board of directors should be composed and controlled by those members most committed to trade with the board. I think this is a reasonable requirement bearing in mind the difficult trading environment in which the board must operate. A failure to trade may result in a loss of a seat on the board, but I do not think that this adverse result (particularily bearing in mind the view of Avonmore's managing director on the subject) outweighs the advantage it confers on Bord Bainne. As no public interest is adversely affected by it I think the rule is valid.

Finally, I should refer to the submissions based on certain views expressed by Lord Diplock in *Schroeder Music Publishing Co. Ltd v. Macauley* [1974] 3 All ER 616 to the effect that the question to be answered in claims that a contract is in restraint of trade is: was the bargain fair? Lord Diplock's approach has certain attractions but as in this case the test of 'fairness' would not produce a result any different to the more traditional test of 'reasonableness' I need not decide which approach is the more correct. What the plaintiffs submit is that this case is different to the usual case where the parties have agreed to a term which subsequently one of them claims is illegal as being in restraint of trade; in this case the plaintiffs have had imposed on them new terms to which they have not agreed (by a majority vote at a members' meeting) and that even though the actual restraints themselves may pass the test of 'fairness' the *mechanism by which* the restraints became a term of the plaintiffs' contracts is unfair and it is thereby illegal.

When members of a co-operative join a registered society they enter into a contract with it, one of whose terms is that the contract may be amended in accordance with procedures to which assent is given by every member; in this case the plaintiffs and all other members have agreed that the terms of their contract can be amended by a two-thirds vote of members at a special general meeting. This seems to me to be a perfectly fair procedure and presumably the plaintiffs thought so also as when they joined Bord Bainne the rules contained this provision. If the amendments validly adopted by the members are not illegal as being in restraint of trade the fact that a dissident minority objects to them does not, in my view, make them so nor does their objection render the mechanism by which the amendment was effected an unfair one.

My conclusion is therefore that none of the rules are illegal as being in restraint of trade.

(b) *Ultra vires*

The contract, as I have said, of every member of the society contains a provision permitting its amendment by a two-thirds vote of the members at a special general meeting. But the law does not allow a majority to abuse its powers. Limitations which have been placed on the power of amendment by the judgments of courts dealing with similar powers in the articles of associations of registered companies and in the rules of building societies apply, I believe, with equal force to the rules of registered industrial societies.

These limitations are well known and I need only refer to two cases. *Stohmenger v. Borough of Finsbury Permanent Investment Building Society* [1897] 2 Ch 469 was a case in which a building society suffered very heavy financial losses. To deal with these losses it was decided that every member was to reduce its shares so that the loss would be shared by all the shareholders and a resolution was passed by the requisite majority to the effect that the amount due by the society to each member in respect of his shares would be deemed to be thirty-three-fiftieths of the net amount paid up on each share. This resolution was challenged on the basis that it was *ultra vires*. The Court of Appeal in England held that it was not. In the course of his judgment Chitty LJ observed that the members could not adopt a rule which changed 'the nature of the constitution of the society' and that the power of making and altering rules 'must be confined to the internal rights of the members of the society', Lopes LJ making comments to the same effect. As the resolution dealt only with internal rights it was valid.

In a later case concerned with an industrial and provident society the House of Lords held that an amendment to the rules adopted by the requisite majority was not binding on dissenting members. In reaching this conclusion Lord Atkin pointed out that a member joining the society only committed himself to be bound by the decision of the majority of his associates on matters within 'the contemplated scope of the venture he had undertaken with them'. Lord Tomlin suggested that the power of amendment should be 'confined to such amendments as can reasonably be considered to have been within the contemplation of the parties when the contract was made having regard to the nature and circumstances of the contract'. If no such principle existed, he pointed out, then a dairy society in Wiltshire could by the exercise of a power of amendment convert itself into a boot manufacturer in Leicester, a development which he considered as being outside the powers conferred by the rules. (See *Hole v. Garnsey* [1930] AC 472 at 493, 503). **8.1.1**

The plaintiffs here have argued that the rules which they challenge are *ultra vires* because they are (a) amendments to the 1972 rules which could not reasonably have been in the contemplated scope of the venture undertaken by them in 1972, and/or (b) because they are not confined to regulating the internal rights of members but effect a change in the nature of Bord Bainne's constitution. The defendants do not deny that the power of amendment is limited by the two principles to which I have referred but say that the 1988 amendments do not infringe them.

Before considering in detail the impugned rules in the light of these principles there are two preliminary points to be made. Firstly, in considering what was the contemplated scope of the venture undertaken by the members in 1972 the test must in my view be an objective one. That is, an objection by a member to a new rule merely because it was not one that he had thought of as a possible future amendment does not mean that the rule is thereby *ultra vires* — if it did, few amendments could be validly adopted by registered societies. The court should look at all the circumstances surrounding the venture jointly undertaken at the time a member joined a society, in this case the venture being the creation of a central marketing organisation for the dairy products of its members produced for sale outside the State. It should then look at the amendments which are challenged and decide whether objectively any of them are outside the scope of the venture undertaken when the member joined.

Secondly, the law should not impute to members of Bord Bainne a prescience which they could not possibly have possessed. When they joined in 1972 the Irish dairy industry was in a state of transition and no one could predict exactly what would happen or how the board's role would change over the years. The plaintiffs knew they were joining an undertaking which subjected them to certain obligations to trade with it. It seems to me that it should have been reasonably within their contemplation that circumstances might evolve which might require (a) the strengthening of the contractual obligations of members to trade with the board (as happened in 1975) or (b) the weakening of those obligations (as happened in 1988). What the court has to consider is whether the members could, in 1972, have reasonably contemplated that if it was decided to relax the contractual trading obligations a future meeting would also adopt the sort of rules which were in fact adopted in 1988 in order to maintain the central marketing organisation their society had established.

Coming, then, to consider whether it can be said that any of the new rules are outside the contemplated scope of the venture undertaken by Kerry Co-op and Avonmore Co-op and their fellow members I conclude as follows:

(a) *Rule 5*. The new rule has reduced the obligation which had previously been imposed on new entrants with regard to the commitment to trade with the society. In 1972 it would have been within the contemplation of the members that changing trading conditions would lead to a reduction in the scope of the obligation of new members and this rule does not alter the scope of their joint venture and does not infringe the principle in *Hole v. Garnsey*.

(b) *Rule 6*. A number of changes were made in the terms on which membership could be terminated which are not relevant to the subject which I am now considering. It seems to be that the change whereby an expelled member may not be repaid the amounts paid up on its shares if the financial circumstances of the company would not justify such repayment does

8.1.1 not infringe the principle I am now considering.

(c) *Rule 8(c)*. This is a new rule in that a power to expel a member who has not traded with the board for two years was not expressly contained in the 1972 or 1975 rules. As I pointed out in section (4) of Part IV under the previous rules a member who had failed to trade with the board in accordance with the more stringent requirements they then contained could have been expelled if it had failed to comply with them over a two year period. It follows that this rule does not infringe the principle I am considering.

(d) *Rule 9(d)* As pointed out in section (4) of Part IV this new rule gives effect to the policy that those who trade with the board should be rewarded for doing so. This policy existed under the 1972 and 1975 rules. Under the 1972 rules a member could be rewarded by the grant of a cash bonus out of current profits; under this rule it can be rewarded by the grant of bonus shares payable out of current profits. I can see no reason why such a change is outside the scope of the 1972 venture, particularly bearing in mind the fact that the 1972 rules made provision for issuing of bonus shares from profits *retained* from trading in previous years.

(e) *Rule 42*. The principle that the voting rights should be weighted had been built into the 1972 rules. The principle was retained in the new rules. Under the 1972 rules voting rights were determined by the milk intake of the members; now they are to be determined by the volume of trade with the board.

As I pointed out in section 3 of Part IV, once the contractual obligation to trade with the board is diminished then an amendment such as this would reasonably be required to give effect to a policy that the control of the board should be in the hands of those most committed to it, as demonstrated by the level of their trade with it. As this rule does not alter in any way the scope of the board as a central marketing organisation it seems to me to have been one well within the amending powers of the members.

(f) *Rule 44*. This rule has altered the weighting system for appointing, and voting for, membership of the board of directors. There is now a more direct link between trade with the board and the power to appoint and vote for directors of the board. However, for reasons given in relation to rule 42 I do not think that this part of the new rule is *ultra vires*. This new rule also provides an eligibility test for board membership based on trade with the board as therein defined. But I think that it would have been reasonably forseeable in 1972 that if the contractual obligations to trade were relaxed an eligibility test such as is contained in this rule might be introduced in order to give effect to the policy that the board's day-to-day affairs should be handled by those who demonstrated their commitment to the board by the level of trading maintained with it. So this part of the rule is not *ultra vires*.

As all these rules deal with the internal rights of members and not with the nature of the constitution of Bord Bainne none infringes the principle established in *Stohmenger* regarding the limits on the amending powers of majorities in general meetings.

There were a number of other arguments advanced in support of the *ultra vires* claim but these have been answered by the conclusions I have reached on the other issues already examined. It was claimed that rule 9(d) was *ultra vires* because it was introduced for an ulterior purpose, namely to transfer the ownership of the shares in the board from, *inter alia*, Kerry Co-op and Avonmore Co-op to other members. But no such ulterior motive lay behind the adoption of this rule and as I pointed out in section 1 of this Part it did not have the effect of transferring ownership as alleged. Indeed there was no ulterior motive of any sort in the adoption of this rule; its purpose was well known and was considered a proper one by the majority of the board's membership. It was also claimed that rule 9(d) was *ultra vires* because it was oppressive in that it involved the expropriation of the shares of dissenting members. I have in the same section shown that this claim is based on a misunderstanding of the legal consequences of the operation of the rule. In the light of my finding that the rules are not illegal as being in restraint of trade the claim that they are *ultra vires* for this reason also fails. And my finding that the rules are not unconstitutional disposes of the argument that the new rules are *ultra vires* the 1893 Act because that argument was based on the proposition that a registered society could not adopt rules which infringed constitutional rights. 8.1.1

I must hold therefore that the new rules are not invalid at common law.

(3) *Community law*

The plaintiffs' claim is that Bord Bainne's new rules breach the rules on competition contained in both Article 85 and Article 86 of the Treaty of Rome, and to that claim I will now turn.

Article 85 provides as follows:

> (1) The following shall be prohibited as incompatible with the common market: all agreements between undertakings, decisions by associations of undertakings and concerted practices which may affect trade between member states and which have as their object or effect the prevention, restriction or distortion of competition within the common market, and in particular those which:
>
> (a) directly or indirectly fix purchase or selling prices or any other trading condition;
> (b) limit or control production, markets, technical development or investment;
> (c) share markets or sources of supply;
> (d) apply dissimilar conditions to equivalent transactions with other trading parties, thereby placing them at a competitive disadvantage;
> (e) make the conclusion of contracts subject to acceptance by the other parties of supplementary obligations which, by their nature or according to commercial usage, have no connection with the subject of such contracts.

Paragraph (2) provides that any agreement or decision which has been prohibited by Article 85 is to be 'automatically void'. But exemptions to the application of sub-article (1) may be permitted in accordance with paragraph (3) which provides:

> (3) The provisions of paragraph 1 may, however, be declared inapplicable in the case of:
>
> — any agreement or category of agreements between undertakings;
>
> — any decision or category of decision by associations of undertakings;
>
> — any concerted practice or category of concerted practices;
>
> which contributes to improving the production or distribution of goods or to promoting technical or economic progress, while allowing consumers a fair share of the resulting benefit, and which does not:
>
> (a) impose on the undertakings concerned restrictions which are not indispensable to the attainment of those objectives;
> (b) afford such undertakings the possibility of eliminating competition in respect of a substantial part of the products in question.

It is for the Commission to declare inapplicable the provisions of paragraph (1) but in the absence of an application to the Commission and a favourable decision on the point any of the agreements etc, referred to in that paragraph are automatically void.

It will be observed that this article (a) prohibits 'agreements', 'decisions' and 'concerted practices' which (b) may affect trade between member states and which (c) either have as their object or their effect the prevention, restriction or distortion of competition within the common market. The plaintiffs' case is that the new rules adopted on 15 November 1988 by Bord Bainne amount to an agreement between undertakings which have either as their object or as their

8.1.1 effect the prevention, restriction and/or distortion of trade or competition and so infringe this article.

Article 86 is a brief article. It provides:

> Any abuse by one or more undertakings of a dominant position within the common market or in a substantial part of it shall be prohibited as incompatible with the common market in so far as it may affect trade between member states. Such abuse may, in particular, consist in:
>
> (a) directly or indirectly imposing unfair purchase or selling prices or unfair trading conditions;
> (b) limiting production, markets or technical development to the prejudice of consumers;
> (c) applying dissimilar conditions to equivalent transactions with other trading parties, thereby placing them at a competitive disadvantage;
> (d) making the conclusion of contracts subject to acceptance by the other parties of supplementary obligations which by their nature or according to commercial usage, have no connection with the subject of such contracts.

I draw attention to two aspects of this article; it is concerned (a) with an undertaking which is in a 'dominant position' and which (b) 'abuses' that dominant position. An undertaking may be in a 'dominant position' in the relevant market without infringing this article (Case 322/81, *Michelin v. Commission* [1983] ECR 3461); what the article prohibits is conduct amounting to an 'abuse' of that position. As has been pointed out, the distinction between what is permissible conduct by a dominant firm and conduct which is prohibited as 'abusive' is often a difficult one and a number of considerations would have to be taken into account. These would include:

> — the kind of conduct: is it plainly restrictive of competition or unfair?;
> — how far the relevant conduct is normal industry practice;
> — how far the market is already dominated;
> — the effect, direct and indirect, of the conduct on competitors or customers;
> — the intention of the dominant firm — is it exclusionary or is it a legitimate response to competition?;
> — the 'proportionality' of the conduct relative to the perceived threat, if any;
> — the connection between the conduct and the general principles of the Treaty . . . (see Bellamy and Child, *Common Market Law of Competition*. 3rd ed (London, 1987) at p. 408)

It is crucial to understand what conduct the plaintiffs in this case impugn. The plaintiffs' claim is that Bord Bainne has abused the dominant position which it is said it enjoys in the relevant market by adopting the new rules in 1988; their adoption and implementation is the conduct challenged as abusive not any other conduct of Bord Bainne's. In short, the plaintiffs' case is that the adoption of the new rules resulted in an infringement of both articles — Article 85 because they amounted to an agreement between undertakings prohibited by that article; Article 86 because their adoption and implementation constitute an abuse of a dominant position.

But Articles 85 and 86 are not the only provisions of Community law relevant to the plaintiffs' claims; special provision has been made in the Treaty and by regulations made under the Treaty for the application of these articles to the agricultural sector which must also be considered.

Article 38 provides that the rules laid down for the establishment of the common market shall apply to agricultural products 'save as otherwise provided in Articles 39 to 46'. Having provided that the operation and development of the common market for agricultural products must be accompanied by the establishment of a common agricultural policy (para. (4) of Article 38) the Treaty goes on, in Article 39, to provide what the objectives of the common agricultural policy are to be. That specifically, in relation to the rules on competition, it provides, in Article 42, that the provisions of the chapter relating to such rules (that is the chapter in the Treaty which includes Articles 85 and 86) shall apply to trade in agricultural products 'only to the extent determined by the Council of Ministers'. The Council made such a determination when on 6 April 1962 it adopted Regulation 26. So Regulation 26 is of central significance in this case. **8.1.1**

Regulation 26 contains a number of important recitals. Having referred to the fact that by virtue of Article 42 of the Treaty one of the matters to be decided under the common agricultural policy is whether the rules on competition laid down in the Treaty are to apply to production of and trade in agricultural products and to the fact that certain rules of competition must be forthwith made applicable to trade in agricultural products, it drew attention to the need for special attention 'in the case of farmers' organisations which are particularly concerned with the joint production or marketing of agricultural products'. A further recital stressed the need for giving the Commission the sole power, subject to review by the Court of Justice, to determine the matters referred to in the regulation. The regulation then provides:

> Article 1.
> From the entry into force of this regulation, Articles 85 to 90 of the Treaty and provisions made in implementation thereof shall, subject to Article 2 below, apply to all agreements, decisions and practices referred to in Articles 85(1) and 86 of the Treaty which relate to production of or trade in the products listed in Annex II to the Treaty:
>
> Article 2.
> (1) Article 85(1) of the Treaty shall not apply to such of the agreements, decisions, and practices referred to in the preceding Article as form an integral part of a national market organisation or are necessary for attainment of the objectives set out in Article 39 of the Treaty. In particular, it shall not apply to agreements, decisions and practices of farmers, farmers' associations, or associations of such associations belonging to a single member state which concern the production or sale of agricultural products or the use of joint facilities for the storage, treatment or processing of agricultural products, and under which there is no obligation to charge identical prices, unless the Commission finds that competition is thereby excluded or that the objectives of Article 39 of the Treaty are jeopardised.

Paragraph (2) of this article gave to the Commission 'sole power' subject to review by the Court of Justice, 'to determine by decision which agreements, decisions and practices fulfil the conditions specified in paragraph (1)' and it is to undertake such a determination either on its own initiative or at the request of the competent authority of a member state at the request of an interested undertaking or association of undertakings.

I draw attention to three aspects of this regulation. Firstly, the exemptions granted by article 2. The first sentence of article 2 provides that Article 85(1) of the Treaty is not to apply to agreements which form an integral part of a national market organisation. Most national market organisations have now been replaced by common organisations of the market and this provision does not apply in the present case. But there are also exempt from Article 85(1) agreements which are 'necessary for the attainment of the objectives set out in Article 39 of the Treaty' and in particular 'agreements, decisions and practices of farmers, farmers' associations, or associations of such associations belonging to a single member state concerned with the sale of agricultural products.' Secondly, the Commission has been given by paragraph (2) of article 2 the 'sole power' (subject to review) to determine which agreements decisions and

8.1.1 practices are exempt under paragraph (1) of article 2. Thirdly, unlike the procedures established in Article 85 of the Treaty, no application to claim exemption is required. The law declares that agreements which meet certain requirements are to be exempt from the operation of Article 85; it is the law which validates the agreements, not their approval by the Commission.

So, an important jurisdictional point arises. How can I in the light of paragraph 2 of article 2 of Regulation 26 adjudicate on the issue which has been raised in these proceedings, namely whether Regulation 26 exempts the association created by the new rules from the provisions of Article 85. I do not think I can. I must apply a law which specifically withdraws from national courts jurisdiction to adjudicate on such an issue and confers jurisdiction on the Commission (and on appeal the Court of Justice) to determine it. I think however that I, like other national courts, would not be required to decline all jurisdiction merely because a claim to exemption is made by a defendant charged with breach of Article 85. I think I should look at the evidence in the case and, without making a final adjudication, consider whether a *prima facie* case for exemption is made out. If *prima facie* it appears that no exemption could arise then I should stay the proceedings provided the applicant for exemption applies for a stay and undertakes to refer the issue for determination by the Commission. If, however, a *prima facie* case for exemption is shown to exist I should allow the exemption unless an application to stay is made and good reason is shown why an application to the Commission to determine the matter had not been brought.

It has been firstly urged on the plaintiffs' behalf that the claimed exemption does not exist because it has not been established that the agreement which constituted Bord Bainne is necessary for the attainment of the objectives set out in Article 39 of the Treaty. Amongst the objectives set out in Article 39 is the rational development of agricultural production so as to bring about an increase in agricultural productivity, and the ensuring of a fair standard of living for the agricultural community. I am quite satisfied on the evidence adduced that a *prima facie* case has been made out that the agreements contained in the 1988 rules constituting Bord Bainne are necessary for the attainment of these objectives. It is secondly argued that Bord Bainne is not an association of farmers' associations because some of its members are commercial firms and not farmers' associations. Again, it seems to me that the board has made out a *prima facie* case that, although it has permitted certain companies which manufacture agricultural products to avail of the central marketing organisation which has been established, this does not detract from the essential features of the undertaking, which are (a) that it was formed by all the dairy co-operatives in the country with a view to providing a marketing organisation for their products and (b) that it is and has been operated in the interests of Irish dairy farmers. Finally, it was urged that Bord Bainne cannot be regarded as an association of farmers' associations because some of the activities of its foreign subsidiaries are not consistent with such an association. But I think that the board has made out a *prima facie* case that it acquired foreign subsidiaries for the purpose of marketing Irish dairy produce abroad and that the existence of commercial activities of those subsidiaries not normally associated with the dairy industry does not deprive the board of the exemption from the provision of Article 85(1) which otherwise it would have.

I conclude therefore that, *prima facie*, Regulation 26 applies to the agreements which are involved by the adoption of the new rules. As no application to stay these proceedings has been made pending an application to the Commission to determine the matter I must dismiss the claim that the new rules infringe Article 85 of the Treaty, in the absence of a contrary ruling on the point by the Commission.

That brings me to the claim under Article 86. The Treaty envisaged in Article 42 that the rules of competition would apply to trade in agricultural products only to the extent determined by the Council and so it seems to me that Article 86 must be construed in the light of Regulation 26 by which such determination was made.

The rules of farmers' co-operatives constitute an agreement between each individual member and his co-operative as well as mutual engagements between the members themselves.

So, article 2(1) of Regulation 26 means that the rules of farmers' co-operatives are not prohibited by Article 85 of the Treaty even though they may in fact restrict or distort competition. Quite clearly the Council in legislating in this way acknowledged that farmers' co-operatives could have rules which strictly speaking restricted or distorted trade but went on to provide that this fact should not invalidate them, for it was also acknowledged that co-operatives could have very beneficial effects, for example, in ensuring a rational development of agricultural production or in raising farmers' living standards. The intent and purpose of this regulation was therefore to allow farmers' co-operatives to develop and flourish. Similar considerations applied to associations of farmers' co-operatives. It is equally clear that the Council must have been aware that, apart from the adoption of rules which were restrictive of competition, farmers' co-operatives (and associations of farmers' co-operatives) might enter into other agreements or engage in other activities which were abusive within the meaning of Article 86. Complete exemption from the application of Article 86 was not, therefore, granted to farmers' co-operatives. But it seems to me that the *rules* of a farmers' co-operative which finds itself in a dominant position cannot be regarded as 'abusive conduct' under Article 86 merely because they restrict competition as this would defeat the whole purpose and intent of Regulation 26, which is to permit the growth of farmers' co-operatives even if their rules restrict competition. And similar considerations apply to associations of farmers' co-operatives. 8.1.1

This construction of Community law is reinforced by the inference that it is one shared by the Commission. Had the Commission considered that the adoption of rules restrictive of competition by a co-operative in a dominant position amounted in itself to an abuse of that dominant position it seems to me that it would have proceeded long ago against Bord Bainne when its position in the market was more dominant than it now is and when its rules were more restrictive of competition than they now are. The fact that it did not do so suggests that the Commission did not consider that any breach of Community law had been committed by Bord Bainne.

It follows therefore that once a *prima facie* case has been established that the rules of an association of farmers' co-operatives are exempted from the provisions of Article 85(1) by Regulation 26, in the absence of a decision of the Commission to the contrary the rules cannot themselves constitute an abuse of a dominant position under Article 86. As this is the position in this case, and as no other abusive conduct has been alleged against the board, the claim under Article 86 also fails.

As in the event of an appeal my views on the issue of fact raised on this part of the case might be required I should briefly outline my conclusions on the plaintiffs' allegation of breach of Article 86. Bord Bainne purchases agricultural products in Ireland and exports them, *inter alia*, into EEC markets. It has not been suggested that in the market of the member states of the Community in which its dairy products are sold Bord Bainne enjoys a dominant position or that it has in that market abused a dominant position. What has been urged is that in the market *in Ireland* for dairy produce, other than milk (which is the relevant market for present purposes, and not the market in offering services to exporters of dairy produce — see section 5 of Part I), the board enjoys a dominant position and that it has abused it. With some considerable hesitation and notwithstanding the liberalisation of the trading rules brought about in 1988 and the drop in Bord Bainne's market share of exports of dairy produce I have come to the conclusion that it can be said that factually Bord Bainne is presently in a dominant position in the market to which I have referred.

But I do not think that the adoption of the new rules constituted an abuse by the board of that dominant position.

As already pointed out the board by its new rules has considerably liberalised its members' contractual obligations to trade with it so that now that obligation is little more than nominal. This means that all the dairy co-operatives in the country are free to dispose of their products on the home market or abroad as they think fit, subject to an insignificant obligation to maintain a regular supply of some dairy product to the board. I do not consider the imposition of this

8.1.1 obligation amounts to abuse of its dominant position. As the rules in practice do not coerce its members to trade no 'abuse' arises because of their operation. The board itself is not guilty of any of the acts which, by Article 86 itself, are deemed to be an abuse. It does not either by the new rules or otherwise impose unfair purchasing or selling prices or unfair trading conditions; it does not limit production or markets or technical development; it does not apply dissimilar conditions to equivalent transactions or make the conclusion of contracts subject to acceptance of supplementary obligations. It does not, either by the new rules or otherwise, refuse to supply products or fix its prices with a view to eliminating or weakening competition and I cannot agree that the rule (rule 9(d)) permitting the allotment of bonus shares can be likened to a fidelity rebate such as was condemned in *Case 85/76, Hoffmann-La Roche v. Commission* [1979] ECR 461. It is to be remembered that the board is a co- operative selling products sold to it by its members and there is an objective justification for the new rule in the policy which the members wished to implement. The members concluded that the interests of the board are best secured if the ownership of the 'A' ordinary shares are held by those utilising the board as a central marketing organisation and the rule gives effect to this view. All the evidence satisfies me that the board is using its position in the market to ensure that Irish dairy farmers get the best possible price for their products and I cannot accept the evidence that its pricing policies result in its members obtaining lower prices than would otherwise be obtained on world markets. Finally, there is no evidence that the new rules will operate to the detriment of the Irish consumer.

I conclude therefore that Bord Bainne has not, in any way, abused its dominant position. It follows that none of the rules are invalid under Community law.

(4) *Implementation of rule 9(d)*

For reasons given earlier the rules adopted on 15 November 1988 are in my view valid. What remains now for consideration is whether the proposed implementation of rule 9(d) is valid.

It will be recalled that under this rule the board is entitled to apply the net profits of the group of companies of which Bord Bainne is parent in issuing additional 'A' shares to the board's existing shareholders rateably according to the value of the sales of dairy products made by shareholders to the board in the immediately preceding financial year. The new rules were registered on 27 April 1987. The group accounts for the financial year ending 31 December 1988 were considered by the board who decided that there should be issued under new rule 9(d) out of the net profits 5 million £1 bonus shares. The draft accounts were then prepared on this basis for presentation to the annual general meeting of the board's members. Pending the determination of the plaintiffs' claim in these proceedings the court ordered that no further steps be taken to issue or allocate the proposed 5 million bonus shares and the sum of £5m proposed to be utilised for this purpose has been included in a suspense account in the accounts as passed.

The proposed allocation of bonus shares is challenged on a number of grounds. The first is that the allocation is not authorised by the rules because the rules were only registered in 1989. But the rule which was in operation after 27 April 1989 is perfectly clear — the board of directors may make the allocation out of the net profits according to the value of sales to the board in the immediately preceding financial year. As the proposed allocation is from the net profits for the year ending 31 December 1988 which is the financial year immediately preceding the impugned allocation I think the rules permit the board to do what is proposed. It is then argued that the rules are in breach of 'natural and/or constitutional justice' because no adequate notice of intention to distribute the 1988 profits in accordance with rule 9(d) was given to the plaintiffs and the decision to make the allocation was made at a time when neither Kerry Co-op or Avonmore Co-op could alter its trading pattern for the year 1988. The complaint is not that the members in adopting the rule acted oppressively but that the board of directors in implementing it failed to give notice of intention to do so thereby depriving members of an opportunity to qualify for bonus shares by trading with the board to a greater extent than they would have otherwise done. In considering this argument I must recall my finding that the rules were adopted *bona fide* by the members and in the interest of the society as they conceived them. I am equally satisfied that the board of directors *bona fide* purported to implement this rule and neither the board now nor, earlier, the members in general meeting, were seeking to take advantage of the poor trading record of any member. All members were in exactly the same position with regard to notice and no unfair discrimination was involved in the decision to operate rule 9(d). I can find no breach of the rules of natural justice or of the constitutional concept of fair procedures in what the directors are proposing to do. All members were aware that the principle of rewarding those who traded with the board was a long established one. A new way of doing this was authorised by the members by the adoption of rule 9(d) and I do not think that there was any unfairness involved in giving effect to it. Indeed the giving of notice might itself involve unfairness in allowing members artificially to increase their allocation by increasing temporarily their trade with the board. The interlocutory order will therefore lapse with the dismissal of the plaintiffs' claim and the board will be at liberty to operate rule 9(d) in the manner proposed. **8.1.1**

(5) *The plaintiffs' claim against the Registrar of Friendly Societies.*
This is the final matter to be considered. The plaintiffs' claim against the Registrar is that he had acted *ultra vires* and/or illegally and/or contrary to the Industrial and Provident Societies Acts and/or in breach of the constitutional rights of Kerry Co-op and Avonmore Co-op and/or in breach of Article 85 and 86 of the EEC Treaty in registering the 1988 rules. As the new rules did not involve any breach of the plaintiffs' constitutional rights and were not illegal at common law or prohibited by Community law then obviously the claim against him fails. But I think I should add that I agree with the submissions made on his behalf and express my view that the authorities to which I was referred (and in particular the judgment of the Supreme Court in *Irish Civil Service Building Society v. Registrar of Friendly Societies* [1985] IR 167 establish that it is not part of the Registrar's functions to consider a claim that rules proposed for registration are contrary to the Constitution or the common law or Community law; that his sole function is to see that they do not conflict with the provisions of the Industrial and Provident Societies Acts; and that even if the plaintiffs had succeeded in their claim that the rules were invalid the Registrar would not have committed an actionable wrong in registering them.

I will therefore dismiss the claims against both defendants in both actions.

Solicitor for the plaintiffs in the Kerry Co-Operative proceedings: *Martin O'Donoghue*
Solicitors for the plaintiffs in the Avonmore Creameries proceedings: *Arthur Cox & Co.*
Solicitors for the first-named defendant: *Binchy & Partners*
Solicitors for the second-named defendant: *Liam Lysaght & Co.*

A.M. Collins
Barrister

8.1.2 Kerry Co-Operative Creameries Ltd and Patrick O'Connell v. An Bord Bainne Co-Operative Ltd *and* Avonmore Creameries Ltd, Avonmore Foods plc and John Duggan v. An Bord Bainne Co-Operative Ltd: Supreme Court 1990 No. 227 and 234 (Finlay CJ, McCarthy and O'Flaherty JJ) 21 March 1991 and 14 May 1991*

Contract – Restraint of trade – Whether rules of an industrial and provident society which benefit members who trade with that society over those who prefer not to do so are in restraint of trade – Whether the existence of an express covenant or condition in a contract is a precondition for the application of the doctrine – Constitution of Ireland 1937, Article 45

European Community – Question of EC law arising – Function of Supreme Court – Whether resolution of the question necessary to enable court to give judgment – Whether question should be referred to Court of Justice – Whether appropriate for court to express any view on such question – EEC Treaty, Article 177

Industrial and Provident Society – Property rights of shareholders – Power of society to amend rules – Whether shareholders a property right in the assets of the society – Whether amendment ultra vires

Facts An Bord Bainne Co-Operative Ltd ('the Bord') was established as an industrial and provident society in 1972 with the purpose of marketing Irish dairy produce abroad. Its membership consisted of co-operative societies of farmer producers. Members made a nominal subscription for shares calculated by reference to the value of milk intake in their respective creameries in the previous year. The rest of the Bord's capital was raised by means of levies, the issue of deferred shares or loans. With the full consent of its members, the Bord never paid any dividends on its members' shares, maximised prices for the produce it bought and adopted a policy of using profits to reward those members who traded with it.

The members of the Bord agreed upon a set of operating principles which provided, *inter alia*, that each member would get the same price for products of similar quality produced at the same time regardless of the ultimate market in which the product was sold and irrespective of when it was sold. Whilst members were obliged to sell export dairy products to the Bord and any breach of this obligation made them liable to have their membership terminated, no member had been expelled and there was no effective sanction to force members to fulfil their obligations. By means of waiver of the 1975 rules rather than any amendment thereof new purchasing arrangements were adopted by the Bord in 1981 to allow members a freer choice as to whether to use the board's services or to export products directly.

In 1987, the directors of the Bord commenced discussions with its members concerning the board's future structure. These led to the adoption of new rules aimed at improving the position of members which traded exclusively with the Bord over those members which chose to dispose of products for export themselves. At a special general meeting held on 15 November 1988 the members adopted certain amendments of the Bord's rules by a two-thirds majority. These provided for changes concerning membership and the expulsion of members, the manner in which bonus

*This report first appeared in [1991] ILRM 851-880.

shares were to be issued, voting rights and the composition and election of the board of directors. 8.1.2

The appellants in both proceedings had traded extensively with the board up until 1987, when they began to reduce the amount of dairy products sold thereto. They unsuccessfully opposed the adoption of the new rules and subsequently sought to prevent them being registered by the Registrar of Friendly Societies. They then instituted proceedings challenging the validity of the new rules against the board and the registrar but their claims were dismissed by Costello J (see [1990] ILRM 664) [8.1.1 of this book]. The decision in respect of the registrar was not appealed.

Held by the Supreme Court (Finlay CJ, McCarthy and O'Flaherty JJ) in dismissing the appeal but in referring certain questions for a preliminary ruling to the Court of Justice of the European Communities:

(1) Where a decision of the High Court involving a determination of questions of European Community law is appealed to the Supreme Court, the function of the court is to reach a decision as to whether the resolution of such questions was necessary to enable the court to give judgment. In a case where the High Court judge had reached a decision on one or more questions of European Community law, the Supreme Court could not affirm, vary or reverse such decision but, if the resolution of such questions is necessary to enable it to give judgment, must refer those questions for a preliminary ruling to the Court of Justice of the European Communities pursuant to Article 177 of the EEC Treaty.

(2) Assets acquired by an industrial and provident society are the property of the society and no shareholder has a legal right to any specific portion thereof. Such a society is also free to issue shares to new members or to allot new shares to existing members even though the effect is to reduce the fractional interest of existing members in the capital of the society. There is no implied term in the contract between a shareholder and the society of which he is a member that the fractional interest he has in the society's share capital will remain constant.

(3) The adoption of the new rules was not invalid as constituting an unreasonable restraint of trade either because (*per* McCarthy J) the restraint was reasonable or because (*per* O'Flaherty J) there was no covenant restraining trade.

Cases referred to in judgment:

Attorney General v. Jameson [1904] 2 IR 644
Attorney General v. Paperlink Ltd [1984] ILRM 373
Borlans's Trustee v. Steel Brothers & Co. Ltd [1901] 1 Ch 279
Buckley v. Attorney General [1950] IR 57
Bull v. Pitney-Bowes Ltd [1967] 1 WLR 273; [1966] 3 All ER 384
Byrne v. Ireland [1972] IR 241
Comyn v. Attorney General [1950] IR 142
Esso Petroleum Co. Ltd v. Harper's Garage (Stourport) Ltd [1968] AC 269; [1967] 2 WLR 871; [1967] 1 All ER 699
Hole v. Garnsey [1930] AC 472; 46 TLR 312, 143 LT 153
Landers v. Attorney General (1975) 109 ILTR 1
McEllistrim v. Ballymacelligott Co-Operative Agricultural and Dairy Society [1919] AC 548
McGee v. Attorney General [1974] IR 284
Maxim Nordenfelt Guns and Ammunition Co. v. Nordenfelt [1894] AC 535
Mulligan v. Corr [1925] 1 IR 169
Murtagh Properties Ltd v. Cleary [1972] IR 330
Mutual Life Insurance Co. of New York v. Rank Organisation Ltd [1985] BCLC 11
Nova Media Services Ltd v. Minister for Posts and Telegraphs [1984] ILRM 161

8.1.2 *O'Brien v. Manufacturing Engineering Co. Ltd* [1973] IR 334
Rodgers v. ITGWU [1978] ILRM 51
Ryan v. Attorney General [1965] IR 294
Schroeder Music Publishing Co. Ltd v. Macaulay [1974] 1 WLR 1308; [1974] 3 All ER 616
Stenhouse Australia Ltd v. Phillips [1974] AC 391;[1974] 2 WLR 134; [1974] 1 All ER 117
Stohmenger v. Borough of Finsbury Permanent Investment Building Society [1897] 2 Ch 469
Wyatt v. Kreglinger [1933] 1 KB 793

T.K. Liston SC, Daniel O'Keeffe SC and Paul Gallagher SC **for the appellants in the Kerry Co-Operative appeal**
Dermot Gleeson SC, Daniel O'Keeffe SC and Paul Gallagher SC **for the appellants in the Avonmore Creameries appeal**
Nial Fennelly SC, John D. Cooke SC and John Trainor **for the respondent**

FINLAY CJ delivered his judgment on 21 March 1991 saying: I have read the judgments which are about to be delivered by McCarthy J and O'Flaherty J, each of which deals with the issues of national law arising in these two appeals, and I am in agreement with the conclusions which they have reached and with their proposed dismissal on all grounds of the appeals by the plaintiffs against the findings and order made by Costello J on those issues.

In relation to the claim that the adoption of the new rules was invalid as constituting an unreasonable restraint of trade, both the judgments decide that the measures were reasonable. With those decisions and with the reasoning underlying them I am in complete agreement.

McCarthy J in his judgment has rejected the submission made on behalf of the respondent that a restraint of trade must be an express covenant or condition in a contract, whereas, O'Flaherty J has concluded that the existence of such covenant or condition in a contract is a precondition for the application of the doctrine concerning restraint of trade.

The resolution of the issue thus arising as between the two judgments is not necessary for the determination of the plaintiffs' claim in the light of our agreed conclusion that any restraint of trade, howsoever arising in the case, was reasonable.

Having regard to the general importance of this issue of law, I would prefer to reserve my decision on it until it arises in a case as a question necessary for the determination of the claim.

The agreed decision of this Court to affirm the dismiss of the entire of the plaintiffs' claim, based on national law, makes potentially relevant issues of European Community law which have been pleaded and debated.

The other members of the court have authorised me in this judgment to state our agreed views on these issues.

Where a decision of the High Court involving (as occurred in this case) a determination of questions of EC law is appealed to this Court, the function of this Court, having regard to the provisions of Article 177 of the Treaty establishing the European Community (the Treaty) is both clear and limited.

It is for this Court to reach a decision as to whether the resolution of any question concerning
(a) the interpretation of the Treaty and/or
(b) the validity and interpretation of acts of the institutions of the Community and/or
(c) the interpretation of the statutes of bodies established by an act of the Council where those statutes so provide is necessary to enable this Court to give judgment.

That decision is, of course, a matter of national law necessarily governed by a consideration of the principles applicable in that law to the issues which must be determined in order for this Court to give judgment on the issues between the parties.

In any case where a judge of first instance has, as he is clearly entitled to do, reached a decision on one or more questions of European Community law, coming within the categories mentioned in Article 177 of the Treaty, this Court as a final court of appeal cannot affirm, vary or reverse such a decision, but must, if the resolution of such questions is necessary to enable it to give its judgment, refer those questions for a preliminary ruling to the Court of Justice of the European Communties pursuant to Article 177. If, of course, this Court decides that the resolution of such questions is not necessary to enable it to give judgment in the case, then no reference is made. In either event it is not appropriate for this Court to express any view on issues of European Community law arising in this manner, except for the particular instance where it may conclude that what was alleged to be an issue of EC law is in fact incapable of any but one resolution, and has so clearly been determined. **8.1.2**

In this case the plaintiffs' claim that the enactment of the new rules is invalid as constituting a breach of Article 85 and Article 86 of the Treaty.

With regard to the allegation of a breach of Article 85, Costello J, having reviewed the provisions of relevant articles of the Treaty and of Regulation No. 26 adopted by the Council of Ministers on 6 April 1962, came to the following conclusion:

> So, an important jurisdictional point arises. How can I in the light of paragraph 2 of Article 2 of Regulation 26 adjudicate on the issue which has been raised in these proceedings, namely whether Regulation 26 exempts the association created by the new rules from the provisions of Article 85? I do not think I can. I must apply a law which specifically withdraws from national courts jurisdiction to adjudicate on such an issue and confers jurisdiction on the Commission (and on appeal the Court of Justice) to determine it.
>
> I conclude, therefore, that *prima facie* Regulation 26 applies to the agreements which are involved by the adoption of the new rules. As no application to stay these proceedings has been made pending an application to the Commission to determine the matter, I must dismiss the claim that the new rules infringe Article 85 of the Treaty, in the absence of a contrary ruling on the point by the Commission.

This Court is satisfied that the conclusion thus reached was correct and, furthermore, that it constitutes a decision concerning the jurisdiction of the court to grant to the plaintiffs relief in respect of a complaint in these proceedings of a breach of Article 85. As such it is a determination not of a question of interpretation of the Treaty, such as is referred to in Article 177, but of the fact that the determination of the question of an alleged breach of Article 85 cannot be made by the national court in this case and, consequently, could not be necessary to enable the court to give judgment in this action.

The court is, therefore, satisfied that the issue of an alleged breach of Article 85 should neither be determined in this appeal nor referred to the Court of Justice of the European Communities pursuant to Article 177 of the Treaty.

With regard to the complaint of a breach of Article 86, the conclusion of Costello J was as follows:

> Complete exemption from the application of Article 86 was not, therefore, granted to farmers' co-operatives. But it seems to me that the rules of a farmers' co-operative which finds itself in a dominant position cannot be regarded as 'abusive conduct' under Article 86 merely because they restrict competition, as this would defeat the whole purpose and intent of Regulation 26 which is to permit the growth of farmers' co- operatives, even if their rules restrict competition. And similar considerations apply to associations of farmers' co-operatives.
>
> It follows, therefore, that once a *prima facie* case has been established that the rules of an association of farmers' co-operatives is exempted from the provisions of Article 85(1) by Regulation 26, in the absence of a decision of the Commission to the contrary, the rules cannot themselves constitute an abuse of a dominant position under Article 86. As this is the position in this case and as no other abusive conduct has been alleged against the board, the claim under Article 86 also fails.

8.1.2 These are conclusions which involve an interpretation of articles of the Treaty which is not a self-evident interpretation. In these circumstances, this Court cannot express any view on them, but if they determine issues which are necessary to enable judgment to be given in this appeal, they must be referred, under Article 177, to the Court of Justice of the European Communities. The respondent in the course of this appeal has, however, submitted, in addition to submissions that the findings of the learned trial judge with regard to Article 86 of European law are so clear as to admit of no question, which submission has been rejected by this Court, that a determination of any question on the pleadings and on the facts under Article 86 does not arise as necessary to enable the court to give judgment in this case. They have made that general contention, largely based, firstly, on an assertion that in the absence of any evidence of distortion or abuse arising from the actual trading operation of An Bord Bainne that the mere introduction of new rules the effect of which in trading has not been established, could not constitute an abuse, nor could it constitute evidence of an abuse fit to raise a question for reference to the Court of Justice. Secondly, they have contended that by reason of the necessity, if an issue under Article 85 is to be determined between the parties, that it should be referred, in the first instance, to the Commission under Regulation 26, that since the Commission must, in considering any such application for exemption from Article 85 also consider the provisions of Article 86, and since its decision on such application is subject to appeal to the Court of Justice, that it is not appropriate nor necessary to enable this Court to give judgment in this case for it to refer any question with regard to Article 86 to the Court of Justice of the European Communities.

In the light of the findings and decision of this Court in regard to the issues of national law and fact which were the subject matter of this appeal, and in the light of the determination which has been reached by this Court that, for the reasons stated, a reference under Article 177 is not appropriate in relation to a complaint concerning a breach of Article 85 of the Treaty, the court would be anxious to have further submissions from the parties directly related to the question as to whether a reference under Article 177 of the complaint of a breach of Article 86 is necessary to enable the court to give judgment, which submissions should be related to the two issues which have been identified as already adumbrated by the respondent on this question and also to any other question touching the necessity for such a reference.

McCARTHY J: This judgment is common to both appeals.

The facts have been detailed in the judgment of Costello J to whom I am indebted for the clear and comprehensive summary of all relevant facts that he has made. I gratefully adopt that summary contained in Parts I to IV of that judgment and the accuracy of which has not been challenged.

It is proper, however, to identify certain features:

(1) From small and diffuse beginnings, as identified in *McEllistrim v. Ballymacelligot Co-operative Agricultural and Dairy Society* [1919] AC 548, the dairy co-operatives in Ireland have combined a massive growth in business with a sharp drop in the numbers of individual co-operatives. Both Kerry and Avonmore are major co-operatives in the Irish dairy industry. There are few others of their size.

(2) A key to this growth has been the establishment and success of Bord Bainne whose flagship is the trademark 'Kerrygold', acknowledged to be itself a most valuable asset.

(3) Both Kerry and Avonmore as well as a small number of other major co-operatives and the dairy farming industry in Ireland generally have made significant contributions to the success of Bord Bainne.

(4) Bord Bainne, like any other co-operative, is bound by rules duly adopted and subject to change. There has always been a limit on the number of shares that may be held by any member.

(5) The profile of supplies by different co-operatives to Bord Bainne has changed and continues to change because of a variety of market considerations. In particular, Kerry, whose turnover increased from £21 million in 1974 to £397 million in 1988, of its product sold to the

Board £16 million in 1975 rising to £47 million in 1986 but falling to £6.6 million (or 1.1% of total purchases made by Bord Bainne) in 1988. Likewise, Avonmore has seen its turnover grow to £295 million in 1988, whilst its sales to Bord Bainne grew from £9 million in 1974 to almost £80 million in 1984 but declined to £33 million in 1988. Both Kerry and Avonmore have invested substantially in the food industry in other countries. **8.1.2**

(6) By reason of the policy adopted by Bord Bainne, a policy decided by the various shareholders, its steadily increasing profits have been largely put back into the co-operative of which the net worth had, by 1988, reached £88.8 million.

(7) Shares in Bord Bainne were issued at par. In the event of a winding up, Kerry and Avonmore as shareholders have a contractual right (i) to be repaid the amount they subscribed for their shares and (ii) to share in the distribution of any surplus assets as provided in the rules — a right vested in the holders in the 'A' and 'B' ordinary shares. Further, in the case of termination of membership for misconduct (Rule 6) or for non- trading (Rule 8) the member expelled is entitled only to a return of the sums subscribed by it for shares. This is in keeping with the practice in other co-operatives, including Kerry and Avonmore; it is reflected in their accounts.

(8) The market believes that co-operative shares have a value which may be unlocked because of winding up or flotation. Viewed as a percentage of the 'A' and 'B' shareholding corresponding to a percentage of the net asset value of Bord Bainne, the value of the shareholdings of Kerry and Avonmore would approximate to £10 million.

(9) There is said to be a possible market for such shares at a sum significantly greater than the par value. I will return to a more detailed consideration of this feature.

(10) One of the effects of the new rules is to enable Bord Bainne, by appropriate resolution, to distribute bonus shares which would rank *pari passu* with the existing'A' and 'B' shares; in the event of winding up, if there had been such a distribution, as in fact resolved by Bord Bainne in 1988, the percentage equivalent payable to the plaintiffs would be significantly reduced, because their percentage of qualifying shares would be reduced.

(11) The objectives of Bord Bainne, however worded, essentially are the promotion of Irish dairy exports. The continuing strength of Bord Bainne is part of that promotion; the channelling of milk product exports through Bord Bainne is part of the same promotion.

(12) After protracted debate, the new rules were adopted by resolution supported by over 70% of the votes cast.

The Complaint

The core of the case, as described by Mr Gleeson SC at the commencement of the hearing, is contained in paragraph 4.2 of the appellants' written submission:

> One of the bundle of rights, (implicit in the ownership of shares as a property right) is an entitlement not to have shares arbitrarily or unfairly devalued, or deprived of their value.

If that be the core, it is at the centre of a much larger case. The attack on the validity of the new rules is on a broad front in which it is alleged:

(a) the dilution is an unconstitutional attack on property rights,

(b) the relevant new rules are *ultra vires* the board,

(c) the relevant new rules amount to oppression of a minority,

(d) the implementation of the relevant new rules constitutes an impermissible restraint of trade — a vertical restraint,

(e) the like implementation constitutes,

(1) an agreement prohibited by Article 85 of the Treaty of Rome,

(2) an abuse of a dominant position prohibited by Article 86 of the Treaty.

Having examined in detail each of the complaints, Costello J rejected the challenge to the

8.1.2 validity of the new rules. The plaintiffs appeal.

The value of the shareholding

Kerry and Avonmore each hold approximately 6% of the relevant ordinary shares which were issued at par and, in the event of the shareholder ceasing to be a member of Bord Bainne, are to be redeemed at par. The rules permit the issuing of such shares to new members — also at par. Such an event would dilute the percentage shareholding of Kerry and Avonmore. Issuing bonus shares under Rule 9(d) the impugned rule — would have the same effect, unless Kerry or Avonmore qualify for such shares in exactly the same proportion as their existing shareholding bears to the total number of issued shares. The argument for Kerry and Avonmore is that each owns part of the equity as that word is used in the affairs of commercial companies. I agree with Costello J that this is a misnomer in respect of the nominal sums paid by members on joining Bord Bainne. The nub of the case on this aspect is that Kerry and Avonmore are not only owners of a particular number of shares of £1 each allotted to them when they became members but that those shares must continue to represent the same percentage of the total number of like shares of the society. If they fail in that contention, then the consequences alleged, as to oppression or unconstitutional expropriation have no actionable base.

The classical definition of a share in a company is that of Farwell J in *Borland's Trustee v. Steel Brothers & Co. Ltd* [1901] 1 Ch 279 at 288:

> A share is the interest of a shareholder in the company measured by a sum of money, for the purpose of liability in the first place, and of interest in the second, but also consisting of a series of mutual covenants entered into by all the shareholders *inter se* in accordance with [the Companies Act]. The contract contained in the articles of association is one of the original incidents of the share. A share is not a sum of money . . . but is an interest measured by a sum of money and made up of various rights contained in the contract, including the right to a sum of money of a more or less amount.

Share capital may be increased by the issue of further shares. There is no legal obligation to issue shares at the best price, for instance, where a company has been trading profitably and built up reserves. In that case the true value of the existing shares will exceed par; yet the effect of dilution of the value of the existing shares is the inevitable consequence of what is perfectly lawful, so long as there is no breach of fiduciary duty or fraud on the minority. Costello J, in dealing with this topic, cited with approval the observations of Kenny J in *Attorney General v. Jameson* [1904] 2 IR 644 at 669, 670. And goes on to state:

> (d) There is no implied term in the contract between a member and the company of which he is a member that the fractional interest he has in the company's issued share capital will remain constant and will not be altered by the issuing of additional shares, citing in support of this principle the judgment of Goulding J in *Mutual Life Insurance Company of New York v. Rank Organisation Ltd* [1985] BCLC 11. In that case, at p. 21, Goulding J said:
>
> to my mind the wide powers and provisions contained in article 7, being themselves an express term of the membership contract which the members have accepted, ought not to be whittled down by any implication beyond what is required in the circumstances of the membership contract by the ordinary principles of the law of contract. That law in such circumstances, and so far as relevant to this action, requires in my judgment but two implied terms. First, the time honoured rule that the directors' powers are to be exercised in good faith in the interests of the company, and secondly, that they must be exercised fairly as between different shareholders. I doubt whether it is possible to formulate either of the stipulations more precisely because of the infinity of circum-

stances in which they may fall to be applied. 8.1.2

Assuming that the rights of members of the co-operative that is Bord Bainne are the same as the rights of members of a company, the principles outlined and justified by Goulding J, and adopted by Costello J, appear to contemplate that where power to allot shares has been conferred in wide terms it is only subject to these two implied terms:

(1) that the power would be exercised by the directors in good faith and in the interests of the society and

(2) that it will be exercised fairly as between different shareholders (which did not require that they be treated identically).

More to the point in the present case is the overriding factor that there is no apparent inequality in the possible or intended distribution of bonus shares save an inequality created by the action or inaction of the relevant members. If Kerry and Avonmore want to qualify for bonus shares in the future, the remedy is in their own hands. That does not answer for those reasons the complaint in respect of the distribution based upon the 1988 trading.

In his judgment ([1990] ILRM at 715) Costello J said:

> (e) The power to increase and reduce the capital of a registered company is subject to considerable statutory regulation. In particular, the recent Companies (Amendment) Act 1983 contains a provision designed to protect existing shareholders against the dilution of their holdings by the issue of new shares by conferring pre-emptive rights on existing shareholders when what are called 'equity securities' are issued (a term which does not include bonus shares). But none of this legislation applies to societies registered under the 1893 Act. There are no statutory restrictions on the manner in which *registered societies* may increase or decrease their share capital. They may decrease their capital, as Kerry Co-op did when it expelled members in the manner to which I have earlier referred and repaid them the capital they had contributed. They may increase their capital by taking in new members, as Avonmore Co-op proposed to do in its takeover battle in relation to Westmeath Co-op. When new shares are paid for, the society may acquire assets and in the event of a winding up existing shareholders who own a smaller percentage of the enlarged issued capital may not suffer financially because of this. But assets may be lost and if so the members whose shareholding has been diluted by the allotment of new shares will be adversely affected. But no legal wrong will have been committed.
>
> (f) The terms 'net worth' and 'net assets' (frequently employed throughout this case) are terms used by accountants to refer to the difference between a company's outside liabilities and the book value of its assets. They refer to an abstract figure and there is no group of assets which can be designated the 'net worth' or the 'net assets' of the company and no property right can reside in a balance sheet figure of a registered society designated in the balance sheet as its 'net worth'.
>
> The application of these principles to the facts of these cases inevitably leads to the conclusion that the claims that Kerry Co-op and Avonmore Co-op have property rights in the assets or in the 'net worth' of Bord Bainne fails. . . .

The plaintiffs identify three factors which they say were not taken into account in the judge's summary:

(a) If members of the society choose to leave profits behind them that is an investment by them in the society.

(b) There may be wholly innocent reasons for not trading with Bord Bainne — fire, strike, infection.

8.1.2 (c) If shares are a bonus they must have a value.

Further, from an empirical point of view, they point to the retrospective application of what they say is an arbitrary criterion.

Costello J in concluding as I have quoted identified his reasons as being:

> (a) There is no term in their contracts as shareholders or members which confers any property rights in any of the underlying assets of Bord Bainne nor in what has been referred to as the board's 'net worth' or 'net assets'. They did not acquire any percentage of the board's net worth by virtue of their ownership of ordinary shares either by reference to the percentage of the ordinary shares they own or otherwise. It follows that by operating Rule 8(c) so as to expel a member and return only the capital it paid up, or by operating Rule 9(d) so as to reduce the percentage shareholding of a member in the total issued share capital of the society, the board does not infringe any property right of the member or involve the expropriation of any member's property.
>
> (b) Nor can it be said that by trading over the years with the board and by contributing at least in part to the net profits made from which assets were acquired that they acquired a proprietorial interest in any of the board's assets. The assets thus acquired became the board's property and no shareholder has any property in them either alone or jointly with others. Rule 9(d), by which profits from foreign subsidiaries may theoretically be used to fund an issue of bonus shares, is not for this reason invalid as it infringes no property right of any member.

I find this reasoning and conclusion of the learned trial judge wholly convincing. Under the rules, the rights of members are not altered by the success or failure of the society. The contention as to market value of shares in Bord Bainne has a superficial attraction; the experience of the last decade or so in the growth of the major co-operatives from relative insignificance to being major factors in the agricultural industry with the consequent interest of big investors from the world of finance and the efforts of self aggrandisement, which may be called greed, in many instances has created a market for shares in co-operatives where the price far exceeds the par value. This is based upon a degree of informed speculation to which I shall return.

The rules of the society contain express provision concerning the manner of dealing with the shares of a member on termination of membership. Rule 6 which enables the society to terminate the membership of any member who shall offend against the rules of the society *etc* provides that the full amount paid or credited upon the shares held by the member, less such sums as may be due by him to the society, shall be paid to him on the termination of his membership provided that such repayment would not jeopardise the financial stability of the society. Rule 15 enables the society to refund the share capital subscribed in the event of a member amalgamating with a society which is not a member of Bord Bainne; that society has other options in regard to issuing the combined amount of all shares in the event of a member amalgamating with another member of the society. Rule 18 should be quoted in full:

> The board may sell and transfer any shares including deferred shares standing in the name of a member who is indebted to the society, provided a fortnight's notice in writing has been given to the defaulting member. The board may apply so much of the proceeds as may be necessary to the discharge of the debt due, together with the necessary incidental expenses, and the balance outstanding of the full amount paid upon the shareholding of such member shall be refunded to him and the shareholding cancelled, whereupon an entry shall be made in the share register accordingly. A member in arrear with the calls duly made on his shares shall forfeit all rights of membership, including attendance at meetings, during the period of his default.

This rule corresponds to Rule 18 of the 1975 rules, as amended, and to Rule 15 of the 1972 rules. 8.1.2

These rules lend further support to the conclusion I have outlined. If the society wished to eliminate a debt due by a member to the society it may transfer the relevant shares for that purpose. On the plaintiffs' argument, it would have to realise the 'market value' of the shares; in doing so it might have to break its own rules by admitting to membership of the society some person or body other than those contemplated by Rule 5.

From time to time in the course of the appeal hearing and during my protracted consideration of the arguments advanced, I have had to remind myself of the fundamental nature of a co-operative society. It contrasts with a company of limited liability in that its shareholders invest their efforts in the betterment of activity in co-operation with each other being persons of a like interest, rather than their seeking a return on investment capital, which is the role of the investor in a company of limited liability; the latter is indifferent to the operation of the company so long as he is assured of an adequate return on his investment. The development of industrial and provident societies, including agricultural co-operatives, is one of the happier features of the Victorian age. In their written submission, the respondents have quoted from a former English Registrar of Societies who, in distinguishing these societies from Friendly Societies, said that their purpose was 'intended to intimate the design that such societies should be industrial as making their profits by the mutual personal exertions of the members and provident as distributing their profits by way of provision for the future.' Such a purpose is reflected in the rules of Bord Bainne, as it is, I believe, in the rules of other agricultural co-operative societies, which are concerned with the promotion of agriculture by self help with a flexible capital; such flexibility does not depend upon bonus shares but may well arise under rules concerning termination of membership, amalgamation and the like.

The share value

It was in the context of the alleged restraint of trade that Costello J considered the plaintiffs' case as to the share value. This was largely derived from the evidence of Christopher G. Glover who is an expert in the valuation, of unquoted securities. He prepared a valuation report on An Bord Bainne Co-operative Ltd; it was dated February 1990 and had appended to it a trading review. The report concluded that Avonmore's shareholding on the basis of the 1975 rules, as amended, had a value in the region of IR £7 million, and on the basis of the impugned rules of 1988 a value of approximately IR £100,000. The calculation of the larger valuation was based on three alternatives; flotation or capitalisation if its shares were listed; purchase of the entire equity — as already indicated, perhaps not an appropriate phrase; the amount receivable in a voluntary winding up. Mr Glover's report was examined in detail in the judgment in the High Court. The shares have no market value but what is called an owner value, dependant upon which of the three alternatives was most probable. Costello J concluded that the shares cannot have any owner value and gave his reasons as follows:

> There are a number of factors which suggest that it is extremely unlikely that the members of Bord Bainne will decide to alter fundamentally the structure and status of the board in the manner envisaged in Mr Glover's evidence or to establish a corporate structure in some other way which would enable it to obtain a stock exchange listing. Firstly, there is no financial reason for it to do so, as there is no evidence to suggest that there is any need for it to raise equity capital by means of a public subscription in order to fund future development. Secondly, to carry out its functions as a central marketing organisation for the export produce of the dairy farmers of this country by means of a listed public company would involve a considerable alteration in the basic policy which has guided the board over the years and there is no evidence to show that the members would agree to such a change. That policy has been to pay the highest possible price for the dairy products of its members and not to operate so as to create profits to pay

8.1.2 dividends to its shareholders. There might, it is true, be some immediate financial gain to the member societies and companies of the board if a decision to adopt the proposed new structure was taken but I think it is very unlikely that members would sacrifice the long-term interest of Irish dairy farmers to obtain it. Thirdly, the whole future of the board was discussed by the members and debated in the media over many months before the decisions were taken at the meeting of 15 November 1988. Those decisions involved the rejection of an option involving the establishment of a public limited company with the stock exchange listing, which would have created a corporate status more beneficial to the individual dairy farmers than would the corporate framework envisaged in the evidence I am now considering. I think it is very unlikely that the question of the future structure of the board will be a live issue again for some considerable time and I believe that the corporate structures established in 1988 will remain in place for the foreseeable future.

The plaintiffs expressly challenge this conclusion inviting this Court to substitute its own conclusion upon the primary facts as found by Costello J. In my judgment, not merely was such a conclusion open to the learned trial judge on the evidence to which he has referred; it was the correct and proper inference to be drawn from those facts. I do not overlook the evidence of transactions of one kind or another in which various cash values well in excess of par have been paid for shares in other societies; we are here not dealing with other societies — we are dealing with a society in whose future the entire dairy agricultural industry in Ireland has an immense stake and for whose future government more than 70% of the qualified shareholding in effect voted to continue its operation on existing lines, save to encourage further the direct participation by its members in the trading activities of the society itself. The alleged dilution of the percentage of shareholding consequent upon the implementation of Rule 9(d) is not a one-way traffic; it affects all the shareholders whose votes added up to the majority voting in favour of the change in rules. They, also, suffer, if that be the appropriate word, the dilution, but they voted in favour of the change. This, itself, must be a consideration in assessing the realities when examining Mr Glover's report and his evidence. Individuals or corporate bodies may speculate and be prepared to wager upon their speculations; such a circumstance does not change the legal position. The forbearance year on year in respect of profits was not a contribution to the value of the individual shareholding. The allocation of shares as a bonus is an incentive to trade with the board; if the shares have an owner or market value, it is itself eroded by the distribution of bonus shares. Apart from prestige for the shareholder the bonus shares also increase, pro rata, the voting strength of the shareholder on any aspect of liquidation. True, the bonus might be paid by cash to the co-operating shareholder, who deals directly with the society, but the continuing of such a scheme would lessen the cash resources of the society and, consequently, its liquidity.

The Alternative Claims

(1) Infringement of Property Rights

Kerry argues that if it were expelled under Rule 8(c) it would be deprived of the value of its share in the net worth; similarly a dilution under Rule 9(d) would also involve an expropriation of the property right — a right of property in the underlying assets of the society, which it contends it has as a shareholder and because of its past trading with the society. I find no support in law for this proposition. The rules of the society constitute the contract between the society and its members; there is no implied term in a contract between a limited company and its shareholders that the fractional interest a shareholder has in the company's issued share capital will remain constant. Is there a term express or implied in the contract between the society and its members that there will be no dilution? It is self evident that there may be dilution if only to admit new members. No more than a shareholder in a limited company has any property right in any of the underlying assets of the company does the member of a co-op have a property right in the assets of the co-op. The argument advanced as detailed in the judgment of the learned trial judge, I find to be contrived and unsustainable. I wholly accept the reasoning of the learned trial judge in this regard. **8.1.2**

(2) Ultra vires

It is not in issue that the restraints placed on the power of amendment of articles of association of a limited company apply to the rules of a society such as Bord Bainne. The shareholders cannot validly adopt a rule which changes the nature and constitution of the society; the alterations 'must be confined to the internal rights of the members of the society' (*Stohmenger v. Borough of Finsbury Permanent Investment Building Society* [1897] 2 Ch 469). In this context, the appellants placed great reliance on the principles outlined in *Hole v. Garnsey* [1930] AC 472. They contend that a member joining a society only committed himself to be bound by the decision of the majority of his associates on matters within 'the contemplated scope of the venture he had undertaken with them' and that the power of amendment should be 'confined to such amendments as can reasonably be considered to have been within the contemplation of the parties when the contract was made, having regard to the nature and circumstances of the contract'. They identify a variety of matters which it is said would not reasonably have been in the contemplation of the members of the board in 1972:

(a) That reserves would be preserved and value accumulated, and profits built up within the organisation for 17 years and that the value represented by such reserves would be released in a flood in a single year in the form of bonus shares.

(b) That in that first year alone the total bonus shares issued (with a right to participate in the surplus assets on a winding up) would be four times as great in number as the whole of the existing shareholding enjoying such rights.

(c) That in a distribution in the 17th year, based on sales, the reserves or value which accumulated over the 17 years by way of sales and patronage or dividends foregone (for the first 16 of those 17 years) would be entirely ignored.

(d) That those members who contributed significantly to the building up of Bord Bainne would be damnified by an issue of bonus shares, at a time when Bord Bainne was financially sound, and when it was no longer necessary to support it.

(e) That the shares in Bord Bainne would have the actual or potential value they have today.

(f) That the members would be encouraged to leave the profits in Bord Bainne until it had a solid financial footing and that the benefit of these profits in a strong Bord Bainne would then be passed to other members without the payment of compensation.

(g) That bonus shares would be issued in a discriminatory way, without giving all the members a chance to participate. (This was identified in oral argument as being in contrast to a chance to participate *pro rata* to capital invested.)

(h) That any bonus share scheme would ever be used as an instrument to bring about a radical and rapid alteration of ownership of Bord Bainne.

I cite this argument in full from the written submission of the appellants. They appear to me to be an instance of the somewhat contrived features that are to be found from time to time in the arguments presented on this appeal, not merely by the appellants. An objective examination of the circumstances prevailing at the time of the adoption of the 1972 rules can be fairly readily made; I reject, however, the submission that regard should be had to the subjective evidence of what was within the contemplation of the parties or to the action of the members of the society in the ensuing years in, for instance, foregoing dividends. In so far as the power of amendment is to be confined to such amendments as can reasonably be considered to have been within the contemplation of the parties when the contract was made, in my judgment the limitation thus imposed must, itself, be limited by the circumstance that there are many events, both national and international, which may effect fundamental changes of circumstance but have to be met within the parameters of existing laws or rules, which themselves provide a machinery for amendment. I find it easier to accept the view of the learned

8.1.2 trial judge that what the court has to consider is whether the members could, in 1972, have reasonably contemplated, for instance, that if it were decided to relax the contractual trading obligations, a future meeting would also adopt the sort of rules which were in fact adopted in 1988 in order to maintain the central marketing organisation that Bord Bainne had established. I put it further. Could the members in 1972 have reasonably contemplated that if the business of the society were to be dramatically successful, as it turned out, but that some of the members might prove less than willing to continue the size of their active participation in the use of the board as a marketing organisation, the rules might validly be altered so as to promote the co-operative feature of the society — that the members would be encouraged to stay together.

Hole v. Garnsey was a case where the purported amendment 'did not simply affect the rights of the member in the capital of the society, but imposed a perfectly new and outside liability upon him' (*per* Viscount Dunedin at 490). In that instance it differed from *Stohmenger*. The amendment was described by Viscount Sumner as being a claim by the society (the Wilts and Somerset Farmers Ltd) 'by the exercise of its power to make regulations and to alter or rescind them, [to] compel members to invest capital in its business against their will without, so far as I can see, any limit at all.' Lord Tomlin gave a graphic instance of what would be an excessive exercise of the power of amendment and rejected a scheme which:

> discriminated between members and has laid on members an obligation to hold more shares. . . . I do not think that it is within the contemplation of the parties to a bargain of this kind that they should be made liable for a compulsory levy or expenditure over and above the contributions payable or to become payable under the original terms. On the contrary I think the basis of such a bargain is that the extent of the members' liability is limited by the original terms and that it cannot be enlarged by any amendment of the rules. (p. 501).

I pose the question: if in 1972 the members of the society had believed that with growth beyond any expectation in the society some of its members would, 16 years down the road, contemplate going it alone or largely alone, would they have said — then we will amend the rules to make more stringent the provisions to secure co-operative trading? There can only be one answer — it lies in the nature of a co-operative society.

I do not construe *Hole v. Garnsey* as stating a principle limiting amendments of rules to what was within the contemplation of the parties when the contract was made. If it does state such a principle, then I do not accept it as part of our law. It would seem to me unworkable particularly in the case of a highly successful organisation that the only changes the members or shareholders might make pursuant to a power of amendment would be those that were contemplated at the time of the making of the contract. Indeed, one might well say that nothing save formal amendments would be permitted under such principle since if it were to be such and only such as was within the contemplation of the parties, why did they not put it in the contract at the start? One may imply terms into a contract on the basis that if the parties had thought of it at the time, such a term would have been inserted. That is not quite the same thing as the restricted interpretation sought to be imposed here. There is no fundamental alteration involved in the 1988 rules; the structure of the society remains the same with the same objects, function and trade. So far as *Hole v. Garnsey* is concerned, there is an essential difference — no new financial burden is placed upon the shareholders — there is no change in the essential nature of the society — there is no conversion of a dairy society into a boot manufacturing society.

The learned trial judge dealt with this submission at considerable length and rejected it. He was correct in doing so.

Costello J referred to two principles touching on the validity of the amendments — (a) reasonable contemplation and (b) change in the nature of the society. These principles must be read in the light of the conclusions that I have expressed.

(3) Oppression 8.1.2

No challenge has been made nor could any be successfully made to the good faith of the majority who adopted the 1988 rules. The fact that the changed operation of the society, including the rewards to its members for trading with the society, will benefit some more than others, largely because of their own choice of operation, cannot constitute a true oppression. There is nothing unfair even though the result may provide inequality.

(4) Restraint of Trade

> A contract which is in restraint of trade cannot be enforced unless
> (a) it is reasonable as between the parties and
> (b) it is consistent with the interests of the public.

McEllistrim v. Ballymacelligott Co-operative Agricultural and Dairy Society [1919] AC 548 at 562.

Here, the contract is contained in the 1988 rules; no relevant restraint is expressed in them. Costello J said 'It is, moreover, well established that although a contract or a term of a contract may not explicitly restrain trade the prohibition against restraints may be infringed if the effect in practice of implementing a contractual term is to restrain trade (*Stenhouse Australia Ltd v. Phillips* [1974] AC 391)'. The respondents 'do not fully adopt' this statement of the law contending that it is too broad, since every commercial contract of any sort whatever would come within that test. We are not concerned with every commercial contract; we are concerned with the rules of 1988. The effect in practice of implementing Rule 9(d) is beyond question to restrain trade; its implementation provides the clearest incentive to trade in one direction and not another, to trade within the society and not outside it. I reject the submission that a restraint of trade must be an express covenant or condition in a contract.

The doctrine of restraint of trade is a classic instance of the application of public policy; it has been part of the common law since the 16th century. It is desirable from the standpoint of the public good, to protect the right to work of weaker parties from abuse and to gain the economic benefits of preventing such abuses. It finds an echo in Article 45 of the Constitution which provides:

> (2) The State shall, in particular, direct its policy towards securing:
>
> (i) That the citizens (all of whom, men and women equally, have the right to an adequate means of livelihood) may through their occupations find the means of making reasonable provision for their domestic needs.
> (ii) That the ownership and control of the material resources of the community may be so distributed amongst private individuals and the various classes as best to subserve the common good.
> (iii) That, especially, the operation of free competition shall not be allowed so to develop as to result in the concentration of the ownership or control of essential commodities in a few individuals to the common detriment.

The exclusion of these directive principles of social policy from being cognisable by any court is in respect of the making of laws.

There have been many judicial definitions of what is restraint of trade. In *Mulligan v. Corr* [1925] 1 IR 169 Fitzgibbon J accepted that the nature of the doctrine had been settled by *Maxim Nordenfelt Guns and Ammunition Co. v. Nordenfelt* [1894] AC 535. There, Lord Macnaghten formulates the doctrine by way of a test:

> The true view at the present time, I think, is this; the public have an interest in every

8.1.2 person carrying on his trade freely; so has the individual. All interference with individual liberty of action in trading, and all restraints of trade of themselves, if there is nothing more, are contrary to public policy, and therefore void. That is the general rule. But there are exceptions: restraints of trade and interference with individual liberty of action may be justified by the special circumstances of a particular case. It is a sufficient justification, and indeed it is the only justification, if the restriction is reasonable — reasonable, that is, in reference to the interests of the parties concerned and reasonable in reference to the interests of the public, so framed and so guarded as to afford adequate protection to the party in whose favour it is imposed, while at the same time it is in no way injurious to the public.

This updating of expression of the doctrine is now nearly a hundred years old; the doctrine is one peculiarly related to the vagaries of economic philosophy and of changing times. In *Esso Petroleum Co. Ltd v. Harper's Garage (Stourport) Ltd* [1968] AC 269 Lord Reid, at 294, said:

> Whenever a man agrees to do something over a period he thereby puts it wholly or partly out of his power to exercise any trade or business he pleases during that period . . . but no-one has ever suggested that such contracts are in restraint of trade except in very unusual circumstances such as those . . . where the servant had agreed not to work for anyone else but might have been given no work and received no remuneration for considerable periods and thus have been deprived of a livelihood . . . but the cases outside these two classes (interference with individual liberty of action in trading, and all restraints of trade of themselves) afford little guidance as to the circumstances in which it should be applied.

In my view, the construction of the doctrine should be informed by the application of Article 45 of the Constitution; some decisions[1] have excluded the application of Article 45, others[2] have applied the article. In my view, the exclusion of the application of the article by any court in respect of the making of laws, does not exclude their consideration in the construction of the common law.

Costello J doubted that the obligation imposed by Rule 8(c), to supply dairy products to the society on a reasonably regular basis, an obligation met by even a small supply, could be regarded as a restraint of trade. I am not convinced that the obligations implied by the new rules or what may be better described as the impact of the new rules on the trading of the members of the society are limited in that fashion. The effect of the new rules in respect of allocation of bonus shares is to make trading with the society at a given level essential to maintaining the proportionate shareholding in the society. This is a far greater indirect obligation; in my view, the implementation of Rule 9(d) in that fashion, as exemplified by the distribution already authorised, is a restraint of trade within the meaning of the doctrine. This conclusion does not help the appellants. The learned trial judge concluded that the obligation as he construed it, if a restraint of trade, was a reasonable one as between the parties. I am satisfied that the restraint as I have outlined it is also a reasonable one; indeed, I have difficulty in understanding any argument that it is unreasonable that a co-operative dairy society may not use every legitimate means available to it to secure that those of its members who trade through it will benefit and greatly benefit by such trading as compared with those of its members

1 *Buckley v. Attorney General* [1950] IR 57; *Byrne v. Ireland* [1972] IR 241 — Walsh J; *Comyn v. Attorney General* [1950] IR 142; *O'Brien v. Manufacturing Engineering Co. Ltd* [1973] IR 334; *McGee v. Attorney General* [1974] IR 284 — Fitzgerald CJ.

2 *Murtagh Properties Ltd v. Cleary* [1972] IR 330; *Ryan v. Attorney General* [1965] IR 294; *Rodgers v. ITGWU* [1978] ILRM 51; *Landers v. Attorney General* (1975) 109 ILTR 1; *Nova Media Services Ltd v. Minister for Posts and Telegraphs* [1984] ILRM 161; *Attorney General v. Paperlink Ltd* [1984] ILRM 373.

who decide to go it alone, in whole or in part. As to the second consideration of public good, it is clear as a legitimate opinion to be held by the majority of the members that the national interests are best served by the promotion and expansion of Bord Bainne. 8.1.2

I reject the case based upon alleged restraint of trade.

Implementation of Rule 9(d)

At first sight, it may seem unfair that no advance notice was given of the intention to implement the rule in respect of a previous years trading; on reflection, however it is clear that the giving of such notice might itself be unfair in that it would allow members artificially to increase their allocation by increasing temporarily their trade with the board (see the judgment of Costello J). The principle of rewarding those who traded with the board was a long established one—this is merely a new way of doing it; there is no suggestion of bad faith and the implementation of the rule cannot be validly challenged.

For these reasons, the appeal based upon the national law should be dismissed.

O'FLAHERTY J: Bord Bainne has grown from small beginnings to a turnover, it may be, of around £1 billion a year but it remains in law an industrial and provident society.

So, too, have Kerry and Avonmore grown and prospered over the years. It may be true, as was said in evidence, that a farmers' co-operative 15 years ago was comprised of a group of farmers at a crossroads creamery but nowadays industrial and provident societies accommodate trading giants — competing, as they must, with the same ferocity as their rivals in the market-place but in law their *co-operative* nature is at the core of their existence. That means such a society exists for the mutual benefit of its members, who control it and use it to trade and to make profits. What is done with those profits is a matter to be resolved by agreement between the parties and the parameters of such agreement may well be delineated in the rules of a society. Such a society must be run *bona fide* by and for its members; such a society requires for its existence a commitment to trade from its members which commitment it is entitled to reward provided it does so in accordance with its rules and the relevant legislation.

It was submitted on behalf of Bord Bainne that the shareholding element in an industrial and provident society is very different from that in a limited liability company; that a share holding in such a society is not intended primarily as a measure of investment but was merely an 'entrance fee'. I think this is a correct analogy. In my judgment, therefore, all the arguments addressed to us in relation to what the plaintiffs say is their 'ownership' in a 'share' of Bord Bainne might have been appropriately addressed to us if we were dealing with a limited liability company and, most certainly, could have been addressed to us if we were dealing with a trading *partnership* but are totally misplaced when applied to the legal entity that Bord Bainne is.

While we have had the benefit of voluminous written submissions and extensive oral argument over many days I have found it astonishing that so little has been said about Bord Bainne's future if all its members were to follow Kerry's example and reduce trade with it to a miniscule amount.

I know it has been submitted that Kerry and Avonmore were 'staunch supporters' of Bord Bainne in the past but that will not secure its present or future and if all members sought their fortunes separately Bord Bainne would simply wither away.

That certainly is not desirable either in the national interest or in the interests of the European Community.

The true position in the past was that all parties enjoyed a truly co-operative relationship; that is not to say, as was proved in evidence, but that there were occasional tensions. The plaintiffs it was who severed or at least diminished that relationship. They, however, while they want to go their own way and trade to their best advantage wish, at the same time, to preserve what they regard as their 'stake' in Bord Bainne. However, if they wish to do that the remedy is in their hands: they should continue to trade with Bord Bainne. Bord Bainne are not saying to Kerry and Avonmore that they have made their beds and must lie in them; they are saying

8.1.2 that if they do not chose to lie in the beds they cannot complain either about their comforts or their constraints.

In justice, it is right to point out, too, that Kerry has the power under its rules to expel a member for conduct detrimental to the society, *e.g.* supplying milk to a rival co-operative and, in those circumstances, the expelled member is entitled only to be returned the capital that he subscribed — which is similar to the Bord Bainne rule. And, in an attempted take-over bid for another co-operative society, Avonmore was prepared to issue to new members shares which would have the same effect as the 'bonus' shares that it was sought to condemn when authorised under the Bord Bainne rule change. The old equitable maxim has some relevance: he who seeks equity must do equity.

I accept the argument advanced on behalf of Bord Bainne that the capital of such a society is not fixed but is flexible and it can increase and reduce according as members join or leave just as the capital of a building society can increase or reduce as members come and go and as they contribute or withdraw their subscription shares. Because the aggregate capital of such a society must necessarily fluctuate all of the time, no individual member can own a permanent fixed fractional interest in that capital.

In my judgment once I accept, as I do, that the taking up of the original shares was merely something akin to the payment of an entrance fee, then the constitutional argument that there has been an expropriation of property rights must fail. Similarly, the suggestion that the rule changes proposed are *ultra vires* the constitution of Bord Bainne and of the relevant legislation is equally untenable. The rule change was not oppressive because the analogy by reference to company law is unsustainable. Company law with reference to oppression of minorities does not apply to industrial and provident societies. I am satisfied that the rule change brought about is required by the circumstances and should be deemed to be well within the contemplation of the parties at the initial contract date; not in the sense that this precise change would be brought about but that changes would have to be brought about, from time to time, to enable Bord Bainne to survive in the market-place. I cannot find anything *ultra vires* about such a rule change. With regard to the element of 'retrospection' I respectfully adopt everything that has been set forth by the learned High Court judge and by McCarthy J.

Indeed, with the fear that the brevity of my judgment on this aspect of the case would involve disrespect to the elaborate learned arguments that were addressed to us at the Bar and in the belief that to over-simplify the complicated may be as bad a vice as to complicate the straightforward, I wish to buttress my judgment by respectfully adopting the lucid reasoning of both the learned High Court judge and McCarthy J on the alleged property right argument; the *ultra vires* argument as well as the oppression and retrospective effect arguments. But, while I agree with the result reached on the restraint of trade argument, by the learned High Court judge and McCarthy J, I do so by a more precipitate route and, therefore, feel justified in giving my views on this aspect of the case.

Restraint of Trade

As noted by Dr Michael Forde in his work: *Commercial Law in Ireland* (at p. 320):

> Generally, those who suffer loss in consequence of admittedly unfair methods of competition are not entitled to damages from or an injunction against their competitor. Provided the competitor does not commit a criminal offence or a tort or a breach of contract, or contravene one or more of the administrative controls, he is legally free to compete in the market in whatever way he chooses. As a judge at the beginning of the fifteenth century put it, 'If I have a mill, and my neighbour builds another mill, by which the profit of my mill is diminished, I have no action against him and yet there is damage to me.' *Gloucester Grammer School case* (1410) YB 11 Hen. IV, fo. 47, pl. 21).

I respectfully adopt the definition of a contract in restraint of trade contained in Cheshire,

Fifoot & Furmston's *Law of Contract* (11th ed.) at p. 380: **8.1.2**

> A contract in restraint of trade is one by which a party restricts his future liberty to carry on his trade, business or profession in such manner and with such persons as he chooses. A contract of this class is *prima facie* void, but it becomes binding upon proof that the restriction is justifiable in the circumstances as being reasonable from the point of view of the parties themselves and also of the community.
>
> Such has long been the legal effect of two familiar types of contract. First, one by which an employee agrees that after leaving his present employment he will not compete against his employer, either by setting up business on his own account or by entering the service of a rival trader. Secondly, an agreement by the vendor of the goodwill of a business not to carry on a similar business in competition with the purchaser.

The history of restraint of trade is recounted in many cases, probably most notably in *Esso Petroleum Co. Ltd v. Harpers Garage (Stourport) Ltd* [1968] AC 269.

In this jurisdiction, as long ago as 1925, FitzGibbon J, delivering the judgment of the Supreme Court in the case of *Mulligan v. Corr* [1925] 1 IR 169 said at 175:

> The principles of law applicable to covenants of this description in restraint of trade may be regarded as now finally settled; the only difficulty is to ascertain the facts to which they are to be applied.

Over the years it became clear that a distinction should be drawn between contracts of services and contracts for the sale of a business. A restraint may be imposed more readily and more widely upon the vendor of a business in the interests of the purchaser, than upon an employee in the interests of an employer. And so into modern times: it is thought that, in general, businessmen are best able to look after their own interests and that the public interest is best guarded by reliance on legislation. However, it appears to me that the protection that the law affords to employees continues with the same force as before. This is a distinction which I think it is important to preserve and to emphasize.

Lord Diplock, in the course of his speech in *Schroeder Music Publishing Co. Ltd v. Macaulay* [1974] 3 All ER 616, said at 623:

> It is, in my view, salutory to acknowledge that in refusing to enforce provisions of a contract whereby one party agrees for the benefit of the other party to exploit or to refrain from exploiting his own earning-power, the public policy which the court is implementing is not some 19th century economic theory about the benefit to the general public of freedom of trade, but the protection of those whose bargaining power is weak against being forced by those whose bargaining power is stronger to enter into bargains that are unconscionable. Under the influence of Bentham and of laissez-faire the courts in the 19th century abandoned the practice of applying the public policy against unconscionable bargains to contracts generally, as they had formerly done to any contract considered to be usurious; but the policy survived in its application to penalty clauses and to relief against forfeiture and also to the special category of contracts in restraint of trade. If one looks at the reasoning of 19th century judges in cases about contracts in restraint of trade one finds lip service paid to current economic theories but if one looks at what they said in the light of what they did, one finds that they struck down a bargain if they thought it was unconscionable as between the parties to it, and upheld it if they thought that it was not.

The case put on behalf of Kerry and Avonmore amounts to this: that the new rules involve

8.1.2 an express or implied form of restraint of trade; that this is not reasonable between the parties and that it is not reasonable in the public interest. To this Bord Bainne respond by saying that the very first and fundamental requirement is that there should be a *covenant* in restraint of trade on which Bord Bainne would be entitled to sue; whether they could sue successfully or not would be a separate question but the very first, basic, requirement is that such a *covenant* should be in existence.

In this regard, counsel for Bord Bainne placed reliance on the definition contained in *Chitty on Contracts* (26th ed.) vol. 1 at para. 1190:

> All covenants in restraint of trade are *prima facie* unenforceable at common law and are enforceable only if they are reasonable with reference to the interests of the parties concerned and of the public. Unless the unreasonable part can be severed by the removal of either part or the whole of the covenant in question, its inclusion renders the covenant or the entire contract unenforceable. The doctrine of restraint of trade is probably one of the oldest applications of the doctrine of public policy; cases go back to the second half of the sixteenth century and as early as 1711 it was laid down in *Mitchel v. Reynolds* 1 P. Wms 181 that a bond to restrain oneself from trading in a particular place, if made upon a reasonable consideration, is good, though if it be upon no reasonable consideration or to restrain a man from trading at all, it is void.

This part of the Bord Bainne argument has the virtue of extreme simplicity; before a party is entitled to sue under the restraint of trade doctrine there must be a *covenant* in restraint of trade. If there is no such covenant, then what is involved may be something that causes damage to the complainants or it may be a form of what they allege is 'unfair' competition but whatever is involved, so the Bord Bainne argument goes, it is not something that is covered by the doctrine of restraint of trade.

Mr Fennelly SC, in the course of his address to this Court, challenged his opponents to produce any authority which said that a cause of action lay without there being an express covenant in existence.

In response to this the appellants relied upon three cases, *viz* the decision of the Privy Council in *Stenhouse Australia Ltd v. Phillips* [1974] AC 391; a decision of the Court of Appeal in England in *Wyatt v. Kreglinger* [1933] 1 KB 793 and a decision of the High Court in England in *Bull v. Pitney-Bowes Ltd* [1966] 3 All ER 384.

In the *Stenhouse* case the facts were that the Stenhouse group carried on an insurance broking business in Australia. The respondent entered into an agreement expressed to continue until he should attain the age of sixty years and thereafter, subject to certain conditions, from year to year until determined by six months notice on either side.

Afterwards, on the respondent's terminating his employment with the brokers, he entered into an agreement containing certain covenants. One was held to be clearly in restraint of trade because it provided that he would not for a period of five years directly or indirectly as principal, servant or agent solicit insurance business from any client of the brokers.

Lord Wilberforce in the course of his opinion dealt with another clause, clause 5, as follows. He said that clause 5 was a stipulation of a different character. He said:

> It is not on the face of it a restraint of trade at all, but a provision for the payment of money: it was described by counsel for the appellant as a profit-sharing agreement. And it was submitted that, as such, the court should not inquire whether it was burdensome, or one-sided. The judge took a different view, holding that it operated in restraint of trade and that it was not shown to be reasonable.
>
> Their Lordships on the whole agree with this view. Whether a particular provision operates in restraint of trade is to be determined not by the form the stipulation wears, but, as the statement of the question itself shows, by its effect in practice.

Lord Wilberforce went on to point out that the clause in question contained no direct covenant to abstain from any kind of competition or business, but the question to be answered is whether in effect, it is likely to cause the employee to refuse business which otherwise he would take: or, looking at it another way, whether the existence of this provision would diminish his prospects of employment. Judged by this test the Privy Council had no doubt that the clause operated in restraint of trade. **8.1.2**

I am of the opinion that this case is authority for the proposition that a court is entitled to look at the effect that a covenant or stipulation has but it is not authority for the proposition that there can be a restraint of trade without such a covenant.

In *Wyatt v. Kreglinger and Fernau* [1933] 1 KB 793 the facts were that in 1923 the defendants wrote to the plaintiff, who had been in their service for many years, intimating that upon his retirement they proposed to give him an annual pension of £200 subject to the condition that he did not compete against them in the wool trade. The plaintiff's reply was lost, but he retired on the following September and received a pension until 1932, when the defendants refused to make further payments. The plaintiff sued them for breach of contract. The defendants denied that any contract existed, and also pleaded that if a contract did exist it was void as being in restraint of trade.

Scrutton LJ was of the view that all that was involved was a gratuitous promise creating no legal obligation. But, in any event, all the appeal judges were agreed that assuming that a contractual obligation was created it was an agreement in restraint of trade and was not binding. The decision was heavily criticised in an article in 49 *Law Quarterly Review* at p. 465 but on grounds not germane to what we have to decide.

However, the decision was followed in *Bull v. Pitney-Bowes Ltd* [1966] 3 All ER 384. In that case the plaintiff was employed by the defendants, manufacturers of postal franking machines. In common with all other eligible employees he had been required by the company to enter a pension scheme which, at the time of the plaintiff's retirement, and for some years previously, was non-contributory. The pension scheme was established by way of a trust fund, held by trustees, and the pension benefits were provided under the trust so constituted. The plaintiff retired from the employment of the defendant company at the age of forty five, having complied with the requirements of the scheme and being entitled to a deferred pension on the normal retirement date. Rule 16 of the scheme provided that any retired member who was employed in any activity in competition with or detrimental to the defendant company's interests, or who failed to discontinue such activity when required, would be liable to forfeit his rights under the scheme. On his retirement the plaintiff entered employment with a competing company which manufactured machines similar in purpose to those manufactured by the defendant company. The defendant company required the plaintiff to discontinue that employment pointing out that if he failed to do so his pension rights would be liable to be cancelled. It was admitted that if rule 16 was to be treated on the same footing as a covenant in restraint of trade, its terms would not in the circumstances be enforceable as reasonably required for the protection of the employers, the defendant company. Thesiger J (at p. 389 of the report) said that the defendants had pointed out that the *Wyatt* case could be distinguished on the ground that Scrutton LJ and Greer LJ implied a promise not to enter a particular trade whereas in the case before him the defendants contended that there was no such promise and no automatic forfeiture, although they had to concede that the loss of the pension depended on the view of the committee. Thesiger J said that one might perhaps summarise the defendants' argument by saying that it is that to discourage is not the same as to restrain.

He went on to mark the distinction relied upon by the defendants between (i) a covenant not to take up certain skilled works and (ii) the discontinuance of a pension if one does choose to take up that work.

At p. 392 the learned judge expressed his conclusions as follows:

> My first conclusion in this case is that the provisions of the pension fund were part of

8.1.2 the terms and conditions of the plaintiff's employment and those provisions include rule 16. My next conclusion is that rule 6 would have been regarded by the Court of Appeal that decided *Wyatt's* case as equivalent from the public point of view to a covenant in restraint of trade.

In my opinion none of the cases cited is authority for the proposition that there can be a restraint of trade *in vacuo*. I believe all the cases suggest that there has to be a covenant in restraint of trade or something akin to a covenant. In so far as the *Wyatt* and *Bull* cases create an anomaly this can be explained, I think, by saying that the courts must continue to pay particular attention to the need to safeguard and protect the rights of employees despite the fact that many of their rights are now, of course, guarded by legislation, too. Historically, the restraint of trade provisions were different as regards employers and employees to that which prevailed between business people and that distinction should remain in the law I believe.

What we are concerned with in this case is a dispute between competing giants of the market-place. I am of the clear opinion that if any such parties wish to invoke the doctrine of restraint of trade then they have an obligation to point to a clear covenant so restraining trade and to its breach.

Leaving aside the question of the necessity to have a *covenant* in restraint of trade, was there in effect, directly or indirectly, any *restraint* of trade here? In my opinion, except in the sense that whenever one takes any course in the business world it will operate as a restraint either on one's own activities or some form of clog on one's competitors, then, except in that very limited sense, there was no question of restraint of trade. Certainly there was no question of such a restraint of trade as has been defined in the various cases through the centuries.

I wish to add that had I reached the conclusion that a restraint of trade was involved as a result of the rule change then my decision would have been that such a restraint was reasonable as between the parties and in the public interest.

FINLAY CJ delivered the Judgment of the Court on 14 May 1991 saying: Having regard to the judgments delivered by the court on 21 March 1991 in this case, the only issue now remaining to be determined on the appeals is the question as to whether for the purpose of giving a decision on the plaintiffs' claim for a declaration of invalidity of the impugned rules by reason of a breach of Article 86 of the Treaty it is necessary for the court to refer any questions of European law, pursuant to Article 177 of the Treaty to the European Court of Justice. The members of the court have carefully considered the submissions made on this issue since the delivery of the judgments in March of 1991, as well as the submissions made at the previous hearing of the appeal. They have come to the unanimous decision that it is necessary for certain questions to be referred.

The topics of these questions are as follows:

1. Can the plaintiff obtain from the national courts, on the facts of this rule, a declaration of invalidity of the impugned rules on the grounds of a breach of Article 86, without having invoked the jurisdiction of the Commission, or, without the Commission having initiated its jurisdiction, to decide pursuant to Article 2(2) of Regulation 26 whether the said rules fulfil the conditions specified in Article 2(1) of that regulation?

2. Can the adoption of the said rules as such amount to an abuse of a dominant position in the Common Market, in breach of Article 86 without proof of

(a) An actual distortion of competition, or

(b) A probability of distortion of competition?

3. Can the distribution of bonus shares in respect of quantities of dairy products sold to the defendant co-operative by its members constitute an abuse of a dominant position in breach of Article 86, where such shares have been determined by the court in accordance with national law not to have an actual value, although there was credible evidence at the hearing of the trial

that in the minds of some individuals they have a perceived value? 8.1.2

4. In arriving at a conclusion as to whether the adoption of the impugned rules constitutes an abuse of a dominant position in breach of Article 86, can the court have regard to a finding, if it were to make one, that the objective of the adoption of the said rules supported by the majority of the members of the defendant co-operative who are the suppliers of dairy products to it, was to maintain and/or strengthen the position of the defendant co-operative as a national dairy marketing organisation by the process of placing the influential control of it in the members who trade most with it, as well as maintaining the supply of dairy products to it.

The court would request counsel for the parties, if possible, to agree the text of questions reflecting these three topics. If agreement cannot be reached the court will consider two alternative drafts of questions prepared by the parties.

Solicitors for the appellants in the Kerry Co-Operative proceedings: *Martin O'Donoghue*
Solicitors for the appellants in the Avonmore Creameries proceedings: *Arthur Cox & Co.*
Solicitors for the respondent: *Binchy and Partners*

Tony Kerr
Barrister

HB Ice-Cream Ltd v Masterfoods Ltd t/a Mars Ireland; Masterfoods Ltd t/a Mars Ireland v HB Ice-Cream Ltd: High Court Nos. 1264P and 3359P (Lynch J) 6 April 1990* 8.1.3

European Communities – Community law – Trade – Restriction – Bailment – Terms – Ice-cream manufacturer – Retailer supplied by manufacturer with freezer cabinets on gratuitous bailments – Bailments made on condition that only manufacturer's goods to be placed in cabinets – Other goods in cabinets – Whether trespass – Whether bailment terms contrary to Community law – Dominant position – Whether abuse of dominant position – Whether conditions of bailment constituted restrictive practice – EEC Treaty, Articles 85 and 86.

Injunction – Trespass – Contravention of Community law – Restrictive trade practice – Whether fair question to be tried – Restrictive Practices (Groceries) Order, 1987 (SI No. 142) – EEC Treaty, Articles 85 and 86

Facts Article 9 of the Restrictive Practices (Groceries) Order, 1987, provides that:

> No supplier, wholesaler or retailer shall be a party to any agreement, arrangement or understanding (whether induced by threat, promise or otherwise) which has or is likely to have the effect of limiting or restricting entry to trade in any grocery goods.

The plaintiff in the first action, HB Ice-Cream Ltd, was a manufacturer of ice-cream

*The headnote had been kindly reproduced with the permission of the Incorporated Council of Law Reporting for Ireland. The judgment is reported in [1990] 2 IR 463.

8.1.3 products and enjoyed the major share of the market in the State. It supplied and serviced freezer cabinets on free loan or hire to retailers on condition *inter alia* that the cabinets be used exclusively for the sale, storage or advertising of the plaintiff's products and not for the sale, storage or advertising of products supplied by anyone else. Retailers who sold the plaintiff's product were not obliged to sell it from a cabinet supplied by the plaintiff nor were they prohibited from selling products supplied by competitors of the plaintiff.

In June 1989, the defendant in the first action, Masterfoods Ltd, entered the ice-cream market for the first time. Some of its products were stored by retailers in the plaintiff's cabinets. The plaintiff objected to the defendant supplying its products for storage in the plaintiff's cabinets as being in breach of the exclusive terms in its cabinet agreements with the retailers. The defendant argued that the exclusive terms in the cabinet agreements constituted a restrictive practice and had the effect or were likely to have the effect of restricting the entry of a new competitor into the market and consequently were in breach of Articles 85 and 86 of the Treaty of Rome and of Article 9 of the Restrictive Practices (Groceries) Order 1987. The plaintiff sought an injunction restraining the defendant *inter alia* allowing products sold or distributed by the defendant to be sold in the plaintiff's cabinets.

The defendant, in separate proceedings, sought an order restricting the plaintiff from enforcing its cabinet agreement with retailers so as to prevent retailers from storing or stocking the defendant's products on the grounds that the agreements constituted a restrictive practice restricting the entry into the retail ice cream market contrary to Art. 85 of the Treaty of Rome and, in the alternative, amounted to a breach of the dominant position enjoyed by the plaintiff in the market for ice cream contrary to Article 86 of the Treaty of Rome and Art. 9 of the Order of 1987.

Held by Lynch J in granting the injunctions sought:

(1) That the plaintiffs had a serious case to be tried on the issue of wrongful interference with its contractual rights *vis-à-vis* the retailers to whom it had supplied cabinets and that the balance of convenience favoured the granting of the interlocutory relief sought.

(2) That the *status quo* to be preserved was that which existed prior to the intrusion of the defendant's products into the plaintiff's cabinets.

(3) That the defendant had raised a fair question to be tried as to whether the plaintiff enjoyed a dominant position in the market in ice-cream products in Ireland but not as to whether the plaintiff's cabinet agreement might affect trade between the member states or might prevent, restrict or distort competition within the market or amount to an abuse of its dominant position contrary to Articles 85 and 86 of the Treaty of Rome and Art. 9 of the Order of 1987.

Notice of motion

By notice of motion dated 12 March 1990, the plaintiff sought injunctions in the following terms:

(1) an interlocutory injunction restraining Mars whether by its directors, officers, servants or agents or any of them or otherwise howsoever from including, inciting, procuring or persuading the plaintiff's customers, that is to say, HB's customers, or any of them to breach the terms of cabinet agreements made between HB and its customers;

(2) an interlocutory injunction restraining Mars whether by its directors, officers, servants or agents or any of them or otherwise howsoever from unlawfully interfering with HB's business; 8.1.3

(3) an interlocutory injunction restraining Mars whether by its directors, officers, servants or agents or any of them or otherwise howsoever from causing, permitting or allowing products sold or distributed by Mars to be sold in refrigerated cabinets, the property of HB.

By notice of Motion dated 5 March 1990, the defendant also sought injunctions in the following terms:

(1) an order restraining HB whether by its servants or howsoever from enforcing or purporting to enforce its standard form of cabinet agreement with retailers so as to prevent retailers from storing or stocking Mars' products;

(2) an order restraining HB whether by its servants or agents or howsoever from removing or threatening to remove freezer cabinets from such retailers or from offering any threat or inducement to such retailers in order to prevent such retailers from stocking or storing products supplied by Mars.

The application was heard by the High Court (Lynch J) on 3, 4, 5, and 6 April 1990.

Peter Shanley SC, Peter Kelly SC and *William Shipsey* **for the plaintiff**
Nial Fennelly SC and *Donal O'Donnell* **for the defendant**

LYNCH J delivered his judgment on 6 April 1990 saying: I shall refer to the parties in the proceedings before me as HB and Mars. The matters before me for decision are applications by each party for interlocutory injunctions against the other.

HB claims in its notice of motion:

(1) an interlocutory injunction restraining Mars whether by its directors, officers, servants or agents or any of them or otherwise howsoever from including, inciting, procuring or persuading the plaintiff's customers, that is to say, HB's customers, or any of them to breach the terms of cabinet agreements made between HB and its customers;

(2) an interlocutory injunction restraining Mars whether by its directors, officers, servants or agents or any of them or otherwise howsoever from unlawfully interfering with HB's business;

(3) an interlocutory injunction restraining Mars whether by its directors, officers, servants or agents or any of them or otherwise howsoever from causing, permitting or allowing products sold or distributed by Mars to be sold in refrigerated cabinets, the property of HB.

By notice of Motion dated 5 March 1990, the defendant also sought injunctions in the following terms:

(1) an order restraining HB whether by its servants or howsoever from enforcing or purporting to enforce its standard form of cabinet agreement with retailers so as to prevent retailers from storing or stocking Mars' products;

(2) an order restraining HB whether by its servants or agents or howsoever from removing or threatening to remove freezer cabinets from such retailers or from offering any threat or inducement to such retailers in order to prevent such retailers from stocking or storing products supplied by Mars.

Undertakings as to damages have been given on behalf of each of the parties.

What these applications mean is that in its action (1990 No. 1264P) HB seeks to restrain Mars from using space in freezer cabinets the property of HB to store Mars' products which cabinets are supplied by HB to retailers for the exclusive storage of HB's products. In its action (1990 No. 3359P) Mars claims a number of declarations concerning the validity of HB's agreement whereby HB supplies freezers to retailers and Mars seeks to restrain HB from

8.1.3 enforcing its freezer agreements to the extent that they should store only HB products therein so that such retailers may be free to store Mars' products therein if they so wish.

The two conflicting applications for interlocutory injunctions were heard by me concurrently on affidavit over the last four days. A great many affidavits were filed on each side raising many disputes on the facts. It is not possible for me to resolve disputed questions on fact on affidavit, but there is enough common ground or undisputed averments on the facts in the affidavits to enable me to get a sufficiently clear picture of the factual situation to decide the matter on the affidavits without the necessity of requiring oral evidence.

HB have invested £7 million in the purchase of freezers which it supplies on free loan or hire for the exclusive storage of HB ice cream products. HB also spends about £1 million per year in servicing and replacing such freezers free of charge to its retailers. The terms on which such free loan or hire is made are:

(a) that the freezers will be used exclusively for storing products for sale supplied by HB and will not be used for the sale or storage of products supplied by anybody else;
(b) that HB has the right to terminate the agreement without notice if there should be any breach of any terms of the agreement by the retailer;
(c) subject to HB's right to terminate without notice for breach of the agreement, either party may terminate the arrangement on two calendar months' notice;
(d) the freezer remains the absolute property of HB;
(e) only HB's advertising material may be put on top of or fixed to the sides of the freezers.

A number of points should be noted about these agreements which are, of course, at the very core of the two cases brought by HB and Mars and at the core of the applications which I now have to decide:

(1) The retailer is not restricted from selling the products of other suppliers in competition with HB. The only restriction is that the HB freezers must not be used for that purpose.
(2) That form of restriction is widespread throughout the State and the European Community and does not seem to have been heretofore challenged either under European law or domestic law, although I recognise that this is not a conclusive point because there can always be a first time.
(3) In many small shops the retailer will wish to accommodate only one freezer and will therefore have to be satisfied to carry only HB ice-cream products if he takes a HB freezer. However, if the retailer has a HB freezer he can negotiate with another supplier to supply a freezer and complete the changeover in two months.
(4) The retailer can provide his own freezer and carry only the brands he wishes to carry. He can also provide a second freezer, if he has room for it, and carry only the brands he likes in that freezer or carry any products in it. There is no requirement that HB ice-cream products can only be sold from HB's freezers, just simply that other brands will not be sold from HB's freezers.

As from the month of June 1989, Mars began an attempt to enter into the Irish ice-cream market with its ice-cream Mars product. HB discovered that some of its retailers were storing this product in HB's freezers contrary to their agreements with HB. I have no doubt that a substantial proportion of retailers were assured by servants of Mars that 'HB would not mind', or words to that effect, and that those assurances were made at least recklessly, not caring whether they were true or false. HB did mind and made its objections clear in correspondence and called upon Mars to desist. Mars denied that it had authorised any servant or agent to give any such assurance as referred to but nevertheless claimed that HB had no right to object to the Mars product being stored in HB's freezers if the retailers so wished, having regard to the provisions of Article 85 and 86 of the Treaty of Rome and Article 9 of the Restrictive Practices (Groceries) Order 1987, as confirmed by the Restrictive Practices (Confirmation of Order) Act 1987. **8.1.3**

Mars claimed that it should be entitled to have retailers, if the retailers so wish, use space in HB's freezers to store and sell Mars' products. Mars does not suggest or concede that it should get the agreement of HB to this use of HB's freezers having regard to the legal provisions referred to above. It contends that it is entitled to this facility absolutely free of charge, that it need not pay one penny to HB for the use of its £7 million worth of freezers or towards the £1 million annual cost of servicing and replacing them.

HB objects that this is an unlawful interference with its property right in its freezers and with its contractual rights *vis-à-vis* its retailers. There is no issue but that what Mars wishes to do is an interference with HB's property and contractual rights, but the issue is whether or not such interference is wrongful or unlawful.

HB says that its bailment by the loan or hire of its freezers to retailers does not entitle retailers nor *a fortiori* anyone else (in this case Mars) to store products therein which have not been supplied by HB. Mars says that the retailer has possession of the freezer and therefore there can be no trespass against HB. HB replies that such possession as the retailer has does not entitle him to store other products in HB's freezers and that storage of other products in HB's freezers is a trespass or is certainly a wrong committed against its property rights in the freezers.

I am satisfied that HB has a serious case to be tried on the issue of wrongful interference with its property rights in its freezers. So far as interference with HB's contractual rights is concerned, again no real issue arises but that interference with its contractual rights has taken place. The question is whether or not that interference is lawful or, at any rate, not unlawful by virtue of Articles 85 and 86 of the Treaty of Rome or article 9 of the Order of 1987. *Prima facie* the interference is unlawful and therefore the onus of establishing that it is not unlawful rests on Mars.

It follows, and I am satisfied, that HB has a serious case to be tried on the issue of wrongful interference with its contractual rights *vis-à-vis* its retailers to whom it has supplied freezer cabinets.

Turning to Mars' case, I shall deal first with Articles 85 and 86 of the Treaty of Rome, Article 85(1) provides:

> The following shall be prohibited as incompatible with the common market: all agreement between agreements, decision by associations of undertakings and concerted practices which may affect trade between Member States and which have as their object or effect the prevention, restriction or distortion of competition within the common market and in particular those which:
>
> (a) directly or indirectly fix purchase or selling prices or any other trading conditions;
> (b) limit or control production, markets, technical development, or investment;
> (c) share markets or sources of supply;
> (d) apply dissimilar conditions to equivalent transactions with other trading parties, thereby placing them at a competitive disadvantage;
> (e) make the conclusion of contracts subject to acceptance by the other parties of supplementary obligations which, by their nature or accordance to commercial usage, have no connection with the subject of such contracts.

As regards the particular examples set out in this article of breaches of it in paragraphs (a) to (e), Mars mainly relies on paragraph (e) without necessarily abandoning the possibility of a contravention of some other paragraph.

I think that a breach of paragraph (e) does not arise at all in this case. The contracts in question are bailments of freezers whether they be on loan or hire. The terms objected to relate

8.1.3 to the very basis of the contract of bailment, namely, the purpose for which the goods (the freezers) are bailed to the bailee (the retailer). The freezers are bailed to the bailees for the purpose of storing, selling and advertising HB ice-cream products only. Those terms are not supplementary obligations nor by their nature or according to commercial usage do they not have an essential connection with the contracts of bailment? They do. It would seem that none of the particular breaches set out in paragraphs (a) to (e) of Article 85(1) apply; certainly, none clearly apply to the facts of this case. That is not, of course, conclusive because there could still be a breach of Article 85 if it was reasonably clear that there was a contravention of the general intention of the article. It is reasonably likely that these contracts of bailment of freezers may affect trade between member states of the European Community and may prevent, restrict or distort competition within the common market? I am not satisfied that Mars has made out a sufficient *prima facie* or serious case to that effect.

The foregoing ruling largely but not wholly governs the case under Article 86 as well. Article 86 provides:

> Any abuse by one or more undertakings of a dominant position within the common market or in a substantial part of it shall be prohibited as incomparable with the common market in so far as it affects trade between Member States. Such abuse may, in particular consist in:
>
> (a) directly or indirectly imposing unfair purchase or selling prices or other unfair trading conditions;
> (b) limited production, markets or technical development to the prejudice of consumers;
> (c) applying dissimilar conditions to equivalent transactions with other trading parties, thereby placing them at a competitive disadvantage;
> (d) making the conclusion of contracts subject to acceptance by the other parties of supplementary obligations which, by their nature or according to commercial usage, have no connection with the subject of the contracts.

The particular breaches set out in paragraphs (a) to (d) of Article 86 are the same as those set out in Article 85, with the omission of paragraphs (c) of Article 86 which relates to sharing of markets or sources of supply. My conclusions about these particular breaches in relation to Article 85 govern the particulars contained in Article 86. However, as in the case of Article 85, this is not conclusive.

I think that Mars has established a serious case to be tried that HB enjoys a dominant position within the Irish ice-cream market. However, I am not satisfied that Mars has established a serious case to be tried that HB has by these contracts of bailment abused its dominant position either so as to affect trade between members states or at all.

I turn now to article 9 of the Restrictive Practices (Groceries) Order 1987, which reads:

> No supplier wholesaler or retailer shall be a party to any agreement, arrangement or understanding (whether induced by threat, promise or otherwise) which has or is likely to have the effect of limiting or restricting entry to trade in any grocery goods.

Ice-cream products are clearly 'grocery goods' within the meaning of this article and therefore article 9 applies to them.

It was submitted by Mars that the exclusivity clause in HB's bailment contracts with its retailers to whom it supplies freezers is illegal and unenforceable by virtue of article 9. I have already drawn attention to a number of points about these agreements. They do not restrict any retailer from selling other brands besides HB's, provided he is equipped to do so, and there is nothing to prevent another supplier who wishes to enter into the ice-cream market in Ireland from canvassing such retailers to take Mars' products and for such retailers, if necessary, to equip themselves to store them or offering the necessary storage to the retailer. Mars may not only canvass retailers of HB's products to do this but it can also canvass other retailers to whom other suppliers of ice-cream bail or lend or hire freezers. **8.1.3**

Mars says that the bailment contracts restrict its entry to the trade in Ireland. However, in this action Mars is seeking terms of entry to the Irish ice-cream trade which are more favourable to it than those available to other suppliers. In the case of HB, Mars is seeking to have available to it the £7 million capital investment and£1 million annual maintenance and replacement costs of freezers free *gratis* and for nothing. Mars could also, of course, seek to use storage space for its products from other suppliers of freezers, and it appears it has done that in the case of Valley Ice Cream Ltd, although it has not disclosed the terms of that arrangement.

I am not satisfied that Mars has established a sufficiently serious case to be tried that the HB bailment contracts limit or restricts its entry into the Irish ice-cream trade within the meaning of article 9 of the Order of 1987.

On the question of balance of convenience as to whether to grant or refuse HB an interlocutory injunction, I think the balance lies in HB's favour. Mars achieved its sales target in 1989 so it has not suffered any real loss to date. On the other hand, HB's property and contractual rights have been set at nought. If I refuse an injunction there must be a danger that other suppliers might seek to poach HB's freezer space on the basis that an injunction was unlikely to be given against them if not given against Mars. The damage suffered by HB is incapable of calculation as also is the element of bad will created thereby between HB and the retailers. Moreover, HB objected to Mars' conduct and there has been no undue delay in bringing the proceedings. In the circumstances I think the proper *status quo* to be preserved is that which existed prior to the month of June 1989, that is to say, the state of affairs existing before the alleged wrongful conduct of Mars. On being satisfied, as I am, with the undertaking as to damages given on behalf of HB, I make the order sought in HB's notice of motion, that is to say, the interlocutory injunction asked for in the terms of paragraphs 1, 2 and 3 of its notice of motion, and I refuse to grant the orders sought by Mars in its notice of motion.

As these are interlocutory applications, this judgment in no way finally determines the issue with which I have dealt. Therefore the costs of both motions will be reserved.

Finally, I am grateful to counsel on both sides for their detailed and helped submissions in these cases. The fact that I have not chosen to refer specifically in the course of my judgment to any of the many authorities does not mean that they have been overlooked.

Solicitors for the plaintiff: *Hayes & Sons*
Solicitors for the defendant: *Arthur Cox & Co.*

Caroline Costello
Barrister

8.1.4 Masterfoods Ltd t/a Mars Ireland v. H.B. Ice Cream Ltd *and* HB Ice Cream v. Masterfoods Ltd t/a Mars Ireland: High Court 1990 Nos. 3359P and 1264P (Keane J) 28 May 1992*

European Community – Competition Law – Whether agreement whereby ice cream manufacturer supplied retailers with freezers on condition that only manufacturer's goods to be placed in cabinets infringed Article 85 of the EC Treaty – Whether terms of the agreement supplying freezers constituted abuse of dominant position within meaning of Article 86 of the EC Treaty – Recognition of property rights protected under laws of national states and Article 222 of the EC Treaty – Burden of proof – Whether higher owing to liability to fines and penalties under Article 85 – Whether necessary to seek interpretation from Court of Justice under Article 177 as to principles of community law applicable – Whether Article 9 of Restrictive Practices (Groceries) Order 1987 was still in force – Whether exclusivity term likely to limit or restrict entry to ice-cream industry contrary to Article 9 – EC Treaty 1957, Articles 85, 86, 177, 222 – Competition Act 1991 (No. 24), sections 2, 22 – Restrictive Practices (Groceries) Order 1987 (SI No. 142 of 1987), Article 9

Facts HB Ice Cream Ltd (HB) is the leading manufacturer of ice-cream on the Irish market and was taken over by Unilever in 1973. Mars is a wholly owned subsidiary of a U.S. corporation. HB had for many years supplied freezer cabinets to retailers for the storage and display of their products. These cabinets were effectively supplied free of charge but remained the property of HB. The agreements under which they were supplied contained a clause prohibiting the retailer from stocking any products other than those of HB in the cabinet. When Mars ice-cream was launched on the Irish market in 1989, many retailers with cabinets supplied by HB on these terms began storing and displaying the Mars produce in those cabinets. HB complained to Mars that the latter's sales' staff were persuading retailers to break their agreements with HB and they also warned a number of traders that they would remove the cabinets if this practice persisted. In response, Mars claimed that the relevant clause in the agreements, referred to as '*the exclusivity term*', was an unfair competitive practice. Thereupon HB instituted the second of the two actions and in early 1990 applied successfully to the court in *HB Ice Cream Ltd v. Masterfoods Ltd* [1990] 2 IR 463, for an interlocutory injunction restraining Mars from inducing the alleged breaches of the exclusivity term.

In the first action Mars claimed that certain provisions of HB's cabinet agreement with retailers infringed Article 85 of the EC Treaty, and that certain activities between HB and retailers constituted an abuse by HB of what was said to be its dominant position in a substantial part of the common market, contrary to Article 86 of the EC Treaty.

Mars also claimed declarations that HB's cabinet agreement with retailers was contrary to Article 9 of the Restrictive Practices (Groceries) Order 1987 and the Restrictive Practices (Confirmation of Order) Act 1987, in that it had, or was likely to have had, the effect of limiting or restricting Mars entry to trade in ice cream products, that the agreement was contrary to Article 85 of the EC Treaty and the relevant provisions were void.

*This text was first printed in [1993] ILRM 145-213. The appeal to the Supreme Court has yet to be heard.

In the second action HB claimed injunctions restraining Mars from inducing or procuring breaches of the terms of the cabinet agreements, from unlawfully interfering with HB's business and restraining Mars from causing or allowing Mars products to be stored in HB cabinets. 8.1.4

Held by the High Court (Keane J) in dismissing the claim by the plaintiff in the first action and granting the plaintiff in the second action the permanent injunctions sought restraining the defendants from inducing or procuring breaches of the terms of the cabinet agreements, from interfering with the plaintiff's business or storing its products in the plaintiff's cabinets.

(1) An agreement between a manufacturer and retailers whereby the latter are supplied with freezer cabinets for the exclusive storage and sale of the manufacturer's products does not infringe Articles 85 and 86 of the EC Treaty or Article 9 of the Restrictive Practices (Groceries) Order 1987.

(2) In order to establish that an undertaking is in breach of Article 86 of the EC Treaty, it is not sufficient to prove that it is in a dominant position, the practices complained of must also constitute an abuse of that position.

(3) In the case of Article 85 of the EC Treaty, a breach may occur even though none of the undertakings concerned is in a dominant position. However, in considering whether actions by a particular undertaking constitute breaches of Article 85, the extent of their market share and, in particular, the question as to whether they enjoy a dominant position in the market is relevant.

(4) In determining whether a particular agreement has an anti- competitive object within the meaning of Article 85, the agreement should be considered objectively and the standard of proof was that normally applicable in civil proceedings.

(5) Attempts by the manufacturer to ensure that competitors did not obtain an advantage by obtaining cabinet space for the display and storage of their products at the expense of the manufacturer could not be regarded as an inherently anti- competitive objective. In this regard the fact that the retailers could terminate the agreements and could sell competitor's products was very important.

(6) It was the generally accepted practice of the industry to include an exclusivity term. This could not be regarded as imposing what could reasonably be described as a supplementary obligation on the retailer, or one that had no connection with the subject of the contracts. There was no question of the manufacturer having adopted this strategy as a means of keeping competitors out of the market and preserving their own dominant position contrary to Article 86.

(7) To compel a supplier to allow its competitors store products in freezer cabinets owned by the supplier and subject to an exclusion term, would constitute an infringement of the supplier's property rights in the cabinets which was so radical in nature as to violate Article 222 of the EC Treaty.

(8) The practices complained of were well established commercial methods used to protect the property rights of the supplier in the cabinets, and it was not an agreement of the sort intended to be captured by Article 9 of the Restrictive Practices (Groceries) Order 1987.

Cases referred to in judgment:

AB Volvo v. Erik Veng (UK) Ltd (Case 238.87) [1988] ECR 6211

AKZO Chemie v. Commission of the EC (Case 62/86), judgment delivered 3 July 1991, not yet reported

Amministrazione delle Finanze dello Stato v. S.a.s. Mediterranea Importazione, Rapppresentanze,

8.1.4 *Esportazione, Commercio (Mireco) (Case 826/79)* [1980] ECR 2559
Banco Ambrosiano v. Ansbacher [1987] ILRM 669
Belgische Radio en Televisie v. SABAM (Case 127/73) [1974] ECR 51; [1974] 2 CMLR 238
Brasserie de Haecht v. Wilkin (No. 1) (Case 23/67) [1967] ECR 407; [1968] CMLR 26
British Broadcasting Corporation v. Commission of the EC (Case T-70/89 [1991] 4 CMLR 669
Camera Care Ltd v. Commission of the EC (Case 792/79R) [1980] ECR 119; [1980] 1 CMLR 334
Campus Oil Ltd v. Minister for Industry and Energy (No. 1) [1983] IR 82
Campus Oil Ltd v. Minister for Industry and Energy (No. 2) [1983] IR 88; [1984] 1 CMLR 465
Chicago Board of Trade v. US (1918) 246 US 231
Circa and Maxicar v. Renault (Case 53/87) [1988] ECR 6039; [1990] 4 CMLR 265
Coditel SA v. Cine-Vøg Films SA (Case 262/81) [1982] ECR 3381; [1983] 1 CMLR 49
Comet BV v. Produktschap voor Siergewassen (Case 45/76) [1976] ECR 2043; [1977] 1 CMLR 533
Commercial Solvents v. Commission of the EC (Joined Cases 6 and 7/73) [1974] ECR 223; [1974] 1 CMLR 309
Consten and Grundig v. Commission of the EC (Joined Cases 56 and 58/64) [1966] ECR 299; [1966] CMLR 418
Delimitis v. Henninger Brau AG (Case C-234/89) [991] 4 CMLR 329; [1992] 5 CMLR 201
Deutsche Grammophon GmbH v. Metro-SB-Grossmarkte GmbH and Co. KG (Case 78/70) [1971] ECR 487; [1971] CMLR 631
Europemballage Corp v. Commission of the EC (Case 6/72) [1973] ECR 215; [1973] CMLR 199
GTE v. Sylvania (1977) 433 US 36
Hauer v. Land Rheinland-Pfalz (Case 44/79) [1979] ECR 3727; [1980] 3 CMLR 42
HB Ice Cream Ltd v. Masterfoods Ltd [1990] 2 IR 463
Hilti AG v. Commission of the EC (Case T-30/90) [1992] 4 CMLR 16
Hoffman-La Roche v. Commission of the EC (Case 85/76) [1979] ECR 791; [1979] 3 CMLR 211
Hornal v. Neuberger Products Ltd [1957] 1 QB 247
Independent Television Productions Ltd v. Commission of the EC (Case T-76/89) [1991] 4 CMLR 745
Irish Association of Distributive Trades Ltd, Retail Grocery Dairy and Allied Trades Association v. 3 Guys Ltd [1979] ILRM 269
Mars/Langnese and Scholler (Case no. IV/34.072), 25 March 1992, not yet reported
Metro SB – Grossmarkte GmbH and Co. KG v. Commission of the EC (Case 26/76) [1977] ECR 1875; [1978] 2 CMLR 1
NV Nederlandsche Banden – Industrie Michelin v. Commission of the EC (Case 322/81) [1983] ECR 3461; [1985] 1 CMLR 282
Parke, Davis & Co. v. Probel (Case 24/67) [1968] ECR 55; [1968] CMLR 47
Pronuptia de Paris GmbH v. Pronuptia de Paris Irmgard Schillgalis (Case 161/84) [1986] ECR 353; [1986] 1 CMLR 414
Radio Telefís Éireann v. Commission of the EC (Case T-69/89) [1991] 4 CMLR 586
R. v. Secretary of State for the Home Department, ex parte Khawaja [1984] 1 AC 74
Shearson Lehman Hutton Inc v. Maclaine Watson & Co. Ltd [1989] 2 Lloyd's Rep 570; [1989] 3 CMLR 429
Sirena SRL v. Eda SRL (Case 262/81) [1971] ECR 69; [1971] CMLR 260
Societe Technique Miniere v. Maschinenbau Ulm GmbH (Case 56/65) [1966] ECR 235; [1966] CMLR 357
Standard Oil v. US (1911) 221 US 1
Tetra Pak Rausing SA v. Commission of the EC (Case T-51/89) [1990] ECR 309; [1991] 4 CMLR 334
United Brands Co. v. Commission of the EC (Case 27/76) [1978] ECR 207; [1978] 1 CMLR 429

Nial Fennelly SC, Paul Gallagher SC and Patrick McCann **for the plaintiff in the first action and the defendant in the second action**
Peter Shanley SC, Peter Kelly SC and William Shipsey **for the defendant in the first action and the plaintiff in the second action**

KEANE J delivered his judgment on 28 May 1992 saying: These two actions have been at hearing for 22 days, during which a vast volume of factual and expert evidence has been adduced and detailed legal submissions advanced. The major issue in the case can, however, be stated in relatively simple terms. Can the defendants in the first action (whom I shall call 'HB') lawfully prevent the plaintiffs in that action (whom I shall call 'Mars') from inducing retailers to stock and display their products in freezer cabinets owned and supplied by HB? **8.1.4**

In the first action, Mars claim declarations that the terms in the written agreements under which such cabinets are supplied prohibiting the retailer from stocking in the cabinets products other than those of HB are void because they contravene certain provisions of European Community law and regulations made under the Restrictive Practices Act 1972. In the second action, HB claim injunctions restraining Mars from inducing breaches by their customers of the relevant clauses of the agreements.

The first part of this unavoidably lengthy judgment is a summary of the history of the dispute. The second part identifies the issues between the parties in the two actions. The third part summarizes the evidence as to conditions in the Irish ice-cream industry as it has emerged during the hearing. The fourth part summarizes the expert evidence adduced as to the economic issues which have arisen in the case. The fifth part sets out the applicable law of the EC and the State. In the sixth part, I set out my conclusions.

I: History of the dispute

It is necessary first to recount the history of the two protagonists. HB are the successors of Hughes Brothers Ltd, a dairy company which was in business in the Dublin area only, when it was formed in 1924. Like other dairy companies in Dublin at that time, they had a surplus of milk and cream which they decided to utilize in the manufacture and sale of ice-cream. Until the 1950s, their ice-cream products consisted almost exclusively of ice-cream bricks and tubs. The bricks were sliced into portions by the shopkeeper who put them between wafers and sold them in the form of the twopenny or fourpenny ice-cream familiar to the older generation. The only addition to this limited product range was the choc-ice, which was introduced in 1936. In the 1950s, a large number of stick line products, as they were called, were produced and throughout the 1960s and 1970s the range of products which they, and their competitors, supplied continued to increase, leading ultimately to the large variety of wrapped ice-cream bars which HB, and other suppliers, now produce.

The other dairy companies in the Dublin area which also produced ice-cream were originally Merville, Lucan, Tel-el-Kebir and Dublin Dairies. In 1965, Hughes Brothers Ltd were taken over by an American company, W.R. Grace, and shortly afterwards they in turn acquired the ice-cream section of Lucan Dairies. In 1967, Merville, Dublin and Tel-el-Kebir Dairies amalgamated to form Premier Dairies and Premier Ice Cream. In 1969, Hughes Brothers Ltd and the newly formed Premier group entered into an arrangement under which the former exchanged its milk business for the ice-cream business of the latter. Hughes Brothers Ltd thus became HB Ice Cream Ltd and since then have been the leading manufacturers of ice-cream on the Irish market. In 1973, they were taken over by Unilever and to this day remain a wholly owned subsidiary of that organization.

Mr Gerard Kilcoyne was appointed managing director of HB in 1969, having joined their predecessor, Hughes Brothers Ltd, as marketing manager in 1967. He left HB in 1973, shortly after their acquisition by Unilever, to become in effect the owner of another company in the ice-cream business based in Thurles and called Valley Ice Cream Ltd (which I shall call 'Valley'). Although Valley's share of the ice-cream market increased significantly under Mr Kilcoyne's proprietorship, its share of the market has always been substantially less than that of HB.

Mars is a wholly owned subsidiary of a U.S. corporation. The parent company has for many years been engaged in the manufacture and supply internationally of a range of confectionery (in addition to other food products), including the well known Mars bar. Until the mid-1980s, however, they were not involved in any way in the manufacture of ice-cream. At that time, they acquired another U.S. company called Dove which had launched a product called the Dove bar on the American market with considerable success. The parent company decided to launch a new ice-cream Mars bar which, as it was hoped, would extend the strong appeal of the Mars bar to the ice-cream market. With a view to marketing the new product in this country, Mars

8.1.4 entered into a distribution arrangement with Valley.

HB, like their predecessors and the other dairies whose ice-cream business they had acquired, had for many years supplied freezer cabinets to retailers for the storage and display of their products. These cabinets were effectively supplied free of charge but remained the property of HB. The agreements under which they were supplied contained a clause prohibiting the retailer from stocking any products other than those of HB in the cabinet. When Mars ice-cream was launched on the Irish market in June 1989, many retailers with cabinets supplied by HB on these terms began storing and displaying the Mars product in those cabinets. HB complained to Mars that the latter's sales staff were persuading retailers to break their agreements with HB and they also warned a number of retailers that they would remove the cabinets if this practice persisted. In response, Mars claimed that the relevant clause in the agreements (which I shall refer to as 'the exclusivity term') was an unfair competitive practice. Thereupon HB instituted the second of the two actions and early in April 1990 applied to the court for an interlocutory injunction restraining Mars from inducing the alleged breaches of the exclusivity term. An injunction in those terms was granted by Lynch J, after a three day hearing (reported *sub nom HB Ice Cream Ltd v. Masterfoods Ltd* [1990] 2 IR 463). In the meantime, on 5 March 1990, Mars had instituted the first action in which they claimed a declaration that the exclusivity provision was void as being in contravention of EC law and orders made under the Restrictive Practices Act 1972.

II: The issues

In the first action, Mars say that, by reason of the position of HB in the Irish ice-cream market, including its dominant market share, its range of products, the number of freezer cabinets which they supply and their position of economic strength generally, or alternatively, by reason of their own terms, the agreements under which the cabinets are supplied, either alone or in combination, infringe Article 85 of the Treaty establishing the European Economic Community (which I shall call 'the Treaty'). They say that the agreements are agreements between undertakings or, alternatively, concerted practices which may affect trade between member states and which have as their object or effect the prevention, restriction or distortion of competition within the common market established by the Treaty.

Particulars of the alleged infringement of Article 85 of the Treaty are then given. Mars say that HB supply ice-cream to a very large proportion of the market subject to the exclusivity term and have removed freezer cabinets from the premises of retailers who have stocked Mars products and threaten to continue to do so. They further say that HB have refused to supply retailers with ice-cream products if they are stored in cabinets supplied by other manufacturers or, alternatively, that HB have made it more difficult for such retailers to obtain supplies of HB's products. They say that HB have participated in agreements or concerted practices with other ice-cream suppliers in Ireland for the purpose of regulating the prices at which ice-cream products will be supplied to retailers and the rebates which would be allowed to them. They also say that HB operate a system of fidelity or other rebates with the object or intent that they should tie retailers to HB's products. They say that HB have threatened to vary the terms of rebates or have refused to allow rebates to retailers who accept or stock products supplied by other manufacturers in the freezer cabinets supplied by HB.

Mars further allege that the activities referred to constitute an abuse by HB of what is said to be its dominant position in a substantial part of the common market, contrary to Article 86 of the Treaty. In support of the claim that HB enjoy a dominant position, it is said that their market share is at least 70% and is even higher in the sector which they describe as the 'impulse' sector and which they identify with retailers who are tobacconists, sweet shops and newsagents (known as, and subsequently referred to as, 'TSNs'). They say that approximately 70% of the retailers in the TSN sector are provided by HB with cabinets free of charge which are tied to HB and its products and that these retailers, or a substantial proportion of them, are unable or unwilling for space, financial or other reasons to place a second cabinet in their retail premises.

All of this, they claim, constitutes a barrier to entry into the trade in ice-cream products in the Irish market. They say that the activities of HB in this area constitute an abuse of its dominant position in the market in a manner which is liable to affect trade between member states of the community. 8.1.4

More particularly, Mars allege that HB are in breach of Articles 85 and 86 by:

(a) directly or indirectly fixing purchase or selling prices and other trading conditions;

(b) limiting or controlling production, markets, technical development or investment;

(c) sharing markets;

(d) making the conclusion of contracts subject to acceptance by other parties of supplementary obligations which, by their nature or according to commercial usage, have no connection with the subject of such contracts.

Mars also claim that the use by HB of the agreements in the manner already described is an agreement or arrangement which has, or is likely to have, the effect of limiting or restricting Mars' entry to trade in ice-cream products and hence is in breach of Article 9 of the Restrictive Practices (Groceries) Order 1987 and the Restrictive Practices (Confirmation of Order) Act 1987.

Mars claim declarations that HB's cabinet agreement with retailers, or certain provisions thereof, is contrary to Article 9 of the 1987 Order and to the 1987 Act, that it is prohibited by Article 85 of the Treaty and that, accordingly, the relevant provisions are void and of no effect. They further claim a declaration that HB, by using its cabinet agreements in the manner alleged, is abusing what is claimed to be its dominant position in the common market and hence is in breach of Article 86 of the Treaty. They further claim an order restraining HB from enforcing or purporting to enforce the cabinet agreements and, in particular, the exclusivity term. They also claim damages and further and other relief.

In their defence, HB deny that they occupy a dominant position within the meaning of Article 86 of the Treaty. They further deny the existence in Ireland of an 'impulse ice-cream market'. They admit that the supply of cabinets is part of their chain of distribution and that they are supplied free of charge or at a nominal rent, subject to certain terms, but they deny that the agreement infringes Article 85 of the Treaty. They deny that the supply of cabinets affects trade between member states or that their object in supplying cabinets subject to the agreements is to prevent and/or restrict and/or distort competition within the common market. They deny that they supplied ice-cream to any customer in Ireland on terms that the customer would only use HB's cabinet and say that they have never removed a freezer from a customer who merely stocked Mars products. They say that they have removed their freezers from retail outlets in circumstances where the customer frequently and persistently breached its agreement with them. They deny that they have refused to supply retailers with ice-cream products, provided that in supplying them HB would not procure the breach of another supplier's agreement. They admit that they operate a quantity rebate system, but not a fidelity rebate system as alleged and they deny that they have varied the terms of rebates or refused to allow rebates to customers who accept or stock Mars products in HB cabinets.

HB deny that they have the alleged share of the relevant product market or that it is higher in the impulse or TSN sector. They further deny that they own 70% of freezer cabinets in TSN outlets or that all retailers, or alternatively a substantial or any portion of them, are unwilling or unable by reason of space to place a second cabinet in their premises. They say that many retailers are unable to afford a cabinet and therefore could not even trade in ice-cream were it not for the cabinets supplied by HB and other suppliers, including Mars' distributor. They say that the supply of cabinets with limited rights, such as are contained in their agreements, enhances competition and permits retailers who are unable to afford cabinets to enter into trade in ice-cream. They say that their principal object in supplying cabinets is to provide a high quality and hygienic cabinet from which its products can be sold. And they also say that Mars has demonstrated by its trading record that it was neither limited nor restricted in entering the Irish market or in competing therein.

8.1.4 In the second action, HB claim that Mars procured and induced a large number of their customers to break their respective cabinet agreements with HB and that in the result they have suffered loss and damage. They claim injunctions restraining Mars from inducing or procuring breaches of the terms of the cabinet agreements, from unlawfully interfering with HB's business and restraining Mars from causing or allowing Mars products to be stored in HB cabinets. In their defence, Mars deny that they procured or induced any breaches of the cabinet agreements and say that, if they did so, their actions were not wrongful, since the relevant provisions of the agreement contravene Articles 85 and 86 of the Treaty, Article 9 of the 1987 Order and the 1987 Act and hence are void and of no effect.

III: The Irish ice-cream industry

(a) *The products*

Ice-cream products in this country, as in a number of other countries, fall into two relatively distinct categories. There are, first, the 'take home' products, *ie*, ice-cream which is sold in blocks, multi-packs or tubs to purchasers who normally bring it home, store it in a refrigerator or freezer and eat it later. There are, secondly, 'impulse' products, *ie*, ice-cream bought in the form of wrapped bars, cones, *etc*, and intended for immediate consumption. This second category in turn is divided into what are called 'premium' products and others, the difference being that the premium products are sold at a significantly higher price, in the region of 60p per item and upwards.

The Mars ice-cream bar, which was launched on the Irish market in June 1989 and whose storage in HB cabinets led to the present proceedings, is an impulse item in the premium range. So also are three other items which Mars have put on the market since June 1989, *ie*, Snickers, Bounty and Milky Way. HB supply a much greater range of impulse products, about 80 in all, ranging from items sold at 10p up to premium items selling at 60p or more. HB also, unlike Mars, are engaged in the supply of ice-cream for sale by retailers in the form of scoops or cones, which can be regarded as part of the impulse market rather than the take-home market.

Another form of product should be referred to which played a prominent part of the proceedings, although not manufactured by either Mars or HB. These are called 'cool pops' or 'freezer pops' and consist essentially of liquid sweets contained in sachets which can be stored at ambient temperatures on shop counters or shelves and sold with a view to being frozen at home and eaten — in the main — by children. The evidence was, however, that they were frequently frozen by the retailers in freezer cabinets supplied for the storage of ice-cream products so as to be available in frozen form for immediate consumption principally by children.

The sales of ice-cream in Ireland are highly seasonal in character, reaching a peak in July/August and a valley in December/January.

(b) *The manufacturers*

In an earlier part of this judgment, some details were given as to the involvement of Mars and HB respectively in the Irish ice-cream market. It will be recalled that HB became the leading manufacturer of ice-cream in that market following the exchange of its milk business for the ice-cream business of the Premier Group in 1969. According to market share estimates prepared by HB for their own purposes and discovered by them in the course of the proceedings, their market share of impulse products during the period from 1986 to 1990 ranged from 75.9% to 78%. Mr Ted Murphy, the managing director of HB, said in evidence that he considered these figures somewhat high and that their share of the impulse market was more in the region of 68/70%. Valley, as already mentioned, increased its market share under Mr Kilcoyne's management from approximately 5% until at one stage in the early 1980s it had approximately 22.5% of the market. At that stage, however, HB were experiencing difficulties with a strike and, when conditions returned to normal, Valley's share started to decline from that peak until it settled down at around 15%. 8.1.4

At the time of the arrangement between HB and the Premier Group, there was another manufacturer in the Dublin area, Palm Grove which had a market share of approximately 12% to 15% but went out of business in 1982. Another company, Leadmore, based in Kilrush, County Clare, have generally enjoyed a share of between 8% and 9%. Finally, the market leaders in Northern Ireland, a company called Dale Farm Ltd, entered the market in this country in the 1970s under the name Northern Foods. They appear to have reached a market share of approximately 10% to 12%, but in recent years their market share has declined significantly so that at present it is relatively small. A company called Meadow Gold in County Cork which also manufactured ice-cream went into liquidation at some point, all their equipment and machinery being purchased by HB from the liquidator.

Mars, as we have seen, launched their ice-cream product for the first time on the Irish market in June 1989, using Valley as their distributor. In their first season, they had hoped that sales of their products would be effected in 40% of the retail outlets and in fact their actual sales slightly exceeded that figure. Following the granting of the interlocutory injunction and, I am satisfied, as a direct result of it, their sales in retail outlets fell to approximately 20% of the total. Their market share is less clear: while it may have risen to 10% in the period prior to the granting of the injunction, it seems unlikely that it is at present more than 5%.

The evidence established that, apart from having the largest market share, HB also enjoyed the best 'brand image', to use the language of marketing. This was due to two factors, the range and quality of their products and the substantial sums which they spend on advertising and other forms of promotion. The extent of their range is in contrast to that of Mars, who, again to use marketing language, are regarded as a 'niche player'. Valley have a significantly wider range of products than Mars, although not as extensive as HB.

It should finally be observed in this section that the figures as to market share are necessarily uncertain. Thus, a survey carried out by Irish Marketing Surveys Ltd for HB in July 1989 as to the consumption of ice-cream in the State indicated that HB's share of the market in terms of purchases by adults was as high as 93%. It declined the following year to 87%, the difference being largely explained by the arrival of Mars. However, while there is clearly some degree of uncertainty as to the precise market share enjoyed by HB, the evidence established beyond doubt that in recent years it has never fallen below 70% and certainly for significant periods hovered at percentages well above that level.

(c) *The outlets*

Impulse ice-cream products are sold in this country in the following retail outlets:

(1) Supermarkets owned by large groups known as 'multiples', such as Messrs Dunnes and Quinnsworth;

(2) Grocery shops, usually with self-service facilities, owned by groups such as Mace, Spar, *etc*;

(3) Smaller independent groceries, usually but not invariably with self-service facilities;

(4) TSNs;

(5) Garage forecourt shops;

(6) Other outlets, such as cinemas, hospitals and sea-side kiosks.

The evidence established that by far the highest volume of sales of impulse ice-cream products was in the outlets other than the multiples and particularly in the TSNs and smaller groceries.

Evidence as to the total number of retail outlets selling impulse ice-cream products in the State varied somewhat during the hearing, but most of the witnesses in the industry considered that it was in the region of 12,000. A survey prepared by the marketing firm, A.C. Nielsen & Co., for HB in 1990 indicated the following totals:

8.1.4

Multiples	154
Groups	999
Independent Grocers	6,069
Independent TSN	1,870
Garage Forecourts	1,187
Total	10,279

This did not include the other outlets to which reference has been made and, accordingly, the suggested figure of 12,000 outlets in total appears to represent a reasonable estimate of the total number of outlets selling impulse ice-cream products.

The Nielsen Survey also indicated that the number of TSNs in the State had declined noticeably from 4,003 in 1966 to 1,870 in 1990. In more recent years, there was a significant rise in the number of garage forecourt shops: between 1988 and 1990, the number increased by 75%.

The pattern in the trade generally is for deliveries to be effected directly by the manufacturers to the retail outlets. However, HB also have eight distributors in different parts of the country, through whom approximately 20% of their total output is distributed to retail outlets.

Retailers and suppliers also avail of a number of 'cash and carry' stores throughout the country.

(d) *Freezers*

Impulse ice-cream products differ from other products sold for immediate consumption in that they must be kept refrigerated. They are stored in the retail outlets in freezer cabinets, the appropriate temperature being -18° centigrade. These cabinets, in the outlets other than the multiples, are usually, but not invariably, supplied by the manufacturers, either free of charge or subject to a nominal rent. It was also the usual practice in this country until recently for the agreements under which they were supplied by the manufacturers to the retailer to include a clause prohibiting the retailer from storing any products other then those of the manufacturer in the cabinet. A change occurred in one company in December 1989: Valley, who, as already noted, were distributing the Mars product, agreed with Mars that the clause would not be included in agreements in the future.

Mr Kilcoyne said that, when he joined HB in 1967 as marketing manager, the cabinets were supplied under agreements which contained an exclusivity term. During his period with HB, a new form of agreement was introduced on the advice of their then solicitors. Mr Ted Murphy said in evidence that, following concern expressed by Mr van den Hoven of Unilever NV in Rotterdam in a letter dated 30 October 1974 as to the possible anti-trust implications of the existing agreements, a new form of agreement approved by their solicitors was introduced. This is basically the agreement under which cabinets are now supplied by HB. It is in the form of a letter to the customer and (slightly abridged) is in the following terms:

> We have pleasure in setting out below the trading arrangements agreed between us as to the supply and sale to you of ice-cream, water ices, frozen confections and any other products which we may supply in your area (hereinafter called 'the products') and to the hire of a conservator. . . .
>
> 1. From this date and while this arrangement is in operation the conservator will be used exclusively for storing products for sale supplied by HB Ice Cream Ltd and there will not be sold or offered for sale from this conservator, or stored in it, any other products whatsoever manufactured or supplied by any other person or company.
> 2. We will do our best to supply you with all the products which we normally distribute in your area at such times and in such quantities as to meet your reasonable requirements. So that you can store our products correctly we shall hire to you while this agreement

is in operation a conservator at an annual rent of £ (plus Value Added Tax payable) to be paid on the . The hiring of this conservator is subject to the terms and conditions set out in this letter. **8.1.4**

3. All our products as so supplied to you will be charged and paid for by you at wholesale prices as fixed by us from time to time. Payment, therefore, shall become due immediately at the time of delivery, unless you have a credit account with us.

4. We shall have the right to terminate this agreement without notice if you commit any breach of the terms of the agreement or if any execution or distress is levied on your premises or anything there or if you commit any act of bankruptcy or being a company go into liquidation or have a receiver appointed or if the ownership of the business changes or if your annual turnover for twelve months is less than £ at wholesale prices.

5. This agreement shall, subject to paragraph 4, continue in force from the date shown overleaf until put an end to by either you or us giving two calendar months notice in writing to the other.

6. The conservator we agree to hire to you for use in connection with this agreement shall remain our absolute property. We shall attach to it an inscription to this effect and this must not be removed, covered up or defaced.

7. The conservator shall be installed by us at our expense (the supply of gas, water, electric current, power point and plug to be the customer's responsibility). We shall be at liberty at all reasonable times to inspect the condition of the conservator. We shall do our best to maintain it in running repair, normal wear and tear excepted. However, as power failure may damage the contents of the conservator we regret that we cannot accept responsibility for any loss which you may suffer if the conservator goes out of order and we suggest that you might insure the contents against loss of this nature. You will refund to us the cost of any repairs made necessary by misuse or negligence by you or your employees or customers, for example: damages of the lid.

8. You shall keep the conservator insured in the joint names of yourself and HB Ice Cream Ltd against all damage and loss howsoever arising against fire and theft in its full value which it is agreed is £ . The current premium receipt for such insurance shall at all times be available for inspection by us.

9. You shall deliver up to us the conservator in a proper, clean and good condition whenever requested to do so by us or at the termination of the agreement. If you fail so to deliver it up, this agreement gives us permission to enter your premises at all reasonable times and remove it.

10. You will keep this conservator at all times in a prominent position in your premises at: and you will not move it or allow it to be moved away from those premises. If it is moved away from those premises for any reason you must notify us at once in writing and tell us where it is. If you sell those premises or sell or cease to be connected with the business now carried on there you or your representative must notify us at once in writing. Only HB advertising material may be put on top of or fixed to the sides of the conservator.

11. You will not allow the conservator to be fixed to your premises in such a way as to become a fixture.

12. We shall be relieved of our obligations under this agreement if it is impossible to carry them out for reasons such as strikes which are beyond our reasonable control.

13. This agreement supersedes and cancels any previous agreement between us relating to this conservator.

14. Our employees and agents have no authority to alter or add to any of the terms of this agreement.

As already noted, the rent normally charged is nominal. The terms of the agreement which

8.1.4 are of particular relevance in these actions are those

(a) enabling the agreement to be terminated on two months' notice on either side;

(b) precluding the retailer from storing any other products in the freezer; and

(c) requiring the freezer to be kept at all times in a prominent position at the retailer's premises.

While there are a number of different types of freezer cabinets, the ones in the TSNs and smaller groceries tend to be about 3 ft. in height and are, of course, familiar to everyone. The evidence was that there were approximately 18,000 of these freezers in the retail outlets, of which approximately 12,000 were owned by HB. HB, however, also deliver to cabinets which are owned by retailers. The evidence of Mr Tony Synnott, the sales director of HB, was that the cabinets ranged in cost from £294 to approximately £2,000. The evidence of Mr O'Rourke, their marketing manager, indicated that the total expenses of maintaining this fleet of cabinets, made up of servicing and control costs, for the year ended December 1991 amounted to £520,097. The estimated current replacement cost of the fleet, *ie*, the cost of replacing them at current prices, for the same year is £8,283,000.

Mr O'Rourke also said that the cabinets were bought in bulk from a firm called Anglo-Irish Refrigeration Co. Ltd and that the discount attributable to the size of their order was between 27% and 30%.

Mr Kilcoyne, in cross-examination, agreed that Valley had spent approximately £600,000 on increasing their fleet of cabinets between the years 1973 and 1983. He also agreed, as did the Mars executives, that Mars were unwilling to provide their own cabinet freezers. In the event, when Mars came on the Irish market, Valley supplied approximately 500 new cabinets to that number of the 1,500 retail outlets which formed, in the view of themselves and Mars, the prime existing outlets for Mars confectionery. Mr Kilcoyne's hope was that Mars might supply the remaining 1,000 cabinets, but in fact, consistent with their policy of not becoming involved in freezer provision on a significant scale, Mars supplied only 200.

Mr Synnott's evidence was that there was what he called a cold chain of distribution of their products, beginning in their factory at Rathfarnham, from where the products were transferred in refrigerated vans to depots with cold stores in various parts of the country. From there they were delivered, again by refrigerated vans, to different retail outlets.

The principal HB witnesses, Mr Murphy, Mr Synnott and Mr O'Rourke, said that a number of advantages flowed from the exclusivity arrangement. First, it protected the property of HB and ensured that it was not available free of charge for the benefit of their competitors. Secondly, it ensured that refrigerated space was available for the storage and display of their products in the retail outlet. Thirdly, it enabled them to display advertising and promotional literature at the point of sale. Fourthly, it facilitated quality control and reduced distribution costs.

So far as the fourth of these factors was concerned, it was said on behalf of Mars that storing competing ice-cream products in the HB freezers could not have any effect on quality control, since they would require to be refrigerated at the same temperature. It appeared from the evidence that the principal cause of concern to HB in the quality control area was not competing ice-cream brands but rather the tendency of some retailers to store other unsuitable products in the freezers. This was particularly so in the case of the cool pops or freezer pops to which I have already referred. There was evidence that, if these were stored in the cabinets for the purpose of supplying them in the frozen state to children, the extra demand on the refrigerating capacity of the cabinet led to a raising of the temperature generally and could cause melting of the HB product.

There was also evidence as to counter-top freezers, one of which was produced in court, and which, it was suggested, might be particularly appropriate to a 'niche player' such as Mars. However, Mr James Holohan, the divisional manager of Mars with responsibility for ice-cream, said that such a cabinet would be impractical, first, because the heat it would generate would adversely affect adjoining displays of confectionery and, secondly, because the profit it would generate for the retailer would be insufficient in terms of the space on the counter which it displaced. 8.1.4

Mr Kieron Murphy, general manager of Mars, and Mr James Holohan gave evidence as to the practice in the confectionery trade in regard to the display of confectionery in retail outlets. The retail unit is normally supplied by the manufacturers but there are no restrictions on the display of competitors' products in the unit. As to soft drinks, there was evidence from retailers that some manufacturers, *eg*, Coca Cola and C & C, who supplied units for the storage of their products, stipulated that only their products were to be stored, although there was no evidence as to how rigidly these provisions were enforced.

The evidence as to frozen food cabinets was that these were normally not subject to any exclusivity term.

A number of proprietors of retail outlets, either TSNs of various sizes or larger independent grocery shops, gave evidence. Most of them had at one stage one or more HB cabinets on their premises. Much of this evidence was directed to the manner in which, and the extent to which, HB enforced the exclusivity term. It is difficult to draw any general conclusions from the evidence: clearly, in some instances, HB (whether in the person of the relevant salesman or someone at a higher level) adopted a relatively relaxed attitude to the presence of cool pops or freezer pops in the cabinets while in other instances action was taken. The evidence did establish clearly, however, and there was indeed no dispute in relation to this, that vigorous action, culminating in the application for an interlocutory injunction, was taken from the summer of 1989 onwards when retailers began to stock Mars' products in significant quantities in HB cabinets.

Mr Synnott also gave detailed evidence as to the increased distribution costs which, it was suggested, HB would incur if retailers were entitled to store Mars' products in their freezers. The calculations were on the assumption that, ideally, the HB delivery van would call to the retail outlet when the cabinet was half full. If a given number of Mars' boxes were in the cabinet, it would mean, the argument went, that a smaller amount of the product could be 'dropped' per visit, thus increasing the number of calls that had to be made at retailers by the vans in each year and thereby increasing distribution costs generally.

(e) *Prices, rebates and discounts*

The prices charged by HB to their customers are the same, irrespective of whether the cabinet is owned by HB. (The evidence indicated that of the cabinets into which HB's products are delivered, approximately 11% are owned by the customer).

HB operate a system of quantity rebates. This is paid in cash to the retailer around the beginning of March in each year, *ie*, just before the beginning of the new high season. It is calculated on the basis of his sales in the previous twelve months of HB's products. The rebate is a percentage of the sales in cash terms in that twelve months period and the percentage increases as the volume of sales increases. Printed notices of the rebate structure for the year are sent to the retailers at the beginning of the year and again in March. In 1990 they provided for a sliding scale of from 2% on sales between £1,080 and £2,200 up to 11% on sales of £21,501 and upwards. Retailers were also notified that the payment of the rebate was subject to their strict adherence to their trading agreement and their attention was particularly drawn to the exclusivity term in the agreement.

Mr Synnott said in evidence that HB did not operate a system of fidelity rebates, *ie*, rebates which were paid to the customer in consideration of his buying his ice-cream requirements exclusively from HB. He agreed that there were some retailers who got a special rebate, generally 5%, but sometimes as much as 10%, irrespective of the volume sold, but that there were normally special reasons for giving these rebates. He instanced the case of kiosks which were open only for ten or eleven weeks of the year at the seaside. He also said that the policy of HB was to get all customers on to the published rebate list and that at this stage approximately 95% of their customers got the published rebate only.

8.1.4 The evidence was that rebates and discounts were a feature of the industry generally, although they were operated in different ways. Thus, in the case of Valley, a discount was generally negotiated individually by the salesmen with the retailers.

All the Irish manufacturers are members of the Irish Ice Cream Federation. This body has existed for many years, but does not appear to have become particularly active until Mr Kilcoyne became managing director of HB. From then on it met regularly, at first under his chairmanship and then under Mr Ted Murphy's chairmanship. While matters of general interest in the business were discussed at these meetings, one of the principal topics was prices. The evidence established that in each year HB, through Mr Kilcoyne and later Mr Murphy, would inform the meeting of their proposed price structures for the following year. While there would be considerable discussion on occasions as to the price structure, in general the smaller companies followed HB's lead in relation to prices. This process appears to have been accentuated by the introduction of price control, particularly after the establishment of the National Prices Commission in 1971. The level of price control was fixed by that body after detailed discussions with the market leader, HB, as to the increases in their various costs of production in the relevant year. Price control came to an end in 1985, but the evidence was that prices in general continued to be fixed by the federation at their meeting at the beginning of the season and that the level of prices was effectively that which was communicated by HB to the other firms in the industry. Mr Murphy's evidence was also to the effect that the average increase in prices over the past number of years was in general below the average rate of inflation.

(f) *Comparisons with other countries*

Companies in the Unilever Group are engaged in the manufacture of ice-cream in a number of European countries. Mr O'Rourke gave evidence that in the United Kingdom, Walls & Co., a Unilever subsidiary, have exclusivity arrangements, as do their principal competitor, Lyons Maid. Similar exclusivity arrangements are operated in Denmark, the Netherlands, Germany, Spain and Greece. He agreed that in most of these countries Unilever was the leading supplier, but said that the exclusivity arrangement was operated by all the suppliers and not merely Unilever.

Three witnesses gave evidence as to the position in the United States. Mr Michael Stefanos is the president of Dove International, which has already been mentioned and is now the North American Ice-Cream Division of Mars. He said his company employed distributors, generally on a state wide basis. He also said that the individual shops owned their cabinets and did not operate any exclusivity arrangements. He said that Unilever operated in the American market in the same manner as in this country, *ie*, supplying cabinets subject to exclusivity arrangements, but that they had a dwindling presence in the market.

Mr Stefanos was called by Mars and it was not suggested to him in cross-examination that his view as to the prevalence of exclusivity arrangements in the United States was mistaken. However, two witnesses called by HB gave a different picture. The first was Mr David McCarthy, who is a vice-president and part owner of a marketing company which was responsible for the marketing originally of the Dove bar and who has extensive experience of the ice-cream market in the United States. He said that there were four national brands in that country in addition to a number of regional brands. He said that the nationai brands were distributed by different independent distributors covering different regions or states. The regional brands were usually distributed by the manufacturers themselves. The majority of sales in the impulse ice-cream market were by independent stores and 90% of these, he said, were supplied with freezer cabinets by either the distributor or the manufacturer. He produced a number of standard agreements which included conditions that the equipment should be used solely for the preservation of ice-cream and other frozen products manufactured by the company or distributor and said that a clause of this nature was invariably included in such agreements. He said that the independent distributor would normally supply the retailer with a number of different lines produced by different manufacturers and that, where such an exclusivity arrangement exists, the distributor normally decides the proportion of different manufacturers' products that should be put in the cabinet at any time. **8.1.4**

A similar picture was given by Mr Joseph Esposito, who is the president of an ice-cream distributing company in New York. He produced a standard form of agreement used by his company, Uneedan Ice Cream Co. Ltd, which included a clause stating that only products distributed by his company were to be stored in the freezer cabinet and that any exceptions to the clause would require the express written permission of the company.

Reference was also made to the report of the United Kingdom Monopolies and Mergers Commission on 'Ice-Cream and Water-Ices' presented to Parliament in 1979 (Cmnd. 7632). This report said that, although the use of such terms excluded other suppliers from retail outlets too small to be expected to sell from more than one cabinet (which outlets were numerous), there were arguments in favour of allowing the condition to continue. In particular, they thought that suppliers might be unwilling to continue to provide at a nominal rent a cabinet that could be used for a competitor's products. If cabinets were no longer provided the number of outlets, particularly those consisting of small retailers selling ice-cream products, might fall significantly. This they thought, would reduce the scope for competition in the retail market, the opportunities for entry to the market or to increase sales on the part of the smaller suppliers and would limit consumer choice. While, for those reasons, they did not find that cabinet exclusivity operated against the public interest, save in certain limited circumstances, they hoped that suppliers would in the longer term adapt their arrangements for supplying retailers so that those customers who wished to buy their own cabinets would find it easier and cheaper to do so than at present was the case. (Paras. 406/7 at p. 144.)

IV: *The economic issues*

A number of professional economists and experts in marketing gave evidence. It was accepted by the parties that only the court could resolve the issues as to whether HB were in breach of either Article 85 or Article 86 of the Treaty or both of them. However, it was also accepted by the parties that, in determining these issues, an economic analysis of the relevant market would be helpful and that this could only be conducted by the court in the light of the principles of economics which would be regarded as generally accepted today. The evidence in question focussed on three main issues, *ie*,

(a) What is the relevant market to which the court should have regard in determining whether HB enjoy a dominant position in the market?

(b) Are HB in a dominant position in the market?

(c) Does the use of the exclusivity term, whether considered in isolation or in conjunction with HB's pricing policies, prevent, distort or restrict competition within the meaning of Article 85 or amount to an abuse of a dominant position, assuming that HB enjoys such a position?

The expert witnesses, in giving evidence in relation to issue (c), were in the main concerned with whether the practices in question could be regarded, in the light of generally accepted economic principles, as creating an unacceptable barrier to entry into the relevant market.

Three independent experts gave evidence on behalf of Mars: Dr William Bishop, an economist who has specialized particularly in the application of economics to questions of competition law and who has held academic posts in the London School of Economics, Oxford and at various universities in Canada, Australia and U.S., Professor Frank Bradley, the Bailey Professor of International Marketing in University College, Dublin and Dr John Fingleton, a lecturer in Trinity College, Dublin in the economics of industrial organisation. In addition, evidence was given by Mrs Jenny Abelman, a research director of an English company called Rosslyn Research Ltd, which carried out a market research survey on behalf of Mars. Evidence was given on behalf of HB by Mr John Moore McDowell, a statutory lecturer in political

8.1.4 economy in University College, Dublin who specializes in micro-economic principles, comparative economic systems and industrial economics in industrial operations, and Mr Rodney Thom, a lecturer in economics at University College, Dublin who specializes in econometrics.

(a) *The relevant market*

It was contended on behalf of Mars that the relevant market was the market in ice-cream impulse products. HB claimed that the relevant market was a wider market in impulse products consisting of ice-cream, crisps, confectionery, snack foods, soft drinks and chewing-gum.

Dr Bishop in evidence said that the basic factor in determining whether a group of products could be regarded as being in the same market was whether the purchasers saw them as being substitutable for one another. He was of the view that all the available evidence suggested that the other products claimed by HB to form part of the market were not substitutable in this sense for ice-cream. He advanced three grounds for this view.

1. First, he said that on a commonsense basis other products would not be regarded as sufficiently close substitutes for ice-cream. It was seen as being cold, sweet and refreshing on a warm day and hence a person who wanted an ice-cream was unlikely to be satisfied with, for example, crisps as an alternative.

2. Second, there was the seasonality factor. Dr Bishop produced graphs demonstrating that sales of confectionery varied hardly at all throughout the year, while sales of ice-cream reached a noticeable peak during the summer months and declined steeply during the autumn and winter. His figures for sales were based on data from the U.K. supplied by the National Market Research Agency, but he said conditions in this country were not noticeably different so far as the sales of ice-cream were concerned.

3. Thirdly, he said that his view was borne out by a study of what economists called the cross-price elasticity of demand. He said that economists were agreed that one could determine whether products were competing in the same market if, when prices change, consumers bought significantly more of the product which had become relatively cheaper and less of the product which had become relatively more expensive. Conversely, if there was no significant systematic change in consumer purchasing patterns, the conclusion could be drawn that the products were not substitutable in the eyes of consumers. The cross-price elasticity of demand could be established, he said, by the use of a sophisticated statistical technique known as 'multiple regression analysis'.

In the present case, this necessitated, Dr Bishop said, the carrying out by him of an econometric study of the ice-cream market by examining consumer buying behaviour in TSNs.

The methodology of this econometric analysis can be briefly summarized. Data was obtained from the National Market Research Agency in the U.K. as to the sales of ice-cream in TSNs over a specified period. The sample group of TSNs was said by him to be carefully selected so as to be representative of Great Britain as a whole. The volume of ice-cream sold in each TSN is described, in the terms of the mathematical calculation which was then made, as 'the dependent variable'. A number of 'explanatory variables' are then identified, including the price of ice-cream and the price of the other items claimed by HB to be in the same market, such as confectionery. A number of other explanatory variables are also identified such as the turnover of the shop, sunshine, rainfall, *etc*. The relationship between the dependent variable and each of the explanatory variables is measured by a logarithmic calculation resulting in a 't' value for each explanatory variable. Where the 't' value is either greater or less than 1.96, the variable, in Dr Bishop's analysis, is treated as significant, since there is only a 5% probability that the variable has a zero value. Using this model, Dr Bishop said that the R^2 factor — *ie* the extent to which the variations in the sales were explained by the variables — is 48.2%. The conclusion from this model — giving a 't' value of 8.84 to the price of ice-cream — was that variations in its price were very significant in determining volumes of sales, whereas in the case of the prices of the allegedly competing products, such as confectionery, the 't' value in each case was less than the 1.96 standard, leading to a conclusion that they had no significance in explaining variations in the volumes of ice-cream sales. 8.1.4

Dr Bishop said that he had confirmed these findings by estimating the model in 'first difference' form. In this form, the dependent variable is no longer the actual sales of ice-cream but the difference between the sales in one period and the sales in the previous period. Similarly, explanatory variables are no longer, for example, the actual price of ice-cream and the actual average hours of sunshine but the changes in these from one period to the next. The point of this exercise is to eliminate characteristics which are specific to individual shops, since obviously they do not change from one period to another. Here, the R^2 factor is substantially less, *ie* 18%, but Dr Bishop suggested that the results of the 'first differences' model would still tend to confirm the findings of the basic model, *ie*, of no significance being attached to the prices of confectionery, *etc*, as an explanatory variable.

Dr Bishop said that the results of this econometric analysis satisfied him that there was no cross-elasticity of demand as between ice-cream and the other products.

Dr Bishop's methodology was criticized by Mr Thom. He said that the log linear model employed by Dr Bishop was defective because in this model the co-efficient representing the degree of price elasticity for each product was constant for all time periods and all regions and as a result the extent of cross-price elasticity which it measured was independent of the data being used, which, he said, greatly reduced its value. Mr Thom referred to criticisms of the model in a standard work called *Economics and Consumer Behaviour* by Deaton and Muellbauer, in which at p. 18 they said they saw little virtue in the use of the model. In particular, Mr Thom said that the model took no account of the fact that the unit price of ice-cream would vary greatly depending on the mix of products in a particular shop. He also said it took no account of such variables as the place or time at which the product was being sold and the extent of surplus income available for expenditure on luxuries at the disposal of the customers of the particular shop.

Dr Bishop relied on two other factors in reaching his conclusion that the relevant products market was the ice-cream impulse products market. The first was evidence provided by a consumer buying behaviour survey carried out by Mars in May 1991. Consumers were asked what they would have purchased if one of the Mars ice-cream products had not been available and four times as many respondents said they would have purchased an alternative ice-cream as said they would have purchased one of the other products, *eg*, soft drinks. Secondly, he said that the minutes of the Ice Cream Federation meetings indicated that each of the suppliers was concerned about the price of competing ice-cream products but not of other products.

The criteria so far mentioned relate to 'demand side' substitutability. So far as 'supply side' substitutability was concerned, Dr Bishop said that it was unlikely that manufacturers in related markets, for example, dairy products and chocolate producers, could switch production to ice-cream within a reasonably short period of time and without incurring significant additional expenses. Hence, he said there was no real supply side substitutability.

Mr McDowell said that the first test used by Dr Bishop — based on the innate characteristics of the product and described by Dr Bishop as the 'commonsense' test — was unreliable. He cited as an example the energy market, where he said that coal, oil and nuclear fuels are very different in characteristics, but that those involved in the energy business would not consider that they should be treated as separate markets rather than as competing energy sources in a single market. As to the second test, of seasonality, he said that this was so flawed as to be virtually worthless. He referred to goods sold at different seasons and yet clearly in the same market, such as chicken and turkey (in the poultry meat market) or lager and stout (in the beer market). Similarly, he said that there were products with similar seasonal patterns, such as petrol and ice-cream, which could not be considered as being in the same market.

As to the measuring of cross-price elasticity of demand, Mr McDowell said that it presented the difficulty as to what was to be considered a convincingly high value for the cross-price elasticity. He said that in any event it could give misleading results. Thus, he said that if cars and bicycles were treated as substitutes as modes of transport, one might expect to find that a

8.1.4 rise in the price of cars would result in an increase in the demand for bicycles. One would be surprised, however, to find that the reverse was the case, *ie* that the price of bicycles had any real impact on the demand for cars. He said that this indicated that the elasticity test was an incomplete mechanism and could result in excluding as substitutes products which should be regarded as substitutes for one another.

A final point made by Mr McDowell in relation to the relevant market should be noted. He said that if the relevant market was to be confined to impulse ice-cream products, there was no reason why it should be confined to wrapped products and that, accordingly, soft ice-cream products, such as whipped cones, should be taken into account. He suggested that this could be a significant factor in determining whether HB were in a dominant position in the relevant market, since it would reduce to some extent their share of the total impulse ice-cream market.

Professor Bradley agreed with Dr Bishop's view that the relevant market was that in impulse ice-cream products. Mr Kilcoyne, however, said that as a supplier he considered that he was in competition with other products, such as soft drinks, snacks, *etc*.

On the whole, there was agreement among those engaged in the ice-cream industry that 'take home' products, such as multi-packs, were not in the same market as the impulse products.

(b) *Has HB a dominant position in the market?*

Dr Bishop was the only economist who expressed a view on this question. In his evidence he avoided the use of the expression 'dominance' on the grounds that this was an issue for the court to decide. He said, however, that HB clearly enjoyed what he described as a position of 'market power'. He said that this was the result of a process he called 'merger to monopoly' which, in the case of HB began with the merger of their ice-cream business with that of the Premier Group in 1969. He said that the subsequent history showed that there was no entry to the market of any significance since then, other than Dale Farm who exited from the market, or partly exited, a few years later: HB, in effect, had 'seen off' all its potential rivals in the market. He said that, whenever a market share gets very high, economists consider it as quite likely that market power results, but there is no generally accepted figure among economists as to what constitutes such market power. Ease of entry into the market was by far the most important factor in determining whether the particular company enjoyed market power. He also said that the length of time for which the firm tended to dominate the market was also a factor in determining whether it enjoyed market power. He concluded that, in the present case, it could be said that HB enjoyed 'substantial power' in the ice-cream market.

(c) *Is freezer exclusivity an unacceptable barrier to entry?*

All three economists referred in their evidence to the principles generally considered in their discipline as applicable to this issue. Not surprisingly, they differed in the emphasis which they laid on particular views attributed to various economists, but I think that there was little disagreement as to the general approach of those writers.

It would appear that, in the period since the Second World War, a number of writers have attempted to identify the factors which enable a firm enjoying market power, amounting in some instances to a monopoly, to maintain that power. Beginning with the premise that any free entry into the market by another profit seeking firm would tend to erode such positions of power and monopoly, they sought to identify the factors which inhibited such entry. These were first defined as 'barriers to entry' by Joe S. Bain writing in the 1950s. Manifestly, legal restrictions imposed by governments, such as licences or patents, could constitute 'barriers to entry', but would be irrelevant in the context in which the expression was being employed. In 1968, G.J. Stigler propounded what was regarded at least for a time as the classical definition of 'barriers to entry', *ie*:

> . . . a cost of producing (at some or every rate of output) which must be borne by a firm which seeks to enter an industry but is not borne by firms already in the industry.

This definition would undoubtedly exclude the legal restrictions I have already mentioned. **8.1.4**
More significantly, it would not extend to barriers which could be regarded as part of the normal costs of production. A firm already in the market might not have the same costs of production as an entrant because of scale economies resulting from technology. But this would not be treated as a barrier to entry which should be restricted as unduly inhibiting competition. The costs referred to in the Stigler definition were what economists describe as 'sunk costs', *ie*, costs of production incurred on entry to a market which in general will not be recouped by the new entrant if he exits from the market.

Subsequently, however, it was accepted by economists that the Stigler definition, although a useful starting point, could not be regarded as a fully comprehensive definition of barriers to entry. In later writings, economists have concentrated on ascertaining whether the activities of incumbents in the market make the market significantly less 'contestable' for potential entrants. In particular, economists have sought to identify what they describe as 'strategic barriers to entry', *ie*, the incurring by the incumbent of costs which are designed to increase the costs which have to be incurred by a new entrant relative to the incumbent's costs.

The question as to whether the use by HB of an exclusivity term, either considered separately or in conjunction with its policy in relation to prices, rebates and discounts, constituted an unacceptable barrier to entry in accordance with these principles was the topic mainly discussed by the expert witnesses. In the case of Dr Bishop and Dr Fingleton, their conclusions on this aspect of the case were based to some extent on the evidence of the market research survey to which reference has already been made and which must now be considered in more detail.

This survey was carried out under the supervision of Mrs Abelman in accordance with instructions she received from Mars and their legal advisers. Five hundred shops were surveyed, a sample representing approximately 6% of the retail outlets in the State which sold ice-cream, excluding the supermarket 'multiples'. Mrs Abelman said that, in marketing terms, this was an extremely substantial sample. She gave details of the methodology employed by her firm so as to ensure that there was a random selection of outlets which were properly representative of the outlets throughout the country. The actual interviewing was carried out by the Market Research Bureau of Ireland and neither they nor the interviewers employed by them were told the purpose of the survey. The survey was carried out early in December 1991. After the results had been received by her firm and collated, a further cross-check was carried out in the form of telephone calls to 24% of the actual respondents, which she said was an unusually high number in a survey of this kind.

The questions asked can be summarized as follows:

(a) whether there were any ice-cream brands which the retailer would like to stock but for some reason could not;

(b) how many retail freezer cabinets for ice-cream products the retailer had in the front of the shop;

(c) who owned the cabinets and, where they were supplied by manufacturers, the terms on which they were supplied;

(d) in the case of cabinets subject to an exclusivity term, whether the retailer had room to install another cabinet or whether he would be prepared to install another cabinet.

The survey demonstrated that 30% of those sampled were 'very interested' in stocking new ice-cream brands and 36% were 'fairly interested'. 400 out of the 502 outlets had HB cabinets. Of those, 302 had one cabinet and 93 had two cabinets. 71% of all the cabinets included in the survey were owned by HB.

408 of the total sample said they would have to install another cabinet to sell other brands of ice-cream. Of those, 65% said they had no room to install such a cabinet. Of the remaining 34% who had room, 22% said they would not be prepared to install another cabinet.

The survey established that of the 613 cabinets included in the sample, 66 were owned by the retailer, 56 by Mars or Valley and 489 by other manufacturers, the latter accordingly amounting to 80% of the total.

8.1.4 Mrs Abelman said that the general picture was that a majority of the shops interviewed would like to stock another brand of ice-cream. The majority had not room for a further cabinet and the vast majority were restricted in what they could stock at the moment. She agreed on cross-examination that she had not included a question in the survey as to whether any retailer with a cabinet subject to an exclusivity term would be prepared to swap that cabinet for another. She was asked for details of the instructions from her clients as to the nature of the survey and produced notes of a meeting held at Heathrow Airport on 19 November 1991 with representatives of Mars and their legal advisers. It appeared from the notes that a question as to the switching of HB cabinets with other cabinets was suggested but later discarded.

The figure that emerged from this survey as to the number of cabinets in each of the sample outlets — 1.22 — was lower than the average suggested by other evidence in the case *ie* 1.50. As already noted, however, this survey confined itself to asking the retailers as to the number of cabinets in the front of the store and the difference may be accounted for by the fact that (particularly in the winter months when the sample was taken) retailers might have a second cabinet at the back of the store which was unplugged and not in use.

Dr Bishop inferred from this survey that .76 of the retail outlets in the State either had no room for a second freezer or were not prepared to take one. Based on the Rosslyn survey finding that 80% of the outlets had cabinets containing an exclusivity term (the overwhelming majority of which, of course, are HB) he concluded that 61% of the market was, as he put it, 'fully foreclosed'. Again basing his conclusion on the survey, he said that .23 of the outlets had room for, and were prepared to take, another cabinet. This led him to the conclusion that, again taking 80% of the cabinets to have an exclusivity term, the market was as to 19% 'partly foreclosed'. Based on the turnover figures produced for outlets by the survey, he then calculated that, in terms of turnover, 53% of the market was fully foreclosed and 26% partly foreclosed.

Dr Bishop gave the following reasons for treating the market as completely foreclosed in the case of outlets where the existing cabinet was subject to the exclusivity term and the retailer had either no room for an additional cabinet or was unwilling to take one. In such cases, a new entrant would have to persuade the retailer to replace their existing cabinets with their own or, if they had room, to take another one. This would involve, in the first place, a large capital investment over a short period of time, an investment which it would not be possible to justify in economic terms. Such expenditure would constitute 'sunk costs'. In the second place, a new entrant would probably encounter significant reluctance from retailers to changing their supplier. He said that retailers would probably exhibit a certain amount of inertia and that the decision to switch to a new entrant would involve several 'transaction costs'. Thus, the existing agreement with HB would have to be terminated, the cabinet removed and a new one installed. Moreover, in the present state of the market, where HB was the main supplier and the only firm offering a large product range, he thought that retailers might be concerned that changing their supplier would jeopardize future supplies from HB or might result in a lower level of service. Additionally, in order to compete with HB, a new entrant would have to supply cabinets free of charge and hence could not recoup its investment by charging a flat annual fee.

Dr Bishop said that in the case of the partly foreclosed outlets, the problem would also arise for the new entrant of a substantial capital investment in new cabinets. This might not be justified in the case of manufacturers with small product ranges and relatively small sales volumes. He also said that a new entrant who produced a smaller range of products — such as Mars — would incur significantly higher costs. Based on the expected level of sales from an average cabinet supplied by HB, he calculated that cabinet costs add about 24p to a litre of ice-cream. In the case of Mars, this figure would rise to approximately 145p in an average TSN.

Dr Bishop was also of the view that HB's pricing practices constituted a barrier to entry. This was because they charged all retailers the same price irrespective of the ownership of the cabinet. Thus, where the cabinet was owned by HB , they 'bundled together' the capital costs of the cabinet, its maintenance costs and the price of the ice-cream. This meant, he said, that the retailers who owned their own cabinets were effectively paying a higher price and hence subsidising the retailers with tied cabinets. It also meant that the larger retailers who were selling above average volumes of ice-cream were subsidising the smaller retailers. The result was to discourage ownership of the cabinets by the retailers and to facilitate HB in maintaining exclusivity. He said that, by contrast, in the U.K., Unilever's subsidiary, Walls, operated a dual price system under which retailers who owned their own cabinets obtained a larger discount on the volume of ice-cream they sold. **8.1.4**

Dr Bishop said that the effect of these practices had been to discourage new entrants into the Irish market and that as a result innovations in the market had been stifled. He concluded that the maintenance of the exclusivity clause in conjunction with the pricing policy constituted an unacceptable barrier to entry and that the maintenance by HB of these practices would, from an economist's viewpoint, constitute an abuse by them of their position of market power. He said that while the lack of space for a second cabinet, in such a large number of the retail outlets was an important factor in making the market difficult to penetrate for a new entrant, the 'bundling' of the price was even more important since, without 'bundling', most retailers would opt for independence. He rejected the argument that HB should not have to provide free storage for the products of their competitors and said that this took no account of the other possibilities which were open to HB *eg*, supplying cabinets without an exclusivity term but charging for them. He also disagreed with the suggestion that the savings, if any, effected by HB in distribution costs as a result of the exclusivity term was a justification for the practice in economic terms.

Dr Fingleton accepted that cabinet exclusivity in itself would not automatically constitute an unacceptable barrier to entry. He said, however, that, coupled with the 'bundling' of which Dr Bishop spoke, it constituted a significant barrier to entry.

Professor Bradley said that a manufacturer bringing a new product to the market had to concern himself with four factors which he said were generally known as the four 'Ps': product, price, promotion and 'place' or distribution. He said that in terms of the Irish ice-cream market the operation of the exclusivity term was a barrier to such distribution. He said that, from the retailer's point of view, space was of paramount importance and hence rendered the taking of a second cabinet an unattractive option. The fact that a new product, such as Mars, was not available in a large number of cabinets would of itself have a damaging effect on the marketing of the product.

Mr McDowell said that there were two critical factors in determining whether the provision of cabinets free of charge by a manufacturer such as HB subject to an exclusivity term constituted a barrier to entry which was unacceptable from an economist's point of view. The first was whether action of this nature would normally be taken by an incumbent firm irrespective of the threat of competition from possible new entrants into the market. If it would, then, in his view, it could not be said to constitute an unacceptable barrier to entry. The second was whether in any event such a practice in fact constituted a credible deterrent to new entrants.

In relation to the first criterion, Mr McDowell said that the available information suggested that in most of the countries of Western Europe, including the U.K., it was normal operating procedure for manufacturers of ice-cream to supply cabinets to retail outlets. He identified a number of factors as contributing to the existence of this practice:

(a) the requirements of market development and penetration;

(b) scale economies in the supply and maintenance of freezers as part of the distribution chain;

(c) the improved ability to guarantee product quality and thus protect the supplier's investment in brand development;

(d) lower distribution costs.

In relation to market development, he said it was clear that, as between the supplier and the retailer, the supplier was in a better position to undertake such risks as were involved in meeting the costs of new cabinets and their subsequent maintenance costs. As to scale economies, he said it was to be expected that a large scale purchaser and operator of equipment such as cabinets

8.1.4 would obtain substantial scale economies which would not be available to a small scale user. He instanced the substantially lower price at which cabinets were supplied to HB. As to product quality maintenance, he pointed to the perishable and unstable nature of ice-cream as a product and to the importance from the supplier's point of view of ensuring that the freezers in which it is stored are kept at the appropriate temperature and in good working order. Finally, in terms of lower distribution costs, he said it was clearly advantageous for HB to own cabinets at the point of sale, as it ensured that less space was left unoccupied by their own products and resulted in fewer delivery 'drops' per unit of sales.

As to the second criterion, *ie*, whether the practice constituted a credible deterrent to entry, Mr McDowell suggested that in the first place it depended on whether the costs which a new entrant would have to incur would be both substantial and 'sunk'. He said that an expenditure of £350 to hold stock for a period of ten years in a retail outlet did not appear to be exorbitant. (The evidence was that HB depreciated their cabinets over a ten year period, while Mars adopted a seven year period). Mr McDowell accepted that the costs could to some limited extent be regarded as 'sunk', but he thought that a reasonable level of sales per cabinet would recoup the cost fairly quickly and that, in the result, Mars could recover the expenditure in a relatively short time if its sales revenues exceeded its direct operating costs.

Mr McDowell said that the available information suggested that the market was not in fact foreclosed. He said that the fact that Mars had achieved a market share of between 6% and 10% and that Valley had installed more than 500 cabinets in retail outlets over the last three years, indicated that it was not foreclosed. He said that, for Mars to sustain their allegation that the market was to a significant extent foreclosed, they would have to establish that:

(a) so many retailers could take only one freezer and have taken that one from HB that Mars are physically precluded from achieving a break-even level of sales by this fact alone: and

(b) that the retailers who take only one freezer could not by any reasonable expenditure be persuaded to change suppliers.

Mr McDowell said that, in the light of the evidence that there was a cabinet population of 18,000 in 12,000 retail outlets, these propositions were unsustainable. He said that it was not simply a question of Mars having a narrow product range, since their marketing strategy had been to combine with Valley who had a larger product range. He said that if their strategy was not working, it could not be because of the joint result of cabinet exclusivity and a narrow product range. He also pointed to the evidence in the Nielsen survey that independent TSNs are declining steeply in importance in the Irish retail market and said that this further weakened the proposition that the exclusivity term was a significant barrier to entry.

Mr McDowell disagreed with the view of Dr Bishop and Dr Fingleton that the 'bundling' of prices created a barrier to entry. He said that the segment of the market in which HB owned the cabinets and there was no room for other cabinets was clearly the market which it was more difficult to enter. Yet it was precisely in this segment, he said, that the 'subsidized' price structure prevailed. He said that, if the 'bundling' was to be viewed as an attempt to exclude competitors, it made no economic sense, since the lower prices prevailed in that part of the market which was least vulnerable to new entrants. He considered that the real explanation of the pricing arrangement was the importance from HB's point of view of encouraging retailers to take their cabinets on an exclusive basis, thereby reducing HB's distribution costs.

V: The applicable law

(a) *General*

The claims made by Mars in these proceedines are based on both EC law and the law of the State. At the outset, it is necessary to consider the position of this Court and the EC institutions so far as both claims are concerned.

Articles 85 and 86 are contained in Chapter I of Part III, Title 1 of the Treaty. This chapter is headed 'RULES ON COMPETITION' and Articles 85 and 86 are in section 1 under the heading 'RULES APPLYING TO UNDERTAKINGS'. Article 85 prohibits agreements and other arrangements between undertakings which are anti- competitive in nature. Article 86 is concerned with the abuse by undertakings in a dominant position of that position. **8.1.4**

Article 87 of the Treaty enables the Council of the Community to adopt any appropriate regulations to give effect to the principles set out in these articles. In pursuance of that power, the Council adopted Regulation No. 17, to the provisions of which it will be necessary to refer in more detail at a later stage. At this point, it is sufficient to note that, under Article 3 of that regulation, the Commission are entitled to bring to an end infringements of Articles 85 and 86 and that this power includes the power to adopt interim measures where the conduct at issue appears *prima facie* to represent an infringement of Articles 85 and 86 and where 'serious and irreparable damage' might be caused to other undertakings if the interim measures were not adopted. (It will be seen that the procedure is not dissimilar to the procedure governing interlocutory injunctions under our law, although the jurisdictional threshold is different and arguably higher: see the judgment of the Court of Justice in *Camera Care Ltd v. Commission of the EC* [1980] ECR 119; *Campus Oil v. Minister for Industry and Energy (No. 2)* [1983] IR 88). The decisions of the Commission may be the subject of an appeal to the Court of First Instance whose decision in turn may be reviewed on points of law by the Court of Justice.

The sister company of Mars in Germany (Mars GmbH) lodged a complaint with the Commission under Article 3 in respect of alleged infringements by two undertakings, one of them the sister company of HB in Germany, in respect of alleged infringements by them of Articles 85 and 86. That complaint, which related in part to the maintenance by the undertakings concerned of cabinet exclusivity, was the subject of a decision by the Commission on 25 March 1992 (while the present action was at hearing), adopting certain interim measures in respect of the complaint. The decision of the Commission is set out in more detail in the next part of this judgment.

Article 85(3), as given effect to by Regulation 17, enables the Commission to declare Article 85 inapplicable in the case of either specific agreements or categories of agreements (the latter being known as 'bloc exemptions'), where their maintenance can be justified on particular grounds. The regulations also enable a 'negative clearance' to be given to individual agreements in the form of a certificate by the Commission that there are no grounds under either Article 85 or Article 86 for action on its part in respect of the agreement.

It will be seen that the Commission has a central role in determining community policy in this area. Its decisions are, accordingly, of value to national courts in cases such as the present. However, ultimately, the decisions which carry most weight with the national court must inevitably be those of the Court of Justice and the Court of First Instance, including, of course, the opinions of the Advocates General.

It is also clear that, under Article 177 of the Treaty, a judge of a national court is entitled to request an interpretation of the Treaty from the Court of Justice. In the present case, neither of the parties have requested me to make such a reference, but I bear in mind the decision of the Supreme Court in *Campus Oil v. Minister for Industry and Energy* [1983] IR 82 that the national judge has, in the words of Walsh J, 'an untrammelled discretion' as to whether he should seek an interpretation of the Treaty from the Court of Justice and that in exercising that discretion he is not in any way subject to the parties.

The provisions of Irish domestic law have also been invoked by Mars in this case. It has not been suggested that any of these provisions are in conflict with EC law, in which case they would have to yield to the primacy of community law over the domestic law of the member states.

(b) *EC law*

It is submitted on behalf of Mars that Articles 85 and 86 of the Treaty have direct effect in the law of member states with the following consequences:

(1) they confer direct rights in favour of individuals;

8.1.4 (2) it is the duty of the national courts to protect and safeguard these rights;

(3) all legal means must be made available by the national courts to give effect to these rights under the same conditions and procedures as apply to domestic legal remedies;

(4) these conditions must not be such as make it impossible in practice to give effect to the direct rights in question.

It is accepted on behalf of HB that the provisions in question have direct effect in national law. It is also submitted on their behalf, however, that the pursuit of these rights before national courts will, subject to certain community safeguards, be governed by national rules where there are no community rules. Since, as it is urged on their behalf, infringement of Article 85(1) or 86 exposes the party in breach to the imposition of fines, which under Irish law would fall to be regarded as penal in nature, it is submitted that the standard applicable in a civil action is inappropriate and that a higher standard of proof is required. On behalf of Mars, this latter proposition is contested and it is submitted that the standard applicable is that appropriate in civil proceedings before the Irish courts.

Article 85 of the Treaty provides that:

> 1. The following shall be prohibited as incompatible with the common market: all agreements between undertakings, decisions by associations of undertakings and concerted practices which may affect trade between member states and which have as their object or effect the prevention, restriction or distortion of competition within the common market, and in particular those which:
>
> > (a) directly or indirectly fix purchase or selling prices or any other trading conditions;
> > (b) limit or control production, markets, technical development, or investments;
> > (c) share markets or sources of supply;
> > (d) apply dissimilar conditions to equivalent transactions with other trading parties, thereby placing them at a competitive disadvantage;
> > (e) make the conclusion of contracts subject to acceptance by the other parties of supplementary obligations which, by their nature or according to commercial usage, have no connection with the subject of such contracts.
>
> 2. Any agreements or decisions prohibited pursuant to this article shall be automatically void.
> 3. The provisions of paragraph 1 may, however, be declared inapplicable in the case of:
>
> > – any agreement or category of agreements between undertakings;
> > – any decision or category of decisions by associations of undertakings;
> > – any concerted practice or category of concerted practices
>
> which contributes to improving the production or distribution of goods or to promoting technical or economic progress, while allowing consumers a fair share of the resulting benefit, and which does not:
>
> > (a) impose on the undertakings concerned restrictions which are not indispensable to the attainment of these objectives;
> > (b) afford such undertakings the possibility of eliminating competition in respect of a substantial part of the products in question.

On behalf of Mars, it is submitted that the agreements which are the subject matter of these actions are clearly 'agreements between undertakings' within the meaning of this article. They also say that the agreements in question may affect trade between member states and that no question of exemption under Article 85 (3) arises. In the result, it is submitted that the only issue which the court has to resolve under Article 85 is whether the cabinet agreements and, in particular, the exclusivity term, have as their object or effect the prevention, restriction or distortion of competition within the common market. **8.1.4**

It is submitted on behalf of Mars that the words 'object or effect' in Article 85(1) are to be read disjunctively. Accordingly, if the court should hold that the agreements in the present case have as their object the prevention, restriction or distortion of competition, it is unnecessary for the court to take into account the actual effects of the agreements. If an agreement by its nature is intended to distort competition, it is void by virtue of Article 85(2), irrespective of its effects.

If, however, the court should find it necessary to take into account the *effects* of the agreements in question, it is submitted on behalf of Mars that the following factors should be taken into account in determining whether those effects amount to the prevention, restriction or distortion of competition, *ie*:

(i) the nature and quantity, limited or otherwise, of the products governed by the agreement;

(ii) the position and importance of the grantor and the concessionaire on the market for the products concerned;

(iii) the isolated nature of the disputed agreement, or, alternatively, its position in a series of agreements;

(iv) the severity of the clauses intended to protect the exclusive dealership.

It is emphasized on behalf of Mars that in order to examine whether it is caught by Article 5(1) an agreement cannot be examined in isolation from its factual and legal context and that the existence of similar contracts may be taken into consideration.

On behalf of HB, it is submitted that Article 85 of the Treaty must be considered in the context of other provisions of the Treaty and, in particular, Article 222 which provides that:

> This Treaty shall in no way prejudice the rules in member states governing the system of property ownership.

It is submitted that, while EC law may intervene to control the use of property, it cannot be availed of to interfere with the substance of a right of property, such as, HB's ownership of the cabinets and, as a necessary consequence of that right of ownership, the right to exclude other suppliers from storing their products in the cabinets.

As to the object of the cabinet agreement being to prevent or distort competition and that, accordingly, its effects need not be considered, HB say that this approach is inappropriate in the case of a 'vertical' agreement such as the present, *ie* one between undertakings which are not in direct competition with one another, such as, in the present case, manufacturers and retailers. Where an agreement is not plainly intended to restrict competition, it is urged, it is necessary to consider the effects of the agreement in order to determine whether it is prohibited by Article 85. In deciding whether the effect of an agreement is to restrict competition, a 'rule of reason' approach should be adopted, *ie* the system of distribution should be examined in order to ascertain whether the contractual terms in question are compatible with Article 85(1). If those provisions are an important component in ensuring the effective operation of the distribution system, they will not be void under Article 85(2). Community law, it is submitted, recognizes that different industries and trades require special forms of distribution, such as 'tied house' agreements in the case of beer and 'solus' agreements in the case of petrol: these may either be accorded exemption as a category under Article 85(3) or, by the application of the 'rule of reason' approach be excluded under Article 85(1). The agreements in this case, it is submitted, fall into the latter category.

As I have already mentioned, Article 85(3) provides that the provisions of Article 85(1) may be declared inapplicable in the case of any agreement or category of agreements. It was accepted that no such exemption had been granted, either in the form of a specific or a 'bloc exemption'. On behalf of HB, it was submitted that the agreements in this case enjoyed what

8.1.4 was called 'provisional validity' until such time as a declaration was made under Article 85(3). It was said that this was the effect of Article 4 of Regulation No. 17, which provided for the notification to the Commission of agreements in respect of which the parties sought the application of Article 85(3).

Article 4 provides that:

> 1. Agreements, decisions and concerted practices of the kind described in Article 85(1) of the Treaty which came into existence after the entry into force of this regulation and in respect of which the parties seek application of Article 85(3) must be notified to the Commission. Until they have been notified, no decision in application of Article 85(3) may be taken.
> 2. Paragraph 1 shall not apply to agreements, decisions or concerted practices where:
>
> > (1) the only parties thereto are undertakings from one member state and the agreements, decisions or practices do not relate either to imports or to exports between member states;
> > (2) not more than two undertakings are party thereto and the agreements only;
> > (a) restrict the freedom of one party to the contract in determining the prices or conditions of business upon which the goods which he has obtained from the other party to the contract may be resold; or
> > (b) impose restrictions on the exercise of the rights of the assignee or user of industrial property rights — in particular patterns, utility models, designs or trademarks — or of the person entitled under a contract to the assignment, or grant, of the right to use a method of manufacture or knowledge relating to the use and to the application of industrial processes;
> >
> > (3) They have as their sole object:
> > (a) the development or uniform application of standards or types; or
> > (b) joint research and development;
> > (c) specialization in the manufacture of products including agreements necessary for achieving this,
> >
> > – where the products which are the subject of specialization do not, in a substantial part of the common market, represent more than 15% of the volume of business done on identical products or those considered by consumers to be similar by reason of their characteristics, price and use, and
> > – where the total annual turnover of the participating undertakings does not exceed 200 million units of account.
>
> These agreements, decisions and practices may be notified to the Commission.

Article 5(1) of the regulation provides:

> 1. Agreements, decisions, and concerted practices of the kind described in Article 85(1) of the Treaty which are in existence at the date of entry into force of this regulation and in respect of which the parties seek application of Article 85(3) shall be notified to the Commission before 1 November 1962. However, notwithstanding the foregoing provisions any agreements, decisions and concerted practices to which not more than two undertakings are party shall be notified before 1 February 1963.

It was accepted on behalf of HB that, *prima facie*, an agreement enjoyed provisional validity pending a decision of the Commission only where notice had been given under Article 4(1). However, it was submitted that, having regard to Article 5(1), this did not apply where agreements were in existence at the date of the coming into force of the regulation, *ie* 13 March 1962. Nor did it apply to agreements in existence at the date of the accession of the State to the European Economic Community, *ie* 1 January 1973. Such agreements, it was said, enjoyed provisional validity whether notice had been given or not and a number of the agreements in issue in this case fall into either or both categories. It was further submitted that the agreements came within Article 4(2) which did not in any event require the giving of notice to the Commission. **8.1.4**

Mars objected to the raising of the issue as to the provisional validity of the agreements, on the ground that it was advanced for the first time during the course of closing submissions and had not been raised in the pleadings. Without prejudice to that objection, it was submitted that no evidence had been directed as to the dates on which the various agreements had been entered into between HB and the retailers and there could obviously be many agreements in existence which would be later in date than 1 January 1973. It was further submitted that Article 4(2) had no application to the agreements in issue in the present actions and that, in any event, the effect of the article was not to confer provisional validity on such agreements, but simply to relieve the parties of the obligation to notify the Commission of their existence.

Article 86 of the Treaty provides that:

> Any abuse by one or more undertakings of a dominant position within the common market or in a substantial part of it shall be prohibited as incompatible with the common market in so far as it may affect trade between member states. Such abuse may, in particular, consist in:
> (a) directly or indirectly imposing unfair purchase or selling prices or unfair trading conditions;
> (b) limiting production, markets or technical development to the prejudice of consumers;
> (c) applying dissimilar conditions to equivalent transactions with other trading parties, thereby placing them at a competitive disadvantage;
> (d) making the conclusion of contracts subject to acceptance by the other parties of supplementary obligations which, by their nature or according to commercial usage, have no connection with the subject of such contracts.

On behalf of Mars, it was submitted that, in reaching a conclusion as to whether HB enjoyed a dominant position within the meaning of this article, the court should have regard to the following principles.

(1) A 'dominant position' describes a position of such economic strength enjoyed by an undertaking that it is able to behave to an appreciable extent independently of its competitors, its customers and its consumers.

(2) The identification of a dominant position derives from consideration of a combination of several factors any one of which may not, taken alone, be necessarily decisive.

(3) Very large market shares are in themselves, save in exceptional circumstances, evidence of the existence of a dominant position.

(4) Although the concept of the abuse of a dominant position is a separate matter, regard may be had to the activity alleged to consist of abuse when consideration is being given to whether a dominant position exists.

(5) The competitive situation in the market must be considered by reference to the particular features of the product with reference to a clearly defined geographic area in which it is marketed.

(6) The geographic area must be defined by reference to an area where conditions of competition are sufficiently homogeneous for the effect of the economic power of the undertaking concerned to be evaluated.

(7) Establishing the relevant product market requires consideration of the nature and characteristics of the product itself, whether it is adapted to satisfy the constant needs of an

8.1.4 important section of the population, its interchangeability with other products, cross-elasticity of prices between it and other potentially substitutable products and conditions of supply and demand in the market.

(8) Behaviour affects trade between member states if it may have an influence, direct or indirect, actual or potential on the pattern of trade between member states such as might prejudice the aim of a single market.

It was further submitted on behalf of Mars that the list of abusive practices contained in Article 86 is not intended to be exhaustive and that, independently of the methods employed, abuse may occur if an undertaking in a dominant position strengthens that position in such a way that the degree of dominance reached substantially fetters competition. Specifically, an undertaking in a dominant position which makes use of that dominant position to create barriers to entry into the market will be held to have abused its dominant position. In particular circumstances, requiring customers to buy their supplies from the undertaking in a dominant position, sometimes, but not exclusively, by the use of rebates or discounts, may be an abuse of such position. So also may a refusal to supply individual customers.

On behalf of HB, it is submitted that a dominant position only arises where the undertaking enjoys a position of economic strength which enables it to prevent effective competition being maintained on the relevant market by affording it the power to behave to an appreciable extent independently of its competitors and ultimately of its customers. It was further submitted that proof of a significant market share was not, of itself, satisfactory evidence of a dominant position. A firm with a large market share might well be influenced in its decisions by potential competitors who have not yet entered the market. An existing market share may fluctuate and may not be maintained into the future. Information as to other factors, besides market share, is necessary, it was said, in determining how the market operates.

It was further submitted on behalf of HB that, even where the court held that an undertaking was in a dominant position, Article 86 could not be invoked so as to deprive the undertaking of its property rights recognized under Article 222. Nor could that article be applied to the exercise of such rights, unless the conduct complained of constitutes a form of abuse additional to the exercise of the right as such.

It was further submitted on behalf of HB that, even if the exercise by HB of its property rights was not a defence to the claim under Article 6, that claim would still fail if the court considered that HB's conduct was objectively justified. It was submitted that the following propositions were relevant in determining whether particular conduct should be characterized as abusive.

(1) No abuse exists where a dominant company pursues its own interest through legitimate competitive means.

(2) Forms of competition which are normal in a particular industry should not generally be treated as abusive.

(3) It is to be presumed that, if a particular practice falls outside Article 85(1) on a 'rule of reason' analysis, it is not to be regarded as abusive when engaged in by a dominant undertaking.

(4) It is to be presumed that a practice is not abusive in the absence of evidence that the same legitimate ends could be achieved with equal cost efficiency in another manner.

(5) A dominant undertaking owes no duty not to compete so long as its competition is fair and proportionate.

(6) Actions to protect rights of property are not to be regarded normally as abusive.

(7) Property and facilities are not required to be made available to competitors without proper remuneration.

It was also submitted on behalf of HB that, in the event of the court holding that the agreements enjoyed provisional validity until such time as a decision of the Commission was pronounced pursuant to Regulation 17, it was not open to Mars to contend that the enforcement of the agreement constituted an abuse of a dominant position within the meaning of Article 86. On behalf of Mars, it was submitted that, even if it were open to HB to advance this case which had not been pleaded, it was not well founded, since an agreement could constitute an abuse of a dominant position irrespective of whether it enjoyed provisional validity by virtue of Regulation 17. 8.1.4

Having carefully considered the submissions of counsel and the many authorities to which they referred, I have come to the following conclusions as to the principles of EC law which are applicable to these two actions.

It has been held by the Court of Justice in *Belgische Radio en Televisie v. SABAM* [1974] ECR 51, that Articles 85 and 86 of the Treaty produce direct effects in relations between individuals and consequently create direct rights in respect of the individuals concerned which the national courts must safeguard. This proposition is not disputed on behalf of HB, but it is urged that, since a finding by this Court in these proceedings which is adverse to them may result in the imposition of a fine on them by the Commission, a higher standard of proof should be required than would normally be applicable in civil actions. They rely on statements by the Court of Justice in *Comet BV v. Produktschap voor Siergewassen* [1976] ECR 2043 and *MIRECO* [1980] ECR 2559 that it is for the domestic legal system of the member state to determine the procedural conditions governing actions intended to safeguard rights flowing from community law and that such conditions must be as favourable as those relating to similar actions of a domestic nature. They further rely on a statement by Webster J in *Shearson Lehman Hutton Inc v. Maclaine Watson & Co. Ltd* [1989] 2 Lloyd's Rep 570 that:

> An infringement of Article 85 carries with it a liability to penalties and fines; and I will, therefore, apply the standard of a high degree of probability, but less than the standard of proof in criminal cases.

They also rely on statements in two other English cases, *Hornal v. Neuberger Products Ltd* [1957] 1 QB 247, and *R. v. Secretary of State for the Home Department, ex parte Khawaja* [1984] 1 AC 74, suggesting that a higher standard of proof is required in civil cases where criminal conduct is alleged.

These are civil proceedings and it follows that the applicable standard of proof is that appropriate to such cases, *ie*, proof on the balance of probabilities. It may well be that that standard should be applied with some degree of flexibility and that the courts should require allegations of particular gravity to be clearly established in evidence. But the Supreme Court have made it clear in *Banco Ambrosiano v. Ansbacher* [1987] ILRM 669 that this does not mean that a different standard of proof is to be applied when, for example, an allegation of fraud is being made.

I am, accordingly, satisfied that I should apply in these actions the standard of proof normally applicable in civil proceedings, *ie*, proof on the balance of probabilities.

The application of Article 85 of the Treaty to these actions must first be considered. It is not in dispute that the cabinet agreements containing the exclusivity term are agreements between undertakings within the meaning of that article. The enforcement of the exclusivity term prevents the storage and display of other manufacturers' products, including products imported from other member states, such as the products made by Mars which are manufactured in France. Thus, it is also clear — and again this is not disputed by HB — that they are agreements that may affect trade between member states within the meaning of Article 85. The question is as to whether the agreements, either separately or taken in conjunction with HB's policies in relation to pricing, discounts and rebates, have as their object or effect the prevention, restriction or distortion of competition within the common market. It is also not in dispute that agreements between undertakings which affect trade between member states may be prohibited under Article 85, either because they are captured by the general prohibition on agreements having the specified object or effects or because they fall under one or more of the categories of agreement specified in paragraphs 1(a) to (e) inclusive.

Article 85 is not to be considered in isolation from the other provisions of the Treaty. In the

8.1.4 first place, Articles 2 and 3 of the Treaty, which set out its principal objectives, may need to be considered. Article 2 provides that:

> The community shall have as its task, by establishing a common market and progressively approximating the economic policies of member states, to promote throughout the Community a harmonious development of economic activities, a continuous and balanced expansion, an increase in stability, an accelerated raising of the standard of living and closer relations between the states belonging to it.

Article 3 provides that, for the purposes set out in Article 2, the activities of the community are to include *inter alia*:

> the institution of a system ensuring that competition in the common market is not distorted.

In *Metro SB-Grossmarkte GmbH & Co. KG v. Commission of the EC* [1977] ECR 1875, the Court of Justice said (at p. 1904):

> The requirement contained in Articles 3 and 85 of the EEC Treaty that competition shall not be distorted implies the existence on the market of workable competition, that is to say the degree of competition necessary to ensure the observance of the basic requirements and the attainment of the objectives of the Treaty, in particular the creation of a single market achieving conditions similar to those of a domestic market.

The competition rules can thus be seen as part of the grand design of the Treaty to achieve a single market.

In addition, regard must be had to the provisions of Article 222, *ie*:

> This Treaty shall in no way prejudice the rules in member states governing the system of property ownership.

As I have already noted, the agreements under attack in this case are vertical in nature, *ie* they govern the relations between manufacturers and retailers and do not directly affect relations between persons who are in direct competition with each other. However, while the vertical nature of the agreements is relevant in assessing their compatibility with Article 85, it is clear that such agreements are not by reason of their vertical nature excluded from the scope of Article 85. (See *Consten and Grundig v. Commission of the EC* [1966] ECR 299).

It is also clear that the words 'object or effect' in the article are to be read disjunctively. The precise purpose of the agreement must first be considered. If an analysis of its provisions does not lead to the conclusion that its purpose was to prevent, restrict or distort competition, the consequences of the agreement must then be considered and, for the agreement to be captured, it must be shown that competition has in fact been prevented, restricted or distorted to an appreciable extent. (See *Societe Technique Miniere v. Maschinenbau Ulm GmbH* [1966] ECR 235). The last mentioned case also indicates a number of factors which should be taken into account in determining whether the agreement is to be considered as prohibited by reason of its object or effect, *ie*,

(1) The nature and quantity, limited or otherwise, of the products governed by the agreement.

(2) The position and importance of the grantor and the concessionaire on the market for the products concerned.

(3) The isolated nature of the disputed agreement, or alternatively its position in a series of agreements.

(4) The severity of the clauses intended to protect an exclusive dealership or, alternatively, the opportunities allowed for other commercial competitors in the same products by way of parallel re-exportation and importation. 8.1.4

The cabinet agreements in issue in these actions do not prevent the retailers from selling other competing products. They do, however, prevent the retailer from selling competing products from a cabinet which is the subject of such an agreement and, to that extent, can be regarded as similar in nature to vertical agreements imposing exclusive purchasing requirements on the distributor. However, such agreements are not by their nature prohibited by Article 85(1). In *Brasserie de Haecht v. Wilkin (No. 1)* [1967] ECR 407, the Court of Justice ruled that:

> Agreements whereby an undertaking agrees to obtain its supplies from one undertaking to the exclusion of all others do not by their very nature necessarily include all the elements constituting incompatibility with the common market as referred to in Article 85(1) of the Treaty. Such agreements may, however, exhibit such elements where, taken either in isolation or together with others, and in the economic and legal context in which they are made on the basis of a set of objective factors of law or of fact, they may affect trade between member states and where they have either as their object or effect the prevention, restriction or distortion of competition.

In a more recent case *Delimitis v. Henninger Brau AG* [1991] 4 CMLR 329, the court indicated in some detail the factors which the national court should take into account in determining whether the object of such agreements is anti-competitive within the meaning of the article, *viz.*:

> 10. Contracts for the supply of beer generally stipulate that the supplier grants to the retailer certain economic and financial advantages such as granting loans on favourable terms, leasing premises for the operation of the bar and making available technical installations, furniture and other items of equipment necessary for the operation of the bar. In consideration of these advantages, the retailer normally undertakes to stock up, for a certain duration, only from the supplier as regards products covered by the contract. To this exclusive purchase undertaking is generally added a prohibition on selling competing products in the bar leased by the supplier.
>
> 11. The conclusion of these contracts presents for the supplier the advantage of having an assured outlet so that, taking account of the exclusive purchase obligation and the prohibition and competition imposed on the retailer, the latter concentrates its sales efforts on the distribution of the products in the contract. The contracts for supply also imply co-operation with the retailer which enables the supplier to plan its sales for the duration of the contract and to organize its production and distribution efficiently.
>
> 12. Contracts for the supply of beer also provide advantages for the retailer in that it enables him to gain access at favourable terms and with guaranteed supply to the beer distribution market. The joint interests of the retailer and the supplier in promoting sales of the products in the contract also provide the retailer with the benefit of the supplier's support with a view to guaranteeing the quality of the products and the service offered to clients.
>
> 13. If agreements of this type do not have the objective of restricting competition, as defined by Article 85(1), it is nevertheless appropriate to verify whether or not they have the effect of hindering it, restricting it or distorting its interplay.

8.1.4 It was made clear by the court in *Brasserie de Haecht v. Wilkin* that, in assessing the *effects* of such an agreement, it was necessary to take into account its economic and legal context and that this included the cumulative effect produced by several similar agreements. However, in *Delimitis v. Henninger Brau AG*, the court emphasized that the existence of such a network of agreements was simply one factor amongst others to be considered in determining whether the agreement had an anti-competitive effect. The court indicated the approach which should be taken as follows:

> 19. In order to assess whether the existence of more than one contract for the supply of beer hinders access to the market thus delimited, it is then necessary to examine the nature and size of all these contracts. This includes all similar contracts tying a large number of points of sale to several national producers. ... The effect of these networks of contracts on market access depends in particular on the number of points of sale tied in this way to national producers in relation to that of bars which are not so tied, on the duration of the undertakings subscribed, on the quantities of beer covered by these undertakings, as well as on the ratio of these quantities to those sold by non-tied distributors.
>
> 20. The existence of a bundle of similar contracts, even if its effect on the opportunities for market access is significant, would not however suffice in itself to conclude that the market in question is inaccessible, in that it only constitutes one element, amongst others, of the economic and legal context in which a contract must be assessed. . . . Taking account of these other elements, in the first place, includes those which also determine these opportunities for access.
>
> 21. In this respect, it is appropriate to examine whether there are real and concrete opportunities for a new competitor to penetrate the bundle of contracts thanks to the acquisition of a brewery already established in the market with its whole chain of points of sale or to circumvent the bundle of contracts by opening new bars. . . .
>
> 22. It is appropriate to take account in the second place of the conditions under which the interplay of competition takes place in the reference market. In this respect it is a question of knowing not only the number and size of producers present in the market, but also the degree of saturation in this market and the loyalty of consumers to existing labels, since it is generally more difficult to penetrate a saturated market that is characterized by the loyalty of consumers to a low number of large producers, than a market undergoing expansion in which a large number of small producers operates which do not have strong labels.

In the United States, where anti-trust legislation was in force long before the establishment of the European Community, the Supreme Court has adopted what has been called the 'rule of reason' approach in certain cases. Section 1 of the Sherman Act 1890 provided that:

> Every contract, combination in the form of trust or otherwise, or conspiracy, in restraint of trade . . . is hereby declared to be illegal.

At an early stage in the development of anti-trust law, it was made clear by the Supreme Court that even the remarkably wide sweep of this provision could not justify the conclusion that every restraint of trade was prohibited. In *Chicago Board of Trade v. U.S.* (1918) 246 US 231 it was said that:

> The legality of an agreement or regulation cannot be determined by so simple a test, as

whether it restrains competition. Every agreement concerning trade, every regulation of trade, restrains. To bind, to restrain, is of their very essence. 8.1.4

Hence, in *Standard Oil v. U.S.* (1911) 221 US 1, White CJ said that the appropriate method of deciding whether a restraint was within the Sherman Act or not was to apply a 'standard of reason' and that only undue or unreasonable restraints should be condemned. Elsewhere in his opinion he referred to this as 'the rule of reason'. As it was subsequently developed by the courts, it meant that agreements which were not illegal *per se* (because, for example, they fixed prices or shared markets), should be subjected to a 'rule of reason' analysis in order to determine whether they were captured by the Sherman Act. The particular importance of the rule of reason approach in U.S. law where vertical distribution agreements are concerned is emphasized by the decision of the Supreme Court in *GTE v. Sylvania* (1977) 433 US 36.

In considering the applicability of the 'rule of reason' approach to Article 85, the differences between the United States and the European Community must be borne in mind. One of the principal objectives — some might say the paramount objective — of the Treaty is the integration of the common market. In the U.S., an integrated market and a single currency already exists. Moreover the bald formula of the Sherman Act has already been noted: it is in stark contrast to the elaborate detail of Article 85. In particular, the machinery operated by the Commission of negative clearances and exemptions, including bloc exemptions, has no parallel in U.S. anti-trust law. There is thus less incentive for the Court of Justice to adopt a 'rule of reason' approach. (See 'Article 85 and the Rule of Reason', by Richard Whish and Brenda Sufrin, 1987 *European Law Year Book* 1).

These considerations may render a 'rule of reason' approach inappropriate in considering agreements effecting territorial partitions of the market, whether by means of horizontal or vertical agreements. But in such cases also, the court has, on occasions, found it neceesary to conduct a 'rule of reason' inquiry: decisions involving intellectual property rights demonstrate that, even in the case of agreements leading to territorial exclusivity, a rule of reason approach may be necessary.

More recently, this has been extended to franchise agreements. Thus, in *Pronuptia de Paris GmbH v. Pronuptia de Paris Irmgard Schillgalis* [1986] ECR 363, the court, having concluded that franchise agreements were not *per se* incompatible with Article 85, went on to examine certain restrictions which the agreement at issue in that case imposed on both the franchisor and the franchisee. To the extent that these provisions had the effect of sharing markets on a territorial basis between the franchisor and the franchisees or between franchisees, they were held to constitute restrictions of competition for the purposes of Article 85(1). However, they were upheld to the extent that:

> (a) they are strictly necessary in order to ensure that the knowhow and assistance provided by the franchisor do not benefit competitors; and
> (b) they establish the control strictly necessary for maintaining the identity and reputation of the network identified by the common name or symbol.

The effect of Article 222 must next be considered. It was made clear by the court in *Consten and Grundig v. Commission of the EC* that the recognition of property rights protected under the laws of member states contained in that article does not prevent community law from restricting the exercise of such rights in order to give effect to the prohibition under Article 85(1). It has also been held, however, that such a restriction must not constitute:

> A disportionate and intolerable interference with the rights of the owner, impinging upon the very substance of the right to property. (*Hayer v. Land Rheinland-Pfalz* [1979] ECR 3727).

8.1.4 The cases in which the interaction of Article 222 with Articles 85 and 86 have been considered are, in the main, cases concerning intellectual property rights. It is emphasized in those cases that the rights of the owners in such cases to grant licences for the use of the particular patent, or whatever may be in issue, and to prevent infringements by third parties constitute the very subject matter of such exclusive rights. Consequently, Article 85(1) cannot be applied so as to deprive the owner of those rights, since that would amount to the abolition of the right of property itself, but can be invoked so as to restrain the *exercise* of the rights in such a manner as to contravene Article 85 (1). (See *Parke, Davis and Co. v. Probel* [1968] ECR 55; *Sirena SRL v. Eda SRL* [1971] ECR 69; *Deutsche Grammophon GmbH v. Metro-SB-Grossmarkte GmbH and Co. KG* [1971] ECR 487; *Coditel SA v. Cine-Vog Films SA* [1982] ECR 3381; *Cicra and Maxicar v. Renault* [1988] ECR 6039; *Tetra Pak Rausing SA v. Commission of the EC* [1991] 4 CMLR 334; *RTE v. Commission of the EC* [1991] 4 CMLR 586, *BBC v. Commission of the EC* [1991] 4 CMLR 669, *ITV v. Commission of the EC* [1991] 4 CMLR 745, judgments delivered by Court of First Instance, 10 July 1991).

As to the submission on behalf of HB that the agreements in issue enjoy provisional validity until such time as the Commission have made a decision under Article 85(3), I am satisfied that, since this issue was not raised in the pleadings or at any stage during the hearing until closing submissions were being made, it should not now be entertained. However, in case the matter should go further, I will indicate what my findings would have been, had it been open to me to entertain the point.

While it may be that some of the agreements were entered into before either of the relevant dates in 1962 or 1973, no evidence was directed to this issue during the hearing and it is, in any event, obvious that many of the agreements must have been later in date than 1973. Accordingly, I would not be prepared to hold that the agreements the subject-matter of these proceedings are entitled to provisional validity as having been entered into before the relevant dates. As to the argument based on Article 4.2 of Regulation No. 17, this seems to me to proceed upon a misconception as to the effect of that paragraph. Paragraph 1 requires that all agreements to which Article 85(1) apply must be notified to the Commission. Paragraph 2 provides that certain agreements are not subject to such compulsory notification, but may be notified to the Commission. If they are notified to the Commission, they then presumably enjoy the same provisional validity as other agreements. Unless they are so notified, there seems no reason why they should enjoy the benefit of provisional validity accorded to agreements which have been notified.

Article 86 of the Treaty must next be considered. While there is a major dispute between the parties as to what constitutes the relevant market for the purpose of ascertaining whether HB enjoys a dominant position therein, it is not in dispute that the relevant market, however composed, constitutes a substantial part of the common market, since it extends to the entire of one of the member states of the community (See *NV Nederlandsche Banden-Industrie Michelin v. Commission of the EC* [1983] ECR 3461). The dispute between the parties is as to what constitutes the relevant market, whether HB enjoys a dominant position within it and, if so, whether the practices complained of by Mars, principally the enforcement of the exclusivity term, amount to an abuse of that position.

No issue therefore arises as to whether the market with which we are concerned constitutes, in geographical terms, a substantial part of the common market for the purposes of Article 85(1). It is clear that it does. A substantial issue has, however, arisen between the parties as to what that market is in terms of the relevant product. Mars contend that it is the impulse ice-cream market. HB contend that it is a larger impulse market consisting of ice-cream, crisps, confectionery, snack foods, soft drinks and chewing-gum. If the relevant product market is as claimed by HB, then it is beyond argument that HB do not enjoy a dominant position in the market.

The factors which should be taken into account in determining the relevant product market were explained by the Court of Justice in *United Brands Co. v. Commission of the EC* [1978] ECR 207. In that case the applicants, who were found by the Commission to have abused their dominant position in the relevant market, challenged the Commission's view that the market in question was in bananas. They maintained that the banana market was part of the fresh fruit market, since bananas were reasonably interchangeable by consumers with other kinds of fresh fruit, such as apples, oranges, grapes, peaches, strawberries, *etc*. In its judgment, the court said that, for the banana to be regarded as forming a market which is sufficiently differentiated from other fruit markets, it must be possible for it to be singled out by such special features distinguishing it from other fruits that it is only to a limited extent interchangeable with them and is only exposed to their competition in a way that is hardly perceptible. **8.1.4**

Having considered seasonal factors, interchangeability with other fruits, cross-elasticity of demand and the characteristics of the fruit itself, the court concluded:

> It follows from all these considerations that a very large number of consumers having a constant need for bananas are not noticeably or even appreciably enticed away from the consumption of this product by the arrival of other fresh fruit on the market and that even the personal (*recte* seasonal) peak periods only affect it for a limited period of time and to a very limited extent from the point of view of substitutability.
>
> Consequently the banana market is a market which is sufficiently distinct from the other fresh fruit markets.

The generally accepted definition of 'dominance' in EC law is to be found in the decision of the Court of Justice in *Hoffman-La Roche v. Commission of the EC* [1979] 3 CMLR 211, *ie*:

> A position of economic strength enjoyed by an undertaking which enables it to prevent effective competition being maintained on the relevant market by affording it the power to behave to an appreciable extent independently of its competitors, its customers and ultimately of the consumers.

While this is the fundamental definition, the court identified a number of factors in *United Brands* as being of relevance in determining whether an undertaking has a dominant position in the relevant market, *ie*:

(1) Whether it has succeeded in winning a large part of the relevant market;

(2) The strength and number of its competitors;

(3) Whether the percentage of the relevant market enjoyed by the undertaking represents *grosso modo* a share several times greater than that of its nearest competitor;

(4) The extent to which the undertaking is vertically integrated, *ie*, the extent to which it owns and controls its own distribution network.

It is also made clear by the judgment in that case that an undertaking does not have to have eliminated all opportunity for competition in order to be in a dominant position. However, it also recognizes that the existence of barriers to competitors entering the market which are almost insuperable is also a feature of a dominant position.

In *Hoffman-La Roche*, the court said, that although the importance of the market share held by the undertaking alleged to be in a dominant position may vary from one market to another, very large shares are in themselves and, save in exceptional circumstances, evidence of the existence of a dominant position.

It said:

> An undertaking which has a very large market share and holds it for some time, by means of the volume of production and the scale of the supply which it stands for — without those having much smaller market shares being able to meet rapidly the demand from those who would like to break away from the undertaking which has the largest market share — is by virtue of that share in a position of strength which makes it an unavoidable

8.1.4 trading partner and which, already because of this secures for it, at the very least during relatively long periods, that freedom of action which is the special feature of a dominant position.

In *AKZO Chemie v. Commission of the EC* (judgment delivered 3 July 1991) the court, applying the principles in *Hoffman-La Roche*, concluded that a market share of 50% was evidence of a dominant position. In *Hilti AG v. Commission of the EC* [1992] 4 CMLR 16, the Court of First Instance concluded that a market share of between 70% and 80% was, in itself, a clear indication of the existence of a dominant position.

If it has been established that HB enjoy a dominant position in the relevant market, the question then arises as to whether any of the practices complained of amount to an abuse of that dominant position within the meaning of Article 86.

Clearly, the existence of a dominant position is not of itself unlawful in EC law. It is also clear from the decision of the Court of Justice in *Europemballage Corp. v. Commission of the EC* [1973] ECR 215 that the list of practices expressly prohibited by Article 86 as abuses of a dominant position are not intended to be exhaustive. That case also contains a frequently cited statement of what constitutes abuse:

> Abuse may therefore occur if an undertaking in a dominant position strengthens such position in such a way that the degree of dominance reached substantially fetters competition, *ie*, that only undertakings remain in the market whose behaviour depends on the dominant one.

This definition was elaborated further by the court in *Hoffman-La Roche* as follows:

> The concept of abuse is an objective concept relating to the behaviour of an undertaking in a dominant position which is such as to influence the structure of a market where, as a result of the very presence of the undertaking in question, the degree of competition is weakened and which, through recourse to methods different from those which condition normal competition in products or services on the basis of the transactions of commercial operators, has the effect of hindering the maintenance of the degree of competition still existing in the market or the growth of that competition.

It is accordingly clear that, if an undertaking in a dominant position adopts strategies which result in the establishment of barriers to competitors entering the market, these will normally be held to amount to an abuse of its dominant position. (See the decision of the Court of First Instance in *Hilti AG v. Commission of the EC*).

Specific strategies have been identified in decisions of the Court of Justice and the Court of First Instance as falling within this prohibition, *eg*, a requirement by the undertaking that purchasers obtain all or most of their requirements from the undertaking. Thus, in *Hoffman-La Roche*, the court said that:

> An undertaking which is in a dominant position on a market and ties purchasers — even if it does so at their request — by an obligation or promise on their part to obtain all or most of their requirements exclusively from the said undertaking abuses its dominant position within the meaning of Article 86 of the Treaty, whether the obligation in question is stipulated without further qualification or whether it is undertaken in consideration of the grant of a rebate.
>
> The same applies if the said undertaking, without tying the purchasers by a formal obligation, applies, either under the terms of agreements concluded with these purchasers or unilaterally, a system of fidelity rebates, that is to say discounts conditional on the customers obtaining all or most of its requirements — whether the quantity of its

> purchases be large or small — from the undertaking in a dominant position. **8.1.4**
>
> Obligations of this kind to obtain supplies exclusively from a particular undertaking, whether or not they are in consideration of rebates or of the granting of fidelity rebates intended to give the purchaser an incentive to obtain his supplies exclusively from the undertaking in a dominant position, are incompatible with the objective of undistorted competition within the common market, because — unless there are exceptional circumstances which may make an agreement between undertakings in the context of Article 85 and in particular of paragraph (3) of that article, permissible — they are not based on an economic transaction which justifies this burden or benefit but are designed to deprive the purchaser of or restrict his possible choice of sources of supply and to deny other producers access to the market.

Similarly, it was held in *United Brands* that a refusal to supply a particular customer may amount to an abuse of a dominant position. (See also *Commercial Solvents v. Commission of the EC* [1974] ECR 223 at p. 250).

It is also clear that, in considering whether particular practices amount to an abuse of a dominant position, it may be relevant to determine whether the practices in question can be objectively justified and, in particular, whether they are normal competitive practices. Thus, in *Michelin*, the Court of Justice said that:

> As regards the application of Article 86 to a system of discounts conditional upon the attainment of sales targets, such as described above, it must be stated first of all that in prohibiting any abuse of a dominant position on the market insofar as it may affect trade between member states, Article 86 covers practices which are likely to affect the structure of a market where, as a direct result of the presence of the undertaking in question, competition has already been weakened and which, through recourse to methods *different from those governing normal competition in products or services based on traders' performance*, have the effect of hindering the maintenance or development of the level of competition still existing in the market. (emphasis added).

The development of community case law in this area is helpfully summarized in the opinion of Advocate General Krischner in *Tetra-Pak Rausing SA v. Commission of the EC*. He says:

> If a restraining effect on competition only is allowed to suffice in order to characterize the conduct of an undertaking in a dominant position as abusive, the danger will arise that Article 86 will be applied to all the profit making activities of the said undertaking. That would at least come close to prohibiting dominant positions, which is not provided for in the Treaty. Consequently, Article 86 must be considered more closely in this regard.
>
> Since Article 86 does not prohibit the existence of a dominant position *per se*, an undertaking in a dominant position may also act in a profit-oriented way and strive to expand its business activities.
>
> It may reinforce its dominant position on the market through competition and drive less efficient competitors from the market, even if that results in its market share reaching 100%. The EEC Treaty does not require the undertaking in a dominant position to act in a way which makes no economic sense and is against its legitimate interest. If it did, community law would conflict with other obligations to which an undertaking in a dominant position — like any other undertaking — is subject. I am thinking of, for instance, the company law obligation on management organs to use the capital entrusted to them by the shareholders in order to make a profit and undertakings' responsibility for safeguarding jobs.

8.1.4 The use of disproportionate means in pursuit of economic advantage may, however, amount to an abuse. The law is thus stated by Advocate General Kirschner in *Tetra Pak*:

> The undertaking in a dominant position may act in a profit oriented way, strive through its efforts to improve its market position and pursue its legitimate interests. But in so doing it may employ only such methods as are necessary to pursue those legitimate aims. In particular it may not act in a way which, foreseeably, will limit competition more than is necessary.

(See also the decision of the court in *United Brands*.)

The relationship between Article 222 of the Treaty, recognizing the systems of property ownership in the member states, and Article 86 must next be considered. The principles which the Court of Justice and the Court of First Instance have applied are similar to those applied in relation to Article 85. Thus, it has been held in a number of cases that the mere exercise by an undertaking in a dominant position of a right of property does not of itself constitute an abuse of a dominant position. If, however, its exercise by the undertaking involves conduct which itself can be considered abusive, then the conduct in question will be held to be an abuse of the dominant position. (See in particular the judgment of the Court of Justice in *Volvo v. Eric Veng (UK) Ltd* and *Cicra v. Renault*).

I should also refer to the Commission decision of 25 March 1992 (*IV/34.072 – Mars/Langnese and Scholler*).

The decision recites the complaint by Mars against the two undertakings, of which one is a member of the Unilever Group. They point out that Mars is not in principle in favour of installing its own freezer cabinets in retail outlets, but that it has departed from this principle in the United Kingdom and the Netherlands. Mars obtained the co-operation of other firms in distributing their products, one of whom made available 20,000 freezer cabinets. However, one of the firms informed Mars in August 1991 that it was terminating their relationship because:

> Sales prospects [were] practically non existent, the market clearly being sewn up as a result of exclusivity agreements operated by Scholler and Langnese-Iglo.

The Commission found that Langnese-Iglo, the Unilever subsidiary, whom I shall call 'L-I', was the market leader in frozen food and ice-cream in Germany. The other respondent company, Scholler, entered into an agreement in September 1991 with Jacobs Suchard with the object of manufacturing and selling ice-cream bars in imitation of the corresponding chocolate confectionery products of Jacobs Suchard. It was said in the trade press that this idea derived from the successful launch of the Mars ice-cream bar.

The Commission give detailed statistics as to the breakdown of the German market which like the Irish market is divided into single items, multi-packs, take-home packs and 'bulk consumption' packs. There is also a segment of the market called 'artisan', which clearly equates to our own soft ice-cream sector. A special situation has arisen in Germany as a result of the achievement of unification in 1990 and the opening up of the market in the former German Democratic Republic.

Freezer cabinet exclusivity exists in the grocery retail trade in Germany and in the 'traditional' retail trade, the latter being described as 'restaurants, service stations, kiosks, cake shops and other outlets.' The composition of the traditional retail sector is thus somewhat different from that in this country, at least in its historic form of TSNs and small independent groceries. There is an even more significant difference, however, between the trading arrangements in the traditional retail sectors in the two countries: in Germany, it is customary for ice-cream manufacturers to operate 'exclusivity agreements', in addition to freezer cabinet tying arrangements. The retailer is required to sell in the way of ice-cream or similar products in his outlet only products bought direct from the manufacturer. 8.1.4

In May 1985, Scholler notified to the Commission, under the procedure already described, a standard form agreement under which the retailer was obliged to sell only their ice-cream. The Commission's Directorate General for Competition originally informed Scholler that this agreement was compatible with the competition principles of the Treaty, but in 1991 informed Scholler that the proceeding was being reopened. It would appear that 90% of all Scholler's customers in the traditional retail area are bound by these agreements.

The Commission found that approximately 60% of the sales of what we would describe as impulse ice-cream products were effected by the traditional retail trade and that between 75% and 90% of all sales outlets in that trade were subject to tying arrangements which would, of course, include the agreements tying the outlets. It was also stated that the average duration of these exclusivity agreements in the case of L-I was two and a half years and in the case of Scholler just more than one year.

The Commission also found that filling stations are an important part of the traditional retail trade and referred to a distribution agreement concluded between L-I and an unnamed body under which the latter became the agent for L-I ice-cream in respect of all the filling stations in Germany. There is no exclusivity clause in that agreement but it would seem that the agreement was interpreted by the parties on a 'partnership basis', whereby only two suppliers were to be allowed in the network, namely, L-I and Scholler. Following the introduction of Mars ice-cream, the distributing agency informed L-I that it no longer felt bound by this interpretation. L-I replied that a departure from the original interpretation might result in their having to reconsider the terms of the agreement.

There was also evidence that fidelity rebates were operated by L- I.

The Commission found that since the second half of 1989, the incumbent manufacturers in the German market had decided to defend their exclusivity agreements against the Mars' products 'using every means at their disposal'. They also found that, since well before the arrival of Mars on the scene, there had been 'close co-operation' between L-I and Scholler.

The Commission found that the relevant product market was that in 'impulse ice-cream'. It also found that the freezer exclusivity arrangements obliged a new competitor entering the market to carry out an investment in the provision of these cabinets which increased the economic risks.

The Commission found that the expansion of the market, and in particular the opening up of the East German market, made market access easier. However this was counterbalanced by the existence of the exclusivity agreements both in relation to the cabinets and the retail outlets. They also found that the domination of the market by L-I and Scholler, consumer preferences for established manufacturers and the 'close co-operation' between L-I and Scholler all constituted additional barriers to entry.

So far as the exclusivity term in relation to cabinets was concerned, the Commission found that its provision and maintenance conferred economic advantages on the retailer which, however, could be forfeited if he gave it back or the manufacturer took it back. They concluded that in this area:

> There is a restriction of competition, though the extent to which it is appreciable can be determined only in the light of special circumstances.

The Commission reject the claim that the ownership of the cabinets carries with it the right to exclude other people from using them. They point out that the tying of the freezer cabinets limits competition in another way, in that retailers may be unwilling to install another freezer because space is limited or for economic reasons. They also say that the overall turnover of a shop selling impulse ice-cream products cannot be expected to increase substantially if competitors' products are sold in addition to the products of an established supplier.

The Commission conclude that:

8.1.4 If the German ice-cream market had a less oligopolistic structure, the system would reduce itself to absurdity. However, the practice seems to ensure its own survival by preventing the development of more intense competition.

They add, however, that a number of outlets in the 'traditional' retail trade would not carry any ice-cream at all if the manufacturers did not provide the freezer cabinets. They also said that it must be assumed that the manufacturers for their part undertake the relevant investment only if it is economically worthwhile. They conclude that:

> As soon as the retailer concerned is persuaded of the profitability of selling ice-cream, he will be prepared to make the appropriate investment and will if necessary also be able to contain the financial resources required. In such cases, therefore, the installation of manufacturers' freezer cabinets tied to a specific use does not, during a certain transitional period at any rate, have the effect of restricting competition.

They go on to consider the sales outlet exclusivity arrangements and the fidelity rebates and to find that they are restrictive of competition.

The Commission find that the cumulative anti-competitive effect of the large number of freezer agreements is appreciable, particularly having regard to the large market shares of L-I and SLG. This conclusion is substantially reinforced in their view by the fact that three quarters of all the sales outlets are also tied by exclusivity agreements to the manufacturers.

The Commission go on to deal with the possibility of individual and bloc exemption. They then conclude that, the combination of the various factors to which they have referred, *ie*, the tying of freezer cabinets, the exclusivity agreements tying retail outlets, the 'duopolistic' structure of the market and the close co-operation between L-I and Scholler all lead to the conclusion that:

> The German market for impulse ice-cream does not display the characteristics of effective competition.

The Commission took the view that 'serious and irreparable damage' could be caused to Mars by maintaining the exclusivity agreements in relation to the outlets. This would deprive them of the 'competitive edge' which they would obtain from the introduction of their new products. The detriment to L-I and Scholler which would result from their being prohibited on an interim basis from enforcing their exclusive rights in respect of sales outlets was more than outweighed, in the Commission's view, by the irreparable harm that would be caused to Mars. However, they considered that no action should be taken against the tying of the freezer cabinets, since:

> there is a danger that a substantial part of the large amount of investment carried out by L-I and [Scholler] in the existing stock of freezer cabinets would be economically destroyed by any such action on the part of the Commission. The interest of Mars in such immediate action by the Commission does not offset the possible damage to the undertakings concerned.

Hence, the interim measures ordered are confined to prohibiting the assertion by L-I and Scholler of their rights to compel the retailers to sell only their products.

The Court of Justice in the *Delimitis* case said that it was open to the national court to contact the Commission where the concrete application of Article 85(1) or Article 86 raises particular difficulties, with a view to obtaining economic and legal data. However, in view of the fact that the detailed interim decision of the Commission on the Mars' application is now available, it does not seem to be necessary to invoke this procedure.

The final question that arises is as to whether it is necessary to seek an interpretation from the Court of Justice as to the principles of EC law applicable to the facts already found. As already noted, this is solely a matter for the discretion of the national judge and he is not bound in any way by the views of the parties. It seems to me that, in the light of the extremely elaborate and helpful arguments of counsel, the legal principles applicable to the present case, although part of an evolving jurisprudence of competition law in the community, are reasonably clear. I do not find it necessary in these circumstances to refer any question to the court under Article 177. **8.1.4**

(b) *National law*

Article 9 of the Restrictive Practices (Groceries) Order 1987 (SI No. 142 of 1987) made by the Minister for Industry and Commerce pursuant to section 8 of the Restrictive Practices Act 1972 provides that:

> No supplier, wholesaler or retailer shall be a party to any agreement, arrangement or understanding (whether induced by threat, promise or otherwise) which has or is likely to have the effect of limiting or restricting entry to trade in any grocery goods.

'Grocery goods' are defined by Article 2(1) and it is accepted that the definition extends to the products which are the subject matter of these proceedings. However, a preliminary point is taken on behalf of HB as to whether this order is still in force and I should consider this point first.

Section 22 of the Competition Act 1991 provides that:

> The provisions of the Act of 1972 and every order made under that Act and sections 5 and 6 and sections 8 to 23 of the Act of 1987 are hereby repealed.

Section 2 of the Act of 1991 provides that:

> (1) This Act shall come into operation on such day or days as may be fixed therefor by order or orders of the Minister, either generally or with reference to a particular purpose or provision, and different days may be so fixed for different purposes and different provisions of this Act.
> (2) An order under subsection (1) may as respects the repeal effected by section 22 of the provisions of the Act of 1972 fix different days for the repeal of different provisions of that Act or for the repeal for different purposes of any provision of that Act.

The minister in question is the Minister for Industry and Commerce. He made an order in purported exercise of the powers conferred on him by that section entitled the Competition Act 1991 (Commencement) Order 1991. Articles 3 and 4 of that order provide *inter alia* that:

> 3. Subject to paragraph 4 of this order, the Act shall come into operation on 1 October 1991. . . .
>
> 4. This order does not apply to . . .
>
> > (b) Section 22 of the Act insofar as it provides for the repeal of —(i) The following order made under section 8(1) of the Act of 1972 – Restrictive Practices (Groceries) Order 1987. . . .

The point made on behalf of HB is that the power conferred on the Minister by section 2(2) of the Act of 1991 is confined to the repeal effected by section 22 of the provisions of the Act of 1972 and does not apply to orders made under that Act. Consequently, the Minister was not entitled to make an order providing for the coming into force of section 22, insofar as it repeals the 1987 Order, on a different day from that fixed for the coming into effect of section 22 as

8.1.4 respects other provisions or other purposes.

I am satisfied that this point is not well taken. It is true that subs. (2) is expressly confined to the repeal effected by section 22 of the provisions of the Act of 1972 and that it does not extend to orders made under that Act. However, subs. (1) expressly empowers the Minister to provide for the coming into operation of the Act on such day or days as he may fix, either generally *or with reference to a particular purpose or provision*. He has made use of that power by the 1991 Order to bring into force section 22 for all its purposes, other than those specified, on 1 October 1991. Among those so specified is the repeal of the 1987 Order. This he was clearly entitled to do.

It is submitted on behalf of Mars that the exclusivity term in the present case has or is likely to have the effect of limiting or restricting entry to the ice-cream industry and that, accordingly, it is in breach of that article. It is submitted on behalf of HB that it does not have any such effect, since any entrant to the trade is free to come to an agreement with any retailer for the supply of a freezer cabinet stocking the entrant's products and is not in any way limited or restricted from so doing by the existence of the exclusivity term in the HB agreements.

It was also submitted that, in determining whether there had been a breach of Article 9, I should have regard to the Third Schedule to the Restrictive Practices Act 1972 under which the relevant order was made and which defines 'unfair practices' as including 'agreements . . . which . . . have or are likely to have the effect of unjustly eliminating a competitor.' I was referred to my decision in *Irish Association of Distributive Trades Ltd, Retail Grocery Dairy and Allied Trades Association v. 3 Guys Ltd* [1979] ILRM 269 where I held that the schedule was a legitimate aid to the construction of an order made under section 8(1) of the Act of 1972, since the Minister was empowered by virtue of the section to make an order prohibiting *inter alia* 'unfair practices'.

I am satisfied, however, that the words in question in the Third Schedule probably add little of significance when one is considering what is at issue in the present case. An agreement which unjustly eliminated a competitor in the ice-cream trade would presumably be, by definition, one which limited or prevented entry to that trade and hence within the scope of Article 9 in any event. Ultimately, the issue that has to be resolved is not dissimilar to the issue which arises in the context of EC law, *ie* whether, having regard to all the relevant circumstances, the exclusivity term constitutes a barrier to entry into the ice-cream trade which Article 9 was designed to render unlawful.

For completeness sake, I should also refer to sections 4 and 5 of the Act of 1991, prohibiting anti-competitive agreements and the abuse of a dominant position respectively. The wording of these two sections which, of course, came into force after the commencement of these proceedings reflects the wording of Articles 85 and 86 of the Treaty.

VI: Conclusions

Despite the length of the hearing, there was no very serious conflict of evidence as to the primary facts. The parties are, however, in certain areas in dispute as to the inferences which should be drawn from the facts. Before proceeding to state my conclusions, I should, accordingly, indicate the inferences that I think should be drawn in these areas.

The first relates to the market share enjoyed by HB. The extent of that share depends, of course, on how one defines the relevant market and it is also obvious that their share of that relevant market must have fluctuated over the period of years which are relevant and which, in this case, can safely be said to have begun when they acquired the ice-cream business of the Premier Group in 1969.

It is not in dispute that the question of market share only arises if the relevant market is that in ice-cream products. Moreover, while there were occasional suggestions during the case that the relevant market, if not the wider market, was the market in ice-cream products as a whole, *ie*, including the 'take home' products and multipacks, I am satisfied that the overwhelming burden of the evidence was that the relevant market, again assuming that one is excluding the wider market, was that in impulse ice-cream products. The evidence clearly established, in my view, that HB's share of that market was in excess of 70% for the four years preceding the institution of the first of these actions on 26 January 1990. I am also satisfied that, in the period since 1969, it has rarely fallen below that level, with the possible exception of a period in the early 1970s when they were affected by a strike. It may be that if one were to treat the soft or home-made ice-creams as part of this market that HB's share might be reduced. These are also undoubtedly impulse products and, on none of the criteria put forward by the experts, could they be regarded as being in a different products market. However, the extent to which HB's market share might be reduced if those ice-cream products were taken into account in addition to the wrapped impulse products was not explored in any depth during the hearing and, accordingly, I do not think it should affect my finding as to the probable market share of HB in the impulse ice-cream market. **8.1.4**

The second factual issue which may be of some significance and on which there was controversy was the number of retail outlets in the State in which there was more than one freezer. As already noted, according to the Rosslyn Research Ltd market survey, the average number of freezers per retail outlet (excluding the multiple supermarkets) was 1.22. This was at variance with the figures given by other witnesses which suggested an average of 1.5 freezers per outlet. This latter figure was based on what appeared to be a generally accepted estimate that there were approximately 18,000 freezers in the retail outlets throughout the State and that the number of relevant retail outlets was approximately 12,000. The discrepancy may be explained by the fact that in the Rosslyn Research Ltd survey, retailers were simply asked how many freezers they had at the front of their shop. However, this survey was carried out in December at a time when other evidence indicated that many retailers who had a second freezer unplugged it and put it in the back of the shop. I am, accordingly, of the view that the more likely ratio is that of 1.5 freezers per relevant retail outlet.

The third factual issue is as to the extent to which HB enforced the exclusivity term. The evidence in this area was necessarily selective and incomplete. Insofar as it can be relied on, it indicated that, while HB made some attempt to secure compliance with the exclusivity term even before the advent of Mars and were particularly concerned to prevent the practice of storing cool pops and similar products in the cabinets, their response was of a different order from their reaction to the challenge of Mars. While individual salesmen drew the attention of retailers to the undesirability in particular of storing cool pops in the cabinets, there was no indication that at management level the matter was treated with anything like the degree of urgency and concern that greeted the 'colonizing' by Mars of HB freezer cabinets in the summer of 1989.

There is one further matter to which I should refer before I come to my conclusions on the legal issues that arise. In the pleadings, it was alleged that HB operated a system of fidelity rebates which because of their anti-competitive nature were in breach of the relevant articles of the Treaty and of the 1987 Order. The evidence established, in my view, that the number of retailers who could be said to have been offered such fidelity rebates was relatively insignificant and certainly not more than 5%. It would also appear that there were special circumstances affecting at least some of them. However that may be, it is perfectly clear that the number of outlets involved was so small that it could not seriously be suggested that this constituted any significant form of anti-competitive practice on the part of HB. I do not think that this aspect of the case was ultimately seriously pressed by Mars and this was almost inevitable in the light of the evidence. They did, of course, maintain that the generally prevailing system of volume rebates, while in itself unexceptionable, was operated under the threat that the rebates would not be forthcoming if the exclusivity term was not observed.

The first issue of law that must be resolved is as to the relevant product market. I am satisfied that the contention advanced on behalf of Mars is correct and that the relevant product market is the market in impulse ice-cream products. I reach that conclusion largely on what has been described as the 'commonsense' or 'innate characteristics' test. I do not think that someone

8.1.4 going into a confectioner's or newsagent to buy an ice-cream who finds the cabinet temporarily empty would treat their appetite as slaked by a can of coke or a bag of crisps. They are far more likely to cross the road to the nearest sweet shop and get their ice-cream there. That conclusion is undoubtedly borne out by some of the marketing surveys to which I have already referred. It is also confirmed, but to a limited extent only, by the seasonal factor, since undoubtedly ice-cream is more evidently a product consumed in large quantities in hot weather than any of the allegedly competing products.

As to the cross-elasticity of demand criterion, to which much expert evidence was directed, it may be that Dr Bishop's econometric study could be said, at least in a negative sense, to confirm the 'commonsense' test. Ultimately, however, I think that the acknowledged incapacity of that procedure to embrace all the significant variables which would have to be taken into account significantly reduces its value.

The next question of law is as to whether the evidence establishes that HB enjoy a dominant position in the relevant market. I am satisfied that they do. I think that the following factors point clearly to that conclusion:

(1) The fact that HB's share of the market has, for nearly a quarter of a century, been rarely less than 70% and may at times have been significantly more, a market share which, on any view, is very substantial indeed;

(2) The small number of competitors with HB and their relatively low market shares;

(3) The fact that HB's market share, on any view, is several times greater than that of its nearest competitor, *ie*, Valley/Mars;

(4) The efficient vertically integrated distribution system operated by HB (I bear in mind, of course, that HB does not actually own any of the retail outlets.)

This combination of factors has enabled HB to behave to an appreciable extent independently of its competitors, its customers and ultimately of the consumers. This is clearly demonstrated by the evidence as to the activities of the Irish Ice Cream Federation. It is clear that HB have at all times effectively dictated the level of prices for all ice-cream products and have never felt the need to reduce prices in order to compete more effectively with others in the market. There is also no indication that they ever felt obliged to reduce their prices so as to enhance the volume of their sales to the retailers and ultimately to the general public. It would seem that the only factors which influenced them in determining prices were their costs of production and — presumably — the degree of profit which was considered appropriate as remuneration for the capital invested in the company. The only body to whom they were obliged to have regard in determining the level of their prices was the National Prices Commission during the period that price control existed.

It is only fair to add that Mr Ted Murphy, in his evidence, said that HB generally succeeded in keeping any price increases below current levels of inflation. There was also no evidence that ice-cream prices in this country were significantly higher than in other comparable economies.

It should also, of course, be pointed out that, while the other manufacturers from time to time disagreed with HB as to the appropriate price level for particular products, it did not appear that any of the members of this federation at any time objected to the procedures by which prices were determined. As against this, representatives of only two of the firms who are members of the federation — HB and Valley gave evidence in these proceedings. I mention this because, while the fixing of selling prices by agreement between undertakings is one of the practices prohibited by Articles 85 and 86 of the Treaty, the question as to whether the procedures followed by the federation are incompatible with Articles 85 and 86 of the Treaty, although raised in the pleadings, was not referred to by counsel during the hearing as being an issue in these proceedings and I refrain from making any finding as to whether they are or not. Their relevance to these proceedings is in determining whether HB enjoy a dominant position in the relevant market and, for the reasons stated, I think they confirm that HB does indeed enjoy such a position.

In order to establish that HB are in breach of Article 86, it is not sufficient for Mars to prove that they are in a dominant position: they must also satisfy the court that the practices complained of constitute an abuse of that dominant position. In the case of Article 85, a breach may occur even though none of the undertakings concerned is in a dominant position. However, in considering whether actions by a particular undertaking constitute breaches of Article 85, the extent of their market share and, in particular the question as to whether they enjoy a dominant position in the market, is plainly relevant. It is for that reason that I have, at the outset, dealt with the question as to whether HB enjoy a dominant position in the relevant market. I next consider the question as to whether they are or have been in breach of the individual articles. 8.1.4

The first question that arises is as to whether the exclusivity term in the HB agreements, either of itself or in conjunction with their pricing and rebates policy, has as its object the prevention, restriction or distortion of competition and, in particular, whether it falls within any of the particular categories specified in Article 85(1).

At the outset, two points should be noted. First, the fact that the impugned term is unarguably intended to prohibit the retailer from stocking other products in the cabinet does not of itself mean that the term is automatically void under Article 85(2). Secondly, the fact that the agreement is a vertical distribution agreement, and is not an agreement between suppliers of the same products restricting competition on a territorial or other basis, while a relevant factor, does not of itself remove the agreement from the ambit of Article 85(1).

In determining whether the object, as distinct from the effect, of the agreements is to prevent, restrict or distort competition, either generally or in any of the specified ways, certain features of the agreements are of critical importance. First, they do not prohibit the sale by the retailer of competing products, provided they are not displayed or stored in the cabinet. Secondly, they do not require the retailer to purchase either all, or a specified proportion, of his requirements of the product from HB. Thirdly, the agreement may be terminated on two months' notice at any time by the retailer.

The agreement is thus not merely outside the category of 'horizontal' agreements between undertakings providing for the partitioning of territories, the fixing of prices, *etc*, which might plainly be regarded as having an anti-competitive object within the meaning of Article 85. They do not come either within any of the categories of 'vertical' distribution agreements which have been recognized as having such an object and which, in some cases, has led to their being accorded either individual or bloc exemptions under Article 85(3). They are thus different in character from the 'tied house' agreements, common in the brewing industries of some EC countries, and which are the subject of some of the EC decisions. Nor are they in any way equivalent to those exclusive distributorship agreements under which a particular supplier agrees not to distribute his products through any other distributor. Nor can they be equated to those selective distributorship agreements which are familiar, for example, in the motor car business. Nor can they be equated to the 'franchise agreements' which, depending on their terms, may be regarded as having an anti-competitive object.

In the case of the agreements in issue here, one of the principal objects is to ensure that HB's competitors do not obtain an advantage over them by obtaining cabinet space for the display and storage of their products for which they have not had to pay and which is provided to them free of charge by HB. This cannot be regarded as an inherently anti-competition objective. Doubtless it could be achieved, as has been suggested, in other ways, *eg*, by charging a commercial rent for the cabinets. But that is not a relevant consideration in the present context where I am concerned solely with what is the actual *object* of the agreements. The agreement has also a number of other objects, *ie*, ensuring that refrigerated space is available for the storage and display of HB's products, enabling advertising material to be displayed at the point of sale and facilitating quality control. Of these, one — ensuring storage and display — could be said to be, in an indirect way, a restriction of competition. But while in that indirect fashion, it could be said to have such an *effect*, that is not to say that it is an *object* of the agreement.

8.1.4 This conclusion would doubtless be reinforced if one were to view the matter subjectively and take into account the probable intention of HB in entering into the agreements. In ascertaining their intention, the history of how the agreements came to include the exclusivity term would be relevant. However, it is clear that, in determining whether a particular agreement has an anti-competitive object within the meaning of Article 85(1), the agreement should be considered objectively and without regard to what the intention of the undertaking concerned may have been.

I next consider whether the exclusivity term, either on its own or in conjunction with HB's pricing and rebates policy, has the *effect* of preventing, restricting and distorting competition generally and, in particular, whether it falls within any of the prohibited categories.

A number of factors must be taken into account in considering this question. I have already found that HB enjoy a dominant position in the relevant market. This is a factor which is clearly relevant in determining whether the relevant agreements have the impugned effect. There is secondly the fact that a network of agreements is involved and not simply one agreement. There is thirdly the relatively weak position of the retailers who are parties to the agreements. There is fourthly the substantial volume of products which is the subject matter of all the agreements involved. All of these factors indicate that the impugned clauses must be scrutinised carefully to ascertain whether they have the effects alleged.

However, these agreements, as I have already indicated, are not *per se*, or of their very nature, contrary to Article 85. Hence, an approach approximating to the 'rule of reason' approach is, in my view, appropriate in determining whether their effects are as contended for. A number of additional factors must therefore be taken into account in considering whether they have those effects.

There is first the fact that the agreements confer significant commercial advantages on HB which are not anti-competitive in their nature, except, of course, to the extent that every practice by a business which increases its sales and maximizes its profits is likely to be to the disadvantage of its competitors. Some of these advantages have already been referred to. First, the agreements are a guarantee to HB that sufficient refrigerated space will be available for the storage and display of their products in the retail outlets in question. Secondly, they enable HB to display advertising and promotional literature at the point of sale. Thirdly, they enable HB to organize its distribution of ice-cream products more efficiently and economically. They also confer advantage on the retailers, since they relieve them of the financial burden of installing and maintaining cabinets and are more likely to ensure them supplies of the leading brand on the market than would be the case if they owned the cabinets themselves.

Again, in this context, the fact that the agreements do not prevent the retailers from selling competing products is of great importance, since in outlets where there is room for more than one cabinet the exclusivity term of itself cannot have the effect of excluding competitors. Even in outlets where there is room for only one cabinet, there is nothing to prevent the retailer from terminating the agreement at any stage and either buying a cabinet himself to stock any brands he wishes or obtaining a cabinet from another supplier.

It is urged on behalf of Mars that the Rosslyn Research Ltd market survey and the evidence of the expert witnesses whom they called demonstrate that, notwithstanding those considerations, the exclusivity term, either on its own or coupled with the pricing and rebates policy, constitutes an unacceptable barrier to entry into the market. However, I think that this issue is more appropriately resolved, in these proceedings, in the context of Article 86. Since I have already held that HB occupy a dominant position in the relevant market, it might well be that the maintenance by them of practices which constitute such an unacceptable barrier would be an abuse of that position. If, on the other hand, one were to resolve the issue in the context of Article 85, it would leave it open to HB to obtain either an individual exemption under paragraph (3) or avail of a bloc exemption if such were to be granted by the Commission. No such exemption is available to an undertaking in a dominant position which abuses that position within the meaning of Article 86.

As to the particular agreements which are specified in Article 85(1) of the Treaty as prohibited because of their effect on competition, two were relied on by Mars. Subparagraph (b) includes agreements which 'limit or control . . . markets' . No doubt agreements which, in the EC jurisprudence, are regarded as anti-competitive *per se*, would be captured by this clause, without any consideration necessarily being given to their effects and their economic and legal context. This would apply, for example, to horizontal agreements partitioning territories between potential competitors and vertical distribution agreements which are exclusive in their nature. As I have already said, the agreements in this case are not of that kind and, on the basis of the analysis already conducted, are not captured by Article 85(1). **8.1.4**

The second category on which Mars relied was subparagraph (e) *ie*, those which:

> make the conclusion of contracts subject to acceptance by the other parties of supplementary obligations which, by their nature or according to commercial usage, have no connection with the subject of such contracts.

The contracts in dispute in this case are of a kind which have been familiar and well recognized in the Irish ice-cream industry for a great many years and, indeed, are familiar in the ice-cream industries of other countries. The overwhelming burden of the evidence was that, whatever differences might exist as to pricing policies (as, for example, between this country and U.K.), it was and is the generally accepted practice to include an exclusivity term. Far from being a supplementary obligation which has no connection with the subject of such a contract, the exclusivity term is of the essence of the contract, since where the cabinet is supplied free of charge the whole purpose of the contract would be frustrated from the supplier's point of view if such a term where not to be included. I am satisfied, accordingly, that the inclusion of the exclusivity term could not be regarded as imposing what could reasonably be described as a 'supplementary' obligation on the retailer or one that had no connection with the subject of the contracts.

I have, accordingly, come to the conclusion that Mars have failed to establish that the agreements in question are prohibited by Article 85(1) and that hence they are not void by reason of Article 85(2).

The second question that arises is as to whether the practices complained of constitute an abuse by HB of their dominant position in the relevant market. This, as I have said, gives rise to the question on which differing views were advanced by the expert witnessees, as to whether the operation of the exclusivity term, either on its own or coupled with the pricing and rebates policy, created an unacceptable barrier to entry.

The economists were agreed that the definition of unacceptable barriers to entry once accepted, *ie*, costs incurred by a new entrant which the incumbent did not have to incur, while acceptable so far as it went, would not be regarded as sufficiently comprehensive today. I accordingly approach this question on the basis that, if the practices complained of create what has been described as a strategic barrier to entry designed to make the market significantly less contestable, they would constitute an abuse of HB's dominant position.

In this context, the history of the exclusivity term is of crucial importance. The uncontested evidence is that prior to the arrangement with the Premier Group which led to the emergence of HB as the dominant manufacturer, their predecessors, Hughes Brothers Ltd, adopted the same policy of cabinet exclusivity. So too did all their competitors in the Irish market. The uncontested evidence also was that this was the position in a number of other European countries and it also would seem to be the generally prevailing approach in the United States. There is, accordingly, no question of HB having adopted this strategy as a means of keeping competitors out of the market and preserving their own dominant position. No convincing reason has been put forward as to why HB should have been expected to abandon unilaterally a practice which was universal in the industry and which would simply have enabled their competitors to make use of HB's capital investment to their own benefit.

8.1.4 The evidence undoubtedly established that a significant number of relevant retail outlets, principally small independent grocers and TSNs, either had room for one freezer only or were unwilling to install a second freezer. It is also clearly established that, in a large proportion of those outlets, perhaps as many as 80%, the existing freezer is tied to HB products. Where the retailer has room for another freezer but is unwilling to install one, it is probably because, as the EC Commission have suggested, he does not think that his sales will be notably increased by selling a competitor's products. There is, however, nothing to prevent that retailer, or one who has room for one freezer only, terminating his agreement with HB and replacing it with a Valley cabinet including the Mars' products. If the retailers are not adopting this course, it is not because of the exclusivity clause, but because of other factors. Inertia may be one reason and, while what were described as 'transaction costs' may be another, these would seem to be relatively trivial. A factor of greater significance, in my view, is that under present circumstances, if the retailer adopts this course, he will not be selling the leading brand with the largest range of products. That situation would only change if HB were prepared to deliver to cabinets owned by Valley and freed from an exclusivity term. The logical outcome of such a development would seem to be a market in which the cost of supplying freezers would ultimately be borne by the retailers either as a capital outlay or by way of a commercial rent paid to the manufacturer.

It may be that such a development would increase competition in the Irish ice-cream market. It might also result in a significant number of retailers dropping out of the sale of ice-cream, because they were unwilling to bear the cost of providing cabinets. Again, if one is endeavouring to predict the future in this particular industry, it could be that a factor dwelt on by L.I. and Scholler in their submission to the Commission might become important, *ie* the development of new retail outlets such as discotheques, off-licences, video libraries and health centres. The possibility of a development of that nature was not raised during the hearing, but it was clear that the pattern of the retail trade in this country was altering significantly with a major decline in the number of TSNs and a corresponding rise in garage forecourt shops. Again one is in the region of speculation, but it may be that if the traditional retail outlets continue to change in character, the significance of HB's exclusivity policy will decline.

Whatever may happen in the future, however, HB's dominant position in the market will continue to present a crucial difficulty for new entrants, at least in the short term. But it does not follow from that inescapable fact that they are required to act in a way which, in the words of Advocate General Kirschner, makes no economic sense and is against their legitimate interest, *ie* by abandoning their exclusivity term and giving free access to competitors to the cabinets in which they have made a huge investment. The evidence undoubtedly established that, before the advent of Mars, HB did not react with any great vigour to the appearance of other products in their cabinets. But that is not a factor of decisive importance in the resolution of the issue in this case. If the presence of such a term in their cabinet agreements was in pursuance of a legitimate objective which involved *inter alia* the exclusion of competing products from their cabinets, it would be the natural consequence that, where a powerful multi-national competitor launched a planned strategy to make use of the HB freezers, the reaction would take the form that it did.

Mars laid stress on the fact that it was not simply the exclusivity term but its use in conjunction with HB's pricing policy which created the barrier to entry. Again, whatever the position is in other countries, there is no suggestion that HB created this pricing stategy in this country in order to protect their position in the market. They simply inherited it from their predecessors. But it is obvious that it has a straightforward commercial justification and is not maintained simply in order to exclude competitors from the market. The objects they wish to achieve, of having guaranteed refrigerated space available for the storage and display of their products and effecting economies in their distribution system, would clearly be at risk it they adopted a new policy of charging the retailer for the cabinet and allowing it to be used for the storage and display of other products.

A new entrant to the market may very well find himself in the position, as Valley and Mars did, of having to make a reasonably substantial investment in cabinets. This may be to some extent what the economists have called a 'sunk cost' in the sense that if Mars/Valley were to exit from the market, the cabinets might have a somewhat problematical resale value. However, it is a fact that Valley and Mars between them have attained a respectable share of the Irish market, although manifestly much smaller than that of HB. It may well be that, in the case of those outlets where they have succeeded in installing their cabinets, the throughput of their products, because of their high quality and market appeal, will lead to the recoupment of this expenditure, in the same manner as HB have over the years recouped their expenditure in the same area. 8.1.4

It has been said by Mars that the Irish ice-cream market has all the indicia of a sluggish or stagnant market which is the result of one dominant firm abusing its position in order to exclude competitors. It is certainly true that, so far as pricing is concerned, HB have effectively dictated the level of prices in the market for many years. Mars' complaint against them, however, is not that they have maintained prices at an artificially high level to the detriment of the consumer, but that they have used their pricing policy in combination with the exclusivity term to exclude competition. As I have already indicated, there is no evidence to indicate that the price level of ice-cream products has been kept at an artificially high level as a result of HB's dominant position.

While it was said that HB's dominant position also resulted in one of the classical features of a stagnant market, *ie*, a lack of innovation and new products, the evidential basis for this assertion was not entirely established. It was not suggested that the Irish consumer was being deprived of new products in the market which were available in other countries with high levels of ice-cream consumption. On the contrary, in the case of the product which is at the heart of this case, the Mars ice-cream bar, not merely have Mars established a foothold in the market: it has also led to the appearance of new HB lines intended to compete with Mars ice-cream.

There is thus no evidence that the interests of consumers have been seriously adversely affected by the practices complained of in these proceedings. Undoubtedly, it would be easier for new entrants to become established in the market, if freezer exclusivity and/or price 'bundling' were abandoned by HB and to that extent consumer choice would be improved. But the same, no doubt, would happen if HB were forced to reduce drastically the huge amounts they spend on advertising and promotion. It may well be that strategies adopted by a firm in a dominant position will prevent competitors from eroding its market power: that is what they are intended to do. But to say that for that reason alone they contravene Article 86 is to treat the existence of the dominant position itself as a contravention of the Treaty.

In my opinion, Mars have not established that these practices constitute an abuse by HB of their dominant position. It also follows that these practices are not prohibited by Article 85(1) of the Treaty.

I am also of the view that the right claimed by Mars to store and display their products in cabinets owned and supplied by HB constitutes an infringement of HB's rights of property in the cabinets which is so radical in nature as to violate Article 222 of the Treaty.

The cabinets are supplied by HB for one purpose alone, the storage and display of their products. If they were available to all comers without restriction, then it seems to me that their property rights would have been very significantly eroded indeed. This is in obvious contrast to the situation that arises in the 'tied houses' system where a brewery owns a chain of public-houses and stipulates that the tenants may sell their products only. The ending of the exclusivity tie in such a case leaves the essential right of ownership intact. It is merely the exercise of the right, in such cases, which is being restricted and, as has been clearly established, such a restriction may well be required under the terms of Articles 85 and 86. Here, however, it is the substance of the right itself which is under attack and this, I think, comes plainly within the ambit of Article 222. It would, of course, be open to HB to meet this attack by terminating the existing agreements and substituting therefor agreements without an exclusivity term subject

8.1.4 to a commercial rent. But I must have regard to the fact that this very substantial capital investment was made by HB in accordance with the normal practice in the industry in order to provide cabinets to retailers on an exclusive basis and it would be contrary to the spirit of Article 222, in my opinion, to require them to make such a change.

In this context, I have noted the view of the EC Commission that:

> The agreements concluded in this respect are not part of the systems of property ownership protected by Article 222 of the EC Treaty.

This appears to be on the basis that:

> Neither ownership rights nor the exercise of such rights by the owner are being questioned in this case. The subject of the proceedings is the contractual transfer of the right of user to third parties.

I am not clear as to how this conclusion was reached, and it may be that it is related in some way to the provisions of German national law. It is, of course, an interim finding only by the Commission and is subject to review by the Commission itself, the Court of First Instance and the Court of Justice. In contrast, Lynch J, in the interlocutory injunction proceedings, said:

> I am satisfied that HB has a serious case to be tried on the issue of wrongful interference with its property rights in the freezers.

He did not, of course, reach any final conclusion on that issue. To the extent, however, that the approach of Lynch J is somewhat different from that adopted by the Commission, I respectfully prefer his view which is more in accordance with the system of property rights under Irish law.

The question of the alleged breaches of Article 9 of the 1987 Order and the 1987 Act must next be considered. This is in theory an entirely separate issue arising solely under national law. Given, however, the somewhat laconic and uninformative nature of Article 9, as contrasted with the great detail of the relevant competition provisions of the Treaty, it would be somewhat surprising if a practice which survived exhaustive analysis and consideration under Articles 85 and 86 would be captured by these provisions. In particular, a 'rule of reason' approach would again seem appropriate. I think that, applying the same detailed economic analysis which has been applied in this case to Articles 85 and 86, I would come to a similar conclusion, *ie*, that the practices complained of are well established commercial methods used to protect the property rights of the supplier in the cabinets, ensuring the storage and display of their products in refrigerated space in the retail outlets and contributing to the efficient distribution of their products generally. It was not, in my view, an agreement of the sort intended to be captured by Article 9, *ie*:

> Any agreement, arrangement or understanding (whether induced by threat, promise or otherwise) which has or is likely to have the effect of limiting or restricting entry to trade in any grocery goods.

There remains the question of damages which were claimed by HB as resulting from the actions of Mars in procuring and inducing breaches of contract. These damages are particularised as follows in the statement of claim:

To value of refrigerated cabinets utilized by the defendants:	IR£830,000
To annual maintenance of the said cabinets:	IR£ 56,000
To loss of profits owing to displacement of the plaintiffs' product in their cabinets:	IR£ 34,000

I have no doubt that HB suffered some loss as a result of the stocking of Mars products in their refrigerators, since it would, on the findings I have made, have interfered with their distribution system and increased their costs. No serious attempt, however, was made in the proceedings to quantify the actual amount of the loss and, since the burden clearly rests on HB of proving on the balance of probabilities the actual financial loss which they sustained as a result of the breaches, they are not entitled to damages. 8.1.4

In the result, the claim by Mars in the first action will be dismissed. HB are entitled to permanent injunctions in terms of paragraph 8(1), (2) and (3), of the statement of claim in the second action.

Solicitors for the plaintiff in the first action and the defendant in the second action: *Arthur Cox & Co.*
Solicitors for the defendant in the first action and the plaintiff in the second action: *Hayes & Sons*

Mary Deane, Nora Cronin, Kathleen Oliver Walsh and Anne Cody v. The Voluntary Health Insurance Board: High Court ,22 April 1993 8.1.5

Body Corporate providing health insurance – 'Undertaking' – duty of statutory board – Abuse of dominant position – Contractual obligations – Quantum meruit *claim – Profits claim of charitable organisation – Health Insurance Act 1957 (No. 1), sections 3 and 4 – Competition Act 1991 (No. 24) section 5*

Facts The Voluntary Health Insurance Board (VHI) was established under the Voluntary Health Insurance Act 1957 (the 1957 Act). The plaintiffs are trustees of a religious order and are the owners of a private hospital.

The 1957 Act was enacted to make available to the public who were not entitled to free medical care, voluntary health insurance administered by a non profit making statutory body under the control of the Minister for Health. The 1957 Act effectively granted a monopoly for the provision of health insurance to the VHI. It was envisaged under the 1957 Act that the Minister could grant licences but no licences were granted or sought in respect of the provision of health insurance. A small number of employer sponsored schemes were operated in the State. VHI enjoyed 92% of the relevant market.

Up to 1989 VHI reimbursed its subscribers for payments which those subscribers made to hospitals and for medical expenses. Escalating health care costs forced VHI to implement a recovery programme. VHI decided that it could not look for increased premiums because that strategy would only diminish the number of subscribers who effectively pay for the subscribers requiring medical treatment. VHI's research shows that the subscribers who would probably not need medical assistance would be the first and largest group of subscribers who would cease subscribing on the implementation of any increase of premiums. The government was also reluctant to sanction any increase in VHI premiums for policy reasons.

8.1.5 Under the VHI's 'Mutual Hospitals Programme' it was arranged that the hospitals would be paid directly by VHI in respect of VHI subscribers attending those hospitals on the basis of rates agreed in advance. Previously VHI had no control over the bills issued by hospitals which were ultimately presented to them by their subscribers. Under this programme a hospital which did not wish to take part was to be called a 'partially participating hospital' and would be reimbursed with a grant in aid towards the cost of a subscriber's medical care and expenses.

The deteriorating position prompted VHI later in 1988 to propose that hospitals which opted for direct payment in respect of agreed advance fees would now enter into a new agreement for the 16 month period beginning on 1 March 1989 and ending on 30 June 1990. The object of the agreement was to freeze the level of hospital charges and the liability of VHI for those charges in respect of that period.

The agreement between the plaintiffs and VHI provided that VHI would not pay to the plaintiff in excess of the 'cash limit' which was a sum calculated by reference to amounts previously paid to the plaintiffs. The 'cash limit' was related to 'a volume of cases' and 'case mix'.

Following the expiration of the 16 month agreement VHI and the plaintiffs could not agree on the terms of a further agreement. The plaintiffs sought damages on a *quantum meruit* basis in respect of the services provided by the plaintiffs to the subscribers of VHI.

On 17 October 1991 Murphy J in the High Court refused an application for an interlocutory injunction restraining VHI from publishing a notice that the plaintiff's hospital was no longer a fully participating hospital within the meaning of the rules of VHI. On 13 November 1991 Lardner J granted an interlocutory injunction to the plaintiffs restraining VHI from informing its subscribers that they need not discharge the charges of the plaintiffs. As and from 2 December 1991 VHI withdrew any indemnity to its subscribers for charges incurred by those subscribers in the hospital of the plaintiffs.

Held by Keane J:

(1) The plaintiffs claim for recovery of sums in excess of the 'cash limit' set for the period 1 March 1989 to 30 June 1990 could not be sustained because the plaintiffs had been notified of VHI's stipulation that a 15% reduction in respect of the same 'case load' and 'case mix' was required.

(2) The plaintiffs were entitled to be paid in respect of the period 1 July 1990 to 31 December 1991 for services provided to VHI subscribers on the basis of rates notified by the plaintiffs to VHI.

(3) VHI was in a dominant position in the health insurance market despite the fact that it was an indirect purchaser of services as opposed to a provider.

(4) The object of section 5 of the 1991 Act was to outlaw two categories of activity by an undertaking in a dominant position:

(i) Those which weaken competition in the relevant market

(ii) Those which directly damage the interest of those dependent on the supply or acquisition of the goods or services in question.

In the present case the actions of VHI complained of by the plaintiffs had no effect on competition in the market for voluntary health insurance. Consequently there was no evidence that they had damaged the interests of purchasers actual or potential, of health insurance.

(5) Even if one accepted that VHI is 'a discriminating monopsonist' parliament has given VHI that particular role. The exercise of VHI's power in withdrawing cover from members attending the plaintiffs' hospital was within its power even though in this particular case it lacked 'reason' and 'equity'. VHI was not guilty of an abuse of its dominant position in the voluntary health insurance market. 8.1.5

(6) VHI's exercise of its powers lacked 'reason and equity' and was thus in breach of its statutory duty. The plaintiffs are entitled to an injunction restraining VHI from refusing to provide indemnity to subscribers in respect of charges incurred by VHI subscribers to the plaintiffs.

(7) The plaintiffs have the onus of proof to prove their claim for substantial damages based upon loss of profit. The claim that a charitable organisation would earn profits of £1m. was unsupported.

Cases referred to in judgment

East Cork Foods v. O'Dwyer Steel [1978] IR 103
Folens & Co. v. Minister for Education and Others [1984] ILRM 265
William Lacy (Hounslow) Ltd v. Davis [1957] 2 AER 712
Brewer Street Investments Ltd v. Barclays Woollen Company Ltd [1954] 1 QB 428
Rover International Ltd and Others v. Cannon Film Sales Ltd (No. 3) [1989] 3 AER 423
Attorney General v. Great Eastern Railway Co. [1880] 5 APP CAS 473
Masterfoods Ltd t/a Mars Ireland v. HB Ice Cream Ltd, 28 May 1992 Keane J [1993] ILRM 145
Hoffmann-La Roche v. EC Commission [Case 85/76] [1979] 3 ECR 461, [1979] 3 CMLR 211
Italian Republic v. Commission of the European Communities(Case 41/83) [1985] ECR 873, [1985] 2 CMLR 368
Centre Belge d'Etudes de Marche-Telemarketing (CBEN) SA v. Compagnie Luxembourgeoise de Telediffusion SA and Information Publicite Benelux SA (Case 311/84) [1985] ECR 3261, [1986] 2 CMLR 558

KEANE J delivered his judgment on 22 April 1993 saying: The greatly increased cost of providing health care has confronted a number of countries, including Ireland, with major problems since these trends began to accelerate in the 1980s. Those problems are at the root of the troubled relationship between the St Francis Medical Centre in Mullingar and the defendants which has led to the present proceedings.

The plaintiffs are trustees of a community known as the Congregation of the Franciscan Missionaries of Our Lady and are the owners of the St Francis Medical Centre which is a private hospital located at Ballinderry, Mullingar. The defendants (whom I shall refer to as 'the VHI') are a statutory body established under the Voluntary Health Insurance Act 1957 for the purpose of providing schemes of voluntary health insurance.

For a significant part of the period to which these proceedings relate a large proportion of the patients attending the plaintiffs' hospital were VHI patients. While the figure would obviously have fluctuated, it was generally about 70%. For many years, patients who were treated at the hospital paid the bills themselves and then sought reimbursement from the VHI. That method of billing VHI patients, which was also in use in the other private hospitals throughout the country, was changed in 1989. In that year, the financial problems being encountered by the VHI as a result of escalating health costs, led to the introduction of what was called the VHI Recovery Programme. A feature of that programme was the conclusion of agreements between the VHI and the individual private hospitals, one of the objects of which was to ensure that the fees charged by the private hospitals were frozen at the level obtaining at that time for a specified period, i.e. the period of 16 months ending on 30 June 1990. The manner in which the VHI has sought to implement that agreement and the events which occurred since it expired on 30 June 1990 have given rise to three different areas of dispute between the plaintiffs and the VHI which constitute the subject matter of the proceedings.

1. The agreement incorporated two elements which were at the heart of much of the

8.1.5 subsequent controversy between the parties, i.e. a 'cash limit' and an 'inclusive daily rate', the latter generally being referred to as the *per diem* rate. In the case of every hospital participating in the agreements, the payments made by the VHI to the relevant hospital were under no circumstances to exceed the cash limit. Subject to a crucial qualification in the case of the plaintiffs' hospital, the figure representing the cash limit was the estimated total of the benefits paid by the VHI in respect of the hospital for the period of 12 months immediately preceding the 16 months period. The hospital could opt for one of two methods of payment: option A, which was chosen by the plaintiffs, substituted a system of direct payment on a fortnightly basis by the VHI to the hospital for the previous method under which the patients paid the bills themselves and were reimbursed by the VHI. Under the old system, the patients were billed separately in respect of maintenance and what were called the 'Ancillary Charges', e.g. drugs, theatre, pathology and X-ray fees. Under option A, they were to be paid the daily inclusive or *per diem* rate already referred to. The crucial qualification in respect of the cash limit figure in the case of the plaintiffs' hospital was that it embodied a reduction of 15% in the total of benefits paid by the VHI for the preceding 12 months period. The plaintiffs say that they were never told by the VHI that the cash limit had been reduced by 15% in this manner and that, in the result, the payments made by the VHI to them in respect of the 16 months period fell short of what they would have been entitled to, had this 15% reduction not been applied, by a sum of £281,629. The VHI say that the plaintiffs were aware of the 15% reduction and that, in the result, there was no shortfall in the payments made. That is the first issue which has to be determined.

2. Following the expiration of the 16 months period on 30 June 1990 negotiations went on between the plaintiffs, the VHI and their respective financial advisers with a view to reaching a new agreement for the period of 18 months ending on 31 December 1991 which would apply retrospectively to the period from 30 June 1990 to whenever the agreement was concluded. In the event, no such agreement was ever concluded between the plaintiffs and the VHI in respect of this period, but VHI patients continued to be treated at the plaintiffs' hospital. Bills were regularly presented by the plaintiffs to the VHI in respect of these patients and the VHI made from time to time what were called 'interim payments' to the plaintiffs. The plaintiffs say that the amounts paid by the VHI during this period fall short substantially of the charges actually made by the plaintiffs in respect of the patients concerned and which the plaintiffs say were, in the circumstances, reasonable charges. The plaintiffs say that the amount due by the VHI to them in respect of this period is the sum of £483,931, the claim being made on a *quantum meruit* basis. The VHI say that these are not reasonable charges and that they have overpaid the plaintiffs in respect of this period by a sum which they calculate at £109,737. That is the second issue which has to be resolved.

3. The negotiations between the plaintiffs and the VHI broke down in June 1991 and the former instructed their solicitors to take legal proceedings for the recovery of what they claimed were the sums due to them by the VHI. On 6 September 1991, the Hospital Administrator of the plaintiffs, Sister Gregory, told the General Manager of the VHI, Mr Tom Ryan, that the plaintiffs proposed to commence billing patients directly with effect from 9 September. Mr Ryan in a letter of 14 October 1991 informed the plaintiffs that, with effect from 21 October 1991 the plaintiffs' hospital would no longer be a 'fully participating hospital' as defined in the rules of the VHI and that notice to their subscribers to that effect would be published, in accordance with the rules, on 15 October 1991. The plaintiffs having failed to obtain an interlocutory injunction to restrain the VHI from giving any such notice to their subscribers, the VHI published an advertisement in the national press on 6 November, which stated that as from 2 December the plaintiffs' hospital would no longer be a fully participating hospital as defined in VHI rules and added that:

> This means that hospital cover will not be provided to VHI members admitted to St Francis Medical Centre from Monday, 2 December next.

Existing patients and patients admitted prior to that date remain covered. 8.1.5

The plaintiffs say that this action by the VHI was in breach of their statutory duty under the Voluntary Health Insurance Act 1957 and was an abuse of what the plaintiffs say is the dominant position of the VHI within the meaning of the Competition Act 1991, and claim injunctive and other relief, including damages, arising out of these alleged breaches. The VHI say that the actions in question were not in breach of any statutory duty owed by them to the plaintiffs and that, on the contrary, these actions were taken by them in pursuance of their statutory duties under the 1957 Act. They further deny that they are in any dominant position within the meaning of the Competition Act 1991, or that, if they are, they have abused that position as alleged. That is the third issue which has to be resolved in these proceedings.

While it is obviously convenient to deal with these three issues in the order already indicated, it should be borne in mind that they were not kept completely segregated during the 22 days hearing of the action. Accordingly, when I turn to the first issue, much of the factual background contained in that part of this Judgment is also relevant to the second and third issues.

The '15%' issue

The VHI was established by the 1957 Act in order to make available to the section of the population who were not entitled to free medical care schemes of voluntary health insurance administered by a non-profit making statutory body appointed by, and subject to the ultimate control of, the Minister for Health. It grew rapidly from the start and at present approximately 1.3 million people are entitled to VHI benefit. Its powers and duties are examined in more detail at a later stage: at this point, it is sufficient to note that the insurance schemes which it has administered since its inception display many of the usual features of commercial insurance schemes, whether related to health care or other areas. Its subscribers obtain cover against the risk of having to pay for health care in consideration of an annual premium and the amount of the premium is related to the degree of cover provided.

At the time the VHI was established, there were three principal categories of hospital in the State: public hospitals owned and funded by the State through its appropriate agencies, now the health boards, public hospitals owned by voluntary institutions, in many instances religious orders, but funded in part at least by the State, and private hospitals. Irish hospitals still fall into one or other of these categories, although there have, of course, been radical changes over the years: some hospitals have closed down, others have merged and new hospitals have appeared in both the public and private sectors. It should be noted that, while public hospitals in both categories have always admitted patients who are entitled to free treatment under the Health Acts 1947 to 1991, they have also at all times maintained 'private' beds for patients not so entitled.

The levels of cover provided by the VHI reflected, as one would expect, these categories. The highest premiums were payable in respect of private treatment in private hospitals, the next highest in respect of semi-private treatment in the same hospitals and the lowest in respect of semi-private and private treatment in public hospitals, the subscriber paying the appropriate premium in respect of one of three equivalent Plans. For a time, this was replaced by a system under which the subscriber opted for a specified number of 'treatment units' which entitled him to a particular level of treatment. The latter system was discontinued in 1979, when the government decided that in future all treatment in public hospitals would be free of charge. To meet what was seen as the danger of a drop off in subscribers, a new system was introduced by the VHI under which full indemnity was guaranteed by the VHI in respect of treatment under the particular plan chosen by the subscriber: Plan A covering private and semi-private treatment in public hospitals, Plan B covering in addition semi-private treatment in private hospitals and Plan C covering in addition private treatment in private hospitals. With the arrival

8.1.5 of two 'high technology' private hospitals in the mid-1980s charging substantially higher fees than other private hospitals, two further plans in respect of these hospitals, Plans D and E, were introduced.

The 1957 Act prohibited anyone other than the VHI from providing voluntary health insurance in the State except under a licence granted by the Minister for Health. It would appear that no such licences have ever been granted and that, in recent years at least, commercial firms have shown no interest in obtaining such licences. This is probably due to two factors, first, the fact that the available market is minuscule, given the huge proportion of potential customers who are already VHI subscribers and who are unlikely to move to a firm operating on a commercial basis and, secondly, the income tax relief afforded to VHI subscribers. The evidence established that the VHI enjoys 92% of the market for voluntary health insurance, the balance being accounted for by small schemes provided for their members by bodies such as the Garda Síochána and the ESB.

The plaintiffs opened their hospital in 1968. At that stage, it was largely confined in its activities to a geriatric nursing home. However, over the years it has expanded, and during the time with which this case is concerned it could accommodate approximately 150 patients, of whom only some were geriatric cases. The hospital was originally called the Sacred Heart Hospital, Ballinderry, but subsequently changed its name to the St Francis Medical Centre.

As has already been pointed out, the majority of patients admitted to the hospital were VHI subscribers, and while the proportions obviously varied, they seem to have generally represented in the region of 70% of the hospital's patients. In common with other hospitals, the plaintiffs furnished bills to their patients when they were being discharged and the patients were then reimbursed by the VHI. In the case of patients other than those admitted on a 'day care' basis, the plaintiffs' practice at one stage was to charge the patient an inclusive fee, the rate depending on whether they were private or semi-private. In 1984, this was replaced by a system under which the patients were charged separately for maintenance and 'ancillaries'.

While relations between the plaintiffs and the VHI did not become significantly acrimonious until the period immediately preceding the litigation, there were undoubtedly areas of disagreement between them from the early 1980's onwards. This was at a time when the VHI was encountering financial problems arising from a number of factors, principally the constantly increasing cost of health care and the opening of the two new private hospitals already mentioned, the Mater Private Hospital and the Blackrock Clinic. The VHI, although not subject to the same statutory constraints as commercial insurers, maintained reserves at a particular level and the various financial pressures to which they were being subjected led to an increasing drain on the reserves.

One of the matters raised from time to time by the VHI with the plaintiffs was their charges. The VHI were concerned by the fact that increases in the charges were introduced by the plaintiffs at irregular intervals and, on occasions, without what they would have regarded as reasonable notice being given to them. This, they said, created difficulties for them, since the rate of premiums charged by them was fixed on a yearly basis and it was not possible for them to pass on increases in charges of this nature until the subscriber's policy was due for renewal. While this part of the problem was ultimately resolved, the VHI also considered that the actual level of charges at the hospital was unduly high and complained on occasions to the plaintiffs that their charges were higher than any other private hospitals with the exception of the Mater Private and the Blackrock Clinic.

Two additional contentious issues which were closely related were the length of stay of patients and the proportion of surgical to medical cases (sometimes referred to as the 'case mix'). The length of stay problem had two aspects. First, the VHI were concerned that individual patients might be kept in the hospital for longer than was justified by strictly medical criteria. Secondly, they claimed that the average length of stay of patients in the plaintiffs' hospital was significantly longer than in other private hospitals.

So far as the latter problem was concerned, it might be thought that the economics of running a hospital are not in this context significantly different from other businesses and that, if all their beds were occupied throughout the year, this would be a desirable situation. However, this was not the case from the VHI's point of view. From their perspective, the higher the volume of VHI cases dealt with by the hospital in a given year in proportion to the number of bed days being paid for, the better. If in one hospital the average length of stay was significantly higher than in others, it would mean that throughout the private hospital system more resources would be required to process the same volume of cases, resulting inevitably in higher charges. Their approach was to ensure that hospitals in which their subscribers were treated were in the nature of acute hospitals rather than nursing homes *simpliciter*. Since, in general, surgical cases were discharged from hospital sooner than medical cases, each private hospital, in their view, should achieve a mix of surgical and medical cases with the proportion of surgical cases being not less than 30%. This, in their view, ensured the optimum utilisation of resources throughout the private hospital system and, in the result, lower charges. They repeatedly emphasised to the plaintiffs the desirability of developing the hospital as an acute facility rather than one orientated, as they saw it, towards lengthy stays. They were also concerned with what they saw as relatively low levels of occupancy which, in their view, led inevitably to higher charges. Although steps were taken during the period now being reviewed to provide operating theatres and the associated equipment and to retain surgeons in different specialties, the slow rate of progress, as the VHI saw it, in this area, was also a source of disagreement between them and the plaintiffs. **8.1.5**

The next issue that arose between the plaintiffs and the VHI was the opening by the plaintiffs of a unit to deal with what were described as 'weight disorders'. The VHI was concerned that this unit was inaugurated by the plaintiffs without prior discussion with them and that they were being asked to reimburse patients who were admitted, not for strictly medical reasons, but for what were in effect weight reducing or slimming courses. The plaintiffs insisted that this unit was introduced in order to deal with strictly medical complaints, particularly the conditions of anorexia nervosa, bulimia and obesity.

A further issue that arose between the plaintiffs and the VHI was the charges made by the former in respect of radiology and pathology. The VHI claimed that the plaintiffs' charges were excessive in these areas and that, in the case of pathology, there was an element of duplication, since the actual work was carried out in UCD where a professional fee was charged, despite which, as the VHI claimed, a professional fee was charged again by the hospital.

Finally, the VHI sought on a number of occasions from the plaintiffs details of their actual accounts so as to enable them (the VHI) to ascertain whether the charges which their subscribers, and ultimately the VHI themselves, were being asked to pay were reasonable. However, it was not until a relatively late stage in the discussions which ultimately led to the present litigation that the plaintiffs were prepared to allow the VHI any access to their accounts.

The extent to which either the plaintiffs or the VHI were justified in their attitude to these matters has in the end only a limited relevance to the resolution of the three substantial issues in the case. They do, however, provide an essential background if one is to understand how the relationship between the plaintiffs and the VHI deteriorated and ultimately culminated in the present litigation. Two facts seem to me to be established clearly by the evidence. First, while the level of charges in the plaintiffs' hospital was undoubtedly high at one time in comparison with the level of charges in comparable private hospitals, this was no longer so in 1989 when the Agreement which led to the first of the legal issues was signed. Over the period from 1984 to 1988, all the private hospitals in respect of which information is available had increased their charges, but the rate of increase in the case of the plaintiffs was significantly lower. In the result, of 20 private hospitals in the country, only 9 had lower rates in respect of both categories than the plaintiffs. Secondly, while the concern of the VHI that patients should not be kept longer in the plaintiffs' hospital than their medical conditions strictly warranted was understandable, the plaintiffs for their part repeatedly offered to submit any cases that the VHI might wish to question to scrutiny by their own medical advisers and, although this offer

8.1.5 was availed of, it would appear from the evidence that the VHI accepted that in no case had it been established that any patient had been detained longer than his or her medical condition required.

As against this, however, it is also clear that the concern of the VHI with the high proportion of medical, as distinct from surgical, cases in the plaintiffs' hospital and the resultant lengthy stays were justified. It was also understandable that they should be concerned by the high level of charges for pathology and radiology. It was also to be expected that they should wish to be fully apprised of the hospital's financial situation and the reluctance of the plaintiffs to furnish them with this information is difficult to understand. Having regard to the fact that the VHI were providing, indirectly, approximately 70% of the plaintiffs' income, it was entirely reasonable that they should seek to satisfy themselves, in the interests of their subscribers, that the maximum value was being obtained by them for this large volume of expenditure.

The financial problems of the VHI became more serious throughout this period as their reserves continued to drop. Their problems were exacerbated by the decision of the government to increase drastically the fees payable for private beds in the public hospitals in order to meet the soaring demands of health care on the exchequer. It might be thought that, since they had a virtual monopoly of private health insurance, they could solve their problems by simply raising premiums. But this created additional difficulties for them. The effects of increasing premiums would in time be to diminish their business generally and experience indicated that the most profitable business, i.e. that resulting in the least volume of claims, would be the first to go. In addition, at a time when the control of inflation was regarded as an economic priority, their capacity to increase their premiums was severely limited by the control exercised by both the Prices Commissioner and the Minister.

The initial response of the VHI was to initiate what was called the Mutual Hospitals Programme in 1988. A crucial feature of this programme was a move away from the existing system of payment under which the private hospitals billed their patients and the latter recovered the appropriate amount from the VHI. It was now envisaged that the hospital would be paid directly by the VHI and that this would be on the basis of inclusive *per diem* rates agreed in advance with the hospital. This was a change from the existing system of 'retrospective payment', under which the VHI had no control over the bills that were ultimately presented to them and were, in the result, as they saw it, carrying most of the financial risk. The alternative now proposed was a system of 'prospective payment' under which both the provider of care and the insurer would know in advance how much the services being provided were going to cost. It was also thought that this new system would provide benefits for the hospitals, in particular in improving their cash flow. A hospital which did not wish to take part in the new programme and became what was called a 'partially participating hospital' was to be reimbursed with a grant-in-aid towards the cost of the patients' accommodation and ancillary charges.

Later that year, the situation of the VHI had worsened to such an extent that the Minister for Health intervened and appointed a financial consultant to prepare what was called a 'VHI Recovery Programme'. The consultant, Mr Noel Fox, in conjunction with the General Manager, Mr Ryan, and the recently appointed Assistant General Manager, Miss Maureen Lynott, prepared a new scheme which it was proposed to submit to each of the private hospitals. Under the scheme, each of the hospitals was invited to sign an Agreement by virtue of which a 'cash limit' would be imposed on the amount of the payments to be made by the VHI in respect of the particular hospital for the period of sixteen months beginning on 1 March 1989 and ending on 30 June 1990. This cash limit was to be based on the actual payments made by the VHI in respect of the hospital for the previous 12 months. As it was envisaged that the Agreements would be signed on 3 February 1989, so that each of the signatory hospitals could be included as 'fully participating hospitals' in the VHI Directory of Hospitals then about to be printed, the actual expenditure for the months January and February 1989 was not available when the agreements were due to be signed. Hence, the Agreement made it clear that for those two months the expenditure was estimated only and that the cash limit might have to be revised when the actual figures became available. 8.1.5

The Agreement enabled the hospital to choose between two methods of payment. Under option A, for which the plaintiffs elected, payments were to be made directly to the hospital on a fortnightly basis calculated by reference to a *per diem* rate, i.e. an inclusive daily rate which did not distinguish between maintenance and ancillaries. (It was also possible for hospitals to avail of this option without direct payment). Option B provided for the existing method of direct billing of the patient by the hospital with direct monthly payments by the VHI to the hospital.

The agreement expressly stated that the cash limit was being imposed on the basis that the hospital disposed of the same volume of cases with the same case mix as in the preceding 12 months. It will be seen that the essential object of the agreement was to freeze the level of the hospital's charges and the VHI's liability for them at the February 1989 level for the period of 16 months ending on 30 June 1990.

On 26 October 1988, a meeting took place between some of the VHI executives and Sister Gregory at the VHI offices in Dublin in order to discuss with her the possibility of her hospital taking part in the Mutual Hospitals Programme. The VHI were represented by Miss Lynott, Mr Diarmuid Fitzsimons, the general manager with responsibility for providers of care, Miss Margaret Shanahan, from their Research Department and Mr Andrew Smith. On behalf of the VHI, the proposal was made that the *per diem* rates effective from 1 January 1989 in the case of her hospital should be as follows:

Private:	IR£85.67
Semi-Private:	IR£64.26
Day Cases:	IR£49.17

The minutes of the meeting record, and those who took part in the discussion agreed in evidence, that a number of the various issues that had arisen between the plaintiffs and the VHI were discussed at this meeting. Sister Gregory said she would need time to think about the Mutual Hospitals Programme concept, but made clear that the *per diem* rates being proposed were, in her view, 'unrealistic'. The day following the meeting she wrote to Mr Ryan indicating new rates, made up on the old basis of maintenance and ancillary charges being separately specified, which would come into force on 1 December 1988.

Mr Ryan replied on 2 November 1988, referring to the Mutual Hospitals Programme and what he stated was the inability of the VHI to absorb any increased charges for the time being. In the event, the plaintiffs did not seek to impose the new charges as of 1 December 1988.

With a view to implementing the VHI Recovery Programme, the VHI Executives had meetings with the various hospitals concerned during the period leading up to the date on which the Agreements were, as the VHI envisaged, due to be signed. A meeting with the plaintiffs took place at the VHI offices in Dublin on 16 January 1989, the VHI being represented by Mr Ryan and Miss Lynott and the hospital by Sister Gregory. (While there was initially some confusion during the hearing as to the date of the meeting, it appears quite clear that it was in fact on the 16th.) There was an important conflict of evidence as to what was said at this meeting to which it will be necessary to return. On 19 January 1989, Sister Gregory wrote a letter in which, having referred to the meeting on the 16th, to her concern with the new Mutual Hospitals Programme and to her desire that the hospital should continue co-operating with the VHI, she said:

> Decision time has arrived and whereas I have some reservations about the operation of this scheme you have requested that I put my proposals to you in writing. These proposals which I enclose relate solely to the adoption by the hospital of a *per diem* rate on the experimental basis for a period to be agreed between us. From a practical viewpoint I feel this period should be for not less than one year.

8.1.5 I enclose my proposals for the implementation of the *per diem* rate on an experimental basis.

The suggestions are in keeping with your views and designed not to interfere greatly with our hospital policy on patient care.

There was enclosed with this letter a document headed 'proposal to the Voluntary Health Insurance Board for hospital charges for one year on an experimental basis'.

Paragraph one provided for the charging of a *per diem* rate as follows:

Private	£122.97
Semi-Private	£110.47
Day Ward	£80.97

There were a number of other proposals in the document relating to matters such as the methods of payment. It also envisaged some agreement being reached as to the maximum length of stay per patient.

Despite reminders, a reply to that letter was not sent until 3 February. In the meantime, however, on 30 January, the plaintiffs, in common with all the other private hospitals, received a letter signed by Mr Ryan which enclosed a draft Agreement. The letter was as follows:

As you are aware, VHI has been involved in extensive discussions with hospitals regarding co-operation in maintaining a cash limit on the total VHI payout to each hospital for eighteen months. This is a vital element in VHI's Recovery Programme. The programme VHI has embarked on includes cost containment, cash limits, modifications in benefits, as well as increases in member subscriptions. The hospital community and VHI have together over the past thirty years built a quality independent health care system in Ireland. We are now seeking broad co-operation for VHI's return to solvency and the continuing strength of independent health care into the future. I want to thank you for your agreement in holding the hospital's charges for the month of January and February and ask your co-operation in operating within an annual cash limit for the next sixteen months from 1 March.

In summary we are asking hospital providers, for an interim sixteen month period only, to operate a cash limit through either of two options:

Option A: The mechanism of a daily inclusive rate with the *option* to the hospital of fortnightly direct payment. The rates for your hospital are shown in the letter of agreement.

OR

Option B: The existing method of billing charges with monthly direct payment *on a non-optional basis* and monthly reconciliation. The maintenance component will be adjusted to achieve the monthly reconciliation.

Agreement will provide indemnity (full cover) for VHI members for the period 1 March 1989 to June 1990 at the same monthly level of volume and case mix as in the present financial year. This will be reviewed with each hospital on a monthly basis. Where necessary, mechanisms will be adjusted upwards or downwards with the hospital to enable the cash limit to be met. If hospitals achieve efficiencies within the cash limit, these are retained by the hospital.

Hospitals accepting this agreement will be designated as fully participating in the VHI directory of hospitals. Non-accepting hospitals will be designated as partially participating and the level of partial benefit will be indicated.

The implementation date for the in-patient elements of the recovery programme is 1 March. At VHI we are finalising the contractual materials for members renewing on or after 1 March and the content of the hospital directory must be finalised by Friday, 3 February. Would you please indicate to us, the hospital's decision as to its desired status as a fully or partially participating hospital. Attached is a letter of agreement for exchange between the chairperson of the Hospital's Board and the chairman of the Voluntary Health Insurance Board. It states the understanding of this agreement and the values specific to the hospital. If there are any details that need further clarification we will arrange an immediate response. **8.1.5**

As we have stated, this is an interim method and we at VHI are committed to progressing a more appropriate financing mechanism with the hospital community immediately beginning 1 March so that feasibility and applications can be ready for implementation at the end of the sixteen month treaty period. Additionally we are committed to progressing new structures through a joint working group representing the hospital and through on-going meetings with the participating hospitals.

The attached letter of agreement is for signature by the chairperson of the Hospital's board. Once received, it will be signed by the chairman of the VHI board and a fully signed copy returned to you.

I look forward to your response and co-operation and thank you in advance for your major contribution to the VHI Recovery Programme.

The agreement itself is a relatively short document and because of its importance should be set out in full.

The St Francis Medical Centre undertakes to contribute to the VHI Recovery Programme by maintaining a cash limit for sixteen months from 1 March 1989 through 30 June 1990. VHI confirms that the cash limit and payment mechanism are viewed as interim measures for implementation of the VHI Recovery Programme and acknowledges with appreciation the hospital's co-operation and significant contribution to the VHI Recovery Programme.

VHI and the St Francis Medical Centre have agreed the following for the sixteen months from 1 March 1989 through 30 June 1990. The hospital will be a fully participating provider in VHI's directory of hospitals and will accept the agreed rate from VHI as full payment for all members covered by the agreement.

The hospital will operate the cash limit through the reimbursement mechanism of: (please sign the preferred method and delete other sections).

OPTION A. Inclusive daily rate with fortnightly direct payment on the 1st and 15th days of the month. Value of inclusive daily rate:

£77.23	Private
£57.92	Semi-Private
£111.98	Day Case
Signed	date

OR

OPTION A Without direct payment

Signed date

OR

8.1.5 OPTION B The existing method of billing charges with monthly direct payment and monthly reconciliation.
Signed date

For the year 1 March 1989 through 28 February 1990 VHI will reimburse the hospital at a cash limit of £1,122,692.00 for a similar volume and case mix of VHI patients treated at the hospital in the year ending 28 February 1989. This commences with all payments from 1 March. The operation of the cash limit will be based on the monthly claims payment experience of the hospital for the year ending February 1989. VHI will provide a monthly report to each hospital identifying results against budget for payments and volumes. As necessary the payment mechanism will be adjusted upwards or downwards in order to achieve the cash limit.

The cash limit for the hospital is based on actual results to December 1988 and projected results for January and February 1989 (in the case of maternity, the cash limit reflects the modified benefit). An adjustment will occur in March 1989 based on the actual yearly outcome. The hospital agrees to provide the following level of services at full cover to VHI members for the stated year:

877 in-patient cases
180 day cases

The hospital agrees to make no increases in bed numbers or technology for potential VHI reimbursement in the period of this agreement and agrees that VHI members will not be charged more for services than non-members and other insured.

VHI will provide a Quarterly Ancillaries Report in order to obtain details on utilisation of ancillary services.

A working group representing the hospital community will be convened immediately after 1 March to work with VHI on the development of a more refined and appropriate payments structure with effect at the end of the treaty period and to communicate difficulties that may arise in operating the cash limit agreement with hospitals. VHI will also convene meetings of participating hospitals to enhance ongoing communication.

On behalf of the Hospital Board Date
On behalf of the Voluntary Health Insurance Board Date

The figure of £1,122,692, stated to be the cash limit, did not represent the total payment by the VHI in respect of the hospital for the ten month period ending on 31 December 1988 and the projected payments in respect of the months of January and February 1989. It was the total and projected payments for those periods reduced by 15%.

Sister Gregory having received the agreement rang the VHI the following day, 31 January, and spoke to Miss Lynott. Following that conversation and, it would seem as a result of it, a meeting took place between Mr Pearse Gilroy, an accountant who at that stage was acting as financial consultant to the plaintiffs, Mr Kieran McGill, also an accountant, who was assisting Mr Fox in relation to the Recovery Programme and Miss Shanahan. The next day Mr Gilroy sent the following letter by fax to Mr Ryan:

I refer to your letter of 30 January 1989 addressed to Sister Gregory re the proposed cash limit scheme for a sixteen months period. Sister Gregory has asked me to deal with this.

Following my meeting with your Margaret Shanahan and Kieran McGill of yesterday, 2 February 1989, St Francis is prepared to operate the cash limit scheme *at the same monthly level of volume and case mix as in the present financial year.*

> I have underlined the above to indicate exactly what you state in your letter. **8.1.5**
>
> However at my meeting yesterday it emerged that the draft contract you forwarded for signing includes a cash limit for the year to 28 February 1989 (yet to be finalised) which is calculated at the present financial year level less 15%.
>
> This is not in keeping with your letter so I would appreciate your confirmation that the 15% levy will not apply. I am aware that the 15% levy is not being applied to other hospitals.
>
> I also note from my discussions that you have placed a ceiling on the number of bed days available to VHI patients at St Francis's for the coming year. Can you confirm my understanding that the bed days offered to VHI members in excess of the agreed limit will not be reimbursed by VHI.
>
> I would appreciate it if you would deal with these points immediately. You are aware that today is the deadline for our indication of participation in your 1989/1990 scheme. We are prepared to commit ourselves to your plan despite the short notice once you have clarified the above points.
>
> I suggest you fax your reply to me.

It would appear that Mr Ryan and Mr Gilroy also spoke on the telephone that day. A letter was sent by Mr Ryan the same day by fax to Mr Gilroy in the following terms:

> I refer to our telephone conversation this evening and regret that I have to confirm that we are not in a position to improve on the arrangements set out for St Francis Medical Centre.
>
> I can say to you however that we have indicated to all hospitals that if an exceptional situation should arise, we would be prepared to meet to examine the problem on the basis of a full disclosure of information by both sides.
>
> Our main purpose in negotiating new arrangements with hospitals is to ensure the recovery of the VHI fund and we feel that this is of paramount importance to the hospitals themselves. In the process however we are also keen to ensure that hospital facilities are used as economically as possible.
>
> I thank you for your understanding and look forward to receiving the Agreement from the hospital.

The agreement was signed by Sister Gregory on the afternoon of 3 February and sent by fax to the VHI office. It was signed on behalf of the VHI on 20 February.

On 3 February Mr Ryan also wrote to Sister Gregory as follows:

> Thank you for your recent letters setting out your proposals.
>
> I am not in a position to go into these in detail at the moment but I understand that discussions on our proposals to you are taking place with your financial advisers. I sincerely hope that we will be able to reach a satisfactory conclusion.

The plaintiffs say that they were never told that the cash limit had been reduced by 15% and that the Agreement should in effect be rectified so as to provide for what they say they reasonably assumed to be the true position, i.e. a cash limit representing 100% of the total payments for the preceding twelve months. The defendants say that it was made clear to the plaintiffs that the cash limit was being reduced by 15% and that this is put beyond doubt by the letter from Mr Gilroy to Mr McGill of 3 February.

As I have already mentioned, there is a conflict of evidence as to what was said at the meeting on 16 January. Sister Gregory said (Volume 5, Q 319)

> The cash limit, the cash reduction was not discussed with me on 16 January.

8.1.5 Mr Ryan said (Volume 16, Q 283) that:

> This meeting was to break the bad news that we were seeking a decrease of 15% and much of the meeting centred around that. I seem to recall that Sister was suggesting some alternative arrangement but our prime purpose in calling the meeting was to announce the fact that we intended to seek a 15% reduction, to discuss this with Sister and to progress it as rapidly as possible, bearing in mind we wanted these Agreements from 1 March and there was a considerable amount of administration to be done.

Miss Lynott also said that the cash limit and the proposed reduction applicable to the plaintiffs' hospital was mentioned at the meeting. She said in cross examination (Volume 13, Q 373/375):

> I told Sister Gregory as well that they would be, that in the case of some hospitals, there was a reduction in the amount and I described the reasons for that and the broad amount of the reduction in per cent terms.
>
> Q. In some hospitals and what per cent did you mention?
> A. In the area of 15%.
>
> Q. Are you telling his Lordship now, as a matter of certainty, you mentioned that?
> A. Yes.

Miss Lynott's note of this meeting indicated that the first item to be covered was 'reduced rate or partial partic.' which she said indicated her intention to raise the matter of the cash limit and to indicate to Sister Gregory the alternative open to the hospital of becoming a partially participating hospital.

As already mentioned, Sister Gregory rang the VHI the day after the agreement had been faxed to her office. It was suggested to her that, when she was told that Mr Ryan was not available, she left a message with his secretary enquiring whether the figure for the cash limit in the Agreement was a typographical error. Sister Gregory said she had no recollection of having said that. She and Miss Lynott were in agreement that Miss Lynott rang her later in the day and that they agreed during the conversation that Mr Gilroy should discuss the amount of the cash limit with the VHI representatives. Miss Lynott said that her recollection was that Sister Gregory was upset by the reduction in the cash limit, but Sister Gregory said that this was not correct as at that stage she was not aware of the reduction.

Mr McGill said that he and Miss Shanahan attended the meeting on 2 February with Pearse Gilroy and that at that meeting he and Miss Shanahan gave details as to how the cash limit had been calculated, specifying in particular the reduction of 15% in the volumes for the previous year. He said that Mr Gilroy asked the reason for the reduction and that he (Mr McGill) indicated to him that there were a number of hospitals where the costs were considered to be 'relatively high', that, accordingly, reductions were being applied and that, in the case of this particular hospital, the reduction was 15% (Volume 11, Q 506.) Mr McGill said that prior to that meeting a member of the research department, Miss Barbara Simons, had worked out the necessary calculations to establish the actual amount of the cash limit, taking into account the reduction of 15%, and that the results of her calculations, giving the figure of £1,122,692, were embodied in a handwritten memorandum which was produced in evidence and was dated 24 January 1989. Mr McGill said that, while he had no specific recollection as to whether this document was produced at the meeting with Mr Gilroy, he assumed that it must have been. Miss Margaret Shanahan, who was also present at the meeting, said that her recollection was that the document was presented to Mr Gilroy and the calculations explained to him. She also said that Mr Gilroy indicated that he would have to report back to the hospital on the meeting. Mr Gilroy did not give evidence.

Sister Gregory said that she recalled Mr Gilroy reporting back to her on this meeting, but said that he certainly did not tell her prior to the agreement being sent back to the VHI that the cash limit which it contained embodied the 15% reduction. She said that the first time she became aware of the 15% reduction was following the receipt by her of a letter from Mr Fitzsimons dated 4 April 1989. That letter set out amended figures for the cash limit and the volume of cases to take account of the actual results for January and February 1989. (It will be recalled that the cash limit and volumes specified in the Agreement were based on the projected figures for those two months.) The figures in Mr Fitzsimons letter were as follows: 8.1.5

Annual cash limit:	£1,213,313
In-patient cases:	941
Day cases:	195

Sister Gregory said that after receiving this letter she spoke to Miss Lynott on the telephone about the cash limit and the *per diem* rate.

She said (Volume 3, Q 35)

> I said that I didn't think it was correct and it was at that stage Miss Lynott said to me, 'but you are reduced by 15%'. I was shocked and I repeated 'by 15%?' 'Yes' I was totally taken aback by it and that's why then I said 'what other hospitals have been reduced? 'Plenty of them'. That was her reply'.

Miss Lynott said that she had no recollection of this conversation, but that in any event she was quite certain that the level of the reduction was discussed with Sister Gregory at the meeting on 16 January. (Volume 13, Q 65.)

In the meantime, there had been correspondence between Mr Gilroy and Mr McGill relating to the Agreement. On 14 February, Mr Gilroy wrote saying that there was a major discrepancy between the figures being used by the VHI for the purpose of the Agreement and the hospital's own figures. He gave details of these suggested discrepancies in a further letter of 21 February. On 28 February, Mr McGill replied, indicating a number of reasons why the figures might not coincide, but expressing surprise that there should be such large discrepancies. On 2 March, Mr Gilroy replied saying that:

> VHI have asked St Francis to agree to a cash limit on claims for sixteen months from March 1st 1989. Despite the fact that this cash limit will cause severe financial problems for the hospital we have agreed to this in order to help VHI in its Recovery Programme.

He went on to deal again with the discrepancies in the figures and to ask for further information. On 2 March Mr McGill replied, expressing dissatisfaction on his part with the information being provided by the hospital. Mr Gilroy responded on 6 March and again claimed that the information being provided by the VHI was inadequate.

In the course of his evidence, Mr Ryan said that a reduction had been imposed in the case of three other private hospitals. He did not wish to give further details unless ordered to do so by the Court because he considered that the VHI were under an obligation of confidentiality so far as the other hospitals were concerned. I ordered that the question should be answered, but that the names of the hospitals concerned should not be published. Mr Ryan said that in the case of one of the hospitals the reduction of the cash limit was in the order of £2,000,000, although he did not express this in percentage terms. In the case of another hospital, the reduction was in the order of 7% and in the case of the third, he was unable to specify a precise figure.

That is a summary of the evidence concerning the state of knowledge of the parties as to the 15% reduction in the cash limit. Whatever else may be in doubt, it is clear beyond

8.1.5 controversy that Mr Gilroy was told on 2 February of the reduction in the cash limit, the manner in which it had been calculated so as to be reflected in the *per diem* rates specified in the agreement and the reason why it was being imposed. The evidence of Mr McGill and Miss Shanahan on these matters was not challenged or contradicted and is in any event corroborated by Mr Gilroy's letter of 2 February. There is, accordingly, no basis whatever in the evidence for the claim advanced on behalf of the plaintiffs that the Agreement was signed on their behalf at a time when the VHI had withheld from them this crucial information. The meeting between Mr Gilroy and Mr McGill was arranged for the express purpose of clarifying the financial implications of the agreement and the VHI were entitled to assume that he had informed his principals of the true position, as indeed he told them he intended to do. It was submitted, on behalf of the plaintiffs, that Mr Gilroy's knowledge of the true state of affairs could not be imputed to his principals if they were in fact unaware of the reduction and they relied in this context on my decision in *Irish Life Assurance Co. Ltd v. Dublin Land Securities Ltd*, [1986] IR 772. However, that case is clearly distinguishable since there the disputed term had never been incorporated in the agreement relied on, whereas in this case the agreement was unquestionably executed giving effect to the 15% reduction. The only basis on which it would be just and equitable to give effect to the Agreement contrary to its express terms would be if the VHI withheld the essential information from the plaintiffs. Since the VHI did everything that could reasonably be asked of them in ensuring that the plaintiffs' financial adviser was fully aware of the 15% reduction before the agreement was executed, the Court must in these circumstances give effect to the actual terms of the agreement.

Apart altogether from those considerations, I think that the probabilities are that Sister Gregory was told of the 15% reduction at the meeting on 19 January. This hospital had been singled out for drastic treatment—it may be more drastic than any of the other three hospitals to which I have referred—and this must have been uppermost in the minds of the VHI executives when they met Sister Gregory on the 19th. Even if the precise figures had not been calculated at that stage, as the memorandum of 24 January might suggest, it is difficult to see what point there was in the VHI executives meeting her without informing her of the very purpose for which the meeting was being called. When it is borne in mind that one of the practical consequences of the reduction in the cash limit was that there would be a reduced *per diem* rate, the significance of the reference in Miss Lynott's note of the meeting to a 'reduced rate' is clear.

It was also a remarkable feature of the account put forward on behalf of the plaintiffs that Mr Gilroy at no stage reported to Sister Gregory that her hospital had been singled out for a 15% reduction, although he was acting as the hospital's financial consultant, had been fully informed of this at the meeting on 2 February and conducted a detailed correspondence with Mr McGill in relation to the cash limit which continued throughout the month of March 1989. It is very difficult to understand how, in these circumstances, Sister Gregory remained in the dark about the 15% reduction until 6 April. She said on a number of occasions in the course of her evidence that she was not a 'figures' person and that she tended to leave these matters to her accountants. It may be that the full financial implications of the 15% reduction did not dawn on her until a significantly later stage and that, when she tried to recall the sequence of events, she confused the telephone conversation of 6 April with Miss Lynott with her earlier conversation the day after she received the Agreement. Whatever the explanation may be, I am satisfied that her account of these matters cannot be relied on as accurate and that she was in fact informed of the 15% reduction at the meeting on 16 January.

The manner in which the agreement was implemented must next be considered.

Mr Malachy Stevens, a chartered accountant, whose firm of M.A. Stevenson & Co. succeeded Oliver Freeney & Co. as the plaintiffs' accountants in 1987 and who ultimately became a member of the board of the plaintiffs' hospital on 1 May 1990, was not involved in the aspects of the agreement so far discussed. However, following correspondence regarding the implementation of the Agreement between the then solicitors for the plaintiffs, Messrs Jones

Walsh & Co. and the solicitors for the VHI, he was asked by the plaintiffs to see if he could assist the plaintiffs in relation to the implementation of the Agreement so as to ensure that the plaintiffs were paid the amounts properly due under that agreement. Mr Stevens took the view that, even allowing for the 15% reduction, the amounts calculated by the VHI as being due to the plaintiffs were erroneous. Ultimately, as I understand the case advanced on behalf of the plaintiffs, they did not claim to be entitled to an adjustment on the basis suggested by Mr Stevens, but they did at a comparatively late stage in the case put forward an alternative claim, which I shall deal with in more detail at a later stage. In relation to both Mr Stevens' suggested adjustments and the plaintiffs' amended claim, it is necessary to consider the figures in some more detail. 8.1.5

On 11 August 1989, the solicitors for the VHI informed the plaintiffs' solicitors that the actual turnout for the year ending 28 February 1989 was £1,411,435. This was reduced by £198,122 to give the revised cash limit specified by Mr Fitzsimons in his letter of 4 April to which I have already referred. The solicitors pointed out in the course of the letter that the reduction was, accordingly, 'slightly less' than the 15%. Mr Stevens considered that the reduction—£198,122. as distinct from £211,715 was in fact significant. Mr Stevens subsequently had meetings with Mr McGill and Mr John Looney, who became Financial Controller of VHI in February 1989, but had not taken any part in the completion of the agreement.

At a meeting on 22 June, between Mr Stevens and Mr Looney, the latter gave Mr Stevens four pages of calculations setting out the basis on which the amounts due to the hospital on foot of the agreement were being calculated. These showed that the figure of the actual cash limit based on the twelve months ending on 28 February 1989 was £1,243,913 and not the figure of £1,213,313 referred to in Mr Fitzsimons' letter of 4 April. The difference in the figures was due to the fact that the original calculation of the cash limit was on the basis of 'assessments', i.e. payments actually made by the VHI to the hospital in the relevant period. The revised figure was based on 'discharges', i.e. payments in respect of patients actually treated in the hospital and discharged during the twelve month period, irrespective of whether the payments were made during the twelve month period. Mr Stevens wrote to Mr Looney on 11 July, pointing out the actual outturn for the year ending February 1990 was less than the cash limit and added:

> Consequently we now feel that the 15% reduction should not have been imposed and we hereby request that you do not impose this 15% reduction on the *per diem* rate.

Mr Stevens also said in evidence that the *per diem* rate had been wrongly calculated by the VHI: they should have taken the original cash limit before the 15% reduction and divided that figure by the number of bed days in order to arrive at the *per diem* rate. On this basis he attached a calculation to his letter of 11 July which added back an increase of 15% to each of the relevant *per diem* rates. However, in a letter of 14 August, Miss Lynott took issue with this approach and said:

> The *per diem* rate was calculated by taking the hospital result for the year ending February 1989, net of the reduction of 15%, and dividing that by the actual bed days/volume result. As the hospital had not billed the VHI via the *per diem* rate previously, there was not a 15% reduction in the hospital charges. Rather, the net cash limit represented a reduction of 15% and the *per diem* rate was calculated on that basis.

On 15 August Mr Stevens wrote again to Mr Looney claiming that the hospital was owed the sum of £231,967.90, a sum which he based on the 15% added back to the *per diem* rates to which I have just referred. Mr Looney wrote on 20 August to Mr Stevens, saying that the revision of the figures based on the discharges rather than the assessments indicated that there was a refund due to the hospital of £27,662, a cheque for which he enclosed.

8.1.5 The actual calculation of the per diem rate should be examined somewhat more closely at this point. The first figure that had to be obtained was the actual payment of benefit to the hospital for the base year, i.e. the year ending 28 February 1989. The hospital's actual charges in respect of their patients for that period amounted to £1,640,580. If this was reduced by 15%, it would give a net figure for the cash limit of £1,394,493. If the cash limit was being assessed by reference to the 'assessments' of charges by the VHI, i.e. the amounts actually paid by the VHI during the period in question, the total of payments made was £1,473,966. From this it was necessary to deduct a sum of £27,448 in respect of 'underinsured' patients i.e. those whose claims were either rejected or reduced. A further sum of £35,083 had then to be deducted in respect of professional fees which previously had been included in the patients' bill but were now being paid directly. This gave a figure of £1,411,435 which, when reduced by 15%, gave the cash limit of £1,213,313 notified by Mr Fitzsimons to the hospital on 4 April. The figure based on the actual discharges of patients during that period was, however, £1,442,035. This figure was reconciled with the 'assessments' figure by taking the difference between the opening debtors and the closing debtors for the same period, giving a cash limit of £1,243,913, the figure used by Mr Looney in order to calculate the amount of the refund due.

That brings us to the computation of the *per diem* rates. A composite rate could be obtained by dividing the number of bed days into the cash limit figure. However, this would not reflect the difference between the private and semi-private rates. This was achieved by taking the number of days occupied at the private rate and at the semi-private rate and dividing the cash limit by the total of the private days and 75% of the semi-private days, to give the figure for the private *per diem* rate. The semi-private *per diem* rate was then calculated at 75% of the private rate.

It should be noted that the calculations being made by Mr Stevens and Mr Looney were in order to ascertain the appropriate payment for the period of 12 months from 1 March 1989 to 28 February 1990. As we have already seen, the Agreement was to run for a period of 16 months from 1 March 1989. There was no cash limit as such for the period from 1 March 1990 to 30 June 1990. However, it was common case that the same *Per diem* rates should apply for the remaining 4 months. Mr Stevens made his assessment of what was due in respect of this period by simply taking one third of what he treated as the underpayment of £231,968 in respect of the previous 12 months. This gave a calculation of £309,291 and, after giving credit for the payment of £27,662, a net sum due to the hospital of £281,629. Mr Looney, whose calculations did not, of course, add back the 15% to the *per diem* rates for the 12 month period, calculated the payments due in respect of the remaining 4 month period by reference to the actual discharges for the period. This gave a total of payments of £398,269 which, when added to the cash limit figure for the period of 12 months, gave a total of £1,642,182. The total of bed days for the whole of this period was 25,007 and, when the calculation as to the *per diem* rates was done for the 16 months period in the manner to which I have already referred, it gave marginally reduced *per diem* rates and a slight increase in the rate for day cases. This indicated, on Mr Looney's approach, that the refund figure should have been £22,040, indicating an overpayment of £5,622.

The accuracy of Mr Looney's calculations, as distinct from their legal validity, was not challenged on behalf of the plaintiffs. Mr Stevens' assessment that the plaintiffs had been underpaid by a sum of £281,629 would, of course, be correct, if the case made on behalf of the plaintiffs that the reduction in the cash limit of 15% was wrongly imposed on the plaintiffs was also correct. I am satisfied, however, for the reasons already stated, that the plaintiffs' case under this heading has not been established. It is also clear that Mr Stevens was in error in thinking that, even if the 15% reduction in the cash limit was enforceable, it should not have resulted in the reduction of the *per diem* rates. The whole object of the agreement, including the mechanism of the cash limit reduced by 15% and the *per diem* rates, was to ensure, in the case of the plaintiffs' hospital, that the hospital was remunerated at a lesser rate in respect of a similar level of activity because of the view taken, rightly or wrongly, by the VHI that their existing charges were too high. 8.1.5

It will be noted that the letter from Mr Ryan enclosing the draft agreement for signature by the hospital stated that:

> Where necessary, mechanisms will be adjusted upwards or downwards with the hospital to enable the cash limit to be met. If hospitals achieve efficiencies within the cash limit, these are retained by the hospital.

As we have seen, the actual out-turn for the year ending 28 February 1990 was less than the cash limit. Miss Lynott, who was principally responsible for the drafting of this letter and the agreement, said that the quoted passage was intended to convey that, if the number of bed days multiplied by the *per diem* rates gave a figure which was less than the cash limit, the hospital would be entitled to the difference, provided that the same or a higher volume of in-patient cases and day cases was dealt with and that the case mix was the same. It was clear that hospitals, by introducing economies of one sort or another, might achieve roughly the same level of activity as the previous year but at a lower cost and that they should be entitled to the benefit of such economies. When this emerged from her evidence, counsel for the plaintiffs said that they had been unaware that this was the construction put by the VHI on the letter and the Agreement and that it would be unjust in these circumstances to deprive the plaintiffs of the difference between the cash limit and the actual payments made to them, if they were in fact entitled to it under that construction. Counsel for the VHI understandably expressed concern at the claim being formulated in this fashion at a very belated stage, but since it was obvious that the issue could be resolved without any injustice to the VHI provided a properly amended statement of claim were delivered and they were allowed the opportunity of considering it and calling any fresh evidence in relation to it, I allowed an amendment of the statement of claim on the lines indicated.

It is undoubtedly the case that the plaintiffs did achieve almost the same volume of in-patient activity in the year ending 28 February 1990, the actual figures being 925 in-patient cases as contrasted with the revised budget figure of 941. Miss Lynott said in cross examination that this would not have been a sufficiently significant difference to exclude an upwards adjustment in the payments to the hospital, provided the case mix was the same. The day cases, according to the same figures, were actually higher, the relevant figures being 195 and 262.

It is thus clear, and conceded on behalf of the VHI, that the same volume of cases was achieved. However, a different picture emerges when one comes to consider the case mix. Health statistics in relation to the plaintiffs' hospital produced by the Research Department of the VHI on 17 December 1992 indicate that the number of claims referable to psychoneurotic illnesses for the year ending February 1989 was 397 as contrasted with 230 for the year ending February 1990. The same statistics show that the corresponding reduction in the number of bed days in respect of these illnesses was from 7,912 to 4,578. The total number of bed days for the year ending February 1989 was 18,286 and for the year ending February 1990, 13,790. It is obvious therefore that the reduction in bed days, leading in turn to a reduction in the total benefit paid, was accounted for to a large extent by the reduction in the number of claims for psychoneurotic illnesses. Hence, the second requirement for adjusting the payment mechanism upwards, i.e. the attainment of the same case mix as in the previous year, was not met.

The plaintiffs sought to meet this difficulty in two ways. First, it was submitted that the reliance by the VHI on the fall in the number of psychoneurotic claims was inconsistent with their stated desire that the plaintiffs' hospital should treat more acute cases and less long term medical cases. That was undoubtedly a frequently expressed desire on the part of the VHI, but is irrevelant to the issue under consideration. If the hospital during the year of the 'standstill' could have the same remuneration for a significantly reduced number of bed days based on a different case mix from that in the previous year, the whole object of the Agreement from the VHI's point of view would have been frustrated. A significant part of the reduction in bed days

8.1.5 was effected, not by the more efficient processing of the same volume and mix of claims, but by treating many less cases of a type which involved lengthy stays.

The second ground on which the plaintiffs take issue with the VHI approach is that the Agreement was not intended to reflect as refined a differentiation between different illness groups as is reflected in the statistics produced in December 1992. However, it is clear from the evidence of Miss Lynott that, within the broad divisions of medical, surgical and psychiatric categories, which were in operation at the time of the agreement, there were also sub-divisions into specialities and it would have been surprising if as broad a speciality as 'psychoneurotic illnesses' had not been included in even the most rudimentary categorisation. It would appear that this form of diagnostic grouping, as it was called, had been a common feature of the administration of hospitals for some time prior to 1989. Construing the agreement as benevolently as possible in favour of the plaintiffs, on the basis that it emanated solely from the VHI and that there was realistically no possibility of the latter accepting any alterations to it, the fact remains that the case mix was markedly different, taking even the broadest categories into consideration, from the case mix for the previous year.

I am, accordingly, satisfied that the plaintiffs have not established their alternative claim to a sum of £221,035 in respect of the period for the year ending 28 February 1990 and £73,678 in respect of the period from 1 March 1990 to 30 June 1990, both of which sums are based on the shortfall between the actual payment of benefit and the cash limit.

The *quantum meruit* issue

(a) *The facts*

It is common case that, following the expiration of the 1989 Agreement on 30 June 1990, the parties were unable to agree on the terms of a further Agreement which it had been hoped would be executed in respect of the period of 18 months from 1 July 1990 to 31 December 1991. It is also not in dispute that, having regard to the previous relationship between the plaintiffs and the VHI, the VHI were obliged to pay the plaintiffs a reasonable sum in respect of the services provided by the plaintiffs to VHI patients from 1 July 1990 onwards. The dispute between the parties is as to what can be regarded as a reasonable rate of remuneration in the circumstances of this case.

As many as six different options as to how the amounts owing might reasonably be calculated were canvassed during the hearing, but ultimately the available options were reduced to three. In order to appreciate the basis on which they were put forward, it is necessary to return to the sequence of events which culminated in the breakdown of negotiations between the parties.

As has been seen, there was considerable correspondence between the parties and their respective legal and financial advisers during the currency of the 1989 Agreement, but this largely reflected disagreement between the plaintiffs and the VHI as to how it should be implemented in financial terms. However, on 22 June 1990 a meeting was held at the VHI offices between executives of the VHI and representatives of the plaintiffs. The VHI was represented by Mr Ryan, Miss Lynott and Mr Looney and the plaintiffs by Sister Gregory, Mr Stevens, Mr Jones, then the plaintiffs' solicitor and Mr Colm Carey, a member of the Board. At that meeting, the VHI representatives indicated seven areas affecting the plaintiffs' hospital with which they were particularly concerned. In respect of them, they indicated certain measures which they thought should be taken by the plaintiffs for the period of the projected new agreement and which were subsequently referred to in correspondence and during the case as the 'seven steps'. Immediately after the agreement, Miss Lynott wrote to Sister Gregory enclosing a draft agreement and a summary of the 'seven steps'. She also said that it had been agreed that Mr Stevens and Mr Looney should review the financial aspects. She added:

> VHI and the hospital undertook to come to a resolution concerning a new agreement as

> soon as possible. As discussed today, if that requires going past 30 June for a short period, then the present agreement will operate and any adjustment will be retroactive to 1 July. 8.1.5

The seven steps may be summarised as follows:

(1) *Length of Stay:* The average length of stay which at sixteen days was stated to be the highest of any private acute hospital, was to be reduced to twelve days in the next year and to ten days in the period to 31 December 1991.

(2) *Case Mix:* The surgical mix was described as 'minimal' and it was proposed that this should increase to 50% over the period of the eighteen month agreement.

(3) *Cost per patient:* These were described as on average higher than any other private acute hospitals, with the exception of the Blackrock Clinic and the Mater Private Hospital. It was proposed that the average cost per claim should reduce by 25%.

(4) *Speciality services:*

> (a) *Psychiatry:* There was to be an identified special Psychiatric Unit with 24 hour psychiatric cover and the length of stay was to be limited to fourteen days with exceptions subject to review by the VHI medical adviser.
>
> (b) *Eating Disorders:* These were to be pre-certified by the medical adviser for insurance cover prior to admission.
>
> (c) An inventory of approved specialities was to be agreed with the hospital and any additions would require VHI approval.

(5) Hospital's Financial Situation: There was to be an 'open books' review of the hospital's financial situation.

(6) The hospital was to provide the VHI Medical Adviser with access to the complete patients' records at the hospital, with the patients' authorisation.

(7) The hospital was to notify VHI if length of stay was beyond 14 days, in which case the VHI would 'medically review for approval of insurance benefit'.

The 'General Terms of Agreement with Hospitals: Version 1', also enclosed with this letter, provided that the plaintiffs' hospital was to be designated in its literature and information as a 'fully participating hospital'. There were also provisions relating to the respective obligations of the VHI and the plaintiffs as to methods of payment etc.

Sister Gregory acknowledged receipt of this letter and the accompanying documents on 28 June in a letter in which she took issue with what she saw as a suggestion by Miss Lynott that some form of agreement had been reached. Having indicated certain matters on which she required further information, she went on:

> On receipt of the above information, we shall carry out a more thorough review of the documents received from you and revert to you on the basis of the agreement which we proposed to enter into.
>
> In this regard, as we indicated to you at our meeting of 22 June, we propose entering into an agreement whereby the basis of our charges from 1 July 1990 shall be a maintenance rate in respect of hospital accommodation and separate charges for all other functions. In order that you can review these for inclusion in the agreement, we enclose herewith a schedule of same.
>
> We look forward to hearing from you by return, as we propose to finalise the Agreement with you next week.

Enclosed with the letter was a schedule of laboratory fees, radiology fees and theatre fees. Maintenance fees were stated to be:

8.1.5

Private	£85.50
Semi-Private	£72.50
Day Care	£35.50

Mr Ryan replied to this letter on 29 June, commenting generally on the points made by Sister Gregory in her letter and adding:

> We note your preference for a system which would separate the maintenance rate and the ancillary charges but you may recall that we expressed some reservations about this. In common with the points which we put forward, it is however a matter for discussion.

It appeared from the evidence of Sister Gregory and Mr Stevens that the schedule of rates enclosed with the letter of 22 June represented the rates which had been charged by the hospital up to the end of 1988 with an increase of 10%. Mr Stevens said that, while the 10% increase, in the absence of more detailed calculations as to possible increases in wages and costs, was 'arbitrary', the increase was necessary in order to bring the hospital back to a 'break-even' situation and might even be inadequate. (Volume 7, QQ 363/5).

Following the expiration of the 1989 Agreement on 30 June 1990 and the notification by Sister Gregory to the VHI of the revised maintenance and ancillary rates which the plaintiffs were proposing, the plaintiffs proceeded to invoice the VHI on the basis of these rates.

The VHI responded to these invoices by making what were described as payments 'on account' which were normally accompanied by a letter making clear that the payments were being made in this fashion pending the completion of a new Agreement. The letter of 16 November 1990 from Mr Looney to Sister Gregory may serve as an example:

> I refer to our telephone conversation of this morning and I confirm having lodged a cheque to the value of IR£60,000 for credit to your account at AIB, 11/13 Oliver Plunkett Street, Mullingar, Account Number 22805025.
>
> This cheque is a further payment on account in lieu of claims received but not yet processed, pending finalisation of a new agreement.

On 17 August, Mr Stevens wrote to Mr Ryan enclosing a statement of account in respect of the period from 1st July 1990 to the date of the letter. He referred to payments on account already made and said that he wished to make it clear that the hospital were not prepared to accept payments on account in future.

He added:

> We also wish to make it clear that the basis of our charges to you with effect from 1 July 1990 is as set out in the schedule of charges enclosed with our letter to you of 28 June 1990. If you do not accept this basis of charge then you should immediately let us have the necessary documentation which will enable our patients who are insured with you to claim our charges direct from you and we can invoice our patients directly.

There does not seem to have been any reply to this letter. Payments on account continued to be made and accepted by the plaintiffs.

The procedure adopted by the VHI in relation to invoices submitted by the hospital to them during the currency of the 1989 Agreement should be noted at this point. The practice was for the VHI to furnish lists to the hospital of the patients whose claims had been admitted and those which were described as 'pended', i.e. awaiting further assessment because the VHI considered that they were not liable to meet the claim in full, or, in some cases, were entitled to reject them in full. When the 1988 Agreement expired on 30 June 1989 and the system of interim payments began, lists were no longer furnished by the VHI to the hospital in this manner.

In the case of certain other hospitals, agreement had not been reached between the VHI and those hospitals as to the terms of a new agreement to replace the 1989 Agreement. The VHI decided that, pending the finalisation of agreements between the VHI, these hospitals and the plaintiffs', the *per diem* rates applicable under the 1989 Agreement should be applied with an increase of 8% followed by a further increase of 4%. It appears from the correspondence, however, that the plaintiffs were never notified in writing by the VHI that this was the basis on which the sum payable to them would be calculated: as has been noted, the VHI simply made payments on account in response to invoices furnished by the plaintiffs without indicating the basis on which they were being made. Miss Lynott had a telephone conversation with Sister Gregory sometime around 1 August 1990 in which, as they agreed in evidence, Miss Lynott referred to the VHI's proposal for a two stage increase in the *per diem* rate (Volume 6, QQ 110/113). Sister Gregory also said in evidence that she spoke to Mr Noel Fox on the telephone sometime early in November. She said that, in the course of the conversation, Mr Fox said 'you are getting 8% Sister' and that she replied 'I understand, Noel, that 8 is not sufficient. Malachy Stevens tells me what's necessary is 10.' She said that Mr Fox said 'I will get back to you or I will see what I can do' and that approximately 10 minutes later Mr Looney rang her to say that 'I just want you to know that there is an increase of 10%' She said, however, that her understanding was that this was an increase of 10% on the pre-1989 maintenance and ancillary charges and not on the 1989 *per diem* rate. Mr Fox did not give evidence, but Mr Looney said he recalled being in the office when Mr Fox had the telephone conversation with Sister Gregory during which he said that he agreed with her that he was prepared to increase the 8% to 10%. (Volume 6, QQ 177/178, Volume 19, Q 326). 8.1.5

At the meeting of 22 June between the VHI executives and the representatives of the plaintiffs, it had been agreed that Mr Stevens and Mr Looney should meet to discuss the financial aspects of the proposed new agreement. As has been seen, the initial discussions and correspondence between them related principally to the differences between the hospital and the VHI as to the implementation of the 1989 Agreement and, specifically, the 15% reduction in the cash limit. However, following a telephone conversation with Miss Looney on 27 August, Mr Stevens on 5 September wrote to Miss Lynott stating that he had agreed that he would finalise the hospital budgets for the forthcoming year and provide them to Miss Lynott, but required statistical information from the VHI for this purpose. He also indicated that the Board of the Hospital were maintaining their attitude that they would not make their accounts available to the VHI. He then went on:

> We also discussed my letter to Mr Ryan of 17 August 1990 and we clarified the rates payable to the hospital with effect from 1 July 1990.
>
> I confirm that on receipt of the statistical reports from you, I shall be in a position to arrange a meeting with Mr Looney, in order to review the hospital budget for the forthcoming year, and hopefully finalise matters between the hospital and the VHI.

Mr Stevens said in evidence that he had intended to convey to Miss Lynott that he had clarified with Mr Looney that the hospital was now charging a rate for maintenance which was equivalent to the pre-1989 rates increased by 10%. (Volume 7, Q 380).

Mr Stevens gave Mr Looney the budgets and projections upon which he had been working at a meeting in Mr Stevens' office on 26 September. He presented Mr Looney with two budgets in respect of the years ending 30 April 1991 and 30 April 1992. Mr Stevens, while conceding that Mr Looney thought that the total level of the budget for a 12 month period was higher than the VHI would be prepared to agree to, said that Mr Looney confirmed to him that neither he nor the VHI would have any difficulty in agreeing to the rates of charge which he had included in the budget. These rates, as calculated by Mr Stevens, were on the basis of separate charges for maintenance and ancillaries and represented a further increase on the rates notified in Sister Gregory's letter of 28 June 1990. Mr Stevens acknowledged that at this meeting in September

8.1.5 Mr Looney insisted that the VHI still required a *per diem* rate, but said that this was irrelevant, because once he and Mr Looney had agreed the rate of charge in the budgets, it was immaterial whether that was charged on a maintenance and ancillary basis or on a *per diem* basis because in either event the rate of charge would produce the same budget figure based on a particular level of activity. (Volume 7, Q386/7). Mr Looney said that he had not formed any impression as to the reasonableness of the figures being put forward by Mr Stevens in respect of the maintenance and ancillary charges: he was concentrating, he said, on trying to arrive at a budget for the 18 months period and took the view that once there was agreement on the budget and the number of bed days, the rates would 'fall out' from that.

Mr Stevens and Mr Looney had a further meeting on 31 October at which the financial basis of the proposed new agreement for the 18 month period was again discussed. At that meeting, Mr Looney indicated that he was prepared to recommend to the VHI that the budget for the hospital for the 18 month period should be approximately £2.1 million. On 1 November 1990, he wrote to Mr Stevens as follows:

> Further to our meeting on Wednesday, 31 October 1990, I now set out hereunder the claims volumes and *per diem* rates appropriate to our budget offer of IR£2,074,000 for the 18 month period 1 July 1990 to 31st December 1991.

The *per diem* rates quoted in the letter were as follows:

Period

(1) 1 July 1990 — 28 February 1991

(2) 1 March 1991 — 31 December 1991

Per Diem Rates

Private	Semi-Private	Day Care
(1) £83.41	£62.55	£120.94
(2) £86.75	£65.05	£125.78

A number of calculations were enclosed with the letter, indicating that these rates were based on an 8% increase on the *per diem* rates payable on 1 July 1990 with an additional increase of 4% payable from 1 March 1991. In his reply of 27 November 1990, Mr Stevens said:

> As I have indicated to you in the course of our subsequent telephone conversations, the rates which you have offered are not acceptable to the hospital and bear no resemblance whatsoever to the rates which we have included in the detailed budgeted accounts which we have already reviewed and discussed fully with you. As I have pointed out to you over the course of the last number of months, it is imperative that the hospital is paid rates equivalent to those set out in its financial projections, as otherwise the hospital will have no option but to deal directly with all patients including patients who have VHI membership, as it cannot operate at a loss.

Mr Stevens went on to say in the course of this letter that, while the board of management of the hospital were 'extremely annoyed at the time being taken to agree the current rates', and were most reluctant to agree to any changes to budgets already approved by them, they had now given approval to an overall budget of IR£2,505,133 for the 18 months period on condition that the hospital be paid a maintenance charge per bed day and separate ancillary charges 'in line with those set out in the budgeted accounts which I have already given to you.' Calculations were enclosed with this letter which set out the maintenance charges and ancillary charges separately. The maintenance charges were as follows:

Private	Semi-Private	Day Care
£92.00	£78.00	£38.00

On 28 November 1990, Mr Looney wrote to Mr Stevens enclosing what was described as a 'revised offer' in the amount of £2,300,000.00 for the 18 month period. He said in the letter that he had found it difficult to obtain the consent of his principals to a budget of this figure and that it was subject to 'satisfactory production of a hospital marketing plan which will set out the steps being taken to achieve the improvements as outlined at our meeting on 22 June 1990 (copy enclosed) and production of audited accounts for the year ended April 1990'. **8.1.5**

The calculations enclosed with this letter indicated new rates which were described as 'effective 1.7.90', i.e.:

Private	£103.02
Semi-Private	£77.27
Day Care	£132.58

These *per diem* rates were obviously substantially in excess of what had previously been proposed by the VHI in respect of the 18 month period.

Mr Stevens said in evidence (Vol. 7 Q420/422) that the principal difference between Mr Looney and himself was not so much as to the level of charges, but as to the projected level of activity. Mr Stevens took the view that, if the budget was being reduced from £2.5 million to £2.3 million, there should be a corresponding reduction in the number of bed days which, in turn, would obviously have given a higher *per diem* rate.

At this stage, however, another problem came to the surface, i.e. the request by VHI for a 'marketing plan'. There appears to have bean a misunderstanding between Mr Looney and Mr Stevens as to what was envisaged by this: the former was thinking in terms of a detailed plan by the hospital to implement the 'seven steps', whereas the latter thought he was referring to a plan for marketing *simpliciter*. Correspondence continued between them in relation to this matter and the question of the budgets generally, Mr Looney drawing attention in a letter of 7 December 1990 to what he said were the very substantial increases in the *per diem* rate being offered by the VHI, and Mr Stevens in his reply of 12 December 1990, disputing Mr Looney's approach:

> I would appreciate if you could let me know as soon as possible whether or not the VHI is in a position to accept the basis of charge and overall budget of IR£2,505,133 as outlined in the enclosed budgets as otherwise it would be necessary for the hospital to withdraw from the direct payment method and invoice the patients directly.

There was also correspondence between the VHI, and Mr Stevens, which did not resolve the impasse that had been reached as to the financial basis of the new agreement. A meeting was then proposed between the VHI and the hospital with a view to reaching agreement, but before that meeting was held—on 21 March 1991—an invoice was furnished by the plaintiffs to the VHI dated 7 March 1991. This set out what were described as the 'old rates' and which were the same in each category as those proposed by the plaintiffs on 28 June 1990. It also set out what is described as 'new rate 1.7.90' as follows:

Private	£92.30
Semi Private	£78.30
Intensive Treatment Unit	£99.80
Day Care	£38.30

It will be seen that the 'new rate' was effectively the same as that proposed by Mr Stevens to Mr Looney in his letter of 27 November 1990. The sum set out in the invoice as being payable by the VHI to the hospital was the difference between the 'old rate' and the 'new rate' multiplied by the relevant number of bed days. Mr Stevens said in evidence that the reason for the delay in furnishing this invoice was the result of a communication problem with the persons in charge of the invoicing procedure. The meeting at which it was hoped to resolve the difficulties that had arisen as to the financial basis for the 18 months agreement was held on 21 March at the

8.1.5 hospital. It was attended on behalf of the VHI by Mr Looney, Dr Buckley and Miss Lynott and on behalf of the hospital by Sister Gregory. Following the meeting, Miss Lynott wrote on 2 April stating that:

> We are prepared to enter into a written agreement with the hospital based on a total budget of £2.3 million for the 18 month period. The budget for volume over this period would be 25,500 bed days equating to 2,258 in-patient claims and 468 day case claims, all charged at the following rates:
>
> | | |
> |---|---|
> | Private | £103.02 |
> | Semi-Private | £77.27 |
> | Day Case | £132.58 |
>
> A major element in our written agreement would be a formal plan by the hospital, outlining the methods to be employed to achieve the terms set out in the attached document. The all inclusive *per diem* rate is also an essential part of an agreement for the time being but this may be reviewed at a future date if targets are met.

Miss Lynott enclosed with this letter a copy of the document outlining the 'seven steps'. Sister Gregory replied on 3 April 1991 and said:

> As a gesture of goodwill and trust, which I now believe is permeating between our respective organisations, we will not insist on our budget as outlined in previous correspondence with you, and agree with the budget level approved by your Board. However, as you were advised in the course of this meeting, we cannot accept a *per diem* rate, and must insist on a maintenance rate plus payment for ancillary services. Our maintenance rates, of which you have already been notified, are as follows:
>
> | | |
> |---|---|
> | Private | £92.00 |
> | Semi-Private | £78.00 |
> | Day Ward | £38.00 |
> | Intensive Care Ward | £100.00 |
>
> Our computers have been programmed for this method of billing and our Ward Managers and Heads of Departments have now become au fait with our method of budgeting.

Sister Gregory said that she was enclosing a plan indicating the manner in which the hospital would attempt to implement the 'seven steps'. This document was in fact omitted in error from her letter but was sent to Miss Lynott on 11 April. The document indicated a number of steps which the hospital were proposing to take or had already taken in order to meet the 'seven steps' required of them. Miss Lynott replied on 20 May 1991 and raised a number of queries in regard to the matters referred to in Sister Gregory's document. She added:

> In your letter you state that the hospital cannot accept the *per diem* rate, but must insist on a maintenance rate plus payment for ancillary services. I must respond that retaining the *per diem* rate is essential in concluding an agreement with the hospital. At various meetings with you and at our meeting at the hospital on 31 March, we discussed and emphasised this as a key requirement.

Miss Lynott then added the following comments on the state of accounts as between the

VHI and the hospital: **8.1.5**

> While discussing the terms of this Agreement and budget with the hospital, VHI has in the period 1 July 1990 to 3 May 1991 paid claims on account totalling £966,098, yet the value of claims assessed amounts to £565,306. This overpayment is explained by the value of claims pended not yet cleared amounting to £400,792.00.
>
> Should these pended claims become rejected then the rejected values will be deducted automatically from the value of new claims as assessed and cleared. In normal circumstances claims pended would not be paid until cleared. Therefore, in the event of failing to reach agreement, we reserve the right to seek repayments of these claims currently pended and subsequently rejected, such that the value of claims payments to the hospital will not exceed the value of claims assessed and cleared.
>
> We also wish to advise that submission of interim claims for payment can no longer be operated. Not only is it an administratively complicated arrangement, but further a claim cannot properly be assessed unless the details of complete length of stay and services rendered are provided.

Miss Lynott enclosed a draft of a letter of agreement which she proposed should be signed by the hospital and the VHI and on which she invited Sister Gregory's comments. Sister Gregory replied on 5 June 1991 as follows:

> I refer to your letter and enclosures dated 20 May 1991.
>
> The points raised in that letter have been discussed on several occasions between our respective organisations since the initial meeting between us on 22 June 1990 at VHI House. They were fully, openly and sincerely dealt with by us at our meeting with you in Mullingar on 21 March 1991. Additional information requested by you at that meeting was vouched for by me in a letter to you dated 3 April 1991. Despite the foregoing, you persist in your same line of questioning in your letter dated 20 May 1991 and delivered by hand to my office in the afternoon of 24 May 1991.
>
> The Managing Board of the St Francis Medical Centre fails to understand your Board's delay in honouring requests for payment in respect of services provided by and for your subscribers since 1 July 1990. Our Mr Malachy Stevens, in a letter faxed to your Mr Ryan on 23 May 1991 called upon your Board to pay all outstanding accounts in full. This letter of his was ignored by your Mr Ryan. Your Board's response has been evasive and at times you have been very selective and discourteous in your dealings with the Management Board of the St Francis Medical Centre.
>
> The extraordinary decency and goodwill of the Sisters of this congregation—the Franciscan Missionaries of Our Lady—towards your Board, as vouched for very positively in my letter to you dated 3 April 1991, has possibly been misconstrued by your Board as being something different. Your Board has, on several occasions, expressed satisfaction in dealing with non-profit making organisations in the provision of health care services. The St Francis Medical Centre falls into this category, yet you refuse to honour requests for payment for services rendered to your subscribers, thus placing the integrity of my congregation and its relationship with its bankers in jeopardy. My congregation cannot continue to be unfairly exposed in this manner, as such exposure prevents it from fulfilling its mission and charism in playing its part in the provision of health care services in this country.
>
> Despite my congregation's best efforts and great personal sacrifice on my part to avoid confrontation, your Board has now forced my congregation to hand the matter to its legal advisers, who will be in contact with you.

The letter of 23 May from Mr Stevens referred to in this letter enclosed a Statement of

8.1.5 Account showing a balance due to the hospital in respect of the period concerned of IR£151,658.43.

The letter from Sister Gregory of 5 June 1991 marked the end of the negotiations between the VHI and the hospital which, it had been hoped, would result in a new 18 month agreement. The subsequent events which culminated in the present proceedings belong more properly to my consideration of the third issue between the parties.

The six possible methods of calculating sums due either by the VHI to the plaintiffs or the plaintiffs to the VHI in respect of this period when there was no agreement between them can now be summarised. Option A is on the basis of the rates as actually invoiced to the VHI by the hospital on 7 March 1991. Option B is on the basis of the rates as set out in the letter from Sister Gregory of 28 June 1990. Option C is on the basis of the rates applicable under the 1989 Agreement but increased by 10%. Option D is on the basis of the rates proposed by Mr Looney in his letter of 28 November 1990 to Mr Stevens. Option E is based on the same rates but embodying the reduction in the average length of stay as proposed in the 'seven steps'. Option F is also on the basis of those rates, but with the reduction in the average length of stay staggered over the period of the agreement.

Depending on which option is appropriate, it might be necessary to make certain adjustments, reflecting an agreed reduction in the level properly payable in respect of radiology and pathology and the patients who were either under insured or rejected in total.

Before I consider the cases made respectively on behalf of the plaintiff and the VHI on this issue, I should indicate my conclusions on such issues of fact as were in dispute. It will be seen from my summary of the evidence that the area of conflict is not extensive and can be reduced to two matters. In relation to the first—Sister Gregory's telephone conversations with Mr Fox and Mr Looney early in November 1990—there was indeed ultimately little conflict; Sister Gregory's version that Mr Fox simply spoke of an 8% increase, without indicating to what rate the 8% was to be added, remained uncontradicted, since Mr Fox did not give evidence. Nor was there anything in the evidence of Mr Looney, who said he was present in the room when Mr Fox was speaking on the telephone to Sister Gregory, to cast doubt on Sister Gregory's account. I think that the probabilities are that Sister Gregory and Mr Fox were at cross purposes; she undoubtedly thought that they were talking about the appropriate increase in the pre-1989 hospital charges, whereas he may well have thought that they were referring to the appropriate increase on the *per diem* rate under the 1989 agreement.

The second area of conflict is as to whether Mr Looney accepted the rates being put forward by Mr Stevens as reasonable at their meeting on 26 September 1990. While I am satisfied that both Mr Stevens and Mr Looney gave, as one would expect, their honest recollection of what had transpired between them, I think that on balance it is unlikely that Mr Looney informed Mr Stevens that he would have no difficulty in recommending the actual rates proposed by Mr Stevens to his principals, since this would seem to be entirely inconsistent with Mr Looney's approach to the negotiations. He appears to be have been concentrating at all stages on arriving at an overall budget figure which was appropriate to the plaintiffs' needs together with an estimate of bed days. The appropriate *per diem* rate would then be a matter of simple arithmethical calculation rather than agreement. I am satisfied that, to the extent that Mr Stevens thought that Mr Looney had actually signalled his agreement to the rates as being reasonable, this was a mistaken although bona fide impression on his part.

(b) *The law*

The basis in law of the plaintiffs' claim to be entitled to the rates as calculated in option A or, at the worst, option B, is as follows. Although the parties failed to reach an agreement as to the rates of charge which the VHI would be prepared to make by way of direct payment to the plaintiffs, it would be unjust to deprive the plaintiffs of payment at anything less than a reasonable rate. Any other approach, it was said, would result in the unjust enrichment of the VHI at the expense of the plaintiffs. Since the parties were unable to agree on what was a reasonable rate, it was for the Court to determine that rate having regard to all the evidence. The plaintiffs' claim was thus essentially a *quantum meruit* claim. **8.1.5**

Since it was not contested on behalf of the VHI that the plaintiffs were entitled to be paid whatever was a reasonable rate in respect of the period in question, it is unnecessary to refer to all the authorities which were opened by counsel. The fundamental principle of law applicable was stated by Henchy J. speaking for the Supreme Court in *East Cork Foods v. O'Dwyer Steel* [1978] IR 103 at p. 110, as follows:

> So far, I have been dealing with the matter on the footing that the second defendant would be entitled, if its claim were resisted, to recover back the £20,000 in an action for money had and received. The basis of such a claim is quasi-contract. It is usually dealt with in the books on contract. The plaintiff succeeds in this type of action because, it is said, the law imputes to the debtor a promise pay the debt. The historical reason for this fiction was to enable the claim to be brought as a form of *indebitatus assumpsit*. It was a pleader's stratagem. In most cases, however, it is in the teeth of the facts to impute to the debtor a promise to pay. So long as the forms of action governed the course of litigation, it was necessary for the courts to go along with this transparent fiction. Nowadays, however, when the forms of action have long since been buried, the concept of implied contract is an unreal and outdated rationale for the action for money had and received. Judges in modern times generally prefer to look at the reality of the situation rather than engage in the pretence that the defendant has promised to pay the debt.
>
> In the present case, while the second defendant (if it were necessary for it to do so) could recover the £20,000 in an action for money had and received, it would be an affront to truth and reality to say that the basis of that cause of action is an implied promise to repay the money. The real reason why the courts would uphold the claim is because it would be unjust and inequitable to allow the first defendant to keep the money. To refuse the claim would mean that the first defendant would be unjustly enriched.

This general principle was applied to a case somewhat analogous to the present by MacWilliam J, in *Folens & Co. v. Minister for Education and Others* [1984] ILRM 265. In that case, there were negotiations between the plaintiff Company and the First Named defendant over the production by the plaintiffs of a children's encyclopaedia in Irish. The plaintiff did certain preliminary work all of which was approved of, or directed by, officials of the Department. No contract was ever in fact executed and the plaintiff claimed that the defendant was liable to recoup the expenditure actually incurred by the plaintiff on the work together with a reasonable profit. It was held that the plaintiffs were entitled to be paid for all the work which had been done at the approval or at the direction of the defendant, including a reasonable profit element, although they were not entitled to any sum calculated on the basis of the loss of profits which would have been made by completing the work. A similar approach had been adopted in two English cases, *William Lacy (Hounslow) Ltd v. Davis* (1957) 2 ALL ER 712, and *Brewer Street Investments Ltd v. Barclays Woollen Co. Ltd* (1954) 1 QB 428.

It was also said on behalf of the plaintiffs that in assessing their *quantum meruit* claim it would be wrong in principle to place a ceiling on the *quantum meruit* by applying the provisions that would in the normal course of events have been contained in the concluded agreement. They relied in support of this proposition on the decision of the Court of Appeal in England in *Rover International Ltd & Ors. v. Cannon Film Sales Ltd (No. 3)* [1989] 3 ALL ER 423. Again it was not suggested on behalf of VHI that the principle relied on was incorrect.

The significant controversy between the parties in this area is as to how these principles should be applied in the circumstances of the present case. For the plaintiffs, it is urged that, in the absence of any agreement between the plaintiffs and VHI, it was for the plaintiffs to determine what were reasonable rates, having regard to the necessity to cover the costs of their operations and, if possible, generate a small surplus. It was said that while the plaintiffs were

8.1.5 a charitable and non profit-making organisation, it was legitimate on their part to fix their rates at such a level as would generate at least some surplus, however small. Unless the rates as so calculated were exorbitant and excessive, they should be accepted by the Court.

On behalf of the VHI, it was submitted that the reasonable rate was the *per diem* rate being paid at the termination of the 1988 Agreement with whatever increase might be regarded as reasonable which, in the circumstances of this case, it was submitted was 10%. The rate of remuneration in a *quantum meruit* was to be assessed, it was urged, in an objective manner having regard to the prevailing rate in the market and not by reference to the particular requirements or difficulties of the person supplying the goods or services. Alternatively, it was submitted on their behalf that the plaintiffs could not recover any higher rates than those notified to the VHI on 28 June 1990. It was said on their behalf that the plaintiffs clearly intended that those rates should be applicable throughout the period of the new agreement and that it would be unjust to treat the VHI as having undertaken any greater liability than that represented by those rates.

(c) *Conclusion*

I have no hesitation in rejecting option C, as representing a reasonable basis of charge in the circumstances of the present case. The plaintiffs had been extremely reluctant to accept the *per diem* rate under the 1989 Agreement, not only because they would have preferred to continue charging for maintenance and ancillary services separately, but also because that *per diem* rate was based on the 15% reduction in the cash limit to which they took such vigorous exception. It would be wholly unjust and inequitable to determine the remuneration for the period which followed by reference to that rate even with the suggested increase of 10%.

The substantial issue between the parties is, in my view, between options A and B. While I appreciate that the rates furnished on 28 June by Sister Gregory were estimates only and were not based on a detailed calculation of what the hospital might require, the fact remains that the VHI were told without any ambiguity that these would be the rates in any new agreement and it was not suggested that they would be increased in any way during the term of that agreement. Had such an agreement been entered into, the VHI would not only have secured stability in the hospital's charges during the period of the agreement: they would also have obtained at least some of the benefits which they envisaged as accruing to them as a result of the implementation to some degree at least of the 'seven steps'. It would seem to me unjust and inequitable to place them in a significantly worse position than they would have been if they had executed the agreement on 28 June in the form proposed by the plaintiffs. I bear in mind the dicta in the English decisions to which I have referred that, in assessing a *quantum meruit* claim in circumstances where a contract has failed to materialise, one should not in general have regard to the terms of the abortive contract. However, as MacWilliam J pointed out in *Folens v. Minister for Education & Ors.*, the relevant principles must be applied having regard to the circumstances of the particular case. In the present case, I am satisfied that it would be unjust and inequitable to allow the plaintiffs an increase on the rates of charge which was not notified to the VHI until the system of invoicing on the basis of 28 June rates and the interim payments by the VHI had been in operation for more than 8 months.

I am, accordingly, satisfied that option is the appropriate basis of charge. Mr Looney in his calculations found that this left a balance due to the plaintiffs of £240,319. This figure reflected a deduction of £36,720 in respect of what were described as overcharges for radiology and pathology. It was agreed towards the end of the hearing that the appropriate deduction was in fact £18,000 and, accordingly, the sum of £240,319 should be increased by £18,720. There remains a significant discrepancy between Mr Looney's calculation of this option and that put forward by Mr Stevens. The principal element in this is the deduction by Mr Looney of charges for patients who had been either under-insured or were not insured at all. The respective figures for each category, as calculated by Mr Looney at the June 1990 rates, are £38,152 and £46,437.

As I have already mentioned, from July 1st onwards, the VHI discontinued their practice of furnishing the plaintiffs with lists of patients indicating claims which had either been rejected or not paid in full. It was said on behalf of the VHI that it would have been possible at any stage for the plaintiffs to get in touch with the VHI and ascertain the position in regard to what were described as 'pended claims'. However, during the period in which the system of interim payments on account was being made by the VHI in response to invoices furnished directly to them by the plaintiffs, I think the obligation was on the VHI in the absence of any formal arrangements between them to let the plaintiffs know what claims were being pended. While it is still in theory possible for the plaintiffs to pursue the patients concerned, in Court proceedings if necessary, for the amounts involved, I think that the practical difficulties are obvious and that, from the plaintiffs' point of view, it is not unreasonable to treat these claims as bad debts which will probably have to be written off. I am, accordingly, satisfied that the sums in question should be added back to Mr Looney's figures. This gives a total of £343,628 in respect of option B, as contrasted with Mr Stevens figure of £364,076 in respect of the same option. However, I do not think that the accuracy of Mr Looney's calculations was challenged on behalf of the plaintiffs save to the extent I have already mentioned. The plaintiffs are, in the result, entitled to the sum of £343,628 in respect of this claim. 8.1.5

The breach of statutory duty issue

(a) *The facts*

The final stages in the relations between the plaintiffs and the VHI can now be summarised. Following Sister Gregory's letter of 5 June 1991, which effectively marked the end of the negotiations for a new agreement, the system of interim payments continued to operate. On 10 June 1991, the then solicitors for the plaintiffs wrote to Mr Ryan claiming that there was an outstanding balance due in respect of the period from 9 August 1990 to 9 May 1991 of £151,658.43 and threatening the institution of proceedings. A summary summons was issued on 25 June and a motion for summary judgment brought before the Master on 6 August. While there was further correspondence between Miss Lynott and Mr Ryan on behalf of VHI and Sister Gregory on behalf of the plaintiffs which reflected the virtually total breakdown of the relationship between the parties, I do not think it is necessary to refer to that correspondence in any detail. Matters ultimately came to a head on the 6th September when Sister Gregory was concerned by the fact that a cheque she was expecting from the VHI for a sum of approximately £83,000 had not arrived. She had a telephone conversation with Mr Ryan that day about the non-payment and he told her that he had been advised by the VHI's lawyers not to pay the money in view of the pending litigation and also because they (the VHI) considered that the hospital had been overpaid. Sister Gregory pointed out that the money was needed to pay staff wages which were due that day, and Mr Ryan said that the VHI would be prepared to put the money on deposit while the legal teams and accountants on both sides met early the following week to reconcile the figures. She said that this was no good to the plaintiffs who needed the money that day, but Mr Ryan again said that he was unable to pay the money having regard to the legal advice he was being given. He also asked Sister Gregory to forward directly to the VHI certain invoices so that they could be reconciled. She had a further conversation with Mr Ryan later in the day in which she told him that the hospital now proposed to revert to the direct billing method with their patients and asked him to make arrangements for the supply to the hospital of the forms required if the direct billing method was to be reintroduced. Mr Ryan said: 'Oh dear, this will make it very awkward for us' but agreed to have the forms sent on.

Two memoranda of the same date by Mr Ryan were also produced. The first recorded advice from Mrs Jane Marshall, a partner in the firm of solicitors acting for the VHI, to the effect that making a payment at this stage would weaken the case being made on behalf of VHI that there had been an overpayment. The second of these memoranda was in the following terms:

> Jane Marshall telephoned me again and we finalised the wording of a letter to be faxed to Sister Gregory. I brought her up to date on the latest conversation with Sister Gregory

8.1.5 and she agreed that her decision to withdraw from the direct payment system is helpful to us as it is a further unilateral distancing of herself from VHI.

> It does, of course, carry the immediate difficulty that she will now be billing patients for treatment in a hospital which remains on the fully approved list, but at rates which we have not agreed. Following some discussion however we agreed that it would be useful to take a couple of days, in order to get Mr Cook's opinion and to do whatever preparatory work of a public relations nature which might be necessary.
>
> It is essential, however, that the situation should not now be allowed to drift.

On the same day, Mr Ryan wrote to Sister Gregory confirming that he had been advised by the solicitors that the VHI should not discharge the latest invoice and also confirming his offer to place the amount in a separate deposit while the accountants and solicitors on both sides met to reconcile the financial matter in dispute.

It would seem that the plaintiffs on receiving the necessary forms from the VHI began to bill the patients directly, as Sister Gregory had indicated they would. They were apparently concerned that the VHI were treating the existing system under which there was no direct billing of the patients as continuing in operation and their solicitor wrote as follows to the solicitors for the VHI on 2 October:

> Please be advised that we require an undertaking in writing from your client today Wednesday, 2 October 1991 by 5 p.m. not to inform its subscribers that they need not discharge the charges for medical and nursing care provided by our client at St Francis Medical Centre, Mullingar and that the cover provided by your client is limited to out-patients only at the said centre.
>
> In default of such undertaking in writing by 5 p.m. today Wednesday, 2 October 1991 we will be applying *ex parte* for proceedings for an injunction to restrain your client from doing so.

That letter was replied to on 4 October as follows:

> We have now had an opportunity to take our clients' instructions regarding your letter of 2 October 1991. We must say that we find your letter confusing if not totally contradictory. Would you please confirm whether your client is now electing to be no longer treated as a direct payment hospital. If so, please confirm that members will be billed only on the agreed *per diem* rate which our client will be liable to reimburse.
>
> By seeking our clients' undertaking that the cover provided is limited to out-patients only, you seem to be inferring (sic) that your client no longer regards itself to be a fully participating hospital. Please confirm whether this is the case.
>
> Please note also that our client will be obliged to make clear to its members any change which your client makes to its status or to payment methods.

On 14 October, Mr Ryan wrote a letter to the plaintiffs in which, having recounted the earlier history of the matter as the VHI saw it, he went on:

> In a telephone conversation on 6 September 1991 between our General Manager, Mr Ryan and your Hospital Administrator, Sister Gregory O'Reilly, it was stated on your behalf that you proposed to commence billing patients directly with effect from the following Monday, 9 September. At your request, we furnished a supply of claim forms appropriate to the direct billing of patients. However, on that occasion we pointed out to you that if you were to commence billing our members in that fashion, an immediate difficulty would arise for VHI, since St Francis Medical Centre is still shown in our rules as a fully participating hospital. Such difficulty arises because the rates at which you

would be billing are not agreed between us. Nonetheless under the terms of our rules, because St Francis Medical Centre is shown as a fully participating hospital we would be obliged to indemnify our members. Our Mr Ryan informed your Sister Gregory that if such a step were to be taken by you, VHI would have to consider its future relationship with you immediately. **8.1.5**

In our solicitor's letter to your solicitors dated 4 October, we sought clarification as to whether you wished to opt out of the direct payment system and we sought confirmation from you that VHI members would only be billed at the agreed *per diem* rate. No such confirmations were received in response to that letter. However, in an Affidavit sworn by your Sister Gregory on 3 October 1991 she has stated that St Francis Medical Centre has informed prospective patients who are subscribers to VHI that they should discharge fees to St Francis Medical Centre and recover them from VHI in accordance with their contracts of indemnity. Further a circular letter dated 24 September 1991 exhibited to an affidavit of Bridie Reilly sworn on behalf of St Francis Medical Centre on 3 October 1991 confirms that the said billing system was implemented with effect from 26 September 1991.

In circumstances where St Francis Medical Centre refuses to bill patients at agreed rates, VHI cannot continue to hold out to its subscribers that it will indemnify them against whatever charges St Francis Medical Centre may choose to make to them, since to do so would expose VHI to a potentially unlimited liability.

In these circumstances, we hereby give you notice that with effect from Monday, 21 October 1991, St Francis Medical Centre will no longer be a fully participating hospital as defined in the rules of VHI and notice to our subscribers to that effect will be published in accordance with the rules of VHI on Tuesday, 15 October 1991.

On the same day Mr Stevens wrote on behalf of the plaintiffs to Mr Ryan protesting against the proposal to publish the notice referred to and stating that the proposed action would cause the hospital 'irreparable damage'. Mr Stevens in that letter, disputed Mr Ryan's statement that the plaintiffs did not wish to accept an interim agreement with the VHI and was not prepared to accept the conditions for a fully participating hospital. He went on:

I wish to make it clear that the hospital wishes to continue as a fully participating hospital and is quite prepared to comply with all your requirements for it to do so. This letter is being sent to you by fax and I should be obliged if you would confirm to me by return fax that you will not proceed with the publication of the notices in tomorrow's daily papers advising VHI's subscribers that St Francis Medical Centre will no longer be a fully participating hospital as defined in the rules of VHI. If you do not give me this confirmation, then you will leave me with no choice but to apply immediately to the Courts for an injunction preventing you from doing so.

A plenary summons had already been issued on 4 October claiming an injunction restraining the VHI from informing its subscribers that they need not discharge the charges made by the hospital. A further plenary summons was issued on 15 October 1991 claiming an injunction restraining the VHI from publishing the notice already referred to in the daily newspapers. On 17 October, Murphy J refused an application for an interlocutory injunction restraining the publication of the notice. On 6 November the notice was published in the national newspapers in the following terms:

TO ALL VHI SUBSCRIBERS

Notice of change in hospital benefit

Pursuant to Rules 8(4) and 8(6) we hereby give you notice of the following amendment

8.1.5 to hospital benefit:

With effect from Monday, 2 December 1991
St Francis Medical Centre
Ballinderry, Mullingar, County Westmeath also known as Ballinderry Hospital will no longer be a fully participating hospital as defined in rules.
This means that hospital cover will not be provided to VHI members admitted to St Francis Medical Centre from Monday, 2 December next.
Existing patients and patients admitted prior to that date remain covered.

On 13 November, Lardner J granted an interlocutory injunction restraining the VHI from informing its subscribers that they need not discharge the charges made by the plaintiffs at their hospital.

As from 2 December 1990, accordingly, all cover was withdrawn by the VHI from patients attending the plaintiff's hospital. The effect on the hospital was described by Sister Gregory as 'Absolutely devastating': while it had managed to remain open, staff had been reduced from about 130 to approximately 30. She estimated that the number of patients had dropped by at least 70%.

Mr Stevens in evidence produced calculations as to the loss of profits which he said the plaintiffs had sustained as a result of the withdrawal of VHI cover and which, up to the year ended 30 November 1992, he calculated in the sum of £1,011,797. He also said that there was a continuing loss per day from 1 December 1992 which he estimated at £2,752.

Evidence was also adduced on behalf of the plaintiffs and the VHI as to the general nature of the operations of the VHI which did not relate directly to the situation of the plaintiffs' hospital. Mr Kevin Heary said that he was the chief executive of Galvia Hospital Holdings Plc which operated the Galvia Hospital in Galway. This hospital was owned and run on a commercial basis. The hospital had been in operation since 1986 and had at all times been recognised as a fully participating hospital by VHI. In 1989, the hospital, like the plaintiffs, had a written agreement with the VHI embodying what he described as an arbitrary reduction of 7% in the rates to be charged by them. He said that in the year 1992, the arrangement was changed with the introduction of a concept of 'marginal pricing' under which, if the quota of patients allowed for the hospital was exceeded, thereafter the VHI would only pay 40% of the bill of each patient. He said that as a result of the financial constraints imposed on the hospital by the VHI, they were obliged to close one theatre in October, an entire floor from October to December and the remaining theatres in December. He said that his hospital had no option other than to agree to whatever VHI determined as financially appropriate in an environment where the latter had 92% of the market. The VHI limited the profitability of his hospital to 3% of its properly incurred costs.

Two economists gave evidence. Mr Moore McDowell, who is a Statutory Lecturer in Economics in University College Dublin, said that, having regard to the fact that approximately 92% of those with private health insurance policies were subscribers to the VHI, private hospitals in Ireland were in the position that as a factual matter they were obliged to deal with a single purchaser of their services. Hence, he said, an economist would describe the VHI as being in a 'monopsonist' position. (The more familiar expression 'monopoly' is, it would appear, only appropriate to suppliers, as distinct from purchasers, of goods and services). Since the evidence established that in recent years the VHI were accustomed to negotiate individually with hospitals and agree rates with them which varied both in terms of the amounts charged and as to whether they were inclusive *per diem* or separate maintenance and ancillary services rates, Mr McDowell said that they were properly described as a 'discriminating monopsonist'. He said that it was very unusual to find such a situation in a competitive market and that, if a similar situation existed in another retail market, it would have the inevitable result of redistributing income from the suppliers to the monopsonist purchaser. He said that Mr Heary's evidence demonstrated that the amount the VHI were paying was less than the marginal cost of supplying health care, because were it greater than that marginal cost, it would not be in the interests of a hospital to shut down a ward. 8.1.5

Mr McDowell was also of the view that, in a truly competitive market, it would not be possible to have the system of full indemnity insurance operated by the VHI under which the hospital cannot recover any difference in charge from the VHI subscriber. He referred to arrangements which exist in the United States called Health Maintenance Organisations, under which the same entity provides insurance and owns a hospital or hospitals. It is, of course, the case, as Mr McDowell pointed out, that in contrast to Ireland, many different insurers compete in the U.S. market. He thought that it would be possible for VHI to introduce a greater element of competition into the Irish situation by indicating to the hospitals rates which they (the VHI) would be prepared to pay. This should lead to a situation in which hospitals would, in effect, be competing with each other in tendering for the supply of their services to the VHI's subscribers.

Mr McDowell agreed in cross-examination that introducing the system just mentioned, to the extent that it would exclude hospitals who were tendering at the higher rate from treating VHI patients, would be at odds with the case advanced on behalf of the plaintiffs that the VHI were not entitled to exclude from cover patients attending any hospital which had been approved under the Health Acts 1947 to 1991. He also agreed that conditions in the health care market were, from an economist's point of view, somewhat peculiar; this was because of what he described as 'physician induced demand'. Because the patient in receipt of treatment normally does not dispute the opinion of the physician that he needs particular services, the supplier of the service has an unusual degree of control over the level of demand generated for the service. He accepted that one of the biggest problems in the health care market was that of 'information and consumer choice'.

Mr McDowell also agreed in the course of cross-examination, and this was later confirmed in evidence by Mr Ryan, that the VHI operate a system of what is called 'community rating'. Essentially this means that, as a general rule, the insurer in determining the level of the premium does not have regard to the experience and characteristics of the individual to be insured which, for example, in the case of motor insurance results in a wide range of different premiums being charged to insured persons. He accepted that, were it not for the community rating system operated by VHI, those who were prone to ill-health and more likely to be in need of medical care, would have to pay increased premiums.

Mr McDowell also accepted that, in determining whether the VHI was behaving as a 'discriminating monopsonist', it was essential to establish that the VHI, was paying different prices for similar services. He also accepted that it was legitimate for the VHI to seek to reduce costs by endeavouring to negotiate terms with different hospitals. He disagreed, however, with views expressed in the report of the Commission on Health Funding published in September 1989 as to the difficulties that might be encountered by the consumer of health services in a private system of health funding.

Dr Miriam Wylie, an Economist who is the head of the Health Policy Research Centre and a senior Research Officer with the Economic and Social Research Institute, gave evidence on behalf of the VHI. She said that the factors which differentiated the health services from other markets were the information problem, the fact that the supply and demand for services may not be independent and the lack of predictability of illness experience. She said that there had been a growing awareness internationally of the importance of containing costs in the health care area. A system under which suppliers of services, such as hospitals, were not subjected to any cost constraints would be the most inefficient of the various possible systems. She thought there would be serious problems in introducing a tendering system such as that suggested by Mr McDowell, since it would be unlikely to take account of the desirability of basing payment on the type of service being provided. Nor did she favour the replacement of full indemnity insurance, as operated by the VHI, with a form of 'co-insurance' under which the potential patient assumes part of the financial risk, since this would penalise the sick.

8.1.5 (b) *The Law*

(i) Voluntary Health Insurance Act 1957
Before considering the submissions advanced on behalf of the plaintiffs and the VHI under this heading, it is necessary to examine the provisions of the 1957 Act more closely. It was enacted following the report of an advisory body which had been appointed by the Minister for Health to advise him as to the feasibility of introducing a scheme of voluntary health insurance in Ireland and, if such a scheme were feasible, as to how best it might be established. According to that report, voluntary health insurance benefits were provided on only a very limited scale at that time in Ireland.

The VHI is established under section 3 of the Act as a body corporate and section 4 then provides as follows:

> (1) The (VHI) shall make and carry out a scheme of voluntary health insurance for defraying, to such extent as the Minister may from time to time specify, the cost to persons paying subscriptions to the (VHI) in respect thereof, and to dependents of such persons, of such medical, surgical, hospital and other health services as the Minister (for Health) may from time to time specify.
> (2) The (VHI) may make and carry out such other schemes of voluntary health insurance as it may think fit, subject to the consent of the Minister in regard to the scope and extent of the benefits.
> (3) A scheme under this section may be amended by a subsequent scheme made by the (VHI), subject to the consent of the Minister in regard to any amendment relating to the scope or extent of benefits.
> (4) The (VHI) shall so fix the subscriptions provided for by schemes under this section that taking one year with another the revenue of the (VHI) from subscriptions together with its other revenues (if any) shall be sufficient, but only sufficient (as nearly as may be), after the (VHI) has made such allowances it thinks proper for reserves, depreciation and other like purposes, to meet the charges (including repayments of loans to the Minister) properly chargeable to revenue.

It will be seen that the VHI was intended to operate as a non-profit making body. It would also appear that the power given to the Minister under section 4(1) to specify from time to time the extent of any scheme or the nature of the services in respect of which the VHI were to provide voluntary insurance has been exercised by the Minister on one occasion only, in 1979, and then in a limited manner. The VHI have, however, invariably sought the approval of the Minister to changes of any significance in the schemes of insurance which they have, from time to time, offered to the public. The only formal statutory instruments made by the Minister under the provisions of the 1957 Act to which I was referred were those bringing the Act into operation in 1957.

I have already summarised the various schemes produced by the VHI from time to time. The rules promulgated by the VHI which govern such schemes contain provisions which are of some relevance to the issues in this case. Those adopted on 1 February 1977, provide for the payment of benefit in respect of treatment or investigation in an 'approved hospital'. The expression is defined in paragraph 1(e) as follows:

> A hospital . . . fully approved by the Minister for Health under section 54 of the Health Act 1970 or a health or mental institution within the State maintained by a health board or any other hospital . . . approved by the (VHI).

In the 1979 Rules, (paragraph 1 (e)), the following definition was substituted:

'Any hospital . . . which is included in the (VHI's) current list of approved hospitals. . . .' 8.1.5

In the 1984 Rules, the expressions 'fully participating hospital' and 'partially participating hospital' appear for the first time. The first is defined as:

> A hospital . . . which is included in the (VHI's) current directory of hospitals and for which full cover is provided under the required plan.

'Partially participating hospital' is defined as:

> A hospital . . . which is included in the (VHI's) current directory of hospitals and for which partial cover is provided under the required plan.

The Rules at present in force and which were also in force during the relevant period contain definitions of 'fully participating' and 'partially participating' hospitals in identical terms.

While the evidence established that the VHI was not subject to day-to-day supervision by the Minister in the exercise of its functions, all the members of the Board, including the Chairman, are appointed by the Minister, who may also remove any member from office. It is clear, accordingly, that the Minister may, if he wishes, determine to a significant extent the policies to be pursued by the VHI.

Material provisions are also contained in sections 22 and 23. Section 23 prohibits, subject to certain exceptions which are not material, the carrying on of a health insurance business without a licence granted by the Minister under section 22. Under section 22 the granting of such a licence is in the 'absolute discretion' of the Minister. As we have seen, no such licence has ever been granted by the Minister.

It was submitted on behalf of the plaintiffs that, under section 4 of the 1957 Act, the VHI was not expressly empowered to enter into the form of contract which it had sought to enter into with all the private hospitals who wished to be treated as fully participating hospitals. While it was conceded that the VHI had power to enter into agreements which were incidental to, or consequential on, the powers expressly conferred on them, this did not necessarily extend to the scheme adopted by the VHI in 1989, under which it was sought to make all hospitals parties to direct contracts with the VHI. It was further submitted on behalf of the plaintiffs that, even if the VHI enjoyed such a power, it was a power to enter into contracts with *all* hospitals who were willing to be fully participating hospitals. If they failed to reach an agreement with one hospital, as had happened in the present case, it was not within their powers to deprive all patients attending that hospital of VHI cover. The consequence of adopting a scheme under which every fully participating hospital was under direct contract with the VHI was that the VHI were obliged to reach agreement with every such hospital. If they failed to reach such agreement in any individual case, it followed inevitably that such a hospital would have to revert to its status as a fully participating private hospital without any direct contract with the VHI.

It was submitted on behalf of the VHI that the arguments advanced on behalf of the plaintiffs were based on a misconception as to the provisions of the 1957 Act and, in particular, section 4 thereof. It was submitted that section 4(1) imposed an obligation on the VHI to carry out a scheme of voluntary insurance where they were required by the Minister so to do. However, whether or not the Minister exercised his powers under that section, it remained open to the VHI to enter into any other schemes of voluntary health insurance they considered appropriate, subject to their obtaining the consent of the Minister to the scope and extent of the benefits which such schemes conferred. This, it was argued, indicated that the intention of the Oireachtas was to confer a wide discretion on the VHI as to the manner in which they provided schemes of voluntary health insurance, subject to the overriding power of the Minister just mentioned.

8.1.5 That, it was said, had been the manner in which the Act had been operated by the VHI since its establishment, i.e. the promulgation from time to time of particular schemes of insurance, divided into different plans and with specific rules. The VHI, moreover, in common with all other corporations, statutory or otherwise, had power to enter into contracts which were incidental to or consequential upon its stated powers and functions. Manifestly, in the case of the VHI, it was said, this included the power to enter into agreements with providers of health care specifying the rates of charges in respect of which the VHI would be prepared to extend cover and, if this was seen as appropriate in the context of their duties towards their subscribers and as prudent insurers, the power to enter into the form of agreements which were actually negotiated by the VHI in 1989 as part of the Recovery Programme. It was submitted that it logically followed from this that the VHI were also clearly entitled *not* to enter into agreements which they considered uneconomic or in some other way not viable. A statutory corporation such as the VHI not merely had power to enter into contracts in pursuit of its statutory functions: it was also under an obligation not to enter into contracts which it considered not to be in its interests.

It was also urged on behalf of the VHI that private hospitals varied greatly in their characteristics and requirements, ranging from the new high technology hospitals to much older hospitals, and that it was reasonable for the VHI to enter into agreements reflecting the different needs and objectives of the individual hospitals.

(ii) *Conclusion*

The uniquely important role of the VHI, not merely in the provision of private health insurance, but in the structure of health care generally in Ireland today, is of central importance when one comes to consider this part of the case. Whether or not sections 22 and 23 of the 1957 Act were enacted originally in order to enable the VHI to provide private health insurance on a non-profit making basis in a near monopoly situation (and there may have been good reasons why the Oireachtas considered that desirable) it is beyond argument that the VHI now enjoys precisely that position, since the evidence established that 92% of the persons who purchase private health insurance are subscribers to the VHI, representing approximately 1.3 million people. The evidence established clearly that the huge share of the market enjoyed by VHI and the tax advantages available to its subscribers make it extremely unlikely that there will be any new entrants to the market, even if the Minister were disposed to grant any licences. (It was pointed out in the course of the hearing that the situation might change in the future as a result of the implementation in this country of EC law, but I must deal with matters as they exist today).

The VHI is not a private commercial organisation: it is a public body established by the Oireachtas with statutorily defined objects and powers. While the enabling Act undoubtedly confers on the VHI a wide discretion, under the ultimate control of the Minister, as to how it carries out those objectives and the manner in which it uses its powers, in common with other bodies of this nature it must use the powers entrusted to it fairly and reasonably. That obligation which must, if necessary, be enforced by the Courts, exists not merely in the case of its subscribers and potential subscribers, but also in the case of the providers of health care, such as the plaintiffs, with whom the VHI may have reason to deal and who, for their part, have no practicable alternative to dealing with the VHI.

It is not in dispute that the VHI can reasonably confine their provision of cover to hospitals which are approved by the Minister under the provisions of the Health Acts 1947 to 1991. It is equally not in dispute that the hospital operated by the plaintiffs is such a hospital. The evidence in this case also demonstrates beyond doubt that a private hospital, such as that operated by the plaintiffs, cannot hope to survive as a viable entity if the VHI are not prepared to extend any form of cover to its patients.

It is against this background that one must consider the legality of the various arrangements entered into by the VHI which have been subjected to such detailed scrutiny in the present case. It is clear that the powers of the VHI are not confined to providing schemes of insurance as such. That is one of the principal powers conferred expressly on them by statute: they also have such powers as are necessarily and properly required for carrying into effect the purposes of incorporation or as may be fairly regarded as incidental to, or consequential upon, those things which the Oireachtas has authorised. (See *Attorney General v. Great Eastern Railway Company* (1880) 5 App Cas 473, 478). 8.1.5

I am satisfied that the VHI were entitled, as a matter of law, to take the various steps which formed part of the Recovery Programme, undertaken, as they undoubtedly were, with a view to ending the erosion of the VHI's reserves without imposing what they regarded as unacceptable and, it might be, economically counter-productive increases in premiums on their subscribers. I have no hesitation in rejecting the submission advanced, admittedly somewhat tentatively, on behalf of the plaintiffs that entering into such contracts was *ultra vires* their powers under the 1957 Act.

The crucial issue is as to whether the actions taken by the VHI in October 1991 following the breakdown in negotiations constituted a fair and reasonable exercise of their statutory powers, whether conferred expressly or by implication. In arriving at a conclusion on that issue, it is not necessary for me to express a concluded view as to where the merits lay in the matters of contention that arose between the parties over the years. In particular, I express no opinion on whether Sister Gregory was justified in regarding Miss Lynott's letter of 20 May 1991, as so unreasonable as to make further negotiations for an agreement at that time futile. It takes two parties to enter into a contract and it may well be that the parties had reached an impasse at that time which made the conclusion of an agreement impractical. That does not mean that the VHI were necessarily within their rights in notifying the public in general in the following October that, as from 2 December, no person attending the hospital as a patient would receive any cover whatever from the VHI.

In determining whether that was a fair and reasonable exercise of the VHI's statutory powers, express or implied, the context in which the decision was taken is of critical importance. The plaintiffs had voluntarily entered into an Agreement with the VHI in February 1989 which not merely imposed a standstill on their charges, but subjected them to a 15% reduction in their budget, which, so far as the evidence goes, was a reduction of a severity not imposed on any other hospital. In addition, the VHI had, as I have already found, wrongfully withheld from the plaintiffs substantial sums which were owing to them during the months following the expiration of the 1989 Agreement. The VHI must have been aware of the adverse effect these actions were having on the finances of the plaintiffs' hospital. I do not think that the plaintiffs can be blamed, in the circumstances, for deciding that only drastic action would produce any amelioration in their financial position. It is, of course, the case that responsibility cannot be exclusively attributed to either the plaintiffs or the VHI for the fact that what was intended to be an interim arrangement of a relatively short duration lasted, in the event, for 14 months. But when one has regard to the previous history and the respective positions of the parties, the VHI in worsening drastically the financial position of the plaintiffs by the action they took in October 1991 cannot be regarded as having acted fairly and reasonably.

The VHI's stated justification for their action was the fact that, if the plaintiffs reverted to the system of direct billing at a stage when they were still listed as a fully participating hospital, the VHI would be obliged to indemnify the subscribers in full in respect of charges over which they had no control. However, this explanation must be viewed with some scepticism. Had the plaintiffs been allowed to revert to their pre-1989 status, it would have presented difficulties for them as well as for the VHI: the latter had repeatedly emphasised when the Mutual Hospitals Programme was produced in 1988 that it provided advantages to the private hospitals as well as to the VHI. One obvious advantage was the guaranteed cash flow at regular intervals. It is much more likely, in my view, that both parties, acting in their own interests, would eventually have had to come to some form of agreement. On the other hand, there are certainly indications in the evidence that the VHI simply used the confrontation between themselves and the plaintiffs in September 1991 as a convenient opportunity for ending any relationship with this

8.1.5 particular hospital.

It must also be said that the request contained in the letter from the solicitors to the VHI dated 4 October that the plaintiffs should confirm that VHI subscribers would be billed 'only on the agreed *per diem* rate which our client would be liable to reimburse' was disingenuous. The VHI and their legal advisers were fully aware throughout this period that the plaintiffs were invoicing them on the basis — at the least — of the charges set out in the letter from Sister Gregory dated 28 June 1990. In these circumstances, the VHI and their solicitors must have known that, if the plaintiffs reverted to a direct billing system, there was simply no 'agreed *per diem* rate' which could form the basis of the VHI's reimbursement of the charges.

The actions of the VHI in October 1991 might have been unexceptional in legal terms in the case of a private commercial firm vigorously protecting its own interests. They were not, however, a fair and reasonable use of the powers entrusted expressly and by implication to the VHI by the Oireachtas for the common good and I am, accordingly, satisfied that the plaintiffs are entitled to appropriate relief in respect of those actions.

I should emphasise that this is not to say that the VHI are under a statutory obligation to extend cover to every approved hospital, as was suggested on behalf of the plaintiffs at the outset. There may be circumstances in which, in the proper and reasonable exercise of their statutory powers, they may decide not to extend any cover to a particular hospital. My finding that they acted unreasonably and unfairly in deciding to withdraw all cover from the plaintiffs' hospital is reached solely on the facts of the present case.

(iii) *The Competition Act 1991*

In view of the conclusions which I have reached in the preceding section, it is not strictly necessary for me to make any findings on this issue. However, in deference to the arguments of Counsel and in case the matter should go further, I think I should set out my conclusions.

(a) *The Law*

Section 5 of the Competition Act 1991 provides as follows:

> (1) Any abuse by one or more undertakings of a dominant position in trade for any goods or services in the State or in a substantial part of the State is prohibited.
> (2) Without prejudice to the generality of subs. (1), such abuse may, in particular, consist in
>
> > (a) directly or indirectly imposing unfair purchase or selling prices or other unfair trading conditions;
> > (b) limiting production, markets or technical development to the prejudice of consumers;
> > (c) applying dissimilar conditions to equivalent transactions with other trading parties, thereby placing them at a competitive disadvantage;
> > (d) making the conclusion of contracts subject to the acceptance by other parties of supplementary obligations which by their nature or according to commercial usage have no connection with the subject of such contracts.

Section 3(1) of the Act provides that:

> In this act, unless the context otherwise requires . . . 'undertaking' means a person being an individual, a body corporate or an unincorporated body of persons engaged for gain in the production, supply or distribution of goods or the provision of a service.

The question as to whether the VHI is an 'undertaking' within the meaning of section 3(1) was determined by Costello J as a preliminary point of law in these proceedings. He answered that question in the negative, but on appeal to the Supreme Court it was held that the VHI was an 'undertaking' within the meaning of the section. (*Deane & Ors .v. Voluntary Health Insurance Board*, unreported; Judgment delivered 29 July 1992). **8.1.5**

On behalf of the plaintiffs, it was submitted that the evidence clearly established that the VHI enjoyed a 'dominant position' within the meaning of section 4(1) in the relevant market, the provision of insurance for health care, and that the actions of the VHI referred to in the preceding section constituted an abuse of that dominant position.

On behalf of the VHI, it was submitted that they were not engaged 'in trade for any goods or services' within the meaning of section 5(1). It was further submitted that the only service which the VHI were providing within the meaning of section 3(1) was that of health insurance and that the Act only affected them in their capacity as suppliers of a service, whereas the case made against them in these proceedings was based on their role as an indirect purchaser of services provided by the plaintiffs. It was further submitted that the VHI could not be in any worse position than purely commercial undertakings who were entitled to protect their own interests by taking objectively justifiable steps into which category, it was submitted, the actions taken by the VHI in the present case fell.

(b) *Conclusion*

The Competition Act 1991 came into force on 1 October 1991. Since the actions complained of by the plaintiffs on the part of the VHI took place after that date and since the VHI have been found by the Supreme Court to be an 'undertaking' within the meaning of section 3(1) of the Act, section 5, which prohibits the abuse of a dominant position in the State, *prima facie* applies to the actions of the VHI. The issues which have to be determined are:

(1) whether the VHI are engaged 'in trade for . . . services' within the meaning of subs. (1);
(2) if so, whether the VHI enjoy a 'dominant position' in that trade; and
(3) whether the actions complained of constitute an 'abuse' of that dominant position.

The long title of the Act indicates that it has been enacted 'by analogy with Articles 85 and 86 of the Treaty establishing the European Economic Community' (usually referred to as 'the Treaty of Rome'). The analogy is necessarily incomplete, since one of the principal objectives the Treaty (some would say the paramount objective) is the establishment of a single integrated market in the community, whereas such a market already exists in the State. Moreover, as was pointed out on behalf of the VHI, the 'Competition Authority' established by section 10 and on which certain powers of enforcement are conferred, enjoys nothing like the wide range of legislative, investigative, policing and adjudicating powers enjoyed by the European Commission in relation to the corresponding provisions of the Treaty of Rome. In addition, while sections 4 and 5 virtually replicate Articles 85 and 86 of the Treaty, there is one material difference in that the words 'in trade' which appear in both sections 4 and 5 do not appear in the Articles. Finally, there is no equivalent in the Act to Article 90 of the Treaty which provides that:

> 1. In the case of public undertakings and undertakings to which Member States grant special or exclusive rights, Member States shall neither enact nor maintain in force any measure contrary to the rules contained in this Treaty, in particular to those rules provided for in Article 7 and Articles 85 to 94.
> 2. Undertakings entrusted with the operation of services of general economic interest or having the character of a revenue producing monopoly shall be subject to the rules contained in this Treaty, in particular to the rules of competition, in so far as the application of such rules does not obstruct the performance, in law or in fact, of the particular tasks assigned to them. The development of trade must not be affected to such an extent as would be contrary to the interests of the community.
> 3. The Commission shall ensure the application of the provisions of this article and shall, where necessary, address appropriate directives or decisions to Member States.

8.1.5 The VHI would appear to be one of the 'undertakings' referred to in this Article and the absence of any provision corresponding to Article 90.2 in the Act might suggest at first sight that a more severe regime is applicable to undertakings such as the VHI under our domestic law than obtains under the Treaty. However, it was not suggested on behalf of the plaintiffs that the provisions of the 1957 Act had been amended, either expressly or by implication, by the 1991 Act and it follows that the VHI remain capable in law of carrying out any functions assigned to them by the 1957 Act notwithstanding any of the provisions of the 1991 Act.

The decision of the Supreme Court is the only decision so far available on the proper construction of the 1991 Act and that decision, as I have indicated, is confined to the single issue as to whether the VHI are captured by the expression 'undertaking' in section 3. There are, however, many decisions on the corresponding provisions of the Treaty of Rome by the European Commission, the Court of First Instance and the Court of Justice of the European Communities, a number of which were considered by me in my Judgment in *Masterfoods Ltd trading as Mars Ireland v. H.B. Ice Cream Ltd* (unreported; judgment delivered, 28 May 1992). While these decisions are of considerable assistance in construing the relevant sections of the 1991 Act, it must be borne in mind that that Act, as was pointed out on behalf of the VHI, is an autonomous Act of the Oireachtas and not one simply giving effect to Directives of the European Community. Moreover, the differences between the provisions of the 1991 Act and the corresponding provisions of the Treaty of Rome, to which I have already referred, must also be borne in mind.

As to the first issue, I am satisfied that the VHI are engaged 'in trade for . . . services' within the meaning of section 5. As I have already mentioned, section 4 is also confined in its operation to 'agreements . . . which have as their object or effect the prevention, restriction or distortion of competition *in trade in* . . . services'. If one were to treat the expression 'in trade' as confined to the carrying on of a business for profit, it would drastically curtail the operation of the Act so far as bodies such as the VHI were concerned and this would not seem to be in harmony with the decision of the Supreme Court. Section 4 admittedly would still be applicable to agreements between a non-profit making body, such as the VHI and other bodies if the result of the agreement was to unduly affect competition 'in trade' in the narrower sense of 'profit making' trade. However, I think that, in the light of the Supreme Court decision, a broader meaning should be given to the words 'in trade' and there seems no reason why they should not be applicable to an activity such as the sale of voluntary health insurance policies, even when carried on by a statutory body precluded from making profits.

The next issue is as to whether the VHI enjoys a dominant position in the relevant trade, i.e. the provision of voluntary health insurance services. Unlike Article 86, which refers to a dominant position 'within the common market or in a substantial part of it', there is no reference in section 5 to any 'market' as such. However, it is clear that in determining whether the VHI are in a dominant position 'in trade for . . . services in the State or a substantial part of the State', one must first establish what the relevant market is within the State by reference to which the issue as to dominance and its possible abuse can then be determined. On behalf of the plaintiffs, it is said that the relevant market is the provision of voluntary health insurance and that the VHI who enjoy 92% of that market are clearly in a dominant position. On behalf of the VHI, it is submitted that there is effectively no relevant market in the present case: the plaintiffs are operating in one market, i.e. the provision of health care, while the VHI are operating in another, the provision of voluntary health insurance. It is pointed out on their behalf that VHI are only captured by sections 4 and 5 of the 1991 Act to the extent that they are engaged in 'the provision of a service' within the meaning of section 3 (1), but that the essential complaint against them by the plaintiffs is in their capacity as indirect purchasers of services provided by the plaintiffs and their allegedly 'monopsonist' status.

I think that it is clear that the only market in which the VHI operate is the voluntary health insurance market. The VHI are not providers, directly or indirectly, of health care services and are not in any sense competing with the plaintiffs in any such market. It is also clear that they enjoy a 'dominant position' within the meaning of section 5(1) in the health insurance market. The classic definition of 'dominant position' to which I referred in *Masterfoods Ltd trading as Mars Ireland v. H.B. Ice Cream Ltd* is that of the Court of Justice of the European Communities in *Hoffman-La Roche v. EC Commission* (1979) 3 CML. 274, i.e. **8.1.5**

> A position of economic strength enjoyed by an undertaking which enables it to prevent effective competition being maintained on the relevant market by affording it the power to behave to an appreciable extent independently of its competitors, its customers and ultimately of the consumers.

The fact that VHI enjoy 92% of the market and is, in the result, virtually without competition makes it clear beyond argument that it enjoys a dominant position in the market. The fact that it enjoys this position because of the relevant provisions of the Voluntary Health Insurance Act 1957 and the manner in which it has been implemented by successive Ministers for Health does not affect this conclusion: indeed, if anything, it reinforces the view that they enjoy a dominant position. (See the decisions of the Court of Justice in *Italian Republic v. Commission of the European Communities* [1985] ECR 873; *Centre Belge D'Etudes de Marche – Telemarketing (CBEM) SA v. Compagnie Luxembourgeoise de Telediffusion SA and Information Publicite Benelux SA* [1984] ECR 3261).

The third issue is as to whether the Acts referred to constitute an abuse of that dominant position. As I indicated in *Masterfoods Ltd trading as Mars Ireland v. H.B. Ice Cream Ltd*, the existence of a dominant position is not of itself unlawful in EC law and this is also true in the case of section 5(1) of the 1991 Act: for the Act to operate there must have been 'an abuse' of that dominant position. As to what constitutes such abuse, there is again a helpful passage in the Judgment of the Court in *Hoffman La-Roche*:

> The concept of abuse is an objective concept relating to the behaviour of an undertaking in a dominant position which is such as to influence the structure of a market where, as a result of the very presence of the undertaking in question, the degree of competition is weakened and which, through recourse to methods different from those which condition normal competition in products or services on the basis of the transactions of commercial operators, has the effect of hindering the maintenance of the degree of competition still existing in the market or the growth of that competition.

The object of section 5 is to outlaw two categories of activity by an undertaking in a dominant position: those which (a) weaken competition in the relevant market or (b) directly damage the interests of those dependent on the supply or acquisition of the goods or services in question. It is clear that in the present case the actions complained of have had no effect on competition in the market for voluntary health insurance. There is also no evidence that they have damaged the interests of purchasers, actual or potential, of health insurance.

The plaintiffs' claim is in essence that the activities of the VHI constituted an abuse of their dominant position in the health insurance market because they caused damage in an indirect manner to the plaintiffs in their capacity as providers of health care. If that contention were correct in law, it would follow that the action of the VHI in requiring the plaintiffs to accept a 15% reduction in their cash limit in 1989 was also an abuse of that position. That was, I think, the view taken by Mr McDowell, although he refrained from stating his opinion in those words on an issue that only the Court could decide. I have, however, already indicated my view that the VHI were entitled as a matter of law to take that action, if they had come to the conclusion that it was necessary in order to protect their reserves and prevent an unacceptably large rise in the level of premiums.

Mr McDowell's description of the VHI's actions in this context as those of a 'discriminating monopsonist' is doubtless accurate from an economist's perspective, but that is the role which

8.1.5 they have been assigned by the Oireachtas. It is not for the Court to substitute its own view for that of the VHI in this area, unless the decision taken was one that no reasonable person could have taken. I have stated my conclusion that their action in October displayed that manifest lack of reason and equity. But it is because of those vitiating factors that the Court's intervention is called for and not because their actions were an abuse of their dominant position in the market for health insurance, as that expression is used in the 1991 Act.

I conclude, accordingly, that while the VHI undoubtedly occupy a dominant position in the market consisting of the provision of voluntary health insurance, the actions complained of, although beyond their powers under the Voluntary Health Insurance Act 1957, were not an abuse of their dominant position in the voluntary health insurance market.

(iv) *Relief*

The next question that arises is as to the relief to which the plaintiffs are entitled, having regard to these findings. While they have advanced a claim for substantial damages based upon loss of profits, the onus of proof rests squarely upon them to establish that they have in fact sustained such damage and I am satisfied that, while their operations have undoubtedly been gravely affected by the actions of the VHI, they have not discharged that onus.

In the first place, the plaintiffs are a charitable organisation and, while they naturally have sought to conduct their operations from year to year so that all their costs are covered and, if possible, a small surplus is generated, the suggestion that they would have earned over £1,000,000 in profits for the year ended 30 November 1992 is almost wholly unsupported by evidence. In fact, this figure seems to be based on a projected loss of payments from the VHI rather than a loss of profits as such. Secondly, if the VHI had not wrongfully withdrawn recognition from the plaintiffs' hospital, they would still have been entitled to insist on cost containment measures in protection of their reserves and their subscribers' interests. This might well have meant that the plaintiffs would ultimately have been obliged either to enter into a new contract as a fully participating hospital or to accept the status of a partially participating hospital. The VHI were perfectly entitled to adopt the attitude that they could not indefinitely afford full indemnity to the plaintiffs' patients in the absence of any agreement on charges and an agreement implementing, to at least some degree, the 'seven steps' or some other regime under which costs would be reduced. Eventually, the plaintiffs might well have been compelled to elect between entering into such an agreement, accepting the status of a partially participating hospital or going their own way in the knowledge that they could not guarantee their patients any degree of VHI cover. The effect on their overall financial position in the event of any of these options being chosen remains unclear so far as the evidence goes. Thirdly, the plaintiffs were obliged to mitigate any losses they might sustain as a result of the VHI's wrongful withdrawal of recognition by reducing such of their overheads as were capable of reduction, in particular, by laying off staff. It would appear from the evidence that they did in fact take some steps in that direction, but no attempt was made in the evidence to establish the savings that had been, or might have been, achieved.

The plaintiffs are, however, entitled to injunctive relief in respect of the actions by the VHI in October and November 1991. It is accepted on their behalf that there would be difficulties in the Court's granting a mandatory injunction requiring the VHI to include the plaintiffs as a fully participating hospital in their Directory of Hospitals in the absence of an agreement between the parties as to the terms on which the plaintiffs' hospital would be fully participating. They are, however, entitled to an injunction restraining the VHI from refusing to provide indemnity to their subscribers in respect of charges incurred by their subscribers to the plaintiffs.

There will, accordingly, be judgment for the plaintiffs in the sum of £343,628 and I will, in addition, grant an injunction in the terms I have indicated.

Deane & Others v. Voluntary Health Insurance Board, Supreme Court, 28 July 1994 **8.1.6**

Terms of Agreement imposing cost control – Proof of contract term breached – Breach of statutory duty of defendant – Allegation of abuse of dominant position – Jurisprudence of the Supreme Court in deciding questions in issue – Voluntary Health Insurance Act 1957 – Competition Act 1991, section 5

Facts The plaintiffs who are the trustees of a community of nuns own a private hospital in a provincial town in Ireland. The Voluntary Health Insurance Board (VHI) is a statutory corporation established by the Voluntary Health Insurance Act 1957 to make and carry out schemes of voluntary health insurance.

In 1988 VHI suffered very substantial losses and a recovery programme was devised and implemented. For the period from 1 March 1989 to 30 June 1990 the plaintiffs agreed with VHI that it would not recover from VHI in respect of subscribers of VHI a sum in excess of a limit set according to payments made during the 12 months preceding 1 March 1989. This agreement terminated on 30 June 1990 and VHI sought to implement a further cost control mechanism. If the plaintiffs did not want to participate in this further cost control proposal their hospital would no longer be a fully participating hospital as defined by VHI. The plaintiffs did not participate in the further proposal and VHI then implemented the conditions under which VHI subscribers would be covered by VHI insurance. In effect VHI subscribers attending at the plaintiffs' hospital were only indemnified in respect of a proportion of the cost incurred by them at the plaintiffs' hospital.

In November 1991 the plaintiffs unsuccessfully sought an interlocutory injunction to prevent VHI from advertising that the plaintiffs' hospital was no longer a fully participating hospital within the meaning of the Rules of VHI. In the plenary hearing Keane J of the High Court found that VHI had breached its statutory duty and for which the plaintiffs could recover damages.[1]

The appeal These proceedings on appeal concerned:

(1) A claim on a *quantum meruit* basis for services provided to the VHI subscribers after 30 June 1990.

(2) A claim for the difference between the limit originally set in the agreement and that sum which was received from the VHI under the agreement.

(3) A claim that the defendant did not exercise its statutory powers fairly and reasonably in refusing to provide indemnity to their subscribers in respect of the plaintiffs' charges.

(4) A claim for damages for an abuse of VHI's dominant position in the provision of Voluntary Health Insurance Services.

Held by the Supreme Court (O'Flaherty, Blayney and Denham JJ):

(1) If VHI wished to deprive the plaintiffs of their *quantum meruit* claim and the difference between the limit and what they received, VHI was required under the principles of contract law to prove that a term of an agreement existed which was

1. See 8.1.5 above.

8.1.6 breached by the plaintiffs and which thereby entitled VHI to refuse the payments sought.

(2) The Supreme Court differed from the trial judge's construction of the relevant term concerning the limit set for the plaintiffs. It was agreed by the parties that the plaintiffs had complied with the limit of hospital beds used in the period in order to maintain the limit. VHI succeeded in its argument in the High Court trial that the plaintiffs had failed to maintain 'a similar case mix' and were therefore not entitled to the difference between the sum of the limit and what they received from VHI. The Supreme Court differed with the trial judge's finding and stated that the 14% difference in the case mix was not such that the requirement of similarity was not met. Furthermore the Supreme Court outlined how the plaintiffs had successfully reduced the average length of stay of patients and increased efficiency which was the purpose of the agreement entered into voluntarily by the plaintiffs with VHI. The Supreme Court stated it was very much the onus of VHI to show what was agreed by the parties in relation to case mix if VHI wished to deprive the plaintiffs of an agreed sum based on a difference of a 'case mix'. The VHI could not rely upon a term which had a clear meaning for both parties in order to avoid its payment obligations.

(3) The claim for services on a *quantum meruit* basis which was allowed by the trial judge was not appealed and the plaintiffs therefore succeeded in recovering sums for the period after the termination of the agreement on a quantum meruit basis and the difference during the period of the agreement between the sums paid by VHI and what was agreed to be the sum payable on a successful operation of the agreement by the plaintiffs.

Breach of statutory duty claim

(1) VHI appealed the determination of the trial judge that VHI had breached its statutory duty to act fairly and reasonably in exercising its powers. The Supreme Court and particularly Flaherty J in his supplementary judgment outlined how the plaintiffs had suffered the highest reduction in income of any private hospital as a result of the cost cutting programme of VHI.

(2) Flaherty J commented disapprovingly of the continuing failure or omission of VHI until the twelfth day of the trial to disclose to the plaintiffs the reason why their hospital was not to be paid the difference between what they were paid and what they would have been paid on a successful compliance by the plaintiffs with the terms of the agreement. Flaherty J also noted the tactics of VHI in the proceedings and commented that the lodgment of money with the Defence which was obviously due to the plaintiffs rather than the payment of those monies to the plaintiffs when it was known that the plaintiffs were in dire need of money, was not 'a principled or seemly course to adopt in relation to the plaintiffs who, after all, were only trying to keep their hospital open and whose chief purpose and mission in life was to see to the care of the patients who would attend their hospital'.

(3) Blayney J termed the tort relied upon by the plaintiff as 'misfeasance in public office'.[2] Counsel for VHI referred to a number of cases in support of the argument that VHI could exercise its powers in order to cut costs and to benefit its subscribers. The authorities cited by VHI's counsel were not considered relevant by Blayney J

2. Blayney J commented that this tort was considered in depth in *Bourgoin SA and Others v. Minister for Agriculture, Fisheries and Food* [1986] 1 QB 716.

because they related to the quashing of decisions by an organ of the State.[3] The members of the Supreme Court were satisfied that VHI was not entitled to refuse to indemnify its subscribers when they attended a particular hospital for the sole reason that that particular hospital is not prepared to enter into an agreement with the VHI on terms proposed by VHI. 8.1.6

(4) The plaintiffs appealed the trial judge's decision that they had failed to prove any damage consequent upon the breach of statutory duty. The Supreme Court commented that an exact sum of damage consequent upon a breach of statutory duty need not be proven in order to recover damages. An order for the assessment of damages was then made so that the High Court could make an award.

Abuse of dominant position claim The trial judge's rejection of this claim was made with the comment that he was dealing with the issue in the event that the proceedings should go further. In declining to make any finding on whether VHI abused a dominant position in a trade for services the Supreme Court relied upon the constant jurisprudence of the Supreme Court that it did not enter upon a consideration of any matter which is not necessary for the resolution of the issues between the parties.

THE JUDGMENT

O'FLAHERTY J delivered his judgment on 28 July 1994 saying: I agree with the judgment that Blayney J is about to deliver and with the order that he proposes. I would like to add brief observations on some aspects of the case only.

This case was at hearing for twenty two days in the High Court and for seven days before this Court. In addition, there were many interlocutory applications. Prior to the hearing of the appeal there was even an application for security for costs brought before this Court by the VHI against the plaintiffs. This, however, was abandoned before it came to hearing.

The litigation was conducted between a mendicant order of nuns on the one hand and a statutory corporation that was so cash-strapped as to require the introduction of a 'rescue package' to save it from possible extinction.

The hospital in debate in this case was singled out for special treatment by the terms of the agreement sent by the VHI to the plaintiffs on 30 January 1989. The full terms of that agreement are reproduced in Blayney J's judgment. Initially the plaintiffs had to suffer a 15% reduction in income from VHI patients as compared with the previous year. This seems to be the highest deduction imposed on any hospital; no such deduction was imposed on any comparable, or near comparable, hospital.

In addition, for the duration of the agreement which ended on 30 June 1990, the plaintiffs were obliged to treat a similar number of patients and to have a similar 'case mix' as had prevailed in the plaintiffs' hospital in the year ending 28 February 1989. It was held in the High Court, indeed conceded, that the plaintiffs had treated a similar number of patients and therefore had complied with the first leg of the requirement. Was the 'case mix' similar? The answer is: it clearly was if one takes these words as bearing the meaning that would occur to one on any reasonable reading of the agreement. It would *prima facie* strike anyone considering the working of this hospital as meaning that there was to be a broad blend or intermingling of cases and, in particular, that this phrase required that the proportion of surgical and medical cases should be in synchronisation with what had prevailed in the twelve months prior to the agreement. That is the plaintiffs' case. The VHI contend, on the other hand, that the plaintiffs are not entitled to the 'cash uplift' since, as proved by computer statistics, there was such a

3. Blayney J cited *Hay v. O'Grady* [1992] ILRM 689 in support.

8.1.6 divergence in a sub-category (there being 17 possible sub-categories) of medical cases from the previous twelve months, which had the effect of reducing the number of bed days in the hospital and, though this was something which the VHI was seeking and for which they praised the plaintiffs, nonetheless, the plaintiffs because of the divergence in the number of cases treated in the sub-category, so the VHI contend, should be disentitled to the 'uplift'. I reject that as a wholly untenable proposition. I regard it as elementary contract law that a party seeking to establish a breach of contract, especially of a contract drafted by the particular party, has a clear obligation to prove what the term allegedly breached means if it is said to bear a more extensive meaning than its plain meaning and then to explain how it was breached. The VHI have satisfied neither requirement in my judgment. If the VHI intended to contract so as to deprive the plaintiff of their cash entitlement because of a failure to meet the requirement of preserving a 'case mix' in the sense that if there was a divergence in the numbers treated in a remote sub- categorisation then that would need to have been spelled out in some detail—it might be in considerable detail —in the actual contract so that it would be made known to the other contracting party the extent to which they were to be bound by this requirement. In any event, I would even go so far as to hold that such divergence in numbers as there was in the particular sub-categorisation, if it had any relevance, which I hold it has not, was not such as to breach the requirement as regards 'case mix'.

One of the many disagreeable aspects of this litigation is that the precise basis on which the plaintiffs were being deprived of this 'uplift' did not become apparent until the twelfth day of the trial. It was during the cross-examination of Ms Maureen Lynott, assistant general manager of the VHI at the relevant time, that Mr Fennelly SC became aware of the basis on which the plaintiffs were being so deprived. This required an amendment of the statement of claim at that stage, leave to do so being granted by the Court.

I find it incomprehensible that the plaintiffs should have been kept in the dark until that stage of the case as to the basis for withholding this cash 'uplift' which came to the not inconsiderable total of £294,713.

A further disagreeable aspect of the case is that the substantial sum of £388,628 (including £45,000 in interest) which was what the learned trial judge found was due on a *quantum meruit* to the plaintiffs was withheld by the defendants. Approximately 80% of the base figure that was ultimately awarded by way of *quantum meruit* by the judge was lodged in Court by the defendants with their defence. So they must have known that at least that much was due to the plaintiffs. In the meantime, of course the plaintiffs were deprived of that money which was sorely needed by them to keep going.

While that was a course of conduct which the defendants were entitled to take under the rules of court, I do not find it was a principled or seemly course to adopt in relation to the plaintiffs who, after all, were only trying to keep their hospital open and whose chief purpose and mission in life was to see to the care of the patients who would attend their hospital.

The further unfortunate aspect of the whole matter is that in September 1991, the parties, having been on the verge of agreement fell out and the extreme action of placing the advertisement in the newspapers (which will be reproduced in the judgment of Blayney J) was taken. I think it is a pity that the chief negotiators, Mr John Looney for the VHI and Mr Malachy Stevens, who was the hospital accountant as well as being on the board of the hospital, could not go, or were not allowed to go, the extra distance to seek a resolution of the differences between the parties. Instead there resulted a lamentable flow of litigation—both in its length and its complexity—and one that must have proved very expensive.

As Blayney J points out in the judgment that he will deliver, the learned trial judge found a breach of statutory duty on the part of VHI. Blayney J gives a full analysis of the jurisprudential significance of this finding and the consequences that should flow from it. I do not wish to add anything to what he will say except that it follows inexorably from the learned trial judge's finding, and the facts established in this regard, that the plaintiffs must have suffered damage and severe damage. A party who suffers damage is required to be put in the same position as he would be if he did not suffer the damage: *restitutio in integrum*. It is obviously not the case that the plaintiffs are in the same position as if the wrong had not been done to them; therefore, they must be entitled to damages. The fact that the actual figure to which they may be entitled may not have been presented to the satisfaction of the judge does not mean that the plaintiffs should not get any damages at all under this heading. As stated in *McCregor on Damages* [15th ed.] at para. 344: **8.1.6**

> . . . where it is clear that some substantial loss has been incurred, the fact that an assessment is difficult because of the nature of the damage is no reason for awarding no damages or merely nominal damages. As Vaughan Williams LJ put it in *Chaplin v. Hicks* [1911] 2 KB 786, the leading case on the issue of certainty: 'The fact that damages cannot be assessed with certainty does not relieve the wrong-doer of the necessity of paying damages.' Indeed if absolute certainty were required as to the precise amount of loss that the plaintiff had suffered, no damages would be recovered at all in the great number of cases.

BLAYNEY J (Denham J concurring): The plaintiffs are the trustees of a community known as The Congregation of the Franciscan Missionaries of Our Lady and are the owners of a private hospital at Ballinderry, Mullingar, Co. Westmeath. The defendant (to which I shall refer as the VHI is a statutory corporation to established by the Voluntary Health Insurance Act 1957 to make and carry out schemes of voluntary health insurance.

This is an appeal by the plaintiffs against part of the order made by Keane J in the High Court and a cross-appeal by the VHI against another part of that order and against some of the findings in the judgment. The case was at hearing for twenty two days before Keane J and his very thorough and careful judgment runs to 114 pages. The appeal raises a number of important and difficult issues, but before referring to it in detail it is necessary to set out a summary of the background to the proceedings.

For a number of years prior to 1989 approximately 70% of the plaintiffs' patients were VHI subscribers and the practice up to then was that the patients paid the plaintiffs directly the amount due for their stay in hospital and were then reimbursed in full by the VHI. Under a scheme which had been introduced by the VHI in 1979, members insured under the appropriate plan were entitled to a complete indemnity in respect of the cost of their maintenance and ancillary services during their stay in the plaintiffs' hospital.

In 1988 the VHI suffered very substantial losses and as a result had acute financial problems so much so that the Minister for Health intervened and appointed a financial consultant, Mr Noel Fox, to prepare what was called the 'VHI Recovery Programme'. Under this scheme each of the private hospitals was requested to enter into a written agreement with the VHI for a period of sixteen months commencing on 1 March 1989 and terminating on 30 June 1990. Under the agreement a 'cash limit' was imposed on the aggregate of the payments to be made by the VHI to each hospital, such cash limit to be based on the actual payments by the VHI to the hospital during the twelve months preceding 1 March 1989.

The plaintiffs received the draft of their agreement enclosed in a letter from the VHI dated 30 January 1989. If the plaintiffs wished to continue as a fully participating hospital under the VHI's existing scheme, the agreement had to be signed by them on or before 3 February. It was signed on that date by Sr Gregory, the Superior of the plaintiffs.

It will be necessary to consider the terms of the agreement later. At this stage it is only necessary to indicate that the agreement provided for a cash limit, an inclusive daily rate and required the plaintiffs to provide services for 941 in-patient cases and 195 day cases during the first twelve months. The method by which the plaintiffs were paid for their services was altered. Instead of being paid by their patients, the agreement provided that the plaintiffs would be paid directly by the VHI, such payments to be made twice monthly in discharge of what was due. It was a term of the agreement that the payment mechanism would be adjusted upwards or

8.1.6 downwards in order to achieve the cash limit.

The cash limit in the plaintiffs' agreement, instead of being the aggregate of the payments made by the VHI to the plaintiffs during the twelve months preceding 1 March 1989, was the amount of that aggregate less 15%. One of the plaintiffs' claims in the High Court was that they were not bound by this reduced figure as they had no notice of it, and accordingly that they were entitled to recover from the VHI the difference between the actual cash limit specified in the agreement and the amount that it ought to have been. This claim failed on the facts found by the learned trial judge and there is no appeal by the plaintiffs against this finding.

When the sixteen month agreement terminated on 30 June 1990, discussions which had commenced between the plaintiffs and the VHI during the currency of the agreement continued with a view to the parties entering into a new agreement. These discussions broke down in September 1991. There is a dispute as to the reason for the breakdown which it is not necessary to resolve. It is clear, however, that one of the sticking points was that the plaintiffs wanted to be paid separately for maintenance and ancillaries (such as X-ray, pathology, etc.) whereas the VHI was insisting on a single *per diem* rate covering both.

The immediate cause of the breakdown was the failure of the VHI in September, 1991 to send the plaintiffs a cheque for £83,000 which they were expecting, a failure which caused the plaintiffs acute financial problems. Sr Gregory immediately informed the VHI that her hospital would have to revert to the old system of billing their patients directly and letting them recover from the VHI. The VHI objected vigorously to this on the ground that they had undertaken with their members to pay the hospital directly and they told the plaintiffs that they would have to remove them from their list of fully participating hospitals. Following on this, the VHI in a letter of 14 October 1991 to the plaintiffs gave them notice that with effect from 21 October 1991 the plaintiffs' hospital would no longer be a fully participating hospital as defined in the rules of the VHI, and that notice to this effect to their subscribers would be published on 15 October, 1991. The plaintiffs unsuccessfully sought an injunction to prevent that notice being published and on 6 November 1991 the notice was published in the national newspapers in the following terms:

> To all VHI subscribers Notice of change in hospital benefit. Pursuant to rules 8(4) and 8(6) we hereby give you notice of the following amendment to hospital benefit:
> With effect from Monday, 2 December 1991 St Francis Medical Centre, Ballinderry, Mullingar, Co. Westmeath also known as Ballinderry Hospital will no longer be a fully participating hospital as defined in VHI rules.
> This means that hospital cover will not be provided to VHI members admitted to St Francis Medical Centre from Monday, 2 December next. Existing patients and patients admitted prior to that date remain covered.

Five separate issues arose in the High Court of which the last three are the subject of this appeal and cross-appeal.

1. The first issue was in regard to the 15% reduction in the amount of the plaintiffs' cash limit to which I have already referred. As indicated earlier, this was decided against the plaintiffs and there is no appeal against that decision.

2. The plaintiffs recovered a decree for £343,628 together with £45,000 interest in respect of a claim on a *quantum meruit* for services provided to the VHI's subscribers after the termination of the sixteen month agreement. This decree has not been appealed by the VHI.

3. During the course of the hearing, the plaintiffs were given leave to amend their statement of claim in order to claim the difference between their actual cash limit in the agreement and the amount that they received from the VHI under the agreement. The amount of the difference for the first twelve months was £221,035 and for the ensuing four months was £73,678. This claim, which was referred to in the argument as the 'uplift' claim was rejected by the learned trial judge and is the first matter appealed by the plaintiffs.

4. The plaintiffs claimed damages and injunctive relief on the ground that the VHI had been in breach of their statutory duty under the Voluntary Health Insurance Act 1957 in refusing as and from 2 December, 1991 to cover any of their subscribers for treatment in the plaintiffs' hospital. The learned trial judge held that the VHI were in breach of their statutory duty in that what they did was not a fair and reasonable exercise of their statutory powers and that the plaintiffs were accordingly entitled to appropriate relief. He found that the plaintiffs were entitled to an injunction restraining the VHI from refusing to provide indemnity to their subscribers in respect of charges incurred by them to the plaintiffs and he made an order that the VHI 'be restrained from refusing to provide all cover to their subscribers in respect of charges incurred by said subscribers to the plaintiffs.' The VHI's cross-appeal is against these findings and against the part of the order just cited. The learned trial judge held that the plaintiffs were not entitled to any damages as they had not discharged the onus of proving damage and the plaintiffs have appealed against this finding. 8.1.6

5. The plaintiffs also claimed damages and injunctive relief on the ground that the VHI, in breach of section 5 of the Competition Act 1991, had abused a dominant position in trade for services. The learned trial judge rejected this claim. He found that the VHI were engaged in trade for services and enjoyed a dominant position in the relevant trade, i.e. the provision of voluntary health insurance services, but that they had not been guilty of any abuse of such dominant position. The plaintiffs' appeal against the rejection of their claim is based on the contention that the learned trial judge failed to find that the VHI, in addition to having a dominant position in the provision of voluntary health insurance services, also enjoyed a dominant position in the market for hospital services, and that they had abused such dominant position thus giving the plaintiffs an entitlement to damages under section 6 of the 1991 Act.

It can be seen from the foregoing that there are essentially three issues raised by the appeal and cross-appeal.

1. Are the plaintiffs entitled to the uplift, that is to say, the difference between the cash limit and the amount actually received from the VHI during the sixteen month period of the rescue agreement?

2. Were the VHI guilty of a breach of statutory duty and, if so, are the plaintiffs entitled to injunctive relief and also to damages?

3. Did the VHI abuse a dominant position in a trade for services and, if so, are the plaintiffs entitled to injunctive relief and also damages?

I will now deal with these issues starting with the first.

1. As a number of findings made by the learned trial judge in regard to this issue have not been appealed, they are not in dispute, with the result that the only point in contention is an extremely narrow one. Firstly, the learned trial judge found that the difference between the actual cash limit and what was received by the plaintiffs from the VHI during the first twelve months was £221,035, and that the difference during the last four months was £73,678. So, if the plaintiffs are entitled to recover the uplift, these are the sums to which they are entitled. Secondly, the learned trial judge held that in order to be entitled to the difference, the plaintiffs had to treat 'a similar volume and case mix of VHI patients' as had been treated at their hospital in the year ending 28 February 1989, and that the plaintiffs had satisfied the first part of this condition, that is to say, that they had treated a similar volume of patients. He held that they had not satisfied the second part of the condition, that is to say, that they had not treated a similar case mix of VHI patients and on that ground he rejected the plaintiffs' claim. The sole point to be determined, accordingly, is whether he was correct in rejecting the plaintiffs' claim on this ground.

Even though the issue is a very narrow one, in order to determine it, it is necessary to set out the entire agreement entered into between the parties. It was in the following terms:

Letter of agreement
The St Francis Medical Centre undertakes to contribute to the VHI Recovery Programme

8.1.6 by maintaining a cash limit for sixteen months from March 1st 1989 through 30 June 1990. VHI confirms that the cash limit and payment mechanism are viewed as interim measures for implementation of the VHI Recovery Programme and acknowledges with appreciation the hospital's co-operation and significant contribution to the VHI Recovery Programme.

VHI and the St Francis Medical Centre have agreed the following for the sixteen months from 1 March 1989 through 30 June 1990: The hospital will be a fully participating provider in VHI's directory of hospitals and will accept the agreed rate from VHI as full payment for all members covered by the agreement.

The Hospital will operate the cash limit through the reimbursement mechanism of . . .

Option A. Inclusive daily rate with fortnightly direct payment on the first and fifteenth days of the month.

Value of inclusive daily rate: £77.23 private, £57.92 semi-private, £111.98 day case.

Signed: Sr Gregory
Date: 3 February 1929.

For the year 1 March 1989 through 28 February 1990 VHI will reimburse the hospital at a cash limit of £1,122,692 for a similar volume and case mix of VHI patients treated at the hospital in the year ending 28 February 1989. This commences with all payments from 1 March. The operation of the cash limit will be based on the monthly claims payment experience of the hospital for the year ending February 1989. VHI will provide a monthly report to each hospital identifying results against budget for payments and volumes. As necessary the payment mechanism will be adjusted upwards or downwards in order to achieve the cash limit.

The cash limit for the hospital is based on actual results to December 1988 and projected results for January and February 1989 (in the case of maternity the cash limit reflects the modified benefit). An adjustment will occur in March 1989 based on the actual yearly outcome. The hospital agrees to provide the following level of services at full cover to VHI members for the stated year:

877 in-patient cases (subsequently adjusted to 941 cases)
180 day cases (subsequently adjusted to 195

The hospital agrees to make no increases in bed numbers or technology for potential VHI reimbursement in the period of this agreement and agrees that VHI members will not be charged more for services than non-members and other insurers.

VHI will provide a quarterly ancillaries report in order to obtain details on utilisation of ancillary services.

A working group representing the hospital community will be convened immediately after 1 March to work with VHI on the development of a more refined and appropriate payments structure with effect at the end of the treaty period and to communicate difficulties that may arise in operating the cash limit agreement with hospitals. VHI will also convene meetings of participating hospitals to enhance on-going communications.

(Signed on behalf of the plaintiffs on 3 February 1989 and on behalf of the VHI on 20 February 1989).

The grounds on which the learned trial judge found that the plaintiffs were not entitled to the cash uplift are set out at p. 45 of his judgment:

It is thus clear, and conceded on behalf of the VHI, that the same volume of cases was

> achieved. However, a different picture emerges when one comes to consider the case mix. Health statistics in relation to the plaintiffs' hospital produced by the research department of the VHI on 17 December, 1992 indicate that the number of claims referable to psychoneurotic illnesses for the year ending February 1989 was 397 as contrasted with 230 for the year ending February 1990. The same statistics show that the corresponding reduction in the number of bed days in respect of these illnesses was from 7,912 to 4,578. The total number of bed days for the year ending February 1989 was 18,286 and for the year ending February 1990, 13,790. It is obvious therefore that the reduction in bed days, leading in turn to a reduction in the total benefit paid, was accounted for to a large extent by the reduction in the number of claims for psychoneurotic illnesses. Hence, the second requirement for adjusting the payment mechanism upwards, i.e., the attainment of the same case mix as in the previous year, was not met. **8.1.6**

The reasoning on which this conclusion is reached is based principally on the assumption that the reduction in the number of bed days for psychoneurotic illnesses resulted in the case mix not being similar to the previous year. While there undoubtedly was a sizeable reduction it seems to me that it was not sufficient to make it correct to say that the case mix had been altered.

The December 1992 statistics show that in both of the years in question the plaintiffs treated seventeen different types of illness. The proportion of psychoneurotic cases in the year ending February 1989 was 35% and in the following year 21% so, while the proportion was reduced, it was still a substantial proportion of the total cases. In my opinion the reduction was not such that the case mix ceased to be similar. The plaintiffs continued to treat all seventeen categories of illness and the psychoneurotic illnesses continued to be the group with the largest proportion of cases.

There is no doubt that the reduction in the number of bed days was accounted for to a considerable extent by the reduction in the number of psychoneurotic cases, but it was also accounted for by the plaintiffs having succeeded in reducing the average length of stay per claim from 16.1 days in the year ending February 1989 to 12.5 days in the year ending February 1990. Were it not for this reduction, the number of bed days in the latter year would have been increased by an additional 3,963 bed days (the total of 1,101 claims multiplied by 3.6 the difference between 16.1 and 12.5). It is also important to note that this reduction in the average length of stay was something which the VHI had been pressing the plaintiffs to achieve and represented in their eyes an increase in efficiency. Furthermore, the managing director of the VHI, Mr Ryan, in his letter to the plaintiffs enclosing the agreement to be signed, stated:

> Where necessary, mechanisms will be adjusted upwards or downwards with the hospital to enable the cash limit to be met. If hospitals achieve efficiencies within the cash limit, these are retained by the hospital.

The savings to the VHI resulting from the plaintiffs having succeeded in reducing the average length of stay was, accordingly, something which the plaintiffs were entitled to retain.

It seems to me also that, in coming to his conclusion, the learned trial judge failed to have regard to the fact that in order to meet the obligation which they had accepted under the agreement to provide services for 941 in-patient cases the plaintiffs were obliged to reduce the number of long stay cases, and psychoneurotic cases fell into that category having an average length of stay of 19.9 days. The plaintiffs had an express obligation under the agreement to provide this level of service and if, in order to achieve it the plaintiffs were obliged to make some reduction in the psychoneurotic cases, as they were, it would be totally unjust that this should be relied upon by the VHI to deprive them of the cash limit.

There was a considerable debate in the course of the argument as to the meaning to be given

8.1.6 to the term 'case mix'. On behalf of the plaintiffs it was submitted that it only referred to the mix between surgical and medical cases, while the VHI contended that it included also psychoneurotic cases and that because of the reduction in the number of such cases the case mix in the first twelve months of the agreement was not similar to that of the previous twelve months. In my opinion, if an alteration in the case mix was to be a ground for depriving the plaintiffs of the right to receive the full cash limit, which otherwise they were clearly entitled to under the terms of the agreement, the onus was on the VHI to show that the term 'case mix' had such a clear meaning that a reduction in the number of psychoneurotic cases plainly came within it, and they failed to do that. The volume of cases which the plaintiffs had to service was specified in precise figures but the reference to 'case mix' was nowhere defined.

There are other considerations also which lead me to the same conclusion. An analysis of the agreement shows the following references to the cash limit:

1. The St Francis Medical Centre undertakes to contribute to the VHI Recovery Programme by maintaining a cash limit for sixteen months from 1 March 1989 through 30 June 1990.

2. VHI confirms that the cash limit and payment mechanism are viewed as interim measures for implementation of the VHI Recovery Programme and acknowledges with appreciation the hospital's co-operation and significant contribution to the VHI Recovery Programme.

3. The hospital will operate the cash limit through the reimbursement mechanism of … Option A. inclusive daily rate with fortnightly direct payment on the first and fifteenth days of the month.

4. The operation of the cash limit will be based on the monthly claims payment experience of the hospital for the year ending February 1989. VHI will provide a monthly report to each hospital identifying results against budget for payments and volumes. As necessary the payment mechanism will be adjusted upwards or downwards in order to achieve the cash limit.

The last two references to the cash limit make it clear that effect was to be given to the cash limit through a monthly payment mechanism. The obligation was on the VHI to adjust the payments upwards or downwards and since the payments they made to the plaintiffs were less than the cash limit their obligation was to adjust the payments upwards, and in failing to do so they were in breach of their obligation.

For all these reasons I am satisfied that the plaintiffs are entitled to the full amount of the cash limit and I would allow the appeal on this issue and give the plaintiffs a decree for £295,713, being the aggregate of the two agreed sums of £221,035 and £73,678.

I now turn to the second issue which is: were the VHI guilty of a breach of statutory duty and, if so, are the plaintiffs entitled to injunctive relief and also to damages?

In formulating the issue in this way, I have followed the formulation used by the learned trial judge who treated it under the heading 'The breach of statutory duty issue'. It seems to me, however, that when this part of the judgment is analysed it can be seen that the ultimate conclusion reached by the learned trial judge, on the basis of which he found that the plaintiffs were entitled to damages (subject to proving damage) and to injunctive relief, was that the VHI had abused their statutory powers. This is clear from the following passages from the judgment dealing with this issue:

> Page 97. The VHI is not a private commercial organisation: it is a public body established by the Oireachtas with statutorily defined objects and powers. While the enabling Act undoubtedly confers on the VHI a wide discretion, under the ultimate control of the Minister, as to how it carries out those objectives and the manner in which it uses its powers, in common with other bodies of this nature it must use the powers entrusted to it fairly and reasonably. That obligation which must, if necessary, be enforced by the courts, exists not merely in the case of its subscribers and potential subscribers, but also in the case of the providers of health care, such as the plaintiffs, with whom the VHI may have reason to deal and who, for their part, have no practicable alternative to dealing with the VHI.

> Page 99. The crucial issue is as to whether the actions taken by the VHI in October 1991 following the breakdown in negotiations constituted a fair and reasonable exercise of their statutory powers, whether conferred expressly or by implication. In arriving at a conclusion on that issue, it is not necessary for me to express a concluded view as to where the merits lay in the matters of contention that arose between the parties over the years. **8.1.6**
>
> Pages 101/102. The actions of the VHI in October 1991 might have been unexceptional in legal terms in the case of a private commercial firm vigorously protecting its own interests. They were not, however, a fair and reasonable use of the powers entrusted expressly and by implication to the VHI by the Oireachtas for the common good and I am, accordingly, satisfied that the plaintiffs are entitled to appropriate relief in respect of those actions.

These passages in the judgment might be summarised as follows:

1. The VHI had a duty to use the powers entrusted to them fairly and reasonably.
2. The action of the VHI in October 1991 in withholding all cover from the plaintiffs' hospital was not a fair and reasonable exercise of their powers.
3. In the circumstances, the plaintiffs were entitled to appropriate relief.

The learned trial judge went on later to deal with what that relief was. He dealt first with the question of damages and held that the plaintiffs were not entitled to damages as they had not discharged the onus of proving damage. But he held that the plaintiffs were entitled to injunctive relief and he granted the two injunctions referred to earlier in this judgment.

The VHI's cross-appeal is confined to two matters: firstly, they contest the finding that they exercised their powers unfairly and unreasonably, and secondly, they claim that the plaintiffs are not entitled to the two injunctions that they were granted. There is no cross-appeal against the finding that the VHI had a duty to exercise their powers reasonably and fairly, nor was there any cross-appeal against the learned trial judge's finding that the plaintiffs would have been entitled to damages if they could have discharged the onus of proving damage. I shall be dealing later with the general issue of damages which was argued at considerable length in the course of the hearing in the context of the plaintiffs' appeal against the refusal of the learned trial judge to award any damages: I only want to note here that there was no contest in the course of the hearing as to the plaintiffs' right to damages if they could prove damage. The submissions of counsel for the VHI were confined to maintaining that the VHI, in taking the action they did in October 1991, had not exercised their powers unreasonably and unfairly and, if this was decided against the VHI, to maintaining that the damages that the plaintiffs were seeking were excessive. Whilst it was not expressly conceded that the plaintiffs were entitled to damages if the learned trial judge's finding that the VHI had used their powers unfairly and unreasonably was correct, provided of course that they could establish that they had suffered damage, neither was it contested, and that being so, it seems to me that the learned trial judge's decision on this issue must stand.

The learned trial judge did not categorise the tort constituted by the VHIs exercising their powers unreasonably and unfairly, but if he had done so, the probability is that having regard to its ingredients he would have classified it as misfeasance in public office, the tort which was considered in depth by the Court of Appeal in England in the case of *Bourgoin SA and Others v. Ministry for Agriculture Fisheries and Food* [1986] 1 QB 716.

It follows that what has to be considered is the VHI's cross-appeal claiming that the learned trial judge was wrong in holding that the VHI had exercised their powers unreasonably and unfairly, and the plaintiffs' appeal claiming that the learned trial judge was wrong in holding that they had not discharged the onus of proving that they had suffered damage.

As to the first of these issues, it was submitted by Mr Cooke on behalf of the VHI that the withholding of cover from the plaintiffs' hospital in October 1991 was a reasonable exercise

8.1.6 of their powers and accordingly perfectly lawful. In support of his submission he referred to *Cassidy v. Minister for Industry and Commerce* [1978] IR 297; *State (Keegan v. Lysaght) v. Stardust Victims Compensation Tribunal* [1986] IR 643 and *O'Keeffe v. An Bord Pleanála* [1992] ILRM 237. He submitted that however unfair and unreasonable the decision may have been, it was not manifestly arbitrary or flagrantly in disregard of reason. It was a business decision which the VHI were entitled to make.

In my opinion the authorities cited by Mr Cooke are not relevant to the particular issue. The Court is not considering whether the decision of the VHI should be quashed. It is considering whether the learned trial judge was justified in finding that their decision was an unfair and unreasonable exercise of their powers. This conclusion was an inference drawn by the learned trial judge from the facts, so what has to be considered is whether there was credible evidence to support the facts from which the inference was drawn and whether the learned trial judge was correct in the conclusion that he reached (see *Hay v. O'Grady* [1992] ILRM 689).

The grounds on which the learned trial judge reached his conclusion are to be found at pp. 98, 99 and 100 of his judgment:

> It is not in dispute that the VHI can reasonably confine their provision of cover to hospitals which are approved by the Minister under the provisions of the Health Acts 1947 to 1991. It is equally not in dispute that the hospital operated by the plaintiffs is such a hospital. The evidence in this case also demonstrates beyond doubt that a private hospital, such as that operated by the plaintiffs, cannot hope to survive as a viable entity if the VHI are not prepared to extend any form of cover to its patients.
>
> In determining whether that was a fair and reasonable exercise of the VHI's statutory powers, express or implied, the context in which the decision was taken is of critical importance. The plaintiffs had voluntarily entered into an agreement with the VHI in February 1989 which not merely imposed a standstill on their charges, but subjected them to a fifteen per cent reduction in their budget, which, so far as the evidence goes, was a reduction of a severity not imposed on any other hospital. In addition, the VHI had, as I have already found, wrongfully withheld from the plaintiffs substantial sums which were owing to them during the months following the expiration of the 1989 agreement. The VHI must have been aware of the adverse effect these actions were having on the finances of the plaintiffs' hospital. I do not think that the plaintiffs can be blamed, in the circumstances, for deciding that only drastic action would produce any amelioration in their financial position. It is, of course, the case that responsibility cannot be exclusively attributed to either the plaintiffs or the VHI for the fact that what was intended to be an interim arrangement of a relatively short duration lasted, in the event, for fourteen months. But when one has regard to the previous history and the respective positions of the parties, the VHI in worsening drastically the financial position of the plaintiffs by the action they took in October 1991 cannot be regarded as having acted fairly and reasonably.

It was not suggested that any of the findings of fact in these passages were not supported by credible evidence. The only issue is whether the conclusion was justified. I have no doubt that it was. Particularly when one takes into account a further finding at p. 101 of the judgment:

> . . . there are certainly indications in the evidence that the VHI simply used the confrontation between themselves and the plaintiffs in September 1991 as a convenient opportunity for ending any relationship with this particular hospital.

What has to be borne in mind is that there was no obligation on the plaintiffs to enter into any agreement with the VHI in regard to their charges. Up to February 1989, when the plaintiffs, at the request of the VHI, entered into the rescue agreement, there had been no agreement between them. Under the terms of their policies with their members, the VHI provided a complete indemnity for treatment in the plaintiffs' hospital, which was a fully participating hospital. The members paid the hospital and were reimbursed by the VHI. But there was no agreement between the plaintiffs and the VHI in regard to the plaintiffs' charges. After the rescue agreement terminated at the end of June in 1990, the VHI wanted to have a new agreement, obviously with a view to controlling the plaintiffs' charges. Throughout the hearing in the High Court, they had claimed to be entitled to impose cost control on the hospitals in which their members were treated. Their right to do so seems to me to be extremely doubtful, but what is clear is that this was the object they had in mind in seeking to reach agreement with the plaintiffs on a new contract. So they were seeking to impose something on the plaintiffs which they had no right to impose on them. I am not suggesting that the VHI have no power to enter into contracts with hospitals—a matter which was debated in particular in the High Court—I am satisfied that they have, but I am equally satisfied that they are not entitled to refuse to cover a particular hospital for the sole reason that the hospital is not prepared to enter into an agreement with the VHI on the VHI's terms. And that is at the root of the VHI's action in October 1991 as well as the other matters to which the learned trial judge referred in his judgment. I am, accordingly, of opinion that the conclusion he reached was correct and I would dismiss the VHI's cross-appeal on this issue. 8.1.6

No submissions were addressed by counsel for the VHI in support of the cross-appeal against the injunctive relief granted in the High Court and, accordingly, I would dismiss that part of the cross-appeal also.

There remains the plaintiffs' appeal against the finding of the learned trial judge that they had not discharged the onus of proving that they had sustained damage. This finding is expressed in the following paragraph (p. 112):

> The next question that arises is as to the relief to which the plaintiffs are entitled, having regard to these findings. While they have advanced a claim for substantial damages based upon loss of profits, the onus of proof rests squarely upon them to establish that they have in fact sustained such damage and I am satisfied that, while their operations have undoubtedly been gravely affected by the actions of the VHI, they have not discharged that onus.

The learned trial judge then went on to give his reasons for reaching this conclusion but having regard to the view I have formed on this issue it is not necessary for me to set them out.

It seems to me that the learned trial judge did not approach this issue in the correct way. There were in effect two issues to be considered:

1. Had the plaintiffs suffered damage? and

2. if so, what is the appropriate measure of damages to compensate them for the damage suffered.

Having regard to the learned trial judge's finding that the plaintiffs' operations had undoubtedly been gravely affected by the actions of the VHI and to his reference at p. 100 of his judgment to the VHI 'worsening drastically the financial position of the plaintiffs by the action they took in October 1991' and to his finding on p. 98 of his judgment that a private hospital, like the plaintiffs, 'cannot hope to survive as a viable entity if the VHI are not prepared to extend any form of cover to its patients', it is difficult to see how he could have failed to take the view that the plaintiffs had suffered damage. The findings that the operations of the hospital had been gravely affected and that the financial position of the plaintiffs had been worsened drastically seem to me to constitute a finding that the plaintiffs had suffered damage and loss and there was ample evidence from both Sr Gregory and Mr Stevens, the hospital's accountant, to support that finding. Sr Gregory's evidence was that the effect on the hospital of the cover being removed was devastating. Amongst other things, the staff of the hospital had to be reduced from 130 persons to 30. The learned trial judge seems to have taken the view

8.1.6 that there was inadequate evidence to support the claim being made by the plaintiffs for a figure in the region of £1 million for loss of profits and it would appear that it was on this basis that he disallowed the claim for any damages. To refer again to the relevant passage in his judgment, he said:

> While they have advanced a claim for substantial damages based upon loss of profits, the onus of proof rests squarely upon them to establish that they have in fact sustained such damage. . .'.

This would seem to suggest that the learned trial judge took the view that because the plaintiffs had not established the full extent of the loss they were claiming, they had not discharged the onus of proving that they had suffered any damage. In my opinion this does not follow.

I am satisfied on the findings of the learned trial judge that the plaintiffs established that they had suffered damage and that, accordingly, the learned trial judge ought to have assessed what was the appropriate measure of damages to compensate them. Since no assessment of damages was in fact made, it is not possible for this Court to deal with the issue and accordingly the case will have to be sent back to the High Court the damages to which the plaintiffs are entitled.

That brings me to the final issue in the appeal which is: Did the VHI abuse a dominant position in a trade for services and, if so, are the plaintiffs entitled to injunctive relief and also damages?

The learned trial judge took the view that it was not necessary for him to deal with this issue having regard to his conclusions on the other issues in the case, but he did deal with it in deference to the arguments of counsel and in case the matter should go further. The situation in this Court is somewhat different. It has been the constant jurisprudence of the Court that it does not enter upon a consideration of any matter which is not necessary for the resolution of the issues between the parties. If the Court were to deal with this third issue it would be in breach of this principle. A conclusion either way on the issue would not alter in any way the decision of the Court on the appeal. Accordingly, in my view notwithstanding the fact that a very considerable time was spent on this issue in the course of hearing the appeal the Court should not express any opinion on it. At the same time, I would like to express my appreciation to counsel on both sides for the very thorough and carefully prepared submissions which they presented to the Court and my regrets that I am prevented from expressing any opinion on them.

The summary of my conclusions on the appeal is as follows. I would allow the appeal of the plaintiffs; give them a decree for £294,713 on the uplift claim; declare that they are entitled to damages and remit the case to the High Court to have the damages assessed. And I would dismiss the cross-appeal of the VHI.

8.2 Interlocutory Reliefs

Leanort Ltd, Hytherm (Ireland) Ltd and Hytherm Ltd v. Southern Chemicals Ltd, Aircell Ltd, CRH plc, Litepac Ltd, Springvale EPS Ltd and BASF Ireland Ltd: High Court No. 5821P of 1988 (Blayney J) 15 August 1988* 8.2.1

Injunction – Apprehended breach of Articles 85 and 86 of the EEC Treaty – Form of order restraining defendants – Unreasonably low prices – Whether Court can fix minimum prices

Facts The parties were manufacturers of expanded polystyrene insulating panels used principally in the construction of new houses for insertion into cavity walls, sold in cartons of 18 sheets, roughly equivalent to 10 square metres.

The plaintiffs commenced the manufacture and sale of the panels in August 1986. They alleged that the defendants had reduced their prices in unison as soon as the plaintiffs entered the market and maintained them at an uneconomically low level with a view to putting the plaintiffs out of business. The plaintiffs, *inter alia*, sought an order restraining the first to fifth named defendants from selling cartons of panels at less than IR£14.50 or UK£13.00. The defendants denied these allegations and contended that prices were reduced as a result of undercutting by the plaintiffs.

Although he refused to determine any disputed issues of fact, Blayney J found that in June 1986 the price per carton in Ireland was between £20 and £22.50. Since May 1987 the price had fallen to between £9.50 and £10.00. The latter price was uneconomical and losses were being sustained by all parties. Although the plaintiffs wished to become members of the Polystyrene Moulders Association (of which the first, second and fourth named defendants were the only members) and appeared to be eligible, they had not succeeded in joining. When another manufacturer of panels went out of business in 1983 it was taken over by a consortium of the first, second and fourth named defendants.

Held by the High Court (Blayney J):

(1) On the uncontested facts the submission that the defendants had acted in breach of Articles 85 and 86 of the EEC Treaty either by means of an agreement between those who controlled the market or because the dominant enterprises therein brought about this situation raised a serious issue to be determined.

(2) The continuance of the current situation would put the plaintiffs into receivership or liquidation. Damages would not be an adequate remedy. Were the injunction to be refused the plaintiffs would run the risk of being put out of business. Were it to be granted the defendants would only continue to compete with the plaintiffs.

(3) In making an order, the court will not accede to a price suggested by one party to the proceedings since it would effectively determine a disputed issue of fact. In

*This is an edited copy of the report in [1992] Irish Journal of European Law, 143-152.

8.2.1 view of Article 85 of the EEC Treaty, were a court to make an order fixing minimum prices, it would be acting contrary to the policy embodied therein as such an order could lead to the prevention, restriction or distortion of competition. An appropriate form of order would be to restrain the first, second, fourth and fifth named defendants from selling or offering for sale expanded polystyrene insulating panels in Ireland and Northern Ireland at unreasonably low prices. *Engineering and Chemical Supplies (Epsom & Gloucester) Ltd v. Akzo Chemie BV* [1986] 3 CMLR 273 applied.

Case referred to in judgment
Engineering and Chemical Supplies (Epsom & Gloucester) Ltd v. Akzo Chemie BV [1986] 3 CMLR 273

John D. Cooke SC and Ian Finlay **for the plaintiffs**
Nial Fennelly SC and Michael M. Collins **for the first, second and third named defendants**
Richard Nesbitt BL **for the fourth named defendants**
Eoghan Fitzsimons SC and James O'Reilly **for the fifth named defendants**
(adjourned as against the sixth named defendant with liberty to re-enter)

BLAYNEY J delivered his judgment on 15 August 1988 saying: This is a difficult and unusual case. The plaintiffs seek an interlocutory injunction with a view to putting an end to a price war which has been going on between the plaintiff and four of the defendants for approximately a year and a half. They base their claim on Articles 85 and 86 of the Treaty of Rome. Numerous lengthy affidavits were filed and the application was at hearing for three and a half days. I now have to decide if the plaintiffs are entitled to the order they are seeking.

While the plaintiffs are three different companies, they form a single unit, the second and third named plaintiffs being wholly owned subsidiaries of the first named plaintiff. I shall not make any distinction between them in the course of this judgement. Only four of the defendants are concerned in the application, and I shall refer to them as Southern Chemicals, Aircell, Litepac and Springvale respectively. Aircell is a wholly owned subsidiary of Southern Chemicals. Any reference I may make to the defendants globally will be a reference to these four defendants only.

The plaintiff and the defendants are all manufacturers of expanded polystyrene insulating panels (which I will refer to as E.P.S. panels) which are used principally in the construction of new houses being inserted into the cavity walls. The E.P.S. panels are sold in cartons containing eighteen sheets which is roughly equivalent to 10 square metres and the price is fixed at so much per carton.

Southern Chemicals, Aircell and Litepac manufacture in the State; Springvale manufactures in Northern Ireland. All have been in this business for a considerable time. The plaintiffs commenced manufacturing in the State in August 1986. The managing director of the three plaintiff companies, Mr Eoghan Hynes, had considerable experience of the business, having been sales director of Aircell in May 1986.

The plaintiffs urged that the defendants reduced their prices in unison as soon as the plaintiff entered the market and have since early 1987 kept them at an uneconomically low level with a view to putting the plaintiff out of business. The defendants deny that they reduced their prices, or have kept them down in order to damage the plaintiffs and contend that the cause of the prices being reduced was undercutting by the plaintiff in order to gain entry to the market.

The first issue that I have to determine is whether the plaintiffs have satisfied me that there is a serious question to be tried in regard to these allegations that the defendants are in breach of Articles 85 and 86 of the Treaty of Rome. And in determining that issue I must refuse to decide any disputed issues of fact since that cannot be done when the only evidence before the court is on affidavit. I make no determination accordingly on the question of what caused the reduction in prices after the plaintiffs entered the market, nor what has caused the prices to remain at an uneconomically low level. 8.2.1

Neither will I make any determination on the other allegations of the plaintiffs which are disputed, namely, that Southern Chemicals influenced BASF (Ireland) Ltd not to supply the plaintiff with raw materials; that Southern Chemicals blocked the plaintiffs' application for membership of the Polystyrene Moulders Association; that Mr Enright of Litepac disrupted the commissioning of the plaintiffs' plant by tellling Mr Lindle that the plaintiffs could not pay the balance of the contract price; that Mr Peter Cooke of Springvale told Mr Flynn in November 1986 that he was joining the other defendants in their agreement to price the plaintiffs out of the market; that Mr Enright and Mr Reilly of Litepac told Mr Hynes in March 1987 that they and the other companies felt they had no option but to force the plaintiffs out of the market as there was no room for another producer. The resolving of these contested issues will have to await the trial of the action.

But certain facts which are undisputed do emerge from the affidavits.

(1) Before the plaintiffs entered the market, the price per carton in the State was somewhere between £22 and £22.50. The graph prepared by Mr Enright shows that this was the price prevailing in June and July of 1986.

(2) Since at least May 1987, the price per carton has been between £9.50 and £10.00.

(3) This price is uneconomical and losses are being suffered. The plaintiffs claim to have lost £68,818.00. Mr Hynes said in paragraph 22 of his first affidavit that Mr Dermot Quirke, a director of Southern Chemicals and Aircell had told his father, Mr John S. Hynes, chairman of the board of the plaintiffs, on 30 November 1987, that heavy losses were being incurred by his company and this was not denied in the affidavit sworn by Mr Jeremiah O'Mahony on behalf of Southern Chemicals and Aircell. Mr Enright, in paragraph 20 of his affidavit sworn on behalf of Litepac, said he told Mr Hynes in February 1987 that the prices at which they had been forced to trade were economically unattractive; and he further stated that he had rung Mr John Nash of Southern Chemicals in March 1987 and he agreed that the prices were uneconomic and unattractive. And as regards the position in Northern Ireland, Mr Peter Cooke said at paragraph 24 of his affidavit that as a result of the market condition which he described, Springvale's margins in the expanded polystyrene wall board market in Northern Ireland had been reduced dramatically. Losses had been sustained as a consequence of this.

(4) Although the plaintiffs wish to become members of the Polystyrene Moulders Association and would appear to be eligible, they have not succeeded in becoming members.

(5) The sole members of the Polysterene Moulders Association are Southern Chemicals, Aircell and Litepac.

(6) When a company called Polyzote Ltd, which formerly manufactured E.P.S. panels went out of business in 1983, it was taken over by a consortium of other manufacturers consisting of Southern Chemicals, Aircell and Litepac.

(7) The volume, in tons, of E.P.S. panels produced by the defendants in 1985 was as follows: Southern Chemicals 700; Aircell 380; Litepac 800 and Springvale 40.

On the facts Mr Cooke submits that the market has been made to operate consistently at loss levels and that this could not have come about without a breach of either Article 85 or 86. The relevant part of Article 85 is as follows: "The following shall be prohibited as incompatible with the Common Market: All agreements between undertakings, decisions by associations of undertakings and concerted practices which may affect trade between Member States and which have at their object of effect the prevention, restriction or distortion of competition within the Common Market, and in particular those which: (a) directly or indirectly fix purchase or selling prices or any other trading conditions". The relevant part of Article 86 is as follows: "Any abuse by one or more undertakings of a dominant position within the Common Market or in a substantial part of it shall be prohibited as incompatible with the Common Market insofar as it may affect trade between member states. Such abuse may, in particular, consist in (a) directly or indirectly imposing unfair purchase or selling prices or other unfair trading conditions".

8.2.1 Mr Cooks submits that the price cutting campaign which has gone on since autumn 1986 would only have been possible if there had been an agreement between those who control the market or alternatively because the dominant enterprise in the market, being Southern Chemicals and Aircell, was forcing it to act that way, and the other parties had no alternative but to go along with it. It is not for the court at the interlocutory stage to determine whether this submission is well founded or not, but whether on the uncontested facts it raises a serious question to be determined and in my opinion it does. Obviously I am not anticipating what may happen at the ultimate trial and the various hotly contested issues of fact have been researched on oral evidence — all I am deciding is that it seems to me as matters stand at the moment that there is a serious question to be tried.

The next question is whether damages would be an adequate remedy because if that is the case, an injunction should not be granted. On this issue I have no doubt. I am satisfied that damages would not be an adequate remedy. The effect of the current situation continuing could be that the plaintiff companies would be put into receivership or wound up; and so would cease to exist. Damages would not be adequate to compensate for such a situation.

I come then to the balance of convenience. Here, equally, I have no doubt. The plaintiffs would clearly be at a greater risk of inconvenience if the injunction was refused than the defendants would be if it were granted. If the injunction was refused the plaintiff companies run the risk of being put out of business and ceasing to exist, whereas if the injunction is granted there would appear to be little risk to the defendants. It seems to me that the only risk of inconvenience they will run is that they will continue to have the plaintiffs as competitors in the market, but that is a risk that they are required to live with in any event.

The first question, and the one which I have found the most difficult is the form that the order should take. While a number of orders are sought in the notice of motion, in the course of the argument Mr Cooke concentrated on that referred to in paragraph (b) namely "an injunction restraining the defendants (other than the sixth named defendant) from selling or offering the products for sale in the State or in Northern Ireland at a price which is less than the economic cost price to the defendants thereof, and particularly at a price which is less than (in the State), IR£14.50 and (in Northern Ireland) £13.00 Sterling per carton".

It seems to me for a number of reasons that the court should not make an order in this form. The evidence in regard to the economic price of a carton was conflicting. While Mr Hynes, on behalf of the plaintiffs, put the price at £14.50, Southern Chemicals say they can sell at £9.48 and Litepac say that they can sell at less than £11.00. To choose the plaintiffs' figure rather than either of the others would be to decide a contested issue of fact without having the material to do so, something which the court should not do at the interlocutory stage. Apart from this, in view of the provisions of Article 85, I would be slow to make such an order. It prohibits agreement etc., which directly or indirectly fix prices or selling prices, and which have as their object of effect the prevention, restriction or distortion of competition within the common market. So if the Court were to make an order fixing minimum prices it seems to me that it would be acting contrary to the public policy embodied in the Article as such an order could lead to the prevention, restriction or distortion of competition.

So what form of order can the Court make which would afford protection to the plaintiffs pending the trial of the action and would not be inconsistent with Art. 85. It seems to me that the furthest the Court can go is to make an order on the lines of that made by the Commission in the case of *Engineering and Chemical Supplies (Epsom and Gloucester) Ltd v. Akzo Chemie BV* [1986] 3 CMLR 273. The Commission there made an order restraining the defendants from offering and supplying certain products at unreasonably low prices and added the qualifying "designed to damage the plaintiffs' business viability"; which it seems to me would not be appropriate here as it would constitute a finding on a particular issue in the case which can only be dealt with at the trial.

I will hear counsel on the form of the order but unless I am persuaded that some alternative form is preferable, I will make an order restraining Southern Chemicals, Aircell, Litepac and

Springvale until the trial of the action, or until further order, from selling or offering for sale expanded polystyrene insulating panels in the State of Northern Ireland at unreasonably low prices. It is with some hesitation I include Springvale in the injunction as it seems its position is different from that of the other defendants, but to omit it would be unjust as it would give Springvale an unfair advantage over them, so on balance I consider they must be included. 8.2.1

It was objected that an injunction should not be granted because the plaintiffs' undertaking as to damages is worthless because of their financial plight. That objection would carry more weight if ther was a real risk of the defendants suffering loss as a result of the order, but in my opinion such risk is minimal, so even if the undertaking as to damages is of little value, it has little relevance in the circumstances.

The undertaking as to damages is imposed in exercise of the court's jurisdiction to impose terms as a condition of granting an interlocutory injunction. In the present case I propose to impose a further condition, that is that the plaintiffs shall not sell the same product at unreasonably low prices either, whether in the State or in Northern Ireland.

Neither an injunction nor the condition imposed on the plaintiffs will apply to existing contracts with customers, otherwise they should take effect immediately.*

Solicitors for the plaintiffs: *L.K. Shields & Partners*
Solicitors for the first, second and third named defendants: *Gerrard Scallan & O'Brien*
Solicitors for the fourth named defendants: *William Fry*
Solicitors for the fifth named defendants: *A. & L. Goodbody*
Solicitors for the sixth named defendants: *Arthur Cox & Co.*

Paramount Pictures Corporation, Rank Film Distributors Ltd, Les Films Ariane SA, Les Films de la Tour SA and Union Generale Cinematographique SC v. Cablelink Ltd: High Court, No. 7179P (Murphy J) 8 March 1990** 8.2.2

Injunction – Interlocutory – Fair question – Balance of convenience – Whether damages an adequate remedy – Defendant operating television diffusion service – Owner of copyright seeking damages for alleging infringement of copyright in cinematography film

European Community law – Invocation – Justification – Defence alleging abuse of dominant position in common market by plaintiffs – Whether plea stateable – EEC Treaty, Arts. 85 and 86

European Communities – Community law – Invocation – Justification – Copyright – Infringement – Damages claimed by plaintiffs – Defendant pleading that plaintiffs abusing dominant position in common market – Plaintiffs' interlocutory motion to

**Editor's Note*: The report in 1992 IJEL includes a copy of the transcript of the exchanges between counsel and Blayney J concerning the effect of the order including the possible enforcement of the order in Northern Ireland under the Brussels Convention. In summary Blayney J did not make any special order concerning enforcement and left the parties to use whatever procedure which might be available in Northern Ireland to enforce his order.

**This report is reproduced with the kind permission of the Incorporated Council of Law Reporting in Ireland. It was first reported in [1991] 1 IR 521-530.

8.2.2 *have defence struck out – Whether reasonable grounds for defendant's plea – EEC Treaty, Arts. 85 and 86*

Intellectual property – Copyright – Cinematograph film – Defendant operating cable diffusion service – Whether infringement of copyright – Copyright Act, 1963 (No. 10)

Facts The plaintiffs were film producers. The defendant operated a television diffusion or relay system throughout the Dublin and other areas in the State and for approximately 20 years had transmitted programmes, including films the copyright of which was claimed by the plaintiffs. No royalty had been paid by the defendant to the plaintiffs or any of their members in respect of the films in which the plaintiffs sought copyright.

The plaintiffs sought an injunction restraining the defendant from infringing the copyright in any cinematograph film which was vested in the plaintiffs or in any member of an association of film producers represented by the plaintiffs, by transmitting any such film through its diffusion service or otherwise. They further sought an injunction restraining the relay by the defendant of any films produced by the plaintiffs.

The defendant argued that the plaintiffs enjoyed a dominant position in respect of films within the European Community and that they abused this position by seeking to obtain from the defendant royalties which discriminated against the defendant as an Irish company or as a company in one Member State of the European Community as against another and consequently it was alleged the plaintiffs were in breach of Arts. 85 and 86 of the EEC Treaty. The injunction was refused on the condition that the defendant lodge certain monies every month in a bank account to be held pending the determination of the action.

Subsequently, the defendant filed a defence which included grounds which had not been relied upon at the hearing of the application for an injunction. The plaintiffs argued that the defendant was not entitled to rely on any defence other than that indicated by them to the court at the interlocutory hearing so that any new grounds of defence should be struck out. They further argued that the defence based on Arts. 85 and 86 was unstatable and so should be struck out as an abuse of the process of the court. The plaintiffs also sought an injunction to restrain the defendant from relaying any films in which the plaintiffs had copyright by means of a new system of transmission, the MMDS system. The defendant sought to vary the terms of the order under which it was obliged to make monthly payments into a holding bank account pending the determination of the action.

Held by Murphy J in refusing the relief sought by the plaintiffs:

(1) That the reliance on a particular defence on earlier occasions did not constitute a waiver of other defences or amount to an estoppel so as to preclude alternative defences being relied on.

(2) That in determining whether or not a stateable defence had been shown the defence had to be reviewed on its merits, whether based upon European law or domestic legislation or traditional considerations. The defendant's case based on Arts. 85 and 86 was that the plaintiffs were abusing a dominant position enjoyed by them by virtue of their rights in respect of films by seeking to recover royalties from the defendant which discriminated against the defendant as an Irish company or as a

company in a member state of the European Community as against another. Their case in this respect was stateable and so accordingly the defence should not be struck out. *Imperial Chemical Industries v. Berk Pharmaceuticals Ltd* [1981] 2 CMLR 91 and *British Leyland Motor Corporation Ltd v. T.I. Silencers Ltd* [1981] 2 CMLR 75 considered. **8.2.2**

(3) That an injunction would issue as of right if the plaintiff established a stateable case to which the defendant could show no defence, without the necessity of considering the balance of convenience or the adequacy of damages as a remedy. *Campus Oil Ltd v. Minister for Industry (No. 2)* [1983] IR 88 considered.

(4) That in determining whether to grant an injunction, once it is established that the plaintiff has a stateable case and the defendant a stateable defence, the question of the balance of convenience and the adequacy of damages as a remedy should be considered together, not as separate issues.

(5) That as the recovery of damages would be an adequate vindication of the plaintiffs' rights and the monies being paid by the defendant into the bank account were sufficient to ensure that there would be funds available to meet any award for damages which might be made in favour of the plaintiffs the injunctions should be refused.

Cases referred to in the judgment

Imperial Chemicals Industries Ltd v. Berk Pharmaceuticals Ltd [1981] 2 CMLR 91; [1981] FSR 1

British Leyland Motor Corporation Ltd v. T.I. Silencers Ltd [1981] 2 CMLR 75; [1981] FSR 213; [1981] CMLR 3

Campus Oil Ltd v. Minister for Industry (No. 2) [1983] IR 88; [1984] ILRM 45

Injunction

By a plenary summons issued on 5 July 1989, and by a notice of motion dated 7 July 1989, the plaintiffs sought an injunction restraining the defendant from infringing the copyright in any cinematograph film, the copyright in which was vested in the plaintiffs or any memer of their association of film producers, on whose behalf the plaintiffs brought the action, by transmitting any such film. On 31 July 1989, Murphy J in the High Court, refused to grant the injunction sought so long as the defendant lodged certain monies in a defined bank account each month. By two notices of motion dated 5 March 1990, and the 16 February 1990, respectively, the plaintiffs sought:

(i) an injunction to restrain the defendant from relaying any of the films in which the plaintiffs claimed copyright by means of a new MMDS system of transmission, and
(ii)to strike out the defence on the grounds that it was unstateable.

By notice of motion dated 16 February 1990, the defendant sought to vary the terms of Murphy J's order of 31 July 1989, by reviewing the monthly judgments into holding bank account.

Article 85 of the European Economic Community Treaty 1957, provides *inter alia* as follows:

(1) The follows shall be prohibited as incompatible with the common market: all agreements between undertakings, decisions by associations of undertakings and concerted practices which may affect trade between Member States and

8.2.2 which have as their object or effect the prevention, restriction or distortion of competition within the common market, and in particular those which:

> (a) directly or indirectly fix purchase or selling prices or any other trading conditions;
> (b) limit or control production, markets, technical development, or investment;
> (c) share markets or sources of supply;
> (d) apply dissimilar conditions to equivalent transactions with other trading parties, thereby placing them at a competitive disadvantage;
> (e) make the conclusion of contracts subject to acceptance by the other parties of supplementary obligations which, by their nature or according to commercial usage, have no connection with the subject of such contracts.
>
> (2) Any agreements or decisions prohibited pursuant to this Article shall be automatically void.

Article 86 of the Treaty provides as follows:

> Any abuse by one or more undertakings of a dominant position within the common market or in a substantial part of it shall be prohibited as incompatible with the common market in so far as it may affect trade between Member States. Such abuse may, in particular consist in:
>
> (a) directly or indirectly imposing unfair purchase or selling prices or any other unfair trading conditions;
> (b) limiting production, markets or technical development to the prejudice of consumers;
> (c) applying dissimilar conditions to equivalent transactions with other trading parties, thereby placing them at a competitive disadvantage;
> (e) making the conclusion of contracts subject to acceptance by the other parties of supplementary obligations which, by their nature or according to commercial usage, have no connection with the subject of such contracts.

The facts and arguments have been summarised in the headnote and are set out in the judgment of Murphy J *infra*.

The application was heard by the High Court (Murphy J) on 8 March 1990.

Peter Kelly SC, John Gallagher SC and Michael M. Collins **for the plaintiffs**
Brian McCracken SC and Peter Finlay **for the defendant**

MURPHY J delivered his judgment on 8 March 1990 saying: The plenary summons in this matter was issued on 5 July 1989. In that summons the plaintiffs claim on their own behalf and on behalf of some nine hundred members of an association which is generally known and referred to by its initials, A.G.I.C.O.A., who are film producers. The plaintiffs claim an injunction to restrain the defendant from infringing the copyright in any cinematograph film the copyright in which is vested in the plaintiffs or in any of the members of their association. In particular, an injunction is claimed to restrain the defendant from transmitting through the defendant's diffusion service or otherwise howsoever, whether such transmission is effected by the use of a multi-point microwave distribution system (MMDs), cable system or otherwise, any such cinematograph film the copyright in which is vested in the plaintiffs or in any member of A.G.I.C.O.A. In addition, certain declarations are sought as to the rights of the plaintiffs and an inquiry as to the damages, if any, to which they may be entitled. **8.2.2**

Earlier today the parties handed in, and the court has received, an agreement between them which governs to some extent the further prosecution of these proceedings. In substance, though not in detail, the effect of the agreement would be to enable an issue as to the rights in principle of the named plaintiffs to be established, postponing to a later date, if necessary, the ascertainment of the damages, if any, to which the plaintiffs may be entitled, depending upon the determination of the issue as to liability. Obviously, this is a prudent and desirable course and in the best interest of both parties.

The defendant is a company which was incorporated in Ireland in the month of August 1970, under the name Marlin Communal Aerials Ltd and which later changed its name to Cablelink Ltd in the month of October 1981. Since its incorporation the defendant has operated a cable diffusion or relay system throughout Dubln and other areas in Ireland. The persons connected to the relay system subscribe an annual charge of £64 to the defendant. No part of that subscription of any other monies are paid by the defendant to the plaintiffs or to any of their members in respect of the copyright claimed by the plaintiffs.

Ordinarily and in general, but subject to certain exceptions, it would be a breach of copyright to relay through a diffusion service any material in respect of where a person owns the copyright without the agreement of that owner; again, ordinarily one would expect that such consent would be forthcoming only on the terms of the payment of a royalty for the use of such material. It is common case that no royalty has been paid by the defendant to the plaintiffs or any of them in respect of the films in which they claim to have a copyright.

It was in those circumstances that the plenary summons was issued and an application made to this court in the month of July 1989, for an injunction to restrain the relay by the defendant of any films produced by the plaintiffs. The matter came before the court on 31 July 1989, and on that occasion I declined to grant the injunction sought but refused it only on the terms that the defendant lodged on or before 15 August 1989, in a defined bank account in the names of the plaintiffs and the defendant and their respective solicitors a sum equal to one-twelfth of 6 percent of the annual subscription income received by the defendant net after certain charges, levies and VAT. I provided that the injunction should be withheld as long as that lodgment was made and a similar lodgment made monthly thereafter. The effect, therefore, has been that the defendant is continuing to lodge this sum to an account and that sum would be available to meet any claim established by the plaintiffs in respect of damages in these proceedings.

There are at present three motions before the court, two brought by the plaintiffs and one by the defendant. The first motion is an application for an injunction to restrain the defendant from relaying by means of an MMDS system any films in which the plaintiff have copyright. The second motion is to strike out part of the defence filed by the defendant herein. Thirdly, there is a motion by the defendant to vary the order made by me on 31 July 1989.

It seems to me that it would be more helpful if I deal with the second of these motions first, that is, the motion to strike out part of the defence. The application requires to be considered under two headings: first, the contention by the plaintiffs that the defendant is not entitled to rely on any defence other than that indicated by it to the court in the course of the hearing in the month of July. That was a defence based upon Articles 86 and 86 of the Treaty of Rome. The second aspect of the matter is the contention of the plaintiffs that the defence aforesaid based upon Articles 85 and 86 is itself wholly unstateable and should be struck out as an abuse of the process of the court.

As to the first of these arguments, I accept that the defendant relied exclusively on Articles 85 and 86 at the hearing in the month of July 1989, as being its defence to the plaintiffs' claim herein; indeed, it does appear that subsequently the defendant in a motion which it brought but did not proceed with, claiming security for costs, indicated Articles 85 and 86 as its defence to the plaintiffs' claim. However, the fact that the defendant did rely on earlier occasions on a particular defence does not, in my view, constitute a waiver of other defences or amount to an

8.2.2 estopel so as to preclude alternative defences being relied on. Indeed, the omission to indicate or rely upon other defences should not even cast doubt on the strength of the case now pleaded. These defences must be considered an evaluated on their merits.

The new defences may be summarised very broadly by saying that they contain, first, a challenge to the constitutionality of certain domestic legislation on which the plaintiffs' claim is based and, secondly, a challenge to the validity of international conventions relating to trade marks which likewise form part of the plaintiffs' case in these proceedings.

It is not suggested that these defences now raised are in themselves unstateable. It is the plaintiffs' contention that the defendant should not be permitted to raise them at this stage. For the reason already mentioned, I refuse that application.

This leaves the issue with regard to whether or not the defence based upon Articles 85 and 86 itself should be struck out. In fact, this argument is made by the plaintiffs and resisted by the defendant on the basis of two English decisions which are relied upon by the respective parties. The plaintiffs rely upon the decision of Megarry VC in *Imperial Chemical Industries Ltd v. Berk Pharmaceuticals Ltd* [1981] 2 CMLR 91. The Vice-Chancellor makes a colourful but helpful analysis of defences based upon the Treaty of Rome at pp. 7 and 8 in the following terms:

> It has of course, long been settled by high authority that this jurisdiction should be exercised only in plain and obvious cases which are clear beyond all doubt. Once the Treaty of Rome and its columinous and complex jurisprudence has entered a case, it often becomes difficult to say that anything is clear. For this reason, many defendants whose contentions have had little substance have tended to encase themselves in portions of the Treaty and its jurisprudence and so hold at bay with the Euro-defences many plaintiffs who otherwise would have had an easy path to prompt litigious success.

Passing on, then, over a reference to *British Leyland Motor Corporation Ltd v. T.I. Silencers Ltd* [1981] 2 CNLR 75, I take up the quotation of the Vice-Chancellor as follows:

> Like Walton J I think that the English courts must be ready to scrutinise a Euro-defence with care, notwithstanding any apparent conmplexity, and should not adopt the attitude, whether overt or covert, that because it is a Euro-defence it must at least be arguable. If at the end of the examination counsel has been unable to demonstrate that there is a viable defence, then the defence, like any other hopeless defence, should be struck out.

I accept in full what the Vice-Chancellor said there, that defences, be they based upon the Treaty of Rome or on domestic legislation or on traditional considerations, must be viewed on their merits with whatever complexities involved examined and a final result achieved as to whether or not a plausible defence or an arguable defence is shown.

Perhaps the importance of *British Leyland Motor Corporation Ltd v. T.I. Silencers Ltd* [1981] 2 CMLR 75, is that it represents the alternative situation, in that the Court of Appeal in the *British Leyland* case came to a different conclusion on the facts than did the Vice-Chancellor in *Imperial Chemical Industries Ltd v. Berk Pharmaceuticals Ltd* [1981] 2 CMLR 91. It does not create any different principle, as I see it; it is merely that one must investigate the defence and see it is viable, stateable or plausible, all different expressions used by the judges was, in my view, amounting to the same thing. The *British Leyland* case was an example of the court being satisfied that the invocation of the Treaty of Rome did provide a stateable defence. It seems to me that that represents the present case as well.

What the defendant says (and, of course, this is merely summarising a complex composition) in regard to the breach alleged against the plaintiffs by reference to Articles 85 and 86 is that they are abusing a dominant position by virtue of their rights in respect of films in that they are seeking to obtain them from the defendant royalties which discriminate against the defendant as an Irish company or as a company in one member state of the EC as against another. 8.2.2

It is not simply a case that the plaintiffs are alleged to be abusing their position but abusing it as against the defendant by claiming and insisting upon, as the defendant contends, a premium royalty which discriinates against an Irish company. It seems to me that that case is stateable. Of course, I express no view whatever as to its prospects of success. That being so, it seems to me that it would be inappropriate for me to prevent the defendant making that case. Accordingly, I refuse the application to strike out any part of the defence.

The second motion which falls for consideration is the application for an injunction to restrain the introduction by the defendant of the MMDS system. The plaintiffs say that the planned introduction of this system is a changing circumstance since July last; that it is an intensification of the user and, of course, that it is an abuse by the defendant of the product in which the plaintiffs claim copyright. Again, the plaintiffs say (and in this no doubt they are correct) that the MMDS system is technically severable from the Cablelink system so that an injunction could be granted in respect of the former without necessarily impinging upon the latter, in that an injunction, oif granted, would not affect the enjoyment of the service by third parties who are not directly involved in these proceedings.

The defendant contends that the introduction of the MMDS system does not involve a change in the *status quo*. It does involve a technical change in the electronic or engineering sense, but the defendant contends that the *status quo* consists of the provision of a diffusion service which has continued for approximately 20 years and that that is the *status quo* which falls to be considered by the court, and whether this service is provided by one technical process or another is immaterial.

Obviously, both of these arguments have substance, but it seems to me that they all fall to be considered by reference to the principles comprehensively laid down by the Supreme Court in *Campus Oil Ltd v. Minister for Industry (No. 2)* [1983] IR 88. Following that decision and those to which it refers, there are three factors to be taken into account:

(1) Have the plaintiffs established a stateable case in support of their claim for an injunction;
(2) Where lies the balance of convenience;
(3) Would damages provide an adequate remedy?

The question whether the plaintiffs have established a stateable case does not and never did cause any problem. The difficulty in this regard was whether or not the defendant showed a stateable defence because clearly an injunction will issue immediately and as a matter of right on an interlocutory application if the plaintiffs' right is not open to challenge. That is so stated and elementary a proposition but it is sometimes overlooked. Because of the fact that other matters are ordinarily considered at the interlocutory stage, including the balance of convenience and the adequacy of damages as a remedy, it does not mean that those considerations would be considered at all unless the defendant had a defence. There is no reason why the plaintiffs' rights or the remedies to vindicate their rights should be postponed if the defendant has no defence.

In the present case I accept, as I have already indicated, that there is a stateable defence so the first question is disposed of. The plaintiffs have shown that they have a stateable case and the defendant has shows that it has a stateable defence and so one must then consider the balance of convenience. In that regard it seems to me that perhaps it is mistaken to view as separate or watertight compartments the questions of the balance of convenience and the adequacy of damages as a remedy because one will necessarily impinge on teh other. Indeed, in the present case it seems to me that the matter is best approached by a consideration of the adequacy of damages as a remedy.

Can the damages in the present case to which the plaintiffs would be entitled if they succeed be ascertained? Would it be an adequate vindication of their rights to recover damages and is

8.2.2 it clear that there would be a mark against which an order of the court could be executed? Would there be a fund available to meet that claim if it was upheld? In that regard, whatever other problems there may be in quantifying the damages, the plaintiffs have themselves estimated their claim as being 6 percent of the annual subscribed income of the defendant after certain charges. That being their own assessment of their loss, it seems to me that, if provision is made to cover that sum and to ensure that that amount will be available in the event of the plaintiffs succeeding both as to their right and as to quantum justice will be achieved. And it is for this reason that on 31 July 1989, I required that such a sum be set aside. The plaintiffs' interest will be safeguarded and they will be fully compensated for their continuing loss if it turns out that they have that right. In that regard one recognises that if, in fact, an injunction were granted there would be no comparable benefit accruing to the plaintiffs because, by definition, the defendant would not have been utilising the plaintiffs' property. It may be, as the plaintiffs have indicated, that they would benefit in other respects, but the obvious benefit of gaining a royalty or compensation for the use of their product would be lost if an injunction is granted. Of course, I am not saying that the plaintiffs would not be entitled to an injunction at the end of the day if they succeed in the case. If their right is established notwithstanding the defences, they would, of course, be at liberty and entitled at that stage to claim a permenant injunction and I would assume that such an order would be made so as to vindicate their property right in that event.

By preserving the *status quo* I will do justice to the plaintiffs without unfairly prejudicing the defendant. It seems to me that the provision of a sufficient sum of money to meet the full amount of the plaintiffs' claims as it is present accruing meets the full justice of the case.

In relation to the third motion, from the defendant's point of view it has been argued that the sums which are required by the defendant to be set aside were excessive, particularly in the light of the fact that other claims are made by other parties which would perhaps, if the same principle was applied, involve setting aside an additional fraction of their subscribed annual income to meet the other claims. Perhaps in that event the matter might require reviewing, but at the present time and on the basis of the information at present available it seems to me that that is not the case.

In so far as the defendant relies on the defence based on Articles 85 and 86 of the Treaty of Rome, it is its own case that it must pay a royalty, an appropriate royalty, not necessarily a modest or unreasonable one, that is, such a royalty as would not involve discrimination between companies in member states. That is the defendant's own case, as I understand it, but only in so far as it is based upon Articles 85 and 86 of the Treaty of Rome. Of course, if it succeeds on other defences it may be relieved from any liability to pay any royalty. But it seems to me that that contingency as to exemptions from royalties or from liability to a lesser sum is adequately covered by the fact that it is not, in fact, paying over any monies; it is merely segregating the monies and depriving itself of the use of them. But the monies remain under their control and ultimately will be available for return to them if they succeed in the case. It does not seem to me that any injustice is perpetrated by continuing that arrangement.

For that reason it seems to me that the application for an injunction should be refused and that the application to vary the order which I made should likewise be refused. I say that subject to certain qualifications in detail.

It seems to me that the order made on 31 July 1989, which has apparently facilitated the parties up to now, could be improved upon, preferably with the agreement of the parties, by arranging that the very substantial sum of money involved be invested in Government securities or by some other procedure which would secure the interests of both parties and ensure that the money would be invested in the best interests of the party ultimately having an interest therein. Subject to that, it seems to me that the injunction application must be refused and that the application to vary the order made last August should likewise be refused.

Solicitors for the plaintiff: *Patrick G. Colfer & Co.*
Solicitors for the defendant: *Eugene F. Collins & Son*

Patrick Dunlea t/a Pat Dunlea & Sons v. Nissan (Ireland) Ltd t/a Nissan Ireland: **8.2.3**
High Court 1990 No. 2065P (Barr J) 24 May 1990*

Injunction – Conditions for grant of interlocutory order – Alleged abuse of a dominant position – EEC Treaty Art. 86 – Commission Regulation 123/85

Facts The plaintiff had been a motor car dealer since 1973. In July 1980 the plaintiff entered into an agreement with the defendant, the exclusive distributor of 'Nissan' motor vehicles in Ireland, whereby he obtained a franchise for the sale of those vehicles in south County Kildare. In July 1989 the plaintiff decided to expand his business by selling used cars imported from Japan, which included 'Nissan' vehicles. After unsuccessfully attempting to persuade the plaintiff to desist such activity, by letter of 8 December 1989 the defendant terminated the plaintiff's franchise with effect from 8 February 1990. Subsequent to the termination of the franchise, the plaintiff segregated his business in second-hand cars imported from Japan from his 'Nissan' franchise and excluded 'Nissan' vehicles from the range of such second-hand cars offered for sale.

On the hearing of a motion for an interlocutory order to restrain the defendant from terminating the aforesaid franchise agreement pending the trial of the action, the plaintiff submitted that the franchise agreement was a motor vehicle distribution and servicing agreement governed by Commission Regulation 123/85/EEC of 12 December 1984 and that he was accordingly entitled to twelve months notice of termination. In the alternative, he argued that the purported termination of the franchise agreement was an abuse of a dominant position and a breach of Art. 86 of the EEC Treaty.

Held by Barr J:

(1) Where it might be shown at the trial of the action that the termination of a franchise agreement would constitute an abuse of a dominant position contrary to Art. 86 of the EEC Treaty and that, as a consequence of that termination, an applicant would suffer unquantifiable loss and irreparable damage, the Court may grant an interlocutory injunction to restrain the termination of such an agreement.

No cases referred to in the judgment

Mary Robinson SC and Brian Lenehan **for the plaintiff**
James O'Reilly SC and Ian Finlay **for the defendant**

BARR J delivered his judgment on 24 May 1990 saying: The plaintiff carries on business as a motor car dealer and repairer at Kilcullen, County Kildare and has done so since 1973. At all times material to this action he has engaged and continues to engage in the business of selling new and second- hand motor cars and light commercial vehicles. The latter aspect of his business comprises not only vehicles traded-in against new vehicles, but also used cars purchased by him at auctions and from other motor dealers.

The defendant is the exclusive distributor in Ireland of a range of motor cars and light commercial vehicles now known and described as 'Nissan' but previously called 'Datsun'. It commands twelve to thirteen per cent of the new passanger car market in Ireland. In or about the month of July 1980 the plaintiff entered into a main dealer agreement with 'Datsun' Ltd, the predecessor in title of the defendant company under which he was granted the Datsun

*This report first appeared in [1993] Irish Journal of European Law, 146-150.

8.2.3 franchise for south County Kildare subject to the terms set out in a letter to him from the general sales manager of Datsun Ltd dated 8 July 1980. These included an embargo on the sale of other makes of new motor vehicles by the plaintiff and a provision that either party might terminate the franchise agreement by giving two months' due notice. It is common case that until in or about the middle of the year 1989 the plaintiff and the defendant had a good and profitable relationship which is illustrated by the fact that in 1988 the plaintiff purchased 125 new motor cars and 40 new light commercial vehicles from Nissan. It is also not in dispute that over the years since the franchise was originally granted to the plaintiff, he has expended substantial sums of money in promoting 'Nissan' products and in carrying stocks of new vehicles and spare parts.

In July 1989 the plaintiff decided to expand his business by selling used cars which had been imported from Japan, including 'Nissan' vehicles. By the end of January 1990 he had sold 200 such cars and he hopes to sell 1,000 of them by August 1990. The plaintiff has deposed on affidavit that the latter business does not interfere with his obligations or his activities as a main dealer on foot of his franchise with Nissan.

In or about the month of October 1989 the plaintiff learned for the first time that the defendant objected to his participation in the business of importing and selling used Japanese cars. Discussions took place between him and and Mr Tony Kelly, the managing director of the defendant company. There is some controversy as to the reasons for Nissan's objections to the plaintiff engaging in such business. The two reasons which have been advanced are that second-hand cars imported from Japan do not conform in every respect with safety standards applicable in Ireland and spare parts may not be available for all such models. Complaint has been made on behalf of the defendant and others to the Department of the Environment about imported Japanese used cars, but no particular regulations have been made and, so far, the Minister does not appear to have interfered with the importation or sale of such vehicles. The defendant takes the point, which may be well-founded, that the sale by their authorized dealers of second-hand Nissan cars imported from Japan has a damaging effect on the defendant's reputation in Ireland which may do them irreparable harm. However, there is controversy as to whether the reasons advanced by Mr Kelly in that regard are well founded or whether they represent the reality of the defendant's attitude in this matter.

Negotiations between the parties were unsuccessful and by letter dated 8 December 1989 the defendant company terminated the plaintiff's 'Nissan' franchise which, in accordance with the original agreement, was to take effect as and from 8 February 1990. These proceedings were commenced by plenary summons dated 12 February 1990. Subsequent to termination of the franchise the plaintiff modified his position by excluding 'Nissan' vehicles from the range of second-hand cars imported from Japan which he offers for sale. He also carries on the latter business under the title 'Tokyo Motor Co.' at premises in Kilcullen which are entirely separate from that relating to the 'Nissan' franchise.

The various affidavits sworn herein make it clear that there is substantial controversy between the parties on certain relevant facts which cannot be determined on affidavit and require oral testimony. It also emerged at the interlocutory hearing that there is substantial controversy on matters of law relating to the purported termination of the plaintiff's dealership by the defendant. It is submitted on the plaintiff's behalf that his 'Nissan' franchise is a motor vehicle distribution and servicing agreement governed by Commission Regulation 123/85/EEC and that it benefits from a group exemption thereunder pursuant to Art. 85(3) of the Treaty of Rome. It is argued that in the premises the plaintiff is entitled to twelve months' notice of termination of the agreement in accordance with the regulation. The defendant disputes that the regulation applies in the plaintiff's case and further submits that, if it does apply, Nissan is entitled to terminate the agreement under the termination clause having regard to the plaintiff's stated intention of building up a major business in the sale of second-hand motor vehicles imported from Japan, the effect of which, it is submitted, would relegate his activities on foot of the 'Nissan' franchise to a minor place.

A further argument advanced on behalf of the plaintiff is that the purported termination by the defendant of the agreement constitutes an abuse by it of a dominant position in the market in new Japanese cars imported into Ireland and is an infringment of Art. 86 of the Treaty of Rome. **8.2.3**

The interlocutory relief sought by the plaintiff on foot of this motion is an injunction restraining the defendant, its servants or agents, from terminating or taking any or any further steps in purported termination of the franchise agreement between the plaintiff and the defendant made on or about 8 July 1980 pending the trial of this action. There are three factors which the court must consider in deciding whether the plaintiff is entitled to the relief which he seeks. First, has he established that there are serious questions to be tried regarding whether the purported termination of the franchise agreement by the defendant is lawful and of binding effect, and whether in the premises the defendant is entitled to terminate the agreement having regard to the provisions of Art. 86 of the Treaty of Rome. I am satisfied that the plaintiff has established that requirement.

Secondly, in the premises, would damages be an adequate remedy? The plaintiff has been a Nissan main dealer for almost ten years. It is common case that since 1980 he has built up a substantial business in the sale of new cars and light commercial vehicles of that mark. It is also established that the defendant company is a major distributor of Japanese vehicles in Ireland and that it has a substantial share of that market. If in essence the only issue between the parties was the period of notice to which the plaintiff is entitled on termination of his franchise agreement in the events which have happened, then damages would be an adequate remedy and the plaintiff would not be entitled to the interlocutory injunction which he seeks. However, as already adverted to, one of the issues between the parties is whether in all the circumstances termination of the franchise agreement with the plaintiff amounts to an abuse by the defendant of a dominant position in the market in new vehicles imported into Ireland from Japan and constitutes an infringement of Art. 86 of the Treaty of Rome. The undisputed evidence presently before the court establishes that the defendant has a large part of the market relating to the distribution of new Japanese cars and light commercial vehicles in Ireland and that it has sought to prevent not only the plaintiff but also other main Nissan dealers from selling used vehicles imported from Japan. It is pointed out by Bellamy and Child in 'Common Market Law of Competition, 3rd ed. at p. 391, that in practice there are four steps which have to be taken to establish that a firm is in a dominant position.

> First, to define the market — the 'relevant product market' — in which conditions of competition and the market power of the dominant firm are to be assessed.
>
> Secondly, to show that the undertaking has a persistently high share of current activity in that market.
>
> Thirdly, to show that there is no real likelihood of actual or potential rivals eroding the position of the dominant firm.
>
> Fourthly, to show that the dominant position exists in the common market or a substantial part thereof.

On the information before me presently it is not possible to reach a firm conclusion as to whether or not the franchise agreement is within the contemplation of Art. 86. Further evidence by way of oral testimony is required in order to reach a conclusion on that issue. What does emerge presently is that that particular issue constitutes a serious question to be determined in due course by the trial judge. Accordingly, I have to take account of the fact that it may be decided ultimately that the agreement in question is within Art. 86 and that in the premises the defendant is not entitled to terminate its franchise contract with the plaintiff for the reasons on which it presently relies. If that is ultimately decided, then in my view damages would not be an adequate remedy. The loss of a major franchise for the sale of new vehicles might be regarded by customers or potential customers of the plaintiff as something of a stigma which would cast

8.2.3 doubt on his status in the motor trade. Even if ultimately the plaintiff succeeded in this action and the 'Nissan' franchise was restored to him by the defendant, there is a real risk that he might never recover the volume of new vehicle sales which he enjoyed previously and it would be impossible to quantify that potential loss. The stigma to which I have referred might also inhibit the plaintiff from obtaining an alternative franchise from some other distributor of comparable vehicles. Furthermore, even if it were possible to obtain an appropriate alternative franchise, it is probable that the plaintiff would require a period of years to build up the new business to the level of the original franchise prior to its termination. I am satisfied that if ultimately the trial judge decides the issue as to Art. 86 in favour of the plaintiff then damages would not be an adequate remedy and on that ground also the plaintiff has established that it is appropriate to grant him the injunction which he seeks.

The third question for consideration relates to the balance of convenience in granting or not granting the relief sought. I have already indicated that if the plaintiff's franchise agreement with the defendant is not preserved pending the trial of the action, then if he is ultimately successful on the issue raised as to Art. 86 of the Treaty of Rome, the likelihood is that he will have suffered significant unquantifiable loss and also some irreparable damage to his status in the motor trade. On the other hand, if the defendant is ultimately successful in the action, loss (if any) which it may have suffered due to the continuance of the franchise agreement up to the date of ultimate judgment is readily quantifiable and would be recoverable on foot of the plaintiff's undertaking as to damages. On this issue I also take into account that the plaintiff has undertaken to desist from the sale of second-hand 'Nissan' vehicles imported from Japan pending the outcome of the trial and that he is conducting his business in the sale of imported used Japanese vehicles under a different name and in premises which are not associated with the property where he carries on business as a main Nissan dealer.

In all the circumstances I am satisfied that the plaintiff is entitled to an interlocutory injunction restraining the defendant, its servants or agents until the trial of this action or further order from terminating or taking any or any further steps in purported termination of the franchise agreement relating to the sale of 'Nissan' vehicles entered into between the plaintiff and the defendant on or about 8 July 1980. This relief is granted, *inter alia*, on the basis of the plaintiff's undertaking that he will not sell used 'Nissan' vehicles imported from Japan and that he will continue to carry on his business in the sale of used vehicles from that country under the style or title 'Toyko Motor Co.' at premises separate and distinctive from the property where he trades in new vehicles as a main 'Nissan' dealer. Both parties shall have liberty to apply and the costs of this motion are reserved.

Solicitors for the plaintiff: *Reidy Stafford & Co.*
Solicitors for the defendant: *A. & L. Goodbody*

Mantruck Services Ltd and Manton & Co. Ltd v. Ballinlough Electrical Refrigeration Co. Ltd: Supreme Court, 30 July 1991, No. 216 of 1991* **8.2.4**

Injunction – Interlocutory – Criteria – Fair case – Alleged breach – Plaintiffs and defendant selling refrigeration units manufactured by a third party – Whether sole distributorship agreement with third party exised in favour of plaintiff – Whether sole distributorship agreement in breach of Article 85 of Treaty of Rome – Whether fair case to be tried where there is prima facie *breach – Balance of convenience – Plaintiff an established company – Defendant a competitor having a growing business – Whether injunction would commercially damage defendant's business – Whether damages could be accurately assessed in respect of commercial damage – Whether inability to assess possible damages tilted balance of convenience in favour of defendant – European Economic Community Treaty 1957, Article 85*

Tort – Passing off – Defendant representing it was sole agent within the State for the sale and supply of refrigeration units manufactured by a third party – Plaintiffs claimed sole distributorship agreement with the third party for sale of the refrigeration units – Whether defendant's actions constituted the tort of passing off – Whether defendants guilty of a conspiracy to interfere with contractual relations – Whether defendants committed tort of injurious falsehood

European Communities – Sole distributorship agreement – Plaintiff claiming sole distributorship agreement with third party for sale of third party's products within the state – Plaintiffs obtained supplies of products from subsidiary of third party – Defendant succeeded in obtaining supplies of third party's products from another subsidiary of the third party – Plaintiffs claimed defendants' actions amounted to breach of plaintiffs' rights under sole distributorship agreement – Whether sole distributorship agreement in breach of EEC Competition law – European Economic Community Treaty 1957, Article 85

Facts Article 85(1) of the European Economic Community Treaty, prohibits agreement between undertakings which prevent, restrict, or distort competition within the common market.

The plaintiffs and the defendant sold refrigeration units manufactured by a third party, C.C. Since 1980 the plaintiffs had held a distributorship agreement through two subsidiaries of C.C., C.T.R. and Frigiking. Since it commenced business in 1986 the defendant had for some time obtained C.C.'s units from the plaintiffs. In 1989 the defendant commenced, and continued thereafter, to buy C.C.'s products from Frigiking through an agent. By this time the plaintiffs were only buying from C.T.R.

By facsimile letter dated 25 April 1991, the director of sales of another subsidiary of C.C., who appeared to be in charge of overall distribution of C.C.'s units, informed the defendant that as soon as prices were agreed, he would arrange for a direct supply to it of the units, thereby enabling the defendant to by-pass their agent. The facsimile also stated that a direct supply of spare parts from C.T.R. to the defendant had been arranged. On 1 May 1991, the director of sales sent another facsimile in which he

*This report is reproduced with the kind permission of the Incorporated Council of Law Reporting for Ireland. It was first reported in [1992] 1 IR 351-360.

8.2.4 referred to the fact that the prices (which had since been agreed) would make the defendants 'absolutely competitive in Ireland'. The facsimile continued:

> We are all very anxious to cement our relationship with you and hope that this may give us that basis.

On 2 May 1991, the plaintiffs wrote to C.T.R. and referred it to a meeting in which, they alleged, an agreement had been made that they 'would continue to retain the sole agency for Ireland'. The letter went on to express dissatisfaction with the level of competition from the defendant, who, they alleged, was undercutting their prices. They asked to be informed as to where the units which the defendants were selling were coming from. On 3 May 1991, C.T.R. sent a letter to the plaintiffs denying that it had entered into any arrangement with the defendant for the sale of units. With respect to the plaintiffs' contention that the defendant had been selling C.C.'s products, C.T.R. stated it would need 'specific evidence to support this claim;.

In June 1991, the defendant circulated a letter to its customers stating that it had 'been appointed to distribute and service C.C.'s units.

On 11 July 1991, the plaintiffs issued a plenary summons seeking an interlocutory injunction and damages for conspiracy to interfere with contractual relations, passing off, injurious falsehood and other unidentified economic torts. On 15 July 1991, the High Court granted an interlocutory injunction restraining the defendants, pending the trial of the proposed action, from, *inter alia*, (i) selling, distributing, exhibiting, advertising, or offering for sale any units under C.C.'s brand name, (ii) holding itself out as an authorised dealer, or distributor of C.C.'s units.

Further orders were made the effect of which was to prevent the defendant from connecting itself in any way with the C.C. brand name prior to the trial of the action. Liberty to issue and serve third party notices on C.T.R. and Frigiking, and other orders appropriate to expediting the trial of the action were granted to the defendant.

The orders disclosed that the court was satisfied that the plaintiffs were the sole distributors of C.C. in Ireland and that the defendant had known this. The court further found that the sole distributorship agreements was valid despite the provisions of Article 85(1) of the European Economic Community Treaty 1957. Therefore on the balance of convenience and to retain the *status quo*, the court granted the interlocutory injunction, being of the view that in the event of the plaintiffs succeeding in their action, damages would not be an adequate remedy for losses suffered through competition pending the hearing of the action.

Notice of appeal from the decision of the High Court was served on 16 July 1991. On that date a formal distributorship agreement was made between the plaintiffs and C.T.R. and Frigiking.

In the Supreme Court it was argued on behalf of the defendant that the High Court was incorrect in finding that the plaintiffs had made out a fair case to be tried. It was submitted that even if the plaintiffs had a sole distributorship agreement such agreement was invalid having regard to the provisions of Article 85(1) of the European Economic Community Treaty 1957, in that the defendant as a parallel importer was directly damaged by such agreement. Further, though contending that it remained entitled to deal in C.C.'s units (which it intended to obtain from any available source including through its original agent) it conceded, for the purposes of the appeal, that it was not an appointed agent or distributor. It undertook, pending the trial of the action, not to display the C.C. logo on its documentation. It argued that the balance of convenience was in its favour in that it would suffer serious commercial damage were the interlocutory injunction continued, in respect of which damages would be an inadequate remedy. It undertook to record the profits from future sales of the units so that, in the event of the plaintiffs winning at the trial, they would recover the amount, it being the amount lost through competition from the defendant. 8.2.4

Held by the Supreme Court (Finlay CJ, Hederman and McCarthy JJ) in allowing the appeal and substituting the orders of the High Court:

(1) That were the injunction to be discharged, the plaintiffs would suffer measurable financial losses through competition from the defendant which could be recovered in the event of their winning at the trial of the action.

(2) That were the injunction to be continued, the defendant would suffer not only measurable financial losses (through competition from the plaintiffs) but also, by reason of the fact that it was a growing business which had only begun to establish itself, immeasurable commercial damage.

(3) That the impossibility of assessing the commercial damage which the defendants would suffer were the injunction to continue until the trial of the action, as opposed to the ability to assess the financial losses of the plaintiffs through competition from the defendant, tilted the balance of convenience in favour of the defendant.

(4) That though the defendant had conceded that it had the right to be described as a dealer in C.C.'s units, its concession that it was not an authorised distributor or agent of C.C. raised the inference that the plaintiffs, insofar as they maintained that they were the sole distributor, had made out a fair case to be tried.

(5) That as Article 85(1) of the European Economic Community Treaty 1957, prohibited the making of exclusive distributorship agreements, *prima facie* the plaintiffs had not in fact made out a fair case to be tried on this point. *Consten and Grundig v. Commission* [1966] ECR 299 and *Distillers Company v. Commission* [1980] ECR 2229 considered.

(6) That the order of the High Court insofar as it granted the injunctions should be substituted with the effect that the defendant should be prohibited from holding itself out as an authorised agent or distributor of C.C.'s units within the State or from utilising the C.C. name on its documentation. However, the defendant was entitled to deal in the units.

(7) That the plaintiffs should undertake to compensate the defendant for any losses which it might suffer up to the trial of the action by reason of the substituted order being made, in the event of the plaintiffs failing to win at the trial of the action.

Cases mentioned in this report

Consten and Grundig v. Commission [1966] ECR 299; [1966] CMLR 418
Distillers Company v. Commission [1980] ECR 2229; [1980] 3 CMLR 121
Duffy Group Ltd v. Quaker Oats Ltd [1989] 4 CMLR 553; [1988] OJL 49/19
Moore and Others v. Attorney General [1927] IR 569
Westman Holdings Ltd v. McCormack [1992] 1 IR 151

Appeal from the court

On 11 July 1991, the plaintiffs issued a plenary summons seeking and interlocutory injunction and damages in tort. On 15 July 1991, the High Court (Denham J) granted an interlocutory injunction whereby it was ordered that, pending the trial of the action, the defendant be restrained *inter alia*:

8.2.4 1. From selling, distributing, exhibiting, advertising, displaying, offering for sale or in any other manner dealing in transport refrigeration equipment or units under the 'Carrier' brand name within the jurisdiction of this honourable court.

2. From holding or purporting to hold itself out as an agent or distributor or dealer in transport refrigeration equipment or units under the 'Carrier' brand name within the jurisdiction of this honourable court.

3. From passing itself off as a dealer or distributor or agent of 'Carrier' products.

4. From utilising the name 'Carrier' within the State.

Further orders were made giving the defendant liberty to issue and serve third party notices and other orders appropriate to expediting the trial of the action. On 16 July 1991, notice of appeal from such orders as granted injunctions to the plaintiffs was filed. The appeal was heard by the Supreme Court (Finlay CJ, Hederman and McCarthy JJ) on 23 and 24 July 1991. The facts are fully set out in the headnote and judgment of McCarthy J, *post*.

Conor Maguire SC and Robert Hastings **for the defendant**
Hugh Geoghegan SC and Edward Walsh **for the plaintiffs**

FINLAY CJ: I agree with the judgment which is about to be delivered by McCarthy J.

HEDERMAN J: I agree also.

McCARTHY J delivered his judgment on 30 July 1991 saying: The defendant (Ballinlough) appeals against an interlocutory injunction granted in the High Court (Denham J) on 15 July whereby it was ordered that the defendant its servants or agents be restrained pending trial of this action:

1. From selling, distributing, exhibiting, advertising, displaying, offering for sale or in any other manner dealing in transport refrigeration equipment or units under the 'Carrier' brand name within the jurisdiction of this honourable court.

2. From holding or purporting to hold itself out as an agent or distributor or dealer in transport refrigeration equipment or units under the 'Carrier' brand name within the jurisdiction of this honourable court.

3. From passing itself off as a dealer or distributor or agent of 'Carrier' products.

4. From utilising the name 'Carrier' within the State.

5. From infringing the registered business name of the second named plaintiff of 'Carrier Ireland' or any such format or description likely to confuse or deceive third parties.

6. From causing, allowing or permitting the defendant to operate the telephone lines and numbers 01-343232 and 088-578481 in the name of or associated with the sales and distribution of the 'Carrier' range of products.

It was further ordered that the defendant be at liberty to issue and serve third party notices upon

Carrier Transport Refrigeration Ltd (CTR) and Carrier Global Transport Refrigeration Frigiking SA (Frigiking); further orders were made appropriate to expediting the trial of the action. 8.2.4

The facts

Since 1980 the plaintiffs have held some form of sole distributorship agreement within the State of Carrier products, such agreement coming either from Frigiking through Manton or from CTR through Mantruck. Since the making of the order under appeal, a further formal agreement has been executed on 16 July 1991. The exact nature of the pre-existing agreement is not clear but, as of today, the terms of the sole distributorship agreement are as set out in the document of that date. Ballinlough, which also handles refrigeration equipment of other manufacturers, has been in business since 1986 and has enjoyed significant success, some presumably at the expense of the plaintiffs. Having dealt initially with the plaintiffs for Carrier products, it has obtained them from a Belgian distributor (Carfrig) having made contact through Frigiking. The result has been that Mantruck has been getting its supplies from CTR, a subsidiary of Carrier Cpn, a United States company, and Ballinlough its supplies from Carfrig through Frigiking which is also a subsidiary of Carrier. The individual at the apex of this commercial triangle appears to be Mr Colin Harrison. By a fax message sent on 25 April 1991, Mr Harrison, as director of sales of Carrier Transicold, European Transcontinental Operations Sales Department, informed Ballinlough that as soon as prices were agreed direct supply from France for units would commence and that he had agreed with Mr Rod Campbell-Stanway of CTR that he would arrange a supply of spare parts from the United Kingdom. On 1 May, Mr Harrison, in a fax message, informed Ballinlough 'as you will realise these prices make you absolutely competitive in Ireland and I would very much like to hear from you as to your immediate plans. We are all very anxious to cement our relationship with you and hope that this may give us that basis'.

On 2 May, Mantruck wrote to Mr Campbell-Stanway at CTR stating, in reference to the meeting in Dublin, 'We confirmed and you agreed at the time that we would continue to retain the sole agency for Ireland . . . we find now that they are attempting to supply Carrier equipment to all our existing customers and undercutting prices with the sales strategy of 'whatever Mantruck's price is we will beat it'. Where are the units coming from?' On 3 May, Mr Campbell-Stanway for CTR by letter stated to Mantruck 'Since the meeting held in Dublin to which you refer we CTR have not entered into any arrangement either directly or indirectly with Ballinlough for the purchase of units . . . you state that they have been attempting to supply Carrier equipment and as such I would need specific evidence of supply before being in a position to investigate your claim.' The correspondence may be thought to lack candour. An affidavit sworn by Mr Campbell- Stanway was filed on this appeal. There he exhibited correspondence with Mantruck and stated 'Neither I, this deponent or anybody on behalf of Carrier Transport Ltd or Frigiking SA ever acknowledged or held out to the defendants that they could act as authorised dealers/agents in respect of the Carrier range of products in Ireland and I further categorically state that the defendants were never so appointed.' No affidavit by Mr Colin Harrison has been filed.

In June 1991, Ballinlough circulated to their customers a letter stating 'In conjunction with distributing the Norfrig bodies for Ireland, we have been appointed to distribute and service the Carrier Transicold Transport Refrigeration Units.' That was untrue and has been so acknowledged on the hearing of the appeal. Whilst Ballinlough appear to have, with the knowledge of the parent concerns, an ample supply of units and parts through its Belgian contact, it certainly has not been appointed to distribute and service the Carrier units.

The claim

Shorn of its surplusage, the claim is that Ballinlough has been selling Carrier refrigerated transport units under the Carrier brand name within the State and that it has held itself out as

8.2.4 a lawful supplier and distributor of the Carrier range of products, and has purported to be an authorised distributor or an appointed agent for Carrier products. Other allegations of what may be termed unidentified economic torts are also made. The plaintiffs claim injunctions in the form granted in the interlocutory order together with damages for passing off, for conspiracy to interfere with the contractual relations of the plaintiffs and for injurious falsehood.

On the interlocutory application, Denham J was satisfied that the plaintiff companies are the sole distributors for Carrier in Ireland and that the defendant knew that. She concluded that on the face of it the sole distributorship agreement was valid, despite the provisions of Art. 85(1) of the Treaty of Rome. Therefore, on the balance of convenience, and to retain the status quo, she granted the interlocutory injunction, being of opinion that damages would not be an adequate remedy to the plaintiffs.

The appeal

The principle governing applications of this kind for an interlocutory injunction is clear — has the plaintiff made out a fair case and where does the balance of convenience lie? Ballinlough contends that in so far as the plaintiffs or either of them had or have a sole distributorship agreement, it is in clear breach of Art. 85(1) of the Treaty of Rome and that Ballinlough, as a parallel importer, is directly damaged by the enforcement of the agreement. It is expressly conceded that Ballinlough is not an appointed agent or an authorised distributor for Carrier products, and an undertaking has been offered to the Court not to describe Balllinlough as such either in its publicity literature or otherwise. It has further undertaken not to show the Carrier logo on its headed paper. This offer of undertaking is made whilst vigorously contending that Ballinlough was entitled and remains entitled to deal in Carrier products which it lawfully obtains from its Belgian source, if not also directly from France. In that sense, it claims the right to be described as a dealer in such products. Having regard to the concession implied by the offer of the undertaking, the concession it is to be emphasised only made for the purpose of this hearing, it is not necessary to examine the claim of Mantruck, as the apparently sole authorised distributor within the State of Carrier products, to maintain this claim without the support as plaintiff by CTR or Frigiking. No such question was raised in the High Court nor does it appear in the notice of appeal.

It would appear, therefore, that in regard to the self- description, a fair case has been made and the making of a restraining order is not opposed, although reference has been made to the decision of the European Court of Justice on a logo point in Case 56/64 *Consten and Grundig* [1966] ECR 429.

The balance of convenience

I turn to this issue before the Art. 85(1) question. The latter clearly has a European law dimension. The plaintiffs are an established company having had the Carrier agency for many years; they have a nationwide distribution and service structure; no doubt it is damaged by every sale or service arrangement that Ballinlough makes in respect of Carrier products. The profits made by Ballinlough in that regard must be recorded for business and taxation reasons. At the commencement of the hearing, Ballinlough volunteered an undertaking to keep ample and accurate records of all such transactions. The other side of the coin is that Ballinlough which is later into the field would not be vulnerable to competition alone but would be significantly impeded by court order if the interlocutory injunction were to continue until trial of action. Its entire operation, of which approximately 50% involves Carrier products, would be set at risk, not by competition, but by legal restraint. In so far as that damages Ballinlough in money terms, this would be recoverable following on the undertaking already given by the plaintiffs; it would be very difficult to assess in money terms the damage to a growing business.

I then turn to the question of a fair case. In the course of argument reference has been made by both sides to a standard textbook on Common Market Law of Competition by Bellamy and Child (3rd ed, 1987); there at para. 6-103, the authors, citing *Consten and Grundig v.*

Commission [1966] ECR 299 and *Distillers v. Commission* [1980] ECR 2229 say: **8.2.4**

> It is a basic principle of Community law that an exclusive distribution agreement falls within the prohibition of Art. 85(1) when it impedes, in law or in fact, either re-export of the contract products by the distributor to other Member States or import of such products by third parties from other Member States. That is so whether the prevention of imports or exports resulted from export bans, discriminatory pricing policies or other measures. . . .

It may be that the plaintiffs can identify in law a construction whereby the prohibition of Art. 85 does not apply. The argument on this interlocutory appeal was necessarily limited. At first sight, however, it appears to me that Art. 85(1) is directly in point. In those circumstances, it would seem that the plaintiffs fall short of establishing a fair case on this second aspect of the claim for injunction; I differ from the view expressed by the learned High Court judge that on the face of it the agreement is valid. In so far as it is appropriate to take this aspect into account on the balance of convenience, there can be no question but that the balance lies in favour of the defendant/appellant. Even without that consideration, in my view the balance lies the same way. It is unnecessary to elaborate further on this aspect.

The proper order

It follows that I would allow the appeal and set aside the order of the High Court in so far as it granted the injunctions. I would substitute for that part of the order of the High Court the following order:

> 1. From holding or purporting to hold itself out as an appointed agent or authorised distributor in transport refrigeration equipment or units under the 'Carrier' brand name within the State.
>
> 2. From utilising the 'Carrier' name or logo on its headed paper or other publicity material, including invoices and statements of account.

Whilst the order made upon the *ex parte* application on 5 July 1991 recited an undertaking by the plaintiffs to abide by any order if the High Court is of opinion that the defendant should have suffered any damages by reason of the order and which the plaintiffs ought to pay this was not recited in the order under appeal. I would require such an undertaking for the purpose of this order. The granting of the injunction, despite the offer of the undertakings made by the defendant, is intended to ensure that enforcement will be by the High Court and that, in the event of the proceedings failing, the defendant will have an adequate remedy.

Solicitors for the plaintiffs: *Michael F. Butler & Co.*
Solicitors for the defendants: *Ó Cléirigh & O'Dwyer*

8.2.5 Curust Financial Services Ltd and Curust Industries Ltd v. Loewe-Lack-Werk Otto Loewe GmbH & Co., K.G. and R.S. Sales Ltd: High Court No. 4108P of 1992 (Barron J) 3 July 1992, Supreme Court, 2 November 1992*

Injunction – Interlocutory injunction – Breach of – Exclusive manufacturing and distribution agreement between plaintiffs and first defendant – Termination – Distribution agreement between defendants – Whether plaintiff's would be adequately compensated by damages – Balance of convenience – Onus of proof

European Communities – Community law – Competition law – Exclusive manufacturing and distribution agreement – Whether void having regard to the Treaty of Rome – Whether agreement one falling outside the provisions of Treaty – Size of share in relevant market – EEC Treaty, Article 85

Words and phrases – 'He who comes to equity must come with clean hands' – Turpitude – Breach of contact – Whether sufficient basis upon which to deny relief sought

Facts Article 85 of the EEC Treaty provides, *inter alia*, that 'all agreements between undertakings . . . which may affect trade between Member States and which have as their object or effect the prevention, restriction or distortion of competition within the common market' shall be automatically void.

The first defendant was the manufacturer of a rust primer paint which was the largest-selling rust primer paint on the Irish retail market. The paint was marketed in Ireland and the United Kingdom by the plaintiffs under the first defendant's trademark, for which they were registered.

In November 1986, the first defendant granted to the plaintiffs the sole and exclusive licence to manufacture, market, sell and distribute its products within Ireland and the United Kingdom. Clause 9 of the agreement provided that either party might assign, sub-licence or sub-contract all or a part of its obligations or benefits under the agreement, subject to the prior written consent of the other party. In addition, the plaintiffs undertook that they would not disclose any information about the methods of manufacture of the products in question to any third party without the consent of the first defendant.

The plaintiffs manufactured, packaged and distributed the rust primer paint in accordance with the agreement of November 1986, until the end of 1988, when manufacture was suspended. An agreement was entered into for the supply by the first defendant to the plaintiffs of the finished product, which was packaged and sold by the plaintiffs as before. This agreement was to expire at the end of December 1991, when it was envisaged that the plaintiffs would recommence manufacture of the paint. A dispute arose in relation to the terms of the agreement. On 5 October 1990, the first defendant declared that all the agreements between the parties, including the agree-

*This report is reproduced with the kind pemission of the Incorporated Council of Law Reporting for Ireland. It was first reported in [1994] 1 IR 450-473.

Editor's Note: A notification to the Competition Authority as of 1 October 1995 entitled: 'CA/50/92E—Curust Financial Services Ltd; Loewe-Lack Werke Otto GmbH & Co. EG. Exclusive Manufacturing and distribution agreement' remains to be decided upon.

ment of November 1986, were at an end, and at the end of 1991 it ceased to supply the plaintiffs with the paint. 8.2.5

In March 1992, the plaintiffs entered into an agreement with a third party for the manufacture of the paint in Ireland, and that paint was placed on the market in tins which were marked 'Loewe rust primer'. While the first defendant was notified of the plaintiffs' intention to take this course of action, its consent thereto was not sought in accordance with clause 9 of the agreement of November 1986. Meanwhile, an agreement was entered into between the defendants whereby the second defendant agreed to sell paint manufactured by the first defendant in Ireland, and in May 1992, the second defendant placed the paint on the market in tins which bore a label stating that the product contained therein was 'Loewe rust primer'.

The plaintiffs applied to the High Court for a declaration that the first defendant was bound by the terms of the agreement of November 1986, together with injunctions restraining the first defendant from, *inter alia*, granting to the second defendant the right to manufacture, sell or distribute its products, including the rust primer paint, within Ireland or the United Kingdom. Further injunctions were sought restraining the second defendant from, *inter alia*, manufacturing, distributing or selling or offering for sale in Ireland or the United Kingdom all or any of the products of the first defendant.

At the hearing of the application the defendants, while disputing the existence of the agreement of November 1986, and submitting in the alternative that the agreement had been validly terminated on 5 October 1990, accepted that the plaintiffs had established a triable argument in relation to the existence of the agreement. It was submitted further that the said agreement was *prima facie* contrary to the provisions of Article 85(1) of the EEC Treaty, and that the plaintiffs had not established a triable issue that the agreement was one to which the provision of that article did not apply; that damages would be an adequate remedy for the plaintiffs; that the plaintiffs were guilty of delay; and that the plaintiffs had disentitled themselves to injunctive relief by reason of their admitted breach of clause 9 of the 1986 agreement.

It was submitted on behalf of the plaintiffs that the onus of showing that the agreement was void having regard to the provisions of the EEC Treaty rested upon the defendants.

Held by Barron J, in granting the relief sought:

(1) That on 5 October 1990, there had been a genuine dispute between the parties in relation to the terms of the supply contract which had arisen out of events which were not of the plaintiffs' making. Before the defendants could successfully argue that they had validly terminated the 1986 agreement, it was necessary for them to show that the plaintiffs had repudiated it. The plaintiffs, however, were only required to show a triable issue that they had not by their conduct repudiated the 1986 agreement and this they had done.

(2) That it was for the defendants to raise the provisions of the EEC Treaty, but once they were raised as a matter of defence, the onus reverted to the plaintiffs to establish a triable issue as to whether they could bring themselves outside the terms of the Treaty. In determining whether the 1986 agreement was void having regard to the provisions of Article 85(1) of the EEC Treaty, the issue was whether that agreement would have an appreciable effect on trade in the product in question. On the evidence before the court, which was slight, it appeared that trade in the product

8.2.5 was small. Accordingly, the plaintiffs had established a triable issue on the point.

(3) That where the damage to the plaintiff was not readily susceptible to accurate measurement, damages were not usually an appropriate remedy, unless the damage was small. There was no difference between the tests for the adequacy of damages at the interlocutory and final stages respectively. Having regard to the difficulties involved in quantifying the effects upon trade of granting, or denying, interlocutory relief, damages would not be an adequate remedy in the instant case. *Westman Holdings Ltd v. McCormick* [1992] 1 IR 151 considered.

(4) That although the second defendant did not induce any breach of contract, but merely filled a void in the market created by the first defendant, it was more reasonable to require the maintenance of the *status quo ante* than to permit the second defendant to continue selling the paint in competition with the plaintiffs.

(5) That since the plaintiffs had asserted their right to continue manufacture of the paint with the assistance of a third party in response to the first defendant's threat to issue proceedings, the obligation to commence proceedings had rested upon the first defendant and not upon the plaintiffs, who were not, in the premises, guilty of delay. The plaintiffs' failure to seek the first defendant's consent to the manufacture of the paint by a third party was understandable, since in the circumstances it was hardly likely that such consent would have been forthcoming.

On appeal by the defendants to the Supreme Court, the defendants did not pursue the contention that the Court should hold that the 1986 agreement was void having regard to Article 85 (1) of the EEC Treaty. They did, however, submit that the trial judge's holding that there was a triable issue as to whether the agreement fell outside the provisions of that article was unsupported by the evidence. It was further submitted that if the Court came to the question of balance of convenience, then it was the date of the issue of the summons, at which time the second defendants had already placed the paint on the market, that was the material date in considering the preservation of the *status quo ante*.

In the High Court the plaintiffs had given evidence by way of an averment on affidavit to the effect that the 1986 agreement was an agreement of minor importance which had no material effect on inter-Community trade; that the plaintiffs enjoyed only a very small share of the sales of rust primer paint in the market in question; and that in the premises the agreement was not one to which the provisions of Article 85(1) of the EEC Treaty applied.

Held by the Supreme Court (Finlay CJ, O'Flaherty and Egan JJ), in allowing the appeal:

(1) That since no cross-appeal had been entered against the trial judge's ruling that the onus lay on the plaintiffs to establish a triable issue that the 1986 agreement fell outside the provisions of Article 85(1) of the EEC Treaty, the Court would proceed on the basis that the ruling was correct without making any decision in that regard. Whilst the evidential value of the averments contained in the plaintiffs' affidavit was slight, they established a triable issue which would require investigation in depth at the trial of the action.

(2) That the Court had a discretion to refuse the equitable relief of injunction where it was satisfied that the plaintiff had come before the Court otherwise than with clean hands. A denial of relief on this ground must of necessity be grounded upon an element of turpitude on the part of the plaintiff, and a mere breach of contract would not

necessarily suffice. In the instant case, it would be unreasonable for the Court to hold that a breach of contract which the plaintiffs might establish at the final hearing to have been provoked by the first defendant's wrongful repudiation of the 1986 agreement, and by its refusal to undertake not to interfere with the plaintiffs' contractual right to enter into negotiations with third parties with a view to sub-contracting the manufacture of the paint, should disentitle the plaintiffs to an injunction. 8.2.5

(3) That difficulty, as distinct from complete impossibility, of assessment was not a ground for characterising the award of damages as an inadequate remedy. The plaintiffs' loss, were they to be denied the relief sought, was exclusively a commercial loss in what had been a stable and well established market. No insuperable difficulties of quantification arose with regard to the assessment of future damages in respect of any period after the trial of the action whilst the plaintiffs were recovering their share of the market; it was reasonable to suppose that evidence could be adduced which would enable the trial judge to assess such future losses.

Per O'Flaherty J: That the crucial matter was that the plaintiff's had not been deprived of access to the market in rust primer, but rather were obliged to share it with the second defendant. Were that not the case, then damages would not be an adequate remedy and the matter would be so finely balanced as to require further enquiry into where the balance of convenience lay.

(4) That the plaintiffs had not established as a matter of probability that there was a real risk of their financial collapse were an injunction to be refused.

(5) That where damages could be quantified, where the loss was clearly a commercial loss, where there was no doubt about the capacity of the defendants to pay any damages awarded against them, and where there was no element of new or expanding business which might make quantification particularly difficult, then as a matter of principle, damages must be deemed to be an adequate remedy.

(6) That so much of the trial judge's judgment as referred to the granting of an injunction as being preferable to the awarding of damages related more correctly to the final decision as to whether the relief being claimed for a continuing breach of contract should be in the form of a permanent injunction or an assessment of damages, and was not strictly relevant to the issues which arose in an application for an interlocutory injunction.

Cases mentioned in this report

American Cyanimid Co. v. Ethicon Ltd [1975] AC 396; [1975] 2 WLR 316; [1975] 1 All ER 504; 119 SJ 135; [1975] FSR 101; [1975] RPC 513
Coatsworth v. Johnson (1886) 55 LJ QB 220
Doherty v. Allman (1878) 3 App Cas 709
Dublin Port and Docks Board v. Britannia Dredging Co. Ltd [1968] IR 136
H.B. Ice Cream Ltd v. Masterfoods Ltd [1990] 2 IR 463
Irish Shell v. Elm Motors [1984] IR 200; [1984] ILRM 595
Kerry Co-Operative Ltd v. An Bord Bainne [1991] ILRM 851
Measure Brothers Ltd v. Measures [1910] 2 Ch 248
Westman Holdings Ltd v. McCormack [1992] 1 IR 151; [1991] ILRM 833

Anthony Aston **for the plaintiffs**
Mary Finlay SC and Niall Beirne **for the first named defendant**
Mary Irvine **for the second defendant**

FINLAY CJ (Egan J concurring) delivered his judgment on 2 November 1992 saying: These are two appeals brought by the first and second named defendants against an order made in the

8.2.5 High Court by Barron J on 3 June 1992, by way of interlocutory injunction.

The proceedings arise out of a dispute originating between the plaintiffs (which I will jointly refer to as Curust), and the first-named defendant (which I will refer to as Loewe) concerning what Curust allege to be a breach by Loewe of an agreement dated 27 November 1986 made between them and Loewe, whereby Loewe granted to Curust the sole and exclusive licence to manufacture, market, sell and distribute the goods manufactured or distributed by them from time to time, in certain areas, including Ireland. The second-named defendant (which I will refer to as Sales Ltd) became involved in the action by reason of accepting appointment as a distributor from Loewe. The particular product with which this case is concerned is a product known as Loewe Rust Primer, a paint sold under the trademark of Loewe in Ireland, being a paint for application to prevent rust on objects to which it is applied. It is stated by all the parties to this action to be the major rust primer sold on the Irish market in the retail shops and in what is described as the DIY trade.

The commercial relationship between Curust and Loewe has existed for over 30 years, and prior to November 1986 it is agreed that Curust manufactured and distributed Loewe Rust Primer in Ireland, using the trade mark of Loewe under a series of licences or agreements.

The plenary summons was issued on 17 June 1992, and claimed a declaration that Loewe was bound by the terms of the agreement of 27 November 1986 and claimed a series of injunctions restraining Loewe, its servants and agents from what were claimed were breaches of that agreement. Further injunctions were sought restraining Sales Ltd from carrying out activities which would, in effect, constitute a breach of the agreement and an invasion of what is alleged to be the sole right of Curust to manufacture, sell and distribute these products. The hearing of the application for an interlocutory injunction was on affidavit, and by his order, Barron J restrained Loewe, pending the trial of the action, from appointing or purporting to appoint Sales Ltd, or any other person as a licensee for the manufacture, distribution or sale in Ireland and in other territories of all or any of the products manufactured by Loewe and from supplying Loewe Rust Primer or any other product manufactured or distributed by them to Sales Ltd, or to any other person for distribution or sale within the territory. The order further restrained Sales Ltd, pending the trial of the action, without permission of Curust, from manufacturing, distributing, selling or offering for sale in Ireland or in the United Kingdom all or any of the products manufactured or distributed by Loewe, including Loewe Rust Primer.

In the order it was provided that the relief granted to Curust was subject to their applying for consent in accordance with the exclusive manufacturing and distribution agreement of 27 November 1986, of Loewe in relation to the manufacture of the product the subject matter of the proceedings, by an agent on behalf of Curust. This condition and the issues arising in it do not form part of the subject matter of this appeal.

Whilst on the affidavits filed and on the submissions made both in the High Court and on this appeal there are a number of disputed issues of both law and fact, it is possible to trace an uncontroversial broad history of the matters arising in this appeal.

From the early 1960s Curust had a sole manufacturing and distribution agreement from Loewe which covered Loewe Rust Primer.

Up to the end of the year 1988, Curust manufactured and put into tins the Loewe Rust Primer in Ireland from formulae provided to them and in accordance with processes of which they were informed and instructed by Loewe, with a raw material sold to them by Loewe at cost price. Curust then paid to Loewe a commission on the products sold by them. At the end of 1988 Curust ceased the manufacture of the primer by reason of the fact that a change in the specification required different methods of production, and it was necessary for them to reorganise their manufacturing process in order to comply with that.

An agreement was then entered into for the supply by Loewe to Curust of the finished product of Loewe Rust Primer to be put into tins and sold and distributed in Ireland. This agreement contained terms with regard to price and with regard to credit, and disputes have arisen with regard to those precise terms. It was expressed, or appears to have been expressed to conclude at the end of the year 1991 when it was anticipated that Curust would have returned to manufacturing of the Loewe Rust Primer. **8.2.5**

During the currency of that agreement and in the years 1990 and 1991, disputes arose between the parties concerning the payments, the amount of credit to be allowed and the date of payments, and eventually Loewe purported to repudiate all agreements, including the agreement of November 1986, and stated that all agreements were at an end between the parties, and that they would, after the expiry of the agreement for the supply of the finished product at the conclusion of 1991, cease to supply any further products or raw materials to Curust.

At some time which is not identified in the affidavits Loewe entered into an agreement with Sales Ltd for the sale and distribution by them of Loewe's product in Ireland, and this was put on the market at the end of May and beginning of June of this year by Sales Ltd, under the name Durabond, in a tin similar to that used by Curust. What is in that tin is, undoubtedly, the Loewe Rust Primer and, on the evidence, it is being sold as such by the retailers to whom it has been distributed.

It was provided by clause 9 of the agreement of November 1986 that either party might assign, sub-license or sub-contract all or part of its obligations or benefits under the agreement, subject to the prior, written consent of the other party. In addition, Curust undertook, by virtue of the agreement that they would not, at any time otherwise than for the purpose of the rights given to them, including, of course, the right of sub-contracting, divulge any information in relation to the goods, methods of manufacture, price structure or the affairs, business or methods of carrying on business of Loewe without written consent of Loewe.

On the evidence before the learned trial judge, which he accepted and which is not disputed on the affidavits, in March 1992, at an interview between Mr Brocklesby representing Curust and Mr Schoening representing Loewe, Mr Brocklesby informed Mr Schoening that it was the intention of Curust, if possible, to enter into an arrangement with a third party involving the resumption of the manufacture in Ireland of the Loewe prime rust product, and he asked (according to his affidavit) Mr Schoening to give him an assurance that if he informed him of the identity of that party that he, Mr Schoening and his company, would not try and intimidate that person from entering into an arrangement. This conversation was in the light of an assertion then being made, and still being made, by Loewe that all contractual relationships between the two companies had ceased, and that Curust had no right to sell, distribute or manufacture the product of Loewe. Mr Schoening refused to give any such assurance, and, accordingly, he was not informed of the identity. Apparently, subsequent to that, an arrangement was entered into between Curust and a company known as International Coating Ltd for the manufacture of the product Loewe Rust Primer in Ireland, and that has been done and Curust has put that on the market in tins clearly marked Loewe Rust Primer.

On these broad facts, Loewe sought in the High Court to resist the making of an interlocutory injunction on a number of grounds.

1. They asserted that an agreement had not been concluded between the parties in November 1986, and in the absence of the production by Curust of the original of that agreement which they say has been mislaid, they challenged the validity of a produced copy of it.

2. They asserted that if the agreement was concluded it was void, having regard to the provisions of Article 85(1) of the Treaty of Rome, and, in the alternative, that Curust had not established a triable issue that the agreement did not have an appreciable effect upon trade and competition in the product the subject matter of the agreement so as to bring it outside the invalidity arising from the said article of the Treaty.

3. That damages would be an adequate remedy for Curust, and that, therefore, they should not be entitled to an injunction.

4. That Curust, by reason of their delay in seeking relief, were disentitled to an injunction.

5. That the admitted breach by Curust of the agreement of 1986, consisting of their entering into arrangements with a third party for the manufacture and supply of Loewe Rust Primer in Ireland without the prior written consent of Loewe, disentitled them to an injunction.

8.2.5 6. That if damages were not an adequate remedy, then the balance of convenience did not favour the granting of relief.

Judgment of the High Court
In deciding to grant the injunction Barron J reached the following conclusions concerning the issues which have been raised before him.

Dealing with the question of the conclusion of the agreement in November 1986, he held that, on the facts, there was a triable issue concerning that. Although in the notice of appeal filed by Loewe a ground was inserted appealing against that decision, this was not pursued on the hearing of the appeal before us.

With regard to the issue arising under the Treaty of Rome, the learned trial judge found as follows:

> In my view the provisions of the treaty are a matter of defence but once raised as a matter of defence the onus reverts to the plaintiffs to establish that they can bring themselves outside the terms of the treaty. On the evidence before me which is slight, it does seem to me that the amount of trade involved is small and that accordingly the plaintiffs have established a triable issue on this point.

Loewe on the hearing of this appeal did not pursue a contention that this Court could or should at this stage hold that the agreement of November 1986 was void, having regard to the provisions of Article 85(1) of the treaty, but did contend that the learned trial judge's finding that there was a triable issue as to the avoidance of that invalidity, by reason of the smallness of the trade, was not supported by the evidence.

The learned trial judge in holding that damages would not be an adequate remedy for the plaintiffs stated as follows:

> The next issue is whether or not damages would be an adequate remedy. Damages are clearly an adequate remedy if they are liquidated in circumstances where there is no particular interest in the plaintiff to maintain the right save to obtain such damages. Save in the situation envisaged by the Lord Cairns' Act where the damage is small, damages which are not readily susceptible to accurate measurements are not usually an appropriate remedy. A rich man has never been entitled to buy out the rights of a poor man just because he wishes to do so. For example the owner of a premises which would be devalued by a readily ascertainable amount cannot be forced to accept that sum in lieu of an injunction to restrain a defendant from infringing that right. In my view that in essence is what the defendants are saying here: if there is a breach of the 1986 agreement, then the first-named defendant can pay the plaintiffs the value of the business which they will lose as a result. I do not accept such a proposition.

Dealing further with the question of adequacy, the learned trial judge stated as follows:

> Where trade is involved as in this case it is always difficult to determine whether trade has been lost by reason of the failure to obtain the injunction, or whether it has been lost through other causes and equally it is difficult if the injunction is ultimately given to establish whether or not all the trade which was lost has come back and if it has not why it has not. In such cases it is also fairly notorious that people once they change over from a product which they have been using do not always return to that product when they are free to do so. Having regard to these views and to what I regard to be the general principles as to the adequacy of damages it seems to me that damages would not be an adequate remedy in the present case.

Dealing with the position of Sales Ltd, who are also appellants and who pursue most of the grounds of appeal pursued by Loewe, the learned trial judge on this issue came to the following conclusion: 8.2.5

> However, as I have indicated I do not regard damages as being an adequate remedy and this would apply as much to the second named defendant as to the plaintiffs. In the circumstances the issue seems to me as to whether or not I should preserve the *status quo ante* rather than to permit these defendants and the plaintiffs to sell the product in competition. It seems to me that it would be more reasonable to require the maintenance of the *status quo ante.*

The learned trial judge rejected the contention made in the High Court that Curust had delayed too long and would be, therefore, disentitled to the relief claimed. This ground was not pursued as a separate ground of appeal, but it was contended that it was the date of the issue of the summons, at which date they had already placed the Loewe Rust Primer under the name of Durabond on the market, that was the material date if the court came to the question of the balance of convenience, and, in particular, if the court was viewing it in the light of trying to deal with the *status quo ante.*

The learned trial judge rejected the contention that Curust by its action in subcontracting the manufacture of the rust primer in March 1992 were disentitled to an injunction.

The decision

Since Sales Ltd, in essence, supported the grounds of appeal put forward by Loewe, merely adding the factual assertion that it was unaware of any difficulty or problem arising from accepting the agreement for the distribution of the rust primer concerned, and was unaware of any subsisting licence to Curust, I deal with all the issues raised by both appellants in a single series of decisions.

(1) *Is there a triable issue concerning the exemption of the agreement of 1986 from the prohibition contained in Article 85(1) of the Treaty of Rome?*

No cross-appeal has been entered against the ruling by the learned trial judge in the High Court that once Loewe had raised the question of the prohibition contained in Article 85(1) as a defence (and presumably had shown *prima facie* that the article applied to the agreement) the onus of establishing an exemption or avoidance of that prohibition rested on Curust. That being so, without making any decision on the question, I proceed on the basis that the onus is on Curust to establish a triable issue as to whether, by reason of the smallness of the market in Ireland for the product concerned, the agreement relating to it is outside Article 85(1). Dealing with this issue which was raised in the affidavit of Mr Schoening, Mr Brocklesby in a supplemental affidavit, at paragraph 6, stated as follows:

> With regard to paragraph 11 of Mr Schoening's affidavit, I do not accept that the 1986 agreement is void, having regard to the provisions of Article 85 of the Treaty of Rome. It is my belief that the agreement is one of minor importance which does not have any material effect on inter community trade. The plaintiffs have only a tiny share of the sales of metal primer paint and rust paint in the relevant part of the territory in the community, that is, Ireland and the United Kingdom. The plaintiffs even have a very small and minor share of that part of the patent market concerned with metal priming and rust protection, being largely confined to the DIY market, rather than the steel industry. In industry generally and in transport, there are significant sales of comparable products. I am unaware of the precise turnover of the first named defendant, but even by Irish standards, and certainly by European standards, the plaintiff companies are extremely small.

8.2.5 I would accept the learned trial judge's classification of these averments as being slight evidence, but at the same time I would also accept his conclusion that they do establish a triable issue which, undoubtedly, at the hearing of the action would have to be gone into in much greater detail. In those circumstances I am satisfied that he was correct in rejecting that ground as a ground for refusing to grant an injunction.

(2) *Does a breach by Curust of the agreement of 1986, consisting of their sub-contracting the manufacture of the product without the prior written consent of Loewe, disentitle them to an injunction?*
On this issue I have come to the following conclusions. I accept that, the granting of an injunction being an equitable remedy, the court has a discretion, where it is satisfied that a person has come to the court, as it is so frequently expressed, otherwise than 'with clean hands' by that fact alone to refuse an equitable relief of injunction. It seems to me, however, that this phrase must of necessity involve an element of turpitude and cannot necessarily be equated with a mere breach of contract.

If Curust are correct in the contention which they are making, Loewe in March 1992 was still bound by the agreement of November 1986 and was prohibited by the terms of that agreement from entering into any arrangement with any other supplier to manufacture or distribute these products in Ireland, and was furthermore obliged not unreasonably to withhold its consent to the sub-contracting by Curust of any part of their rights or obligations under that agreement. It must be on the basis that Curust may succeed in establishing such a case finally at the hearing that the question of an interlocutory injunction must be viewed. If they do, then, obviously Loewe in March 1992 was quite wrong in asserting that it had no obligation to Curust, and quite wrong in proceeding, as it obviously was proceeding, to enter into arrangements with another party to sell this product in Ireland. Having regard to those facts, it seems to me that it was entirely justifiable for the representative of Curust to seek an assurance from the representative of Loewe that he would not interfere with or, presumably, intimidate any person with whom Curust were negotiating in order to sub-contract the manufacturing of this product. Having regard to that view, I conclude that it would be unreasonable to say that what may be established as a breach by Curust of the agreement not to sub-contract without prior consent, which may also be established as having been provoked by a repudiation which was wrongful on the part of Loewe, of the existence of contractual obligations subsisting under the 1986 agreement, and a refusal which would also have been wrongful to undertake not to interfere with what would appear to be almost certainly a right on the part of Curust at least to negotiate in general terms with other parties, should disentitle them to an injunction if they were otherwise entitled to it. I would, therefore, agree with the view of the learned trial judge that this did not constitute a ground for rejecting the claim for an injunction.

(3) *Are damages an adequate remedy for Curust?*
I am satisfied the following considerations apply to this issue which, in my view, is the most difficult issue arising on this appeal.

(a) No suggestion has been made that if Curust were to obtain a decree for damages arising out of Loewe's breach of contract, that Loewe would not be in a position to pay the amount of such damages.

(b) Whilst the loss likely to be sustained by Curust in the event of an injunction not being granted, is purely and simply a commercial loss arising from a diminution in trade and, therefore, ostensibly capable of quantification and assessment, they assert that there would be considerable difficulty in such quantification and a real risk that damages assessed in accordance with the evidence would not be adequate. This assertion largely consists of an assertion that whilst it might be possible to calculate between the time of the advent into the market of Sales Ltd up to the time of the successful conclusion by Curust of their action and the obtaining of a permanent injunction, the loss of trade and, therefore, the loss of profits sustained by

Curust, that it would be extremely difficult, if not impossible to quantify into the future the loss of profits which would continue to be sustained until such time as Curust recovered their pre-1992 share of the market. **8.2.5**

(c) It is asserted on behalf of Curust that if they lose the substantial market in these products, which they had up to the end of 1991 and continue to suffer that loss up to the date of the determination of the action, that having regard to the proportion which the sales of this product constituted of both their turnover and gross profits, that they might not survive as a solvent, trading unit.

To these issues the following general principles apply. The loss to be incurred by Curust if they succeed in the action and no interlocutory injunction is granted to them, is clearly and exclusively a commercial loss, in what had been, apparently, a stable and well established market. In those circumstances, *prima facie* it is a loss which should be capable of being assessed in damages both under the heading of loss actually suffered up to the date when such damages would fall to be assessed and also under the heading of probable future loss. Difficulty, as distinct from complete impossibility, in the assessment of such damages should not, in my view, be a ground for characterising the awarding of damages as an inadequate remedy.

With regard to the particular question of the assessment of damages in respect of any period after the granting of a permanent injunction to Curust while their share of the market is being recovered, it does not seem to me that insuperable difficulties of quantification could arise. The extent of the market to which Curust were accustomed before an interruption in their exclusive rights of sale and distribution is ascertainable, the quantity sold by Sales from April 1992 until the conclusion of the action would also be ascertainable, as would its value. Evidence in such a situation could surely be adduced which would permit a judge to make a reasonable forecast of the period during which Curust may suffer a continued diminution of trade and the approximate extent of that. In those circumstances, I do not see, by reason of difficulties in quantification, any ground for holding that damages are not an adequate remedy. So much of the learned trial judge's judgment on this issue as refers to Lord Cairns' Act and the question of an injunction being in many ways preferable to the awarding of damages, except in cases where damages are very small, relates more correctly, in my view, to the final decision as to whether relief being claimed for breach of contract which is continuing, should be in the form of a permanent injunction or in the form of an assessment of damages, but is not strictly relevant to the issues which arise with regard to an interlocutory injunction.

There remains the question as to whether on the evidence which was before the learned trial judge it was open to him to conclude that damages would not constitute an adequate remedy by reason of a real risk that the postponement of their payment necessarily involved until after the determination of the action, would lead to the collapse, from a financial point of view, of Curust. Although this issue was submitted in the High Court and is the subject matter of certain averments in the affidavits, it was not decided by the learned trial judge because, for other reasons, he concluded that damages would not be an adequate remedy and proceeded on to consider the balance of convenience.

The factual information contained in the affidavits which is relevant to this issue is as follows. Mr Brocklesby in his affidavit of 15 June 1992 stated as follows:

> 31. Further, although Curust sells a range of hardware products, including turpentine, brush cleaner, teak oil, penetrating oil and a range of branded locks and door catches, Curust's principal business is with Loewe Rust Primer and with white spirits. The rust primer not only gives the best margin but sales of rust primer also tend to lead to sales of all other products.
>
> 32. In the circumstances, I am extremely concerned that if R. S. Sales is allowed to continue sales of rust primer pending the hearing of the action, there will not only be very serious direct results as a result of loss of sales of Loewe Rust Primer, but there will be consequential reduction in turnover of other products. This would be likely to

8.2.5 prejudice the viability of both Curust Industries and Curust Financial Services. Loewe Rust Primer has been a mainstay of Curust's business since the early 1960s and considerable advance planning would be required to build up other aspects of the business or introduce new products to replace it without doing very great longterm damage to the viability of both the plaintiff companies. Further, the paint market is seasonal, and the prime selling period is April to October.

In the same affidavit Mr Brocklesby stated a turnover figure for the plaintiff companies of £650,000 per annum.

In paragraph 20 of Mr Schoening's affidavit, dated 25 June 1992, he stated as follows:

> I beg to refer to paragraph 32 of Mr Brocklesby's said affidavit wherein he avers that the loss of sale of Loewe Rust Primer 'would be likely to prejudice the viability of both Curust Industries and Curust Financial Services'. Having regard to both the turnover figure of £650,000 per annum given at paragraph 4 of Mr Brockleby's said affidavit and the sales figures in relation to the supply of primer by the first named defendant to the plaintiffs for the past three years I am at a loss to understand this averment.

The deponent then went on, in the form of Deutsch Marks converted to Irish pounds, to give the figure for supply of primer for the three years as follows:

1989 DM 104,828 = IR £39,155.83
1990 DM 61,814 = IR £23,089.04
1991 DM 157,920 = IR £58,987.01

He further explained that the figures were somewhat deceptive in that those for 1991 included both an item which would ordinarily have been costed into the 1990 year, and an item which would have been costed into the 1992 year. The average for the three years would appear to be slightly more than £40,000. In the supplemental affidavit of Mr Brocklesby, dated 26 June 1992, he dealt with this issue at paragraph 12, in the following terms:

> With regard to paragraph 20, I have not had time to check the figures which are given by Mr Schoening in respect of the value to Loewe of sales for the years 1989 to 1991, but I am able to say that in 1988 Curust's turnover was £575,000 of which £145,000 was attributable to Loewe Rust Primer. In 1989 the turnover was £632,000 of which £153,700 was attributable to Loewe Rust Primer. In the same year the total gross profit of Curust was £259,000 of which £88,000 (more than a quarter) is attributable to Loewe Rust Primer. In 1990 the proportion was even higher. The total gross profit was £200,606, of which £92,000 was attributable to Loewe. In 1991 the total gross profit was £220,000, of which £99,000 was attributable to Loewe.

Considering these facts, it is necessary to add in as a relevant factor that it is anticipated that the substantive action in which a statement of claim has been filed and in which, we are informed, a defence is almost ready, is likely to be heard, on the state of the High Court list, some time in the Spring of 1993. If the injunction were now set aside Curust would not be deprived of access to the market in rust primer, but rather would be obliged to share it in competition with Sales Ltd.

Since this issue on affidavit and the inferences to be drawn from it was not decided in the High Court, by reason of the learned trial judge's view that damages were for other reasons not an adequate remedy, and since I find myself in disagreement with that view, it is necessary that I should reach a conclusion on the affidavit evidence as to whether it has, as a matter of probability been established at this stage for the purpose of the interlocutory injunction that

damages would not be an adequate remedy, by reason of the real risk of the financial collapse 8.2.5
of the Curust companies. In my view, having regard to all the factors which I have outlined, there has not been established such a case as a matter of probability. No information is forthcoming about the general position of the companies with regard to their indebtedness or net assets situation. No attempt has been made to assess the probable result of competition between Curust and Sales Ltd in relation to this market for rust primer, except an averment in affidavit that Sales Ltd is underselling Curust with regard to the cost of the rust primer being offered for sale. In these circumstances, where damages can be quantified and where the loss is quite clearly a commercial loss and there is no doubt about the capacity of the defendants to pay any damages awarded against them and where there is no element of new or expanding business which may make quantification particularly difficult, as a matter of principle, I conclude that damages must be deemed to be an adequate remedy in this case, and I would therefore allow the appeal and set aside the order made in the High Court. In so doing, however, I have as a factor taken into consideration an estimate of the probable date on which this case will come on for hearing and, having regard to that fact, would request that all parties should inform the High Court of a request emanating from this Court that the proceedings should be given a speedy trial, and that both parties should expedite the completion of pleadings to facilitate such an event.

O'FLAHERTY J: It was found by the learned High Court judge and not disputed before us that Curust had made out a fair case to be tried concerning the binding effect of the 1986 agreement. Further evidence, slight though the learned trial judge held it to be at this stage of the case, went to show that there was no breach of Article 85 of the Treaty of Rome.

In general, the court's function at the hearing of the application for an interlocutory injunction is to determine whether there is a fair question to be tried and, if there is, where the balance of convenience lies. In my judgment, there are cases, however, where the breach of contract, which is the matter in issue in this case, is so clear or the party attempting to resist the application for an injunction so devoid of merits that the court should immediately provide a remedy by way of injunction: *Doherty v. Allman* (1878) 3 App Cas 709; *Dublin Port & Docks Board v. Brittania Dredging Co. Ltd* [1968] IR 136 and *Irish Shell Ltd v. Elm Motors Ltd* [1984] IR 200 at 225.

As I understand the submissions made to us it is not asserted that this is such a case. It seems to be agreed by both sides that complex questions of law and fact remain outstanding. Perhaps that is so and, therefore, I must abstain from offering any view on the strength of the case for the enforcement by Curust of the 1986 agreement.

I then turn to the question of the balance of convenience. That involves as a first inquiry whether damages would be an adequate remedy for Curust should Curust ultimately succeed at the plenary hearing. I agree with the Chief Justice's reasoning that it would be in the circumstances of this case. The crucial matter, in my judgment, is that Curust are not to be deprived of access to the market in rust primer, but rather would be obliged to share it in competition with Sales Ltd.

Were it not for that factor I would hold that the matter was so finely balanced as to require a further inquiry as to where the balance of convenience lay. I would not, except for that circumstance, regard damages as an adequate remedy. Then I would look to the *status quo ante* which I would regard as comprising the long trading relationship that existed between the parties and the equilibrium of which was affected not by any direct default by Curust in relation to the 1986 agreement (on which agreement Curust rely) but on alleged tardiness in making payments in relation to a subsidiary agreement or agreements. In that situation I would have upheld the order of the High Court. However, in the conclusion that I have reached, in concurring with the Chief Justice on the matter of the adequacy of damages, I would allow the appeal and I would join with the Chief Justice in the proposal that he has made in relation to the early disposal of the substantive case.

8.2.5 **Solicitors for the plaintiffs/respondents:** *A. & L. Goodbody*
Solicitors for the first-named defendant/appellant: *Donal O'Kelly & Co.*
Solicitors for the second-named defendant/appellant: *Peter Morrissey & Co.*

Notifications to the Competition Authority in 1991

(1 October 1991 – 31 December 1991)

Legend	Number	Title
A = Acquisition AR = Annual Report of the Competition Authority C = Certificate CL = Category Licence D = Distribution EP = Exclusive Purchasing main subject FR = Franchising IO = Iris Oifigiúil IT = *Irish Times* J = Joint Decision L = Licence LPG = Liquid Petroleum Gas M = Mentioned and Listed Category Licence MF = Motor Fuel NC = Notification changed P = Property R = Rejection/Refusal S = Decision summarised in text T = More than one subject W(N) = Withdrawn no reason given W(T) = Withdrawn because of termination of agreement	CA/1/91E	Performing Right Society (PRS); Irish Music Rights Organisation (IMRO). Copyright licence (assignment).
	CA/2/91E	PRS; Creators (Composers and Lyricists), Publishers. Assignment of copyright.
	CA/3/91E	IMRO; Users (Pubs, Cinemas, Discos, Shops etc.). Copyright licence.
	CA/4/91E	IMRO; RTE. Copyright licence.
	CA/5/91E	IMRO; Independent radio stations. Copyright licence.
	CA/6/91E	IMRO; BBC, ITA and others. Copyright licence.
	CA/7/91E	IMRO; Foreign television stations; Cablelink and other cable television companies. Copyright licence.
	CA/8/91	Thomas Nallen; Edward O'Toole (Belmullet). Non-competition clause and sale of business interest.
	CA/9/91	ACT Group plc; Kindle Group Ltd. Non-competition clause and other restrictions in sale of business interest.
	CA/10/91	Blackrock Clinic Ltd; Voluntary Health Insurance Board. Provision of health care services in return for remuneration by VHI.
	CA/11/91E	ESSO Ireland Ltd; Independent dealers. Deed of charge/mortgage.
	CA/12/91E	ESSO Ireland Ltd; Independent dealers. Dealer loan agreements.
	CA/13/91E	ESSO Ireland Ltd; Independent dealers. Dealer equipment loan agreement.
	CA/14/91E	ESSO Ireland Ltd; Independent dealers. Exclusive purchase (Solus) agreement.

Decision No.	Date	Type of Decision	Subject of Decision	Relevant Decision in Book	Number
5	30 June 1992	C		S 1.3.2	CA/1/91E
326	18 May 1994	R		S 6.3	CA/2/91E
IT 10 Nov. 1995	Intention to licence				CA/3/91E
					CA/4/91E
IT 10 Nov. 1995	Intention to licence				CA/5/91E
384	16 Dec. 1994	L			CA/6/91E
383 NC	16 Dec. 1994	L		S 6.4	CA/7/91E
1	2 April 1992	C	A	S 3.3	CA/8/91
8 NC	4 Sept. 1992	C	A	S 3.6	CA/9/91
IT 13 March 1992		W(N)			CA/10/91
4 J + 25 J	25 June 1992 + 9 July 1993 (IO)	L + M	MF	S 4.1 + CL	CA/11/91E
4 J + 25 J	25 June 1992 + 9 July 1993 (IO)	L + M	MF	S 4.1 + CL	CA/12/91E
4 J + 25 J	25 June 1992 + 9 July 1993 (IO)	L + M	MF	S 4.1 + CL	CA/13/91E
4 J + 25 J	25 June 1992 + 9 July 1993 (IO)	L + M	MF	S 4.1 + CL	CA/14/91E

Notifications to the Competitition Authority 1992

Legend	Number	Title
A = Acquisition AR = Annual Report of the Competition Authority C = Certificate CL = Category Licence D = Distribution EP = Exclusive Purchasing main subject FR = Franchising IO = Iris Oifigiúil IT = *Irish Times* J = Joint Decision L = Licence LPG = Liquid Petroleum Gas M = Mentioned and Listed Category Licence MF = Motor Fuel NC = Notification changed P = Property R = Rejection/Refusal S = Decision summarised in text T = More than one subject W(N) = Withdrawn no reason given W(T) = Withdrawn because of termination of agreement	CA/1/92	Phil Fortune; Budget Travel Ltd. Sale of business agreement with non-competition clause.
	CA/2/92E	Texaco (Ireland) Ltd; Licensees. Licence for operation of a company-owned station.
	CA/3/92E	Texaco (Ireland) Ltd; Independent Dealers. Exclusive purchase (solus) agreement.
	CA/4/92E	Texaco (Ireland) Ltd; Lessees. Lease for operation of a company-owned station.
	CA/5/92E	Texaco (Ireland) Ltd; Independent Dealers. Dealer equipment loan agreement.
	CA/6/92E	Texaco (Ireland) Ltd; Independent Dealers. Agreement to repay advances on cessation of agreement.
	CA/7/92	AGF-Irish Life Holdings plc; Church and General Insurance plc; Insurance Corporation of Ireland plc. Parent/subsidiary arrangements.
	CA/8/92E	Cambridge Investments Ltd; Mr. T.J. O'Neill; Imari Ltd; Allied Combined Trust Ltd. Restrictive covenants in a shareholding agreement.
	CA/9/92E	Association of Optometrists, Ireland. Memorandum, Articles and Code of Ethics.
	CA/10/92	Woodchester Investments plc and Woodchester Bank Ltd; UDT Bank Ltd. Sale of business agreement with non-competition clauses.
	CA/11/92	Waterford Harbour Commissioners; Bell Lines Ltd. Priority use of harbour facilities.
	CA/12/92	Athlone Travel Ltd; Michael Stein Travel Ltd. Restrictive clause in sale of business.
	CA/13/92E	Estuary Fuels Ltd; Independent dealers. Exclusive purchase (solus) agreement.
	CA/14/92E	Flogas Ireland Ltd; authorised dealers. Exclusive purchase agreement.
	CA/15/92E	Flogas Ireland Ltd; authorised distributors. Exclusive purchase agreement.
	CA/16/92E	Flogas Ireland Ltd; bulk customers. Exclusive purchase agreement.
	CA/17/92E	Capitol Holdings Ltd./Abbey Sun; customers.

NOTIFICATIONS TO THE COMPETITION AUTHORITY IN 1992

Decision No.	Date	Type of Decision	Subject of Decision	Relevant Decision in Book	Number
9 NC	14 Sept. 1992	C	A	S 3.7	CA/1/92
25 J	9 July 1993 (IO)	M	MF	CL (4.2)	CA/2/92E
25 J	9 July 1993 (IO)	M	MF	CL (4.2)	CA/3/92E
25 J	9 July 1993 (IO)	M	MF	CL (4.2)	CA/4/92E
25 J	9 July 1993 (IO)	M	MF	CL (4.2)	CA/5/92E
25 J	9 July 1993 (IO)	M	MF	CL (4.2)	CA/6/92E
2	14 May 1992	C		S 1.3.1	CA/7/92
24 NC	21 June 1993	C	A	S 3.12	CA/8/92E
16 NC	29 April 1993	C		S 1.7.2	CA/9/92E
6	4 Aug. 1992	C	A	S 3.5	CA/10/92
7	4 Aug. 1992	C			CA/11/92
3	4 June 1992	C	A	S 3.4	CA/12/92
25 J	9 July 1993 (IO)	M	MF	CL (4.8)	CA/13/92E
364	11 Nov. 1994 (IO)	R	LPG	CL (4.9)	CA/14/92E
					CA/15/92E
388					CA/16/92E
IT 10 July 1992		R			CA/17/92E

Legend	Number	Title
A = Acquisition AR = Annual Report of the Competition Authority C = Certificate CL = Category Licence D = Distribution EP = Exclusive Purchasing main subject FR = Franchising IO = Iris Oifigiúil IT = *Irish Times* J = Joint Decision L = Licence LPG = Liquid Petroleum Gas M = Mentioned and Listed Category Licence MF = Motor Fuel NC = Notification changed P = Property R = Rejection/Refusal S = Decision summarised in text T = More than one subject W(N) = Withdrawn no reason given W(T) = Withdrawn because of termination of agreement	CA/18/92E	Musgrave Ltd; licensees. SuperValu and Centra licences for retailers.
	CA/19/92E	Musgrave Ltd; franchisees. SuperValue and Centra franchises for managers.
	CA/20/92E	Musgrave Ltd; toy retailers. Franchise and joint purchasing agreement for SuperToys.
	CA/21/92	ESB Industrial Holdings Ltd; Irish Cement Ltd. Sale and purchase agreement for pulverised fuel ash.
	CA/22/92E	Irish Seafood Producers Group Ltd; Producers. Exclusive marketing agency agreement
	CA/23/92E	Book Publishers. Net Book Agreement 1957 (Members' and non-members' versions).
	CA/24/92E	Book Publishers; Book Retailers. Standard conditions of sale of net books.
	CA/25/92E	The Publishers Association. Book Club Regulations 1985.
	CA/26/92E	The Publishers Association. Library Licence.
	CA/27/92E	The Publishers Association. Book Agent's Licence.
	CA/28/92E	The Publishers Association. Quantity Book Buying Scheme.
	CA/29/92E	The Publishers Association. National Book Sale Conditions.
	CA/30/92E	The Publishers Association. Primary and Secondary School Licence.
	CA/31/92E	Falcon Holidays; Ben McArdle Ltd; Travel Agents. Exclusive dealing in package holiday insurance.
	CA/32/92E	Burmah Castrol (I) Ltd; Independent Dealers. Exclusive purchasing (solus) agreement.
	CA/33/92E	Burmah Castrol (I) Ltd; Independent Dealers. Equipment loan agreement.
	CA/34/92E	Burmah Castrol (I) Ltd; Licensees. Licence agreement.
	CA/35/92E	Burmah Castrol (I) Ltd; Lessees. Lease
	CA/36/92E	Burmah Castrol (I) Ltd; Lubricating oil resellers. Loan agreement.
	CA/37/92E	Burmah Castrol (I) Ltd; Motor fuel dealers. Hire purchase agreement.
	CA/38/92E	Burmah Castrol (I) Ltd; Independent dealers. Lubricating equipment loan agreement.
	CA/39/92E	Burmah Castrol (I) Ltd; Independent dealers. Mortgage.
	CA/40/92	Burmah Castrol (I) Ltd; Independent dealers. Exclusive purchasing (solus) agreement—new version.

NOTIFICATIONS TO THE COMPETITION AUTHORITY IN 1992

Decision No.	Date	Type of Decision	Subject of Decision	Relevant Decision in Book	Number
354 J NC	19 Sept. 1994	R	EP	S 4.5	CA/18/92E
354 J NC	19 Sept. 1994	R	EP	S 4.5	CA/19/92E
304 NC	21 April 1994	C	EP	S 4.3	CA/20/92E
390	12 April 1995	C	EP		CA/21/92
					CA/22/92E
336 J	10 June 1994	R		S 1.7.4	CA/23/92E
336 J	10 June 1994	R		S 1.7.4	CA/24/92E
336 J	10 June 1994	R		S 1.7.4	CA/25/92E
336 J	10 June 1994	R		S 1.7.4	CA/26/92E
336 J	10 June 1994	R		S 1.7.4	CA/27/92E
336 J	10 June 1994	R		S 1.7.4	CA/28/92E
336 J	10 June 1994	R		S 1.7.4	CA/29/92E
336 J	10 June 1994	R		S 1.7.4	CA/30/92E
274 NC	4 Feb. 1994	C		S 1.2	CA/31/92E
25 J	9 July 1993 (IO)	M	MF	CL (4.2)	CA/32/92E
25 J	9 July 1993 (IO)	M	MF	CL (4.2)	CA/33/92E
25 J	9 July 1993 (IO)	M	MF	CL (4.2)	CA/34/92E
25 J	9 July 1993	M	MF	CL (4.2)	CA/35/92E
324	5 May 1994	C	MF	S 4.4	CA/36/92E
361 J	13 Oct. 1994	R	MF	S 4.6	CA/37/92E
361 J	13 Oct. 1994	R	MF	S 4.6	CA/38/92E
25 J	9 July 1993 (IO)	M	MF	CL (4.2)	CA/39/92E
25 J	9 July 1993 (IO)	M	MF	CL (4.2)	CA/40/92

Legend	Number	Title
A = Acquisition AR = Annual Report of the Competition Authority C = Certificate CL = Category Licence D = Distribution EP = Exclusive Purchasing main subject FR = Franchising IO = Iris Oifigiúil IT = *Irish Times* J = Joint Decision L = Licence LPG = Liquid Petroleum Gas M = Mentioned and Listed Category Licence MF = Motor Fuel NC = Notification changed P = Property R = Rejection/Refusal S = Decision summarised in text T = More than one subject W(N) = Withdrawn no reason given W(T) = Withdrawn because of termination of agreement	CA/41/92	Burmah Castrol (I) Ltd; Independent dealers. Equipment loan agreement—new version.
	CA/42/92	Burmah Castrol (I) Ltd; Licensees. Licence agreement–new version.
	CA/43/92	Burmah Castrol (I) Ltd; Lubricating oil resellers. Loan agreement–new version.
	CA/44/92	Burmah Castrol (I) Ltd; Motor fuel dealers. Hire purchase agreement–new version.
	CA/45/92	Burmah Castrol (I) Ltd; Independent dealers. Lubricating equipment loan agreement—new version.
	CA/46/92	Burmah Castrol (I) Ltd; Independent dealers. Mortgage—new version.
	CA/47/92	Home Choice Videos (I) Ltd; Franchisees. Franchise agreement.
	CA/48/92	Cerestar UK Ltd; Betco Marketing Ltd. Sole agency agreement.
	CA/49/92E	Esso (I) Ltd; Licensees. Licence agreement.
	CA/50/92E	Curust Financial Services Ltd; Loewe-Lack-Werk Otto Loewe GmbH & Co. KG. Exclusive manufacturing and distribution agreement.
	CA/51/92	GI Corporation; General Semiconductor Industries Inc. Acquisition of business.
	CA/52/92	GI Corporation; General Semiconductor Industries Inc. Restrictive clauses in sale of business agreement.
	CA/53/92E	Crown Equipment Ireland; Hydraulic Services Ltd. Distribution agreement.
	CA/54/92	Natelex Natioal Electronics Society Ltd; Members. Franchise agreement.
	CA/55/92	Premier Tir Laighean Society Ltd; Midland Dairies Ltd; and Dealgan Milk Products Ltd; distribution contractors. Exclusive distribution agreement.
	CA/56/92	Hickson International plc; Angus Fine Chemicals Ltd. Sale of business agreement with non-competition clauses.
	CA/57/92	Edberg Ltd; D.P. Scully and Others. Sale of business and related agreements with restrictive clauses.
	CA/58/92E	NCB Group Ltd; Mr. Anthony J. Waters. Shareholders' agreement and employment contract.
	CA/59/92	Rank Xerox (Ireland) Ltd; concessionaires. Exclusive dealing agreement.
	CA/60/92	Lithographic Universal Ltd; C.C.A. Ireland Ltd. Joint venture.

NOTIFICATIONS TO THE COMPETITION AUTHORITY IN 1992

Decision No.	Date	Type of Decision	Subject of Decision	Relevant Decision in Book	Number
25 J	9 July 1993 (IO)	M	MF	CL (4.2)	CA/41/92
25 J	9 July 1993 (IO)	M	MF	CL (4.2)	CA/42/92
380 NC	15 Dec. 1994	L	EP/MF	S 4.7	CA/43/92
IT 26 Nov. 1993	17 Nov. 1993 (AR)	R			CA/44/92
IT 26 Nov. 1993	217Nov. 1993 (AR)	R			CA/45/92
25 J	9 July 1993 (IO)	M	MF	CL (4.2)	CA/46/92
	IT 10 Feb. 1995	W(T)			CA/47/92
374	21 Nov. 1994	C	Agency		CA/48/92
25 J	9 July 1993 (IO)	M	MF	CL (4.2)	CA/49/92E
					CA/50/92E
10 J	23 Oct. 1992	C	A	S 3.8	CA/51/92
10 J	23 Oct. 1992	C	A	S 3.8	CA/52/92
144 J	19 Nov. 1993 (IO)	L	D	CL (4.2)	CA/53/92E
					CA/54/92
391 NC	12 April 1995	C	D	See footnote 7 at 3.0	CA/55/92
353 NC	7 Sept. 1994	C + L	A/EP	S 3.22	CA/56/92
12 NC	29 Jan. 1993	C	A	S 3.10	CA/57/92
	IT 8 Sept. 1995	W (T)			CA/58/92E
144 J	19 Nov. 1993 (IO)	L	D	CL (5.1)	CA/59/92
					CA/60/92

Legend	Number	Title
A = Acquisition AR = Annual Report of the Competition Authority C = Certificate CL = Category Licence D = Distribution EP = Exclusive Purchasing main subject FR = Franchising IO = Iris Oifigiúil IT = *Irish Times* J = Joint Decision L = Licence LPG = Liquid Petroleum Gas M = Mentioned and Listed Category Licence MF = Motor Fuel NC = Notification changed P = Property R = Rejection/Refusal S = Decision summarised in text T = More than one subject W(N) = Withdrawn no reason given W(T) = Withdrawn because of termination of agreement	CA/61/92	NM Life Assurance Ireland Ltd; Mr. Gerard Murphy. Director's non-competition covenant.
	CA/62/92	NM Life Assurance Ireland Ltd; Ms. Brenda Murphy. Non-competition covenant by wife of director.
	CA/63/92	Castlecomer Woodwork Co. Ltd; Patrick J. Kelly. Consultancy agreement with non-competition clauses.
	CA/64/92	Flor Griffin; Teddy O'Connor. Franchise agreement.
	CA/65/92	Group 91 Architects. Shareholders' agreement for joint venture.
	CA/66/92E	Chanel Ltd; Harwood Brothers Ltd. Exclusive distribution agreement.
	CA/67/92	Harwood Brothers Ltd; retailers. Selective retail distribution agreement for Chanel products.
	CA/68/92	Beamish & Crawford Ltd; publicans. Beer supply joint venture agreement.
	CA/69/92	Toyota Ireland; motor dealers. Selective distribution agreement.
	CA/70/92E	Conoco Ireland Ltd; independent dealers. Exclusive purchase (solus) agreement.
	CA/71/92E	Conoco Ireland Ltd; consignees. Consignee agreement.
	CA/72/92E	Conoco Ireland Ltd; licensees. Licence agreement.
	CA/73/92E	Conoco Ireland Ltd; distributors. Exclusive distribution agreement.
	CA/74/92E	Cranford Properties Ltd; lessees. Restrictive covenants in shopping centre lease.
	CA/75/92E	Henry Ford & Son Ltd; motor dealers. Selective distribution.
	CA/76/92E	Darrigowen Ltd; Donnybrook Mall Ltd. Shopping centre lease.
	CA/77/92E	Texaco (Ireland) Ltd; licensees. Licence agreement (new version).
	CA/78/92E	Irish Pension Fund Property Unit Trust; Power Supermarkets Ltd. Shopping centre leases.
	CA/79/92E	IPFPUT; lessees. Shopping centre lease.
	CA/80/92E	IPFPUT; Power Supermarkets Ltd. Shopping centre lease.
	CA/81/92E	Rover Ireland Ltd; motor dealers. Selective distribution.
	CA/82/92E	Rover Ireland Ltd; Rover Ireland Finance Ltd; motor dealers. Finance agreement associated with selective distribution agreement.

NOTIFICATIONS TO THE COMPETITION AUTHORITY IN 1992

Decision No.	Date	Type of Decision	Subject of Decision	Relevant Decision in Book	Number
IT 13 Nov. 1992		R			CA/61/92
IT 13 Nov. 1992		R			CA/62/92
	IT 8 Sept. 1995	W (T)			CA/63/92
416	4 Sept. 1995	R			CA/64/92
433	20 Oct. 1995	C	Shareholder agreement		CA/65/92
IT 10 June 1994	3 June 1994 (AR)	W(T)			CA/66/92E
IT 8 July 1994	3 June 1994 (AR)	W(T)			CA/67/92
					CA/68/92
					CA/69/92
25 J	9 July 1993 (IO)	M	MF	CL (4.2)	CA/70/92E
286 NC	25 Feb. 1994	C	MF/ Agency	S 1.6.1	CA/71/92E
25 J	IT 26 Nov. 1993	L	MF	CL (4.2)	CA/72/92E
413 J NC	25 Aug. 1995	L	MF/D		CA/73/92E
197	3 Dec. 1993	C	P		CA/74/92E
					CA/75/92E
96	13 Oct. 1993	C	P		CA/76/92E
25 J	9 July 1993 (IO)	M	MF	CL (4.2)	CA/77/92E
93 J	13 Oct. 1993	C	P		CA/78/92E
162	3 Dec. 1993	C	P		CA/79/92E
161 J	3 Dec. 1993	C	P		CA/80/92E
					CA/81/92E

<table>
<tr><th>Legend</th><th>Number</th><th>Title</th></tr>
<tr><td rowspan="24">A = Acquisition
AR = Annual Report of the Competition Authority
C = Certificate
CL = Category Licence
D = Distribution
EP = Exclusive Purchasing main subject
FR = Franchising
IO = Iris Oifigiúil
IT = Irish Times
J = Joint Decision
L = Licence
LPG = Liquid Petroleum Gas
M = Mentioned and Listed Category Licence
MF = Motor Fuel
NC = Notification changed
P = Property
R = Rejection/Refusal
S = Decision summarised in text
T = More than one subject
W(N) = Withdrawn no reason given
W(T) = Withdrawn because of termination of agreement</td><td>CA/83/92E</td><td>Maxol Ltd; independent dealers. Exclusive purchase (new version)</td></tr>
<tr><td>CA/84/92E</td><td>Maxol Ltd; independent dealers. Bailment equipment agreement.</td></tr>
<tr><td>CA/85/92E</td><td>Maxol Ltd; independent dealers. Exclusive purchase.</td></tr>
<tr><td>CA/86/92E</td><td>Maxol Ltd; independent dealers. Loan agreement.</td></tr>
<tr><td>CA/87/92E</td><td>Maxol Ltd; independent dealers. Deed of charge.</td></tr>
<tr><td>CA/88/92E</td><td>Maxol Ltd; independent dealers. Hire purchase agreement.</td></tr>
<tr><td>CA/89/92E</td><td>Maxol Ltd; independent dealers. Licence agreement.</td></tr>
<tr><td>CA/90/92E</td><td>Maxol Ltd; lessees. Lease agreement.</td></tr>
<tr><td>CA/91/92E</td><td>Maxol Ltd; distributors. Exclusive distribution.</td></tr>
<tr><td>CA/92/92E</td><td>Maxol Ltd; consumers. Exclusive purchase.</td></tr>
<tr><td>CA/93/92E</td><td>Maxol Ltd; consumers. Exclusive purchase.</td></tr>
<tr><td>CA/94/92E</td><td>Maxol Ltd; consumers. Exclusive purchase.</td></tr>
<tr><td>CA/95/92E</td><td>Maxol Ltd; distributors. Licence agreement.</td></tr>
<tr><td>CA/96/92E</td><td>Maxol Ltd; distributors. Deed of charge.</td></tr>
<tr><td>CA/97/92</td><td>Patrick Kennedy; Michael and Bridget Brady. Sale of shopping centre unit.</td></tr>
<tr><td>CA/98/92</td><td>Rhone Poulenc Ireland Limited; Shell Chemicals Ireland Limited. Sale of business and exclusive distribution agreement.</td></tr>
<tr><td>CA/99/92E</td><td>The Elkinson Trust; Damien and Mary Burke. User restrictions in use of shop.</td></tr>
<tr><td>CA/100/92</td><td>Lee & Co.; Musgrave Limited. Sale of business.</td></tr>
<tr><td>CA/101/92</td><td>Esso/Artane Service Station Ltd; contractors. Exclusive purchase.</td></tr>
<tr><td>CA/102/92</td><td>Chem-Dry Ireland Ltd; franchisees. Franchise agreement.</td></tr>
<tr><td>CA/103/92</td><td>Peter Wong; The Park Shopping Centre Ltd. Shopping centre lease.</td></tr>
<tr><td>CA/104/92E</td><td>Marspel Ltd; Melcorpo Ltd; Bray Shopping centre leases.</td></tr>
<tr><td>CA/105/92E</td><td>Killiney Management Shopping Centre Company; Marspel Ltd. Shopping centre lease.</td></tr>
<tr><td>CA/106/92E</td><td>Conoco Ireland Limited; independent dealers. Exclusive purchase (image agreement).</td></tr>
<tr><td></td><td>CA/107/92E</td><td>Conoco Ireland Limited; independent dealers. Support and loan agreement.</td></tr>
<tr><td></td><td>CA/108/92E</td><td>Conoco Ireland Limited; independent dealers. Mortgage.</td></tr>
</table>

NOTIFICATIONS TO THE COMPETITION AUTHORITY IN 1992

Decision No.	Date	Type of Decision	Subject of Decision	Relevant Decision in Book	Number
					CA/82/92E
25 J	9 July 1993 (IO)	M	MF	CL (4.2)	CA/83/92E
25 J	9 July 1993 (IO)	M	MF	CL (4.2)	CA/84/92E
25 J	9 July 1993 (IO)	M	MF	CL (4.2)	CA/85/92E
25 J	9 July 1993 (IO)	M	MF	CL (4.2)	CA/86/92E
25 J	9 July 1993 (IO)	M	MF	CL (4.2)	CA/87/92E
25 J	9 July 1993 (IO)	M	MF	CL (4.2)	CA/88/92E
25 J	9 July 1993 (IO)	M	MF	CL (4.2)	CA/89/92E
25 J	9 July 1993 (IO)	M	MF	CL (4.2)	CA/90/92E
144 J	19 Nov. 1993	L	D	CL (5.1)	CA/91/92E
IT 10 Dec. 1993	7 Dec. 1993 (AR)	R			CA/92/92E
IT 10 Dec. 1993	7 Dec. 1993 (AR)	R			CA/93/92E
IT 10 Dec. 1993	7 Dec. 1993 (AR)	R			CA/94/92E
320 J + 144 J	21 April 1994	L	MF	CL (5.1)	CA/95/92E
320 J+ 144 J	21 April 1994	L	MF	CL (5.1)	CA/96/92E
238	15 Dec. 1993	C	P		CA/97/92
273	3 Feb. 1994	C	A + D	S 5.4	CA/98/92
276	4 Feb. 1994	C	P	S 7.9	CA/99/92E
147 NC	18 Nov. 1993	C	A		CA/100/92
328	19 May 1994	C	Agency	S 1.6.5	CA/101/92
IT + 372 J NC	IT 9 June 1995	L	FR	CL (4.9)	CA/102/92
113	13 Oct 1993	C	P		CA/103/92
89	5 Oct. 1993	C	P		CA/104/92E
106	13 Oct. 1993	C	P		CA/105/92E
25 J	9 July 1993 (IO)	M	MF	CL (4.2)	CA/106/92E
25 J	9 July 1993 (IO)	M	MF	CL (4.2)	CA/107/92E

Legend	Number	Title
A = Acquisition AR = Annual Report of the Competition Authority C = Certificate CL = Category Licence D = Distribution EP = Exclusive Purchasing main subject FR = Franchising IO = Iris Oifigiúil IT = *Irish Times* J = Joint Decision L = Licence LPG = Liquid Petroleum Gas M = Mentioned and Listed Category Licence MF = Motor Fuel NC = Notification changed P = Property R = Rejection/Refusal S = Decision summarised in text T = More than one subject W(N) = Withdrawn no reason given W(T) = Withdrawn because of termination of agreement	CA/109/92E	Conoco Ireland Limited; independent dealers. Franchise agreement (retail shop).
	CA/110/92E	Conoco Ireland Limited; distributors. Bulk storage loan agreement.
	CA/111/92E	Conoco Ireland Limited; distributors. Distributor depot licence.
	CA/112/92E	The Irish Times Newspapers Ltd; newsagents. Supply agreement (minimum orders).
	CA/113/92E	The Irish Times Newspapers Ltd; newsagents. Supply agreement (method of payment).
	CA/114/92E	The Irish Times Newspapers Ltd; newsagents. Supply agreement (method of payment).
	CA/115/92E	British Shoe Corporation Ltd; retailers. Concessionaire agreement.
	CA/116/92E	Levi Strauss UK Ltd; franchisees. Franchise agreement.
	CA/117/92E	Baron Craft Co. Ltd; Deerpark Ltd. Shopping centre lease.
	CA/118/92E	Irish Permanent Building Society; agents. Agency agreement.
	CA/119/92E	Irish Permanent Building Society; agents. Agency agreement.
	CA/120/92E	Patrick G. Flynn; Wardell Roberts plc. Agency agreement.
	CA/121/92E	SWIFT (Ireland). Worldwide data communications network in banking.
	CA/122/92E	Dublin Bankers Clearing Committee. Agreement on payment clearing system.
	CA/123/92E	The Eurocheque Committee. Agreement on operation of the Eurocheque system.
	CA/124/92E	The Cheque Card Committee. Agreement on cheque guarantee cards.
	CA/125/92E	The Direct Debiting Committee; originators. Agreement on direct debiting arrangements.
	CA/126/92	Irish Country Bacon Ltd; Mr Paschal Phelan. Acquisition of shares in business.
	CA/127/92	Irish Country Bacon Ltd; Mr Paschal Phelan. Sale of business.
	CA/128/92E	Esso Ireland Ltd; distributors. Exclusive distribution.
	CA/129/92E	Associated Marketing Ltd; James Halstead Ltd. Marketing services agreement.
	CA/130/92E	Associated Marketing Ltd; Waterford Carpets Ltd. Marketing services agreement.

Decision No.	Date	Type of Decision	Subject of Decision	Relevant Decision in Book	Number
					CA/109/92E
413 J NC	25 Aug. 1995	L	MF/D		CA/110/92E
413 J NC	25 Aug. 1995	L	MF/D		CA/111/92E
					CA/112/92E
					CA/113/92E
					CA/114/92E
					CA/115/92E
IT + 372 J NC	IT 9 June 1995	L	FR	CL (4.9)	CA/116/92E
54	5 Oct. 1993	C	P		CA/117/92E
IT 9 June 1995		W(N)			CA/118/92E
IT 9 June 1995		W(N)			CA/119/92E
303	7 April 1994	C	Agency	S 1.6.2	CA/120/92E
IT 10 Nov. 1995		R			CA/121/92E
	IT 13 Oct. 1995	Intention to certify			CA/122/92E
NC	IT 10 Nov. 1995	Intention to licence			CA/123/92E
427	2 Oct. 1995	C			CA/124/92E
	IT 13 Oct. 1995	Intention to certify			CA/125/92E
		W*			CA/126/92
		W*			CA/127/92
144 J	19 Nov. 1993 (IO)	L	D	CL (5.1)	CA/128/92E
IT 11 August 1995		W(T)			CA/129/92E
435	20 Oct. 1995	R	D		CA/130/92E

*The list of notifications disposed of in the 1993 and 1994 annual reports indicate that CA/126/92 and CA/127/92 were withdrawn.

Legend	Number	Title
A = Acquisition AR = Annual Report of the Competition Authority C = Certificate CL = Category Licence D = Distribution EP = Exclusive Purchasing main subject FR = Franchising IO = Iris Oifigiúil IT = *Irish Times* J = Joint Decision L = Licence LPG = Liquid Petroleum Gas M = Mentioned and ListedCategory Licence MF = Motor Fuel NC = Notification changed P = Property R = Rejection/Refusal S = Decision summarised in text T = More than one subject W(N) = Withdrawn no reason given W(T) = Withdrawn because of termination of agreement	CA/131/92E	Associated Marketing Ltd; Joseph Hamilton & Seaton Ltd. Marketing services agreement.
	CA/132/92E	Irish Telephone Rentals Ltd; subscribers. Standard contract for rental of time control equipment.
	CA/133/92E	Cable and Wireless Ltd; subscribers. Telephone rental contract.
	CA/134/92E	Irish Telephone Rentals Ltd; subscribers. Telephone rental contract.
	CA/135/92E	Irish Telephone Rentals Ltd; subscribers. Contract for rental of staff location equipment.
	CA/136/92E	Sound Systems plc; subscribers. Contract for telephone rental.
	CA/137/92E	Cable and Wireless Ltd; subscribers. Contract for rental of staff location equipment.
	CA/138/92E	Cable and Wireless Ltd; subscribers. Contract for rental of time control equipment.
	CA/139/92E	Irish Telephone Rentals Ltd; subscribers. Contract for rental of security equipment.
	CA/140/92E	Esso Ireland Ltd; Irish Tar & Bitumen Suppliers. Exclusive distribution.
	CA/141/92E	Esso Ireland Ltd; Blugas Ltd. Exclusive distribution.
	CA/142/92E	Allied Distributive Merchants Ltd; retailers. Franchise/exclusive purchase agreement.
	CA/143/92E	Bewley's Franchising Ltd; franchisees. Franchise agreement.
	CA/144/92E	Chem-Dry Irealnd Ltd; Devere Internation plc. Master franchise agreement.
	CA/145/92E	Sketchley Recognitrion Express Ltd; Mr Don Wallace. Franchise agreement.
	CA/146/92E	Response System International (Europe) Ltd; Lifetime Assurance Co. Ltd. Exclusive agreement to market insurance services.
	CA/147/92E	Irish Permanent Building Society; Prudential Life of Ireland Ltd. Insurance sales joint venture.
	CA/148/92E	Irish Handcrafts Ltd; AIB Investment Nominees, etc. Shopping centre lease.
	CA/149/92E	HSI Ltd; Hoover plc. Exclusive distribution.
	CA/150/92E	Dimpco Ltd; Sharp Electronics (UK) Ltd. Exclusive distribution.
	CA/151/92E	Frederick and Mary Cleary; Rita Power. Restrictive covenant in shop lease.
	CA/152/92	Vendo plc; Commercial Vehicle Cleaning Services Ltd. Master franchise agreement.

NOTIFICATIONS TO THE COMPETITION AUTHORITY IN 1992

Decision No.	Date	Type of Decision	Subject of Decision	Relevant Decision in Book	Number
436	20 Oct. 1995	R	D		CA/131/92E
356 J NC	19 Sept. 1994	C	D	S 5.8	CA/132/92E
356 J NC	19 Sept. 1994	C	D	S 5.8	CA/133/92E
356 J NC	19 Sept. 1994	C	D	S 5.8	CA/134/92E
356 J NC	19 Sept. 1994	C	D	S 5.8	CA/135/92E
356 J NC	19 Sept. 1994	C	D	S 5.8	CA/136/92E
356 J NC	19 Sept. 1994	C	D	S 5.8	CA/137/92E
356 J NC	19 Sept. 1994	C	D	S 5.8	CA/138/92E
356 J NC	19 Sept. 1994	C	D	S 5.8	CA/139/92E
IT + 144 J NC	IT 13 Jan. 1995	L		CL (5.1)	CA/140/92E
144 J	19 Nov. 1993 (IO)	L	D	CL (5.1)	CA/141/92E
IT 8 Oct. 1993	21 Sept. 1993 AR	R			CA/142/92E
IT + 372 J NC	IT 9 June 1995	L		CL (4.9)	CA/143/92E
IT + 372 J NC	IT 9 June 1995	L		CL (4.9)	CA/144/92E
IT 10 Nov. 1995		W(T)			CA/145/92E
					CA/146/92E
					CA/147/92E
246	15 Dec. 1993	C	P		CA/148/92E
144 J	19 Nov. 1993 (IO)	L	D	CL (5.1)	CA/149/92E
144 J	19 Nov. 1993 (IO)	L	D	CL (5.1)	CA/150/92E
277	4 Feb. 1994	C	P		CA/151/92E
					CA/152/92

<table>
<tr><th>Legend</th><th>Number</th><th>Title</th></tr>
<tr><td rowspan="23">A = Acquisition
AR = Annual Report of the Competition Authority
C = Certificate
CL = Category Licence
D = Distribution
EP = Exclusive Purchasing main subject
FR = Franchising
IO = Iris Oifigiúil
IT = Irish Times
J = Joint Decision
L = Licence
LPG = Liquid Petroleum Gas
M = Mentioned and Listed Category Licence
MF = Motor Fuel
NC = Notification changed
P = Property
R = Rejection/Refusal
S = Decision summarised in text
T = More than one subject
W(N) = Withdrawn no reason given
W(T) = Withdrawn because of termination of agreement</td><td>CA/153/92E</td><td>The Irish League of Credit Unions; ECCU Assurance Co. Ltd. Compulsory insurance requirement.</td></tr>
<tr><td>CA/154/92E</td><td>Calor Teo; Industrial customers. Standard contract for the supply of LPG.</td></tr>
<tr><td>CA/155/92E</td><td>Calor Teo; Industrial customers. Standard contract for the supply of bulk LPG.</td></tr>
<tr><td>CA/156/92E</td><td>Beaver Distribution Ltd; Balay SA. Exclusive distribution.</td></tr>
<tr><td>CA/157/92E</td><td>Beaver Distribution Ltd; Scintilla AG. Exclusive distribution.</td></tr>
<tr><td>CA/158/92E</td><td>Beaver Distribution Ltd; Robert Bosch GmbH. Trademark licence.</td></tr>
<tr><td>CA/159/92E</td><td>Beaver Distribution Ltd; Blaupunkt-Werke GmbH. Exclusive distribution.</td></tr>
<tr><td>CA/160/92E</td><td>Beaver Distribution Ltd; Robet Bosch HG GmbH. Exclusive distribution.</td></tr>
<tr><td>CA/161/92E</td><td>Beaver Distribution Ltd; Robet Bosch GmbH. Exclusive distribution.</td></tr>
<tr><td>CA/162/92E</td><td>Una and Jim Flanagan; Balally Investments Ltd. Shopping centre lease.</td></tr>
<tr><td>CA/163/92E</td><td>Burgess Galvin & Co. Ltd; Deb Group Ltd. Exclusive manufacturing licence and use of trademark.</td></tr>
<tr><td>CA/164/92E</td><td>Cybury Ltd. Shopping centre lease.</td></tr>
<tr><td>CA/165/92E</td><td>Baytrust Ltd. Street Shopping centre lease.</td></tr>
<tr><td>CA/166/92E</td><td>Dartgate Ltd; Shankill Shopping centre leases.</td></tr>
<tr><td>CA/167/92E</td><td>Ola Teo; independent dealers. Exclusive purchase.</td></tr>
<tr><td>CA/168/92E</td><td>Ola Teo; independent dealers. Equipment loan agreement.</td></tr>
<tr><td>CA/169/92E</td><td>Ola Teo; independent dealers. Bailment Equipment agreement.</td></tr>
<tr><td>CA/170/92E</td><td>Ola Teo; independent dealers. Mortgage agreement.</td></tr>
<tr><td>CA/171/92E</td><td>Ola Teo; authorised distributors. Exclusive purchase distribution agreement.</td></tr>
<tr><td>CA/172/92E</td><td>Sisk Properties Ltd; Capwell Investments Ltd; and others. Property investment agreement.</td></tr>
<tr><td>CA/173/92E</td><td>Shannon Town Centre Co. Ltd; tenants. Shopping centre lease.</td></tr>
<tr><td>CA/174/92E</td><td>D.G. Cook Ltd; franchisees. Franchise agreement.</td></tr>
<tr><td>CA/175/92E</td><td>Irish Telephone Rentals Ltd; subscribers. Contract for rental of telephones.</td></tr>
</table>

NOTIFICATIONS TO THE COMPETITION AUTHORITY IN 1992

Decision No.	Date	Type of Decision	Subject of Decision	Relevant Decision in Book	Number
IT 13 Oct. 1995		Intention to certify			CA/153/92E
IT 10 Feb. 1995		W(T)			CA/154/92E
408 NC	22 June 1995	L	LPG		CA/155/92E
144 J	19 Nov. 1993 (IO)	L	D	CL (5.1)	CA/156/92E
144 J	19 Nov. 1993 (IO)	L	D	CL (5.1)	CA/157/92E
					CA/158/92E
144 J	19 Nov. 1993 (IO)	L	D	CL (5.1)	CA/159/92E
IT + 144 J NC	IT 24 June 1994	L	D	CL (5.1)	CA/160/92E
144 J	19 Nov. 1993 (IO)	L	D	CL (5.1)	CA/161/92E
198	3 Dec. 1993	C	P		CA/162/92E
					CA/163/92E
125	13 Oct. 1993	C	P		CA/164/92E
268	15 Dec. 1993	C	P		CA/165/92E
117	13 Oct. 1993	C	P		CA/166/92E
25 J	9 July 1993 (IO)	M	MF	CL (4.2)	CA/167/92E
25 J	9 July 1993 (IO)	M	MF	CL (4.2)	CA/168/92E
25 J	9 July 1993 (IO)	M	MF	CL (4.2)	CA/169/92E
25 J	9 July 1993 (IO)	M	MF	CL (4.2)	CA/170/92E
IT 26 Nov. 1993	24 Nov. 1993 (AR)	R			CA/171/92E
					CA/172/92E
126	13 Oct. 1993	C	P		CA/173/92E
IT 10 Nov. 1995		W(T)			CA/174/92E
356 J NC	19 Sept. 1994	C	EP	S 5.8	CA/175/92E

Legend	Number	Title
A = Acquisition AR = Annual Report of the Competition Authority C = Certificate CL = Category Licence D = Distribution EP = Exclusive Purchasing main subject FR = Franchising IO = Iris Oifigiúil IT = *Irish Times* J = Joint Decision L = Licence LPG = Liquid Petroleum Gas M = Mentioned and Listed Category Licence MF = Motor Fuel NC = Notification changed P = Property R = Rejection/Refusal S = Decision summarised in text T = More than one subject W(N) = Withdrawn no reason given W(T) = Withdrawn because of termination of agreement	CA/176/92E	Irish Telephone Rentals Ltd; subscribers. Contract for rental of telephones.
	CA/177/92E	Sound Systems plc; subscribers. Contract for rental of time control equipment.
	CA/178/92E	Sound Systems plc; subscribers. Contract for telephone rental.
	CA/179/92E	Irish Telephone Rentals Ltd; subscribers. Contract for telephone rental.
	CA/180/92E	Irish Telephone Rentals Ltd; subscribers. Contract for security service rental.
	CA/181/92E	Irish Telephone Rentals Ltd; subscribers. Contract for rental of staff location equipment.
	CA/182/92E	Irish Telephone Rentals Ltd; subscribers. Contract for rental of time control equipment.
	CA/183/92E	Sound Systems plc; subscribers. Contract for rental of security service equipment.
	CA/184/92E	Irish Telephone Rentals Ltd; subscribers. Contract for rental of staff location equipment.
	CA/185/92E	Irish Telephone Rentals Ltd; subscribers. Contract for rental of security service equipment.
	CA/186/92E	Irish Telephone Rentals Ltd; subscribers. Contract for rental of time control equipment.
	CA/187/92E	Sound Systems plc; subscribers. Contract for rental of telephones.
	CA/188/92E	Sound Systems plc; subscribers. Contract for rental of telephones.
	CA/189/92E	Sound Systems plc; subscribers. Contract for rental of telephones.
	CA/190/92E	Sound Systems plc; subscribers. Contract for rental of telephones.
	CA/191/92E	Irish Telephone Rentals Ltd; subscribers. Contract for rental of staff location equipment.
	CA/192/92E	Motor Import Ltd; motor dealers. Selective distribution.
	CA/193/92E	Linabbey Ltd; Santa Anita Estates Ltd. Shopping centre lease.
	CA/194/92E	Barlo Heating Ltd; Igote Ltd; Acquisition of business.
	CA/195/92E	Player & Wills (Ireland) Ltd; Henri Wintermans Sigarenfabrieken B.V. Exclusive distribution.
	CA/196/92E	Player & Wills (Ireland) Ltd; R.J. Reynolds Tobacco (GB) Ltd. Exclusive distribution.
	CA/197/92E	Francis Spaight & Sons Ltd; Mr Seamus Canty. Shopping centre lease.

Decision No.	Date	Type of Decision	Subject of Decision	Relevant Decision in Book	Number
356 J NC	19 Sept. 1994	C	EP	S 5.8	CA/176/92E
356 J NC	19 Sept. 1994	C	EP	S 5.8	CA/177/92E
356 J NC	19 Sept. 1994	C	EP	S 5.8	CA/178/92E
356 J NC	19 Sept. 1994	C	EP	S 5.8	CA/179/92E
356 J NC	19 Sept. 1994	C	EP	S 5.8	CA/180/92E
356 J NC	19 Sept. 1994	C	EP	S 5.8	CA/181/92E
356 J NC	19 Sept. 1994	C	EP	S 5.8	CA/182/92E
356 J NC	19 Sept. 1994	C	EP	S 5.8	CA/183/92E
356 J NC	19 Sept. 1994	C	EP	S 5.8	CA/184/92E
356 J NC	19 Sept. 1994	C	EP	S 5.8	CA/185/92E
356 J NC	19 Sept. 1994	C	EP	S 5.8	CA/186/92E
356 J NC	19 Sept. 1994	C	EP	S 5.8	CA/187/92E
356 J NC	19 Sept. 1994	C	EP	S 5.8	CA/188/92E
356 J NC	19 Sept. 1994	C	EP	S 5.8	CA/189/92E
356 J NC	19 Sept. 1994	C	EP	S 5.8	CA/190/92E
356 J NC	19 Sept. 1994	C	EP	S 5.8	CA/191/92E
					CA/192/92E
123	13 Oct. 1993	C	P		CA/193/92E
IT 6 May 1994	21 April 1994 (AR)	W(N)			CA/194/92E
144 J	19 Nov. 1993 (IO)	L	D	CL (5.1)	CA/195/92E
144 J	19 Nov. 1993 (IO)	L	D	CL (5.1)	CA/196/92E
136	13 Oct. 1993	C	P		CA/197/92E

Legend	Number	Title
A = Acquisition AR = Annual Report of the Competition Authority C = Certificate CL = Category Licence D = Distribution EP = Exclusive Purchasing main subject FR = Franchising IO = Iris Oifigiúil IT = *Irish Times* J = Joint Decision L = Licence LPG = Liquid Petroleum Gas M = Mentioned and Listed Category Licence MF = Motor Fuel NC = Notification changed P = Property R = Rejection/Refusal S = Decision summarised in text T = More than one subject W(N) = Withdrawn no reason given W(T) = Withdrawn because of termination of agreement	CA/198/92E	Cassidy's Family Pharmacies Ltd; Mall Holdings Ltd. Shopping centre lease.
	CA/199/92E	The Irish Stock Exchange; member firms. Rules in relation to dealings in Irish Government securities.
	CA/200/92E	North Western Cattle Breeding Society Ltd; Mr John Doherty. Exclusive distribution.
	CA/201/92E	North Western Cattle Breeding Society Ltd; Mr Michael Tarpey. Exclusive distribution.
	CA/202/92E	North Western Cattle Breeding Society Ltd; Mr John O'Loughlin. Exclusive distribution.
	CA/203/92E	North Western Cattle Breeding Society Ltd; Mr Sean McHugh. Exclusive distribution.
	CA/204/92E	Sedgwick Dineen Ltd; Legal and Commerical Insurances Ltd; and others. Sale of Business.
	CA/205/92E	Brendan Doherty and others; Arden Heath Co. Ltd. Shopping centre lease.
	CA/206/92	Levi Strauss UK Ltd; franchisees. Franchise agreement (amended).
	CA/207/92E	Wilhelmina McCormak; Max Developments Ltd. Shopping centre lease.
	CA/208/92E	Gallaher (Dublin) Ltd; The World Professional Billiards and Snooker Association Ltd. Exclusive sports promotion agreement and restrictive covenants.
	CA/209/92E	Gallaher (Dublin) Ltd; Fintra Computers Ltd. Restrictions in computer software agreement.
	CA/210/92E	Gallaher (Dublin) Ltd; Digital Telephone Co. Ltd. Restrictions in computerised telesales system agreement.
	CA/211/92E	Mary Jo Duffy; Power Supermarkets Ltd. Shopping centre lease.
	CA/212/92E	Clada Soft Drinks Ltd; Murphy Brewery Ireland Ltd. Exclusive distribution.
	CA/213/92E	Calor Teo; authorised dealers. Exclusvie purchase.
	CA/214/92E	Marspel Ltd; Town and Country Ltd. Shopping centre lease.
	CA/215/92E	Pride & Joy Ltd; Max Developments Ltd. Shopping centre lease.
	CA/216/92E	C and A Lonergan; N.J. Kelly Ltd. Shopping centre lease.
	CA/217/92E	Wardell Roberts plc; United Biscuits Ltd. Exclusive distribution.
	CA/218/92E	Wardell Roberts plc; Williams & Humbert Ltd. Exclusive distribution.

Decision No.	Date	Type of Decision	Subject of Decision	Relevant Decision in Book	Number
250	15 Dec. 1993	C	P		CA/198/92E
335	10 June 1994	R		S 1.7.3	CA/199/92E
NC	IT 10 Nov. 1995	Intention to licence	A.I. Agent		CA/200/92E
NC	IT 10 Nov. 1995	Intention to licence	A.I. Agent		CA/201/92E
NC	IT 10 Nov. 1995	Intention to licence	A.I. Agent		CA/202/92E
NC	IT 10 Nov. 1995	Intention to licence	A.I. Agent		CA/203/92E
332	27 May 1994	R			CA/204/92E
92	13 Oct. 1993	C	P		CA/205/92E
IT + 372 J NC	IT 9 June 1995	L	FR	CL (4.9)	CA/206/92
40	5 Oct. 1993	C	P		CA/207/92E
423	12 Sept. 1995	C			CA/208/92E
					CA/209/92E
					CA/210/92E
221	15 Dec. 1993	C	P		CA/211/92E
362 J	13 Oct. 1994	C	D	S 5.10	CA/212/92E
364	11 Nov. 1994 (IO)	R	LPG	CL (4.8)	CA/213/92E
41	5 Oct. 1993	C	P		CA/214/92E
39	5 Oct. 1993	C	P		CA/215/92E
241	15 Dec. 1993	C	P		CA/216/92E
IT 6 May 1994	8 April 1994 (AR)	W(T)			CA/217/92E
144 J	19 Nov. 1993 (IO)	L	D	CL (5.1)	CA/218/92E

Legend	Number	Title
A = Acquisition AR = Annual Report of the Competition Authority C = Certificate CL = Category Licence D = Distribution EP = Exclusive Purchasing main subject FR = Franchising IO = Iris Oifigiúil IT = *Irish Times* J = Joint Decision L = Licence LPG = Liquid Petroleum Gas M = Mentioned and Listed Category Licence MF = Motor Fuel NC = Notification changed P = Property R = Rejection/Refusal S = Decision summarised in text T = More than one subject W(N) = Withdrawn no reason given W(T) = Withdrawn because of termination of agreement	CA/219/92E	Wardell Roberts plc; Lofthouse of Fleetwood Ltd. Exclusive distribution.
	CA/220/92E	Century Management; Brian Tracy Learning Systems Ltd. Exclusive distribution.
	CA/221/92E	Riga Ltd; Cork Shopping centre lease.
	CA/222/92E	Doncove Ltd; Berryvale Ltd; AIBI Nominees Ltd. Arthur's Quay Shopping centre lease.
	CA/223/92E	Riga Ltd; Douglas Shopping centre lease.
	CA/224/92E	Nitrigín Éireann Teo; Irish Fertilizer Industries Ltd. Purchase agreement for natural gas.
	CA/225/92E	Nitrigín Eireann Teo; Bord Gais Éireann. Purchase agreement for natural gas.
	CA/226/92E	Thomas Wixted; Patrick Healy. Shop lease.
	CA/227/92E	Sociedad Espanola de Automoviles de Turismo SA; Hispano Cars Ltd. Selective distribution.
	CA/228/92E	Sanbra Fyffe Ltd; Enfield Rolling Mills and others. Agreement on trade marks, agencies, purchasing, manufacture and sale of products under licence.
	CA/229/92E	R and B Kelly; Noonan Developments Ltd. Shopping centre lease.
	CA/230/92E	National Trust and Investment Co. Ltd; tenants. Shopping centre lease.
	CA/231/92E	National Trust and Investment Co. Ltd; Clondalkin Shopping centre lease.
	CA/232/92E	Irish National Insurance Co. plc; ARAG. Joint venture company.
	CA/233/92	Irish National Insurance Co. plc; GESA. Joint venture company.
	CA/234/92E	AIB Investment Nominees; The Square Shopping centre lease.
	CA/235/92E	Bookneeds Ltd; Mall Holdings Ltd. Shopping centre lease.
	CA/236/92E	Richard O'Rourke, N.J. Kelly Ltd. Shopping centre lease.
	CA/237/92E	International Coatings Ltd; Power Adhesives Ltd. Exclusive distribution.
	CA/238/92E	International Coatings Ltd; ISF Group. Exclusive distribution.
	CA/239/92E	International Coatings Ltd; System Devpack Ltd. Exclusive distribution.
	CA/240/92	Riga Ltd; Douglas Eye Care Ltd. Shopping centre lease.

NOTIFICATIONS TO THE COMPETITION AUTHORITY IN 1992

Decision No.	Date	Type of Decision	Subject of Decision	Relevant Decision in Book	Number
144 J	19 Nov. 1993 (IO)	L	D	CL (5.1)	CA/219/92E
IT 24 June 1994	16 June 1994 (AR)	W(T)			CA/220/92E
227	15 Dec. 1993	C	P		CA/221/92E
247	15 Dec. 1993	C	P		CA/222/92E
59	5 Oct. 1993	C	P		CA/223/92E
					CA/224/92E
					CA/225/92E
337	14 June 1994	C	P		CA/226/92E
					CA/227/92E
					CA/228/92E
258	15 Dec. 1993	C	P		CA/229/92E
159	3 Dec. 1993	C	P		CA/230/92E
160	3 Dec. 1993	C	P		CA/231/92E
					CA/232/92E
424	12 Sept. 1995	C			CA/233/92
213	3 Dec. 1993	C	P		CA/234/92E
134	13 Oct. 1993	C	P		CA/235/92E
71	5 Oct. 1993	C	P		CA/236/92E
144 J	19 Nov. 1993 (IO)	L	D	CL (5.1)	CA/237/92E
144 J	19 Nov. 1993 (IO)	L	D	CL (5.1)	CA/238/92E
144 J	19 Nov. 1993 (IO)	L	D	CL (5.1)	CA/239/92E
58	5 Oct. 1993	C	P		CA/240/92

<table>
<tr><th>Legend</th><th>Number</th><th>Title</th></tr>
<tr><td rowspan="23">A = Acquisition
AR = Annual Report of the Competition Authority
C = Certificate
CL = Category Licence
D = Distribution
EP = Exclusive Purchasing main subject
FR = Franchising
IO = Iris Oifigiúil
IT = Irish Times
J = Joint Decision
L = Licence
LPG = Liquid Petroleum Gas
M = Mentioned and Listed Category Licence
MF = Motor Fuel
NC = Notification changed
P = Property
R = Rejection/Refusal
S = Decision summarised in text
T = More than one subject
W(N) = Withdrawn no reason given
W(T) = Withdrawn because of termination of agreement</td><td>CA/241/92E</td><td>Edson Investments Ltd; Mullingar Shopping centre lease.</td></tr>
<tr><td>CA/242/92E</td><td>Moralto Investments Ltd; Island House Office leases.</td></tr>
<tr><td>CA/243/92E</td><td>Quality Hotels Ltd; franchisees. Franchise agreement.</td></tr>
<tr><td>CA/244/92E</td><td>Drakebury Construction Ltd; Eyre Square Shopping centre and office leases.</td></tr>
<tr><td>CA/245/92E</td><td>A & K O'Donovan; Edward Drennan; and others. Shopping centre lease.</td></tr>
<tr><td>CA/246/92E</td><td>Packaging Inks and Coatings Ltd; James Lacey. Contract of employment with director.</td></tr>
<tr><td>CA/247/92E</td><td>Johnson Brothers Ltd; United Biscuits (UK) Ltd. Exclusive distribution.</td></tr>
<tr><td>CA/248/92E</td><td>Ciga-Geigy Ireland Ltd; Cahill May Roberts Ltd. Exclusive distribution.</td></tr>
<tr><td>CA/249/92E</td><td>Ciga-Geigy Ireland Ltd; Pemberton Marketing International Ltd. Exclusive distribution.</td></tr>
<tr><td>CA/250/92E</td><td>Ciga-Geigy Ireland Ltd; SDS Biotech. Exclusive distribution.</td></tr>
<tr><td>CA/251/92E</td><td>Bandai UK Ltd; customers. Standard terms and conditions of sale.</td></tr>
<tr><td>CA/252/92E</td><td>Johnson Brothers Ltd; Combe International Ltd. Exclusive distribution.</td></tr>
<tr><td>CA/253/92E</td><td>Nissan Ireland; motor dealers. Selective distribution.</td></tr>
<tr><td>CA/254/92E</td><td>Town and Country Investments plc; Coffee Garden (Drogheda) Ltd. Shopping centre lease.</td></tr>
<tr><td>CA/255/92E</td><td>Town and Country Investments plc; Ballybrack Shopping centre lease.</td></tr>
<tr><td>CA/256/92E</td><td>Town and Country Investments plc; H. Williams (Tallaght) Ltd; 3 Guys Ltd; Ballybrack Shopping centre lease.</td></tr>
<tr><td>CA/257/92E</td><td>Town and Country Investments plc; Coffee Garden Ltd. Navan Shopping centre lease.</td></tr>
<tr><td>CA/258/92E</td><td>Irish Shell Ltd; independent dealers. Equipment loan agreement.</td></tr>
<tr><td>CA/259/92E</td><td>Irish Shell Ltd; authorised distributors. Exclusive distribution.</td></tr>
<tr><td>CA/260/92E</td><td>Irish Shell Ltd; independent dealers. Exclusive purchase.</td></tr>
<tr><td>CA/261/92E</td><td>Irish Shell Ltd; licensees. Licence agreement.</td></tr>
<tr><td>CA/262/92E</td><td>Irish Shell Ltd; independent dealers. Loan agreement for tank storage.</td></tr>
<tr><td>CA/263/92E</td><td>Irish Shell Ltd; licensees. Licence agreement.</td></tr>
</table>

NOTIFICATIONS TO THE COMPETITION AUTHORITY IN 1992

Decision No.	Date	Type of Decision	Subject of Decision	Relevant Decision in Book	Number
264	15 Dec. 1993	C	P		CA/241/92E
305	21 April 1994	C	P		CA/242/92E
372 J	9 Dec. 1994 (IO)	L	FR	CL (4.9)	CA/243/92E
232	15 Dec. 1993	C	P		CA/244/92E
224	15 Dec. 1993	C	P		CA/245/92E
IT 13 Oct. 1995			W(T)		CA/246/92E
144 J	19 Nov. 1993 (IO)	L	D	CL (5.1)	CA/247/92E
144 J	19 Nov. 1993 (IO)	L	D	CL (5.1)	CA/248/92E
144 J	19 Nov. 1993 (IO)	L	D	CL (5.1)	CA/249/92E
144 J	19 Nov. 1993 (IO)	L	D	CL (5.1)	CA/250/92E
	IT 8 Sept. 1995	W(N)			CA/251/92E
144 J	19 Nov. 1993 (IO)	L	D	CL (5.1)	CA/252/92E
					CA/253/92E
77	5 Oct. 1993	C	P		CA/254/92E
90	13 Oct. 1993	C	P		CA/255/92E
152	3 Dec. 1993	C	P		CA/256/92E
78	5 Oct. 1993	C	P		CA/257/92E
25 J	9 July 1993 (IO)	M	MF	CL (4.2)	CA/258/92E
144 J	19 Nov. 1993 (IO)	L	D	CL (5.1)	CA/259/92E
25 J	9 July 1993 (IO)	M	MF	CL (4.2)	CA/260/92E
325	5 May 1994	C	Agency	S 1.6.3	CA/261/92E
25 J	9 July 1993 (IO)	M	MF	CL (4.2)	CA/262/92E
327	19 May 1994	C	Agency	S 1.6.4	CA/263/92E

Legend	Number	Title
A = Acquisition	CA/264/92E	Irish Shell Ltd; independent dealers. Publicity allowance agreement.
AR = Annual Report of the Competition Authority	CA/265/92E	Irish Shell Ltd; licensees. Temporary licence agreement.
C = Certificate	CA/266/92E	Irish Shell Ltd; licensees. Licence agreement (old).
CL = Category Licence	CA/267/92	Burke Egan & Co. Ltd; retailers. Selective distribution agreement for Lancome products.
D = Distribution	CA/268/92	Lee Strand Co-operative Creamery Ltd; distributors. Exclusive purchase and distribution agreement.
EP = Exclusive Purchasing main subject	CA/269/92E	Europlex Holdings Ltd; Shareholders and investors. Shareholding agreement.
FR = Franchising	CA/270/92E	John Sutton, William Neville & Sons Ltd. Shopping centre lease.
IO = Iris Oifigiúil	CA/271/92E	W and A. Dolan, Richfield Investments Ltd. Shopping centre lease.
IT = *Irish Times*	CA/272/92E	Vincent Walsh; McGee Land Trust Shopping centre lease.
J = Joint Decision	CA/273/92E	P and M Byrne, L and C Power. Shopping centre lease.
L = Licence	CA/274/92E	Moulinex S.A.; Glen Dimplex; Irish Sugar plc. Joint venture.
LPG = Liquid Petroleum Gas	CA/275/92E	Asha Clothing Ltd; Firmount Ltd. Shopping centre lease.
M = Mentioned and Listed Category Licence	CA/276/92E	James Daly & Sons Ltd; Alfred Bird & Sons (Ireland) Ltd. Exclusive supply.
MF = Motor Fuel	CA/277/92E	Greencore Foodsales Ltd; Major International Ltd. Exclusive distribution.
NC = Notification changed	CA/278/92E	KP (Ireland) Ltd; UB Investments and others. Joint venture.
P = Property	CA/279/92	Combined Performance Measurement Services Ltd; William M. Mercer Fraser; Noble Lowndes Irish Pensions. Joint venture.
R = Rejection/Refusal	CA/280/92E	Súicre Éireann cpt; Farmline International Ltd. Exclusive distribution.
S = Decision summarised in text	CA/281/92E	Wessel Industries Ltd; Volex Group plc. Exclusive distribution and manufacturing licence agreement.
T = More than one subject	CA/282/92E	Wessel Industries Ltd; BICC Cables Ltd. Exclusive distribution
W(N) = Withdrawn no reason given	CA/283/92E	Tedcastle Engineering Ltd; MAN N.A. Exclusive distribution.
W(T) = Withdrawn because of termination of agreement	CA/284/92E	Tedcastle Engineering Ltd; Atlas Weyhausen GmbH. Exclusive distribution.

NOTIFICATIONS TO THE COMPETITION AUTHORITY IN 1992

Decision No.	Date	Type of Decision	Subject of Decision	Relevant Decision in Book	Number
25 J	9 July 1993 (IO)	M	MF	CL (4.2)	CA/264/92E
25 J	9 July 1993 (IO)	M	MF	CL (4.2)	CA/265/92E
25 J	9 July 1993 (IO)	M	MF	CL (4.2)	CA/266/92E
					CA/267/92
					CA/268/92
IT 13 Oct. 1995		W(N)			CA/269/92E
88	5 Oct. 1993	C	P		CA/270/92E
251	15 Dec. 1993	C	P		CA/271/92E
69	5 Oct. 1993	C	P		CA/272/92E
194	3 Dec. 1993	C	P		CA/273/92E
					CA/274/92E
119	5 Oct. 1993	C	P		CA/275/92E
					CA/276/92E
IT + 144 J	IT 4 Feb. 1994	L	D	CL (5.1)	CA/277/92E
					CA/278/92E
					CA/279/92
IT 11 Feb. 1994	4 Feb. 1994 (AR)	W(N)			CA/280/92E
					CA/281/92E
					CA/282/92E
144 J	19 Nov. 1993 (IO)	L	D	CL (5.1)	CA/283/92E
144 J	19 Nov. 1993 (IO)	L	D	CL (5.1)	CA/284/92E

Legend	Number	Title
A = Acquisition AR = Annual Report of the Competition Authority C = Certificate CL = Category Licence D = Distribution EP = Exclusive Purchasing main subject FR = Franchising IO = Iris Oifigiúil IT = *Irish Times* J = Joint Decision L = Licence LPG = Liquid Petroleum Gas M = Mentioned and Listed Category Licence MF = Motor Fuel NC = Notification changed P = Property R = Rejection/Refusal S = Decision summarised in text T = More than one subject W(N) = Withdrawn no reason given W(T) = Withdrawn because of termination of agreement	CA/285/92E	Tedcastle Engineering Ltd; Orienstein and Koppel Ltd. Exclusive distribution.
	CA/286/92E	Tedcastle Engineering Ltd; J.J. Case Europe Ltd. Exclusive distribution.
	CA/287/92	Tedcastle Engineering Ltd; Jacty Engineering Ltd. Exclusive distribution.
	CA/288/92E	The Nestle Co. Ltd; Clayton Love Distribution Ltd. Exclusive distribution.
	CA/289/92E	Thomas O'Connor; Riga Ltd. Shopping centre lease.
	CA/290/92E	Johnson Brothers Ltd; Campbell Grocery Products Ltd. Exclusive distribution.
	CA/291/92E	Johnson Brothers Ltd; Cussons (UK) Ltd. Exclusive distribution.
	CA/292/92E	H & R Johnson Tiles Ltd; Oxley Keartland & Co. Ltd. Agency agreement.
	CA/293/92E	Irish Ropes Ltd; Koltec B.V. Exclusive distribution.
	CA/294/92E	Irish Ropes Ltd; Nentec UK Ltd. Agency agreement.
	CA/295/92E	Mentec Ltd; Online Computing Ltd; shareholders. Sale of business
	CA/296/92E	Ipodec SA; GKN United Kingdom plc and others. Sale of business.
	CA/297/92E	Northern Telecom (Ireland) Ltd; Sound Systems Ltd. Exclusive distribution.
	CA/298/92E	Northern Telecom (Ireland) Ltd; Telecom Éireann Information Systems Ltd. Exclusive distribution.
	CA/299/92E	Applied Micro Electronics Ltd; Industrial Development Authority. Shareholding agreement.
	CA/300/92E	Hoorn & Winkel (Irl) Ltd; tenants. Shopping centre lease.
	CA/301/92E	Hoorn & Winkel (Irl) Ltd; Esmonde Motors Ltd. Warehouse lease with restrictive covenant.
	CA/302/92E	Cantrell and Cochrane Group Ltd; GIE Perrier Export. Exclusive distribution.
	CA/303/92E	Grants of Ireland Ltd; M & R Martini & Rossi Ltd. Exclusive distribution.
	CA/304/92E	Grants of Ireland Ltd; Marchesi L & P Antinori Distribuzione SPA. Exclusive distribution.
	CA/305/92E	Cantrell and Cochrane (Dublin) Ltd; Pepsi Co. Ltd. Exclusive bottling and distribution agreement.
	CA/306/92E	Grants of Ireland Ltd; Bewleys Ltd. Exclusive purchase.
	CA/307/92E	Federation of Irish Chemical Industries; Department of Health. Terms and conditions of supply.

NOTIFICATIONS TO THE COMPETITION AUTHORITY IN 1992

Decision No.	Date	Type of Decision	Subject of Decision	Relevant Decision in Book	Number
144 J	19 Nov. 1993 (IO)	L	D	CL (5.1)	CA/285/92E
144 J	19 Nov. 1993 (IO)	L	D	CL (5.1)	CA/286/92E
144 J	19 Nov. 1993 (IO)	L	D	CL (5.1)	CA/287/92
144 J	19 Nov. 1993 (IO)	L	D	CL (5.1)	CA/288/92E
57	5 Oct. 1993	C	P		CA/289/92E
368	28 Oct. 1994	C	D	S 5.12	CA/290/92E
IT 9 Sept. 1994	22 Aug. 1994 (AR)	W(T)			CA/291/92E
					CA/292/92E
IT + 144 J	IT 15 April 1994	L	D	CL (5.1)	CA/293/92E
397	26 April 1995	C	Agency		CA/294/92E
141	27 Oct. 1993	C	A		CA/295/92E
342	14 June 1994	R	A		CA/296/92E
					CA/297/92E
					CA/298/92E
					CA/299/92E
150	3 Dec. 1993	C	P		CA/300/92E
306	21 April 1994	C	P		CA/301/92E
IT 11 Feb. 1994	21 Dec. 1993 (AR)	W(N)			CA/302/92E
144 J	19 Nov. 1993 (IO)	L	D	CL (5.1)	CA/303/92E
144 J	19 Nov. 1993 (IO)	L	D	CL (5.1)	CA/304/92E
					CA/305/92E
					CA/306/92E
					CA/307/92E

Legend	Number	Title
A = Acquisition AR = Annual Report of the Competition Authority C = Certificate CL = Category Licence D = Distribution EP = Exclusive Purchasing main subject FR = Franchising IO = Iris Oifigiúil IT = *Irish Times* J = Joint Decision L = Licence LPG = Liquid Petroleum Gas M = Mentioned and Listed Category Licence MF = Motor Fuel NC = Notification changed P = Property R = Rejection/Refusal S = Decision summarised in text T = More than one subject W(N) = Withdrawn no reason given W(T) = Withdrawn because of termination of agreement	CA/308/92E	Hanford Ltd; tenants of Poplar House, Naas.
	CA/309/92E	Maeldoon Ltd; FBD House Limerick. Office and shop lease.
	CA/310/92E	Boreenmannu Investments Ltd; tenants of Elm Court, Cork.
	CA/311/92E	FBD Developments (Cork) Ltd; tenants. Office leases.
	CA/312/92E	Comeragh Properties Ltd; tenants. Office and shop leases.
	CA/313/92E	Power Leisure Ltd; M. and V. Grant. Shop lease.
	CA/314/92E	Power Leisure Ltd; Ventnor Developments Ltd. Shopping centre lease.
	CA/315/92E	Power Leisure Ltd; R. and M. Tweedy. Shopping centre lease.
	CA/316/92E	Irish Refrigeration Enterprises Association; Department of Agriculture and Food. Arrangements for cold storage of intervention beef.
	CA/317/92E	Irish Commercials (Sales) Ltd; Volvo Trucks (GB) Ltd. Exclusive distribution.
	CA/318/92E	Divillys (Galways Leading Butchers) Ltd; G.D. Investments Ltd. Shopping centre lease.
	CA/319/92E	Edward Dillons & Co.; Jas Hennessy & Co. Ltd. Exclusive distribution.
	CA/320/92E	Irish Nurseries Ltd; Uniplumo Ltd; Give Joy Ltd and others. Sale of business.
	CA/321/92E	Addis Ltd; Addis BV; FII plc; Gillespie & Co. Ltd. Shareholding agreement.
	CA/322/92E	Masterfoods Ltd; Shamrock Foods (Distributors) Ltd. Exclusive distribution.
	CA/323/92E	Bank of Ireland; James Davey. Shopping centre lease.
	CA/324/92E	Bank of Ireland; Townparks Ltd. Shopping centre lease.
	CA/325/92E	Bank of Ireland; Cornelscourt Shopping Centre. Shopping centre lease.
	CA/326/92E	Bank of Ireland; Institute of Chartered Accountants in Ireland. Property lease.
	CA/327/92E	Bank of Ireland; Hotel & Motel Enterprises Ltd. Property lease.
	CA/328/92E	Bank of Ireland; Beaumont Hospital Board. Property lease.
	CA/329/92E	Bank of Ireland; University College, Cork. Property lease.

NOTIFICATIONS TO THE COMPETITION AUTHORITY IN 1992

Decision No.	Date	Type of Decision	Subject of Decision	Relevant Decision in Book	Number
243	15 Dec. 1993	C	P		CA/308/92E
269	15 Dec. 1993	C	P		CA/309/92E
307	21 April 1994	C	P		CA/310/92E
358	12 Oct. 1994	C	P	S 7.16	CA/311/92E
270	15 Dec. 1993	C	P		CA/312/92E
278	4 Feb. 1994	C	P	S 7.10	CA/313/92E
157	3 Dec. 1993	C	P		CA/314/92E
86	5 Oct. 1993	C	P		CA/315/92E
					CA/316/92E
					CA/317/92E
66	5 Oct. 1993	C	P		CA/318/92E
					CA/319/92E
300	24 March 1994	C	A		CA/320/92E
	IT 8 Sept. 1995	W(T)			CA/321/92E
IT + 144 J NC	IT 10 Mar. 1995	L	D	CL (5.1)	CA/322/92E
248	15 Dec. 1993	C	P		CA/323/92E
67	5 Oct. 1993	C	P		CA/324/92E
50	5 Oct. 1993	C	P		CA/325/92E
291	10 March 1994	C	P		CA/326/92E
292	10 March 1994	C	P		CA/327/92E
IT 8 July 1994	24 June 1994 (AR)	W(T)			CA/328/92E
IT 18 Mar. 1994	10 March 1994 (AR)	W(T)			CA/329/92E

Legend	Number	Title
A = Acquisition AR = Annual Report of the Competition Authority C = Certificate CL = Category Licence D = Distribution EP = Exclusive Purchasing main subject FR = Franchising IO = Iris Oifigiúil IT = *Irish Times* J = Joint Decision L = Licence LPG = Liquid Petroleum Gas M = Mentioned and Listed Category Licence MF = Motor Fuel NC = Notification changed P = Property R = Rejection/Refusal S = Decision summarised in text T = More than one subject W(N) = Withdrawn no reason given W(T) = Withdrawn because of termination of agreement	CA/330/92E	Bank of Ireland; University of Limerick. Property lease.
	CA/331/92E	Bank of Ireland; University College, Galway. Property lease.
	CA/332/92E	Bank of Ireland; University College, Dublin. Property lease.
	CA/333/92E	Bank of Ireland; Salix Trust. Shopping centre lease.
	CA/334/92E	Bank of Ireland; Cranford Properties Ltd. Shopping centre lease.
	CA/335/92E	Bank of Ireland; Waterford Shopping Centre. Shopping centre lease.
	CA/336/92E	Bank of Ireland; Royal Liver Trustees Ltd. Shopping centre lease.
	CA/337/92E	Bank of Ireland; Superior Drug Co. Ltd. Shopping centre lease.
	CA/338/92E	Bank of Ireland; Richfield Investments Ltd. Shopping centre lease.
	CA/339/92E	Bank of Ireland; Drakebury Construction Ltd. Shopping centre lease.
	CA/340/92E	Bank of Ireland; Spearhill Co. Ltd. Shopping centre lease.
	CA/341/92E	Cartron Management Co. Ltd; Stateline Enterprises Ltd. Shopping centre lease.
	CA/342/92E	Manzares Ltd; Dorcorn Developments Ltd. Shopping centre lease.
	CA/343/92E	Morningford Ltd,; Mahon Shopping Centre tenants. Shopping centre lease.
	CA/344/92E	Colthurst Ltd; Elan Corporation plc. Research and development licence agreement.
	CA/345/92E	Percom Ltd; CHL Software Ltd. Exclusive distribution.
	CA/346/92E	Wexford Mushrooms Ltd; mushroom growers. Production licence.
	CA/347/92E	Carbury Mushrooms Ltd; mushroom growers. Production licence.
	CA/348/92E	Allied Combined Trust Ltd; Etos International Ltd. Shareholding agreement.
	CA/349/92E	ACT Ltd; Barronstown Bloodstock shareholders. Shareholding agreement.
	CA/350/92E	ACT Ltd; B.M. Browne Holdings Ltd; and shareholders. Shareholding agreement.
	CA/351/92E	ACT Ltd; Emdee Holdings Ltd. and shareholders. Shareholding agreement.

NOTIFICATIONS TO THE COMPETITION AUTHORITY IN 1992

Decision No.	Date	Type of Decision	Subject of Decision	Relevant Decision in Book	Number
289	10 March 1994	C	P	S 7.13	CA/330/92E
290	10 March 1994	C	P		CA/331/92E
288	10 March 1994	C	P	S 7.12	CA/332/92E
202	3 Dec. 1993	C	P		CA/333/92E
195	3 Dec. 1993	C	P		CA/334/92E
84	5 Oct. 1993	C	P		CA/335/92E
127	13 Oct. 1993	C	P		CA/336/92E
109	13 Oct. 1993	C	P		CA/337/92E
76	5 Oct. 1993	C	P		CA/338/92E
233	15 Dec. 1993	C	P		CA/339/92E
75	5 Oct. 1993	C	P		CA/340/92E
83	5 Oct. 1993	C	P		CA/341/92E
47	5 Oct. 1993	C	P		CA/342/92E
225	15 Dec. 1993	C	P		CA/343/92E
					CA/344/92E
					CA/345/92E
IT 13 Oct. 1995		W(N)			CA/346/92E
IT 13 Oct. 1995		W(T)			CA/347/92E
IT 11 August 1995		W(N)			CA/348/92E
IT 9 Dec. 1994	5 Dec. 1994 (AR)	W(T)			CA/349/92E
					CA/350/92E
IT 8 Sept. 1995		W(N)			CA/351/92E

Legend	Number	Title
A = Acquisition AR = Annual Report of the Competition Authority C = Certificate CL = Category Licence D = Distribution EP = Exclusive Purchasing main subject FR = Franchising IO = Iris Oifigiúil IT = *Irish Times* J = Joint Decision L = Licence LPG = Liquid Petroleum Gas M = Mentioned and Listed Category Licence MF = Motor Fuel NC = Notification changed P = Property R = Rejection/Refusal S = Decision summarised in text T = More than one subject W(N) = Withdrawn no reason given W(T) = Withdrawn because of termination of agreement	CA/352/92E	ACT Ltd; Screen Scene (I) Ltd. and shareholders. Shareholding agreement.
	CA/353/92E	ACT Ltd; My Kinda Baile Ltd and My Kinda Town Group Ltd. Shareholding agreement.
	CA/354/92E	ACT Ltd; Odenberg Investments Ltd. and shareholders. Shareholding agreement.
	CA/355/92E	ACT Ltd; Colour Books Ltd; John Harold. Shareholding agreement.
	CA/356/92E	ACT Ltd; Dublin Plant Hire; John Kelly. Shareholding agreement.
	CA/357/92E	ACT Ltd; Top Shot Publishers Ltd; shareholders. Shareholding agreement.
	CA/358/92E	AIB Capital Markets plc; Data Packaging Ltd; Coster Corporation; Nadcorp Ltd. Shareholding agreement.
	CA/359/92E	AIB Capital Markets plc; Woodland Investments Group Ltd; shareholders. Shareholding agreement.
	CA/360/92E	Allied Venture Capital Ltd; Trintech Ltd; shareholders. Shareholding agreement.
	CA/361/92E	First Venture Fund Ltd; Matrix Group; shareholders. Shareholding agreement.
	CA/362/92E	ACT Ltd; Odenberg Investments Ltd; shareholders. Shareholding agreement.
	CA/363/92E	ACT Ltd; Odenberg Investments Ltd; shareholders. Shareholding agreement.
	CA/364/92E	Sigma Wireless Communications Ltd; Motorola Ireland Ltd. Sale of business.
	CA/365/92E	Sigma Wireless Communications Ltd; Motorola Ireland Ltd. Exclusive distribution.
	CA/366/92E	Sigma Wireless Communications Ltd; Motorola Ltd. Exclusive distribution
	CA/367/92E	Prontaprint plc; franchisees. Franchise agreement, with property lease.
	CA/368/92E	Prontaprint plc; franchisees. Franchise agreement.
	CA/369/92E	ITT World Directories Inc; ITT Information Services Ltd; Golden Pages Ltd. Technical services agreement.
	CA/370/92E	Bord Telecom Éireann; Golden Pages Ltd. Directory agreement (copyright)
	CA/371/92E	Bord Telecom Éireann; ITT World Directories Inc. Share option agreement
	CA/372/92E	Bord Telecom Éireann; Golden Pages Ltd. ITT World Directories (Ireland) Ltd. M.V. Murphy; Bord Telecom Éireann. Shareholding agreement

NOTIFICATIONS TO THE COMPETITION AUTHORITY IN 1992

Decision No.	Date	Type of Decision	Subject of Decision	Relevant Decision in Book	Number
IT 8 Sept. 1995		W(N)			CA/352/92E
IT 13 Jan. 1995	23 Dec. 1994 (AR)	W(T)			CA/353/92E
					CA/354/92E
428 NC	19 Oct. 1995	C	Share subscription		CA/355/92E
IT 13 Jan. 1995		W(T)			CA/356/92E
IT 11 August 1995		W(N)			CA/357/92E
IT 10 Nov. 1995		W(N)			CA/358/92E
IT 8 Sept. 1995		W(N)			CA/359/92E
IT 8 Sept. 1995		W(N)			CA/360/92E
IT 13 Jan. 1995	23 Dec. 1994 (AR)	W(T)			CA/361/92E
IT 10 Nov. 1995		W(N)			CA/362/92E
IT 10 Nov. 1995		W(N)			CA/363/92E
143	27 Oct. 1993	C	A + D	S 5.3	CA/364/92E
144 J	19 Nov. 1993 (IO)	L	D	CL (5.1)	CA/365/92E
IT + 144 J	IT 9 Sept. 1994	L	D	CL (5.1)	CA/366/92E
IT + 372 J NC	IT 9 June 1995	L	FR	CL (4.9)	CA/367/92E
IT 6 May 1994	29 Apr. 1994 (AR)	W(T)			CA/368/92E
					CA/369/92E
					CA/370/92E
					CA/371/92E
					CA/372/92E

Legend	Number	Title
A = Acquisition AR = Annual Report of the Competition Authority C = Certificate CL = Category Licence D = Distribution EP = Exclusive Purchasing main subject FR = Franchising IO = Iris Oifigiúil IT = *Irish Times* J = Joint Decision L = Licence LPG = Liquid Petroleum Gas M = Mentioned and Listed Category Licence MF = Motor Fuel NC = Notification changed P = Property R = Rejection/Refusal S = Decision summarised in text T = More than one subject W(N) = Withdrawn no reason given W(T) = Withdrawn because of termination of agreement	CA/373/92E	Combined Insurance Company of Ireland Ltd; agents. Agency agreement.
	CA/374/92E	Combined Life Assurance Co. of Ireland Ltd; agents. Agency agreement.
	CA/375/92E	Independent Newspapers Marketing Ltd; wholesalers and newsagents. Newspaper distribution agreement.
	CA/376/92E	Independent Newspapers Marketing Ltd; wholesalers and newsagents. Newspaper distribution agreement-transfer.
	CA/377/92E	Chevron Mineral Corporation of Ireland; Ivernia West plc. Joint venture.
	CA/378/92E	Amax Exploration (Ireland) Inc; Chevron Mineral Corporation of Ireland; Preussag AM. Joint venture.
	CA/379/92E	Guinness Ireland Ltd; United Breweries International Ltd. Exclusive production and distribution.
	CA/380/92E	Guinness Ireland Ltd; Anheuser-Busch Inc. Exclusive production and distribution.
	CA/381/92E	Guinness Ireland Ltd; Furstlich Furstenbergische Brauerie KG. Exclusive production and distribution.
	CA/382/92E	Natureline Ltd; Jackel International Ltd. Exclusive distribution.
	CA/383/92E	Minister for Tourism, Transport and Communications; Dublin Airport Restaurants Ltd. Exclusive right to provide catering services.
	CA/384/92E	Salix Trust Ltd; tenants. Stillorgan Shopping centre lease.
	CA/385/92E	Salix Trust Ltd; Lorcan O'Sullivan. Shopping centre lease.
	CA/386/92	Salix Trust Ltd; Huntbrook Ltd. Shopping centre lease.
	CA/387/92E	Unifood Ltd; DCL (Yeast) Ltd. Exclusive distribution.
	CA/388/92E	Unifood Ltd; John F. Renshaw and Co. Ltd. Exclusive distribution.
	CA/389/92E	Irish Biscuits Ltd; Jacobs Suchard Manufacturing GmbH. Exclusive distribution.
	CA/390/92E	Unifood Ltd; DCA Industries Ltd. Exclusive distribution.
	CA/391/92	Premier Dairies Group; distributors. Exclusive purchase agreement—country agency.
	CA/392/92	Premier Dairies Group; distributors. Exclusive purchase agreement—city agency.

NOTIFICATIONS TO THE COMPETITION AUTHORITY IN 1992

Decision No.	Date	Type of Decision	Subject of Decision	Relevant Decision in Book	Number
					CA/373/92E
IT 9 June 1995		W(T)			CA/374/92E
					CA/375/92E
					CA/376/92E
IT 13 Oct. 1995		W(T)			CA/377/92E
IT 13 Oct. 1995		W(T)			CA/378/92E
					CA/379/92E
					CA/380/92E
					CA/381/92E
144 J	19 Nov. 1993 (IO)	L	D	CL (5.1)	CA/382/92E
					CA/383/92E
203	3 Dec. 1993	C	P		CA/384/92E
201	3 Dec. 1993	C	P		CA/385/92E
200	3 Dec. 1993	C	P		CA/386/92
144 J	19 Nov. 1993 (IO)	L	D	CL (5.1)	CA/387/92E
IT + 144 J	IT 27 May 1994	L	D	CL (5.1)	CA/388/92E
IT + 144 J NC	IT 6 May 1994	L	D	CL (5.1)	CA/389/92E
144 J	19 Nov. 1993 (IO)	L	D	CL (5.1)	CA/390/92E
					CA/391/92
					CA/392/92

<table>
<tr><th>Legend</th><th>Number</th><th>Title</th></tr>
<tr><td rowspan="22">A = Acquisition
AR = Annual Report of the Competition Authority
C = Certificate
CL = Category Licence
D = Distribution
EP = Exclusive Purchasing main subject
FR = Franchising
IO = Iris Oifigiúil
IT = Irish Times
J = Joint Decision
L = Licence
LPG = Liquid Petroleum Gas
M = Mentioned and Listed Category Licence
MF = Motor Fuel
NC = Notification changed
P = Property
R = Rejection/Refusal
S = Decision summarised in text
T = More than one subject
W(N) = Withdrawn no reason given
W(T) = Withdrawn because of termination of agreement</td><td>CA/393/92</td><td>Dealgan Milk Products Ltd; distributors. Exclusive purchase agreement—Dealgan agency.</td></tr>
<tr><td>CA/394/92E</td><td>Premier Dairies Group; contractors. Exclusive distribution.</td></tr>
<tr><td>CA/395/92E</td><td>Power Leisure Ltd; Shannon Town Centre Co. Ltd. Shopping centre lease.</td></tr>
<tr><td>CA/396/92E</td><td>Masterfoods Ltd; J.C. Distribution Ltd. Exclusive distribution.</td></tr>
<tr><td>CA/397/92E</td><td>Masterfoods Ltd; Valley Ice Cream (Distribution) Ltd. Exclusive distribution.</td></tr>
<tr><td>CA/398/92E</td><td>Masterfoods Ltd; Valley Ice Cream (Ireland) Ltd. Delamont Ltd; shareholders. Non-disposal of shares agreement.</td></tr>
<tr><td>CA/399/92E</td><td>Cahill May Roberts. Societe d'Hygiene Dermatologique de Vichy. Joint venture.</td></tr>
<tr><td>CA/400/92E</td><td>Michael Breen; GD Investments (Galway) Ltd. Shopping centre lease.</td></tr>
<tr><td>CA/401/92E</td><td>Michael Breen; GD Investments (Galway) Ltd. Shopping centre lease.</td></tr>
<tr><td>CA/402/92E</td><td>Iveco Fiat SpA; McCormick MacNaughton Commercials Ltd. Selective distribution.</td></tr>
<tr><td>CA/403/92E</td><td>Cahill May Roberts Ltd; Societe d'Hygiene Dermatologique de Vichy. Shareholding agreement.</td></tr>
<tr><td>CA/404/92E</td><td>Cahill May Roberts Ltd; Merck Sharp & Dohme Ltd. Exclusive distribution.</td></tr>
<tr><td>CA/405/92E</td><td>Cahill May Roberts Ltd; Mates Healthcare Ltd. Exclusive distribution.</td></tr>
<tr><td>CA/406/92E</td><td>Cahill May Roberts Ltd; Kabipharmacia Ireland Ltd. Exclusive distribution.</td></tr>
<tr><td>CA/407/92E</td><td>Cahill May Roberts Ltd; Janssen Pharmaceuticals Ltd. Exclusive distribution.</td></tr>
<tr><td>CA/408/92E</td><td>Cahill May Roberts Ltd; Fisons Pharmaceuticals Ireland Ltd. Exclusive distribution.</td></tr>
<tr><td>CA/409/92E</td><td>Cahill May Roberts Ltd; Fisons Pharmaceuticals Ireland Ltd. Exclusive distribution.</td></tr>
<tr><td>CA/410/92E</td><td>Cahill May Roberts Ltd; Elizabeth Arden Ltd. Exclusive distribution.</td></tr>
<tr><td>CA/411/92E</td><td>Cahill May Roberts Ltd; Eurocetus UK Ltd. Exclusive distribution.</td></tr>
<tr><td>CA/412/92E</td><td>Cahill May Roberts Ltd; Cilag Ltd. Exclusive distribution.</td></tr>
<tr><td>CA/413/92E</td><td>Cahill May Roberts Ltd; Clini-Med Ltd. Exclusive distribution.</td></tr>
</table>

NOTIFICATIONS TO THE COMPETITION AUTHORITY IN 1992

Decision No.	Date	Type of Decision	Subject of Decision	Relevant Decision in Book	Number
					CA/393/92
392 NC	12 April 1995	C	D	See footnote 7 at 3.0	CA/394/92E
56	5 Nov. 1993	C	P		CA/395/92E
144 J	19 Nov. 1993 (IO)	L	D	CL (5.1)	CA/396/92E
					CA/397/92E
					CA/398/92E
					CA/399/92E
234	15 Dec. 1993	C	P		CA/400/92E
235	15 Dec. 1993	C	P		CA/401/92E
	IT 8 Sept. 1995	W(T)			CA/402/92E
					CA/403/92E
IT 8 July 1994	24 June 1994 (AR)	W(T)			CA/404/92E
144 J	19 Nov. 1993 (IO)	L	D	CL (5.1)	CA/405/92E
144 J	19 Nov. 1993 (IO)	L	D	CL (5.1)	CA/406/92E
					CA/407/92E
144 J	19 Nov. 1993 (IO)	L	D	CL (5.1)	CA/408/92E
					CA/409/92E
IT 10 June 1994	1 June 1994 (AR)	W(T)			CA/410/92E
144 J	19 Nov. 1993 (IO)	L	D	CL (5.1)	CA/411/92E
IT 6 May 1994	25 April 1994 (AR)	W(T)			CA/412/92E
144 J	19 Nov. 1993 (IO)	L	D	CL (5.1)	CA/413/92E

Legend	Number	Title
A = Acquisition AR = Annual Report of the Competition Authority C = Certificate CL = Category Licence D = Distribution EP = Exclusive Purchasing main subject FR = Franchising IO = Iris Oifigiúil IT = *Irish Times* J = Joint Decision L = Licence LPG = Liquid Petroleum Gas M = Mentioned and ListedCategory Licence MF = Motor Fuel NC = Notification changed P = Property R = Rejection/Refusal S = Decision summarised in text T = More than one subject W(N) = Withdrawn no reason given W(T) = Withdrawn because of termination of agreement	CA/414/92E	Cahill May Roberts Ltd; Merck Sharp & Dohme Ltd (Agvet). Exclusive distribution.
	CA/415/92E	Mall Holdings Ltd; John Ryan. Shopping centre lease.
	CA/416/92E	Wiggins Teape Ireland Ltd; KNP Fine Paper Division. Exclusive distribution.
	CA/417/92E	Wiggins Teape Ireland Ltd; Collins Stationery and Diary Ltd. Exclusive distribution.
	CA/418/92E	Irish Ropes Ltd; Mobil Plastics Europe Inc. Exclusive distribution.
	CA/419/92E	Irish Ropes Ltd; Rosenlew Emballage AB. Exclusive distribution.
	CA/420/92E	Irish Ropes Ltd; Werra Plastics GmbH. Exclusive distribution.
	CA/421/92E	Irish Ropes Ltd; Itipack S.R.L. Exclusive distribution.
	CA/422/92E	Irish Ropes Ltd; British Twines Ltd. Exclusive distribution.
	CA/423/92	Green Property plc; Northside Shopping centre lease.
	CA/424/92	Green Property plc; Waterford Shopping centre lease.
	CA/425/92	Adidas (Ireland) Ltd; The Football Association of Ireland. Exclusive right to use FAI crest, and supply of sportswear.
	CA/426/92E	Adidas (Ireland) Ltd; sports stars. Agreement to sponsor a 'Sports Star'.
	CA/427/92E	Murphy Brewery Ireland Ltd; Clada Mineral Water Co. Ltd. Exclusive distribution.
	CA/428/92	Murphy Brewery Ireland Ltd; distributors. Exclusive distribution.
	CA/429/92E	AIB Investment Managers Ltd; Foxfield Mushrooms Ltd; shareholders. Shareholding agreement.
	CA/430/92E	AIB Investment Managers Ltd; Kingspan Veha Ltd; shareholders. Shareholding agreement.
	CA/431/92E	AIB Investment Managers Ltd; Prince of Wales Hotel Ltd; shareholders. Shareholding agreement.
	CA/432/92E	AIB Investment Managers Ltd; Seletar Ltd; shareholders. Shareholding agreement.
	CA/433/92E	AIB Investment Managers Ltd; Baroncastle Ltd; Ramville Ltd; Green Isle Foods Ltd. Shareholding agreement.
	CA/434/92E	Allied Irish Banks plc; Veritate Ltd. Shopping centre lease.

NOTIFICATIONS TO THE COMPETITION AUTHORITY IN 1992

Decision No.	Date	Type of Decision	Subject of Decision	Relevant Decision in Book	Number
144 J	19 Nov. 1993 (IO)	L	D	CL (5.1)	CA/414/92E
249	15 Dec. 1993	C	P		CA/415/92E
144 J	19 Nov. 1993 (IO)	L	D	CL (5.1)	CA/416/92E
144 J	19 Nov. 1993 (IO)	L	D	CL (5.1)	CA/417/92E
144 J	19 Nov. 1993 (IO)	L	D	CL (5.1)	CA/418/92E
144 J	19 Nov. 1993 (IO)	L	D	CL (5.1)	CA/419/92E
144 J	19 Nov. 1993 (IO)	L	D	CL (5.1)	CA/420/92E
144 J	19 Nov. 1993 (IO)	L	D	CL (5.1)	CA/421/92E
144 J	19 Nov. 1993 (IO)	L	D	CL (5.1)	CA/422/92E
283	4 Feb. 1994	C	P	S 7.11	CA/423/92
85	5 Oct. 1993	C	P		CA/424/92
421	12 Sept. 1995	C			CA/425/92
422	12 Sept. 1995	C			CA/426/92E
362 J	13 Oct. 1994	C	D	S 5.10	CA/427/92E
363	13 Oct. 1994	C	D		CA/428/92
IT 12 May 1995		W(T)			CA/429/92E
IT 13 April 1995		W(T)			CA/430/92E
396	25 April 1995	C	A		CA/431/92E
					CA/432/92E
399	27 April 1995	C	A		CA/433/92E
192	3 Dec. 1993	C	P		CA/434/92E

<table>
<tr><th>Legend</th><th>Number</th><th>Title</th></tr>
<tr><td rowspan="22">A = Acquisition
AR = Annual Report of the Competition Authority
C = Certificate
CL = Category Licence
D = Distribution
EP = Exclusive Purchasing main subject
FR = Franchising
IO = Iris Oifigiúil
IT = Irish Times
J = Joint Decision
L = Licence
LPG = Liquid Petroleum Gas
M = Mentioned and Listed Category Licence
MF = Motor Fuel
NC = Notification changed
P = Property
R = Rejection/Refusal
S = Decision summarised in text
T = More than one subject
W(N) = Withdrawn no reason given
W(T) = Withdrawn because of termination of agreement</td><td>CA/435/92</td><td>AIB plc. Shannon Aerospace. Property lease.</td></tr>
<tr><td>CA/436/92E</td><td>AIB plc. Dublin City University. Property lease.</td></tr>
<tr><td>CA/437/92E</td><td>AIB plc. Douglas Developments Ltd. Shopping centre lease.</td></tr>
<tr><td>CA/438/92E</td><td>AIB plc. Mastercard International Inc. Licence and interchange fee agreement.</td></tr>
<tr><td>CA/439/92E</td><td>AIB plc. Eurocard International SA. Licence and interchange fee agreement.</td></tr>
<tr><td>CA/440/92E</td><td>AIB Finance Ltd; General Motors Distribution Ireland Ltd. Car purchase financing agreement.</td></tr>
<tr><td>CA/441/92E</td><td>Statoil Ireland Ltd; independent dealers. Exclusive purchase.</td></tr>
<tr><td>CA/442/92E</td><td>Statoil Ireland Ltd; independent dealers. Equipment loan agreement.</td></tr>
<tr><td>CA/443/92E</td><td>Statoil Ireland Ltd; independent dealers. Hire purchase agreement.</td></tr>
<tr><td>CA/444/92E</td><td>Statoil Ireland Ltd; independent dealers. Exclusivity payment agreement.</td></tr>
<tr><td>CA/445/92E</td><td>Statoil Ireland Ltd; licensees. Licence and trial licence.</td></tr>
<tr><td>CA/446/92E</td><td>Statoil Ireland Ltd; lessees. Lease.</td></tr>
<tr><td>CA/447/92E</td><td>Statoil Ireland Ltd; independent dealers. Deed of charge/mortgage.</td></tr>
<tr><td>CA/448/92E</td><td>Statoil Ireland Ltd; distributors. Exclusive distribution.</td></tr>
<tr><td>CA/449/92E</td><td>Statoil Ireland Ltd; distributors. Distibutor loan agreements.</td></tr>
<tr><td>CA/450/92E</td><td>Statoil Ireland Ltd; distributors and commerical customers. Equipment loan agreement.</td></tr>
<tr><td>CA/451/92E</td><td>Statoil Ireland Ltd; independent dealers. Franchise agreement for BP Card.</td></tr>
<tr><td>CA/452/92E</td><td>Statoil Ireland Ltd; distributors. Loan to distributors.</td></tr>
<tr><td>CA/453/92E</td><td>Goodbody Stockbrokers; Elvetham Ltd; Grand Hotel Malahide Ltd; shareholders. Shareholding agreement.</td></tr>
<tr><td>CA/454/92E</td><td>AIB Investment Managers Ltd; Hamptoncove Holdings Ltd; Erin Executor & Trustee Co. Ltd; shareholders. Shareholding agreement.</td></tr>
<tr><td>CA/455/92E</td><td>Warner Lambert (Ireland) Ltd; Tennant & Ruttle Distribution Ltd. Exclusive distribution.</td></tr>
<tr><td>CA/456/92E</td><td>Warner Lambert Distributors (Ireland) ltd.; Johnson Brothers Ltd. Exclusive distribution.</td></tr>
</table>

NOTIFICATIONS TO THE COMPETITION AUTHORITY IN 1992

Decision No.	Date	Type of Decision	Subject of Decision	Relevant Decision in Book	Number
294	10 March 1994	C	P		CA/435/92
293	10 March 1994	C	P		CA/436/92E
60	5 Oct. 1993	C	P		CA/437/92E
					CA/438/92E
					CA/439/92E
IT 13 Oct. 1995		W(T)			CA/440/92E
25 J	9 July 1993 (IO)	M	MF	CL (4.2)	CA/441/92E
25 J	9 July 1993 (IO)	M	MF	CL (4.2)	CA/442/92E
25 J	9 July 1993 (IO)	M	MF	CL (4.2)	CA/443/92E
25 J	9 July 1993 (IO)	M	MF	CL (4.2)	CA/444/92E
25 J	9 July 1993 (IO)	M	MF	CL (4.2)	CA/445/92E
25 J	9 July 1993 (IO)	M	MF	CL (4.2)	CA/446/92E
25 J	9 July 1993 (IO)	M	MF	CL (4.2)	CA/447/92E
144 J	19 Nov. 1993 (IO)	L	D	CL (5.1)	CA/448/92E
321 J + 144 J	21 April 1994	L	D	CL (5.1)	CA/449/92E
357	20 Sept. 1994	L	D	S 5.9	CA/450/92E
					CA/451/92E
321 J + 144 J	21 April 1994	L	D	CL (5.1)	CA/452/92E
403	22 June 1995	C	A		CA/453/92E
398	26 April 1995	C	A		CA/454/92E
IT 25 Feb. 1994	23 Feb. 1994 (AR)	W(T)			CA/455/92E
IT 25 Feb. 1994	23 Feb. 1994 (AR)	W(T)			CA/456/92E

NOTIFICATIONS TO THE COMPETITION AUTHORITY IN 1992

Legend	Number	Title
A = Acquisition	CA/457/92E	Warner Lambert Distributors (Ireland) ltd.; Robert Roberts Ltd. Exclusive distribution.
AR = Annual Report of the Competition Authority	CA/458/92E	Carlow Developments Ltd; Naas Holdings Ltd. Transfer of property agreement.
C = Certificate	CA/459/92E	Power Meats Ltd; Albafare Ltd; Cranford Properties Ltd. Shopping centre lease.
CL = Category Licence	CA/460/92E	Light Bite; Crumlin Investments Ltd. Shopping centre lease.
D = Distribution	CA/461/92	Warner Music Ireland Ltd; Sony Music. Exclusive distribution.
EP = Exclusive Purchasing main subject	CA/462/92	J.C. Distribution Ltd; The Prestige Group plc. Exclusive distribution.
FR = Franchising	CA/463/92	J.C. Distribution Ltd; Kopex International Ltd. Exclusive distribution.
IO = Iris Oifigiúil	CA/464/92	J.C. Distribution Ltd; H. Vesshoff & Co. GmbH. Exclusive distribution.
IT = *Irish Times*	CA/465/92E	J.C. Distribution Ltd; Jordan AS. Exclusive distribution.
J = Joint Decision	CA/466/92E	J.C. Distribution Ltd; Vileda LP. Exclusive distribution.
L = Licence	CA/467/92	J.C. Distribution Ltd; Application Des Gaz. Exclusive distribution.
LPG = Liquid Petroleum Gas	CA/468/92	J.C. Distribution Ltd; Dietzel GmbH. Exclusive distribution.
M = Mentioned and Listed Category Licence	CA/469/92E	The Agricultural Trust; Newspread Ltd. Exclusive distribution.
MF = Motor Fuel	CA/470/92E	Coca-Cola Bottling Co. (Dublin) Ltd; Kiely's Bottling Co. Ltd; Seven-Up International. Exclusive manufacturing and distribution.
NC = Notification changed	CA/471/92E	Westlake Estates Ltd; Mullingar Shopping centre lease.
P = Property	CA/472/92E	D.F. O'Neill (Chemist) Ltd; Superquinn. Shopping centre lease.
R = Rejection/Refusal	CA/473/92E	Volvo Trucks (GB) Ltd; McCarthy Commericals Ltd. Exclusive distribution.
S = Decision summarised in text	CA/474/92E	Volvo Trucks (GB) Ltd; McCarthy Commericals Ltd. Distribution agreement.
T = More than one subject	CA/475/92E	Volvo Trucks (GB) Ltd; Irish Commericals (Sales) Ltd. Exclusive distribution.
W(N) = Withdrawn no reason given	CA/476/92E	Volvo Trucks (GB) Ltd; Irish Commericals (Sales) Ltd. Distribution agreement.
W(T) = Withdrawn because of termination of agreement	CA/477/92	Wexford Farmers Co-operative Society Ltd; Irish Agricultural Wholesale Society Ltd. Joint venture.

NOTIFICATIONS TO THE COMPETITION AUTHORITY IN 1992

Decision No.	Date	Type of Decision	Subject of Decision	Relevant Decision in Book	Number
IT 25 Feb. 1994	23 Feb. 1994 (AR)	W(T)			CA/457/92E
382 NC	16 Dec. 1994	C	P	S. 7.20	CA/458/92E
196	3 Dec. 1993	C	P		CA/459/92E
279	4 Feb. 1994	C	P		CA/460/92E
					CA/461/92
144 J	19 Nov. 1993 (IO)	L	D	CL (5.1)	CA/462/92
144 J	19 Nov. 1993 (IO)	L	D	CL (5.1)	CA/463/92
144 J	19 Nov. 1993 (IO)	L	D	CL (5.1)	CA/464/92
IT 9 Dec. 1994	10 Nov. 1994 (AR)	W(N)			CA/465/92E
144 J	19 Nov. 1993 (IO)	L	D	CL (5.1)	CA/466/92E
					CA/467/92
144 J	19 Nov. 1993 (IO)	L	D	CL (5.1)	CA/468/92
369	28 Oct. 1994	C	D	S 5.13	CA/469/92E
					CA/470/92E
87	5 Oct. 1993	C	P		CA/471/92E
44	5 Oct. 1993	C	P		CA/472/92E
					CA/473/92E
					CA/474/92E
					CA/475/92E
					CA/476/92E
					CA/477/92

Legend	Number	Title
A = Acquisition AR = Annual Report of the Competition Authority C = Certificate CL = Category Licence D = Distribution EP = Exclusive Purchasing main subject FR = Franchising IO = Iris Oifigiúil IT = *Irish Times* J = Joint Decision L = Licence LPG = Liquid Petroleum Gas M = Mentioned and Listed Category Licence MF = Motor Fuel NC = Notification changed P = Property R = Rejection/Refusal S = Decision summarised in text T = More than one subject W(N) = Withdrawn no reason given W(T) = Withdrawn because of termination of agreement	CA/478/92E	B.M. Browne Ltd; Roche Products Ltd. Exclusive distribution.
	CA/479/92E	B.M. Browne Ltd; ACT Medisys Ltd. Exclusive distribution (agency).
	CA/480/92E	B.M. Browne Ltd; Fujinon (Europe) GmbH. Exclusive distribution.
	CA/481/92E	B.M. Browne Ltd; Dia Med Ag. Exclusive distribution
	CA/482/92E	B.M. Browne Ltd; Straumann (GB) Ltd. Exclusive distribution
	CA/483/92E	Mechanical Copyright Protection Society Ireland Ltd. (MCPSA); Mechanial Copyright Protection Society (MCPS); composers. Membership agreement.
	CA/484/92E	MCPS; production music members. Production music membership agreement.
	CA/485/92E	MCPS; record producers. Agreement on royalties.
	CA/486/92E	MCPSI; Radio Telefís Éireann. Copyright licence.
	CA/487/92E	MCPSI; users. Royalties for production music library catalogue.
	CA/488/92E	MCPSI; broadcast production companies. Synchronisation licence.
	CA/489/92E	MCPSI; film makers. Code of practice.
	CA/490/92E	MCPSI; videogram producers. Producers and duplication agreement.
	CA/491/92E	MCPSI; radio programme producers. Radio programming agreements.
	CA/492/92E	MCPSI; recording contractors. In-flight entertainment agreements.
	CA/493/92E	MCPSI; makers of recordings. Background music operators agreement.
	CA/494/92E	MCPSI; telephone recording producers. Premium telephone agreement.
	CA/495/92E	MCPSI; education institutions. Music and education agreements.
	CA/496/92E	MCPSI; amateur cinematographers. Amateur cinematographers agreement.
	CA/497/92E	MCPSI; operators. Recording booths agreement.
	CA/498/92E	MCPSI; facility houses. Code of conduct.
	CA/499/92E	MCPSI; production companies. Code of conduct.
	CA/500/92E	MCPSI; radio stations. Radio station licence.
	CA/501/92E	V. Jackson Ltd; D. Horkan Ltd. Shopping centre lease.

NOTIFICATIONS TO THE COMPETITION AUTHORITY IN 1992

Decision No.	Date	Type of Decision	Subject of Decision	Relevant Decision in Book	Number
144 J	19 Nov. 1993 (IO)	L	D	CL (5.1)	CA/478/92E
					CA/479/92E
IT 14 Oct. 1994	29 Sept. 1994 (AR)	W(T)			CA/480/92E
144 J	19 Nov. 1993 (IO)	L	D	CL (5.1)	CA/481/92E
IT + 144 J NC	IT 24 June 1994	L	D	CL (5.1)	CA/482/92E
					CA/483/92E
					CA/484/92E
					CA/485/92E
					CA/486/92E
					CA/487/92E
					CA/488/92E
					CA/489/92E
					CA/490/92E
					CA/491/92E
					CA/492/92E
					CA/493/92E
					CA/494/92E
					CA/495/92E
					CA/496/92E
					CA/497/92E
					CA/498/92E
					CA/499/92E
					CA/500/92E
103	13 Dec. 1993	C	P		CA/501/92E

<table>
<tr><th>Legend</th><th>Number</th><th>Title</th></tr>
<tr><td rowspan="21">A = Acquisition
AR = Annual Report of the Competition Authority
C = Certificate
CL = Category Licence
D = Distribution
EP = Exclusive Purchasing main subject
FR = Franchising
IO = Iris Oifigiúil
IT = Irish Times
J = Joint Decision
L = Licence
LPG = Liquid Petroleum Gas
M = Mentioned and Listed Category Licence
MF = Motor Fuel
NC = Notification changed
P = Property
R = Rejection/Refusal
S = Decision summarised in text
T = More than one subject
W(N) = Withdrawn no reason given
W(T) = Withdrawn because of termination of agreement</td><td>CA/502/92E</td><td>New Irish Assurance Co. plc; Nutgrove Shopping centre lease.</td></tr>
<tr><td>CA/503/92E</td><td>Irish Coal Importers; Weglokoks. Joint purchasing agreement.</td></tr>
<tr><td>CA/504/92E</td><td>Broderick Bros. Ltd; Niedecker GmbH. Exclusive distribution.</td></tr>
<tr><td>CA/505/92E</td><td>Chivers & Sons Ltd; Tate & Lyle Industries Ltd. Exclusive distribution.</td></tr>
<tr><td>CA/506/92E</td><td>Chivers & Sons Ltd; Cadbury Beverages Ltd. Exclusive distribution.</td></tr>
<tr><td>CA/507/92</td><td>Lucas Automotive Ltd; distributors. Exclusive distribution.</td></tr>
<tr><td>CA/508/92</td><td>Salix Trust Ltd; IBI Nominees Ltd; Merchant's Quay Shopping centre lease.</td></tr>
<tr><td>CA/509/92E</td><td>Cadbury Beverages Ltd; Chivers & Sons Ltd. Exclusive distribution.</td></tr>
<tr><td>CA/510/92</td><td>Cadbury Beverages Ltd; Batchelors Ltd. Exclusive production and distribution.</td></tr>
<tr><td>CA/511/92</td><td>Cadbury Beverages Ltd; Batchelors Ltd. Exclusive production and distribution.</td></tr>
<tr><td>CA/512/92E</td><td>W. & J. Donovan; Civil Engineers (Ireland) Ltd. Shopping centre lease.</td></tr>
<tr><td>CA/513/92E</td><td>Michael Reilly & Sons Ltd (now Nabola Ltd). Phoenix Newsagents. Shopping centre lease.</td></tr>
<tr><td>CA/514/92E</td><td>Sports Locker Ltd; M.P. O'Brien (Maynooth) Ltd. Shopping centre lease.</td></tr>
<tr><td>CA/515/92E</td><td>Virgin Enterprises Ltd; Virgin Retail (Ireland) Ltd. Trademark licence.</td></tr>
<tr><td>CA/516/92E</td><td>Dalgety Agriculture Ltd; Spillers Ltd; Thomas Hill & Co. Ltd. Know-how and trademark licence.</td></tr>
<tr><td>CA/517/92E</td><td>Dalgety Agriculture Ltd; Spillers Ltd; Thomas Hill & Co. Ltd. Know-how and trademark licence.</td></tr>
<tr><td>CA/518/92E</td><td>Dalgety Agriculture Ltd; Spillers Ltd; E. Morrin & Son Ltd. Know-how and trademark licence.</td></tr>
<tr><td>CA/519/92E</td><td>Dalgety Agriculture Ltd; Spillers Ltd; E. Morrin & Son Ltd. Know-how and trademark licence.</td></tr>
<tr><td>CA/520/92E</td><td>Pig Improvement Co. Ltd; Master Pork Packers Ltd. Know-how and trademark licence.</td></tr>
<tr><td>CA/521/92E</td><td>Cadbury Ireland Ltd; Chivers & Sons Ltd. Exclusive distribution.</td></tr>
<tr><td>CA/522/92E</td><td>Cadbury Ireland Ltd; Premier Brands UK Ltd. Exclusive distribution.</td></tr>
</table>

NOTIFICATIONS TO THE COMPETITION AUTHORITY IN 1992

Decision No.	Date	Type of Decision	Subject of Decision	Relevant Decision in Book	Number
186	3 Dec. 1993	C	P		CA/502/92E
IT 9 June 1995		R*			CA/503/92E
IT 9 Dec. 1994	7 Dec. 1994 (AR)	W(T)			CA/504/92E
144 J	19 Nov. 1993 (IO)	L	D	CL (5.1)	CA/505/92E
144 J	19 Nov. 1993 (IO)	L	D	CL (5.1)	CA/506/92E
					CA/507/92
226	15 Dec. 1993	C	P		CA/508/92
144 J	19 No. 1993 (IO)	L	D	CL (5.1)	CA/509/92E
					CA/510/92
					CA/511/92
70	5 Oct. 1993	C	P		CA/512/92E
240	15 Dec. 1993	C	P		CA/513/92E
133	13 Oct. 1993	C	P		CA/514/92E
IT 17 Sept. 1993	9 Sept. 1993 (AR)	W(N)			CA/515/92E
					CA/516/92E
					CA/517/92E
					CA/518/92E
					CA/519/92E
IT 10 Feb. 1995		W(T)			CA/520/92E
219	3 Dec. 1993	R	D	S 2.2.2	CA/521/92E
					CA/522/92E

*Rejected as not notifiable because European Commission authorised the agreement under Article 65 of ECSC Treaty.

NOTIFICATIONS TO THE COMPETITION AUTHORITY IN 1992

Legend	Number	Title
A = Acquisition AR = Annual Report of the Competition Authority C = Certificate CL = Category Licence D = Distribution EP = Exclusive Purchasing main subject FR = Franchising IO = Iris Oifigiúil IT = *Irish Times* J = Joint Decision L = Licence LPG = Liquid Petroleum Gas M = Mentioned and Listed Category Licence MF = Motor Fuel NC = Notification changed P = Property R = Rejection/Refusal S = Decision summarised in text T = More than one subject W(N) = Withdrawn no reason given W(T) = Withdrawn because of termination of agreement	CA/523/92E	Cadbury Ltd; Cadbury Schweppes plc; Premier Brands Ltd; Premier brands UK Ltd. Trademark and franchise agreement.
	CA/524/92	Sunkist Soft Drinks (British Isles) Ltd; Batchelors Ltd; Sunkist Growers Inc. Know-how and trademark licence.
	CA/525/92E	Canada Dry Corporation Ltd; Cantrell & Cochrane Group Ltd. Exclusive manufacture and distribution.
	CA/526/92E	Sunkist Soft Drinks (British Isles) Ltd; Cantrell & Cochrane Group Ltd. Exclusive manufacture and distribution.
	CA/527/92E	Schweppes International Ltd; Cantrell & Cochrane Group Ltd. Exclusive manufacture and distribution.
	CA/528/92E	Gilbeys of Ireland Sales Ltd; Hermann Kendermann GmbH. Exclusive distribution.
	CA/529/92E	Gilbeys of Ireland Sales Ltd; Davide Campari–Milano SPA. Exclusive distribution.
	CA/530/92E	Gilbeys of Ireland Sales Ltd; Veuve Clicquot Ponsardin. Exclusive distribution.
	CA/531/92E	Newspaper Publishing; The Irish Times Newspaper service syndication agreement.
	CA/532/92E	Guardian Assurance plc; The Square Shopping centre leases.
	CA/533/92E	Caledonian Insurance Co.; Grafton Shopping arcade leases.
	CA/534/92E	Trustees of Telecom Éireann Superannuation Fund; Bord Telecom Éireann. Office lease.
	CA/535/92E	Trustees of Telecom Éireann Superannuation Fund; Bord Telecom Éireann. Office lease.
	CA/536/92E	Trustees of Telecom Éireann Superannuation Fund; Bord Telecom Éireann. Office lease.
	CA/537/92	Raleigh Ireland Ltd; cycle dealers. Trading terms and conditions.
	CA/538/92E	Blugas Ltd; dealers. Exclusive purchase.
	CA/539/92E	Blugas Ltd; distributors. Exclusive distribution.
	CA/540/92E	Blugas Ltd; bulk customers. Exclusive purchase.
	CA/541/92E	Caledonian Insurance Co; Grafton Shopping arcade leases.
	CA/542/92E	Guardian Assurance plc; tenants. The Square Shopping centre lease.
	CA/543/92E	Gilbeys of Ireland Ltd; Matthew Gloag (UK) Ltd. Exclusive distribution.

NOTIFICATIONS TO THE COMPETITION AUTHORITY IN 1992

Decision No.	Date	Type of Decision	Subject of Decision	Relevant Decision in Book	Number
					CA/523/92E
					CA/524/92
					CA/525/92E
					CA/526/92E
					CA/527/92E
144 J	19 Nov. 1993 (IO)	L	D	CL (5.1)	CA/528/92E
IT 6 May 1994	22 Apr. 1994 (AR)	W(N)			CA/529/92E
IT + 144 J	IT 4 Feb. 1994	L	D	CL (5.1)	CA/530/92E
420 NC	12 Sept. 1995	C			CA/531/92E
209	3 Dec. 1993	C	P		CA/532/92E
166	3 Dec. 1993	C	P		CA/533/92E
338 J	14 June 1994	C	P		CA/534/92E
338 J	14 June 1994	C	P		CA/535/92E
339 J	14 June 1994	C	P		CA/536/92E
IT 8 April 1994	29 March 1994 (AR)	W(N)*			CA/537/92
364 J	11 Nov. 1994 (IO)	R	LPG	CL (4.8)	CA/538/92E
439	27 Oct. 1995	C	LPG		CA/539/92E
389	10 April 1995	L	LPG		CA/540/92E
167	3 Dec. 1993	C	P		CA/541/92E
208	3 Dec. 1993	C	P		CA/542/92E
144 J	19 Nov. 1993 (IO)	L	D	CL (5.1)	CA/543/92E

*The 1994 Annual Report of the Authority notes that a Statement of Objections was sent to Raleigh which later withdrew the notification.

Legend	Number	Title
A = Acquisition AR = Annual Report of the Competition Authority C = Certificate CL = Category Licence D = Distribution EP = Exclusive Purchasing main subject FR = Franchising IO = Iris Oifigiúil IT = *Irish Times* J = Joint Decision L = Licence LPG = Liquid Petroleum Gas M = Mentioned and Listed Category Licence MF = Motor Fuel NC = Notification changed P = Property R = Rejection/Refusal S = Decision summarised in text T = More than one subject W(N) = Withdrawn no reason given W(T) = Withdrawn because of termination of agreement	CA/544/92E	Gilbeys of Ireland Ltd; Pedrotti Interdrink S.A.S. Trademark and exclusive purchase agreement.
	CA/545/92E	Kitchen Assessories Ltd; Franke UK Ltd. Exclusive distribution.
	CA/546/92E	Royal Liver Trustees Ltd; Deanstown Investments Ltd. Shopping centre lease.
	CA/547/92E	Royal Liver Trustees Ltd; Texas Homecare (Ireland) Ltd. Shopping centre lease.
	CA/548/92E	Royal Liver Trustees Ltd; Carpet & Bedding Home Ltd. Shopping centre lease.
	CA/549/92E	Royal Liver Trustees Ltd; Anika Enterprises. Shopping centre lease.
	CA/550/92	Royal Liver Trustees Ltd; Naas Road Shopping centre lease.
	CA/551/92E	United Drug plc; British Cod Liver Oil Ltd. Exclusive distribution.
	CA/552/92E	United Drug plc; Pentax Europe N.V. Exclusive distribution.
	CA/553/92E	United Drug plc; Norgine Ltd. Exclusive distribution.
	CA/554/92E	United Drug plc; 3 M Health Care Ltd. Exclusive distribution.
	CA/555/92E	United Drug plc; Seven Seas Ltd. Exclusive distribution.
	CA/556/92E	United Drug plc; Brocades (GB) Ltd. Exclusive distribution.
	CA/557/92E	United Drug plc; Trinity Instruments Ltd; Dixon Hempenstall Ltd; vendors. Sale of business.
	CA/558/92E	United Drug plc; Roc International. Exclusive distribution.
	CA/559/92E	United Drug plc; Astra Phamaceuticals Ltd. Exclusive distribution.
	CA/560/92E	United Drug plc; Du Pont (UK) Ltd. Non-exclusive distribution.
	CA/561/92E	United Drug plc; Kodak Ireland Ltd. Distribution agreement.
	CA/562/92E	United Drug plc; Nycomed (UK) Ltd Ltd. Sole distributor agreement.
	CA/563/92E	United Drug plc; Coloplast Ltd. Exclusive distribution.
	CA/564/92E	United Drug plc; The Boots Co. (Ireland) Ltd. Sole distributor agreement.
	CA/565/92E	United Drug plc; Reckitts & Coleman Ireland Ltd. Sole distributor agreement.

Decision No.	Date	Type of Decision	Subject of Decision	Relevant Decision in Book	Number
					CA/544/92E
144 J	19 Nov. 1993 (IO)	L	D	CL (5.1)	CA/545/92E
182	3 Dec. 1993	C	P		CA/546/92E
180	3 Dec. 1993	C	P		CA/547/92E
183	3 Dec. 1993	C	P		CA/548/92E
181	3 Dec. 1993	C	P		CA/549/92E
184	3 Dec. 1993	C	P		CA/550/92
IT 10 June 1994	27 May 1994 (AR)	W(T)			CA/551/92E
144 J	19 Nov. 1993 (IO)	L	D	CL (5.1)	CA/552/92E
					CA/553/92E
					CA/554/92E
					CA/555/92E
					CA/556/92E
IT 10 June 1994	25 May 1994 (AR)	W(N)			CA/557/92E
IT 17 June 1994	27 May 1994 (AR)	W(N)			CA/558/92E
					CA/559/92E
IT 10 Nov. 1995		W(T)			CA/560/92E
367	28 Oct. 1994	C	D		CA/561/92E
144 J	19 Nov. 1993 (IO)	L	D	CL (5.1)	CA/562/92E
					CA/563/92E
					CA/564/92E
					CA/565/92E

Legend	Number	Title
A = Acquisition AR = Annual Report of the Competition Authority C = Certificate CL = Category Licence D = Distribution EP = Exclusive Purchasing main subject FR = Franchising IO = Iris Oifigiúil IT = *Irish Times* J = Joint Decision L = Licence LPG = Liquid Petroleum Gas M = Mentioned and Listed Category Licence MF = Motor Fuel NC = Notification changed P = Property R = Rejection/Refusal S = Decision summarised in text T = More than one subject W(N) = Withdrawn no reason given W(T) = Withdrawn because of termination of agreement	CA/566/92E	United Drug plc; Bayer (Ireland) Ltd. Sole distributor agreement.
	CA/567/92E	United Drug plc; Lilly Industries Ltd. Exclusive distribution.
	CA/568/92E	United Drug plc; The Boots Co. (Ireland) Ltd. Exclusive distribution.
	CA/569/92E	United Drug plc; Warner Lambert Ireland Ltd. Sole distributor agreement.
	CA/570/92E	United Drug Distributors Ltd; Novo Industri A/S. Exclusive distribution.
	CA/571/92E	United Drug Distributors Ltd; Cow & Gate Ireland Ltd. Exclusive distribution.
	CA/572/92E	United Drug Distributors Ltd; Mundipharma Pharmaceutical Co. Exclusive distribution.
	CA/573/92E	United Drug Distributors Ltd; Squibb (Ireland) Ltd. Exclusive distribution.
	CA/574/92E	United Drug Distributors Ltd; Boehringer Mannheim UK (Pharmaceuticals) Ltd. Exclusive distribution.
	CA/575/92E	United Drug Distributors Ltd; Pharma Services. Exclusive distributor agreement.
	CA/576/92	United Medical Ltd; Clement Clarke International Ltd. Sole distributor agreement.
	CA/577/92	United Medical Ltd; Haag-Streit AG. Sole distributor agreement.
	CA/578/92E	United Medical Ltd; Bausch & Lomb UK Ltd. Exclusive distribution.
	CA/579/92E	Pemberton Marketing International Ltd; Nicholas Laboratories Ltd. Sole distributor agreement.
	CA/580/92E	Pemberton Marketing International Ltd; Nevinar Ltd. Sole distributor agreement.
	CA/581/92E	Pemberton Marketing International Ltd; Orlane SA. Exclusive distribution.
	CA/582/92E	Pemberton Marketing International Ltd; Parfums Nina Ricci. Exclusive distribution.
	CA/583/92E	Pemberton Marketing International Ltd; Ilford Ltd. Exclusive distribution.
	CA/584/92E	Pemberton Marketing International Ltd; Cupal Ltd. Exclusive distribution.
	CA/585/92E	Pemberton Marketing International Ltd; Ciba-Geigy Ireland Ltd. Exclusive distribution.
	CA/586/92E	Pemberton Marketing International Ltd; Bausch & Lomb UK Ltd. Exclusive distribution.

NOTIFICATIONS TO THE COMPETITION AUTHORITY IN 1992

Decision No.	Date	Type of Decision	Subject of Decision	Relevant Decision in Book	Number
					CA/566/92E
					CA/567/92E
					CA/568/92E
					CA/569/92E
IT 10 June 1994	27 May 1994 (AR)	W(T)			CA/570/92E
					CA/571/92E
					CA/572/92E
					CA/573/92E
					CA/574/92E
144 J	19 Nov. 1993 (IO)	L	D	CL (5.1)	CA/575/92E
144 J	19 Nov. 1993 (IO)	L	D	CL (5.1)	CA/576/92
IT + 144 J	IT 15 April 1994	L	D	CL (5.1)	CA/577/92
IT 10 June 1994	27 May 1994 (AR)	W(T)			CA/578/92E
IT 18 March 1994	27 May 1994 (AR)	W(T)			CA/579/92E
144 J	19 Nov. 1993 (IO)	L	D	CL (5.1)	CA/580/92E
					CA/581/92E
					CA/582/92E
144 J	19 Nov. 1993 (IO)	L	D	CL (5.1)	CA/583/92E
IT 25 Feb. 1994	23 Feb. 1994 (AR)	W(T)			CA/584/92E
144 J	19 Nov. 1993 (IO)	L	D	CL (5.1)	CA/585/92E
IT 8 April 1994	16 March 1994 (AR)	W(T)			CA/586/92E

Legend	Number	Title
A = Acquisition AR = Annual Report of the Competition Authority C = Certificate CL = Category Licence D = Distribution EP = Exclusive Purchasing main subject FR = Franchising IO = Iris Oifigiúil IT = *Irish Times* J = Joint Decision L = Licence LPG = Liquid Petroleum Gas M = Mentioned and Listed Category Licence MF = Motor Fuel NC = Notification changed P = Property R = Rejection/Refusal S = Decision summarised in text T = More than one subject W(N) = Withdrawn no reason given W(T) = Withdrawn because of termination of agreement	CA/587/92E	Power Supermarkets Ltd; Arthur's Quay Developments Ltd; Colossus Management Services Ltd. Shopping centre lease.
	CA/588/92E	Power Supermarkets Ltd; Town and Country Investments plc. Shopping centre lease.
	CA/589/92E	Power Supermarkets Ltd; Navan Shopping Centre Ltd. Shopping centre lease.
	CA/590/92E	Power Supermarkets Ltd; Feresant Ltd. Shopping centre lease.
	CA/591/92E	Power Supermarkets Ltd; McMullan Bros. Ltd. Property purchase agreement.
	CA/592/92E	Power Supermarkets Ltd; Riga Ltd; Modred Ltd. Shopping centre lease.
	CA/593/92E	Power Supermarkets Ltd; Mayfield Investments Ltd. Shopping centre lease.
	CA/594/92E	Power Supermarkets Ltd; Todd Burns & Co. Ltd. Shop lease.
	CA/595/92E	Power Supermarkets Ltd; MEPC Ireland Ltd; Erin Executor and Trustee Co. Ltd. Shopping centre lease.
	CA/596/92E	Power Supermarkets Ltd; Kerrib Ltd; IPFPUT; Northern Bank Development Corp. Ltd. Shopping centre lease.
	CA/597/92E	Power Supermarkets Ltd; L. & C. Properties Ltd and others. Shopping centre lease.
	CA/598/92E	Power Supermarkets Ltd; tenants. Shopping centre leases.
	CA/599/92E	Power Supermarkets Ltd; tenants. Shopping centre leases.
	CA/600/92E	Outlandus Ltd; tenants. Shopping centre leases.
	CA/601/92E	Power Supermarkets Ltd; tenants. Phibsboro Shopping centre leases.
	CA/602/92E	Quinnsworth; H. Williams. Greystones Shopping centre lease.
	CA/603/92E	Quinnsworth Ltd; Omni Park Ltd. Ennis Shopping centre lease.
	CA/604/92E	Quinnsworth Ltd; Park Shopping Centre Ltd. Industrial Credit Corporation Ltd. Shopping centre lease.
	CA/605/92E	Grittar; David J. Bolger. Shopping centre lease.
	CA/606/92E	Grittar; Light Bite. Ballyfermot Shopping centre lease.
	CA/607/92E	Five Star Supermarkets; Richfield Investments Ltd. Thomond Shopping centre lease.

Decision No.	Date	Type of Decision	Subject of Decision	Relevant Decision in Book	Number
245	15 Dec. 1993	C	P		CA/587/92E
386	22 Dec. 1994	C	P		CA/588/92E
79	5 Oct. 1993	C	P		CA/589/92E
131	13 Oct. 1993	C	P		CA/590/92E
308	21 Apr. 1994	C	P	S 7.14	CA/591/92E
228	15 Dec. 1993	C	P		CA/592/92E
168	3 Dec. 1993	C	P		CA/593/92E
309	21 Apr. 1994	C	P		CA/594/92E
161 J	3 Dec. 1993	C	P		CA/595/92E
93 J	13 Oct. 1993	C	P		CA/596/92E
207	3 Dec. 1993	C	P		CA/597/92E
149	3 Dec. 1993	C	P		CA/598/92E
112	3 Dec. 1993	C	P		CA/599/92E
265	15 Dec. 1993	C	P		CA/600/92E
220	15 Dec. 1993	C	P		CA/601/92E
153	3 Dec. 1993	C	P		CA/602/92E
188	3 Dec. 1993	C	P		CA/603/92E
114	13 Oct. 1993	C	P		CA/604/92E
345	23 June 1994	C	P	S 7.15	CA/605/92E
154	3 Dec. 1993	C	P		CA/606/92E
252	15 Dec. 1993	C	P		CA/607/92E

Legend	Number	Title
A = Acquisition AR = Annual Report of the Competition Authority C = Certificate CL = Category Licence D = Distribution EP = Exclusive Purchasing main subject FR = Franchising IO = Iris Oifigiúil IT = *Irish Times* J = Joint Decision L = Licence LPG = Liquid Petroleum Gas M = Mentioned and Listed Category Licence MF = Motor Fuel NC = Notification changed P = Property R = Rejection/Refusal S = Decision summarised in text T = More than one subject W(N) = Withdrawn no reason given W(T) = Withdrawn because of termination of agreement	CA/608/92E	Five Star Supermarkets; Mall Holdings Ltd. Crescent Shopping centre lease.
	CA/609/92E	Five Star Supermarkets; Drumcondra Shop leases.
	CA/610/92E	Five Star Supermarkets; Sligo Shopping centre leases.
	CA/611/92E	Clondalkin Properties; Thomas Farren. Shopping centre lease.
	CA/612/92E	Albafare. H. O'Doherty. Shopping centre lease.
	CA/613/92E	Quinnsworth; Revoclife Ltd. Shopping centre lease.
	CA/614/92E	Five Star Supermarkets; Clonmel Shopping centre leases.
	CA/615/92E	Power Supermarkets Ltd; Dungoyne Ltd. Shopping centre lease.
	CA/616/92E	Telecom Éireann Information Systems Ltd; Landis & Gyr Lake Ltd. Exclusive distribution.
	CA/617/92E	TEIS Ltd; Case Communications plc. Exclusive distribution.
	CA/618/92E	TEIS Ltd; Infotron Systems Ltd. Exclusive distribution.
	CA/619/92E	TEIS Ltd; MDS Telelphone Systems Ltd. Exclusive distribution.
	CA/620/92E	TEIS Ltd; Sharptext Ltd. Exclusive distribution.
	CA/621/92E	TEIS Ltd; Siemens Ltd. Exclusive distribution.
	CA/622/92E	TEIS Ltd; Northern Telecom (Ireland) Ltd. Exclusive distribution.
	CA/623/92E	TEIS Ltd; Alcatel Business Systems Ltd. Exclusive distribution.
	CA/624/92E	Gowan Distributors Ltd; Automobiles Peugeot S.A. Selective distribution.
	CA/625/92E	Gowan Distributors Ltd; dealers. Dealer loan agreement.
	CA/626/92E	Gowan Distributors Ltd; dealers. Deed of charge/mortgage.
	CA/627/92	Adam F. Torrie Ltd; Dungarvan, Tramore, Waterford and Wexford Shopping centre leases.
	CA/628/92E	Gilbeys of Ireland Sales Ltd; Baron Philippe de Rothschild S.A. Exclusive distribution.
	CA/629/92E	Estuary Fuel Ltd; distributors. Exclusive distribution.
	CA/630/92E	Estuary Fuel Ltd; distributors. Exclusive distribution.
	CA/631/92E	Estuary Fuel Ltd; distributors. Retention of title.
	CA/632/92E	Estuary Fuel Ltd; distributors. Specific chattel mortgage.

NOTIFICATIONS TO THE COMPETITION AUTHORITY IN 1992

Decision No.	Date	Type of Decision	Subject of Decision	Relevant Decision in Book	Number
74	5 Oct. 1993	C	P		CA/608/92E
280	4 Feb. 1994	C	P		CA/609/92E
80	5 Oct. 1993	C	P		CA/610/92E
158	3 Dec. 1993	C	P		CA/611/92E
97	13 Oct. 1993	C	P		CA/612/92E
128	13 Oct. 1993	C	P		CA/613/92E
259	15 Dec. 1993	C	P		CA/614/92E
73	5 Oct. 1993	C	P		CA/615/92E
144 J	19 Nov. 1993 (IO)	L	D	CL (5.1)	CA/616/92E
144 J	19 Nov. 1993 (IO)	L	D	CL (5.1)	CA/617/92E
144 J	19 Nov. 1993 (IO)	L	D	CL (5.1)	CA/618/92E
IT + 144 J NC	IT 24 June 1994	L	D	CL (5.1)	CA/619/92E
IT + 144 J NC	IT 24 June 1994	L	D	CL (5.1)	CA/620/92E
IT + 144 J NC	IT 24 June 1994	L	D	CL (5.1)	CA/621/92E
					CA/622/92E
IT 10 June 1994	27 May 1994 (AR)	W(T)			CA/623/92E
					CA/624/92E
					CA/625/92E
					CA/626/92E
262	15 Dec. 1993	C	P		CA/627/92
144 J	19 Nov. 1993 (IO)	L	D	CL (5.1)	CA/628/92E
IT + 144 J NC	IT 24 June 1994	L	D	CL (5.1)	CA/629/92E
IT 10 June 1994	27 May 1994 (AR)	W(N)			CA/630/92E
IT 10 June 1994	27 May 1994 (AR)	W(N)			CA/631/92E
IT 10 June 1994	27 May 1994 (AR)	W(N)			CA/632/92E

Legend	Number	Title
A = Acquisition	CA/633/92E	Estuary Fuel Ltd; distributors. Debenture.
AR = Annual Report of the Competition Authority	CA/634/92E	Estuary Fuel Ltd; distributors. Debenture.
C = Certificate	CA/635/92E	Estuary Fuel Ltd; distributors. Guarantee and indemnity.
CL = Category Licence D = Distribution	CA/636/92E	Estuary Fuel Ltd; distributors. Guarantee and indemnity.
EP = Exclusive Purchasing main subject	CA/637/92E	Sony (UK) Ltd; dealers. Selective distribution.
	CA/638/92E	Universal Honda Ltd; dealers. Selective distribution.
FR = Franchising IO = Iris Oifigiúil	CA/639/92E	Honda Motor Co. Ltd; Universal Honda Ltd; Selective distribution.
IT = *Irish Times* J = Joint Decision	CA/640/92E	Gowan Distributors Ltd; dealers. Selective distribution.
L = Licence	CA/641/92E	TEIS LTD.; Mitel Telecom Ltd; Excl. distribution.
LPG = Liquid Petroleum Gas	CA/642/92E	Doyle Donnelly Flynn Hanlon & Brannelly Ltd; Eastcastle Ltd; J. Walter Thompson Group. Shareholding agreement.
M = Mentioned and Listed Category Licence	CA/643/92E	C. & J. Clarke International Ltd; Torlink Ltd; Franchise agreement with shop lease.
MF = Motor Fuel NC = Notification changed	CA/644/92E	Visa International Service Association. Arrangements for Visa Card International.
P = Property R = Rejection/Refusal	CA/645/92E	Oglesby and Butler Ltd; directors; shareholders of Portagas Ltd. Merger agreement, employment contracts and exclusive know-how licence.
S = Decision summarised in text	CA/646/92E	Oglesby and Butler Ltd; D. Butler. Employment contract.
T = More than one subject	CA/647/92E	Dublin Aluminium Ltd; S. Hughes. Employment contract.
W(N) = Withdrawn no reason given W(T) = Withdrawn because of termination of agreement	CA/648/92E	Unidare plc; B. Mills and D. Kenny, and others. Share purchase agreement and employment contracts.
	CA/649/92E	Odlum Group Ltd; Readibake Ltd. Exclusive purchase.
	CA/650/92E	Odlum Group Ltd; Readibake Ltd. Joseph Brennan Bakery Ltd. Exclusive purchase.
	CA/651/92E	P.J.D. Investment Co.; investors and shareholders. Share purchase agreement.
	CA/652/92E	Hornsea Ltd. (Parke Davis/Elan Ltd.); Elan Corporation plc. Exclusive purchase.
	CA/653/92E	Siúicre Éireann cpt; Talmino Ltd; Gladebrook Co. Ltd; Charles Lyons, Michael Tully, Thomas Keleghan and Charles Garavan. Share purchase agreement.
	CA/654/92E	Siúicre Éireann cpt; Charles Garavan. Employment contract.

NOTIFICATIONS TO THE COMPETITION AUTHORITY IN 1992

Decision No.	Date	Type of Decision	Subject of Decision	Relevant Decision in Book	Number
334 J	10 June 1994	L	D		CA/633/92E
IT 10 June 1994	27 May 1994 (AR)	W(N)			CA/634/92E
334 J	10 June 1994	L	D		CA/635/92E
IT 10 June 1994	27 May 1994 (AR)	W(N)			CA/636/92E
					CA/637/92E
					CA/638/92E
					CA/639/92E
					CA/640/92E
144 J	19 Nov. 1993 (IO)	L	D	CL (5.1)	CA/641/92E
					CA/642/92E
IT 27 May 1994	10 May 1994 (AR)	W(T)			CA/643/92E
					CA/644/92E
IT 11 Feb. 1994	30 Nov. 1993 (AR)	W(N)			CA/645/92E
IT 8 Sept. 1995		W(N)			CA/646/92E
					CA/647/92E
IT 6 May 1994	28 April 1994 (AR)	W(N)			CA/648/92E
					CA/649/92E
					CA/650/92E
142 NC	27 Oct 1993	C	A	S 3.14	CA/651/92E
					CA/652/92E
344 J NC	14 June 1994	C	A		CA/653/92E
344 J NC	14 June 1994	C	A		CA/654/92E

Legend	Number	Title
A = Acquisition AR = Annual Report of the Competition Authority C = Certificate CL = Category Licence D = Distribution EP = Exclusive Purchasing main subject FR = Franchising IO = Iris Oifigiúil IT = *Irish Times* J = Joint Decision L = Licence LPG = Liquid Petroleum Gas M = Mentioned and Listed Category Licence MF = Motor Fuel NC = Notification changed P = Property R = Rejection/Refusal S = Decision summarised in text T = More than one subject W(N) = Withdrawn no reason given W(T) = Withdrawn because of termination of agreement	CA/655/92E	Siúicre Éireann cpt; Charles Lyons. Employment contract.
	CA/656/92E	Siúicre Éireann cpt; Thomas Keleghan. Employment contract.
	CA/657/92E	Siúicre Éireann cpt; Michael Tully. Employment contract.
	CA/658/92E	The Technical Equipment Co. Ltd; Holec Nederland B.V. Exclusive distribution.
	CA/659/92E	The Technical Equipment Co. Ltd; The Leyland and Birmingham Rubber Co. Ltd. Exclusive distribution.
	CA/660/92E	The Technical Equipment Co. Ltd; BTR Hose Ltd. Exclusive distribution.
	CA/661/92E	The Technical Equipment Co. Ltd; Digi Table (UK) Ltd. Exclusive distribution.
	CA/662/92E	The Technical Equipment Co. Ltd; Jumo Instrument Co. Ltd. Exclusive distribution.
	CA/663/92E	The Technical Equipment Co. Ltd; Eaton Ltd. Exclusive distribution.
	CA/664/92E	The Technical Equipment Co. Ltd; suppliers. Exclusive distribution.
	CA/665/92E	Norish Eirfreeze Ltd; Green Isle Foods Ltd. Rental of cold storage space.
	CA/666/92E	Norish plc; grantees. Fee farm grant for cold storage units.
	CA/667/92E	Norish plc; Viking Frozen Products Ltd. Fee farm grant for cold storage units.
	CA/668/92E	Norish plc; Biko Farm Ltd. Fee farm grant for cold storage units.
	CA/669/92E	Norish plc; Avonmore Creameries Ltd; Standby Manufacturing Ltd. Joint venture.
	CA/670/92E	Norish plc; Goodman International Ltd. Trading agreement.
	CA/671/92E	Norish plc; Food Industries plc. Trading agreement.
	CA/672/92E	Norish plc; Food Industries plc. Share purchase agreement.
	CA/673/92E	Thoroughbred Promotion & Development Co. Ltd; B. and D. Firestone. Share purchase.
	CA/674/92E	B. and D. Firestone; Karim Agan Khan. Purchase of stud farms.
	CA/675/92E	Allied Foods Ltd; Spendgrade Ltd. Exclusive distribution.
	CA/676/92E	Allied Foods Ltd; Van den Broeke (Foods) (UK) Ltd. Exclusive distribution.

NOTIFICATIONS TO THE COMPETITION AUTHORITY IN 1992

Decision No.	Date	Type of Decision	Subject of Decision	Relevant Decision in Book	Number
344 J NC	14 June 1994	C	A		CA/655/92E
344 J NC	14 June 1994	C	A		CA/656/92E
344 J NC	14 June 1994	C	A		CA/657/92E
IT + 144 J NC	IT 15 April 1994	L	D	CL (5.1)	CA/658/92E
144 J	19 Nov. 1993 (IO)	L	D	CL (5.1)	CA/659/92E
144 J	19 Nov. 1993 (IO)	L	D	CL (5.1)	CA/660/92E
144 J	19 Nov. 1993 (IO)	L	D	CL (5.1)	CA/661/92E
IT + 144 J	IT 4 Feb. 1994	L	D	CL (5.1)	CA/662/92E
IT + 144 J NC	IT 15 April 1994	L	D	CL (5.1)	CA/663/92E
144 J	19 Nov. 1993 (IO)	L	D	CL (5.1)	CA/664/92E
					CA/665/92E
429 NC	19 Oct. 1995	C	P		CA/666/92E
430 NC	19 Oct. 1995	C	P		CA/667/92E
431 NC	19 Oct. 1995	C	P		CA/668/92E
					CA/669/92E
					CA/670/92E
					CA/671/92E
138	20 Oct. 1993	C	A	S 3.13	CA/672/92E
11 J	5 Nov. 1992	C	A + P	S 3.9	CA/673/92E
11 J	5 Nov. 1992	C	A + P	S 3.9	CA/674/92E
144 J	19 Nov. 1993 (IO)	L	D	CL (5.1)	CA/675/92E
144 J	19 Nov. 1993 (IO)	L	D	CL (5.1)	CA/676/92E

Legend	Number	Title
A = Acquisition AR = Annual Report of the Competition Authority C = Certificate CL = Category Licence D = Distribution EP = Exclusive Purchasing main subject FR = Franchising IO = Iris Oifigiúil IT = *Irish Times* J = Joint Decision L = Licence LPG = Liquid Petroleum Gas M = Mentioned and Listed Category Licence MF = Motor Fuel NC = Notification changed P = Property R = Rejection/Refusal S = Decision summarised in text T = More than one subject W(N) = Withdrawn no reason given W(T) = Withdrawn because of termination of agreement	CA/677/92E	Allied Foods Ltd; U.B. (Ross Young's) International Ltd. Exclusive distribution.
	CA/678/92E	Allied Foods Ltd; Goosens B.V. Exclusive distribution.
	CA/679/92E	Allied Foods Ltd; Moy Park Ltd. Exclusive distribution.
	CA/680/92E	Snowcream Ltd; milkmen. Exclusive purchase.
	CA/681/92E	Sony (UK) Ltd; dealers. Exclusive purchase.
	CA/682/92E	Eirtrade Ltd; International Network Services Ltd. Exclusive distribution.
	CA/683/92E	Bord Telecom Éireann; L.R. Ericsson Holdings Ltd. Shareholding agreement.
	CA/684/92E	BTE; Alcatel Ireland Ltd. Bulk supply agreement.
	CA/685/92E	BTE; L.M. Ericsson Ltd. Bulk supply agreement.
	CA/686/92E	BTE; Post GEM Ltd. Joint venture and operating agreement.
	CA/687/92E	BTE; Unidare plc/Unidare Cables plc. Cable supply agreement.
	CA/688/92E	BTE; Wessel Industries Ltd; Wessel Cables Ltd. Cable supply agreement.
	CA/689/92E	IAWS Group; First National Bakery Co. Ltd; shareholders. Shareholding agreement.
	CA/690/92E	IAWS Sales Ltd; Dock Milling Ltd; S. & A.G. Davis Ltd; Katowice Ltd; and others. Sharehholding agreement.
	CA/691/92E	IAWS-Agri Society Ltd; Unigrain Dublin Ltd. and others. Merger.
	CA/692/92E	IAWS Group plc; Shamrock Foods Ltd; shareholders. Shareholding agreement.
	CA/693/92E	First National Bakery Co. Ltd; Clianthus Ltd. and others. Merger.
	CA/694/92E	Shamrock Foods Ltd; Brookline Ltd. and others. Merger.
	CA/695/92E	Warner Lambert Ireland Ltd; Hornsea Ltd. Joint venture-management services.
	CA/696/92E	Warner Lambert Ireland Ltd; Elan Pharma Ltd; Horsea Ltd. Joint venture.
	CA/697/92E	J. Brierley, R. Downer. J. Hamilton. M. McDonough. D. McNeill and M. Magnier; Plangrove Ltd. Trademark licence.
	CA/698/92	FBH Ltd; FBH Distributors Ltd; Harty Security Ltd; Harty Holdings Ltd. Purchase of assets.

NOTIFICATIONS TO THE COMPETITION AUTHORITY IN 1992

Decision No.	Date	Type of Decision	Subject of Decision	Relevant Decision in Book	Number
144 J	19 Nov. 1993 (IO)	L	D	CL (5.1)	CA/677/92E
144 J	19 Nov. 1993 (IO)	L	D	CL (5.1)	CA/678/92E
IT + 144 J NC	IT 8 July 1994	L	D	CL (5.1)	CA/679/92E
					CA/680/92E
					CA/681/92E
					CA/682/92E
					CA/683/92E
					CA/684/92E
					CA/685/92E
					CA/686/92E
IT 13 Oct. 1995		R			CA/687/92E
IT 13 Oct. 1995		R			CA/688/92E
379	21 Nov. 1994	C	A/T		CA/689/92E
343	14 June 1994	C	A		CA/690/92E
351	6 Sept. 1994	R	A	S 3.20	CA/691/92E
299	24 March 1994	C	A		CA/692/92E
146 NC	18 Nov. 1993	C	A		CA/693/92E
32	9 Sept. 1993	C	A		CA/694/92E
					CA/695/92E
					CA/696/92E
					CA/697/92E
					CA/698/92

<table>
<tr><th>Legend</th><th>Number</th><th>Title</th></tr>
<tr><td rowspan="22">A = Acquisition
AR = Annual Report of the Competition Authority
C = Certificate
CL = Category Licence
D = Distribution
EP = Exclusive Purchasing main subject
FR = Franchising
IO = Iris Oifigiúil
IT = Irish Times
J = Joint Decision
L = Licence
LPG = Liquid Petroleum Gas
M = Mentioned and Listed Category Licence
MF = Motor Fuel
NC = Notification changed
P = Property
R = Rejection/Refusal
S = Decision summarised in text
T = More than one subject
W(N) = Withdrawn no reason given
W(T) = Withdrawn because of termination of agreement</td><td>CA/699/92E</td><td>Gallic Distributors Ltd; dealers. Selective distribution.</td></tr>
<tr><td>CA/700/92</td><td>Gallic Distributors Ltd; Automobiles Citroen. Selective distribution.</td></tr>
<tr><td>CA/701/92E</td><td>Gallic Distributors Ltd; dealers. Deed of charge/mortgage.</td></tr>
<tr><td>CA/702/92</td><td>Gallic Distributors Ltd; dealers. Dealer loan.</td></tr>
<tr><td>CA/703/92E</td><td>The Association of Consulting Engineers of Ireland; Institution of Engineers of Ireland. Recommended scales of fees and charges.</td></tr>
<tr><td>CA/704/92</td><td>Tennant & Ruttle Distribution Ltd; United Biscuits (UK) Ltd. Exclusive distribution.</td></tr>
<tr><td>CA/705/92E</td><td>Tennant & Ruttle Distribution Ltd; Ferrero Ltd. Exclusive distribution.</td></tr>
<tr><td>CA/706/92E</td><td>Tennant & Ruttle Distribution Ltd; Kinnerton. Exclusive distribution.</td></tr>
<tr><td>CA/707/92E</td><td>Tennant & Ruttle Distribution Ltd; Duracell UK Ltd. Exclusive distribution.</td></tr>
<tr><td>CA/708/92</td><td>Tennant & Ruttle Distribution Ltd; Greensleeves Confectionery Ltd. Exclusive distribution.</td></tr>
<tr><td>CA/709/92E</td><td>Tennant & Ruttle Distribution Ltd; Lindt & Sprungli UK Ltd. Exclusive distribution.</td></tr>
<tr><td>CA/710/92E</td><td>Tennant & Ruttle Distribution Ltd; Tipperary Candy Ltd. Exclusive distribution.</td></tr>
<tr><td>CA/711/92E</td><td>Tennant & Ruttle Distribution Ltd; The Wrigley Co. Ltd. Exclusive distribution.</td></tr>
<tr><td>CA/712/92E</td><td>Tennant & Ruttle Distribution Ltd; Jacobs Suchard Cote d'Or Export. Exclusive distribution.</td></tr>
<tr><td>CA/713/92</td><td>Tennant & Ruttle Distribution Ltd; Jacobs Suchard. Exclusive distribution.</td></tr>
<tr><td>CA/714/92</td><td>General Motors Distribution Ireland Ltd; motor dealers. Selective distribution.</td></tr>
<tr><td>CA/715/92</td><td>General Motors Distribution Ireland Ltd; motor dealers. Selective distribution.</td></tr>
<tr><td>CA/716/92E</td><td>Tennant & Ruttle Ltd; Masterfoods Ltd. Exclusive distribution.</td></tr>
<tr><td>CA/717/92</td><td>Apex Fire Protection Ltd; William Brennan. Employment contract.</td></tr>
<tr><td>CA/718/92E</td><td>Dairygold Cooperative Society Ltd; Sean Bohan. Exclusive purchase.</td></tr>
<tr><td>CA/719/92E</td><td>Dairygold Cooperative Society Ltd; Eugene O'Sullivan. Exclusive purchase.</td></tr>
<tr><td>CA/720/92E</td><td>Dairygold Cooperative Society Ltd; Michael Cotter. Exclusive purchase and sale of business.</td></tr>
</table>

Decision No.	Date	Type of Decision	Subject of Decision	Relevant Decision in Book	Number
					CA/699/92E
					CA/700/92
					CA/701/92E
					CA/702/92
					CA/703/92E
144 J	19 Nov. 1993 (IO)	L	D	CL (5.1)	CA/704/92
IT 9 Dec. 1994	6 Dec. 1994 (AR)	W(T)			CA/705/92E
144 J	19 Nov. 1993 (IO)	L	D	CL (5.1)	CA/706/92E
144 J	19 Nov. 1993 (IO)	L	D	CL (5.1)	CA/707/92E
IT + 144 J	4 Feb. 1994	L	D	CL (5.1)	CA/708/92
144 J	19 Nov. 1993 (IO)	L	D	CL (5.1)	CA/709/92E
IT 18 March 1994	3 March 1994 (AR)	W(T)			CA/710/92E
IT + 144 J	15 April 1994	L	D	CL (5.1)	CA/711/92E
IT 18 March 1994	3 March 1994 (AR)	W(T)			CA/712/92E
IT 18 March 1994	3 March 1994 (AR)	W(T)			CA/713/92
					CA/714/92
					CA/715/92
					CA/716/92E
27	2 July 1993 (AR)	W		Noted by Editor at 1.4.3 & 2.1.4	CA/717/92
IT 14 July 1995		W(N)			CA/718/92E
IT 14 July 1995		W(N)			CA/719/92E
373	17 Nov. 1994	R	A	S 3.23	CA/720/92E

<table>
<tr><th>Legend</th><th>Number</th><th>Title</th></tr>
<tr><td rowspan="22">A = Acquisition
AR = Annual Report of the Competition Authority
C = Certificate
CL = Category Licence
D = Distribution
EP = Exclusive Purchasing main subject
FR = Franchising
IO = Iris Oifigiúil
IT = Irish Times
J = Joint Decision
L = Licence
LPG = Liquid Petroleum Gas
M = Mentioned and Listed Category Licence
MF = Motor Fuel
NC = Notification changed
P = Property
R = Rejection/Refusal
S = Decision summarised in text
T = More than one subject
W(N) = Withdrawn no reason given
W(T) = Withdrawn because of termination of agreement</td><td>CA/721/92E</td><td>Dairygold Cooperative Society Ltd; Michael Kearney. Exclusive purchase.</td></tr>
<tr><td>CA/722/92E</td><td>Dairygold Cooperative Society Ltd; C. and A. O'Brien. Sale of property.</td></tr>
<tr><td>CA/723/92E</td><td>Irish Life Assurance plc; Noel Woods. Agency agreement.</td></tr>
<tr><td>CA/724/92</td><td>Irish Life Assurance plc; registered Irish Life insurance brokers. Agency agreement.</td></tr>
<tr><td>CA/725/92</td><td>Irish Life Assurance plc; registered Irish Life insurance agents. Agency agreement.</td></tr>
<tr><td>CA/726/92E</td><td>Beaumark Ltd; Moulinex S.A. Exclusive distribution.</td></tr>
<tr><td>CA/727/92E</td><td>Beaumark Ltd; Russell Hobbs Tower Ltd. Exclusive distribution.</td></tr>
<tr><td>CA/728/92E</td><td>Beaumark Ltd; suppliers. Exclusive distribution.</td></tr>
<tr><td>CA/729/92E</td><td>Waterford Foods Ireland Ltd; Avondale Foods Ltd. Exclusive distribution.</td></tr>
<tr><td>CA/730/92E</td><td>Caddens Pharmacy Ltd; National Carways Ltd. Shopping centre lease.</td></tr>
<tr><td>CA/731/92E</td><td>Ballybrack Pharmacy Ltd; Galway Homes Ltd; Martin O'Toole. Shopping centre lease.</td></tr>
<tr><td>CA/732/92E</td><td>J. and E. Murray; Rathmines Properties Ltd. Shopping centre lease.</td></tr>
<tr><td>CA/733/92E</td><td>Colm Stanley; Arden Heath Co. Ltd. Shopping centre lease.</td></tr>
<tr><td>CA/734/92E</td><td>Irish Life Assurance plc; Irish Life Building Society. Agency agreement.</td></tr>
<tr><td>CA/735/92E</td><td>Clayton Love Distribution Ltd; The Nestle Co. Ltd. Exclusive distribution.</td></tr>
<tr><td>CA/736/92E</td><td>Eight to Twelve Ltd. and others; franchisees. Franchise agreement.</td></tr>
<tr><td>CA/737/92</td><td>Walker Air Conditioning Ltd; Vokes Ltd. Exclusive distribution.</td></tr>
<tr><td>CA/738/92E</td><td>Walker Air Conditioning Ltd; Condair A.G. Exclusive distribution.</td></tr>
<tr><td>CA/739/92E</td><td>Abbey Life Assurance (Ireland) Ltd; Merrion Shopping centre leases.</td></tr>
<tr><td>CA/740/92E</td><td>Abbey Life Assurance (Ireland) Ltd; Holland Brooklands Ltd. Shopping centre lease.</td></tr>
<tr><td>CA/741/92E</td><td>Abbey Life Assurance (Ireland) Ltd; Merrion Shopping Centre Ltd; Hayes Bookshops Ltd; Shopping centre lease.</td></tr>
<tr><td>CA/742/92E</td><td>Abbey Life Assurance (Ireland) Ltd; Power Supermarkets Ltd. Merrion Shopping centre lease.</td></tr>
</table>

NOTIFICATIONS TO THE COMPETITION AUTHORITY IN 1992

Decision No.	Date	Type of Decision	Subject of Decision	Relevant Decision in Book	Number
IT 14 July 1995		W(T)			CA/721/92E
346	23 June 1994	C	P		CA/722/92E
IT 26 Nov. 1993	23 Nov. 1993 (AR)	W(N)			CA/723/92E
					CA/724/92
					CA/725/92
IT 4 March 1994	23 Feb. 1994 (AR)	W(T)			CA/726/92E
IT + 144 J	4 Feb. 1994	L	D	CL (5.1)	CA/727/92E
144 J	19 Nov. 1993 (IO)	L	D	CL (5.1)	CA/728/92E
144 J	19 Nov. 1993 (IO)	L	D	CL (5.1)	CA/729/92E
95	13 Oct. 1993	C	P		CA/730/92E
231	15 Dec. 1993	C	P		CA/731/92E
116	13 Oct. 1993	C	P		CA/732/92E
91	13 Oct. 1993	C	P		CA/733/92E
	IT 10 Feb. 1995	W(N)			CA/734/92E
144 J	19 Nov. 1993 (IO)	L	D	CL (5.1)	CA/735/92E
					CA/736/92E
144 J	19 Nov. 1993 (IO)	L	D	CL (5.1)	CA/737/92
144 J	19 Nov. 1993 (IO)	L	D	CL (5.1)	CA/738/92E
174	3 Dec. 1993	C	P		CA/739/92E
172	3 Dec. 1993	C	P		CA/740/92E
173	3 Dec. 1993	C	P		CA/741/92E
175	3 Dec. 1993	C	P		CA/742/92E

Legend	Number	Title
A = Acquisition AR = Annual Report of the Competition Authority C = Certificate CL = Category Licence D = Distribution EP = Exclusive Purchasing main subject FR = Franchising IO = Iris Oifigiúil IT = *Irish Times* J = Joint Decision L = Licence LPG = Liquid Petroleum Gas M = Mentioned and Listed Category Licence MF = Motor Fuel NC = Notification changed P = Property R = Rejection/Refusal S = Decision summarised in text T = More than one subject W(N) = Withdrawn no reason given W(T) = Withdrawn because of termination of agreement	CA/743/92E	Irish Life plc; Eason & Son Ltd; Shopping centre lease.
	CA/744/92E	Poldy's Fresh Foods (Portumna) Ltd; Birds Eye Walls Ltd. Exclusive manufacture and supply.
	CA/745/92E	Thomas De La Rue and Co. Ltd; Smurfit Print and Packaging Ltd; Bayleaf Ltd. Joint venture.
	CA/746/92E	P. and R. Murphy; Reflex Investments plc. Merger.
	CA/747/92E	P. Murphy and others; Reflex Investments plc. Merger.
	CA/748/92E	G. Merrick and others; Reflex Investments plc. Merger.
	CA/749/92E	Reflex Investments plc; Harris Adacom Ltd. Distribution agreement.
	CA/750/92E	Reflex Investments plc; Storage Technology plc. Exclusive distribution.
	CA/751/92E	Campus Oil Ltd; licensee. Licence.
	CA/752/92	Campus Oil Ltd; independent dealers. Mortgage.
	CA/753/92E	Campus Oil Ltd; independent dealers. Loan agreement.
	CA/754/92E	Campus Oil Ltd; independent dealers. Equipment loan agreement.
	CA/755/92E	Campus Oil Ltd; independent dealers. Petrol pump agreement.
	CA/756/92E	Campus Oil Ltd; independent dealers. Exclusive purchase.
	CA/757/92E	Hospicare Ltd; Scott Paper Co. Exclusive manufacture.
	CA/758/92E	Hospicare Ltd; Smith & Nephew Medical Ltd. Exclusive manufacture.
	CA/759/92E	Campus Oil Ltd; distributors. Guarantee.
	CA/760/92E	Campus Oil Ltd; distributors. Licence for distributors.
	CA/761/92E	Campus Oil Ltd; licensor. Licence.
	CA/762/92E	Campus Oil Ltd; distributors. Debenture.
	CA/763/92	Campus Oil Ltd; distributors. Debenture.
	CA/764/92E	Campus Oil Ltd; distributors. Equipment agreement.
	CA/765/92	Campus Oil Ltd; distributors. Exclusive distribution.
	CA/766/92E	Tanning Research Laboratories Inc; Gillespie & Co. Ltd. Exclusive distribution.
	CA/767/92E	J. Donohoe Ltd; Pepsi-Cola Co. Exclusive bottling and distribution.

NOTIFICATIONS TO THE COMPETITION AUTHORITY IN 1992

Decision No.	Date	Type of Decision	Subject of Decision	Relevant Decision in Book	Number
105	13 Oct. 1993	C	P		CA/743/92E
					CA/744/92E
					CA/745/92E
139 NC	20 Oct. 1993	C	A(T)		CA/746/92E
140 NC	20 Oct. 1993	C	T		CA/747/92E
298 NC	11 March 1994	C	A		CA/748/92E
					CA/749/92E
329	19 May 1994	R	D	S 5.6	CA/750/92E
25 J	9 July 1993 (IO)	M	MF	CL (4.2)	CA/751/92E
25 J	9 July 1993 (IO)	M	MF	CL (4.2)	CA/752/92
25 J	9 July 1993 (IO)	M	MF	CL (4.2)	CA/753/92E
25 J	9 July 1993 (IO)	M	MF	CL (4.2)	CA/754/92E
25 J	9 July 1993 (IO)	M	MF	CL (4.2)	CA/755/92E
25 J	9 July 1993 (IO)	M	MF	CL (4.2)	CA/756/92E
IT 13 Oct. 1995		W(T)			CA/757/92E
					CA/758/92E
319 J + 144 J	21 April 1994	L	D	S 5.5 + CL (5.1)	CA/759/92E
319 J + 144 J	21 April 1994	L	D	S 5.5 + CL (5.1)	CA/760/92E
319 J + 144 J	21 April 1994	L	D	S 5.5 + CL (5.1)	CA/761/92E
319 J + 144 J	21 April 1994	L	D	S 5.5 + CL (5.1)	CA/762/92E
319 J + 144 J	21 April 1994	L	D	S 5.5 + CL (5.1)	CA/763/92
319 J + 144 J	21 April 1994	L	D	S 5.5 + CL (5.1)	CA/764/92E
144 J	19 Nov. 1993 (IO)	L	D	CL (5.1)	CA/765/92
IT 6 May 1994	18 April 1994 (AR)	W(T)			CA/766/92E
					CA/767/92E

Legend	Number	Title
A = Acquisition AR = Annual Report of the Competition Authority C = Certificate CL = Category Licence D = Distribution EP = Exclusive Purchasing main subject FR = Franchising IO = Iris Oifigiúil IT = *Irish Times* J = Joint Decision L = Licence LPG = Liquid Petroleum Gas M = Mentioned and Listed Category Licence MF = Motor Fuel NC = Notification changed P = Property R = Rejection/Refusal S = Decision summarised in text T = More than one subject W(N) = Withdrawn no reason given W(T) = Withdrawn because of termination of agreement	CA/768/92E	J. Donohoe Ltd; The Monarch Co. Inc. Exclusive bottling and distribution.
	CA/769/92E	Minitel Communications Ltd; Philips Electronics (Ireland) Ltd. Exclusive distribution.
	CA/770/92E	Bord Telecom Éireann; Allied Irish Banks plc; Intelmatique S.A.; La Societe Rhodanienne Mobiliere et Immobiliere. Joint venture (Minitel).
	CA/771/92E	Minitel Communications Ltd; Intelmatique S.A. Technical and marketing agreement.
	CA/772/92E	Ministere des Postes Telecommunications et de l'Espace; Intelmatique S.A.; Minitel Communications Ltd. Trademark licence.
	CA/773/92E	Bord Telecom Éireann; Minitel Communications Ltd. Operating agreement.
	CA/774/92E	Bord Telecom Éireann; Motorola Ireland Ltd. Joint venture (Eirpage).
	CA/775/92E	Eirpage Ltd; agents. Agency agreement.
	CA/776/92E	Bord Telecom Éireann; Motorola Ireland Ltd. Marketing and development agreement.
	CA/777/92E	Bord Telecom Éireann; Eirpage Ltd. Operating agreement.
	CA/778/92E	Eirpage Ltd; subscribers. Subscriber agreement.
	CA/779/92E	Bord Telecom Éireann; information dealers. Information dealer agreement.
	CA/780/92E	MMC Commercials Ltd; motor dealers. Selective distribution.
	CA/781/92E	MMC Commercials Ltd; motor dealers. Selective distribution.
	CA/782/92E	Lillington Ltd. and others. Glenageary Shopping centre leases.
	CA/783/92E	NEC Electronics (UK) Ltd; Mr. T. Fingleton. Employment contract.
	CA/784/92E	Manor Park Homebuilders Ltd; Trident Homes Ltd; David Daly. Licence to build houses.
	CA/785/92E	Development Capital Corporation. Fannin Group Ltd; shareholders. Shareholding agreement.
	CA/786/92E	DCC; Direct Marketing Technologies Group Ltd; shareholders. Shareholding agreement.
	CA/787/92E	DCC; Allied Foods Ltd; shareholders. Shareholding agreement.
	CA/788/92E	DCC; Capco Holdings Ltd; shareholders. Shareholding agreement.
	CA/789/92E	DCC; John Hinde Ltd; shareholders. Shareholding agreement.

Decision No.	Date	Type of Decision	Subject of Decision	Relevant Decision in Book	Number
IT 13 Oct. 1995		W(T)			CA/768/92E
					CA/769/92E
					CA/770/92E
					CA/771/92E
					CA/772/92E
					CA/773/92E
					CA/774/92E
					CA/775/92E
					CA/776/92E
					CA/777/92E
					CA/778/92E
					CA/779/92E
					CA/780/92E
					CA/781/92E
165	3 Dec. 1993	C	P		CA/782/92E
					CA/783/92E
IT 13 Oct. 1995		W(N)			CA/784/92E
					CA/785/92E
					CA/786/92E
					CA/787/92E
					CA/788/92E
					CA/789/92E

Legend	Number	Title
A = Acquisition AR = Annual Report of the Competition Authority C = Certificate CL = Category Licence D = Distribution EP = Exclusive Purchasing main subject FR = Franchising IO = Iris Oifigiúil IT = *Irish Times* J = Joint Decision L = Licence LPG = Liquid Petroleum Gas M = Mentioned and Listed Category Licence MF = Motor Fuel NC = Notification changed P = Property R = Rejection/Refusal S = Decision summarised in text T = More than one subject W(N) = Withdrawn no reason given W(T) = Withdrawn because of termination of agreement	CA/790/92E	DCC; Sharptext Ltd; shareholders. Shareholding agreement.
	CA/791/92E	DCC; Emo Oil Ltd; shareholders. Shareholding agreement.
	CA/792/92E	Bord Telecom Éireann; Nynex Security Systems Ltd. Joint venture (PhoneWatch).
	CA/793/92E	Bord Telecom Éireann; Nynex Security Systems Ltd; Telecom PhoneWatch Ltd. Technical information agreement.
	CA/794/92E	Nynex Corporation; Telecom PhoneWatch Ltd. Trademark licence.
	CA/795/92E	BTE; Telecom PhoneWatch Ltd. Telecom agreement.
	CA/796/92E	Telecom PhoneWatch Ltd; licencee. UK licence.
	CA/797/92E	Telecom PhoneWatch Ltd; customers. System sales and installation agreement.
	CA/798/92E	Telecom PhoneWatch Ltd; customers. Monitoring and maintenance agreement.
	CA/799/92E	Omnitron Ltd; Crytovision A/S. Exclusive distribution.
	CA/800/92E	Omnitron Ltd; Crytovision A/S. Tandberg A/S. Exclusive manufacture and distribution.
	CA/801/92E	Omnitron Ltd; Crytovision A/S. Tandberg A/S. Cablelink Ltd. Exclusive supply contract.
	CA/802/92E	Tedcastle Oil Products Ltd; distributors. Exclusice distribution.
	CA/803/92E	Heron (Suzuki) Ltd; motor dealers. Selective distribution.
	CA/804/92E	Gill & MacMillan Ltd; Attic Press. Exclusive distribution.
	CA/805/92E	Gill & MacMillan Ltd; Brandon Book Publishers Ltd. Exclusive distribution.
	CA/806/92E	Gill & MacMillan Ltd; The Lilliput Press. Exclusive distribution.
	CA/807/92E	Gill & MacMillan Ltd; Irish Academic Press. Exclusive distribution.
	CA/808/92E	Gill & MacMillan Ltd; Four Courts Press. Exclusive distribution.
	CA/809/92E	Gill & MacMillan Ltd; The Round Hall Press. Exclusive distribution.
	CA/810/92E	Gill & MacMillan Ltd; The O'Brien Press. Exclusive distribution.
	CA/811/92E	Gill & MacMillan Ltd; Wolfhound Press. Exclusive distribution.

NOTIFICATIONS TO THE COMPETITION AUTHORITY IN 1992

Decision No.	Date	Type of Decision	Subject of Decision	Relevant Decision in Book	Number
					CA/790/92E
					CA/791/92E
					CA/792/92E
					CA/793/92E
					CA/794/92E
					CA/795/92E
					CA/796/92E
					CA/797/92E
					CA/798/92E
393 NC	12 April 1995	L	D		CA/799/92E
					CA/800/92E
					CA/801/92E
					CA/802/92E
					CA/803/92E
366 J	28 Oct. 1994	C	D	S 5.11	CA/804/92E
366 J	28 Oct. 1994	C	D	S 5.11	CA/805/92E
366 J	28 Oct. 1994	C	D	S 5.11	CA/806/92E
366 J	28 Oct. 1994	C	D	S 5.11	CA/807/92E
366 J	28 Oct. 1994	C	D	S 5.11	CA/808/92E
366 J	28 Oct. 1994	C	D	S 5.11	CA/809/92E
366 J	28 Oct. 1994	C	D	S 5.11	CA/810/92E
366 J	28 Oct. 1994	C	D	S 5.11	CA/811/92E

Legend	Number	Title
A = Acquisition AR = Annual Report of the Competition Authority C = Certificate CL = Category Licence D = Distribution EP = Exclusive Purchasing main subject FR = Franchising IO = Iris Oifigiúil IT = *Irish Times* J = Joint Decision L = Licence LPG = Liquid Petroleum Gas M = Mentioned and Listed Category Licence MF = Motor Fuel NC = Notification changed P = Property R = Rejection/Refusal S = Decision summarised in text T = More than one subject W(N) = Withdrawn no reason given W(T) = Withdrawn because of termination of agreement	CA/812/92E	Gill & MacMillan Ltd; Townhouse & Countryhouse Publishers Ltd. Exclusive distribution.
	CA/813/92E	Gill & MacMillan Ltd; booksellers. Standard terms and conditions.
	CA/814/92E	D. Horkan Ltd; Michael Kavanagh. Shopping centre lease.
	CA/815/92E	D. Horkan Ltd; Michael Kavanagh. Shopping centre lease.
	CA/816/92E	D. Horkan Ltd; Eder Trust Co. Shopping centre lease.
	CA/817/92E	D. Horkan Ltd; Malincourt Ltd. Shopping centre lease.
	CA/818/92E	Power Supermarkets Ltd; D. Horkan Ltd. Shopping centre lease.
	CA/819/92E	D. Horkan Ltd; Erin Executor and Trustee Co. Ltd. Shopping centre lease.
	CA/820/92E	Texaco (Ireland) Ltd; bulk buyers. Sale agreement-exclusive purchase.
	CA/821/92E	Texaco (Ireland) Ltd; distributors and bulk buyers. Equipment loan agreement.
	CA/822/92E	Texaco (Ireland) Ltd; distributors. Exclusive purchase.
	CA/823/92E	Texaco (Ireland) Ltd; bulk buyers. Terms and conditions of sale.
	CA/824/92E	Coillte Teo; sawmills. Coillte Allocation Scheme.
	CA/825/92E	Miller Brewing Co.; Showerings Ltd. Exclusive distribution.
	CA/826/92E	The Institute of Chartered Accountants in Ireland. Bye-laws.
	CA/827/92E	The Institute of Chartered Accountants in Ireland. Rules of Professional Conduct.
	CA/828/92	The Institute of Chartered Accountants in Ireland. Ethical Guide for Members.
	CA/829/92E	Service Master Ltd; franchisees. Contract services franchise agreement.
	CA/830/92E	Service Master Ltd; franchisees. On-location franchise agreement.
	CA/831/92E	The Wardens and Commonalty of Goldsmiths of the City of Dublin. Charter.
	CA/832/92E	Bewleys Coffee Ltd; customers. Coffee machines loan agreement.
	CA/833/92E	Bewleys Coffee Ltd; large customers. Coffee machine loan agreement.

NOTIFICATIONS TO THE COMPETITION AUTHORITY IN 1992

Decision No.	Date	Type of Decision	Subject of Decision	Relevant Decision in Book	Number
366 J	28 Oct. 1994	C	D	S 5.11	CA/812/92E
365 NC	28 Oct. 1994	C	D		CA/813/92E
191	3 Dec. 1993	C	P		CA/814/92E
190	3 Dec. 1993	C	P		CA/815/92E
46	5 Oct. 1993	C	P		CA/816/92E
179	3 Dec. 1993	C	P	S 7.6	CA/817/92E
102	13 Oct. 1993	C	P		CA/818/92E
94	13 Oct. 1993	C	P		CA/819/92E
IT 10 Nov. 1995		R	Notification incomplete		CA/820/92E
IT 10 Nov. 1995		R	Notification incomplete		CA/821/92E
IT 10 Nov. 1995		R	Notification incomplete		CA/822/92E
IT 10 Nov. 1995		R	Notification incomplete		CA/823/92E
					CA/824/92E
					CA/825/92E
					CA/826/92E
					CA/827/92E
					CA/828/92
					CA/829/92E
					CA/830/92E
IT 12 May 1995		R			CA/831/92E
					CA/832/92E
					CA/833/92E

<table>
<tr><th>Legend</th><th>Number</th><th>Title</th></tr>
<tr><td rowspan="22">A = Acquisition
AR = Annual Report of the Competition Authority
C = Certificate
CL = Category Licence
D = Distribution
EP = Exclusive Purchasing main subject
FR = Franchising
IO = Iris Oifigiúil
IT = Irish Times
J = Joint Decision
L = Licence
LPG = Liquid Petroleum Gas
M = Mentioned and Listed Category Licence
MF = Motor Fuel
NC = Notification changed
P = Property
R = Rejection/Refusal
S = Decision summarised in text
T = More than one subject
W(N) = Withdrawn no reason given
W(T) = Withdrawn because of termination of agreement</td><td>CA/834/92E</td><td>Brooks Thomas Ltd; franchisees. Franchise agreement.</td></tr>
<tr><td>CA/835/92E</td><td>Unislim (Ireland) Ltd; franchisees. Franchise agreement.</td></tr>
<tr><td>CA/836/92</td><td>Electricity Supply Board; electrical contractors. Register of Electricity Contractors Ireland Ltd.</td></tr>
<tr><td>CA/837/92E</td><td>An Post; postmasters. Appointment of postmaster, and General Rules.</td></tr>
<tr><td>CA/838/92E</td><td>Nostex Properties Ltd; Bishopstown Shopping centre leases.</td></tr>
<tr><td>CA/839/92E</td><td>Castlebrook Investments Ltd; Newbridge Shopping centre leases.</td></tr>
<tr><td>CA/840/92E</td><td>Oakville Ltd; Clonmel Shopping centre leases.</td></tr>
<tr><td>CA/841/92</td><td>Salix Trust Ltd; The Square Management Ltd; tenants. Shopping centre leases.</td></tr>
<tr><td>CA/842/92</td><td>B. and J. McCormack; The Square Management Ltd; tenants. Shopping centre lease.</td></tr>
<tr><td>CA/843/92E</td><td>T. O'Muire. J. Smyth and D. Kavanagh; Toscorva Rest Ltd. Property lease.</td></tr>
<tr><td>CA/844/92E</td><td>Crumlin Investments Ltd; tenants. Crumlin Shopping centre leases.</td></tr>
<tr><td>CA/845/92E</td><td>Cornelscourt Shopping Centre Ltd; tenants. Shopping centre leases.</td></tr>
<tr><td>CA/846/92E</td><td>Interfit Ltd; Portmarnock Shopping centre leases.</td></tr>
<tr><td>CA/847/92E</td><td>ICC Bank plc; Cornell Electronics and others. Shareholding agreement.</td></tr>
<tr><td>CA/848/92E</td><td>ICC Bank plc; Mentec Ltd and others. Shareholding agreement.</td></tr>
<tr><td>CA/849/92E</td><td>ICC Bank plc; Navenby Ltd and others. Shareholding agreement.</td></tr>
<tr><td>CA/850/92E</td><td>ICC Bank plc; Largo Food Exports Ltd and others. Shareholding agreement.</td></tr>
<tr><td>CA/851/92E</td><td>ICC Bank plc; Astra Group (Holdings) Ltd and others. Shareholding agreement.</td></tr>
<tr><td>CA/852/92E</td><td>ICC Bank plc; Irish Conference and Leisure Holdings Ltd and others.
Shareholding agreement.</td></tr>
<tr><td>CA/853/92E</td><td>ICC Bank plc; IDA; SFADCO; CTT.
Joint venture.</td></tr>
<tr><td>CA/854/92E</td><td>ICC Bank plc; Acquaporte Ltd and others. Shareholding agreement.</td></tr>
<tr><td>CA/855/92E</td><td>ICC Bank plc; Kleerex Licensing Ltd and others. Shareholding agreement.</td></tr>
</table>

Decision No.	Date	Type of Decision	Subject of Decision	Relevant Decision in Book	Number
410 NC	30 June 1995	C	Agency		CA/834/92E
					CA/835/92E
IT 9 Dec. 1994		Intention to certify			CA/836/92
400	27 April 1995	C	Agency		CA/837/92E
223	15 Dec. 1993	C	P		CA/838/92E
244	15 Dec. 1993	C	P		CA/839/92E
260	15 Dec. 1993	C	P		CA/840/92E
215	3 Dec. 1993	C	P		CA/841/92
216	3 Dec. 1993	C	P		CA/842/92
340	14 June 1994	C	P		CA/843/92E
48	5 Oct. 1993	C	P		CA/844/92E
51	5 Oct. 1993	C	P		CA/845/92E
193	3 Dec. 1993	C	P		CA/846/92E
					CA/847/92E
395	12 April 1995	C	A		CA/848/92E
IT 9 June 1995		W(N)			CA/849/92E
IT 9 June 1995		W(N)			CA/850/92E
IT 9 June 1995		W(N)			CA/851/92E
IT 9 June 1995		W(N)			CA/852/92E
IT 14 July 1995		W(N)			CA/853/92E
IT 9 June 1995		W(N)			CA/854/92E
					CA/855/92E

Legend	Number	Title
A = Acquisition AR = Annual Report of the Competition Authority C = Certificate CL = Category Licence D = Distribution EP = Exclusive Purchasing main subject FR = Franchising IO = Iris Oifigiúil IT = *Irish Times* J = Joint Decision L = Licence LPG = Liquid Petroleum Gas M = Mentioned and Listed Category Licence MF = Motor Fuel NC = Notification changed P = Property R = Rejection/Refusal S = Decision summarised in text T = More than one subject W(N) = Withdrawn no reason given W(T) = Withdrawn because of termination of agreement	CA/856/92E	ICC Bank plc; Kleerex International Ltd; Carroll Products and Designs Ltd and others. Intellectual property licence.
	CA/857/92E	ICC Bank plc; Kleerex International Ltd and others. Shareholding agreement.
	CA/858/92E	ICC Bank plc; Kleerex International Ltd; Carroll Products and Designs Ltd and others. Intellectual property licence.
	CA/859/92E	ICC Bank plc; Carroll Products and Designs Ltd and others. Shareholding agreement.
	CA/860/92E	ICC Bank plc; Noontec Ltd and others. Shareholding agreement and patent licence.
	CA/861/92E	Navenby Ltd; I. Gracie and R. Fearnley. Merger.
	CA/862/92E	ICC Bank plc; Mosney Irish Holidays plc and others. Shareholding agreement.
	CA/863/92E	ICC Bank plc; Hemera & Cie S.C.P.A.; Rochglen Holdings Ltd and V.R. (Spideal) Teo and others. Shareholding agreement.
	CA/864/92E	Navenby Ltd; Savage Plastic Packaging and Savpack Ltd and others. Merger.
	CA/865/92E	ICC Bank plc; Irish Fencing and Products Ltd and others. Shareholding agreement.
	CA/866/92E	ICC Bank plc; Corcoran's Management Ltd and others; Isbauch Ltd; Cambridge Investments Ltd. Shareholding agreement.
	CA/867/92E	ICC Bank plc; Marine Computation Service plc; Dental Laboratories (Drumshambo) Ltd and others. Shareholding agreement.
	CA/868/92E	ICC Bank plc; Etos Investments Ltd; Allied Combined Trust Ltd and First Venture Fund Ltd; Allied Irish Investment Bank plc and others. Shareholding agreement.
	CA/869/92E	ICC Bank plc; L. & P. Financial Trustees of Ireland Ltd and others. Shareholding agreement.
	CA/870/92E	AIB Finance Ltd and AIB Leasing Ltd; Combined Insurance Co. of America; Pat Ryan & Associates; Sedgwick Dineen Ltd. Memorandum of Agreement on Creditor Insurance.
	CA/871/92E	Aviette Ltd; Firhouse Shopping centre leases.
	CA/872/92E	E. and A. Gorman; A. Elkinson. Property lease.
	CA/873/92	Aviette Ltd; Musgraves Ltd. Tallaght Shopping centre lease.
	CA/874/92	Airspace Investments Ltd; The Square Management Ltd; tenants. Shopping centre lease.

NOTIFICATIONS TO THE COMPETITION AUTHORITY IN 1992

Decision No.	Date	Type of Decision	Subject of Decision	Relevant Decision in Book	Number
438	23 Oct. 1995	C	Manufac. licence		CA/856/92E
					CA/857/92E
437	23 Oct. 1995	C	Manufac. licence		CA/858/92E
					CA/859/92E
IT 9 June 1995		W(N)			CA/860/92E
36	24 Sept. 1993	R	A/T		CA/861/92E
IT 9 June 1995		W(N)			CA/862/92E
IT 9 June 1995		W(N)			CA/863/92E
35	24 Sept. 1993	R		S 2.2.1	CA/864/92E
IT 9 June 1995		W(N)			CA/865/92E
IT 14 July 1995		W(N)			CA/866/92E
IT 9 June 1995		W(N)			CA/867/92E
IT 14 July 1995		W(N)			CA/868/92E
IT 9 June 1995		W(N)			CA/869/92E
					CA/870/92E
267	15 Dec. 1993	C	P	S 7.8	CA/871/92E
341	14 June 1994	C	P		CA/872/92E
218	3 Dec. 1993	C	P		CA/873/92
210	3 Dec. 1993	C	P		CA/874/92

Legend	Number	Title
A = Acquisition AR = Annual Report of the Competition Authority C = Certificate CL = Category Licence D = Distribution EP = Exclusive Purchasing main subject FR = Franchising IO = Iris Oifigiúil IT = *Irish Times* J = Joint Decision L = Licence LPG = Liquid Petroleum Gas M = Mentioned and Listed Category Licence MF = Motor Fuel NC = Notification changed P = Property R = Rejection/Refusal S = Decision summarised in text T = More than one subject W(N) = Withdrawn no reason given W(T) = Withdrawn because of termination of agreement	CA/875/92E	G.D. Investments (Galway) Ltd; tenants. Shopping centre lease.
	CA/876/92E	Dunnes Properties Ltd; Castlebrook Investments and others; tenants. Ballilna Shopping centre leases.
	CA/877/92E	Tallaght Shopping Centre Ltd; tenants. Kilmanagh Shopping centre leases.
	CA/878/92E	Dunnes Stores (Headford Road) Ltd. and others; tenants. Shopping centre leases.
	CA/879/92E	Ballyvolane Ltd; tenants. Shopping centre leases.
	CA/880/92E	Dunnes Stores (Limerick) Ltd; tenants. Sarsfield Shopping centre leases.
	CA/881/92E	Quinnsworth; Trikkala Ltd; Janelle Shopping centre leases.
	CA/882/92E	Bararnca; Nutgrove Shopping Centre (Management) Ltd; Tesco Stores (Ireland) Ltd. Shopping centre lease.
	CA/883/92E	Power Supermarkets Ltd; Letterkenny Shopping Centre Ltd. Shopping centre lease.
	CA/884/92E	Merrion Shopping Centre and others; tenants. Shopping centre leases.
	CA/885/92E	Pesenta; Power Supermarkets Ltd; tenants. Merrion Shopping centre leases.
	CA/886/92E	The Square Management Ltd; investors; tenants. Shareholders agreement, shopping centre leases etc.
	CA/887/92E	Superquinn Ltd; AIB Capital Markets plc; tenants. Blackrock Shopping centre leases.
	CA/888/92E	Superquinn Ltd; tenants. Blanchardstown Shopping centre leases.
	CA/889/92E	Superquinn Ltd; tenants. Swords Shopping centre leases.
	CA/890/92E	Superquinn Ltd; tenants. Ballinteer Shopping centre leases.
	CA/891/92	The Square Management Ltd; IBI Nominees Ltd; tenants. Shopping centre leases.
	CA/892/92	The Square Management Ltd; IBI Property Nominees Ltd; tenants. Shopping centre leases.
	CA/893/92E	Emo Oil Ltd; Canvale Ltd; F. O'Sullivan. Exclusive distribution.
	CA/894/92E	Atlas Oil Laboratories Ltd; G. Dunne. Collection agreement for waste oil.
	CA/895/92E	Adam F. Torrie (Properties) Ltd; tenants. Waterford Shopping centre and office leases.
	CA/896/92	Abrakebabra Ltd; franchisees. Franchise agreement.

Decision No.	Date	Type of Decision	Subject of Decision	Relevant Decision in Book	Number
68	5 Oct. 1993	C	P		CA/875/92E
256	15 Dec. 1993	C	P		CA/876/92E
171	3 Dec. 1993	C	P		CA/877/92E
236	15 Dec. 1993	C	P		CA/878/92E
222	15 Dec. 1993	C	P		CA/879/92E
135	13 Oct. 1993	C	P		CA/880/92E
163	3 Dec. 1993	C	P		CA/881/92E
187	3 Dec. 1993	C	P		CA/882/92E
229	15 Dec. 1993	C	P		CA/883/92E
178	3 Dec. 1993	C	P		CA/884/92E
177	3 Dec. 1993	C	P		CA/885/92E
206	3 Dec. 1993	C	P	S 7.7	CA/886/92E
43	5 Oct. 1993	C	P		CA/887/92E
45	5 Oct. 1993	C	P		CA/888/92E
122	13 Oct. 1993	C	P		CA/889/92E
151	3 Dec. 1993	C	P		CA/890/92E
212	3 Dec. 1993	C	P		CA/891/92
211	3 Dec. 1993	C	P		CA/892/92
IT 9 Sept. 1994	6 Sept. 1994 (AR)	W(N)			CA/893/92E
IT 13 Jan. 1995	23 Dec. 1994 (AR)	W(T)			CA/894/92E
261	15 Dec. 1993	C	P		CA/895/92E
					CA/896/92

Legend	Number	Title
A = Acquisition AR = Annual Report of the Competition Authority C = Certificate CL = Category Licence D = Distribution EP = Exclusive Purchasing main subject FR = Franchising IO = Iris Oifigiúil IT = *Irish Times* J = Joint Decision L = Licence LPG = Liquid Petroleum Gas M = Mentioned and Listed Category Licence MF = Motor Fuel NC = Notification changed P = Property R = Rejection/Refusal S = Decision summarised in text T = More than one subject W(N) = Withdrawn no reason given W(T) = Withdrawn because of termination of agreement	CA/897/92	Jotun Henry Clark Ltd; Marinco Ltd; J. O'Riordan. Exclusive distribution.
	CA/898/92	Fiat Auto (Ireland) Ltd; dealers. Selective distribution.
	CA/899/92E	Fiat Auto (Ireland) Ltd; J. Donohoe Ltd. Selective distribution.
	CA/900/92E	Burmah Castrol (Ireland) Ltd; distributors. Exclusive distribution.
	CA/901/92	Burmah Castrol (Ireland) Ltd; distributors. Loan equipment agreement.
	CA/902/92E	Burmah Castrol (Ireland) Ltd; Liffey Oil Ltd. Exclusive distribution.
	CA/903/92E	Burmah Castrol (Ireland) Ltd; Kingdom Oil Ltd. Exclusive distribution.
	CA/904/92E	The Booksellers Association of Great Britain and Ireland–Irish Branch. Currency conversion rates for English books.
	CA/905/92E	Brown Thomas & Co. Ltd,; Extravert Design Ltd. Exclusive distribution.
	CA/906/92E	Wanze Properties (Ireland) Ltd; Janelle Shopping centre leases.
	CA/907/92E	Wanze Properties (Ireland) Ltd; Drogheda Shopping centre leases.
	CA/908/92E	Wanze Properties (Ireland) Ltd; Athlone Shopping centre leases.
	CA/909/92E	Wanze Properties (Ireland) Ltd; Dundalk Shopping centre leases.
	CA/910/92E	Wanze Properties (Ireland) Ltd; Greystones Shopping centre leases.
	CA/911/92E	Wanze Properties (Ireland) Ltd; Hartstown Shopping centre leases.
	CA/912/92E	Wanze Properties (Ireland) Ltd; Navan Shopping centre leases.
	CA/913/92E	Wanze Properties (Ireland) Ltd; AnCO. Office and light industrial lease.
	CA/914/92E	Lombard & Ulster Banking Ltd; car dealers. Provision of loan facilities for car dealers.
	CA/915/92E	Bewleys Manufacturing Ltd; Butler Irish Confectionery Ltd. and others. Joint venture.
	CA/916/92E	Four Star Pizza (Ireland) Ltd; franchisees. Franchise agreement.
	CA/917/92E	Brooke Thomas Ltd; Servicised Ltd. Exclusive distribution.

NOTIFICATIONS TO THE COMPETITION AUTHORITY IN 1992

Decision No.	Date	Type of Decision	Subject of Decision	Relevant Decision in Book	Number
144 J	19 Nov. 1993 (IO)	L	D	CL (5.1)	CA/897/92E
					CA/898/92E
					CA/899/92E
IT + 144 J NC	IT 11 March 1994	L	D	CL (5.1)	CA/900/92E
322 + 144 J	21 April 1994	L	D	CL (5.1)	CA/901/92
IT + 144 J NC	IT 11 March 1994	L	D	CL (5.1)	CA/902/92E
IT + 144 J	IT 4 Feb. 1994	L	D	CL (5.1)	CA/903/92E
348	2 Sept. 1994	R		S 1.7.5	CA/904/92E
144 J	19 Nov. 1993 (IO)	L	D	CL (5.1)	CA/905/92E
164	3 Dec. 1993	C	P		CA/906/92E
253	15 Dec. 1993	C	P		CA/907/92E
263	15 Dec. 1993	C	P		CA/908/92E
255	15 Dec. 1993	C	P		CA/909/92E
266	15 Dec. 1993	C	P		CA/910/92E
100	13 Oct. 1993	C	P		CA/911/92E
257	15 Dec. 1993	C	P		CA/912/92E
359	12 Oct. 1994	C	P		CA/913/92E
IT 9 Dec. 1994	15 Nov. 1994 (AR)	W(N)			CA/914/92E
					CA/915/92E
IT + 372 J NC	IT 8 Sept. 1995	L	FR	CL (4.9)	CA/916/92E
IT + 144 J NC	IT 4 Feb. 1994	L	D	CL (5.1)	CA/917/92E

Legend	Number	Title
A = Acquisition AR = Annual Report of the Competition Authority C = Certificate CL = Category Licence D = Distribution EP = Exclusive Purchasing main subject FR = Franchising IO = Iris Oifigiúil IT = *Irish Times* J = Joint Decision L = Licence LPG = Liquid Petroleum Gas M = Mentioned and Listed Category Licence MF = Motor Fuel NC = Notification changed P = Property R = Rejection/Refusal S = Decision summarised in text T = More than one subject W(N) = Withdrawn no reason given W(T) = Withdrawn because of termination of agreement	CA/918/92E	Brooks Haughton Ltd; franchisees. Franchise agreement.
	CA/919/92E	Cannon Hygienic Products (Ireland) Ltd; Initial Services (Ireland) Ltd. Agreement for the provision and service of disposal units and vending machines.
	CA/920/92E	Power Supermarkets Ltd; Carmel Feeney; Shopping centre lease.
	CA/921/92E	Fitzwilliam Trust Co.; Fitzpatrick Associates Economic Consultants Ltd. Office lease.
	CA/922/92E	Fitzwilliam Trust Co.; Linen Supply of Ireland Ltd. and Texas Homecare (Ireland) Ltd. Office and shop leases.
	CA/923/92E	Nabola Development Ltd; tenants. Maynooth Shopping centre leases.
	CA/924/92E	Naas Mall Ltd; tenants. Shopping centre leases.
	CA/925/92E	Bridtron Ltd; Bridge Street; AIB Corporation plc; tenants. Office leases.
	CA/926/92E	Liam O'Farrell and others; Merchant's Hall Office leases.
	CA/927/92E	Liam O'Farrell and others; Bridtron Ltd; Merchant's House Office leases.
	CA/928/92E	O. McDermott and L. O'Farrell; Merchant's Court Office leases.
	CA/929/92E	L. & C. Properties Ltd. and others; The Square Management Ltd; tenants. Shopping centre leases.
	CA/930/92E	K. Rohan; The Square Management Ltd; tenants. Shopping centre leases.
	CA/931/92E	Worldwide Refinishing Systems Inc; Halton Business Systems Ltd. Franchise agreement.
	CA/932/92E	Halton Business Systems Ltd; P. Burns. Franchise agreement.
	CA/933/92E	Levi Strauss (UK) Ltd; Lasater Ltd. Franchise agreement.
	CA/934/92E	Levi Strauss (UK) Ltd; Limington Ltd. Franchise agreement.
	CA/935/92E	Levi Strauss (UK) Ltd; B. & S. Fashions Ltd. Franchise agreement.
	CA/936/92E	Prontaprint plc; Kippure Business Services Ltd; B. O'Brien. Franchise agreement.
	CA/937/92E	Euroscreen Ltd; International Screen Ltd; J. Delves Shareholding agreement.
	CA/938/92E	P.J. Carroll & Co. Ltd., Dakota Ltd. Exclusive supply agreement.

Decision No.	Date	Type of Decision	Subject of Decision	Relevant Decision in Book	Number
411 NC	30 June 1995	C	Agency		CA/918/92E
					CA/919/92E
101	13 Oct. 1993	C	P		CA/920/92E
296	10 March 1994	C	P		CA/921/92E
271	15 Dec. 1993	C	P		CA/922/92E
132	13 Oct. 1993	C	P		CA/923/92E
242	15 Dec. 1993	C	P		CA/924/92E
310	21 April 1994	C	P		CA/925/92E
311	21 April 1994	C	P		CA/926/92E
312	21 April 1994	C	P		CA/927/92E
313	21 April 1994	C	P		CA/928/92E
214	3 Dec. 1993	C	P		CA/929/92E
217	3 Dec. 1993	C	P		CA/930/92E
IT + 372 J NC	IT 9 June 1995	L	FR	CL (4.9)	CA/931/92E
IT 9 Dec. 1994		R			CA/932/92E
IT + 372 J NC	IT 9 June 1995	L	FR	CL (4.9)	CA/933/92E
IT + 372 J NC	IT 9 June 1995	L	FR	CL (4.9)	CA/934/92E
IT + 372 J NC	IT 9 June 1995	L	FR	CL (4.9)	CA/935/92E
IT + 372 J NC	IT 9 June 1995	L	FR	CL (4.9)	CA/936/92E
IT 17 Sept. 1993	14 Sept. 1993 (AR)	W(N)			CA/937/92E
IT 13 Oct. 1995		W(T)			CA/938/92E

<table>
<tr><th>Legend</th><th>Number</th><th>Title</th></tr>
<tr><td rowspan="23">A = Acquisition
AR = Annual Report of the Competition Authority
C = Certificate
CL = Category Licence
D = Distribution
EP = Exclusive Purchasing main subject
FR = Franchising
IO = Iris Oifigiúil
IT = Irish Times
J = Joint Decision
L = Licence
LPG = Liquid Petroleum Gas
M = Mentioned and Listed Category Licence
MF = Motor Fuel
NC = Notification changed
P = Property
R = Rejection/Refusal
S = Decision summarised in text
T = More than one subject
W(N) = Withdrawn no reason given
W(T) = Withdrawn because of termination of agreement</td><td>CA/939/92E</td><td>P.J. Carroll & Co. Ltd., Burger Sohne A.G. Exclusive distribution.</td></tr>
<tr><td>CA/940/92E</td><td>P.J. Carroll & Co. Ltd., Le S.E.I.T.A. Exclusive distribution.</td></tr>
<tr><td>CA/941/92E</td><td>P.J. Carroll & Co. Ltd., B.V. Willem II Sigarenfabrieken. Exclusive distribution.</td></tr>
<tr><td>CA/942/92E</td><td>Duffy Group Old Bawn Ltd; Timebrock Ltd. Shopping centre leases.</td></tr>
<tr><td>CA/943/92E</td><td>B. Duffy; Timebrock Ltd. Shopping centre leases.</td></tr>
<tr><td>CA/944/92E</td><td>Superquinn; Sutton Shopping centre leases.</td></tr>
<tr><td>CA/945/92</td><td>Superquinn; Lucan Shopping centre leases.</td></tr>
<tr><td>CA/946/92E</td><td>Superquinn; Sundrive Shopping centre leases.</td></tr>
<tr><td>CA/947/92E</td><td>Superquinn; Knocklyon Shopping centre leases.</td></tr>
<tr><td>CA/948/92E</td><td>Solicitors Financial and Property Services (Ireland) Ltd; Sedgwick Dineen Personal Financial Management Ltd. Exclusive supply of services.</td></tr>
<tr><td>CA/949/92E</td><td>Cable Management (Ireland) Ltd; the Minister for Communications. Exclusive licence for cable television.</td></tr>
<tr><td>CA/950/92E</td><td>Maguire & Paterson Ltd; G. & M. Ltd. Exclusive distribution.</td></tr>
<tr><td>CA/951/92E</td><td>Maguire & Paterson Ltd; Irish Dog Foods Ltd. Exclusive distribution.</td></tr>
<tr><td>CA/952/92E</td><td>Maguire & Paterson Ltd; Jade Cosmetics GmbH. Exclusive distribution.</td></tr>
<tr><td>CA/953/92E</td><td>Maguire & Paterson Ltd; LRC Products Ltd. Exclusive distribution.</td></tr>
<tr><td>CA/954/92E</td><td>Maguire & Paterson Ltd; Seerys Biscuits Ltd. Exclusive distribution.</td></tr>
<tr><td>CA/955/92E</td><td>Maguire & Paterson Ltd; Wilkinson Sword GmbH. Exclusive distribution.</td></tr>
<tr><td>CA/956/92E</td><td>Maguire & Paterson Ltd; Conros Corporation. Exclusive distribution.</td></tr>
<tr><td>CA/957/92E</td><td>Fannin Ireland Ltd; Vernon & Co. (Pulp Products) Ltd. Exclusive distribution.</td></tr>
<tr><td>CA/958/92E</td><td>Fannin Hospital Enterprises Ltd; Portex Ltd. Exclusive distribution.</td></tr>
<tr><td>CA/959/92E</td><td>Fannin Health Care Ltd; Hospicare Ltd. Exclusive distribution.</td></tr>
<tr><td>CA/960/92E</td><td>Fannin Hospital Enterprises Ltd; Kendall Co. (UK) Ltd. Exclusive distribution.</td></tr>
<tr><td>CA/961/92E</td><td>Fannin Hospital Enterprises Ltd; Eschmann Bros. & Walsh Ltd. Exclusive distribution.</td></tr>
</table>

Decision No.	Date	Type of Decision	Subject of Decision	Relevant Decision in Book	Number
IT 11 Feb. 1994	3 Dec. 1993 (AR)	W(N)			CA/939/92E
IT + 144 J	IT 4 Feb. 1994	L	D	CL (5.1)	CA/940/92E
IT 11 Feb. 1994	3 Dec. 1993 (AR)	W(N)			CA/941/92E
111	13 Oct. 1993	C	P		CA/942/92E
110	13 Oct. 1993	C	P		CA/943/92E
121	13 Oct. 1993	C	P		CA/944/92E
107	13 Oct. 1993	C	P		CA/945/92E
120	13 Oct. 1993	C	P		CA/946/92E
55	5 Oct. 1993	C	P		CA/947/92E
					CA/948/92E
					CA/949/92E
144 J	19 Nov. 1993 (IO)	L	D	CL (5.1)	CA/950/92E
IT + 144 J	IT 9 Sept. 1994	L	D	CL (5.1)	CA/951/92E
IT + 144 J NC	IT 13 Jan. 1995	L	D	CL (5.1)	CA/952/92E
IT 9 Sept. 1994	5 Sept. 1994 (AR)	W(T)			CA/953/92E
IT 11 Feb. 1994	8 Dec. 1993 (AR)	W(N)			CA/954/92E
IT + 144 J NC	IT 16 Sept. 1994	L	D	CL (5.1)	CA/955/92E
144 J	19 Nov. 1993 (IO)	L	D	CL (5.1)	CA/956/92E
IT + 144 J NC	IT 11 March 1994	L	D	CL (5.1)	CA/957/92E
144 J	19 Nov. 1993 (IO)	L	D	CL (5.1)	CA/958/92E
144 J	19 Nov. 1993 (IO)	L	D	CL (5.1)	CA/959/92E
144 J	19 Nov. 1993 (IO)	L	D	CL (5.1)	CA/960/92E
144 J	19 Nov. 1993 (IO)	L	D	CL (5.1)	CA/961/92E

Legend	Number	Title
A = Acquisition AR = Annual Report of the Competition Authority C = Certificate CL = Category Licence D = Distribution EP = Exclusive Purchasing main subject FR = Franchising IO = Iris Oifigiúil IT = *Irish Times* J = Joint Decision L = Licence LPG = Liquid Petroleum Gas M = Mentioned and Listed Category Licence MF = Motor Fuel NC = Notification changed P = Property R = Rejection/Refusal S = Decision summarised in text T = More than one subject W(N) = Withdrawn no reason given W(T) = Withdrawn because of termination of agreement	CA/962/92E	Irish Life Assurance plc; Irish Intercontinental Bank Ltd; Irish Life Finance Group Ltd; Irish Life Finance Ltd. Shareholding agreement.
	CA/963/92	Swintron Ltd; Design Factory Ltd. Office lease.
	CA/964/92E	Wexford Creamery Ltd; Wexford Milk Producers Ltd; Unigate Foods Ltd. Exclusive supply agreement.
	CA/965/92E	ESM Paper Ltd; Du Pont (UK) Ltd. Exclusive distribution.
	CA/966/92E	ESM Paper Ltd; Iggesund Paperboard (Workington) Ltd. Exclusive distribution.
	CA/967/92E	ESM Paper Ltd; Berghuizer Papierfabriek N.V. Exclusive distribution.
	CA/968/92E	Lanes Group Ltd; Dipetane International Ltd. Exclusive distribution.
	CA/969/92E	Tedcastle Oil Products Ltd; independent dealers. Exclusive distribution.
	CA/970/92E	Irish Distillers Group plc; P. O'Lionaird. Trademark usership agreement.
	CA/971/92E	Irish Distillers Ltd; Lakeshore Foods Ltd. Trademark usership agreement.
	CA/972/92E	Irish Distillers Ltd; Celtic Glass Ltd. Trademark usership agreement.
	CA/973/92	Irish Distillers Ltd; Celtic Glass Ltd. Trademark usership agreement.
	CA/974/92E	The 'Old Bushmills' Distillery Co. Ltd; Celtic Glass Ltd. Trademark usership agreement.
	CA/975/92E	Irish Distillers Ltd; P. Thompson. Trademark usership agreement.
	CA/976/92E	The 'Old Bushmills' Distillery Co. Ltd; J.B. Casey. Trademark usership agreement.
	CA/977/92E	Irish Distillers Ltd; J.B. Casey. Trademark usership agreement.
	CA/978/92E	Irish Distillers Ltd; Tobler Suchard Ltd. Trademark usership agreement.
	CA/979/92E	Irish Distillers Ltd; Lough Derg Handcrafts Ltd. Trademark usership agreement.
	CA/980/92E	Irish Distillers Ltd; Mileeven Ltd. Trademark usership agreement.
	CA/981/92	Irish Distillers Ltd; LLEDO Ltd. Trademark usership agreement.
	CA/982/92E	Spar (Ireland) Ltd; BWG Foods Ltd; Sancroft Ltd. Equipment, supply and merchandising agreement.

Decision No.	Date	Type of Decision	Subject of Decision	Relevant Decision in Book	Number
					CA/962/92E
314	21 April 1994	C	P		CA/963/92
					CA/964/92E
144 J	19 Nov. 1993 (IO)	L	D	CL (5.1)	CA/965/92E
144 J	19 Nov. 1993 (IO)	L	D	CL (5.1)	CA/966/92E
					CA/967/92E
					CA/968/92E
25 J	9 July 1993 (IO)	M	MF	CL (4.2)	CA/969/92E
287 J	25 Feb. 1994	C		S 6.2	CA/970/92E
287 J	25 Feb. 1994	C		S 6.2	CA/971/92E
284 J	7 Feb. 1994	C		S 6.1	CA/972/92E
284 J	7 Feb. 1994	C		S 6.1	CA/973/92
284 J	7 Feb. 1994	C		S 6.1	CA/974/92E
287 J	25 Feb. 1994	C		S 6.2	CA/975/92E
15	19 Feb. 1993	W(T)		S 2.1.2	CA/976/92E
IT 26 Nov. 1993	23 Nov. 1993 (AR)	W(N)			CA/977/92E
284 J	7 Feb. 1994	C		S 6.1	CA/978/92E
284 J	7 Feb 1994	C		S 6.1	CA/979/92E
287 J	25 Feb. 1994	C		S 6.2	CA/980/92E
284 J	7 Feb. 1994	C		S 6.1	CA/981/92
23	11 June 1993	W(T)		S 2.1.3	CA/982/92E

Legend	Number	Title
A = Acquisition AR = Annual Report of the Competition Authority C = Certificate CL = Category Licence D = Distribution EP = Exclusive Purchasing main subject FR = Franchising IO = Iris Oifigiúil IT = *Irish Times* J = Joint Decision L = Licence LPG = Liquid Petroleum Gas M = Mentioned and Listed Category Licence MF = Motor Fuel NC = Notification changed P = Property R = Rejection/Refusal S = Decision summarised in text T = More than one subject W(N) = Withdrawn no reason given W(T) = Withdrawn because of termination of agreement	CA/983/92E	BWG Foods Ltd; Eight to Twelve Ltd; Kingsbrook Investments Ltd; Sancroft Ltd. Shareholding agreement.
	CA/984/92E	BWG Foods Ltd; Sancroft Ltd. Loan agreement.
	CA/985/92E	Malting Co. of Ireland Ltd; Beamish & Crawford plc. Exclusive purchase.
	CA/986/92E	Spar (Ireland) Ltd; BWG Foods Ltd; Eight to Twelve Ltd. Equipment, supply and merchandising agreement.
	CA/987/92E	Ewos Agriculture Ab; Cross Vetpharm Group Ltd. Exclusive distribution.
	CA/988/92E	NV Medicopharma; The Cross Chemical Group; Clonmel Chemical Co. Ltd. Shareholding agreement.
	CA/989/92	Cross Vetpharm Group Ltd; agents. Agency agreement.
	CA/990/92	Green Science Ltd; Micro-Bac International Inc. Agreement for the purchase of technology and exclusive manufacture and distribution.
	CA/991/92E	Clonmel Chemicals Co. Ltd; Ethical Pharmaceuticals Ltd. Know-how licence.
	CA/992/92	Franklin Pharmaceuticals Ltd; Cross Vetpharm Group Ltd. Secrecy agreement.
	CA/993/92E	Clonmel Chemicals Co. Ltd; Ethical Pharmaceuticals Ltd. Exclusive distribution.
	CA/994/92E	Bimeda Chemicals Ltd; Orion-Yhtyma Oy. Exclusive distribution.
	CA/995/92E	Clonmel Chemicals Co. Ltd; Ethical Generics Ltd. Exclusive distribution.
	CA/996/92E	Clonmel Chemicals Co. Ltd; Waterford Pharmaceuticals Ltd. Exclusive distribution.
	CA/997/92	Glenberg; Winchurch Investments Ltd. Finglas Shopping centre lease.
	CA/998/92E	Glenberg; City Properties (Cork) Ltd. Shopping centre lease.
	CA/999/92E	Glenberg; Westport Developments Ltd. Shopping centre lease.
	CA/1000/92E	Glenberg; K. Coogan. Earl Street Shop lease.
	CA/1001/92E	Glenberg; Associated Restaurants Ltd. Restaurant lease.
	CA/1002/92E	Glenberg; Wilton Securities Ltd. Shopping centre lease.
	CA/1003/92E	Glenberg; Wanze Properties Ltd. Shopping centre lease.

Decision No.	Date	Type of Decision	Subject of Decision	Relevant Decision in Book	Number
					CA/983/92E
					CA/984/92E
					CA/985/92E
26 Nov. 1993	23 Nov. 1993 (AR)	W(N)			CA/986/92E
					CA/987/92E
					CA/988/92E
412	25 Aug. 1995	R	Agency		CA/989/92
					CA/990/92
					CA/991/92E
					CA/992/92
					CA/993/92E
					CA/994/92E
					CA/995/92E
					CA/996/92E
53	5 Oct. 1993	C	P		CA/997/92
63	5 Oct. 1993	C	P		CA/998/92E
130	13 Oct. 1993	C	P		CA/999/92E
281	4 Feb. 1994	C	P		CA/1000/92E
295	10 March 1994	C	P		CA/1001/92E
64	5 Oct. 1993	C	P		CA/1002/92E
254	15 Dec. 1993	C	P		CA/1003/92E

<table>
<tr><th>Legend</th><th>Number</th><th>Title</th></tr>
<tr><td rowspan="23">A = Acquisition
AR = Annual Report of the Competition Authority
C = Certificate
CL = Category Licence
D = Distribution
EP = Exclusive Purchasing main subject
FR = Franchising
IO = Iris Oifigiúil
IT = Irish Times
J = Joint Decision
L = Licence
LPG = Liquid Petroleum Gas
M = Mentioned and Listed Category Licence
MF = Motor Fuel
NC = Notification changed
P = Property
R = Rejection/Refusal
S = Decision summarised in text
T = More than one subject
W(N) = Withdrawn no reason given
W(T) = Withdrawn because of termination of agreement</td><td>CA/1004/92E</td><td>Glenberg; H. Williams & Co. Ltd. Shankill Shopping centre lease.</td></tr>
<tr><td>CA/1005/92E</td><td>Glenberg; Glenhest Developments Ltd. Sutton Shopping centre lease.</td></tr>
<tr><td>CA/1006/92E</td><td>Glenberg; Tallaght Shopping Centre Ltd. Shopping centre lease.</td></tr>
<tr><td>CA/1007/92E</td><td>Glenberg; Urban Development Ltd. Stillorgan Shopping centre leases.</td></tr>
<tr><td>CA/1008/92E</td><td>N.M. Life Assurance Ireland Ltd; tied agents. Agency agreement.</td></tr>
<tr><td>CA/1009/92E</td><td>Rowe Mark Holdings and Peter Holdings; Bally London Shoe Co. Ltd. Shop lease.</td></tr>
<tr><td>CA/1010/92E</td><td>Cosine Ltd; C. O'Sullivan. Shop lease.</td></tr>
<tr><td>CA/1011/92E</td><td>Peter Mark; Majella Stapleton. Employment contract.</td></tr>
<tr><td>CA/1012/92E</td><td>Peter Mark; Dunloe House Group plc. Shopping centre lease.</td></tr>
<tr><td>CA/1013/92E</td><td>Peter Mark; Irish Life Assurance plc. Shopping centre lease.</td></tr>
<tr><td>CA/1014/92E</td><td>Peter Mark; Erin Executor and Trustee Co. Ltd. Shopping centre lease.</td></tr>
<tr><td>CA/1015/92E</td><td>Peter Mark; Cornelscourt Shopping Centre Ltd. Shopping centre lease.</td></tr>
<tr><td>CA/1016/92E</td><td>Peter Mark; Roches Stores Dublin Ltd. Shopping centre lease.</td></tr>
<tr><td>CA/1017/92E</td><td>Peter Mark; Firmount Ltd. Shopping centre lease.</td></tr>
<tr><td>CA/1018/92E</td><td>Peter Mark; Merchant's Quay Developments Ltd. Shopping centre lease.</td></tr>
<tr><td>CA/1019/92E</td><td>Peter Mark; Douglas Developments Ltd. Shopping centre lease.</td></tr>
<tr><td>CA/1020/92E</td><td>Peter Mark; D. Farrell. Shopping centre lease.</td></tr>
<tr><td>CA/1021/92E</td><td>Peter Mark; Roches Stores Limerick Ltd. Shopping centre lease.</td></tr>
<tr><td>CA/1022/92E</td><td>Peter Mark; Superquinn. Shopping centre lease.</td></tr>
<tr><td>CA/1023/92E</td><td>Peter Mark; L. & C. Properties Ltd. Shopping centre lease.</td></tr>
<tr><td>CA/1024/92E</td><td>Motor Distributors Ltd; Daimler-Benz A.G. Selective distribution.</td></tr>
<tr><td>CA/1025/92E</td><td>Motor Distributors Ltd; Mazda Motor Corporation; Sumitomo Corporation; Mazda Motor Europe SA/NV. Selective distribution.</td></tr>
<tr><td>CA/1026/92E</td><td>Motor Distributors Ltd; Volkswagenwerk A.G. Selective distribution.</td></tr>
</table>

NOTIFICATIONS TO THE COMPETITION AUTHORITY IN 1992

Decision No.	Date	Type of Decision	Subject of Decision	Relevant Decision in Book	Number
199	3 Dec. 1993	C	P		CA/1004/92E
205	3 Dec. 1993	C	P		CA/1005/92E
170	3 Dec. 1993	C	P		CA/1006/92E
204	3 Dec. 1993	C	P		CA/1007/92E
IT 9 June 1995		W(N)			CA/1008/92E
315	21 April 1994	C	P		CA/1009/92E
282	4 Feb. 1994	C	P		CA/1010/92E
13	18 Feb. 1993	R		S 1.4.2	CA/1011/92E
176	3 Dec. 1993	C	P		CA/1012/92E
104	13 Oct. 1993	C	P		CA/1013/92E
98	13 Oct. 1993	C	P		CA/1014/92E
49	5 Oct. 1993	C	P		CA/1015/92E
37	5 Oct. 1993	C	P	S 7.4	CA/1016/92E
118	13 Oct. 1993	C	P		CA/1017/92E
62	5 Oct. 1993	C	P		CA/1018/92E
61	5 Oct. 1993	C	P		CA/1019/92E
72	5 Oct. 1993	C	P		CA/1020/92E
129	13 Oct. 1993	C	P		CA/1021/92E
108	13 Oct. 1993	C	P		CA/1022/92E
124	13 Oct. 1993	C	P		CA/1023/92E
					CA/1024/92E
					CA/1025/92E
					CA/1026/92E

Legend	Number	Title
A = Acquisition AR = Annual Report of the Competition Authority C = Certificate CL = Category Licence D = Distribution EP = Exclusive Purchasing main subject FR = Franchising IO = Iris Oifigiúil IT = *Irish Times* J = Joint Decision L = Licence LPG = Liquid Petroleum Gas M = Mentioned and Listed Category Licence MF = Motor Fuel NC = Notification changed P = Property R = Rejection/Refusal S = Decision summarised in text T = More than one subject W(N) = Withdrawn no reason given W(T) = Withdrawn because of termination of agreement	CA/1027/92E	Motor Distributors Ltd; Mazda Motor Corporation; Sumitomo Corporation. Selective distribution.
	CA/1028/92E	Motor Distributors Ltd; Mazda dealers. Selective distribution.
	CA/1029/92E	Motor Distributors Ltd; Mazda dealers. Selective distribution.
	CA/1030/92E	Motor Distributors Ltd; Volkswagen and Audi dealers. Selective distribution.
	CA/1031/92E	Motor Distributors Ltd; Mercedes-Benz dealers. Selective distribution.
	CA/1032/92E	Musicmaker Ltd; Vic Firth Inc. Exclusive distribution.
	CA/1033/92E	Musicmaker Ltd; Roland UK Ltd. Exclusive distribution.
	CA/1034/92E	Musicmaker Ltd; Pearl Musical Instrument Co. Exclusive distribution.
	CA/1035/92E	Musicmaker Ltd; Young Chang Akki Europe GmbH. Exclusive distribution.
	CA/1036/92E	Musicmaker Ltd; Paul Reed Smith Guitars. Exclusive distribution.
	CA/1037/92E	Musicmaker Ltd; Marshall Amplification Ltd. Exclusive distribution.
	CA/1038/92E	Musicmaker Ltd; Freestyle Music Products. Exclusive distribution.
	CA/1039/92E	Musicmaker Ltd; D'Andrea Mfg. Co. Inc. Exclusive distribution.
	CA/1040/92E	Musicmaker Ltd; GMS Corp. Exclusive distribution.
	CA/1041/92E	Musicmaker Ltd; Sabian Ltd. Exclusive distribution.
	CA/1042/92E	Musicmaker Ltd; Teac UK Ltd. Exclusive distribution.
	CA/1043/92E	Musicmaker Ltd; Trace Elliott Ltd. Exclusive distribution.
	CA/1044/92	Tedcastle Engineering Ltd; MS Commercials Ltd. Selective distribution.
	CA/1045/92	Irish Life Assurance plc; First National Building Society. Tied agency agreement.
	CA/1046/92E	Irish Life; Irish Insurance Federation. Agreement on maximum rates of remuneration for life business.
	CA/1047/92E	Musicmakers Ltd; retailers. Retailer agreement on discounts.
	CA/1048/92E	Phonographic Performance (Ireland) Ltd; record companies. Assignment of copyright.

Decision No.	Date	Type of Decision	Subject of Decision	Relevant Decision in Book	Number
					CA/1027/92E
					CA/1028/92E
					CA/1029/92E
					CA/1030/92E
					CA/1031/92E
144 J	19 Nov. 1993 (IO)	L	D	CL (5.1)	CA/1032/92E
144 J	19 Nov. 1993 (IO)	L	D	CL (5.1)	CA/1033/92E
144 J	19 Nov. 1993 (IO)	L	D	CL (5.1)	CA/1034/92E
144 J	19 Nov. 1993 (IO)	L	D	CL (5.1)	CA/1035/92E
144 J	19 Nov. 1993 (IO)	L	D	CL (5.1)	CA/1036/92E
144 J	19 Nov. 1993 (IO)	L	D	CL (5.1)	CA/1037/92E
144 J	19 Nov. 1993 (IO)	L	D	CL (5.1)	CA/1038/92E
144 J	19 Nov. 1993 (IO)	L	D	CL (5.1)	CA/1039/92E
144 J	19 Nov. 1993 (IO)	L	D	CL (5.1)	CA/1040/92E
144 J	19 Nov. 1993 (IO)	L	D	CL (5.1)	CA/1041/92E
144 J	19 Nov. 1993 (IO)	L	D	CL (5.1)	CA/1042/92E
144 J	19 Nov. 1993 (IO)	L	D	CL (5.1)	CA/1043/92E
					CA/1044/92
					CA/1045/92
IT 17 Sept. 1993	9 Sept. 1993 (AR)	W(N)			CA/1046/92E
					CA/1047/92E
					CA/1048/92E

Legend

A = Acquisition
AR = Annual Report of the Competition Authority
C = Certificate
CL = Category Licence
D = Distribution
EP = Exclusive Purchasing main subject
FR = Franchising
IO = Iris Oifigiúil
IT = *Irish Times*
J = Joint Decision
L = Licence
LPG = Liquid Petroleum Gas
M = Mentioned and Listed Category Licence
MF = Motor Fuel
NC = Notification changed
P = Property
R = Rejection/Refusal
S = Decision summarised in text
T = More than one subject
W(N) = Withdrawn no reason given
W(T) = Withdrawn because of termination of agreement

Number	Title
CA/1049/92E	PPI Ltd; record companies. Assignment of copyright (videograms).
CA/1050/92E	PPI Ltd; record companies. Standard dubbing mandate.
CA/1051/92E	PPI Ltd; users. Copyright licence.
CA/1052/92E	PPI Ltd; users. Music video licence.
CA/1053/92E	PPI Ltd; background music system suppliers. Dubbing licence.
CA/1054/92E	Palace Video Ltd; Abbey films. Exclusive distribution.
CA/1055/92E	Allegro Ltd; Clara Candy Ltd. Exclusive distribution.
CA/1056/92E	Allegro Ltd; Bewleys Coffee Ltd. Exclusive distribution.
CA/1057/92E	Allegro Ltd; Bewleys Tea Ltd. Exclusive distribution.
CA/1058/92E	Allegro Ltd; Wander Ltd. Exclusive distribution.
CA/1059/92E	Allegro Ltd; Novo Enzyme Products Ltd. Exclusive distribution.
CA/1060/92E	Allegro Ltd; Northern Foods Grocery Group Ltd. Exclusive distribution.
CA/1061/92E	Allegro Ltd; Del Monte Foods International Ltd. Exclusive distribution.
CA/1062/92E	Allegro Ltd; Kimberley-Clark Corporation. Exclusive distribution.
CA/1063/92E	Allegro Ltd; Albright & Wilson Ltd. Exclusive distribution.
CA/1064/92E	Sherwin Williams; Simgrove Investments Ltd; Indou Investments Ltd; Dev Ltd; J.F. Walsh. Joint venture.
CA/1065/92E	Business and Trading House Investment Co. Ltd; Tara Meats and others. Shareholding agreement.
CA/1066/92E	Business and Trading House Investment Co. Ltd; Tara Meats and others. Shareholding agreement.
CA/1067/92E	Business and Trading House Investment Co. Ltd; Curragh Carpel Holdings Ltd. and others. Shareholding agreement.
CA/1068/92E	Business and Trading House Investment Co. Ltd; Parade Biscuits and others. Shareholding agreement.
CA/1069/92E	Business and Trading House Investment Co. Ltd; Premier International Trading House Ltd; Bank of Ireland. Shareholding agreement.
CA/1070/92E	Business and Trading House Investment Co. Ltd; Prince of Wales Hotel Ltd. and others. Shareholding agreement.

Decision No.	Date	Type of Decision	Subject of Decision	Relevant Decision in Book	Number
					CA/1049/92E
					CA/1050/92E
					CA/1051/92E
					CA/1052/92E
					CA/1053/92E
144 J	19 Nov. 1993 (IO)	L	D	CL (5.1)	CA/1054/92E
IT 8 April 1994	22 Mar. 1994 (AR)	W(T)			CA/1055/92E
					CA/1056/92E
					CA/1057/92E
IT + 144 J	15 April 1994	L	D	CL (5.1)	CA/1058/92E
IT 24 June 1994	10 June 1994 (AR)	W(N)			CA/1059/92E
IT + 144 J NC	IT 13 Jan. 1995	L	D	CL (5.1)	CA/1060/92E
144 J	19 Nov. 1993 (IO)	L	D	CL (5.1)	CA/1061/92E
144 J	19 Nov. 1993 (IO)	L	D	CL (5.1)	CA/1062/92E
144 J	19 Nov. 1993 (IO)	L	D	CL (5.1)	CA/1063/92E
					CA/1064/92E
418 NC	8 Sept. 1995	C	Shareholder agreement		CA/1065/92E
419 NC	8 Sept. 1995	C	Shareholder agreement		CA/1066/92E
IT 10 March 1995		W(N)			CA/1067/92E
IT 12 May 1995		W(T)			CA/1068/92E
IT 17 Sept. 1993	13 July 1993 (AR)	W(N)			CA/1069/92E
417	8 Sept. 1995	R	Shareholder agreement		CA/1070/92E

Legend	Number	Title
A = Acquisition AR = Annual Report of the Competition Authority C = Certificate CL = Category Licence D = Distribution EP = Exclusive Purchasing main subject FR = Franchising IO = Iris Oifigiúil IT = *Irish Times* J = Joint Decision L = Licence LPG = Liquid Petroleum Gas M = Mentioned and Listed Category Licence MF = Motor Fuel NC = Notification changed P = Property R = Rejection/Refusal S = Decision summarised in text T = More than one subject W(N) = Withdrawn no reason given W(T) = Withdrawn because of termination of agreement	CA/1071/92E	Pentos Retailing Group Ltd; Optel Ltd; N. McCreesh. Franchise agreement.
	CA/1072/92E	Pentos Retailing Group Ltd; Vogue Management Ltd; N. McCreesh. Franchise agreement.
	CA/1073/92E	T.P. Whelehan Son & Co. Ltd; American Cyanamid Co. Exclusive distribution.
	CA/1074/92E	T.P. Whelehan Son & Co. Ltd; American Cyanamid Co. Exclusive distribution.
	CA/1075/92E	T.P. Whelehan Son & Co. Ltd; Carter-Wallace Ltd. Exclusive distribution.
	CA/1076/92	T.P. Whelehan Son & Co. Ltd; Rohm & Haas (UK) Ltd. Exclusive distribution.
	CA/1077/92E	M., T. and P.J. McGrath; Kilbarrack Shopping centre leases.
	CA/1078/92E	M., T. and P.J. McGrath; Finglas Shopping centre leases.
	CA/1079/92E	M., T. and P.J. McGrath; Ballyfermot Shopping centre leases.
	CA/1080/92E	Eason & Son Ltd; Newspread Ltd. Agreement on forward purchasing of foreign currency and its application to resale prices.
	CA/1081/92E	B. and J. Moran; A. P. and M. Dargan; Universal Travel Agency Ltd; Hewitts Travel Agency Ltd. Merger.
	CA/1082/92E	Edward Dillon & Co. Ltd; Jas Hennessy & Co. Ltd. Exclusive distribution.
	CA/1083/92E	Edward Dillon & Co. Ltd; The Old Bushmills Distillery Co. Ltd. Exclusive distribution.
	CA/1084/92E	Edward Dillon & Co. Ltd; Grants of St. James's. Exclusive distribution.
	CA/1085/92E	Edward Dillon & Co. Ltd; United Distillers plc. Exclusive distribution.
	CA/1086/92	Edward Dillon & Co. Ltd; Maison Bouchard Pere et Fils. Exclusive distribution.
	CA/1087/92E	Edward Dillon & Co. Ltd; Hedges & Butler Ltd. Exclusive distribution.
	CA/1088/92E	Edward Dillon & Co. Ltd; Vintners International Co. Inc. Exclusive distribution.
	CA/1089/92E	Edward Dillon & Co. Ltd; Seagram U.K. Ltd. Exclusive distribution.
	CA/1090/92E	Edward Dillon & Co. Ltd; H. Sichel Sohne GmbH. Exclusive distribution.
	CA/1091/92E	Edward Dillon & Co. Ltd; Bacardi International Ltd. Exclusive distribution.

NOTIFICATIONS TO THE COMPETITION AUTHORITY IN 1992

Decision No.	Date	Type of Decision	Subject of Decision	Relevant Decision in Book	Number
					CA/1071/92E
					CA/1072/92E
144 J	19 Nov. 1993 (IO)	L	D	CL (5.1)	CA/1073/92E
144 J	19 Nov. 1993 (IO)	L	D	CL (5.1)	CA/1074/92E
144 J	19 Nov. 1993 (IO)	L	D	CL (5.1)	CA/1075/92E
144 J	19 Nov. 1993 (IO)	L	D	CL (5.1)	CA/1076/92
38	5 Oct. 1993	C	P		CA/1077/92E
52	5 Oct. 1993	C	P		CA/1078/92E
42	5 Oct. 1993	C	P		CA/1079/92E
IT 11 Feb. 1994	22 Dec. 1993 (AR)	W(N)		S 2.3.1	CA/1080/92E
26	1 July 1993	C	A		CA/1081/92E
IT + 144 J	IT 9 Sept. 1994	L	D	CL (5.1)	CA/1082/92E
IT + 144 J NC	IT 8 April 1994	L	D	CL (5.1)	CA/1083/92E
144 J	19 Nov. 1993 (IO)	L	D	CL (5.1)	CA/1084/92E
IT + 144 J NC	IT 15 April 1994	L	D	CL (5.1)	CA/1085/92E
144 J	19 Nov. 1993 (IO)	L	D	CL (5.1)	CA/1086/92
144 J	19 Nov. 1993 (IO)	L	D	CL (5.1)	CA/1087/92E
144 J	19 Nov. 1993 (IO)	L	D	CL (5.1)	CA/1088/92E
144 J	19 Nov. 1993 (IO)	L	D	CL (5.1)	CA/1089/92E
144 J	19 Nov. 1993 (IO)	L	D	CL (5.1)	CA/1090/92E
144 J	19 Nov. 1993 (IO)	L	D	CL (5.1)	CA/1091/92E

Legend	Number	Title
A = Acquisition AR = Annual Report of the Competition Authority C = Certificate CL = Category Licence D = Distribution EP = Exclusive Purchasing main subject FR = Franchising IO = Iris Oifigiúil IT = *Irish Times* J = Joint Decision L = Licence LPG = Liquid Petroleum Gas M = Mentioned and Listed Category Licence MF = Motor Fuel NC = Notification changed P = Property R = Rejection/Refusal S = Decision summarised in text T = More than one subject W(N) = Withdrawn no reason given W(T) = Withdrawn because of termination of agreement	CA/1092/92	Mothercare Ireland Ltd; Mothercare UK Ltd. Franchise agreement.
	CA/1093/92E	Moremiles Tyre Services Ltd; The Goodyear Tyre and Rubber Co. (GB) Ltd. Exclusive distribution.
	CA/1094/92E	N. MacManus; Arch Properties Ltd. Rathmines Shopping centre lease.
	CA/1095/92	Conoco Ireland Ltd; Reckitt & Colman. Exclusive purchase.
	CA/1096/92E	C. Collins; E. Stokes. Celbridge Shopping centre lease.
	CA/1097/92E	Ballymun Developments Ltd; tenants. Shopping centre leases.
	CA/1098/92E	Ballymun Developments Ltd; tenants. Shopping centre leases.
	CA/1099/92E	Lager Distributors Ltd; Tennants Ireland Ltd. Exclusive distribution.
	CA/1100/92E	Doyles Shoe Centre Ltd; Michael Reilly & Sons Ltd. Maynooth Shopping centre lease.
	CA/1101/92E	Friends Provident Life Assurance Co. Ltd; Dawson Street Office and shopping centre leases.
	CA/1102/92	Omni Park Ltd; tenants. Office and shopping centre leases.
	CA/1103/92E	Tambrands Inc; David Mayrs Ltd. Exclusive distribution.
	CA/1104/92E	Killiney Shopping Centre Management Co. Ltd., tenants. Shopping centre leases.
	CA/1105/92E	AIB Investment Nominees Ltd., Nutgrove Shopping centre leases.
	CA/1106/92E	Cambridge Investments Ltd; Industrial Credit Corporation; covenantors. Standard shareholding agreement.
	CA/1107/92E	Carton Bros. Ltd; Carton Bros. (Processing) Ltd; Kantoher Food Products Ltd. Acquisition of business.
	CA/1108/92E	Cambridge Business Expansion Fund Ltd; covenantors. Standard shareholding agreement.
	CA/1109/92E	DCC Business Expansion Fund Ltd; covenantors. Standard shareholding agreement.
	CA/1110/92E	P. Sweeney; P. and K. Dunleavy. Dungloe Shopping centre lease.
	CA/1111/92E	Palace Video Ltd; Abbey Films. Exclusive distribution.
	CA/1112/92E	G. and M. Conway; Five Star Supermarket. Sligo Shopping centre leases.

NOTIFICATIONS TO THE COMPETITION AUTHORITY IN 1992

Decision No.	Date	Type of Decision	Subject of Decision	Relevant Decision in Book	Number
372 J	9 Dec. 1993 (IO)	L	FR	CL (4.9)	CA/1092/92
					CA/1093/92E
115	13 Oct. 1993	C	P		CA/1094/92E
					CA/1095/92
237	15 Dec. 1993	C	P		CA/1096/92E
156	3 Dec. 1993	C	P		CA/1097/92E
155	3 Dec. 1993	C	P		CA/1098/92E
IT 9 Sept. 1994	9 Aug. 1994 (AR)	W(N)			CA/1099/92E
239	15 Dec. 1993	C	P		CA/1100/92E
99	13 Oct. 1993	C	P		CA/1101/92E
189	3 Dec. 1993	C	P		CA/1102/92
144 J	19 Nov. 1993 (IO)	L	D	CL (5.1)	CA/1103/92E
169	3 Dec. 1993	C	P		CA/1104/92E
185	3 Dec. 1993	C	P		CA/1105/92E
					CA/1106/92E
352	7 Sept. 1994	R	A	S 3.2.1	CA/1107/92E
404	22 June 1995	C	A		CA/1108/92E
					CA/1109/92E
65	5 Oct. 1993	C	P		CA/1110/92E
14	19 Feb. 1993 (AR)	W(T)		S 2.1.1	CA/1111/92E
82	5 Oct. 1993	C	P		CA/1112/92E

Legend	Number	Title
A = Acquisition AR = Annual Report of the Competition Authority C = Certificate CL = Category Licence D = Distribution EP = Exclusive Purchasing main subject FR = Franchising IO = Iris Oifigiúil IT = *Irish Times* J = Joint Decision L = Licence LPG = Liquid Petroleum Gas M = Mentioned and Listed Category Licence MF = Motor Fuel NC = Notification changed P = Property R = Rejection/Refusal S = Decision summarised in text T = More than one subject W(N) = Withdrawn no reason given W(T) = Withdrawn because of termination of agreement	CA/1113/92E	M. Conway; Five Star Supermarket. Sligo hopping centre lease.
	CA/1114/92E	Power Supermarkets Ltd; P. Owens. Sale of property agreement.
	CA/1115/92E	Power Supermarkets Ltd; R. and S. Whyte. Sale of property agreement.
	CA/1116/92E	Toyota (Ireland) Ltd; motor vehicles. Selective distribution.
	CA/1117/92	Toyota Ltd; motor vehicles. Selective distribution.
	CA/1118/92E	Aer Lingus. IATA Passenger Agency Programme-Europe.
	CA/1119/92E	Aer Lingus. IATA Cargo Agency Programme-Europe.
	CA/1120/92E	Aer Lingus. IATA Passenger Services Conference Resolutions.
	CA/1121/92E	Aer Lingus. IATA Cargo Services Conference Resolutions.
	CA/1122/92E	Aer Lingus. IATA Passenger and Cargo Agency Programmes-Worldwide and other than Europe.
	CA/1123/92E	Aer Lingus. Consultations on passenger tariffs.
	CA/1124/92E	Aer Lingus. Consultations on cargo tariffs.
	Noticications Post 30 September 1992[1]	
	CA/1125/92	JCB Sales Ltd; Earthmover Commercial Industrial Ltd. Exclusive distribution agreement.
	CA/1126/92	Belfield Management Ltd; Usit Ireland Ltd. Property Management agreement.
	CA/1127/92E	David Allen Holdings Ltd; Adsites Ltd; Campaign Post Sites Ltd; Adsites (N.I.) ltd. Option to purchase poster sites.
	CA/1128/92E	David Allen Holdings Ltd; Adsites Ltd; Exclusive licence to market and sell advertising space.
	CA/1129/92E	Dairygold Co-operative Society Ltd; Muileann Ui Luasa Teo; IAWS Group plc. Asset acquisition agreement.

1. Sections 6(7) and 7(2) precludes the application of section 6 to agreements, decisions or concerted practices which were in existence on 1 October 1991 and which were notified to the Authority before 1 October 1992 under the Competition Act until a decision to grant or to refuse a Certificate of Licence as has been made the Competition Authority or by the High Court in the event of an appeal.

NOTIFICATIONS TO THE COMPETITION AUTHORITY IN 1992

Decision No.	Date	Type of Decision	Subject of Decision	Relevant Decision in Book	Number
81	5 Oct. 1993	C	P		CA/1113/92E
316	21 April 1994	C	P		CA/1114/92E
377	21 Nov. 1994	C	P	S 7.17	CA/1115/92E
					CA/1116/92E
					CA/1117/92
					CA/1118/92E
					CA/1119/92E
					CA/1120/92E
					CA/1121/92E
					CA/1122/92E
					CA/1123/92E
					CA/1124/92E
IT + 144 J NC	IT 14 Oct. 1994	L	D	CL (5.1)	CA/1125/92
387	22 Dec. 1994	C	P		CA/1126/92
381	15 Dec. 1994	R	P+A	S 7.19	CA/1127/92E
378	21 Nov. 1994	R	R	S 7.18	CA/1128/92E
22 NC	11 June 1993	C	A		CA/1129/92E

<table>
<tr><th>Legend</th><th>Number</th><th>Title</th></tr>
<tr><td rowspan="8">A = Acquisition
AR = Annual Report of the Competition Authority
C = Certificate
CL = Category Licence
D = Distribution
EP = Exclusive Purchasing main subject
FR = Franchising
IO = Iris Oifigiúil
IT = Irish Times
J = Joint Decision
L = Licence
LPG = Liquid Petroleum Gas
M = Mentioned and Listed Category Licence
MF = Motor Fuel
NC = Notification changed
P = Property
R = Rejection/Refusal
S = Decision summarised in text
T = More than one subject
W(N) = Withdrawn no reason given
W(T) = Withdrawn because of termination of agreement</td><td>CA/1130/92E</td><td>Apex Fire Protection Ltd; Noel Murtagh. Employment Contract.</td></tr>
<tr><td>CA/1131/92E</td><td>Precision Heating Equipment Ltd; Bentone Electro Oil AB. Exclusive distribution agreement.</td></tr>
<tr><td>CA/1132/92E</td><td>Giltsharp Technology (UK) Ltd; Michael McPhillips Ltd; Michael McPhillips. Franchise agreement.</td></tr>
<tr><td>CA/1133/92E</td><td>Martin Andrew Doyle; Joseph Moffitt. Partnership and sale of business.</td></tr>
<tr><td>CA/1134/92E</td><td>P. Reynolds; J. Reynolds; M. Hegarty; Aquis Estates Ltd., Letterkenny Shopping centre lease.</td></tr>
<tr><td>CA/1135/92E</td><td>Spring Grove Ireland Ltd; Initial Services (International) Ltd; BET plc and the P & O Services Group Ltd. Merger.</td></tr>
<tr><td>CA/1136/92E</td><td>J.D. Carroll and M.T.B. Carroll; Sutcliffe Ireland Ltd. Merger.</td></tr>
<tr><td></td><td></td></tr>
</table>

NOTIFICATIONS TO THE COMPETITION AUTHORITY IN 1992

Decision No.	Date	Type of Decision	Subject of Decision	Relevant Decision in Book	Number
20	10 June 1993	R		S 1.4.3	CA/1130/92E
144 J	19 Nov. 1993 (IO)	L	D	CL (5.1)	CA/1131/92E
IT 11 Aug. 1995		W(T)			CA/1132/92E
333	10 June 1994	R		S 1.5	CA/1133/92E
230	15 Dec. 1993	C	P		CA/1134/92E
148 NC	18 Nov. 1993	C	A	S 3.15	CA/1135/92E
29 NC	9 Sept. 1993	C	A		CA/1136/92E

Notifications to the Competition Authority in 1993

Legend	Number	Title
A = Acquisition AR = Annual Report of the Competition Authority C = Certificate CL = Category Licence D = Distribution EP = Exclusive Purchasing main subject FR = Franchising IO = Iris Oifigiúil IT = *Irish Times* J = Joint Decision L = Licence LPG = Liquid Petroleum Gas M = Mentioned and Listed Category Licence MF = Motor Fuel NC = Notification changed P = Property R = Rejection/Refusal S = Decision summarised in text T = More than one subject W(N) = Withdrawn no reason given W(T) = Withdrawn because of termination of agreement	CA/1/93	Galvia Hospital Ltd/VHI Board; provision of health care services and payment by VHI.
	CA/2/93	Butler Manufacturing Services Ltd/Melvin Pumps Ltd; distribution agreement.
	CA/3/93	Ove Arkil A.S./James Kelly and Patrick Kennedy; takeover and service agreements.
	CA/4/93	Irish Fertiliser Industries Ltd/Pioneer Hi-Bred (UK) Ltd; exclusive distribution agreement.
	CA/5/93	Warner Lambert Ireland Ltd/Fraxinor Anstalt; acquisition of minority shareholding.
	CA/6/93	Sigma Wireless Technologies Ltd/Philips Electronics U.K. Ltd; exclusive purchase agreement.
	CA/7/93	Gillespie & Co. Ltd/Milupa Ltd; exclusive distribution agreement.
	CA/8/93	RHM Ltd/Naresa Ltd; property lease.
	CA/9/93	Smith & Nephew Ltd/Beiersdorf U.K. Ltd; exclusive distribution agreement.
	CA/10/93	Chemical International Finance Ltd/Irish Life Assurance plc; deed of covenant pursuant to a share purchase agreement.
	CA/11/93	Unisolutions & Associates/Dascom Services Ltd and Manix Systems Ltd; non-exclusive distribution agreement.
	CA/12/93	AGF-Irish Life Holdings plc/AGF International S.A., AFG Holdings (UK) Ltd; transfer of subsidiary within a group.
	CA/13/93	Rotterdamsche Margarine Industrie/Betco Marketing Ltd; agency agreement.
	CA/14/93	Viva Travel Dun Laoghaire Ltd/G. McDonald Travel Ltd/J & M. O'Donohue & W Murphy; acquisition of business.
	CA/15/93	Rohan Construction Ltd/Rohcon Ltd/K Rohan; acquisition of assets.
	CA/16/93	Omni Med Ltd/Omni Park Ltd; shopping centre lease.
	CA/17/93	Irish Life Building Society/First National Building Society; takeover (transfer of engagements).

NOTIFICATIONS TO THE COMPETITION AUTHORITY IN 1993

Decision No.	Date	Type of Decision	Subject of Decision	Relevant Decision in Book	Number
					CA/1/93
144J	19 Nov. 1993 (IO)	L	D	CL (5.1)	CA/2/93
350 NC	6 Sept. 1994	C	A		CA/3/93
1 Oct. 1993 (AR)	IT 8 Oct. 1993	W(N)			CA/4/93
370	28 Oct. 1994	C	A		CA/5/93
					CA/6/93
28 Oct. 1994 (AR)	IT 11 Nov. 1994	W(T)			CA/7/93
394	12 April 1995	R	P	S 7.21	CA/8/93
					CA/9/93
17	29 April 1993	C	A	S 3.11	CA/10/93
					CA/11/93
18	9 June 1993	C	A		CA/12/93
375	21 Nov. 1994	C	D		CA/13/93
34 NC	24 Sept. 1993	C	A		CA/14/93
301 NC	25 March 1994	C	A	S 3.15	CA/15/93
317	21 April 1994	C	P		CA/16/93
19	9 June 1993	C	A		CA/17/93

NOTIFICATIONS TO THE COMPETITION AUTHORITY IN 1993

Legend	Number	Title
A = Acquisition AR = Annual Report of the Competition Authority C = Certificate CL = Category Licence D = Distribution EP = Exclusive Purchasing main subject FR = Franchising IO = Iris Oifigiúil IT = *Irish Times* J = Joint Decision L = Licence LPG = Liquid Petroleum Gas M = Mentioned and Listed Category Licence MF = Motor Fuel NC = Notification changed P = Property R = Rejection/Refusal S = Decision summarised in text T = More than one subject W(N) = Withdrawn no reason given W(T) = Withdrawn because of termination of agreement	CA/18/93	Executive Towel Rental Ltd/Bright & Clean Ltd/ J & A Clark; sub-contracting agreement to provide laundry services.
	CA/19/93	Sutcliffe Ireland Ltd/National Catering Ltd; Merger.
	CA/20/93	Circa Group Europe Ltd/shareholders; shareholders agreement.
	CA/21/93	Commercial Vehicle Cleaning Services Ltd/James Nolan; franchise agreement.
	CA/22/93	Commercial Vehicle Cleaning Services Ltd/McCarthy Motor Clean Ltd; franchise agreement.
	CA/23/93	A. Whittaker & A.M. Whittaker t/a Computa Tune/Computa Tune Services Ltd; franchise agreement.
	CA/24/93	Gillespie & Co. Ltd/Seven Seas (Ireland) Ltd; distribution agreement.
	CA/25/93	Cassidy's Family Pharmacies Ltd/Valbury Ltd; sale of shop premises.
	CA/26/93	Betco Marketing Ltd/Holland Sweetener Co VOF; agency agreement.
	CA/27/93	J Murray/L & J O'Connell; tenancy agreement.
	CA/28/93	ESBI Consultants Ltd/Maritz Inc/Murray Financial Services Ltd; joint venture.
	CA/29/93	Tate & Lyle Industries Ltd/Cooperative Animal Health Ltd; exclusive distribution agreement.
	CA/30/93	Members of Irish Insurance Federation; agreement on maximum rates of remuneration for life business.
	CA/31/93	Energy Control Systems Ltd/Erinova Ltd; exclusive distribution agreement.
	CA/32/93	Energy Control Systems Ltd/Belton Engineering Works Ltd; exclusive distribution agreement.
	CA/33/93	Grant Engineering Ltd/Ecoflam S P A; exclusive distribution agreement.
	CA/34/93	Dairygold Cooperative Society Ltd/J W Green & Co (Cork) Ltd; asset acquisition agreement.
	CA/35/93	Gallaher (Dublin) Ltd/Ritmeester BV; exclusive distribution agreement.
	CA/36/93	Heating Replacement Parts & Controls Ltd/ Windsor Motors Ltd/Gas & Oil Parts Ltd/T MacGee, M. O'Reilly & T. Daly; share acquisition agreement.
	CA/37/93	Tennents Ireland Ltd/publicans; loan and mortgage agreements.
	CA/38/93	Mac Publishing Ltd/D. McAuliffe; serviee contract.

NOTIFICATIONS TO THE COMPETITION AUTHORITY IN 1993

Decision No.	Date	Type of Decision	Subject of Decision	Relevant Decision in Book	Number
					CA/18/93
275 NC	4 Feb. 1993	C	A		CA/19/93
425	22 Sept. 1995	C	Shareholder Agreement		CA/20/93
					CA/21/93
					CA/22/93
					CA/23/93
IT 9 June 1995		W(T)			CA/24/93
318	21 April 1994	C	P		CA/25/93
376	21 Nov. 1994	C	Agency		CA/26/93
30	9 Sept. 1993	C	P	S 7.2	CA/27/93
					CA/28/93
144 J NC	IT 4 Feb. 1994	L	D	CL (5.1)	CA/29/93
					CA/30/93
31 J	9 Sept. 1993	C	D	S 5.2	CA/31/93
31 J	9 Sept. 1993	C	D	S 5.2	CA/32/93
					CA/33/93
33	9 Sept. 1993	C	A		CA/34/93
					CA/35/93
297 NC	11 March 1994	C	A		CA/36/93
					CA/37/93
					CA/38/93

<table>
<tr><th>Legend</th><th>Number</th><th>Title</th></tr>
<tr><td rowspan="20">A = Acquisition
AR = Annual Report of the Competition Authority
C = Certificate
CL = Category Licence
D = Distribution
EP = Exclusive Purchasing main subject
FR = Franchising
IO = Iris Oifigiúil
IT = Irish Times
J = Joint Decision
L = Licence
LPG = Liquid Petroleum Gas
M = Mentioned and Listed Category Licence
MF = Motor Fuel
NC = Notification changed
P = Property
R = Rejection/Refusal
S = Decision summarised in text
T = More than one subject
W(N) = Withdrawn no reason given
W(T) = Withdrawn because of termination of agreement</td><td>CA/39/93</td><td>Irish Distillers Group plc/J. Hennessy & Co SA/Guinness Distillers Holdings BV; restructuring of issued share capital of E Dillon & Co Ltd.</td></tr>
<tr><td>CA/40/93</td><td>Celmac Ltd/Protim (Ireland) Ltd; exclusive distribution agreement.</td></tr>
<tr><td>CA/41/93</td><td>Kiddie Products Inc/UPC Co. Ltd; exclusive distribution agreement.</td></tr>
<tr><td>CA/42/93</td><td>Sedgwick Group plc/TSB Group plc; takeover.</td></tr>
<tr><td>CA/43/93</td><td>Toyota Ireland/dealers; selective distribution agreement.</td></tr>
<tr><td>CA/44/93</td><td>General Electric Capital Corporation/GPA Group plc; omnibus agreement.</td></tr>
<tr><td>CA/45/93</td><td>General Electric Capital Corporation/GPA Group plc; master aircraft sale agreement & master deferred payment agreement.</td></tr>
<tr><td>CA/46/93</td><td>General Electric Capital Corporation/GPA Group plc; subscription option agreement.</td></tr>
<tr><td>CA/47/93</td><td>General Electric Capital Corporation/GPA Group plc; management agreement.</td></tr>
<tr><td>CA/48/93</td><td>General Electric Capital Corporation/GPA Group plc; Air Tara option agreement.</td></tr>
<tr><td>CA/49/93</td><td>General Electric Capital Corporation/GPA Group plc, asset purchase agreement.</td></tr>
<tr><td>CA/50/93</td><td>General Electric Capital Corporation/GPA Group plc; treasury MIS license agreement.</td></tr>
<tr><td>CA/51/93</td><td>General Electric Capital Corporation/GPA Group plc; license agreement.</td></tr>
<tr><td>CA/52/93</td><td>General Electric Capital Corporation/GPA Group plc; shareholders agreement.</td></tr>
<tr><td>CA/53/93</td><td>General Electric Capital Corporation/GPA Group plc; sublease.</td></tr>
<tr><td>CA/54/93</td><td>General Electric Capital Corporation/GPA Group plc, interested party agreement.</td></tr>
<tr><td>CA/55/93</td><td>General Electric Capital Corporation/GPA Group plc; GPA management assets consent & Boeing consents.</td></tr>
<tr><td>CA/56/93</td><td>General Electric Capital Corporation/GPA Group plc; deferral agreements.</td></tr>
<tr><td>CA/57/93</td><td>General Electric Capital Corporation/GPA Group plc; loan stock trust deed, security trust deed & the security instruments.</td></tr>
<tr><td>CA/58/93</td><td>Warner Lambert Distributors (Ireland) Ltd/Johnson Brothers Ltd; exclusive distribution agreement.</td></tr>
</table>

NOTIFICATIONS TO THE COMPETITION AUTHORITY IN 1993

Decision No.	Date	Type of Decision	Subject of Decision	Relevant Decision in Book	Number
					CA/39/93
144 J	19 Nov. 1993 (IO)	L	D	CL (5.1)	CA/40/93
144 J	19 Nov. 1993 (IO)	L	D	CL (5.1)	CA/41/93
415 NC	25 Aug. 1995	C			CA/42/93
					CA/43/93
137 J	20 Oct. 1993	C	A(T)		CA/44/93
28	9 Sept. 1993	C	A		CA/45/93
137 J	20 Oct. 1993	C	A(T)		CA/46/93
137 J	20 Oct. 1993	C	A(T)		CA/47/93
137 J	20 Oct. 1993	C	A(T)		CA/48/93
137 J	20 Oct. 1993	C	A(T)		CA/49/93
22 Sept. 1993 (AR)	IT 8 Oct. 1993	W(N)			CA/50/92
137 J	20 Oct. 1993	C	A(T)		CA/51/93
137 J	20 Oct. 1993	C	A(T)		CA/52/93
137 J	20 Oct. 1993	C	A(T)		CA/53/93
137 J	20 Oct. 1993	C	A(T)		CA/54/93
137 J	20 Oct. 1993	C	A(T)		CA/55/93
22 Sept. 1993 (AR)	IT 8 Oct. 1993	W(N)			CA/56/93
137 J	20 Oct. 1993	C	A(T)		CA/57/93
144 J NC	IT 12 Aug. 1994	L	D	CL (5.1)	CA/58/93

Legend	Number	Title
A = Acquisition AR = Annual Report of the Competition Authority C = Certificate CL = Category Licence D = Distribution EP = Exclusive Purchasing main subject FR = Franchising IO = Iris Oifigiúil IT = *Irish Times* J = Joint Decision L = Licence LPG = Liquid Petroleum Gas M = Mentioned and Listed Category Licence MF = Motor Fuel NC = Notification changed P = Property R = Rejection/Refusal S = Decision summarised in text T = More than one subject W(N) = Withdrawn no reason given W(T) = Withdrawn because of termination of agreement	CA/59/93	Canada Life Assurance Co. of Great Britain Ltd/Lloyds Abbey Life plc; acquisition agreement with non-compete clauses.
	CA/60/93	Aldwych Investment Co Ltd/E Kinsella, D Collins, J Curley & B Daly/Jones Engineering Ltd; shareholders agreement.
	CA/61/93	Fuel Distributors Ltd/J. Enright; restrictive covenant in sale of business.
	CA/62/93	Irish Distillers Group plc/Cooley Distillery plc; takeover.
	CA/63/93	The Round Hall Press Ltd/Bart Daly; service agreement.
	CA/64/93	Rochglen Holdings Ltd/Foreign Exchange Co. of Ireland and others; share purchase and related agreements.
	CA/65/93	Irish Shell Limited/users; lubrication bay equipment loan agreement.
	CA/66/93	Wm. Miller & Sons Ltd/David Galavan; employment contract.
	CA/67/93	Eastern Health Board; Cyanamid of Great Britain Ltd. Exclusive supply agreement for vaccines.

Decision No.	Date	Type of Decision	Subject of Decision	Relevant Decision in Book	Number
323 NC	5 May 1994	C	A		CA/59/93
371 NC	28 Oct. 1994	C	A		CA/60/92
145	18 Nov. 1993	C	P	S 7.5	CA/61/93
285	25 Feb. 1994	R	A	S 3.16	CA/62/93
					CA/63/93
272	20 Jan. 1994	C	A		CA/64/93
					CA/65/93
					CA/66/93
					CA/67/93

Notifications to the Competition Authority in 1994

<table>
<tr><th>Legend</th><th>Number</th><th>Title</th></tr>
<tr><td rowspan="17">A = Acquisition
AR = Annual Report of the Competition Authority
C = Certificate
CL = Category Licence
D = Distribution
EP = Exclusive Purchasing main subject
FR = Franchising
IO = Iris Oifigiúil
IT = Irish Times
J = Joint Decision
L = Licence
LPG = Liquid Petroleum Gas
M = Mentioned and Listed Category Licence
MF = Motor Fuel
NC = Notification changed
P = Property
R = Rejection/Refusal
S = Decision summarised in text
T = More than one subject
W(N) = Withdrawn no reason given
W(T) = Withdrawn because of termination of agreement</td><td>CA/1/94</td><td>Chanel Ltd; Gaelgate Ltd. Selectibe distribution agreement.</td></tr>
<tr><td>CA/2/94</td><td>Barlo Group plc; Kingspan Group plc. Asset purchase agreement.</td></tr>
<tr><td>CA/3/94</td><td>T. Sheridan Sales & Marketing Ltd; St Ives Laboratories Inc. Exclusive distribution agreement.</td></tr>
<tr><td>CA/4/94</td><td>T. Sheridan Sales & Marketing Ltd; Giorgio Beverly Hills Inc. Selective distribution agreement.</td></tr>
<tr><td>CA/5/94</td><td>T. Sheridan Sales & Marketing Ltd; Beauty International Ltd. Exclusive distribution agreement.</td></tr>
<tr><td>CA/6/94</td><td>Halton Business Systems Ltd; Peter Burns. Franchise agreement.</td></tr>
<tr><td>CA/7/94</td><td>J. & H. Underwood; Ye Olde Coopers Inns Ltd. Purchase of premises.</td></tr>
<tr><td>CA/8/94</td><td>Mount Juliet; David Ledbetter Golf Academy Inc. Sole provision of golf tuition.</td></tr>
<tr><td>CA/9/94</td><td>Clubman Omega Ltd; Enterprise Equity (Ireland) Ltd; Forfas; The Directors. Subscription and shareholders agreement.</td></tr>
<tr><td>CA/10/94</td><td>VDU Services Franchising Ltd; Franchisees. Franchise agreement.</td></tr>
<tr><td>CA/11/94</td><td>EBS Building Society; Midland & Western Building Society; Transfer of engagements.</td></tr>
<tr><td>CA/12/94</td><td>Suttons Ltd; Dairygold Co-operative Society Ltd. Asset purchase agreement/sale of business.</td></tr>
<tr><td>CA/13/94</td><td>Estuary Fuel Ltd; Collins Oil Products Ltd. Exclusive purchase (Solus) agreement.</td></tr>
<tr><td>CA/14/94</td><td>Sedgwick Overseas Group Ltd; P.J. Dineen. Option/share purchase agreement.</td></tr>
<tr><td>CA/15/94</td><td>Bank of Ireland; Careerline Ltd. Exclusive supply and purchase of corporate clothing agreement.</td></tr>
<tr><td>CA/16/94</td><td>Fexco Innovations Ltd; BIG Estates Ltd; Foreign Exchange Company of Ireland. Share sale agreement.</td></tr>
<tr><td>CA/17/94</td><td>Foreign Exchange Company of Ireland; BIG Estates Ltd. Agreement for the sale of assets.</td></tr>
</table>

Decision No.	Date	Type of Decision	Subject of Decision	Relevant Decision in Book	Number
					CA/1/94
302	25 March 1994	C	A	S 3.18	CA/2/94
IT 13 Jan. 1995 144 J NC		L	D	CL (5.1)	CA/3/94
					CA/4/94
IT 11 Nov. 1994 144 J NC		L	D	CL (5.1)	CA/5/94
IT 9 Dec. 1994			R		CA/6/94
330 NC	19 May 1994	C	A + P		CA/7/94
355	19 Sept. 1994	C	EP	S 5.7	CA/8/94
					CA/9/94
IT + 372 J NC	IT 9 June 1995	L	FR	CL (4.9)	CA/10/94
331	19 May 1994	C	A		CA/11/94
347	1 July 1994	C	A		CA/12/94
					CA/13/94
349	6 Sept. 1994	C	A	S 3.19	CA/14/94
					CA/15/94
405 J	22 June 1995	C	A		CA/16/94
405 J	22 June 1995	C	A		CA/17/94

<table>
<tr><th>Legend</th><th>Number</th><th>Title</th></tr>
<tr><td rowspan="18">A = Acquisition
AR = Annual Report of the Competition Authority
C = Certificate
CL = Category Licence
D = Distribution
EP = Exclusive Purchasing main subject
FR = Franchising
IO = Iris Oifigiúil
IT = Irish Times
J = Joint Decision
L = Licence
LPG = Liquid Petroleum Gas
M = Mentioned and Listed Category Licence
MF = Motor Fuel
NC = Notification changed
P = Property
R = Rejection/Refusal
S = Decision summarised in text
T = More than one subject
W(N) = Withdrawn no reason given
W(T) = Withdrawn because of termination of agreement</td><td>CA/18/94</td><td>Bank of Ireland; Abt Association Inc. Customer satisfaction measurement programme agreement.</td></tr>
<tr><td>CA/19/94</td><td>Daelgate Ltd; Retailers. Selective distribution agreement.</td></tr>
<tr><td>CA/20/94</td><td>Lyne/Paul. Sale of Business.</td></tr>
<tr><td>CA/21/94</td><td>Office Team Supplies Ltd; Kelly Office Supplies Ltd. Franchise agreement.</td></tr>
<tr><td>CA/22/94</td><td>Allied Distributive Merchants Ltd. Retailers. Exclusive purchase agreement.</td></tr>
<tr><td>CA/23/94</td><td>Robert William Sandys; Mary Angela and Dermot Ward. Sale of general practice.</td></tr>
<tr><td>CA/24/94</td><td>Tedcastle McCormick & Co. Ltd/Star Oil East Ltd. Exclusive purchase agreement.</td></tr>
<tr><td>CA/25/94</td><td>Tedcastle McCormick & Co. Ltd/Aidan McCrystal. Exclusive purchase agreement.</td></tr>
<tr><td>CA/26/94</td><td>Tedcastle McCormick & Co. Ltd/McCrystal Oil (Bellurgan) Ltd. Exclusive purchase agreement.</td></tr>
<tr><td>CA/27/94</td><td>H. & K. International Inc. Shareholder's agreement.</td></tr>
<tr><td>CA/28/94</td><td>Odenberg Engineering Ltd; Inspection Ltd; J. Mallon, W. Mallon and P. O'Dowd. Research and development — general services agreement.</td></tr>
<tr><td>CA/29/94</td><td>Fuel Distributors Ltd; Brendan Cleary. Termination of employment contract.</td></tr>
<tr><td>CA/30/94</td><td>Fuel Distributors Ltd; Brendan Cleary. Consultancy agreement.</td></tr>
<tr><td>CA/31/94</td><td>Odenberg Engineering Ltd; Inspectron Ltd; J. Mallon, W. Mallon and P. O'Dowd. Research and development — special projects agreement.</td></tr>
<tr><td>CA/32/94</td><td>Irish Potato Marketing Ltd; P. Keating liquitator. Share purchase agreement.</td></tr>
<tr><td>CA/33/94</td><td>Maxol Ltd; Mulfield Co. Ltd. Non-exclusive distribution agreement.</td></tr>
<tr><td>CA/34/94</td><td>Tedcastle McCormick & Co. Ltd/Clarke Oil Products Ltd. Exclusive purchase agreement.</td></tr>
<tr><td></td><td></td></tr>
</table>

NOTIFICATIONS TO THE COMPETITION AUTHORITY IN 1994

Decision No.	Date	Type of Decision	Subject of Decision	Relevant Decision in Book	Number
					CA/18/94
					CA/19/94
360	12 Oct. 1994	C	A + P		CA/20/94
372 J	9 Dec. 1994 (IO)	L	FR	CL (4.9)	CA/21/94
					CA/22/94
IT 14 July 1995		W(N)			CA/23/94
					CA/24/94
					CA/25/94
					CA/26/94
401	April 1995	C	Shareholder agreement		CA/27/94
					CA/28/94
					CA/29/94
					CA/30/94
					CA/31/94
385	22 Dec. 1994	C	A		CA/32/94
432	19 Oct. 1995	L	MF/D		CA/33/94
					CA/34/94

Notifications to the Competition Authority in 1995

(1 January to 30 September 1995)

Legend	Number	Title
A = Acquisition AR = Annual Report of the Competition Authority C = Certificate CL = Category Licence D = Distribution EP = Exclusive Purchasing main subject FR = Franchising IO = Iris Oifigiúil IT = *Irish Times* J = Joint Decision L = Licence LPG = Liquid Petroleum Gas M = Mentioned and Listed Category Licence MF = Motor Fuel NC = Notification changed P = Property R = Rejection/Refusal S = Decision summarised in text T = More than one subject W(N) = Withdrawn no reason given W(T) = Withdrawn because of termination of agreement	CA/1/95	Toyota Ireland. Motor dealers; selective distribution agreement.
	CA/2/95	Irish Music Rights Organisation Ltd. Writers; assignment of copyright in musical works.
	CA/3/95	Irish Music Rights Organisation Ltd. Individual publishers; assignment of copyright in musical works.
	CA/4/95	Irish Music Rights Organisation Ltd. Publishers (limited company); assignment of copyright in musical works.
	CA/5/95	Eureko Ireland Holdings Ltd.; Mr John F. Bourke; Stellar International Ltd. The shareholders; sale of business (Celtic International Insurance Co. Ltd.).
	CA/6/95	Stellar International Ltd.; Dotinga Investments D.V., Celtic International Insurance Co. Ltd. Computer programme licence agreement.
	CA/7/95	Azinger Ltd.; Fispak Holdings; Mr George McNulty. Deed of covenant with shareholder.
	CA/8/95	Bell Freight Transport Group Ltd/H.E.S. Beheer N.V./H.E.S. Transport BV/Oranet Ltd. Acquisition of shares in Bell Lines.
	CA/9/95	Bell Freight Transport Group Ltd/F.C. Hucker and Others/Natwest Ventures. Subscription and shareholders agreement in Bell Freight Transport Group Ltd.
	CA/10/95	Sumitomo Electric Hardmetal Ltd. Fengarin Engineering Ltd. Non-exclusive distribution agreement.
	CA/11/95	Azinger Ltd/David Gray/Fispak Holdings Ltd. Deed of covenant with shareholder.
	CA/12/95	Azinger Ltd/Ray McNally/Fispak Holdings Ltd. Deed of covenant with shareholder.
	CA/13/95	Azinger Ltd/Kieron Hayes/Fispak Holdings Ltd. Deed of covenant with shareholder.
	CA/14/95	AG (Ireland) Ltd/AG Holdings plc/John and Alice Neill. Takeover.
	CA/15/95	An Post/Customers. Standard franking machine agreement.
	CA/16/1995	An Post/Ascom Hasler Mailing Systems Ltd/Zurich Insurance Company. Agreement for the supply of postal franking machines.

Decision No.	Date	Type of Decision	Subject of Decision	Relevant Decision in Book	Number
					CA/1/95
IT 13 Oct. 1995		Intention to licence			CA/2/95
IT 13 Oct. 1995		Intention to licence			CA/3/95
IT 13 Oct. 1995 (NC)		Intention to licence			CA/4/95
409 NC	23 June 1995	C	A		CA/5/95
					CA/6/95
414 J NC	25 Aug. 1995	C	A		CA/7/95
					CA/8/95
					CA/9/95
					CA/10/95
414 J NC	25 Aug. 1995	C	A		CA/11/95
414 J NC	25 Aug. 1995	C	A		CA/12/95
414 J NC	25 Aug. 1995	C	A		CA/13/95
406	22 June 1995	C	A		CA/14/95
					CA/15/95
					CA/16/95

Legend	Number	Title
A = Acquisition AR = Annual Report of the Competition Authority C = Certificate CL = Category Licence D = Distribution EP = Exclusive Purchasing main subject FR = Franchising IO = Iris Oifigiúil IT = *Irish Times* J = Joint Decision L = Licence LPG = Liquid Petroleum Gas M = Mentioned and Listed Category Licence MF = Motor Fuel NC = Notification changed P = Property R = Rejection/Refusal S = Decision summarised in text T = More than one subject W(N) = Withdrawn no reason given W(T) = Withdrawn because of termination of agreement	CA/17/95	An Post/Pitney Bowes plc/Barclays Bank plc. Agreement for the supply of postal franking machines.
	CA/18/95	An Post/Neopost Ltd/Banque Nationale de Paris. Agreement for the supply of postal franking machines.
	CA/19/95	Burmah Castrol (Ireland) Ltd/Customers. Hire purchase agreement.
	CA/20/95	Burmah Castrol (Ireland) Ltd. Equipment loan agreement.
	CA/21/95	Lister Tubes Ltd/Jonava Properties Ltd. Sale of property agreement.
	CA/22/95	Carlton Cards Ltd/Balladeer Ltd. Purchase and revolving credit agreement.
	CA/23/95	Fiat Auto (Ireland) Ltd/Main dealers. Selective distribution agreement.
	CA/24/95	Cahill May Roberts Ltd/Guertain Ltd. Selective distribution agreement.
	CA/25/95	Bord na Mona/Fuel Distributors Ltd. Asset purchase agreement.
	CA/26/95	Bristow Helicopters Ltd/Petroleum Helicopters Inc. Joint venture agreement.
	CA/27/95	Roche Professional Products Ltd/Allphan Services Ltd. Exclusive Distribution agreement.
	CA/28/95	Professional Golfers Association. Constitution.
	CA/29/95	Iveco Ford Truck Ltd/Truck dealers. Exclusive distribution agreement.
	CA/30/95	Collins/Butler/O'Brien. Partnership.
	CA/31/95	Warner Lambert/Plaistow Ltd. Manufacturing partnership.
	CA/32/95	Warner Lambert/Plaistow Ltd. Patent, trademark and know-how licence agreement.
	CA/33/95	Warner Lambert/Plaistow Ltd. Exclusive purchase agreement.
	CA/34/95	Bride and Blackwater Valley Co-Op Dairy Society. Rules of Society.
	CA/35/95	Irish Insurance Federation. Registration Scheme for life assurance sales people.
	CA/36/95	Aer Lingus Shannon plc/Aer Lingus plc/Bristow Helicopters Ltd/Petroleum Helicopters Ltd. Share purchase agreement.
	CA/37/95	Bristow Helicopters Ltd/Petroleum Helicopters Inc. Joint venture shareholders agreement.

Decision No.	Date	Type of Decision	Subject of Decision	Relevant Decision in Book	Number
					CA/17/95
					CA/18/95
407 J	22 June 1995	L	EP		CA/19/95
407 J	22 June 1995	L	EP		CA/20/95
426	22 Sept. 1995	C	P		CA/21/95
434	20 Oct. 1995	C	EP		CA/22/95
					CA/23/95
					CA/24/95
					CA/25/95
IT	10 Nov. 1995	R	Notification incompletre		CA/26/95
					CA/27/95
					CA/28/95
					CA/29/95
					CA/30/95
					CA/31/95
					CA/32/95
					CA/33/95
					CA/34/95
					CA/35/95
					CA/36/95
					CA/37/95

Notifications to the Competitition Authority (in alphabetical order)

1 October 1991 — 30 September 1995

CA/739/92E	Abbey Life Assurance (Ireland) Ltd. Merrion Shopping centre leases.
CA/740/92E	Abbey Life Assurance (Ireland) Ltd; Holland Brooklands Ltd. Shopping centre lease.
CA/741/92E	Abbey Life Assurance (Ireland) Ltd; Merrion Shopping Centre Ltd; Hayes Bookshops Ltd; Shopping centre lease.
CA/742/92E	Abbey Life Assurance (Ireland) Ltd; Power Supermarkets Ltd. Merrion Shopping centre lease.
CA/896/92	Abrakebabra Ltd; franchises. Franchise agreement.
CA/9/91	ACT Group plc; Kindle Group Ltd. Non-competition clause and other restrictions in sale of business interest.
CA/349/92E	ACT Ltd; Barronstown Bloodstock shareholders. Shareholding agreement.
CA/350/92E	ACT Ltd; B.M. Browne Holdings Ltd; and shareholders. Shareholding agreement.
CA/351/92E	ACT Ltd; Emdee Holdings Ltd. and shareholders. Shareholding agreement.
CA/352/92E	ACT Ltd; Screen Scene (I) Ltd. and shareholders. Shareholding agreement.
CA/353/92E	ACT Ltd; My Kinda Baile Ltd and My Kinda Town Group Ltd. Shareholding agreement.
CA/354/92E	ACT Ltd; Odenberg Investments Ltd. and shareholders. Shareholding agreement.
CA/355/92E	ACT Ltd; Colour Books Ltd; John Harold. Shareholding agreement.
CA/356/92E	ACT Ltd; Dublin Plant Hire; John Kelly. Shareholding agreement.
CA/357/92E	ACT Ltd; Top Shot Publishers Ltd; shareholders. Shareholding agreement.
CA/362/92E	ACT Ltd; Odenberg Investments Ltd; shareholders. Shareholding agreement.
CA/363/92E	ACT Ltd; Odenberg Investments Ltd; shareholders. Shareholding agreement.
CA/321/92E	Addis Ltd; Addis BV; FII plc; Gillespie & Co. Ltd. Shareholding agreement.
CA/425/92	Adidas (Ireland) Ltd; The Football Association of Ireland. Exclusive right to use FAI crest, and supply of sportswear.
CA/426/92E	Adidas (Ireland) Ltd; sports stars. Agreement to sponsor a 'Sports Star'.
CA/1118/92E	Aer Lingus. IATA Passenger Agency Programme-Europe.
CA/1119/92E	Aer Lingus. IATA Cargo Agency Programme-Europe.
CA/1120/92E	Aer Lingus. IATA Passenger Services Conference Resolutions.
CA/1121/92E	Aer Lingus. IATA Cargo Services Conference Resolutions.

CA/1122/92E	Aer Lingus. IATA Passenger and Cargo Agency Programmes-Worldwide and other than Europe.
CA/1123/92E	Aer Lingus. Consultations on passenger tariffs.
CA/1124/92E	Aer Lingus. Consultations on cargo tariffs.
CA/14/95	AG (Ireland) Ltd/AG Holdings plc/John and Alice O'Neill. Takeover.
CA/7/92	AGF-Irish Life Holdings plc.; Church and General Insurance plc.; Insurance Corporation of Ireland plc. Parent/subsidiary arrangements.
CA/12/93	AGF-lrish Life Holdings plc/AGF International S.A., AFG Holdings (UK) Ltd. Transfer of subsidiary within a group.
CA/469/92E	The Agricultural Trust; Newspread Ltd. Exclusive distribution.
CA/358/92E	AIB Capital Markets plc; Data Packaging Ltd; Coster Corporation; Nadcorp Ltd. Shareholding agreement.
CA/359/92E	AIB Capital Markets plc; Woodland Investments Group Ltd; shareholders. Shareholding agreement.
CA/440/92E	AIB Finance Ltd; General Motors Distribution Ireland Ltd. Car purchase financing agreement.
CA/870/92E	AIB Finance Ltd adn AIB Leasing Ltd; Combined Insurance Co. of America; Pat Ryan & Associates; Sedgwick Dineen Ltd. Memorandum of Agreement on Creditor Insurance.
CA/234/92E	AIB Investment Nominees; The Square Shopping centre leases.
CA/429/92E	AIB Investment Managers Ltd; Foxfield Mushrooms Ltd; shareholders. Shareholding agreement.
CA/430/92E	AIB Investment Managers Ltd; Kingspan Veha Ltd; shareholders. Shareholding agreement.
CA/431/92E	AIB Investment Managers Ltd; Prince of Wales Hotel Ltd; shareholders. Shareholding agreement.
CA/432/92E	AIB Investment Managers Ltd; Seletar Ltd; shareholders. Shareholding agreement.
CA/433/92E	AIB Investment Managers Ltd; Baroncastle Ltd; Ramville Ltd; Green Isle Goods Ltd. Shareholding agreement.
CA/454/92E	AIB Investment Managers Ltd; Hamtoncove Holdings Ltd; Erin Executor & Trustee Co. Ltd; shareholders. Shareholding agreement.
CA/1105/92E	AIB Investment Nominees Ltd., Nutgrove Shopping centre leases.
CA/874/92	Airspace Investments Ltd; The Square Management Ltd; tenants. Shopping centre lease.
CA/60/93	Aldwych Investment Co. Ltd/E Kinsella, D. Collins, J Curley & B. Daly/Jones Engineering Ltd; shareholders agreement.
CA/22/94	Allied Distributive Merchants Ltd. Retailers. Exclusive purchase agreement.
CA/434/92E	Allied Irish Banks plc; Veritate Ltd. Shoppince centre lease.
CA/435/92	AIB plc. Shannon Aerospace. Property lease.
CA/436/92E	AIB plc. Dublin City University. Property lease.
CA/437/92E	AIB plc. Douglas Developments Ltd. Shopping centre lease.
CA/438/92E	AIB plc. Mastercard International Inc. Licence and interchange fee agreement.
CA/439/92E	AIB plc. Eurocard International SA. Licence and interchange fee agreement.

CA/1055/92E	Allegro Ltd; Clara Candy Ltd. Exclusive distribution.
CA/1056/92E	Allegro Ltd; Bewleys Coffee Ltd. Exclusive distribution.
CA/1057/92E	Allegro Ltd; Bewleys Tea Ltd. Exclusive distribution.
CA/1058/92E	Allegro Ltd; Wander Ltd. Exclusive distribution.
CA/1059/92E	Allegro Ltd; Novo Enzyme Products Ltd. Exclusive distribution.
CA/1060/92E	Allegro Ltd; Northern Foods Grocery Group Ltd. Exclusive distribution.
CA/1061/92E	Allegro Ltd; Del Monte Foods International Ltd. Exclusive distribution.
CA/1062/92E	Allegro Ltd; Kimberley-Clark Corporation. Exclusive distribution.
CA/1063/92E	Allegro Ltd; Albright & Wilson Ltd. Exclusive distribution.
CA/348/92E	Allied Combined Trust Ltd; Etos investors. Shareholding agreement.
CA/142/92E	Allied Distributive Merchants Ltd; retailers. Franchise/exclusive purchase agreement.
CA/675/92E	Allied Foods Ltd; Spendgrade Ltd. Exclusive distribution.
CA/676/92E	Allied Foods Ltd; Van den Broeke (Foods) (UK) Ltd. Exclusive distribution.
CA/677/92E	Allied Foods Ltd; U.B. (Ross Young's) International Ltd. Exclusive distribution.
CA/678/92E	Allied Foods Ltd; Goosens B.V. Exclusive distribution.
CA/679/92E	Allied Foods Ltd; Moy Park Ltd. Exclusive distribution.
CA/360/92E	Allied Venture Capital Ltd; Trintech Ltd; shareholders. Shareholding agreement.
CA/612/92E	Albafar. H. O'Doherty. Shopping centre leases.
CA/378/92E	Amax Exploration (Ireland) Inc; Chevron Mineral Corporation of Ireland; Preussag AM. Joint venture.
CA/837/92E	An Post; postmasters. Appointment of postmaster, and General Rules.
CA/15/95	An Post/Customers. Standard franking machine agreement.
CA/16/95	An Post/Ascom Hasler/Zurich Insurance. Supply agreement for postal franking machines.
CA/17/95	An Post/Pitney Bowes/Barclays Bank. Supply agreement for postal franking machines.
CA/18/95	An Post/Neopost/Banque Nationale de Paris. Supply agreement for postal franking machine.
CA/1130/92E	Apex Fire Protection Ltd; Noel Murtagh. Employment Contract.
CA/717/92	Apex Fire Protection Ltd; William Brennan. Employment contract.
CA/299/92E	Applied Micro Electronics Ltd; Industrial Development Authority. Shareholding agreement.
CA/275/92E	Asha Clothing Ltd; Firmount Ltd. Shopping centre lease.
CA/129/92E	Associated Marketing Ltd; James Halstead Ltd. Marketing services agreement.
CA/130/92E	Associated Marketing Ltd; Waterford Carpets Ltd. Marketing services agreement.
CA/131/92E	Associated Marketing Ltd; Joseph Hamilton & Seaton Ltd. Marketing services agreement.
CA/9/92E	Association of Optometrists, Ireland. Memorandum, Article and Code of Ethics.

CA/12/92	Athlone Travel Ltd; Michael Stein Travel Ltd. Restrictive clause in sale of business.
CA/894/92E	Atlas Oil Laboratories Ltd; G. Dunne. Collection agreement for waste oil.
CA/871/92E	Aviette Ltd; Firhouse Shopping centre leases.
CA/873/92	Aviette Ltd; Musgraves Ltd. Tallaght Shopping centre lease.
CA/7/95	Azinger Ltd; Fispak Holdings; Mr George McNulty. Deed of covenant with shareholder.
CA/11/95	Azinger Ltd/David Gray/Fispak Holidays. Deed of covenant with shareholder.
CA/12/95	Azinger Ltd/Rory McNally/Fispak Holidays. Deed of covenant with shareholder.
CA/13/95	Azinger Ltd/Kieron Hayes/Fispak Holidays. Deed of covenant with shareholder.
CA/1097/92E	Ballymun Developments Ltd; tenants. Shopping centre leases.
CA/1098/92E	Ballymun Developments Ltd; tenants. Shopping centre leases.
CA/879/92E	Ballyvolane Ltd; tenants. Shopping centre leases.
CA/251/92E	Bandai UK Ltd; customers. Standard terms and conditions of sale.
CA/323/92E	Bank of Ireland; James Davey. Shopping centre lease.
CA/324/92E	Bank of Ireland; Townparks Ltd. Shopping centre lease.
CA/325/92E	Bank of Ireland; Cornelscourt Shopping Centre. Shopping centre lease.
CA/326/92E	Bank of Ireland; Institute of Chartered Accounts in Ireland. Property lease.
CA/327/92E	Bank of Ireland; Hotel & Motel Enterprises Ltd. Property lease.
CA/328/92E	Bank of Ireland; Beaumont Hospital Board. Property lease.
CA/329/92E	Bank of Ireland; University College, Cork. Property lease.
CA/330/92E	Bank of Ireland; University of Limerick. Property lease.
CA/331/92E	Bank of Ireland; University College, Galway. Property lease.
CA/332/92E	Bank of Ireland; University College, Dublin. Property lease.
CA/333/92E	Bank of Ireland; Salix Trust. Shopping centre lease.
CA/334/92E	Bank of Ireland; Cranford Properties Ltd. Shopping centre lease.
CA/335/92E	Bank of Ireland; Waterford Shopping Centre. Shopping centre lease.
CA/336/92E	Bank of Ireland; Royal Liver Trustees Ltd. Shopping centre lease.
CA/337/92E	Bank of Ireland; Superior Drug Co. Ltd. Shopping centre lease.
CA/338/92E	Bank of Ireland; Richfield Investments Ltd. Shopping centre lease.
CA/339/92E	Bank of Ireland; Drakebury Construction Ltd. Shopping centre lease.
CA/340/92E	Bank of Ireland; Spearhill Co. Ltd. Shopping centre lease.
CA/18/94	Bank of Ireland; Abt Association Inc. Customer satisfaction measurement programme agreement.
CA/15/94	Bank of Ireland; Careerline Ltd. Exclusive supply and purchase of corporate clothing agreement.
CA/731/92E	Ballybrack Pharmacy Ltd; Galway Homes Ltd; Martin O'Toole. Shopping centre lease.
CA/882/92E	Bararnca; Nutgrove Shopping Centre (Management) Ltd; Tesco Stores (Ireland) Ltd. Shopping centre lease.

CA/2/94	Barlo Group plc; Kingspan Group plc. Asset purchase agreement.
CA/194/92E	Barlo Heating Ltd; Igote Ltd; Acquisition of business.
CA/117/92E	Baron Craft Co. Ltd; Deerpark Ltd. Shopping centre lease.
CA/165/92E	Baytrust Ltd; Wexford Street Shopping centre leases.
CA/68/92	Beamish & Crawford Ltd; publicans. Beer supply joint venture agreement.
CA/726/92E	Beaumark Ltd; Moulinex S.A. Exclusive distribution.
CA/727/92E	Beaumark Ltd; Russell Hobbs Tower Ltd. Exclusive distribution.
CA/728/92E	Beaumark Ltd; suppliers. Exclusive distribution.
CA/156/92E	Beaver Distribution Ltd; Balay SA. Exclusive distribution.
CA/157/92E	Beaver Distribution Ltd; Scintilla AG. Exclusive distribution.
CA/158/92E	Beaver Distribution Ltd; Robert Bosch GmbH. Trademark licence.
CA/159/92E	Beaver Distribution Ltd; Blaupunkt-Werke GmbH. Exclusive distribution.
CA/160/92E	Beaver Distribution Ltd; Robet Bosch HG GmbH. Exclusive distribution.
CA/161/92E	Beaver Distribution Ltd; Robet Bosch GmbH. Exclusive distribution.
CA/1126/92	Belfield Management Ltd; Usit Ireland Ltd. Property Management agreement.
CA/8/95	Bell Freight Transport Group Ltd/H.E.S. Beheer N.V./H.E.S. Transport BV/Oranet Ltd. Acquisition agreemetn for shares in Bell Lines.
CA/9/95	Bell Freight Transprt Group Ltd/Oranet Ltd/F.C. Hucket and Others/Natwest ventures and others. Subscription and shareholder's agreement in Bell Freight Transport Group Ltd.
CA/26/93	Betco Marketing Ltd/Holland Sweetener Co. VOF; agency agreement;
CA/832/92E	Bewleys Coffee Ltd; customers. Coffee machines loan agreement.
CA/833/92E	Bewleys Coffee Ltd; large customers. Coffee machines loan agreement.
CA/143/92E	Bewley's Franchising Ltd; franchisees. Franchise agreement.
CA/915/92E	Bewleys Manufacturing Ltd; Butler Irish Confectionery Ltd. and others. Joint venture.
CA/994/92E	Bimeda Chemicals Ltd; Orion-Yhtyma Oy. Exclusive agreement.
CA/10/91	Blackrock Clinic Ltd; Voluntary Health Insurance Board. Provision of health care services in return for remuneration by VHI.
CA/538/92E	Blugas Ltd; dealers. Exclusive purchase.
CA/539/92E	Blugas Ltd; distributors. Exclusive distribution.
CA/540/92E	Blugas Ltd; bulk customers. Exclusive purchase.
CA/235/92E	Bookneeds Ltd; Mall Holdings Ltd. Shopping centre lease.
CA/23/92E	Book Publishers. Net Book Agreement 1957 (Members' and non-members' versions).
CA/24/92E	Book Publishers; Book Retailers. Standard conditions of sale of net books.
CA/904/92E	The Booksellers Association of Great Britain and Ireland–Irish branch. Currency conversion rates for English books.
CA/25/95	Bord na Mona/Fuel Distributors Ltd. Asset purchase agreement.
CA/770/92E	Bord Telecom Éireann; Allied Irish Banks plc; Intelmatique S.A.; La Societe Rhodanienne Mobiliere et Immobiliere. Joint venture (Minitel).

CA/370/92E	Bord Telecom Éireann; Golden Pages Ltd. Directory agreement (copyright).
CA/371/92E	Bord Telecom Éireann; ITT World Directories Inc. Share option agreement
CA/372/92E	Bord Telecom Éireann; Golden Pages Ltd. ITT World Directories Ltd. M.V. Murphy; Bord Telecom Éireann. Shareholding agreement
CA/683/92E	Bord Telecom Éireann; L.R. Ericsson Holdings Ltd. Shareholding agreement.
CA/773/92E	Bord Telecom Éireann; Minitel Communications Ltd. Operating agreement.
CA/774/92E	Bord Telecom Éireann; Motorola Ireland Ltd. Joint venture (Eirpage).
CA/776/92E	Bord Telecom Éireann; Motorola Ireland Ltd. Marketing and development agreement.
CA/777/92E	Bord Telecom Éireann; Eirpage Ltd. Operating agreement.
CA/779/92E	Bord Telecom Éireann; information dealers. Information dealer agreement.
CA/792/92E	Bord Telecom Éireann; Nynex Security Systems Ltd. Joint venture (PhoneWatch).
CA/793/92E	Bord Telecom Éireann; Nynex Security Systems Ltd; Telecom PhoneWatch Ltd. Technical information agreement.
CA/310/92E	Boreenmannu Investments Ltd; tenants. Office lease.
CA/400/92E	Michael Breen; GD Investments (Galway) Ltd. Shopping centre lease.
CA/401/92E	Michael Breen; GD Investments (Galway) Ltd. Shopping centre lease.
CA/925/92E	Bridtron Ltd; Bridge Street; tenants. Office leases.
CA/697/92E	J. Brierley, R. Downer. J. Hamilton. M. McDonough. D. McNeill and M. Magnier; Plangrove Ltd. Trademark licence.
CA/26/95	Bristow Helicopters Ltd./Petroleum Helicopters Inc. Joint venture agreement.
CA/115/92E	British Shoe Corporation Ltd; retailers. Concessionaire agreement.
CA/504/92E	Broderick Bros. Ltd; Niedecker GmbH. Exclusive distribution.
CA/918/92E	Brooks Haughton Ltd; franchises. Franchise agreement.
CA/834/92E	Brooks Thomas Ltd; franchises. Franchise agreement.
CA/905/92E	Brown Thomas & Co. Ltd,; Extravert Design Ltd. Exclusive distribution.
CA/917/92E	Brooke Thomas Ltd; Servicised Ltd. Exclusive agreement.
CA/478/92E	B.M. Browne Ltd; Roche Products Ltd. Exclusive distribution.
CA/479/92E	B.M. Browne Ltd; ACT Medisys Ltd. Exclusive distribution (agency).
CA/480/92E	B.M. Browne Ltd; Fujinon (Europe) GmbH. Exclusive distribution.
CA/481/92E	B.M. Browne Ltd; Dia Med Ag. Exclusive distribution
CA/482/92E	B.M. Browne Ltd; Straumann (GB) Ltd. Exclusive distribution
CA/684/92E	BTE; Alcatel Ireland Ltd. Bulk supply agreement.
CA/685/92E	BTE; L.M. Ericsson Ltd. Bulk supply agreement.
CA/686/92E	BTE; Post GEM Ltd. Joint venture and operating agreement.
CA/795/92E	BTE; Telecom PhoneWatch Ltd. Telecom agreement.
CA/687/92E	BTE; Unidare plc/Unidare Cables plc. Cable supply agreement.
CA/688/92E	BTE; Wessel Industries Ltd, Wessel Cables Ltd. Cable supply agreement.
CA/163/92E	Burgess Galvin & Co. Ltd; Deb Group Ltd. Exclusive manufacturing licence and use of trademark.

CA/267/92	Burke Egan & Co. Ltd; retailers. Selective distribution agreement for Lancome products.
CA/32/92E	Burmah Castrol (I) Ltd; Independent Dealers. Exclusive purchasing (solus) agreement.
CA/33/92E	Burmah Castrol (I) Ltd; Independent Dealers. Equipment loan agreement.
CA/34/92E	Burmah Castrol (I) Ltd; Licensees. Licence agreement.
CA/35/92E	Burmah Castrol (I) Ltd; Lessees. Lease
CA/36/92E	Burmah Castrol (I) Ltd; Lubricating oil resellers. Loan agreement.
CA/37/92E	Burmah Castrol (I) Ltd; Motor fuel dealers. Hire purchase agreement.
CA/38/92E	Burmah Castrol (I) Ltd; Independent dealers. Lubricating equipment loan agreement.
CA/39/92E	Burmah Castrol (I) Ltd; Independent dealers. Mortgage.
CA/40/92	Burmah Castrol (I) Ltd; Independent dealers. Exclu- sive purchasing (solus) agreement—new version.
CA/41/92	Burmah Castrol (I) Ltd; Independent dealers. Equipment loan agreement—new version.
CA/42/92	Burmah Castrol (I) Ltd; Licensees. Licence agreement–new version.
CA/43/92	Burmah Castrol (I) Ltd; Lubricating oil resellers. Loan agreement—new version.
CA/44/92	Burmah Castrol (I) Ltd; Motor fuel dealers. Hire purchase agreement–new version.
CA/45/92	Burmah Castrol (I) Ltd; Independent dealers. Lubricating equipment loan agreement—new version.
CA/46/92	Burmah Castrol (I) Ltd; Independent dealers. Mortgage—new version.
CA/900/92E	Burmah Castrol (Ireland) Ltd; distributors. Exclusive distribution.
CA/901/92	Burmah Castrol (Ireland) Ltd; distributors. Loan equipment agreement.
CA/902/92E	Burmah Castrol (Ireland) Ltd; Liffey Oil Ltd. Exclusive distribution.
CA/903/92E	Burmah Castrol (Ireland) Ltd; Kingdom Oil Ltd. Exclusive distribution.
CA/19/95	Burmah Castrol (Ireland) Ltd/Customers. Hire purchase agreement.
CA/20/95	Burmah Castrol (Ireland) Ltd/Customers. Equipment loan agreement.
CA/1065/92E	Business and Trading House Investment Co. Ltd; Tara Meats and others. Shareholding agreement.
CA/1066/92E	Business and Trading House Investment Co. Ltd; Tara Meats and others. Shareholding agreement.
CA/1067/92E	Business and Trading House Investment Co. Ltd; Curragh Carpel Holdings Ltd. and others. Shareholding agreement.
CA/1068/92E	Business and Trading House Investment Co. Ltd; Parade Biscuits and others. Shareholding agreement.
CA/1069/92E	Business and Trading House Investment Co. Ltd; Premier International Trading House Ltd; Bank of Ireland. Shareholding agreement.
CA/1070/92E	Business and Trading House Investment Co. Ltd; Prince of Wales Hotel Ltd. and others. Shareholding agreement.
CA/2/93	Butler Manufacturing Services Ltd/Melvin Pumps Ltd. Distribution agreement;
CA/983/92E	BWG Foods Ltd; Eight to Twelve Ltd; Kinsbrook Investments Ltd; Sancroft Ltd. Shareholding agreement.

CA/984/92E	BWG Foods Ltd; Sancroft Ltd. Loan agreement.
CA/273/92E	P and M Byrne, L and C Power. Shopping centre lease.
CA/137/92E	Cable and Wireless Ltd; subscribers. Contract for rental of staff location equipment.
CA/138/92E	Cable and Wireless Ltd; subscribers. Contract for rental of time control equipment.
CA/133/92E	Cable and Wireless Ltd; subscribers. Telephone rental contract.
CA/949/92E	Cable Management (Ireland) Ltd; the Minister for Communications. Exclusive licence for cable television.
CA/509/92E	Cadbury Beverages Ltd; Chivers & Sons Ltd. Exclusive distribution.
CA/510/92	Cadbury Beverages Ltd; Batchelors Ltd. Exclusive production and distribution.
CA/511/92	Cadbury Beverages Ltd; Batchelors Ltd. Exclusive production and distribution.
CA/521/92E	Cadbury Ireland Ltd; Chivers & Sons Ltd. Exclusive distribution.
CA/522/92E	Cadbury Ireland Ltd; Premier Brands UK Ltd. Exclusive distribution.
CA/523/92E	Cadbury Ltd; Cadbury Schweppes plc; Premier Brands Ltd; Premier brands UK Ltd. Trademark and franchise agreement.
CA/347/92E	Cadbury Mushrooms Ltd; mushroom growers. Production licence.
CA/730/92E	Caddens Pharmacy Ltd; National Carways Ltd. Shopping centre lease.
CA/399/92E	Cahill May Roberts. Societe d'Hygiene Dematologique de Vichy. Joint venture.
CA/403/92E	Cahill May Roberts Ltd. Societe d'Hygiene Dematologique de Vichy. Shareholdingagreement.
CA/404/92E	Cahill May Roberts Ltd. Merck Sharp & Dohme Ltd. Exclusive distribution.
CA/405/92E	Cahill May Roberts Ltd. Mates Healthcare Ltd. Exclusive distribution.
CA/406/92E	Cahill May Roberts Ltd. Kabipharmacia Ireland Ltd. Exclusive distribution.
CA/407/92E	Cahill May Roberts Ltd. Janssen Pharmaceuticals Ltd. Exclusive distribution.
CA/408/92E	Cahill May Roberts Ltd. Fisons Pharmaceuticals Ireland Ltd. Exclusive distribution.
CA/409/92E	Cahill May Roberts Ltd. Fisons Pharmaceuticals Ireland Ltd. Exclusive distribution.
CA/410/92E	Cahill May Roberts Ltd. Elizabeth Arden Ltd. Exclusive distribution.
CA/411/92E	Cahill May Roberts Ltd. Eurocetus UK Ltd. Exclusive distribution.
CA/412/92E	Cahill May Roberts Ltd. Cilag Ltd. Exclusive distribution.
CA/413/92E	Cahill May Roberts Ltd. Clini-Med Ltd. Exclusive distribution.
CA/414/92E	Cahill May Roberts Ltd. Merck Sharp & Dohme Ltd (Agvet). Exclusive distribution.
CA/24/95	Cahill May Roberts Ltd/Guertain Ltd. Selective distribution agreement.
CA/533/92E	Caledonian Insurance Co.; Grafton Shopping arcade leases.
CA/541/92E	Caledonian Insurance Co; Grafton Shopping arcade leases.
CA/213/92E	Calor Teo; authorised dealers. Exclusvie purchase.
CA/154/92E	Calor Teo; Industrial customers. Standard contract for the supply of LPG.

CA/155/92E	Calor Teo; Industrial customers. Standard contract for the supply of bulk LPG.
CA/8/92E	Cambridge Investments Ltd; Mr. T.J. O'Neill; Imari Ltd; Allied Combined Trust Ltd. Restrictive covenants in a shareholding agreement.
CA/1106/92E	Cambridge Investments Ltd; Industrial Credit Corporation; covenantors. Standard shareholding agreement.
CA/1108/92E	Cambridge Business Expansion Fund Ltd; covenantors. Standard shareholding agreement.
CA/751/92E	Campus Oil Ltd; licensee. Licence.
CA/752/92	Campus Oil Ltd; independent dealers. Mortgage.
CA/753/92E	Campus Oil Ltd; independent dealers. Loan agreement.
CA/754/92E	Campus Oil Ltd; independent dealers. Equipment loan agreement.
CA/755/92E	Campus Oil Ltd; independent dealers. Petrol pump agreement.
CA/756/92E	Campus Oil Ltd; independent dealers. Exclusive purchase.
CA/759/92E	Campus Oil Ltd; distributors. Guarantee.
CA/760/92E	Campus Oil Ltd; distributors. Licence for distributors.
CA/761/92E	Campus Oil Ltd; licensor. Licence.
CA/762/92E	Campus Oil Ltd; distributors. Debenture.
CA/763/92	Campus Oil Ltd; distributors. Debenture.
CA/764/92E	Campus Oil Ltd; distributors. Equipment agreement.
CA/765/92	Campus Oil Ltd; distributors. Exclusive distribution.
CA/525/92E	Canada Dry Corporation Ltd; Cantrell & Cochrane Group Ltd. Exclusive manufacture and distribution.
CA/59/93	Canada Life Assurance Co. of Great Britain Ltd/Lloyds Abbey Life plc; acquisition agreement with non-compete clauses.
CA/919/92E	Cannon Hygienic Products (Ireland) Ltd; Initial Services (Ireland) Ltd. Agreement for the provision and service of disposal units and vending machines.
CA/305/92E	Cantrell and Cochrane (Dublin) Ltd; Pepsi Co. Ltd. Exclusive bottling and distribution agreement.
CA/302/92E	Cantrell and Cochrane Group Ltd; GIE Perrier Export. Exclusive distribution.
CA/17/92E	Capitol Holdings Ltd./Abbey Sun; customers.
CA/458/92E	Carlow Developments Ltd; Naas Holdings Ltd. Transfer of property agreement.
CA/22/95	Carlton Cards Ltd/Balladeer Ltd. Purchase and revolving credit agreement.
CA/1136/92E	J.D. Carroll and M.T.B. Carroll; Sutcliffe Ireland Ltd. Merger.
CA/938/92E	P.J. Carroll & Co. Ltd., Dakota Ltd. Exclusive supply agreement.
CA/939/92E	P.J. Carroll & Co. Ltd., Burger Sohne A.G. Exclusive distribution.
CA/940/92E	P.J. Carroll & Co. Ltd., Le S.E.I.T.A. Exclusive distribution.
CA/941/92E	P.J. Carroll & Co. Ltd., B.V. Willem II Sigarenfabrieken. Exclusive distribution.
CA/1107/92E	Carton Bros. Ltd; Carton Bros. (Processing) Ltd; Kantoher Food Products Ltd. Acquisition of business.
CA/341/92E	Cartron Management Co. Ltd; Stateline Enterprises Ltd. Shopping centre lease.
CA/198/92E	Cassidy's Family Pharmacies Ltd; Mall Holdings Ltd. Shopping centre lease.

CA/25/93	Cassidy's Family Pharmacies Ltd/Valbury Ltd; sale of shop premises.
CA/63/92	Castlecomer Woodwork Co. Ltd; Patrick J. Kelly. Consultancy agreement with non-competition clauses.
CA/839/92E	Castlebrook Investments Ltd; Newbridge Shopping centre leases.
CA/40/93	Celmac Ltd/Protim (Ireland) Ltd; exclusive distribution agreement.
CA/220/92E	Century Management; Brian Tracy Learning Systems Ltd. Exclusive distribution.
CA/48/92	Cerestar UK Ltd; Betco Marketing Ltd. Sole agency agreement.
CA/66/92E	Chanel Ltd; Harwood Brothers Ltd. Exclusive distribution agreement.
CA/1/94	Chanel Ltd; Gaelgate Ltd. Selectibe distribution agreement.
CA/144/92E	Chem-Dry Ireland Ltd; Devere Internation plc. Master franchise agreement.
CA/102/92	Chem-Dry Ireland Ltd; franchises. Franchise agreement.
CA/10/93	Chemical International Finance Ltd/Irish Life Assurance plc; deed of covenant pursuant to a share purchase agreement;
CA/124/92E	The Cheque Card Committee. Agreement on cheque guarantee cards.
CA/377/92E	Chevron Mineral Corporation of Ireland; Ivernia West plc. Joint venture.
CA/506/92E	Chivers & Sons Ltd; Cadbury Beverages Ltd. Exclusive distribution.
CA/505/92E	Chivers & Sons Ltd; Tate & Lyle Industries Ltd. Exclusive distribution.
CA/248/92E	Ciga-Geigy Ireland Ltd; Cahill May Roberts Ltd. Exclusive distribution.
CA/249/92E	Ciga-Geigy Ireland Ltd; Pemberton Marketing International Ltd. Exclusive distribution.
CA/250/92E	Ciga-Geigy Ireland Ltd; SDS Biotech. Exclusive distribution.
CA/20/93	Circa Group Europe Ltd/shareholders; shareholders agreement;
CA/212/92E	Clada Soft Drinks Ltd; Murphy Brewery Ireland Ltd. Exclusive distribution.
CA/643/92E	C. & J. Clarke International Ltd; Torlink Ltd; Franchise agreement with shop lease.
CA/897/92	John Henry Clark Ltd; Marinco Ltd; J. O'Riordan. Exclusive distribution.
CA/735/92E	Clayton Love Distribution Ltd; The Nestle Co. Ltd. Exclusive distribution.
CA/611/92E	Clondalkin Properties; Thomas Farren. Shopping centre lease.
CA/991/92E	Clonmel Chemicals Co. Ltd; Ethical Pharmaceuticals Ltd. Know-how licence.
CA/993/92E	Clonmel Chemicals Co. Ltd; Ethical Pharmaceuticals Ltd. Exclusive agreement.
CA/995/92E	Clonmel Chemicals Co. Ltd; Ethical Generics Ltd. Exclusive agreement.
CA/996/92E	Clonmel Chemicals Co. Ltd; Waterford Pharmaceuticals Ltd. Exclusive agreement.
CA/9/94	Clubman Omega Ltd; Enterprise Equity (Ireland) Ltd; Forfas; The Directors. Subscription and shareholders agreement.
CA/470/92E	Coca-Cola Bottling Co. (Dublin) Ltd; Kiely's Bottling Co. Ltd; Seven-Up International. Exclusive manufacturing and distribution.
CA/824/92E	Coillte Teo; sawmills. Coillte Allocation Scheme.
CA/1096/92E	C. Collins; E. Stokes. Celbridge Shopping centre lease.
CA/30/95	Collins/Butler/O'Brien. Partnership.
CA/344/92E	Colthurst Ltd; Elan Corporation plc. Research and development licence agreement.

CA/373/92E	Combined Insurance Company of Ireland Ltd; agents. Agency agreement.
CA/374/92E	Combined Life Assurance Co. of Ireland Ltd; agents. Agency agreement.
CA/279/92	Combined Performance Measurement Services Ltd; William M. Mercer Fraser; Noble Lowndes Irish Pensions. Joint venture.
CA/312/92E	Comeragh Properties Ltd; tenants. Office and shop lease.
CA/312/92E	Comeragh Properties Ltd; tenants. Office and shop lease.
CA/21/93	Commercial Vehicle Cleaning Services Ltd/James Nolan; franchise agreement;
CA/22/93	Commercial Vehicle Cleaning Services Ltd/McCarthy Motor Clean Ltd; franchise agreement;
CA/71/92E	Conoco Ireland Ltd; consignees. Consignee agreement.
CA/110/92E	Conoco Ireland Limited; distributors. Bulk storage loan agreement.
CA/111/92E	Conoco Ireland Limited; distributors. Distributor depot licence.
CA/73/92E	Conoco Ireland Ltd; distributors. Exclusive distribution agreement.
CA/106/92E	Conoco Ireland Limited; independent dealers. Exclusive purchase (image agreement).
CA/70/92E	Conoco Ireland Ltd; independent dealers. Exclusive purchase (solus) agreement.
CA/107/92E	Conoco Ireland Limited; independent dealers. Support and loan agreement.
CA/108/92E	Conoco Ireland Limited; independent dealers. Mortgage.
CA/109/92E	Conoco Ireland Limited; independent dealers. Franchise agreement (retail shop).
CA/72/92E	Conoco Ireland Ltd; licensees. Licence agreement.
CA/1095/92	Conoco Ireland Ltd; Reckitt & Colman. Exclusive purchase.
CA/1112/92E	G. and M. Conway; Five Star Supermarket. Sligo Shopping centre leases.
CA/1113/92E	M. Conway; Five Star Supermarket. Sligo hopping centre lease.
CA/174/92E	D.G. Cook Ltd; franchises. Franchise agreement.
CA/845/92E	Cornelscourt Shopping Centre Ltd; tenants. Shopping centre leases.
CA/1010/92E	Cosine Ltd; C. O'Sullivan. Shop lease.
CA/74/92E	Cranford Properties Ltd; lessees. Restrictive covenants in shopping centre lease.
CA/989/92	Cross Vetpharm Group Ltd; agents. Agency agreement.
CA/53/92E	Crown Equipment Ireland; Hydraulic Services Ltd. Distribution agreement.
CA/844/92E	Crumlin Investments Ltd; tenants. Shopping centre leases.
CA/50/92E	Curust Financial Services Ltd; Loewe-Lack-Werk Otto Loewe GmbH & Co. KG. Exclusive manufacturing and distribution agreement.
CA/164/92E	Cybury Ltd; Walkinstown Shopping centre leases.
CA/19/94	Daelgate Ltd; Retailers. Selective distribution agreement.
CA/718/92E	Dairygold Cooperative Society Ltd; Sean Bohan. Exclusive purchase.
CA/719/92E	Dairygold Cooperative Society Ltd; Eugene O'Sullivan. Exclusive purchase.
CA/720/92E	Dairygold Cooperative Society Ltd; Michael Cotter. Exclusive purchase and sale of business.
CA/721/92E	Dairygold Cooperative Society Ltd; Michael Kearney. Exclusive purchase.
CA/722/92E	Dairygold Cooperative Society Ltd; C. and A. O'Brien. Sale of property.

CA/1129/92E	Dairygold Co-operative Society Ltd; Muileann Ui Luasa Teo; IAWS Group plc. Asset acquisition agreement.
CA/34/93	Dairygold Cooperative Society Ltd/J W Green & Co. (Cork) Ltd; asset acquisition agreement.
CA/516/92E	Dalgety Agriculture Ltd; Spillers Ltd; Thomas Hill & Co. Ltd. Know-how and trademark licence.
CA/517/92E	Dalgety Agriculture Ltd; Spillers Ltd; Thomas Hill & Co. Ltd. Know-how and trademark licence.
CA/518/92E	Dalgety Agriculture Ltd; Spillers Ltd; E. Morrin & Son Ltd. Know-how and trademark licence.
CA/519/92E	Dalgety Agriculture Ltd; Spillers Ltd; E. Morrin & Son Ltd. Know-how and trademark licence.
CA/276/92E	James Daly & Sons Ltd; Alfred Bird & Sons (Ireland) Ltd. Exclusive supply.
CA/76/92E	Darrigowen Ltd; Donnybrook Mall Ltd. Shopping centre lease.
CA/166/92E	Dartgate Ltd; Shankill Shopping centre leases.
CA/1127/92E	David Allen Holdings Ltd; Adsites Ltd; Campaign Post Sites Ltd; Adsites (N.I.) ltd. Option to purchase poster sites.
CA/1128/92E	David Allen Holdings Ltd; Adsites Ltd; Exclusive licence to market and sell advertising space.
CA/1109/92E	DCC Business Expansion Fund Ltd; covenantors. Standard shareholding agreement.
CA/745/92E	Thomas De La Rue and Co. Ltd; Smurfit Print and Packaging Ltd; Bayleaf Ltd. Joint venture.
CA/786/92E	DCC; Direct Marketing Technologies Group Ltd; shareholders. Shareholding agreement.
CA/787/92E	DCC; Allied Foods Ltd; shareholders. Shareholding agreement.
CA/788/92E	DCC; Capco Holdings Ltd; shareholders. Shareholding agreement.
CA/789/92E	DCC; John Hinde Ltd; shareholders. Shareholding agreement.
CA/790/92E	DCC; Sharptext Ltd; shareholders. Shareholding agreement.
CA/791/92E	DCC; Emo Oil Ltd; shareholders. Shareholding agreement.
CA/393/92	Dealgan Milk Products Ltd; distributors. Exclusive purchase agreement—Dealgan agency.
CA/785/92E	Development Capital Corporation. Fannin Group Ltd; shareholders. Shareholding agreement.
CA/319/92E	Edward Dillons & Co.; Jas Hennessy & Co. Ltd. Exclusive distribution.
CA/1082/92E	Edward Dillon & Co. Ltd; Jas Hennessy & Co. Ltd. Exclusive distribution.
CA/1083/92E	Edward Dillon & Co. Ltd; The Old Bushmills Distillery Co. Ltd. Exclusive distribution.
CA/1084/92E	Edward Dillon & Co. Ltd; Grants of St. James's. Exclusive distribution.
CA/1085/92E	Edward Dillon & Co. Ltd; United Distillers plc. Exclusive distribution.
CA/1086/92	Edward Dillon & Co. Ltd; Maison Bouchard Pere et Fils. Exclusive distribution.
CA/1087/92E	Edward Dillon & Co. Ltd; Hedges & Butler Ltd. Exclusive distribution.
CA/1088/92E	Edward Dillon & Co. Ltd; Vintners International Co. Inc. Exclusive distribution.

CA/1089/92E	Edward Dillon & Co. Ltd; Seagram U.K. Ltd. Exclusive distribution.
CA/1090/92E	Edward Dillon & Co. Ltd; H. Sichel Sohne GmbH. Exclusive distribution.
CA/1091/92E	Edward Dillon & Co. Ltd; Bacardi International Ltd. Exclusive distribution.
CA/150/92E	Dimpco Ltd; Sharp Electronics (UK) Ltd. Exclusive distribution.
CA/318/92E	Divillys (Galway Leading Butchers) Ltd; G.D. Investments Ltd. Shopping centre lease.
CA/205/92E	Brendan Doherty and others; Arden Heath Co. Ltd. Shopping centre lease.
CA/271/92E	W and A. Dolan, Richfield Investments Ltd. Shopping centre lease.
CA/767/92E	J. Donohoe Ltd; Pepsi-Cola Co. Exclusive bottling and distribution.
CA/768/92E	J. Donohoe Ltd; The Monarch Co. Inc. Exclusive bottling and distribution.
CA/512/92E	W. & J. Donovan; Civil Engineers (Ireland) Ltd. Shopping centre lease.
CA/1133/92E	Martin Andrew Doyle; Joseph Moffitt. Partnership and sale of business.
CA/642/92E	Doyle Donnelly Flynn Hanlon & Brannelly Ltd; Eastcastle Ltd; J. Walter Thompson Group. Shareholding agreement.
CA/1100/92E	Doyles Shoe Centre Ltd; Michael Reilly & Sons Ltd. Maynooth Shopping centre lease.
CA/244/92E	Drakebury Construction Ltd; Eyre Square Shopping centre and office leases.
CA/647/92E	Dublin Aluminium Ltd; S. Hughes. Employment contract.
CA/122/92E	Dublin Bankers Clearing Committee. Agreement on payment clearing system.
CA/211/92E	Mary Jo Duffy; Power Supermarkets Ltd. Shopping centre lease.
CA/942/92E	Duffy Group Old Bawn Ltd; Timebrock Ltd. Shopping centre leases.
CA/943/92E	B. Duffy; Timebrock Ltd. Shopping centre leases.
CA/876/92E	Dunnes Properties Ltd; Castlebrook Investments and others; tenants. Ballilna Shopping centre leases.
CA/880/92E	Dunnes Stores (Limerick) Ltd; tenants. Shopping centre leases.
CA/125/92E	The Direct Debiting Committee; originators. Agreement on direct debiting arrangements.
CA/222/92E	Doncove Ltd; Berryvale Ltd; AIBI Nominees Ltd. Arthur's Quay Shopping centre leases.
CA/878/92E	Dunnes Stores (Headford Road) Ltd. and others; tenants. Shopping centre leases.
CA/1080/92E	Eason & Son Ltd; Newspread ltd. Agreement on forward purchasing of foreign currency and its application to resale prices.
CA/67/93	Eastern Health Board; Cyanamid of Great Britain Ltd. Exclusive supply agreement for vaccines.
CA/11/94	EBS Building Society; Midlands & Western Building Society; The Directors. Transfer of engagements.
CA/57/92	Edberg Ltd; D.P. Scully and Others. Sale of business and related agreements with restrictive clauses.
CA/241/92E	Edson Investments Ltd; Mullingar Shopping centre lease.
CA/736/92E	Eight to Twelve Ltd. and others; franchises. Franchise agreement.
CA/775/92E	Eirpage Ltd; agents. Agency agreement.

CA/778/92E	Eirpage Ltd; subscribers. Subscriber agreement.
CA/682/92E	Eirtrade Ltd; International Network Services Ltd. Exclusive distribution.
CA/836/92	Electricity Supply Board; electrical contractors. Register of Electricity Contractors Ireland Ltd.
CA/99/92E	The Elkinson Trust; Damien and Mary Burke. User restrictions in use of shop.
CA/893/92E	Emo Oil Ltd; Canvale Ltd; F. O'Sullivan. Exclusive distribution.
CA/31/93	Energy Control Systems Ltd/Erinova Ltd; exclusive distribution agreement;
CA/32/93	Energy Control Systems Ltd/Belton Engineering Works Ltd; exclusive distribution agreement;
CA/21/92	ESB Industrial Holdings Ltd; Irish Cement Ltd. Sale and purchase agreement for pulverised fuel ash.
CA/28/93	ESBI Consultants Ltd/Maritz Inc/Murray Financial Services Ltd; joint venture;
CA/18/93	Executive Towel Rental Ltd/Bright & Clean Ltd/ J & A Clark; sub-contracting agreement to provide laundry services;
CA/965/92E	ESM Paper Ltd; Du Pont (UK) Ltd. Exclusive distribution.
CA/966/92E	ESM Paper Ltd; Iggesund Paperboard (Workington) Ltd. Exclusive distribution.
CA/967/92E	ESM Paper Ltd; Berghuizer Papierfabriek N.V. Exclusive distribution.
CA/11/91E	Esso Ireland Ltd; Independent dealers. Deed of Charge/Mortgage.
CA/12/91E	Esso Ireland Ltd; Independent dealers. Dealer equipment loan agreement.
CA/13/91E	Esso Ireland Ltd; Independent dealers. Exclusive purchase solus agreement.
CA/101/92	Esso Ireland Ltd/Artane Service Station Ltd; contractors. Exclusive purchase.
CA/141/92E	Esso Ireland Ltd; Blugas Ltd. Exclusive distribution.
CA/140/92E	Esso Ireland Ltd; Irish Tar & Bitumen Suppliers. Exclusive distribution.
CA/128/92E	Esso Ireland Ltd; distributors. Exclusive distribution.
CA/49/92E	Esso Ireland Ltd; Licensees. Licence agreement.
CA/13/92E	Estuary Fuels Ltd; Independent dealers. Exclusive purchase (solus) agreement.
CA/629/92E	Estuary Fuel Ltd; distributors. Exclusive distribution.
CA/630/92E	Estuary Fuel Ltd; distributors. Exclusive distribution.
CA/631/92E	Estuary Fuel Ltd; distributors. Retention of title.
CA/632/92E	Estuary Fuel Ltd; distributors. Specific chattel mortgage.
CA/633/92E	Estuary Fuel Ltd; distributors. Debenture.
CA/634/92E	Estuary Fuel Ltd; distributors. Debenture.
CA/635/92E	Estuary Fuel Ltd; distributors. Guarantee and indemnity.
CA/636/92E	Estuary Fuel Ltd; distributors. Guarantee and indemnity.
CA/13/94	Estuary Fuel Ltd; Collins Oil Products Ltd. Exclusive purchase (Solus) agreement.
CA/5/95	Eureko Ireland Holdings Ltd; Mr John F. Bourke; Stellar Internationa Ltd; The Shareholders, sale of business (Celtic International Insurance Co. Ltd.)
CA/123/92E	The Eurocheque Committee. Agreement on operation of the Eurocheque system.
CA/269/92E	Europlex Holdings Ltd; Shareholders and investors. Shareholding agreement.
CA/937/92E	Euroscreen Ltd; International Screen Ltd; J. Delves Shareholding agreement.

CA/987/92E	Ewos Agriculture Ab; Cross Vetpharm Group Ltd. Exclusive distribution.
CA/31/92E	Falcon Holidays; Ben McArdle Ltd; Travel Agents. Exclusive dealing in package holiday insurance.
CA/957/92E	Fannin Ireland Ltd; Vernon & Co. (Pulp Products) Ltd. Exclusive distribution.
CA/958/92E	Fannin Hospital Enterprises Ltd; Portex Ltd. Exclusive distribution.
CA/959/92E	Fannin Health Care Ltd; Hospicare Ltd. Exclusive distribution.
CA/960/92E	Fannin Hospital Enterprises Ltd; Kendall Co. (UK) Ltd. Exclusive distribution.
CA/961/92E	Fannin Hospital Enterprises Ltd; Eschmann Bros. & Walsh Ltd. Exclusive distribution.
CA/311/92E	FBD Developments (Cork) Ltd; tenants. Office lease.
CA/698/92	FBH Ltd; FBH Distributors Ltd; Harty Security Ltd; Harty Holdings Ltd. Purchase of assets.
CA/307/92E	Federation of Irish Chemical Industries; Department of Health. Terms and conditions of supply.
CA/16/94	Fexco Innovations Ltd; BIG Estates Ltd; Foreign Exchange Company of Ireland. Share sale agreement.
CA/898/92	Fiat Auto (Ireland) Ltd; dealers. Selective distribution.
CA/899/92E	Fiat Auto (Ireland) Ltd; J. Donohoe Ltd. Selective distribution.
CA/23/95	Fiat Auto (Ireland) Ltd; main dealers. Selective distribution agreement.
CA/674/92E	B. and D. Firestone; Karim Agan Khan. Purchase of stud farms.
CA/693/92E	First National Bakery Co. Ltd; Clianthus Ltd. and others. Merger.
CA/361/92E	First Venture Fund Ltd; Matrix Group; shareholders. Shareholding agreement.
CA/921/92E	Fitzwilliam Trust Co.; Fitzpatrick Associates Economic Consultants Ltd. Office lease.
CA/922/92E	Fitzwilliam Trust Co.; Linen Supply of Ireland Ltd. and Texas Homecare (Ireland) Consultants Ltd. Office and shop leases.
CA/607/92E	Five Star Supermarkets; Richfield Investments Ltd. Thomond Shopping centre lease.
CA/608/92E	Five Star Supermarkets; Mall Holdings Ltd. Crescent Shopping centre lease.
CA/609/92E	Five Star Supermarkets; Drumcondra Shop leases.
CA/610/92E	Five Star Supermarkets; Sligo Shopping centre leases.
CA/614/92E	Five Star Supermarkets; Clonmel Shopping centre leases.
CA/162/92E	Una and Jim Flanagan; Balally Investments Ltd. Shopping centre lease.
CA/14/92E	Flogas Ireland Ltd; authorised dealer. Exclusive purchase agreement.
CA/15/92E	Flogas Ireland Ltd; authorised distributors. Exclusive purchase agreement.
CA/16/92E	Flogas Ireland Ltd; bulk customers. Exclusive purchase agreement.
CA/64/92	Flor Griffin; Teddy O'Connor. Franchise agreement.
CA/151/92E	Frederick and Mary Cleary; Rita Power. Restrictive covenant in shop lease.
CA/120/92E	Patrick G. Flynn; Wardell Roberts plc. Agency agreement.
CA/75/92E	Henry Ford & Son Ltd; motor dealers. Selective distribution.

CA/17/94	Foreign Exchange Company of Ireland; BIG Estates Ltd. Agreement for the sale of assets.
CA/1/92	Phil Fortune; Budget Travel Ltd. Sale of business agreement with non-competition clause.
CA/916/92E	Four Star Pizza (Ireland) Ltd; franchises. Franchise agreement.
CA/992/92	Franklin Pharmaceuticals Ltd; Cross Vetpharm Group Ltd. Secrecy agreement.
CA/1101/92E	Friends Provident Life Assurance Co. Ltd; Dawson Street Office and shopping centre leases.
CA/29/94	Fuel Distributors Ltd; Brendan Cleary. Termination of employment contract.
CA/30/94	Fuel Distributors Ltd; Brendan Cleary. Consultancy agreement.
CA/61/93	Fuel Distributors Ltd/J. Enright. Restrictive covenant in sale of business.
CA/25/95	Fuel Distributors Ltd/Bord na Mona. Asset purchase agreement.
CA/208/92E	Gallaher (Dublin) Ltd; The World Professional Billiards and Snooker Association Ltd. Exclusive sports promotion agreement and restrictive covenants.
CA/209/92E	Gallaher (Dublin) Ltd; Fintra Computers Ltd. Restrictions in computer software agreement.
CA/210/92E	Gallaher (Dublin) Ltd; Digital Telephone Co. Ltd. Restrictions in computerised telesales system agreement.
CA/35/93	Gallaher (Dublin) Ltd/Ritmeester BV; exclusive distribution agreement;
CA/699/92E	Gallic Distributors Ltd; dealers. Selective distribution.
CA/700/92	Gallic Distributors Ltd; Automobiles Citroen. Selective distribution.
CA/601/92E	Gallic Distributors Ltd; dealers. Deed of charge/mortgage.
CA/702/92	Gallic Distributors Ltd; dealers. Dealer loan.
CA/1/93	Galvia Hospital Ltd/VHI Board. Provision of health care services and payment by VHI.
CA/875/92E	G.D. Investments (Galway) Ltd; tenants. Shopping centre lease.
CA/44/93	General Electric Capital Corporation/GPA Group plc. Omnibus agreement.
CA/45/93	General Electric Capital Corporation/GPA Group plc. Master aircraft sale agreement & master deferred payment agreement.
CA/46/93	General Electric Capital Corporation/GPA Group plc;. Subscription option agreement.
CA/47/93	General Electric Capital Corporation/GPA Group plc. Management agreement.
CA/48/93	General Electric Capital Corporation/GPA Group plc; Air Tara option agreement.
CA/49/93	General Electric Capital Corporation/GPA Group plc. Asset purchase agreement.
CA/50/93	General Electric Capital Corporation/GPA Group plc. Treasury MIS license agreement.
CA/51/93	General Electric Capital Corporation/GPA Group plc. License agreement.
CA/52/93	General Electric Capital Corporation/GPA Group plc. Shareholders agreement.
CA/53/93	General Electric Capital Corporation/GPA Group plc. Sub lease.
CA/54/93	General Electric Capital Corporation/GPA Group plc. Interested party agreement.

CA/55/93	General Electric Capital Corporation/GPA Group plc. GPA management assets consent & Boeing consents.
CA/56/93	General Electric Capital Corporation/GPA Group plc; deferral agreements.
CA/57/93	General Electric Capital Corporation/GPA Group plc. Loan stock trust deed, security trust deed & the security instruments.
CA/714/92	General Motors Distribution Ireland Ltd; motor dealers. Selective distribution.
CA/715/92	General Motors Distribution Ireland Ltd; motor dealers. Selective distribution.
CA/51/92	GI Corporation; General Semiconductor Industries Inc. Acquisition of business.
CA/52/92	GI Corporation; General Semiconductor Industries Inc. Restrictive clauses in sale of business agreement.
CA/628/92E	Gilbeys of Ireland Sales Ltd; Baron Philippe de Rothschild S.A. Exclusive distribution.
CA/543/92E	Gilbeys of Ireland Ltd; Matthew Gloag (UK) Ltd. Exclusive distribution.
CA/544/92E	Gilbeys of Ireland Ltd; Pedrotti Interdrink S.A.S. Trademark and exclusive purchase agreement.
CA/528/92E	Gilbeys of Ireland Sales Ltd; Hermann Kendermann GmbH. Exclusive distribution.
CA/529/92E	Gilbeys of Ireland Sales Ltd; Davide Campari–Milano SPA. Exclusive distribution.
CA/530/92E	Gilbeys of Ireland Sales Ltd; Veuve Clicquot Ponsardin. Exclusive distribution.
CA/804/92E	Gill & MacMillan Ltd; Attic Press. Exclusive distribution.
CA/805/92E	Gill & MacMillan Ltd; Brandon Book Publishers Ltd. Exclusive distribution.
CA/806/92E	Gill & MacMillan Ltd; The Lilliput Press. Exclusive distribution.
CA/807/92E	Gill & MacMillan Ltd; Irish Academic Press. Exclusive distribution.
CA/808/92E	Gill & MacMillan Ltd; Four Courts Press. Exclusive distribution.
CA/809/92E	Gill & MacMillan Ltd; The Round Hall Press. Exclusive distribution.
CA/810/92E	Gill & MacMillan Ltd; The O'Brien Press. Exclusive distribution.
CA/811/92E	Gill & MacMillan Ltd; Wolfhound Press. Exclusive distribution.
CA/812/92E	Gill & MacMillan Ltd; Townhouse & Countryhouse Publishers Ltd. Exclusive distribution.
CA/813/92E	Gill & MacMillan Ltd; booksellers. Standard terms and conditions.
CA/7/93	Gillespie & Co. Ltd/Milupa Ltd; exclusive distribution agreement.
CA/24/93	Gillespie & Co. Ltd/Seven Seas (Ireland) Ltd; distribution agreement.
CA/1132/92E	Giltsharp Technology (UK) Ltd; Michael McPhillips Ltd; Michael McPhillips. Franchise agreement.
CA/997/92	Glenberg; Winchurch Investments Ltd. Finglas Shopping centre lease.
CA/998/92E	Glenberg; City Properties (Cork) Ltd. Shopping centre lease.
CA/999/92E	Glenberg; Westport Developments Ltd. Shopping centre lease.
CA/1000/92E	Glenberg; K. Coogan. Earl Street Shop lease.
CA/1001/92E	Glenberg; Associated Restaurants Ltd. Restaurant lease.
CA/1002/92E	Glenberg; Wilton Securities Ltd. Shopping centre lease.
CA/1003/92E	Glenberg; Wanz Properties Ltd. Shopping centre lease.

CA/1004/92E	Glenberg; H. Williams & Co. Ltd. Shankill Shopping centre lease.
CA/1005/92E	Glenberg; Glenhest Developments Ltd. Sutton Shopping centre lease.
CA/1006/92E	Glenberg; Tallaght Shopping Centre Ltd. Shopping centre lease.
CA/1007/92E	Glenberg; Urban Development Ltd. Stillorgan Shopping centre leases.
CA/453/92E	Goodbody Stockbrokers; Elvetham Ltd; Grand Hotel Malahide Ltd; shareholders. Shareholding agreement.
CA/872/92E	E. and A. Gorman; A. Elkinson. Property lease.
CA/624/92E	Gowan Distributors Ltd; Automobiles Peugeot S.A. Selective distribution.
CA/625/92E	Gowan Distributors Ltd; dealers. Dealer loan agreement.
CA/626/92E	Gowan Distributors Ltd; dealers. Deed of charge/mortgage.
CA/640/92E	Gowan Distributors Ltd; dealers. Selective distribution.
CA/33/93	Grant Engineering Ltd/Ecoflam S P A; exclusive distribution agreement;
CA/303/92E	Grants of Ireland Ltd; M & R Martini & Rossi Ltd. Exclusive distribution.
CA/304/92E	Grants of Ireland Ltd; Marchesi L & P Antinori Distribuzione SPA. Exclusive distribution.
CA/306/92E	Grants of Ireland Ltd; Bewleys Ltd. Exclusive purchase.
CA/423/92	Green Property plc; Northside Shopping centre lease.
CA/424/92	Green Property plc; Waterford Shopping centre lease.
CA/990/92	Green Science Ltd; Micro-Bac International Inc. Agreement for the purchase of technology and exclusive manufacture and distribution.
CA/277/92E	Greencore Foodsales Ltd; Major International Ltd. Exclusive distribution.
CA/605/92E	Grittar; David J. Bolger. Shopping centre lease.
CA/606/92E	Grittar; Light Bite. Ballyfermot Shopping centre lease.
CA/65/92	Group 91 Architects. Shareholders' agreement for joint venture.
CA/532/92E	Guardian Assurance plc; The Square Shopping centre leases.
CA/379/92E	Guinness Ireland Ltd; United Breweries International Ltd. Exclusive production and distribution.
CA/380/92E	Guinness Ireland Ltd; Anheuser-Busch Inc. Exclusive production and distribution.
CA/381/92E	Guinness Ireland Ltd; Furstlich Fursternbergische Bruaerie KG. Exclusive production and distribution.
CA/542/92E	Guardian Assurance plc; tenants. Shopping centre lease.
CA/27/94	H. + K. International Inc. Shareholder's agreement.
CA/932/92E	Halton Business Systems Ltd, P. Burns. Franchise agreement.
CA/6/94	Halton Business Systems Ltd; Peter Burns. Franchise agreement.
CA/308/92E	Hanford Ltd; tenants. Office and shop leases.
CA/67/92	Harwood Brothers Ltd; retailers. Selective retail distribution agreement for Chanel products.
CA/36/93	Heating Replacement Parts & Controls Ltd/ Windsor Motors Ltd/Gas & Oil Parts Ltd/T MacGee, M O'Reilly & T Daly; share acquisition agreement.
CA/803/92E	Heron (Suzuki) Ltd; motor dealers. Selective distribution.

CA/56/92	Hickson International plc.; Angus Fine Chemicals Ltd. Sale of business agreement with non-competition clauses.
CA/47/92	Home Choice Videos (I) Ltd; Franchises. Franchise agreement.
CA/639/92E	Honda Motor Co. Ltd; Universal Honda Ltd; Selective distribution.
CA/300/92E	Hoorn & Winkel (Irl) Ltd; tenants. Shopping centre lease.
CA/301/92E	Hoorn & Winkel (Irl) Ltd; Esmonde Motors Ltd. Warehouse lease with restrictive covenant.
CA/814/92E	D. Horkan Ltd; Michael Kavanagh. Shopping centre lease.
CA/815/92E	D. Horkan Ltd; Michael Kavanagh. Shopping centre lease.
CA/816/92E	D. Horkan Ltd; Eder Trust Co. Shopping centre lease.
CA/817/92E	D. Horkan Ltd; Malincourt Ltd. Shopping centre lease.
CA/818/92E	D. Horkan Ltd; Power Supermarkets Ltd. Shopping centre lease.
CA/819/92E	D. Horkan Ltd; Erin Executor and Trustee Co. Ltd. Shopping centre lease.
CA/652/92E	Hornsea Ltd. (Parke Davis/Elan Ltd.); Elan Corporation plc. Exclusive purchase.
CA/757/92E	Hospicare Ltd; Scott Paper Co. Exclusive manufacture.
CA/758/92E	Hospicare Ltd; Smith & Nephew Medical Ltd. Exclusive manufacture.
CA/149/92E	HSI Ltd; Hoover plc. Exclusive distribution.
CA/691/92E	IAWS-Agri Society Ltd; Unigrain Dublin Ltd. and others. Merger.
CA/689/92E	IAWS Group; First National Bakery Co. Ltd; shareholders. Shareholding agreement.
CA/692/92E	IAWS Group plc; Shamrock Foods Ltd; shareholders. Shareholding agreement.
CA/690/92E	IAWS Sales Ltd; Dock Milling Ltd; S. & A.G. Davis Ltd; Katowice Ltd; and others. Sharehholding agreement.
CA/847/92E	ICC Bank plc; Cornell Electronics and others. Shareholding agreement.
CA/848/92E	ICC Bank plc; Mentec Ltd and others. Shareholding agreement.
CA/849/92E	ICC Bank plc; Navenby Ltd and others. Shareholding agreement.
CA/850/92E	ICC Bank plc; Largo Food Exports Ltd and others. Shareholding agreement.
CA/851/92E	ICC Bank plc; Astra Group (Holdings) Ltd and others. Shareholding agreement.
CA/852/92E	ICC Bank plc; Irish Conference and Leisure Holdings Ltd and others. Shareholding agreement.
CA/853/92E	ICC Bank plc; IDA; SFADCO; CTT. Joint venture.
CA/854/92E	ICC Bank plc; Acquaporte Ltd and others. Shareholding agreement.
CA/855/92E	ICC Bank plc; Kleerex Licensing Ltd and others. Shareholding agreement.
CA/856/92E	ICC Bank plc; Kleerex International Ltd; Carroll Products and Designs Ltd and others. Intellectual property licence.
CA/857/92E	ICC Bank plc; Kleerex Licensing Ltd and others. Shareholding agreement.
CA/858/92E	ICC Bank plc; Kleerex International Ltd; Carroll Products and Designs Ltd and others. Intellectual property licence.
CA/859/92E	ICC Bank plc; Carroll Products and Designs Ltd and others. Shareholding agreement.
CA/860/92E	ICC Bank plc; Noontec Ltd and others. Shareholding agreement and patent licence.

CA/862/92E	ICC Bank plc; Mosney Irish Holidays plc and others. Shareholding agreement.
CA/863/92E	ICC Bank plc; Hemera & Cie S.C.P.A.; Rochglen Holdings Ltd adn V.R. (Spideal) Teo and others. Shareholding agreement.
CA/865/92E	ICC Bank plc; Irish Fencing and Products Ltd and others. Shareholding agreement.
CA/866/92E	ICC Bank plc; Corcoran's Management Ltd and others; Isbauch Ltd; Cambridge Investments Ltd. Shareholding agreement.
CA/867/92E	ICC Bank plc; Marine Computation Service plc; Dental Laboratories (Drumshambo) Ltd and others. Shareholding agreement.
CA/868/92E	ICC Bank plc; Etos Investments Ltd; Allied Combined Trust Ltd and First Venture Fund Ltd; Allied Irish Investment Bank plc and others. Shareholding agreement.
CA/869/92E	ICC Bank plc; L. & P. Financial Trustees of Ireland Ltd and others. Shareholding agreement.
	IMRO = See listings for Irish Music Rights Organisation.
CA/375/92E	Independent Newspapers Marketing Ltd; wholesalers and newsagents. Newspaper distribution agreement.
CA/376/92E	Independent Newspapers Marketing Ltd; wholesalers and newsagents. Newspaper distribution agreement-transfer.
CA/826/92E	The Institute of Chartered Accountants in Ireland. Bye-laws.
CA/827/92E	The Institute of Chartered Accountants in Ireland. Rules of Professional Conduct.
CA/828/92	The Institute of Chartered Accountants in Ireland. Ethical Guide for Members.
CA/846/92E	Interfit Ltd; Portmarnock Shopping centre leases.
CA/27/94	H. & K. International Inc. Shareholder's agreement.
CA/237/92E	International Coatings Ltd; Power Adhesives Ltd. Exclusive distribution.
CA/238/92E	International Coatings Ltd; ISF Group. Exclusive distribution.
CA/239/92E	International Coatings Ltd; System Devpack Ltd. Exclusive distribution.
CA/79/92E	IPFPUT; lessees. Shopping centre lease.
CA/80/92E	IPFPUT; Power Supermarkets Ltd. Shopping centre lease.
CA/296/92E	Ipodec SA; GKN United Kingdom plc and others. Sale of business.
CA/389/92E	Irish Biscuits Ltd; Jacobs Suchard Manufacturing GmbH. Exclusive distribution.
CA/503/92E	Irish Coal Importers; Weglokoks. Joint purchasing agreement.
CA/317/92E	Irish Commercials (Sales) Ltd; Volvo Trucks (GB) Ltd. Exclusive distribution.
CA/126/92	Irish County Bacon Ltd; Mr Paschal Phelan. Acquisition of shares in business.
CA/127/92	Irish County Bacon Ltd; Mr Paschal Phelan. Sale of business.
CA/970/92E	Irish Distillers Group plc; P. O'Lionaird. Trademark usership agreement.
CA/971/92E	Irish Distillers Ltd; Lakeshore Goods Ltd. Trademark usership agreement.
CA/972/92E	Irish Distillers Ltd; Celtic Glass Ltd. Trademark usership agreement.
CA/973/92	Irish Distillers Ltd; Celtic Glass Ltd. Trademark usership agreement.
CA/974/92E	The 'Old Bushmills' Distillery Co. Ltd; Celtic Glass Ltd. Trademark usership agreement.
CA/975/92E	Irish Distillers Ltd; P. Thompson. Trademark usership agreement.

CA/977/92E	Irish Distillers Ltd; J.B. Casey. Trademark usership agreement.
CA/978/92E	Irish Distillers Ltd; Tobler Suchard Ltd. Trademark usership agreement.
CA/979/92E	Irish Distillers Ltd; Lough Derg Handcrafts Ltd. Trademark usership agreement.
CA/980/92E	Irish Distillers Ltd; Mileeven Ltd. Trademark usership agreement.
CA/981/92	Irish Distillers Ltd; LLEDO Ltd. Trademark usership agreement.
CA/62/93	Irish Distillers Group plc/Cooley Distillery plc. Takeover.
CA/39/93	Irish Distillers Group plc/J Hennessy & Co. SA/Guinness Distillers Holdings BV. Restructuring of issued share capital of E. Dillon & Co. Ltd.
CA/4/93	Irish Fertiliser Industries Ltd/Pioneer Hi-Bred (UK) Ltd. Exclusive distribution agreement
CA/148/92E	Irish Handcrafts Ltd; AIB Investment Nominees, etc. Shopping centre lease.
CA/723/92E	Irish Life Assurance plc; Noel Woods. Agency agreement.
CA/724/92	Irish Life Assurance plc; registered Irish Life insurance brokers. Agency agreement.
CA/725/92	Irish Life Assurance plc; registered Irish Life insurance brokers. Agency agreement.
CA/734/92E	Irish Life Assurance plc; Irish Life Building Society. Agency agreement.
CA/962/92E	Irish Life Assurance plc; Irish Intercontinental Bank Ltd; Irish Life Finance Group Ltd; Irish Life Finance Ltd. Shareholding agreement.
CA/1045/92	Irish Life Assurance plc; First National Building Society. Tied agency agreement.
CA/1046/92E	Irish Life; Irish Insurance Federation. Agreement on maximum rates of remuneration for life business.
CA/17/93	Irish Life Building Society/First National Building Society; takeover (transfer of engagements);
CA/743/92E	Irish Life plc; Eason & Son Ltd; Shopping centre lease.
CA/153/92E	The Irish League of Credit Unions; ECCU Assurance Co. Ltd. Compulsory insurance requirement.
CA/1/91E	Irish Music Rights Organisation (IMRO); Performing Right Society. Copyright licence (assignment).
CA/2/91E	IMRO/PRS; Creators (Composers and Lyricists); Publishers. Assignment of copyright.
CA/3/91E	IMRO; Users (Pubs, Cinemas, Discos, Shops etc.). Copyright licence.
CA/4/91E	IMRO; RTE. copyright licence.
CA/2/95	Irish Music Rights Organisation Ltd; Writers. Assignment of copyright in musical works.
CA/3/95	Irish Music Rights Organisation Ltd; Individual publishers. Assignment of copyright in musical works.
CA/4/95	Irish Music Rights Organisation Ltd; Publishers (Limited Company). Assignment of copyright in musical works.
CA/232/92E	Irish National Insurance Co. plc; ARAG. Joint venture company.
CA/233/92	Irish National Insurance Co. plc; GESA. Joint venture company.
CA/320/92E	Irish Nurseries Ltd; Uniplumo Ltd; Give Joy Ltd and others. Sale of business.

CA/78/92E	Irish Pension Fund Property Unit Trust; Power Supermarkets Ltd. Shopping centre lease.
CA/118/92E	Irish Permanent Building Society; agents. Agency agreement.
CA/119/92E	Irish Permanent Building Society; agents. Agency agreement.
CA/147/92E	Irish Permanent Building Society; Prudential Life of Ireland Ltd; Insurance sales joint venture.
CA/32/94	Irish Potato Marketing Ltd; P. Keating liquitator. Share purchase agreement.
CA/316/92E	Irish Refrigeration Enterprises Association; Department of Agriculture and Food. Arrangements for cold storage of intervention beef.
CA/293/92E	Irish Ropes Ltd; Koltec B.V. Exclusive distribution.
CA/294/92E	Irish Ropes Ltd; Nentec UK Ltd. Agency agreement.
CA/418/92E	Irish Ropes Ltd; Mobil Plastics Europe Inc. Exclusive distribution.
CA/419/92E	Irish Ropes Ltd; Rosenlew Emballage AB. Exclusive distribution.
CA/420/92E CA/421/92E	Irish Ropes Ltd; Werra Plastics GmbH. Exclusive distribution. Irish Ropes Ltd; Itipack S.R.L. Exclusive distribution.
CA/422/92E	Irish Ropes Ltd; British Twines Ltd. Exclusive distribution.
CA/22/92E	Irish Seafood Producers Group Ltd; Producers. Exclusive marketing agency agreement
CA/258/92E	Irish Shell Ltd; independent dealers. Equipment loan agreement.
CA/259/92E	Irish Shell Ltd; authorised distributors. Exclusive distribution.
CA/260/92E	Irish Shell Ltd; independent dealers. Exclusive purchase.
CA/261/92E	Irish Shell Ltd; licensees. Licence agreement.
CA/262/92E	Irish Shell Ltd; independent dealers. Loan agreement for tank storage.
CA/263/92E	Irish Shell Ltd; licensees. Licence agreement.
CA/264/92E	Irish Shell Ltd; independent dealers. Publicity allowance agreement.
CA/265/92E	Irish Shell Ltd; licensees. Temporary licence agreement.
CA/266/92E	Irish Shell Ltd; licensees. Licence agreement (old).
CA/65/93	Irish Shell Ltd./users; lubrication bay equipment loan agreement;
CA/199/92E	The Irish Stock Exchange; member firms. Rules in relation to dealings in Irish Government securities.
CA/132/92E	Irish Telephone Rentals Ltd; subscribers. Standard contract for rental of time control equipment.
CA/134/92E	Irish Telephone Rentals Ltd; subscribers. Telephone rental contract.
CA/135/92E	Irish Telephone Rentals Ltd; subscribers. Contract for rental of staff location equipment.
CA/139/92E	Irish Telephone Rentals Ltd; subscribers. Contract for rental of security equipment.
CA/175/92E	Irish Telephone Rentals Ltd; subscribers. Contract for rental of telephones.
CA/176/92E	Irish Telephone Rentals Ltd; subscribers. Contract for rental of telephones.
CA/179/92E	Irish Telephone Rentals Ltd; subscribers. Contract for telephone rental.
CA/180/92E	Irish Telephone Rentals Ltd; subscribers. Contract for security service rental.

CA/181/92E	Irish Telephone Rentals Ltd; subscribers. Contract for rental of staff location equipment.
CA/182/92E	Irish Telephone Rentals Ltd; subscribers. Contract for rental of time control equipment.
CA/184/92E	Irish Telephone Rentals Ltd; subscribers. Contract for rental of staff location equipment.
CA/185/92E	Irish Telephone Rentals Ltd; subscribers. Contract for rental of security service equipment.
CA/186/92E	Irish Telephone Rentals Ltd; subscribers. Contract for rental of time control equipment.
CA/191/92E	Irish Telephone Rentals Ltd; subscribers. Contract for rental of staff location equipment.
CA/112/92E	The Irish Times Newspapers Ltd; newsagents. Supply agreement (minimum orders).
CA/113/92E	The Irish Times Newspapers Ltd; newsagents. Supply agreement (method of payment).
CA/114/92E	The Irish Times Newspapers Ltd; newsagents. Supply agreement (method of payment).
CA/369/92E	ITT World Directories Inc; ITT Information Services Ltd; Golden Pages Ltd. Technical services agreement.
CA/402/92E	Iveco Fiat SpA; McCormick MacNaughton Commercials Ltd. Selective distribution.
CA/29/95	Iveco Road Truck Ltd. Exclusive distribution agreement.
CA/462/92	J.C. Distribution Ltd; The Prestige Group plc. Exclusive distribution.
CA/463/92	J.C. Distribution Ltd; Kopex International Ltd. Exclusive distribution.
CA/464/92	J.C. Distribution Ltd; H. Vesshoff & Co. GmbH. Exclusive distribution.
CA/465/92E	J.C. Distribution Ltd; Jordan AS. Exclusive distribution.
CA/466/92E	J.C. Distribution Ltd; Vileda LP. Exclusive distribution.
CA/467/92	J.C. Distribution Ltd; Application Des Gaz. Exclusive distribution.
CA/468/92	J.C. Distribution Ltd; Dietzel GmbH. Exclusive distribution.
CA/1125/92	JCB Sales Ltd; Earthmover Commercial Industrial Ltd. Exclusive distribution agreement.
CA/501/92E	V. Jackson Ltd; D. Horkan Ltd. Shopping centre lease.
CA/290/92E	Johnson Brothers Ltd; Campbell Grocery Products Ltd. Exclusive distribution.
CA/252/92E	Johnson Brothers Ltd; Combe International Ltd. Exclusive distribution.
CA/291/92E	Johnson Brothers Ltd; Cussons (UK) Ltd. Exclusive distribution.
CA/247/92E	Johnson Brothers Ltd; United Biscuits (UK) Ltd. Exclusive distribution.
CA/292/92E	H & R Johnson Tiles Ltd; Oxley Keartland & Co. Ltd. Agency agreement.
CA/229/92E	R and B Kelly; Noonan Developments Ltd. Shopping centre lease.
CA/97/92	Patrick Kennedy; Michael and Bridget Brady. Sale of shopping centre unit.
CA/41/93	Kiddie Products Inc/UPC Co. Ltd; exclusive distribution agreement;
CA/1104/92E	Killiney Shopping Centre Management Co. Ltd., tenants. Shopping centre leases.

CA/545/92E	Kitchen Assessories Ltd; Franke UK Ltd. Exclusive distribution.
CA/278/92E	KP (Ireland) Ltd; UB Investments and others. Joint venture.
CA/1099/92E	Lager Distributors Ltd; Tennants Ireland Ltd. Exclusive distribution.
CA/968/92E	Lanes Group Ltd; Dipetane International Ltd. Exclusive distribution.
CA/929/92E	L. & C. Properties Ltd. and others; The Square Management Ltd; tenants. Shopping centre leases.
CA/100/92	Lee & Co.; Musgrave Limited. Sale of business.
CA/268/92	Lee Strand Co-operative Creamery Ltd; distributors. Exclusive purchase and distribution agreement.
CA/116/92E	Levi Strauss UK Ltd; franchises. Franchise agreement.
CA/206/92	Levi Strauss UK Ltd; franchises. Franchise agreement (amended).
CA/933/92E	Levi Strauss (UK) Ltd; Lasalter Ltd. Franchise agreement.
CA/934/92E	Levi Strauss (UK) Ltd; Limington Ltd. Franchise agreement.
CA/935/92E	Levi Strauss (UK) Ltd; B. & S. Fashions Ltd. Franchise agreement.
CA/460/92E	Light Bite; Crumlin Investments Ltd. Shopping centre lease.
CA/782/92E	Lillington Ltd. and others. Glenageary Shopping centre leases.
CA/193/92E	Linabbey Ltd; Santa Anita Estates Ltd. Shopping centre lease.
CA/21/95	Lister Tubes Ltd/Jonava Properties. Property sale agreement.
CA/60/92	Lithographic Universal Ltd; C.C.A. Ireland Ltd. Joint venture.
CA/914/92E	Lombard & Ulster Banking Ltd; car dealers. Provision of loan facilities for car dealers.
CA/216/92E	C and A Lonergan; N.J. Kelly Ltd. Shopping centre lease.
CA/507/92	Lucas Automotive Ltd; distributors. Exclusive distribution.
CA/20/94	Lyne/Paul. Sale of Business.
CA/1094/92E	N. MacManus; Arch Properties Ltd. Rathmines Shopping centre lease.
CA/38/93	Mac Publishing Ltd/D McAuliffe; serviee contract;
CA/309/92E	Maeldoon Ltd; FBD House Limerick. Office and shop leases.
CA/950/92E	Maguire & Paterson Ltd; G. & M. Ltd. Exclusive distribution.
CA/951/92E	Maguire & Paterson Ltd; Irish Dog Foods Ltd. Exclusive distribution.
CA/952/92E	Maguire & Paterson Ltd; Jade Cosmetics GnbH. Exclusive distribution.
CA/953/92E	Maguire & Paterson Ltd; LRC Products Ltd. Exclusive distribution.
CA/954/92E	Maguire & Paterson Ltd; Seerys Biscuits Ltd. Exclusive distribution.
CA/955/92E	Maguire & Paterson Ltd; Wilkinson Sword GmbH. Exclusive distribution.
CA/956/92E	Maguire & Paterson Ltd; Conros Corporation. Exclusive distribution.
CA/415/92E	Mall Holdings Ltd; John Ryan. Shopping centre lease.
CA/985/92E	Malting Co. of Ireland Ltd; Beamish & Crawford plc. Exclusive purchase.
CA/784/92E	Manor Park Homebuilders Ltd; Trident Homes Ltd; David Daly. Licence to build houses.
CA/342/92E	Manzares Ltd; Dorcorn Developments Ltd. Shopping centre lease.
CA/104/92E	Marspel Ltd; Melcorpo Ltd; Bray Shopping centre leases.

CA/105/92E	Marspel Ltd; Killiney Management Shopping Centre Company. Shopping centre lease.
CA/214/92E	Marspel Ltd; Town and Country Ltd. Shopping centre lease.
CA/322/92E	Masterfoods Ltd; Shamrock Foods (Distributors) Ltd. Exclusive distribution.
CA/396/92E	Masterfoods Ltd; J.C. Distribution Ltd. Exclusive distribution.
CA/397/92E	Masterfoods Ltd; Valley Ice Cream (Distribution) Ltd. Exclusive distribution.
CA/398/92E	Masterfoods Ltd; Valley Ice Cream Ltd. Delamont Ltd; shareholders. Non-disposal of shares agreement.
CA/92/92E	Maxol Ltd; consumers. Exclusive purchase.
CA/93/92E	Maxol Ltd; consumers. Exclusive purchase.
CA/94/92E	Maxol Ltd; consumers. Exclusive purchase.
CA/91/92E	Maxol Ltd; distributors. Exclusive distribution.
CA/95/92E	Maxol Ltd; distributors. Licence agreement.
CA/96/92E	Maxol Ltd; distributors. Deed of charge.
CA/83/92E	Maxol Ltd; independent dealers. Exclusive purchase (new version)
CA/84/92E	Maxol Ltd; independent dealers. Bailment equipment agreement.
CA/85/92E	Maxol Ltd; independent dealers. Exclusive purchase.
CA/86/92E	Maxol Ltd; independent dealers. Loan agreement.
CA/87/92E	Maxol Ltd; independent dealers. Deed of charge.
CA/88/92E	Maxol Ltd; independent dealers. Hire purchase agreement.
CA/89/92E	Maxol Ltd; independent dealers. Licence agreement.
CA/90/92E	Maxol Ltd; lessees. Lease agreement.
CA/33/94	Maxol Ltd; Mulfield Co. Ltd. Non-exclusive distribution agreement.
CA/842/92	B. and J. McCormack; The Square Management Ltd; tenants. Shopping centre lease.
CA/207/92E	Wilhelmina McCormak; Max Developments Ltd. Shopping centre lease.
CA/928/92E	O. McDermott and L. O'Farrell; Merchant's Court Office leases.
CA/1077/92E	M., T. and P.J. McGrath; Kilbarrack Shopping centre leases.
CA/1078/92E	M., T. and P.J. McGrath; Finglas Shopping centre leases.
CA/1079/92E	M., T. and P.J. McGrath; Ballyfermot Shopping centre leases.
CA/484/92E	MCPS; production music members. Production music membership agreement.
CA/485/92E	MCPS; record producers. Agreement on royalties.
CA/486/92E	MCPSI; Radio Telefís Éireann. Copyright licence.
CA/487/92E	MCPSI; users. Royalties for production music library catalogue.
CA/488/92E	MCPSI; broadcast production companies. Synchronisation licence.
CA/489/92E	MCPSI; film makers. Code of practice.
CA/490/92E	MCPSI; videogram producers. Producers and duplication agreement.
CA/491/92E	MCPSI; radio programme producers. Radio programming agreements.
CA/492/92E	MCPSI; recording contractors. In-flight entertainment agreements.

CA/493/92E	MCPSI; makers of recordings. Background music operators agreement.
CA/494/92E	MCPSI; telephone recording producers. Premium telephone agreement.
CA/495/92E	MCPSI; education institutions. Music and education agreements.
CA/496/92E	MCPSI; amateur cinematographers. Amateur cinematographers agreement.
CA/497/92E	MCPSI; operators. Recording booths agreement.
CA/498/92E	MCPSI; facility houses. Code of conduct.
CA/499/92E	MCPSI; production companies. Code of conduct.
CA/500/92E	MCPSI; radio stations. Radio station licence.
CA/483/92E	Mechanical Copyright Protection Society Ireland Ltd. (MCPSA); Mechanial Copyright Protection Society (MCPS); composers. Membership agreement.
CA/988/92E	NV Medicopharma; The Cross Chemical Group; Clonmel Chemical Co. Ltd. Shareholding agreement.
CA/30/93	Members of Irish Insurance Federation; agreement on maximum rates of remuneration for life business;
CA/748/92E	G. Merrick and others; Reflex Investments plc. Merger.
CA/295/92E	Mentec Ltd; Online Computing Ltd; shareholders. Sale of business
CA/884/92E	Merrion Shopping Centre and others; tenants. Shopping centre leases.
CA/825/92E	Miller Brewing Co.; Showerings Ltd. Exclusive distribution.
CA/66/93	Wm. Miller & Sons Ltd/David Galavan; employment contract.
CA/383/92E	Minister for Tourism, Transport and Communications; Dublin Airport Restaurants Ltd. Exclusive right to provide catering services.
CA/769/92E	Minitel Communications Ltd; Philips Electronics (Ireland) Ltd. Exclusive distribution.
CA/771/92E	Minitel Communications Ltd; Intelmatique S.A. Technical and marketing agreement.
CA/772/92E	Ministere des Postes Telecommunications et de l'Espace; Intelmatique S.A.; Minitel Communications Ltd. Trademark licence.
CA/780/92E	MMC Commercials Ltd; motor dealers. Selective distribution.
CA/781/92E	MMC Commercials Ltd; motor dealers. Selective distribution.
CA/242/92E	Moralto Investments Ltd; Island House Office leases.
CA/1081/92E	B. and J. Moran; A. P. and M. Dargan; Universal Travel Agency Ltd; Hewitts Travel Agency Ltd. Merger.
CA/1093/92E	Moremiles Tyre Services Ltd; The Goodyear Tyre and Rubber Co. (GB) Ltd. Exclusive distribution.
CA/343/92E	Morningford Ltd,; Mahon Shopping Centre tenants. Shopping centre lease.
CA/1092/92	Mothercare Ireland Ltd; Mothercare UK Ltd. Franchise agreement.
CA/1024/92E	Motor Distributors Ltd; Daimler-Benz A.G. Selective distribution.
CA/1025/92E	Motor Distributors Ltd; Mazda Motor Corporation; Sumitomo Corporation; Mazda Motor Europe SA/NV. Selective distribution.
CA/1026/92E	Motor Distributors Ltd; Volkswagenwerk A.G. Selective distribution.
CA/1027/92E	Motor Distributors Ltd; Mazda Motor Corporation; Sumitomo Corporation. Selective distribution.

CA/1028/92E	Motor Distributors Ltd; Mazda dealers. Selective distribution.
CA/1029/92E	Motor Distributors Ltd; Mazda dealers. Selective distribution.
CA/1030/92E	Motor Distributors Ltd; Volkswagen and Audi dealers. Selective distribution.
CA/1031/92E	Motor Distributors Ltd; Mercedes-Benz dealers. Selective distribution.
CA/192/92E	Motor Import Ltd; motor dealers. Selective distribution.
CA/274/92E	Moulinex S.A.; Glen Dimplex; Irish Sugar plc. Joint venture.
CA/8/94	Mount Juliet; David Ledbetter Golf Academy Inc. Sole provision of golf tuition.
CA/427/92E	Murphy Brewery Ireland Ltd; Clada Mineral Water Co. Ltd. Exclusive distribution.
CA/428/92	Murphy Brewery Ireland Ltd; distribution. Exclusive distribution.
CA/746/92E	P. and R. Murphy; Reflex Investments plc. Merger.
CA/747/92E	P. Murphy and others; Reflex Investments plc. Merger.
CA/732/92E	J. and E. Murray; Rathmines Properties Ltd. Shopping centre lease.
CA/27/93	J Murray/L & J O'Connell; tenancy agreement;
CA/18/92E	Musgrave Ltd; licensees. SuperValu and Centra licences for retailers.
CA/19/92E	Musgrave Ltd; franchises. SuperValue and Centra franchises for managers.
CA/20/92E	Musgrave Ltd; toy retailers. Franchise and joint purchasing agreement for SuperToys.
CA/1032/92E	Musicmaker Ltd; Vic Firth Inc. Exclusive distribution.
CA/1033/92E	Musicmaker Ltd; Roland UK Ltd. Exclusive distribution.
CA/1034/92E	Musicmaker Ltd; Pearl Musical Instrument Co. Exclusive distribution.
CA/1035/92E	Musicmaker Ltd; Young Chang Akki Europe GmbH. Exclusive distribution.
CA/1036/92E	Musicmaker Ltd; Paul Reed Smith Guitars. Exclusive distribution.
CA/1037/92E	Musicmaker Ltd; Marshall Amplification Ltd. Exclusive distribution.
CA/1038/92E	Musicmaker Ltd; Freestyle Music Products. Exclusive distribution.
CA/1039/92E	Musicmaker Ltd; D/Andrea Mfg. Co. Inc. Exclusive distribution.
CA/1040/92E	Musicmaker Ltd; GMS Corp. Exclusive distribution.
CA/1041/92E	Musicmaker Ltd; Sabian Ltd. Exclusive distribution.
CA/1042/92E	Musicmaker Ltd; Teac UK Ltd. Exclusive distribution.
CA/1043/92E	Musicmaker Ltd; Trace Elliott Ltd. Exclusive distribution.
CA/1047/92E	Musicmakers Ltd; retailers. Retailer agreement on discounts.
CA/924/92E	Naas Mall Ltd; tenants. Shopping centre leases.
CA/8/91	Thomas Nallen; Edward O'Toole (Belmullet). Non-competition clause and sale of business interests.
CA/923/92E	Nabola Development Ltd; tenants. Shopping centre leases.
CA/54/92	Natelex National Electronics Society Ltd; Members. Franchise agreement.
CA/230/92E	National Trust and Investment Co. Ltd; tenants. Shopping centre lease.
CA/231/92E	National Trust and Investment Co. Ltd; Clondalkin Shopping centre leases.
CA/382/92E	Natureline Ltd; Jackel International Ltd. Exclusive distribution.
CA/861/92E	Navenby Ltd; I. Gracie and R. Fearnley. Merger.

CA/864/92E	Navenby Ltd; Savage Plastic Packaging and Savpack Ltd and others. Merger.
CA/58/92E	NCB Group Ltd; Mr. Anthony J. Waters. Shareholders' agreement and employment contract.
CA/783/92E	NEC Electronics (UK) Ltd; Mr. T. Fingleton. Employment contract.
CA/288/92E	The Nestle Co. Ltd; Clayton Love Distribution Ltd. Exclusive distribution.
CA/502/92E	New Irish Assurance Co. plc; Nutgrove Shopping centre leases.
CA/531/92E	Newspaper Publishing; The Irish Times Newspaper service syndication agreement.
CA/253/92E	Nissan Ireland; motor dealers. Selective distribution.
CA/224/92E	Nitrigín Éireann Teo; Irish Fertilizer Industries Ltd. Purchase agreement for natural gas.
CA/225/92E	Nitrigín Eireann Teo; Bord Gais Éireann. Purchase agreement for natural gas.
CA/61/92	NM Life Assurance Ireland Ltd; Mr. Gerard Murphy. Director's non-competition covenant.
CA/62/92	NM Life Assurance Ireland Ltd; Ms. Brenda Murphy. Non-competition covenant by wife of director.
CA/1008/92E	NM Life Assurance Ireland Ltd; tied agents. Agency agreement.
CA/665/92E	Norish Eirfreeze Ltd; Green Isle Foods Ltd. Rental of cold storage space.
CA/666/92E	Norish plc; grantees. Fee farm grant for cold storage units.
CA/667/92E	Norish plc; Viking Frozen Products Ltd. Fee farm grant for cold storage units.
CA/668/92E	Norish plc; Bico Farm Ltd. Fee farm grant for cold storage units.
CA/669/92E	Norish plc; Avonmore Creameries Ltd; Standby Manufacturing Ltd. Joint venture.
CA/670/92E	Norish plc; Goodman International Ltd. Trading agreement.
CA/671/92E	Norish plc; Food Industries plc. Trading agreement.
CA/672/92E	Norish plc; Food Industries plc. Share purchase agreement.
CA/200/92E	North Western Cattle Breeding Society Ltd; Mr John Doherty. Exclusive distribution.
CA/201/92E	North Western Cattle Breeding Society Ltd; Mr Michael Tarpey. Exclusive distribution.
CA/202/92E	North Western Cattle Breeding Society Ltd; Mr John O'Loughlin. Exclusive distribution.
CA/203/92E	North Western Cattle Breeding Society Ltd; Mr Sean McHugh. Exclusive distribution.
CA/297/92E	Northern Telecom (Ireland) Ltd; Sound Systems Ltd. Exclusive distribution.
CA/298/92E	Northern Telecom (Ireland) Ltd; Telecom Éireann Information Systems Ltd. Exclusive distribution.
CA/838/92E	Nostex Properties Ltd; Bishopstown Shopping centre leases.
CA/794/92E	Nynex Corporation; Telecom PhoneWatch Ltd. Trademark licence.
CA/840/92E	Oakville Ltd; Clonmel Shopping centre leases.
CA/289/92E	Thomas O'Connor; Riga Ltd. Shopping centre lease.
CA/28/94	Odenberg Engineering Ltd; Inspection Ltd; J. Mallon, W. Mallon and P. O'Dowd. Research and development — general services agreement.

CA/31/94	Odenberg Engineering Ltd; Inspectron Ltd; J. Mallon, W. Mallon and P. O'Dowd. Research and development — special projects agreement.
CA/649/92E	Odlum Group Ltd; Readibake Ltd. Exclusive purchase.
CA/650/92E	Odlum Group Ltd; Readibake Ltd. Joseph Brennan Bakery Ltd. Exclusive purchase.
CA/245/92E	A & K O'Donovan; Edward Drennan; and others. Shopping centre lease.
CA/926/92E	Liam O'Farrell and others; Merchant's Hall Office leases.
CA/927/92E	Liam O'Farrell and others; Bridtron Ltd; Merchant's House Office leases.
CA/21/94	Office Team Supplies Ltd; Kelly Office Supplies Ltd. Franchise agreement.
CA/645/92E	Oglesby and Butler Ltd; directors; shareholders of Portagas Ltd. Merger agreement, employment contracts and exclusive know-how licence.
CA/646/92E	Oglesby and Butler Ltd; D. Butler. Employment contract.
CA/167/92E	Ola Teo; independent dealers. Exclusive purchase.
CA/168/92E	Ola Teo; independent dealers. Equipment loan agreement.
CA/169/92E	Ola Teo; independent dealers. Bailment Equipment agreement.
CA/170/92E	Ola Teo; independent dealers. Mortgage agreement.
CA/171/92E	Ola Teo; authorised distributors. Exclusive purchase distribution agreement.
CA/976/92E	The 'Old Bushmills' Distillery Co. Ltd; J.B. Casey. Trademark usership agreement.
CA/16/93	Omni Med Ltd/Omni Park Ltd; shopping centre lease;
CA/1102/92	Omni Park Ltd; tenants. Office and shopping centre leases.
CA/799/92E	Omnitron Ltd; Crytovision A/S. Exclusive distribution.
CA/800/92E	Omnitron Ltd; Crytovision A/S. Tandberg A/S. Exclusive manufacture and distribution.
CA/801/92E	Omnitron Ltd; Crytovision A/S. Cablelink Ltd. Exclusive supply contract.
CA/843/92E	T. O'Muire. J. Smyth and D. Kavanagh; Toscorva Rest Ltd. Property lease.
CA/472/92E	D.F. O'Neill (Chemist) Ltd; Superquinn. Shopping centre lease.
CA/236/92E	Richard O'Rourke, N.J. Kelly Ltd. Shopping centre lease.
CA/600/92E	Outlandus Ltd; tenants. Shopping centre leases.
CA/3/93	Ove Arkil A.S./James Kelly and Patrick Kennedy. Takeover and service agreements.
CA/246/92E	Packaging Inks and Coatings Ltd; James Lacey. Contract of employment with director.
CA/1111/92E	Palace Video Ltd; Abbey Films. Exclusive distribution.
CA/579/92E	Pemberton Marketing International Ltd; Nicholas Laboratories Ltd. Sole distributor agreement.
CA/580/92E	Pemberton Marketing International Ltd; Nevinar Ltd. Sole distributor agreement.
CA/581/92E	Pemberton Marketing International Ltd; Orlane SA. Exclusive distribution.
CA/582/92E	Pemberton Marketing International Ltd; Parfums Nina Ricci. Exclusive distribution.
CA/583/92E	Pemberton Marketing International Ltd; Ilford Ltd. Exclusive distribution.

CA/584/92E	Pemberton Marketing International Ltd; Cupal Ltd. Exclusive distribution.
CA/585/92E	Pemberton Marketing International Ltd; Ciba-Geigy Ireland Ltd. Exclusive distribution.
CA/586/92E	Pemberton Marketing International Ltd; Bausch & Lomb UK Ltd. Exclusive distribution.
CA/1071/92E	Pentos Retailing Group Ltd; Optel Ltd; N. McCreesh. Franchise agreement.
CA/1072/92E	Pentos Retailing Group Ltd; Vogue Management Ltd; N. McCreesh. Franchise agreement.
CA/345/92E	Percom Ltd; CHL Software Ltd. Exclusive distribution.
CA/885/92E	Pesenta; Power Supermarkets Ltd; tenants. Merrion Shopping centre leases.
	Performing Right Society — See listing for Irish Music Rights Organisation (IMRO)
CA/1011/92E	Peter Mark; Majella Stapleton. Employment contract.
CA/1012/92E	Peter Mark; Dunloe House Group plc. Shopping centre lease.
CA/1013/92E	Peter Mark; Irish Life Assurance plc. Shopping centre lease.
CA/1014/92E	Peter Mark; Erin Executor and Trustee Co. Ltd. Shopping centre lease.
CA/1015/92E	Peter Mark; Cornelscourt Shopping Centre Ltd. Shopping centre lease.
CA/1016/92E	Peter Mark; Roches Stores Dublin Ltd. Shopping centre lease.
CA/1017/92E	Peter Mark; Firmount Ltd. Shopping centre lease.
CA/1018/92E	Peter Mark; Merchant's Quay Developments Ltd. Shopping centre lease.
CA/1019/92E	Peter Mark; Douglas Developments Ltd. Shopping centre lease.
CA/1020/92E	Peter Mark; D. Farrell. Shopping centre lease.
CA/1021/92E	Peter Mark; Roches Stores Limerick Ltd. Shopping centre lease.
CA/1022/92E	Peter Mark; Superquinn. Shopping centre lease.
CA/1023/92E	Peter Mark; L. & C. Properties Ltd. Shopping centre lease.
CA/1048/92E	Phonographic Performance (Ireland) Ltd; record companies. Assignment of copyright.
CA/520/92E	Pig Improvement Co. Ltd; Master Pork Packers Ltd. Know-how and trademark licence.
CA/651/92E	P.J.D. Investment Co.; investors and shareholders. Share purchase agreement.
CA/195/92E	Player & Wills (Ireland) Ltd; Henri Wintermans Sigarenfabrieken B.V. Exclusive distribution.
CA/196/92E	Player & Wills (Ireland) Ltd; R.J. Reynolds Tobacco (GB) Ltd. Exclusive distribution.
CA/744/92E	Poldy's Fresh Foods (Portumna) Ltd; Birds Eye Walls Ltd. Exclusive manufacture and supply.
CA/313/92E	Power Leisure Ltd; M. and V. Grant. Shop lease.
CA/314/92E	Power Leisure Ltd; Ventnor Developments Ltd. Shopping centre lease.
CA/315/92E	Power Leisure Ltd; R. and M. Tweedy. Shopping centre lease.
CA/395/92E	Power Leisure Ltd; Shannon Town Centre Co. Ltd. Shopping centre lease.
CA/459/92E	Power Meats Ltd; Albafare Ltd; Cranford Properties Ltd. Shopping centre lease.

CA/587/92E	Power Supermarkets Ltd; Arthur's Quay Developments Ltd; Colossu Management Services Ltd. Shopping centre lease.
CA/588/92E	Power Supermarkets Ltd; Town and Country Investments plc. Shopping centre lease.
CA/589/92E	Power Supermarkets Ltd; Navan Shopping Centre Ltd. Shopping centre lease.
CA/590/92E	Power Supermarkets Ltd; Feresant Ltd. Shopping centre lease.
CA/591/92E	Power Supermarkets Ltd; McMullan Bros. Ltd. Property purchase agreement.
CA/592/92E	Power Supermarkets Ltd; Riga Ltd; Modred Ltd. Shopping centre lease.
CA/593/92E	Power Supermarkets Ltd; Mayfield Investments Ltd. Shopping centre lease.
CA/594/92E	Power Supermarkets Ltd; Todd Burns & Co. Ltd. Shop lease.
CA/595/92E	Power Supermarkets Ltd; MEPC Ireland Ltd; Erin Executor and Trustee Co. Ltd. Shopping centre lease.
CA/596/92E	Power Supermarkets Ltd; Kerrib Ltd; IPFPUT; Northern Bank Development Corp. Ltd. Shopping centre lease.
CA/597/92E	Power Supermarkets Ltd; L. & C. Properties Ltd and others. Shopping centre lease.
CA/598/92E	Power Supermarkets Ltd; tenants. Shopping centre leases.
CA/599/92E	Power Supermarkets Ltd; tenants. Shopping centre leases.
CA/601/92E	Power Supermarkets Ltd; tenants. Shopping centre leases.
CA/615/92E	Power Supermarkets Ltd; Dungoyne Ltd. Shopping centre lease.
CA/883/92E	Power Supermarkets Ltd; Letterkenny Shopping Centre Ltd. Shopping centre lease.
CA/1114/92E	Power Supermarkets Ltd; P. Owens. Sale of property agreement.
CA/1115/92E	Power Supermarkets Ltd; R. and S. Whyte. Sale of property agreement.
CA/920/92E	Power Supermarkets Ltd; Carmel Feeney. Shopping centre lease.
CA/1049/92E	PPI Ltd; record companies. Assignment of copyright (videograms).
CA/1050/92E	PPI Ltd; record companies. Standard dubbing mandate.
CA/1051/92E	PPI Ltd; users. Copyright licence.
CA/1052/92E	PPI Ltd; users. Music video licence.
CA/1053/92E	PPI Ltd; background music system suppliers. Dubbing licence.
	PRS — See listings for Irish Music Rights Organisation (IMRO)
CA/1054/92E	Palace Video Ltd; Abbey films. Exclusive distribution.
CA/1131/92E	Precision Heating Equipment Ltd; Bentone Electro Oil AB. Exclusive distribution agreement.
CA/391/92	Premier Dairies Group; distributors. Exclusive purchase agreement—country agency.
CA/392/92	Premier Dairies Group; distributors. Exclusive purchase agreement—city agency.
CA/394/92E	Premier Dairies Group; contractors. Exclusive distribution.
CA/55/92	Premier Tir Laighean Society Ltd; Midland Dairies Ltd; and Dealgan Milk Products Ltd; distribution contractors. Exclusive distribution agreement.
CA/215/92E	Pride & Joy Ltd; Max Developments Ltd. Shopping centre lease.
CA/28/95	Professional Golfers Association. Constitution.
CA/367/92E	Prontaprint plc; franchises. Franchise agreement, with property lease.

CA/368/92E	Prontaprint plc; franchises. Franchise agreement.
CA/936/92E	Prontaprint plc; Kippure Business Services Ltd; B. O'Brien. Franchise agreement.
CA/25/92E	The Publishers Association. Book Club Regulations 1985.
CA/26/92E	The Publishers Association. Library Licence.
CA/27/92E	The Publishers Association. Book Agent's Licence.
CA/28/92E	The Publishers Association. Quantity Book Buying Scheme.
CA/29/92E	The Publishers Association. National Book Sale Conditions.
CA/30/92E	The Publishers Association. Primary and Secondary School Licence.
CA/243/92E	Quality Hotels Ltd; franchises. Franchise agreement.
CA/602/92E	Quinnsworth; H. Williams. Shopping centre lease.
CA/603/92E	Quinnsworth Ltd; Omni Park Ltd. Shopping centre lease.
CA/613/92E	Quinnsworth; Revoclife Ltd. Shopping centre lease.
CA/881/92E	Quinnsworth; Trikkala Ltd; Janelle Shopping centre leases.
CA/604/92E	Quinnsworth Ltd; Park Shopping Centre Ltd. Industrial Credit Corporation Ltd. Shopping centre lease.
CA/59/92	Rank Xerox (Ireland) Ltd; concessionaires. Exclusive dealing agreement.
CA/537/92	Raleigh Ireland Ltd; cycle dealers. Trading terms and conditions.
CA/749/92E	Reflex Investments plc.; Harris Adacom Ltd. Distribution agreement.
CA/750/92E	Reflex Investments plc.; Storage Technology plc. Exclusive distribution.
CA/513/92E	Michael Reilly & Sons Ltd (now Nabola Ltd). Phoenix Newsagents. Shopping centre lease.
CA/146/92E	Response System International (Europe) Ltd; Lifetime Assurance Co. Ltd. Exclusive agreement to market insurance services.
CA/1134/92E	P. Reynolds; J. Reynolds; M. Hegarty; Aquis Estates Ltd., The Four Lanterns (Sligo) Ltd. Shopping centre lease.
CA/8/93	RHM Ltd/Naresa Ltd; property lease;
CA/221/92E	Riga Ltd; Cork Shopping centre leases.
CA/223/92E	Riga Ltd; Douglas Shopping centre leases.
CA/240/92	Riga Ltd; Douglas Eye Care Ltd. Shopping centre lease.
CA/98/92	Rhone Poulenc Ireland Limited; Shell Chemicals Ireland Limited. Sale of business and exclusive distribution agreement.
CA/27/95	Roche Products Ltd/AllPhar Services Ltd. Exclusive distribution agreement.
CA/64/93	Rochglen Holdings Ltd/Foreign Exchange Co. of Ireland and others; share purchase and related agreements;
CA/15/93	Rohan Construction Ltd/Rohcon Ltd/K Rohan. Acquisition of assets.
CA/930/92E	K. Rohan; The Square Management Ltd; tenants. Shopping centre leases.
CA/13/93	Rotterdamsche Margarine Industrie/Beteo Marketing Ltd. Agency agreement.
CA/63/93	The Round Hall Press Ltd/Bart Daly. Service agreement.
CA/81/92E	Rover Ireland Ltd; motor dealers. Selective distribution.
CA/82/92E	Rover Ireland Ltd; Rover Ireland Finance Ltd; motor dealers. Finance agreement associated with selective distribution agreement.

CA/1009/92E	Rowe Mark Holdings and Peter Holdings; Bally London Shoe Co. Ltd. Shop lease.
CA/546/92E	Royal Liver Trustees Ltd; Deanstown Investments Ltd. Shopping centre lease.
CA/547/92E	Royal Liver Trustees Ltd; Texas Homecare (Ireland) Ltd. Shopping centre lease.
CA/548/92E	Royal Liver Trustees Ltd; Carpet & Bedding Home Ltd. Shopping centre lease.
CA/549/92E	Royal Liver Trustees Ltd; Anika Enterprises. Shopping centre lease.
CA/550/92	Royal Liver Trustees Ltd; Naas Road Shopping centre lease.
CA/384/92E	Salix Trust Ltd; tenants. Shopping centre lease.
CA/385/92E	Salix Trust Ltd; Lorcan O'Sullivan. Shopping centre lease.
CA/386/92	Salix Trust Ltd; Huntbrook Ltd. Shopping centre lease.
CA/508/92	Salix Trust Ltd; IBI Nominees Ltd; Merchant's Quay Shopping centre leases.
CA/841/92	Salix Trust Ltd; The Square Management Ltd; tenants. Shopping centre lease.
CA/228/92E	Sanbra Fyffe Ltd; Enfield Rolling Mills and others. Agreement on trade marks, agencies, purchasing, manufacture and sale of products under licence.
CA/23/94	Robert William Sandys; Mary Angela and Dermot Ward. Sale of general practice.
CA/527/92E	Schweppes International Ltd; Cantrell & Cochrane Group Ltd. Exclusive manufacture and distribution.
CA/204/92E	Sedgwick Dineen Ltd; Legal and Commerical Insurances Ltd; and others. Sale of Business.
CA/42/93	Sedgwick Group plc/TSB Group plc; takeover;
CA/14/94	Sedgwick Overseas Group Ltd; P.J. Dineen. Option/share purchase agreement.
CA/829/92E	Service Master Ltd; franchises. Contract services franchise agreement.
CA/830/92E	Service Master Ltd; franchises. On-location franchise agreement.
CA/694/92E	Shamrock Foods Ltd; Brookline Ltd. and others. Merger.
CA/3/94	T. Sheridan Sales & Marketing Ltd; St Ives Laboratories Inc. Exclusive distribution agreement.
CA/4/94	T. Sheridan Sales & Marketing Ltd; Giorgio Beverly Hills Inc. Selective distribution agreement.
CA/5/94	T. Sheridan Sales & Marketing Ltd; Beauty International Ltd. Exclusive distribution agreement.
CA/1064/92E	Sherwin Williams; Simgrove Investments Ltd; Indou Investments Ltd; Dev Ltd; J.F. Walsh. Joint venture.
CA/364/92E	Sigma Wireless Communications Ltd; Motorola Ireland Ltd. Sale of business.
CA/365/92E	Sigma Wireless Communications Ltd; Motorola Ireland Ltd. Exclusive distribution.
CA/366/92E	Sigma Wireless Communications Ltd; Motorola Ltd. Sale of business.
CA/6/93	Sigma Wireless Technologies Ltd/Philips Electronics U.K. Ltd; exclusive purchase agreement;
CA/172/92E	Sisk Properties Ltd; Capwell Investments Ltd; and others. Property investment agreements.
CA/280/92E	Siúcre Éireann cpt; Farmline International Ltd. Exclusive distribution.

CA/653/92E	Siúicre Éireann cpt; Talmino Ltd; Gladebrook Co. Ltd; Charles Lyons, Michael Tully, Thomas Keleghan and Charles Garavan. Share purchase agreement.
CA/654/92E	Siúicre Éireann cpt; Charles Garavan. Employment contract.
CA/655/92E	Siúicre Éireann cpt; Charles Lyons. Employment contract.
CA/656/92E	Siúicre Éireann cpt; Thomas Keleghan. Employment contract.
CA/657/92E	Siúicre Éireann cpt; Michael Tully. Employment contract.
CA/173/92E	Shannon Town Centre Co. Ltd; tenants. Shopping centre lease.
CA/145/92E	Sketchley Recognitrion Express Ltd; Mr Don Wallace. Franchise agreement.
CA/9/93	Smith & Nephew Ltd/Beiersdorf U.K. Ltd; exclusive distribution agreement;
CA/680/92E	Snowcream Ltd; milkmen. Exclusive purchase.
CA/227/92E	Sociedad Espanola de Automoviles de Turismo SA; Hispano Cars Ltd. Selective distribution.
CA/637/92E	Sony (UK) Ltd; dealers. Selective distribution.
CA/681/92E	Sony (UK) Ltd; dealers. Exclusive purchase.
CA/136/92E	Sound Systems plc.; subscribers. Contract for telephone rental.
CA/177/92E	Sound Systems plc.; subscribers. Contract for rental of time control equipment.
CA/178/92E	Sound Systems plc.; subscribers. Contract for telephone rental.
CA/183/92E	Sound Systems plc.; subscribers. Contract for rental of security service equipment.
CA/187/92E	Sound Systems plc.; subscribers. Contract for rental of telephones.
CA/188/92E	Sound Systems plc.; subscribers. Contract for rental of telephones.
CA/189/92E	Sound Systems plc.; subscribers. Contract for rental of telephones.
CA/190/92E	Sound Systems plc.; subscribers. Contract for rental of telephones.
CA/948/92E	Solicitors Financial and Property Services (Ireland) Ltd; Sedgwick Dineen Personal Financial Management Ltd. Exclusive supply of services.
CA/197/92E	Francis Spaight & Sons Ltd; Mr Seamus Canty. Shopping centre lease.
CA/982/92E	Spar (Ireland) Ltd; BWG Foods Ltd; Sancroft Ltd. Equipment, supply and merchandising agreement.
CA/986/92E	Spar (Ireland) Ltd; BWG Foods Ltd; Eight to Twelve Ltd. Equipment, supply and merchandising agreement.
CA/514/92E	Sports Locker Ltd; M.P. O'Brien (Maynooth) Ltd (now Nabola Ltd). Shopping centre lease.
CA/1135/92E	Spring Grove Ireland Ltd; Initial Services (International) Ltd; BET plc and the P & O Services Group Ltd. Merger.
CA/6/95	Stellar International Ltd; Dotinga Investments DV; Celtic International Insurance Co. Ltd. computer programme licence agreement.
CA/886/92E	The Square Management Ltd; investors; tenants. Shareholders agreement, shopping centre leases etc.
CA/891/92	The Square Management Ltd; IBI Nominees Ltd; tenants. Shopping centre leases.
CA/892/92	The Square Management Ltd, IBI Property Nominees Ltd; tenants. Shopping centre leases.
CA/733/92E	Colm Stanley; Arden Heath Co. Ltd. Shopping centre lease.

CA/441/92E	Statoil Ireland Ltd; independent dealers. Exclusive purchase.
CA/442/92E	Statoil Ireland Ltd; independent dealers. Equipment loan agreement.
CA/443/92E	Statoil Ireland Ltd; independent dealers. Hire purchase agreement.
CA/444/92E	Statoil Ireland Ltd; independent dealers. Exclusivity payment agreement.
CA/445/92E	Statoil Ireland Ltd; licensees. Licence and trial licence.
CA/446/92E	Statoil Ireland Ltd; licensees. Lease.
CA/447/92E	Statoil Ireland Ltd; independent dealers. Deed of charge/mortgage.
CA/448/92E	Statoil Ireland Ltd; distributors. Exclusive distribution.
CA/449/92E	Statoil Ireland Ltd; distributors. Distibutor loan agreements.
CA/450/92E	Statoil Ireland Ltd; distributors and commerical customers. Equipment loan agreement.
CA/451/92E	Statoil Ireland Ltd; independent dealers. Franchise agreement for BP Card.
CA/452/92E	Statoil Ireland Ltd; distributors. Loan to distributors.
CA/10/95	Sumitomo Electric Hardmetal Ltd/Fengrin Engineering Ltd.Non-exclusive distribution agreement.
CA/524/92	Sunkist Soft Drinks (British Isles) Ltd; Batchelors Ltd; Sunkist Growers Inc. Know-how and trademark licence.
CA/526/92E	Sunkist Soft Drinks (British Isles) Ltd; Cantrell & Cochrane Group Ltd. Exclusive manufacture and distribution.
CA/944/92E	Superquinn; Sutton Shopping centre leases.
CA/945/92	Superquinn; Lucan Shopping centre leases.
CA/946/92E	Superquinn; Sundrive Shopping centre leases.
CA/947/92E	Superquinn; Knocklyon Shopping centre leases.
CA/887/92E	Superquinn Ltd; tenants. Blackrock Shopping centre leases.
CA/888/92E	Superquinn Ltd; tenants. Swords Shopping centre leases.
CA/889/92E	Superquinn Ltd; tenants. Ballinteer Shopping centre leases.
CA/890/92E	Superquinn Ltd; tenants. Shopping centre leases.
CA/19/93	Sutcliffe Ireland Ltd/National Catering Ltd; Merger
CA/270/92E	John Sutton, William Neville & Sons Ltd. Shopping centre lease.
CA/12/94	Suttons Ltd; Dairygold Co-operative Society Ltd. Asset purchase agreement/sale of business.
CA/1110/92E	P. Sweeney; P. and K. Dunleavy. Dungloe Shopping centre lease.
CA/121/92E	SWIFT (Ireland). Worldwide data communications network in banking.
CA/963/92	Swintron Ltd; Design Factory Ltd. Office lease.
CA/877/92E	Tallaght Shopping Centre Ltd; tenants. Kilmanagh Shopping centre leases.
CA/1103/92E	Tambrands Inc; David Mayrs Ltd. Exclusive distribution.
CA/766/92E	Tanning Research Laboratories Inc; Gillespie & Co. Ltd. Exclusive distribution.
CA/29/93	Tate & Lyle Industries Ltd/Cooperative Animal Health Ltd. Exclusive distribution agreement;
CA/283/92E	Tedcastle Engineering Ltd; MAN N.A. Exclusive distribution.

CA/284/92E	Tedcastle Engineering Ltd; Atlas Weyhausen GmbH. Exclusive distribution.
CA/285/92E	Tedcastle Engineering Ltd; Orienstein and Koppel Ltd. Exclusive distribution.
CA/286/92E	Tedcastle Engineering Ltd; J.J. Case Europe Ltd. Exclusive distribution.
CA/287/92	Tedcastle Engineering Ltd; Jacty Engineering Ltd. Exclusive distribution.
CA/34/94	Tedcastle McCormick & Co. Ltd/Clarke Oil Products Ltd. Exclusive purchase agreement.
CA/24/94	Tedcastle McCormick & Co. Ltd/Star Oil East Ltd. Exclusive purchase agreement.
CA/25/94	Tedcastle McCormick & Co. Ltd/Aidan McCrystal. Exclusive purchase agreement.
CA/26/94	Tedcastle McCormick & Co. Ltd/McCrystal Oil (Bellurgan) Ltd. Exclusive purchase agreement.
CA/802/92E	Tedcastle Oil Products Ltd; distributors. Exclusice distribution.
CA/969/92E	Tedcastle Oil Products Ltd; independent dealers. Exclusive distribution.
CA/1044/92	Tedcastle Engineering Ltd; MS Commercials Ltd. Selective distribution.
CA/796/92E	Telecom PhoneWatch Ltd; licence. UK licence.
CA/797/92E	Telecom PhoneWatch Ltd; customers. System sales and installation agreement.
CA/798/92E	Telecom PhoneWatch Ltd; customers. Monitoring and maintenance agreement.
CA/704/92	Tennant & Ruttle Distribution Ltd; United Biscuits (UK) Ltd. Exclusive distribution.
CA/705/92E	Tennant & Ruttle Distribution Ltd; Ferrero Ltd. Exclusive distribution.
CA/706/92E	Tennant & Ruttle Distribution Ltd; Kinnerton. Exclusive distribution.
CA/707/92E	Tennant & Ruttle Distribution Ltd; Duracell UK Ltd. Exclusive distribution.
CA/708/92	Tennant & Ruttle Distribution Ltd; Greensleeves Confectionery Ltd. Exclusive distribution.
CA/709/92E	Tennant & Ruttle Distribution Ltd; Lindt & Sprungli UK Ltd. Exclusive distribution.
CA/710/92E	Tennant & Ruttle Distribution Ltd; Tipperary Candy Ltd. Exclusive distribution.
CA/711/92E	Tennant & Ruttle Distribution Ltd; The Wrigley Co. Ltd. Exclusive distribution.
CA/712/92E	Tennant & Ruttle Distribution Ltd; Jacobs Suchard Cote d'Or Export. Exclusive distribution.
CA/713/92	Tennant & Ruttle Distribution Ltd; Jacobs Suchard. Exclusive distribution.
CA/37/93	Tennents Ireland Ltd/publicans; loan and mortgage agreements;
CA/617/92E	TEIS Ltd; Case Communications plc. Exclusive distribution.
CA/618/92E	TEIS Ltd; Infotron Systems Ltd. Exclusive distribution.
CA/619/92E	TEIS Ltd; MDS Telelphone Systems Ltd. Exclusive distribution.
CA/620/92E	TEIS Ltd; Sharptext Ltd. Exclusive distribution.
CA/621/92E	TEIS Ltd; Siemens Ltd. Exclusive distribution.
CA/622/92E	TEIS Ltd; Northern Telecom (Ireland) Ltd. Exclusive distribution.
CA/623/92E	TEIS Ltd; Alcatel Business Systems Ltd. Exclusive distribution.
CA/641/92E	TEIS LTD.; Mitel Telecom Ltd; Exclusive distribution.

CA/616/92E	Telecom Éireann Information Systems Ltd; Landis & Gyr Lake Ltd. Exclusive distribution.
CA/716/92E	Tennant & Ruttle Ltd; Masterfoods Ltd. Exclusive distribution.
CA/2/92E	Texaco (Ireland) Ltd; Licensees. Licence for operation of a company-owned station.
CA/3/92E	Texaco (Ireland) Ltd; Independent Dealers. Exclusive purchase (solus) agreement.
CA/4/92E	Texaco (Ireland) Ltd; Lessees. Lease for operation of a company-owned station.
CA/5/92E	Texaco (Ireland) Ltd; Independent Dealers. Dealer equipment loan agreement.
CA/6/92E	Texaco (Ireland) Ltd; Independent Dealers. Agreement to repay advances on cessation of agreement.
CA/77/92E	Texaco (Ireland) Ltd; licensess. Licence agreement (new version).
CA/820/92E	Texaco (Ireland) Ltd; bulk buyers. Sale agreement- exclusive purchase.
CA/821/92E	Texaco (Ireland) Ltd; distributors and bulk buyers. Equipment loan agreement.
CA/822/92E	Texaco (Ireland) Ltd; distributors. Exclusive purchase.
CA/823/92E	Texaco (Ireland) Ltd; distributors. Terms and conditions of sale.
CA/703/92E	The Association of Consulting Engineers of Ireland; Institution of Engineers of Ireland. Recommended scales of fees and charges.
CA/658/92E	The Technical Equipment Co. Ltd; Holec Nederland B.V. Exclusive distribution.
CA/659/92E	The Technical Equipment Co. Ltd; The Leyland and Birmingham Rubber Co. Ltd. Exclusive distribution.
CA/660/92E	The Technical Equipment Co. Ltd; BTR Hose Ltd. Exclusive distribution.
CA/661/92E	The Technical Equipment Co. Ltd; Digi Table (UK) Ltd. Exclusive distribution.
CA/662/92E	The Technical Equipment Co. Ltd; Jumo Instrument Co. Ltd. Exclusive distribution.
CA/663/92E	The Technical Equipment Co. Ltd; Eaton Ltd. Exclusive distribution.
CA/664/92E	The Technical Equipment Co. Ltd; suppliers. Exclusive distribution.
CA/673/92E	Thoroughbred Promotion & Development Co. Ltd; B. and D. Firestone. Share purchase.
CA/627/92	Adam F. Torrie Ltd; Waterford and Wexford Shopping centre leases.
CA/895/92E	Adam F. Torrie (Properties) Ltd; tenants. Waterford Shopping centre and office leases.
CA/254/92E	Town and Country Investments plc; Coffee Garden (Drogheda) Ltd. Shopping centre lease.
CA/255/92E	Town and Country Investments plc; Ballybrack Shopping centre leases.
CA/256/92E	Town and Country Investments plc; H. Williams (Tallaght) Ltd; 3 Guys Ltd; Ballybrack Shopping centre leases.
CA/257/92E	Town and Country Investments plc; Coffee Garden Ltd. Navan Shopping centre leases.
CA/69/92	Toyota Ireland; motor dealers. Selective distribution agreement.
CA/1/95	Toyota Ireland; motor dealers. Selective distribution agreement.
CA/1116/92E	Toyota (Ireland) Ltd; motor vehicles. Selective distribution.
CA/1117/92	Toyota Ltd; motor vehicles. Selective distribution.

CA/43/93	Toyota Ireland/dealers; selective distribution agreement;
CA/11/93	Unisolutions & Associates/Dascom Services Ltd and Manix Systems Ltd; non-exclusive distribution agreement;
CA/534/92E	Trustees of Telecom Éireann Superannuation Fund; Bord Telecom Éireann. Office lease.
CA/535/92E	Trustees of Telecom Éireann Superannuation Fund; Bord Telecom Éireann. Office lease.
CA/536/92E	Trustees of Telecom Éireann Superannuation Fund; Bord Telecom Éireann. Office lease.
CA/7/94	J. & H. Underwood; To Olde Coopers Inns Ltd. Purchase of premises.
CA/648/92E	Unidare plc; B. Mills and D. Kenny, and others. Share purchase agreement and employment contracts.
CA/387/92E	Unifood Ltd; DCL (Yeast) Ltd. Exclusive distribution.
CA/388/92E	Unifood Ltd; John F. Renshate and Co. Ltd. Exclusive distribution.
CA/390/92E	Unifood Ltd; DCA Industries Ltd. Exclusive distribution.
CA/835/92E	Unislim (Ireland) Ltd; franchises. Franchise agreement.
CA/570/92E	United Drug Distributors Ltd; Novo Industri A/S. Exclusive distribution.
CA/571/92E	United Drug Distributors Ltd; Cow & Gate Iralend Ltd. Exclusive distribution.
CA/572/92E	United Drug Distributors Ltd; Mundipharma Pharmaceutical Co. Exclusive distribution.
CA/573/92E	United Drug Distributors Ltd; Squibb (Ireland) Ltd. Exclusive distribution.
CA/574/92E	United Drug Distributors Ltd; Boehringer Mannheim UK (Pharmaceuticals) Ltd. Exclusive distribution.
CA/575/92E	United Drug Distributors Ltd; Pharma Services. Exclusive distributor agreement.
CA/576/92	United Medical Ltd; Clement Clarke International Ltd. Sole distributor agreement.
CA/577/92	United Medical Ltd; Haag-Streit AG. Sole distributor agreement.
CA/578/92E	United Medical Ltd; Bausch & Lomb UK Ltd. Exclusive distribution.
CA/551/92E	United Drug plc; British Cod Liver Oil Ltd. Exclusive distribution.
CA/552/92E	United Drug plc; Pentax Europe N.V. Exclusive distribution.
CA/553/92E	United Drug plc; Norgine Ltd. Exclusive distribution.
CA/554/92E	United Drug plc; 3 M Health Care Ltd. Exclusive distribution.
CA/555/92E	United Drug plc; Seven Seas Ltd. Exclusive distribution.
CA/556/92E	United Drug plc; Brocades (GB) Ltd. Exclusive distribution.
CA/557/92E	United Drug plc; Trinity Instruments Ltd; Dixon Hempenstall Ltd; vendors. Sale of business.
CA/558/92E	United Drug plc; ROC International. Exclusive distribution.
CA/559/92E	United Drug plc; Astra Phamaceuticals Ltd. Exclusive distribution.
CA/560/92E	United Drug plc; Du Pont (UK) Ltd. Non-exclusive distribution.
CA/561/92E	United Drug plc; Kodak Ireland Ltd. Distribution agreement.
CA/562/92E	United Drug plc; Nycomed (UK) Ltd Ltd. Sole distributor agreement.

CA/563/92E	United Drug plc; Coloplast Ltd. Exclusive distribution.
CA/564/92E	United Drug plc; The Boots Co. (Ireland) Ltd. Sole distributor agreement.
CA/565/92E	United Drug plc; Reckitts & Coleman Ireland Ltd. Sole distributor agreement.
CA/566/92E	United Drug plc; Bayer (Ireland) Ltd. Sole distributor agreement.
CA/567/92E	United Drug plc; Lilly Industries Ltd. Exclusive distribution.
CA/568/92E	United Drug plc; The Boots Co. (Ireland) Ltd. Exclusive distribution.
CA/569/92E	United Drug plc; Warner Lambert Ireland Ltd. Sole distributor agreement.
CA/638/92E	Universal Honda Ltd; dealers. Selective distribution.
CA/10/94	VDU Services Franchising Ltd; Franchisees. Franchise agreement.
CA/152/92	Vendo plc.; Commercial Vehicle Cleaning Services Ltd. Master franchise agreement.
CA/272/92E	Vincent Walsh; McGee Land Trust Shopping centre lease.
CA/515/92E	Virgin Enterprises Ltd; Virgin Retail (Ireland) Ltd. Trademark licence.
CA/644/92E	Visa International Service Association. Arrangements for Visa Card International.
CA/14/93	Viva Travel Dun Laoghaire Ltd/G. McDonald Travel Ltd/J. & M. O'Donohue & W. Murphy Acquisition of business.
	Voluntary Health Insurance Board — see Blackrock Clinic.
CA/473/92E	Volvo Trucks (GN) Ltd; McCarthy Commericals Ltd. Exclusive distribution.
CA/474/92E	Volvo Trucks (GN) Ltd; McCarthy Commericals Ltd. Distribution agreement.
CA/475/92E	Volvo Trucks (GN) Ltd; Irish Commericals (Sales) Ltd. Exclusive distribution.
CA/476/92E	Volvo Trucks (GN) Ltd; Irish Commericals (Sales) Ltd. Distribution agreement.
CA/737/92	Walker Air Conditioning Ltd; Vokes Ltd. Exclusive distribution.
CA/738/92E	Walker Air Conditioning Ltd; Condair A.G. Exclusive distribution.
CA/906/92E	Wanze properties (Ireland) Ltd; Janelle Shopping centre leases.
CA/907/92E	Wanze properties (Ireland) Ltd; Drogheda Shopping centre leases.
CA/908/92E	Wanze properties (Ireland) Ltd; Athlone Shopping centre leases.
CA/909/92E	Wanze properties (Ireland) Ltd; Dundalk Shopping centre leases.
CA/910/92E	Wanze properties (Ireland) Ltd; Greystones Shopping centre leases.
CA/911/92E	Wanze properties (Ireland) Ltd; Hartstown Shopping centre leases.
CA/912/92E	Wanze properties (Ireland) Ltd; Navan Shopping centre leases.
CA/913/92E	Wanze properties (Ireland) Ltd; AnCO. Office and light industrial lease.
CA/217/92E	Wardell Roberts plc; United Biscuits Ltd. Exclusive distribution.
CA/218/92E	Wardell Roberts plc; Williams & Humbert Ltd. Exclusive distribution.
CA/219/92E	Wardell Roberts plc; Lofthouse of Fleetwood Ltd. Exclusive distribution.
CA/831/92E	The Wardens and Commonalty of Goldsmiths of the City of Dublin. Charter.
CA/455/92E	Warner Lambert (Ireland) Ltd; Tennant & Ruttle Distribution Ltd. Exclusive distribution.

CA/456/92E	Warner Lambert Distributors (Ireland) Ltd; Johnson Brothers Ltd. Exclusive distribution.
CA/457/92E	Warner Lambert Distributors (Ireland) Ltd; Robert Roberts Ltd. Exclusive distribution.
CA/695/92E	Warner Lambert Ireland Ltd; Hornsea Ltd. Joint venture-management services.
CA/696/92E	Warner Lambert Ireland Ltd; Elan Pharma Ltd; Horsea Ltd. Joint venture.
CA/5/93	Warner Lambert Ireland Ltd/Fraxinor Anstalt; acquisition of minority shareholding;
CA/58/93	Warner Lambert Distributors (Ireland) Ltd/Johnson Brothers Ltd; exclusive distribution agreement;
CA/31/95	Warner Lambert Export Ltd/Plaistow Ltd. Manufacturing partnership.
CA/32/95	Warner Lambert Export Ltd/Plaistow Ltd/Parke Pauis & Co. Patent, trademark and know-how licence.
CA/33/95	Warner Lambert Export Ltd/Company/Plaistow Ltd. Exclusive purchase agreement.
CA/461/92	Warner Music Ireland Ltd; Sony Music. Exclusive distribution.
CA/729/92E	Waterford Foods Ireland Ltd; Avondale Foods Ltd. Exclusive distribution.
CA/11/92	Waterford Harbour Commissioners; Bell Lines Ltd. Priority use of harbour facilities.
CA/281/92E	Wessel Industries Ltd; Volex Group plc. Exclusive distribution and manufacturing licence agreement.
CA/282/92E	Wessel Industries Ltd; BICC Cables Ltd. Exclusive distribution.
CA/471/92E	Westlake Estates Ltd; Mullingar Shopping centre lease.
CA/964/92E	Wexford Creamery Ltd; Wexford Milk Producers Ltd; Unigate Foods Ltd. Exclusive supply agreement.
CA/477/92	Wexford Farmers Co-operative Society Ltd; Irish Agricultural Wholesale Society Ltd. Joint venture.
CA/346/92E	Wexford Mushrooms Ltd; mushroom growers. Production licence.
CA/1073/92E	T.P. Whelehan Son & Co. Ltd; American Cyanamid Co. Exclusive distribution.
CA/1074/92E	T.P. Whelehan Son & Co. Ltd; American Cyanamid Co. Exclusive distribution.
CA/1075/92E	T:P. Whelehan Son & Co. Ltd; Carter-Wallace Ltd. Exclusive distribution.
CA/1076/92	T.P. Whelehan Son & Co. Ltd; Rohm & Haas (UK) Ltd. Exclusive distribution.
CA/23/93	A. Whittaker & A.M. Whittaker t/a Computa Tune/Computa Tune Services Ltd; franchise agreement;
CA/416/92E	Wiggins Teape Ireland Ltd; KNP Fine Paper Division. Exclusive distribution.
CA/417/92E	Wiggins Teape Ireland Ltd; Collins Stationery and Diary Ltd. Exclusive distribution.
CA/226/92E	Thomas Wixted; Patrick Healy. Shop lease.
CA/103/92	Peter Wong; The Park Shopping Centre Ltd. Shopping centre lease.
CA/10/92	Woodchester Investments plc and Woodchester Bank Ltd; UDT Bank Ltd. Sale of business agreement with non competition clauses.
CA/931/92E	Worldwide Refining Systems Inc; Halton Business Systems Ltd. Franchise agreement.

Annex

Competition Act 1991
Number 24 of 1991

AN ACT TO PROHIBIT, BY ANALOGY WITH ARTICLES 85 AND 86 OF THE TREATY ESTABLISHING THE EUROPEAN ECONOMIC COMMUNITY, AND IN THE INTERESTS OF THE COMMON GOOD, THE PREVENTION, RESTRICTION OR DISTORTION OF COMPETITION AND THE ABUSE OF DOMINANT POSITIONS IN TRADE IN THE STATE, TO ESTABLISH A COMPETITION AUTHORITY, TO AMEND THE MERGERS, TAKE-OVERS AND MONOPOLIES (CONTROL) ACT 1978, AND TO PROVIDE FOR OTHER MATTERS CONNECTED WITH THE MATTERS AFORESAID. [*22nd July*, 1991]

BE IT ENACTED BY THE OIREACHTAS AS FOLLOWS:

PART I
PRELIMINARY

1.—This Act may be cited as the Competition Act 1991. Short title

2.—(1) This Act shall come into operation on such day or days as may be based therefor by order or orders of the Minister, either generally or with reference to a particular purpose or provision, and different days may be so fixed for different purposes and different provisions of this Act. Commenceme

(2) An order under subsection (1) may as respects the repeal effected by section 22 of the provisions of the Act of 1972 fix different days for the repeal of different provisions of that Act or for the repeal for different purposes of any provision of that Act.

Interpretation

3.—(1) In this Act, unless the context otherwise requires–

"the Act of 1972" means the Restrictive Practices Act 1972;

"the Act of 1978" means the Mergers, Take-overs and Monopolies (Control) Act 1978;

"the Act of 1987" means the Restrictive Practices (Amendment) Act 1987;

A.1 "authorised officer" means a person appointed under *section 20*;

"the Authority" means the Competition Authority established by *section 10*;

"the Court" means the High Court or, in the case of an appeal, the Supreme Court;

"the Minister" means the Minister for Industry and Commerce;[1]

"prescribed" means prescribed by regulations made by the Minister;

"undertaking" means a person being an individual, a body corporate or an unincorporated body of persons engaged for gain in the production, supply or distribution of goods or the provision of a service.

(2) In this Act a reference to a section or Schedule is to a section of, or Schedule to, this Act unless it is indicated that a reference to some other provision is intended.

(3) In this Act a reference to a subsection or paragraph is to the subsection or paragraph of the provision in which the reference occurs unless it is indicated that reference to another provision is intended.

(4) In this Act a reference to any other enactment is to that enactment as amended by any other enactment including this Act.

PART II
Rules of Competition

Anti-competitive agreements, decisions and concerted practices

4.—(1) Subject to the provisions of this section, all agreements between undertakings, decisions by associations of undertakings and concerted practices which have as their object or effect the prevention, restriction or distortion of competition in trade in any goods or services in the State or in any part of the State are prohibited and void, including in particular, without prejudice to the generality of this subsection, those which—

(*a*) directly or indirectly fix purchase or selling prices or any other trading conditions;

(*b*) limit or control production, markets, technical development or investment;

(*c*) share markets or sources of supply;

(*d*) apply dissimilar conditions to equivalent transactions with other trading parties thereby placing them at a competitive disadvantage;

(*e*) make the conclusion of contracts subject to acceptance by the other parties of supplementary obligations which by their nature or according to commercial usage have no connection with the subject of such contracts.

(2) The Competition Authority established by this Act ("the Authority") may in accordance with *section 8* grant a licence for the purposes of this section in the case of—

(*a*) any agreement or category of agreements,

(*b*) any decision or category of decisions,

(*c*) any concerted practice or category of concerted practices,

which in the opinion of the Authority, having regard to all relevant market conditions contributes to improving the production or distribution of goods or provision of services or to promoting technical or economic progress, while allowing consumers

1. SI No. 19 of 1993 changed the Minster's name to the Minister for Enterprise and Employment.

a fair share of the resulting benefit and which does not—

(i) impose on the undertakings concerned terms which are not indispensable to the attainment of those objectives;

(ii) afford undertakings the possibility of eliminating competition in respect of a substantial part of the products or services in question.

(3)(*a*) A licence under *subsection (2)* shall, while it is in force, and in accordance with its terms, permit the doing of acts which would otherwise be prohibited and void under *subsection (1)*.

(*b*)Where a licence under *subsection (2)* covers a category of agreements, decisions or concerted practices, any agreements, decisions or concerted practices (as the case may be) within that category which comply with the terms of the licence need not be notified under *section 7* to benefit from the licence while it is in force.

(4) The Authority may certify that in its opinion, on the basis of the facts in its possession, an agreement, decision or concerted practice notified under *section 7* does not offend against *subsection (1)*.

(5) Before granting a licence or issuing a certificate under this section, the Authority may invite any Minister of the Government concerned with the matter to offer such observations as he may wish to make.

(6) On granting a licence or issuing a certificate under this section, the Authority shall forthwith give notice in the prescribed manner to every body to which it relates stating the terms and the date thereof and the reasons therefor and cause the notice to be published in *Iris Oifigiúil* and cause notice of the grant of the licence or issue of the certificate, as the case may be, to be published in one daily newspaper published in the State.

(7) The prohibition in *subsection (1)* shall not prevent the Court, in exercising any jurisdiction conferred on it by this Act concerning an agreement, decision or concerted practice which contravenes that prohibition and which creates or, but for this Act, would have created legal relations between the parties thereto, from applying, where appropriate, any relevant rules of law as to the severance of those terms of that agreement, decision or concerted practice which contravene that prohibition from those which do not.

(8) In respect of an agreement, decision or concerted practice such as is referred to in *subsection (7)* a court of competent jurisdiction may make such order as to recovery, restitution or otherwise between the parties to such agreement, decision or concerted practice as may in all the circumstances seem just, having regard in particular to any consideration or benefit given or received by such parties on foot thereof.

5.—(1) Any abuse by one or more undertakings of a dominant position in trade for any goods or services in the State or in a substantial part of the State is prohibited. Abuse of dominant position

(2) Without prejudice to the generality of *subsection (1)*, such abuse may, in particular, consist in—

(*a*) directly or indirectly imposing unfair purchase or selling prices or other unfair trading conditions;

(*b*) limiting production, markets or technical development to the prejudice of consumers;

A.1 (*c*) applying dissimilar conditions to equivalent transactions with other trading parties, thereby placing them at a competitive disadvantage;

(*d*) making the conclusion of contracts subject to the acceptance by other parties of supplementary obligations which by their nature or according to commercial usage have no connection with the subject of such contracts.

Right of action

6.—(1) Any person who is aggrieved in consequence of any agreement, decision, concerted practice or abuse which is prohibited under *section 4* or *5* shall have a right of action for relief under this section against any undertaking which is or has at any material time been a party to such agreement, decision or concerted practice or has been guilty of such abuse.

(2)(*a*) Subject to *paragraph (b)*, an action under this section shall be brought in the High Court.

(*b*) An action under this section may be brought in the Circuit Court in respect of any abuse which is prohibited under *section 5* but any relief by way of damages, including exemplary damages, shall not, except by consent of the necessary parties in such form as may be provided for by rules of court, be in excess of the limit of the jurisdiction of the Circuit Court in an action founded on tort.

(3) The following reliefs, or any of them, may be granted to the plaintiff in an action under this section:

(*a*) relief by way of injunction or declaration,

(*b*) subject to *subsection (6)*, damages, including exemplary damages.

(4) The Minister shall have a right of action, in respect of an agreement, decision or concerted practice or an abuse which is prohibited under *section 4* or *5*, for the reliefs specified in *subsection (3)(a)*.

(5)(*a*) Where in proceedings under this section it is finally decided by the Court that an agreement, decision or concerted practice which is in question infringes the prohibition in *section 4(1)*, any certificate in force under *section 4(4)* in relation to that agreement, decision or concerted practice shall thereupon cease to have force and effect as from the date of the order of the Court and the Court shall cause a certified copy of the said order to be served on the Authority.

(*b*) The Authority shall, as soon as may be, cause notice of the fact that, pursuant to *paragraph (a)*, its certificate has ceased to have force and effect to be published in *Iris Oifigiúil*.

(6) Where there is or has been in force a certificate pursuant to *section 4(4)* in relation to an agreement, decision or concerted practice, and that certificate has not been revoked under *section 8(6)(b)*, a claimant shall not be entitled to damages pursuant to this section for a contravention of the prohibition in *section 4(1)* in any proceedings under this section commenced after the issue of that certificate for loss suffered in consequence of that agreement, decision or concerted practice in respect of the period during which the certificate is or has been in force, but this subsection shall not prejudice any right to damages for a contravention of the prohibition in *section 5*.

(7) This section shall not apply to any agreement, decision or concerted practice to which *section 7(2)* applies which has been duly notified to the Authority until the

Authority has decided to grant or refuse to grant a licence under *section 4(2)*, or to issue a certificate or not to issue a certificate under *section 4(4)*, in relation thereto and any appeal to the Court under *section 9* in relation to the licence or the certificate has been concluded. **A.1**

(8) The Authority shall as soon as may be cause to be published in *Iris Oifigiúil* any decision of the Authority referred to in *subsection (7)* and a copy of any such notice shall be *prima facie* evidence of the making and content of such decision and of the date thereof in any action under this section.

Notification of agreements, decisions and concerted practices to Authority

7.—(1) Every agreement, decision and concerted practice of a kind described in *section 4(1)* which comes into existence after the commencement of that section in respect of which the parties thereto concerted practices request a licence under *section 4(2)* or a certificate under *section 4(4)* of that section shall be notified to the Authority.

(2) Every agreement, decision and concerted practice of a kind described in *section 4(1)* which is in existence at the commencement of that section and in respect of which the parties seek a licence under *section 4(2)* or a certificate under *section 4(4)* shall be notified to the Authority within one year of such commencement.

(3) A licence under *section 4(2)* or a certificate under *section 4(4)* shall not be granted until the agreement, decision or concerted practice (as the case may be) has been notified to the Authority but any such licence may in the case of an agreement, decision or concerted practice to which *subsection (1)* applies be made retrospective to the date of notification under that subsection.

(4) A notification in accordance with this section shall be accompanied by such fee as may be prescribed.

(5) For the purpose of the exercise of its functions in relation to licences under *section 4(2)* and certificates under *section 4(4)* the Authority may accept such observations or submissions from persons claiming to be interested as it may think proper.

(6) The functions of the Authority under this Act shall be carried out in accordance with such procedures, if any, as may be prescribed.

Licence of Authority under section 4(2) and certificate of Authority under section 4(4)

8.—(1) A licence of the Authority under *section 4(2)* shall be granted for a specified period subject to such conditions as may be attached to and specified in the licence.

(2) The Authority may from time to time, on the application of a party to a request under *section 7*, extend the period of a licence if it is of opinion that the requirements of *section 4(2)* continue to be fulfilled and the Authority shall, as soon as may be, cause to be published in *Iris Oifigiúil* notice of any such extension.

(3) Where the Authority is of the opinion that, having regard to the requirements of *section 4(2)* and to the basis upon which a licence under that subsection was granted—

(*a*) there has been a material change in any of the circumstances on which the decision was based,

(*b*) any party commits a breach of any obligation attached to the decision,

(*c*) the licence was based on materially incorrect or misleading information, or

(*d*) any party abuses the permission granted to it by the licence,

the Authority may revoke or amend the licence and, without prejudice to the generality of this subsection, may in particular insert in a licence conditions the effect of which

A.1 is to prohibit specific acts by any party thereto which would otherwise be authorised pursuant to such a licence.

(4) The Authority shall as soon as may be cause to be published in *Iris Oifigiúil* notice of every revocation or amendment of a licence under *section 4(2)*.

(5) Every licence under *section 4(2)* shall have effect in accordance with its terms, subject to any amendment thereof including any conditions inserted therein under *subsection (3)* of this section.

(6) The Authority may revoke a certificate under *section 4(4)* where it is of opinion that—

(*a*) there has been a material change in any of the circumstances on which the certificate was based, or

(*b*) the certificate was based on materially incorrect or misleading information.

(7) The Authority shall as soon as may be cause to be published in *Iris Oifigiúil* notice of every revocation under *subsection (6)*.

Appeal to High Court

9.—(1) Any undertaking or association of undertakings concerned, or any other person aggrieved by a licence or a certificate of the Authority under *section 4(2)* or (4), or the Minister, may appeal to the High Court within 28 days of publication pursuant to this Act of the licence or certificate and on the hearing of any such appeal the Court may confirm, amend or revoke the licence so appealed against, or, in the case of such a certificate, may cancel or refuse to cancel the certificate.

(2) The right of appeal in relation to a licence under *section 4(2)* includes the right to appeal against the insertion or exclusion of conditions attaching to any exemption granted.

(3) The Court may order that a licence or certificate in respect of which an appeal has been brought under this section shall be suspended pending the hearing and conclusion of the appeal.

(4) Any undertaking or association of undertakings concerned or the Minister may within 28 days of the notification or publication pursuant to this Act of a revocation or amendment by the Authority, pursuant to *section 8(3)*, of a licence under *section 4(2)*, or of a revocation by the Authority, pursuant to *section 8(6)*, of a certificate under *section 4(4)*, appeal to the High Court.

(5) The Court may extend the time specified in *subsection (1)* or *(4)* in any case where it seems just and convenient to do so.

PART III
The Competition Authority

Establishment of Competition Authority

10.—(1) There shall be a body to be known as the Competition Authority to exercise the functions assigned to it by this Act.

(2) The Authority shall stand established on such day as the Minister may by order appoint.

(3) The Authority shall in particular discharge any function of the Fair Trade Commission under the Act of 1972 not completed at the commencement of this

section and, accordingly, *sections 7* and *8* of the Act of 1978 are amended by the substitution of references to the Authority for references to the Fair Trade Commission. A.1

(4) The provisions of the *Schedule* shall have effect in relation to the Authority.

Studies and analyses of Authority

11.—The Authority may, at the request of the Minister, study and analyse and, when requested by the Minister, report to him the results of any such study or analysis, any practice or method of competition affecting the supply and distribution of goods or the provision of services. A study or analysis may consist of, or include, a study or analysis of any development outside the State.

Reports

12.—(1) The Authority shall submit to the Minister an annual report of its activities within four months of the end of each year.

(2) The Minister shall lay before each House of the Oireachtas a copy of every such report within four months of receiving the report.

PART IV
MERGERS, TAKE-OVERS AND MONOPOLIES

Construction with Act of 1978

13.—This Part shall be construed as one with the Act of 1978 and with the other Parts of this Act.

Investigation of abuse of dominant position

14.—(1) Where the Minister is of the opinion that there is, contrary to *section 5*, an abuse of a dominant position he may request the Authority to carry out an investigation and the Authority shall comply with the request.

(2) Where the Authority holds an investigation pursuant to a request under *subsection (1)* it shall report thereon to the Minister and the report shall state whether in the opinion of the Authority

(*a*) a dominant position exists, and

(*b*) if it does, whether that dominant position is being abused.

(3) The Minister, having considered a report of the Authority under subsection (2), may, if the interests of the common good so warrant, after consultation with any other Minister of the Government concerned, by order either—

(*a*) prohibit the continuance of the dominant position except on conditions specified in the order, or

(*b*) require the adjustment of the dominant position, in a manner and within a period specified in the order, by a sale of assets or otherwise as he may specify.

(4) An order under this section shall state the reasons for making the order.

(5) The Minister may by order revoke an order under this section and may, with the agreement of every enterprise concerned, amend an order under this section.

(6) An order under this section shall not have effect unless and until it is confirmed by a resolution of each House of the Oireachtas.

(7) References in *sections 12* and *13* of the Act of 1978 to *section 11* of that Act shall be construed as references to this section and the expression monopoly shall be construed as a reference to an abuse of a dominant position.

A.1 (8) Compliance with an order under this section shall be a good defence to an action under *section 6* in respect of any period after such compliance, in so far as such action is in respect of any matter which is the subject of such compliance.

(9) A right of action for relief under *section 6* includes a right of action for contravention of an order under this section.

(10) The Minister shall publish a report under *subsection (2)*, with due regard to commercial confidentiality, within two months of its being furnished to him by the Authority.

(11) *Sections 10* and *11* of the Act of 1978 are hereby repealed.

Definitions in Act of 1978

15.—(1) "Service" in *section 1(1)* of the Act of 1978 shall not include the owning and transfer of land where this activity is the sole activity of the enterprise in which control is being sought.

(2) *Section 1(3)* of the Act of 1978 is hereby amended by the substitution for paragraph (*c*) of the following:

"(c) Without prejudice to *paragraph (b)*, where an enterprise (in this paragraph referred to as 'the first enterprise'), whether by means of acquisition or otherwise, obtains the right in another enterprise (in this paragraph referred to as 'the second enterprise') which is a body corporate—

(i) to appoint or remove a majority of the board or committee of management of the second enterprise, or

(ii) to shares of the second enterprise which carry voting rights, except where the voting rights in the second enterprise which are controlled by the first enterprise—

(I) are not after the acquisition more than 25 per cent of the total of such voting rights, or

(II) are before the acquisition more than one half of the total of such voting rights,

the said enterprises shall be deemed to have been brought under common control."

(3) Section 1(3)(*e*) of the Act of 1978 is hereby amended by the insertion after "acquisition" at the end of the paragraph of "and the value of those assets or the value of the turnover generated therefrom, exceeds the thresholds referred to in section 2(1)(*a*)."

Notification of proposed merger or take-over

16.—The Act of 1978 is hereby amended by the substitution, for *section 5*, of the following section:

"5.—(1) Each of the enterprises involved in a proposed merger or take-over shall notify the Minister in writing of the proposal, and provide full details thereof within the specified period of the offer capable of acceptance having been made, the effect of which would bring the enterprises under common control.

(2) Where, having received a notification under this section from each of the enterprises involved, the Minister is of opinion that in order to consider for the purposes of this Act a proposed merger or take-over he requires further information he may, within one month of the date of receipt by him of the notification, or of the last of such notifications, as the case may

be, request such further information in writing from any one or more of the enterprises concerned, each of which shall provide the information within a period to be stated to them by the Minister in writing. **A.1**

(3)(*a*) Where there is a contravention of *subsection (1)* or *(2)* the person in control of an enterprise failing to notify the Minister within the specified period or failing to supply the information requested within the period stated by the Minister shall be guilty of an offence and shall be liable—

(i) on summary conviction, to a fine not exceeding £1,000 and, for continued contravention, to a daily default fine not exceeding £100, or

(ii) on conviction on indictment, to a fine not exceeding £200,000 and, for continued contravention, to a daily default fine not exceeding £20,000.

(*b*) Where a person is liable to a daily default fine he shall be guilty of contravening the provision on every day on which the contravention continues after the specified period has elapsed.

(*c*) For the purposes of this subsection the person in control of an enterprise is—

(i) in the case of a body corporate, any officer of the body corporate who knowingly and wilfully authorises or permits the contravention,

(ii) in the case of a partnership, each partner who knowingly and wilfully authorises or permits the contravention,

(iii) in the case of any other form of enterprise, any individual in control of that enterprise who knowingly and wilfully authorises or permits the contravention.

(4) For the purposes of this section the specified period shall be one month, or such other period as the Minister may specify.

(5) A notification for the purposes of *subsection (1)* shall not be valid where any information provided or statement made under *subsection (1)* or *(2)* is false or misleading."

Amendments of sections 6, 7 and 8 of the Act of 1978

17.—(1) *Section 6* of the Act of 1978 is hereby amended by the insertion after "*section 3*" of "or *section 7*".

(2) The Act of 1978 is hereby amended by the substitution of the following for *section 7*:

"7.—Upon receipt of a notification under *section 5* the Minister shall—

(*a*) as soon as practicable inform the enterprises which made the notification and any other enterprise involved which enquires of him that he has decided not to make an order under *section 9* in relation to the proposed merger or take-over, or

(*b*) within 30 days of the commencement of the relevant period refer the notification to the Authority for investigation."

(3) *Section 8(1)* of the Act of 1978 is hereby amended by the insertion after the word "date" of "not being less than 30 days after the reference".

(4) *Section 8* of the Act of 1978 is hereby amended by the substitution for *subsection (2)* of the following:

"(2) (*a*) A report of the Authority under *subsection (1)* shall state its opinion as to whether or not the proposed merger or take-over concerned would

A.1 be likely to prevent or restrict competition or restrain trade in any goods or services and would be likely to operate against the common good.

(*b*) The Authority shall give its views on the likely effect of the proposed merger or take-over on the common good in respect of:
(i) continuity of supplies or services,
(ii) level of employment,
(iii) regional development,
(iv) rationalisation of operations in the interests of greater efficiency,
(v) research and development,
(vi) increased production,
(vii) access to markets,
(viii) shareholders and partners,
(ix) employees,
(x) consumers."

(5) The Minister shall publish any such report, with due regard to commercial confidentiality, within two months of its being furnished to him by the Authority.

(6) The Schedule to the Act of 1978 is hereby repealed.

Amendments of section 9 of the Act of 1978

18.—*Section 9(1)(a)* of the Act of 1978 is hereby amended by the insertion after "so warrant", of the following, "which shall include, but is not confined to, the criteria in *section 8*."

Control of concentrations

19.—(1) The transmission to the Minister by the Commission of the European Communities of a copy of a notification made under Council Regulation (EEC) No. 4064/89 on the control of concentrations between undertakings shall constitute a notification under *section 5* of the Act of 1978 (as inserted by *section 16* of this Act).

(2) The relevant period in respect of such a notification shall not commence until the Commission of the European Communities makes a decision under either Article 9 or 21(3) of that Regulation.

PART V
General

Authorised officers

20.—The Minister and the Authority with the consent of the Minister may appoint persons to be authorised officers for the purposes of this Act.

Powers of authorised officers

21.—(1) For the purpose of obtaining any information necessary for the exercise by the Authority or the Minister of any of their functions under this Act, an authorised officer may, on production of a warrant issued by a Justice of the District Court expressly authorising him to do so—

(*a*) enter and inspect premises at or vehicles in or by means of which any activity in connection with the business of supplying or distributing goods or providing a service, or in connection with the organisation or assistance of persons engaged in any such business, is carried on,

(*b*) require the person who carries on such activity and any person employed in connection therewith to produce to the authorised officer any books, documents or records relating to such activity which are in that person's power or control, and to give to the authorised officer such information as he may reasonably require in regard to any entries in such books, documents and records, A.1

(c) inspect and copy or take extracts from any such books, documents and records,

(d) require a person mentioned in *paragraph (b)* to give to the authorised officer any information he may require in regard to the persons carrying on such activity (including in particular, in the case of an unincorporated body of persons, information in regard to the membership thereof and its committee of management or other controlling authority) or employed in connection therewith,

(e) require a person mentioned in *paragraph (b)* to give to the authorised officer any information which the officer may reasonably require in regard to such activity.

(2) A Justice of the District Court may issue a warrant under *subsection (1)*, if satisfied by information on oath that it is proper for him to do so for the purposes of that subsection.

(3) A person who obstructs or impedes an authorised officer in the exercise of a power conferred by this section or does not comply with a requirement under this section shall be guilty of an offence and shall be liable on summary conviction to a fine not exceeding £1,000 or imprisonment for a period not exceeding twelve months or, at the discretion of the Court, to both such fine and imprisonment.

Repeals

22.—The provisions of the Act of 1972 and every order made under that Act and *sections 5* and *6* and *sections 8* to *23* of the Act of 1987 are hereby repealed.

Regulations

23.—(1) The Minister may by regulations provide for any matter referred to in this Act as prescribed or to be prescribed.

(2) Every regulation made by the Minister under this section shall be laid before each House of the Oireachtas as soon as may be after it is made and, if a resolution annulling the regulation is passed by either House within the next 21 days on which that House has sat after the regulation is laid before it, the regulation shall be annulled accordingly, but without prejudice to the validity of anything previously done thereunder.

Expenses

24.—Any expenses incurred by the Minister in the administration of this Act shall, to such extent as may be sanctioned by the Minister for Finance, be paid out of moneys provided by the Oireachtas.

A.1

SCHEDULE

Competition Authority

1. (1) The permanent members of the Authority shall consist of a chairman and not less than two and not more than four other members each of whom shall be appointed by the Minister.

(2) Whenever it appears to the Minister that a permanent member is temporarily unable to discharge his duties, the Minister may appoint a temporary member to act in his place during such inability or for such shorter period as the Minister thinks proper.

(3) The Minister may also appoint additional temporary members for such period and on such terms and conditions as he may specify in the appointment.

2. (1) The term of office of a permanent member shall be fixed by the Minister when appointing him and shall not exceed five years.

(2) An outgoing permanent member shall be eligible for re-appointment.

(3) Each member shall hold office on such conditions as may be fixed by the Minister after consultation with the Minister for Finance.

(4) A member may be paid such remuneration as the Minister with the consent of the Minister for Finance determines.

(5) The Civil Service Commissioners Act 1956 and the Civil Service Regulation Acts, 1956 and 1958, shall not apply to the office of member.

3. If a member is personally interested in a particular matter with which the Authority is dealing, he shall inform the Minister accordingly and shall not act as a member during the consideration of the matter, unless the Minister, being of opinion that the member's interest is not such as to interfere with the impartial performance of his duties, authorises him to act.

4. (1) The Minister may remove from office a member who has become incapable through ill-health of performing efficiently his duties as such member or whose removal appears to the Minister to be necessary in the interests of the effective and economical performance of the functions of the Authority.

(2) Where the Minister removes a member from office he shall lay before each House of the Oireachtas a statement in writing of the reasons for such removal.

(3) A member may resign his office.

(4) Where a member of the Authority is—

(*a*) nominated as a member of Seanad Éireann, or

(*b*) elected as a member of either House of the Oireachtas or of the European Parliament, or

(*c*) regarded pursuant to section 15 (inserted by the European Assembly Elections Act 1984) of the European Assembly Elections Act 1977, as having been elected to the European Parliament to fill a vacancy,

he shall thereupon cease to be a member of the Authority.

(5) A person who is, for the time being, entitled under the Standing Orders of either House of the Oireachtas to sit therein or who is a member of the European Parliament shall be disqualified from being a member of the Authority.

(6) A member shall be disqualified from holding and shall cease to hold office if he is adjudged bankrupt or makes a composition or arrangement with his creditors, or is sentenced by a court of competent jurisdiction to suffer imprisonment or penal servitude or ceases to be ordinarily resident in the State.

5. (1) The Minister shall, with the consent of the Minister for Finance, as soon as may be make and carry out a scheme for the granting of pensions, gratuities or other allowances to or in respect of members of the Authority ceasing to hold office other than members in respect of whom an award under the Superannuation Acts, 1934 to 1963, may be made. **A.1**

(2) A scheme under this paragraph may provide that the termination of the appointment of a member of the Authority during the member's term of office shall not preclude the award to him of a pension, gratuity or other allowance.

(3) The Minister may, with the consent of the Minister for Finance, amend a scheme made by him under this paragraph.

6. (1) The quorum for a meeting of the Authority shall be—

(*a*) three permanent members unless the Minister otherwise authorises,

(*b*) three permanent members for decisions on requests for a licence or certificate under *section 4*.

(2) The Authority may act notwithstanding vacancies in its membership.

(3) Subject to this Act, the Authority may regulate its own procedure.

(4) The Authority may, with the consent of the Minister, appoint officers of the Minister to be authorised officers for the purposes of this Act.

7. (1) The Authority may, for the purposes of its functions under this Act and the Act of 1978, do all or any of the following things—

(*a*) summon witnesses to attend before it,

(*b*) examine on oath (which any member is hereby authorised to administer) the witnesses attending before it,

(*c*) require any such witness to produce to the Authority any document in his power or control,

(*d*) perform such of its functions as it deems proper through or by any officer of the Minister duly authorised by it in that behalf.

(2) A witness before the Authority shall be entitled to the same immunities and privileges as if he were a witness before the High Court.

(3) A summons shall be signed by at least one member.

(4) Any person who—

(*a*) on being duly summoned as a witness before the Authority makes default in attending, or

(*b*) being in attendance as a witness refuses to take an oath legally required by the Authority to be taken, or to produce any document in his power or control legally required by the Authority to be produced by him, or to answer any question to which the Authority may legally require an answer, or

(*c*) does any other thing which would, if the Authority were a court, having power to commit for contempt of court, be contempt of such court,

shall be guilty of an offence and shall be liable on summary conviction to a fine not exceeding £1,000 or imprisonment for a period not exceeding six months or, at the discretion of the court, to both such fine and imprisonment.

8. Any person may make a submission to the Authority in the manner prescribed by its rules in relation to the subject matter of any investigation.

9. (1) No person shall disclose information available to him by virtue of the powers of obtaining information conferred by this Act or by any other enactment conferring functions on the Authority or through being present at a meeting of the Authority held

A.1 in private.

(2) *Subparagraph (1)* shall not apply to—

(i) a communication made by a member of the Authority in the execution of his functions under this Act, or

(ii) the disclosure of information in a report of the Authority or for the purpose of legal proceedings under this Act or pursuant to an order of a court of competent jurisdiction for the purposes of any proceedings in that court.

(3) If any person contravenes this paragraph he shall be guilty of an offence and shall be liable on summary conviction to a fine not exceeding £1,000 or imprisonment for a period not exceeding six months or, at the discretion of the court, to both such fine and imprisonment.

10. (1) The Minister, with the consent of the Minister for Finance, may appoint such officers and servants as he thinks necessary to assist the Authority in the performance of its functions.

(2) The officers and servants so appointed shall hold office on such terms and receive such remuneration as the Minister for Finance determines.

11. The Authority shall be entitled, in any proceedings, to the same privilege in respect of a communication to or by the Authority, any member of the Authority or any of its officers or servants as any Minister of the Government.

Competition Act 1991 (Commencement) Order 1991 [SI No. 249 of 1991]

A.2

I, Desmond O'Malley, Minister for Industry and Commerce, in exercise of the powers conferred on me by section 2 of the Competition Act 1991 (No. 24 of 1991), hereby order as follows;

1. This Order may be cited as the Competition Act 1991 (Commencement) Order 1991.
2. In this Order, "the Act" means the Competition Act 1991.
3. Subject to paragraph 4 of this Order, the Act shall come into operation on the 1st day of October, 1991, and the Competition Authority shall stand established on that day.
4. This Order does not apply to —
   (*a*) section 6(2)(b) of the Act,
   (*b*) section 22 of the Act in so far as it provides for the repeal of —
      (i) the following order made under section 8(1) of the Act of 1972 — Restrictive Practices (Groceries) Order 1987 (SI No. 142 of 1987), and
      (ii) for the purposes only of the said order the following provisions of the Act of 1972, as amended by the Act of 1987, namely, sections 1, 8(2), 13(2), 14(1)(b), 14(3), 14(4), 15, 19, 20, 22, 23, 24 and 27 and paragraphs 3, 6, 7 and 8 of the Second Schedule,
      (iii) section 6 of the Act of 1987.

GIVEN under my Official seal,
this 23rd day of September, 1991.

DESMOND O'MALLEY
Minister for Industry and Commerce

Competition (Notification Fee) Regulations 1991 [SI No. 250 of 1991]

I, Desmond O'Malley, Minister for Industry and Commerce, in exercise of the powers conferred on me by section 23 of the Competition Act 1991 (No. 24 of 1991), hereby make the following Regulations:

1. (*a*) These Regulations may be cited as the Competition (Notification Fee) Regulations 1991.
   (*b*) These Regulations shall come into operation on the 1st day of October, 1991.
2. Every agreement, decision and concerted practice to be notified to the Authority under section 7 of the Competition Act 1991 (No. 24 of 1991), shall be accompanied by a fee of £100.00.

GIVEN under my official seal,
this 23rd day of September, 1991.

DESMOND O'MALLEY
Minister for Industry and Commerce

A.2 Competition Act 1991 (Section 6(2)(b)) (Commencement) Order 1992
[SI No. 299 of 1992]

I, Desmond O'Malley, Minister for Industry and Commerce, in exercise of the powers conferred on me by section 2 of the Competition Act 1991 (No. 24 of 1991), hereby order as follows:

1. This Order may be cited as the Competition Act 1991 (Section 6(2)(b)) (Commencement) Order 1992.
2. In this Order, 'the Act' means the Competition Act 1991.
3. Section 6(2)(b) of the Act shall come into operation on the 2nd day of November, 1992.

Given under my Official Seal,
this 19th day of October, 1992.

DESMOND O'MALLEY
Minister for Industry and Commerce

EXPLANATORY NOTE

(This Note is not part of the Instrument and does not purport to be a legal interpretation).

This Order gives the Circuit Court jurisdiction for actions in respect of any abuse which is prohibited by section 5 of the Competition Act 1991, with effect from 2 November, 1992.

Competition Act 1991 (Notice of Licences and Certificates) Regulations 1992
[SI No. 76 of 1992]*

I, Desmond O'Malley, Minister for Industry and Commerce, in exercise of the powers conferred on me by section 23 of the Competition Act 1991 (No. 24 of 1991), hereby make the following Regulations:

1. (*a*) These Regulations may be cited as the Competition Act 1991 (Notice of Licences and Certificates) Regulations 1992
   (*b*) These Regulations shall come into operation on the 13th day of April, 1992.
2. Notice of the grant of a licence or the issue of a certificate under section 4 shall be given to every body to which it relates by being sent by registered post to that body at the address indicated in the relevant notification under section 7 as the address of that body.

GIVEN under my official seal,
this 6th day of April, 1992.

DESMOND O'MALLEY
Minister for Industry and Commerce

*Amended by SI No. 293 of 1993 on next page of this book.

Competition Act 1991 (Notice of Licences and Certificates) Regulations 1993 [SI No. 293 of 1993]

A.2

I, Ruairi Quinn, Minister for Enterprise and Employment, in exercise of the powers conferred on me by section 23 of the Competition Act 1991 (No. 24 of 1991), hereby make the following Regulations:

1. (*a*) These Regulations may be cited as the Competition Act 1991 (Notice of Licences and Certificates) Regulations 1993.

(*b*) These Regulations shall come into operation on the 18th day of October, 1993.

2. (1) Notice of the grant of a licence or the issue of a certificate under section 4 in respect of an agreement, decision or concerted practice shall be given to every party thereto seeking the licence or certificate by being sent by registered post to that party at the address indicated in the relevant notification under section 7 as its address.

(2) Where a licence or certificate under section 4 covers a category of agreements, decisions or concerted practices, publication of the notice in *Iris Oifigiúil* as provided for by subsection (6) shall, for the purposes of that subsection, be sufficient notice to every body to which the licence or certificate relates.

3. The Competition Act 1991 (Notice of Licences and Certificates) Regulations 1992 (SI No. 76 of 1992) are hereby revoked.

GIVEN under the Official Seal of the Minister for Enterprise and Employment this 12th day of October, 1993.

L.S.

J. Corcoran

A person authorised by the Minister for Enterprise and Employment to authenticate the Official Seal of the Minister.

EXPLANATORY NOTE

(This note is not part of the Instrument and does not purport to be a legal interpretation).

These Regulations prescribe the appropriate manner in which the Competition Authority shall give notice of its decisions.

A.3 **Restrictive Practices (Groceries) Order 1987**
[SI No. 142 of 1987]

I, Albert Reynolds, Minister for Industry and Commerce, having considered the report of the Restrictive Practices Commission being a special review under section 10 of the Restrictive Practices Act 1972 (No. 11 of 1972) of the operation of the Restrictive Practices (Groceries) Order 1981, in exercise of the powers conferred on me by section 8 of the said Act, hereby order as follows:

1. This Order may be cited as the Restrictive Practices (Groceries) Order 1987.

2. (1) In this Order—

"authorised officer" means a person authorised in writing by the Examiner for the purposes of Section 15 of the Restrictive Practices Act 1972 "best list price", in relation to grocery goods, means the lowest price of the goods which having regard to the statement which for the time being stands prepared and maintained by the relevant supplier in accordance with the requirements of Article 13 of this Order (no account being taken of any supplementary term, or of any allowance or discount which is not calculated by reference to the purchase concerned), may be obtained by a purchaser taking the maximum advantage of the terms and conditions specified in the said statement;

"date of minimum durability" in relation to grocery goods shall be the date marked on the goods, preceded by the words 'best before' or 'best before end' (being a date until which the grocery goods retain their specific properties when properly stored);

"discount" and "mark-up" include, respectively, a discount or mark-up however expressed;

"the Examiner" means the Examiner of Restrictive Practices;

"grocery goods" means grocery goods for human consumption (excluding fresh fruit, fresh vegetables, fresh and frozen meat, fresh fish and frozen fish, ice cream which has undergone no processing other than freezing with or without the addition of preservatives) and intoxicating liquors not for consumption on the premises and such household necessaries (other than foodstuffs) as are ordinarily sold in grocery shops, and includes grocery goods designated as "own label", "generic" or other similar description;

"like goods" means similar goods which do not differ one from another as regards their nature, grade, brand, quantity per pack or packaging,

"retailer" means any person who resells grocery goods to the public;

"supplementary term" means any term or condition providing for a rebate or discount in relation to the amount payable in respect of the sale of any grocery goods by a supplier to a wholesaler or retailer or an allowance by a supplier to a wholesaler or retailer, in consideration of—

(*a*) the making of purchases by the wholesaler or retailer from the supplier of those goods over specified period of time, whether or not in excess of specified quantities, or **A.3**

(*b*) the promotion of sales of those goods by means of special arrangements carried out for a limited period by or on behalf of the wholesaler or retailer, or

(*c*) any other arrangement relating to price not indicated in the terms and conditions published under Article 13 of this Order;

"seasonal goods" means Christmas cakes, Easter eggs and Halloween bracks;

"supplier" means a manufacturer or importer of grocery goods for sale to wholesalers or retailers and includes any person who processes, blends, cans, packs or otherwise prepares grocery goods for sale to wholesalers or retailers and also includes any person who acts as the sole distributor of such goods to wholesalers or retailers;

"wholesaler" means any person who purchases from a supplier grocery goods for resale to retailers;

(2) For the purposes of this Order the net invoice price of grocery goods supplied by a supplier or a wholesaler to a retailer or by a supplier to a wholesaler shall be calculated having regard to an invoice relating to the delivery of like goods by the supplier or wholesaler to the warehouse or retail store concerned which is of the same date with the sale of goods or with the relevant advertisement, and, in case there is not in existence such an invoice, then such net invoice price shall be calculated having regard to the invoice which relates to such a delivery and which is that issued most recently prior to the sale of goods or the advertisement's publication, and such price shall be calculated net of any allowance or refund that is allowable on the return of the goods' container, and no account shall be taken of discounts, rebates or other deductions which are not entered on the invoice in cash terms as deductions from the sum due to the supplier or wholesaler.

3. (1) Subject to paragraphs (2), (3) and (4) of this Article, a supplier or wholesaler shall not require or induce or attempt to require or induce any person (whether directly or indirectly, by withholding supplies from that other person or otherwise discriminating against him or by threatening to do so, or by any other threat or by any agreement, promise or any other means) to resell or offer for resale grocery goods—

(*a*) at a fixed price specified by the supplier or wholesaler or established by agreement or otherwise, or

(*b*) at a price not less than a fixed or minimum price specified by the supplier or wholesaler or established by agreement or otherwise, or

(*c*) at a fixed mark-up or a fixed discount specified by the supplier or wholesaler or established by agreement or otherwise, or

(*d*) at a mark-up not less than a fixed or minimum mark-up specified by the supplier or wholesaler or established by agreement or otherwise, or

(*e*) at a discount not greater than a fixed or maximum discount specified by the supplier or wholesaler or established by agreement or otherwise.

(2) Subject to paragraph (3) of this Article, nothing in paragraph (1) of this Article shall be construed as preventing supplier —

(*a*) from advertising, or otherwise specifying, resale prices for any grocery goods: provided such prices are maximum prices, or

A.3 (*b*) from withholding grocery goods from a wholesaler or retailer who—

(i) has sold or offered for sale, grocery goods supplied by the supplier—

(I) at a price that exceeded the maximum resale price specified by the supplier, or

(II) at a price (not being a maximum price fixed for the time being by an order under the Prices Acts, 1958 to 1972) that is less than the net invoice price of the goods (including value-added tax) payable to the supplier, and

(ii) fails to give to the supplier an acceptable undertaking to discontinue so selling, or offering for sale, such grocery goods.

(3) Where the grocery goods are sold by a retailer more than four weeks after the date on which a price list provided by a supplier for like goods has been altered and no delivery of like goods accompanied by an invoice has been made to the retailer concerned since the date of the alteration, then, in relation to the goods, paragraph (2)(b)(i)(II) of this Article shall be construed and have effect as if "best list price" were substituted for "net invoice price".

(4) A supplier may request a wholesaler to withhold supplies of grocery goods supplied by him from a retailer in any circumstances in which, under this Order, the supplier would be entitled to withhold supplies from the retailer and, if the wholesaler fails or refuses to comply with the request, the supplier may withhold supplies of such goods from that wholesaler.

4. Where a supplier indicates or recommends a resale price of grocery goods such price shall not be binding on any person as a minimum resale price.

5. Save as hereinafter provided, there shall not be any arrangements, agreements or understandings between two or more persons, each of them being a supplier, a wholesaler or a retailer, which has or is likely to have the effect of ensuring that goods will be resold or offered for resale—

(*a*) at a fixed price or at a price not less than a specified minimum price, or

(*b*) at a fixed mark-up or at a mark-up not less than a specified minimum mark-up, or

(*c*) at a fixed discount or at a discount not greater than a specified maximum discount, or

(*d*) on any other basis which involves eliminating or limiting competition in price between suppliers or between wholesalers or between retailers.

6. There shall not be any agreement, arrangement or understanding (whether induced by threat, promise or otherwise) between two or more suppliers or between two or more wholesalers as to the prices at which they will supply grocery goods to other persons or as to the discount to be allowed or the mark-up to be applied in respect of such goods.

7. A supplier or wholesaler shall not withhold grocery goods from any person or discriminate against any person as to the terms on which such goods are supplied, because that person is or is not a member of a trade association or is not approved of by a trade association or because that person's name appears or does not appear on any list prepared, maintained, published or issued by a trade association or because representations that supplies should be withheld from such person or be made available to him only on specified terms have been made by or on behalf of any trade association.

8. (1) No trade association or other combination of persons shall, as respects grocery goods, coerce or induce or attempt to coerce or induce a supplier or wholesaler to withhold supplies from any wholesaler or retailer or discriminate against any wholesaler or retailer as to the terms on which goods may be supplied to them. **A.3**

(2) Paragraph (1) of this Article shall not be construed as preventing a trade association from notifying a supplier of any circumstances that, in the belief of the association, would, under this Order, entitle the supplier to withhold goods from a wholesaler or retailer.

9. No supplier, wholesaler or retailer shall be a party to any agreement, arrangement or understanding (whether induced by threat, promise or otherwise) which has or is likely to have the effect of limiting or restricting entry to trade in any grocery goods.

10. No person or combination of persons shall prepare, maintain, publish or issue any lists, or do any other act, designed—

(*a*) to secure a boycott of any person in relation to grocery goods because—

(i) if such person is a supplier or a wholesaler, of the prices charged by him for such goods or the other terms or conditions on which such goods are supplied by him, or

(ii) if such person is a retailer, of the prices charged by him, or

(*b*) to affect adversely the terms of supply of such goods to any person because that person has refused to do any act which he is prohibited from doing by this Order.

11. (1) Subject to the paragraphs (2), (3), (4), (5) and (6) of this Article, a retailer shall not sell grocery goods (other than grocery goods whose date of minimum durability has expired) at a price that (after the deduction of the cost to the retailer of any discount or other benefit given by him on the sale of the goods), is less than whichever of the following is applicable—

(*a*) in case charges in respect of carriage, insurance or other costs not included in the relevant invoice have to be paid by the retailer to the supplier or any other person to obtain the delivery of the goods to his premises, the amount obtained when the said charges or costs are added to the net invoice price of the goods (including value added tax), or

(*b*) in any other case, the net invoice price of the goods (including value added tax).

(2) Where a sale is effected to a purchaser of two or more items at a price which is less than the amount which he would have to pay to the retailer concerned if the items were bought from him singly, then, for the purposes of paragraph (1) of this Article, the price of each item shall be the amount obtained by dividing the amount paid by the number of items.

(3) Where a sale is effected more than four weeks after the date on which a supplier's list price for like goods has been altered and no delivery of like goods accompanied by an invoice has been made to the retailer concerned since the date of the said alteration, then paragraph (1) of this Article shall, in relation to the sale, be construed and have effect as if "best list price" were substituted for "net invoice price" in both places where it occurs.

A.3 (4) The selling at a price which is a maximum price fixed for the time being by an Order under the Prices Acts, 1958 to 1972, shall not be regarded as contravening paragraph (1) of this Article.

(5) Where goods are invoiced in a foreign currency, then, for the purposes of this Article, the equivalent in Irish currency shall be calculated at the exchange rate quoted by the Central Bank as the official exchange rate for the Irish pound on the date of the relevant invoice or, if no official rates are declared on that date, at the latest previous mid-closing exchange rate.

(6) For the purposes of this Article, the net value added tax to be included in the net invoice price (including value added tax) of grocery goods shall be the value added tax in respect of the goods payable by the retailer and in the case of grocery goods invoiced in a foreign currency, for the purposes of this Order the value added tax in respect of the goods shall be that payable on the equivalent amount in Irish currency calculated in accordance with paragraph (5) of this Article.

12. (1) Subject to the paragraphs (2), (3), (4), (5), (6) and (7) of this Article, a retailer, or any wholesaler or other person acting on behalf of a retailer, shall not publish or display, or cause to be published or displayed, an advertisement for the sale of grocery goods at a price that (after the deduction of the cost to the retailer of any discount or other benefit given by him on a sale of any of the goods) is less than whichever of the following is applicable:

(*a*) in case charges in respect of carriage, insurance or other costs not included in the relevant invoice have to be paid by the retailer to the supplier or any other person to obtain the delivery of the goods to his premises, the amount obtained when the said charges or costs are added to the net invoice price of the goods (including value added tax), or

(*b*) in any other case, the net invoice price of the goods (including value added tax).

(2) Paragraph (1) of this Article shall apply in relation to an advertisement whether or not it contains an indication of the price of the goods to which it relates and whether or not it contains an indication that the price of the goods to which it relates is below either:

(i) the amount obtained when the charges or costs referred to in subparagraph (a) of paragraph (1) of this Article are added to the net invoice price of the goods (including value added tax) or

(ii) the net invoice price of the goods (including value added tax).

(3) Where an advertisement makes an offer pursuant to which a purchaser may purchase two or more items at a price which is less than the amount which he would have to pay to the retailer concerned if the items were bought from him individually then for the purposes of paragraph (1) of this Article, the price of each item shall be the amount obtained by dividing the price specified in the offer by the number of items.

(4) Where an advertisement for the retail sale of grocery goods is published or displayed more than four weeks after the date on which a supplier's list price for like goods has been altered and no delivery of like goods accompanied by an invoice has been made to the retailer concerned since the date of the alteration, then paragraph (1) of this Article shall, in relation to the advertisement, be construed and have effect as if "best list price" were substituted for "net invoice price" in both places where it occurs.

(5) The advertising of a price which is a maximum price fixed for the time being by an Order under the Prices Acts, 1958 to 1972, shall not be regarded as contravening paragraph (1) of this Article. A.3

(6) Nothing in this Article shall be construed as imposing any criminal liability on—

(*a*) Radio Telefís Éireann or any person participating in any sound or television broadcast,

(*b*) the proprietor, publisher, or editor or seller of any newspaper, magazine or other periodical,

by reason only of the publication in such a broadcast or periodical of an advertisement in contravention of this Article.

(7)(*a*) In this Article "advertisement" includes any catalogue, price list, notice, circular, photograph, film, sound broadcast, television broadcast or personal canvass.

(*b*) Where goods are invoiced in a foreign currency then, for the purposes of this Article, the equivalent in Irish currency shall be calculated at the exchange rate quoted by the Central Bank as the official exchange rate on the date of the relevant invoice or, if no official rates are declared on that date, at the latest previous mid-closing exchange rate.

(*c*) For the purposes of this Article, the net value added tax to be included in the net invoice price (including value added tax) of grocery goods shall be the value added tax in respect of the goods payable by the retailer and in the case of grocery goods invoiced in a foreign currency, for the purposes of this Order the value added tax in respect of the goods shall be that payable on the equivalent amount in Irish currency calculated in accordance with sub-paragraph (b) of this paragraph.

13. (1) (*a*) A supplier shall prepare and maintain a statement in writing prescribing the terms and conditions upon and subject to which he sells grocery goods (including supplementary terms, if any, and, if he grants credit in respect of the purchase price of any grocery goods the terms and conditions of such grant), and the supplier shall effect a sale of grocery goods of any kind to wholesalers or retailers upon and subject to those terms and conditions (in so far as they apply in relation to that sale of that kind of goods).

(*b*) Where a statement under this Article in relation to supplementary terms contains a general indication of the nature and extent of those terms, the statement shall be deemed, in so far as those terms are concerned, to comply with the provisions of this Article.

(*c*) Sub-paragraph (a) of this paragraph does not apply to the sale of goods that have been processed, blended, canned, packed or otherwise prepared in accordance with the specification and requirements of the purchaser, and, for the purposes of resale, are not given the name or a brand name of the purchaser.

(2) The terms and conditions aforesaid may make provision for discounts or rebates of different amounts on the price of goods sold on the basis of—

(*a*) the different functions in relation to the sale and distribution of the goods performed by purchasers of the goods,

A.3 (*b*) the quantity or value of the goods,

(*c*) other objective criteria which are designed to promote efficiency in supply or distribution and which are necessary in the legitimate interests of the supplier's business.

(3) The terms and conditions aforesaid —

(*a*) shall not discriminate unfairly against purchasers and, having regard to the legitimate interests of the supplier's business, shall take reasonable account of the economies of supply and distribution to different purchasers,

(*b*) shall not provide for any variation in the rates of discounts or rebates to any persons by reference to sales of goods to those persons by other suppliers, whether the other suppliers are members of any trade association or not, and

(*c*) shall not be such as unfairly or unjustly to prevent a person from commencing business as a wholesaler or retailer.

(4) Where the terms and conditions referred to in paragraph (1) of this Article include supplementary terms relating to the promotion of sales in the manner specified in the definition of "supplementary term" in Article 2 of this Order, the supplementary terms may be made available to different wholesalers and retailers at different times within a period which is of reasonable duration having regard to all the circumstances.

14. (1) A supplier shall, if so requested by the Examiner, furnish to the Examiner, within 14 days of the receipt of the request, a copy of the statement prepared by him pursuant to Article 13 of this Order together with any amendments thereof.

(2) A supplier shall furnish to the Examiner such information as the Examiner may from time to time request in relation to the supply of goods of a kind referred to in Article 13(1)(b) and (c) of this Order.

(3) Any retail grocer with more than five grocery outlets, and any wholesaler, if so requested by the Examiner, shall furnish to the Examiner a statement of supplementary terms negotiated with the suppliers during each month by the seventh day of the following month.

(4) Each supplier shall maintain a register of supplementary terms and such register shall be made available to the Examiner, if the Examiner so requests.

(5) A supplier shall, if requested by any person carrying on or proposing to carry on business as a wholesaler or retailer, furnish to such person, within fourteen days after the date of the making of the request, a copy of the statement which at the date of the request stands prepared and maintained by him in accordance with the requirements of Article 13 of this Order together with any amendments thereof.

15. If the Examiner is satisfied that the operation by a supplier of the terms and conditions contained in the statement prepared by him pursuant to Article 13 of this Order constitutes unfair discrimination in favour of or against any wholesaler or retailer or any section of the grocery trade comprising the business carried on by wholesalers and retailers, the supplier shall, at the request of the Examiner, make such amendments of the terms and conditions aforesaid as may be specified by the Examiner being amendments calculated to eliminate the alleged unfair discrimination.

16. (1) (a) A wholesaler or retailer shall not, whether by the use of threats or

inducements or otherwise, cause a supplier to sell grocery goods to him on and subject to terms and conditions other than those contained or referred to in the statement prepared by the supplier pursuant to the requirements of Article 13 of this Order. **A.3**

(*b*) A wholesaler or retailer who purchases goods from a supplier shall comply with any terms or conditions as to credit in relation to the purchase contained in the statement prepared by the supplier pursuant to Article 13 of this Order.

(c) Where a person is charged with an offence in relating to a failure to comply with sub-paragraph (b) of this paragraph, it shall be a defence for him to prove that the failure was due to his inability to pay for the goods purchased in accordance with the relevant terms or conditions as to credit.

(2) Nothing in this Article shall be construed as prohibiting a wholesaler or retailer from requesting a supplier to amend, vary or delete any of the terms or conditions contained or referred to in the statement prepared by the supplier pursuant to the requirements of Article 13 of this Order.

17. (1) Subject to paragraph (2) of this Article, a supplier, wholesaler or retailer who purchases grocery goods outside the State and imports them into the State for sale shall, within 14 days after such importation, furnish to the Examiner a statement containing the terms and conditions upon and subject to which the goods were purchased and imported.

(2) It shall not be necessary for a supplier, wholesaler or retailer to furnish a statement to the Examiner under this Article in relation to goods purchased outside the State and imported into the State for sale if the goods are of the same kind as other goods in respect of which such a statement has been furnished to the Examiner by the wholesaler or retailer and the terms and conditions on which the first-mentioned goods were purchased and imported are the same as those contained in the statement furnished as aforesaid.

18. (1) A supplier shall not make any payment or allowance to a person who is a wholesaler or retailer, or give a reduction of or discount on the price of grocery goods sold to that person by him or give to that person any other benefit, in consideration of —

(*a*) the carrying out by that person of advertising of the goods aforesaid,

(*b*) the making available of selling space or additional selling space—

(i) on the opening of a new retail outlet;

(ii) on the extension of an existing outlet;

(iii) after the change of ownership of an existing outlet.

(2) A retailer or wholesaler shall not receive from a supplier any payment or allowance, or reduction of or discount on the prices of grocery goods, or any other benefit in consideration of any of the matters referred to in paragraph (1) of this Article.

19 When an authorised officer acting in the course of his duties visits the premises of any retailer or wholesaler and finds therein (or receives later from the retailer or wholesaler) any invoices, documents or other records purporting to indicate, or appearing to indicate, the net invoice price of any goods, then, in any proceedings

A.3 under this Order against that retailer or wholesaler, these invoices, documents or other records or anything shown to be a true copy of or extract from such invoices, documents or records shall, unless the contrary is shown, be sufficient evidence as to the net invoice price of the relevant goods.

20. Articles 11 and 12 of this Order shall not apply to seasonal goods.

21. The Restrictive Practices (Groceries) Order 1981 is hereby revoked.

GIVEN under my Official Seal this 25th day of May, 1987

Albert Reynolds
Minister for Industry and Commerce

EXPLANATORY NOTE

(This note is not part of the Instrument and does not purport to be a legal interpretation).

The effect of this Order is to prohibit the selling, or advertising for sale, of grocery goods (including alcoholic beverages), below cost price. The provisions in relation to the withholding of supply of grocery goods are outlined and the payment or receipt of 'Hello Money' is prohibited. The Order requires to be confirmed by an Act of the Oireachtas before it will have the force of law.

Mergers, Takeovers and Monopolies (control) Act 1978 [No. 17] **A.4**

[As amended, *inter alia*, by Part II of the Restrictive Practices (Amendment) Act 1987 and Part IV of the Competition Act 1991]

AN ACT TO PROVIDE FOR THE CONTROL BY THE MINISTER FOR INDUSTRY, COMMERCE AND ENERGY IN THE INTERESTS OF THE COMMON GOOD OF CERTAIN TAKEOVERS, MERGERS AND MONO-POLIES, TO EXTEND THE RESTRICTIVE PRACTICES ACT 1972, AND TO PROVIDE FOR OTHER MATTERS CONNECTED WITH THE AFORESAID MATTERS. [3*rd July*, 1978]

BE IT ENACTED BY THE OIREACHTAS AS FOLLOWS:

Interpretation

1.—(1) In this Act:

'the Act of 1972' means the Restrictive Practices Act 1972;[1]

'the Act of 1987' means the Restrictive Practices (Amendment) Act 1987;[1]

'the Competition Act 1991' means the Competition Act 1991;[2]

'the Authority' means the Competition Authority established by section 10 of the Competition Act 1991;[3]

'Conditional Order' means an order under section 9 prohibiting a proposed merger or takeover except on conditions specified in the order;

'enterprise' means:

(i) a person or partnership engaged for profit in the supply or distribution of goods or the provision of services, including:

(*a*) a society, including a credit union, registered under the Industrial and Provident Societies Acts 1893 to 1978;[4]

(*b*) a society registered under the Friendly Societies Acts 1896 to 1977; and[5]

1. Section 3(1) of the Competition Act 1991 sets out these meanings. The Act of 1972 as amended by the Act of 1987 was repealed with effect from 1 October 1991 by section 22 of the Competition Act 1991 as commenced by SI No. 249 of 1991 which commencement 'order does not apply' to Restrictive Practices (Groceries) Order 1987 and 'for the purposes only of the said Order the following provisions of the Act of 1972, as amended by the Act of 1987 namely, sections 1, 8(2), 13(2), 14(1)(b), 14(3), 14(4), 15, 19, 20, 22, 23, 24 and 27 and paragraphs 3, 6, 7, and 8 of the second schedule and 'section 6 of the Act of 1987' continue to apply.
2. Section 1 of the Competition Act 1991 creates this citation.
3. 'The Commission' was the original definition, but now see section 3(1) and section 10(3) of the Competition Act 1991. 'the Commission' where translated in this consolidation is noted.
4. See section 1(2) of the Industrial and Provident Societies (Amendment) Act 1978 (No. 23) which provides that the 1978 Act shall be read with the earlier Acts.
5. Note that section 8 of the Friendly Societies Act 1896 concerning restriction on registration was supplemented by section 28 of Insurance Act 1989 which refers to Council Directives 73/237/EEC, 79/237/EEC and EC (Life Assurance) Regulations, 1984.

A.4 (*c*) a society established under the Building Societies Act 1989; or[6]

(ii) a holding company within the meaning of section 155 of the Companies Act 1963.

'the Examiner' means the Authority;[7]

'the Minister' means the Minister for Enterprise and Employment;[8]

'Monopoly'[9] means an enterprise or two or more enterprises under common control, which supply or provide, or to which is supplied or provided, not less than one-half of goods or services of a particular kind supplied or provided in the State in a particular year, according to the most recent information available on an annual basis, but does not include any enterprise at least 90 per cent of whose output is exported from the State or any enterprise at least 90 per cent of whose output comprises components for products which are exported from the State;

'the scheduled criteria' means the matters specified in the Schedule to this Act;[10]

'service'[11] includes any professional service, but does not include:

(i) any service provided by the holder of a licence under section 9 of the Central Bank Act 1971 [as amended by section 32 of the Central Bank Act 1989];[12]

(ii) any service provided by a trustee savings bank certified under the Trustee Savings Banks Act 1989;[13]

(iii) any service provided under a contract of employment;

(iv) any service provided by a local authority within the meaning of section 2 of the Local Government Act 1941.

'service' shall not include the owning and transfer of land where this activity is the sole activity of the enterprise in which control is being sought.[14]

6. See section 6 of the Building Societies Act 1989 (No. 17).
7. Section 7(1) of the Act of 1987 substantially transfers the functions of the Examiner to the Commission in respect of functions under the Act of 1978. Section 10(3) of the Competition Act 1991 substitutes 'the Authority' for 'the Commission' in respect of section 7 and section 8 of the Act of 1978.
8. The title of the Minister originally had 'Energy', subsequently had 'Tourism' and reverted to 'Industry, Trade and Commerce' before being changed to its present name. The Act of 1987 and the Competition Act 1991 refers to the Minister for Industry and Commerce. SI No. 295 and 306 of 1977, SI No. 10 of 1980, SI 384 and 385 of 1983, SI No. 41 of 1986 and SI No. 19 of 1993 gave effect to the name changes for the Department and title of the Minister.
9. Section 14(7) of the Competition Act 1991 provides: 'References in sections 12 and 13 of the Act of 1978 to section 1 of that Act shall be construed as references to this section and the expression '*monopoly*' shall be construed as a reference to an abuse of a dominant position'. See also footnote 40 later. See section 5 of the Competition Act 1991 for abuse of Dominant Position.
10. This definition is no longer relevant because the criteria are set out in section 8(2) of the Act of 1978 as inserted by section 17(2) of the Competition Act 1991 and the Schedule is repealed by section 17(6) of the Competition Act 1991.
11. This inclusive definition was reduced by section 24 of the Act of 1987.
12. The Central Bank Act 1971 was supplemented and amended by the Central Bank Act 1989 (No. 16) and section 9 of the 1971 Act in particular by section 32 of the 1989 Act. Council Directive 77/780/EEC defines credit institution for the purpose of section 32.
13. The Trustee Savings Banks Acts were consolidated and repealed by the Trustee Savings Banks Act 1989 (No. 21) in which section 3(2) provides that references to enactments shall be amended enactments and section 7 repeals Acts set out in the Schedule to the Act.
14. This sentence was added by section 15(1) of the Competition Act 1991.

(2) For the purposes of this Act, a merger or takeover shall be deemed to be proposed when an offer capable of acceptance is made. **A.4**

(3)(*a*) For the purposes of this Act, but subject to section 3, a merger or takeover shall be taken to exist when two or more enterprises, at least one of which carries on business in the State, come under common control.

(*b*) Enterprises shall be deemed to be under common control if the decision as to how or by whom each shall be managed can be made either by the same person, or the same group of persons acting in concert.

(*c*)[15] Without prejudice to paragraph (b), where an enterprise (in this paragraph referred to as 'the first enterprise') whether by means of acquisition or otherwise, obtains the right in another enterprise (in this paragraph referred to as 'the second enterprise') which is a body corporate:

(i) to appoint or remove a majority of the board or committee of management of the second enterprise; or

(ii) to shares of the second enterprise which carry voting rights, except where the voting rights in the second enterprise which are controlled by the first enterprise:

(I) are not after the acquisition more than 25 percent of the total of such voting rights, or

(II) are before the acquisition more than one half of the total of such voting rights,

the said enterprises shall be deemed to have been brought under common control.

(*d*) For the purposes of paragraph (*c*):

(i) 'voting rights' do not include voting rights which arise only in specified circumstances; and

(ii) voting rights shall be deemed to be controlled by an enterprise when it can determine how the votes concerned shall be cast;

(*e*) Subject to section 3, where the assets, including goodwill, (or a substantial part of the assets) of an enterprise are acquired by another enterprise, the acquisition shall be deemed to constitute a merger or takeover for the purposes of this Act if upon the acquisition a result of the acquisition is to place the second mentioned enterprise in a position to replace (or substantially to replace) the first mentioned enterprise in the business in which that enterprise was engaged immediately before the acquisition[16] and the value of those assets or the value of the turnover generated therefrom exceeds the thresholds referred to in section 2(1)(a).

(*f*) This subsection does not apply to a case where enterprises come under common control (or are deemed to come under common control) either because the person referred to in paragraph (*b*) is a receiver or liquidator acting as such or because the person making an acquisition referred to in paragraph (*c*) is an underwriter or jobber acting as such, or because the person making an acquisition referred to in paragraph (*e*) is a receiver or liquidator acting as such.

(*g*) This subsection does not apply to two or more bodies corporate, each of which is a wholly owned subsidiary of the same body corporate.

15. This is the substitute section 1(3)(c) contained in section 15(2) of the Competition Act 1991.
16. The following words of this sentence were inserted by section 15(3) of the Competition Act 1991.

A.4 (4) In this Act a reference to a section is to a section of this Act unless it is indicated that reference to some other enactment is intended.

(5) In this Act a reference to a subsection, paragraph, subparagraph or clause is to the subsection, paragraph, subparagraph or clause of the provision in which the reference occurs, unless it is indicated that reference to some other provision is intended.

Application of the Act

2.—(1) (*a*) This Act shall apply to a proposed merger or takeover if in the most recent financial year the value of the gross assets of each of two or more of the enterprises to be involved in the proposal is not less than £10,000,000 or the turnover of each of those two or more enterprises is not less than £20,000,000.[17]

(*b*) For the purposes of this subsection, 'turnover' does not include any payment in respect of value added tax on sales or in respect of duty of excise.

(2) This Act shall apply to a monopoly where in the most recent financial year the monopoly's sales or purchase of the goods or services concerned exceed £6,000,000.[18]

(3) This Act shall not apply to enterprises coming under common control where this occurs solely as a result of a testamentary disposition or an intestacy.

(4) The Minister may from time to time by order amend subsection 1 or subsection (2) by the substitution for an amount mentioned in that subsection of another amount, not being in any case a smaller amount than the amount for which it is substituted.[17] [18]

(5)(*a*) Where he is of opinion that the exigencies of the common good so warrant, the Minister may by order declare that notwithstanding subsection 1, this Act shall apply to a proposed merger or takeover of a particular class specified in the order and upon the making of such an order, this Act shall apply to a proposed merger or takeover of that class.[19]

(*b*) The Minister may by order amend or revoke an order under this sub- section.

(6) Every order under this section shall have effect on and from the date on which it was made and shall be laid before each House of the Oireachtas as soon as may be after it is made and, if a resolution confirming the order is not passed by each such

17. These figures of £10,000,000 and £20,000,000 were originally £1,250,000 and £2,500,000 respectively, but were increased to £5,000,000 and £10,000,000 by SI No. 230 of 1985 pursuant to section 2(4) of the Act of 1978 which took effect from 8 July 1985 and increased to £10,000,000 and £20,000,000 by SI No. 135 of 1993 with effect from 21 May 1993. Footnote 30 on p. 112 of *The Irish Constitution*, J.M. Kelly, 3rd edition, Gerard Hogan and Gerry Whyte states that this sub- section 'would seem to be constitutionally objectionable in that (i) it allows the Minister to amend the law by statutory order and (ii) the subsection contains no adequate principles and policies'.

18. SI No. 230 of 1985 by Regulation 2(*b*) increased the original figure of £1,500,000 to £6,000,000. This subsection is irrelevant because 'monopoly' shall be construed as a a reference to an abuse of a dominant position according to section 14(7) of the Competition Act 1991.

19. SI No. 17 of 1979 which is the only order made pursuant to section 2(5) provides that this 'Act shall apply to proposed mergers or take-overs of the following class, namely, proposed mergers or take-overs involving enterprises at least one of which is engaged in the printing or publication (or printing and publication) of one or more than one newspaper.' 'Newspaper means any periodical consisting substantially of news and comment on current affairs, but does not include a newspaper intended for circulation only to members of a particular trade, profession or occupation.' In effect SI No. 17 of 1979 provides that no thresholds apply to mergers or takeovers involving a newspaper enterprise.

House within the next 21 days after each House has laid before it, the order shall lapse, without prejudice to the validity previously done thereunder.[20] **A.4**

Limitation on commencement of merger or takeover

3.—(1) In relation to a proposed merger or takeover, title to any shares or assets concerned shall not pass until:

(*a*) the Minister, in pursuance of section 7(a), has stated in writing that he has decided not to make an order under section 9 in relation to the proposed merger or takeover, or

(*b*) the Minister has stated in writing that he has made a conditional order in relation to the proposed merger or takeover, or

(*c*) the relevant period within the meaning of section 6 has elapsed without the Minister having made any order under section 9 in relation to the proposed merger or takeover,

whichever first occurs.

(2) A statement under subsection (1)(a) shall cease to have effect at the end of the period of 12 months beginning on the date of the statement if the enterprises the subject of the proposed merger or takeover referred to in the statement have not come under common control during that period.

Right of purported vendor of shares to damages

4.—Where a purported sale of shares is rendered invalid under section 3, the purported vendor shall be entitled to recover from the purported purchaser any damages the purported vendor suffers by reason only of the invalidity, unless the purported purchaser satisfies the court that before the purported sale he had notified the purported vendor of circumstances relating to the proposed sale which gave rise to the possibility of such an invalidity.

Notification of proposed merger or takeover to Minister[21]

5.—(1) Each of the enterprises involved in a proposed merger or takeover shall notify[22] the Minister in writing of the proposal, and provide full details thereof within the specified period of the offer capable of acceptance having been made, the effect of which would bring the enterprises under common control.

(2) Where, having received a notification under this section from each of the enterprises involved, the Minister is of opinion that in order to consider for the purpose of this Act a proposed merger or takeover he requires further information he may, within one month of the date of receipt by him of the notification, or of the last of such notifications, as the case may be, request such further information in writing from any one or more of the enterprises concerned, each of which shall provide the information within a period to be stated to them by the Minister in writing.

(3)(*a*) Where there is a contravention of subsection (1) or (2) the person in control

20. The Dáil library has records of such resolutions.
21. This is the substitution for section 5 as provided in section 16 of the Competition Act 1991.
22. Section 19 of the Competition Act 1991 provides: '(1) The transmission to the Minister by the Commission of the European Communities of a copy of a notification made under Council regulation (EEC) No. 4064/89 on the control of concentrations between undertakings shall constitute a notification under section 5 of the Act of 1978.'

A.4 of an enterprise failing to notify the Minister within the specified period or failing to supply the information requested within the period stated by the Minister shall be guilty of an offence and shall be liable:

(i) on summary conviction, to a fine not exceeding £1,000 and, for continued contravention, to a daily default fine not exceeding £100, or

(ii) on conviction on indictment, to a fine not exceeding £200,000 and, for continued contravention, to a daily default fine not exceeding £20,000.

(*b*) Where a person is liable to a daily default fine he shall be guilty of contravening the provision on every day on which the contravention continues after the specified period has elapsed.

(*c*) For the purposes of this subsection, the person in control of an enterprise is—

(i) in the case of a body corporate, any officer of the body corporate who knowingly and wilfully authorises or permits the contravention;

(ii) in the case of a partnership, each partner who knowingly and wilfully authorises or permits the contravention;

(iii) in the case of any other form of enterprise, any individual in control of that enterprise who knowingly and wilfully authorises or permits the contravention.

(4) For the purposes of this section the specified period shall be one month, or such other period as the Minister may specify.

(5) A notification for the purposes of subsection (1) shall not be valid where any information provided or statement made under subsection (1) or (2) is false or misleading.

Relevant period for purpose of section 3 and section 7

6.—(1) For the purpose of section 3 or section 7.[23] the relevant period in relation to a particular merger or takeover shall be the period,[24] of three months beginning on the date on which the Minister first receives a notification under section 5(1) or, where the Minister requests further information under section 5(2), the date of receipt by him of such information.

(2) Where a person involved in a proposed merger or takeover which is being investigated by the Authority[25] under section 8 applies, by virtue of that section, to the High Court for a declaration under section 15 of the Act of 1972,[26] the period beginning on the date of the application and ending on the date of the decision of the High Court, or (where that decision is appealed) the date of the decision of the Supreme Court, on the application shall, notwithstanding any other provision of this

23. 'Or section 7' was inserted by section 17(1) of the Competition Act 1991.
24. Section 19(2) of the Competition Act 1991 provides: 'The relevant period in respect of such a notification shall not commence until the Commission of the European Communities makes a decision under either Article 9 or 21(3) of that regulation'. Section 19(1) of the Competition Act 1991 applies as described in footnote 22 above.
25. Section 10(3) of the Competition Act 1991 substitutes 'the Authority' for 'the Commission'. The original word 'Examiner' had been translated to 'the Commission' by section 7(2) of the Act of 1987.
26. Section 15 of the Act of 1972 relates to the powers of inspection of premises and records — interestingly section 15 of the Act of 1972 was amended by section 18 of the Act of 1987 which latter provision together with all of the Act of 1972 was repealed by section 22 of the Competition Act 1991.

section, not be reckoned in calculating the relevant period for the purposes of this section.[27] **A.4**

Reference to Authority[28] of proposed merger or takeover

7.—[29] Upon receipt of a notification under section 5, the Minister shall:

(*a*) as soon as practicable inform the enterprises which made the notification and any other enterprise involved which enquiries of him that he has decided not to make an order under section 9 in relation to the proposed merger or takeover; or

(*b*) within 30 days of the commencement of the relevant period refer the notification to the Authority for investigation.

Report by Authority[30] to Minister

8.—(1) As soon as practicable after reference to {it} under section 7, the Authority[30] shall investigate the proposal so referred and shall, before such date,[31] not being less than 30 days after the reference, if any, as the Minister specifies furnish the Minister with a report of {its} investigation.

(2)(*a*)[32] A report of the Authority under subsection (1) shall state its opinion as to whether or not the proposed merger or takeover concerned would be likely to prevent or restrict competition or restrain trade in any goods or services and would be likely to operate against the common good.

(*b*) The Authority shall give its views on the likely effect of the proposed merger and takeover on the common good in respect of:

(i) continuity of supplies or services,
(ii) level of employment,
(iii) regional development,
(iv) rationalisation of operations in the interests of greater efficiency,
(v) research and development,
(vi) increased production,
(vii) access to markets,
(viii) shareholders and partners,
(ix) employees,
(x) consumers.

[33]The Minister shall publish any such report, with due regard to commercial confidentiality, within two months of its being furnished to him by the Authority.

27. This section 6(2) is rendered ineffective by virtue of the subsequent Acts. The powers of the Authority and the rights of persons now arise under section 8(4) below as transferred by section 10(3) of the Competition Act 1991 and supplemented by section 7 of the Schedule to the Competition Act 1991;
28. Authority has been translated from Examiner of Restrictive Practices by reference to section 10(3) of the Competition Act 1991 and section 7 of the Act of 1987.
29. This is a substitute paragraph by virtue of section 17(2) of the Competition Act 1991.
30. The change from 'Examiner' to the 'Authority' can be traced to section 7 of the Act of 1987 and then to section 10(3) of the Competition Act 1991; 'him' and 'his' has been changed by the Editor to {it} and {its} consequently.
31. 'Not being less than 30 days after the reference' was inserted by section 17(3) of the Competition Act 1991
32. This is a complete substitute for section 8(2) as inserted by section 17(4) of the Competition Act 1991.
33. This sentence is provided for in section 17(5) of the Competition Act 1991, but does not mention whether the sentence is in addition or in substitution for any other previous sentence.

A.4 (3)[34] Section 15 of the Act of 1972, which relates to inspection of premises and records, shall, for the purposes of an investigation under this section, apply to a person authorised in writing by the Examiner.

(4)[35] The Authority[36] may, for the purpose of this section, delegate one or more of their members to carry out an investigation and to report thereon in accordance with this section and may make different delegations for different investigations and may revoke a delegation.

Order by Minister prohibiting proposed merger or takeover

9.—(1) (*a*) The Minister having considered a report of the Authority[37] under section 8(1), may, if he thinks that the exigencies of the common good so warrant, which shall include, but is not confined to, the criteria in section 8[38] after consultation with any other Minister of the Government appearing to him to be concerned, by order prohibit a proposed merger or takeover either absolutely or except on conditions specified in the order.

(*b*) The conditions referred to in paragraph (a) shall include a condition requiring the proposed merger or takeover to be effected within 12 months of the making of the order.

(2) An order under this section shall state the reasons for making the order and, in the case of a conditional order, may have retrospective effect.

(3) Before making an order under this section the Minister shall have regard to any relevant international obligations of the State.[39]

(4) The Minister may by order revoke an order under this section and may, with the agreement of the enterprise or enterprises concerned, amend an order under this section.[40]

(5) Every order under this section shall be laid before each House of the Oireachtas as soon as may be after it is made and, if a resolution annulling the order is passed by either such House within the next 21 days on which that House has sat after the order is laid before it, the order shall be annulled accordingly, but without prejudice to the validity of anything previously done thereunder.

Equiry and report on monopoly[40]

10.

34. Section 22 of the Competition Act 1991 repeals all of the Act of 1972 and section 18 of the Act of 1987 which amended section 15. Therefore, this subsection 8(3) has no effect.
35. This subsection 8(4) was added to the Act of 1978 by section 25 of the Act of 1987.
36. 'The Authority' was substituted for the Commission by section 10(3) of the Competition Act 1991.
37. The word 'Examiner' was substituted by 'the Commission' by section 27(1) of the Act of 1987 and one can only surmise that this changed to 'the Authority' by the Competition Act 1991 despite no specific translation.
38. 'Which shall include but is not confined to, the criteria in section 8' As inserted by section 18 of the Competition Act 1991.
39. An example is SI No. 115 of 1990 which revoked the Proposed Merger or Take-over Prohibition Order, 1990 SI No. 42 of 1990 which concerned the merger of British Steel plc and C. Walker & Sons (Holdings) Ltd. because the European Commission on 8 May 1990 under Article 66 of the ECSC authorised the merger subject to conditions.
40. Section 14(11) of the Act of 1991 repeals section 10 and section 11 of the Act of 1978. Section 5 and section 14 of the Competition Act 1991 makes provisions to prohibit and control abuses of a dominant position and how they may be investigated, controlled and adjusted by the Minister.

11. A.4

12.—(1) Where the Minister makes an order under section 9(1) or section 14 of the Competition Act 1991,[41] an appeal on a point of law may be made to the High Court against the order within one month of the coming into effect of the order by any enterprise referred to in the order. Order by Minister relating to monopoly[40]

(2) Where the High Court allows an appeal under this section, the Minister shall by order amend or revoke (as may be appropriate) the order the subject of the appeal as soon as practicable. Appeal to High Court against orders of Minister

(3) Where pursuant to subsection 2 the Minister makes an order following an appeal, section 9(5) (in the case of an appeal against an order under section 9(1)) or section 14(6) of the Competition Act 1991[41] [in the case of an appeal against an order under section 14(3) of the Competition Act 1991] shall not apply to the order under subsection 2.

(4) An appeal against a decision of the High Court under this section shall not lie to the Supreme Court.[42]

13.—(1) (*a*) It shall be lawful for a court of competent jurisdiction to grant an injunction on the motion[46] of the Director or of the Minister or of any other person to enforce compliance with the terms of an order under section 9 or section 14 of the Competition Act 1991[45] for the time being in force. Provisions relating to order under[43] section 9[44] and section 14 of the Competition Act 1991[45]

(*b*) This subsection shall not affect any other right of the Minister or other person to bring proceedings (whether civil or criminal) for the enforcement of compliance with the terms of an order under section 9 or section 14 of the Competition Act 1991.[45]

(2) A person who contravenes (whether by act or omission) a provision of an order under section 9 or section 14 of the Competition Act 1991[45] for the time being in force shall be guilty of an offence under this section and shall be liable:

(*a*) on summary conviction, to a fine not exceeding £500 (together with, in the case of a continuing offence, a fine not exceeding £100 for every day on which the offence is continued) or, at the discretion of the court, to imprisonment for a term not exceeding 6 months, or to both such fine and such imprisonment; or

(*b*) on conviction on indictment, to a fine not exceeding £5,000 (together with, in the case of a continuing offence, a fine not exceeding £500 for every day on which the offence is continued) or, at the discretion of the court, to imprisonment for a term not exceeding 2 years, or to both such fine and such imprisonment.

41. Inserted by section 14(7) of the Competition Act 1991.
42. Article 34(4) of Bunreacht na hÉireann provides: 'No law shall be enacted excepting from the appellate jurisdiction of the Supreme Court cases which involve questions as to the validity of any law having regard to the provisions of this Constitution'
43. This is a substitute by section 26 of the Act of 1987.
44. Of the Act of 1978.
45. Section 14(7) of the Competition Act 1991 states that all references in section 12 and section 13 of the Act of 1978 to section 11 of the Act of 1978 shall be to section 14 of the Competition Act 1991.

A.4 (3)(*a*) Where a person is convicted of an offence under this section by reason of his failure, neglect or refusal to comply with a provision in an order requiring him to perform a specified act within a specified period or before a specified date, and the act remains, after the date of conviction, unperformed by him, the person shall be guilty of an offence and shall be liable on summary conviction to a fine not exceeding £100, or on conviction on indictment to a fine not exceeding £500, for each day, after the date of the first mentioned conviction, on which the act remains unperformed by him or, at the discretion of the court, to imprisonment for a term not exceeding 6 months.

(*b*) An offence under this section shall be a continuing offence and, accordingly, fresh proceedings in respect thereof may be taken from time to time.

(4) Every person who aids, abets or assists another person, or conspires with another person, to do anything (whether by way of act or of omission), the doing of which is an offence by virtue of subsection (2) or (3) shall himself be guilty of an offence under this section and shall be liable on conviction to the penalties specified in subsection (2) or (3).

(5)(*a*) Summary proceedings in relation to an offence under this section may be prosecuted by the Director;[47]

(*b*) Notwithstanding section 10(4) of the Petty Sessions (Ireland) Act 1851, summary proceedings for an offence under this section may be instituted within 12 months from the latest day on which the offence was committed.

(6) Where an offence under this section which is committed by a body corporate or by a person purporting to act on behalf of a body corporate or an unincorporated body of persons is proved to have been so committed with the consent or connivance of, or to be attributable to any neglect on the part of, any person who is a director, manager, secretary, member of the committee of management or other controlling authority of any such body, or who is any other similar officer of any such body, that person shall also be guilty of the offence and shall be liable to be preceded against and punished accordingly.

Application of certain statutory provisions relating to amalgamation

14.—(1) Nothing in the Companies Acts 1963 to 1990,[48] the Industrial and Provident Societies Acts 1893 to 1978,[49] the Building Societies Act 1989,[50] or the Friendly Societies Acts 1896 to 1978,[51] shall be construed as relieving an enterprise of the obligation to comply with section 5.

(2) An order under section 201 or 203 of the Companies Act 1963, shall not be

46. The words 'of the Director' were inserted by section 26 of the Act of 1987
47. Section 26(b) of the Act of 1987 inserted the 'Director' for the 'Minister'.
48. Section 1 of the Companies Act 1990 provides that all of the Companies Acts since 1963 shall be cited and construed together.
49. Section 1(2) of the Industrial and Provident Societies (Amendment) Act 1978 (No. 23) provides that the 1978 Act shall be read with earlier Acts.
50. Section 6 of the Building Societies Act 1989 (No. 17) repeals the Building Societies Act 1976 which Act was mentioned in the original 1978 version of this Act.
51. Section 8 of the Friendly Societies Act 1896 was supplemented by section 28 of the Insurance Act 1989 which refers to Council Directives 73/237/EEC and EC (Life Assurance) Regulations, 1984.

made in respect of a proposed amalgamation (being a proposed merger or takeover to which this Act applies) until either: **A.4**

(*a*) the Minister has stated in writing that he has decided not to make an order under section 9 in relation to the proposed amalgamation; or

(*b*) the Minister has stated in writing that he has made a conditional order in relation to the proposed amalgamation; or

(*c*) the relevant period within the meaning of section 6 has elapsed without the Minister's having made an order under section 9 in the relation to the proposed amalgamation,

whichever first occurs.

(3)(*a*) A copy of a special resolution under section 53 of the Act of 1893, providing for the amalgamation of, or the transfer of engagements between, two or more societies, registered under that Act (being a proposed merger or takeover to which this Act applies) shall not be registered under section 56 of the Act of 1893 until either:

(i) the Minister has stated in writing that he has decided not to make an order under section 9 in relation to the proposed amalgamation or transfer of engagements; or

(ii) the Minister has stated in writing that he has made a conditional order in relation to the proposed amalgamation or transfer of engagements; or

(iii) the relevant period within the meaning of section 6 has elapsed without the Minister's having made an order under section 9 in relation to the proposed amalgamation or transfer of engagements,

whichever first occurs.

(*b*) In this subsection 'the Act of 1893' means the Industrial and Provident Societies Act 1893.[49]

(4)(*a*) A copy of a special resolution under section 70 of the Act of 1896, providing for the amalgamation of, or the transfer of engagements between, two or more societies, registered under that Act (being a proposed merger or takeover to which this Act applies) shall not be registered under section 75 of the Act of 1896 until either:

(i) the Minister has stated in writing that he has decided not to make an order under section 9 in relation to the proposed amalgamation or transfer of engagements; or

(ii) the Minister has stated in writing that he has made a conditional order in relation to the proposed amalgamation or transfer of engagements; or

(iii) the relevant period within the meaning of section 6 has elapsed without the Minister's having made an order under section 9 in relation to the proposed amalgamation or transfer of engagements,

whichever first occurs.

(*b*) In this subsection 'the Act of 1896' means the Friendly Societies Act 1896.

(5)(*a*) A union of two or more societies which are registered under the Act of 1989,[52] a transfer of engagements between two such societies or an

52. The regulation of Building Societies was transferred from the Registrar of Building Societies to the Central Bank by the Building Societies Act 1989.

A.4

undertaking by one such society to fulfil the engagements of another such society (being in each case a proposed merger or takeover to which this Act applies) shall not be registered under Part X of the Building Societies Act 1989[53] until either:

(i) the Minister has stated in writing that he has decided not to make an order under section 9 in relation to the proposed union, transfer or undertaking; or

(ii) the Minister has stated in writing that he has made a conditional order in relation to the proposed union, transfer or undertaking; or

(iii) the relevant period within the meaning of section 6 has elapsed without the Minister having made an order under section 9 in relation to the proposed union, transfer or undertaking,

whichever first occurs.

(*b*) In this subsection 'the Act of 1989' means the Building Societies Act 1989.[50]

Annual Report by Minister

15.—(1) The Minister shall furnish to each House of the Oireachtas an annual report stating the number and the nature of investigations under section 8.

(2) It shall be lawful for the Minister to omit from an annual report under this section any information the publication of which would in his opinion materially injure the legitimate interests of an enterprise, if the information is not essential to the full understanding of the investigation to which it relates, and a statement indicating the general character of information so omitted shall be included in the report.

Amendment of Second Schedule to Act of 1972[54]

16.

Expenses

17. Any expenses incurred by the Minister in the administration of this Act shall to such extent as may be sanctioned by the Minister for Finance be paid out of monies provided by the Oireachtas.

Short Title

18.—(1) This Act may be cited as the Mergers, Takeovers and Monopolies (Control) Act 1978.

SCHEDULE

[This was repealed by section 17(6) of the Competition Act 1991]

53. Part X of Building Societies Act 1989 now governs amalgamations and transfers of engagements.
54. Section 22 of the Competition Act 1991 repeals all of the Act of 1972.

List of Statutory Instruments made pursuant to the Mergers, Take-Overs and Monopolies (Control) Act 1978

A.5

1. Mergers, Take-Overs and Monopolies (Newspapers) Order 1979 **(SI No. 17 of 1979)** [Removes thresholds for enterprises engaged in newspapers].

2. Proposed Merger or Take-Over Conditional Order 1981 **(SI No. 331 of 1981)** [prohibits merger or take-over by Smurfit Investments (Ireland) Ltd of Bedstone Ltd until the ownership of the right to publish the magazine 'Irish Business' is divested by Smurfit Investments (Ireland) Ltd].

3. Proposed Merger or Take-Over Conditional Order 1982 **(SI No. 130 of 1982)** [extension of 6 months within which Smurfit Investments (Ireland) Ltd may comply with the condition in SI No. 331 of 1981].

4. Proposed Merger or Take-Over Conditional Order 1981 (Revocation) Order 1982 **(SI No. 317 of 1982)** [revokes SI No. 331 of 1981 which allows Smurfit Investments (Ireland) Ltd to acquire Bedstone Ltd, the sole asset of which is the magazine 'Irish Business'].

5. Proposed Merger or Take-Over Conditional Order 1984 **(SI No. 217 of 1984)** [prohibition of merger or take-over involving Bank of Ireland and Irish Civil Service Building Society until rules of building society are changed in accordance with this statutory instrument].

6. Proposed Merger or Take-Over Conditional Order 1984 (Revocation) Order 1989 **(SI No. 220 of 1989)** [revokes SI No. 217 of 1984].

7. Mergers, Take-Overs and Monopolies (Control) Act 1978 (Section 2) Order 1985 **(SI No. 230 of 1985)** [increases thresholds in section 2 by substituting £5m. and £10m. for £1,250,000 and £2,500,000 and £6m. for £1,500,000.

8. Proposed Merger or Take-Over Prohibition Order 1988 **(SI No. 301 of 1988)** [prohibits merger or take-over involving GC & C Brands plc and Irish Distillers Group plc].

9. Proposed Merger or Take-Over Conditional Order 1988 **(SI No. 302 of 1988)** [prohibits merger or take-over involving Pernod Ricard and Irish Distillers Group plc except in certain conditions].

10. Proposed Merger or Take-Over Prohibition Order 1990 **(SI No. 42 of 1990)** [prohibits proposed merger or take-over involving British Steel plc and C. Walker & Sons (Holdings Ltd].

11. Proposed Merger or Take-Over Prohibition Order 1990 **(SI No. 93 of 1990)** [prohibits proposed merger or take-over involving Anglo-Irish Beef Processors and the undertaking of Master Meat Packers (Bandon) Ltd except in certain conditions].

12. Proposed Merger or Take-Over Conditional Order (No. 2) 1990 **(SI No. 94 of 1990)** [prohibits merger/take-over involving Anglo-Irish Beef Processors and DJS Meats Ltd].

13. Proposed Merger or Take-Over Prohibition Order 1990 **(SI No. 115 of 1990)** [revokes SI No. 42 of 1990 and allows proposed merger or take-over involving British Steel plc and C. Walker & Sons (Holdings Ltd].

14. Proposed Merger or Take-Over Prohibition Order 1992 **(SI No. 56 of 1992)**

A.5 [prohibits Independent Newspaper plc from increasing its shareholding in Tribune Group from 29.9% to 53.09%].

15. Mergers, Take-Overs and Monopolies (Control) Act 1978 (Section 2) Order 1993 (**SI No. 135 of 1993**) [substitutes £10m. and £20m. and £10m. respectively as inserted by SI No. 230 of 1985].

Mergers, Takeovers and Monopolies (Control) Act 1978
Notifications under Section 5
[Notice published by Department of Enterprise and Employment]

The following note sets out, in general terms, the information needed in order to examine a proposed merger or takeover requiring to be notified under Section 5(1) of the above Act.

(1) Details of each of the enterprises to be involved in the proposal including ownership, current activities/numbers employed and financial performance in recent years.

Note: In the case of public companies such information may be contained in annual report and accounts.

(2) Details of the proposed transaction including means of control (share, asset acquisition etc.), consideration involved and period within which transaction is to take place.

Note: Copy of draft legal contract (or offer document in the case of publicly-quoted companies) will generally suffice for this purpose.

(3) Estimated national market share of each of the enterprises involved in the sector(s) in which they are engaged and details of any further acquisitions which may be planned by them in these or any other sector(s) in the foreseeable future.

(4) Reasons for the proposal insofar as each of the enterprises involved is concerned.

(5) Details of any changes planned in the operation of any of the enterprises as a result of the proposal (e.g. change of product or production methods, management practices, purchase/distribution patterns, level of employment, terms and conditions of employees or geographical location).

(6) Details of any other agreement (e.g. option purchase, exclusive dealing) which is being entered into in conjunction with, or at the same time as, the proposal.

Where non-Irish enterprises are involved:

- Details of any legal sanctions or clearances which may be necessary in other jurisdictions in relation to the proposal.
- Details of any investigations or prosecutions instituted in respect of the enterprise(s) concerned by other national authorities in relation to antitrust or other competition law matters.

Full disclosure, on the basis set out above, will normally be sufficient to allow a notified proposal to be examined without a formal request for information as provided for under Section 5(2) of the Act. However, emphasis on the various points obviously vary from case to case and different issues may well arise in individual instances.

Notifying parties should, of course, feel free to submit any other information which is felt to have a bearing on the case or which is considered relevant, particularly in relation to the criteria scheduled in the Act.

PART IV
Acquiring Transactions

Interpretation

74.— In this Chapter,

"acquiring transactions" shall be construed in accordance with section 75;

"prescribed percentage" means 10 per cent of the total shares or of the total voting rights attaching to shares.

Application

75.—(1) This Chapter applies to the following transactions (in this Part referred to as "acquiring transactions"):

(*a*) any acquisition by a person or more than one person acting in concert of shares or other interest in a holder of a licence but does not apply to an acquisition where—

(i) if after the proposed acquisition the proportion of shares would not exceed the prescribed percentage, and

(ii) if the holder of the licence concerned as a body incorporated in the State, the acquisition, together with any other interest already held or controlled (either directly or indirectly) by the acquiring person or persons, would not confer a right to appoint or remove some or all of the board of directors or committee of management of the holder of that licence;

(*b*) any acquisition by the holder of a licence of shares or other interest in any other undertaking or business (whether or not the undertaking or business is controlled by another holder of a licence) but does not apply to an acquisition where either—

(i) the acquisition relates to an undertaking or business outside the State and is made by a holder of a licence which is incorporated outside the State, or

(ii) after such acquisition, the proportion of shares in the undertaking or business concerned would not exceed the prescribed percentage and the acquisition, together with any other interest already held or controlled (either directly or indirectly) by the holder of the licence so acquiring, would not confer a right to appoint or remove some or all of the board of directors or committee of management of that undertaking or business.

(2) The Bank may, subject to such conditions as it sees fit, exempt an acquiring transaction, or any class of acquiring transaction, from the requirements of this Chapter where it is satisfied that—

(*a*) the acquiring transaction is being, or has been entered into, by a holder of a licence as part of the bona fide underwriting of a share issue, or

(*b*) the interest in shares is not being beneficially acquired by a holder of a licence as or is being acquired only in the course of its normal business to secure the issue of a loan to be made by the holder of the undertaking or business concerned.

Limitation on validity of acquiring transactions

76.— An acquiring transaction shall only be valid where it is entered into within 12 months after—

(*a*) the Bank has given its approval in writing to the transaction, or

(*b*) the relevant period within the meaning of section 83 has elapsed without the Bank refusing its approval to the transaction.

and, accordingly, any purported acquiring transaction which does not comply with either paragraph (*a*) or (*b*) shall be invalid and—

(i) title to any shares or other interest concerned shall not pass, and

(ii) any consequential purported exercise of powers shall be void.

Consent of Minister to certain acquiring transactions required

77.—(1) Where—

(*a*) the holder of a licence proposes to participate in an acquiring transaction and that holder controls, or would control as a consequence of the proposed transaction, whether alone or with any subsidiary or associated company, not less than 20 per cent of the total assets in the State of all holders of licences, or

(*b*) a person proposes to participate in an acquiring transaction which involves the acquisition of shares or other interest in a holder of a licence which controls, whether alone with any subsidiary or associated company, not less than 20 per cent of the total assets in the State of all holders of licences,

then the Bank shall neither give nor refuse to give its approval without the prior consent of the Minister.

(2) The Minister shall not give his consent under subsection (1) unless—

(*a*) he is satisfied that the Bank's proposal to give or refuse to give its approval, as the case may be, would be in the interests of the orderly and proper regulation of banking, and

(*b*) where the proposed acquiring transaction is of such a nature that the provisions of the Mergers, Takeovers and Monopolies (Control) Act 1978, apply, he has consulted with—

(i) the Minister for Industry and Commerce, and

(ii) such other Minister of the Government appearing to the Minister to be concerned,

and he shall refuse to give his consent where he considers that the exigencies of the common good so warrant.

(3) A consent by the Minister to a proposal of the Bank to approve a proposed acquiring transaction shall be subject to the imposition by the Bank of conditions (being such conditions, if any, which in the opinion of the Minister are necessary for the orderly and proper regulation of banking) as the Minister may specify in the consent.

Requirement on bank before refusal to approve acquiring transaction

78.—(1) Subject to subsection (2), the Bank shall not refuse its approval to a proposed acquiring transaction unless it is satisfied that the transaction would not be in the interests of the orderly and proper regulation of banking.

A.7 (2) In the case of a proposed acquiring transaction to which section 77 relates, the Bank shall refuse its approval—

(*a*) where the proposal of the Bank is to refuse to give its approval and the Minister consents to that proposal, or

(*b*) where the proposal of the Bank is to give its approval and the Minister refuses to consent to that proposal.

Alteration of prescribed percentage

79.—(1) The Minister may, where he is satisfied after consultation with the Bank that it would be in the interest of the orderly and proper regulation of banking, by order amend the definition of "prescribed percentage" in section 74 by altering the percentage amount therein specified including an amount for the time being so specified by virtue of this section.

(2) Whenever an order is proposed to be made under subsection (1) a draft of that order shall be laid before each House of the Oireachtas and the order shall not be made until a resolution approving of the draft has been passed by each such House.

Conditions no approval of proposed acquiring transaction

80.—(1) An approval given by the Bank to a proposed acquiring transaction shall be subject to such conditions, if any, as the Bank—

(*a*) may impose (being conditions which in the opinion of the Bank are necessary for the orderly and proper regulation of banking), and

(*b*) shall impose (being conditions specified by the Minister under section 77).

(2) The Bank may, at any time, amend or revoke a condition with, in the case of a condition to which subsection (1)(b) relates, the consent of the Minister.

Right of purported vendor to damages

81.—Where a purported acquiring transaction is rendered invalid under section 76, the purported vendor of shares shall be entitled, in any court of competent jurisdiction, to recover from the purported purchaser any damages the purported vendor suffers by reason only of the invalidity, unless the purported purchaser satisfies such court that before the purported transaction he had notified the purported vendor of circumstances relating to the purported transaction which gave rise to the possibility of such an invalidity.

Notification of proposed acquiring transactions to bank

82.—(1) Where an acquiring transaction is proposed, each of the undertakings involved and having knowledge of the existence of the proposal shall notify the Bank in writing of the proposal as soon as may be.

(2) Where, having received a notification under this section from any of the undertakings involved, the Bank is of opinion that in order to consider for the purposes of this Chapter a proposed acquiring transaction it requires further information it may, within one month of the date of receipt by it of a notification, request such further information in writing from any one or ore of the undertakings concerned.

(3)(*a*) Where there is a contravention of subsection (1) the person in control of an undertaking failing to notify the Bank shall be guilty of an offence and shall be liable—

(i) on summary conviction, to a fine not exceeding £1,000 or, at the discretion of the court, to imprisonment for a term not exceeding 12 months, or to both, or

(ii) on conviction on indictment, to a fine not exceeding £50,000 or, at the discretion of the court, to imprisonment for a term not exceeding 5 years, or to both.

(*b*) For the purposes of this subsection the person in control of the undertaking shall, in the case of an incorporated body or an unincorporated body, be any officer of the body concerned who knowingly and willingly authorises or permits the contravention. **A.7**

Relevant period for purpose of sections 76, 86 and 88

83.—For the purposes of sections 76, 86 and 88, the relevant period in relation to a particular acquiring transaction shall, subject to section 82(2), be—

(*a*) where the Minister's consent is required by virtue of section 77 to a proposal of the Bank to approve or not to approve the transaction, the period of 6 months, and

(*b*) in every other case, the period of 3 months,

such period beginning on the date on which the Bank first receives a notification under section 82 or, where the Bank requests further information from an undertaking concerned under section 82, the date of receipt by the Bank of such information.

Inquiries by bank

84.—(1) The Bank may carry out such inquiries and obtain such information as it considers necessary to enable it to consider the proposed acquiring transaction.

(2) Where the provisions of section 77 apply, the Minister may require the Bank to carry out such inquiries and provide him with such information as he considers necessary to enable him to decide or give or not to give his consent for the purposes of that section.

(3) Any person who wilfully and knowingly impedes the Bank's inquiries under this section or provides false or misleading information shall be guilty of an offence and shall be liable—

(*a*) on summary conviction, to a fine not exceeding £1,000 or, at the discretion of the court, to imprisonment for a term not exceeding 12 months, or to both, or

(*b*) on conviction on indictment, to a fine not exceeding £50,000 or, at the discretion of the court, to imprisonment for a term not exceeding 5 years, or to both.

Communication of bank's approval or refusal to approve

85.—(1) Where the Bank approves or approves subject to conditions or refuses to approve a proposed acquiring transaction, it shall communicate the approval and conditions (if any) or the refusal, as the case may be, to the undertakings concerned which had notified the Bank of the proposal under section 82 and, where such a communication is not in writing, the Bank shall confirm in writing the approval or refusal to approve, as the case may be, as soon as possible thereafter.

(2) Where the Bank refuses to approve the proposed acquiring transaction, it shall state its reasons in writing and, subject to section 16, shall send them to the persons concerned as soon as possible thereafter.

Appeal to High Court against refusal, etc., of bank

86.—(1) Where the Bank communicates with an undertaking concerned in accordance with section 85 that it—

(*a*) refuses to give its approval, or

(*b*) gives its approval subject to conditions,

an appeal on a point of law may be made by the undertaking to the Court against the refusal or approval, as the case may be, within one month of that refusal or approval being so communicated.

A.7 (2) Where the Court allows the appeal it shall direct the Bank to make a new decision in accordance with the Court's determination and the Bank shall made its decision within the relevant period beginning on the date of the Court's determination and, in a case to which section 77 relates, consult with the Minister before making its decision.

(3) Where on an appeal under this section the Minister requests to be made a party to the proceedings, the Court shall order that he shall be added as a party.

(4) Where any costs are incurred by the Minister in connection with an appeal under this section, the Court may make such order as it considers just as to the payment of those costs by other parties to the proceedings.

(5) Where the Court is satisfied, because of the nature or the circumstances of the case or otherwise in the interests of justice, that it is desirable, the whole or any part of proceedings under this section may be heard otherwise than in public.

(6) An appeal against a decision of the Court under this section shall not lie to the Supreme Court.

(7) In this section "Court" means the High Court.

Contravention of approval, etc.

87.—(1) Where an acquiring transaction is entered into subsequent to approval being given by the Bank, any person who contravenes (whether by act or omission) the approval or any condition of the approval shall be guilty of an offence and shall be liable—

(*a*) on summary conviction, to a fine not exceeding £1,000 or, at the discretion of the court, to imprisonment for a term not exceeding 12 months, or to both, or

(*b*) on conviction on indictment, to a fine not exceeding £50,000 or, at the discretion of the court, to imprisonment for a term not exceeding 5 years, or to both.(2) Where a person is convicted of an offence under this section by reason of his failure, neglect or refusal to comply with a condition of the approval requiring him to perform a specified act within a specified period or before a specified date, and the act remains, after the date of the conviction, unperformed by him, the person shall be guilty of contravening this section on every day on which the contravention continues after that conviction and for each such offence he shall be liable on summary conviction to a fine not exceeding £100 or on conviction on indictment to a fine not exceeding £5,000.

(3) Notwithstanding the paragraph numbered 4 of section 10 of the Petty Sessions (Ireland) Act 1851, summary proceedings for an offence under this section may be instituted within 12 months from—

(*a*)in the case of an offence to which subsection (1)(a) relates, the latest day on which the offence was committed, and

(*b*)in the case of an offence to which subsection (2) relates, the day on which the offence was committed.

Application of certain other enactments

88.—(1) Nothing in any other enactment shall be construed as relieving a holder of a licence or other person or any obligation of his to comply with section 82.

(2) An order under section 201 or 203 of the Companies Act 1963, in respect of a

proposed amalgamation or under section 33 of the Act of 1971 in respect of a proposed transfer of business of a holder of a licence (being in each case an acquiring transaction) shall not be made until the Bank has given its approval to the acquiring transaction or the relevant period referred to in section 83 has elapsed without the Bank having given or refused to give such approval. A.7

Notes:
(a) This form must be accompanied by an Annex containing the information specified in the attached note 'Information to be annexed to form CA'.
(b) This form must also be accompanied by the relevant notification fee (£100).
(c) Please complete the enclosed Acknowledgement of Receipt.
(d) If space is insufficient on this form, please use extra pages, specifying clearly the relevant items on the form.

Competition Authority
Irish Life Centre
Talbot Street
Dublin 1

Form CA

Notification under section 7 of the Competition Act, 1991 to the Competition Authority of an agreement, decision or concerted practice for the purpose of obtaining a certificate under section 4(4) or a licence under section 4(2).

Purpose of notification

1. State whether the notification is for the purpose of obtaining (Please tick appropriate box)

    a certificate only (section 4(4)) ☐

    a licence only (section 4(2)) ☐

    a certificate or, in the event of refusal by the Authority to issue a certificate, a licence ☐

Identity of the party/parties

2. Full name and address, telephone, telex and telefax numbers, and brief description of the undertaking(s) or association(s) of undertakings on whose behalf the notification is submitted.

3. Where a notification is submitted by a representative of the undertaking(s) concerned, the name, address and position of the representative must be given. Where notification is submitted by or on behalf of more than one person they should appoint a joint representative.

Form CA (continued) **A.8**

4. Full name and address and brief description of any other parties to the agreement, decision or concerted practice (hereinafter referred to as 'the arrangements').

5. State what steps have been taken to inform these other parties of this notification.

(This information is not necessary in respect of standard contracts which an undertaking submitting the notification has concluded or intends to conclude with a number of parties (e.g. a contract appointing dealers)).

Brief description of arrangements

6. Give a brief description of the arrangements, e.g. nature, purpose and duration. (Full details must be annexed to this form).

Declaration and Signature(s)

7. The undersigned declare that the information given above and in the pages annexed hereto is correct to the best of their knowledge and belief, that all estimates are identified as such and are their best estimates of the underlying facts and that all the opinions expressed are sincere.

Date: ....

Signature(s): ....

....

A.8 Form CA (continued)

....

Competition Authority
Irish Life Centre
Talbot Street
Dublin 1

ACKNOWLEDGEMENT OF RECEIPT OF NOTIFICATION AND FEE

Part 1
(To be completed by person submitting notification)
Name and address to which acknowledgement is to be sent

Your notification under section 7 of the Competition Act 1991 concerning:

Arrangements relating to ....

Parties:

1. ....

2. .... and other

(There is no need to name the other undertakings party to the arrangements here)

Your Reference: ....

Part 2
(To be completed by the Authority)

was received on: ...., together with fee of £.......................

and registered under No. ....

Please quote this number in all correspondence

Signed: ______________________
Secretary

Information to be annexed to Form CA

Introduction

Further information is to be given under the following headings and reference numbers. Wherever possible, give exact information. If this is not readily available, give your best estimate, and identify what you give as an estimate. If you believe any detail asked for is unavailable or irrelevant, please explain why. This may, in particular, be the case if one party is notifying arrangements alone without the cooperation of other parties. Officials of the Authority are available to discuss what detail is relevant, and to give guidance in preparing the notification.

1. *Market*

The nature of the goods or services affected by the arrangements or behaviour. A brief description of the structure of the market (or markets) for these goods or services — e.g. who sells in it, who buys in it, its geographical extent, market turnover, how competitive it is, whether it is easy for new suppliers to enter the market, whether there are substitute products. If you are notifying a standard contract (e.g. a contract appointing dealers), say how many you expect to conclude. If you know of any studies of the market, it would be helpful to refer to them.

2. *Details of the party or parties*

2.1 Do any of the parties form part of a group of companies? A group relationship is deemed to exist where a firm:

— owns more than half the capital or business assets, or
— has the power to exercise more than half the voting rights, or
— has the power to appoint more than half the members of the board of directors or bodies legally representing the undertaking, or
— has the right to manage the affairs of another.

If the answer is yes, give:

— the name and address of the ultimate parent company,
— a brief description of the business of the group (and one copy of the latest set of group accounts),
— the name and address of any other company in the group competing in a market affected by the arrangements or in any related market, that is to say any other company competing directly or indirectly with the parties ('relevant associated company').

2.2 The most recently available total turnover of each of the parties and, as the case may be, of the group of which it forms part (attach one copy of the latest set of accounts).

2.3 The sales or turnover of each party in the goods or services affected by the arrangements in the State. Provide the same figures for any relevant associated company.

A.8 [Information to be annexed to Form CA continued]

2.4 In relation to the market (or markets) for the goods or services described at para. 1 above, give, for each of the sales or turnover figures in para. 2.3, your estimate of the market share it represents.

2.5 If you have a substantial interest falling short of control (more than 25% but less than 50%) in some other company competing in a market affected by the arrangements, or if some other such company has a substantial interest in yours, give its name and address and brief details.

3. *Full details of the arrangements*

3.1 If the contents are in writing give a brief description of the purpose of the arrangements and attach a copy of the text.

If the contents are not, or are only partially, in writing, give a full description.

3.2 Detail any provisions contained in the arrangements which may restrict the parties in their freedom to take independent commercial decisions, for example regarding:

- — buying or selling prices, discounts or other trading conditions;
- — the quantities of goods to be manufactured or distributed or services to be offered;
- — technical development or investment;
- — the choice of markets or sources of supply;
- — purchases from or sales to third parties;
- — whether to apply similar terms for the supply of equivalent goods or services;
- — whether to offer different goods or services separately or together.

4. *Arguments in support of request for the issuing of a certificate*

Explain why the arrangements do not have the object or effect of preventing, restricting or distorting competition in the State or in any part of the State.

5. *Arguments in support of request for the granting of a licence*

Explain how the arrangements

(a) contribute to improving the production or distribution of goods or the provision of services or to promoting technical or economic progress,

(b) allow consumers a fair share of the resulting benefit,

(c) do not impose on the undertakings concerned terms which are not indispensable to the attainment of those objectives,

(d) do not afford undertakings the possibility of eliminating competition in respect of a substantial part of the products or services in question.

[Information to be annexed to Form CA continued] **A.8**

6. *Other Information*

6.1 Have the arrangements been the subject of a notification to, or in any other proceedings before, the European Commission in connection with Articles 85 and 86 of the Treaty establishing the European Economic Community'? If so, please give details.

6.2 Have the arrangements been the subject of any competition law proceedings involving a national authority or Court in any other EC Member State? If so, please give details.

6.3 Are you aware of any EC Decisions, block exemption regulations or notices, or EC Court judgments relevant to this notification? If so, please give details.

6.4 Give any other information that you think would he helpful in enabling the Authority to assess the arrangements.

A.8

Form CA
EXPLANATORY NOTE

Introduction

This note has been prepared for the assistance of persons who wish to submit a notification under the Competition Act, 1991 to the Competition Authority. It does not purport to be a legal interpretation of the relevant provisions of the Act and has no binding force.

Any undertaking which is uncertain about how to complete a notification or wishing further explanation may contact the Competition Authority.

Anti-Competitive Agreements

The Competition Act came into operation on 1 October 1991. The purpose of the provisions in the Act on anti-competitive agreements is to prevent the distortion of competition in the State or in any part of the State; they apply to any undertaking engaged for gain in the production, supply or distribution of goods or the provision of a service within the State. Section 4(1) of the Competition Act prohibits and renders void anti-competitive agreements, decisions or concerted practices (referred to in this Note as arrangements). There is a right of action in the Courts which may be brought by aggrieved persons in respect of prohibited arrangements. Section 4(2) gives the Competition Authority power to issue a licence exempting arrangements with beneficial effects from the prohibition. In addition, the Competition Authority is empowered, under section 4(4), to issue a certificate stating that an arrangement does not offend against section 4(1). (The text of sections 4(1), (2) and (4) is reproduced in the Annex to this note). In order to obtain a licence or certificate, the arrangements must be notified to the Competition Authority, established by the Act. Notification should be made on Form CA which is enclosed.

Issue of a certificate under section 4(4)

The purpose of the procedure for the issue of a certificate is to allow undertakings to ascertain whether or not the Authority considers that any of their arrangements or behaviour are prohibited under section 4(1) of the Competition Act. Clearance takes the form of a decision by the Authority certifying that in its opinion, on the basis of the facts in its possession, a notified agreement, decision or concerted practice does not offend against section 4(1).

Issue of a licence under section 4(2)

The purpose of the procedure for the issue of a licence under section 4(2) is to allow undertakings to enter into arrangements which, in fact, offer economic advantages but which, without a licence, would be prohibited under section 4(1). Section 8 requires the Authority to specify the period of validity of any such licence, allows the Authority to attach conditions and provides for licences to be amended or revoked in certain circumstances, notably if the licences were based on incorrect or misleading information or if there is any material change in the facts.

[Form CA Explanatory Note continued] **A.8**

The Act makes a distinction between agreements which were in existence at the commencement of section 4(1) and agreements coming into existence after 1 October 1991. Existing agreements must be notified to the Authority within one year, i.e. before I October 1992. In the case of such an agreement, it is provided that no legal action under section 6 may be brought against the agreement concemed while the notification is under consideration by the Authority (or by the Court in respect of any appeal under section 9).

New agreements may be notified at any time, including before they come into effect. Early notification is recommended, since a licence for a new agreement may be made retrospective to the date of notification.

Besides permitting arrangements which would otherwise be prohibited and void under section 4(1), a licence ensures that, while it is in force, an aggrieved party shall not be entitled to damages in respect of any action under section 6.

Purpose of the Form

The purpose of Form CA is to allow undertakings, or associations of undertakings, to notify the Authority of arrangements and to request a certificate under section 4(4), or a licence to exempt such arrangements from the prohibition of section 4(1) of the Act by virtue of section 4(2). The form allows undertakings notifying to apply for a certificate, or for a licence, or for a licence failing the grant of a certificate.

Notification should be made on Form CA. The notification must be accompanied by the relevant fee. (£100)

A notification may be made by any undertaking(s) party to the arrangements being notified. It is not necessary that the consent of any other parties be obtained prior to notification although they should be informed of the notification.

The form consists of a single sheet calling for the identity of the parties concerned and a brief description of the arrangements. This must be supplemented by further information given under the headings and references detailed in the accompanying Note — 'Information to be annexed to Form CA'. The paper used should be A4 (the same size as the form). Leave a margin of at least 25mm or one inch on the left-hand side of the page and, if you use both sides, on the right-hand side of the reverse.

The need for complete and accurate information

It is important that the notification contain all the relevant facts. Any decision taken on the basis of materially incorrect or misleading information could lead to revocation of the certificate, or to revocation or amendment of the licence. For the same reason, it is also important to inform the Authority of any material changes to your arrangements made after your notification.

The key words are 'materially incorrect or misleading information'. It often remains, however, a matter of judgment how much detail is relevant; the Authority accepts estimates where accurate information is not readily available in order to facilitate notifications, and the Authority calls for opinions as well as facts.

It is important to note that the party or parties notifying have a responsibility for adequately justifying their case for the issue of a certificate or licence, by demonstrating that the arrangements or behaviour either do not prevent, restrict or distort competition, or, if they do so, they satisfy all the requirements of section 4(2). In this

A.8 [Form CA Explanatory Note continued]

regard, notifying parties might find it helpful to refer to appropriate decisions, block exemptions or notices of the EC Commission in respect of cases involving Article 85 of the Treaty establishing the European Community (upon which sections 4(1) and (2) are closely based), and to any relevant judgments by the Court of Justice.

Procedure subsequent to Notification

The notification is registered by the Competition Authority. The date of receipt by the Authority is the effective date of notification. The notification might be considered invalid if obviously incomplete or not on Form CA. A receipt will be issued for the notification fee, which will also serve as an acknowledgement of the notification.

A list of notifications will be published by the Competition Authority. Further information or observations might be sought from notifying parties or from third parties. The Authority might suggest amendments to the arrangements which would make them acceptable.

In addition the Authority may accept such observations or submissions from persons claiming to be interested as it may think proper.

Secrecy

The work of the Competition Authority in considering requests for a licence or a certificate will normally involve a detailed examination of the circumstances of each case. The matters to be considered include the likely effects of the arrangements on competition in the market in question, whether the arrangements are likely to contribute to technical or economic progress and the likely effects on consumers. It is, therefore, to be expected that the information required by the Authority to enable it to carry out its functions will in many cases include information which is commercially sensitive. In this connection, attention is drawn to the provisions of paragraph 9 of the Schedule of the Competition Act which prohibits the improper disclosure of information obtained pursuant to the Act and provides for penalties.

When granting a licence or a certificate, the Authority is required under section 4(6) to publish notice of the decision, including the terms, date and reasons therefore, in *Iris Oifigiúil*. This will involve the disclosure of certain information contained in the notification or obtained subsequently. Attention is also drawn to section 7(5) of the Act which empowers the Authority to 'accept such observations or submissions from persons claiming to be interested as it may think proper'. To facilitate this, the Authority may make available to such parties a summary of the notification.

In preparing the notice or summary, the Authority will have due regard to matters covered by commercial confidentiality. Any information, the disclosure of which to other parties might be harmful to the notifying parties, should be included in a second annex, with each page clearly marked 'Business Secrets' (with appropriate cross-references to the principal annex). The second annex should also contain a statement of the reasons for seeking confidentiality for the information concerned. Before making available to any third party a summary of a notification, a copy of the proposed text will be shown to the undertakings concerned.

Annex

Text of sections 4(1), (2) and (4) of the Competition Act, 1991

4. (1) Subject to the provisions of this section, all agreements between undertakings, decisions by associations of undertakings and concerted practices which have as their object or effect the prevention, restnction or distortion of competition in trade in any goods or services in the State or in any part of the State are prohibited and void, including in particular, without prejudice to the generality of this subsection, those which:—

(a) directly or indirectly fix purchase or selling prices or any other trading conditions;

(b) limit or control production, markets, technical development or investment;

(c) share markets or sources of supply;

(d) apply dissimilar conditions to equivalent transactions with other trading parties thereby placing them at a competitive disadvantage;

(e) make the conclusion of contracts subject to acceptance by the other parties of supplementary obligations which by their nature or according to commercial usage have no connection with the subject of such contracts.

(2) The Competition Authority established by this Act ('the Authority') may in accordance with section 8 grant a licence for the purposes of this section in the case of—

(a) any agreement or category of agreements,

(b) any decision or category of decisions,

(c) any concerted practice or category of concerted practices,

which in the opinion of the Authority, having regard to all relevant market conditions, contributes to improving the production or distribution of goods or provision of services or to promoting technical or economic progress, while allowing consumers a fair share of the resulting benefit and which does not—

(i) impose on the undertakings concerned terms which are not indispensable to the attainment of those objectives;

(ii) afford undertakings the possibility of eliminating competi-tion in respect of a subitantial part of the products or services in question

(4) The Authority may certify that in its opinion, on the basis of the facts in its possession, an agreement, decision or concerted practice notified under section 7 does not offend against subsection (1)

A.9

Procedures of the Competition Authority under s. 4

[Chapter 3 of 'A Guide to Irish Legislation on Competition']*

Introduction

3.1 The primary function of the Competition Authority under the Competition Act is to decide upon notifications of agreements, decisions of associations and concerted practices under section 4 of the Act. The Authority may issue a certificate of negative clearance or a licence of exemption. Conversely, the Authority may refuse a request for a certificate or for a licence. The Competition Act gives power to the Authority to devise its own procedures. The Minister may prescribe procedures for the carrying out of the Authority's functions under the Act. Each such regulation must be laid before each House of the Oireachtas and is subject to negative resolution. The Authority has devised procedures for dealing with notifications and so far there has been no need for the Minister to make regulations.

Notification—Requirements and Benefits

3.2 Section 7(1) of the Act provides that every agreement, decision and concerted practice of a kind described in section 4(1) which comes into existence after 1 October 1991, in respect of which the parties involved request a licence or certificate, shall be notified to the Authority. In the case of arrangements which were in effect before the Act came into force, section 7(2) provides that they may be notified within one year of that date, i.e. by 30 September 1992. No action may be taken against such an 'old' arrangement under section 6 which has been duly notified, until such time as the Authority has decided whether or not to grant a certificate or licence and any Court appeal against such a decision has been concluded. An arrangement concluded after 1 October 1991 does not receive such protection on notification, although a licence may be made retrospective to the date of notification.

3.3 A licence or certificate cannot he granted until an arrangement has been notified to the Authority (section 7(3)) (but see para 3.31 on category licences). A certificate is a statement that, in the opinion of the Authority, an agreement is not in breach of section 4(1). A certificate may be challenged in the Courts (section 6(5)(a)), but a claimant is not entitled to damages in respect of a breach of section 4(1), for the period during which the certificate was in force (section 6(6)). A licence, while it is in force, permits actions which would otherwise be prohibited and void (section 4(3)(a)). A licence shall have effect in accordance with its terms, subject to any amendment including conditions inserted when a licence is amended under section 8(3).

Pre-Notification Stage

3.4 There may be pre-notification contacts with the Authority by persons seeking information and advice. The staff may provide general information about the Act, notification

*This is an extracted chapter, Chapter 3 of 'A Guide to Irish Legislation on Competition', which was published by the Government Publications Service and prepared by the Competition Authority.

and Authority procedures. No views can be given, however, about an individual arrangement, or whether it should be notified or not. The Authority cannot deal with suspected infringements, unless an arrangement has been notified. The Authority cannot offer views on whether a private action under section 6 should be brought in any case. A.9

3.5 The Authority makes available on request the notification form, Form CA, and an Explanatory Note. (These are reproduced in the Annex*). While the staff can give guidance, they cannot help people to complete Form CA. Responsibility for completing the notification, making sure it is complete, truthful and valid, and providing the necessary reasoning, lies with notifying parties and their representatives. Where undertakings have a large number of identical agreements, only one need be notified, and the licence, if granted, may cover the category of those agreements.

Notification Procedures

3.6 A notification is made by submitting a completed Form CA together with the detailed supplementary information required. It must be accompanied by the fee for each notification, which is currently £100. Form CA is based on the comparable form (A/B) used by the EEC Commission. Form CA itself seeks certain basic information such as the identity of the parties and a brief description of the arrangements. Notification may be made requesting a certificate only, a licence only, or a licence if a certificate is refused.

3.7 The further information which must be annexed to the Form is more comprehensive. This seeks from the applicant a full description of the arrangements being notified, whether they have been reduced to writing or not, a full description of the economic setting in which the arrangements exist as well as certain other relevant information. The following specific matters must be covered:—

(a) The market—the nature of the goods or services involved. A description of the structure of the market, e.g. who sells in it, who buys in it, its geographical extent, market turnover, how competitive it is, whether it is easy for new suppliers to enter the market, whether there are substitute products.

(b) Details of the parties involved, including parent and subsidiary companies, i.e. accounts, turnover and estimates of market shares. Interests involving less than control of other relevant companies must also be disclosed.

(c) Full details of the arrangements—a description of the arrangements and a complete copy of any written agreement; if the contents are not, or are only partially, in writing, a full description is required; any provisions which may restrict freedom to take independent commercial decisions should be outlined.

(d) Arguments in support of the request for a licence or certificate.

(e) Other information—have the arrangements been notified to the EC, or been the subject of any proceedings, under Articles 85 and 86; or the subject of any competition law proceedings in a national court of a Member State; draw attention to any relevant EC decisions, block exemption regulations or notices, or EC Court judgments.

3.8 Where there is genuine doubt about whether an arrangement is caught by section 4(1), or where firms consider that an anti-competitive arrangement has benefits which merit an exemption from the prohibition, notification to the Authority is the appropriate course.

**Editor's Note*: These are set out in this book in Annex A.8.

A.9 3.9 When a notification is received, it is checked to see if the main documents are present—Form CA, the annex, the agreement and the fee. The effective date of a valid notification is the date on which the completed Form CA, together with all relevant accompanying documents and the appropriate fee, are received by the Authority.

Requests for Information and Investigations

3.10 Each month the Authority publishes a list of the notifications it has received in a daily newspaper. This notice simply gives the notification number, the names of the parties and the type of agreement involved, e.g. a distribution agreement. It invites any third parties who may wish to do so to submit observations on the agreements. The Authority will not supply any further information concerning a notified agreement to any third party at this time.

3.11 After being allocated to a member of the Authority, each notification is examined for completeness and accuracy. If additional information or explanation is required, it is requested in writing or at a meeting with the parties, and, in all cases, the notifying parties are informed that consideration of the case has commenced. The Authority has various powers to obtain information. The principle of proportionality suggests that no more onerous a procedure should be adopted than is strictly necessary. It should, therefore, seldom prove necessary to invoke the Authority's formal investigatory powers:

— to summon witnesses and examine them on oath,

— to appoint authorised officers to carry out investigations.

3.12 Should information not be submitted on request, or should a party refuse a request to attend a meeting, the Authority must decide whether to invoke its formal powers. Under para 7(1) of the Schedule to the Competition Act 1991, the Authority may do all or any of the following things:

(a) summon witnesses to attend before it,

(b) examine on oath (which any member is hereby authorised to administer) the witnesses attending before it,

(c) require any such witness to produce to the Authority any document in his power or control.

3.13 Under para 7(2), a witness before the Authority is entitled to the same immunities and privileges as if he were a witness before the High Court. Under para 7(3), a summons shall be signed by at least one member. According to para 7(4), a person summoned who refuses to attend, take an oath, produce a document, answer a question, etc., is guilty of an offence, and may be fined up to £1,000 or imprisoned for up to six months, or both.

3.14 In addition to the power to summon witnesses, there is the power of the Authority to appoint authorised officers, with the consent of the Minister, under section 20.

3.15 Section 21 provides that an authorised officer may, on production of a warrant issued by a Judge of the District Court,

(a) enter and inspect premises at or vehicles in or by means of which any activity in connection with the business of supplying or distributing goods or providing a service, or in connection with the organisation or assistance of persons engaged in any such business, is carried on,

(b) require the person who carries on such activity and any persons employed in connection therewith to produce to the authorised officer any books, documents or records relating to such activity which are in that person's power or control, and to give to the authorised officer such information as he may reasonably require in regard to any entries in such books, documents and records, **A.9**

(c) inspect and copy or take extracts from any such books documents and records,

(d) require a person mentioned in paragraph (b) to give to the authorised officer any information he may require in regard to the persons carrying on such activity (including in particular, in the case of an unincorporated body of persons, information in regard to the membership thereof and its committee of management or other controlling authority) or employed in connection therewith,

(e) require a person mentioned in paragraph (b) to give to the authorised officer any information which the officer may reasonably require in regard to such activity.

3.16 The Judge of the District Court may issue a warrant if he is satisfied by information on oath that it is proper to do so. Any person who obstructs or impedes an authorised officer, or who does not comply with a requirement under section 21, is guilty of an offence, and is liable, on summary conviction, to a fine of up to £1,000 or imprisonment for up to 12 months, or both a fine and imprisonment.

3.17 If it is considered necessary, the Authority will decide that an investigation by authorised officers is required, including an unannounced 'dawn raid'. Having obtained the approval of the Minister for the appointment of an authorised officer, a warrant must be issued by a District Court Judge. The authorised officers visit the premises or vehicle concerned, and show to the person concerned the warrant and an explanatory note. The undertaking may consult a legal adviser, but the presence of a lawyer is not necessary for the investigation to be valid, and it must not unduly delay or impede the investigation. The authorised officers are entitled to take copies of documents, and the cost of photocopies will be reimbursed if requested. A note is taken of any oral explanations, and a copy will be given to the undertaking.

3.18 Finally, under section 41 of the 1987 Act, the Authority may apply to the High Court for an order to examine accounts maintained by a financial institution.

3.19 Information may also be sought orally or in writing from third parties. They will be allowed to make observations on the case, although they will not be given any details of the arrangements at this stage.

Issue of a Certificate

3.20 The first question to be considered in the assessment is whether the arrangements notified are in breach of section 4(1) of the Act, i.e. do they 'have as their object or effect the prevention, restriction or distortion of competition in trade in any goods or services in the State or in any part of the State'? If the arrangements are not, in the Authority's opinion, in breach of section 4(1) then the Authority issues a certificate in accordance with section 4(4).

Grant of a Licence

3.21 When, in the opinion of the Authority, the arrangements notified are in breach of section 4(1), consideration is given to the question of whether the arrangements qualify for a licence under section 4(2). The Act sets out strict criteria which an agreement which infringes section 4(1) must satisfy in order to gain a licence of exemption. To qualify, the agreement must:

A.9

(i) contribute to improving the production or distribution of goods or provision of services or to promoting technical or economic progress;

(ii) while allowing consumers a fair share of the resulting benefit;

and must not:

(iii) impose on the undertakings concerned terms which are not indispensable to the attainment of those objectives;

(iv) afford undertakings the possibility of eliminating competition in respect of a substantial part of the products or services in question.

It is important to note that all four conditions must be satisfied in order to obtain a licence.

3.22 A licence is granted for a specific period and may be subject to such conditions as may be attached to and specified in the licence (section 8(1)). The Authority may extend the period of a licence at the request of one of the notifying parties (see para 3.39).

Decision to Grant a Certificate or Licence

3.23 An initial assessment of the case is prepared, consisting of the facts, an analysis and suggested conclusions. The initial assessment is considered by the Authority. If the decision is favourable, notice of the Authority's intention to grant a certificate or licence is published in a daily newspaper, and interested third parties will be able to obtain a summary of the case from the Authority for a small fee. They will be given time to submit observations. This is in line with EC procedures. Prior to this, the notifying parties are shown a copy of the document which is to be made available to third parties. As required by the Act, Ministers concerned are also invited to make such observations as they may wish.

3.24 In the absence of any observations which raise serious concerns regarding the notification, the Authority proceeds to its final Decision. Where observations received do raise concerns regarding the notification, further discussions are held with the notifying parties to secure amendment, after which a final Decision is taken. If conditions are to be attached to the grant of a licence, they will be discussed with the notifying parties. (EC practice is that these are usually reporting conditions).

3.25 As required under the Act, the Authority transmits a copy of the notice to be published, together with the full Decision, to the parties to which it relates. A Ministerial regulation requires the notice to be sent by registered post. The Authority must publish a notice of the grant of a certificate or a licence in *Iris Oifigiúil*. It must also publish notice of the grant in a daily newspaper. The *Iris Oifigiúil* notice is generally likely to be fairly brief and the full decision will be available to third parties from the Authority, for a small fee. It would appear to be impossible to give the reasons of the Authority unless relevant parts of the arrangements, that is those which raise issues under section 4, are made public. Since they also have a right of appeal against a Decision to grant a certificate or licence, third parties must be entitled to obtain the full Decision.

Refusal to Grant a Certificate or Licence

3.26 Where the initial assessment is unfavourable, the procedure is more lengthy. The Authority decides to refuse a certificate or licence unless offensive clauses are deleted or amended. The Authority member dealing with the arrangements then initiates written or oral negotiations with the parties. If this results in arrangements which satisfy the Authority, a favourable Decision is taken in the manner described.

3.27 If the Authority is not satisfied, a Statement of Objections is approved by the Authority, and transmitted to the parties. The parties are given time to respond in writing, and they may request an oral hearing. Concerned Ministers are invited to make submissions at this stage. The oral hearing is before the full Authority. Following written or oral proceedings, the Authority may be satisfied, usually after amendments, and a favourable Decision can then be taken.

3.28 If, on the other hand, the Decision remains negative, a final Decision to refuse a certificate or licence is taken by the Authority. The parties are informed of the refusal, and, for agreements in existence at the time the Act came into force, notice of the Decision must be published in *Iris Oifigiúil.* The Authority intends to publish notice of refusal for agreements concluded after 1 October 1991 also, and to publish brief notice of all refusals in a daily newspaper. Copies of the full decision will be available to interested third parties from the Authority, for a fee.

Content of Decisions

3.29 In each case the decision includes an outline of the relevant facts, i.e. a description of the product(s) involved, the market, the undertakings and the arrangements. This is followed by an assessment of whether or not the arrangements are in breach of section 4(1). If they are in breach of section 4(1), an assessment of whether or not the arrangements qualify for a licence under section 4(2) is outlined. The Authority's conclusions are then presented. The certificate or licence, including in the latter case, its commencement and termination dates, together with any relevant conditions, is annexed to the decision. Where a certificate or licence is refused, the decision will contain the Authority's reasons for so doing.

Category Licences

3.30 The Authority may grant licences to categories of agreements. There are two types of category licence. The first relates to a standard form of agreement which an undertaking may enter into with a number of other undertakings. In this case the undertaking notifies the standard form agreement and the Authority considers it in accordance with the procedures already outlined.

3.31 The second type of category licence is the equivalent of the 'block exemption' given by the EC. Such licences are designed to cover similar types of agreements, e.g. distribution agreements. Provided an individual agreement meets the requirements set out in the category licence, it will be covered by that licence, and there will be no need to notify the agreement separately (section 4(3)(b)). The Authority, however, cannot issue a category licence until an agreement has been notified (section 7(3)). In effect at least one of the agreements to be covered by the category licence must be notified before the licence can be given. In practice the Authority will require several notifications of similar arrangements before deciding that a category licence is justified. In this case the notification is considered in accordance with the procedures described. If the initial assessment is that a category licence is to be issued, the Authority will publish notice of this intention together with the details of the proposed category licence. Interested parties will then be allowed make observations on the proposal before the category licence is finalised.

Business Secrets

3.32 Notifying parties are asked to indicate 'business secrets' in their notification, and to

A.9 justify any claim for confidentiality. The Authority must decide whether to accept the arguments. Improper disclosure of information is prohibited under para. 9 of the Schedule, and may be penalised, but the Authority will have to disclose certain information regarded as confidential, especially the restrictive clauses of an agreement. This is necessary in seeking observations from third parties and in publishing decisions. Disclosure is most unlikely, however, in the case of unpublished accounts, sales figures, cost data, market shares, and secret know-how.

Revocation of a Licence or Certificate

3.33 The Authority may, under section 8(3), revoke or amend a licence, and may insert in a licence conditions whose effect is to prohibit acts which would otherwise be authorised by the licence. This section provides that the Authority may take such action where it is of the opinion that:

(a) there has been a material change in any of the circumstances on which the decision to issue the licence was based;

(b) any party commits a breach of any obligation attached to the licence decision;

(c) the licence was based on materially incorrect or misleading information; or

(d) any party abuses the permission granted to it by the licence.

3.34 Similarly section 8(6) provides that the Authority may revoke a certificate where it is of the opinion that:

(a) there has been a material change in any of the circumstances on which the certificate was based; or

(b) the certificate was based on materially incorrect or misleading information.

3.35 Notice of any decision to revoke or amend a licence or revoke a certificate must be published in *Iris Oifigiúil*. Before taking such a decision, the Authority will investigate the arrangements on the basis of the procedures already outlined. A full copy of any such decision will be available for a small fee.

Appeal to the High Court

3.36 A party aggrieved by a licence or certificate has a right to appeal to the High Court under section 9(1). The Court may confirm, amend or revoke the licence or cancel or refuse to cancel a certificate. Pursuant to the Act, an appeal must be made within 28 days of publication of notice of the licence or certificate. Section 9(5), however, provides that the Court may extend this time limit in any case where it seems just and convenient to do so. The right of appeal includes the right to appeal against the insertion or exclusion of conditions attaching to any licence granted.

3.37 A party may also appeal against the revocation or amendment of a licence or revocation of a certificate. While section 9(4) provides that an appeal should be within 28 days of publication of the decision, section 9(5) again allows the Court to extend this time limit in any case where it seems just and convenient to do so. The Court can also order the suspension of a licence or certificate in respect of which an appeal has been brought pending the hearing and conclusion of the appeal (section 9(3)).

3.38 The Minister for Industry and Commerce may also appeal against a licence or certificate and against any decision to revoke or amend a licence or revoke a certificate. No appeal procedure is provided in the Act against a refusal by the Authority to issue a certificate or grant a licence.

Extension of a Licence

A.9

3.39 The Authority may extend the period of a licence at the request of one of the notifying parties, if it is of the opinion that the requirements of section 4(2) continue to be fulfilled (section 8(2)). Upon receiving such a request, the Authority will have to investigate whether, in fact, this is the case. While such an investigation may not prove as lengthy as an examination of an initial notification, the procedures adopted are likely to be broadly similar to those which apply in the latter case and which are described above. Notice of extension of a licence must be published in *Iris Oifigiúil*.

[illegible]

Index